UNIVERSITY CASEBOOK SERIES®

CASES AND MATERIALS

FOOD AND DRUG LAW

FOURTH EDITION

by

PETER BARTON HUTT
Senior Counsel, Covington & Burling LLP, Washington, D.C.
Lecturer on Food and Drug Law, Harvard Law School

RICHARD A. MERRILL
Daniel Caplin Professor of Law Emeritus, University of Virginia
Retired Senior Of Counsel, Covington & Burling LLP

LEWIS A. GROSSMAN
Professor of Law
Washington College of Law, American University

FOUNDATION
PRESS

© 1980, 1991 FOUNDATION PRESS
© 2007 by FOUNDATION PRESS
© 2014 LEG, Inc. d/b/a West Academic
    444 Cedar Street, Suite 700
    St. Paul, MN 55101
    1-877-888-1330
Printed in the United States of America

ISBN: 978-1-60930-175-0

Mat #41290158

Dedicated to
Louise Fraser Hutt (1905–2013)
Elizabeth D. Merrill
and
Lisa M. Rabin

And to the thousands of dedicated women and men
who have worked at the Food and Drug Administration
since its creation

In memory of our colleague and friend, Eugene I. Lambert

PREFACE

Food and Drug Law is the oldest field of consumer protection legislation in the United States. City, county, and state food and drug laws have existed since colonial times. The Federal Food and Drugs Act of 1906, and the Federal Meat Inspection Act of the same year, were Congress's first major efforts to protect consumers on a national level. Lawyers have thus been involved in advising and representing private clients and government officials on federal food and drug law matters for more than a century. The 1906 Act predated the creation of the Federal Trade Commission by nearly a decade and the establishment of other agencies with a consumer protection role—such as the Environmental Protection Agency and the Consumer Product Safety Commission—by a full half-century.

Notwithstanding this comparatively ancient lineage, until the 1970s, food and drug law did not command the attention of a large number of lawyers or legal academics. The relatively small number of practitioners specializing in this area could be attributed to the geographic concentration of the practice in Washington, D.C. and to the comparatively modest resources of the Food and Drug Administration. Prior to the 1980s, food and drug law was taught in only a few law schools (primarily by adjunct faculty) and generated little serious scholarship. The inattention of legal academia was, we suspect, a function not only of the limited size of the practice community, but also of a failure of law professors to recognize the richness of the issues presented by FDA regulation.

Today, after more than three decades of steadily increasing attention, food and drug law may finally be on the verge of becoming a core subject of the legal academy. A new generation of professors, having themselves taken food and drug law classes in law school, is now teaching the subject. Growing numbers of law schools are offering not only the survey class on food and drug law, but also specialized courses such as food law and biotechnology law. Law schools are also establishing centers and LLM degrees focusing on food law and on health law, and such programs serve as incubators for creative food and drug law scholarship. In 2008, the *Cornell Law Review* published an entire issue devoted to food and drug regulation. In 2013, Harvard Law School's Petrie-Flom Center for Health Law Policy, Biotechnology, and Bioethics held the first-ever major academic conference devoted exclusively to food and drug law. This event represented a "coming out party" for food and drug law as an independent academic field. It also reflected the growing recognition that food and drug law is a fundamental component of the broader subject of health law.

Various legal, economic, scientific, and cultural trends have contributed to the burgeoning of the food and drug law field. Health care is perhaps the great policy issue of our age, and academic and popular interest in food has also soared. In addition, food and drug law touches on many of the most exciting, cutting-edge areas of science and technology, including bioengineering, gene therapy, nanotechnology, personalized medicine, mobile computing, and 3-D printing.

Moreover, the study and practice of food and drug law has recently been enriched by the "constitutionalization" of the field. The most prominent example of this phenomenon is the striking rise of successful First-Amendment challenges to FDA labeling regulation, on commercial free speech grounds. The last decade has also witnessed a series of extremely important federal preemption cases concerning the asserted preemption of state-law tort suits regarding FDA-regulated products.

As an area of practice, food and drug law has proved to be largely immune to the economic tribulations of recent years—a fact not overlooked by law school administrators, professors, and students. The introduction of user fees has supported substantial growth in the size of FDA itself; in 2012, the agency had about 26.5% more employees than it did in 2005, 52.4% more than it did in 2000, and 75.5% more than it did in 1990. Meanwhile, food and drug regulatory experts employed by law firms, trade associations, in-house counsel offices, public interest organizations, and Congress have remained extremely busy. Transactional lawyers and litigators often encounter food and drug law issues as well.

Since the release of the Third Edition of this casebook in 2007, food and drug practitioners have been occupied not only with their usual work, but also with the enactment, interpretation, and implementation of a steady stream of major amendments to the Food, Drug, and Cosmetic Act and Public Health Service Act. These amendments include the Food and Drug Administration Amendments Act of 2007, the Family Smoking Prevention and Tobacco Control Act of 2009, the biosimilars provisions of the Patient Protection and Affordable Care Act of 2010, the Food Safety Modernization Act of 2011, and the Food and Drug Administration Safety and Innovation Act of 2012.

The already impressive scope of commercial activities regulated by FDA has increased even further since the 2007 publication of the previous edition. In the preface to that volume, we offered a rough estimate that 25 cents of every consumer dollar was spent on products within categories regulated by FDA: food (including dietary supplements), drugs, cosmetics, medical devices, biological products, animal food, animal drugs, and radiation-emitting products. Since then, Congress has added tobacco products to the agency's bailiwick, and the health care sector of the economy has continued to grow. Consequently, it may be time to reconsider this "25 cents per dollar" estimate.

As a society, the United States is evincing an ever-growing interest in FDA-related issues. Almost every week, numerous food-and-drug-related headlines appear in the press. A search of "FDA" and "Food and Drug Administration" in Google's wonderful Ngram Viewer function shows that the relative frequency of references to the agency in American books (i.e., mentions as a percentage of the total words published) has climbed almost inexorably since 1960. Indeed, in 2004 (the last year with a relatively reliable dataset), the agency was mentioned in American books more than seven times as frequently as in 1960 and almost twice as frequently as in 1980, the year the First Edition of this casebook was published.

Even apart from all these recent developments, food and drug law is a compelling law school subject for a variety of other reasons. First, it is a matter of great personal importance to consumers—including students. Few if any Americans escape daily exposure to multiple products regulated by FDA. Professor Grossman opens his course by telling his students: "If you are interested in food, beauty, sex, sickness, and death, then you'll find this to be a fascinating class."

In addition, FDA's continuing efforts to come to grips with its regulatory responsibilities offer a fascinating window into American administrative law. Many judicial decisions that are accepted as part of the corpus of administrative law have involved FDA. The agency has been responsible for major innovations in administrative procedure, and in the agency's experience one can discern the intimate interrelationship between administrative procedure and regulatory substance.

Finally, the story of federal efforts to regulate the marketing of food and drugs is fascinating as history. The creation and experience of any regulatory agency undoubtedly mirrors strong political and economic currents, but few other agencies regulate products or activities that play so intimate a role in the daily lives of citizens. The visibility of food and drugs, the concern of individuals for their health, and the expectations citizens have for those charged with protecting them, have made FDA a resonant amplifier of American social history.

The Audience for this Book

This is a coursebook on food and drug law, intended primarily for law students. The materials included, the organization used, and the issues addressed reflect this focus. We expect, however, that the book will also prove useful in teaching students and professionals in other fields, such as nutrition, medicine, public health, and public administration.

We are confident that food and drug law practitioners will continue to find the book extremely helpful in clarifying legal requirements, framing pertinent questions, and identifying relevant sources. In most instances, the statutory provisions referred to and the cases reproduced reflect legal requirements prevailing in 2013. The changes in this field are rapid, however, and no careful lawyer should fail to consult other sources that can provide the most recent legal and policy developments.

Changes from the Third Edition

The Fourth Edition is completely updated through the early fall of 2013. It includes a new chapter on tobacco regulation to reflect the responsibilities FDA acquired under the Family Smoking Prevention and Tobacco Control of 2009. It also incorporates the other statutory amendments since 2007 (for example, the Food and Drug Administration Act, the Food Safety Modernization Act, and the Food and Drug Administration Safety and Innovation Act). Every major development of the past six years—judicial, legislative, regulatory, and scientific—is addressed.

We have reorganized and edited the book to make it more useful for students and professors. Much important contextual material has been moved to the front of the book, so students will grasp essential administrative, jurisdictional, federalism, and enforcement issues before mastering the intricacies of the product-specific chapters. The casebook thus provides an introductory window into administrative law for upper-level students who have not yet taken the basic Administrative Law course, as well as for first-year students taking Food and Drug Law as an elective. (The more specialized administrative law issues surrounding advisory committees, public information, and environmental assessments continue to be treated in the book's final chapter). We have thoroughly rearranged the chapter on human drugs to improve its comprehensibility. Throughout the book, we have made other changes to organization and presentation with professors and students in mind.

Selection of Materials

Various types of primary source materials are excerpted in this book, including judicial opinions; administrative documents published in the Federal Register, such as proposed regulations and final regulations; administrative documents not published in the Federal Register, such as guidances and warning letters; articles from law reviews and other academic and professional journals; congressional sources; reports by various entities; and articles from the popular press.

Obviously, economy of space has been one important criterion in our choice of materials. A major problem for the editors of a casebook in any regulatory field is the sheer volume of printed pages available. Legal requirements that administrative agencies be more explicit in explaining their decisions, and that they analyze the environmental, economic, and other effects of their actions, have generated challenges for scholars and practitioners alike. Not only are there more words to read and evaluate, but it is also increasingly difficult to capture the reality of the regulatory process in a single book.

Judicial opinions, too often maligned as teaching materials, provide one way of responding to this problem. The opinions of conscientious judges engaged in reviewing administrative action are often the best summaries of the labyrinthine proceedings and complex factual and legal issues underlying regulators' decisions. In an opinion concerning FDA, a judge frequently has to condense the entire history of a regulatory question to explain how the case should be decided. Another important reason to feature judicial decisions in a coursebook on food and drug law is that from the earliest days of federal food and drug regulation until about 1970, most substantive law was reflected in court rulings. Moreover, ground-breaking judicial decisions have continued to appear in recent decades, and because most manufacturers of food and drugs strive to avoid adverse publicity, these decisions generate a high degree of voluntary compliance. Thus, in many areas, the substance of food and drug law is expressed in a series of well-accepted judicial precedents.

As discussed in detail in Chapter 2, FDA's regulatory style changed starting about 1970. Confronted with increasingly complex substantive issues and a growing number of firms making regulated products, FDA turned toward rulemaking as the principal technique for explaining and defining legal requirements. The Federal Register thus became the primary vehicle for official discussion and resolution of food and drug problems. Accordingly, we have included numerous excerpts from this source. More recently, FDA has relied increasingly on the promulgation of informal guidance documents. We have thus also included numerous examples of this modern substitute for notice-and-comment regulation.

Our use of congressional materials cannot be explained in terms of economy, for committee reports and hearing records tend to be prolix and unfocused. But they can provide useful summaries of problems and, more important, they reflect legislative perceptions that significantly influence FDA officials and courts.

We have also included some excerpts from the popular press. FDA began to be the subject of general public interest and scrutiny in the 1960s, largely as the result of increasing congressional hearings about food and drug issues. Today it is almost impossible to read any newspaper without finding an article that directly mentions or at least relates to an FDA matter. Although we cannot convey the true extent and impact of this press coverage in this book, we have included examples of these materials to remind students that research on food and drug law extends far beyond traditional legal sources.

Throughout the book, in addition to excerpts from original sources, we have included extensive text and notes written by us. Our own contributions to the book contain substantive information and analysis that we have concluded can be related more effectively in our own voices than by excerpting other sources. The notes in particular have various goals. First, they attempt to bring the reader up to date on a subject. Second, they supply historical background missing from primary sources. Third, they raise questions about the policies reflected in agency decisions or judicial rulings. Finally, the notes attempt to provide bibliographic assistance to the reader who wishes to pursue a subject in depth. In comparison with the previous edition, however, the notes in this edition contain less purely bibliographical information. We reduced this content so as to control the size of the volume, in view of the fact that printed listings of sources are less important in this age of electronic research.

The full text of the Federal Food, Drug, and Cosmetic Act of 1938, 21 U.S.C. 302 *et seq.* (the Act or FD&C Act) and other statutes referred to in the book are reproduced separately in a paperback supplement.

Citation Format

Though our citation forms generally follow *The Bluebook: A Uniform System of Citation*, we have adopted some distinctive practices of our own, sometimes to save space that would be wasted if we endlessly repeated the prescribed form.

Our statutory references are to sections of the FD&C Act of 1938, as amended, and not to the United States Code. We have not, however, substituted FD&C Act references for U.S. Code citations in original sources, such as judicial opinions. Determining the proper U.S. Code citation for older sections of the FD&C Act is straightforward. By dropping the middle digit and inserting a "3" in front of the two remaining digits, one can often derive the U.S. Code section. For example, section 402 of the Act is codified as 21 U.S.C. 342. This simple translation method does not work for more recently enacted sections, however.

We sometimes use short forms for agencies and organizations that are cited or mentioned frequently. For example, "GAO" is our colloquial, as well as official, reference to the Government Accounting Office, and "NAS" frequently substitutes for the National Academy of Sciences.

In excerpted primary sources, such as cases, we have routinely omitted citations and footnotes without any notation in the text. The footnotes that remain retain their original numbering. We have also deleted, again without notation, many organizational designations, such as headings. All omissions of substantive text are disclosed by ellipses appearing at the beginning, in the middle, or at the end of sentences or paragraphs, with the exception of omissions of text from the beginning of an excerpted source, which are not always indicated in this manner. A three-dot ellipsis at the end of a paragraph denotes the omission of the balance of that paragraph and perhaps of additional paragraphs. A stand-alone four-dot ellipsis denotes the omission of at least one full paragraph. Errors in spelling or grammar are generally, but not always, denoted by [sic].

FDA has one of the most comprehensive websites in the federal government. It can be accessed at www.fda.gov. Most information available from FDA under the Freedom of Information Act is now routinely posted on this website, which we refer to throughout this volume simply as the "FDA website." Because recent agency documents with known titles are almost always easily accessible from the FDA website using basic word-search techniques, we usually do not provide the URL address for them.

Since 1994, Mr. Hutt has taught a full course on Food and Drug Law each year during Winter Term at Harvard Law School. *See* Peter Barton Hutt, *Food and Drug Law: Journal of an Academic Adventure*, 46 J. LEGAL EDUC. 1 (1996). Each student prepares a course paper, and most combine it with Harvard's third-year written work requirement. Virtually all of these hundreds of papers have been compiled in FOOD AND DRUG LAW: AN ELECTRONIC BOOK OF STUDENT PAPERS, which can be accessed online at http://www.law.harvard.edu/faculty/hutt. Throughout this casebook, we refer to this resource as the "Electronic Book."

Disclosure of Interests

Two of us have served as Chief Counsel to the Food and Drug Administration. Mr. Hutt occupied that position from 1971 to 1975, when he was succeeded by Mr. Merrill, who served until 1977. With the exception of his period of government service, Mr. Hutt has been engaged in the private practice of food and drug law with Covington & Burling LLP since 1962. Professor Merrill was an associate of Covington & Burling from 1965 to 1969. He rejoined the firm as Senior Of Counsel in 1991. He is now Retired Senior Of Counsel. Professor Grossman was an associate at Covington & Burling from 1993 to 1997 and has been Of Counsel to the firm on a part-time basis since 2004. Professor Grossman was a member of the Institute of Medicine's Committee on the Review of the FDA's Role in Ensuring Safe Food, which produced the report excerpted in Chapter 6 titled ENHANCING FOOD SAFETY: THE ROLE OF THE FOOD AND DRUG ADMINISTRATION.

Appreciation

Two Covington & Burling paralegals, Marilynn Whitney, who assisted with all four editions, and Katherine MacRae, who worked on the Second Edition, retrieved and helped organize materials that cannot be found in conventional libraries. The founding librarian of the Covington & Burling Food and Drug Law Library, Meg Gleason, and her successors, Dorothy Donahoe and Jennifer Korpacz, have facilitated our work by maintaining the country's most comprehensive collection of food and drug legal materials. Portions of the current manuscript were prepared by Cheryl Parsons at Covington & Burling.

We owe a considerable debt to many law students at American University's Washington College of Law who worked on this Fourth Edition. Invaluable research assistance was provided by Joanna Hess Kunz, Amy Gaither Speros, Kathleen Scott, Heather Dorsey, Kyu Min Lee, Samantha Dietle, and Charlotte McKiver.

Before his passing in 2013, Eugene Lambert of Covington & Burling, a gentleman with encyclopedic knowledge of all things food and drug law, was always available to share his insights and wisdom. Dean Claudio Grossman of the Washington College of Law has generously supported Professor Grossman's work on this project.

PETER BARTON HUTT
Washington, D.C.

RICHARD A. MERRILL
Charlottesville, Virginia

LEWIS A. GROSSMAN
Washington, D.C.

November 2013

ACKNOWLEDGMENTS

We acknowledge the courtesy of the following publishers, journals, law reviews and authors who have permitted us to reprint excerpts from their publications:

1. Food and Drug Law Institute: FDLI gave us blanket permission to reproduce or quote from articles appearing in the Food and Drug Law Journal, the Food Drug Cosmetic Law Journal, and the Food and Drug Law Quarterly. For this, we owe FDLI a special debt of thanks.

2. American Bar Association: Todd Rakoff, *The Choice Between Formal and Informal Modes of Administrative Regulation*, published in ADMINISTRATIVE LAW REVIEW, Volume 52, No. 1, Winter 2000. © 2000 by the American Bar Association. Reprinted with permission.

3. Annual Review of Nutrition: Peter Barton Hutt, *Government Regulation of the Integrity of the Food Supply*, 4 Annual Review of Nutrition 1 (1984).

4. American Academy of Dermatology: Bergfeld et al., *Safety of Ingredients Used in Cosmetics*, 52 Journal of the American Academy of Dermatology 125 (2005); Robert L. Elder, *The Cosmetic Ingredient Review: A Safety Evaluation Program*, 11 Journal of the American Academy of Dermatology 1168 (1984).

5. BMJ Books: Peter Barton Hutt, *The Regulation of Drug Products by the United States Food and Drug Administration*, in John P. Griffin & John O'Grady, the Textbook of Pharmaceutical Medicine (5th edition 2006).

6. BioCentury Publications: Steve Usdin, *Diminishing Returns*, BioCentury February 13, 2006, at A1.

7. A. Larry Branen: Peter Barton Hutt, *Regulation of Food Additives in the United States*, in Food Additives (2d ed. 2001).

8. Columbia Law Review: Richard A. Merrill and Earl M. Collier, *"Like Mother Used to Make": An Analysis of FDA Food Standards of Identity,* 74 Colum. L. Rev. 561 (1974).

9. Cornell Law Review: Lewis A. Grossman, *Food, Drugs, and Droods*, 93 Cornell L. Rev. 1091 (2008).

10. Marcel Dekker: Peter Barton Hutt, *A History of Government Regulation of Adulteration and Misbranding of Cosmetics*, in Norman F. Estrin & James M. Akerson, eds., Cosmetic Regulation in a Competitive Environment (2000).

11. Peter Elsner & Howard I. Maibach: Peter Barton Hutt, *The Legal Distinction in the United States Between a Cosmetic and a Drug*, in Cosmeceuticals (2000).

12. Environmental Lawyer: Allison D. Carpenter, *Impact of the Food Quality Protection Act of 1996,* 3 Envtl. Law. 479 (1997).

13. FDC Reports: FDA Examples of Acceptable and Unacceptable Dietary Supplement Claims, 8 The Tan Sheet, No. 3, at 12–13 (January 17, 2000).

14. Florida Law Review: Lars Noah, Assisted Reproductive Technologies and the Pitfalls of Unregulated Biomedical Innovation, 55 Fla. L. Rev. 603 (2003).

15. Malcolm Gladwell: *High Prices*, The New Yorker, October 25, 2004, at 86.

16. Harvard Law Review: Thomas W. Merrill & Kathryn Tongue Watts, *Agency Rules with the Force of Law: The Original Convention*, 116 Harv. L. Rev. 467 (2002).

17. Health Scan: Peter Barton Hutt, *Landmark Pharmaceutical Law Enacted*, 1 Health Scan, No. 3, p. 11 (1984).

18. Houston Journal of Health Law & Policy: Richard A. Merrill, *Human Tissues and Reproductive Cloning: New Technologies Challenge FDA*, 3 Hous. J. Health Law & Pol'y 1 (2002).

19. Journal of Health Care Law & Policy: Michael Greenberger, The 800 Pound Gorilla Sleeps: The Federal Government's Lackadaisical Liability and Compensation Policies in the Context of Pre-Event Vaccine Immunization Programs, 8 J. of Health Care L. & Pol'y 7 (2005).

20. Journal of Law and Economics: Peter Temin, *The Origin of Compulsory Drug Prescriptions*, 22 J. L. & Econ. 91 (1979).

21. Law & Contemporary Problems: Lauffer Hayes & Frank Ruff, *The Administration of the Federal Food and Drugs Act*, 1 Law & Contemp. Probs. 16 (1933).

22. Law & Society Review: Cary Coglianese & David Laezer, *Management-Based Regulation: Prescribing Private Management to Achieve Public Goals*, 37 Law & Soc'y Rev. 691 (2003).

23. Los Angeles Times: Jerry Hirsch, *The Courage of their Convections*, Apr. 14, 2007, at A1.

24. National Academy Press: Enhancing Food Safety: The Role of the Food and Drug Administration (2010); Stem Cells and the Future of Regenerative Medicine (2001); Food and Drug Administration Advisory Committees (1992).

25. New England Journal of Medicine: Marlene E. Haffner, *Adopting Orphan Drugs—Two Dozen Years of Treating Rare Diseases*, 354 New Eng. J. Med. 445 (2006); Frank A. Sloan, et al., *The Fragility of the U.S. Vaccine Supply*, 351 New Eng. J. Med. 23 (2004); Robert Steinbrook, *Financial Conflicts of Interest and the Food and Drug Administration's Advisory Committees*, 353 New Eng. J. Med. 126 (2005).

26. New York Sun: Scott Gottlieb, *The Price of Too Much Caution*, Dec. 22, 2004, at 8.

27. Pharmacogenomics Journal: Larry J. Lesko & Janet Woodcock, *Pharmacogenomic-Guided Drug Development: Regulatory Perspective*, 2 Pharmacogenomics J. 20 (2002).

28. Public Health Reports: Marion Nestle, *The Selling of Olestra*, 113 Pub. Health Rep. 508 (1998).

29. Quarterly Bulletin of the Association of Food and Drug Officials: Peter Barton Hutt, *Public Information and Public*

Participation in the Food and Drug Administration, 36 Q. Bull. Ass'n Food & Drug Officials 212 (1972).

30. Science, copyright by the American Association for the Advancement of Science: Edward Mortimer, *Immunization Against Infectious Disease,* 200 Science 902 (1978).

SUMMARY OF CONTENTS

PREFACE...V

ACKNOWLEDGMENTS... XIII

TABLE OF CASES... LVII

Chapter 1. History and Context..1
A.   Global Precedents 1
B.   The Development of FDA as an Institution 3
C.   The Development of American Food and Drug Legislation 5
D.   FDA's Mission 14
E.   FDA's Structure and Organization 16
F.   FDA's Relationship With Other Agencies 20
G.   FDA's Relationship With Regulated Industry 21
H.   FDA's Resources.. 24
I.   The Regulatory Environment.. 25

Chapter 2. FDA Rulemaking, Judicial Review, and the
Administrative Procedure Act 29
A.   FDA's Reliance on Regulations: History and Analysis.......................29
B.   Rulemaking Procedures... 43
C.   The Decline of Notice-and-Comment Rulemaking and the Rise of
     Guidance 55
D.   Direct Final Rulemaking and Interim Rulemaking 60
E.   Legislative Rule or Interpretive Rule? 61
F.   Judicial Review of Agency Action 62
G.   Judicial Review of Agency Inaction 69

Chapter 3. FDA Jurisdiction: A Matter of Definitions 77
A.   Introduction.. 77
B.   Food....... 79
C.   Drugs and Devices 89
D.   The Food–Drug Spectrum Adjusted: Health Claims and Dietary
     Supplements... 101
E.   Cosmetics... 109
F.   The Cosmetic–Drug Spectrum 110
G.   Exploring the Outer Limits of the Drug and Device Definitions........121
H.   Human Biological Products... 135
I.   Tobacco Products... 139
J.   "Label," "Labeling," and "Advertising" 151

Chapter 4. FDA Enforcement 163
A.   Introduction.. 163
B.   Enforcement Consistency, Selectivity, and Discretion 168
C.   Factory Inspection 176
D.   Seizure.. 193
E.   Injunctions.. 211
F.   Recalls... 230
G.   Criminal Liability 237

H. Debarment and Exclusion 252
I. Civil Money Penalties...262
J. Informal Compliance Correspondence...263
K. Publicity...268

Chapter 5. FDA's Place in Our Federal System..............................**271**
A. The Scope of Federal Power 271
B. The Elusive Goal of Uniformity of State Laws 289
C. Federal Preemption and the Limits of State Power 292

Chapter 6. Food **317**
A. Subcategories of Food 317
B. Historical Overview of FDA Regulation of Food Identity, Quality,
    and Labeling..325
C. What's in a Name? Regulation of Food Identity and Quality 332
D. Regulation of Food Labeling 379
E. Food Sanitation and Aesthetic Adulteration 469
F. The Presence of Poisonous or Deleterious Substances......................489
G. Regulation of Food Production and the Problem of Pathogenic
    Microorganisms..521
H. Intentional Functional Ingredients 552

Chapter 7. Human Drugs..**641**
A. Historical Background..641
B. The Definition of "New Drug" 660
C. Drug Development and FDA Licensure of New Drugs 669
D. Variations and Exceptions to the Standard Drug Development,
    Investigation, and Approval Process 751
E. Restrictions on Distribution and Prescribing 802
F. Postapproval Issues 834
G. Physician Labeling and Patient Labeling of Prescription Drugs 860
H. Advertising and Promotion of Prescription Drugs 907
I. Regulating Off-Label Promotion 925
J. Over-the-Counter Drugs..957
K. Generic Drugs 996
L. The Cost of Drugs 1023
M. Counterfeit, Imitation, Street Alternative, and Diverted
    Prescription Drugs 1028
N. Present and Future Challenges 1035

Chapter 8. Food and Drugs for Animals..**1045**
A. Introduction..1045
B. Animal Food and Feed 1045
C. Animal Drugs 1059

**Chapter 9. Biological Products: Vaccines, Blood, Tissue
Transplants, and Cellular Therapies** **1123**
A. Historical Background...1123
B. FDA Acquires Responsibility for Biologics.....................................1124
C. FDA Regulation of Therapeutic Biologics 1127

D. Regulating and Promoting Vaccines..1137
E. Blood and Blood Products..1153
F. Human Tissues and Cells...1165
G. Other Cellular Technologies..1175

Chapter 10. Medical Devices **1193**
A. Historical Background..1193
B. Regulation of Devices Under the FD&C Act before 1976.................1194
C. Introduction to the Modern Device Regulatory Regime 1202
D. The Definition of "Device" Since 1976 1205
E. Classification of Devices into Class I, Class II, and Class III..........1212
F. Changeover Issues: The 1976 Medical Device Amendments and
    the Regulation of Preamendments Devices.......................................1215
G. Regulation of Market Entry 1218
H. Special Controls for Class II Devices..1251
I. General Controls Applicable to All Devices 1254
J. Mobile Medical Devices 1277
K. Preemption of State Law by the Medical Device Amendments of
    1976…..1280
L. Radiation Control...1292

Chapter 11. Cosmetics.. **1301**
A. Historical and Statutory Background 1301
B. Definition of "Cosmetic"..1311
C. Adulterated Cosmetics...1311
D. Coal-Tar Hair Dyes...1322
E. Misbranded Cosmetics...1325
F. Cosmetic Ingredient Labeling 1335
G. Voluntary "Regulation" of Cosmetics...1338
H. The Present and Future of Cosmetics Regulation 1348

Chapter 12. Tobacco Products **1351**
A. Introduction..1351
B. Tobacco Product Review 1353
C. Tobacco Product Standards..1362
D. Tobacco Product Labeling and Advertising.....................................1363

Chapter 13. Regulation of Carcinogens.. **1373**
A. Historical Background..1373
B. Early FDA Policy 1374
C. Evolution of Legislative Policy...1375
D. Regulation of Diethylstilbestrol 1382
E. FDA Embraces Quantitative Risk Assessment 1387
F. Deciding Whether an Additive "Induces Cancer" 1417
G. Resolving the "Delaney Paradox"...1425
H. Other Efforts to Identify or Regulate Carcinogens..........................1431
I. Issues 1435

Chapter 14. Regulation of Foreign Commerce **1439**
A. Importation Into the United States...1439
B. Exportation From the United States..1468
C. Import for Export...1483

Chapter 15. Other Agency Procedures **1487**
A. Regularizing Agency Procedures 1487
B. Advisory Committees...1488
C. Public Information 1503
D. Environmental Assessment...1526

INDEX 1531

TABLE OF CONTENTS

PREFACE...V

ACKNOWLEDGMENTS... XIII

TABLE OF CASES.. LVII

Chapter 1. History and Context..1
A.   Global Precedents 1
     Peter Barton Hutt, *Government Regulation of the Integrity of the
     Food Supply*..1
B.   The Development of FDA as an Institution 3
     Peter Barton Hutt, *A Historical Introduction*..................................3
     Richard A. Merrill, *The Architecture of Government Regulation of
     Medical Products*..4
C.   The Development of American Food and Drug Legislation 5
     1.   State and Local Laws in the 19th Century 5
     2.   National Developments Leading Up to 1906 6
     3.   The 1906 Pure Food and Drugs Act..8
          Lauffer Hayes & Frank Ruff, *The Administration of the
          Federal Food and Drugs Act*..8
          1917 Report of the USDA Bureau of Chemistry 9
          Note..10
     4.   The Federal Food, Drug, and Cosmetic Act of 1938 10
          1933 Report of the Food and Drug Administration 10
     5.   The Growth of the FD&C Act: Amendments Since 1938 11
     6.   Other Laws Enforced by FDA 14
D.   FDA's Mission 14
     Agriculture, Rural Development, Food and Drug Administration,
          and Related Agencies Appropriations Bill, 2014 15
E.   FDA's Structure and Organization...16
     1.   Legal Basis for the Agency 16
     2.   The FDA Commissioner..17
     3.   FDA's Place Within the Federal Government............................17
     4.   FDA's Size and Internal Organization 19
F.   FDA's Relationship With Other Agencies 20
G.   FDA's Relationship With Regulated Industry 21
     Review Panel on New Drug Regulation, Final Report 22
     Final Report of the National Committee to Review Procedures for
          Approval of New Drugs for Cancer and Aids 23
     Note...24
H.   FDA's Resources...24
     Note...25
I.   The Regulatory Environment...25

**Chapter 2. FDA Rulemaking, Judicial Review, and the
Administrative Procedure Act** 29
A.   FDA's Reliance on Regulations: History and Analysis...........................29
     1.   Introduction...29
     2.   APA "Rulemaking" 29

        3.   FDA's Embrace of Notice-and-Comment Rulemaking 30
           a.   Background 30
           b.   The Statutory Framework 32
           c.   Judicial Acknowledgment of FDA's Rulemaking
               Authority 33
               Abbott Laboratories v. Gardner 34
               Notes 36
               National Association of Pharmaceutical Manufacturers
                   v. Food and Drug Administration 37
           d.   The Debate Reopened 41
               Thomas W. Merrill & Kathryn Tongue Watts, *Agency Rules*
                   With the Force of Law: The Original Convention 41
   B.   Rulemaking Procedures 43
        1.   APA Notice-and-Comment Requirements 43
           United States v. Nova Scotia Food Products Corp. 44
           Notes 46
        2.   HHS Oversight of FDA Rulemaking 47
        3.   OMB Oversight of FDA Rulemaking 47
        4.   Formal Rulemaking 49
           a.   When Is an Evidentiary Hearing Required? 49
               Dyestuffs and Chemicals, Inc. v. Flemming 49
               Notes 50
           b.   Formal Hearing Procedures 52
           c.   The Public Board of Inquiry Alternative to a Trial–
               Type Hearing 53
               Notice of Proposed Rulemaking: Administrative Practices
                   and Procedures 53
   C.   The Decline of Notice-and-Comment Rulemaking and the Rise of
       Guidance 55
       Todd D. Rakoff, *The Choice Between Formal and Informal*
           Modes of Administrative Regulation 56
       Notes 59
   D.   Direct Final Rulemaking and Interim Rulemaking 60
   E.   Legislative Rule or Interpretive Rule? 61
       Notes 61
   F.   Judicial Review of Agency Action 62
        1.   Introduction 62
           Note 63
        2.   Standards of Review 63
           Note 64
        3.   The Limits of Judicial Power 65
           a.   Justiciability 65
                Notes 65
           b.   Primary Jurisdiction 66
               Notes 67
           c.   Exhaustion of Remedies 68
   G.   Judicial Review of Agency Inaction 69
        1.   Enforcement Discretion 69
        2.   Unreasonable Delay 70

Center for Food Safety v. Hamburg 70
Notes 73

Chapter 3. FDA Jurisdiction: A Matter of Definitions **77**
A.   Introduction 77
     Food, Drugs, and Cosmetics 77
          United States v. An Article of Drug . . . Bacto–Unidisk 78
B.   Food 79
     United States v. Tuente Livestock 80
     Notes 84
     Nutrilab, Inc. v. Schweiker 85
     Notes 88
C.   Drugs and Devices 89
     1.   Inclusion in Official Compendia 90
     2.   Establishing "Intended Use" 92
          National Nutritional Foods Ass'n v. Mathews 93
          Notes 96
          United States v. Travia 97
     3.   Diagnostic Products 98
          United States v. 25 Cases, More or Less, of an Article of
               Device . . . "Sensor Pad for Breast Self–Examination" 99
          Notes 100
D.   The Food–Drug Spectrum Adjusted: Health Claims and
     Dietary Supplements 101
     Letter from Felicia B. Satchell, Director, FDA CFSAN Office of
          Nutritional Products, Labeling and Dietary Supplements,
          Division of Standards and Labeling Regulations,
          to Jason S. Crush 104
     Notes 105
E.   Cosmetics 109
     Notes 109
F.   The Cosmetic–Drug Spectrum 110
     1.   Cosmetic Claims Versus Drug Claims 111
          United States v. An Article . . . Sudden Change 111
          Notes 113
          Letter From John M. Taylor, FDA Associate Commissioner
               for Regulatory Affairs, to Various Attorneys
               Representing the Cosmetic Industry 114
          Notes 115
     2.   The "Active Ingredient" Approach 118
          Notes 120
G.   Exploring the Outer Limits of the Drug and Device
     Definitions 121
     1.   Cosmetic Devices 121
          Letter From Rep. Henry A. Waxman to Tommy Thompson,
               Secretary of Health and Human Services 122
          Notes 123
     2.   Common Sense Limits? 124

Letter From Daniel E. Troy, FDA Chief Counsel, to Jeffrey N.
            Gibbs 125
        Notes 128
    3. First Amendment Limits 131
        United States v. 23 . . . Articles 131
        United States v. Undetermined Quantities of Article of
            Device 132
H. Human Biological Products 135
    David M. Dudzinski, *Reflections on Historical, Scientific, and Legal
        Issues Relevant to Designing Approval Pathways for Generic
        Versions of Recombinant Protein–Based Therapeutics and
        Monoclonal Antibodies* 136
    Notes 138
I. Tobacco Products 139
    1. Struggles Over FDA Jurisdiction Before the Family Smoking
        Prevention and Tobacco Control Act of 2009 139
        Food and Drug Administration v. Brown & Williamson
            Tobacco Corp. 141
    2. The Family Smoking Prevention and Tobacco Control Act 145
        Sottera, Inc. v. FDA 146
        Notes 150
J. "Label," "Labeling," and "Advertising" 151
    1. Introduction 151
        Note 151
    2. Labeling 152
        Kordel v. United States 152
        Note 153
        United States v. 24 Bottles "Sterling Vinegar & Honey," etc. 154
        Notes 155
    3. Advertising 156
    4. The Internet 157
        Letter From Margaret M. Dotzel, Assoc. Comm. for Policy,
            FDA, to Daniel J. Popeo and Paul D. Kamenar,
            Washington Legal Foundation 157
        Notes 158
        Promotion of Food and Drug Administration–Regulated
            Medical Products Using the Internet and Social Media
            Tools; Notice of Public Hearing 159
        Note 162

Chapter 4. FDA Enforcement 163
A. Introduction 163
    1. Section 301: Prohibited Acts 163
    2. Tools of Enforcement 163
    3. FDA Enforcement Statistics 164
        Prescription for Harm: The Decline in FDA Enforcement
            Activity 165
    4. FDA Enforcement Policy 166

Remarks by Margaret A. Hamburg, Commissioner of Food and Drugs, on "Effective Enforcement and Benefits to Public Health" 166

5. Policy-Making Through Rulemaking Versus Policy-Making Through Case-by-Case Enforcement 167

B. Enforcement Consistency, Selectivity, and Discretion 168

1. Administrative Consistency and Selective Enforcement 168

United States v. Undetermined Quantities of an Article of Drug Labeled as Exachol 168

Note 170

2. Enforcement Discretion 171

Heckler v. Chaney 171

Notes 175

C. Factory Inspection 176

1. Introduction 176

FDA Investigations Operations Manual 2012, Chapter 5: Establishments Inspection 177

Notes 178

2. Constitutional Limitations 179

United States v. Jamieson–McKames Pharmaceuticals, Inc. 179

Notes 183

3. Scope of Inspections 184

a. Records 184

Notes 185

b. Samples and Photographs 188

Triangle Candy Co. v. United States 188

Note 189

Frederick H. Branding & James M. Ellis, *Underdeveloped: FDA's Authority to Take Photographs During an FDA Establishment Inspection Under Section 704* 189

Notes 191

4. The USDA Inspection Regime 192

D. Seizure 193

1. The Seizure Process 194

United States of America v. Argent Chemical Laboratories, Inc. 194

Notes 198

2. Pre-Condemnation Release 198

United States v. Undetermined Quantities of Drugs 198

Notes 201

3. Multiple Seizures 201

Ewing v. Mytinger & Casselberry, Inc. 202

Notes 204

4. Proof Required for Condemnation 204

United States v. 43 1/2 Gross Rubber Prophylactics Labeled in Part "Xcello's Prophylactics" 205

Notes 206

5. Final Condemnation Decrees and Salvaging 207

United States v. 1,638 Cases of Adulterated Alcoholic
        Beverages...207
    Notes 209
6. Effectiveness of Seizures 210
    Peter Barton Hutt, *Philosophy of Regulation Under the
        Federal Food, Drug and Cosmetic Act* 210
    Note..211
7. Administrative Detention..211
E. Injunctions...211
    1. Introduction..211
        Note..213
    2. Preliminary Injunctions...213
        United States v. Nutri-cology, Inc....................................213
    3. Permanent Injunctions 215
        United States v. Laerdal Manufacturing Corp. 215
        Note..218
        United States v. Articles of Drugs, et al., Midwest
            Pharmaceuticals, Inc...218
        Note..220
    4. Consent Decrees, Restitution, and Disgorgement 221
        Department of Justice Press Release 221
        William W. Vodra & Arthur N. Levine, *Anchors Away: The
            Food and Drug Administration's Use of Disgorgement
            Abandons Legal Moorings* 222
        United States v. Lane Labs–USA Inc. 225
        Notes 230
F. Recalls...230
    1. Voluntary Recalls...230
        Enforcement Policy, Practices and Procedures: Recall Policy
            and Procedures...231
        Notes 234
    2. Mandatory Recalls 235
        Note..237
G. Criminal Liability 237
    1. The Decision to Prosecute...237
        Sam D. Fine, *The Philosophy of Enforcement* 237
        Notes 238
    2. Standard of Liability...240
        a. Criminal Liability of Responsible Corporate Officials.........240
            United States v. Dotterweich 240
            United States v. Park...243
            Notes 248
        b. The Defense of Impossibility 250
    3. The Guaranty Clause...251
        Notes 251
H. Debarment and Exclusion 252
    1. Debarment..252
        Bae v. Shalala..253
        Notes 256

        2.   Exclusion...257
              Friedman v. Sebelius 257
              Note..261
I.   Civil Money Penalties..262
      Notes 263
J.   Informal Compliance Correspondence.......................................263
      FDA Regulatory Procedures Manual, Chapter 4
              ("Advisory Actions") 264
      Notes 266
K.   Publicity...268
      Hoxsey Cancer Clinic v. Folsom..268
      Notes 269

Chapter 5. FDA's Place in Our Federal System 271
A.   The Scope of Federal Power 271
        1.   Introduction...271
        2.   "Introduction Into Interstate Commerce".........................273
              United States v. 7 Barrels . . . Spray Dried Whole Egg.............273
              Notes 275
              United States v. Sanders...275
              Notes 276
        3.   "Held for Sale After Shipment in Interstate Commerce" 277
              Note..277
              United States v. Geborde...278
              Notes 280
        4.   Components Shipped in Interstate Commerce 282
              Baker v. United States..282
              Notes 284
        5.   Medical Devices...285
              United States v. Undetermined Quantities of an Article of
                      Device . . . "Depilatron Epilator" 285
              Note..286
        6.   Biologics..286
              United States v. Calise 287
              Notes 288
B.   The Elusive Goal of Uniformity of State Laws 289
      Melvin Hinich & Richard Staelin, Regulation of the U.S. Food
              Industry 291
C.   Federal Preemption and the Limits of State Power 292
        1.   Introduction...292
        2.   Historical Background 292
        3.   Field Preemption..294
              Hillsborough County v. Automated Medical Laboratories,
                      Inc...294
              Notes 298
        4.   Conflict Preemption 299
              a.   Obstacle Preemption 299
                    Florida Lime & Avocado Growers, Inc. v. Paul 299
                    Jones v. Rath Packing Co. 302

Notes 307
b. Impossibility Preemption 308
Grocery Manufacturers of America v. Gerace 308
Notes 310
5. Statutory Preemption 310
a. Medical Devices 311
Notes 312
b. Food Labeling 313
Notes 314
c. Nonprescription Drugs and Cosmetics 314
Notes 315
d. Tobacco Products 315

Chapter 6. Food 317
A. Subcategories of Food 317
1. Food Regulated Primarily by Agencies Other Than FDA 317
2. Dietary Supplements and Other FDA-Regulated Foods With
Special Requirements 319
Warning Letter From Michael W. Roosevelt, Acting Director,
CFSAN Office of Compliance, to Terry Harris, HBB,
LLC dba Baked World 320
Notes 321
Notes: Other Special Categories of Food 324
B. Historical Overview of FDA Regulation of Food Identity, Quality,
and Labeling 325
C. What's in a Name? Regulation of Food Identity and Quality 332
1. Food Standards of Identity 333
a. Strong Standards of Identity: The Filled Milk Act 334
Carolene Products Co. v. United States 334
Notes 336
Milnot Co. v. Richardson 337
Notes 338
b. The Formation and Zenith of the FD&C Act Food
Standards Regime 339
Federal Security Administrator v. Quaker Oats Co. 340
Notes 343
Richard A. Merrill & Earl M. Collier, *"Like Mother Used
to Make": An Analysis of FDA Food Standards of
Identity* 344
Notes 345
62 Cases of Jam v. U.S. 348
Notes 349
c. The Decline of Food Standards 350
i. "Safe and Suitable Ingredients" 350
ii. Redefinition of "Imitation" 351
iii. New Understanding of "Purports to Be" 352
iv. The Abandonment of Food Standards as a Primary
Vehicle for Fortification and Vitamin/Mineral
Supplement Policy 353

      d.   The Persistence of Food Standards 355

          Food Standards; General Principles and Food Standards

              Modernization 355

          Jerry Hirsch, *The Courage of Their Confections* 358

          Notes 359

  2.   The Modern Food-Naming Regime 362

      a.   Regulation of Common or Usual Food Names....................362

          Common or Usual Names for Nonstandardized Foods........363

          21 C.F.R. Part 102—Common or Usual Name for

              Nonstandardized Foods..363

          American Frozen Food Institute v. Mathews 365

          Notes 367

      b.   Redefinition of "Imitation"...369

          Imitation Foods, Application of Term "Imitation":

              Proposed Rulemaking 369

          Notes 370

          Federation of Homemakers v. Schmidt 371

          Notes 372

      c.   The Use of Nutrient Descriptors ("Nutrient Content

          Claims") in Food Names 372

          21 C.F.R. § 130.10. Requirements for Foods Named by

              Use of a Nutrient Content Claim and a Standardized

              Term......... 373

          Notes 375

  3.   Economic Adulteration 375

      United States v. 88 Cases . . . Bireley's Orange Beverage 376

      Notes 378

D. Regulation of Food Labeling..379

  1.   "False or Misleading in Any Particular"....................................379

      United States v. Ninety–Five Barrels of . . . Apple Cider

          Vinegar..380

      United States v. 432 Cartons . . . Candy Lollipops 381

      Notes 382

      United States v. Farinella 383

      Notes 386

  2.   Mandatory Information and Disclosures....................................389

      a.   Prominence and Conspicuousness 389

          21 C.F.R. Part 101—Food Labeling 389

      b.   Net Quantity of Contents...390

          Note 391

      c.   Ingredient Labeling...391

          Notes 392

          FDA Response to Petition From Corn Refiners

              Association to Authorize "Corn Sugar" as an

              Alternate Common or Usual Name for High

              Fructose Corn Syrup (HFCS)..394

          Notes 396

      d.   Allergen Disclosure 397

      e.   Mandatory Warning Statements..399

Food, Drug and Cosmetic Products, Warning Statements
(Final Rule) 400
Notes 401
f.   Nutrition Facts 403
Notes 404
g.   Mandatory Country of Origin Labeling 408
3.   Voluntary Claims 409
a.   Introduction 409
Lewis A. Grossman, *Food, Drugs, and Droods: A
Historical Consideration of Definitions and
Categories in American Food and Drug Law* 409
b.   Nutrient Content Claims 413
21 C.F.R. § 101.62 Nutrient Content Claims for Fat,
Fatty Acid, and Cholesterol 414
Notes 416
c.   Disease Prevention Claims ("Health Claims") 418
i.   Unqualified Health Claims 419
Food Labeling; General Requirements for Health
Claims for Food 420
Notes 423
Warning Letter from W. Charles Becoat, Director,
FDA Minneapolis District, to Ken Powell, CEO,
General Mills 426
Notes 428
ii.   The First Amendment and Qualified Health Claims ... 428
Pearson v. Shalala 430
Whitaker v. Thompson 433
Fleminger v. HHS 437
Notes 440
d.   Dietary Guidance Statements 441
Food Labeling: Health Claims; Dietary Guidance 441
Notes 442
e.   Structure/Function Claims 443
Regulations on Statements Made for Dietary Supplements
Concerning the Effect of the Product on the Structure
or Function of the Body 445
21 CFR 101.93. Certain Types of Statements for
Dietary Supplements 447
Notes 448
f.   Other Common Voluntary Food Claims 451
Notes 454
g.   FTC Regulation of Food Advertising 456
4.   Labeling of Genetically Modified Foods 458
Food and Drug Administration, Statement of Policy: Foods
Derived From New Plant Varieties 459
Alliance for Bio-Integrity v. Shalala 461
Note 463

Draft Guidance for Industry: Voluntary Labeling Indicating
Whether Foods Have or Have Not Been Developed Using
Bioengineering; Draft Guidance 463
International Dairy Foods Association v. Amestoy 466
Notes 469

E.   Food Sanitation and Aesthetic Adulteration 469
1.   "Filthy, Putrid, or Decomposed Substance" 470
United States v. 1,500 Cases More or Less,
Tomato Paste 471
Notes 473
Natural or Unavoidable Defects in Food for Human Use That
Present No Health Hazard: Public Availability of
Information 474
Notes 475
Melvin J. Hinich & Richard Staelin, *Regulation of the U.S.
Food Industry* 477
Notes 478
United States v. 1,200 Cans . . . Pasteurized Whole Eggs,
etc. 479
Note 481
2.   "Prepared Under Insanitary Conditions . . . Whereby it
May Have Become Contaminated With Filth" 482
Berger v. United States 482
Notes 485
3.   "Otherwise Unfit for Food" 486
United States v. 298 Cases . . . Ski Slide Brand
Asparagus 486
Notes 486

F.   The Presence of Poisonous or Deleterious Substances 489
1.   Introduction to FDA's Regulation of the Safety of Food
Constituents 489
2.   Nonadded Substances and the "Ordinarily Injurious"
Standard 492
United States v. 1232 Cases American Beauty Brand
Oysters 492
Notes 494
3.   Added Substances and the "May Render Injurious"
Standard 495
United States v. Lexington Mill & Elevator Co. 495
Notes 497
United States v. Anderson Seafoods, Inc. 498
Notes 500
Continental Seafoods v. Schweiker 502
Notes 505
4.   Tolerances and Action Levels for Unavoidable Poisonous or
Deleterious Substances 507
a.   Section 406 Tolerances 507
b.   Action Levels: Legal Basis and Procedure 509

Poisonous or Deleterious Substances in Food: Notice of
   Proposed Rulemaking 510
Note...512
Young v. Community Nutrition Institute............................512
Note...515
  c. Action Levels: The Example of Mercury...............................515
Action Level for Mercury in Fish and Shellfish: Notice of
   Proposed Rulemaking 516
Notes 517
  d. The Question of Blending 518
Aflatoxin–Contaminated Corn: Limited Exemption From
   Blending Prohibition 519
Notes 520
G. Regulation of Food Production and the Problem of Pathogenic
Microorganisms..521
  1. Introduction...521
Enhancing Food Safety: The Role of the Food and Drug
   Administration 524
Notes 525
  2. Good Manufacturing Process (GMP) Regulations 528
United States v. Nova Scotia Food Products Corp........................529
Notes 532
  3. Mandatory Pasteurization...533
Requirements Affecting Raw Milk for Human Consumption
   in Interstate Commerce: Final Rule 534
Notes 537
  4. Emergency Permit Control..539
Notes 540
  5. Hazard Analysis and Critical Control Points (HACCP).............540
Food and Drug Administration Development of Hazard
   Analysis Critical Control Points for the Food Industry:
   Advanced Notice of Proposed Rulemaking 541
Notes 546
Cary Coglianese & David Lazer, *Management–Based
   Regulation: Prescribing Private Management to Achieve
   Public Goals* 547
Notes 552
H. Intentional Functional Ingredients 552
  1. Introduction...552
Investigation of the Use of Chemicals in Foods and
   Cosmetics 553
Food Additives Amendment of 1958 554
Note...555
  2. Food Additive Approval 555
21 C.F.R. § 172.867   Olestra..557
Marion Nestle, *The Selling of Olestra* 558
Henry I. Miller, *Who Is Trying to Kill Olestra? and Why?* 561
Notes 562
Notes: Specific Additives 564

3.   The Meaning of "Food Additive" 566
United States v. An Article of Food . . . FoodScience Labs..........568
United States v. Two Plastic Drums . . . Black Currant Oil 570
Notes 571
National Nutritional Foods Ass'n v. Kennedy.............................572
Notes 573
4.   Generally Recognized as Safe (GRAS) Substances.....................574
a.   Procedures for Establishing GRAS Status 574
1.   FDA GRAS Lists..574
2.   Voluntary GRAS Notification 575
3.   Self-Determination of GRAS Status.......................576
Notes...576
b.   Substantive Criteria for GRAS Status................................577
United States v. An Article of Food . . . Coco Rico, Inc. 577
Note 579
General Recognition of Safety and Prior Sanctions for
Food Ingredients..579
Notes 580
Fmali Herb, Inc. v. Heckler 581
Note 583
Substances Generally Recognized as Safe: Proposed
Rule 583
Agency Response Letter GRAS Notice No. 000227, From
Laura M. Tarantino, Director, CFSAN Office of Food
Additive Safety to Donald L. Wilke, Procter
& Gamble 586
Note 587
Warning Letter from Joann M. Givens, Acting Director,
CFSAN Office of Compliance, to Jaisen Freeman
et al., Phusion Projects, LLC 588
Notes 590
5.   The GRAS Presumption for Genetically Modified Ingredients...592
FDA Statement of Policy: Foods Derived From New Plant
Varieties...592
Notes 596
Alliance for Bio-Integrity v. Shalala 596
Notes 597
6.   Prior Sanctioned Substances..599
Proposal Regarding Regulation of Prior–Sanctioned Food
Ingredients...599
Notes 600
7.   The Deterioration of the Food Additive Approval Process 603
Peter Barton Hutt, *Regulation of Food Additives in the
United States* 603
Note...607
8.   Food Packaging and Processing Substances 607
Natick Paperboard Corp. v. Weinberger.....................................608
Monsanto Co. v. Kennedy...610
Notes 614

9. Color Additive Regulation 617
  a. Historical Background 617
  b. The Color Additives Amendment 618
    Notes 619
    Kalsec, Inc., Citizen Petition Requesting FDA to Enforce
        Ban on Carbon Monoxide Gas in Fresh Meat
        Packaging.. 620
    Notes 624
    FD&C Yellow No. 5: Labeling in Food and Drugs for
        Human Use 625
    Notes 626
10. Dietary Ingredients in Dietary Supplements........................... 627
    Notes 628
    Nutraceutical Corporation v. Von Eschenbach 629
    Notes 633
11. Animal Drug Residues.. 633
12. Pesticide Residues... 634
    Notes 634
    Notes 637
13. Recent Safety Enhancements... 638
    Note... 639

Chapter 7. Human Drugs 641
A. Historical Background... 641
  1. Drug Regulation Before the 1938 FD&C Act 641
  2. Drug Regulation Under the 1938 FD&C Act 642
  3. Regulation of Drug Efficacy: History and Policy....................... 644
    American School of Magnetic Healing v. McAnnulty 645
    Research Laboratories, Inc. v. United States............................. 647
    Note... 649
    Rutherford v. United States 650
    Notes 652
    Abigail Alliance v. Von Eschenbach.. 654
B. The Definition of "New Drug" 660
  1. GRAS/GRAE Status.. 661
    Weinberger v. Hynson, Westcott & Dunning, Inc....................... 662
    Note... 665
  2. The "Grandfather" Clauses 666
  3. Jurisdiction to Determine New Drug Status 667
    Weinberger v. Bentex Pharmaceuticals, Inc. 667
    Notes 668
C. Drug Development and FDA Licensure of New Drugs 669
  1. Nonclinical Formulation and Testing 669
    a. Synthesis and Purification 669
      Preclinical Research: Synthesis and Purification 669
    b. Nonclinical Testing 670
      Preclinical Research 670
      Notes 671
    c. Good Laboratory Practices... 672

      d.   Request for Designation 672

          Note 673

2. Clinical Testing: Investigational New Drug

    Application (IND) 673

      a.   Purpose and Form of the IND 674

          Notes 674

      b.   Meetings With FDA 676

          Guidance for Industry: Formal Meetings With Sponsors

              and Applicants for PDUFA Products 677

          Notes 677

      c.   Phases of Clinical Testing 678

          i.   Phase Zero 678

              Guidance for Industry, Investigators, and

                  Reviewers: Exploratory IND Studies 678

          ii.   Phase I 680

              Phase I Clinical Studies 680

              Notes 680

          iii. Phase II 681

              Phase II Clinical Studies 681

          iv. Phase III 681

              Phase III Clinical Studies 681

              21 C.F.R. § 314.126 Adequate and Well-Controlled

                  Studies 682

              Notes 683

      d.   Institutional Review Board Approval and Human Subject

          Protection 686

          21 C.F.R. § 50.25 Elements of Informed Consent 687

          Notes 687

      e.   Protocol Amendments 690

      f.   The Clinical Hold 690

          Clinical Hold Decision 690

          Notes 691

      g.   Special Protocol Assessment 691

          Guidance for Industry: Special Protocol Assessment 692

          Notes 694

      h.   Clinical Endpoints, Surrogate Endpoints, and

          Biomarkers 694

          James Bilstad, M.D., Surrogate Endpoints 694

          Notes 696

      i.   Clinical Testing on Subpopulations 697

          i.   Children 697

              Notes 698

          ii.   The Elderly 699

          iii. Women 699

          iv. Ethnic and Racial Groups 700

              Note 700

      j.   GMP for Investigational Drugs 700

          Note 701

      k.   Data Monitoring Committee 701

Guidance for Clinical Trial Sponsors: Establishment and
Operation of Clinical Trial Data Monitoring
Committees 702
Notes 702
l. Clinical Testing Conducted Overseas 703
m. Investigator Fraud 704
n. Clinical Trials Databank (ClincialTrials.gov) 705
o. FDA/SEC Cooperation 706
FDA and SEC Work to Enhance Public's Protection From
False and Misleading Statements 706
Notes 707
3. The New Drug Application 707
Richard A. Merrill, *The Architecture of Government
Regulation of Medical Products* 707
a. Purpose and Form of the NDA 709
Peter Barton Hutt, *The Regulation of Drug Products
by the United States Food and Drug
Administration* 709
Notes 710
b. User Fees 712
FDA White Paper, Prescription Drug User Fee Act
(PDUFA): Adding Resources and Improving
Performance in FDA Review of New Drug
Applications 714
Steve Usdin, *Diminishing Returns* 717
c. Meetings With FDA 717
Booz Allen Hamilton, Inc., *Independent Evaluation of
FDA's First Cycle Review Performance—
Retrospective Analysis* 718
d. Refusal to File 720
e. The Safety Standard 720
Testimony of FDA Commissioner George Larrick 721
Note 722
Bernadine Healy, M.D., *What Is a 'Safe' Drug?* 722
Notes 723
f. The Effectiveness Standard 724
Notes 725
g. Balancing Benefit and Risk 729
Testimony of FDA Commissioner George Larrick 729
Notes 730
Thomas M. Burton, *Risk vs. Benefit: FDA Weighs
Antipsychotic* 731
Notes 732
h. Internal Agency Review Process 733
Notes 734
i. Advisory Committee Review 735
Peter Barton Hutt, *The Regulation of Drug Products by
the United States Food and Drug Administration* 735
Notes 735

      j.   Labeling Review 736

         House of Representatives 737

         Note 738

      k.   Final Approval or Denial 738

         Ubiotica Corp. v. FDA 739

         Notes 740

         Richard J. Crout, *The Nature of Regulatory Choices* 743

         Scott Gottlieb, M.D., *The Price of Too Much Caution* 744

   4.   The Effects of the NDA Requirement 744

      a.   The "Drug Lag" 744

         Statement of Sam Peltzman 745

         Notes 747

      b.   IND/NDA Statistics.. 747

         i.   Cost of an Approved NME Drug.................... 748

         ii.   Number of Approved NME NDAs 748

         iii.   Time Devoted to IND Testing and NDA Review 749

D. Variations and Exceptions to the Standard Drug Development,

Investigation, and Approval Process 751

   1.   Expedited Development of Lifesaving Drugs and Drugs for

     Serious Conditions 751

      a.   Fast Track.. 751

         i.   The FDA Regulations.................................... 751

           Investigational New Drug, Antibiotic, and Biological

           Drug Product Regulations: Procedures for Drugs

           Intended to Treat Life–Threatening and

           Severely Debilitating Illnesses 751

         ii.   The Congressional Statute............................. 752

           Note 753

      b.   Breakthrough Therapy 753

      c.   Accelerated Approval 754

         i.   The FDA Regulations.................................... 754

           (a) Approval Based on a Surrogate Endpoint.............. 754

              Ramzi Dagher et al., *Accelerated Approval of*

              Oncology Products: A Decade of Experience 754

           (b) Approval Conditioned on Restricted

              Distribution.. 755

              Notes.. 756

         ii.   The Congressional Statute............................. 756

      d.   Priority Review 756

         CDER Manual of Policies and Procedures 6020.3,

           Priority Review Policy 757

         Notes 758

   2.   Orphan Drugs... 758

     Genentech, Inc. v. Bowen 759

     Notes 761

     Marlene E. Haffner, *Adopting Orphan Drugs—Two Dozen*

       Years of Treating Rare Diseases 762

     Note 763

3. Use of Investigational Drugs for Therapy 763
    a. Introduction 763
    b. The Variety of Expanded Access Programs 765
        i.   Individual Patient IND or Protocol 765
        ii. Emergency Use IND or Protocol 765
             Notes 766
        iii. Treatment IND or Protocol 766
             Notes 767
        iv. Intermediate-Size Patient Population IND
             or Protocol 767
             Notes: Other Early Access Programs 768
    c. Charging for Expanded Access 771
    d. Importation of Investigational Drugs for Personal Use 771
        Coverage of Personal Importations 772
        Notes 773
4. Pre-1962 DESI Drugs 775
    Note 784
5. Non-DESI Unapproved New Drugs 784
    Notes 787
6. Special Categories of Drugs 788
    a. Radiopharmaceutical Drugs 788
        Syncor International Corporation v. Shalala 789
        Notes 791
    b. Insulin and Antibiotic Drugs 791
        Notes 792
    c. Medical Gas 793
7. The Practice of Pharmacy 793
    FDA's Oversight of NECC and Ameridose: A History of
        Missed Opportunities 794
    Compliance Policy Guides Section 460.200: Pharmacy
        Compounding 797
    Notes 798
8. NDA-Exempt Products 799
    a. Homeopathic Drugs 799
        Note 800
    b. Traditional Chinese Medicine 800
        Notes 801
    c. Specifically Excluded Products 801
E. Restrictions on Distribution and Prescribing 802
    1. Limitation to Prescription Sale 802
        a. Legal Basis 802
            Peter Temin, *The Origin of Compulsory Drug
            Prescriptions* 802
            United States v. El–O–Pathic Pharmacy 804
            Note 805
            Notes 805
        b. Authority to Prescribe and the Requirement of a Valid
            Prescription 807
            Notes 810

2.   Prescription Drug Controlled Substances 810
     Notes 811
3.   The (Non–)Regulation of the Practice of Medicine 814
     a.   Off-Label Prescribing Practices...814
          Notes 815
     b.   FDA Authority Over Off-Label Prescribing.........................815
          New Drugs Used for Nonapproved Purposes
               (Methotrexate for Psoriasis) 816
          Legal Status of Approved Labeling for Prescription
               Drugs; Prescribing for Uses Unapproved by the
               Food and Drug Administration: Notice of Proposed
               Rule Making..817
          Notes 819
          United States v. Evers 822
4.   Controls Over Prescription Drug Distribution............................825
     a.   Pre-2007 825
          American Pharmaceutical Association v. Weinberger.........825
          Notes 827
     b.   Risk Evaluation and Mitigation Strategies (REMS)............829
          Risk Evaluation and Mitigation Strategy (REM) for
               NDA 21–775 Entereg (alvimopan) 830
          Note 832
          Speech by Scott Gottlieb, M.D., Before the American
               Medical Association..832
          Note 834
F.   Postapproval Issues 834
1.   Postapproval Submissions to FDA...834
     a.   Drug Establishment Registration and Drug Product
          Listing 834
     b.   Supplemental NDAs (SNDAs)..835
          i.   Labeling Changes 835
          ii.   Manufacturing Changes...835
     c.   Adverse Event Reporting..836
          Notes 836
2.   Postapproval Testing Commitments...837
3.   Current Good Manufacturing Practice (CGMP) 838
     a.   Background..839
          United States v. An Article of Drug . . . White
               Quadrisect...839
          Human and Veterinary Drugs: Current Good
               Manufacturing Practice in Manufacture, Processing,
               Packing, or Holding...840
          Notes 842
     b.   CGMP Enforcement 843
          United States v. Barr Laboratories, Inc. 843
          Notes 845
     c.   CGMP Modernization 846
          Pharmaceutical CGMPs for the 21st Century:
               A Risk–Based Approach...846

Note 847
    4.   Withdrawal of NDA Approval and Voluntary Withdrawal
        From the Market 848
        a.   Involuntary Withdrawal of NDA 848
              Weinberger v. Hynson, Westcott & Dunning, Inc. 848
              Notes 851
        b.   Voluntary Withdrawal From Market 851
              Statement of Sandra L. Kweder, Deputy Director,
                  CDER Office of New Drugs 852
              Notes 853
        c.   Summary Ban of an "Imminent Hazard" Drug 855
              Forsham v. Califano 855
              Notes 858
G.   Physician Labeling and Patient Labeling of Prescription Drugs 860
    1.   Physician Labeling (Prescribing Information) 860
        a.   Content 860
              Notes 862
        b.   Drug Names 864
              Administered Prices—Drugs 864
              Notes 865
        c.   Warnings 866
              Bradley v. Weinberger 867
              Notes 869
              Labeling: Failure to Reveal Material Facts 870
              Notes 871
        d.   Revisions to Warnings Based on Postmarket Safety
              Information 874
    2.   Patient Labeling for Prescription Drugs 876
        a.   Introduction 876
        b.   The Introduction of Mandatory Patient Labeling: Patient
              Package Inserts (PPIs) 877
              Statement of Policy Concerning Oral Contraceptive
                  Labeling Directed to Users 877
              Notes 879
              Pharmaceutical Manufacturers Association v. FDA 880
              Note 882
        c.   The Rise of Voluntary Patient Labeling 883
              Prescription Drug Products: Patient Labeling
                  Requirements 883
              Prescription Drug Products: Revocation of Patient
                  Package Insert Requirements 884
              Notes 886
        d.   Mandatory Patient Medication Guides 886
              Notes 887
    3.   FDA Regulation of Prescription Drug Labeling and "Failure
        to Warn" Tort Suits 888
        a.   The Learned Intermediary Doctrine and Exceptions 888
              MacDonald v. Ortho Pharmaceutical Corporation 889
              Notes 893

       b.   Federal Preemption of Private Tort Suits 894
             Wyeth v. Levine..894
             PLIVA, Inc. v. Mensing...901
             Notes 906

H.   Advertising and Promotion of Prescription Drugs............................907
   1.   Introduction...907
   2.   Print Advertising to Professionals 908
       21 C.F.R. § 202.1 Prescription-Drug Advertisements................908
       Notes 910
   3.   Other Forms of Promotion to Professionals 911
       a.   FDA's Legal Authority..912
       b.   Controversies Regarding the Content of Drug
             Promotion..912
             Note 913
       c.   Material Inducements to Physicians.......................................913
             1.   Statutory Responses...914
             2.   Organizational Responses...914
   4.   Direct to Consumer Advertising...915
       a.   Print Advertising to Consumers..915
             Direct-to-Consumer Advertising of Prescription Drugs;
                Withdrawal of Moratorium 915
             Notes 916
       b.   Broadcast Advertising...916
             Draft Guidance for Industry: Consumer-Directed
                Broadcast Advertisements 917
             Guidance for Industry: Consumer–Directed Broadcast
                Advertisements..918
             Notes 919
             Warning Letter From Thomas Abrams, Dir., DDMAC to
                Reinhard Franzen, Pres. & CEO, Bayer HealthCare
                Pharmaceuticals, Inc..920
       c.   General Issues Surrounding DTC Advertising 923
             Keeping Watch Over Direct-to-Consumer Ads 923
             Notes 924

I.   Regulating Off-Label Promotion 925
   1.   Introduction...925
   2.   The Legal Bases for Prohibiting Off-Label Promotion Under
       the FD&C Act 926
       a.   Off-Label Promotion in Labeling..926
       b.   Off-Label Promotion in Advertising......................................927
       c.   Off-Label Promotion Through Oral Statements and
             FDA's "Squeeze Play"...927
             i.   The "Squeeze Play" in the OTC Context......................928
                  United States v. Articles of Drug . . . Foods
                     Plus, Inc...928
                  Notes...930
             ii.   The "Squeeze Play" in the Prescription Context 932
                  Memorandum of Law in Support of Motion for
                     Preliminary Injunction...932

          d.   The Government's Use of Other Statutes to Enforce the
               Prohibition Against Off-Label Promotion 934
               United States ex. rel. Franklin v. Parke–Davis 934
               Notes 937
       3.   Permissible Off-Label Communications by Drug
          Manufacturers 939
          a.   Responses to Unsolicited Requests for Information 939
               Draft Guidance for Industry: Responding to Unsolicited
                 Requests for Off-Label Information About
                 Prescription Drugs and Medical Devices (2011) 939
               Note 942
          b.   Manufacturer-Initiated Distribution of Scientific
               Information 942
               Washington Legal Foundation v. Henney 943
               Final Amended Order Granting Summary Judgment
                 and Permanent Injunction 946
               Notes 947
               Guidance for Industry: God Reprint Practices for the
                 Distribution of Medical Journal Articles and Medical
                 or Scientific Reference Publications on Unapproved
                 New Uses of Approved Drugs and Approved or
                 Cleared Medical Devices 948
          c.   Other Speech About Unapproved Uses Protected by the
               First Amendment 951
               United States v. Caronia 951
       4.   Preapproval Promotion 957
   J. Over-the-Counter Drugs 957
       1.   Distinguishing Between Prescription and Nonprescription
          Drugs 957
          United States v. Article of Drug . . . "Decholin" 958
          Note 960
       2.   Switch From Prescription to Nonprescription Status 960
          Peter Barton Hutt, *A Legal Framework for Future Decisions
               on Transferring Drugs From Prescription to
               Nonprescription Status* 961
          Notes 964
          Tummino v. Hamburg 966
          Notes 972
       3.   The OTC Drug Review 973
          a.   Rationale and Procedures of the Review 973
               Over-the-Counter Drugs: Proposal Establishing Rule
                 Making Procedures for Classification 973
               Over-the-Counter Human Drugs Which Are Generally
                 Recognized as Safe and Effective and Not
                 Misbranded 975
               Notes 977
          b.   Completion of the OTC Drug Review 979
               Note 980
          c.   Final Monographs 980

Topical Acne Drug Products 980
Notes 982
    d.   Inactive Ingredients 984
4.   OTC Drug Labeling..985
    a.   OTC Drug Review Restrictions 985
Labeling of Drug Products for Over-the-Counter
Human Use..985
Note 986
    b.   OTC "Drug Facts" Format 987
Over-the-Counter Human Drugs; Proposed Labeling
Requirements...987
    c.   OTC Drug Label Warnings.................................989
Notes 989
5.   FTC Regulation of OTC Drug Advertising 990
Notes 991
6.   OTC Drug Product Packaging..993
Tamper-Resistant Packaging Requirements for Certain
Over-the-Counter Human Drug and Cosmetic Products.....993
Notes 995
K.   Generic Drugs 996
1.   FDA and Generic Drugs Before Hatch-Waxman (1984)......996
Hoffman–LaRoche, Inc. v. Weinberger 997
United States v. Generix Drug Corp. 999
Notes 999
2.   The Drug Price Competition and Patent Term
Restoration Act of 1984 (Hatch–Waxman) 1000
    a.   The Hatch–Waxman Scheme.................................1000
Peter Barton Hutt, *Landmark Pharmaceutical
Law Enacted* 1001
Notes...1004
    b.   The Orange Book 1006
Note 1007
    c.   The ANDA and "Bioequivalence" 1007
Notes...1009
    d.   Section 505(b)(2) NDAs.......................................1012
Notes...1012
    e.   Hatch-Waxman, Drug Prices, and Industry Profits...1013
    f.   Patent Infringement Litigation Under
Hatch Waxman 1014
        i.   The Commencement of Litigation and the
30-Month Stay 1014
Notes...1015
        ii.   180-Day First-Filer Generic Exclusivity and
"Pay-to-Delay"...1016
FTC v. Actavis, Inc. 1016
Notes...1023
L.   The Cost of Drugs 1023
1.   Introduction..1023
Malcolm Gladwell, *High Prices* 1024

Notes 1026
2. Importation of Cheaper Drugs 1026
3. Promotion of the Use of Generics.......................... 1027
M. Counterfeit, Imitation, Street Alternative, and Diverted
Prescription Drugs.. 1028
1. Counterfeit Drugs 1028
Prescription Drug Marketing Act Pedigree Requirements;
Effective Date and Compliance Policy Guide; Request
for Comment 1029
Notes 1030
2. Diverted Drug Samples 1031
Notes 1032
3. Internet Pharmacy... 1032
Jody Feder, *Legal Issues Related to Prescription Drug
Sales on the Internet*.. 1033
Notes 1034
4. Imitation Drugs and Street Drug Alternatives.......... 1034
N. Present and Future Challenges 1035
1. Restoring Innovation 1035
"The FDA and the Next Generation of Drug Development" 1036
2. Genetics, Genomics, and Personalized Medicine 1039
Larry J. Lesko & Janet Woodcock, *Pharmacogenomic–
Guided Drug Development: Regulatory Perspective* 1039
Notes 1042
3. Drug Shortages 1043
Executive Order 13588—Reducing Prescription Drug
Shortages 1043
Note 1044

Chapter 8. Food and Drugs for Animals..1045
A. Introduction... 1045
Notes 1045
B. Animal Food and Feed... 1045
Notes 1046
1. Pet Food 1047
Indictment in United States v. Sally Miller, Stephen S.
Miller, and ChemNutra, Inc. 1047
Note 1051
2. Livestock Feed and the Mad Cow Disease Crisis 1051
Substances Prohibited From Use in Animal Food or Feed 1052
Notes 1058
C. Animal Drugs 1059
1. New Animal Drug Approval 1059
Animal Drug Amendments... 1060
Eugene I. Lambert, *The Reformation of Animal Drug Law:
The Impact of 1996*.. 1061
Notes 1064
2. The Effectiveness Standard.. 1066
3. The Safety Standard 1067

Notes 1068
4. Prescription Status and Veterinary Feed Directives.................1069
    Note...1071
5. Extralabel Use of Animal Drugs and Use of Human Drugs
    in Animals..1071
    United States v. Scenic View Dairy, L.L.C...............................1073
    Notes 1079
6. The Safety of Antibiotics Used in Livestock Production 1081
    Harold C. Hopkins, *Keeping the Kick in Antibiotics* 1081
    Antibiotic and Sulfonamide Drugs in the Feed of Animals.......1082
    Natural Resources Defense Council, Inc. v. Food and Drug
        Administration 1084
    Guidance for Industry: The Judicious Use of Medically
        Important Antimicrobial Drugs in Food–Producing
        Animals..1092
    Notes 1094
    Natural Resources Defense Council v. Food and Drug
        Administration 1095
    Note...1097
    Withdrawal of Approval of the New Animal Drug Application
        for Enrofloxacin in Poultry: Final Decision of the
        Commissioner 1098
7. Bioengineered Animals..1105
    Guidance for Industry: Regulation of Genetically Engineered
        Animals Containing Heritable Recombinant DNA
        Constructs..1105
    Notes 1112
8. Animal Drug Compounding..1112
    United States v. Franck's Lab, Inc..1112

**Chapter 9. Biological Products: Vaccines, Blood, Tissue
Transplants, and Cellular Therapies.. 1123**
A. Historical Background...1123
B. FDA Acquires Responsibility for Biologics 1124
    Notes 1127
C. FDA Regulation of Therapeutic Biologics 1127
    1. The Biologics Review 1127
        Biological Products: Procedures for Review of Safety,
            Effectiveness, and Labeling..1127
        Biological Products: Bacterial Vaccines and Toxoids;
            Implementation of Efficacy Review..................................1128
        Note...1130
    2. FDA Approval of New Biologics 1130
        Reinventing Regulation of Drugs Made From
            Biotechnology..1131
        Elimination of Establishment License Application for
            Specified Biotechnology and Specified Synthetic
            Biological Products 1132

Biological Products Regulated Under Section 351 of the Public
Health Service Act; Implementation of Biologics License;
Elimination of Establishment License and Product
License 1133
Note.. 1134
3.   FDA Review of BLAs 1135
4.   Biosimilar Biological Products 1135
5.   User Fees 1137
D.   Regulating and Promoting Vaccines.. 1137
Edward Mortimer, *Immunization Against Infectious Disease*.......... 1137
1.   Government Support for Immunization 1138
Frank A. Sloan, et al., *The Fragility of the U.S. Vaccine
Supply* 1139
Institute of Medicine, Financing Vaccines in the 21st
Century: Assuring Access and Availability 1140
2.   Manufacturer Liability for Vaccine Injuries 1141
Reyes v. Wyeth Laboratories....................................... 1141
Note.. 1145
3.   Government Liability for Vaccine Injuries...................... 1145
Berkovitz v. United States 1146
Notes 1148
4.   Compensating Vaccine Injuries 1149
Michael Greenberger, *The 800 Pound Gorilla Sleeps: The
Federal Government's Lackadaisical Liability and
Compensation Policies in the Context of Pre-Event
Vaccine Immunization Programs*...................................... 1149
Note.. 1153
E.   Blood and Blood Products.. 1153
1.   Regulatory Jurisdiction 1153
2.   The Regulatory Mechanism.. 1154
United States General Accounting Office, Blood Supply:
FDA Oversight and Remaining Issues of Safety................ 1155
3.   Protecting the Safety of the Blood Supply...................... 1157
Blood Donor Classification Statement, Paid or Volunteer
Donor.. 1158
R.F. and R.F. v. Abbott Laboratories............................. 1159
Snyder v. American Association of Blood Banks 1162
Notes 1164
F.   Human Tissues and Cells... 1165
1.   Whole Organs 1165
Statement by the Food and Drug Administration Concerning
Its Legal Authority to Regulate Human Organ
Transplants and to Prohibit Their Sale............................. 1165
Notes 1167
2.   FDA's Regulation of Tissues and Cells............................ 1167
a.   Introduction 1167
Richard A. Merrill, *Human Tissues and Reproductive
Cloning: New Technologies Challenge FDA*................ 1169

      b.   Distinguishing Between "Section 361 HCT/Ps" and
           HCT/Ps Regulated as Biological Drugs or Devices 1172
           Notes 1173
      c.   Section 361 Regulation of HCT/Ps 1174
           Current Good Tissue Practice for Human Cell, Tissue,
              and Cellular and Tissue–Based Product
              Establishments; Inspection and Enforcement............1174
           Note 1175
G.   Other Cellular Technologies..1175
    1.   Gene Therapy 1176
        Joseph M. Rainsbury, *Biotechnology on the RAC:*
           FDA/NIH Regulation of Human Gene Therapy.........1176
    2.   Stem Cells 1178
        Stem Cells and the Future of Regenerative Medicine 1178
        United States v. Regenerative Sciences, LLC 1179
        Notes 1184
    3.   Assisted Reproduction...1185
        Lars Noah, *Assisted Reproductive Technologies and the*
           Pitfalls of Unregulated Biomedical Innovation 1185
    4.   Reproductive Cloning..1186
        Richard A. Merrill, *Human Tissues and Reproductive*
           Cloning: New Technologies Challenge FDA...............1186
        FDA's Jurisdiction Over Human Cloning Activities.........1187
    5.   Xenotransplantation 1189
        Jodi K. Frederickson, *He's All Heart . . . and a Little Pig*
           Too: A Look at the FDA Draft Xenotransplant
           Guideline 1190
        Notes 1192

Chapter 10. Medical Devices **1193**
A.   Historical Background...1193
    Wallace F. Janssen, *The Gadgeteers*......................................1193
    Note..1194
B.   Regulation of Devices Under the FD&C Act before 1976.................1194
    1.   Background..1195
        Medical Device Legislation—1975 1195
    2.   Diapulse Litigation 1195
    3.   Scientology's E-Meter 1196
        Founding Church of Scientology v. United States 1197
        Notes 1199
    4.   The Drug–Device Distinction Before 1976 1200
C.   Introduction to the Modern Device Regulatory Regime....................1202
    1.   Background to the 1976 Medical Device Amendments 1202
        Medical Device Amendments of 1976 1202
        Study Group on Medical Devices, Medical Devices:
           A Legislative Plan 1203
        Notes 1203
    2.   Overview of the Modern Regime 1204
D.   The Definition of "Device" Since 1976 1205

1. The Line Between a "Drug" and a "Device" 1205
2. Drug–Device Combinations 1206
    Prevor v. Food and Drug Administration 1207
3. Diagnostic Devices 1211
E. Classification of Devices into Class I, Class II, and Class III 1212
1. Procedure 1212
    Medical Devices: Classification Procedures 1212
2. The Classification Regulations 1213
    21 C.F.R. Part 872—Dental Devices 1214
    Note 1215
F. Changeover Issues: The 1976 Medical Device Amendments and
    the Regulation of Preamendments Devices 1215
1. Equitable Treatment of Old and New Devices 1215
2. The Still-Unfinished Implementation of the 1976
    Amendments With Respect to Preamendments Class III
    Devices 1216
3. "Transitional" Devices Previously Regulated as Drugs 1217
G. Regulation of Market Entry 1218
1. Introduction 1218
    Jonathan S. Kahan, *Premarket Approval Versus Premarket
    Notification: Different Routes to the Same Market* 1219
    Notes 1220
2. The 510(k) Review Process and "Substantial Equivalence" 1221
    a. Background 1221
    b. Meaning of "Substantial Equivalence" 1222
    c. "Piggybacking" 1223
    d. Exemptions From the PMN Requirement 1223
    e. Revoking a 510(k) Clearance 1223
        Ivy Sports Medicine, LLC v. Sebelius 1224
        Notes 1227
    f. 510(k) and Reprocessed Single-Use Devices 1229
3. Investigational Devices 1230
    a. General Requirements 1230
    b. Feasibility Studies 1231
    c. "Research Use Only" Exemption for Diagnostic Devices ... 1232
        Notes 1232
    d. Emergency Investigational Use 1233
        Cristine Russell, *Temporary Heart Implanted:
        Tucson Operation Lacked FDA Approval* 1233
        Information Sheet Guidance For IRBs, Clinical
            Investigators, and Sponsors, Frequently Asked
            Questions About Medical Devices (2006) 1235
4. Premarket Approval Applications 1236
    a. Comparison of PMAs and NDAs 1236
        Note 1238
    b. Advisory Committee Review 1238
    c. FDA Action on PMAs 1239
        Notes 1239
    d. Efforts to Quicken the PMA Review Process 1241

Notes 1242
e. Postapproval Requirements..................................1243
5. Regulation of In Vitro Diagnostic Devices...............................1243
6. Humanitarian Device Exemptions...............................1245
Note 1246
7. Custom Devices 1246
8. Reclassification and *De Novo* Classification of Novel Device....1247
Lake v. FDA..1249
Notes 1251
H. Special Controls for Class II Devices.................................1251
1. Performance Standards 1251
a. Introduction 1251
b. Voluntary Medical Device Standards 1252
2. Other Special Controls...1254
I. General Controls Applicable to All Devices 1254
1. Traditional Adulteration and Misbranding..................1254
United States v. An Article . . . Acu–Dot...........................1255
Medical Devices; Labeling for Menstrual Tampons; Ranges
of Absorbency; Reproposed Rule...........................1258
Note...1259
2. Establishment Registration and Product Listing 1259
3. Adverse Event Reporting..1260
4. Good Manufacturing Practice/Quality System.........................1261
Medical Devices; Current Good Manufacturing Practice
(CGMP) Regulations; Proposed Revisions; Request for
Comments 1262
Notes 1263
5. Restricted Devices 1264
a. Introduction 1264
b. Hearing Aids..1265
American Speech and Hearing Ass'n v. Califano...............1266
c. In Vitro Diagnostic Devices 1267
d. Cigarettes..1268
Coyne Beahm, Inc. v. United States Food & Drug
Administration.. 1269
Notes... 1270
6. Banned Devices 1271
7. Administrative Detention..1271
8. Notification and Repair, Replacement, or Refund 1271
In re Procter & Gamble Co.: Consent Agreement....................1272
Notes 1273
9. Postmarket Surveillance 1274
10. Device Tracking..1274
11. Mandatory Recalls 1275
12. Reports of Removals and Corrections 1276
13. Civil Penalties 1276
J. Mobile Medical Devices 1277
Guidance for Industry and FDA Staff: Mobile Medical
Applications 1277

K.   Preemption of State Law by the Medical Device Amendments
        of 1976...1280
    Exemptions From Federal Preemption of State and Local Device
        Requirements 1281
    Notes..1282
    Medtronic, Inc. v. Lohr 1283
    Notes..1289
    Riegel v. Medtronic, Inc..1290
L.   Radiation Control...1292
    1.   Performance Standards 1293
        Electronic Products; Performance Standard for Diagnostic
            X–Ray Systems and Their Major Components;
            Final Rule 1294
        Notes 1295
        Sunlamp Products; Performance Standard....................1296
        Notes 1297
    2.   Enforcement of Radiation Standards 1298
    3.   Collection and Dissemination of Information 1299
    4.   Other Federal Radiation Control Programs....................1300

Chapter 11. Cosmetics..1301
A.   Historical and Statutory Background 1301
    Peter Barton Hutt, *A History of Government Regulation of
        Adulteration and Misbranding of Cosmetics*...........................1301
    Senate Report No. 361 1302
    Notes..1303
    George P. Larrick, *Some Current Problems in the Regulation of
        Cosmetics Under the Federal Food, Drug, and Cosmetic Act* 1303
    Investigation of the Use of Chemicals in Foods and Cosmetics........1304
    S. L. Mayham, *Chemicals in Cosmetics*..................................1306
    U.S. General Accounting Office, Lack of Authority Hampers
        Attempts to Increase Cosmetic Safety 1307
    Statement of the Cosmetic, Toiletry and Fragrance
        Association, Inc. 1309
    Notes..1310
B.   Definition of "Cosmetic"..1311
C.   Adulterated Cosmetics 1311
    United States v. An Article of Cosmetic . . . "Beacon Castile
        Shampoo" 1311
    Notes..1314
    Aerosol Drug and Cosmetic Products Containing Zirconium 1317
    Notes..1318
    Nitrosamine-Contaminated Cosmetics; Call for Industry Action;
        Request for Data 1319
    Notes..1320
D.   Coal-Tar Hair Dyes..1322
    Toilet Goods Association v. Finch 1322
    Notes..1324
E.   Misbranded Cosmetics..1325

    1.   Label Warnings 1325
        Preservation of Cosmetics Coming in Contact With the Eye:
           Intent to Propose Regulations and Request for
           Information 1325
           Notes 1326
        Food, Drug, and Cosmetic Products: Warning Statements 1326
           Notes 1329
    2.   Misleading Labeling..1330
        Almay, Inc. v. Califano..1330
        Note..1332
        Peter Barton Hutt, *The Legal Distinction in the United States Between a Cosmetic and a Drug* 1332
           Notes 1334
F. Cosmetic Ingredient Labeling..1335
    21 C.F.R. § 701.3 Designation of Ingredients..1336
    Notes 1337
G. Voluntary "Regulation" of Cosmetics..1338
    Voluntary Registration of Cosmetic Product Establishments; Voluntary Filing of Cosmetic Product Ingredient and Cosmetic Raw Material Composition Statements 1339
    Voluntary Filing of Cosmetic Product Experiences.....................1339
    Notes 1341
    Robert L. Elder, *The Cosmetic Ingredient Review—A Safety Evaluation Program*..1342
    Statement of Robert L. Elder, SC.D. 1343
    Wilma F. Bergfeld et al., *Safety of Ingredients Used in Cosmetics* 1344
    Letter From Ronald G. Chesemore, Associate Commissioner for Regulatory Affairs, FDA, to Consumer Federation of America..1345
    Note..1346
    Letter From Robert E. Brackett, Director, FDA Center for Food Safety and Applied Nutrition, to CTFA..1346
    Notes 1347
H. The Present and Future of Cosmetics Regulation 1348
    Peter Barton Hutt, "*Examining the Current State of Cosmetics*"..1348

Chapter 12. Tobacco Products 1351
A. Introduction..1351
B. Tobacco Product Review 1353
    1.   Substantial Equivalence Reports..1353
        Guidance for Industry and FDA Staff; Section 905(j) Reports: Demonstrating Substantial Equivalence for Tobacco Products 1354
           Notes 1355
    2.   Exemption From Demonstration of Substantial Equivalence 1356
    3.   Premarket Tobacco Product Application (PMTA)..................1356

Draft Guidance for Industry Applications for Premarket
Review of New Tobacco Products 1356
Note 1358
4. Modified Risk Tobacco Product Application (MRTPA) 1358
a. Definition of Modified Risk Tobacco Product 1358
Letter From Lawrence R. Deyton, Dir., Center for
Tobacco Products, to Tobacco Manufacturers on
Tobacco Products Labeled or Advertised With the
Descriptors "Light," "Low," "Mild," or Similar
Descriptors 1359
Note 1360
b. Standards for Approval of an MRTPA 1360
Scientific Standards for Studies on Modified Risk
Tobacco Products 1360
C. Tobacco Product Standards 1362
Notes 1363
D. Tobacco Product Labeling and Advertising 1363
Discount Tobacco City & Lottery, Inc. v. United States 1364
Notes 1367
R.J. Reynolds Tobacco Co. v. Food & Drug Administration 1368

Chapter 13. Regulation of Carcinogens 1373
A. Historical Background 1373
B. Early FDA Policy 1374
Arnold Lehman et al., *Procedures for the Appraisal of the Toxicity
of Chemicals in Foods* 1374
C. Evolution of Legislative Policy 1375
1. The Incidence and Causes of Cancer 1375
2. The Original Delaney Clause 1376
3. The Color Additives Delaney Clause 1379
D. Regulation of Diethylstilbestrol 1382
Diethylstilbestrol: Withdrawal of Approval of New Animal Drug
Application 1385
Notes 1386
E. FDA Embraces Quantitative Risk Assessment 1387
1. Applied to Animal Drugs (the "DES Proviso") 1388
Chemical Compounds in Food-Producing Animals: Criteria
and Procedures for Evaluating Assays for Carcinogenic
Residues 1388
Notes 1391
Sponsored Compounds in Food–Producing Animals; Criteria
and Procedures for Evaluating the Safety of
Carcinogenic Residues 1392
Notes 1393
2. Applied to Contaminants of Food 1395
Aflatoxins in Shelled Peanuts and Peanut Products Used as
Human Foods: Proposed Tolerance 1395
Notes 1396
3. Applied to "Constituents" of Additives 1397

　　　　Policy for Regulating Carcinogenic Chemicals in Food and
　　　　　　Color Additives: Advance Notice of Proposed
　　　　　　Rulemaking...1398
　　　　Scott v. Food and Drug Administration.....................................1401
　　　　Notes 1402
　　4.　Applied to Additives "Straight Up".......................................1402
　　　　a.　Artificial Sweeteners...1402
　　　　　　Notes 1404
　　　　b.　Color Additive (Lead Acetate) in Hair Dye...........................1405
　　　　　　Lead Acetate; Listing as a Color Additive in Cosmetics
　　　　　　　That Color the Hair on the Scalp 1405
　　　　　　Note 1407
　　　　c.　Color Additive (Orange No. 17) in Externally Applied
　　　　　　Drugs and Cosmetics...1407
　　　　　　Listing of D&C Orange No. 17 for Use in Externally
　　　　　　　Applied Drugs and Cosmetics...1407
　　　　　　Correction of Listing of D&C Orange No. 17 for Use in
　　　　　　　Externally Applied Drugs and Cosmetics................1410
　　　　　　Public Citizen v. Young..1410
　　　　　　Notes 1414
　　5.　Applied to Natural Foods...1416
F.　Deciding Whether an Additive "Induces Cancer" 1417
　　1.　Carcinogenicity Thresholds 1417
　　　　Selenium in Animal Feed; Proposed Food Additive
　　　　　Regulation..1417
　　　　Notes 1419
　　2.　FDA Scientific Assessment..1420
　　　　Notes 1424
G.　Resolving the "Delaney Paradox"...1425
　　Les v. Reilly 1426
　　James Smart, *All the Stars in the Heavens Were in the Right
　　　Places: The Passage of the Food Quality Protection Act of
　　　1996*..1428
　　Allison D. Carpenter, *Impact of the Food Quality Protection Act
　　　of 1996*...1429
　　Note...1430
H.　Other Efforts to Identify or Regulate Carcinogens..........................1431
　　1.　IARC and NTP 1431
　　2.　Agency Cancer Guidelines..1432
　　3.　Government-Wide Policies 1434
I.　Issues 1435
　　Peter Barton Hutt, *Food and Drug Law: A Strong and
　　　Continuing Tradition*...1435
　　Notes 1436

Chapter 14. Regulation of Foreign Commerce 1439
A.　Importation Into the United States...1439
　　1.　FDA's General Authority Over Importation 1439
　　　　Sugarman v. Forbragd...1439

Notes 1440
Cook v. FDA 1441
Notes 1447
2. Reconditioning, Destroying, or Reexporting Goods Refused
   Admission 1447
   Carl Borchsenius Co. v. Gardner 1448
3. Refusal of Admission Compared to Seizure 1450
   United States v. Food, 2,998 Cases 1451
   Notes 1454
4. Importation of Food 1455
   Notes 1457
5. Importation of Prescription Drugs and Devices 1458
   a. Commercial Importation 1458
      Warning Letter From David J. Horowitz, Dir., CDER
         Office of Compliance, to Harry Lee Jones, Store
         Manager, Rx Depot, Inc. 1458
      United States of America v. Rx Depot, Inc. 1460
      Notes 1463
   b. Importation for Personal Use 1464
   c. Importation Pursuant to Waiver 1464
      State of Vermont v. Leavitt 1465
      Notes 1467
B. Exportation From the United States 1468
   1. Exportation Pursuant to FD&C Act § 801(e)(1) 1468
      a. General 1468
         United States v. An Article . . . Enriched Rice 1468
         United States v. Kanasco, Ltd. 1469
         Compliance Policy Guide Sec. 587.200: Uncertified or
            Delisted Colors in Food for Export—
            (e.g., FD&C Red #2) 1471
         Notes 1472
      b. Exportation of Unapproved New Drugs and Unlicensed
         Biologics 1472
         United States v. An Article of Drug . . . Ethionamide–
            INH 1473
         Notes 1474
      c. Exportation of Unapproved New Animal Drugs 1474
      d. Exportation of Unapproved Medical Devices 1475
   2. Exportation of Unapproved Medical Products Pursuant to
      FD&C Act § 802 1476
      Guidance for Industry: Exports Under the FDA Export
         Reform and Enhancement Act of 1996 1476
      Notes 1481
   3. International Trade Agreements 1482
C. Import for Export 1483
   FDA Regulatory Procedures Manual, Chapter 9–15: Import for
      Export 1483

Chapter 15. Other Agency Procedures **1487**
A.   Regularizing Agency Procedures 1487
B.   Advisory Committees..1488
     1.   FDA's Reliance on Advisory Committees 1488
          Food and Drug Administration Advisory Committees 1488
          Notes 1490
     2.   Statutory Requirements for Advisory Committees....................1491
          Consumers Union of United States, Inc. v. Department of
               HEW 1491
          National Nutritional Foods Ass'n v. Califano 1494
          Notes 1496
          Public Citizen v. National Advisory Committee 1498
          Robert Steinbrook, M.D., *Financial Conflicts of Interest and
               the Food and Drug Administration's Advisory
               Committees*..1501
          Notes 1503
C.   Public Information 1503
     1.   The Freedom of Information Act (FOIA) 1503
          Peter Barton Hutt, *Public Information and Public
               Participation in the Food and Drug Administration* 1504
          Notes 1505
          Pharmaceutical Manufacturers Association v. Weinberger......1506
          Notes 1508
          Judicial Watch, Inc. v. Food & Drug Administration 1508
     2.   The Confidentiality of Trade Secrets and Confidential
          Commercial Information...1514
          a.   General Issues 1514
               Notes 1516
          b.   The Scope of Exemption 4 of FOIA 1517
               Public Citizen Health Research Group v. Food & Drug
                    Administration...1517
               Note 1521
          c.   Non-FOIA Disclosure of Clinical Information...................1522
               Notes 1523
     3.   Other Relevant Statutes...1524
          a.   The Shelby Amendment...1524
          b.   The Information Quality Act 1524
               Note 1525
D.   Environmental Assessment...1526
     Environmental Defense Fund, Inc. v. Mathews 1526
     Notes 1527

INDEX 1531

TABLE OF CASES

The principal cases are in bold type.

62 Cases of Jam v. U.S.
-------------------------- 327, 334, **348**
A.E. Staley Mfg. Co. v. Secretary
of Agriculture --------------------52
A.O. Andersen & Co. v. United
States------------------------------ 480
Abbott Laboratories v.
Celebrezze ------------------------ 865
**Abbott Laboratories v.
Gardner** ------------------33, **34**, 865
Abigail Alliance v. Von
Eschenbach------------------- 654, 771
Abney v. Amgen, Inc.---------------- 684
Abruzzi Foods, Inc. v. Pasta
& Cheese, Inc. --------------- 383, 453
Action on Smoking and Health v.
Harris -------------------------- 98, 140
Action v. Bureau of Land
Mgmt. ----------------------------------71
Agri-Tech, Inc. v. Richardson ----- 780,
1066
Ajay Nutrition Foods, Inc. v.
FDA--------------------------------- 269
Alabama Power Co. v. Costle ---- 1408
Alberty Foods Products v.
United States ---------------------- 930
**Alliance for Bio-Integrity v.
Shalala**----------------**461**, **596**, 1528
Alliance for Cannabis Therapeutics
v. DEA ------------------------------ 811
Alliance for Natural Health U.S.
v. Sebelius ------------------------ 438
Almay, Inc. v. Califano ---- 65, **1330**
American Cyanamid Co. v.
FDA------------------------------- 1071
American Cyanamid Co. v.
Richardson--------------------------- 779
American Federation of Government
Employees v. Glickman---- 193, 526
American Frozen Food Institute v.
Califano------------------------------ 367
**American Frozen Food Institute
v. Mathews**------------------------**365**
American Grain Products Processing
Institute v. Department of Public
Health---------------------------- 290
American Health Products Co., Inc.
v. Hayes ------------------------------ 443
American Home Products Corp. v.
Finch ----------------------------- 778
American Judicial School of Magnetic
Healing v. McAnnulty------ 644, 646
American Meat Institute v.
Bergland---------------------------- 1528
American Meat Institute v. United
States Dept. of Agriculture ------ 361
American Medical Association v.
Mathews--------------------------- 1028

American Methyl Corp. v.
EPA----------------------------------1225
**American Pharmaceutical
Association v.
Weinberger**------------------755, **825**
American Public Health Ass'n v.
Veneman------------------------ 75, 780
**American School of Magnetic
Healing v. McAnnulty** -------- **645**
American Sumatra v. SEC -------1507
American Trucking Ass'ns v. United
States ------------------------------ 40
AMP, Inc. v. Gardner ------- 740, 1201
Animal Health Institute v.
USDA ------------------------------1066
Animal Legal Defense Fund Boston,
Inc. v. Provimi Veal Corp. ------1083
Archambault v. United States ---- 277
Arent v. Shalala ---------------------- 404
Armour & Co. v. Freeman --------- 361
Armour & Co. v. North
Dakota --------------------------- 294
ASARCO, Inc. v. Occupational Safety
and Health Administration ----1434
Asbestos Information
Association/North America v.
Occupational Safety and Health
Administration--------------------1434
Ass'n of American Physician &
Surgeons, Inc. v. FDA----------- 698
Auer v. Robbins ------------------ 64, 903
Autin v. Solvay Pharmaceuticals,
Inc.-------------------------------- 787
Auvil v. CBS --------------------------- 636
Bae v. Shalala ---------------------- **253**
**Baker v. United
States** ---------------------**282**, 1182
BankAmerica Corp v. U.S. -------- 227
Bd. of Trustees of the State Univ.
of N.Y. v. Fox ---------------------- 429
Beaty v. FDA -------------------------- 175
Bell v. Goddard --------------------1383
Bellarno International Ltd. v.
FDA -------------------- 61, 1032, 1447
Benten v. Kessler -------------------- 774
Berger v. United States--------- **482**
**Berkovitz v. United
States** --------------------------- **1146**
Berlex Laboratories, Inc. v. Food and
Drug Administration------------- 761
Biodiversity Legal Found. v.
Badgley-------------------------- 72, 73
Biotics Research Corp. v.
Heckler ------------------------ 66, 267
Blank v. United States ------------1153
Bordenkircher v. Hayes ------------ 170
Bourjois, Inc. v. Chapman---------1303
Bowen v. Georgetown Univ.
Hosp. -------------------------------- 82

Bracco Diagnostics, Inc. v.
    Shalala -------------- 673, 1206, 1210
Bradley v. Weinberger ------- 69, **867**
Bristol Laboratories v.
    Richardson --------------------------- 779
Bristol–Myers Squibb Co. v.
    Shalala ----------------------------- 1009
Brown & Williamson Tobacco
    Corp. v. FDA ----------------------- 141
Brown v. United States ------------- 808
Brown–Forman Distillers
    Corp. v. Mathews ------------ 319, 393
Bruce's Juices, Inc. v. United
    States--------------------------------- 481
Bruesewitz v. Wyeth LLC --------- 1153
Buckman Co. v. Plaintiffs'
    Legal Comm. ----------------------- 819
Building and Construction Trades
    Department, AFL–CIO v.
    Brock ------------------------------ 1434
Burke Pest Control Inc. v. Joseph
    Schlitz Brewing Co. --------------- 614
Burroughs Wellcome Co. v.
    Schweiker -------------------- 782, 1000
Byrd v. United States ------------- 1324
California v. Tri–Union
    Seafoods ----------------------------- 402
Campaign for Responsible
    Transplantation v. U.S. Food
    and Drug Administration ------ 1192
Campbell v. Department of
    HHS------------------------------------ 1517
Capital Cities Cable, Inc. v.
    Crisp ---------------------------------- 307
Carey v. Population Services
    International ----------------------- 966
Caribbean Produce Exchange, Inc. v.
    Secretary of HHS ------------------ 61
**Carl Borchsenius Co. v.
    Gardner** ----------------------------- **1448**
Carnohan v. United States --------- 653
**Carolene Products Co. v.
    United States** ------- **334**, 342, 387
Carolina Brown, Inc. v.
    Weinberger ---------------------------- 67
Carson Prods. Co. v. Califano ---- 1337
Carter v. Carter Coal Co.----- 272, 274
Center for Science in the Public
    Interest v. Department of the
    Treasury----------------------------- 394
Center for Science in the Public
    Interest v. Novitch ----------------- 62
Central Hudson Gas & Elec. Corp. v.
    Public Serv. Commission of
    New York------   428, 431, 467, 944,
    1364, 1366
Certified Color Manufacturers
    Association v. Mathews----------- 619
Chaney v. Heckler ------------- 279, 280
Chevron U.S.A. Inc. v.
    NRDC, Inc.----- 63, 80, 81, 100, 142,
    296, 462, 514, 597, 630, 1287, 1414,
    1518

Chocolate Mfrs. Ass'n of the
    United States v. Block ------------- 46
Christensen v. Harris County ------- 64
Chrysler Corp. v. Brown ----------- 1508
Ciba Corp. v. Weinberger -----668, 779
Ciba–Geigy Corp. v.
    Richardson -------------------------- 779
Citizens to Preserve Overton
    Park v. Volpe ----------------------- 172
City of New York v. FCC------------ 307
Clinton Foods, Inc. v. United
    States -------------------------------- 206
Colonnade Catering Corp. v.
    United States-----------------180, 195
Columbia Cheese v. McNutt ------- 343
Commonwealth of Massachusetts v.
    Hayes ------------------------312, 1282
Community Nutrition Institute v.
    Block -------------------------------- 397
Community Nutrition Institute v.
    Butz --------------------------------- 397
Community Nutrition Institute v.
    Novitch ----------------------------- 1397
Community Nutrition Institute v.
    Young ---- 51, 61, 63, 175, 501, 1397
**Consumers Union of United
    States, Inc. v. Department of
    HEW** ----------------------- 1347, **1491**
Contact Lens Manufacturers Ass'n v.
    FDA----------------- 1246, 1247, 1249
**Continental Seafoods v.
    Schweiker**------------------------- **502**
Cook Chocolate Co. v. Miller--------- 51
Cook v. FDA----------------------- **1441**
Copanos and Sons, Inc. v. Food and
    Drug Administration-------------- 842
Corn Products Co. v. Department of
    HEW --------------------------------343, 345
Corn Products Refining Co. v.
    Federal Trade Commission------ 483
Cosmetic, Toiletry and Fragrance
    Ass'n v. Minnesota ---------------- 307
Cosmetic, Toiletry and Fragrance
    Ass'n, Inc. v. Schmidt ------------1329
Cowan v. United States ------------ 684
Cowdin v. Young----------------------1080
Coyne Beahm, Inc. v. U.S. Food and
    Drug Administration ------------- 141
**Coyne Beahm, Inc. v. United
    States Food & Drug
    Administration** ---------------- **1269**
CropLife America v. EPA ---------- 636
**Ctr. for Food Safety v.
    Hamburg** ---------------------------**70**
Cutler v. Hayes ---------------------- 979
Cutler v. Kennedy------------------- 979
Dahl v. HEM Pharmaceuticals
    Corp.------------------------------------ 684
Dahnke–Walker Milling Co. v.
    Bondurant -------------------------- 276
Dainty–Maid, Inc. v. United
    States -------------------------------- 204
Davis v. Wyeth Laboratories -----1143

Dean Rubber Mfg. Co. v.
    United States ----------------- 175
DeFreese v. United States --------- 808
Del Labs., Inc. v. United
    States--------------------------------- 1337
Designated B–Complex
    Cholinos Capsules----------------- 931
Diamond Laboratories, Inc. v.
    Richardson------------------------ 1066
DiCola v. FDA ------------------------ 256
Dimethyl Dicarbonate------------- 1415
**Discount Tobacco City &
    Lottery, Inc. v. United
    States**---------------------------**1364**, 1368
Doe v. Bolton ----------------------------- 650
Doe v. Rumsfeld-------------------- 1130
Doe v. Sullivan ----------------------- 689
Doe v. United States----------------- 809
Dole v. United Steelworkers of
    America----------------------------48, 71
Dow Chemical v. United
    States--------------------------------- 190
Dowhal v. Smithkline Beecham
    Consumer Healthcare------------- 990
Drown v. United States------------- 276
Drug Review ----------------------------980
**Dyestuffs and Chemicals, Inc.
    v. Flemming** ----------------------- **49**
Dyson v. Miles Laboratories,
    Inc. ---------------------------------- 310
E.R. Squibb & Sons, Inc. v.
    Bowen ------------------------- 117, 783
E.R. Squibb & Sons, Inc. v.
    Weinberger -------------------------- 780
Edison Pharmaceutical Co., Inc. v.
    FDA---------------------------------- 740
Eli Lilly & Co. v. Medtronic, Inc.
    ------------------------1005, 1006, 1221
Employment Div. v. Smith --------- 812
Environmental Defense Fund v.
    Environmental Protection
    Agency -------------------------------- 857
**Environmental Defense Fund,
    Inc. v. Mathews** ---------------- **1526**
Evart v. Suli------------------------------ 494
**Ewing v. Mytinger & Casselberry,
    Inc.**---------------------------- **202**, 204
F.T.C. v. Simeon Management
    Corp.------------------------------------ 821
Fagan v. Amerisourcebergen
    Corp. ---------------------------------- 1031
Far East Conference v.
    United States -----------------------66
FDA v. Brown & Williamson Tobacco
    Corp.----------------------- 62, 78, 1118
Federal Election Comm'n v.
    Furgatch----------------------------- 216
**Federal Security Administrator
    v. Quaker Oats Co.** ------------- **340**
**Federation of Homemakers v.
    Schmidt** --------------------------- **371**
Ferndale Laboratories, Inc. v.
    Cavendish----------------- 1031, 1032
Fertilizer Institute v. U.S.
    Department of Health and Human
    Services --------------------------- 1432

Fidelity Federal Savings & Loan
    Association v. de la Cuesta ----- 307,
    309, 310
Fisons Corp. v. Shalala------------1010
Fisons Plc v. Quigg -----------------1005
Fleminger v. HHS ---------------- **437**
Flemming v. Florida Citrus
    Exchange --------------- 497, 617, 618
Florida Breckenridge, Inc. v. Solvay
    Pharmaceuticals, Inc.------------- 787
**Florida Lime & Avocado
    Growers, Inc. v.
    Paul**----------------------**299**, 307, 309
Fmali Herb, Inc. v. Heckler---- **581**
**Food and Drug Administration v.
    Brown & Williamson Tobacco
    Corp.** -------------- **141**, 146, 147, 148
Food Chemical News v.
    Young -----------------------------1497
Food Chemical News, Inc. v.
    Davis ---------------- 1491, 1492, 1496
**Forsham v.
    Califano**-------------- **855**, 869, 1506
Forsham v. Harris ------------------1506
Forsyth v. Eli Lilly & Co. ---------- 742
**Founding Church of Scientology
    v. United States** --------- 198, **1197**
FPC v. Texaco, Inc. ----------------- 850
Freightliner Corp. v. Myrick------1289
Fresh Grown Preserve Corp. v. FTC
    --- 456
Fresh Grown Preserve Corp. v.
    United States----------------------- 209
Friedman v. Sebelius ------------ **257**
FTC v. Actavis, Inc.-------------- **1016**
FTC v. Algoma Lumber
    Co. --------------------------------383, 387
FTC v. Good–Grape Co. ------------ 456
FTC v. Mandel Brothers, Inc. ----- 142
FTC v. Pantron I Corp. ------------- 116
FTC v. Universal–Rundle
    Corp. --------------------------------- 167
Gardner v. Toilet Goods Ass'n------- 36
Garlic v. FDA--------------------742, 774
Geier v. American Honda Motor
    Co. ------------------------------------- 900
Genentech, Inc. v. Bowen------- **759**
General Medical Co. v. United
    States Food and Drug
    Admin.------------------------------1250
Gerber Products Co. v. Fisher
    Tank Co. ---------------------------- 614
Glaxo Operations UK Limited v.
    Quigg----------------------------------1009
Gonzales v. O Centro Esprita
    Beneficente Uniao Do
    Vegetal ------------------------------- 812
Gonzales v. Raich -----------------271, 812
Goodwin v. United States --------1440
Grand Laboratories, Inc. v.
    Harris-------------------------------- 1066
Granholm v. Heald ----------------- 299
Greenberg v. FDA-------------------1517
Griffin v. United States -----------1149

Grocery Manufacturers of
    America, Inc. v.
    Gerace------------------------ **308**, 372
Gulf South Insulation v. U.S.
    Consumer Product Safety
    Commission-------------------------- 1434
Gustafson v. Alloyd Co. -------------- 142
Hartz v. Bensinger ------------------- 811
Harvey v. Veneman ------------------- 454
Hawkins v. Upjohn Company------ 724
Health Plan, Inc. v. Pfizer, Inc.---- 938
Hebe Co. v. Shaw -------------- 294, 334
Heckler v. Chaney ----- 69, 129, 171,
    279, 1441
Hemp Industries Association v.
    DEA-------------------------------------812
Hess & Clark, Division of Rhodia,
    Inc. v. FDA--------- 1099, 1104, 1384
Heterochemical Corp. v.
    FDA -----------------------------64, 175
**Hillsborough County v.
    Automated Medical
    Laboratories, Inc.**------- 294, 1161
Hines v. Davidowitz----- 297, 300, 309
Hipolite Egg Co. v. United
    States-------------------------- 275, 279
Hi–Tech Pharmaceuticals v.
    Crawford -------------------------------633
Hoffman v. Sterling Drug, Inc. ----- 68
**Hoffman–LaRoche, Inc. v.
    Weinberger** ------------------ 781, **997**
Hoffmann–LaRoche, Inc. v.
    Califano---------------------------- 1028
Holk v. Snapple Beverage
    Corp. ------------------------------------298
Home Box Office, Inc. v. FCC ------- 24
**Hoxsey Cancer Clinic v.
    Folsom** --------------------------------**268**
Idaho Association of Naturopathic
    Physicians, Inc. v. FDA ----------- 808
Immuno International, A.G. v.
    Hillsborough County, Florida --- 298
In re Barr Laboratories-------------- 742
In re Canadian Import Antitrust
    Litigation---------------------------- 1027
In re Sabin Polio Vaccine Products
    Liability Litigation --------------- 1149
Independent Cosmetic Mfrs. &
    Distribs., Inc. v. Califano------- 1337
Indictment in United States v. Sally
    Miller, Stephen S. Miller, and
    ChemNutra, Inc. ------------------ **1047**
Industrial Union Department
    Industrial Union Department,
    AFL–CIO v. American Petroleum
    Institute ------------------------------ 1433
INS v. Yang------------------------------969
Int'l Ctr. for Tech. Assessment v.
    Thompson --------------------------- 1107
Int'l Dairy Foods Ass'n v.
    Boggs --------------------------------469
International Center for Technology
    Assessment v. Thompson---------176

International Dairy Foods
    Association v. Amestoy ------- **466**
International Union, United
    Automobile, Aerospace and
    Agricultural Implement Workers of
    America v. Pendergrass ---------1433
Israel v. Baxter Laboratories,
    Inc.-------------------------------------- 740
**Ivy Sports Medicine, LLC v.
    Sebelius** ----------------------------- **1224**
Jacob Siegel Co. v. FTC ------------- 383
Jacobson v. Commonwealth of
    Massachusetts----------------------1138
Jarboe–Lackey Feedlots, Inc. v.
    United States----------------------- 201
Jerome Stevens Pharmaceuticals,
    Inc. v. FDA -------------------------- 788
Jin Fuey Moy v. United States---- 808
Jones v. Rath Packing Co.----- 296,
    302, 309
**Judicial Watch, Inc. v. Food &
    Drug Administration** -------- **1508**
Katzenbach v. McClung------------- 271
Kehm v. Procter & Gamble--------1273
Keys v. U.S. Dep't of Justice ------1510
Knight v. FDA----------------------- 639
**Kordel v. United
    States** ------------------------- **152**, 158
Kos Pharmaceuticals, Inc. v. Andrx
    Corp.----------------------------------- 865
Kraemer–Katz v. Public Health
    Service ------------------------------- 684
Kuromiya v. United States--------- 765
K–V Pharm. Co. v. United States
    FDA----------------------------------- 176
L&M Industries, Inc. v.
    Kenter ------------------------------1441
Lake v. FDA ----------------------- **1249**
Land O'Lakes Creameriess, Inc. v.
    McNutt -------------------------------52
Larkin v. Pfizer, Inc. --------------- 888
Lee v. United States----------------- 198
Leedom v. Kyne--------------------- 740
Lefaivre v. KV Pharm. Co. -------- 298
Leo Winter Associates, Inc. v.
    Department HHS ----------------- 186
Les v. Reilly ----------------------- **1426**
Lever Brothers Co. v. Maurer ----- 310
Lombardo v. Handler --------------1497
Love v. Wolf----------------------------- 911
**MacDonald v. Ortho
    Pharmaceutical
    Corporation**----------------------- **889**
Marshall Minerals, Inc. v. FDA---- 51,
    1527
Marshall v. Barlow's, Inc.-----180, 181
Maryland Pest Control Ass'n v.
    Montgomery County,
    Maryland ---------------------------- 635
Maryland v. Louisiana-------------- 298
Masti–Kure Products Co. v.
    Califano ------------------------------1066
Matter of American Home
    Products Corp. --------------------- 992

Matter of Bristol–Myers Co. ------- 992
Matter of Establishment Inspection
    of: Wedgewood Village Pharmacy,
    Inc. --------------------------------- 798
McDermott v. Wisconsin ----- 293, 294
McIlwain v. Hayes-------------------- 619
Medical Center Pharmacy v.
    Mukasey----------------------------- 796
Medical Center v. Mukasey ------ 1117
Medtronic, Inc. v.
    Lohr----------- 312, 896, 1228, **1283**
Merck KGaA v. Integra Lifesciences
    I, Ltd.------------------------------- 1006
Meserey v. United States ---------- 984
Millet, Pit and Seed Co., Inc. v.
    United States ---------------- 488, 494
Milnot Co. v. Richardson--------**337**
Mitchell v. Robert de Mario
    Jewelry, Inc.------------------ 227, 230
Monsanto Co. v.
    Kennedy---------------**610**, 614, 1397
Montgomery County v.
    Leavitt ----------------------------- 1468
Moog Industries, Inc. v. FTC------- 167
Moore v. East Cleveland------------ 654
Morissette v. United States -------- 260
Mourning v. Family Publications
    Service, Inc. ----------------------- 400
Murdock v. Pennsylvania ---------- 428
Mutual Pharmaceutical Co., Inc.
    v. Bartlett ------------------------- 906
Mylan Laboratories, Inc. v.
    Matkar------------------------------ 1011
Nader v. Baroody ----------- 1492, 1496
Nader v. EPA ------------------------ 636
Nat'l Cable & Telecomms. Ass'n v.
    Brand X Internet Servs. --------- 149
Natick Paperboard Corp. v.
    Weinberger ------------ 84, 509, **608**
National Association of
    Pharmaceutical Manufacturers
    v. Food and Drug
    Administration--------------**37**, 842
National Broadcasting Co. v.
    United States -------------------------40
National Confectioners' Ass'n v.
    Califano----------------------------- 528
National Ethical Pharmaceutical
    Ass'n v. Weinberger------------------67
National Milk Producers
    Federation v. Harris -------------- 372
National Nutritional Foods
    Ass'n v. Califano ------------ 69, **1494**
National Nutritional Foods
    Ass'n v. FDA ---------------------91, 95
National Nutritional Foods
    Ass'n v. Kennedy ----------------**572**
National Nutritional Foods Ass'n
    v. Mathews---- 65, 91, **93**, 127, 330
National Nutritional FoodsAss'n
    v. Weinberger-----31, 36, 40, 42, 93,
    400, 807
National Nutritional Foods
    Association v. FDA---------------- 330
National Nutritional Foods
    Association v. Goyan------------- 401
National Nutritional Foods
    Association v. Young ------------- 401
National Petroleum Refiners
    Ass'n v. FTC -------------- 39, 40, 400
National Pharmaceutical Alliance v.
    Henney ------------------------------ 698
National Pork Producers Council v.
    Bergland -------------------- 362, 1528
National Wildlife Federation v.
    Secretary of HHS--------------- 62, 69
National Women's Health Network,
    Inc. v. A.H. Robins Co., Inc.----1273
Natural Resources Defense
    Council, Inc. v. FDA----- 74, 1083,
    1084, 1094, **1095**
Navel Orange Admin. Comm. v.
    Exeter Orange Co. ---------------- 214
New Jersey Guild of Hearing Aid
    Dispensers v. Long-------- 312, 1282
New Mexico v. Castleman --------1034
New York v. Burger ----------- 183, 195
New York v. U.S. E.P.A. -----------1431
Nijhawan v. Holder----------------- 259
NLRB v. Jones & Laughlin Steel
    Corp. ------------------------------- 272
Norcal/Crosetti Foods, Inc. v.
    United States---------------------- 408
NORML v. Bell----------------------- 811
NORML v. DEA --------------------- 811
NORML v. Ingersoll----------------- 811
Northwest Connection, Inc. v.
    Board of Pharmacy --------------- 966
Norton v. S. Utah Wilderness
    Alliance------------------------71, 1088
Novartis Corp. v. FTC -------------- 992
Novartis v. Leavitt------------------- 865
Nutraceutical Corporation v. Von
    Eschenbach -----------------**629**, 633
Nutrilab, Inc. v. Schweiker 83, **85**,
    422, 443
Nutritional Health Alliance v.
    FDA ----------------------------639, 995
Nutritional Health Alliance v.
    Shalala ----------------------------- 441
NVE Inc. v. Department of Health
    and Human Services ------------- 628
Odgers v. Ortho Pharm. Corp. ---- 889
Olsen v. DEA ----------------------- 812
Ortho Pharmaceutical Corp. v.
    Amgen, Inc. ----------------------- 711
Otis McAllister & Co. v. United
    States ------------------------------- 84
Pacific Gas & Electric Co. v. State
    Energy Resources Conservation &
    Development Commission ------- 309
Pactra Industries, Inc. v. Consumer
    Product Safety Comm'n ----------- 51
Palmer v. United States------------ 284
Parke, Davis & Co. v.
    Califano ---------------------------- 204
Parke–Davis & Co. v. Ricci-------1032
PDK Laboratories, Inc. v.
    DEA -------------------------------- 813
Pearson v. Shalala -----63, **430**, 431,
    434, 911
Pearson v. Thompson -------------- 434

Pennsylvania Employee Benefit Trust Fund v. Zeneca, Inc. ------924
People v. Privitera--------------------653
Perez v. Wyeth Laboratories, Inc. ------------------------------------889
Peyote Way Church of God, Inc. v. Smith--------------------------------812
Pfizer, Inc. v. Richardson------------779
Pfizer, Inc. v. Shalala----------65, 1010
Pharmaceutical Manufacturers Ass'n v. Gardner---------------------------- 47
Pharmaceutical Manufacturers Association v. FDA-------------**880**
Pharmaceutical Manufacturers Association v. Finch----------------778
Pharmaceutical Manufacturers Association v. Kennedy --------- 1028
Pharmaceutical Manufacturers Association v. Richardson--------778
Pharmaceutical Manufacturers Association v. Weinberger ----------------------**1506**
Pharmanex v. Shalala---------------108
Pineapple Growers Ass'n of Hawaii v. FDA----------------------- 51
Planned Parenthood of Southeastern Pennsylvania v. Casey -----------659
PLIVA, Inc. v. Mensing------------**901**
Plumley v. Massachusetts --- 298, 299
Porter v. Warner Holding Company -----------------------------226
Potato Chip Institute v. General Mills, Inc.------------------------------383
Powell v. Pennsylvania --------------335
Premo Pharmaceutical Laboratories, Inc. v. United States --------------- 67
Prevor v. Food and Drug Administration------------ 672, **1207**
Price v. Illinois-------------------------294
Processed Apples Institute, Inc. v. Department of Public Health --------------------------- 290, 636
Professionals and Patients for Customized Care v. Shalala ------ 62
Public Citizen Health Research Group v. Commissioner, FDA----62, 69, 74, 990
Public Citizen Health Research Group v. FDA----------------- 1515, 1516, **1517**
Public Citizen Health Research Group v. Tyson -------------------1434
Public Citizen v. Bowen-------------1415
Public Citizen v. Department of HHS--------------------------------------619
Public Citizen v. Foreman --- 601, 624
Public Citizen v. Goyan---------------- 69
Public Citizen v. Heckler--------62, 534
Public Citizen v. National Advisory Committee----------**1498**
Public Citizen v. United States Department of Justice-----------1497
Public Citizen v. Young----------------------**1410**, 1427

Public Citizen, Inc. v. Shalala ----- 407
R. J. Reynolds Tobacco Co. v. FDA 63
R.F. and R.F. v. Abbott Laboratories--------------------**1159**
R.J. Reynolds Tobacco Co. v. Food & Drug Administration ----------------**1368**
Reade v. Ewing-------------------------52
Research Laboratories, Inc. v. United States ---------------------**647**
Reyes v. Wyeth Laboratories----------------889, **1141**
Rhone–Poulenc, Inc. v. FDA -----1099, 1104, 1386, 1528
Rice v. Santa Fe Elevator Corp.------------------------------------ 301
Riegel v. Medtronic, Inc. ---------------------------312, **1290**
Roe v. Wade--------650, 651, 659, 1257
Rosado v. Wyman --------------------- 740
Royal Baking Powder Co. v. FTC------------------------------------ 456
Rubin v. Coors Brewing Co.-------- 418
Rutherford v. American Medical Ass'n ------------------------52
Rutherford v. United States -------------- 67, 650, 652, 1257
Salt Institute v. Leavitt -----------1525
Samuels v. Health & Hospital Corp. of the City of New York---------- 298
Sandoz, Inc. v. Leavitt---------- 75, 742
Savage v. Jones -----------------293, 299
Schechter Poultry v. United States --------------------------------- 272
Schering Corp. v. FDA-------------1010
Schor v. Abbott Laboratories Inc.------------------------------------1026
Schuck v. Butz ------------------------ 601
Scott v. Food and Drug Administration --------- **1401**, 1413
Serono Laboratories, Inc. v. Shalala ------------------------------1009
Seven Cases of Eckman's Alterative v. U.S. ------------------------------ 646
Sharp v. Artifex----------------------1246
Shepard v. United States ----------- 259
Sifre v. Robles -----------------------774
Sigma–Tau Pharmaceuticals, Inc. v. Schwetz -------------------------- 761
Skidmore v. Swift & Co.-------------- 64
Smith v. Pingree--------------312, 1282
Smith v. Shalala ---------------------- 765
SmithKline Beecham Consumer Healthcare v. Watson Pharmaceuticals, Inc. ------------1006
Snyder v. American Association of Blood Banks------------------ **1162**
Somerset Pharmaceuticals, Inc. v. Shalala ------------------------------1010
Sorrell v. IMS Health, Inc.------------------------------429, 954
Sottera, Inc. v. FDA----------------- **146**
State of Louisiana v. Mathews -------------------------288, 538

State of Vermont v. Leavitt----------------------**1465**, 1467

State v. Interstate Blood Bank, Inc. ---------------------------- 298, 299

Stauber v. Shalala------ 462, 469, 1528

Stenberg v. Carhart------------------659

Stinson Canning Co. v. United States-------------------------------- 209

Sugarman v. Forbragd --------- **1439**

Supreme Beef Processors Inc. v. USDA ---------------------- 505, 532

Syncor International Corporation v. Shalala------------------------------61, **789**

Synthetic Organic Chemical Mfrs. Ass'n v. Secretary, Dept. of HHS--------------------------------- 1432

Takhar v. Kessler-------------------- 1073

Telecommunications Res. & Action Ctr. v. F.C.C. ------------------------72

Telecommunications Research & Action Center v. FCC----------- 1096

Teva Pharmaceuticals USA, Inc. v. Pfizer, Inc. ------------------------ 1015

Teva Pharmaceuticals, Inc. v. Crawford ------------------------- 1023

TGA v. Gardner --------------------- 1325

Thompson Hine LLP v. Smoking Everywhere, Inc.------------------- 150

Thompson v. Western States Medical Center --------------------- 796

Toilet Goods Ass'n v. Finch--------- 619

Toilet Goods Ass'n v. Gardner------------------------------36, 39

Toilet Goods Ass'n v. Finch ----------------------------- **1322**

Tozzi v. U.S. Department of Health and Human Services----- 1432, 1437

Triangle Candy Co. v. United States --------------------**188**

Tri–Bio Laboratories, Inc. v. United States --------------------- 1516

Tummino v. Hamburg--------------- 966

Tummino v. Torti --------------------- 966

Turkel v. Food and Drug Administration --------------------- 739

Tutoki v. Celebrezze -------------------52

Ubiotica Corp. v. FDA ------------ **739**

Unimed, Inc. v. Richardson--------- 740

United States v. 4 Cases . . . Slim–Mint Chewing Gum -------- 204

United States v. 7 Barrels . . . Spray Dried Whole Egg -------**273**

United States v. 7 Cartons . . . "Ferro–Lac Swine Formula Concentrate (Medicated)" ---- 1064

United States v. 7 Jugs, etc., of Dr. Salsbury's Rakos ------------- 648

United States v. 8 Cartons, Containing " 'Plantation' 'The Original' etc., Molasses"---------------------- 156, 198

United States v. 9/1 Kg. Containers ------------------------ 1116

United States v. 14 105 Pound Bags . . . Mineral Compound---------- 1059

United States v. 22 Rectangular or Cylindrical Devices . . . "The Ster–O–Lizer MD–200"----------------- 129

United States v. 22 Rectangular or Cylindrical Finished Devices -----------------------220, 221

United States v. 23 . . . Articles------------------------------ **131**

United States v. 24 Bottles . . . "Sterling Vinegar & Honey," etc. -- 89, **154**

United States v. 24 Cases More or Less---------------------------------- 486

United States v. 25 Cases, More or Less, of an Article of Device . . . "Sensor Pad for Breast Self-Examination" ----------------------**99**

United States v. 29 Cartons of . . . An Article of Food----------------571, 577

United States v. 36 Drums of Pop'n Oil ----------------------------- 378

United States v. 39 Cases . . . Michigan Brand Korleen Tablets----------------------------- 284

United States v. 40 Cases . . . "Pinocchio Brand 75% Corn, Peanut Oil and Soya Bean Oil Blended With 25% Pure Olive Oil"----------------------------------- 285

United States v. 43 1/2 Gross Rubber Prophylactics Labeled in Part "Xcello's Prophylactics" ------------------- **205**

United States v. 46 Cartons . . . Fairfax Cigarettes ----------------- 139

United States v. 50 Boxes More or Less ---------------------------- 666

United States v. 52 Drums of Maple Syrup ---------------------- 275

United States v. 55 Cases Popped Corn ---------------------- 378

United States v. 60 28–Capsule Bottles . . . "Unitrol"-------------- 204

United States v. 62 Packages . . . Marmola Prescription Tablets----------------------------- 386

United States v. 71/55 Gallon Drums . . . Stuffed Green Olives in Brine --------------------- 486, 529, 567

United States v. 75 Cases . . . Peanut Butter, Labeled . . . "Top Notch Brand" -------------------------184, 185

United States v. 88 Cases . . . Bireley's Orange Beverage ------------------------- **376**

United States v. 91 Packages . . . Nutrilite Food Supplement------ 207

United States v. 116 Boxes . . . Arden Assorted Candy Drops ----------- 387

United States v. 119 Cases . . . "New Dextra Brand Fortified Cane Sugar" ---------------------- 353

United States v. 133 Cases of Tomato Paste ---------------------- 471

United States v. 174 Cases . . . "Delson Thin Mints"-------------- 388

United States v. 225 Cartons . . .
  Fiorinal ------------------------------666
United States v. 250 Jars . . . "Cal's
  Tupelo Blossom U.S. Fancy Pure
  Honey" -------------------------------- 89
**United States v. 298 Cases . . . Ski
  Slide Brand Asparagus**--------**486**
United States v. 302 Cases . . .
  Frozen Shrimp-------------------- 1454
United States v. 354 Bulk Cartons
  Trim Reducing–Aid
  Cigarettes -----------------------------139
**United States v. 432 Cartons . . .
  Candy Lollipops** -----------------**381**
**United States v. 449 Cases,
  Containing Tomato
  Paste**-------------------------- 205, **471**
United States v. 484 Bags,
  More or Less------------------- 175, 473
United States v. 600 Units . . . "Nue–
  Ovo"---------------------------------207
United States v. 651 Cases . . .
  Chocolate
  Chil-Zert---------------- 327, 369, 376
United States v. 716 Cases . . . Del
  Comida Brand Tomatoes . . . ----379
United States v. 738 Cases . . . Jiffy–
  Lou Vanilla Flavor Pudding-----387
United States v. 856 Cases . . .
  "Demi"--------------------------------350
United States v. 893 One–Gallon
  Cans, More or Less, . . . Labeled
  Brown's Inhalant ------------------201
**United States v. 1,200 Cans . . .
  Pasteurized Whole Eggs,
  etc.**------------------------------------**479**
**United States v. 1232 Cases
  American Beauty Brand
  Oysters**--------------------------------**492**
United States v. 1,322 Cans, More
  or Less, of Black Raspberry
  Puree --------------------------------209
United States v. 1500 90–Table
  Bottles . . . Genendo
  Pharmaceutical N.V.--------------835
**United States v. 1,500 Cases More
  or Less, Tomato Paste** ---------**471**
**United States v. 1,638 Cases of
  Adulterated Alcoholic
  Beverages** --------------------------**207**
United States v. 2,116 Boxes of
  Boned Beef------------- 201, 488, 497
United States v. 76,552 Pounds
  of Frog Legs ----------------------- 1454
United States v. 1,800,2625 Wine
  Gallons of Distilled Spirits-------319
**United States of America v.
  Argent Chemical Laboratories,
  Inc.**------------------------------------**194**
**United States of America v. Rx
  Depot, Inc.**----------------------- **1460**
United States v. Abbott
  Laboratories--------------------------270
United States v. Acklen-------------183

United States v. Acri Wholesale
  Grocery Company ----------------- 190
United States v. Agnew ------------ 474
United States v. Alcon
  Labs ----------------------67, 200, 1116
United States v. Algon
  Chemical, Inc. --------------------- 684
United States v. Allan
  Drug Corp.----------------------209, 667
United States v. Allbrook Freezing
  & Cold Storage --------------------- 284
United States v. An Article of Drug
  . . . Ova II ----------------------------1211
**United States v. An Article . . .
  Acu–Dot**-------------------------- **1255**
**United States v. An Article . . .
  Enriched Rice**------------------ **1468**
United States v. An Article . . .
  "Line Away"------------------------ 113
**United States v. An Article
  . . . Sudden
  Change** -----------------**111**, 134, 144
United States v. An Article of
  Device . . . "Hubbard
  Electrometer"-----------------------1199
United States v. An Article of
  Device . . . Diapulse--------------1196
United States v. An Article of Device
  . . . Diapulse Manufacturing Corp.
  of America ----------------------------1195
United States v. An Article of
  Drug (Bentex Ulcerine)----------- 666
**United States v. An Article of
  Drug . . . Bacto–
  Unidisk**---------------- **78**, 1188, 1194
United States v. An Article of
  Drug . . . "Tutag Pharmaceuticals
  . . . X–Otag Plus Tablets" ----------- 67
United States v. An Article of
  Drug . . . "Cap–Chur–Sol" ------1064
United States v. An Article of Drug
  . . . Ova II -----------------------------91
**United States v. An Article of
  Drug . . . White
  Quadrisect**------------------------- **839**
United States v. An Article of
  Drug Consisting of 4,680
  Pails -------------------- 206, 210, 1064
United States v. An Article of Food
  . . . "Manischewitz . . . Diet
  Thins"------------- 383, 387, 481, 568
**United States v. An Article of
  Food . . . Coco Rico,
  Inc.** -----------------------283, **577**, 602
**United States v. An Article of
  Food . . . FoodScience
  Labs**---------------------------- **568**, 579
United States v. An Article or
  Device Consisting of 31
  Units (Gonsertron)-----------283, 284
United States v. Anderson
  Seafoods, Inc. ----------- 498, 503, 517
United States v. Antosh------------ 834

United States v. Argent Chemical
  Laboratories, Inc. ------------------ 183
United States v. Arnold's Pharmacy,
  Inc. ---------------------------------- 185
United States v. Article Consisting of
  216 Cartoned Bottles . . . "Sudden
  Change"------------------------------- 387
United States v. Articles of Drug . . .
  Century Food Co. ------------------ 156
United States v. Article of Device . . .
  "The Ster–O–Lizer MD–200" --- 201
United States v. Article of
  Drug ---------------------------------- 210
**United States v. Article of Drug
  . . . "Decholin"** -------------------**958**
United States v. Article of Drug . . .
  United States Cane Sugar
  Refiners' Ass'n v. McNutt --------- 52
United States v. Article of Food . . .
  Orotic Acid-------------------------- 579
United States v. Articles of Device
  . . . Diapulse --------------------- 1196
United States v. Articles of
  Drug -------------------------------- 1034
**United States v. Articles of
  Drug . . . Foods Plus, Inc.** -----**928**
United States v. Articles of Drug . . .
  Promise Toothpaste for
  Sensitive Teeth--------------------- 983
United States v. Articles of
  Drug . . . Wans--------------------- 280
United States v. Articles of Drug
  Consisting of the Following:
  5,906 Boxes -------------------------- 666
United States v. Articles of Drug
  for Veterinary Use--------------- 1045
United States v. Articles of Drug
  in Possession of Nip-Co Mfg.,
  Inc. ---------------------------------- 1065
United States v. Articles of Drugs
  Consisting of 203 Paper
  Bags-------------------------- 1447, 1454
United States v. Articles of Drugs
  Consisting of 203 Paperbags ------61
**United States v. Articles of
  Drugs, et al., Midwest
  Pharmaceuticals, Inc.** ---------**218**
United States v. Articles of Food
  Consisting . . . of Pottery --------- 616
United States v. Articles of
  Hazardous Substance ------ 198, 223
United States v. Atropine Sulfate 1.0
  Mg. (Article of Drug)-------------- 999
United States v. Bacto–
  Unidisk ---------------------530, 1471
United States v. Balanced
  Foods -------------------------------- 252
United States v. Ballard---------- 1198
**United States v. Barr
  Laboratories, Inc.**-------- 236, **843**
United States v. Baxter
  Healthcare Corp.------------- 792, 799
United States v. Bel–Mar
  Laboratories, Inc.----------------- 840
United States v. Bhutani----------- 842

United States v. Bioclinical
  Systems, Inc. ----------------------- 61
United States v. Biswell ------180, 195
United States v. Borjesson --------- 256
United States v. Boston Farm
  Center, Inc.------------------------- 501
United States v. Bowen ------------ 129
United States v. Bradshaw--------- 238
United States v. Brewer ----------- 483
United States v. Burzynski Cancer
  Research Institute ---------------- 770
United States v. C.E.B. Prods.,
  Inc.----------------------------236, 237
United States v. Calise----------- **287**
United States v. Cambra, Jr. -----1031
United States v. Carolene
  Products Co. ---------------------- 336
United States v. Caronia------- 63, **951**
United States v. Cassaro, Inc.----- 284
United States v. Cataldo----------- 387
United States v. Coca Cola
  Company----------------------------- 502
United States v. Colahan ---------1070
United States v. Commonwealth
  Brewing Corp. --------------------- 319
United States v. Crown Rubber
  Sundries Co. ---------------------- 251
United States v. Dakota Cheese,
  Inc.----------------------------------- 346
United States v. Dean Rubber
  Mfg. Co. ---------------------------- 221
United States v. Del Campo Baking
  Mfg. Co. ---------------------------- 183
United States v. Deremus --------- 808
United States v. Detroit Vital
  Foods, Inc. ------------------------- 284
United States v. Device
  Labeled ----------------------------- 197
United States v. Dianovin
  Pharmaceuticals, Inc.-------283, 842
United States v. Diapulse
  Corp. of America------ 170, 187, 221,
  1196
United States v.
  Dotterweich ------------ 175, 239, 240
**United States v.
  Dotterweich**---------------------- **240**
United States v. Dr. David
  Roberts Veterinary Co. ---------1059
United States v. Durbin------------ 178
United States v. Dino -------------1032
United States v. Eight
  Unlabeled Cases . . . "French
  Bronze Tablets"-------------------- 619
United States v. Ellis Research
  Laboratories, Inc. ----------------- 213
**United States v. El–O–Pathic
  Pharmacy** ------------------------- **804**
**United States v.
  Evers** ------------------ 821, **822**, 1183
United States v. Ewig
  Brothers Co. ----------------------- 637
**United States ex. rel. Franklin v.
  Parke–Davis** ---------------**934**, 937
United States v. Fabro, Inc.-------- 378
United States v. Farinella ------ **383**

United States v. Food, 2,998 Cases-------------------- **1451**

United States v. Franck's Lab, Inc. -------------------- 798, **1112**

United States v. Farinella ---------- 164

United States v. Garnett ------------ 995

United States v. Geborde-------- **278**

United States v. Gel Spice Co., Inc. ------------ 183, 191, 239, 250

United States v. General Foods Corp. ------------------------ 485

United States v. General Nutrition, Inc. ---------------------- 960

United States v. Generix Drug Corp. ------------- 284, 781, **999**

United States v. Green-------------- 810

United States v. Guerrero---------- 810

United States v. H.B. Gregory Co. ----------------------------------- 84

United States v. Haas -------------- 774

United States v. Halper------------ 254

United States v. Herold------ 185, 798

United States v. Hiland------------ 819

United States v. Hohensee---------- 89

United States v. Hoxsey Cancer Clinic ---------------------------- 770

United States v. Hunter Pharmacy, Inc.---------------------- 267

United States v. I. D. Russell Laboratories------------------------ 221

United States v. Industrial Laboratories Co.--------------------- 163

United States v. International Exterminator Corp. --------- 163, 275

United States v. Jamieson–McKames Pharmaceuticals, Inc.--------------- **179**, 191, 842, 1029

United States v. Kanasco, Ltd. --------------------------------- **1469**

United States v. Kaplan ------------- 809

United States v. Kaybel, Inc.----- 1031

United States v. Kent Food Corp. --------------------------------- 1471

United States v. Keplinger ---------- 672

United States v. Kim ---------- 810, 813

United States v. K–N Enterprises, Inc. -------------------- 236

United States v. Kohlbach ---------- 346

United States v. Kordel------------- 239

United States v. Laerdal Manufacturing Corp.----------- **215**

United States v. Lane Labs–USA Inc. -------------- 108, **225**

United States v. Leal ---------------- 810

United States v. Levine------------- 639

United States v. Lexington Mill & Elevator Co.-------------- **495**

United States v. Line Material Co. ---------------------- 1019

United States v. Lit Drug Co. ------ 221

United States v. Lopez -------------- 271

United States v. Lyon Drug Co. ----------------------------------- 185

United States v. Marcus------------- 835

United States v. Mead Corp.---------------------------- 64, 149

United States v. Midwest Pharmaceuticals, Inc. ------------1034

United States v. Milstein ---------1031

United States v. Morrison --------- 271

United States v. Mosinee Research Corp. ---------------------- 67

United States v. Moyer ------------- 995

United States v. Munoz ------------ 810

United States v. Nelson ----- 809, 1034

United States v. New England Grocers Supply Co. --- 183, 250, 251

United States v. Ninety–Five Barrels of . . . Apple Cider Vinegar----------------------- **380**, 462

United States v. Nova Scotia Food Products Corp.------------------- 40, **44**, 64, **529**

United States v. Nutri-cology, Inc.---------------------------- 170, **213**

United States v. O.F. Bayer & Co. -----------------------------81, 83

United States v. Odessa Union Warehouse Co-op------------------ 214

United States v. Olsen-------------- 281

United States v. One Article of Device Labeled Spectrochrome --------------------- 281

United States v. Parfait Powder Puff Co. ----------------------------- 249

United States v. Park --------------------175, **243**, 258

United States v. Parkinson -------- 229

United States v. Phelps Dodge Mercantile Co.----------------277, 817

United States v. Pinaud, Inc. ------ 386

United States v. Pro–Ag, Inc.-----1045

United States v. Regenerative Sciences, LLC ------ 285, 288, **1179**

United States v. Rosen ------------- 809

United States v. Roux Labs., Inc.-------------------- 189, 1325

United States v. Rutherford----------------68, 142, 652

United States v. Rx Depot, Inc.--------------------230, 1027, 1463

United States v. Sage Pharmaceuticals, Inc. ------------ 785

United States v. Sanders-------- **275**

United States v. Sars of Louisiana --------------------------- 218

United States v. Scenic View Dairy, L.L.C. -------------------- **1073**

United States v. Schlicksup Drug Co., Inc. ----------------------- 220

United States v. Sene X Eleemosynary Corp., Inc. -------- 798

United States v. Shapiro------------ 249

United States v. Shimer------------- 307

United States v. Shock ------------- 807

United States v. Starr -------------- 251

United States v. Steinschreiber ---------------------1153

United States v. Storer
  Broadcasting Co. -------------- 40, 850
United States v. Sullivan --- 124, 175,
  277, 805
United States v. Superpharm
  Corp. ---------------------------------- 236
United States v. Syntrax
  Innovations, Inc. ------------------ 220
United States v. Technical Egg
  Prods., Inc. --------------------------- 87
United States v. Themy–
  Kotronakis ------------------- 220, 221
United States v. Tomahara
  Enterprises, Ltd. ------------------- 318
United States v. Torigian Labs,
  Inc. ---------------------------------- 279
United States v. Travia----------- **97**
United States v. Tri–Bio
  Laboratories, Inc. ----------------- 179
**United States v. Tuente
  Livestock** -------------------- **80**, 1074
**United States v. Two Plastic
  Drums . . . Black Currant
  Oil**---------------------------------------**570**
United States v. Undetermined
  Number of Unlabeled Cases----- 101
**United States v. Undetermined
  Quantities of an Article of
  Device . . . "Depilatron
  Epilator"**---------------------------**285**
**United States v. Undetermined
  Quantities of an Article of Drug
  Labeled as Exachol** ------ **168**, 170
United States v. Undetermined
  Quantities of Article of
  Device ----------------------------- 132
United States v. Undetermined
  Quantities of Articles of
  Drug -------------------------- 107, 110
United States v. Undetermined
  Quantities of Articles of Drug,
  Street Drug Alternatives------- 1035
United States v. Undetermined
  Quantities of Drugs --------------**198**
United States v. Undetermined
  Quantities of Various Articles of
  Drug . . . Equidantin
  Nitrofurantoin Suspension ---- 1064
United States v. United States v.
  Articles of Drug . . . Manufactured
  or Labeled by *Goshen* Laboratories,
  Inc. ---------------------------------- 1065
United States v. Universal
  Management Services, Inc. ------ 130
United States v. Universal Mgmt.
  Servs.---------------------------------- 228
United States v.
  Urbuteit ----------------------153, 1200
United States v. v. Universal Mgmt.
  Servs., Inc. ------------------------- 223
United States v. "Vitasafe
  Formula M"------------------------- 328
United States v. Wiesenfeld
  Warehouse -------------------- 280, 281
United States v. Vale---------------- 220

United States v. Various Articles of
  Drugs Consisting of Unknown
  Quantities of Prescription
  Drugs -------------------------------1031
United States v. Vital Health
  Products, Ltd. --------------------- 666
United States v. Vitasafe
  Corp. --------------------------------- 198
United States v. W. T. Grant
  Co. ----------------------------------- 216
United States v. Walsh ------------- 252
United States v. Western
  Serum Co., Inc.----------------67, 1064
United States v. Wiesenfeld
  Warehouse Co. ---------------246, 250
United States v. Wood ------------1517
United States v. Writers &
  Research, Inc. --------------------- 800
United States v. Y. Hata &
  Co., Ltd. ---------------------------- 250
United States v. Yaron
  Laboratories, Inc. -------- 1474, 1476
United States v. Youngblood ------ 813
Upjohn Co. v. Finch ---------------- 778
Upjohn Co. v. Kessler --------------1005
Upjohn Co. v. Medtron
  Labs., Inc.--------------------------- 220
Upjohn Manufacturing Co. v.
  Schweiker--------------------782, 1000
USV Pharmaceutical Corp. v.
  Secretary of HEW ----------------- 778
USV Pharmaceutical Corp. v.
  Weinberger--------------------665, 779
V.E. Irons, Inc. v. United
  States ------------------------------- 328
Valentine v. Chrestensen----------- 428
Van Liew v. United States -------- 378
Vaughn v. Rosen--------------------1509
Vermont Pure Holdings, Ltd. v.
  Nestle Waters North
  America, Inc. ---------------------- 383
Virginia State Pharmacy Board v.
  Virginia Citizens Consumer
  Council -------------------------428, 915
Warner–Lambert Co. v. FTC ------ 992
Warner–Lambert Co. v.
  Heckler ------------------------------ 783
Washington Legal Foundation v.
  Friedman --------------------------- 943
**Washington Legal Foundation v.
  Henney** -----------------------**943**, 948
Washington Post Co. v. HHS -----1521
Washington Post v. Department
  of Justice----------------------------1517
Washington State Apple Advertising
  Comm'n v. Federal Security
  Adm'r -------------------------------- 508
Washington v. Glucksberg -------- 654
Wayte v. United States------------- 170
Weaver v. Graham------------------- 254
Webb v. Department of HHS ---- 1516,
  1517
Webb v. United States -------------- 808
Wedgewood Village Pharmacy,
  Inc. v. United States -------186, 798
Weeks v. United States------------- 382

Weigle v. Curtice Bros. Co. --------- 294

Weinberger v. Bentex Pharmaceuticals, Inc. ---- 66, 665, **667**, 779, 977

Weinberger v. Hynson, Westcott & Dunning, Inc. ------ 51, 400, **662**, 669, 779, **848**

Western States ---------------- 435, 1114

Whalen v. Roe ------------------------- 882

Whitaker v. Thompson -------------- 424, 433, 953

White v. United States -------------- 808

Wickard v. Filburn ------------------- 271

Williamson v. Mazda Motor of America, Inc. ------------------------ 307

Wisconsin v. Mitchell ---------------- 953

Wolfe v. Department of HHS -------- 48

Wolfe v. Weinberger ---------------- 1497

Woodard Laboratories, Inc. v. United States ----------------------- 843

Wooley v. Maynard ---------- 1366, 1369

Wyeth v. Levine ------- 862, 875, 903, 904, 905

Wyeth v. Levine --------------------- **894**

Young v. Community Nutrition Institute --------------------- **512**, 1397

Young v. Community Nutrition Institute ------------------------------- 61

Zauderer v. Office of Disciplinary Counsel of the Sup. Ct. of Ohio ---------- 1364, 1365, 1366, 1369

Zeneca Inc. v. Eli Lilly & Co. ------- 993

Zotos Int'l, Inc. v. Kennedy ------ 1517

Zotos Int'l, Inc. v. Young ----------------------- 1337, 1517

CASES AND MATERIALS

FOOD AND DRUG LAW

FOURTH EDITION

CHAPTER 1

HISTORY AND CONTEXT

A. GLOBAL PRECEDENTS

Peter Barton Hutt, *Government Regulation of the Integrity of the Food Supply*

4 ANNUAL REVIEW OF NUTRITION 1 (1984).

For centuries, government has had an essential role in assuring the integrity of the food supply. The focus of the regulatory function has, of course, evolved over the years. It originated essentially as a means to protect against fraud in the marketplace. Very quickly, it expanded into a mechanism for preventing the sale of unsafe food. As the science of nutrition has developed, it has assumed the role of protecting the nutritional integrity of the food supply as well. . . .

Ancient Times. . . .

The first great botanical treatise on plants as a source of food and medicine, the Enquiry Into Plants written by Theophrastus (370–285 BC), reported on the use of artificial preservatives and flavors in the food supply even at that early date. Theophrastus noted that "even uncompounded substances have certain odors which men endeavor to assist by artificial means even as they assist nature in producing palatable tastes." He reported that items of commerce, such as balsam gum, were mixed with adulterants for economic reasons. The treatise On Agriculture by Cato (234–149 BC) recommended the addition to wine of boiled-down must, salt, marble dust, and resin, and included a method "to determine whether wine has been watered."

Pliny the Elder (23–79 AD) found widespread adulteration throughout the food supply. He described, for example, the adulteration of bread with chalk, vegetable meals, and even cattle fodder. He pointed out that pepper was commonly adulterated with juniper berries. Indeed, his Natural History is replete with so many references to adulteration of the natural food and drug supply that he observed: "So many poisons are employed to force wine to suit our taste—and we are surprised that it is not wholesome!" Pliny, describing "the remedies that are in the control of a man's will," stated that "the greatest aid to health is moderation in food." He urged the value of a kitchen garden for "harmless" market supplies. Galen (131–201 AD), a renowned Roman physician who followed the philosophical tradition of the School of Hippocrates, similarly warned against the adulteration of common food products, such as pepper. . . .

The Roman civil law reflected the concern expressed by these early writers about preserving the integrity of the food supply. Fraud in the sale of merchandise not only gave rise to a private right of action, but also constituted the offense of stellionatus, which included the adulteration of food: "And, where anyone has substituted some article for another; or has put aside goods which he was obliged to deliver, or has spoiled them, he is also liable for this offense." Although stellionatus was technically not a crime, it was comparable to a civil offense under present law, subject to government prosecution, and resulted in such punishment as condemnation to the mines or temporary exile.

The English Experience, 1200–1875

. . . At the end of the Dark Ages . . . concern about the food supply once again emerged. Nowhere is this more evident than in the experience reflected in the laws of England at that time.

Initial governmental concern came in the form of regulating the price of bread, and perhaps other staple food products as well. It did not take long for the English government to realize that the price of food could be regulated only in relation to the quality of that food. Accordingly, the early English regulatory statutes prohibited the adulteration of any staple food that was also subject to price controls.

These regulatory enactments, called assizes, were codified by Parliament in 1266. The 1266 statutes prohibited the sale of any "corrupted wine" or of any meat, fish, bread, or water that was "not wholesome for Man's body" or that was kept so long "that it loseth its natural wholesomeness." These laws, with periodic amendments, continued in effect throughout England until 1844. They were supplemented, from time to time, with additional statutes directed at other food commodities that became a source of commerce, such as butter, cheese, and spices.

In addition to the statutes enacted by Parliament, local cities enacted their own ordinances to prevent food adulteration. The judicially-created common law, reflecting the principles underlying the statutes and ordinances, created both a civil cause of action for damages for any aggrieved party, and a criminal offense as well. Numerous examples of early enforcement actions against the purveyors of adulterated food may be found in the records of the City of London.

Finally, the trade guilds . . . also performed a major regulatory function. These guilds covered every important food category, including the bakers, butchers, cooks, grocers, fruiters, poulters, and salters. Using their power to search all premises and to seize all unwholesome products, the guilds exercised a relatively strong regulatory power in policing the marketing of food to the public.

The Development of Chemistry and the Accum Treatise

As the Renaissance emerged out of the Middle Ages, a few pioneers in the newly developing discipline of "chymistry" broke away from the philosophic mysticism of alchemy and initiated modern scientific inquiry. While earlier analyses of food adulteration depended almost completely upon taste and sight, the new science of chemistry, led particularly by Boyle, slowly began to develop chemical methods of analysis. . . .

By the beginning of the 19th century . . . chemical analysis had advanced to the point where at least qualitative methods had become available for detecting many common food adulterants. In 1820, a German-born chemist, Frederick Accum, working in England, published his landmark Treatise on Adulterations of Food and Culinary Poisons. . . . Accum undertook to describe both the numerous kinds of adulteration practiced at that time and the various methods available to detect them. His treatise was an immediate and worldwide success. . . . The treatise spawned a generation of books on food adulteration in England, the United States, and Europe. Ultimately, it resulted in the modern era of food regulatory statutes.

. . . [T]he English Parliament enacted statutes in 1860, 1872, and 1875, replacing the assizes that had been repealed in 1844, to assure strong regulatory authority to protect the integrity of the food supply.

As would be expected, these English statutes reflect only the state of scientific, medical, and nutritional knowledge at that time. There is no specific mention in those statutes of nutrition. Instead, they broadly prohibited any form of food adulteration, thus assuring that food would reach the marketplace and the consumer in its natural and most nutritious state. Indeed, the prohibitions against adulteration contained in these statutes encompass the same prohibitions contained in our most modern food regulatory statutes, and were in fact the models for the 1906 and 1938 legislation enacted in the United States.

B. THE DEVELOPMENT OF FDA AS AN INSTITUTION

The history of food and drug regulation in the United States is chronicled both in congressional enactments and in the establishment and growth of an institution, the Food and Drug Administration (FDA).

Peter Barton Hutt, *A Historical Introduction*

45 FOOD DRUG COSMETIC LAW JOURNAL 17 (1990).

In his 1837 annual report, Patent Commissioner Henry L. Ellsworth recommended a national agency for the encouragement of agriculture. Congress responded in 1839 by an appropriation of $1000 to the Commissioner of Patents for "the collection of agricultural statistics, and for other agricultural purposes." From then on, the Patent Office collected and reported agricultural statistics, sponsored or conducted chemical investigations on agricultural matters, monitored agricultural developments, and reported on all of these in its annual reports. Beginning in 1849, a separate report was made by the Patent Commissioner to Congress on agricultural matters. An Agricultural Division was established in the Patent Office and a chemical laboratory was created in that Division.

In 1846, Professor Lewis C. Beck, M.D., of Rutgers College and Albany Medical College, published the first American treatise on adulteration of food and drugs. Two years later, at the request of Patent Commissioner Edmund Burke, Congress appropriated $1000 for the Commissioner of Patents to conduct chemical analyses of "vegetable substances produced and used for the food of man and animals in the United States." Commissioner Burke recruited Dr. Beck to do this work for the Patent Office. Dr. Beck submitted his Report on the Breadstuffs of the United States in 1849 and a second report in 1850.

When the United States Department of Agriculture (USDA) was created by Congress in 1862, it included authorization to employ chemists. The Agricultural Division of the Patent Office, including its chemical laboratory, was transferred to the new department and the USDA occupied the office space in the basement of the Patent Office that previously had belonged to that Division. The first Commissioner of Agriculture, Isaac Newton, immediately established the Chemical Division from the former Patent Office chemical laboratory, which became the Division of Chemistry in 1890; the Bureau of Chemistry in 1901; the Food, Drug, and Insecticide Administration in 1927; and the Food and Drug Administration (FDA) in 1930. The FDA was transferred from the USDA to the Federal Security Agency in 1940 and to the Department of Health, Education, and Welfare in 1953, which became the Department of Health and Human Services in 1979. . . .

————

Throughout its history FDA has had essentially the same assignment: to assure that the products it regulates are safe and truthfully labeled. This statement, however, oversimplifies the agency's current responsibilities, which encompass a much larger role in the development, testing, introduction, and marketing of these products. By Washington, D.C., standards, FDA is a venerable institution, whose employees have long memories and a tradition of dedicated, often single-minded public service—in sum, a strong commitment to the job of regulation. As science has advanced, and as the FD&C Act has been amended to transfer the burden of proof from FDA to the regulated industry by requiring premarket approval of products, the agency's activities have changed from court enforcement of clear-cut statutory prohibitions to approval of products based upon an administrative choice among closely balanced alternatives in controlling advanced technologies.

Richard A. Merrill, *The Architecture of Government Regulation of Medical Products*
82 Virginia Law Review 753 (1996).

. . . Under the 1906 law, FDA had relatively little influence over the therapeutic claims made for drugs. Its authority was exerted, if at all, after a drug was on the market and evidence had accumulated that it might not work. The 1938 Act gave the agency a gatekeeper role, which permitted officials to examine and sometimes question a drug's clinical utility. The 1962 Amendments completed the law's reversal of the burden of proof. Since the passage of the Amendments, FDA has been responsible for judging, on the basis of evidence that it prescribed and makers supplied, whether new drugs worked. This shift in responsibility transformed the way in which drugs are developed, tested and marketed.

With this shift came a more subtle change in FDA's own view of its consumer protection role. Citizens may complain when local police fail to curtail unlawful or violent activity, but few believe that even the best functioning police force can solve, much less prevent, all crimes. FDA is believed to have a different role, a responsibility to prevent harm before it occurs. The law makes it unlawful, without proof of intent or demonstration of actual injury or deception, to market drugs that the agency has not approved. In some sense, the agency becomes a warrantor of manufacturer compliance with the rules that govern drug development and marketing. This responsibility is implicitly acknowledged in the agency's own publications, is frequently referred to in press accounts of its performance, and historically has permeated the dialogue between the agency and congressional oversight committees. FDA is repeatedly reminded, and often reminds us, that it shares responsibility for any drug that causes harm. Many observers claim that this perception of FDA's role has made agency officials responsible for allowing drugs to reach the market exceptionally, and inappropriately, cautious. . . .

Over FDA's long history of evaluation and approval of drugs and devices the familiar artifacts of law have often been hard to detect. With the notable exception of Congress's decision to require premarket proof of safety and effectiveness for virtually all new drugs and many medical devices, legal rules have not been a dominant determinant of FDA behavior. The FD&C Act provides formal procedures for challenging agency decisions, but these administrative safeguards are almost never invoked. Nor are FDA's decisions—to grant, withhold, or delay approval—commonly challenged in court. Statutory directives do not materially affect the conduct or pace of agency review, nor do they control its evolving requirements for the data product sponsors must submit to gain marketing approval. The FDA product approval system is, in short, remarkably free from conventional legal constraint. . . .

C. THE DEVELOPMENT OF AMERICAN FOOD AND DRUG LEGISLATION

A single statute, the 1938 FD&C Act, as amended, provides the basic legal framework controlling the activities of producers of food, drugs, cosmetics, medical devices, and tobacco products. The 1938 Act replaced an earlier law, the Federal Food and Drugs Act of 1906, 34 Stat. 768 (also known as the "Pure Food and Drugs Act" and the "Wiley Act.") FDA has also been delegated responsibility for administering other important regulatory laws applicable to these categories of products. Thus, FDA's current statutory armamentarium is an ensemble of laws enacted by Congress over a hundred years in more than a hundred statutes.

1. STATE AND LOCAL LAWS IN THE 19TH CENTURY

Colonial America was an agrarian society. People consumed the food and herbal drugs they produced at home. Even those who lived in small towns kept livestock and maintained their own gardens. As urban centers grew, local food markets were established to serve them. In a classic study published in 1862, T. F. De Voe traced the history of the public markets of the City of New York from the establishment of the West India Company's store in the 1630s through the 1840s. THE MARKET BOOK: A HISTORY OF THE PUBLIC MARKETS OF THE CITY OF NEW YORK (1862). As these markets were established, the City of New York adopted various requirements to regulate them. These requirements largely reflected the English common and statutory law.

Although many of these early laws were aimed at specific commodities or narrow problems, a number were directed more generally at preventing any form of adulteration. As cities grew larger, concern about public health expanded. Lemuel Shattuck's landmark report on public health in 1850 documented the decrease in average life expectancy in America's large urban centers and identified the adulteration of food and drugs as a matter of public health concern. REPORT OF THE SANITARY COMMISSION OF MASSACHUSETTS (1850). Shattuck recommended the establishment of local boards of health which would "endeavor to prevent the sale and use of unwholesome, spurious, and adulterated articles, dangerous to the public health, designed for food, drink, or medicine." *Id.* at 220.

In 1867, De Voe published another study in which he noted the great expansion in public trade and the need for increased regulation to protect both the producer and the consumer:

> The producer is often hundreds of miles in one direction, while the consumer may be as many hundred in another, from the mart at which the productions were sold and purchased. . . .

> A great trade has imperceptibly grown upon us (particularly in New York), which I have sometimes thought, would have been more profitable to both producer and consumer, if proper laws, and practical, honest heads, had been placed over these vast interests, which so much affect the general health and comfort, as well as the pockets of our over-taxed citizens. . . .

THE MARKET ASSISTANT 9 (1867). Around this time, cities, counties, and states throughout the nation started to establish boards of health. Congress initially enacted food and drug legislation for the District of Columbia in 1888 and substantially strengthened it in 1898.

2. NATIONAL DEVELOPMENTS LEADING UP TO 1906

Congress enacted a short-lived statute during the early 1800s to assure a safe and effective supply of smallpox vaccine. 2 Stat. 806 (1813), repealed 3 Stat. 677 (1822). During the nineteenth century, Congress also passed several statutes to regulate foreign commerce in food and drugs. E.g., 9 Stat. 237 (1848) (imported drugs); 22 Stat. 451 (1883) and 29 Stat. 604 (1897) (imported tea); 26 Stat. 414 (1890), 26 Stat. 1089 (1891), 30 Stat. 151, 210 (1897), and 30 Stat. 947, 951 (1899) (imported and exported food). However, no pre-1900 federal law dealt generally with the safety or utility of domestically marketed food and drugs.

At the same time that De Voe was documenting the growth of public food markets, English and American authors influenced by the German chemist Accum, were warning the public about adulteration of food and drugs. In the 1850s and 1860, publications such as Frank Leslie's *Illustrated Newspaper* and the *New York World* mounted campaigns to publicize this problem. By 1879, there was a full-fledged public outcry against adulteration of food and drugs in the United States. Dr. E.R. Squibb, in an address to the Medical Society of the State of New York, proposed the enactment of a national food and drug statute patterned after the English law of 1875. Only 10 days later, Congressman Wright introduced the first comprehensive federal food legislation in Congress. It would take 27 years before such a law ultimately would be enacted by Congress as the Pure Food and Drugs Act of 1906.

Meanwhile, in December 1879, the National Board of Trade adopted a resolution establishing a "$1000 Competition for the Draft of a Food Adulteration Act." The prize-winning entry was submitted by G.W. Wigner, a public analyst in England. The model pure food statute he drafted was highly influential at the state level. In 1881, for example, New York and New Jersey adopted the model legislation wholesale. Wigner's proposal also helped shape the various federal bills proposed (and rejected) in the 1880s and 1890s and the Pure Food and Drugs Act finally enacted by Congress in 1906.

The appeal of national uniformity was an important argument in favor of federal legislation. The director of New York's food and drug regulatory body supported federal regulation of food and drugs on this basis:

> . . . [I]t is very certain that the widely differing statutes relating to our food supply in the different States have worked much mischief, been the cause of much confusion, and seriously embarrassed some useful industries. I think all who have studied the matter will be inclined to admit that uniformity in our food laws is much to be desired. . . .

W. TUCKER, FOOD ADULTERATION: ITS NATURE AND EXTENT, AND HOW TO DEAL WITH IT 21 (1903).

However, because of strong sentiment that food and drug regulation was properly a matter for state and local regulation, federal legislation languished in Congress until 1906. In what would become a longstanding pattern, the enactment of the first national food and drug statute required the impetus of a tragedy. The Biologics Act of 1902, 32 Stat. 728, was passed in response to the distribution in St. Louis of a tetanus-infected diphtheria antitoxin, which resulted in the death of several children. The 1902 law required that biological drugs sold in interstate commerce be produced in licensed establishments. Administration of this statutory scheme was the responsibility of the National Institutes of Health (and its predecessors) before being transferred to FDA in 1972.

The United States Department of Agriculture (USDA) Division of Chemistry played an important role in the investigation of food adulteration that ultimately led to enactment of the Federal Food and Drugs Act of 1906. When Peter Collier became Chief Chemist in 1879, the Division began a major investigation of food and drug adulteration. Collier was succeeded by Dr. Harvey W. Wiley, who served from 1883 to 1912 and is generally considered to be the father of American food and drug law. Under his leadership, the Division of Chemistry began, in 1883, to publish bulletins containing the results of its investigations. This publication, titled "Technical Bulletin 13, *Foods and Food Adulterants*" issued in 10 parts and 1417 pages from 1887 to 1902. After the Department of Agriculture was given Cabinet status in 1889, Congress appropriated funds "to enable the Secretary of Agriculture to extend and continue the investigation of the adulteration of food, drugs, and liquors." The appropriations continued through enactment of the 1906 Act and permitted USDA to conduct extensive work in this area.

Perhaps the most dramatic work of the Division of Chemistry involved food preservatives. Congress specifically appropriated funds in 1900 "to investigate the character of proposed food preservatives and coloring matters; to determine their relation to digestion and health; and to establish the principles which should guide their use." During 1902–1904, a "poison squad" of twelve USDA employees acted as human volunteers to test the safety of boric acid and borax, salicylic acid and salicylates, sulfurous acid and sulfites, benzoic acid and benzoates, and formaldehyde. Each member of the squad complied with a strict, carefully recorded dietary regimen and was subject to extensive examination respecting the effects of the preservatives included in the diet. The results, published in five parts during between 1904 and 1908, drew interest throughout the country.

But the event that finally precipitated enactment of the Food and Drugs Act of 1906 was publication that year of Upton Sinclair's THE JUNGLE, the work of a twenty-seven-year-old author who hoped to convert America to socialism and had no particular interest in legislation to regulate food and drugs. His description of the Chicago meat industry captured nationwide attention and inexorably resulted in the enactment both the Federal Meat Inspection Act of 1906 and the Federal Food and Drugs Act of the same year. Upton Sinclair claimed to have been bitterly disappointed that "I aimed at the public's heart and by accident I hit it in the stomach," but he will forever be remembered as the person who galvanized Congress and the country to bring federal food and drug legislation to fruition after 27 years of consideration.

3. THE 1906 PURE FOOD AND DRUGS ACT

Lauffer Hayes & Frank Ruff, *The Administration of the Federal Food and Drugs Act*

1 LAW & CONTEMPORARY PROBLEMS 16 (1933).

The [1906] Act forbids interstate commerce in adulterated and misbranded food and drugs. It provides criminal penalties for violation and also authorizes the seizure of offending products. In the case of standard drugs, the United States Pharmacopoeia and the National Formulary were resorted to by Congress for the purpose of establishing standards of purity and quality which the drug manufacturers were enjoined to follow—unless they declared standards of their own on the labels of their products. . . . In the case of foods, standards were not available, and in their stead, the draftsmen of the Act resorted to generalities proscribing the intermixture or substitution of substances reducing quality, the abstraction of valuable constituents, the concealment of damage or inferiority, the addition of deleterious ingredients, and the use of spoiled animal or vegetable products. Misbranding was confined chiefly to the making of false or misleading statements regarding a food or drug on the package or label thereof. The sale of an imitation was forbidden, but this was accompanied by provisos which relieved mixtures or compounds not in themselves harmful when sold under "their own distinctive names" or when labeled with the word "compound," "imitation" or "blend," from the operation of both the misbranding and adulteration provisions of the Act. Aside from the latter, the only affirmative labeling requirements were the disclosure of the presence and quantity of enumerated narcotic drugs and the declaration of the net weight of foods when sold in package form.

———

After a decade of implementing the 1906 Act, FDA talked openly about the statute's weaknesses as well as its strengths.

1917 Report of the USDA Bureau of Chemistry

It is perhaps impossible for any one correctly to estimate the general effect of the Food and Drugs Act. To state that more than six thousand cases have been terminated in the courts during the first decade since the enactment of the act; that manufacturers have been cited to hearing more than forty thousand times, that many thousands of factory inspections have been made, that more than seven hundred and fifty thousand shipments of food and drugs, both domestic and imported, have been examined, gives but an imperfect indication of results. . . .

The Food and Drugs Act was among the first of that group of laws which today would be classed as laws for the prevention of unfair competition. The suppression of fraud upon the consumer and of unfair competition among business rivals are but the two faces of the same coin. In consequence the food industries are sincerely and effectively supporting and helping the Bureau of Chemistry to enforce the law. Indeed, the Bureau is not infrequently appealed to by the industries to compel the cessation of unfair practices and to encourage the standardization of products when the industry is incapable by itself of bringing about these results. . . .

The Food and Drugs Act's chief contributions to the safeguarding of the peoples' health have been its effect upon the drug and patent medicine industry, upon the control of the traffic in polluted, decomposed or filthy foods and upon the elimination from foodstuffs of contamination with poisons such as lead and arsenic which entered the product because of the use of impure reagents in the process of manufacture, or of utensils constructed of improper materials.

While the accomplishments of the Food and Drugs Act have been considerable, it must be admitted that it has its serious limitations. Especially conspicuous ones are the lack of legal standards for foods, of authority to inspect warehouses, and of any restriction whatever upon the use of many of the most virulent poisons in drugs; the limitations placed upon the term "drug" by definition which render it difficult to control injurious cosmetics, fraudulent mechanical devices used for therapeutic purposes, as well as fraudulent remedies for obesity and leanness; the limitation of dangerous adulterants to those that are added so that the interstate shipment of a food that naturally contains a virulent poison is unrestricted. Furthermore, the law fails to take cognizance of fraudulent statements covering foods or drugs which are not in or upon the food or drug package. Greater flexibility to prescribe the disposition of imports is also desirable. The Secretary of Agriculture has at one time or another recommended legislation to fill most of these gaps in the law. It should also be noted that at present there is no Federal law which prohibits unregistered or unlicensed persons from sending into interstate commerce medicinal agents, poisons, and the like, although they can not be sold locally by them nor indiscriminately even by registered or licensed pharmacists or physicians.

NOTE

Decisions Under the 1906 Act. FDA's administrative decisions under the 1906 Act were issued by FDA in periodic regulations, Food Inspection Decisions, and Service and Regulatory Announcements, which were compiled through mid-1914 in C. A. GWINN, FOOD AND DRUGS ACT (1914). Court decisions under the 1906 Act were compiled through mid-1934 in MASTIN G. WHITE & OTIS H. GATES, DECISIONS OF COURTS IN CASES UNDER THE FEDERAL FOOD AND DRUGS ACT (1934).

4. THE FEDERAL FOOD, DRUG, AND COSMETIC ACT OF 1938

In the early days of the New Deal, FDA convinced the new Roosevelt Administration to sponsor a complete revision of the 1906 Act.

1933 Report of the Food and Drug Administration

Demand for a complete overhauling of the outworn mechanism of 1906 received a new impetus during the year through the interest of the President of the United States and the sympathy and cooperation of the Secretary and Assistant Secretary of Agriculture. A bill to supplant the present measure was drafted in the Department, reviewed and approved by the Department of Justice, and introduced in the Senate on June 12, by Senator Royal S. Copeland, of New York, as S. 1944.

The new draft preserves all of the worthy features of the present law. Its principal additional features are as follows:

1. Cosmetics are brought within the scope of the statute.

2. Mechanical devices intended for curative purposes, and devices and preparations intended to bring about changes in the structure of the body are also included within the purview of the law.

3. False advertising of foods, drugs, and cosmetics is prohibited.

4. Definitely informative labeling is required.

5. A drug which is, or may be, dangerous to health under the conditions of use prescribed in its labeling is classed as adulterated.

6. The promulgation of definitions and standards for foods, which will have the force and effect of law, is authorized.

7. The prohibition of added poisons in foods or the establishment of safe tolerances therefor is provided for.

8. The operation of factories under Federal permit is prescribed where protection of the public health cannot be otherwise effected.

9. More effective methods for the control of false labeling and advertising of drug products are provided.

10. More severe penalties, as well as injunctions in the case of repeated offenses, are prescribed.

———

The FD&C Act as passed in 1938 differed in two important ways from Copeland's 1933 bill. First, FDA was given authority over the labeling of the products it regulated, but not the advertising. A contemporaneous revision to the Federal Trade Commission Act, known as the Wheeler–Lea Amendments of 1938, confirmed the authority of the FTC to regulate advertising for these products. Second, drug manufacturers were required to demonstrate the safety of their new products to FDA before marketing them. This important power was added in response to a tragic 1937 episode in which more than 100 people died after consuming Elixir Sulfanilamide, a medicine containing the deadly poison diethylene glycol (widely used as automotive antifreeze). It is quite possible that Congress would not have passed the FD&C Act, let alone given FDA premarket review powers over drugs, if not for this highly publicized calamity.

In Chapter 4, we examine the enforcement remedies available to FDA. Today, the principal statutorily authorized sanctions remain those Congress provided the government in 1938: criminal prosecution of individuals and firms guilty of prohibited acts, injunction against such acts, and seizure of adulterated or misbranded goods. More recently, Congress has authorized civil penalties for some violations of the FD&C Act. From the beginning, however, FDA has also relied on informal remedies not explicitly provided in the Act, such as publicity, recalls, and warning letters, which now comprise the primary routine enforcement tools of the agency.

5. THE GROWTH OF THE FD&C ACT: AMENDMENTS SINCE 1938

The FD&C Act has been amended on more than a hundred occasions since its original passage, and it has inexorably grown throughout this period. The FD&C Act today is more than *30 times* the length it was in 1938.

Some of the changes made by Congress can fairly be described as technical or remedial. The more noteworthy amendments have either extended the coverage of the Act or, more commonly, enlarged FDA's substantive authority over products already within its jurisdiction. Notable early examples of the latter type of legislation include the Miller Pesticides Amendment of 1954, which empowered FDA to establish tolerances for pesticides on agricultural commodities; the Food Additives Amendment of 1958, which required premarket approval of new food ingredients and many food contact articles; and the Color Additive Amendments of 1960, which established a premarket approval system for colors used in food, drugs, and cosmetics.

Major amendments to the basic Act were enacted in 1962 and 1976. The Drug Amendments of 1962 fundamentally restructured the way in which FDA regulated new medicines, transforming a system of premarket notification into one that requires individual premarket approval of the safety and effectiveness of every new drug. The 1962 Amendments also thrust FDA into significant roles in regulating prescription drug promotion and clinical testing of new agents. With the passage of this legislation, the regulation of drugs became the single most controversial, and probably the most important, of FDA's activities.

In 1976 Congress made fundamental changes in the way that medical devices are regulated under the FD&C Act. The Medical Device Amendments were the culmination of fifteen years of careful study and debate, not only within Congress and the agency, but also among representatives of clinical medicine, biomedical engineering, device manufacturers, and consumer groups. While the 1976 Amendments did not significantly enlarge FDA's jurisdiction, they transformed its approach to regulation of these products and substantially enlarged the array of regulatory tools available to it.

The 1980s were punctuated by additional but more narrowly focused amendments, including the Infant Formula Amendments of 1980, the Orphan Drug Act of 1983, the Drug Price Competition and Patent Term Restoration Act of 1984, the Drug Export Amendments of 1986, the Prescription Drug Marketing Act of 1987, and the Generic Animal Drug and Patent Term Restoration Act of 1988. In 1988, Congress created FDA by statute.

The 1990s and 2000s produced a plethora of important amendments to the FD&C Act, some narrow and others very broad. In 1990, Congress passed the Nutrition Labeling and Education Act and the Safe Medical Devices Act, as well as a statute to control food transportation. Legislation regarding pediatric testing of new drugs was enacted in 1997, 2002, and 2003. As part of the 1990 medical device legislation, Congress incorporated the 1967 Radiation Control for Health and Safety Act into the FD&C Act. Narrowly drawn statutes in 1994, 1996, and 2004 also amended animal drug provisions of the Act relating, respectively, to the limitations imposed on unapproved uses of prescription animal drugs, the new animal drug approval process, and animal drugs for minor species. The drug export provisions enacted in 1986 were replaced by more lenient provisions in the FDA Export Reform and Enhancement Act of 1996, and new drug import provisions were enacted in 2000, 2003, and 2006. Following the September 11, 2001 terrorist attack, Congress passed the Public Health Security and Bioterrorism Preparedness and Response Act of 2002 to strengthen food security and to promote the development of drug and device products to counter bioterrorism.

Just since the publication of the last edition of this casebook, Congress has passed the Food and Drug Administration Amendments Act of 2007 (FDAAA), which, among other things, increased FDA's postmarket authority over the safety of human drugs; the 2009 Family Smoking Prevention and Tobacco Control Act, which gave FDA the power to regulate tobacco products; the 2011 Food Safety Modernization Act (FSMA), which represents the most significant increase in FDA's regulatory power over food since at least 1958, and the 2012 Food and

Drug Administration Safety and Innovation Act, which revises the drug and device provisions in potentially important ways.

The past two decades have also witnessed an explosion in Congressional authorization for FDA to charge user fees to help finance FDA's ever-increasing responsibilities for premarket approval, Congress enacted user fee authority for prescription drugs in 1992, 1997, 2002, 2007, and 2012; for medical devices in 2002, 2004, 2005, 2007, and 2012; for animal drugs in 2003, 2008, and 2013; and for tobacco products in 2009. Congress also authorized user fees for animal generic drugs in 2008 and 2013, and for human generic drugs and biosimilars in 2012.

FDA has inherited entire programs from other agencies. The seafood, milk, and food service sanitation programs were transferred from the Public Health Service in 1968. The National Center for Toxicological Research was made part of FDA in 1971. Responsibility for the Radiation Control for Health and Safety Act of 1968 was transferred to FDA in 1971 and the Biologics Act of 1902 came to FDA in 1972.

The history of federal food and drug legislation has not, however, been an unbroken succession of enlargements of regulatory power. Congress transferred primary jurisdiction over poultry to USDA in 1957, over pesticides to the Environmental Protection Agency in 1970, over controlled substances to the Drug Enforcement Agency in 1970, and over hazardous household products to the Consumer Product Safety Commission in 1972. In 1976, FDA also saw the first of a series of enactments intended to curtail its authority under the FD&C Act, perhaps reflecting growing congressional skepticism of regulation generally as well as specific solicitude for the targets of FDA attention. The Vitamin–Mineral Amendments of 1976 limited FDA's authority to regulate the composition and promotion of dietary supplements— marking a rejection of the agency's decade-long efforts to control high-potency nutritional products and health foods. A year later, Congress passed the first of a series of laws forestalling any FDA action to ban the use of saccharin in food. In 1977, it also adopted a rider to unrelated legislation that directed FDA to refrain from implementing a proposed system for controlling the sanitation of shellfish harvested in U.S. waters until the Department of Commerce had completed what was expected to be an alarming assessment of the economic impact. In 1994, Congress enacted the Dietary Supplement Health and Education Act to prevent FDA from taking stringent regulatory action against dietary supplements. And in 1997, Congress enacted the Food and Drug Administration Modernization Act, which reformed several facets of FDA regulation.

While these and other expressions of congressional disagreement on specific issues depart from the general trajectory of federal food and drug legislation, they do not appear to represent a fundamental shift in legislative policy. Over the past several decades, both parties in both houses of Congress have generally displayed support for vigorous regulation of food, drugs, and other medical products.

6. OTHER LAWS ENFORCED BY FDA

While the much-amended FD&C Act forms the agency's basic legal framework, FDA also administers several other statutes applicable to one or more categories of products within its jurisdiction. It has been delegated authority to enforce the Biologics Act, originally enacted in 1902 and now codified in Section 351 of the Public Health Service Act, 42 U.S.C. 262. The Biologics Act provides the agency's primary authority to regulate biological products, such as vaccines, products derived from human blood, and drugs produced by the recent advances in biotechnology. FDA relies on section 361 of the Public Health Service Act, 42 U.S.C. 264 ("Regulations to control communicable diseases"), to regulate sanitation in food service establishments and on interstate carriers and to prevent the transmission of disease by blood, human tissue, and more unusual products such as pet turtles. Specific aspects of food packaging and labeling are regulated by FDA under the Fair Packaging and Labeling Act of 1966. FDA enforces pesticide tolerances for food as required by the Environmental Protection Agency and child resistant packaging as required by the Consumer Product Safety Commission under the Poison Prevention Packaging Act of 1970. Another important law delegated to FDA is the Radiation Control for Health and Safety Act of 1968, now recodified by the Safe Medical Devices Act of 1990 as Section 531 et seq. of the FD&C Act, under which it regulates X-ray machines, microwave ovens, ultrasound equipment, and other products capable of emitting potentially harmful radiation. Finally, the 2009 Family Smoking Prevention and Tobacco Control Act gave FDA enforcement power over the warnings provisions of section 4 of the Federal Cigarette Labeling and Advertising Act and section 3 of the Comprehensive Smokeless Tobacco Health Education Act.

D. FDA'S MISSION

The FD&C Act, like its 1906 predecessor, consists of statutory prohibitions against adulterated and misbranded products. From the time of its origin, FDA—reflecting the constant pressure from Congress and the media—has regarded its mission as protecting the public against unsafe and mislabeled products. In the past two decades, however, advocates for seriously ill patients have argued that FDA has a corresponding responsibility to promote health by rapid review and approval of new medical products. This issue was directly addressed in the Food and Drug Administration Modernization Act of 1997, which added Section 903(b) to the FD&C Act:

(b) MISSION.—The [Food and Drug] Administration shall—

(1) promote the public health by promptly and efficiently reviewing clinical research and taking appropriate action on the marketing of regulated products in a timely manner;

(2) with respect to such products, protect the public health by assuring that [they are not adulterated or misbranded].

Notwithstanding the clear decision by Congress to put health promotion first and health protection second, FDA, reflecting its heritage, has reversed this order in the mission statement that appears on the agency's website.

Congress describes the agency in the following terms:

Agriculture, Rural Development, Food and Drug Administration, and Related Agencies Appropriations Bill, 2014
Senate Report No. 113–046, 113th Congress, 1st Session (2013).

The Food and Drug Administration [FDA] is a scientific regulatory agency whose mission is to promote and protect the public health and safety of Americans. FDA's work is a blend of science and law. The Food and Drug Administration Modernization Act of 1997 [FDAMA] (Public Law 105–115) reaffirmed the responsibilities of the FDA; to ensure safe and effective products reach the market to a timely way, and to monitor products for continued safety after they are in use. In addition, FDA is entrusted with two critical functions in the Nation's war on terrorism; preventing willful contamination of all regulated products, including food, and improving the availability of medications to prevent or treat injuries caused by biological, chemical or nuclear agents.

The FDA Foods program has the primary responsibility for assuring that the food supply, quality of foods, food ingredients and dietary supplements are safe, sanitary, nutritious, wholesome, and honestly labeled, and that cosmetic products are safe and properly labeled. The variety and complexity of the food supply has grown dramatically while new and more complex safety issues, such as emerging microbial pathogens, natural toxins, and technological innovations in production and processing, have developed. This program plays a major role in keeping the United States food supply among the safest in the world.

. . . .

The FDA Drugs programs are comprised of four separate areas, Human Drugs, Animal Drugs, Medical Devices, and Biologics. FDA is responsible for the life cycle of the product, including premarket review and postmarket surveillance of human, animal and biological products to ensure their safety and efficacy. For Human Drugs this includes assuring that all drug products used for the prevention, diagnosis and treatment of disease are safe and effective. Additional procedures include the review of investigational new drug applications; evaluation of market applications for new and generic drugs, labeling and composition of prescription and over-the-counter drugs; monitoring the quality and safety of products manufactured in, or imported into, the United States; and, regulating the advertising and promotion of prescription drugs. The Animal Drugs and Feeds Program ensures only safe and beneficial veterinary drugs, intended for the treatment and/or prevention of diseases in animals and the improved production of food-producing animals, are approved for marketing.

The FDA Biologics program assures that blood and blood products, blood test kits, vaccines, and therapeutics are pure, potent, safe, effective, and properly labeled. The program inspects blood banks and blood processors, licenses and inspects firms collecting human source plasma, evaluates and licenses biologics manufacturing firms and products; lot releases licensed products; and monitors adverse events associated with vaccine immunization, blood products, and other biologics.

The FDA Devices and Radiological program ensures the safety and effectiveness of medical devices and eliminates unnecessary human exposure to manmade radiation from medical, occupational, and consumer products. In addition, the program enforces quality standards under the Mammography Quality Standards Act (Public Law 108–365). Medical devices include thousands of products from thermometers and contact lenses to heart pacemakers, hearing aids, and MRIs. Radiological products include items such as microwave ovens and video display terminals.

FDA's National Center for Toxicological Research in Jefferson, Arkansas, serves as a specialized resource, conducting peer-review scientific research that provides the basis for FDA to make sound science-based regulatory decisions through its premarket review and postmarket surveillance. The research is designed to define and understand the biological mechanisms of action underlying the toxicity of products and lead to developing methods to improve assessment of human exposure, susceptibility and risk of those products regulated by FDA.

In 2009, Congress granted FDA new authority to regulate the manufacture, distribution, and marketing of tobacco products. FDA exercises this responsibility by protecting the public health from the health effects of tobacco, setting scientific standards and standards for tobacco product review, conducting compliance activities to enforce its authority over tobacco, and conducting public education and outreach about the health effects of tobacco products.

E. FDA'S STRUCTURE AND ORGANIZATION

1. LEGAL BASIS FOR THE AGENCY

While FDA's legal authority is outlined in the FD&C Act and related laws, the agency's structure is described in regulations, which are subject to change. 21 C.F.R. 5.1100. In fact, although it has a long institutional history, FDA was a creature of administrative action until it was finally recognized in legislation in 1988. 102 Stat. 3048, 3120–3122 (1988). Similarly, the agency's top official, the Commissioner of Food and Drugs, was not recognized by statute until that year. As a formal matter, legal responsibility for implementing the FD&C Act and the other statutes that the agency administers continues to lie with the Secretary of Health and Human Services (HHS). The Secretary delegates this authority to the Commissioner of Food and Drugs. These delegations used to be listed in 21 C.F.R. 5.10, but they are now found on the FDA website. See 64 Fed. Reg. 17285 (Apr. 2, 2004).

2. THE FDA COMMISSIONER

Every FDA Commissioner who took office before 1988, though perhaps approved by the White House, was appointed by the Secretary of HHS or its predecessor departments and thus was not subject to Senate confirmation. Under Section 903(b)(1) of the FD&C Act, added in 1988, the Commissioner must now be appointed by the President with the advice and consent of the Senate. In formal organizational terms, the Commissioner ranks in the third tier of the Department, below the Assistant Secretaries of HHS. In fact, the job is more prominent than many ostensibly higher-ranking HHS offices, and it attracts individuals of national reputation. Because of the agency's visibility and the potential sensitivity of its decisions, FDA Commissioners have always had a direct line to the Secretary of HHS and sometimes to the White House as well.

During President George W. Bush's first six years in office (2001–2006), there was a confirmed FDA Commissioner in office for a total of only 18 months. Two of the individuals Bush nominated were subject to lengthy delays, imposed by both Democrats and Republicans. However, the current commissioner under President Obama, Margaret Hamburg, was confirmed easily and served in the position since May 2009.

3. FDA'S PLACE WITHIN THE FEDERAL GOVERNMENT

FDA is an operating division of the U.S. Department of Health and Human Services, along with other entities including The Centers for Disease Control and Prevention (CDC), the Centers for Medicare and Medicaid Services (CMS), the Health Resources and Service Administration (HRSA), the Indian Health Service (HIS), the National Institutes of Health (NIH), and the Office of Public Health and Science (OPHS) (which itself includes the Office of the Surgeon General, the Public Health Service Commissioned Corps, the National Vaccine Program Office, and various other agencies). Before it was made a part of HHS, FDA was within the U.S. Department of Agriculture (origins to 1940), the Federal Security Agency (1940 to 1953), and the Department of Health, Education, and Welfare (1953 to 1979).

As the FDA organizational location reveals, the agency does not have the same independence from presidential control that independent regulatory commissions like the Federal Trade Commission (FTC), Securities and Exchange Commission (SEC), and Consumer Product Safety Commission (CPSC) ostensibly enjoy. A Commissioner of Food and Drugs is subject to direction and may be removed by the Secretary (now by the President) for any or no reason. The agency is headed by a single administrator. Its decisions represent collegial judgments only to the extent that the Commissioner has collegial support. Deliberative meetings among agency officials are frequent, informal, unannounced, and closed to the public. The Government in the Sunshine Act, 90 Stat. 1241 (1976), has no application to FDA's internal major deliberations. However, the agency's numerous expert advisory committees hold open meetings as required by the Federal Advisory Committee Act, 86 Stat. 770 (1972).

FDA's location in the Department of HHS might suggest that the agency is subject to pervasive political influence. For several reasons, however, this has not been the historical pattern. First, the evident scientific basis for most of FDA's decisions has helped insulate it from many of the customary forms of political pressure. Second, the visibility of FDA's programs has given the agency a public standing that often blunts pressure from within any administration. Finally, the agency's relatively low rank in the bureaucratic hierarchy means that few other jobs within it are subject to political appointment. As a technical matter, only two positions in FDA—the Commissioner and the Deputy Commissioner—have been formally subjected to Secretarial or Presidential appointment. Other top positions, such as the Chief Counsel and the Associate Commissioners are now also usually regarded as political appointees (although the Chief Counsel position was recently returned to nonpolitical status). But the Directors of the Centers for Food, Drugs, Biologics, Devices, Veterinary Medicine, and Tobacco Products are not political appointees. A change in administration therefore does not result in resignations or reassignments among the agency's middle and upper level managers, even though it may abruptly terminate the service of a Commissioner and some Associate Commissioners.

Accordingly, for most of its existence, FDA has operated with considerable decisional independence and enjoyed continuity in the service of employees who hold managerial positions and staff its several field offices. When FDA abruptly changes its position or delays a decision on a controversial issue—as has happened under both Democratic and Republican Administrations—it is usually unclear whether this reflects policy changes or political considerations, if indeed there is a difference. Recently, however, both the George W. Bush Administration and the Obama administration have generated controversy by interfering in the FDA decision making process regarding petitions to institute and expand over-the-counter availability of Plan B emergency contraceptives. *See infra* p. 966. For discussion of the politicization of FDA under President Clinton, see Kathryn R. Cook, *The Presidential FDA: Politics Meet Science* (2001), in Chapter 1(E) of the Electronic Book. *See generally* Alex S. Gordon, *The Delicate Dance of Immersion and Insulation: The Politicization of the FDA Commissioner* (2003), in Chapter 1(C) of the Electronic Book.

The structure and location of FDA within the executive branch have been the subject of continuous study and debate. Over the years, various commissions and bodies have recommended that FDA be divided into two agencies, one regulating food and cosmetics and the other regulating medical products; indeed, a number of bills have been introduced in Congress to implement such a plan. Others have advocated transferring FDA's food regulatory functions to another existing agency, such as USDA or CPSC. Still others have proposed expanding FDA's authority by giving it USDA's food regulatory responsibilities, which extend primarily to meat and poultry. However, every such proposal has ultimately been defeated by some combination of bureaucratic inertia, congressional committee territoriality, a feeling of shared mission within FDA itself, and a general feeling that the costs and burden of a major reorganization would outweigh any ultimate gains.

4. FDA's SIZE AND INTERNAL ORGANIZATION

FDA's total full-time workforce numbered 10,826 in 2010 and now undoubtedly exceeds 11,000, a majority of whom are located in the Washington, D.C. area. Most of the remainder—inspectors, compliance officers, and laboratory scientists—work in one of five Regional Offices, 20 District Offices, 13 laboratories, or more than 150 Resident Posts around the country, or at approximately 13 foreign posts in Europe, Latin America, China, India, the Middle East, and Sub–Saharan Africa. FDA's headquarters personnel are dispersed among about three dozen different buildings in and around Washington. They are divided among eight primary components. First, there is the Commissioner's office and central administrative staff, which includes several Associate Commissioners, budget officers, and personnel experts. Second, there are the field operations, which consist of regional, district, and local offices throughout the country that carry on FDA's inspectional and enforcement activities, all of which are coordinated by the Associate Commissioner for Regulatory Affairs. Third, there is the National Center for Toxicological Research, established in 1971 in the converted facilities of the former biological warfare project in Jefferson, Arkansas. Finally, there are six Centers (formerly "Bureaus") responsible for one or more categories of products within FDA's jurisdiction: the Center for Drug Evaluation and Research (CDER), the Center for Biologics Evaluation and Research (CBER), the Center for Food Safety and Applied Nutrition (CFSAN), the Center for Devices and Radiological Health (CDRH), the Center for Veterinary Medicine (CVM), and the Center for Tobacco Products (CTP). The heads of each of these entities—Center directors—report to the Commissioner.

A key organization in FDA's regulatory operations, but not formally a part of the agency, is the Chief Counsel's office—officially the Food and Drug Division of the Office of the General Counsel of the Department of Health and Human Services. FDA's Chief Counsel is thus an employee of the Secretary of HHS, not of the Commissioner of Food and Drugs. In practice, however, the office generally functions more as an active component of the agency than as a representative of the Department. The FDA Chief Counsel essentially functions as the Commissioner's lawyer.

One other important organizational development deserves attention. Throughout the first 70 to 80 years of FDA's history, regulatory policy was made by the Office of the Commissioner and the Office of the Chief Counsel and carried out through the lower levels of the headquarters staff and the field force. Within the past generation, this dynamic has changed dramatically. Today, policy is largely made at the lowest levels of FDA rather than at the top. There are a number of interrelated reasons for this development. First, the vast bulk of FDA's daily decisions now come in the form of action taken with respect to applications for FDA approval of drugs, biologics, devices, and other products that require FDA approval prior to marketing. The Office of the Commissioner almost never reviews these decisions and may not even know about them. It is these decisions that determine FDA policy, not the FD&C Act or the implementing regulations. Second, the Office of the Commissioner and the Office of Chief Counsel are occupied with establishing very broad policy, overseeing the operations of the agency, and managing relations with HHS, the Office of Management and Budget (OMB), other government agencies, Congress, the media, trade associations, professional societies, and a host of other interested domestic and international organizations and individuals. To the extent that they consider specific regulatory issues, it is almost always in the context of a crisis or emotionally-charged matter that commands national interest, such as a major recall; the approval of a controversial product like RU–486, Plan B, or breast implants; or another question that demands prompt and complete attention at a high level. Third, the agency has now grown so large that the Office of the Commissioner could not oversee all of the agency's activities even if it had the resources and desire to do so. For example, more than 2000 informal guidances have been issued in the past decade governing in minute detail thousands of issues relating to new drug regulation alone. It is doubtful that the Office of the Commissioner has the expertise, much less the staff, to review, understand, and comment on even a small fraction of them. Accordingly, the actions of low-level FDA employees almost always prevail within the agency and thus constitute the true agency policy with regard to the matters involved.

During the 1970s, the Office of the Commissioner conducted a comprehensive review of all agency actions through weekly three-hour meetings with each Center (then called Bureaus). Few important issues took longer than seven days to be considered and resolved under this intensive scrutiny. But this approach was abandoned by the 1990s, and it would be difficult to revive it today. One former Center Director famously confided that he had not met with the Commissioner in over a year and had not even been in his presence in more than six months. Today the Center Directors, rather than the Commissioner, largely run the agency.

Even at the Centers, however, review and supervision of the low level employees is attenuated, and in many situations nonexistent. An issue that rises to the level of the Center Director is inherently a very difficult one, and it is only under extraordinary circumstances that the top management of the Center will overrule a decision made below. Thus, again, low level agency employees frequently make the most important decisions, with major impact on the country's health and economy.

F. FDA'S RELATIONSHIP WITH OTHER AGENCIES

Since 1970, the proliferation of new regulatory statutes and agencies has enlarged the need for FDA to coordinate activities with other agencies. Numerous memoranda of understanding (MOU) and interagency agreements (IAG) have been published in the Federal Register.

Mutually Exclusive Jurisdiction. FDA-regulated products are often explicitly excluded from other regulatory statutes. For example, the Toxic Substances Control Act (TSCA), 15 U.S.C. 2602(2)(B)(vi), excludes FDA-regulated products, and EPA has interpreted this exclusion as extending to all aspects of these products, including raw materials. *See, e.g.,* 42 Fed. Reg. 64572 (Dec. 23, 1977) ; 43 Fed. Reg. 11318 (Mar. 17, 1978). Because jurisdictional lines are not always easy to draw, however, FDA has on occasion entered into agreements with other regulatory agencies to allocate responsibilities. For instance, FDA and the Consumer Product Safety Commission (CPSC) have agreed that, to the extent that food containers and utensils that do not become components of food present a hazard, they are subject to regulation by CPSC. 41 Fed. Reg. 34342 (Aug. 13, 1976).

Overlapping and Concurrent Jurisdiction. FDA-regulated products are not always exempt from other regulatory statutes. Congress has often addressed the jurisdictional issue ambiguously or not at all. For example, the jurisdictional divisions between USDA and FDA for meat, and between BATF (now TTB) and FDA for alcoholic beverages, have been the subject of intense controversy and not even now definitively resolved. To guide agency officials and regulated firms following the creation of EPA by Executive Order in 1970, FDA and EPA entered into a series of agreements regarding matters of mutual responsibility. 36 Fed. Reg. 24234 (Dec. 22, 1971); 38 Fed. Reg. 24233 (Sept. 6, 1973); 40 Fed. Reg. 25078 (June 12, 1975). FDA and BATF (TTB) have entered into an MOU defining their responsibilities for adulterated alcoholic beverages. 52 Fed. Reg. 45502 (Nov. 30, 1987). FDA and the Patent and Trademark Office (PTO) have entered into an MOU establishing procedures for their mutual responsibilities under the Drug Price Competition and Patent Term Restoration Act of 1984. 52 Fed. Reg. 17830 (May 12, 1987). An intriguing example of such an MOU is the agreement entered into between FDA (which administers the Radiation Control Act) and the Federal Aviation Administration to cooperatively regulate the risk that laser light shows present to aviation by potentially harming the vision of aircraft pilots, crew, and passengers. MOU 225–99–6000 (1998).

FDA and the Customs Service of the Department of Treasury (now Customs and Border Protection of the Department of Homeland Security), which jointly enforce the import provisions of the FD&C Act, have signed MOUs and established a working relationship on sampling and refusal of imports. 44 Fed. Reg. 53577 (Sept. 14, 1979); 69 Fed. Reg. 924 (Jan. 7, 2004).

Service to Other Agencies. FDA provides services to several other agencies as a part of its regulatory activities. For example, FDA has agreed to inspect toxicology testing laboratories for compliance with EPA's Good Laboratory Practice requirements, 43 Fed. Reg. 14124 (Apr. 4, 1978), and has assumed the responsibility to assure that drugs and biologics procured by Department of Defense are of appropriate quality, FDA Compliance Policy Guide No. 7155d.02 (Oct. 1, 1980).

Cooperation with States. FDA also works extensively with state regulatory bodies. For example, the agency is a participant in multiple cooperative food sanitation programs. *See infra* p. 527.

G. FDA's Relationship With Regulated Industry

Throughout its history the relationship that does, or should, prevail between agency officials and organizations that market regulated products has been a source of controversy. Academic theorists have argued that the relationship would become too conciliatory with the passage of time. Relations between FDA and the firms it regulates have been more contentious than this "capture" theory predicts. Nevertheless, concerns that FDA may be too receptive to industry claims have persisted. Because compliance with the FD&C Act requires voluntary action by regulated firms, frequent informal communications are inevitable.

One well known episode is illustrative of this controversy. In August 1974, eleven employees of the Bureau of Drugs (now CDER), testified at a Senate hearing that FDA officials had harassed them when they made decisions adverse to drug manufacturers. "Examination of the Pharmaceutical Industry, 1973–74," Joint Hearings Before the Subcomm. on Health of the Senate Comm. on Labor and Public Welfare and the Subcomm. on Administrative Practice and Procedure of the Senate Comm. on the Judiciary, 93rd Cong., 1st & 2nd Sess., Pt. 7 (1974). Commissioner Alexander Schmidt vigorously disputed the charges. "Regulation of New Drug R & D by the Food and Drug Administration, 1974," 93rd Cong., 2nd Sess. (1974). Nonetheless, HEW Secretary David Mathews was persuaded to appoint a panel of outside experts to investigate the charges that FDA was too close to regulated firms and that the industry exerted undue influence over agency decisions.

Review Panel on New Drug Regulation, Final Report

Department of Health, Education and Welfare, 1977.

. . . FDA employees and industry representatives frequently discuss INDs and NDAs in telephone conversations and at meetings. Industry representatives also make numerous unscheduled visits to FDA reviewers to drop off materials, chat, and check on the status of their companies' applications. . . .

FDA employees and industry representatives have stated that oral communications are essential because many scientific issues are not easily resolved through written correspondence. Nevertheless, such a system has led to questions about the influence exerted by the pharmaceutical industry on agency decisions, especially in light of FDA's trade secrets policy.

The . . . Panel agrees that non-written communication at times can be a more efficient means of resolving complex scientific questions than written communication. . . . However, the Panel found no justification for much of the informal, non-written contact which takes place between FDA staff and industry representatives. . . .

. . . Because the system is *ad hoc*, Bureau procedures for communicating with industry vary from division to division and sometimes from reviewer to reviewer. Although FDA staff are required to prepare memoranda of their communications with industry representatives, the Panel found that reviewers differed in the extent to which they documented such contacts and in the amount of detail they provided in memoranda.

The Panel recommends that FDA institute a more formalized system of contact, in which written correspondence is the preferred means of communication. Such a system, using a minimum of oral, informal communications, is appropriate for FDA to assure both its regulatees and the public that it is performing its function fairly and objectively. It also is necessary to produce a well-documented record of FDA decision-making. Finally, written correspondence is consistent with the Bureau of Drugs' duty to approve or disapprove new drugs solely on the basis of the scientific data presented. . . .

———

Several years later, a similar advisory body, chartered to identify ways to expedite the development of new drugs, offered a different view.

Final Report of the National Committee to Review Procedures for Approval of New Drugs for Cancer and Aids

Department of Health and Human Services, 1990.

If the drug development and approval process is to proceed expeditiously, it is essential that there be free and open communication between FDA and drug sponsors at all times. The relationship between FDA reviewers and drug sponsors must be informal, highly interactive, and foster a spirit of mutual cooperation. An atmosphere of arms-length formality will slow down the process, raise artificial barriers to drug development and approval, and seriously harm the public health. The development and approval of AIDS and cancer drugs depends upon helpful cooperation, not adversarial isolation. Communications should most frequently be by telephone, fax, and computer, to provide current information, quick responses to important questions, and a feeling of genuine partnership. The artificial barriers that have been erected through years of criticism on the part of both the regulators and the regulated have created a serious threat to rapid development and approval of new drugs, and can no longer be tolerated. . . .

———

A similar theme was sounded during a 2005 conference sponsored by the FDA and Association of American Medical Colleges on "Drug Development Science." The conference was inspired by a March 2005 white paper issued by the agency on the need to improve the system for developing and regulating medical products, titled "Innovation or Stagnation: Challenge and Opportunity on the Critical Path to New Medical Products." The conference dealt with a wide range of issues, among them the now-familiar debate over the appropriate relationship between regulators and the regulated. While the AAMC/FDA report called for earlier and faster collaboration, it acknowledged a continuing concern about agency capture, a concern fueled by the controversy over FDA's handling of the Cox–2 inhibitor, VIOXX.

> In exploring novel preclinical research approaches, industry would like to improve the level of dialogue with FDA on the design and implementation of innovative early study designs. Some industry researchers find that discussions with FDA during the pre-approval research process tend to be highly orchestrated. Multiple rules of engagement across different CDER and CBER offices and

differing toxicology requirements in FDA review divisions make it needlessly difficult for industry to address the dynamic process of moving from pre-clinical animal testing to human experimentation. . . .

The report went on to recommend that communication between sponsors and FDA be improved.

NOTE

Ex Parte Communications. FDA's regulations, 21 C.F.R. 10.65, 10.70, and 10.80, permit essentially unlimited contact between agency employees and private individuals, including representatives of regulated firms, but at the same time require that all significant communications be summarized and disclosed. All memoranda summarizing meetings or telephone conversations are available to the public and are required to be made part of the pertinent administrative record. *Cf. Home Box Office, Inc. v. FCC,* 567 F.2d 9 (D.C. Cir. 1977). If a draft regulation is made available to any outside person, it is available to everyone. *See, e.g.,* 37 Fed. Reg. 24117 (Nov. 14, 1972); 40 Fed. Reg. 12535 (Mar. 19, 1975).

H. FDA'S RESOURCES

The more than 10,000 employees at FDA are responsible for regulating the products of numerous large and diverse industries. FDA has fared relatively well in maintaining its budget. For FY 2010, the agency budget was $3.291 billion (plus $922 million in user fees), compared with $1.777 billion in 2005, $567 million in 1990 and $313 million in 1980. As large as this figure sounds, however, it is not sufficient to fund the agency's ever-growing portfolio of responsibilities. *See* Peter Barton Hutt, *The State of Science at the Food and Drug Administration,* 60 ADMIN. L. REV. 431 (2008). Approximately 20 to 25 cents of every consumer retail sales dollar is spent for products within the agency's jurisdiction (the latter figure is probably more accurate since the agency gained regulatory authority over tobacco products in 2009). As the following chapters reveal, the scope of FDA's authority over this heterogeneous universe of products varies widely, ranging from comprehensive premarket approval responsibility for new drugs, food additives, life-supporting medical devices, and tobacco products to the policing activities applicable to most food products, nonprescription drugs, and cosmetics. Within the several industries over which FDA has some measure of regulatory control, there is enormous diversity among individual firms. They range in size from giant nationwide food processors and distributors to small warehousemen, from multinational chemical companies to small partnerships of biomedical engineers engaged in the development of a single type of device, and from the nation's largest cattle feed lots to contract laboratories engaged in preclinical testing of new food ingredients. And FDA performs its manifold obligations with an annual budget less than half the size of that of Montgomery County, Maryland.

There is at present no validated historical statistical series reflecting the resources and work of FDA throughout its history. The following table represents the best available data on the growth of the agency budget (including user fees) from 1890 to the present.

YEAR	APPROPRIATION	EMPLOYEES (FTEs)
1890	12,000	
1900	17,100	
1910	880,560	70
1920	1,391,571	374
1930	1,537,300	
1940	2,741,000	719
1950	4,802,500	955
1960	13,800,000	1660
1970	72,352,000	4363
1980	312,796,000	7517
1990	567,079,000	7692
1995	897,104,000	9264
2000	1,183,095,000	8857
2005	1,776,784,000	10,668
2010	3,291,676,000	12,381

In the years prior to 1906, there was increasing investigation of food and drug adulteration but no direct regulatory functions. From 1906 to 1927, FDA combined regulatory work with continuing research on agricultural chemistry. Since 1927, the entire FDA budget has been devoted, directly or indirectly, to regulation.

NOTE

Citizens Committees. On three occasions, the Secretary of HEW/HHS has appointed a Citizens Committee to review the FDA mission, resources, and programs. See Report of the Citizens Advisory Committee on the Food and Drug Administration to the Secretary of Health, Education, and Welfare (June 1955); Report of the Citizens Advisory Committee to the Secretary of Health, Education, and Welfare on the Food and Drug Administration (Oct. 1962); Final Report of the Advisory Committee on the Food and Drug Administration (May 1991). See also "Food and Drug Administration Oversight," Hearings before the Subcomm. on Health and the Environment of the House Comm. on Energy and Commerce, 102d Cong., 1st Sess. (1991). On each occasion the report has resulted in a substantial increase in FDA appropriations.

I. THE REGULATORY ENVIRONMENT

Experienced practitioners in any regulatory field appreciate the need to understand the background and motives of the agency with which they are dealing, and sophisticated observers of federal regulation have commented on the influence of history, personality, and style on the regulatory process. Though it is not possible to describe the style or atmosphere of a century-old agency in a few pages, our account of FDA's formulation and enforcement of substantive legal requirements in this book attempts to convey a sense of the forces that drive FDA and the political and scientific environment in which it functions. It is therefore appropriate at the outset to identify some features of the FDA landscape that cast long shadows over its administration of the law.

While many federal agencies come under close public and journalistic scrutiny, FDA has been watched intensely even by Washington standards. It is unlikely that any other agency has been the subject of more internal and external study during the last five decades. The number of studies of FDA's performance is certainly evidence of the high degree of public interest in its work, but it also betrays the persistence of a belief in some quarters that the agency is not doing its job well enough or fast enough. This skepticism contributes to the self-doubt that periodically besets FDA employees. The public at large does not generally share this skepticism, however; according to repeated surveys, it ranks FDA among the federal agencies in which it has the greatest confidence.

FDA's attraction as a subject of study mirrors congressional interest in its work. Beginning in the late 1950s, FDA has been the subject of a degree of congressional attention unmatched by the amount focused on any other regulatory agency. Both Republican and Democratic members of Congress interrogate the agency regardless of which party holds the White House.

The sheer number of congressional hearings involving FDA tells only part of the story. Fewer than 20 percent of its appearances deal with legislation affecting the agency, and in most years, no more than two appearances concern the agency's budget. The remainder of hearings, almost thirty a year, are "oversight" hearings in the conventional sense. Our purpose is not to argue that FDA should be left alone to do its work, but simply to document that it is not left alone. The agency is controversial. Its decisions affect every citizen and are closely watched. Many congressional committees are interested in its performance, frequently concluding that it has been either reckless or tardy in approving new products or insufficiently vigorous in acting against old ones. The message conveyed by both the intensity and frequency of congressional oversight has substantially influenced both the content of FDA's requirements and the thrust of the agency's enforcement efforts.

FDA's modern duties have forced the agency to become less suspicious and more inventive. As we discuss more fully in Chapter 2, *infra* pp. 30–43, the agency has shifted its emphasis from court enforcement against individual violators to the establishment of generic requirements through rulemaking, guidance, and other informal processes. In the process, FDA has assumed a larger role in determining the content of regulatory policy. Whenever Congress establishes a regulatory program, it necessarily must allow the responsible agency discretion to fashion the precise requirements applicable to regulated firms. But while administrative discretion is inherent in the regulatory process, FDA has enjoyed unusual freedom to adopt and revise regulatory approaches. Other health regulatory agencies are creatures of modern organic statutes, which typically express more explicit legislative choices among available regulatory techniques. The FD&C Act, by contrast, is comparatively old-fashioned. Though it is quite lengthy, many of its most important provisions are couched in general language, which FDA has had the responsibility and opportunity to adapt to contemporary problems.

CHAPTER 2

FDA RULEMAKING, JUDICIAL REVIEW, AND THE ADMINISTRATIVE PROCEDURE ACT

A. FDA's RELIANCE ON REGULATIONS: HISTORY AND ANALYSIS

1. INTRODUCTION

Various modes exist by which administrative agencies enforce and interpret the statutes they administer. They can often do so by bringing civil and criminal enforcement actions in court (ordinarily through the proxy of the U.S. Department of Justice). In addition, the Administrative Procedure Act (APA) sets forth two primary mechanisms for agency action: rulemaking (5 U.S.C. 553) and administrative (as opposed to judicial) adjudication (5 U.S.C. 554).

Formal administrative adjudication has always represented a miniscule percentage of FDA's activities. This is not to say that the agency does not perform adjudicatory functions; every product licensing decision can be viewed as a form of informal, non-APA adjudication. But unlike the Social Security Administration, for example, which has more than 1,300 Administrative Law Judges (ALJs) constantly performing formal hearings, FDA's single ALJ frequently has nothing to do at all.

— product licensing as informal adjudication

Ever since 1938, FDA has advanced its mission primarily through a combination of enforcement actions in court (*i.e.*, judicial adjudication) and administrative rulemaking, in combination with more informal actions. As described below, the importance of court proceedings has diminished dramatically over the past 75 years, while the importance of rulemaking has correspondingly surged. But it is also important to understand that FDA's approach to rulemaking itself has changed considerably over the past few decades.

2. APA "RULEMAKING"

The APA defines "rule" broadly to include

the whole or a part of an agency statement of general or particular applicability and future effect designed to implement, interpret, or prescribe law or policy or describing the organization, procedure or practice requirements of an agency.

5 U.S.C. 551(4). It defines "rule making" to mean simply "agency process for formulating, amending, or repealing a rule." *Id.* 551(5).

Section 553 sets out the requirements for notice-and-comment rulemaking, the best known mode for creating administrative regulations. The essential elements of this procedure (which is often more complicated in practice) are the publication of a proposed rule in the Federal Register, the opportunity for any interested person to comment on the proposed rule, and the publication of the final rule, first in the Federal Register and then in the Code of Federal Regulations. As discussed below, notice-and-comment rulemaking was FDA's most important method for disseminating rules during the 1970s and early 1980s.

In fact, however, section 553 also refers to two other mechanisms for establishing rules. It mentions "rules . . . required by statute to be made on the record after opportunity for an agency hearing." 5 U.S.C. 553(c). This process—commonly known as "formal rulemaking"—is governed by sections 556 and 557 of the APA. FD&C Act 701(e) specifies certain types of regulations that FDA must create through formal rulemaking. Although FDA conducted some formal rulemaking earlier in its history, the procedure is so burdensome and lengthy that the agency today assiduously avoids it.

Section 553 of the APA also designates certain categories of rules that are exempt from the notice-and-comment requirements altogether, most notably "interpretive rules, general statements of policy, or rules of agency organization, procedure, or practice." As notice-and-comment rulemaking has itself become progressively more onerous in the past few decades, FDA has increasingly made use of these exempt rules, often called "guidances." Although guidances, which ordinarily are not published in the Code of Federal Regulations, are not formally binding on industry, they have become the agency's principal method for exerting its will. Although the promulgation of guidance documents is technically "rule making" under the APA, in common usage the term *rulemaking* is not used to describe the issuance of such unenforceable interpretive rules and policy statements.

3. FDA'S EMBRACE OF NOTICE-AND-COMMENT RULEMAKING

a. BACKGROUND

For most regulatory agencies, the number and scope of their regulations grow over time. For much of its history FDA fit this pattern. The agency's regulations, which occupied not even 250 pages in the Code of Federal Regulations in 1948, reached 585 pages in 1956, 1,718 pages in 1969 and 1,951 pages in 1979. By the time of the publication of the second edition of our casebook in 1991, FDA regulations had ballooned to nearly 3,790 pages. Then, however, what had seemed to be inexorable growth in regulatory text slowed dramatically. On July 1, 2006, shortly before the release of our third edition, FDA's regulations occupied only 3800 CFR pages. In the summer of 2013, on the verge of the release of this fourth edition, the number of pages occupied by FDA regulations had edged up only slightly, to 4045 pages.

This explosion, then stabilization, of the volume of FDA regulations reflects an evolution in the agency's approach to enforcing the FD&C

Act. For three decades following the 1938 passage of the Act, FDA relied on case-by-case court enforcement as its main method for establishing policy and assuring compliance. This approach was feasible because the issues facing the agency were typically less complex and its ambitions were more modest.

By the early 1970s, however, the breadth and complexity of the agency's duties were growing dramatically because of changing public and congressional expectations. Court enforcement was not adequate to this expanding task. Starting around 1970, therefore, FDA implemented the FD&C Act primarily through rulemaking. It continued to rely on court enforcement to deal with traditional problems such as filth in food and fraudulent labeling, and also to assure compliance with already-promulgated regulations. But new substantive law and policy were rarely made through court action. The Second Circuit endorsed the agency's approach.

> [O]ver the last decade rule-making has been increasingly substituted for adjudication as a regulatory technique, with the support and encouragement of courts, at least where the regulation involves specialized scientific knowledge. Where the objective is essentially legislative, *i.e.*, to establish rules or principles by which an entire industry may be governed, the case-by-case adversary proceeding, in which the agency confronts a single alleged offender selected for suit with respect to a specific factual situation, has frequently proved to be an unsuitable method of enforcing the law, since it often resolves narrow issues of importance only to the immediate adversaries rather than broad questions of interest to the industry or the public. The rule-making proceeding, on the other hand, provides the agency with an opportunity first to receive a wide spectrum of views proffered by all segments affected by the proposed rule (*e.g.*, manufacturers, vendors, doctors, consumers) and then in a legislative fashion to consider and choose from several alternatives or options rather than limit its decisions to narrow issues controlling a particular case. Furthermore, once binding regulations are promulgated, the industry and public are put on notice and may be guided accordingly rather than speculate as to the outcome of a seizure or enforcement suit.

National Nutritional Foods Ass'n v. Weinberger, 512 F.2d 688 (2d Cir. 1975).

FDA pioneered rulemaking as the primary instrument of regulation, issuing numerous new rules to particularize the FD&C Act's substantive requirements. An example was the regulation establishing the required type, size and location for mandatory information on food labels, 38 Fed. Reg. 6950 (Mar. 14, 1973). Previously, the agency had relied on enforcement actions in court to implement section 403(f)'s requirement that this information appear "prominently" and "with such conspicuousness (as compared with other words, statements, designs, or devices in the labeling) and in such terms as to render it likely to be read and understood by the ordinary individual under customary conditions of purchase and use." The 1973 rule, by mandating a specific type size and establishing requirements for placement of information on the label, eliminated uncertainty and thus obviated court action except against firms that did not follow the clearly prescribed standards. *See generally* Stephen McNamara, *The New Age of FDA Rule–Making*, 31 FOOD DRUG COSM. L.J. 393 (1976); Richard A. Merrill, *Administrative Rule–Making*, 30 FOOD DRUG COSM. L.J. 478 (1975).

In addition to promulgating such substantive rules, FDA in the 1970s also designed—by regulation—a variety of nonstatutory procedures for resolving issues that were not foreseen when the FDCA was passed. A good example of this use of rulemaking is the OTC Drug Review, discussed *infra* in Chapter 7. During this decade, FDA also issued detailed regulations specifying how it interprets and applies laws of government-wide applicability, such as the Freedom of Information Act, the National Environmental Policy Act, and the Federal Advisory Committee Act. *See infra* Chapter 15. FDA's Public Information Regulations, for example, list all of the numerous types of documents in its files and specify exactly how each type will be dealt with under the FOIA.

b.   THE STATUTORY FRAMEWORK

FDA's reliance on rulemaking to implement the FD&C Act beginning in the 1970s assumed that the statute conferred authority to adopt regulations that have the force of law. By the end of that decade, the agency could point to several court victories that supported this proposition. Previously, however, FDA's authority to adopt binding rules was uncertain. To appreciate this uncertainty, we must examine the text of the original 1938 Act.

The core of the Act was a series of descriptions of conditions that would render an article—a food, drug, device, or cosmetic— "adulterated" or "misbranded." For example, section 403(a) provided (and still does) that a food is misbranded "if its labeling is false or misleading in any particular." Elsewhere the statute provided remedies for this and other forms of adulteration or misbranding—specifically seizure, injunction, or criminal prosecution.

Certain of the Act's misbranding or adulteration provisions, however, specifically provided that FDA had to adopt regulations to make the law's obligations concrete. Thus, for example, section 403(j) provided that a food intended for special dietary use would be misbranded unless its label conveyed information about its dietary properties that FDA prescribed by regulation. In short, for section 403(j), and nine other misbranding or adulteration definitions, the 1938 Act conferred on FDA the authority to determine—by regulation—what the law required. Agency regulations implementing these specific definitions were understood to have the force of law. Furthermore, because such regulations would be binding, Congress prescribed special procedures for their adoption. Section 701(e) required FDA to establish the factual and legal bases for these regulations in a formal evidentiary hearing, using the process known as "formal rulemaking." *See infra* p. 49. These procedures were intended to give persons subject to binding regulations an opportunity to contest the factual assumptions and policy judgments embodied in the regulations.

Thus, the 1938 FD&C Act's substantive requirements—embodied in its definitions of misbranding and adulteration—took two forms. Most imposed obligations or prohibited conduct described in the text of the statute itself. But ten misbranding or adulteration provisions did not impose primary obligations; instead they directed FDA to issue regulations to carry out the policies set forth in the statute. And in fulfilling this responsibility, FDA was required to conduct a trial-type hearing.

Most of the 1938 Act's self-sufficient misbranding and adulteration. provisions were couched in general language which did not clearly describe the conduct that Congress meant to prescribe or prohibit. For example, the statutory directive to avoid label statements that might mislead provided little concrete guidance. An obvious issue, then, was whether FDA had the authority to promulgate regulations translating this and other broad prohibitions into concrete obligations. And if it could, would such regulations be binding, too?

From the time of the Act's passage, few doubted that FDA could issue regulations interpreting statutory provisions that did not themselves call for regulations. After all, section 701(a) gives FDA "the authority to promulgate regulations for the efficient enforcement of this Act." But until 1967, this language was assumed, by both agency counsel and industry, to authorize only "interpretative" regulations (*i.e.*, regulations that could influence but could not bind) and procedural regulations. This assumption rested on those provisions of the Act like section 403(j) that specifically authorized the agency to issue substantive regulations but required that they be the product of formal rulemaking. In short, section 701(e)'s procedural obligations were thought to be Congress's indispensable condition for its delegation of authority to adopt binding regulations.

c.   JUDICIAL ACKNOWLEDGMENT OF FDA'S RULEMAKING AUTHORITY

In a series of decisions, commencing with the Supreme Court's opinion in *Abbott Laboratories v. Gardner*, 387 U.S. 136 (1967), set forth below, FDA won judicial acceptance for the proposition that section 701(a) was a general grant of authority to adopt binding notice-and-comment regulations implementing any of the FD&C Act's substantive requirements for which the statute did not mandate formal rulemaking.

In *Abbott Laboratories*, pharmaceutical manufacturers sought a declaratory judgment that particular FDA regulations issued pursuant to section 701(a) exceeded the agency's authority. FDA countered that because the regulations were only interpretive, they were not "ripe" for review and could only be challenged by way of defense in a court enforcement action brought by the government. The Supreme Court held that the regulations were immediately reviewable under the Administrative Procedure Act and in so doing implied, without analysis, that section 701(a) regulations could have the force of law.

Abbott Laboratories v. Gardner

387 U.S. 136 (1967).

■ MR. JUSTICE HARLAN delivered the opinion of the Court.

In 1962 Congress amended the Federal Food, Drug, and Cosmetic Act to require manufacturers of prescription drugs to print the "established name" of the drug "prominently and in type at least half as large as that used thereon for any proprietary name or designation for such drug," on labels and other printed material. . . . After inviting and considering comments submitted by interested parties the Commissioner promulgated the following regulation for the "efficient enforcement" of the Act, § 701(a):

> "If the label or labeling of a prescription drug bears a proprietary name or designation for the drug or any ingredient thereof, the established name, if such there be, corresponding to such proprietary name or designation, shall accompany each appearance of such proprietary name or designation."

A similar rule was made applicable to advertisements for prescription drugs.

The present action was brought by a group of 37 individual drug manufacturers and by the Pharmaceutical Manufacturers Association. . . . They challenged the regulations on the ground that the Commissioner exceeded his authority under the statute by promulgating an order requiring labels, advertisements, and other printed matter relating to prescription drugs to designate the established name of the particular drug involved every time its trade name is used anywhere in such material.

    . . . .

The first question we consider is whether Congress by the Federal Food, Drug, and Cosmetic Act intended to forbid pre-enforcement review of this sort of regulation promulgated by the Commissioner. The question is phrased in terms of "prohibition" rather than "authorization" because a survey of our cases shows that judicial review of a final agency action by an aggrieved person will not be cut off unless there is persuasive reason to believe that such was the purpose of Congress. . . .

In this case the Government has not demonstrated such a purpose. . . .

We conclude that nothing in the Food, Drug, and Cosmetic Act itself precludes this action.

A further inquiry must, however, be made. The injunctive and declaratory judgment remedies are discretionary, and courts traditionally have been reluctant to apply them to administrative determinations unless these arise in the context of a controversy "ripe" for judicial resolution. Without undertaking to survey the intricacies of the ripeness doctrine it is fair to say that its basic rationale is to prevent the courts, through avoidance of premature adjudication, from entangling themselves in abstract disagreements over administrative policies, and also to protect the agencies from judicial interference until an administrative decision has been formalized and its effects felt in a concrete way by the challenging parties. The problem is best seen in a twofold aspect, requiring us to evaluate both the fitness of the issues for judicial decision and the hardship to the parties of withholding court consideration.

As to the former factor, we believe the issues presented are *ripe* appropriate for judicial resolution at this time. First, all parties agree that the issue tendered is a purely legal one: whether the statute was properly construed by the Commissioner to require the established name of the drug to be used *every time* the proprietary name is employed.... It is suggested that the justification for this rule might vary with different circumstances, and that the expertise of the Commissioner is relevant to passing upon the validity of the regulation. This of course is true, but the suggestion overlooks the fact that both sides have approached this case as one purely of congressional intent, and that the Government made no effort to justify the regulation in factual terms.

Second, the regulations in issue we find to be "final agency action" within the meaning of § 10 of the Administrative Procedure Act, 5 U.S.C. 704, as construed in judicial decisions. An "agency action" includes any "rule," defined by the Act as "an agency statement of general or particular applicability and future effect designed to implement, interpret, or prescribe law or policy," §§ 2(c), 2(g). The cases dealing with judicial review of administrative actions have interpreted the "finality" element in a pragmatic way....

... The regulation challenged here, promulgated in a formal manner after announcement in the Federal Register and consideration of comments by interested parties is quite clearly definitive. There is no hint that this regulation is informal, or only the ruling of a subordinate official, or tentative. It was made effective upon publication, and the Assistant General Counsel for Food and Drugs stated in the District Court that compliance was expected.

The Government argues, however, that the present case can be distinguished on the ground that in [prior cases] ... the agency involved could implement its policy directly, while here the Attorney General must authorize criminal and seizure actions for violations of the statute. In the context of this case, we do not find this argument persuasive. These regulations are not meant to advise the Attorney General, but purport to be directly authorized by the statute. Thus, if within the Commissioner's authority, they have the status of law and violations of them carry heavy criminal and civil sanctions. Also, there is no representation that the Attorney General and the Commissioner disagree in this area; the Justice Department is defending this very suit.... Moreover, the agency does have direct authority to enforce this regulation in the context of passing upon applications for clearance of new drugs, § 505....

This is also a case in which the impact of the regulations upon the petitioners is sufficiently direct and immediate as to render the issue appropriate for judicial review at this stage. These regulations purport to give an authoritative interpretation of a statutory provision that has a direct effect on the day-to-day business of all prescription drug companies; its promulgation puts petitioners in a dilemma that it was the very purpose of the Declaratory Judgment Act to ameliorate. . . . The regulations are clear-cut, and were made effective immediately upon publication; as noted earlier the agency's counsel represented to the District Court that immediate compliance with their terms was expected. If petitioners wish to comply they must change all their labels, advertisements, and promotional materials; they must destroy stocks of printed matter; and they must invest heavily in new printing type and new supplies. The alternative to compliance—continued use of material which they believe in good faith meets the statutory requirements, but which clearly does not meet the regulation of the Commissioner—may be even more costly. That course would risk serious criminal and civil penalties for the unlawful distribution of "misbranded" drugs. . . .

NOTES

1. *Companion Cases.* Two companion cases were decided the same day as *Abbott Laboratories.* In *Toilet Goods Ass'n v. Gardner,* 387 U.S. 158 (1967), a regulation authorizing FDA to suspend color additive certification for a cosmetic manufacturer who refused agency inspectors access to the firm's manufacturing facilities, processes, and formulae was held not ripe for review prior to implementation. In *Gardner v. Toilet Goods Ass'n,* 387 U.S. 167 (1967), however, the Court permitted preenforcement review of other regulations implementing the Color Additives Amendments of 1960.

2. *Interpretive or Legislative Rules?* Justice Harlan's statement that FDA's regulations, if within the scope of the agency's substantive authority, "have the status of law" was extremely significant. The government, seeking to strengthen its contention that the suit was not ripe, suggested throughout the litigation that the challenged regulations were not binding rules. Though the Supreme Court's ruling was an immediate defeat for the agency, FDA quickly recognized that the decision held the seeds of a larger victory. The agency soon began churning out rules under 701(a) that were meant to be legislative, not merely interpretive. Years later, William W. Goodrich, the agency's lead lawyer at the time of *Abbott,* opined:

> [W]e really had more to win by . . . making those regulations a binding regulation than we had to lose. You know, it wouldn't really help us much to open the rules up for challenge at some undefined time, when we could get it all settled and have it as force and effect of law. So I consider the *Abbott* and *Toilet Goods* case . . . as cases that gave us a very strong leg up on making our general regulations have force and effect of law. And as things turned out later, that, of course, has been an important development in administration of the law.

Interview with William W. Goodrich, FDA Chief Counsel, 1959–1971, in Rockville, MD (Oct. 15, 1986).

———

Later decisions read *Abbott Laboratories* as supporting FDA's authority under section 701(a) to adopt regulations implementing other requirements of the Act. An early influential opinion was *National*

Nutritional Foods Ass'n v. Weinberger, 512 F.2d 688 (2d Cir. 1975), in which the Second Circuit wrote:

> Congress did not expressly spell out the authoritative effect that should be given to regulations promulgated under §§ 701(a) and 701(e). This naturally leads one to wonder, in view of the care with which Congress spelled out the elaborate § 701(e) procedure, whether it intended any limits on the apparently expansive delegation of rule-making power granted by § 701(a), and specifically whether (as appellants urge) the latter was meant merely to grant authority to issue interpretive, non-binding advisory opinions with respect to matters of lesser importance. . . .

> . . . We have come to recognize that, if the administrative process is to be practically effective, specific regulations promulgated pursuant to a general statutory delegation of authority must be treated as authoritative, whether labeled "substantive" or "interpretive", especially in areas where the agency possesses expertise not shared by the courts. In that event its views are unlikely to be disturbed by the court in an enforcement proceeding. Where once we may have demanded proof of specific delegation of legislative authority to an agency purporting to promulgate substantive rules we have learned from experience to accept a general delegation as sufficient in certain areas of expertise.

> . . . .

> Our attention has not been directed to anything in the legislative history of §§ 701(a) and (e) that militates against these conclusions. . . .

Six years later, the same court elaborated further on these principles in the following case:

National Association of Pharmaceutical Manufacturers v. Food and Drug Administration

637 F.2d 877 (2d Cir. 1981).

■ FRIENDLY, CIRCUIT JUDGE:

In 1962 Congress enacted various amendments to the Federal Food, Drug, and Cosmetic Act of 1938 (the Act) to "strengthen and broaden existing laws in the drug field so as to bring about better, safer medicine and to establish a more effective system of enforcement of the drug laws." Among the amendments was a section by which a drug is deemed <u>adulterated</u> if its packaging, processing, holding or manufacturing fail to conform to "current good manufacturing practice (CGMP) to assure that such drug meets the requirements of this chapter as to safety and has the identity and strength, and meets the quality and purity characteristics, which it purports or is represented to possess". § 501(a)(2)(B).

The Food and Drug Administration (FDA) issued its first regulations under this section in 1963. In February, 1976, FDA announced a proposal to revise and update the then current CGMP regulations. This proposal, which provided for the notice and comment procedures contemplated by 5 U.S.C. 553, announced:

> The Commissioner intends for CGMP regulations to become binding specific requirements that must be complied with; failure to do so shall render a drug product adulterated under section 501(a)(2)(B) of the (Act) ... Binding regulations will ... serve to inform courts of FDA's expert judgments regarding current good manufacturing practice for drugs in the United States; this will expedite and assist enforcement proceedings to assure compliance with section 501(a)(2)(B) of the act.

The FDA received numerous comments both upon the substance of its requirements and upon its proposal that the new CGMP regulations should have the force of law.[1] In an extensive preamble to the new regulations it set forth a legal analysis supporting its view that it had power to issue binding regulations, and the reasons why it believed binding rather than merely interpretive regulations would be in the public interest.[2] The regulations ... were published on September 29, 1978, to be effective March 28, 1979, 43 F.R. 45014. They cover a broad spectrum of affairs, including requirements for personnel practices, record keeping, building design, and procedures for the control of drug production, packaging and labeling.

Administrative rule-making ... includes the formulation of both legally binding regulations and interpretative regulations. The former receive statutory force upon going into effect. The latter do not receive statutory force and their validity is subject to challenge in any court proceeding in which their application may be in question. The statutes themselves and not the regulations remain in theory the sole criterion of what the law authorizes or compels and what it forbids.

In this action ... the National Association of Pharmaceutical Manufacturers and the National Pharmaceutical Alliance, both trade associations, sought a declaration that FDA's attempt to give binding effect to the new CGMP Regulations was beyond its authority. . . .

Two different subsections of § 701 confer rulemaking authority upon the FDA. Section 701(a) provides:

> The authority to promulgate regulations for the efficient enforcement of this chapter, except as otherwise provided in this section, is vested in the Secretary (of Health and Human Services).

---

[1] A concise formulation of the distinction between "binding" and "interpretive" rules is supplied by the Final Report of the Attorney General's Committee on Administrative Procedure 100 (1941):

> Administrative rule-making ... includes the formulation of both legally binding regulations and interpretative regulations. The former receive statutory force upon going into effect. The latter do not receive statutory force and their validity is subject to challenge in any court proceeding in which their application may be in question. The statutes themselves and not the regulations remain in theory the sole criterion of what the law authorizes or compels and what it forbids.

[2] The most significant justification for having the regulations binding is to minimize the burden on the government and on the courts in a case where a violation does occur. When the regulations are merely interpretive, the agency must provide expert testimony in each trial to demonstrate what the current good manufacturing practice in the industry is, notwithstanding the regulation. The cost of locating and preparing such expert witnesses and bringing them to the trial, as well as the judicial time taken in hearing these witnesses, would be eliminated by having binding regulations.

The effect of § 4 of the Administrative Procedure Act of 1946 (APA), now 5 U.S.C. 553, is to require that rulemaking under § 701(a), with certain exceptions, including "interpretative rules", follow an informal notice and comment procedure, which was done here. Section 701(e) provides that "(any) action for the issuance, amendment, or repeal of any regulation" under various sections of the Act of which § 501(a)(2)(B) is not one, shall follow a complex procedure which has been read to include a trial-type hearing. . . . Admittedly § 701(e) procedures were not followed here and the FDA's authority to give binding effect to the CGMP regulations at issue must rest on § 701(a).

Reading the language of that subsection, which comes from the Act of 1938, with the eyes of 1980, one would have little difficulty in concluding that the words suffice to empower the Commissioner of the FDA . . . to issue regulations, substantive as well as procedural, having the force of law. The comprehensive opinion of Judge J. Skelly Wright in *National Petroleum Refiners Ass'n v. FTC*, 482 F.2d 672 (D.C. Cir.1973), catalogued the many instances in which general statutory provisions not differing essentially from § 701(a) have been held to endow agencies with power to issue binding rules and regulations. In the interest of historical accuracy, it should be noted that at one time it was widely understood that generalized grants of rulemaking authority conferred power only to make rules of a procedural or an interpretative nature, and not binding substantive regulations, for which a specific delegation was thought necessary. . . .

As documented by Judge Wright in *National Petroleum Refiners*, th[e] generous construction of agency rulemaking authority has become firmly entrenched. Beyond this there is formidable authority to the effect that § 701(a) itself is a grant of power to issue binding regulations. The first is the statement in *Abbott Laboratories* [*supra* p. 34] adverting to certain drug labeling regulations issued pursuant to § 701(a):

> These regulations are not meant to advise the Attorney General, but purport to be directly authorized by the statute. Thus, if within the Commissioner's authority, they have the status of law and violations of them carry heavy criminal and civil sanctions.

The Court also spoke of the regulations as "self-operative" rules "that must be followed by an entire industry". It can be argued that the Court could not really have meant to decide whether the regulations there at issue had the "status of law" since the Government had urged throughout the case that they were merely interpretive, the court of appeals had so held, and the petitioner had not seriously challenged this, and also because in *Toilet Goods Ass'n v. Gardner*, 360 F.2d 677, heard and decided in the Supreme Court, together with *Abbott Laboratories*, we had said that we saw "little profit in debating the point, much discussed by the parties, whether the Regulations are 'interpretative' or 'legislative'," since "the interpretative character of a regulation does not necessarily make it unripe for review". However, the Court's remarks are at least impressive dicta operating in the Government's favor here.

. . . .

[T]his court, in *National Nutritional Foods Ass'n v. Weinberger*, 512 F.2d 688 (1975), . . . said: "(our) attention has not been directed to anything in the legislative history of §§ 701(a) and (e) that militates against [the conclusion that rules issued under § 701(a) are legislative rules]", and correctly stated that "over the last decade rule-making has been increasingly substituted for adjudication as a regulatory technique, with the support and encouragement of the courts, at least where the regulation involves specialized scientific knowledge", citing, among other cases, Judge Wright's opinion in *National Petroleum Refiners Ass'n v. FTC*. The decision in *National Nutritional Foods* . . . thus reinforced our earlier reliance on *Abbott Laboratories* as supporting the Commissioner's power to issue § 701(a) regulations that are binding. In *United States v. Nova Scotia Food Products Corp.*, 568 F.2d 240 (1977), we again read the 1938 Act as authorizing the issuance of binding substantive regulations under § 701(a). . . .

Appellants' claim is that, whether or not the FDA may generally issue binding substantive regulations under § 701(a), although they obviously think it may not, it cannot do so with respect to the CGMP Regulations. In support of this position they rely on the legislative history of the portion of the 1962 amendments that added § 501(a)(2)(B). . . .

Plaintiffs' . . . argument . . . is that when the 1962 Congress decided to rely on the Secretary's rulemaking authority under § 701(a), it was to that authority as then understood; that the pre-1962 case law established that any substantive regulations issued under § 701(a) could be interpretive only; that the legislative history of the 1938 Act strongly corroborates this; and that the Supreme Court's statements in *Abbott Laboratories* in 1967 . . . and our own still later decisions are thus not dispositive of the problem in hand. . . .

We do not find the pre-1962 decisions with respect to the extent of the Secretary's power under § 701(a) to be so conclusive as plaintiffs assert. . . .

An indication of the intent of the 1962 Congress with respect to the scope of the regulatory power conferred by § 701(a) far more persuasive than this inconclusive smattering of cases under § 701(a) itself is furnished by well-known pre-1962 Supreme Court decisions which had held that rulemaking provisions similar to § 701(a) empowered [other agencies] to issue binding rules. We cite as examples *National Broadcasting Co. v. United States*, 319 U.S. 190 (1943); *United States v. Storer Broadcasting Co.*, 351 U.S. 192 (1956); and *American Trucking Ass'ns v. United States*, 344 U.S. 298 (1953).

On the other hand plaintiffs seem on solid ground when they contend that if the 1962 Congress had made the detailed examination of the legislative history and contemporary understanding of the 1938 Act, which plaintiffs' counsel have now made at long last, it might well have concluded that § 701(a) in fact very likely was not intended to confer power to issue binding substantive rules. . . . Plaintiffs supplement this history with references to instances, not necessary here to recount, wherein the FDA at various times had represented that § 701(a) did not empower it to issue binding substantive regulations, and with citations to secondary sources supporting that view.

A principal difficulty with plaintiffs' argument is that there is no evidence that these arcana concerning the legislative history of the 1938 Act were known to the 1962 Congress. Much water had flowed under the bridge since 1938. The principal consideration in 1938 against permitting the FDA to issue binding substantive rules except by following the complex procedures of § 701(e), namely the absence of any statutorily prescribed procedures under § 701(a), was radically changed when Congress enacted the APA in 1946. Pursuant to § 4 of that Act, now 5 U.S.C. 553, the FDA . . . cannot issue a binding substantive rule under § 701(a) without complying with notice and comment procedures that give affected parties an adequate opportunity to be heard. While the Federal Food, Drug, and Cosmetic Act has not been completely reenacted since 1946, it has been repeatedly amended to give the Secretary new powers. Many of these provisions have expressly authorized him to make implementing regulations. When it has provided for regulations but has not required this or, as in the case of the current good manufacturing practice provisions, it has said nothing about regulations, it is more reasonable to believe that Congress meant the FDA to have the same power to issue binding substantive regulations as the Supreme Court had recognized for other agencies.

. . . Moreover, the FDA, since the decision in *Abbott Laboratories*, has issued a substantial number of binding substantive regulations under § 701(a). A decision at this late date denying such power to it would thus create turmoil throughout numerous areas subject to regulation by the FDA. . . .

d.   THE DEBATE REOPENED

Thomas W. Merrill & Kathryn Tongue Watts, *Agency Rules With the Force of Law: The Original Convention*

116 HARVARD LAW REVIEW 467 (2002).

. . . Statutes typically give agencies the power "to make, amend, and rescind such rules and regulations as may be necessary to carry out the provisions of this title," or "to make such rules and regulations . . . as may be necessary in the administration of this Act." The phrase "rules and regulations" in these statutes could refer to legislative rules—that is, rules that have legally binding effect on the general public—or it could refer to interpretive rules that do not have such binding effect. . . .

Although the language of most rulemaking grants is facially ambiguous, we argue in this Article that these grants were not ambiguous during the formative years of the modern administrative state—up to and beyond the enactment of the Administrative Procedure Act (APA) in 1946. Throughout the Progressive and New Deal eras, Congress followed a drafting convention that signaled to agencies whether particular rulemaking grants conferred authority to make rules with the force of law as opposed to mere housekeeping rules. That convention was simple and easy to apply in most cases: If Congress specified in the statute that a violation of agency rules would subject

If C granted A sanction authority if violations = authority for binding (legislative) rules

auth. for sanction auth

if no sanction auth = interpretive rules only

the offending party to some sanction—for example, a civil or criminal penalty; loss of a permit, license, or benefits; or other adverse legal consequences—then the grant conferred power to make rules with the force of law. Conversely, if Congress made no provision for sanctions for rule violations, the grant authorized only procedural or interpretive rules. . . .

. . . In the 1960s, courts and commentators began to urge an expanded use of rulemaking by agencies and a reduced emphasis on adjudication. Eventually, two influential federal appellate judges who strongly favored greater use of rulemaking—Judges J. Skelly Wright of the D.C. Circuit and Henry Friendly of the Second Circuit—authored important opinions construing facially ambiguous rulemaking grants to the FTC and FDA as authorizing legislative rulemaking. These holdings were inconsistent with what Congress had intended, as measured by the convention. . . .

. . . Section 701(a) [of the FD&C Act] granted general rulemaking power to the Secretary, stating that the Secretary could "promulgate regulations for the efficient enforcement of this Act." Then sections 701(e), (f), and (g) set forth detailed procedures, including procedures for public hearings and judicial review of regulations, that the Secretary was required to follow when promulgating regulations under certain enumerated, specific rulemaking grants. Notably, section 701(e) does not refer to section 701(a), and therefore rules promulgated under section 701(a) are not subject to section 701(e)'s procedural safeguards.

Under the convention, the specific rulemaking provisions that were subject to the procedural safeguards of sections 701(e), (f) and (g) conferred legislative rulemaking authority. For example, section 401 gave the Secretary the power to promulgate regulations fixing standards of identity for food. Those regulations are given legislative effect by various sections that expressly make violations of section 401 regulations unlawful and subject to criminal penalties.

author's arg's

701(a) silent as to sanctions = should only be legislative

In contrast to the regulations subjected to the procedural safeguards of section 701(e), nothing in the Act indicated that a regulation issued under the authority of section 701(a) would subject the violator to any sanction, penalty, or other legal consequence. This silence suggests Congress's intent to withhold legislative rulemaking powers under that section.

. . . The FDA's "belated discovery" of general rulemaking powers in section 701(a) stemmed largely from the entrepreneurial efforts of Peter Barton Hutt during his tenure as the FDA's chief counsel. In a paper presented to the Food and Drug Law Institute in 1972, Hutt expounded the theory that the FDCA should be viewed as a "constitution" that gave the FDA broad authority to implement "a set of fundamental objectives." Specifically, he argued that the Act gave the FDA power to do anything not excepted or withheld by the Act, and he cited the general rulemaking clause in section 701(a) to support his conclusion that the Act "provide[d] ample legal authority" for the FDA to adopt procedures for the enforcement of FDCA requirements. . . .

Hutt's prediction [that FDA would prevail on this point in court] came true in *National Nutritional Foods Ass'n v. Weinberger* [512 F.2d 688 (2d Cir. 1975)]. . . .

One factor that did not significantly influence the Second Circuit's *Nutritional Foods* was the legislative history of the FDCA, which . . . provides strong evidence that Congress intended to grant legislative rulemaking authority to the FDA only pursuant to specific rulemaking grants. Judge Mansfield made just one brief reference to the legislative history in his opinion, observing that the court's attention had not been directed to anything in the legislative history of sections 701(a) or (e) that militated against the court's decision. . . .

B. RULEMAKING PROCEDURES

1. APA NOTICE-AND-COMMENT REQUIREMENTS

As discussed above, the FD&C Act provides for rulemaking in two circumstances: (1) informal rulemaking under section 701(a), which requires compliance with the notice-and-comment procedures of the APA, and (2) formal rulemaking under section 701(e), which requires an evidentiary hearing. Ten provisions of the 1938 Act expressly authorized FDA to adopt implementing regulations and, directly or by cross-reference, mandated adherence to section 701(e)'s procedures. The procedure prescribed by section 701(e) has proved so burdensome, for FDA and for private parties, that the agency has either abandoned the authorities to which section 701(e) applies or persuaded Congress to amend the law to permit a simpler procedure for particular substantive provisions.

Unlike the explicit grants of rulemaking authority subject to section 701(e), section 701(a) is not confined by text or context to specific products or addressed to specific regulatory goals. Any regulation that will facilitate implementation of any part of the Act is presumably within the agency's authority to adopt. But the FD&C Act says nothing at all about the procedure FDA must follow in exercising the power section 701(a) confers. One must look elsewhere for Congress's directions, namely, the Administrative Procedure Act. It is universally understood that section 553 of the APA describes the default procedure for the exercise of rulemaking authority conferred to any agency by any statute that does not itself prescribe a particular procedure for adopting rules. This default—informal rulemaking— governs almost all rulemaking in which FDA engages, and so we explore its requirements here.

The procedure that the APA mandates seems straightforward on its face. Section 553 imposes only three requirements: (1) An agency must first publish in the Federal Register the rule it proposes to adopt. (2) The agency must invite, and allow reasonable time for, the submission of data, views, or arguments—"comments" in administrative law vernacular—from persons or organizations interested in the subject. (3) Then, after considering the comments, the agency—if it is still determined to issue a rule—must publish the text of the rule it is adopting along with a "concise general statement of [its] basis and purpose." The APA text seems to permit a reasonably informal and expeditious process, but courts have read it as demanding a fair degree of formality, substantial factual support, and rigorous analysis of both supporting and opposing comments. Moreover, section 553's procedures are only minimum procedures. An agency can do more than the APA requires to collect and analyze evidence in favor of its proposal, it can take account of issues and objections in addition to those raised by comments, and it can provide multiple opportunities for critics to question its proposal.

Beginning in 1971, FDA adopted the practice of explaining and justifying its regulations in lengthy and detailed preambles to both proposed and final rules. This practice was later incorporated in the agency's procedural regulations. Reviewing courts subsequently interpreted the spare requirements of the APA as imposing the approach pioneered by FDA, thus compelling all agencies conducting informal rulemaking to take steps previously associated with more formal proceedings. Indeed, the procedural obligations mandated by the courts were so rigorous that sometimes FDA itself failed to satisfy them—as illustrated by the case below.

United States v. Nova Scotia Food Products Corp.
568 F.2d 240 (2d Cir. 1977).

■ GURFEIN, CIRCUIT JUDGE:

This appeal involving a regulation of the Food and Drug Administration is not here upon a direct review of agency action. It is an appeal from a judgment of the District Court for the Eastern District of New York ... enjoining the appellants, after a hearing, from processing hot smoked whitefish except in accordance with time-temperature-salinity (T–T–S) regulations contained in 21 C.F.R. Part 122 (1977). . . .

The regulations cited above require that hot-process smoked fish be heated by a controlled heat process that provides a monitoring system positioned in as many strategic locations in the oven as necessary to assure a continuous temperature through each fish of not less than 180 F° for a minimum of 30 minutes for fish which have been brined to contain 3.5% water phase salt or at 150 F° for a minimum of 30 minutes if the salinity was at 5% water phase. Since *each* fish must meet these requirements, it is necessary to heat an entire batch of fish to even higher temperatures so that the lowest temperature for *any* fish will meet the minimum requirements. . . .

[The public health rationale for the regulations and FDA's authority to issue binding regulations to implement section 402(a)(4) are discussed in portions of the opinion reproduced at p. 529, *infra*. EDS.]

The Commissioner ... issued the final regulations in which he adopted certain suggestions made in the comments, including a suggestion by the National Fisheries Institute, Inc. . . . the intervenor herein. The original proposal provided that the fish would have to be cooked to a temperature of 180 F° for at least 30 minutes, if the fish have been brined to contain 3.5% water phase salt, with no alternative. In the final regulation, an alternative suggested by the intervenor "that the parameter of 150 F° for 30 minutes and 5% salt in the water phase be established as an alternate procedure to that stated in the proposed regulation for an interim period until specific parameters can be established" was accepted, but as a permanent part of the regulation rather than for an interim period. . . .

The Commissioner did not answer the suggestion by the Bureau of Fisheries that nitrite and salt as additives could safely lower the high temperature otherwise required, a solution which the FDA had accepted in the case of chub. Nor did the Commissioner respond to the claim of Nova Scotia through its trade association . . . that "[t]he proposed process requirements suggested by the FDA for hot processed smoked fish are neither commercially feasible nor based on sound scientific evidence obtained with the variety of smoked fish products to be included under this regulation."

[handwritten margin note: did not respond to comments re: other methods + how burdensome rgs were]

Nova Scotia, in its own comment, wrote to the Commissioner that "the heating of certain types of fish to high temperatures will completely destroy the product." . . .

When, after several inspections and warnings, Nova Scotia failed to comply with the regulation, an action by the United States Attorney for injunctive relief was filed on April 7, 1976, six years later, and resulted in the judgment here on appeal. . . .

Appellants contend that . . . the failure to disclose to interested persons the factual material upon which the agency was relying vitiates the element of fairness which is essential to any kind of administrative action. Moreover, they argue that the "concise general statement of . . . basis and purpose" by the Commissioner was inadequate.

. . . .

The keys issues were (1) whether, in the light of the rather scant history of botulism in whitefish, that species should have been considered separately rather than included in a general regulation which failed to distinguish species from species; (2) whether the application of the proposed T–T–S requirements for smoked whitefish made the whitefish commercially unsaleable; and (3) whether the agency recognized that prospect, but nevertheless decided that the public health needs should prevail even if that meant commercial death for the whitefish industry. The procedural issues were whether, in the light of these key questions, the agency procedure was inadequate because (i) it failed to disclose to interested parties the scientific data and the methodology upon which it relied; and (ii) because it failed utterly to address itself to the pertinent question of commercial feasibility. . . .

[handwritten margin note: (I)]

[handwritten margin note: Whether Procedure Inadequate s/c ① failed to provide data on which it relied ② failed to address issue of commercial feasibility]

Interested parties were not informed [by FDA's notice of proposed rulemaking] of the scientific data, or at least of a selection of such data deemed important by the agency, so that comments could be addressed to the data. Appellants argue that unless the scientific data relied upon by the agency are spread upon the public records, criticism of the methodology used or the meaning to be inferred from the data is rendered impossible. . . .

[handwritten margin note: need to provide scientific data relied upon for meaningful c+n period]

We think that the scientific data should have been disclosed to focus on the proper interpretation of "insanitary conditions." When the basis for a proposed rule is a scientific decision, the scientific material which is believed to support the rule should be exposed to the view of interested parties for their comment. One cannot ask for comment on a scientific paper without allowing the participants to read the paper. Scientific research is sometimes rejected for diverse inadequacies of methodology; and statistical results are sometimes rebutted because of a lack of adequate gathering technique or of supportable extrapolation. Such is the stuff of scientific debate. To suppress meaningful comment by failure to disclose the basic data relied upon is akin to rejecting comment altogether. . . .

Appellants additionally attack the "concise general statement" required by [the] APA as inadequate. We think that, in the circumstances, it was less than adequate. It is not in keeping with the rational process to leave vital questions, raised by comments which are of cogent materiality, completely unanswered. The agencies certainly have a good deal of discretion in expressing the basis of a rule, but the agencies do not have quite the prerogative of obscurantism reserved to legislatures. . . .

The Secretary was squarely faced with the question whether it was necessary to formulate a rule with specific parameters that applied to all species of fish, and particularly whether lower temperatures with the addition of nitrite and salt would not be sufficient. Though this alternative was suggested by an agency of the federal government, its suggestion, though acknowledged, was never answered.

Moreover, the comment that to apply the proposed T–T–S requirements to whitefish would destroy the commercial product was neither discussed nor answered. We think that to sanction silence in the face of such vital questions would be to make the statutory requirement of a "concise general statement" less than an adequate safeguard against arbitrary decision-making. . . .

One may recognize that even commercial infeasibility cannot stand in the way of an overwhelming public interest. Yet the administrative process should disclose, at least, whether the proposed regulation is considered to be commercially feasible, or whether other considerations prevail even if commercial unfeasibility is acknowledged. This kind of forthright disclosure and basic statement was lacking in the formulation of the T–T–S standard made applicable to whitefish. . . .

We cannot, on this appeal, remand to the agency to allow further comments by interested parties, addressed to the scientific data now disclosed at the trial below. We hold in this enforcement proceeding, therefore, that the regulation, as it affects non-vacuum-packed hot-smoked whitefish, was promulgated in an arbitrary manner and is invalid. . . .

NOTES

1.   *Procedural Regulation.* Even before this decision, FDA's own regulations, 21 C.F.R. 10.40(b) & (c), required essentially the procedures that the Second Circuit held were mandated by the APA. But the practice of FDA did not meet this standard.

2.   *Adequate Notice.* When an agency contemplates major changes in a proposed regulation, it may be obligated to provide an additional opportunity for public comment. *Compare Chocolate Mfrs. Ass'n of the United States v. Block*, 755 F.2d 1098 (4th Cir. 1985), *and Animal Health*

Inst. v. FDA, Food Drug Cosm. L. Rep. (CCH) ¶ 38,154 (D.D.C. 1978), *with Pharmaceutical Mfrs. Ass'n v. Gardner*, 381 F.2d 271 (D.C. Cir. 1967).

2.   HHS OVERSIGHT OF FDA RULEMAKING

The authority conferred by the FD&C Act is expressly lodged in the Secretary of HHS. Indeed, prior to 1988, the Act did not mention either FDA or the office of Commissioner of Food and Drugs.

Before 1981, Secretaries of HHS formally delegated authority to implement the FD&C Act to the Commissioner. This delegation implicitly included the authority to propose and promulgate all regulations without specific HHS approval. Commissioners generally kept Secretaries and their staffs informed about important FDA actions, including regulations, but no formal process for HHS review existed. The degree of HHS influence largely depended on the desires of the incumbent Secretary.

In 46 Fed. Reg. 26052 (May 11, 1981), HHS Secretary Richard Schweiker promulgated a regulation, codified in 21 C.F.R. 5.11, stating that "the Secretary reserves the authority to approve [FDA] regulations" which establish general rules applicable to a class of products or present highly significant public issues. Regulations promulgated under section 701(e) were excluded from this reservation of authority. In 47 Fed. Reg. 16010 (Apr. 14, 1982), the regulation was modified to permit, but not require, the Secretary to approve regulations promulgated through formal rulemaking as well. Accordingly, since 1981, all significant FDA regulations have been reviewed and formally or tacitly approved at the departmental level. In 2004, FDA deleted the information regarding delegations of authority from Part 5 of the C.F.R. and moved it Staff Manual Guide (SMG) 1410.10, which is available on the agency website. 69 Fed. Reg. 17285 (Apr. 2, 2004).

3.   OMB OVERSIGHT OF FDA RULEMAKING

The imposition by courts, in cases like *Nova Scotia*, of rigorous requirements on notice-and-comment rulemaking began a process known by administrative law academics as the "ossification" of rulemaking. One of the most important aspects of this accretion of additional obligations during the 1970s and 1980s was the creation of an elaborate system for close supervision of most agency rulemaking by the Office of Management and Budget (OMB) in the Executive Office of the President.

First, President Ford's Executive Order 11821, 39 Fed. Reg. 41501 (Nov. 29, 1974), requires that every federal agency proposing a "major" regulation prepare an inflation impact statement (IIS). The Office of the Federal Register subsequently required that the inflation impact analysis be referenced in the preamble to every proposed or final major regulation. 40 Fed. Reg. 26312 (June 23, 1975); 40 Fed. Reg. 48979 (Oct. 20, 1975); 41 Fed. Reg. 43476 (Oct. 1, 1976).

President Carter, whose election platform promised regulatory reform, issued Executive Order 12174, 44 Fed. Reg. 69609 (Dec. 4, 1979), requiring a reduction in the paperwork burden imposed by the federal government. Based upon this executive order, Congress enacted the Paperwork Reduction Act of 1980, 94 Stat. 2812, which created the OMB Office of Information and Regulatory Affairs (OIRA) and authorized it to reduce the federal paperwork burden. OMB promulgated regulations to implement the Paperwork Reduction Act, and its 1986 reauthorization, in 48 Fed. Reg. 13666 (Mar. 31, 1983) and 53 Fed. Reg. 16618 (May 10, 1988) respectively. 5 C.F.R. Part 1320. In a decision that has obvious implications for FDA, the Supreme Court held in *Dole v. United Steelworkers of America*, 494 U.S. 26 (1990), that the Paperwork Reduction Act does not grant OIRA authority to review and disapprove agencies' regulations mandating disclosures by private enterprises directly to their employees or to the public.

President Carter also issued Executive Order 12044, 43 Fed. Reg. 12661 (Mar. 24, 1978), requiring an economic analysis of significant regulations and a review of existing regulations. Congress then enacted the Regulatory Flexibility Act, 94 Stat. 1164 (1980), requiring each agency to publish a semiannual regulatory agenda, to perform regulatory flexibility analysis for each proposed and final regulation, and to conduct periodic reviews of regulations.

President Ronald Reagan took these initiatives several steps further. He issued Executive Order 12291, 46 Fed. Reg. 13193 (Feb. 19, 1981) and Executive Order 12498, 50 Fed. Reg. 1036 (Jan. 8, 1985), requiring a regulatory impact analysis (*i.e.*, cost/benefit analysis) for each major proposed and final regulation, a yearly regulatory program from each agency, and OMB review of these documents. In 1993, President Clinton issued Executive Order 12866, which amended but continued the requirement that OIRA perform a cost/benefit analysis of every "significant regulatory action," a phrase that the order defines as including rules that have an annual effect on the economy of $100 million or more, as well as various other categories of rules.

Operating under these executive orders, OMB has had a major impact on FDA's (and other agencies') regulations. An attempt under the Freedom of Information Act to obtain records that would reveal the status of FDA regulations under review in OMB was denied in *Wolfe v. Department of HHS*, 839 F.2d 768 (D.C. Cir. 1988) (en banc). *See also* GAO, Regulatory Review: Information on OMB's Review Process, No. GGD–89–101FS (July 1989). Recently, the delay in OMB's release of FDA rules implementing the Food Safety Modernization Act prompted a 2012 *New York Times* editorial titled "Rules Delayed, Governing Denied."

It has been 19 months since President Obama signed into law the Food Safety Modernization Act, the first overhaul of the Food and Drug Administration's food safety laws since the 1930s. But if you think the food supply has become markedly safer since then, think again.

The F.D.A. rules needed to carry out the law are still held up as a review by the White House's Office of Management and Budget enters its eighth month. While coordinating suggestions from various agencies can take time, a delay of eight months and counting lends credence to the suspicions of consumer advocates who think election-year politics are at play, with Democrats trying to avoid Republican charges that rules kill jobs.

... [S]everal important rules, like those on food safety, remain in limbo. Such delays call into question the Obama administration's commitment to reforms that are needed to make government work better and more effectively.

N.Y. TIMES, Aug. 12, 2012, at 12.

4. FORMAL RULEMAKING

As discussed above, section 701(e) provides that specified regulations (*e.g.*, prescribing labeling for special dietary foods, rulings on food additive and color additive petitions) may be issued only after the agency has provided affected persons an opportunity for a formal evidentiary hearing. Hearings held pursuant to these provisions must comply with the applicable provisions of the Administrative Procedure Act, 5 U.S.C. 556 and 557.

FDA's frustration with this process, highlighted by its decade-long effort to establish labeling requirements for dietary supplements and other foods pursuant to section 403(j) and by increasingly protracted hearings on food standards of identity proposed pursuant to section 401, have led the agency either to abandon use of the authorities that require formal hearings or to construe hearing requests strictly.

a. WHEN IS AN EVIDENTIARY HEARING REQUIRED?

Dyestuffs and Chemicals, Inc. v. Flemming

271 F.2d 281 (8th Cir. 1959).

■ VOGEL, CIRCUIT JUDGE.

Petitioner is a producer of food colors, including certain coal tar colors known as FD&C Yellows 3 and 4 which have been widely used in the coloring of edible fat products, principally butter and oleomargarine. FD&C Yellows 3 and 4 have been certified by the respondent and his predecessors under § 346(b) as safe for such use for approximately the past 40 years. On January 24, 1957, the Deputy Commissioner of Food and Drugs published in the Federal Register a notice of his proposal to amend the Food and Drug Administration regulations by removing FD&C Yellow Nos. 1, 2, 3 and 4 from the approved list for unrestricted use. ... After receiving comments, including those of the Certified Color Industry Committee of which petitioner is a member, the Commissioner on May 4, 1957, published an order removing the colors in question from the approved list, because they "are not harmless and suitable for use within the meaning of" 21 U.S.C. 346(b). ... On May 27, 1957, within the time provided by law, the Certified Color Industry Committee filed objections to the order and requested a hearing thereon in accordance with the provisions of 21 U.S.C. 371(e)(2, 3) [FD&C Act 701(e)(2, 3)]. ...

... Petitioner contends that [Sections 701(e)(2) and (3)] ... constitute an unconditional statutory requirement for a hearing upon the filing of objections and that they were wholly disregarded by the order deleting the colors from the harmless list, with the result that no chance was afforded petitioner and others to raise any objections that might be available or to question and refute the pharmacological evidence referred to in the Secretary's order.

Respondent counters by claiming that the grounds set forth in petitioner's objections were wholly insufficient to warrant a hearing in that they sought the promulgation of regulations that were beyond the Department's authority. . . .

It seems to us obvious, as it did to the respondent, that . . . each of the objections set forth by the petitioner must be held inadequate to prevent the removal of the coal tar colors in question from the "harmless" list. . . . We thus conclude that the four grounds set forth in the petitioner's objections to the order were legally insufficient and turn next to the question of whether a hearing must be held even though the prerequisite objections fail to state valid or legal grounds for the requested action.

It will be noted that 21 U.S.C. 371(e)(2) provides that objections may be filed ". . . stating the grounds therefor, and requesting a public hearing upon such objections . . ." and (3) ". . . the Secretary, after due notice, *shall hold such a public hearing for the purpose of receiving evidence relevant and material to the issues raised by such objections.*" (Emphasis supplied.) It is only after filing objections and ". . . stating the grounds therefor, and requesting a public hearing upon such objections . . ." that an interested party is entitled to a hearing. The hearing is solely for the purpose of receiving evidence "relevant and material to the issues raised by such objections." Certainly, then, the objections, in order to be effective and necessitate the hearing requested, must be legally adequate so that, if true, the order complained of could not prevail. The objections must raise "issues." The issues must be material to the question involved; that is, the legality of the order attacked. They may not be frivolous or inconsequential. Where the objections stated and the issues raised thereby are, even if true, legally insufficient, their effect is a nullity and no objections have been stated. Congress did not intend the governmental agencies created by it to perform useless or unfruitful tasks. If it is perfectly clear that petitioner's appeal for a hearing contains nothing material and the objections stated do not abrogate the legality of the order attacked, no hearing is required by law. . . .

NOTES

1. *FDA Regulations.* 21 C.F.R. 12.24(b), sets forth criteria that must be satisfied to warrant a hearing on objections to regulations that are subject to section 701(e):

(1) There is a genuine and substantial issue of fact for resolution at a hearing. A hearing will not be granted on issues of policy or law.

. . . .

(3) The data and information submitted, if established at a hearing, would be adequate to justify resolution of the factual issue in the way sought by the person. . . .

(4) Resolution of the factual issue in the way sought by the person is adequate to justify the action requested. . . .

2.   *Hearing Denials.* In *Community Nutrition Institute v. Young,* 773 F.2d 1356 (D.C. Cir. 1985), the Court of Appeals upheld FDA's approval of beverage uses of aspartame and denial of a formal hearing. *See also Pineapple Growers Ass'n of Hawaii v. FDA,* 673 F.2d 1083 (9th Cir. 1982). In *Cook Chocolate Co. v. Miller,* 72 F. Supp. 573 (D.D.C. 1947), 1938–1964 FDLI Jud. Rec. 985 (D.D.C. 1949), a food processor petitioned to amend a food standard and, when FDA declined to hold an evidentiary hearing, brought suit contending that he had demonstrated the statutorily required "reasonable grounds." The District Court concluded, after a trial, that the evidence failed to show that FDA had abused its discretion.

3.   *Contrary Authority. Pactra Industries, Inc. v. Consumer Product Safety Comm'n,* 555 F.2d 677 (9th Cir. 1977), overturned a ban on the use of vinyl chloride as a propellant in consumer products issued by the CPSC under the Hazardous Substances Act, which incorporates the formal rulemaking requirements of the FD&C Act. The Commission had declined to hold a hearing on objections to its "final" rule, concluding in substance that there were no facts the objectors could prove which would alter its judgment. The court of appeals rejected this reasoning:

> We hold that section 371(e) leaves the agency no discretion to rule on the quality and validity of the objections prior to the formal hearing, so long as they are made in good faith and draw in question in a material way the underpinnings of the regulation at issue. It is inconsistent with the statutory scheme to require the objecting party to allege anything more.
>
> The Commission's summary procedure may be justified where, as was the case in *Dyestuffs,* the issues raised by the objecting party have been authoritatively determined to be legally irrelevant. But a different case is presented where, merely because the agency has concluded that the scientific evidence is adequate to support its order, a hearing is denied on the assumption that it would serve no purpose. . . .

Id. at 684. *See also Marshall Minerals, Inc. v. FDA,* 661 F.2d 409 (5th Cir. 1981) (overturning FDA's denial of a request for a public hearing on a food additive petition).

4.   *Entitlement to a Formal Hearing under Sections 505 and 512.* Sections 505(d) and (e) of the FD&C Act require FDA to provide a New Drug Application (NDA) filer or holder an opportunity for an evidentiary hearing when the agency declines to approve, or proposes to revoke, an NDA. Parallel provisions require the agency to provide an opportunity for an evidentiary hearing upon denial or withdrawal of approval of a New Animal Drug Application. FD&C Act 512(d), (e). It is unclear whether such proceedings are properly characterized as formal rulemaking or formal adjudication. In *Weinberger v. Hynson, Westcott & Dunning,* 412 U.S. 609 (1973), excerpted *infra* p. 662, the Supreme Court upheld the agency's authority to deny a hearing and enter summary judgment when the party

seeking a hearing fails to demonstrate that material factual issues are in dispute.

5. *Standing to Demand a Hearing of an NDA Decision.* Because an NDA is a private license, section 505 permits only the applicant or holder to request a hearing on an adverse agency action. Thus, FDA has declared that "a physician has no legal right to a hearing to contest withdrawal of approval of a new drug." 40 Fed. Reg. 22950, 22967 (May 27, 1975). *See also Rutherford v. American Medical Ass'n*, 379 F.2d 641 (7th Cir. 1967); *Tutoki v. Celebrezze*, 375 F.2d 105 (7th Cir. 1967) (cancer patients have no standing to contest FDA's prohibition of Krebiozen except by filing their own new drug application and appealing its denial).

6. *Food Standards.* FD&C 701(e) used to require formal rulemaking for the promulgation, amendment, or repeal of any food standard of identity under section 401 of the Act. This original requirement was amended in the 1950s to require a hearing only upon the filing of objections. 68 Stat. 54 (1954), 70 Stat. 919 (1956). It was further amended in 1990 to remove most food standards from the scope of the formal rulemaking requirement altogether—with the exception of standards "for any dairy product . . . or maple sirup [sic]." 104 Stat. 2353, 2365 (1990) Apart from these exceptions, FDA today is permitted to adopt, amend, or repeal standards through notice and comment rulemaking under section 701(a). *See infra* p. 343, note 2.

7. *Adversely Affected by a Food Standard.* The issue of *who* can be "adversely affected" under sections 701(e) and (f), and thus be entitled to demand a hearing and later seek court review, arose soon after FDA first began to promulgate food standards. *See Reade v. Ewing*, 205 F.2d 630 (2d Cir. 1953) (consumer of food may be adversely affected by a food standard); *United States Cane Sugar Refiners' Ass'n v. McNutt*, 138 F.2d 116 (2d Cir. 1943) (ingredient supplier is not adversely affected by a food standard that excludes an ingredient it markets); *Land O'Lakes Creameries, Inc. v. McNutt*, 132 F.2d 653 (8th Cir. 1943) (producer of a competitive product has standing to seek review of a food standard); *A.E. Staley Mfg. Co. v. Secretary of Agriculture*, 120 F.2d 258 (7th Cir. 1941) (food processor is adversely affected by a food standard that excludes an ingredient he uses).

b. Formal Hearing Procedures

FDA's detailed procedures for conducting a formal evidentiary public hearing are set forth at 21 C.F.R. Part 12. Such proceedings do not necessarily conclude with the decision by the administrative law judge (ALJ); indeed, that determination is called the "initial decision." The regulations also provide for appeal to and the issuance of a "final decision" by the FDA Commissioner. 21 C.F.R. Part 12, Subpart G.

Many formal hearings conducted by FDA have been protracted, some famously so. Several have been cited as evidence of the need to reform or dispense with formal rulemaking. President Jimmy Carter once stated: "It should not have taken 12 years and a hearing record of over 100,000 pages for the FDA to decide what percentage of peanuts there ought to be in peanut butter. . . . I would have used that example even if I had grown soybeans and wheat, by the way." 15 Weekly

COMP. PRES. DOC. 482, 484 (Mar. 25, 1979). The most cogent criticisms of the FDA experience include Ben G. Fisher, *Procedural Techniques in Food and Drug Administration Proceedings*, 17 FOOD DRUG COSM. L.J. 724 (1962); Robert Hamilton, *Rulemaking on a Record by the Food and Drug Administration*, 50 TEX. L. REV. 1132 (1972); Note, *FDA Rulemaking Hearings: A Way Out of the Peanut Butter Quagmire*, 40 GEO. WASH. L. REV. 726 (1972). *See also* Administrative Conference of the United States, Recommendation No. 71–7, 2 RECOMMENDATIONS AND REPORTS OF THE ADMINISTRATIVE CONFERENCE OF THE UNITED STATES 42 (1973).

On the premise that repetitive cross examination is a major cause of delay at hearings, FDA has attempted to limit cross examination to the extent permitted by the Administrative Procedure Act. *See* 41 Fed. Reg. 51706 (Nov. 23, 1976), 21 C.F.R. 12.87, 12.94. For discussions of other procedural aspects of FDA's formal hearings, see Selma Levine, *Separation of Functions in FDA Administrative Proceedings*, 23 FOOD DRUG COSM. L.J. 132 (1968); William Pendergast, *The Nature of Section 701 Hearings and Suggestions for Improving the Procedures for the Conduct of Such Hearings*, 24 FOOD DRUG COSM. L.J. 527 (1969); *FDA Procedures*, 25 FOOD DRUG COSM. L.J. 191 (1970).

c.   THE PUBLIC BOARD OF INQUIRY ALTERNATIVE TO A TRIAL–TYPE HEARING

Because formal adversary hearings are often not well-suited to resolving the types of scientific issues that the agency regularly confronts, FDA has experimented with the use of an alternative process based on scientific peer review. This alternative is codified at 21 C.F.R. 12.32 and Part 13 ("Public Hearing before Public Board of Inquiry").

Notice of Proposed Rulemaking: Administrative Practices and Procedures

40 Fed. Reg. 40682 (September 3, 1975).

. . . Proposed § 2.117 [now 21 C.F.R. 12.32] would provide that a person who had a right to an opportunity for a formal evidentiary hearing could waive that opportunity and, in lieu thereof, request a public hearing before a Public Board of Inquiry . . .

. . . [T]he proposed regulations would establish . . . an informal public hearing before a Public Board of Inquiry that would be conducted in the form of a scientific inquiry rather than as a legal trial. . . . Proposed § 2.202 [now 21 C.F.R. 13.10] would require that the members of a Board have medical, technical, scientific, or other qualifications relevant to the issues to be considered at the hearing. The members would be [designated] special government employees and thus subject to the conflict of interest rules applicable to such employees. . . .

Within 30 days after the notice of the hearing before the Board was published in the FEDERAL REGISTER, each of the parties to the proceeding and any person whose petition was the subject of the hearing would submit a list of five nominees for members of the Board. Such persons could agree upon a single list of nominees. Following receipt of such lists, such persons could submit comments on the other lists submitted. The Commissioner would then review the lists and comments and select one member of the Board from the lists submitted by the director of the agency bureau involved and any person whose petition was the subject of the hearing, one member from the lists submitted by the other parties, and one member of his own choosing from any source whatever who would serve as the Chairman of the Board. . . .

Proposed § 2.206(a) [now 21 C.F.R. 13.30] would make it clear that the purpose of a Board is to review complex technical issues in a reasonably short time by using the informal approach of a scientific inquiry rather than the formal procedures of a legal trial. Accordingly, it is anticipated that there will be little, if any, need for participation by attorneys. . . .

The Chairman of the Board would determine the order in which the parties and participants make their presentations. Such order of presentation could well be the subject of a prior agreement. Each participant could then proceed with his presentation, which would be made without interruptions and without objection or other legalistic procedures. At the conclusion of a participant's presentation, each of the other participants could briefly state questions or criticism and suggest further questioning with respect to specific matters. The members of the Board could interrupt a participant at any time to ask questions, and could conduct further questioning at the conclusion of the participant's full presentation either on their own initiative or at the suggestion of the other participants.

In addition to hearing the views of the participants, the Board could independently consult with any other person who it concluded may have useful information. All such consultation would have to be at an announced hearing of the Board unless all participants agreed that it could be done in writing. Moreover, any participant in the proceeding could submit to the Board a request that it consult with specific persons who could have useful information.

The administrative record of the public hearing would constitute the exclusive record for decision on the matter. . . .

———

FDA has established a Public Board of Inquiry in two cases. *See* 44 Fed. Reg. 31716 (June 1, 1979) (aspartame); 44 Fed. Reg. 44274 (July 27, 1979) (Depo Provera). Professor Sidney Shapiro offered the following assessment of these experiments:

The FDA's experiences with the PBOI confirm the value of the "science court" idea for resolving issues of scientific judgment. Its scientific seminar format is conducive to scientific analysis and debate. As a practical matter, however, the costs of merging the PBOI and the regulatory process will limit the use of these boards. Although the two PBOIs that have been convened did engage in the type of scientific inquiry that the FDA anticipated at the hearing stage, delays and other problems in the pre- and post-hearing stages revealed the need to integrate the PBOI into the normal regulatory process. Many of these problems can be alleviated, but

PBOIs will continue to be expensive. As a result, they will be cost-effective only in cases involving issues that for sophisticated scientific judgment and stimulate great public interest. In those cases, the benefits of the PBOI—enhanced accuracy and legitimacy—are likely to outweigh the costs of the process.

Even if the use of the PBOI is limited, the process offers the FDA a unique option with several important advantages over the agency's advisory committee system. One key difference is that the PBOI convenes after the agency has decided whether to license a new drug or food additive. Because the PBOI can focus on the key issues in the agency's decision, it can serve as an independent check on the validity of that decision. Another key difference is that the PBOI emphasizes data analysis and is more accountable than other processes for its conclusions. As a result, the PBOI process enhances the accuracy and legitimacy of an agency's decision making.

In an analysis of whether a "scientific" or "adversarial" process better resolves issues of scientific judgment, the results are mixed. The FDA's experience does indicate that the PBOI can be the more effective process, but at a higher price than the conventional approach. Thus, the PBOI is unlikely to be cost-effective except when it is used to resolve significant issues of scientific judgment.

Scientific Issues and the Function of Hearing Procedures: Evaluating the FDA's Public Board of Inquiry, 1986 DUKE L.J. 288.

C. THE DECLINE OF NOTICE-AND-COMMENT RULEMAKING AND THE RISE OF GUIDANCE

As suggested previously, the production of legislative rules through the "ossified" notice-and-comment process is not easy. Even before the "proposed rule" stage, agencies not infrequently request comments through advance notices of proposed rulemaking (ANPRs), hold public meetings, or both. Agency officials must then reach agreement on the policy they wish to adopt, as well as the words they will use to express it. In light of cases like *Nova Scotia, supra* p. 44, the agency must approach both the notice and comment steps with great rigor, and consequently, the preambles to proposed and final rules are often extremely lengthy. Moreover, pursuant to Executive Order 12866, the agency must submit both the proposed and final versions of "significant" rules to cost/benefit review by OMB's Office of Information and Regulatory Affairs (OIRA). *See supra* p. 48. For many rules, FDA can expect questions and perhaps opposition from OIRA. Federal law also requires that the agency give consideration to the implications of a rule for small business, for the environment, for the reporting and record keeping burdens on citizens, and for federal-state relations. Finally, the possibility always exists that somebody will challenge the regulation in court.

All this takes time. FDA's location within the Department of Health and Human Services creates additional obstacles which potentially can duplicate those implicit in OMB review. The frequent turnover in agency leadership means that the average Commissioner often cannot expect to see the rulemaking process through from start to finish. It is little wonder that FDA, and many other agencies, have increasingly turned to less formal ways of describing their expectations for regulated industry. Besides representing savings in time and resources, the less formal route also preserves the agency's future flexibility; after all, a policy embodied in an APA-compliant rule can only be changed or abandoned by commencing anew the onerous process that produced the rule in the first place.

The pace of rulemaking at FDA has slackened in recent decades. According to Professor Todd Rakoff, FDA's annual output of regulations declined by approximately 50 percent between the early 1980s and the mid-1990s. *The Choice Between Formal and Informal Modes of Administrative Regulation*, 52 ADMIN. L. REV. 159, 168 (2000) (excerpted immediately below). An examination of annual indices of the Federal Register from 1970 to 2005 reveals the following:

• From 1970 to 1978, FDA produced roughly 700 proposed and final rules each year.

• After 1978 its annual production of proposed and final rules never again passed 600 and exceeded 500 only once (in 1983).

• The agency's rulemaking productivity declined further after the mid-1980s; FDA's annual output of proposed and final rules averaged 270 through the end of the century.

• FDA's production of proposed and final rules fell below 200 in 2001—where it has remained every year since.

These statistics do not demonstrate that FDA is less inclined than it once was to articulate and publicize its policies in written form, but only that notice-and-comment rulemaking is no longer the agency's preferred mechanism for doing so. Instead, it has turned to the issuance of guidance documents.

In its 1975 procedural regulations, FDA identified a category of official but nonbinding documents intended to reflect the agency's position on regulatory matters but not purporting to be legal requirements. As "interpretive rules" or "general statements of policy," such publications were not subject to the APA's notice-and-comment requirements. 5 U.S.C. 553(b)(A). The agency initially labeled these documents "guidelines" but later named them "guidance." Originally, most guidance documents were developed to help the pharmaceutical industry meet the agency's expectations for adequate NDAs, but today FDA uses them for almost every purpose imaginable.

The agency's preference for guidance has produced its own internal logic—the increasing formalization of the process by which guidances themselves are developed and adopted. In other words, the production of guidance documents, too, has ossified somewhat in recent years.

Todd D. Rakoff, *The Choice Between Formal and Informal Modes of Administrative Regulation*

52 ADMINISTRATIVE LAW REVIEW 159 (2000).

On February 8, 1997, the United States Food and Drug Administration (FDA) issued a document entitled "Good Guidance

Practices" that set forth the agency's "policies and procedures for the development, issuance, and use of guidance documents." The details are, of course, of special interest to lawyers who practice food and drug law. From a broader standpoint, the document is important because it frankly recognizes and treats a category of administrative action called "guidance."

"Guidance" as a named, identified legal category is something new in American administrative law. . . .

During the 1950s and 1960s, most major regulation took place through formal adjudicatory proceedings. This emphasis on developing law by deciding individual cases proved deficient in three respects. First, it was costly. Second, even though American lawyers are skilled in handling case law, the law that could be extracted from agency decisions often proved to be vague or contradictory. Third, the newer goals of regulation that developed in the 1960s, such as protection of the environment, depended on establishing generally applicable standards with precise contours. Such standards are difficult to establish in the context of a single case.

The response was to shift the emphasis of the system from adjudicating cases to promulgating rules. This was done partly by Congress when it mandated rulemaking in various environmental, health, and safety statutes.

The upshot of these developments was a surge of administrative rulemaking. . . .

With so much regulating being done by rulemaking rather than by adjudication, one might think that the system as a whole had become less formal. Indeed, if one reads the plain text of the APA [Administrative Procedure Act], it does seem that the less formal rulemaking process, while certainly not left entirely to agency discretion, is not too demanding.

. . . The American legal culture, however, could not tolerate such lack of formality once rulemaking of this sort became the paradigmatic case of agency action. In light of the large substantive discretion many agencies had been given, doing so would seem to authorize highhanded agency behavior. As a result, partly through legislative and executive action, but primarily led by judges, these provisions were given increasingly burdensome interpretations.

For example, agencies were required to provide the public from the start, not only the substance of the proposed rule, but also the data on which the agency relied to justify the rule. Agencies were also required to explain why they rejected at least the most forceful comments made by regulated parties or the public; otherwise, they had not adequately explained the basis for the rule. And on review, judges increasingly ask the agency to justify the specific regulatory choice it had made, rather than merely showing that the agency had not been, in the ordinary sense of the term, arbitrary.

These developments were exacerbated by the new political culture that developed after the inauguration of Ronald Reagan as President in 1981. The organized bureaucracy of the government—the administrative agencies—were seen by many in the Reagan

Administration as the representatives of entrenched interests that opposed the Chief Executive's program of deregulation. Further procedural requirements were imposed in order to give the President's close advisors more control over the agencies. That these requirements made rulemaking yet more cumbersome did not dissuade an administration interested in less, not more, regulation. . . .

In short, notice-and-comment rulemaking—already more formal than the rulemaking process in some other countries—has now become (even though still known as "informal" rulemaking) an even more formal, more burdensome, and more expensive process. . . . Promulgating a major rule often takes years and represents a substantial commitment of an agency's resources. . . .

If we compare the mid-1990s with the late 1970s or early 1980s, we find that the number of FDA regulations adopted each year in accordance with the APA's rulemaking procedures declined by about fifty percent. By contrast, since the start of this decade [the 1990s] there has been a striking increase in the number of FDA-issued documents intended to give guidance to the regulated industry but not adopted through public procedures. . . . This decrease in the number of enacted rules, and this increase in the number of guidance documents led to cries that the required procedures were being subverted. Under pressure from industry, and to some extent from the courts as well, the FDA responded with a substantial, public proceeding—much like a rulemaking proceeding—in order to develop the very procedures by which this new process would be carried out.

The scope of the matter can be seen from the definition of the term "guidance documents" that the agency ultimately adopted. While speeches or warning letters were not included, the term does cover documents directed either to the agency's own staff or to the public that relate to: the evaluation or approval of proposed new drugs; the production and testing of regulated products; the agency's inspection and enforcement procedures; or documents that broadly describe "the agency's policy and regulatory approach to an issue." At the same time, the FDA takes pains to state that guidance documents "are not legally binding on the public or the agency. Rather, they explain how the agency believes the statutes and regulations apply to certain regulated activities." . . . In short, guidance documents are meant to be statements of no legal consequence but immense practical consequence about virtually everything the agency regulates.

. . . .

The "Good Guidance Practices" statement divides guidance documents into two groups. The documents in the first, more important, group "set forth first interpretations of statutory or regulatory requirements, changes in interpretation or policy that are of more than a minor nature, unusually complex scientific issues, or highly controversial issues." The stipulated procedures for this group provide that the agency will publish a notice of the draft guidance in the Federal Register, accept written comments and perhaps hold public meetings regarding the draft, review the comments, and "make changes to a guidance document in response to comments as appropriate." It would not be far-fetched to rephrase these matters by saying that the

FDA now proposes to issue its important regulations mostly in accordance with the notice-and-comment rulemaking procedure set forth in the APA, as it was understood before 1970.

The only difference is that, at least in the agency's view, the entire matter will be beyond the purview of the courts. The promulgated policies will not legally bind the agency or regulated parties, and the stipulated procedures are not intended to confer procedural rights. But is that such a difference? The FDA appears to thinks it is not, as it proposes to set forth new interpretations of statutory requirements and other regulatory changes "of more than a minor nature" in this fashion. It appears that the industry thinks it is not a great difference either, since it participated extensively in the proceeding to establish these "good guidance practices." In this highly regulated industry, in which all the players—including the agency, the drug companies, and even the representatives of consumers—are repeat players, it may well be that "the force of law," in the strict sense of enforceability in court, is of little value compared to "the force of law" in the practical sense as dictated by existing relationships. . . .

NOTES

1. *Codification.* After FDA published its Good Guidance Practice (GGP) document in 2007, 62 Fed. Reg. 8961 (1997), the agency's approach received congressional approval in the Food and Drug Administration Modernization Act of 1997 (FDAMA). FD&C Act 701(h), added by FDAMA, sets forth general requirements for guidance documents regarding public participation, publication, and content. In an uncodified provision, 111 Stat. 2369, FDAMA also instructed FDA to promulgate a good guidance practices regulation informed by the 2007 GGP document and consistent with new section 701(h). The agency published this regulation in 65 Fed. Reg. 7321 (Feb. 14, 2000), codified at 21 C.F.R. 10.115.

2. *OMB Standardization and Oversight of Agency Guidance.* The FDA's "good guidance" approach proved to be extremely influential. In late 2005, the Office of Management and Budget released a draft bulletin describing the process that, in OMB's view, all agencies should follow in issuing new guidances. "Proposed Bulletin for Good Guidance Practice," 70 Fed. Reg. 71866 (Nov. 30, 2005). OMB issued the final bulletin at 72 Fed. Reg. 3432 (Jan. 25, 2007). In doing so, it explicitly acknowledged FDA's pioneering activities in this area. *Id.* at 3433.

Major guidances are now also subjected to cost/benefit review by OMB's OIRA. In Executive Order 13422 (2007), President George W. Bush amended E.O. 12866 to mandate such review for all "significant guidance documents." In E.O. 13497 (2009), President Obama revoked these amendments, but in a March 4, 2009 Memorandum (M–09–13), Peter Orszag, the Director of OMB, made clear that OIRA would continue to review all significant policy and guidance documents.

3. *Rulemaking vs. Guidance.* Important differences remain between a legislative rule and a guidance document. For example, a guidance requires no preamble and no publication in the Federal Register. The notice-and-comment process generating a major guidance is not governed

by the APA and is thus usually less rigorous. Moreover, guidances are not subject to some of the non-APA review requirements imposed by legislation on regulations. Most important, a guidance document, unlike a regulation, does have the force of law.

NOT

4. *Commentary.* For analyses of FDA's reliance on and production of guidances, *see, e.g.*, Lars Noah, *The FDA's New Policy on Guidelines: Having Your Cake and Eating It Too*, 47 CATH. U.L. REV. 113 (1997); Erica Seiguer & John J. Smith, *Perception and Process at the Food and Drug Administration: Obligations and Trade–Offs in Rules and Guidances*, 60 FOOD & DRUG L.J. 17 (2005). For discussion of the "guidance phenomenon" across the government, *see, e.g.*, Andrew P. Morriss, Bruce Yandle & Andrew Dorchak, *Choosing How to Regulate*, 29 HAR. ENVTL. L. REV. 179 (2005); David Zaring, *Best Practices*, 81 N.Y.U. L. REV. 294 (2006); "Use of Alternatives to Conventional Notice and Comment Rulemaking," Symposium at the American University Center for the Study of Rulemaking, March 16, 2005.

D. DIRECT FINAL RULEMAKING AND INTERIM RULEMAKING

The Administrative Procedure Act, in addition to exempting interpretative rules, general policy statements, and procedural rules from the notice and comment requirements, also allows an agency to skip notice and comment "when the agency for good cause finds [and explains] that notice and public procedure thereon are impracticable, unnecessary, or contrary to the public interest." 5 U.S.C. 553(b)(B). There are two main varieties of rulemaking under this this provision: "direct final rulemaking" and "interim rulemaking."

"Direct final rulemaking" is used if an agency determines at the outset that a rulemaking is expected to be uncontroversial and thus generate no significant adverse comment. Under FDA's version of this procedure, described in a guidance published at 62 Fed. Reg. 62466 (Nov. 21, 1997), the agency publishes a direct final rule with a statement of basis and purpose and simultaneously promulgates a proposed rule. If the agency receives no significant adverse comment, the direct final rule goes into effect. If, however, the agency receives any significant adverse comment during the comment period, the agency withdraws the direct final rule and reverts to ordinary notice-and-comment procedures. According to one recent study, between November 1997 and April 2008, FDA commenced direct rulemaking on 38 occasions, and on fifteen of these, the agency withdrew the direct final rules because the agency received significant adverse comments. Michael Kolber, *Rulemaking without Rules: An Empirical Study of Direct Final Rulemaking*, 72 ALB. L. REV. 79 (2009).

In "interim rulemaking," an agency issues a final rule that is effective immediately, without first publishing a notice of proposed rulemaking. The agency announces that it will, after the rule becomes effective, receive comments, modify the interim final rule in light of these comments, and then adopt a final rule. *See generally* Michael Asimow, *Interim–Final Rules: Making Haste Slowly*, 51 ADMIN. L. REV. 703 (1999). Interim final rulemaking is often used in situations of exigency, where an agency deems it important to put a rule into effect as quickly as possible. *Id.* at 710. FDA uses the procedure most frequently to conform existing regulations to recent court decisions and to provisions of recent legislation. FDA has issued approximately 25 interim rules since the inception of the approach in 1992. *See, e.g.*, 66 Fed. Reg. 20589 (Apr. 24, 2001) ("Additional Safeguards for Children in Clinical Investigations of FDA–Regulated Product").

E. LEGISLATIVE RULE OR INTERPRETIVE RULE?

If FDA publishes a position without first affording members of the public an opportunity to comment, it may be accused of violating the notice and comment provisions of the Administrative Procedure Act. A court must then determine whether the agency's pronouncement constitutes a legislative rule to which the APA applies or represents only the agency's interpretation of established law. For an example of such a dispute, see *Syncor International Corp. v. Shalala*, 127 F.3d 90 (D.C. Cir. 1997) (excerpted *infra* p. 789).

NOTES

1. *Action Levels for Contaminants.* The majority in *Syncor* relied on the Court of Appeals' own earlier ruling in *Community Nutrition Institute v. Young*, 818 F.2d 943 (D.C. Cir. 1987), on remand from the Supreme Court. The Supreme Court had ruled that FDA had discretion to determine whether binding tolerances issued pursuant to formal rulemaking under section 406 were necessary to regulate the levels of aflatoxin on corn and other affected crops, but it then remanded the case to the court of appeals to determine whether the informal action levels that FDA had actually issued were subject to the notice-and-comment rulemaking requirements of the APA. *Young v. Community Nutrition Institute*, 476 U.S. 974 (1986). The Court of Appeals concluded that FDA's action levels—which it had issued without notice or opportunity for comment—functioned as rules because, though they did not formally bind growers or sellers of corn, they effectively constrained the agency's enforcement discretion. The action levels thus required compliance with section 553 of the APA. Judge Starr dissented. He thought the Court's ruling, by requiring compliance with the APA's increasingly burdensome requirements for rulemaking, would discourage the agency from sharing with the public its assessment of the levels at which aflatoxin posed a health threat that could warrant regulatory action. Following this decision, FDA acquiesced and announced that action levels for poisonous or deleterious substances in food constitute only guidance and not binding requirements. 53 Fed. Reg. 5043 (Feb. 19, 1988).

2. *Supporting Authority.* The courts have sometimes invalidated, or refused to enforce, FDA guidelines that have not been subjected to notice and comment. *See, e.g., Caribbean Produce Exchange, Inc. v. Secretary of HHS, Food Drug Cosm. L. Rep.* (CCH) ¶¶ 38,100, 38,110 (D.P.R. 1988), *rev'd and remanded*, 893 F.2d 3 (1st. Cir. 1989); *Bellarno International Ltd. v. FDA*, 678 F. Supp. 410 (E.D.N.Y. 1988); *United States v. Bioclinical Systems, Inc.*, 666 F. Supp. 82 (D. Md. 1987); *United States v. Articles of*

Drugs Consisting of 203 Paperbags, 634 F. Supp. 435 (N.D. Ill. 1985), *vacated* 818 F.2d 569 (7th Cir. 1987).

3.   *Contrasting Authority.* In *Professionals and Patients for Customized Care v. Shalala*, 56 F.3d 592 (5th Cir. 1995), the Fifth Circuit rejected a claim that an FDA's Compliance Policy Guide's description of the practices that would make a compounding pharmacist a manufacturer of drugs constituted a rule whose announcement had to comply with the APA. The Court of Appeals considered the text, form, and context of the agency's guide in arriving at the conclusion that it was not meant to establish a binding norm.

4.   *Discretion as to Whether to Issue Rules.* Courts generally leave the decision whether to issue a legislative rule to FDA's discretion *See, e.g., National Wildlife Federation v. Secretary of HHS*, 808 F.2d 12 (6th Cir. 1986); *Center for Science in the Public Interest v. Novitch*, Food Drug Cosm. L. Rep. (CCH) ¶ 38,275 (D.D.C. 1984). The only cases in which a court has required FDA to promulgate a regulation not specifically mandated by Congress are *Public Citizen v. Heckler*, 602 F. Supp. 611 (D.D.C. 1985), 653 F. Supp. 1229 (D.D.C. 1986), and *Public Citizen Health Research Group v. Commissioner, FDA*, 724 F. Supp. 1013 (D.D.C. 1989).

F. JUDICIAL REVIEW OF AGENCY ACTION

1. INTRODUCTION

As subsequent chapters of this book will make clear, FDA actions are frequently challenged in court. The FD&C Act expressly authorizes suits to review several dozen types of FDA decisions, including the approval of a food or color additive, the approval or revocation of approval of a human or animal drug, and the promulgation of any regulation subject to the formal rulemaking requirements of section 701(e) of the Act. And for the many rules and decisions about which the Act is silent regarding reviewability, the Administrative Procedure Act, coupled with relevant language in the FD&C Act, afford manifold opportunities for private parties to contest the legality of FDA's actions in court.

There was a time that FDA seemed to fare better in court than its counterpart health and safety agencies, such as EPA and OSHA. During the 1970s and early 1980s, when FDA was vigorously engaged in rulemaking, it was usually successful in fending off suits that threatened important agency policies. For example, on a single day in 1973, FDA's positions on the application of the 1962 Drug Amendments were upheld, with just one dissent, in a quartet of decisions by the Supreme Court. *See infra* p. 665, note 3. In recent years, however, FDA has not been as consistently successful in court. Reviewing courts have overturned a significant number of the agency's policies and actions. The agency has met some particularly dramatic defeats, such as the Supreme Court's rejection of its attempt to regulate tobacco products as drug delivery devices, *FDA v. Brown & Williamson Tobacco Corp.*, 529 U.S. 120 (2000) (*infra* p. 141), and a series of cases striking down FDA regulation and enforcement on commercial free speech grounds under the First Amendment of the United States Constitution. *See, e.g.,*

Pearson v. Shalala, 164 F.3d 650 (D.C. Cir. 1999) (*infra* p. 430); *R. J. Reynolds Tobacco Co. v. FDA*, 696 F.3d 1205 (D.C. Cir. 2012); *United States v. Caronia*, 703 F.3d 149 (2d Cir. 2012) (*infra* p. 951). For other recent examples of instances in which courts have blocked, or even compelled, FDA action, see *infra* pp. 70, 966, & 1441.

NOTE

Which Court? In general, challenges to FDA action must be brought in U.S. District Court. The FD&C Act states some exception, however. For example, an adversely affected party who challenges an FDA order regarding a food additive petition must bring suit "in the United States Court of Appeals for the circuit wherein such person resides or has his principal place of business, or in the United States Court of Appeals for the District of Columbia Circuit." FD&C Act 409(g)(1). *See, e.g., Community Nutrition Institute v. Young*, 773 F.2d 1356 (D.C. Cir. 1985).

2. STANDARDS OF REVIEW

The APA provides that a reviewing court shall:

> (2) hold unlawful and set aside agency action, findings, and conclusions found to be—
>
>> (A) arbitrary, capricious, an abuse of discretion, or otherwise not in accordance with law;
>>
>> (B) contrary to constitutional right, power, privilege, or immunity;
>>
>> (C) in excess of statutory jurisdiction, authority, or limitations, or short of statutory right;
>>
>> (D) without observance of procedure required by law;
>>
>> (E) unsupported by substantial evidence in a case subject to sections 556 and 557 of this title or otherwise reviewed on the record of an agency hearing provided by statute; or
>>
>> (F) unwarranted by the facts to the extent that the facts are subject to trial de novo by the reviewing court.

5 U.S.C. 706.

We cannot hope in this text to offer a discussion of the enormous and complex body of court decisions addressing the appropriate standard of review of agency action. Nonetheless, a student not familiar with this case law should be aware of several important precedents that are cited repeatedly throughout this book.

In *Chevron USA v. Natural Resources Defense Council, Inc.*, 467 U.S. 837 (1984), the Supreme Court established a seminal two-part test for determining the legality of an agency's interpretation of a statute that it is charged with administering (as FDA has been charged with administering the FD&C Act):

> First, always, is the question whether Congress has directly spoken to the precise question at issue. If the intent of Congress is clear, that is the end of the matter; for the court, as well as the agency, must give effect to the unambiguously expressed intent of

Congress. If, however, the court determines Congress has not directly addressed the precise question at issue, the court does not simply impose its own construction on the statute, as would be necessary in the absence of an administrative interpretation. Rather, if the statute is silent or ambiguous with respect to the specific issue, the question for the court is whether the agency's answer is based on a permissible construction of the statute.

Id. at 842–843. In other words, under "step one" of *Chevron*, the reviewing court grants *no* discretion to the agency's interpretation if "Congress has spoken directly to the precise question at issue." But if the statute is "silent or ambiguous with respect to the specific issue," a court will, under "step two," defer to the agency's interpretation so long as it is based on a "permissible construction of the statute." (The word "reasonable" is often used an alternative to "permissible.") Agency actions almost always survive "step two," but courts not inclined to grant deference to an agency have occasionally evinced creativity in denying the presence of ambiguity in the first place and thus categorizing a case as "step one." *See, e.g., Brown & Williamson, infra* p. 141.

Courts sometimes apply a lower level deference, derived from *Skidmore v. Swift & Co.*, 323 U.S. 134 (1944). *Skidmore* provided that the amount of deference due to an agency action depends on "the thoroughness evident in [the agency's] consideration, the validity of its reasoning, its consistency with earlier and later pronouncements, and all those factors which give it power to persuade. . . ." *Id.* at 139–40. A series of fairly recent Supreme Court cases has set forth situations, sometimes called "*Chevron* step zero" in which an agency action without the "force of law" should receive only *Skidmore* deference. Although *Chevron* applies to notice-and-comment rulemaking, formal rulemaking, and formal adjudication, the Supreme Court has said *Skidmore* deference is appropriate with respect to many less formal actions, such as a National Labor Relations Board opinion letter, *Christensen v. Harris County*, 529 U.S. 576 (1999), or a Customs Service tariff ruling letter, *United States v. Mead Corporation*, 533 U.S. 218 (2011). Consequently, FDA interpretations of the FD&C Act embodied in guidance documents, warning letters, preambles to proposed and final rules, and amicus briefs are ordinarily accorded the less deferential, *Skidmore* deference.

Finally, according to a doctrine known as *Auer* deference, a court should defer to an agency's interpretation of its own ambiguous regulations unless the interpretation is "plainly erroneous or inconsistent with the regulation." *Auer v. Robbins*, 519 U.S. 452, 461 (1997).

NOTE

Record for Judicial Review. In *Nova Scotia, supra* p. 44, FDA successfully argued that review of its smoked fish regulations should be confined to the record of its original rulemaking. The agency's regulations also reflect this position. 21 C.F.R. 10.45(f). *See also Heterochemical Corp. v. FDA*, Food Drug Cosm. L. Rep. (CCH) ¶ 38,074 (E.D.N.Y. 1987). When an agency's reasoning on a critical issue is not apparent from the rulemaking record, a reviewing court ordinarily will remand the matter to the agency for further elaboration or reopening of the record. On rare occasions, a district court may allow the submission of additional testimony or accept affidavits to clarify the agency's position. *See National Nutritional Foods Ass'n v. Mathews*, 557 F.2d 325 (2d Cir. 1977). *Cf.* Almay, Inc. v. Califano, 569 F.2d 674 (D.C. Cir. 1977).

3.   THE LIMITS OF JUDICIAL POWER

a.   JUSTICIABILITY

The concept of "justiciability" comprises a set of principles constraining the authority of the courts in our constitutional structure. Justiciability doctrines include, among others, standing, ripeness, finality, and mootness. This book will not attempt to analyze or even summarize these doctrines; the reader should simply be aware that there are limits to who can challenge FDA actions, what types of actions they can challenge, and when they can do so. Many of the cases excerpted in this book originally contained substantial discussions of justiciability issues that have been edited out.

NOTES

1.   *Ripeness. Abbott Laboratories*, excerpted earlier in this chapter, *supra* p. 34, is the leading case on ripeness in all of administrative law.

2.   *The Implications of Pre-Enforcement Review.* The Supreme Court's ruling in *Abbott Laboratories* that section 701(a) regulations could be challenged in a pre-enforcement suit led logically to the conclusion that review should be based on the rulemaking record compiled by the agency. The posture of a pre-enforcement suit makes it difficult for a court to visualize a regulation's impact in the various contexts to which it might apply. The question presented, essentially, is whether the regulation is authorized by law and supported by the facts relied on by the agency. So framed, it is difficult for a reviewing court to conclude that the regulation is invalid unless the agency committed some procedural error or made an obvious error in judgment. The regulation is thus likely to be upheld, and thereby given "substantive" effect, even though it might later be applied in some contexts where a court—were it still free to do so—might consider it "arbitrary." *See* Richard A. Merrill, *FDA and the Effects of Substantive Rules*, 35 FOOD DRUG COSM. L.J. 270 (1980).

3.   *Ripeness Again.* In *Pfizer Inc. v. Shalala*, 182 F.3d 975 (D.C. Cir. 1999), Pfizer challenged FDA's acceptance for processing of an abbreviated new drug application (ANDA) submitted by Mylan Laboratories for a product that delivered the same active ingredient as Pfizer's "pioneer" drug, though by a different mechanism. Prior to Mylan's submission of the ANDA, Pfizer had petitioned FDA to rule that Mylan's product was ineligible for ANDA treatment. After accepting the ANDA for processing, FDA denied Pfizer's petition. The Court of Appeals dismissed the case on the ground that Pfizer would not suffer any real harm until, and unless, FDA approved Mylan's ANDA and Pfizer faced actual competition in the marketplace. Even the discovery, at oral argument, that FDA had given

tentative approval to the Mylan product did not convert Pfizer's distress into a justiciable law suit. Nor was the court moved by FDA's regulation, 21 C.F.R. 10.45(d), which states that the agency will consider the denial of any citizen petition to be "final" for purposes of judicial review. It pointed out that an agency's action—such as FDA's rejection of Pfizer's petition—may be "final" but yet still not yet ripe for judicial review.

4.   *Ripeness and Warning Letters.* When FDA began using regulatory letters (later renamed warning letters) as an alternative to court enforcement, it intended that they represent the agency's definitive position and thus final action that could be the subject of a declaratory judgment action. The agency later retreated from this position, arguing that regulatory letters are only advisory, and the courts have accordingly held that they are not subject to pre-enforcement review. *See, e.g., Biotics Research Corp. v. Heckler,* 710 F.2d 1375 (9th Cir. 1983).

b.   PRIMARY JURISDICTION

The doctrine of primary jurisdiction arises from the following principle: "in cases raising issues of fact not within the conventional experience of judges or cases requiring the exercise of administrative discretion, agencies created by Congress for regulating the subject matter should not be passed over." *Far East Conference v. United States,* 342 U.S. 570, 574–75 (1952). The Supreme Court has thus consistently recognized that when Congress creates an agency vested with expertise and power over a certain regulatory subject, that agency's primary jurisdiction must be respected. The usual application of the doctrine requires courts to stay their hand so that an agency may consider an issue in the first instance, but it is also sometimes invoked to require a court to respect a prior determination by an agency.

The 1938 FD&C Act consisted of definitions of adulteration and misbranding applicable to food, drugs, devices, or cosmetics, coupled with a trio of remedies (seizure, injunction, criminal penalties) the government could pursue in U.S. district court. For three decades, FDA saw its role as that of a specialized police force, responsible for discovering violations and assembling the evidence needed to prevail in court. In such cases the agency performed the role of advocate; whether the conduct charged constituted a violation of the Act was for the courts to decide.

In later amendments to the Act, exemplified by the 1962 Drug Amendments, Congress gave FDA new responsibilities that required the agency to determine how the law applied to particular facts. Was the product a "new drug" for which the law required proof of effectiveness? Did the evidence demonstrate that the drug was effective? As FDA's responsibilities expanded, the agency increasingly sought judicial endorsement for its role as the primary interpreter of the statute's requirements.

The Supreme Court acknowledged such a role in four 1973 decisions upholding FDA's implementation of the 1962 Amendments' effectiveness standard. The key opinion was *Weinberger v. Bentex Pharmaceuticals, Inc.,* 412 U.S. 645 (1973) (excerpted *infra* at p. 667). FDA had announced that it regarded generic copies of a pioneer drug for which it had approved a New Drug Application (NDA) as "new drugs" whose legal status depended on the status of the pioneer. Manufacturers of generic versions of the drug, pentylenetrazol, insisted that only a court could determine a product's "new drug" status. The Supreme Court rejected this claim:

> . . . Whether a particular drug is a "new drug" depends in part on the expert knowledge and experience of scientists based on controlled clinical experimentation and backed by substantial support in scientific literature. One function is not peculiar to judicial expertise, the other to administrative expertise. The two types of cases overlap and strongly suggest that Congress desired that the administrative agency make both kinds of determination. . . .

> We think that it is implicit in the regulatory scheme, not spelled out in *haec verba*, that FDA has jurisdiction to decide with administrative finality, subject to the types of judicial review provided, the "new drug" status of individual drugs or classes of drugs. . . .

Peter Barton Hutt, FDA's chief counsel at the time, considered the Court's ruling in *Bentex* the most significant of its four opinions. In affirming FDA's primary jurisdiction to determine how the Act applied to particular products, the Court implicitly endorsed a host of regulatory initiatives, including the OTC Drug Review, FDA's nutrition labeling requirements for food, the Biologics Review, and the regulation of in vitro diagnostic products. *See FDA Court Actions and Recent Developments*, 39 Q. BULL. ASS'N OF FOOD & DRUG OFFICIALS 11 (1975).

NOTES

1. *Supporting Authority. Carolina Brown, Inc. v. Weinberger*, 365 F. Supp. 310 (D.S.C. 1973), and *National Ethical Pharmaceutical Ass'n v. Weinberger*, 365 F. Supp. 735 (D.S.C. 1973), *aff'd per curiam*, 503 F.2d 1051 (4th Cir. 1974), dismissed suits seeking a judicial declaration of a product's new drug status on the ground that this issue lay within FDA's primary jurisdiction and that judicial review should be available only after the agency ruled. *See also United States v. Western Serum Co., Inc.*, 666 F.2d 335 (9th Cir. 1982); *Premo Pharmaceutical Laboratories, Inc. v. United States*, 629 F.2d 795 (2d Cir. 1980); *United States v. An Article of Drug . . . "Tutag Pharmaceuticals . . . X–Otag Plus Tablets,"* 602 F.2d 1387 (10th Cir. 1979); *United States v. Mosinee Research Corp.*, 583 F.2d 930 (7th Cir. 1978). *But see United States v. Alcon Labs,* 636 F.2d 876 (1st Cir. 1981) (rejecting application of primary jurisdiction on a particular determination of "new drug" status, invoked by company to oppose seizure action in court).

2. *Court–Mandated Primary Jurisdiction.* In *Rutherford v. United States*, 542 F.2d 1137 (10th Cir. 1976), the Court of Appeals instructed FDA to hold an administrative hearing to document its announced position that the alleged cancer treatment Laetrile was a new drug that required formal agency approval. The plaintiff was a cancer patient who sought a judicial ruling that the agency's position was inconsistent with the statute and violated the Constitutional rights of cancer patients. In a decision excerpted *infra* at p. 650, the District Court had ruled in the plaintiff's

favor, enjoining FDA from interfering with his right to obtain Laetrile for his personal use. The Court of Appeals remanded the matter to FDA for development of an administrative record in a hearing, and it allowed the injunction to remain in effect pending FDA's completion of this procedure.

> ... Nothing in the record suggests that the FDA has dealt with Laetrile in a rule-making proceeding under Section 701 of the Act. Hence, if this is true the appropriate procedure for the district court is to remand the case back to the FDA for proceedings adequate to develop a record supportive of the agency's determination; the proceedings should give Laetrile proponents an opportunity to express their views. . . .

Id. at 1143. After holding the mandated hearing, the FDA Commissioner ruled that Laetrile could not lawfully be marketed as either a food or drug. 42 Fed. Reg. 39768 (Aug. 5, 1977). That decision was ultimately upheld by the Supreme Court in *United States* v. *Rutherford*, 442 U.S. 544 (1979).

3. *Primary Jurisdiction in Private Litigation.* Suits between private parties can raise issues that fall within FDA's special competence. In *Purdue Frederick Co. v. Acme United Corp.*, Civ. No. N–74–115 (D. Conn. 1975), the plaintiff alleged violation of the false advertising provision of the Lanham Act and unfair competition. It claimed that the defendant's antiseptic drug, formulated in a novel fashion, should not be marketed under the same generic name as its own product. It suggested that FDA be asked for its views on a series of questions, most of which revolved around the issue of whether the defendant's drug was lawfully marketed under the FD&C Act. The trial court declined to refer the matter to FDA because it appeared clear that the agency's OTC Drug Review had several years to run, but it invited the agency to submit answers to specific questions respecting the bioequivalence of the defendant's formulation. The agency answered those questions. The matter was subsequently settled out of court.

4. *FDA Regulation.* Following the *Purdue Fredrick* experience, FDA adopted a regulation providing that it will institute an administrative proceeding whenever a court holds in abeyance or refers to the agency any matter on which an administrative determination "is feasible in light of agency priorities and resources." 42 Fed. Reg. 4680 (Jan. 25, 1977), codified at 21 C.F.R. 10.25(c). Reference of issues in private litigation to FDA can be important in product liability suits, where the status of a product or ingredient under the FD&C Act is often in dispute. *See, e.g., Hoffman v. Sterling Drug, Inc.*, 485 F.2d 132 (3d Cir. 1973).

c.   EXHAUSTION OF REMEDIES

The administrative law doctrine of "exhaustion of remedies" prevents a person from appealing an agency's action to a court before that person has attempted every means of redress provided within the agency itself. In various instances, the FD&C Act provides for internal agency appeals. For example, a person protesting FDA's denial of a New Drug Application can request a formal evidentiary hearing before an Administrative Law Judge (ALJ) and then appeal that decision to the FDA Commissioner. *See infra* p. 848. A disappointed applicant thus cannot appeal FDA's decision immediately upon denial of the application, but must first attempt to reverse the decision using these agency procedures.

A court may also use the exhaustion doctrine to dismiss a case if a litigant raises argument in court that it did not previously raise during the administrative process within the agency. For example, in *Bradley v. Weinberger*, 483 F.2d 410 (1st Cir. 1973), the Court of Appeals vacated an injunction against FDA on such grounds, and it remanded the matter to the agency. The court explained:

> . . . The exhaustion requirement, as it applies to administrative agencies, is no mere technical rule to enable courts to avoid difficult decisions. It is grounded in substantial concerns not only of fairness and orderly procedure, but also of competence. Courts are not best equipped . . . to judge the merits of the scientific studies and the objections to them. Specialized agencies like the FDA are created to serve that function.

Id. at 415. *See also Public Citizen Health Research Group v. Commissioner*, 740 F.2d 21 (D.C. Cir. 1984); *National Nutritional Foods Ass'n v. Califano*, 603 F.2d 327 (2d Cir. 1979); *Public Citizen v. Goyan*, 496 F. Supp. 364 (D.D.C. 1980).

G. JUDICIAL REVIEW OF AGENCY INACTION

The Administrative Procedure Act states that a "reviewing court shall . . . compel agency action unlawfully withheld or unreasonably delayed." 5 U.S.C. 706(a). Parties have invoked this provision against FDA in two broad sets of circumstance: (1) situations in which the agency has determined, for policy or resource reasons, not to enforce the law in a particular instance and (2) situations in which the agency has failed to meet statutory deadlines for mandatory action.

1. ENFORCEMENT DISCRETION

One aspect of FDA discretion that courts have generally viewed as sacrosanct is the agency's freedom *not* to undertake enforcement action in particular instances. We will explore the doctrine of administrative enforcement discretion in detail in Chapter 4, where *Heckler v. Chaney*, 470 U.S. 821, the leading case, is excerpted. *Infra* p. 171.

Because of *Chaney*, courts usually will not interfere when FDA rejects pleas by companies, public interest organization, or individual citizens to enforce provisions of the FD&C Act or agency regulations. *See, e.g., National Wildlife Federation v. Secretary of Health and Human Services*, 808 F.2d 12 (6th Cir. 1986). There are exceptions, however. Indeed, in 2012, a U.S. district judge rejected an exercise of this type of discretion in a context strikingly similar to that of *Chaney* itself, and the D.C. Circuit upheld his decision. *Cook v. FDA*, 2013 WL 3799987 (D.C. Cir. 2013) (excerpted *infra* p. 1441).

2.   Unreasonable Delay

Center for Food Safety v. Hamburg

___ F.Supp.2d ___ 2013 WL 1741816 (N.D. Cal. 2013).

■ Phyllis J. Hamilton, United States District Judge

The parties' cross-motions for summary judgment came on for hearing before this court on March 27, 2013. . . . [T]he court hereby GRANTS plaintiffs' motion and DENIES defendant's motion as follows.

This is an action brought by plaintiffs Center for Food Safety and Center for Environmental Health against Margaret Hamburg, M.D., Commissioner of the U.S. Food and Drug Administration, pursuant to the Administrative Procedures Act. Plaintiffs seek declaratory and injunctive relief regarding the failure of the FDA to promulgate final regulations by mandatory deadlines contained in the FDA Food Safety and [sic] Modernization Act of 2010 (FSMA), 124 Stat. 3885 (2011) (codified in scattered sections of 21 U.S.C. § 301 *et seq.*, as amended).

Congress enacted the FSMA . . . to modernize food safety laws and regulations by mandating science-based standards and controls; by providing the FDA with greater authority to prevent and address food safety hazards by taking steps to prevent them from occurring; by strengthening the FDA's inspection and enforcement powers; and by improving coordination among federal, state, and foreign food safety agencies. . . . To this end, Congress directed the FDA to promulgate new regulations in seven areas, within 18 months of the effective date of the FSMA.

In the complaint . . . plaintiffs allege that certain proposed and final regulations have not been issued within the time frame set forth in the FSMA. Plaintiffs seek a judicial declaration that the FDA has violated the FSMA and the APA by failing to issue the regulations by the statutory deadlines, and continues to be in violation of the FSMA and the APA for failing to promulgate the regulations. Plaintiffs also seek an order ordering the FDA to issue the regulations as soon as reasonably possible, according to a court-ordered timeline. In addition, plaintiffs request that the court retain jurisdiction over the case to ensure compliance with the order.

Each side now seeks summary judgment. The issues to be decided are whether the FDA has "unlawfully withheld" or "unreasonably delayed" action in violation of the APA by failing to promulgate the FSMA regulations by the statutory deadlines, and whether the court must grant plaintiffs the relief they seek.

DISCUSSION

. . . .

In a "failure to act" case, a court can "compel agency action unlawfully withheld or unreasonably delayed." 5 U.S.C. § 706(1). Judicial review is appropriate if the plaintiff makes a showing of "agency recalcitrance . . . in the face of clear statutory duty or . . . of such a magnitude that it amounts to an abdication of statutory responsibility." *Action v. Bureau of Land Mgmt.*, 150 F.3d 1132, 1137 (9th Cir. 1998) (citation and quotation omitted).

In *Norton v. Southern Utah Wilderness Alliance*, 542 U.S. 557 (2004), the Supreme Court explained that a "failure to act" within the meaning of the APA is the failure of the agency to issue an "agency rule, order, license, sanction or relief." *Id.* at 62. That is, judicial review of a failure to act under § 706(1) "is properly understood to be limited . . . to a discrete action" such as "the failure to promulgate a rule or take some decision by a statutory deadline." *Id.* at 63.

However, even discrete agency action cannot be compelled under § 706(1) unless that action is "demanded by law." *Id.* at 65. Statutory goals that are "mandatory as to the object to be achieved" but leave the agency with "discretion in deciding how to achieve" those goals are insufficient to support a "failure to act" claim because such discretionary actions are not "demanded by law." *Id.* at 66.

The sole remedy available under § 706(1) is for the court to "compel agency action," such as by issuing an order requiring the agency to act, without directing the substantive content of the decision. . . .

. . . The FDA argues that the regulations that it was directed to promulgate under the FSMA are novel and complex, and the complexity is increased by the need to build a cohesive system of regulatory controls integrating different regions and countries, as well as different food types, and also coordinate with other regulations (such as regulations relating to small businesses) and other federal and state agencies.

. . . .

To carry out this complex and difficult task, the FDA first established an implementation committee, which in turn established six implementation teams, with a number of working groups under those teams. The working groups were assigned the hands-on responsibility for developing the regulations, reports, guidance, and processes required by FSMA.

The FDA asserts that even with this organizational structure specifically directed at the expedited implementation of the FSMA, the aggressive timelines set forth in the statute have proven to be unachievable. In addition, because promulgating the new regulations requires the participation and input of individuals with specific expertise . . . and because the FDA employs only a limited number of such individuals (particularly those having the relevant subject matter expertise), the FDA has found it difficult to staff the simultaneous development of such a large number of major rules in the same general subject area.

For this reason, the FDA determined that it needed to prioritize, and decide which regulations to develop first. . . .

The FDA contends that it has been working diligently to develop the required regulations. . . .

. . . [A]fter the FDA filed the present motion, it issued two complex and major proposed rules—"Current Good Manufacturing Practice and Hazard Analysis and Risk–Based Preventive Controls for Human Food," and "Standards for Growing, Harvesting, Packing, and Holding of Produce for Human Consumption"—which set out extensive new proposals for preventing problems that can cause foodborne illness. The FDA asserts that these proposals are concrete steps taken to implement three of the seven statutory requirements identified in plaintiffs' complaint.

The FDA concedes that FSMA provides specific deadlines for the promulgation of the regulations, but argues that because the issue under the APA is whether it has "unreasonably delayed" in issuing the regulations, the matter that needs to be resolved is the reasonableness of the FDA's administrative timeline. The FDA asserts that it has responded to FSMA by making its implementation a top priority, but still has not been able to complete rules of such magnitude and complexity within the statute's timeframes.

The FDA agrees that these regulations are important to public health and safety, but argues that is just as important that any regulations that are promulgated be carefully developed, given the scope and magnitude of what is called for by the statute. The FDA argues that a particular administrative timetable should be evaluated under the six-factor test set forth in *Telecommunications Res. & Action Ctr. v. F.C.C.*, 750 F.2d 70 ("*TRAC*").

In their motion, plaintiffs submit that the FSMA resulted from Congress' recognition of the prevalence and severity of the food-borne illness problem, and argue that it was because of the need to remedy this problem that Congress instructed the FDA to act quickly to promulgate the needed regulations. . . .

Plaintiffs disagree with the FDA's argument that the court should apply the *TRAC* balancing test to this case. They contend that the *TRAC* test applies only where the issue is whether a delay is unreasonable in the absence of express Congressional deadlines. Here, however, because Congress included mandatory deadlines in the FSMA, plaintiffs argue that the FDA cannot be excused for its per se violation of the law (failing to meet those deadlines).

. . . .

The court finds that given that the FDA has admittedly failed to comply with the mandatory rulemaking schedule, declaratory relief is proper. . . . The FDA asserts that the court should evaluate this case under the TRAC factors. . . . However, because the FSMA includes specific deadlines, the failure to comply with those deadlines constitutes a "failure to act" under the APA. Moreover, where Congress has specifically provided a deadline for performance by an agency, "no balancing of factors is required or permitted." *Biodiversity Legal Found. v. Badgley*, 309 F.3d 1166, 1177–78 & n.11 (9th Cir. 2002).

The question with regard to injunctive relief is less straightforward. Plaintiffs seek an order compelling the FDA to complete the rulemaking process by a date certain. That is, they contend that having found that the FDA has violated the FSMA and the APA by failing to complete the regulations by the statutory deadlines, the court is required to issue an order compelling the FDA to act.

The APA provides that a court "shall" compel unlawfully withheld agency action. *See* 5 U.S.C. § 706. The question is whether the court has any discretion in this regard. . . .

The Ninth Circuit addressed this issue in *Biodiversity*, concluding that "a statutory violation does not always lead to the automatic issuance of an injunction." *Id.*, 309 F.3d at 1177. "[W]hen federal statutes are violated, the test for determining if equitable relief is appropriate is whether an injunction is necessary to effectuate the congressional purpose behind the statute." *Id.* . . .

Here, the parties are in agreement that the "purpose" of the FSMA is to protect human health by ensuring that the food supply is safe from contaminants. Plaintiffs contend that the regulations are essential to that purpose, and the FDA counters that the issuance of the required regulations on a rushed or hurried basis would not help protect human health and safety. . . .

Beyond the evident purpose of the FSMA—to ensure the safety of the food supply—Congress also intended that the implementing regulations be promulgated and finalized by a date certain. The dates set for completion of the regulations in the seven areas identified in the complaint have passed. . . . While the FSMA vests the FDA with discretion regarding the substance of the mandated regulations, endless delay does not serve any purpose of the FSMA. At a minimum, it seems clear that by setting deadlines, Congress signaled its intention that the process be closed-ended, rather than open-ended. Thus, the court finds that imposition of an injunction imposing deadlines for finalization of the regulations would be consistent with the underlying purposes of the FSMA.

Nevertheless, the FDA is correct that the purpose of ensuring food safety will not be served by the issuance of regulations that are insufficiently considered, based on a timetable that is unconnected to the magnitude of the task set by Congress. The court issues the following order in the hope that the parties will themselves arrive at a mutually acceptable schedule. It will behoove the parties to attempt to cooperate on this endeavor, as any decision by the court will necessarily be arbitrary.

The parties are hereby ORDERED to meet and confer, and prepare a joint written statement setting forth proposed deadlines, in detail sufficient to form the basis of an injunction. The joint statement shall be submitted no later than May 20, 2013. After reviewing the statement, the court will determine whether any further written submissions would be helpful or necessary.

     . . . .

NOTES

1. *Subsequent Order.* In June 2013, Judge Hamilton rejected FDA's proposed timeline for completion of the FSMA regulations. The court ordered the agency to publish all the proposed regulations not yet promulgated by November 30, 2013, and to publish all seven of the final regulations implementing the statute by June 30, 2015. The following month, the agency moved for reconsideration of this order, maintaining

that it could not comply with the court's order with respect to publication of the proposed rules regarding intentional adulteration and sanitary transport because of the complexity of the issues, the amount of work required, and other reasons the agency had previously advanced. In response, Judge Hamilton extended the deadline for publication of the proposed sanitary transport rule by 60 days, but only because the plaintiffs agreed to such an extension. She flatly denied FDA's request for extension of the deadline for publication of the proposed intentional adulteration rule, remarking: "The court understands the FDA's position, and is in sympathy with it, but remains of the opinion that the dispute here is between the FDA and Congress." *Ctr. for Food Safety v. Hamburg*, 2013 WL 4396563, at *11 (N.D. Cal. Aug. 13, 2013).

2.   *Other Successful Challenges.* Various provisions of the FD&C Act prescribe time limits for agency action. Like many other agencies, FDA has often missed such statutory deadlines. One of the few other successful legal challenges to FDA's failure to meet a statutory deadline is *Southeastern Minerals, Inc. v. Califano* (M.D. Ga. 1978), where the agency failed to satisfy the statutory 180-day deadline for acting on a food additive petition. The court enjoined FDA from interfering with the firm's marketing of the ingredient in question until there was final action on the petition. And in *Natural Resources Defense Council, Inc. v. FDA*, 884 F. Supp. 2d 108 (S.D.N.Y. 2012) (excerpted *infra* p. 1084), the court held that FDA's failure to hold hearings on its proposed withdrawal of certain animal antibiotics, despite the passage of a quarter century since the issuance of a notice of opportunity for a hearing, constituted agency action "unlawfully withheld or unreasonably delayed" in violation of the APA. In this instance, the court found an APA violation despite the absence of a specific statutory deadline. *See also Public Citizen Health Research Group v. Commissioner, FDA*, 724 F. Supp. 1013 (D.D.C. 1989) (holding FDA's seven-year delay in promulgating regulations specifying tampon absorbency to be unreasonable).

3.   *Responding to Citizen Petitions.* In 1975 FDA voluntarily established a six-month deadline for responding to citizen petitions, 21 C.F.R. 10.30(e)(2). In practice, however, this deadline is seldom met, and, when it is, the agency's initial response often states simply that a substantive determination is not yet feasible.

4.   *Ruling on Product Applications.* Section 505(d) of the Act specifies that the agency must act on an application to market a new drug within 180 days. This time limit had been routinely ignored by both the industry and the agency, For decades it has been standard practice for FDA to conduct a preliminary review of any application for approval, and then to notify the applicant that it is "incomplete" and thus not eligible for "filing." Although FDA regulations may require the agency to send an "incomplete" letter within 15 days of receipt of the application, often it is sent just before the end of the period set by statute for review of the application. FDA thereby avoids "filing" the application and, on its theory, the statutory time limit does not begin to run. The initial submission of an application is therefore only the beginning of a negotiation process between the applicant and agency reviewers leading ultimately toward official "filing" several months, or sometimes even years, later. Applicants for marketing approval

have generally been unwilling to contest the legality of this process out of fear that a court challenge might precipitate a premature negative decision on the merits, further delay ultimate FDA approval, or prejudice the agency's attitude toward other pending or future applications in which the applicant is interested.

In 2006, the United States District Court for the District of Columbia ordered FDA to rule on a company's NDA, rejecting the agency's argument that the statutory timetable is an aspiration rather than a requirement. *Sandoz v. Leavitt*, 427 F. Supp. 2d 29 (D.D.C. 2006).

5. *Prominent Incomplete Mandates.* Some striking examples exist of FDA's failure to complete regulatory processes decades after their commencement, sometimes in violation of explicit statutory deadlines. For example, section 107(c)(3) of the 1962 Drug Amendments provided a two-year "grace period" before the new proof of effectiveness requirement could be applied to new drugs for which NDA's became effective during the period 1938–1962. In *American Public Health Ass'n v. Veneman*, 349 F. Supp. 1311 (D.D.C. 1972), discussed *infra* at p. 780, the court concluded that FDA had failed to implement the Amendments as rapidly as Congress had mandated and issued a detailed order requiring staged implementation by October 10, 1976. *See* 37 Fed. Reg. 26623 (Dec. 14, 1972). FDA still has not yet completed implementation of the 1962 Amendments to prescription drugs. In addition, FDA has not yet finished applying the 1962 Drug Amendments to nonprescription drugs biologics, or unapproved new drugs. Other programs that remain unfinished are the implementation of the 1958 Food Additives Amendments, the 1960 Color Additives Amendments, and the 1976 Medical Device Amendments.

CHAPTER 3

FDA JURISDICTION:
A MATTER OF DEFINITIONS

A. INTRODUCTION

The 1938 Food, Drug, and Cosmetic Act gave FDA authority over four broad categories of products, all of which the agency still regulates: food, drugs, cosmetics, and medical devices. In the ensuing decades, the agency assumed or was given responsibility for additional classes of products, some of which (human biological products, electronic radiation-emitting products, tobacco products) it continues to regulate today, while others (toys, pesticides) it later ceded to other agencies. In addition, Congress has repeatedly tweaked the FD&C Act definitions, in some instances establishing entire subcategories with their own definitions, such as "food additives" and "dietary supplements" (both subcategories of "food").

The scope of FDA's power is defined almost entirely by the list of product categories over which it has jurisdiction.[*] The statutory definitions of these categories thus delineate the outer boundaries of the arena within which the agency operates. The definitions are also important for another reason. FDA has different degrees of power over different categories of products. In general, the agency has greater authority over drugs, devices, and biological products than over food and cosmetics. The category to which FDA—or Congress—assigns an article thus largely controls the shape of the regulatory regime the agency will impose on it.

Food, Drugs, and Cosmetics
Senate Report No. 361, 74th Congress, 1st Session (1935).

It has not been considered necessary to specify that the definitions of food, drug, and cosmetic shall not be construed, other than to the extent expressly provided, as mutually exclusive. The present law does not have such a clause relating to the definitions of food and drug and there has never been a court decision to the effect that these definitions are mutually exclusive, despite the fact that repeated actions have been brought, for example, against filthy foods bearing unwarranted therapeutic claims, alleging these products to be adulterated as food because of their filth, and misbranded as drugs because of their false and fraudulent therapeutic claims.

---

[*] The most important exception to this principle is the power FDA shares with the Centers for Disease Control under Section 361 of the Public Health Service Act (measures to control the spread of communicable diseases.

The use to which the product is to be put will determine the category into which it will fall. If it is to be used only as a food it will come within the definition of food and none other. If it contains nutritive ingredients but is sold for drug use only, as clearly shown by the labeling and advertising, it will come within the definition of drug, but not that of food. If it is sold to be used both as a food and for the prevention or treatment of disease it would satisfy both definitions and be subject to the substantive requirements for both. The manufacturer of the article, through his representations in connection with its sale, can determine the use to which the article is to be put. For example, the manufacturer of a laxative which is a medicated candy or chewing gum can bring his product within the definition of drug and escape that of food by representing the article fairly and unequivocally as a drug product.

————

As the materials in this chapter show, the product definitions are strikingly broad and thus confer jurisdiction over a vast range of goods. Furthermore, the definitions, which are often not mutually exclusive, are remarkably plastic, providing the agency with great flexibility to decide whether and how to regulate products. Sometimes FDA has interpreted the definitions expansively, so as to expand its power. On other occasions, the agency has construed the definitions narrowly, so as to avoid taking responsibility for products it does not want to regulate or to minimize the burdensomeness of the requirements it does impose. For an extended consideration of the product definitions in the FD&C Act, their regulatory significance, and their relationship with cultural understandings of these terms, see Lewis A. Grossman, *Food, Drugs, and Droods: A Historical Consideration of Definitions and Categories in American Food and Drug Law*, 93 CORNELL L. REV. 1091 (2008).

Occasionally, when FDA interprets the definitions flexibly so as to achieve particular policy objectives, the courts will rein in the agency, as the Supreme Court did with respect to FDA's attempts in the 1990s to regulate cigarettes as medical devices. *See FDA v. Brown & Williamson Tobacco Corp.*, 529 U.S. 120 (2000), *infra* p. 141. In general, however, as the next case illustrates, courts have granted the agency considerable latitude in applying the product definitions.

United States v. An Article of Drug . . . Bacto–Unidisk

394 U.S. 784 (1969).

■ MR. CHIEF JUSTICE WARREN delivered the opinion of the court.

At issue here is the scope of the statutory definition of drug contained in the Federal Food, Drug, and Cosmetic Act and the extent of the Secretary of Health, Education, and Welfare's regulatory authority under that definition. The specific item involved in this definitional controversy is a laboratory aid known as an antibiotic sensitivity disc, used as a screening test for help in determining the proper antibiotic drug to administer to patients. If the article is a "drug" . . . then the Secretary can subject it to pre-market clearance regulations promulgated pursuant to § 507 of the Act. . . . If, on the other hand, the article is merely a "device" under the Act, it is subject only to the misbranding and adulteration proscriptions of the Act and does not have to be pretested before marketing; and, of course, if the disc does not fall under either definition, the Act itself is totally inapplicable. . . .

At the outset, it is clear from § 201 that the word "drug" is a term of art for the purposes of the Act, encompassing far more than the strict medical definition of that word. . . .

The historical expansion of the definition of drug, and the creation of a parallel concept of devices, clearly show, we think, that Congress fully intended that the Act's coverage be as broad as its literal language indicates and equally clearly, broader than any strict medical definition might otherwise allow. Strong indications from legislative history that Congress intended the broad coverage the District Court thought "ridiculous" should satisfy us that the lower courts erred in refusing to apply the Act's language as written. But we are all the more convinced that we must give effect to congressional intent in view of the well-accepted principle that remedial legislation such as the Food, Drug, and Cosmetic Act is to be given a liberal construction consistent with the Act's overriding purpose to protect the public health, and specifically, § 507's purpose to ensure that antibiotic products marketed serve the public with "efficacy" and "safety."

Respondent's alternative contention, that even if its product does fall within the purview of the Act, it is plainly a "device" and therefore by definition necessarily not a "drug," must also be rejected, we believe, in light of the foregoing analysis. At the outset, it must be conceded that the language of the statute is of little assistance in determining precisely what differentiates a "drug" from a "device": to the extent that both are intended for use in the treatment, mitigation and cure of disease, the former is an "article" and the latter includes "instruments," "apparatus," and "contrivances." Despite the obvious areas of overlap in definition, we are not entirely without guidance in determining the propriety of the Secretary's decision below, given the overall goals of the Act and its legislative history.

More specifically, . . . the "natural way" to draw the line "is in light of the statutory purpose." Since the patient will tend to derive less benefit and perhaps some harm from a particular antibiotic if, though the drug itself was properly batch-tested, it was not the proper antibiotic to use, it was entirely reasonable for the Secretary to determine that the discs, like the antibiotics they serve, are drugs and similarly subject to pre-clearance certification under § 507. An opposite conclusion might undercut the value of testing the antibiotics themselves, for such testing would be a useless exercise if the wrong drug were ultimately administered, even partially as the result of an unreliable disc. . . .

Reversed.

B. FOOD

Section 201(f) of the FD&C Act defines "food" as follows: "The term 'food' means (1) articles used for food or drink for man or other animals,

(2) chewing gum, and (3) articles used for components of any such article." Not surprisingly, this tautological definition ("food" means "food") leaves many open questions.

The following opinion considers the scope of this sparse definition. Observe the district court's deferential posture toward FDA's interpretation of section 201(f). The court implements this deference through application of *Chevron, U.S.A., Inc. v. Natural Resources Defense Council, Inc.*, 467 U.S. 837 (1984), a seminal administrative law case decided outside the food and drug context. *Chevron* bolstered and formalized the deference courts were already supposed to grant FDA pursuant to *Bacto–Unidisk*.

United States v. Tuente Livestock

888 F. Supp. 1416 (S.D. Ohio 1995).

■ RICE, DISTRICT JUDGE.

The Defendants in this case . . . buy hogs from farmers (producers) and sell them to slaughterhouses, which, in turn, slaughter and process the animals for ultimate consumption. The Defendants are accused by the United States Food and Drug Administration ("FDA") of delivering to the slaughterhouses swine whose edible tissues are tainted with illegal levels of residue of a certain animal drug known as sulfamethazine. . . . [T]he United States seeks an injunction to prevent these Defendants from engaging in their business, unless and until they have taken certain actions to ensure the purity of their porkers. The Defendants now seek dismissal of the suit, arguing that live swine are not "food" within the meaning of the Act . . . .

. . . The Defendants purchase live hogs from producers and sell those hogs (still breathing) to slaughterhouses. When the hogs reach the slaughterhouses, they are slaughtered and their edible tissues are shipped in interstate commerce. . . .

There is *absolutely no* allegation that the Defendants, themselves, introduce sulfamethazine into the hogs. Rather, the allegations are that the Defendants purchase swine from producers without obtaining guaranties that the producers have taken the appropriate measures to ensure that the edible tissues of the swine are not contaminated (*i.e.*, that the swine have not been given the drug for the appropriate withdrawal period), and, additionally, that the Defendants do not appropriately mark the swine that they purchase to enable the identification of producers of hogs that are found (in testing after slaughter) to contain illegal residues. . . .

The Act, with brazen circularity, defines "food" as:

> (1) articles used for food or drink for man or other animals, (2) chewing gum, and (3) articles used for components of any such article.

21 U.S.C. § 321(f). Thus, within the meaning of the Act, food is food. Food is also drink, chewing gum, and components of food, drink, and chewing gum; but, primarily, and in the portion of the definition relevant to this case, food is food. Nothing in the language of statute itself explicitly indicates that live animals raised for slaughter and

consumption (such as the hogs in question in this case) either are or are not food (or "articles used for food") within the meaning of the statute.

Only one published case, relied upon by the Government, deals directly with the question whether live animals are food within the meaning of the Act. In *United States v. Tomahara Enterprises, Ltd.*, Food Drug Cosm. L. Rep. (CCH) ¶ 38,217 (N.D.N.Y. March 29, 1983), the court determined that live veal calves raised for food were food within the meaning of the statute. Unfortunately, that case is utterly without persuasive value because the court simply decided to take "judicial notice" that the live animals were food within the meaning of the Act. . . .

It appears that the *Tomahara* court based its decision on the opinion of the Second Circuit Court of Appeals in *United States v. O.F. Bayer & Co.*, 188 F.2d 555, 557 (2d Cir. 1951), in which that Court of Appeals took judicial notice that coffee (the drink) is made from green coffee beans that have been roasted. On that basis, the Court of Appeals found that there was no evidence required to show that green coffee beans are food within the meaning of the Act. However, it is the opinion of this Court that green coffee beans analogize more appropriately to the carcasses of food producing animals than to the living animals themselves. That is to say, if the *O.F. Bayer* court had found that *live* coffee *plants* were food within the meaning of the act, then the conclusion of the *Tomahara* court (that live veal calves are food) would be supported. Instead, the *Tomahara* court took the *O.F. Bayer* analysis a step further, defining as food not only the harvested (*i.e.*, dead) raw product, but the living creature itself. In the opinion of this Court, that is a significant additional step, and the dealer in pre-harvested (*i.e.*, living) food producing creatures deserves a better explanation for the extension . . . .

The Government's strongest (and, ultimately, compelling) argument is the one based on *Chevron U.S.A. Inc. v. Natural Resources Defense Council, Inc.*, 467 U.S. 837 (1984). In *Chevron*, the Supreme Court explained:

> When a court reviews an agency's construction of the statute which it administers, it is confronted with two questions. First, always, is the question whether Congress has directly spoken to the precise question at issue. If the intent of Congress is clear, that is the end of the matter; for the court, as well as the agency, must give effect to the unambiguously expressed intent of Congress. If, however, the court determines Congress has not directly addressed the precise question at issue, the court does not simply impose its own construction of the statute, as would be necessary in the absence of an administrative interpretation. Rather, if the statute is silent or ambiguous with respect to the specific issue, the question for the court is whether the agency's answer is based on a permissible construction of the statute.

Chevron, 467 U.S. at 842–843.

In this instance, nothing in the language of the statute, nor in its legislative history, directly addresses the precise question at issue: whether live animals may be considered food within the meaning of the Act. That being the case, "the question for the [C]ourt is whether the

agency's answer is based on a permissible construction of the statute." *Id.*

. . . [I]n beginning the second phase of a *Chevron* analysis, [the] Court must determine whether it is presented with an agency position worthy of consideration for deference, as opposed to a position taken only for the purpose of litigation. . . . [H]as the agency clearly made an administrative determination that live animals fall within the Act's definition of food, if not by formal published pronouncement, then by established practice? If the agency has engaged in no such administrative practice, then the position taken by the Government herein could be described as one asserted solely for the purposes of litigation, and not entitled to deference. . . .

. . . [I]t appears that the FDA began to take enforcement action against the purveyors of *live animals* as long ago as 1970. Specifically, the FDA has held for approximately 25 years the position that it now takes, that the offering for slaughter of live animals whose edible tissues contain above-tolerance residues exposes the offeror to liability for introducing adulterated food into interstate commerce, and has taken action against other purveyors of live animals in accordance with that position. Accordingly, the Court finds that the interpretation of the FDCA asserted by the Government herein is not an "agency litigating position[ ] that [is] wholly unsupported by regulations, rulings, or administrative practice[,]" and is, therefore, subject to deference if it meets the standard governing the second step of *Chevron* analysis (*i.e.*, if it is "based on a permissible construction of the statute"). *Bowen v. Georgetown Univ. Hosp.*, 488 U.S. 204, 212 (1988).

There is practically no legislative history regarding the definition of "food" as used in the Act. The current definition, which has remained unchanged since 1938, "is simply a clarification of the definition in the Food and Drugs Act of June 30, 1906." H.R. Rep. No. 2139, 75th Cong., 3d Sess. 3 (1938). Thus . . . it is not inappropriate to cast an eye upon the 1906 statute and its history.

The 1906 Act defined "food" as including "all articles used for food, drink, confectionery, or condiment by man or other animals, whether simple, mixed, or compound." That statutory definition is no clearer with respect to the question herein than is the current definition. As to legislative history directly concerning that definition, there are only the comments of Mr. Gill of Maryland, speaking in opposition to the bill:

> This provision is so comprehensive, so all-embracing that in its application it affects the business operations of a large class of our people and all kinds of articles of food and drugs. It includes the products of our fisheries, the products of almost every garden and farm in the land, and every modification of the natural product when these products enter into interstate commerce. . . .

40 Cong. Rec. 8981 (1906). Obviously, Mr. Gill's understanding that the statutory definition was "all-embracing" is not binding on this Court, yet there do not appear to be any statements on the record, in either house, that would tend to assuage his fears. . . .

The statutory scheme . . . supports an inference that the Act is meant to be effective as early in the commercial chain as the adulteration or mislabeling is accomplished, regardless of where in the chain—from farmer to slaughterhouse to ultimate consumer—responsibility rests. . . . Given that it is reasonable to read one purpose of the statute to be the prosecution of those responsible for the adulteration of food, it is not unreasonable for the FDA to interpret the statute to grant to the agency the authority to pursue dealers in living animals, when it appears that, to reach those responsible for the adulteration of food, the agency must reach those who deal in the animals even before they are slaughtered.

One other point, although not definitive in itself, favors the FDA in this matter. . . . [T]he Congress has been aware of the FDA's understanding and practice concerning live animals for almost twenty-five years, yet has in no way acted to limit the agency's jurisdiction (or prevent its exercise of authority) over dealers in live animals. . . .

Accordingly, the Court concludes that, in light of the structure of the FDCA and the legislative history of the Act, it is permissible for the FDA to interpret of the term "food". . . to include live animals raised for food and intended to be offered for slaughter.

Certain arguments of the Defendants contrary to this position require comment. *First*, the Defendants' argument that this is a question of the "plain meaning" of the language of the statute is not well taken. In providing a circular definition (food is food), the Congress built into the statute, whether intentionally or not, a measure of ambiguity. It is not intuitively obvious to this Court that "food" cannot mean live animals raised for food. . . .

Second, the Defendants' argument that it is logically inconsistent for the FDA to classify as food both living animals and their edible tissues is not well taken. An article that consists only in part of edible tissue—a rack of pork ribs, for example, which contains both edible tissue (flesh) and inedible tissue (bone)—may certainly be classified as food for purposes of the statute. The sale of tainted pork ribs to the public cannot be allowed to escape regulation merely because only a portion of the article offered actually consists of edible tissue. . . .

. . . Defendants concede that none of the cases that they cite are factually similar to the case presented herein. The question presented herein does not concern an end-product derived from the processing of food items. *See, e.g., Nutrilab v. Schweiker*, 713 F.2d 335 (7th Cir. 1983) (starch blocker extracted from bean is a drug, not food). Rather, this case goes in the opposite direction—the Court is concerned with how far *back* in the processing of food, toward the "raw material," the statute reaches, rather than how far *forward* an item can be processed before it loses its quality as food. There are, indeed, cases that have extended the reach of the statute backward to preprocessed items. *See, e.g., O.F. Bayer*, 188 F.2d 555 (green coffee beans, not yet fully processed, are food). The Defendants have cited no case in which the backward (preprocessing) extent of the statute has been limited. On the other hand, no case (aside from *Tomahara*) has held that the statute actually extends all the way back to the living creature. Thus, this Court is of the opinion that it writes on a relatively blank slate . . . .

The Defendants also present certain arguments that adoption of the agency's interpretation would yield absurd results. They cite 9 CFR §§ 325.1(a) and (c), which require "any product which is capable of use as human food" that is moved in commerce to "bear[ ] the official inspection legend[,]," and require transportation of "meat or meat food products capable of use as human food" only in tightly sealed packages or containers. The Court does not take the Government's argument in this case to be that the USDA should be permitted to apply those regulations to live animals, and any attempt by the USDA to do so would be subject to challenge under *Chevron* as an unreasonable interpretation of the Congress' intent.

Similarly, the Defendants' argue that if live swine were to fall within the definition of "food" for purposes of § 331(a), they would all be adulterated, *per se*, because they carry dirt and manure with them, have digestive tracts containing decomposed substances, and produce excrement. Again, the Court does not understand the Government to be arguing that all live swine are adulterated for purposes of the Act, or that such an interpretation of the statute would be a reasonable one under *Chevron*.

. . . The FDA's interpretation of § 331(a) to permit it to act against persons who introduce or deliver for introduction into interstate commerce live swine, intended for slaughter and subsequent use as food, the edible tissues of which contain above-tolerance residues of sulfamethazine, is a permissible interpretation of the statute, and, thus, is entitled to deference under *Chevron*.

Hogs are food.

. . . [T]he Defendants' Motion to Dismiss is overruled. . . .

NOTES

1. *Migrating Food-Contact Materials.* The statutory definition of food includes substances that migrate to food from food packaging and dinnerware, even before such migration takes place. *Natick Paperboard Corp. v. Weinberger*, 525 F.2d 1103 (1st Cir. 1975).

2. *Condiments, Candy, and Chewing Gum.* Because condiments and confectionery were not universally considered to be "food" in common parlance in the early 20th Century, the definition of "food" in the 1906 Act explicitly listed these items. By 1938, this ambiguity had apparently disappeared, and the drafters of the FD&C Act did not find it necessary to expressly include these items. But to resolve another potential ambiguity, they drafted the definition so as to explicitly embrace "chewing gum." FD&C Act 201(f)(2).

3. *No Longer "Fit" Food.* A product is a food under the Act if it is generally regarded as food when sold in food form, even if it is decomposed or otherwise unfit for food at the time FDA institutes legal action against it. *See, e.g., United States v. H.B. Gregory Co.*, 502 F.2d 700 (7th Cir. 1974); *Otis McAllister & Co. v. United States*, 194 F.2d 386 (5th Cir. 1952).

4. *Other Agencies' Roles in Regulating Food.* Food is regulated by numerous agencies in addition to the FDA. Indeed, there are entire subcategories of food primarily under the jurisdiction of other agencies. Most notably, the United States Department of Agriculture has primary authority over meat, poultry, and some egg products, and the United States Department of the Treasury is the chief regulator of most alcoholic

beverages. Nonetheless, these products are "food" under the FD&C Act, and (as discussed *infra* at pp. 317–319), FDA has a role in regulating them.

―――――

Tuente Livestock concerned a situation in which the product in question (live hogs) were either "food" or fell outside FDA's authority altogether. On other occasions, as in the case excerpted below, disputes over the correct interpretation of the "food" definition have come up when FDA has tried to regulate as a drug a product that the manufacturer claims is only a food. Because new drugs are subject to premarket approval by the agency for safety and effectiveness, whereas foods are not, the resolution of such a dispute over application of the food definition frequently determines the fate of the product.

Nutrilab, Inc. v. Schweiker

713 F.2d 335 (7th Cir. 1983).

■ CUMMINGS, CHIEF JUDGE.

Plaintiffs manufacture and market a product known as "starch blockers" which "block" the human body's digestion of starch as an aid in controlling weight. On July 1, 1982, the Food and Drug Administration ("FDA") classified starch blockers as "drugs" and requested that all such products be removed from the market until FDA approval was received. . . .

The only issue on appeal is whether starch blockers are foods or drugs under the Federal Food, Drug, and Cosmetic Act. Starch blocker tablets and capsules consist of a protein which is extracted from a certain type of raw kidney bean. That particular protein functions as an alpha-amylase inhibitor; alpha-amylase is an enzyme produced by the body which is utilized in digesting starch. When starch blockers are ingested during a meal, the protein acts to prevent the alpha-amylase enzyme from acting, thus allowing the undigested starch to pass through the body and avoiding the calories that would be realized from its digestion.

Kidney beans, from which alpha-amylase inhibitor is derived, are dangerous if eaten raw. By August 1982, FDA had received seventy-five reports of adverse effects on people who had taken starch blockers, including complaints of gastro-intestinal distress such as bloating, nausea, abdominal pain, constipation and vomiting. Because plaintiffs consider starch blockers to be food, no testing as required to obtain FDA approval as a new drug has taken place. If starch blockers were drugs, the manufacturers would be required to file a new drug application pursuant to 21 U.S.C. § 355 and remove the product from the marketplace until approved as a drug by the FDA.

The statutory scheme under the Food, Drug, and Cosmetic Act is a complicated one. Section 321(g)(1) provides that the term "drug" means

> . . . (B) articles intended for use in the diagnosis, cure, mitigation, treatment, or prevention of disease in man or other animals; and (C) articles (other than food) intended to affect the structure or any function of the body of man or other animals; and (D) articles intended for use as a component of any article specified in clauses

(A), (B), or (C) of this paragraph; but does not include devices or their components, parts, or accessories.

The term "food" as defined in Section 321(f) means

(1) articles used for food or drink for man or other animals, (2) chewing gum, and (3) articles used for components of any such article.

Section 321(g)(1)(C) was added to the statute in 1938 to expand the definition of "drug." The amendment was necessary because certain articles intended by manufacturers to be used as drugs did not fit within the "disease" requirement of Section 321(g)(1)(B). Obesity in particular was not considered a disease. Thus "anti-fat remedies" marketed with claims of "slenderizing effects" had escaped regulation under the prior definition. . . .

It is well established that the definitions of food and drug are normally not mutually exclusive; an article that happens to be a food but is intended for use in the treatment of disease fits squarely within the drug definition in part B of Section 321(g)(1) and may be regulated as such. Under part C of the statutory drug definition, however, "articles (other than food)" are expressly excluded from the drug definition (as are devices) in Section 321(g)(1).* In order to decide if starch blockers are drugs under Section 321(g)(1)(C), therefore, we must decide if they are foods within the meaning of the part C "other than food" parenthetical exception to Section 321(g)(1)(C). And in order to decide the meaning of "food" in that parenthetical exception, we must first decide the meaning of "food" in Section 321(f).

Congress defined "food" in Section 321(f) as "articles used as food." This definition is not too helpful, but it does emphasize that "food" is to be defined in terms of its function as food, rather than in terms of its source, biochemical composition or ingestibility. Plaintiffs' argument that starch blockers are food because they are derived from food—kidney beans—is not convincing; if Congress intended food to mean articles derived from food it would have so specified. Indeed some articles that are derived from food are indisputably not food, such as caffeine and penicillin. In addition, all articles that are classed biochemically as proteins cannot be food either, because for example, insulin, botulism toxin, human hair and influenza virus are proteins that are clearly not food.

Plaintiffs argue that 21 U.S.C. § 343(j) specifying labeling requirements for food for special dietary uses indicates that Congress intended products offered for weight conditions to come within the statutory definition of "food." Plaintiffs misinterpret that statutory section. It does not define food but merely requires that if a product is a food and purports to be for special dietary uses, its label must contain certain information to avoid being misbranded. If all products intended to affect underweight or overweight conditions were *per se* foods, no diet product could be regulated as a drug under Section 321(g)(1)(C), a result clearly contrary to the intent of Congress that "anti-fat remedies" and "slenderizers" qualify as drugs under that Section.

---

*   [Authors' Note: The definition of "drug" at 21 U.S.C. § 321(g)(1) no longer explicitly excludes devices.]

If defining food in terms of its source or defining it in terms of its biochemical composition is clearly wrong, defining food as articles intended by the manufacturer to be used as food is problematic. When Congress meant to define a drug in terms of its intended use, it explicitly incorporated that element into its statutory definition. For example, Section 321(g)(1)(B) defines drugs as articles "intended for use" in, among other things, the treatment of disease; Section 321(g)(1)(C) defines drugs as "articles (other than food) intended to affect the structure or any function of the body of man or other animals." The definition of food in Section 321(f) omits any reference to intent. . . . Further, a manufacturer cannot avoid the reach of the FDA by claiming that a product which looks like food and smells like food is not food because it was not intended for consumption. In *United States v. Technical Egg Prods., Inc.*, 171 F. Supp. 326 (N.D. Ga. 1959), the defendant argued that the eggs at issue were not adulterated food under the Act because they were not intended to be eaten. The court held that there was a danger of their being diverted to food use and rejected defendant's argument.

Although it is easy to reject the proffered food definitions, it is difficult to arrive at a satisfactory one. In the absence of clearcut Congressional guidance, it is best to rely on statutory language and common sense. The statute evidently uses the word "food" in two different ways. The statutory definition of "food" in Section 321(f) is a term of art and is clearly intended to be broader than the common-sense definition of food, because the statutory definition of "food" also includes chewing gum and food additives. Food additives can be any substance the intended use of which results or may reasonably [be expected to] result in its becoming a component or otherwise affecting the characteristics of any food. *See* 21 U.S.C. § 321(s). Paper food-packaging when containing polychlorinated biphenyls (PCB's), for example, is an adulterated food because the PCB's may migrate from the package to the food and thereby become a component of it. . . . Yet the statutory definition of "food" also includes in Section 321(f)(1) the common-sense definition of food. When the statute defines "food" as "articles used for food," it means that the statutory definition of "food" includes articles used by people in the ordinary way most people use food—primarily for taste, aroma, or nutritive value. To hold as did the district court that articles used as food are articles used solely for taste, aroma or nutritive value is unduly restrictive since some products such as coffee or prune juice are undoubtedly food but may be consumed on occasion for reasons other than taste, aroma, or nutritive value.

This double use of the word "food" in Section 321(f) makes it difficult to interpret the parenthetical "other than food" exclusion in the Section 321(g)(1)(C) drug definition. As shown by that exclusion, Congress obviously meant a drug to be something "other than food," but was it referring to "food" as a term of art in the statutory sense or to foods in their ordinary meaning? Because all such foods are "intended to affect the structure or any function of the body of man or other animals" and would thus come within the part C drug definition, presumably Congress meant to exclude common-sense foods. Fortunately, it is not necessary to decide this question here because starch blockers are not food in either sense.* The tablets and pills at issue are not consumed primarily for taste, aroma, or nutritive value under Section 321(f)(1); in fact, as noted earlier, they are taken for their ability to block the digestion of food and aid in weight loss. In addition, starch blockers are not chewing gum under Section 321(f)(2) and are not components of food under Section 321(f)(3). To qualify as a drug under Section 321(g)(1)(C), the articles must not only be articles "other than food," but must also be "intended to affect the structure or any function of the body of man or other animals." Starch blockers indisputably satisfy this requirement for they are intended to affect digestion in the people who take them. Therefore, starch blockers are drugs under Section 321(g)(1)(C) of the Food, Drug, and Cosmetic Act.

Affirmed.

NOTES

1. *Food Additives.* As explained by the *Nutrilab* court, the distinction between a food and a drug is critical because new drugs, unlike conventional foods, are subject to the requirement of premarket approval by FDA. The manufacturer of a new drug must establish to FDA that its product is safe and effective before the agency will approve it. Observe, however, that there is a subcategory of foods, called "food additives," that are subject to premarket safety approval by the agency. The definition of food in section 201(f) includes "articles used for components" of food or drink. As set forth in section 201(s) of the FD&C Act, "The term 'food additive' means any substance the intended use of which results or may reasonably be expected to result, directly or indirectly, in its becoming a component or otherwise affecting the characteristics of any food . . . if such substance is not generally recognized, among experts qualified by scientific training and experience to evaluate its safety, . . . to be safe under the conditions of its intended use." The exemption for foods that are generally recognized as safe (GRAS) frees most conventional food ingredients from the requirement of premarket approval. Section 201(s) also lists a number of specific exceptions to the definition of "food additive." This section is examined in detail *infra* in Chapter 6.

2. *The Impact of DSHEA.* The Dietary Supplement Health and Education Act of 1994 (DSHEA) amended the FD&C Act in a way that dramatically changed the categorization question for products such as starchblockers. A product that satisfies DSHEA's definition of a "dietary supplement" is now automatically classified as a food, regardless of

---

* The FDA urges an interpretation of the statute that would allow drug regulation of a product if, for example, an appetite suppressant were added to a recognized food. According to the FDA, addition of the drug might make it a "component" and therefore subject to regulation as a statutory "food". As such, the literal language of Section 321(g)(1)(C) would preclude regulation as a drug because the product would qualify as a statutory "food". Even if Section 321(g)(1)(C) meant only to exclude common-sense foods, an article might still be considered food unless addition of an appetite suppressant so changed its nature that it was no longer used primarily for taste, aroma or nutritional value. The FDA submits that a drug manufacturer could easily escape drug regulation by simply adding the drug to a food.

It is not necessary to resolve this problem in order to resolve this case. We merely note the possibility that the word "component" might be interpreted to exclude substances specifically added to a food to avoid bringing the substance within the drug definition, and, as noted above, a food may lose its food character if a drug is added.

whether it satisfies *Nutrilab*'s "common sense" test. Indeed, "starch-blocking" amylase inhibitors derived from kidney beans are currently marketed as dietary supplements, and thus as foods. Nonetheless, for products that do not qualify as dietary supplements under DSHEA, *Nutrilab*'s "common sense" definition of food still applies. DSHEA is addressed in detail below, *infra* p. 101.

3. *Dual Classification.* Although a product cannot simultaneously be both a structure/function drug under section 201(g)(1)(C) and food under 201(f), a product can be dual-classified as a therapeutic drug under section 201(g)(1)(B) and as a food. *See* Senate Rep. No. 361, 74th Cong., 1st Sess. 4 (1935). Courts have repeatedly upheld FDA's reliance on the Act's broad definition of "drug" to regulate products that were concededly also subject to the food provisions of the Act. *See, e.g., United States v. 250 Jars . . . "Cal's Tupelo Blossom U.S. Fancy Pure Honey"*, 344 F.2d 288 (6th Cir. 1965); *United States v. 24 Bottles . . . "Sterling Vinegar and Honey"*, 338 F.2d 157 (2d Cir. 1964) (excerpted *infra* p. 154); *United States v. Hohensee*, 243 F.2d 367 (3d Cir. 1957) (tea). Indeed, a product currently marketed as a food may at the same time undergo clinical investigation for drug uses, in compliance with the FDA investigational drug requirements. *See, e.g.,* "Nutrition Education—1973: Phosphate Research and Dental Decay," Hearings before the Senate Select Comm. on Nutrition and Human Needs, 93d Cong., 1st Sess. 549 (1973). In 2007, however, Congress amended the FD&C Act to prohibit the addition to food of an approved drug or a drug for which substantial, publicly known clinical investigations have been instituted, unless (among some other exceptions) the drug was previously "marketed in food." FD&C Act 301(ll).

4. *Structure/Function Claims Versus Disease Claims.* The line between structure/function claims and disease claims can be a maddeningly indistinct one. Nevertheless, FDA did not set forth a comprehensive analysis of the distinction until 2000. We consider the agency's assessment of the difference between the types of claims *infra* at pp. 443–444.

5. *Caffeine.* FDA regulates over-the-counter stimulants in which caffeine is the active ingredient as drugs. 21 C.F.R. Part 340. However, when caffeine is added to food, such as a soft drink, the agency does not regulate the product as a drug even if the manufacturer promotes the food's high level of caffeine and its "energizing" qualities. Apparently, in FDA's view, such products fall within the food exception to the structure/function drug definition in section 201(g)(1)(C).

C. DRUGS AND DEVICES

In general, drugs and devices are subject to much more rigorous regulatory regimes than food or cosmetics. Most important, since 1938, "new drugs" have been subject to premarket approval, and since 1976, many medical devices have been subject to either premarket approval or to the requirement that their manufacturers demonstrate that they are substantially equivalent to products already on the market. Consequently, a determination that a product is a drug or device is often tantamount to a determination that the product cannot be sold at all until FDA approves it for marketing.

Section 201(g)(1) of the FD&C Act defines "drug" as follows:

The term "drug" means

(A) articles recognized in the official United States Pharmacopoeia, official Homeopathic Pharmacopoeia of the United States, or official National Formulary, or any supplement to any of them; and

(B) articles intended for use in the diagnosis, cure, mitigation, treatment, or prevention of disease in man or other animals; and

(C) articles (other than food) intended to affect the structure or any function of the body of man or other animals; and

(D) articles intended for use as a component of any article specified in clause (A), (B), or (C). . . .

Section 201(h) of the FD&C Act defines "device" as follows:

The term "device" . . . means an instrument, apparatus, implement, machine, contrivance, implant, in vitro reagent, or other similar or related article, including any component, part, or accessory, which is—

(1) recognized in the official National Formulary, or the United States Pharmacopeia, or any supplement to them,

(2) intended for use in the diagnosis of disease or other conditions, or in the cure, mitigation, treatment, or prevention of disease, in man or other animals, or

(3) intended to affect the structure or any function of the body of man or other animals, and

which does not achieve its primary intended purposes through chemical action within or on the body of man or other animals and which is not dependent upon being metabolized for the achievement of its primary intended purposes.

The Act's definitions of drug and device are parallel in many respects. This chapter focuses primarily on their common elements, while the distinctions between drugs and devices are considered in Chapter 10, which examines device regulation.

1. INCLUSION IN OFFICIAL COMPENDIA

Section 321(g)(1)(A) of the Act includes within the definition of "drug" any article "recognized in the official United States Pharmacopoeia, official Homeopathic Pharmacopoeia of the United States, or official National Formulary, or any supplement to any of them." The definition of "device" contains a parallel provision. *See* FD&C Act 321(h)(1).

The *United States Pharmacopeia and National Formulary* (*USP–NF*) is a compendium of standards for drug strength, quality, purity, packaging, labeling, and storage, published by the United States Pharmacopeial Convention (USP), a nongovernmental organization more than a century old. The *National Formulary* (*NF*) was published separately by the American Pharmaceutical Association until 1975, when USP acquired the NF and combined the two publications under one cover. In addition to products universally viewed as drugs, the *USP–NF* also contains standards for most vitamins and minerals. The Homeopathic Pharmacopeia contains many herbal products.

Although section 321(g)(1)(A) appears on its face to give FDA the power to treat any item listed in these compendia as a drug, the agency generally has not viewed this provision so expansively. When FDA has attempted to regulate products as drugs based solely on their inclusion in the *USP* or *NF*, courts have usually thwarted these efforts. *Compare National Nutritional Foods Ass'n v. FDA*, 504 F.2d 761, 788–89 (2d Cir. 1974) (rejecting argument that vitamins and minerals are drugs because of their recognition in the official compendia); *National Nutritional Foods Ass'n v. Mathews*, 557 F.2d 325, 337–38 (2d Cir. 1977) (rejecting the argument with regard to high potency vitamins); and *United States v. An Article of Drug . . . Ova II*, 414 F. Supp. 660 (D.N.J. 1975), *aff'd without op.* 535 F.2d 1248 (3d Cir. 1976) (rejecting the argument with regard to pregnancy test kit), *with United States v. Articles of Drug . . . Beuthanasia*, Food Drug Cosm. L. Rep. (CCH) ¶ 38,265 (D. Neb. 1979) (accepting the argument with regard to animal euthanasia drug).

In *United States v. Ova II*, a federal district court considering the regulatory status of a pregnancy test concluded that the official compendia provision of the drug definition "cannot be taken literally," because a literal interpretation would "run[ ] afoul of the principle that a legislative body may not lawfully delegate its functions to a private citizen or organization." Nonetheless, the court observed that the inclusion of a product in such a compendium has real, if limited, legal significance:

> [T]he first definition, *i.e.*, recognition in the U.S.P. or other named compendium must be read to mean that:

> (a) an article put into the stream of interstate commerce with the intention that it be used for medicinal purposes, as evidenced by the label designation "U.S.P.," "N.F.," and the like, must meet the privately designated standards for quality and strength, or else be subject to appropriate action for misbranding or adulteration;

> (b) the recognition of an item in the U.S.P., etc., by a monograph, coupled with a label indicating compliance with standards, constitutes evidence that the item is a "drug" as a matter of prima facie proof only, calling on the opposing party to come forward with contrary evidence or else risk an adverse ruling; . . .

> (d) an item recognized in U.S.P., etc., such as sodium hydroxide, hydrochloric acid, or whatever, by name, is not a drug if it is put into the channels of interstate commerce without a label such as "U.S.P.," "N.F." and the like, to imply that it is intended for medicinal use.

414 F. Supp. at 665–66.

For a further analysis of the official compendia provision of the drug definition, see *National Nutritional Foods Ass'n v. Mathews, infra* p. 93.

2.   ESTABLISHING "INTENDED USE"

The most important similarity between the definitions of "drug" and "device" is their common reference to "intended" use. In most instances, if a product is "intended for use in the diagnosis, cure, mitigation, treatment, or prevention" of disease or is "intended to affect the structure or function of the body," it is either a drug or a device. Not surprisingly, there have been countless disputes over the meaning of "intent" and over the types of evidence required to establish intent.

For both drugs and devices, FDA has used the following regulatory definition of "intended use" since 1952:

> The words *intended uses* or words of similar import . . . refer to the objective intent of the persons legally responsible for the labeling of drugs. The intent is determined by such persons' expressions or may be shown by the circumstances surrounding the distribution of the article. This objective intent may, for example, be shown by labeling claims, advertising matter, or oral or written statements by such persons or their representatives. It may be shown by the circumstances that the article is, with the knowledge of such persons or their representatives, offered and used for a purpose for which it is neither labeled nor advertised. The intended uses of an article may change after it has been introduced into interstate commerce by its manufacturer. If, for example, a packer, distributor, or seller intends an article for different uses than those intended by the person from whom he received the drug [or device], such packer, distributor, or seller is required to supply adequate labeling in accordance with the new intended uses. But if a manufacturer knows, or has knowledge of facts that would give him notice, that a drug [or device] introduced into interstate commerce by him is to be used for conditions, purposes, or uses other than the ones for which he offers it, he is required to provide adequate labeling for such a drug [or device] which accords with such other uses to which the article is to be put.

21 C.F.R. 201.128 (drugs); 21 C.F.R. 801.4 (devices). This definition articulates an extremely broad view of the types of evidence the agency can rely upon to establish a product's intended use. However, FDA has rarely attempted to classify a product as a drug or device in the absence of relevant representations by the manufacturer or distributor. The following, seminal case concerns one of the rare instances in which the agency attempted to do so.

The case involves high-dose vitamin supplements. FDA traditionally classified vitamin and mineral products as foods unless therapeutic claims were made for them. In the early 1970s, however, the agency was confronted with reports of people experiencing toxic effects from large doses of vitamins A and D. Adelle Davis, a self-proclaimed nutritional expert who advocated a "natural" approach to good health, recommended megadoses of these vitamins in her books. Vitamins A and D are fat-soluble nutrients (which accumulate in fatty tissue), and FDA thus concluded that ingestion of excess quantities of these vitamins could lead to serious harm.

To meet this problem, FDA promulgated regulations, 37 Fed. Reg. 26618 (Dec. 14, 1972), 38 Fed. Reg. 20723 (Aug. 2, 1973), classifying preparations providing more than 10,000 international units (IU) of vitamin A or 400 IU of vitamin D per daily serving as drugs and requiring further that they be sold only on prescription. Vitamin manufacturers challenged these regulations in court. The District Court initially upheld the regulations, *National Nutritional Foods Ass'n v. Weinberger*, 376 F. Supp. 142 (S.D.N.Y. 1974), but the Court of Appeals concluded that the administrative record was incomplete. It remanded the case with instructions that the district court inquire into the FDA Commissioner's reasoning. 512 F.2d 688 (2d Cir. 1975). After conducting the mandated hearing, the District Court once again upheld the regulations, 418 F. Supp. 394 (S.D.N.Y. 1976), and the plaintiffs appealed for a second time.

National Nutritional Foods Ass'n v. Mathews

557 F.2d 325 (2d Cir. 1977).

■ ROBERT P. ANDERSON, CIRCUIT JUDGE:

. . . When this case was previously remanded by us to the district court, we said, ". . . a serious question is raised as to whether the Commissioner, in concluding that the higher level dosage forms of Vitamins A and D are 'drugs,' acted 'in accordance with law.'" *. . .* In the statement announcing the proposal of the Vitamins A and D regulations and in the one accompanying their adoption, the Commissioner did not rely upon the recognition of these preparations in the [official compendia] as the basis of the drug classification. Rather, the Commissioner determined that the circumstances surrounding the use of Vitamins A and D at the regulated levels indicated an intended therapeutic use under § 201(g)(1)(B). The vendors' intent in selling the product to the public is the key element in this statutory definition.

In determining whether an article is a "drug" because of an intended therapeutic use, the FDA is not bound by the manufacturer's subjective claims of intent but can find actual therapeutic intent on the basis of objective evidence. Such intent also may be derived or inferred from labeling, promotional material, advertising, and "any other relevant source." [Case citations omitted.] In remanding this case, this court expressly indicated that evidence that Vitamins A and D at the regulated levels were used "almost exclusively for therapeutic purposes" when coupled with lack of a recognized nutritional use, would be sufficient to show that high dosage Vitamins A and D products were intended for use in the treatment of disease.

In proposing the regulations, the Commissioner emphasized the potential for toxicity and the widespread promotion of the intake of high doses of Vitamins A and D to cure a variety of ills. To show objective therapeutic intent, the Commissioner's affidavit submitted on remand relied upon three factors: (1) widespread promotion to the public in the use of high potency Vitamins A and D preparations for the treatment of various ailments; (2) lack of recognized nutritional usefulness; and (3) potential for toxicity from the ingestion of large doses of these vitamins over extended periods of time. . . .

Plaintiffs assert that toxicity is irrelevant to the issue of therapeutic intent and, although the key element in determining that a drug should be limited to prescription use under § 503(b) of the Act, it has no bearing upon whether an article is a drug. The Government argues, on the other hand, that toxicity is relevant to therapeutic intent and that the Commissioner must make the decision of whether there should be a regulation which classifies an article as a food or as a drug, for the purposes of the Act. Although an article may be recognized as a food, this does not preclude it from being regulated as a drug. The determination that an article is properly regulated as a drug, however, is not left to the Commissioner's unbridled discretion to act to protect the public health but must be in accordance with the statutory definition. Toxicity is not included as an element in the statutory definition of a drug. It is relevant as a factor supporting the Commissioner's classification under § 201(g)(1)(B), but only to the extent that it constitutes objective evidence of therapeutic intent. Toxicity is cited by the Commissioner as constituting objective evidence of "something more" than lack of nutritional usefulness. . . . Such evidence, however, only presents a further indication that the excessive intake of Vitamins A and D may not be nutritionally useful and does not provide the objective evidence of therapeutic intent necessary to support these regulations.

There is no evidence in the administrative record that the manufacturers and vendors of Vitamins A and D preparations, at the regulated dosages, represent through labeling, promotional materials, or advertising that these products are effective in the cure or treatment of disease. They are sold as "dietary supplements." . . .

The main issue on this appeal is whether the evidence of the extensive use of large doses of Vitamins A and D to treat or prevent diseases and the promotion of such usage by persons not associated with the manufacturers or vendors establishes such widespread therapeutic use at the regulated levels as to overcome the plaintiffs' claim of the lack of an intended use to cure or prevent disease and thus justifies the Commissioner's determination.

The Commissioner admits that below the stated levels of potency, Vitamins A and D are foods. The evidence relied upon to show therapeutic intent, therefore, must be related to the potency level chosen to differentiate between the use of Vitamins A and D as foods and the use of these vitamins as drugs. The administrative record clearly establishes that the factors involved in choosing the levels at which Vitamins A and D become drugs were solely related to the Commissioner's fear of potential toxic effect and his belief that the ingestion of vitamins at levels above the U.S. RDA is not nutritionally useful. No further record evidence has been produced on the remand to show that the 10,000 IU and 400 IU levels were chosen because at those potencies, consumption of them is almost exclusively for therapeutic purposes. A sampling of the comments submitted to the FDA after publication of the proposed regulations reveals that people believe that a wide range of doses of these vitamins are therapeutically useful. A large group of individuals indicated that they ingested these vitamins at various dosages solely to supplement their daily diet in the belief that more Vitamins A and D were needed to maintain optimal health than the upper limits in the U.S. RDA.

In remanding this case, this court suggested that proof in the record demonstrating that, at the 10,000 IU and 400 IU levels, respectively, these vitamins were taken "almost exclusively" for therapeutic purposes, would tend to show that the regulations were not arbitrary or capricious. There was no evidence, however, supporting the Commissioner's conclusion that, when sold at the regulated, *i.e.* prescription, levels, therapeutic usage of these vitamins so far outweighed their use as dietary supplements, it showed an objective intent that these products were used in the mitigation and cure of diseases. This claim furnished no contradiction to the charge that the FDA's regulations are arbitrary and capricious and not in accordance with law. . . .

The Commissioner also seeks to justify the Vitamins A and D regulations on the basis of § 201(g)(1)(A), which defines as drugs, articles "recognized" in the United States Pharmacopoeia (USP) or National Formulary (NF). . . . To construe § 201(g)(1)(A) so as to grant the Commissioner the power to regulate as drugs every item mentioned in the USP and NF solely on the basis of such inclusion would give the FDA virtually unlimited discretion to regulate as drugs a vast range of items. . . . An administrator's decision under a regulatory statute, such as the Food, Drug, and Cosmetic Act, must be governed by an intelligible statutory principle. If § 201(g)(1)(A) defines as drugs every item included in the USP and NF, the FDA is not being consistent in its treatment of other items similarly recognized. The Commissioner, therefore, has not applied the § 201(g)(1)(A) definition to every item in the compendia. Rather he has singled out for drug classification items included in the USP and NF on the basis of factors, such as toxicity in this case, that are not relevant to the statutory criteria in § 201(g).

The Commissioner admitted in his affidavit that mere inclusion in the USP and NF is an insufficient basis for drug classification after the decision in *National Nutritional Foods Ass'n v. FDA* [504 F.2d 761 (2d Cir. 1974)]. He attempts to distinguish that case on the ground that Vitamins A and D are recognized at therapeutic dosages in the compendia and are regulated as drugs in this case only at levels in excess of the recognized food levels in the USP. Other articles, however, are recognized in the compendia at therapeutic levels and not regulated as drugs, for example Vitamin C. The Commissioner must, therefore, show that the conflicting treatment in the regulations of items similarly classified in the USP and NF is not arbitrary under the applicable criteria. The FDA regulates Vitamin C preparations at the USP's therapeutic level as food. To justify the regulation of Vitamins A and D as drugs by relying on § 201(g)(1)(A) the Commissioner would have to distinguish his treatment of Vitamin C as food.

In proposing and adopting these regulations for Vitamins A and D, the Commissioner did not rely upon or cite the recognition of these vitamins in the USP and NF. He may not at this late hour on appeal rely upon them as the basis for his drug classification because it is sheer post hoc rationalization. . . .

The district court's dismissal of this action is reversed and the case is remanded with directions to enter an order granting summary judgment in plaintiffs' favor declaring 21 C.F.R. §§ 250.09 and 250.10 invalid as arbitrary and capricious and not in accordance with law. . . .

NOTES

1. *Subsequent Developments.* Following this decision, FDA revoked the challenged regulations. 43 Fed. Reg. 10551 (Mar. 14, 1978).

2. *The 1976 Vitamin–Mineral Amendments.* Even before *Mathews*, Congress had acted to limit FDA's power over vitamin-mineral products in the Vitamin–Mineral Amendments of 1976, 90 Stat. 401. Section 411 of the FD&C Act, added by this measure, provides, among other things, that the agency "may not classify any natural or synthetic vitamin or mineral (or combination thereof) as a drug solely because it exceeds the level of potency which [FDA] determines is nutritionally rational or useful." FD&C Act 411(a)(1)(B).

3. *Once a Drug?* In *United States v. Articles of Drug . . . Neptone*, Food Drug Cosm. L. Rep. (CCH) ¶ 38,240 (N.D. Cal. 1983), FDA contended that the seized product (freeze-dried, powdered green mussel in capsule form) was a drug, and the agency was granted summary judgment. However, the opinion also noted:

> The Court does not view this opinion as establishing for all time that Neptone is a drug. The determination that Neptone is a drug rests entirely on the pattern of promotion used by claimant in the several years immediately preceding the instant seizure. Should Neptone again be marketed after some hiatus and a change in labelling, this order will not necessarily work an estoppel on whether that batch of Neptone is a drug. The answer will turn on the relationship between the future sales and the offensive labelling.

———

Since the decision in *Mathews*, FDA has rarely asserted its drug or device jurisdiction over a product unless the manufacturer or distributor has made representations about product's disease or structure/function effects. But neither has the agency unequivocally disclaimed its authority to establish intended use based on the "circumstances surrounding the distribution of the article." 21 C.F.R. 201.128, 801.4.

The most famous instance in which FDA attempted to declare a product to be a drug (or device) in the absence of relevant manufacturer claims was its 1996 rulemaking on cigarettes and smokeless tobacco. 61 Fed. Reg. 44396 (Aug. 28, 1996). FDA argued that tobacco products were "intended" to affect the structure/function of the body based solely on evidence concerning the foreseeable and actual use of the products for stimulation, tranquilization, weight control, and satisfaction of nicotine addiction and on internal company statements confirming the manufacturers' awareness of these uses. The Supreme Court ultimately denied FDA jurisdiction without reaching the "intended use" issue. *FDA v. Brown & Williamson Tobacco Corp.*, 529 U.S. 120 (2000) (excerpted *infra* p. 141). In the Family Smoking Prevention and Tobacco Control Act of 2009, Congress gave FDA explicit authority over tobacco products as a distinct product category. *See infra* p. 145.

Throughout the *Brown & Williamson* litigation, the tobacco industry asserted that no court had ever found that a product was "intended for use" or "intended to affect" absent manufacturer claims regarding that product's use. Because of the following case, this assertion would no longer be true if made today.

United States v. Travia
180 F. Supp. 2d 115 (D.D.C. 2001).

■ THOMAS F. HOGAN, CHIEF JUDGE.

Memorandum Opinion

Pending before the Court is the government's appeal from the Magistrate Judge's bench ruling of July 31, 2001, dismissing with prejudice the criminal informations and complaints filed in these cases. In each information, the government charged the defendants with distributing nitrous oxide, commonly known as laughing gas at a rock concert at RFK Stadium on June 9, 2001. The government specifically charged the defendants with unlawful distribution of misbranded prescription drugs, in violation of the Food, Drug, and Cosmetic Act ("FDCA"). The Magistrate Judge dismissed the criminal complaints and informations after opining that the FDCA did not cover these individual defendants. . . .

According to the government, members of the D.C. Metropolitan Police Department ("MPD") and Special Agents from the Food and Drug Administration ("FDA") engaged in a joint investigation of illegal distribution of nitrous oxide at a rock concert at RFK Stadium on June 9, 2001. An undercover officer approached the defendants in the parking lot, handed them pre-recorded MPD funds, and in exchange received balloons containing nitrous oxide gas. The undercover officer then left the area and signaled arrest teams. The arrest teams moved into the area and arrested the defendants, who were subsequently identified by the undercover officer.

. . . [T]wo of the defendants appeared before the Magistrate Judge to enter pleas of guilty. Rather than taking the guilty pleas, however, the Magistrate Judge *sua sponte* raised a question concerning whether nitrous oxide was a "drug" within the meaning of the FDCA. . . .

The FDCA defines the term "drug" to mean "articles (other than food) *intended to affect the structure or any function of the body of man or other animals.*" 21 U.S.C. § 321(g)(1)(C) (emphasis added). The intended use of an article thus determines whether it is classified as a "drug" for purposes of the FDCA.

The parties[ ] dispute how to properly discern the "intended use" of the nitrous oxide in this case. The government argues that the Court should look to the objective intent of the sellers in this case, which would permit the Court to view the totality of the circumstances— namely, the selling of balloons of laughing gas in the parking lot at a rock concert—surrounding the sale of the nitrous oxide here. *See, e.g.,*

21 C.F.R. § 201.128 ("The words 'intended uses' . . . refer to the objective intent of the persons legally responsible for the labeling of drugs. The intent is determined by such persons' expressions or may be shown by the circumstances surrounding the distribution of the article.").

The defendants rejoin that "it is well established 'that the intended use of a product, within the meaning of the [FDCA], is determined from its label, accompanying labeling, promotional claims, advertising, and any other relevant source.'" *Action on Smoking and Health v. Harris*, 655 F.2d 236, 239 (D.C. Cir. 1980). But, contend the defendants, the gravamen of the charge against them here is that there was no labeling on the balloons they sold. By the defendants' logic, therefore, without at least an allegation that representations were made by them in labeling or advertising the balloons, the nitrous oxide they sold cannot be considered a "drug" for the purposes of the FDCA.

The Court can find no support for the defendants' position. Labeling is not exclusive evidence of the sellers' intent. Rather, as the very language quoted by the defendants themselves states, "it is well established 'that the intended use of a product, within the meaning of the [FDCA], is determined from its label, accompanying labeling, promotional claims, advertising, *and any other relevant source.*'" The court in *Action on Smoking* went on to acknowledge that even *consumer* intent could be relevant, so long as it was pertinent to demonstrating the seller's intent: "Whether evidence of consumer intent is a 'relevant source' for these purposes depends upon whether such evidence is strong enough to justify an inference as to the vendors' intent." *Id*. Thus, while it may be true that "'the vendors' intent in selling the product to the public is the key element in this statutory definition,'" *id*., nothing limits the attempt to discern that intent to labeling or advertising. Moreover, the focus on the seller's intent is premised, at least in part, upon the fact that the FDCA generally is concerned with protecting the public against false or misleading representations of the healing power of various articles placed into the stream of interstate commerce. This case is obviously unique in that, if the government's allegations are true, the sellers did not need to label or advertise their product, as the environment provided the necessary information between buyer and seller. In this context, therefore, the fact that there was no labeling may actually bolster the evidence of an intent to sell a mind-altering article without a prescription—that is, a misbranded drug. The Court thus concludes that from the surrounding circumstances of the sales alleged in this case that the government has made a sufficient showing that the defendants' intent to sell the nitrous oxide was to affect "the structure or any function of the body of man," and thus, the nitrous oxide involved in this case is a "drug" for the purposes of the FDCA. . . .

. . . [T]he Court will reverse the Magistrate Judge's ruling and reinstate these cases. . . .

3. DIAGNOSTIC PRODUCTS

The device definition includes articles (including "in vitro reagent[s]") "intended for use in the diagnosis of disease or other conditions." FD&C Act 201(h). This provision raises its own interpretive problems.

United States v. 25 Cases, More or Less, of an Article of Device . . . "Sensor Pad for Breast Self–Examination"

942 F.2d 1179 (7th Cir. 1991).

■ CUDAHY, CIRCUIT JUDGE.

In this case we are called on to interpret the word "device" as used in the Federal Food, Drug and Cosmetic Act, 21 U.S.C. § 321(h)(2) (1988) (the Act). The government brought this action to seize the appellant's inventory, believing it to consist of adulterated devices in interstate commerce. The district court granted summary judgment for the government. . . .

In the mid-1980s, Earl Wright developed a product which he believed would aid women in conducting self-examinations for the early detection of breast cancer. This product, descriptively named the "Sensor Pad," consists of a flat, circular latex bag filled with a layer of silicone lubricant. It is intended to be placed over the breast during self-examinations to improve the woman's ability to feel abnormalities beneath the skin. Wright and his associates believed the Pad was not a "device" under the Act. . . .

According to the Act, the term device "means an instrument, apparatus, implement, machine, contrivance, implant, in vitro reagent, or other similar or related article, including any component, part, or accessory, which is . . . (2) intended for use in the diagnosis of disease or other conditions, or in the cure, mitigation, treatment, or prevention of disease. . . ." 21 U.S.C. § 321(h). . . . Although agreeing that its Pad aids in the detection and screening of breast cancer, Inventive Products nevertheless argues that the word diagnosis does not encompass the function of the Sensor Pad. Diagnosis, the appellant suggests, includes only examinations to "determine the nature and circumstances of a diseased condition." Because the Sensor Pad merely helps the woman in detecting abnormalities that could be symptoms of a disease, strictly speaking it is used *before* actual diagnosis.

The distinction appellant attempts to draw between screening and diagnosis is an untenable one. In its opening brief, Inventive Products appears to argue that diagnosis occurs only at the last step in the process of discovering a disease, that step which ultimately determines the nature and circumstances of a diseased condition. Thus, because the Sensor Pad only detects irregularities which may or may not be cancerous growths, it does not diagnose the disease. Indeed appellant agrees with one of its expert physicians, who averred that "biopsy is the only means of diagnosing breast cancer." By proposing that medical inquiries change from screening to diagnosis only at the final determination, the appellant's theory would apparently exclude even a mammography unit from being classified as diagnostic, because it too cannot confirm the presence of cancer. . . .

The obscurity of the line appellant would draw between diagnosis and screening . . . well illustrates the arbitrariness of the line-drawing. Pursuing this fruitless inquiry is irrelevant in any event since we believe Congress had no such screening/diagnosing distinction in mind when it wrote section 321(h).

The current description of "device" in the Act was adopted essentially in the original version of the Federal Food, Drug and Cosmetic Act, 52 Stat. 1040 (1938), the development of which is discussed in *United States v. Article of Drug . . . Bacto–Unidisk*, 394 U.S. 784, 793–98 (1969). The bill emerged from committee in the Senate with several amendments, one of which proposed broadening the definition of "device" to include tools used in diagnosis of disease. At that time one senator, with the voiced approval of the bill's sponsor, summarized the amendment on the floor of the chamber: "the word 'diagnosis' merely adds to their uses, namely, their use in looking into a situation prior to the time when the cure or mitigation shall begin." 79 Cong. Rec. 4843 (1935) (statement of Sen. Barkley). Another senator meanwhile offered the view that weight scales used during the diagnosis of a patient would come within the bill's regulation. *Id.* (statement of Sen. Clark).

Moreover, even if Congress' intentions with regard to the scope of "diagnosis" were not clear from its debate, the FDA's position in this matter would still prevail. It would be entirely plausible to suggest that Congress intended the FDA to decide for itself which devices are used for diagnosing disease. One senator opined on the floor of the Senate that "the language [of the bill] is broad enough to cover any device of which the Food and Drug Bureau of the Agricultural Department chooses to take jurisdiction." *Id.* at 4841. Such a delegation to the FDA would require a court to give considerable deference to the agency's decision. . . .

Second, even had Congress never considered the question before us, we might allow the FDA room to decide the question itself. Courts often will defer to an agency's reasonable interpretation of an ambiguous provision within the agency's own organic statute. *Chevron U.S.A., Inc. v. Natural Resources Defense Council, Inc.*, 467 U.S. 837, 843 (1984). . . .

Our approach in this case has been further reinforced by the Supreme Court, which reminded litigants that "[r]emedial legislation such as the Food, Drug and Cosmetic Act is to be given a liberal construction consistent with the Act's overriding purpose to protect the public health. . . ." *Bacto–Unidisk*, 394 U.S. at 798. A broad definition of "diagnosis" allows for greater authority in the agency to oversee developments in health care, and thus to better protect the public health.

For each of the above reasons, the district court was correct to grant the government's motion for summary judgment in this case. . . .

NOTES

1. *Diagnostic Drugs.* The definition of "drug" at FD&C Act 201(g)(1) includes "articles intended for use in the diagnosis . . . of disease." Unlike the definition of "device," this provision does not embrace products intended for the diagnosis of "conditions" other than diseases. Since 1976, FDA has regulated most diagnostic products (whether for diseases or "other conditions") as medical devices. *See infra* p. 98.

2. *"Diagnosis" for What Purpose?* FDA regulates as devices "OTC test sample collection systems for drugs of abuse testing." These products, according to the regulation, are intended to "[c]ollect biological specimens (such as hair, urine, sweat, or saliva), outside of a medical setting and not on order of a health care professional *(e.g.,* in the home, insurance, sports, or workplace setting); maintain the integrity of such specimens during storage and transport in order that the matter contained therein can be tested in a laboratory for the presence of drugs of abuse or their metabolites; and provide access to test results and counseling." 21 C.F.R. 864.3260. When it finalized this regulation, FDA rejected a comment which asserted that kits for detecting drugs of abuse in hair are not medical devices under section 201(h) of the FD&C Act because they are not for medical diagnosis and treatment. 65 Fed. Reg. 18230, 18232 (Apr. 7, 2000).

In *United States v. Undetermined Number of Unlabeled Cases*, 21 F.3d 1026 (10th Cir. 1994), the Tenth Circuit held that containers used to collect urine and saliva specimens for HIV testing were devices, even though the laboratory-defendant that distributed the containers performed the testing for insurance risk-assessment purposes rather than for medical treatment.

D. THE FOOD–DRUG SPECTRUM ADJUSTED: HEALTH CLAIMS AND DIETARY SUPPLEMENTS

The definition of "drug" in section 201(g)(1) of the FD&C Act concludes with the following proviso:

> A food or dietary supplement for which a claim, subject to sections 403(r)(1)(B) and 403(r)(3) of this title or sections 403(r)(1)(B) and 403(r)(5)(D) of this title, is made in accordance with the requirements of 403(r) of this title is not a drug solely because the label or the labeling contains such a claim. A food, dietary ingredient, or dietary supplement for which a truthful and not misleading statement is made in accordance with section 403(r)(6) of this title is not a drug under clause (C) solely because the label or the labeling contains such a statement.

This language reflects dramatic changes in the relationship between food and drugs made by two important statutes passed in the 1990s: the Nutrition Labeling and Education Act of 1990 (NLEA) and the Dietary Supplement Health and Education Act of 1994 (DSHEA).

DSHEA established a new subcategory of food called "dietary supplements." The first sentence in the paragraph quoted above refers to the fact that under the NLEA and subsequent amendments, either a conventional food or a dietary supplement may, with approval by FDA (or in accordance with an authoritative statement by a federal scientific body or the National Academy of Sciences), make a claim "which expressly or by implication . . . characterizes the relationship of any nutrient . . . to a disease or a health-related condition." FD&C Act 403(r)(1)(B). Such claims have come to be known as "health claims." The second sentence refers to the fact that pursuant to section 403(r)(6), added by DSHEA, dietary supplements (many of which are not "common sense" foods) may make structure and function claims.

FDA began to permit explicit disease prevention claims on food labels in the 1980s, following the lead of the Federal Trade Commission, which started to allow such claims in food advertisements in the 1970s. *See infra* p. 418. By establishing the NLEA health claims regime in 1990, Congress was thus authorizing a lenient regulatory approach that FDA had, in broad terms, already embraced. By contrast, before the passage of DSHEA, FDA demonstrated a willingness to regulate dietary supplements aggressively, particularly through the imposition of the FD&C Act's premarket approval requirements for drugs and food additives. In short, DSHEA represented an effort by Congress to rein in the agency. At this early stage, it is thus important to recognize that the desire to subject certain classes of products to more or less regulation not only shapes FDA's interpretation of the statutory definitions, but sometimes leads Congress to revise the definitions.

The regulatory regimes for health claims and dietary supplements are discussed at length in Chapter 6, which addresses food regulation. Here, we will briefly examine the new product category, "dietary supplement," that DSHEA added to the list of definitions in the FD&C Act.

Section 201(ff) of the FDCA defines "dietary supplement" as follows:

The term "dietary supplement"—

(1) means a product (other than tobacco) intended to supplement the diet that bears or contains one or more of the following dietary ingredients:

(A) a vitamin;

(B) a mineral;

(C) an herb or other botanical;

(D) an amino acid;

(E) a dietary substance for use by man to supplement the diet by increasing the total dietary intake; or

(F) a concentrate, metabolite, constituent, extract, or combination of any ingredient described in clause (A), (B), (C), (D), or (E);

(2) means a product that—

(A)(i) is intended for ingestion in a form described in section 411(c)(1)(B)(i) of this title; or

(ii) complies with section 411(c)(1)(B)(ii) of this title;

(B) is not represented for use as a conventional food or as a sole item of a meal or the diet; and

(C) is labeled as a dietary supplement . . . .

Section 411(c)(1)(B), mentioned within the definition of "dietary supplement," refers to a product which "(i) is intended for ingestion in tablet, capsule, powder, softgel, gelcap, or liquid form, or (ii) if not intended for ingestion in such a form, is not represented as conventional food and is not represented for use as a sole item of a meal or of the diet."

DSHEA declares that, for most purposes, "a dietary supplement shall be deemed to be a food within the meaning of this Act." FD&C Act 201(ff). Since many dietary supplements are not "common sense" foods as elaborated in *Nutrilab, supra* 85, DSHEA in effect greatly expanded the definition of "food." For present purposes, the most important aspect of DSHEA is that it permits a dietary supplement to make a structure/function claim without rendering itself a drug, even if the supplement is not a "common sense" food.

Vitamins and minerals, which are consumed primarily for their nutritive value, have always been permitted to make such structure/function claims, because of the parenthetical exception for "food" in the structure/function arm of the drug definition. FD&C Act 201(g)(1)(C). By contrast, before DSHEA, supplements that were not common sense foods, such as botanicals (and the "starch blockers" in *Nutrilab*) were drugs if they made structure/function claims. DSHEA added FD&C Act 403(r)(6), explicitly permitting all dietary supplements to make statements that, among other things, "describe[] the role of a nutrient or dietary ingredient intended to affect the structure or function in humans, [or] characterize[] the documented mechanism by which a nutrient or dietary ingredient acts to maintain such structure or function . . . ." Moreover, as noted above, DSHEA amended the FD&C Act to exclude supplements making such statements from the definition of drug. Consequently, today, all dietary supplements, even those that do not satisfy the common sense definition of food, can make structure/function claims without being subject to the premarket approval requirements for new drugs.

As mentioned above, the first sentence of the drug definition's proviso excludes from that definition dietary supplements making the same types of pre-approved "health claims" (disease prevention claims) that conventional foods may make. *See supra* p. 101. You can see what a large chunk DSHEA carved out of the drug definition when you consider the fact that today, a capsule containing the extract of a foul-tasting herb, sold in a pill bottle bearing a structure/function claim or an approved disease prevention claim, is treated as a dietary supplement (and thus a type of food) and not as a drug. *See* Lewis A. Grossman, *Food, Drugs, and Droods: A Historical Consideration of Definitions and Categories in American Food and Drug Law*, 93 CORNELL L. REV. 1091, 1134–48 (2008).

Although DSHEA mandates that dietary supplements be deemed food for most purposes, dietary supplements are not regulated identically to conventional food. For example, section 201(s)(6) of the Act specifically excludes dietary supplement ingredients from the definition of "food additive," thus releasing them from the requirement of premarket approval under the food additive provisions of the Act. *See infra* p. 568. Various other safety provisions in the FD&C Act apply to dietary supplements, but not to food generally. *See infra* p. 627. In addition, section 403(r)(6) imposes certain conditions on structure/function claims for dietary supplements that do not apply to similar claims for conventional food, including the requirement of a disclaimer. *See infra* p. 444. The distinction between a conventional food and a dietary supplement is thus sometimes quite important. We will save this aspect of the dietary supplement definition for later, however. *See infra* pp. 319–323. For now, focus your attention not on the line dividing conventional foods from dietary supplements, but rather on the line separating dietary supplements from products that are not foods at all.

The following letter offers an opportunity to consider exactly what non-commonsense foods the definition of "dietary supplement" embraces. DSHEA requires the manufacturer of a dietary supplement containing a "new dietary ingredient" to submit to FDA, at least 75 days prior to marketing, a notification setting forth its basis for concluding that the dietary ingredient will reasonably be expected to be safe. *See infra* p. 627. The following is a letter sent by FDA to a lawyer who had belatedly submitted such a 75-day notification on behalf of a client.

Letter from Felicia B. Satchell, Director, FDA CFSAN Office of Nutritional Products, Labeling and Dietary Supplements, Division of Standards and Labeling Regulations, to Jason S. Crush

August 29, 2002.

Dear Mr. Crush,

This letter is in response to your notification, dated June 10, 2002, submitted to the Food and Drug Administration for a new dietary ingredient pursuant to 21 U.S.C. 350b(a)(2) [section 413(a)(2) of the Federal Food, Drug, and Cosmetic Act (the Act)]. . . . Your letter notified FDA that your client, Natural ASA . . . has been marketing conjugated linoleic acid (CLA) products in the United States since 1998. . . .

Your notification . . . stated that CLA is a naturally occurring ingredient, which is available in meat and dairy products, and chemically equivalent to the CLA in Natural ASA's products. . . .

However, your notification also stated that the products marketed by Natural ASA contain CLA that is isolated and purified from safflower oil and contain higher concentrations of CLA than those found in meat and dairy products. Your notification stated that this is the basis for the present notification. . . .

CLA is a term that refers to a group of polyunsaturated fatty acids that exist as positional and stereoisomers of conjugated dienoic octadecadienoate. Plant oils do not contain significant amounts of CLA. However, CLA can be produced synthetically by exposing plant oils rich in linoleic acid, such as safflower and soybean, to base and heat. . . . The isomeric ratio and profile of synthetic preparations of CLA vary significantly from the naturally occurring CLA of meat and dairy products. . . .

FDA has carefully evaluated your submission and has concerns about the evidence on which you rely to support your conclusion that CLA is a new dietary ingredient and conforms to the statutory definition of a dietary supplement. The CLA that your client produces is not a dietary ingredient under section 21 U.S.C. 321(ff)(1) of the Act. . . .

The CLA that is produced by your client is not a vitamin, mineral, or amino acid under 21 U.S.C. 321(ff)(1)(A), (B), or (D). Because it is not a plant or a physical part of a plant (*e.g.*, a leaf, stem, or root) it is not an herb or other botanical under 21 U.S.C. 321(ff)(l)(C). Nor does FDA believe that this chemical is a "dietary substance for use by man to supplement the diet by increasing the total dietary intake" under 21 U.S.C. 321(ff)(1)(E). The term "dietary substance" is not defined in the Act. FDA interprets it with its common or usual meaning. *Webster's II New Riverside University Dictionary* defines "dietary" as "of or pertaining to the diet" and "diet" as "an organism's usual food or drink." Therefore, a "dietary substance" means a substance that is commonly used as human food or drink. The statutory language "for use by man to supplement the diet by increasing the total dietary intake" supports this interpretation; and one cannot increase the total dietary intake of something that is not customarily part of the diet in the first place. Humans do not commonly use chemically manufactured or synthetic CLA as food or drink.

Moreover, synthetic CLA is not a dietary ingredient as defined by 21 U.S.C. 321(ff)(1)(F) because it is not a concentrate, metabolite, constituent, extract, or combination of any of the other types of dietary ingredients. This synthetic group of compounds cannot be obtained by concentrating, metabolizing, or combining vitamins, minerals, amino acids, botanicals, or dietary substances. Nor is the substance in question a constituent or extract of any other type of dietary ingredient. . . . Although some forms of synthetic CLA compounds may be chemically indistinguishable from naturally occurring CLA compounds, a substance that has never been physically a part of a whole cannot be a constituent or an extract of that whole, irrespective of the starting material as the source.

Further, synthetic CLA is not a constituent of a dietary substance because it is not an inherent component of anything commonly used as human food or drink. Likewise, it is not an extract of any dietary substance. Therefore, synthetically produced CLA is not a dietary ingredient under 21 U.S.C. 321(ff)(l).

. . . For the reasons discussed above, the Agency concludes that synthetic CLA . . . does not meet the definition of a dietary supplement. Introduction of such a product into interstate commerce is prohibited under 21 U.S.C. 331(a). In addition, because the Agency concluded that the subject of your notification cannot be marketed as a dietary supplement, FDA did not review the evidence of safety information you submitted on CLA. . . .

Sincerely yours,

_____

Felicia B. Satchell

NOTES

1. *"Dietary Substance."* The dietary supplement definition's references to minerals, botanicals, and amino acids at 201(ff)(1)(B)–(D) clearly embrace many substances not contained in common foodstuffs. In

the letter above, however, FDA asserts that the "catch-all" provision at 201(ff)(1)(E) ("a dietary substance for use by man to supplement the diet by increasing the total dietary intake") applies only to substances commonly used as human food or drink. The agency has advanced narrow interpretations of this provision in other contexts, as well. For example, the agency denied that products containing freeze-dried bacteria and bacterial lysates are dietary supplements. In a letter to one manufacturer, FDA stated: "These ingredients in your product . . . are not 'dietary substances' that increase the 'total dietary intake' because they cannot reasonably be viewed as part of man's usual food or drink. . . . Pathogens are not substances that are food or that are used for food." Letter from Lynn A. Larsen, Director, CFSAN Office of Special Nutritionals, Division of Programs and Enforcement Policy, to David Balzer (Nov. 15, 1999).

While this narrow interpretation of 201(ff)(1)(E) would embrace popular dietary supplement ingredients such as fish oil and garlic extract, it would exclude from the definition of "dietary supplement" products containing many other widely marketed ingredients, such as EPO, glucosamine, and chondroitin. In other contexts, however, FDA has suggested that the provision is not limited to dietary ingredients commonly used in human food or drink. For example, FDA has allowed non-botanical enzymes to be marketed as dietary supplements. Letter from James Tanner, Acting Director, CFSAN Office of Special Nutritionals, Division of Programs and Enforcement Policy, to Vic Rathi (July 30, 1996) (accepting the company's position that Enzyme–Peptidase, an enzyme derived from bacteria, is a dietary supplement ingredient.) The agency has also declined opportunities to declare that melatonin—a hormone produced in the pineal gland—is not a dietary ingredient. *See, e.g.*, Letter from Lynn A. Larsen to R. Doug Metz (Oct. 1, 1999) (denying that the company's melatonin product was a dietary supplement, but only because it was not "intended for ingestion").

2. *Synthetic Counterparts.* The letter above also asserts that synthetic CLA compounds do not qualify as dietary ingredients even if "chemically indistinguishable from naturally occurring CLA compounds." Today, FDA continues to maintain that synthetically produced equivalents of naturally occurring dietary substances are not dietary ingredients under 201(ff)(1)(E) unless they are themselves commonly used as food or drink. *See., e.g.*, Letter from Michael W. Roosevelt, Acting Director, CFSAN Office of Compliance, to USP Labs (Apr. 24, 2012) (declaring synthetic DDMA to be not a dietary ingredient). But elsewhere, FDA has stated that Coenzyme Q_{10}, a commonly synthesized substance, falls within the broad range of dietary ingredients that Congress contemplated in 201(ff)(1). 62 Fed. Reg. 49859, 49860 (Sept. 23, 1997) (quoting from the legislative history of "other nutritional substances," a precursor to "dietary ingredients"). And the agency has acknowledged new dietary ingredient notifications for some synthetic equivalents to botanical ingredients without objection. *See, e.g.,* Letter from A. Davidovich, Roche Vitamins, to CFSAN Office of Nutritional Products, Labeling, and Dietary Supplements (Mar. 21, 2001) (synthetic zeaxanthin).

3. *Interpretations of "Botanical."* FDA has embraced a broad understanding of the term "botanical." For example, the agency has stated

that fungi and algae are botanicals. 21 C.F.R. 101.4(h). In a recent draft guidance, FDA stated its current thinking of the meaning of the term "botanical or herbal" for purposes of applying the new dietary ingredient provisions: "A plant, alga, or fungus; a part of a plant, alga, or fungus (*e.g.*, bark, leaves, stems, roots, flowers, fruits, seeds, berries, or parts thereof); or an exudate (secretion) of a plant, alga, or fungus." DRAFT GUIDANCE FOR INDUSTRY: DIETARY SUPPLEMENTS: NEW DIETARY INGREDIENT NOTIFICATIONS AND RELATED ISSUES (July 2011).

4. *Metabolites*. It is not clear when a substance can properly be designated a "metabolite" of another dietary ingredient. An entire open meeting of the Dietary Supplements Subcommittee of FDA's Food Advisory Committee was devoted to this complex scientific question. *See* Summary Minutes, Meeting of the Dietary Supplements Subcommittee (Mar. 25, 2003). In the draft guidance mentioned in the previous note, FDA published its current thinking of the meaning of the terms "concentrate," "metabolite," "constituent," and "extract" in the context of the new dietary ingredient provisions. DRAFT GUIDANCE FOR INDUSTRY: DIETARY SUPPLEMENTS: NEW DIETARY INGREDIENT NOTIFICATIONS AND RELATED ISSUES (July 2011).

5. *"Intended to Supplement the Diet"*. Regardless of what type of ingredient a product contains, it is not a "dietary supplement" under section 201(ff)(1) unless it is "intended to supplement the diet." FDA has stated that products marketed as alternatives to illicit street drugs are unapproved new drugs, and not dietary supplements, even if they are composed of vitamins, minerals, herbs, other botanicals, or amino acids. In a guidance on the topic, the agency declared:

> FDA does not consider street drug alternatives to be dietary supplements. The term dietary supplement as defined in section 201(ff) of the Act means, inter alia, a product "intended to supplement the diet." While the Act does not elaborate on the meaning of this phrase, many congressional findings, set forth in the Dietary Supplement Health and Education Act of 1994, suggest that dietary supplements are intended to be used to augment the diet to promote health and reduce the risk of disease. FDA does not believe that street drug alternatives are intended to be used to augment the diet to promote health or reduce the risk of disease. Moreover, FDA considers the diet to be composed of usual food and drink that may be designed to meet specific nutritional requirements. Illicit street drugs are not food or drink, and neither they, nor alternative street drugs, can be said to supplement the diet. Rather, these products are intended to be used for recreational purposes to effect psychological states (*e.g.*, to get high, to promote euphoria, or to induce hallucinations). Accordingly, street drug alternatives are not intended to supplement the diet and are not dietary supplements.

FDA CENTER FOR DRUG EVALUATION AND RESEARCH, GUIDANCE FOR INDUSTRY: STREET DRUG ALTERNATIVES (Mar. 2000). *See also United States v. Undetermined Quantities of Articles of Drug*, 145 F. Supp. 2d 692 (D. Md. 2001) (herbs sold as alternatives to marijuana, psychotropic mushrooms, and ecstasy are not dietary supplements). The agency has referred to the 2000 policy guidance and the *Undetermined Quantities of Articles of Drug* case in issuing subsequent warning letters regarding street drug substitutes marketed as dietary supplements. *See, e.g.,* Warning Letter from Alonza E. Cruse, FDA Los Angeles District Director, to James Kirby, Senior Partner, Redux Beverages (Apr. 4, 2007) (beverage called "Cocaine" is not a dietary supplement and is an unapproved and misbranded drug).

6.   *Use of Previously Designated Drugs.* Section 201(ff)(3)(B) excludes from the definition of a dietary supplement a drug that was the subject of an investigational new drug exemption (IND), new drug application (NDA), or biologics license application (BLA) prior to its marketing as a dietary supplement. Thus, red rice yeast—which has the same active ingredient, lovastatin, as the prescription drug Mevacor—was held to be a drug and not a dietary supplement. *Pharmanex v. Shalala,* 221 F.3d 1151 (10th Cir. 2000), *rev'g* 35 F. Supp. 2d 1341 (D. Utah 1999). On the authority of section 201(ff)(3)(B), FDA took the position that nicotine, which is found naturally in various foods, is not a dietary ingredient because it was the subject of an NDA for investigation as a new drug beginning in 1987, before it was added to food or dietary supplements. Letter from Vasilios H. Frankos, Acting Director, CFSAN Office of Nutritional Products, Labeling and Dietary Supplements Division of Dietary Supplement Programs, to Joseph R. Knight (June 29, 2006).

7.   *Method of Administration.* In *United States v. Ten Cartons . . . Ener–B Nasal Gel,* the District Court found that Ener–B, a Vitamin B–12 gel designed to be applied to the inside of the nose and absorbed into the bloodstream, was a drug and not a dietary supplement because it was not "intended for ingestion," as required by section 201(ff)(2)(A). 888 F. Supp. 381, 395 (E.D.N.Y. 1995), *aff'd on other grounds,* 72 F.3d 285 (2d Cir. 1995). The court remarked that the "ordinary and plain meaning of the term 'ingestion' means to take into the stomach and gastrointestinal tract by means of enteral administration." Citing the District Court opinion in *Ener–B,* FDA later denied dietary supplement status to a melatonin product in the form of "a sublingual lozenge (to be placed under the tongue) for rapid absorption" and to an herbal throat drop. Letters from Lynn A. Larson, Director, FDA CFSAN Office of Special Nutritionals Division of Programs and Enforcement Policy, to R. Doug Metz (Oct. 1, 1999) and to Bryan J. Simmons (Nov. 4, 1999). In each instance, the agency explained that the product in question was not a dietary supplement because it was intended to deliver its contents prior to introduction into the gastrointestinal tract. Similarly, a skin cream does not qualify as a dietary supplement because it is not ingested. *United States v. Lane Labs–USA, Inc.,* 324 F. Supp. 2d 547, 569 (D.N.J. 2004). And in a 2012 warning letter to the C.E.O. of Breathable Foods, FDA made clear that the company's Aeroshot "caffeine inhaler" could not be a dietary supplement if it was in fact intended for inhalation rather than ingestion. Letter from Michael W. Roosevelt, Acting Director, FDA CFSAN Office of Compliance, to Thomas Hadfield (Mar. 5, 2012).

8.   *Combination of Drug and Dietary Supplement.* In a letter from Melinda K. Plaisier, FDA Associate Commissioner for Legislation, to Representative Dan Burton, Chairman of the House Committee on

Government Reform (Feb. 1, 2002), FDA took the position that a combination product containing a dietary supplement and an over-the-counter drug would be illegal because the added dietary ingredient becomes a drug ingredient. This position directly conflicts with the FDA position that the addition of a cosmetic ingredient to an OTC drug does not convert the cosmetic ingredient into a drug. Nevertheless, on October 28, 2008, FDA sent warning letters to Bayer HealthCare concerning two new OTC aspirin products, Bayer Women's Low Dose Aspirin + Calcium and Bayer Aspirin with Heart Advantage, both of which were labeled as combinations of a drug and a dietary supplement. In these letters, FDA took the position that "the presence of aspirin . . . renders the *entire* product a drug." Letters from Deborah M. Autor, Director, FDA CDER Office of Compliance, to Gary S. Balkema (Oct. 27, 2008) (emphasis in original).

E. COSMETICS

Section 201(i) of the FD&C Act defines "cosmetic" as "(1) articles intended to be rubbed, poured, sprinkled, or sprayed on, introduced into, or otherwise applied to the human body or any part thereof for cleansing, beautifying, promoting attractiveness, or altering the appearance, and (2) articles intended for use as a component of any such articles; except that such term shall not include soap." Cosmetics are the least intensively regulated of all the product categories under FDA's jurisdiction. There is no premarket approval requirement for any cosmetic or cosmetic ingredient, with the exception of color additives. But, like foods, cosmetics may be simultaneously classified as drugs. Moreover, because the structure/function leg of the drug definition, section 201(g)(1)(C), does not contain an exception for cosmetics, as it does for food, a cosmetic may be dual-classified as a drug even if it is a nontherapeutic product intended only to affect the structure or any function of the body. The question of when a cosmetic is also a drug is addressed in the next section of this chapter, *infra* p. 110.

Section 201(i)—the "cosmetic" definition itself—has raised relatively few interpretive questions. Even so, several features of this provision deserve further discussion.

NOTES

1.   *Odors.* FDA considers products intended to mask or prevent body odors, such as mouthwashes and underarm deodorants, to be cosmetics.

2.   *Soap Exemption.* The FD&C Act does not define "soap." FDA has defined the scope of the soap exemption by regulation. According to the agency, the exemption applies only to articles that meet the following conditions: "(1) The bulk of the nonvolatile matter in the product consists of an alkali salt of fatty acids and the detergent properties of the article are due to the alkali-fatty acid compounds; and (2) The product is labeled, sold, and represented only as soap." 23 Fed. Reg. 7483 (Sept. 26, 1958), codified at 21 C.F.R. 701.20. In *United States v. An Article of Cosmetic . . . Beacon Castile Shampoo*, 1969–1974 FDLI Jud. Rec. 149 (N.D. Ohio 1973), the court held that the claimant had the burden of proving the product fell within the soap exemption. The court acknowledged that a shampoo made from soap would fall within that exemption, but concluded that the

claimant's shampoo did not qualify because it contained a synthetic detergent.

If a product is intended not only for cleansing but also for other cosmetic uses, such as beautifying, moisturizing, or deodorizing, FDA will regulate it as a cosmetic. The exemption is thus quite narrow, and most products on the soap shelves of stores are cosmetics. A soap-like product may also be a drug if it is intended to cure, treat or prevent disease or to affect the structure or any function of the human body. It remains unclear whether simply calling a soap product "antibacterial" renders it a drug, *see infra* p. 116, note 4, but any explicit therapeutic claims indisputably place a soap product in the drug category.

    3.   *Tattoos.* FDA regulates the inks used in tattoos and permanent makeup as cosmetics and the pigments used in these inks as color additives. Office of Cosmetics & Colors Fact Sheet: *Tattoos & Permanent Makeup*, Nov. 29, 2000. FDA, however, does not regulate the actual practice of tattooing; instead, oversight is left to local laws and jurisdictions.

    4.   *Animal Cosmetics.* The FD&C Act's definition of "cosmetic" is limited to articles intended to be applied to the "human body." Products intended to cleanse or promote the attractiveness of animals thus fall outside FDA's control. *Cf. United States v. Articles of Drug for Veterinary Use . . . Goshen Laboratories, Inc.*, Food Drug Cosm. L. Rep. (CCH) ¶ 38,174 (S.D.N.Y. 1982) (claimant argued that the veterinary products involved were "canine cosmetics" not subject to the FD&C Act, but court concluded the articles were animal drugs under FDA control). By contrast, the FD&C Act's definitions of "food," "drug," and "device" (but not the definition of "biological product" in the Public Health Service Act) refer to "man or other animals."

    5.   *Cosmetic Foods.* Because breath freshening is a cosmetic effect, the line between foods and cosmetics can sometimes be elusive. For example, some dissolvable "breath strips" were once labeled as foods, whereas most are now labeled as cosmetics. FDA apparently has not voiced its opinion on the proper categorization of these products.

F. THE COSMETIC–DRUG SPECTRUM

An article may fall under the FD&C Act's definition of "drug" or "medical device" even if it has no therapeutic purpose, so long as it is "intended to affect the structure or any function of the body." FD&C Act 201(g)(1)(C) & 201(h). The definitions thus raise the question of how much, and in what way, a nontherapeutic product must be intended to alter the body to be considered a drug or device.

Just as an article may be both a "food" and a "drug," a product may simultaneously fall within the definitions of "cosmetic" and "drug" and be subject to the requirements of both categories. Cosmetics are the least intensively regulated of any of the products under FDA's jurisdiction. The agency thus has sometimes reached for greater authority over particular cosmetic products by trying to categorize them as new drugs subject to premarket review for safety and effectiveness.

1. COSMETIC CLAIMS VERSUS DRUG CLAIMS

United States v. An Article . . . Sudden Change
409 F.2d 734 (2d Cir. 1969).

■ ANDERSON, CIRCUIT JUDGE:

This is an appeal in a seizure action from an order of the United States District Court for the Eastern District of New York . . . granting summary judgment for the claimant. The seizure concerned 216 bottles of a cosmetic product called "Sudden Change" which is a clear liquid lotion consisting primarily of two ingredients: bovine albumen (15%) and distilled water (over 84%). It is meant to be applied externally to the surface of the facial skin, and it is claimed, *inter alia*, in its labeling and advertising that it will provide a "Face Lift Without Surgery." The court below described the effects of the product as follows:

> Allowed to dry on the skin, it leaves a film which (1) masks imperfections, making the skin look smoother and (2) acts mechanically to smooth and firm the skin by tightening the surface. Both effects are temporary. There is apparently no absorption by, or changes in, skin tissue resulting from its applications; it washes off.

The central issue presented in this appeal is whether Sudden Change is, within the meaning of the Federal Food, Drug and Cosmetic Act, 21 U.S.C. § 321(g)(1), a "drug." . . .

It is well settled that the intended use of a product may be determined from its label, accompanying labeling, promotional material, advertising and any other relevant source. Regardless of the actual physical effect of a product, it will be deemed a drug for purposes of the Act where the labeling and promotional claims show intended uses that bring it within the drug definition. . . .

The mere statement of this rule poses a crucial issue: by what standards are these claims to be evaluated? Or, to put it another way, what degree of sophistication or vulnerability is to be ascribed to the hypothetical potential consumer in order to understand how these claims are understood by the buying public? . . . [W]e conclude that the purposes of the Act will best be effected by postulating a consuming public which includes "the ignorant, the unthinking and the credulous. . . ."

While it is not altogether clear what standard the court below applied, the reasoning appears to assume something like a "reasonable woman" standard. Thus, the District Court assumes that the "constant exposure to puffing and extravagant claims" has induced "some immunity in the beautifiers' hyperbole" which is such that the court "cannot believe" that the potential consumer of Sudden Change "expects anything other than a possibility that she may look better." We agree that certain claims which arguably would bring the product within § 321(g)(1)(C) have so drenched the potential consumer that even the "ignorant, the unthinking and the credulous" must be presumed able to discount their promises as typical of cosmetic advertising puffery. We cannot agree, however, with the conclusion that such immunity or skepticism somehow transfers to the promise to "lift out puffs" or give a "face lift without surgery." The references to "face lift" and "surgery" carry distinctly physiological connotations, suggesting, at least to the vulnerable consumer, that the product will "affect the structure . . . of the body . . ." in some way other than merely temporarily altering the appearance. We do not accept the concept that skepticism toward familiar claims necessarily entails skepticism toward unfamiliar claims; the theory of the legislation is that someone might take the claim literally.

In other words, with the exception of those claims which have become so associated with the familiar exaggerations of cosmetics advertising that virtually everyone can be presumed to be capable of discounting them as puffery,[10] the question of whether a product is "intended to affect the structure . . . of the body of man . . ." is to be answered by considering, first, how the claim might be understood by the "ignorant, unthinking or credulous" consumer, and second, whether the claim as so understood may fairly be said to constitute a representation that the product will affect the structure of the body in some medical—or drug-type fashion, *i.e.*, in some way other than merely "altering the appearance."

We hold, therefore, that so long as Sudden Change is claimed to give a "face lift without surgery" and to "lift out puffs" it is to be deemed a drug within the meaning of 21 U.S.C. § 321(g)(1)(C). It should be understood, however, that if the claimant ceases to employ these promotional claims and avoids any others which may fairly be interpreted as claiming to affect the structure of the skin in some physiological, though temporary, way, then, assuming *arguendo* that no actual physical effect exists, the product will not be deemed a drug for purposes of the Act. While there may be merit in the cause of those who seek to require pretesting of new cosmetics, it is not for the courts to legislate such a requirement; rather it must rest in the hands of Congress to decide whether such an amendment to the statute should be enacted or not.

Reversed . . . .

■ MANSFIELD, DISTRICT JUDGE (dissenting): . . .

In view of the existence of ample authority for regulation of cosmetics, it strikes me as unnecessary, in the absence of some imminent danger to public health—and none is suggested here—for the Court to adopt new standards of construction for the purpose of determining whether an article is intended as a "drug" rather than to follow time-proven rules. Yet that is exactly what the Court does here, with the result that it opens up a new—and in my view, unnecessary—avenue for regulation of cosmetics as drugs. If Congress believes that protection of the public requires pretesting and clearance of cosmetics

---

[10] . . . We agree that the legislative history and the language of the Act require rejection of any rule which would convert all cosmetics into drugs. We believe, however, that the test which we have applied draws the necessary line while at the same time protecting the public. For example, promises that a product will "soften" or "moisturize" a woman's skin are so thoroughly familiar that constant exposure can be presumed to have induced sufficient immunity even in our hypothetical vulnerable consumer (this assumes, *arguendo*, that these promises have exactly the same degree of drug-type connotations as the "face lift without surgery" claim—an assumption which we reject).

by the Food and Drug Administration . . . and that their components be listed on the label, it has the power to act. I do not think the Court should do so by a process of tortuous construction. . . .

It may well be that the existence of fraud upon consumers of such products (whether drugs or cosmetics) should depend upon whether "the ignorant, the unthinking and credulous" would be deceived. The issue before us, however, is not whether consumers may be defrauded by the labelling [sic] and enclosures used in connection with the sale of "Sudden Change." The issue is whether the product must be classified as a "drug" which must be pre-tested, cleared and bear a label listing its components. Since that issue turns upon whether the article is "*intended* to affect the structure of the body" (emphasis added), it seems to me that the "gullible" woman standard is both irrelevant and unnecessary, and that the standard should be whether a reasonable person would construe the labeling and advertising as showing that the product was so intended. . . .

NOTES

1. *Parallel Cases.* In *United States v. An Article . . . "Line Away,"* 415 F.2d 369 (3d Cir. 1969), the FDA seized as an unapproved and misbranded new drug a product called "Line Away Temporary Wrinkle Smoother." In labeling and advertising, the manufacturer declared that this product was "not a face lift, not a treatment" and that it "contains no hormones or harmful drugs." The court nonetheless upheld the seizure, noting: "[T]he repeated statements that Line Away is made in a 'pharmaceutical laboratory' and packaged under 'biologically aseptic conditions' imply that the product itself is a pharmaceutical. Characterizing the lotion as 'super-active' and 'amazing,' creating a 'tingling sensation' when 'at work,' 'tightening' the skin and 'discouraging new wrinkles from forming' strongly reinforces the impression that this is a therapeutic product, the protein content of which has a tonic or otherwise wholesome physiological effect on the skin itself." *Id.* at 372. But in *United States v. An Article . . . "Helene Curtis Magic Secret . . .",* 331 F. Supp. 912 (D. Md. 1971), a district court held that Helene Curtis's wrinkle smoother was a cosmetic and not a drug, despite its claims of "astringent activity" and "tightening skin." The court concluded: "[T]he promotional claims made for 'Magic Secret' are less exaggerated than those reported in *Line Away* and *Sudden Change.* It cannot be said that they carry the same drug connotations as found by the Second and Third Circuits." *Id.* at 917.

2. *"Vulnerable Consumer" Versus "Reasonable Consumer."* Neither FDA nor any court has ever explicitly abandoned the *Sudden Change* majority's "vulnerable consumer" approach in the specific context of assessing the line between a cosmetic claim and drug claim. However, as discussed in greater detail *infra* at p. 386, note 1, FDA in 2002 embraced the "reasonable consumer" standard in a different context—the assessment of whether labeling is "misleading." 67 Fed. Reg. 78002, 78003–04 (Dec. 20, 2002). The agency would be unlikely to apply a more protective standard when determining "intended use" than when interpreting "misleading." It is thus probably safe to assume that today FDA, as a formal matter, analyzes the difference between cosmetic claims and drug claims through

the lens of a "reasonable consumer." As a practical matter, this possible change in standard has not been reflected in any reduction in the rigor with which FDA deems even quite modest cosmetic claims to be drug claims.

Attempting to formulate a hard and fast rule differentiating between cosmetic claims and drug claims is virtually impossible. Some cosmetics are intended merely to color some part of the body in order to promote attractiveness, and they present no problem of proper classification. On the other end of the scale, some products are represented to effect a physiological change in the body, and these clearly fall into the drug category as well as the cosmetic category. But in between these two extremes is the difficult area of judgment—the cosmetics that claim to promote attractiveness through a slight, and usually temporary, physical but not physiological, effect upon the skin.

Beginning in April 1987, FDA sent regulatory letters to dozens of cosmetic manufacturers alleging that products with "wrinkle remover" claims were illegal new drugs. A series of meetings and correspondence between an industry coalition and FDA on this matter was abruptly terminated on November 19, 1987 by the following letter from the FDA Associate Commissioner for Regulatory Affairs. This letter represents the agency's view of the line between separating cosmetics from cosmetic drugs to the current day.

Letter From John M. Taylor, FDA Associate Commissioner for Regulatory Affairs, to Various Attorneys Representing the Cosmetic Industry
November 19, 1987.

Re: Cosmetic Regulatory Letters

We have carefully reviewed your letter of September 11, 1987. We recognize that you and the other attorneys who participated in the drafting of this letter tried in good faith to devise a set of principles for distinguishing cosmetic products from drug products. . . . After fully considering your letter, however, we find that the principles that you suggest would permit manufacturers to make drug claims on products that would be regulated as cosmetics. Such a situation would be inconsistent with the Food, Drug, and Cosmetic Act (the Act). Therefore, we cannot accept the great majority of these principles.

. . . We consider a claim that a product will affect the body in some physiological way to be a drug claim, even if the claim is that the effect is only temporary. Such a claim constitutes a representation that the product is intended to affect the structure or function of the body and thus makes the product a drug under 21 U.S.C. 321(g)(1)(C). Therefore, we consider most of the anti-aging and skin physiology claims that you outline in your letter to be drug claims. For example, claims that a product "counteracts," "retards," or "controls" aging or the aging process, as well as claims that a product will "rejuvenate," "repair," or "renew" the skin, are drug claims because they can be fairly understood as claims that a function of the body, or that the structure of the body, will be affected by the product. For this reason also, all of the examples that you use to allege an effect within the epidermis as the basis for a temporary beneficial effect on wrinkles, lines, or fine lines are unacceptable. A claim such as "molecules absorb . . . and expand, exerting upward pressure to 'lift' wrinkles upward" is a claim for an inner, structural change.

. . . [W]e would not object to claims that products will temporarily improve the appearance of such outward signs of aging. The label of such products should state that the product is intended to cover up the signs of aging, to improve the appearance by adding color or luster to skin, or otherwise to affect the appearance through physical means.

In addition, any product that makes a sunscreen claim, or that makes certain skin protection claims is a drug. These claims are evidence that the product is intended to mitigate or to prevent a disease, and that it is a drug under 21 U.S.C. 321(g)(1)(B). . . .

However, we would consider a product that claims to improve or to maintain temporarily the appearance or the feel of the skin to be a cosmetic. For example, a product that claims to moisturize or soften the skin is a cosmetic.

We recognize that advances in science and technology enable the cosmetic and health care industries to introduce skin care and beauty aid products to the public. Some formulas for these products may safely achieve both drug and cosmetic effects. Notwithstanding this fact, . . . [p]roducts that affect the structure and the function of the body in the ways that you describe . . . are drugs and must be scrutinized by FDA in the manner prescribed by the Act. Any additional cosmetic benefit to consumers that may be derived from such drug products may be communicated through appropriate labeling.

The physiological effects that you allege in . . . your proposal reinforce our concern. Products that actually affect the structure and any function of the body in the many ways you describe surely require a close and careful scrutiny by FDA to assure their safety. . . .

Sincerely,

John M. Taylor

NOTES

1. *Recent Warning Letters on Antiwrinkle Products.* After a lull, FDA resumed taking action against antiwrinkle products in the mid-2000s. It issued warning letters to two manufacturers of skin creams, stating that the companies were selling unapproved drugs. *See Warning Letters Address Claims Made for Topical Skincare Preparations,* Office of Cosmetics and Colors Press Release (Mar. 1, 2005). The objectionable claims cited by FDA with respect to one of these products, Collagen5, included: "Collagen5™ is proven to reduce deep wrinkles up to . . . 70%," "Stimulates your skin's own collagen building network," "Reduces deep wrinkles from within the skin's surface," and "Visible results that won't fade away." Warning Letter from Alonza E. Cruse, Director, Los Angeles District, FDA, to University Medical Products USA, Inc. (Jan. 22, 2004). The other warning letter cited (among many other statements) the manufacturers' reference to "Pal–KTTKS solution's effectiveness at reducing the appearance of fine lines and

wrinkles." Warning Letter from B. Belinda Collins, Director, Denver District Office, FDA, to Basic Research, LLC (Jan. 14, 2005). It is unclear why FDA took issue with this particular claim; perhaps it objected to the manufacturer's failure to declare that the effects were only "temporary."

In a 2011 warning letter to the manufacturer of antiwrinkle products, FDA listed, among numerous more obviously problematic claims, the statement: "I have been using your wrinkle cream for six weeks now. The skin around my eyes . . . [has] less wrinkles." Letter from Michael W. Roosevelt, Acting Director, FDA CFSAN Office of Compliance, to Joe Adams, JabaLabs, LLC (Mar. 1, 2011). And in a 2012 letter to Avon, the agency objected to a variety of statements on the company's website regarding its line of Anew® products, including, for example, the following: "The at-home answer to wrinkle-filling injections. Start rebuilding collagen in just 48 hours." "[H]elp tighten the connections between skin's layers." "Designed to boost Activin, ANEW's Activinol Technology helps reactivate skin's repair process to recreate fresh skin & help dramatically reverse visible wrinkles." Letter from Roosevelt to Andre Jung, CEO, Avon Products (Oct. 5, 2012).

2.   *Thigh Creams.* The warning letters discussed above in Note 1 also informed companies that products claiming to combat cellulite, stretch marks, and breast sag and shrinkage and to reduce thigh circumference and overall weight were unapproved drugs. Warning Letter from Alonza E. Cruse, Director, Los Angeles District, FDA, to University Medical Products USA, Inc. (Jan. 22, 2004); Warning Letter from B. Belinda Collins, Director, Denver District, FDA, to Basic Research, LLC. FDA has suggested that it views all thigh creams promoted for cellulite reduction as drugs. *See Thigh Creams*, Office of Cosmetics and Colors Fact Sheet (Feb. 24, 2000) ("Thigh creams may more appropriately be classified as drugs under the Food, Drug, and Cosmetic Act since removal or reduction of cellulite affects the 'structure or function' of the body.")

3.   *Hair Growth Products.* In *United States v. Kasz Enterprises, Inc.,* the U.S. District Court found that the distributor's products, promoted for hair growth and hair loss prevention, were drugs under the FD&C Act. The court rejected the defendant's assertion that the government had to demonstrate that a product be intended both to treat disease and to affect the structure or function of the body. 855 F. Supp. 534, 540 (D.R.I. 1994). In *FTC v. Pantron I Corp.*, 33 F.3d 1088 (9th Cir. 1994), the Court of Appeals held that "representations that the product will cause the body to generate new hair in parts of the scalp where no hair currently exists" render a product a drug under the identical structure/function provision of the "drug" definition in the Federal Trade Commission Act, 15 U.S.C. 55(c).

4.   *Antimicrobial Deodorant Products.* Describing a product as a deodorant is indisputably a cosmetic claim, and deodorant products that merely mask odor with perfumes are clearly cosmetics and not drugs. But what of products that attack odors with antimicrobial ingredients? It was long assumed that a mouthwash or deodorant soap could make a claim like "kills germs that cause odor" without becoming a drug for regulatory purposes. In the early 1990s, however, the preambles to the tentative final monographs for various types of OTC antiseptic drug products firmly stated

that claims of this sort would subject a product to regulation as a drug. 56 Fed. Reg. 33644, 33648–49 (July 22, 1991) (first aid antiseptics); 59 Fed. Reg. 6084, 6088–89 (Feb. 9, 1994) (oral antiseptics); 59 Fed. Reg. 31402, 31440 (June 17, 1994) (health care antiseptics). *But see E.R. Squibb & Sons, Inc. v. Bowen*, 870 F.2d 678, 682 (D.C. Cir. 1989) (a claim that a product suppresses the growth of a fungus in the body does not implicate the drug definition's structure/function provision, in part because "it is questionable whether a drug that acts only upon non-human organisms that happen to reside within the human body can properly be understood as affecting the 'body of man'").

5.   *Approved Cosmetic Drugs and Devices.* In recent years, FDA has approved new drug applications (NDAs) and device premarket approval applications (PMAs) for antiwrinkle products. Renova (tretinoin) is a prescription drug approved to reduce fine wrinkles, discoloration, and roughness on facial skin. BOTOX Cosmetic (Botulinum Toxin Type A) is a prescription drug approved to treat frown lines between the eyebrows. The agency has approved collagen and hyaluronic acid gel, both injectable antiwrinkle products, as medical devices, as well as lasers making antiwrinkle claims. The agency has approved NDAs for two types of hair regrowth products: Rogaine (minoxidil), a topical solution, and Propecia (finasteride), a drug in pill form. Most recently, FDA approved an NDA for Latisse, an eyelash lengthener and thickener. *See infra* p. 119.

6.   *Other Products on the Cosmetic–Drug Line.* There are a variety of common claims that can turn a product with cleansing or beautifying uses into a drug in addition to, or instead of, a cosmetic. The following is a list of important examples of this phenomenon, based on decades of FDA literature and practice:

A suntan product is a cosmetic but a sunscreen product is a drug.

A deodorant is a cosmetic but an antiperspirant is a drug.

A shampoo is a cosmetic but an antidandruff shampoo is a drug.

A toothpaste is a cosmetic but an anticaries toothpaste is a drug.

A skin exfoliant is a cosmetic but a skin peel is a drug.

A mouthwash is a cosmetic but an antigingivitis mouthwash is a drug.

A hair bulking product is a cosmetic but a hair growth product is a drug.

A skin product to hide acne is a cosmetic but an antiacne product is a drug.

An antibacterial deodorant soap is a cosmetic but an antibacterial anti-infective soap is a drug.

A skin moisturizer is a cosmetic but a wrinkle remover is a drug.

A lip softener is a cosmetic but a product for chapped lips is a drug.

Peter Barton Hutt, *The Legal Distinction in the United States Between a Cosmetic and a Drug*, in COSMECEUTICALS: DRUGS VS. COSMETICS 223, 228 (Peter Elsner & Howard I. Maibach, eds., 2000).

2. THE "ACTIVE INGREDIENT" APPROACH

Recent developments have reinforced many of these traditional positions taken by the agency. With regard to some products, however, FDA has manifested an inclination to categorize articles containing pharmacologically active ingredients as drugs even when their manufacturers make only cosmetic claims.

FDA scientists recognized very early that all cosmetics penetrate the skin and thus affect the body. As one wrote: "[T]here are few if any substances which are not absorbed through the intact skin, even though the idea is prevalent that the skin is a relatively effective barrier to its environment." H.O. Calvery, *Safeguarding Foods and Drugs in Wartime*, 32 AM. SCIENTIST No. 2, at 103, 119 (1944). There are some skin care products marketed as cosmetics, however, that clearly have more significant effects on the body than do traditional cosmetics. These products are often referred to as "cosmeceuticals." Although FDA does not itself assign the word "cosmeceutical" any legal or regulatory significance, the agency recognizes on its website that cosmetic manufacturers use the term "to refer to cosmetic products that have medicinal or drug-like benefits."

When discussing the term "cosmeceutical" on its website, the FDA remarks, "If a product has drug properties, it must be approved as a drug." This statement is one of several instances in which the agency has suggested that the presence of an ingredient with pharmacological effects may render a product a drug, regardless of the claims made by the manufacturer. In 1996, John Bailey, the Director of FDA's Office of Cosmetics and Colors, stated, "If an active ingredient is present in a therapeutic concentration, the product is a drug, even if that product does not claim to produce the effect that will result from the action of the therapeutically effective ingredient." Anita H. Shaw, *The News in Skin Care*, SOAP–COSM.–CHEM. SPECIALTIES, Oct. 1, 1996, at 72. More recently, Michael Landa, the FDA CFSAN Director, took a slightly less aggressive position before a Congressional committee, testifying that many cosmeceuticals "are advertised as containing 'active ingredients,' which, by virtue of the ingredients themselves or the claims made for the product, may cause the product to be classified under the FD&C Act as a drug." Michael M. Landa, "Examining the Current State of Cosmetics," Testimony before the Subcommittee on Health of the Committee on Energy and Commerce, U.S. House of Representatives (Mar. 27, 2012).

In the world of "cosmeceuticals," the question of whether the mere presence of active ingredients can establish intent has been raised with regard to various types of products, as discussed below.

Hormone–Containing Cosmetics

In 1993, FDA proposed a rule declaring that any cosmetic product containing more than a specified amount of the hormones pregnenolone acetate or progesterone was an unapproved drug, regardless of manufacturer claims. The agency observed that, above these amounts, the ingredients affected the structure or function of the body. 58 Fed Reg. 47,611 (Sept. 9, 1993). The agency also proposed banning "natural estrogens" from cosmetics altogether, unless manufacturers provided adequate data on the safety and exact chemical identity of such estrogens. "[T]he agency concludes at this time that any use of natural estrogens in cosmetic products makes the product an unapproved new drug. The conclusion is based on available data stating conclusively that at some levels the ingredients affect the structure or function of the body, and a concomitant lack of data establishing at what level, if any, the drug effect ceases." Finally, FDA also proposed that the use of the word "hormone" in the labeling or ingredient statement of any cosmetic product was an implied drug claim. In 2004, the agency withdrew this proposed rule but remarked that "this withdrawal neither affirms nor rejects statements contained in the preamble [to the proposed rule]." 69 Fed. Reg. 68833 (Nov. 26, 2004). Although the rule was never finalized, FDA did finalize a drug regulation, proposed simultaneously, providing that the use of the word "hormone" in the labeling or ingredient statement of any topically applied product is an implied drug claim. 58 Fed. Reg. 47610 (Sept. 9, 1993), codified at 21 C.F.R. 310.530(a).

Alpha Hydroxy Acids

Alpha hydroxy acids (AHAs) are chemicals that cause the skin to lose its outer layer. Manufacturers of cosmetics containing AHAs claim their products will smooth fine lines, reduce spots, and improve skin condition in general. In a 1994 speech, FDA official John Bailey stated: "In the final analysis, it is well established that AHAs exert an effect on the skin. I don't think that there is any doubt that, under some conditions of formulation and use, AHA containing products are affecting the structure and function of the body and that they should be regulated as drugs." *Quoted in* Jacqueline A. Greff, *Regulation of Cosmetics That Are Also Drugs*, 51 FOOD DRUG COSM. L.J. 243, 257 (1997). Nonetheless, FDA has not, to this point, charged a manufacturer with selling an unapproved drug based solely on the fact that the product contains AHAs. It has addressed safety issues raised by AHA-containing skin care products based solely on its authority over cosmetics. *See* 70 Fed. Reg. 1721 (Jan. 10, 2005) (announcing availability of final guidance advising manufacturers of AHA-containing cosmetics to label them so as to alert consumers of the need to limit sun exposure and apply sunscreen). For further discussion on AHAs, see Laura A. Heymann, *The Cosmetic/Drug Dilemma: FDA Regulation of Alpha–Hydroxy Acids*, 52 FOOD & DRUG L.J. 357 (1997).

Eyelash Lengthener

In 2008, FDA approved a prescription drug, Latisse®, to treat eyelash hyoptrichosis (inadequate growth) by making eyelashes longer, thicker and darker. In 2011, the agency sent a warning letter to Lifetech Resources, which sold, as cosmetics, products claiming to lengthen and thicken eyelashes and eyebrows. The agency could have based its conclusion that these products were unapproved drugs solely on explicit structure/function claims such as "After 84 days of daily use, RapidLash induced a significant increase in the length of eyelashes." Instead, FDA went further and stated that even assertions concerning only the appearance of eyelashes and eyebrows were structure/function claims because of the presence of an active ingredient:

> As currently formulated, [the products] contain the active ingredient isopropyl cloprostenate. Isopropyl cloprostenate is a synthetic prostaglandin analog in the same class of compounds as

the active ingredients in FDA-approved drugs indicated to lower intraocular pressure in glaucoma patients and to treat hypotrichosis of the eyelashes. Prostaglandin analogs are well known to have an effect on the structure or function of the body. The presence of the prostaglandin analog, isopropyl cloprostenate, along with appearance claims such as "enhance the appearance of your lashes and brows," "fuller healthier-looking lashes," and "fuller healthier-looking brows" indicate that your products are intended to affect the structure or function of the body. Accordingly, "RapidLash", "NeuLash", and "NeuveauBrow" are drugs as defined by section 201(g)(1)(C) of the Act.

Warning Letter from Alonza E. Cruse, Los Angeles District Director, FDA, to Richard Carieri, Lifetech Resources (Apr. 18, 2011).

NOTES

1.   *Tanning Aids.* When issuing its tentative final monograph for sunscreen drug products, FDA stated unambiguously that "a product containing a sunscreen ingredient, even when labeled solely as a tanning aid, is both intended and understood to be a sunburn preventative. Such a product, therefore, is a drug under the act." 58 Fed. Reg. 28194, 28204 (May 12, 1993). Perhaps because of the absence of such products on the current market, FDA did not address this issue at all when it promulgated the final sunscreen monograph. 76 Fed. Reg. 35620 (June 17, 2011).

2.   *Pets Smellfree.* While maintaining that antimicrobial deodorant claims were drug claims with respect to OTC antiseptic drug product, FDA explicitly disclaimed any intention to regulate deodorant products without such claims as drugs merely because they contained antimicrobial ingredients. 56 Fed. Reg. 33644, 33648 (July 22, 1991); 59 Fed. Reg. 6084, 6088 (Feb. 9, 1994). About the same time, however, FDA initiated a seizure action against a product called Pets Smellfree. The agency contended that the product, a pet food additive containing a subtherapeutic dose of an antibiotic, was an adulterated and misbranded animal drug. The manufacturer claimed the product "stops those awful odors associated with feces, urine, gas and BAD BREATH." *United States v. Undetermined Quantities of Bottles of . . . "Pets Smellfree"*, 1991 WL 11666517 (D. Utah 1991). The District Court accepted the company's argument that the product was not a drug, but the Court of Appeals reversed. *United States v. Undetermined Quantities of Bottles of . . . "Pets Smellfree"*, 22 F.3d 235 (10th Cir. 1994). Interestingly, the Court of Appeals did not refer to even one instance in which the manufacturer mentioned the product's antibacterial properties. Instead, the court seemed to hold that Pets Smellfree could properly be deemed a drug simply because of common knowledge that bacterial contamination causes those odors the product claimed to stop. *Id.* 239–40.

3.   *OTC Drug Review.* As discussed in Chapter 7, the Over-the-Counter (OTC) Drug Review is the primary process by which the agency has assessed the safety and effectiveness of active ingredients in OTC drug products. In this context, the relationship between the Act's definitions of "cosmetic" and "drug" has frequently been at issue. The agency has frequently evaded the question of whether a particular use of a substance is

solely a cosmetic use or also a drug use by simply restricting the use of the substance in both cosmetics and drugs. *E.g.*, 21 C.F.R. 250.250(d) & (c) (limiting the use of hexacholorophene in OTC drugs and cosmetics). *Cf.* 21 C.F.R. 310.545(a)(17) (skin-bleaching OTC drug products containing ammoniated mercury are not generally recognized as safe and effective), 700.13 (mercury-containing skin-bleaching agents are drugs as well as cosmetics and are misbranded and adulterated).

G. EXPLORING THE OUTER LIMITS OF THE DRUG AND DEVICE DEFINITIONS

1. COSMETIC DEVICES

The section above on the cosmetic-drug spectrum discussed the categorization of products intended to cleanse, beautify, or promote attractiveness. Some articles intended for cosmetic use operate through physical, rather than chemical, action and thus raise similar issues with respect to the device definition. As with cosmetic drugs, the question of whether a cosmetic device is a "device" under the FD&C Act hinges on how much, and in what way, the article is "intended to affect the structure or any function of the body." FD&C Act 201(h)(3).

FDA does not consider most nonmechanical household cosmetic implements to be "devices" under the Act. The following products, for example, fall outside the device requirements unless they make medical claims: toothpicks, hair brushes, combs, nail files, nail clippers, nail scissors, razors, tweezers, and loofah sponges (used to exfoliate the skin). On the other hand, FDA regulates breast implants and chin prostheses as medical devices, regardless of whether they are intended to be used for reconstructive or cosmetic purposes. 21 C.F.R. 878.3530, 3540, 3550. In addition, the agency treats collagen used to correct wrinkles and acne scars as a medical device, defined as "dermal collagen implants for aesthetic use." *See* PMA Approval for CosmoDerm 1 Human–Based Collagen, CosmoDerm 2 Human–Based Collagen, and CosmoPlast Human–Based Collagen (Mar. 11, 2003). FDA also treats tanning lamps, epilators (used for hair removal), and tongue scrapers (used to treat bad breath) as medical devices. 21 C.F.R. 878.5350 ("needle-type epilator"); 878.5360 ("tweezer-type epilator"); 868.4635 ("ultraviolet lamp for tanning"); 872.6855 ("manual toothbrushes," which is how FDA categorizes tongue scrapers).

Decorative contact lenses are products that do not correct vision but change the apparent color of the iris, seem to add a design to it, or give the eye a nonhuman or otherwise abnormal appearance. They present the same significant risks of eye injury that corrective contact lenses do. Corrective contact lenses are regulated as prescription medical devices, and it had long been assumed that noncorrective lenses were devices, as well. In 2002, however, Daniel Troy, the FDA Chief Counsel, informed the agency's Center for Devices and Radiological Health (CDRH) that he was considering declaring that noncorrective decorative contact lenses are not medical devices. Megan Garvey, *Health Concerns Tinge Use of Cosmetic Lenses*, L.A. TIMES, Aug. 26, 2002, at 1. This information motivated California Congressman Henry Waxman, the ranking minority member of the House of Representatives

Committee on Government Reform, to write the following letter to Tommy Thompson, the Secretary of Health and Human Services.

Letter From Rep. Henry A. Waxman to Tommy Thompson, Secretary of Health and Human Services

August 26, 2002.

... I am writing to alert you to a plan apparently set in motion by the Chief Counsel of the Food and Drug Administration (FDA) to reclassify colored contact lenses that do not correct vision as cosmetics instead of medical devices, essentially deregulating these products. Under current law, manufacturers of colored lenses must meet federal standards of hygiene and sterility and can sell their products only with a prescription. FDA's new plan, however, would eliminate these rules, make colored lenses available over-the-counter without adequate directions for safe use, and depend on an underfunded cosmetics enforcement division with limited safety authority to protect consumers. It would also establish a precedent that could lead to the deregulation of many more potentially hazardous prescription drugs and devices.

Because poor-quality or misused contact lenses can cause severe eye infections, painful corneal disease, and even blindness, the FDA plan virtually guarantees serious medical complications.... Ophthalmologists and optometrists find no justification to treat colored lenses differently from corrective contact lenses. I urge you to intervene personally and stop what is a legally unsound and medically dangerous policy....

Contact lenses all qualify as medical devices under the third part of the [medical device definition at section 201(h)], as a product that is "intended to affect the structure or any function of the body of man." Lenses unavoidably alter the structure of the body by profoundly altering the biology of the eye. As one leading ophthalmology textbook states:

A contact lens may be considered to be an optical patch and bandage. As a patch it reduces the availability of oxygen to and the dissipation of carbon dioxide from the cornea. As a bandage it creates pressure on the underlying tissues and reduces wetting of the ocular surface and dissipation of material from between the contact lens and the cornea.

These effects are unavoidable and foreseeable. Any manufacturer of contact lenses that intends for users to place the products in the eye must also intend for these effects to occur.

This longstanding and fair reading of the law, however, has apparently been rejected by the Chief Counsel of FDA, Daniel Troy. Mr. Troy appears to believe that a product is only a "medical device" if it is marketed expressly as something that will affect the structure or function of the body. His argument seems to be that since colored noncorrective contact lenses are not marketed as something to correct a problem (like poor vision), these products cannot be classified as medical devices.

This reasoning is both wrong and dangerous. It is wrong because of legislative history, administrative precedent, and legal precedent, including cases in which courts have acknowledged FDA's ability to regulate products on the basis of evidence other than express marketing claims. Indeed, two such cases have expressly found that colored noncorrective contact lenses are medical devices. It is dangerous because of its logical consequence. If a medical device or a drug (which is defined using similar terms) must be expressly marketed as a treatment to fall under the FDCA, then manufacturers can simply use their marketing claims to evade regulation altogether. Breast implants and collagen injections marketed for aesthetic appeal and condoms marketed for pleasure would not be medical devices. Botox marketed for cosmetic purposes would not be a drug. A company might even attempt to market valium as "fun" to evade drug regulation. . . .

NOTES

1.   *Subsequent Events.* In April 2003, FDA officially stated that it considered noncorrective decorative contact lenses to be cosmetics, but not devices. *See* GUIDANCE FOR FDA STAFF ON SAMPLING OR DETENTION WITHOUT PHYSICAL EXAMINATION OF DECORATIVE CONTACT LENSES (Import Alert 86–10); 68 Fed. Reg. 16520, 16521 (Apr. 4, 2003). Subsequently, Rep. Waxman—with support from the major manufacturers of colored lenses, advocacy organizations dedicated to eye health and safety, and eye health professionals—cosponsored legislation requiring FDA to regulate decorative contact lenses as medical devices. In November 2005, Congress amended the FD&C Act by adding a new subsection 520(n), "Regulation of Contact Lens [sic] as Devices." This new provision provides: "All contact lenses shall be deemed to be devices under section 201(h)." 119 Stat. 2119. It also, however, declares: "Paragraph (1) shall not be construed as bearing on or being relevant to the question of whether any product other than a contact lens is a device as defined by section 201(h) or a drug as defined by section 201(g)."

2.   *Stretching the Definition of "Cosmetic"?* It is also interesting to consider whether FDA was justified in determining that decorative contact lenses fall within the definition of "cosmetic." The requirement that a cosmetic be "rubbed, poured, sprinkled, or sprayed on, introduced into, or otherwise applied to the human body" arguably excludes many devices and device-like implements from the definition, despite their cosmetic uses. Indeed, prior to the passage of the FD&C Act, a Senate report considering this language declared, "[T]he definition of the term cosmetic does not include devices. . . ." S. Rep. No. 361, 74th Cong., 1st Sess. 3 (1935). Nevertheless, until the early 1960s, FDA, on rare occasions, took legal action against household devices such as hair brushes, stockings, and toothpicks under the cosmetic provisions of the Act. Between the early 1960s and the early 2000s, the agency generally declined to assert jurisdiction over such products, although it never explicitly disclaimed its authority to classify them as cosmetics. In 2003, when FDA asserted that decorative contact lenses were cosmetics, it observed: "Decorative contact lenses are articles intended to be introduced into the eye, which is a part of the body, to beautify the wearer, promote the attractiveness of the wearer, or alter the wearer's appearance. . . . The fact that contact lenses are

'devices' in the colloquial sense does not preclude cosmetic status under the act. FDA has previously determined that section 201(i) of the act applies to appearance-enhancing devices such as wigs, hair brushes, stockings and toothpicks." 68 Fed. Reg. 16520, 16521 (Apr. 4, 2003).

2. COMMON SENSE LIMITS?

FDA's effort in the 1990s to regulate tobacco products as drug-delivery devices raised fascinating issues concerning the definitions of "device" and "drug," which the agency explored at length in the preambles to the proposed and final rules. *See* 60 Fed. Reg. 41314 (Aug. 16, 1995); 61 Fed. Reg. 44396 (Aug. 28, 1996). We have already mentioned FDA's expansive approach to establishing the "intended use" of cigarettes and smokeless tobacco in the absence of representations by the manufacturers. *Supra* p. 96. Another important interpretive issue was whether there are unstated common sense limitations on the categories of "drug" and "device" as defined by the FD&C Act.

As discussed at the beginning of this chapter, courts use a "common sense" approach in interpreting the FD&C Act's definition of "food." The circular brevity of that definition leaves them with little other choice. By contrast, the more detailed definitions of "drug" and "device" are less obvious candidates for the imposition of implied limitations. However, the plain language of these definitions encompasses an enormous range of products not traditionally viewed as being within FDA's authority. This is particularly true of the definition of "device," which embraces products that do not act primarily through chemical action or metabolization. As the tobacco manufacturers pointed out repeatedly in attacking FDA's jurisdiction over its products, the device definition, applied literally, would include guns and ammunition, thermal pajamas, air conditioners, scuba diving gear, automobile airbags, and roller coasters. The industry thus argued that a product could be treated as a device only if its intended effects on structure or function were "therapeutic," "medical," or "beneficial." *See* 61 Fed. Reg. 44619, 44674–75 (Aug. 28, 1996). FDA emphatically opposed reading such limitations into the statute. The agency also observed that, in any event, tobacco products achieve their effects pharmacologically and are thus indistinguishable from products that the agency has traditionally regulated as drugs and devices. *Id.* at 44675–85.

The federal district court hearing the challenge to the tobacco rule rejected the industry's argument that the structure/function provisions must be construed narrowly to avoid absurd implications for other types of products. The court remarked that a statute's scope "is not to be judicially narrowed . . . by envisioning extreme possible applications." *Coyne Beahm v. FDA*, 966 F. Supp. 1374, 1393 (M.D.N.C. 1997) (quoting *United States v. Sullivan*, 332 U.S. 689, 694 (1948)). Ultimately, however, the Supreme Court ruled for the tobacco industry without reaching the issue of the precise meaning of "affect the structure or any function of the body." *FDA v. Brown & Williamson Tobacco Corp.*, 529 U.S. 120 (2000) (excerpted *infra* p. 141). Justice Breyer addressed the issue in his dissent, however:

> . . . Taken literally, [the structure/function] definition might include everything from room air conditioners to thermal pajamas.

The companies argue that, to avoid such a result, the meaning of "drug" or "device" should be confined to medical or therapeutic products, narrowly defined.

The companies may well be right that the statute should not be read to cover room air conditioners and winter underwear. But I do not agree that we must accept their proposed limitation. For one thing, such a cramped reading contravenes the established purpose of the statutory language. For another, the companies' restriction would render the other two "drug" definitions superfluous. *See* 21 U.S.C. §§ 321(g)(1)(A), (g)(1)(B) (covering articles in the leading pharmacology compendia and those "intended for use in the diagnosis, cure, mitigation, treatment, or prevention of disease").

Most importantly, the statute's language itself supplies a different, more suitable, limitation: that a "drug" must be a *chemical* agent. The FDCA's "device" definition states that an article which affects the structure or function of the body is a "device" only if it "does *not* achieve its primary intended purposes through chemical action within . . . the body," and "is *not* dependent upon being metabolized for the achievement of its primary intended purposes." § 321(h) (emphasis added). One can readily infer from this language that at least an article that *does* achieve its primary purpose through chemical action within the body and that *is* dependent upon being metabolized is a "drug," provided that it otherwise falls within the scope of the "drug" definition. And one need not hypothesize about air conditioners or thermal pajamas to recognize that the chemical nicotine, an important tobacco ingredient, meets this test. . . .

Id. at 168–69 (Breyer, J., dissenting).

Breyer's opinion was a dissent, however, so the question of whether any unstated limits on the definition of "device" exist remains an open one. In the following 2002 letter, FDA Chief Counsel Daniel Troy—who had represented Brown & Williamson in its challenge to the agency's regulation of cigarettes—firmly embraced the notion that the device definition encompasses consumer products only if they are marketed with claims of therapeutic or medical utility. He also advanced a narrow interpretation of what types of evidence can establish "intended use."

Letter From Daniel E. Troy, FDA Chief Counsel, to Jeffrey N. Gibbs

October 17, 2002.

. . . This responds to your letters concerning Applied Digital Solutions (ADS)'s two separate written requests submitted to the Center for Devices and Radiological Health under Section 513(g) of the Federal Food, Drug, and Cosmetic Act (FD&C Act) requesting a determination that the VeriChip is not a medical device under the FD&C Act for the intended uses described in the requests. Your requests cover two different intended uses of the product. The first is for use of the VeriChip in health information applications ("health information VeriChip"). The second is for security, financial, and personal identification\safety applications ("personal ID\security

VeriChip"). For the reasons discussed below, FDA believes that the health information VeriChip is a medical device subject to FDA's jurisdiction. FDA agrees, however, that the personal ID/security VeriChip is not covered by the FD&C Act.

Background

Since 1986, Digital Angel Corporation, which is working with VeriChip Corporation, has sold more than 20 million implantable RFID transponders for animals. . . . The transponders provide access to information necessary to identify the animal.

In January of 1984, the Center for Veterinary Medicine (CVM) within FDA issued a letter to the manufacturer of this product stating: ". . . The device does not have a medical\therapeutic function. Therefore, we have no objection to marketing of this identification device for use in animals." . . .

ADS has determined to market in the United States a version of the microminiature transponder, known by the trade name "VeriChip," for a variety of uses in human beings. We understand from ADS that the VeriChip is a microminiature transponder that is encapsulated in medical grade glass that may be inserted by hypodermic needle under the skin of the upper arm in humans. The chip\transponder stores a unique identification number only. A small, handheld introducer is used to place the chip subcutaneously. A small, handheld battery-powered scanner can read the identification number on the chip. That number enables access to a database. . . . The personal\security VeriChip would allow access, via the database, to information related to security, financial, and personal safety applications only. You have represented that it will not contain any medical information. By contrast, ADS and its representatives have explained, the health information VeriChip would allow access, via the database, to medical history and other information to assist medical personnel in diagnosing or treating an injury or illness.

Regulatory Status of the VeriChip

We believe that the health information product, which facilitates access to information for use by medical professionals in treating the individual with the VeriChip embedded in his or her arm, is "intended for use in the diagnosis of disease or other conditions, or in the cure [or] mitigation of disease." The information in the database is meant to be used by medical professionals in diagnosing a disease or other condition. Indeed, the entire purpose of this product is for a medical professional to employ it when treating a stricken individual. For example, information about whether the person is allergic to a particular medicine, or has an implanted pacemaker, which is accessed in connection with the VeriChip, is intended for use in treating the person. Accordingly, FDA has determined that the health information VeriChip is a medical device within the meaning of Section 201(h)(2) of the FD&C Act.

By contrast, as CVM recognized with respect to the use of the VeriChip predecessor in animals, it does not appear that the personal ID\security VeriChip is a medical device, even though it is an "implant." It is of course true that virtually any product that comes into contact with the body—and many that do not—could be said to have an effect on the structure or a function of the body. However ... FDA's medical device jurisdiction under Section 201(h)(2) extends only to such products that are marketed by their manufacturers or distributors with claims of effects on the structure or a function of the body. In the language of the statute itself, the product must be "intended to" affect the structure or a function of the body. It is well settled that intended use is determined with reference to marketing claims. . . .

In [its brief in] a 1994 case, FDA stated that it "does not claim that a device which has no *medical* application could 'qualify as a device under the FD&CA.'" Courts have held that Section 201(h)(3) only encompasses products claimed to affect the body "in some *medical*—or drug-type fashion, *i.e.*, in some way other than merely altering the appearance." *An Article ... "Sudden Change,"* 409 F.2d at 742 (emphasis added).

The pertinent legislative history supports this interpretation. Specifically, the Senate Report accompanying the legislation that became the Federal Food, Drug, and Cosmetic Act of 1938 states:

> The use to which the product is to be put will determine the category into which it will fall. . . . The manufacturer of the article, *through his representations in connection with its sale*, can determine the use to which the article is to be put.

S. Rep. No. 74–361, at 240 (1935) (emphasis added). . . .

Accordingly, assuming that no medical claims are made for the personal ID\security VeriChip, and the product marketed for that purpose contains no health information, FDA can confirm that it is not a medical device.

It is, of course, foreseeable that any implant, such as the personal ID\security VeriChip, will have an effect on the structure and function of the body; indeed, it will be permanently embedded under a person's skin. However, as the Fourth Circuit recently held, a foreseeable effect on the structure or function of the body does not establish an intended use. If the foreseeability theory had been accepted by the courts, FDA would have won several cases that it lost. *See, e.g., National Nutritional Foods Ass'n v. Mathews*, 557 F.2d 325 (2d Cir. 1977).

Also, if foreseeability were a permissible basis for finding an intended use as that term is used in Section 201(h)(3), FDA's jurisdiction would encompass many articles having foreseeable physical effects. Yet FDA only regulates products if they are marketed with claims of medical or therapeutic utility. For example, FDA only regulates exercise equipment as a medical device when it is marketed with claims to prevent, treat, or rehabilitate injury or disability. Otherwise, it is a consumer product.

In addition, if foreseeable effects were cognizable under Section 201(h)(3), FDA's legal authority would intrude into consumer product regulation—an area of responsibility delegated by Congress to another federal agency[, the Consumer Product Safety Commission (CPSC)]. CPSC's jurisdiction extends to "consumer products," which means "any article, or component part thereof, produced or distributed (i) for sale to a consumer for use in or around a permanent or temporary household or residence, a school, in recreation, or otherwise, or (ii) for the personal use, consumption or enjoyment of a consumer in or around a permanent or temporary household or residence, a school, in recreation, or otherwise. . . ." 15 U.S.C. § 2052(a)(1). The definition expressly excludes "drugs, devices, or cosmetics (as such terms are defined in sections 201(g), (h), and (i) of the Federal Food, Drug, and Cosmetic Act . . .)." *Id.* § 2052(a)(1)(H).

Similarly, if Section 201(h)(3) of the FD&C Act were interpreted to give FDA jurisdiction over any product foreseeably having an effect on the structure or a function of the body, then regulatory authority would shift from the CPSC to FDA for a host of non-health-related products. Hiking boots; shirts, pants, and coats; exercise equipment; insulated gloves; airbags; and chemical sprays can be said to affect bodily structure or function. Clothing and gloves, for example, keep the body warm. . . .

NOTES

1.   *Subsequent Regulatory Treatment.* FDA now regulates the health information VeriChip and similar products as class II medical devices under the name "Implantable radiofrequency transponder system for patient identification and health information." 21 C.F.R. 880.6300 (Dec. 10, 2004).

2.   *"Behind-the-Wall" Medical Gas Pipeline Systems.* Most hospitals and many other health care facilities have permanently installed medical gas pipeline systems as part of their architectural infrastructure. These systems deliver medical gases such as oxygen and nitrous oxide from remote tanks to wall outlets throughout the facility. Medical gases are prescription drugs, and medical gas delivery products on the patients' side of the wall (such as flowmeters, gauges, tubing, and masks) are indisputably devices. But what about the "behind-the-wall" pipes, manifolds, valves, and connectors, typically installed by plumbing contractors? FDA originally took the position that such systems were "part of the physical plant" rather than medical devices. *See* Letter from Franklin K. Coombs, P.E., Biomedical Engineering Branch, Division of Classification and Scientific Classification, FDA, to Larry R. Pilot, Director of the Division of Compliance, FDA (Jan. 3, 1977); Memorandum from Pilot to Coombs (Jan. 10, 1977) (response confirming that oxygen supply systems "are not devices as that term is defined in the Act"). More recently, however, the agency has indicated that medical gas delivery distribution systems are in fact devices under the statute. Letter from Eugene M. Berk, Center for Devices and Radiological Health, FDA, to Howard Holstein (May 11, 1993). Nevertheless, FDA has said it will use its regulatory discretion to exempt such systems from the legal requirements for devices, with the exception of the general misbranding and adulteration regulations, which still apply.

3.   *Computer Products.* FDA has stated, "Products that are built with, or consist of, computer and/or software components are subject to regulation as devices if they meet the definition of a device contained in section 201(h) of the FD&C Act." 76 Fed. Reg. 8637, 8638 (Feb. 15, 2011). The agency once embraced a unified approach to determining whether computer- and software-based products were devices and how to regulate them. DRAFT FDA POLICY FOR THE REGULATION OF COMPUTER PRODUCTS

(Nov. 13, 1989). In 2005, however, FDA concluded that the diversity and complexity of computer systems and controlling software had evolved to the point where it was infeasible to maintain a single approach, and it thus withdrew the draft guidance. 70 Fed. Reg. 824 (Jan. 5, 2005). Since then, FDA has promulgated regulations regarding a particular category of computer and software devices called "Medical Device Data Systems." 76 Fed. Reg. 8637 (Feb. 15, 2011), codified at 21 C.F.R. 880.6310. This rule downclassified devices intended to be used for the electronic transfer, storage, display, and format conversion of medical device data from Class III (high-risk) to Class I (low-risk).

Related issues concerning the definition and regulation of "mobile medical applications" are explored in Chapter 10, *infra* p. 1277.

4. *Leeches and Maggots*. FDA treats maggots and leeches marketed for medicinal purposes as medical devices. Maggots, or fly larvae, are normally associated with corpses and adulterated food, but they also help heal wounds and burns in living patients' tissue by liquefying dead tissue. Leeches, the bloodsucking aquatic animals with cameo roles in the films *The African Queen* and *Stand By Me*, have been used in medicine for thousands of years. Today, doctors use them primarily to remove pooled blood in skin grafts and reattachment surgery. In 2004, FDA cleared separate 510(k) applications to market each of these products as a medical device substantially equivalent to a device sold prior to the enactment of the Medical Device Amendments in 1976. *See* FDA Talk Paper, No. T04–19 (June 28, 2004).

5. *Sterilizers*. Federal courts have held that machines used to sterilize other medical devices are themselves medical devices. *See* United States v. 22 Rectangular or Cylindrical Devices . . . "The Ster–O–Lizer MD–200", 714 F. Supp. 1159 (D. Utah 1989) (surgical instruments); United States v. Bowen, 172 F.3d 682 (9th Cir. 1999) (dental handpieces).

6. *Lethal Drugs*. In *United States v. Beuthanasia D Regular*, Food Drug Cosm. L. Rep. (CCH) ¶ 38,265 (D. Neb. 1979), the court upheld an FDA seizure of products intended for euthanasia of animals, rejecting the company's argument that the products were not drugs and thus were outside the jurisdiction of the FD&C Act. Two years later, FDA rejected a petition to assert jurisdiction over the use of approved pharmaceuticals by state prison officials to execute prisoners sentenced to death. Letter from FDA Commissioner A.H. Hayes, Jr., to D.E. Kendall, FDA Dkt. No. 80P–0513 (July 7, 1981). The Supreme Court ultimately held that the agency's refusal to take enforcement action in this instance was unreviewable. *Heckler v. Chaney*, 470 U.S. 821 (1985).

7. *Drugs of Abuse*. Prior to 1970, federal control of narcotic drugs, marijuana, and other drugs used for recreational and nonmedical purposes was shared among several agencies and rested on a haphazard cluster of laws enacted since 1900. For example, FDA was responsible for enforcement of the Drug Abuse Control Amendments of 1965, 79 Stat. 226, to prevent abuse of depressant and stimulant drugs that also have legitimate medical uses, such as amphetamines and barbiturates.

In 1970, Congress repealed the earlier statutes and enacted a new comprehensive law, the Controlled Substances Act, 84 Stat. 1236, 1242, codified at 21 U.S.C. 801 *et seq.* The CSA establishes five "schedules" of substances with strong potential for abuse, calibrated according to their degree of danger. Responsibility for enforcement of the distribution controls of the Controlled Substances Act rests with the Drug Enforcement Administration (DEA) of the Department of Justice. DEA has the obligation to consult with FDA on the scheduling of controlled substances. FDA's recommendations on scientific and medical matters are binding, and DEA may not schedule a drug if FDA recommends against it. Moreover, FDA regulates the legitimate medical uses of scheduled substances the same way it regulates other drugs. Schedule I drugs—that is, illegal drugs with no approved medical use, such as heroin, cocaine, and marijuana—are under the exclusive jurisdiction of DEA.

8.   *Dual Use Products.* FDA has set forth the following policy for products that have both medical and nonmedical uses.

> FDA will regulate a multi-purpose product as a medical device if it is intended for a medical purpose . . . . FDA will determine the intended use of a product based upon the expressions of the person legally responsible for its labeling and by the circumstances surrounding its distribution. The most important factors the agency will consider in determining the intended use of a particular product are the labeling, advertising, and other representations accompanying the product. Products that have medical uses only are clearly intended for medical purposes, and, therefore, will be regulated as medical devices whether or not medical claims are made for them.

45 Fed. Reg. 60576, 60579 (Sept. 12, 1980).

FDA has taken the position that exercise equipment used in recreational and sporting activities will be regulated as medical devices only where those products are intended for medical purposes and thus are properly classified as "therapeutic equipment." 48 Fed. Reg. 53032, 53043–44 (Nov. 23, 1983). Similarly, the agency has concluded that "electrostatic air cleaners are not inherently medical devices," because they have other uses as well, and that the fact that FDA regulates the emission of ozone from medical devices in 21 C.F.R. 801.415 does not mean that all products emitting ozone are medical devices. Letter from FDA Chief Counsel R.M. Cooper to CPSC Assistant General Counsel S. Lemberg (May 14, 1979).

FDA considers magnets marketed with medical claims, including treatment of cancer or arthritis, to be medical devices. CDRH Consumer Information (Mar. 1, 2000). Similarly, the FDA website states that the agency considers clothes that are labeled or promoted as providing protection against the sun or limiting exposure to the sun's UVA/UVB rays to be medical devices. FDA imposed unapproved device status on an electric gas grill igniter advertised to relieve various kinds of pain when used to send an electric current into acupressure points on the body. A federal appeals court upheld this determination. *United States v. Universal Management Services, Inc.*, 191 F.3d 750 (6th Cir. 1999).

9.   *Hand Sanitizers.* Under the Federal Insecticide, Rodenticide, and Fungicide Act (FIFRA), 7 U.S.C. 136 *et seq.*, the Environmental Protection Agency (EPA) regulates all "pesticides." Although a pesticide is defined under 7 U.S.C. 136(t) and (u) as any substance that destroys

microorganisms, EPA has issued regulations in 40 C.F.R. 152.8(a) excluding microorganisms "in or on living man or animals." Thus, EPA has narrowed its jurisdiction to exclude FDA-regulated products. FDA has regulated antimicrobial soap and other topical antimicrobial products as drugs under section 201(g)(1)(B) of the FD&C Act.

3. FIRST AMENDMENT LIMITS

United States v. 23 . . . Articles

192 F.2d 308 (2d Cir. 1951).

■ WOODBURY, CIRCUIT JUDGE.

The United States of America filed a libel . . . seeking the seizure and condemnation of certain phonograph records, and various accompanying items of printed and graphic matter, all of which were moving or had moved in interstate commerce. The phonograph records were entitled in part "Time To Sleep," and their accompanying literature consists of (1) an album in part entitled, "De Luxe Records Presents Time To Sleep a Tested Method of Inducing Sleep Conceived and Transcribed by Ralph Slater," (2) a leaflet in part reading: "Sleep With This Amazing Record 'Time to Sleep,'" (3) a certificate entitled "Sleep Guaranteed," (4) display cards entitled "De Luxe Records Presents Time to Sleep," and (5) a poster headed "A 'Dream Girl' Shows a New Way to Dreamland." . . .

Section 201(h) of the Act under consideration provides in material part that "[t]he term 'device' . . . means instruments, apparatus, and contrivances, including their components, parts, and accessories, intended (1) for use in the diagnosis, cure, mitigation, treatment, or prevention of disease in man or other animals; or (2) to affect the structure or any function of the body of man or other animals."

Certainly a phonograph record, if not itself an instrument or an apparatus, is a contrivance. And moreover, it is without question a component, part or accessory of a phonograph, or like record playing machine, which in its turn is without any doubt at all an instrument, apparatus or contrivance. The real question therefore is whether the libeled records were intended for either of the uses described in (1) or (2) of § 201(h), *supra*. Obviously the records were intended for use in the cure, mitigation, treatment or perhaps prevention of insomnia. But the medical experts who testified at the trial were agreed that insomnia is not a disease, but is a symptom of a disease, usually although not necessarily a neurological one, or of an emotional disturbance of some kind. Thus it may be argued that the records do not fall within the coverage of (1) above.

However, all the expert witnesses who testified on the point were unanimous that sleep is a function of the body, or body and mind, of man and other animals, and this testimony brings the records within the terms of (2), *supra*, for their intended use was to affect that function, *i.e.* to induce sleep in those who needed it but had difficulty in obtaining enough. Without further laboring the point it will suffice to say that the records involved are "devices within the meaning of § 201(h)(2) of the Act. . . ."

United States v. Undetermined Quantities of Article of Device

Med. Devices Rep. (CCH) ¶ 15,055 (W.D. Mich. 1982).

This is an action by the United States ... seeking the condemnation and forfeiture of thirty-two different tape recordings, marketed by the claimant, Potentials Unlimited, Inc. under various titles. These tape recordings were initially seized, pursuant to warrant, on January 6, 1981. The tapes sought to be condemned include:

1. "Relief of Back Pain" or "Back Pain"
2. "Removal of Warts"
3. "Bust Enlargement" or "Natural Bust Enlargement"
4. "Migraine Relief" or "Headaches"

... [28 additional titles suggesting disease or structure/function effects]

Although the claimant disputes whether the labeling of the tapes is false or misleading and whether they lack adequate directions for use, it does not dispute that the tapes were manufactured in an unregistered establishment, that the tapes themselves are not registered as medical devices, or that there was no premarket notification of their manufacture and sale. It follows that if, in fact, the tapes are medical devices, they are in violation of the Act and are subject to forfeiture. Therefore, the resolution of this action turns upon one question; are these tapes medical devices within the meaning of the Act? ...

In January, 1981 Potentials Unlimited marketed over 100 tape recordings. Most of these are unrelated to health or medical problems, as evidenced by the fact that only 32 of the tapes are under seizure. ...

The Potentials Unlimited catalogue comprises the most significant and detailed promotional literature used to market the tapes. ... The introduction refers to the tape recordings, at one point, as "learning"; however, read as a whole, the introduction leaves the impression that the positive suggestions contained on the tapes will act upon the "subconscious mind" to automatically bring about the changes which a person desires. Any teaching and learning aspects of the tapes are deemphasized or negated by the reference to "magic" and the implication that the tapes will work better, "without any interference from your conscious mind." Indeed, the introduction suggests that the tapes will be more beneficial if played during sleep, rather than actually being listened to and assimilated.

. . . .

The general introduction applies to all of the self-hypnosis tapes. The separate descriptive paragraphs contained in the catalogue refer by title and content to specific tapes and the specific problem or aspect of a person's life which that tape is designed to improve. ... When combined with the general introduction, the individual descriptions generally leave the impression that the tapes will cure or treat the specific health-related problem indicated by the title of the tape.

Generally there is no dispute that the tapes purport to effect [sic] structures or functions of the body or to mitigate the effects of diseases. . . .

The tape recordings themselves are very similar in style, structure, and content. They begin with brief instructions regarding the use and purpose of the particular tape, a standard hypnotic induction, and a series of statements, descriptions of visual images, and suggestions designed to influence the listener's thinking. . . .

All of the tapes clearly convey a number of related ideas revolving around a central theme, *i.e.* that a person's thoughts can influence their health or physical characteristics. This central theme is developed through an emphasis on the benefits of relaxation, the elimination of negative feelings such as anger, hate and jealousy, the creation of a positive self-image, and the idea that reality is a reflection of one's own perceptions. Thus, according to the tapes, if a person thinks of himself in a particular, desired way, such as thin, free of allergies or pain, or generally healthy, the person will actually take on those desired characteristics. The tapes are clearly designed to communicate both this central tenet, and a method for putting it into practice.

The court does not find that the tapes themselves are, apart from the claims made in the catalogue, designed or intended to be used in the cure or treatment of the physical and mental conditions indicated by their titles. Each tape is designed to teach a method of mental therapy which it is claimed will have beneficial effects on a particular aspect of a person's life. Any therapeutic results flow from the listener's successful implementation of the lessons contained on the tape. The purported "treatment", therefore, consists of the new thought patterns, beliefs, and behaviors which the listener has learned and adopted. The lessons contained on the tapes are communicated linguistically, and can be understood as well by reading transcripts of the tapes as by listening to the tapes. The contents of the tapes could also be transmitted directly between two individuals, using speech, without the use of tape recording devices. Therefore, the court finds that the mechanical components of these tape recordings are not part of any medical treatment and are used only as a means of communicating the verbal ideas and methods found on the tapes.

. . . .

The fundamental finding regarding hypnosis, as it impacts upon this case, is that hypnosis is an ill defined and little understood concept which it is at least possible to view as a special form of communication or as a teaching device. . . . Since hypnosis can be considered a form of communication, the fact that the tapes use hypnosis techniques, does not prevent their classification as communication or teaching devices. The court rejects Dr. Reyher's testimony that communication must be logical, rational, or objectively purposeful. His definition of communication . . . would exclude poetry, art, music, and drama from the area of communication. Whatever the merits of such a restricted definition for some purposes, it does not comport with the ordinary concept of communication and is irrelevant for First Amendment purposes.

. . .

This case illustrates the difficulty which inevitably arises in balancing the ideal of philosophical and economic freedom against the practical need to protect unwary and vulnerable individuals from the claims of rapacious and unethical businessmen. . . .

Fortunately, the court need not confront the problem presented in this case from the fundamental level of balancing the costs and benefits of the two competing perspectives suggested above. Congress has already engaged in such a balancing process and has determined that "medical devices" should be regulated by the FDA for the protection and benefit of the consuming public seeking medical treatment. In doing so, Congress has adopted a broad definition of medical device which is to be liberally construed in order to effectuate the purpose of the Act. *United States v. Bacto–Unidisk*, 394 U.S. 784 (1969).

There is no doubt that a tape recording is an implement, apparatus, or contrivance [as required by the FD&C Act definition]. However, a distinction must be made in this case between the tapes themselves, and the ideas that are contained on the tapes. Congress did not intend to regulate an article or device, the sole function of which is to serve as a means of communicating health related ideas or information. Had Congress had such an intent it would have expressly included books, the quintessential communication device, in the definition of "medical device." It did not do so.

. . . [T]he tape recordings under seizure in this case are designed and intended to communicate and to teach certain ideas, beliefs, and mental processes which are claimed to have health benefits when adopted and practiced by the listener. Congress did not purport to regulate quack medical ideas or beliefs when it drafted the definition of medical device contained in the Act. By no stretch of language can an idea or a mental process be considered an instrument, apparatus, implement, machine, contrivance, implant, or in vitro reagent, or a similar or related article.

The "liberal interpretation" to be accorded the Act must yield somewhat when it comes into conflict with First Amendment freedoms. . . . Since ideas, beliefs and mental processes do not come within the statutory definition they are outside the jurisdiction of the FDA. Mechanical devices which do no more than communicate or expound such ideas, beliefs and mental processes are likewise outside the jurisdiction of the FDA. To include such devices within the definition would have grave First Amendment implications and would, by implication, bring health related books, magazines, and publications within the agency jurisdiction. That is a result Congress clearly did not contemplate or intend.

The fact that the tapes in issue do no more than communicate certain ideas using hypnosis as a tool in that communication does not end the inquiry into whether these tapes, as marketed by Potentials Unlimited, are subject to regulation as medical devices. Articles and devices which have no intended therapeutic qualities may be regulated if they are sold by the vendor accompanied by therapeutic claims. Thus, the seller's objective manifestation of a therapeutic intent brings otherwise medically benign articles within the purview of the Act. . . .

The therapeutic claims contained in promotional literature can convert the most innocent of articles into drugs or devices within the meaning of the Act. . . . The conduct of Potentials Unlimited in marketing these tapes as therapeutic medical devices is subject to regulation by Congress, even if the tapes themselves communicate ideas.

As stated in the court's findings of fact, the catalogue distributed by Potentials Unlimited tells the reader through its general introduction, that the self-hypnosis tapes will work "like magic," by "saturating the subconscious mind with positive suggestions." This language creates the expectation of an automatic and mechanical process by which suggestions will be implanted in the brain, much like a drug, and miraculous cures will result from the therapeutic effects of these suggestions. The whole introduction is designed to imply a therapeutic result from listening to the tapes, rather than a simple act of communication. Hypnosis is regarded, in the catalogue, as a treatment rather than a form of communication. Coupled with the titles of the seized tapes, an intended therapeutic use for the tapes is objectively manifested. This objective manifestation makes the tapes, as they are presently marketed, medical devices, to the extent they are used in treating disease or to affect body function. . . .

The petition for condemnation against the . . . tapes . . . is granted. . . .

H. HUMAN BIOLOGICAL PRODUCTS

The Public Health Service Act gives FDA jurisdiction to regulate "biological products." Under the PHS Act, most biological products are subject to a regulatory regime similarly rigorous to that for drugs, including premarket review by FDA for safety and effectiveness. Section 262(i)(1) of the PHS Act defines "biological product" as follows:

> [T]he term "biological product" means a virus, therapeutic serum, toxin, antitoxin, vaccine, blood, blood component or derivative, allergenic product, protein (except any chemically synthesized polypeptide), or analogous product, or arsphenamine or derivative of arsphenamine (or any other trivalent organic arsenic compound), applicable to the prevention, treatment, or cure of a disease or condition of human beings.

This definition, with its list of examples and reference to "analogous" products, is of a different character from the FD&C Act's product definitions. It presents its own interpretive problems.

David M. Dudzinski, *Reflections on Historical, Scientific, and Legal Issues Relevant to Designing Approval Pathways for Generic Versions of Recombinant Protein–Based Therapeutics and Monoclonal Antibodies*

60 FOOD & DRUG LAW JOURNAL 143 (2005).

. . . Concurrent with rising demand for treatments for the major nineteenth century diseases, private entities began to manufacture vaccine and antitoxin. Especially after the introduction of diphtheria antitoxin in 1894 from Germany, many small outfits run by pharmacies and physicians, as well as two large pharmaceutical ventures, H.K. Mulford Co. and Parke Davis, moved to produce antitoxins and supplant the government suppliers. While Mulford and Parke Davis had devoted significant resources to quality control and standardization of their antitoxin products, other smaller entities manufacturing antitoxins did not. Instances of unscrupulous behavior by some smaller firms had previously resulted in a fake smallpox vaccine being sold in the early 1800s. Instances of contamination of commercial products also became a frequently recognized problem: large outbreaks of tetanus allegedly occurred via contamination of diphtheria antitoxin in the late 1890s and contamination of smallpox vaccine in 1901.

Though numerous investigations revealed that the tetanus outbreak in 1901 was most likely not associated with the smallpox vaccine, the "report[s] did not silence public outcry." The major manufacturers of biologics, pitted against each other by the assignment of blame for the tetanus outbreaks, found themselves under increasing scrutiny of the state governments and public. In response, the majors buried their disputes and redoubled their efforts to attack the smaller biologics manufacturers who were more likely to have "unsanitary and outmoded" facilities. Ultimately, it was deaths of thirteen children from tetanus-contaminated vaccine that "convinced Congress and the public that producing antitoxin or vaccine was not a simple matter like weighing out a dose of a drug on a scale" and provided an impetus for legislation.

Congress responded to the recent outbreaks as well as to the companies' lobbying by enacting the Biologics Act of 1902, the first enduring scheme of national regulation for any pharmaceutical product. The Biologics Act was groundbreaking in part because it set new precedents both in terms of shifting from retrospective post-market to prospective pre-market government review, and modifying the common law notion of punishing conduct only of intentional or reckless actors, in favor of moving toward pro-active safety measures for all entities.

The Biologics Act exerted jurisdiction over "viruses, therapeutic serums, toxins, antitoxins, or analogous products" as "biologics" that were intended for the "prevention, and cure of diseases of man." Each of the categories of regulated biologics represent immunologic agents, and Congress seemed to select these particular substances out of particular concern for immunologic, allergenic, and (at least what was then perceived to be) possibly contagious side effects. Viruses and toxins function to stimulate development of active immunity and antibody production when introduced into humans. Vaccines had been made for decades by exposing patients to a relatively non-pathogenic strain of bacteria or killed or inactivated pathogens. Antitoxins and therapeutic serums confer passive immunity simply by providing preformed antibodies, often developed by another animal like horse or goat in response to the toxin. All of these products—even in their final form after "manufacturing"—remained relatively crude mixtures; in fact, most of the products regulated in 1902 had a purity less than 1%. The Congressional concern for immunologic side effects was heightened especially in light of the biologics' animal origin and their parenteral, or injectable route of administration; compared to oral administration, where the digestive system provided some barriers protecting the body, injection gave the biologics direct access to the inner body. . . .

. . . In 1963 *United States v. Steinschreiber* held blood plasma and other components derived from processing of blood were subject to biologics regulations as analogues to serum. 219 F. Supp. 373, 382–83 (S.D.N.Y. 1963), *aff'd*, 326 F.2d 759 (2d Cir. 1964) (per curiam). In contrast, in 1968 *Blank v. United States* held blood and red blood cells were drugs but exempt from biologics regulation. 400 F.2d at 305 (5th Cir. 1968). Individual adjudications are a poor means to develop any comprehensive regulatory scheme because of the lack of a guiding principle and the resultant fragmented, confusing system. Recognizing that every "[f]ederal court . . . has held that blood is a drug" but diverged on the issue of blood as a biologic, Congress unified the law by amending the PHSA § 351 to include the classes of "blood, blood components or derivatives". Heart Disease, Cancer, Stroke, and Kidney Disease Amendments [to the Public Health Service Act] of 1970, 84 Stat. 1297, 1308 (Oct. 30, 1970). . . .

The very notion of a biologic has changed many times over the last century, and has deviated far from the root concern of grouping and regulating non-human organism (virus, bacteria, or large animal) immunogenic molecules. By statute, biological products are now "defined" as including viruses, therapeutic sera, toxins and antitoxins, vaccines, blood, blood components or derivatives, allergenic products, any analogous products, and arsphenamines used treating disease. Though several of these terms (*e.g.* therapeutic sera, antitoxin) lack crisp scientific meaning, no actual definition of "biologic" is offered in the statute or its regulations.

However, no definition is probably preferable to the alternative of a scientifically invalid definition, such as for virus, which is "interpreted to be a product containing the minute living cause of an infectious disease and includes but is not limited to filterable viruses, bacteria, rickettsia, fungi, and protozoa." 21 C.F.R. § 600.3(h)(1). It is also far from clear that the earliest premise of biologics regulation was even internally consistent, as many of the first substances considered to be biologics were not really immunogenic per se, but designed to confer passive immunity. The more modern additions to the family of designated biologics are also questionable. Arsphenamines, while toxic, do no more to affect the immune process or cause immunogenic toxicities than do other well-known antibiotics and anti-microbials. Moreover the "analogous" language greatly amplifies the specter of biologics: for example, a product is analogous to 1) a virus if it is merely prepared from any "potentially infectious agent", 2) a therapeutic serum if it contains "some organic constituent" from blood (amino acids and hormones, like insulin and human growth hormone, excepted), or 3) a toxin or antitoxin if it addresses human disease "through a specific immune process." 21 C.F.R. § 600.3(h)(5)(i)–(iii). When one considers that virtually every chemical, including small molecules, can be an allergen to a certain fraction of the population, and that "products analogous to blood" has been theorized to encompass everything from the most well-characterized and well-purified serum protein all the way to whole organs, bewilderment about the definition of a biologic is understandable.

NOTES

1. *"[P]rotein (except any chemically synthesized polypeptide)."* The Biologics Price Competition and Innovation Act of 2009 ("BPCI Act"), enacted as part of the Patient Protection and Affordable Care Act on March 23, 2010, amended the Public Health Service Act to create an abbreviated pathway to market for biological products that are "biosimilar" to approved biologics. *See infra* p. 1135. The BPCI Act amended the definition of "biological product" in § 351(i) of the PHS Act to include a "protein (except any chemically synthesized polypeptide)." FDA defines "protein" as "any alpha amino acid polymer with a specific defined sequence that is greater than 40 amino acids in size," while a "chemically synthesized polypeptide" constitutes "any alpha amino acid polymer that (1) is made entirely by chemical synthesis[ ] and (2) is less than 100 amino acids in size." DRAFT GUIDANCE FOR INDUSTRY ON BIOSIMILARS: QUESTIONS AND ANSWERS REGARDING IMPLEMENTATION OF THE BIOLOGICS PRICE COMPETITION AND INNOVATION ACT OF 2009 (Feb. 2012). Accordingly, peptides of less than 41 amino acids and "chemically synthesized polypeptides" are regulated as "drugs" unless a peptide otherwise meets the statutory definition of a "biological product" (*i.e.*, a peptide vaccine). *See id.*; WENDY H. SCHACHT & JOHN R. THOMAS, CONG. RESEARCH SERV., R41270, P.L. 111–148: INTELLECTUAL PROPERTY PROVISIONS FOR FOLLOW–ON BIOLOGICS (2010).

2. *Human Cellular and Tissue–Based Products.* Human tissue products have been used by doctors for decades. Skin, tendons, bones, heart valves, and corneas that are damaged or diseased are replaced by tissues removed from the body of a donor. Semen, ova, and embryos are transferred to aid reproduction. Recent years have seen an explosion of research into human cellular products for therapeutic purposes, including somatic cell therapy products and gene therapy products. FDA deems some human cellular and tissue-based products to be biologics, as well as medical devices or drugs. The agency's regulation of these products is discussed in Chapter 9, *infra*.

3. *Dual Classification.* Because the definition of "biological products" refers exclusively to articles "applicable to the prevention, treatment, or cure of a disease or condition of human beings," all biologics are simultaneously also drugs or devices. This dual classification raises many issues regarding the appropriate application of the requirements of PHS Act and the FD&C Act to biologics, as well as the division of responsibility

over these products among FDA's biologics, drug, and device centers. These issues are addressed in Chapter 9, *infra*.

4.   *Combination Products.* The issue of "dual classification" that has arisen throughout this chapter concerns situations in which a product, in its entirety, simultaneously falls within more than one product definition in the FD&C Act. A distinct issue is that of "combination products," different components of which satisfy different product definitions. The Act includes special provisions dedicated to the regulation of "products that constitute a combination of a drug, device, or biological product." *See* FD&C Act 503(g). The most common combination products are drug/device combinations, examples of which include prefilled syringes, transdermal patches, and drug-eluting stents. Regulation of such products will be considered later in this book. *See infra* p. 1206.

I. TOBACCO PRODUCTS

1.   STRUGGLES OVER FDA JURISDICTION BEFORE THE FAMILY SMOKING PREVENTION AND TOBACCO CONTROL ACT OF 2009

In 1995, FDA announced that it was going to assert jurisdiction over cigarettes and smokeless tobacco and regulate their manufacture, labeling, and advertising. 60 Fed. Reg. 41314 (Aug. 11, 1995). For legal authority, the agency invoked the FD&C Act. Contending that tobacco products were responsible for as many as 400,000 American deaths annually, the agency mounted what it considered a compelling case for government intervention. The agency's goal was to protect adolescents who had not yet begun to smoke. Its plan was designed to obstruct their access to tobacco and discourage manufacturer promotional efforts to attract new smokers. FDA's notice of proposed rulemaking immediately precipitated litigation that probed the boundaries of the agency's legal authority. The eventual failure of FDA's initiative in the United States Supreme Court, in *FDA v. Brown & Williamson Tobacco Corp.*, 529 U.S. 120 (2000) (excerpted below), exposed new limits of the Act's definitions as measures of its regulatory jurisdiction.

Decades before the 1995 announcement, FDA had asserted its authority over at least some tobacco products that made explicit disease prevention or weight-loss claims, asserting that such claims rendered the products "drugs." *United States v. 46 Cartons . . . Fairfax Cigarettes*, 113 F. Supp. 336 (D.N.J. 1953) (disease claims); *United States v. 354 Bulk Cartons Trim Reducing–Aid Cigarettes*, 178 F. Supp. 847 (D.N.J. 1959) (weight-loss claims).

In 1964 the Surgeon General released a ground-breaking report which documented the heavy price smokers paid for the pleasure of smoking. *See* SMOKING AND HEALTH: REPORT OF THE ADVISORY COMMITTEE OF THE SURGEON GENERAL OF THE PUBLIC HEALTH SERVICE (1964). The report inspired several proposals to regulate the manufacture, labeling, and sale of cigarettes and, later, of smokeless tobacco. During congressional hearings on these bills, FDA officials were asked what, if any, role their agency could play. Their uniform response was that FDA had no authority over cigarettes unless they bore claims that they could prevent or relieve disease.

Ultimately, suggestions that FDA be given authority to regulate cigarettes were rejected in favor of statutes passed in 1965 and 1969 curbing the labeling and, later, the advertising of cigarettes and requiring their labels to bear mild warnings about their health effects. The 1960s came to an end with no material change in the marketing of cigarettes despite mounting evidence of their adverse effects.

Advocates of tobacco control, however, never lost hope that FDA might be persuaded to acknowledge, and then exercise, jurisdiction over tobacco. In 1977, Action on Smoking and Health (ASH), a citizen action group, filed a petition urging the agency to assert jurisdiction over cigarettes under the FD&C Act and impose restrictions on their advertising and distribution. The petition cited evidence that smokers smoked to gain the physiological effects of nicotine, and it contended that these effects were thus "intended." FDA declined to exercise jurisdiction. The D.C. Circuit upheld the agency's refusal to regulate cigarettes in the following words:

> . . . [B]y failing to introduce any evidence of vendors' intent— whether based upon subjective vendor claims or objective evidence such as labeling, promotional material, and advertising—ASH placed itself in the position of having to meet the high standard established in cases where the statutory "intent" is derived from consumer use alone. . . .
>
> In cases such as the one at hand, consumers must use the product predominantly—and in fact nearly exclusively—with the appropriate intent before the requisite statutory intent can be inferred. . . . ASH did not establish, and arguably cannot establish, the near-exclusivity of consumer use of cigarettes with the intent "to affect the structure or any function of the body of man. . . ."

Action on Smoking and Health v. Harris, 655 F.2d 236, 239–40 (D.C. Cir. 1980). *See also* Letter from Deputy Commissioner M. Novitch to J.F. Banzhaf, III, FDA Dkt. Nos. 77P–0185 & 78P–0338/CP (Nov. 25, 1980) (denying petitions by ASH asking FDA to assert jurisdiction over attached and detached cigarette filters as medical devices).

Both FDA and the D.C. Circuit in *ASH* left open the possibility that the agency might be able to assert jurisdiction over cigarettes if there were evidence that the manufacturers themselves intended their products to "affect the structure or function of the body." Events soon reopened this line of analysis. In the early 1990s, several states sued the major manufacturers of cigarettes to recover the costs of state-funded medical care provided to smokers suffering from tobacco-related illness. In the course of discovery in these cases, some of the defendants disgorged documents that strongly suggested, and in the view of many proved beyond question, that the companies knew their customers smoked to gain the effects of nicotine and designed their products to satisfy this desire.

FDA Commissioner David Kessler launched an extensive investigation into the cigarette business—how these products were made and marketed, and what the manufacturers knew or intended about their effects. In 1995, FDA published a notice of proposed rulemaking in which it asserted jurisdiction over cigarettes and smokeless tobacco as "devices" for delivering the "drug" nicotine. 60 Fed. Reg. 41314 (Aug. 11, 1995). The agency proposed measures to make cigarettes difficult for young people to obtain and less appealing to consumers generally, including mandatory carding of youthful customers, relocation of cigarette displays, and outright bans on the industry's favorite promotions, including sponsorship of concerts, art exhibits, and sporting events. To support this proposal, FDA contended that the evidence from company files made clear that the cigarette manufacturers did "intend" their products to affect the bodily functions of their customers. In addition, the agency asserted that the FD&C Act allowed a range of remedial options short of an outright ban. FDA issued its final rule in 1996. 61 Fed. Reg. 44396 (Aug. 28, 1996). In its preamble to the final rule, the agency made some adjustments to its defense of its jurisdiction and more significant revisions to its regulatory scheme, but its fundamental claims remained the same.

Meanwhile, the cigarette and smokeless tobacco manufacturers, along with representatives of advertising interests who saw FDA's proposed curbs on promotion as an assault on the First Amendment, had challenged the agency's assertion of jurisdiction. In 1997, a district court rendered a decision that upheld FDA's jurisdiction to regulate these products. *Coyne Beahm, Inc. v. U.S. Food and Drug Administration*, 966 F. Supp. 1374 (M.D.N.C. 1997). The court held that both foreseeable consumer use and actual consumer use were valid bases for the agency to conclude that tobacco products were "intended" to affect the structure or function of the body. *Id.* at 49–53. A year later, the Fourth Circuit overturned this ruling. *Brown & Williamson Tobacco Corp. v. FDA*, 153 F.3d 155 (4th Cir. 1998). Predictably, the Supreme Court granted the government's Petition for Certiorari.

Food and Drug Administration v. Brown & Williamson Tobacco Corp.

529 U.S. 120 (2000).

■ JUSTICE O'CONNOR delivered the opinion of the Court.

. . . .

The FDA's assertion of jurisdiction to regulate tobacco products is founded on its conclusions that nicotine is a "drug" and that cigarettes and smokeless tobacco are "drug delivery devices." Again, the FDA found that tobacco products are "intended" to deliver the pharmacological effects of satisfying addiction, stimulation and tranquilization, and weight control because those effects are foreseeable to any reasonable manufacturer, consumers use tobacco products to obtain those effects, and tobacco manufacturers have designed their products to produce those effects. As an initial matter, respondents take issue with the FDA's reading of "intended," arguing that it is a term of art that refers exclusively to claims made by the manufacturer or vendor about the product. That is, a product is not a drug or device under the FDCA unless the manufacturer or vendor makes some express claim concerning the product's therapeutic benefits. We need not resolve this question, however, because assuming, *arguendo*, that a product can be "intended to affect the structure or any function of the body" absent claims of therapeutic or medical benefit, the FDA's claim to jurisdiction contravenes the clear intent of Congress.

A threshold issue is the appropriate framework for analyzing the FDA's assertion of authority to regulate tobacco products. Because this case involves an administrative agency's construction of a statute that it administers, our analysis is governed by *Chevron U.S.A. Inc. v. Natural Resources Defense Council, Inc.*, 467 U.S. 837 (1984). Under *Chevron*, a reviewing court must first ask "whether Congress has directly spoken to the precise question at issue." *Id.*, at 842. If Congress has done so, the inquiry is at an end; the court "must give effect to the unambiguously expressed intent of Congress." *Id.*, at 843. But if Congress has not specifically addressed the question, a reviewing court must respect the agency's construction of the statute so long as it is permissible. . . .

In determining whether Congress has specifically addressed the question at issue, a reviewing court should not confine itself to examining a particular statutory provision in isolation. The meaning—or ambiguity—of certain words or phrases may only become evident when placed in context. A court must therefore interpret the statute "as a symmetrical and coherent regulatory scheme," *Gustafson v. Alloyd Co.*, 513 U.S. 561, 569 (1995), and "fit, if possible, all parts into an harmonious whole," *FTC v. Mandel Brothers, Inc.*, 359 U.S. 385, 389 (1959). Similarly, the meaning of one statute may be affected by other Acts, particularly where Congress has spoken subsequently and more specifically to the topic at hand. In addition, we must be guided to a degree by common sense as to the manner in which Congress is likely to delegate a policy decision of such economic and political magnitude to an administrative agency.

With these principles in mind, we find that Congress has directly spoken to the issue here and precluded the FDA's jurisdiction to regulate tobacco products.

Viewing the FDCA as a whole, it is evident that one of the Act's core objectives is to ensure that any product regulated by the FDA is "safe" and "effective" for its intended use. This essential purpose pervades the FDCA. . . . Thus, the Act generally requires the FDA to prevent the marketing of any drug or device where the "potential for inflicting death or physical injury is not offset by the possibility of therapeutic benefit." *United States v. Rutherford*, 442 U.S. 544, 556 (1979).

In its rulemaking proceeding, the FDA quite exhaustively documented that "tobacco products are unsafe," "dangerous," and "cause great pain and suffering from illness." It found that the consumption of tobacco products presents "extraordinary health risks," and that "tobacco use is the single leading cause of preventable death in the United States." . . .

These findings logically imply that, if tobacco products were "devices" under the FDCA, the FDA would be required to remove them from the market. . . . [F]irst, . . . in light of the FDA's findings, two distinct FDCA provisions would render cigarettes and tobacco misbranded devices. . . .

Second, the FDCA requires the FDA to place all devices that it regulates into one of three classifications. *See* § 360c(b)(1). . . . Given the FDA's findings regarding the health consequences of tobacco use, the agency would have to place cigarettes and smokeless tobacco in Class III because, even after the application of the Act's available controls, they would "present a potential unreasonable risk of illness or injury." 21 U.S.C. § 360c(a)(1)(C). As Class III devices, tobacco products would be subject to the FDCA's premarket approval process. *See* 21 U.S.C. § 360c(a)(1)(C); 21 U.S.C. § 360e. Under these provisions, the FDA would be prohibited from approving an application for premarket approval without "a showing of reasonable assurance that such device is safe under the conditions of use prescribed, recommended, or suggested on the labeling thereof." 21 U.S.C. § 360e(d)(2)(A). In view of the FDA's conclusions regarding the health effects of tobacco use, the agency would have no basis for finding any such reasonable assurance of safety. Thus, once the FDA fulfilled its statutory obligation to classify tobacco products, it could not allow them to be marketed.

The FDCA's misbranding and device classification provisions therefore make evident that were the FDA to regulate cigarettes and smokeless tobacco, the Act would require the agency to ban them. . . .

Congress, however, has foreclosed the removal of tobacco products from the market. A provision of the United States Code currently in force states that "[t]he marketing of tobacco constitutes one of the greatest basic industries of the United States with ramifying activities which directly affect interstate and foreign commerce at every point, and stable conditions therein are necessary to the general welfare." 7 U.S.C. § 1311(a). More importantly, Congress has directly addressed the problem of tobacco and health through legislation on six occasions since 1965. When Congress enacted these statutes, the adverse health consequences of tobacco use were well known, as were nicotine's pharmacological effects. Nonetheless, Congress stopped well short of ordering a ban. Instead, it has generally regulated the labeling and advertisement of tobacco products, expressly providing that it is the policy of Congress that "commerce and the national economy may be . . . protected to the maximum extent consistent with" consumers "be[ing] adequately informed about any adverse health effects." 15 U.S.C. § 1331. . . .

In adopting each statute, Congress has acted against the backdrop of the FDA's consistent and repeated statements that it lacked authority under the FDCA to regulate tobacco absent claims of therapeutic benefit by the manufacturer. In fact, on several occasions over this period, and after the health consequences of tobacco use and nicotine's pharmacological effects had become well known, Congress considered and rejected bills that would have granted the FDA such jurisdiction. Under these circumstances, it is evident that Congress' tobacco-specific statutes have effectively ratified the FDA's long-held position that it lacks jurisdiction under the FDCA to regulate tobacco products. Congress has created a distinct regulatory scheme to address the problem of tobacco and health, and that scheme, as presently constructed, precludes any role for the FDA. . . .

. . . Reading the FDCA as a whole, as well as in conjunction with Congress' subsequent tobacco-specific legislation, it is plain that

Congress has not given the FDA the authority that it seeks to exercise here. For these reasons, the judgment of the Court of Appeals for the Fourth Circuit is affirmed.

It is so ordered.

■ Justice Breyer, with whom Justice Stevens, Justice Souter, and Justice Ginsburg join, dissenting.

. . . .

The Food and Drug Administration (FDA) has the authority to regulate "articles (other than food) intended to affect the structure or any function of the body . . . ." Unlike the majority, I believe that tobacco products fit within this statutory language.

In its own interpretation, the majority nowhere denies the following two salient points. First, tobacco products (including cigarettes) fall within the scope of this statutory definition, read literally. Cigarettes achieve their mood-stabilizing effects through the interaction of the chemical nicotine and the cells of the central nervous system. Both cigarette manufacturers and smokers alike know of, and desire, that chemically induced result. Hence, cigarettes are "intended to affect" the body's "structure" and "function," in the literal sense of these words.

Second, the statute's basic purpose—the protection of public health—supports the inclusion of cigarettes within its scope. *See United States v. Article of Drug . . . Baco-Unidisk*, 394 U.S. 784, 798 (1969). Unregulated tobacco use causes "[m]ore than 400,000 people [to] die each year from tobacco-related illnesses, such as cancer, respiratory illnesses, and heart disease." 61 Fed. Reg. 44398 (1996). Indeed, tobacco products kill more people in this country every year "than . . . AIDS . . . , car accidents, alcohol, homicides, illegal drugs, suicides, and fires, *combined.*" *Ibid.* (emphasis added). . . .

. . . Taken literally, [the structure/function] definition might include everything from room air conditioners to thermal pajamas. The companies argue that, to avoid such a result, the meaning of "drug" or "device" should be confined to *medical* or *therapeutic* products, narrowly defined.

The companies may well be right that the statute should not be read to cover room air conditioners and winter underwear. But I do not agree that we must accept their proposed limitation. For one thing, such a cramped reading contravenes the established purpose of the statutory language. For another, the companies' restriction would render the other two "drug" definitions superfluous. *See* 21 U.S.C. §§ 321(g)(1)(A), (g)(1)(B) (covering articles in the leading pharmacology compendia and those "intended for use in the diagnosis, cure, mitigation, treatment, or prevention of disease").

Most importantly, the statute's language itself supplies a different, more suitable, limitation: that a "drug" must be a *chemical* agent. The FDCA's "device" definition states that an article which affects the structure or function of the body is a "device" only if it "does *not* achieve its primary intended purposes through chemical action within . . . the body," and "is not dependent upon being metabolized for the achievement of its primary intended purposes." § 321(h) (emphasis added). One can readily infer from this language that at least an article that *does* achieve its primary purpose through chemical action within the body and that *is* dependent upon being metabolized is a "drug," provided that it otherwise falls within the scope of the "drug" definition. And one need not hypothesize about air conditioners or thermal pajamas to recognize that the chemical nicotine, an important tobacco ingredient, meets this test. . . .

The tobacco companies' principal definitional argument focuses upon the statutory word "intended." The companies say that "intended" in this context is a term of art. They assert that the statutory word "intended" means that the product's maker has made an *express claim* about the effect that its product will have on the body. Indeed, according to the companies, the FDA's inability to prove that cigarette manufacturers make such claims is precisely why that agency historically has said it lacked the statutory power to regulate tobacco.

The FDCA, however, does not use the word "claimed"; it uses the word "intended." And the FDA long ago issued regulations that say the relevant "intent" can be shown not only by a manufacturer's "expressions," *but also* "by the circumstances surrounding the distribution of the article." 21 CFR § 801.4. Thus, even in the absence of express claims, the FDA has regulated products that affect the body if the manufacturer wants, and knows, that consumers so use the product. . . .

Nor is the FDA's "objective intent" interpretation unreasonable. It falls well within the established scope of the ordinary meaning of the word "intended." And the companies acknowledge that the FDA can regulate a drug-like substance in the ordinary circumstance, *i.e.*, where the manufacturer makes an express claim, so it is not unreasonable to conclude that the agency retains such power where a product's effects on the body are so well known (say, like those of aspirin or calamine lotion), that there is no need for express representations because the product speaks for itself. . . .

The majority nonetheless reaches the "inescapable conclusion" that the language and structure of the FDCA as a whole "simply do not fit" the kind of public health problem that tobacco creates. That is because, in the majority's view, the FDCA requires the FDA to ban outright "dangerous" drugs or devices (such as cigarettes); yet, the FDA concedes that an immediate and total cigarette-sale ban is inappropriate. . . .

In my view, where linguistically permissible, we should interpret the FDCA in light of Congress' overall desire to protect health. That purpose requires a flexible interpretation that both permits the FDA to take into account the realities of human behavior and allows it, in appropriate cases, to choose from its arsenal of statutory remedies. . . .

2. THE FAMILY SMOKING PREVENTION AND TOBACCO CONTROL ACT

In 2009, Congress passed the Family Smoking Prevention and Tobacco Control Act (FSPTCA), Pub. L. No. 111–31, which amended the FD&C Act to give the agency explicit power over "tobacco products" pursuant to a new Chapter IX of the Act dedicated to these products.

The FSPTCA added the following definition of "tobacco product" to the FD&C Act as section 201(rr):

> (1) The term "tobacco product" means any product made or derived from tobacco that is intended for human consumption, including any component, part, or accessory of a tobacco product (except for raw materials other than tobacco used in manufacturing a component, part, or accessory of a tobacco product).

> (2) The term "tobacco product" does not mean an article that is a drug under subsection (g)(1), a device under subsection (h), or a combination product described in section 353(g) of this title.

The details of FDA's recently acquired authority over tobacco products will be examined in Chapter 12.

At first glance, the enactment of the FSPTCA seemed to render *Brown & Williamson* largely irrelevant to current food and drug law. But almost immediately, the new statutory definition of "tobacco product" raised its own interpretive questions which turned on the precise meaning of the *Brown & Williamson* decision.

<h2 style="text-align:center">Sottera, Inc. v. FDA</h2>

627 F.3d 891 (D.C. Cir. 2010).

■ WILLIAMS, SENIOR CIRCUIT JUDGE:

Sottera, Inc., which does business as NJOY, is an importer and distributor of "electronic cigarettes" or "e-cigarettes," a product that enables users to inhale vaporized nicotine. The question before us is whether Congress has authorized the Food and Drug Administration to regulate e-cigarettes under the drug/device provisions of the Federal Food, Drug, and Cosmetic Act ("FDCA"), or under the Family Smoking Prevention and Tobacco Control Act of 2009 (the "Tobacco Act"), Pub. L. 111–31. We think that the statutes, properly read in light of the Supreme Court's decision in *FDA v. Brown & Williamson*, 529 U.S. 120 (2000), locate the product under the Tobacco Act.

Electronic cigarettes are battery-powered products that allow users to inhale nicotine vapor without fire, smoke, ash, or carbon monoxide. Designed to look like a traditional cigarette, each e-cigarette consists of three parts: the nicotine cartridge, the atomizer or heating element, and the battery and electronics. . . .

NJOY has imported and distributed e-cigarettes since 2007. The liquid nicotine in each e-cigarette is derived from natural tobacco plants, and NJOY claims that its product is marketed and labeled for "smoking pleasure," rather than as a therapeutic or smoking cessation product. On April 15, 2009 the FDA ordered that a shipment of NJOY's e-cigarettes be denied entry into the United States, asserting that the e-cigarettes appeared to be adulterated, misbranded, or unapproved drug-device combinations under the FDCA.

Also in April 2009, another importer and distributor of e-cigarettes, Smoking Everywhere, Inc., sought a preliminary injunction barring the FDA and various officials from denying their products entry into the United States and from regulating e-cigarettes under the drug/device provisions of the FDCA. NJOY joined as an intervenor-plaintiff and filed its own complaint and request for a preliminary injunction.

Smoking Everywhere and NJOY argued that the FDA can regulate electronic cigarettes, as they propose to market them, only under the Tobacco Act, claiming that the Supreme Court's opinion in *Brown & Williamson* foreclosed FDCA drug/device jurisdiction over tobacco products marketed without claims of therapeutic effect. The district court agreed and granted the injunction. While this appeal was pending, Smoking Everywhere voluntarily dismissed its complaint against the FDA, leaving NJOY as the sole appellee.

. . .

To fill the regulatory gap identified in *Brown & Williamson*, Congress in 2009 passed the Tobacco Act, providing the FDA with authority to regulate tobacco products. The act defines tobacco products so as to include all consumption products derived from tobacco except articles that qualify as drugs, devices, or drug-device combinations under the FDCA . . . . 21 U.S.C. § 321(rr).

. . . The question before us . . . is whether the FDA can regulate electronic cigarettes under the FDCA's drug/device provisions or whether it can regulate them only under the Tobacco Act's provisions.

The FDA at one point argues that its decision to regulate electronic cigarettes under the FDCA's drug/device provisions is entitled to *Chevron* deference. But in fact the case does not turn on matters of statutory interpretation. . . . [W]ith respect to tobacco products, the breadth of [FDA's authority under the drug, device, and combination products provisions of the FDCA] is governed by the Supreme Court's decision in *Brown & Williamson*. We therefore turn to that case.

In *Brown & Williamson* the Supreme Court . . . began by noting that . . . [i]f tobacco products were drug/device combinations under the FDCA, the FDA would have no choice but to ban them.

Clearly that could not be the case, the Court reasoned. After all, Congress had declared, in a provision of the U.S. Code then in force, that tobacco was "one of the greatest basic industries of the United States," *id.* at 137 (quoting 7 U.S.C. § 1311(a)), and it had also passed six separate statutes relating to tobacco since 1965. . . . So the Court held that the FDA's claim of FDCA jurisdiction failed.

. . . The FDA argues that *Brown & Williamson* takes a statute-specific approach, excluding the FDA from regulating only those tobacco products that at the time of *Brown & Williamson* had been the subject of specific federal legislation. Though *Brown & Williamson* is not crystal clear, we think the better reading is that the FDA lacks FDCA drug/device authority to regulate all tobacco products marketed without claims of therapeutic effect, *i.e.*, as customarily marketed.

Brown & Williamson's focus was not on the particular products that the six statutes cover or even on the six statutes themselves. . . . Rather, *Brown & Williamson* considered the context of each statute to show that Congress was actively thinking about "the tobacco problem." 529 U.S. at 145. In situating the statutes, *Brown & Williamson* found that "[i]n adopting each statute, Congress has acted against the backdrop of the FDA's consistent and repeated statements that it lacked authority under the FDCA to regulate tobacco absent claims of therapeutic benefit by the manufacturer." *Id.* at 144.

. . . .

In this light, *Brown & Williamson* interprets the six statutes not as a particular carve-out from the FDCA for cigarettes and smokeless tobacco (plus any additional products covered in the six statutes, which the FDA briefs make no effort to itemize), but rather as "a distinct regulatory scheme to address the problem of tobacco and health"—one that Congress intended would "preclude[ ] any role for the FDA" with respect to "tobacco absent claims of therapeutic benefit by the manufacturer." *Id.* . . .

Brown & Williamson therefore did not preclude the FDA from regulating only those products for which Congress had passed specific statutes. Rather, it recognized that Congress had consciously developed a statutory scheme for tobacco and health that distinguished tobacco products as customarily marketed from ones marketed for therapeutic purposes. "Thus, what Congress ratified was the FDA's plain and resolute position that the FDCA gives the agency no authority to regulate tobacco products as customarily marketed." *Id.* at 159.

At oral argument the FDA observed with some justice that the regulatory scheme before the Court in *Brown & Williamson* addressed only cigarettes and smokeless tobacco; it would have us infer that the Court used the incessantly repeated phrase "tobacco products" as a shorthand, confined to the products before the Court (supplemented by whatever additional products were reached by the six statutes). We find no evidence of any such restrictive intent. . . .

The Tobacco Act is wholly consistent with this reading of *Brown & Williamson*. Written to address the regulatory gap that the case identified, the Tobacco Act provides the FDA with regulatory authority over tobacco products without requiring therapeutic claims. Besides leaving the FDA's authority under the drug/device provisions of the FDCA undisturbed, . . . the act broadly defines tobacco products as extending to "*any* product made *or derived from* tobacco," 21 U.S.C. § 321(rr)(1) (emphasis added). To be sure, this definition could align with a variety of interpretations of *Brown & Williamson's* scope (including the one FDA proffers here), but our reading is squarely within that range.

The FDA responds that its treatment of the Favor Smokeless Cigarette in 1987 supports its reading of *Brown & Williamson*. We think not. Favor was a small tube containing a nicotine solution, enabling the user to inhale nicotine vapor without smoke. Though the Smokeless Cigarette was marketed without therapeutic claims, the FDA warned Favor that it was an unapproved new drug. The FDA's claimed authority over Favor was, however, never challenged or adjudicated in court. . . .

The FDA has also offered a consequentialist argument, namely, that understanding *Brown & Williamson* in this fashion leaves the FDA severely thwarted in any effort to nudge e-cigarettes toward relatively healthful forms (or at least away from relatively unhealthful ones). Whether such a consequentialist argument should play any role in our interpretation of *Brown & Williamson* is questionable, but no matter. In fact the Tobacco Act gives the FDA broad regulatory authority over tobacco products, including, for instance, authority to impose restrictions on their sale, and on the advertising and promotion of such products, to regulate the mode of manufacture of tobacco products, and to establish standards for tobacco products. To the extent that Congress believed *Brown & Williamson* left an insufficiently regulative environment for cigarettes, smokeless tobacco, cigars, and other tobacco products, it found the Tobacco Act an adequate remedy.

. . . Given the likelihood of NJOY's success on the merits, the irreparable harm to NJOY's business, and the FDA's unquestioned Tobacco Act authority to mitigate any public harm, the district court did not abuse its discretion in granting the preliminary injunction.

. . . The judgment of the district court is

Affirmed.

■ GARLAND, CIRCUIT JUDGE, concurring in the judgment:

Although I join my colleagues in the disposition of this case, I do so based on different reasoning. I do not read *FDA v. Brown & Williamson* as barring the FDA from regulating "electronic cigarettes" under the Food, Drug, and Cosmetic Act (FDCA), because I do not believe the Supreme Court intended its use of the term "tobacco products" to extend to products that do not contain tobacco. The Tobacco Control Act of 2009, however, expressly extends to products that are merely "derived from" tobacco. Accordingly, at least in the absence of a contrary agency interpretation entitled to *Chevron* deference, I read the Tobacco Control Act as requiring the FDA to regulate products like electronic cigarettes under that Act, rather than under the FDCA. . . .

In the usual circumstance, of course, a judge's view of the "better" reading of a statute administered by an agency is not necessarily dispositive. "If a statute is ambiguous, and if the implementing agency's construction is reasonable, *Chevron* requires a federal court to accept the agency's construction of the statute, even if the agency's reading differs from what the court believes is the best statutory interpretation." *Nat'l Cable & Telecomms. Ass'n v. Brand X Internet Servs.*, 545 U.S. 967, 980 (2005). In *United States v. Mead Corp.*, 533 U.S. 218 (2001), however, the Supreme Court held *Chevron* deference appropriate only for statutory interpretations with the "force of law," *id.* at 229, and ruled that an agency's litigation briefs—unlike, for example, its regulations—do not warrant such deference, *id.* at 238 n.19.

In this case, there is no agency pronouncement that calls for *Chevron* deference. Other than its briefs, which do not qualify, the only expression of the FDA's view regarding electronic cigarettes is the agency's 2008 detention order barring the importation of NJOY's products. But that order was issued before Congress passed the Tobacco Control Act in 2009 and hence does not construe it at all. . . .

In the absence of an authoritative agency interpretation, I conclude that, unless a product derived from tobacco is marketed for therapeutic purposes, the FDA may regulate it only under the provisions of the Tobacco Control Act. Accordingly, because NJOY's electronic cigarettes are derived from tobacco, I join my colleagues' disposition. What the result would be were the FDA to offer a contrary statutory interpretation in the form of a regulation, I leave for the day the agency decides to take that step.

NOTES

1. *Subsequent History. Rev'd on other grounds sub nom., Thompson Hine LLP v. Smoking Everywhere, Inc.*, 840 F. Supp. 2d 138 (D.D.C. 2012). In 2011, FDA announced: "The government has decided not to seek further review of this decision, and FDA will comply with the jurisdictional lines established by Sottera." "Regulation of E–Cigarettes and Other Tobacco Products," Letter from Lawrence R. Deyton, Director, FDA CTP, and Janet Woodcock, Director, FDA CDER, to Stakeholders (Apr. 25, 2011).

2. *Extension of FSPTCA to E-Cigarettes and Other Products.* FDA's new tobacco authorities apply automatically to "all cigarettes, cigarette tobacco, roll-your-own tobacco, and smokeless tobacco," but they will also apply to other sorts of tobacco products (e.g., cigars, pipe tobacco, and e-cigarettes) only if and when FDA deems them by regulation to be subject to the law. FD&C Act 901(b). FDA has announced its intention to promulgate such a regulation. "Regulation of E–Cigarettes and Other Tobacco Products," *supra* note 1. As of summer 2013, FDA still had not yet issued this rule, and a bill was under committee consideration in the House and Senate that would explicitly exempt "traditional large and premium cigars" from FDA's jurisdiction. H.R. 792, 113th Cong. (2013). In September 2013, in view of the dramatically rising popularity of e-cigarettes (including among mniors), a group of Democratic members of the House of Representatives sent a letter to FDA asking it "to act quickly" to issue rules for these products. Letter from Reps. Henry A. Waxman et al. to Margaret A. Hamburg, FDA Commissioner (Sept. 16, 2013).

3. *"Components, Parts, and Accessories."* With respect to the definition's reference to "any component, part, or accessory of a tobacco product," FDA has explained: "Thus, the term ["tobacco product"] is not limited to products containing tobacco, but also includes components, parts, and accessories of tobacco products, whether they are sold for further manufacturing or for consumer use. For example, tobacco, papers, and filters are tobacco products, whether they are sold to consumers for use with roll-your-own tobacco or are sold for further manufacturing into a product sold to a consumer, such as a cigarette." FINAL GUIDANCE FOR INDUSTRY: LISTING OF INGREDIENTS IN TOBACCO PRODUCTS 3 (Nov. 2009).

4. *FDA Approval of Smoking Cessation Products.* In 1984, FDA approved a new drug application (NDA) for Nicorette chewing gum, which was indicated "as a temporary aid to the cigarette smoker seeking to give up his or her smoking habit while participating in a behavior modification program under medical or dental supervision." Nicorette, originally approved as a prescription drug but now sold over-the-counter, contains either 2 mg or 4 mg nicotine in each piece of chewing gum. FDA considered, but ultimately rejected, establishing an over-the-counter monograph for smoking deterrent drug products. 58 Fed. Reg. 31236 (June 1, 1993). Consequently, any drug product that is labeled, represented, or promoted as a smoking deterrent is a new drug subject to the NDA process. 21 C.F.R. 310.544.

FDA has since approved NDAs for nicotine transdermal patches, lozenges, oral sprays, and inhalers to aid in smoking cessation. The first two are now available over-the-counter, whereas the latter two remain available only by prescription. In 2002, FDA found that "nicotine lollipops" and "lip balm," promoted to assist smoking cessation were intended for use as drugs. The FDA based its decision on the manufacturers' claims that these products are a "convenient, tasty way" to replace cigarettes and helped to decrease the "hand to mouth" fixation associated with smoking. FDA Talk Paper No. T02–17, FDA Warns Sellers of Nicotine Lollipops & Lip Balm that their Products are Illegal (Apr. 10, 2002). The Family Smoking Prevention and Tobacco Control Act explicitly states that a product "intended for the treatment of tobacco dependence, including smoking cessation" is regulated as a drug or device, rather than as a "modified risk tobacco product" under FD&C Act 911, if it has been approved as a drug or device by FDA. FD&C Act 911(c).

J. "LABEL," "LABELING," AND "ADVERTISING"

1. INTRODUCTION

FDA has authority over the "label" and "labeling" of every product within categories it regulates. Accordingly, the FD&C Act sets forth a definition for each these terms that applies throughout the statute. According to section 201(k) of the Act: "The term 'label' means a display of written, printed, or graphic matter upon the immediate container of any article." Section 201(m) provides: "The term 'labeling' means all labels and other written, printed, or graphic matter (1) upon any article or any of its containers or wrappers, or (2) accompanying such article." The significance of the word "accompanying" in section 201(m)(2) is the most analyzed and disputed aspect of these definitions.

The FD&C Act nowhere defines the term "advertisement" or "advertising." This is unfortunate, in light of the fact that the statute gives the agency authority to regulate the "advertising" of certain products, namely, prescription drugs, "restricted" medical devices, tobacco products, and vitamin and mineral supplements. *See* FD&C Act 403(a), 502(n) & (r), 900. Importantly, FDA's authority over advertising is exclusive only with respect to prescription drugs; it shares jurisdiction with the Federal Trade Commission over the advertising of restricted medical devices, tobacco products, and vitamin and mineral supplements, and it has in practice ceded control over the last of these entirely to the FTC. The FTC has exclusive authority over the advertising of food, over-the-counter drugs, non-restricted medical devices, and cosmetics, although, as discussed above, the content of advertising sometimes plays an indirect role in FDA's regulation of these products by helping to establish their "intended use." This bifurcation of authority has meant that considerable attention has been focused on defining the outer limits of FDA jurisdiction over "labeling."

NOTE

FDA (Non–)Regulation of Vitamin/Mineral Supplement Advertising. In the Vitamin–Mineral Amendments of 1976, Congress significantly limited FDA's authority over vitamin and mineral supplements. *See supra* p. 13, *infra* p. 323. At the same time, as partial compensation, Congress gave the agency limited power to regulate the advertising of these products. FD&C Act 403(a)(2). But the 1976 legislation also added a new section 707 to the FD&C Act, which, in substance, requires FDA to defer to the FTC before seeking to enforce its authority over vitamin and mineral advertising. FDA has not used this authority since it was conferred, and the procedural restrictions imposed by section 707 make it unlikely that it will ever be invoked.

2.　LABELING

The cases immediately following deal with the jurisdictional reach of FDA's labeling requirements. All of them involve health food products against which FDA took action because of their therapeutic claims.

Kordel v. United States
335 U.S. 345 (1948).

■ Opinion of the Court by MR. JUSTICE DOUGLAS, announced by MR. JUSTICE REED.

Kordel was charged by informations containing twenty counts of introducing or delivering for introduction into interstate commerce misbranded drugs. He was tried without a jury, found guilty, and fined two hundred dollars on each count. This judgment was affirmed on appeal.

. . . Since 1941 [Kordel] has been marketing his own health food products, which appear to be compounds of various vitamins, minerals and herbs. The alleged misbranding consists of statements in circulars or pamphlets distributed to consumers by the vendors of the products, relating to their efficacy. The petitioner supplies these pamphlets as well as the products to the vendors. Some of the literature was displayed in stores in which the petitioner's products were on sale. Some of it was given away with the sale of products; some sold independently of the drugs; and some mailed to customers by the vendors.

It is undisputed that petitioner shipped or caused to be shipped in interstate commerce both the drugs and the literature. Seven of the counts charged that the drugs and literature were shipped in the same cartons. The literature involved in the other counts was shipped separately from the drugs and at different times—both before and after the shipments of the drugs with which they were associated. The question whether the separate shipment of the literature saved the drugs from being misbranded within the meaning of the [FD&C] Act presents the main issue in the case.

. . . The term labeling is defined in § 201(m) to mean "all labels and other written, printed, or graphic matter (1) upon any article or any of its containers or wrappers, or (2) accompanying such article." . . . In this case the drugs and the literature had a common origin and a common destination. The literature was used in the sale of the drugs. It explained their uses. Nowhere else was the purchaser advised how to use them. It constituted an essential supplement to the label attached to the package. Thus the products and the literature were interdependent. . . .

It would, indeed, create an obviously wide loophole to hold that these drugs would be misbranded if the literature had been shipped in the same container but not misbranded if the literature left in the next or in the preceding mail. The high purpose of the Act to protect consumers who under present conditions are largely unable to protect themselves in this field would then be easily defeated. The administrative agency charged with its enforcement has not given the Act any such restricted construction. . . . Accordingly, we conclude that the phrase "accompanying such article" is not restricted to labels that are on or in the article or package that is transported. . . .

One article or thing is accompanied by another when it supplements or explains it, in the manner that a committee report of the Congress accompanies a bill. No physical attachment one to the other is necessary. It is the textual relationship that is significant. . . .

The false and misleading literature in the present case was designed for use in the distribution and sale of the drug, and it was so used. The fact that it went in a different mail was wholly irrelevant whether we judge the transaction by purpose or result. And to say that the prior or subsequent shipment of the literature disproves that it "is" misbranded when introduced into commerce within the meaning of § 301(a) is to overlook the integrated nature of the transactions established in this case. . . .

Petitioner points out that in the evolution of the Act the ban on false advertising was eliminated, the control over it being transferred to the Federal Trade Commission. We have searched the legislative history in vain, however, to find any indication that Congress had the purpose to eliminate from the Act advertising which performs the function of labeling. Every labeling is in a sense an advertisement. The advertising which we have here performs the same function as it would if it were on the article or on the containers or wrappers. As we have said, physical attachment or contiguity is unnecessary under § 201(m)(2). . . .

NOTE

The defendant in *Kordel* was responsible for the shipment of both the products and the descriptive pamphlets, even though the two acts were separated in time. The Court's expansive interpretation of the Act's definition of "labeling" was reiterated the same day by its decision in *United States v. Urbuteit*, 335 U.S. 355 (1948). In *Urbuteit*, a seizure action, the Court similarly found that leaflets shipped at a different time than medical devices nonetheless accompanied the devices:

> [T]he common sense of the matter is to view the interstate transaction in its entirety—the purpose of the advertising and its actual use. In this case it is plain to us that the movements of machines and leaflets in interstate commerce were a single interrelated activity, not separate or isolated ones. The Act is not concerned with the purification of the

stream of commerce in the abstract. The problem is a practical one of consumer protection, not dialectics. The fact that the false literature leaves in a separate mail does not save the article from being misbranded. Where by functional standards the two transactions are integrated, the requirements of § 304(a) are satisfied, though the mailing or shipments are at different times.

335 U.S. at 357–58.

United States v. 24 Bottles "Sterling Vinegar & Honey," etc.

338 F.2d 157 (2d Cir. 1964).

■ LUMBARD, CHIEF JUDGE.

. . . .

Balanced Foods, Inc., appeals from an order of the District Court for the Southern District of New York condemning a number of bottles of Sterling Vinegar and Honey and a number of copies of two books, "Folk Medicine" and "Arthritis and Folk Medicine." Balanced Foods wholesales health foods and related products. The books and Vinegar and Honey were seized in its warehouse in New York City and condemned as misbranded drugs . . . on the ground that the books were "labeling" for the Vinegar and Honey and are misleading. . . .

Vinegar and Honey seems to have been one of the minor ephemera characteristic of the health and diet food trade. That it gained shelf space among boxes of sunflower seed, wheat germ and healing grasses can be attributed to the wide reading of Dr. D. C. Jarvis' first book, "Folk Medicine," subtitled "A Vermont Doctor's Guide to Good Health." . . .

Prominent among Dr. Jarvis' remedies is a mixture of cider vinegar and honey, which is prescribed for a wide variety of maladies. Inevitably some people found it burdensome to mix the vinegar with the honey, and, true to the traditions of free enterprise, several companies responded by producing a pre-mixed product. Among them was Sterling. "Folk Medicine" and its sequel, "Arthritis and Folk Medicine," mention Sterling cider vinegar by name as suitable for medicinal use, and the two books certainly have promoted the sale of Sterling's Honey and Vinegar. In addition, Balanced Foods stocked both and sold both to a number of retailers. The question is whether the sum of these relationships constitutes labeling. We do not think that it does.

The Vinegar and Honey bottles bear a label, which claims no more than that they contain one pint of "aged in wood cider vinegar blended with finest honey." The labeling subject to the Act is not limited to this common form of label. . . . On the other hand, labeling does not include every writing which bears some relation to the product. There is a line to be drawn, and, if the statutory purpose is to be served, it must be drawn in terms of the function served by the writing.

. . . Advertising and labeling overlap; most labels advertise as well. They are not identical, however, and material which serves only as an advertisement is not covered by the Act.

The distinguishing characteristic of a label is that, in some manner or another, it is presented to the customer in immediate connection with his view and his purchase of the product. Such a connection existed at both wholesale and retail levels in Kordel: Although the pamphlets and drugs were mailed to retailers separately, they were mailed in "integrated transactions"; the vendors in turn gave the pamphlets away with the sale of the drugs in some cases. . . .

We need not consider whether or under what circumstances integrated use of written material and a drug product by a retailer would by itself allow condemnation of the goods in the hands of the wholesaler, for there is no evidence of such use of "Folk Medicine" or "Arthritis and Folk Medicine" with Vinegar and Honey at either level. Balanced Foods sold both, and the government presented some evidence that it took special steps to promote "Folk Medicine." There was no evidence of any joint promotion of either book with Vinegar and Honey, however. It perhaps could be inferred that the officers of Balanced Foods realized that sale of the books would tend to promote sale of Vinegar and Honey. But there can be no inference that it sold the books for that purpose. It first ordered "Folk Medicine" almost two years before it began carrying Vinegar and Honey; it sold over 7,000 copies of "Folk Medicine" at $2.00 each wholesale and fewer than 2,000 pint bottles of Vinegar and Honey. There was, in sum, no basis for finding that Balanced Foods did more than carry two related products. . . .

"Folk Medicine" . . . made broad claims for a vinegar and honey mixture, which led ultimately to Sterling's marketing Vinegar and Honey. It is not disputed that these claims were misleading, but the Federal Food, Drug and Cosmetic Act was not intended to deal generally with misleading claims. . . .

The judgment of the district court is reversed.

NOTES

1. *"Written, printed, or graphic matter."* Section 201(m)'s limitation of "labeling" to "written, printed, or graphic" matter could be read to significantly restrict the range of materials that fall within the definition. But in its regulation defining "labeling" with respect to prescription drugs, FDA construes the word extremely broadly:

> Brochures, booklets, mailing pieces, detailing pieces, file cards, bulletins, calendars, price lists, catalogs, house organs, letters, motion picture films, film strips, lantern slides, sound recordings, exhibits, literature, and reprints and similar pieces of printed, audio, or visual matter descriptive of a drug and references published (for example, the "Physicians Desk Reference") for use by medical practitioners, pharmacists, or nurses, containing drug information supplied by the manufacturer, packer, or distributor of the drug and which are disseminated by or on behalf of its manufacturer, packer, or distributor are hereby determined to be labeling as defined in section 201(m) of the act.

21 C.F.R. 202.1(l)(2). As suggested by the references to "film strips" and "lantern slides," this regulation dates back to 1975.

2.   *Books and Articles as Labeling.* As *Sterling Vinegar & Honey* makes clear, independently-produced books and articles may constitute labeling if they are distributed as part of an integrated distribution program in conjunction with a product they discuss. In several cases in which the government deemed books to be labeling and seized the books along with the product, the authors or publishers of the books intervened in the seizure actions and alleged—unsuccessfully—that such seizures violated the First Amendment of the U.S. Constitution, guaranteeing freedom of the press and of speech. *See, e.g., United States v. 8 Cartons, Containing "'Plantation' 'The Original' etc., Molasses"*, 103 F. Supp. 626, 627 (W.D.N.Y. 1951); *United States v. Articles of Drug . . . Century Food Co.*, 32 F.R.D. 32 (S.D. Ill. 1963). Although these decisions upheld the government's power to seize particular copies of independently-written materials distributed in a manner that rendered them labeling, in 1982, FDA embraced a policy of not seizing labeling in the form of books, but only the violative product itself. Compliance Policy Guide No. 7153.13 (Dec. 1, 1982). The current version of the CPG states:

> Where labeling other than books renders a product to be violative, and the labeling is closely associated with the product in question (e.g., brand name, proximity at point of sale) the agency will continue to recommend recommend seizure of both the product and the labeling.

> Where labeling is in the form of a book and the agency believes that the use of the book to promote the product creates a significant consumer deception, the agency will consider filing a complaint for forfeiture against the product and an injunction to halt, after a hearing, misuse of the book.

CPG Sec. 140.100 (Rev. Aug. 31, 1989).

3.   *Dietary Supplement Labeling Exemption.* Section 403B of the FD&C Act, added by the Dietary Supplement Health and Education Act of 1994, exempts from section 201(m)'s definition of "labeling" certain publications used in connection with the sale of dietary supplements. Materials reprinted in their entirety qualify for this exemption if they (1) are not false or misleading; (2) do not promote a particular manufacturer or brand of a dietary supplement; (3) are displayed or presented so as to present a balanced view of the available scientific information; (4) are, if displayed in an establishment, physically separate from the dietary supplements; and (5) do not have appended to them any additional information. FD&C Act 403B(a). Moreover, FD&C Act 403B(b) provides that these five conditions of subsection 403B(a) "shall not apply to or restrict a retailer or wholesaler of dietary supplements in any way whatsoever in the sale of books or other publications as a part of the business of such retailer or wholesaler." Thus, books or other publications that are offered for sale by a retailer or wholesaler of dietary supplements do not become labeling for those dietary supplements simply because they fail to meet one or more of the five criteria of section 403B(a).

3.   ADVERTISING

As noted above, the FD&C Act, somewhat surprisingly, does not contain a definition of "advertising" or "advertisement." Most of the bills introduced prior to mid-1937 during the flurry of legislative activity culminating in the passage of the 1938 FD&C Act included a definition of "advertisement." Early bills gave the word a broad meaning. For example, one bill provided: "The term 'advertisement' includes all representations of fact or opinion disseminated in any manner or by any means other than by labeling." S. 2800, 73d Cong. § 2(j) (1934).

Later bills included a narrower definition of "advertisement." For example, S. 5, the bill that ultimately passed, included in its early iterations the following definition (which varied slightly in different versions): "The term 'advertisement' means all representations of fact or opinion disseminated in any manner or by any means, other than by the labeling, for the purpose of inducing, directly or indirectly, the purchase of food, drugs, devices, or cosmetics." S. 5, 75th Cong. § 2(o) (as introduced in the Senate, Jan. 6, 1937).

The definition of "advertisement" disappeared entirely from the final versions of the bill, and thus from the FD&C Act itself. This deletion likely occurred because in 1938, Congress amended the Federal Trade Commission Act (FTCA) of 1914 to give the FTC, rather than FDA, authority over food, drug, device, and cosmetic advertising. Neither the FD&C Act nor the FTCA as amended included a definition of "advertising" or "advertisement." When FDA ultimately acquired authority over prescription drug advertising from FTC in 1962, no statutory definition of "advertising" came along with the new power.

To this day, FDA still has not filled this statutory gap with a regulatory definition of "advertisement" or "advertising." The closest the agency has come is a regulation stating: "Advertisements subject to section 502(n) of the act [the subsection giving FDA power over prescription drug advertisements] include advertisements in published journals, magazines, other periodicals, and newspapers, and advertisements broadcast through media such as radio, television, and telephone communication systems." 21 C.F.R. 202.1(l)(1).

4. THE INTERNET

Letter From Margaret M. Dotzel, Assoc. Comm. for Policy, FDA, to Daniel J. Popeo and Paul D. Kamenar, Washington Legal Foundation

Nov. 1, 2001.

Dear Messers Popeo and Kamenar:

This letter responds to your citizen petition . . . filed on behalf of the Washington Legal Foundation. Your petition asked FDA to "formally adopt a rule, policy, or guidance stating that information presented or available on a company's Internet website, including hyperlinks to other third party sites, does not constitute 'labeling,'" as defined by the Federal Food, Drug, and Cosmetic Act (FDCA) at 21 U.S.C. § 321(m). In your petition, you further requested that the rule, policy, or guidance specify that such information may, but does not necessarily, constitute advertising. . . .

. . . The agency . . . agrees that it has not issued a specific rule, policy, or guidance that addresses whether information posted on a company's website is considered advertising, labeling, neither, or both. However, FDA disagrees that information presented or available on a company's website could never constitute labeling.

"Labeling" is defined in section 201(m) of the FDCA as "all labels and other written, printed or graphic matter upon any article . . . or accompanying such article." In *Kordel v. United States*, 335 U.S. 345 (1948), the Supreme Court concluded that the phrase "accompanying such article" included literature that was shipped separately and at different times from the drugs with which they were associated. "One article or thing is accompanied by another when it supplements or explains it, in the manner that a committee report of the Congress accompanies a bill. No physical attachment one to the other is necessary. It is the textual relationship that is significant." *Id.* at 350. . . .

. . . In addition, the courts have considered whether the information and the product are part of an integrated distribution program, where, for example, the information and the product originate from the same source or the information is designed to promote the distribution and sale of the product, even if such sale is not immediate.

Accordingly, FDA believes that, in certain circumstances, information about FDA regulated products that is disseminated over the Internet by, or on behalf of, a regulated company can meet the definition of labeling in section 201(m) of the FDCA. For example, if a company were to promote a regulated product on its website and allow consumers to purchase the product directly from the website, the website is likely to be "labeling." The website, in that case, would be written, printed, or graphic matter that supplements or explains the product and is designed for use in the distribution and sale of the product.

To provide an example from the other end of the spectrum, some product-specific promotion presented on non-company websites that is very much similar, if not identical to messages the agency has traditionally regulated as advertisements in print media (*e.g.*, advertisements published in journals, magazines, periodicals, and newspapers) would be viewed as advertising. These are just examples at the extremes and . . . the agency will proceed on case-by-case basis in determining what is "labeling."

. . . [F]or the reasons stated above, FDA has decided to deny your petition. . . .

Sincerely yours,

Margaret M. Dotzel

NOTES

1. *2007 Guidance.* One of the few other instances where FDA has identified particular circumstances in which information available through the internet may constitute "labeling" is a 2007 guidance document to food

manufacturers regarding labeling claims. In that document, which cites the letter excerpted above, the agency explains:

> In certain circumstances, information that is disseminated over the Internet by, or on behalf of, a regulated company meets the definition of labeling in section 201(m) of the Act and is subject to the requirements of the Act. For example, if a company were to promote a regulated product on its website and allow consumers to purchase the product directly from the website, the website is likely to be "labeling." As another example, if the label for a product contained a statement that referred the consumer to a specific website for additional information about a claim for the product, the website is likely to be "labeling." The websites, in these cases, are considered written, printed, or graphic matter that supplements or explains the product and is designed for use in the distribution and sale of the product.

GUIDANCE FOR INDUSTRY AND FDA: DEAR MANUFACTURER LETTER REGARDING FOOD LABELING (Jan. 2007).

2.   *FDA and FTC.* With respect to prescription drugs and biologics, restricted devices, and tobacco products, not much is at stake in the precise demarcation between "labeling" and "advertising" on the internet because the agency has authority over both. By contrast, FDA has no direct authority over the advertising of food, cosmetics, over-the-counter drugs, or non-restricted devices—the FTC has exclusive jurisdiction in these areas. Consequently, the classification of internet promotion of these products as "labeling" or "advertising" determines which agency has jurisdiction and which statute (the FD&C Act or the Federal Trade Commission Act) applies. In practice, however, the two agencies have cooperated in policing the internet in a fairly *ad hoc* manner without offering firm guidance on the boundaries of their respective authority.

With respect to products for which FDA has jurisdiction over both labeling and advertising (tobacco products and many medical products), the most important unanswered questions regarding the internet concern issues unrelated to the dividing line between labeling and advertising.

Promotion of Food and Drug Administration– Regulated Medical Products Using the Internet and Social Media Tools; Notice of Public Hearing

74 Fed. Reg. 48083 (Sept. 21, 2009).

The Food and Drug Administration . . . is announcing a public hearing to discuss issues related to the promotion of FDA-regulated medical products (including prescription drugs for humans and animals, prescription biologics, and medical devices) using the Internet and social media tools. FDA is seeking participation in the public hearing and written comments from all interested parties. . . .

FDA regulates the labeling of all drugs and devices under its jurisdiction. . . .

FDA also regulates the advertising for prescription drugs and biologics. Although the act does not define what constitutes an "advertisement," FDA generally interprets the term to include information (other than labeling) that is issued by, or on behalf of, a manufacturer, packer, or distributor and is intended to promote a product. . . .

FDA similarly regulates advertising for restricted devices. . . .

Although FDA has not comprehensively addressed when Internet promotion of prescription drugs and medical devices is labeling versus advertising, the agency has jurisdiction over all prescription drug and biologic product promotion as well as all restricted device advertising and all device promotional labeling when conducted by or on behalf of a manufacturer, packer, or distributor. There are no regulations that specifically address Internet promotion separately from the other types of promotion . . . , nor are there any regulations that prohibit the use of certain types of media to promote drugs and medical devices. Although no rule has specifically addressed Internet promotion, it is fairly clear that some promotional efforts are substantially similar in presentation and content to promotional materials in other media or publications. At the same time, FDA recognizes that the Internet possesses certain unique technological features and that some online tools that may be used for promotion offer novel presentation and content features. . . .

Questions have arisen regarding the application of the prescription drug and device advertising and labeling provisions, regulations, and policies of promotion on the Internet, especially with regard to the use of emerging technologies such as blogs, microblogs, podcasts, social networks and online communities, video sharing, widgets, and wikis. . . .

1.   For what online communications are manufacturers, packers, or distributors accountable?

FDA regulates promotion of medical products that is conducted by or on behalf of a manufacturer, packer, or distributor. In determining whether a manufacturer, packer, or distributor is accountable for a communication about its product(s), the agency considers whether the manufacturer, packer, or distributor or anyone acting on behalf of the manufacturer, packer, or distributor, such as an ad agency, created the promotional communication. In addition, the agency considers whether the manufacturer, packer, or distributor or anyone acting on behalf of the manufacturer, packer, or distributor is influencing or controlling the promotional activity or communication in whole or in part.

Manufacturers, packers, and distributors may have a variety of options for how much control they exert over activities on the Internet, regardless of whether the promotional activity occurs on company-sponsored venues or on third-party venues. . . . For example, in setting up a program about its product(s) through a chatroom, a manufacturer, packer, or distributor may allow comments to be posted in real time with no editing or review by the manufacturer, packer, or distributor; alternatively, the manufacturer, packer, or distributor may have the option of reviewing and editing comments before they are posted. . . .

Similarly, a manufacturer, packer, or distributor posting a video on a video-sharing site such as YouTube may choose whether or not to allow viewers to post comments.

In addition, various Web sites and tools can allow manufacturers, packers, or distributors to prompt others to communicate about their products. For example, a manufacturer, packer, or distributor may ask or otherwise encourage users to post their own videos about its product(s) on sites such as YouTube. A manufacturer, packer, or distributor may also send out packets of information to prominent bloggers with the aim of prompting the blogger to write about its product(s). Alternatively, a manufacturer, packer, or distributor may create an online community for patients or health care professionals to discuss disease states, which may prompt discussion about the manufacturer's, distributor's, or packer's product(s). The agency is interested in hearing the views of the public on the following topics:

- What parameters or criteria should be applied to determine when third-party communications occurring on the Internet and through social media technologies are subject to substantive influence by companies that market products related to the communication or discussion?
- In particular, when should third-party discussions be treated as being performed by, or on behalf of, the companies that market the product, as opposed to being performed independent of the influence of the companies marketing the products?
- How should companies disclose their involvement or influence over discussions or material, particularly discussions or material on third-party sites? . . .

2.   How can manufacturers, packers, or distributors fulfill regulatory requirements (*e.g.*, fair balance, disclosure of indication and risk information, postmarketing submission requirements) in their Internet and social media promotion, particularly when using tools that are associated with space limitations and tools that allow for real-time communications (*e.g.*, microblogs, mobile technology)? . . .

3.   What parameters should apply to the posting of corrective information on Web sites controlled by third parties?

Some manufacturers, packers, or distributors have expressed a desire to correct what are, in their belief, misconceptions or misinformation about their products, including unapproved uses of their products that are being conveyed on a Web site outside their control, such as on a blog, social networking site, or a wiki Web site (*i.e.*, Wikipedia). Other companies have stated that they have not corrected what they believe is misinformation in the belief that they could be viewed by such an action as being responsible for all the information on the target Web site rather than just the information that they post or submit. . . .

4.   When is the use of links appropriate?

The Internet allows users to move easily between Web sites or sources that provide information on many related topics. Under the act, companies are prohibited from promoting approved human and animal drugs, biologics, and medical devices for unapproved uses. However, sponsors sometimes provide links from their branded (*e.g.*, mentions a product) Web sites to other informational sources about diseases, such as support groups, some of which may contain information about unapproved disease conditions or unapproved uses of approved products. Furthermore, some companies are using unbranded (*e.g.*, does not mention a product) uniform resource locators (URLs) that, when clicked on, take users directly to branded information.

The agency is interested in any comments about the appropriateness of various techniques regarding the use of links (including between various social media tools) and data or research about whether or not users find these approaches to be misleading. . . .

NOTE

No Subsequent Action. As of the date of publication of this book, FDA had not yet issued a guidance or other document clarifying its views regarding the questions presented above.

CHAPTER 4

FDA ENFORCEMENT

A. INTRODUCTION

1. SECTION 301: PROHIBITED ACTS

Section 301, which enumerates the acts prohibited by the FD&C Act, is the heart of the enforcement provisions of the Act. These prohibitions are in turn enforceable in courts by the judicial remedies provided elsewhere in the Act and by other less formal mechanisms. Broadly speaking, section 301 prohibits the violation of any of the Act's substantive proscriptions or requirements. One or more provisions of section 301 is thus involved in every enforcement suit initiated by FDA.

One feature of section 301 deserves separate consideration. The section's opening phrase provides that the "causing" of any prohibited act, as well as the act itself, is prohibited. Neither the legislative history of the Act nor any judicial opinion discusses the scope of this provision. It had no counterpart in the 1906 Act, and Congress gave no reason for its inclusion in the 1938 Act. The provision is most often cited in holding corporate officers criminally liable for violations of the Act, although such liability had also been sustained under the 1906 Act. *See generally* George E. Harding, The "Causing" Provision and Jurisdictional Limits, 6 FOOD DRUG COSM. L.J. 594 (1951). In *United States v. Industrial Laboratories Co.*, 456 F.2d 908 (10th Cir. 1972), it was assumed without discussion that a consulting laboratory that failed to perform proper tests on a drug "caused" the adulteration of the product. Presumably any person involved in a violation is brought within the Act under this "causing" language. *See, e.g., United States v. International Exterminator Corp.*, 294 F.2d 270 (5th Cir. 1961) (assuming the potential liability of a pest control service for causing the introduction of contaminated food into interstate commerce).

2. TOOLS OF ENFORCEMENT

Sections 302 to 309 of the FD&C Act set forth specific mechanisms available to the government to enforce the Act: injunction proceedings, criminal prosecution, seizure and condemnation, debarment, civil money penalties, and informal compliance correspondence. Additional enforcement tools are contained elsewhere in the statute, most importantly the power to inspect facilities where regulated products are manufactured, processed, and held and the authority to publicize violations of the Act. FD&C Act 704, 705. All of these enforcement mechanisms will be examined in detail in this chapter.

Two critical points must be made at the outset of this discussion. First, private citizens do not have a right to sue to enforce the Act. Section 310(a) declares that except in a few instances in which states (though not individuals) may take action, "all ... proceedings for the enforcement, or to restrain violations, of this Act shall be by and in the name of the United States." Consequently, in virtually every formal enforcement action discussed in this book, the plaintiff (or prosecutor) is the United States government. It should be noted, however, that various ways exist for private plaintiffs to *indirectly* invoke the FD&C Act in lawsuits.

Second, like almost all other federal agencies, FDA must rely on the Department of Justice and local U.S. Attorneys to initiate suits to enforce the FDCA. The office within the Department of Justice that handles FDA referrals is the Civil Division's Office of Consumer Protection Litigation (OCPL), formerly known as the Office of Consumer Litigation. The FDA Chief Counsel sends referrals of proposed seizures, injunction cases, and criminal prosecutions to this office. With respect to FDA-developed and referred cases, the relationship between FDA and the Department of Justice (both OCPL and the U.S. Attorney offices) generally works quite smoothly. When breakdowns in cooperation and communication occur, they most frequently involve matters that the Chief Counsel's Office has not referred. The starkest recent example of this phenomenon was the ultimately failed criminal prosecution of an individual for the alleged misbranding of salad dressing. *U.S. v. Farinella*, 558 F.3d 695 (7th Cir. 2009). The Office of the U.S. Attorney in Chicago pursued this case against the advice of the FDA Chief Counsel's office. The Seventh Circuit's disdainful reversal of the jury conviction is excerpted *infra* at p. 383. *See generally* John R. Fleder, *The Role of the Department of Justice in Enforcement Matters Relating to the Food and Drug Administration*, 46 FOOD DRUG COSM. L.J. 781–92 (1991). In 1972, Congress considered, but failed to enact, a bill that would have authorized FDA's counsel to represent the agency in court. *See Hearings on H.R. 15315 Before the Subcomm. on Public Health and Env't of the H. Comm. on Interstate and Foreign Commerce*, 92d Cong. (1972).

3. FDA ENFORCEMENT STATISTICS

The 1906 Pure Food and Drugs Act provided the government only two formal means of enforcement: product seizures and criminal prosecution. The 1938 FD&C Act added the important enforcement tools of inspection and injunction and also included, in section 306 (now section 309) the statutory basis for what would decades later become a robust system of regulatory/warning letters. Over the years, the Act has been amended to give the government still more means of enforcement: civil penalties, mandatory recall, administrative detention, and debarment. We will examine all of these modes of enforcement below. But before studying these formal tools, it is important to understand two critical facts. First, FDA has immense informal power to impose its will on regulated industry. This informal authority is based both on the agency's ability to cripple a company through the use of adverse publicity and on the incentive for industries (especially those subject to FDA premarket approval) to remain in the agency's good graces. Second, the frequency with which the government has used the various formal enforcement tools has varied tremendously over time. The table below provides some insight into these trends:

Activity	1939	1951	1963	1976	1989	1994	2003	2007	2011	2012
Criminal Prosecution	626	347	248	43	16	8	1	344*	255*	262*
Seizure	1,861	1,341	1,049	317	144	98	25	6	15	8
Injunction	0	4	30	39	13	16	22	12	16	17
Regulatory/ Warning Letters	N.A.	N.A.	N.A.	982	370	1,594	545	471	1,720	4,882
Recalls†	0	54	101	837	2,183	3,236	4,627	5,585	3,640	4,075
Factory Inspections	N.A.	13,357	35,539	39,870	17,740	15,179	22,543	15,581	17,635	21,051
Samples	39,746	40,853	10,316	57,495	71,932	22,502	15,590	13,047	48,280	20,210
Import Inspections	16,352	39,942	30,985	71,643	102,617	93,323	139,310	N.A.	243,400	N.A.

Data derived from FDA: A CENTURY OF CONSUMER PROTECTION 116 (2006) and FDA website

*Convictions only

†Almost all recalls have been FDA-supervised, but not mandated

. . . .

Prescription for Harm: The Decline in FDA Enforcement Activity

Minority Staff of House Committee on Government Reform, 109th Cong.,
2d Sess., 2006.

. . . The report finds that there has been a dramatic decline in FDA enforcement actions over the last five years. Enforcement statistics show that FDA sent far fewer warning letters and conducted fewer seizures in 2005 than in 2000. One reason for the decline in enforcement actions is revealed in the internal FDA files reviewed in the investigation: FDA officials in Washington repeatedly rejected the recommendations of career field officials urging enforcement actions, even in cases involving death and serious injury. . . .

. . . The overall number of warning letters issued by the agency decreased from 1,154 in fiscal year 2000 to 535 in fiscal year 2005, a drop of over 50%. . . .

The decline in the number of FDA warning letters has been consistent throughout the Bush Administration, with the number of letters declining in four of the last five years. The number of warning letters declined by 11% in 2001, 27% in 2002, and 28% in 2003. After increasing slightly in 2004, the number of warning letters again declined (by 26%) in 2005, reaching a 15-year low.

A similar trend characterizes agency seizures. The number of seizures of unsafe products conducted by FDA fell by 44%, from 36 in 2000 to 20 in 2005.

Only one enforcement measure has shown a significant increase over the last five years: the number of FDA-regulated products on the market that had to be recalled increased by 44%, from 3,716 in 2000 to 5,338 in 2005. Since one of the goals of an enforcement system is to deter violations and keep dangerous products off of the market, the increase in recalls is not a hallmark of effective enforcement.

Increased compliance by manufacturers does not appear to account for the decline in FDA enforcement activity under the Bush Administration. Whenever FDA field inspectors observe violations during an inspection, the inspectors give the firm a notice to inform them of the violations observed. These notices, referred to as "483 forms," are an indication of the number of violations observed during a given year. In 2000, FDA issued 6,334 such forms. The number of "483 forms" issued was higher for the next four years: 7,683 in 2001; 7,180 in 2002; 7,813 in 2003, and 7,137 in 2004. In 2005, FDA issued 6,268 "483 forms," almost identical to the number issued in 2000. . . .

Internal FDA documents indicate that in at least 138 cases involving drugs or biological products over the last five years, FDA failed to take enforcement actions recommended by the agency's own field inspectors. . . .

In nearly half of these cases (67 cases), FDA took no enforcement action at all against the firm identified by field inspectors. In the remaining cases, the agency took action that was weaker than recommended by the field inspectors. . . .

4.   FDA ENFORCEMENT POLICY

Remarks by Margaret A. Hamburg, Commissioner of Food and Drugs, on "Effective Enforcement and Benefits to Public Health"

Food and Drug Law Institute (August 6, 2009).

A strong FDA has credibility with the public.

A strong FDA is transparent in explaining its decisions.

A strong FDA pursues creative solutions to longstanding problems and is always looking for novel ways to prevent illness and promote health.

And a strong FDA enforces the law.

. . . I have been impressed by the commitment to compliance that many companies have made—both in terms of their corporate culture and their investment in compliance systems.

Our goal is for all companies to make and implement such a commitment in order to prevent harm to the American people. We have a responsibility to clearly articulate and explain our rules and regulations, but a key part of the strategy to support private sector compliance is effective enforcement against violations of the law.

Effective enforcement has many clear benefits to public health.

It enables FDA to intercept unsafe or fraudulent products promptly . . . and prevent additional harm.

By holding violators accountable, enforcement deters others who would put the public at risk or prey upon vulnerable consumers.

Visible and clearly explained enforcement actions inform members of the public about potential dangers.

And enforcement helps industry too—by maintaining a level playing field for safe products. Making sure that offenders are held legally accountable prevents companies from having to choose between doing the right thing and staying competitive.

Ultimately, an effective enforcement strategy creates public confidence in FDA oversight . . . which in turn keeps trust in the safety of FDA-regulated products from eroding. Such confidence is critical to the long-term interest of both consumers and industry.

. . . .

An effective enforcement strategy depends on several key elements.

The FDA must be *vigilant*. Through regular inspections and follow-up on signals indicating problems, the FDA must work to identify and resolve problems early. . . . Companies must have a realistic expectation that if they are crossing the line, they will be caught, and that if they fail to act . . . we will.

The FDA must be *strategic*. The agency must place greater emphasis on significant risks and violations, and use meaningful penalties to send a strong message to discourage future offenses.

The FDA must be *quick*. The agency must be able to respond rapidly to egregious violations or violations that jeopardize public health.

And the FDA must be *visible*. The agency must show industry and consumers that we are on the job. We must publicize our enforcement actions—and the rationale for those actions—widely and effectively. This will increase public confidence, encourage compliance, and educate patients and consumers about potential risks. . . .

5. POLICY-MAKING THROUGH RULEMAKING VERSUS POLICY-MAKING THROUGH CASE-BY-CASE ENFORCEMENT

It is well established that a regulatory agency has discretion to initiate enforcement action against fewer than all of the firms engaged in similar unlawful conduct. *See Moog Industries, Inc. v. FTC*, 355 U.S. 411 (1958); *see also FTC v. Universal–Rundle Corp.*, 387 U.S. 244 (1967). Yet there are strong arguments favoring more comprehensive regulation. When FDA embraced the approach of generally-applicable regulation rather case-by-case enforcement in the early 1970s (as discussed in Chapter 2, *supra* p. 30), Peter Barton Hutt (then Chief Counsel) explained:

> . . . Standing alone, institution of legal enforcement action, resulting in costly and time-consuming litigation on a case-by-case basis, is an inadequate method of regulation. It fails to inform the regulated industry of its obligations, it involves years of delay, and the end results are often uncertain. Worst of all, it inevitably results in invidious selective enforcement, whereby one or two

individuals or companies must be singled out as the test cases while the rest of the industry is left alone. By contrast, the promulgation of regulations informs an entire industry of all applicable requirements and has proved to be far more likely to induce widespread compliance. . . .

Peter Barton Hutt, *Philosophy of Regulation Under the Federal Food, Drug and Cosmetic Act,* 28 FOOD DRUG COSM. L. J. 177, 183 (1973). Ever since the agency embraced this regulatory philosophy in the early 1970s, it has announced and advanced policies applicable to whole industries through the promulgation of rules (both notice-and-comment rules and, increasingly, informal guidance documents) rather than through case-by-case enforcement.

B. ENFORCEMENT CONSISTENCY, SELECTIVITY, AND DISCRETION

1. ADMINISTRATIVE CONSISTENCY AND SELECTIVE ENFORCEMENT

United States v. Undetermined Quantities of an Article of Drug Labeled as Exachol

716 F. Supp. 787 (S.D.N.Y. 1989).

■ SWEET, DISTRICT JUDGE:

Plaintiff the United States Federal Food and Drug Administration moves for summary judgment pursuant to Rule 56, Fed. R. Civ. P. against defendant U.S. Health Club, Inc. ("Health Club") seeking to condemn the seized Exachol as a misbranded and unapproved new drug. Because Exachol is entitled to be considered under the Health Claims for Food Policy, the motion for summary judgment is denied. . . .

Health Club manufactures and sells a product . . . distributed under the name "Exachol." . . . According to Health Club, the ingredients used in Exachol are commonly available as food supplements for which scientific data as to their effectiveness is publicly available.

. . . According to the FDA, an inspection conducted on December 8, 1986, revealed that the labelling and promotion of Exachol asserts that Exachol is effective in the prevention and treatment of coronary thrombosis, arteriosclerosis, atherosclerosis and angina. . . .

On August 4, 1987, the FDA published the Health Claims for Food Policy in the form of a Notice of Proposed Rulemaking concerning the content of health-related claims or information placed on food labelling and the criteria applied to evaluate the propriety of such labelling. Pending the rulemaking proceeding, the FDA decided to apply the proposed criteria to any questioned labelling:

(1) Information on the labelling must be truthful and not misleading to the consumer.

(2) The claims should be supported by valid, reliable, scientific evidence that is publicly available (prior to any health related claim being made).

(3) The claims must be consistent with generally recognized medical and nutritional principles.

(4) Food labels containing a health-related claim must also contain the nutrition labelling information required by 21 CFR § 101.9.

The FDA also indicated that it would apply the same criteria to dietary supplements, noting that it may be more difficult for dietary supplements to meet the criteria.

Under the health claims policy, a company is permitted to label its food or food supplement with appropriate health related messages without the product being rendered "misbranded" or a "drug" under the Act. . . .

According to the FDA, this policy is inapplicable to Exachol because Exachol is a drug. The correct inquiry, however, is whether the labelling accompanying Exachol is consistent with the criteria discussed by FDA for the type of health claim which does not trigger the drug provisions of the Act.

. . . [T]he FDA's application of the health claims rule to Kellogg's All Bran and various fish oil products before determining whether they will be regulated as drugs indicates that Health Club has been treated in a manner inconsistent with the FDA's established policy.

. . . The FDA has declined to regulate All–Bran as a drug until it has developed and applied one standard for considering health related information on food labels. As a result, the Health Claims for Food Policy, which applies to foods, should be applied to both products since the effect of the current labelling of each is virtually indistinguishable.

The FDA claims that Health Club has not submitted evidence similar to Kellogg's scientific evidence upon which the FDA based its decision indicating that its labels were not misleading. However, this did not constitute grounds for the prosecution of the fish oil manufacturers. The FDA has withheld review of the scientific evidence submitted by the fish oil manufacturers and classification of the fish oil products until after the health claims policy is applied. Further the FDA has given the fish oil manufacturers additional time to compile their evidence. . . .

. . . The FDA has apparently already reviewed Exachol's scientific evidence without awaiting the formalization of the health claims policy. There is no evidence offered here that the fish oil companies are compiling scientific data that will substantiate their claims of the health benefits of fish oils any more than the evidence which Health Club may present to substantiate its claims. Further the FDA has given no indication that the scientific evidence which Kellogg submitted . . . will significantly differ from that which Health Club has provided or may provide. Because the FDA makes no clear distinction between the scientific evidence presented for each product it has not sufficiently disputed health Club's claim that Exachol is similarly situated to All–Bran and the fish oil products.

Finally the FDA has not set forth its criteria for distinguishing which products are similar to Exachol and which are not. . . .

Courts reviewing administrative action require consistency from the government—whether the context be the denial of a regulatory exemption; the denial of a license; or the issuance of a cease and desist order. In every context, the overriding principle of fairness is always the same: the government must govern with an even hand.

In *United States v. Diapulse Corp. of America*, 748 F.2d 56 (2d Cir. 1984), the same standard of evenhandedness was required. There, the Diapulse Corporation of America sought to modify an injunction issued several years earlier in an enforcement action by the FDA, which prohibited Diapulse from marketing one of its products. Diapulse had moved to modify the injunction because the FDA has subsequently approved the same product for sale by a different company. Despite FDA objection, the district court agreed to a modification of the injunction. This decision was affirmed by the Second Circuit.

In explaining its affirmance, the Second Circuit declared that the government must act "evenhandedly" and that it could "not 'grant to one person the right to do that which it denies to another similarly situated.'" In the future, the Court instructed, the government could not continue "to treat like cases differently," and "must apply to [Diapulse] the same scientific and legal standards it applies to [Diapulse's] competitors."

Because the FDA has not treated Exachol under its Health Claims for Food Policy, it has applied an uneven regulatory policy, requiring denial of the requested summary judgment. . . .

NOTE

Selective Prosecution. Compare *U.S. v. Nutri–Cology, Inc.*, 1993 WL 13585505 (N.D. Cal. 1993), in which defendant, a dietary supplement manufacturer, advanced an affirmative defense of "selective prosecution" in an action in which FDA sought to enjoin it from distributing several products the agency deemed to be unapproved new drugs.

> Defendants primarily rely upon *United States v. Undetermined Quantities of an Article of Drug Labeled as "Exachol"*, 716 F. Supp. 787 (S.D.N.Y. 1989), which they claim supports the view that an uneven regulatory approach by the FDA precludes summary judgment. . . . Since this decision, however, the FDA has withdrawn its Health Claims for Food Policy. As a result, it appears that defendants' reliance on a so-called uneven regulatory approach defense lacks relevant case support. Defendants are thus left with their more traditional selective prosecution defense.

> A defense of selective prosecution requires two factors: First, defendants must show that others similarly situated have not been prosecuted. Second, defendants must show that the decision to prosecute was motivated by a discriminatory purpose, such as race, religion, or other arbitrary classification. *See Wayte v. United States*, 470 U.S. 598 (1985) (citing *Bordenkircher v. Hayes*, 434 U.S. 357 (1978)).

Although the evidence may support a conclusion that the FDA is more aggressively prosecuting Nutri–Cology than other similarly-situated companies, there is a total lack of credible evidence that the government's prosecution is motivated by a discriminatory purpose. Moreover, the FDA has broad prosecutorial discretion. See *Heckler v. Chaney*, 470 U.S. 821 (1985).

As a result, the Court finds that defendants' affirmative defense of selective prosecution is without basis.

2. ENFORCEMENT DISCRETION

Heckler v. Chaney

470 U.S. 821 (1985).

■ JUSTICE REHNQUIST delivered the opinion of the Court.

This case presents the question of the extent to which a decision of an administrative agency to exercise its "discretion" not to undertake certain enforcement actions is subject to judicial review under the Administrative Procedure Act, 5 U.S.C. § 501 et seq. (APA). Respondents are several prison inmates convicted of capital offenses and sentenced to death by lethal injection of drugs. They petitioned the Food and Drug Administration (FDA), alleging that under the circumstances the use of these drugs for capital punishment violated the Federal Food, Drug, and Cosmetic Act (FDCA) and requesting that the FDA take various enforcement actions to prevent these violations. The FDA refused their request. We review here a decision of the Court of Appeals for the District of Columbia Circuit, which held the FDA's refusal to take enforcement actions both reviewable and an abuse of discretion, and remanded the case with directions that the agency be required "to fulfill its statutory function." 718 F.2d 1174, 1191 (1983). . . .

The Court of Appeals' decision addressed three questions: (1) whether the FDA had jurisdiction to undertake the enforcement actions requested, (2) whether if it did have jurisdiction its refusal to take those actions was subject to judicial review, and (3) whether if reviewable its refusal was arbitrary, capricious, or an abuse of discretion. In reaching our conclusion that the Court of Appeals was wrong, however, we need not and do not address the thorny question of the FDA's jurisdiction. For us, this case turns on the important question of the extent to which determinations by the FDA *not to exercise* its enforcement authority over the use of drugs in interstate commerce may be judicially reviewed. That decision in turn involves the construction of two separate but necessarily interrelated statutes, the APA and the FDCA. *[handwritten: Court of Appeals Issues]*

The APA's comprehensive provisions for judicial review of "agency actions" are contained in 5 U.S.C. §§ 701–706. Any person "adversely affected or aggrieved" by agency action, *see* § 702, including a "failure to act," is entitled to "judicial review thereof," as long as the action is a "final agency action for which there is no other adequate remedy in a court," *see* § 704. The standards to be applied on review are governed by the provisions of § 706. But before any review at all may be had, a party must first clear the hurdle of § 701(a). That section provides that the *[handwritten: APA Judicial Review Sections]* chapter on judicial review "applies, according to the provisions thereof, except to the extent that—(1) statutes preclude judicial review; or (2) agency action is committed to agency discretion by law." Petitioner urges that the decision of the FDA to refuse enforcement is an action "committed to agency discretion by law" under § 701(a)(2). . . .

This Court first discussed § (a)(2) in *Citizens to Preserve Overton Park v. Volpe*, 401 U.S. 402 (1971). . . .

[*Overton Park*] answers several of the questions raised by the language of § 701(a), although it raises others. First, it clearly separates the exception provided by § (a)(1) from the § (a)(2) exception. The former applies when Congress has expressed an intent to preclude judicial review. The latter applies in different circumstances; even where Congress has not affirmatively precluded review, review is not to be had if the statute is drawn so that a court would have no meaningful standard against which to judge the agency's exercise of discretion. In such a case, the statute ("law") can be taken to have "committed" the decisionmaking to the agency's judgment absolutely. This construction avoids conflict with the "abuse of discretion" standard of review in § 706—if no judicially manageable standards are available for judging how and when an agency should exercise its discretion, then it is impossible to evaluate agency action for "abuse of discretion." In addition, this construction satisfies the principle of statutory construction mentioned earlier, by identifying a separate class of cases to which § 701(a)(2) applies. . . .

Overton Park did not involve an agency's refusal to take requested enforcement action. It involved an affirmative act of approval under a statute that set clear guidelines for determining when such approval should be given. Refusals to take enforcement steps generally involve precisely the opposite situation, and in that situation we think the presumption is that judicial review is not available. This Court has recognized on several occasions over many years that an agency's decision not to prosecute or enforce, whether through civil or criminal process, is a decision generally committed to an agency's absolute discretion. This recognition of the existence of discretion is attributable in no small part to the general unsuitability for judicial review of agency decisions to refuse enforcement.

The reasons for this general unsuitability are many. First, an agency decision not to enforce often involves a complicated balancing of a number of factors which are peculiarly within its expertise. Thus, the agency must not only assess whether a violation has occurred, but whether agency resources are best spent on this violation or another, whether the agency is likely to succeed if it acts, whether the particular enforcement action requested best fits the agency's overall policies, and, indeed, whether the agency has enough resources to undertake the action at all. An agency generally cannot act against each technical violation of the statute it is charged with enforcing. The agency is far better equipped than the courts to deal with the many variables involved in the proper ordering of its priorities. Similar concerns animate the principles of administrative law that courts generally will defer to an agency's construction of the statute it is charged with implementing, and to the procedures it adopts for implementing that statute.

In addition to these administrative concerns, we note that when an agency refuses to act it generally does not exercise its coercive power over an individual's liberty or property rights, and thus does not infringe upon areas that courts often are called upon to protect. . . .

We of course only list the above concerns to facilitate understanding of our conclusion that an agency's decision not to take enforcement action should be presumed immune from judicial review under § 701(a)(2). For good reasons, such a decision has traditionally been "committed to agency discretion," and we believe that the Congress enacting the APA did not intend to alter that tradition. In so stating, we emphasize that the decision is only presumptively unreviewable; the presumption may be rebutted where the substantive statute has provided guidelines for the agency to follow in establishing its enforcement powers.[4] Thus, in establishing this presumption in the APA, Congress did not set agencies free to disregard legislative direction in the statutory scheme that the agency administers. Congress may limit an agency's exercise of enforcement power if it wishes, either by setting substantive priorities, or by otherwise circumscribing an agency's power to discriminate among issues or cases it will pursue. . . .

Rebuttable Presumption

To enforce the various substantive prohibitions contained in the FDCA, the Act provides for injunctions, 21 U.S.C. § 332, criminal sanctions, §§ 333 and 335, and seizure of any offending food, drug, or cosmetic article, § 334. The Act's general provision for enforcement, § 372, provides only that "[t]he Secretary is *authorized* to conduct examinations and investigations . . ." (emphasis added) . . . § 332 gives no indication of when an injunction should be sought, and § 334, providing for seizures, is framed in the permissive—the offending food, drug, or cosmetic "shall be liable to be proceeded against." The section on criminal sanctions states baldly that any person who violates the Act's substantive prohibitions "shall be imprisoned . . . or fined." Respondents argue that this statement mandates criminal prosecution of every violator of the Act but they adduce no indication in case law or legislative history that such was Congress' intention in using this language, which is commonly found in the criminal provisions of Title 18 of the United States Code. We are unwilling to attribute such a sweeping meaning to this language, particularly since the Act charges the Secretary only with recommending prosecution; any criminal prosecutions must be instituted by the Attorney General. The Act's enforcement provisions thus commit complete discretion to the Secretary to decide how and when they should be exercised.

FDCA Provision

Respondents nevertheless present three separate authorities that they claim provide the courts with sufficient indicia of an intent to circumscribe enforcement discretion. Two of these may be dealt with summarily. First, we reject respondents' argument that the Act's substantive prohibitions of "misbranding" and the introduction of "new drugs" absent agency approval supply us with "law to apply." These provisions are simply irrelevant to the agency's discretion to refuse to initiate proceedings.

Arguments Against

---

4 We do not have in this case a refusal by the agency to institute proceedings based solely on the belief that it lacks jurisdiction. Nor do we have a situation where it could justifiably be found that the agency has "consciously and expressly adopted a general policy" that is so extreme as to amount to an abdication of its statutory responsibilities. . . .

We also find singularly unhelpful the agency "policy statement" on which the Court of Appeals placed great reliance [37 Fed. Reg. 16503 (August 15, 1972), excerpted *infra* p. 817]. We would have difficulty with this statement's vague language even if it were a properly adopted agency rule. . . . But in any event the policy statement was attached to a rule that was never adopted. Whatever force such a statement might have, and leaving to one side the problem of whether an agency's rules might under certain circumstances provide courts with adequate guidelines for informed judicial review of decisions not to enforce, we do not think the language of the agency's "policy statement" can plausibly be read to override the agency's express assertion of unreviewable discretion contained in the above rule.

Respondents' third argument, based upon § 306 [now 309] of the FDCA, merits only slightly more consideration. That section provides:

> "Nothing in this chapter shall be construed as requiring the Secretary to report for prosecution, or for the institution of libel or injunction proceedings, minor violations of this chapter whenever he believes that the public interest will be adequately served by a suitable written notice or ruling."

Respondents seek to draw from this section the negative implication that the Secretary is *required* to report for prosecution all "major" violations of the Act, however, those might be defined, and that it therefore supplies the needed indication of an intent to limit agency enforcement discretion. We think that this section simply does not give rise to the negative implication which respondents seek to draw from it. The section is not addressed to agency proceedings designed to discover the existence of violations, but applies only to a situation where a violation has already been established to the satisfaction of the agency. We do not believe the section speaks to the criteria which shall be used by the agency for investigating *possible* violations of the Act.

We therefore conclude that the presumption that agency decisions not to institute proceedings are unreviewable under 5 U.S.C. § 701(a)(2) is not overcome by the enforcement provisions of the FDCA. The FDA's decision not to take the enforcement actions requested by respondents is therefore not subject to judicial review under the APA. . . . In so holding, we essentially leave to Congress, and not to the courts, the decision as to whether an agency's refusal to institute proceedings should be judicially reviewable. No colorable claim is made in this case that the agency's refusal to institute proceedings violated any constitutional rights of respondents, and we do not address the issue that would be raised in such a case. The fact that the drugs involved in this case are ultimately to be used in imposing the death penalty must not lead this Court or other courts to import profound differences of opinion over the meaning of the Eighth Amendment to the United States Constitution into the domain of administrative law.

The judgment of the Court of Appeals is *Reversed*.

[The concurring opinions of Justice Brennan and Justice Marshall are omitted.]

NOTES

1.   *Section 309 and Enforcement Discretion. Chaney* is not the only case in which the United States Supreme Court has cited section 309 (formerly section 306) in rejecting arguments for literal interpretation of the FD&C Act's broader provisions. *See, e.g., United States v. Dotterweich,* 320 U.S. 277 (1943); *United States v. Sullivan,* 332 U.S. 689 (1948); *United States v. Park,* 421 U.S. 658 (1975). FDA itself has cited section 309 as authority for the issuance of informal tolerances for filth and other contaminants in food, and courts have accepted this argument. *See, e.g., United States v. 484 Bags, More or Less,* 423 F.2d 839, 841 (5th Cir. 1970); *Dean Rubber Mfg. Co. v. United States,* 356 F.2d 161, 164 (8th Cir. 1966). But in 1979, when the Attorney General was asked about the legality of phasing out the presence of carcinogenic nitrates in food instead of immediately banning them, he rejected that suggestion that section 309 conferred such discretion. 43 Op. Att'y Gen. 19 (1979). This opinion was issued prior to the Supreme Court's decision in *Chaney,* however.

2.   *Heterochemical Corp. v. FDA.* In one of the first cases after *Chaney* in which FDA asserted nonreviewable discretion not to take an enforcement action, the district court rejected the agency's argument. In *Heterochemical Corp. v. FDA,* 644 F. Supp. 271 (E.D.N.Y. 1986), the plaintiff petitioned FDA to take regulatory action against three competitors who sold vitamin K for use in animal feed without FDA approval. The agency denied the petition seven years later in 48 Fed. Reg. 16748 (April 19, 1983), and the plaintiff sought judicial review. FDA took the position that *Chaney* was dispositive. The court refused to dismiss the action, however. It held that the Supreme Court had excluded from FDA's unreviewable discretion those situations in which the agency has already conducted an investigation and determined that there is a violation of the FD&C Act, particularly when FDA regulations themselves establish a required course of agency action. The court later determined that the agency's own regulations required it to take action with regard to the vitamin K substances, and it thus granted the plaintiff's motion for summary judgment and required the agency to proceed with its established procedures. *Heterochemical Corp. v. FDA,* 741 F. Supp. 382 (E.D.N.Y. 1990).

3.   *Cook v. FDA.* Years passed before FDA's exercise of enforcement discretion was again judicially thwarted. In *Beaty v. FDA,* 853 F. Supp. 2d 30 (D.D.C. 2012), a judge limited the agency's discretion in a situation strikingly similar to that addressed by *Chaney* itself. The district court required FDA to bar importation of an unapproved drug used in executions, over the agency's objection that its policy not to do so was unreviewable. The D.C. Circuit opinion upholding this decision, *Cook v. FDA,* 2013 WL 3799987 (D.C. Cir. 2013), is excerpted in Chapter 14. *Infra* p. 1441.

4.   *Other Cases.* Notwithstanding *Heterochemical* and *Cook,* FDA's failure to take a particular enforcement action has rarely been challenged in court post-*Chaney,* and the few suits that have been brought have generally been unsuccessful. For example, in *Community Nutrition Institute v. Young,* 818 F.2d 943, 949–50 (D.C. Cir. 1987), the D.C. Circuit, citing *Chaney,* refused to review the agency's decision not to commence

enforcement proceedings against corn into which aflatoxin-contaminated corn had been intentionally blended. In *International Center for Technology Assessment v. Thompson*, 421 F. Supp. 2d 1, 7 (D.D.C. 2006) the court rejected the plaintiff's claim that FDA was required to impose the Act's new animal drug application (NADA) provisions on the Glofish, an ornamental, glowing zebra fish for home aquariums. Citing *Chaney*, the court observed: "[T]he FDA was not acting on the basis of a mistaken belief as to its regulatory jurisdiction. . . . [T]he FDA is simply exercising its discretion not to take enforcement actions against these particular fish." In *K–V Pharm. Co. v. United States FDA*, 889 F. Supp. 2d 119 (D.D.C. 2012), the court held that FDA's decision not to enforce the FD&C Act against pharmacies compounding cheaper me-too versions of Makena®, a drug for prevention of premature birth, was unreviewable under *Chaney*. For further details on this case, see *infra* p. 1026, note 3.

   5.   *Program Priorities.* In light of budget and personnel constraints, FDA always has to prioritize some enforcement goals over others, and the agency does not disguise its choices. For example, the Center for Food Safety and Applied Nutrition (CFSAN) annually publishes a "Program Priorities" report, which categorizes some activities as higher priorities than others and fails to mention other activities altogether.

   6.   *Systematic Exercise of Enforcement Discretion.* FDA has designed several entire initiatives explicitly around the principle of enforcement discretion. For example, as discussed in Chapter 6, *infra* p.474, the agency uses a system of "defect action levels" for aesthetic (nonharmful) contamination of food with filth; FDA will not take enforcement action against a food containing less filth than is allowed by the relevant action level, even though that food is adulterated as a formal matter. As also discussed in Chapter 6, *infra* p. 430, after the D.C. Circuit declared that the First Amendment limits FDA's authority to reject petitions for health claims on food, *Pearson v. Shalala*, 64 F.3d 650 (D.C. Cir. 1999), the agency established a framework to permit qualified health claims pursuant to its "enforcement discretion." The agency issued a guidance which, citing *Heckler*, laid out the circumstances "under which FDA will consider exercising its enforcement discretion to permit health claims that do not meet the 'significant scientific agreement' standard of evidence by which the health claims regulations require FDA to evaluate the scientific validity of claims." GUIDANCE FOR INDUSTRY, QUALIFIED HEALTH CLAIMS IN THE LABELING OF CONVENTIONAL FOODS AND DIETARY SUPPLEMENTS (Dec. 18, 2002). The agency calls the letters it sends to petitioners stating its intention not to object to the use of a qualified health claim "letters of enforcement discretion," even though it is not exercising "discretion" in these instances, but rather complying with a constitutional mandate.

C. FACTORY INSPECTION

1. INTRODUCTION

   The 1906 Act contained no provision authorizing FDA to inspect the establishments in which food and drugs were manufactured, processed, or stored. Section 704 of the 1938 Act therefore represented a major increase in the agency's enforcement authority. Section 704 provides, in part:

> (a)(1) For purposes of enforcement of this chapter, officers or employees duly designated by the Secretary, upon presenting appropriate credentials and a written notice to the owner, operator, or agent in charge, are authorized (A) to enter, at reasonable times, any factory, warehouse, or establishment in which food, drugs, devices, or cosmetics are manufactured, processed, packed, or held, for introduction into interstate commerce or after such introduction, or to enter any vehicle being used to transport or hold such food, drugs, devices, or cosmetics in interstate commerce; and (B) to inspect, at reasonable times and within reasonable limits and in a reasonable manner, such factory, warehouse, establishment, or vehicle and all pertinent equipment, finished and unfinished materials, containers, and labeling therein.

Section 301(f) of the FD&C Act makes the "refusal to permit entry or inspection as authorized by section 704" a prohibited act. Consequently, it is illegal for the owner of an establishment to refuse entry to an inspector who arrives at a "reasonable time" and presents appropriate credentials and notice.

FDA's inspection force is contained within the Office of Regulatory Affairs (ORA) and is dispersed throughout the United States. The inspectors are almost all generalists who work in all of the product areas under FDA jurisdiction.

FDA Investigations Operations Manual 2012, Chapter 5: Establishments Inspection

SUBCHAPTER 5.1—INSPECTION INFORMATION

5.1.1—AUTHORITY TO ENTER AND INSPECT

. . . .

It is your obligation to fulfill these requirements because failure to do so may prevent use of evidence and information obtained during the inspection.

. . . .

5.1.1.1—FDA Investigator's Responsibility

Your authority to enter and inspect establishments is predicated upon specific obligations to the firm as described below. It is your responsibility to conduct all inspections at reasonable times and within reasonable limits and in a reasonable manner. Proceed with diplomacy, tact and persuasiveness.

5.1.1.2—Credentials

Display your credentials to the top management official be it the owner, operator, or agent in charge.

. . . .

5.1.1.3—Written Notice

After showing the firm's representative your credentials, issue the original, properly executed, and signed FDA 482, Notice of Inspection, to the top management official. Keep the carbon copy for submission with your report.

5.1.1.4—Written Observations

Upon completing the inspection and before leaving the premises, provide the highest management official available your inspectional findings on an FDA 483—Inspectional Observations. See Section 704(b) of the FD&C Act.

5.1.1.5—Receipts

Furnish the top management official the original of the FDA–484— Receipt for Samples describing any samples obtained during the inspection.

. . . .

5.1.1.8—Business Premises

Authority to inspect firms operating at a business location . . . requires issuing management an FDA 482, Notice of Inspection, and presenting your credentials. A warrant for inspection is not necessary unless a refusal or partial refusal is encountered or anticipated.

. . . .

5.2.5.1—Refusal of Entry

When you are faced with a refusal of entry, call the person's attention to the pertinent sections of the Acts. . . . If entry is still refused, leave the completed FDA 482, leave the premises and telephone your supervisor immediately for instructions.

5.2.5.3—Refusal after Serving Warrant

If you have been refused entry, obtained a warrant, tried to serve or execute it and are refused entry under the warrant, inform the person, the warrant is a court order and such refusal may constitute contempt of court. If the warrant is not then immediately honored (entry and inspection permitted), leave the premises and promptly telephone the facts to your supervisor.

5.2.6—Inspection Warrant

A refusal to permit inspection invokes a criminal provision of section 301(f) of the FD&C Act [21 U.S.C. 331(f)]. Depending on the individual situation, instances of refusal may be met by judicious use of inspection warrants. . . .

NOTES

1.   *Duration of Inspection.* In *United States v. Durbin*, 373 F. Supp. 1136 (E.D. Okl. 1974), the court observed: "[D]efendant's interpretation of 21 U.S.C. § 374(a) as requiring a separate notice for each day of a multiple day inspection is incorrect. . . . [T]he Notice was dated May 31, 1973 and was effective until the inspection was completed and the required Report submitted."

2.   *Time of Day. In re Establishment Inspection of New England Medical Center Hospital*, 1969–1974 FDLI Jud. Rec. 622 (D. Mass. 1974), authorized FDA investigators and a local medical examiner to enter the

hospital any time except between 6:00 a.m. and 1:00 p.m. in order to determine what caused a radiation therapy stretcher assembly to rise and crush a patient against the ceiling. The judge concluded that the investigation could proceed more rapidly if access to the device were granted at all other times in a closed room so as not to disturb other patients.

3. *Inspection Costs*. In *United States v. Tri–Bio Laboratories, Inc.*, 700 F. Supp. 223 (M.D. Pa. 1988), the court held that it has inherent equitable power to order defendants to bear the cost of FDA inspection to enforce an injunction, but it declined to exercise that authority under the circumstances of this case, which presented no reasonable likelihood of future violations.

4. *Third–Party Inspections*. The Medical Device User Fee and Modernization Act of 2002 added a new subsection "g" to section 704 (Factory Inspection) of the FD&C Act. This subsection requires FDA to accredit third parties to perform inspections of eligible manufacturers of Class II or III devices. Manufacturers who meet certain conditions have the option of requesting inspection by one of these accredited third parties. This program is entirely voluntary.

2. CONSTITUTIONAL LIMITATIONS

United States v. Jamieson–McKames Pharmaceuticals, Inc.

651 F.2d 532 (8th Cir. 1981).

■ ARNOLD, CIRCUIT JUDGE. . . .

Jamieson–McKames Pharmaceuticals, Inc. (Jamieson–McKames) is a Missouri corporation with its principal place of business in St. Louis, Missouri. The company manufactured, purchased, packaged, labeled, distributed, and sold drugs from before June 1972 until November 1975. . . .

On October 29, 30, and 31, and November 3, 1975, federal and state agents entered and searched the premises of Jamieson–McKames Pharmaceuticals, Inc., and Pharmacare, Inc. . . . Samples of drugs were taken, documents were taken, quantities of drugs were embargoed, the premises and contents photographed, and machinery seized. On October 29 and 30, 1975, defendant's premises [in] Wentzville, Missouri, were also searched, and similar items were seized.

. . . .

Thereafter, on May 12, 1977, defendants were charged in an 11–count indictment with counterfeiting, adulterating, and misbranding drugs and conspiracy to counterfeit, adulterate, and misbrand drugs. The indictment also charged that the defendants committed all of these acts with the intent to defraud and mislead, rendering such felonies punishable under 21 U.S.C. § 333(b).

The appellants contend that their Fourth Amendment rights were violated by the failure of the court to suppress evidence seized by government agents from the defendants' business premises. . . .

The seizures at the Wentzville pharmacy were conducted on the authority of a notice to inspect authorized by 21 U.S.C. § 374(a). The employee in charge was given a copy of the notice to inspect, but no warrant to inspect was obtained.

The Supreme Court has held that warrantless searches are generally unreasonable, and that commercial premises as well as homes are within the Fourth Amendment's protection. *Marshall v. Barlow's, Inc.*, 436 U.S. 307 (1978). An exception from the search-warrant requirement has, however, been delineated for industries "long subject to close supervision and inspection," *Colonnade Catering Corp. v. United States,* 397 U.S. 72 (1970), and "pervasively regulated business[es]," *United States v. Biswell,* 406 U.S. 311 (1972). *Colonnade* involved the liquor industry, and *Biswell* the interstate sale of firearms. The threshold question therefore is whether the drug-manufacturing industry should be included within this class of closely regulated businesses.

The appellants argue that the drug-manufacturing industry is no more closely regulated than any number of industries involved in interstate commerce, and that therefore the rule of *Marshall v. Barlow's, Inc., supra,* requiring a warrant in the absence of consent before an administrative search can take place, should apply. In *Barlow's*, the Supreme Court held that warrantless searches authorized by § 8(a) of the Occupational Safety and Health Act violated the Fourth Amendment. There, however, the government sought to inspect work areas not open to the public on the premises of an electrical and plumbing contractor. In *Barlow's* the argument that all businesses involved in interstate commerce had "long been subject to close supervision" of working conditions was urged by the Secretary of Labor but explicitly rejected by the Court. In rejecting this argument and others the Court specifically preserved the *Colonnade–Biswell* exception to the warrant requirement. The Court indicated that there were other industries, covered by regulatory schemes applicable only to them, where regulation might be so pervasive that a *Colonnade–Biswell* exception to the warrant requirement could apply. Such warrantless searches are upheld because "when an entrepreneur embarks on such a business, he has chosen to subject himself to a full arsenal of governmental regulation," and "in effect consents to the restrictions placed on him." Further, in the face of a long history of government scrutiny, such a proprietor has no "reasonable expectation of privacy."

We think the drug-manufacturing industry is properly within the *Colonnade–Biswell* exception to the warrant requirement. The drug-manufacturing industry has a long history of supervision and inspection. The present Food, Drug, and Cosmetic Act has its origins in the Food and Drug Act of 1906. . . .

The *Biswell* Court acknowledged that the history of regulation of interstate firearms traffic was "not as deeply rooted" as the history of liquor regulation, but included firearms within the warrant exception because their regulation was of "central importance to federal efforts to prevent violent crime and to assist the states in regulating the firearms traffic within their borders." This passage teaches that the nature of the federal or public interest sought to be furthered by the regulatory scheme is important to our analysis. It is difficult to overstate the urgent nature of the public-health interests served by effective regulation of our nation's drug-manufacturing industry. Furthermore, virtually every phase of the drug industry is heavily regulated, from packaging, labeling, and certification of expiration dates, to prior FDA approval before new drugs can be marketed. The regulatory burdens on the drug-manufacturing industry are weighty, and that weight indicates that the drug manufacturer accepts the burdens as well as the benefits of the business and "consents to the regulations placed on him." *Marshall v. Barlow's, Inc.*, 436 U.S., at 313.

The final lesson of *Barlow's* is that the reasonableness of warrantless searches is dependent on the "specific enforcement needs and privacy guarantees of each statute." In *Barlow's* the Court was unconvinced that requiring OSHA officials to obtain administrative warrants when consent to inspect was withheld would cripple the effectiveness of the enforcement scheme. . . .

Regulation of the drug industry differs from the OSHA situation in another significant way. The class sought to be protected by OSHA regulation of safety of work areas is made up of employees, who are in the work place itself and free to report violations at any time. The protected class in the area of drug manufacturing is the consuming public, which has no way of learning of violations short of illness resulting from the consumption of defective drug products. In this sense the enforcement needs of drug-industry regulation are considerably more critical than those before the Court in *Barlow's*.

As for privacy guarantees, the Supreme Court points out that a warrant provides assurances that the proposed "inspection is reasonable under the Constitution, is authorized by statute, and is pursuant to an administrative plan containing specific neutral criteria." *Id.* at 323 (footnote omitted). The notice of inspection used in this case satisfies at least some of these criteria. It informs the "owner or agent in charge" (§ 374(a)) of the "scope and objects of the search." *Id.* at 323. Although the notice of inspection makes no express reference to reasonableness under the Constitution, it clearly states that notice is given pursuant to 21 U.S.C. § 374, which is enacted by the Congress. The name of the firm and address is also prominently listed. Further, the notice of inspection reproduces large portions of § 374(a), stating the areas and objects to be searched; that the inspection is to take place at reasonable times; that certain records are to be made available to the inspector; that each inspection must be made with reasonable promptness; that each inspection must be accompanied by a separate notice; and that the purpose of any inspection of a prescription-drug operation is discovery of information "bearing on whether prescription drugs (are being) adulterated or misbranded within the meaning of" the Act or on other violations of the Act. 21 U.S.C. § 374(a). Equally important, the Notice of Inspection informs the owner of what cannot be examined by the inspector. Inspections relating to prescription drugs do not extend to financial data, pricing data, and certain data regarding sales, personnel, and research.

In sum, the authorizing statute now before the Court was not painted with so broad a brush as the one rejected in *Barlow's*, the enforcement needs are more critical in the drug-manufacturing field, and the interests of the general public are more urgent. We hold that inspections authorized by § 374 are "reasonable" and therefore not inconsistent with the Fourth Amendment. Thus, this case falls within the "carefully defined classes of cases" which are an exception to the search-warrant requirement. We share, to a degree, the fears expressed by appellants that many businesses are thoroughly regulated by the United States, and that an undue extension of our rationale might obliterate much of the Fourth Amendment's protection. On balance, however, we are persuaded that the capacity for good or ill of the manufacture of drugs for human consumption is so great that Congress had power to enact § 374(a).

Having concluded that drug manufacturing is a "pervasively regulated" industry does not end our inquiry, but establishes only that Congress has broad authority to place restrictions on that industry that might otherwise violate the Fourth amendment. A question remains as to whether the conduct of the government in this case conforms with the statutory scheme provided by the Congress. . . .

The Federal Food, Drug, and Cosmetic Act contains provisions, similar to those addressed in *Colonnade*, which punish refusals to permit inspections by imprisonment up to one year, or a fine of not more than $1,000, or both. It follows, therefore, as in *Colonnade*, that an inspection pursuant to a § 374 notice to inspect is authorized only when there is a valid consent. If consent is withheld, a separate violation of the Act occurs, and the FDA inspectors are required to obtain a warrant before the inspection can proceed. . . .

This brings us to the problem presented by the search at the Wentzville site. Here, as in *Colonnade*, the critical issue is whether there was consent to the inspection. Unfortunately this issue was not expressly resolved in the court below. . . . Therefore, as to . . . the counts as to which evidence was taken from the Wentzville site, the judgments of conviction will be vacated, and the cause remanded for the making of further findings on the issue of consent. . . .

We add a word of clarification as to the meaning of the term "consent" as we intend it in this context. We do not mean, by imposing a requirement of "consent," to require a factual determination as to whether appellants, with respect to the Wentzville site, knowingly and understandingly relinquished a known right. The question is whether appellants refused to permit entry or inspection, thereby violating 21 U.S.C. § 331(f). If they did so refuse, then FDA was obliged to obtain an administrative warrant in order to effect the inspection, and could also seek a separate criminal prosecution for the refusal itself. If appellants did not refuse to permit entry or inspection, then they "consented" to the search and seizure, as we use that term here. This formulation, while it may not answer every question that may arise with respect to searches and seizures pursuant to § 374 notices of inspection, seems to us to be the most logical way to harmonize *Biswell* and *Colonnade*. . . .

The inspection and seizures conducted at the [St. Louis] site were supported not only by a statutory notice, but also by a Warrant for Inspection issued by a United States Magistrate . . . and a Warrant for Arrest of Property issued by the clerk of the district court. . . .

Appellants . . . argue that the inspections were part of an ongoing criminal investigation, and that therefore a warrant issued on less than criminal probable cause was not sufficient to authorize a search. It is our view that a warrant based on an administrative showing of probable cause is valid in this pervasively regulated industry. To hold otherwise would be inconsistent with our conclusion, already expressed, that warrantless entry under a notice of inspection does not violate the Fourth Amendment in the drug-manufacturing field. Probable-cause standards are relaxed because the business person engaged in this industry has a lesser expectation of privacy. . . .

Appellants next argue that certain statements made by the defendants to FDA agents during the searches were inadmissible at trial because *Miranda* warnings were not given. The district court held that *Miranda* was not applicable because "the evidence failed to establish that defendants . . . were in a custodial situation, subject to arrest."

Evidence presented at trial showed that FDA agents are without authority to make arrests, that the defendants' movements were not restricted during the time of the search, and that there were no threats or coercion. Evidence also indicated that appellants' employees were free to go about their business, and that consultation with attorneys was not limited. There is ample evidence to support the district court's finding, and the statements were therefore properly admitted at trial. . . .

NOTES

1. *Supporting Authority.* The Sixth and Ninth Circuits have also found the pharmaceutical industry to be so "pervasively regulated" that a warrantless search is permissible under the Fourth Amendment. *See United States v. Acklen*, 690 F.2d 70, 75 (6th Cir. 1982); *United States v. Argent Chemical Laboratories, Inc.*, 93 F.3d 572 (9th Cir. 1996). Several lower courts have applied the "pervasively regulated" reasoning to the food industry. *See, e.g., U.S. v. Del Campo Baking Mfg. Co.*, 345 F. Supp. 1371 (D. Del. 1972); *United States v. New England Grocers Supply Co.*, 488 F. Supp. 230, 238 (D. Mass. 1980).

2. *Clinical Investigators. United States v. Fogari*, 1987–1988 FDLI Jud. Rec. 144 (D.N.J. 1988), upheld a warrantless inspection of a physician conducting clinical investigations whose results were to be submitted to FDA. The court applied criteria set forth in *New York v. Burger,* 482 U.S. 691 (1987), a Supreme Court decision upholding the warrantless inspection of an automobile junkyard under a statute regulating such businesses: (1) Does the government have a substantial interest in regulating the industry? (2) Are warrantless inspections necessary to further the regulatory scheme? (3) Does the certainty and regularity of the statutory inspection program provide a constitutionally adequate substitute for a warrant?

3. *Criminal Investigation.* An argument that FDA improperly used its section 704 inspection authority to gather evidence for a criminal prosecution was rejected in *United States v. Gel Spice Co., Inc.*, 773 F.2d 427 (2d Cir. 1985), based on a lack of evidence of bad faith. The court held that the mere fact that FDA was pursuing criminal enforcement of the FD&C Act at the same time that it conducted a section 704 inspection did

not evidence bad faith because the agency has concurrent civil and criminal enforcement responsibilities. Under 28 C.F.R. 60.3, FDA officials are authorized to request the issuance of a search warrant under Rule 41 of the Federal Rules of Criminal Procedure.

3.   SCOPE OF INSPECTIONS

a.   RECORDS

As enacted, section 704 did not generally empower FDA to inspect establishment records. Over time, however, Congress has repeatedly amended the FD&C Act to grant the agency the authority to inspect an increasingly broad array of records. The Drug Amendments of 1962 and the Device Amendments of 1976 revised section 704(a) to authorize FDA to inspect "records, files, papers, processes, controls, and facilities," except for "financial data, sales data other than shipment data, pricing data, personnel data ... and research data" for prescription drugs, human OTC drugs, and restricted devices. The 1976 device amendments also added Section 704(e), a provision giving FDA access to any records that device manufacturers, user facilities, and investigators are required to maintain under the FD&C Act. The 1980 Infant Formula Act required manufacturers to retain records and gave FDA authority to inspect these records. FD&C Act 412(b)(4); 704(a)(3). The Bioterrorism Act of 2002 gave the agency access to records relating to an article of food when the agency has a reasonable belief that the article is adulterated and presents a threat of serious adverse health consequences or death to humans or animals. FD&C Act 414; 704(a)(1). The Family Smoking Prevention and Tobacco Control Act of 2009 added tobacco products facilities to the list of establishments in section 704(a) that must provide access to records, files, and papers.

Moreover, there are sections of the Act other than 704 that give FDA authority to inspect records. For example, under section 703, titled "Records of Interstate Shipment," the agency may inspect the records of shippers and receivers of FDA-regulated articles, so far as those records show "the movement in interstate commerce" of such articles, "the holding thereof after such movement," or the "quantity, shipper, and consignee thereof." Most recently, the Food Safety Modernization Act of 2011 added a provision stating that a food facility must, "upon oral or written request," make "promptly available" to an FDA representative its written hazard analysis and preventive control plan and its records documenting the monitoring of preventive controls, the implementation of corrective actions, and other specified information. FD&C Act 418(h).

However, in some situations, and for some whole product categories (cosmetics and nonrestricted devices, for example), FDA does not have—and acknowledges that it does not have—explicit authority under the FD&C Act to inspect the records. However, the absence of explicit statutory authority has not prevented FDA inspectors from requesting access to pertinent records, and often getting it. And courts have not stood in the way of the agency obtaining such voluntary access. For example, in *United States v. 75 Cases ... Peanut Butter, Labeled ... "Top Notch Brand,"* 146 F.2d 124 (4th Cir. 1944), a manufacturer not covered by section 703 ("Records of Interstate Shipment") produced invoices to an FDA investigator on request. The

Court of Appeals agreed with the District Court below that "the prescribing of certain compulsory methods of investigation does not exclude permissive investigation." *Id.* at 127. Furthermore, the appeals court rejected the lower court's conclusion that the government is obligated when requesting permission to "make a full and complete disclosure" and "make sure that [the] consent is not due in any respect to a failure to understand the fullest use to which the records might be put by the Government." *Id.* at 126.

NOTES

1. *Voluntary Disclosure.* Section 703 provides that "evidence obtained under this section . . . shall not be used in a criminal prosecution of the person from whom obtained. . . ." In *United States v. Arnold's Pharmacy, Inc.*, 116 F. Supp. 310 (D.N.J. 1953), the defendants were convicted of dispensing prescription drugs without a physician's authorization. The government's evidence included the pharmacy's shipping and prescription records, which the defendant had voluntarily shown to FDA inspectors. At trial, the defendants sought to suppress this evidence on the ground that it had been "obtained under" section 703 of the Act and therefore could not be used to support their prosecution. The court rejected this claim:

> . . . [T]he purpose of the provision here in question was to close an earlier loophole in the enforcement provisions of the act, which handicapped its enforcement, this handicap being caused by the refusal of certain carriers, if not others, to permit the copying of essential records. In other words, where, as was generally the case, these records were willingly made available to the Government, so that the Act could readily be enforced, the previous law was effective. But, in cases where this access and copying was refused, the section in question would apply to overcome such refusal, and eliminate such "handicap to its (the Act's) enforcement." . . .

> Since the evidence here was voluntarily turned over to the Government by its owners, the conditions for the applicability of the statutory provision in question did not exist, and the statute does not apply. And since the evidence was not obtained unconstitutionally, defendant's motion for the suppression, impounding and return of the evidence, is denied.

For other cases holding that section 703—and thus the bar against using records in a criminal prosecution—applies only where the person refused to provide the requested records voluntarily and FDA requested them in writing, see *United States v. Herold*, 136 F. Supp. 15 (E.D.N.Y. 1955); *United States v. Lyon Drug Co.*, 122 F. Supp. 597 (E.D. Wis. 1954). As a result of these decisions, FDA rarely makes a written request for records under section 703.

2. *Pharmacy Exemption.* Section 704(a)(2)(A) explicitly exempts from FDA records inspection "pharmacies which maintain establishments in conformance with any applicable local laws regulating the practice of pharmacy . . . and which do not . . . manufacture, prepare, propagate, compound, or process drugs or devices for sale other than in the regular

course of their business of dispensing or selling drugs or devices at retail." In *Wedgewood Village Pharmacy v. United States*, 421 F.3d 263 (3d Cir. 2005), FDA obtained an administrative warrant to inspect a pharmacy's "production and distribution records to determine the extent to which [its] activities are consistent with those of a drug manufacturer rather than a retail pharmacy, and to evaluate the extent of violations of the [FD&C Act]." *Id.* at 265. The Third Circuit rejected the pharmacy's assertion that it was eligible for the 704(a)(2)(A) exemption and that the inspection was therefore illegal. FDA's Compliance Policy Guide 460.200 sets forth a nine-factor approach for distinguishing manufacturing activities subject to FD&C Act enforcement from compounding activities outside the scope of the FDCA. *Wedgewood* held that CPG 460.200's factors are reasonable and that, given the averments of the warrant application, "it was therefore reasonable for the FDA to conclude that Wedgewood may be engaged in activity inconsistent with its status as a retail pharmacy." *Id.* at 273.

3. *Medical Practitioner's Exemption.* Section 704(a)(2)(B) exempts from records inspection any practitioner who is licensed by law to prescribe or administer drugs and who manufactures those drugs solely for use in his professional practice. In *United States v. Jacobs*, Food Drugs Cosm. L. Rep. (CCH) ¶ 38,123 (E.D. Cal. 1989), the court ruled against suppression of evidence despite the failure of an FDA inspector either to request the defendant physician's permission to inspect the records or to inform him that the agency's inspection authority did not extend to the records of a licensed physician. Because the physician did not object to the inspection, the court concluded that he had consented.

4. *Contract Laboratories.* Where a contract research organization assumed responsibilities for clinical trials regulated by FDA, the court held that the organization was subject to FDA inspection of its records under section 704. *Leo Winter Associates, Inc. v. Department HHS*, 497 F. Supp. 429 (D.D.C. 1980).

5. *FDA Assertions of Implied Records Inspection Authority.* FDA has a long history of creatively establishing record inspection powers outside the explicit grant in section 704. For example, in the early 1970s, the agency was concerned about the contamination of acidified foods and low-acid canned foods with *Clostridium botulinum* toxin. It wanted processors of these products to submit detailed information about their manufacturing processes and to provide FDA inspectors with access to processing records and other documents. Since section 704 did not authorize inspection of records in food establishments, FDA turned instead to section 404 ("Emergency Permit Control"), which authorizes the agency to require permits for foods that might be dangerous because of contamination with microorganisms. Instead of directly mandating recordkeeping and access, FDA by regulation required producers of acidified foods and low-acid canned foods to disclose processing records as a condition for avoiding the imposition of emergency permit controls. 21 C.F.R. 108.25(c)(3)(ii) & (g); 108.35(c)(3)(ii) and (h).

In 1974, before section 704 was amended by the Medical Device Amendments to allow inspection of records in certain device establishments, FDA sought and was granted a permanent injunction by a federal court authorizing the agency to inspect the records of the manufacturer of the Diapulse, a misbranded device. The manufacturer appealed the injunction, contending that the fact that the 1962 amendment to section 704 specifically allowed inspection of the records of prescription drug manufacturers implied that such authority did not exist with respect to other products. The Second Circuit rejected this argument and upheld the injunction. *United States v. Diapulse Corp.*, 514 F.2d 1097 (2d Cir. 1975).

In the 1990s, as discussed *infra* at p. 540, FDA decided to establish a Hazard Analysis and Critical Control Point (HACCP) approach to regulating seafood safety. The very concept of HACCP is premised on the assumption that an establishment will maintain accurate records of its production operations and make them available to regulators. When FDA proposed its seafood HACCP regulations in 1994, some comments suggested that the agency should once again base its claim to records access on section 404, as it had with when issuing the acidified food and low-acid canned food regulations of the 1970s. 60 Fed. Reg. 65096, 65101–02 (Dec. 18, 1995). The agency, however, rejected this approach, observing that the permit system applied only in emergency situations and only to hazards from micro-organisms. Instead, FDA found broader authority to demand access to seafood establishment records under section 402 (the food adulteration provisions) and section 701(a) (the provision giving the agency "authority to promulgate regulations for the efficient enforcement of this Act"). *Id.* at 65101. The agency rejected the contention that the explicit grant of records access for drugs and devices in section 704 precluded the agency from extending its access to other types of records.

> FDA has concluded . . . that these regulations are consistent with section 704 of the act and with the act as a whole. Because the preventive controls required by HACCP are essential to the production of safe food as a matter of design, the statutory scheme is benefited by agency access to records that demonstrate that these controls are being systematically applied. The case law supports FDA's authority to require such recordkeeping and to have access to such records.

Nobody has challenged the records access provision of the seafood HACCP regulations (21 C.F.R. 123.10(c)) in court. Nor has anybody challenged an essentially identical provision in FDA's 2001 HACCP regulations for juices. 21 C.F.R. 120.12(d)(1). In both situations, the industries were under severe public criticism and could not risk the consequences of opposing FDA. Because the section 418(h) records inspection provision of the 2011 Food Safety Modernization Act does not apply to facilities required to comply with the seafood or juice HACCP rules, *see* FD&C Act 418(j), the records access requirements of these rules apparently remain based on sections 402 and 701(a).

b.   SAMPLES AND PHOTOGRAPHS

Triangle Candy Co. v. United States
144 F.2d 195 (9th Cir. 1944).

■ DENMAN, CIRCUIT JUDGE.

This is an appeal by defendants and appellants, Triangle Candy Company, a corporation, and Bernard G. Kennepohl, from judgments rendered against them after appellants were found guilty on six counts of violation of the Federal Food, Drug, and Cosmetic Act. . . .

There were seven counts in the information. . . . Alleged in each count was adulteration under 21 U.S.C. § 342(a)(4), providing that a food shall be deemed adulterated "if it has been prepared, packed, or held under insanitary conditions whereby it may have become contaminated with filth, or whereby it may have been rendered injurious to health." In all counts save the first it was additionally alleged that there was adulteration of the candy involved under 21 U.S.C. § 342(a)(3), providing that a food shall be deemed to be adulterated "if it consists in whole or in part of any filthy, putrid, or decomposed substance, or if it is otherwise unfit for food." . . .

It is the contention of the appellants that Congress made the supplying to them of part of the samples whose analysis provided the basis for the charges a condition precedent to the maintenance of a prosecution under the Act. It was stipulated at trial that though seasonable written request was made for such samples as to each count, it was not complied with as to samples involved in [four of the counts].

The sample provision requirement of the Act [FD&C Act 702] is as follows:

> (b) Where a sample of a food, drug, or cosmetic is collected for analysis under this chapter the [Secretary] shall, upon request, provide a part of such official sample for examination or analysis by any person named on the label of the article, or the owner thereof, or his attorney or agent; except that the [Secretary] is authorized, by regulations, to make . . . reasonable exceptions from, and impose . . . reasonable terms and conditions relating to the operation of this subsection . . . .

[The FDA regulation pursuant to this provision, 21 C.F.R. 2.10(b), provides:] "When an officer or employee collects an official sample . . . he shall collect at least twice the quantity estimated by him to be sufficient for analysis, unless [one of the subsequent listed exceptions applies]," none of them pertinent to the facts of this case. . . .

. . . [T]he government's chief chemist of the Los Angeles station to whom the collector sent the collected samples . . . nowhere testified that double the amount deemed needed for analysis was received. . . . All he testified to is that "the reason why samples were not furnished which the candy company requested was because all the samples at the Los Angeles station were used in the course of the analyses by the chemists involved; that there was no candy left over after the analyses [which] could be sent to them."

It is thus apparent that the government, failing to supply the demanded samples, has not brought itself within the exceptions of the regulations created under the statute. The problem thus becomes one of the effect of such failure to obey the mandate that the [Secretary] "shall . . . provide" the samples. . . .

We hold that the provision is not merely directory—for the guidance of the [Secretary]—but mandatorily gives the right to samples to the accused manufacturers, unless the [Secretary] brings himself within the excepting regulations. . . .

. . . If those accused under the Act are not given a portion of the sample, their power to make a complete defense is substantially curtailed. Intent is no part of the crime with which they are charged. If they have introduced the food into interstate commerce, and if it is adulterated, they are guilty, regardless of their intent or lack of knowledge as to adulteration. It may frequently happen that the single factual issue is that of adulteration. Without access to a portion of the sample, they are confronted by a government analysis of that sample which they cannot refute but at best, and with difficulty, impeach by challenging the government's method of sampling and testing.

Section [702(b)], then, must have been intended to provide defendants with an opportunity for independent analysis; and it is clear that the results of such analysis may be among the most important pieces of evidence defendants can offer in their own behalf. Deprival of the chance to make this test . . . prejudices defendants' substantial rights. This consideration, added to the statute's mandatory wording, and the analogy of cases under other acts, lead us to the conclusion that provision of a portion of the sample, save in properly excepted cases, is a condition precedent to prosecution.

Since, despite seasonable written request, no samples of the food involved . . . were furnished defendants, nor any reason offered for this failure, the convictions on these counts must be reversed. . . .

NOTE

Sample Size. In *United States v. Roux Laboratories, Inc.*, 456 F. Supp. 973 (M.D. Fla. 1978), the court rejected the contention that FDA inspectors' demand for an eight-ounce total sample of expensive cosmetic ingredients was unreasonable. The court also rejected Roux's claim that the agency should be required to disclose in advance what tests it intended to conduct.

Frederick H. Branding & James M. Ellis,
Underdeveloped: FDA's Authority to Take
Photographs During an FDA Establishment
Inspection Under Section 704
58 FOOD & DRUG LAW JOURNAL 9 (2003).

As a guide to FDA investigators, FDA maintains an Investigations Operations Manual (IOM). The IOM describes to its field personnel the procedures to follow in conducting establishment inspections.

. . . IOM [5.3.4] . . . discusses the taking of photographs . . . during inspections:

> Since photographs are one of the most effective and useful forms of evidence, every one should be taken with a purpose. Photographs should be related to insanitary conditions contributing or likely to contribute filth to the finished product, or to practices likely to render it injurious or otherwise violative.

The IOM cites seven examples of conditions or practices that may be "effectively documented by photographs.". . . .

IOM [5.3.4.1] . . . directs investigators to assume that they have authority to take photographs. Inspectors are instructed as follows:

> Do not request permission from management to take photographs during an inspection. Take your camera into the firm and use it as necessary just as you use other inspectional equipment.

> If management objects to the taking of photographs, explain that photos are an integral part of an inspection and present an accurate picture of plant conditions. Advise management that the U.S. courts have held photographs may lawfully be taken as part of an inspection.

Section 704 of the FDCA states that the inspection must be conducted during "reasonable times," "within reasonable limits," and in a "reasonable manner." . . . The scope of an establishment inspection (i.e., "reasonable time," "reasonable limits," and "reasonable manner") is rarely litigated. When an inspection is challenged, courts usually favor the agency.

When an investigator complies with the statutory requirements of section 704, FDA's right to inspect is extremely broad. Refusal to permit FDA investigators access to inspect a facility, assuming the investigator presents proper identification and a valid inspection notice, is a violation of section 301(f) of the FDCA. The refusal may be partial or total. . . .

Whether a refusal to allow photographs is an actual refusal of the inspection under section 704 is not settled. . . . In the absence of explicit legal authority in the statute . . . such nonconsent should not, as a matter of legal interpretation, be referred to as a refusal of the inspection. Nevertheless, if the refusal is of such a character that the investigator determines that he or she cannot conduct a satisfactory inspection or obtain information to which FDA is entitled under the Act, the investigator is instructed to contact his or her supervisor to determine whether an administrative inspection warrant should be requested . . . from a federal magistrate judge. If FDA feels compelled to obtain such an order from the court, it is probable that the inspection warrant will contain language specifically authorizing the taking of photographs. . . .

FDA cites two cases in the IOM to support its authority to take photographs: *Dow Chemical v. United States*, 476 U.S. 227 (1986), and *United States v. Acri Wholesale Grocery Company*, 409 F. Supp. 529 (S.D. Iowa 1976). If management continues to refuse the taking of photographs, investigators are instructed to provide management with references to the *Dow Chemical* and *Acri Wholesale Grocery Co.* cases as support for FDA's authority to take photographs during inspections. Neither *Dow Chemical* nor *Acri Wholesale Grocery Co.* specifically addresses FDA's authority to take photographs during inspections and, more importantly, neither case addresses whether a company may refuse the taking of photographs during an inspection.

In *Dow*, the taking of aerial photographs by the Environmental Protection Agency (EPA), pursuant to the Clean Air Act, was upheld as a valid exercise of EPA's inspectional powers and not a violation of Dow Chemical's Fourth Amendment privacy rights. In support of its interpretation that photographs may lawfully be taken as part of an inspection, the IOM quotes, in part, the Supreme Court: "When Congress invests an agency with enforcement and investigatory authority, it is not necessary to identify explicitly each and every technique that may be used in the course of executing the statutory mission." The *Dow* case did not deal with FDA's authority under the FDCA, nor did the *Dow* case deal with the taking of photographs inside a plant during an establishment inspection. . . .

In *Acri*, the court admitted into evidence photographs taken by FDA investigators while inside a food warehouse. FDA's authority to take the photographs, however, was not at issue. In *Acri*, no objection was made to the taking of the photographs at the time of the inspection, so the court determined the company had consented to the taking of photographs. Thus, *Acri* does not support FDA's claimed right to take photographs during an establishment inspection, absent consent from the establishment.

In addition to *Dow* and *Acri*, two other cases address FDA's inspectional authority where photographs were taken during the inspections. . . .

Although neither [*United States v. Jamieson–McKames Pharmaceuticals, Inc.*, 651 F.2d 532 (8th Cir. 1981) (excerpted *supra* p. 179)] nor [*United States v. Gel Spice Co., Inc.*, 601 F. Supp. 1214 (E.D.N.Y. 1985)], addressed the specific issue of whether section 704 authorized the taking of photographs, both decisions appear to support FDA's broad inspectional authority, based on a flexible standard of reasonableness, once consent to the inspection is given.

It also appears from the case law that once consent is given to inspect the facility, it may be too late to refuse the taking of the photographs. Under such circumstances, the issue then becomes whether the inspection (and the taking of the photographs) was reasonable. Such determinations, perhaps made at a later time by a court, are heavily influenced by the particular facts and circumstances associated with the inspection, including a firm's regulatory history. . . .

NOTES

1. *Procedure when Photographing Refused.* In the wake of the enactment of the Food Safety Modernization Act of 2011, FDA revised its Investigations Operations Manual (IOM) to state:

> [If management refuses to allow the taking of photographs,] obtain name and contact information for the firm's legal counsel, and advise

your district management immediately. If the firm does not have legal counsel on retainer, collect the name and contact information for the most responsible individual. . . . [Office of Chief Counsel] will then contact the firm's legal counsel or most responsible individual to discuss FDA's legal right to take pictures during inspections.

In comments it recently submitted to the agency, the American Bakers Association, in addition to maintaining that the use of warrantless in-plant photography exceeds FDA's statutory authority, also objected to the above amendment to the IOM in particular. The Association argued, "[T]he procedure sets a hostile tone for the interaction between inspector and management that is likely to pervade the entire inspection. ABA strongly encourages FDA to reconsider or decline to enforce this policy in order ensure accurate and fair inspections, as well as to preserve positive relations between FDA and regulated industries." Letter from Lee Sanders, Sr. V.P., Am. Bakers Assoc., to Elizabeth H. Dickinson, Chief Counsel, FDA and Dara Corrigan, Assoc. Comm'r for Reg. Affairs, FDA, re. "Comments on FDA Authority to Take In–Plant Photographs During Inspections" (June 25, 2012) (available on Am. Bakers Assoc. website).

2. *Recording During Inspections.* Section 5.3.5 of the IOM states, "Under normal circumstances recording devices will not be used while conducting inspections and investigations." However, the Manual goes on to provide that if the inspected firm records or videotapes "the discussion with management portion of the inspection," it "should be advised we do not object to this procedure, but we will also record the discussion to assure the accuracy of our records."

4.   THE USDA INSPECTION REGIME

The FDA method of intermittent random factory inspections, coupled with occasional "for cause" inspections, differs markedly from the continuous factory inspection by resident inspectors conducted by USDA's Food Safety and Inspection Service (FSIS). In accordance with the Federal Meat Inspection Act and the Poultry Products Inspection Act, FSIS inspectors not only conduct sanitary inspections of slaughtering and packing establishments, but also perform mandatory carcass-by-carcass inspections, apply inspection marks to carcasses and parts that pass inspection, and require the destruction of those found to be adulterated. The labor-intensiveness of this inspection regime explains why the number of inspectors at FSIS dwarfs the number available to FDA's Center for Food Safety and Applied Nutrition.

Critics have long questioned the merits of this approach. Continuous inspection of the type conducted by FSIS is extremely costly. Moreover, USDA's continuous inspection programs, with their resident inspectors, have sometimes been vulnerable to compromise by inspected firms. The *Report of the USDA Food Safety and Quality Service Task Force on Program Quality* (Oct. 1979) concluded that continuous factory inspection "because of its structure and functions is inherently vulnerable to corruption" and recommended a new "integrity program" to combat this problem.

By the 1970s, the traditional "poke-and-sniff" approach used by FSIS inspectors began to seem inadequate in light of growing concern about the dangers of microbial pathogens undetectable by organoleptic (sight, touch, and smell) methods. USDA thus began to experiment with different forms of continuous inspection for meat and poultry, including total quality control (TQC) and partial quality control (PQC) systems that gave meat and poultry establishments more responsibility to control their own production under FSIS oversight. *See* 45 Fed. Reg. 54310 (Aug. 15, 1980), 51 Fed. Reg. 32301 (Sept. 11, 1986). These precursors to Hazard Analysis and Critical Control Point (HACCP) led finally, in 1996, to the issuance of an FSIS rule imposing HACCP requirements on meat and poultry establishments, with the stated goal of reducing pathogenic microorganisms in meat and poultry products. 61 Fed. Reg. 38806 (July 25, 1996), codified at 9 C.F.R 417. The rule required first large plants, then small plants, then very small plants to adopt HACCP, and by 2000 the approach was mandatory for the entire industry.

Congress might have used the adoption of HACCP as an occasion to end FSIS "continuous inspection" and severely reduce the number of meat and poultry inspectors. Indeed, during the implementation of the FSIS rule, the inspectors' union warned of this result. *See* George Anthan, *Inspectors Decry New Meat System*, DES MOINES REG., Jan. 21, 1999, at B9. But to this point, carcass-by-carcass inspection remains required by law, the massive force reductions predicted by the union have not come to pass, and the primary change confronted by the inspectors has been the incorporation of HACCP-related document inspection into their traditional duties. See *American Fed. Gov't Emps. v. Glickman*, 215 F.3d 7 (D.C. Cir. 2000) (federal employees must inspect every carcass, despite implementation of HACCP); Richard A. Merrill & Jeffrey K. Francer, *Organizing Federal Food Safety Regulation*, 31 SETON HALL L. REV. 61, 100–04 (2000). FSIS has implemented pilot programs in pork and chicken plants that reduce the number of USDA inspectors in half and replace them with private inspectors employed by the industry. Although the agency has announced a goal of expanding this approach nationwide, its plans may be disrupted by a recent USDA Inspector General finding that pork plants participating in the pilot program were among the worst offenders in the country with respect to health and safety violations. *See New Meat Inspection System Has Safety Gaps*, WASH. POST, Sept. 9, 2013, at A01.

D. SEIZURE

Section 304 of the FD&C Act, titled "Seizure," sets forth a two-step process. First, it authorizes the United States to proceed against adulterated or misbranded articles (or unapproved drugs) "on libel of information" and seize the articles. Second, the section empowers the federal district courts, after trial, to decree the "condemnation" of such articles and order them destroyed, sold, or returned to the owner for destruction, reconditioning, or, in some instances, export.

1. THE SEIZURE PROCESS

United States of America v. Argent Chemical Laboratories, Inc.

93 F.3d 572 (9th Cir. 1996).

■ CANBY, CIRCUIT JUDGE.

Under procedures authorized by Congress, the Food and Drug Administration ("FDA") seized allegedly adulterated products from the premises of a regulated veterinary drug manufacturer, without obtaining a warrant from a judicial officer issued upon a finding of probable cause. The question before us is whether that seizure violated the Fourth Amendment. We conclude that it did not, and we reverse the judgment of the district court.

I. The Factual Background

Argent Chemical Laboratories manufactures and repackages veterinary drugs. FDA agents inspected Argent several times between the summer of 1993 and May 1994 to ensure compliance with the Food, Drug, and Cosmetic Act ("Act"). The FDA cited Argent for certain deficiencies. Several months after the last inspection, the FDA agents secured from the Deputy Clerk of the District Court, without the intervention of a judicial officer or a showing of probable cause, an in rem arrest warrant for various veterinary drugs alleged to violate the Act. FDA agents and United States Marshals then seized over $100,000 worth of veterinary drugs from Argent's premises. This condemnation action followed. Argent appeared as claimant and contested the constitutionality of the seizure. The district court held that the seizure violated the Fourth Amendment; it accordingly granted Argent's motion to quash the *in rem* arrest warrant and ordered the government to return the property. The government appealed, and the district court stayed its order pending the appeal.

II. The Statutory Scheme of Seizure

The warrant in this case was issued in accordance with the Act. Under the Act, an article "proceeded against shall be liable to seizure by process pursuant to the libel, and the procedures in cases under this section shall conform, as nearly as may be, to the procedure in admiralty...." 21 U.S.C. § 334(b). Under the Supplemental Rules for Certain Admiralty and Maritime Claims ("Supplemental Rules"), an *in rem* action begins with a complaint that must "be verified on oath or solemn affirmation" and that must "describe with reasonable particularity the property that is the subject of the action." Supplemental Rule C(2). Upon filing of the complaint, the clerk issues a warrant:

> Except in actions by the United States for forfeitures for federal statutory violations, the verified complaint and any supporting papers shall be reviewed by the court and, if the conditions for an action in rem appear to exist, an order so stating and authorizing a warrant for the arrest of the vessel or other property that is the

subject of the action shall issue and be delivered to the clerk who shall prepare the warrant.

. . . .

> *In actions by the United States for forfeitures for federal statutory violations, the clerk, upon filing of the complaint, shall forthwith issue a summons and warrant for the arrest of the vessel or other property. . . .*

Supplemental Rule C(3) (emphasis added). Thus, because this was an action by the United States for a forfeiture for federal statutory violations, FDA agents were able to obtain a warrant without review by a judicial officer or a finding of probable cause.

III. *The Fourth Amendment and the Colonnade–Biswell Exception*

Argent argues that, although the drugs were seized pursuant to a warrant issued in accordance with the Act, the seizure violated the Fourth Amendment's prohibition of unreasonable searches and seizures and its requirement that warrants issue upon probable cause. We conclude, however, that Argent's argument is defeated by the nature of its business and the regulation to which it is subject.

The Fourth Amendment applies to commercial premises as well as to private homes, but under the so-called *Colonnade–Biswell* exception, warrantless searches and seizures on commercial property used in "closely regulated" industries are constitutionally permissible. *Colonnade Catering Corp. v. United States*, 397 U.S. 72 (1970); *United States v. Biswell*, 406 U.S. 311 (1972). Persons engaging in pervasively regulated industries have a diminished expectation of privacy. With regard to such industries, "Congress has broad authority to fashion standards of reasonableness for searches and seizures." *Colonnade*, 397 U.S. at 77. . . .

Argent asserts that it is not subject to the *Colonnade–Biswell* exception for two reasons: first, its veterinary drug business is not the kind of industry that is subject to the *Colonnade–Biswell* exception; and second, the *Colonnade–Biswell* exception does not extend to a separate and particularized seizure of misbranded or adulterated goods. We reject both contentions.

IV. *Manufacture of Veterinary Drugs as a Closely Regulated Industry*

In *New York v. Burger*, 482 U.S. 691 (1987), the Supreme Court set forth the standards for determining when the *Colonnade–Biswell* exception applies. A warrantless inspection will be deemed reasonable only if the business is closely regulated and if three criteria are met:

> First, there must be a "substantial" government interest that informs the regulatory scheme pursuant to which the inspection is made. . . .

> Second, the warrantless inspections must be "necessary to further [the] regulatory scheme." . . .

> Finally, "the statute's inspection program, in terms of the certainty and regularity of its application, [must] provide a constitutionally adequate substitute for a warrant."

We conclude that all of these standards are met in this case.

As a threshold matter, the veterinary drug industry is "closely regulated." . . .

FDA regulation of Argent's industry also meets the three enumerated criteria of *Burger*. First, there is "a 'substantial' government interest that informs the regulatory scheme pursuant to which the inspection is made." . . . Congress has seen fit, either for human safety or for economic reasons, to regulate animal drugs to ensure their safety and effectiveness. Whether the interest is human health, economic health, or both, we conclude that it is substantial.

Second, "the warrantless inspections [are] 'necessary to further [the] regulatory scheme.'" *Burger*, 482 U.S. at 702. Unannounced inspections have a deterrent effect; forcing inspectors to obtain a warrant before inspection might frustrate the purpose of the Act by alerting owners to inspections. Moreover, this court has recognized the "need for swift governmental action to remove misbranded products from the stream of commerce." . . .

Finally, the regulatory scheme, "'in terms of the certainty and regularity of its application, [provides] a constitutionally adequate substitute for a warrant,'" thereby satisfying the third *Burger* requirement. "The regulatory statute must perform the two basic functions of a warrant: it must advise the owner of the commercial premises that the search is being made pursuant to the law and has a properly defined scope, and it must limit the discretion of the inspecting officers." *Id*. Taken as a whole, the Act, the accompanying regulations, and the Supplemental Rules for Certain Admiralty and Maritime Claims provide a constitutionally adequate substitute for a warrant. Inspections are conducted with notice furnished at the time, and their scope is limited by statute. 21 U.S.C. § 374(a)(1). Seizures are limited to drugs that are adulterated or misbranded, 21 U.S.C. § 334(a)(1), the articles to be seized must be described "with reasonable particularity," Supplemental Rules C(2), and the government's complaint must be "verified on oath or solemn affirmation." Moreover, in most cases, the seizure is subject to the approval of one of the Food and Drug Administration's district offices, the appropriate office (or "center") in the Food and Drug Administration headquarters, the Food and Drug Administration's Office of Enforcement, the Office of the Chief Counsel, and the Department of Justice. See FDA REGULATORY PROCEDURES MANUAL, ch. 6, at 173–85 (Aug. 1995).

We conclude, therefore, that Argent's operation, as regulated by the FDA, falls within the *Colonnade–Biswell* exception to the Fourth Amendment's warrant requirement.

V. *The Particularized Seizure and the Warrant Requirement of the Theramatic Case*

Argent next contends that, even if it is a "closely regulated" industry for purposes of the *Colonnade–Biswell* exception, that exception does not apply to the seizure in this case. To the extent that Argent's argument suggests that the *Colonnade–Biswell* exception applies only to inspections and not to seizures, the argument is untenable. It is true that *Burger* discussed its criteria for "closely regulated" industries in terms of "inspections," but it also approved the use of evidence seized in the course of the inspection. Moreover, both *Colonnade* and *Biswell* involved seizures of contraband discovered during the unwarranted inspections. . . . Thus, *Colonnade–Biswell* extends to seizure without warrant of what may be inspected without warrant, when Congress so authorizes.

The argument that Argent most vigorously asserts, and the one that was accepted by the district court, is based on our decision in *United States v. Device Labeled "Theramatic"*, 641 F.2d 1289 (9th Cir. 1981) ("*Theramatic I*"). In *Theramatic I*, we held that the Fourth Amendment was violated by the FDA's seizure from a physician's office of an allegedly misbranded medical device pursuant to a warrant issued under the Supplemental Rules. We emphasized that the physician was entitled to the protection of the Fourth Amendment in his office just as he was in his home. We recognized that some administrative searches could be conducted on the strength of a warrant issued on less than probable cause, but the government in *Theramatic I* was not conducting random inspections to enforce administrative standards; it was "searching a particular physician's office to seize a particular, identified device." Finally, we said that the *Colonnade–Biswell* exception to the warrant requirement did not apply because "the search at issue here was not part of any statutory program to inspect physicians' offices."

We do not draw from *Theramatic I* the same lessons that Argent and the district court did. The problem with the seizure in *Theramatic I* was that it was effectuated by an impermissible invasion of the physician's right of privacy. That is why we were careful in *Theramatic I* to point out that the case involved not only a seizure, "but a paradigmatic search—a physical intrusion by the U.S. Marshal into [the physician's] office." *Id*. at 1291. We also stated:

> It is one thing to seize without a warrant property resting in an open area or seizable by levy without an intrusion into privacy, and it is quite another thing to effect a warrantless seizure of property, even that owned by a corporation, situated on private premises to which access is not otherwise available for the seizing officer.

The *Colonnade–Biswell* exception did not apply because it is based largely on the diminished expectation of privacy in a closely-regulated industry, and the physician in *Theramatic I* was not closely regulated by the FDA.

The district court, however, accepted Argent's interpretation of *Theramatic I,* concluding that "although a well-defined scheme for inspecting pervasively regulated businesses may survive Fourth Amendment scrutiny, the protection against unreasonable searches and seizures may nevertheless prevent government agents from returning to conduct a particularized search and seizure without first obtaining an ordinary warrant." The District Court held that *Theramatic I* forbade agents from searching "a particular business to seize particular, identified chemicals and drugs." . . .

. . . [I]t is the invasion of privacy, not the particularity of the seizure, that is the relevant difference between Argent's case and *Theramatic I* for purposes of the *Colonnade–Biswell* exception. Argent, being closely regulated by the FDA, has a diminished expectation of privacy that was not violated by the seizure. We attach no significance to the fact that the FDA "returned" to execute its *in rem* warrant some time after its last inspection. If a random, unannounced inspection does not violate Argent's Fourth Amendment right of privacy, we see no reason why the unannounced execution of a warrant under the Supplemental Rules would do so. The seizure is from the premises of a closely regulated manufacturer and is conducted within the regulatory scheme in the manner Congress has authorized. There is no need to brigade the seizure with an inspection in order to legitimize it; Argent's expectation of privacy has not been violated.

. . . .

REVERSED.

NOTES

1. *Seizures from Non–Closely–Regulated Industries.* In the *Theramatic* decision, distinguished by the court in Argent Chemical, the Ninth Circuit struck down a section 304 seizure of a diathermy machine and accompanying leaflets from a neurosurgeon's office because the seizure did not satisfy Fourth Amendment requirements. 641 F.2d 1289 (9th Cir. 1981). As the *Theramatic* court itself acknowledged, however, this decision was in tension with decisions by two other circuits: *Founding Church of Scientology v. United States*, 409 F.2d 1146 (D.C. Cir. 1969) (seizure of devices from church facilities); *United States v. Articles of Hazardous Substance*, 588 F.2d 39 (4th Cir. 1978) (seizure of pajamas from retail store).

2. *Seizure of Labeling.* The power of seizure extends to product labeling as well as to the article itself. *E.g., United States v. 8 Cartons, Containing "Plantation 'The Original' . . . Molasses,"* 103 F. Supp. 626 (W.D.N.Y. 1951). But promotional materials for an illegal product cannot be condemned unless they "accompany" the product in interstate commerce and thus qualify as "labeling" under FD&C Act 201(m). *United States v. Vitasafe Corp.*, 345 F.2d 864 (3d Cir. 1965), held that

3. *Removal of Labeling. Lee v. United States*, 187 F.2d 1005 (10th Cir. 1951), held that if a device was misbranded when introduced into interstate commerce, while in interstate commerce, or when held for sale after shipment in interstate commerce, the removal of the illegal labeling before seizure does not render the device immune from seizure and condemnation.

2. PRE-CONDEMNATION RELEASE

United States v. Undetermined Quantities of Drugs
675 F. Supp. 1113 (N.D. Ill. 1987).

■ DUFF, JUDGE.

The $500,000 of drugs at issue here are "sterile active ingredients"—principally freeze-dried powders or concentrated liquids—that have been subject to Food & Drug Administration review and approval and are therefore perfectly lawful; *provided* they are packaged and sold in accordance with applicable regulations. According to the government, however, since the mid-1980s, Travenol has been engaged in a program ("the TRC program") in which it alters these "sterile active ingredients" to produce different drugs—"finished product"—and the TRC program does violate the Act.

On May 22, 1987, the government sought and obtained an order for the seizure of approximately $680,000 worth of drugs from the TRC. Of these drugs, approximately $180,000 worth was "finished product"; the other approximately $500,000 worth were "sterile active ingredients." The government admits that the "sterile active ingredients" were not misbranded nor mislabeled and would thus be perfectly lawful drugs, were it not for their intended use in producing the allegedly unlawful "finished product."

On December 11, 1987, Travenol sought release of the "sterile active ingredients" on the condition that they would not be used in the TRC program but would instead be sold and/or distributed in a lawful manner. Travenol noted that the "sterile active ingredients" have a limited "shelf-life" and argued that the continued forced storage of these products was resulting in undue waste of beneficial drugs as well as unnecessary storage costs.

The government responded that, even conceding everything Travenol said, this court lacks the power to order the release of the sterile active ingredients at this time. According to the government, these drugs were properly seized as the intended ingredients of unlawful drugs; accordingly, they may only be released in accordance with 21 U.S.C. § 334(d), which provides that a court may, in its discretion, order the release of products seized under the Act *after* a condemnation proceeding has been held and any issues regarding the lawfulness of the products resolved. Such condemnation proceedings have not yet been held.

. . . .

21 U.S.C. § 334, sets out a coherent scheme for the seizure, condemnation and final disposition of products which allegedly violate the Act. When the FDA believes that a drug violates the Act, it may seek condemnation of the drugs "on libel of information." 21 U.S.C. § 334(a). The drug may be seized pre-trial "by process pursuant to the libel." 21 U.S.C. § 334(b). The procedures employed by the court in resolving the motion for libel and any other pre-trial matters "shall conform, as nearly as may be, to the procedures in admiralty." 21 U.S.C. § 334(b).

Once a trial is held, and the drugs condemned, the district court may do any one of three things. It may order the drugs destroyed; it may order them sold; or it may order them "delivered to the owner thereof to be destroyed or brought into compliance with the provisions of this chapter under the supervision of an officer or employee duly designated by the Secretary." 21 U.S.C. § 334(d).

Thus, the statute does not directly address the question of whether drugs may be released prior to the completion of condemnation procedures. The defendant claims that, because it does not, this court may invoke its equitable powers to order the pre-condemnation release of the "sterile active ingredients."

. . . .

The government insists that ... the statute's comprehensive scheme for condemning allegedly unlawful drugs gives rise to the "unescapable and necessary inference" that *pre-condemnation* release is always improper. In so arguing, the government ignores entirely the Act's instruction that admiralty procedures should inform the disposition of seizures pursuant to the Act. Admiralty Rule E(9) specifically provides for situations in which perishable goods have been seized:

> (b) *Interlocutory Sales.* If property that has been attached or arrested is perishable, or liable to deterioration, decay or injury by being detained in custody pending the action, or if the expense of keeping the property is excessive or disproportionate, or if there is unreasonable delay in securing the release of property, the court, on application of any party to the marshall, may order the property or any portion thereof to be sold; and the proceeds, or so much thereof as shall be adequate to satisfy any judgment, may be ordered brought into court to abide the event of the action; *or the court may, on motion of the defendant or claimant, order delivery of the property to the defendant or claimant, upon the giving of security in accordance with these rules.* (Emphasis supplied).

Thus, the Admiralty Rules specifically authorize the pre-condemnation release of certain seized goods. To be sure, the difference between the purposes of the Act and those of admiralty law may necessitate adjusting the Rules when applying them to seizures pursuant to the Act. Nevertheless, the Act's specific reference to the Rules strongly suggests that Congress did not intend to strictly limit the court's authority over seizure proceedings to those procedures specifically delineated on the face of the statute. . . .

In *United States v. Alcon Labs*, 636 F.2d 876 (1st Cir. 1981), *cert. denied*, 451 U.S. 1017 (1982), the court held, on the basis of its reading of § 334, that "articles seized in an FDA enforcement action may not be released by the court prior to a judicial determination of whether they violate the Act." *Id*. at 883. The court agreed that "the Supplemental Rules for Certain Admiralty and Maritime Claims [Admiralty Rules] . . . were intended to inform seizure procedure under the Act," and that "Rule E(5) implies some general grant of authority to a court to order the release of seized property." *Id*. Nevertheless, it held that the district court erred when it released drugs which the FDA maintained were in violation of the Act's "new drug" provisions. *Id*.

Two aspects of that case render it inapposite the instant one. First, the drugs in that case were not perishable. Thus, the Court was forced to rely solely on Admiralty Rule E(5). That rule provides for the pre-trial release of property upon an order of the court after the giving of security; it does not, however, provide any guidance for determining when a court may properly grant such an order. Accordingly, the court saw "little in Rule E(5) by way of a general grant of authority permitting courts to countermand administratively instituted seizures without first adjudicating the merits of the agency's claim." *Id*. This conclusion does not apply to the instant case, where Rule E(9) provides specific authority for the pre-condemnation release of *perishable goods*.

Second, and perhaps more importantly, the district court in that case had ordered the release of drugs which the government continued to maintain were harmful. In such situations, the court of appeals reasoned, strict application of the Admiralty Rules to § 334 proceedings would be improper. When the harmfulness of drugs remains at issue, "preliminary and necessarily tentative findings cannot serve as a substitute for a determination on the merits." *Id.*

That decision does not preclude an order releasing the "sterile active ingredients" prior to condemnation. Since no determination as to the harmfulness of these drugs will be made at trial, an order releasing them to Travenol on the condition that they not be used in the TRC program does not require this court to make the sort of "preliminary and tentative findings" that the *Alcon Labs* court feared would circumvent the statute's purposes.

. . . .

The $500,000 worth of "sterile active ingredients" seized by the government on May 22, 1987, are released to claimant Travenol Laboratories for use in accordance with law and other than in the TRC program. Travenol must post security of $500,000 prior to release.

NOTES

1. *Reimbursement for Perishable Commodities.* Seizure of perishable commodities may result in the articles' destruction, or a reduction in their value, even if the claimant ultimately prevails. If the seizure was reasonable, however, the claimant is not entitled to reimbursement for any loss in the commodity's value during storage. For example, in *United States v. 2,116 Boxes of Boned Beef,* 516 F. Supp. 321 (D. Kan. 1981), *aff'd,* 726 F.2d 1481 (10th Cir. 1984), the claimant prevailed in the court proceedings following a seizure of beef containing DES. Nevertheless, the claimant's attempt to recover the lost value of the food under the Tucker Act, 28 U.S.C. § 1491(a)(1), which creates a cause of action for uncompensated takings, was rejected because the Tenth Circuit had determined that the seizure was reasonable. *Jarboe–Lackey Feedlots, Inc. v. United States,* 7 Cl. Ct. 329 (1985).

2. *Nonperishable Commodities.* The courts are apparently unanimous that nonperishable commodities are not eligible for pretrial release. In addition to the *Alcon* case discussed in the decision excerpted above, see also, e.g., *United States v. 893 One–Gallon Cans, More or Less, . . . Labeled Brown's Inhalant,* 45 F. Supp. 467 (D. Del. 1942); *United States v. Article of Device . . . "110 V Vapozone . . .",* 194 F. Supp. 332 (N.D. Cal. 1961).

3. MULTIPLE SEIZURES

Section 304(a)(1) of the Act contains no restrictions against multiple seizures of adulterated articles. With respect to misbranded articles, however, it prohibits the institution of any libel for condemnation (i.e., any seizure) "if there is pending in any court a libel for condemnation proceeding . . . based on the same alleged misbranding." Moreover, even if no seizure proceeding has commenced with respect to a misbranding allegation, the statute prohibits the simultaneous institution of multiple libel for condemnation proceedings, unless a court has already determined in another enforcement action that the labeling in question constitutes misbranding or if "the

Secretary has probable cause to believe from facts found, without hearing, by him or any officer or employee of the Department that the misbranded article is dangerous to health, or that the labeling of the misbranded article is fraudulent, or would be in a material respect misleading to the injury or damage of the purchaser or consumer." In the following case, the United States Supreme Court addresses the constitutionality of the latter exception.

Ewing v. Mytinger & Casselberry, Inc.
339 U.S. 594 (1950).

■ MR. JUSTICE DOUGLAS delivered the opinion of the Court.

This is an appeal from a three-judge District Court specially constituted on appellee's application for an injunction to restrain enforcement of a portion of an Act of Congress for repugnance to the Due Process Clause of the Fifth Amendment.

Section 304(a) of the Federal Food, Drug, and Cosmetic Act . . . permits multiple seizures of misbranded articles "when the Administrator has probable cause to believe from facts found, without hearing, by him or any officer or employee of the Agency that the misbranded article is dangerous to health, or that the labeling of the misbranded article is fraudulent, or would be in a material respect misleading to the injury or damage of the purchaser or consumer."

Appellee is the exclusive national distributor of Nutrilite Food Supplement, an encapsulated concentrate of alfalfa, water cress, parsley, and synthetic vitamins combined in a package with mineral tablets. There is no claim that the ingredients of the preparation are harmful or dangerous to health. The sole claim is that the labeling [a booklet touting the curative powers of Nutrilite] was, to use the statutory words, "misleading to the injury or damage of the purchaser or consumer" and that therefore the preparation was "misbranded" when introduced into interstate commerce.

This was indeed the administrative finding behind eleven seizures resulting in that number of libel suits, between September and December, 1948. . . . Shortly thereafter the present suit was instituted to have the multiple seizure provision of § 304(a) declared unconstitutional and to dismiss all libel cases except the first one instituted. The District Court held that appellants had acted arbitrarily and capriciously in violation of the Fifth Amendment in instituting multiple libel suits without first affording the appellee a hearing on the probable cause issue; that the multiple seizure provision of § 304(a) was unconstitutional under the Due Process Clause of the Fifth Amendment; and that appellants should be permanently enjoined from instituting any action raising a claim that the booklet accompanying the preparation was a misbranding since it was not fraudulent, false, or misleading.

First. The administrative finding of probable cause required by § 304(a) is merely the statutory prerequisite to the bringing of the lawsuit. When the libels are filed the owner has an opportunity to appear as a claimant and to have a full hearing before the court. This hearing, we conclude, satisfies the requirements of due process. . . .

It is said that these multiple seizure decisions of the Administrator can cause irreparable damage to a business. And so they can. The impact of the initiation of judicial proceedings is often serious. . . . Yet it has never been held that the hand of government must be stayed until the courts have an opportunity to determine whether the government is justified in instituting suit in the courts. Discretion of any official may be abused. Yet it is not a requirement of due process that there be judicial inquiry before discretion can be exercised. It is sufficient, where only property rights are concerned, that there is at some stage an opportunity for a hearing and a judicial determination. . . .

Second. The District Court had no jurisdiction to review the administrative determination of probable cause.

[FDA's] determination of probable cause in and of itself had no binding legal consequence. . . . It took the exercise of discretion on the part of the Attorney General . . . to bring it into play against appellee's business. Judicial review of such a preliminary step in a judicial proceeding is so unique that we are not willing easily to infer that it exists. . . .

The purpose of the multiple seizure provision is plain. It is to arrest the distribution of an article that is dangerous, or whose labeling is fraudulent or misleading, pending a determination of the issue of adulteration or misbranding. The public therefore has a stake in the jurisdictional issue before us. If the District Court can step in, stay the institution of seizures, and bring the administrative regulation to a halt until it hears the case, the public will be denied the speedy protection which Congress provided by multiple seizures. It is not enough to say that the vitamin preparation in the present case is not dangerous to health. This preparation may be relatively innocuous. But the statutory scheme treats every "misbranded article" the same in this respect— whether it is "dangerous to health," or its labeling is "fraudulent," or materially "misleading to the injury or damage of the purchaser or consumer." . . . Congress weighed the potential injury to the public from misbranded articles against the injury to the purveyor of the article from a temporary interference with its distribution and decided in favor of the speedy, preventive device of multiple seizures. We would impair or destroy the effectiveness of that device if we sanctioned the interferences which a grant of jurisdiction to the District Court would entail. . . .

Reversed.

■ MR. JUSTICE JACKSON, dissenting.

. . . .

The trial court of three judges wrote no opinion but made forty-three detailed findings of fact. . . . The substance of these is to find that the Government instituted a multiplicity of court actions, with seizures in widely separated parts of the country, with a purpose to harass appellee and its dealers and intending that these actions and the attendant publicity would injure appellee's business *before any of the issues in such cases could be tried*. This, the court held, was justified by no emergency, the product being, at worst, harmless and having been marketed for years with knowledge of the Department.

Assuming as I do that the Act on its face is not constitutionally defective, the question remains whether it has been so misused by refusal of administrative hearing, together with such irreparable injury in anticipation of judicial hearing, as to deny appellee due process of law or to amount to an abuse of process of the courts.

. . . The holding of the court below and the contention of the appellee here that the Government is not entitled to so apply the statute as to bring multiple actions designed to destroy a business before it can be heard in its own defense is not frivolous, to say the least.

I am constrained to withhold assent to a decision that passes in silence what I think presents a serious issue.

NOTES

1. *Multiple Misbranding Seizures.* In *Dainty–Maid, Inc. v. United States*, 216 F.2d 668 (6th Cir. 1954), claimant sought dismissal of multiple seizures for misbranding, on the ground that the labeling involved was not identical to the labeling held illegal in an earlier default judgment. The court refused, holding that whether the new labeling involved the same misbranding as the earlier judgment was a factual question for the district court.

2. *The Unavailability of Injunctions Against Seizures.* In addition to upholding the particular provision in question, *Ewing* also stands for the broader proposition that the decision of the government to institute a seizure action cannot be enjoined, because the proper forum in which to challenge the government's justification for the seizure is in the subsequent condemnation proceeding in a U.S. district court. In *Parke, Davis & Co. v. Califano*, 564 F.2d 1200 (6th Cir. 1977), the court extended this reasoning to a seizure situation in which a "probable cause" finding was not required. In ordering the reversal of an injunction against the government, the Court of Appeals explained:

> We conclude that the district court had no jurisdiction to review the decision of the FDA to initiate enforcement actions. That decision is indistinguishable from the finding of probable cause which the Supreme Court has held may not be challenged in a separate action. *Ewing v. Mytinger & Casselberry,* 339 U.S. 594 (1950).
>
> . . . Parke Davis had an adequate remedy, and the district court erred in holding that it did not. Parke Davis had the same remedy which was available to the distributor in *Ewing*—the statutory right to contest the seizure of its property in the libels. . . . [I]t was an abuse of discretion to enjoin the FDA in the circumstances of this case where pending enforcement actions provided an opportunity for a full hearing before a court. . . .

4. PROOF REQUIRED FOR CONDEMNATION

In a civil seizure action the government must prove its case by a preponderance of the evidence. *See, e.g., United States v. 60 28–Capsule Bottles . . . "Unitrol,"* 325 F.2d 513 (3d Cir. 1963); *United States v. 4*

Cases ... Slim–Mint Chewing Gum, 300 F.2d 144 (7th Cir. 1962); *United States v. 449 Cases, Containing Tomato Paste,* 212 F.2d 567 (2d Cir. 1954). It is not required, however, to offer such proof with respect to every article in a seized shipment.

United States v. 43 1/2 Gross Rubber Prophylactics Labeled in Part "Xcello's Prophylactics"

65 F. Supp. 534 (D. Minn. 1946).

■ NORDBYE, DISTRICT JUDGE.

. . . .

The government inspection has established that the devices tested were defective in the number indicated, and there can be no serious doubt that the strength and quality of these particular defective articles fell below that which they purported or were represented to possess. . . .

The problem presented, however, pertains to the right of the Government to condemn the entire shipment. . . . The average defects . . . of all the tests [made on samples randomly drawn from the shipment] is approximately 7.37 per cent. But of the entire shipment seized a fraction of one per cent is definitely shown to be defective, and claimant contends that the Government has failed to sustain the burden of proof which rests on it in these proceedings in its attempt to condemn the entire shipment. It should be pointed out that apparently the only practical tests which the government representatives are able to make with the facilities available to them results in the article's being rendered useless after the test has been made. Concededly, the burden of proof rests upon the Government. But it does not follow that each individual article in the shipment must be tested. Inspection and condemnation on the basis of samples tested is clearly contemplated by the Act. In fact, the Act speaks of samples and their availability for testing. 21 U.S.C.C. § 334(c) . . . No serious question is raised in this proceeding as to the samples taken being representative. But claimant contends that the Court cannot order the condemnation of good articles, and concededly some of the remaining articles are in all probability free from defects. However, in urging this contention, claimant fails to distinguish between condemnation and the confiscation or sale of goods. Condemnation only sustains the Government's position that the goods as they were composed in interstate shipment violate the provision and purpose of the Federal Food, Drug, and Cosmetic Act. After the decree, the claimant can separate the good from the defective if it posts a bond, and thereby will be able to retain the balance of the goods. 21 U.S.C.A. § 334(d). . . . But it is urged that the number of defectives are so low in proportion to the total number of articles involved in this proceeding that a grave injustice would result to the claimant if the entire shipment is condemned. Again, it may be reiterated that condemnation is not confiscation. . . . Moreover, the Court is not required or permitted to establish any formula as to what tolerance of defects should be allowed, if any, in every type of libel proceeding before it determines that the Government has sustained the burden of proof as to any particular shipment. Suffice it to say that, on the state of the facts herein, and assuming that the same ratio of defectives would be found in the entire shipment, it would follow that over 1,500 defective articles would be found in this shipment. Such a number, if sold on the market, would constitute a potential menace to public health, and, in view of the claimed purpose and object of the devices, that is, the prevention of disease, are sufficient to sustain the libel proceedings herein.

. . . .

NOTES

1.   *Jurisdiction in Condemnation Proceedings.* According to section 304(a), condemnation proceedings must be brought within the federal district in which the articles in question were seized. In such actions, the court obtains *in rem* jurisdiction (over the articles seized) rather than *in personam* jurisdiction (over the owner of the articles). Consequently, the court does not have jurisdiction to hear an injunction claim directly against the owner. However, the owner may intervene in the case and claim the goods. By doing so, the claimant submits to the personal jurisdiction of the court, and FDA may move to amend the complaint to add a request for an injunction. Moreover, the court retains *in personam* jurisdiction over a claimant even if the government later releases the seized articles. *United States v. An Article of Drug Consisting of 4,680 Pails*, 725 F.2d 976, 982–84 (5th Cir. 1984).

2.   *In Rem Jurisdiction.* In *United States v. An Article of Drug Consisting of 4,680 Pails*, 725 F.2d 976 (5th Cir. 1984), the United States Marshall released a seized animal drug after a jury in the district court ruled against the government. When the judge then granted a new trial, Pfizer, the claimant, contended that the court no longer had *in rem* jurisdiction because of the release and removal of the drug (the *res*). The Court of Appeals rejected this argument, finding a substitute basis of *in personam* jurisdiction over the parties. It noted the inappropriateness of strictly applying the rule requiring the presence of the *res*, in view of the fact that *in rem* jurisdiction is a legal fiction that exists to effectuate the adjudication of disputes. *Id.* at 983. Pfizer also contended that the release of the drugs rendered the case moot, because the relief sought in the seizure and condemnation action was the forfeiture and destruction of the drugs. The Court rejected this argument as well, refusing to "elevate form over substance" and observing that while in form the suit sought condemnation of a specific lot of drugs, "the substantive character of the remedy sought is . . . a declaration that [the drug] is or is not a new animal drug"—a declaration that would be *res judicata* in any future action. *Id.* at 984.

3.   *Venue in Condemnation Proceedings.* The seizure of articles not only establishes jurisdiction over condemnation proceedings but also usually determines the venue of the action. Because section 304(a) requires condemnation proceedings to be brought within the district where the article is found, a claimant may not ordinarily use the federal change of venue statute, 28 U.S.C. § 1404, to transfer such an action for the convenience of the parties and witnesses. *Clinton Foods, Inc. v. United States*, 188 F.2d 289, 292 (4th Cir. 1951). Nonetheless, when multiple seizures are filed in different jurisdictions, the claimant may, pursuant to section 304(b), request that the actions be consolidated in "a district of

reasonable proximity to the claimant's principal place of business." The court is required to grant such a request for consolidation "unless good cause to the contrary is shown." FD&C Act 304(b). *See, e.g., United States v. 91 Packages . . . Nutrilite Food Supplement*, 93 F. Supp. 763 (D.N.J. 1950). Seizure actions for misbranding are sometimes limited to a single proceeding, FD&C Act 304(a), and in such instances, the claimant may similarly request transfer of that one proceeding to a district in reasonable proximity to its principal place of business. Interestingly, the phrase "a district of reasonable proximity to the claimant's principal place of business" excludes the district within which the principal place of business is actually located. *See, e.g., United States v. 600 Units . . . "Nue–Ovo"*, 60 F. Supp. 144, 145 (W.D. Mo. 1945).

5. FINAL CONDEMNATION DECREES AND SALVAGING

Section 304(d) of the FD&C Act, governing final decrees in seizure and condemnation actions, provides, in part, as follows:

> Any [article] condemned under this section shall, after entry of the decree, be disposed of by destruction or sale as the court may . . . direct and the proceeds thereof, if sold, less the legal costs and charges, shall be paid into the Treasury of the United States. . . . After entry of the decree and upon the payment of the costs of such proceedings and the execution of a good and sufficient bond conditioned that such article shall not be sold or disposed of contrary to the provisions of this Act or the laws of any State or Territory in which sold, the court may by order direct that such article be delivered to the owner thereof to be destroyed or brought into compliance with the provisions of this Act, under the supervision of an officer or employee duly designated by the Secretary. . . .

United States v. 1,638 Cases of Adulterated Alcoholic Beverages

624 F.2d 900 (9th Cir. 1980).

■ THORNBERRY, CIRCUIT JUDGE.

K&L Distributors, Inc. brings this appeal from a judgment for the destruction of 1,638 cases of alcoholic beverages entered by the United States District Court for the District of Alaska under the authority of the Federal Food, Drug and Cosmetic Act (Act). . . . K&L asserts that the district court erred in ruling that appellant's method of reconditioning the articles must be rejected in favor of the method approved by the Food and Drug Administration (FDA). . . .

On November 11, 1974, a flood swept through the City of Nome, Alaska. . . . The flood waters caused extensive damage to the commercial district of Nome. Included in the commercial district is the Bering Sea Saloon, the location of the articles that are the subject of this controversy. The flood waters apparently burst through the back door of the saloon, resulting in merchandise being thrown to the ground and being exposed to various amounts of sea water.

The flood also destroyed the city's sewage disposal plant. . . . It is possible that the raw sewage was washed into the commercial district of Nome and into the Bering Sea Saloon. . . .

This action was initiated by the United States on March 27, 1975, by filing a Complaint for Forfeiture seeking the seizure and condemnation of liquor and other articles, claiming that the items had been held under insanitary conditions which may have caused them to become contaminated with filth or may have rendered them injurious to health. The articles were seized by the United States Marshal pursuant to an arrest warrant on April 1, 1975.

. . . On June 9, 1976, K&L entered into [a] consent decree with respect to the cases of alcohol. First, K&L admitted that the articles under seizure were adulterated in violation of 21 U.S.C. § 342(a)(4). They were therefore condemned pursuant to 21 U.S.C. § 334(a). Second, the consent decree provided that the goods were to be released from custody for the purpose of reconditioning the articles pursuant to 21 U.S.C. § 334(d) under the supervision of the FDA. Because the alcohol may have been contaminated by raw sewage, the FDA would only approve a reconditioning plan that included redistillation of the alcohol. Appellant claimed that this plan would be economically disastrous and brought an action seeking approval and implementation of its reconditioning plan. The district court approved the FDA's plan. . . . The district court then ordered the condemned articles destroyed [because K&L would not recondition them in accordance with FDA's plan] but stayed the order during the pendency of this appeal.

K&L initially contends that the owner of seized goods should have the right to choose the method of reconditioning that is to be used to bring adulterated articles in compliance with the Act.

In assessing this claim, we must first examine the statutory framework surrounding this type of situation. . . . After it is determined that an article is "adulterated," . . . [t]he article is then disposed of by destruction or sale unless, upon payment of the costs of the proceeding and execution of a sufficient bond, the court orders the articles to be delivered to the owner to be destroyed or brought into compliance with the provisions of the Act under the supervision of an officer designated by the Secretary of Health, Education and Welfare. 21 U.S.C. § 334(d)(1).

K&L admitted in the consent decree that the articles were adulterated. The consent decree provided that they were to be returned to K&L to be reconditioned under the supervision of the FDA. The only remaining question then is whether "under the supervision of" the FDA requires appellant to adopt the FDA's recommended method of reconditioning the articles. K&L suggested a plan of reconditioning that included a soap and water washing of the bottles followed by a hypochlorite dip. . . . K&L's proposal was found unacceptable because it would not solve the problem of the filth under the caps. If a cap was removed for additional cleaning, there would be further contamination. Therefore, the FDA provided that the only acceptable method for remedying the insanitary condition would be through a complete reprocessing of the product by redistillation.

It is the duty of the FDA to protect the health and welfare of the general public. Therefore, the courts that have dealt with the issue presented in this case have held that it is proper to rely on the scientific expertise of the FDA in determining the acceptability of a reconditioning proposal and to require FDA approval of a reconditioning plan. *United States v. Allan Drug Co.*, 357 F.2d 713 (10th Cir.), *cert. denied*, 385 U.S. 899 (1966); *United States v. 1,322 Cans, More or Less, of Black Raspberry Puree*, 68 F. Supp. 881 (N.D. Ohio 1946). In *Allan*, the Tenth Circuit addressed the meaning of the language of § 334(d)(1) as it applies to misbranded drugs. The court stated that once a district court delivers a misbranded (or adulterated) article to the owner to bring it into compliance with the law under the supervision of an officer designated by the Secretary of HEW,

> the supervisory powers committed to the Secretary undoubtedly carry broad authority to determine whether and in what manner the labeling may be brought within compliance with the act. The judicial function is concerned with the end product of the labeling process. While the final decision lies with the courts, great weight must be given to the administrative decision.

357 F.2d at 719. The district court in *1,322 Cans* reached a similar conclusion with respect to articles of adulterated food when it stated that

> The Food and Drug Administration has determined that distillation is the only process which would recondition this puree for human consumption and which it would approve. I see no abuse of discretion in making this determination. To interfere would be substituting the judgment of the court for that of the Food and Drug Administration upon a matter which it is better able to decide upon an issue which I think is not properly joined in this case.

68 F. Supp. at 881.

The district court properly deferred to the expertise of the FDA. While this court is not bound by *Allan* or *1,322 Cans*, we choose to follow the reasoning of those cases. A district court may rely on and give great weight to the FDA's finding that a reconditioning plan is not scientifically acceptable. The FDA did not abuse its discretion, even in light of the economic hardship imposed on appellants by its reconditioning plan. The district court, in its discretion, properly adopted the determination of the FDA.

AFFIRMED.

NOTES

1. *Forfeiture of Bond.* Violation of a court decree permitting salvaging after condemnation will result in forfeiture of the bond posted by the claimant. *See Stinson Canning Co. v. United States*, 170 F.2d 764 (4th Cir. 1948); *Fresh Grown Preserve Corp. v. United States*, 143 F.2d 191 (6th Cir. 1944). *See generally* Thomas Haskins Jacobs, *An Analysis of the Application of the Salvaging Provision of the Food, Drug, and Cosmetic Act of 1938*, 26 FOOD DRUG COSM. L.J. 240 (1971).

2. *Costs of Litigation.* Section 304(e) provides: "When a decree of condemnation is entered against the article, court costs and fees, and

storage and other proper expenses, shall be awarded against the person, if any, intervening as claimant of the article." If the claimant withdraws its claim for seized articles prior to judgment, the claimant is nonetheless properly charged for court costs and storage. *See, e.g., United States v. 374 100 Pound Burlap Bags . . . Cocoa Beans*, Food Drug Cosm. L. Rep. (CCH) ¶ 38,119 (E.D. Pa. 1989). The costs imposed on a claimant under section 304(e) may not include the costs the government incurred in proving its case. *United States v. Article of Drug*, 428 F. Supp. 278, 281–82 (E.D. Tenn. 1976).

   3.   *Re-export.* Section 304(d)(1) provides that an article that violates the FD&C Act at the time it is imported into the United States may be delivered to the importer for exportation in lieu of destruction, but only if the importer had no cause to believe the article was illegal before it was released from customs custody. As *United States v. An Article of Food . . . "Basmati Rice,"* Food Drug Cosm. L. Rep. ¶ 38,009 (N.D. Cal. 1986), illustrates, a claimant has a heavy burden to prove it lacked cause to believe that the product was illegal when imported.

6. EFFECTIVENESS OF SEIZURES

Peter Barton Hutt, *Philosophy of Regulation Under the Federal Food, Drug and Cosmetic Act*
28 FOOD DRUG COSMETIC LAW JOURNAL 177 (1973).

   . . . [A] seizure represents a substantial expenditure of governmental resources. . . . Many seizures, involving relatively minor violations, include only a small amount of the total goods involved. During the past ten years 13% of our seizure recommendations were never executed because the product had been moved or consumed during the time taken to complete these procedures. And during this same period, 99.7% of all seizures were adjudicated by default or consent, and were not litigated through to trial. . . .

   There is no question that, in many instances, the traditional seizure mechanism remains very useful. Where an entire carload or grain elevator of food is found adulterated, seizure obviously does accomplish its intended purpose. In an unfortunately large number of instances, however, seizure is a wholly ineffective and inappropriate remedy that needs to be supplemented by more efficient approaches. One particularly disturbing aspect is that, as any food and drug lawyer knows, the impact of a single seizure of a small amount of a product can be effectively blunted simply by filing a claim and engaging in the usual pre-trial discovery. The inventory of the offending product can then be relabeled, or exhausted without change, and at that point a consent decree can be accepted or the claim withdrawn and the case forfeited. In the meantime, the public is subjected to the illegal product, and the entire purpose of the seizure is substantially delayed and subverted.

   There is no easy solution to these problems. Whether or not statutory changes occur, it is clear that the Food and Drug Administration will continue its use of recall and detention, in lieu of seizure, where this is the most appropriate means of enforcement available. Another approach that I favor is the increased use of a regulatory letter to a company under section 306 of the Act where relatively minor violations are involved (e.g., FPLA violations, some misbranding charges, and perhaps instances of esthetic adulteration), requiring compliance with the law within a specified period of time. Failure to comply would then be subject to injunction and/or criminal action, and in some instances also seizure. . . .

NOTE

In the early 1970s, based on the above analysis, FDA began frequently to use regulatory letters (now called warning letters) in lieu of seizures, particularly in cases involving no danger to health. Seizure actions, which approached two thousand annually in the years immediately following the passage of the 1938 FD&C Act, numbered only 15 in 2011 and 8 in 2012. *See supra* p. 165 (chart).

7. ADMINISTRATIVE DETENTION

To prevent illegal articles from being moved or consumed while FDA is taking the steps necessary to accomplish a seizure, the agency often requests state officials to use their statutory powers to embargo or detain the articles by administrative order.

The agency shares with USDA the authority to detain by administrative order meat, poultry, and egg products under 21 U.S.C. 679(b), 467f(b), and 1052(d), respectively. (For USDA regulations implementing this authority, see 9 C.F.R. Part 329.) The Bioterrorism Act Preparedness of Response Act of 2002 amended the FD&C Act to provide that an officer or qualified employee of FDA may order the detention of any article of food found during an inspection, examination, or investigation under the Act if he or she "has credible evidence or information indicating that such article presents a threat of serious adverse health consequences or death to humans or animals." FD&C Act 304(h)(1)(A). The agency has published a final rule implementing this provision. 69 Fed. Reg. 31660 (June 4, 2004), codified in 21 C.F.R. Part 1, Subpart K.

Under the Medical Device Amendments, FDA has administrative detention authority for medical devices. FD&C Act 304(g). *See* 21 C.F.R. 800.55; *Life Design Systems, Inc. v. Sullivan*, Civ. No. CA3–90–701–D (N.D. Tex. 1990). Section 304(g) was amended to extend this power to tobacco products in the Family Smoking Prevention and Tobacco Control Act of 2009 and to drugs in the Food and Drug Administration Safety and Innovation Act of 2012. By terms of the legislation, the latter amendment will not take effect until FDA issues final implementing regulations. 126 Stat. 993, 1069 (2012).

E. INJUNCTIONS

1. INTRODUCTION

The 1906 Act did not authorize FDA to seek injunctive relief against violators. The legislative history of the 1938 Act reveals various reasons for including injunction authority. During Senate hearings on an early version of the legislation, FDA Chief Campbell testified:

> The next section . . . provides for the suppression of repetitious offenses. In the present circumstances there is no way by which that can be done effectively. If an article is misbranded or adulterated the manufacturer can continue for a protracted period its production and shipment in interstate commerce because of the delay incident to the conclusion of a [criminal] prosecution. Even though a conviction were obtained, it would be impossible to bring the matter at issue to a definite determination without the lapse of an inordinate period. This section by expediting action and suppressing continued offenses is for the more adequate protection of the public. . . .

"Food, Drugs, and Cosmetics," Hearings before a Subcomm. of the Senate Comm. on Commerce, 73d Cong., 2d Sess. 78 (1933).

The House Report on the final version of the FD&C Act discussed another benefit of adding the option of enforcement by injunction.

> Section 302 provides a new enforcement procedure for food and drug legislation by authorizing the courts to enjoin violations. This procedure will be particularly advantageous in border-line cases that cannot be settled without litigation. In many such cases it is unfair to the manufacturer to subject him to criminal trial and likewise unfair to the public to have the issue determined under the restrictions necessarily prevailing in criminal procedure. This remedy should reduce litigation. In some cases it should avoid the hardship and expense to litigants in seizure cases. . . . A seizure case finally decided in favor of a defendant leaves him without recourse for his losses, including court costs, storage, and other charges.

House Rep. No. 2139, 75th Cong., 3d Sess. (1938).

FDA was slow to start taking advantage of this new enforcement tool, and it has not frequently sought injunctions. *See supra* p. 165 (chart). Nevertheless, the agency does occasionally file civil actions seeking injunctions, sometimes as the sole remedy, other times in combination with seizure. An injunction has several distinct advantages as an enforcement mechanism. The government has a lower burden of proof in an injunction suit than in a criminal prosecution. An injunction can prohibit further violations, whereas a condemnation decree after a seizure cannot, because it is issued against the seized product itself, not against any person. Moreover, FDA can seek a preliminary injunction, or even a temporary restraining order (TRO), to put a halt to violative conduct immediately, before the court decides whether to award a permanent injunction. Most injunction actions are resolved by consent decree.

The issuance of temporary restraining orders and injunctions by federal courts is regulated by Rule 65 of the Federal Rules of Civil Procedure.

NOTE

Jury Trial. A defendant is not entitled to a jury trial in an injunction suit under the Act. *See United States v. Ellis Research Laboratories, Inc.,* 300 F.2d 550 (7th Cir. 1962). Under section 302(b), however, a charge of violation of an injunction may be triable to a jury, if the violation also constitutes a violation of the FD&C Act.

2. Preliminary Injunctions

United States v. Nutri-cology, Inc.

982 F.2d 394 (9th Cir. 1992).

■ Pregerson, Circuit Judge: . . .

I. *Background*

Nutri-cology distributes and promotes a number of products labelled as nutritional or dietary supplements. These products are allegedly promoted as useful to prevent and treat numerous diseases and conditions.

The Food and Drug Administration began monitoring Nutri-cology's activities in 1982. The FDA notified defendants in writing— three times in 1982, twice in 1985, and twice in 1988—that the FDA considered Nutri-cology's products to be unapproved "drugs" and "new drugs" under the FDCA. . . .

Since 1982, Nutri-cology has maintained that its products are not "drugs" or "new drugs," under the FDCA, but are herbs, oils, vitamins, and other "foods." The FDA sent its last communication to Nutri-cology on June 16, 1988. The government filed this action three years later on May 2, 1991.

On May 8, 1991, the district court granted the government's ex parte request for a temporary restraining order enjoining Nutri-cology from further marketing nine of its products, which constituted 80% of Nutri-cology's business.

On May 23, 1991, the district court denied the government's motion for a preliminary injunction. The district court applied the following preliminary injunction standard: " 'the moving party must show either (1) a combination of probable success on the merits and the possibility of irreparable harm, or (2) that serious questions are raised and the balance of hardships tips sharply in the moving party's favor.' "

The district court made the following findings: (1) the government made a threshold evidentiary showing that Nutri-cology intended its products to be perceived as beneficial in preventing or treating diseases; (2) the government created some showing that Nutri-cology's products were "drugs" falling under the auspices of 21 U.S.C. § 321(g)(1)(B); and (3) the government made a colorable showing that Nutri-cology was violating 21 U.S.C. § 331(d) by marketing unapproved "new drugs." The court further concluded that a rebuttable presumption of irreparable harm arose from the colorable showing of an FDCA violation.

The district court then concluded that the presumption of irreparable harm was rebutted by Nutri-cology's extensive showing, through the petition signed by sixty physicians and nutritionists, in support of the merit and reliability of its products. Nutri-cology's showing was particularly persuasive because the government failed to demonstrate any harm to consumers. The district court found that two other factors weighed against granting the preliminary injunction: the FDA's nine-year delay in bringing the action, and the likelihood that an injunction would destroy Nutri-cology's business.

On July 19, 1991, the district court denied the government's motion for reconsideration. On September 10, 1991, the government filed its notice of appeal. . . .

IV. Standard for Issuing Preliminary Injunctions

The principal issue in this appeal is whether the district court applied the correct legal standard in denying the government's motion for preliminary injunction. Generally, to obtain a preliminary injunction, "the moving party must show either (1) a combination of probable success on the merits and the possibility of irreparable injury or (2) that serious questions are raised and the balance of hardships tips in its favor." *United States v. Odessa Union Warehouse Co-op*, 833 F.2d 172, 174 (9th Cir. 1987). "These two formulations represent two points on a sliding scale in which the required degree of irreparable harm increases as the probability of success decreases." *Id*.

A. Probability of Success on the Merits

. . . .

In its preliminary determination regarding the merits of the government's claims, the district court . . . found that the government had made merely a colorable showing that Nutri-cology was violating the FDCA by marketing its products. We cannot say that the district court erred.

B. Irreparable Injury

The government relies on our opinion in *Odessa Union* when it contends that, because this is a statutory enforcement action, it was not required to make a showing of irreparable harm. We disagree.

In *Odessa Union*, the parties conceded that the FDCA was violated. We therefore found that the conventional requirement of showing the possibility of irreparable injury was inapplicable. Specifically, we held that "[w]here an injunction is authorized by statute, *and the statutory conditions are satisfied as in the facts presented here*, the agency to whom the enforcement of the right has been entrusted is not required to show irreparable injury." (emphasis added). . . . In *Navel Orange Admin. Comm. v. Exeter Orange Co.*, 722 F.2d 449, 453 (9th Cir.1983), we did not require a showing of irreparable harm where . . . the evidence supported the conclusion that the government was likely to prevail on the merits.

In this case, the FDCA violation is substantially disputed, and has been disputed since 1982. The district court found that the government submitted "sufficient evidence to survive a motion for a directed verdict," but did not submit sufficient evidence to show that it was "likely to succeed on the merits of the case." Thus, the government's showing did not reach the level of the showing in *Odessa Union*, i.e., of an undisputed statutory violation. Moreover, it did not even match the government's showing in *Navel Orange*, i.e., that it was likely to prevail on the merits. Consequently, the government is not entitled to a presumption, rebuttable or otherwise, of irreparable injury.

In statutory enforcement cases where the government has met the "probability of success" prong of the preliminary injunction test, we presume it has met the "possibility of irreparable injury" prong because the passage of the statute is itself an implied finding by Congress that violations will harm the public. Therefore, further inquiry into irreparable injury is unnecessary. However, in statutory enforcement cases where the government can make only a "colorable evidentiary showing" of a violation, the court must consider the possibility of irreparable injury.

Here, the government did not show that it would probably prevail on the merits. Therefore, it was not entitled to a presumption of irreparable injury.

Relying on language in *Odessa Union*, the district court gave the government the benefit of a rebuttable presumption of irreparable injury. This was error. However, the district court would have reached the same result had it not initially presumed irreparable injury. Because the government failed to demonstrate any harm to consumers and because Nutri-cology submitted extensive evidence to the contrary, the district court did not abuse its discretion in finding that the government did not make the requisite showing of irreparable harm. The district court, moreover, did not abuse its discretion in denying the government's motions for preliminary injunction and for reconsideration.

Affirmed.

3. PERMANENT INJUNCTIONS

United States v. Laerdal Manufacturing Corp.

73 F.3d 852 (9th Cir. 1995).

■ D.W. NELSON, CIRCUIT JUDGE:

Appellant Laerdal Manufacturing Corp. appeals the order of the district court that Laerdal be "perpetually restrained and enjoined from directly or indirectly . . . (f)ailing or refusing to furnish information required by or under 21 U.S.C. § 360i, in accordance with" Medical Device Reporting ("MDR") regulations, 21 C.F.R. § 803. Laerdal is a manufacturer of automated external defibrillators ("AEDs"), which are applied to cardiac arrest victims in order to convert ventricular fibrillation back into regular heartbeats. In its findings of fact, the court determined that Laerdal had violated 21 C.F.R. § 803(a)(1)(i), which requires a manufacturer to file a report with the Food and Drug Administration "whenever information is received that reasonably suggests that a patient care device . . . may have caused or contributed to a death or serious injury."

Laerdal argues that the court improperly imposed this injunction, because there was no cognizable danger that Laerdal would violate the MDR regulation in the future. Laerdal claims that (a) the violation found by the court was an isolated incident, (b) the violation was unintentional, and (c) Laerdal has taken the necessary steps to prevent future violations. In addition, Laerdal contends that the balance of the parties' interests dictates that no injunction is warranted. We . . . affirm [the district court].

We review the scope of injunctive relief for an abuse of discretion or application of erroneous legal principles.

The Permanent Injunction and the "Cognizable Danger of Recurrent Violation"

A district court cannot issue an injunction unless "there exists some cognizable danger of recurrent violation." *United States v. W. T. Grant Co.*, 345 U.S. 629, 633 (1953). The determination that such danger exists must "be based on appropriate findings supported by the record." *Federal Election Comm'n v. Furgatch*, 869 F.2d 1256, 1263 (9th Cir. 1989); Fed. R. Civ. P. 65(d). Factors that a district court may consider in making this finding include the degree of scienter involved; the isolated or recurrent nature of the infraction; the defendant's recognition of the wrongful nature of his conduct; the extent to which the defendant's professional and personal characteristics might enable or tempt him to commit future violations; and the sincerity of any assurances against future violations.

. . . We find . . . that the district court did make findings that indicated a cognizable danger of recurrent violations.

We review the scope of injunctive relief for an abuse of discretion or application of erroneous legal principles.

The Number of Violations

Laerdal asserts that the court found only one isolated violation of the MDR regulation. This assertion does not accurately represent the whole of the court's findings. The district court specifically found that "at least one violation of the MDR regulations has occurred." The court developed at length the facts surrounding the incident in Grand Rapids that first brought Laerdal's reporting practices to the FDA's attention, but the court also found testimony in the record that Laerdal had received complaints of other instances in which a Laerdal AED failed to work properly.

On the basis of these findings the court concluded that while Laerdal's official reporting policy incorporated the language of FDA regulations, in actual practice Laerdal had an ongoing history of not implementing these procedures. . . .

Even if the district court had found evidence of only one violation, Laerdal is in error in asserting that one violation provides insufficient grounds for granting an injunction. The Supreme Court has determined that if a court has found a cognizable danger of recurrent future violations, an injunction "can be utilized even without a showing of past wrongs." *W. T. Grant Co.*, 345 U.S. at 633. . . .

Intention and the Likelihood of Recurrence

Laerdal further argues that it did not intend to violate the MDR regulations, and thus, no degree of scienter was involved. In this context, Laerdal also argues that the district court made a clearly erroneous factual finding in its determination that Laerdal had received information reasonably suggesting that in the Grand Rapids incident a Laerdal AED may have caused or contributed to a death. As Laerdal concedes, 21 C.F.R. § 803 is a strict liability provision. For purposes of determining whether Laerdal violated the MDR regulations, the district court was not required to develop the issue of Laerdal's intent; however, Laerdal contends that its intent is pertinent to the likelihood of its committing future violations.

Laerdal has repeatedly argued that its actions in violating the MDR regulations were justifiable. Though Laerdal decided to file a report concerning the Grand Rapids incident two weeks before trial, the court noted that Laerdal continued to argue at trial that the circumstances of the incident did not make filing a report necessary. . . .

Though Laerdal does not appeal the court's finding that it violated the MDR regulations, Laerdal nonetheless continues to argue that its actions were justifiable. Laerdal cites as support for its failure to file a report "the ambiguous language of the regulation" and numerous unique aspects of the Grand Rapids incident that warranted its decision not to file a report. . . .

Laerdal's intransigent insistence on its own blamelessness also manifests itself in hostility toward the MDR system. At trial and on appeal, Laerdal has attempted to demonstrate the "foibles of the MDR system." It claims that "MDR reports languish for several months in a bureaucratic limbo" and that the consequences of its Grand Rapids violation were "merely trifling." . . .

Laerdal's repeated self-justification is sufficient to show a likelihood of future violation. Even if Laerdal had not intended to violate the regulation, its continued insistence on justifying its actions in committing the violation "is an important factor in deciding whether future violations are sufficiently likely to warrant an injunction." . . . That Laerdal's self-justification extends to indicting the MDR system itself reflects "the sort of extraordinary intransigence and hostility" toward the FDA and the MDR regulations that support the inference of a likelihood to commit future violations.

. . . .

Balancing the Interests of the Parties

Laerdal asserts that the district court failed to balance the interests of the parties. Furthermore, Laerdal contends that its own interests—the reputational damage caused by the injunction and the losses due to sanctions imposed when Laerdal next violates the regulation—outweigh the public interest served by the regulation. The record shows otherwise. In the first paragraph of the "Conclusion" of the findings, the court implicitly balances the public health against the burden placed upon Laerdal, namely, that it comply with government regulations. The court's ruling in favor of the public interest is consistent with the legal standards governing the exercise of equitable discretion.

Laerdal argues that the public interest was not harmed, because FDA allegedly suffers from a backlog in filing its reports and the Grand Rapids report would have languished for several months before being filed. However, the public interest addressed by the MDR regulations centers not on the efficiency of the FDA, but on the attention manufacturers pay to evidence that their products could be causing or contributing to needless deaths. That Laerdal regards its own reputational and financial interests to be more important only reinforces the need for the injunction.

NOTE

Injunction Denied. Compare *United States v. Sars of Louisiana*, 324 F. Supp. 307 (E.D. La. 1971), in which the court denied an injunction. Though the defendants did not dispute that when inspected in 1968 and 1970 their animal food product contained *Salmonella* microorganisms, by the time the case came to trial they had complied with all the recommendations of FDA inspectors.

> Thus, the critical determination in this case is whether or not it is reasonable to expect that the defendants will commit violative acts in the future. It is the conclusion of this Court, from the evidence at trial, that there is simply no showing that such violations are likely to reoccur. . . .

Id. at 310

United States v. Articles of Drugs, et al., Midwest Pharmaceuticals, Inc.

825 F.2d 1238 (8th Cir. 1987).

■ McMILLIAN, CIRCUIT JUDGE.

Midwest Pharmaceuticals, Inc., Steven F. Sommers and Robert S. Leibert (collectively referred to as Midwest) appeal from a final judgment entered in the District Court for the District of Nebraska condemning as "misbranded" certain drug products seized from Midwest in April 1984. The district court held that the Midwest drugs were imitations of other drugs in violation of 21 U.S.C. §§ 331(b), 352(i)(2) and enjoined Midwest under 21 U.S.C. § 332(a) from selling or marketing any drug product similar in appearance and in effect to drugs seized in April 1984 by the Food and Drug Administration (FDA or the government).

For reversal, Midwest argues that . . . the injunction is overly broad and lacks specificity. . . .

Midwest is both a wholesale and retail distributor of generic, over-the-counter drug products containing caffeine, ephedrine . . . , and phenylpropanolamine. Midwest also sells powdery and sticky substances, which Midwest markets as "incense."

Midwest . . . usually sells its products in bulk containers of 1,000 dosage units (caplets or tablets). The drugs are shipped by mail in response to mail or telephone orders and payment is usually C.O.D. According to the government, Midwest sold over 245 million dosage units during 1984. . . . Midwest advertises its drug products in print media that the government characterizes as "subculture," "porno," "drug," and "biker" magazines. . . . Midwest in advertisements describes its drug products as "legal body stimulants" and "sleep aids." The advertisements contain pictures or photographs of the drugs, but contain no information about the ingredients or indications or contraindications, and describe the drug products by names such as "357 Magnum," "20/20," "30/30," "White Mole," "Mini–White" and "Incense." Some of these names are "street names" for various illegal drugs. . . .

On April 5, 1984, the FDA seized approximately 15 tons of drug products from Midwest. . . .

On the day of the seizure, the FDA filed a complaint alleging that Midwest drug products were "misbranded" because they were "imitations" of other drugs in violation of 21 U.S.C. § 352(i)(2) and were thus subject to *in rem* seizure under 21 U.S.C. § 334. The FDA also sought an order enjoining Midwest and its president, Sommers, under 21 U.S.C. § 332(a), from selling or marketing the same or similar products in the future. . . .

The case was tried in February 1986. . . . The government introduced evidence that Midwest's drug products were purchased in bulk, then repackaged without any information about the ingredients, and sold as "real drugs" to "youthful and unsophisticated" junior high and high school students at "real drug" prices. Midwest "dealers" thus realized a tremendous profit, approximately 20 times the actual cost of the drugs. . . .

The government also presented evidence that Midwest markets only drug products that are similar in appearance and effect to controlled substances and that the many different shapes, sizes and colors of Midwest drugs are non-functional. . . .

The district court held that the Midwest drugs, which had been seized in April 1984, were imitations of other drugs and enjoined Midwest from selling or marketing any drug similar in appearance and in effect to those seized. This appeal followed. . . .

Midwest . . . contends that the permanent injunction issued by the district court is both defective and grossly overbroad. Midwest argues that the injunction violates Fed. R. Civ. P. 65(d) because it fails to enumerate the drug products Midwest is enjoined from marketing. In addition, Midwest argues that the injunction is overbroad because it prohibits the sale of Midwest products for legal uses.

We consider first Midwest's contention that the injunction violates Fed. R. Civ. P. 65(d) which provides: "Every order granting an injunction and every restraining order shall set forth the reasons for its issuance; shall be specific in terms; shall describe in reasonable detail, and not by reference to the complaint or other document, the act or acts sought to be restrained." We agree that the injunction violates Rule 65(d). The district court order enjoins Midwest from

> selling or marketing in any way products described in CV. 84–0–206 and further are enjoined from employing marketing techniques to sell drug products identical or similar to those described in CV. 84–0–206. . . .

The injunction fails to identify the specific drug products that Midwest is prohibited from selling or marketing and fails to specify the marketing techniques that Midwest may not employ. On remand the district court should revise the injunction so that the specific acts which are prohibited are clearly defined within the order as required by Fed. R. Civ. P. 65(d).

Midwest also argues that the injunction is overbroad because it is not tailored to remedy the alleged specific harm, that is, the passing off of Midwest drug products as controlled substances. Midwest argues that there is no legal basis to enjoin the otherwise lawful sale of drug products that are capable of a lawful use to customers who act lawfully in reselling or consuming these products.

The government responds that the injunction is not overbroad because the injunction, as drafted, is necessary in order to prevent Midwest from continuing its illegal conduct. According to the government, a narrower injunction would not be effective because, even without future advertising, Midwest could continue to sell these drug products as a result of residual orders and repeat business. Thus, Midwest would reap future profits from its past illegal conduct.

Under § 332, the district court is authorized to restrain acts that are in violation of 21 U.S.C. § 331. Good faith is not a defense to the issuance of an injunction. Nor may a defendant successfully defend against the issuance of an injunction by asserting that the injunction would drive it out of business. A district court may issue an injunction if it concludes that the injunction is necessary to prevent future violations. . . .

The government presented evidence that Midwest had a pattern of noncompliance with federal drug laws. For example, the government showed that Midwest continued to sell imitation drug products, without change, after the FDA advised Midwest in regulatory letters that Midwest drug products were being passed off and after several seizures of Midwest products by the FDA. The district court could reasonably conclude that Midwest would continue the illegal acts unless restrained. We hold that the district court did not abuse its discretion in issuing an injunction barring Midwest from marketing and selling drugs in violation of 21 U.S.C. §§ 331, 352(i)(2).

NOTE

Suits for Contempt. Violation of an injunction may lead to a suit for contempt under section 302(b) of the Act. See, e.g., United States v. Vale, 140 Fed. Appx. 302 (2d Cir. 2005) (upholding criminal contempt conviction); United States v. Syntrax Innovations, Inc., 149 F. Supp. 2d 880 (E.D. Mo. 2001) (denying motion for civil contempt); United States v. Themy–Kotronakis, 140 F.3d 858 (10th Cir. 1998) (upholding criminal contempt conviction); United States v. 22 Rectangular or Cylindrical Finished Devices, 941 F. Supp. 1086 (D. Utah 1996) (finding of criminal contempt); Upjohn Co. v. Medtron Labs., Inc., 894 F. Supp. 126 (S.D.N.Y. 1995) (granting motion for civil contempt).

As discussed below, infra p. 240, the government does not have to prove criminal intent to establish criminal liability under the FD&C Act. Whether FDA must prove intent to sustain a charge of criminal contempt of an injunction issued under the FD&C Act has not been resolved. Cf. United States v. Schlicksup Drug Co., Inc., 206 F. Supp. 801 (S.D. Ill. 1962) (no proof of intent or willfulness required); *United States v. Lit Drug Co.*, 333 F. Supp. 990, 996–97 (D.N.J. 1971) (no proof of specific intent required); *with United States v. I. D. Russell Laboratories*, 439 F. Supp. 711 (W.D. Mo. 1977) (proof of willfulness required); *United States v. Themy–Kotronakis*, 140 F.3d at 864 (same).

FD&C Act 302(b) provides a right to a jury in some contempt proceedings. For discussions of some of the more technical aspects of this provision, see *United States v. 22 Rectangular or Cylindrical Finished Devices*, 941 F. Supp. 1086, 1093 (D. Utah 1996); *United States v. Dean Rubber Mfg. Co.*, 72 F. Supp. 819 (W.D. Mo. 1947); *United States v. Diapulse Corp.*, 365 F. Supp. 935 (E.D.N.Y. 1973).

4. CONSENT DECREES, RESTITUTION, AND DISGORGEMENT

A consent decree is a settlement ratified by the court, and thus enforceable by it. FDA frequently enters "consent decrees of permanent injunction." See, for example, the following press release:

Department of Justice Press Release

Jan. 24, 2012.

Office of Public Affairs

FOR IMMEDIATE RELEASE

U.S. Files Consent Decree for Permanent Injunction Against Pharmaceutical Ranbaxy Laboratories

The United States has filed a consent decree for permanent injunction against the generic drug manufacturer Ranbaxy Laboratories Ltd., an Indian corporation, in the U.S. District Court for the District of Maryland, the Department of Justice announced today. The Justice Department filed the consent decree at the request of the Food and Drug Administration (FDA).

Through investigation by the department and the FDA, the government uncovered numerous problems with Ranbaxy's drug manufacturing and testing in India and at facilities owned by its U.S. subsidiary, Ranbaxy Inc. These problems include failure to keep written records showing that drugs had been manufactured properly; failure to investigate evidence indicating that drugs did not meet their specifications; failure to adequately separate the manufacture of penicillin drugs from non-penicillin drugs in order to prevent cross-contamination; failure to have adequate procedures to prevent contamination of sterile drugs; and inadequate testing of drugs to ensure that they kept their strength and effectiveness until their expiration date.

The government also determined that Ranbaxy submitted false data in drug applications to the FDA, including the backdating of tests and the submitting of test data for which no test samples existed. All of these actions constituted violations of the federal Food, Drug and Cosmetic Act, making many of Ranbaxy's drugs adulterated, potentially unsafe and illegal to sell in the United States.

. . . .

The consent decree filed today is unprecedented in its scope, and requires Ranbaxy to take a wide range of actions to correct its violations and ensure that they do not happen again. Among other things, the consent decree prevents Ranbaxy from manufacturing drugs for the U.S. market at certain of its facilities until those facilities can do so according to U.S. standards. To remove false data contained in Ranbaxy's past drug applications and to prevent Ranbaxy from submitting false data to FDA in the future, the consent decree requires Ranbaxy to take actions such as: hire an outside expert to conduct a thorough internal review at the affected facilities and to audit applications containing data from those facilities; withdraw any applications found to contain false data; set up a separate office of data reliability within Ranbaxy; and hire an outside auditor to audit the affected facilities in the future.

Once the consent decree is approved by the court, it becomes a court order with which Ranbaxy must comply or face contempt.

"Submitting false data to the FDA in drug applications will not be tolerated," said Mr. [Tony] West [the Assistant Attorney General for the Justice Department's Civil Division]. "The Department of Justice, in partnership with the FDA, will use all available tools, including civil injunction actions and consent decrees, to ensure the integrity of drug applications, and to ensure that all drugs sold in the U.S. meet U.S. standards."

. . . .

Assistant Attorney General West thanked the FDA for referring this matter to the Department of Justice. Allan Gordus, Trial Attorney, of the Consumer Protection Branch of the Justice Department, in conjunction with the U.S. Attorney's Office for the District of Maryland and Marci Norton, Senior Counsel at FDA's Office of the Chief Counsel, brought this case on behalf of the United States.

———

In recent years, consent decrees in injunction suits involving violations of the FD&C Act have not only ordered defendants to take and not take various actions, but have also required them to pay large amounts of money under the theories of disgorgement and restitution.

William W. Vodra & Arthur N. Levine, *Anchors Away: The Food and Drug Administration's Use of Disgorgement Abandons Legal Moorings*

59 FOOD & DRUG LAW JOURNAL 1 (2004).

During the past several years, the Food and Drug Administration (FDA) has renewed a decades-old pursuit of restitution and disgorgement to enforce alleged violations of the Federal Food, Drug, and Cosmetic Act (FDCA). This effort has produced three consent decrees containing multi-million dollar payments to the U.S. Treasury that purport to represent disgorgement of ill-gotten gains.[2] To date, at least $759,000,000 has been paid under these three decrees. . . .

FDA first attempted to marshal the equitable powers of federal courts in the enforcement of the FDCA over fifty years ago. After the Ninth Circuit rejected the use of restitution in FDA actions in 1956,[6] the agency did not attempt to seek either restitution or disgorgement for almost forty years. Then, in the 1990s, FDA sought equitable monetary remedies in three consecutive cases. The first two resulted in judicial rejections of FDA's theories. On the agency's third try, a district court denied the agency's request for disgorgement but awarded restitution as part of an injunction. The Court of Appeals for the Sixth Circuit affirmed.[9]

Why has FDA now returned to the pursuit of disgorgement? We believe that the agency is attempting to solve a dilemma in regulatory law enforcement that emerged in the 1990s. The FDCA provides three judicial mechanisms to address violations: seizure, injunction, and criminal prosecution. The first removes noncompliant products from the market; the second prohibits the further manufacture or distribution of such products; the last punishes the wrongdoer with fines and (in the case of individuals) imprisonment. In practice, FDA has rarely used criminal penalties for violations that were not willful and did not result in death or serious injury to, or blatant fraud upon, consumers. Instead, it has relied on civil actions to compel a wrongdoer to cease operations "unless and until" the alleged deficiencies are cured. . . .

After a series of actions in the early 1990s, however, FDA found that these tools were not always appropriate or effective. Seizures and traditional prohibitory injunctions in these cases would have removed products or services that were essential, such as therapeutic drugs for which there were no adequate alternatives, blood and blood products, and food service on long-distance passenger railroads. Instead, FDA turned to "forward-looking" consent decrees of mandatory injunction that allowed necessary goods and services to continue to be provided while ordering that the defendants remediate the alleged noncompliance within time periods specified under the decree.

This response, however, produced other regulatory challenges. By its initial action that permitted the continued distribution of necessary products, FDA had effectively signaled to the defendant that, even if remediation were not accomplished under the decree, the agency would be extremely reluctant to block future sales of those products to compel compliance. The only tools left were contempt citations (which FDA has rarely sought) or criminal prosecutions (which are enormously costly for the government). The agency was frustrated by this lack of credible judicial remedies to compel full and timely compliance under the "going-forward" decrees. At the same time, FDA was repeatedly encountering

---

[2] The three consent decrees are United States v. Abbott Labs., Consent Decree of Permanent Injunction (N.D. Ill. filed Nov. 2, 1999); United States v. Various Articles of Drug Identified in Attachment A & Wyeth–Ayerst Labs., Consent Decree of Condemnation and Permanent Injunction (E.D. Tenn. filed Oct. 4, 2000); and United States v. Schering–Plough Corp., Consent Decree of Permanent Injunction (D.N.J. filed May 20, 2002).

[6] United States v. Parkinson, 240 F.2d 918 (9th Cir. 1956).

[9] United States v. Universal Mgmt. Servs., Inc., 191 F.3d 750 (6th Cir. 1999), *cert. denied*, 530 U.S. 1274 (2000).

claims from companies targeted for enforcement actions that their products also were "medically necessary," such that the supply could not be safely interrupted. These companies wanted "going-forward" injunctions too. How could FDA both increase the effectiveness of such injunctions and also convince future targets that having a "medically necessary" or otherwise essential product would not be a free pass for business as usual?

FDA's creative solution to this dual challenge emerged in the Abbott consent decree and has been repeated in the Wyeth and Schering decrees. The answer was disgorgement payments of significant size. All of these decrees involved alleged violations of current good manufacturing practice (GMP) requirements in the production of medical products (i.e., drugs, biologics, and medical devices). The decrees contain three separate types of payments:

(1) A "lump-sum payment" to the U.S. Treasury at the time the decree is entered. . . .

(2) "Percentage of sales" payments required if remediation is not achieved by the deadline established under the decree. The amount of these payments would be based on revenues generated by any "medically necessary" product between the expiration of the deadline and the date when, in FDA's view, compliance was finally achieved. . . .

(3) "Daily payments" required for each product or process not brought into compliance within specific deadlines determined pursuant to the decree, from the date of the deadline until compliance is actually achieved. . . .

The legal rationale for *all* of these payments was the doctrine of disgorgement, which FDA has described as a "long-recognized equitable remedy developed to prevent unjust enrichment and to deprive a defendant of ill-gotten gains." FDA's premise was that the sale of any product not made in compliance with GMP requirements generated profits to which the manufacturer was not entitled. The agency distinguished between restitution and disgorgement on the basis of where the money goes and which remedy is appropriate when the aggrieved party cannot be identified. . . .

Although often treated interchangeably, the concepts of "disgorgement" and "restitution" frequently are distinguished from each other on the basis of the primary intended purpose of each equitable remedy. The goal of restitution is to restore losses to a victim. In contrast, the objective of disgorgement is to divest from wrongdoers the gains flowing from their wrong. "The purpose of disgorgement is to deter violations by making them unprofitable. . . ."

The term "disgorgement" does not carry any specific meaning regarding the ultimate disposition of the assets divested. These monies can be—and very often are—used to offset the losses of victims. For example, when other federal agencies seek disgorgement, they have insofar as it is possible applied the funds to compensate victims for losses. The Federal Trade Commission (FTC), the Securities and Exchange Commission (SEC), and the Commodities Futures Trading Commission (CFTC) usually place recovered monies into escrow accounts for distribution to claimants who can demonstrate financial loss as a result of the wrongdoing alleged as the basis for the decrees. . . .

FDA's approach is quite different from these sister government bodies. The agency makes no attempt to compensate alleged victims. Rather, FDA relies on a restricted interpretation of "disgorgement" under which the proceeds are *intended from the outset* of the proceeding to be kept by the government. . . .

United States v. Lane Labs–USA Inc.

427 F.3d 219 (3d Cir. 2005).

■ RENDELL, CIRCUIT JUDGE.

In this case, we are called upon to decide whether a district court has the power under the Federal Food, Drug and Cosmetic Act to order a defendant found to be in violation of the Act to pay restitution to consumers. Because a district court's equitable powers in such a situation are broad, we hold that an order of restitution is properly within the jurisdiction of the court.

. . . Three products are the subject of this action: (1) BeneFin, sold in powder or tablet form as a dietary supplement and containing shark cartilage; (2) SkinAnswer, a skin cream containing glycoalkaloid; and (3) MGN–3, a dietary fiber produced by the hydrolysis of rice bran with the enzymatic extract of Shiitake mushroom, and whose main ingredient is arabinoxylan. . . .

Investigations revealed that Appellants specifically promoted the products . . . as cancer and HIV treatments. . . .

On December 10, 1999, the FDA filed a Complaint for Permanent Injunction, alleging that Labs' promotional claims brought their products under 21 U.S.C. § 321(g)(1)(B)'s definition of "drugs" and that they were "new drugs" . . . being distributed without requisite FDA approval. . . . It also alleged that the products were misbranded . . . because they lacked adequate directions for use. . . .

. . . FDA [sought] both a permanent injunction and equitable relief in the form of restitution for purchasers of the products . . . and disgorgement of profits, if such profits were not exhausted through restitution.

On July 12, 2004, the District Court granted the government's motion for summary judgment, issued a permanent injunction against the future sales of the products until a new drug application was approved for them, and ordered restitution to all purchasers of the products since September 22, 1999. . . .

Appellants contend that the District Court did not have the authority to order restitution under the FDCA. This is a question of law, which we review de novo. Appellants urge that restitution cannot be awarded in this case because the FDCA does not expressly provide for such a remedy and restitution is inconsistent with the policy, purpose, and legislative history of the FDCA.

The District Court based its power to order restitution on 21 U.S.C. § 332(a), which states:

The district courts of the United States and the United States courts of the Territories shall have jurisdiction, for cause shown, to restrain violations of section 331 of this title, except paragraphs (h), (i), and (j).

It is undisputed that this provision invokes the equitable jurisdiction of the District Court. Appellants claim that the specific language of § 332 that permits the District Court "to restrain violations" also limits its jurisdiction to injunctive orders that would require them to cease their offensive conduct. They argue, further, that the remedial structure of the FDCA and principles of statutory construction require us to find such a limitation to the court's power.

While arguably a close call, we conclude that applicable Supreme Court jurisprudence has mapped out the contours of a district court's equitable powers in much more expansive terms than Appellants recognize. Though the FDCA does not specifically authorize restitution, such specificity is not required where the government properly invokes a court's equitable jurisdiction under this statute. . . .

Our review of the case law begins with the Supreme Court's opinion in *Porter v. Warner Holding Company*, 328 U.S. 395 (1946). In *Porter*, the Office of Price Administration sought an injunction against the Warner Holding Company under § 205(a) of the Emergency Price Control Act of 1942 to prevent Warner from collecting rents from tenants in excess of those permitted by the applicable maximum rent regulations issued under the Act. The complaint was later amended to seek, in addition, an order of restitution to certain tenants who were entitled to a refund of any rent that exceeded the regulatory maximum. . . .

The Supreme Court held that, although the language of Section 205(a) did not explicitly grant the power to order restitution, such power was within a district court's equitable jurisdiction. The Court explained:

> Unless otherwise provided by statute, all the inherent equitable powers of the District Court are available for the proper and complete exercise of that jurisdiction. . . . Power is thereby resident in the District Court, in exercising this jurisdiction to do equity and to mould [sic] each decree to the necessities of the particular case. It may act so as . . . to accord full justice to all the real parties in interest. . . . Only in that way can equity do complete rather than truncated justice.

> Moreover, the comprehensiveness of this equitable jurisdiction is not to be denied or limited in the absence of a clear and valid legislative command. Unless a statute in so many words, or by a necessary and inescapable inference, restricts the court's jurisdiction in equity, the full scope of that jurisdiction is to be recognized and applied.

Based on such clear and sweeping language, it would appear that a district court sitting in equity may order restitution unless there is an explicit statutory limitation on the district court's equitable jurisdiction and powers. . . . Yet, Appellants urge that the statutory language in *Porter* is distinguishable from the language of 21 U.S.C. § 332(a) in such a way as to merit a different result here. In Porter, § 205(a) of the Emergency Price Control Act granted jurisdiction to enter a "permanent or temporary injunction, restraining order, *or other order*" (emphasis added). Since § 332(a) makes no mention of any "other order" nor includes any language that suggests alternative equitable remedies may be available under the FDCA, Appellants claim that restitution is not authorized by the statute. This argument, however, was foreclosed by the Supreme Court in *Mitchell v. Robert de Mario Jewelry, Inc.*, 361 U.S. 288 (1960).

In *Mitchell*, the Supreme Court not only reinforced its ruling in *Porter*, but expanded its scope as well. There ... the Secretary [of Labor] sought reimbursement for wages lost by the employee-victims of ... discrimination based on § 17 of the Fair Labor Standards Act, which grants the district courts jurisdiction "for cause shown, to restrain violations of section 15." ... The Court noted that the absence of language that could be said to support an affirmative confirmation of the power to order restitution, such as the "other order" provision in *Porter*, did not preclude the district court from ordering reimbursement.... The Court thus held that when a statutory provision gives the courts power to "enforce prohibitions" contained in a regulation or statute, Congress will be deemed to have granted as much equitable authority as is necessary to further the underlying purposes and policies of the statute.

... Thus, we must now examine the scope of the grant of equitable authority under the FDCA and the policies and purposes underlying the statute to ensure that ordering restitution furthers such purposes.

The statutory grant of equitable power of 21 U.S.C. § 332(a) at issue here is identical to the language the Supreme Court considered in *Mitchell*. Consequently, the Supreme Court's reasoning in *Mitchell* applies with equal force in the instant case. Since nothing in the FDCA creates a "necessary and inescapable inference" that the equitable power of district courts under § 332(a) is limited, we conclude that the authority given is broad enough to encompass all equitable remedies that would further the purposes of the Act.

Appellants and amicus argue that the FDA's failure to seek restitution for long periods of time, including during the first thirteen years after the FDCA's enactment, is strong evidence that such power is not granted by the statute.... However, " 'authority granted by Congress ... cannot evaporate through lack of administrative exercise.' " *BankAmerica Corp v. U.S.*, 462 U.S. 122, 131 (1983). That the FDA has rarely sought restitution under § 332(a) does not create a "necessary and inescapable inference" that Congress stripped district courts of their equitable power to award it.

Appellants argue that ordering restitution does not further the purpose of the FDCA, which they contend is limited to protecting consumers from dangerous and harmful products. They distinguish *Porter* and *Mitchell* in this regard, claiming that restitution supported the statutory purposes of the violated Acts in each of those cases in a way that it does not here. . . .

We agree that protecting consumer health and safety is a primary purpose of the FDCA. Appellants argue that since this purpose is not of a financial nature, restitution should not be ordered in equity. We are not convinced, however, that the purposes of the FDCA are as limited as Appellants suggest. The FDCA and its legislative history make it clear that Congress intended the statute to protect the financial interests of consumers as well their health.

The economic purposes of the FDCA are evidenced in part by the statute itself. . . . Indeed, the FDCA explicitly prohibits labeling and advertising that may deceive consumers as to the quality or content of products. See 21 U.S.C. § 331 (prohibiting the misbranding of food, drugs, devices, or cosmetics); 21 U.S.C. § 352 (defining "misbranded drugs" to include any drugs labeled or packaged in a misleading manner). Preventing such deception has as much to do with ensuring customers receive the value they expect from products as it does ensuring their safety. . . .

The legislative history likewise supports the view that one purpose of the FDCA is to protect consumers' financial interests. During its deliberations about the Act, Congress stated that prevention of deceit upon the purchasing public and protection of consumers from unscrupulous competition were among its purposes. The statute was aimed at protecting both "the consumer's health and pocketbook." H.R. Rep. No. 74–2755 at 2 (1936). . . .

Appellants and amicus argue that § 332(a) was designed only to fill a gap in the previous enactment by allowing a prompt injunctive action to prevent products from entering commerce. . . . Appellants and amicus argue that nothing in the legislative history suggests that Congress viewed § 332 as granting courts authority to order restitution, or any other backward-looking relief . . .

They also argue that construing § 332 to encompass backward-looking monetary relief such as restitution would turn Congress's intent on its head because one reason Congress added § 332 was to provide an option that was less punitive to manufacturers than the seizure provisions and criminal sanctions already in the Act. . . .

The Court of Appeals for the Sixth Circuit properly rejected this argument in *Universal Management*, reasoning that "even if Congress expressed some concern that seizure should remain the harshest relief available, there is no convincing argument that, in all cases, restitution creates a more harsh result than seizure, procedurally or substantively." *United States v. Universal Mgmt. Servs.*, 191 F.3d 750, 762 (6th Cir. 1999). The court went on to find that "even accepting the references to legislative concerns . . . these concerns are far from a clear statement of Congress's intent to exclude restitution, recalls, disgorgement, or any other traditional form of equitable relief." *Id.* . . .

Thus, both the FDCA and its legislative history support the view that protecting consumers' economic interests is an important objective of the Act. Though this economic purpose is not as central to the FDCA as protecting public health, one objective need not be the sole guide for how a court constructs a statute that has multiple purposes.

Restitution that reimburses consumers who paid for unapproved drugs, and may have been defrauded or deceived about their effectiveness, restores aggrieved parties to the same economic position they enjoyed before the Act was violated. This strengthens the financial protection offered to the public by the FDCA and enhances consumer confidence in the drug market. Whether or not Congress specifically contemplated restitution under the FDCA, the ability to order this remedy is within the broad equitable power granted to the district courts to further the economic protection purposes of the statute.

Restitution also serves a deterrent function embodied in the district court's authority to "restrain violations of section 331." 21 U.S.C. § 332(a). . . . Such a forward-looking deterrent effect is an important ancillary consequence of restitution. Given Appellants' repeated violations of the FDCA, committed despite numerous warnings from the FDA, it was within the District Court's equitable discretion to award restitution in order to prevent further violations.

. . . [T]here is case law and commentary that discusses how we should apply *Porter* and *Mitchell* to the specific context of the FDCA. . . .

Nearly fifty years ago, in *United States v. Parkinson*, 240 F.2d 918 (9th Cir. 1956), the Court of Appeals for the Ninth Circuit rejected the government's request to collect restitution under the FDCA. . . . *Parkinson* does not survive *Porter* and *Mitchell*. . . .

More recently, the Court of Appeals for the Sixth Circuit rejected the reasoning in *Parkinson* and ordered a party to pay restitution under the FDCA. *Universal Mgmt. Servs., Inc.*, 191 F.3d at 764. In that case, the defendant sold electric gas grill lighters equipped with finger grips as pain reliving devices without obtaining FDA approval. The court held that the grant of equitable power in § 332(a) was so broad that it was within the district court's authority to order restitution. . . .

In the years since *Universal Management*, the FDA has negotiated three consent decrees with drug companies that included significant disgorgement amounts. . . .

Amicus and other commentators have responded vigorously to these consent decrees and to the *Universal Management* decision. The authors of several recent articles have raised numerous arguments as to why *Porter* and *Mitchell* do not, or should not, authorize courts to order restitution or disgorgement under the FDCA. To the extent that the arguments of commentators are relevant to the instant case, their central claim is that awarding restitution under the FDCA would rewrite or improperly expand the remedies available under the statute. They argue that the ability under § 332(a) "to restrain violations" contemplates only forward-looking remedies and that this mandate excludes restitution. . . .

. . . Since Congress has placed no unambiguous restriction on equity jurisdiction under § 332(a), the arguments of amicus and other commentators are little more than entreaties that we ignore or overrule *Porter* and *Mitchell*, neither of which we have the power to do.

Also, we view amicus and the commentators as making a fundamental error in analyzing whether restitution is available: they view this primarily as a question of what remedies are provided by the FDCA rather than, as we have emphasized, a question of the scope of the express legislative grant of equitable power under § 332(a). The District Court did not "discover" an implied remedy, but rather exercised the equitable power that Congress explicitly granted to it under the FDCA. . . . [T]here is a presumption that "when Congress entrusts to an equity court the enforcement of prohibitions contained in a regulatory enactment, it must be taken to have acted cognizant of the historic power of equity to provide complete relief in light of the statutory purposes." *Mitchell*, 361 U.S. at 291–92. . . .

. . . Until the Court overrules *Porter* and *Mitchell*, we are bound by the reasoning of those cases. Given the breadth and open-ended nature of § 332(a), and the direct correlation between the language of that provision and the directives in *Porter* and *Mitchell*, we hold that the District Court here did have the power to grant restitution. We will therefore AFFIRM its order.

NOTES

1. *Restitution vs. Disgorgement.* In *United States v. Rx Depot, Inc.*, 438 F.3d 1052 (10th Cir. 2006), the Tenth Circuit extended the reasoning of *Lane Labs* to hold that a court may, pursuant to its equity power under the FD&C Act, impose the remedy of disgorgement. The court saw no distinction of legal significance between restitution and disgorgement. The government has continued to invoke this disgorgement power in constructing consent decrees. *See, e.g., Genzyme Corp. Signs Consent Decree to Correct Violations at Allston, Mass., Manufacturing Plant and Give up $175 Million in Profits*, FDA News Release (May 24, 2010).

2. *Repair, replacement, and refund.* The Medical Device Amendments, at section 518(b) of the FD&C Act, gave FDA restitution ("refund") authority respecting medical devices that present an "unreasonable risk of substantial harm to the public health." As an alternative, FDA can order repair or replacement of the device in question. FD&C Act 518(b). Section 535 of the Act requires manufacturers of electronic products to notify purchasers when they discover safety defects related to the emission of radiation and to repair the defect, replace the product, or refund the cost. FD&C Act 535(f). Regulations implementing this provision appear in 21 C.F.R. Part 1004.

F. RECALLS

1. VOLUNTARY RECALLS

Since before passage of the 1938 Act, FDA has used its own resources, and encouraged manufacturers, to recall illegal products from the market. The recall of the infamous Elixir Sulfanilamide in 1937 accounted for 99.2 percent of the product manufactured. In 1947 the agency explained its practice:

> As soon as the [Food and Drug] Administration learns that a potentially injurious product has been distributed, its efforts to retrieve the suspect batches are abated only when every unit is accounted for. As far as possible this is accomplished through instigating adequate recalls by the shippers and checking upon their effectiveness and the safe disposition of the returned goods. When necessary, the goods are removed from consumer channels by individual visits to wholesale houses, retail drug stores, hospitals, and other consignees, with the very real assistance of State and local enforcement agencies whose efforts have been an

important factor in the success of every major round-up. After the dangerous drugs have been accounted for, the firm involved is cited to a hearing with a view to criminal prosecution if the error was one which could have been avoided by good manufacturing practice or could have been corrected at an earlier stage.

FEDERAL SECURITY AGENCY, ANNUAL REPORT 525 (1947).

In the early 1970s, FDA became concerned about various aspects of its recall policy. First, the failure to distinguish between the severity of violations behind recalls was diminishing the public's sense of urgency with respect to recalls of products that presented serious health hazards. Second, the agency was devoting an inordinate amount of its resources and personnel to implementing recalls. *See* Fred H. Degnan, FDA'S CREATIVE APPLICATION OF THE LAW 108–09 (2000).

In 1976, FDA thus proposed regulations setting forth new uniform procedures for voluntary recalls overseen by FDA. These regulations both established a hierarchized structure based on the severity of the hazard and shifted more of the burden of conducting recalls to manufacturers. *Id.* FDA's final recall regulations, 43 Fed. Reg. 26202 (June 16, 1978), codified at 21 C.F.R. Part 7, Subpart C, continue to this day to undergird a highly successful voluntary recall system—a system that Fred H. Degnan has been moved to dub "A Regulatory Masterpiece." *Id.* at 107. The following document is the preamble to the 1976 proposed regulations.

Enforcement Policy, Practices and Procedures: Recall Policy and Procedures

41 Fed. Reg. 26924 (June 30, 1976).

. . . .

LEGAL AUTHORITY . . .

Most manufacturers and distributors of products subject to the jurisdiction of FDA have long recognized their responsibility to market safe and properly labeled products and to take measures to protect the public from adulterated and misbranded products that have already reached the marketplace. Indeed, it is not unusual for a firm, when it learns that a distributed product is defective, to take steps to correct the situation by removing the product from commerce or by remedying the defect. The Commissioner generally regards such responsible, voluntary action as an acceptable alternative to an agency-initiated seizure of the defective product.

Most firms honor FDA requests to recall violative foods, drugs, devices, cosmetics, or biologics. . . . Thus, the recall policy and procedures of FDA are, in part, founded upon the cooperation of firms and their willingness to remove violative products from the marketplace. . . .

The Commissioner is proposing these regulations to define more clearly FDA recall policy and procedures and to provide guidance to the regulated industry so that firms may more effectively discharge their responsibility to remove or correct violative products in commerce. The proposed regulations are authorized by section 701(a) of the Federal

Food, Drug, and Cosmetic Act . . . and sections 301, 351, and 361 of the Public Health Service Act (42 U.S.C. §§ 241, 262, and 264) relating to cooperative programs for the protection of the public health, to biological products, and to interstate quarantine. The provisions of the proposed regulations that describe responsibilities of recalling firms consist of guidelines rather than enforceable requirements. In this respect, the proposed regulations do not exhaust the authority of FDA to prevent the introduction of violative products into commercial channels, facilitate recalls by manufacturers, and enable the agency to monitor recalls. If experience under the final regulations proves that mandatory requirements are necessary, the Commissioner will propose appropriate revisions.

. . . .

SCOPE AND POLICY . . .

FDA-initiated recalls. There are two types of FDA-initiated recalls. First, when the agency determines that a marketed product violates the law and so informs the responsible firm, a later recall of the product by that firm is considered an "FDA-initiated recall," even though such action has not been specifically requested by the agency. Second, when use of the product presents a danger to health or significant consumer deception and immediate action is necessary, the Commissioner or his designee will formally notify the firm of this determination and of the need to begin immediately a recall of the product. Because the latter type of FDA-initiated recall is an urgent matter and must be used judiciously, the decision to request a recall shall be made only by the Commissioner or his designee.

Firm-initiated recall. A firm may, for a variety of reasons, on its own initiative remove, correct or otherwise dispose of an illegal product that it has distributed in commerce. FDA has clear authority to require notification [to the agency] that a firm has initiated a recall of new drugs, new animal drugs, biologics, foods subject to emergency permit control, electronic products subject to the Radiation Control for Health and Safety Act, and articles subject to interstate quarantine regulations.[*] However, the Commissioner also believes it serves the public interest for firms to notify FDA when a recall of any other FDA-regulated product is initiated. . . .

The proposed regulations also provide that the Commissioner will continue the policy of making available to the public information on all recalls by routinely issuing the weekly "FDA Enforcement Report." . . . The report is not, however, intended to serve, nor is it used by the agency, as a form of public warning or as a means of seeking publicity in the news media. . . .

RECALL PROCEDURES

A recall involves several separate but related steps that are taken by recalling firms and by FDA. These include: evaluation of the health hazard associated with the product being recalled or being considered for recall; developing and following a recall strategy (described below in

---

[*]   [FDA now also has such authority with regard to infant formula and medical devices.]

this preamble); recall communications to a firm's customers; periodic reports on the progress of the recall; and finally, termination of the recall and proper disposition or correction of the violative product. The combined purpose of these steps is to assure that a recall is conducted in a manner that achieves the orderly removal or correction of a violative product to the extent necessary to protect public health.

Health Hazard Evaluation and Classification. The Commissioner believes that any violation of the laws administered by FDA is a serious matter. Obviously, however, some violations are more serious than others, and the relative seriousness of the violation has a bearing on the course of regulatory action the agency will pursue and what actions it expects of the responsible manufacturer or distributor. . . . For this reason, the agency carefully evaluates the seriousness of the health consequences or the economic deception that results from individuals using a product. . . .

The result of a health hazard evaluation generally dictates whether the agency will request a firm to recall its product. If a recall is requested, the results of the evaluation will, in part, also determine the strategy of conducting the recall. . . .

On the basis of the health hazard evaluation, a numerical classification is assigned to the recall, *e.g.*, Class I, Class I, or Class III. The sole purpose of this classification system is to convey in lay terms the relative seriousness of the hazard associated with a specific recall. The class assigned to a recall does not dictate a specific course of action the agency and the recalling firm are to follow. . . .

Recall strategy. Each recall, whether FDA-initiated or firm-initiated, requires devising a specific course of action to implement the recall. . . .

The elements of a recall strategy include:

1. **Depth of recall.** This element refers to the level of product distribution to which the recall is to extend. There are three basic options: (1) Consumer or user level (which may vary with product); (2) retail level; or (3) wholesale level. . . .

2. **Public warnings.** This element of the recall strategy refers to FDA-issued warnings to the public about a product in consumer channels that is being recalled. The purpose of a public warning is to alert consumers or users that a product presents a serious hazard to health. . . .

3. **Effectiveness checks.** The third element of recall strategy involves verification that consignees (recipients of a product being recalled) have been notified of the recall and have taken appropriate action . . . [which is] a vital part of the overall responsibility of recalling firms. For FDA to routinely carry out industry's task of assuring recall effectiveness would represent misuse of public funds. However . . . FDA will monitor the efforts of a firm to effect a recall, and where necessary, will initiate its own effectiveness checks. . . .

SUMMARY

Because the Commissioner considers recalls to be primarily the responsibility of manufacturers and distributors of regulated products, this notice describes ways in which they should carry out this responsibility, which can be summarized in the following steps:

1.   Develop a contingency plan for a recall.

2.   Develop the capability of tracing product distribution and identifying the product being recalled.

3.   Promptly notify FDA when products are being removed or corrected . . . and provide the agency with pertinent information on these actions.

4.   Initiate a recall when it is requested by FDA.

5.   Develop and follow a recall strategy for handling any recall situation.

6.   Assume the responsibility and expense of conducting all aspects of a recall, including effectiveness checks.

7.   Notify all consignees of initiated recalls.

8.   Evaluate the circumstances causing the violation and take steps to prevent recurrence of violations and future recalls.

9.   Provide periodic reports to FDA on the progress of the recall.

10. When a recall is completed, certify to FDA that the recall has been effective and that final disposition of the recalled product has been made. . . .

NOTES

1.   *Recall Procedures.* Chapter Seven of FDA's Regulatory Procedures Manual, titled "Recall Procedures," implements the recall regulations set forth at 21 C.F.R. 7.40 et seq. The manual provides FDA personnel with detailed policy, definitions, responsibilities, and procedures for recall actions. FDA Regulatory Procedures Manual (Ch. 7 rev. Aug. 4, 2011). In addition, FDA has published a guidance document for regulated industry on its website. GUIDANCE FOR INDUSTRY: PRODUCT RECALLS, INCLUDING REMOVALS AND CORRECTIONS (Nov. 3, 2003).

2.   *USDA Recall Policy.* FDA and USDA have entered into a Memorandum of Understanding to coordinate their responsibilities for food recalls, published in 40 Fed. Reg. 25079 (June 12, 1975). USDA subsequently announced in 44 Fed. Reg. 56732 (Oct. 2, 1979) the availability of its own internal directive concerning recalls.

3.   *"Phantom Recall."* In 2010, McNeil Consumer Healthcare was the target of much criticism in the press and on Capitol Hill for conducting what came to be known as a "phantom recall" of subpotent Motrin tablets in 2009. The company paid a contractor to purchase all of the available product from retail stores around the country without revealing to either the stores or FDA that the purchases were part of a recall. In Congressional testimony, the FDA Principal Deputy Commissioner expressed concern about this procedure, but he acknowledged that it was not illegal. "FDA urges and expects firms to notify the Agency when initiating a drug recall, but firms have no legal requirement to provide this type of notification." "Johnson and Johnson's Recall of Children's Tylenol and Other Children's Medicines and the Phantom Recall of Motrin (Part

2)," Statement of Joshua Sharfstein, FDA Principal Deputy Comm'r, before the House Comm. on Oversight and Governmental Reform (Sept. 30, 2010) (available on FDA website).

2. MANDATORY RECALLS

The question of whether a court or FDA itself can order a manufacturer to recall a product does not often arise. FDA's prevailing practice, on learning about an illegal product in commercial distribution, is to informally encourage the manufacturer to recall it from commercial channels. Almost all FDA-initiated recalls are thus denominated "voluntary." Only if the manufacturer refuses to conduct a recall, or if a voluntary recall proves to be inadequate, will FDA seek a court order or issue a mandatory administrative recall order.

Why do manufacturers almost always comply with FDA recall requests? The threat of creating adverse publicity is a powerful club for the agency in such situations. *See* Lars Noah, *Administrative Arm–Twisting in the Shadow of Congressional Delegations of Authority*, 1997 WISC. L. REV. 873 (1997). Moreover, regulated industries dependent on FDA approval of their products are wary about incurring the agency's wrath. Finally, behind every FDA informal request for a recall lies an implied threat that the agency might take formal legal action if the manufacturer does not cooperate. It is thus important to understand the parameters of mandatory recall authority under the FD&C Act, even though this authority is rarely invoked.

Originally, the FD&C Act itself said nothing about recalls. Today, because of various amendments and transfers of administrative responsibility, FDA has explicit statutory authority to mandate recalls in certain limited circumstances.

In 1971, FDA assumed responsibility for implementing the Radiation Control for Health and Safety Act of 1968, 82 Stat. 1173. The Radiation Act, which was originally codified as part of the Public Health Services Act (PHSA), was recodified by 104 Stat. 4511, 4529 (1990) as §§ 531–42 of the FD&C Act. Section 535(f) gives FDA power to mandate the repurchase, repair, or replacement of radiation-emitting electronic products. Although this provision does not explicitly mention recall, FDA has always interpreted it to authorize recall orders as well. *See, e.g.*, 21 C.F.R. 1004.4 (requiring plans for refund to include the "procedure for obtaining possession of the product for which the refund is to be made" and the "steps which the manufacturer will take to insure that the defective products will not be reintroduced into commerce").

In 1972, responsibility for administering the Biological Products portion of the Public Health Service Act (PHSA) was transferred from the National Institutes of Health to FDA. Section 351(d) of the PHSA, as then written and as amended in 1999, gives FDA the power to order recall of a biological product that presents an "imminent or substantial hazard to public health." 42 U.S.C. § 262(d).

The Infant Formula Act of 1980, 94 Stat. 1190, added current section 412(f) to the FD&C Act, directing FDA to prescribe the scope and extent of recalls of infant formulas. The 1980 statute was further strengthened by the Alcohol and Drug Abuse Amendments of 1986, 100

Stat. 3207, 3207, which added the provision now found in section 412(e)(1), requiring a manufacturer to take all actions necessary to recall an infant formula if FDA determines that it presents a risk to human health.

The Safe Medical Devices Act of 1990, 104 Stat. 4511, amended the device provisions in the FD&C Act by adding section 518(e), titled "Recall Authority." This section requires FDA to order cessation of the distribution of a device and notification of health professionals and user facilities if the agency finds that the device would cause serious health consequences or death. After an opportunity for informal hearing, the agency may amend the order to include a recall of the device.

Finally, the Food Safety Modernization Act of 2011 added new section 423, which gives FDA mandatory recall authority over foods other than infant formula (which is already covered by section 412(f)). Although FDA asked Congress for this addition to its power, the agency likely will have only rare occasions to use it, because manufacturers almost always cooperate with FDA-requested food recalls. Moreover, section 423 requires FDA to provide the responsible party with an opportunity to voluntarily cease distribution and recall an article before the agency may invoke the mandatory provisions. *See* FD&C Act 423(a), (b). FDA's sparse use of the Act's other mandatory recall provisions may offer some indication of the ultimate importance (or lack of importance) of the new mandatory food recall provision. For example, although FDA has had mandatory recall authority over medical devices since 1990, an agency representative stated in 2009 that it had invoked this power only ten times, and never since 1994. ENHANCING FOOD SAFETY: THE ROLE OF THE FDA 301 (IOM–NRC 2010).

In some situations in which it has not possessed formal power to demand recalls, FDA has successfully sought court orders to recall illegal products by invoking section 302(a), the injunction provision. The case law is split on the question of whether district courts have the power to order recalls under this section. *Cf. United States v. C.E.B. Prods., Inc.*, 380 F. Supp. 664 (N.D. Ill. 1974) (denying authority to require recall); *United States v. Superpharm Corp.*, 530 F. Supp. 408 (E.D.N.Y. 1981) (same) *with United States v. Barr Laboratories, Inc.*, 812 F. Supp. 458, 489 (D.N.J. 1993) (affirming authority to require recall); *United States v. K–N Enterprises, Inc.*, 461 F. Supp. 988, 990–91 (N.D. Ill. 1978) (same). The trend seems to be toward recognizing the courts' authority to require recalls. As the *Barr Laboratories* court observed: "Although not authorized expressly in the Act, this remedy [recall] is consistent with the broad equitable relief powers district courts enjoy."

Moreover, the reasoning of *Lane Labs, supra* p. 225, in which the Third Circuit recognized the district courts' implicit power to order restitution, seems also to apply to recall. Indeed, *United States v. Universal Mgmt. Servs.*, 191 F.3d 750 (6th Cir. 1999), the other recent Court of Appeals case affirming the remedy of restitution under section 302(a), treated the questions of restitution and recall identically. Thus, interwoven with the Sixth Circuit's discussion of the remedy of restitution was the following dictum on recalls.

Appellants also rely on a number of district court cases that determine that recalls ... are unavailable under the FDCA.

Portions of the legislative history relating to the FDCA indicates [sic] that Congress was concerned about the harshness and seriousness of the remedy of seizure. Injunctive procedures, it is argued, "were viewed as a means to alleviate the hardships seizures might cause to manufacturers." *C.E.B. Prods.*, 380 F. Supp. at 668. Based on that legislative history, the court in *C.E.B. Products* reasoned that a recall provision was probably not within the court's power because it would, in the court's opinion, make an injunction as harsh as a seizure, contrary to the intent of Congress. See *C.E.B. Prods.* 380 F. Supp. at 668. . . .

We reject the holdings in the . . . *C.E.B. Products* line of cases. First, the existence of the remedy of seizure exists alongside an explicit authorization for injunctive relief to cure violations of the FDCA. The express provision for general equitable relief without the enumeration of any exceptions makes it difficult for this court to find any legitimate means for implicitly carving out such exceptions as we see fit. . . . [E]ven accepting the references to legislative concerns relied upon by the . . . *C.E.B. Products* line, these concerns are far from a clear statement of Congress's intent to exclude . . . recalls. . . .

Id. at 761–62.

NOTE

Recalls in Consent Decrees. Consent decrees entered in district court by FDA and defendants sometimes require recall by the defendant. For example, the 2002 Schering–Plough consent decree, discussed above in the Vodra & Levine excerpt, *supra* p. 222, included a number of recall provisions. *United States v. Schering–Plough*, Consent Decree of Permanent Injunction 8, 23, 36 (D.N.J. filed May 20, 2002). In November 2002, FDA entered into a consent decree with a distributor of large gel candies that presented a choking hazard for children. The consent decree provided not only that FDA would supervise the destruction of candies already seized by the United States, but also that the company would withdraw the product still on the market. *See Press Release, FDA, New Choice Agrees to Withdraw Remaining Gel Snacks on U.S. Market* (Nov. 6, 2002).

G. CRIMINAL LIABILITY

1. THE DECISION TO PROSECUTE

Sam D. Fine,* *The Philosophy of Enforcement*
31 FOOD DRUG COSM. L.J. 324 (1976).

. . . .

In considering whether or not prosecution action should be forwarded to the next reviewing authority, and eventually to a United

---

* [Mr. Fine was FDA Associate Commissioner for Compliance from 1969 to 1976.]

States Attorney, one or more of the following general conditions must exist. In most cases, more than one of the conditions does exist.

(1) The violations ordinarily are shown to be of a continuing nature; that is, previous inspections or documented incidents indicate management of the firm is aware of the problem and has failed to take steps to correct the violations. This situation requires a showing of awareness. . . .

(2) The violation is so gross that any reasonable person would conclude management must have known of the conditions. Examples include a heavily insect or rodent-infested warehouse or an obvious fraud. . . .

(3) The violations are such that it is obvious that normal attention by management could have prevented them; for example, those situations where violations develop because management delegates authority and does not exercise normal care. . . .

(4) The violations are such that they are life-threatening or injuries have occurred; for example, botulism in improperly prepared products or serious drug mix-ups. . . .

(5) The violations are deliberate attempts to circumvent the law; for instance, submission of false data, falsification of records, or deliberate short weight or subpotency. . . .

What this means is that continuation or repetition of violations over a period of time, or a single gross or deliberate violation, generally will trigger consideration for prosecution. . . .

NOTES

1. *Authorized Criminal Penalties.* Under FD&C Act 303(a), violations of the Act are generally misdemeanors, but they may be felonies if they constitute second offenses or are committed "with the intent to defraud or mislead." Such "intent" includes the intent to defraud or mislead not only ultimate consumers, but also state and federal government enforcement agencies. *See United States v. Bradshaw*, 840 F.2d 871 (11th Cir. 1988), *cert. denied*, 488 U.S. 924 (1988).

Section 303(a) provides criminal penalties of $1,000 or up to one year imprisonment for any misdemeanor violation of the Act and $10,000 or up to three years imprisonment for a felony violation. Section 303(b)(1) establishes criminal penalties of not more than 10 years imprisonment or a fine of not more than $250,000 for violation of the Act's prescription drug sample requirements or the drug reimportation prohibition. In the Sentencing Reform Act of 1984, 98 Stat. 1837, Congress enacted new criminal fines in 18 U.S.C. § 3571, which were made applicable to any offense under any federal statute by 18 U.S.C. § 3551. In the Criminal Fines Improvement Act of 1987, Congress amended section 3571 to raise the maximum fines. 101 Stat. 1279. The current provisions impose maximum fines for individuals of $100,000 for a misdemeanor that does not result in death and $250,000 for a misdemeanor resulting in death or for a felony. For corporations, the maximums are $200,000 for a misdemeanor that does not result in death and $500,000 for a misdemeanor resulting in death or a felony.

2. *Office of Criminal Investigations.* In 1992, FDA established an Office of Criminal Investigations (OCI) in the Office of Regulatory Affairs to conduct and coordinate criminal investigations of violations of the FD&C Act and related statutes, including various provisions of Title 18 of the U.S. Code (the general criminal and penal code of the federal government), such as conspiracy, mail and wire fraud, and false claims. OCI special agents are hired from other federal enforcement agencies. The creation of this office led eventually to a notable increase in criminal prosecutions. *See supra* p. 165 (chart). Nonetheless, OCI has been criticized for focusing on complex cases and neglecting investigations into simple and direct violations of the FD&C Act (the classic "dirty warehouse" cases). A 2010 GAO report criticized FDA for lack of sufficient oversight of the OCI. FOOD AND DRUG ADMINISTRATION: IMPROVED MONITORING AND DEVELOPMENT OF PERFORMANCE MEASURES NEEDED TO STRENGTHEN OVERSIGHT OF CRIMINAL AND MISCONDUCT INVESTIGATIONS (GAO 2010).

3. *Other Statutes Invoked in Criminal Enforcement of the FD&C Act.* The provisions of Title 18 of the United States that are potentially available for ancillary enforcement of the FD&C Act include, among others, conspiracy to defraud the government (18 U.S.C. 286), general conspiracy (18 U.S.C. 371), false statements (18 U.S.C. 1001), mail fraud (18 U.S.C. 1341), wire fraud (18 U.S.C. 1343), and health care fraud (18 U.S.C. 1347).

4. *Section 305 Notice and Hearing.* Section 305 of the Act provides: "Before any violation of this Act is reported by the Secretary to any United States attorney for institution of a criminal proceeding, the person against whom such proceeding is contemplated shall be given appropriate notice and an opportunity to present his views, either orally or in writing, with regard to such contemplated proceeding." The regulations implementing this section are at 21 C.F.R. 7.84. This provision is rarely used, however, for various reasons. First, as the United States Supreme Court has made clear, the failure to provide an opportunity for a section 305 hearing is not a bar to prosecution of persons who violate the act. *United States v. Dotterweich*, 320 U.S. 277, 278–79 (1943). Moreover, the section does not apply at all to criminal violations of statutes other than the FD&C Act itself. Finally, the agency's liberal use of warning letters since the 1970s has served the same function as section 305, namely, providing potential criminal defendants with notice and an opportunity for discussion with the agency.

5. *Interaction of Civil and Criminal Proceedings.* In *United States v. Kordel*, 397 U.S. 1 (1970), FDA instituted a seizure, served interrogatories, and then issued a notice under section 305 of the Act that the agency also contemplated criminal prosecution. The defendant objected to answering the interrogatories while the possibility of a criminal action existed, but it ultimately complied and supplied the answers, which were then used in the criminal prosecution. The Supreme Court held that this did not violate the privilege against self-incrimination or basic standards of fairness, concluding that FDA should not be required to choose between civil and criminal enforcement proceedings. *See also United States v. Gel Spice Co., Inc.*, 773 F.2d 427 (2d Cir. 1985).

2. STANDARD OF LIABILITY

a. CRIMINAL LIABILITY OF RESPONSIBLE CORPORATE OFFICIALS

Most violations of the FD&C Act potentially carry criminal penalties. The Act's standard of criminal liability, as articulated by the *United States Supreme Court in United States v. Dotterweich*, excerpted below, does not include the mens rea (guilty mind) element typically required in Anglo–American criminal law. According to Dotterweich, the FD&C Act criminalizes the conduct of individuals without consciousness of wrongdoing if they bear a "responsible relation" to the violation. This strict liability standard has proved to be one of the most controversial features of the statute.

United States v. Dotterweich
320 U.S. 277 (1943).

■ MR. JUSTICE FRANKFURTER delivered the opinion of the Court.

This was a prosecution begun by two informations, consolidated for trial, charging Buffalo Pharmacal Company, Inc., and Dotterweich, its president and general manager, with violations of the . . . Federal Food, Drug, and Cosmetic Act. The Company, a jobber in drugs, purchased them from their manufacturers and shipped them, repacked under its own label, in interstate commerce. . . . The informations were based on § 301 of that Act, paragraph (a) of which prohibits "The introduction or delivery for introduction into interstate commerce of any . . . drug . . . that is adulterated or misbranded." "Any person" violating this provision is, by paragraph (a) of § 303, made "guilty of a misdemeanor." Three counts went to the jury—two, for shipping misbranded drugs in interstate commerce, and a third, for so shipping an adulterated drug. The jury disagreed as to the corporation and found Dotterweich guilty on all three counts. . . .

. . . The Circuit Court of Appeals, one judge dissenting, reversed the conviction on the ground that only the corporation was the "person" subject to prosecution unless, perchance, Buffalo Pharmacal was a counterfeit corporation serving as a screen for Dotterweich. . . .

The court below drew its conclusion not from the provisions defining the offenses on which this prosecution was based (§§ 301(a) and 303(a)), but from the terms of § 303(c). That section affords immunity from prosecution if certain conditions are satisfied. The condition relevant to this case is a guaranty from the seller of the innocence of his product. So far as here relevant, the provision for an immunizing guaranty is as follows:

> No person shall be subject to the penalties of subsection (a) of this section . . . (2) for having violated section 301(a) . . . if he establishes a guaranty or undertaking signed by, and containing the name and address of, the person residing in the United States from whom he received in good faith the article, to the effect, in case of an alleged violation of section 301(a), that such article is not adulterated or misbranded, within the meaning of this Act, designating this Act. . . .

The Circuit Court of Appeals found it "difficult to believe that Congress expected anyone except the principal [*i.e.*, in this case, the corporation itself] to get such a guaranty, or to make the guilt of an agent depend upon whether his employer had gotten one." And so it cut down the scope of the penalizing provisions of the Act to the restrictive view, as a matter of language and policy, it took of the relieving effect of a guaranty.

The guaranty clause cannot be read in isolation. . . . The purposes of this legislation . . . touch phases of the lives and health of people which, in the circumstances of modern industrialism, are largely beyond self-protection. Regard for these purposes should infuse construction of the legislation if it is to be treated as a working instrument of government and not merely as a collection of English words. The prosecution to which Dotterweich was subjected is based on a now familiar type of legislation whereby penalties serve as effective means of regulation. Such legislation dispenses with the conventional requirement for criminal conduct—awareness of some wrongdoing. In the interest of the larger good it puts the burden of acting at hazard upon a person otherwise innocent but standing in responsible relation to a public danger. . . .

The Act is concerned not with the proprietory relation to a misbranded or an adulterated drug but with its distribution. In the case of a corporation such distribution must be accomplished, and may be furthered, by persons standing in various relations to the incorporeal proprietor. . . . To read the guaranty section, as did the court below, so as to restrict liability for penalties to the only person who normally would receive a guaranty—the proprietor—disregards the admonition that "the meaning of a sentence is to be felt rather than to be proved." It also reads an exception to an important provision safeguarding the public welfare with a liberality which more appropriately belongs to enforcement of the central purpose of the Act.

The Circuit Court of Appeals was evidently tempted to make such a devitalizing use of the guaranty provision through fear that an enforcement of § 301(a) as written might operate too harshly by sweeping within its condemnation any person however remotely entangled in the proscribed shipment. But that is not the way to read legislation. Literalism and evisceration are equally to be avoided. To speak with technical accuracy, under § 301 a corporation may commit an offense and all persons who aid and abet its commission are equally guilty. Whether an accused shares responsibility in the business process resulting in unlawful distribution depends on the evidence produced at the trial and its submission—assuming the evidence warrants it—to the jury under appropriate guidance. The offense is committed, unless the enterprise which they are serving enjoys the immunity of a guaranty, by all who do have such a responsible share in the furtherance of the transaction which the statute outlaws, namely, to put into the stream of interstate commerce adulterated or misbranded drugs. Hardship there doubtless may be under a statute which thus penalizes the transaction though consciousness of wrongdoing be totally wanting. Balancing relative hardships, Congress has preferred to place it upon those who have at least the opportunity of informing themselves of the existence of conditions imposed for the protection of consumers before sharing in illicit commerce, rather than to throw the hazard on the innocent public who are wholly helpless.

It would be too treacherous to define or even to indicate by way of illustration the class of employees which stands in such a responsible relation. To attempt a formula embracing the variety of conduct whereby persons may responsibly contribute in furthering a transaction forbidden by an Act of Congress, to wit, to send illicit goods across state lines, would be mischievous futility. In such matters the good sense of prosecutors, the wise guidance of trial judges, and the ultimate judgment of juries must be trusted. Our system of criminal justice necessarily depends on "conscience and circumspection in prosecuting officers," even when the consequences are far more drastic than they are under the provision of law before us. For present purpose it suffices to say that in what the defense characterized as "a very fair charge" the District Court properly left the question of the responsibility of Dotterweich for the shipment to the jury, and there was sufficient evidence to support its verdict.

Reversed.

■ MR. JUSTICE MURPHY, dissenting.

. . . There is no evidence in this case of any personal guilt on the part of the respondent. There is no proof or claim that he ever knew of the introduction into commerce of the adulterated drugs in question, much less that he actively participated in their introduction. Guilt is imputed to the respondent solely on the basis of his authority and responsibility as president and general manager of the corporation.

It is fundamental principle of Anglo–Saxon jurisprudence that guilt is personal and that it ought not lightly to be imputed to a citizen who, like the respondent, has no evil intention or consciousness of wrongdoing. It may be proper to charge him with responsibility to the corporation and the stockholders for negligence and mismanagement. But in the absence of clear statutory authorization it is inconsistent with established canons of criminal law to rest liability on an act in which the accused did not participate and of which he had no personal knowledge. Before we place the stigma of a criminal conviction upon any such citizen the legislative mandate must be clear and unambiguous. . . .

The dangers inherent in any attempt to create liability without express Congressional intention or authorization are illustrated by this case. Without any legislative guides, we are confronted with the problem of determining precisely which officers, employees and agents of a corporation are to be subject to his Act by our fiat. To erect standards of responsibility is a difficult legislative task and the opinion of this Court admits that it is "too treacherous" and a "mischievous futility" for us to engage in such pursuits. But the only alternative is a blind resort to "the good sense of prosecutors, the wise guidance of trial judges, and the ultimate judgment of juries." Yet that situation is precisely what our constitutional system sought to avoid. Reliance on the legislature to define crimes and criminals distinguishes our form of jurisprudence from certain less desirable ones. The legislative power to restrain the liberty and to imperil the good reputation of citizens must not rest upon the variable attitudes and opinions of those charged with the duties of interpreting and enforcing the mandates of the law. I therefore cannot approve the decision of the Court in this case.

■ MR. JUSTICE ROBERTS, MR. JUSTICE REED and MR. JUSTICE RUTLEDGE join in this dissent.

United States v. Park

421 U.S. 658 (1975).

■ MR. CHIEF JUSTICE BURGER delivered the opinion of the Court.

Acme Markets, Inc., is a national retail food chain with approximately 36,000 employees, 874 retail outlets, 12 general warehouses, and four special warehouses. Its headquarters, including the office of the president, respondent Park, who is chief executive officer of the corporation, are located in Philadelphia, Pa. In a five-count information filed in the United States District Court for the District of Maryland, the Government charged Acme and respondent with violations of the Federal Food, Drug, and Cosmetic Act. Each count of the information alleged that the defendants had received food that had been shipped in interstate commerce and that, while the food was being held for sale in Acme's Baltimore warehouse following shipment in interstate commerce, they caused it to be held in a building accessible to rodents and to be exposed to contamination by rodents. These acts were alleged to have resulted in the food's being adulterated within the meaning of 21 U.S.C. §§ 342(a)(3) and (4). . . .

Acme pleaded guilty to each count of the information. Respondent pleaded not guilty. The evidence at trial demonstrated that in April 1970 the Food and Drug Administration (FDA) advised respondent by letter of insanitary conditions in Acme's Philadelphia warehouse. In 1971 the FDA found that similar conditions existed in the firm's Baltimore warehouse. An FDA consumer safety officer testified concerning evidence of rodent infestation and other insanitary conditions discovered during a 12-day inspection of the Baltimore warehouse in November and December 1971. He also related that a second inspection of the warehouse had been conducted in March 1972. On that occasion the inspectors found that there had been improvement in the sanitary conditions, but that "there was still evidence of rodent activity in the building and in the warehouses and we found some rodent-contaminated lots of food items."

The Government also presented testimony by the Chief of Compliance of the FDA's Baltimore office, who informed respondent by letter of the conditions at the Baltimore warehouse after the first inspection. There was testimony by Acme's Baltimore division vice president, who had responded to the letter on behalf of Acme and respondent and who described the steps taken to remedy the insanitary conditions discovered by both inspections. The Government's final witness, Acme's vice president for legal affairs and assistant secretary, identified respondent as the president and chief executive officer of the company and read a bylaw prescribing the duties of the chief executive officer. He testified that respondent functioned by delegating "normal operating duties," including sanitation, but that he retained "certain things, which are the big, broad, principles of the operation of the company," and had "the responsibility of seeing that they all work together." . . .

Respondent was the only defense witness. He testified that, although all of Acme's employees were in a sense under his general direction, the company had an "organizational structure for responsibilities for certain functions" according to which different phases of its operation were "assigned to individuals who, in turn, have staff and departments under them." He identified those individuals responsible for sanitation, and related that upon receipt of the January 1972 FDA letter, he had conferred with the vice president for legal affairs, who informed him that the Baltimore division vice president "was investigating the situation immediately and would be taking corrective action and would be preparing a summary of the corrective action to reply to the letter." Respondent stated that he did not "believe there was anything [he] could have done more constructively than what [he] found was being done."

On cross-examination, respondent conceded that providing sanitary conditions for food offered for sale to the public was something that he was "responsible for in the entire operation of the company," and he stated that it was one of many phases of the company that he assigned to "dependable subordinates." Respondent was asked about and, over the objections of his counsel, admitted receiving the April 1970 letter addressed to him from the FDA regarding insanitary conditions at Acme's Philadelphia warehouse. He acknowledged that, with the exception of the division vice president, the same individuals had responsibility for sanitation in both Baltimore and Philadelphia. Finally, in response to questions concerning the Philadelphia and Baltimore incidents, respondent admitted that the Baltimore problem indicated the system for handling sanitation "wasn't working perfectly" and that as Acme's chief executive officer he was responsible for "any result which occurs in our company."

At the close of the evidence, respondent's renewed motion for a judgment of acquittal was denied. The relevant portion of the trial judge's instructions to the jury challenged by respondent is set out in the margin.[9] Respondent's counsel objected to the instructions on the ground that they failed fairly to reflect our decision in *United States v.*

---

[9]   "In order to find the Defendant guilty on any count of the Information, you must find beyond a reasonable doubt on each count. . . .

. . . . .

"Thirdly, that John R. Park held a position of authority in the operation of the business of Acme Markets, Incorporated.

". . . The main issue for your determination is only with the third element, whether the Defendant held a position of authority and responsibility in the business of Acme Markets.

. . . . .

"The statute makes individuals, as well as corporations, liable for violations. An individual is liable if it is clear, beyond a reasonable doubt, that . . . the individual had a responsible relation to the situation, even though he may not have participated personally.

"The individual is or could be liable under the statute, even if he did not consciously do wrong. However, the fact that the Defendant is pres[id]ent and is a chief executive officer of the Acme Markets does not require a finding of guilt. Though, he need not have personally participated in the situation, he must have had a responsible relationship to the issue. The issue is, in this case, whether the Defendant, John R. Park, by virtue of his position in the company, had a position of authority and responsibility in the situation out of which these charges arose."

Dotterweich, and to define " 'responsible relationship.' " The trial judge overruled the objection. The jury found respondent guilty on all counts of the information, and he was subsequently sentenced to pay a fine of $50 on each count.

The Court of Appeals reversed the conviction and remanded for a new trial. . . . The Court of Appeals concluded that the trial judge's instructions "might well have left the jury with the erroneous impression that Park could be found guilty in the absence of 'wrongful action' on his part," and that proof of this element was required by due process. It . . . directed that on retrial the jury be instructed as to "wrongful action," which might be "gross negligence and inattention in discharging . . . corporate duties and obligations or any of a host of other acts of commission or omission which would 'cause' the contamination of food."

The Court of Appeals also held that the admission in evidence of the April 1970 FDA warning to respondent was error warranting reversal, based on its conclusion that, "as this case was submitted to the jury and in light of the sole issue presented," there was no need for the evidence and thus that its prejudicial effect outweighed its relevancy. . . .

We granted certiorari because of an apparent conflict among the Courts of Appeals with respect to the standard of liability of corporate officers under the Federal Food, Drug, and Cosmetic Act as construed in *United States v. Dotterweich*, and because of the importance of the question to the Government's enforcement program. We reverse. . . .

The rationale of the interpretation given the Act in *Dotterweich*, as holding criminally accountable the persons whose failure to exercise the authority and supervisory responsibility reposed in them by the business organization resulted in the violation complained of, has been confirmed in our subsequent cases. Thus, the Court has reaffirmed the proposition that "the public interest in the purity of its food is so great as to warrant the imposition of the highest standard of care on distributors." . . . Similarly, in cases decided after *Dotterweich*, the Courts of Appeals have recognized that those corporate agents vested with the responsibility, and power commensurate with that responsibility, to devise whatever measures are necessary to ensure compliance with the Act bears a "responsible relationship" to, or have a "responsible share" in, violations.

Thus *Dotterweich* and the cases which have followed reveal that in providing sanctions which reach and touch the individuals who execute the corporate mission—and this is by no means necessarily confined to a single corporate agent or employee—the Act imposes not only a positive duty to seek out and remedy violations when they occur but also, and primarily, a duty to implement measures that will insure that violations will not occur. The requirements of foresight and vigilance imposed on responsible corporate agents are beyond question demanding, and perhaps onerous, but they are no more stringent than the public has a right to expect of those who voluntarily assume positions of authority in business enterprises whose services and products affect the health and well-being of the public that supports them.[15]

The Act does not, as we observed in *Dotterweich*, make criminal liability turn on "awareness of some wrongdoing" or "conscious fraud." The duty imposed by Congress on responsible corporate agents is, we emphasize, one that requires the highest standard of foresight and vigilance, but the Act, in its criminal aspect, does not require that which is objectively impossible. The theory upon which responsible corporate agents are held criminally accountable for "causing" violations of the Act* permits a claim that a defendant was "powerless" to prevent or correct the violation to "be raised defensively at a trial on the merits." *United States v. Wiesenfeld Warehouse Co.*, 376 U.S. 86, 91 (1964). If such a claim is made, the defendant has the burden of coming forward with evidence, but this does not alter the Government's ultimate burden of proving beyond a reasonable doubt the defendant's guilt, including his power, in light of the duty imposed by the Act, to prevent or correct the prohibited condition. Congress has seen fit to enforce the accountability of responsible corporate agents dealing with products which may affect the health of consumers by penal sanctions cast in rigorous terms, and the obligation of the courts is to give them effect so long as they do not violate the Constitution.

We cannot agree with the Court of Appeals that it was incumbent upon the District Court to instruct the jury that the Government had the burden of establishing "wrongful action" in the sense in which the Court of Appeals used that phrase. The concept of a "responsible relationship" to, or a "responsible share" in, a violation of the Act indeed imports some measure of blameworthiness; but it is equally clear that the Government establishes a prima facie case when it introduces evidence sufficient to warrant a finding by the trier of the facts that the defendant had, by reason of his position in the corporation, responsibility and authority either to prevent in the first instance, or promptly to correct, the violation complained of, and that he failed to do so. The failure thus to fulfill the duty imposed by the interaction of the corporate agent's authority and the statute furnishes a sufficient causal link. The considerations which prompted the imposition of this duty, and the scope of the duty, provide the measure of culpability. . . .

Our conclusion . . . suggests as well our disagreement with [the Court of Appeals] concerning the admissibility of evidence demonstrating that respondent was advised by the FDA in 1970 of insanitary conditions in Acme's Philadelphia warehouse. We are satisfied that the Act imposes the highest standard of care and permits conviction of responsible corporate officials who, in light of this standard of care, have the power to prevent or correct violations of its provisions. . . .

Respondent testified in his defense that he had employed a system in which he relied upon his subordinates, and that he was ultimately

---

[15] We note that in 1948 the Senate passed an amendment to § 303(a) of the Act to impose criminal liability only for violations committed "willfully or as a result of gross negligence." 94 Cong. Rec. 6760–6761 (1948). However, the amendment was subsequently stricken in conference.

* [The first sentence of FD&C Act 301 prohibits not only the listed acts, but also the "causing thereof."—EDS.]

responsible for this system. He testified further that he had found these subordinates to be "dependable" and had "great confidence" in them. By this and other testimony respondent evidently sought to persuade the jury that, as the president of a large corporation, he had no choice but to delegate duties to those in whom he reposed confidence, that he had no reason to suspect his subordinates were failing to insure compliance with the Act, and that, once violations were unearthed, acting through those subordinates he did everything possible to correct them.

Although we need not decide whether this testimony would have entitled respondent to an instruction as to his lack of power, had he requested it, the testimony clearly created the "need" for rebuttal evidence. That evidence was not offered to show that respondent had a propensity to commit criminal acts or that the crime charged had been committed; its purpose was to demonstrate that respondent was on notice that he could not rely on his system of delegation to subordinates to prevent or correct insanitary conditions at Acme's warehouses, and that he must have been aware of the deficiencies of this system before the Baltimore violations were discovered. The evidence was therefore relevant since it served to rebut respondent's defense that he had justifiably relied upon subordinates to handle sanitation matters. And, particularly in light of the difficult task of juries in prosecutions under the Act, we conclude that its relevance and persuasiveness outweighed any prejudicial effect.

Reversed.

■ MR. JUSTICE STEWART, with whom MR. JUSTICE MARSHALL and MR. JUSTICE POWELL join, dissenting.

Although agreeing with much of what is said in the Court's opinion, I dissent from the opinion and judgment, because the jury instructions in this case were not consistent with the law as the Court today expounds it.

As I understand the Court's opinion, it holds that in order to sustain a conviction under § 301(k) of the Federal Food, Drug, and Cosmetic Act the prosecution must at least show that by reason of an individual's corporate position and responsibilities, he had a duty to use care to maintain the physical integrity of the corporation's food products. A jury may then draw the inference that when the food is found to be in such condition as to violate the statute's prohibitions, that condition was "caused" by a breach of the standard of care imposed upon the responsible official. This is the language of negligence, and I agree with it. . . .

The trial judge instructed the jury to find Park guilty if it found beyond a reasonable doubt that Park "had a responsible relation to the situation. . . . The issue is, in this case, whether the Defendant, John R. Park, by virtue of his position in the company, had a position of authority and responsibility in the situation out of which these charges arose." Requiring, as it did, a verdict of guilty upon a finding of "responsibility," this instruction standing alone could have been construed as a direction to convict if the jury found Park "responsible" for the condition in the sense that his position as chief executive officer gave him formal responsibility within the structure of the corporation. But the trial judge went on specifically to caution the jury not to attach such a meaning to his instruction, saying that "the fact that the Defendant is pres[id]ent and is a chief executive officer of the Acme Markets does not require a finding of guilt." "Responsibility" as used by the trial judge therefore had whatever meaning the jury in its unguided discretion chose to give it.

The instructions therefore, expressed nothing more than a tautology. They told the jury: "You must find the defendant guilty if you find that he is to be held accountable for this adulterated food." In other words: "You must find the defendant guilty if you conclude that he is guilty." . . .

. . . The instructions given by the trial court in this case . . . were a virtual nullity, a mere authorization to convict if the jury thought it appropriate. Such instructions—regardless of the blameworthiness of the defendant's conduct, regardless of the social value of the Food, Drug, and Cosmetic Act, and regardless of the importance of convicting those who violate it—have no place in our jurisprudence.

The *Dotterweich* case stands for two propositions, and I accept them both. First, "any person" within the meaning of 21 U.S.C. § 333 may include any corporate officer or employee "standing in responsible relation" to a condition or transaction forbidden by the Act. Second, a person may be convicted of a criminal offense under the Act even in the absence of "the conventional requirement for criminal conduct—awareness of some wrongdoing."

But before a person can be convicted of a criminal violation of this Act, a jury must find—and must be clearly instructed that it must find—evidence beyond a reasonable doubt that he engaged in wrongful conduct amounting at least to common-law negligence. There were no such instructions, and clearly, therefore, no such finding in this case. . . .

NOTES

1.   Park *Doctrine Prosecution Criteria and Possible Increased Use.* On March 4, 2010, FDA Commissioner Margaret Hamburg generated consternation among officials of regulated companies when she told Senator Charles Grassley that misdemeanor prosecutions were a "valuable enforcement tool . . . to hold responsible corporate officials accountable" and that FDA had developed "criteria . . . for consideration in selection" of such prosecutions. Letter from Margaret A. Hamburg, Commissioner of FDA, to Sen. Charles Grassley (Mar. 4, 2010) (available on FDA website). In January 2011, FDA revised the Regulatory Procedures Manual to set forth these criteria.

> When considering whether to recommend a misdemeanor prosecution against a corporate official, consider the individual's position in the company and relationship to the violation, and whether the official had the authority to correct or prevent the violation. Knowledge of and actual participation in the violation are not a prerequisite to a misdemeanor prosecution but are factors that may be relevant when deciding whether to recommend charging a misdemeanor violation.
>
> Other factors to consider include but are not limited to:

1.   Whether the violation involves actual or potential harm to the public;

2.   Whether the violation is obvious;

3.   Whether the violation reflects a pattern of illegal behavior and/or failure to heed prior warnings;

4.   Whether the violation is widespread;

5.   Whether the violation is serious;

6.   The quality of the legal and factual support for the proposed prosecution; and

7.   Whether the proposed prosecution is a prudent use of agency resources.

As the Supreme Court has recognized, it would be futile to attempt to define or indicate by way of illustration either the categories of persons that may bear a responsible relationship to a violation or the types of conduct that may be viewed as causing or contributing to a violation of the Act. In addition, these factors are intended solely for the guidance of FDA personnel, do not create or confer any rights or benefits for or on any person, and do not operate to bind FDA. Further, the absence of some factors does not mean that a referral is inappropriate where other factors are evident.

FDA, REGULATORY PROCEDURES MANUAL 6–5–3 ("Special Procedures and Considerations for *Park* Doctrine Prosecutions"). Since Hamburg's speech, there appears to have been a slight uptick in *Park* prosecutions, including the very high profile conviction of the three Purdue Pharma executives whose subsequent exclusion from health programs is discussed in *Friedman v. Sebelius, infra* p. 257. *See also Former Drug Company Executive Pleads Guilty in Oversized Drug Tablets Case*, Justice Department Press Release (Mar. 10, 2011); *Three Former Synthes Officials Sentenced to Prison*, PHIL. INQUIRER, Nov. 22, 2011, at A13.

2.   *Lack of Knowledge. United States v. Parfait Powder Puff Co.*, 163 F.2d 1008 (7th Cir. 1947), affirmed the defendant's conviction for introducing an adulterated cosmetic product into interstate commerce. The defendant, a cosmetics company, had entered into a contract with Helfrich Laboratories under which Helfrich would manufacture and distribute hair lacquer pads with the Parfait Powder Puff Company label. Defendant tested the first sample submitted by Helfrich and found it satisfactory. When shellac supplies became difficult to obtain, however, Helfrich made a substitution in the lacquer formula without the defendant's knowledge. Subsequently, the defendant learned of the substitution and immediately forbade its use. The defendant's argument that Helfrich was an independent contractor for whose acts it was not responsible was rejected by the court of appeals, which reasoned that the defendant incurred liability when it voluntarily selected Helfrich to manufacture and distribute a product it knew would become part of interstate commerce. *Id.* at 1010.

3.   *Responsible Officer.* A district court's revocation of a suspended sentence for violation of the Act was sustained in *United States v. Shapiro*, 491 F.2d 335 (6th Cir. 1974). The defendant, convicted for operating the Tasty Cookie Company under unsanitary conditions, was given a probated sentence contingent upon his rectifying those conditions before continuing production. The defendant also agreed to sell the plant as soon as a buyer

could be found. Within several months the defendant entered into a formal "operations and management" agreement giving a newly found buyer complete production control until the final closing. Several days prior to that closing, FDA inspected the plant and found it infested with vermin. Acting upon the FDA's petition, the district court revoked probation and imposed a 6-month sentence. The district court was unpersuaded by the defendant's arguments that he was no longer the responsible officer because equitable title and plant control had passed to his purchaser. The court of appeals found that the trial judge had not abused his discretion in revoking probation under these circumstances because the defendant still had legal title at the time of inspection.

    4.   *Record of Conviction.* Where individual defendants were acquitted on all charges of intent to violate the FD&C Act, but were convicted under the *Park* doctrine, which does not require proof of intent, the court reluctantly denied the defendants' motion to expunge their criminal records in *United States v. Purity Condiments, Inc.,* Food Drug Cosm. L. Rep. (CCH) ¶ 38,276 (S.D. Fla. 1984). The court concluded that the rationale underlying the FD&C Act and the applicable precedent left it no choice but to deny the motion for expungement, but the judge characterized this lack of discretionary power as amounting to "an unreasonable and impermissible restraint on judicial authority."

b.   THE DEFENSE OF IMPOSSIBILITY

    In *Park*, the Court observed: "The duty imposed by Congress on responsible corporate agents is, we emphasize, one that requires the highest standard of foresight and vigilance, but the Act, in its criminal aspect, does not require that which is objectively impossible." The Supreme Court had earlier held that a defendant in a criminal action under the FD&C Act can introduce evidence at trial that he was "powerless" to prevent or correct the violation. *United States v. Weisenfeld Warehouse Co.,* 376 U.S. 86, 91 (1964). To advance the impossibility defense, the defendant must come forward with sufficient evidence of impossibility to warrant placing an additional burden on the government, namely, the burden of establishing beyond a reasonable doubt that the defendant could have prevented or corrected the prohibited condition through the exercise of extraordinary care. *See United States v. Gel Spice Co.,* 773 F.2d 427, 434–35 (2d Cir. 1985).

    In practice, defendants have had trouble sustaining the impossibility defense. For example, in *United States v. Certified Grocers Co–Op,* 1968–1974 FDLI Jud. Rec. 299 (W.D. Wis. 1974), the court denied defendants' motion to dismiss the information charging violation of the Act by the holding and contamination of foods in a rodent-infested warehouse. The court refused to accept the defense of impossibility even though the prosecution stipulated that the defendant was doing everything possible to maintain sanitary conditions in the warehouse. The court reasoned that the defendants were helpless only for as long as they continued to use that particular warehouse.

    In the wake of *Park*, courts continued to rein in the impossibility defense. The Ninth Circuit, applying the *Park* standard of "foresight and vigilance," upheld the convictions of corporate officers in two cases decided the same day in 1976. By *per curiam* opinion in *United States v.*

Y. Hata & Co., Ltd., 535 F.2d 508 (9th Cir. 1976), the court rejected the defense tendered by the company's president that he had done everything possible to correct the unsanitary warehouse conditions. Having discovered the violations months before FDA inspection, the company had attempted unsuccessfully, through various methods, to prevent access of birds to stored food. At the time of inspection, the company was awaiting shipment of materials with which it would build a huge wire cage enclosing the warehouse. The court concluded that since "a wire cage is scarcely a novel preventive device," it would not have been "objectively impossible" for the defendant to implement this effective solution earlier. Consequently, the defendant was not excused.

Rodent infestation and contamination of stored food resulted in the conviction of the corporation's secretary-treasurer in *United States v. Starr*, 535 F.2d 512 (9th Cir. 1976). The defendant advanced a two-pronged argument of objective impossibility. First, the defendant asserted that he was helpless to prevent contamination resulting from the natural flow of rodents seeking sanctuary from the plowing of a nearby field. The court rejected this argument, remarking, "One with only a minimum of foresight would recognize that rodents and insects would flee from freshly plowed fields." Second, the defendant claimed that he had instructed the janitor to correct the situation, and the janitor deliberately failed to do so. The Court of Appeals denied that this situation obligated the trial judge to give an "objective impossibility" instruction to the jury, because the defendant worked in close proximity to the scene of the violations and was therefore in a position to observe for himself whether the necessary corrections were being made.

The impossibility defense does not invariably fail, however. For example, the court in *United States v. New England Grocers Supply Co.*, 488 F. Supp. 230 (D. Mass. 1980), set aside a magistrate's finding of guilt. The court held that if a defendant introduced sufficient evidence that he had exercised "extraordinary care" and still could not prevent the violation, the burden shifted to the government affirmatively to establish, beyond a reasonable doubt, that the defendant could have prevented the violation through the exercise of extraordinary care. The court remanded the case so the magistrate could apply this standard properly.

3. THE GUARANTY CLAUSE

Under section 303(c)(1) of the Act, a person who in good faith merely receives and later delivers an illegal article is exempt from criminal liability. Furthermore, under section 303(c)(2), a person who introduces an illegal article into commerce is also exempt from liability if he has received the article in good faith and obtained a written guaranty that it is not in violation of the Act. In turn, the giving of a false guaranty is prohibited by section 301(h) and is thus itself a criminal offense.

NOTES

1. *Eligibility for Guaranty Clause Immunity.* In *United States v. Crown Rubber Sundries Co.*, 67 F. Supp. 92 (N.D. Ohio 1946), the court

held that a repackager of condoms was subject to criminal prosecution despite having received a guaranty from the manufacturer.

> It is the judgment of this court that no person may rely upon any guaranty unless, in introducing the product into interstate commerce, he has acted merely as a conduit through which the merchandise reaches the consumer. . . . The guaranty can be received in good faith, within the meaning of the statute, only if the shipper passes the product on in the same form as he received it, without repacking it or subjecting it to any new hazards of adulteration or failure which were not present when the original guaranty upon which he relies was given.

Id. at 93.

2.   *Guaranty with Assurances.* In *United States v. Balanced Foods,* 146 F. Supp. 154 (S.D.N.Y. 1955), government agents informed a food shipper, who had received a guarantee, that the product in question was misbranded. The defendant shipper communicated this fact to the guarantor and was given assurances that the charge was a mistake. The court held that the defendant could justifiably rely on such assurances until there was an adjudication or authoritative determination that the merchandise was misbranded.

3.   *No Specific Interstate Nexus Required for False Guaranty Offense.* The United States Supreme Court has held that section 301(h) "proscribes the giving of a false guaranty to one engaged wholly or partly in an interstate business irrespective of whether that guaranty leads in any particular instance to an illegal shipment in interstate commerce." *United States v. Walsh,* 331 U.S. 432, 437 (1947).

H. Debarment and Exclusion

1. Debarment

Section 306 of the FD&C Act gives FDA power to debar companies or individuals who have been convicted of certain crimes (or have conducted certain other misconduct) related to the development, approval, or regulation of a drug. Debarment for a corporation, partnership, or association means the entity may not submit any abbreviated drug applications (ANDAs) to the agency for generic drugs. FD&C Act 306(a)(1), (b)(1)(A). Because FDA has never debarred a firm, this text will focus on debarment of individuals. For an individual, debarment means that he or she may not "provid[e] services *in any capacity* to a person [including a firm] who has an approved or pending drug product application [whether or not an abbreviated application]." FD&C 306(a)(2), (b)(1)(B) (emphasis added). Permanent debarment of an individual is mandatory when FDA finds that he or she has been convicted of a federal felony for conduct "relating to the development or approval . . . of any drug product" or "otherwise relating to the regulation of any drug product under this Act." *Id.* 306(a)(2), 306(c)(2)(A)(ii). FDA may seek permissive debarment of individuals for no more than five years in various other situations, including when the individual has been convicted of a state felony or a federal misdemeanor relating to the regulation of a drug or biologic. *Id.* 306(b)(2)(B), (c)(2)(A)(iii).

Although Congress gave FDA its debarment power in the Generic Drug Enforcement Act of 1992, Pub. L. No. 102–282, enacted following the generic drug scandal, both the violations and penalties in section 306 with respect to individual debarment extend to all drugs and drug applications, not merely generic drugs and ANDAs. Moreover, as applied by FDA, the word "drug" in section 306 encompasses biologics and the term "drug product application" includes Biologics License Applications (BLAs).

In 2002, the Bioterrorism Act extended FDA's permissive debarment power to any person who "has been convicted of a felony for conduct related to the importation into the United States of any food" or who "has engaged in a pattern of importing... adulterated food that presents a threat of serious adverse health consequences or death to humans or animals." FD&C Act 306(b)(1)(C), (b)(3).

Bae v. Shalala

44 F.3d 489 (7th Cir. 1995).

■ COFFEY, CIRCUIT JUDGE.

Petitioner Kun Chae Bae, the former president of a generic drug manufacturing company, appeals the final order of the Food and Drug Administration under the Generic Drug Enforcement Act of 1992 ("GDEA"), 21 U.S.C. §§ 335a–335c, permanently debarring him from "providing services in any capacity to a person that has an approved or pending drug product application." . . . This case presents the question of whether and under what circumstances a civil debarment penalty may constitute retroactive punishment prohibited by the *Ex Post Facto* Clause of the United States Constitution. We affirm.

I. Background

While president of My–K Laboratories, Bae submitted several abbreviated new drug applications to the FDA's Division of Generic Drugs. . . . Charles Y. Chang, the Branch Chief of the FDA's chemistry review branch in Maryland, was responsible for supervising the chemists who evaluated My–K Laboratories' abbreviated new drug applications. . . .

. . . In 1990, Bae was charged with and pleaded guilty to one felony count of aiding and abetting interstate travel in aid of racketeering. . . . The Information alleged that on or about August 21, 1987, Bae caused . . . Chang to travel from Maryland to Illinois with the intent to provide Chang with an "unlawful gratuity." The Information further alleged that during Chang's visit to Illinois, Bae gave Chang $10,000 "for and because of official acts performed and to be performed" by Chang. The statement of facts accompanying the Information asserted that Chang provided Bae "with several formulations for generic drugs which Chang had gleaned from other companies' [applications]."

By certified letter dated March 30, 1993, the FDA notified Bae that it proposed to debar him from participation in the generic drug industry pursuant to 21 U.S.C. § 335a(a)(2) based on his prior felony conviction for conduct relating to the development or approval of a generic drug product. The FDA notified Bae that he would have the opportunity for an evidentiary hearing, should he desire to contest his debarment, if he presented specific facts, in writing, demonstrating a genuine and substantial issue of fact relevant to his debarment. Bae requested a hearing, but submitted no specific facts, and instead raised the argument that the GDEA's debarment provision was punitive in nature, and that its retroactive application to him violated the constitutional prohibition against ex post facto laws. The FDA, after reviewing Bae's request for a hearing, denied the request, finding that Bae had failed to raise any genuine or substantial issue of fact relevant to his debarment. On December 30, 1993, the FDA issued a final order permanently debarring Bae from providing services in any capacity to a person with a pending or approved drug product application.

II. *Discussion*

. . . .

The *Ex Post Facto* Clause of the United States Constitution, Article I, § 9, clause 3, prohibits the enactment of any law "which imposes a punishment for an act which was not punishable at the time it was committed; or imposes additional punishment to that then prescribed." "[F]or a criminal or penal law to be ex post facto . . . it must be retrospective, that is, it must apply to events occurring before its enactment, and it must disadvantage the offender affected by it." *Weaver v. Graham*, 450 U.S. 24, 28 (1981).

A civil sanction, like the debarment provision of the GDEA, will implicate ex post facto concerns only if it can fairly be characterized as punishment. *United States v. Halper*, 490 U.S. 435, 447–48 (1989). . . .

In *Halper*, the Supreme Court described the proper analysis to determine whether a given civil sanction constitutes punishment in the constitutional sense:

> . . . We have recognized in other contexts that punishment serves the twin aims of retribution and deterrence. . . . [I]t follows that a civil sanction that cannot fairly be said solely to serve a remedial purpose, but rather can only be explained as also serving either retributive or deterrent purposes, is punishment, as we have come to understand the term. . . . We therefore hold that under the Double Jeopardy Clause a defendant who already has been punished in a criminal prosecution may not be subjected to an additional civil sanction to the extent that the second sanction may not fairly be characterized as remedial, but only as a deterrent or retribution.

The aim of the GDEA was to restore consumer confidence in generic drugs by eradicating the widespread corruption in the generic drug approval process. The preamble to the GDEA focuses exclusively on its remedial purpose, i.e., "to restore and to ensure the integrity of the abbreviated drug application approval process and to protect the public health." Pub.L. 102–282, § 1(c). Enactment of the GDEA was prompted by the 1988 investigation that revealed the crimes of Bae and others in connection with the FDA's generic drug approval process. . . .

With these objective goals, the GDEA can fairly be said solely to serve a remedial purpose.

Bae argues that a civil sanction that serves both remedial and punitive goals must be characterized as punishment. Bae contends that debarment cannot be said to serve solely remedial purposes because debarment is triggered only by a criminal conviction, and the only basis for limiting or terminating an otherwise permanent debarment is to provide substantial assistance to the government in other criminal prosecutions. We refuse to read *Halper* so broadly. A civil sanction that can fairly be said solely to serve remedial goals will not fail under *ex post facto* scrutiny simply because it is consistent with punitive goals as well. . . . Without question, the GDEA serves compelling governmental interests unrelated to punishment. The punitive effects of the GDEA are merely incidental to its overriding purpose to safeguard the integrity of the generic drug industry while protecting public health.

Our inquiry does not end here. We must also determine whether the legislative history of the GDEA evinces an intent to punish. Bae points out that the legislators who sponsored the GDEA repeatedly sought support for the bill in the name of deterrence.

Even though the legislative history of the GDEA is replete with references to its deterrent objective, we are unconvinced that Congress, as a whole, intended the mandatory debarment provision of the GDEA to serve solely punitive goals. . . . The Supreme Court has consistently required "unmistakable evidence of punitive intent" to characterize a sanction as punishment. . . .

. . . [A] deterrent purpose does not automatically mark a civil sanction as a form of punishment. General deterrence is the foremost and overriding goal of all laws, both civil and criminal, and transcends the nature of any sanction. General deterrence aims to dissuade all persons from violating the laws. . . .

Bae finally argues that his permanent debarment is overwhelmingly disproportionate to the remedial goals of the GDEA. . . . [W]e must determine whether Bae's permanent debarment from participation in the generic drug industry "reasonably can be viewed as a remedial measure commensurate with his wrongdoing." *Furlett*, 974 F.2d at 844.

A number of appellate courts have upheld debarments and other similar employment restrictions to serve nonpunitive, remedial goals. The employment restrictions imposed in [these cases] were of limited duration. . . . In contrast, petitioner Bae's debarment is permanent. However, the duration or severity of an employment restriction will not mark it as punishment where it is intended to further a legitimate governmental purpose. This court has twice upheld permanent employment bans against double jeopardy and *ex post facto* challenges. . . .

In enacting the GDEA, Congress adopted a bright-line rule excluding from the generic drug industry all individuals with prior felony convictions relating to the approval or regulation of any generic drug product. Although Bae's permanent debarment from providing services in any capacity to a person with an approved or pending drug product application is undoubtedly harsh, it is not disproportionate to the remedial goals of the GDEA or to the magnitude of his wrongdoing. Bae's actions were both unlawful and unscrupulous. Bae lined the pockets of a high-ranking FDA official with thousands of dollars in exchange for information or preferential treatment. His contribution to the widespread corruption in the generic drug industry was by no means slight. We agree with the Tenth Circuit that

> [i]t is the clear intent of debarment to purge government programs of corrupt influences and to prevent improper dissipation of public funds. Removal of persons whose participation in these programs is detrimental to public purposes is remedial by definition. While those persons may interpret debarment as punitive, and indeed feel as though they have been punished, debarment constitutes the "rough remedial justice" permissible as a prophylactic governmental action.
>
>   . . . .

III. Conclusion

By enacting the mandatory debarment provision of the GDEA, Congress sought not to punish Kun Chae Bae but to safeguard the integrity of the generic drug industry. The clear and unambiguous intent of Congress in passing the GDEA was to purge the generic drug industry of corruption and to restore consumer confidence in generic drug products. The GDEA's civil debarment penalty is solely remedial, even though it "carries the sting of punishment" in the eyes of petitioner Bae. Accordingly, the FDA's final order permanently debarring Bae from providing services in any capacity to a person with an approved or pending drug product application is

Affirmed.

NOTES

1. *Subsequent Cases.* The reasoning of *Bae* was embraced in *DiCola v. FDA*, 77 F.3d 504 (D.C. Cir. 1996) and *United States v. Borjesson*, 92 F.3d 954 (9th Cir. 1996).

2. *Publication.* A list of debarments is available on the FDA website. Each debarment is also announced in the Federal Register.

3. *Frequency of Debarment.* FDA's use of the drug application debarment procedure has increased in recent years. In the fifteen year period between the start of 1993 and end of 2008, it issued approximately 85 debarment orders. In the time since, less than five years later, the agency has issued almost 50 such orders. The agency has issued approximately one dozen debarment orders against food importers since it obtained this authority in 2002, although two of these orders were subsequently withdrawn following vacation of the importers' convictions.

4. *Disqualification* 21 CFR 312.70. Clinical investigators are among the individuals who can be debarred under FD&C Act 306. But by regulation, FDA has also created a less severe penalty for clinical investigators, known as disqualification. According to 21 C.F.R. 312.70, if the agency finds that a clinical investigator (including a sponsor) has "repeatedly or deliberately failed to comply" with the investigational new drug application (IND) regulations or has submitted false information to

FDA or the sponsor, it may disqualify the investigator from receiving investigational drugs or biologics in any investigation until reinstated by the agency.

5. *Medical Devices.* A 2009 GAO report criticized the fact that FDA's debarment authority does not extend to medical devices with regard to either the violations or the punishment. OVERSIGHT OF CLINICAL INVESTIGATORS: ACTION NEEDED TO IMPROVE TIMELINESS AND ENHANCE SCOPE OF FDA'S DEBARMENT AND DISQUALIFICATION PROCESSES FOR MEDICAL PRODUCT INVESTIGATORS 39–40 (GAO 2009).

2. EXCLUSION

Under 42 U.S.C. 1320a–7, the Secretary of HHS (acting through the HHS Inspector General) may exclude from participation in federal health care programs individuals and entities who have been convicted of crimes "relating to" health care fraud. In many instances, the practical effect of such exclusion of an individual is to preclude employment of that individual in any capacity by an entity that receives reimbursement, indirectly or directly, from any federal health care program.

Friedman v. Sebelius

686 F.3d 813 (D.C. Cir. 2012).

■ GINSBURG, SENIOR CIRCUIT JUDGE: Michael Friedman, Paul Goldenheim, and Howard Udell were executives at the Purdue Frederick Company when it misbranded a drug, to wit, the painkiller OxyContin, a schedule II controlled substance. The Company was convicted of fraudulent misbranding, a felony, whilst the executives were convicted under the "responsible corporate officer" doctrine of the misdemeanor of misbranding a drug. Based upon their convictions, the Secretary of Health and Human Services later excluded the individuals from participation in Federal health care programs for 12 years, pursuant to 42 U.S.C. § 1320a–7(b). They sought review of the Secretary's decision in the district court, arguing section 1320a–7(b) does not authorize their exclusion and, in any event, the Secretary's decision was unsupported by substantial evidence and was arbitrary and capricious because she failed to give a reasoned explanation for the allegedly unprecedented length of their exclusions. The district court granted summary judgment for the Secretary.

We hold the statute authorized the Secretary's exclusion of the three executives but her decision was arbitrary and capricious for want of a reasoned explanation for the length of their exclusions. We therefore reverse the judgment of the district court and direct it to remand the matter to the Secretary for further proceedings.

I. Background

The Appellants were senior corporate officers at Purdue when the Company developed and marketed OxyContin. According to the Information initiating the criminal cases against the Appellants and the Company, the "misbranding" occurred when unnamed employees at Purdue, "with the intent to defraud or mislead, marketed and promoted

OxyContin as less addictive, less subject to abuse and diversion, and less likely to cause tolerance and withdrawal than other pain medications." Purdue pleaded guilty to felony misbranding, in violation of 21 U.S.C. § 331(a) and § 333(a)(2). Pursuant to the plea agreement, the district court put the Company on probation for five years, fined it $500,000, and imposed other monetary sanctions totaling approximately $600 million. . . . At the same time, the Appellants pleaded guilty to misdemeanor misbranding, in violation of 21 U.S.C. § 331(a) and § 333(a)(1), for their admitted failure to prevent Purdue's fraudulent marketing of OxyContin; each was sentenced to do 400 hours of community service, fined $5,000, and put on probation for three years. The sentencing court also ordered the Appellants to disgorge compensation they had received from Purdue totaling approximately $34.5 million.

Under the "responsible corporate officer" (RCO) doctrine, a "corporate agent, through whose act, default, or omission the corporation committed a crime" in violation of the Food, Drug, and Cosmetic Act may be held criminally liable for the wrongdoing of the corporation "whether or not the crime required 'consciousness of wrongdoing'" by the agent. *United States v. Park*, 421 U.S. 658 (1975). Criminal liability under the RCO doctrine extends "not only to those corporate agents who themselves committed the criminal act, but also to those who by virtue of their managerial positions or other similar relation to the actor could be deemed responsible for its commission." *Id.* A corporate officer may therefore be guilty of misdemeanor misbranding without "knowledge of, or personal participation in," the underlying fraudulent conduct. *Id.* The Appellants, as part of their plea agreements, admitted having "responsibility and authority either to prevent in the first instance or to promptly correct" the misrepresentations certain unnamed Purdue employees made regarding OxyContin and thereby, under the RCO doctrine, admitted being guilty of misdemeanor misbranding.

Several months after the Appellants had been convicted, the Office of the Inspector General (OIG) of the Department of Health and Human Services determined the Appellants should be excluded from participation in Federal health care programs for 20 years, pursuant to 42 U.S.C. § 1320a–7(b)(1). . . .*

The executives appealed the OIG's determination to an Administrative Law Judge and ultimately to the Departmental Appeals Board [DAB], to which the Secretary had delegated authority to review decisions to exclude an individual. . . . The DAB . . . reduced the length of the exclusion to 12 years. . . .

---

* Section 1320a–7(b)(1)(A) authorizes the Secretary to exclude any "individual . . . [who] has been convicted . . . of a criminal offense consisting of a misdemeanor relating to fraud, theft, embezzlement, breach of fiduciary responsibility, or other financial misconduct . . . in connection with the delivery of a health care item or service." . . . The length of an exclusion predicated upon a conviction for a misdemeanor "shall be 3 years, unless the Secretary determines in accordance with published regulations that a shorter period is appropriate because of mitigating circumstances or that a longer period is appropriate because of aggravating circumstances." 42 U.S.C. § 1320a–7(c)(3)(D). 42 C.F.R. § 1001.2 provides "items and services furnished, ordered, or prescribed by [an excluded person] will not be reimbursed under Medicare, Medicaid and all other Federal health care programs until [that person] is reinstated by the OIG."

II. *Analysis*

. . . .

The Appellants first argue misdemeanor misbranding is not a "criminal offense consisting in a misdemeanor relating to fraud" [as required by section 1320a–7(b)(1)] because it lacks the allegedly requisite " 'generic' relationship to fraud." On their view, it is not enough for the conduct underlying a particular conviction to be factually related to fraud; the generic misdemeanor must comprise the "core elements" of fraud, one of which is *scienter*. Misdemeanor misbranding does not necessarily require a culpable mental state because a conviction for the offense may be, and in this case was, predicated upon the responsible corporate officer doctrine, which entails strict liability. The Secretary defends her interpretation by arguing that . . . the Appellants' convictions . . . 'relate to' fraud . . . because there is a 'nexus' or 'common sense connection' between their convictions and those statutory bases for exclusion."

This case therefore presents the question whether the phrase "misdemeanor relating to fraud" in section 1320a–7(b)(1)(A) refers to a generic criminal offense or to the facts underlying the particular defendant's conviction. As the Supreme Court has pointed out, "in ordinary speech words such as 'crime,' 'felony,' 'offense,' and the like sometimes refer to a generic crime, say, the crime of fraud or theft in general, and sometimes refer to the specific acts in which an offender engaged on a specific occasion, say, *the* fraud that the defendant planned and executed last month." *Nijhawan v. Holder*, 557 U.S. 29, 33–34 (2009). The "categorical approach," according to which the statutory term refers to the generic criminal offense, "prohibits the later court from delving into particular facts disclosed by the record of conviction" and directs that court to "look only to the fact of conviction and the statutory definition of the prior offense," including the elements of that offense. *Shepard v. United States*, 544 U.S. 13, 17 (2005). Under the "circumstance-specific" approach, by contrast, the statutory term refers to the particular conduct giving rise to the conviction and so the court "must look to the facts and circumstances underlying an offender's conviction" to determine whether that conviction is covered by the statute. *Nijhawan*, 557 U.S. at 34. Whether the Congress intended the categorical or the circumstance-specific approach is to be discerned from the text, structure, and purpose of the particular statute at issue.

. . . The text, structure, and purpose of the statute, *viz.*, to protect Federal health care programs from financial harm wrought by untrustworthy providers, all indicate the Secretary's circumstance-specific approach is proper; *i.e.*, the statute authorizes exclusion of an individual whose conviction was for conduct factually related to fraud. . . .

The key phrase in this provision is "relating to," the "ordinary meaning of [which] is a broad one—'to stand in some relation; to have bearing or concern; to pertain; refer; to bring into association with or connection with.' " *Morales*, 504 U.S. at 383 (quoting Black's Law Dictionary 1158 (5th ed. 1979)) . . . . Accordingly, just as the Secretary contends, a misdemeanor "relat[es] to" fraud "in the normal sense of the phrase, if it has a connection with, or reference to" fraud.

The rest of section 1320a–7(b)(1)(A) confirms its broad scope. . . .

The text and structure of the provisions adjoining section 1320a–7(b)(1)(A) further confirm this interpretation. . . .

Finally, the Appellants and their amici argue, because the Secretary's interpretation permits her to impose "career-ending disabilities" upon someone whose criminal conviction required no *mens rea*, it raises a serious question of validity under the Due Process Clause of the Fifth Amendment to the Constitution of the United States. Quoting *Morissette v. United States*, 342 U.S. 246, 256 (1952), they note the Supreme Court upheld the constitutionality of strict liability crimes "in part, because their associated penalties 'commonly are relatively small, and conviction does no grave damage to an offender's reputation.'" Section 1320a–7(b)(1), however, is not a criminal statute and, although exclusion may indeed have serious consequences, we do not think excluding an individual under 42 U.S.C. § 1320a–7(b) on the basis of his conviction for a strict liability offense raises any significant concern with due process. Exclusion effectively prohibits one from working for a government contractor or supplier. Surely the Government constitutionally may refuse to deal further with senior corporate officers who could have but failed to prevent a fraud against the Government on their watch.

For the foregoing reasons, we hold section 1320a–7(b)(1)(A) authorizes the Secretary to exclude from participation in Federal health care programs an individual convicted of a misdemeanor if the conduct underlying that conviction is factually related to fraud. The Appellants do not dispute they are excludable under this circumstance-specific approach: Their convictions for misdemeanor misbranding were predicated upon the company they led having pleaded guilty to fraudulently misbranding a drug and they admitted having "responsibility and authority either to prevent in the first instance or to promptly correct" that fraud; they did neither. Accordingly, section 1320a–7(b)(1)(A) authorized the Secretary to exclude them for a time from participation in Federal health care programs.

The Appellants also challenge the Secretary's decision to exclude them for fully 12 years . . . .

. . . We . . . review the Secretary's decision to exclude the Appellants according to the arbitrary and capricious standard, which requires that the Secretary provide a reasoned explanation for departing from agency precedent.

. . . Research reveals the longest period of exclusion the DAB had ever approved under section 1320a–7(b)(1) was four years. . . . [T]he agency had never excluded anyone for more than ten years based upon a misdemeanor—a departure the agency does not even acknowledge, much less explain.

We do not suggest the Appellant's exclusion for 12 years based upon a conviction for misdemeanor misbranding might not be justifiable; we express no opinion on that question. Our concern here is that the DAB did not justify it in the decision under review. Simply pointing to prior cases with the same bottom line but arising under a different law and [*40] involving materially different facts does not provide a reasoned explanation for the agency's apparent departure from precedent. Therefore we hold the decision of the DAB was arbitrary and capricious with respect to the length of the Appellants' exclusion.

III. Conclusion

For the reasons set out above, we hold section 1320a–7(b)(1) authorizes the exclusion of the Appellants on the basis of their convictions for misdemeanor misbranding. The Secretary's decision, however, was arbitrary and capricious with respect to the length of their exclusion because it failed to explain its departure from the agency's own precedents. The judgment of the district court is therefore reversed and the matter shall be remanded to the district court with instructions to remand it to the agency for further consideration consistent with this opinion.

So ordered.

NOTE

Role of the HHS Inspector General. In 90 Stat. 2429 (1976), Congress created the Office of Inspector General in the Department of HEW (the predecessor of HHS) for the purpose of "preventing and detecting fraud and abuse" in departmental programs and operations. Two years later, in the Inspector General Act of 1978, 92 Stat. 1101, Congress created an Office of Inspector General in other departments and agencies as well. As part of the Inspector General Act Amendments of 1988, 102 Stat. 2515, the 1976 statute was repealed, and the HHS Office of Inspector General was made subject to the 1978 statute.

In 1989, the Office of Legal Counsel in the Department of Justice issued an opinion that under the 1978 statute, inspectors general do not have authority to investigate violations of regulatory statutes but rather are limited to investigating the employees and operations of a department and its contractors, grantees, and other recipients of federal funds in order to "root out waste and fraud." Memorandum from Assistant Attorney General D.W. Kmiec to Department of Labor Acting Solicitor J.G. Thorn (Mar. 9, 1989), reprinted in 3 CORP. CRIME REP., No. 32, at 18 (Aug. 14, 1989). Nonetheless, on the heels of a corruption scandal regarding the approval of generic drugs, the HHS Inspector General was delegated "the responsibility for conducting investigations of criminal violations of the Federal Food, Drug and Cosmetic Act for which the penalty is a felony," excluding matters that "should remain a function of the Food and Drug Administration." Memorandum from HHS Secretary L.W. Sullivan to HHS Inspector General R.P. Kusserow (July 24, 1989). This action was reported to have precipitated the resignation of the FDA Chief Counsel. Linda Hemelstein, *Top FDA Lawyer Resigns Over Policy Dispute*, LEGAL TIMES OF WASH., Aug. 7, 1989, at 6. In the face of substantial criticism, Secretary Sullivan rescinded the delegation on December 28, 1989, on the stated basis that the generic drug "emergency" was over and its need had "passed." See "Naked Reverse: Secretary Sullivan's Rescission of his Delegation of Investigative Authority to the Inspector General," Staff Report Prepared for the Use of the Subcomm. on Oversight and Investigations of the House Comm. on Energy and Commerce, 101st Cong.,

2d Sess., Comm. Print 101–S (1990). Not coincidentally, the creation of the OCI, *supra* p. 239, note 2, closely followed this move.

Today, in addition to investigating cases involving FDA employees, the HHS Inspector General also participates in investigating FDA-regulated entities when HHS funds or programs are involved.

I. CIVIL MONEY PENALTIES

The 1938 FD&C Act contained no provisions authorizing civil money penalties. For many years, the only authority FDA had to seek such penalties was under the Radiation Control for Health and Safety Act of 1968, which amended the Public Health Service Act to regulate radiation-emitting electronic products. (FDA assumed responsibility for administering the Radiation Act in 1971.) Former section 360(C) of the PHS Act, now codified as section 539 of the FD&C Act, empowers FDA to seek the imposition of civil penalties for violations of the Radiation Act in federal district court. FD&C Act 539(b), (c).

Beginning in the late 1980s, Congress repeatedly amended the FD&C Act and the PHS Act to give FDA authority to impose civil money penalties for various types of violations. The National Childhood Vaccine Injury Act of 1986 added civil penalties to the PHS Act for violations of the biological product recall provision and the vaccine manufacturer recordkeeping requirements. 42 U.S.C. 262(d)(2), 300aa–28(b)(1). The Prescription Drug Marketing Act of 1987 authorizes FDA to seek civil penalties from manufacturers or distributors convicted of violations of the drug sample provisions of the FD&C Act or parallel state laws. FD&C Act 333(b)(2). *See also* FD&C Act 332(b)(3) (civil penalty for failing to report conviction under state law).

The Safe Medical Devices Act of 1990 (SMDA) authorizes FDA to impose civil penalties on "any person who violates a requirement of this Act which relates to devices." FD&C Act 303(f)(1)(A). See also FD&C Act 303(f)(1)(B) (exempting certain violations from civil money penalties). The Generic Drug Enforcement Act of 1992 added civil penalties for various categories of misconduct in connection with an Abbreviated New Drug Application. FD&C Act 307. The Food Quality Protection Act of 1996 authorizes FDA to seek civil penalties from people other than growers who introduce food containing unsafe pesticide chemicals into interstate commerce. FD&C Act 303(f)(2). The Mammography Quality Standards Acts of 1992 and 1998, amending the PHSA, include civil penalties for various violations regarding mammography facilities. 42 U.S.C. § 263b(h)(2). *See* 58 Fed. Reg. 30,680, 30,680–82 (May 26, 1993) (summarizing the civil money penalty provisions enacted to that point).

Most of the important recent amendments to the FD&C Act have included additional civil money penalties. With respect to drugs and biologics, the Food and Drug Administration Amendments Act of 2007 (FDAAA) authorizes the imposition of civil money penalties for violations of requirements regarding submission of clinical trial information, failure to conform to mandatory risk evaluation and mitigations strategies (REMS), and dissemination of false or misleading direct-to-consumer advertisements for prescription products. FD&C Act 303(f)(4), 303(g). The Food Safety Modernization Act of 2010 provides for civil penalties for failure to comply with a mandatory recall order. *Id.* 303(f)(2). Most dramatically, the Family Smoking Prevention and Tobacco Control Act of 2009 creates civil penalties for any violation of any requirement of the FD&C Act relating to tobacco products. *Id.* 303(f)(9).

Under the Radiation Act, the United States must file an action in federal district court to obtain an order imposing civil money penalties. Under all of the later civil penalty provisions, by contrast, FDA can impose the monetary penalties itself, through administrative order, after notice and an administrative hearing. Some of the statutory provisions in question explicitly provide for administrative imposition of the civil money penalties, but even with regard to those that are "silent on whether Congress intended civil money penalties to be judicially or administrative imposed," FDA has declared that it has "the authority to choose which [approach] it believes best." 58 Fed. Reg. at 30,680. In 1995, the agency issued final regulations establishing the hearing procedures for the imposition of civil money penalty provisions. 21 C.F.R. Part 17.

NOTES

1. *Frequency of Civil Penalties.* Until very recently, FDA rarely sought civil money penalties under any of the FD&C Act provisions that authorized them. However, with the passage of the Family Smoking Prevention and Tobacco Control Act, civil money penalties may now take on a more prominent role in FDA enforcement strategies. In April 2012 alone, FDA filed 147 civil money penalties against tobacco product retailers not in compliance with tobacco product requirements. *See* Cumulative number of Civil Money Penalties filed for the FY as a result of retailer compliance check inspections (available on FDA website).

2. *Inflation Adjustment.* The Federal Civil Penalties Inflation Adjustment Act of 1990 Pub. L. 101–410, requires agencies to issue regulations every four years to adjust for inflation each civil money penalty provided by statutes within their jurisdiction. Therefore, the maximum amounts stated in the older civil penalty provisions of the FD&C Act and the PHSA are no longer in force. The higher, adjusted current amounts are listed at 21 C.F.R. 17.2.

J. INFORMAL COMPLIANCE CORRESPONDENCE

Section 309 of the FD&C Act (formerly section 306) permits FDA to decline to institute formal enforcement proceedings for "minor violations of this Act whenever [it] believes that the public interest will be adequately served by a suitable written notice or warning." Historically, FDA relied primarily upon seizure and other formal court proceedings to enforce the FD&C Act. Beginning in the early 1970s, however, the agency developed regulatory letters and other informal compliance correspondence as alternatives to court enforcement. The agency established a two-tiered approach to such correspondence. A "Regulatory Letter" warned a violator that formal enforcement was likely in the absence of voluntary compliance. By contrast, a "Report of Investigational Finding" (also known as an "Information Letter") requested voluntary correction but made no representation that formal enforcement action was imminent. This two-tiered approach continues today, although the nomenclature has evolved: "Regulatory Letters" are now known as "Warning Letters," and "Information Letters" are now denominated "Untitled Letters."

FDA Regulatory Procedures Manual, Chapter 4 ("Advisory Actions")

July 2012.

4–1 WARNING LETTERS

4–1–1 Warning Letter Procedures

When it is consistent with the public protection responsibilities of the agency and depending on the nature of the violation, it is the Food and Drug Administration's (FDA's) practice to give individuals and firms an opportunity to take voluntary and prompt corrective action before it initiates an enforcement action. Warning Letters are issued to achieve voluntary compliance and to establish prior notice. . . . The use of Warning Letters and the prior notice policy are based on the expectation that most individuals and firms will voluntarily comply with the law.

The agency position is that Warning Letters are issued only for violations of regulatory significance. Significant violations are those violations that may lead to enforcement action if not promptly and adequately corrected. A Warning Letter is the agency's principal means of achieving prompt voluntary compliance with the Federal Food, Drug, and Cosmetic Act (the Act).

The Warning Letter was developed to correct violations of the statutes or regulations. Also available to the agency are enforcement strategies which are based on the particular set of circumstances at hand and may include sequential or concurrent FDA enforcement actions such as recall, seizure, injunction, administrative detention, civil money penalties and/or prosecution to achieve correction. Despite the significance of the violations, there are some circumstances that may preclude the agency from taking any further enforcement action following the issuance of a Warning Letter. For example, the violation may be serious enough to warrant a Warning Letter and subsequent seizure; however, if the seizable quantity fails to meet the agency's threshold value for seizures, the agency may choose not to pursue a seizure. In this instance, the Warning Letter would document prior warning if adequate corrections are not made and enforcement action is warranted at a later time.

Responsible officials in positions of authority in regulated firms have a legal duty to implement whatever measures are necessary to ensure that their products, practices, processes, or other activities comply with the law. Under the law such individuals are presumed to be fully aware of their responsibilities. Consequently, responsible individuals should not assume that they would receive a Warning Letter, or other prior notice, before FDA initiates enforcement action.

FDA is under no legal obligation to warn individuals or firms that they or their products are in violation of the law before taking enforcement action, except in a few specifically defined areas. . . .

A Warning Letter is informal and advisory. It communicates the agency's position on a matter, but it does not commit FDA to taking enforcement action. For these reasons, FDA does not consider Warning Letters to be final agency action on which it can be sued.

There are instances when issuing a Warning Letter is not appropriate, and, as previously stated, a Warning Letter is not a prerequisite to taking enforcement action. Examples of situations where the agency will take enforcement action without necessarily issuing a Warning Letter include:

1. The violation reflects a history of repeated or continual conduct of a similar or substantially similar nature during which time the individual and/or firm has been notified of a similar or substantially similar violation;

2. The violation is intentional or flagrant;

3. The violation presents a reasonable possibility of injury or death;

4. The violations, under Title 18 U.S.C. 1001 [criminalizing "Fraud and False Statements"], are intentional and willful acts that once having occurred cannot be retracted. Also, such a felony violation does not require prior notice. Therefore, Title 18 U.S.C. 1001 violations are not suitable for inclusion in Warning Letters; and,

5. When adequate notice has been given by other means and the violations have not been corrected, or are continuing. . . .

. . . .

4–1–10 Warning Letter Format

Warning Letters can vary in form, style, and content to provide the flexibility needed to accurately and effectively state the nature of the violation(s) found and the response expected. However, the elements listed below are common to Warning Letters:

1. Title: "WARNING LETTER."

. . . .

3. The Warning Letter should be addressed to the highest known official in the corporation that includes the facility that was inspected, and a copy should be sent to the highest known official at the facility that was inspected. . . .

4. The dates of the inspection and a description of the violative condition, practice, or product in brief but sufficient detail to provide the respondent the opportunity to take corrective action. Include citation of the section of the law and, where applicable, the regulation violated. . . .

5. A request for correction and a written response within a specific period of time after the date of receipt of the letter, usually fifteen (15) working days. At the district's discretion, the recipient may be offered an opportunity to discuss the letter with district officials or, when appropriate, with center officials.

6.   A warning statement that failure to achieve prompt correction may result in enforcement action without further notice. Examples of such actions may be cited. Do not include a commitment to take enforcement action.

9.   Instructions, as appropriate, that the response include:

a.   each step that has been or will be taken to completely correct the current violations and to prevent similar violations;

b.   the time within which correction will be completed;

c.   any reason the corrective action has not been completed within the response time; and,

d.   any documentation necessary to show that correction has been achieved.

. . . .

11. Issued by the district director, division director, or higher agency official. Some program areas will require center concurrence before issuance.

. . . .

4–2 UNTITLED LETTERS

An Untitled Letter cites violations that do not meet the threshold of regulatory significance for a Warning Letter. Therefore, the format and content of an Untitled Letter should clearly distinguish it from a Warning Letter. For example:

1.   The letter is not titled.

. . . .

3.   The letter does not include a warning statement that failure to take prompt correction may result in enforcement action.

. . . .

5.   The letter requests (rather than requires) a written response from the firm within a reasonable amount of time (e.g., "Please respond within 30 days"), unless more specific instructions are provided in a relevant compliance program.

Any appropriate agency compliance official may issue an Untitled Letter.

. . . .

NOTES

1.   *OCC Clearance of Enforcement Correspondence* On November 29, 2001, the Deputy Secretary of the Department of Health and Human Services in the new Bush administration directed FDA to submit all Warning Letters and Untitled Letters to FDA's Office of Chief Counsel (OCC) prior to their issuance so that they could be reviewed for legal sufficiency and consistency with agency policy. These procedures were implemented in March 2002. Following the institution of the OCC review policy, the number of FDA warning letters dropped sharply. Following the election of President Obama, the new FDA commissioner announced that to speed the issuance of warning letters, "I have approved a new policy

brought forward by the FDA's Chief Counsel to limit warning letter review to significant legal issues." She noted that this approach "is consistent with the FDA's longstanding historical practice." "Effective Enforcement and Benefits to Public Health," Remarks by Margaret A. Hamburg, FDA Commissioner, to the Food and Drug Law Institute (Aug. 6, 2009) (available on FDA website).

2.   *Legal Status of Warning Letters.* When FDA devised Regulatory Letters (now called Warning Letters) in the early 1970s, the agency intended them to represent final statements of enforcement policy subject to court challenge. FDA later retreated from this position, characterizing Regulatory Letters as informal correspondence, which did not constitute final agency action, and the courts agreed. *E.g., Biotics Research Corp. v. Heckler,* 710 F.2d 1375 (9th Cir. 1983). This policy change occurred because OCC had no control over the issuance of Regulatory Letters and thus was not prepared routinely to defend them in court. Nevertheless, the second Bush administration's institution of mandatory OCC review of Warning Letters did not lead to a change in FDA's position regarding their lack of finality. Even during the years of mandatory OCC clearance, the Regulatory Procedures Manual stated, as it continues to state today: "FDA does not consider Warning Letters to be final agency action on which it can be sued." FDA Reg. Proc. Manual 4–1–1 (available on FDA website).

3.   *Other Recent Warning Letter Policy.* In the same 2009 speech discussed *supra* in note 1, Commissioner Hamburg also stated that FDA would emphasize prompt follow-up of warning letters with inspections or investigations to assess whether the company has taken corrective action. She announced that the agency would no longer issue multiple warning letters to noncompliant firms before taking enforcement action. Finally, she also introduced the creation of a formal warning letter "close-out process." Under this procedure, when FDA determines that a firm has fully corrected the violations raised in a warning letter, it provides the company with a "close-out" letter indicating that the problems appear to have been successfully addressed. As of the publication of this book, FDA has issued more than 750 close-out letters, all of which are published on the agency website.

4.   *Section 309 and Agency Discretion.* As discussed earlier, *supra* p. 175, section 309 of the FD&C Act (previously section 306) has frequently been invoked by the government as support for the exercise of its discretion not to bring formal enforcement actions. Conversely, courts have also held that section 309 does not fetter FDA's discretion to pursue formal enforcement rather than issue a warning. For example, in *United States v. Hunter Pharmacy, Inc.,* 213 F. Supp. 323 (S.D.N.Y. 1963), the court stated:

> . . . The determination of whether a violation is of such a nature as not to require criminal prosecution to vindicate the public interest is entrusted to the judgment of the Secretary. In the instant case, the reference of the matter to the United States Attorney for prosecution is indication that he deems the offenses as other than "minor," or that he believes the public interest will not be adequately safeguarded by a warning. The statute nowhere commands, with respect to this section, that he establish rules and regulations for procedures to determine

whether a warning instead of a prosecution of injunction serves to vindicate the public interest. The statute itself indicates the matter rests in his discretion.

Id. at 324.

K. PUBLICITY

The FD&C Act, in section 705 ("Publicity"), expressly authorizes the issuance of information to the public. Section 705(a) obligates FDA to publish "from time to time" summaries of all formal enforcement actions resolved in court. Section 705(b) permits FDA also to disseminate information regarding regulated products "in situations involving . . . imminent danger to health, or gross deception of the consumer." *See also* PHS Act 301(b), 42 U.S.C. 242o (requiring Secretary, from time to time, to issue "information related to public health" for the public and to publish weekly reports of "health conditions . . . and other pertinent health information" for health care deliverers). The explicit or implicit threat of adverse publicity is an extraordinarily powerful enforcement tool that FDA routinely uses to persuade regulated industries to "voluntarily" undertake corrective actions.

Hoxsey Cancer Clinic v. Folsom

155 F. Supp. 376 (D.D.C. 1957).

■ HOLTZOFF, DISTRICT JUDGE.

The Food and Drug Administration has issued a circular, copies of which are being posted in post offices throughout the country, warning the public that the so-called Hoxsey cancer treatment has been found worthless insofar as internal cancer is concerned. It also warns those afflicted with cancer not to be misled by the false promise that the Hoxsey cancer treatment will cure or alleviate their condition. This action is brought by Harry M. Hoxsey who claims to have treated patients afflicted with cancer, to enjoin the Secretary of the Department of Health, Education, and Welfare, and the Commissioner of the Food and Drug Administration, against the dissemination of this poster.

The defendants claim that they are acting pursuant to the authority of [Section 705(b) of the FD&C Act]. . . .

It is claimed in behalf of the plaintiff that the statute to which reference has just been made is unconstitutional as a denial of due process of law in that it does not provide for any notice or hearing, administrative or otherwise, before the Secretary disseminates information of the type described in the statute. It is elementary law, of course, that an order of an administrative agency adjudicating rights or directing someone to do or refrain from doing something must be based on a hearing after due notice. Here, however, the situation is entirely different. The defendants have made no order; they are issuing no directions. What they are doing is disseminating information and warning the public against the use of certain medicines and of a certain treatment for internal cancer. There is no basis for requiring a hearing before information can be disseminated.

But beyond that, even in the absence of this statute there would be nothing to prevent the defendants from disseminating information to the public. . . . The defendants are performing a public duty when they are urging the use of certain treatments or warning the public against the use of certain treatments. The only purpose of this statute is to place within the express scope of the duties of the Secretary something that was one of his implied functions.

If, however, the contents of the poster were erroneous then the question might arise whether they were libelous. It is a well settled rule of equity that equity does not enjoin a libel or slander, and that the only remedy for libel or slander is an action for damages if the libelous character of a statement to which objection is made can be established. . . . Naturally in a libel suit the question would arise whether there is absolute or conditional privilege, and those questions are not before the Court at this time. . . .

NOTES

1. *Privilege in Defamation Suits Against FDA Officials.* Two years after the decision in *Hoxsey Cancer Clinic*, the United States Supreme Court addressed the question that *Hoxsey* explicitly declined to address, namely, the extent of the privilege enjoyed by government officials against common law defamation suits. In *Barr v. Mateo*, a case involving a libel suit brought against the Director of the Office of Rent Stabilization, the Court embraced a broad version of the privilege, holding that executive officers are absolutely immune from defamation claims if they issued the allegedly defamatory statements in the appropriate discretionary exercise of their official duties. 360 U.S. 564, 570–74 (1959). *Barr v. Mateo* also made clear that the privilege attaches not just to high-ranking officials, but to officers anywhere in the executive hierarchy.

The *Barr v. Mateo* doctrine poses a virtually unconquerable obstacle to individuals contemplating an action against FDA officials for the dissemination of allegedly libelous information. In *Barr*, the Court assigned importance to the fact that the "issuance of press releases was standard agency practice" for the agency in question. *Id.* at 574. For FDA, publicity is not only "standard agency practice," but a practice explicitly authorized by section 705 of the FD&C Act. Unsurprisingly, in light of this legal background, defamation claims against FDA officers are extremely rare and none has been successful. In one of the few instances, post-Barr, in which such a claim was advanced, the court brushed it away effortlessly, based on the plaintiffs' failure to overcome the absolute privilege. *Ajay Nutrition Foods, Inc. v. FDA*, 378 F. Supp. 210 (D.N.J. 1974), *aff'd*, 513 F.2d 625 (3d Cir. 1975).

2. *Publicity Policy Regulations.* In 1973, based upon Ernest Gellhorn, *Adverse Publicity By Administrative Agencies*, 86 HARV. L. REV. 1380 (1973), the U.S. Administrative Conference adopted recommendations respecting the use of publicity by regulatory agencies. The primary recommendation was that agencies should adopt regulations describing the circumstances and appropriate content of agency publicity, particularly publicity related to pending administrative or judicial proceedings, and providing a procedure for retraction or correction of erroneous publicity. *See*

Recommendation 73–1: Adverse Agency Publicity, 38 Fed. Reg. 16839 (June 27, 1973). Subsequently, FDA issued proposed regulations on its publicity policy. 42 Fed. Reg. 12436 (March 4, 1977). The agency never finalized this rule, however, and it withdrew it along with 88 other pre-1986 proposed rules at 56 Fed. Reg. 42668 (Aug. 28, 1991). FDA has issued no other guidelines governing agency publicity.

3.   *Pollution of Jury Pool.* In *U.S. v. Abbott Laboratories*, 505 F.2d 565 (5th Cir. 1974), the federal district court had dismissed the indictment of Abbott officials responsible for the shipment of contaminated intravenous drugs, in part because prejudicial publicity precluded a fair trial. This prejudicial publicity included an FDA press release that not only reported the indictment, but also mentioned a Center for Disease Control determination that fifty deaths were associated with use of the contaminated drugs. The Fourth Circuit reversed the dismissal of the indictment, instructing the district court to attempt to impanel an impartial jury before concluding that a fair trial was impossible. Nonetheless, the court castigated FDA for issuing "a press release containing such prejudicial material." 505 F.2d at 571 (4th Cir. 1974).

CHAPTER 5

FDA's Place in Our Federal System

FDA and its partner federal agencies are not the sole regulators of food, drugs, and related products. State and local governments also play an important role. In many instances they share responsibility with FDA, and they act cooperatively with the federal authorities in various ways. Moreover, as explored below, state and local regulators have exclusive jurisdiction over much purely intrastate commerce. Conversely, state authority in the food and drug field is sometimes restricted by the doctrine of federal preemption, which applies to negate state regulation that is explicitly preempted by Congress or is deemed to conflict or otherwise interfere with federal regulation.

Space does not permit close examination of the law of any one state or locality, much less a survey of them all. Instead, this chapter explores the broad contours of the overlapping spheres of federal and state power in the food and drug field.

A. THE SCOPE OF FEDERAL POWER

1. INTRODUCTION

The United States Constitution grants Congress power "[t]o regulate commerce with foreign nations, and among the several States, and with the Indian tribes." U.S. CONST., Art. I, § 3. Since the early 1940s, the Supreme Court has construed the commerce clause extremely broadly. For example, the Court famously upheld Congress' authority to impose a marketing penalty on home-grown, home-consumed wheat, *Wickard v. Filburn*, 317 U.S. 111 (1942), and to prohibit racial discrimination in a restaurant frequented only by local customers, *Katzenbach v. McClung*, 379 U.S. 294 (1964).

Around the turn of the present century, the Court, in two decisions, ruled for the first time in decades that Congress had exceeded its commerce power. *United States v. Lopez*, 514 U.S. 549 (1995); *United States v. Morrison*, 529 U.S. 598 (2000). These decisions led some analysts to predict a new era of more limited federal authority over intrastate activities. But in 2005, the Court ringingly affirmed *Wickard* when it upheld the enforcement of the federal Controlled Substances Act against parties using home-grown or locally-grown marijuana for medical purposes, as permitted by California law. *Gonzales v. Raich*, 545 U.S. 1 (2005). As a constitutional matter, Congress thus appears to retain virtually unlimited power to regulate even the wholly intrastate production and sale of food, drugs, devices, and cosmetics.

Importantly, however, FDA's jurisdiction over such activities is restricted *as a statutory matter*. The scope of the FD&C Act is largely limited to products that have moved, are moving, or will be moving in interstate commerce. This is hardly surprising, for when the Act was enacted in 1938, the Supreme Court had only just begun to breathe life into the commerce power. See *NLRB v. Jones & Laughlin Steel Corp.*, 301 U.S. 1 (1937). At the time, controlling Supreme Court precedents still maintained formalistic distinctions between "commerce" and "production" and between "direct" and "indirect" effects on commerce. *See Carter v. Carter Coal Co.*, 298 U.S. 238 (1936). Moreover, the year before the enactment of the FD&C Act, the Supreme Court had held that a product was no longer in interstate commerce after "it had come to a permanent rest within [a] State." *Schechter Poultry v. United States*, 295 U.S. 495, 543 (1935). Therefore, even if Congress had desired to regulate purely local commerce in food, drugs, and cosmetics, it would have been constrained by this older commerce clause jurisprudence.

In the years since *Wickard*, Congress has expanded FDA's power over intrastate activities. For example, as discussed below, the FD&C Act was amended in 1947 to make clear that its prohibitions apply to a product that was previously shipped in interstate commerce, even if the article has changed hands numerous times within a state after its arrival there. FD&C Act 301(k), 304(a). In 1976, Congress revised the Act to permit FDA to seize misbranded or adulterated devices without proving interstate commerce at all. FD&C Act 304(a)(2). Moreover, in 1972 FDA assumed responsibility for implementing the biological product provisions of the Public Health Service Act, and that statute's prohibition against the false labeling of biological products is not restricted to articles moving in interstate commerce. PHS Act 351(b). FDA also has authority to prevent the spread of communicable diseases under section 361 of the PHSA, a provision with no interstate commerce limitations whatsoever.

Even in instances where the FD&C Act still requires there be a nexus to interstate commerce, the agency no longer has the initial burden to demonstrate this nexus in court. In 1997, Congress amended section 709 of the FD&C Act to state: "In any action to enforce the requirements of this Act respecting a device, food, drug, or cosmetic the connection with interstate commerce required for jurisdiction in such action shall be presumed to exist." (Prior to 1997, this section applied only to devices.) This is, however, a rebuttable presumption and not a delegation to FDA of complete authority over intrastate commerce.

Thus, FDA still does not have the full degree of power Congress could constitutionally give it under the commerce clause as interpreted today. All of the "prohibited acts" listed in section 301 of the FD&C Act are (either explicitly or by reference to other provisions) limited to articles that were, are, or will be in interstate commerce. Furthermore, the agency's basic authority to seize adulterated or misbranded articles under section 304 remains (with a few exceptions, including devices) limited to articles "introduced into or while in interstate commerce or while held for sale (whether or not the first sale) after shipment in interstate commerce." FD&C Act 304(a). In short, FDA cannot exercise many of the enforcement powers discussed in this chapter unless it can, if challenged, demonstrate a connection with interstate commerce.

2. "INTRODUCTION INTO INTERSTATE COMMERCE"

United States v. 7 Barrels . . . Spray Dried Whole Egg

141 F.2d 767 (7th Cir. 1944).

■ SPARKS, CIRCUIT JUDGE.

The Government appeals from a judgment dismissing its libel for want of jurisdiction. The libel, alleging adulteration, had been filed against one lot of seven barrels of dried eggs which it sought to condemn under the provisions of § 304(a) of the Federal Food, Drug, and Cosmetic Act. The claimant . . . interposed [the defense] that the libel failed to state facts indicating that the article seized was introduced into or was in interstate commerce, at the time of the seizure. . . .

The statute relied upon to confer jurisdiction provides: "Any article of food . . . that is adulterated or misbranded when introduced into or while in interstate commerce . . . shall be liable to be proceeded against while in interstate commerce, or at any time thereafter, on libel of information and condemned in any district court of the United States within the jurisdiction of which the article is found. . . ." [FD&C Act 304(a).]

The subject of the libel was part of 150 barrels of spray-dried whole eggs tendered by appellee to the Federal Surplus Commodities Corporation in part performance of a contract between the parties. . . .

. . . [T]he 7 libeled barrels . . . were rejected by the FSCC. . . . The libeled product has never been removed from appellee's plant.

Appellant contends that the contract was a transaction in interstate commerce; that the barrels were marked and set aside as the property to be used in fulfillment of the contract, thus being brought within the exclusive dominion of the out-of-state purchaser, and thereby introduced into commerce within the meaning of the statute. It further contends that the subsequent rejection of the eggs did not remove them from the jurisdiction of the Act or divest them of their interstate character.

We are not in accord with these contentions. It is clear that the contract is quite conditional in its character. It consists of an accepted offer to deliver at appellee's plant, on or before a certain date, a prescribed amount of eggs of a described character. The eggs here libeled were part of a lot intended for delivery, if accepted, within the time, and at the place named in the contract, in part performance thereof. True, they were marked and set aside in seller's plant. However, they were not thus segregated as the property to be used in fulfillment of the contract, but for inspection and testing to determine whether they complied with the required specifications. This was necessary before there could be an acceptance of the delivery, and before acceptance there could be no dominion of the FSCC over the property.

The contract provided that the product should be considered ready for delivery on the date the inspection certificate was issued, and not sooner. . . . It seems to us that the only reasons for the required preliminary marking and segregation of the barrels before the inspection and test was [sic] that actual delivery might be expedited after the acceptance, and the probability of substitution for any part of the tendered produce, without the knowledge of the FSCC, would be greatly minimized.

It is quite apparent that the object of the statute is to prevent adulterated articles of food from entering interstate commerce. That object seems to have been fully accomplished long before this libel suit was filed. After the inspection certificate was issued neither party insisted upon a delivery of the seven barrels, and that was as early as a delivery could be made under Article 7 of the contract. Appellee thereupon substituted seven other barrels in their stead and the FSCC accepted them, whereupon the State of Indiana placed an embargo upon the rejected barrels, the effect of which was to prevent their removal from the plant. Hence they could never become a part of interstate commerce.

We recognize the legal principle that goods may become a part of interstate commerce before transportation begins, and may remain such after transportation ends. The cases bearing on the former enunciate the rule that where goods are purchased in one State for transportation to another, the commerce includes the purchase quite as much as it does the transportation. . . .

In the instant case, however, the contract did not provide, nor did the parties intend that the eggs segregated and marked prior to the test would then and there become a part of interstate commerce, or that such acts would amount to a sale or delivery of them. . . .

. . . Appellant also relies on *Carter v. Carter Coal Co.*, 298 U.S. 238, where the distinction was drawn in regard to federal jurisdiction between goods which were part of a contract of sale in interstate commerce and goods merely intended to be sold in another state. There the Court said: "One who produces or manufactures a commodity, subsequently sold and shipped by him in interstate commerce, whether such sale and shipment were originally intended or not, has engaged in two distinct and separate activities. So far as he produces or manufactures a commodity, his business is purely local. So far as he sells and ships, or contracts to sell and ship, the commodity to customers in another state, he engages in interstate commerce. In respect to the former, he is subject only to regulation by the state; in respect to the latter, to regulation only by the federal government."

We have never questioned the soundness of that principle. It constitutes the basis of our conclusion. We are convinced that if appellee had sold and shipped, or contracted to ship, the seven barrels of eggs to customers in another state it would be held to have engaged in interstate commerce. However, our conclusion is that appellee never sold nor shipped, nor did it contract to sell or ship, to customers in another state the seven barrels of eggs in question.

Affirmed.

NOTES

1.   *Other Authorities. See also Hipolite Egg Co. v. United States*, 220 U.S. 45 (1911) (1906 Act's provision for seizure of an adulterated food "transported from one state . . . to another for sale" applies to food shipped for use in the manufacture of another food product); *United States v. 52 Drums of Maple Syrup*, 110 F.2d 914 (2d Cir. 1940) (adulterated food shipped in commerce is illegal even though intended for processing to bring it into compliance).

2.   *Holding Prior to Shipment. See United States v. International Exterminator Corp.*, 294 F.2d 270 (5th Cir. 1961):

> . . . [T]he defendants operate an exterminator and pest-control service for establishments such as warehouses, mills and dryers which store and sell foods such as beans, rice, flour, sugar, meal, salt, bakery supplies and also animal and poultry feed. In so doing, it is averred, the defendants are causing quantities of a poisonous liquid known as compound 1080 to be placed in the establishments in uncovered paper bait cups in close proximity to the foods. This, the complaint alleged, results in the foods being adulterated within the meaning of the Act "because of being held under insanitary conditions whereby they may have been rendered injurious to health prior to being introduced or delivered for introduction into interstate commerce." . . .

> There seems to us no question but that the complaint brings the case within the interstate commerce requirements of the Act.

United States v. Sanders

196 F.2d 895 (10th Cir. 1952).

■ HUXMAN, CIRCUIT JUDGE.

On October 17, 1951, an injunction was entered against appellee . . . enjoining him from directly or indirectly introducing or causing to be introduced, and delivering or causing to be delivered, for introduction into interstate commerce, in violation of 21 U.S.C. § 331(a), a drug which was misbranded. . . . Thereafter this action was filed in the nature of an application for an order to show cause why he should not be prosecuted for criminal contempt for a violation of the injunction. . . . [The district court] denied the application for a show cause order on the ground that the allegations of the application were insufficient to state an offense.

It is admitted that the drug in question was misbranded. Appellee's position adopted by the court is that his activities do not constitute interstate commerce as prohibited by the injunction. Prior to the injunction, appellee engaged " 'runners' or 'drummers' " who went into states other than Oklahoma and solicited orders for the drug. After the injunction . . . [a]ppellee sold only to those who came to his place of business at Wanette, Oklahoma, and delivered the drugs to them there. Many of these customers came from states other than Oklahoma.

The application for the order to show cause . . . alleged that since the issuance of the injunction appellee had . . . on January 24, 1951 . . .

sold and delivered to Loyd Mangan of Garden City, Kansas, for introduction into interstate commerce two one quart jars of said misbranded drug, with the knowledge that Mangan intended to and would return to Garden City, Kansas, with said article of drug. The complaint alleged five other specific sales made to out of state customers and alleged that all of said sales were made with the knowledge that the purchaser was from out of the state and intended to and would return to his place of residence out of the state with said drugs. It alleged that . . . appellee . . . had adopted the practice of selling and delivering his products at Wanette, Oklahoma, directly to out of state customers, soliciting them to return at later dates for more of the product, knowing that at all times said misbranded drug would be transported in interstate commerce by said purchasers for use in other states. . . .

. . . The Act must be given a reasonable construction to effectuate its salutary purposes. It prohibits not only the introduction into interstate commerce of adulterated articles but also the delivery thereof for introduction into commerce. One is as much a violation of the Act as the other. There is a long line of cases beginning with *In re Dahnke–Walker Milling Co. v. Bondurant*, 257 U.S. 282 (1921), holding that where one purchases goods in one state for transportation to another the interstate commerce transaction includes the purchase as well as the transportation. . . . The decisions . . . make it clear that whether delivery for transportation is made to a common carrier, a private carrier, or even to the purchaser for transportation by himself is immaterial.

To be guilty of violating the Act, it was not necessary that appellee be engaged in interstate commerce with respect to a misbranded drug. It was sufficient if he was engaged in delivering such a drug for introduction into interstate commerce. If appellee knowingly and regularly sold misbranded drugs and delivered them, knowing that they were purchased for transportation in interstate commerce, and solicited customers to return for future purchases and deliveries, he was guilty of a violation of the Act. . . .

The judgment is Reversed and the cause is Remanded with directions to proceed in conformity with the views expressed herein.

NOTES

1. *Supporting Authority*. See *Drown v. United States*, 198 F.2d 999 (9th Cir. 1952) (sale to buyer known to be returning to Illinois constituted delivery for introduction into interstate commerce).

2. *Dispensing of Rx Drugs*. Compare Trade Correspondence No. 183 (March 15, 1940), in which FDA provided the following reply to a physician who treated patients in several states:

> With reference to medicines given to your patients at your hospital and transported by them to their homes in some other states for use by themselves, it is our opinion that such a transaction is not interstate commerce as that term is defined in Section 201(b) of the Act. We are still of the opinion, however, that the shipment of drugs by you to patients in other states, whether by mail, express, messenger,

or otherwise, is interstate commerce, and that products so shipped are required by the statute to comply with its terms.

3. "HELD FOR SALE AFTER SHIPMENT IN INTERSTATE COMMERCE"

Whereas the cases excerpted above address when interstate commerce begins, this discussions concerns when, if ever, it ends.

As enacted in 1938, section 304(a) of the FD&C Act authorized the seizure of articles that were adulterated or misbranded "when introduced into or while in interstate commerce." FD&C Act 304(a) (pre-1948). The plain language of this provision appeared not to reach articles after they completed their interstate journey and came to rest within a state. In 1946, the Ninth Circuit Court of Appeals affirmed this interpretation, holding that section 304(a) did not empower the government to seize pasta that was adulterated while sitting in a warehouse after transmission in interstate commerce. *United States v. Phelps Dodge Mercantile Co.*, 157 F.2d 453 (9th Cir. 1946). In reaction to this decision, Congress amended section 304(a) in 1948 to also permit the seizure of an article that is adulterated or misbranded "while held for sale (whether or not the first sale) after shipment in interstate commerce." 62 Stat. 882 (1948).

In contrast to section 304(a), the original version of section 301(k) outlawed (and thus permitted injunctive and criminal proceedings with respect to) acts resulting in the misbranding of an article "if such act [was] done while such article [was] held for sale after shipment in interstate commerce." FD&C Act 301(k) (pre-1948). Some argued that this provision applied only to acts taken while an article was held for its *first* intrastate sale after shipment in interstate commerce. In the same 1948 legislation in which it revised section 304(a), Congress also amended section 301(k), both to clarify that the provision extended to intrastate sales subsequent to the first sale and to apply the provision to adulterated as well as misbranded articles. Interestingly, by the time the legislation passed, the Supreme Court had already held that section 301(k) in its original form "broadly and unqualifiedly prohibits misbranding articles held for sale after shipment in interstate commerce, without regard to how long after the shipment the misbranding occurred, how many intrastate sales had intervened, or who had received the articles at the end of the interstate shipment." *United States v. Sullivan*, 332 U.S. 689, 696 (1948). In any event, the amended version of 301(k), still in effect, leaves no doubt as to this question, prohibiting any act that results in an article being adulterated or misbranded "if such act is done while such article is held for sale (whether or not the first sale) after shipment in interstate commerce." FD&C Act 301(k).

NOTE

Proof of Shipment. Archambault v. United States, 224 F.2d 925 (10th Cir. 1955), held that interstate commerce could be proved simply by the fact that a drug produced in one state was subsequently found in another.

United States v. Geborde

278 F.3d 926 (9th Cir. 2002).

■ SILVERMAN, CIRCUIT JUDGE.

Defendant Lindley Geborde manufactured and gave away to several teenagers a home-made designer drug called gamma hydroxy butyrate, commonly known as GHB [or the "date-rape drug."]. Geborde's concoction killed one of the teenage boys who drank the stuff. Geborde was convicted of manslaughter in state court and sentenced to prison. The present case involves the efforts of federal authorities to prosecute Geborde on drug charges arising out of the same events. Although GHB is now a controlled substance as defined by federal law, it wasn't at the time, and therefore, wasn't covered by the usual federal statutes dealing with illegal drugs. Unable to bring a conventional drug case, the government charged Geborde with various violations of the Food, Drug, and Cosmetic Act ("FDCA") . . . . The problem is that the FDCA was not designed to deal with the wholly gratuitous distribution of homemade substances. We now have to decide whether the square pegs of Geborde's conduct can be pounded into the round holes of the FDCA.

Geborde was convicted of . . . seven counts of misbranding of drugs held for sale after receipt in interstate commerce, with the intent to defraud or mislead, in violation of 21 U.S.C. §§ 331(k), 333(a)(2). . . .

. . . [T]he government failed to prove an essential statutory element of the offense—that the misbranding occurred while the drug was "held for sale." The undisputed evidence established that Geborde did not sell the GHB or hold it for sale; he gave it away, free of charge, to the ultimate users with whom he socialized. Accordingly, we reverse Geborde's convictions of Counts Two through Eight and remand with directions to enter a judgment of acquittal as to those counts.

I.   Facts

In the fall of 1995, Geborde was a 25-year old aspiring disc jockey and musician from Los Angeles who moved to Yucca Valley, California and soon became something of a Pied Piper among a group of young locals. According to the testimony, he was admired as a deejay and regarded as cool. . . .

On seven different occasions between September, 1995 and January, 1996, Geborde gave his homemade GHB to his young friends. . . . [I]n each instance, at a party or in some other social setting, Geborde gave his teenage groupies GHB, either straight or mixed with vodka. . . . Count Eight is the instance in which Geborde, while partying with his young friends . . . in North Landers, California, gave GHB to 15-year-old Lucas Bielat. Bielat died from ingesting a toxic level of GHB. It is undisputed, however, that Geborde never sold or offered to sell GHB. . . .

II.   Sufficiency of the evidence

. . . .

B.   Counts II through VIII—Misbranding of drugs held for sale after receipt in interstate commerce in violation of 21 U.S.C. §§ 331(k) and 333(a)(2)

In Counts Two through Eight, Geborde was charged with misbranding of a drug after receiving it in interstate commerce, in violation of 21 U.S.C. § 331(k). The indictment also contained an allegation under 21 U.S.C. § 333(a)(2) that the offense was committed with the intent to defraud or mislead, enhancing it to a felony.

21 U.S.C. § 331(k) provides as follows:

The following acts and the causing thereof are prohibited:. . . .

(k) The alteration, mutilation, destruction, obliteration, or removal of the whole or any part of the labeling of, or the doing of any other act with respect to, a food, drug, device, or cosmetic, *if such act is done while such article is held for sale (whether or not the first sale)* after shipment in interstate commerce and results in such article being adulterated or misbranded.

(Emphasis added.)

The government does not contend that Geborde actually sold GHB or held it for sale in the usual sense. Rather, the government's position is that "held for sale" means "not for personal consumption." At the government's request, the district court instructed the jury as follows:

"All articles, including drugs, not intended for the sole consumption by the producer are deemed to be held for sale under the Federal Food, Drug and Cosmetic Act. If a producer possesses a drug with the intent of selling or giving it away to others, even if she or he also possess it in addition for his or her own personal consumption, he or she holds the drug for sale.". . . .

The government's main case is the 1911 decision in *Hipolite Egg Co. v. United States*, 220 U.S. 45 (1911), in which the Supreme Court held that eggs intended for use by a commercial bakery rather than for sale in unbroken packages were nevertheless "held for sale." The government also relies on *United States v. Torigian Labs, Inc.*, 577 F. Supp. 1514 (E.D.N.Y.), aff'd 751 F.2d 373 (2d Cir.1984), a case in which the defendants' laboratory received intra-ocular lenses from their manufacturer in order to sterilize, package, and label them before returning the lenses to the manufacturer for distribution to customers. The court rejected the defendants' argument that the lab wasn't holding the lenses for sale, but was just sterilizing and packaging them for the manufacturer. Both *Hipolite Egg* and *Torigian Labs.* clearly involve commercial transactions, commercial actors, and commercial products. The eggs and lenses, respectively, were products held for sale, in one form or another, to consumers who would buy them. They were not homemade items distributed free of charge to friends.

The government also cites *Chaney v. Heckler*, 718 F.2d 1174 (D.C. Cir. 1983) (rev'd on other grounds, *Heckler v. Chaney*, 470 U.S. 821 (1985)). This odd case was brought by prison inmates in Texas and Oklahoma seeking to require FDA regulation of lethal drugs used in executions. The court held that the drugs were subject to regulation even though they were not "held for sale" to the condemned inmate, described by the court as the "ultimate consumer." "Inquiry into the statutory scheme and legislative history of the FDCA and subsequent amendments reveals a specific congressional intent to prevent misbranding of drugs at each stage of the distribution process from manufacturer to patient." *Chaney*, 718 F.2d at 1181. *Chaney* sheds little light on the problem before us because it, too, involved the distribution of commercial drugs by an entity (to wit, a prison) that was in the business of administering them to the "ultimate consumer."

All of the FDCA "held for sale" cases of which we are aware involve individuals or entities who are in the business of distributing or handling the drug or product in question. We know of no case, much less a criminal case, in which the "held for sale" language of the FDCA has been applied to an individual who gave away a homespun drug or product in a wholly non-commercial setting.

. . . It seems clear to us that the phrase "held for sale" plainly contemplates a sale. But even if "held for sale" could somehow mean something else, in a criminal case due process requires that ambiguity be resolved against the government. The government did not have to prove that Geborde sold GHB; it would have been sufficient if the government proved that Geborde simply held the drug for sale. In this case, the government proved neither, and therefore, Geborde's convictions of Counts Two through Eight must be reversed.

By way of epilogue, we note that in March, 2000, pursuant to the Hillory J. Farias and Samantha Reid Date-Rape Drug Prohibition Act of 1999, GHB is now listed as a Schedule I controlled substance. Law enforcement authorities can now prosecute GHB cases just as they do other illegal drug cases, under the Drug Abuse Prevention and Control statutes, 21 U.S.C. § 801 et seq.

NOTES

1. *Shipment of Components in Interstate Commerce.* Although the home-brewed GHB distributed by Geborde did not itself move in interstate commerce, the ingredients he used to make the GHB (lye and common industrial solvent) apparently had so moved. As will be discussed *infra* at p. 282, an article may be deemed "held for sale after shipment in interstate commerce" based solely on the prior movement of one or more of its components across state lines.

2. *New Drugs.* Whereas the adulteration and misbranding provisions of the FD&C Act apply to actions taken subsequent to shipment of an article in interstate commerce, the new drug provisions apply only at the moment of shipment in interstate commerce. See FD&C Act 301(d), 505(a). (As discussed *infra* at p. 817, FDA has predicated its conclusion that the FD&C Act does not apply to a physician who prescribes an approved drug for an unapproved use in part on this stricter interstate commerce requirement applicable to new drugs.) On occasion, FDA loses sight of its own construction of the Act and seizes products as illegal new drugs that have not themselves been shipped in commerce. E.g., *United States v. Articles of Drug . . . Wans*, 526 F. Supp. 703 (D.P.R. 1981).

3. *Goods in Possession of Bailee.* In *U.S. v. Wiesenfeld Warehouse*, 376 U.S. 86 (1964), a warehouse was charged under amended section 301(k) for allowing food in its possession to become contaminated with filth. Among other defenses, the warehouse contended that it was a bailee of the food, not a seller, and thus that it was not holding the food "for sale" within

the meaning of section 301(k). The United States Supreme Court rejected this argument:

> The language of § 301(k) does not limit its application to one holding title to the goods, and since the danger to the public from insanitary storage of food is the same regardless of the proprietary status of the person storing it, the purpose of the legislation—to safeguard the consumer from the time the food is introduced into the channels of interstate commerce to the point that it is delivered to the ultimate consumer—would be substantially thwarted by such an unwarranted reading of the statutory language.

Id. at 92.

4. *Goods in Possession of Ultimate Consumer. United States v. Olsen,* 161 F.2d 669 (9th Cir. 1947), reversed the district court's dismissal of the government's seizure under section 304 of a misbranded device in the appellee's private home. The undisputed facts indicated that the article was misbranded when introduced into interstate commerce.

> It is immaterial, if true, that appellee had purchased and paid for the article, had it in his home, was satisfied with it and desired to keep it; that the article was not inherently dangerous or harmful; that appellee did not intend to use it commercially or permit its use by persons other than himself and his mother and brothers. . . .

Id. at 671. In compliance with the court of appeals' mandate, the same district judge that had originally dismissed the seizure reluctantly issued a seizure order. *United States v. One Article of Device Labeled Spectrochrome,* 77 F. Supp. 50 (D. Or. 1948). In doing so, the judge deplored the adoption of a country-wide "policy of entering private homes to seize articles . . . [as] governmental madness."

It is important to recognize that the basis for the section 304 seizure in this case was not that the device was misbranded by the appellee "while held for sale after shipment in interstate commerce," but rather that it had already been misbranded by others "when introduced into [and] while in interstate commerce." Consequently, although the government could seize the misbranded device in the appellee's home, it could not have penalized him under section 301(k). After all, he did not misbrand the device himself nor was he holding it for sale.

5. *FDA Jurisdiction over Restaurants and Food Stores.* Because section 301(k) of the FD&C Act prohibits the adulteration of an article "while such article is held for sale (whether or not the first sale) after shipment in interstate commerce," FDA's legal power to enforce food sanitation requirements clearly extends to restaurants, grocers, and food vending machines. Nonetheless, in light of the overwhelming number of retail food operations in the United States, and their traditional supervision by local authorities, FDA has ceded the regulation of such establishments to state and local governments. FDA's primary contribution has been to draft model ordinances and codes for voluntary adoption by state agencies and local departments. Starting in 1934, when the agency published recommended Restaurant Sanitation Regulations, it issued and

periodically revised separate model sanitation codes for restaurants, food stores, and vending establishments.

In 1974, the agency, concerned about the lack of uniformity in federal, state, and local regulation, proposed to make the restaurant code mandatory by issuing a revision of it in the form of an administrative rule. 39 Fed. Reg. 35438 (October 1, 1974). State officials opposed this action, primarily because "it abridged a long-term understanding between the States and the Federal government regarding the regulation of the food service industry. . . ." 42 Fed. Reg. 15428 (March 22, 1977). In response to these comments, FDA withdrew the proposal, declaring that "it was never [the agency's] intention to supersede State and local regulation of food service sanitation. . . ." *Id.*

Since 1993, FDA has combined the model sanitation codes for restaurants, food stores, and vending establishments into one model "Food Code," which the agency revises every two years. As of 2011, 49 states and three territories have adopted a version of the Food Code. See "Real Progress in Food Code Adoptions," FDA CFSAN (July 1, 2011).

4. Components Shipped in Interstate Commerce

Even if a food, drug, or cosmetic is itself not shipped in interstate commerce, it is almost always made from ingredients that have been so shipped.

Baker v. United States

932 F.2d 813 (9th Cir. 1991).

■ Boochever, Circuit Judge

OVERVIEW

. . . Baker was convicted of misbranding certain drugs, in violation of the Federal Food, Drug, and Cosmetic Act (FDCA). He moved to vacate his sentence under 28 U.S.C. § 2255, for lack of federal jurisdiction, arguing that the transactions set out in the information charging him were wholly intrastate in nature. The district court found a sufficient nexus to interstate commerce. We AFFIRM.

BACKGROUND

Baker manufactured a drug that was sold as synthetic heroin. As sold, the package contained no labels identifying the drug, its effects, or the proper dosage. Baker and others entered a *nolo* plea to a seven-count superseding indictment charging them with violating 21 U.S.C. § 331(k) as they

> caused an act to be done, and aided and abetted the act being done with respect to a drug, an analog of fentanyl, while such drug was held for sale, after components of the drug were shipped in interstate commerce, which act resulted in the drug being misbranded.

Baker was sentenced to three consecutive one-year terms on the first three counts, and a four-year term of probation in exchange for a suspended sentence on the remaining four counts.

Baker filed . . . a motion to vacate his sentence. . . . The motion was denied and this appeal was taken.

DISCUSSION

Essentially, Baker's argument . . . is that notwithstanding that the component parts of the synthetic heroin traveled in interstate commerce, the manufacture and distribution of the end product all occurred in California, so that the interstate commerce link is missing. In other words, he reads § 331(k) to require that the misbranded drug . . . and not the components alone travel in interstate commerce.

A plain reading of § 331(k) supports affirmance. Reading only the part of the relevant subsection, the question is whether Baker did anything with respect to the drug, while it was held for sale and after shipment in interstate commerce, that results in the drug being misbranded. He did. There was a failure to label, done while or before the synthetic heroin was held for sale, which occurred after a shipment in interstate commerce.

The shipment in interstate commerce, of course, did not involve the synthetic heroin but the ingredients combined to make it. The FDCA defines the term "drug," however, to include "articles intended for use as a component of" a recognized drug. See 21 U.S.C. § 321(g)(1)(A) & (D). Thus, the "shipment in interstate commerce" requirement is satisfied even when only an ingredient is transported interstate. . . .

. . . [T]he better-reasoned cases are consistent with this reading, concluding that the "shipment in interstate commerce" requirement of § 331(k) is satisfied when the misbranded drug held for intrastate sale contains ingredients shipped in interstate commerce. *See United States v. An Article of Food . . . Coco Rico,* 752 F.2d 11, 14 (1st Cir. 1985) ("Because it is undisputed that the potassium nitrate added to the seized beverages was shipped in interstate commerce, those beverages[, although mixed and sold only intrastate,] clearly fall within the scope of statutory forfeiture jurisdiction."); *United States v. Dianovin Pharmaceuticals, Inc.,* 475 F.2d 100, 103 (1st Cir.), *cert. denied,* 414 U.S. 830 (1973) ("The appellants' use of components shipped in interstate commerce to make vitamin K for injection brought their activities within § 331(k). . . . ").

Baker's whole argument relies on a thirty-year old case from the Eastern District of Michigan, *United States v. An Article or Device Consisting of 31 Units (Gonsertron),* 180 F. Supp. 52 (E.D. Mich. 1959). There, the district court, in a six-paragraph decision, dismissed the government's motion to seize a misbranded device. Nine component parts, apparently all of which traveled in interstate commerce, were used in manufacturing the device. The court concluded that 21 U.S.C. § 321(h)—defining "device"—"does not attempt to regulate devices solely by reason of the fact that they contain component parts shipped in interstate commerce." *Id.* at 53.

The government attempts to distinguish *Gonsertron* on the ground that it "involved a device, not drugs" and that "the Act specifically includes within its definition the *components* of a drug." (emphasis added). This distinction is of no help as the definition of "device," albeit with slightly different language, also includes *components* of devices. 21 U.S.C. § 321(h). The better distinction is simply that, as the government points out, *Gonsertron* was incorrectly decided, and, in any case, does not represent the current state of the law. Indeed, a subsequent case in its own jurisdiction has thrown the result in *Gonsertron* into doubt.

In *United States v. 39 Cases . . . Michigan Brand Korleen Tablets,* 192 F. Supp. 51 (E.D. Mich. 1961) the same district judge who wrote *Gonsertron* held that tablets compounded in Michigan from ingredients that moved in interstate commerce were properly seizable, reasoning that "it would be a strained interpretation to say that each 'drug' component falls within the jurisdiction of the Act, being shipped in interstate commerce, but, when compounded together to form another 'drug,' the finished product is not being held for sale after shipment in interstate commerce." *Id.* at 52. The judge offered the following distinction between the cases:

> In [*Gonsertron*], the Court[] held that . . . [a] device is not subject to the jurisdiction of the Act where the only components shipped in interstate commerce were either a minor ingredient of the final product or several commonly used components which lost their identity within the newly manufactured device. In contrast, in the case at bar, the 'drugs' comprising the Korleen Tablets are the very heart of the manufactured and tableted 'drug' and were proclaimed as such to the public.

Korleen Tablets, 192 F. Supp. at 52.

This distinction, heavily relied upon by *Baker,* seems fairly strained . . . . Baker's theory cannot withstand the Supreme Court's opinion in *United States v. Generix Drug Corp.,* 460 U.S. 453, 457–61 (1983). In *Generix,* the Court decided that the term "drug" as used in the FDCA includes both active and inactive ingredients of chemical compounds. *Id.* Thus, whether the ingredient is a main one or minor one, or whether it is identifiable or unidentifiable after combination is inconsequential.

CONCLUSION

We hold that wholly intrastate manufactures and sales of drugs are covered by 21 U.S.C. § 331(k) as long as an ingredient used in the final product travelled in interstate commerce. . . .

AFFIRMED.

NOTES

1. *Supporting Authority.* For other cases holding that shipment of product ingredients in interstate commerce is sufficient to confer jurisdiction on FDA, see *United States v. Cassaro, Inc.,* 443 F.2d 153 (1st Cir. 1971); *Palmer v. United States,* 340 F.2d 48 (5th Cir. 1964); *United States v. Detroit Vital Foods, Inc.,* 330 F.2d 78 (6th Cir. 1964); *United States v. Allbrook Freezing & Cold Storage,* 194 F.2d 937 (5th Cir. 1952). Most recently, the United States District Court for the District of Columbia held that a procedure in which stem cells are isolated from a patient's bone marrow, grown to greater numbers, and then injected back into the same patient is subject to FDA jurisdiction, because the defendant doctors combine the cell product with an antibiotic shipped from out of state before

administering it to the patient. *United States v. Regenerative Sciences*, 878 F. Supp.2d 248 (D.D.C. 2012) (excerpted *infra* p. 1179).

2. *Food Components and Loss of Identity.* In *United States v. 40 Cases . . . "Pinocchio Brand 75% Corn, Peanut Oil and Soya Bean Oil Blended With 25% Pure Olive Oil"*, 289 F.2d 343 (2d Cir. 1961), the court held that FDA had jurisdiction over a blended oil that was sold only intrastate because the component oils were imported from other states and from foreign nations. Nevertheless, the court remarked on the fact that both the components and the final product were "oil," and it held out the possibility that FD&C Act 301(k) would not apply in "a case in which oil which was transported interstate was used as one of many ingredients in a finished product which in no way resembled the food which had crossed state lines." *Id.* at 345–46. This apparent embrace, in *dictum*, of the "loss of identity" approach for food components is almost certainly contrary to the law today, in light of *Baker* and other cases cited above. Note that the definition of "food," like those of "drug" and "device," includes "components" of the article. FD&C Act 201(f).

5. MEDICAL DEVICES

The Medical Device Amendments of 1976 amended section 304(a) of the FD&C Act to authorize seizure (but not criminal penalties or injunctive action) against misbranded or adulterated devices without proof of interstate commerce.

United States v. Undetermined Quantities of an Article of Device . . . "Depilatron Epilator"

473 F. Supp. 913 (S.D.N.Y. 1979).

■ SAND, DISTRICT JUDGE.

This action is an in rem proceeding . . . for forfeiture and condemnation of a depilatory device. Claimant has moved to dismiss the complaint on the grounds that 21 U.S.C. § 334(a)(2) "is unconstitutional on its face as a violation of the commerce clause of the United States Constitution.". . .

Section 334(a) provides for the seizure of, inter alia, adulterated or misbranded devices. Prior to 1976, it was a requirement of such seizures that the device in question have been introduced into interstate commerce. Subsection 334(a) was amended in 1976, however, so as to include adulterated or misbranded devices in the class of articles which are "liable to be proceeded against at any time on libel of information" without regard to interstate commerce.

Claimant concedes that "Congress may regulate not only interstate commerce, but also those wholly intrastate activities which it concludes have an affect [sic] upon interstate commerce." Claimant's contention is, rather, that where Congress seeks to regulate intrastate activities, "a proper nexus to interstate commerce must be made by Congress in order to justify [the] departure from the Commerce Clause," and that Congress has failed to make the required findings.

The legislative history of the 1976 amendment contains no express consideration of the impact of the intrastate sale and distribution of medical devices on interstate commerce. It was, however, the clear intent of Congress

> to authorize the seizure of devices which are distributed wholly in intrastate commerce. This provision will be applicable to all devices and will assist enforcement by doing away with the cumbersome and time consuming task of establishing interstate shipment. This provision will be particularly useful against quack devices.

S.Rep.No. 94–33, 94th Cong.1st Sess. 14 (1976). . . .

The Government argues that § 334(a)(2) is a valid exercise of Congress' power under the Commerce Clause, and that its legislative history "plainly implies [that] effective protection of the public health and safety would be sacrificed were Congress to have required that the source and destination of all allegedly adulterated or misbranded devices be determined in seizure cases." Moreover, the Government argues that

> [w]ith respect to the absence of express legislative history regarding the impact of the intrastate sale and distribution of medical devices on interstate commerce, it is enough that this Court perceive a basis upon which Congress could have predicated a judgment that such a nexus exists. . . .

We agree that the absence of formal findings as to the nexus between intrastate sale and distribution of medical devices and interstate commerce is not fatal, as long as Congress had a rational basis for finding such a nexus. Congress alluded to the proliferation of medical devices and to the danger posed by unsafe and ineffective devices to the public health and safety. In light of the extensive hearings held by Congress with respect to the 1976 legislation, we find that Congress did have a sufficient basis for concluding that the regulation of the intrastate sale and distribution of medical devices was necessary for the proper regulation of interstate commerce. . . .

NOTE

Presumption of Interstate Nexus. In addition to permitting FDA to seize misbranded or adulterated devices without proving interstate commerce, the Device Amendments added a new section 709 to the Act, which provided: "In any action to enforce the requirements of this Act respecting a device the connection with interstate commerce required for jurisdiction in such action shall be presumed to exist." (Emphasis added.) This provision was intended to establish a rebuttable presumption in order to relieve FDA of the burden of demonstrating a connection with interstate commerce in criminal and injunction proceedings. See H.R. Rep. No. 94–853, 94th Cong., 2nd Sess. 15 (1976). In 1997, as noted previously, this provision was amended to embrace foods, drugs, and cosmetics, as well.

6. BIOLOGICS

The licensing requirement for biological products, like the new drug approval process, applies only to articles "introduce[ed] or deliver[ed] for introduction into interstate commerce." *Compare* section 351(a) of the Public Health Service Act, 42 U.S.C. 262(a), *with* FD&C Act 505(a).

Unlike the FD&C Act's prohibitions against drug misbranding, however, the PHS Act's prohibition against "falsely labeling or marking" a biological product is not limited to articles in interstate commerce. *Compare* PHS Act 351(b), 42 U.S.C. 262(b), *with* FD&C Act 301(a)–(c), (k). Moreover, FDA's power under section 361 of the PHSA to issue regulations to prevent the introduction, transmission, or spread of communicable diseases has no interstate commerce restrictions. 42 U.S.C. 264.

United States v. Calise

217 F. Supp. 705 (S.D.N.Y. 1962).

■ CASHIN, DISTRICT JUDGE.

The voluminous eighty count indictment in the above entitled action charges defendants, John P. Calise and Westchester Blood Service, Inc., with several types of violations of the Public Health Service Act and the Federal Food, Drug and Cosmetic Act, and a conspiracy to violate those statutes. . . .

The defendants . . . assert that counts . . . alleging violations of the mislabeling provisions of 42 U.S.C. § 262(b), are not within the jurisdiction of this court because the acts complained of occurred entirely within the boundaries of the State of New York. The subsection reads as follows:

> "(b) No person shall falsely label or mark any package or container of any virus, serum, toxin, antitoxin, or other product aforesaid; nor alter any label or mark on any package or container of any virus, serum, toxin, antitoxin, or other product aforesaid so as to falsify such label or mark."

The language in subsection (b) does not indicate that Congress intended the effect of the statute to be confined merely to products moving in interstate commerce. The restrictive interpretation of subdivision (b) which the defendants urge is not persuasive, in view of the fact that Congress could very easily have expressed such an intention in the Public Health Service Act, as it was cautious to do in 21 U.S.C. § 331(k) where such an intention actually existed. Furthermore, the manner in which Congress separated the mislabeling ban of Section 262(b) from the labeling requirements of Section [262(a)(1)(B)] would seem to be indicative of an intention that Section 262(b) was to reach further in its scope from Section 262(a). To restrict Section 262(b) exclusively to products moving in interstate commerce would also be inconsistent with the general purpose of the Public Health Service Act as a whole, because such an interpretation would encourage unscrupulous distributors to sell falsely labeled products on the local market which have been marked so as to apparently meet federal standards, but which do not meet those standards. This would grant such distributors a definite advantage in competing with those who sell interstate products which fulfill the licensing and labeling requirements of 42 U.S.C. § 262(a).

. . . .

NOTES

1.   *Joint Reliance on FD&C Act and Biologics Act*. In the preambles to its proposed and final GMP regulations for the collection, processing, and storage of human blood and blood components, 39 Fed. Reg. 18614 (May 28, 1974), 40 Fed. Reg. 53532 (Nov. 18, 1975), FDA invoked both the drug provisions of the FD&C Act and sections 351(b) and 361 of the Biologics Act, thus exerting regulatory control over both interstate and intrastate blood banks. More recently, FDA has followed a similar approach in designing its system for the regulation of human cellular and tissue-based products, invoking both the drug and device provisions of the FD&C Act and section 361 of the PHS Act. E.g., 63 Fed. Reg. 26744, 26747–48 (May 14, 1998) (proposed establishment registration rule and summary of overall approach); 69 Fed. Reg. 68612, 68613–14 (Nov. 24, 2004) (current good tissue practice final rule).

2.   *Turtle Ban. State of Louisiana v. Mathews*, 427 F. Supp. 174 (E.D. La. 1977), upheld FDA's ban on intrastate as well as interstate commerce in small turtles to prevent the spread of communicable disease under section 361 of the Public Health Service Act.

3.   *FDA Jurisdiction over Human Cloning*. As discussed *infra* at p. 1186, FDA has asserted jurisdiction over "clinical research using cloning technology to create a human being." See "Dear Colleague" Letter from Stuart L. Nightingale, Associate Commissioner, FDA (Oct. 26, 1998). Without citing specific provisions, the agency claimed power under both the PHS Act and the FD&C Act to require an approved investigational new drug application (IND) for such research. *Id.* FDA has not, however, publicly addressed how these statutes authorize it to regulate human cloning that is conducted entirely intrastate.

A scientist cloning a human being would fuse an enucleated egg with the nucleus of a regular adult cell, for example a skin cell, taken from the person to be cloned. The scientist would then implant the resulting embryo in a woman. If the enucleated egg and nucleic DNA were both obtained from local people (or one local woman), and the resulting embryo were carried by a local woman (perhaps the same woman), the physician or researcher would not be introducing an unapproved drug into interstate commerce in violation of section 301(d) of the FD&C Act or an unlicensed biological product into interstate commerce in violation of section 351(a) of the PHSA. However, as illustrated by FDA's recent successful exertion of authority over a stem cell procedure in *United States v. Regenerative Sciences, infra* p. 1179, the agency would likely gain a jurisdictional hook if the enucleated egg, the nucleic DNA, or the embryo were combined with a substance that had been shipped in interstate commerce.

Section 361 of the PHSA does not have any interstate commerce limitations, and, indeed, FDA based its general regulations on human cellular and tissue-based products in part on this provision. But this section is relevant only to measures designed to prevent the spread of communicable diseases and thus does not seem to empower the agency to impose an IND requirement for human cloning. FDA could clearly demand investigational device exemptions (IDEs) for the devices used in cloning experiments, assuming they moved in interstate commerce. But this tactic would only work with respect to instruments that were represented for use in cloning, or were in fact used almost exclusively for that purpose. Perhaps for this reason, the "Dear Colleague" letter on human cloning does not even mention FDA's medical device authorities.

In short, the interstate commerce limitations in the FD&C Act and PHSA raise important unanswered questions about the agency's asserted authority to prevent human cloning experiments.

4. *Oleomargarine.* The Oleomargarine Act of 1950. 20 (1950), added section 407 to the FD&C Act, regulating all "colored" (yellow) margarine sold at retail establishments or used in public eating places. The legislation mandates prominent label disclosure on all packages of colored margarine. FD&C Act 407(b). Moreover, the law requires restaurants serving colored margarine to disclose this fact on a prominent placard or menu statement, and it directs that they serve it only in triangular portions with labeling identifying the food as margarine. FD&C Act 407(c). Because of the FD&C Act's interstate commerce language, Congress was concerned that margarine produced and sold intrastate would evade these requirements designed to prevent consumer confusion. The legislation thus also added Section 407(a), which explicitly provides, "Colored oleomargarine or colored margarine which is sold in the same State or Territory in which it is produced shall be subject in the same manner and to the same extent to the provisions of this Act as if it had been introduced in interstate commerce."

B. THE ELUSIVE GOAL OF UNIFORMITY OF STATE LAWS

As has been noted elsewhere:

> The 1906 [Pure Food and Drugs] Act and its successor, the Federal Food, Drug, and Cosmetic Act of 1938, were a reflection of the emerging nationwide food marketing system in this country. Nonetheless, in spite of a [long] tradition of a single federal statute governing the food supply, and a marketing system that knows no political bounds, there remain today the persistent vestiges of inconsistent state and local laws and regulations reflecting the piecemeal approach to food regulation that characterized the 1800's. . . .

Peter Barton Hutt, *The Basis and Purpose of Government Regulation of Adulteration and Misbranding of Food*, 33 FOOD DRUG COSM. L. J. 505 (1978).

State regulatory officials have long been troubled by the diversity of state laws. In 1897, representatives from ten states met "for the purpose of forming a national association . . . with the end in view of producing, as nearly as conditions and laws would permit, uniformity of action in the enforcement of such [food and drug] laws." The 1897 constitution of the resulting organization, the Association of Food and Drug Officials (AFDO), declared that its purpose was "to promote and foster such legislation as would tend to protect public health and prevent deception . . . also to promote uniformity in legislation and rulings. . . ." William F. Reindollar, *The Association of Food and Drug Officials*, 6 FOOD DRUG COSM. L.J. 52, 53, 54 (1951).

Promotion of uniform laws continues to be a primary goal of the AFDO. According to the organization's mission statement, available on its website, the AFDO "successfully fosters uniformity in the adoption and enforcement of science-based food, drug, medical devices, cosmetics and product safety laws, rules, and regulations." This statement states that one of ways AFDO pursues this mission is by "[p]romoting the adoption and uniform enforcement of laws and regulations at all levels of government." For our purposes, the most important effort by AFDO to promote uniformity is its promulgation of the Uniform State Food, Drug, and Cosmetic Act, which is based on the 1938 federal statute. As of 2012, 42 of the 50 states have adopted the Uniform FD&C Act. *See* FDA Investigations Operations Manual 3.3.3 (rev. 2012) (describing the laws of each state).

Despite the widespread adoption of the Uniform FD&C Act, significant variation remains among the food and drug laws of the different states. This lack of uniformity exists for several reasons. First, of all, a few states have adopted only part of the Uniform Act. Secondly, a few other states have not enacted any of the Uniform FD&C Act and have instead adopted the 1906 Pure Food and Drugs Act. Third, and importantly, although the Uniform FD&C Act includes a provision for automatic adoption of ongoing amendments to the federal FD&C Act, fewer than half of the states that have adopted all or part of the Uniform Act have adopted this automatic adoption provision. Finally, even states that have adopted the Uniform FD&C Act sometimes pass additional statutes that affect the food and drug arena.

Another problematic issue is the uniformity of regulations, as opposed to statutes. The Uniform State Food, Drug, and Cosmetic Act authorizes states "to make the regulations promulgated under this Act conform, insofar as practicable, with those promulgated under the Federal Act." Most state laws contain a provision that urges or requires consistency with FDA regulations. Enforcing compliance with these provisions, however, has not proved easy. For example, in *American Grain Products Processing Institute v. Department of Public Health*, 467 N.E.2d 455 (Mass. 1984), the court decided (4–3) that, even though a state statute provided that any state standard or tolerance must conform to a federal standard or tolerance, Massachusetts could establish a tolerance for ethylene dibromide (EDB) in food in the face of a federal EPA "exemption from tolerance." In *Processed Apples Institute, Inc. v. Department of Public Health*, 522 N.E.2d 965 (Mass. 1988), the court held (5–1) that the same statute was intended to set a floor and not a ceiling and that Massachusetts could "conform" to the federal tolerance by imposing a more stringent limit on residues of the pesticide daminozide on apple products. Complicating matters is the fact that some states prohibit prospective adoption of regulations. In these states, the legislature may incorporate by reference only those FDA regulations in effect at the time it enacts legislation. *See* Thomas Christopher, *May a State Adopt Prospective Federal Regulations*, 15 Food Drug Cosm. L.J. 373 (1960).

Melvin Hinich & Richard Staelin, *Regulation of the U.S. Food Industry*

Appendix, VI Study on Federal Regulation, S. Doc. No. 96–14 (1st Session 1978).

Why does food regulation differ among the states? We suggest two factors: local special interest groups use their influence in state legislatures to secure a competitive advantage, and special features exist between differing locales, leading to a heterogeneity of preferences across regions. In other words the economic and social forces which affect food regulation at the national level are also present at the state and even local level. Just as U.S. producers profit from Federal regulations which raise the costs of foreign producers, local producers profit from regulations which give them a competitive edge over their competitors in other regions. The consumers pay for any profits which result from constraints on free trade, although they also get the benefits of being protected by the regulatory actions of the Government. Not all the profits, however, go to the producers; labor unions and local suppliers can also benefit at the expense of others. Since there are fewer special interest groups in a state or local region as compared to the nation as a whole, it is probably easier for these groups to organize to exert effective pressure for restrictive regulations. . . .

Arguments made for uniformity of legislation stress the desirability of modernizing food laws, regulations, and standards. Uniform legislation is said to be needed to protect consumers' health, assure high quality food, and eliminate objectionable trade barriers. . . .

Another argument for uniformity of state food laws by the food industry is that concerning productivity. Non-uniform statutes are said to necessitate additional production lines for the same product to meet different requirements, thereby reducing productivity. Some other arguments for uniformity stress that the legal interpretation of acts in state courts are [sic] unpredictable—adding more uncertainty to the business. With uniform legislation, a state can coordinate state enforcement efforts with the FDA (e.g., supplementing field forces, exchange of laboratory results, and use of FDA resources where expert testimony is needed). State scientific resources can be devoted to enforcement of federally established standards, revising them as special circumstances or doubt[s] arise.

While there is general support for uniformity, this does not necessarily translate into proof that Federal pre-emption of state food and drug law is best for the consumer. States have provided much impetus for food and drug legislation and uniformity in law and regulation, have played a crucial part in enforcing Federal pre-emptive legislation, and have shown a willingness to adopt uniform regulations (e.g., the Interstate Milk Shippers Program). Moreover, without any say, state legislators may be more reluctant to appropriate state funds to enforce Federal laws and regulations. Also, states have expressed a desire to retain the authority to require nutritional standards and maintain enforcement ability over and above that of the Federal government. Differing regulations also allow for different sensibilities among geographic areas in regard to ingredients in meat or other products.

As with Federal agencies, state and local units can regulate either by banning or providing information. In our opinion it seems reasonable for a local government, whose citizens have very different risk preferences from the rest of the nation, to exercise its judgment and ban a product from its region, since this does not impose costs on other consumer groups. Jurisdictional duplication and conflict about product labeling, on the other hand, cause economic losses to everyone, since there normally exist economies of scale in production and marketing which are unrealized if labeling regulations vary by region. For example, if label requirements vary by area, major food producers can not advantageously use the low mass distribution systems now available. This implies a significant economic advantage for a uniform national labeling code which would allow firms to market their products without having to worry about specific labels for individual areas. . . .

C. FEDERAL PREEMPTION AND THE LIMITS OF STATE POWER

1. INTRODUCTION

A court may find that a federal statute preempts a particular state law in a variety of circumstances. First is the situation known as "express preemption," where the federal statute in question includes a preemption provision explicitly declaring that some or all state law is displaced. Second, under the theory of "implied field preemption," a court may find that the comprehensiveness of a federal scheme demonstrates congressional intent to occupy the field exclusively, despite the absence of express statutory language to this effect. Third, a court may find that there is "conflict preemption." This third type of preemption contains two subcategories; (1) "impossibility" preemption, when it is physically impossible for a party to comply with both the federal and state requirements and (2) "obstacle preemption," where a court deems a state law to be an obstacle to the accomplishment and execution of Congress' full purposes and objectives. This section will explore each of these theories in the food and drug context, although not in the order presented above. The application of preemption doctrine becomes more complicated in the context of private suits for damages; this topic will be explored later in the book. *Infra* pp. 894, 1280.

2. HISTORICAL BACKGROUND

Early support for comprehensive federal food and drug legislation was driven largely by the desire for uniformity. In an 1879 address to the Medical Society of the State of New York, Dr. E. R. Squibb advocated the enactment of a nationwide food and drug law, asserting: "It is self-evident that a law to be most effective in preventing the adulteration of food and medicine should be general or national in order to secure universality and uniformity of action. . . ." E.R. SQUIBB, PROPOSED LEGISLATION ON THE ADULTERATION OF FOOD AND MEDICINE 3 (1879). About twenty years later, the Chief of the USDA Food Laboratory argued for national legislation because "[b]y no other means can we hope to secure laws uniform in their scope, requirements and penalties among ourselves. . . ." Willard Bigelow, *The Development of*

Pure Food Legislation, 7 SCIENCE 505, 512 (1898). Five years after that, Harvey Wiley, the renowned Chief of the USDA Bureau of Chemistry, stated that federal legislation was necessary "to secure uniformity in the composition of drugs. . . ." Harvey Wiley, *Drugs and Their Adulteration and The Laws Relating Thereto*, 2 WASH. MED. ANNALS205 (1903).

Because of strong feelings in Congress that food and drug regulation was properly a matter for states and localities, supporters of federal legislation faced an uphill battle. At first glance, they may have appeared to have triumphed with the passage of the 1906 Pure Food and Drugs Act. The House Report accompanying the 1906 Act stated:

> The laws and regulations of the different States are diverse, confusing, and often contradictory. What one State now requires the adjoining State may forbid. Our food products are not raised principally in the States of their consumption.

> State boundary lines are unknown in our commerce, except by reason of local regulations and laws, such as State pure-food laws. It is desirable, as far as possible, that the commerce between the States be unhindered. One of the hoped-for good results of a national law on the subject of pure foods is the bringing about of a uniformity of laws and regulations on the part of the States within their own several borders.

H.R. Rep. No. 5056, 59th Cong., 1st Sess. 8–9 (1906).

Nonetheless, the 1906 Act did not establish a comprehensive national regulatory scheme. The effectiveness of a federal statute in creating national uniformity depends on two factors: (1) the extension of the federal requirements to local, as well as interstate, transactions, and (2) the preemptive force of the statute over state laws. The 1906 statute fell short in both respects. As explored above, the 1938 FD&C Act's reach into local affairs is even today somewhat limited by its provisions restricting the application of the statute, in many instances, to articles that will be, are, or were in interstate commerce. *See supra* pp. 271–289. As is also discussed above, *supra* p. 277, until 1948, the FD&C Act did not clearly apply to articles after they came to rest in a state. (1948 was the year that the Supreme Court decided *U.S. v. Sullivan* and that Congress enacted amendments to rectify the *Phelps Dodge* decision). In this respect, the 1906 Pure Food and Drugs Act was even more modest than the original 1938 statute; according to section 2 of the 1906 legislation, the only intrastate transactions covered by the law were deliveries of articles "in original unbroken packages" by people who had received these articles in interstate commerce. 21 U.S.C. 2 (1906). This limitation may have reflected Congress's doubt about the reach of its jurisdiction.

The 1906 statute, as interpreted by the Supreme Courts, also did little to preempt state laws. In *Savage v. Jones*, 225 U.S. 501 (1912), the Court held that the Pure Food and Drugs Act did not preempt an Indiana statute regulating the sale and labeling of animal feed. The Court declared: "[T]he intent to supersede the exercise by the State of its police power as to matters not covered by the Federal legislation . . . is not to be implied unless the act of Congress fairly interpreted in actual conflict with the law of the State." *Id.* at 539. In *McDermott v.*

Wisconsin, 228 U.S. 115 (1913), the Court rejected the contention that 1906 Act "passed under the authority of the Constitution has taken possession of this field of regulation and that the state act is a wrongful interference with the exclusive power of Congress over interstate commerce . . . ." *Id.* at 127. The Court explained: "While these regulations are within the power of Congress, it by no means follows that the State is not permitted to make regulations, with a view to the protection of its people against fraud or imposition by impure food or drugs." *Id.* at 131.

The Court was willing to find that the 1906 Act preempted state laws when there was a direct conflict—as indeed it did in *McDermott* itself. But following the *McDermott* decision, the Supreme Court repelled effort after effort to demonstrate that other state laws conflicted with the Pure Food and Drugs Act. *See Price v. Illinois*, 238 U.S. 446 (1915); *Armour & Co. v. North Dakota*, 240 U.S. 510 (1916); *Weigle v. Curtice Bros. Co.*, 248 U.S. 285 (1919); *Hebe Co. v. Shaw*, 248 U.S. 297 (1919).

Leading up to the passage of the 1938 statute, senators debated whether the better path to national uniformity was amendment of the 1906 Act or the enactment of an entirely new law. *See* S. Rep. No. 74–361 (1st Sess. 2–3 1935). The latter approach prevailed, but as the materials below illustrate, the preemptive force of the 1938 FD&C Act and other federal food and drug-related statutes have never been powerful enough to squelch the continued enactment and enforcement of state and local food and drug laws.

3. FIELD PREEMPTION

Although federal food and drug statutes contain a few explicit preemption provisions relating to particular products or topics, *see infra* p. 310, the FD&C Act does not contain a general preemption clause. Consequently, litigants contending that state statutes and regulations are preempted by federal law in this area usually must rely on one of the other theories of preemption. One of these arguments—the contention that Congress has impliedly "occupied the field" of food and drug regulation—has apparently failed in every case in which it has been advanced.

In the following case, involving the biologics provisions of the Public Health Service Act (which lack an explicit preemption provision), the United States Supreme Court rejected both a field preemption argument and a secondary claim of obstacle preemption.

Hillsborough County v. Automated Medical Laboratories, Inc.

471 U.S. 707 (1985).

■ JUSTICE MARSHALL delivered the opinion of the Court.

The question presented is whether the federal regulations governing the collection of blood plasma from paid donors pre-empt certain local ordinances.

Appellee Automated Medical Laboratories, Inc., is a Florida corporation that operates, through subsidiaries, eight blood plasma centers in the United States. One of the centers, Tampa Plasma Corporation (TPC), is located in Hillsborough County, Florida. Appellee's plasma centers collect blood plasma from donors by employing a procedure called plasmapheresis. . . . Appellee sells the plasma to pharmaceutical manufacturers.

Vendors of blood products, such as TPC, are subject to federal supervision. Under § 351(a) of the Public Health Service Act, such vendors must be licensed by the Secretary of Health and Human Services (HHS). Licenses are issued only on a showing that the vendor's establishment and blood products meet certain safety, purity, and potency standards established by the Secretary. HHS is authorized to inspect such establishments for compliance.

Pursuant to § 351 of the Act, the Food and Drug Administration (FDA), as the designee of the Secretary, has established standards for the collection of plasma. 21 C.F.R. §§ 640.60–640.76 (1984). . . .

In 1980, Hillsborough County [in Florida] adopted Ordinances 80–11 and 80–12. . . .

Ordinance 80–12 establishes a countywide identification system, which requires all potential donors to obtain from the County Health Department an identification card, valid for six months, that may be used only at the plasmapheresis center specified on the card. The ordinance incorporates by reference the FDA's blood plasma regulations, but also imposes donor testing and recordkeeping requirements beyond those contained in the federal regulations. Specifically, the ordinance requires that donors be tested for hepatitis prior to registration, that they donate at only one center, and that they be given a breath analysis for alcohol content before each plasma donation. . . .

The county has promulgated regulations to implement Ordinance 80–12. . . .

In arguing that the Hillsborough County ordinances and regulations are pre-empted, appellee faces an uphill battle. The first hurdle that appellee must overcome is the FDA's statement, when it promulgated the plasmapheresis regulations in 1973, that it did not intend its regulations to be exclusive. In response to comments expressing concern that the regulations governing the licensing of plasmapheresis facilities "would pre-empt State and local laws governing plasmapheresis," the FDA explained in a statement accompanying the regulations that "[t]hese regulations are not intended to usurp the powers of State or local authorities to regulate plasmapheresis procedures in their localities."

The question whether the regulation of an entire field has been reserved by the Federal Government is, essentially, a question of ascertaining the intent underlying the federal scheme. In this case, appellee concedes that neither Congress nor the FDA expressly preempted state and local regulation of plasmapheresis. Thus, if the county ordinances challenged here are to fail they must do so either because Congress or the FDA *implicitly* pre-empted the whole field of plasmapheresis regulation, or because particular provisions in the local ordinances conflict with the federal scheme. . . .

The FDA's statement is dispositive on the question of implicit intent to pre-empt unless either the agency's position is inconsistent with clearly expressed congressional intent, *see Chevron U.S.A. Inc. v. NRDC, Inc.,* 467 U.S. 837, 842–845, or subsequent developments reveal a change in that position. Given appellee's first argument for implicit pre-emption—that the comprehensiveness of the FDA's regulations evinces an intent to pre-empt—any pre-emptive effect must result from the change since 1973 in the comprehensiveness of the federal regulations. To prevail on its second argument for implicit pre-emption—the dominance of the federal interest in plasmapheresis regulation—appellee must show either that this interest became more compelling since 1973, or that, in 1973, the FDA seriously underestimated the federal interest in plasmapheresis regulation.

The second obstacle in appellee's path is the presumption that state or local regulation of matters related to health and safety is not invalidated under the Supremacy Clause. Through the challenged ordinances, Hillsborough County has attempted to protect the health of its plasma donors by preventing them from donating too frequently. It also has attempted to ensure the quality of the plasma collected so as to protect, in turn, the recipients of such plasma. "Where . . . the field that Congress is said to have pre-empted has been traditionally occupied by the States 'we start with the assumption that the historic police powers of the States were not to be superseded by the Federal Act unless that was the clear and manifest purpose of Congress.'" *Jones v. Rath Packing Co.,* 430 U.S. 519, 525 (1977). Of course, the same principles apply where, as here, the field is said to have been pre-empted by an agency, acting pursuant to congressional delegation. . . .

Given the clear indication of the FDA's intention *not to pre-empt* and the deference with which we must review the challenged ordinances, we conclude that these ordinances are not pre-empted by the federal scheme.

We reject the argument that an intent to pre-empt may be inferred from the comprehensiveness of the FDA's regulations at issue here. . . . The FDA has not indicated that the new regulations affected its disavowal in 1973 of any intent to pre-empt state and local regulation, and the fact that the federal scheme was expanded to reach other uses of plasma does not cast doubt on the continued validity of that disavowal.

We are even more reluctant to infer pre-emption from the comprehensiveness of regulations than from the comprehensiveness of statutes. As a result of their specialized functions, agencies normally deal with problems in far more detail than does Congress. To infer pre-emption whenever an agency deals with a problem comprehensively is virtually tantamount to saying that whenever a federal agency decides to step into a field, its regulations will be exclusive. . . .

Moreover, because agencies normally address problems in a detailed manner and can speak through a variety of means, including regulations, preambles, interpretive statements, and responses to comments, we can expect that they will make their intentions clear if they intend for their regulations to be exclusive. Thus, if an agency does not speak to the question of pre-emption, we will pause before saying that the mere volume and complexity of its regulations indicate that the agency did in fact intend to pre-empt. . . .

Appellee's second argument for pre-emption of the whole field of plasmapheresis regulation is that an intent to pre-empt can be inferred from the dominant federal interest in this field. We are unpersuaded by the argument. Undoubtedly, every subject that merits congressional legislation is, by definition, a subject of national concern. That cannot mean, however, that every federal statute ousts all related state law. Neither does the Supremacy Clause require us to rank congressional enactments in order of "importance" and hold that, for those at the top of the scale, federal regulation must be exclusive.

Instead, we must look for special features warranting pre-emption. Our case law provides us with clear standards to guide our inquiry in this area. For example, in the seminal case of *Hines v. Davidowitz*, 312 U.S. 52 (1941), the Court inferred an intent to pre-empt from the dominance of the federal interest in foreign affairs because "the supremacy of the national power in the general field of foreign affairs . . . is made clear by the Constitution," and the regulation of that field is "intimately blended and intertwined with responsibilities of the national government." Needless to say, those factors are absent here. Rather, as we have stated, the regulation of health and safety matters is primarily, and historically, a matter of local concern.

. . . .

Appellee's final argument is that even if the regulations are not comprehensive enough and the federal interest is not dominant enough to pre-empt the entire field of plasmapheresis regulation, the Hillsborough County ordinances must be struck down because they conflict with the federal scheme. Appellee argues principally that the challenged ordinances impose on plasma centers and donors requirements more stringent than those imposed by the federal regulations, and therefore that they present a serious obstacle to the federal goal of ensuring an "adequate supply of plasma." We find this concern too speculative to support pre-emption. . . .

. . . [E]ven if the Hillsborough County ordinances had, in fact, reduced the supply of plasma in that county, it would not necessarily follow that they interfere with the federal goal of maintaining an adequate supply of plasma. Undoubtedly, overly restrictive local legislation could threaten the national plasma supply. Neither Congress nor the FDA, however, has struck a particular balance between safety and quantity. . . . Moreover, the record in this case does not indicate what supply the Federal Government considers "adequate," and we have no reason to believe that any reduction in the quantity of plasma donated would make that supply "inadequate."

Finally, the FDA possesses the authority to promulgate regulations pre-empting local legislation that imperils the supply of plasma and can do so with relative ease. Moreover, the agency can be expected to monitor, on a continuing basis, the effects on the federal program of local requirements. Thus, since the agency has not suggested that the county ordinances interfere with federal goals, we are reluctant in the absence of strong evidence to find a threat to the federal goal of ensuring sufficient plasma. . . .

NOTES

1. *State Regulation of Blood Products.* On remand, the *Hillsborough* ordinances were upheld. *Immuno International, A.G. v. Hillsborough County, Florida,* 775 F.2d 1430 (11th Cir. 1985). Compare *State v. Interstate Blood Bank, Inc.,* 222 N.W.2d 912 (Wis. 1974), which overturned the defendant's conviction for operating a commercial blood bank in violation of a Wisconsin law prohibiting the operation of a blood bank for commercial profit. In addition to declaring the state statute unconstitutional under the Commerce Clause, s*ee infra* note 4, the court also ruled that the Wisconsin statute was preempted because it directly conflicted with the federal government's licensing scheme. *Id.* at 917–18. *See also Samuels v. Health & Hospital Corp. of the City of New York,* 432 F. Supp. 1283 (S.D.N.Y. 1977) (holding that classification of blood as a "drug" under the FD&C Act does not preempt a different classification for purposes of state product liability law).

2. *Field Preemption and the FD&C Act.* In view of the states' traditional role in regulating food and drugs, and the strong presumption against inferring that Congress intended to displace state laws, *see Maryland v. Louisiana,* 451 U.S. 725, 746 (1981), courts have uniformly resisted finding field preemption in areas covered by the FD&C Act. *See, e.g., Holk v. Snapple Beverage Corp.,* 575 F.3d 329, 337 (3rd Cir. 2009) ("It does not appear that Congress has regulated so comprehensively in either the food and beverage or juice fields that there is no role for the states."); *Lefaivre v. KV Pharm. Co.,* 636 F.3d 935, 941 (8th Cir. 2010) (concluding that the federal scheme of drug regulation "is *not* so pervasive in scope that it occupies the field" (emphasis in original)).

3. *Pennsylvania Bakery Legend.* One of the most notorious state food labeling provisions was 43 Pennsylvania Statutes § 405, which required every "bakery product" to bear a "Registered with Pennsylvania Department of Agriculture" legend in full text or an approved abbreviated form. Enacted in 1933, this statute was never judicially challenged before it was repealed in the last years of the 20th century. What if other states had followed Pennsylvania's example?

4. *Dormant Commerce Clause.* The dormant commerce clause is another federalism theory, in addition to field preemption, that a court might use to strike down a state law in the absence of either a conflict with federal law or an express Congressional intent to preempt. Under this approach, a state law is deemed unconstitutional if it unduly burdens or discriminates against interstate commerce, an area over which the Constitution grants Congress plenary power. More often than not, state food and drug laws have survived dormant commerce clause challenges. For example, in *Plumley v. Massachusetts,* 155 U.S. 461 (1894), decided prior to the passage of any comprehensive federal food and drug statute, the plaintiff contended unsuccessfully that a Massachusetts law prohibiting the sale of his oleomargarine product was invalid because it intruded into the federal government's enumerated constitutional power to regulate

interstate commerce. The Supreme Court rejected the application of the dormant commerce clause approach in this instance, opining:

> If there be any subject over which it would seem the States ought to have plenary control, and the power to legislate in respect to which it ought not to be supposed was intended to be surrendered to the general government, it is the protection of the people against fraud and deception in the sale of food products. Such legislation may, indeed, indirectly or incidentally affect trade in such products transported from one State to another State. But that circumstance does not show that laws of the character alluded to are inconsistent with the power of Congress to regulate commerce among the States. . . .

Id. at 472. *Accord Savage v. Jones*, 225 U.S. 501, 524 (1912) (upholding state statute regulating animal feed against dormant commerce clause argument). *Cf. Granholm v. Heald*, 544 U.S. 460 (2005) (state laws prohibiting out-of-state, but not in-state, wineries to ship wine directly to consumers violated the dormant commerce clause despite the states' explicit power under the 21st Amendment to regulate liquor); *State v. Interstate Blood Bank, Inc.*, 22 N.W.2d 912, 916–17 (Wis. 1974) (state law prohibiting the operation of a blood bank for commercial profit violated the commerce clause because it unduly burdened interstate commerce, particularly in light of the fact that the defendant sold all of its blood out-of-state).

4.   CONFLICT PREEMPTION

a.   OBSTACLE PREEMPTION

Florida Lime & Avocado Growers, Inc. v. Paul
373 U.S. 132 (1963).

■ MR. JUSTICE BRENNAN delivered the opinion of the Court.

Section 792 of California's Agricultural Code, which gauges the maturity of avocados by oil content, prohibits the transportation or sale in California of avocados which contain "less than 8 per cent of oil, by weight . . . excluding the skin and seed." In contrast, federal marketing orders approved by the Secretary of Agriculture gauge the maturity of avocados grown in Florida by standards which attribute no significance to oil content. This case presents the question of the constitutionality of the California statute insofar as it may be applied to exclude from California markets certain Florida avocados which, although certified to be mature under the federal regulations, do not uniformly meet the California requirement of 8% of oil.

Appellants . . . brought this action . . . to enjoin the enforcement of § 792 against Florida avocados certified as mature under the federal regulations. Appellants challenged the constitutionality of the statute on [the ground] that under the Supremacy Clause, Art. VI, the California standard must be deemed displaced by the federal standard for determining the maturity of avocados grown in Florida. . . .

The federal marketing regulations were adopted pursuant to the Agricultural Adjustment Act. . . .

In 1954, after proceedings in compliance with the statute, the Secretary promulgated orders governing the marketing of avocados grown in South Florida. . . . The maturity test for the South Florida fruit is based upon a schedule of picking dates, sizes and weights . . .

The experts who testified at the trial disputed whether California's percentage-of-oil test or the federal marketing orders' test of picking dates and minimum sizes and weights was the more accurate gauge of the maturity of avocados. In adopting his calendar test of maturity for the varieties grown in South Florida the Secretary expressly rejected physical and chemical tests as insufficiently reliable guides for gauging the maturity of the Florida fruit.

. . . Whether a State may constitutionally reject commodities which a federal authority has certified to be marketable depends upon whether the state regulation "stands as an obstacle to the accomplishment and execution of the full purposes and objectives of Congress," *Hines v. Davidowitz*, 312 U.S. 52, 67 (1941). By that test, we hold that § 792 is not such an obstacle; there is neither such actual conflict between the two schemes of regulation that both cannot stand in the same area, nor evidence of a congressional design to preempt the field.

. . . .

The principle to be derived from our decisions is that federal regulation of a field of commerce should not be deemed preemptive of state regulatory power in the absence of persuasive reasons—either that the nature of the regulated subject matter permits no other conclusion, or that the Congress has unmistakably so ordained.

A holding of federal exclusion of state law is inescapable and requires no inquiry into congressional design where compliance with both federal and state regulations is a physical impossibility for one engaged in interstate commerce. That would be the situation here if, for example, the federal orders forbade the picking and marketing of any avocado testing more than 7% oil, while the California test excluded from the State any avocado measuring less than 8% oil content. No such impossibility of dual compliance is presented on this record, however. As to those Florida avocados . . . which were actually rejected by the California test, . . . Florida growers might have avoided such rejections by leaving the fruit on the trees beyond the earliest picking date permitted by the federal regulations. . . .

The issue under the head of the Supremacy Clause is narrowed then to this: Does either the nature of the subject matter, namely the maturity of avocados, or any explicit declaration of congressional design to displace state regulation, require § 792 to yield to the federal marketing orders? The maturity of avocados seems to be an inherently unlikely candidate for exclusive federal regulation. . . .

On the contrary, the maturity of avocados is a subject matter of the kind this Court has traditionally regarded as properly within the scope of state superintendence. Specifically, the supervision of the readying of foodstuffs for market has always been deemed a matter of peculiarly local concern. . . .

. . . Federal regulation by means of minimum standards of the picking, processing, and transportation of agricultural commodities, however comprehensive for those purposes that regulation may be, does not of itself import displacement of state control over the distribution and retail sale of those commodities in the interests of the consumers of the commodities within the State. . . . Congressional regulation of one end of the stream of commerce does not, ipso facto, oust all state regulation at the other end. Such a displacement may not be inferred automatically from the fact that Congress has regulated production and packing of commodities for the interstate market. . . .

Since no irreconcilable conflict with the federal regulation requires a conclusion that § 792 was displaced, we turn to the question whether Congress has nevertheless ordained that the state regulation shall yield. The settled mandate governing this inquiry, in deference to the fact that a state regulation of this kind is an exercise of the "historic police powers of the States," is not to decree such a federal displacement "unless that was the clear and manifest purpose of Congress," *Rice v. Santa Fe Elevator Corp.*, 331 U.S. 218, 230. In other words, we are not to conclude that Congress legislated the ouster of this California statute by the marketing orders in the absence of an unambiguous congressional mandate to that effect. We search in vain for such a mandate.

. . . .

Nothing in the language of the Agricultural Adjustment Act . . . discloses a . . . comprehensive congressional design. There is but one provision of the statute which intimates any purpose to make agricultural production controls the monitors of retail distribution—the reference to a policy of establishing such "minimum standards of quality and maturity and such grading and inspection requirements . . . as will effectuate . . . orderly marketing . . . in the public interest." 7 U. S. C. § 602(3). That language cannot be said, without more, to reveal a design that federal marketing orders should displace all state regulations. By its very terms, in fact, the statute purports only to establish minimum standards.

. . . [W]e conclude that Congress has not attempted to oust or displace state powers to enact the regulation embodied in § 792. The most plausible inference from the legislative scheme is that the Congress contemplated that state power to enact such regulations should remain unimpaired.

[Justice White, in a dissenting opinion joined by Justices Black, Douglas, and Clark, concluded that California's statute conflicted with, and thus preempted by, federal law. EDS.]

———

The following case interprets two express preemption provisions—those in the Federal Meat Inspection Act and the Fair Packaging and Labeling Act—while also considering an obstacle preemption argument with respect to the latter statute. As the dissenters point out, the Court's conclusion that obstacle preemption exists in this case is in tension with the Court's contrary holding in *Florida Lime and Avocado Growers.*

Jones v. Rath Packing Co.

430 U.S. 519 (1977).

■ Mr. Justice Marshall delivered the opinion of the Court.

Petitioner Jones is Director of the Department of Weights and Measures in Riverside County, Cal. In that capacity he ordered removed from sale bacon packaged by respondent Rath Packing Co. and flour packaged by three millers, respondents General Mills, Inc., Pillsbury Co., and Seaboard Allied Milling Corp. (hereafter millers). Jones acted after determining by means of procedures set forth in 4 Cal. Admin. Code c. 8, Art. 5, that the packages were contained in lots whose average net weight was less than the net weight stated on the packages. The removal orders were authorized by Cal. Bus. & Prof. Code § 12211 (West Supp. 1977). . . .

I

. . . We are required to decide . . . whether the federal laws which govern respondents' packing operations preclude California from enforcing § 12211, as implemented by Art. 5.

. . . .

II

Section 12211 . . . applies to both Rath's bacon and the millers' flour. The standard it establishes is straightforward: "[T]he average weight or measure of the packages or containers in a lot of any . . . commodity sampled shall not be less, at the time of sale or offer for sale, than the net weight or measure stated upon the package." . . .

III

Rath's bacon is produced at plants subject to federal inspection under the Federal Meat Inspection Act (FMIA or Act). . . . Among the requirements imposed on federally inspected plants, and enforced by Department of Agriculture inspectors, are standards of accuracy in labeling. On the record before us, we may assume that Rath's bacon complies with these standards. . . .

. . . As relevant here, [section 1(n) of the FMIA] provides that meat or a meat product is misbranded

> "(5) if in a package or other container unless it bears a label showing . . . (B) an accurate statement of the quantity of the contents in terms of weight, measure, or numerical count: Provided, That . . . reasonable variations may be permitted, and exemptions as to small packages may be established, by regulations prescribed by the Secretary." 81 Stat. 586.

. . . .

The Secretary of Agriculture has used his discretionary authority to permit "reasonable variations" in the accuracy of the required statement of quantity:

"The statement [of net quantity of contents] as it is shown on a label shall not be false or misleading and shall express an accurate statement of the quantity of contents of the container exclusive of wrappers and packing substances. Reasonable variations caused by loss or gain of moisture during the course of good distribution practices or by unavoidable deviations in good manufacturing practice will be recognized. Variations from stated quantity of contents shall not be unreasonably large." 9 CFR § 317.2(h)(2) (1976).

. . . .

Section 408 of the FMIA prohibits the imposition of "[m]arking, labeling, packaging, or ingredient requirements in addition to, or different than, those made under" the Act. This explicit pre-emption provision dictates the result in the controversy between Jones and Rath. California's use of a statistical sampling process to determine the average net weight of a lot implicitly allows for variations from stated weight caused by unavoidable deviations in the manufacturing process. But California makes no allowance for loss of weight resulting from moisture loss during the course of good distribution practice. Thus, the state law's requirement—that the label accurately state the net weight, with implicit allowance only for reasonable manufacturing variations— is "different than" the federal requirement, which permits manufacturing deviations and variations caused by moisture loss during good distribution practice. . . .

We therefore conclude that with respect to Rath's packaged bacon, § 12211 and Art. 5 are pre-empted by federal law.

IV

The federal law governing net-weight labeling of the millers' flour is contained in two statutes, the Federal Food, Drug, and Cosmetic Act (FDCA) and the Fair Packaging and Labeling Act (FPLA), 15 U.S.C. §§ 451–1461. For the reasons stated below, we conclude that the federal weight-labeling standard for flour is the same as that for meat.

. . . [The net weight labeling requirement in FDCA 403(e)] is identical to [section 1(n)] in the FMIA, except that the FDCA mandates rather than allows the promulgation of implementing regulations. The regulation issued in response to this statutory mandate is also substantially identical to its counterpart under the FMIA.

"The declaration of net quantity of contents shall express an accurate statement of the quantity of contents of the package. Reasonable variations caused by loss or gain of moisture during the course of good distribution practice or by unavoidable deviations in good manufacturing practice will be recognized. Variations from stated quantity of contents shall not be unreasonably large." 21 CFR § 1.8b (q) (1976).

Since flour is a food under the FDCA, its manufacture is also subject to the provisions of the FPLA. That statute states a congressional policy that '(p)ackages and their labels should enable consumers to obtain accurate information as to the quantity of the contents and should facilitate value comparisons.' 15 U.S.C. § 1451. To accomplish these goals . . . the FPLA bans the distribution in commerce of any packaged commodity unless it complies with regulations

"which shall provide that—. . . .

"(2) The net quantity of contents (in terms of weight, measure, or numerical count) shall be separately and accurately stated in a uniform location upon the principal display panel of [the required] label." § 1453(a).

The FPLA also contains a saving clause which specifies that nothing in the FPLA "shall be construed to repeal, invalidate, or supersede" the FDCA. § 1460. [Although] [n]othing in the FPLA explicitly permits any variation between stated weight and actual weight . . . [w]e can only conclude that under the FPLA, as under the FDCA, a manufacturer of food is not subject to enforcement action for violation of the net-weight labeling requirements if the label accurately states the net weight, with allowance for the specified reasonable variations.

The FDCA contains no pre-emptive language. The FPLA, on the other hand, declares that

"it is the express intent of Congress to supersede any and all laws of the States or political subdivisions thereof insofar as they may now or hereafter provide for the labeling of the net qua[nt]ity of contents of the package of any consumer commodity covered by this chapter which are less stringent than or require information different from the requirements of section 1453 of this title or regulations promulgated pursuant thereto." 15 U.S.C. § 1461. . . .

The Court of Appeals . . . concluded that § 12211, as implemented by Art. 5, is pre-empted because it is less stringent than the Federal Acts.

The basis for the Court of Appeals' holding is unclear. . . . [T]he Court of Appeals may have found California's approach less stringent because the State takes no enforcement action against lots whose average net weight *exceeds* the weight stated on the label, even if that excess is not a reasonable variation attributable to a federally allowed cause.

We have some doubt that by pre-empting less stringent state laws, Congress intended to compel the States to expend scarce enforcement resources to prevent the sale of packages which contain more than the stated net weight. We do not have to reach that question, however, because in this respect California law apparently differs not at all from federal law, as applied. The inspectors responsible for enforcing the netweight labeling provisions of the Federal Acts are officially informed that "[f]ield weighing for net weight is primarily to determine the likelihood of short weight units in the lots." Moreover, they are not required to submit samples to headquarters "if the average net is not below the amount declared on the label." . . . Since neither jurisdiction is concerned with overweighting in the administration of its weights and measures laws, we cannot say that California's statutory lack of concern for that "problem" makes its laws less stringent than the federal.

Respondents argue that California's law is pre-empted because it requires information different from that required by federal law. The meaning of the statutory pre-emption of laws that require "information different from" the federal net weight labeling provisions, like the meaning of the phrase "less stringent," is unclear. Respondents attribute to the ban on requiring different information a broad meaning, similar in scope to the pre-emption provision of the FMIA. They contend that since California law requires the label to state the minimum net weight, it requires "information different from" the federal laws, which demand an accurate statement with allowance for the specified reasonable variations. The legislative history, however, suggests that the statute expressly pre-empts as requiring "different information" only state laws governing net quantity labeling which impose requirements inconsistent with those imposed by federal law.[34] Since it would be possible to comply with the state law without triggering federal enforcement action we conclude that the state requirement is not inconsistent with federal law. We therefore hold that 15 U.S.C. § 1461 does not pre-empt California's § 12211 as implemented by Art. 5.

That holding does not, however, resolve this case, for we still must determine whether the state law "stands as an obstacle to the accomplishment and execution of the full purposes and objectives of Congress." As Congress clearly stated, a major purpose of the FPLA is to facilitate value comparisons among similar products. Obviously, this goal cannot be accomplished unless packages that bear the same indicated weight in fact contain the same quantity of the product for which the consumer is paying. The significance of this requirement for our purposes results from the physical attributes of flour.

Flour is composed of flour solids and moisture. The average water content of wheat kernels used to make flour is 12.5% by weight, with a range from 10% to 14.5%. Efficient milling practice requires adding water to raise the moisture content to 15% to 16%; if the wheat is too wet or too dry, milling will be hindered. During milling, the moisture content is reduced to 13% to 14%.

The moisture content of flour does not remain constant after milling is completed. If the relative humidity of the atmosphere in which it is stored is greater than 60%, flour will gain moisture, and if the humidity is less than 60%, it will lose moisture. The federal net-weight labeling standard permits variations from stated weight caused by this gain or loss of moisture.

Packages that meet the federal labeling requirements and that have the same stated quantity of contents can be expected to contain the same amount of flour solids. Manufacturers will produce flour with a moisture content fixed by the requirements of the milling process. Since manufacturers have reason not to pack significantly more than is required and federal law prohibits underpacking, they will pack the same amount of this similarly composed flour into packages of any given size. Despite any changes in weight resulting from changes in moisture content during distribution, the packages will contain the

---

[34] The language of 15 U.S.C. § 1461 ... accepted by the House was adopted by the conference committee, along with the House committee's explanation that "preemption would take place to the extent that '8tate laws or State regulations with respect to the labeling of net quantity of contents of packages impose inconsistent or less stringent requirements than are imposed under section 4 of this legislation.'" H.R.Rep.No.2286, 89th Cong., 2d Sess., 11 (1966).

same amount of flour solids when they reach the consumer. This identity of contents facilitates consumer value comparisons.

The State's refusal to permit reasonable weight variations resulting from loss of moisture during distribution produces a different effect. In order to be certain of meeting the California standard, a miller must ensure that loss of moisture during distribution will not bring the weight of the contents below the stated weight. Local millers, which serve a limited area, could do so by adjusting their packing practices to the specific humidity conditions of their region. For example, a miller in an area where the humidity is typically higher than 60% would not need to overpack at all. By contrast, a miller with a national marketing area would not know the destination of its flour when it was packaged and would therefore have to assume that the flour would lose weight during distribution. The national manufacturer, therefore, would have to overpack.

Similarly, manufacturers who distributed only in States that followed the federal standard would not be concerned with compensating for possible moisture loss during distribution. National manufacturers who did not exclude the nonconforming States from their marketing area, on the other hand, would have to overpack. Thus, as a result of the application of the California standard, consumers throughout the country who attempted to compare the value of identically labeled packages of flour would not be comparing packages which contained identical amounts of flour solids. Value comparisons which did not account for this difference—and there would be no way for the consumer to make the necessary calculations—would be misleading.

We therefore conclude that with respect to the millers' flour, enforcement of § 12211, as implemented by Art. 5, would prevent "the accomplishment and execution of the full purposes and objectives of Congress" in passing the FPLA. Under the Constitution, that result is impermissible, and the state law must yield to the federal. . . .

■ MR. JUSTICE REHNQUIST, with whom MR. JUSTICE STEWART joins, concurring in part and dissenting in part.

I agree that with respect to Rath's packaged bacon, § 12211 of the Cal. Bus. & Prof. Code and Art. 5 of 4 Cal. Admin. Code, c. 8, are pre-empted by the express pre-emptive provision of the Federal Meat Inspection Act. . . . I am unable to agree, however, with the implicit pre-emption the Court finds with respect to the flour. . . .

. . . It is virtually impossible to say, as the Court does, that "neither the State nor the Federal Government is concerned with overweighting," and yet conclude that state-induced overweighting conflicts with a "value comparison" purpose, while, presumably, other overweighting does not. In viewing such a purpose to be sufficient to require pre-emption while the very purpose is ignored in practice by the administering federal agency reverses the normal presumption against finding pre-emption. The reasoning process which leads the Court to conclude that there is no express pre-emption leads me to conclude that there is no implied pre-emption. . . .

The assumptions in the Court's opinion not only are insufficient to compel a finding of implied pre-emption, they suggest an approach to the question of pre-emption wholly at odds with that enunciated in *Florida Lime & Avocado Growers, Inc. v. Paul*, 373 U.S. 132 (1963). There, this Court . . . rejected a test which looked to the similarity of purposes, and noted instead that a manufacturer could have complied with both statutes by modifying procedures somewhat, which demonstrated that there was "no inevitable collision between the two schemes of regulation, despite the dissimilarity of the standards." Nothing has been shown to demonstrate that this conclusion is not equally justified in the instant case. . . .

NOTES

1. *Chlorofluorocarbon Propellants.* In *Cosmetic, Toiletry and Fragrance Ass'n v. Minnesota*, 440 F. Supp. 1216 (D. Minn. 1977), *aff'd per curiam* 575 F.2d 1256 (8th Cir. 1978), the District Court struck down as preempted a Minnesota statute that required the following label warning on products using chlorofluorocarbon propellants:

> Warning: Contains a chlorofluorocarbon that may harm the public health and environment by reducing ozone in the upper atmosphere.

Inspired by the same scientific findings that had animated the Minnesota legislators, FDA had previously adopted a regulation under the FD&C Act that mandated the very same warning on foods, drugs, and cosmetics that incorporated chlorofluorocarbon propellants. The FDA rule required the warning to appear on a panel on which it was likely to be seen by the purchaser at the time of purchase. The state statute, by contrast, required the warning to appear on the immediate container, even if it was not visible at the time of purchase.

The District Court began with the conclusion that FDA's decision to address the risk of ozone damage by requiring a label warning effectively precluded the state from requiring any other measure or form of words. It credited FDA's repeated statements that "uniformity in labeling is required to meet the dual national goal of the most effective warning at the least possible cost." And it was not persuaded by the state's argument that placement of the warning on the product's immediate container, in addition to the mandated federal placement on a visible panel, would be both more effective than and not incompatible with federal policy. The district court concluded: "The responsible federal administrative agency has determined that the federal policy is purchase awareness and that a policy of use awareness would require more time and expense and cause more disruption." The state's labeling requirement, therefore, was "an obstacle to full effectuation of the federal purpose," and accordingly unconstitutional under the Supremacy Clause of the Constitution.

2. *Preemption by Agencies.* The Supreme Court, relying upon *United States v. Shimer*, 367 U.S. 374 (1961), has frequently emphasized that an agency's intent to preempt state regulation, if clear, will usually be decisive. *See, e.g., City of New York v. FCC*, 486 U.S. 57, 64 (1988); *Capital Cities Cable, Inc. v. Crisp*, 467 U.S. 691, 698–700 (1984); *Fidelity Federal Savings & Loan Association v. de la Cuesta*, 458 U.S. 141, 152–54 (1982). *Cf. Williamson v. Mazda Motor of America, Inc.*, 131 S. Ct. 1131 (2011) (relying on agency's view that a regulation did *not* preempt state law).

Nonetheless, as one scholar has asserted, Congress was, until quite recently, the "leading actor" in the mechanics of preemption. Catherine M. Sharkey, *Inside Agency Preemption*, 110 Mich. L. Rev. 521, 523 (2012). Courts focused "almost exclusively on the precise wording of [Congress'] statutory directives as a clue to its intent to displace state law," and federal agencies were "if not ignored, certainly no more than supporting players." *Id.* This scholar continues:

> But the twenty-first century has witnessed a role reversal. Federal agencies now play the dominant role in statutory interpretation. While Congress, with the stroke of a pen, could definitively resolve preemption questions by specifying the impact of its legislation on state law, in reality it often does not, but rather leaves open a wide interpretive space for courts to fill. And while courts reiterate that congressional intent is the touchstone of preemption analysis, they increasingly rely on the views propounded by federal agencies either in regulations or else in preambles or litigation briefs.

Id. During the George W. Bush administration, from 2001 to 2008, FDA was the second most active agency in issuing notices of preemption. *Id.* at 546. For an analysis of FDA's most controversial assertion of preemption during this period, *see infra* p. 894 (discussion of *Wyeth v. Levine*).

b.   Impossibility Preemption

A finding of preemption based on the physical impossibility of complying with both state law and federal law tends to be more straightforward than a finding of obstacle preemption. Today, preemption in the case below would be mandated by an express preemption provision added to the FD&C Act five years later by the 1990 Nutrition Labeling and Education Act. *See infra* p. 313. At the time it was decided, however, the decision pivoted on the question of impossibility preemption.

Grocery Manufacturers of America v. Gerace

755 F.2d 993 (2d Cir. 1985).

■ Meskill, Circuit Judge. . . .

This litigation involves state and federal regulatory schemes that require descriptive labeling of cheese alternatives: products composed wholly or partly of food that looks, smells and tastes like cheese, but is not, in fact, cheese. The major focus of the dispute concerns the use and meaning of the modifier "imitation" as applied to these products. . . .

The text of New York's section 63, enacted in 1982, . . . requires that alternative cheese products feature labels that display prominently the descriptive term "imitation." . . .

Section 63 does not define imitation. The regulations promulgated pursuant to the statute define "imitation cheese" as any food simulating "cheese" as described or standardized by regulation but failing to meet that description or standard. Neither the statute nor any of its regulations is concerned with nutritional values.

. . . Under the FDCA, a food is misbranded if it is sold under the name of any other food, 21 U.S.C. § 343(b), or if it purports to be a food, such as cheese, for which a standard of identity has been prescribed by regulation and it does not conform exactly to that standard, 21 U.S.C. § 343(g). In addition, a food that "is an imitation of another food" is misbranded unless its label contains the word "imitation" in prominent letters immediately preceding the name of the food imitated. 21 U.S.C. § 343(c).

The FDCA does not define imitation; that task was accomplished by regulation in 1973. An imitation food is defined as a food which "is a substitute for and resembles another food but is nutritionally inferior to that food." 21 C.F.R. § 101.3(e)(1). Nutritional inferiority is determined by comparing the percentages of so-called "essential nutrients" in the substitute to those in the food for which it substitutes. 21 C.F.R. § 101.3(e)(4). . . .

A nutritionally equivalent or superior substitute food would be misbranded under federal law if it was labeled with the term "imitation." Such foods must be identified by an appropriate common or usual name or, if none exists, a descriptive term. The fact that such foods are substitute foods would thus be evident from the foods' labels, albeit less so than if the word "imitation" was used.

. . . .

[T]he court below . . . held that New York's labeling requirements as applied to alternative cheese were preempted by the FDCA because the federal requirements, as applied in compliance with the FDA's definition of imitation, and the state requirements were in actual conflict. Further, . . . the district court held that the sign, menu and container provisions were invalid because they placed an undue burden on interstate commerce in violation of the Commerce Clause.

Any state law intruding upon an area that Congress intended to control exclusively is preempted, "whether Congress' command is explicitly stated in the statute's language or implicitly contained in its structure and purpose." *Jones v. Rath Packing Co.*, 430 U.S. 519, 525 (1977). Absent explicit preemption language, congressional intent to occupy the field regulated may nevertheless be inferred on the basis of the pervasiveness of the federal scheme, the dominance of the federal interest involved or because the federal statute in combination with the nature of its directives reveals the purpose to preclude state action. *Fidelity Federal Savings & Loan Association v. de la Cuesta*, 458 U.S. 141, 153 (1982).

"Even where Congress has not entirely displaced state regulation in a specific area, state law is pre-empted to the extent that it actually conflicts with federal law." *Pacific Gas & Electric Co. v. State Energy Resources Conservation & Development Commission*, 461 U.S. 190, 204 (1983). An actual conflict exists when it is impossible to comply with both state and federal law, *Florida Lime & Avocado Growers, Inc. v. Paul*, 373 U.S. 132, 142–143 (1963), or where the state law stands as an obstacle to the accomplishment of the full purposes and objectives of Congress, *Hines v. Davidowitz*, 312 U.S. 52, 67 (1941).

Moreover, preemption is compelled not only when the conflict involves a federal statute, but also when it involves valid federal regulations. Provided that they are reasonable exercises of an agency's duly authorized discretion and not in conflict with congressional intent, "federal regulations have no less preemptive effect than federal statutes." *Fidelity Federal Savings & Loan*, 458 U.S. at 153.

The preemptive effect of the FDCA depends entirely on whether the FDA's definition of imitation is valid and therefore entitled to our deference. . . .

If we were addressing the validity of the FDA regulation in or about 1973, the year of its promulgation, we might be inclined to reject it. But the regulation has been in effect for eleven years. Congress' failure during this period to alter the relevant statutory language or to otherwise condemn the regulatory definition, while not a fail-safe guide, allows us at least to infer that it has acquiesced in the FDA's construction. . . .

Thus, as applied to alternative cheese, the New York labeling scheme is in direct conflict with its federal counterpart. Including the term imitation on the label of a nutritionally superior alternative cheese in order to comply with New York law, would render the product misbranded under federal law. Compliance with both the state and federal requirements is impossible. To the extent that it attempts to regulate the labeling of alternative cheese, the New York Law is preempted.

NOTES

1. *Decision in Tension with Gerace.* In *Dyson v. Miles Laboratories, Inc.*, 57 A.D.2d 197 (N.Y. 1977), New York State charged that Morningstar Farms Breakfast Links and similar soy-based substitutes for sausage and bacon were misbranded under an "imitation" labeling requirement in New York's Agriculture and Markets Law because they failed to bear the term "imitation." The court refused to dismiss New York's complaint. It acknowledged the existence of the 1973 FDA regulation, but it concluded that New York could constitutionally apply its own standard.

2. *Impossibility Preemption and Failure to Warn Claims.* In recent years, assertions of impossibility preemption have occurred most frequently in cases concerning the relationship between federal drug labeling requirements and state tort suits for failure to warn. That topic will be considered in detail later in this book. *See infra* p. 894.

3. *Another Case on Preemption in Dairy Labeling.* Relying on both obstacle and impossibility preemption, as well as the dormant commerce clause, *Lever Brothers Co. v. Maurer*, 712 F. Supp. 645 (S.D. Ohio 1989) invalidated a state statute precluding use of the word "butter" on the label or in the labeling of any substitute for butter.

5. STATUTORY PREEMPTION

As originally enacted in 1938, the FD&C Act contained no express preemption provisions. Subsequent amendments made prior to 1976, including the revolutionary 1958 Food Additives Amendments and 1962 Drug Amendments, failed to add any explicit preemption language. Starting with the passage of the 1976 Medical Device Amendments, however, Congress has added a series of preemption provisions applicable to specific product categories. Each of these is examined below.

a.   MEDICAL DEVICES

In the 1976 Medical Device Amendments, Congress attempted to define the federal and state roles in the regulation of medical instrumentation. The result is section 521 of the FD&C Act, which reads:

> Sec. 521(a) Except as provided in subsection (b), no State or political subdivision of a State may establish or continue in effect with respect to a device intended for human use any requirement—
>
> (1) which is different from, or in addition to, any requirement applicable under this Act to the device, and
>
> (2) which relates to the safety or effectiveness of the device or to any other matter included in a requirement applicable to the device under this Act.
>
> (b) Upon application of a State or a political subdivision thereof, the Secretary may, by regulation promulgated after notice and opportunity for an oral hearing, exempt from subsection (a), under such conditions as may be prescribed in such regulation, a requirement of such State or political subdivision applicable to a device intended for human use if
>
> (1) the requirement is more stringent than a requirement under this Act which would be applicable to the device if an exemption were not in effect under this subsection; or
>
> (2) the requirement
>
> (A) is required by compelling local conditions, and
>
> (B) compliance with the requirement would not cause the device to be in violation of any applicable requirement under this Act.

The House Report on the 1976 Amendments explained:

> In the absence of effective Federal regulation of medical devices, some States have established their own programs. The most comprehensive State regulation of which the Committee is aware is that of California, which in 1970 adopted the Sherman Food, Drug, and Cosmetic Law. This law requires premarket approval of all new medical devices, requires compliance of device manufacturers with good manufacturing practices and authorizes inspection of establishments which manufacture devices. . . .
>
> Because there are some situations in which regulation of devices by States and localities would constitute a useful supplement to Federal regulation, the reported bill authorizes a State or political subdivision thereof to petition the Secretary for exemptions from the bill's general prohibition of non-Federal regulation. . . .
>
> In the Committee's view, requirements imposed under the California statute serve as an example of requirements that the

Secretary should authorize to be continued (provided any application submitted by a State meets requirements pursuant to the reported bill). . . .

H.R. No. 94–853 (1976).

Soon after passage of the Amendments, FDA promulgated regulations describing its understanding of section 521. 43 Fed. Reg. 18661 (May 2, 1978), codified at 21 C.F.R. Part 808. The most important disputes regarding the scope of section 521 have occurred with respect to its preemptive effect on private state tort suits, a topic that will be examined in detail later in the book. *See infra* p. 1283 (excerpting *Medtronic, Inc. v. Lohr*, 518 U.S. 470 (1996) and *Riegel v. Medtronic*, 552 U.S. 312 (2008)).

NOTES

1. *FDA Exemption Regulations.* FDA's regulations governing exemptions from preemption of state medical device laws, and the specific exemptions that have been granted, are codified in 21 C.F.R. Part 808. Twenty-two states have had one or more requirements restored through this exemption process. FDA has not promulgated new or amended exemption regulations since the 1980s, however.

2. *Hearing Aid Controls.* In response to the applications of Massachusetts and Rhode Island for exemptions from preemption of state hearing aid requirements, FDA issued proposed regulations in 44 Fed. Reg. 22119 (Apr. 13, 1979) and, after a public hearing, promulgated final regulations in 45 Fed. Reg. 67325 (Oct. 10, 1980). Massachusetts challenged FDA's denial of its application for an exemption for two provisions of its statute governing the sale of hearing aids, contending that the agency's published criteria for exemptions were invalid because they permit broad consideration of "the best interest of public health, taking into account the potential burden on interstate commerce." 21 C.F.R. 808.25(g)(3). The First Circuit approved both FDA's criteria for exemptions from preemption and its action on the Massachusetts application. *Commonwealth of Massachusetts v. Hayes*, 691 F.2d 57 (1st Cir. 1982). For a discussion of the circumstances under which state hearing aid requirements are not preempted, see 55 Fed. Reg. 23984 (June 13, 1990). State hearing aid requirements were upheld in *Smith v. Pingree*, 651 F.2d 1021 (5th Cir. 1981); *New Jersey Guild of Hearing Aid Dispensers v. Long*, 384 A.2d 795 (N.J. 1978).

3. *Advisory Opinions.* In 1988, in response to a request for an advisory opinion on whether a city may ban the use of indoor commercial tanning equipment, FDA said it had to consider both section 521 of the FD&C Act and the preemption provisions applicable to radiation-emitting electronic products under section 360F of the Public Health Service Act (now FD&C Act section 541). FDA advised that section 521 does not preempt the city ordinance because the agency had not promulgated any requirements under the FD&C Act applicable to the use of sun tanning equipment, and that section 360F does not preempt because the ordinance does not establish a standard applicable to the performance of suntanning equipment. Letter from J. M. Taylor to D. R. Kalins, FDA Dkt. No. 87A–0201 (June 20, 1988).

In 2004, FDA issued an advisory opinion to the city of Arlington, Texas, concluding that proposed city ordinances regarding the provision and use of automatic external defibrillators (AEDs) in nonhospital settings would not be preempted by section 521, and thus did not need exemptions. The advisory opinion explained that each of the ordinances either "would not establish any requirements with respect to the device itself" or imposed requirements without FDA counterparts. Thus, the opinion concluded, none of the proposed ordinances would "establish any requirements with respect to AEDs that are different from or in addition to any FDA requirement with respect to AEDs." Letter from Linda S. Kahan, CDRH Dep. Dir., to Ivan Bland (May 15, 2005).

b. FOOD LABELING

The 1990 Nutrition Labeling and Education Act (NLEA), 104 Stat. 2353, expressly prohibits any state or local government from "directly or indirectly" establishing any food labeling requirement of the type governed by sections 403(b)–(k), (q), and (r) of the FD&C Act that is not identical to FDA requirements. FD&C Act 403A.

In response to members of Congress who believed FDA had been slow to require nutrition information on food labels, NLEA's drafters offered the states a role in enforcing the statute's new requirements. NLEA added a new paragraph (b) to what had been section 307 and is now section 310 of the FD&C Act. That section in its entirety now reads:

SEC. 310 [337]. PROCEEDINGS IN NAME OF UNITED STATES; PROVISION AS TO SUBPOENAS.

(a) Except as provided in subsection (b), all such proceedings for the enforcement, or to restrain violations, of this Act shall be by and in the name of the United States. Subpoenas for witnesses who are required to attend a court of the United States, in any district, may run into any other district in any proceeding under this section.

(b)(1) A State may bring in its own name and within its jurisdiction proceedings for the civil enforcement, or to restrain violations, of section 401, 403(b), 403(d), 403(e), 403(f), 403(g), 403(h), 403(i), 403(k), 403(q), or 403(r) if the food that is the subject of the proceedings is located in the State.

(2) No proceeding may be commenced by a State under paragraph (1)—

(A) before 30 days after the State has give notice to the Secretary that the State intends to bring such proceeding,

(B) before 90 days after the State has given notice to the Secretary of such intent if the Secretary has, within such 30 days, commenced an informal or formal enforcement action pertaining to the food which would be the subject of such proceeding, or

(C) if the Secretary is diligently prosecuting in court pertaining to such food, has settled such proceeding, or has settled the informal or formal enforcement action pertaining to such food.

In any court proceeding described in subparagraph (C), a State may intervene as a matter of right.

Section 310(b) draws on the model of the "citizen suit" provisions found in the nation's major environmental laws, including the Clean Air Act and Federal Water Pollution Control Act. These laws authorize suits by individuals and organizations who are affected by polluting conduct that violates statutory requirements. Section 310(b) confers on state officials, but not private citizens, the authority to sue to enforce federal labeling requirements. FDA must be given notice of any such suit, however, and has the right to take over responsibility for the case. No state or state official has brought suit pursuant to this authority.

NOTES

1. *Restaurant and Retail Food.* Because foods consumed in restaurants and foods prepared in retail stores (*e.g.*, bread baked on the premises in a grocery store) are exempt from the food labeling requirements of sections 403(q) and (r), state and local requirements governing such foods are not subject to preemption.

2. *State Petitions.* Under FD&C section Act 403A(b), a state or local government may petition FDA to exempt a specific requirement from preemption by the NLEA. FDA may grant the petition if the requirement would not cause any food to be in violation of the FD&C Act, would not unduly burden interstate commerce, and is designed to address a particular need for information that is not met by the FD&C Act. The agency has established procedural regulations pertaining to the submission of such petitions at 21 C.F.R. 100.1. Since 1990, only six state petitions have been submitted to FDA (none recently) and the agency has never granted such a petition.

c.   NONPRESCRIPTION DRUGS AND COSMETICS

The 1997 Food and Drug Administration Modernization Act (FDAMA) mandated "national uniformity" for the regulation of nonprescription (over-the-counter) drugs and cosmetics, but Congress approached the two product categories differently. Section 751 of the FD&C Act, added by FDAMA, prohibits states from establishing "any requirement . . . that is different from or in addition to, or that is otherwise not identical with, a requirement under this Act, the Poison Prevention Packaging Act of 1970 . . . or the Fair Packaging and Labeling Act. . . ." FD&C Act 751(a)(2). This section permits states to apply for exemptions from preemption, includes various limitations on scope and exceptions, and explicitly disclaims any effect on product liability law. FD&C Act 751(b)–(e).

Section 752, also added by FDAMA, sets forth essentially identical preemption language for cosmetics, with one critical difference—it applies only to requirements "for labeling or packaging" of cosmetics, and thus excludes state cosmetic safety requirements from the scope of the provision.

NOTES

1. *Reason for Difference.* The OTC drug and cosmetic national uniformity provisions in the FDA Modernization Act were the result of classic political bargaining. FDA agreed to support national uniformity only if the regulated industry agreed to a provision giving the agency the authority to inspect records that FDA has sought for half a century. The OTC drug industry agreed to this deal. However, the cosmetic industry rejected the bargain and still pressed for national uniformity over FDA's opposition. The food industry likewise spurned the compromise and decided to pursue national uniformity in separate legislation.

2. *Food Uniformity Legislation.* Local interest group politics and special geographical considerations have encouraged divergent food regulations among the fifty states. Food processors have been urging Congress to pass legislation to prohibit states from requiring warnings for ingredients that FDA deems safe. They contend the uniformity legislation would "ensure consumers have access to the same accurate, science-based food safety information regardless of where they live," while state regulators and consumer groups contend such legislation would gut state food safety laws. Legislation providing for national uniformity for food was reported favorably in 2000, S. Rep. No. 106–504, 106th Cong., 2d Sess., but was not considered on the Senate floor. Similar legislation was endorsed in H.R. Rep. No. 108–770, 108th Cong., 2d Sess. (2004), but was not taken up by the House. Most recently, uniformity legislation was endorsed in H.R. Rep. No. 109–379, 109th Cong., 2d Sess. (2006), and passed by the House but was not considered by the Senate.

d. TOBACCO PRODUCTS

The 2009 Family Smoking Prevention and Tobacco Control Act, which gave FDA authority over tobacco products, contains a preemption provision, codified at FD&C Act 916, but it also expressly preserves state power over certain aspect of tobacco regulation. Section 916(a)(2) provides:

(2) Preemption of certain State and local requirements

(A) In general

No State or political subdivision of a State may establish or continue in effect with respect to a tobacco product any requirement which is different from, or in addition to, any requirement under the provisions of this subchapter relating to tobacco product standards, premarket review, adulteration, misbranding, labeling, registration, good manufacturing standards, or modified risk tobacco products.

(B) Exception

Subparagraph (A) does not apply to requirements relating to the sale, distribution, possession, information reporting to the State, exposure to, access to, the advertising and promotion of, or use of, tobacco products by individuals of any age, or relating to fire safety standards for tobacco products.

Section 916(a)(1), titled "Preservation," reinforces this "Exception" by declaring that a state may, with respect to any of the same aspects of tobacco regulation listed in 916(a)(2)(B), enact laws and regulations "in addition to, or more stringent than, requirements established under this chapter." Finally, section 916 expressly states that the new tobacco chapter of the FD&C Act has no effect on product liability law. FD&C Act 916(b).

CHAPTER 6

FOOD

In recent years, the volume of writing about food has exploded, both in academia, where a multidisciplinary field called "food studies" has arisen, and in the public arena, where the nonfiction bestseller list seems to reserve at least one place for a book about food. In light of food's central place in our culture and economy, not to mention our biology, the topic certainly deserves the attention it is receiving. And because of the prominent role law plays in every aspect of food production and consumption, it lies near the center of much of this analysis.

Food studies scholar Warren Belasco has proposed that people decide what to eat "based on a rough negotiation—a pushing and tugging" between three factors: identity, convenience, and responsibility. "Identity" involves considerations such as personal preference, pleasure, creativity, and cultural values and ideas. "Convenience" embraces variables such as price, availability, and ease of preparation. Finally, "responsibility" (which Belasco suggests is not the strongest factor but perhaps should be) encompasses concerns including the consumer's short and long-term health and the impact of food production on the environment, animals, and the distribution of social power and resources. WARREN BELASCO, FOOD: THE KEY CONCEPTS 7–10 (2008).

As will become apparent in this chapter, food law shapes and is shaped by all three of these factors.

A. SUBCATEGORIES OF FOOD

A food is a food is a food—except when it is not. For the most part, food is subject to a fairly uniform regulatory regime. But some important segments of the conventional food supply—most importantly, meat and poultry—are regulated largely pursuant to statutes other than the FD&C Act and, indeed, primarily by agencies other than FDA. Moreover, a few subcategories of nonconventional food—most importantly, dietary supplements—are exempt from some FD&C Act provisions applicable to "food" generally and subject to their own, special requirements.

1. FOOD REGULATED PRIMARILY BY AGENCIES OTHER THAN FDA

Numerous agencies in addition to the FDA regulate various components and aspects of the food supply. Altogether, as many as fifteen different agencies administer about thirty federal laws related to food safety and labeling. Recent reports from organizations such as the Government Accountability Office and the National Academy of Sciences Institute of Medicine have recommended that Congress address the fragmented state of food regulation. Some specific food categories with regulatory or enforcement authority assigned to other agencies are detailed below.

Meat, Poultry, and Eggs

Meat, poultry, and unshelled egg products are regulated primarily by the United States Department of Agriculture (USDA) under the Federal Meat Inspection Act (FMIA), 21 U.S.C. 601 *et seq.*, the Poultry Products Inspection Act, 21 U.S.C. 451 *et seq.*, and the Egg Products Inspection Act, 21 U.S.C. 1031 *et seq.* USDA has ceded jurisdiction to FDA over any food that is less than two percent meat or poultry. Consequently, a food plant manufacturing both plain cheese pizza and pepperoni pizza may be subject to regulation by both agencies.

The jurisdiction of USDA and FDA over these three categories of food products is complex and uncertain. FDA has exclusive regulatory jurisdiction over live animals intended to be used for food. *United States v. Tomahara Enterprises, Ltd.*, Food Drug Cosm. L. Rep. (CCH) ¶ 38,217 (N.D.N.Y. 1983). USDA has exclusive jurisdiction over the slaughter of food animals and over the subsequent processing of meat and poultry, except that USDA and FDA have joint jurisdiction over the use of food additives in meat and poultry. After processing, USDA and FDA have joint jurisdiction over the distribution of meat and poultry up to the retail establishment where it is sold. FDA has exclusive jurisdiction over retail food establishments.

The FMIA long applied to the meat of only five named species (cattle, sheep, swine, goats, and equines), and not to the meat of other species such as rabbit, deer, or bison, which remained within FDA's purview. *See, e.g.*, 21 U.S.C. 601(j) (definition of "meat food product"). In 2005, however, Congress amended the FMIA to extend the USDA inspection system to all "amenable species," defined as the five listed species plus "any additional species of livestock that the Secretary considers appropriate." 119 Stat. 2120 (2006); 21 U.S.C. 601(w)(3). In 2008, Congress amended the term "amenable species" to also include "catfish, as defined by the Secretary." 122 Stat. 651 (2008), Sec. 10016(b); 21 U.S.C. 601(w)(2).

FDA has primary responsibility for the safety and labeling of shell eggs, although the voluntary grading of shell eggs is done under USDA supervision. Egg processing plants that wash, sort, break, and pasteurize eggs are under USDA jurisdiction, as are processed products known for their egg content.

Alcoholic Beverages

The Alcohol and Tobacco Tax and Trade Bureau (TTB) of the Department of the Treasury has jurisdiction over distilled spirits, wines, and malt beverage products under the Federal Alcohol Administration Act (FAA), codified in 27 U.S.C. 201 *et seq.* The Bureau of Alcohol, Tobacco and Firearms (BATF) in the Department of the Treasury performed this function until 2002, when the Homeland Security Act of 2002 divided BATF into two new agencies: the Bureau of Alcohol, Tobacco, Firearms, and Explosives (now called ATF), which became part of the Department of Justice, and the Alcohol and Tobacco Tax and Trade Bureau (now called TTB), which was left in the Department of the Treasury. TTB is responsible for administration of the Federal Alcohol Administration Act and related statutes, whereas ATF is a law enforcement agency.

TTB has primary regulatory responsibility under the FAA over all wine products that contain 7 percent alcohol or more, while FDA regulates wine products containing less than 7 percent alcohol (such as wine coolers and dealcoholized wines) pursuant to the FD&C Act. TTB also is the chief regulator of all malt beverage products regardless of their alcohol content, although beers that do not qualify as malt beverages fall within FDA's bailiwick. FDA Compliance Policy Guide 510.400 (May 2005); 510.450 (Aug. 1996); DRAFT GUIDANCE FOR INDUSTRY: LABELING OF CERTAIN BEERS SUBJECT TO THE LABELING JURISDICTION OF THE FOOD AND DRUG ADMINISTRATION (Aug. 2009).

The FAA's product-specific requirements regarding the labeling of alcoholic beverages supplant the labeling requirements of the FD&C Act. *See Brown–Forman Distillers Corp. v. Mathews*, 435 F. Supp. 5 (W.D. Ky. 1976). Consequently, TTB has exclusive jurisdiction over the labeling of those alcoholic beverages subject to the FAA. However, the adulteration provisions of FD&C Act 402(a) do apply to alcoholic beverages. *United States v. 1,800,2625 Wine Gallons of Distilled Spirits*, 121 F. Supp. 735 (W.D. Mo. 1954); *United States v. Commonwealth Brewing Corp.*, Food Drug Cosm. L. Rep. (CCH) ¶ 50,051.43 (D. Mass. 1945). According to a still-observed 1987 memorandum of understanding (MOU) between BATF and FDA, TTB has primary responsibility for overseeing voluntary recalls of adulterated products. MOU 225–88–2000. In other respects, the adulteration of FAA alcoholic beverages is jointly regulated by TTB and FDA, as set forth in the MOU.

Water and Ice

Under the Safe Drinking Water Act, 88 Stat. 1660 (1974), general responsibility for the purity of drinking water was placed in the Environmental Protection Agency (EPA), but section 410 was added to the FD&C Act to preserve FDA's jurisdiction over bottled drinking water. The agency also has jurisdiction over ice. Water used to process food or as an ingredient in food is subject to the same requirements under the FD&C Act as any other food constituent.

2. DIETARY SUPPLEMENTS AND OTHER FDA-REGULATED FOODS WITH SPECIAL REQUIREMENTS

The FD&C Act has always recognized the existence of special categories of food. Section 403(j), unchanged since 1938, provides that a food that "purports to be or is represented for special dietary uses" is misbranded "unless its label bears such information concerning its vitamin, mineral, and other dietary properties as the Secretary determines to be, and by regulations prescribes as, necessary in order to fully inform purchasers as to its value for such uses." The first regulations FDA issued pursuant to 403(j) established special requirements for "infant food," "food used in control of body weight or in dietary management with respect to disease," and "hypoallergenic food." These regulations also set forth requirements for food "purport[ed] to be or ... represented for special dietary use by man by reason of its vitamin property [or] . . . mineral property," a category of products eventually understood to encompass vitamin and mineral supplements as well as conventional food. 6 Fed. Reg. 5921 (Nov. 22, 1941); Lewis A. Grossman, *Food, Drugs, and Droods: A Historical Consideration of Definitions and Categories in American Food and Drug Law* 93 CORNELL L. REV. 1091, 1119–23 (2008).

Over the years, the "foods for special dietary use" regulations have become less important, as statutes and implementing regulations have been enacted addressing infant formulas, medical foods, and dietary supplements in particular, as well as nutrient content claims and health claims in general. Certainly, the most important of the subcategory-specific food regulation schemes is that established by the Dietary Supplement Health and Education Act of 1994 (DSHEA). As noted in Chapter 3, *supra* p. 102, DSHEA's definition of "dietary supplement" ends with the statement that for most purposes, "a dietary supplement shall be deemed to be a food within the meaning of this Act." FD&C Act 201(ff). Nonetheless, as will be discussed in detail at relevant points throughout this chapter, dietary supplements are in some important respects treated differently from conventional foods. For example, the dietary ingredients in dietary supplements are exempt from the definition of "food additive" and thus from the preapproval regime applicable to such substances. FD&C Act 201(s)(6). *See infra* p. 627.

The Act thus maintains a distinction between dietary supplements and conventional food. The definition of "dietary supplement" states that it "is not represented for use as a conventional food or as a sole item of a meal or the diet." FD&C Act 201(ff)(2)(B). Moreover, section 411(c)(1)(B), incorporated by reference in the definition, allows a supplement to be intended for ingestion "in tablet, capsule, powder, softgel, gelcap or liquid form," or in another form if it "is not represented as conventional food and is not represented for use as a sole item of a meal or of the diet." Finally, the Act requires that a dietary supplement be "labeled as a dietary supplement," which means, most importantly, that it bear a "Supplement Facts" label instead of a "Nutrition Facts" label. *See infra* p. 407, note 10.

As shown by the warning letter below, some manufacturers have tested the line between dietary supplements and conventional food.

Warning Letter From Michael W. Roosevelt, Acting Director, CFSAN Office of Compliance, to Terry Harris, HBB, LLC dba Baked World

July 28, 2011.

Dear Mr. Harris:

The Food and Drug Administration (FDA) has reviewed the regulatory status of your product, "Lazy Larry" (formerly "Lazy Cakes"). Your "Lazy Larry" product is adulterated under section 402(a)(2)(C) of the Federal Food, Drug, and Cosmetic Act (FDCA) because it bears or contains an unsafe food additive. Specifically, it contains melatonin (5-methoxy–N–acetyltryptamine), which is a neurohormone and is an unapproved food additive under section 409 of the FDCA. . . .

Your "Lazy Larry" product is represented for use as a conventional food, and accordingly is not a dietary supplement, as defined under Section 201(ff) of the FDCA. The FDCA excludes from the definition of a dietary supplement a product represented for use as a conventional food or as a sole item of a meal or the diet [201(ff)(2)(B)]. Your use of the term "dietary supplement" in the statement of identity and your use of a "Supplement Facts" panel for nutrition labeling do not make your product a dietary supplement, because your "Lazy Larry" product is represented for use as a conventional food. Examples of factors and information that establish that the product is represented as a conventional food are as follows:

— the product is marketed alongside snack foods;

— the name of a URL ... that directs people to your product website, refers to a conventional food (cake);

— the product is described on your website as having "the same ingredients your mother uses to make brownies," which is a conventional food;

— the use of a combination of ingredients particular to a brownie (including sugar, flour, oil, cocoa, egg, and salt, in order of predominance by weight);

— the appearance and packaging of the product as a brownie.

As previously sold, your "Lazy Cakes" product additionally was represented for use as conventional food, for example, by the use of the words "cakes" in the product name and use of the word "brownie" in the statement of identity on the package label.

Any substance added to a conventional food, such as your "Lazy Larry" product must be used in accordance with a food additive regulation, unless the substance is the subject of a prior sanction or is generally recognized as safe (GRAS) among qualified expert for its use in foods. There is no food additive regulation that authorizes the use of melatonin. We are not aware of any information to indicate that melatonin is the subject of a prior sanction. As explained below, we are not aware of any basis to conclude that melatonin is GRAS for use in conventional foods.

... [M]elatonin added to a conventional food is a food additive under section 201(s) of the FDCA and is subject to the provisions of section 409 of the FDCA. Under section 409, a food additive is deemed unsafe unless it is approved by FDA for its intended use prior to marketing. Melatonin is not approved for use in any food, including brownies. Therefore, your "Lazy Larry" product is adulterated within the meaning of section 402(a)(2)(C) of the FDCA. . . .

Sincerely,

Michael W Roosevelt

NOTES

1. *Dietary Supplement/Conventional Food Distinction.* DSHEA's definition of "dietary supplement" expressly incorporates section 411(c)(1)(B), which in turn lists permissible forms for supplements (tablet, capsule, powder, softgel, gelcap, liquid) and also provides that a

supplement may take another form if it "is not represented as conventional food and is not represented for use as a sole item of a meal or of the diet." FD&C Act 411(c)(1)(B) (incorporated by reference in section 201(ff)(2)(A)). Because 201(ff)(2)(B) itself contains almost equivalent language, the FD&C Act effectively distinguishes dietary supplements from conventional foods twice.

2. *"Either Way" Product Forms.* Although marketing brownies as dietary supplements may have been too bold, some product forms legitimately can be sold as either dietary supplements or conventional foods, depending on their labeling and marketing. The most obvious examples are liquids, teas, and bars. Such products are legitimately categorized as dietary supplements if they are designated as dietary supplements on the principal display panel, bear a "Supplement Facts" (rather than a "Nutrition Facts") label, and are not "represented for use as a conventional food or as a sole item of a meal or the diet."

In 1997, FDA observed that cranberry juice cocktail may be marketed as either a conventional food or a dietary supplement. 60 Fed. Reg. 67194, 67196 (Dec. 28, 1995), 62 Fed. Reg. 49826, 49937, 49860 (Sept. 23, 1997). In a recent guidance document, however, FDA indicated that it will strictly limit when liquids may be marketed as dietary supplements.

> . . . Beverages are conventional foods under the FFDCA. Even when the label of a liquid product characterizes it as a dietary supplement, the product may not in fact be a dietary supplement. Liquid products can be represented as conventional foods as a result of factors such as their packaging, the volume in which they are intended to be consumed, their product or brand name, and statements about the product in labeling or advertising. For example, the packaging of liquid products in bottles or cans similar to those in which single or multiple servings of beverages like soda, bottled water, fruit juices, and iced tea are sold, suggests that the liquid product is intended for use as a conventional food.

> . . . Liquid products that suggest through their serving size, packaging, or recommended daily intake that they are intended to be consumed in amounts that provide all or a significant part of the entire daily drinking fluid intake of an average person in the U.S., are represented as beverages. In addition, the name of a product can represent the product as a conventional food. Product or brand names that use conventional food terms such as "beverage," "drink," "water," "juice," or similar terms represent the product as a conventional food.

DRAFT GUIDANCE FOR INDUSTRY: FACTORS THAT DISTINGUISH LIQUID DIETARY SUPPLEMENTS FROM BEVERAGES, CONSIDERATIONS REGARDING NOVEL INGREDIENTS, AND LABELING FOR BEVERAGES AND OTHER CONVENTIONAL FOODS (Dec. 2009). Just before issuing this guidance, FDA issued several untitled letters informing manufacturers of bottled water products that they were not properly categorized as dietary supplements. *See, e.g.*, Letter from Vasilios H. Frankos, Dir., Div. of Dietary Supplement Programs, to Ronald D. Wilson, President and CEO, Skinny Nutritional Corp. (Nov. 30, 2009).

3.   *Other Product Forms.* In concluding that melatonin brownies were conventional foods, one of the factors FDA listed was "the appearance and packaging of the product as a brownie." This statement shows that with respect to products other than liquids, teas, and bars, FDA may deem the very use of a conventional food form, particularly in combination with other factors, to constitute an inherent representation that the product is a conventional food. For example, after McNeil informed FDA that it intended to market Benecol®, a margarine-like spread containing plant stanol esters and labeled for use in maintaining cholesterol at a healthy level, as a dietary supplement, FDA cautioned the company not to do so. In a letter to McNeil, FDA stated: "The [prototype] label for the Benecol spread, through statements that the product replaces butter or margarine, *vignettes picturing the product in common butter or margarine uses,* statements promoting the flavor and texture of the product, and statements such as '. . . help(s) you manage your cholesterol naturally through foods you eat,' represents this product for use as a conventional food. Therefore, the product is not a dietary supplement." Letter from Joseph A. Levitt, Director, CFSAN, FDA, to Brian D. Perkins (Oct. 28, 1998) (emphasis added). McNeil strongly disagreed with FDA but chose not to contest the matter. Today, McNeil markets Benecol as a conventional food with an approved health claim.

On occasion, FDA has suggested that a properly named product can legally be marketed as a dietary supplement despite its conventional food form. For example, in a 1998 letter, FDA took the position that describing a dietary supplement as a "chewing gum" would require that it be labeled as a conventional food, but that it could be marketed as a dietary supplement if it were described as a dietary ingredient in a chewing gum base. Letter from James T. Tanner, Acting Director, FDA CFSAN Office of Special Nutritionals Division of Programs and Enforcement Policy, to John P. Vernardos (June 28, 1998). Similarly, FDA objected to the use of stevia represented as a sugar substitute but not as a dietary ingredient. *See* Warning Letter from Tyler H. Thornberg, Acting Director, FDA Denver District Office, to D. Gary Young (Apr. 26, 2002).

4.   *Section 411 (the Vitamin–Mineral Amendments).* The fact that section 411 of the FD&C Act contained a list of permissible supplement forms prior to the 1994 passage of DSHEA reflects the fact that DSHEA was not Congress's first measure establishing special requirements for dietary supplements. In 1976, in response to efforts by FDA to stringently regulate vitamin and mineral supplements, Congress amended the FD&C Act by adding section 411, which significantly curtailed FDA's authority to restrict the composition of these products. Vitamin–Mineral Amendments of 1976, 90 Stat. 401 (1976). Section 411, still in effect, prohibits FDA from establishing maximum limits on the potency of vitamin and mineral products, from classifying a vitamin or mineral supplement as a drug solely because it exceeds nutritionally useful levels, and from limiting the combination or number of vitamin, mineral, and other food ingredients in supplements. FD&C Act 411(a)(1).

NOTES: OTHER SPECIAL CATEGORIES OF FOOD

1. *Infant Foods.* Until 1980, FDA promulgated special requirements for infant food (including infant formulas) pursuant solely to FD&C Act 403(j), the "special dietary use" provision. In mid-1979, Syntex Laboratories recalled three soy protein-based infant formulas that, because of an inadequate level of chlorine, resulted in a number of cases of metabolic alkalosis, an abnormal condition generally characterized in infants by a failure to thrive. "Infant Formulas Being Recalled," FDA Talk Paper No. T79–34 (Aug. 2, 1979). The following year, Congress, impelled by dissatisfaction with FDA's response to this crisis, enacted the Infant Formula Act of 1980, 94 Stat. 1190. This law added FD&C Act section 412, which significantly enhanced the agency's power over infant formulas. In 1986, Congress amended section 412 to add additional requirements. 100 Stat. 3207, 3207–116.

FDA has implemented its section 412 authority over infant formula by issuing regulations setting forth quality control procedures, reporting and record retention requirements, recall procedures (for both voluntary and mandatory recalls), labeling requirements, and nutrient requirements. The infant formula regulations are codified in 21 C.F.R. Parts 106 & 107. Moreover, the special dietary food regulations still contain a couple of labeling requirements for infant foods, now rendered largely redundant by statutory requirements and regulations applicable to all foods. 35 Fed. Reg. 16737 (Oct. 29, 1970), 36 Fed. Reg. 23555 (Dec. 10, 1971), codified at 21 C.F.R. 105.65.

2. *Medical Foods.* FDA initially created the category of medical food administratively, without express statutory authority. "Medical food" was subsequently defined as follows in the Orphan Drug Act Amendments of 1988: "a food which is formulated to be consumed or administered enterally [i.e., by way of the intestine] under the supervision of a physician and which is intended for the specific dietary management of a disease or condition for which distinctive nutritional requirements, based on recognized scientific principles, are established by medical evaluation." Section 5(b) of the Orphan Drug Act, codified at 21 U.S.C. 360ee(b)(3). FDA has clarified:

> FDA considers the statutory definition of medical foods to narrowly constrain the types of products that fit within this category of food. Medical foods are distinguished from the broader category of foods for special dietary use and from foods that make health claims by the requirement that medical foods be intended to meet distinctive nutritional requirements of a disease or condition, used under medical supervision, and intended for the specific dietary management of a disease or condition. Medical foods are not those simply recommended by a physician as part of an overall diet to manage the symptoms or reduce the risk of a disease or condition, and all foods fed to sick patients are not medical foods. Instead, medical foods are foods that are specially formulated and processed (as opposed to a naturally occurring foodstuff used in a natural state) for a patient who is seriously ill or who requires use of the product as a major component of a disease or condition's specific dietary management.

DRAFT GUIDANCE FOR INDUSTRY: FREQUENTLY ASKED QUESTIONS ABOUT MEDICAL FOODS; SECOND EDITION 4 (rev. Aug. 2013). FDA has issued regulations clarifying the statutory definition of "medical food" at 21 C.F.R. 101.9(j)(8).

Medical foods are subject to almost all of the requirements applicable to food generally. *Id.* The only—but significant—exception is a statutory exemption from the provisions governing nutrition labeling, nutrient descriptors, and disease prevention claims for food. FD&C Act 403(q)(5)(A)(iv).

3. *Hypoallergenic Foods.* In addition to the infant food labeling requirements mentioned above, *supra* note 1, FDA's remaining "Foods for Special Dietary Use" regulations, issued pursuant to FD&C Act 403(j), include label requirements for hypoallergenic foods, 37 Fed. Reg. 9763 (May 17, 1972), codified at 21 C.F.R. 105.62. Manufacturers rarely make such claims, however. In early 1989, when FDA undertook a review of the labeling claims for existing infant formulas in accordance with the Infant Formula Act of 1980, 94 Stat. 1190, codified at FD&C Act 412, the agency concluded that claims for hypoallergenicity, i.e., "usefulness in the management of severe food allergies, sensitivity to intact protein and galactosemia (inability to metabolize one milk sugar)," were not supported by "a convincing body of evidence." "Infant Formula Claims," FDA Talk Paper No. T89–18 (Mar. 27, 1989); "Update on Good Start Formula," FDA Talk Paper No. T89–31 (May 10, 1989). The Food Allergen Labeling and Consumer Protection Act of 2004 requires the disclosure of the presence of eight major allergens. *See infra* p. 397.

4. *Diet Foods.* The special dietary food regulations also include labeling requirements for foods represented for usefulness in reducing or maintaining body weight (including food labeled with terms such as "diet," "dietetic," and "artificially sweetened"). 43 Fed. Reg. 43248 (Sept. 22, 1978), codified at 21 C.F.R. 105.66. Most of the concerns regarding the labeling of such products are addressed by the Nutrition Labeling and Education Act of 1990, and these provisions were thus revised as part of the NLEA regulations. A low sodium food rule promulgated under 403(j) was completely superseded by the NLEA and thus revoked by the NLEA regulations.

5. *Nutrigenomics.* Nutrigenomics is the emerging field that studies how an individual's unique genetic makeup determines the appropriate nutrients and food for that individual. Although this field is in its infancy, nutrigenomics will undoubtedly have a substantial impact on the labeling and formulation of personalized conventional food and dietary supplements in the future.

B. HISTORICAL OVERVIEW OF FDA REGULATION OF FOOD IDENTITY, QUALITY, AND LABELING

Section 403 of the FD&C Act itemizes the circumstances under which a food will be considered "misbranded" and thus subject to enforcement action. Most of the forms of "misbranding" specified in section 403 relate to information included in, or omitted from, the "label" or "labeling" of food products. In various ways, these definitions of misbranding are designed to force food suppliers to tell the truth about their products. Section 403(a)(1) thus prohibits label statements that are "false or misleading in any particular." Additional provisions prohibit other types of affirmative deceptions respecting quality, quantity, or identity. Other provisions force manufacturers to provide information that they might otherwise omit—such as the complete ingredients or the nutrient content of a product. These affirmative requirements thus make assumptions about the types of information that consumers require to make wise food choices.

The history of FDA regulation of food labeling under the FD&C Act can be divided into three eras. The first era lasted from passage of the FD&C Act in 1938 until the White House Conference on Food, Nutrition, and Health in December 1969, the second extended from this conference until the passage of the Nutrition Labeling and Education Act in 1990, and the third has continued to the present. Most of the specific developments discussed in general terms in this historical summary will be addressed in detail subsequently in this Chapter. Much of the content of the summary derives from Peter Barton Hutt, *Regulating the Misbranding of Food*, 43 FOOD TECHNOLOGY 288 (Sept. 1989).

Period I: 1938–1969

During this period, FDA, while taking enforcement actions against false and misleading content in food labeling, also relied largely on controlling the composition of foods to prevent consumer deception and to ensure adequate nutrition.

Following enactment of the FD&C Act in 1938, FDA relied primarily upon five (still extant) statutory provisions to regulate food misbranding: (1) the mandatory information required by the statute to appear on all food labels, (2) the mandatory standards of identity for food products, (3) the labeling of imitation food, (4) the nutrition information for special dietary food, and (5) the prohibition against any false or misleading claims.

Under section 403 of the 1938 FD&C Act, every food label was required to bear, at the very minimum, the following four categories of information: the name of the food; a statement of the ingredients (or of the optional ingredients for standardized foods); the net quantity of contents; and the name and address of the manufacturer or distributor. The agency vigorously enforced these requirements, although they (particularly the "name" requirement) sometimes presented complex interpretive problems.

Standards of identity played a major role in FDA regulation during Period I. Even before enactment of the 1906 statute, FDA had established some 200 informal food standards. Although Congress declined to include legal authority for mandatory food standards in the 1906 Act, FDA continued with this work until the FD&C Act was enacted in 1938. Section 401 of the Act authorized FDA to promulgate definitions and standards of identity for any food product in order to "promote honesty and fair dealing in the interest of consumers." Because of its long interest in food standards, FDA promptly moved to implement this new authority. By 1970, approximately half of the American food supply was subject to an FDA food standard.

When the agency promulgated the earliest food standards under the Act, modern food technology was just beginning to flourish. Some functional food ingredients (e.g., preservatives, emulsifiers, thickeners, and so forth) were in use, but many staple foods remained quite simple and had not yet undergone the transformation that later occurred. Moreover, until 1958, FDA had no independent statutory authority to require premarket testing and approval of new food additives for safety. Accordingly, FDA adopted the policy of establishing strict "recipe" standards of identity, under which every permitted ingredient was specifically listed in the standard. Under this policy, no new ingredient could be used until the standard was amended to include it. Accordingly, all progress in food technology for standardized foods depended upon amendment of the applicable food standards. In the 1960s, FDA started to experiment with a new, broader form of standard that permitted any "safe and suitable" functional ingredient, although the agency did not move to broaden all of the existing standards.

FDA initially sought to use food standards to ban the development of new substitute food products. It argued that any imitation of a standardized product was inherently illegal, no matter how it was labeled. In 1951, however, the United States Supreme Court ruled in *62 Cases of Jam v. U.S.*, 340 U.S. 593 (excerpted *infra* p. 348]), that the FD&C Act did not prohibit the sale of a food that violated an applicable standard so long as it was labeled as an "imitation" of the standardized food, pursuant to section 403(c). Immediately following this decision, FDA successfully compelled a soy-based frozen desert to be unappealingly labeled "imitation ice cream." *United States v. 651 Cases . . . Chocolate Chil-Zert*, 114 F. Supp. 430 (N.D.N.Y. 1953). The agency thus indicated that it would vigorously enforce the imitation provision to inhibit the marketing of new food products. This was the high point of FDA's use of the imitation labeling requirement to try to control food composition.

FDA also used standards of identity to establish appropriate levels of vitamin and mineral fortification and to control which foods could be fortified. Developing knowledge about essential vitamins and minerals during the 1930s led the American Medical Association's Council on Food and Nutrition to adopt a policy that food fortification should be reserved for exceptional cases where there was convincing evidence of a need for the vitamin or mineral and where the food to be fortified was a suitable carrier. When FDA announced public hearings in 1940 to establish a standard of identity for flour, both AMA and the National Academy of Sciences recommended that the standard establish appropriate levels for enrichment with vitamins and minerals. The enriched flour standard of identity became effective on January 1, 1942, and set a pattern for numerous subsequent standards for enriched food. Following World War II, as food fortification continued to grow, FDA became convinced that a more restrictive regulatory approach was necessary to prevent overfortification of the American food supply. In 1960s, FDA proposed to limit fortification to eight classes of food with 12 essential nutrients. 27 Fed. Reg. 5815 (June 20,1962).

Period I also saw significant agency activity pursuant to section 403(j) of the FD&C Act, which authorized FDA to promulgate regulations mandating label information concerning the vitamin, mineral, and other dietary properties of food represented for special dietary uses. In November 1941, following a public hearing, FDA promulgated regulations governing vitamin-mineral supplements, fortified food products, and other special dietary foods such as infant food, hypo-allergenic food, and food used in weight control. Because these regulations imposed no limit on other types of claims or on permissible formulations, the number of special dietary products proliferated, along with the claims made for them. In spite of numerous court actions and educational approaches, FDA could not bring these products under control. As a result, FDA concluded that the only reasonable approach to this matter would be through revision of the 1941 regulations. As part of the proposed regulations to restrict food fortification discussed above, FDA proposed to limit the number of permitted formulations of vitamin and mineral supplements and to ban common labeling claims for these products that the agency regarded as false or misleading.

Finally, Period I saw the agency actively enforcing section 403(a)'s prohibition on any "false or misleading statement" in food labeling, a provision carried over from the 1906 Act. Most fraudulent or outrageous food claims had long since disappeared as a result of regulatory action under the 1906 Act. However, with the advent of food fortification and vitamin-mineral supplements, and the gradual unfolding of scientific evidence about the relationship between diet and health, new regulatory problems emerged. During this period, FDA sought to prohibit any specific claim that a food or food component would prevent a particular disease. Following publication of a major report by the American Heart Association in August 1957 recommending a reduction in dietary cholesterol and saturated fats, labeling and advertising claims for common food products made reference to this new information. Faced with these claims, FDA sought to forbid any mention of cholesterol or saturated fat, considering such references to be "nutritional quackery." As time wore on, however, and the scientific evidence became more compelling, the agency faced increased pressure to change its position. By the late 1960s, FDA continued to adhere to this policy in public, but took relatively little legal action to enforce it.

During this period, FDA also brought numerous court actions against vitamin and mineral supplements under both the food and drug sections of the FD&C Act. *See, e.g., V.E. Irons, Inc. v. United States,* 244 F.2d 34 (1st Cir. 1957); *United States v. "Vitasafe Formula M",* 226 F. Supp. 266 (D.N.J. 1964). These enforcement actions were directed not only at claims to prevent, treat, and cure specific diseases, but also at labeling assertions regarding basic nutritional requirements that the agency deemed to be false or misleading. Prior to 1970, FDA (along with the Federal Trade Commission) undoubtedly expended more enforcement resources in the area of nutrition than in any other single field.

Period II: 1969–89

In 1969, President Richard M. Nixon convened a White House Conference on Food, Nutrition, and Health. Although the conference was organized in response to charges of hunger and malnutrition in America, not to consider regulatory issues, its conclusions had a dramatic and unexpected impact on FDA policy toward food misbranding. The White House Conference report thoroughly criticized and rejected the highly restrictive approach to food regulation embraced by the agency through the 1960s. Rather than stress the problems of nutrition quackery, the report emphasized the need for sound nutrition, the capacity of modern food technology to fulfill that need, and the benefits of increased public information about nutrition. The release of the report coincided, moreover, with the start of a major turnover in FDA personnel. Many who formed the new leadership in FDA during the early 1970s had participated in the White House Conference and were ready to implement the regulatory recommendations of the report.

The White House Conference thus represented the end of FDA's restrictive approach to food regulation. In its place emerged an approach based largely on labeling requirements rather than on rigid standards for product composition. Although standardized foods were required at the time to list only their optional ingredients on the label, FDA took steps to encourage full ingredient listing on such products. FDA also promulgated new regulations governing the names to be used on the labels of food products. The new regulations emphasized that a food name must accurately identify or describe the basic nature of the food or its characterizing properties or ingredients, state the percentage of any characterizing ingredients, and distinguish the food from different products.

The Food Additives Amendment of 1958 and the Color Additives Amendment of 1960 provided for premarket safety review of many food ingredients. In light of these laws, and the rapid development of food technology, the use of recipe standards was no longer warranted by the early 1970s. FDA thus began a systematic amendment of all existing food standards to eliminate the old "recipe" approach and to permit any "safe and suitable" functional ingredient. Moreover, in 1970, FDA stopped proposing and promulgating new food standards, and it has not issued a single new standard since. The agency also abandoned its old position that any resemblance of a new food to a traditional standardized food, or any reference to a standardized food's name in the name of a new food, automatically rendered the new food illegal unless it was called an "imitation" of its standardized counterpart. FDA began instead to emphasize the accurate descriptive naming of modified standardized foods. In 1973, FDA promulgated a regulation defining "imitation" solely in terms of nutritional inferiority. 38 Fed. Reg. 2138 (Jan. 19, 1973) (excerpted *infra* p. 369).

In the early 1970s, FDA also adopted new regulations governing nutrition labeling for all food. The agency promulgated a requirement that, if any nutrient was added to a food, or any nutrition claim was made for a food, the product had to bear full nutrition labeling in the format established by FDA. Meanwhile, the agency totally abandoned its regulations allowing vitamin and mineral fortification only in specified foods at specified levels.

FDA made a conscious trade-off in adopting this new approach to food regulation. It substantially reduced the restrictions on formulation and composition imposed by food standards and other regulations, and it correspondingly increased the labeling requirements for all food. The food industry was thus free to pursue the benefits of modern food technology, but only at the price of providing far more information to consumers through food labeling.

As part of this new approach, FDA adopted a distinction between the provision of specific information relating to food composition, on the one hand, and the use of specific health claims based on that composition, on the other hand. FDA took the position that information concerning product composition was lawful, but that any specific claim that the composition of a product would help prevent a particular disease was unlawful. Thus, FDA permitted cholesterol and fatty acid information as an optional part of nutrition labeling, but it prohibited any claims linking that information to a potential reduction in heart disease.

In 1985, however, a year after industry forced the issue by beginning to use disease prevention claims in food labeling, FDA announced a major change in this policy. Under the new policy, specific claims about prevention of disease were permitted if they were recognized as valid by qualified experts, emphasized that good nutrition is a function of the total diet, were reasonably uniform within the marketplace, and did not result in dietary "power" races.

Overall, however, FDA lagged behind congressional and public expectations in addressing food labeling issues throughout the 1980s. The agency defined nutrient descriptors for sodium and proposed to define some nutrient descriptors for cholesterol, but it did not address this area systemically. Moreover, FDA gave no consideration to performing a substantial reconsideration of nutrition labeling to reflect new information on diet and health. As a result, FDA came under increasing criticism from Congress and the public. Congress, as described in the next section, ultimately took the matter into its own hands in 1990 through passage of the Nutritional Labeling and Education Act.

Finally, even while abandoning its restrictive approach to food fortification, FDA attempted to retain limitations on the composition and potency of vitamin-mineral supplements. In the same 1973 regulations in which the agency deserted any limits on food fortification, it also established composition-restricting standards of identity for four types of combination dietary supplements and ruled that any product containing an amount in excess of 150 percent of the RDA of a vitamin or mineral would be a drug. 38 Fed. Reg. 20708, 20730 (Aug. 2, 1973). These regulations were immediately challenged in court. Before the courts had their final say, however, President Ford, on April 22, 1976, signed the Vitamin–Mineral Amendments of 1976, which were intended to constrict the authority on which FDA had relied in adopting its controversial vitamin and mineral regulations. The Amendments added a new section 411 to the FD&C Act, which significantly curtailed FDA's power to restrict the composition of dietary supplements under sections 201(n), 401, or 403.

Meanwhile, the Second Circuit invalidated parts of the 1973 regulations and stayed the regulations in their entirety pending further consideration and rulemaking by FDA. *National Nutritional Foods Association v. FDA*, 504 F.2d 761 (2d Cir. 1974); *National Nutritional Foods Ass'n v. Mathews*, 557 F.2d 325 (2d Cir. 1977) (excerpted *supra* p.

93). In 1976 and 1977, FDA issued final revised regulations that it believed responded to the Court of Appeals' ruling and complied with section 411, but following a further remand of the rules to the agency on procedural grounds, FDA revoked the vitamin-mineral regulations altogether in 1978 and 1979—even those aspects that had been upheld by the court and were consistent with section 411. When FDA resumed aggressive enforcement against dietary supplements in the early 1990s, Congress intervened once again by passing the Dietary Supplement Health and Education Act of 1994.

Period III: 1990-Present

The history of FDA regulation of conventional food labeling since 1990 has been overwhelmingly dominated by the enactment that year of an important new statute, the Nutrition Labeling and Education Act (NLEA). This law extensively amended and expanded section 403 of the FD&C Act, the section dealing with misbranded food. The NLEA dealt with various matters, all of which involved, directly or indirectly, FDA regulation relating to the nutrient content of food.

First, section 403(q) was added to the FD&C Act to require nutrition labeling for virtually all food products. This was not a controversial issue. FDA had belatedly proposed to do this by regulation in 1989, and the industry had supported it. The statute required a shift in emphasis from micronutrients to macronutrients and authorized FDA to set standards for serving sizes. Because FDA could have taken these measures under existing law, however, this aspect of NLEA represented little change.

Second, FDA was required to define the nutrient descriptors commonly in use throughout the food industry—high fiber, low fat, reduced cholesterol, and so forth. FDA had begun this task in the 1970s, but it had not nearly completed it. Although the agency could have done so under existing law, the NLEA compelled it to finish the process.

Third, FDA was required to review petitions for use of disease prevention claims on food labeling. (These claims are generally but confusingly now called "health claims.") The NLEA empowered FDA to promulgate regulations authorizing those claims supported by "significant scientific agreement." This provision was quite controversial because it reflected some of the same criteria that had earlier been proposed by FDA and strongly criticized by the food industry. This provision of the NLEA would ultimately produce the most serious controversy. One aspect of this controversy that may not have been fully anticipated in 1990 was the question of whether government restrictions on the use of health claims could infringe the First Amendment of the United States Constitution, protecting freedom of speech. In the early 2000s, court decisions regarding this issue compelled FDA to adjust its health claims regime so as not to violate the First Amendment.

The NLEA also contained several new food labeling and food standards provisions. For example, vegetable and fruit juice beverages were required to bear the percent of each juice on the information panel. All ingredients in standardized food products were required to be included in the statement of ingredients. Food standards (except for dairy products and "maple sirup") were permitted to be promulgated, amended, and repealed using informal notice-and-comment rulemaking, rather than the formal trial-type administrative hearing procedure that prevailed (and effectively prevented agency action) in the past.

Finally, most of the labeling requirements under the FD&C Act were explicitly made subject to national uniformity (federal preemption). By requiring national uniformity, the NLEA effectively removed state and local government from establishing regulatory requirements relating to the nutrient content of food. This represented a major change in national food policy, one that had been sought by the food industry for a century.

Meanwhile, the regulation of dietary supplements during the modern period has been dominated by the Dietary Supplement Health and Education Act of 1994 (DSHEA). FDA took relatively little regulatory action that focused on dietary supplements for a decade following its late-1970s revocation of the 1973 vitamin-mineral regulations. When the agency began to implement the Nutrition Labeling and Education Act of 1990, however, it saw an opportunity to revive its earlier, thwarted effort to tighten the regulatory controls over dietary supplements. This strategy backfired, however, and resulted in DSHEA, a second congressional rejection of FDA's approach to dietary supplement regulation.

DSHEA establishes a new, broad category called "dietary supplement," which includes substances such as botanicals as well as vitamins and minerals. DSHEA requires all such products—including those that are not common sense "food"—to be regulated as food for most purposes. It mandates that dietary supplements bear a "Supplement Facts" label similar to the "Nutrition Facts" label required for conventional foods. DSHEA also permits manufacturers of all such products to make structure/function claims without subjecting them to regulation as drugs. In accordance with the NLEA, dietary supplements may also make health claims. Furthermore, First Amendment limitations on the regulation of food labeling also apply to dietary supplements—indeed, the seminal cases were decided in the supplement context. *See infra* p. 430. Overall, therefore, the modern system for regulating the labeling of dietary supplements is extremely similar to that applicable to conventional food.

C. WHAT'S IN A NAME? REGULATION OF FOOD IDENTITY AND QUALITY

Regulation of food labeling and regulation of food content are linked issues. The interaction between them is particularly important with respect to food names. The commercial viability of a product depends largely on what the manufacturer is permitted to call it. Food names are not limited to brand names; every food label must include a "common or usual name," an FDA-regulated term. FD&C Act 403(i)(1). The agency can indirectly control food composition by allowing only products of preferred composition to bear the most appealing common or usual names, which are often basic, unmodified terms such as *milk* or *macaroni*. For the first few decades of the life of the FD&C Act, FDA actively attempted to control food composition through just this method. As the materials below show, however, we are now in an era in which

FDA generally does not seek to inhibit the sale of disfavored products through draconian naming rules.

Section 403(i) requires that a food label bear "the common or usual name of the food, if any there be." According to section 403(g) of the FD&C Act, if a food "purports to be or is represented as" a type of food for which FDA has issued a standard of identity regulation, the label must bear "the name of the food specified in the definition and standard." Section 401 states that the name that FDA assigns a food in a standard of identity regulation is required to be "its common or usual name so far as practicable." In the absence of an applicable standard of identity, the common or usual name of a food may be established "by common usage" or by other regulation. 21 C.F.R. 102.5(d). FDA regulations implement these requirements as follows, at 21 C.F.R. 101.3:

§ 101.3   Identity labeling of food in packaged form.

(a) The principal display panel of a food in package form shall bear as one of its principal features a statement of the identity of the commodity.

(b) Such statement of identity shall be in terms of:

(1) The name now or hereafter specified in or required by any applicable Federal law or regulation; or, in the absence thereof,

(2) The common or usual name of the food; or, in the absence thereof,

(3) An appropriately descriptive term, or when the nature of the food is obvious, a fanciful name commonly used by the public for such food.

. . . .

(d) This statement of identity shall be presented in bold type on the principal display panel, shall be in a size reasonably related to the most prominent printed matter on such panel, and shall be in lines generally parallel to the base on which the package rests as it is designed to be displayed.

1.   FOOD STANDARDS OF IDENTITY

Ancient botanists, beginning with Theophrastus (370–285 B.C.), established "standards" by describing the available food supply and warning against its adulteration with other substances. Standards of identity for bread were established in the Roman Empire and in medieval England to assure the integrity of the food supply. The same approach has been pursued in the United States, although with varying vigor. As the materials below will show, standards of identity now play a relatively limited function in the food regulatory system. Nonetheless, an examination of the history of food standards in America provides a good introduction to different possible modes of regulation of food identity and quality, and it casts light on the regulatory choices ultimately made by FDA.

a.   STRONG STANDARDS OF IDENTITY: THE FILLED MILK ACT

Section 401 of the FD&C Act gives the agency power to issue by regulation a definition and standard of identity for any food. However, as will be explored below, section 403 of the Act, as interpreted by the United States Supreme Court, does not altogether prohibit the sale of a food that purports to be a standardized food but fails to conform to the relevant food standard regulation. *62 Cases of Jam v. U.S.*, 340 U.S. 593 (1951) (excerpted *infra* p. 348), Instead, section 403 requires that the food be called an "imitation" version of the standardized food. 21 U.S.C. 403(c). Over the past forty years, even this requirement has been applied sparingly. *See infra* p. 368.

It should be noted that there is a stronger version of food standardization that actually prohibits the sale of products that do not satisfy the legal "recipe," regardless of how these substitutes are labeled. This approach is embodied in the Federal Filled Milk Act, 42 Stat. 1486 (1923), 21 U.S.C. 61–64, which bans products that blend milk with any fat or oil other than milk fat "in imitation or semblance of milk." FDA administered this statute until 1973, when the agency stopped enforcing it following a court's determination that it was unconstitutional. *See infra* p. 338, note 1. Earlier, however, the Filled Milk Act had been upheld by the United States Supreme Court in one of the more famous cases of the New Deal era:

Carolene Products Co. v. United States
304 U. S. 144 (1938).

■ MR. JUSTICE STONE delivered the opinion of the Court.

The question for decision is whether the "Filled Milk Act" of Congress of March 4, 1923 (21 U.S.C. § 61–63), which prohibits the shipment in interstate commerce of skimmed milk compounded with any fat or oil other than milk fat, so as to resemble milk or cream . . . infringes the Fifth Amendment.

Appellee was indicted in the district court for southern Illinois for violation of the Act by the shipment in interstate commerce of certain packages of "Milnut," a compound of condensed skimmed milk and coconut oil made in imitation or semblance of condensed milk or cream. . . .

. . . Appellee . . . complains that the statute denies to it equal protection of the laws, and in violation of the Fifth Amendment, deprives it of its property without due process of law, particularly in that the statute purports to make binding and conclusive upon appellee the legislative declaration that appellee's product "is an adulterated article of food, injurious to the public health, and its sale constitutes a fraud on the public."

. . . The prohibition of shipment of appellee's product in interstate commerce does not infringe the Fifth Amendment. Twenty years ago, this Court, in *Hebe Co. v. Shaw*, 248 U. S. 297, held that a state law which forbids the manufacture and sale of a product assumed to be wholesome and nutritive, made of condensed skimmed milk, compounded with coconut oil, is not forbidden by the Fourteenth

Amendment. The power of the legislature to secure a minimum of particular nutritive elements in a widely used article of food and to protect the public from fraudulent substitutions was not doubted, and the Court thought that there was ample scope for the legislative judgment that prohibition of the offending article was an appropriate means of preventing injury to the public.

We see no persuasive reason for departing from that ruling here, where the Fifth Amendment is concerned, and since none is suggested, we might rest decision wholly on the presumption of constitutionality. But affirmative evidence also sustains the statute. In twenty years, evidence has steadily accumulated of the danger to the public health from the general consumption of foods which have been stripped of elements essential to the maintenance of health. The Filled Milk Act was adopted by Congress after committee hearings, in the course of which eminent scientists and health experts testified. An extensive investigation was made of the commerce in milk compounds in which vegetable oils have been substituted for natural milk fat, and of the effect upon the public health of the use of such compounds as a food substitute for milk. . . . Both committees concluded, as the statute itself declares, that the use of filled milk as a substitute for pure milk is generally injurious to health and facilitates fraud on the public.

There is nothing in the Constitution which compels a legislature, either national or state, to ignore such evidence, nor need it disregard the other evidence which amply supports the conclusions of the Congressional committees that the danger is greatly enhanced where an inferior product, like appellee's, is indistinguishable from a valuable food of almost universal use, thus making fraudulent distribution easy and protection of the consumer difficult.

Here, the prohibition of the statute is inoperative unless the product is "in imitation or semblance of milk, cream, or skimmed milk, whether or not condensed." Whether in such circumstances the public would be adequately protected by the prohibition of false labels and false branding imposed by the Pure Food and Drugs Act, or whether it was necessary to go farther and prohibit a substitute food product thought to be injurious to health if used as a substitute when the two are not distinguishable, was a matter for the legislative judgment, and not that of courts. It was upon this ground that the prohibition of the sale of oleomargarine made in imitation of butter was held not to infringe the Fourteenth Amendment in *Powell v. Pennsylvania*, 127 U.S. 678.

Appellee raises no valid objection to the present statute by arguing that its prohibition has not been extended to oleomargarine or other butter substitutes in which vegetable fats or oils are substituted for butter fat. The Fifth Amendment has no equal protection clause, and even that of the Fourteenth, applicable only to the states, does not compel their legislatures to prohibit all like evils, or none. A legislature may hit at an abuse which it has found, even though it has failed to strike at another.

. . . . [R]egulatory legislation affecting ordinary commercial transactions is not to be pronounced unconstitutional unless in the light of the facts made known or generally assumed it is of such a character as to preclude the assumption that it rests upon some rational basis within the knowledge and experience of the legislators. . . .

The prohibition of shipment in interstate commerce of appellee's product, as described in the indictment, is a constitutional exercise of the power to regulate interstate commerce. As the statute is not unconstitutional on its face the demurrer should have been overruled, and the judgment will be reversed.

NOTES

1. *Related Case.* In a subsequent decision, *United States v. Carolene Products Co.*, 323 U.S. 18 (1944), the Supreme Court upheld the application of the Filled Milk Act to a version of the same product that was fortified with vitamins to make it as nutritious as milk. The Court explained: "While . . . the vitamin deficiency was an efficient cause in bringing about the enactment of the Filled Milk Act, it was not the sole reason for its passage. A second reason was that the compounds lend themselves readily to substitution for or confusion with milk products." *Id.* at 22–23.

2. *Substantive Due Process.* Since the Supreme Court dismantled economic substantive due process during the 1930s and 1940s in cases like *Carolene Products*, courts have routinely validated a wide range of both federal and state laws that regulate the composition and naming of food. However, some have criticized judicial doctrines that, in the name of consumer protection, allow legislative schemes whose primary effect, and perhaps purpose, is to protect established producers from competition. *See, e.g.* Jerry L. Mashaw, *Constitutional Deregulation: Notes Toward a Public, Public Law*, 54 TUL. L. REV. 849 (1980).

3. *Industry Use of Regulation.* In *The Theory of Economic Regulation*, 2 BELL J. OF ECON. & MGT. SCI. 3 (1971), Professor George Stigler argues:

> . . . as a rule, regulation is acquired by the industry and is designed and operated primarily for its benefit. . . .

> The most obvious contribution that a group may seek of the government is a direct subsidy of money. . . .

> The second major public resource commonly sought by an industry is control over entry by new rivals. . . .

> We propose the general hypothesis: every industry or occupation that has enough political power to utilize the state will seek to control entry. In addition, the regulatory policy will often be so fashioned as to retard the rate of growth of new firms. . . .

> A third general set of powers of the state which will be sought by the industry are those which affect substitutes and complements. Crudely put, the butter producers wish to suppress margarine and encourage the production of bread. . . .

The following 1972 case signaled somewhat closer judicial scrutiny of statutes designed to protect traditional food products against new products made through modern food technology. The decision effectively spelled the end of the Filled Milk Act, related statutes, and the "strong" version of food standards generally. The plaintiff corporation in this case was the same as the one in *Carolene Products*; it changed the name of its filled milk product from Milnut to Milnot in the late 1930s and the name of the corporation itself to Milnot in the early 1950s.

Milnot Co. v. Richardson

350 F. Supp. 221 (N.D. Ill. 1972).

■ MORGAN, DISTRICT JUDGE.

This is an action for declaratory judgment . . . asking the court to declare that the product known as "Milnot," manufactured by the plaintiff, is not within the purview of the provisions of 21 U.S.C. §§ 61–64 [The Filled Milk Act]; or, in the alternative, to declare that Act unconstitutional on the ground that it violates the provisions of the Fifth Amendment to the Constitution of the United States. . . .

. . . The substance involved in this case, Milnot, is a food product which basically is a blend of fat free milk and vegetable soya oil, to which are added vitamins A and D. In the production of this product cream is skimmed from whole fresh milk. The cream contains the butterfat content of the milk including the fat-soluble vitamins A, D and E. To the portion of the milk which remains after the skimming process, plaintiff adds, *inter alia,* soybean oil as well as vitamins A and D. This restores the liquid to a milk-like consistency and composition. The mixture is then evaporated so as to remove a portion of the water content. That Milnot is wholesome, nutritious, and useful as a food source is clear from the record.

The Filled Milk Act, promulgated by Congress in 1923, prohibits interstate shipment of filled milk products. Following enactment of that statute, plaintiff, then known as Carolene Products Company, violated it and was convicted. After much litigation, the United States Supreme Court twice upheld the validity of the statute. . . . At least since affirmance of its second conviction, plaintiff has limited its distribution of Milnot to intrastate commerce in the several states where it is produced. . . .

. . . Plaintiff suggests, and this court agrees, that the appearance and continued existence of new products on the market and in interstate commerce which are quite similar in composition to and competitive with Milnot, and also in imitation or semblance of milk as fully as is Milnot (even though perhaps not "filled milk" in a technical sense under the statutory definition), creates a new factual situation upon which the court should reconsider the constitutionality of the Filled Milk Act as applied to Milnot. . . .

The measuring stick to which legislative acts must conform in order to satisfy due process has been stated in the previous *Carolene* decisions. That is, regulatory legislation affecting ordinary commercial transactions is not to be pronounced unconstitutional unless, in light of the known facts, it is of such a character as to preclude the assumption that it rests upon some rational basis within the knowledge and experience of the legislators. And as previously stated, the constitutionality of a statute predicated upon the existence of a particular state of facts may be challenged by showing to the court that those facts have ceased to exist.

From the undisputed facts in the record here, it appears crystal clear that certain imitation milk and dairy products are so similar to Milnot in composition, appearance, and use that different treatment as to interstate shipment caused by application of the Filled Milk Act to Milnot violates the due process of law to which Milnot Company is constitutionally entitled. No useful purpose is served by listing such products here by name or otherwise, or by discussing the dairy market conditions and dangers of confusion which led to the passage and judicial upholding of the Filled Milk Act many years ago. Suffice it to say that this court finds that the latter have long since ceased to exist.[1]

. . . The possibility of confusion, or passing off, in the marketplace, which justified the statute in 1944, can no longer be used rationally as a constitutional prop to prevent interstate shipment of Milnot. There is at least as much danger in this regard with imitation milk as with filled milk, and actually no longer any such real danger with either. . . .

NOTES

1. *Agency Response.* Following the *Milnot* decision, FDA published this announcement in 38 Fed. Reg. 20748 (Aug. 2, 1973):

> The court in the *Milnot* case concluded that, since other substitute milk and dairy products may lawfully be shipped in interstate commerce, the prohibition against interstate shipment of filled milk products was an unconstitutional discrimination against these products. The White House Conference on Food, Nutrition and Health recommended in 1969 that the Filled Milk Act be repealed, and the Food and Drug Administration has concurred in that recommendation. Accordingly, it has been concluded that the decision in the *Milnot* case will not be appealed. . . .

> This notice will serve to inform the public that, pursuant to the court decision in this case, the Filled Milk Act will no longer be enforced. Henceforth, filled milk products may lawfully be shipped in interstate commerce and will be regulated under the provisions of the Federal Food, Drug, and Cosmetic Act, just as any other foods.

In conjunction with this statement of enforcement policy, FDA proposed the establishment of a common or usual name for "filled milk" in 38 Fed. Reg. 20743 (Aug. 2, 1973). The agency subsequently withdrew the proposed common or usual name regulation and proposed a standard of identity for filled milk and other substitute dairy products in 43 Fed. Reg. 42118 (Sept. 19, 1978), which was withdrawn in 48 Fed. Reg. 37666 (Aug. 19, 1983).

---

[1] It is not insignificant in this regard that some eleven states which passed filled milk acts have since discarded them—five by repeal and six by court action. By far the majority of states now permit wholesome and properly labeled filled milk products. It is worth noting, also, that when the Federal Filled Milk Act was passed by Congress and upheld by the Supreme Court, the presently accepted dangers of "cholesterol" in animal fat were almost unknown.

2.   *Other Dairy Protection Statutes.* The Oleomargarine Act, 24 Stat. 209 (1886), was repealed and replaced by section 407 of the FD&C Act in 64 Stat. 20 (1950). The Filled Cheese Act, 29 Stat. 253 (1896), 68A Stat. 576 (1939), was repealed by 88 Stat. 1466 (1974). The Renovated Butter Act, 32 Stat. 193 (1902), was repealed by 90 Stat. 1520, 1814 (1976).

3.   *Tea Quality Standards.* Under the Tea Importation Act of 1883, 22 Stat. 451, repealed and replaced in 1897, 29 Stat. 604, FDA established a Board of Tea Experts to establish uniform quality standards for imported tea. In *Buttfield v. Stranahan*, 192 U.S. 470 (1904), the Supreme Court upheld FDA's constitutional authority to ban importation of substandard tea. Fearful of this precedent, the food industry successfully opposed FDA authority to promulgate food standards under the 1906 Pure Food and Drugs Act. The Tea Importation Act was repealed in 110 Stat. 1198 (1996) on the ground of regulatory reform.

b.   THE FORMATION AND ZENITH OF THE FD&C ACT FOOD STANDARDS REGIME

As noted by one author: "One of the greatest weaknesses of the 1906 [Pure Food and Drugs] Act was its failure to provide for mandatory standards of identity and quality for food, which would have the force of law in prosecutions for adulteration and misbranding. The Secretary could and did establish standards for his own guidance in deciding when to proceed against a food as adulterated or misbranded, but in each prosecution he had to reestablish the validity and reasonableness of the standard from which he claimed the offending food departed." *Developments in the Law—The Federal Food, Drug, and Cosmetic Act*, 67 HARV. L. REV. 632 (1954).

Recognizing this weakness, Congress included the following (still extant) provision in the 1938 FD&C Act:

> Whenever in the judgment of the Secretary such action will promote honesty and fair dealing in the interest of consumers, he shall promulgate regulations fixing and establishing for any food, under its common or usual name so far as practicable, a reasonable definition and standard of identity. . . .

FD&C Act 401.

As described in the history related earlier in this chapter, *supra* p. 325, FDA enthusiastically embraced this new authority. By 1970, the agency had issued almost 300 standards, largely for staple food products. At their broadest reach, these standards covered nearly 45 percent of the wholesale value of food shipped in interstate commerce, excluding fresh fruits and vegetables. 44 Fed. Reg. 75990 (Dec. 21, 1979). Most of these food standards remain in effect today, although many have been amended.

FDA initially viewed the FD&C Act as giving it the authority to promulgate "strong" standards with the same prohibitory effect as the Filled Milk Act. Section 403(g) declares a food to be misbranded "[i]f it purports to be or is represented as a food for which a definition and standard of identity has been prescribed by regulations as provided by section 401, unless . . . it conforms to such definition and standard." Early on, the agency interpreted this provision to completely ban the development of new substitute food products. It argued that any imitation of a standardized product was inherently illegal, no matter how it was labeled.

Most of the standards of identity promulgated by FDA included requirements designed to uphold the quality of the standardized food, such as minimum amounts of important constituents. Vitamin fortification was another principal focus of the agency's early activity in this area. Developing knowledge about essential vitamins and minerals during the 1930s led the American Medical Association's Council on Food and Nutrition to adopt a policy that food fortification should be reserved for exceptional cases where there was convincing evidence of a need for the vitamin or mineral and where the food to be fortified was a suitable carrier. In the early 1940s, as World War II loomed and then commenced, the physicians of the AMA maintained this stance, whereas nutritional scientists on the National Research Council's Food and Nutrition Board began to warn of population-wide vitamin and mineral deficiencies and their potential impairment of the national defense. HARVEY LEVENSTEIN, PARADOX OF PLENTY: A SOCIAL HISTORY OF EATING IN MODERN AMERICA 64–79 (2003). What the doctors and nutritionists agreed on was that fortification of food was a matter of great public concern. When FDA announced public hearings in 1940 to establish a standard of identity for flour, both the AMA (which supported fortification of flour and milk) and the NRC recommended that the agency establish appropriate levels for enrichment with vitamins and minerals. The enriched flour standard of identity became effective on January 1, 1942, and set a pattern for numerous subsequent standards for enriched food.

The following case concerns FDA's application of the enriched farina standard and illustrates the FD&C Act food standards regime at the height of its rigor. The Federal Security Administration was, at the time, the name of the umbrella agency containing FDA. Farina is a milled cereal grain, today exemplified by Cream of Wheat®.

Federal Security Administrator v. Quaker Oats Co.

318 U.S. 218 (1943).

■ MR. CHIEF JUSTICE STONE delivered the opinion of the Court.

The Federal Security Administrator, acting under §§ 401 and 701(e), promulgated regulations establishing "standards of identity" for various milled wheat products, excluding vitamin D from the defined standard of "farina" and permitting it only in "enriched farina," which was required to contain Vitamin B1, riboflavin, nicotinic acid and iron. The question is whether the regulations are valid as applied to respondent. The answer turns upon (a) whether there is substantial evidence in support of the Administrator's finding that indiscriminate enrichment of farina with vitamin and mineral contents would tend to confuse and mislead consumers; (b) if so, whether, upon such a finding, the Administrator has statutory authority to adopt a standard of identity, which excludes a disclosed non-deleterious ingredient, in order to promote honesty and fair dealing in the interest of consumers; and (c) whether the Administrator's treatment, by the challenged regulations, of the use of vitamin D as an ingredient of a product sold as "farina" is within his statutory authority to prescribe "a reasonable definition and standard of identity." . . .

Any food which "purports to be or is represented as a food for which a definition and standard of identity has been prescribed" pursuant to § 401 is declared by § 403(g) to be misbranded "unless (1) it conforms to such definition and standard, and (2) its label bears the name of the food specified in the definition and standard, and, insofar as may be required by such regulations, the common names of optional ingredients . . . present in such food." . . .

. . . Regulation 15.130 defined "farina" as a food prepared by grinding and bolting cleaned wheat, other than certain specified kinds, to a prescribed fineness with the bran coat and germ of the wheat berry removed to a prescribed extent. The regulation made no provision for the addition of any ingredients to "farina." Regulation 15.140 defined "enriched farina" as conforming to the regulation defining "farina," but with added prescribed minimum quantities of vitamin B1, riboflavin, nicotinic acid . . . and iron. The regulation also provided that minimum quantities of vitamin D, calcium, wheat germ or disodium phosphate might be added as optional ingredients of "enriched farina," and required that ingredients so added be specified on the label. . . .

Respondent, The Quaker Oats Company, has for the past ten years manufactured and marketed a wheat product commonly used as a cereal food, consisting of farina as defined by the Administrator's regulation, but with vitamin D added. Respondent distributes this product in packages labeled "Quaker Farina Wheat Cereal Enriched with Vitamin D," or "Quaker Farina enriched by the Sunshine Vitamin." The packages also bear the label "Contents 400 U.S.P. units of Vitamin D per ounce, supplied by approximately the addition of 1/5 of 1 percent irradiated dry yeast."

Respondent asserts, and the Government agrees, that the Act as supplemented by the Administrator's standards will prevent the marketing of its product as "farina" since, by reason of the presence of vitamin D as an ingredient, it does not conform to the standard of identity prescribed for "farina," and that respondent cannot market its product as "enriched farina" unless it adds the prescribed minimum quantities of vitamin B1, riboflavin, nicotinic acid and iron. Respondent challenges the validity of the regulations on the grounds sustained below and others so closely related to them as not to require separate consideration. . . .

In recent years millers of wheat have placed on the market flours and farinas which have been enriched by the addition of various vitamins and minerals. The composition of these enriched products varies widely. There was testimony of weight before the Administrator, principally by expert nutritionists, that such products, because of the variety and combination of added ingredients, are widely variable in nutritional value; and that consumers generally lack knowledge of the relative value of such ingredients and combinations of them.

These witnesses also testified, as did representatives of consumer organizations which had made special studies of the problems of food standardization, that the number, variety and varying combinations of the added ingredients tend to confuse the large number of consumers who desire to purchase vitamin-enriched wheat food products but who lack the knowledge essential to discriminating purchase of them; that because of this lack of knowledge and discrimination they are subject to exploitation by the sale of foods described as "enriched," but of whose inferior or unsuitable quality they are not informed. Accordingly, a large number of witnesses recommended the adoption of definitions and standards for "enriched" wheat products which would ensure fairly complete satisfaction of dietary needs, and a somewhat lesser number recommended the disallowance, as optional ingredients in the standards for unenriched wheat products, of individual vitamins and minerals whose addition would suggest to consumers an adequacy for dietary needs not in fact supplied.

. . . Taking into account the evidence of public demand for vitamin-enriched foods, their increasing sale, their variable vitamin composition and dietary value, and the general lack of consumer knowledge of such values, there was sufficient evidence of "rational probative force" to support the Administrator's judgment that, in the absence of appropriate standards of identity, consumer confusion would ensue. . . .

We have recognized that purchasers under such conditions are peculiarly susceptible to dishonest and unfair marketing practices. In *United States v. Carolene Products Co.*, 304 U. S. 144, 149, 150, we upheld the constitutionality of a statute prohibiting the sale of "filled milk" . . . although honestly labeled and not, in itself, deleterious. Decision was rested on the ground that Congress could reasonably conclude that the use of the product as a milk substitute deprives consumers of vitamins requisite for health and "facilitates fraud on the public" by "making fraudulent distribution easy and protection of the consumer difficult."

Both the text and legislative history of the present statute plainly show that its purpose was not confined to a requirement of truthful and informative labeling. False and misleading labeling had been prohibited by the Pure Food and Drugs Act of 1906. But it was found that such a prohibition was inadequate to protect the consumer from "economic adulteration," by which less expensive ingredients were substituted, or the proportion of more expensive ingredients diminished, so as to make the product, although not in itself deleterious, inferior to that which the consumer expected to receive when purchasing a product with the name under which it was sold. The remedy chosen was not a requirement of informative labeling. Rather it was the purpose to authorize the Administrator to promulgate definitions and standards of identity "under which the integrity of food products can be effectively maintained," and to require informative labeling only where no such standard had been promulgated, where the food did not purport to comply with a standard, or where the regulations permitted optional ingredients and required their mention on the label.

The provisions for standards of identity thus reflect a recognition by Congress of the inability of consumers in some cases to determine, solely on the basis of informative labeling, the relative merits of a variety of products superficially resembling each other. We cannot say that such a standard of identity, designed to eliminate a source of confusion to purchasers—which otherwise would be likely to facilitate unfair dealing and make protection of the consumer difficult—will not "promote honesty and fair dealing" within the meaning of the statute.

Respondent's final and most vigorous attack on the regulations is that they fail to establish reasonable definitions and standards of identity, as § 401 requires, in that they prohibit the marketing, under the name "farina," of a wholesome and honestly labeled product consisting of farina with vitamin D added, and that they prevent the addition of vitamin D to products marketed as "enriched farina" unless accompanied by the other prescribed vitamin ingredients which do not co-act with or have any dietary relationship to vitamin D. Stated in another form, the argument is that it is unreasonable to prohibit the addition to farina of vitamin D as an optional ingredient while permitting its addition as an optional ingredient to enriched farina, to the detriment of respondent's business.

. . . We must reject at the outset the argument earnestly pressed upon us that the statute does not contemplate a regulation excluding a wholesome and beneficial ingredient from the definition and standard of identity of a food. The statutory purpose to fix a definition of identity of an article of food sold under its common or usual name would be defeated if producers were free to add ingredients, however wholesome, which are not within the definition. . . .

We cannot say that the Administrator made an unreasonable choice of standards. . . . Consumers who buy farina will have no reason to believe that it is enriched. Those who buy enriched farina are assured of receiving a wheat product containing those vitamins naturally present in wheat, and, if so stated on the label, an additional vitamin D, not found in wheat. . . .

NOTES

1. *Forced Name Changes.* FDA's early food standards, in addition to banning some foods from the market altogether, also forced some products that were permitted to remain on the market to change their names. For example, the agency defined "cream cheese" in such a way that, among major manufacturers, only Kraft's product satisfied the standard of identity and thus could call itself "cream cheese." FDA required manufacturers of lower-fat, higher-moisture products that had long been sold as "cream cheese" to redub them "neufchatel cheese." The Second Circuit upheld FDA's actions in *Columbia Cheese v. McNutt,* 137 F.2d 576 (2d Cir. 1943).

2. *Formal Rulemaking Requirement.* The deference that courts granted to FDA's early implementation of its food standards authority is even more striking in light of the fact that the FD&C Act then mandated that such standards be supported by "substantial evidence of record" after a trial-type administrative hearing. Such formal rulemaking was required for all section 401 food standard regulation by section 701(e) of the Act. This requirement led to some agonizingly protracted proceedings, most famously those establishing the standard of identity for peanut butter, in which the manufacturers of Skippy, Peter Pan, and Jiff clashed over the mandatory percentage of peanuts before the agency and in court from 1959 until 1970. *See Corn Products Co. v. Department of HEW,* 427 F.2d 511 (3d Cir. 1970) (upholding the peanut butter standard). The administrative proceedings for

orange juice took almost seven years to complete, and those for jelly, almost five years. The advantages and disadvantages of the formal hearing requirement of section 701(e) are explored in Chapter 2, *supra* p. 49.

The original requirement of formal rulemaking under section 701(e) for every food standard was amended by 68 Stat. 54 (1954) and 70 Stat. 919 (1956) to require a hearing only upon the filing of objections. Later, in 104 Stat. 2353, 2365 (1990), Congress removed most food standards from the scope of the formal rulemaking requirement altogether. In a striking illustration of the rent-seeking nature of lawmaking emphasized by public choice theorists, however, the 1990 amendments preserved formal rulemaking, if requested, for the amendment or repeal of a standard "for any dairy product . . . or maple syrup." Can you guess what state's Senator ensured the inclusion of this provision? Apart from this exception, FDA today is permitted to adopt, amend, or repeal standards through notice-and-comment rulemaking under section 701(a) and the Administrative Procedure Act.

Richard A. Merrill & Earl M. Collier, *"Like Mother Used to Make": An Analysis of FDA Food Standards of Identity*
74 COLUMBIA LAW REVIEW 561 (1974).

. . . From the very beginning, Congress conceived that standards of identity would resemble "recipes" for foods. Legislators explicitly analogized processed foods purchased in the market to their home-made counterparts. . . . Starting from this initial conception—that standards of identity should define foods in terms of "time-honored" home recipes—the FDA began promulgating standards that prescribed the composition of foods in detail. The first standards fixed every ingredient in a food, but gradually FDA "recipes" began not only to specify mandatory ingredients but to allow certain optional ingredients as well. Nevertheless, until the early 1960's virtually all identity standards faithfully followed the basic "recipe" concept, leaving manufacturers comparatively little choice among ingredients and affording consumers practically no information about the composition of standardized foods. . . .

Two objectives explain the FDA's prolonged adherence to its original recipe format: (1) a desire to preclude any modifications of basic food formulas that could contribute to consumer deception, and (2) a concern to restrain the growing use in food production of chemical additives whose safety had not been demonstrated. . . .

. . . Recipe standards would not have dramatically affected the availability of substitutes for traditional foods if the FDA had not simultaneously espoused an expansive reading of the "purports to be or is represented as" language in section 403(g). A broad reading obviously imperils more products than a narrow one, for any product that "purports to be or is represented as" a standardized food must meet FDA's compositional requirements. . . . An expansive reading thus contributes to product homogeneity in those food markets for which standards have been adopted.

. . . The few reported cases . . . demonstrate an early consistency of purpose by the FDA to apply section 403(g) to reach most substitutes for standardized foods, sometimes even when there was no risk that consumers would confuse a challenged product with the standard item. Moreover, they reflect the courts' willingness to support the FDA's initial broad reading of that provision. . . .

Even if the FDA had read "purports to be" more narrowly, however, the use of recipe standards would itself have significantly restricted the range of substitutes for standard foods. For instance, by fixing the amount of fruit that "jam" must contain, the FDA's recipe standard for that food prevents marketing as "jam" other products that contain less fruit. Of course, a relaxed construction of section 403(g) would allow a manufacturer of a low-fruit product to establish a separate market identity without altering its labeling or appearance so substantially that it could not compete with "jam." . . .

NOTES

1. *Peanut Butter.* In *Corn Products Co. v. Department of HEW*, 427 F.2d 511 (3d Cir. 1970), the court upheld FDA's infamous standard, 21 C.F.R. 164.150, requiring 90% peanut ingredients in peanut butter. The agency rejecting the claim that 87% peanuts should be sufficient. This rulemaking demonstrates how a standard of identity may raise the "quality" of existing foods.

2. *Mayonnaise.* For an example of a classic "recipe-style" standard of identity, see the following:

§ 169.140   Mayonnaise

(a) *Description.* Mayonnaise is the emulsified semisolid food prepared from vegetable oil(s), one or both of the acidifying ingredients specified in paragraph (b) of this section, and one or more of the egg yolk-containing ingredients specified in paragraph (c) of this section. One or more of the ingredients specified in paragraph (d) of this section may also be used. The vegetable oil(s) used may contain an optional crystallization inhibitor as specified in paragraph (d)(7) of this section. All the ingredients from which the food is fabricated shall be safe and suitable. Mayonnaise contains not less than 65 percent by weight of vegetable oil. Mayonnaise may be mixed and packed in an atmosphere in which air is replaced in whole or in part by carbon dioxide or nitrogen.

(b) *Acidifying ingredients.* (1) Any vinegar or any vinegar diluted with water to an acidity, calculated as acetic acid, of not less than 2 ½ percent by weight, or any such vinegar or diluted vinegar mixed with an optional acidifying ingredient as specified in paragraph (d)(6) of this section. For the purpose of this paragraph, any blend of two or more vinegars is considered to be a vinegar.

(2) Lemon juice and/or lime juice in any appropriate form, which may be diluted with water to an acidity, calculated as citric acid, of not less than 2 ½ percent by weight.

(c) *Egg yolk-containing ingredients.* Liquid egg yolks, frozen egg yolks, dried egg yolks, liquid whole eggs, frozen whole eggs, dried whole eggs, or any one or more of the foregoing ingredients listed in this paragraph with liquid egg white or frozen egg white.

(d) *Other optional ingredients.* The following optional ingredients may also be used:

(1) Salt.

(2) Nutritive carbohydrate sweeteners.

(3) Any spice (except saffron or turmeric) or natural flavoring, provided it does not impart to the mayonnaise a color simulating the color imparted by egg yolk.

(4) Monosodium glutamate.

(5) Sequestrant(s), including but not limited to calcium disodium EDTA (calcium disodium ethylenediamine-tetraacetate) and/or disodium EDTA (disodium ethylenediaminetetraacetate), may be used to preserve color and/or flavor.

(6) Citric and/or malic acid in an amount not greater than 25 percent of the weight of the acids of the vinegar or diluted vinegar, calculated as acetic acid.

(7) Crystallization inhibitors, including but not limited to oxystearin, lecithin, or polyglycerol esters of fatty acids.

(e) *Nomenclature.* The name of the food is "Mayonnaise".

(f) *Label declaration.* Each of the ingredients used in the food shall be declared on the label as required by the applicable sections of parts 101 and 130 of this chapter.

Kraft's Miracle Whip® falls outside the mayonnaise standard because it does not contain at least 65 percent vegetable oil by weight. Rather, it satisfies the standard of identity for salad dressing, 21 C.F.R. 169.150. Therefore, the common and usual name for Miracle Whip is "salad dressing," not "mayonnaise." The label for the product calls it "dressing," even though 21 C.F.R. 169.150 does not explicitly permit this truncated nomenclature.

3. *Challenges to Nonconforming Products.* Cases involving the failure of a product to conform to a standard of identity have been litigated infrequently. A rare illustration is *United States v. Articles of Food ... [Concentrated Orange Juice]*, Food Drug Cosm. L. Rep. (CCH) ¶ 38,152 (W.D. Tex. 1981), which held that products labeled "concentrated orange juice for manufacturing" or "orange juice" failed to comply with applicable standards. For a description of a complex fraudulent scheme to adulterate orange juice in violation of the standard of identity for "orange juice from concentrate," resulting in criminal prosecution of the responsible individuals, see *United States v. Kohlbach*, 38 F.3d 832 (6th Cir. 1994). In

United States v. Dakota Cheese, Inc., 906 F.2d 335 (8th Cir. 1990), the defendants were found guilty of illegally using calcium caseinate to fortify raw milk used to make cheese. In *Stauffer Chemical Co. v. FDA*, Food Drug Cosm. L. Rep. (CCH) ¶ 38,065 (C.D. Cal. 1980), the court declined to entertain a challenge to a letter from FDA stating that use of a processing aid for the canning of tuna would violate the standard of identity for canned tuna. The court held that the matter was not yet ripe for judicial review and that the company had failed to exhaust its administrative remedies. The court indicated, however, that it agreed with FDA's position on the merits.

4.   *Statutory Standards of Identity.* In 2002, Congress effectively established two food standards of identity by statute. It added to the FD&C Act sections 403(t) and (u), which respectively declare a food to be misbranded if "[i]t purports to be or is represented as catfish, unless it is fish classified within the family Ictaluridae" or "[i]f it purports to be or is represented as ginseng, unless it is an herb or herbal ingredient derived from a plant classified within the genus Panax." Uncodified provisions of the law clearly stated that Congress was limiting the organisms for which the terms "catfish" and "ginseng" may be "considered to be a common or usual name." Farm Security & Rural Investment Act § 10806(a)(1)(A), (b)(1)(A), 116 Stat. 134, 526 (2002). The catfish provision was directed against the use of the name "catfish" for cheaper whiskered, bottom-feeding freshwater fish from the family Pangasiidae imported from Vietnam. *See* Philip Brasher, *When is a Catfish Not a Catfish? When it Comes from Vietnam and Cuts into U.S. Sales, Hill Says*, WASH. POST, Dec. 27, 2001, at A21.

Congress has defined at least three additional food products by statute outside the FD&C Act: butter, 42 Stat. 1500 (1923), 21 U.S.C. 321a; oleomargarine, 64 Stat. 20 (1950), 15 U.S.C. 55(f); and nonfat dry milk, 70 Stat. 486 (1956), 21 U.S.C. 321c.

5.   *Temporary Marketing Permits.* To facilitate the development of new foods that deviate from a standard of identity, FDA established a system of temporary permits for test marketing of such products pending amendment of the standard. 21 C.F.R. 130.17. Recognizing the difficulty of amending existing standards, the agency has increasingly liberalized this temporary permit system to allow continuous marketing during consideration of a pending amendment. 37 Fed. Reg. 26340 (Dec. 9, 1972), 40 Fed. Reg. 21721 (May 19, 1975). However, the temporary permit system itself remains an impediment to product innovation because FDA has adopted the policy that when the agency approves a permit, it must also approve the entire product label and not just the deviation from the standard. Many temporary permits involve trivial variations from a standard and illustrate the need to amend standards to make them more flexible. *See, e.g.*, 70 Fed. Reg. 57607 (Oct. 3, 2005) (temporarily permitting the use of icebergs as a source of bottled water rather than the sources specified in 21 C.F.R. 165.110).

———

Section 403(c) of the FD&C Act provides that any food that is an imitation of another food is misbranded "unless its label bears . . . the word 'imitation' and, immediately thereafter, the name of the food imitated." This provision, which allows the marketing of substitute versions of foods so long as they are accurately (though unappealingly) labeled as "imitation," was in tension with FDA's initial "strong" reading of section 403(g), according to which any food closely resembling a standardized food "purport[ed] to be" or was "represented as" that food and thus was misbranded if it violated the standard of identity. After the Supreme Court decided the case below, the agency had to operate under the assumption that properly-labeled "imitation" variants of standardized food could, in fact, legally exist on the market.

62 Cases of Jam v. U.S.

340 U.S. 593 (1951).

■ MR. JUSTICE FRANKFURTER delivered the opinion of the Court.

. . . .

The proceeding before us was commenced in 1949 in the District Court for the District of New Mexico. By it the United States seeks to condemn 62 cases of "Delicious Brand Imitation Jam," manufactured in Colorado and shipped to New Mexico. The Government claims that this product "purports" to be fruit jam, a food for which the Federal Security Administrator has promulgated a "definition and standard of identity." The regulation specifies that a fruit jam must contain "not less than 45 parts by weight" of the fruit ingredient. The product in question is composed of 55% sugar, 25% fruit, 20% pectin, and small amounts of citric acid and soda. These specifications show that pectin, a gelatinized solution consisting largely of water, has been substituted for a substantial proportion of the fruit required. The Government contends that the product is therefore to be deemed "misbranded" under § 403(g). . . .

. . . In some instances, products similar to those seized were sold at retail to the public in response to telephone orders for jams, and were served to patrons of restaurants, ranches and similar establishments, who had no opportunity to learn the quality of what they received. . . .

The Court of Appeals . . . held that, since the product seized closely resembled fruit jam in appearance and taste, and was used as a substitute for the standardized food, it "purported" to be fruit jam, and must be deemed "misbranded" notwithstanding that it was duly labeled an "imitation." The court therefore remanded the case with instructions to enter a judgment for condemnation. . . .

Our decision in the *Quaker Oats* case [*supra* p. 340] does not touch the problem now before us. In that case, it was conceded that, although the Quaker product did not have the standard ingredients, it "purported" to be a standardized food. We did not there consider the legality of marketing properly labeled "imitation farina." That would be the comparable question to the one now here.

According to the Federal Food, Drug, and Cosmetic Act, nothing can be legally "jam" after the Administrator promulgated his regulation in 1940, unless it contains the specified ingredients in prescribed proportion. Hence the product in controversy is not "jam." It cannot lawfully be labeled "jam" and introduced into interstate commerce, for to do so would "represent" as a standardized food a product which does not meet prescribed specifications.

But the product with which we are concerned is sold as "imitation jam." Imitation foods are dealt with in § 403(c) of the Act. In that section Congress did not give an esoteric meaning to "imitation." It left it to the understanding of ordinary English speech. . . .

In ordinary speech there can be no doubt that the product which the United States here seeks to condemn is an "imitation" jam. It looks and tastes like jam; it is unequivocally labeled "imitation jam." The Government does not argue that its label in any way falls short of the requirements of § 403(c). Its distribution in interstate commerce would therefore clearly seem to be authorized by that section. We could hold it to be "misbranded" only if we held that a practice Congress authorized by § 403(c) Congress impliedly prohibited by § 403(g).

We see no justification so to distort the ordinary meaning of the statute. Nothing in the text or history of the legislation points to such a reading of what Congress wrote. In § 403(g) Congress used the words "purport" and "represent"—terms suggesting the idea of counterfeit. But the name "imitation jam" at once connotes precisely what the product is: a different, an inferior preserve, not meeting the defined specifications. . . . A product so labeled is described with precise accuracy. It neither conveys any ambiguity nor emanates any untrue innuendo, as was the case with the "Bred Spred" considered by Congress in its deliberation on § 403(g). It purports and is represented to be only what it is—an imitation. It does not purport nor represent to be what it is not—the Administrator's genuine "jam." . . .

■ MR. JUSTICE DOUGLAS, with whom MR. JUSTICE BLACK concurs, dissenting.

The result reached by the Court may be sound by legislative standards. But the legal standards which govern us make the process of reaching that result tortuous to say the least. We must say that petitioner's "jam" purports to be "jam" when we read § 403(g) and purports to be not "jam" but another food when we read § 403(c). Yet if petitioner's product did not purport to be "jam" petitioner would have no claim to press and the Government no objection to raise.

NOTES

1. *Mandatory Nomenclature as Regulatory Enforcement Mechanism.* The Supreme Court's decision in *62 Cases of Jam* ensured that food standards promulgated under the FD&C Act would not be strong, prohibitory standards like the Filled Milk Act. The case established the principle that an analogue to a standardized product could avoid being deemed as "purporting to be" that product through adequate labeling. Subsequently, regulation of nomenclature would be FDA's primary tool for policing the food standards regime.

2. *The Market Potential of "Imitation" Products.* While a loss for the government, *62 Cases* nevertheless left FDA with ample practical power— through vigorous application of the "imitation" provision—to coerce

industry to comply with standards of identity. Unlike the claimant in *62 Cases*, which appears to have sold its "imitation jam" primarily to institutions, companies that sold their food products directly to consumers tended to view the term "imitation" as a commercial death sentence and thus wanted desperately to avoid it.

3. *Imitation Margarine.* In *United States v. 856 Cases . . . "Demi"*, 254 F. Supp. 57 (N.D.N.Y. 1966), the government seized as misbranded the claimant's "imitation margarine," a product that failed to conform to FDA's standard of identity for margarine. The government unsuccessfully attempted to distinguish *62 Cases of Jam* by arguing that Congress intended all products made in semblance of butter to be called "margarine," and that FDA had in effect defined the only marketable imitation of butter in its standard of identity for margarine.

c. THE DECLINE OF FOOD STANDARDS

In the early 1970s, in response to the proliferation of new foods that did not conform to established standard of identity, FDA adopted a revised policy on food names based on the Report of the White House Conference. Various components of this policy limited or reduced the impact of food standards of identity on the composition of the American food supply. First, FDA officials concluded that the agency should cease adopting new standards of identity. Second, the agency amended many existing standards to permit a wider range of optional ingredients. Third, FDA issued a new interpretation of "imitation" in section 403(c) so as to significantly limit the number of modified standardized foods that were required to be labeled "imitation." Fourth, the agency decided to interpret the "purports to be" language in section 403(g) narrowly, thus restricting the reach of the standards of identity. As a result of the latter two changes, modified standardized foods today are usually named straightforwardly by informative descriptions that include the standard name, and the food industry is thus not discouraged from marketing such modified products.

i. *"Safe and Suitable Ingredients"*

The enactment of the 1958 Food Additives Amendment and the 1960 Color Additives Amendment, both of which established premarket safety review requirements for food ingredients, led FDA to conclude that it could permit greater flexibility in food standards. In 1965, FDA promulgated a food standard for frozen raw breaded shrimp, 21 C.F.R. 161.175, the first to permit the use of any "safe and suitable" functional ingredients (in this case, "batter and breading ingredients") rather than specifying every permissible ingredient. 30 Fed. Reg. 2860 (Mar. 5, 1965). In 1969, the New Foods Panel of White House Conference on Food, Nutrition and Health praised the breaded shrimp standard while criticizing the deadening effect on food technology and the unnecessary constraints on consumer choice caused by traditional "recipe" standards. Beginning in 1972, FDA, inspired in part by the final report of the conference, undertook to modernize important food standards by (1) requiring full labeling of optional ingredients, (2) permitting use of any safe and suitable food ingredients to perform designated functions, and (3) adopting any appropriate aspects of the international food standards developed by the FAO/WHO Codex Alimentarius Commission, discussed *infra* at p. 359, note 2. *See, e.g.*, 37 Fed. Reg. 18392 (Sept. 9, 1972); 38 Fed. Reg. 27924 (Oct. 10, 1973) (revision of milk and cream standards). In 1974, FDA established a uniform definition of "safe and suitable" food ingredients for all food standards. 39 Fed. Reg. 17304 (May 15, 1974), now codified at 21 C.F.R. 130.3(d).

ii. Redefinition of "Imitation"

As will be discussed in detail below, *infra* p. 369, in 1973 FDA established the current interpretation of section 403(c)'s "imitation" labeling requirement, according to which a substitute food is deemed to be subject to the requirements of section 403(c) *only* if it is "nutritionally inferior" to the food it resembles. 38 Fed. Reg. 2138 (Jan. 19, 1973) (now codified at 21 C.F.R. 101.3(e)).

After the Supreme Court's 1951 decision in *62 Cases of Jam*, excerpted *supra* at p. 348, mandatory "imitation" labeling under 403(c) was FDA's primary tool to prevent manufacturers from selling substitute products for standardized foods. Given a choice between complying with FDA standards of identity or labeling their foods "imitation," uncounted numbers of food manufacturers chose the former course. Consequently, when FDA backed away from its strong imitation labeling policy in 1973, food standards lost much of their power. *See* 38 Fed. Reg. 2138 (Jan. 19, 1973) (excerpted *infra* p. 369). Under its new policy, still in effect today, the common or usual name for a modified standardized food may include the name of the standardized food that it copies, as long as the difference between the products is made clear. Indeed, in 1979, FDA stated that "in some cases it may be necessary to include a standardized name in the name of a substitute food in order to provide the consumer with accurate, descriptive, and fully informative labeling." 44 Fed. Reg. 3964 (Jan. 19, 1979). The 1973 policy was intended to prevent standards of identity from operating as barriers to the development of new food products, especially new versions of traditional foods whose macronutrient composition was modified to meet national nutrition goals.

The path to uninhibited marketing and accurate, descriptive naming of modified standardized foods was not a smooth one. During the 1980s, FDA required modified versions of standardized foods—even if not nutritionally inferior—to be designated as "alternative" or "substitute," unless the substitute product had its own standard of identity. *See, e.g.*, Letter from Sanford A. Miller, Director, FDA, CFSAN, to J. E. Thompson (July 9, 1987) ("[T]he product may not bear both a reduced fat claim and the unmodified standardized name because it would no longer be cheddar cheese. In order to assure that consumers are not confused, some further modification of the name such as "substitute" or "alternative" after the standardized name is necessary.") In effect, the agency replaced the term "imitation" with "alternative" or "substitute" as a way of differentiating between standardized and nonstandardized versions of foods. In 1993, however, the agency—in rules implementing the Nutrition Labeling and Education Act—effectively abandoned this "substitute" and "alternative" nomenclature, at least for foods modified to satisfy a regulation defining a permissible nutrient content claim, such as "nonfat" or "low sodium." (The current scheme for labeling standardized foods modified to satisfy NLEA nutrient content claims will be examined in detail *infra* at p. 373.) Although FDA has never explicitly abandoned the substitute/alternative labeling requirement for standardized foods modified for other reasons, its practice of accepting accurate statements describing such modifications without imposing use of these terms suggests that it has in fact done so.

It remains the case that a nutritionally inferior substitute for a standardized product must be labeled as "imitation." *See* 21 C.F.R. 101.3(e)(1).

iii. New Understanding of "Purports to Be"

A food standard applies only to a product that "purports to be or is represented as" the standardized food. FD&C Act 403(g). Since the 1970s, FDA has been less likely than it was before to conclude that an accurately and descriptively named modified product is "purporting to be" a standardized product. To see how this approach lessens the force of food standards, compare the fate of "Farina Wheat Cereal Enriched with Vitamin D" (at issue in the *Quaker Oats* case, *supra* p. 340) to FDA's later treatment of enriched raisin bread.

In 41 Fed. Reg. 46851 (Oct. 26, 1976), FDA issued a final standard of identity for "enriched raisin bread." The standard mandated the same quantity of nutrients required by the standard for "enriched bread" (which did not provide for the use of raisins) and the same quantity of raisins required by the standard for "raisin bread" (which did not provide for the use of enriched flour). Formal objections to the new standard were filed, resulting in a stay of its effective date. Rather than hold the necessary evidentiary hearing to resolve the objections, FDA concluded that the new standard could be rendered unnecessary by "providing advice" on the appropriate labeling for raisin bread made with enriched flour:

> The Commissioner . . . advises that a raisin bread conforming to the requirements of § 136.160 except that it is made with enriched flour, enriched brominated flour, or a combination, as the sole farinaceous ingredient may be sold as a nonstandardized bread under a suitable name, *e.g.*, "raisin bread made with enriched flour." Many breads are sold as nonstandardized foods when they contain and are named to identify ingredients not provided for in the standard for bread that provide a distinctive flavor, color, or other feature important to consumers, *e.g.*, rye bread. If a raisin bread has been enriched to the nutrient levels in § 136.115, (with additional amounts of nutrients added to compensate for the flour displaced by the raisins), the food may be sold as "enriched raisin bread." Either raisin bread so labeled must also bear nutrition labeling in accordance with § 101.9.

43 Fed. Reg. 43456 (Sept. 26, 1978). *See also* 43 Fed. Reg. 11695 (Mar. 21, 1978) ("enriched macaroni with fortified protein" does not purport to be standardized "enriched macaroni"); 39 Fed. Reg. 31898 (Sept. 3, 1974) ("tomato juice enriched with vitamin C" does not purport to be standardized "tomato juice").

*iv. The Abandonment of Food Standards as a Primary Vehicle for
Fortification and Vitamin/Mineral Supplement Policy*

From 1941, when FDA issued the standards of identity for various types of enriched flour, 6 Fed. Reg. 2574 (May 27, 1941), through the early 1970s, food standards were FDA's primary tool for shaping vitamin and mineral fortification policy in the United States. The agency believed that enrichment of a few standardized, staple foods was the best way to ensure nutritional welfare while promoting honesty and fair dealing. In 1943, the agency explained: "[A]ppropriate enrichment of a few foods widely consumed by the population in general or by significant population groups will contribute substantially to the nutritional welfare of consumers and to meeting their expectations of benefit." 8 Fed. Reg. 9170 (July 3, 1943). Accordingly, in the 1950s, FDA added standards of identity for enriched foods in addition to flour, such as bread (17 Fed. Reg. 4453 (May 15, 1952)), macaroni and noodle products (20 Fed. Reg. 9575 (Dec. 20, 1955)), and dairy products (20 Fed. Reg. 9580 (Dec. 20, 1955)). *See* 21 C.F.R. Parts 131, 136, 137, 139.

In the same 1943 statement, FDA observed: "Enrichment of those foods which are *not* a substantial part of the diet of any significant group tends to confuse and mislead consumers through giving rise to conflicting claims of nutritional values and by creating an exaggerated impression of the benefits to be derived from the consumption of such foods." 8 Fed. Reg. at 9170 (emphasis added). For the subsequent two decades, however, the agency did nothing to regulate the fortification of nonstandardized foods except to take action against misleading or false claims.

In the early 1960s, FDA's increasing concern about possible excessive fortification of food led it to take action. It proposed to revise the special dietary food regulations so as to permit fortification of food only with specific listed nutrients recognized as both essential in human nutrition and appropriate for supplementation. 27 Fed. Reg. 5815 (June 20, 1962). Comments on this proposal (and a court decision striking down the agency's seizure action against fortified sugar, *United States v. 119 Cases . . . "New Dextra Brand Fortified Cane Sugar"*, 231 F. Supp. 551 (S.D. Fla. 1963)) convinced FDA that an even more restrictive approach was necessary to stem the tide of indiscriminate food fortification. Thus, the agency published regulations that included a novel "standard of identity" for "vitamin and mineral-fortified foods." 31 Fed. Reg. 15730 (Dec. 14, 1966). This standard would have drastically limited the vitamins and minerals that could be added to foods for nutritive value, the permissible quantity of these nutrients, and the types of food that could be fortified. At the same time, FDA promulgated a standard of identity limiting the nutrients and their levels in dietary supplements. 31 Fed. Reg. 8525 (June 18, 1966). FDA's actions in 1966 precipitated an avalanche of objections, which automatically stayed the regulations and led to an evidentiary hearing lasting much of 1968 and 1969.

Ultimately, a political event transformed public attitudes about food fortification. The Report of the White House Conference on Food, Nutrition and Health publicized the problems of hunger and malnutrition in America and contained several recommendations for fortification of existing and new food products that cut directly against FDA's prevailing approach of restricting fortification. By the early 1970s, the officials who had designed the restrictive strategy of the 1960s had left FDA and been succeeded by individuals who had helped prepare the Report of the White House Conference. Accordingly, FDA in 1973 explicitly deserted its attempt to control food fortification by fiat, abandoning the "vitamin and mineral-fortified foods" standard proposed in 1966. 38 Fed. Reg. 20708, 20716 (Aug. 2, 1973).

FDA issued its final food fortification policy in 45 Fed. Reg. 6314 (Jan. 25, 1980), codified at 21 C.F.R. 104.20. The agency expressed concern that, in the absence of a unifying set of principles, random and arbitrary fortification of foods would be likely. This could result in overfortification with nutrients that are inexpensive and easy to add and underfortification with others. Yet FDA concluded that promulgation of standards of identity for fortification of all foods would be unnecessarily inflexible. The policy statement enunciates the five circumstances in which food fortification is appropriate: (1) to correct a dietary insufficiency recognized by the scientific community; (2) to restore nutrients lost in storage, handling, and processing (3) to balance total caloric content of the food with nutrients; (4) to avoid nutritional inferiority of substitute food products so as to avoid the "imitation" label; and (5) to comply with other regulations, such as existing standards of identity. 21 C.F.R. 104.20(b)–(f). The fortification policy also states that it is not appropriate to fortify fresh produce; meat, poultry, or fish products; sugars; or snack foods such as candies and carbonated beverages. 21 C.F.R. 104.20(a).

But this policy statement represents only a set of guidelines that are not directly enforceable as legal requirements. When FDA originally proposed the policy in 1974, it incorporated enforcement mechanisms to assure compliance with the fortification principles. 39 Fed. Reg. 20900 (June 14, 1974). The agency's final policy statement, however, eliminated these restrictions. FDA has never initiated formal compliance action to enforce its food fortification policy. *But see* 21 C.F.R. 101.54(e)(2)(ii) and (f)(2) (incorporating 21 C.F.R. 104.20 as a requirement for "more" and "high potency" claims for added nutrients).

FDA clung to the food standards approach a bit longer in its attempt to control the vitamin/mineral content of dietary supplements (as opposed to conventional foods). The 1973 rulemaking established standards of identity for four broad types of combination dietary supplements. 38 Fed. Reg. 20730 (Aug. 2, 1973). (FDA also ruled that any product containing amounts in excess of 150 percent of the RDA of a vitamin or mineral would be a drug. *Id.* at 20708, 20717–18.) In 1976, Congress responded with the Vitamin–Mineral Amendments of 1976, 90 Stat. 401 (1976). This statute added FD&C Act section 411, still in effect, which prohibits FDA from establishing maximum limits on the potency of vitamin and mineral products, from classifying a vitamin or mineral supplement as a drug solely because it exceeds nutritionally useful levels, and from limiting the combination or number of vitamins, minerals, and other food ingredients in supplements. FD&C Act 411(a)(1). Section 411 explicitly prohibits the use of section 401 food standards either to establish maximum potency or to control the composition of vitamin-mineral supplements. FD&C Act 411(a)(1)(A), (C).

d. THE PERSISTENCE OF FOOD STANDARDS

In 1995, FDA published an advance notice of proposed rulemaking (ANPRM) to invite public comment on whether food standards are still needed and, if so, whether they should be modified or streamlined. 60 Fed. Reg. 67492 (Dec. 29, 1995). The Food Safety Inspection Service (FSIS) of the USDA, which has established approximately 80 meat and poultry product standards of identity, published a similar ANPRM soon thereafter. 61 Fed. Reg. 47453 (Sept. 9, 1996). Almost a decade later, FDA and FSIS jointly published proposed regulations to establish general principles for the modernization of food standards. This rule, though not yet finalized, seems to ensure that food standards will continue to play a real, if diminished, role in the regulation of food identity and quality.

Food Standards; General Principles and Food Standards Modernization

70 Fed. Reg. 29214 (May 20, 2005).

. . . Most comments to both ANPRMs strongly supported the concept of food standards, while a few requested that standards be eliminated. However, very few comments to both ANPRMs supported the existing food standards as currently written. . . .

Many of the comments that supported retaining food standards stated that they protect consumers from fraudulent and substandard products by establishing the basis upon which similar products are formulated. Others argued that food standards ensure that products meet consumers' nutritional expectations and needs. . . .

Several industry comments that supported food standards also stated that the Federal food standards ensure a level playing field for industry because they provide direction to industry members producing standardized products. Several industry comments and one comment from the USDA FCS also stated that, in the absence of Federal food standards, the States would be able to establish their own food standards and manufacturers would be confronted with the challenge of meeting different States' requirements. In addition, many industry comments stated that the food standards provide a basis for negotiations related to the international harmonization of standards and facilitate international trade. One comment stated that, without a U.S. food standards system, food standards development could shift to international bodies, which may not be sensitive to the American consumer or industry. Another comment stated that the absence of food standards could pose a barrier to exports and international markets.

Although most comments supported retaining food standards in some form, they requested that food standards be simplified, be made more flexible, or be clarified. For example, one industry comment stated that food standards should not include manufacturing methods, prohibitions regarding classes of ingredients, or product-specific labeling (other than the acceptable product name). This comment also stated that standardized and nonstandardized food product labeling should be the same. Similarly, other industry comments requested that the food standards be made more flexible to allow for alternative safe and suitable ingredients and alternative technologies that do not change the basic nature or basic characteristics of the food. Several industry comments recommended limiting food standards to the name of the product and the essential characterizing properties of the product. . . .

On September 12, 1996, FDA convened an internal agency task force to discuss the current and future role of food standards and to draft a set of principles for reviewing and revising FDA's food standards regulations. The task force agreed that the food standards should protect consumers without unduly inhibiting technological advances in food production and marketing.

To ensure that FSIS and FDA were consistent as the food standards reform process continued, in January 1997, a joint FDA and FSIS Food Standards Work Group (the Work Group) was convened. . . .

In addition to developing these general principles, the Work Group considered five options, as the next step in the process of food standards reform, and analyzed the advantages and disadvantages of each option. The first option the Work Group considered was not proceeding any further with the review of the food standards regulations. The advantage of this option is that, in the short run, it would require little or no increase in the agencies' use of resources.

A major disadvantage of this option is that there is very little industry or consumer support for it. As noted previously, the majority of comments supported revising the existing system of food standards to simplify them and to make them more flexible. . . .

The second option the Work Group considered was removing all food standards from the regulations and treating all foods as nonstandardized foods. One advantage of this option is that, in most cases, fewer agency resources would be required to eliminate food standards than to review and revise them. Also, under this option, we no longer would devote resources to responding to petitions requesting an amendment to an existing standard or the establishment of a new food standard.

As with the first option, however, very few comments on the ANPRMs supported eliminating food standards completely. We agree with the comments that stated that States might establish their own food standards in the absence of Federal food standards. . . . Without Federal food standards, there would be no reference point for ensuring consistency of products for national commodity programs or feeding programs, such as the National School Lunch Program. In addition, as comments stated, without Federal food standards, the United States would have no reference point for negotiating international food standards, or facilitating international trade.

Another disadvantage of this option is the loss of enforcement efficiency. Without food standards, we would have to rely solely on the general adulteration and misbranding provisions of our statutes rather than upon the specified requirements of a food standard to determine if a product were economically adulterated (i.e., adulterated under Sec.

402(b)(1)) or misbranded. This would likely require more enforcement resources than a food standards system would require.

The third option the Work Group considered was using our resources to review and revise food standards to make them internally consistent, more flexible for manufacturers and consumers, and easier to administer. . . . The disadvantage of this option is competing priorities would make it unlikely we could do this in a timely manner.

The fourth option the Work Group considered was to request external industry groups to review, revise, and administer the food standards (private certification). This option would require little or no use of the agencies' resources. In addition, the revised food standards would provide the level of flexibility that industry desires. However, for private organizations to review, revise, and administer the food standards, the [FD&C Act, the Federal Meat Inspection Act, and the Poultry Products Inspection Act] would have to be amended, so that these standards would have the force of law. . . .

The fifth option the Work Group considered was to rely on external groups—consumer, industry, commodity, or other groups—to draft recommended revisions to existing Federal food standards but retain the agencies' authority to establish the final food standards. . . .

One major advantage of this option is that it would require the use of fewer of our agencies' resources than would be required if we were to review and propose amendments to the food standards without the benefit of petitions. . . .

The disadvantage to this fifth option is that, if a consumer, industry, or commodity group does not feel strongly about revising a particular group of food standards, we might not receive a petition and would then need to commit resources to reviewing the food standards without the benefit of a petition. . . .

For the reasons discussed previously, we have tentatively determined that the fifth option is the most appropriate course of action. The Work Group preliminarily determined that we could rely on external groups to suggest new food standards, revisions to existing food standards, or elimination of certain food standards that are consistent with the proposed general principles. The general principles approach would allow us to chart the basic course of food standards review and modernization. Moreover, it would allow consumer and industry groups to participate in the development of new and revised food standards and to identify food standards that should be eliminated. In addition, it would provide an opportunity for consumer and industry groups to submit data to support any claims made in petitions relating to consumer expectations or beliefs, and hence, protect consumer interests. . . .

————

The following year, a dozen major food industry associations submitted a citizen petition to FDA and FSIS proposing that both agencies' food standards be amended, through a regulation of general applicability, to allow various types of variation from the standards "to provide needed flexibility." These variations included, among others, the addition of ingredients for technical effects; the use of advanced technologies and alternative manufacturing processes; changes in product shape and form; and, most controversially, "the [u]se of safe and suitable flavors and flavor enhancers in foods generally, and use of safe and suitable ingredients such as salt substitutes, sweeteners, and vegetable fats and oils where appropriate." Food Industry Associations' Citizen Petition to Modernize Food Standards 3–4 (Oct. 25, 2006). A public outcry ensued when chocoholics—incited by gourmet chocolate manufacturers—learned that Appendix C to the petition provided as an example of the last type of variation the replacement of cacao fat with other vegetable fat.

Jerry Hirsch, *The Courage of Their Confections*
LOS ANGELES TIMES, Apr. 14, 2007, at A1.

Calling all chocoholics. Put down the truffles and power up the PC. It's time to weigh in on a fundamental question: What "is" chocolate?

Two of California's oldest confectioners, See's Candies Inc. and Guittard Chocolate Co., are battling an attempt to loosen government rules that dictate what ingredients go into the sweet stuff.

Legally, the candy that melts hearts and comforts the brokenhearted is made with cocoa butter and, in the case of milk chocolate, whole milk. But the Grocery Manufacturers of America, a trade group, wants to let confectioners substitute cheaper ingredients—vegetable oils and milk protein concentrates.

Gary Guittard, president of his eponymous, family-owned business, sees this as a battle for the soul of the popular confection.

"Anybody who has a passion for chocolate doesn't want to see it adulterated," said Guittard. . . .

But the trade group, which has the support of the Chocolate Manufacturers of America, says it's just thinking outside the old chocolate box. The petition is part of a broad effort to give its members more flexibility in choosing the ingredients that go into many food products. A spokeswoman said the proposed rules would not prevent companies such as See's and Guittard from adhering to the current standards for chocolate.

Nevertheless, Guittard and See's Chief Executive Brad Kinstler want America's chocoholics to complain loudly to the Food and Drug Administration before April 25, the day the agency will stop taking public comments on the issue.

It's a big constituency. . . . All told, the U.S. consumes 3.6 billion pounds of chocolate annually—that's 12 pounds per person. . . .

The idea of substituting vegetable oil for cocoa butter, a natural component of the cocoa bean that is the traditional source of chocolate, irks Andrea Langston of Long Beach.

"I would feel like I was being duped," said Langston. . . .

Langston and other self-respecting lovers of what the Mayans called the food of the gods should be worried about producers' substituting oils for cocoa butter, said Kristy Choo, artisan chocolatier at Jin Patisserie in Venice.

"It won't be as intense as a real chocolate. It will have a waxy taste," said Choo. . . .

Price is at the heart of the argument over whether manufacturers should be allowed to change the ingredients of chocolate, said Kinstler of See's. . . .

"You can make chocolate a lot cheaper with vegetable oil," he said. . . .

Hershey Co., which supports the Grocery Manufacturers' petition, said the standards were created decades ago and should be modernized.

By adopting the proposal, the FDA would be providing "flexibility to make changes based on consumer taste preferences, ingredient costs and availability and shelf life," said Kirk Saville, spokesman for the Hershey, Pa.-based company.

Saville said it could be years before the FDA issued a decision. . . .

The proposed rule change is part of a strategy by Hershey and other large producers to segment the industry, lowering the quality and expense of everyday candy bars while marketing high-quality, high-priced premium chocolate, said Marcia Mogelonsky, an analyst with market research firm Mintel International.

"If you take the cocoa butter out of an inexpensive candy bar, most people probably won't notice," Mogelonsky said. . . .

Gary Guittard believes that in proposing to change the rules, the food industry is overthinking what he believes should be one of the simple joys of life.

"Why add ingredients to something that is just fine the way it is?" he asked.

NOTES

1. *Recent Petitions.* FDA still has not acted on the food trade associations' petition to modernize food standards, and chocolate thus remains subject to the same requirements as before. While high-grade chocolate manufacturers have sought to keep in place standards that inhibit the sale of cheap substitutes, another segment of the food industry has requested the creation of a *new* standard of identity for the same reason. In 2006, American honey producers, losing market share to less expensive imported products in which the honey was blended with other sweeteners, filed a citizen petition with FDA to reserve the name "honey" for the pure version of the food. The American Beekeeping Federation, invoking the Codex standard review process of 21 C.F.R. 130.6, requested that FDA, pursuant to FD&C Act 401, adopt (with some deviations) the 2001 Revised Codex Standard for Honey. Citizen Petition, Submitted by the American Beekeeping Federation et al. (Mar. 3, 2006). (For a discussion of Codex standards, see *infra* note 2.) To date, the agency has not acted on this petition, either.

2. *Codex Alimentarius Food Standards.* A theme that recurred throughout the Food Standard Modernization proceedings discussed above is the relationship between U.S. and international food standards. The Food and Agriculture Organization (FAO) and the World Health

Organization (WHO) created the Codex Alimentarius Commission in 1961 with the objective of establishing food standards that will protect consumer expectations, public health, and facilitate international trade. In 1973, FDA adopted a procedure for review of all Codex Alimentarius commodity food standards. 38 Fed. Reg. 12396 (May 11, 1973), codified at 21 C.F.R. 130.6. Under this procedure, any person may petition FDA to adopt a Codex standard, with or without deviations, by proposing a new standard or an appropriate amendment of an existing standard pursuant to section 401 of the FD&C Act. 21 C.F.R. 130.6(b)(1). FDA may also propose such an action on its own initiative. *Id.* 130.6(b)(2). Codex standards not handled in one of these two ways may be published for review and public comment in the Federal Register. *Id.* 130.6(b)(2). As of 1995, FDA had considered 83 Codex standards for adoption. 60 Fed. Reg. 67492, 67499 (Dec. 29, 1995).

The Codex standards have had a larger impact on dairy products than in any other area. The agency has also adopted or amended standards for vegetables in response to Codex standards. Consideration of virtually all other Codex standards has been terminated by FDA without action, but their publication in the Federal Register has served the useful purpose of informing United States food producers about the existence and content of food standards that are often adopted and enforced in other countries. No Codex standard has been published by FDA in the Federal Register since 1989.

The principal international trade agreement is the General Agreement on Tariffs and Trade (GATT), which became effective on January 1, 1948. The GATT Agreement on Technical Barriers to Trade (TBT) became effective on January 1, 1980. The Uruguay Round that created the World Trade Organization, a new TBT agreement, and an agreement on the application of sanitary and phytosanitary measures (SPS) became effective on January 1, 1995. The SPS agreement defers specifically to standards established by the Codex Alimentarius. *See* Julie D. Cromer, *Before and After the Uruguay Round: How GATT Affects the Import Policy of the FDA*, 36 HARV. INT'L L.J. 557 (1995).

As required by the U.S. statute implementing the Uruguay Round agreements, 19 U.S.C. 2548, 108 Stat. 4809, 4970 (1994), President Clinton designated USDA as the lead agency for the Codex Alimentarius, with the obligation to publish in the Federal Register yearly reports on Codex standard-setting activities. 60 Fed. Reg. 15845 (Mar. 27, 1995). USDA has published informative reports each year since.

In 60 Fed. Reg. 53078 (Oct. 11, 1995), FDA published a policy statement on the conditions under which it would participate with outside standards bodies, domestic or international, in the development of standards applicable to products regulated by the agency. The policy also covered the conditions under which FDA would use the resulting standards, or other available domestic or international standards, in fulfilling its statutory mandates. In 60 Fed. Reg. 67492, 67499 (Dec. 29, 1995), as part of the ANPR on food standards reform discussed above, *supra* p. 355, the agency specifically asked for comment on the relationship between domestic food standards and international food standards. *See* Joseph A. Levitt and H. Michael Wehr, *The Importance of International*

Activities to the Work of the Food and Drug Administration's Center for Food Safety and Applied Nutrition, 56 FOOD & DRUG L.J. 1 (2001).

In addition to food commodity standards, Codex adopts standards regarding food additives, food contaminants, animal drug residues, food labeling, and a host of other food regulatory policies. FDA and USDA participate in these standard-setting activities as well, and they are covered in the yearly report published by USDA in the Federal Register.

3.   *Continued Utility of Section 403(g)(1)*. FDA still sometimes brings enforcement actions based on an assertion that a nonstandardized product "purports to be" a standardized food under section 403(g)(1). For example, in 2011, FDA sent a Warning Letter to CytoSport, Inc., alleging, among other violations, that:

> Your "Chocolate Muscle Milk Protein Nutrition Shake" and "Vanilla Crème Muscle Milk Light Nutritional Shake" products are misbranded within the meaning of section 403(g)(1) of the Act because they purport to be a food for which definition and standard of identity has been prescribed by regulation but they fail to conform to such definition and standard. Specifically, these products purport to be milk by prominently featuring the word "MILK" on the labels. Milk is a food for which a definition and standard of identity has been prescribed by regulation. The standard of identity for milk (21 CFR 131.110) describes milk as "the lacteal secretion, practically free from colostrum, obtained by the complete milking of one or more healthy cows" and it lists the vitamins and other ingredients that may be added. According to the ingredient list on your product labels, your products contain no milk and contain numerous ingredients not permitted by the standard; therefore, your products do not conform to the standard of identity for milk.

Warning Letter from Darlene Almogela, Director, Compliance Branch, FDA San Francisco District, to Michael Pickett, C.E.O., CytoSport, Inc. (June 29, 2011).

4.   *Meat Food Names*. USDA exercises primary jurisdiction in the area of meat food labeling, and many important meat food names are established in standards of identity that it has promulgated in 9 C.F.R. Parts 317 and 319. *Armour & Co. v. Freeman*, 304 F.2d 404 (D.C. Cir. 1962), held invalid a USDA regulation that required meat packers who added moisture to ham during the curing process to use the label "Imitation Ham." The Court of Appeals concluded that the required labeling was false and deceptive and thus inconsistent with USDA's own statute, the Federal Meat Inspection Act. Judge Prettyman, concurring with the court's decision, declared: "Everybody knows that a ham made of the cured thigh of a hog and otherwise unaltered save by the addition of a bit of water is not an imitation of some product other than ham. . . . As a matter of plain fact, such a ham is not even an imitation ham. It is a real ham, a ham by definition and by universal common acceptance." In *American Meat Institute v. United States Dept. of Agriculture*, 646 F.2d 125 (4th Cir. 1981) (per curiam), the court, reversing the district court, upheld a USDA regulation permitting cured turkey to be labeled as "turkey ham" with the additional qualifying phrase "cured turkey thigh meat." In

National Pork Producers Council v. Bergland, 631 F.2d 1353 (8th Cir. 1980), *cert. denied*, 450 U.S. 912 (1981), the Court of Appeals upheld a USDA regulation permitting nitrate-free and nitrite-free meat products to be sold under the product names traditionally reserved for food containing these preservatives as long as the word "uncured" appeared as part of the product name and the label stated that no nitrate or nitrite had been added and that refrigeration was required.

2. THE MODERN FOOD-NAMING REGIME

The report of the New Foods Panel of the 1969 White House Conference on Food, Nutrition, and Health called for a straightforward naming scheme in which every food bore "an informative and descriptive generic name." In the early 1970s, inspired by the recommendations of the Conference, FDA established the core elements of the food-naming regime that, in essence, still governs food nomenclature today. This regime was effectively completed in 1990 by the NLEA's nutrient content claims provisions and FDA's regulations implementing them. *See infra* pp. 372, 413. The main features of the modern food-naming regime are (1) the embrace of general principles for establishing the common or usual names of nonstandardized foods, (2) liberalized naming requirements for variants of standardized foods, and (3) a generally uniform approach to the naming of both standardized and nonstandardized products—an approach that stresses the use of descriptive and informative nomenclature. Today's food-naming requirements—which permit the use of traditional food names within descriptive names of modified products and do not generally impose unappealing modifiers (such as "imitation") on these appellations—do little to discourage the development of new food products.

a. REGULATION OF COMMON OR USUAL FOOD NAMES

In 1973, FDA promulgated a new 21 C.F.R. Part 102, "Common or Usual Name for Nonstandardized Foods." This regulation set forth the important "general principles" for common or usual names that still apply today. 21 C.F.R. 102.5. Perhaps the most important of these principles is that the common or usual name must include the percentage of any "characterizing ingredients." Part 102 also establishes a procedure by which FDA can promulgate regulations prescribing the common or usual name for particular foods. 21 C.F.R. 102.19. As originally published, Part 102 contained common and usual name regulations for four particular foods, all seafood products. FDA has since added only twelve additional common and usual name regulations for particular nonstandardized foods. (Two examples of specific common or usual name regulations are excerpted below.) The vast majority of nonstandardized foods are thus named by manufacturers according to the general principles set forth in 21 C.F.R. 102.5, rather than pursuant to specific regulations.

Common or Usual Names for
Nonstandardized Foods

38 Fed. Reg. 6964 (March 14, 1973).

In the FEDERAL REGISTER of June 22, 1972 (37 FR 12327), the Commissioner of Food and Drugs proposed a procedure for the establishment by regulation of common or usual names for foods. . . .

Twenty-eight requests were made that the proposal be expanded to include additional labeling requirements such as the percentage of all ingredients for all foods; the percentage of primary ingredients for all foods; the percentage of fats, carbohydrates, and proteins; the vitamin and mineral content; and the specific source of ingredients.

The Commissioner concludes that percentage labeling of ingredients should be restricted to situations where this information has a material bearing on price or consumer acceptance of the food, or where such information may prevent deception. Labeling the percentage of all ingredients would be extremely costly and would provide no proven benefits to consumers. A mechanism for establishing a regulation requiring labeling of the percentage of all "primary" ingredients that have a material bearing on the price or consumer acceptance is provided for in this regulation. . . .

Several objections were made on the ground that authority for establishing the common or usual name does not exist outside section 401 of the act. . . .

The Commissioner agrees that a name may be determined by regulation through the establishment of a standard of identity under section 401 of the act. . . . Section 401 does not, however, preclude the establishment of a common or usual name under other sections of the act. . . .

Common or usual names will not be established . . . for all non-standardized foods. Such names will be established by such regulation only when it is necessary fully to inform the consumer, or where different names are used for the same product by different manufacturers.

Common or usual names for "like" or "similar" products, where none now exists, may be proposed under the provisions of this regulation and will reflect the reasonable expectations of consumers. The name itself will accurately identify or describe the basic nature or characterizing properties of the food in a way that will distinguish it from other foods. . . .

21 C.F.R. Part 102—Common or Usual Name for
Nonstandardized Foods

Subpart A—General Provisions

§ 102.5   General principles

(a) The common or usual name of a food, which may be a coined term, shall accurately identify or describe, in as simple and direct terms as possible, the basic nature of the food or its characterizing properties or ingredients. The name shall be uniform among all identical or similar products and may not be confusingly similar to the name of any other food that is not reasonably encompassed within the same name. Each class or subclass of food shall be given its own common or usual name that states, in clear terms, what it is in a way that distinguishes it from different foods.

(b) The common or usual name of a food shall include the percentage(s) of any characterizing ingredient(s) or component(s) when the proportion of such ingredient(s) or component(s) in the food has a material bearing on price or consumer acceptance or when the labeling or the appearance of the food may otherwise create an erroneous impression that such ingredient(s) or component(s) is present in an amount greater than is actually the case. . . .

(c) The common or usual name of a food shall include a statement of the presence or absence of any characterizing ingredient(s) or component(s) and/or the need for the user to add any characterizing ingredient(s) or component(s) when the presence or absence of such ingredient(s) or component(s) in the food has a material bearing on price or consumer acceptance or when the labeling or the appearance of the food may otherwise create an erroneous impression that such ingredient(s) or component(s) is present when it is not, and consumers may otherwise be misled about the presence or absence of the ingredient(s) or component(s) in the food. . . .

Subpart B—Requirements for Specific Nonstandardized Foods

. . . .

§ 102.26 Frozen "heat and serve" dinners

(a) A frozen "heat and serve" dinner:

(1) Shall contain at least three components, one of which shall be a significant source of protein and each of which shall consist of one or more of the following: meat, poultry, fish, cheese, eggs, vegetables, fruit, potatoes, rice, or other cereal based products (other than bread or rolls).

(2) May also contain other servings of food (*e.g.*, soup, bread or rolls, beverage, dessert).

(b) The common or usual name of the food consists of all of the following:

(1) The phrase "frozen 'heat and serve' dinner," except that the name of the predominant characterizing ingredient or other appropriately descriptive term may immediately precede the word "dinner" (*e.g.*, "frozen chicken dinner" or "frozen heat and serve beef dinner"). The words "heat and serve" are optional. The word "frozen" is also optional, provided that the words "Keep Frozen" or the equivalent are prominently and conspicuously placed on the principal display panel. . . .

(2) The phrase "containing (or contains) _____" the blank to be filled in with an accurate description of each of the three or more dish components listed in paragraph (a)(1) of this section in their order of descending predominance by weight (*e.g.*, ham, mashed potatoes, and peas), followed by any of the other servings specified in paragraph (a)(2) of this section contained in the package (*e.g.*, onion soup, enriched white bread, and artificially flavored vanilla pudding) in their order of

descending predominance by weight. This part of the name shall be placed immediately following or directly below the part specified in paragraph (b)(1) of this section. . . . The words "contains" or "containing" are optional.

(3) If the labeling implies that the package contains other foods and these foods are not present in the package, *e.g.*, if a vignette on the package depicts a "serving suggestion" which includes any foods not present in the package, the principal display panel shall bear a statement that such foods are not present. . . .

. . . .

§ 102.54 Seafood cocktails

The common or usual name of a seafood cocktail in package form fabricated with one or more seafood ingredients shall be:

(a) When the cocktail contains only one seafood ingredient, the name of the seafood ingredient followed by the word "cocktail" (*e.g.*, shrimp cocktail, crabmeat cocktail) and a statement of the percentage by weight of that seafood ingredient in the product. . . .

(b) When the cocktail contains more than one seafood ingredient, the term "seafood cocktail" and a statement of the percentage by weight of each seafood ingredient in the product. . . .

———

In the case below, the plaintiff challenged FDA's promulgation of common or usual name regulations for particular foods using notice-and-comment rulemaking as an illegal evasion by the agency of the then-applicable formal rulemaking requirement for establishing food standards of identity. (The formal rulemaking requirement has since been abandoned for the issuance of food standards.) The plaintiff also advanced specific complaints against the "frozen 'heat and serve' dinners" and "seafood cocktails" regulations.

American Frozen Food Institute v. Mathews

413 F. Supp. 548 (D.D.C. 1976).

■ ROBINSON, JR., DISTRICT JUDGE.

By this action Plaintiff American Frozen Food Institute (AFFI) challenges the innovative attempt by the Food and Drug Administration (FDA) to regulate labeling in certain areas of the food industry through establishing "common and usual names" for nonstandardized foods. AFFI contends that two recent rulings from FDA which establish common and usual names for seafood cocktails and frozen heat and serve dinners must be set aside by this Court on the grounds that they were promulgated in a manner excessive of agency authority, establish an unlawful presumption, violate the First Amendment and are arbitrary and capricious without sufficient support in the record. . . . [T]he Court concludes that the FDA acted within its statutory authority and that the defendants are entitled to summary judgment. . . .

. . . FDA has established common and usual names for certain of these foods under its general rulemaking authority, Section 701(a) of the Act. The regulations were prompted by a concern expressed by the White House Conference on Food Nutrition and Health, regarding the lack of informative food labeling. . . .

The Plaintiff contends that FDA lacks authority to *create* common and usual names through substantive rulemaking. . . . In the alternative, AFFI contends that even if FDA has authority to establish common and usual names through its general rulemaking authority, these two specific regulations exceed that authority. . . .

. . . Under the general rulemaking provision of the governing statute set forth in 21 U.S.C. § 371(a) [FD&C Act 701(a)], FDA is authorized to "promulgate regulations for the efficient enforcement of [the Act]." Plaintiff contends that despite the broad mandate reflected by this provision, FDA is restricted to two methods for establishing common and usual names. AFFI's position is that FDA can either recognize an already established common and usual name in the context of a Section 701[(e)] proceeding (establishing a definition and standard of identity) or may bring a judicial action pursuant to the sanctions set forth in 21 U.S.C. §§ 331–334 for violations of the Act, during which the Court can recognize the common and usual name of a particular food. . . .

The Court is not persuaded that the Act should be read so narrowly. Plaintiff[ ] . . . ignores significant case law which by analogy supports the FDA's authority to proceed by substantive lawmaking in this case. The cases are legion in which Courts have recognized the preference of substantive rulemaking by an agency over the time consuming and often unfair process of case by case adjudication. . . .

By the action challenged herein, FDA is attempting to provide consumers with relevant buying information on food labels of nonstandardized products. It is not attempting to eradicate economic adulteration nor to prescribe food composition. As stated earlier, the label of a standardized food bears only optional ingredients. The nonstandardized foods for which FDA has established common and usual names by the procedure challenged herein will bear on the label such information deemed appropriate by the agency in light of the purpose of the Act.

Although there is nothing in the legislative history which clearly indicates that FDA has the authority to provide this consumer information pursuant to its rulemaking authority by establishing common and usual names, there is nothing in the legislative history of Section 701(a) or (e) which indicates that it cannot. . . .

Next the Court must determine whether the two specific regulations challenged by this action have additional infirmities requiring this Court to set them aside. The thrust of Plaintiff's attack directed at the common and usual name for frozen heat and serve dinners is that this regulation . . . is actually a definition and standard of identity because it includes components as part of the name. Plaintiff contends that it must be set aside because it was not promulgated pursuant to a Section 701(e) proceeding. . . .

Although the Court recognizes that this name [frozen "heat and serve" dinner] appears to be more than just a name, Plaintiff's argument that it is a definition and standard of identity is not persuasive. This regulation controls use of the term "dinner" and requires an accurate description of each component in order of descending predominance. As the regulation makes clear, all the specific ingredients are optional. Only categories are mandatory. Therefore, to require a definition and standard of identity, which normally sets forth a "recipe" for a food, would be inappropriate since there *are* no specific mandatory ingredients for frozen heat and serve dinners. Therefore, it cannot be said that this particular regulation is actually a definition and standard of identity.

Lastly, Plaintiff challenges that portion of the regulation for seafood cocktails . . . which requires that the percentage of seafood ingredients be plainly stated on the label. Plaintiff argues strongly that FDA's authority to enforce such percentage of ingredient labeling requirements was specifically deleted from the statute when originally enacted. However, the Court is influenced by the subsequent inclusion of Section 201(n) which authorizes the Commissioner to consider "the extent to which the labeling fails to reveal facts material in the light of such representations" in determining whether a label is false or misleading.

FDA's reasoning for the general principle of requiring disclosure of the percentage of characterizing ingredients for certain foods is that such information may be a "material fact" which must be disclosed to prevent a food label from being misleading. . . .

The Court also notes that the record support for this regulation indicates the materiality of the percentage of characterizing ingredient in this particular product. Virtually all of the consumer responses heartily supported the general principle proposed, and several consumers indicated express approval of disclosure of percentage of ingredients for seafood cocktails as a necessary device for comparative food shopping. In light of the materiality of the information required to be disclosed by this regulation, the Court is not persuaded that the Commissioner has exceeded his statutory authority in requiring that the label of seafood cocktail reveal the percentage of seafood ingredients therein. . . .

NOTES

1. *Affirmed on Appeal.* The District Court was affirmed on appeal *sub nom. American Frozen Food Institute v. Califano*, 555 F.2d 1059 (D.C. Cir. 1977).

2. *Peanut Butter versus Peanut Spread.* Compare the standard of identity for "peanut butter" in 21 C.F.R. 164.150, which requires at least 90 percent peanuts, *see supra* p. 345, note 1, with the FDA-prescribed common or usual name for "peanut spread" in 21 C.F.R. 102.23, which merely requires label declaration of the percent of peanuts in products containing between 10 percent and 90 percent. Most reduced fat versions of standardized foods can call themselves "Reduced Fat [Standard Name]." *See infra* p. 373. Because of the existence of this common or usual name

regulation, however, the correct name for reduced fat peanut butter (which contains less than 90 percent peanuts) is "Peanut Spread Containing [ ] Percent Peanuts." Many of these products avoid highlighting this unappealing name by giving the name less conspicuousness and prominence on the principal display panel than is actually required by regulation. *See* 21 C.F.R. 101.2(c), 101.3(a), 101.15.

3.   *Juices.* Like standards of identity, common or usual name rules can generate significant controversy. Following the 1973 promulgation of a regulation requiring that any diluted orange juice beverage declare the percent of orange juice, 38 Fed. Reg. 6968 (Mar. 14, 1973), FDA promulgated a similar regulation for all other diluted fruit or vegetable juices. 45 Fed. Reg. 39247 (June 10, 1980), codified at 21 C.F.R. 102.33. After the agency rejected a petition for reconsideration, 45 Fed. Reg. 80497 (Dec. 5, 1980), and repeatedly extended the time for compliance, *see* 49 Fed. Reg. 26541 (June 27, 1984), a court upheld the rule. *See Processors Council of the California–Arizona Citrus League v. FDA*, Food Drug Cosm. L. Rep. (CCH) ¶ 38,186 (C.D. Cal. 1982). Opponents of the regulation persisted, however, and FDA proposed amendments to the common or usual name rule for diluted fruit and vegetable juices, 49 Fed. Reg. 22831 (June 1, 1984), and then proposed its revocation, 52 Fed. Reg. 26690 (July 16, 1987). This proposal, in turn, provoked efforts to salvage the regulation. 55 Fed. Reg. 3266 (Jan. 31, 1990). Finally, the 1990 Nutrition Labeling and Education Act amended section 403(i) to require that a beverage containing a fruit or vegetable juice must declare the percent of juice on the label. In 1993, FDA revoked the separate regulation for diluted orange juice beverages, revised 102.33 (now the rule for naming all beverages containing fruit or vegetable juice), and promulgated 21 C.F.R. 101.30 to implement the NLEA requirement requiring the prominent declaration of percent juice on the label. 58 Fed. Reg. 2897 (Jan. 6, 1993).

4.   *Other Names.* In addition to the regulations discussed above, FDA has also established common or usual names by regulation for protein hydrolysates, 21 C.F.R. 102.22; foods packaged for use in the preparation of "main dishes" or "dinners," 21 C.F.R. 102.28; mixtures of edible fat or oil and olive oil, 21 C.F.R. 102.37; onion rings made from diced onion, 21 C.F.R. 102.39; potato chips made from dried potatoes, 102.41; fish sticks or portions made from minced fish, 21 C.F.R. 102.45; pacific whiting, 21 C.F.R. 102.46; bonito, 21 C.F.R. 102.47; fried clams made from minced clams, 21 C.F.R. 102.49; crabmeat, 21 C.F.R. 102.50; nonstandardized breaded composite shrimp units, 21 C.F.R. 102.55; and Greenland turbot, 21 C.F.R. 102.57.

5.   *Other Proposed Names.* FDA proposed names for main dish products, 39 Fed. Reg. 20906 (June 14, 1974); formulated meal replacements, 39 Fed. Reg. 20905 (June 14, 1974); fruit-flavored sweetened spreads, 40 Fed. Reg. 52616 (Nov. 11, 1975); and substitutes for margarine and butter, 41 Fed. Reg. 36509 (Aug. 30, 1976). However, all of these proposals were withdrawn in 51 Fed. Reg. 15653 (Apr. 25, 1986), and no new common or usual names have been proposed since then.

b.   REDEFINITION OF "IMITATION"

Section 403(c) of the FD&C Act provides that a food is misbranded "[i]f it is an imitation of another food, unless its label bears, in type of uniform size and prominence, the word 'imitation' and immediately thereafter, the name of the food imitated." As discussed above, *supra* p. 351, this provision was, for many years, the primary source of FDA's practical power to deter the manufacture of substitutes for standardized foods. The agency could also use this provision to inhibit the marketing of substitutes of traditional foods for which it had not issued standards of identity. For example, prior to the 1960 publication of the initial standard of identity for ice cream, 25 Fed. Reg. 7126, FDA required the manufacturer of "Chil-Zert," a chocolate-flavored frozen dessert made from soy fat and protein rather than milk fat and protein, to call the product "imitation ice cream." The company objected, but a district court upheld FDA's position. *United States v. 651 Cases . . . Chocolate Chil-Zert*, 114 F. Supp. 430 (N.D.N.Y. 1953). The *Chil-Zert* case was, however, the first and only enforcement action that FDA brought based solely on section 403(c).

The 1969 Report of the White House Conference on Food, Nutrition and Health criticized the blanket use of the term "imitation" for substitute foods. It remarked: "The 'imitation' label has been regarded as equally applicable when the new product is inferior to the old as it is when the new product is superior to the old. Thus, the use of such over simplified and inaccurate words [is] potentially misleading to consumers, and fail[s] to inform the public about the actual characteristics and properties of the new product." Following the Conference's lead, FDA dramatically constrained its use of this term in 1973. It established the current approach, codified at 21 C.F.R. 101.3(e), that limits mandatory "imitation" labeling to substitute products that are nutritionally inferior to the foods they resemble.

Imitation Foods, Application of Term "Imitation": Proposed Rulemaking

38 Fed. Reg. 2138 (January 19, 1973).

. . . .

Vast strides in food technology have taken place since section 403(c) of the act was enacted, and there are now on the market many new wholesome and nutritious food products, some of which resemble and are substitutes for other, traditional foods. Significantly, it is no longer the case that such products are necessarily inferior to the traditional foods for which they may be substituted.

There has been some uncertainty as to the proper scope of the term "imitation" in this modern context. The term clearly fails to inform the public of the actual characteristics and properties of a new food product. . . . To apply automatically the term "imitation" to new substitute food products which are not nutritionally inferior would be a disservice to consumers and would be contrary to the common understanding that the word "imitation" connotes inferiority. Section 403(c) of the act would then present a serious obstacle to the development and marketing of modified products with improved nutritional content. Indeed, because of the traditional connotation of inferiority, application of the term "imitation" to a substitute food product which is not inferior could be misleading to the consumer, in violation of section 403(a) of the act.

Accordingly, the Commissioner of Food and Drugs has concluded that it is in the interest of consumers and consistent with the general intent of Congress to restrict required application of the term "imitation" to a substitute food which is nutritionally inferior to the food for which it is a substitute.

The consumer, however, must be protected from unwitting purchase of a product which is different, although not inferior, from what he may reasonably expect. The Commissioner concurs with the further recommendation of the White House Conference that the "name of a food should accurately describe, in as simple and direct terms as possible, the basic nature of the food or its characterizing properties or ingredients." Accordingly, in order to avoid "imitation" status, a substitute food product which is not nutritionally inferior must also bear a label which clearly states the common or usual name of the product and which is not false or misleading. . . .

The Commissioner has considered whether there may be basis for imitation labeling other than nutritional inferiority. In reviewing this matter, it appears that nutritional inferiority is the only type of inferiority that is quantifiable on an objective basis. All other potential aspects of inferiority involve essentially subjective judgment which may vary from person to person. . . . The Commissioner has concluded that it is not the function of the Food and Drug Administration to attempt to arbitrate between the likes and dislikes of different individuals or between the different economic considerations that motivate different producers of agricultural commodities or different manufacturers and distributors of foods. The function of the Food and Drug Administration is solely to assure the safety of all foods and to prevent misleading labeling. . . .

NOTES

1.   *Final Regulation.* In promulgating the final regulation, 21 C.F.R. 101.3(e), FDA noted, "No comment was able to articulate or even suggest objective standards constituting inferiority in addition to nutritional inferiority." 38 Fed. Reg. 20702 (Aug. 2, 1973).

2.   *Meaning of "Nutritional Inferiority."* Under the regulation, "nutritional inferiority" is defined as a reduction of 2 percent or more of the U.S. Daily Reference Value (DRV) of protein or potassium or a reduction of 2 percent or more of the Reference Daily Intake (RDI) of most of the essential vitamins and minerals. 21 C.F.R. 101.3(e)(4)(ii). It explicitly does not include a reduction in the caloric or fat content of the food. *Id.* 101.3(e)(4)(i).

———

FDA's new approach to "imitation" labeling was challenged unsuccessfully in court:

Federation of Homemakers v. Schmidt

539 F.2d 740 (D.C. Cir. 1976).

■ TAMM, CIRCUIT JUDGE.

The Food and Drug Administration (FDA) recently promulgated a regulation which, for the first time, attempted to define an imitation food subject to section 403(c) of the Federal Food, Drug, and Cosmetic Act. The appellants in this case challenge the new regulation as contrary to the terms of the Act and as arbitrary and capricious. We affirm the district court's finding that the regulation fulfills the objectives of the statute in question and is a reasonable exercise of the regulatory power of the FDA. . . .

The Federation of Homemakers, a national consumer group, filed suit to enjoin enforcement of the new definition by the FDA, but on cross motions for summary judgment, District Judge Joseph C. Waddy held that the regulation is consistent with the statute and Congressional intent. *Federation of Homemakers v. Schmidt*, 385 F. Supp. 362 (D.D.C. 1974). . . .

. . . Beginning with the Supreme Court's admonition in *62 Cases of Jam v. United States* [excerpted *supra* p. 348] that "imitation" must be "left . . . to the understanding of ordinary English speech," appellants call our attention to cases in which texture, smell, taste, appearance, manufacture, packaging and marketing all contribute to a determination of whether the food in question must be labeled an imitation.[8] While it is true that these judicial definitions may be reasonable ones, we do not believe that they prevent the promulgation of an equally reasonable definition by the agency charged with administering the Act. Congress chose not to define the parameters of its imitation label requirements; our deference to the enforcing agency's interpretation limits our review to determining only whether the regulation violates the language of the statute or is arbitrary and capricious. Neither the legislative history of the companion section regarding standardized foods, 21 U.S.C. § 341 (1970), nor the undefined use of "imitation" in the statute leads us to conclude that a food nutritionally equivalent to the ordinary food and clearly labeled with a common name established by regulation or with a descriptive term violates Congressional objectives if it is marketed without the imitation label. Indeed, the new regulation successfully reconciles the need to alert the public to inferior products with the proscription in subsection 343(a) against false or misleading labels.

As to the arbitrary and capricious issue raised by the Federation of Homemakers, we are convinced that the FDA regulation is well within the zone of reasonableness required of agency rulemaking. We note first that appellant's primary complaint with the regulation is that the FDA

---

[8] In response to criticisms that the new regulation considers only nutritional equivalency, the FDA pointed out that by defining an imitation as a substitute, the characteristics previously noted by courts are still applicable in reaching this threshold finding.

Nutritional inferiority is not the only criterion involved in defining "imitation" status. An evaluation of the over-all impression conveyed by the food must first establish that the food is a substitute for and resembles another food.

Response to Comments, 38 Fed. Reg. 20202 (1973). . . .

has not decided to issue standards of identity for all new foods, but instead has promulgated regulations which provide for developing new common names as well as for employing standards of identity and imitation labeling. . . .

This regulatory scheme satisfies prior criticisms that the imitation requirement as interpreted by courts had unduly deterred the development of new food products, desirable for consumers, because the manufacturer's product, even if superior, was subject to the disparagement intimated by the imitation label. *See, e.g.,* Report of Panel III–2; White House Conference on Food and Nutrition, *Final Report* (Dec. 24, 1969). In addition, the FDA reasonably expects this more flexible approach to encourage greater emphasis on nutritional value and consumer knowledge about purchased food products. Furthermore, the regulation provides a safety valve for specific cases arising later in which nutritional equivalency and descriptive labeling do not adequately protect consumers from food substitutes which are inferior in other ways.

This regulation, directed at the laudable aims of encouraging manufacture of nutritional food products and of better informing consumers so that they may exercise a knowledgeable choice of differing foods within general categories, lies well within the bounds of discretion which the FDA may exercise. . . .

NOTES

1. *Preservation of the "Nutritionally Inferior" Test.* A decade after it promulgated its regulation defining "imitation" in terms of nutritional inferiority, FDA reaffirmed that decision and rejected alternative approaches. 48 Fed. Reg. 37665 (Aug. 19, 1983).

2. *Collateral Challenges.* In *National Milk Producers Federation v. Harris*, 653 F.2d 339 (8th Cir. 1981), the court rejected the plaintiffs' claim that FDA violated section 403(c) by failing to require cheese substitutes to be labeled as imitations and upheld the agency's definition of "imitation." In *Grocery Manufacturers of America, Inc. v. Gerace*, 755 F.2d 993 (2d Cir. 1985) (excerpted *supra* p. 308), the court, citing the *Federation of Homemakers* case, held that FDA's definition of "imitation" was reasonable, in addition to finding that FDA's definition preempted the New York "imitation cheese" statute.

c.   THE USE OF NUTRIENT DESCRIPTORS ("NUTRIENT CONTENT CLAIMS") IN FOOD NAMES

As discussed in more detail below, *infra* p. 413, FD&C Act 403(r) (added by the Nutrition Labeling and Education Act of 1990) instructs FDA to issue regulations defining claims that "characterize[ ] the level of any nutrient." FD&C Act 403(r)(1)(A). Pursuant to this provision, the agency has issued detailed and complex rules defining and regulating the use of "nutrient content claims." 21 C.F.R. Part 101, Subpart D. Many of the nutrient descriptors thus defined by regulation are frequently used in food names, including general terms such as "light" and "healthy" and terms characterizing the amount (e.g., "free," "low," "reduced") of particular nutrients (e.g., calories, sodium, fat, cholesterol). The NLEA nutrient content claim regulations ensure that claims such as "low fat" and "zero cholesterol" now mean the same thing across the food supply.

Because FDA allowed the liberal use of such claims in the names of nonstandardized foods even before 1990, incorporating the nutrient content claims regulations into the naming system for nonstandardized foods was relatively straightforward. The relationship between the nutrient content claims regulations and the naming requirements for standardized foods was more problematic, however. First of all, FDA in the 1980s still required the use of "alternative" or "substitute" in the names of modified standardized foods, even if they were not nutritionally inferior. Second, changing a standardized food to make it, for example, "sodium free" or "reduced fat," often required a variance from the requirements of the standard itself. Finally, some food standards existed for foods named with a nutrient descriptor (for example, lowfat milk), and these standards were not always consistent with the new nutrient content claims regulations.

Following the enactment of the NLEA in 1990, FDA was thus forced to reconcile its already weakened policy of protecting standardized food names with its new mandate to define and permit nutrient descriptors. Congress's instruction to the agency to establish a nutrient descriptors regime took precedence, thus further undermining the stature of standardized food names. In 1993, FDA issued the current rule, excerpted below, permitting the use of any nutrient descriptor defined by FDA as part of the common or usual name of a modified version of a standardized food (e.g., "low calorie ice cream," "high fiber enriched white bread," or "nonfat French dressing"). 58 Fed. Reg. 2446 (Jan. 6, 1993), codified at 21 C.F.R. 130.10. The use of the term "substitute" or "alternative" is not required. In an attempt to reconcile the new rule with its prior approach, FDA described the regulation as a "general definition and standard of identity." Importantly, the regulation permits deviations from both the ingredient and noningredient provisions of the standard to permit preservation of the "performance characteristics" of the standardized food.

21 C.F.R. § 130.10. Requirements for Foods Named by Use of a Nutrient Content Claim and a Standardized Term

(a) *Description.* The foods prescribed by this general definition and standard of identity are those foods that substitute for a standardized food defined in parts 131 through 169 of this chapter and that use the name of that standardized food in their statement of identity but that do not comply with the standard of identity because of a deviation that is described by an expressed nutrient content claim that has been defined by FDA regulation. The nutrient content claim shall comply with the requirements of § 101.13 of this chapter and with the requirements of the regulations in part 101 of this chapter that define the particular nutrient content claim that is used. The food shall comply with the relevant standard in all other respects except as provided in paragraphs (b), (c), and (d) of this section.

(b) *Nutrient addition.* Nutrients shall be added to the food to restore nutrient levels so that the product is not nutritionally inferior . . . to the standardized food as defined in parts 131 through 169 of this chapter. . . .

(c) *Performance characteristics.* Deviations from noningredient provisions of the standard of identity (*e.g.*, moisture content, food solids content requirements, or processing conditions) are permitted in order that the substitute food possesses performance characteristics similar to those of the standardized food. Deviations from ingredient and noningredient provisions of the standard must be the minimum necessary to qualify for the nutrient content claim while maintaining similar performance characteristics as the standardized food, or the food will be deemed to be adulterated under section 402(b) of the act. The performance characteristics (e.g., physical properties, flavor characteristics, functional properties, shelf life) of the food shall be similar to those of the standardized food as produced under parts 131 through 169 of this chapter, except that if there is a significant difference in performance characteristics that materially limits the uses of the food compared to the uses of the standardized food, the label shall include a statement informing the consumer of such difference (e.g., if appropriate, "not recommended for cooking"). . . . The modified product shall perform at least one of the principal functions of the standardized product substantially as well as the standardized product.

(d) *Other ingredients.* (1) Ingredients used in the product shall be those ingredients provided for by the standard as defined in parts 131 through 169 of this chapter and in paragraph (b) of this section, except that safe and suitable ingredients may be used to improve texture, add flavor, prevent syneresis, extend shelf life, improve appearance, or add sweetness so that the product is not inferior in performance characteristics to the standardized food defined in parts 131 through 169 of this chapter.

(2) An ingredient or component of an ingredient that is specifically required by the standard (*i.e.*, a mandatory ingredient) as defined in parts 131 through 169 of this chapter, shall not be replaced or exchanged with a similar ingredient from another source unless the standard, as defined in parts 131 through 169 of this chapter, provides for the addition of such ingredient (*e.g.*, vegetable oil shall not replace milkfat in light sour cream).

(3) An ingredient or component of an ingredient that is specifically prohibited by the standard as defined in parts 131 through 169 of this chapter, shall not be added to a substitute food under this section.

(4) An ingredient that is specifically required by the standard as defined in parts 131 through 169 of this chapter, shall be present in the product in a significant amount. A significant amount of an ingredient or component of an ingredient is at least that amount that is required to achieve the technical effect of that ingredient in the food. . . .

(e) *Nomenclature.* The name of a substitute food that complies with all parts of this regulation is the appropriate expressed nutrient content claim and the applicable standardized term. . . .

NOTES

1. *Implications of the General Standard of Identity.* With the enactment of 21 C.F.R. 130.10, FDA effectively abandoned its "substitute" and "alternative" nomenclature, at least for foods modified to satisfy a nutrient content claim regulation. Note, however, that according to 130.10(b), the general standard does not apply to nutritionally inferior substitutes for a standardized food, and FDA may thus still require that such products be labeled "imitation."

2. *Dairy Products.* The market for dairy products has long been a major battlefield in the war over names for modifications of or substitutes for traditional foods. Prior to the enactment of the NLEA, FDA had established numerous standards of identity for dairy products with reduced amounts of fat, such as lowfat and skim milk, lowfat and nonfat yogurt, and lowfat cottage cheese. The amount of fat permitted by these standards did not correspond to the amount allowed by the corresponding NLEA nutrient content claim regulations. In response to a petition filed jointly by the milk industry and a public interest group, the agency revoked the standards of identity for lowfat and nonfat dairy products while preserving the standards of identity for whole-fat dairy products. 60 Fed. Reg. 56541 (Nov. 9, 1995), 61 Fed. Reg. 58991 (Nov. 20, 1996). Consequently, modified-fat dairy products are now named in accordance with 21 C.F.R. 130.10, the general standard of identity, and the fat content descriptors have the same meaning when applied to dairy products as when applied to other foods. The application of the general standard of identity also allows producers to improve the performance characteristics of reduced fat, lowfat, and nonfat dairy products by adding ingredients that were not permitted by the now-revoked standards of identity. For example, milk processors now can add ingredients such as cellulose gel, carrageenan (a seaweed extract), and flavor to skim milk to better approximate the taste, appearance, and mouthfeel of whole milk.

3. ECONOMIC ADULTERATION

Section 402(b)(4) of the FD&C Act provides that a food is adulterated:

> (1) If any valuable constituent has been in whole or in part omitted or abstracted therefrom; or (2) if any substance has been substituted wholly or in part therefore; or (3) if damage or inferiority has been concealed in any manner; or (4) if any substance has been added thereto or mixed or packed therewith so as to increase its bulk or weight, or reduce its quality or strength, or make it appear better or of greater value than it is.

In practice, this section has been of limited use to FDA in policing food identity and quality.

United States v. 88 Cases . . . Bireley's Orange Beverage

187 F.2d 967 (3d Cir. 1951).

■ HASTIE, CIRCUIT JUDGE.

Pursuant to its libel charging economic adulteration of certain food within the meaning of Section 402(b)(4) of the Federal Food, Drug and Cosmetic Act, the United States seized for condemnation 88 cases of an article of food labeled "Bireley's Orange Beverage." The charges thus asserted were tried to a jury in the District Court for the District of New Jersey with a resultant finding of adulteration and a decree of condemnation. . . .

In this case the United States charged and undertook to prove that the "food" in question—Bireley's Orange Beverage—was "adulterated" within the meaning of the statute in that "substances[']—particularly, yellow coal tar dyes, sugar, lactic acid, and orange oil—had been "added thereto or mixed therewith . . . so as to make it appear better or of greater value than it is." . . .

Preliminarily, we consider an argument that the types of processing and manufacture covered by Section 402(b)(4) should be limited by a strict grammatical application of the words of the statute. Such an approach suggests that the noun "food" used in the introductory line of the section, and the articles and adverbs referring back to it be applied precisely and consistently to denote either an adulterated end product or an unadulterated original food. Further, it is argued that the statutory description of adulteration in terms of substances "mixed with" or "added to" a "food" limits the application of the section to situations in which the process of manufacture has been the modification of a basic identifiable and unadulterated article of food through the introduction of some additive.

We reject this restrictive analysis. In Section 402(b)(4) we think Congress has employed a very brief text, informally phrased in non-technical language, to cover generally a very considerable and diverse, but not precisely delimited, field of processing and fabrication. We view the language of the section as a comprehensive, if not always grammatically precise and consistent, description applicable to the manufacture and processing of foods generally, whether a recognized food is altered or sundry ingredients are combined or compounded to make what is essentially a new article of manufacture. . . .

More difficult questions arise in construing and applying the requirement of the statute that admixture shall have made the food "appear better than it is." . . . [H]ow is it to be determined whether the food "appears better than it is"? . . .

The parties agree that Bireley's orange drink contains about 6% orange juice, 2% lemon juice, 87% water, and small quantities of various other harmless substances. Undoubtedly, any percentage increase in the orange juice content with a corresponding decrease in water content would represent some improvement in food value. Hence, literally the product appears better than it is if it appears to the consumer to contain more than 6% orange juice.

But here we encounter serious difficulties of vagueness. The statutory test in Section 402(b)(4) is unreasonable and unenforceable if it requires manufacturers in first instance to anticipate and the trier of fact thereafter to measure anything so speculative or even whimsical as the customer's guess whether an artificial beverage contains five, six, seven, or some other percentage of orange juice. Popular judgments as to degree of dilution, more or less than actuality, are in our view too vague and speculative for meaningful guidance or fair and practical administration of a prohibition against the introduction of otherwise unobjectionable food into commerce. The difficulty with this entire approach is that the "adulterated" food is made to serve as its own only standard.

The solution to the problem and the correct construction of the statutory language are to be found in the rationale of the legislative exclusion of products from commerce for economic adulteration where no hygienic adulteration exists. In such cases a product is recognized as wholesome but is excluded from commerce because of the danger of confusing it with something else which is defined, familiar, and superior. There is no evidence to indicate a legislative intent to bar from the market foods which are wholesome merely because they may in fact be of relatively little value. So long as they are not confused with more wholesome products, their presence does no harm. Without a finding that a marketable inferior product is likely to be confused with a specified superior counterpart, we think there can be no appearing "better than it is" within the scope of disapproval of a section patently concerned only with confusion. Thus, in the case before us, proof of violation of the statute requires first description and definition of the superior counterpart, and second, proof that the consumer is likely to mistake the inferior for the superior. . . .

In the instant case, undiluted orange juice is the only defined and familiar food pointed out in the libel and in evidence as possibly to be confused with Bireley's Orange Beverage. We therefore agree with the claimant that the issue on this aspect of the case is squarely this: Would the ordinary consumer confuse claimant's product with undiluted orange juice? . . .

Questions of various permissible degrees of dilution which were regarded below as relevant and in issue are peculiarly appropriate for disposition by [the establishment of section 401 food standards by formal rulemaking]." Under the required administrative procedure, the whole industry can participate in the determination whether orange-flavored soft drinks are capable of satisfactory definition, how their composition should be restricted, and even whether such a food as orange drink, or any of its variants, should be permitted in commerce.

However, we agree with the government that it is not necessary that this channel be used. We agree that the statute does not foreclose the procedure used here. But as already indicated, we think the procedure used here permits condemnation only where there is confusion with a defined superior product. If the government would go further it must undertake the formulation of standards of identity in this area.

The trial court's instruction to the jury did not ask simply and directly whether the Bireley product could be confused with undiluted orange juice. Nor did it ask anything sufficiently close so that we can say that the issue was in effect determined. . . . In a new trial that issue should be made entirely clear to the jury. . . .

For the reasons heretofore given, the decree of condemnation will be vacated and the case remanded to the district court for further proceedings not inconsistent with this opinion.

NOTES

1. *Common or Usual Name Regulation.* In 1973, FDA issued a common or usual name regulation for diluted orange juice beverages. This regulation required the name to include a statement of the percent of orange juice contained in the product. 38 Fed. Reg. 6968 (Mar. 14, 1973), codified at 21 C.F.R. 102.9, later 102.32. Today, the naming and labeling of such a beverage is regulated by 21 C.F.R. 102.33 (common or usual name regulation for beverages that contain fruit or vegetable juice) and 101.30 (percentage juice declaration for foods purporting to be beverages that contain fruit or vegetable juice.). *See supra* p. 368, note 3.

2. *Unconstitutional Vagueness.* The court in *United States v. Fabro, Inc.*, 206 F. Supp. 523 (M.D. Ga. 1962), declared section 402(b)(1), prohibiting the omission of a "valuable constituent," to be unconstitutionally vague as applied to a nonstandardized food. *Van Liew v. United States*, 321 F.2d 664 (5th Cir. 1963), held that an indictment charging a violation of sections 402(b)(2) and (4) was impermissibly vague because it did not specify in detail what valuable constituent was omitted from the defendants' orange drink product, what substance was substituted for that constituent, or how the beverage was made to appear better or of greater value than it was.

3. *Concealment of Inferiority.* Section 402(b)(3) of the FD&C Act prohibits the concealment "in any manner" of a food's "damage or inferiority." In *United States v. 36 Drums of Pop'n Oil*, 164 F.2d 250 (5th Cir. 1947), the majority sustained a charge of economic adulteration under sections 402(b)(3) and (b)(4) against mineral oil marketed principally to movie theaters for use with popcorn. The oil—conceded by the government to be safe to consume—was artificially colored yellow to resemble melted butter. The majority opinion concluded that the product's truthful labeling did not cure the economic adulteration because "the ultimate consumer of the popcorn probably never sees the labeling." *Id.* at 252. The concurring judge, though agreeing with the dissent's assertion that "zeal for enforcement . . . is here outrunning common sense and the true intent of the law," reluctantly concluded that the product was adulterated under section 402(b)(3) because its inferiority had been concealed by making it look like butter, and under section 402(b)(4) because the mineral oil had been colored to make it appear of greater value than it was.

If ingredient information had been provided to the consumers in this case, should the result have been different? Consider *United States v. 55 Cases Popped Corn*, 62 F. Supp. 843 (D. Idaho 1943), posing the same issue as *Pop'n Oil* in the context of a popcorn product that bore full ingredient labeling disclosing the presence of mineral oil and coloring. FDA contended the product was not properly called "popcorn" because neither melted butter nor vegetable oil was used. The court rejected this contention because "there is no exact formula used in the preparation of popcorn for the market" and "the consumer was fully advised as to the contents of the various packages." *But see United States v. 716 Cases ... Del Comida Brand Tomatoes ...*, 179 F.2d 174 (10th Cir. 1950) (holding that truthful labeling cannot cure economic adulteration).

4. *Nonenforcement of Section 402(b).* Applied literally, the economic adulteration provisions of the FD&C Act would render most modern food technology problematic. Many functional ingredients—color additives, preservatives, emulsifiers—are intended to improve the appearance of the product and thus could be challenged as making food appear "better than it is." Food producers would claim that these ingredients in fact improve the food and only make it appear to be as good as it genuinely is. Without purporting to resolve this debate, FDA has virtually abandoned enforcement of section 402(b) except in cases of outright fraud, which are rare. The agency has embraced, though never publicized, the philosophy that, notwithstanding the proper legal interpretation of the statute, informative labeling can cure "economic adulteration."

D. REGULATION OF FOOD LABELING

1. "FALSE OR MISLEADING IN ANY PARTICULAR"

Section 403(a) prohibits statements in labeling that are "false or misleading in any particular." Proponents of the 1938 Act were successful in resisting the addition of qualifying terms, such as the insertion of the word "material" before "particular," although one has difficulty finding a case in which the FDA successfully attacked labeling representations to which that qualifier would not have applied.

Section 201(n) is an extraordinarily important supplement to section 403(a)—and to other provisions throughout the FD&C Act that prohibit misleading representations. Section 201(n) provides:

> If an article is alleged to be misbranded because the labeling or advertising is misleading, then in determining whether the labeling or advertising is misleading there shall be taken into account (among other things) not only representations made or suggested by statement, word, design, device, or any combination thereof, but also the extent to which the labeling or advertising fails to reveal facts material in the light of such representations or material with respect to consequences which may result from the use of the article to which the labeling or advertising relates under the conditions of use prescribed in the labeling or advertising thereof or under such conditions of use as are customary or usual.

With respect to FDA's authority over food, the only relevance of this subsection's references to "advertising" (as opposed to "labeling") is FDA's unexercised power over the advertising of vitamin and mineral supplements. FD&C Act 403(a)(2).

Section 403(a), alone or in combination with 201(n), is frequently cited in FDA's enforcement actions regarding food labeling. Moreover, using its power under section 701(a) "to promulgate regulations for the efficient enforcement of this Act," *see supra* pp. 30–32, the agency has issued a variety of regulations implementing 403(a) and 201(n). These regulations either forbid particular representations or mandate particular disclosures. Thus, even though section 403 of the FD&C Act contains numerous provisions governing particular labeling issues— many of which have been added in recent decades—FDA's general power under 403(a) and 201(n) is important.

––––––

As shown by the following three cases, one aspect of labeling that may be "false and misleading" is the name itself. Thus, FDA may allege violations of 403(a) in combination with violations of the various naming and economic adulteration provisions examined in the previous section. Note that although the first excerpted case was decided under the 1906 Pure Food and Drugs Act, that statute contained the equivalent "false or misleading in any particular" language as the current law.

United States v. Ninety–Five Barrels of . . . Apple Cider Vinegar

265 U.S. 438 (1924).

■ MR. JUSTICE BUTLER delivered the opinion of the Court.

This case arises under the Food and Drugs Act of June 30, 1906. The United States filed information in the District Court for the Northern District of Ohio, Eastern Division, for the condemnation of 95 barrels of vinegar. Every barrel seized was labeled:

> "Douglas Packing Company
> Excelsior Brand Apple Cider Vinegar
> Made from Selected Apples
> Reduced to 4 Percentum
> Rochester, N.Y."

The information alleged . . . that the vinegar was made from dried or evaporated apples, and was misbranded in violation of § 8 [of the Act], in that the statements on the label were false and misleading, and in that it was an imitation of and offered for sale under the distinctive name of another article, namely apple cider vinegar. . . .

Section 8 provides:

> "That the term 'misbranded,' as used herein, shall apply to all . . . articles of food, or articles which enter into the composition of food, the package or label of which shall bear any statement, design, or device regarding such article, or the ingredients or substances contained therein which shall be false or misleading in any particular. . . . That for the purpose of this Act an article shall also be deemed to be misbranded: . . . In the case of food: First. If it be an imitation of or offered for sale under the distinctive name of another article. Second. If it be labeled or branded so as to deceive or mislead the purchaser, . . . Fourth. If the package containing it or its label shall bear any statement, design, or device regarding

the ingredients or the substances contained therein, which statement, design, or device shall be false or misleading in any particular. . . ."

The statute is plain and direct. Its comprehensive terms condemn every statement, design and device which may mislead or deceive. Deception may result from the use of statements not technically false or which may be literally true. The aim of the statute is to prevent that resulting from indirection and ambiguity, as well as from statements which are false. It is not difficult to choose statements, designs and devices which will not deceive. Those which are ambiguous and liable to mislead should be read favorably to the accomplishment of the purpose of the act. The statute applies to food, and the ingredients and substances contained therein. It was enacted to enable purchasers to buy food for what it really is. . . .

If an article is not the identical thing that the brand indicates it to be, it is misbranded. The vinegar in question was not the identical thing that the statement "Excelsior Brand Apple Cider Vinegar made from selected apples," indicated it to be. . . . [T]he words, "apple cider vinegar made from selected apples" are misleading. Apple cider vinegar is made from apple cider. Cider is the expressed juice of apples and is so popularly and generally known. It was stipulated that the juice of unevaporated apples when subjected to alcoholic and subsequent acetous fermentation is entitled to the name "apple cider vinegar." The vinegar in question was not the same as if made from apples without dehydration. The name "apple cider vinegar" included in the brand did not represent the article to be what it really was; and, in effect, did represent it to be what it was not—vinegar made from fresh or unevaporated apples. The words "made from selected apples" indicate that the apples used were chosen with special regard to their fitness for the purpose of making apple cider vinegar. They give no hint that the vinegar was made from dried apples, or that the larger part of the moisture content of the apples was eliminated and water substituted therefor. As used on the label, they aid the misrepresentation made by the words "apple cider vinegar."

The misrepresentation was in respect of the vinegar itself, and did not relate to the method of production merely. When considered independently of the product, the method of manufacture is not material. The act requires no disclosure concerning it. And it makes no difference whether vinegar made from dried apples is or is not inferior to apple cider vinegar.

The label was misleading as to the vinegar, its substance and ingredients. The facts admitted sustain the charge of misbranding.

United States v. 432 Cartons . . . Candy Lollipops

292 F. Supp. 839 (S.D.N.Y. 1968).

■ MANSFIELD, DISTRICT JUDGE. . . .

The article of food in question consists of about 432 cartons each containing six lollipops. On the outside the carton is labeled on top "Candy . . . for one with Sophisticated Taste," on one side, "A. Freed Novelty, Inc., N.Y.C.," and on the other side, "Ingredients: Sugar, corn syrup, citric acid, natural and artificial flavors." The inside of the box contains the legend, "Liquor Flavored Lollypops," and the slogan, "Take Your Pick of a Liquor Stick." In addition the lollipops themselves are labeled, both in the box and on the cellophane in which they are individually wrapped as "Scotch," "Bourbon," and "Gin."

The Government contends that the internal labeling is false or misleading [in violation of section 403(a)] in that it implies and represents that "the article is flavored with liquor, which it is not." In response claimant does not allege that the lollipops are flavored with liquor, but by way of affirmative defenses contends that they are not misbranded because the cartons are clearly labeled "candy" and the ingredients are distinctly set forth, and that the ordinary purchaser would not read or understand it to represent that the lollipops contain any alcohol or liquor.

In approaching the question of whether the labeling here was false and misleading within the meaning of the statute, we recognize that the statute does not provide for much flexibility in interpretation, since it requires only that the labeling be false or misleading *"in any particular."* (emphasis supplied). This represents a stricter substantive standard than that applied with respect to false advertising, which in order to be prohibited must be "misleading in a *material respect."* (emphasis supplied) 15 U.S.C. § 55(a). Furthermore the statute says "false *or* misleading." . . .

The issue of whether a label is false or misleading may not be resolved by fragmentizing it, or isolating statements claimed to be false from the label in its entirety, since such statements may not be deemed misleading when read in the light of the label as a whole. However, even though the actual ingredients are stated on the outside of a carton, false or misleading statements inside the carton may lead to the conclusion that the labeling is misleading, since a true statement will not necessarily cure or neutralize a false one contained in the label. Furthermore, the fact that purchasers of a product have not been misled, while admissible on the issue of whether the label is false or misleading, would not constitute a defense.

Applying these principles here, it cannot be concluded as a matter of law that no material issue exists with respect to the alleged false and misleading character of the label here before us. Although the labeling on the inside of each box of "candy," when read alone, might be misleading, the detailed description of the contents of the box listed on the outside of the carton could convince a jury, when the labeling or literature is read as a whole, that it is not "misleading in any particular." . . .

. . . The Government's motion for a judgment on the pleadings is therefore denied.

NOTES

1. *Subsequent Resolution.* On remand, "an order for the discontinuance of the action was entered pursuant to stipulation of the parties." 5 FDA Papers, No. 3, at 42 (Apr. 1971).

2. *Oral Representations.* In *Weeks v. United States*, 245 U.S. 618 (1918), the Court held that oral misrepresentations could constitute misbranding under the 1906 Act's prohibition against offering a food for sale under the name of another article. Under the FD&C Act, by contrast, only misrepresentations in a food product's label or labeling constitute misbranding.

3. *Disclaimers Ineffective.* Prior to recent elaboration of commercial free speech doctrine, *see infra* p. 428, disclaimers were often held insufficient to cure otherwise misleading labeling. *E.g., United States v. 24 Unlabeled Cans . . . "Compound Vegetable Butter Brand . . . "*, 1969–1974 FDLI Jud. Rec. 32 (E.D. Mich. 1969) ("Not a dairy product" insufficient to overcome misleading use of the word "butter").

4. *Misleading Brand Name.* While a product's brand name may be misleading, *United States v. 70 1/2 Dozen Bottles . . . "666"*, 1938–1964 FDLI Jud. Rec. 89 (M.D. Ga. 1944), courts are reluctant to sustain orders that would require abandonment of a brand name. *See Jacob Siegel Co. v. FTC*, 327 U.S. 608 (1946); *FTC v. Algoma Lumber Co.*, 291 U.S. 67 (1934). Nonetheless, they sometimes will do so. *E.g., United States v. An Article of Food . . . "Manischewitz . . . Diet Thins"*, 377 F. Supp. 746 (E.D.N.Y. 1974).

5. *Private Enforcement.* Although there is no private right of enforcement under the FD&C Act, *see supra* p. 163, a company can sue a competitor for false or misleading labeling or advertising under the Lanham Act, 15 U.S.C. 1125(a). *E.g., Potato Chip Institute v. General Mills, Inc.*, 461 F.2d 1088 (8th Cir. 1972); *Abruzzi Foods, Inc. v. Pasta & Cheese, Inc.*, 986 F.2d 605 (1st Cir. 1993); *Vermont Pure Holdings, Ltd. v. Nestle Waters North America, Inc.*, 2004 WL 2030254 (D. Mass. 2004), 2006 WL 839486 (D. Mass. 2006).

United States v. Farinella

558 F.3d 695 (2009).

■ POSNER, CIRCUIT JUDGE

The defendant was convicted by a jury . . . of introducing into interstate commerce a misbranded food with intent to defraud or mislead. 21 U.S.C. §§ 331(a), 333(a)(2). The judge sentenced him to five years' probation (including six months of home confinement) and to pay a $75,000 fine and forfeit the net gain from the offense, which was in excess of $400,000. . . . The defendant's appeal primarily argues that there was insufficient admissible evidence to convict him of misbranding. . . .

The facts, stated as favorably to the government as the record permits . . . are as follows. In May 2003 the defendant bought 1.6 million bottles of "Henri's Salad Dressing" from ACH Foods, which in turn had bought it from Unilever, the manufacturer. The label on each bottle said "best when purchased by" followed by a date, which had been picked by Unilever, ranging from January to June 2003. ACH had purchased Henri's Salad Dressing from Unilever when the "best when purchased by" date was approaching. The intention was to sell the salad dressing to consumers through discount outlets. The defendant accordingly resold the salad dressing he bought from ACH to "dollar stores," which are discount stores, but before doing so he pasted, over the part of the label that contains the "best when purchased by" date, on each bottle, a new label changing the date to May or July 2004. The government calls these the dates on which "the dressing would expire." That is itself false and misleading, and is part of a pattern of improper argumentation in this litigation that does no credit to the Justice Department. . . . [I]n her opening argument the principal prosecutor said that "it's a case about taking nearly two million bottles of old, expired salad dressing and relabeling it with new expiration dates to pass it off as new and fresh. . . . [N]obody wants to eat foul, rancid food." The term "expiration date" (or "sell by" date, another date that the government's brief confuses with "best when purchased by" date) on a food product, unlike a "best when purchased by" date, has a generally understood meaning: it is the date after which you shouldn't eat the product. Salad dressing, however, or at least the type of salad dressing represented by Henri's, is what is called "shelf stable"; it has no expiration date. . . .

It is important to understand what else this case does not involve, and also what is not in the record—the omissions are more interesting than the scanty contents of the government's threadbare case. There is no suggestion that selling salad dressing after the "best when purchased by" date endangers human health; so far as appears, Henri's Salad Dressing is edible a decade or more after it is manufactured. There is no evidence that the taste of any of the 1.6 million bottles of Henri's Salad Dressing sold by the defendant had deteriorated by the time of trial—four years after the latest original "best when purchased by" date—let alone by the latest relabeled "best when purchased by" date, which was 18 months after Unilever's original "best when purchased by" date. There is no evidence that any buyer of any of the 1.6 million bottles sold by the defendant has ever complained about the taste.

The term "misbranded food" is defined in some detail in 21 U.S.C. § 343, but there is nothing there about dates on labels, so that the defendant's conduct if illegal is so only if it can be said to be "false or misleading in any particular." § 343(a)(1). No regulation issued by the Food and Drug Administration, or, so far as we are informed, by the Federal Trade Commission or any other body, official or unofficial, defines "best when purchased by" or forbids a wholesaler (as here) or retailer to change the date. There is evidence that Unilever picked the "best when purchased by" dates on the basis of tests that it conducted, but the tests were not described at the trial and we do not know whether for example they are taste tests.

There is also and critically nothing in the record concerning consumers' understanding of the significance of "best when purchased by." Without evidence of that understanding, whether the defendant's redating was misleading cannot be determined. No consumer evidence was presented, whether as direct testimony or in survey form. . . . Conceivably consumers understand the "best when purchased by" date to refer to a date picked by the manufacturer, but there is no evidence of that and it is not, as the government believes, self-evident.

No evidence was presented that "best when purchased by" has a uniform meaning in the food industry. The government wants us to believe that it is a synonym for "expires on" but presented no evidence for this interpretation, and indeed argues the point by innuendo, simply by substituting in its brief, as in the indictment and in the prosecution's statements at the trial in the hearing of the jury, "expires on" for "best when purchased by."

The parties have found no previous case, either criminal or civil, and no administrative proceeding, in which alteration of the "best when purchased by" date was challenged as unlawful. As far as the evidence shows, any firm in the chain of production and distribution that leads from the manufacturer to the ultimate consumer can make its own judgment of when the taste of the product is likely to deteriorate. For all we know, the date is determined less by a judgment about taste than about concern with turnover. The manufacturer might want to affix an early "best when purchased by" date so that his distributors would be more inclined to repurchase the product within a reasonably short time, so that he has more sales. Admittedly, this is speculation, for while a date in the near future will increase turnover it will do so at the cost of making each bottle less likely to be sold at retail, and hence less valuable. Grocery stores pay less for bottles that are less likely to be sold. The cost of restocking shelves more frequently also would drive down the price to the manufacturer.

Another possibility is that labeling a product with a "best when purchased by" date is a method of price discrimination. After that date, products are not destroyed, for they are not only safe but also, as far as the record shows, of undiminished quality for an indefinite time. But well-off consumers prefer to buy before that date, and after the date passes the product will be sold at a discount in dollar stores or their equivalent, catering to less well-off consumers. In economic lingo, the label invites consumers to sort themselves into two groups, one of less-elastic demanders willing to pay a higher price for what may or may not be a higher-quality good and the others preferring the discount.

So was the defendant ripping off the consumer by selling salad dressing after its "best when purchased by" date had passed, without disclosing the fact? Apparently not, because it sold the salad dressing to dollar stores rather than to stores that cater to consumers who would not buy a product after its "best when purchased by" date.

Still another possibility is that "best when purchased by" is just a guarantee by the seller, in this case by the defendant—a time-limited warranty. If so, then a consumer who had a bad experience with a bottle of salad dressing used before the "best when purchased by date" affixed by the defendant would be entitled to a refund because the defendant, and the retailers to whom he sold the salad dressing and who we assume (though again there is no evidence) did not alter the date, had implicitly guaranteed "bestness" up to that date.

All this is speculation, but it is less implausible speculation than the government's that consumers think "best when purchased by" means "expires on," so that if they knew that the manufacturer's "best when purchased by" date had passed they would not dream of buying the product no matter how steeply it was discounted. . . .

The prosecutor told the judge that if there is a "best when purchased by" date on the label of a food product "and it's changed[,] that is a violation of the Food, Drug and Cosmetic Act." That is false.

The government is left to argue that any change on the label of a food product is misbranding, whatever consumers understand. . . .

We do not suggest that a novel fraud can never be punished as a crime. But to prove a person guilty of having made a fraudulent representation, a jury must be given evidence about the meaning (unless obvious) of the representation claimed to be fraudulent, and that was not done here. . . . [O]ne possible meaning of "best when purchased by" is that it is a guarantee by the seller that if purchased by then (and, presumably, eaten within a reasonable time afterward) it will taste as good as when it was first sold; if this is the meaning that consumers attach to the phrase, there was no misrepresentation.

Because the government presented insufficient evidence that the defendant engaged in misbranding, he is entitled to be acquitted. But since there was insufficient evidence, why did the jury convict? Perhaps because of a series of improper statements by [the] prosecutor . . . in her rebuttal closing argument. . . .

. . . The prosecutor told the jury that the "best when purchased by" date "allows a manufacturer to trace the product if there is a consumer complaint, if there is illness, if there is a need to recall the product." The implication is that by altering the "best when purchased by" date the defendant had prevented the manufacturer from tracing the product in order to prevent it from causing illness. If that were true, the FDA presumably would require that the date not be altered, and it does not require that; in any event there was no evidence that a bottle of Henri's Salad Dressing consumed before or for that matter after the altered "best when purchased by" date could make anybody ill.

In like vein the prosecutor told the jury that if what the defendant "did was business as usual in the food industry, I suggest we stop going to the store right now and start growing our own food." That was a veiled reference to the nonexistent issue of safety, which she pressed further when she said that "in spite of all this talk about the quality of the dressing, I don't see them opening any of these bottles and taking a whiff." . . . She also called the bottles of salad dressing "truckfulls of nasty, expired salad dressing," which was another groundless comment about quality and safety. . . .

REVERSED.

NOTES

1. *The "Reasonable Consumer" Test.* Prior to 2002, the courts articulated a variety of standards for determining whether statements in labeling are "misleading." In *United States v. 62 Packages . . . Marmola Prescription Tablets*, 48 F. Supp. 878 (W.D. Wis. 1943), the court stated that the purpose of the FD&C Act is "to protect the public, the vast multitude which includes the ignorant, the unthinking and the credulous who, when making a purchase, do not stop to analyze." By contrast the court in *United States v. Pinaud, Inc.*, 1938–1949 FDLI Jud. & Admin. Rec. 526, 529 (S.D.N.Y. 1949), stated that the proper standard was "purchasers

who are of normal capacity and use that capacity in a common sense way." The correct standard was characterized as the "ordinary person" in *United States v. 1 Device . . . Radiant Ozone Generator*, 1949–1950 FDLI Jud. & Admin. Rec. 139, 143 (W.D. Mo. 1949), and *United States v. Vrilium Products, Co.*, 1949–1950 FDLI Jud. & Admin. Rec. 210, 214 (N.D. Ill. 1950). But in *United States v. Article Consisting of 216 Cartoned Bottles . . . "Sudden Change"*, 409 F.2d 734 (2d Cir. 1969) (excerpted *supra* p. 111), the court concluded that the law should protect "the ignorant, the unthinking and the credulous." Another court characterized the standard as the "often unthinking and gullible consumer" in *United States v. An Article of Food . . . "Schmidt's Blue Ribbon"*, 1969–1974 FDLI Jud. Rec. 139 (D. Md. 1973).

FDA resolved this confusion in December 2002 by announcing, "In assessing whether food labeling is misleading, FDA will use a 'reasonable consumer' standard. . . ." 67 Fed. Reg. 78002, 78003 (Dec. 20, 2002). The agency explained:

> The reasonable consumer standard more accurately reflects FDA's belief that consumers are active partners in their own health care who behave in health promoting ways when they are given accurate health information. In addition, the reasonable consumer standard is consistent with the governing first amendment case law precluding the Government from regulating the content of promotional communication so that it contains only information that will be appropriate for a vulnerable or unusually credulous audience.

Id. at 78004. In adopting the "reasonable consumer" standard, FDA explicitly embraced the test used by the Federal Trade Commission since 1984. *Id.* at 78003; 103 F.T.C. 100, 174, 177 (1984).

Although FDA's statement was limited on its face to food labeling, it certainly also applies to cosmetics, which the Center for Food Safety and Applied Nutrition regulates as well. Moreover, FDA has declared that the same "reasonable consumer" standard applies to promotional materials for prescription drugs and medical devices. DRAFT GUIDANCE FOR INDUSTRY: PRESENTING RISK INFORMATION IN PRESCRIPTION DRUG AND MEDICAL DEVICE PROMOTION (May 2009).

2. *Slack Fill and Deceptive Packaging.* Section 403(d) provides that a food is misbranded "[i]f its container is so made, formed, or filled as to be misleading." This prohibition against misleading packaging has rarely been the basis for FDA enforcement proceedings. Between 1938 and the enactment of the Fair Packaging and Labeling Act in 1966, the agency had not prevailed in a single contested case under section 403(d). *See, e.g., United States v. 116 Boxes . . . Arden Assorted Candy Drops*, 80 F. Supp. 911 (D. Mass. 1948); *United States v. 738 Cases . . . Jiffy–Lou Vanilla Flavor Pudding*, 71 F. Supp. 279 (D. Ariz. 1946).

One obstacle to successful enforcement was the lack of legislatively prescribed criteria of deception and FDA's failure to develop such criteria by regulation. Thus, according to one court, "There is no hard and fast rule as to what would constitute slack-filling. Whether or not over 50 per cent space in a particular package of candy was slack-filling is a question of fact for the district court to decide." *United States v. Cataldo*, 157 F.2d 802, 804

(1st Cir. 1946). Furthermore, courts vacillated over whether it was incumbent upon the FDA to introduce evidence of actual consumer deception. Courts appeared reluctant to find a package misleading without such evidence, perhaps because the Act requires the net contents to be disclosed on the label. Finally, one court emphasized that "a showing by the United States that the ordinary purchaser, on viewing a container, will believe that it contains significantly more food than in fact it does contain, and was deceived, cannot be dispositive. . . . A claimant may go forward and show . . . that the circumstantial deception was forced upon it by other considerations such as packaging features necessary to safeguard its product." *United States v. 174 Cases . . . "Delson Thin Mints,"* 287 F.2d 246, 248 (3d Cir. 1961). On remand, the District Court in this case held that the package was not deceptive, and that even if it were, the available alternative means of packaging were no less deceptive and the efficacy of the present package outweighed any deception. 195 F. Supp. 326 (D.N.J. 1961).

In 1966, Congress enacted the Fair Packaging and Labeling Act, 80 Stat. 1296, 15 U.S.C. 1451–1461, a law primarily designed to facilitate price comparisons by consumers between competing products. The core of the FPLA is a requirement that packages of consumer commodities bear a legible, prominent label statement of net quantity of contents (in terms of weight, measure or numerical count). In addition, section 5(c)(4) of the FPLA authorizes FDA to adopt regulations to "prevent the nonfunctional-slack-fill of packages containing" food, drugs, devices, or cosmetics. In 1994, FDA belatedly promulgated regulations establishing general principles on nonfunctional slack fill. 59 Fed. Reg. 536 (Jan.5, 1994), codified at 21 C.F.R. 100.100. The agency issued these regulations under section 403(d) of the FD&C Act rather than under the FPLA because reliance on the latter would have required compliance with the formal rulemaking requirements of section 701(e) of the FD&C Act. Since the publication of these regulations, FDA has essentially ignored the issue of slack fill and deceptive packaging.

3. *Fill of Container Standards.* Section 401 authorizes FDA to issue "reasonable standards of fill of container," and the agency has issued such standards, as a component of its food standards regulations, for many canned foods. 21 C.F.R. Parts 145 *et seq.*

4. *Package Size.* Section 5(d) of the FPLA authorizes the Secretary of Commerce to establish voluntary product standards governing the sizes of retail packages to prevent "undue proliferation" in package sizes that "impairs the reasonable ability of consumers to make value comparisons." This provision, designed to preclude odd package sizes that hinder price comparison, requires use of the voluntary product standard procedures in 15 C.F.R. Part 10. Following an opinion of the Department of Justice that permitted the private formulation of package size standards without adherence to the Department of Commerce's formal procedures, several industries voluntarily established standard package sizes.

2. MANDATORY INFORMATION AND DISCLOSURES

In addition to the common and usual name, discussed above, section 403 of the FD&C Act requires that four other types of information appear on all food labels (with a few narrow exceptions): the name and place of business of the manufacturer, the net quantity of contents, a statement of ingredients, and nutrition information. FD&C Act 403(e), (i), (k), (q). In addition, section 403(w) mandates the disclosure of the presence of major food allergens. Finally, using its section 701(a) authority to "promulgate regulations for the efficient enforcement" of the Act, FDA has issued various requirements for affirmative disclosure of information in food labeling based on the "failure to reveal material facts" language of section 201(n).

a. PROMINENCE AND CONSPICUOUSNESS

Section 403(f) mandates that any information required by section 403 to appear on the label or labeling be "prominently placed thereon with such conspicuousness . . . and in such terms as to render it likely to be read and understood by the ordinary individual under customary conditions of use." From 1938 until 1973, FDA enforced this requirement based solely on the subjective impressions and informed judgment of agency compliance personnel. In 1973, the agency relied on section 403(f) to promulgate the following regulation. 38 Fed. Reg. 6950 (Mar. 14, 1973).

21 C.F.R. Part 101—Food Labeling
Subpart A—General Provisions

§ 101.1 Principal display panel of package form food

The term *principal display panel* as it applies to food in package form and as used in this part, means the part of a label that is most likely to be displayed, presented, shown, or examined under customary conditions of display for retail sale. The principal display panel shall be large enough to accommodate all the mandatory label information required to be placed thereon by this part with clarity and conspicuousness and without obscuring design, vignettes, or crowding. Where packages bear alternate principal display panels, information required to be placed on the principal display panel shall be duplicated on each principal display panel. . . .

§ 101.2 Information panel of package form food

(a) The term *information panel* as it applies to packaged food means that part of the label immediately contiguous and to the right of the principal display panel as observed by an individual facing the principal display panel with the following exceptions. . . .

(b) All information required to appear on the label of any package of food under [most relevant provisions of] this chapter shall appear either on the principal display panel or on the information panel, unless otherwise specified by regulations in this chapter.

(c) All information appearing on the principal display panel or the information panel pursuant to this section shall appear prominently and conspicuously, but in no case may the letters and/or numbers be less than one-sixteenth inch in height unless an exemption pursuant to paragraph (f) of this section is established. . . .

(d)(1) Except as provided in [various provisions regarding small packages and insufficient panel space], all information required to appear on the principal display panel or on the information panel pursuant to this section shall appear on the same panel unless there is insufficient space. In determining the sufficiency of the available space . . . any vignettes, designs, and other nonmandatory label information shall not be considered. . . .

(e) All information appearing on the information panel pursuant to this section shall appear in one place without other intervening material.

(f) If the label of any package of food is too small to accommodate all of the information required by . . . this chapter, the Commissioner may establish by regulation an acceptable alternative method of disseminating such information to the public, *e.g.,* a type size smaller than one-sixteenth inch in height, or labeling attached to or inserted in the package or available at the point of purchase. . . .

b.   NET QUANTITY OF CONTENTS

Section 403(e)(2) of the FD&C Act mandates that a food label contain "an accurate statement of the quantity of the contents in terms of weight, measure, or numerical count." This provision originated with the Gould Amendment to the 1906 Act, 37 Stat. 732 (1913) (codified at § 8 of the Pure Food and Drugs Act). Net weight labeling, although straightforward in principle, presents two difficult problems, both of which involve the moisture content of food.

The first problem is gain and loss of moisture. Food packaged in a dry climate will gain moisture, and thus weight, when it is stored and marketed in a moister climate. Conversely, food packaged in a moist climate will lose weight when marketed in a dry climate. Accordingly, rules must be developed to govern the gain or loss of moisture during transportation and storage. FDA regulations state: "Reasonable variations caused by loss or gain of moisture during the course of good distribution practice or by unavoidable deviations in good manufacturing practice will be recognized." 21 C.F.R. 101.105(q). For many years, the National Bureau of Standards (now the National Institute of Standards and Technology, or NIST) in the Department of Commerce has published handbooks explaining how to determine the net weight of consumer products, and one of these handbooks establishes maximum allowable variances for moisture loss for products. NIST HANDBOOK 133, CHECKING THE CONTENTS OF PACKAGED GOODS. USDA has explicitly incorporated this handbook by reference. 55 Fed. Reg. 49826 (Nov. 30, 1990), codified at 9 C.F.R. 381.121b. FDA has not done so, although the agency has expressed its desire to harmonize its regulations with this and other NIST handbooks. 58 Fed. Reg. 2462, 2463–64 (Jan. 6, 1993).

The other challenging issue in weight labeling is that of "drained weight." Many canned fruits and vegetables naturally contain juice or moisture or are traditionally packed in some type of liquid. The net weight of these products thus does not reflect the actual amount of fruit or vegetable, and unless regulated, the latter amount can vary from packer to packer or even from shipment to shipment by the same packer. In the mid-1970s, FDA issued proposals to require label declaration of the drained weight of most canned fruits or vegetables or, alternatively, either the drained weight or the solid content weight. 40 Fed. Reg. 52172 (Nov. 7, 1975); 42 Fed. Reg. 62282 (Dec. 9, 1977). However, in light of the successful implementation of a voluntary solid content labeling program by the National Canners Association (now the Grocery Manufacturers Association), FDA withdrew its proposal in 56 Fed. Reg. 67440, 67446 (Dec. 30, 1991). Some of the canned fruit standards of identity have provisions regulating the proportions of certain size pieces or certain ingredients according to drained weight, and this part of the regulations thus contains both a definition of "drained weight" and a procedure for determining drained weight. 21 C.F.R. 145.3(n), (o)(4).

NOTE

Metric Labeling. Prior to 1992, FDA regulations governing label declaration of the net quantity of contents required that the declaration be expressed in terms of avoirdupois (English) rather than metric units, although a separate statement of the net quantity of contents in terms of the metric system was also permitted. In early 1992, however, Congress enacted the American Technology Preeminence Act of 1991, which contained an amendment to the Fair Packaging and Labeling Act to require that consumer commodities declare the net quantity of contents using the metric system "as the primary system for measuring quantity." 106 Stat. 7, 13 (1992). This provision caught the regulated industry completely by surprise. Congress quickly enacted legislation to amend the FPLA to repeal the metric requirement of the American Technology Preeminence Act and to replace it with a requirement for dual declaration of both the avoirdupois and metric content. 106 Stat. 847 (1992).

c. INGREDIENT LABELING

Section 403(i) of the FD&C Act requires that a food label bear not only the common or usual name of the food itself, but also, "in case it is fabricated from two or more ingredients, the common or usual name of each such ingredient." FD&C Act 402(i)(2). FDA has issued numerous regulations to explain and amplify the requirements for ingredient labeling. 21 C.F.R. 101.4, 101.22–35. The basic rule can be stated simply: All of the ingredients of a food must be listed in descending order of predominance by weight. *See* 21 C.F.R. 101.4(a)(1). Listing is to be by chemical name, rather than by class or function (e.g., "sweeteners" or "emulsifiers"), except that spices, flavorings, and uncertified colorings *may* be listed generically. Chemical preservatives are the only class of food ingredient that must be declared both by chemical name and by function.

Section 403(i) has required the complete listing of the ingredients of nonstandardized foods ever since 1938. Until 1990, however, the FD&C Act exempted standardized foods from section 403(i) and subjected them only to the special ingredient labeling provision at

403(g)(2). Under this provision, the label of a standardized food did not have to declare any mandatory ingredients. It was instead required to bear only the common name of those optional ingredients that the standard required to be declared. In 1990, NLEA amended 403(i) to remove the exemption for standardized foods, and all foods are thus now required to provide full ingredient labeling.

NOTES

1. *Purpose of Ingredient Labeling.* In recent years, discussions of ingredient labeling have focused on the consumer's ability to identify and avoid specific ingredients. In 1938, however, the new requirement of ingredient declaration was also viewed as a matter of economics—that is, preventing food producers from "creating the impression that a product is a commonly-known food when it does not in fact contain the ingredients which may properly be expected of that food." David F. Cavers, *The Food, Drug, and Cosmetic Act of 1938: Its Legislative History and Its Substantive Provisions*, 6 LAW AND CONTEMPORARY PROBLEMS 2 (1939).

2. *Flavorings.* Section 403(i)(2) of the Act permits generic declaration of spices and flavors in the ingredient statement. Thus, under 21 C.F.R. 101.22(h)(1), flavors can be listed as "spice," "natural flavor," "artificial flavor," or any combination of them, although FDA has promulgated complex additional requirements governing specific issues regarding the disclosure of natural and artificial flavoring. 21 C.F.R. 101.22 Section 403(k) mandates the declaration of the presence of artificial flavoring, and FDA requires that this declaration be placed so as to be "likely to be read by the ordinary person under customary conditions of purchase and use." 21 C.F.R. 101.22(c). See also the USDA flavor regulations for meat food products at 7 C.F.R. 317.2(f)(1)(i).

3. *Colors.* Section 403(i)(2), as enacted in 1938, also permitted generic declaration of all colors. The Nutrition Labeling and Education Act of 1990 (NLEA) amended section 403(i)(2) to require the declaration by name of all colors required to be certified under section 721(c), i.e., all FD&C color additives (such as "Yellow 5" or "Blue 1"). *See* 21 C.F.R. 101.22(k)(1). (For further discussion on certification of color additives, see *infra* p. 617.) FDA does not require the use of the "FD&C" prefix in the declaration of a certified color, nor the term "No." In 2009, FDA revised its regulations to also require the declaration by name of cochineal extract and carmine, two certification-exempt color additives to which some consumers have allergic reactions. 74 Fed. Reg. 207 (Jan. 5, 2009). All other colors additives can be declared generally with a phrase such as "Color Added," or "Artificial Color Added." Under section 403(k) of the Act and 21 C.F.R. 101.22(c), the presence of artificial colors, as well as artificial flavors, must be prominently declared. Section 403(k) specifically exempts artificial coloring in butter, cheese, and ice cream from the ingredient labeling and "artificial color" declaration requirements.

4. *Chemical Preservatives.* FDA has interpreted section 401(k) to require that a preservative be declared in the statement of ingredients both by its chemical name and by a separate description of its specific function. 39 Fed. Reg. 5627 (Feb. 14, 1974), codified at 21 C.F.R. 101.22(j).

5. *Varying Predominance of Ingredients.* With respect to its requirement that food ingredients be labeled in descending order of predominance by weight, FDA has addressed the practical difficulties confronting manufacturers who adjust the ingredients in their products in response to changes in the price and seasonal fluctuations in the characteristics of basic ingredients. In 1978, at the behest of the American Bakers Association, FDA amended its designation of ingredients regulations to provide that ingredients that act as dough conditioners, yeast nutrients, or leavening agents may be listed by their specific common or usual names in the ingredient statement in parentheses following the appropriate collective names "leavening," "yeast nutrients," or "dough conditioners." To address the problem of raw material variation, the regulation further provides that these types of ingredients need not be listed in descending order of predominance and that the parenthetical list may include all such ingredients that are sometimes used, whether or not they are present in the particular item, with clarifying language such as "contains one or more of the following." 43 Fed. Reg. 24518 (June 6, 1978), codified at 21 C.F.R. 101.4(b)(16)–(18). A similar rule exists for the labeling of firming agents. 48 Fed. Reg. 8053 (Feb. 25, 1983), codified at 21 C.F.R. 101.4(b)(19).

6. *No Order of Predominance Requirement for Minor Ingredients.* The ingredient labeling rule provides that the "descending order of predominance" requirement does not apply to ingredients present in the amount of 2 percent or less by weight, so long as they are listed at the end of the ingredient statement with an appropriate qualifying statement, such as "Contains ___ percent or less of ___." 21 C.F.R. 101.4(a)(2).

7. *Exempt Incidental Ingredients.* Incidental additives that are present in a food at insignificant levels and do not achieve any technical or functional effect in the food are exempt from label declaration under 21 C.F.R. 101.100(a)(3). In the only reported case interpreting this provision, *Sea Snack Foods, Inc. v. United States*, Food Drug Cosm. L. Rep. (CCH) ¶ 38,062 (D.D.C. 1987), the court upheld FDA's determination that the processing aid at issue served a functional purpose in the finished food and therefore must be declared on the label.

8. *Ingredient Labeling for Alcoholic Beverages.* As noted previously, *supra* p. 318, the Federal Alcohol Administration Act (FAA), administered by the Department of Treasury's Alcohol and Tobacco Tax and Trade Bureau (TTB) (formerly the Bureau of Alcohol, Tobacco, and Firearms (BATF)), governs the labeling of alcoholic beverages. Regulations to implement this authority have been promulgated in 27 C.F.R. Parts 4, 5, and 7.

For a long while, it remained unclear whether the labeling provision of the FD&C Act also applied to alcoholic beverages. Until the early 1970s, FDA did not object to BATF's failure to require the labeling of ingredients in distilled spirits, wine, or beer. However, as FDA became convinced of the desirability of complete ingredient labeling of foods, it began to pressure BATF to require such labeling for alcoholic beverages. When BATF concluded that ingredient labeling was likely to be costly for the industry and not useful for consumers, FDA announced that it was abandoning its historical posture and would require compliance by all alcoholic beverages with the labeling requirements of the FD&C Act, including section 403(i), the ingredient labeling provision. 40 Fed. Reg. 54455 (Nov. 24, 1975).

The following year, in a suit brought by producers of distilled spirits and wine, alcoholic beverages were held to be exempt from the labeling requirements of the FD&C Act. *Brown–Forman Distillers Corp. v. Mathews*, 435 F. Supp. 5 (W.D. Ky. 1976). The Department of Justice declined to allow FDA to appeal this ruling after BATF agreed to initiate rulemaking to require at least partial ingredient labeling of alcoholic beverages. 44 Fed. Reg. 6740 (Feb. 2, 1979). After years of administrative and judicial wrangling, BATF ultimately determined, at 48 Fed. Reg. 45549 (Oct. 6, 1983), that the only ingredient whose labeling could be justified on health grounds was FD&C Yellow No. 5. This determination was upheld in the D.C. Circuit in *Center for Science in the Public Interest v. Department of the Treasury*, 797 F.2d 995 (D.C. Cir. 1986). Subsequently, BATF also required the disclosure of sulfites on alcoholic beverage labels based on a health concern. 51 Fed. Reg. 34706 (Sept. 30, 1986). Most recently, TTB mandated the declaration of the presence of the color additives cochineal extract and carmine for the benefit of people allergic to these ingredients. 77 Fed. Reg. 22485 (Apr. 16, 2012). To date, these are the only ingredients that must be disclosed on the labels of products subject to the FAA.

————

FDA regulations mandate that a food ingredient be declared on the label by a "specific" common or usual name. 21 C.F.R. 101.4(a) & (b). FDA has over the years issued various types of regulations, such as standards of identity, food additive approvals, and "generally recognized as safe" (GRAS) affirmations for food substances, that have established common or usual names for food ingredients. *See* 21 C.F.R. 102.5(d) (providing that a common or usual name may best established "by common usage," by a common or usual name regulation, by a standard of identity, or "in other regulations in this chapter").

During the past several years, high fructose corn syrup (HFCS), a sweetening substance extremely prevalent in processed foods, has developed a negative reputation among certain segments of the population. In 2010, the Corn Refiners Association attempted to gain FDA approval of "corn sugar" as an alternative common or usual name for HFCS. The agency's response follows.

FDA Response to Petition From Corn Refiners Association to Authorize "Corn Sugar" as an Alternate Common or Usual Name for High Fructose Corn Syrup (HFCS)

May 30, 2012

Ms. Audrae Erickson
President
Corn Refiners Association

Dear Ms. Erickson:

This letter responds to your citizen petition filed on September 14, 2010, as supplemented on July 29, 2011. After careful review of your citizen petition and for the reasons described below, the Food and Drug Administration (FDA) is denying your petition. . . .

In your petition, you asked us to authorize "corn sugar" as an alternate common or usual name for high fructose corn syrup (HFCS). Specifically, you requested that we amend (1) the generally recognized as safe (GRAS) affirmation regulation for HFCS (21 CFR 184.1866) to designate "corn sugar" as an optional name for HFCS; (2) the standard of identity for dextrose monohydrate (21 CFR 168.111) to eliminate "corn sugar" as an alternate name for dextrose; and (3) the GRAS affirmation regulation for corn sugar (21 CFR 184.1857) to replace all references to "corn sugar" with "dextrose.

As explained below, your petition does not provide sufficient grounds for the agency to authorize "corn sugar" as an alternate common or usual name for HFCS.

First, you contend consumers are confused by the name "high fructose corn syrup" and that the proposed alternate name "corn sugar" more closely reflects consumer expectations and more accurately describes the basic nature of HFCS and its characterizing properties. You base this on the following: You state that HFCS and sugar are equivalent by every parameter of relevance to consumers, for example, that they have equivalent ratios of fructose and glucose and both are metabolized similarly in the body. Based on a consumer research study, you state that many consumers are confused by the name "high fructose corn syrup," that consumers incorrectly believe that HFCS is significantly higher in calories, fructose, and sweetness than sugar, and that the term "corn sugar" more accurately reflects the properties of HFCS based on consumer ratings of this alternative name on these attributes compared to sugar. You cite other evidence of consumer confusion regarding the characteristics of HFCS. You also state that the name "corn sugar" as an alternate common or usual name for HFCS fully satisfies the criteria for common or usual names under 21 CFR 102.5(a) because "corn sugar" accurately reflects the source of the food (corn), identifies the basic nature of the food (a sugar), and discloses the food's function (a sweetener).

However, FDA's regulatory approach for the nomenclature of sugar and syrups is that sugar is a solid, dried, and crystallized food; whereas syrup is an aqueous solution or liquid food. FDA's regulations permit the term "sugar" as part of the name for food that is solid, dried, and crystallized, specifically the standards of identity for dextrose monohydrate (21 CFR 168.111) and lactose (21 CFR 168.122), and the GRAS regulation for sucrose (21 CFR 184.1854). FDA's regulations provide for the terms "syrup" or "sirup" for food that is liquid or is an aqueous solution, specifically the standards of identity for glucose sirup (21 CFR 168.120), cane sirup (21 CFR 168.130), maple sirup (21 CFR 168.140), sorghum sirup, (21 CFR 168.160), and table sirup (21 CFR 168.180). FDA's approach is consistent with the common understanding of sugar and syrup as referenced in a dictionary.

Consequently, the use of the term "corn sugar" for HFCS would suggest that HFCS is a solid, dried, and crystallized sweetener obtained from corn. Instead, HFCS is an aqueous solution sweetener derived from corn after enzymatic hydrolysis of cornstarch, followed by enzymatic conversion of glucose (dextrose) to fructose. Thus, the use of the term "sugar" to describe HFCS, a product that is a syrup, would not accurately identify or describe the basic nature of the food or its characterizing properties. As such, using the term "sugar" would not be consistent with the general principles governing common or usual names under 21 CFR 102.5.

Second, with regard to your request to amend both the standard of identity for dextrose monohydrate (21 CFR 168.111) to eliminate "corn sugar" as an alternative name, and the GRAS affirmation regulation for corn sugar (21 CFR 184.1857) to replace the term "corn sugar" with "dextrose," your petition states that consumers do not commonly associate the term "corn sugar" with dextrose. You also contend that there is strong evidence that the term "dextrose" is widely used on food labels to describe ingredients covered by the dextrose standard of identity, and that the terms "corn sugar" and "corn sugar monohydrate" are seldom used on food labels.

However, the petition does not support amending FDA's longstanding regulations, which describe and define corn sugar as "dextrose," to instead identify corn sugar as an alternative name for a sweetener that is different from dextrose. We are not persuaded by the arguments in the petition that consumers do not associate "corn sugar" with dextrose. . . .

For the reasons discussed above, we conclude that your petition does not provide sufficient grounds for the agency to authorize "corn sugar" as an alternate common or usual name for HFCS. Therefore, FDA is denying your petition in accordance with 21 CFR 10.30(e)(3).

Sincerely yours,

Michael M. Landa

Director Center for Food Safety
and Applied Nutrition

NOTES

1.   *Successful Changes in Ingredient Nomenclature.* Other efforts to change the common or usual name of food ingredients have been more fruitful. Where a food manufacturer wishes to shorten or simplify the chemical name of a food ingredient, FDA has customarily permitted use of the shortened version in parentheses following the full chemical or biological name for a period of time, and eventually allowed use of the shortened version alone. For example, the agency's initial GRAS affirmation regulation for rapeseed oil with a low erucic acid content, 50 Fed. Reg. 3745 (Jan. 28, 1985), specified the name "low erucic acid rapeseed oil." The petitioners requested use of the specific name "canola oil," but FDA replied that this term had no meaning in the United States and suggested that it be used in parentheses following the name the agency had

designated. Several years later, FDA amended the regulation to include the alternate name "canola oil." 53 Fed. Reg. 52681 (Dec. 29, 1988), codified at 21 C.F.R. 184.1555(c). See also 49 Fed. Reg. 22796 (June 1, 1984), establishing the specific name "cocoa butter substitute primarily from palm oil" for "1–palmitoy/1–2–oleoyl–3–stearin" without ever requiring that the former be used in parentheses following the latter.

2. *Alternative Naming Procedures.* Because food ingredient nomenclature has a low priority at FDA, it has been suggested that the designation of specific names should be undertaken by the National Academy of Sciences (which publishes the Food Chemicals Codex) or a consortium of organizations like those responsible for designating United States Adopted Names (USAN) for drugs, *see infra* p. 865, note 1, but no action has been taken to implement this approach.

3. *Mechanically Separated Meat.* USDA promulgated a standard of identity for "Mechanically Processed (Species) Product" in 1978. 43 Fed. Reg. 26416 (June 20, 1978). The agency initially determined that this product, mechanically deboned meat, could lawfully be used in processed meat food products without any special labeling. After *Community Nutrition Institute v. Butz*, 420 F. Supp. 751 (D.D.C. 1976) overturned this ruling, USDA promulgated regulations requiring that the product be identified in the ingredient statement as "mechanically processed [species] product" and that the presence of the ingredient also be emphasized by two prominent qualifying phrases next to the common or usual name of the food: "With mechanically processed [species] product" and "Contains up to _____ percent powdered bone." On the basis of an industry petition, and following the change in administration produced by the 1980 presidential election, USDA revised the regulations to require that the product be declared in the ingredient statement as "mechanically separated [species]," to repeal the requirement that the common or usual name refer to the ingredient, and to replace the powdered bone statement with a mandatory statement of the percent of the U.S. RDA of calcium in a serving. 47 Fed. Reg. 28214 (June 29, 1982). These changed requirements, 9 C.F.R. 317.2(j)(13), were upheld in *Community Nutrition Institute v. Block*, 749 F.2d 50 (D.C. Cir. 1984). During the scare over Bovine Spongiform Encephalopathy ("Mad Cow" Disease) in the mid-2000s, USDA revised the standard of identity for mechanically separated meat to state: "Mechanically Separated (Beef) is inedible and prohibited for use as human food." 69 Fed. Reg. 1874 (Jan. 12, 2004), codified at 9 C.F.R. 319.5(b).

Mechanically separated beef is not the same as "lean finely textured beef," which was the subject of controversy in the media in 2012 under the derogatory name "pink slime."

d. ALLERGEN DISCLOSURE

Allergic reactions to food are common. In the late 1980s, food allergies were estimated to affect up to 8 percent of children and 2 percent of adults. Dean D. Metcalfe, *Diseases of Food Hypersensitivity*, 321 NEW ENG. J. MED. 255 (July 27, 1989). Fifteen years later, the estimate for adults had doubled to 4 percent.

A principal reason that the FD&C Act required ingredient labeling on all nonstandardized foods was to enable allergic consumers to "protect themselves from the consumption of foods to which they are allergic by the information made available to them" under the ingredient labeling provisions of the new law. S. Rep. No. 493, 73d Cong. 2d Sess. 12 (1934). But even after Congress extended the ingredient labeling requirement to standardized foods in 1990, other ingredient labeling policies made it difficult for some consumers to detect the presence of allergens. For example, the source of some ingredients was not apparent from the common or usual name itself, incidental additives were exempt from label declaration, spices and flavorings were declared only by collective terms, and some labels declared that the food "may contain" ingredients because formulations varied from batch to batch.

In the mid-1990s, faced with an apparent increase in food allergy, the food industry, as well as FDA, recognized that more informative labeling was needed. In June 1996, the agency issued a notice to food manufacturers directly addressing the labeling of food allergens. FDA Center for Food Safety and Applied Nutrition, Notice to Manufacturers: Label Declarations of Allergic Substances in Foods (June 10, 1996). Reversing prior policy, FDA declared that an incidental additive must be declared as an ingredient when the additive contains a "known allergen;" that ambiguous declarations such as "may contain" should not be used to deal with avoidable cross-contamination; and that allergens present in spices, flavor, and color should also be declared. A 2001 public meeting on allergen labeling, announced at 66 Fed. Reg. 38591 (July 25, 2001), was followed by a notice proposing a regulation to require the labeling of the eight most prevalent food allergens. 68 Fed. Reg. 72889 (Dec. 22, 2003). In response, the food industry established voluntary guidelines for label disclosure of the so-called "big eight" allergens beginning in the early 2000s.

These efforts resulted in enactment of the Food Allergen Labeling and Consumer Protection Act of 2004 (FALCPA), 118 Stat. 891, 905. The statute added section 201(qq) to the FD&C Act, defining the term "major food allergen" to include eight foods: milk, egg, fish, crustacean shell fish, tree nuts, wheat, peanuts, and soy beans. New section 403(w) requires the label of a food that contains a major food allergen to declare the presence of the allergen unless FDA issues an exemption. A flavoring, coloring, or incidental additive that contains a major food allergen is subject to the same requirement.

Section 403(w) is self-executing with respect to the eight "major food allergens" and does not require the promulgation of regulations. In 70 Fed. Reg. 35258 (June 17, 2005), FDA published a draft report on approaches to establish thresholds for major food allergens, below which they would be exempt from label declaration under the new statute. Section 206 of FALCPA directed FDA to issue a regulation defining the term "gluten-free" and permitting its use. Accordingly, in 78 Fed. Reg. 47154 (Aug. 5, 2013), FDA published a final rule defining "gluten-free" and three synonymous phrases and setting forth the conditions necessary for the voluntary use of this claim in food labeling. Under the regulation, specific grains (wheat, rye, and barley) and proteins (prolamins and glutelins) are prohibited at levels greater than

20 parts per million in foods bearing "gluten-free" labeling claims. *See* 21 C.F.R. 101.91 (2013).

The Allergen Act did not deal with the issue of labeling to disclose the possible cross-contamination of a food with another food that contains a major allergen, but it did require FDA to report back to Congress on this issue. The FDA report, issued in July 2006, found that the food industry uses a variety of labeling approaches to communicate potential cross-contamination and that consumers preferred "Allergy Information: May contain _____." In August of 2008, FDA announced a public hearing on the use of advisory labeling of allergens in food. 73 Fed. Reg. 46302. The hearing was to discuss current trends in the use of allergen advisory labeling and its usefulness, effectiveness, and consumer perceptions of the labeling. FDA was soliciting comments in order to develop "a long-term strategy to assist manufacturers in using allergen advisory labeling that is truthful and not misleading, conveys a clear and uniform message, and adequately informs food-allergic consumers and their caregivers."

The "big eight" are not the only food ingredients that present allergy risks. Although FDA has made no attempt to specify the frequency of adverse reactions that warrants declaration of an ingredient or justifies a ban, the agency has, over the years, mandated the specific disclosure of various food ingredients because of concerns about allergic reactions. *See, e.g.* 21 C.F.R. 74.405(d)(2) (FD&C Yellow No. 5 must be declared in all foods, including butter, cheese, and ice cream, which are ordinarily exempt from artificial color listing); 21 C.F.R. 73.100(d), 73.2087(c) (requiring the label declaration of the certification-exempt color additives cochineal extract and carmine); 21 C.F.R. 101.100(a)(4) (requiring label declaration of incidental sulfiting agents present at more than 10 ppm); 21 C.F.R. 101.22 (requiring label declaration of flavor enhancer monosodium glutamate). FD&C Act 403(x), added by the Allergen Act, confirms that a spice, flavor, color, or incidental additive that contains a food allergen other than a major food allergen must disclose its presence as determined by FDA regulations.

For a complete history of the development of food labeling policy to address food allergen labeling, see Laura E. Derr, *When Food is Poison: The History, Consequences, and Limitations of the Food Allergen Labeling and Consumer Protection Act of 2004*, 61 FOOD & DRUG L.J. 65 (2006).

e.   MANDATORY WARNING STATEMENTS

The FD&C Act contains no specific authority for FDA to require warning statements on food labels, and until the 1970s such warnings were rare. In 1975, FDA promulgated its first warning statement regulation, which prescribes warnings against unsafe use of self-pressurized containers for food (as well as drug and cosmetic) products by inhaling the propellant, spraying in eyes, or incinerating the container. 40 Fed. Reg. 8912 (Mar. 3, 1975), codified (for food) at 21 C.F.R. 101.17(a), (b). In issuing the final rule, the agency established the legal framework for establishing mandatory warnings for all categories of FDA-regulated products under FD&C Act 201(n).

Food, Drug and Cosmetic Products, Warning Statements (Final Rule)

40 Fed. Reg. 8912 (Mar. 3, 1975).

... Several comments [in response to the proposed rule, 38 Fed. Reg. 6191] questioned the legality of the proposal, asserting that there is no statutory authority for the proposed provisions in the Federal Food, Drug, and Cosmetic Act. The comments argued that there is no indication in the legislative history or elsewhere that Congress intended to grant general authority to promulgate substantive regulations.

The Commissioner concludes that there is ample authority for the establishment of warning statements as proposed. These regulations are intended to provide the consumer with adequate warning against possible hazards associated with the use of food, drugs, and cosmetics. Regarding the Food and Drug Administration's authority under section 701 (a) of the act, the Commissioner concludes that it authorizes promulgation of substantive regulations. The Supreme Court recently reiterated its earlier holdings that similar language in other statutes grants broad authority to issue regulations reasonably related to the purposes of the legislation. (*See Mourning v. Family Publications Service, Inc.*, 411 U.S. 356 (1973); *see also National Petroleum Refiners Association v. F.T.C.*, 482 F.2d 672 (D.C. Cir. 1973).)

The application of this general rule to the Federal Food, Drug, and Cosmetic Act is indicated by decisions that have upheld regulations issued under the authority of section 701(a). (*See, e.g., Weinberger v. Hynson, Westcott & Dunning, Inc.*, 412 U.S. 609 (1973); *National Nutritional Foods Ass'n v. Weinberger*, [512 F.2d 688 (2d Cir. 1975)]. ...

Several comments questioned the legal basis for the application of section 201(n) of the act to the establishment of a warning against deliberate misuse of a commodity, on the ground that section 201(n) refers to those uses of an article that are prescribed in the labeling, or which are customary or usual.

The Commissioner concludes that section 201(n) of the act applies in those situations where abuse has become sufficiently frequent to constitute a hazard of widespread public concern. Section 201(n) of the act is applicable to require affirmative disclosures in the light of representations and also to reveal consequences of customary or unusual [sic] conditions of use. The very act of representing a product for food, drug, or cosmetic use constitutes an inherent implied representation of its safety. Warnings to ensure safe use are therefore within the scope of section 201(n) of the act. Moreover, the customary or usual conditions of use of such products often involve little or no protection against their misuse, where no warning exists. Accordingly, section 201(n) of the act is applicable to assure that consumers will understand, and guard against, the potential consequences of inadvertent misuse under conditions of such customary or usual conditions of use. In addition, the Commissioner advises that "conditions of use" is not a narrow term limited to the active handling, operation, and application of a product, but rather includes the entire setting and circumstances in which a product is used. The usual conditions of use of aerosol products are, that one [sic] purchased, they are freely available to all members of a household. Thus, warnings against misuse of aerosol products may alert parents of, adolescent children to take precautions to ensure that such products in the household are not misused.

NOTES

1. *Other Mandatory Warnings.* Since FDA issued the self-pressurized container warning requirement in 1975, the number of warnings required on food labels by regulation or by statute, as well as the number provided voluntarily by manufacturers, has increased significantly, and this trend can be expected to continue. The additional FDA-mandated statements enumerated in 21 C.F.R. 101.17 ("Food labeling warning, notice, and safe handling statements") concern: food containing or manufactured with a chlorofluorocarbon or other ozone-depleting substance; the risk of low calorie protein diets (discussed further *infra* note 2); the danger of accidental overdose by children of iron-containing dietary supplements; the choking hazard associated with consuming foods containing psyllium husk without sufficient liquid; the risk of bacterial illness from unpasteurized juices; and safe handling instructions for shell eggs. 21 C.F.R. 101.17(c)–(h).

FDA requires other warning statements in its regulations approving specific food additives. For example, 21 C.F.R. 172.804(e)(2) requires that any food containing the sweetener aspartame must bear the following prominent statement: "Phenylketonurics: contains phenylalanine." Many food ingredients produce undesirable but temporary physiological effects in some consumers, and food labels bear warnings about many of these side effects. For example, 21 C.F.R. 184.1835(e) requires that any food whose reasonably foreseeable consumption may result in a daily ingestion of 50 grams of sorbitol shall bear the statement: "Excess consumption may have a laxative effect." When FDA approved the food additive Olestra in 1996, the agency required the following label warning statement: "Olestra may cause abdominal cramping and loose stools." 61 Fed. Reg. 3118 (Jan. 30, 1996), codified at 21 C.F.R. 172.867. Following the conduct of studies which demonstrated that this warning was not supported by the evidence, FDA revoked this requirement. 69 Fed. Reg. 29428 (May 24, 2004).

2. *Protein Diet Products.* In the mid-1970s, low calorie protein-based diets were marketed for rapid weight loss. Following reports of illness and death associated with these products, FDA required label warnings on protein products. 45 Fed. Reg. 22904 (Apr. 4, 1980). Two courts determined that FDA failed to justify the specific warnings. *National Nutritional Foods Association v. Goyan*, 493 F. Supp. 1044 (S.D.N.Y. 1980) (highlighting the lack of an evidentiary foundation of a causal relationship between the protein products at issue and deaths caused by a very low protein calorie diet); *Council for Responsible Nutrition v. Goyan*, Food Drug Cosm. L. Rep. (CCH) ¶ 38,057 (D.D.C. 1980) (noting a lack of evidentiary support for claims of serious illness or death related to the protein product being regulated). On remand, FDA amended the regulations. 49 Fed. Reg. 13679 (Apr. 6, 1984), codified at 21 C.F.R. 101.17(d). Both the required warnings

and the requirement that they appear on the principal display panel were subsequently upheld. *Council for Responsible Nutrition v. Novitch*, Food Drug Cosm. L. Rep. (CCH) ¶ 38,281 (D.D.C. 1984); *National Nutritional Foods Association v. Novitch*, 589 F. Supp. 798 (S.D.N.Y. 1984); *National Nutritional Foods Association v. Young*, 598 F. Supp. 1107 (S.D.N.Y. 1984).

3. *Saccharin*. Following the results of studies indicating that saccharin may be an animal carcinogen, FDA proposed in 42 Fed. Reg. 19996 (Apr. 15, 1977) to prohibit saccharin in food. Congress responded by enacting the Saccharin Study and Labeling Act, 91 Stat. 1451 (1977), adding Sections 403(o) and 403(p) to the FD&C Act. Section 403(o) required the following statement on the labels and labeling of food containing saccharin:

Use of This Product May Be Hazardous to Your Health.

THIS PRODUCT CONTAINS SACCHARIN WHICH HAS BEEN
DETERMINED TO CAUSE CANCER IN
LABORATORY ANIMALS

Section 403(p) required a notice containing the same saccharin statement at every retail establishment selling food containing saccharin for other than immediate consumption. This remains the only instance where Congress or FDA has imposed the requirement of a retail establishment warning for an FDA-regulated product. Congress repealed section 403(p) almost two decades later. 110 Stat. 882 (1996). The section 403(o) labeling requirement survived until 2000, when Congress repealed the provision based on accumulated scientific tests demonstrating that the original concern about the carcinogenicity of saccharin was unfounded. 114 Stat. 2763, 2763A–73 (2000). For more discussion of the regulation of saccharin, see *infra* p. 1403.

4. *Alcoholic Beverages*. In the Alcoholic Beverage Labeling Act of 1988, 102 Stat. 4181, 4518, 27 U.S.C. 213 *et seq.*, Congress required the following statement on the container of every alcoholic beverage: "GOVERNMENT WARNING: (1) According to the Surgeon General, women should not drink alcoholic beverages during pregnancy because of the risk of birth defects. (2) Consumption of alcoholic beverages impairs your ability to drive a car or operate machinery, and may cause health problems." BATF implemented this statute with regulations published in 55 Fed. Reg. 5414 (Feb. 14, 1990).

5. *California Proposition 65*. Proposition 65 was adopted as an Initiative Measure under Article II, section 8, of the California Constitution by the voters of California on November 4, 1986. It is codified in chapter 6.6 of the California Health and Safety Code, Sections 25249.5–25249.13. Proposition 65 requires the California Governor to publish, and periodically revise, a list of natural and synthetic chemicals "known to the State to cause cancer or reproductive toxicity." Any listed chemical is presumed to be a health hazard, and any individual exposed to a listed chemical must be given a "clear and reasonable warning" about the exposure by the person responsible for the exposure, unless it is preempted by federal law or the person responsible for the exposure can show "no significant risk" for a carcinogen or "no observable effect" for a reproductive toxicant. Proposition

65 is enforceable both by the California Attorney General and by private citizens. Cases have been brought against a wide variety of food products, including alcoholic beverages, the lead content of calcium and of candy, acrylamide in a variety of food products, polycyclic aromatic hydrocarbons in broiled meat, and mercury in fish. In the only litigated case on Proposition 65, which involved mercury in fish, the California Superior Court determined both that the State failed to prove a violation of Proposition 65 and that specific FDA action regarding mercury in fish preempts State action. California v. *Tri–Union Seafoods*, 2006 WL 1544384 (San Francisco Super, Ct., 2006).

f.   NUTRITION FACTS

The 1969 White House Conference on Food, Nutrition and Health recommended that FDA place greater emphasis on label information about the nutritional characteristics of food. The cornerstone of the agency's new policy was the initial version of nutrition labeling that has evolved into the label format that appears today on almost all packaged food. In 1973, FDA required nutrition labeling on a large portion of the food supply by relying on its power under section 201(n) regarding the "failure to reveal material facts." The agency took the position that when a manufacturer either added a nutrient to a food or made any representation about the nutrient content of the food in labeling or advertising, full nutrition labeling was required. 38 Fed. Reg. 2125 (Jan. 19, 1973), 38 Fed. Reg. 6951 (Mar. 14, 1973). The foods to which the 1973 nutrition labeling requirements applied—that is, foods to which a nutrient was added or for which a representation about nutritional content was made—constituted approximately 60 percent of FDA-regulated packaged foods by 1989. 54 Fed. Reg. 32610, 32612 (Aug. 8, 1989).

In the late 1980s, support emerged for new legislation to establish a firm legal basis for nutrition labeling of all food, as well as to mandate related labeling reforms. In 1989, FDA indicated that it was considering requiring labeling for all foods under its present authority, but that legislation explicitly mandating nutrition labeling "would probably be most desirable." 54 Fed. Reg. 32610, 32612 (Aug. 8, 1989).

In 1990, Congress passed the Nutrition Labeling and Education Act (NLEA) which, in addition other provisions discussed throughout this chapter, added section 403(q) to the FD&C Act to mandate comprehensive nutrition labeling for virtually all food products. A dramatic confrontation between FDA and USDA ensued over the appropriate format for nutrition labeling, until President George H. W. Bush personally chose a final version. *See* Peter Barton Hutt, *A Brief History of FDA Regulation Relating to the Nutrient Content of Food*, in Ralph Shapiro, ed., NUTRITION LABELING HANDBOOK, Ch. 1 (1995). President Bush's version was incorporated into FDA's final nutrition labeling regulations, which required the now familiar "Nutrition Facts" label to appear on all foods not explicitly exempted. 58 Fed. Reg. 2079 (Jan. 6, 1993), codified at 21 C.F.R. 101.9.

FDA's lengthy nutrition labeling regulations at 21 C.F.R. 101.9 address a large variety of issues, including both the content and the format of the "Nutrition Facts" label. What follows is the sample standard label currently presented at 21 C.F.R. 101.9(d)(12):

Nutrition Facts
Serving Size 1 cup (228g)
Servings Per Container 2

Amount Per Serving

Calories 260   Calories from Fat 120

% Daily Value*

Total Fat 13g   20%
　Saturated Fat 5g   25%
　Trans Fat 2g
Cholesterol 30mg   10%
Sodium 660mg   28%
Total Carbohydrate 31g   10%
　Dietary Fiber 0g   0%
　Sugars 5g
Protein 5g

Vitamin A 4%   •   Vitamin C 2%
Calcium 15%   •   Iron 4%

* Percent Daily Values are based on a 2,000 calorie diet. Your Daily Values may be higher or lower depending on your calorie needs:

	Calories:	2,000	2,500
Total Fat	Less than	65g	80g
Sat Fat	Less than	20g	25g
Cholesterol	Less than	300mg	300mg
Sodium	Less than	2,400mg	2,400mg
Total Carbohydrate		300g	375g
Dietary Fiber		25g	30g

Calories per gram:
Fat 9   •   Carbohydrate 4   •   Protein 4

NOTES

1. *Alternative Formats.* FDA rules also establish alternative "Nutrition Facts" formats to address various situations, such as packages containing multiple separately packaged foods and small packages. 21 C.F.R. 101.9(d)(13), (j)(13)(ii). The regulations also permit the use of multiple columns to present information for two or more forms of the same food (e.g., both "as purchased" and "as prepared," or both "mix" and "baked," or both "alone" and "with ½ cup of skim milk"). *See* 21 C.F.R. 101.9(e).

2. *Exempted Foods.* Certain categories of foods are exempt from the nutrition information labeling requirements, so long as they bear no nutrition claims or other nutrition information. These exempted foods include, for example, food sold directly to consumers by smaller businesses; food served in restaurants or in other establishments for immediate consumption; food containing insignificant amounts of any of the nutrients required to be declared; raw fruits, vegetables, and fish; and food sold in very small packages. 21 C.F.R. 101.9(j)(1), (2), (4), (10), (13).

The exception for fresh fruits and vegetables reflects a legislative compromise. Section 403(q)(4) provides that nutrition labeling for the 20 most frequently consumed raw fruits, vegetables, and fish shall be furnished voluntarily in retail food stores based on FDA guidelines. FDA has implemented this provision at 21 C.F.R. 101.42–45 & Appendix C & D. The agency is required to issue a report on this program every two years. If there is substantial compliance, the voluntary system will remain in place. If there is not substantial compliance, the voluntary system shall become mandatory. The first FDA report, published in 58 Fed. Reg. 28985 (May 18, 1993), found substantial compliance. A subsequent report repeated this finding, 62 Fed. Reg. 25635 (May 9, 1997), but FDA has not had sufficient funds to prepare any reports since 1997. In *Arent v. Shalala*, 70 F.3d 610 (D.C. Cir. 1995), *aff'g* 866 F. Supp. 6 (D.D.C. 1994), the courts determined that the FDA implementing regulations in 21 C.F.R. 101.43, which define "substantial compliance" as 90 percent compliance in 60 percent of all stores, are not arbitrary or capricious.

3. *Nutrients Listed.* In the NLEA, Congress left it to FDA to determine which nutrients must be included in the Nutrition Facts Label. FD&C Act 403(q)(2). Currently, in 21 C.F.R. 101.9(c), the agency requires the amount of the following nutrients to be listed: calories, total fat, saturated fat, trans fat, cholesterol, sodium, total carbohydrate, dietary fiber, sugars, protein, vitamin A, vitamin C, calcium, iron, and any other vitamins and minerals with listed RDIs "when they are added as a nutrient supplement, or when a claim is made about them." 21 C.F.R. 101.9(c)(8)(ii). Food manufacturers have the option of also listing polyunsaturated fat, potassium, soluble fiber, insoluble fiber, sugar alcohol, other carbohydrates, and any of the other vitamins and minerals with listed RDIs "when they are naturally occurring in the food." 21 C.F.R. 101.9(c)(2)(iii)–(iv), (5), (6)(i)(A)–(B), 6(iii)–(iv), (8)(ii)(B).

4. *Daily Value.* In a 1993 final rule, 58 Fed. Reg. 2206 (Jan. 6, 1993), FDA established a "Daily Value" (DV) for every nutrient that must or may be declared in the "Nutrition Facts" label. 21 C.F.R. 101.9(c)(8), (9). The "% Daily Value" required to be stated for most of the nutrients included in a "Nutrition Facts" label (or in a "Supplement Facts" label mandated for dietary supplements, 21 C.F.R. 101.36) is calculated based on these DVs. (These DVs are also the basis for various mandatory nutrient amounts set forth in the nutrient content regulations and the fortification regulations.) Although FDA amended its regulations in 1995 to establish RDIs for some additional nutrients, 60 Fed. Reg. 67164 (Dec. 28, 1995), it has never revised the DVs it set in 1993. In 2007, the agency promulgated an advance notice of proposed rulemaking in which it suggested that it was considering revising the DVs in light of reports issued by the NAS's Institute of Medicine after 1993. 72 Fed. Reg. 62149, 62150, 62168 (Nov. 2, 2007). The agency has not taken any further action on this notice.

5. *Serving Size.* The NLEA requires the food label to provide "the serving size which is an amount customarily consumed and which is expressed in a common household measure that is appropriate to the food." FD&C Act 403(q)(1)(A)(i). The entire nutrition labeling regime (both with respect to the "Nutrition Facts" label and nutrient content claims) is affected greatly by these serving sizes. FDA has established by regulation the "reference amounts customarily consumed per eating occasion" for well over 100 categories of food. 21 C.F.R. 101.12, Table 2. The agency derived these values primarily from the 1977–78 and 1987–88 Nationwide Food Consumption Surveys conducted by the USDA. *Id.* n. 1. FDA has also promulgated procedures for determining serving size in light of these reference amounts. 21 C.F.R. 101.9(b). Nutritionists and others have criticized the serving sizes established by the regulations (and thus stated on food labels) as outdated and unrealistically small. *See, e.g.*, William Neuman, *One Bowl = 2 Servings. Puzzled?*, N.Y. TIMES, Feb. 6, 2010, at A1. In 2005, FDA requested comment on whether it should amend the serving size regulations in view of evidence that average portion sizes have grown

since the 1970s and 1980s. 70 Fed. Reg. 17010 (Apr. 4, 2005). Five years later, the agency reaffirmed its commitment to addressing this issue, but it has not taken any formal action. *See* Neuman, *One Bowl*.

6.   *Trans Fat*. Mandatory label declarations can not only impart information to consumers, but also indirectly influence the content of food. A dramatic example of this effect occurred with respect to trans fat. In the late 1980s and early 1990s, a growing body of evidence suggested that trans-fatty acids, which are present in partially hydrogenated vegetable oils and fats, raise cholesterol levels and thus increase the risk of coronary heart disease. 64 Fed. Reg. 62746, 62749–62753 (Nov. 17, 1999). Trans fat was present in a vast number of processed foods, including margarine, baked goods, chips, and fried potatoes. In 2003, FDA amended the nutrition labeling regulations to require that trans fatty acids be declared in the nutrition label. 68 Fed. Reg. 41434 (July 11, 2003), codified at 21 C.F.R. 101.9(c)(2)(ii). Many food processors—most famously Oreo® cookies—subsequently changed their recipes so as to be able to declare zero grams of trans fat per serving. (The rule, to the consternation of some nutritionists, permits a declaration of zero trans fat if the food contains any amount less than 0.5 grams per serving.) In 2012, the Center for Disease Control reported that blood levels of trans fat declined 58 percent in white adult Americans. *See* David Brown, *Blood Levels of Trans Fats Plunge After Food Labeling Decree*, WASH. POST, Feb. 9, 2012, at A3. Various state and local bans on the use of trans fat in restaurant food may have contributed to this decline. *Id.*

7.   *Front of Package Nutrition Labeling*. In recent years, the food industry has increasingly presented summary nutritional information about products on easy-to-read front-of-package (FOP) labels. In 2008–09, major food producers underwrote the creation and implementation of a "Smart Choices" program that issued a green stamp of approval for use on the front of packaging to indicate healthy food choices. FDA responded by issuing a guidance in which it expressed skepticism about current FOP label formats, reminded industry that such labeling is subject to the FD&C Act and existing FDA regulations, and stated that it was "assessing the criteria established by food manufacturers for such symbols and comparing them to our regulatory criteria." GUIDANCE FOR INDUSTRY: LETTER REGARDING POINT OF PURCHASE FOOD LABELING (Oct. 2009). Although this guidance did not specifically mention the Smart Choices program, the program voluntarily halted operations within days of its issuance. In the guidance document, FDA stated that it was "developing a proposed regulation that would define the nutritional criteria that would have to be met by manufacturers making broad FOP or shelf label claims concerning the nutritional quality of a food, whether the claim is made in text or in symbols. FDA's intent is to provide standardized, science-based criteria on which FOP nutrition labeling must be based." *Id.* The agency has not yet issued such a rule.

In August 2011, FDA received a letter from the Grocery Manufacturers Association and the Food Marketing Institute requesting that the agency exercise enforcement discretion with respect to the Nutrition Keys ("Facts Up Front") voluntary labeling program developed by these organizations. This program includes the front-of-package use of four

"Nutrition Keys Basic Icons" for calories, saturated fat, sodium, and total sugar and the additional use of "Optional Icons" for potassium, dietary fiber, protein, vitamins A, D, and C, calcium, and iron. In December 2011, FDA agreed to exercise such enforcement discretion with respect to firms that follow the program and use the four basic icons on virtually all eligible products (rather than only on those with positive nutrition profiles). Letter from Michael R. Taylor, FDA Deputy Commission for Foods, to James H. Sikes, V.P. and General Counsel, Grocery Manufacturers Association and Erik R. Lieberman, Regulatory Counsel, Food Marketing Institute (Dec. 13, 2011).

8. *Dietary Guidelines for Americans.* Under 7 U.S.C. 5341, enacted by the National Nutritional Monitoring and Related Research Act of 1990, HHS and USDA are required jointly to publish guidelines every five years that reflect sound nutrition and dietary habits. In past years, the Dietary Guidelines could easily be summarized with fewer than ten clear and concise rules. The 2005 edition of Dietary Guidelines for Americans, however, expanded to 70 pages, and the 2010 version ballooned to 95 pages. The 2010 iteration of this report gives special focus to the problem of obesity and, for the first time, unambiguously recommends that Americans eat less. It also urges Americans to drink fewer sugary beverages; eat more fruits, vegetables, fish, and whole grains; and reduce consumption of sodium, solid fat, and added sugar. DIETARY GUIDELINES FOR AMERICANS (2010). In a related initiative, in 2011, USDA replaced its well-known "food pyramid" with MyPlate, a simpler image of a plate divided into basic food groups.

9. *Nutrition Labeling in Restaurants.* Under section 403(q)(5)(A)(1) of the FD&C Act, restaurants are exempt from the nutrition information labeling requirements applicable to most other foods. In promulgating its regulations on nutrient descriptors and health claims, FDA made these requirements applicable to restaurant signs, placards, and posters, but not to menus. 58 Fed. Reg. 2302, 2386–90 & 58 Fed. Reg. 2478, 2515–19 (Jan. 6, 1993). After the menu exemption was declared unlawful in *Public Citizen, Inc. v. Shalala*, 932 F. Supp. 13 (D.D.C. 1996), FDA published a regulation deleting the exemption. 61 Fed. Reg. 40320 (Aug. 2, 1996), codified at 21 C.F.R. 101.10. Under the regulation, nutrition labeling "shall be provided upon request for any restaurant food or meal for which" a nutrient descriptor or health claim is made. Nutrient levels may be determined by nutrient databases rather than by analyses, and may be provided in any reasonable form.

Section 4205 of the Patient Protection and Affordable Care Act of 2010 added section 403(q)(5)(H) to the FD&C Act. These new provisions require chain restaurants and similar retail food establishments with 20 or more locations to post calorie information on the menu or menu board for every standard item and to provide additional, written information about such items to consumers on request.

10. *Supplement Facts.* In the Dietary Supplement Health and Education Act of 1994 (DSHEA), Congress included an amendment to section 403(q)(5)(F) of the FD&C Act to require FDA to establish different nutrition labeling requirements for dietary supplements. The agency

implemented this provision in 62 Fed. Reg. 49826 (Sept. 23, 1996), codified at 21 C.F.R. 101.36. The regulation includes a number of sample "Supplement Facts" labels, including the following:

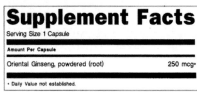

11. *Alcoholic Beverages.* In 1993, BATF issued an advance notice of proposed rulemaking to determine whether FDA's nutrition labeling requirements should be adopted, but did not take further action on the matter. 58 Fed. Reg. 42517 (Aug. 10, 1993). More recently, in response to a petition, TTB proposed mandatory labeling rules for alcoholic beverages, which would require a standardized "Serving Facts" panel stating alcohol content (expressed as a percentage of alcohol by volume), calories, carbohydrates, fat, and protein. 72 Fed. Reg. 41860 (July 31, 2007). To date, TTB has not finalized this rule.

g. MANDATORY COUNTRY OF ORIGIN LABELING

U.S. Customs and Border Protection (CBP) (formerly known as the United States Customs Service) has long required, under section 304 of the Tariff Act of 1930, 19 U.S.C. 1304, that food imported into the United States be labeled to indicate the country of origin to the "ultimate purchaser" (the last person who will receive the article in the form in which it is imported). 19 C.F.R. 134.1(d), 134.11. In general, CBP country-of-origin labeling requirements apply only to food that is not further processed or changed in the United States after importation; products that have been "substantially transformed" in the U.S. are excepted. 19 C.F.R. 134.35(a). In *Norcal/Crosetti Foods, Inc. v. United States*, 963 F.2d 356 (Fed. Cir. 1992), the Court of Appeals determined that the country of origin does not need to appear on the principal display panel of a food.

CBP has always exempted perishable agricultural commodities and meat products from its country-of-labeling requirements as "J-list" exceptions under 19 U.S.C. 1304(a)(3)(J). 21 C.F.R. 134.33. However, in the Farm Bills of 2002 and 2008, Congress applied a new country-of-origin labeling requirement to fish, shellfish, beef, pork, lamb, chicken, goat meat, perishable agricultural commodities, macadamia nuts, pecans, peanuts, and ginseng. Country-of-origin labeling (COOL) for these products is regulated separately by the USDA, which issued final regulations at 74 Fed. Reg. 2658, 2658 (Jan. 15, 2009), codified at 7 C.F.R. Parts 60 & 65. USDA amended these regulations in 2013, in part to comply with a World Trade Organization (WTO) ruling that certain COOL requirements were inconsistent with the United States' obligations under the WTO Agreement on Technical Barriers to Trade. 78 Fed. Reg. 31367 (May 24, 2013). As this book went to press, various organizations representing the meat industry were challenging USDA's COOL regulations on First Amendment grounds.

3. VOLUNTARY CLAIMS

a. INTRODUCTION

Lewis A. Grossman, *Food, Drugs, and Droods: A Historical Consideration of Definitions and Categories in American Food and Drug Law*

93 CORNELL LAW REVIEW 1091 (2008).

. . . .

V

THE AMENDMENTS OF THE EARLY 1990'S: FOOD IMPERIALISM

Through the 1970s and 1980s, growing societal and political pressure was aimed at lifting the rigorous requirement of premarket drug review from foods and "natural" products making health-related claims. In the early 1990s, Congress responded to these demands with two important amendments to the FD&C Act: the Nutrition Labeling and Education Act of 1990 (NLEA) and the Dietary Supplement Health and Education Act of 1994 (DSHEA). The former permitted conventional foods, under certain conditions, to make explicit disease prevention claims without subjecting themselves to the drug regime. The latter recharacterized various types of products that did not satisfy the *Nutrilab* "taste, aroma, or nutritive value" test as food and permitted them to make structure-function claims, and sometimes disease-prevention claims, without falling into the "drug" category. These changes to the FD&C Act have significantly reshaped the legal categories of "food" and "drug"; many products that formerly would have been classified as drugs, or as both food and drugs, are now considered solely foods. . . .

A.   The NLEA and Disease Prevention Claims

. . . [U]ntil the mid-1980s, the FDA obstinately stuck to its position that if a food's labeling made a claim regarding a particular disease state, that food was also a drug. In 1984, however, the FTC (which regulates food advertising) not only permitted, but actually lauded, a Kellogg's campaign for All–Bran® cereal that highlighted the relationship between dietary fiber and reduced cancer risk. Discomfited by the inconsistency in the agencies' positions, and under pressure from scientific groups to permit disease prevention claims on food, the FDA reversed course in 1985, publicly stating that it would permit such claims. The FDA then published proposed regulations and an interim enforcement policy that allowed food manufacturers to make disease prevention claims on food, subject to certain conditions. The agency confusingly termed these "health claims."

In 1990, before the FDA could complete its health-claims rulemaking, Congress enacted the NLEA, which explicitly permitted claims characterizing the relationship between a nutrient and "a disease or health-related condition." The statute amended the FD&C Act to provide that a disease prevention claim may be made with respect to food if the FDA authorizes the claim, by regulation, on the basis of "significant scientific agreement." The NLEA also amended the FD&C Act's definition of "drug" to include an exemption for foods with statements made in accordance with the NLEA.

Pursuant to NLEA regulations promulgated in 1993, the FDA has approved petitions for twelve disease claims based on a demonstration of "significant scientific agreement," including, for example, calcium and osteoporosis, sodium and hypertension, and dietary saturated fat and cholesterol. In 1999, the D.C. Circuit held in *Pearson v. Shalala* that the FDA is obligated under the First Amendment to permit some claims with less than significant scientific agreement if they contain appropriate disclaimers. Four years later, in response to a related subsequent decision by the district court, the FDA embraced a "credible scientific evidence" standard for "qualified" disease claims. The FDA also established a premarket notification process whereby the agency exercises "enforcement discretion" to permit such claims if they include obligatory qualifying language that corresponds to the strength of the scientific evidence.

The disease-prevention claims permitted on food do not resemble typical drug claims. Even unqualified claims, approved by the FDA pursuant to a petition, are couched in qualifying language ("may reduce the risk of") and presented, as required by the statute, "in the context of a total daily diet." Nonetheless, the NLEA represented a partial return to an earlier era, in which the labels of both food and drugs explicitly claimed effectiveness against disease, thus blurring the difference between the categories of "food" and "drug." The NLEA also empowered the FDA to issue regulations authorizing implied disease claims, in the form of standardized statements characterizing the level of nutrients such as fat, cholesterol, sodium, and fiber in food. The resulting nutrient content claim regulations contributed to a proliferation of statements such as "low fat" and "cholesterol free" on food labels. The NLEA labeling regime has undoubtedly influenced Americans' conception of food. As eloquently stated by Michael Pollan:

It was in the 1980s that food began disappearing from the American supermarket, gradually to be replaced by "nutrients," which are not the same thing. Where once the familiar names of recognizable comestibles—things like eggs or breakfast cereal or cookies—claimed pride of place on the brightly colored packages crowding the aisles, now new terms like "fiber" and "cholesterol" and "saturated fat" rose to large-type prominence. More important than mere foods, the presence or absence of these invisible substances was now generally believed to confer health benefits on their eaters. Foods by comparison were coarse, old-fashioned and decidedly unscientific things—who could say what was in them, really?[337]

The very presence of disease claims on food, along with the atmosphere of chemical reductionism and scientific certainty surrounding the entire NLEA approach, rendered the difference between food and drugs more indistinct than it was in the pre-NLEA era.

B.   DSHEA: Where's Herb?

Perhaps no class of product presents a starker challenge to the notion of a clear food-drug dichotomy than the herbal and other botanical supplements traditionally used for medicinal purposes. . . .

Until the very end of the twentieth century, the FDA seems never to have taken a systematic approach to herbs, botanical products, fish and plant oils, and other "natural" supplement ingredients. . . . The FDA apparently never maintained that herbal products listed in the USP or NF were automatically drugs, but it almost always treated herbal supplements as drugs if their labeling contained disease claims. . . .

In the 1980s . . . the natural products business grew rapidly and was increasingly dominated by larger corporations. Herbal products were advertised more widely and became available in grocery stores and drugstores as well as health food and specialty nutrition stores. The herbal supplement industry was thus capable of mounting an organized and well-funded defense if the FDA abandoned its haphazard and largely nonintrusive approach.

The agency did so in the late 1980s, commencing an aggressive enforcement campaign against herbal and other natural supplements, such as evening primrose oil. When such products bore disease claims, the FDA used its drug authorities against them. In the absence of such claims, the agency did not hesitate to employ its food additive powers, even against those supplements that did not obviously provide any "taste, aroma, or nutritive value." . . .

The NLEA of 1990 authorized disease prevention claims (so-called "health claims") for dietary supplements as well as conventional foods. However, instead of subjecting claims for supplements to the same approval procedure and "significant scientific agreement" standard that the statute established for conventional foods, Congress provided that supplements would "be subject to a procedure and standard, respecting the validity of such claim, established by [FDA regulation]." The FDA, under new Commissioner David Kessler, did not accept the invitation to

---

[337]   Michael Pollan, *Unhappy Meals,* N.Y. TIMES, Jan. 28, 2007, (Magazine), at 41.

establish a more liberal standard for dietary supplement claims. Instead, it proposed that disease prevention claims for supplements be subject to the same "significant scientific agreement" standard that applied with respect to conventional foods. This proposal provoked an unprecedented flood of irate mail and telephone calls to the agency and Congress. After a one-year moratorium imposed by Congress, the FDA once again proposed to apply the same approach to health claims for dietary supplements as was used for conventional foods. Congress stepped in again, this time with the Dietary Supplement Health and Education Act of 1994 (DSHEA).

DSHEA created a new regulatory regime for supplements, and, in some ways, significantly reduced the FDA's power over them. . . .

Several aspects of the regulation of dietary supplements under DSHEA are important to note. First, a dietary supplement is now "deemed to be a food" for most purposes under the FD&C Act, even if it is not a "common sense" food under *Nutrilab*. Second, dietary supplement ingredients are nonetheless excluded from the definition of "food additive." This releases them from the premarket approval requirement applicable to most conventional food ingredients that are not generally recognized as safe. Third, DSHEA excludes supplements that make structure-function claims from the definition of "drug" and thus from the new drug premarket approval requirements. This exclusion applies to all dietary supplements, not just those that are "common sense" foods such as vitamins and minerals. However, instead of simply relying on the parenthetical food exception from the structure-function branch of the drug definition, DSHEA added a new section significantly titled "Statements of Nutritional Support." This section requires a supplement manufacturer, unlike a conventional food manufacturer, to have "substantiation" of a structure-function claim, to accompany the statement with a prominent disclaimer, and to notify the FDA of its use of the claim within 30 days after the commencement of marketing. Although the legislative process leading to the enactment of DSHEA was triggered largely by controversy over the FDA's refusal to create a separate NLEA health claims procedure for dietary supplements, the enacted statute did not require the FDA to do so. To date, the agency, using a process equivalent to that used for conventional foods, has approved only two unqualified health claims for dietary supplements.

Denied the right to liberally communicate the benefits of their products through disease prevention claims (health claims), supplement manufacturers turned instead to structure-function claims. Before 1994, there was no hint of how creatively such claims could be used. After the enactment of DSHEA, the dietary supplement industry re-imagined structure-function claims, expanding them well beyond the "helps weight loss" and "builds strong bones" statements that had occasionally been used with conventional foods. St. John's Wort, used overseas as a remedy for depression, might be labeled "Promotes Positive Mood & Healthy Emotional Balance." Saw Palmetto, a well-known European treatment for enlarged prostate, might claim "Supports Healthy Prostate Function." The FDA endorsed just such an approach in its DSHEA regulations, allowing the use of terms such as "stimulate," "maintain," "support," "regulate," and "promote." The agency also ruled that statements concerning nonserious "natural life state" conditions, such as noncystic acne, morning sickness, hot flashes, and mild geriatric memory loss, were permissible subjects of structure-function claims. Grocery and drugstores shelves are now filled with dietary supplements that make structure-function claims with a wink at consumers interested in using them to fight disease.

DSHEA dramatically expands the legal category of "food" far beyond *Nutrilab*'s "common sense" notion of articles used primarily for taste, aroma, or nutritive value. Vitamin and mineral pills, which were treated as food even before DSHEA, have indisputable nutritive value. By contrast, many of the amino acids, herbs, and botanicals that are now classified as "food" by DSHEA do not have significant nutritive value, at least in the traditional sense of the term "nutritive." Moreover, DSHEA encompasses concentrates, metabolites, constituents, and extracts of each of these ingredients. The statute thus challenges the common cultural understanding of "food" and further obscures the distinction between "food" and "drugs." Today, a capsule containing the extract of a foul-tasting herb, sold in a pill bottle with barely disguised disease claims on its label is, for legal purposes, a "food." At the beginning of this story, such a product was a prototypical drug. . . .

————

b. NUTRIENT CONTENT CLAIMS

As we have already discussed in connection with food names, the Nutrition Labeling and Education Act of 1990 instructed FDA to define, and thus regularize, claims characterizing the content of nutrients. But FDA had some experience in defining nutrient descriptors even before the enactment of the NLEA. In the late 1970s, following years of administrative proceedings (including formal hearings) regarding its regulation of special dietary foods, FDA promulgated regulations respecting label statements for "special dietary foods used in reducing or maintaining body weight or caloric intake." 43 Fed Reg. 43248 (Sept. 22, 1978). These regulations prescribed requirements for the nutrient descriptors "low calorie," "reduced calorie," and "for calorie restricted diets," as well as for related terminology such as "diet," "dietetic," and "artificially sweetened." These were the first nutrient descriptors defined by FDA by regulation, and they set a template for those that followed.

In 1984, the agency defined the nutrient descriptors "sodium free," "very low sodium," "low sodium," and "reduced sodium." 49 Fed. Reg. 15510 (Apr. 18, 1984). Following that, FDA proposed to define the nutrient descriptors "cholesterol free," "low cholesterol," and "cholesterol reduced," 51 Fed. Reg. 42584 (Nov. 25, 1986), but it did not take final action on that matter prior to enactment of the NLEA.

In section 403(r)(1)(A) of the FD&C Act, as added by the NLEA, Congress ordered FDA to complete the job of defining nutrient descriptors. This provision addresses claims that "characterize[ ] the level of any nutrient which is of the type required by paragraph (q)(1) or (q)(2) [the provisions mandating nutrition information labeling] to be in the label or labeling of food." For reasons that remain unclear, FDA chose in its regulations to use the term "nutrient content claims" instead of "nutrient descriptors." The latter would have been more apt; it is clear from the statutory language that a nutrient content claim that merely provides factual information regarding the level of a nutrient, without in any way *characterizing* (i.e., describing) that level, does not fall within section 403(r)(1)(A). Indeed, FDA's regulations explicitly recognize that a mere factual statement about nutrient content (*e.g.*, "100 calories" or "5 grams of fat") is not covered by the nutrient content claims regulations. 21 C.F.R. 101.13(i)(3). Our efforts in prior editions of this book to steer the terminology back toward "nutrient descriptor" appear to have utterly failed, however, so in this edition we surrender and treat "nutrient content claims" as the official name of section 403(r)(1)(A) claims (although we continue to use "descriptors" as an unofficial alternative term).

The regulations promulgated by FDA at 58 Fed. Reg. 2302 (Jan. 6, 1993) to implement the nutrient content claim provisions of the NLEA are detailed and complex. The general principles applicable to this category of claims are found in 21 C.F.R. 101.13, and the specific nutrient content claims that have been defined by the agency are set forth in 21 C.F.R. Part 101, Subpart D. The nutrients for which such claims have been defined are calories; sodium; fat, fatty acid, and cholesterol; and fiber. General descriptors such as "high" and "good source" are defined for purposes of protein, vitamins, minerals, dietary fiber, and potassium. The term "high potency" is defined specifically for vitamins and minerals. Comparative claims such as "less" and "more" are also defined, as are general terms such as "light" and "healthy." This summary barely skims the surface of these regulations and does not begin to explore the details that govern how nutrient descriptors can be used in food labeling.

To provide an example of a nutrient content claims regulation, we have excerpted below the main provisions concerning claims for "fat" from the rule governing claims about the levels of fat, saturated fat, and cholesterol.

21 C.F.R. § 101.62 Nutrient Content Claims for Fat, Fatty Acid, and Cholesterol

. . . .

(b) *Fat content claims.* (1) The terms "fat free," "free of fat," "no fat," "zero fat," "without fat," "negligible source of fat," or "dietarily insignificant source of fat" or, in the case of milk products, "skim" may be used on the label or in labeling of foods, provided that:

(i) The food contains less than 0.5 gram (g) of fat per reference amount customarily consumed and per labeled serving or, in the case of a meal product or main dish product, less than 0.5 g of fat per labeled serving; and

(ii) The food contains no added ingredient that is a fat or is generally understood by consumers to contain fat unless the listing of the ingredient in the ingredient statement is followed by an asterisk that refers to the statement below the list of ingredients, which states "adds a trivial amount of fat," "adds a negligible amount of fat," or "adds a dietarily insignificant amount of fat;" and

(iii) As required in § 101.13(e)(2), if the food meets these conditions without the benefit of special processing, alteration, formulation, or reformulation to lower fat content, it is labeled to disclose that fat is not usually present in the food (e.g., "broccoli, a fat free food").

(2) The terms "low fat," "low in fat," "contains a small amount of fat," "low source of fat," or "little fat" may be used on the label or in labeling of foods . . . provided that:

(i)(A) The food has a reference amount customarily consumed greater than 30 g or greater than 2 tablespoons and contains 3 g or less of fat per reference amount customarily consumed; or

(B) The food has a reference amount customarily consumed of 30 g or less or 2 tablespoons or less and contains 3 g or less of fat per reference amount customarily consumed and per 50 g of food . . . ; and

(ii) If the food meets these conditions without the benefit of special processing, alteration, formulation, or reformulation to lower fat content, it is labeled to clearly refer to all foods of its type and not merely to the particular brand to which the label attaches (e.g., "frozen perch, a low fat food").

. . . .

(4) The terms "reduced fat," "reduced in fat," "fat reduced," "less fat," "lower fat," or "lower in fat" may be used on the label or in the labeling of foods . . . provided that:

(i) The food contains at least 25 percent less fat per reference amount customarily consumed than an appropriate reference food as described in § 101.13(j)(1); and

(ii) As required in § 101.13(j)(2) for relative claims:

(A) The identity of the reference food and the percent (or fraction) that the fat differs between the two foods and [sic] are declared in immediate proximity to the most prominent such claim (e.g., "reduced fat—50 percent less fat than our regular brownies"); and

(B) Quantitative information comparing the level of fat in the product per labeled serving with that of the reference food that it replaces (e.g., "Fat content has been reduced from 8 g to 4 g per serving.") is declared adjacent to the most prominent claim or to the nutrition label. . . .

(iii) Claims described in paragraph (b)(4) of this section may not be made on the label or in the labeling of a food if the nutrient content of the reference food meets the definition for "low fat."

. . . .

(6) The term "___ percent fat free" may be used on the label or in the labeling of foods, provided that:

(i) The food meets the criteria for "low fat" in paragraph (b)(2) or (b)(3) of this section;

(ii) The percent declared and the words "fat free" are in uniform type size; and

(iii) A "100 percent fat free" claim may be made only on foods that meet the criteria for "fat free" in paragraph (b)(1) of this section, that contain less than 0.5 g of fat per 100 g, and that contain no added fat.

NOTES

1.   *Carbohydrate Descriptors.* FDA has consistently declined to define nutrient content claims for carbohydrates. 58 Fed. Reg. 2302, 2343 (Jan. 6, 1993). Even in the early 2000s, at the height of the popularity of diet programs based upon a restricted carbohydrate intake, FDA adhered to its policy of not proposing regulations to clarify the various carbohydrate claims made by the food industry.

2.   *Whole Grains.* When consumer interest shifted from carbohydrates to whole grains, FDA again declined to propose regulations or guidance to define the descriptors for this category of food components. *See e.g.,* Letter from Margaret O'K. Glavin, Associate Commissioner for Regulatory Affairs, FDA, to Stuart M. Pape (Nov. 8, 2005), FDA Docket No. 2004P–0223/CPI. Subsequently, in a draft guidance, the agency stated that manufacturers could make "factual statements" like "10 grams of whole grains" provided that the statements did not "imply a particular level of the ingredient." DRAFT GUIDANCE FOR INDUSTRY AND FDA STAFF: WHOLE GRAIN LABEL STATEMENTS (Feb. 2006).

3.   *Restriction on Terms.* Section 403(r)(2)(A)(i) restricts the use of nutrient content claims to those terms defined in FDA regulations. FDA has declined to expand defined terminology other than to allow creative spelling (*e.g.,* "lo" rather than "low"). 58 Fed. Reg. 2302, 2319–2320, 2343–2344 (Jan. 6, 1993). The food industry has argued that the prohibition against using terms not defined by FDA raises constitutional questions under commercial free speech doctrine. In 60 Fed. Reg. 66206 (Dec. 21, 1995) and 69 Fed. Reg. 24541 (May 4, 2004), FDA reopened the record to reconsider additional synonyms for nutrient descriptors.

4.   *Descriptor Bans.* Section 403(r) contains outright bans against the use of nutrient content claims in specified circumstances, with the details and exceptions left to FDA. For example, 403(r)(2)(A)(iii) generally prohibits nutrient content claims for the level of cholesterol "if the food contains, as determined by the Secretary by regulation, fat or saturated fat in an amount which increases . . . the risk of disease. . . ." In turn, 21 C.F.R. 101.62(d)(i)(C) and (ii)(C) set forth a ban on any cholesterol descriptor if the food contains more than 2 grams of saturated fat. The food industry has argued that in such circumstances, disclosure of the health risk, rather than an outright ban of the claim, is required under commercial free speech doctrine.

5.   *Disclosure Levels.* FDA regulations require a food bearing a nutrient content claim but also containing more than 13.0 g of fat, 4.0 g of saturated fat, 60 mg of cholesterol, or 480 mg of sodium per serving to disclose the presence of the nutrient exceeding the specified level as follows: "See nutrition information for _____ content." 21 C.F.R. 101.13(h)(1). These levels are thus known as "disclosure levels."

6. *Factual "Amount" Statements.* Despite FDA's previous allowance of claims such as "5 grams of fat" and "10 grams of whole grains," the agency contended in a recent series of warning letters that a front-of-package claim of "0g Trans Fat" *characterizes* the level of a nutrient in a product, akin to a claim that the product is "Trans Fat Free." *E.g.*, Letter to Mike Mitchell, CEO & President, Dreyer's Grand Ice Cream from Roberta Wagner, Dir., Office of Compliance, CFSAN (Feb. 22, 2010). The distinction between factual "amount" statements, on one hand, and claims that "characterize" the level of a nutrient, on the other hand, is important because manufacturers lawfully may make characterizing claims only about those nutrients for which FDA has authorized nutrient content claims by regulation. Further, characterizing claims are subject to the disclosure rules described in the previous note. The lack of such disclosure was the basis for FDA's warning letters to the manufacturers using "0g trans fat" claims. While the agency may have been particularly concerned about the appearance of "0g Trans Fat" claims on products, such as ice cream, containing high levels of fat and saturated fat, FDA's reasoning in the letters suggests that the agency might take the same position with regard to factual "amount" statements in other circumstances.

7. *Nutrient Content Claim Determined by Scientific Body.* Because of concern about FDA's restrictive implementation of the nutrient content claim provisions, Congress included in the Food and Drug Administration Modernization Act of 1997 a new section 403(r)(2)(G) of the FD&C Act, which permits a food manufacturer to make a nutrient content claim based upon a published authoritative statement by (i) a scientific body of the United States Government with official responsibility for public health protection or for research directly relating to human nutrition or (ii) the National Academy of Sciences. This provision has been invoked on relatively few occasions. FDA action under the provision is published on its website, not in the Federal Register. The agency has not proposed regulations to implement this provision. When FDA published interim final rules prohibiting nine claims based on the parallel "authoritative body" provision for health claims in section 403(r)(3)(C), it expressed a very narrow and restrictive interpretation of what constitutes an "authoritative statement." 63 Fed. Reg. 34083 (June 22, 1998).

8. *The "Jelly Bean Rule" for "Healthy" Claims.* As part of its NLEA regulations, FDA established requirements for using the term "healthy" as an "implied nutrient content claim." 21 C.F.R. 101.65(d). According to this regulation, most foods may use the term "healthy" in labeling only if they are "low" in fat and saturated fat; do not exceed the disclosure levels of cholesterol and sodium; and provide at least 10 percent of the daily value of vitamin A, vitamin C, calcium, iron, protein, or fiber. 21 C.F.R. 101.65(d)(2)(i). When the agency initially proposed this rule, it did not include the last requirement, regarding minimum contribution of essential nutrients. 58 Fed. Reg. 2944 (Jan. 6, 1993). FDA added this prerequisite to the final rule in response to various comments, including one observing that without it, "jelly beans, soda, and certain candies could qualify to bear the term ['healthy']." 59 Fed. Reg. 24232, 24242 (May 10, 1994). This minimum nutrient contribution requirement (along with a similar provision for health claims, *see infra* p. 424, note 4) thus became known as

the "jelly bean rule." In the final rule, FDA provided an exception to the "10 percent daily value" provision for raw fruits and vegetables, in response to another comment remarking that these foods were inherently "healthy" even if they did not satisfy such a requirement, 59 Fed. Reg. at 24244. Four years later, three trade associations persuaded FDA to extend this exception to certain processed fruits and vegetables and enriched cereal-grain products. 63 Fed. Reg. 14349 (Mar. 25, 1998). The "healthy" rule now presents this complicated set of requirements and exceptions in table form. 21 C.F.R. 101.65(d)(2)(i)–(ii).

9.   *Nutrient Descriptor in Brand Name.* Section 403(r)(4)(A)(iii) of the FD&C Act, as added by the NLEA, provides a unique procedure for a company to petition FDA for permission to use an implied nutrient descriptor in a brand name. After publishing a notice in 67 Fed. Reg. 72963 (Dec. 9, 2002) requesting comment on the use of "Carbolite" as a brand name, FDA denied the petition. Letter from L. Robert Lake, Director, FDA, CFSAN Office of Regulations and Policy, to Carbolite Foods, Inc. (Jan. 15, 2003), FDA Docket No. 02P–0462.

10.   *Alcohol Content Labeling.* In *Rubin v. Coors Brewing Co.*, 514 U.S. 476 (1995), the Supreme Court struck down as unconstitutional, in violation of the First Amendment's freedom of speech provision, a prohibition in the Federal Alcohol Administration Act against voluntary alcohol content statements on beer labels.

c.   DISEASE PREVENTION CLAIMS ("HEALTH CLAIMS")

Since 1938, the definition of a "drug" in section 201(g)(1)(B) has included any article intended for use in the prevention or treatment of disease. Accordingly, for almost half a century after passage of the FD&C Act, FDA unfailingly maintained that no disease claim could be made for a food without also subjecting the food to regulation as a drug and, more important, as a new drug that required premarket approval prior to marketing.

As mentioned earlier, the agency reversed its traditional ban on specific disease prevention claims for food in the 1980s. A combination of trends and events combined to force FDA's hand: the mounting evidence of the important relationships between diet and disease; the growing wave of misinformation about these relationships disseminated in media outside government control; and the Federal Trade Commission's 1984 endorsement of Kellogg's use of a cancer prevention claim in advertising for All–Bran® cereal. To effect its own subsequent change in position regarding disease prevention claims for food, FDA published proposed regulations on permissible "Public Health Messages on Food Labels and Labeling," followed by a revised reproposal of this rule along with an interim enforcement policy explaining its continued use of enforcement discretion with respect to health messages in food labeling. 52 Fed. Reg. 28843 (Aug. 4, 1987); 55 Fed. Reg. 5176 (Feb. 13, 1990).

These events were overtaken by enactment of FD&C Act provisions authorizing disease claims for food in the Nutrition Labeling and Education Act of 1990, and their later amendment by the Food and Drug Administration Modernization Act of 1997. Section 403(r)(1)(B) of the FD&C Act explicitly permits claims that characterize the relationship of a nutrient to "a disease or health related condition." Two kinds of disease prevention claims for food may be made that do not result in the food being classified as a drug: (1) those approved by FDA under section 403(r)(3)(B) of the FD&C Act on the basis of "significant scientific agreement," and (2) those approved in "authoritative statements" by other federal health agencies or the National Academy of Sciences, as provided in section 403(r)(3)(C). The NLEA also authorizes disease prevention claims for dietary supplements, but provides that such claims will be subject to their own procedure and standard, as established by FDA regulation. FD&C Act 403(r)(5)(D). Nevertheless, the agency has never accepted the invitation to treat health claims for dietary supplements differently from health claims for conventional food, and they are subject to the same regulatory regime.

Before examining this regime in detail, we must provide a note on terminology. In its Federal Register notices published since 1987 on claims about the relation of diet to disease and health, FDA has used inconsistent and conflicting terminology that does not conform to the statutory language and congressional intent. In its first recognition that disease claims could properly be used for food products, FDA used the terms "health messages" and "health claims" interchangeably and never once admitted that they were in fact disease claims. 52 Fed. Reg. 28843 (Aug. 4, 1987). FDA's reluctance to admit that the agency was permitting disease claims was undoubtedly because it had banned all disease claims from food labeling for the prior 80 years. By failing to address the matter directly, FDA set an unfortunate pattern that continues to plague the agency to this day.

When Congress addressed the matter in the NLEA of 1990, it left no question that it was authorizing disease claims for food. Section 403(r)(1)(B) of the FD&C Act allows claims relating a nutrient to "a disease or health-related condition." It is only because Congress recognized them as disease claims that section 201(g)(1) had to be amended to exclude them from the definition of a drug. Rather than designate these as "disease claims," however, FDA calls them "health claims" in its NLEA regulations. 21 C.F.R. 101.14 & 101.70 et seq.

Faced with this continuing confusion in FDA terminology, we attempted in the previous edition of this book to steer the food and drug field toward consistent use of the phrase "disease prevention claims" when discussing the unqualified or qualified claims authorized by section 403(r)(1)(B) and the First Amendment. This attempt has been unsuccessful, however, so in this edition we capitulate to established usage and call such claims "health claims," as the agency itself virtually always does.

i.   *Unqualified Health Claims*

The general requirements for NLEA health claims were promulgated by FDA in 1993. 58 Fed. Reg. 2478 (Jan. 6, 1993), codified at 21 C.F.R. 101.14. Echoing the language of FD&C Act 403(r)(3)(B)(i), these regulations provide:

> FDA will promulgate regulations authorizing a health claim only when it determines, based on the totality of publicly available

scientific evidence (including evidence from well-designed studies conducted in a manner which is consistent with generally recognized scientific procedures and principles), that there is significant scientific agreement, among experts qualified by scientific training and experience to evaluate such claims, that the claim is supported by such evidence.

21 C.F.R. 101.14(c).

Under this standard, FDA has promulgated regulations approving 12 unqualified health claims, including, for example, calcium and osteoporosis; sodium and hypertension; dietary saturated fat and cholesterol and risk of coronary heart disease; and fiber-containing grain products, fruits, and vegetables and cancer. 21 C.F.R. Part 101, Subpart E. Originally, these were simply known as "authorized health claims." As examined in detail below, however, *infra* p. 428, the *Pearson/Whitaker* litigation of the late 1990s and early 2000s required FDA, on First Amendment grounds, to permit some claims supported by less than "significant scientific agreement." Since then, the 12 "significant scientific agreement" claims have been known as "unqualified health claims," whereas claims allowed with less support have been known as "qualified health claims." Although the former claims are *less* qualified than the latter, it is actually a misnomer to call them "unqualified," for each contains a version of a phrase that actually contains two qualifications: "[substance *x*] *may* reduce the *risk* of [disease *y*]." Perhaps for this reason, the public has difficulty distinguishing between unqualified and qualified health claims. The agency has requested comment on the propriety of the use of "may" and "might" in unqualified health claims as recently as 2004, but it has not taken any further action. 69 Fed. Reg. 24541, 24544 (May 4, 2004).

The NLEA provides that "[a]ny person" may petition FDA to issue a regulation authorizing a health claim. FD&C Act 403(r)(4)(A)(i). The detailed requirements for this petition process are set out at 21 C.F.R. 101.70. Although the agency could, in theory, issue a health claims regulation in the absence of a petition, it has not done so.

Excerpted below is the preamble to FDA's final 1993 regulations setting forth the general requirements for health claims (21 C.F.R. 101.14).

Food Labeling; General Requirements for Health Claims for Food

58 Fed. Reg. 2478 (January 6, 1993).

. . . .

The proposed definition [of "health claim"] establishes that a claim must have at least two basic elements for it to be regulated as a "health claim." First, the claim must be about a "substance" as that term is defined in proposed § 101.14(a)(2). Secondly, the claim must characterize the relationship of the substance to a "disease or health-related condition." . . .

Substance—The First Basic Element

... FDA does not agree that section 403(r)(1)(B) of the act addresses health claims for only those nutrients required to be on the label of a food and does not include claims about other types of nutrients. The language of section 403(r)(1)(B) of the act is clear in that it pertains to a claim that "... characterizes the relationship of any nutrient which is *of the type* required by paragraph (q)(1) or (q)(2) to be in the label or labeling of a food" (emphasis added). Thus, claims relating to a broad range of substances are potentially subject to regulation under section 403(r)(1)(B) of the act. ...

... FDA agrees with the comments that contended that the proposed rule interpreted the 1990 amendments too narrowly with respect to the regulation of claims about [whole] foods. ...

... The agency has reviewed the legislative history of the 1990 amendments and concluded that this history does indeed contain evidence to support the conclusion that Congress intended that [whole] foods could be the subject of claims that are regulated under section 403(r) of the act. However, this legislative history also makes clear that, to be subject to section 403(r) of the act, a claim about a food must be, at least by implication, a claim about a substance in the food. ...

Thus when a consumer could reasonably interpret a claim about the relationship of a food to a disease or health-related condition to be an implied claim about a substance in that food, that claim would satisfy the first element of a health claim.

However, a claim about the benefits of a broad class of foods that does not make an express or implied connection to any of the substances that are found in foods that comprise that class would not constitute an implied claim. Such claims about classes of foods (*e.g.*, fruits and vegetables) are not health claims because they are not about a substance.

Accordingly, FDA has revised the definition of "substance" in new § 101.14(a)(2) to include a specific food as well as a component of food. ...

Under the revised definition of a substance that FDA has included in new § 101.14(a)(2), phrases on labeling such as "eat apples to _____," "eat low sodium foods to _____," "eat fruits high in fiber to _____," or "cook with garlic to _____" would constitute references to a substance and would thereby satisfy one of the two essential elements of a health claim. ...

Disease or Health–Related Condition—Second Basic Element

... One comment asserted that the statutory phrase "a disease or health-related condition" does not set up two categories and maintained that the phrase "health-related" as used in the law appears to be nothing more than an expansion of the word "disease." ...

However, the inclusion of the phrase "health-related condition" in section 403(r)(1)(B) of the act in addition to the term "disease" leaves no question that Congress intended that claims about conditions other than diseases be regulated under this provision. ...

... Accordingly, the agency concludes that the inclusion of "a health-related condition" in the coverage of section 403(r)(1)(B) of the act means that claims about risk factors related to disease, as well as claims about a disease, can be health claims. . . .

Therefore, to assist affected parties in clearly understanding what the second element of a health claim encompasses, FDA is adopting the following definition of "disease or health-related condition" in new § 101.14(a)(6):

> *Disease or health-related condition* means damage to an organ, part, structure, or system of the body such that it does not function properly (e.g., cardiovascular disease), or a state of health leading to such dysfunctioning (e.g., hypertension); except that diseases resulting from essential nutrient deficiencies (e.g., scurvy, pellagra) are not included in this definition (claims pertaining to such diseases are thereby not subject to §§ 101.14 or 101.70).

This definition does not differentiate between a "disease" and a "health-related condition." The two states are often so closely related that no bright-line distinction is practicable. Further, both states are regulated under section 403(r) of the act. Thus, there is no reason to separate one state from the other as long as both are covered.

. . . .

Components of Food . . .

New § 101.14(b)(2) and (b)(3)(i) contain provisions requiring that the substance be a component of food. If the substance is present at decreased dietary levels, under new § 101.14(b)(2), it must be a nutrient that is required to be included in nutrition labeling (e.g., cholesterol, total fat). If the substance is present at other than decreased dietary levels, under new § 101.14(b)(3)(i), it must contribute taste, aroma, or nutritive value, or any technical effect listed in § 170.3(o) to the food, and must retain that attribute when consumed at levels that are necessary to justify a claim.

Some comments stated that the eligibility restrictions on the term "substance" in proposed § 101.14(b)(3)(i) are too restrictive and asked that they be removed. One comment asserted that the agency is creating needless procedural confusion by having a broad definition of the term "substance" in proposed § 101.14(a)(2), which it then immediately narrows in proposed § 101.14(b)(3)(i). . . . Another comment stated that although the phrase "taste, aroma, or nutritive value" is borrowed from the Seventh Circuit's opinion in *Nutrilab, Inc. v. Schweiker*, 713 F.2d 335, 338 (7th Cir. 1983), the court noted in that decision that these food characteristics were only the primary reasons why people consume food. The court, according to the comment, did not intend to give an all-inclusive list. . . .

FDA disagrees with the comments' interpretation of the *Nutrilab* decision and believes that the agency's reliance on the case is justified. The *Nutrilab* court adopted a "common sense" definition under section 201(f)(1) of the act: "When the statute defines 'food' as 'articles used for food,' it means that the statutory definition of 'food' includes articles used by people in the ordinary way most people use food—primarily for taste, aroma, or nutritive value." *Nutrilab*, 713 F.2d at 338. . . . By describing taste, aroma, and nutritive value as the "primary" reasons for consuming food, the *Nutrilab* court acknowledged that a food consumed for one of these reasons might sometimes also be consumed for an additional purpose. 713 F.2d at 338 (giving prune juice and coffee as examples of foods that "may be consumed on occasion for reasons other than taste, aroma, or nutritive value"). Under *Nutrilab*, a substance whose uses do not include taste, aroma, or nutritive value is not a food. . . .

NOTES

1. *Meaning of "Nutritive Value."* FDA defines "nutritive value" succinctly as "a value in sustaining human existence by such processes as promoting growth, replacing loss of essential nutrients, or providing energy." 21 C.F.R. 101.14(a)(3). In practice, the line between a product's nutritive value and nonnutritive value is not clear. For example, in approving a health claim for plant sterol/stanol esters and the risk of coronary heart disease, FDA characterized the ability of these substances to *block* the absorption of dietary cholesterol as a nutritive value. *See* 21 C.F.R. 101.83. The agency observed simply that the cholesterol-lowering effect of these esters is achieved through "an effect on the digestive process" and that the phrase "nutritive value" should be interpreted flexibly. 65 Fed. Reg. 54685, 54688 (Sept. 8, 2000).

2. *Health Claims for Dietary Supplements.* As noted previously, FDA imposes the same health claims regime on dietary supplements that it does on conventional foods. The regulations provide that, regardless of whether the food is a conventional food or a dietary supplement, a substance must "contribute taste, aroma, or nutritive value," or a listed "technical effect" to be eligible for a health claim. 21 C.F.R. 101.14(b)(3)(i). Because dietary supplements ordinarily do not contain ingredients that contribute to taste, aroma, or one of the listed technical characteristics, dietary supplement health claims apparently are limited to substances that provide "nutritive value."

Most permitted health claims for dietary supplements appear to conform to this restriction. For example, FDA has approved unqualified health claims for dietary supplements regarding calcium/osteoporosis and folate/neural tube defects claim. 21 C.F.R. 101.72, 101.79. FDA has also announced it will permit the use of a number of qualified health claims for dietary supplement ingredients, including selenium and cancer; antioxidant vitamins and cancer; omega-3 fatty acids and coronary heart disease; folic acid, vitamin B[6], and vitamin B[12] and vascular disease. The "nutritive value" of some other dietary supplement ingredients with permitted claims is less apparent, however. The unqualified plant sterol/stanol ester health claim discussed *supra* in note 1 applies to dietary supplements as well as conventional foods. FDA has also allowed qualified dietary supplement health claims for phosphatidylserine/dementia and phosphatidylserine/cognitive dysfunction. *See* Letter Regarding Dietary Supplement Health Claim for Phosphatidylserine and Cognitive Dysfunction and Dementia, from Christine Taylor, Dir., Off. Nutritional Products, Labeling, and Dietary Supplements, CFSAN, FDA, to Jonathan W. Emord (Feb. 24, 2003). Phosphatidylserine is a structural component of biological membranes of plants, animals and other life forms, in this case derived from either bovine brain cortex or soy lecithin.

As discussed *infra* at p. 450, FDA has explicitly agreed that dietary supplements may make structure/function claims (as opposed to health claims) for ingredients that have no nutritive value.

3.   *Disease Treatment Claims.* Section 403(r)(1)(B) authorizes claims relating to "a disease or a health-related condition." On its face, this language is not limited to disease prevention claims and could permit disease treatment claims if they are adequately supported. The courts have held, however, that it is within FDA's discretion to interpret the health claims provision in section 403(r)(1)(B) to relate only to disease prevention and not to disease treatment, and that this does not violate the free speech provisions of the First Amendment. *E.g., Whitaker v. Thompson*, 239 F. Supp. 2d 43 (D.D.C. 2003), *aff'd* 353 F.3d 947 (D.C. Cir. 2004).

only for prevention and not disease

4.   *The "Jelly Bean Rule" for Health Claims.* Under 21 C.F.R. 101.14(e)(6), no food may make a health claim unless it contains ten percent or more of the reference daily intake or the daily reference value for vitamin A, vitamin C, iron, calcium, protein, or fiber per reference amount customarily consumed *prior* to any nutrient addition. The requirement does not apply to dietary supplements or when waived or modified in specific health claims regulations. FDA intends this provision to preclude health claims for foods of little nutritional value, hence the moniker "jelly bean rule." In practice, however, the provision also precludes health claims for some fruits and vegetables and other foods that many people regard as nutritious. As has already been mentioned, *supra* p. 417, note 8, FDA imposes an identical minimum nutrient content requirement on foods using the descriptor "healthy," but in that context the agency exempts fruits and vegetables from the requirement and furthermore allows minimum nutrient content to be achieved through fortification.

The industry has strongly objected to the health claims jelly bean rule on both policy and legal grounds. In 60 Fed. Reg. 66206 (Dec. 21, 1995), FDA discussed the rule in detail and proposed to create an exemption for fruits and vegetables and allow claims with full disclosure that the nutrients are added through fortification. FDA subsequently reopened this proposed rule for reconsideration. 69 Fed. Reg. 24541, 24543 (May 4, 2004).

5.   *Disqualifying Macronutrient Levels.* FD&C Act 403(r)(3)(A)(ii) states that a health claim may not generally be made for a food that contains "any nutrient in an amount which increases to persons in the general population the risk of a disease. . . ." Under the implementing regulation, 21 C.F.R. 101.14(a)(4), a food is prohibited from any health claim if it contains any of the following disqualifying nutrient levels per reference amount customarily consumed or per label serving size: 13 grams of fat, 4 grams of saturated fat, 60 milligrams of cholesterol, or 480 milligrams of sodium. Industry has strongly argued that this ban on health claims violates commercial free speech doctrine and should be replaced with a disclosure requirement. FDA has reopened the record to reconsider this matter. 69 Fed. Reg. 24541, 24543–44 (May 4, 2004).

6. *Health Claim Determined by Scientific Body.* The "authoritative statement" provision for health claims under section 403(r)(3)(C)–(D) of the FD&C Act is comparable to the same provision for nutrient descriptors. *See supra* p. 417, note 7. Manufacturers may make health claims based on authoritative statements published by a scientific body of the U.S. government so long as they notify FDA at least 120 days in advance and the agency does not object. FDA rejected the first nine authoritative body health claims submitted to the agency, 63 Fed. Reg. 34083 (June 22, 1998), but has since agreed to a few other health claims under this provision. Because section 403(r)(3)(C) of the FD&C Act, which governs "authoritative body" health claims, does not by its terms embrace the "jelly bean" rule, and because FDA has not promulgated regulations imposing it, this restrictive rule is not applicable to health claims authorized under this provision. FDA letters agreeing to authoritative body health claims are available only on the FDA website and are not published in the Federal Register.

———

Because FDA requires unqualified health claims to include lengthy, detailed, and complex information and limits their precise language, the food industry does not frequently use them. Take, for example, the sodium/hypertension claim. The regulation governing this claim at 21 C.F.R. 101.74(c)(2) imposes the following specific requirements with respect to wording:

(2) Specific requirements—(i) *Nature of the claim.* A health claim associating diets low in sodium with reduced risk of high blood pressure may be made on the label or labeling of a food described in paragraph (c)(2)(ii) of this section, provided that:

(A) The claim states that diets low in sodium "may" or "might" reduce the risk of high blood pressure;

(B) In specifying the disease, the claim uses the term "high blood pressure";

(C) In specifying the nutrient, the claim uses the term "sodium";

(D) The claim does not attribute any degree of reduction in risk of high blood pressure to diets low in sodium; and

(E) The claim indicates that development of high blood pressure depends on many factors.

In addition, the general requirements for all health claims in 21 C.F.R. 101.14 apply to sodium/hypertension claims. *See* 21 C.F.R. 101.74(c)(1). Among other labeling conditions listed in 21 C.F.R. 101.14(d)(2) are the following:

(ii) The claim is limited to describing the value that ingestion (or reduced ingestion) of the substance, as part of a total dietary pattern, may have on a particular disease or health-related condition;

. . . .

(iv) All information required to be included in the claim appears in one place without other intervening material, except that the principal display panel of the label or labeling may bear the reference statement, "See ___ for information about the relationship between ___ and ___," with the blanks filled in with the location of the labeling containing the health claim, the name of the substance, and the disease or health-related condition . . . with the entire claim appearing elsewhere on the other labeling, . . . ;

    (v) The claim enables the public to comprehend the information provided and to understand the relative significance of such information in the context of a total daily diet; . . . .

As illustrated by the following warning letter, food manufacturers face significant consequences if they are deemed to have contravened the multifarious requirements applicable to unqualified health claims

Warning Letter from W. Charles Becoat, Director, FDA Minneapolis District, to Ken Powell, CEO, General Mills

May 5, 2009.

Dear Mr. Powell:

The Food and Drug Administration (FDA) has reviewed the label and labeling of your Cheerios® Toasted Whole Grain Oat Cereal. FDA's review found serious violations of the Federal Food, Drug, and Cosmetic Act (the Act) and the applicable regulations in Title 21, Code of Federal Regulations (21 CFR). . . .

Unapproved New Drug

Based on claims made on your product's label, we have determined that your Cheerios® Toasted Whole Grain Oat Cereal is promoted for conditions that cause it to be a drug because the product is intended for use in the prevention, mitigation, and treatment of disease. Specifically, your Cheerios® product bears the following claims on its label:

- "you can Lower Your Cholesterol 4% in 6 weeks"

- "Did you know that in just 6 weeks Cheerios can reduce bad cholesterol by an average of 4 percent? Cheerios is . . . clinically proven to lower cholesterol. A clinical study showed that eating two 1 1/2 cup servings daily of Cheerios cereal reduced bad cholesterol when eaten as part of a diet low in saturated fat and cholesterol."

These claims indicate that Cheerios® is intended for use in lowering cholesterol, and therefore in preventing, mitigating, and treating the disease hypercholesterolemia. Additionally, the claims indicate that Cheerios® is intended for use in the treatment, mitigation, and prevention of coronary heart disease through, [sic] lowering total and "bad" (LDL) cholesterol. Elevated levels of total and LDL cholesterol are a risk factor for coronary heart disease and can be a sign of coronary heart disease. Because of these intended uses, the product is a drug within the meaning of section 201(g)(1)(B) of the Act. The product is also a new drug under section 201(p) of the Act because it is not generally recognized as safe and effective for use in preventing or treating hypercholesterolemia or coronary heart disease. Therefore, under section 505(a) of the Act, it may not be legally marketed with the above claims in the United States without an approved new drug application.

FDA has issued a regulation authorizing a health claim associating soluble fiber from whole grain oats with a reduced risk of coronary heart disease (21 CFR 101.81). Like FDA's other regulations authorizing health claims about a food substance and reduced risk of coronary heart disease, this regulation provides for the claim to include an optional statement, *as part of* the health claim, that the substance reduces the risk of coronary heart disease through the intermediate link of lowering blood total and LDL cholesterol. See 21 CFR 101.81(d)(2)–(3). Although the lower left corner of the Cheerios® front label contains a soluble fiber/coronary heart disease health claim authorized under 21 CFR 101.81, the two claims about lowering cholesterol are not made as part of that claim but rather are presented as separate, stand-alone claims through their location on the package and other label design features. . . .

Additionally, . . . [t]o use the soluble fiber health claim, a product must comply with the claim specific requirements in 21 CFR 101.81, including the requirement that the claim not attribute any degree of risk reduction for coronary heart disease to diets that include foods eligible to bear the claim. See 21 CFR 101.81(c)(2)(E). However, the label of your Cheerios® cereal claims a degree of risk reduction for coronary heart disease by stating that Cheerios® can lower cholesterol by four percent in six weeks. . . . [T]he cholesterol-lowering claims on the Cheerios® label attribute a degree of risk reduction for coronary heart disease because if total and LDL cholesterol levels decline, the risk of coronary heart disease declines as well.

Misbranded Food

Your Cheerios® product is misbranded within the meaning of section 403(r)(1)(B) of the Act because it bears unauthorized health claims in its labeling. We have determined that your website www.wholegrainnation.com is labeling for your Cheerios® product under section 201(m) of the Act because the website address appears on the product label. This website bears the following unauthorized health claim[ ]:

- "Heart-healthy diets rich in whole grain foods, [sic] can reduce the risk of heart disease."

. . . Although FDA has issued a regulation authorizing a health claim associating fiber-containing grain products with a reduced risk of coronary heart disease (21 CFR 101.77), the claim on your website does not meet the requirements for this claim. For example, under section 101.77(c)(2), the claim must state that diets low in saturated fat and cholesterol and high in fiber-containing fruit, vegetable, and grain products may reduce the risk of heart disease. The claim on your website leaves out any reference to fruits and vegetables, to fiber content, and to keeping the levels of saturated fat and cholesterol in the diet low. Therefore, your claim does not convey that all these factors together help to reduce the risk of heart disease and does not enable the public to understand the significance of the claim in the context of the total daily diet (see section 343(r)(3)(B)(iii) of the Act). . . .

Failure to promptly correct the violations specified above may result in enforcement action without further notice. Enforcement action may include seizure of violative products and/or injunction against the manufacturers and distributors of violative products.

Please advise this office in writing 15 days from your receipt of this letter of the specific steps you have taken to correct the violations noted above and to ensure that similar violations do not occur. . . .

Sincerely,

W. Charles Becoat

NOTES

1. *General Mills Response.* For General Mills' comprehensive response to FDA's contentions, see Letter from Janice L. Marturano, V.P. and Deputy General Counsel, to Tyra S. Wisecup, Compliance Officer, FDA Minneapolis Dist. Office (May 14, 2009).

2. *Abbreviated Health Claims.* Under 21 C.F.R. 101.14(d)(2)(iv), all information required to be in a health claim must appear together in one place without other intervening material. This condition substantially reduces the number of health claims used in food labeling. In light of industry concerns, FDA reopened the record to reconsider this matter. 60 Fed. Reg. 66206 (Dec. 21, 1995), 69 Fed. Reg. 24541 (May 4, 2004). The industry has also complained that the FDA-prescribed health claims are lengthy and detailed, and are not written in a way designed to attract consumer attention. It has been suggested that FDA-prescribed health claims should be guidelines, not requirements, and that industry should be permitted to creatively structure these claims in ways best suited to reach consumers. Thus far, however, FDA has not given serious consideration to this approach.

ii. *The First Amendment and Qualified Health Claims*

Opponents of FDA regulation began to contend only quite recently that restrictions on labeling are restrictions on speech and thus protected by the First Amendment. The late appearance of this argument is due largely to the fact that until the 1970s, commercial speech was generally viewed as ineligible for First Amendment protection, except perhaps when the primary motive of the speaker was noncommercial. *See Valentine v. Chrestensen,* 316 U.S. 52, 54 (1942) ("the Constitution imposes no [heightened scrutiny] as respects purely commercial advertising"). *But see Murdock v. Pennsylvania*, 319 U.S. 105, 111 (1943) ("the mere fact that . . . religious literature is 'sold' by itinerant preachers rather than 'donated' does not transform evangelism into a commercial enterprise"). Notably, the first case in which the United States Supreme Court unambiguously stated that commercial speech is covered by the First Amendment was a food and drug law matter. In *Virginia State Board of Pharmacy v. Virginia Citizens Consumer Council,* the Court struck down a state statute declaring it unprofessional conduct for licensed pharmacists to advertise the prices of prescription drugs. 425 U.S. 748 (1976). In doing so, the Court held that the First Amendment extends even to speech that does no more than propose a commercial transaction. *Id.* at 762.

Although commercial speech now incontrovertibly receives constitutional protection, it receives less than noncommercial speech. The seminal case in the area is *Central Hudson Gas & Elec. Corp. v. Public Serv. Comm'n of New York*, 447 U.S. 557 (1980). *Central Hudson* lays out a four-step test (sometimes framed as an initial inquiry followed by a three-part test) that is a variety of intermediate scrutiny. A court reviewing the constitutionality of a restriction on commercial speech must, first, determine whether the speech is false or misleading or concerns an unlawful activity, in which case the First Amendment does not apply. Second, if the speech is truthful, not inherently misleading, and concerns a lawful activity, the government restriction is constitutional only if it advances a *substantial* governmental interest. Third, the restriction must *directly advance* this substantial interest. Finally, and critically, the suppression of speech must be *no more extensive than necessary* to advance the interest. *Id.* at 569–70. In later cases, the Court has explained that the fourth step is not as strict as it might appear. "What our decisions require is a 'fit' between the legislature's ends and the means chosen to accomplish those ends, a fit that is not necessarily perfect, but reasonable; . . . that employs not necessarily the least restrictive means but . . . a means narrowly tailored to achieve the desired objective." *Bd. of Trustees of the State Univ. of N.Y. v. Fox*, 492 U.S. 469, 480 (1989).

Since the 1990s, First Amendment arguments have become more and more common in the food and drug law field—to the point where it is now impossible to be a well-informed food and drug lawyer without being familiar with commercial speech doctrine. Recently, the Supreme Court injected confusion into the area by suggesting—in yet another food and drug case—that the First Amendment requires heightened, rather than intermediate, scrutiny for "content- and speaker-based" burdens on commercial speech. *Sorrell v. IMS Health Inc.*, 131 S. Ct. 2653 (2011) (striking down state statute prohibiting the sale of prescriber-identifying information for marketing purposes). If *Sorrell* is ultimately interpreted broadly, the First Amendment will pose an even greater challenge to FDA labeling regulation than it does now.

The following litigation, an assault on FDA's administration of the NLEA health claims regime, was among the first successful commercial free speech challenges to the agency's regulation of product labeling. (This litigation occurred almost simultaneously with the Washington Legal Foundation's claim that the First Amendment protects scientific communications about unapproved uses of drugs. *See infra* p. 943.) Following enactment of the NLEA in 1990, FDA promulgated regulations construing the statutory standard of "significant scientific agreement." In particular, FDA required mature science—a virtual scientific consensus—for approval of a health claim and rejected all claims, however truthful, based on emerging science that had not yet reached maturity. As reflected in the materials below, a dietary supplement marketer and its supporters challenged the agency's disapproval of four claims in court. Although the case involved claims for dietary supplements, the decision of the Court of Appeals is equally applicable to conventional food.

Pearson v. Shalala

164 F.3d 650 (D.C. Cir. 1999).

■ SILBERMAN, CIRCUIT JUDGE.

Marketers of dietary supplements must, before including on their labels a claim characterizing the relationship of the supplement to a disease or health-related condition, submit the claim to the Food and Drug Administration for preapproval. The FDA authorizes a claim only if it finds "significant scientific agreement" among experts that the claim is supported by the available evidence. Appellants failed to persuade the FDA to authorize four such claims and sought relief in the district court, where their various constitutional and statutory challenges were rejected. We reverse.

. . . Each of appellants' four claims links the consumption of a particular supplement to the reduction in risk of a particular disease:

(1) "Consumption of antioxidant vitamins may reduce the risk of certain kinds of cancers."

(2) "Consumption of fiber may reduce the risk of colorectal cancer."

(3) "Consumption of omega-3 fatty acids may reduce the risk of coronary heart disease."

(4) ".8 mg of folic acid in a dietary supplement is more effective in reducing the risk of neural tube defects than a lower amount in foods in common form."

 Rule

. . . The FDA authorizes a claim only "when it determines, based on the totality of publicly available scientific evidence (including evidence from well-designed studies conducted in a manner which is consistent with generally recognized scientific procedures and principles), that there is significant scientific agreement among experts qualified by scientific training and experience to evaluate such claims, that the claim is supported by such evidence. 21 C.F.R. § 101.14(c). . . .

In [issuing 21 C.F.R. 101.14(c)], the agency rejected arguments asserted by commenters . . . that the "significant scientific agreement" standard violates the First Amendment because it precludes the approval of less-well supported claims accompanied by a disclaimer and because it is impermissibly vague. The FDA explained that, in its view, the disclaimer approach would be ineffective because "there would be a question as to whether consumers would be able to ascertain which claims were preliminary [and accompanied by a disclaimer] and which were not," and concluded that its prophylactic approach is consistent with applicable commercial speech doctrine. . . .

Then the FDA rejected the four claims supported by appellants. The problem with these claims, according to the FDA, was not a dearth of supporting evidence; rather, the agency concluded that the evidence was inconclusive for one reason or another and thus failed to give rise to "significant scientific agreement." . . . The agency refused to approve the dietary fiber-cancer claim because "a supplement would contain *only* fiber, and there is no evidence that any specific fiber itself caused the effects that were seen in studies involving fiber-rich [foods]." The FDA gave similar reasons for rejecting the antioxidant vitamins-cancer claim and the omega-3 fatty acids-coronary heart disease claim. As for the claim that 0.8 mg of folic acid in a dietary supplement is more effective in reducing the risk of neural tube defects than a lower amount in foods in common form, the FDA merely stated that "the scientific literature does not support the superiority of any one source over others." The FDA declined to consider appellants' suggested alternative of permitting the claim while requiring a corrective disclaimer such as "The FDA has determined that the evidence supporting this claim is inconclusive."

. . . .

Appellants sought relief in the district court, raising APA and other statutory claims as well as a constitutional challenge, but were rebuffed. *Pearson v. Shalala*, 14 F. Supp. 2d 10 (D.D.C. 1998). . . .

It is undisputed that FDA's restrictions on appellants' health claims are evaluated under the commercial speech doctrine. . . . The government makes two alternative arguments in response to appellants' claim that it is unconstitutional for the government to refuse to entertain a disclaimer requirement for the proposed health claims: first, that health claims lacking "significant scientific agreement" are *inherently* misleading and thus entirely outside the protection of the First Amendment; and second, that even if the claims are only *potentially* misleading, under *Central Hudson Gas & Elec. Corp. v. Public Serv. Comm'n of New York*, 447 U.S. 557, 566 (1980), the government is not obliged to consider requiring disclaimers in lieu of an outright ban on all claims that lack significant scientific agreement.

If such health claims could be thought inherently misleading, that would be the end of the inquiry. . . . As best we understand the government, its first argument runs along the following lines: that health claims lacking "significant scientific agreement" are inherently misleading because they have such an awesome impact on consumers as to make it virtually impossible for them to exercise any judgment *at the point of sale*. It would be as if the consumers were asked to buy something while hypnotized, and therefore they are bound to be misled. We think this contention is almost frivolous. . . . We reject it. But the government's alternative argument is more substantial. It is asserted that health claims on dietary supplements should be thought at least potentially misleading because the consumer would have difficulty in independently verifying these claims. We are told, in addition, that consumers might actually assume that the government has approved such claims.

Under *Central Hudson*, we are obliged to evaluate a government scheme to regulate potentially misleading commercial speech by applying a three-part test. First, we ask whether the asserted government interest is substantial. The FDA advanced two general concerns: protection of public health and prevention of consumer fraud. . . . [A] substantial governmental interest is undeniable . . .

The more significant questions under *Central Hudson* are the next two factors: "whether the regulation *directly* advances the governmental interest asserted," and whether the fit between the government's ends and the means chosen to accomplish those ends "is not necessarily perfect, but reasonable." We think that the government's regulatory approach encounters difficulty with both factors.

It is important to recognize that the government does not assert that appellants' dietary supplements in any fashion *threaten* consumer's health and safety. The government simply asserts its "common sense judgment" that the health of consumers is advanced *directly* by barring any health claims not approved by the FDA. Because it is not claimed that the product is harmful, the government's underlying—if unarticulated—premise must be that consumers have a limited amount of either attention or dollars that could be devoted to pursuing health through nutrition, and therefore products that are not indisputably health enhancing should be discouraged as threatening to crowd out more worthy expenditures. We are rather dubious that this simplistic view of human nature or market behavior is sound, but, in any event, it surely cannot be said that this notion—which the government does not even dare openly to set forth—is a *direct* pursuit of consumer health; it would seem a rather indirect route, to say the least.

On the other hand, the government would appear to advance directly its interest in protecting against consumer *fraud* through its regulatory scheme. If it can be assumed—and we think it can—that some health claims on dietary supplements will mislead consumers, it cannot be denied that requiring FDA pre-approval and setting the standard extremely, perhaps even impossibly, high will surely prevent any confusion among consumers. . . .

The difficulty with the government's consumer fraud justification comes at the final *Central Hudson* factor: Is there a "reasonable" fit between the government's goals and the means chosen to advance those goals? The government insists that it is never obliged to utilize the disclaimer approach, because the commercial speech doctrine does not embody a preference for disclosure over outright suppression. Our understanding of the doctrine is otherwise. . . .

Our rejection of the government's position that there is no general First Amendment preference for disclosure over suppression, of course, does not determine that any supposed weaknesses in the claims at issue can be remedied by disclaimers and thus does not answer whether the subregulations are valid. The FDA deemed the first three claims . . . to lack significant scientific agreement because existing research had examined only the relationship between consumption of *foods* containing these components and the risk of these diseases. . . . But certainly this concern could be accommodated, in the first claim for example, by adding a prominent disclaimer to the label along the following lines: "The evidence is inconclusive because existing studies have been performed with *foods* containing antioxidant vitamins, and the effect of those foods on reducing the risk of cancer may result from other components in those foods." A similar disclaimer would be equally effective for the latter two claims.

The FDA's concern regarding the fourth claim . . . is different from its reservations regarding the first three claims; the agency simply concluded that "the scientific literature does not support the superiority of any one source [of folic acid] over others." But it appears that credible evidence did support this claim, and we suspect that a clarifying disclaimer could be added to the effect that "The evidence in support of this claim is inconclusive." . . .

We do not presume to draft precise disclaimers for each of appellants' four claims; we leave that task to the agency in the first instance. Nor do we rule out the possibility that where evidence in support of a claim is outweighed by evidence against the claim, the FDA could deem it incurable by a disclaimer and ban it outright.[10] . . .

———

Following this landmark decision, FDA construed the mandate of the Court of Appeals narrowly and continued to disapprove proposed health claims. In particular, FDA stated that it would apply a "weight of the evidence" test in determining whether to permit a qualified health claim—that is, it would disallow such a claim unless the scientific evidence in support of the claim outweighed the evidence against. 65 Fed. Reg. 59855 (Oct. 6, 2000). This strategy provoked further litigation.

Whitaker v. Thompson

248 F. Supp. 2d 1 (D.D.C. 2002).

■ KESSLER, DISTRICT JUDGE. . . .

Plaintiffs challenge the FDA decision prohibiting dietary supplements' labels from including the health claim that "Consumption of antioxidant vitamins may reduce the risk of certain kinds of cancers." . . .

The Court of Appeals in *Pearson I* strongly suggested, without explicitly holding, that Plaintiffs' Antioxidant Vitamin Claim was only "potentially misleading," not "inherently misleading," and therefore the FDA's refusal to authorize the Antioxidant Vitamin Claim (or to propose a disclaimer to accompany the Claim) violated the First Amendment. Specifically, while *Pearson I* recognized the FDA's concern that the antioxidant health claim lacked "significant scientific agreement because existing research had examined only the relationship between consumption of *foods* containing these components and the risk of these diseases," the Court stated that the FDA's concern "could be accommodated . . . by adding a prominent disclaimer to the label." . . .

On October 3, 2000, over 18 months after the *Pearson I* decision, the FDA published a notice revoking the four rules held unconstitutional by the Court of Appeals. 65 Fed. Reg. 58917, 58918 (Oct. 3, 2000). However, the FDA continued to refuse to authorize the health claims at issue in *Pearson I*, including Plaintiffs' Antioxidant Vitamin Claim.

———

[10] Similarly, we see no problem with the FDA imposing an outright ban on a claim where evidence in support of the claim is *qualitatively* weaker than evidence against the claim—for example, where the claim rests on only one or two old studies.

On November 13, 2000, the *Pearson* Plaintiffs filed a lawsuit in this Court challenging the FDA's decision to prohibit inclusion of the folic acid/neural tube defect health claim at issue in *Pearson I* on dietary supplement labels. The folic acid/neural tube effects health claim was denied because the FDA thought the claim was inherently misleading even with clarifying disclaimers. *See Pearson v. Shalala*, 130 F. Supp. 2d 105, 111–12 (D.D.C. 2001) ("*Pearson II*"). The Court found that the FDA had failed to comply with *Pearson I* and granted the *Pearson* Plaintiffs' request for a preliminary injunction, remanding the case to the FDA with instructions to draft one or more accurate disclaimers.

. . . .

The FDA then moved for reconsideration of the *Pearson II* decision, claiming that the decision . . . created a legal standard inconsistent with *Pearson I*. In denying the motion, this Court noted that:

> . . . the philosophy underlying *Pearson I* is perfectly clear: that First Amendment analysis applies in this case, and that if a health claim is not inherently misleading, the balance tilts in favor of disclaimers rather than suppression.

Pearson v. Thompson, 141 F. Supp. 2d 105, 112 (D.D.C. 2001) (*Pearson III*). The Court clarified the import of the previous *Pearson* decisions on the FDA's decision to suppress health claims by stating that both *Pearson I* and *Pearson II* "established a very heavy burden which [Defendants] must satisfy if they wish to totally suppress a particular health claim." Accordingly, the Court indicated that the FDA "*must* 'demonstrate with empirical evidence that disclaimers similar to [those] suggested . . . would bewilder consumers and fail to correct for deceptiveness.'" Accordingly, on June 4, 2001, the case was dismissed after an agreement was reached that allowed the labels of dietary supplements containing folic acid to display the folic acid/neural tube defect health claim with a disclaimer proposed by the FDA and chosen by the *Pearson* Plaintiffs. . . .

On May 4, 2001, the FDA issued a letter decision in which it declared that it would not authorize Plaintiffs' Antioxidant Vitamin Claim given the agency's review of new antioxidant vitamin/cancer relationship studies. . . . The FDA found a lack of significant scientific agreement as to the relationship between antioxidant vitamin intake and reduction in the risk of developing cancer. The FDA also found that the weight of the scientific evidence against the relationship was greater than the weight of evidence in favor of the relationship, and therefore concluded that Plaintiffs' Antioxidant Vitamin Claim was "inherently misleading and cannot be made non-misleading with a disclaimer or other qualifying language." . . .

Plaintiffs contend that the FDA's Antioxidant Vitamin Decision fundamentally misread and misapplied the legal standard articulated by the Court of Appeals in *Pearson I,* in violation of the First Amendment. . . .

. . . [T]he Court concludes that a preliminary injunction is warranted in this case. Upon reviewing the FDA's Antioxidant Vitamin Decision conclusion that the Claim is "misleading and incurable by a disclaimer," the Court concludes that the FDA has failed to comply with the Court of Appeals decision in *Pearson I* and that Plaintiffs have demonstrated a substantial likelihood of success on the merits of their First Amendment claim.

The Court finds, as a matter of law, that Plaintiffs' Antioxidant Vitamin Claim is not "inherently misleading," and that the FDA, therefore erred in not considering disclaimers to accompany the Claim. The FDA has failed to carry its burden of showing that suppression of Plaintiffs' Antioxidant Vitamin Claim is the least restrictive means of protecting consumers against the potential of being mislead [sic] by the Claim. As explained below, it is clear that the FDA has once again failed to comply with the constitutional guidelines outlined in *Pearson I*. . . .

The Court of Appeals established clear guidelines for the FDA in determining whether a particular health claim may be deemed "inherently misleading" and thus subject to total suppression. The Court implied, though it did not declare explicitly, that when "credible evidence" supports a claim, that claim may not be absolutely prohibited. While the Court did not "rule out the possibility that where evidence in support of a claim is outweighed by evidence against the claim, the FDA could deem it incurable by a disclaimer and ban it outright," it is clear that the Court was alluding to a very narrow set of circumstances in which suppression would be permissible under the First Amendment.

Specifically, *Pearson I* identified two situations in which a complete ban would be reasonable. First, when the "FDA has determined that no evidence supports [a health] claim," it may ban the claim completely. Second, when the FDA determines that "evidence in support of the claim is qualitatively weaker than evidence against the claim—for example, where the claim rests on only one or two old studies," it may impose an outright ban. Even in these two situations, a complete ban would only be appropriate when the government could demonstrate with empirical evidence that disclaimers similar to the ones [the Court] suggested above ["The evidence in support of this claim is inconclusive" or "The FDA does not approve this claim"] would bewilder consumers and fail to correct for deceptiveness. . . .

Thus, two conclusions emerge from a close reading of *Pearson I*. First, the Court of Appeals did not rule out the possibility that disclaimers would not be able to correct the inherent misleadingness of some health claims. Second, the Court stated that any complete ban of a claim would be approved only under narrow circumstances, *i.e.*, when there was almost no qualitative evidence in support of the claims and where the government provided empirical evidence proving that the public would still be deceived even if the claim was qualified by a disclaimer.

As the FDA has satisfied the second and the third steps of the *Central Hudson* test in the present case, the key analysis comes under *Central Hudson*'s final step—whether there is a reasonable fit between the government's goals and the means it has chosen to achieve them. In determining whether there is a reasonable fit between the FDA's goals of consumer protection and its decision to ban Plaintiffs' Antioxidant Vitamin Claim, the Supreme Court has clearly stated that "if the Government could achieve its interests in a matter that does not restrict speech, or that restricts less speech, the Government *must* do so." In its review of the relevant Supreme Court decisions, our Court of Appeals also concluded—even before issuance of *Western States* [535 U.S. 357 (2002)]—that disclaimers were "constitutionally preferable to outright suppression." In other words, more disclosure rather than less is the preferred approach, so long as commercial speech is not inherently misleading.

Given that the First Amendment "means that regulating speech must be a last—not first—resort," the burden in this case is on the FDA to prove that suppression of the Antioxidant Vitamin Claim "was a *necessary* as opposed to *merely convenient* means of achieving its interests." The Court of Appeals' earlier review of the FDA's denial of the Plaintiffs' Antioxidant Vitamin Claim found that the FDA's justifications for suppression were merely "conclusory assertions [that fell] far short" of satisfying its burden and concluded that the FDA had not chosen a less restrictive means of protecting its interests, *i.e.*, a disclaimer.

Once again in its 2001 decision, the FDA has failed to recognize that its decision to suppress the Plaintiffs' Antioxidant Vitamin Claim does not comport with the First Amendment's clear preference for disclosure over suppression of commercial speech. . . .

———

Following the *Whitaker* decision, FDA recognized that it had no choice but to change its strategy. The agency announced the availability of two final guidance documents, one establishing an interim evidence-based ranking system and the other setting forth interim health claims procedures. 68 Fed. Reg. 41387 (July 11, 2003). It then issued an advanced notice of proposed rulemaking to request comments on alternatives for regulating qualified health claims. 68 Fed. Reg. 66040 (Nov. 25, 2003). In these documents and notices, the agency concluded that it would have two separate and different standards for health claims for food: (1) significant scientific agreement for "unqualified" health claims and (2) "credible scientific evidence" (rather than "weight of the evidence") for "qualified" health claims. These guidances and notices also established two other important interim policies: (1) an evidence-based ranking system to evaluate the scientific evidence relevant to a health claim and (2) four levels of health claims based upon the degree of supporting evidence. The highest-grade health claims were unqualified NLEA health claims backed by "significant scientific agreement." Below them were three levels of qualified claims with corresponding standardized qualifying language:

A.   High: significant scientific agreement

B.   Moderate: . . . "although there is scientific evidence supporting the claim, the evidence is not conclusive."

C.   Low: "Some scientific evidence suggests . . . however, FDA has determined that this evidence is limited and not conclusive."

D.   Extremely low: "Very limited and preliminary scientific research suggests . . . FDA concludes that there is little scientific evidence supporting this claim."

GUIDANCE FOR INDUSTRY INTERIM PROCEDURES FOR QUALIFIED HEALTH CLAIMS (July 2003). The agency stated: "If the scientific evidence to support the substance/disease relationship is below that described in the fourth level *no claim will be appropriate.*" GUIDANCE FOR INDUSTRY AND FDA: INTERIM EVIDENCE-BASED RANKING SYSTEM FOR SCIENTIFIC DATA (July 2003).

Using this approach, FDA began to issue "enforcement discretion" letters with respect to qualified health claims. It issued some of these letters in conjunction with the rejection of petitions for unqualified claims and others in direct response to "qualified health claim petitions." In each instance, FDA—sometimes in negotiation with the petitioner—fashioned specific qualified claims over which it would "consider the exercise of its enforcement discretion." Because the agency composed qualifying statements specific to each product, the standardized language corresponding to the "B," "C," and "D"-grade analysis had limited direct impact. In 2009, FDA withdrew the July 2003 "Interim Evidence–Based Ranking System" guidance as "obsolete," 74 Fed. Reg. 3060, 3061 (Jan. 16, 2009), and replaced it with a new GUIDANCE FOR INDUSTRY: EVIDENCE–BASED REVIEW SYSTEM FOR THE SCIENTIFIC EVALUATION OF HEALTH CLAIMS (Jan. 2009). This new guidance document does not refer to the graded levels at all, although the other 2003 interim procedural guidance, not yet withdrawn, still lists them.

As of September 2013, FDA had issued active "enforcement discretion" letters with respect to 17 qualified health claims. A summary of the qualified health claims allowed by FDA is published on the agency's website (along with the enforcement discretion letters themselves).

As the case reproduced below illustrates, FDA has not had complete success in defending its implementation of this regime.

Fleminger v. HHS

854 F. Supp. 2d 192 (D. Conn. 2012).

■ BRYANT, DISTRICT JUDGE. . . .

Plaintiff, Fleminger, Inc. ("Fleminger"), a manufacturer and retailer of green tea . . . filed a petition with the FDA for authorization of . . . its qualified health claim that drinking green tea "may reduce the risk of breast or prostate cancer." Fleminger alleges that Defendants violated its commercial speech rights under the First Amendment by requiring Fleminger to include [a] modified disclaimer. . . . Both Fleminger and Defendants have moved for summary judgment. . . .

In response to the decisions rendered in *Pearson I, Pearson II* and *Whitaker,* the FDA developed a system for evaluating proposed health claims. Under this system, the FDA first determined whether the proposed health claim was supported by significant scientific agreement (SSA). If it was, the FDA considered the claim to be "unqualified" and it approved the claim without requiring the addition of any corrective disclaimers. However, if the claim was not supported by significant scientific agreement, but there was credible evidence in support of the claim, the FDA considered the claim to be "qualified" and would require the addition of corrective disclaimers to the claim to reflect the scientific record. Since the FDA is only authorized to approve claims that are supported by significant scientific agreement under NLEA and the FDA's regulations, it does not "approve" qualified health claims but instead "exercises enforcement discretion" to allow such claims to made with the additional of corrective disclaimers.

According to the [2009 "Evidence–Based Review System" guidance] ... "When the evidence for a substance-disease relationship is credible but does not meet the SSA standard, then the proposed health claim for the relationship should include qualifying language that identifies limits to the level of scientific evidence to support the relationship." *Id.* . . . .

In *Alliance for Natural Health U.S. v. Sebelius,* 714 F.Supp.2d 48, 51 (D.D.C. 2010) ("*Alliance I*") ... [ANH] argued that the FDA's decision to modify one of their proposed claims by entirely replacing the proposed language with its own language violated the Supreme Court's mandate there be a reasonable fit between the government's goal and the restrictions it imposes on commercial speech. [ANH] had proposed the following claim "Selenium may reduce the risk of prostate cancer. Scientific evidence supporting this claim is convincing but not yet conclusive." ... [T]he FDA, in exercising its enforcement discretion, modified the claim to the following: 'Two weak studies suggest that selenium intake may reduce the risk of prostate cancer. However, four stronger studies and three weak studies showed no reduction in risk. Based on these studies, FDA concludes that it is highly unlikely that selenium supplements reduce the risk of prostate cancer."

The court agreed with [ANH] that there was not "a reasonable fit" because the "Agency has not drafted a precise disclaimer designed to qualify plaintiffs' claim while adhering to the First Amendment preference for disclosure over suppression as mandated." The Court emphasized that the FDA had "replaced the plaintiffs' claim entirely. And the Agency's qualification effectively negates any relationship between prostate cancer risk and selenium intake. Indeed, the FDA's language is an example of a disclaimer that contradicts the claim and defeats the purpose of making it in the first place." The Court suggested that where there is some credible evidence for a substance-disease relationship the FDA "is obligated to at least consider the possibility of approving plaintiffs' proposed language with the addition of 'short, succinct, and accurate disclaimers.' ". . . .

Fleminger originally submitted a health claim petition to the FDA dated January 27, 2004. . . .

On June 30, 2005, the FDA issued a response letter informing Fleminger that . . . it would consider exercising enforcement discretion for the following qualified health claims:

(i) Two studies do not show that drinking green tea reduces the risk of breast cancer in women, but one weaker, more limited study suggests that drinking green tea may reduce this risk. Based on these studies, FDA concludes that it is highly unlikely that green tea reduces the risk of breast cancer; and

(ii) One weak and limited study does not show that drinking green tea reduces the risk of prostate cancer, but another weak and limited study suggests that drinking green tea may reduce this risk. Based on these studies, FDA concludes that it is highly unlikely that green tea reduces the risk of prostate cancer.

. . . .

Subsequently . . . the *Alliance I* decision prompted the FDA to reconsider Fleminger's . . . claim. After such reconsideration, the FDA issued an amended response on February 24, 2011. . . .

[In that response,] the FDA considered exercising its enforcement discretion for the following claim: "Green tea may reduce the risk of breast or prostate cancer. FDA does not agree that green tea may reduce the risk because there is very little scientific evidence for the claim." . . . The FDA indicated that the language "FDA does not agree" will prevent "consumers from erroneously assuming that the health claim reflects FDA's determination that scientific evidence, taken as a whole, shows that green tea is likely to reduce the risk of breast or prostate cancer." In addition, the language "there is very little scientific evidence" according to the FDA "accurately conveys the strength of the scientific evidence because it helps consumers distinguish among claims that are supported by different levels of scientific evidence. . . ."

After the FDA issued its amended response, Fleminger filed the instant action in federal court alleging that the FDA violated the First Amendment when it rejected Fleminger's proposed health claim that "Green tea may reduce the risk of breast and prostate cancers. The FDA has concluded that there is credible evidence supporting this claim although the evidence is limited". . . .

. . . [T]he Court's analysis with respect to whether the FDA violated Fleminger's commercial speech rights under the First Amendment is evaluated under the analytical framework articulated in *Central Hudson* . . .

Fleminger principally argues that the FDA violated its commercial speech rights because the FDA's interests in regulating its speech are not substantial. . . . There are two asserted governmental interests at stake the first being the interest in "accurately conveying the strength of the scientific evidence" and second in "preventing the mistaken assumption that the FDA endorses the claim." . . .

The Court finds that the FDA has asserted a substantial interest in ascertaining the validity and truthfulness of health-related claims on food and in drafting appropriate disclaimers which reflect the level of scientific evidence for a particular health claim in order to prevent consumer confusion and protect public health. . . .

Since the statutory and regulatory framework for health claims made on food is pervasive and long established, the Court [also] finds that the FDA's concern that consumers might mistakenly assume that the FDA approves such health claims to be more than well founded. . . .

Since Fleminger's proposed disclaimer is inaccurate and misleading, under the applicable FDA nomenclature, the FDA is not obligated under the First Amendment to allow Fleminger to use such language in its marketing. . . .

The portion of the FDA's modified disclaimer stating that "there is very little scientific evidence" for the proposed health claim reflects a reasonable fit between the FDA's goal of preventing consumer confusion and protecting public health and the means chosen to accomplish that end as it permits the claim to be made while disclosing to the consumer contrary sound scientific evidence. . . .

Although the portion of the FDA's disclaimer conveying the strength of scientific evidence supporting the health claim is appropriate under the First Amendment, the portion of the disclaimer stating that the "FDA does not agree that green tea may reduce that risk" suffers from the same constitutional infirmities as the modified disclaimers at issue in *Alliance I*. . . . The placement of this language immediately after Fleminger's claim that "drinking green tea may reduce the risk of breast or prostate cancer" has the effect of negating any relationship between green tea and the reduction of breast or prostate cancer and therefore effectively swallows the entire claim. . . .

While the FDA does have a substantial interest in preventing the assumption that it has approved the health claim, the FDA's language burdens substantially more speech than is necessary to further that interest since the language effectively negates the substance-disease relationship claim altogether. There are less burdensome ways in which the FDA could indicate in a short, succinct and accurate disclaimer that it has not approved the claim without nullifying the claim altogether. . . . As the *Pearson I* court suggested the "agency could require the label to state that 'the FDA does not approve this claim.' " . . .

The Court also suspects that the FDA's concern that consumers will assume it has approved the health claim could also be accommodated by changing the disclaimer along the following lines: "Green tea may reduce the risk of breast or prostate cancer although the FDA has concluded that there is very little scientific evidence to support the claim." Such a disclaimer would not have the effect of negating the substance-disease claim and would therefore represent a lesser restriction on Fleminger's commercial speech but also accommodate the FDA substantial interest in preventing the assumption that it has approved the claim. . . .

As the *Pearson I* court acknowledged it is not the role of the courts to draft precise declaimers but instead "leave[s] that task to the agency in the first instance." The Court accordingly remands Fleminger's health claim to the FDA for the purpose of drafting appropriate disclaimers consistent with this Memorandum Opinion. . . .

NOTES

1. *FDA Response.* Pursuant to this decision, FDA issued a letter stating that it intends to consider exercising enforcement discretion for either of the following qualified health claims:

> Green tea may reduce the risk of breast or prostate cancer although the FDA has concluded that there is very little scientific evidence for this claim.

> Green tea may reduce the risk of breast or prostate cancer. FDA has concluded that there is very little scientific evidence for this claim.

Letter Updating the Green Tea and Risk of Breast Cancer and Prostate Cancer Health Claim (Apr. 17, 2012).

2. *Enforcement "Discretion."* FDA continues to refer to "enforcement discretion" rather than forthrightly stating that the qualified claims referred to in its letters are constitutionally protected and that the agency thus has no discretion in permitting their use.

3. *Constitutional Limitations on Time Frame for FDA Consideration.* In the mid-1990s, the National Health Alliance brought a facial First Amendment challenge to the NLEA provisions regarding health claims. The District Court upheld the premarket approval requirement against the argument that it was an unconstitutional prior restraint, but it ordered FDA to impose a reasonable limit on the time within which the agency would approve or disapprove any health claim. *Nutritional Health Alliance v. Shalala*, 953 F. Supp. 526 (S.D.N.Y. 1997). The Court of Appeals affirmed the District Court. It concluded that a 540 day limit for final FDA action (imposed by statute in 1997) was not an unconstitutional prior restraint of commercial free speech. 144 F.3d 220 (2d Cir. 1998).

d.   DIETARY GUIDANCE STATEMENTS

In the preamble to the final regulations on health claims under the NLEA, FDA stated that a health claim contains two basic elements: (1) a particular substance and (2) a disease-related condition. FDA stated that it would use the term "dietary guidance" to refer to general health claims that do not contain both of these basic elements. 58 Fed. Reg. 2478, 2487 (Jan. 6, 1993). Unlike disease-prevention claims, dietary guidance statements are not subject to the requirements of section 403(r)(1)(B) of the FD&C Act. Because that 1993 preamble discussion provoked little food industry response, a decade later FDA explained the importance of general health claims/dietary guidance in the following notice.

Food Labeling: Health Claims; Dietary Guidance

68 Fed. Reg. 66040 (November 25, 2003).

. . . Unlike health claims, which target a specific substance and a specific disease or health-related condition, dietary guidance statements focus instead on general dietary patterns, practices, and recommendations that promote health. . . . [S]uch statements can be made on conventional food and dietary supplement labels without FDA review or authorization before use. . . . An example of a dietary guidance statement is: "Diets rich in fruits and vegetables may reduce the risk of some types of cancer and other chronic diseases." As part of a cooperative effort with the National Cancer Institute (NCI), FDA recently encouraged the produce industry and food manufacturers to use this statement in the labeling of fruits, vegetables, and foods that meet the criteria for NCI's 5 A Day for Better Health Program.

. . . FDA recognizes the importance of dietary guidance in assisting and encouraging the U.S. population to make better food choices and establish healthier eating patterns. Although these types of statements are not health claims, consistent and scientifically sound dietary guidance statements can be useful to consumers when they are truthful and nonmisleading. As previously mentioned, FDA has no regulatory authority to review or authorize dietary guidance statements before use. When used in labeling for foods, however, such statements must be truthful and not misleading under sections 201(n) and 403(a)(1) of the act. The agency generally has viewed most dietary guidance for the general U.S. population as originating from Federal agencies with public health missions related to diet and disease. For example, major Federal documents such as the Dietary Guidelines for Americans issued by USDA and U.S. Department of Health and Human Services exemplify government consensus about dietary recommendations. Given the important role that information on food labels can play in affecting consumers' health and dietary decisions, FDA sees a need to foster enhanced federal cooperative efforts to identify and agree upon dietary guidance that is appropriate for food labels and how such guidance may be used. . . .

FDA is seeking comment on dietary guidance statements on food labels generally and on approaches appropriate for FDA to consider under its statutory authorities. As part of this consideration, FDA is requesting comments on whether providing a list of dietary guidance statements that FDA recommends for inclusion on food labels would be desirable or useful to manufacturers. In addition, FDA is requesting comments on these topics: (1) Whether and how the agency should partner with other Federal agencies to identify and agree upon recommended dietary guidance statements for food labeling, (2) the appropriate criteria for evaluating the scientific validity of dietary guidance statements that appear on products in the marketplace, and (3) whether and how the agency should address dietary guidance statements from non-federal sources (*e.g.*, States, trade associations, professional associations, etc.). . . .

NOTES

1.   *The Obesity Epidemic.* In the 2000s, it became clear that obesity was reaching epidemic levels in the United States. In August 2003, FDA established an Obesity Working Group, which in March 2004 issued a comprehensive report on combatting obesity. CALORIES COUNT: REPORT OF THE FOOD AND DRUG ADMINISTRATION WORKING GROUP ON OBESITY (Mar. 12, 2004). FDA's principal regulatory authority applicable to obesity is its control over food labeling. In 2005, FDA published two advance notices of proposed rulemaking, one focused on changing nutrition labeling to increase the emphasis on the caloric content and the other focused on updating serving sizes. 70 Fed. Reg. 17008 & 17010 (Apr. 4, 2005). The same year, a citizen petition relied upon both the food additive and the food labeling provisions of the FD&C Act to request that FDA require that sweetened soft drinks bear a variety of rotating health messages to help reduce obesity and related diseases. Citizen Petition No. 2005P–0282/CPI (July 13, 2005). No action has been taken by FDA on this petition.

Many agencies have a role in combatting the obesity epidemic, including the CDC (which supports obesity prevention programs), the USDA (which administers a variety of food and nutrition programs and, jointly with HHS, issues the National Dietary Guidelines), and the FTC (which regulates food advertising). Many nutrition programs are beyond the FDA budget or legal authority to implement. Yet the agency's regulatory policies can affect the success of other programs. *See, e.g.*, Peter Barton Hutt, *Regulatory Implementation of Dietary Recommendations*, 36 FOOD DRUG COSM. L.J. 66 (1981).

2.   *Television Advertising to Children.* Thirty years ago, as part of a broad approach to regulation of food advertising that was ultimately abandoned, the FTC proposed to restrict television advertising to children of sugared food products. 43 Fed. Reg. 17967 (Apr. 22, 1978). This effort culminated in Congress enacting the Federal Trade Commission Improvements Act of 1980, 94 Stat. 374, 15 U.S.C. 57a(h), to prohibit the FTC from regulating children's advertising as an "unfair act or practice." On May 2, 2006, the Department of HHS and the FTC issued a joint report titled MARKETING, SELF–REGULATION, AND CHILDHOOD OBESITY. *See also* INSTITUTE OF MEDICINE, FOOD MARKETING TO CHILDREN AND YOUTH: THREAT OR OPPORTUNITY? (2005). In 2007, in response to such attention and threats of regulation, eleven major food companies voluntarily ceased advertising products that do not meet certain nutritional standards to children under 12, although cereals such as Cocoa Puffs® meet these standards, and the policy does not apply to television shows deemed to be directed to families, rather than just children. *Limiting Ads of Junk Food for Children*, N.Y. TIMES, July 18, 2007, at C1.

e.   STRUCTURE/FUNCTION CLAIMS

As discussed in Chapter 3, *supra* p. 85, the FD&C Act defines "drug" to include "articles intended for use in the diagnosis, cure, mitigation, treatment, or prevention of disease" and "articles (other than food) intended to affect the structure or any function of the body." FD&C Act 201(g)(1)(B)–(C). Because of the parenthetical exclusion of food from the structure/function portion of the drug definition, structure/function claims may be made for a food without the effect of classifying the food as a drug. Nevertheless, for many years, FDA took the position that any structure/function claim was an implied drug claim that would render a food an illegal unapproved drug. Although this position was declared "untenable" by a court in the starch blocker cases, *American Health Products Co., Inc. v. Hayes*, 574 F. Supp. 1498, 1507 (S.D.N.Y. 1983), the food industry is very conservative and thus generally did not—until recently—pursue structure/function claims for conventional food products.

At least in theory, dietary supplements that were common sense food—that is, vitamin and mineral supplements used for their nutritive value—were, like conventional food, always permitted to make structure/function claims pursuant to the parenthetical in section 201(g)(1)(C). When Congress passed the Dietary Supplement Health and Education Act of 1994, it extended the right to make structure/function claims to all supplements, including those that are not common sense foods used primarily for their "taste, aroma, or nutritive value." *See Nutrilab v. Schweiker*, *supra* p. 85. Congress could have accomplished this goal simply by making all dietary supplements—now considered "food" for most purposes according to FD&C Act 201(ff)—eligible for the parenthetical exception to the structure/function component of the drug definition. Instead, DSHEA added section 403(r)(6) to the FD&C Act to authorize four types of statements for dietary supplements: (1) a claimed benefit related to a classical nutrient deficiency disease; (2) a description of the role of a nutrient or dietary ingredient intended to affect the structure or function in humans (a "structure/function" claim); (3) a characterization of the documented mechanism by which a nutrient or dietary ingredient acts to maintain the structure or function in humans; and (4) a description of general well-being from consumption of a nutrient or dietary ingredient. FD&C Act 403(r)(6)(A). DSHEA itself referred to these claims as "statements of nutritional support," but FDA has abandoned that terminology "because many of the substances that can be the subject of this type of claim do not have nutritional value." 62 Fed. Reg. 49859, 49863 (Sept. 23, 1997).

Congress imposed special requirements on structure/function claims and other 403(r)(6) claims made for dietary supplements. Section 403(r)(6)(C) requires that the label of any dietary supplement bearing such a claim must also bear the following disclaimer: "This statement has not been evaluated by the Food and Drug Administration. This product is not intended to diagnose, treat, cure, or prevent any disease." In addition, section 403(r)(6) states that within 30 days after the first marketing of a dietary supplement with such a claim, the manufacturer must notify FDA that the claim is being made. The agency has implemented these provisions at 21 C.F.R. 101.93. When structure/function claims are made in conventional food labeling, they are subject to neither of these requirements.

The Act also requires a dietary supplement manufacturer making a section 403(r)(6) claim to have "substantiation that such statement is truthful and not misleading." FD&C Act 403(r)(6)(B). However, the statute does not require the manufacturer to submit information substantiating the claim to FDA, nor does it provide the agency with special access to this information. It thus is not clear how and whether this requirement differs from the section 403(a) prohibition on "false or misleading" labeling applicable to all food manufacturers.

Whereas the FD&C Act now permits dietary supplement manufacturers to make structure/function claims pursuant to section 403(r)(6) without prior FDA approval, a claim that a dietary supplement prevents or treats a disease remains illegal unless the agency approves it as an unqualified health claim, exercises its "enforcement discretion" over it as a qualified health claim, or approves a new drug application for the product. Not surprisingly, therefore, one of the most controversial issues following the enactment of DSHEA was the line between structure/function claims and disease claims. And although there are some technical differences between the structure/function claim regimes for dietary supplements and conventional food, FDA has indicated that the dividing line between structure/function claims and disease claims is identical for both. *See* 65 Fed. Reg. 1000, 1034 (Jan. 6, 2000).

FDA's first systematic attempt to differentiate valid structure/function claims from disease claims appeared in proposed regulations it issued in 1998.

Regulations on Statements Made for Dietary Supplements Concerning the Effect of the Product on the Structure or Function of the Body

63 Fed. Reg. 23624 (April 29, 1998).

The Dietary Supplement Health and Education Act of 1994 (the DSHEA) authorizes manufacturers of dietary supplements to make certain types of statements about the uses of their products. Among the types of permitted statements are certain claims that, prior to enactment of the DSHEA, could have rendered the product a "drug" under the Federal Food, Drug, and Cosmetic Act (the act). Specifically, section 403(r)(6) of the act, added by the DSHEA, allows dietary supplement labeling to bear a statement that "describes the role of a nutrient or dietary ingredient intended to affect the structure or function in humans" or that "characterizes the documented mechanism by which a nutrient or dietary ingredient acts to maintain such structure or function." . . .

Certain other types of statements about dietary supplements continue, under the DSHEA, to cause the product to be regulated as a drug. Statements permitted under section 403(r)(6) of the act "may not claim to diagnose, mitigate, treat, cure, or prevent a specific disease or class of diseases," except that such statements may claim a benefit related to a classical nutrient deficiency disease, provided that they also disclose the prevalence of the disease in the United States. Such statements are generally referred to as "disease claims." FDA notes that certain statements that pertain to a disease or health-related condition are permitted on food products, including dietary supplements. These statements are known as health claims and describe the relationship between a nutrient and a disease or health-related condition. Unlike structure/function claims, health claims must be authorized by FDA before they may be used on the label or in the labeling of a food or dietary supplement. Thus, certain claims about disease may be made for foods and dietary supplements without causing these products to be regulated as drugs, provided the claim has been authorized for use by FDA in accordance with the applicable regulations. . . .

Diseases, by definition, adversely affect some structure or function of the body, and it is possible to describe most products intended to treat or prevent disease in terms of their effects on the structure or function of the body. The DSHEA, thus, does not authorize the use of all claims that describe the effect of a dietary supplement on the structure or function of the body. Instead, section 403(r)(6) of the act authorizes only those structure/function claims that describe an effect of a product on the structure or function of the body but that are not also disease claims. Because the distinction between allowable structure/function claims and disease claims is not always obvious, the dietary supplement industry has requested clarification from FDA on structure/function claims that can be made for dietary supplements under section 403(r)(6) of the act. To develop clarifying criteria for such claims, FDA has reviewed the notification letters that have been submitted to FDA under section 403(r)(6) of the act. In addition, FDA has reviewed the report of the Commission [on Dietary Supplement Labels], which was established by the DSHEA to provide guidance and recommendations for the regulation of label claims and statements for dietary supplements.

The Commission's final report contains the following guidance (the guidance) on the scope of permissible structure/function claims:

GUIDANCE

While the Commission recognizes that the context of a claim has to be considered on a case-by-case basis, the Commission proposes the following general guidelines:

. . . .

3. Statements indicating the role of a nutrient or dietary ingredient in affecting the structure or function of humans may be made when the statements do not suggest disease prevention or treatment.

4. Statements that mention a body system, organ, or function affected by the supplement using terms such as "stimulate," "maintain," "support," "regulate," or "promote" can be appropriate when the statements do not suggest disease prevention or treatment or use for a serious health condition that is beyond the ability of the consumer to evaluate.

5. Statements should not be made that products "restore" normal or "correct" abnormal function when the abnormality implies the presence of disease. An example might be a claim to "restore" normal blood pressure when the abnormality implies hypertension.

6. Health claims are specifically defined under NLEA as statements that characterize the relationship between a nutrient or a food component and a specific disease or health-related condition. [Section 403(r)(6) claims] should be distinct from NLEA health claims in that they do not state or imply a link between a supplement and prevention of a specific disease or health-related condition.

7. [Section 403(r)(6) claims] are not to be drug claims. They should not refer to specific diseases, disorders, or classes of diseases and should not use drug-related terms such as "diagnose," "treat," "prevent," "cure," or "mitigate."

The guidance thus focuses on the distinction between allowable structure/function claims and claims that a product can diagnose, treat, prevent, cure, or mitigate disease (disease claims), and makes clear that structure/function claims made for dietary supplements should not imply treatment or prevention of disease. The guidance also provides examples of types of structure/function claims that do and do not imply disease claims. . . .

. . . FDA believes that the Commission's guidelines provide a useful framework for clarifying the sometimes difficult distinction between structure/function claims and disease claims. Based upon the Commission's advice and the agency's experience in reviewing notification letters submitted under section 403(r)(6) of the act, FDA has developed proposed regulations to define the types of claims that are "disease claims" and thus not acceptable as structure/function claims. . . .

———

In 2000, FDA promulgated a final rule on structure/function statements for dietary supplements. 65 Fed. Reg. 1000 (Jan. 6, 2000), codified at 21 C.F.R. 101.93(f)–(g). In the preamble, the agency observed: "FDA received over 235,000 submissions in response to the proposed rule. Many of these were form letters, but over 22,000 were individual letters from the dietary supplement industry, trade associations, health professional groups, and consumers. Almost all the comments from the dietary supplement industry and from individuals, which made up the vast majority of the comments, objected to all or part of the proposed rule, arguing that it inappropriately restricted the structure/function claims that could be made for dietary supplements."

The preamble to the final rule filled fifty pages in the Federal Register, while the regulation itself occupied only one page. The final rule made several significant changes to the proposed version, but it continued to follow the same general approach laid out by the Commission on Dietary Supplement Labels.

21 CFR 101.93 Certain Types of Statements for Dietary Supplements

. . . .

(f) *Permitted structure/function statements.* Dietary supplement labels or labeling may . . . bear statements that describe the role of a nutrient or dietary ingredient intended to affect the structure or function in humans or that characterize the documented mechanism by which a nutrient or dietary ingredient acts to maintain such structure or function, provided that such statements are not disease claims under paragraph (g) of this section. If the label or labeling of a product marketed as a dietary supplement bears a disease claim as defined in paragraph (g) of this section, the product will be subject to regulation as a drug unless the claim is an authorized health claim for which the product qualifies.

(g) *Disease claims.* (1) For purposes of 21 U.S.C. 343(r)(6), a "disease" is damage to an organ, part, structure, or system of the body such that it does not function properly (e.g., cardiovascular disease), or a state of health leading to such dysfunctioning (e.g., hypertension); except that diseases resulting from essential nutrient deficiencies (e.g., scurvy, pellagra) are not included in this definition.

(2) FDA will find that a statement about a product claims to diagnose, mitigate, treat, cure, or prevent disease (other than a classical nutrient deficiency disease) under 21 U.S.C. 343(r)(6) if it meets one or more of the criteria listed below. These criteria are not intended to classify as disease claims statements that refer to the ability of a product to maintain healthy structure or function, unless the statement implies disease prevention or treatment. In determining whether a statement is a disease claim under these criteria, FDA will consider the context in which the claim is presented. A statement claims to diagnose, mitigate, treat, cure, or prevent disease if it claims, explicitly or implicitly, that the product:

(i) Has an effect on a specific disease or class of diseases;

(ii) Has an effect on the characteristic signs or symptoms of a specific disease or class of diseases, using scientific or lay terminology;

(iii) Has an effect on an abnormal condition associated with a natural state or process, if the abnormal condition is uncommon or can cause significant or permanent harm;

(iv) Has an effect on a disease or diseases through one or more of the following factors:

(A) The name of the product;

(B) A statement about the formulation of the product, including a claim that the product contains an ingredient (other than an ingredient that is an article included in the definition of "dietary supplement" under 21 U.S.C. 321(ff)(3)) that has been regulated by FDA as a drug and is well known to consumers for its use or claimed use in preventing or treating a disease;

(C) Citation of a publication or reference, if the citation refers to a disease use, and if, in the context of the labeling as a whole, the citation implies treatment or prevention of a disease, e.g., through placement on the immediate product label or packaging, inappropriate prominence, or lack of relationship to the product's express claims;

(D) Use of the term "disease" or "diseased," except in general statements about disease prevention that do not refer explicitly or implicitly to a specific disease or class of diseases or to a specific product or ingredient; or

(E) Use of pictures, vignettes, symbols, or other means;

(v) Belongs to a class of products that is intended to diagnose, mitigate, treat, cure, or prevent a disease;

(vi) Is a substitute for a product that is a therapy for a disease;

(vii) Augments a particular therapy or drug action that is intended to diagnose, mitigate, treat, cure, or prevent a disease or class of diseases;

(viii) Has a role in the body's response to a disease or to a vector of disease;

(ix) Treats, prevents, or mitigates adverse events associated with a therapy for a disease, if the adverse events constitute diseases; or

(x) Otherwise suggests an effect on a disease or diseases.

NOTES

1. *Examples of Acceptable and Unacceptable Claims.* A trade publication, THE TAN SHEET, Vol. 8, No. 3, pp. 12–13 (Jan. 17, 2000), extracted from the preamble all of the examples of permitted structure/function claims and prohibited disease claims for dietary supplements. The resulting list is reproduced *infra* at p. 450.

2. *The "Natural State" Exception.* In the preamble to the final rule, FDA concluded that it is not appropriate to treat common nonserious conditions associated with "natural states" as diseases. These natural

states include adolescence, the menstrual cycle, pregnancy, menopause, and aging. The agency therefore permitted, as valid structure/function claims, such conditions as "(1) Morning sickness associated with pregnancy; (2) leg edema associated with pregnancy; (3) mild mood changes, cramps, and edema associated with the menstrual cycle; (4) hot flashes; (5) wrinkles; (6) other signs of aging on the skin, *e.g.*, liver spots, spider veins; (7) presbyopia (inability to change focus from near to far and vice versa) associated with aging; (8) mild memory problems associated with aging; (9) hair loss associated with aging; and (10) noncystic acne." The following are examples of conditions that remain disease claims: "(1) Toxemia of pregnancy; (2) hyperemesis gravidarum; (3) acute psychosis of pregnancy; (4) osteoporosis; (5) Alzheimer's disease, and other senile dementias; (6) glaucoma; (7) arteriosclerotic diseases of coronary, cerebral or peripheral blood vessels; (8) cystic acne; and (9) severe depression associated with the menstrual cycle." 65 Fed. Reg. 1000, 1020 (Jan. 6, 2000).

3. *Pregnancy and the "Natural State" Exception.* Immediately upon issuing its dietary supplement structure/function rule, FDA received comments expressing concern about the agency's statement that common and mild conditions associated with the "natural state" of pregnancy, such as morning sickness, would not be treated as diseases. These comments pointed out the significant risks that dietary supplements might pose to unborn children. FDA quickly responded to these concerns by advising dietary supplement manufacturers "not to make any claims related to pregnancy on their products based on the agency's recently issued structure/function rule." *FDA Statement Concerning Structure/Function Rule and Pregnancy Claims* (Feb. 9, 2000).

4. *Substantiation.* In January of 2009, FDA issued guidance for the industry with regards to SUBSTANTIATION FOR DIETARY SUPPLEMENT CLAIMS MADE UNDER SECTION 403(R)(6) OF THE FEDERAL FOOD, DRUG, AND COSMETIC ACT. 74 FED. REG. 304 (Jan. 5, 2009). The guidance describes the amount, type, and quality of evidence FDA recommends a manufacturer to have to substantiate a claim under 403(r)(6). The agency recommends that firms consider the following four factors in making their assessment of substantiation: (1) the meaning of the claim(s) being made; (2) the relationship of the evidence to the claim; (3) the quality of the evidence; and (4) the totality of the evidence.

5. *Structure/Function Claims for Dietary Supplements vs. Conventional Food.* In the preamble to its final rule on structure/function claims under DSHEA, FDA stated: "This rule applies to claims for dietary supplements only.... FDA advises, however, that for consistency, the agency is likely to interpret the dividing line between structure/function claims and disease claims in a similar manner for conventional foods as for dietary supplements." 65 Fed. Reg. at 1034. In other particulars, however, structure/function claims on dietary supplements and conventional foods are subject to different requirements. These differences are one reason why the distinction between conventional foods and dietary supplements can be important.

For example, as explained *supra* at p. 444, DSHEA imposes notification and disclaimer requirements on structure/function claims for dietary supplements that do not apply to identical claims for conventional food. A dietary supplement manufacturer cannot avoid these requirements by making a claim pursuant to the "other than food" exclusion from the structure/function prong of the drug definition (201(g)(1)(C)) rather than pursuant to section 403(r)(6), because FDA has stated (against industry opposition) that dietary supplements may bear a structure/function claim only under the latter provision. *See* 65 Fed. Reg. at 1033–34 (Jan. 6, 2000); *see also* 62 Fed. Reg. 49859, 49860–61 (Sept. 23, 1997). The practical impact of this interpretation is that all dietary supplements bearing a structure/function claim must comply with the notification and disclaimer requirements of 403(r)(6).

In another respect, however, dietary supplements are advantaged over conventional foods with respect to structure/function claims. FDA has stated that structure/function claims may be made for dietary ingredients in dietary supplements that have no nutritive value, but that such claims may be made for conventional food only if based on the nutritive value of the food. The agency observed: "[A] claim that cranberry products help to maintain urinary tract health may be permissible on both cranberry products in conventional food form and dietary supplement form if it . . . derives from the nutritional value of cranberries." But if the claimed benefit "did not derive from the nutritional value of cranberries . . . the claim could appear on a dietary supplement but not a conventional food." 62 Fed. Reg. at 49860–61.

Conventional foods for which structure/function claims are made are often called "functional" foods. This is a marketing term, not a separate regulatory category of food. FDA for the first time acknowledged the existence of functional foods, discussed their regulatory status under the FD&C Act, and posed questions about potential future regulatory initiatives to be discussed in a public hearing announced in 71 Fed. Reg. 62400 (Oct. 25, 2006).

FDA EXAMPLES OF ACCEPTABLE AND UNACCEPTABLE DIETARY SUPPLEMENT CLAIMS

Structure/Function Claim Examples

"Helps promote digestion"
"For relief of occasional constipation"
Laxative
"Improves absentmindedness"
Stress and frustration
"Helps support cartilage and joint function"
"Maintains healthy lung function"
"Helps to maintain cholesterol levels that are already within the normal range"

Morning sickness associated with pregnancy
Leg edema associated with pregnancy
Mild mood changes, cramps and edema associated with the menstrual cycle
Hot flashes

Wrinkles
Other signs of aging on the skin, *e.g.*, liver spots, spider veins
Presbyopia (inability to change focus from near to far and vice versa) associated with aging
Mild memory problems associated with aging
Hair loss associated with aging
Noncystic acne
"Supports a normal, healthy attitude during PMS"
"Supportive for menopausal women"
"A good diet promotes good health and prevents the onset of disease"

"Better dietary and exercise patterns can contribute to disease prevention and better health"
"Appetite suppressant"
"Tonic"
"Antispasmodic"
"Supports the immune system"
"Helps maintain intestinal flora"
Pain associated with nondisease states, *e.g.*, muscle pain following exercise

"Relief of sour stomach"
"Upset stomach"
"Occasional heartburn"
"Occasional acid indigestion"
"Alleviates the symptoms referred to as gas"
"Alleviates bloating"
"Alleviates pressure"
"Alleviates fullness"
"Alleviates stuffed feeling"
"For the prevention and treatment of the nausea, vomiting or dizziness associated with motion"
"For the relief of occasional sleeplessness"
"Helps restore mental alertness or wakefulness when experiencing fatigue or drowsiness"
"Occasional simple nervous tension"
"Nervousness due to common every day overwork and fatigue"
"A relaxed feeling"
"Calming down and relaxing"
"Gently soothe away the tension"
"Calmative"
"Resolving that irritability that ruins your day"
"Helps you relax"
"Restlessness"
"Nervous irritability"
"When you're under occasional stress, helps you work relaxed"
"Arouses or increases sexual desire and improves sexual performance"
"Digestive aid"
"Stool softener"
"Weight control"
"Menstrual"

"Boosts stamina, helps increase muscle size and helps enhance muscle tone"

"Smoking alternative"; "Temporarily reduces your desire to smoke"; "Mimics the oral sensations of cigarette smoke" if context does not imply treatment of nicotine addiction

"Treatment and/or prevention of nocturnal leg muscle cramps, *i.e.*, a condition of localized pain in the lower extremities usually occurring in middle life and beyond with no regular pattern concerning time or severity"

"Helps maintain regularity"

"Calcium helps build strong bones"

Disease Claims Examples

"Promotes low blood pressure"

"Relieves crushing chest pain" (angina or heart attack)

"Improves joint mobility and reduces joint inflammation and pain" (rheumatoid arthritis)

"Heals stomach or duodenal lesions and bleeding" (ulcers)

"Anticonvulsant" (epilepsy)

"Relief of bronchospasm" (asthma)

"Prevents wasting in persons with weakened immune systems" (AIDS)

"Prevents irregular heartbeat" (arrhythmias)

"Prevents shortness of breath, an enlarged heart, inability to exercise, generalized weakness and edema" (congestive heart failure)

"Maintaining a tumor-free state"

"Maintain normal bone density in post-menopausal women"

"Maintains healthy lungs in smokers"

"Lowers cholesterol"

"Promotes cholesterol clearance"

Toxemia of pregnancy

Hyperemesis gravidarum

Acute psychosis of pregnancy

Osteoporosis

Alzheimer's disease and other senile dementia

Glaucoma

Arteriosclerotic diseases of coronal, cerebral or peripheral blood vessels

Cystic acne

Severe depression associated with the menstrual cycle

"Helps to maintain normal urine flow in men over 50 years old"

"Promotes good health and prevents the onset of disease"

"Anti-inflammatory"

"To maintain a healthy blood sugar level"

"Controls blood sugar in persons with insufficient insulin" (diabetes)

"Prevents the spread of neoplastic cells" (prevention of cancer metastases)

"Antibiotic" (infections)

"Herbal Prozac" (depression)

Alcohol intoxication

"According to the National Cancer Institute, ingredient X protects smokers' lungs"

"Inhibits platelet aggregation"

"Joint pain"

"Supports the body's antiviral capabilities"

"Helps individuals using antibiotics to maintain normal intestinal flora"

"Deters bacteria from adhering to the wall of the bladder and urinary tract"

"Dietary support during the cold and flu season"

"Promotes general well-being during the cold and flu season"

"To be used as a dietary adjunct in conjunction with your smoking cessation plan"

"Relief of heartburn"; Recurrent" or "persistent" heartburn

"Relief of acid indigestion"

"Helps to reduce difficulty falling asleep"

"Nervous tension headache"

"Helps restore sexual vigor, potency and performance"

"Improves performance, staying power and sexual potency"

"Builds virility and sexual potency"

"To relieve the symptoms of benign prostatic hypertrophy, *e.g.*, urinary urgency and frequency, excessive urinating at night and delayed urination"

"Relieve excessive secretions of the nose and eyes" (hay fever)

"Nasal decongestant" (colds, flu and hay fever)

"Expectorant" (colds, flu and bronchitis)

"Bronchodilator" (asthma)

f. OTHER COMMON VOLUNTARY FOOD CLAIMS

"Natural"

As processed food has become more prevalent, claims that a product is "natural," or contains only "natural ingredients," have become common.

FDA initially took the position that the only food products that could lawfully be characterized as "natural" were raw agricultural commodities sold in their natural state, without any processing. Faced with growing numbers of such claims, however, the agency chose not to expend the resources necessary to enforce this policy or to promulgate regulations defining the term "natural." Beginning in the mid-1970s, FDA concluded that it would prohibit the use of the term "natural" only on products containing artificial color, artificial flavor, or synthetic ingredients such as chemical additives. Later, in the preamble to its final regulations implementing the NLEA, FDA stated that it would construe "natural" to mean that "nothing artificial or synthetic (including all color additives regardless of source) has been included in, or has been added to, a food that would not normally be expected to be in the food." FDA said that it would delay rulemaking to formally define the term. 58 Fed. Reg. 2302, 2407 (Jan. 6, 1993). Although it has never issued a final rule, the agency continues today to cite this 1993 language.

For many years, USDA simply banned any claim using the term "natural." Then, in Policy Memorandum No. 055, issued on November 22, 1982, the department provided that the term "natural" could be used if the product did not contain any artificial flavor, color, chemical preservative, or other artificial or synthetic ingredient, and the product and its ingredients were not more than "minimally processed" (as defined in the document). This policy memorandum required that all products that claimed to be "natural" had to be accompanied by a brief statement explaining what is meant by the term "natural,"—i.e., that it contains no artificial ingredients and is only minimally processed. Today, USDA continues to apply essentially the same policy. *See* USDA, FOOD STANDARDS AND LABELING POLICY BOOK (Rev. Nov./Dec. 2006) ("Natural Claims").

On February 28, 2006, the Sugar Association submitted a citizen petition requesting FDA to define the term "natural" based on the USDA definition. The association was hoping to position cane and beet sugar (as opposed to high fructose corn syrup) as "natural" sweeteners. About a year later, on April 9, 2007, the Sara Lee Corporation filed its own citizen petition asking FDA, jointly with USDA, to adopt the following definition of "natural" as a statement of policy:

> Use of the term "natural" may be used to describe a food or food ingredient that does not contain any artificial flavor or flavoring, coloring ingredient (regardless of source), or any artificial or synthetic ingredient that is included within or not normally expected to be in the product. The degree of processing necessary to produce the food or food ingredient should be considered in determining consumer expectation.

Sara Lee Corp., Citizen Petition Requesting FDA to Develop Requirements for the Use of the term "Natural" Consistent with USDA's Food Safety and Inspection Service at 2, 6 (Apr. 9, 2007). Sara Lee was particularly desirous that the requested new uniform policy reject the position embraced by USDA (but not FDA) that "natural" foods may not contain any ingredients that exhibit antimicrobial (i.e. preservative) effects, even if the preservative in question is naturally derived. *Id.* at 8–9.

In January 2008, a trade publication reported that an FDA representative had stated in an interview that the agency would not be considering the two petitions or the definition of "natural" in the near future because of resource limitations and because the agency did not view the issue as a high priority for consumers. Lorraine Heller, *'Natural' Will Remain Undefined, Says FDA*, FOODNAVIGATOR–USA.COM (Jan. 4, 2008). Nonetheless, FDA has recently sent warning letters to food manufacturers asserting section 403(a)(1) violations for "false and misleading" use of the term "natural." *See, e.g.*, Warning Letter from Alonza E. Cruse, Dist. Dir., FDA L.A. Dist., to Cyrus Teadolmanesh, Pres., Shemshad Food Prods. (Mar. 11, 2011) (synthetic chemical preservative sodium benzoate in lime juice); Warning Letter from Michael W. Roosevelt, Acting Dir., FDA Office of Compliance, to Alex Dzieduszycki, CEO and Pres., Alexia Foods, Inc. (Nov. 16, 2011) (synthetic chemical preservative disodium dihydrogen pyrophosphate in potatoes and mushroom product). Despite the fuzziness of the legal definition of "natural," consumer lawyers have recently brought a spate of lawsuits against food companies alleging the fraudulent use of the term. *See* Ashby Jones, *Is Your Dinner "All Natural"?*, WALL ST. J. (ONLINE), Sept. 20, 2011.

"Fresh"

FDA issued a final regulation defining the term "fresh" in 58 Fed. Reg. 2302, 2401 (Jan. 6, 1993), codified at 21 C.F.R. 101.95. Under the regulation, the term "fresh" may be used only on the label of a raw food that has not been frozen or subjected to any form of thermal processing or any other form of preservation. When the baking industry protested, FDA stated that it "would not object to the use of terms such as 'freshly baked' or 'freshly prepared' on bread that has been preserved. . . ." Letter from Elizabeth Campbell, Acting Dir., FDA CFSAN Office of Food Labeling, to Paul C. Abenante (May 15, 1998). The regulation provides that pasteurized milk is exempt from the ban on the use of "fresh" on thermally processed foods because consumers recognize that milk is nearly always pasteurized. This pasteurization exemption applies only to milk, however. When FDA requested comments on First Amendment issues, Tropicana submitted a letter contending that the agency violated the company's commercial free speech rights by not permitting it to call its pasteurized Pure Premium® not-from-concentrate juices "fresh." Letter from Thomas J. Ryan, Senior Vice President and General Counsel, Tropicana Prods., Inc., to Dockets Management Branch (HFA–305), FDA (Jan. 29, 2003).

In *Abruzzi Foods, Inc. v. Pasta & Cheese, Inc.*, 986 F.2d 605 (1st Cir. 1993), the court held that the plaintiff in a Lanham Act case failed to sustain its argument that a competitor's use of the term "fresh" for refrigerated pasta in extended shelf-life packaging is unfair or deceptive. The National Advertising Division of the Council of Better Business Bureaus has determined that the term "fresh" may describe the ingredients used to prepare a processed product if they refer only to the ingredients and do not imply that the final product is unprocessed. *Del Monte Foods, Inc.*, 28 NAD Case Reports 21 (Mar. 1998).

The USDA policy of allowing chilled but unfrozen poultry to be labeled as "fresh" was severely criticized at a congressional hearing on June 16, 1994. In 1995, USDA issued final regulations providing that poultry products ever held at temperatures below 0° must be labeled as "frozen," that those held between 0°F and 26°F must be labeled as "hard chilled," and that those above 26°F may be labeled as "fresh." 60 Fed. Reg. 44396 (Aug. 25, 1995). In the 1997 appropriations legislation, however, Congress ordered USDA to delete the term "hard chilled" and not impose any specific alternative labeling on these mid-range poultry products. USDA subsequently issued revised regulations complying with these congressional instructions. 61 Fed. Reg. 66198 (Dec. 17, 1996), codified at 9 C.F.R. 381.129(b)(6).

"Organic"

In the Organic Foods Production Act of 1990, 104 Stat. 3359, 3935, Congress directed USDA to establish national standards for the certification of foods as "organic." The statute set forth three objectives: (1) to establish national standards for the marketing of agricultural products as organically produced products, (2) to assure consumers that such products meet a consistent standard, and (3) to facilitate improved interstate commerce in food that is organically produced. After lengthy meetings of the National Organic Standards Board, USDA proposed regulations to establish the National Organic Program in 62 Fed. Reg.

65850 (Dec. 16, 1997). Attacked as allowing excessive nonorganic content, including genetically modified organisms (GMOs), that proposal was withdrawn and a new proposal was published in 65 Fed. Reg. 13512 (Mar. 13, 2000). Final regulations were promulgated in 65 Fed. Reg. 80548 (Dec. 21, 2000), 7 C.F.R. Part 205.

The National Organic Program regulations describe approved methods of production and handling of organic crops and livestock that foster cycling of resources, promote ecological balance, and conserve biodiversity. See 7 C.F.R. pt. 205 Subpart C. In general, the regulations also prohibit the use of synthetic ingredients and substances (including synthetic pesticides and petroleum-based fertilizers) unless they are explicitly permitted, and they allow the use of nonsynthetic substances unless they are specifically forbidden. 7 CFR 205.105(a)–(d).The regulations ban the use of ionizing radiation and sewage sludge. *Id.* (f)–(g). In addition, "organic" foods must be produced without the use of "excluded methods," which are defined to include a variety of nontraditional methods used to genetically modify organisms. 21 C.F.R. 105(e), 205.2. Organic producers must implement measures to prevent contact with nonorganic products and prohibited substances. 7 C.F.R. 205.272. The USDA has made clear that organic certification is process-based and that inadvertent contamination with GMOs thus does not constitute their prohibited "use." Miles McEvoy, USDA Deputy Adm'r, Policy Memorandum on "Genetically modified organisms" (Apr. 15, 2011).

The USDA regulations recognize four organic product categories: (1) "100 percent organic," (2) "organic" (95–99 percent organic), (3) "made with organic ingredients" (70–90 percent organic), and (4) products for which the organic status of particular ingredients may be indicated only in the ingredients statement (below 70 percent organic). To be labeled as organic a product must be produced and handled only by operations certified by an accredited certifying agent. Use of the term "organic" was further narrowed by the decision in *Harvey v. Veneman*, 396 F.3d 28 (1st Cir. 2005), which held that the statute precludes designating any food product as organic if it contains any synthetic ingredient. However, Congress overruled this aspect of *Harvey* in 119 Stat. 2120, 2153, 2165 (2005), and USDA thus did not revise its regulations to prohibit the use of all synthetic ingredients in organic products. USDA implemented other aspects of the *Harvey* decision and the new statutory provisions in 71 Fed. Reg. 32803 (June 7, 2006).

NOTES

1. *USDA Grade.* Under the Agricultural Marketing Act of 1946, 60 Stat. 1082, 1087, codified in 7 U.S.C. 1621 *et seq.*, USDA is authorized to establish a voluntary system of food grading, inspection, and certification. The regulations governing this program appear at 7 C.F.R. Part 51 *et seq.* Producers who desire to participate must request, and pay for, the USDA inspection and grading service. The USDA's Agricultural Marketing Service (AMS) quality standards, which are established by notice-and-comment rulemaking, relate to food quality and include such factors as color, size, shape, flavor, texture, maturity, and defects. The USDA grade

assigned to a lot of food can then be used by the producer in labeling. Thus, the USDA grading system serves two purposes. First, it allows an independent quality determination on the basis of which wholesale buyers can establish prices. Second, it provides useful information to retail consumers. *See* GAO, FOOD LABELING: GOALS, SHORTCOMINGS, AND PROPOSED CHANGES, Ch. 5, No. NWD–75–19 (Jan. 19, 1975). Although use of USDA grade labeling is subject to section 403(a) of the Act, FDA has never participated in this program or objected to inclusion of grade information in food labels.

2. *USDA Production/Marketing Claims.* In 74 Fed. Reg. 3541 (Jan. 21, 2009), the Agricultural Marketing Service established a voluntary standard for a "naturally raised" marketing claim that applies to livestock that were raised without growth promotants or antibiotics and that were not fed animal byproducts. Livestock producers may request to have their "naturally raised" claims verified by the USDA.

In 67 Fed. Reg. 79552 (Dec. 30, 2002), USDA proposed to establish minimum requirements for a number of other claims commonly used for livestock, including "no added hormones," "grass fed," and "free range." Final action has not been taken on this proposal, and a USDA "Fact Sheet" for consumers on meat and poultry labeling terms defines some of these claims in ways not entirely consistent with the proposed rule. For example, "free range" is defined in the 2002 proposal to include only "[l]ivestock that have had continuous and unconfined access to pasture throughout their life cycle," whereas the Fact Sheet states merely, "Producers must demonstrate to the Agency that the poultry has been allowed access to the outside." *Id.* at 79554; USDA–FSIS, "Fact Sheet: Meat and Poultry Labeling Terms" (rev. Apr. 12, 2011).

3. *Kosher Labeling.* Section 403(a)'s prohibition against false or misleading labeling applies to any statement made in food labeling. FDA initially stated in 21 C.F.R. 101.29 that a food may lawfully be described as "kosher" only if it meets the applicable religious dietary requirements. The agency discouraged use of the phrase "kosher style" because it may mislead purchasers into believing that the product is in fact kosher. It explained the two symbols used to signify compliance with Jewish dietary laws in FDA, SYMBOLS ON FOOD LABELS, DHEW Pub. No. (FDA) 76–2021 (rev. Dec. 1975):

The symbol consisting of the letter "J" inside the letter "O" is one whose use is authorized by the Union of Orthodox Jewish Congregations of America, more familiarly known as the Orthodox Union, for use on foods which comply with the Jewish dietary laws. Detailed information regarding the significance and use of this symbol may be obtained from the headquarters of that organization at 116 E. 27th St., New York, New York 10016.

The symbol comprising the letter "K" inside the letter "O" is one whose use is authorized by "O.K." Laboratories, 105 Hudson St., New York, New York 10013, to indicate that the food is "kosher," that is, that it complies with the Jewish dietary laws and its processing has been under the direction of a rabbi.

Because of concern about the constitutionality of its regulation of kosher labeling, FDA revoked 21 C.F.R. 101.29 in 1997. 62 Fed. Reg. 43071, 43072 (Aug. 12, 1997). State laws governing kosher labeling have been struck down as an unconstitutional violation of the separation of church and state. *See* Gerald F. Masoudi, *Kosher Food Regulation and the Religion Clauses of the First Amendment*, 60 U. CHI. L. REV. 667 (1993); Stephen F. Rosenthal, *Food for Thought: Kosher Fraud Laws and the Religion Clauses of the First Amendment*, 65 G.W. L. REV. 951 (1997).

4.   *Voluntary Geographic Designation Labeling.* For over a century, federal regulatory officials have worried about false or misleading claims regarding the geographic origin of food products. A 1902 statute provided that no person may sell "any dairy or food product which shall be falsely labeled or branded as to the State or Territory in which they are made, produced, or grown . . ." 32 Stat. 632 (1902), 21 U.S.C. 16. FDA found it unnecessary to issue regulations implementing this statute prior to the early 1970s, when it proposed and finalized a rule regarding geographical origin labeling in response to both domestic and foreign complaints. 36 Fed. Reg. 9444 (May 25, 1971), codified at 21 C.F.R. 101.18(c). States and foreign nations have independently sought to protect the use of their geographic designations. *See* H. David Gold, *Legal Strategies to Address the Misrepresentation of Vermont Maple Syrup*, 58 FOOD & DRUG L.J. 93 (2004); Raffi Melkonian, *The History and Future of Geographical Indications in Europe and the United States* (2005), in Chapter V(B)(1) of the Electronic Book.

5.   *Size and Weight Descriptors.* Section 4(b) of the Fair Packaging and Labeling Act prohibits the use of "qualifying words or phrases" in conjunction with the net quantity of contents statement, but permits such words to be used elsewhere in labeling. Section 5(c)(1) of the FPLA authorizes FDA to establish standards for characterizing the size of packages, but the agency has not exercised this authority. Congress designed both provisions to deal with the common practice of characterizing the size of consumer product packages with such terms as "giant" or "jumbo."

g.   FTC REGULATION OF FOOD ADVERTISING

Section 5 of the Federal Trade Commission Act provides that "unfair or deceptive acts or practices in or affecting commerce, are declared unlawful." 15 U.S.C. 45 (2000), 38 Stat. 717 (1914). The Wheeler–Lea Amendments of 1938 added sections 14 and 15, which expressly prohibit any food advertisement, other than labeling, which is "misleading in a material respect." 52 Stat. 111 (1938). From its inception, the FTC has regarded false or misleading labeling and advertising of food products as unfair acts or practices that violate section 5, and the courts have upheld that position. *E.g., Fresh Grown Preserve Corp. v. FTC*, 125 F.2d 917 (2d Cir. 1942), *FTC v. Good–Grape Co.*, 45 F.2d 70 (6th Cir. 1930); *Royal Baking Powder Co. v. FTC*, 281 F. 744 (2d Cir. 1922). For an overview of the FTC regulation of food advertising, see Peter Barton Hutt, *Government Regulation of Health Claims in Food Labeling and Advertising*, 41 FOOD DRUG COSM. L.J. 3, 9–20 (1986).

The FTC has issued three important policy statements describing the circumstances under which an advertising claim will be found to violate the FTC Act. In a letter to Congress in December 1980, reprinted in 104 F.T.C. 1070 (1984), the Commission stated that, to constitute an illegal "unfair act or practice," an advertisement must be evaluated to determine whether it results in substantial consumer injury, violates public policy, or constitutes unethical or unscrupulous conduct. In October 1983, in another letter to Congress, reprinted in 103 F.T.C. 174 (1984), FTC stated that, in evaluating whether an advertisement violates the Act, the Commission will examine the advertisement "from the perspective of a consumer acting reasonably in the circumstances." And in a 1984 policy statement, reprinted in 104 F.T.C. 839 (1984), the Commission reaffirmed the requirement that advertisers must "have a reasonable basis for advertising claims before they are disseminated" and stated that "what constitutes a reasonable basis depends, as it does in an unfairness analysis, on a number of factors relevant to the benefits and costs of substantiating a particular claim."

Based upon these policies, the FTC encouraged what it regarded as nondeceptive disease prevention claims when they first appeared in food advertising in the mid-1980s. The preamble to FDA's reproposed regulations on disease prevention claims for food attempted to reconcile the obvious disparity between the flexible FTC "reasonable basis" standard for advertising claims and FDA's more stringent standard of scientific proof for labeling claims in the following terms:

> FDA is not convinced that [FTC's "reasonable basis"] standard is adequate for determining the appropriateness of claims on the food label. As several comments pointed out, it is important that consumers maintain confidence in the food label. Consumers view food labeling as more reliable and trustworthy than food advertising. The existence of this dichotomy in consumer perception of the information from these two sources is supported by the results of several surveys and confirmed by a number of experts in the area of advertising and communication.

> Food labeling has a high degree of acceptance among the general public. For example, when asked in a 1984 Roper Survey what sources of information about the nutritional content of food they thought most useful, labels on food packages were the most widely used source, mentioned by 57 percent of the public. Advertisements were considered the most useful source by only 4 percent. These results are essentially unchanged from a 1976 survey. Similarly, a 1980 FDA survey indicated that the perceived honesty/integrity/truthfulness of the food label is very high. Only 1 percent of respondents reported ever having bought a food product that was falsely labeled. In a 1981 survey about what FDA activities were most worthwhile, the two highest rated activities (tied for first) were "making sure food is safe to eat" and "making sure food labeling is honest."

55 Fed. Reg. 5176, 5186 (Feb. 13, 1990).

Following enactment of the Nutrition Labeling and Education Act of 1990, the FTC published its *Enforcement Policy Statement on Food*

Advertising to emphasize that it would follow FDA's lead on nutrient descriptors and disease prevention claims for food. 59 Fed. Reg. 28388 (June 1, 1994). Some influence still runs in the opposite direction, however. FDA has adopted the FTC's "reasonable person" standard, and it has also raised the question whether the FTC "competent and reliable scientific evidence" standard should be used in evaluating health claims. 67 Fed. Reg. 78002, 78003–04 (Dec. 20, 2002), 69 Fed. Reg. 64962 (Nov. 9, 2004).

Recently, FTC embraced an extremely rigorous health claims substantiation standard in a widely publicized dispute concerning heart disease and prostate cancer claims made in advertising for POM Wonderful® products. *In the Matter of POM Wonderful*, 2013–1 Trade Cases P 78220 (Jan. 16, 2013). The Commission held that two well-designed, well-conducted, double-blind, randomized controlled clinical trials are required to substantiate claims that a food can treat, prevent or reduce the risk of a "serious disease." FDA has never articulated such a demanding standard, at least for NLEA disease prevention claims. In a concurring statement, Commissioner Ohlhausen pointed to another apparent difference between FTC's and FDA's approach: "I am concerned that the majority's interpretation of certain exhibits blurs [the boundaries between health claims and structure/function claims] and creates an inconsistency between FTC advertising requirements and FDA food labeling and advertising requirements by concluding that the mere mention of 'health' or healthy functioning can imply a disease-related efficacy (*i.e.*, a health claim in FDA terms) and that the mere mention of scientific evidence can imply a related establishment claim."

4. LABELING OF GENETICALLY MODIFIED FOODS

In 1953, James Watson and Francis Crick discovered and described the double-helix structure of deoxyribonucleic acid (DNA) and thus opened the field of molecular biology. In the early 1970s, scientists developed the techniques for cutting DNA molecules with a restriction enzyme, inserting foreign DNA, placing the recombined (recombinant) DNA into a host microorganism, and then replicating (cloning) the recombined DNA through fermentation of the microorganism. These remarkable technical achievements laid the foundations for commercial biotechnology. Since 1996, genes have been transferred into a growing number of commercially-available food crops from bacteria, other plants, and even animals. This technology is used to impart various traits to food plants, most commonly resistance to pests and viruses and resistance to pesticides and herbicides. Genetic modification of plants can also be used, for example, to increase tolerance to environmental conditions and to increase nutritive value and productivity. More than 90 percent of the American soybean crop is now genetically modified. The same is true for cotton, and corn is close behind. We also appear to be on the verge of the legal sale of food derived from transgenic food animals. *See infra* p. 1529.

FDA's regulation of the safety of genetically modified organisms (GMOs) will be considered in detail below. *See infra* p. 592. Here, we will address the legal issues surrounding proposed and actual government requirements to disclose the presence of GMOs in food and also examine the question of whether the government can prohibit voluntary claims like "GMO free." The topic of GMO labeling presents a good review of various general issues of food labeling, including mandatory statements, voluntary statements, and the role of the First Amendment.

————

In 1992, FDA issued a comprehensive policy statement on the regulation of genetically modified plant varieties—a statement that still describes the agency's thinking on this subject more than twenty years later. Although this document focused primarily on safety issues, it also addressed GMO labeling.

Food and Drug Administration, Statement of Policy: Foods Derived From New Plant Varieties

57 Fed. Reg. 22984 (May 29, 1992).

. . . .

Under this policy, foods, such as fruits, vegetables, grains, and their byproducts, derived from plant varieties developed by the new methods of genetic modification are regulated within the existing framework of the act, FDA's implementing regulations, and current practice, utilizing an approach identical in principle to that applied to foods developed by traditional plant breeding. The regulatory status of a food, irrespective of the method by which it is developed, is dependent upon objective characteristics of the food and the intended use of the food (or its components). . . .

Plant breeding is the science of combining desirable genetic traits into a variety that can be used in agriculture. The desired traits can be broadly divided into two classes: Those that affect agronomic characteristics of the plant, and those that affect quality characteristics of the food. Agronomic characteristics include those affecting yield; resistance to diseases, insects, and herbicides; and ability to thrive under various adverse environmental conditions. Quality characteristics include those affecting processing, preservation, nutrition, and flavor.

The genetic modification techniques used to develop new plant varieties constitute a continuum. Traditional breeding typically consists of hybridization between varieties of the same species and screening for progeny with desired characteristics. Such hybridizations only can introduce traits found in close relatives. Breeders have developed or adopted a number of techniques to expand the range of genetic variation available to them. These techniques introduce variation either by using mutagenesis to alter the genome or by introducing or modifying DNA segments, including DNA segments derived from other organisms. . . .

Recombinant DNA techniques involve the isolation and subsequent introduction of discrete DNA segments containing the gene(s) of interest into recipient (host) plants. The DNA segments can come from any organism (microbial, animal, or plant). In theory, essentially any trait whose gene has been identified can be introduced into virtually any plant, and can be introduced without extraneous unwanted genetic material. Since these techniques are more precise [than mutagenic techniques and other gene transfer techniques], they increase the potential for safe, better-characterized, and more predictable foods.

DNA segments introduced using the new techniques insert semi-randomly into the chromosome, frequently in tandem multiple copies, and sometimes in more than one site on the chromosome. Both the number of copies of the gene and its location in the chromosome can affect its level of expression, as well as the expression of other genes in the plant. To ensure homozygosity and to enhance the stability of the line and the ability to cross the trait into other lines, the breeder will often perform a limited number of back crosses to ensure that the plant line has the new trait inserted in only one location in the chromosome.

Additionally, as with other breeding techniques, the phenotypic effects of a new trait may not always be completely predictable in the new genetic background of the host. Therefore, it is common practice for breeders using recombinant DNA techniques to cross the new trait into a number of hosts to find the best genetic background for expression of the new trait. Currently, for most crops only a few lines or varieties of any species are amendable to the use of recombinant DNA techniques. Once the desired trait is introduced into a line amenable to the technique, it must then be crossed by traditional means to other desired lines or varieties. . . .

Recombinant DNA techniques are used to achieve the same types of goals as traditional techniques: The development of new plant varieties with enhanced agronomic and quality characteristics. . . .

FDA has received several inquiries concerning labeling requirements for foods derived from new plant varieties developed by recombinant DNA techniques. Section 403(j) of the act requires that a producer of a food product describe the product by its common or usual name or in the absence thereof, an appropriately descriptive term and reveal all facts that are material in light of representations made or suggested by labeling or with respect to consequences which may result from use. [FD&C Act 403(a), 201(n).] Thus, consumers must be informed, by appropriate labeling, if a food derived from a new plant variety differs from its traditional counterpart such that the common or usual name no longer applies to the new food, or if a safety or usage issue exists to which consumers must be alerted.

For example, if a tomato has had a peanut protein introduced into it and there is insufficient information to demonstrate that the introduced protein could not cause an allergic reaction in a susceptible population, a label declaration would be required to alert consumers who are allergic to peanuts so they could avoid that tomato, even if its basic taste and texture remained unchanged. Such information would be a material fact whose omission may make the label of the tomato misleading under section 403(a) of the act.

FDA has also been asked whether foods developed using techniques such as recombinant DNA techniques would be required to bear special labeling to reveal that fact to consumers. To date, FDA has not considered the methods used in the development of a new plant variety (such as hybridization, chemical and radiation-induced mutagenesis, protoplast fusion, embryo rescue, somaclonal variation, or any other method) to be material information within the meaning of section 201(n) of the act. As discussed above, FDA believes that the new techniques are extensions at the molecular level of traditional methods and will be used to achieve the same goals as pursued with traditional plant breeding. The agency is not aware of any information showing that foods derived by these new methods differ from other foods in any meaningful or uniform way, or that, as a class, foods developed by the new techniques present any different or greater safety concern than foods developed by traditional plant breeding. For this reason, the agency does not believe that the method of development of a new plant variety (including the use of new techniques including recombinant DNA techniques) is normally material information within the meaning of [FD&C Act 201(n)] and would not usually be required to be disclosed in labeling for the food. . . .

————

A coalition of consumer advocates brought suit to challenge the legality of the May 1992 FDA policy statement with respect to labeling.

Alliance for Bio-Integrity v. Shalala

116 F. Supp. 2d 166 (D.D.C. 2000).

■ KOLLAR–KOTELLY, DISTRICT JUDGE.

Technological advances have dramatically increased our ability to manipulate our environment, including the foods we consume. One of these advances, recombinant deoxyribonucleic acid (rDNA) technology, has enabled scientists to alter the genetic composition of organisms by mixing genes on the cellular and molecular level in order to create new breeds of plants for human and animal consumption. These new breeds may be designed to repel pests, retain their freshness for a longer period of time, or contain more intense flavor and/or nutritional value. Much controversy has attended such developments in biotechnology, and in particular the production, sale, and trade of genetically modified organisms and foods. The above-captioned lawsuit represents one articulation of this controversy. . . .

Plaintiffs have . . . challenged the [FDA May 1992] Statement of Policy's failure to require labeling for genetically engineered foods, for which FDA relied on the presumption that most genetically modified food ingredients would be GRAS [generally recognized as safe]. Plaintiffs claim that FDA should have considered the widespread consumer interest in having genetically engineered foods labeled, as well as the special concerns of religious groups and persons with allergies in having these foods labeled.

The FDCA, 21 U.S.C. § 321(n) [FD&C Act 201(n)], grants the FDA limited authority to require labeling. In general, foods shall be deemed misbranded if their labeling "fails to reveal facts . . . material with respect to consequences which may result from the use of the article to which the labeling . . . relates under the conditions of use prescribed in the labeling . . . or under such conditions of use as are customary or usual." Plaintiffs challenge the FDA's interpretation of the term "material." Thus, the question is . . . one of statutory interpretation. As is apparent from the statutory language, Congress has not squarely addressed whether materiality pertains only to safety concerns or whether it also includes consumer interest. Accordingly, interpretation of the § 321(n)'s broad language is left to the agency.

Because Congress has not spoken directly to the issue, this Court must determine whether the agency's interpretation of the statute is reasonable. *See Chevron, U.S.A. v. Natural Resources Defense Council,* 467 U.S. 837, 864 (1984). . . . Even if the agency's interpretation is not "the best or most natural by grammatical or other standards," if the interpretation is reasonable, then it is entitled to deference.

The FDA takes the position that no "material change," under § 321(n), has occurred in the rDNA derived foods at issue here. Absent unique risks to consumer health or uniform changes to food derived through rDNA technology, the FDA does not read § 321(n) to authorize an agency imposed food labeling requirement. More specifically irksome to the Plaintiffs, the FDA does not read § 321(n) to authorize labeling requirements solely because of consumer demand. The FDA's exclusion of consumer interest from the factors which determine whether a change is "material" constitutes a reasonable interpretation of the statute. Moreover, it is doubtful whether the FDA would even have the power under the FDCA to require labeling in a situation where the sole justification for such a requirement is consumer demand.

Plaintiffs fail to understand the limitation on the FDA's power to consider consumer demand when making labeling decisions because they fail to recognize that the determination that a product differs materially from the type of product it purports to be is a factual predicate to the requirement of labeling. Only once materiality has been established may the FDA consider consumer opinion to determine whether a label is required to disclose a material fact. Thus, "if there is a [material] difference, and consumers would likely want to know about the difference, then labeling is appropriate. If, however, the product does not differ in any significant way from what it purports to be, then it would be misbranding to label the product as different, even if consumers misperceived the product as different." *Stauber v. Shalala,* 895 F. Supp. 1178, 1193 (W.D. Wis. 1995). The FDA has already determined that, in general, rDNA modification does not "materially" alter foods, and as discussed, *supra,* this determination is entitled to deference. Given these facts, the FDA lacks a basis upon which it can legally mandate labeling, regardless of the level of consumer demand.

Plaintiffs also contend that the process[10] of genetic modification is a "material fact" under § 321(n) which mandates special labeling, implying that there are new risks posed to the consumer. However, the FDA has determined that foods produced through rDNA techniques do not "present any different or greater safety concern than foods developed by traditional plant breeding," and concluded that labeling was not warranted. That determination, unless irrational, is entitled to deference. Accordingly, there is little basis upon which this Court could

---

[10] Disclosure of the conditions or methods of manufacture has long been deemed unnecessary under the law. The Supreme Court reasoned in 1924, "When considered independently of the product, the method of manufacture is not material. The act requires no disclosure concerning it." *U.S.* v. *Ninety–Five Barrels (More or Less) Alleged Apple Cider Vinegar,* 265 U.S. 438, 445. . . .

find that the FDA's interpretation of § 321(n) is arbitrary and capricious. . . .

NOTE

New Petition for Mandatory Labeling. In October 2011, a coalition of consumer and environmental organizations and organic food producers filed a petition with FDA requesting that the agency abandon its 1992 Statement of Policy, issue a new policy declaring that the production of food by genetic engineering is "material" under FD&C Act 201(n), and promulgate a new regulation requiring several types of labeling disclosure of "genetic engineering." Petition Seeking Mandatory Labeling for Genetically Engineered Foods, http://gmolabeling.files.wordpress.com /2011/10/ge-labeling-petition–10–11–2011–final.pdf. The petition cited a number of recent polls in which over 90 percent of respondents supported mandatory labeling of genetically modified foods. Encouraged by an associated "Just Label It" internet campaign, more than a million people have expressed their support for this petition online. To date, FDA has not acted on the petition. But prospects for the success of this campaign seemed to improve in early 2013, when reports emerged that executives from Wal-mart and approximately 20 major food companies suggested, in a meeting with FDA and the co-chair of the "Just Label It" campaign, that they would no longer oppose a federal GMO labeling requirement. *See* Stephanie Strom, *Companies Weigh Federal Labels for Gene–Engineered Ingredients*, N.Y. TIMES, Feb. 1, 2013, at B1.

————

Despite FDA's failure to mandate special labeling of foods developed using bioengineering, many manufacturers want to voluntary disclose the presence or (especially) the absence of genetically modified ingredients. In 2011, following three public meetings, the agency issued the following draft guidance. Although the guidance addresses both voluntary disclosures of the use of biotechnology and voluntary claims of the absence of such use, this excerpt includes the discussion only of the latter.

Draft Guidance for Industry: Voluntary Labeling Indicating Whether Foods Have or Have Not Been Developed Using Bioengineering; Draft Guidance

Jan. 2001.

. . . The agency is still not aware of any data or other information that would form a basis for concluding that the fact that a food or its ingredients was produced using bioengineering is a material fact that must be disclosed under sections 403(a) and 201(n) of the act. FDA is therefore reaffirming its decision to not require special labeling of all bioengineered foods. . . .

While the use of bioengineering is not a material fact, many consumers are interested in the information, and some manufacturers may want to respond to this consumer desire. . . .

In determining whether a food is misbranded, FDA would review label statements about the use of bioengineering to develop a food or its ingredients under sections 403(a) and 201(n) of the act. . . .

Terms that are frequently mentioned in discussions about labeling foods with respect to bioengineering include "GMO free" and "GM free." . . . Consumer focus group data indicate that consumers do not understand the acronyms "GMO" and "GM" and prefer label statements with spelled out words that mean bioengineering.

Terms like "not genetically modified" and "GMO free," that include the word "modified" are not technically accurate unless they are clearly in a context that refers to bioengineering technology. "Genetic modification" means the alteration of the genotype of a plant using any technique, new or traditional. "Modification" has a broad context that means the alteration in the composition of food that results from adding, deleting, or changing hereditary traits, irrespective of the method. . . . Most, if not all, cultivated food crops have been genetically modified. Data indicate that consumers do not have a good understanding that essentially all food crops have been genetically modified and that bioengineering technology is only one of a number of technologies used to genetically modify crops. Thus, while it is accurate to say that a bioengineered food was "genetically modified," it likely would be inaccurate to state that a food that had not been produced using biotechnology was "not genetically modified" without clearly providing a context so that the consumer can understand that the statement applies to bioengineering.

The term "GMO free" may be misleading on most foods, because most foods do not contain organisms (seeds and foods like yogurt that contain microorganisms are exceptions). It would likely be misleading to suggest that a food that ordinarily would not contain entire "organisms" is "organism free."

There is potential for the term "free" in a claim for absence of bioengineering to be inaccurate. Consumers assume that "free" of bioengineered material means that "zero" bioengineered material is present. Because of the potential for adventitious presence of bioengineered material, it may be necessary to conclude that the accuracy of the term "free" can only be ensured when there is a definition or threshold above which the term could not be used. FDA does not have information with which to establish a threshold level of bioengineered constituents or ingredients in foods for the statement "free of bioengineered material." . . . The agency suggests that the term "free" either not be used in bioengineering label statements or that it be in a context that makes clear that a zero level of bioengineered material is not implied. However, statements that the food or its ingredients, as appropriate, was not developed using bioengineering would avoid or minimize such implications. For example,

- "We do not use ingredients that were produced using biotechnology;"

- "This oil is made from soybeans that were not genetically engineered;" or

- "Our tomato growers do not plant seeds developed using biotechnology."

A statement that a food was not bioengineered or does not contain bioengineered ingredients may be misleading if it implies that the labeled food is superior to foods that are not so labeled. FDA has concluded that the use or absence of use of bioengineering in the production of a food or ingredient does not, in and of itself, mean that there is a material difference in the food. Therefore, a label statement that expresses or implies that a food is superior (e.g., safer or of higher quality) because it is not bioengineered would be misleading. The agency will evaluate the entire label and labeling in determining whether a label statement is in a context that implies that the food is superior. . . .

Further, a statement may be misleading if it suggests that a food or ingredient itself is not bioengineered, when there are no marketed bioengineered varieties of that category of foods or ingredients. For example, it would be misleading to state "not produced through biotechnology" on the label of green beans, when there are no marketed bioengineered green beans. . . . "[T]he statement "green beans are not produced using biotechnology" would not imply that this manufacturer's product is different from other green beans.

A manufacturer who claims that a food or its ingredients, including foods such as raw agricultural commodities, is not bioengineered should be able to substantiate that the claim is truthful and not misleading. . . . Because appropriately validated testing methods are not currently available for many foods, it is likely that it would be easier to document handling practices and procedures to substantiate a claim about how the food was processed than to substantiate a "free" claim.

In the absence of federal laws or regulations requiring mandatory labeling of foods produced with the use of genetic engineering, states have stepped in. Labeling bills were proposed in more than a dozen states in 2011 and 2012. In November 2012, the voters of California, by 53.1 percent to 46.9 percent, rejected Proposition 37, a ballot initiative that would have mandated labeling of genetically modified foods. Mark Lifsher, *Prop. 37 Backers Eye Other States; Despite Defeat They Will Seek Food Labeling Rules in Washington, Oregon and the U.S.*, L.A. TIMES, Nov. 8, 2012, at B1. In June 2013, Connecticut became the first state to pass a bill that would require GMO labeling—but only if four other states do likewise. Stephanie Strom, *Connecticut Approves Genetic Labeling*, N.Y. TIMES, June 4, 2013, at B4. If and when any state GMO labeling requirement goes into effect, however, it is likely to be subject to First Amendment challenges. In the following case, presenting a similar issue, the court struck down a state labeling mandate.

In 1993, when FDA approved the use of a recombinant bovine growth hormone (BGH) called Bovine Somatotropin (BST) to increase milk production in cows, the agency took the position that because BST is safe and undetectable in the milk itself, its use need not be labeled.

The State of Vermont, however, enacted a law to require disclosure of the use of BST. *See* 6 V.S.A. § 2760 (West 1997). A group of dairy and other food associations challenged the state law on First Amendment grounds.

International Dairy Foods Association v. Amestoy
92 F.3d 67 (2d Cir. 1996).

■ ALTIMARI, CIRCUIT JUDGE. . . .

In 1993, the federal Food and Drug Administration ("FDA") approved the use of recombinant Bovine Somatotropin ("rBST") (also known as recombinant Bovine Growth Hormone ("rBGH")), a synthetic growth hormone that increases milk production by cows. It is undisputed that the dairy products derived from herds treated with rBST are indistinguishable from products derived from untreated herds; consequently, the FDA declined to require the labeling of products derived from cows receiving the supplemental hormone.

In April 1994, defendant-appellee the State of Vermont ("Vermont") enacted a statute requiring that "[i]f rBST has been used in the production of milk or a milk product for retail sale in this state, the retail milk or milk product shall be labeled as such." The State of Vermont's Commissioner of Agriculture ("Commissioner") subsequently promulgated regulations giving those dairy manufacturers who use rBST four labeling options, among them the posting of a sign to the following effect in any store selling dairy products:

rBST Information

THE PRODUCTS IN THIS CASE THAT CONTAIN OR MAY CONTAIN MILK FROM rBST–TREATED COWS EITHER (1) STATE ON THE PACKAGE THAT rBST HAS BEEN OR MAY HAVE BEEN USED, OR (2) ARE IDENTIFIED BY A BLUE SHELF LABEL LIKE THIS *[BLUE RECTANGLE]* OR (3) A BLUE STICKER ON THE PACKAGE LIKE THIS.
[BLUE DOT]

The United States Food and Drug Administration has determined that there is no significant difference between milk from treated and untreated cows. It is the law of Vermont that products made from the milk of rBST-treated cows be labeled to help consumers make informed shopping decisions.

(6 V.S.A. Section 2754)

Appellants filed suit in April 1994, asserting that the statute was unconstitutional. In June 1995, the dairy manufacturers moved for preliminary injunctive relief, seeking to enjoin enforcement of the statute. The dairy manufacturers alleged that the Vermont statute (1) infringed their protected rights under the First Amendment to the Constitution and (2) violated the Constitution's Commerce Clause, U.S. Const., Art. 1, § 8. Following an extensive hearing, the United States District Court for the District of Vermont (Murtha, C.J.), denied appellants' motion. *See* 898 F. Supp. at 254. The dairy manufacturers now appeal.

Because we find that the dairy manufacturers are entitled to an injunction on First Amendment grounds, we do not reach their claims made pursuant to the Commerce Clause. . . .

The right not to speak inheres in political and commercial speech alike, and extends to statements of fact as well as statements of opinion. If, however, as Vermont maintains, its labeling law compels appellants to engage in purely commercial speech, the statute must meet a less rigorous test. . . .

It is not enough for appellants to show as they have, that they were irreparably harmed by the statute; because the dairy manufacturers challenge government action taken in the public interest, they must also show a likelihood of success on the merits. We find that such success is likely.

In [*Central Hudson Gas & Elec. Corp. v. Public Serv. Comm'r*, 447 U.S. 557 (1980)], the Supreme Court articulated a four-part analysis for determining whether a government restriction on commercial speech is permissible. . . . We need not address the controversy concerning the nature of the speech in question—commercial or political—because we find that Vermont fails to meet the less stringent constitutional requirements applicable to compelled commercial speech.

Under *Central Hudson*, we must determine: (1) whether the expression concerns lawful activity and is not misleading; (2) whether the government's interest is substantial; (3) whether the labeling law directly serves the asserted interest; and (4) whether the labeling law is no more extensive than necessary.

In our view, Vermont has failed to establish the second prong of the *Central Hudson* test, namely that its interest is substantial. In making this determination, we rely only upon those interests set forth by Vermont before the district court. As the district court made clear, Vermont "does not claim that health or safety concerns prompted the passage of the Vermont Labeling Law," but instead defends the statute on the basis of "strong consumer interest and the public's 'right to know'. . . ." These interests are insufficient to justify compromising protected constitutional rights.

Vermont's failure to defend its constitutional intrusion on the ground that it negatively impacts public health is easily understood. After exhaustive studies, the FDA has "concluded that rBST has no appreciable effect on the composition of milk produced by treated cows, and that there are no human safety or health concerns associated with food products derived from cows treated with rBST." Because bovine somatotropin ("BST") appears naturally in cows, and because there are no BST receptors in a cow's mammary glands, only trace amounts of BST can be detected in milk, whether or not the cows received the supplement. Moreover, it is undisputed that neither consumers nor scientists can distinguish rBST-derived milk from milk produced by an untreated cow. Indeed, the already extensive record in this case contains no scientific evidence from which an objective observer could conclude that rBST has any impact at all on dairy products. It is thus plain that Vermont could not justify the statute on the basis of "real" harms.

We do not doubt that Vermont's asserted interest, the demand of its citizenry for such information, is genuine; reluctantly, however, we conclude that it is inadequate. We are aware of no case in which consumer interest alone was sufficient to justify requiring a product's manufacturers to publish the functional equivalent of a warning about a production method that has no discernable impact on a final product.

Although the Court is sympathetic to the Vermont consumers who wish to know which products may derive from rBST-treated herds, their desire is insufficient to permit the State of Vermont to compel the dairy manufacturers to speak against their will. Were consumer interest alone sufficient, there is no end to the information that states could require manufacturers to disclose about their production methods. For instance, with respect to cattle, consumers might reasonably evince an interest in knowing which grains herds were fed, with which medicines they were treated, or the age at which they were slaughtered. Absent, however, some indication that this information bears on a reasonable concern for human health or safety or some other sufficiently substantial governmental concern, the manufacturers cannot be compelled to disclose it. Instead, those consumers interested in such information should exercise the power of their purses by buying products from manufacturers who voluntarily reveal it.

Accordingly, we hold that consumer curiosity alone is not a strong enough state interest to sustain the compulsion of even an accurate, factual statement. Because Vermont has demonstrated no cognizable harms, its statute is likely to be held unconstitutional.

Because appellants have demonstrated both irreparable harm and a likelihood of success on the merits, the judgment of the district court is reversed, and the case is remanded for entry of an appropriate injunction.

■ LEVAL, CIRCUIT JUDGE, dissenting:

I respectfully dissent. Vermont's regulation requiring disclosure of use of rBST in milk production was based on substantial state interests, including worries about rBST's impact on human and cow health, fears for the survival of small dairy farms, and concerns about the manipulation of nature through biotechnology. The objective of the plaintiff milk producers is to conceal their use of rBST from consumers. The policy of the First Amendment, in its application to commercial speech, is to favor the flow of accurate relevant information. The majority's invocation of the First Amendment to invalidate a state law requiring disclosure of information consumers reasonably desire stands the Amendment on its ear. In my view, the district court correctly found that plaintiffs were unlikely to succeed in proving Vermont's law unconstitutional. . . .

I am comforted by two considerations: First, the precedential effect of the majority's ruling is quite limited. By its own terms, it applies only to cases where a state disclosure requirement is supported by no interest other than the gratification of consumer curiosity. In any case in which a state advanced something more, the majority's ruling would have no bearing.

Second, Vermont will have a further opportunity to defend its law. The majority's conclusion perhaps results from Vermont's failure to put forth sufficiently clear evidence of the interests it sought to advance. If so, the failure is remediable because it occurred only at the preliminary injunction stage. Trial on the merits has yet to be held. The majority has found on the basis of the evidence presented at the hearing that the plaintiffs are likely to succeed on the merits; it has of course not ruled on the ultimate issue. If Vermont succeeds at trial in putting forth clear evidence that its laws were in fact motivated by the concerns discussed above (and not merely by consumer curiosity), it will have shown a substantial interest sufficient to satisfy the requirements of the First Amendment.

NOTES

1. *Remand.* On remand, Vermont made no attempt to show that BST is harmful.

2. *Earlier Case.* In *Stauber v. Shalala*, 895 F. Supp. 1178 (W.D. Wis. 1995), the District Court held that FDA did not act arbitrarily and capriciously in not requiring the labeling of dairy products derived from cows treated with BST. The District Court concluded, "In the absence of evidence of a material difference between rBST-derived milk and ordinary milk, the use of consumer demand as the rationale for labeling would violate the Food, Drug, and Cosmetic Act." *Id.* at 1193.

3. *Sixth Circuit Decision in Tension with Amestoy.* In 2008, in response to the appearance of claims like "rbST free" [sic] on milk labels, the Ohio Department of Agriculture adopted a regulation prohibiting dairy processors from making such claims for their dairy products. In *Int'l Dairy Foods Ass'n v. Boggs*, 622 F.3d 628 (6th Cir. 2010), the Court of Appeals accepted the contention of two trade associations that this regulation violated their First Amendment rights. In stark contrast to the Second Circuit in *Amestoy*, the Sixth Circuit pointed to evidence in the record that "a compositional difference does exist between milk from cows not treated with rbST and milk from treated cows." *Id.* at 636–37. In addition, the court stressed that "the failure to discover rbST in [milk from treated cows] is not necessarily because the artificial hormone is absent in such milk, but rather because scientists have been unable to perfect a *test* to detect it." *Id.* The court concluded that a complete ban on "rbST free" claims, rather than the mandatory use of an appropriate disclaimer, could not withstand *Central Hudson. Id.* at 639.

E. FOOD SANITATION AND AESTHETIC ADULTERATION

The 1906 Pure Food and Drugs Act was the result largely of the development of extensive documentation of the adulteration of the American food and drug supply. This evidence (reinforced by Upton Sinclair's vivid depiction of insanitary conditions in the meatpacking industry in his muckraking 1906 novel *The Jungle*) ultimately overwhelmed the congressional reluctance to enact the legislation.

Problems persisted in the 1930s, however. In 1936, Ruth deForest Lamb, the chief education officer of FDA, published a book titled *American Chamber of Horrors* and organized an FDA exhibit with the same name. The book and exhibit brought wide attention to the continuing presence of unsafe and deceptive products in the food and drug market. As an example of inadequate sanitary regulation of food production, the book highlighted conditions in the butter industry:

> . . . Butter that looked perfectly clean and wholesome to the naked eye disclosed a history of filth leading all the way back to the farm. Hay; fragments of chicken feathers; maggots; clumps of mold— blue, green, white and black; grasshoppers; straw chaff; beetles; cow, dog, cat and rodent hairs; moths; grass and other vegetable matter; cockroaches; dust; ants; fly legs; broken fly wings; metallic filings; remains of rats, mice and other animals were revealed to the astonished eye—all impregnated with yellow dye from the butter. . . . In a single pound of packing-stock butter consigned to a candy factory, so many maggots were found that if they had been placed end to end their length would have approximated eleven feet, nine inches. . . . Examination of the cream at stations everywhere—North, East, South and West—yielded some strange and wonderful prizes. Flies and their maggots were the most common find; but mice, rats, cats and chickens in various stages of decomposition were by no means rare. . . .

Ruth deForest Lamb, AMERICAN CHAMBER OF HORRORS 258 (1936).

The 1938 Act enhanced FDA's power in various ways relevant to food sanitation. For example, it provided the agency with authority to conduct inspections of factories and other facilities manufacturing, processing, packing, or holding FDA-regulated products, and it gave the government power to seek injunctions to restrain violations of the Act. FD&C Act 703, 302. Moreover, the 1938 Act declares food to be adulterated "if it consists in whole or in part of any filthy, putrid, or decomposed substance or is otherwise unfit for food" or "if it has been prepared, packed, or held under insanitary conditions whereby it may have become contaminated with filth, or whereby it may have been rendered injurious to health." FD&C Act 402(a)(3), (4).

The problem of food sanitation has two distinct aspects. First, there is the aesthetic problem of "filth" in food. Although filth was once regarded as a potential indicator of contamination by pathogenic microorganisms, and thus evidence of a potential health hazard, modern food technology allows products to be processed in a way that eliminates the risk of disease even in the presence of filth. Nonetheless, even sterilized filth, however harmless, is prohibited on aesthetic grounds alone. Second, insanitation can facilitate the growth of pathogenic microorganisms that present a substantial risk to human health. This section will deal primarily with the aesthetic problem. Issues surrounding health risks from pathogens will be addressed later in this chapter. *See infra* p. 521.

1. "FILTHY, PUTRID, OR DECOMPOSED SUBSTANCE"

Section 402(a)(3) of the Act declares a food to be adulterated "if it consists in whole or part of any filthy, putrid, or decomposed substance, or if it is otherwise unfit for food." As the case below discusses, this provision presents interesting questions of statutory interpretation and agency discretion.

United States v. 1,500 Cases More or Less, Tomato Paste

236 F. 2d 208 (7th Cir. 1956).

■ SWAIM, CIRCUIT JUDGE.

This is an appeal by the United States from the judgments in the combined prosecution of four libels . . . condemning approximately 10,370 cases of tomato paste as "adulterated". . . .

[Two of the] libels . . . charged that the paste involved . . . was adulterated . . . because it consisted wholly or in part of a "Filthy, putrid, or decomposed substance" as defined by 21 U.S.C.A. § 342(a)(3) [FD&C Act 402(a)(3)]: decomposed tomato material in [one libel], and decomposed tomato material and insect parts in [the other].

After an extensive hearing . . . the trial judge found the issues against the Government with regard to all but a small amount of tomato paste seized. . . .

[Section 402(a)(3)] provides the following definition of "adulterated": "A food shall be deemed to be adulterated . . . if it consists in whole or in part of any filthy, putrid, or decomposed substance, or if it is otherwise unfit for food . . . "

Despite the plain language of the section it has been generally held that the two "if" clauses in subsection (3) above are disjunctive, and that the words "otherwise unfit for food" do not limit the first part of the subsection which bans food in whole or in part filthy, etc., as adulterated.

. . . . It has . . . been suggested that Congress wanted to protect "the aesthetic tastes and sensibilities of the consuming public," and therefore intended that food containing "any filthy, putrid, or decomposed substance" be deemed adulterated whether it was "unfit for food" or not. *United States v. 133 Cases of Tomato Paste*, 22 F. Supp. 515, 516 (E.D. Penn. 1938). Congress may also have wanted to set a standard or purity well above what was required for the health of the consuming public, knowing that not every food product can be individually inspected. If the standard is set at the level of what is "fit for food" or not injurious to health, the occasional substandard item that slips by both industry and Government scrutiny will be hazardous to the health of the consumer. A minimum standard of purity above what is actually the level of danger will, however, allow fewer products to drop below that level. A high standard will also have the same effect by encouraging more careful industry inspection. Therefore, we prefer to follow the general rule in interpreting Section 342(a)(3), although admitting that we are unable to answer Judge Frank as to why Congress put the word 'otherwise' in the section. [*See United States v. 449 Cases, etc.*, 212 F.2d 567, 575 (2d Cir. 1954) (Frank, dissenting).]

The interpretation we have chosen has one serious disadvantage which most courts have recognized. It sets a standard that if strictly enforced, would ban all processed food from interstate commerce. A scientist with a microscope could find filthy, putrid, and decomposed substances in almost any canned food we eat. (The substances which it is claimed render the respondent "adulterated" were visible only through a microscope.) The conclusion is inescapable that if we are to follow the majority of the decisions which have interpreted 21 U.S.C.A. § 342(a)(3), without imposing some limitation, the Pure Food and Drug Administration [sic] would be at liberty to seize this or any other food it chose to seize. And there could be no effective judicial review except perhaps for fraud, collusion, or some such dishonest procedure. Such a position is not indefensible. Congress has obviously found it difficult, if not impossible, to express a definite statutory standard of purity that will receive uniform interpretation. And this court is acutely aware of the fact that it is not the proper body to more narrowly define broad standards in this area so that they can be applied in a particular case. Courts know neither what is necessary for the health of the consuming public nor what can reasonably be expected from the canning industry. Furthermore, this is not a determination that should be made individually for each case on the basis of expert testimony. . . .

Despite our limitations as a court and the fact that Section 342(a)(3) does not give us any power to limit the inescapable force of the words, "if it consists in whole or in part of any filthy, putrid, or decomposed substance," we do not think that Congress intended to let the acts of the agency under this subsection go completely without limitation. In 21 U.S.C. 346 (FD&C Act 406], Congress directed that the administrator provide tolerances for amounts of poisonous or deleterious substances that cannot be avoided and are not injurious to health. It would not be reasonable to think that Congress would direct the administrator to set tolerances for the allowance of safe amounts of poisons in food and then declare that the presence of small amounts of filth, etc., which would admittedly have no effect upon health "adulterates" food and justifies its seizure. We believe that if the fact that almost all food contains some filthy, putrid, and decomposed substances had been called to the attention of Congress, that body would have directed the administrator to provide reasonable and acceptable tolerances for these substances just as it did in the case of poisons.

The spirit of 21 U.S.C.A. §§ 346 . . . demands that we give effect to what reasonable standards have been set by the Food and Drug Administration in the area involved in this case, and determine them as best we can where they have not yet been established. The decomposed tomato material which the respondent is accused of containing is commonly referred to as rot. A tomato containing rot is simply a tomato parts of which have begun to decompose. This is not at all uncommon and such fruits are perfectly good if all of the decomposed portions can be cut out. Several different things cause tomatoes to decompose but by far the most common cause is mold. . . . The Food and Drug Administrator with industry cooperation has arrived at a tolerance for tomato paste which is expressed as 40 per cent under the Howard Mold Count method of measurement. The Administration has announced that it will not seize tomato paste on the basis of mold count alone unless that count is over 40 per cent. We, in our search for standards in this area, accept this administrative tolerance as a proper measure of what approximated amount of decomposition is allowable in tomato paste. A properly obtained mold count of over 40 per cent will, therefore, be considered sufficient grounds for seizing tomato paste if the Food and Drug Administrator chooses to do so.

The record in this case does not disclose any established tolerances for what is termed 'filth' in tomato paste: worm fragments, insects and insect fragments, fly eggs, etc. We can only judge on the basis of the testimony of experts as to what amounts are usual or unavoidable.

. . . . This court holds that as a matter of law all tomato paste having a mold count (or an average mold count where several valid counts are taken) of over 40 per cent of positive fields found, is adulterated under 21 U.S.C.A. § 342(a)(3). . . . The Government should be allowed to seize these [cans]. . . .

[handwritten margin note: mold court standard]

. . . The tolerance is admittedly a somewhat arbitrary standard, but one that has been agreed upon by all the parties involved. The line must be drawn somewhere, and it has been validly drawn at 40 per cent. . . .

. . . Although there do not seem to be any acceptable norms for insect and worm fragments, we can get a good idea of how the [tomato paste] here compare[s] with other tomato paste from the testimony of Emil Cassidy, a research chemist with the American Can Company. . . . The witness . . . testified: ". . . Well . . . your worm fragments are very low. I don't know what the tolerance is, but there isn't any tolerance that I know of. This is low compared to a lot of them I have seen."

The highest worm fragment count shown on exhibit 102 is 6. Insect fragments were in the same general range. . . . The record fully supports the trial court's finding that these counts 'were so low that they are regarded by this Court as insignificant and of no consequence.'

The same is true of other foreign bodies found (fly eggs, etc.). . . .

For the reasons discussed above, we hold that the codes . . . identified by the code letter 'I' are not adulterated, and as to them the judgments below are affirmed. . . .

NOTES

1. *Interpretation of "otherwise" in 402(a)(3).* Fourteen years after the decision in *1,500 Cases*, the Second Circuit similarly observed: "[T]he majority, in fact almost unanimous, rule is that the Act confers the power to exclude from commerce all food products which contain in any degree filthy, putrid or decomposed substances. . . ." *United States v. 484 Bags, More or Less,* 423 F.2d 839, 841 (5th Cir. 1970). The disjunctive reading of the two clauses in section 402(a)(3) continues to be the prevailing one.

2. *Availability of Tolerances.* In *1,500 Cases,* the Seventh Circuit upholds the district court's refusal to condemn the tomato paste harmlessly adulterated with insect fragments in the absence of an administrative tolerance setting an enforcement level. The court's unstated concern seems to be the arbitrariness of seizures for aesthetic adulteration without firm guidelines. A related issue is whether such guidelines must be made public. In *U.S. v. 484 Bags,* cited in the note above, the government seized moldy coffee with mold in excess of its working tolerance. The court observed:

It is undisputed that the claimant had no actual notice of the administrative tolerance and that it had not been published in the Federal Register. The claimant insists that the government may not employ in support of condemnation an unpublished standard of allowable tolerances, known only to itself and sprung upon the unsuspecting merchant at a condemnation hearing and after efforts to rehabilitate the food substance. His complaint is not without equity. . . .

Id. at 841. Nevertheless, the court in that case did not formally reach the issue of publication.

3. *Constitutionality.* The constitutionality of the statutory terms "filthy," "putrid," "decomposed," and "unfit for food" was upheld against a claim of unconstitutional vagueness in the context of a criminal prosecution under the Federal Meat Inspection Act. *United States v. Agnew*, 931 F.2d 1397 (10th Cir. 1991).

———

In 1972, faced with a request under the Freedom of Information Act, FDA made public all of its "filth guidelines," which it renamed "unavoidable natural defect guidelines." The Director of the FDA Bureau of Foods was quoted as stating, somewhat defensively, that if food were required to be totally pure, "there would be no food sold in the United States." WASH. POST, Mar. 29, 1972, at B2. The rule proposed by FDA in the excerpt below remains in force today, in essentially the same language, under the rubric "Defect Action Levels."

Natural or Unavoidable Defects in Food for Human Use That Present No Health Hazard: Public Availability of Information
37 Fed. Reg. 6497 (March 30, 1972).

. . . Objective findings of [the presence of natural or unavoidable defects above the stated defect levels] without evidence of the history of the production of the food render the product adulterated, even though no health hazard is presented. Thus, appropriate regulatory action is taken whenever the stated defect levels are exceeded. Whether the level of defect in the food was acquired during the growth, processing, storage, or shipment is immaterial. When evidence of insanitary conditions of production or storage is known, action may be taken against products with lower defect levels. . . .

Few foods contain no natural or unavoidable defects. Even with modern technology, all defects in goods cannot be eliminated. Foreign material cannot be wholly processed out of foods, and many contaminants introduced into foods through the environment can be reduced only by reducing their occurrence in the environment. . . .

The defect levels set by the Commissioner of Food and Drugs represent a level below which the defect is both unavoidable under current technology and presents no health hazard. The Commissioner has concluded that the public is entitled to this information. . . .

Therefore . . . the Commissioner of Food and Drugs proposes to . . . add[ ] the following new section:

§ 128.10 [now 110.110] Natural or Unavoidable Defects in Food for Human use that Present no Health Hazard

(a) Some foods, even when produced under current good manufacturing practice, contain natural or unavoidable defects at low levels that are not hazardous to health. The Food and Drug Administration establishes maximum levels for these defects in foods produced under current good manufacturing practice and uses these levels in deciding whether to recommend regulatory actions. . . .

(c) Compliance with defect action levels does not excuse violation of the requirement in section 402(a)(4) of the act that food not be prepared, packed, or held under unsanitary conditions or the requirements in this part that food manufacturers distributors, and holders shall observe current good manufacturing practice. Evidence indicating that such a violation exists causes the food to be adulterated ... even though the amounts of natural or unavoidable defects are lower than the currently established defect action levels. . . .

(e) Current levels for natural or unavoidable defects in foods may be obtained upon request [from FDA]. . . .

NOTES

1. *Illustrative Action Levels.* The Defect Levels Handbook, containing all current defect action levels, is now available on the FDA website. The following defect action levels are illustrative:

Product	*Defect*	*Action Level*
BAY (LAUREL) LEAVES	Mold	Average of 5% or more pieces by weight are moldy
	Insect filth	Average of 5% or more pieces by weight are insect-infested
	Mammalian excreta	Average of 1 mg or more mammalian excreta per pound after processing
BROCCOLI, FROZEN	Insects and mites	Average of 60 or more aphids and/or thrips and/or mites per 100 grams
CINNAMON, GROUND	Insect filth	Average of 400 or more insect fragments per 50 grams
	Rodent filth	Average of 11 or more rodent hairs per 50 grams
CORN: SWEET CORN, CANNED	Insect larvae	Insect larvae (corn ear worms, corn borers) 2 or more 3mm or longer larvae, cast skins, larval or cast skin fragments of corn ear worms or corn borer and the aggregate

		length of such larvae, cast skins, larval or cast skin fragments exceeds 12 mm in 24 pounds
MACARONI AND NOODLE PRODUCTS	Insect filth	Average of 225 insect fragments or more per 225 grams in 6 or more subsamples
	Rodent filth	Average of 4.5 rodent hairs or more per 225 grams in 6 or more subsamples
POTATO CHIPS	Rot	Average of 6% or more pieces by weight contain rot Average of 6% or more pieces by weight contain rot

The Handbook also lists the source for each defect in each product. For example, for macaroni and noodle products, the Handbook states: "*DEFECT SOURCE:* Insect fragments—preharvest and/or post harvest and/or processing infestation. Rodent hair—post harvest and/or processing contamination with animal hair or excreta."

2. *Procedure for Adoption.* In 47 Fed. Reg. 41637 (Sept. 21, 1982), FDA announced that it would allow a one-year period for comment on any new or revised defect action levels, during which the announced levels would be effective on an interim basis. The agency later revised this procedure, shortening the time for comment to 60 days but suspending enforcement of new or revised levels during this period. 51 Fed. Reg. 12931 (Apr. 16, 1986).

3. *The Issue of "Blending."* Section 110.110(d) of the FDA regulations provides:

> The mixing of a food containing defects above the current defect action level with another lot of food is not permitted and renders the final food adulterated . . . regardless of the defect level of the final food.

FDA's longstanding opposition to "blending" of above-tolerance and below-tolerance lots of contaminated food has continually been subject to reexamination. See *infra* p. 518.

4. *E. coli in Bottled Water.* In its bottled water regulations, FDA explicitly provides: "If *E. coli* is present in bottled water, then the bottled water will be deemed adulterated under section 402(a)(3) of the act." 21 C.F.R. 165.110(d). One comment to the proposed rule contended that because not all strains of *E. coli* are pathogenic, water with *E. coli* is not necessarily contaminated. The agency responded: "FDA agrees that not all strains of *E. coli* are pathogenic. However, FDA disagrees that water with *E. coli* in it is not contaminated and that testing bottled water products for specific pathogenic strains would be more effective than testing for generic *E. coli.* . . . Because *E. coli* is indicative of fecal contamination, . . . bottled water containing *E. coli* would be considered adulterated under section

402(a)(3) of the act, in that it 'consists in whole or in part of any filthy, putrid, or decomposed substance, or . . . is otherwise unfit for food.' Because testing for generic *E. coli* is sufficient to determine whether bottled water is fecally contaminated, it is not necessary to require testing for specific strains."

————

Two University of Chicago economists proposed a very different approach to controlling filth in food.

Melvin J. Hinich & Richard Staelin, *Regulation of the U.S. Food Industry*

In Study on Federal Regulation, Volume VI. (Senate Document No. 96–14, 96th Congress, 1st Session (1978)).

. . . How much effort should be spent guaranteeing that our food is processed using ingredients and under conditions which are "sanitary" (even though bacteria associated with unsanitary conditions are rendered harmless when the food is later processed correctly), versus guaranteeing that the food is free from substances which cannot be rendered harmless by the proper processing by the manufacturer or consumer? Instead of taking legal action related to aesthetic adulteration, what would happen if all producers were required to affix a label which indicated the level of aesthetically unpleasant contamination? This label probably would be in terms of grades although it could also be more explicit by detailing the exact levels of contamination. If a firm felt that a lower grade label would be detrimental to the marketability of its produce, it would take the necessary steps to insure that its ingredients and manufacturing process met the higher standards. On the other hand, the firm might believe that consumers did not want to pay for extra protection since the food is safe (this occurs during the normal processing). In this case the firm may want to reduce costs (and price) and not meet the higher FDA sanitation grading standards. Consequently, consumers could use the presence or absence of such a label as an indication of the level of sanitation in the plant. . . .

. . . [C]onsumers are not now getting "pure" food since such food would be prohibitively expensive. The question then is should the FDA ban food when it exceeds the admittedly arbitrary defect action levels or should they allow "informed" consumers to make the choice? (Remember exceeding the allowable levels does not usually imply any safety hazard.) This is particularly important if the FDA tightens the sanitation standards since they would in effect be banning foods which before the new standards were acceptable to both the FDA and the consumer. Moreover, these limits can have deleterious side effects. For instance Professor Donald Kennedy of Stanford University [later FDA Commissioner] after a four year study on insecticide adulteration sponsored by the National Research Council pointed out that the FDA's DAL [defect action level] requirements for insect infestation in fruits and vegetables have caused farmers to use increased amounts of insecticide. . . .

In summary then there would seem, on theoretical grounds, to be some benefit to the labeling approach versus banning since the labeling would allow the consumer to make the ultimate choice with respect to aesthetic adulteration. However, the approach has some drawbacks. First as mentioned above, the lower grades may not be in high demand, thus consumers would in reality still be offered just one grade. Also institutions, etc. may buy the lower-graded product and serve unknowing customers. . . . Finally, unless the FDA was given the power to require the producer to affix such a label without going through a legal procedure, the label probably would not be any more cost effective than present regulatory procedures which now require the FDA to go to the judiciary to confiscate contaminated foods. However, it represents an interesting combination of standards and consumer information. . . .

NOTES

1.   *Update.* FDA has never proposed or even discussed the Hinich and Staelin labeling approach.

2.   *Intentional Addition of Insects.* Initially, when confronted with the intentional use of predacious insects to kill other insects in food, FDA declared the practice to be illegal in the absence of either an approved pesticide tolerance from the EPA or an approved food additive petition from FDA. In July 1988, the Director of Compliance of FDA's Center for Food Safety and Applied Nutrition informed a Texas grain storage facility of this position and remarked:

> We recognize that certain low levels of natural and unavoidable defects such as field insects may be present in certain foods even if handled in a sanitary manner. The deliberate addition of insects to food is, however, neither natural nor unavoidable. We have not, therefore, endorsed the practice of intentionally adding "beneficial" insects to foods to control insect pests. Indeed we have considered this simply as either substituting one adulterant for another. . . .

Following a highly critical story on March 25, 1990 on CBS's *60 Minutes*, FDA reversed this decision. With the concurrence of FDA and USDA, EPA then also exempted parasitic and predaceous insects used to control insect pests from the requirement of a pesticide tolerance. *See* 57 Fed. Reg. 14644 (Apr. 22, 1992), codified at 40 C.F.R. 180.1101.

In a Warning Letter issued to the manufacturer of "Sugar–Free Hotlix Tequila Flavored Candy with Genuine Worm," FDA objected to the failure to include "insect larva" in the statement of ingredients, but not to the inclusion of the worm itself. Letter from Elaine C. Messa, Director of the FDA Los Angeles District Office, to Larry Peterman, Warning Letter WL–56–3 (Apr. 28, 1993). *See also* Michael E. Ruane, *Insects in Suckers, Bugs in a Bag: Company Has Six Legs Up on the Candy Competition*, Wash. Post, Nov. 5, 1999, at B1.

3.   *Fish Protein.* In 1961, FDA published a proposal to establish a standard of identity for "fish protein concentrate, whole fish flour," a product made by processing intact fish. 26 Fed. Reg. 8641 (Sept. 15, 1961). Many commenters objected that the product would include the viscera, intestines, and other portions of the fish that are not normally used for food

and that they would thus "regard the finished product as filthy." *Id.* The agency's final standard of identity permitted the product to be made only from edible species of cleaned fish, after discarding "the heads, tails, fins, viscera, and intestinal contents." 27 Fed. Reg. 740 (Jan. 25, 1962). Objections to the standard resulted in a stay pending a public hearing. Before a hearing could be held, the entire matter was referred to a committee of the National Academy of Sciences, which eventually endorsed the concept of making protein concentrate, or flour, from whole fish for human consumption. Its report implied that requiring the cleaning of the fish prior to processing would be so expensive as to jeopardize the economic viability of this technology for producing a very cheap source of protein. Accordingly, in 1967 FDA published a regulation under the Food Additives Amendment authorizing the production and sale of whole fish protein concentrate:

> The Commissioner of Food and Drugs, taking cognizance of the findings relative to the suitability of fish protein concentrate . . . deems it desirable to make this economical source of protein available for consumers. Individual consumers are entitled to the opportunity of choice in the matter of whether they desire to include this item in their diets; therefore, the product, to be readily distinguishable, should be more properly identified as "whole fish protein concentrate," and for domestic distribution it should be packaged for household use in consumer sized units not exceeding 1 pound net weight.

The regulation, still in effect, permits processing "without removal of heads, fins, tails, viscera, or intestinal contents." 32 Fed. Reg. 1173 (Feb. 2, 1967), codified at 21 C.F.R. 172.385.

————

United States v. 1,200 Cans . . . Pasteurized Whole Eggs, etc.

339 F. Supp. 131 (N.D. Ga. 1972).

■ SMITH, CHIEF JUDGE.

These five actions were brought in different parts of the United States . . . to condemn and destroy as adulterated various lots of pasteurized frozen whole eggs and sugar yolks processed and introduced into interstate commerce by the Golden Egg Products, Inc. . . .

Golden Egg is a so-called frozen egg breaking plant, the purpose of which is to remove eggs from their shells, process the egg magma, and package and freeze it in a variety of combinations for sale to manufacturers. Its principal use is in the baking, dairy products and vegetable oil industries. . . .

. . . At the outset, it should be noted that [FD&C Act 402(a)(3)] is worded in the absolute. Thus, the question presented is not whether a particular lot "may" be filthy, putrid, or decomposed, but whether it actually is. Nonetheless, in arriving at a proper standard, the courts readily agree that such conditions are not necessarily related to the food's fitness or unfitness for human consumption. Thus, a food substance may be condemned under the present statute as decomposed, filthy, or putrid even though it is not unfit for food. . . . In any event, under the absolute language of the statute, there must exist actual filth, putridity, or decomposition. As to the last, which is the issue here, the Act means more than the beginning of decomposition, it means a state of decomposition. And, in this respect, the courts endeavor to employ "a reasonable interpretation to carry out legislative policy or intent." In this connection, the courts recognize that Section (a)(3) sets a standard that if literally enforced would ban virtually all processed food from interstate commerce in that a scientist with a microscope could find filthy, putrid, and decomposed substances in almost any food we eat. . . . [I]n this instance, the facts must be judged in the absence of [a] workable standard of fitness for food . . . or a measurable tolerance. . . .

Without these tools, the task is not easy. What, then, is decomposition and how do you measure it? Other courts have apparently grappled with the riddle without definitive success. . . .

. . . [A]ll agree that decomposition involves a bacterial separation or breakdown in the elements of the food so as to produce an undesirable disintegration or rot. That in itself is close to the dictionary definition and will have to suffice. Perhaps the term is similar to drunkenness—it is easy to detect, but hard to define.

Indicative of this attribute is the almost universal acceptance of organoleptic tests for determining decomposition. All of the experts in this case agree that, honestly administered, they are valid. . . . Organoleptic smell tests have worked extremely well on unpasteurized egg products for years. The product is either "passable" or "rejected." However, the pasteurization process, which basically arrests decomposition, has posed a new problem.

The pasteurization process, universal since 1966, plus refinements in the freezing process have masked decomposition odors and made the test much more difficult. . . . Thus, it is extremely difficult to effect a satisfactory organoleptic test on lots of pasteurized frozen eggs. Conversely, however, the presence of a test failure under these conditions would be strong evidence of decomposition.

In this case, only two lots (Can Codes 1935 and 1937) were subjected to and failed such tests. In most lots, two subsamples . . . were taken from ten random cans for a total of 20 subsamples in each lot. Lot 1935 had two such series taken. . . . In them, a competent organoleptic examiner found two clear rejects in each series. Out of ten subsamples in Lot 1937, another competent examiner found two passable, five rejects, and three possibles [sic], or borderlines.

Recognizing the validity of the tests and the accuracy of the results, the court is concerned only with the quantum of the proof. . . . What, if any, percent of the total lot must be shown to be decomposed to condemn the entire lot? . . . This is a fine line. Perhaps the soundest approach is an early one: . . . "where the entire product is not inspected or tested, the proof must go far enough to satisfy the court or jury that the adulteration extends to the whole product sought to be condemned." *A.O. Andersen & Co. v. United States*, 284 F. 542 at 545 (9th Cir. 1922). Recognizing that the trend is to order condemnation if the lot is decomposed "to any degree", the court is still not satisfied that the organoleptic evidence is sufficient to conclude that the entire lots in question are decomposed. . . .

This is not to say that the organoleptic test is no longer viable. To the contrary, a consistent showing of organoleptic failure in a reasonable quantity would subject these or any other lots to forfeiture.

Because of these difficulties and the fact that not all decomposition is discoverable under organoleptic tests, interested parties have for years sought a more scientific method for establishing and measuring decomposition. . . .

There can be little dispute that the presence of large numbers of bacteria in a product indicates a greater possibility of activity than a small number. Accordingly, the DMC tests proceed on the basis of ascertaining the actual count in any given product by random sampling. Under acceptable AOAC [Association of Official Analytical Chemists] methods, a precise amount of the product is spread on a slide over a given area, stained, and placed under a high-powered microscope. . . . Years of testing has indicated that DMC counts of 5,000,000 or more coupled with the presence of certain acid measurements are proof of decomposition in unpasteurized eggs.

Here, however, the government seeks to establish the reliability of a DMC count alone. The evidence presented at trial convinces the court that this standard is not acceptable.

Firstly, the DMC count if scientifically accurate only measures the presence of both live and dead bacteria and not their activity (as do the acid tests). Thus the total numbers of bacteria by themselves, while useful . . . in conjunction with acid tests, are not exclusively significant in determining the presence of actual decomposition. Moreover, by reason of the irregular distribution of bacteria throughout frozen eggs and the inherent difficulty in counting those actually observed through the microscope, the DMC is subject to significant variances in different tests run on the same sample. . . . Thus on the unconvincing original premise that a DMC result may prove actual decomposition under Section (a)(3) and on the substantial test variances on the lots in question, the court concludes that the government's case on this basis fails. . . .

NOTE

Organoleptic Testing. In *Bruce's Juices, Inc. v. United States*, 194 F.2d 935 (5th Cir. 1952), the Court of Appeals held that in a decomposition case, the claimant had no right to have the jury taste and smell the product because decomposition "was not a matter cognizable by the senses." *See also* K. L. Bett & C. P. Dionigi, *Detecting Seafood Off–Flavors: Limitations of Sensory Evaluation*, 51 FOOD TECH., No. 8, at 70 (Aug. 1997). Nonetheless, FDA has traditionally relied upon organoleptic examination to detect decomposition. *See, e.g. U.S. v. An Article of Food . . . 915 Cartons of Frog Legs*, Food Drug Cosmetic Law Report (CCH) ¶ 38, 102 (S.D.N.Y. 1981). Food technologists have sought to replace organoleptic evaluation of decomposition with modern technology. *E.g.*, Linda L. Leake, *Electronic Noses and Tongues*, 60 FOOD TECH., No. 6, at 96 (June 2006). At this writing, however, FDA regards such devices as research tools that are not yet ready to aid regulatory decision making.

2.   "PREPARED UNDER INSANITARY CONDITIONS . . . WHEREBY IT MAY HAVE BECOME CONTAMINATED WITH FILTH"

Section 402(a)(4) provides that a food is adulterated "if it has been prepared, packed, or held under insanitary conditions whereby it may have become contaminated with filth, or whereby it may have been rendered injurious to health." The following discussion deals primarily with the first clause, regarding filth; FDA's power to prevent insanitary conditions that pose a direct threat to health will be dealt with later. *Infra* p. 528.

In many cases, the application of section 402(a)(4) raises primarily "aesthetic issues" rather than specific health risks. As observed in another portion of the *Pasteurized Whole Eggs* case excerpted above:

> . . . [T]he (a)(4) section allows the condemnation of foods processed under insanitary conditions, whether they have actually decomposed or become dangerous to health or not. The objective of (a)(4) is to "require the observance of a reasonably decent standard of cleanliness in handling of food products" and to insure "the observance of those precautions which consciousness of the obligation imposed upon producers of perishable food products should require in the preparation of food for consumption by human beings." It almost reaches the aim of removing from commerce those products produced under circumstances which would offend a consumer's basic sense of sanitation and which would cause him to refuse them had he been aware of the conditions under which they were prepared. . . .

The case below illustrates how the application of section 402(a)(4) in filth cases presents its own interpretive challenges.

Berger v. United States
200 F.2d 818 (8th Cir. 1952).

■ COLLET, CIRCUIT JUDGE.

Defendant was charged in three counts with unlawfully causing to be introduced and delivered for introduction into interstate commerce a number of cases of pickles and pickle relish in jars, which were adulterated within the meaning of 21 U.S.C.A. § 342(a)(4) in that they had been prepared and packed under insanitary conditions whereby they may have become contaminated with filth. . . . The case was submitted to a jury which returned a verdict of guilty. . . . Only two questions are presented on this appeal. Defendant challenges (1) the constitutionality of the statute, and, [sic] (2) the sufficiency of the evidence.

Unconstitutionality of the statute is asserted upon the ground that it is so indefinite, uncertain and obscure that it does not inform one accused thereunder of the nature and cause of the accusation in violation of the Sixth Amendment to the United States Constitution.

The constitutional test of definiteness and certainty of the language used in a statute defining a criminal offense has been frequently stated. . . .

In *United States v. Brewer,* 139 U.S. 278, 288 (1891), [the Court stated:] "Laws which create crime ought to be so explicit that all men subject to their penalties may know what acts it is their duty to avoid." . . .

It should be noted that the statute in question is designed to prohibit the introduction or delivery for introduction into interstate commerce of food, etc., which is adulterated. In aid of that objective it defines an adulterated food as that which: ". . . has been prepared, packed, or held under insanitary conditions whereby it may have become contaminated with filth, . . . "

It is clear that the congressional intent is to make it a criminal offense for a person to prepare, pack or hold food under such insanitary conditions that it may become contaminated. It is not necessary that it actually become contaminated. States [sic] in the language of Chief Justice Stone in *Corn Products Refining Co. v. Federal Trade Commission,* 324 U.S. 726, 738 (1945), the statute is designed to prevent adulterations 'in their incipiency' by condemning insanitary conditions which may result in contamination.

It is clear from an examination of [various Supreme Court cases including *Corn Products Refining*] that the clause—"whereby it may have become contaminated"—is not to be construed to mean that criminality may be predicated upon proof of an insanitary condition which gives rise to a 'mere possibility' of contamination. The condition condemned by the statute, which must be proved to support a conviction, is one which would with reasonable possibility result in contamination. . . .

In the light of the foregoing construction of the statue, does it convey a sufficiently definite warning of what conduct will constitute a crime? Its plain meaning is that no one shall prepare, pack or hold food, in this instance pickle relish, for introduction or delivery for introduction into interstate commerce under conditions which would with reasonable possibility result in the food becoming contaminated with filth.

It is contended that because the statute leaves open for determination the degree of insanitation which would possibly or probably result in contamination, it does not meet the test of definiteness. . . . But the law is full of instances where a man's fate depends on his estimating rightly, that is, as the jury subsequently estimates it, some matter of degree. The criterion of criminality is to examine whether common social duty would, under the circumstances, have suggested a more circumspect conduct. . . .

The argument is advanced that the statute is void for indefiniteness and uncertainty because it contains no definition of 'insanitary conditions' and without such a definition no intelligent person can tell in advance when a condition violates the statue. We do not agree. . . . Impossible standards of specificity are not required. It is difficult to think of a more apt way to say that one should not prepare food under conditions whereby it would probably be filthy. Any reasonably intelligent person should know what that means. The statute is not subject to this attack.

Defendant contends that the evidence was insufficient to sustain the verdict. . . . [T]he seized shipments were . . . made at defendant's plant and shipped therefrom on May 3, 1951, and May 17, 1951. . . . Defendant's argument is based on the fact that no government witness saw the shipments in question prepared, canned in glass jars and shipped, and that the testimony relative to the conditions existing on May 21, 22, and 23 [the dates of the inspections], and the analysis of the contents of the shipment was insufficient to show beyond a reasonable doubt that the plaint [sic] was in an insanitary condition on . . . May 3 and May 17.

The evidence shows the following facts. The plant is housed in a brick building. . . . The brick walls contain approximately 200 unscreened glass windows. The glass in 20 or 25 has been broken out. Pigeons fly in and out. Sometimes they are shot and killed inside the plant. . . . At the time of the inspections on May 21 and 22 . . . [t]he hopper of the pickle chopper was rusted and corroded, the shaft rusted and grease was running down the shaft onto the cutting blades of the chopper. . . . In the relish-making area was a wooden table covered with dust, stained material, and its supporting structure was encrusted with spider webbing. . . . Vinegar flies were flying over . . . uncovered barrels, spider webbing partially covered the openings of six barrels approximately full of pickles, a spider was in the webbing above one barrel, houseflies rested on pickles in another barrel, on each pickle floating on top of the solution in another barrel there were two or three vinegar flies, bird feathers floating in the solution in another barrel, moldy pickles in two barrels, and a spider climbing over the pickles in another. . . . In two . . . vats were pickles . . . covered with a whitish and grayish mold approximately one-half inch thick. . . . On the railroad car [inside the plant] there were wooden vats and in the vats were pickles in solution. In this solution were particles of sticks, grass, muddy pickles, and particles which resembled insects. . . . The pigeons heretofore referred to appear to have had access to a large part if not all of the area inside the plant. They were not trained pigeons and were not housebroken. The result of their habitation in the plant was what would reasonably be expected.

It is defendant's theory of the law that these conditions cannot be presumed to have existed when the seized shipments were canned and shipped. . . . The evidence describing the conditions on May 21, 22, and 23, in some particulars justified an inference that those conditions had existed for a considerable period of time. But there was additional and more direct evidence of what the conditions were in the plant at the time the shipments in question were canned and shipped. The analysis of the contents of the seized shipments showed that the jars contained, in addition to pickle relish, fragments of a fly skin, part of a fly's leg, a number of mites, part of a beetle wing, a moth scale, fragments of feathers and fragments of rodent hair. The evidence was not insufficient to support the verdict.

The judgment is affirmed.

NOTES

1. *Government's Burden of Proof.* For an illustration of the difficulty of demonstrating that particular sanitation practices violate section (a)(4) in the absence of regulations prescribing specific good manufacturing practices, see *United States v. General Foods Corp.*, 446 F. Supp. 740 (N.D.N.Y.), *aff'd* 591 F.2d 1332 (2d Cir. 1978). There the District Court refused to find that geotrichum mold found on equipment used to process canned green beans demonstrated that the beans had been processed under such conditions as to present a reasonable possibility that they could have become contaminated with filth. The District Court relied on testimony that mold is common in such facilities.

In *United States v. 155/137 Pound Burlap Bags*, 4 FDLI Food and Drug Rep. 784 (E.D. Va. 1993), the District Court denied a government motion for summary judgment in a section 402(a)(4) case. The District Court held that FDA must only prove a reasonable possibility of contamination rather than actual contamination, but concluded that there were genuine issues of fact as to (i) whether the threshold level of possible contamination of the cocoa beans had been achieved, in light of the fact that the beans are necessarily cleaned and processed before human consumption and (ii) whether there was a reasonable possibility that each separate cell in the warehouses was contaminated.

2. *Compliance Policy.* Following adverse rulings in the *General Foods* case, *supra* note 1, and a similar case, FDA sent a directive to its field force in January 1979 limiting future legal action under section 402(a)(4):

> . . . Inspections that do not involve pathogens can be developed as 402(a)(4) cases based on observed sanitary conditions concerning visible filth. . . .

> In all 402(a)(4) situations other than those involving pathogens, inspections will be conducted using inspectional observations of organoleptically detectable (by sight and/or smell) filth and collection of physical filth exhibits. For the present, we are not prepared to approve cases based on conditions demonstrable only by bacteriological analysis. . . .

3. *Reconditioning.* FDA announced a guideline for reconditioning food adulterated under section 402(a)(4) in 54 Fed. Reg. 32395 (Aug. 7, 1989). Damaged food is often sold to the food salvage industry, which either reconditions it for human use or sells it for other purposes. In cooperation with the Association of Food and Drug officials, FDA developed a model food salvage code. 44 Fed. Reg. 74921 (Dec. 18, 1979), 49 Fed. Reg. 31952 (Aug. 9, 1984).

4. *Transport Sanitation.* The Sanitary Food Transportation Act of 2005, 119 Stat. 1144, 1911, added section 416 to the FD&C Act to require FDA to promulgate regulations for the safe and sanitary transportation of food. In 2010, FDA promulgated an advance notice of proposed rulemaking

on implementing the law. 75 Fed. Reg. 22713 (Apr. 30, 2010). *See also*
GUIDANCE FOR INDUSTRY: SANITARY TRANSPORTATION OF FOOD (Apr. 2010).

3. "OTHERWISE UNFIT FOR FOOD"

United States v. 298 Cases . . . Ski Slide Brand Asparagus

88 F. Supp. 450 (D. Ore. 1949).

■ McCULLOCH, DISTRICT JUDGE.

Defendant is an asparagus packer. One of his products is the center cut of the asparagus. This retails for 20 cents per can (1 lb. 3 oz.) containing 95 to 100 cuts, as compared with 40 to 45 cents per can for the choicer tips. The Government contends that defendant's center cuts are fibrous and woody beyond the permissible limits set up by the Federal Food, Drug and Cosmetic Administration. Three witnesses for the Government said that they had eaten a can (or attempted to) of defendant's cuts. The composite of their testimony was that 25% or more of the cuts were inedible, and the Government's witnesses condemned them as a food product.

On the other hand, the Director of Mary Cullen's Cottage found only 5 or 6 pieces out of 100 that she had to lay aside. Confronted with this conflict in testimony, I obtained counsels' consent to eat a can. This I have done, although I confess had I understood all the difficulties of the undertaking, I might not have been so bold.

To eat a can of asparagus, hand-running, as the saying is, is quite a chore. I took three days to eat the can. That, I can now state, is as much as an old protein user should attempt on his first venture into herbalism. I suspect the Government witnesses tried to eat their cans all at one time, and that may explain the severity of their judgment about defendant's asparagus. I can see where after 50 or 60 cuts, eaten without spelling oneself, one might become very particular.

My test more than confirmed Miss Laughton's good opinion of the cuts. She found 5 or 6 per cent inedible, whereas I ate all of my can, and felt that I was helped by it. There was one runty, tough piece and two or three slivers, but I treated them as de minimis. I agree with the Director of Mary Cullen's Cottage that this is an excellent product, particularly considering its low price. Not everybody in this country can "keep up with the Joneses" and eat only asparagus tips. Indeed it seems strange to me that the Government should be interested in keeping from the market a moderately priced, wholly nutritious food product. I should think in this period of declining income the Government's interest would be the other way. If Mr. Prendergast [the lawyer for the defendant] will prepare appropriate findings, I will give his client's center cuts a clean bill of health. They deserve it.

NOTES

1. *Judicial Standards.* In *United States v. 24 Cases, More or Less*, 87 F. Supp. 826 (D. Me. 1949), the District Court held that for food to be unfit, it "must be proved to be so tough and rubbery that the average, normal

person, under ordinary conditions, would not chew and swallow it." In *United States v. 71/55 Gallon Drums . . . Stuffed Green Olives in Brine*, 790 F. Supp. 1379 (N.D. Ill. 1992), FDA seized olives on the ground that they were "unfit for food." FDA demonstrated that the products contained yeast, but the claimant argued that this is normal and harmless. Claimant asserted that all olives are in this condition when stored in bulk but are cleaned prior to consumer sale. The District Court rejected this argument, holding that a food which is adulterated may be condemned even though it is intended to have the adulteration eliminated by a future process. But the District Court held that an "unfit for food" decision rests upon consumer perception of the article, and it denied motions for summary judgment on the ground that whether the olives were unfit for food was a triable issue of fact.

> In cases such as these, where the condemnation of an article of food is sought even though the article has not been alleged to be injurious to the public, the decision hinges on consumer perception. While the product's appearance is a factor in consumer perception, the decisive factor rests on the taste and expectations of the consumer.

The court ordered a bench trial at which time a taste test would be conducted. The parties then entered into a consent decree that "condemned the article and authorized its release to the claimant for bringing into compliance with the law." 28 FDA CONSUMER, No. 3, at 33 (Apr. 1994).

2.   *Worms.* FDA has frequently been confronted with proposals to market foods from sources that may affront the sensibilities of many consumers. On April 26, 1977, FDA's Bureau of Foods replied to an inquiry that probed the limits of the "otherwise unfit for food" language of section 402(a)(3):

> Pat L. Smith
> Smitty's Worm Hatchery
> 1005 S. College Avenue
> College Place, WA 99324

> . . . .

> Worms are not commonly recognized as a source of food in the United States. We believe the vast majority of consumers would view them as aesthetically objectionable in food or as food, just as insects are viewed as aesthetically objectionable by most people. There are certain specialty items, such as fried agave worms, baby beees [sic], and chocolate covered fried ants that have been sold in this country for many years, but such products are not widely accepted or consumed and are viewed primarily as novelty items. We have not objected to the sale of such items when properly labaled [sic] and otherwise in compliance with the law, because the purchaser is aware of the nature of the items purchased and because they have been consumed with apparent safety. . . .

> From an aesthetic viewpoint, we would probably view the sale of worms or products derived from them in the same manner we view these spacialty [sic] items mentioned above. However, before worms or products derived from them could be marketed as food in this country, we would have to insist that they be considered under the food

additive provisions of the FD&C Act to assure that consumption of these products would be safe. . . .

As the letter indirectly acknowledges, the "disgustingness" of different foodstuffs is culturally contingent. For a fascinating discussion of the accepted role of insects in the diets of cultures around the world (and their potential place in the American diet), see Dana Goodyear, *Grub: Eating Bugs to Save the Planet*, NEW YORKER, Aug. 15 & 22, 2011, at 38.

3. *DES Residues*. Faced with the difficulty of proving that a trace amount of the synthetic nonsteroidal estrogen DES present in beef from supplemented cattle feed was an added poisonous or deleterious substance that may render the food injurious to health, the government tried the additional argument that the DES residue rendered the product "unfit for food." In *United States v. 2,116 Boxes of Boned Beef*, 516 F. Supp. 321 (D. Kan. 1981), the District Court ruled that "[t]he allegation of unfitness must be independent of the allegation of injuriousness" and that "unfit for food" includes such conditions as discoloration or a bad smell but does not include intentional additions of substances to food. The government did not appeal. *See also Millet, Pit and Seed Co., Inc. v. United States*, 436 F. Supp. 84 (E.D. Tenn. 1977) (holding that apricot kernels naturally containing amygdalin are not "unfit for food" because FDA failed to prove that they were "inedible for the average person under ordinary conditions").

4. *Candy Choking Hazard*. Sometimes, FDA deems a product to be "unfit for food" for reasons that implicate safety. For example, starting with "FDA Warns Consumers About Imported Jelly Cup Type Candy that Poses a Potential Choking Hazard," Talk Paper No. T01–38 (Aug. 17, 2001), the agency issued more than a dozen press releases and talk papers on the choking hazard caused by "konjac" jelly cups imported from Asia, which do not readily dissolve when placed in the mouth. The product caused the death of several children. When one company refused to recall its konjac candy products, FDA brought a seizure action alleging that the products were "unfit for food because they pose a serious choking hazard." *See* "FDA Seizes New Choice Food Gel Candies," Press Release P02–16 (May 22, 2002). The company entered into a consent decree of condemnation and destruction.

5. *Cattle Materials*. In another example of safety-related "unfitness," FDA banned specified cattle materials as unfit for use in human food because of concern about transmission of "mad cow disease" (bovine spongiform encephalopathy), and it promulgated recordkeeping requirements to enforce the ban. 69 Fed. Reg. 42256 (July 14, 2004), 70 Fed. Reg. 53063 (Sept. 7, 2005), 71 Fed. Reg. 59653 (Oct. 11, 2006), codified at 21 C.F.R. 189.5. To buttress its legal authority, FDA also relied on sections 402(a)(2)(C), 402(a)(4), 402(a)(5), and 409. The mad cow disease crisis is addressed in detail in Chapter 8, *infra* p. 1051.

F. THE PRESENCE OF POISONOUS OR DELETERIOUS SUBSTANCES

1. INTRODUCTION TO FDA'S REGULATION OF THE SAFETY OF FOOD CONSTITUENTS

One of FDA's most controversial activities is the regulation of the safety of food constituents—materials that occur naturally in agricultural commodities, that are intentionally added to food during processing, or that migrate to food as the result of industrial activity. There is no single food safety standard. The food safety provisions of the FD&C Act are an aggregation of authorities enacted over a period of 100 years, each directed at a distinct category of constituents.

The Pure Food and Drugs Act of 1906 declared adulterated any food that contained "any added poisonous or other added deleterious ingredient which may render such article injurious to health." This law did not deal with hazards posed by constituents that were not "added" to food. The concept "added" was not defined in the 1906 Act but was understood to embrace substances incorporated as ingredients or used during processing.

When Congress wrote the present FD&C Act in 1938, it expanded the 1906 Act's controls over toxicants in food. Section 402(a)(1) declares to be adulterated any food that "bears or contains any poisonous or deleterious substance which may render it injurious to health . . . ." Although this clause contains no reference to the added/nonadded status of the substance, Congress, late in the legislative process, qualified this standard by appending: "but in case the substance is not an added substance such food shall not be considered adulterated under this clause if the quantity of such substance in such food does not ordinarily render it injurious to health." The FD&C Act thus retained the 1906 Act's distinction between substances that are "added" and those that are not, but made the latter subject to FDA regulation for the first time.

Both the "may render injurious" standard for added substances and the "ordinarily injurious" standard for nonadded substances have remained unchanged since 1938. The "ordinarily injurious" test is more permissive of potentially toxic food constituents than any other provision of the Act. Moreover, because the Act does not define "added," FDA has broad discretion in determining which food constituents qualify for evaluation under the "ordinarily injurious" test.

In 1938, Congress also recognized that certain added substances required more comprehensive control than would be achieved under the "may render injurious" test of section 402(a)(1). Section 406 was therefore included in the 1938 Act to empower FDA to establish tolerances sufficient to protect the public health for unavoidable or necessary added "poisonous or deleterious" substances, such as pesticide residues on raw agricultural commodities.

The 1938 Act thus contained three standards applicable to potentially toxic substances in food: (1) The section 402(a)(1) "ordinarily injurious" standard applied to constituents that were not added. (2) The section 402(a)(1) "may render injurious" standard applied to added constituents that were neither necessary nor unavoidable. (3) Under section 406, FDA could set tolerances "for the protection of public health" for added constituents whose use was "necessary in the production of a food" or whose occurrence was "unavoidable by good manufacturing practice."

This original triad of controls has been augmented by several subsequent amendments to the 1938 Act. Each of these amendments deals with a specific category of added food constituents and establishes a system under which FDA is empowered to limit the use, or the occurrence, of potentially toxic substances in or on food. Each of these amendments establishes a standard for safety distinct from those in sections 402(a)(1) and 406.

The first of these amendments was the Miller Pesticide Amendments of 1954, which added section 408 of the Act. This provision was intended to complement the authority then residing in the Department of Agriculture to register pesticides under the Federal Insecticide, Rodenticide, and Fungicide Act (FIFRA). The Amendments provide that a raw agricultural commodity shall be deemed adulterated if it bears any residue of a pesticide that does not conform to a tolerance established under section 408 for use on that food. The Amendments create an elaborate procedure for the establishment of tolerances—a task that FDA originally performed, but that EPA has conducted since the early 1970s. The standard for safety stated in section 408 is "a reasonable certainty that no harm will result from aggregate exposure to the pesticide chemical residue, including all anticipated dietary exposures and all other exposures for which there is reliable information." FD&C Act 408(b)(2)(A)(ii).

In 1958 Congress carved out another category of added constituents of food for special treatment. The Food Additives Amendment, which added section 409 of the Act, establishes a licensure scheme, similar to that for pesticide residues, for substances that are intended to be used as ingredients in formulated foods. Section 409 also applies to substances such as packaging materials that, through use in contact with food, become or "may reasonably be expected to become" components of food. A food that bears or contains a food additive whose use FDA has not approved as "safe," or that contains an approved food additive in a quantity exceeding the limits specified by the agency, is adulterated under section 402(a)(2)(C). Although the literal standard for the safety in section 409 is simply "safe," FD&C Act 409(c)(3)(A), the agency applies the standard as elaborated in the legislative history of the Food Additives Amendment, which requires a demonstration that, with "reasonable certainty," the additive will not harm the health of consumers.

Because of explicit exceptions to the definition of "food additive" in section 201(s), the food additive provisions do not apply to all intentional ingredients of food or to all substances that may migrate to food. Excepted from its coverage are (1) substances whose use in food is "generally recognized as safe by qualified experts" (GRAS)—an exception that embraces a large number of familiar substances such as sugar and salt (as well as many less familiar substances)—and (2) substances that either FDA or USDA approved for use in food prior to 1958, the so-called "prior sanctioned" substances.

standard for "safe"

The famous Delaney Clause was added to the FD&C Act as part of the Food Additives Amendment. This clause (contained within section 409(c)(3)(A)) precludes FDA from approving as "safe" any food additive found to induce cancer in man or in animals when administered by ingestion or other appropriate test. Because the Delaney Clause is drafted as a limitation on FDA's approval authority under section 409, however, it technically applies only to substances that fall within the statutory definition of a "food additive." The issues involved in the regulation of carcinogens are examined in detail in Chapter 13.

In 1960 Congress addressed the issue of substances used to color foods—as well as colorings for drugs and cosmetics. The Color Additives Amendment, at FD&C Act 721, applies to all substances used primarily for the purpose of imparting color to food. Unlike the definition of "food additive," the definition of "color additive" at section 201(t) contains no GRAS or "prior sanction" exception. Section 721 requires FDA approval, or "listing," for use of a color additive. A food that bears or contains a color additive whose use has not been approved by FDA, or whose use deviates from the terms of any approval, is adulterated. The standard for color additive listing, like that for food additive approval, is "safe," FD&C Act 721(b)(4), interpreted in practice as "reasonable certainty of no harm." A second Delaney Clause prohibits the listing of any color additive that has been shown to induce cancer in man or animals. FD&C Act 721(b)(5)(B).

The next relevant modification of the 1938 Act occurred as part of the Animal Drug Amendments of 1968. After the enactment of the Food Additives Amendment of 1958, drugs for food-producing animals that "could reasonably be expected" to leave residues in human food were regulated under a combination of the section 409 food additives provisions and the section 505 new drug approval provisions. In 1968 Congress simplified the procedure for evaluating animal drugs by prescribing a unified licensure system under section 512 of the Act. The same "reasonable certainty of no harm" standard applicable to food additives and color additives is used for residues of new animal drugs in food. Section 512 also has its own Delaney Clause. FD&C Act 512(d)(1)(I).

Section 402 explicitly provides that a food is adulterated if it is or contains a pesticide chemical residue, a food additive, a new animal drug, or a color additive that is "unsafe within the meaning" of the sections specifically regulating these substances. FD&C Act 402(a)(2)(B), (C); 402(c).

In the Dietary Supplement Health and Education Act of 1994 (DSHEA), Congress recognized dietary supplements as a distinct subcategory of food and established separate safety criteria for "dietary ingredients." Dietary ingredients are excluded from the definition of food additive and thus from section 409 premarket approval scheme. FD&C Act 201(s)(6). Dietary supplements and dietary ingredients continue, however, to be subject to section 402(a)(1)'s "may render injurious" and "ordinarily injurious" standards for poisonous or deleterious substances—with the condition that this adulteration be "under the conditions of use recommended or suggested in the labeling." FD&C Act 402(f)(1)(D). DSHEA also prohibits the marketing of any dietary supplement or dietary ingredient that presents a "significant or unreasonable risk of illness or injury" under recommended or suggested conditions of use, and it authorizes the Secretary of HHS to impose an immediate ban of a product or ingredient that poses an imminent hazard. FD&C Act 402(f)(1)(A), (C). Anyone who proposes to market a new (post-1994) dietary ingredient must notify FDA at least 75 days in advance unless the ingredient has been present in the food supply as an article used for food in a form in which the food has not been chemically altered. FD&C Act 402(f)(1)(B), 413. There is no GRAS exception from premarket notification for a new dietary ingredient.

Thus, Congress through its amendments has subdivided the universe of added food constituents into several categories, each of which is subject to distinct regulatory requirements and each of which will be discussed in turn below. However, the categories of food constituents that Congress has dealt with in specific legislation do not embrace nonadded substances and do not exhaust the universe of added substances, so it is still necessary to master the relevant provisions of the original 1938 Act, sections 402(a)(1) and 406.

2. NONADDED SUBSTANCES AND THE "ORDINARILY INJURIOUS" STANDARD

As enacted in 1938, and unchanged since, section 402(a)(1) defines as adulterated any food that contains an added poisonous or deleterious substance which *may render* it injurious to health or a nonadded poisonous or deleterious substance which *ordinarily renders* it injurious to health.

United States v. 1232 Cases American Beauty Brand Oysters

43 F. Supp. 749 (W.D. Mo. 1942).

■ REEVES, DISTRICT JUDGE.

This is a proceeding by the process of libel to condemn an alleged adulterated food product. Such food consists of 1232 cases of oysters, each case containing 24 cans, marked "American Beauty Brand Oysters."

As a basis for condemnation, it is alleged by the government that said article "contains shell fragments, many of them small enough to be swallowed and become lodged in the esophagus, and that said shell fragments are sharp and capable of inflicting injury in the mouth."

The provision of the law invoked by the government is section [402(a)(1)]. . . .

The claimant appeared to deny the averments of the libel and assert ownership of the product. The evidence in the case showed that in the processing of oysters for food there is a constant effort to eliminate shells and fragments thereof from the product. For this purpose many means and devices are used to reduce as nearly to a minimum as possible such shells and fragments in the product. The evidence, however, on behalf of both the government and the defense was that with present known means and devices it was impossible to

[handwritten margin note: libel suit over adding shells during processing]

free the product entirely from the presence of part shells and shell fragments. Moreover, it not only appeared, but it is a matter of common knowledge, that an oyster is a marine bivalve mollusk with a rough and an irregular shell wherein it develops and grows, and that, in the processing of the food produce, it is necessary to remove this irregular, rough shell so far as that may be accomplished. The shells, therefore, are not artificially added. . . .

There was evidence on behalf of the claimant that its processing operations were in accord with the best manufacturing practice and there was even some testimony that the means employed by it for the elimination of shell fragments were superior to the means employed by other processors engaged in similar operations. . . . Claimant . . . proved that over 50 million cans had been processed by it and distributed in its trade territory and that no complaints had ever been made of the presence of part shells or shell fragments. . . .

. . . There was a contention by the government that the shells as a deleterious substance were added to the product while being processed. There was no evidence to support this contention.

The . . . statute . . . contemplates that there may be of necessity food products containing deleterious substances. No one who has had the experience of eating either fish or oysters is unfamiliar with the presence of bones in the fish (a deleterious substance) and fragments of shell in the oysters (also a deleterious substance). The Congress, however, withdrew such foods from the adulterated class "if the quantity of such substance in such food does not ordinarily render it injurious to health."

The evidence on both sides was that by the greatest effort, and in the use of the most modern means and devices, shell fragments could not be entirely separated from an oyster food product. The government, in its brief, quite aptly and concisely stated its point by using the following language: "It is the character, not the quantity of this substance that controls its ability to injure."

This concession on the part of the government . . . removes the case immediately from that portion of the statute which says: ". . . such food shall not be considered adulterated under this clause if the quantity of such substance in such food does not ordinarily render it injurious to health."

Since it is the "character, not the quantity of this substance that controls its ability to injure," as stated by the government, then in the view that it is impossible to eliminate shell fragments in toto from the product, the use of oysters as a food must be entirely prohibited or it must be found that the presence of shell fragments is not a deleterious substance within the meaning of the law and must be tolerated. [T]o reject oyster products as a food is unthinkable. It would be as reasonable to reject fish because of the presence of bones. Even if a greater percentage of shells and shell fragments were found in claimant's product than in that of other processors, yet this fact, under the theory of the government, would not add to the deleterious nature of claimant's product. . . .

Upon the evidence in this case it must be found that the presence of shell fragments in the article sought to be condemned does not ordinarily render it injurious to health. . . .

. . . The claimant, therefore, should have restored to it the articles seized and the libel should be dismissed. . . .

NOTES

1.   *Other Authority.* In *Evart v. Suli*, 259 Cal. Rptr. 535 (Cal. Ct. App. 1989), a private tort suit, the court held that a hamburger containing a piece of bone is not unadulterated as a matter of law under a California provision similar to FD&C Act 402(a)(1). The court explained that even though the bone was a naturally occurring substance, "we are not prepared to state that it is a matter of common knowledge that hamburgers contain pieces of beef bone large enough to cause injury to a consumer." *See also Millet, Pit and Seed Co., Inc. v. United States*, 436 F. Supp. 84 (E.D. Tenn. 1977) (holding that the amygdalin that occurs naturally in apricot kernels is a nonadded substance and that FDA failed to carry its burden of proving that the amount present was sufficient to render the apricot kernels ordinarily injurious to health).

2.   *Legislative History.* The legislative history of the 1938 Act provides little guidance on the interpretation of the second ("ordinarily injurious") clause of section 402(a)(1). Congress evidently was aware that some foods naturally contain substances that, if consumed in excess, can be harmful, and it obviously intended to establish a demanding standard for FDA enforcement. The court's ruling in *American Beauty Brand Oysters* assumes that, notwithstanding the risk of choking or other injury from oyster shell fragments, Congress would value oysters highly enough to preclude a finding of adulteration. While the Act does not explicitly authorize any weighing of "benefits," the court's approach is consistent with the few illustrations contained in the legislative history of the second clause of section 401(a)(1).

The 1906 Act declared food adulterated "[i]f it contain[s] any added poisonous or other added deleterious ingredient which may render such article injurious to health." The earliest proposed bills to reform the law in the 1930s deleted the word "added" from the language of the 1906 Act to allow the FDA to regulate any food that might present a risk to consumers, whether the deleterious constituent occurred naturally or was put in food by artifice. "Federal Foods, Drugs and Cosmetics," Hearing on S. 2800 before the Senate Committee on Commerce, 73d Cong., 2d Sess. (1934). FDA's Walter G. Campbell pointed out that the 1906 Act left foods which acquire their injurious properties naturally, such as poisonous mushrooms and particularly toxic varieties of West Coast mussels, beyond federal control. "Foods, Drugs, and Cosmetics," Hearing before a Subcommittee of the House Committee on Interstate and Foreign Commerce, 74th Cong., 1st Sess. 58 (1935).

So as to reach naturally occurring poisons, the final wording of section 402(a)(1) includes the second clause, which applies if "the substance is not an added substance." But to prevent over-zealous enforcement against foods that naturally contained a deleterious substance, the House

Committee added the proviso requiring the Government to prove that a substance is harmful when consumed in ordinary quantities by consumers with ordinary sensitivities. Statements during the hearings indicate that foods such as coffee, tea, rhubarb (which naturally contains oxalic acid), and cocoa were not to be declared adulterated. Congress wanted to reach only foods that are highly toxic in their natural state, such as the poisonous mushrooms, certain mussels, and Burma beans that FDA witnesses had cited as examples.

3. ADDED SUBSTANCES AND THE "MAY RENDER INJURIOUS" STANDARD

In contrast to the second clause of section 402(a)(1), regarding nonadded substances, the first clause provides that a food is adulterated if it contains an added poisonous or deleterious substance that "may render it injurious to health." An important interpretive question regarding this clause is whether the presence of *any* amount of an added poisonous or deleterious substance, no matter how little, allows the conclusion that the food is adulterated. This question was answered by the United States Supreme Court in the case below, interpreting virtually identical language in the 1906 Pure Food and Drugs Act. Today, the type of substance at issue in this case, a flour bleaching agent, would likely be addressed under the food additive provisions of section 409 rather than under section 402(a). *See* 21 C.F.R. 170.3(o)(13).

United States v. Lexington Mill & Elevator Co.
232 U.S. 399 (1914).

■ MR. JUSTICE DAY delivered the opinion of the court.

The petitioner, the United States of America, proceeding under § 10 of the Food and Drugs Act (June 30, 1906), . . . sought to seize and condemn 625 sacks of flour in the possession of one Terry. . . . The amended libel charges that the flour had been treated by the "Alsop Process," so called, by which nitrogen peroxide gas, generated by electricity, was mixed with atmospheric air and the mixture then brought in contact with the flour, and that it was thereby adulterated under . . . § 7 of the act . . . in that the flour had been caused to contain added poisonous or other added deleterious ingredients, to-wit, nitrites or nitrite reacting material, nitrogen peroxide, nitrous acid, nitric acid and other poisonous and deleterious substances which might render the flour injurious to health. . . .

A special verdict to the effect that the flour was adulterated was returned and judgment of condemnation entered. . . .

The case requires a construction of the Food and Drugs Act. Parts of the statute pertinent to this case are:

"Sec. 7. That for the purposes of this act an article shall be deemed to be adulterated: . . .

"In the case of food: . . .

"Fifth. If it contain any added poisonous or other added deleterious ingredient which may render such article injurious to health". . . .

Without reciting the testimony in detail it is enough to say that for the Government it tended to show that the added poisonous substance introduced into the flour by Alsop Process, in the proportion of 1.8 parts per million, calculated as nitrogen, may be injurious to the health of those who use the flour in bread and other forms of food. On the other hand, the testimony for the respondent tended to show that the process does not add to the flour any poisonous or deleterious ingredients which can in any manner render it injurious to the health of a consumer. On these conflicting proofs the trial court was required to submit the case to the jury. . . .

It is evident . . . that the trial court regarded the addition to the flour of any poisonous ingredient as an offense within this statute, no matter how small the quantity, and whether the flour might or might not injure the health of the consumer. . . . The testimony shows that the effect of the Alsop Process is to bleach or whiten the flour and thus make it more marketable. If the testimony introduced on the part of the respondent was believed by the jury they must necessarily have found that the added ingredient, nitrites of a poisonous character, did not have the effect to make the consumption of the flour by any possibility injurious to the health of the consumer. . . .

. . . [I]n considering this statute, we find that the fifth subdivision of § 7 provides that food shall be deemed to be adulterated: "If it contain any added poisonous or other added deleterious ingredient *which may render such article injurious to health.*" The [jury] instruction of the trial court permitted this statute to be read without the final and qualifying words, concerning the effect of the article upon health. If Congress had so intended the provision would have stopped with the condemnation of food which contained any added poisonous or other added deleterious ingredient. In other words, the first and familiar consideration is that, if Congress had intended to enact the statute in that form, it would have done so by choice of apt words to express that intent. It did not do so, but only condemned food containing an added poisonous or other added deleterious ingredient when such addition might render the article of food injurious to the health. . . .

. . . The act has placed upon the Government the burden of establishing, in order to secure a verdict of condemnation under this statute, that the added poisonous or deleterious substances must be such as may render such article injurious to health. The word "may" is here used in its ordinary and usual signification, there being nothing to show the intention of Congress to affix to it any other meaning. . . . In thus describing the offense Congress doubtless took into consideration that flour may be used in many ways, in bread, cake, gravy, broth, etc. It may be consumed, when prepared as a food, by the strong and the weak, the old and the young, the well and the sick; and it is intended that if any flour, because of any added poisonous or other deleterious ingredient, may possibly injure the health of any of these, it shall come within the ban of the statute. If it cannot by any possibility, when the facts are reasonably considered, injure the health of any consumer, such flour, though having a small addition of poisonous or deleterious ingredients, may not be condemned under the act. This is the plain meaning of the words and in our view needs no additional support by reference to reports and debates, although it may be said in passing that the meaning which we have given to the statute was well expressed by Mr. Heyburn, chairman of the committee having it in charge upon the floor of the Senate:

> "As to the use of the term 'poisonous,' let me state that everything which contains poison is not poison. It depends on the quantity and the combination. A very large majority of the things consumed by the human family contain, under analysis, some kind of poison, but it depends upon the combination, the chemical relation which it bears to the body in which it exists as to whether or not it is dangerous to take into the human system." . . .

It follows that the judgment of the Circuit Court of Appeals reversing the judgment of the District Court must be affirmed, and the case remanded to the District Court for a new trial.

NOTES

1. *Codification of Lexington Mill.* In 1938, when Congress reproduced the language of the 1906 statute in the first clause of FD&C Act 402(a)(1), it clearly intended to incorporate the Supreme Court's interpretation of the "may render injurious" standard in *Lexington Mill. See Flemming v. Florida Citrus Exchange*, 358 U.S. 153, 161 (1958).

2. *Proof of Hazard.* In accordance with *Lexington Mill,* the key issue under the "may render injurious" standard is the quantity of the added substance in the food. In *United States v. Commonwealth Brewing Corp.*, 1938–1964 F.D.L.I. Jud. Rec. 310 (D. Mass. 1945), the court observed that the quantity of a substance is likely to determine whether it may be harmful and therefore concluded that "quantity would be the test" under section 402(a)(1). The plain language of section 402(a) provides that quantity is an essential element under the "ordinarily injurious" standard as well. The chief distinctions between the two standards in section 402(a)(1) appear to be the greater probability of harm that the government must show to restrict a natural constituent and the government's ability, under the "may render injurious" standard, to take account of specially vulnerable segments of the population.

3. *DES Residues.* Even after FDA banned diethylstilbestrol (DES) in food-producing animals, *see infra* p. 1382, some ranchers continued to implant cattle with the drug. The government seized the beef from treated cattle, contending that it contained an added poisonous or deleterious substance in violation of the Federal Meat Inspection Act, 21 U.S.C 601(m)(1), whose language is identical to Section 402(a)(1). In *United States v. 2,116 Boxes of Boned Beef*, 516 F. Supp. 321 (D. Kan. 1981), however, the court ruled that the government failed to carry its burden of proving that the levels of DES present in the beef could render the beef injurious to health under the *Lexington Mill* standard, or that the beef was otherwise adulterated. The government did not appeal.

———

Even in light of *Lexington Mill*, the government can satisfy the "may render injurious" standard applicable to added substances much more easily than the "ordinarily injurious" standard applicable to nonadded substances. To facilitate enforcement, FDA has thus sought to regulate a number of naturally-occurring environmental contaminants of food as added rather than nonadded. Beginning in 1970, FDA established and began to enforce an action level of 0.5 ppm mercury in fish, resulting in a virtual ban on swordfish. In 1974, FDA promulgated this action level as a proposed rule, explaining its justification for treating mercury as "added" to seafood. 39 Fed. Reg. 42743 (December 6, 1974) (excerpted *infra* p. 510). To clarify the distinction between added and nonadded substances, FDA later promulgated regulations which took the position that only a substance "that is an inherent natural constituent of the food and is not the result of environmental, agricultural, industrial, or other contamination" is a "nonadded" substance. 42 Fed. Reg. 52814 (Sept. 30, 1977), codified at 21 C.F.R. 109.3(c).

Meanwhile, a swordfish vendor was challenging the 0.5 action level in court. In *United States v. Anderson Seafoods, Inc.*, 447 F. Supp. 1151 (N.D. Fla. 1978), the district court determined that mercury in fish was an "added" substance and thus eligible for an action level. However, the court rejected both FDA's 0.5 ppm mercury action level and the industry-proposed 2.0 ppm safe level and determined instead that mercury concentrations of 1.0 ppm or less would not be considered adulterated. Before the Fifth Circuit issued the following decision on appeal, the government accepted the 1.0 ppm action level set by the district court.

United States v. Anderson Seafoods, Inc.

622 F.2d 157 (5th Cir. 1980).

■ WISDOM, CIRCUIT JUDGE

This appeal poses the question whether mercury in the tissues of swordfish is an "added substance" within the meaning of the Food, Drug, and Cosmetic Act, 21 U.S.C. 342(a)(1), and is, therefore, subject to regulation under the relaxed standard appropriate to added substances. Only part of that mercury has been added by man.

In April 1977, the United States sought an injunction against Anderson Seafoods, Inc., and its president, Charles F. Anderson, to prevent them from selling swordfish containing more than 0.5 parts per million (ppm) of mercury, which it considered adulterated under the meaning of § 342(a)(1). . . . Anderson responded in May 1977 by seeking a declaratory judgment that fish containing 2.0 ppm of mercury or less are not adulterated. . . .

The district court denied the injunction that the government sought. In Anderson's suit, the court also denied an injunction, but issued a declaratory judgment that swordfish containing more than 1.0 ppm mercury is adulterated under § 342(a)(1). In doing so, the court determined that mercury is an "*added* substance" under the Act and rejected Anderson's contention that a level of 2.0 ppm is acceptable. . . .

In the trial of this case three theories about the meaning of the term "added" emerged. The Food and Drug Administration sponsored the first theory. It argues that an "added substance" is one that is not "inherent". According to FDA regulations:

> (c) A "naturally occurring poisonous or deleterious substance" is a poisonous or deleterious substance that is an inherent natural constituent of a food and is not the result of environmental, agricultural, industrial, or other contamination.

> (d) An "added poisonous or deleterious substance" is a poisonous or deleterious substance that is not a naturally occurring poisonous or deleterious substance. . . .

21 C.F.R. §§ 109.3(c), (d). Under this theory, all the mercury in swordfish is an added substance, because it results not from the creature's bodily processes but from mercury in the environment, whether natural or introduced by man.

Anderson put forward a second theory. A substance, under this theory, is not an added substance unless it is proved to be present as a result of the direct agency of man. Further, only that amount of a substance the lineage of which can be so traced is "added". If some mercury in swordfish occurs naturally, and some is the result of man-made pollution, only that percentage of the mercury in fish proved to result directly from pollution is an added substance.

The district court adopted a third theory. Under the court's theory, if a de minimis amount of the mercury in swordfish is shown to result from industrial pollution, then all of the metal in the fish is treated as an added substance and may be regulated under the statute's "may render injurious" standard. The legislative history and case law, though sparse, persuade us that this is the proper reading of the statute.

The distinction between added and not-added substances comes from the "adulterated food" provisions of the original Food, Drug, and Cosmetic Act of 1906. The legislative history shows that "added" meant attributable to acts of man, and "not-added" meant attributable to events of nature. . . .

The Food and Drug Administration argues that there need not be any connection between man's acts and the presence of a contaminant for it to be considered an added substance. The Agency points to the rule it recently promulgated interpreting § 342(a)(1) . . . which defines an added substance as one which is not "an inherent natural constituent of the food", but is instead the "result of an environmental, agricultural, industrial, or other contamination." 21 C.F.R. §§ 109.3(c), (d) (1977). Under the rule, mercury in swordfish tissue deriving from the mercury naturally dissolved in sea water would be an added substance, as would any substance not produced by or essential for the life processes of the food organism. . . . [H]owever, we agree with the district court that the term "added" as used in § 342(a)(1) means artificially introduced, or attributable in some degree to the acts of man. . . .

Determining that man must appear on the stage before a substance is an added one does not determine the size of the role he must play before it is. The dichotomy in § 342(a)(1) is between two clear cases that bracket the present case. The Act considers added things such as lead in coloring agents or caffeine in Coca Cola. It considers not-added things like oxalic acid in rhubarb or caffeine in coffee. The Act did not contemplate, however, the perhaps rare problem of a toxin, part of which occurs "naturally", and part of which results from human acts. . . .

Anderson argues that when a toxin derives in part from man and in part from nature, only that part for which man is responsible may be considered added and so regulated under the "may render injurious" standard. In such a case, however, neither the statute nor FDA regulations suggest that the amount of an added toxic substance be quantified and shown to have a toxic effect of its own if the total amount of the substance in a food is sufficient to render the food potentially hazardous to health. It may be possible as in this case to prove that man introduced some percentage of a toxin into a food organism, but difficult or impossible to prove that percentage.

Since the purpose of the "may render injurious" standard was to facilitate regulation of food adulterated by acts of man, we think that it should apply to all of a toxic substance present in a food when any of that substance is shown to have been introduced by man. Anderson argues that this reading of the statute would result "in the anomalous situation where a substance in a food can be 90 percent natural and 10 percent added [but] the entire substance is considered as added". There is no anomaly, however, in such a situation. The Act's "may render it injurious to health" standard is to be applied to the food, not to the added substance . . . Anderson's argument proves too much. Anderson would argue that if a swordfish contained 0.99 ppm of natural mercury, and 0.99 ppm of mercury from human sources, the fish could be sold although it contained nearly twice as much mercury as the district court found to be a safe level. . . .

In sum, we hold that where some portion of a toxin present in a food has been introduced by man, the entirety of the substance present in the food will be treated as an added substance and so considered under the "may render injurious to health" standard of the Act. . . .

. . . Under our reading of the statute . . . the amount of mercury that man contributes need not be "substantial". The FDA need show only that some portion of the mercury is attributable to acts of man, and that the total amount may be injurious to health.

There was sufficient evidence to show that some mercury is attributable to the acts of man. There was evidence that mercury is dumped into rivers and washes onto the continental shelf, where some of it is methylated by bacteria and taken up by plankton. It thereby enters the food chain of swordfish, for the plankton is consumed by small organisms and fish, such as copepods, herring, and hake, which are in turn eaten by larger organisms, and eventually by swordfish, a peak predator. This evidence was enough to trigger the Act's "may render injurious to health" standard. . . .

NOTES

1. *Regulatory Definition of "Added"*. Following the District Court's decision in *Anderson*, the agency stated that it would adhere to its own

definition of an "added" substance in 21 C.F.R. 109.3 pending the Court of Appeals' decision. Even though the Fifth Circuit rejected the definition as too broad, FDA still has not amended it.

2. *Aflatoxins.* In the same issue of the Federal Register in which FDA proposed 21 C.F.R. 109.3, setting forth its understanding of "added" versus "naturally occurring" poisonous or deleterious substances, the agency also proposed a tolerance level for the carcinogenic substances known as aflatoxins in peanuts and peanut products. 39 Fed. Reg. 42743 (Dec. 6, 1974), 39 Fed. Reg. 42748 (December 6, 1974). As FDA explained: "The aflatoxins are chemically related substances produced by the common molds *Aspergillus flavus* . . . and by *Aspergillus parasiticus*. . . . Aflatoxins may contaminate foods whenever the producing molds grow on foods under favorable conditions of temperature and humidity. . . . Corn, barley, copra, cassava, tree nuts, cottonseed, peanuts, rice, wheat, and grain sorghum are subject to natural aflatoxin contamination." *Id.* at 42748.

In the preamble to the proposed aflatoxin tolerance, FDA asserted: "Aflatoxins are present in peanuts and peanut products because of these contaminating molds. They are, therefore, added substances within the meaning of [section 402(a)(1) of the] Act." This interpretation was consistent with 21 C.F.R. 109.3, which provides that a substance is "added" if it is "the result of environmental, agricultural, industrial, or other contamination." However, aflatoxins are not necessarily "added" substances under the reasoning of the Fifth Circuit in *Anderson Seafoods*, which asserted in 1980 that "added" means "attributable to the acts of man." Nonetheless, in 1979, the same court, when considering an action level for aflatoxins in corn, did not question the assumption that aflatoxins were "added." *United States v. Boston Farm Center, Inc.*, 590 F.2d 149 (5th Cir. 1979). Nor did the D.C. Circuit in decisions subsequent to *Anderson* concerning the action level for aflatoxins in corn. *See Community Nutrition Institute v. Young*, 757 F.2d 354 (D.C. Cir. 1985); *Community Nutrition Institute v. Young*, 818 F.2d 943 (D.C. Cir. 1987).

3. *Unintentional Formation of Poisonous and Deleterious Substances.* Poisonous and deleterious ingredients not intentionally added to food can sometimes form during or after processing. Two examples of such substances are benzene and acrylamides.

Beginning about 1990, the soft drink industry informed FDA that trace levels of benzene, a carcinogen, could form under certain storage conditions in soft drinks containing both benzoate preservatives and vitamin C. Later laboratory results, including those gathered by FDA's Total Diet Study (TDS) from 1995 to 2001, indicated the presence of benzene in soft drinks at levels of potential concern. Because subsequent studies by FDA in the mid-2000s showed that the vast majority of sampled beverages contained either no detectable benzene or levels below the 5 ppb limit for drinking water, FDA has taken no action on this matter. Indeed, the agency has concluded that the TDS results were unreliable. *See* FDA Statement, Benzene in Soft Drinks (Apr. 13, 2006); Total Diet Study— Analytical Results (updated Feb. 2, 2012) (both available on FDA website).

In April 2002, Swedish researchers announced that they had detected acrylamide in a number of fried and baked foods, including French fries, potato chips, cookies, breakfast cereals, and bread. Acrylamide is toxic at high doses, and its safety (including carcinogenicity) at low doses is uncertain. The substance forms by chemical reaction in some plant-based foods when they are heated. FDA has concluded that there is insufficient information for the agency to issue a public warning or take other regulatory action until additional scientific information becomes available. In 2009, the agency requested such data in a Federal Register notice. 74 Fed. Reg. 43134 (Aug. 26, 2009).

FDA has not indicated how it would regulate these substances if it were to take action—as nonadded substances under section 402(a), as added substances under section 402(a) (subject perhaps to an action level or section 406 tolerance), or as food additives under section 409. The last option seems to be off the table for acrylamide if it is shown to be carcinogenic, because this chemical is unavoidable in heated foods, and the Delaney Clause of section 409 prohibits the approval of any carcinogenic additive. *See* Chapter 13.

4. *"Added" Under the 1906 Act.* In *United States v. Coca Cola Company,* 241 U.S. 265, 279–80 (1916), the Supreme Court, construing similar language in the 1906 Act ("added poisonous or other added deleterious ingredient"), held that caffeine was an "added" substance in Coca Cola®, rejecting the defendant's assertion that a usual and normal constituent of a food sold under its own distinctive name was not "added."

As discussed above, *supra* p. 489–492, various types of substances that were once regulated pursuant to section 402(a)(1)—pesticide residues, intentional food additives, color additives, and animal drugs—have been removed from the scope of that provision through the creation of dedicated statutory regimes. As illustrated by *Anderson Seafoods,* environmental contaminants are one important category of poisonous and deleterious substances to which section 402(a)(1) still applies. Another such category is pathogenic microorganisms.

Continental Seafoods v. Schweiker

674 F.2d 38 (D.C. Cir. 1982).

■ BAZELON, CIRCUIT JUDGE.

We must decide whether the Food and Drug Administration (FDA) acted lawfully in concluding that Indian shrimp contaminated with poisonous bacteria was "adulterated" within the meaning of the Food, Drug and Cosmetic Act. The district court answered yes. We affirm.

The Act permits the FDA to prohibit the importation of food that "appears" to be adulterated.[1] In defining "adulterated," the Act focuses

---

[1]   Section 801(a) of the Act, 21 U.S.C. § 381(a) (1976) provides in pertinent part:

The Secretary of Treasury shall deliver to the Secretary of Health, Education, and Welfare, upon his request, samples of food . . . which are being imported or offered for import into the United States, giving notice thereof to the owner or consignee, who may appear before the Secretary of Health, Education, and Welfare and have the right to introduce testimony. . . . If it *appears* from the examination of such samples or otherwise that . . . such article is adulterated . . . then such article shall be refused admission. . . .

on the origin and dangers of "poisonous or deleterious substance(s)" in the food. When such substances are "added" to the food, the food is adulterated if the substance "*may* render it injurious to health." 21 U.S.C. 342(a)(1) (emphasis added). When, on the other hand, the substance is not added, the food is considered adulterated only if the substance would "*ordinarily* render it injurious to health." 21 U.S.C. 342(a)(1) (emphasis added).

Beginning in late 1978, the FDA observed that a significant proportion of shrimp arriving from India contained salmonella. Without proper cooking and storage, food containing that bacteria can cause salmonellosis, a communicable disease that produces a number of serious bodily impairments and sometimes results in death. After officials of the Indian government acknowledged that insanitary processing facilities were responsible for the high rate of contamination of Indian shrimp, the FDA decided to sample all such shrimp arriving in the United States.

In the spring of 1979, appellants offered two lots of raw, frozen Indian shrimp for import into the United States. The FDA sampled the shrimp and discovered salmonella in both lots. . . . FDA issued a Notice of Refusal of Admission. . . .

Appellants concede that the two lots of shrimp at issue contain salmonella. The FDA, in turn, acknowledges that salmonella is not "ordinarily injurious" since its dangers can be averted through proper cooking and storage. The only issue before us, then, is whether the FDA properly concluded that the shrimp met the more relaxed standard of adulteration for "added" substances. Specifically, we must evaluate the FDA's determinations that (A) salmonella was "added" to the Indian shrimp, and (B) that the bacteria "may render" the shrimp unhealthy.

A.   *Is salmonella "added" to shrimp?*

. . . [W]e must determine whether the FDA's conclusion that salmonella is an "added" substance in shrimp is consistent with the provisions of the FDCA. The parties urge different interpretations of the word "added." A regulation promulgated by the FDA in 1977 defines the word to include any substance that is not an inherent, natural constituent of the food.[14] Appellants, on the other hand, argue that "added" describes only those substances which are present due to human intervention. Citing cases that have employed that definition, appellants contend that the FDA was required to demonstrate that human intervention introduced salmonella to the shrimp at issue here. The district court declined to resolve this definitional dispute. Instead, the court held that the FDA could have deemed the salmonella "added" under either standard.

Appellants' contention that "added" refers only to substances introduced by humans was recently adopted by the Fifth Circuit in

---

(Emphasis added.)

[14]   21 C.F.R. § 109.3 (1977). The FDA states that under its " 'inherent' test, a substance is 'added' to a food if its presence therein is attributable to man or, if the substance is not an inherent, natural constituent of the food." Brief for Appellees. Since we conclude that the FDA has a sufficient basis for determining that salmonella is at least partly "attributable to man," we need not decide whether the agency could apply the more relaxed standard of adulteration to foods which contain dangerous substances due to unusual acts of nature.

United States v. Anderson Seafoods, Inc., 622 F.2d 157 (1980) [*supra* p. 498]. The court there concluded that the more relaxed standard for adulteration "should apply to all of a toxic substance present in a food when any of that substance is shown to have been introduced by man." The court further held that a showing of human intervention could be based on general scientific knowledge about the origin of the additive in question. *Anderson Seafoods* thus implicitly rejected the notion advanced by appellants here that the FDA must demonstrate human intervention with respect to the particular articles of food it wishes to regulate. We reject the argument explicitly. In light of the FDA's broad authority to prohibit import of any food that "appears" to be adulterated, the agency need not prove that substances present in a particular lot were introduced by man.

We agree with the district court that the FDA's decision in this case satisfied appellants' definition of "added" as elaborated in *Anderson Seafoods*. The evidence offered by both parties indicated that salmonella in shrimp can result from human acts and can frequently be attributed to insanitary processing procedures.[17] The FDA had ample reason to believe that the salmonella frequently observed in Indian shrimp in 1978 and 1979 resulted from insanitary conditions. Representatives of the Indian government acknowledged to the FDA that the salmonella contamination was a result of unclean handling. And several months before the administrative hearing in this case, FDA officials visited processing facilities in India and determined the nature of conditions there first hand. . . .

Together with the FDA's understanding of the cause of salmonella in shrimp generally, these observations provided more than enough support for the agency's conclusions that the bacteria had been at least partly introduced by man.

B. *Did the FDA show that salmonella "may render" shrimp unhealthy?*

Appellants claim the evidence does not support the FDA's determination that salmonella "may render (shrimp) injurious to health." This complaint is groundless. The record indicates that ingestion of even small amounts of the bacteria can cause serious cases of food poisoning in some people. Appellants do not dispute the medical evidence; indeed, their own expert witness confirmed the danger. Instead, they rely on (1) the fact that few, if any, cases of salmonellosis traced to shrimp have been reported and (2) their expectation that consumers will properly cook and store the shrimp and thus prevent contraction of the disease.

The FDA offered several reasonable explanations for the low number of reported cases of salmonellosis from shrimp: The sources of information on which appellants rely report only a small proportion of salmonella cases; reporting of "home episodes" is rare; specific cases

---

[17] *See, e.g.,* J.A. 40–41 (plaintiffs' expert testifies that salmonella is introduced to shrimp through waters contaminated, for example, by fecal matter; notes that water far from land is not generally contaminated); . . . *id.* at 175–76 (FDA official testifies that . . . "when salmonella(e) are found in seafood, including shrimp, their presence is almost always attributable to insanitary and improper processing procedures"); *id.* at 251 (defendants' expert states that salmonella does not ordinarily occur in shrimp and is usually caused by "insanitary handling and/or processing practices or harvesting from polluted waters").

may often be attributed to the wrong sources; and shrimp products are consumed in much smaller quantities than other foods which may contain salmonella. These explanations were supported by the record and adopted by the district court. Accordingly, we agree with the court that the "absence of documentation does not foreclose the (FDA's) discretion to determine that salmonella in shrimp may be injurious to the health of those who consume it."

Nor are we comforted by appellants' sanguine assurances that consumers will properly cook and store the shrimp. The FDA has authority to ban contaminated articles from import notwithstanding promises that the deleterious condition will be corrected. Moreover, there was evidence in the record that many people either do not cook shrimp properly or, like the patrons of Japanese restaurants, eat it raw. Under these circumstances, the FDA was well within its authority in concluding that salmonella "may render" shrimp injurious to health.

Affirmed.

NOTES

1. *402(a)(3) and (a)(4).* FDA can, and sometimes does, also base enforcement actions against the presence of pathogenic organisms on section 402(a)(3), declaring a food adulterated "if it consists in whole or in part of any filthy, putrid, or decomposed substance, or if it is otherwise unfit for food." As will be discussed in detail below, *infra* p. 528, another important provision for the control of pathogenic contamination is section 402(a)(4), declaring a food adulterated "if it has been prepared, packed, or held under insanitary conditions . . . whereby it may have been rendered injurious to health."

2. *Contradictory Decision for Meat Products.* The Federal Meat Inspection Act contains an adulteration provision effectively identical to FD&C Act 402(a)(1). *See* 21 U.S.C. 601(m)(1). Nonetheless, the Fifth Circuit has held that salmonella is not an adulterant under this provision. The Court explained:

> The difficulty in this case arises, in part, because *Salmonella,* present in a substantial proportion of meat and poultry products, is not an adulterant *per se* [*i.e.*, a 601(m)(1) adulterant], meaning its presence does not require the USDA to refuse to stamp such meat "inspected and passed." This is because normal cooking practices for meat and poultry destroy the *Salmonella* organism, and therefore the presence of *Salmonella* in meat products does not render them "injurious to health" for purposes of § 601(m)(1). *Salmonella*-infected beef is thus routinely labeled "inspected and passed" by USDA inspectors and is legal to sell to the consumer.

Supreme Beef Processors v. U.S.D.A., 275 F.3d 432, 439 (5th Cir. 2001). The court cited but did not distinguish *Continental Seafoods. Id.* at 339 n. 24.

3. *Recordkeeping, Records Access, and Tracing.* Section 414(b) of the FD&C Act, added by the Bioterrorism Act of 2002, authorizes FDA to issue regulations requiring food facilities, excluding farms and restaurants, to establish and maintain "records . . . needed by the Secretary for inspection

to allow the Secretary to identify the immediate previous sources and the immediate subsequent recipients of food . . . in order to address credible threats of serious adverse health consequences or death to humans or animals." FDA has issued such regulations, which are codified at 21 C.F.R. Part 1, Subpart J. Section 204 of the FDA Food Safety Modernization Act (FSMA), 124 Stat. 3885 (2011) requires FDA to improve its capacity to trace and track food during a foodborne illness outbreak. Within two years of enactment, FDA is required to issue proposed regulations requiring the maintenance of records, in addition to those covered by FD&C Act 414, that will allow FDA to trace high risk foods (specified by the agency) during an outbreak. The agency has not yet promulgated these regulations. In addition, FSMA section 204 requires FDA, within 270 days of the bill's passage, to establish pilot projects to evaluate the efficacy of different systems for tracing packaged foods and fruits and vegetables. On September 7, 2011, FDA announced the launch of two such pilot projects, carried out by the Institute of Food Technologists, a nonprofit scientific society.

Section 101 of FSMA also amends section 414(a) of the Act to significantly expand FDA's access to food records. The Bioterrorism Act of 2002 gives FDA access to records relating to any food article that the agency reasonably believes "is adulterated and presents a risk of serious adverse health consequences or death." FDA promulgated regulations implementing these provisions at 69 Fed. Reg. 71561 (Dec. 9, 2004), codified at 21 C.F.R. Part 1, Subpart J. FSMA expands this access to records concerning "any other article of food that the Secretary reasonably believes is likely to be affected in a similar manner." FD&C Act 414(a). Records access under this provision is limited to records needed to assist the agency in determining whether the food is adulterated and may cause "serious adverse health consequences or death."

4.   *Reporting of Adulteration.* In 2007, Congress amended the FD&C Act to require all registered food facilities to report to the FDA, through an electronic portal into a Reportable Food Registry, "any article of food . . . for which there is a reasonable probability that the use of, or exposure to, such article of food will cause serious adverse health consequences or death to humans or animals." FD&C Act 417. FDA's Reportable Food Registry became operational on September 8, 2009.

5.   *Administrative Detention and Mandatory Recall.* The Bioterrorism Act of 2002 added section 304(h) to Act, authorizing FDA to administratively detain any article of food if it "has credible evidence or information indicating that such article presents a threat of serious adverse consequences or death to humans or animals." FDA promulgated regulations governing this authority at 69 Fed. Reg. 31659 (June 4, 2004), codified at 21 C.F.R. Part 1, Subpart K. In 2011, FSMA expanded FDA's power to order administrative detentions by lowering the standards for an administrative detention and expanding the circumstances in which detention may be ordered. FDA is now authorized to order the administrative detention of a food article if there is "reason to believe" that the food article is "adulterated or misbranded." FD&C Act 304(h)(1)(A). FDA issued a rule reflecting FSMA's changed criteria for ordering

304

administrative detention at 78 Fed. Reg. 7994 (Feb. 5, 2013) (adopting 2011 interim final rule).

FSMA also, for the first time, provides FDA with mandatory recall authority over food. FDA may use this new power only if it determines that "there is a reasonable probability" that the food is "adulterated or misbranded under section 403(w) [the allergen disclosure provision]" and will cause "serious adverse health consequences or death to humans or animals." FD&C Act 423(a). The agency can issue an immediate cease distribution order and, following an opportunity for a hearing, amend the order to require a recall. *Id.* 423(b)–(d). Because the Act still allows the use of agency-supervised voluntary recalls—a procedure which has almost always been adequate to the agency's needs—FDA will probably invoke its new mandatory recall authority only on rare occasions.

6. *Confectionery.* Section 402(d) contains special provisions concerning adulteration of confectionery (candy). This section declares an article of confectionery to be adulterated (with exceptions) if a nonnutritive object is imbedded in it, if it contains any nonnutritive substance, or if it contains alcohol not derived in small amounts from flavoring extracts.

FDA initially took the position that the sale of trinkets mixed with candy and sold in vending machines violated section 402(a), which provides that food is adulterated "if it bears or contains any poisonous or deleterious substance which may render it injurious to health." This interpretation was overruled in *Cavalier Vending Corp. v. United States*, which held that the mingling of candy and trinkets in a vending machine did not fall within section 402(a)(1) because the candy did not "contain" the trinkets. 190 F.2d 386, 387–88 (4th Cir. 1951). Subsequent legislative proposals to ban the practice were unsuccessful. When section 402(d)(1) was enacted in its present form, 80 Stat. 231 (1966), it prohibited only those trinkets that are partially or completely imbedded in a confectionary. Nonetheless, FDA continues to express concern about the mixing of trinkets with confectionery in vending machines and recommends that the trinkets be "physically separated from candy or gum by some form of wrapping as a safety precaution." Compliance Policy Guide Sec. 515.350 (Oct. 1, 1980).

The alcohol provision, section 402(d)(2), was amended by the Comprehensive Smokeless Tobacco Health Education Act of 1986, 100 Stat. 30, 35, to permit confectionery containing alcohol to be shipped to states where such products are lawful. By 1986, eleven states had enacted laws specifically permitting the sale of candy containing alcohol, 132 Cong. Rec. 1862 (Feb. 6, 1986). For FDA enforcement policy in states that have not legalized candy containing alcohol, see 48 Fed. Reg. 18896 (Apr. 26, 1983), 50 Fed. Reg. 8677 (Mar. 4, 1985).

4. TOLERANCES AND ACTION LEVELS FOR UNAVOIDABLE POISONOUS OR DELETERIOUS SUBSTANCES

a. SECTION 406 TOLERANCES

No provision of the FD&C Act explicitly provides a mechanism for regulating substances that become constituents of food through environmental contamination. Yet such materials—which include mercury, polychlorinated biphenyls (PCBs), polybrominated biphenyls (PBBs), and aflatoxins—may pose serious risks to human health. Controlling their occurrence in food raises difficult scientific and economic, as well as administrative, issues. Similar issues arise with respect to pesticide residues on nontarget crops (i.e., crops other than those for which the pesticide is approved), which are not covered by section 408 (the Miller Pesticide Amendments) and potentially also with respect to other types of added poisonous and deleterious substances unavoidably present in foods. *See supra* p. 501, note 3 (discussion of benzene and acrylamide).

FDA might have relied on the "ordinarily injurious" language of section 402(a)(1) as the basis for court actions to control environmental contaminants and other unavoidable substances, on the premise that since such contaminants are not purposely incorporated in or intentionally used in proximity with food, they should not be considered "added." An alternative would have been to rely exclusively on the first clause of section 402(a)(1), which condemns food containing an added poisonous or deleterious substance if the food "may" be injurious to health. The agency has rejected both approaches. Its objective has been to find a statutory rationale that allows it to determine administratively what level of contamination renders food adulterated. Achievement of this objective promises uniformity in enforcement and contributes to certainty among sellers of food. Furthermore, it assigns responsibility for evaluation of the health risks posed by a contaminant to the agency's scientific experts rather than to the district courts.

The obvious statutory route to such an approach is section 406 of the FD&C Act. Enacted in 1938, section 406 authorizes FDA to establish tolerances for added poisonous or deleterious substances that are "required" in the production of food or "cannot be avoided by good manufacturing practice." The level of a tolerance must be set "for the protection of public health." The primary purpose of this provision was to permit FDA to set tolerances for pesticide residues in food. *E.g.*, H.R. REP. NO. 2139, 75th Cong., 3rd Sess. 6 (1938). To promulgate a tolerance under section 406, however, the agency is obliged to proceed under section 701(e), which requires that objectors to any regulation be given an opportunity for a formal administrative hearing. The rigors of this procedure have led FDA to more frequently resort to a less obvious basis for setting enforcement levels, namely, the establishment of informal "action levels" for enforcement of section 402(a)(1). We will first examine section 406 tolerances and then section 402(a)(1) action levels.

As its first action under section 406, FDA initiated a major rulemaking in 1944 to determine appropriate tolerances for residues of fluorine that remained in food treated with pesticide compounds containing this element. Although the resulting tolerance was upheld, the court effectively nullified it by interpreting it to apply only to elemental fluorine and not to compounds containing fluorine. *Washington State Apple Advertising Comm'n v. Federal Security Adm'r*, 156 F.2d 589 (9th Cir. 1946).

After World War II, FDA, joined by the American Medical Association, voiced growing concern about the safety of pesticide residues in the food supply, and the agency decided to conduct further hearings to establish appropriate tolerances under section 406. When the ensuing hearings ended in the early 1950s, however, FDA decided that the toxicological evidence was so poor and the record so confusing that the tolerances should be withdrawn. The agency made no other efforts to set tolerances for pesticides until after the enactment of the Miller Pesticide Amendments of 1954, discussed *infra* p. 634, when the agency began acting pursuant to new section 408 rather than section 406.

Beginning in the 1960s, however, evidence of a variety of other unavoidable contaminants in food began to accumulate. The contaminants that raised the greatest concern were mercury in fish (resulting from both industrial pollution and natural sources), aflatoxin in nuts, grain, and other food crops (resulting from the growth of a fungus on the crops before harvest or during storage), and polychlorinated biphenyls (PCBs) in a variety of foods (resulting from industrial disposal and accidents). Remembering its prior unsuccessful efforts to set formal tolerances under section 406, FDA chose instead to establish informal "action levels," i.e., levels of contamination that would trigger court enforcement action. FDA began to rely on action levels in the mid-1960s and refined their use through regulations that will be discussed further below.

Nevertheless, confronting growing concern over the widespread contamination of food with PCBs, FDA established formal section 406 tolerances for this compound in animal feeds, foods (milk and other dairy products, poultry, eggs, fish, infant food), and paper food packaging materials. *See* 38 Fed. Reg. 18096 (July 6, 1973). After objections to FDA's tolerance for PCBs present in paper food packaging material were filed, the agency stayed the tolerance pending a formal hearing, but also announced that it would seize as adulterated under section 402(a)(1) any packaging material shipped in interstate commerce containing higher than the specified level. 38 Fed. Reg. 22794 (Aug. 24, 1973). This policy was subsequently upheld in *Natick Paperboard Corp. v. Weinberger*, 525 F.2d 1103 (1st Cir. 1975) (excerpted *infra* p. 608). FDA ultimately settled the formal hearing and adopted the tolerance for PCBs in paper food packaging material as amended to comply with this settlement. 48 Fed. Reg. 37020 (Aug. 16, 1983).

While this administrative proceeding was ongoing, FDA amended the regulations to reduce the tolerance for PCBs in fish. 44 Fed. Reg. 38330 (June 29, 1979). After receiving objections, it conducted a formal hearing, following which it issued a final regulation reducing the tolerance in 49 Fed. Reg. 21514 (May 22, 1984). The tolerances for PCBs, codified in 21 C.F.R. 109.30, remain the only formal tolerances ever adopted under section 406.

b.   ACTION LEVELS: LEGAL BASIS AND PROCEDURE

Section 402(a)(1) does not specifically provide for the promulgation of implementing regulations. It is a "policing" provision that appears to call for court enforcement. In the early 1970s, however, FDA embraced the systematic establishment of section 402(a)(1) tolerances, known as "action levels," to supplement its use of 406 with respect to environmental contaminants. While not a formal tolerance, an action level assures food producers that the FDA ordinarily will not enforce the Act's general adulteration provisions against them if the quantity of the harmful substance in food is less than a specified quantity. The following is the preamble to the proposed rule setting forth the agency's general approach to the regulation of poisonous and deleterious substances in food.

Poisonous or Deleterious Substances in Food: Notice of Proposed Rulemaking

39 Fed. Reg. 42743 (December 6, 1974).

. . . .

"Added" is a statutory term of art encompassing all ingredients which are not inherent and intrinsic parts of a food. . . . Although the word chosen implies that the statute is concerned with the act of addition, the legislative history makes clear that the term seeks rather to establish a standard based upon the necessary and inherent normal condition of the food. . . .

The legislative history . . . identifies examples of foods naturally containing poisonous or deleterious substances and thus not subject to the "added" provisions of section 402(a)(1) of the act. These examples are Burma beans, which contain a glucoside that yields prussic or hydrocyanic acid; rhubarb, which contains oxalic acid; and coffee and tea. Except for substances whose deleterious nature is inherent to the natural state of the food, and thus similar in origin to these examples, all poisonous and deleterious components are "added" within the meaning of the act. Moreover, when a naturally occurring poisonous or deleterious substance is increased to abnormal levels through mishandling or other intervening act, it is "added" to the extent of such increase. . . .

Section 406 was included in the 1938 act to permit the establishment of tolerances for added poisonous or deleterious substances which are required in the production of food or otherwise cannot be avoided by good manufacturing practice. . . . Although formal tolerances under section 406 have not been used by the Food and Drug Administration, except for the tolerance for PCB's published in the FEDERAL REGISTER of July 6, 1973 (38 FR 18096), informal action levels have frequently been utilized to implement this provision of the law and a number of those action levels exist today. In the past, such action levels have . . . not been published in the FEDERAL REGISTER or codified as regulations. . . .

When the Food Additives Amendment of 1958 was enacted, the provisions of section 406 of the act were not repealed. Although all added poisonous or deleterious ingredients are food additives, except when they appear in food accidentally and unforeseeably or are exempted under section 201(s) of the act because they are otherwise regulated under the act, the tolerance-setting provisions of section 406 of the act were left intact to deal with those unavoidably added poisonous or deleterious ingredients that could not meet the high standards for issuance of a regulation under the authority of section

409 of the act. A number of added poisonous or deleterious substances, which are also food additives within the meaning of section 201(s) of the act, are unavoidable but cannot meet the requirements for a section 409 regulation because their safety cannot be demonstrated and because they serve no functional purpose. . . . Section 406 of the act, therefore, remains in force to control the use of such substances, since there would otherwise be no statutory means available to recognize their unavoidability and to exercise reasonable control over their presence. . . .

The Commissioner proposes to establish procedures for controlling all poisonous or deleterious substances. Basic reliance on the provisions of section 409 for regulating use of such substances remains unchanged. . . . However, when a food contaminant is unavoidable but cannot be approved under the criteria of section 409 of the act, a formal procedure is being proposed to control its use under authority of sections 306 [now section 309], 402(a), and 406 of the act.

. . . .

At times it will not be appropriate to establish a formal tolerance. The Commissioner is not required to establish a tolerance for every added poisonous or deleterious substance, as is indicated by the language of section 406 of the act recognizing that an adulteration charge can be made under section 402(a)(1) of the act when no tolerance is in effect. Section 306 of the act [now section 309, providing that the agency is not required to bring formal enforcement action against "minor violations"] has long been interpreted to permit the Food and Drug Administration to establish action levels in implementing the adulteration provisions of the act. . . .

When the factors required to be considered prior to promulgation of a section 406 tolerance are rapidly changing, it would be inappropriate to set such a formal tolerance. The procedures required by section 406 of the act, including a public hearing and requirement of substantial evidence to support the tolerance, contemplate ample evidence to consider, and a relatively stable situation where the evidence will be of more than transient significance and where the tolerance eventually promulgated will be appropriate for a relatively long period of time. . . .

When it is not appropriate to promulgate a tolerance under section 406 . . . the Commissioner will consider promulgating an action level under authority of sections 306 [309], 402(a), and 406 of the act.

Such action levels are similar to a formal tolerance in basis and effect. In setting an action level, the Commissioner considers evidence indicating when the presence of an added poisonous or deleterious substance may render food injurious to health, which is the standard in section 402(a)(1) of the act. In addition, the Commissioner takes into account the question of its unavoidability, a policy embodied in section 406 of the act. Thus, an action level is based on the same criteria as a tolerance, except that an action level is temporary until the appearance of more stable circumstances makes a formal tolerance appropriate. . . .

NOTE

Contaminant or Food Additive. The preamble to the final regulations also set forth FDA's theory of the relationship between Section 406 tolerances (or action levels) and Section 409 food additive regulations. The agency stated that a tolerance or action level should generally not be established for an intentionally added food ingredient or for a component of a food-contact article that serves a functional purpose in the article (except when the substance is unavoidable in a particular food). The agency added, however, that an action level or tolerance may be established for an intentionally added GRAS or prior sanctioned substance based on new questions about the safety of the substance, pending the issuance of an interim food additive regulation or an amended prior sanction regulation. 42 Fed. 52817–18, codified at 21 C.F.R. 180.1(f), 181.1(c). For example, as discussed *infra* at p. 616, action levels have been established to control lead migration from pottery and from soldered cans, where the substances containing the lead are intentionally used in the food-contact surface.

———

FDA's final regulations, issued in 1977, reflected no significant change in the agency's interpretation of the applicable statutory provisions. 42 Fed. Reg. 52813 (Sept. 30, 1977), codified at 21 C.F.R. Part 109 ("Unavoidable Contaminants in Food for Human Consumption and Food Packaging Material"). But the agency abandoned its intention stated in the proposed rule to establish all action levels by notice-and-comment rulemaking. It decided instead simply to set each action level administratively and then publish a notice of its availability (along with supporting data) and an invitation for public comments in the Federal Register. *Id.* at 52817.

Through the 1970s, FDA continued to use an informal action level for aflatoxin in corn of 20 parts per billion (ppb) that it had set in 1969. But FDA began to relax its enforcement of this action level when substantial portions of the corn crops of various states were found to be contaminated with aflatoxin. In 1981, FDA extended an exemption from the 20 ppb action level to the 1980 corn crops of three southeastern states. The agency permitted the use of corn containing up to 100 ppb aflatoxin as animal feed, 46 Fed. Reg. 7447 (Jan. 23, 1981). This decision triggered a legal challenge by public interest groups against the agency's very use of informal action levels instead of formal tolerances. The legality of this approach was ultimately resolved by the Supreme Court in the following case:

Young v. Community Nutrition Institute
476 U.S. 974 (1986).

■ JUSTICE O'CONNOR delivered the opinion of the Court.

We granted certiorari in this case to determine whether the Court of Appeals for the District of Columbia Circuit correctly concluded that the Food and Drug Administration's longstanding interpretation of 21 U.S.C. § 346 [FD&C Act 406] was in conflict with the plain language of that provision. We hold that, in light of the inherent ambiguity of the statutory provision and the reasonableness of the Food and Drug Administration's interpretation thereof, the Court of Appeals erred. We therefore reverse. . . .

Section 346 states:

"Any poisonous or deleterious substance added to any food, except where such substance is required in the production thereof or cannot be avoided by good manufacturing practice shall be deemed to be unsafe for purposes of the application of clause (2)(A) of section 342(a) of this title; but when such substance is so required or cannot be so avoided, the Secretary shall promulgate regulations limiting the quantity therein or thereon to such extent as he finds necessary for the protection of public health, and any quantity exceeding the limits so fixed shall also be deemed to be unsafe for purposes of the application of clause (2)(A) of section 342(a) of this title. While such a regulation is in effect . . . food shall not, by reason of bearing or containing any added amount of such substance, be considered to be adulterated. . . . "

. . . .

The parties do not dispute that, since the enactment of the Act in 1938, the FDA has interpreted 21 U.S.C. § 346 to give it the discretion to decide whether to promulgate a regulation, which is known in the administrative vernacular as a "tolerance level." Tolerance levels are set through a fairly elaborate process, similar to formal rulemaking, with evidentiary hearings. On some occasions, the FDA has instead set "action levels" through a less formal process. In setting an action level, the FDA essentially assures food producers that it ordinarily will not enforce the general adulteration provisions of the Act against them if the quantity of the harmful added substance in their food is less than the quantity specified by the action level.

The substance at issue in this case is aflatoxin, which is produced by a fungal mold that grows in some foods. Aflatoxin, a potent carcinogen, is indisputedly "poisonous" or "deleterious" under §§ 342 and 346. The parties also agree that, although aflatoxin is naturally and unavoidably present in some foods, it is to be treated as "added" to food under § 346. As a "poisonous or deleterious substance added to any food," then, aflatoxin is a substance falling under the aegis of § 346, and therefore is at least potentially the subject of a tolerance level.

The FDA has not, however, set a § 346 tolerance level for aflatoxin. It has instead established an action level for aflatoxin of 20 parts per billion (ppb). In 1980, however, the FDA stated in a notice published in the Federal Register:

"The agency has determined that it will not recommend regulatory action for violation of the Federal Food, Drug, and Cosmetic Act with respect to the interstate shipment of corn from the 1980 crop harvested in North Carolina, South Carolina, and Virginia and which contains no more than 100 ppb aflatoxin. . . ." 46 Fed. Reg. 7448 (1981).

The notice further specified that such corn was to be used only as feed for mature, nonlactating livestock and mature poultry. *Id.* at 7447.

In connection with this notice, two public-interest groups and a consumer (respondents here) brought suit against the Commissioner of the FDA. . . . Respondents alleged that the Act requires the FDA to set a tolerance level for aflatoxin before allowing the shipment in interstate commerce of food containing aflatoxin. . . .

The FDA's longstanding interpretation of the statute that it administers is that the phrase "to such extent as he finds necessary for the protection of public health" in § 346 modifies the word "shall." The FDA therefore interprets the statute to state that the FDA shall promulgate regulations to the extent that it believes the regulations necessary to protect the public health. Whether regulations are necessary to protect the public health is, under this interpretation, a determination to be made by the FDA.

Respondents, in contrast, argue that the phrase "to such extent" modifies the phrase "the quantity therein or thereon" in § 346, not the word "shall." Since respondents therefore view the word "shall" as unqualified, they interpret § 346 to require the promulgation of tolerance levels for added, but unavoidable, harmful substances. The FDA under this interpretation of § 346 has discretion in setting the particular tolerance level, but not in deciding whether to set a tolerance level at all.

Our analysis must begin with *Chevron U.S.A. Inc. v. Natural Resources Defense Council, Inc.*, 467 U.S. 837 (1984). . . .

While we agree with the Court of Appeals that Congress in § 346 was speaking directly to the precise question at issue in this case, we cannot agree with the Court of Appeals that Congress unambiguously expressed its intent through its choice of statutory language. The Court of Appeals' reading of the statute may seem to some to be the more natural interpretation, but the phrasing of § 346 admits of either respondents' or petitioner's reading of the statute. As enemies of the dangling participle well know, the English language does not always force a writer to specify which of two possible objects is the one to which a modifying phrase relates. . . .

. . . We find the FDA's interpretation of § 346 to be sufficiently rational to preclude a court from substituting its judgment for that of the FDA.

To read § 346 as does the FDA is hardly to endorse an absurd result. Like any other administrative agency, the FDA has been delegated broad discretion by Congress in any number of areas. To interpret Congress' statutory language to give the FDA discretion to decide whether tolerance levels are necessary to protect the public health is therefore sensible. . . .

The premise of the Court of Appeals is of course correct: the Act does provide that when a tolerance level has been set and a food contains an added harmful substance in a quantity below the tolerance level, the food is legally not adulterated. But one cannot logically draw from this premise, or from the Act, the Court of Appeals' conclusion that food containing substances *not* subject to a tolerance level *must be* deemed adulterated. The presence of a certain premise (*i.e.*, tolerance levels) may imply the absence of a particular conclusion (*i.e.*, adulteration) without the absence of the premise implying the presence of the conclusion. . . . The Act is silent on what specifically to do about food containing an unavoidable, harmful, added substance for which there is no tolerance level; we must therefore assume that Congress intended the general provisions of § 342(a) to apply in such a case. Section 342(a) thus remains available to the FDA to prevent the shipment of any food "[if] it bears or contains any poisonous or deleterious substance which may render it injurious to health." . . .

Finally, we note that our interpretation of § 346 does not render that provision superfluous, even in light of Congress' decision to authorize the FDA to "promulgate regulations for the efficient enforcement of [the] Act." 21 U.S.C. § 371(a). Section 346 gives the FDA the authority to choose whatever tolerance level is deemed "necessary for the protection of public health," and food containing a quantity of a required or unavoidable substance less than the tolerance level "shall not, by reason of bearing or containing any added amount of such substance, be considered to be adulterated." Section 346 thereby creates a specific exception to § 342(a)'s general definition of adulterated food as that containing a quantity of a substance that renders the food "ordinarily . . . injurious to health."* Simply because the FDA is given the choice between employing the standard of § 346 and the standard of § 342(a) does not render § 346 superfluous. . . .

NOTE

Notice-and-Comment Rulemaking Requirement? The plaintiffs also contended that if FDA were allowed to enforce the Act by means of action levels, these levels must be established by notice-and-comment rulemaking. The Supreme Court remanded this claim to the Court of Appeals, which ruled that FDA action levels for poisonous or deleterious substances operated as legislative rules that constrained the agency rather than as general statements of policy, and therefore that these levels must be promulgated through informal rulemaking. *Community Nutrition Institute v. Young*, 818 F.2d 943 (D.C. Cir. 1987). In response, FDA published a notice declaring that in the future it would regard action levels as prosecutorial guidelines and not binding rules. 53 Fed. Reg. 5043 (Feb. 19, 1988). FDA later amended its regulations to incorporate this policy. 55 Fed. Reg. 20782 (May 21, 1990).

c.   ACTION LEVELS: THE EXAMPLE OF MERCURY

In the same December 6, 1974 Federal Register in which it proposed the procedure for establishing action levels for unavoidable contaminants, FDA published the following proposed action level for mercury in fish, 39 Fed. Reg. 42738 (later withdrawn in 44 Fed. Reg. 3990 (Jan. 19, 1979)). In accordance with the proposed procedure, FDA intended to establish this 0.5 ppm action level by notice-and-comment rulemaking. (As noted above, the agency would soon afterward cease using notice-and-comment rulemaking for establishing action levels.) FDA's application of this proposed action level precipitated the

---

*   [Because aflatoxin is treated here as an "added" substance, the relevant standard from 21 U.S.C. 342(a) (section 402(a) of the FDCA) is actually "may render [the food] injurious to health."—Eds.]

Anderson Seafood litigation, which culminated in the Court of Appeals decision excerpted *supra* at p. 498.

Action Level for Mercury in Fish and Shellfish: Notice of Proposed Rulemaking

39 Fed. Reg. 42738 (December 6, 1974).

. . . .

Most of man's exposure to mercury arises from the contamination of food and possibly drinking water. . . . Except in occupational exposure, the contribution of inhaled mercury is insignificant in relation to intake from food. The amount of methylmercury (the most toxic organic form of mercury) found in fruits, vegetables, grains, meat and dairy products is very small. Of all the commodities analyzed for mercury by the Food and Drug Administration (FDA) in a survey of 10 basic foods and in the food commodity classes of the FDA total diet study, fish was the only commodity shown to present a potential hazard to man. Other data show levels of mercury in shellfish (mollusks and crustaceans) similar to the levels in some vertebrate fish. The total human intake of mercury from food sources other than fish and shellfish is insignificant. . . .

Methylmercury and other forms of mercury serve no essential function in fish and shellfish. They are not normal inherent constituents, but are found in aquatic species because of environmental, industrial, and agricultural contamination. . . . The mercury that contaminates the aquatic environment has come from two principal sources, leaching or volatilization from natural geological sources and human activities. Significant amounts of mercury enter the environment from man's agricultural and industrial use. . . .

Methylmercury poisoning may lead to progressive blindness, deafness, incoordination, intellectual deterioration, and death. . . . In all mammals, concentrations of 5 to 10 micrograms per gram (mcg/g) of brain tissue may be associated with neurological symptoms. . . .

. . . [A]n action level of 0.5 ppm [parts per million] permits a daily consumption of 60 grams of fish and shellfish contaminated to that extent, while still maintaining a tenfold margin of safety over the level of mercury intake known to be toxic. The 60 g/day figure is based on a mercury concentration of 0.5 ppm in all fish and shellfish consumed, but because actual concentrations are much less in most fish and shellfish, there is an additional safety margin. In addition, the average consumption of fish and shellfish in this country is regarded as considerably less than 60 grams per day.

A National Marine Fisheries Service (NMFS) survey determined that only 1.8 percent of the population consumes an average of more than 60 grams of fish and shellfish per day. The vast majority of the population is therefore protected by the tenfold margin of safety. Additional protection is provided by the fact that actual concentrations in most fish and shellfish are below 0.5 ppm mercury and the fact that consumption is less than an average of 60 grams per day.

It is not possible, however, to provide this same high level of protection to every person without excluding a great amount of fish and shellfish from the market. The NMFS survey indicated that 1 percent of the participants in the survey consumed an average of 77 grams daily and 0.1 percent consumed 165 grams daily. At the very high consumption of 165 grams per day, the tenfold margin of safety is reduced to less than four; although, it may be increased above that figure by the additional margin resulting from consumption of fish and shellfish with less contamination than 0.5 ppm mercury. . . .

In balancing the unavoidability of mercury in fish and shellfish against the need for protection of the public health, the Commissioner concludes that it would be inappropriate to exclude a vast amount of fish and shellfish from the market in order to provide a large margin of safety for those who consume far more than the average person. The Commissioner notes that a person would have to consume every day the extraordinarily high amount of 600 grams of fish and/or shellfish contaminated at the full 0.5 ppm level to reach the blood levels where symptoms have been known to occur. Thus some margin of safety is still provided for even the largest consumers of these foods. . . .

NOTES

1. *Judicial Review.* In *United States v. Anderson Seafoods, Inc.*, 447 F. Supp. 1151 (N.D. Fla. 1978), the court determined that mercury in fish was an "added" substance and thus eligible for an action level. But it rejected both FDA's 0.5 ppm mercury action level and the industry-proposed 2.0 ppm safe level and determined instead that mercury concentrations of 1.0 ppm or less would not be considered adulterated. While the case was pending appeal, FDA withdrew its December 1974 proposal of a 0.5 action level and accepted the court-determined level of 1.0 ppm as its new action level. In accordance with the revised procedure established by final rule at 42 Fed. Reg. 52813, 52817 (Sept. 30, 1977), *see supra* p. 512, the agency adopted by this 1.0 level "administratively" without prior notice and comment. 44 Fed. Reg. 3990 (Jan. 19, 1979). In *United States v. Anderson Seafoods, Inc.*, 622 F.2d 157 (5th Cir. 1980) (excerpted *supra* p. 498), the Court of Appeals upheld the 1.0 ppm action level and also affirmed the district court's theory that if any of the mercury was shown to result from industrial pollution, then all of it could be treated as "added."

2. *Subsequent History.* Based upon new methodology, FDA subsequently revised the 1.0 ppm action level to encompass only methyl mercury and not total mercury. 49 Fed. Reg. 45663 (Nov. 19, 1984). Section 413 of the Food and Drug Administration Modernization Act of 1997 required FDA to conduct a study of mercury compounds in food and drugs. In 63 Fed. Reg. 68775 (Dec. 14, 1998) and 64 Fed. Reg. 23083 (Apr. 29, 1999), FDA requested data and information in order to prepare this report.

In January 2001, FDA issued a Consumer Advisory to women of childbearing age and pregnant women concerning fish consumption and mercury, and in March 2004, FDA and EPA jointly announced a revised Consumer Advisory directed to women who may become pregnant, pregnant women, nursing mothers, and young children. "FDA and EPA

Announce the Revised Consumer Advisory on Methylmercury in Fish," FDA Press Release No. PO4–33 (Mar. 19, 2004). For high risk groups, the advisory recommended against any consumption of shark, swordfish, king mackerel, and tilefish because of their high mercury levels. The announcement caused substantial public controversy. In June 2006, the two agencies announced that "the 2004 advisory remains current and that FDA and EPA stand behind it." The agencies deliberately issued their recommendations in the form of a consumer advisory rather than a warning because "fish and shellfish are an important part of a healthy diet and can contribute to heart health and children's proper growth and development." *See* Dariush Mozaffarian & Eric R. Rimm, *Fish Intake, Contamination, and Human Health*, 296 J.A.M.A. 1885 (2006).

3. *Lead Contamination.* Like mercury, lead is both ubiquitous in the environment and toxic to humans. Lead occurs in food as a result of natural background levels, environmental pollution, food processing and packaging (e.g., soldered cans), and foodware. FDA has sought to reduce lead residues in food chiefly by focusing on packaging materials and foodware. *See infra* p. 616.

4. *Detection of Dioxin.* As the result of improvements in detection methodology and more comprehensive sampling of the food supply, environmental contaminants are often found unexpectedly. For example, although FDA had been monitoring the dioxin content of fish, *see* "Dioxin in Fish," FDA Talk Paper No. T81–32 (Aug. 28, 1981), the agency learned in 1985 that trace amounts were also detectable in paper food packaging and discovered in 1988 that dioxin could migrate from paperboard cartons into milk. FDA's own tests confirmed that the dioxin contamination was "well below 1 part per trillion," and it announced that production changes undertaken by the paper industry would reduce this level so that paper would "contribute essentially no dioxin to the milk and other foods they packaged." HHS News No. P89–38 (Sept. 1, 1989). As a result of production changes undertaken by the paper industry, FDA announced that a new survey of milk conducted during 1991–1992 found no samples with a detectable level of dioxin using analytical methods with detection limits in the range of 2–10 ppt. 59 Fed. Reg. 17384 (Apr. 12, 1994). The results of FDA's dioxin food surveys in the mid-1990s, 2002–03, and 2008 are available on the FDA website.

d.   THE QUESTION OF BLENDING

FDA's longstanding position has been that the intentional blending of product that violates a tolerance or action level with product not sufficiently contaminated to be considered adulterated is prohibited, even if the resulting mix satisfies the tolerance or action level. In 1978, however, FDA relaxed this policy in response to a dire situation: heavy rains during the 1977 harvesting season led to above-action-level amounts of aflatoxin on as much as 40 percent of the region's corn crop. In the Federal Register notice excerpted below, the agency thus extended a temporary exemption from its prohibition on blending. This decision was issued without prior notice or opportunity for comment. The exemption notice excerpted below preceded the broader 1981 exemption from the 20 ppb action level upheld by the Supreme Court in

Young v. Community Nutrition Institute (excerpted *supra* p. 512). That later exemption also permitted blending.

Aflatoxin–Contaminated Corn: Limited Exemption From Blending Prohibition
43 Fed. Reg. 14112 (Apr. 4, 1978).

The Food and Drug Administration is establishing a limited exemption to its prohibition against blending a food (corn) containing a poisonous or deleterious substance (aflatoxin) in amounts above the tolerance or action level (20 parts per billion (20 ppb)) with less contaminated food to obtain a mixture within the tolerance or action level. This exemption applies to corn harvested in 1977 in the States of Alabama, Florida, Georgia, Mississippi, North Carolina, South Carolina, and Virginia. The blending must be done in accordance with a technically feasible plan approved by the FDA Regional Office in Atlanta, Ga., before blending operations begin. The exemption does not apply to corn that contains more than 20 ppb aflatoxin if the corn has been shipped in interstate commerce. The blended corn must not exceed the action level of 20 parts per billion (ppb) aflatoxin and must be used only for animal feed for mature poultry and swine, and mature, non-milk-producing beef cattle. This exemption does not apply to corn or mixed feeds used for rations for dairy animals, or starter rations for very young animals, or to corn for human consumption.

Corn that contains aflatoxin in excess of the established FDA action level of 20 parts per billion (ppb) is an adulterated food under section 402(a)(1) of the Federal Food, Drug, and Cosmetic Act (21 U.S.C. 342(a)(1)). Use of an adulterated food as an ingredient in another food ordinarily causes the finished food to be deemed adulterated, even if the finished product itself does not violate an established tolerance or action level.

The action level for aflatoxin applies only to unavoidable contamination of corn. Intentional blending of a violative article with an uncontaminated article is wholly avoidable and not authorized by the action level. . . .

Section 509.8 (21 CFR 509.8), issued in the FEDERAL REGISTER of September 30, 1977 (42 FR 52822), provides for exemptions from established action levels if the Commissioner of Food and Drugs determines that (1) based on all available evidence, the food is safe for consumption, and (2) destruction or diversion of the food involved would result in a substantial adverse impact on the national food supply.

The Commissioner has reviewed all available evidence concerning the safety of aflatoxin in feed corn and has determined that the limited exemption to permit blending established by this notice will not result in any perceivable increased risk to the health of mature poultry and swine and mature non-milk-producing beef cattle fed such corn, or to humans consuming edible tissues derived from those animals.

The Commissioner has determined that the destruction or diversion of corn that would be required by the continued prohibition of blending of the subject feed corn would result in a substantial impact on the national food supply.

Based on data recently compiled by FDA, over half the 1977 corn crop in parts of the Southeast United States . . . may exceed the 20 ppb action level and thus may not be shipped in interstate commerce. Since it may be difficult for farmers in this area to find adequate supplies of corn for use in feeding animals if the law is enforced fully, the Commission[er] has determined that he will not recommend regulatory action for violation of the [FD&C Act] with respect to blending of such corn for use as animal feed if conditions of this notice are met. . . .

The Commissioner is not altering the agency's longstanding position that it is ordinarily unlawful to blend corn containing aflatoxin above the action level with less contaminated corn. But the Commissioner is permitting blending on a one-time basis only because of the severity of this emergency situation. . . .

NOTES

1. *Judicial Affirmation.* In the suit culminating in the Supreme Court's decision in *Community Nutrition Institute v. Young* (excerpted *supra* p. 512), CNI claimed that blending was a violation of the FD&C Act. On remand, the Court of Appeals addressed this question, and it held:

> . . . The *intentional* blending of contaminated corn obviously cannot in reason be considered unavoidable. Surely there can be little doubt that blended corn therefore stands branded as "adulterated" for purposes of the FDC Act. . . . But as FDA goes on to point out, a conclusion that a particular food product is "adulterated," in the abstract, means little other than that FDA could choose to initiate enforcement proceedings . . .

> Upon analysis, therefore, the gravaman of CNI's complaint is that FDA failed to initiate enforcement proceedings. But as the Supreme Court held in *Heckler v. Chaney* [excerpted *supra* p. 171], FDA enjoys complete discretion not to employ the enforcement provisions of the FDC Act, and those decisions are not subject to judicial review.

Community Nutrition Institute v. Young, 818 F.2d 943, 949–50 (D.C. Cir. 1987).

2. *1989 Exemption.* When the southeast was again faced with widespread aflatoxin contamination of the corn crop, FDA announced that it was retaining its 20 ppb action level for human food but raising its action levels for animal feed. *See* "Aflatoxin Contamination," FDA Talk Paper No. T88–73 (Oct. 4, 1988); "Drought Increases Aflatoxin Problem for Farmers, Processors," FDA Talk Paper No. T89–13 (Feb. 27, 1989). Explaining that action levels constitute only guidance and not binding requirements, FDA again announced that blending would be permitted. 54 Fed. Reg. 22622 (May 25, 1989).

3. *Aesthetic Adulteration.* When FDA promulgated its final food GMP regulations, it specifically declined to revise 21 C.F.R. § 110.110(d) (excerpted *supra* p. 474), which prohibits the blending of food to comply with an action level for defects presenting no health hazard. 51 Fed. Reg. 22458, 22474 (June 19, 1986).

4. *Continuation of Anti-Blending Policy.* As a general matter, FDA still refuses to permit blending except in exceptional circumstances. Section 555.200 of the Compliance Policy Guide Manual, unchanged since 1980, states, "In our opinion, the deliberate mixing of adulterated food with good food renders the finished product adulterated under the Federal Food, Drug, and Cosmetic Act, regardless of the final concentration of contaminant in the finished food. We, therefore, cannot agree to a plan which incorporates this concept."

5. *Repeal of Rule Providing for Exemptions.* Until 1990, FDA regulations contained a provision—cited in the document excerpted above—explicitly providing for exemptions from tolerances and action levels for animal food in times of potential food shortages. 21 C.F.R. 509.8. An identical provision existed with respect to tolerances and action levels for human food. 21 C.F.R. 109.8. FDA revoked these provisions in 1990 as part of its effort (following the D.C. Circuit's remand decision in *Community Nutrition Institute v. Young*, 818 F.2d 943 (D.C. Cir. 1987)) to make clear that action levels constituted prosecutorial guidance rather than substantive rules and thus were not required to be issued pursuant to notice-and-comment rulemaking. 55 Fed. Reg. 20782 (May 21, 1990). The removal of the regulatory provisions expressly allowing exemptions from action levels would almost certainly not inhibit FDA from permitting blending in special circumstances in the future. *See* Presentation, Mycotoxins in Feeds: CVM's Perspective (Aug. 23, 2006) ("CVM may permit 'blending' under special provisions").

6. *Aflatoxin in Peanuts.* On the same day in 1974 that FDA proposed the 0.5 ppm action level for mercury in fish, it also proposed a formal section 406 tolerance for aflatoxin in shelled peanuts and peanut products, 39 Fed. Reg. 42748 (Dec. 6, 1974). The agency withdrew this proposed tolerance in 1991. 56 Fed. Reg. 67440, 46 (Dec. 30, 1991). Today, action levels for aflatoxin in peanuts in animal feed are stated in Compliance Policy Guide (CPG) 683.100, and the action level for peanut products in human food is stated in CPG 570.375.

G. REGULATION OF FOOD PRODUCTION AND THE PROBLEM OF PATHOGENIC MICROORGANISMS

1. INTRODUCTION

All food contains microorganisms. Most are harmless. Nonpathogenic microorganisms are an essential part of the bacterial fermentation process needed to produce such common food products as cheese, yogurt, and pickles.

The scientific study of food poisoning through pathogenic contamination of food began with the publication of G.M. DACK, FOOD POISONING (1943). With rare exceptions, FDA has always taken regulatory action against any food containing any detectable level of a pathogenic microorganism. For example, Compliance Policy Guide No. 7106.08 (Oct. 10, 1980, as amended) authorizes seizure of any dairy product containing any detectable amount of salmonella, campylobacter jejuni, campylobacter coli, yersinia enterocolitica, or listeria monocytogenes, or greater than a specified level of enteropathic escherichia coli. The following table of typical illnesses caused by common food pathogens, from David W. K. Acheson & Anthony E. Fiore, *Preventing Foodborne Disease—What Clinicians Can Do*, 350 NEW ENG. J. MED. 437, 439 (2004), illustrates the impact of pathogens in food.

Table: Selected Clinical and Epidemiological Characteristics of Typical Illnesses Caused by Common Foodborne Pathogens*				
Pathogen	**Typical Incubation Period†**	**Duration**	**Typical Clinical Presentation‡**	**Associated Foods§**
Bacterial				
Salmonella species	1–3 Days	4–7 Days	Gastroenteritis	Undercooked eggs or poultry, produce
Campylobacter jejuni	2–6 Days	2–10 Days	Gastroenteritis	Undercooked poultry, unpasteurized dairy products
Escherichia coli O157:H7	1–8 Days	5–10 Days	Gastroenteritis	Undercooked beef, produce, unpasteurized dairy products
E. coli, enterotoxigenic	1–3 Days	3–7 Days	Gastroenteritis	Many foods
Shigella species	1–2 Days	Variable	Gastroenteritis	Produce, egg salad
Listeria monocytogenes	2–6 Weeks	Variable	Gastroenteritis, meningitis, abortion¶	Deli meat, hot dogs, unpasteurized dairy products
Bacillus cereus	1–6 Hours	<24 Hours	Vomiting, gastroenteritis	Fried rice, meats
Clostridium botulinum	12–72 Hours	Days-months	Blurred vision, paralysis	Home-canned foods, fermented fish
Staphylococcus aureus	1–6 Hours	1–2 Days	Gastroenteritis, particularly nausea	Meats, potato and egg salads, cream pastries
Yersinia enterocolitica	1–2 Days	1–3 Weeks	Gastroenteritis, appendicitis-like syndrome	Undercooked pork, unpasteurized dairy products

Viral				
Norovirus	1–2 Days	12–60 Hours	Gastroenteritis	Undercooked shellfish
Hepatitis A virus	15–50 Days	Weeks-months	Hepatitis	Produce, undercooked shellfish
Parasitic				
Cryptospori-dium parvum	2–10 Days	Weeks	Gastroenteritis	Produce, water
Cyclospora cayetanensis	1–11 Days	Weeks	Gastroenteritis	Produce, water
Toxoplasma gondii	5–23 Days	Months	Influenza-like illness, lymphadeno-pathy	Food contaminated by cat feces, undercooked meat
Giardia lamblia	1–4 Weeks	Weeks	Gastroenteritis	Water
Taenia solium	Variable	Variable	Asymptomatic cysticercosis	Raw pork

* Adapted from "Diagnosis and Management of Foodborne Illnesses: A Primer for Physicians" (available at http://www.ama-assn.org/ama/pub/category/3629.html).

† Incubation periods may vary; the average periods are given, but wider ranges have been reported.

‡ Gastroenteritis typically includes nausea, vomiting, diarrhea (which may be bloody), fever, and abdominal pain.

§ These foods are among those most commonly implicated in epidemiologic investigations. For some pathogens, person-to-person transmission or transmission through foods prepared by an infected person is more common.

¶ *L. monocytogenes* may also cause gastroenteritis with a short (two-to-three-day) incubation period.

In the past thirty years, four events, more than any others, have led FDA and the public to focus on foodborne illness caused by pathogens: (1) the unexpected discovery in 1982 that *Listeria* contamination can be found in many common food products through the use of more sensitive detection methodology; (2) the January 1993 contamination of undercooked hamburgers by a new strain of *E. coli*, 0157:47, at a Jack in the Box restaurant in Washington State, which caused the death of four children and the hospitalization of many others; (3) the October 1996 contamination with *E. coli* 0157:47 of Odwalla fresh unpasteurized apple cider marketed on the west coast, which led to the death of one child and the hospitalization of many others; and (4) a massive nationwide *Salmonella* outbreak in 2008 and 2009 leading to at least nine deaths and over 700 illnesses (including many children) that was traced to contaminated peanut products distributed by the Peanut Corporation of America from its Blakely, Georgia processing plant.

As discussed in the excerpt below, the increased attention to food poisoning outbreaks has undermined the public's confidence in FDA's ability to ensure a safe food supply. This concern led Congress to pass the Food Safety Modernization Act (FSMA), which was signed into law in 2011. This statute represents the most important and thoroughgoing amendment of the FD&C Act's food safety provisions since 1938. Some of the changes introduced by FSMA have already been mentioned, and others will be examined in detail later in this chapter.

Enhancing Food Safety: The Role of the Food and Drug Administration

Institute of Medicine and National Research Council of the National Academies (2010).

Chapter 1 ("Introduction")

Study Context

Increasing Discussion and Controversies About the FDA's Ability to Ensure Safe Food

Many recent changes in the nation's food system have prompted increasing discussion of the FDA's ability to ensure safe food. The 1998 Institute of Medicine (IOM)/National Research Council (NRC) report *Ensuring Safe Food: From Production to Consumption* identifies some of these changes, such as the food safety implications of emerging pathogens, the trend toward the consumption of more fresh produce, the trend toward eating more meals away from home, and changing demographics, with a greater proportion of the population being immunocompromised or otherwise at increased risk of foodborne illness. These developments must be understood in the context of a wide range of global and societal changes that greatly increase the complexity of the food safety system and the challenges faced by those responsible for implementing the system. These changes . . . include changes in the food production landscape, climate change, evolving consumer perceptions and behaviors (e.g., the growing demand for fresh produce and for its availability year-round), globalization and increased food importation, the role of labor—management relations and workplace safety, heightened concern about bioterrorism, increased levels of pollution in the environment, and the increasing role of international trade agreements. Food production is changing as well, with the number of firms involved with food having increased by roughly 28 percent since 2001. The importation of food is also increasing; roughly $49 billion worth of food was imported to the United States in 2007.

A number of high-profile food-related outbreaks have occurred in recent years, including *E. coli* O157:H7 in spinach in 2006, melamine in pet food in 2007, *Salmonella* in produce and in peanut butter in 2008, and *E. coli* O157:H7 in cookie dough in 2009. In 1999, Mead and colleagues estimated that foodborne infections caused about 76 million illnesses, 325,000 hospitalizations, and 5,000 deaths each year in the United States. It should be emphasized that these data were reported in 1999, and the morbidity, mortality, and hospitalization estimates would likely be different today; new estimates are in preparation but were not available at the time of this writing. Nonetheless, data for

2008 from the U.S. Centers for Disease Control and Prevention (CDC) suggest that there has been no significant change in the incidence of foodborne infections by the major bacterial agents transmitted through food over the last several years. . . . CDC therefore concludes that problems with bacterial contamination through food are not being resolved. According to CDC, the lack of recent progress toward national health objectives for food safety and the continual occurrence of large multistate outbreaks point to gaps in the food safety system. . . .

During the last two decades, many organizations and individuals, including the IOM, have devoted effort to identifying needed improvements in food safety. Attention has been focused in particular on the FDA's food safety program. According to a number of reports [between 2004 and 2008 by GAO and the Food Science Board], although the FDA is working to ensure safer food, problems with its capacities, functions, and processes persist. . . .

An important factor influencing the FDA's ability to fulfill its mission is the resources available to the agency given that, in addition to food, it is required to regulate cosmetics, drugs, biologics, medical devices, and tobacco. Although the agency is responsible for the safety of more than 80 percent of the nation's food supply, its budget accounts for only 24 percent of expenditures on food safety. Moreover, after the events of September 11, 2001, the FDA was given additional responsibilities related to bioterrorism, stretching its funds even thinner. For example, even though the number of domestic food establishments was increasing, the numbers of inspectors and inspections (both domestic and abroad) and the amount of funding allocated to food safety both decreased during the period 2003–2006.

In the face of its decreasing resources, the FDA must continue to make decisions about both appropriate short-term responses to a food crisis and longer-term prevention functions focused on continued improvements in the public health. While the need to respond to a crisis is clear, the agency has been criticized as responding only reactively to food problems, to the neglect of its preventive functions. . . .

NOTES

1. *FSMA.* The Food Safety Modernization Act of 2011 contained various enhancements to FDA authority recommended by the IOM report excerpted above. As discussed previously in Chapter 2, *supra* p. 70, FDA failed to meet the Congressional deadline for issuing seven FSMA implementing regulations, and a consumer group sought a court order compelling the agency to promulgate the rules. While this litigation was in process, FDA issued two major proposed rules: Current Good Manufacturing Practice and Hazard Analysis and Risk–Based Preventive Controls for Human Food, 78 Fed. Reg. 3646 (Jan. 16, 2013), and Standards for Growing, Harvesting, Packing, and Holding of Produce for Human Consumption, 78 Fed. Reg. 3504 (Jan. 16, 2013). On July 29, 2013, the agency published two additional proposed FSMA rules: Foreign Supplier Verification Programs for Importers of Food for Humans and Animals, 78 Fed. Reg. 45730 (July 29, 2013), and Accreditation of Third-Party Auditors/Certification Bodies to Conduct Food Safety Audits and to Issue Certifications, 78 Fed. Reg. 45782 (July 29, 2013). On October 29, 2013, the

agency proposed Current Good Manufacturing Practice and Hazard Analysis and Risk-Based Preventive Controls for Food for Animals, 78 Fed. Reg. 64736 (Oct. 29, 2013).

2. *Inspection Force.* While the size of the FDA inspection force has periodically been expanded, it clearly has not kept pace with the growing number of facilities and the expansion of the agency's responsibilities. FDA inspectors are, for the most part, generalists who perform inspections of all types of FDA-regulated products. It is thus difficult to assess trends in the amount of inspector time devoted to food inspections in particular. Nonetheless, it is clear that the frequency of food inspections plummeted dramatically prior to the passage of FSMA. According to a 2007 report to the FDA Science Board, the rate of inspection had declined by 78 percent in the past 35 years, and food facilities were being inspected only about once every ten years—an "appallingly low inspection rate." FDA SCIENCE AND MISSION AT RISK: REPORT OF THE SUBCOMMITTEE ON SCIENCE AND TECHNOLOGY (FDA SCIENCE BOARD 2007). FSMA requirements concerning inspection frequency are discussed *infra* at p. 547, note 4.

3. *USDA/FSIS Continuous Factory Inspection for Meat and Poultry.* Since 1906, USDA has imposed a system of continuous premarket inspection for meat and poultry, whereas FDA has relied on periodic factory inspection and postmarket surveillance for the rest of the food supply. For more than four decades, there has been controversy about whether the federal meat and poultry statutes require continuous factory inspection and individual carcass examinations, and whether there are more effective and efficient ways to assure the safety of meat and poultry. In 1996, the Food Safety Inspection Service (FSIS) of USDA introduced a system under which meat and poultry processors would perform the organoleptic inspections themselves, and USDA inspectors would monitor the processors to ensure that they were complying with the inspection requirements. The American Federation of Government Employees challenged the USDA's new approach, contending that the federal inspection statutes require USDA inspectors personally to inspect each and every carcass, not just to oversee others performing such a task. The District Court held that the USDA program was lawful. *American Federation of Government Employees v. Glickman*, 127 F. Supp. 2d 243 (D.D.C. 2001). On appeal, however, the Court of Appeals reversed the District Court and held that USDA was illegally "inspecting people not carcasses" and thus in violation of the statutory requirements. *American Fed'n of Gov't Employees v. Glickman*, 215 F.3d 7 (D.C. Cir. 2000). In response, USDA modified its inspection programs to assure that at least one government inspector, in addition to industry inspectors, is responsible for examining each carcass. The District Court then upheld the revised USDA inspection program, 127 F. Supp. 2d 243 (D.D.C. 2001), and the Court of Appeals affirmed, 284 F.3d 125 (D.C. Cir. 2002). The USDA inspection regime is discussed further in Chapter 4, *supra* p. 192.

4. *FDA/USDA Cooperation.* In AN EVALUATION OF THE ROLE OF MICROBIOLOGICAL CRITERIA FOR FOODS (1985), the National Academy of Sciences recommended establishment of a committee to review microbiological quality standards for food. In 52 Fed. Reg. 43216 (Nov. 10, 1987), USDA, in cooperation with FDA, announced the establishment of

this committee, now named the National Advisory Committee on Microbiological Criteria for Foods (NACMCF), which has been meeting ever since and has played an important role in advising FDA on microbiological matters.

5. *Other Federal Agencies.* The role of the Centers for Disease Control (CDC) in monitoring foodborne illness is also a critical part of the federal government's food safety program. Overall, at least 24 federal agencies have some role in ensuring the safety of the American food supply. *See* ENHANCING FOOD SAFETY: THE ROLE OF THE FOOD AND DRUG ADMINISTRATION 44–50 (Table 2–1) (IOM/NRC 2010).

6. *FDA Cooperative Food Sanitation Programs.* Even with respect to foods clearly within its primary jurisdiction, FDA does not act alone in attempting to prevent the sale of articles contaminated with pathogenic microorganisms. The agency participates in a variety of cooperative programs and activities with state and local governments and industry. These programs conform with FDA's responsibility under 42 U.S.C. 243 to provide assistance to state and local governments with respect to the prevention of communicable disease. Some of the more important cooperative agreements are described below.

The FDA's Cooperative Milk Safety Program assists the states in efforts to prevent milk-borne illness. Along with the U.S. Public Health Service, FDA publishes and regularly updates a model "Grade 'A' Pasteurized Milk Ordinance (PMO)," which has been in adopted in most states, counties, and cities. The ordinance includes provisions governing the processing, packaging, and sale of Grade "A" milk and milk products. FDA has a Memorandum of Understanding in place with the National Conference on Interstate Milk Shipments, an independent nonprofit entity that rates farms and milk processing plants for compliance with the PMO.

In the National Shellfish Sanitation Program (NSSP), FDA works with state regulatory agencies and the shellfish industry to ensure the safety of molluscan shellfish (such as oysters, clams, and mussels). The states take the leading role in implementing and enforcing the program, which classifies growing areas based on water quality, inspects facilities, patrols prohibited waters to deter illegal harvesting, and conducts laboratory testing of samples. FDA's main role is to provide training, guidance, and technical assistance. FDA continues periodically to revise and make available the NSSP Manual of Operations. In addition, FDA and the shellfish industry have developed an Interstate Shellfish Sanitation Conference (ISSC), patterned after the National Conference on Interstate Milk Shipments.

FDA's Retail Food Protection Program assists the state and local government agencies that regulate restaurants, grocery stores, and other retail food facilities. FDA's most important function in this program is the development of the model FDA Food Code, which state and local regulators use to develop their own rules. The vast majority of states and territories have adopted food codes modeled after different iterations of the FDA Food Code. In addition, FDA, with input by many stakeholders, has established Voluntary National Retail Food Regulatory Program Standards for the entities that administer the Food Code. Because section 301(k) of the

FD&C Act extends FDA jurisdiction to the adulteration of food while held for sale after shipment in interstate commerce, FDA technically has jurisdiction over all restaurants, food vendors, automatic vending machines, and retail food stores in the United States. Lacking the resources to police the hundreds of thousands of establishments involved, however, the agency concentrates its efforts on food manufacturing, processing, and wholesale warehouses, and relies on state and local enforcement of the model ordinances and codes to protect against insanitary food conditions at the retail level.

Finally, to supplement its own inspection force, FDA contracts with about 41 states to perform more than 10,000 inspections of food facilities per year. These FDA-sponsored state contract inspections represent only 0.4 percent of the more than 2.5 million food safety inspections conducted by state and local officials each year. ENHANCING FOOD SAFETY at 524.

2. GOOD MANUFACTURING PROCESS (GMP) REGULATIONS

Although the presence of pathogenic microorganisms in food can be the basis for regulatory action under sections 402(a)(1) and 402(a)(3), probably the most important pre-FSMA statutory provision for addressing pathogenic contamination of food is section 402(a)(4), which states that a food is adulterated "if it has been prepared, packed, or held under insanitary conditions . . . whereby it may have been rendered injurious to health."

During the 1960s, FDA experimented with a number of techniques to standardize its enforcement of section 402(a)(4) and to provide food producers better guidance about the requirements of this provision. The agency developed a plant evaluation (PEV) system in which inspectors used standardized forms to evaluate particular segments of the food industry. These forms focused on the sanitation practices about which FDA was principally concerned. Later, FDA issued good manufacturing practice guidelines for specific commodities to advise both its inspectors and food manufacturers.

In 1969, following two rounds of comments, FDA promulgated the first "umbrella" current good manufacturing practice (CGMP) regulations for the food industry. 34 Fed. Reg. 6977 (Apr. 26, 1969), codified at 21 C.F.R. Part 110. These regulations addressed plants and grounds; equipment and utensils; sanitary facilities and controls; sanitary operations; and processes and controls. The agency issued these regulations pursuant to sections 402(a)(4) and 701(a) of the FD&C Act. When FDA proposed to amend the regulations in 1979, it explained its legal authority as follows:

> [T]he CGMP regulations identify the applicable criteria for implementing the requirements of section 402(a)(3) and (4) of the act. . . .

> Under section 701(a) of the act, FDA has the authority to promulgate regulations for the efficient enforcement of that act, and such regulations have been held to have the force and effect of law. The courts have also expressly held that FDA has the authority to promulgate substantive regulations defining current good manufacturing practices for the food industry. *National*

Confectioners Ass'n v. Califano, 569 F.2d 690 (D.C. Cir. 1978). Furthermore, since the promulgation of the CGMP regulations in 1969, the Secretary of Health, Education, and Welfare has delegated authority to exercise the functions vested in the Secretary under section 361 of the Public Health Service Act (42 U.S.C. 264) to the Commissioner of Food and Drugs. Under this provision, the Commissioner is authorized to issue and enforce regulations for any measures that, in the Commissioner's judgment, are necessary to prevent the introduction, transmission, or spread of food-borne communicable diseases from one State to another. Because this authority is designed to eliminate the introduction of diseases such as typhus from one State to another, this authority must of necessity be exercised upon the disease-causing substance within the State where the food is manufactured, processed, or held. Due to the nationwide, interrelated structure of the food industry, communicable diseases may, without proper intrastate food controls, easily spread interstate. . . . The Commissioner therefore assumes authority to promulgate regulations under the Public Health Service Act to assure that foods are manufactured, processed, packed, or held under sanitary conditions so as to be safe, wholesome, and otherwise fit for food. Regulations promulgated under that statute also have the force and effect of law.

44 Fed. Reg. 33238, 33239 (June 8, 1979). Final regulations based upon this proposal were promulgated in 51 Fed. Reg. 22458 (June 19, 1986).

The umbrella GMP regulations, codified at 21 C.F.R. Part 110, are necessarily quite general; at its longest, Part 110 filled barely more than six pages of the Code of Federal Regulations. These rules have not been challenged in court. However, after issuing the 1969 CGMP regulations, FDA also adopted and sought to enforce GMP regulations for specific commodities, and the agency was forced to defend the legality of these more specific rules.

United States v. Nova Scotia Food Products Corp.

568 F.2d 240 (2d Cir. 1977).

■ GURFEIN, CIRCUIT JUDGE.

This appeal involving a regulation of the Food and Drug Administration is not here upon a direct review of agency action. It is an appeal from a judgment of the District Court for the Eastern District of New York . . . enjoining the appellants, after a hearing, from processing hot smoked whitefish except in accordance with time-temperature-salinity (T–T–S) regulations contained in 21 C.F.R. Part 122 (1977). . . .

The regulations cited above require that hot-process smoked fish be heated by a controlled heat process that provides a monitoring system positioned in as many strategic locations in the oven as necessary to assure a continuous temperature through each fish of not less than 180 degree F. for a minimum of 30 minutes for fish which have been brined to contain 3.5% water phase salt or at 150 degree F. for a minimum of 30 minutes if the salinity was at 5% water phase. . . .

Government inspection of appellants' plant established without question that the minimum T–T–S requirements were not being met. There is no substantial claim that the plant was processing whitefish under "insanitary conditions" in any other material respect. Appellants, on their part, do not defend on the ground that they were in compliance, but rather that the requirements could not be met if a marketable whitefish was to be produced. They defend upon the grounds that the regulation is invalid (1) because it is beyond the authority delegated by the statute; (2) because the FDA improperly relied upon undisclosed evidence in promulgating the regulation and because it is not supported by the administrative record; and (3) because there was no adequate statement setting forth the basis of the regulation. We reject the contention that the regulation is beyond the authority delegated by the statute, but we find serious inadequacies in the procedure followed in the promulgation of the regulation and hold it to be invalid as applied to the appellants herein.[*]

The hazard which the FDA sought to minimize was the outgrowth and toxin formation of Clostridium botulinum Type E spores of the bacteria which sometimes inhabit fish. . . .

The argument that the regulation is not supported by statutory authority cannot be dismissed out of hand. The sole statutory authority relied upon is § 342(a)(4) [FD&C Act 402(a)(4)]. . . . Nor is the Commissioner's expressed reliance solely on § 342(a)(4) a technicality which might be removed by a later and wiser reliance on another subsection. For in this case, as the agency recognized, there is no other section or subsection that can pass as statutory authority for the regulation. . . .

Appellants contend that the prohibition against "insanitary conditions" embraces conditions only in the plant itself, but does not include conditions which merely inhibit the growth of organisms already in the food when it enters the plant in its raw state. They distinguish between conditions which are insanitary, which they concede to be within the ambit of § 342(a)(4), and conditions of sterilization required to destroy micro-organisms, which they contend are not.

It is true that on a first reading the language of the subsection appears to cover only "insanitary conditions" "*whereby* it [the food] may have been rendered injurious to health" (emphasis added). And a plausible argument can, indeed, be made that the references are to insanitary conditions in the plant itself, such as the presence of rodents or insects.

Yet, when we are dealing with the public health, the language of the Food, Drug and Cosmetic Act should not be read too restrictively, but rather as "consistent with the Act's overriding purpose to protect the public health". *United States v. Bacto-Unidisk*, 394 U.S. 784, 798 (1969). . . .

Appellant's argument, . . . fairly construed, is that Congress did not mean to go so far as to require sterilization sufficient to kill bacteria

---

[*]   [The portion of the court's opinion discussing the agency's procedure in promulgating the T–T–S regulation is set out *supra* p. 44.]

that may be in the food itself rather than bacteria which accreted in the factory through the use of insanitary equipment.

There are arguments which can indeed be mustered to support such a broad-based attack. . . .

. . . [S]o far as the category of harmful micro-organisms is concerned, there is only a single provision, 21 U.S.C. § 344, which directly deals with "micro-organisms." That provision is limited to emergency permit controls dealing with any class of food which the Secretary finds, after investigation, "may, by reason of contamination with micro-organisms *during* the manufacture, processing or packing thereof in any locality, be injurious to health, and that such injurious nature cannot be adequately determined after such articles have entered interstate commerce, [in which event] he then, and in such case only, shall promulgate regulations providing for the issuance . . . of permits. . . ." (Emphasis added.) It may be argued that the failure to mention "micro-organisms" in the "adulteration" section of the Act, which includes § 342(a)(4), means that Congress intended to delegate no further authority to control micro-organisms than is expressed in the "emergency" control of Section 344.

On the other hand . . . the manner of processing can surely give rise to the survival, with attendant toxic effects on humans, of spores which would not have survived under stricter "sanitary" conditions. In that sense . . . the interpretation of the District Court . . . is a fair reading, emphasizing that the food does not have to be actually contaminated during processing and packing but simply that "it may have been rendered injurious to health," § 342(a)(4), by inadequate sanitary conditions of prevention. . . .

We do not discount the logical arguments in support of a restrictive reading of § 342(a)(4), but we perceive a larger general purpose on the part of Congress in protecting the public health.

We come to this conclusion, aside from the general rules of construction noted above, for several reasons: First, until this enforcement proceeding was begun, no lawyer at the knowledgeable Food and Drug bar ever raised the question of lack of statutory delegation or even hinted at such a question. Second, the body of data gathered by the experts, including those of the Technical Laboratory of the Bureau of Fisheries manifested a concern about the hazards of botulism. . . .

Lastly, a holding that the regulation of smoked fish against the hazards of botulism is invalid for lack of authority would probably invalidate, to the extent that our ruling would be followed, the regulations concerning the purity of raw materials before their entry into the manufacturing process in 21 C.F.R. Part 113 (1977) (inspection of incoming raw materials for microbiological contamination before thermal processing of low-acid foods packed in hermetically sealed containers), in 21 C.F.R. Part 118 (1977) (pasteurization of milk and egg products to destroy Salmonella micro-organisms before use of the products in cacao products and confectionery), and 21 C.F.R. Part 129 (1977) (product water supply for processing and bottling of bottled drinking water must be of a safe, sanitary quality when it enters the process).

The public interest will not permit invalidation simply on the basis of a lack of delegated statutory authority in this case. A gap in public health protection should not be created in the absence of a compelling reading based upon the utter absence of any statutory authority, even read expansively. Here we find no congressional history on the specific issue involved, and hence no impediment to the broader reading based on general purpose. We believe, nevertheless, that it would be in the public interest for Congress to consider in the light of existing knowledge, a legislative scheme for administrative regulation of the processing of food where hazard from micro-organisms in food in its natural state may require affirmative procedures of sterilization. . . .

NOTES

1. *Contradictory Decision for Meat and Poultry.* The identical "insanitary conditions" language in section 402(a)(4) of the FD&C Act was enacted in the Federal Meat Inspection Act, 21 U.S.C. 601(m)(4). In *Supreme Beef Processors, Inc. v. USDA,* the District Court struck down a section of the USDA meat HACCP regulations that established a salmonella performance standard, and the Court of Appeals affirmed. 113 F. Supp. 2d 1048 (N.D. Tex. 2000), *aff'd* 275 F.3d 432 (5th Cir. 2001). In addition to holding that salmonella is not a per se adulterant, *see supra* p. 505, note 2, the court also held that the statute's insanitary conditions provision may not be used to regulate the characteristics of raw materials. The Court of Appeals distinguished the *Nova Scotia Food Products* decision on the ground that the FDA regulation involved in that case required the use of processing procedures whereas the USDA regulation was directed at pre-existing characteristics of raw materials before they are processed.

2. *Revocation of Certain Product–Specific GMP Regulations.* FDA later revoked its GMP regulations for smoked fish, 49 Fed. Reg. 20484 (May 15, 1984); for cacao products and confectionary, 51 Fed. Reg. 22481 (June 19, 1986); and for frozen raw breaded shrimp, 51 Fed. Reg. 41615 (Nov. 18, 1986).

3. *Egg Safety.* In 2009, FDA issued a final rule requiring specific *Salmonella* enteritis preventive measures during the production of shell eggs in poultry houses. 74 Fed. Reg. 33095 (July 9, 2009), codified at 21 C.F.R. Part 118. The rule also contains testing, recordkeeping, and registration requirements. The regulations apply to almost all egg producers with more than 3,000 laying hens. These requirements join other egg-specific regulations directed at preventing *Salmonella* infection. A rule promulgated in 2000 requires refrigeration of shell eggs held for retail distribution, 21 C.F.R. Part 115. Another rule, published in 2000, requires that all shell eggs bear the following statement: "SAFE HANDLING INSTRUCTIONS: To prevent illness from bacteria: keep eggs refrigerated, cook eggs until yolks are firm, and cook foods containing eggs thoroughly." 21 C.F.R. 101.17(h).

4. *AIDS–Infected Personnel.* Section 110.10(a) of FDA's GMP regulations states that any person who has an illness or infection by which there is a "reasonable possibility of food, food-contact surfaces, or food-packaging materials becoming contaminated" must be excluded from any

food operation. Soon after acquired immune deficiency syndrome (AIDS) was first identified in this country, in the late 1970s, the question was raised whether individuals infected with the human immunodeficiency virus (originally HTLV and now HIV) should be excluded from employment in food manufacturing and service establishments. CDC responded by issuing *Recommendations for Preventing Transmission of Infection with Human T-lymphotropic Virus Type III/lymphadenopathy-associated Virus in the Workplace*, 34 MORBIDITY & MORTALITY WEEKLY REP. 682, 693–94 (Nov. 15, 1985). This publication stated: "All epidemiologic and laboratory evidence indicates that bloodborne and sexually transmitted infections are not transmitted during the preparation or serving of food or beverages, and no instances of HBV or HTLV–III/LAV transmission have been documented in this setting. . . . FSWs [Food Service Workers] known to be infected with HTLV–III/LAV need not be restricted from work unless they have evidence of other infection or illness for which any FSW should also be restricted. Routine serologic testing of FSWs for antibody to HTLV–III/LAV is not recommended. . . ." This recommendation has not since been changed, and there has been no evidence of AIDS transmission through food.

5. *Infant Formula GMPs.* FD&C Act 412(b)(2)(A) states: "The Secretary shall by regulation establish good manufacturing practices for infant formulas, including quality control procedures that the Secretary determines are necessary to assure that an infant formula provides nutrients in accordance with [relevant provisions] and is manufactured in a manner designed to prevent adulteration of the infant formula." Section 412 was added to the statute by the Infant Formula Act of 1980, 94 Stat. 1190, and amended by the Anti–Drug Abuse Act of 1986, 100 Stat. 3207, 3207–116. The quality control and recordkeeping regulations implementing section 412(b)(2)(A) are codified at 21 C.F.R. Part 106.

6. *Dietary Supplement GMPs.* DSHEA added Section 402(g) to the FD&C Act to authorize FDA to promulgate GMP regulations for dietary supplements, modeled after the food GMP regulations. In 68 Fed. Reg. 12157 (Mar. 13, 2003), FDA proposed dietary supplement GMP regulations, which the industry criticized as being modeled on the drug GMP regulations rather than the food GMP regulations. A final rule establishing the minimum current good manufacturing practices (CGMPs) necessary for manufacturing, packaging, labeling, and holding dietary supplements to ensure their quality was issued by the FDA in July of 2007. 72 Fed. Reg. 34752 (June 25, 2007). The rule, at 21 C.F.R. Part 111, outlines minimum standards for personnel, plant, equipment, and utensils, as well as written procedures for operations.

3. MANDATORY PASTEURIZATION

Even basic food products may be the source of pathogenic microorganisms. Milk was consumed raw until, following Louis Pasteur's discovery that heat treatment destroys bacteria, the dairy industry began in the 1920s to embrace this principle through pasteurization of milk. Over the ensuing decades, pasteurized milk gradually drove raw milk out of the market. Still, some raw milk distributors remained, and in the 1987 rulemaking excerpted below, FDA banned all interstate sales of raw milk.

Requirements Affecting Raw Milk for Human Consumption in Interstate Commerce: Final Rule
52 Fed. Reg. 29509 (Aug. 10, 1987).

In the Federal Register of June 11, 1987 (52 FR 22340), FDA issued a notice of proposed rulemaking in response to a decision by the United States District Court for the District of Columbia ordering "that the Food and Drug Administration and the Secretary of Health and Human Services publish in the Federal Register, a proposed rule banning the interstate sale of all raw milk and raw milk products, both certified and non-certified . . . and complete all rulemaking proceedings in accordance with this Court's opinion within one hundred eighty (180) days." *Public Citizen v. Heckler,* 653 F. Supp. 1229, 1242 (D.D.C. 1986). The notice proposed a pasteurization requirement for all milk and milk products in final package form in interstate commerce.

. . . In this notice, the agency is issuing a final rule based on the proposal.

The provisions of the Public Health Service Act that relate to communicable disease . . . form the legal basis for the final rule. The Public Health Service Act authorizes the Department of Health and Human Services (HHS) to make and enforce such regulations as "are necessary to prevent the introduction, transmission, or spread of communicable diseases from foreign countries into the States . . . or from one State . . . into any other State" (42 U.S.C. 264(a)). Five regulations banning the distribution of products have been published under this section: § 1240.60 *Shellfish* (21 CFR 1240.60); § 1240.62 *Turtles, intrastate and interstate* (21 CFR 1240.62); § 1240.65 *Psittacine birds* (21 CFR 1240.65); § 1240.70 *Lather brushes* (21 CFR 1240.70); and § 1240.75 *Garbage* (21 CFR 1240.75). Additional support for the final rule is found in sections 402(a) (1), (3), and (4) and 701(a) of the Federal Food, Drug, and Cosmetic Act. Under these sections, FDA is authorized to promulgate regulations for preventing adulterated or contaminated food, such as unpasteurized milk containing harmful microorganisms, from entering interstate commerce.

I.   *Background*

Over the years, FDA regulation of milk and milk products, in conjunction with State and local dairy associations, has been pervasive. A brief history of this proceeding reveals that the final rule is consistent with past agency action and will not have a burdensome impact on milk producers.

In the Federal Register of September 9, 1972 (37 FR 18392), FDA, under section 401 of the act, proposed to revise existing standards of identity and to establish new standards of identity for certain milk and cream products. This notice included an FDA proposal to require that each of the listed milk and cream products be pasteurized.

In the Federal Register of October 10, 1973 (38 FR 27924), FDA published a final rule which included the requirement that fluid milk products moving in interstate commerce be pasteurized. In deciding upon the pasteurization requirement, FDA reasoned that pasteurization was the only way to assure the destruction of pathogenic microorganisms that might be present.

Following publication of the final rule, FDA received one request for a hearing and an accompanying set of objections on the pasteurization requirement for certified raw milk. The procedures used in producing certified raw milk are significantly different from those used in producing raw milk in general in that they must comport with the methods and standards established by the American Association of Medical Milk Commissions, a private organization that provides to its members guidelines for the production of certified raw milk. Only dairies that employ the Association's techniques have the right to use the term "certified" on their products. The objections, which pertained only to certified raw milk, were based on two premises: (1) Certified raw milk is a safe product, and (2) section 401 of the act does not provide authority to establish a standard of identity solely for health reasons.

In the Federal Register of December 5, 1974 (39 FR 42351), FDA announced that the objections raised a substantial issue of fact with regard to whether pasteurization is needed for certified raw milk and that a hearing would be conducted. Accordingly, FDA stayed this requirement for certified raw milk.

The requirement for pasteurization for all other milk and milk products covered by the new standards of identity was made final in the December 5, 1974, final rule. Therefore, since December 1974 any such milk product that is in final package form for human consumption moving in interstate commerce, but that is not pasteurized, is misbranded. See section 403(g) of the act. Most milk and milk products [sic] in final package form for human consumption in intrastate commerce are also required by various State laws to be pasteurized.

On April 10, 1984, the Health Research Group (HRG) of Public Citizen . . . petitioned the Secretary of HHS to "promulgate a regulation banning all sales, interstate and intrastate, of raw (unpasteurized) milk and raw milk products in the United States."

In the Federal Register of August 3, 1984 (49 FR 31065), FDA announced a public hearing [held on Oct. 11–12, 1984] to receive information on whether milk and milk products sold for human consumption should be pasteurized. . . .

By letter dated March 15, 1985, the Commissioner of Food and Drugs denied the petition, stating that the agency would not ban either interstate or intrastate sales of raw milk. The letter acknowledged that "raw milk, including certified raw milk, is a vehicle for the transmission and spread of communicable diseases," but concluded that a Federal ban on the interstate shipment of raw milk would not be the most appropriate means of dealing with the health problems posed by unpasteurized milk and milk products, and would have minimal public health benefit, given the current patterns of distribution and sale of these products. The letter further explained that FDA's authority to prohibit the intrastate sale of raw milk was at least questionable and that, in any case, State and local authorities were fully able to take action to ban the product should they consider it appropriate to do so.

In *Public Citizen v. Heckler*, 653 F. Supp. 1229 (D.D.C. 1986), the Court ruled that the agency's denial of the HRG petition was arbitrary and capricious in light of the record compiled in the proceeding before the agency. The Court concluded that the record presents "overwhelming evidence of the risks associated with the consumption of raw milk, both certified and otherwise . . ." and is "replete with credible evidence of the danger of raw milk consumption. . . ." . . . According to the Court, "There is no longer any question of fact as to whether the consumption of raw milk is unsafe." The Court ruled that FDA should propose a rule "banning the interstate sale of all raw milk and raw milk products, both certified and noncertified. . . ." The Court also found that there was no indication that a rule banning the intrastate shipment of raw milk would be necessary to carry out an interstate ban.

II. Comments on the Proposed Regulation

. . . .

In its comments opposing a final rule, Stueve's Natural (Stueve) urged FDA not to ban certified raw milk because it is safe and has never been shown to cause illness. Stueve also suggested that individuals have the right to freely choose whether the benefits of raw milk outweigh its potential risks. . . . Stueve also questioned whether pasteurization would kill *Salmonella dublin* (*S. dublin*) microorganisms. . . .

Based on its review and evaluation of all data and information submitted, FDA has concluded that these contentions are unconvincing when considered in light of the known, documented health risks associate [sic] with the consumption of raw milk, as discussed below.

The administrative record compiled as a result of the hearing and rulemaking process demonstrates that there is an association between the consumption of raw milk and the outbreak of disease. The record also demonstrates an association between the consumption of certified raw milk and the outbreak of disease, particularly among consumers who are young, elderly, or infirm. . . .

The record of this proceeding reveals that on the basis of epidemiological evidence "the role of unpasteurized dairy products, including raw and certified raw milk, in the transmission of disease has been established repeatedly" . . .

. . . [I]n FDA's view, "certification" does not provide a reliable index of whether milk or milk products are contaminated with pathogenic bacteria. . . .

Stueve also contended that heating milk at 80 C for 30 minutes (one form of pasteurization) would not completely kill *S. dublin* microorganisms. . . . All information available to the agency documents that pasteurization, when performed as prescribed in the final rule, effectively eliminates *S. dublin* as well as numerous other harmful microorganisms.

The theoretical health benefits of raw milk have never withstood scientific scrutiny. Conversely, the fact that raw milk presents a substantially greater inherent risk of infectious disease has been documented repeatedly. Numerous articles have reported that pasteurization has either no effect or practically no effect on the major nutrients in milk. . . . Also, a recent investigation found that pasteurization of human milk profoundly reduces the number of bacteria but does not significantly affect the milk's immunological factors. . . . FDA concludes that pasteurization does not significantly change the nutritive or immunologic value of milk and that the risks associated with the consumption of raw milk, including certified raw milk, outweigh any alleged health benefits that may arise from consuming raw milk and certified raw milk.

III. Alternatives to a Ban

In proposing to require raw milk and raw milk products in final package form for direct human consumption, including certified raw milk, to be pasteurized before being shipped in interstate commerce, the agency requested comments on possible alternatives to such a requirement. The overwhelming majority of the comments that addressed alternatives opposed any approach other than ban.

One alternative the agency suggested for comment was the use of labeling to ensure that consumers who voluntarily choose to consume raw milk are informed as to the risks inherent in that choice. . . . The effectiveness of labeling to address a public health problem like that presented by the consumption of raw milk and raw milk products was questioned on several grounds. For example, the risk of infection from consuming raw milk and raw milk products does not arise from the misuse or abuse of the product but rather from its customary food use. Consumers . . . are poorly equipped to assess the likelihood of infection. . . . For these reasons, the agency concludes that labeling is not an acceptable alternative approach.

The agency also requested comments on whether available laboratory methods and analytical methodologies would permit rapid detection of harmful bacteria and could be used either alone or in conjunction with labeling as an alternative to banning raw milk and raw milk products in interstate commerce.

. . . Regarding this subject, the agency agrees with the comment of the American Academy of Pediatrics: "The fact is that there is no laboratory test available that will simultaneously and instantaneously screen for brucellosis, tuberculosis, salmonellosis, listeriosis. . . ." Existing screening technologies are an inadequate alternative to pasteurization as a means of ensuring the safety of milk and milk products.

IV. Conclusion

. . . In light of the opinions expressed in the comments; the documented risks presented by raw milk, including raw milk and raw milk products; the fact that such products are, indeed, shipped in interstate commerce; and the likelihood that a pasteurization requirement for such products in interstate commerce will result in some benefit to the public health, FDA has concluded that the use of Federal authority and resources to eliminate health problems caused by the interstate shipment of raw milk is justifiable. Accordingly, the agency believes that a final rule requiring the pasteurization of all raw milk and raw milk products in interstate commerce should issue in this proceeding. . . .

NOTES

1. *Final Rule.* The final rule, "Mandatory pasteurization for all milk and milk products in final package form intended for direct human

consumption," 21 C.F.R. 1240.61, is still in effect. This federal ban remains limited to interstate commerce in raw milk.

2. *Jurisdiction Over Intrastate Sales.* As FDA remarks in the preamble, when it initially denied the HRG petition to ban all sales of raw milk, interstate and intrastate, the agency did so in part because it believed "that FDA's authority to prohibit the intrastate sale of raw milk was at least questionable." Even though the final rule covers only interstate shipments, the agency found a legal basis for the rule—section 361 of the Public Health Service Act (42 U.S.C. 264)—that would almost certainly authorize the agency to regulate intrastate sales as well. After all, FDA regulations already contained a rule based on this section—the rule banning the sale of turtles of less than 4 inches (to prevent salmonella infection)—that prohibits both intrastate and interstate sales. And when FDA promulgated HACCP regulations in 2001 to ensure the safe and sanitary processing of juice, *see infra* p. 545, it applied the requirements to intrastate sales, explaining:

> Under section 361 of the Public Health Service Act (42 U.S.C. 264), the Surgeon General is authorized to issue and enforce regulations to prevent the introduction, transmission, or spread of communicable diseases from one State to another State. (This authority has been delegated to the Commissioner of Food and Drugs, 5 CFR 5.10(a)(4).) Activities that are wholly intrastate in character, such as the production and final sale to consumers of a regulated article within one State, are subject to regulation under section 361 of the PHS Act. *State of Louisiana v. Mathews*, 427 F. Supp. 174, 176 (E.D. La. 1977). The record in this rulemaking amply demonstrates that juice can function as a vehicle for transmitting foodborne illness caused by pathogens such as *Salmonella* and *E. coli* O157:H7. Similarly, the record demonstrates that consumers (particularly out-of-State tourists and other travelers) are likely to purchase and/or consume "intrastate" juice. These consumers subsequently take the juice back to their home State where the juice is consumed or carry a communicable disease back to their home State, thereby creating the risk that foodborne illness may occur in the home State as a result of such consumption.

66 Fed. Reg. 6138, 6148 (Jan. 19, 2001).

In the juice HACCP rulemaking, FDA declined to impose mandatory pasteurization on all juice. *Id.* at 6142. Shortly before, however, the agency had issued a regulation mandating the following warning statement on fruit and vegetable juice products that have not been processed to prevent, reduce, or eliminate pathogenic microorganisms: "WARNING: This product has not been pasteurized and, therefore, may contain harmful bacteria that can cause serious illness in children, the elderly, and persons with weakened immune systems." 63 Fed. Reg. 37030 (July 8, 1998), codified at 21 C.F.R. 101.17(g).

3. *State Laws.* In light of the fact that the federal prohibition on raw milk applies only to interstate sales, state law remains important in this area. According to a recent survey by the National Association of State Departments of Agriculture (NASDA), 20 states prohibit the sale of raw milk to consumers while 30 allow raw milk sales. Of these 30 states, 13

restrict legal sales to the farm where the milk is produced, 12 others allow the sale of raw milk at retail stores separate from the farm, and the remaining five restrict sales in some other way. News Release, *NASDA Releases Raw Milk Survey* (July 19, 2011).

4. *Continuing Controversy.* Legal restrictions on sales of raw milk remain an extremely contentious topic. *See, e.g., Raw Milk Debate Remains Contentious; Panelists on both sides of issue square off at Harvard Law Forum,* BOSTON GLOBE, Feb. 22, 2012, at G15.

5. *Review of Inaction.* The District Court's decision in *Public Citizen v. Heckler,* 653 F. Supp. 1229 (D.D.C. 1986), which precipitated the mandatory pasteurization rulemaking, is one of only two judicial decisions directing FDA to issue a regulation of specified content.

4. EMERGENCY PERMIT CONTROL

When *Clostridium botulinum,* a normally harmless bacterium, breeds in an airless, low-acid environment, it can transform into botulin toxin, a highly-concentrated poison. One situation potentially conducive to the growth of botulism is the improper cooking of food in canning operations. Following a series of botulin scares in the early 1970s, the National Canner's Association, concerned about a loss of consumer confidence, sought stricter FDA regulations.

FDA decided to act under section 404 of the FD&C Act. This section, titled "Emergency Permit Control," provides:

> Whenever the Secretary finds after investigation that the distribution in interstate commerce of any class of food may, by reason of contamination with micro-organisms during the manufacture, processing, or packing thereof ... be injurious to health, and that such injurious nature cannot be adequately determined after such articles have entered interstate commerce, he then ... shall promulgate regulations providing for the issuance, to manufacturers, processors, or packers of such class of food ... of permits to which shall be attached such conditions governing the manufacture, processing, or packing of such class of food, for such temporary period of time, as may be necessary to protect the public health; and after the effective date of such regulations, and during such temporary period, no person shall introduce or deliver for introduction into interstate commerce any such food manufactured, processed, or packed by any such manufacturer, processor, or packer unless such manufacturer, processor, or packer holds a permit issued by the Secretary as provided by such regulations.

In 1974, FDA promulgated emergency permit control regulations at 21 C.F.R. Part 108, which are still in effect. 39 Fed. Reg. 3748 (Jan. 29, 1974). Subpart A contains definitions and procedures to govern implementation of FDA's emergency control authority. Subpart B at 21 C.F.R. 108.35 contains specific enforcement provisions for thermally processed, low-acid foods in hermetically sealed containers and incorporates by reference 21 C.F.R. Part 113, which contains detailed good manufacturing process procedures for these products.

Subpart A of FDA's emergency permit regulations states that a "manufacturer, processor, or packer of a [class of] food for which a regulation has been promulgated in subpart B . . . shall be exempt from the requirement for a permit . . . if he meets all of the mandatory requirements and conditions established in that regulation." 21 C.F.R. 108.19(b). Consequently, ever since 1974, food processors who follow the requirements for thermal processing of low-acid canned foods set forth at 21 C.F.R. 108.35 (including the mandatory Part 113 GMP regulations incorporated by reference) have been deemed exempt from any requirement for an emergency permit. FDA subsequently extended this approach to include acidified food, which is also a potential host for botulin toxin. 44 Fed. Reg. 16204, 16230 (Mar. 16, 1979), codified at 21 C.F.R. 108.25 and Part 114.

NOTES

1.   *Pet Food.* The requirements for low-acid canned food apply to pet food as well. *See* 44 Fed. Reg. 48598 (Aug. 17, 1979), codified at 21 C.F.R. Part 507.

2.   *USDA Processing Requirements.* USDA has established similar requirements for canned meat and poultry products. 51 Fed. Reg. 45602 (Dec. 19, 1986).

3.   *Handling in the Home.* Virtually all botulism contamination of food occurs through improper home canning or refrigeration. *See, e.g.,* "FDA Consumer Advisory on Refrigeration of Carrot Juice: Three Cases of Botulism Possibly Caused by Improper Refrigeration," FDA News No. P06–135 (Sept. 17, 2006).

5.   HAZARD ANALYSIS AND CRITICAL CONTROL POINTS (HACCP)

During the past decade or so, scholars have devoted increasing attention to "new governance" models of regulation. While the "new governance" approach has multiple strands (and alternate labels), it is generally rejects government-centered, command-and-control regulation and favors experimental, flexible, and collaborative public-private partnerships that depend largely on local stakeholders for the implementation of legal norms and for innovation in law and policy.

Interestingly, as a few scholars have recognized, food safety regulation provides one of the most important examples of new government approaches in action. *See, e.g.,* Charles F. Sabel & William H. Simon, *Minimalism and Experimentalism in the Administrative State,* 100 GEO. L.J. 53 (2011). New governance in the food safety realm usually appears in the form of Hazard Analysis and Critical Control Points (HACCP). As discussed below, *infra* p. 545, the enactment of the Food Safety Modernization Act of 2011 represents the ultimate triumph of HACCP, which is now on the verge of being mandatory for almost the entire food supply.

The HACCP concept is described in the following 1994 advanced notice of proposed rulemaking, published when the agency was about to finalize HACCP requirements for seafood and was contemplating extending the approach to other segments of the food industry under its jurisdiction.

Food and Drug Administration Development of Hazard Analysis Critical Control Points for the Food Industry: Advanced Notice of Proposed Rulemaking

59 Fed. Reg. 39888 (August 4, 1994).

. . . .

Although the current food safety assurance program has generally functioned effectively, it currently faces new stresses and challenges. New food processing and packaging technologies, new food distribution and consumption patterns, increasing public health concerns about low levels of certain chemical contaminants, and new microbial pathogens all contribute to today's food safety challenge. . . .

One of the most important challenges to FDA's current food safety assurance program is the increasing number of new food pathogens. Although food borne illness has always been a public health problem, such illness appears to be on the rise, and new pathogens are appearing. In addition, because foods are more extensively processed and handled, there is now a greater opportunity for food to be contaminated. . . .

Pathogens are not the only potential contaminants of food, however. The extensive use of industrial chemicals, coupled with past failures to deal adequately with chemical waste, have resulted in significant chemical pollution of the environment in some regions. Many of these chemicals have found their way into the food chain. The legal use of pesticides in agriculture may also result in residues in food. Naturally occurring chemicals, such as toxic elements and mycotoxins, can also be found in food at levels of concern. . . .

The size and diversity of the food industry adds to the stress on the current food safety assurance program. FDA's current inventory lists over 30,000 food manufacturers and processors, and in excess of 20,000 food warehouses. The number of foreign manufacturers and processors shipping food products to the United States continues to increase. In 1992, there were well over 1 million food import entries into the United States. . . .

For all of these reasons, FDA believes that it is appropriate at this time for the agency to consider improvements to its food safety assurance program to focus the program on prevention of food safety risks and problems. . . .

Although the agency has reached no final conclusions about how its regulatory programs should be revised to make food as safe as possible, FDA has tentatively concluded that the improvements in the agency's current food safety assurance program should be based on a state-of-the-art preventive approach known as HACCP. . . . HACCP is a science based, systematic approach to preventing food safety problems by anticipating how such problems are most likely to occur and by installing effective measures to prevent them from occurring. HACCP thus requires that the processor and the regulatory authority be aware of the state-of-the-art science relative to food safety and processing technology. HACCP appropriately affirms that the food industry has primary responsibility for producing safe food, and it provides an important opportunity to link the food industry's system for producing safe food with the Government's system of regulatory oversight. . . .

The HACCP concept is a systematic approach to the identification, assessment of risk (likelihood of occurrence and severity), and control of the biological, chemical, and physical hazards associated with a particular food production process or practice. HACCP is a preventive strategy. It is based on development by the food producer of a plan that anticipates food safety hazards and identifies the points in the production process where a failure would likely result in a hazard being created or allowed to persist; these points are referred to as critical control points (CCP's). Under HACCP, identified CCP's are systematically monitored, and records kept of that monitoring. Corrective actions are taken when control of a CCP is lost, including proper disposition of the food produced during that period; and these actions are documented. . . .

HACCP has been endorsed by the National Advisory Committee on Microbiological Criteria for Foods (NACMCF) as an effective and rational means of ensuring food safety from harvest to table. . . .

The NACMCF has developed the following seven principles that describe the HACCP concept:

1.   Hazard Analysis

The first step in the establishment of a HACCP system for a food process or practice is the identification of the hazards associated with the product. The NACMCF defines a hazard as a biological, chemical, or physical property that may cause a food to be unsafe for consumption. The hazard analysis step should include an assessment of both the likelihood that such a hazard will occur and its severity if it does occur. This analysis should also involve the establishment of preventive measures to control identified hazards.

2.   Identification of CCP's

A CCP is a point, step, or procedure at which control can be applied, the result being that a potential food safety hazard can be prevented, eliminated, or reduced to acceptable levels. Points in the manufacturing process that may be CCP's include cooking, chilling, specific sanitation procedures, product formulation control, prevention of cross contamination, and certain aspects of employee and environmental hygiene.

3.   Establishment of Critical Limits for Preventive Measures Associated with Each Identified CCP

This step involves establishing a criterion that must be met for each preventive measure associated with a CCP. Critical limits can be thought of as boundaries of safety for each CCP and may be set for preventive measures such as temperature, time, physical dimensions, moisture level, water activity, pH, and available chlorine.

4.   Establishment of Procedures to Monitor CCP's

Monitoring is a planned sequence of observations or measurements to assess whether a CCP is under control and to produce an accurate record for use in future verification procedures. Continuous monitoring is possible with many types of physical and chemical methods. When it is not possible to monitor a critical limit on a continuous basis, monitoring intervals must be frequent enough to permit the manufacturer to determine whether the step/process/procedure designed to control the hazard is under control.

5.   Establishment of Corrective Actions To Be Taken When Monitoring Shows That a Critical Limit Has Been Exceeded

While the HACCP system is intended to prevent deviations in a planned process from occurring, total prevention can rarely, if ever, be achieved. Therefore, there must be a corrective action plan in place to ensure appropriate disposition of any food produced during a deviation, to fix or correct the cause of noncompliance to ensure that the CCP is once again under control, and to maintain records of corrective actions taken.

6.   Establishment of Effective Recordkeeping Systems That Document the HACCP System

This principle requires the preparation and maintenance of a written HACCP plan that lists the hazards, CCP's, and critical limits identified by the firm, as well as the monitoring, recordkeeping, and other procedures that the firm intends to use to implement the plan. This principle also requires the maintenance of records generated during the operation of the plan.

7.   Establishment of Procedures to Verify That the HACCP System is Working

This process involves verifying that the critical limits are adequate to control the hazards identified, ensuring that the HACCP plan is working properly and verifying that there is documented, periodic revalidation of the plan to confirm that the plan is still performing its intended function under existing plant conditions at any point in time. . . .

. . . Two principal alternatives to HACCP exist; end-product testing and comprehensive current good manufacturing practice (CGMP) regulations. End-product testing does not address the root causes of food safety problems; it is not preventive by design and requires that a large number of samples be analyzed to ensure product integrity. Similarly, CGMP's are not a practical approach because of the breadth and diversity of the food industry, the limited resources available within FDA to prepare the many specific CGMP regulations that would be needed to cover effectively such a diverse industry, and the time required to implement such regulations. . . .

A HACCP system for food safety assurance has numerous distinct advantages including the following: (1) HACCP focuses on prevention and is designed to prevent hazards from entering food; (2) HACCP permits more effective and efficient Government oversight; (3) HACCP places primary responsibility for ensuring food safety appropriately on the food manufacturer/distributor; and (4) HACCP assists food companies in competing more effectively in the world market.

The primary purpose of any HACCP system is to prevent problems through the systematic analysis and control of the production system by industry. This analysis and control would be confirmed by Government verification of the industry's monitoring. As such, a HACCP approach provides an appropriate balance between the responsibilities of industry and Government in ensuring food safety. A HACCP based program will also allow FDA and its State and local government counterparts to conduct more efficient and focused inspections of food facilities.

. . . HACCP allows the regulator to monitor more effectively a firm's compliance with food safety laws. With its current system of inspection, FDA can determine the conditions at a food plant only during the period of inspection. . . .

With an HACCP-based program in place, an investigator can determine and evaluate both current and past conditions critical to ensuring the safety of food produced by the facility. . . . [A]n essential part of a HACCP system is maintenance of monitoring records. By examining such records, the Government inspector can, in effect, look back through time at the conditions of a facility. . . . Government monitoring under a HACCP system would provide assurance that systems of preventive controls are in place and functioning properly and thus afford greater public assurance of food safety.

. . . [T]he current inspection system places a great deal of responsibility on Government regulators to uncover problems and to take regulatory action to address those problems. Under a HACCP-based inspection system, it would be the responsibility of the company to develop a plan for producing safe food, and the role of Government inspectors would be to verify that the company is carrying out its plan.

Finally, adopting a HACCP system could potentially enhance international trade opportunities for the United States. . . . HACCP will improve FDA's ability to monitor . . . imports. . . . Also, HACCP is becoming the world-wide standard to ensure the safety of food and will thus serve as basis for harmonizing U.S. food safety regulations with those of other nations.

———

The quality control personnel of a major food manufacturer devised HACCP in the early 1960s as a new science-based system for quality control. Subsequently, some food manufacturers voluntarily applied HACCP as part of their GMP programs. The federal government's formal embrace of HACCP occurred gradually over the next four decades. The low acid canned food and acidified food regulations that FDA issued in the 1970s pursuant to section 404 (Emergency Permit Control) utilized aspects of the HACCP approach. *See supra* p. 539. When FDA revised its general GMP regulations in June 1986, it referred to "careful monitoring of physical factors . . . and manufacturing operations" as one permissible approach to GMP, although this regulation does not elaborate on the components of a comprehensive HACCP system. 21 C.F.R. 110.80(b)(2).

As concern about pathogenic contamination of the food supply increased during the early 1990s, both FDA and USDA promulgated regulations explicitly requiring HACCP for particular types of food. To allay consumer concerns about fish safety, FDA promulgated HACCP regulations for fish and fishery products in 1995, with the support and cooperation of the seafood industry. 60 Fed. Reg. 65096 (Dec. 18, 1995), codified at 21 C.F.R. Part 123. The agency also announced the availability of a Fish and Fishery Products Hazards and Controls Guide, incorporating the seafood HACCP principles. 59 Fed. Reg. 12949 (Mar. 18, 1994). FDA found its legal authority to promulgate these regulations primarily in sections 402(a)(4) and 701(a), rejecting various objections, including, for example, the assertion that a failure to have a HACCP plan and maintain HACCP records could not be considered an "insanitary condition" under 402(a)(4). 60 Fed. Reg. at 65098–99.

The next developments were triggered by the Jack in the Box and Odwalla contaminations. USDA promulgated regulations requiring HACCP for meat and poultry. 61 Fed. Reg. 38806 (July 25, 1996), codified at 9 C.F.R. Part 417. FDA then published HACCP regulations for fruit and vegetable juices. 66 Fed. Reg. 6137 (Jan. 19, 2001), codified at 21 C.F.R. Part 120. As noted previously, FDA rested its authority for the juice HACCP regulations on section 361 of the Public Health Service Act ("Regulations to Control Communicable Diseases") as well as on section 402(a)(4) of the FD&C Act.

Meanwhile, in the 1994 ANPRM excerpted above, FDA suggested that it was considering imposing HACCP on most of the food industry within its purview. In general, manufacturers supported voluntary adoption of HACCP but opposed its mandatory imposition. Both the seafood and juice trade associations had requested FDA to develop HACCP programs after their industries lost public confidence and suffered economically due to media focus on the contamination of their products with pathogenic microorganisms. But segments of the food industry that did not have similar problems saw no compelling need for additional regulation.

However, following the Peanut Corporation of America salmonella tragedy of 2008–09, and a series of food poisoning crises involving produce around the same time, the food industry for the most part supported Congress's extension of mandatory HACCP to most food facilities in the Food Safety Modernization Act of 2011.

Section 103 of FSMA adds new section 418 ("Hazard Analysis and Risk–Based Preventive Controls") to the FDCA, which requires facilities to conduct a hazard evaluation to identify hazards that are reasonably likely to occur, including "biological, chemical, physical, and radiological hazards, natural toxins, pesticides, drug residues, decomposition, parasites, and unapproved food or color additives." FD&C Act 418(b). Facilities must then establish and implement preventive controls to provide assurances that the identified hazards will be significantly minimized and that food will not be adulterated. *Id.* 418(c). These controls may include sanitation, training, environmental controls, allergen controls, a recall plan, GMPs, and supplier verification activities. *Id.* 418(o)(3). Facilities are required to monitor the controls; establish corrective actions; verify that the plan is working; and maintain records of monitoring, instances of nonconformance, and corrective actions taken. *Id.* 418(d)–(g). The Act also requires that the hazard evaluation and preventive control plan be reduced to writing and made available to FDA (along with the other documentation) upon written request. *Id.* 418(h). A reevaluation of the controls is required every three years or when a significant change is made in the activities conducted at the facility. *Id.* 418(i). Various types of facilities are exempt from section 418, including, for example: seafood and juice facilities already required to comply with extant HACCP regulations; low-acid canned foods (with respect to those microbiological hazards addressed by the existing emergency permit control regulations); dietary supplement facilities; and farms, restaurants, and other retail food establishments. *See* FD&C Act 415(c)(1), 418(l), (j); FSMA 103(g).

FSMA required FDA, within 18 months after enactment, to promulgate "flexible" regulations implementing section 418—a deadline the agency failed to meet. *Id.* 418(n). In early 2013, the agency finally issued a proposed rule implementing these provisions. 78 Fed. Reg. 3646 (Jan. 16, 2013).

Section 105 of FSMA, creating new section 419 ("Standards for Produce Safety") of the FDCA, directs FDA to issue separate regulations establishing safety standards for fresh produce, and it prioritizes regulations for raw fruits and vegetables that have been associated with food borne illness outbreaks. Section 419 does not explicitly require that these standards embody HACCP principles, but they must be "science-based," "based on known safety risks," "provide sufficient flexibility to be practicable for all sizes and types of businesses," and "set forth . . . procedures, processes, and practices that the Secretary determines to be reasonably necessary to prevent the introduction of known or reasonably foreseeable biological, chemical, and physical hazards, including hazards that occur naturally, may be unintentionally introduced, or may be intentionally introduced, including by acts of terrorism, into fruits and vegetables . . . and to provide reasonable assurances that the produce is not adulterated under section 402." FD&C Act 419(b), (c). Section 419 exempts certain small farms that sell primarily to consumers and nearby restaurants and retailers, and FDA may wholly or partially exempt other small businesses that produce and harvest low-risk commodities. FD&C Act 419(a)(1)(B), (f). FDA published a proposed produce safety rule on the same day that it issued the proposed hazard analysis and risk-based preventive control rule cited above. 78 Fed. Reg. 3504 (Jan. 16, 2013).

NOTES

1. *Importers.* FSMA also created new section 805 of the FDCA, which requires importers of food to have a program in place to verify that imported food is produced in accordance with U.S. requirements (including the new preventative controls and produce safety standards required by the Act) and is not otherwise adulterated or misbranded. This aspect of FSMA will be examined in detail in Chapter 14, *infra* p. 1455.

2. *Fresh–Cut Produce Industry.* In 1996, the USDA Agricultural Marketing Service established a HACCP-based voluntary program for the fresh-cut industry. Under this "Qualified by Verification" program, AMS

helps develop, reviews, and certifies the HACCP plans for minimally processed fruits and vegetables that have been freshly cut, washed, and packaged. *See* 63 Fed. Reg. 47220 (Sept. 4, 1998). In 2008, FDA issued a guidance document, GUIDANCE FOR INDUSTRY: GUIDE TO MINIMIZE MICROBIAL FOOD SAFETY HAZARDS OF FRESH–CUT FRUITS AND VEGETABLES (Feb. 2008). The guidance recommends the use of HACCP principles.

3. *Canned Meat and Poultry.* When USDA promulgated its meat and poultry HACCP regulations, the agency exempted canned meat and poultry products that are subject to the emergency permit requirements for canned food on the premise that the emergency permit requirements provide protection against pathogenic microorganisms. A proposal by USDA in 66 Fed. Reg. 12590 (Feb. 27, 2001) to replace the canned meat and poultry requirements with a new performance standard was greeted by a storm of protest from the industry, which argued that the emergency permit regulations have been spectacularly successful for some thirty years and should not be replaced.

4. *Overall Risk–Based System.* One of the main recommendations of the 2010 IOM/NRC report on Enhancing Food Safety was that FDA embrace "a comprehensive, systematic vision for a risk-based safety system." ENHANCING FOOD SAFETY at 4. In certain ways, FSMA mandates a general risk-based decision-making approach. The preventive controls required by section 418 are only one example of this. For example, FSMA requires FDA to inspect those domestic facilities it classifies as "high-risk" (according to designated criteria) more frequently than those it classifies as "low-risk." (After a transition period, the former must be inspected once every three years and the latter, once every five years.) FD&C Act 421(a). The determination of which food shipments to inspect at ports of entry is also required to be based on risk assessment. *Id.* 421(b). Moreover, section 204(d) of FSMA requires FDA to impose additional recordkeeping requirements on facilities that manufacture, process, pack, or hold food that the agency designates as "high risk food" in accordance with listed criteria.

———

The following is an article by two "new governance" scholars that discusses HACCP. It was published prior to the enactment of FSMA and refers to the USDA's HACCP requirements for meat and poultry as well as FDA's seafood and juice regulations.

Cary Coglianese & David Lazer, *Management– Based Regulation: Prescribing Private Management to Achieve Public Goals*
37 LAW & SOCIETY REVIEW 691, 696–98 (2003).

The problem of regulatory instrument choice has typically been framed as a choice between technology-based or performance-based regulation. Regulators can craft rules that either mandate specific technologies or behaviors (technology-based regulation) or require that certain outcomes will be achieved or avoided (performance-based regulation). Even market-based regulatory instruments, around which an important literature has emerged, are still linked either to technologies or, more frequently, to the outcomes of firm behavior. . . .

. . . [M]issing from the traditional emphasis on technology-based and performance-based regulation has been much systematic attention to a third type of regulatory instrument that we call "management-based regulation." Management-based regulation does not specify the technologies to be used to achieve socially desirable behavior, nor does it require specific outputs in terms of social goals. Rather, a management-based approach requires firms to engage in their own planning and internal rule-making efforts that are supposed to aim toward the achievement of specific public goals. . . .

Regulation may intervene at one of three stages of any organization's activities: the planning, acting, or output stages. . . .

. . . Technology-based approaches intervene in the acting stage, specifying technologies to be used or steps to be followed. Performance-based approaches intervene at the output stage, specifying social outputs that must (or must not) be attained. By contrast, management-based approaches intervene at the planning stage, compelling regulated organizations to improve their internal management so as to increase the achievement of public goals.

. . . .

Management-based approaches hold a number of potential advantages over traditional regulation. They place responsibility for decisionmaking with those who possess the most information about risks and potential control methods. Thus, the actions that firms take under a management-based approach may prove to be less costly and more effective than under government-imposed regulatory standards. By allowing firms to make their own decisions, managers and employers are more likely to view their own organization's rules as reasonable, and as a result there may be greater compliance than with government-imposed rules. In this way, as well as by enlisting the assistance of private, third-party certifiers, management-based regulatory strategies may help mitigate the problems associated with limited governmental enforcement resources. Finally, by giving firms flexibility to create their own regulatory approaches, management-based approaches enable firms to experiment and seek out better, more innovative solutions.

. . . . [N]ew food safety challenges have emerged as faster, more innovative production processes in the food industry have placed new demands on inspectors' time. In addition, heightened public expectations and the new processing methods have contributed to increasing concerns about microbial food contamination, which is difficult to detect by the traditional "poke and sniff" methods. In response to these challenges, regulatory authorities around the world have developed an alternative regulatory strategy, Hazards Analysis and Critical Control Points (HACCP). . . .

HACCP first requires firms to identify the potential hazards associated with all stages of food processing and to assess the risks of these hazards occurring. Food processors are expected to use a flow chart to aid them in analyzing the risks at every stage of production after the food enters the plant in question. HACCP next requires firms to identify the best methods for addressing food safety hazards. The firm must identify all "critical control points" (CCPs), or points in the production process at which hazards can likely be eliminated, minimized, or reduced to an acceptable level. For each CCP, the firm must establish a minimum value at which the point must be controlled in order to eliminate or minimize the hazard. Having developed a methodology for dealing with hazards, the firm is required to ensure that it complies with that methodology. The firm must list the procedures that will be used to verify that each CCP does not exceed its critical limit, and it must determine and indicate how frequently each procedure will be performed.

Each firm's HACCP plan should also indicate the actions the firm proposes to use to correct its operating procedures if a CCP is discovered to have exceeded its limit. As part of its corrective action, the firm must ensure that the cause of the deviation is identified and eliminated, that the CCP is "under control" after the corrective action is taken, that steps are taken to prevent recurrence, and that products adulterated by the deviation are not placed on the market. The firm is expected to develop a methodology for monitoring and evaluating the effectiveness of its HACCP plan. Furthermore, in order to permit effective self-evaluation and government oversight, HACCP imposes extensive record-keeping requirements on firms.

The Food Safety Inspection Service (FSIS) of the USDA verifies the firm's compliance with the agency's HACCP requirements. The FSIS has the right to review the HACCP plan and all records pertaining to it. In addition, it may also collect samples and make its own direct observations and measurements. Firms need not get the FSIS's pre-approval for their HACCP plans, although they can later be found to be in violation of the HACCP regulation if their plans fail to meet the government's requirements or if they ship contaminated or spoiled food.

Regulators have produced nonbinding guides that describe how to develop HACCP plans, but the regulations themselves provide firms with substantial latitude in managing their food safety risks—providing examples of possible hazards and responses, but not requiring any particular action. . . .

. . . . A management-based regulatory regime may be complemented with a set of technological mandates or performance targets. For example, with respect to food safety, the USDA complements its HACCP regulation with a sampling and testing regimen that contains performance standards for levels of *E. coli* and *Salmonella*. . . . These performance standards are considered inadequate by themselves to provide the main strategy for regulating food safety. . . . But management-based regulation may be used in conjunction with performance or technology standards in order to compensate for limitations in the effectiveness of the latter, more conventional forms of regulation.

. . . . [H]ow are plans negotiated between the regulator and regulated? One might imagine several alternatives: (1) the regulator reviews all management plans in advance and the regulated firm must receive preapproval of its plan before implementing it, (2) the regulated firm must submit a management plan to the regulator which the regulator keeps on file but does not preapprove, or (3) the regulator checks to see if the firm has completed the appropriate plan ex post, either during periodic inspections of the firm's facilities or following an accident or incident. For example, with respect to the application of HACCP to the processing of fish, regulators in the United States do not have a preapproval process, but in Canada they do.

Beyond requiring preapproval, there is the question of how to monitor and enforce planning and implementation mandates. To facilitate such monitoring, management-based regulation will typically be accompanied by record-keeping requirements. For example, the FDA requires juice-processing facilities to maintain onsite documentation of their entire HACCP plans, including hazards analysis, testing, and documentation of implementation of procedures, so that the FDA inspectors can "determine whether the HACCP system or systems are properly implemented and effective."

Regulatory agencies also need to decide how frequently to inspect facilities governed by management-based regulation. They can require a continuous or occasional presence at processing locations. For example, USDA inspectors are onsite continuously at meat processing plants, whereas the FDA visits fish processors only once a year. . . .

An additional choice is whether the regulator should delegate the inspection function to third-party auditors, allowing firms to choose and pay for their own private auditing services. . . .

Third-party audits offer several potential advantages. First, they may create incentives for the inspections themselves to be as efficient as possible. Second, if there are economies of scale in understanding the relevant management systems, third-party certifiers specializing in different types of facilities or processes may better capture those scale effects. Finally, third-party auditing can help offset or augment the limited resources of government regulators. For example . . . the FDA and USDA have very constrained inspection capacities. Even if third-party auditing is voluntary, the availability of such auditing may help the regulatory agency more efficiently allocate its limited inspection resources, since firms' choices about whether to get an audit may reveal something about the nature of the risk they pose. Firms not choosing to be audited on their own may be assumed to be firms with higher risks, and government inspections of these firms will likely yield greater marginal benefits to society.

The challenge of third-party certification is that it creates another layer of agency problems . . . Relative to government inspectors, third-party certifiers probably face incentives to satisfy their clients through at least marginally more lax enforcement . . .

The critical question regarding management-based regulatory approaches is whether they can overcome the design challenges. . . . In many cases, firms will underinvest in safety measures absent government intervention. This typically means that regulators need to monitor firms' planning in some way and enforce appropriate levels of implementation. In the food safety area, new regulations grant inspectors access to essentially all records related to the HACCP, including the firm's choice of CCPs, its plans of action to ensure that safety is maintained at each CCP, and the records indicating whether the CCP has exceeded the critical limit. Furthermore, regulatory inspectors evaluate the processes that they actually observe during site visits. . . .

Do regulators have the capacity to evaluate planning and implementation? . . . [U]nder its main HACCP program, the FDA has been able to inspect fish processors only *once* a year, examining firms' plans, their records, and the actual processes associated with a *single* product line (usually one of the high-risk product lines). Further, in about half of these cases, the product line selected to be inspected is not active at the time of inspection, and the inspection is limited to paperwork review. This inspection process therefore does not reveal the effectiveness of the HACCP plans of noninspected product lines. It also does not directly reveal whether the firm carries out its plan in the various contingencies specified in the plan that do not occur while the inspector is watching. Instead, inspectors must rely on the firm's records of what occurred.

This leads to the question of whether firms will maintain an accurate record of their actions in those instances where damaging information may lead to the agency penalizing the firm. One critic of HACCP warns that firms have little reason not to falsify records, particularly in the absence of whistleblower protections or other incentives for someone knowledgeable to verify what went on in the production line. Even if firms are not outright untruthful, they may conclude that they would do themselves little good by including in their plan any hazards that government inspectors are unlikely to spot on their own, particularly if these cannot be remedied cheaply. Since management-based regulatory strategies are designed to incorporate a firm's specialized expertise in its product and processes into its safety practices, the very instances in which a firm's expertise would help it to identify hidden hazards may well be some of the same ones in which the firm has the opportunity and incentive to keep its hazards hidden. . . .

Of course, regulatory compliance is usually less than perfect, regardless of what type of regulatory instrument a regulator chooses. The key question, therefore, is whether management-based regulation makes a difference in terms of the achievement of social goals. . . . [T]he USDA has sampled the incidence of *Salmonella* in the meat it inspects before and after it implemented HACCP. It found substantial overall reductions—in the range of about 10 to 60% compared to baseline data, depending on the product line—of *Salmonella* prevalence in poultry, beef, pork, and turkey. While the FDA has not similarly tracked the incidence of pathogens in seafood, it did find an improvement in sanitary practices after it implemented HACCP. Of course, the ultimate metric for evaluating the impact of HACCP is the incidence of foodborne illness. CDC surveillance data are suggestive of an overall decrease in major bacterial foodborne illnesses, where the combined incidence of the seven bacterial pathogens that the CDC tracks dropped by 23% between 1996 and 2001.

. . . .

NOTES

1. *Whistleblower Protections.* FSMA added section 1012 to the FD&C Act, making it illegal for any entity in the food industry to discharge or "otherwise discriminate against . . . with respect to compensation, terms, conditions, or privileges of employment" an employee because that employee provides information to his employer or to the federal or state government about violations of the FD&C Act; testifies about such violations; assists an investigation into such activity; or objects to or refuses to participate in practices he or she reasonably believes to violate the Act.

2. *CDC Estimates.* According to 2011 Centers for Disease Control estimates reported on the CDC website, each year approximately 1 in 6 Americans (or 48 million people) gets sick, 128,000 are hospitalized, and 3000 die of foodborne illnesses. According to CDC's Foodborne Diseases Active Surveillance Network (FoodNet), between 1996–98 and 2010, the number of laboratory-confirmed bacterial infections transmitted by food have dropped overall, but not uniformly. The 2010 FoodNet report card (also available on the CDC website) states that during this period, infections caused by five key pathogens (Campylobacter, Listeria, E. coli, Shigella, and Yirsinia) dropped significantly (between 27 and 44 percent), whereas Salmonella infections increased three percent, and Vibrio infections increased 115 percent. Some important food-borne pathogens, including norovirus, Clostridium, and Taxoplasma, are not tracked on FoodNet because of the lack of generally available testing methods.

3. *Risk Assessments for Pathogens.* Increasingly sensitive analytical methodology can detect pathogens at increasingly lower levels. Although FDA has not altered its zero tolerance policy, the agency has prepared risk assessments on pathogens. *E.g.*, 68 Fed. Reg. 61006 (Oct. 24, 2003) (listeria); 70 Fed. Reg. 41772 (July 20, 2005) (vibrio parahaemolyticus in raw oysters).

H. INTENTIONAL FUNCTIONAL INGREDIENTS

1. INTRODUCTION

Before World War II, relatively few functional ingredients were used in food. Even then, however, they were viewed with suspicion and concern. *See, e.g.*, O. FOLIN, PRESERVATIVES AND OTHER CHEMICALS IN FOODS: THEIR USE AND ABUSE (1914); Wallace F. Janssen, *Inside the Poison Squad*: *How Food Additive Regulation Began*, 51 J. AFDO, No. 2, at 68 (Apr. 1987). The immediate post-war period saw a proliferation of functional food ingredients and a revolution in food technology. In 1950, Representative Frank B. Keefe (R–Wisc.) introduced a resolution to establish a select committee to investigate the use of chemicals in food products. 96 CONG. REC. 8933. Because he was in the minority party and in poor health, Keefe persuaded Representative James Delaney (D–N.Y.) to sponsor the resolution and serve as chairman of the committee. The Report of the Delaney Committee was released in 1952.

Investigation of the Use of Chemicals in Foods and Cosmetics

House of Representatives Report No. 2356, 82d Congress, 2d Session (1952).

At this stage of our civilization, there is a genuine need for the use of many chemicals in connection with our food supply. Many of the chemicals directly added to foods have proved to be of substantial value to the consumer, and constitute a necessary adjunct to modern civilization. Few would quarrel now with the advisability of enriching various staple foods with certain vitamins and minerals, or with the addition of other chemicals which enhance the nutritive value of the products in which they are incorporated. . . . The progress that has been made in food technology, however, has been attended by a certain degree of hazard, since some quantity of many of the new chemicals utilized in the production and processing of foods is inevitably ingested by the consuming public. It is essential that this risk be kept to a minimum.

. . . Chemical substances are being introduced into the production, processing, storage, packaging and distribution of food at an ever-increasing rate. There is hardly a food sold in the market place today which has not had some chemicals used on or in it at some state in its production, processing, packaging, transportation, or storage. . . .

The indirect addition of chemicals to our food supply also raises serious problems. For example, cattle are being treated with antibiotic drugs in the control of mastitis, anthrax, and other diseases. There is a question whether the presence of small amounts of antibiotics in milk and milk products has any effect on the consumer; that is, whether the consumer develops a sensitivity or resistance to these chemicals. . . .

The United States Food and Drug Administration, in collaboration with the United States Public Health Service, revealed that approximately 842 chemicals are used, have been used, or have been suggested for use in foods. Of this total, it was estimated that 704 are employed today, and that of these 704 only 428 are definitely known to be safe. Thus, there are approximately 276 chemicals being used in food today, the safety of which has not been established to the satisfaction of many groups concerned with the health and safety of the public.

The Surgeon General of the Public Health Service pointed out that the extent of this problem cannot be fully visualized, because of a lack of adequate information on the chronic effects of chemical substances currently in use. He testified that the toxic effects of many of these chemicals, and of the compounds which they form when introduced into food, are unknown. . . .

———

Stimulated by the Delaney Committee, Congress enacted the Food Additives Amendment, 72 Stat. 1784 (1958), which inserted sections 201(s) and 409 into the FD&C Act. The following excerpt from the legislative history is particularly important, because it established the "reasonable certainty of no harm" standard that would come to govern FDA safety assessments for food additives, as well as color additives and animal drugs.

Food Additives Amendment of 1958

Senate Report No. 2422, 85th Congress, 2d Session (1958)

. . . [U]nder existing law the Federal Government is unable to prevent the use in foods of a poisonous or deleterious substance until it first proves that the additive is poisonous or deleterious. To establish this proof through experimentation with generations of mice or other animals may require 2 years or even more on the part of the relatively few scientists the Food and Drug Administration is able to assign to a particular problem. Yet, until that proof is forthcoming, an unscrupulous processor of foodstuffs is perfectly free to purvey to millions of our people foodstuffs containing additives which may or may not be capable of producing illness, debility, or death.

. . . This huge loophole is 1 of 2 flaws in existing law which, through this measure, we are attempting to fill. This bill, if enacted, will require the processor who wants to add a new and unproven additive to accept the responsibility now voluntarily borne by all responsible food processors of first proving it to be safe for ingestion by human beings.

The second flaw in existing law which has proved detrimental to consumers, to processors, and to our national economy and which this bill seeks to remove is a provision [section 402(a)] which has inadvertently served to unnecessarily proscribe the use of additives that could enable the housewife to safely keep food longer, the processor to make it more tasteful and appetizing, and the Nation to make use of advances in technology calculated to increase and improve our food supplies. Your committee agrees with the Food and Drug Administration that existing law should be changed to permit the use of such additives as our technological scientists may produce and which may benefit our people and our economy when the proposed usages of such additives are in amounts accepted by the Food and Drug Administration as safe. . . .

The legislation also covers substances which may reasonably be expected to become a component of any food or to affect the characteristics of any food. These substances are generally referred to as "incidental additives." . . .

On the other hand, substances which may accidentally get into a food, as for example, paints or cleaning solutions used in food processing plants, are not covered by the legislation. . . . If accidental additives do get into food, the provisions of the Food, Drug, and Cosmetic Act dealing with poisonous and deleterious substances would be applicable. . . .

The concept of safety used in this legislation involves the question of whether a substance is hazardous to the health of man or animal. Safety requires proof of a reasonable certainty that no harm will result from the proposed use of an additive. It does not—and cannot—require proof beyond any possible doubt that no harm will result under any conceivable circumstances. . . .

In determining the "safety" of an additive, scientists must take into consideration the cumulative effect of such additive in the diet of man or animals over their respective life spans together with any chemically or pharmacologically related substances in such diet. Thus, the safety of a given additive involves informed judgments based on educated estimates by scientists and experts of the anticipated ingestion of an additive by man and animals under likely patterns of use. . . .

NOTE

Transitional Provisions. The 1958 Amendment contained transitional provisions under which all food additives were required to be subject to a food additive regulation within two and a half years. Congress later extended this transitional period in the Food Additives Transitional Provisions Amendment of 1961, 75 Stat. 42, and the Food Additives Transitional Provisions Amendment of 1964, 78 Stat. 1002, to December 31, 1965.

2. FOOD ADDITIVE APPROVAL

The definition of a "food additive" in section 201(s) of the FD&C Act is the key to understanding the operation of the premarketing licensure system that Congress established. The term broadly includes all substances that may reasonably be expected to become components of food, but then expressly excludes a substantial portion, probably the majority, of such substances. The substances excluded are those that (1) are generally recognized as safe ("GRAS"), (2) are subject to an approval (a "prior sanction") given before 1958 by FDA under the FD&C Act or by USDA under the Federal Meat Inspection Act or the Poultry Products Inspection Act, or (3) fall within specific exceptions for pesticides, color additives, new animal drugs, and dietary ingredients used in dietary supplements. Each of these excluded categories is explored below.

[handwritten margin note: excluded: 1. generally regarded as safe 2. already safe 3. specific exceptions]

Manufacturers have a great incentive to classify substances as GRAS or prior sanctioned, because the rigorous premarket approval process imposed by section 409 of the FD&C Act applies only to substances formally categorized as "food additives" under section 201(s). The section 409 requirements for direct food additives have remained unchanged since 1958. (The provisions governing indirect food additives, or food contact substances, have been amended. *See infra* p. 607). Section 402(a)(2)(C)(i) provides that a food is adulterated if it bears or contains "any food additive that is unsafe within the meaning of section 409." Section 409(a) in turn states that a food additive (other than an exempt investigational additive or a food contact substance) is "unsafe for the purposes of the application of clause (2)(C) of section 402(a)" unless "there is in effect, and it and its use or intended use are in conformity with, a regulation issued under this section prescribing the conditions under which such additive may be safely used." The subsequent provisions establish the process by which a person may petition FDA for approval of a food additive and by which the agency must either deny such a petition or issue "a regulation (whether or not in accord with that proposed by the petitioner) prescribing . . . the conditions under which such additive may be safely used." FD&C Act 409(b) & (c).

Section 409(c)(3)(A) provides, "No such regulation shall issue if a fair evaluation of the data before the Secretary . . . fails to establish that the proposed use of the food additive, under the conditions of use to be specified in the regulation, will be safe." The relevant FDA regulation, drawing on the language of the legislative history quoted above, defines "safe" as follows:

> *Safe* or *safety* means that there is a reasonable certainty in the minds of competent scientists that the substance is not harmful under the intended conditions of use. It is impossible in the present state of scientific knowledge to establish with complete certainty the absolute harmlessness of the use of any substance.

21 C.F.R. 170.3. FDA is empowered by Section 409(c)(1)(A) to prescribe conditions necessary to assure that an additive's use will be safe. Such conditions typically include limitations on the levels of use and can also include restrictions on the foods to which it is added or on the purposes for which it may be used. And the Act explicitly permits the agency to prescribe labeling for the additive, apparently to provide information to commercial users. In addition, FDA has occasionally prescribed special labeling requirements for the finished foods in which an additive is used. *E.g.*, 21 C.F.R. 172.110(c) (BHA); 21 C.F.R. 172.175(b) (sodium nitrite); 21 C.F.R. 172.375(b) (potassium iodide).

Food additive petitions, in the relatively rare instances in which they are still used (*see infra* p. 603), are ordinarily supported with lifetime animal feeding studies. Section 409(c)(5)(C) of the Act requires FDA to identify appropriate safety factors, and the agency has done so at 21 C.F.R. 170.22:

> Except where evidence is submitted which justifies use of a different safety factor, a safety factor in applying animal experimentation data to man of 100 to 1, will be used; that is, a food additive for use by man will not be granted a tolerance that will exceed 1/100th of the maximum amount demonstrated to be without harm to experimental animals.

Finally, section 409 contains the famous "Delaney Clause," which states: "no additive shall be deemed to be safe if it is found to induce cancer when ingested by man or animal, or if it is found, after tests which are appropriate for the evaluation of the safety of food additives, to induce cancer in man or animal." When it applies, this absolutist provision—original to the 1958 Act—precludes any use of quantitative risk analysis and simply bans the approval of additives shown to be at all carcinogenic. The Delaney Clause will be examined in detail in Chapter 13.

Section 21 C.F.R. Part 172 contains all the regulations permitting the use of direct food additives.* The approximately 150 approved additives are classified as preservatives; coatings, films, and related substances; special dietary and nutritional additives; anticaking agents; flavoring agents and related substances; gums, chewing gum bases, and related substances; other specific usage additives; and multipurpose additives. The regulations actually contain many more than 150

---

* Part 173 contains the approval regulations for so-called "secondary direct food additives," whose functionality is required during the manufacture or processing of food, but which are not ordinarily expected to be present in the final product. (Although residues might remain in the final product, they are not expected to exhibit any technical effect in food.) Parts 175–179 list approved "indirect food additives", which will be discussed further below. *See infra* p. 607.

approved additives, because the subpart on flavoring agents lists literally hundreds of specific natural and synthetic substances, and the subpart on gums lists dozens of specific masticatory substances. At 21 C.F.R. 170.3(o), FDA regulations list 32 "physical or technical functional effects for which direct human food ingredients may be added to food."

Reproduced below, as an example, is the food additive regulation for olestra, a synthetic fat replacement. Observe how, instead of simply approving the use of the substance, the regulation, in accordance with section 409(c)(1)(A), specifies "the conditions under which such additive may be safely used (including, but not limited to, specifications as to the particular food or classes of food in or on which such additive may be used, the maximum quantity which may be used. . . . , the manner in which such additive may be added to or used in or on such food, and any directions or other labeling or packaging requirements for such additive deemed necessary . . . to assure the safety of such use)."

When FDA originally approved olestra, it mandated that the label of any product containing olestra bear the following warning: "This Product Contains Olestra. Olestra may cause abdominal cramping and loose stools. Olestra inhibits the absorption of some vitamins and other nutrients." 21 C.F.R. 172.867(e)(1) (1997). FDA eliminated this requirement in 2003, in response to a petition by the manufacturer, Procter & Gamble. 68 Fed. Reg. 46363 (Aug. 5, 1972).

21 C.F.R. § 172.867 Olestra.

Olestra, as identified in this section, may be safely used in accordance with the following conditions:

(a) Olestra is a mixture of octa-, hepta-, and hexa-esters of sucrose with fatty acids derived from edible fats and oils or fatty acid sources that are generally recognized as safe or approved for use as food ingredients. The chain lengths of the fatty acids are no less than 12 carbon atoms.

(b) Olestra meets the specifications of the *Food Chemicals Codex*, 4th edition, 1st supplement (1997), pp. 33–35, which is incorporated by reference. . . .

(c) Olestra may be used in place of fats and oils in prepackaged ready-to-eat savory (i.e., salty or piquant but not sweet) snacks and prepackaged, unpopped popcorn kernels that are ready-to-heat. In such foods, the additive may be used in place of fats and oils for frying or baking, in dough conditioners, in sprays, in filling ingredients, or in flavors.

(d) To compensate for any interference with absorption of fat soluble vitamins, the following vitamins shall be added to foods containing olestra: 1.9 milligrams alpha-tocopherol equivalents per gram olestra; 51 retinol equivalents per gram olestra (as retinyl acetate or retinyl palmitate); 12 IU vitamin D per gram olestra; and 8 µg vitamin K1 per gram olestra.

(e)(1) Vitamins A, D, E, and K present in foods as a result of the requirement in paragraph (d) of this section shall be declared in the listing of ingredients. Such vitamins shall not be considered in determining nutrient content for the nutritional label or for any nutrient claims, express or implied.

(i) An asterisk shall follow vitamins A, D, E, and K in the listing of ingredients;

(ii) The asterisk shall appear as a superscript following each vitamin;

(iii) Immediately following the ingredient list an asterisk and statement, "Dietarily insignificant" shall appear prominently and conspicuously as specified in § 101.2(c) of this chapter;

(2) Olestra shall not be considered as a source of fat or calories for purposes of §§ 101.9 and 101.13 of this chapter.

[61 FR 3171, Jan. 30, 1996; 61 FR 11546, Mar. 21, 1996, as amended at 68 FR 46402, Aug. 5, 2003; 69 FR 29432, May 24, 2004.]

Marion Nestle, *The Selling of Olestra*
113 PUBLIC HEALTH REPORTS 508 (1998).

On June 17, 1998, the Food Advisory Committee of the Food and Drug Administration (FDA) confirmed its earlier judgments that the Procter & Gamble (P&G) company's fat substitute, olestra, was reasonably certain to cause no harm as a food additive and that foods containing this substance should carry a warning statement. This peculiar decision—judging olestra "safe" while alerting consumers to its potential hazards—was only the latest episode in a 30-year struggle to bring olestra to market. The elements of this struggle are useful to review, as they illustrate much larger societal concerns about the relationships of corporations to government and health professionals and the conflicts of interest inherent in such relationships.

P&G's persistence in that struggle is easily understood. Olestra, the company's name for sucrose polyester, retains the sensory and physical properties of natural food fats but is not digested or absorbed by the human body. In theory, substitution of olestra for natural fats could help people reduce their intake of calories, fat, saturated fat, and cholesterol and, therefore, reduce the risk of obesity and related diseases. . . . The potential uses of olestra in commonly consumed foods—and the potential economic returns to P&G investors—are enormous.

The reasons for the long delay in FDA approval are also readily apparent. Olestra raises at least two health concerns that have been difficult to resolve: first, olestra might be expected to behave in the body like mineral oil, with similar laxative effects and interference with the absorption of fat-soluble nutrients, and, second, as a replacer of cooking fat, olestra could be consumed in large amounts. P&G's many studies of the effects of olestra have been of short duration and, therefore, unable to address the long-term risk of gastrointestinal problems or nutrient depletion. Under current laws, petitioners must demonstrate that food additives are safe before the FDA grants approval; Congress has not granted the FDA a mandate or funds for independent evaluation of additives under review. Furthermore, because the laws do not require P&G to demonstrate long-term improvements in caloric balance or chronic disease risk, any benefits of olestra also remain uncertain.

. . . . [O]lestra is the first "macro-additive": a 1 oz serving of chips contains up to 10 g of olestra. In contrast, diet soft drinks contain only milligram amounts of artificial sweeteners. On quantitative grounds alone, olestra raises unprecedented public health and regulatory issues. . . .

To demonstrate the safety and potential efficacy of olestra, P&G invested upwards of a half billion dollars in research, development, and activities targeted to the FDA, professional societies, health scientists, practitioners, and consumers. P&G also worked to convince a reluctant Congress to extend protection on a key olestra patent. The company's comprehensive and persistent campaign to bring olestra to market deserves attention as an especially visible example of the ways large corporations gain support for their products from government agencies and health professionals . . .

P&G researchers discovered sucrose polyester accidentally during an unsuccessful 1968 search for fats that could be more easily digested by premature infants. . . . The potential for olestra to be consumed in much larger quantities than any other food additive explains the FDA's regulatory predicament. Food additives are usually consumed in tiny amounts but tested in animals at hundred-fold higher levels; this method could not be used to determine whether olestra affected intestinal function or depleted fat-soluble nutrients because animals could not eat that much. Thus, P&G needed to develop different safety testing methods and the FDA needed to establish new regulatory standards; over the years, they "learned together" how to approach these tasks.

The regulatory history of olestra began in 1971, when P&G obtained its first patent and met with the FDA to explore approval of olestra as a food additive. . . .

[In 1987], P&G petitioned the FDA to permit substitution of olestra for up to 35% of the fat used in home cooking and up to 75% of that used for commercial purposes. Because the petition did not include table spreads and ice cream, P&G presented the request as "a conservative first step." The FDA, however, viewed the potentially vast scope of uses as posing safety issues that required further testing. To expedite approval, P&G then narrowed its request just to use of olestra in savory (salty and spicy) snacks.

Over the years, P&G submitted 150 animal and human studies and 150,000 pages of data on the effects of olestra on absorption and excretion of drugs, vitamins, carotenoids (plant precursors of vitamin A that have antioxidant properties), and minerals and on hormone levels, intestinal function, and certain gastrointestinal diseases. Late in 1995, the FDA provided a summary of this information and a substantial critical analysis to a subcommittee of the FDA Food Advisory Committee and to the Committee itself. Both recommended approval of olestra, although some Committee members sharply dissented. On January 24, 1996, the FDA announced approval of olestra for use in savory snacks provided that . . . users fortify their products with fat-soluble vitamins A, D, E, and K and include a warning notice on packages. Recognizing that P&G planned to conduct post-market surveys of consumer responses to olestra, the FDA also announced that it would review new data in 30 months and reconsider approval at that time.

Current food additive regulations do not demand demonstration of absolute safety but only "reasonable certainty in the minds of competent scientists that the substance is not harmful under the intended conditions of use." In practice, the rules do not require P&G to demonstrate, nor is the FDA permitted to consider, whether olestra might actually be beneficial. As explained by then-FDA Commissioner David Kessler, questions about whether olestra might make sense or contribute to the nutritional health of the nation were irrelevant to the FDA's approval processes.

In June 1998, the FDA asked the Food Advisory Committee to evaluate whether P&G's post-market studies had raised any significant public health concerns and to advise the agency about changes that might be needed in labeling requirements. The Committee reviewed data presented by P&G scientists and sponsored researchers and listened to testimony from about 30 individuals, at least half of them supported by or otherwise connected to P&G. The Committee also heard testimony from representatives of the Washington, DC-based consumer advocacy group, the Center for Science in the Public Interest (CSPI) and independent scientists about reported and potential adverse effects. Most of the Committee members again viewed such concerns as minor and voted to reaffirm their original decisions, thus concluding a matter that had required substantial FDA attention for 27 years.

. . . .

Some scientists and consumer groups have opposed olestra on safety grounds for more than a decade. The most organized opposition has come from CSPI, which first challenged the safety of olestra in a response to P&G's 1987 food additive petition. In preparation for the 1995 meeting of the Food Advisory Committee, CSPI provided a detailed analysis of P&G-sponsored studies that found olestra to deplete carotenoids and fat-soluble vitamins and to cause significant gastrointestinal disturbances. On that basis, and because olestra appeared to be associated with precancerous liver lesions in animals, CSPI asked the FDA to deny approval. Studies conducted or supported by P&G, however, invariably conclude that olestra poses no health risks, but the company obviously has a vested interest in producing such results. CSPI has criticized these studies on methodological grounds. That the FDA cannot require confirmation by disinterested investigators troubles critics. . . .

The FDA approved olestra because P&G's research found it safe, the Advisory Committee judged gastrointestinal effects to be trivial, and critics could not prove demonstrable harm from depletion of fat soluble nutrients. The shift of the burden of proof from industry to critics highlights weaknesses in the current regulatory system. In the case of olestra, research by independent investigators would have been highly desirable, especially since P&G's study designs may have been "years behind" current clinical and epidemiologic methods for evaluating risk, as suggested by one member of the FDA Advisory Committee. If the FDA were adequately funded or if petitioners were required to provide funds to the FDA to conduct or sponsor high quality research by independent investigators, the agency would not need to work hand-in-glove with industry to regulate new products. . . .

Henry I. Miller, *Who Is Trying to Kill Olestra? and Why?*

WASHINGTON TIMES, July 25, 1996, at A19.

Government agencies ranging from the Federal Aviation Administration to the Food and Drug Administration (FDA) often seek the advice of independent advisers to critique and improve their decision-making. Complementing the agencies' own staffs, these extramural experts allow decision-makers to have the benefit of competing advice. . . .

Over the years, extramural advisers, often working without pay, have made real contributions to government efficiency and public safety. . . .

After an eight-year review, the FDA concluded in January that the fat substitute called olestra is safe for use in certain foods. As part of the decision-making process, last year the FDA asked a panel of independent advisers, the Olestra Working Group, to review the finding of Procter and Gamble's 25 years of research on the product. After intense discussion and debate, the panel came back with a positive recommendation. They concluded that—after decades of animal experiments, and trials with more than 8,000 adults and children— olestra is safe. However, since FDA's approval of olestra, the agency and its system of independent advisers have been subjected to a shrill campaign of intimidation and disinformation by a Washington-based Naderite lobbying group, the Center for Science in the Public Interest (CSPI).

As a conservative critic (and former official) of FDA, I have often chided the agency for taking too long to evaluate and review products. I believe reform of many of its procedures and policies are long overdue. But never have FDA and its extramural advisers been accused of the perfidy of having a "conflict of interest" or of "bowing to economic clout." CSPI contends that in approving olestra, the FDA, so often the bane of food and pharmaceutical companies, is a corporate lap dog. . . .

It is time to set the record straight, give the FDA its due and defend the integrity and independence of the advisory system. The agency, under withering fire, has done the right thing (albeit after unconscionable delay). Olestra is a potential boon to public health in the United States, where one person in three is obese, diets are dominated by fat, and most people die from fat-related diseases. Since the FDA's approval, CSPI has abandoned objectivity and common sense in all-out war on olestra. Its executive director, Michael Jacobson, called it a "public health time bomb," adding that FDA Commissioner David Kessler "has lit the fuse." . . .

. . . So how did such a "dangerous" product get on the market? Mr. Jacobson speaks darkly of the FDA and its Olestra Working Group as being "pro-industry," and of some of its members as having a "conflict of interest."

In fact two non-voting members of the more than 20 members of the advisory panel were from industry—something you would expect, even welcome. The panel also included the nation's leading academics in nutrition, food science and gastroenterology. True, some of the panel members had worked as consultants to industry in the past, but the FDA stringently screens its advisers for any conflict of interest. . . .

[G]iven the safety of the product, the marketplace should be the ultimate judge of its fate. The product's success or failure should depend on consumers' willingness to pay for fat-free, lower-calorie olestra foods. Why should CSPI—or other self-anointed experts—decide what goes on the supermarket shelves?. . . .

NOTES

1. *Subsequent History of Olestra.* FDA eliminated the "abdominal cramping and loose stools" warning requirement in 2003, noting: "[T]he petitioner's postapproval studies show that customary or usual consumption of olestra in savory snacks causes only a minor increase in the frequency of loose stools." 68 Fed. Reg. 46364, 46389 (Aug. 5, 2003). Following this development, Frito–Lay rebranded its olestra-containing line of Wow® chips as its "Light" line. In 2004, FDA further revised the olestra approval regulation to permit the use of the substance in unpopped popcorn kernels. 69 Fed. Reg. 29428 (May 24, 2004). In 2008, FDA issued a "No Objection" letter to a Generally Recognized as Safe (GRAS) affirmation notification from Procter & Gamble for use of olestra in cookies (excerpted *infra* p. 586), and in 2008 the agency sent a similar letter to the company regarding olestra's use in many additional types of food. The topic of GRAS status will be examined in detail below.

2. *Consideration of Utility.* A major issue during congressional consideration of the 1958 Amendment was whether an additive should be approved for use if it did not convey some benefit to consumers. The Administration bill would have required a finding by FDA that a food additive has "functional value" in order to be approved if the additive was a poisonous or deleterious substance. H.R. 6747, 85th Cong., 1st Sess. (1957). Industry opposed this approach. The House Committee adopted a compromise suggested in Bernard L. Oser, *The Functional Value of Food Additives*, 13 FOOD DRUG COSM. L.J. (1958), under which FDA must find that the additive accomplishes its intended physical or other technical effect. H.R. REP. NO. 2284, 85th Cong., 2d Sess. 5–6 (1958). Section 409, as enacted, requires a food additive petition to contain "all relevant data bearing on the physical or other technical effect such additive is intended to produce, and the quantity of such additive required to produce such effect." FD&C Act 409(b)(2)(C). If a tolerance limitation is required to assure the safety of the proposed additive, FDA "shall not fix such tolerance limitation at a level higher than [it] finds to be reasonably required to accomplish the "physical or other technical effect for which the additive is intended." *Id.* 409(c)(4)(A). If the agency determines that the additive will not accomplish the intended physical or technical effect at a safe tolerance level, it will not approve the additive. *Id.* 409(c)(4)(B). If no quantitative limitation is required to assure that the use of the additive will be safe, FDA may not consider functionality.

The House Committee stated that this functionality requirement referred to "the objective effect" of the additive and "does not involve any judgment on the part of the Secretary of whether such effect results in any added value to the consumer of such food or enhances the marketability from a merchandising point of view."

3.   *Investigational Exemptions.* Section 409(j) requires the Secretary to issue regulations exempting food additives intended solely for investigational use by qualified experts. FDA has never issued such regulations, but has not objected to the investigational use of food additives under conditions similar to those for investigational new drugs. It is now common for new food additives intended to be directly added to food to be tested in humans prior to FDA approval of a food additive petition.

4.   *Patent Term Extension.* Unlike New Drug Application (NDA) approvals, for example, food additive petition approvals are not granted to a particular applicant. Therefore, under the FD&C Act, any manufacturer can begin to sell a food additive upon publication of the final rule approving the additive. The petitioner's sole possible protection from competition (and from free-riding on the petition process by competitors) lies in patent law. Under the Patent Term Restoration and Drug Price Competition Act of 1984, food additives are, like new drugs, eligible for patent term extension to compensate for the regulatory review period. 35 U.S.C. 156(d)(5). *See, e.g.*, 54 Fed. Reg. 38289 (Sept. 15, 1989) (extension of the patent life of anionic polyurethane); 69 Fed. Reg. 40946 (July 7, 2004) (neotame).

5.   *Specifications for Food Additives.* Many food additive regulations contain chemical specifications. FDA has supported the National Academy of Sciences' development of the Food Chemicals Codex, a compilation of monographs establishing food grade specifications for food substances. FDA occasionally publishes notices providing an opportunity for public comment on changes to Codex monographs. *E.g.*, 67 Fed. Reg. 39999 (June 11, 2002). The agency also adopts specific Codex specifications for particular substances—including, for example, olestra, as shown in the regulation excerpted above, *supra* p. 557.

6.   *Interim Food Additives.* In 35 Fed. Reg. 12062 (July 28, 1970), FDA permitted the continued use of a food additive, brominated vegetable oil (BVO), in fruit-flavored beverages on what was characterized as an interim basis pending additional testing to resolve issues about its safety. This order was upheld in *Jacobson v. Edwards*, Food Drug Cosm. L. Rep. (CCH) ¶ 40,817 (D.D.C. 1971). The D.C. Circuit affirmed the District Court in an unpublished order on December 15, 1972. Subsequently, FDA promulgated criteria and procedures for issuing interim food additive regulations. 37 Fed. Reg. 25705 (Dec. 2, 1972), codified at 21 C.F.R. Part 180. Section 180.1 of these regulations provides: "An interim food additive regulation ... may be promulgated ... when new information raises a substantial question about the safety or functionality of the substance but there is a reasonable certainty that the substance is not harmful and that no harm to the public health will result from the continued use of the substance for a limited period of time while the question raised is being resolved by further study." The interim food additive order for brominated

vegetable oil, codified at 21 C.F.R. 180.30, remains in effect more than thirty years after it was promulgated.

7.   *Testing Guidelines.* Although FDA established general principles governing toxicity testing for food ingredients as early as the 1940s, *see* Arnold J. Lehman et al., *Procedures for the Appraisal of the Toxicity of Chemicals in Foods*, 4 Food Drug Cosm. L.Q. 412 (1949), for many years it resisted issuing specific toxicology guidelines. In 1982, however, the agency published under the name "Redbook" a set of toxicological standards for safety evaluation of food additives and color additives. 47 Fed. Reg. 46141 (Oct. 15, 1982). The updated "Redbook 2000" is now issued as a guidance document available on the FDA website. TOXICOLOGICAL PRINCIPLES FOR THE SAFETY ASSESSMENT OF FOOD INGREDIENTS ("Redbook 2000") (rev. July 2007).

8.   *Competitive Objections.* On occasion competitors will object to new food additive regulations in an attempt to maintain a commercial advantage. *E.g.*, 70 Fed. Reg. 15756 (Mar. 29, 2005).

NOTES: SPECIFIC ADDITIVES

1.   *Cyclamate.* After 1958, FDA considered the noncaloric sweetener cyclamate to be Generally Recognized as Safe (GRAS) and thus exempt from the food additive definition and the food additive approval process. When the agency removed cyclamate from the GRAS list because of evidence of carcinogenicity in animals, 34 Fed. Reg. 17063 (Oct. 21, 1969), the manufacturer continued to test it and eventually petitioned for approval of its use under section 409. The agency denied the petition, 41 Fed. Reg. 43754 (Oct. 4, 1976), but granted the manufacturer's demand for a hearing, 42 Fed. Reg. 12515 (Mar. 4, 1977). The Administrative Law Judge (ALJ) ruled that the petition was properly denied, Food Drug Cosm. L. Rep. (CCH) ¶ 38,199 (1978), but the Commissioner remanded the matter to the ALJ for development of further evidence, 44 Fed. Reg. 47620 (Aug. 14, 1979).

The ALJ reopened the administrative hearing, took additional evidence, and issued a revised initial decision, again upholding the denial of the food additive petition. Food Drug Cosm. L. Rep. (CCH) ¶ 38,026 (1980). Meanwhile, the U.S. District Court rejected the petitioner's assertions that the agency's deliberations had been based on political rather than scientific factors and conducted in bad faith. *Abbott Laboratories v. Harris*, Food Drug Cosm. L. Rep. (CCH) ¶ 38,046 (N.D. Ill. 1980). The Commissioner issued a final decision denying the food additive petition for cyclamate in 45 Fed. Reg. 61474 (Sept. 16, 1980).

Rather than appeal this ruling, the manufacturer undertook additional studies and analysis and submitted a new food additive petition. 47 Fed. Reg. 51227 (Nov. 12, 1982). In 1984, FDA announced that the National Academy of Sciences would hold hearings and issue a report on the matter. 49 Fed. Reg. 24953 (June 18, 1984). In "Cyclamate Update," FDA Talk Paper No. T89–35 (May 16, 1989), FDA acknowledged that both its own Cancer Assessment Committee and the NAS had concluded that cyclamate is not a carcinogen, but it also reported that the NAS was unable to determine whether it may be a tumor promoter or a co-carcinogen. FDA has taken no further action on this matter. As of January 1, 1996, under European Union Directive 94/35/EC (June 30, 1994), cyclamates became lawful throughout Europe. In the United States, they remain explicitly banned from foods. 21 C.F.R. 189.135.

2. *Saccharin.* After FDA proposed to ban saccharin, under the Delaney Clause, based on carcinogenicity in rats, 42 Fed. Reg. 19996 (Apr. 15, 1977), Congress enacted legislation in November 1977 to suspend any further action. For a discussion of subsequent events, including the eventual repeal of the November 1977 legislation, see *infra* p. 1403. This statutory moratorium represents the only time Congress has enacted legislation to prevent FDA from banning a food additive.

3. *Aspartame.* The food additive petition for aspartame as a sugar substitute for table use and for use in certain dry food applications was filed in 1973. FDA approved the petition and published a food additive regulation in 39 Fed. Reg. 27317 (July 26, 1974). Though FDA initially declined to stay its approval in response to demands for an evidentiary hearing, the agency later reversed itself because of suspicions about the reliability of the studies submitted by the manufacturer. 40 Fed. Reg. 56907 (Dec. 5, 1975). After an independent audit validated the study results, FDA announced a hearing before a public board of inquiry. 44 Fed. Reg. 31716 (June 1, 1979). The board's decision recommended that aspartame not be approved because of unresolved questions regarding its capacity to cause brain tumors in rodents. *See* Food Drug Cosm. L. Rep. (CCH) ¶ 38,072 (1980). The Commissioner, however, reversed the public board of inquiry and approved the additive. 46 Fed. Reg. 38284 (July 24, 1981).

In the years since, FDA has approved additional uses of aspartame in food, which are codified in 21 C.F.R. 172.804. After approving the sweetener for use in soft drinks, 48 Fed. Reg. 31376 (July 8, 1983), the agency denied requests for an administrative hearing. 49 Fed. Reg. 6672 (Feb. 22, 1984). Its decision was upheld in *Community Nutrition Institute v. Young,* 773 F.2d 1356 (D.C. Cir. 1985). CNI continued to object to aspartame's approval and FDA continued to overrule those objections and to deny a public hearing. *E.g.,* 53 Fed. Reg. 6595 (Mar. 2, 1988). In 2005, the European Ramazzini Foundation concluded from a long-term feeding study in rats that aspartame causes cancer, but in 2007, FDA determined that the design and interpretation of the study were flawed and therefore that no reason existed to reconsider the approved status of aspartame. FDA–CFSAN, FDA Statement on European Aspartame Study (Apr. 20, 2007).

4. *Sucralose.* In 1998, FDA approved sucralose, a sweetening ingredient (the key component of Splenda®), after extensive testing. *See* 63 Fed. Reg. 16417 (Apr. 3, 1998), codified at 21 C.F.R. 172.831. On April 3, 2006, Citizens for Health submitted a citizen petition, FDA Docket No. 2006P–0158, requesting that FDA revoke this approval or investigate its safety further. The agency has not ruled on this petition.

5. *Radiation.* The definition of a food additive in section 201(s) specifically includes "any source of radiation" in food processing. FDA has

promulgated a number of food additive regulations approving food irradiation in 21 C.F.R. Part 179. The regulations, as amended over the years, permit the use of ionizing radiation for a growing list of specified uses (with corresponding radiation limits). The twelve currently approved uses include, for example, microbial disinfection of herbs, seeds, and spices; control of food-borne pathogens in poultry and meat; control of Salmonella in fresh shell eggs; and control of food-borne pathogens and extension of shelf-life in iceberg lettuce and fresh spinach. 21 C.F.R. 179.26(b).

In 1986, FDA determined that although food containing an irradiated ingredient would not require special labeling, food which itself had been irradiated would require both the international "Radura" logo and, in addition, for two years, a statement that the product has been "treated with radiation" or "treated by irradiation." 51 Fed. Reg. 13376 (Apr. 18, 1986). In 1990, FDA made the radiation statement a permanent requirement, at least until it can be shown that the logo alone is sufficient to convey to consumers that the product has been irradiated. 55 Fed. Reg. 14413 (Apr. 18, 1990). Under section 403C of the FD&C Act, as added by the Food and Drug Administration Modernization Act of 1997, Congress determined that the FDA-required radiation disclosure statement could not be required to be more prominent than the statement of ingredients. FDA amended its labeling requirement to comply with this requirement. 63 Fed. Reg. 43875 (Aug. 17, 1998).

Under an April 2007 FDA proposal, only irradiated foods in which the irradiation causes a change in the foods' organoleptic, nutritional, or functional properties that the consumer cannot identify in the absence of appropriate labeling would need to bear the international "Radura" logo and the term "irradiated." The proposal would also allow firms to petition to use a term other than "irradiated," and allow a firm to use the term "pasteurized" instead of "irradiated" if the firm provides FDA with effectiveness data. 72 Fed. Reg. 16291 (Apr. 4, 2007). The agency has not taken further action on this proposal.

The fact that radiation is specifically included within the definition of a food additive does not mean that it could not be found to be GRAS and thus excluded from the requirement for a food additive regulation. The GRAS exclusion from the requirement of a food additive regulation applies to all substances that fall within the broad definition of food additive in section 201(s).

6.   *Fluoride.* The safety of fluoride added to water has long been controversial. EPA sets the standards for fluoride in drinking water under the Safe Drinking Water Act, 42 U.S.C. 300f et seq. *See also* 50 Fed. Reg. 47142 (Nov. 14, 1985), 51 Fed. Reg. 11396 (Apr. 2, 1986). Under 21 C.F.R. 170.45, FDA prohibits all fluorine-containing compounds from food except as permitted by EPA for drinking water and by FDA (at 21 C.F.R. 165.110(d)) for bottled water.

3.   THE MEANING OF "FOOD ADDITIVE"

As noted previously, the challenges and expenses of the food additive approval process, and the extreme barrier to market entry represented by the Delaney Clause, lead food manufacturers to strive to escape the category of "food additive" as defined in section 201(s) of FD&C Act. Manufacturers frequently try to use one of the definition's explicit exemptions (e.g., GRAS, prior sanctioned, or dietary supplement ingredient), but they sometimes alternatively contend that a food ingredient falls outside the core meaning of "food additive" in 201(s): "any substance the intended use of which results or may result, directly or indirectly, in its becoming a component of or otherwise affecting the characteristics of any food."

[handwritten note: approval of food additive is expensive. Try to be exempted.]

Consider, for example, the question of raw agricultural commodities. The 1958 Food Additives Amendment focused on manmade chemicals added to food to perform specific technological functions. There is little evidence suggesting how Congress expected the Amendment to apply to agricultural commodities. Presumably, an apple, sold as such, is not within the reach of the Amendment because it is itself a distinct food, and it does not become a "component" of any other food when it is sold in its unprocessed form. When an apple is incorporated into applesauce or an apple pie, however, it presumably becomes subject to the same analysis under the 1958 Amendment as any other "added" food constituent.

FDA has not published a definitive regulation on this issue, and there is no pertinent case law. However, during the hearings on the 1958 Amendment, "Food Additives," Hearings before a Subcommittee of the House Committee on Interstate and Foreign Commerce, 85th Cong., 2d Sess. 461–462 (1958), FDA submitted a partial list of GRAS substances, which included such common food items as butter, coffee, lemon juice, olive oil, salt, and sugar. In "Nutrition and Human Needs—1972," Hearings before the Senate Select Committee on Nutrition and Human Needs, 92d Cong., 2d Sess., Part 4B (1972), FDA officials stated that when raw agricultural commodities are used in processed food they become subject to the food additive provisions of the law and thus must be GRAS, prior sanctioned, or the subject of a food additive regulation.

The issue has arisen most directly in FDA's attempts to regulate sassafras tea. In the 1950s, agency scientists determined that safrole, which was widely used as a flavor ingredient in root beer and other soft drinks, is an animal carcinogen. The agency therefore prohibited its addition to food. 25 Fed. Reg. 12412 (Dec. 3, 1960). Sassafras tea is made by stripping the bark from the roots of sassafras trees and steeping the bark in hot water for several minutes. One of the principal constituents of sassafras bark is safrole. Following ineluctable logic from its 1960 rule, FDA concluded that sassafras bark should no longer be permitted to be marketed for use in making sassafras tea. It thus banned the product. *See* 41 Fed. Reg. 19207 (May 11, 1976), codified at 21 C.F.R. 189.180.

In *United States v. Articles of Food . . . Select Natural Herb Tea, Sassafras, etc.* (C.D. Cal.), 12 FDA CONSUMER, No. 9, at 32 (Nov. 1978), FDA contended that the product was a food that was, or contained, an unsafe food additive within the meaning of sections 201(s) and 409(a) of the Act. But the agency's claim raised a problem. Safrole in sassafras bark is a natural constituent of a vegetable substance. Many natural foodstuffs contain substances that, if extracted and added to other food, would be both unhealthful and illegal. Spinach, for example, contains

[handwritten margin note: Substances that occur naturally would not be considered as additive]

oxalic acid. If oxalic acid were extracted from spinach and added to another food, it would be a food additive, rendering the food to which it was added adulterated. Yet oxalic acid in spinach is not regulated as a food additive. Nor had the agency previously suggested that the addition of spinach to other foods raised food additive issues with respect to the oxalic acid that is necessarily added as part of the spinach.

FDA nonetheless insisted that safrole in sassafras tea is a food additive. While the agency conceded that safrole is not a food additive as long as it remains in the bark, it maintained that the substance becomes a food additive when it emerges into the water. Even if confined to safrole, this view poses problems. Safrole is a natural constituent of a number of food substances, including nutmeg. When nutmeg is added to eggnog, the safrole must emerge from the nutmeg to flavor the eggnog. If safrole were regarded as a food additive in eggnog, presumably cholesterol would be considered a food additive in every food containing milk.

*[handwritten margin note: * distinction between tea and nutmeg; milk]*

To avoid this result, FDA took the position that sassafras bark is not a food in its own right, but serves essentially as a vehicle to convey safrole into water. Nutmeg, although not a food that can be eaten alone, does have food value independent of its safrole content. Likewise spinach and milk are independent foods that can be consumed as such. The components of these foods have no separate legal status in the regulatory scheme for food additives.

[handwritten margin note: FDA has NOT enforced the Safafras tea.]

Although FDA vigorously pressed these distinctions in the *Select Natural Herb Tea* case, the court declined to rule on the agency's summary judgment motion. In 1977, the judge ordered the case to be tried. The claimant, over the government's objections, thereupon successfully moved to withdraw its claim. On June 12, 1978, the judge defaulted the tea. Thus, the sassafras tea regulation remains unchallenged, perhaps because FDA has not enforced it since.

The next two cases, which address the regulatory status of substances in dietary supplement products, were decided prior to the passage of the Dietary Supplement Health and Education Act (DSHEA). Today, the ingredients in question would indisputably be exempt from the definition of "food additive" under section 201(s)(6), added by DSHEA, which excludes dietary supplement ingredients from the scope of the term. Nevertheless, the cases, by analogy, raise interesting issues with respect to conventional foods.

United States v. An Article of Food . . . FoodScience Labs

678 F.2d 735 (7th Cir. 1982).

■ CUMMINGS, CHIEF JUDGE.

. . . The defendant food comprises numerous cases containing tablets of Aangamik 15. . . . According to the government's complaint, the tablets are an adulterated food under 21 U.S.C. § 342(a)(2)(C) of the Federal Food, Drug and Cosmetic Act in that they contain a food additive—N,N–Dimethylglycine hydrochloride ("DMG")—which allegedly is unsafe under 21 U.S.C. § 348(a). . . .

Even though DMG is quite clearly a "substance" that has become a "component" of Aangamik 15, FoodScience [the claimant] would have us read into the definition of "food additive" an exception for substances that become "principal ingredients" of the food to which they are added. Although DMG is the lesser of two active components of the tablets and accounts for less than 4% of each tablet's weight, FoodScience argues that DMG is a "principal ingredient" because the tablets' consumers are particularly hopeful of "the potential usefulness of DMG as a metabolic enhancer (whether or not it is a nutrient in the strict sense). . . ." Since many ordinary additives come in relatively small quantities and food manufacturers often attempt to make their presence inconspicuous, an exception from the definition for "principal ingredients" might agree with the notion of "food additive" used in common parlance. But had Congress intended the Food and Drug Administration and the courts to rely on common parlance it would not have so carefully crafted the foregoing definition of the term.

FoodScience argues it is apparent from the statutory definition that Congress intended to limit the definition of "food additive" to substances that become a component of or affect food in some subtle or incidental fashion, such as substances "intended for use in producing, manufacturing, packing, processing etc." . . . FoodScience's argument is that because Congress was concerned with small amounts of unsafe substances, Congress could not similarly be concerned with unsafe substances present in relatively larger quantities. But the definition itself shows the absurdity: "[t]he term 'food additive' means any substance the intended use of which results . . . in its becoming a component . . . of any food. . . ." The term "component" of course includes large quantities of unsafe substances as well as small quantities. . . .

The practical effect of holding that DMG is an additive is to place the burden of showing safety upon FoodScience. In order to avoid the label "food additive," FoodScience must now show that DMG is "generally recognized as safe," whereas if DMG were not an "additive," the Food and Drug Administration would have the burden under 21 U.S.C. § 342 of proving by a preponderance of the evidence that DMG is "injurious to health.". . . .

■ CUDAHY, CIRCUIT JUDGE, concurring.

I concur fully in Chief Judge Cummings' conclusion that the government in this case properly condemned defendant's "Aangamik 15" tablets as an adulterated food because they contain an unsafe "food additive"—DMG—for which no exempting regulations have been issued. I write separately only to emphasize that, in my view, characterizing DMG as a "food additive" depends critically on its being added to or sold in combination with other active ingredients. Because FoodScience consistently represented to the public, and maintained throughout the pre-trial stages of this proceeding, that its "Aangamik 15" tablets contained *two* active and beneficial ingredients—DMG and calcium gluconate—I agree that the district court properly found DMG to be a "food additive" within the meaning of 21 U.S.C. § 321(s) (1976). I believe, however, as did the district court, that this would be a far different case if DMG were being marketed as a single food ingredient. In that case, the FDA would not be entitled to rely on the "food additive" presumption to condemn plaintiff's product but would instead be obligated to shoulder its normal burden of proving, by a preponderance of the evidence, that DMG was an "adulterated food" within the meaning of 21 U.S.C. § 342(a)(1) (1976) or that the product was "misbranded" under the standards set forth in 21 U.S.C. § 343 (1976). . . .

———

A decade later Judge Cudahy was presented with the opportunity to elaborate upon his concurring opinion.

United States v. Two Plastic Drums . . . Black Currant Oil

984 F.2d 814 (7th Cir. 1993).

■ CUDAHY, CIRCUIT JUDGE.

The Food and Drug Administration ("FDA") brings this in rem seizure action under the Food, Drug and Cosmetic Act seeking to condemn and destroy two drums of black currant oil as adulterated under 21 U.S.C. § 342(a)(2)(C) for being a food additive not recognized as safe. The district court granted summary judgment against the FDA, and the government appeals. We affirm.

Black currant oil ("BCO") is extracted from the seeds of the black currant berry and is marketed as a dietary supplement for its unique fatty-acid structures. The FDA argues that BCO is a food additive not generally recognized as safe ("GRAS") and seeks to seize and condemn two drums of BCO pursuant to sections 334 and 342 of the Act. A food is adulterated and subject to seizure under section 334 "if it is, or it bears or contains, any food additive which [the Secretary has not recognized as safe pursuant to section 348]." The determination of whether a substance is a food additive is critical in establishing the safety of the substance because, if the substance is deemed a food additive, it is presumed to be unsafe, and the processor has the burden of showing that the substance is GRAS. On the other hand, if a substance is not a food additive, but food in the generic sense, then the substance is presumed safe and the FDA has the burden of showing that the substance is injurious to health. . . .

The FDA contends that BCO is a food additive because it is a "component" of food when it is combined with the gelatin and glycerin used to market the BCO in capsules. The gelatin and glycerin encase the BCO to prevent it from becoming rancid. The FDA concedes that if the BCO alone was marketed in bottles for teaspoon consumption, it would not be a food additive, and the FDA would bear the burden of proving that BCO is injurious to health. But the combination of BCO with glycerin and gelatin, the FDA maintains, creates a food consisting of three components, and thus, three food additives. . . .

Although we are mindful of the deference due the FDA in construing the statute it administers, deference here is unwarranted since its interpretation is contrary to the language and intent of the

Act. As an initial matter, we question whether BCO can even be considered a "component" under the Act. The term "component," commonly understood and defined as . . . "a constituent part" or "ingredient," loses its meaning when applied to foods used in conjunction with inactive ingredients, as this case amply evidences. There, the dietary supplement (the food) is nothing but BCO combined with glycerin and gelatin—two inactive substances used for marketing the BCO in capsule form. The gelatin and glycerin do not interact with or change the character of the BCO, but merely act as a container comparable to a bottle containing liquids marketed for teaspoon consumption. The BCO in question is the dietary supplement and the dietary supplement is the BCO. Therefore, to hold that BCO is a component of the dietary supplement would be to find that BCO is a component of itself. Such an interpretation would defy logic and common sense.

But even assuming that a single active "ingredient" of food can be considered a component of the food, the statutory language does not indicate that every component of food is necessarily a food additive. The Act defines "food additive" as a substance "becoming a component *or otherwise affecting the characteristics of any food.*" The FDA interpretation of this provision implies that the language "or otherwise" is used disjunctively in such a way that a substance is a food additive if it (1) is a component of any food, or (2) affects the characteristics of a food. We think that this interpretation, however, distorts the plain meaning of the provision. The phrase "or otherwise," as employed here, is not used to express two alternative definitions of a food additive. Rather, it is used in a way to clarify or elaborate, such that "otherwise" is correctly read as "similarly." . . . Therefore, simply becoming a "component" of food does not, in and of itself, satisfy the definition of a food additive. To be a food additive, a substance must not only be added to food, but it must also have the purpose or effect of altering a food's characteristics.

When two or more active ingredients comprise a food, each component is arguably different from the food in such a way that the addition of each has affected the characteristics of the other components and of the food. . . . But when there is only one active component, as is the case here, that single component does not affect the characteristics of the food in question—rather, it constitutes the food. Thus, even if we were to find that BCO was a component of the BCO dietary supplement capsules, the language of the Act indicates that it is not a food additive because, as the single active ingredient, it does not affect the characteristics of any food. . . .

NOTES

1. *Second Case.* Shortly thereafter, the First Circuit reached the same decision in another black current oil case. *United States v. 29 Cartons of . . . An Article of Food*, 987 F.2d 33 (1st Cir. 1993).

2. *Continued Relevance?* While the precise issues in these cases were made moot by DSHEA and its exemption of all dietary supplement ingredients from the food additive provisions of the FD&C Act, it is interesting to consider whether the reasoning of these decisions has any

continuing relevance for conventional foods. Imagine, for example, a new synthetic meat product. Presumably, a pure slab of this meat sold as steak would not be a "food additive," because it would not be a "component" of any other food. But would this analysis change if the synthetic meat were sold salted, or with food coloring added? How would Judge Cudahy address this issue? *See Burger a la Jetsons? Lab Patty Tastes "Almost" Like Beef*, WASH. POST, Aug. 6, 2013, at A1.

~

In 1975 regulations, FDA included a provision, since revoked, which asserted the power to regulate vitamins and minerals in dietary supplements under the food additive provisions of the FD&C Act. This provision came under sharp attack by supplement manufacturers. The following decision was preceded by *National Nutritional Foods v. Mathews*, 557 F.2d 325 (2d Cir. 1977) (excerpted *supra* p. 93), in which the same court, as part of the same litigation, rejected FDA's attempt to classify high-potency vitamins as drugs. The decision excerpted below also came after the 1976 passage of section 411 of the FD&C Act, which prohibits FDA from establishing limits on the potency of any vitamin or mineral and from classifying a vitamin or mineral as a drug solely because of its high potency. Today, vitamins and minerals in dietary supplements, along with all other dietary ingredients in dietary supplements, are exempted from the definition of food additive at FD&C Act 201(s)(6), added by DSHEA in 1994. But the case is still relevant with respect to the addition of vitamins and minerals to conventional food, as well as to the broader question of whether a commonsense "food" may also be a "food additive."

National Nutritional Foods Ass'n v. Kennedy
572 F.2d 377 (2d Cir. 1978).

■ FRIENDLY, CIRCUIT JUDGE. . . .

A[n] . . . important controversy relates to what is now [21 C.F.R.] § 105.85(f). . . .

Petitioners focus on the [following] paragraph:

(8) Any vitamin or mineral which is included in a dietary supplement and which is not generally recognized, among experts qualified by scientific training and experience to evaluate its safety, as having been adequately shown to be safe under the conditions of its intended use is a food additive within the meaning of section 201(s) of the act; and pursuant to sections 402(a)(2)(C) and 409 of the act, such inclusion is illegal in the absence of a food additive regulation approving such inclusion. A listing of some of the vitamins [and] minerals . . . which are generally recognized as safe, and which thus may lawfully be included in a dietary supplement without a food additive regulation, appears at Subpart F of Part 182 of this chapter.

Petitioners say that having been foiled by us [in *National Nutritional Foods v. Mathews*], and by Congress [in FD&C Act 411], in his effort to classify high potency vitamins and minerals as drugs, the

Commissioner is now seeking to reach essentially the same goal by threatening to treat added quantities as food additives. . . .

Petitioners contend that vitamins and minerals are foods within § 201(f), . . . and that in the nature of things a "food" cannot be a "food additive," especially when it is just more of the same. Recognizing that the Commissioner must have power to prevent the sale of vitamin and mineral preparations of such high potency as to be dangerous, they say the Commissioner must proceed under more general provisions relating to adulteration on a case by case basis, *see, e.g.* § 402(a)(1), (3)–(7), (b), rather than the more readily enforceable provisions relating to food additives. . . .

. . . The sole criterion for identifying a food additive is whether a substance which may become a component of or affect the characteristics of any food be not generally recognized among qualified experts as having been shown to be safe. We do not believe a substance gains immunity from this criterion merely because it also qualifies as a food. . . . Congress has vested the Commissioner with broad "authority to promulgate regulations for the efficient enforcement" of the Food, Drug and Cosmetic Act, § 701(a), and we see no reason why we cannot determine that too much of even a good thing may come within the definition of a "food additive."

Still more important, Congress, which most likely was aware of the May 1975 regulations, seems to have held that view. The Senate decided not to include in the 1976 legislation [adding FD&C Act 411] a provision prohibiting FDA from regulating safe vitamins, minerals, and associated ingredients as food additives. . . . And the House Conference Report observed:

> Similarly, if any vitamin, mineral or other food ingredient is not generally recognized as safe by qualified experts and meets the other criteria of the definition of a "food additive" under section 201(s) of the Act, it would be subject to regulation under section 409 of the Act. If such a vitamin, mineral or other ingredient is intentionally added to a food, such food is adulterated (within the meaning of section 402(a)(2)(C) of the Act) unless its use is in conformity with a regulation issued by the Secretary which prescribes the conditions under which it may be safely used or exempts it for investigational use by qualified experts. It is on precisely this basis that the Secretary has, by regulation, restricted the potency of the vitamin folic acid that may be added to a food.

H.R. Rep. No. 94–1005, 94th Cong., 2d Sess. (1976).

We therefore find no infirmity in § 105.85(f). . . .

NOTES

1. *Nutrients as Food Additives.* FDA has restricted the use of several nutrients because of their toxicity. *See* 21 C.F.R. 170.45 (flourine); 21 C.F.R. 172.345 (folic acid). Most recently, FDA issued food additive regulations permitting but restricting the use of vitamins D^2 and D^3 in certain food products. 74 Fed. 11019 (Mar. 16, 2009), codified at 21 C.F.R. 172.379 (D^2 for use in soy-based food products); 68 Fed. Reg. 9000 (Feb. 27, 2003), as codified with later amendments at 21 C.F.R. 172.380 (D^3 for use

in various foods). When it issued these regulations, FDA had already affirmed vitamin D as GRAS for use in other specified foods. *See* 21 C.F.R. 184.1950. In the 1960s, FDA denied a food additive petition for menadione (vitamin K), thus precluding its use in dietary supplements or in food. 28 Fed. Reg. 3051 (Mar. 28, 1963), 28 Fed. Reg. 7262 (July 16, 1963). Vitamins D and K (as well as vitamins A and E) are fat soluble and stored in the body. FDA has long been concerned about the indiscriminate use of fat soluble vitamins.

2.   *Herbs in Food.* FDA has objected to the use of herbs as dietary ingredients or even as conventional food ingredients in common food products. It has issued warning letters against such products but has not taken court enforcement action. *E.g.*, Letter from John B. Foret, Dir., CFSAN Office of Food Labeling Division of Programs and Enforcement Policy, to Myron Cooper (June 21, 1999) (soups containing St. John's Wort and echinacea); Warning Letter from Charles M. Breen, Director, FDA Seattle District Office, to Jerry L. Smith (Jan. 14, 2004) (herbal tea) and to Judd A. Pindell (Dec. 3, 2004) (juices containing herbs). Because herbs are exempt from the food additive provisions, and thus legal, when present in dietary supplements, the FD&C Act gives manufacturers a strong incentive to market products containing functional herbal ingredients as dietary supplements rather than as conventional foods. *See supra* p. 320.

4.   GENERALLY RECOGNIZED AS SAFE (GRAS) SUBSTANCES

Section 201(s) of the FD&C Act, the definition of "food additive," states that a substance is not a food additive if it is "generally recognized, among experts qualified by scientific training and experience to evaluate its safety, as having been adequately shown through scientific procedures (or, in the case of a substance used in food prior to January 1, 1958, through either scientific procedures or experience based on common use in food) to be safe under the conditions of its intended use." The date referred to in the parenthetical reflects the fact that the Food Additives Amendments were enacted in 1958. The distinction between food additives and GRAS substances is critical, for the latter are not subject to the premarket approval mechanism required for the former.

a.   PROCEDURES FOR ESTABLISHING GRAS STATUS

1.   FDA GRAS Lists

Shortly after the passage of the Food Additives Amendment, FDA issued a nonexclusive list (that it has from time to time amended) of ingredients that the agency is prepared to acknowledge are GRAS—and therefore that manufacturers may lawfully use without affirmative approval. *E.g.*, 24 Fed. Reg. 9368 (Nov. 20, 1959); 26 Fed. Reg. 938 (Jan. 31, 1961). This GRAS list is now codified at 21 C.F.R. Part 182.

Following FDA's removal of the artificial sweetener cyclamate from GRAS status in 1969, President Nixon ordered a complete review of the GRAS list in his Consumer Message of October 30, 1969. "Consumer Protection," 5 WEEKLY COMP. PRES. DOC. 1516 (Nov. 3, 1969). In response, FDA contracted with the Life Sciences Research Office

(LSRO) of the Federation of American Societies for Experimental Biology (FASEB) to conduct initial safety reviews. The agency also established procedures by which, on its own initiative, it could affirm a conclusion by LSRO either that a particular substance was GRAS or that it was not GRAS and thus a food additive. 37 Fed. Reg. 25705 (Dec. 2, 1972), codified at 21 C.F.R. 170.35(a) & (b); 170.38. Between 1972 and 1982, LSRO produced 151 detailed reports containing safety reviews of over 400 substances, not all of which were previously listed in the C.F.R. If, following its review of these reports, FDA agreed with the LSRO that a substance was GRAS, the agency would, in accordance with its 1972 regulations, "affirm" the GRAS status of the substance by notice-and-comment rulemaking. Substances ultimately affirmed by FDA as GRAS under these procedures were (if necessary) deleted from the old GRAS list in 21 C.F.R. Part 182 ("Substances Generally Recognized as Safe") and identified instead in 21 C.F.R. Part 184 ("Direct Food Substances Affirmed as Generally Recognized as Safe") or Part 186 ("Indirect Food Substances Affirmed as Generally Recognized as Safe").

FDA's 1972 rulemaking also included a mechanism—the GRAS affirmation petition process—by which an individual could petition FDA to review the GRAS status of a substance not being considered as part of the agency's GRAS review. 21 C.F.R. 170.35(c). Although the GRAS affirmation petition procedure remains in the FDA regulations, it has not been used since 1997, as explained below. Before 1997, FDA, took one of three actions upon receiving a GRAS affirmation petition: (1) it determined that the substance was GRAS and indicated this GRAS affirmation in Part 184 or 186 of the C.F.R., (2) it determined that the substance was a safe food additive and promulgated a regulation under section 409, or (3) it determined that the substance was a food additive for which there was inadequate evidence of safety and banned its use. *See, e.g.*, 42 Fed. Reg. 26467 (May 24, 1977) (determining that a high intensity sweetener, miracle fruit, is not GRAS and is an unapproved food additive); 50 Fed. Reg. 3890 (Jan. 29, 1985) (determining that a quaternary ammonium chloride combination is not GRAS but is a safe and approved food additive).

Initially, all of the regulations promulgated in Parts 184 and 186 affirming particular substances as GRAS were required to contain specific use limitations. Later, FDA revised its regulations to allow flexibility in deciding whether explicit details regarding conditions of use should be included in GRAS affirmation regulations. *See* 48 Fed. Reg. 48457 (Oct. 19, 1983).

2. Voluntary GRAS Notification

Because of the deterioration of the GRAS affirmation process, discussed *infra* at p. 605, FDA issued proposed regulations in 62 Fed. Reg. 18938 (Apr. 17, 1997) to convert that process to a simple premarket notification procedure for virtually all substances for which a company seeks GRAS affirmation. The agency immediately implemented the proposal and has not promulgated final regulations. Under this procedure, which has been in effect since 1997, the company submits a notice stating its determination that the substance involved is GRAS for its intended use. If FDA does not disagree, the agency

[handwritten marginal note: FDA has process for them to review listings]

[handwritten marginal note: approval is NOT actually required]

sends a letter to the company stating that it has "no questions" regarding the company's GRAS determination but has not made its own GRAS determination. The FDA letter is then placed on the agency's website but is not published in the Federal Register.

3.   Self-Determination of GRAS Status

Neither the GRAS affirmation petition procedure nor the GRAS notification procedure has ever been mandatory. FDA has always acknowledged that a food manufacturer can self-determine that a substance is GRAS and sell it on this basis without receiving approval, affirmation, or a "no questions" letter from FDA.

The introductory language to the "old" GRAS list at Part 182 observes: "It is impracticable to list all substances that are generally recognized as safe for their intended use. However, by way of illustration, the Commissioner regards such common food ingredients as salt, pepper, vinegar, baking powder, and monosodium glutamate as safe for their intended use." 21 C.F.R. 182.1(a). Elsewhere, FDA states that the GRAS lists in Parts 182, 184, and 186 of the regulations

> do not include all substances that are generally recognized as safe for their intended use in food. Because of the large number of substances the intended use of which results or may reasonably be expected to result, directly or indirectly, in their becoming a component or otherwise affecting the characteristics of food, it is impracticable to list all such substances that are GRAS. A food ingredient of natural biological origin that has been widely consumed for its nutrient properties in the United States prior to January 1, 1958, without known detrimental effects, which is subject only to conventional processing as practiced prior to January 1, 1958, and for which no known safety hazard exists, will ordinarily be regarded as GRAS without specific inclusion in [one of the lists].

21 C.F.R. 170.30(d).

Consistent with this language, FDA has acknowledged that a food manufacturer may determine for itself whether an ingredient that it desires to use can be considered GRAS. *See* 50 Fed. Reg. 27294 (July 2, 1985); 53 Fed. Reg. 16544 (May 10, 1988); 62 Fed. Reg. 18938, 18941–18942 (Apr. 17, 1997). The freedom of food processers to self-determine GRAS status is not limited to common food ingredients of natural biological origin, but as a practical matter, it is of limited practical significance for other types of ingredients. Very few processors will purchase ingredients for which the supplier cannot provide documentation of FDA approval or acknowledgement as GRAS. Moreover, many manufacturers fear that if they independently conclude that an ingredient is GRAS, they run the risk that FDA might disagree and initiate regulatory action against their products—as occurred in *United States v. An Article of Food . . . Coco Rico*, the next excerpt.

NOTES

1.   *Change in Status.* Under section 201(s), a food additive can acquire GRAS status and thus no longer require a food additive regulation.

FDA has not yet revoked any food additive regulation on this ground, and it is unlikely ever to do so. FDA and food manufacturers have, however, concluded that new uses of approved food additives are GRAS. *E.g.*, 21 C.F.R. 175.105 and GRAS Notice No. GRN 000003 (sodium bisulfite); 21 C.F.R. 173.350 and GRAS Notice No. GRN 000083 (carbon monoxide); 21 C.F.R. 177.1670 and GRAS Notice No. GRN 000141 (polyvinyl alcohol); 21 C.F.R. 172.867 and GRAS Notice No. GRN 000227 (olestra). Conversely, GRAS status does not permanently exempt a substance from the definition of "food additive." FDA has revoked a GRAS determination on the basis of new data relating to safety. *E.g.*, 34 Fed. Reg. 17063 (Oct. 21, 1969) (cyclamate). Citizen Petition No. 2005P–0459/CPI (Nov. 15, 2005) requests that FDA revoke its acceptance of the GRAS notification for the use of carbon monoxide in fresh meat packaging on the ground that it helps simulate the red color of fresh meat.

2.   *Procedural Rights.* An approved food additive enjoys greater procedural protection than does a GRAS ingredient. Revocation of a substance's GRAS status can be accomplished summarily by court enforcement action or by informal rulemaking adding it to the list of banned food substances. 39 Fed. Reg. 34172 (Sept. 23, 1974), codified at 21 C.F.R. Part 189. In contrast, any revocation of a food additive regulation is subject to objection and a demand for a formal evidentiary hearing under section 409.

3.   *Indirect Uses.* To avoid duplicative listing, FDA has clarified that any substance affirmed as GRAS for direct food use is also regarded as GRAS for indirect food use. 48 Fed. Reg. 48456 (Oct. 19, 1983).

4.   *GAO Report.* In 2010, the U.S. Government Accounting Office released a report concluding that FDA's current GRAS oversight is insufficient. FDA SHOULD STRENGTHEN ITS OVERSIGHT OF FOOD INGREDIENTS DETERMINED TO BE GENERALLY RECOGNIZED AS SAFE (GRAS), GAO–10–246 (Feb. 2010). GAO observed that FDA's ability to strengthen its oversight is limited by its lack of legal authority to require companies to report GRAS findings. GAO made various suggestions for improvement, including, among others, a requirement that any company making a GRAS determination provide FDA with basic information about the substance's identity and intended uses; the use of random audits of companies' GRAS determinations; and the finalization of the 1997 rule governing the voluntary notification program. In FDA's comments on an earlier draft that were summarized in the final report, the agency expressed general agreement with the recommendations, but noted that it lacked the legal authority and/or resources to implement most of them. *Id.* at 36–38.

b.   SUBSTANTIVE CRITERIA FOR GRAS STATUS

United States v. An Article of Food . . . Coco Rico, Inc.

752 F.2d 11 (1st Cir. 1985).

■ WEIGEL, SENIOR DISTRICT JUDGE.

This is an appeal from the district court's grant of summary judgment. Appellant Coco Rico, Inc., manufactures in Puerto Rico a coconut concentrate called Coco Rico for use as an ingredient in soft drinks. The Coco Rico concentrate sold to beverage bottlers in Puerto Rico contains potassium nitrate, added for the purpose of developing and fixing a desirable color and flavor. On March 10, 1982, the United States instituted *in rem* proceedings against three lots of bottled soft drinks located on the premises of Puerto Rican bottlers. The soft drinks contained Coco Rico concentrate. The government charged that potassium nitrate constitutes an "unsafe" food additive, making the beverages "adulterated" and subject to forfeiture. . . .

Coco Rico submitted one affidavit in opposition to the motion for summary judgment, that of food chemist Algeria B. Caragay. . . . Caragay's affidavit makes the following points:

    . . .

    3.   Although some studies have cast suspicion on nitrates and nitrites as possible carcinogens, she knows of no conclusive scientific evidence that the use of potassium nitrate in beverages is unsafe;

    4.   Nitrates have been approved by the FDA for use in curing meat; and

    5.   She knows of no difference in health effects between potassium nitrate as used in meat and as used in beverages.

    . . . [T]he district court granted summary judgment for the government. . . .

First, Coco Rico claims that Caragay's affidavit is sufficient to show the existence of a factual issue as to whether potassium nitrate is "generally recognized" by qualified experts as having been scientifically shown to be safe. To fall within this exception, the substance must be generally recognized as safe *under the conditions of its intended use.* [FD&C Act 201(s).] The burden of proving general recognition of safe use is placed on the proponent of the food substance in question. Caragay's affidavit contained only statements to the effect that she knows of no conclusive scientific evidence that the use of potassium nitrate in beverages is *unsafe*, or that the health effects of potassium nitrate when used in beverages differ from those caused by its use in meats. Even if these allegations are true, they are insufficient to meet Coco Rico's burden of proving that the use of potassium nitrate in beverages is generally recognized by experts as *safe* based on scientific evidence.

For similar reasons, Coco Rico's second argument based on "common use" of potassium nitrate must also fail. Again, a substance may be excluded from classification as a "food additive" only if experience based on common use provides a basis for general recognition by scientists that the substance is safe *under the conditions of its intended use.* The evidence submitted by Coco Rico tends to show that nitrates are naturally present in many foodstuffs, particularly vegetables, and that they have been used for many centuries to cure meats. No evidence was submitted to show that potassium nitrate has long been added to beverages. Consequently, there is no issue of fact as to whether common experience could show that potassium nitrate is not a "food additive" when used in beverages. . . .

The district court's grant of summary judgment is affirmed.

NOTE

Different Conditions of Use. In *United States v. Articles of Food . . . Buffalo Jerky*, the trial and appellate courts concluded that patties made from buffalo (bison) meat, sodium nitrate, sodium nitrite, and other ingredients violated section 409 because nitrate and nitrite are not GRAS and no food additive regulation permitted their use for this purpose, even though they recognized that FDA had approved these substances for use in pork products. 456 F. Supp. 207 (D. Neb. 1978), *aff'd per curiam*, 594 F.2d 869 (8th Cir. 1979). *See also United States v. An Article of Food*, 678 F.2d 735 (7th Cir. 1982); *United States v. Article of Food . . . Orotic Acid*, 414 F. Supp. 793 (E.D. Mo. 1976).

The agency initially adopted criteria for GRAS status in 36 Fed. Reg. 12093 (June 25, 1971). Five years later, in the Federal Register document excerpted below, FDA promulgated revised regulations, now codified at 21 C.F.R. 170.30.

General Recognition of Safety and Prior Sanctions for Food Ingredients
41 Fed. Reg. 53600 (December 7, 1976).

. . . .

In the FEDERAL REGISTER of September 23, 1974 (39 FR 34194) . . . [t]he Commissioner proposed to (1) Require that general recognition of safety through scientific procedures must ordinarily be based upon published literature; (2) Recognize that GRAS status based on scientific procedures requires the same quality and quantity of scientific evidence as would be required for approval of a food additive regulation; (3) Define "common use in food" as used in section 201(s) of the act to mean a substantial history of consumption of a substance by a significant number of consumers in the United States; (4) Recognize that GRAS status based upon common use in food does not require the same quality or quantity of scientific evidence that would be required for approval of a food additive regulation; (5) Recognize three categories of ingredients affirmed as GRAS; (6) Recognize that GRAS affirmation proceedings should consider the manufacturing process involved; and (7) Provide for procedures for considering the applicability of prior sanctions. . . .

One comment . . . argued that longtime use by consumers does not establish safety, and that FDA should not permit use of a substance in food unless it had been established as safe by appropriate scientific studies. . . . The Commissioner notes that the criteria set forth in [§ 170.30] interpret section 201(s) of the act as requiring the same quantity and quality of scientific evidence to establish that a substance is GRAS as is required to establish the safety of a newly used food additive, if the substance was first used in food after January 1, 1958. For substances in common use in food before January 1, 1958, however, the act is explicit in requiring FDA to consider experience based on such use in determining whether a substance is GRAS. Indeed, the act permits a manufacturer to determine that a substance is GRAS considering only experience based on common use in food if the substance was used in food before January 1, 1958. Thus, for those substances that were widely used before 1958, under the terms of the statute FDA must consider available data and may not prohibit use of a substance merely because tests that would be required for new food additives have not been performed. . . .

NOTES

1.   *Consideration of Benefits.* The proposed rule would have defined "safe" and "safety" to include consideration of "[t]he benefit contributed by the substance." 39 Fed. Reg. at 34195. Comments to the proposed rule opposed this criterion. In the preamble to the final rule, FDA responded to these comments as follows:

> The Commissioner concludes that it is appropriate to recognize that the benefit contributed by a substance is inevitably a factor to be considered in determining whether a particular substance is "safe" (or generally recognized as "safe") for its intended use. The term "safe" is to be given its ordinary meaning, and in its common usage the term is understood to carry an assessment of benefits and risks. It is true, as the comment states, that minor food additives are not approved at levels that may present a hazard to the normal consumer. This result is required by the act because the benefit of a minor food additive is too small to justify the imposition of a known risk to normal consumers; use of such ingredient at levels that may present a hazard to the normal consumer would not be "safe." However, this result does not necessarily follow in the case of important food additives. For example, if it were found that a major food source such as meat or grain was associated with the development of chronic diseases in normal individuals, it would not necessarily follow that the food was unsafe within the meaning of the act. The ordinary understanding of the term "safe" would require some benefit-to-risk analysis in such circumstances. . . .

> The Commissioner has, however, deleted from the regulations the reference to consideration of benefits on the ground that this separate consideration is legitimately included within the concept of safety as used in the act. Furthermore, explicitly retaining the criterion of benefit in the regulations might be construed as requiring routine formal analysis of a factor that the agency will only occasionally need to take into account, because the agency's general guidelines will result in disapproval of food additives that may cause toxic effects in normal individuals.

41 Fed. Reg. at 53601.

Three years later, however, in his first decision on the animal drug DES, FDA Commissioner Donald Kennedy quoted this language in full "because I am, on behalf of the FDA, disavowing it." Quoting FDA's 1977 proposed revocation of the food additive regulation for saccharin, Kennedy maintained that "under the provisions of the law relating to food additives, FDA is not empowered to take into account the asserted benefits of any food additive in applying the basic safety standard of the act" 44 Fed. Reg. 54852, 54882–83 (Sept. 21, 1979) (excerpted *infra* p. 1385).

2. *Legislative History.* In Congressional testimony two years before the Food Additives Amendment was enacted, FDA Commissioner Larrick explained that "[t]here are hundreds of substances in our diet that have been used for 40, 50, 60, 70, or 80 years, but they have never been tested. There has been no occasion to test them because the common acceptance of them as safe has come about through long usage, but you could not prove through scientific methods whether they are safe or not. . . ." "Federal Food, Drug, and Cosmetic Act (Chemical Additives in Food)," Hearings before a Subcommittee of the House Committee on Interstate and Foreign Commerce, 84th Cong., 2d Sess. 204 (1956).

3. *Applicability of Delaney Clause.* Because GRAS ingredients do not fall within the definition of a food additive, they are not technically subject to the Delaney Clause. In practice, before the mid-1970s, the Delaney principle prevented the introduction or continued use of a GRAS ingredient that was found in appropriate tests to induce cancer in experimental animals. Such a finding was regarded as undermining any basis for general expert recognition of the safety of the ingredient, thereby rendering it a food additive for which affirmative FDA approval was required. This analysis explains FDA's actions in the case of cyclamate, which prior to 1970 had been widely used based on FDA's determination that it was GRAS. A report by the principal manufacturer that cyclamate might be an animal carcinogen was viewed as destroying its GRAS status, making its continued use unlawful overnight.

Beginning in the mid-1970s, however, as evidence accumulated that virtually all food contains at least one substance that is carcinogenic in test animals, FDA began to rethink this approach. Although officials continued to state publicly that a carcinogenic food substance would not be regarded as GRAS, the agency has never challenged the GRAS status of ingredients that have been shown to contain carcinogenic constituents. *See, e.g.,* "Agriculture, Rural Development and Related Agencies Appropriations for 1984," Hearings before a Subcommittee of the House Committee on Appropriations, 98th Cong., 1st Sess., Part 4, at 473–77 (1983) (listing FDA's responses to questions relating to natural carcinogens in the food supply).

Fmali Herb, Inc. v. Heckler
715 F.2d 1385 (9th Cir. 1983).

■ FLETCHER, CIRCUIT JUDGE. . . .

In 1974, the FDA promulgated a regulation defining the term "common use in food" for purposes of section 201(s). The regulation states that "'common use in food' means a substantial history of consumption of a substance by a significant number of consumers *in the*

United States." 21 C.F.R. § 170.3(f)(1982) (emphasis added). Thus, according to the regulation, no substance may be newly introduced into the United States without either pretesting satisfactory to the FDA or general recognition among experts, based solely on scientific evidence, that the substance is safe for the intended use, no matter how widespread or prolonged the history of use of the substance in food in regions outside the United States.

Appellant Fmali Herb, Inc., is an importer of Chinese food products. In its business, Fmali wishes to import foods containing herbs traditional in China that have never been widely used in the United States. One such food is a jelly or honey-like product, known as renshenfengwangjiang, which normally contains schizandra seed. The FDA has ruled that renshenfengwangjiang may be sold in the United States only if it does not contain schizandra seed, because schizandra seed has not been scientifically tested and because it was not commonly used in the United States prior to 1958. The FDA held that evidence of long and widespread use of schizandra seed in China is not admissible in aid of establishing that schizandra seed is safe for human consumption.

Fmali filed an action in district court seeking a declaratory judgment that the FDA regulation codified at 21 C.F.R. § 170.3(f) is invalid as an erroneous interpretation of section 201(s). . . . The district court, agreeing with the FDA that evidence of use of a substance in food in a foreign country may be unreliable to show safety, dismissed Fmali's action.

. . . Under the statute, "common use in food" of an ingredient does not automatically exempt the substance from pretesting requirements. Instead, "common use in food" merely describes one form of evidence that may be introduced by a proponent for the purpose of meeting the ultimate standard, which is whether the ingredient is safe for human consumption. . . . [N]either the language of the statute nor its history indicate that only "common use" within the United States may be cited as evidence of safety.

By promulgating the regulation defining "common use in food" to mean only common use within the United States, the FDA has imposed a restriction not required by the literal terms of the statute. The FDA's reasons for doing so were expressed at the time the regulation was issued:

> The Commissioner believes that the type of experience based on common use in food that will support a GRAS determination must involve use in the United States, and not solely in foreign countries. Reported use in foreign countries often cannot be verified, and in any event the experience based on such use cannot be monitored or evaluated. Food consumption patterns and differences between cultures make it impossible to assess whether a history of use abroad would be comparable to a history of use in the United States.

39 Fed. Reg. 34,195 (1974).

We agree for the most part with the concerns expressed by the FDA. Many residents of areas outside the United States have shorter life expectancies than do Americans. Foreign populations also suffer from higher incidences of some diseases, so that generalizations about the safety of their dietary habits may be unreliable. But it is an illogical and, we think, unwarranted constriction of the statute to rule that evidence of long use of a substance in food outside the United States can *never provide probative evidence* of safety. Counsel for the FDA admitted this point in argument before the district court, when he stated that "there are countries in the world, like West Germany or something, where one might be able to accept" prior use of an ingredient to establish safety, but added that the FDA does not believe that evidence of use in "Guam" or "Southeast Asia" could be accepted. The statute provides no basis for a purely ethnocentric distinction of this kind, divorced from demographic considerations. . . .

Because 21 C.F.R. § 170.3(f) is not a permissible interpretation of 21 U.S.C. § 321(s), the judgment sought by Fmali declaring the regulation invalid should have been granted. . . .

NOTE

FDA Response. Following the *Fmali Herb* case, FDA revised its GRAS regulations to recognize that a substance that was used in food prior to 1958 can be shown to be GRAS through experience based on its common use in food outside, as well as inside, the United States. 50 Fed. Reg. 27294 (July 2, 1985), 53 Fed. Reg. 16544 (May 10, 1988), codified in 21 C.F.R. 170.30(c)(2). The preambles to the proposed and final rules, however, left little doubt about the agency's continued reluctance to accept foreign use as adequate evidence of GRAS status.

In 1997, FDA proposed to revise the regulations concerning GRAS criteria so as to provide greater flexibility in GRAS determinations. Although this rule was never finalized, FDA's practice since 1997 demonstrates that it has implemented the core concepts of the proposal. This is the same proposed rulemaking in which the agency established the GRAS notification procedure that, though never formally finalized, is now the method (replacing the GRAS affirmation petition process) by which manufacturers inform FDA about GRAS determinations. *See* supra p. 575.

Substances Generally Recognized as Safe: Proposed Rule

62 Fed. Reg. 18938 (April 17, 1997).

The Food and Drug Administration (FDA) is proposing to clarify the criteria for exempting the use of a substance in human food or in animal feed from the premarket approval requirements of the Federal Food, Drug, and Cosmetic Act (the act) because such use is generally recognized as safe (GRAS). . . .

Under section 201(s) of the act, a substance is exempt from the definition of food additive and thus, from premarket approval requirements, if its safety is generally recognized by qualified experts. Accordingly, a determination that a particular use of a substance is

GRAS requires both technical evidence of safety and a basis to conclude that this technical evidence of safety is generally known and accepted. In contrast, a determination that a food additive is safe requires only technical evidence of safety. Thus, a GRAS substance is distinguished from a food additive on the basis of the common knowledge about the safety of the substance for its intended use rather than on the basis of what the substance is or the types of data and information that are necessary to establish its safety. To emphasize this distinction between a GRAS substance and a food additive, and to simplify discussion about the standard for general recognition of safety, in this document, FDA uses the term "technical element" when discussing technical evidence of safety and "common knowledge element" when discussing general knowledge and acceptance of safety.

The technical element of the GRAS standard requires that information about the substance establish that the intended use of the substance is safe. . . . FDA has defined "safe" as a reasonable certainty in the minds of competent scientists that the substance is not harmful under its intended conditions of use. Current § 170.30(b) provides that general recognition of safety through scientific procedures requires the same quantity and quality of scientific evidence as is required to obtain approval of the substance as a food additive. Similarly, current § 170.30(c)(1) provides that general recognition of safety through experience based on common use in food prior to January 1, 1958, may be determined without the quantity or quality of scientific procedures required for approval of a food additive regulation and must be based solely on food use of the substance prior to that date. . . .

The common knowledge element of the GRAS standard includes two facets: (1) The data and information relied on to establish the technical element must be generally available; and (2) there must be a basis to conclude that there is consensus among qualified experts about the safety of the substance for its intended use. . . .

The usual mechanism to establish that scientific information is generally available is to show that the information is published in a peer-reviewed scientific journal. However, mechanisms to establish the basis for concluding that there is expert consensus about the safety of a substance are more varied. In some cases, publication in a peer-reviewed scientific journal . . . has been used to establish expert consensus in addition to general availability. In other cases, such publication of data and information in the primary scientific literature has been supplemented by: (1) Publication of data and information in the secondary scientific literature, such as scientific review articles, textbooks, and compendia; (2) documentation of the opinion of an "expert panel" that is specifically convened for this purpose; or (3) the opinion or recommendation of an authoritative body such as the National Academy of Sciences (NAS) . . . on a broad or specific issue that is related to a GRAS determination.

. . . Such consensus does not require unanimity among qualified experts. For example, FDA would evaluate a single published report questioning the safety of use of a substance in food in the context of all the publicly available and corroborative information rather than conclude that such a report automatically disqualifies the substance from satisfying the GRAS standard.

. . . . FDA is proposing to [amend 21 C.F.R. § 170.30(b)] to clarify the types of technical evidence of safety (currently described only as "studies") that could form the basis of a GRAS determination. FDA is proposing this change because the quantity and quality of scientific evidence required to obtain approval of a substance as a food additive vary considerably depending upon the estimated dietary exposure to the substance and the chemical, physical, and physiological properties of the substance; there can likewise be a comparable variation in the scientific evidence that forms the basis of a GRAS determination . . .

Specifically, FDA is proposing to revise § 170.30(b) to provide that general recognition of safety through scientific procedures be based upon generally available and accepted scientific data, information, methods, or principles, which ordinarily are published. Thus, under proposed § 170.30(b), "studies" would be one of several types of scientific "data and information" that could support the technical element of a scientific procedures GRAS determination. However, depending on the circumstances, other scientific data and scientific information such as that relating to chemical identity or characteristic properties of a substance, as well as methods of manufacture, could support, and in some cases be sufficient to satisfy that element.

. . . .

FDA is proposing to clarify the role of publication in satisfying the common knowledge element of the GRAS standard by adding the phrase[ ] . . . "which ordinarily are published" as [a] descriptor[ ] of "scientific data, information, methods, or principles" in proposed § 170.30(b). Thus, under proposed § 170.30(b), publication of data and information about a GRAS substance is usually necessary, but may not always be sufficient, to satisfy the common knowledge element of the GRAS standard.

The descriptor "which ordinarily are published" reflects that the usual mechanism to establish that scientific information is generally available is to show that the information is published in a peer-reviewed scientific journal. This descriptor maintains the explicit emphasis of current § 170.30(b) on the importance of publication in satisfying the common knowledge element. However, current § 170.30(b) does not explicitly emphasize the second facet of the common knowledge element (i.e., that there is a basis to conclude that there is the requisite expert consensus that the generally available data and information establish the safety of the substance for its intended use). . . . [T]he published results of a particular safety study may not be sufficient to satisfy the common knowledge element if the study raises safety questions that require additional data to be resolved. In such cases, the general recognition standard usually requires more than a publication in the primary scientific literature. . . . [T]he basis for concluding that there is expert consensus historically has included publication in secondary sources, convening an expert panel, or relying on an opinion or recommendation of an authoritative body.

The body of information published in secondary sources (such as review articles, articles describing scientific methods, general reference materials, and textbooks) can be more useful than the primary scientific literature for showing a basis for a conclusion that the necessary expert consensus exists because the existence of the secondary sources implies that the primary scientific literature has been evaluated after its publication. . . .

The opinion of a specially-convened expert panel can provide a basis for showing expert consensus when an individual published study raises safety questions. The opinion of an expert panel is also useful when multiple studies bearing on the safety of a substance are published but there are no secondary sources that evaluate these studies and draw general conclusions based on this comprehensive body of knowledge. . . .

In FDA's view, the common knowledge element of the GRAS standard precludes a GRAS determination if the data and information evaluated by such an expert panel are only available in files that are not publicly accessible, such as in confidential industry files. . . .

What follows are two recent FDA applications of the GRAS criteria. The first is a standard agency response letter in which it expresses "no questions" regarding a GRAS notification. The second is a warning letter rejecting a manufacturer's self-determination of GRAS status.

Agency Response Letter GRAS Notice No. 000227, From Laura M. Tarantino, Director, CFSAN Office of Food Additive Safety to Donald L. Wilke, Procter & Gamble

October 9, 2008.

Dear Dr. Wilke:

The Food and Drug Administration (FDA) is responding to the notice, dated June 15, 2007, that you submitted in accordance with the agency's proposed regulation, proposed 21 CFR 170.36 (62 FR 18938; April 17, 1997). . . .

The subject of the notice is olestra. The notice informs FDA of the view of The Procter & Gamble Company (P&G) that olestra is GRAS, through scientific procedures, for use as a total replacement for fats and oils in pre-packaged ready-to-eat cookies. FDA previously approved food additive petitions for olestra as a fat substitute in savory snacks and in ready-to-heat popcorn. . . .

As part of its notice, P&G includes the report of a panel of individuals (P&G's GRAS panel) who evaluated the data and information that are the basis for P&G's GRAS determination. P&G considers the members of its GRAS panel to be qualified by scientific training and experience to evaluate the safety of substances added to food. P&G's GRAS Panel evaluated publicly available scientific information and data about olestra pertaining to the method of manufacture and product specifications, analytical data, intended use levels in specified food products, consumption estimates, multiple safety studies (including in vitro and in vivo genotoxicity studies, metabolic studies, chronic and 2–generation feeding studies in animals), and potential nutritional issues. In addition, P&G's GRAS panel reviewed the results of human studies and post-marketing surveillance studies. Based on this review, P&G's GRAS panel concluded that olestra containing the added vitamins A, D, E, and K that meets its established food grade specifications is GRAS under the conditions of its intended use.

. . . .

P&G summarizes the results of published safety studies for olestra. Metabolic studies in rats and weanling pigs demonstrate that greater than 99% of olestra was unabsorbed. P&G concludes that subchronic toxicological studies in rats, chronic toxicological studies in mice, dogs, and monkeys, and a reproductive and developmental study in rats showed no treatment related effects.

P&G evaluates nutritional issues including a review of published studies on gastrointestinal (GI) physiology and function, olestra's interaction in the digestive tract with lipophilic compounds, as well as effects on appetite regulation and the absorption of nutrients. On the basis of these data, P&G concludes that olestra does not adversely impact GI physiology and function.

. . . .

Based on the information provided by P&G, as well as other information available to FDA, the agency has no questions at this time regarding P&G's conclusion that olestra is GRAS for use as a total replacement for fats and oils in pre-packaged ready-to-eat cookies provided that olestra conforms to the conditions listed in [the food additive regulation for olestra at 21 CFR 172.867, *supra* p. 557]. The agency has not, however, made its own determination regarding the GRAS status of the subject use of olestra. As always, it is the continuing responsibility of P&G to ensure that food ingredients that the firm markets are safe, and are otherwise in compliance with all applicable legal and regulatory requirements.

In accordance with proposed 21 CFR 170.36(f), a copy of the text of this letter responding to GRN 000227, as well as a copy of the information in this notice that conforms to the information in the proposed GRAS exemption claim (proposed 21 CFR 170.36(c)(1)), is available for public review and copying on the homepage of the Office of Food Additive Safety.

Sincerely,

Laura M. Tarantino, Ph.D.

NOTE

Extension of Olestra GRAS Status to Other Host Products. In 2010, FDA sent a similar "no questions" letter to Procter & Gamble regarding a separate notification in which the company stated its view that olestra is also GRAS for use in a wide variety of additional foods, including, among many others, all ready-to-eat baked goods, mayonnaise, ice cream, and chocolate confections. Agency Response Letter GRAS Notice No. GRN 00325, from Mitchell A. Cheeseman, Acting Dir., Office of Food Additive Safety, to Robert Enouen, Procter & Gamble (Aug. 30, 2010).

Warning Letter from Joann M. Givens, Acting Director, CFSAN Office of Compliance, to Jaisen Freeman et al., Phusion Projects, LLC

November 17, 2010.

Dear Messrs. Freeman, Hunter, and Wright:

The Food and Drug Administration (FDA) has reviewed the regulatory status of the ingredients declared on the label of your product, "Four Loko" which contains caffeine that has been directly added to an alcoholic beverage and packaged in combined caffeine and alcohol form. As it is used in your product, caffeine is an unsafe food additive, and therefore your product is adulterated under section 402(a)(2)(C) of the Federal Food, Drug, and Cosmetic Act. . . .

. . . There is no food additive regulation authorizing the use of caffeine as a direct addition to alcoholic beverages, and we are not aware of any information to establish that caffeine added directly to alcoholic beverages is the subject of a prior sanction. Likewise, we are not aware of any basis to conclude that caffeine is GRAS under these conditions of use.

. . . By letter dated November 12, 2009, FDA requested that . . . your company provide evidence of the rationale, along with supporting data and information, for concluding that the use of caffeine in your product is GRAS or prior sanctioned. . . .

. . . The agency received your GRAS Notice, dated June 25, 2010, and filed it on June 30, 2010. But, as discussed in more detail below, FDA has reviewed that notice and continues to have safety concerns about your caffeinated alcoholic beverage product. Accordingly, the agency is issuing this warning letter.

To establish that the use of a substance in food is GRAS under its specific conditions of use . . . there must be consensus among qualified experts that the substance is safe under its conditions of use, based on publicly available data and information. FDA is aware that, based on the publicly available literature, a number of qualified experts have concerns about the safety of caffeinated alcoholic beverages. Moreover, the agency is not aware of data or other information to establish the safety of the relevant conditions of use for your product. Therefore, the criteria for GRAS status have not been met for the caffeine in your beverage.

Based upon the publicly available literature, FDA has the following specific concerns about the safety of caffeine when used in the presence of alcohol.

- Reports in the scientific literature have described behavioral effects that may occur in young adults when energy drinks are consumed along with alcoholic beverages.

- Studies suggest that the combined ingestion of caffeine and alcohol may lead to hazardous and life-threatening situations because caffeine counteracts some, but not all, of alcohol's adverse effects. In one study, a mixture of an energy drink and alcohol reduced subjects' subjective perception of intoxication but did not improve diminished motor coordination or slower visual reaction times using objective measures. . . .

- Because caffeine alters the perception of alcohol intoxication, the consumption of pre-mixed products containing added caffeine and alcohol may result in higher amounts of alcohol consumed per drinking occasion, a situation that is particularly dangerous for naive drinkers.

GRAS status is not an inherent property of a substance, but must be assessed in the context of the intended conditions of use of the substance (section 201(s) of the Act. The assessment includes a consideration of the population that will consume the substance (21 CFR 170.30(b); section 409(b) of the Act). . . . FDA is concerned that the young adults to whom these pre-mixed, added caffeine and alcohol products are marketed are especially vulnerable to the adverse behavioral effects associated with consuming caffeine added to alcohol, a concern reflected in the publicly available literature.

. . . The agency is unaware of any data that address the complex, potentially hazardous behaviors that have been identified in the scientific literature as associated with these beverages or that otherwise alleviate our concerns about the effects of consuming these pre-mixed caffeine and alcohol beverages. Moreover, FDA is not aware of any publicly available data to establish affirmatively safe conditions of use for caffeine added directly to alcoholic beverages and packaged in a combined form.

. . . FDA notes that the GRAS Notice did not cite any scientific literature of which the agency was not already aware. Furthermore, we wish to comment generally on two lines of argument presented in your GRAS Notice.

First, your GRAS Notice relies primarily upon safety studies of caffeine alone (i.e., not in the presence of alcohol) to support your view that caffeine is safe under the relevant conditions of use (that is, in combination with alcohol). Importantly, however, the current scientific literature, which we cite above, establishes that significant safety concerns are raised by the co-consumption of caffeine and alcohol. Accordingly, data and information addressing the safety of caffeine alone are not sufficient to establish the safety, and the general recognition of the safety, of beverages that combine caffeine with alcohol.

Second, we note that one section of your GRAS Notice reviews some of the studies that have reported the adverse behavioral effects elicited by the co-consumption of caffeine and alcohol and identifies purported deficiencies in the design and interpretation of these studies. Even if certain studies in the scientific literature have limitations due to their design or the interpretation of their results, the peer-reviewed literature as a whole is sufficient to raise, among qualified experts, safety concerns about alcoholic beverages to which caffeine has been directly added. . . .

In light of the safety concerns identified above, the use of added caffeine in the alcoholic beverage product "Four Loko" does not satisfy the criteria for GRAS status outlined above. Further, FDA is aware of no other exemption from the food additive definition that would apply to caffeine when used as an ingredient in an alcoholic beverage product. Therefore, caffeine as used in your product is a food additive under section 201(s) of the Act and is subject to the provisions of section 409 of the Act. Under the latter, a food additive is required to be approved by FDA for its proposed conditions of use prior to marketing. Because caffeine is not an approved food additive for its use in your product, "Four Loko," this product is adulterated within the meaning of section 402(a)(2)(C) of the Act.

. . . .

Please advise this office in writing within fifteen (15) days from your receipt of this letter as to the specific steps you have taken to correct the violation identified above and to assure that similar violations do not occur. . . .

Sincerely,

Joann M. Givens

NOTES

1. *Caffeine.* FDA placed caffeine on the original GRAS list when used in "cola-type beverages," and it remains listed there to this day. 26 Fed. Reg. 938 (Jan.31, 1961), codified at 21 C.F.R. 182.1180. Following a report from FASEB recommending that caffeine no longer be considered GRAS in cola beverages, FDA proposed to revoke its GRAS status, to declare that no prior sanction exists, and to promulgate an interim food additive regulation requiring additional studies. 45 Fed. Reg. 69816 (Oct. 21, 1980). The agency withdrew this proposal in 2003. 68 Fed. Reg. 19766, 19767 (Apr. 22, 2003). Following the issuance of the proposed rule, users of caffeine, with the aid of the Freedom of Information Act, scoured FDA archives for correspondence relating to caffeine and found several FDA documents that they claimed supported a prior sanction. On May 20, 1987, FDA proposed to recognize a prior sanction for caffeine in nonalcoholic carbonated beverages, 52 Fed. Reg. 18923, but this proposal was withdrawn in 69 Fed. Reg. 68831, 68833 (Nov. 26, 2004).

In March 2013, a group of health experts wrote to FDA Commissioner Hamburg, requesting that the agency limit the amount of caffeine in energy drinks and require that manufacturers of these products include caffeine content on the labels. Letter from Amelia M. Arria et al. to Margaret Hamburg, FDA Commissioner (Mar. 19, 2013). Soon afterward, Monster Energy announced that it would begin stating the amount of caffeine on the label of its energy drinks.

In May 2013, in light of an industry trend of adding caffeine to a wide variety of foods, from Cracker Jack® to oatmeal, FDA announced that the agency will investigate the safety of caffeine in food products. *See FDA to Investigate Caffeine* (May 3, 2013) (available on FDA website). This announcement followed quickly on Wrigley's introduction of Alert Energy

Caffeine Gum, each piece of which has as much caffeine as half a cup of coffee. Wrigley subsequently announced it would pull the product from the market in deference to FDA's inquiry.

2. *Sulfites.* Sulfites are sulfur-based preservatives. Based upon a FASEB evaluation, FDA proposed in 47 Fed. Reg. 29956 (July 9, 1982) to affirm the GRAS status of sulfiting agents in food. After receiving reports of allergic reactions to sulfites, however, the agency announced that it would reconsider the GRAS status of sulfites on the basis of a report to be prepared by the Ad Hoc Review Panel on the Reexamination of the GRAS Status of Sulfiting Agents. 49 Fed. Reg. 27994 (July 9, 1984). After receiving the final report of the Ad Hoc Review Panel, FDA amended Part 182 GRAS listings for sulfites to revoke their GRAS status for use on fruits and vegetables intended to be served or sold raw to consumers. 51 Fed. Reg. 25021 (July 9, 1986). When FDA also revoked the GRAS status of sulfites for use on "fresh" potatoes in 55 Fed. Reg. 9826 (Mar. 15, 1990), the potato industry initiated litigation seeking an injunction to prohibit FDA from enforcing this rulemaking. In an unreported decision in 1990, the U.S. District Court for the Middle District of Pennsylvania granted summary judgment in favor of the industry on administrative procedural grounds, based on FDA's failure to make the entire record available for public inspection. After the Third Circuit upheld the District Court in an unreported *en banc* decision, FDA withdrew the 1990 regulations. 59 Fed. Reg. 65938 (Dec. 22, 1994). *See Hanover Potato Products, Inc. v. Shalala,* 989 F.2d 123 (3d Cir. 1993) (attorney's fee decision relating the complete history of the dispute).

FDA requires any added sulfite that is detectable at 10 ppm or more to be labeled as an ingredient. 51 Fed. Reg. 25012 (July 9, 1986), codified at 21 C.F.R. 101.100(a)(4). TTB imposes a similar requirement for alcoholic beverages. 51 Fed. Reg. 34706 (Sept. 30, 1986). In 1983, the members of the National Restaurant Association abandoned use of sulfites for salad bars and other related purposes. "Sulfiting Agents—Update," FDA Talk Paper No. T83–15 (Apr. 5, 1983).

3. *Salt.* In 2005, the Center for Science in the Public Interest (CSPI) submitted a petition to FDA asking the agency to revoke the GRAS status of salt, to use its food additive authorities to set a ceiling on the amount of sodium in processed foods, and to take additional measures to reduce sodium consumption. Petition to Revoke the GRAS Status of Salt, to Set Ceilings on the Amount of Sodium in Processed Foods, to Require a Health Warning on Packaged Salt, and to Reduce the Daily Value for Sodium (Nov. 8, 2005), Docket 2005P–0450. CSPI asserted the existence of a broad consensus among scientists that sodium increases blood pressure. FDA has not ruled on this petition.

4. *Caloric Sweeteners.* Shortly before submitting the salt petition discussed above, CSPI submitted another petition requesting that FDA mandate health messages regarding weight gain and tooth decay on soft drinks containing caloric sweeteners. Petition to Require Health Messages on Soft Drinks Containing High–Fructose Corn Syrup and other Caloric Sweeteners (July 13, 2005), Docket 2005P–0282. CSPI asserted that FDA could require such messages under the FD&C Act's misbranding provisions

at sections 403(a) and 201(n). Nevertheless, the organization's primary suggestion was that the agency proceed by (1) revoking the Part 184 regulations affirming the GRAS status of sucrose, high fructose corn syrup, and other caloric sweeteners; (2) reclassifying these sweeteners as food additives; and (3) pursuant to section 409, requiring health messages on soft drinks as a condition of use of these substances. FDA has not ruled on this petition, either.

5. THE GRAS PRESUMPTION FOR GENETICALLY MODIFIED INGREDIENTS

Background information on the development and uses of genetic engineering of food is presented earlier in this chapter, *supra* p. 458, and it will not be repeated here. That earlier portion of the chapter discusses the *labeling* of genetically modified food. This subsection concerns its *safety*.

Regulation of the safety of genetically modified food is divided between USDA and FDA. The Animal and Plant Inspection Service (APHIS) within USDA has jurisdiction over the planting of all genetically modified raw agricultural commodities. FDA has jurisdiction to determine whether those commodities, and any other genetically modified food ingredients, may be marketed in the United States. In addition, EPA has a role in regulating food genetically modified for purposes of pest control.

The initial FDA policy statement on the regulation of biotechnology products, issued in 1986, made it clear that "FDA proposes no new procedures or requirements" for the safety evaluation of genetically modified food ingredients, and it broadly described existing GRAS and food additive provisions. 51 Fed. Reg. 23302, 23310 (June 26, 1986). In its subsequent Statement of Policy on Foods Derived from New Plant Varieties, excerpted below, FDA established an unequivocal presumption that a genetically modified version of a raw agricultural commodity would be GRAS and thus would not require a food additive regulation, absent the introduction of toxic material into the food.

FDA Statement of Policy: Foods Derived From New Plant Varieties

57 Fed. Reg. 22984 (May 29, 1992).

. . . .

Under this policy, foods, such as fruits, vegetables, grains, and their byproducts, derived from plant varieties developed by the new methods of genetic modification are regulated within the existing framework of the act, FDA's implementing regulations, and current practice, utilizing an approach identical in principle to that applied to foods developed by traditional plant breeding. The regulatory status of a food, irrespective of the method by which it is developed, is dependent upon objective characteristics of the food and the intended use of the food (or its components). The method by which food is produced or developed may in some cases help to understand the safety or nutritional characteristics of the finished food. However, the key factors in reviewing safety concerns should be the characteristics of the food product, rather than the fact that the new methods are used.

. . . Substances that are expected to become components of food as result of genetic modification of a plant and whose composition is such or has been altered such that the substance is not generally recognized as safe (GRAS) or otherwise exempt are subject to regulation as "food additives" under section 409 of the act. Under the act, substances that are food additives may be used in food only in accordance with an authorizing regulation.

In most cases, the substances expected to become components of food as a result of genetic modification of a plant will be the same as or substantially similar to substances commonly found in food, such as proteins, fats and oils, and carbohydrates. As discussed in more detail [below], FDA has determined that such substances should be subject to regulation under section 409 of the act in those cases when the objective characteristics of the substance raise questions of safety sufficient to warrant formal premarket review and approval by FDA. . . .

. . . Most foods derived from plants predate the establishment of national food laws, and the safety of these foods has been accepted based on extensive use and experience over many years (or even centuries). Foods derived from new plant varieties are not routinely subjected to scientific tests for safety. . . . The established practices that plant breeders employ in selecting and developing new varieties of plants, such as chemical analyses, taste testing, and visual analyses, rely primarily on observations of quality, wholesomeness, and agronomic characteristics. Historically, these practices have proven to be reliable for ensuring food safety. The knowledge from this past experience coupled with safe practices in plant breeding has contributed to continuous improvements in the quality, variety, nutritional value, and safety of foods derived from plants modified by a range of traditional and increasingly sophisticated techniques. Based on this record of safe development of new varieties of plants. FDA has not found it necessary to conduct, prior to marketing, routine safety reviews of whole foods derived from plants.

Nevertheless, FDA has ample authority under the act's food safety provisions to regulate and ensure the safety of foods derived from new plant varieties, including plants developed by new techniques. . . . Under section 402(a)(1) of the act, a food is deemed adulterated and thus unlawful if it bears or contains an added poisonous or deleterious substance that may render the food injurious to health or a naturally occurring substance that is ordinarily injurious. . . .

FDA has relied almost exclusively on section 402(a)(1) of the act to ensure the safety of whole foods. . . .

FDA regards any substance that is not an inherent constituent of food or whose level in food has been increased by human intervention to be "added" within the meaning of section 402(a)(1) of the act. Added substances are subject to the . . . "may render [the food] injurious" safety standard. . . . The "may render injurious" standard would apply to a naturally occurring toxin in food if the level of the toxin in a new plant variety were increased through traditional plant breeding or some other human intervention. . . .

... Until 1958, [402(a)(1)] was the principal tool relied upon by FDA to regulate the safety of food and food ingredients. In 1958, in response to public concern about the increased use of chemicals in foods and food processing and with the support of the food industry, Congress enacted the Food Additives Amendment (the amendment) to the act. Among other provisions, the amendment established a premarket approval requirement for "food additives." . . .

In enacting the amendment, Congress recognized that many substances intentionally added to food do not require a formal premarket review by FDA to assure their safety, either because their safety had been established by a long history of use in food or because the nature of the substances and the information generally available to scientists about the substance are such that the substance simply does not raise a safety concern worthy of premarket review by FDA. Congress thus . . . exclude[d] from the definition of food additive substances that are GRAS. It is on the basis of the GRAS exception of the "food additive" definition that many ingredients derived from natural sources (such as salt, pepper, vinegar, vegetable oil, and thousands of spices and natural flavors), as well as a host of chemical additives (including some sweeteners, preservatives, and artificial flavors), are able to be lawfully marketed today without having been formally reviewed by FDA and without being the subject of a food additive regulation. The judgment of Congress was that subjecting every intentional additive to FDA premarket review was not necessary to protect public health and would impose an insurmountable burden on FDA and the food industry.

Congress' approach to defining food additives means, however, that companies developing new ingredients, new versions of established ingredients, or new processes for producing a food or food ingredient must make a judgment about whether the resulting food substance is a food additive requiring premarket approval by FDA. In many cases, the answer is obvious, such as when the ingredient is a man made chemical having no widely recognized history of safe use in food. Such an ingredient must be approved prior to its use by the issuance of a food additive regulation, based on information submitted to FDA in a food additive petition.

In other cases, the answer is less obvious, such as when an established ingredient derived from nature is modified in some minor way or produced by a new process. In such cases, the manufacturer must determine . . . whether the ingredient is exempt from regulation as a food additive because it is GRAS. . . .

FDA considers the existing statutory authority under sections 402(a)(1) and 409 of the act, and the practical regulatory regime that flows from it, to be fully adequate to ensure the safety of new food ingredients and foods derived from new varieties of plants, regardless of the process by which such foods and ingredients are produced. . . .

. . . The following paragraphs explain briefly how the current framework will apply specifically to foods derived from new plant varieties, including plants developed by recombinant DNA techniques. . . .

The statutory definition of "food additive" makes clear that it is the intended or expected introduction of a substance into food that makes the substance potentially subject to food additive regulation. Thus, in the case of foods derived from new plant varieties, it is the transferred genetic material and the intended expression product or products that could be subject to food additive regulation, if such material or expression products are not GRAS.

In regulating foods and their byproducts derived from new plant varieties, FDA intends to use its food additive authority to the extent necessary to protect public health. Specifically, consistent with the statutory definition of "food additive" and the overall design of FDA's current food safety regulatory program, FDA will use section 409 of the act to require food additive petitions in cases where safety questions exist sufficient to warrant formal premarket review by FDA to ensure public health protection.

With respect to transferred genetic material (nucleic acids), generally FDA does not anticipate that transferred genetic material would itself be subject to food additive regulation. Nucleic acids are present in the cells of every living organism, including every plant and animal used for food by humans or animals, and do not raise a safety concern as a component of food. In regulatory terms, such material is presumed to be GRAS . . . FDA does not expect that there will be any serious question about the GRAS status of transferred genetic material.

FDA expects that the intended expression product or products present in foods derived from new plant varieties will typically be proteins or substances produced by the action of protein enzymes, such as carbohydrates, and fats and oils. When the substance present in the food is one that is already present at generally comparable or greater levels in currently consumed foods, there is unlikely to be a safety question sufficient to call into question the presumed GRAS status of such naturally occurring substances and thus warrant formal premarket review and approval by FDA. Likewise, minor variations in molecular structure that do not affect safety would not ordinarily affect the GRAS status of the substances and, thus, would not ordinarily require regulation of the substance as a food additive.

It is possible, however, that the intended expression product in a food could be a protein, carbohydrate, fat or oil, or other substance that differs significantly in structure, function, or composition from substances found currently in food. Such substances may not be GRAS and may require regulation as a food additive. For example, if a food derived from a new plant variety contains a novel protein sweetener as a result of the genetic modification of the plant, that sweetener would likely require submission of a food additive petition and approval by FDA prior to marketing. FDA invites comments on substances, in addition to proteins, carbohydrates, and fats and oils, that in the future may be introduced into foods by genetic modification. . . .

FDA has long regarded it to be a prudent practice for producers of foods putting new technologies to work cooperatively with the agency to ensure that the new products are safe and comply with applicable legal requirements. It has been the general practice of the food industry to seek informal consultation and cooperation, and this practice should continue with respect to foods produced using the newer techniques of genetic modification. . . .

NOTES

1. *Consultation Process.* FDA issued Consultation Procedures to implement this Statement of Policy in June 1996. FDA has stated that, although consultation is not mandatory, the agency is not aware that any genetically modified food has been marketed in the United States without prior consultation. The agency proposed to make such consultation mandatory in 66 Fed. Reg. 4706 (Jan. 18, 2001), but no further action has been taken on the proposal. Such a requirement would constitute a mandatory GRAS notification, and FDA has disclaimed the legal authority to impose such a requirement in other contexts. *See, e.g., supra* p. 577, note 4 (GAO Report).

2. *Safety Evaluation.* In 71 Fed. Reg. 35688 (June 21, 2006), FDA announced the availability of GUIDANCE FOR INDUSTRY: RECOMMENDATIONS FOR THE EARLY FOOD SAFETY EVALUATION OF NEW NON–PESTICIDAL PROTEINS PRODUCED BY NEW PLANT VARIETIES INTENDED FOR FOOD USE (June 2006).

3. *Food from Bioengineered Animals.* For a discussion of FDA's approach to foods derived from genetically modified and cloned animals, see Chapter 8, *infra* p. 1105.

The GRAS presumption for genetically modified food, as stated in the May 1992 Federal Register notice excerpted above, was challenged in court.

Alliance for Bio-Integrity v. Shalala

116 F.Supp.2d 166 (D.D.C. 2000).

■ KOLLAR–KOTELLY, DISTRICT JUDGE. . . .

In their challenge to the FDA's Statement of Policy, Plaintiffs . . . claim that the Statement of Policy's presumption that rDNA-engineered foods are GRAS violates the GRAS requirements of the Federal Food, Drug, and Cosmetic Act and is therefore arbitrary and capricious. . . .

In the Statement of Policy, FDA indicated that, under § 321(s),

it is the intended or expected introduction of a substance into food that makes the substance potentially subject to food additive regulation. Thus, in the case of foods derived from new plant varieties, it is the transferred genetic material and the intended expression product or products that could be subject to food additive regulation, if such material or expression products are not GRAS.

Accordingly, FDA reasoned that the only substances added to rDNA engineered foods are nucleic acid proteins, generally recognized as not only safe but also necessary for survival. ("Nucleic acids are present in the cells of every living organism, including every plant and animal

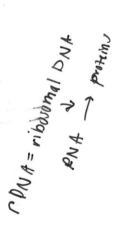

rDNA = ribosomal DNA
DNA → proteins

used for food by humans or animals, and do not raise a safety concern as a component of food"). Therefore, FDA concluded that rDNA engineered foods should be presumed to be GRAS unless evidence arises to the contrary. . . .

This Court's evaluation of the FDA's interpretation of § 321(s) is framed by *Chevron U.S.A. v. Natural Resources Defense Council.* . . .

. . . To resolve the issue, "the question for the reviewing court is whether the agency's construction of the statute is faithful to its plain meaning, or, if the statute has no plain meaning, whether the agency's interpretation 'is based on a permissible construction of the statute.' " . . .

When Congress passed the Food Additives Amendment in 1958, it obviously could not account for the late twentieth-century technologies that would permit the genetic modification of food. . . .

Nonetheless, the statute exempts from regulation as additives substances that are "generally recognized . . . to be safe under the conditions of its intended use. . . ." § 321(s). Plaintiffs have not disputed FDA's claim that nucleic acid proteins are generally recognized to be safe. Plaintiffs have argued, however, that significant disagreement exists among scientific experts as to whether or not nucleic acid proteins are generally recognized to be safe when they are used to alter organisms genetically. Having examined the record in this case, the Court cannot say that FDA's decision to accord genetically modified foods a presumption of GRAS status is arbitrary and capricious. . . .

To be generally recognized as safe, a substance must meet two criteria: (1) it must have technical evidence of safety, usually in published scientific studies, and (2) this technical evidence must be generally known and accepted in the scientific community. *See* 21 C.F.R. § 170.30(a–b); 62 Fed. Reg. 18940. Although unanimity among scientists is not required, "a severe conflict among experts . . . precludes a finding of general recognition." Plaintiffs have produced several documents showing significant disagreements among scientific experts. However, this Court's review is confined to the record before the agency at the time it made its decision. Therefore, the affidavits submitted by Plaintiffs that are not part of the administrative record will not be considered.

. . . Plaintiffs have failed to convince the Court that the GRAS presumption is inconsistent with the statutory requirements.

NOTES

1. *The Fruits of Biotechnology.* The biotechnology industry has been criticized on the ground that genetically engineered crops have primarily benefited farmers by controlling weeds and pests but have not produced healthier foods for consumers. *See, e.g.,* Andrew Pollack, *Biotech's Sparse Harvest,* N.Y. TIMES, Feb. 14, 2006, at C1.

2. *Earlier Applications of Biotechnology.* In 51 Fed. Reg. 10571 (Mar. 27, 1986), FDA published a notice of the filing of a GRAS affirmation petition for alpha-analyse enzyme made from recombinant DNA techniques, for use as an ingredient of human food. The first substance

made through recombinant DNA processes that FDA cleared for use was chymosin, an enzyme for use in making cheese and other food products, which the agency affirmed as GRAS in 1990. *See* 55 Fed. Reg. 10932 (Mar. 23, 1990), codified at 21 C.F.R. 184.1685.

3.   *The Role of USDA/APHIS.* USDA established regulations in 1987, which are still in effect, regarding "the introduction of genetically engineered organisms and products which are plant pests or for which there is reason to believe are plant pests." 52 Fed. Reg. 22892 (June 16, 1987), codified at 7 C.F.R. Part 340. The regulations apply only to "regulated articles," defined as any product of genetic engineering when the donor organism, recipient organism, or vector agent is a "plant pest." 21 C.F.R. 340.1. "Plant pests" are, for purposes of the rule, organisms "which can directly or indirectly injure or cause disease or damage in or to any plants or parts thereof, or any processed, manufactured, or other products of plants." *Id.* "Introduction" of a genetically engineered organism encompasses importation, interstate transportation, and release into the environment outside the constraints of physical confinement (most importantly, in the context of field tests). *Id.*

For genetically modified organism that are "regulated articles" (i.e., actual or potential plant pests), the regulations provide two processes for introduction. First, there is a simple notification process for plants that meet six listed characteristics suggesting low risk and satisfy six performance standards intended to prevent cross-contamination. 7 C.F.R. 340.3. For other regulated genetically engineered plants, a more complex permit process applies that requires submission of an application to USDA with substantial supporting scientific data and proposed containment measures, a detailed risk assessment by USDA, and ultimately the requirement by USDA of all conditions appropriate for approval of the permit for field testing. 7 C.F.R. 340.4(b). In addition to full permits for field testing, the regulations establish limited permits for importation and interstate movement. 7 C.F.R. 340.4(c)–(d). Recognizing the need for transparency, USDA makes all records of notifications and permits publicly available on its website. 60 Fed. Reg. 27490 (May 24, 1995).

Finally, the USDA regulations provide for the submission of petitions for a determination of nonregulated status, which USDA may grant when the petitioner provides sufficient information to substantiate that the article in question is unlikely to pose a greater plant pest risk than the unmodified organism from which it was derived. 7 C.F.R. 340.6.

Prior to June 2000, USDA regulated agricultural biotechnology under the statutory authority provided by a number of old laws, principally the Plant Quarantine Act of 1912, the Federal Pest Act of 1957, and the Federal Noxious Weed Act of 1974. In June 2000, Congress enacted the Plant Protection Act, 114 Stat. 358,438, 7 U.S.C. 7701 *et seq.*, as part of the Agriculture Risk Protection Act, to consolidate and supersede these three earlier laws and a number of other related statutory provisions. Accordingly, all USDA authority to regulate agricultural biotechnology is now concentrated in this single statute. To make certain that there would be no loss of continuity, Congress explicitly provided that regulations issued under the prior statutory authority will remain in effect until USDA issues superseding regulations. With the exception of some technical amendments, 72 Fed. Reg. 43523 (Aug. 6, 2007), USDA has not, since enactment of the new Plant Protection Act, changed either its regulations regarding agricultural biotechnology or the way that it implements these regulations.

4. *EPA's Role.* The Environmental Protection Agency takes the lead in regulating bioengineered plants when the modification is pesticidal in nature. The agency regulates genetically engineered pesticides pursuant to the Federal Insecticide, Fungicide, and Rodenticide Act (FIFRA) as well as the FD&C Act. EPA's regulations governing such products, dubbed the "Plant–Incorporated Protectant" (PIP) rules, are published at 21 C.F.R. Parts 152 and 174.

5. *Interagency Cooperation.* In late 2008, a GAO report recommended that the USDA, EPA, and FDA share more information and develop a strategy for monitoring the widespread use of genetically-engineered crops. GENETICALLY ENGINEERED CROPS: AGENCIES ARE PROPOSING CHANGES TO IMPROVE OVERSIGHT BUT COULD TAKE ADDITIONAL STEPS TO ENHANCE COORDINATION AND MONITORING, GAO–09–60 (November 2008). In response to the report, FDA stated it will post results of food safety evaluations on its website.

6. PRIOR SANCTIONED SUBSTANCES

Section 201(s)(4) constitutes a genuine "grandfather" clause for food substances that FDA or USDA had affirmatively approved before the 1958 enactment of section 409. These "prior sanctions" can be under the 1938 FD&C Act (but not the 1906 Act), the Poultry Products Inspection Act, or the Federal Meat Inspection Act. While prior to 1958, FDA lacked statutory authority to license food ingredients for general use, it routinely responded, as did USDA, to requests for opinions about the safety of individual ingredients. In addition, FDA exercised premarket control over, and thus approved, ingredients permitted to be used in foods covered by standards of identity. USDA issued formal regulations describing permitted uses of many ingredients in meat and poultry products, and in some instances FDA formally acknowledged that USDA had approved certain substances for food use. An ingredient's prior sanction status does not depend upon a current evaluation of its utility or its safety, but rests solely on its prior approval by one of the two agencies. FDA lists the food ingredients for which it recognizes prior sanctions at 21 C.F.R. Part 181.

Proposal Regarding Regulation of Prior–Sanctioned Food Ingredients

37 Fed. Reg. 16407 (August 12, 1972).

. . . [A] food ingredient subject to a prior sanction may not be regulated under the food additive provisions of the law. Such an ingredient may, however, be regulated under the general adulteration and misbranding provisions of the Act, and in particular may be banned from food if found to be a "poisonous or deleterious substance" in violation of Section 402(a)(1) of the Act.

The Food and Drug Administration, between 1938 and 1958, reaffirmed many sanctions or approvals granted under the Federal Food and Drugs Act of 1906, and also granted additional sanctions and approvals. The U.S. Department of Agriculture has similarly granted many sanctions and approvals. Not all of these sanctions and approvals can be ascertained because of the destruction of old records and the retirement of personnel involved in these matters. The Food and Drug Administration has requested information on prior sanctions (35 F.R. 5810) in an effort to make its files on these matters more complete.

Whether or not a food ingredient is used as a result of a determination that it is GRAS, or pursuant to a food additive regulation, or as a result of a prior sanction, the basis for such use should be a matter of public record. The Commissioner has therefore determined to . . . establish[ ] regulations governing all prior-sanctioned direct and indirect food ingredients known to the Commissioner.

New scientific information requires, on occasion, that additional limitations be placed on the use of prior-sanctioned ingredients. Accordingly, the Commissioner has concluded that a procedure should also be established under which a regulation . . . stating the existence of a prior sanction may be established or amended to impose limitations upon the use of the ingredient when scientific data justify such limitations. . . .

NOTES

1. *Final Regulations.* FDA's final regulations, promulgated in 38 Fed. Reg. 12737 (May 15, 1973), afford the agency substantial control over prior-sanctioned food ingredients:

§ 181.1   General

(a) An ingredient whose use in food or food packaging is subject to a prior sanction or approval within the meaning of section 201(s)(4) of the act is exempt from classification as a food additive. The Commissioner will publish in this part all known prior sanctions. Any interested person may submit to the Commissioner a request for publication of a prior sanction, supported by evidence to show that it falls within section 201(s)(4) of the act.

(b) Based upon scientific data or information that shows that use of a prior-sanctioned food ingredient may be injurious to health, and thus in violation of section 402 of the act, the Commissioner will establish or amend an applicable prior sanction regulation to impose whatever limitations or conditions are necessary for the safe use of the ingredient, or to prohibit use of the ingredient.

(c) Where appropriate, an emergency action level may be issued for a prior-sanctioned substance, pending the issuance of a final regulation in accordance with paragraph (b) of this section. Such an action level shall be issued pursuant to section 402(a) of the act to identify, based upon available data, conditions of use of the substance that may be injurious to health. Such an action level shall be issued in a notice published in the FEDERAL REGISTER and shall be followed as soon as practicable by a proposed regulation in accordance with paragraph (b) of this section. Where the available data demonstrate that the substance may be injurious at any level, use of the substance may be prohibited. The identification of a prohibited substance may be made in Part 189 of this chapter when appropriate.

2. *Caffeine.* Although FDA proposed in 45 FR 69817 (Oct. 21, 1980) to find that there was no prior sanction for caffeine in soft drinks, it reversed that position and proposed to find such a prior sanction in 52 Fed. Reg. 18923 (May 20, 1987). The agency withdrew both of these proposals, with little explanation, in 69 Fed. Reg. 68831, 68833 (Nov. 26, 2004). Caffeine continues to be treated as GRAS. *See supra* p. 590.

3. *Nitrate and Nitrite.* The most protracted and prominent dispute regarding the prior sanction status of a food ingredient concerned nitrate and nitrite. These substances (referred to here by the single term "nitrite") are two of the oldest functional food ingredients. Nitrite has been used to preserve meat since prehistoric times. Early in the 20th century, it gained popularity as an agent to impart flavor and color. Nitrite also inhibits the growth of the bacterial spores that cause botulism. In the 1960s, it was discovered that nitrite can combine with amines, substances naturally found in many food products, to produce nitrosamines, some of which cause cancer in laboratory animals. Indeed, the nitrates that occur naturally throughout the human food supply are converted to nitrite and combine with naturally occurring amines to produce nitrosamines in the human gut.

FDA proposed to prohibit nonessential uses of nitrite in 1972. 37 Fed. Reg. 23456 (Nov. 3, 1972). In this notice, however, the agency stated that "nitrite and nitrate . . . have prior sanction for use as curing agents in meat and poultry products." A decade later, the FDA Commissioner responsible for this action acknowledged that nitrite had not been banned in 1972 not only because of its usefulness in preventing botulism, but also "because of its importance in maintaining the characteristics of cured meat that are expected and demanded by consumers." "Oversight of Food Safety, 1983," Hearings before the Senate Committee on Labor and Human Resources, 98th Cong., 1st Sess. (1983).

Following USDA's denial of a 1972 petition by consumer groups to ban or restrict the use of nitrite in meat (a decision upheld in *Schuck v. Butz*, 500 F.2d 810 (D.C. Cir. 1974)), that department changed course. In 1978, it issued a final regulation restricting the use of nitrite in bacon and, more importantly, prohibiting any detectable amount of nitrosamines. 43 Fed. Reg. 20992 (May 16, 1978). Consumer groups challenged this action as inadequate, because it did not ban the use of nitrites altogether, but in *Public Citizen v. Foreman*, 631 F.2d 969 (D.C. Cir. 1980), the Court of Appeals upheld the USDA regulations on the basis that nitrite had a prior sanction as a preservative in cured meat products.

Meanwhile, based on advice from USDA, FDA proposed to determine that no prior sanction exists for nitrite in poultry. 44 Fed. Reg. 75662 (Dec. 21, 1979). After a change in administration, however, FDA withdrew this proposal, as well as its November 1972 proposal to ban nonessential uses of nitrite. 48 Fed. Reg. 9299 (Mar. 4, 1983). FDA's withdrawal of these proposals was based on USDA's conclusion that a prior sanction did in fact exist for use of nitrite in both cured meat and cured poultry products. *See*

48 Fed. Reg. 1702 (Jan. 14, 1983). The prior sanctions for nitrite in the production of cured red meat and poultry products are codified at 21 C.F.R. 181.33, 181.34. In *United States v. An Article of Food . . . Coco Rico, Inc.*, 752 F.2d 11 (1st Cir. 1985), excerpted *supra* p. 577, the Court of Appeals determined that potassium nitrate is not subject to a prior sanction for use in soft drinks.

4.   *Waiver of Prior Sanction.* The prior sanction regulations state: "Any food additive or GRAS regulation promulgated after a general evaluation of use of an ingredient constitutes a determination that excluded uses would result in adulteration of the food. . . . , and the failure of any person to come forward with proof of . . . an applicable prior sanction in response to a proposal will constitute a waiver of the right to assert or rely on such sanction at any later time." 21 C.F.R. 181.5(d). In rejecting a comment opposing this provision, FDA remarked: "[I]t is inequitable if one manufacturer who knows of a prior sanction is permitted to take advantage of it, while his competitors are restrained by regulations arising from the agency's review of ingredient safety. If the prior-sanctioned use is safe, all users should be permitted to rely upon it. If it is not safe, it should be brought to the agency's attention so that appropriate conclusions can be made." 41 Fed. Reg. 53600, 53603 (Oct. 7, 1976).

5.   *Prior Sanction versus GRAS.* The cyclamate episode, *supra* p. 564, in which the GRAS status of a substance was withdrawn, illustrates an important distinction between ingredients that are excepted from the food additive definition because they are GRAS and ingredients that are permanently exempt because FDA or USDA sanctioned their use prior to 1958. An ingredient's status as GRAS is always vulnerable to the discovery of new evidence casting doubt on its safety. An ingredient that ceases to be GRAS falls automatically within the definition of a food additive, and must then be approved by FDA for its use to be lawful. A prior sanction, however, is a permanent exemption from food additive status. FDA may regulate a prior sanction ingredient that "may be injurious to health" under section 402(a), but the burden is on the agency to demonstrate this risk.

6.   *Wisdom of GRAS and Prior Sanction Exceptions.* More than one critic has proposed that the regulation of direct food additives should be tightened by eliminating the exclusion of GRAS and prior sanctioned substances from the food additive definition. *E.g.*, GAO, NEED FOR MORE EFFECTIVE REGULATION OF DIRECT ADDITIVES TO FOOD, REP. NO. HRD–80–90 (Aug. 14, 1980). When closely scrutinized, however, support for this proposition has faded in the face of the vast number of raw agricultural commodities and other common food substances that would have to be subjected to animal toxicity tests, the resulting thousands of petitions requiring safety evaluations, and the development of food additive regulations specifying safe conditions of use.

7. THE DETERIORATION OF THE FOOD ADDITIVE APPROVAL PROCESS

Peter Barton Hutt, *Regulation of Food Additives in the United States*

In Larry Branen et al., eds., FOOD ADDITIVES, Ch. 8 (2d ed. 2001).

Four decades ago, the United States explored and ultimately adopted a new and untried approach under the Federal Food, Drug, and Cosmetic Act (FD&C Act). Congress divided the food supply into two different regulatory categories. The first regulatory category remained subject only to the same policing controls that had been used for centuries. This category included food itself (*e.g.*, raw agricultural commodities) and functional substances added to the food supply that were either approved by the United States Department of Agriculture (USDA) or the Food and Drug Administration (FDA) during 1938–1958 or that were generally recognized as safe (GRAS) for their intended uses. The second regulatory category required the obtaining of premarket approval from FDA prior to marketing for all new food additives that did not fall within the first category and all color additives.

Now we find that half of the system has been a complete success, and the other half is a complete failure. The GRAS process has worked extraordinarily well. The food additive and color additive approval process has broken down completely and requires fundamental reform. . . .

. . . [F]or those pre-1958 substances that were not prior-sanctioned or GRAS, and thus properly fell within the definition of a food additive, Congress included a transitional period within which the manufacturers were required to submit and obtain FDA approval of a food additive petition. . . .

The handling of all of the pre-1958 direct human food additive petitions in seven years reflected a heroic effort by FDA. It required the development and organization of a group of dedicated scientists within FDA, close daily cooperation between FDA and the regulated industry, and a commitment by everyone involved to work through the inevitable problems that arose in a practical and realistic way. No one either in industry or in FDA had the luxury of sitting around for months or years on end, debating theoretical issues. There was a job to be done, and it was done extraordinarily efficiently and with unprecedented success. Not a single additive that was approved during that time has since been removed from the market for lack of safety. The people who participated in that effort, many of whom still are alive today, deserve far greater recognition than they have been given to date.

By the time this transitional process was completed, FDA had promulgated 185 separate direct human food additive regulations, along with an additional 93 indirect food additive regulations, five regulations governing radiation of food, the lists of GRAS substances, and additional lists of prior-sanctioned substances, and effective dates were confirmed. It was an extraordinary outpouring of regulatory science. The productivity of FDA at that time in history stands in stark contrast to the inefficiency and paralysis of today. . . .

Once FDA completed its work on pre-1958 transitional food additives, it seems the agency lost heart on food additive matters. Since that time the record of FDA approval of new food additives is appalling. It is useful to review the FDA record on approving new direct human food additives over the past thirty years, from 1970 to the present. Research indicates only eight new direct human food additives during that time: (1) TBHQ, 1972 (2) Aspartame, 1981 (3) Polydextrose, 1981 (4) Acesulfame K, 1988 (5) Gellan gum, 1990 (6) Olestra, 1996 (7) Sucralose, 1998 (8) Sucrose acetate isobutyrate, 1999.[*]

Eight direct human food additives in thirty years. That is embarrassing. It represents a serious problem for food technology in the United States. Just at the time when we are learning more about the relationship between diet and health, and new food ingredients could contribute greatly to healthy improvements in our daily diet, we have adopted a regulatory system that has virtually destroyed the incentive to innovate and the ability to get new food additives to the market.

Let us also examine the history of one of the new food additives that languished in the FDA pipeline almost nine years prior to FDA approval: olestra. Information published on olestra shows that it was invented in 1968, the first meetings with FDA were held in the early 1970s, and it was the subject of continuing testing and negotiations with FDA until approved in 1996. . . .

The lesson taught by the problems encountered by these hapless compounds has been learned by the entire food industry. The food additive approval process in America is dead. It has been killed by FDA. No food company of which I am aware would even consider beginning research today on a new food additive.

The lesson learned is that there is only one type of food substance worth considering: a GRAS substance that can immediately be marketed. If a new food substance cannot be determined to be GRAS, it is simply discarded. Only if it can be regarded as GRAS will it be pursued. . . .

When FDA established its GRAS affirmation procedures as part of the GRAS List Review in the early 1970s, the agency recognized that it did not have the statutory authority either to preclude self-determination of GRAS status or to prevent marketing while the agency reviewed a self-determination of GRAS. . . . The purpose of the agency was to encourage submission of GRAS affirmation petitions to FDA in order to assist the agency in its surveillance of the food supply and to settle any safety issues that might arise with the use of new food substances. This was a purposeful tradeoff. FDA gave industry the assurance that it could market products after a self-determination of GRAS, and in return industry began to submit GRAS affirmation petitions in order to demonstrate to potential customers and to FDA that the new substance had been thoroughly evaluated and was in fact GRAS.

---

[*]   [Since the publication of this article, FDA has also approved several others. See the note immediately following this excerpt.—EDS.]

While reasonable in concept, FDA implementation of this program broke down almost from the beginning. GRAS affirmation was a process created by FDA, not by statute. There was no statutory deadline for FDA action and thus no priority within FDA. In many instances, FDA seemed to be more intent upon receiving a GRAS affirmation petition than it was upon evaluating and acting upon it. As a result, FDA became simply a dumping ground for GRAS affirmation petitions. The backlog of GRAS affirmation petitions for direct food substances, in various stages of consideration, grew every year. . . .

Nonetheless, the program was still a resounding success from the standpoint of public policy, precisely because FDA involvement was not needed to make it work. Self-determination of GRAS permits immediate marketing, whether or not a GRAS affirmation petition is filed and whether or not FDA ever acts on it. . . .

Perhaps there is no better example of the success of the GRAS approach than the history of high fructose corn syrup. High fructose corn syrup was the subject of a thorough scientific evaluation and a self-determination of GRAS in the mid-1960s. It was immediately marketed, without asking FDA for an opinion or even informing the agency. Once one manufacturer began to market it, others followed suit. By the early 1970s, it was in widespread use throughout the food industry. It proved to have excellent functional properties and to be an extremely important addition to the food supply. . . .

One should stop to consider what would have happened if high fructose corn syrup had been handled through a food additive petition rather than a self-determination of GRAS. . . . High fructose corn syrup was a contemporary of olestra. These two macronutrients were subject to initial research and development at the same time, during the mid-1960s. One took the GRAS superhighway to market, and the other followed the meandering food additive path through the FDA woods. One was freely marketed more than 25 years for unlimited food use before the other was allowed to be marketed for very limited food use. In many ways, this simple comparison tells the entire story.

. . . As of June 1995, there was a backlog of 295 pending petitions . . . approximately 70 direct food additive petitions, 150 indirect food additive petitions, and 75 GRAS affirmation petitions. The oldest food additive petition was filed in 1971 and the oldest GRAS affirmation petition was filed in 1972. . . .

Partly as a response to the findings about the deterioration of the FDA process for review of food petitions, Congress included in the Food and Drug Administration Modernization Act of 1997 a new section 909 of the FD&C Act, explicitly authorizing FDA to enter into contracts with outside experts to review and evaluate any application or submission (including a petition or notification) submitted under the FD&C Act, including those for food additives and GRAS substances. . . .

In 1997, FDA proposed to replace the entire GRAS affirmation process with a GRAS notification procedure. . . . Although FDA has not yet promulgated a final regulation for this procedure, it has declined to accept new GRAS affirmation petitions, has encouraged those who submitted old GRAS affirmation petitions to convert them to GRAS determination notifications, and has accepted new GRAS determination notifications and taken action on them. In short, FDA is already implementing this proposal. . . .

Looking back on the past four decades, it is easy to discern areas of success and areas of failure in the regulation of food substances, food additives, and color additives.

Regulation of GRAS substances under the Food Additives Amendment of 1958 has been an enormous success, largely because it has been implemented outside FDA. It is a classic free market approach. The Food and Drug Administration is not the only access to the market. There are alternative approaches, through equally competent and respected scientific organizations that are much more efficient, less costly, and thus far preferable. Individual companies are free to make their own determinations based upon their own scientific expertise; independent academic experts are available; private companies that specialize in GRAS determinations can be used; and FASEB itself has now, after completing the FDA GRAS List Review, agreed to conduct private GRAS evaluations for the food industry. These compete among each other and with FDA. Under the inexorable rules of competition, in a free enterprise environment, the most effective and efficient organization will ultimately be used.

One must question whether leaving these issues to the free market compromises public health and safety. The evidence over the past four decades provides unequivocal testimony that the public health and safety has been fully protected and not in any way compromised. Not a single food substance that has been added to the food supply under a private GRAS determination based on a thorough and well-documented scientific evaluation since 1958 has been taken off the market by FDA because of a public health or safety problem. The program, in short, has been a complete success.

The failure of the food additive approval process during the past four decades scarcely needs further elaboration. It is a closed process within FDA, not subject to public scrutiny even through an FDA advisory committee, and is solely within the control of the agency. Because there is no other lawful route to the marketplace for a food additive or color additive, manufacturers have no alternative but to do whatever FDA commands. And for the same reason, FDA can demand whatever it wishes, with or without sound scientific justification, without fear of peer review, public scrutiny, or accountability to anyone else. The resulting statistics, documented earlier, are the inevitable result.

One might consider retaining such an approach if it produced better results—that is, safer food—than other approaches might achieve. A comparison with the GRAS self-determination approach, however, demonstrates that this is not true. Far more new direct human food substances have been marketed since 1970 after an industry self-determination of GRAS than after FDA approval of a food additive or color additive petition. No product in either category has proved to present a public health hazard. The highly conservative approach of FDA thus contributes nothing more than delay, higher costs to the public for those products that eventually are approved, and a more restricted choice for consumers because the entire process has choked off innovation in this very important field. . . .

NOTE

Update. In this excerpt, Hutt refers to the fact that FDA approved only eight new direct food additives between 1970 and 2000. In the dozen years since this article was published, FDA has approved three additional direct or secondary direct human food additives that are arguably new: (1) alpha-acetolactate decarboxylase (α-ALDC) enzyme preparation derived from a recombinant Bacillus subtilis, 66 Fed. Reg. 27022 (May 16, 2001), codified at 21 C.F.R. 173.115 (a processing aid for malt beverages and distilled liquors), (2) neotame, 67 Fed. Reg. 45300 (July 9, 2002) (an artificial sweetener), and (3) *Listeria*-specific bacteriophage preparation, 71 Fed. Reg. 47731 (Aug. 18, 2006), codified at 21 C.F.R. 172.785 (an antimicrobial for ready-to-eat meat and poultry products). Like aspartame, neotame is a derivative of phenylalamine and thus could well have been the subject of a self-determination of GRAS status. Although the agency has published and amended numerous other direct food additive regulations since 1970, most of these regulations have been obtained for commercial reasons—to satisfy the requests of customers for some type of FDA approval—rather than because they represent a truly unique new technology.

8. FOOD PACKAGING AND PROCESSING SUBSTANCES

More than 10,000 substances are used in proximity with food (e.g., in food packaging, in equipment used to process or store food, and in compounds used to clean such equipment) in ways that permit small amounts to migrate to, and thus become a part of, food. For about forty years after the passage of the Food Additives Amendment of 1958, the same premarket approval requirements that applied to direct food additives were also applicable to food additives that migrated to food from food-contact surfaces. In 1997, however, Congress—in view of the deterioration of the FDA food additive approval process—included in the Food and Drug Administrative Modernization Act of 1997 (FDAMA) an entirely new approach for handling indirect food additives. As a result of a successful negotiation between FDA and regulated industry, FDAMA established, under section 409(h) of the FD&C Act, a new premarket notification procedure for indirect food additives to replace the old premarket approval procedure.

Section 409(h) provides that a manufacturer of an indirect food additive (a "food contact substance") may, at least 120 days prior to shipment, notify FDA of the identity and intended use of the substance and of the manufacturer's determination that it is safe for its intended use. All pertinent scientific information must be submitted with this notification. The notification becomes effective 120 days after its receipt by FDA. The substance may then be shipped unless the agency determines that use of the substance has not been shown to be safe. FDA maintains a list of effective food contact notifications on its website and does not publish them in the Federal Register.

In other respects, the FD&C Act treats direct and indirect food additives identically. A migrating food contact material is excluded from food additive classification if it is GRAS or if it is the subject of a prior sanction. Some established packaging materials fall within these exceptions. The basic statutory safety criteria are the same for indirect and direct food additives. Thus, an indirect food additive must be shown, with reasonable certainty, to be safe, and no weight may be accorded the benefits of its use. Similarly, the Delaney Clause applies to indirect food additives.

Pre-1997 indirect food additive regulations and GRAS affirmations, published at 21 C.F.R. Parts 175–78 and 186, continue in effect. Even under the new regime, the agency may require that a food additive petition, rather than a notification, be submitted for a food contact substance if it concludes that this procedure is necessary to assure safety. It seems likely, however, that a food additive petition will rarely be required.

FDA promulgated final regulations to implement the new procedure in 2002. 67 Fed. Reg. 35724 (May 21, 2002), codified at 21 C.F.R. Part 170, Subpart D. The availability of final guidance documents on chemistry and toxicology information to be included in a food contact notification (FCN) were announced in 67 Fed. Reg. 17703 (Apr. 11, 2002). The new FCN procedure has substantially reduced FDA resources needed to handle indirect food additive petitions—a development no doubt welcomed by the agency, in light of the fact that the review of food additive petitions is not supported by user fees, as the reviews of other types of product applications are.

————

Following enactment of the 1958 Food Additives Amendment, it was a matter of dispute whether food packaging material falls within the jurisdiction of the FD&C Act before it is actually used to package food. After FDA became aware of the widespread contamination of paper food packaging with PCBs, it took the position that food packaging materials constitute "food" that can be regulated even before they are put to that use. This position was upheld in the case excerpted below.

Natick Paperboard Corp. v. Weinberger

525 F.2d 1103 (1st Cir. 1975).

■ THOMSEN, SENIOR DISTRICT JUDGE. . . .

PCB's are a group of toxic chemical compounds, which find their way into industrial waste, and thence into various products, including recycled paper products. If such a product is used for packaging food, PCB's are likely to migrate into the food unless the food is protected from such migration by an impermeable barrier.

The affidavits before the district court justify the conclusions that PCB's are toxic, that they tend to migrate from paper packaging material to the contained food by a vapor phase phenomenon, that paper packaging material containing PCB's in excess of 10 ppm is not generally recognized as safe for packaging food for human consumption unless the food is protected from such migration by an impermeable barrier, and that if so used, without such barrier, paper food packaging containing PCB's "may reasonably be expected to result, directly or indirectly, in its becoming a component or otherwise affecting the characteristics of . . . food" within the meaning of sec. 321(s).

Since, therefore, paper food packaging material containing PCB's in excess of 10 ppm will in many instances be an "unsafe food additive" within the meaning of the Act, we proceed to the central issue of this case: whether such material is "adulterated food" under sec. 342 and thus, under sec. 334(a)(1) and (b), subject to seizure by FDA.

. . . Plaintiffs argue that, although PCB's may be introduced into food by migration from the packaging, such introduction is not intentional and therefore the packaging is not "used for components" of food within sec. 321(f)(3). FDA replies that intentional introduction is not required to meet the definition, and refers to the "food additive" definition in sec. 321(s), . . . and to the legislative history. . . .

It would defeat the policy of the Act to require, as plaintiffs contend, that FDA must wait until the unsafe food additive has actually entered or come in contact with food before it can be seized; it is enough that FDA has reasonable cause to expect that the additive will be used in such a way as to enter or otherwise come in contact with food. To wait until actual contamination occurs, in the warehouse of the food processor, on the shelf of a grocery store, or in a family kitchen would effectively deny FDA the means to protect the public from adulterated food.

We do not hold, however, that FDA can properly take steps to seize any and all paperboard containing PCB's in excess of 10 ppm wherever it is located and whatever its intended use may be. The district court properly limited its judgment to paper *food packaging* material. We interpret this to mean that the FDA must be able to prove that any paperboard intended to be seized before it has actually been used as a container for food is either in the hands of the packager of food or in transit to, ordered by, or being produced with the intention that it be sold to a packager of food, or that its intended use otherwise meets the test of sec. 321(s). If the packager or other claimant can show that the food placed in or to be placed in the paper container is or will be insulated from PCB migration by a barrier impermeable to such migration, so that contamination cannot reasonably be expected to occur, the paperboard would not be a food additive and would not be subject to seizure under the Act. . . .

————

With the increasing sensitivity of analytical detection methodology, migration of substances from food-contact articles can be found or reliably predicted at levels as low as 1 part per trillion (ppt) or even lower. As detection methodology improved, FDA was forced to reevaluate both its interpretation of the "may reasonably be expected to result . . . in its becoming a component" phrase in section 201(s) and its application of the safety criteria in section 409.

The following landmark court decision on the statutory definition of "food additive" as it applies to materials used in contact with food involved acrylonitrile copolymers used to fabricate plastic beverage bottles. Acrylonitrile was prior sanctioned for some food packaging uses and also came into wide use in a variety of food contact applications pursuant to food additive regulations issued by FDA. In 40 Fed. Reg. 6489 (Feb. 12, 1975), the agency approved a petition to use acrylonitrile/styrene copolymer in the production of bottles for nonalcoholic beverages. The following year, because of increased concern about the potential migration of residual acrylonitrile monomer into foods, FDA issued an interim food additive regulation pursuant to which it required further toxicological study as a condition of continued approval for all uses of all acrylonitrile copolymers. 41 Fed. Reg. 23940 (June 14, 1976).

In early 1977, after preliminary reports of the ongoing toxicological studies suggested that acrylonitrile might be unsafe, FDA stayed the regulations approving the use of acrylonitrile copolymers in producing plastic beverage bottles pending evaluation of the tests in progress. 42 Fed. Reg. 13546 (Mar. 11, 1977). In compliance with a court order, *Monsanto Co. v. Gardner*, Food Drug Cosm. L. Rep. (CCH) ¶ 38,098 (D.C. Cir. 1977), the agency then convened a formal evidentiary hearing requested by the manufacturers. The hearing dealt with two principal issues: (1) whether beverage containers fabricated from acrylonitrile copolymers were properly considered food additives and (2) whether such containers had been shown, with reasonable certainty, to be safe. *See* 42 Fed. Reg. 17529 (Apr. 1, 1977). The FDA Commissioner's final decision upheld the ALJ's determination that acrylonitrile was a food additive when used to make plastic beverage bottles and that it had not been shown to be safe for this use. 42 Fed. Reg. 48528 (Sept. 23, 1977). The manufacturers appealed this decision to the Court of Appeals. They requested that the matter be remanded to FDA on the basis of the pending introduction of a new Monsanto bottle from which the company said there was no migration of residual acrylonitrile monomer.

Monsanto Co. v. Kennedy

613 F.2d 947 (D.C. Cir. 1979).

■ LEVENTHAL, CIRCUIT JUDGE.

This case arises on a petition for review of a Final Decision and Order of the Commissioner of Food and Drugs in which he ruled that a substance used to fabricate unbreakable beverage containers, acrylonitrile copolymer, is a "food additive," within the meaning of section 201(s) of the Federal Food, Drug, and Cosmetic Act. He further concluded that the data of record failed to provide the demonstration of safety established by section 409(c)(3)(A) of the Act as a precedent to FDA approval for use of any "food additive." The Commissioner's Final Order amended the pertinent FDA regulations to provide: "Acrylonitrile copolymers (of the type identified in the regulations) are not authorized to be used to fabricate beverage containers."

. . . .

The FDA determination that acrylonitrile copolymers used in beverage containers are "food additives" within the statute is based on the finding that such containers invariably retain a residual level of acrylonitrile monomer that has failed to polymerize completely during the manufacturing process and that will migrate from the wall of the container into the beverage under the conditions of intended use. Although the administrative proceedings focused on beverage containers with a residual acrylonitrile monomer (RAN) level equal to or greater than 3.3 parts per million (ppm), the Commissioner made findings and conclusions applicable to all beverage containers manufactured with acrylonitrile, and the Final Order prohibited manufacture of such containers irrespective of their RAN levels. . . .

At the administrative hearing, petitioners introduced results from tests on a[n] . . . acrylonitrile beverage container having an RAN level of approximately 3.3 ppm. Tests on the container, employing a detection method sensitive to 10 ppb, detected no migration of acrylonitrile monomer. Nevertheless, the administrative law judge found that acrylonitrile copolymer was a "food additive," since migration had been detected from beverage containers composed of the same chemical compounds, though with higher RAN levels than those present in the [3.3 ppm RAN level] container. The Final Order prohibited manufacture of beverage containers containing acrylonitrile copolymer irrespective of their RAN levels.

This case brings into court the second law of thermodynamics, which C. P. Snow used as a paradigm of technical information well understood by all scientists and practically no persons of the culture of humanism and letters. That law leads to a scientifically indisputable prediction that there will be *some* migration of *any* two substances which come in contact. The Commissioner's Final Decision, which upheld the ALJ's determination, is unclear on whether and to what extent reliance was placed on this "diffusion principle" rather than on a meaningful projection from reliable data. At one point in the Final Decision the Commissioner stated: "the migration of any amount of a substance is sufficient to make it a food additive"—a passage evocative of the diffusion principle. Elsewhere, the Commissioner stated that he was able to make a finding of migration based on a projection from actual data—on the assumption that a roughly linear relationship (as a function of time and temperature) existed between the RAN levels in a container and the concentration of acrylonitrile that would migrate into a test fluid. On this premise, though migration from the 3.3 ppm RAN container was itself below the threshold of detectability (10 ppb), it could be projected from the testing data obtained from containers with higher RAN levels.

This was a troublesome aspect of the case. As it was presented to us, the Commissioner had made a projection of migration from 3.3 ppm RAN containers without the support of any actual data showing that migration had occurred from such containers. One of petitioner's experts put it that the relationship might not be linear at very low RAN levels; but this was dismissed by the Commissioner as "speculative." . . .

. . . [T]his court requested post-argument memoranda from the parties on whether tests had been performed, or would be feasible, to confirm by actual data the hypothesis that migration occurs from containers with an RAN level of 3.3 ppm.

The responses to our inquiry have revealed the probable existence of data unavailable to counsel during the administrative proceedings that bear importantly upon the assumptions made by the Commissioner in reaching his findings and conclusions. . . .

. . . [W]e remand this proceeding for further consideration.

The proceedings at hand are dramatic testimony to the rapid advance of scientific knowledge in our society. At the time of the administrative proceedings, the lowest concentration of acrylonitrile in a test fluid that could be detected with an acceptable degree of confidence was 10 ppb. There are now analytical techniques available that can detect acrylonitrile concentration of 0.1 ppb, an improvement of two orders of magnitude. Thus, on the issue of migration of acrylonitrile monomer it is now possible to generate "hard" data previously unobtainable.

In his post-argument testimony, Monsanto's expert claims, on the basis of such "hard" data, that the hypothesis which the Commissioner labeled as "speculative" may accurately describe the migration characteristics of containers with very low RAN levels, to wit, that in such containers the acrylonitrile monomer is so firmly affixed within the structure of the copolymer that no migration will occur under the conditions of intended use. If these assertions can be demonstrated to the satisfaction of the Commissioner, a modification of the current regulation is a likely corollary. The actual issuance of a regulation approving the production of a beverage container with an acceptable RAN level would presumably require both a container that had been developed and the appropriate petition. However, the Commissioner would have latitude to issue a statement of policy based upon the results of the proceeding on remand that would specify what in his review was an acceptable RAN level. This would serve a technology-forcing objective.[19]

FDA opposes petitioners' post-argument motion for remand, asserting that the proffered new evidence will not affect the Commissioner's order insofar as that order precludes manufacture of beverage containers with RAN levels equal to or greater than 3.3 ppm[,] the type of container already tested. FDA points out that the material submitted in response to this court's inquiry affirmatively supports the validity of the Commissioner's findings and conclusions.[20]

. . . . The Court is . . . concerned that the Commissioner may have reached his determination [banning all use of acrylonitrile copolymers in beverage bottles] in the belief that he was constrained to apply the strictly literal terms of the statute irrespective of the public health and safety considerations. As we discuss below, there is latitude inherent in the statutory scheme to avoid literal application of the statutory definition of "food additive" in those *de minimis* situations that, in the informed judgment of the Commissioner, clearly present no public health or safety concerns.

---

[19] The submission by Monsanto is that no migration can be expected to occur from containers with RAN levels lower than 0.1 ppm. There is a further indication that the manufacture of beverage containers with RAN levels of less than 0.1 ppm is technologically feasible.

[20] In view of the new data generated in response to the Court's inquiry, petitioners no longer contest that migration does occur from Monsanto's "Cycle–Safe" container (RAN level of 3.3 ppm) under the conditions of its intended use.

. . . The statutory definition of "food additive" . . . contains a two part test. First, the *component* element of the definition states that the intended use of the substance must be reasonably expected to result in its becoming a component of any food. Second, the *safety* element of the definition states that the substance must be not *"generally recognized [as] safe* under the conditions of its intended use."

. . . Congress did not intend that the component requirement of a "food additive" would be satisfied by a mere recitation of the diffusion principle, a mere finding of any contact whatever with food. . . .

For the component element of the definition to be satisfied, Congress must have intended the Commissioner to determine with a fair degree of confidence that a substance migrates into food in more than insignificant amounts. We do not suggest that the substance must be toxicologically significant; that aspect is subsumed by the safety element of the definition. Nor is it necessary that the level of migration be significant with reference to the threshold of direct detectability, so long as its presence in food can be predicted on the basis of a meaningful projection from reliable data. Congress has granted to the Commissioner a limited but important area of discretion. Although as a matter of theory the statutory net might sweep within the term "food additive" a single molecule of any substance that finds its way into food, the Commissioner is not required to determine that the component element of the definition has been satisfied by such an exiguous showing. The Commissioner has latitude under particular circumstances to find migration "insignificant" even giving full weight to the public health and welfare concerns that must inform his discretion.

Thus, the Commissioner may determine based on the evidence before him that the level of migration into food of a particular chemical is so negligible as to present no public health or safety concerns, even to assure a wide margin of safety. This authority derives from the administrative discretion, inherent in the statutory scheme, to deal appropriately with *de minimis* situations. However, if the Commissioner declines to define a substance as a "food additive," though it comes within the strictly literal terms of the statutory definition, he must state the reasons for exercising this limited exemption authority. In context, a decision to apply the literal terms of the statute, requires nothing more than a finding that the elements of the "food additive" definition have been satisfied.[27]

In the case at hand, the Commissioner made specific rulings that the component element of the definition was satisfied with respect to acrylonitrile beverage containers having an RAN level of 3.3 ppm or more. . . . In light of the supplementary submission made in response to the post-argument inquiry of this court, we find that the determination can be made for the 3.3 ppm RAN containers with an appropriate degree of confidence, and with the support of the required quantum of evidence.

---

[27] Absent a showing of bad faith or other extraordinary circumstances, a court will not consider meritorious the claim that the Commissioner has abused his discretion in declining to exercise his exemption authority for *de minimis* situations. This is an area of discretion by its nature committed to the informed discretion of the Commissioner.

Turning to the safety element of the definition, the Commissioner determined that the scientific community had insufficient experience with acrylonitrile to form a judgment as to safety. Based on this lack of opinion, the Commissioner made a finding that acrylonitrile was not generally recognized as safe within the meaning of the statute. The Commissioner acted within his discretion in making such a finding, but we note that the underlying premise may be affected, perhaps weakened, perhaps strengthened, with time and greater experience with acrylonitrile. This finding on the safety element will be open to reexamination on remand at the discretion of the Commissioner. He would have latitude to consider whether acrylonitrile is generally recognized as safe at concentrations below a certain threshold, even though he has determined for higher concentrations that in the view of the scientific community acrylonitrile is not generally recognized as safe.

. . . .

The decision of the Commissioner is affirmed in part, and in part is remanded to provide the opportunity for reconsideration.

NOTES

1.   *Subsequent Proceedings.* Following this decision, FDA, after evaluating the supplemented data and arguments, concluded that it was reasonable to expect some migration of acrylonitrile monomer, even from Monsanto's new acrylonitrile/styrene copolymer beverage bottle with a RAN level of only 0.10 ppm, and that the new bottle was thus a food additive. But the agency effectively invited Monsanto to submit a food additive petition for the new bottle, which it approved in 1984. 49 Fed. Reg. 36635 (Sept. 19, 1984), codified at 21 C.F.R. 1040. The agency later also issued a food additive regulation for the use of acrylonitrile/styrene copolymer for containers containing alcoholic beverages. 52 Fed. Reg. 33802 (Sept. 8, 1987).

2.   *Threshold of Regulation.* For many years, even prior to the 1979 decision in *Monsanto v. Kennedy*, the food packaging industry concluded that migration of a component of food packaging into food at "trace" levels (which ranged at various times from 2 ppm to 2 ppb to the low ppt) should be regarded as "toxicologically insignificant" and thus not subject to the Food Additives Amendment. FDA initially declined to accept this approach, although it acknowledged that some approach to determining a "threshold of regulation" should be established.

In 1995, FDA decided that a substance migrating into food from a food contact article is exempt from the requirement of obtaining a food additive regulation if (1) it is not a carcinogen, and (2) it results in dietary concentrations at or below 0.5 ppb. 60 Fed. Reg. 36582 (July 17, 1995), codified at 21 C.F.R. 170.39. Although the procedure established by the rule is based on requests for written FDA exemptions, any migration at this low level could clearly also be the subject of a self-determination of GRAS status.

3.   *Accidental Additives.* Compare *Gerber Products Co. v. Fisher Tank Co.*, 833 F.2d 505 (4th Cir. 1987) (holding that a liner on the interior of a

hot water storage tank used in processing baby foods was an indirect and unapproved food additive, thereby rendering all processed products adulterated), with *Burke Pest Control, Inc. v. Joseph Schlitz Brewing Co.*, 438 So. 2d 95 (Fla. Dist. Ct. App. 1983) (holding that a pesticide introduced into food during fumigation of the food plant was not a food additive but an accidental additive, whose legal status must be determined under section 402(a)(1) rather than under section 409).

4. *Heat Susceptors.* New technology may force FDA to reevaluate existing requirements for indirect food additives. Following the development of microwave ovens, makers of food packaging began to incorporate "heat susceptor" components into their products. These components resulted in a higher temperature than used in conventional ovens, thus raising the possibility that previously-approved food packaging materials might migrate into food at higher levels than the agency had anticipated or that migrating substances could degrade into unanticipated byproducts. In 54 Fed. Reg. 37340 (Sept. 8, 1989), FDA requested information on the use and safety of this form of packaging. The agency has taken no further action on this matter.

5. *Shopping Bags.* Although shopping bags come into contact with food and thus are within FDA jurisdiction, the agency does not regard food contact for such a short period of time to require regulation. *See* "Degradable Commodity Plastics Procurement and Standards Act of 1989," Hearing before the Senate Committee on Governmental Affairs, 101st Cong., 1st Sess. 21, 23 (1989).

6. *Bisphenol A (BPA).* The chemical BPA has been used for decades in the manufacture of hard plastic food containers and other food contact materials, but concerns have been raised about its effect on the brain and prostate gland of fetuses, infants, and children. In 2008, a subcommittee of FDA's Science Board recommended further study of the safety of BPA, following FDA's original conclusion that BPA is safe for humans. The Science Board approved the subcommittee report, agreeing that FDA should reconsider its conclusion. The agency agreed that due to uncertainties raised by some studies relating to the potential effects of low-dose exposure to BPA, additional research was warranted. *See* "FDA Statement on Release of Bisphenol A (BPA) Subcommittee Report," October 28, 2008 (available on FDA website). On the same day as the issuance of this statement, the Natural Resources Defense Council (NRDC) submitted a citizen petition requesting that FDA issue a regulation prohibiting the use of BPA in all human food and food packaging. When FDA failed to respond to the petition in a timely manner, NRDC sued the agency. In December 2011, the agency settled this suit by agreeing to respond to the petition by March 31, 2012. One day before this deadline, FDA denied the petition, stating that the most appropriate course of action was further study. Letter from David H. Dorsey, Acting Assoc. Comm'r for Policy and Planning, FDA, to Sarah Janssen and Aaron Colangelo, NRDC (Mar. 30, 2012) (available on FDA website). But on July 17, 2012, the agency amended the relevant food additive regulation to prohibit the use of BPA in baby bottles and children's drinking cups—a decision it framed as merely a codification of current industry practice. 77 Fed. Reg. 41899 (July 17, 2012), codified at 21 C.F.R. 177.1580.

7.   *The "Housewares Exemption."* Many household articles come into contact with food. These include pots, pans, cooking and eating utensils, home food preparation machines such as blenders and grinders, plates and glasses, and even the surfaces on which food is often laid during the stages of its preparation, such as counter tops. Under a longstanding policy, FDA generally has chosen not to regulate these articles as food additives. For more than twenty years after the enactment of the Food Additives Amendment of 1958, the agency followed this policy in both word (letters and oral opinions) and practice. However, in 1971, when the agency learned that high levels of lead were leaching from ceramic pottery into food, it initiated a formal compliance program to enforce a limit of 7 ppm on lead migration from pottery to food. Following a seizure on this basis, a U.S. District Court rejected the claimant manufacturer's assertions that the pottery in question was not "food" and that the lead could not be considered a "food additive." *United States v. Articles of Food Consisting . . . of Pottery,* 370 F. Supp. 371 (E.D. Mich. 1974).

In 1974, following this decision, FDA proposed to revoke the "housewares exemption." The agency explained: "Section 201(s) provides . . . no basis for an exemption for any houseware, food service, or food dispensing article or cleaning agent. . . . [T]o exempt [such articles] which may reasonably be expected to contribute significant amounts of harmful additives at the final and, arguably, most critical stage of food processing (*i.e.,* immediately before being ingested by the consumer) at the very time when technological advancements have vastly improved methods of detection and evaluation of their effect in man, would be in direct conflict with the express mandate of section 409(c)(5)(B) of the act." 39 Fed. Reg. 13285–86 (Apr. 12, 1974). But concern about the burden of processing several hundred food additive petitions caused FDA to vacillate about this proposal and ultimately to withdraw it. 69 Fed. Reg. 68833 (Nov. 26, 2004).

8.   *Lead in Housewares.* Despite its failure ever to formally revoke the "housewares exemption," FDA has continued to take regulatory actions against cookware and ceramic dinnerware containing leachable lead or cadmium. In 1979, it issued administrative guidelines for migration of lead and cadmium from ceramic ware that lowered the 1971 action levels mentioned in the previous note. 44 Fed. Reg. 47162 (Aug. 10, 1979). In 1992, the agency published a Compliance Policy Guide on lead contamination of ceramics that lowered the action levels (called "release levels") further still. 57 Fed. Reg. 29734 (July 6, 1992). Two years later, it mandated a "Not for Food Use" warning on ornamental and decorative ceramicware. 59 Fed. Reg. 1638 (Jan. 12, 1994), codified at 21 C.F.R. 109.16.

9.   *Other Lead Regulation.* Around the same time FDA started to address the problem of lead in housewares, it also acted to reduce lead residues in food by regulating lead-soldered cans. *See, e.g.,* 39 Fed. Reg. 42740 (Dec. 6, 1974) (proposed tolerance for lead in canned evaporated milk) (withdrawn 58 Fed. Reg. 33871 (June 21, 1983)); 58 Fed. Reg. 17233 (Apr. 1, 1993) (emergency action level for food packed in lead-soldered cans). Following widespread voluntary industry embrace of lead-free welded cans, the agency amended its food additive regulations to ban the use of lead soldered food cans altogether in 1995. 60 Fed. Reg. 33106 (June

27, 1995), codified at 21 C.F.R. 189.240. *See also* 61 Fed. Reg. 4816 (Feb. 8, 1996), codified at 21 C.F.R. 189.301 (banning lead foil for wine bottles).

In June 1995, FDA issued a letter warning about lead in candy wrappers, stating that lead levels exceeding 0.5 ppm in a candy product "would constitute a basis for regulatory action." In July 2004, the Consumer Product Safety Commission sent letters warning that lead in candy wrappers violated the Federal Hazardous Substances Act, 15 U.S.C. 1261. FDA released a draft guidance in December 2005 recommending that lead levels in candy likely to be consumed frequently by small children not exceed 0.1 ppm. In addition, FDA has determined that children's lunchboxes made from lead-contaminated polyvinyl chloride (PVC) violate the FD&C Act. Letter from Linda Tarantino, Director, FDA CFSAN Office of Food Additive Safety (July 20, 2006).

9. COLOR ADDITIVE REGULATION

a. HISTORICAL BACKGROUND

Official concern about the safety of food colorings surfaced as early as 1900, when Congress appropriated funds for USDA "to investigate the character of proposed food preservatives and coloring matters; to determine their relation to digestion and to health, and to establish the principles which should guide their use." 31 Stat. 191, 196 (1900). Dr. Bernhard Hesse, a German dye expert working under commission for the USDA, determined that little was known about the safety of the approximately 695 coal-tar colors then available. (Hesse later published his ongoing findings in a remarkable report, *Coal Tar Colors Used in Food Products*, USDA BUREAU OF CHEMISTRY BULL. No. 147 (1912).) Following passage of the 1906 Act, FDA acknowledged only seven coal-tar colors as safe for use in food. "Dyes, Chemicals, and Preservatives in Food," Food Inspection Decision (FID) No. 76 (June 18, 1907). The agency established a program to certify that individual batches of these colors met specifications. "Certificate and Control of Dyes Permissible for Use in Coloring Foods and Foodstuffs," FID No. 77 (Sept. 16, 1907). FDA took the position that its certification program was mandatory, but the issue was never tested in court. By 1938, the agency had recognized 15 colors as certifiable for use in food.

Section 406(b) of the original 1938 Act provided that "[t]he Secretary shall promulgate regulations providing for the listing of coal-tar colors which are harmless and suitable for use in foods." Following the Act's enactment, unfavorable publicity stemming from the association in the public mind of food colors with "thick, black, sticky" coal tars and from the Delaney Committee's 1950 investigation of the use of chemicals in foods caused FDA to tighten its enforcement of this provision. The agency promulgated regulations that required more animal studies with higher feeding levels before it would certify a color additive. More importantly, it redefined "harmless" to mean "substances incapable of producing harm in test animals in any quantity under any conditions." Under this unrealistic definition, eight color additives were delisted between 1956 and 1960, and the status of 19 others was placed in jeopardy. Pressure for a change in the law grew after the Supreme Court upheld the FDA definition of "harmless" and its ban on three popular color additives in *Flemming v. Florida Citrus Exchange*, 358 U.S. 153 (1958).

In response to the *Florida Citrus Exchange* decision, Congress enacted the Color Additives Amendment of 1960, 74 Stat. 397, codified primarily in section 721 (formerly 706) of the FD&C Act. While the Amendment also applies to substances used to color drugs, cosmetics, and devices, the following discussion focuses on colors that are used in food.

b.   THE COLOR ADDITIVES AMENDMENT

Section 201(t)(1)(B) defines a color additive as any material that, when added to food, is capable of imparting color, "except . . . any material which the Secretary, by regulation, determines is used (or intended to be used) solely for a purpose or purposes other than coloring." Soon after the enactment of the 1960 Amendment, FDA adopted a regulation limiting the circumstances in which the "except" clause might apply:

> For a material otherwise meeting the definition of "color additive" to be exempt from section 706 of the act, on the basis that it is used (or intended to be used) solely for a purpose or purposes other than coloring, the material must be used in a way that any color imparted is clearly unimportant insofar as the appearance, value, marketability, or consumer acceptability is concerned. (It is not enough to warrant exemption if conditions are such that the primary purpose of the material is other than to impart color.)

28 Fed. Reg. 6439 (June 22, 1963), codified at 21 C.F.R. 70.3(g).

The regulatory requirements applicable to color additives resemble those applicable to food additives, with important differences. The Color Additives Amendment requires premarket safety testing and FDA approval of all color additives, with no exceptions for GRAS or prior-sanctioned colors. The manufacturer or would-be user of a color additive may petition the agency for the issuance of a regulation permitting the color to be used in food. Before it may approve, or "list," a color additive, FDA must find, with reasonable certainty, that it poses no risk to human health (the same safety standard applicable to food additives), that it accomplishes the intended effect, and that its use will not result in deception of consumers. The agency is authorized to impose restrictions on the use of a color additive to assure that these criteria are satisfied. These restrictions may include limitations on levels of use, a requirement that individual batches of the color be certified by FDA to assure that the color additive used is identical to the substance tested, and specification of the products in which a color may be used.

The Color Additives Amendment contains an anti-cancer Delaney Clause very similar to the clause that appears in section 409. The color additives Delaney Clause is studied closely in Chapter 13, *infra* pp. 1405–1416. Because the 1960 Amendment does not recognize any GRAS colors or exclude substances that were sanctioned or used prior to 1960, Section 721 applies to all food coloring agents except those that are only provisionally listed while further safety testing is being conducted.

NOTES

1. *Provisional Listing.* While Congress did not "grandfather" color additives that were already in use in 1960, it did accord them special, though ostensibly temporary, status. Section 203 of the Color Additives Amendment, 74 Stat. 397, 404 (1960), which is not part of the codified FD&C Act, authorized FDA "provisionally" to list colors then in use that were believed to be safe, so as to allow manufacturers time to conduct the kind of toxicological testing required to support approval under the new law. Only colors that were in use in 1960 were eligible for provisional listing. FDA has maintained a list of provisionally approved color additives for more than 50 years, deleting those whose safety has come under serious challenge, and permanently listing others as scientific data have been submitted to confirm their safety. *See, e.g., Certified Color Manufacturers Association v. Mathews*, 543 F.2d 284 (D.C. Cir. 1976) (upholding the termination of the provisional listing of Red No. 2).

Following FDA's decision to require that most provisionally listed color additives be retested using modern protocols, 42 Fed. Reg. 6992 (Feb. 4, 1977), the Health Research Group began a continuous but unsuccessful effort to force the agency to remove from the market all those colors for which it had concluded that the existing safety data were inadequate. *See McIlwain v. Hayes*, 690 F.2d 1041 (D. C. Cir. 1982) (upholding continued provisional listing); *Public Citizen v. Department of HHS*, 632 F. Supp. 220 (D.D.C. 1986), *aff'd sub nom. Public Citizen v. Young*, 831 F.2d 1108 (D.C. Cir. 1987) (rejecting claim that the continued provisional listing for color additives found to be carcinogenic in test animals was illegal). The *McIlwain* Court remarked: "Undoubtedly, in 1960 many members of Congress anticipated that color additive testing would be completed more rapidly than has been the case with respect to some additives. Just as certainly, however, Congress foresaw that unavoidable delays were possible and provided a statutory mechanism for the Commissioner to cope with such problems." 690 F.2d at 1043. One explanation for FDA's long delay in resolving the status of color additives on the provisional list was its attempt to use the Color Additives Amendment to strengthen its controls over the safety of cosmetics. Industry challenges to this attempt took nine years to resolve. *See Toilet Goods Ass'n v. Finch*, 419 F.2d 21 (2d Cir. 1969) (excerpted *infra* p. 1322).

The last remaining color additive provisional listing, for FD&C Red No. 3, was terminated in 55 Fed. Reg. 3516 (Feb. 1, 1990), but even today the FD&C lakes (water-insoluble form of the dyes) remain provisionally listed. 21 C.F.R. 81.1. Nine FD&C colors subject to certification are now permanently listed for use in food. 21 C.F.R. 74.101, Subpart A.

2. *Approval by Product Category.* A color additive must have approval for each product category in which it is to be used. For example, an additive approved for cosmetic use cannot be used in a product that is both a cosmetic and a drug until it has also been approved for drug use. *See, e.g., United States v. Eight Unlabeled Cases . . . "French Bronze Tablets,"* 888 F.2d 945 (2d Cir. 1989); 52 Fed. Reg. 29664 (Aug. 11, 1987). The combination of letters "F," "D," and "C" in the name of a color additive (e.g., D&C Yellow No. 10 or FD&C Red. No. 3) indicates the approved uses

for that color. In 1993, however, FDA revised 21 C.F.R. 101.22(k)(1) to no longer require the use of the "FD&C" prefix (or the term "No.") on food labels. 58 Fed. Reg. 2850 (Jan. 6, 1993).

3. *Power to Allocate Uses.* Section 721(b)(8) authorizes FDA to ration the use of a color additive among competing products if safety data do not establish that exposure from all products in combination would be safe. The only time that FDA has considered this provision potentially applicable, it requested submissions on all uses of FD&C Red No. 3 as a first step toward allocating the allowable safe uses if this should become necessary. 52 Fed. Reg. 44485 (Nov. 19, 1987). FDA ultimately did not use this approach, however.

4. *Colors Used in Food Packaging.* Color additives used in food packaging are subject to the food additive provisions of the law. *See, e.g.,* 44 Fed. Reg. 7149 (Feb. 6, 1979); 53 Fed. Reg. 11402 (Apr. 6, 1988).

————————

In 2005, Kalsec, the manufacturer of rosemary extracts used to slow the browning of raw meat, filed the following citizen petition to ban the use of carbon monoxide gas to keep meat looking red and fresh. The document raises interesting questions regarding the definition of "color additive," the relationship between food additive and color additive regulation, and the standards for listing a color additive.

Kalsec, Inc., Citizen Petition Requesting FDA to Enforce Ban on Carbon Monoxide Gas in Fresh Meat Packaging

November 15, 2005.

. . . By this Citizen's Petition, Kalsec requests that FDA take immediate action to prohibit the use of carbon monoxide in the packaging of fresh meat, including to terminate the agency's unlawful responses to the Generally Recognized As Safe ("GRAS") notifications submitted by Pactiv Corp. and Precept Foods, Inc., and taking all such further actions as are necessary to effectively implement and enforce an immediate ban on carbon monoxide in fresh meat packaging, in coordination with USDA Food Safety and Inspection Service ("FSIS"). Kalsec advocates the actions requested to prevent serious harms to public health and consumer confidence in the integrity of the U.S. meat supply.

FDA has failed to object to [the] GRAS notifications for the unlawful use of carbon monoxide to impart color to fresh meat products. . . .

The use of carbon monoxide in fresh meat packaging presents serious food safety and consumer deception concerns of the same kinds that historically justified the broad-based ban on color additives in fresh meat products. Carbon monoxide obscures the natural coloration of meat that is indicative of freshness and safety, by reacting with the natural myoglobin in meat to produce carboxymyoglobin, a bright red substance that hides the true colors of meat, simulating the appearance of freshness and masking meat spoilage. This color-masking effect is particularly dangerous in anaerobic packaging environments such as those described in the Pactiv and Precept GRAS notifications, which potentially allow the proliferation of pathogens such as *Clostridium botulinum* but inhibit the growth of aerobic spoilage organisms that provide the tell-tale signs of spoilage upon which consumers rely, in addition to color change, to determine that meat is no longer safe to consume. . . .

. . . . Under FDCA requirements, food ingredients that constitute either "food additives" or "color additives" are prohibited, including in fresh meat products, except where FDA has determined the ingredient to be safe under the conditions of intended use and has promulgated regulations authorizing such use. Food ingredients that are established to be GRAS under the conditions of intended use are excluded from the FDCA premarket clearance requirements that apply to "food additives" but not from those that apply to "color additives." This means that, for a food ingredient that is established to be GRAS under certain conditions of use, the food ingredient may lawfully be used under such conditions without an authorizing food additive regulation. In contrast, for the same ingredient to be used for color additive purposes, FDA must promulgate regulations listing the food ingredient for specified conditions of color additive use. For example, while the established GRAS status of paprika for seasoning purposes eliminates the need for a food additive regulation to authorize seasoning uses, paprika could not be used under similar conditions for coloring purposes in the absence of the FDA regulations listing paprika specifically for color additive purposes.

. . . . Under . . . new coordinated FDA/FSIS [the Food Safety Inspection Service of USDA] procedures for expedited food ingredient review, petitions for food additives and color additives must be submitted to FDA, which is responsible for promulgating regulations authorizing these substances when they are safe under the intended conditions of use. Where the intended conditions of use encompass fresh meat products, the MOU provides that FDA and FSIS will jointly review petitions, and final FDA regulations will specify appropriate restrictions concerning such uses, as recommended by FSIS. . . .

Under FDCA section 721, adopted under the Color Additives Amendment of 1960, color additives are prohibited from use in food except under the defined conditions of use specified in by [sic] FDA regulations "listing" the particular color additive. Currently, there are no FDA regulations authorizing the use of carbon monoxide in fresh meat, as required by FDCA section 721.

Section 201(t)(1) of the FDCA defines "color additive" to mean any "substance made by a process of synthesis . . . or otherwise derived, with or without intermediate or final change of identity, . . . and when added or applied to a food. . . is capable (alone or through reaction with other substance) of imparting color thereto . . . "

Under well established FDA policy, "color additives" include substances that impart color through chemical reactions occurring after the substance is applied under the intended conditions of use. FDA has explained that "any chemical that reacts with another substance and causes formation of a color may be a color additive." For example, FDA has regulated colorless ingredients of sunless tanning lotions and hair dyes as color additives where these substances participate in color imparting reactions with chemicals naturally present in skin and hair during application.

FDA has also regulated ingredients of food as color additives when the ingredient subsequently participates in color-imparting chemical reactions under the conditions of intended use. For example, ingredients of animal feed intended for consumption by poultry and salmon have been regulated as color additives where the ingredients participate in metabolic reactions which intensify the color of the animal tissues intended for use as human food (e.g., intensified gold in egg yolks and red in salmon fillets).

. . . [C]arbon monoxide in fresh meat packaging imparts color to meat through chemical reactions with the myoglobin naturally occurring in meat tissues. . . .

When the oxygen in fresh meat packaging is displaced by carbon monoxide, the natural coloration provided by meat pigments is masked. Carbon monoxide binds firmly to myoglobin sites that otherwise would be bound more gently by oxygen, forming carboxymyoglobin in place of oxymyoglobin. . . . Carboxymyoglobin imparts a sustained bright red color to meat that simulates the appearance of freshness and safety in meat when the natural pigments would warn consumers otherwise.

. . . .

Section 721(b)(l) of the FDCA authorizes FDA to promulgate a regulation listing a color additive for use in food only "if and to the extent that such additives are suitable and safe for any such use when employed in accordance with such regulations." Further, section 721(b)(6) prohibits FDA from listing a color additive for a proposed use if that use "would promote deception of the consumer in violation of this Act or would otherwise result in misbranding or adulteration within the meaning of this Act." These provisions operate both independently and in conjunction to prohibit the listing of carbon monoxide for use in fresh meat packaging, for this use is neither safe nor suitable precisely because it promotes deception that results in serious food safety concerns.

Ensuring prevention of deception was an overarching principle behind the Color Additives Amendment, as revealed in the text and legislative history of those amendments, FDA implementing regulations, and interlocking FSIS meat additive regulations and suitability determinations. Significantly, Congress and FDA's predecessor agency were particularly concerned about the use of deceptive colorants in meat. . . .

. . . Carbon monoxide has . . . been shown to mask spoilage and color change due to aging by imparting an artificial red color that mimics that of fresh meat. The chemical thereby conceals damage and inferiority and makes meat appear to be of greater value than it is, within the meaning of the adulteration provisions of the FDCA and FMIA. As such, carbon monoxide in fresh meat packaging would promote consumer deception. Accordingly, FDA is prohibited by section

721(b)(6) of the FDCA from listing carbon monoxide for use in fresh meat packaging as a color additive.

. . . .

A central intent of Congress in enacting the Color Additive Amendments was to ensure that such additives will be safe under actual conditions of use. . . . FDA is required to consider actual conditions of consumer use when evaluating a color additive, and must have concrete evidence that the additive will be used safely. The House Report explains that a color additive may be listed for use only when it is shown that it may be safely used under the conditions prescribed by regulation. Moreover, the regulatory definition of "safe" with respect to color additives "means that there is convincing evidence that establishes with reasonable certainty that no harm will result from the intended use of the color additive." [21 C.F.R. 70.3(i).]

Neither FDA nor FSIS have evidence establishing that carbon monoxide in fresh meat packaging is safe under the actual conditions of use. To the contrary the evidence demonstrates that the use of carbon monoxide in anaerobic packaging systems for fresh meat poses genuine food safety risks under real-world conditions. . . .

The serious food safety concerns about, anaerobic packaging are substantially magnified when carbon monoxide is included among the oxygen-displacing gases. In such packaging systems, not only does the anaerobic environment inhibit aerobic spoilage organisms that provide the indications of spoilage to which consumers are accustomed, but the color-imparting effect of the carbon monoxide also masks the natural color change of meat due to aging and deceptively suggests freshness well past the microbial shelf life of the meat.

. . . .

FDA lacks authority to permit the use of carbon monoxide in fresh meat under FDCA requirements for food additives. Under well established FDA food additive regulations specifying the conditions in which carbon monoxide may be used to displace oxygen in food and beverage packaging, such use is expressly prohibited in fresh meat. Section 173.350 of FDA regulations prescribes the conditions under which "combustion product gas," including carbon monoxide gas, can be used to displace oxygen in food packaging. . . . The rule authorizes the use of carbon monoxide gas in food packaging at levels up to 4.5 percent by volume, provided that "[i]t is used or intended for use to displace or remove oxygen in . . . the packaging of beverage products and other food, except fresh meats" and other conditions are satisfied.

. . . [S]ection 173.350 is properly construed as a food additive regulation that encompasses and regulates the conditions of use concerning carbon monoxide in food packaging to remove or displace oxygen. . . . Clearly, where conditions of use have been established for a "food additive," these conditions of use cannot at the same time be excluded from the scope of food additive regulation as "GRAS." On this ground, the conditions of use of carbon monoxide in fresh meat packaging defined in the Pactiv and Precept GRAS notifications cannot qualify as "GRAS," as a matter of law, since these have already been established as "food additive" uses that are regulated directly and explicitly prohibited by section 173.350.

. . . Under FDCA section 201(s), "GRAS" substances are distinguished from and excluded from the scope of the "food additive" definition. Accordingly, under the same specified conditions of intended use, a substance cannot qualify at once as both a "GRAS" substance and a "food additive." . . . [T]he fresh meat prohibition in section 173.350 is best explained as a reflection of the overlapping premarket clearance requirements for color additives. Since FDA has not listed carbon monoxide in fresh meat as required by the FDCA color additive provisions, FDA reasonably codified the prohibition as a specification in the relevant food additive regulation. Notably, GRAS status provides no insulation from FDA premarket clearance requirements for a color additive. . . .

More fundamentally, despite the FDA responses to the Pactiv and Precept GRAS notifications, the sizable body of scientific evidence makes clear that the safety of carbon monoxide is not "generally recognized" as required by the FDCA. To the contrary, the safety of carbon monoxide in fresh meat has been widely challenged in the United States and internationally because of its capacity to mask spoilage and promote consumer deception. . . .

NOTES

1.   *Subsequent Events.* The Kalsec petition still has not been either acted on by the agency or withdrawn by the company. In October and November 2007, a subcommittee of the House Agriculture Committee and a subcommittee of the House Energy and Commerce Committee held competing hearings on the use of carbon monoxide in packaging meat. As recently as January 2012, in response to two GRAS notifications for carbon monoxide in different systems for treating meat, FDA sent letters stating "no questions at this time," thus implicitly suggesting that the agency still does not deem carbon monoxide to be a color additive ineligible for a GRAS notification. *See* Agency Response Letters re. GRN 000194 & GRN 000251 (January 25, 2012) (available on FDA website).

2.   *Deceptive Coloring of Human Food.* Section 721(b)(6) prohibits the listing of colors if the proposed use would "promote deception of the consumer." Deceptive use of color additives in human food has been a persistent concern. When FDA updated the standards of identity for bakery products, a major issue was the use of color additives, and of colored butter, margarine, and spices, to impart a yellow color to final bakery products that would suggest a higher butter or egg content. After conducting a full administrative hearing, *see* 41 Fed. Reg. 6242 (Feb. 12, 1976); Food Drug Cosm. L. Rep. (CCH) ¶ 38,239 (1979); 48 Fed. Reg. 51448 (Nov. 9, 1983); 49 Fed. Reg. 13690 (Apr. 6, 1984), FDA determined that, except for such color as is naturally present in spices, butter, or margarine, coloring may not be added as such or as part of another ingredient to standardized bakery products. 21 C.F.R. 136.110(c)(16), (17).

3.   *Nitrite.* The plaintiffs in *Public Citizen v. Foreman, supra* p. 601, also petitioned FDA to declare nitrite a color additive (and thus unlawful because it lacked either a provisional or permanent listing). FDA concluded that nitrite is not a color additive because, although "fixing" color to bacon and other red meat, it does not "impart" that color. 45 Fed. Reg. 77043

(Nov. 21, 1980). This conclusion was eventually upheld. *Public Citizen v. Hayes*, Food Drug Cosm. L. Rep. (CCH) ¶ 38,161 (D.D.C. 1982).

4. *Animal Drugs Used to Color Poultry.* The use of new animal drugs to provide pigmentation to poultry and egg yolks poses similar issues. *See, e.g.*, 47 Fed. Reg. 31429 (July 20, 1982), 49 Fed. Reg. 38193 (Sept. 27, 1984).

5. *Colors Used in Pet Food.* In 44 Fed. Reg. 28418 (May 15, 1979), FDA denied a petition to prohibit color additives in dog and cat food. The petition alleged that use of color in these products promotes consumer deception by masking the amount of meat these products contain. FDA stated that section 721(b)(6) generally applies only "where the use of color cannot be readily discerned and the use of a label declaration of its presence would not prevent deception of the consumer." The agency found no evidence that use of color in pet food was deceptive. FDA's subsequent denial of a formal evidentiary hearing, 46 Fed. Reg. 7443 (Jan. 23, 1981), was not challenged.

Under the Color Additives Amendment, FDA can impose conditions of use on a listed color, including "directions or other labeling or packaging requirements." FD&C Act 721(b)(3).

FD&C Yellow No. 5: Labeling in Food and Drugs for Human Use

44 Fed. Reg. 37212 (June 26, 1979).

In the FEDERAL REGISTER of May 8, 1969, the Food and Drug Administration (FDA) issued an order listing FD&C Yellow No. 5 (also commonly known as tartrazine) for use in foods under § 74.705 and for use in ingested drugs under § 74.1705. This action was supported by safety data in a color additive petition and other relevant data.... At the time of listing for food and ingested drug use, no specific restrictions were placed on the use of FD&C Yellow No. 5 other than that it be subject to batch certification by FDA.... Because of mounting evidence of allergic-type reactions to FD&C Yellow No. 5, the agency believes it is now appropriate to require that the presence of the color be specifically identified on the label of products in which it is used.

. . . .

This final rule requires the label of all foods containing FD&C Yellow No. 5 to declare the presence of the color additive as FD&C Yellow No. 5. In the case of drugs, a slightly different label declaration is required. The presence of FD&C Yellow No. 5 must be declared by both names by which it is known (FD&C Yellow No. 5 and tartrazine) for OTC and prescription drug products which are administered orally, nasally, rectally, or vaginally, but not for topical or other externally applied drug products. In addition, labeling for the prescription drug products subject to the rule will be required to contain a precautionary statement on possible allergic reactions to the use of FD&C Yellow No. 5. . . .

Since FD&C Yellow No. 5 was listed for use in food and ingested drugs, evidence has accumulated of allergic-type responses in humans, not rats, caused by ingestion of foods or drugs containing the color. There have been increasing numbers of reports that these responses to FD&C Yellow No. 5 occur primarily in patients who also have aspirin intolerance. The phenomenon of aspirin intolerance in certain persons with underlying allergic disorders, including bronchial asthma, nasal polyposis, vasomotor rhinitis, and skin allergies to various substances, has been known for over 50 years. Both the aspirin and the FD&C Yellow No. 5 reactions are manifested by asthmatic symptoms, urticaria, angioedema, or nasal symptoms. . . .

. . . . Several comments contended that color additives provide no "benefit" to the public and that their use is purely cosmetic and concluded, therefore, that their use should not be sanctioned by FDA. . . . Congress has made the judgment that color additives that have been shown to be safe should be permitted in food. The role of FDA under the act is not to make the value judgment about whether color additives are "beneficial," but rather to evaluate the data submitted in support of color additive petitions and to approve for use in foods, drugs, cosmetics, and devices those colors that the agency is reasonably certain are safe. Congress has made the collective judgment that color additives are "beneficial" and should be permitted to be used if shown to be safe. . . .

The primary basis for this action is section 706(b)(3) [now 721(b)(3)] of the Federal Food, Drug, and Cosmetic Act, which provides that regulations for the listing of a color additive shall "prescribe the conditions under which such additive may be safely employed for such use or uses (including, but not limited to . . . and directions or other labeling or packaging requirements for such additive)." . . .

NOTES

1. *Yellow No. 6.* FDA's efforts to require label declaration of FD&C Yellow No. 6 because of similar allergic reactions were unsuccessful.

2. *Color Additives and Hyperactivity in Children.* In the early 1970s, an allergist, Ben F. Feingold, concluded that synthetic colors, synthetic flavors, and salicylates were causing hyperactivity in children. Feingold developed a diet free of such substances and reported that 50 percent of hyperactive children dramatically improved their behavior when following it. In 1977, however, a controlled clinical trial by a group of researchers at the University of Wisconsin failed to confirm such an effect. *See Food Additives and Hyperactivity*, 199 SCIENCE 516 (1978). The theory survives, however, and received new attention after a 2007 British study concluded that food colorings worsened hyperactive behavior in children diagnosed with attention deficit and hyperactivity disorder (ADHD) and also affected other children. In 2008, the Center for Science in the Public Interest (CSPI) submitted a petition (dedicated to Feingold) asking FDA to ban eight of the nine currently listed certified FD&C food dyes and, in the interim, to require a warning regarding hyperactivity and behavioral problems on foods containing these dyes. CSPI, Petition to Ban the use of Yellow 5 and Other Food Dyes (June 3, 2008). In September 2010, FDA concluded, based

on a literature review, that "a causal relationship between exposure to color additives and hyperactivity in children in the general population has not been established" but that "for certain susceptible children with ADHD and other problem behavior, the data suggest that their condition may be exacerbated." Interim Toxicology Review Memorandum, Docket No. FDA–2008–P–0349 (Sept. 1, 2010) (performed in connection with CSPI petition). The FDA Food Advisory Committee held hearings on the issue on March 30–31, 2011, but the agency has not taken any action on the petition.

10. DIETARY INGREDIENTS IN DIETARY SUPPLEMENTS

In addition to broadly defining dietary supplements and explicitly authorizing strong new claims for these products, the Dietary Supplement Health and Education Act of 1994 significantly altered the statutory scheme for regulating their safety. These changes are embodied in three main amendments to the FD&C Act. First, DSHEA revised the definition of "food additive" to exclude "an ingredient described in paragraph (ff) [the definition of "dietary supplement"] in, or intended for use in, a dietary supplement." FD&C Act 201(s)(6). Dietary ingredients in dietary supplements are thus automatically exempt from the premarket approval mechanism for food additives, whether or not they would qualify as GRAS or as prior-sanctioned. Second, Congress enacted a special adulteration provision for dietary supplements at section 402(f), which provides that a food is adulterated:

(1) If it is a dietary supplement or contains a dietary ingredient that—

(A) presents a significant or unreasonable risk of illness or injury under—

(i) conditions of use recommended or suggested in labeling, or

(ii) if no conditions of use are suggested or recommended in the labeling, under ordinary conditions of use;

(B) is a new dietary ingredient for which there is inadequate information to provide reasonable assurance that such ingredient does not present a significant or unreasonable risk of illness or injury;

(C) the Secretary *& HHS* declares to pose an imminent hazard to public health or safety, except that the authority to make such declaration shall not be delegated . . . ; or

(D) is or contains a dietary ingredient that renders it adulterated under paragraph (a)(1) under the conditions of use recommended or suggested in the labeling of such dietary supplement.

In any proceeding under this subparagraph, the United States shall bear the burden of proof on each element to show that a dietary supplement is adulterated. The court shall decide any issue under this paragraph on a de novo basis.

Third, as reflected in paragraph B, DSHEA established a new review mechanism for "new dietary ingredients." FD&C Act 413, also added by DSHEA, defines "new dietary ingredient" as "a dietary ingredient that was not marketed in the United States before October 15, 1994 [ten days prior to the enactment of DSHEA]." FD&C Act 413(d). Section 413 further provides that new dietary ingredients are required to be the subject of a premarket notification submitted to FDA at least 75 days before marketing. (This requirement does not apply to new dietary ingredients in dietary supplements that "contain[ ] only dietary ingredients which have been present in the food supply as an article used for food in a form in which the food has not been chemically altered." *Id.* 413(a)(2).) The 75-day notification must provide information "which is the basis on which the manufacturer . . . has concluded that a dietary supplement containing [the new] dietary ingredient will reasonably be expected to be safe." *Id.* 413(a)(2). The failure to submit a required 75-day notification constitutes adulteration in and of itself. *Id.* 413(a). Moreover, as stated in section 402(f)(1)(B), FDA may take action against a dietary supplement containing a new dietary ingredient if it can prove "that there is inadequate information to provide reasonable assurance that the ingredient does not present a significant or unreasonable risk of illness or injury." Thus, for new dietary supplement ingredients, Congress has effectively repealed the premarket approval requirements of the 1958 Amendment and replaced it with a premarket notification process.

NOTES

1.   *Limitation to Dietary Ingredients.* The safety provisions of the Dietary Supplement Health and Education Act of 1994 apply only to the dietary ingredients in a dietary supplement, not to the accompanying functional ingredients such as preservatives, fillers, stabilizers, and other components.

2.   *De Novo Judicial Review.* The final sentence of section 402(f)(1), as added by DSHEA, provides that in a court enforcement action under this provision the court shall decide the issue of adulteration of a dietary supplement "on a de novo basis." In *NVE Inc.* v. *Department of Health and Human Services*, 436 F.3d 182 (3d Cir. 2006), the Court of Appeals held that this provision does not apply to a challenge to rulemaking brought under the Administrative Procedure Act. *Nutraceutical Corporation v. Eschenbach*, excerpted below, similarly held: "[I]t is appropriate to limit the de novo standard of review, which affords the FDA no deference, to enforcement proceedings. Challenges by private parties to FDA rules promulgated under DSHEA are reviewed pursuant to the Administrative Procedure Act, and the normal rules for judicial deference regarding agency action apply." 459 F.3d 1033, 1037 (10th Cir. 2006).

3.   *New Dietary Ingredient Notifications.* In 1997, FDA promulgated a final regulation implementing the FD&C Act's premarket notification requirements for dietary supplements that contain a new dietary ingredient. 62 Fed. Reg. 49886 (September 23, 1997), codified at 21 C.F.R. 190.6.

4.   *New Dietary Ingredient "Present in the Food Supply."* As mentioned above, under section 413(a)(1), a new dietary ingredient is not required to submit a notice to FDA 75 days before marketing if it has been "present in the food supply as an article used for food in a form in which the

food has not been chemically altered." This provision applies to ingredients marketed in the form of dietary supplements with a history of use in conventional food. In a letter from Lynn A. Larsen, Director, FDA CFSAN Office of Special Nutritionals Division of Programs and Enforcement Policy, to John C. Young (Nov. 20, 1998), FDA took the position that the mere incidental presence of components of a dietary ingredient as inherent components of a food marketed in the United States before October 15, 1994 does not satisfy this requirement. The letter stated that the company would have to show that the dietary ingredient itself has been used as a food or as an ingredient in a food without chemical alteration. The dietary supplement industry, however, interprets this provision to exempt inherent constituents in food from the requirement of a new dietary ingredient notification. FDA held a public meeting to consider the proper interpretation of this provision, but has not taken further action on the matter. 69 Fed. Reg. 61680 (Oct. 20, 2004) (announcing meeting).

5. *Guidance.* For a detailed exposition of FDA's understanding of the requirements for new dietary ingredients, see DRAFT GUIDANCE FOR INDUSTRY: DIETARY SUPPLEMENTS: NEW DIETARY INGREDIENT NOTIFICATIONS AND RELATED ISSUES (July 2011).

6. *Compared to Food Safety Provisions.* Even in light of the changes made by DSHEA in 1994, the FD&C Act arguably provides somewhat greater regulatory authority over the safety of dietary supplements than over the safety of conventional food—or at least conventional food containing only GRAS substances. For example, there is no GRAS exception to the required premarket notification of new dietary ingredients in dietary supplements. Furthermore, FDA has authority to declare a dietary supplement but not a conventional food to be an imminent hazard. *See* Peter Barton Hutt, *FDA Statutory Authority to Regulate the Safety of Dietary Supplements*, 31 AM. J. OF LAW & MED. 155 (2005). It is important to remember, however, that because dietary ingredients are explicitly excluded from the food additive definition, FD&C Act 201(s)(6), they are exempted from the requirement of premarket approval. In this respect, FDA has less authority to regulate the safety of dietary supplements than the safety of conventional foods.

Nutraceutical Corporation v. Von Eschenbach

459 F.3d 1033 (10th Cir. 2006).

■ EAGAN, DISTRICT JUDGE (sitting by designation).

Plaintiffs-appellees, Nutraceutical Corporation and its wholly-owned subsidiary . . . manufacture and sell Ephedra, a product containing ephedrine-alkaloid dietary supplements ("EDS"). In 2004, the FDA issued a regulation which banned all EDS sales in the United States market. Nutraceutical brought this action challenging the regulation as unlawful. The district court agreed with Nutraceutical. . . . [W]e reverse.

. . . .

The issues raised by this appeal are: (1) whether the FDA correctly interpreted the relevant statute to require a risk-benefit analysis in determining if a dietary supplement presents an "unreasonable risk of illness or injury"; and (2) whether the FDA satisfied its burden of proving that dietary supplements containing EDS present an unreasonable risk of illness or injury when doses of 10 mg or less per day are suggested or recommended in labeling.

. . . In 1994, Congress amended the FDCA with the Dietary Supplement Heath and Education Act ("DSHEA"). Under DSHEA . . . a dietary supplement is "adulterated":

If it is a dietary supplement or contains a dietary ingredient that—

(A) presents a significant or unreasonable risk of illness or injury under—

(i) conditions of use recommended or suggested in labeling, or

(ii) if no conditions of use are suggested or recommended in the labeling, under ordinary conditions of use; . . .

21 U.S.C. § 342(f)(1). The FDA argues that EDS are adulterated and points to the "unreasonable risk of illness or injury" provision of DSHEA as the primary source of statutory authority for its EDS ban. 21 U.S.C. § 342(f)(1)(A).

Ephedrine alkaloids are a class of structurally-related chemical stimulants that occur naturally in some botanicals. In the 1980s and 1990s, manufacturers promoted the sale of EDS for weight loss and athletic performance enhancement. In the 1990s, the FDA received numerous Adverse Event Reports ("AERs") which documented harmful side effects, including heart attacks, strokes, seizures, and death, associated with EDS intake. Based on the circumstantial evidence of the AERs, the FDA began to investigate the effects of EDS. . . .

After seven years of investigating EDS, the FDA adopted a regulation which banned EDS at all dosage levels from the national market. 69 Fed. Reg. 6788 (Feb. 11, 2004) ("Final Rule"). In the Final Rule, the FDA concluded that "[t]he best clinical evidence for a benefit . . . supports only a modest short-term weight loss, insufficient to positively affect cardiovascular risk factors or health conditions associated with being overweight or obese." Based on this risk-benefit analysis, the FDA determined that all EDS present an "unreasonable risk of illness or injury" under all ordinary or recommended conditions of use. As such, the Final Rule classified EDS adulterated within the meaning of DSHEA.

The district court held that "the FDA's requirement that EDS demonstrate a benefit is contrary to the clear intent of Congress" and found the agency's definition of "unreasonable" as entailing a risk-benefit analysis to be improper. The district court also found that the FDA failed "to prove by a preponderance of the evidence that a dosage of 10 mg or less of ephedrine alkaloids presents a significant or unreasonable risk of illness or injury." Based on these findings, the district court granted summary judgment for plaintiffs and denied summary judgment for defendants.

. . . .

A court reviewing the FDA's construction of the FDCA must determine: whether Congress has directly spoken to precise question at issue; and if not, then whether agency's construction of statute is a permissible one. *Chevron U.S.A., Inc. v. Natural Res. Def. Council, Inc.*, 467 U.S. 837 (1984). . . .

"Unreasonable Risk"

In this case, we must determine whether Congress unambiguously manifested its intent to restrict the FDA from weighing benefits when determining the risk posed by a dietary supplement. The district court was correct to proceed under *Chevron* step one in deciding the question of whether the FDA properly used a risk-benefit analysis in determining whether EDS pose an "unreasonable risk." We nevertheless reverse the district court after finding that Congress unambiguously required the FDA to conduct a risk-benefit analysis under DSHEA.

. . . DSHEA classifies a dietary supplement as adulterated if it "presents a significant or unreasonable risk of illness or injury." 21 U.S.C. § 342(f)(1). The FDA understood "[t]he plain meaning of 'unreasonable' . . . [to] connote[ ] comparison of the risks and benefits of the product." 69 Fed. Reg. 6788, 6823 (2004). We agree. The plain language of the statute directs the FDA to restrict distribution of dietary supplements which pose any risk that is unreasonable in light of its potential benefits. . . .

. . . The FDCA should not be read too restrictively but in manner consistent with the statute's overriding purpose to protect public health. Accordingly, DSHEA should receive a liberal construction where the FDA has taken remedial steps in response to a perceived public health problem.

According to the district court, by injecting a risk-benefit analysis, the FDA required Nutraceutical to make a showing of the benefits of its product. However, at no time has the FDA required manufacturers of EDS to provide data on the benefits of their products. Rather, the FDA has assumed its responsibility of gathering data, soliciting comments, and conducting the risk-benefit analysis. Congress expressly placed the burden of proof on the government to determine whether a dietary supplement is adulterated. Accordingly, EDS were allowed to enter the market without findings of safety or effectiveness. The FDA did not impose a pre-market requirement for the sale of EDS. . . . [A]s dictated by the statutory scheme, the FDA assumed the duty of post-market surveillance and imposed the EDS ban following numerous AERs, public notice and comment, and significant scientific review. Based on the record, we disagree with the district court and find that the FDA did not shift the burden of proof to manufacturers. . . .

. . . The rule [of statutory construction] against surplusage encourages courts to give meaning to every word used in a statute to realize congressional intent. In effect, this rule embodies the belief that Congress would not have included superfluous language. Thus, in DSHEA, an "unreasonable risk" has a meaning independent from a "significant risk." The plain meaning of a "significant risk" is a great danger. "Unreasonable risk" is a distinct term and requires more than evaluation of the significance of risk. "A risk could be significant but reasonable if the benefits were great enough to outweigh the risks." 69 Fed. Reg. at 6823. In other words, an "unreasonable risk" is relative to the circumstances; the potential risk is more "unreasonable" if the potential benefit is smaller. The district court erred by conflating the terms "significant" and "unreasonable," thereby rendering "unreasonable" superfluous. . . . The use of "unreasonable" to qualify risk in addition to "significant" makes it clear that Congress intended to integrate a risk-benefit analysis in the former. . . .

"Conditions of Use"

Under DSHEA, the government bears the burden of proof to show that, "under conditions of use recommended or suggested in labeling," a dietary supplement is adulterated. 21 U.S.C. § 342(f)(1)(A)(i). It is undisputed that the FDA must consider the dosage recommended in a dietary supplement's labeling when making an adulteration determination under section 342(f)(1)(A). The district court held that the FDA failed "to prove by a preponderance of the evidence that a dosage of 10 mg or less of ephedrine alkaloids presents a significant or unreasonable risk of illness or injury, [and] has failed to give effect to the dose-specific language of [ ] § 342(f)(1)(A)(I).".

In determining that EDS pose an "unreasonable risk of illness or injury," the FDA found that the weight loss and other health benefits possible from the use of EDS were dwarfed by the potential long-term harm to the user's cardiovascular system. The agency went on to enact a complete ban on the product after making a finding that any amount of EDS had negative ramifications on the cardiovascular system and, based on the FDA's analysis, EDS provided no benefits so great as to justify such risk.

. . . The evidence relied on by the FDA to enact its ban of EDS covers over seven years of agency review, public notice and comment, peer-reviewed literature, and scientific data. It is the purview of the FDA to weigh the evidence, including the evidence submitted by Nutraceutical and other manufacturers during public notice and comment.

. . . .

The majority of data in the administrative record suggests that EDS pose an unreasonable threat to the public's health. . . . The evidence in the administrative record was sufficiently probative to demonstrate by a preponderance of the evidence that EDS at any dose level pose an unreasonable risk. . . .

The FDA's extensive research identified the dose level at which ephedrine alkaloids present unreasonable risk of illness or injury to be so minuscule that no amount of EDS is reasonably safe. . . . The FDA was not arbitrary or capricious in its Final Rule; the FDA met its statutory burden of justifying a total ban of EDS by a preponderance of the evidence.

We find that the FDA correctly followed the congressional directive to analyze the risks and benefits of EDS in determining that there is no dosage level of EDS acceptable for the market. Summary judgment for plaintiffs was therefore improper, and summary judgment for defendants should have been entered. . . .

NOTES

1. *Subsequent History.* Nutraceutical filed a petition for writ of certiorari with the Supreme Court in January 2007, asking the Court to determine the appropriate adulteration standard for FDA to utilize under DSHEA. However, the Court denied certiorari on May 14, 2007, thus preserving the Tenth Circuit's holding. *Nutraceutical Corp. v. Von Eschenbach,* 550 U.S. 933 (2007). The Eleventh Circuit similarly held that the FDA regulation declaring dietary supplements containing ephedrine alkaloids to be adulterated was valid. *Hi–Tech Pharmaceuticals v. Crawford,* 544 F.3d 1187 (11th Cir. 2008).

2. *Section 411.* As discussed previously, *supra* p. 323, note 4, FD&C Act 411 was enacted in 1976 in response to efforts by FDA to stringently regulate vitamin and mineral supplements. Among the ways in which section 411 limits FDA's authority to restrict the composition of these products is a provision stating that FDA "may not establish, under section 201(n), 401, or 403, maximum limits on the potency of any synthetic or natural vitamin or mineral" within a supplement. FD&C Act 411(a)(1)(A). Note, however, that this provision does not restrict FDA's authority to establish potency limits on vitamin and mineral supplements pursuant to section 402, governing adulteration.

3. *Adverse Event Reporting.* In December 2006, Congress enacted the Dietary Supplement and Nonprescription Drug Consumer Protection Act (DSNDCPA), 120 Stat. 3469, which added sections 760 and 761 to the FD&C Act to require serious adverse event reporting to FDA for both dietary supplements and nonprescription drugs. The law provides that such a report does not constitute an admission that the product caused the adverse event, and it preempts any non-identical state law. In March 2009, the GAO stated that under-reporting of serious adverse events has presented an obstacle to educating consumers about dietary supplements. The report highlighted several factors which limit FDA's ability to further identify and act on safety concerns. These factors include a lack of information from companies, the fact that companies are not required to provide FDA with information on products they sell, and FDA's relatively few resources devoted to dietary supplement oversight activities. DIETARY SUPPLEMENTS: FDA SHOULD TAKE FURTHER ACTIONS TO IMPROVE OVERSIGHT AND CONSUMER UNDERSTANDING, GAO–09–250 (Jan. 2009). FDA has published guidance on dietary supplement adverse event reporting. GUIDANCE FOR INDUSTRY: QUESTIONS AND ANSWERS REGARDING ADVERSE EVENT REPORTING AND RECORDKEEPING FOR DIETARY SUPPLEMENTS AS REQUIRED BY THE DIETARY SUPPLEMENT AND NONPRESCRIPTION DRUG CONSUMER PROTECTION ACT (rev. June 2009).

11. ANIMAL DRUG RESIDUES

When a drug is used in a food producing animal (e.g., a cow), some residue of that drug, or a metabolite of the drug, may appear in the food produced by the animal (i.e., the milk or meat). Regulation of animal drugs combines features of both food safety regulation and drug regulation. This subject is considered in detail in Chapter 8, and the animal drug anti-cancer Delaney Clause is examined in Chapter 13.

12. PESTICIDE RESIDUES

The 1910 Insecticide Act, 36 Stat. 331, regulated the labeling of insecticides. The core of the current Federal Insecticide, Fungicide, and Rodenticide Act (FIFRA), 7 U.S.C. 136 *et seq.*, was enacted in 61 Stat. 163 (1947) to replace the 1910 Act. FIFRA requires premarket approval ("registration") of all pesticides distributed or sold in the United States. Like the FD&C Act, FIFRA has been amended on several occasions, including three times in the 1970s, again in 1988, and most recently in 1996, and it has become an environmental and health protection statute.

Regulation of pesticide residues in food implicates both FIFRA and the FD&C Act. First, no pesticide may be sold for use on food crops or in food processing unless it has been registered under FIFRA. Second, any pesticide intended for use on a raw agricultural commodity must be the subject of a tolerance established under section 408 of the FD&C Act, which was added by the Miller Pesticides Amendment, 68 Stat. 511 (1954). Section 402(a)(2)(B) provides that a food is adulterated "if it bears or contains a pesticide residue that is unsafe within the meaning of section 408(a)." Third, as a result of the Food Quality Protection Act of 1996, 110 Stat. 1489, 1513, a pesticide approved for use in or on a raw agricultural commodity is exempt from the requirement of a food additive regulation under section 409 of the Act when the raw commodity is used in a processed food. FD&C Act 408(a)(2). Accordingly, "pesticide chemicals," whether in processed foods or raw commodities, are excluded from the Food Additives Amendment, including the Delaney Clause. *See* FD&C Act 201(s)(1)–(2) (exempting both "a pesticide chemical residue in or on a raw agricultural commodity or processed food" and "a pesticide chemical" from the definition of "food additive"). *See also infra* pp. 1425–1429 (discussion of the "Delaney Paradox"). Fourth, where a pesticide is lawfully applied to a "target" commodity but a residue also occurs in another "nontarget" food—e.g., because the wind has transported it or it has been absorbed from the soil in a later growing season—a section 406 action level must be established to control it.

Administration of FIFRA and the FD&C Act is bifurcated. Prior to 1970, USDA was responsible for implementing FIFRA. Reorganization Plan No. 3 of 1970, 84 Stat. 2086, established the Environmental Protection Agency and transferred primary responsibility for pesticide functions to the new agency. EPA and FDA have reached agreement on their mutual responsibilities. 38 Fed. Reg. 24233 (Sept. 6, 1973), 40 Fed. Reg. 25078 (June 12, 1975). Briefly summarized, EPA registers pesticides under FIFRA, establishes pesticide tolerances under section 408, and recommends action levels for pesticide contaminants to FDA, while FDA establishes action levels under section 406 and enforces the limits EPA has established for pesticide residues in food.

NOTES

1.   *EPA Pesticide Registration.* EPA registration of pesticides for food use under FIFRA resembles FDA premarket approval of food additives, color additives, and new drugs. Some notable distinctive features exist, however. For example, FIFRA applies to all pesticides distributed or sold in

the United States, including those sold in intrastate commerce. Furthermore, FIFRA contains complex provisions governing the disclosure of registration data submitted by the pioneer manufacturer and its use by subsequent "me too" manufacturers. 7 U.S.C. 136a(c)(1)(D). The "me too" registrant must in some instances compensate the originator for use of the data under 40 C.F.R. Part 152, Subpart E.

Another unique characteristic of pesticide registration is that under 7 U.S.C. 136v, a state may forbid the sale or use of a pesticide registered by EPA, although it may not impose any labeling or packaging requirements in addition to or different from those established by EPA and may not allow any use of the pesticide on food or animal feed that is not lawful under the FD&C Act. Political subdivisions are barred from any form of pesticide regulation. *See Maryland Pest Control Ass'n v. Montgomery County, Maryland*, 646 F. Supp. 109 (D. Md. 1986), *aff'd without opinion*, 822 F.2d 55 (4th Cir. 1987). Finally, when EPA suspends and subsequently cancels registration of a pesticide, any person who owned any quantity of the pesticide immediately before the suspension notice is entitled to be indemnified under 7 U.S.C. 136m. *See, e.g.*, 49 Fed. Reg. 49796 (Dec. 21, 1984).

EPA imposes user fees for pesticide registration activities. 40 C.F.R. Part 152, Subpart U.

2. *Distinctive Features of Section 408 Tolerances for Pesticide Residues.* The standard under section 408(b)(2)(A)(i) for approval of a pesticide residue in food is that the residue must be safe, which is defined as a reasonable certainty of no harm. This standard was borrowed from the Food Additives Amendment. EPA must specifically find under section 408(b)(2)(C) that any pesticide tolerance is safe for infants and children. Under section 408(b)(2)(B), EPA is authorized to retain an existing tolerance for a pesticide residue posing more than a negligible risk if the pesticide protects consumers from a greater health risk than that posed by the pesticide itself, or if use of the pesticide is necessary to avoid a significant disruption in domestic production of an adequate, wholesome, and economical food supply.

3. *The Effect of Cancelled Registrations.* EPA used to retain the relevant section 408 tolerances and section 409 food additive regulations following cancellation of a FIFRA pesticide registration for as long as residues of the pesticide could occur in food as a result of environmental contamination. EPA abandoned this practice in 1982, however. It explained:

> When a pesticide's registration for a food or feed use is cancelled because of concern about the safety of the pesticide, the associated tolerance for use or food additive regulation is no longer justified and logically should be revoked. . . . For pesticides which degrade rapidly in the environment, particularly in the soil, revoking the tolerance should cause no problem because any pesticide residues remaining from applications prior to the cancellation action would not be expected to be present at detectable levels. However, for pesticides which persist in the environment, *i.e.*, which take long periods of time to degrade, crops may contain detectable residues of these pesticides, perhaps

even at or near the tolerance levels, for many years after the application of the cancelled pesticide has ceased. Similarly, the meat of animals fed crops containing such residues may also contain such residues. If the formal tolerances for persistent pesticides were revoked and no other action were taken, land to which the cancelled pesticides have been applied could be unavailable for crop use for many years to come. Therefore, in order to avoid unfairly penalizing food producers whose commodities may still contain unavoidable residues of persistent pesticides which can no longer be legally applied, the agencies have agreed to establish action levels to replace formal tolerances that will be revoked. The action levels will be reviewed periodically and lowered as the chemicals dissipate from the environment. . . .

47 Fed. Reg. 42956 (September 29, 1982).

4.   *The Impact of Public Pressure.* In the latter part of the 1980s, the Natural Resources Defense Council (NRDC) targeted daminozide (Alar®), a plant growth regulator, as a health hazard. EPA's denial of a petition to ban the pesticide in 1986 was upheld on procedural grounds in *Nader v. EPA*, 859 F.2d 747 (9th Cir. 1988). In response to claims that it was not protecting the public health, EPA reduced the tolerance for daminozide on apples. 52 Fed. Reg. 1909 (Jan. 16, 1987), 54 Fed. Reg. 6392 (Feb. 10, 1989). Still not satisfied, Massachusetts banned daminozide residues in apples. *See Processed Apples Institute, Inc. v. Department of Public Health*, 522 N.E.2d 965 (Mass. 1988). Public concern about Alar exploded when a public relations firm retained by NRDC launched a major media campaign with a story on the television show "60 Minutes" on February 26, 1988. Despite FDA and EPA's efforts to reassure the public, *see, e.g.*, "Little Pesticide Residue Found In Foods Children Eat," FDA Talk Paper No. T89–14 (Feb. 27, 1989); "Extremely Low Levels Of Alar Found By Consumers Union," FDA Talk Paper No. T89–19 (Mar. 30, 1989), reaction to the NRDC campaign caused EPA to ban daminozide. *See* 54 Fed. Reg. 6392 (Feb. 10, 1989), 54 Fed. Reg. 22558 (May 24, 1989), 54 Fed. Reg. 37278 (Sept. 7, 1989), 54 Fed. Reg. 47492 (Nov. 14, 1989), 55 Fed. Reg. 10218 (Mar. 19, 1990). Washington State apple growers unsuccessfully sought damages in an action against CBS for false statements the network allegedly made about the cancer risk from Alar. *Auvil v. CBS "60 Minutes,"* 67 F.3d 816 (9th Cir. 1995).

5.   *Human Testing.* When EPA issued a press release reversing a longstanding policy by banning consideration of the results of human testing in its evaluation of pesticide safety, there was a sharp division of opinion on the matter. In *CropLife America v. EPA*, 329 F.3d 876 (D.C. Cir. 2003), the Court of Appeals invalidated the new policy on the ground that it could only be adopted through notice-and-comment rulemaking.

6.   *Pesticides in Imported Food.* In 65 Fed. Reg. 35069 (June 1, 2000) EPA published detailed guidance on applying current data requirements for pesticide residue tolerances in imported food. EPA later made available a NAFTA Guidance Document on the same subject. 65 Fed. Reg. 17099 (Apr. 5, 2006).

7. *Nonfood Application of FIFRA.* FIFRA regulates all pesticides and thus potentially applies to all FDA-regulated products. Congress twice addressed this FDA/EPA regulatory overlap, in 110 Stat. 1489, 1502 (1996) and 112 Stat. 3035 (1998), and the two agencies have worked together on this issue.

———

Controlling pesticide residues that occur in food as a result of environmental contamination, rather than through purposeful application, has proved difficult. Generally, FDA has relied upon enforcement of section 406 action levels. On two occasions, FDA formulated a legal position that it could enforce an action level for the pesticide DDT in fish, and it did not provoke the sort of challenge that it later encountered with respect to its action level for mercury in swordfish. *See supra* p. 498. In *United States v. Goodman*, 486 F.2d 847 (7th Cir. 1973), the agency successfully argued that, in the absence of a section 408 tolerance, any residue of DDT in raw fish was illegal and that it could lawfully establish an action level of 5 ppm as an exercise of enforcement discretion under section 306 [now 309], "Report of Minor Violations." In the related case of *United States v. Ewig Brothers Co.*, 502 F.2d 715 (7th Cir. 1974), the agency charged that a residue of DDT in smoked fish (a processed food) in excess of the 5 ppm action level was an unapproved "food additive" that was automatically illegal because it was not the subject of an approved food additive regulation. Because the Food Quality Protection Act of 1996 excluded pesticides in both raw and processed food from the definition of a food additive, however, FDA is now left with section 406 action levels as its sole enforcement authority for environmental contamination from pesticides. *Community Nutrition Institute*, 818 F.2d 943 (D.C. Cir. 1987) (discussed *supra* p. 515), forced the agency to characterize action levels as enforcement guidelines rather than binding limits.

NOTES

1. *FDA Action Levels.* FDA's section 406 action levels for pesticide residues in food are contained in Compliance Policy Guide Sec. 575.100, which has been updated periodically to reflect EPA recommendations. *See, e.g.*, 51 Fed. Reg. 11349 (Apr. 2, 1986)(revocation of action levels for DBCP); 52 Fed. Reg. 18025 (May 13, 1987) (new action levels for aldrin and dieldrin, chlordane, DDT, TDE, and DDE) 54 Fed. Reg. 50025 (Dec. 4, 1989)(new action levels for heptachlor). In 55 Fed. Reg. 14359 (Apr. 17, 1990), FDA listed all existing pesticide action levels and announced that they represent only enforcement guidelines.

2. *Monitoring and Enforcement.* Enforcement of pesticide residue limits on imported and domestic food requires analysis of thousands of products. This resource-intensive effort is subject to ongoing reassessment by FDA and is the target of critics who claim the agency is not doing enough. *See, e.g.*, GAO, PESTICIDES: BETTER SAMPLING AND ENFORCEMENT NEEDED ON IMPORTED FOOD, No. RCED–86–219 (Sept. 26, 1986); GAO, PESTICIDES: NEED TO ENHANCE FDA'S ABILITY TO PROTECT THE PUBLIC FROM ILLEGAL RESIDUES, No. RCED–87–7 (Oct. 27, 1986); "Pesticides in Food," Hearing before the Subcommittee on Oversight and Investigations of

the House Committee on Energy and Commerce, 100th Cong., 1st Sess. (1987).

13. RECENT SAFETY ENHANCEMENTS

Some recent enhancements of FDA's authority to protect the safety of food were motivated by fears of bioterrorism. Following the attacks of September 11, 2001, Congress focused on the fact that food is susceptible to intentional contamination with pathogenic microorganisms and other highly toxic chemicals. As part of the Public Health Security and Bioterrorism Preparedness and Response Act of 2002 (the "Bioterrorism Act"), Congress included several provisions to protect the food supply. 116 Stat. 594, 662–675 (2002). The legislation contained various provisions relevant to FDA, including the following (some of which have already been discussed): (a) Section 304 of the Act was amended to give FDA administrative detention authority for any food upon "credible evidence" that the food "presents a threat of serious adverse health consequences or death." (b) The existing permissive debarment provisions in section 306 of the Act were expanded to include debarment for repeated or serious food import violations. (c) A new section 415 requires the registration of all food establishments, both domestic and foreign. (d) A new section 414 authorizes FDA to require maintenance and retention of records needed to identify the immediate previous sources and immediate subsequent recipients of food and to allow FDA to inspect records relating to any food that it reasonably believes presents a threat of serious adverse health consequences or death. (e) To help FDA manage inspection of imported food, section 801 of the Act was amended to require that FDA be given prior notice of imported food shipments. (f) The import provisions in section 801 of the Act were amended to provide that any food that has been refused admission must be labeled "United States: Refused Entry," and section 402 was amended to prohibit the import of food that has previously been refused admission unless it can be established that the food now complies with the applicable requirements of the Act. (g) FDA is required to provide notices to states regarding any food that presents a threat of serious adverse health consequences or death and is authorized to make grants to states to conduct inspections and other food safety surveillance work.

The Food Safety Modernization Act of 2011 (FSMA), motivated by general concerns about food safety rather than about bioterrorism in particular, strengthened these enforcement mechanisms in various ways. For instance: (a) The law expands FDA's power to order administrative detentions by allowing such detentions if there is "reason to believe" that the food article is "adulterated or misbranded." FD&C Act 304(h). (b) It empowers FDA to suspend a food facility's registration if the facility was responsible for an adulteration that creates a reasonable probability of causing serious adverse health consequences or death, or if the facility held the food and knew or should have known of such a probability. FD&C Act 415(b)(1). (c) With oral or written notice, FDA may request records of a facility's food safety plan and access to information concerning preventative controls and corrective actions. FD&C Act 418(h). (d) Whistleblowers who report violations of the FD&C Act are protected. FD&C Act 1012. (e) FSMA provides FDA with mandatory recall authority over food and authorizes civil penalties for failure to follow a recall order. FD&C Act 303(f)(2), 423. (f) As discussed *infra* in Chapter 14, the statute also enhances the agency's power in various ways over the safety of food imports.

NOTE

Food Tampering. Ever since the well-publicized Tylenol poisoning incident of 1982, discussed *infra* at p. 993, there have been numerous examples of food product tampering. FDA has adopted the policy of not publicizing these incidents for fear that publicity will only encourage copycats. One exception involved the tampering in June 1993 of Diet Pepsi with a syringe containing a needle, an incident in which the perpetrator engaged in substantial publicity. *See United States v. Levine*, 41 F.3d 607 (10th Cir. 1994); *Knight v. FDA*, 938 F. Supp. 710 (D. Kan. 1996). Although FDA once administered the Poison Prevention Packaging Act, that responsibility was transferred to the Consumer Product Safety Commission (CPSC) by the Consumer Product Safety Act in 1972. Mandatory tamper resistant packaging can be ordered only by the CPSC, not by FDA. *See Nutritional Health Alliance v. FDA*, 318 F.3d 92 (2d Cir. 2003). Many food companies have voluntarily adopted tamper resistant packaging to assure the integrity of their products.

CHAPTER 7

HUMAN DRUGS

A. HISTORICAL BACKGROUND

1. DRUG REGULATION BEFORE THE 1938 FD&C ACT

The Federal Food and Drugs Act of 1906 was the first law providing for national regulation of all human drugs, but Congress had been concerned about the safety and performance of medications for nearly a century. In 1813, it enacted legislation to assure the dissemination of genuine smallpox vaccine. 2 Stat. 806. In 1902, it enacted the Biologics Act to regulate all "biological products," defined to include articles such as vaccines, serums, and antitoxins. *See infra* Chapter 9.

Before 1906, Congress also took one significant concrete step to regulate drugs other than biological drugs. In 1848, Congress passed the following law to prevent the importation of "adulterated and spurious drugs and medicines."

> *Be it enacted by the Senate and House of Representatives of the United States of America in Congress assembled,* That from and after the passage of this act, all drugs, medicines, medicinal preparations, including medicinal essential oils, and chemical preparations used wholly or in part as medicine, imported into the United States from abroad, shall, before passing the custom-house, be examined and appraised, as well in reference to their quality, purity, and fitness for medical purposes, as to their value and identity specified in the invoice.

9 Stat. 237 (1848). The 1848 law was not supplanted by the 1906 Food and Drugs Act, 36 Op. Att'y Gen. 311 (July 17, 1907), but it ultimately was repealed as part of the enactment of the Tariff Act of 1922, 42 Stat. 858, 989. *See* Wesley J. Heath, *America's First Drug Regulation Regime: The Rise and Fall of the Import Drug Act of 1848*, 59 Food Drug Cosm. L.J. 169 (2004).

The first legislation to establish comprehensive nationwide regulation of all food and drugs was introduced in Congress in 1879. Largely because regulation of food and drugs was thought to be a matter for state and local control, Congress debated this legislation for 27 years before ultimately enacting the Federal Food and Drugs Act of 1906 (hereinafter the 1906 Pure Food and Drug Act). 34 Stat. 768. This law broadly prohibited any adulteration or misbranding of drugs marketed in interstate commerce. Although it was quite short, and very broad and general in nature, it was extremely progressive for its time and included sufficient authority to permit FDA to take strong enforcement action against the unsafe, ineffective, and mislabeled drugs that flooded the United States market in early 1900s. Unlike the Biologics Act of 1902, however, the 1906 Pure Food and Drug Act contained no provisions requiring premarket testing or approval for new drug products. An attempt by FDA to obtain this type of authority in 1912 was unsuccessful. Thus, between 1902 and 1938, the federal government had premarket approval authority over biological drugs but not over other drugs.

2. DRUG REGULATION UNDER THE 1938 FD&C ACT

As is typical in the history of American food and drug law, FDA gained enhanced authority over drugs in 1938 in response to a calamity.

> [In 1937] . . . a tragedy occurred which was directly responsible for adding a new and important proviso to the drug control legislation. At least 73, perhaps over 90, persons in various parts of the country, although chiefly in the South, died as a result of taking a drug known as "Elixir Sulfanilamide," manufactured and sold by the S. E. Massengill Company of Bristol, Tennessee. This product had been prepared in order to render the valuable new drug, sulfanilamide, available in liquid form. Diethylene glycol was used as a solvent. Investigation later showed that the pharmacist on the manufacturer's staff checked the product merely for appearance, flavor, and fragrance. Tests on animals or even an investigation of the published literature would have revealed the lethal character of the solvent. . . . Yet the only legal basis for the F&DA's intervention was the fact that the preparation was not an "elixir" since that term may properly be applied only to an alcoholic solution. The product was therefore misbranded. The label, incidentally, did not mention the presence of the fatal ingredient, diethylene glycol.
>
> . . . Accordingly, Senator Copeland introduced a bill . . . which forbade the introduction into interstate commerce of "any drug . . . not generally recognized as safe for use" under the conditions prescribed in the labeling thereof "unless the packer of such drug holds a notice of finding by the Secretary that such drug is not unsafe for use."

David F. Cavers, *The Food, Drug, and Cosmetic Act of 1938: Its Legislative History and Its Substantive Provisions*, 6 LAW & CONTEMPORARY PROBLEMS 2 (1939). Copeland's bill was enacted as the 1938 Food, Drug, and Cosmetic Act. Therefore, since 1938, federal law has required some premarket review by FDA for all new drugs. The FD&C Act created the modern system under which the submission of a New Drug Application (NDA) to the agency must precede the introduction of a new drug onto the market. Notably, however, the 1938 statute did not create a true premarket *approval* process; rather, it created a premarket *notification* process; a New Drug Application would automatically "become effective" after 60 days unless FDA intervened and affirmatively disapproved it.

Another drug tragedy emerged in the early 1960s, when it was discovered that thalidomide, a drug approved for marketing in various European countries (where it was used widely for morning sickness in pregnant women) was a teratogen, i.e., it resulted in babies with various types of deformities. Although the pending NDA in the United States was not allowed to become effective, Congress, in 1962, promptly amended the FD&C Act to strengthen the licensure system for new drugs.

. . . First, the definition of new drug was extended to comprise drugs not generally recognized as safe *and effective*. Second . . . [t]he data reporting requirements of the new drug procedure were amended to require submission of data showing efficacy. Furthermore, in place of automatic approval of NDAs not disapproved, a positive act of approval is required to make an NDA approved.

. . . Under [section 505(d)], the Secretary . . . is now required to refuse approval of any NDA if, after notice and opportunity for hearing, he determines that on the basis of information before him with respect to the drug in question "there is a lack of substantial evidence that the drug will have the effect it purports or is represented to have under the conditions of use prescribed, recommended or suggested in the proposed labeling thereof. . . ." Furthermore, section 505(e) was modified to require the Secretary to withdraw approval of any drug after notice and opportunity for hearing if he finds that "on the basis of new information before him" substantial evidence of efficacy is lacking. . . .

Note, *Drug Efficacy and the 1962 Drug Amendments,* 60 Georgetown Law Journal 185 (1971) (emphasis added).

In short, under the Drug Amendments of 1962, premarket approval replaced premarket notification, and applicants were required to demonstrate the efficacy, as well as the safety, of a drug to earn approval. These requirements have remained in effect ever since. Since 1962, no new drug can be marketed until FDA specifically approves it as safe, effective, and properly labeled.

On average, it now takes 10 to 15 years to develop a new chemical entity (NCE) new drug, from initial chemical synthesis to FDA approval of an NDA. Of every 5,000 chemicals that enter preclinical testing, only five proceed to clinical testing and only one ultimately gains FDA approval. Averaging the total costs of all this research as well as the opportunity costs, an approved NDA for an NCE drug today costs over $2 billion. In short, the FDA licensure process is extremely lengthy and expensive.

The modern drug approval process leads to more extensive agency involvement in the decisionmaking of private manufacturers than any other provision of the Act. FDA's performance of this function has been the target of persistent criticism, both from those who have regarded the agency as insufficiently rigorous, and more recently, from advocates of reduced regulation who contend that the agency—or the statutory premarket approval requirement itself—adds excessively to the cost of drug development and delays the introduction of important new therapies.

Following the Republican takeover of the House and Senate in November 1994, Congress enacted the FDA Modernization Act of 1997 (FDAMA) with the avowed intent of reforming and speeding up the drug investigation and approval process. Different parties disagreed as to the success of that effort. Following the resurgence of the Democrats, Congress enacted the Food and Drug Administration Amendments Act of 2007 (FDAAA) with the avowed intent of strengthening the FDAs administrative authority and control in the drug arena. This effort had greater success and has had a major impact.

Although the drug provisions of the FD&C Act have been amended multiple times since 1962, the basic outline of the drug approval process has remained the same since then.

3.   REGULATION OF DRUG EFFICACY: HISTORY AND POLICY

The requirement that a manufacturer demonstrate to FDA that a new drug is effective as well as safe prior to marketing was the most revolutionary aspect of the Drug Amendments of 1962. Nonetheless, by 1962, FDA and its predecessor agencies had already been involved in assessing the accuracy of therapeutic claims for more than half a century. FDA exercised this power through its enforcement of the drug misbranding provisions of both the 1906 Pure Food and Drugs Act and the 1938 FD&C Act.

The 1906 Act prohibited any drug claim that was ". . . false or misleading in any particular. . . ." The Supreme Court was soon called upon to interpret this provision, in connection with the prosecution of a dealer of an ineffective cancer cure. In *U.S. v. Johnson*, the Supreme Court interpreted the language so as to embrace only statements "as determine the identity of the article, possibly, including its strength, quality and purity." 221 U.S. 488, 497 (1911). In other words, the Court found that false claims of effectiveness did not constitute misbranding.

Congress responded to the decision in *Johnson* by enacting the Sherley Amendment to the 1906 Pure Food and Drug Act, 37 Stat. 416 (1912). This amendment added a new provision to section 8 of the Act making "false and fraudulent" claims regarding "curative or therapeutic effect" a misbranding violation.

Today, a reader may wonder why Congress in 1906 would have excluded false therapeutic claims from its ban on "false or misleading" drug labeling. The answer lies in that period's very different views regarding the possibility of objective scientific measurement of therapeutic efficacy. The following 1902 Supreme Court opinion illustrates this earlier vision.

The plaintiff in the case, the American Judicial School of Magnetic Healing, was engaged in the business of curing human diseases through appeals to the mind. A large part of the plaintiff's business consisted of providing "treatment" by letter to people throughout the United States. The Postmaster General directed the local postmaster to return all letters addressed to the school to the original senders with the word "fraudulent" stamped on the outside, and to refuse payment of any postal order drawn to the order of the school. A federal statute, 26 Stat. 465, 466 (1890), granted the Postmaster General discretion to instruct local postmasters to take such steps against any person found to be engaged in a ". . . scheme or device for obtaining money through the mail by means of false or fraudulent pretenses, representations or promises. . . ." The plaintiff sought to enjoin the local postmaster from continuing to comply with the Postmaster General's order.

American School of Magnetic Healing v. McAnnulty

187 U.S. 94 (1902).

■ MR. JUSTICE PECKHAM . . . delivered the opinion of the court.

. . . .

As the case arises on demurrer, all material facts averred in the bill are of course admitted. It is, therefore, admitted that the business of the complainants is founded "almost exclusively on the physical and practical proposition that the mind of the human race is largely responsible for its ills, and is a perceptible factor in the treating, curing, benefiting and remedying thereof, and that the human race does possess the innate power, through proper exercise of the faculty of the brain and mind, to largely control and remedy the ills that humanity is heir to. . . . "

. . . . [T]he question is whether the complainants who are conducting the business upon the basis stated thereby obtain money and property through the mails by means of false or fraudulent pretenses, representations or promises. Can such a business be properly pronounced a fraud within the statutes of the United States?

. . . Just exactly to what extent the mental condition affects the body, no one can accurately and definitely say. One person may believe it of far greater efficacy than another, but surely it cannot be said that it is a fraud for one person to contend that the mind has an effect upon the body and its physical condition greater than even a vast majority of intelligent people might be willing to admit or believe. . . . The claim of the ability to cure may be vastly greater than most men would be ready to admit, and yet those who might deny the existence or virtue of the remedy would only differ in opinion from those who assert it. There is no exact standard of absolute truth by which to prove the assertion false and a fraud. We mean by that to say that the claim of complainants cannot be the subject of proof as of an ordinary fact; it cannot be proved as a fact to be a fraud or false pretense or promise, nor can it properly be said that those who assume to heal bodily ills or infirmities by a resort to this method of cure are guilty of obtaining money under false pretenses, such as are intended in the statutes, which evidently do not assume to deal with mere matters of opinion upon subjects which are not capable of proof as to their falsity. We may not believe in the efficacy of the treatment to the extent claimed by complainants, and we may have no sympathy with them in such claims, and yet their effectiveness is but matter of opinion in any court. . . . [T]hose who have business with complainants . . . seem to have faith in the efficacy of the complainants' treatment and in their ability to heal as claimed by them. If they fail, the answer might be that all human means of treatment are also liable to fail, and will necessarily fail when the appointed time arrives. There is no claim that the treatment by the complainants will always succeed.

. . . As the effectiveness of almost any particular method of treatment of disease is, to a more or less extent, a fruitful source of difference of opinion, even though the great majority may be of one way of thinking, the efficacy of any special method is certainly not a matter for the decision of the Postmaster General within these statutes relative to fraud. Unless the question may be reduced to one of fact as distinguished from mere opinion, we think these statutes cannot be invoked for the purpose of stopping the delivery of mail matter.

. . . [T]here are many persons who do not believe in the homeopathic school of medicine, and who think that such doctrine, if practised precisely upon the lines set forth by its originator, is absolutely inefficacious in the treatment of diseases. Are homeopathic physicians subject to be proceeded against under these statutes and . . . to be found guilty of obtaining money under false pretenses . . . ? And, turning the question around, can physicians of what is called the "old school" be thus proceeded against? Both of these different schools of medicine have their followers, and many who believe in the one will pronounce the other wholly devoid of merit. But there is no precise standard by which to measure the claims of either, for people do recover who are treated according to the one or the other school. And so, it is said, do people recover who are treated under this mental theory. By reason of it? That cannot be averred as matter of fact. Many think they do. Others are of the contrary opinion. Is the Postmaster General to decide the question under these statutes?

. . . . [T]he admitted facts show no violation of the statutes cited above, but an erroneous order given by the Postmaster General to defendant. . . .

———

The *McAnnulty* view that the truth of a therapeutic claim was too indeterminate to be the basis for a legal enforcement action was an influential notion that would have to be overcome in subsequent decades whenever the government sought to regulate such claims. For example, in *U.S. v. Johnson*, discussed *supra* at p. 644, the Supreme Court cited *McAnnulty* to support its holding that the "false or misleading in any particular" language of the 1906 Act did not cover claims of efficacy.

> [A] word as to what Congress was likely to attempt. It was much more likely to regulate commerce in food and drugs with reference to plain matter of fact, so that food and drugs should be what they professed to be, when the kind was stated, than to distort the uses of its constitutional power to establishing criteria in regions where opinions are far apart. *See School of Magnetic Healing v. McAnnulty.* . . .

221 U.S. 488, 498 (1911).

Even after Congress enacted the 1912 Sherley Amendment, explicitly banning "false and fraudulent" curative claims, a defendant charged with violating this provision cited *McAnnulty* in asserting that the statute violated its constitutional rights. In *Seven Cases of Eckman's Alterative v. U.S.*, 239 U.S. 510 (1916), the Supreme Court rejected this defense, but only by emphasizing the narrowness of the Sherley Amendment's prohibition.

> . . . [T]he statute is attacked upon the ground that it enters the domain of speculation (*American School of Magnetic Healing v. McAnnulty*, 187 U.S. 94 (1902)) and by virtue of consequent uncertainty operates as a deprivation of liberty and property

without due process of law in violation of the Fifth Amendment of the Constitution, and does not permit of the laying of a definite charge as required by the Sixth Amendment. We think that this objection proceeds upon a misconstruction of the provision. Congress deliberately excluded the field where there are honest differences of opinion between schools and practitioners. It was, plainly, to leave no doubt upon this point that the words "false *and fraudulent*" were used. This phrase must be taken with its accepted legal meaning, and thus it must be found that the statement contained in the package was put there to accompany the goods with actual intent to deceive—an intent which may be derived from the facts and circumstances, but which must be established. . . . It is said that the owner has the right to give his views regarding the effect of his drugs. But state of mind is itself a fact, and may be a material fact, and false and fraudulent representations may be made about it. . . .

When Congress enacted the Federal Food, Drug and Cosmetic Act in 1938 to replace the 1906 Act, it omitted the requirement of a showing of fraud. Instead, section 502(a) of the FD&C Act declares simply that a drug is misbranded if "its labeling is false or misleading in any particular." Although *U.S. v. Johnson* ruled that this same language in the 1906 Act did not embrace therapeutic claims, the legislative history of the 1938 Act makes clear that Congress now intended the provision to cover false or misleading efficacy claims. *See* David Cavers, *The Food, Drug and Cosmetic Act of 1938: Its Legislative History and Its Substantive Provisions*, 6 LAW & CONTEMPORARY PROBLEMS 2 (1939). Moreover, section 502(a) was supplemented by section 201(n), which mandates that the misleadingness of labeling be determined in light of "not only representations made or suggested," but also "the extent to which the labeling . . . fails to reveal facts material in light of such representations. . . ."

In sum, the 1938 FD&C Act was written to enable FDA to proceed against false or misleading claims of therapeutic value masquerading as assertions of opinion. This new approach reflected advances in the science of therapeutics; by the late 1930s, the controlled clinical trial was emerging as a widely accepted objective standard for determining drug efficacy. This scientific development was accompanied by an evolution in societal attitudes regarding the propriety of government regulation of therapeutic claims. The following case illustrates the significance for American drug regulation of the decline of the *McAnnulty* approach.

Research Laboratories, Inc. v. United States

167 F.2d 410 (9th Cir. 1948).

■ GARRECHT, CIRCUIT JUDGE. . . .

In November, 1944, a libel was filed in the United States District Court for the Western District of Missouri . . . pursuant to which there were seized by the United States Marshal about 600 units of Nue–Ovo, each unit containing three bottles. . . . Pursuant to the same libel there were also seized at the same time stocks of circulars entitled "information on Nue–Ovo and its value in Arthritic and other Rheumatoid symptoms." . . .

The libel alleges that:

The article is misbranded within the meaning of 21 U.S.C. 352(a) (21 U.S.C.A. § 352(a)) in that the statements . . . which appear in the labeling of the article * * * are false and misleading in this, that such statements represent and suggest and create in the mind of the reader thereof the impression that the article of drug, Nue–Ovo, is effective in the treatment of arthritis, rheumatism, neuritis, sciatica, and lumbago, whereas, the article is not effective in the treatment of such conditions.

. . . .

Summarized, the [appellant company's] attacks upon the judgment below are as follows:

1.   The court below erred in submitting issues to the jury, since every statement in the labeling as to the effectiveness of the product is a statement of opinion, and at the conclusion of the case the record showed nothing more than a difference of opinion among qualified medical experts as to the effectiveness of the product. . . .

3.   The court erred in instructing the jury as to the elements to be taken into account in determining whether the labeling is misleading, under 21 U.S.C.A § 321(n) [FD&C Act 201(n)].

. . . .

The appellant bases its first contention upon a line of decision commencing with *American School of Magnetic Healing v. McAnnulty.* . . .

Three Limitations to the McAnnulty Rule

It should be borne in mind, however, that the *McAnnulty* case . . . involved the Postmaster General's power to decide what was in reality a medical question, as to which he would presumably have no professional training.

It cannot be assumed that the Supreme Court [in *McAnnulty*] intended to reach out a dead hand over the power of Congress to pass legislation in the future setting up a well-equipped Federal agency capable of arriving at a professional conclusion as to the adulteration or misbranding of drugs. . . . In the *McAnnulty* case . . . throughout the opinion doubt was expressed as to the qualifications of a *postmaster general* to pass on medical questions. . . .

In contrast to the meager technical facilities for the determination of medical questions possessed by the Postmaster General—at least at the time that the *McAnnulty* case was decided—we find that the Federal Security Agency [the agency encompassing FDA] has at its disposal almost unlimited professional resources with which to carry out its investigations in the enforcement of the Federal Food, Drug, and Cosmetic Act. . . .

As was said in *United States v. 7 Jugs, etc., of Dr. Salsbury's Rakos,* 53 F. Supp. 746, 759 (D. Minn. 1944) . . .

Moreover, it must be obvious that tremendous advancements in scientific knowledge and certainty have been made since the rule in the *McAnnulty* case was first announced. Questions which previously were subjects only of opinion have now been answered with certainty by the application of scientifically known facts. In the consideration of the *McAnnulty* rule, courts should give recognition to this advancement.

(a) Jury May Consider Testimony as to Actual Experiments

Much of the appellee's [i.e., the government's] evidence in the instant case consisted of "controlled clinical studies" conducted by eminently qualified physicians and surgeons. . . .

Dr. Frances Baker, Director of the Department of Physical Medicine at the University of California . . . as the result of her studies . . . testified that she thought that Nue–Ovo "offers us nothing that is of value in the treatment of arthritis." She expressed similar opinions as to Nue–Ovo's effectiveness in cases of lumbago, sciatica, neuritis, and rheumatism. . . .

Testimony of experts that is based upon tests or experiments made by them does not come within the ambit of the *McAnnulty* rule. . . .

(b) Testimony of Experts as to Consensus of Scientific Opinion Is Also Relevant. . . .

It is generally agreed that testimony as to the consensus of medical opinion may [also] be considered in drug-misbranding cases. . . .

(c) Even Opinion Testimony as to Therapeutic Value Is Admissible

In this circuit and elsewhere, it has been held that expert testimony even in its broadest sense—i.e., where the witness has neither tested the product nor purports to report the consensus of medical opinion—is admissible on the question of therapeutic value. . . .

The evidence in this case included the three types that we have discussed hereinabove. . . . Altogether, there was ample evidence to support the verdict of the jury. . . .

NOTE

The Role of Section 502(a). Court enforcement of FD&C Act 502(a) (21 U.S.C. 352(a)), exemplified by *Research Laboratories,* no longer plays a major role in FDA's efforts to combat false or misleading therapeutic claims for drugs. This is because the Drug Amendments of 1962 require proof of the effectiveness of all "new drugs," defined as drugs not generally recognized as safe and effective "for use under the conditions prescribed, recommended, or suggested in the labeling." FD&C Act 201(p). FDA court enforcement actions since 1962 have uniformly charged a violation of the new drug provisions of the Act, rather than, or occasionally in addition to, the misbranding provisions.

———

The 1962 Drug Amendments added section FD&C Act 505(d), which explicitly requires manufacturers of new drugs, prior to marketing, to establish the efficacy of their products to FDA by "substantial evidence," defined as "evidence consisting of adequate and well-controlled investigations." FD&C Act 505(d). This new mandate that an NDA contain proof of efficacy generated controversy, particularly over the question of whether it was appropriate for FDA to prevent desperately ill patients with no other treatment options from purchasing unapproved drugs.

This dispute reached a climax in the 1970s, when cancer patients sought the right to use Laetrile (amygdalin), a poorly-characterized natural constituent of apricot kernels. In 1975, two cancer victims sued to enjoin FDA from interfering with their personal use of Laetrile. The District Court determined that the plaintiffs were entitled to an injunction against the agency to preserve their free choice of treatment. *Rutherford v. United States,* 399 F. Supp. 1208 (W.D. Okla. 1975). Following further judicial and administrative proceedings, the District Court issued the following opinion. You should recognize in advance that this decision did not survive subsequent review; it is included here to encourage consideration of the underlying issues.

Rutherford v. United States

438 F. Supp. 1287 (W.D. Okla. 1977).

■ BOHANON, UNITED STATES DISTRICT JUDGE. . . .

FDA asserts authority to preclude Laetrile's importation or interstate transportation on the basis that it is a "new drug" within the Act's meaning. "No person shall introduce or deliver for introduction into interstate commerce any new drug," unless an application on its behalf has been approved. 21 U.S.C. § 355(a). . . .

In plaintiffs' constitutional challenge of FDA's proscription they invoke rights fundamental to a free society and inextricably related to enumerated constitutional concepts.

While the Constitution does not explicitly mention a right of personal privacy, it is unchallengeable "that a right of personal privacy, or a guarantee of certain areas or zones of privacy, does exist under the Constitution." *Roe v. Wade,* 410 U.S. 113, 152 (1973). This right has been discerned within the penumbras of the Bill of Rights, and specifically within the language of the First, Fourth, Fifth, Ninth and Fourteenth Amendments to the Constitution, *Roe v. Wade, supra.* . . .

Mr. Justice Douglas referred to "the freedom to care for one's health and person" as coming within the purview of this right. *Doe v. Bolton,* 410 U.S. 179 (1973) (concurring opinion). "The right of privacy," Justice Douglas proceeded, "has no more conspicuous place than in the physician-patient relationship. . . ." *Doe, supra* at 219. He concluded: "The right to seek advice on one's health and the right to place reliance on the physician of one's choice are basic. . . ." *Doe, supra.*

. . . .

Many knowledgable [sic] and concerned individuals are questioning the effectiveness and wisdom of our orthodox approaches to combatting cancer. The correctness of their criticisms may not be determined for many years, and in any event such discussion provokes controversies largely beyond the realm of the courts' function. Nonetheless, it appears uncontrovertible that a patient has the right to refuse cancer treatment altogether, and should he decide to forego conventional treatment does he not possess a further right to enlist such nontoxic treatments, however unconventional, as he finds to be of comfort, particularly where recommended by his physician?

. . . .

Plaintiffs seek to exercise final control over the handling of their own individual health-care problems. Numerous cancer patients possess extensive first-hand experience with Laetrile which has led them to believe, correctly or not, that the substance has eased their pain and prolonged their lives. Such personal convictions are not readily dispelled by government pronouncements or affidavits to the contrary. When deprived of treatment in this country, they go elsewhere, and in so doing are denied close contact with their families and family doctors.

Unintentionally FDA has wrought needless hardship and expense to countless individuals required to travel to Mexico or Germany in order to utilize Laetrile. If it were more readily available in this country, perhaps many patients currently obtaining the treatment abroad could be persuaded to remain under their doctor's care here and use the substance in conjunction with conventional treatments.

The final consequences are ultimately borne by those whose bodies are the battleground on which cancer's war is waged. Many perceive the drug's acquisition as a life and death matter, and are understandably frustrated and enraged over attempts by their own government to deny them the right to decide for themselves questions of such a personal and grave nature.

Doubtless FDA desires to protect the public. Such good intention, however, is not the overriding issue. Many of us allocate time and money and other resources in ways susceptible to just criticism by many standards. Nonetheless, our political ideals emphasize that the right to freely decide is of much greater significance than the quality of those choices actually made. It is never easy for one who is concerned and feels himself particularly knowledgable [sic] to observe others exercise their freedom in ways that to him appear unenlightened.

As a nation, however, historically and continuously, we are irrevocably committed to the principle that the individual must be given maximum latitude in determining his own personal destiny.

To be insensitive to the very fundamental nature of the civil liberties at issue in this case, and the fact that making the choice, regardless of its correctness, is the sole prerogative of the person whose body is being ravaged, is to display slight understanding of the essence of our free society and its constitutional underpinnings. This is notably true where, as here, there are no simple answers or obvious solutions, uncertainty is pervasive, and even the best efforts leave so much to be desired.

When certain "fundamental rights" are invoked, such as the right of privacy involved herein, regulation may be justified only by a "compelling state interest," and legislative enactments "must be narrowly drawn to express only the legitimate state interests at stake." *Roe v. Wade,* 410 U.S. at 155. By denying the right to use a nontoxic substance in connection with one's own personal health-care, FDA[28] has offended the constitutional right of privacy.

This court's decision in this case in no way portends the return of the traveling snake oil salesman. . . . [T]he right to use a harmless, unproven remedy is quite distinct from any alleged right to promote such. FDA is fully empowered under other statutory provisions to combat false or fraudulent advertising of ineffectual or unproven drugs. *See* the Food, Drug and Cosmetic Act, Misbranded Drugs and Devices, 21 U.S.C. § 352 (1976); and the Federal Trade Commission Act, Dissemination of False Advertisements, 15 U.S.C. § 52 (1975).

The Commissioner's "Laetrile" Decision of July 29, 1977, must be vacated. An appropriate Order will accordingly be entered herein.

NOTES

1. *Subsequent History.* On appeal, the Tenth Circuit held, without reaching the constitutional issue, that the new drug requirements of the FD&C Act have no application to terminally ill cancer patients. It asked:

> What meaning can "effective" have in the absence of anything which may be used as a standard? . . . What can "effective" mean if the person, by all prevailing standards, and under the position the Commission takes, is going to die of cancer regardless of what may be done. Thus there has been no standard here advanced by the Commission against which to measure the safeness [sic] or effectiveness of the drug as to the plaintiffs. Clearly the terms have no meaning under these circumstances, and certainly not the abstract meaning sought to be applied by the Commission. . . .

582 F.2d 1234, 1237 (10th Cir. 1978).

A unanimous Supreme Court reversed this decision, holding that the FD&C Act "makes no special provision for drugs used to treat terminally ill patients." *United States v. Rutherford*, 442 U.S. 544 (1979). The Supreme Court accepted FDA's arguments that it was important to protect individuals suffering from a potentially fatal disease from rejecting conventional therapy in favor of a drug with no demonstrable curative properties, and to protect the public generally from "the vast range of self-styled panaceas that inventive minds can devise." *Id.* at 558. The Court remanded the case to the Court of Appeals.

When the case returned to the Tenth Circuit, it rejected the District Court's constitutional ruling. "It is apparent in the context with which we are here concerned that the decision by the patient whether to have treatment or not is a protected right, but his selection of a particular treatment, or at least a medication, is within the area of governmental interests in protecting public health." *Rutherford v. United States*, 616 F.2d 455, 457 (10th Cir. 1980). The Tenth Circuit later reversed an attempt by

---

[28] Even if no such right existed generally, it would appear that Laetrile's use by terminally ill cancer patients who have exhausted orthodox approaches or cancer patients interested in using Laetrile only in conjunction with conventional methods would be constitutionally protected. While certain problems may attend exact definitions of "terminally ill," the term has a well understood meaning and is of practical significance to our discussion.

the District Court to reinstate the injunction against FDA interference in the use of Laetrile. 806 F.2d 1455 (10th Cir. 1986). *See also Carnohan v. United States,* 616 F.2d 1120 (9th Cir. 1980) (rejecting as premature a constitutional claim of a right to obtain and use Laetrile); *People v. Privitera,* 591 P.2d 919 (Cal. 1979) (holding, 5–2, that the constitutional right to privacy does not protect a cancer patient's desire to obtain and use Laetrile).

2. *Extrajudicial Developments.* In July 1977, a poll showed that 58 percent of Americans believed Laetrile should be sold legally, versus only 28 percent who opined that it should remain illegal. Roper Report 77–7 (July 1977). In 1977, U.S. Representative Steven D. Symms, citing "grass roots support" deriving from outrage over the Laetrile situation, introduced federal legislation titled the "Medical Freedom of Choice Bill." This law would have repealed the power FDA acquired in 1962 to review the efficacy as well as the safety of new drugs prior to marketing. The Symms bill ultimately gained 140 co-sponsors in the House of Representatives.

Supporters of Laetrile also sought its legalization through state legislation. By the early 1980s, half of the states had legalized the use of the drug within their borders. *See* JAMES HARVEY YOUNG, AMERICAN HEALTH QUACKERY 221 (1992).

The public's interest in Laetrile faded after the 1980 death from cancer of movie star Steve McQueen, the world's most prominent Laetrile user, and the 1981 announcement that National Cancer Institute trials had failed to demonstrate Laetrile's effectiveness and had also produced evidence of potential cyanide toxicity. *Id.* at 232–33.

———

Even as interest in Laetrile itself diminished, the question of whether terminally ill patients have a right to access unapproved therapies remained hotly debated, especially with the rise of AIDS in the 1980s. Modern assertions of such a right have largely focused on remedies currently under investigation in FDA-regulated trials.

Individuals afflicted with serious or life-threatening diseases have, since 1962, been frustrated by their inability to obtain investigational new drugs that offer the promise, or at least the hope, of useful therapy. Small companies with limited funds and a supply of an experimental drug sufficient only to conduct FDA-required animal and clinical studies usually cannot afford to provide the drug free to terminally ill patients. And the demand for such drugs is often great. For example, between the time that FDA initially determined the cancer drug Erbitux to be approvable and the time that the agency finally actually approved the drug for marketing, the manufacturer received 8500 requests for compassionate use. Justin Gillis, *Patients Press Pleas for Cancer Drugs: Experimental Medicine in Short Supply*, WASH. POST, April 7, 2002, at A1.

Congress sought to address this problem in the FDA Modernization Act of 1997 by providing, in new section 561(b) of the FD&C Act, that any person acting through a licensed physician may obtain an investigational drug from the sponsor if all the requirements of an individual patient IND are met. This provision did nothing more than codify longstanding FDA policy, however. Most important, it stopped short of overruling FDA's ban on the sale of investigational drugs without the prior written approval of the agency or the agency's blanket prohibition against earning profits from the sale of investigational drugs.

The Abigail Alliance, a patient group, brought suit against FDA to contest the constitutionality of these restrictions. In 2006, a panel of the United States Court of Appeals for the D.C. Circuit held, 2–1, that patients have a substantive due process right to access potentially life-sustaining medications when there are no alternative treatment options. *Abigail Alliance for Better Access to Developmental Drugs v. Von Eschenbach*, 445 F.3d 470 (D.C. Cir. 2006). This decision was vacated for rehearing *en banc*. In the decision below, the D.C. Circuit rejected the existence of such a right, with only the two judges who supported the initial opinion voting in dissent.

Abigail Alliance v. Von Eschenbach

495 F.3d 695 (D. C. Cir. 2007), cert. denied *Abigail Alliance v. Eschenbach*,
128 S. Ct. 1069 (2008).

■ GRIFFITH, CIRCUIT JUDGE

This case presents the question whether the Constitution provides terminally ill patients a right of access to experimental drugs that have passed limited safety trials but have not been proven safe and effective. The district court held there is no such right. A divided panel of this Court held there is. Because we conclude that there is no fundamental right "deeply rooted in this Nation's history and tradition" of access to experimental drugs for the terminally ill, *see Washington v. Glucksberg*, 521 U.S. 702, 720–21(1997) (quoting *Moore v. East Cleveland*, 431 U.S. 494 (1977) (plurality opinion)), we affirm the judgment of the district court.

The Abigail Alliance for Better Access to Developmental Drugs (the "Alliance") is an organization of terminally ill patients and their supporters that seeks expanded access to experimental drugs for the terminally ill. The Food, Drug, and Cosmetic Act, however, generally prohibits access to new drugs unless and until they have been approved by the Food and Drug Administration ("FDA"). *See* 21 U.S.C. § 355(a). Gaining FDA approval can be a long process. . . .

Terminally ill patients need not, however, always await the results of the clinical testing process. The FDA and Congress have created several programs designed to provide early access to promising experimental drugs when warranted. . . .

Concluding that the FDA's current process for early access to new drugs was inadequate to meet the needs of its terminally ill members, the Alliance submitted its own proposals to the FDA. Those proposals culminated in a "citizen petition" to the FDA, arguing that there is a "different risk-benefit tradeoff facing patients who are terminally ill and who have no other treatment options." Although the Alliance agreed that "[e]xtensive marshalling of evidence regarding drug interactions, dose optimization, and the like" is "appropriate for new drugs to treat patients with other alternatives . . . [,] these steps may well entail a delay that is fatal" for terminally ill patients. The Alliance contended that these patients "should have the ability to opt for a new treatment that has met a lower evidentiary hurdle with respect to safety and efficacy." The Alliance's proposal suggested that the FDA allow early access based upon "the risk of illness, injury, or death from the disease in the absence of the drug." Accordingly, the Alliance requested that the FDA promulgate new regulations that would allow sponsors to market experimental drugs, under some circumstances, after the completion of Phase I trials*. . . .

Having . . . been rejected by the FDA, the Alliance turned to the courts, arguing that the United States Constitution provides a right of access to experimental drugs for its members. . . .

. . . .

As framed by the Alliance, we now consider:

> Whether the liberty protected by the *Due Process Clause* embraces the right of a terminally ill patient with no remaining approved treatment options to decide, in consultation with his or her own doctor, whether to seek access to investigational medications that the [FDA] concedes are safe and promising enough for substantial human testing.

That is, we must determine whether terminally ill patients have a fundamental right to experimental drugs that have passed Phase I clinical testing. If such a right exists, the Alliance argues that both 21 C.F.R. § 312.34(b)(3) (preventing access to experimental drugs for terminally ill patients where there is insufficient evidence of effectiveness or where there is an unreasonable risk of injury) and 21 C.F.R. § 312.7 (prohibiting drug manufacturers from profiting on the sale of experimental drugs) must be subjected to strict scrutiny because they interfere with a fundamental constitutional right. We do not address the broader question of whether access to medicine might ever implicate fundamental rights.

The Due Process Clause of the Fifth Amendment provides that "[n]o person shall be . . . deprived of life, liberty, or property, without due process of law." . . . The Court has stated that "[t]he Clause . . . provides heightened protection against government interference with certain fundamental rights and liberty interests," including "the rights to marry, to have children, to direct the education and upbringing of one's children, to marital privacy, to use contraception, to bodily integrity, and to abortion," *Glucksberg*, 521 U.S. at 719–20.

As such rights are not set forth in the language of the Constitution, the Supreme Court has cautioned against expanding the substantive rights protected by the Due Process Clause. . . . [T]he Supreme Court has directed courts to "exercise the utmost care whenever we are asked to break new ground in this field, lest the liberty protected by the Due

---

* [Phase I is the first of three standard phases in the clinical investigation of a drug. During this phase, the drug is tested in a small group of usually healthy volunteers and is normally assessed only for safety. *See infra* p. 680. EDS.]

Process Clause be subtly transformed into the policy preferences of the [courts' members]." *Glucksberg,* 521 U.S. at 720. . . .

In *Glucksberg,* the Supreme Court described its "established method of substantive-due-process analysis" as having "two primary features." *Glucksberg,* 521 U.S. at 720.

> First, we have regularly observed that the Due Process Clause specially protects those fundamental rights and liberties which are, objectively, deeply rooted in this Nation's history and tradition and implicit in the concept of ordered liberty, such that neither liberty nor justice would exist if they were sacrificed. Second, we have required in substantive-due-process cases a careful description of the asserted fundamental liberty interest.

Id. at 720–21.

We will assume *arguendo* that the Alliance's description of its asserted right would satisfy *Glucksberg*'s "careful description" requirement. Looking to whether the Alliance has demonstrated that its right is deeply rooted in this Nation's history, tradition, and practices, the Alliance's claim for constitutional protection rests on two arguments: (1) that "common law and historical American practices have traditionally trusted individual doctors and their patients with almost complete autonomy to evaluate the efficacy of medical treatments"; and (2) that FDA policy is "inconsistent with the way that our legal tradition treats persons in all other life-threatening situations." More specifically, the Alliance argues that the concepts of self-defense, necessity, and interference with rescue are broad enough to demonstrate the existence of the fundamental right they seek—a right for "persons in mortal peril" to "try to save their own lives, even if the chosen means would otherwise be illegal or involve enormous risks."

. . . The Alliance argues that its right can be found in our history and legal traditions because "the government never interfered with the judgment of individual doctors about the medical *efficacy* of particular drugs until 1962," *i.e.,* when major amendments were made to the Food, Drug, and Cosmetic Act.

The Alliance has little to say, however, about our Nation's history of regulating the *safety* of drugs. . . . The Alliance's effort to focus on efficacy regulation ignores one simple fact: it is unlawful for the Alliance to procure experimental drugs not only because they have not been proven effective, but because they have not been proven safe. Although the Alliance contends that it only wants drugs that "are safe and promising enough for substantial human testing," *i.e.,* drugs that have passed Phase I testing, current law bans access to an experimental drug on safety grounds until it has successfully completed all phases of testing. *See* 21 C.F.R. § 312.21(b) (requiring that Phase II studies examine "*common short-term side effects and risks*" of new drugs) (emphasis added); *id.* § 312.21(c) (requiring Phase III studies to "gather . . . additional information about effectiveness and *safety* that is needed to evaluate the overall benefit-risk relationship of the drug") (emphasis added). Thus, to succeed on its claim of a fundamental right of access for the terminally ill to experimental drugs, the Alliance must show not only that there is a tradition of access to drugs that have not yet been proven effective, but also a tradition of access to drugs that have not yet been proven safe.

Examining, as we are required to do under *Glucksberg*, our Nation's history, legal traditions, and practice with respect to the regulation of drugs for efficacy and safety, we conclude that our Nation has long expressed interest in drug regulation, calibrating its response in terms of the capabilities to determine the risks associated with both drug safety and efficacy.

Drug regulation in the United States began with the Colonies and States when the Colony of Virginia's legislature passed an act in 1736 that addressed the dispensing of more drugs than was "necessary or useful" because that practice had become "dangerous and intolerable." The Territory of Orleans (Louisiana) passed an act in 1808 requiring a diploma and an examination before permitting pharmacists to dispense drugs; Louisiana also prohibited the sale of deteriorated drugs and restricted the sale of poisons. South Carolina enacted legislation in 1817 requiring pharmacists to obtain licenses, followed by Georgia in 1825 and Alabama in 1852. By 1870, at least twenty-five states or territories had statutes regulating adulteration (impure drugs), and a few others had laws addressing poisons. In the early history of our Nation, we observe not a tradition of protecting a right of access to drugs, but rather governments responding to the risks of new compounds as they become aware of and able to address those risks.

Nor were the States the only regulators of access to drugs. Although early federal regulation was not extensive . . . there are early examples of federal government intervention. In 1848, the Import Drug Act banned "imported adulterated drugs". . . . Congress acted again when it passed the Biologics Controls Act of 1902, in response to a series of deadly reactions to a tainted diphtheria vaccine that killed children in New Jersey and Missouri. Congress followed with the Pure Food and Drugs Act of 1906, which prohibited the manufacture of any drug that was "adulterated or misbranded."

The current regime of federal drug regulation began to take shape with the Food, Drug, and Cosmetic Act of 1938. The Act required that drug manufacturers provide proof that their products were safe before they could be marketed. The new Act also prohibited false therapeutic claims. Notably, the drug industry "strenuously objected" to the 1938 Act "ostensibly on the ground that it would deprive the American people of the right to self-medication,"—an argument not unlike the Alliance's position of today.

We end our historical analysis where the Alliance would prefer it begin—with the 1962 Amendments to the FDCA. Undoubtedly, as the Alliance argues at length, Congress amended the FDCA in 1962 to explicitly require that the FDA only approve drugs deemed effective for public use. Thus, the Alliance argues that, prior to 1962, patients were free to make their own decisions whether a drug might be effective. But even assuming *arguendo* that efficacy regulation began in 1962, the Alliance's argument ignores our Nation's history of drug safety regulation described above. Nor can the Alliance override current FDA regulations simply by insisting that drugs which have completed Phase I testing are safe enough for terminally ill patients. Current law bars public access to drugs undergoing clinical testing on safety grounds. The fact that a drug has emerged from Phase I with a determination that it is safe for limited clinical testing in a controlled and closely-monitored environment after detailed scrutiny of each trial participant does not mean that a drug is safe for use beyond supervised trials. FDA regulation of post-Phase I drugs is entirely consistent with our historical tradition of prohibiting the sale of unsafe drugs.

But even setting the safety issue to one side, the Alliance's argument that effectiveness was not required before 1962 also fails under closer scrutiny. First, as a matter of history, at least some drug regulation prior to 1962 addressed efficacy. More importantly, an arguably limited history of efficacy regulation prior to 1962 does not establish a fundamental right of access to unproven drugs. The amendments made to the FDCA by Congress throughout the twentieth century demonstrate that Congress and the FDA have continually responded to new risks presented by an evolving technology. Recent government efficacy regulation has reflected Congress's exercise of its well-established power to regulate in response to scientific, mathematical, and medical advances.[12]

True, a lack of government interference throughout history might be some evidence that a right is deeply rooted. But standing alone, it cannot be enough. . . . Indeed, creating constitutional rights to be free from regulation based solely upon a prior lack of regulation would undermine much of the modern administrative state, which, like drug regulation, has increased in scope as changing conditions have warranted.

In keeping with those decisions, we conclude that the Alliance has not provided evidence of a right to procure and use experimental drugs that is deeply rooted in our Nation's history and traditions. . . .

Because the Alliance's claimed right is not fundamental, the Alliance's claim of a right of access to experimental drugs is subject only to rational basis scrutiny. . . .

   . . . .

Applying the rational basis standard to the Alliance's complaint, we cannot say that the government's interest does not bear a rational relation to a legitimate state interest. That conclusion is compelled by the Supreme Court's decision in *United States v. Rutherford,* 442 U.S. 544 (1979). . . .

Although terminally ill patients desperately need curative treatments, as *Rutherford* holds, their deaths can certainly be hastened

---

[12] In exercising the caution the Supreme Court demands when analyzing claims of fundamental rights, we note a more plausible explanation for the limited efficacy regulation— the government was not previously able to systematically regulate effectively for efficacy: "The history of the effectiveness requirement in drug regulation is inextricably linked to the advent of the randomized, controlled clinical trial as the cornerstone of medical research . . . , [which] would not become widely recognized until the twentieth century." . . . In fact, "World War II ushered in the era of the modern clinical trial. . . . The ability of scientists to "detect, identify, and understand" the components of various drugs has contributed to "new regulatory approaches [that] would not have been feasible and could never have occurred" without these scientific advances. Further, the need for efficacy regulation became more pressing "[a]fter World War II [as] the number of drugs available, the range of diseases and conditions amenable to drug therapy, and the power of drugs all increased dramatically."

by the use of a potentially toxic drug with no proven therapeutic benefit. Thus, we must conclude that, prior to distribution of a drug outside of controlled studies, the Government has a rational basis for ensuring that there is a scientifically and medically acceptable level of knowledge about the risks and benefits of such a drug. We therefore hold that the FDA's policy of limiting access to investigational drugs is rationally related to the legitimate state interest of protecting patients, including the terminally ill, from potentially unsafe drugs with unknown therapeutic effects.

. . . .

For the foregoing reasons, the judgment of the district court is affirmed.

■ ROGERS, CIRCUIT JUDGE, with whom CHIEF JUDGE GINSBURG joins, dissenting:

. . . .

In the end, it is startling that the oft-limited rights to marry, to fornicate, to have children, to control the education and upbringing of children, to perform varied sexual acts in private, and to control one's own body even if it results in one's own death or the death of a fetus have all been deemed fundamental rights covered, although not always protected, by the Due Process Clause, but the right to try to save one's life is left out in the cold despite its textual anchor in the right to life. This alone is reason the court should pause about refusing to put the FDA to its proof when it denies terminal patients with no alternative therapy the only option they have left, regardless of whether that option may be a long-shot with high risks. . . . The court commits a logical error of dramatic consequence by concluding that the investigational drugs are somehow not "necessary." While the potential cures may not prove *sufficient* to save the life of a terminally ill patient, they are surely *necessary* if there is to be any possibility of preserving her life.

. . . .

Although the Supreme Court has not squarely addressed the right to use potentially life-saving *medications*, it has developed a sizable body of law regarding the right to a potentially life-saving medical *procedure* when the life or health of a pregnant woman is on the line. In *Roe v. Wade,* 410 U.S. at 164–65, and again in *Planned Parenthood of Southeastern Pennsylvania v. Casey,* 505 U.S. 833, 846, 880, the Court held that even after fetal viability, a state cannot constitutionally proscribe abortion "where it is necessary, in appropriate medical judgment, for the preservation of the life or health of the mother." . . .

In *Stenberg v. Carhart,* 530 U.S. 914 (2000), the Supreme Court . . . held that . . . the State of Nebraska could not constitutionally ban particular abortion procedures, notwithstanding the state's "interest in the potentiality of human life," even though the state claimed that there were adequate alternatives. Here, the situation is even starker: The Alliance's terminally ill members have no remaining alternatives except the medications to which the FDA denies them access. . . .

. . . The court holds that because the Alliance seeks access only to "*potentially* life-saving drugs," the abortion cases are distinguishable. Nowhere in the Supreme Court's jurisprudence has it intimated that the government may ban procedures that represent a patient's only chance of survival because they might not be successful. The fundamental right does not accrue only upon a demonstration of surefire actualization; the trigger is the *necessity*, which is crucially different from the sufficiency to which the court repeatedly refers. . . .

. . . .

For more than half of this Nation's history . . . until the enactment of the 1906 Act, a person could obtain access to any new drug without any government interference whatsoever. Even after enactment of the FDCA in 1938, Congress imposed no limitation on the commercial marketing of new drugs based upon the drugs' efficacy. Rather, at that time, the FDA could interrupt the sale of new drugs only if it determined that the new drug was unsafe. Government regulation of such drugs premised on concern over a new drug's efficacy, as opposed to its safety, is of very recent origin. Even today, a patient may use a drug for unapproved purposes where the drug may be unsafe or ineffective for the off-label purpose. In short, encumbrances on the treatment decisions of a patient and her physician lack the historical pedigree of the rights that the Alliance seeks to vindicate.

Instead of confronting this history, the court relies on statutory restrictions that address misbranded or adulterated drugs, sales of poisons, and fraudulent curative claims, government restrictions that are not inconsistent with the right of a person to attempt to save her own life. None of the cited restrictions, focusing largely on the licensing of pharmacists, suggest a physician could not prescribe a new medication for a terminal patient. . . . [T]he FDA does not regulate physicians, and off-label prescription of medications is a long-standing practice that has not been outlawed. . . .

. . . . [T]he claimed right also falls squarely within the realm of rights implicit in ordered liberty. . . . It is difficult to imagine any context in which this liberty interest would be stronger than in trying to save one's own life.

. . . .

For these reasons, I have serious disagreements with the court's assessment of the Alliance's claim to a fundamental right protected by the Fifth Amendment to the Constitution. . . . Denying a terminally ill patient her only chance to survive without even a strict showing of governmental necessity presupposes a dangerous brand of paternalism. . . .

B. THE DEFINITION OF "NEW DRUG"

Section 505(a)'s requirement that a drug not be marketed without an approved application is limited to "new drugs." Because the scope of FDA's power, the costs of testing the drug, and the timing of the drug's release are all largely determined by its "new drug" status, the statutory definition of this term at FD&C Act 201(p) has been the focus of much debate and litigation.

Section 201(p)(1) defines a "new drug" as:

> Any drug . . . the composition of which is such that such drug is not generally recognized, among experts qualified by scientific training and experience to evaluate the safety and effectiveness of drugs, as safe and effective for use under the condition prescribed, recommended, or suggested in the labeling thereof, except that such a drug not so recognized shall not be deemed to be a "new drug" if at any time prior to the enactment of this Act [1938] it was subject to the Food and Drugs Act of June 30, 1906 . . . and if at such time its labeling contained the same representations concerning the conditions of its use.

This definition contains two exceptions to the definition of "new drug": the "generally recognized as safe and effective" (GRASE) exception and the 1938 "grandfather clause." Moreover, the 1962 Drug Amendments contained a second grandfather clause, not made part of the FD&C Act itself, which exempts a drug from the effectiveness requirements if its composition and labeling has not changed since 1962 and if, on the day before the 1962 law became effective, the drug was (a) used or sold commercially in the United States, (b) not a new drug as defined by the FD&C Act at that time, and (c) not covered by an effective application. See 76 Stat. 180.

At first glance, the definition of "new drug" appears similar to the definition of "food additive" at FD&C Act 201(s), discussed in the previous chapter. In each instance, the FD&C Act establishes a category of product subject to premarket approval and then creates exceptions to that category. The "generally recognized as safe and effective" (GRAS/GRAE) exception to "new drug" parallels the "GRAS" exception to "food additive," and the 1938 "grandfather clause" calls to mind the "prior sanction" provision for food ingredients at 201(s)(4).

Making too much of the similarity between the definitions of "new drug" and "food additive" is bound to confuse rather than clarify matters, however. The GRAS exception to section 201(s) has become a robust—indeed the dominant—classification for food ingredients, and food manufacturers successfully invoke the prior sanction exception as well. By contrast, the GRAS/GRAE exception and the grandfather clauses applicable to drugs embrace few if any actual prescription drug products. (FDA has deemed numerous over-the-counter drugs to be GRAS/GRAE, and thus exempt from the NDA requirement, through the mechanism of the OTC Drug Review, discussed *infra* p. 973.) In 2011, FDA declared: "the Agency believes it is not likely that any currently marketed prescription drug product is grandfathered or is otherwise not a *new drug*. However, the Agency recognizes that it is at least theoretically possible." GUIDANCE FOR FDA STAFF AND INDUSTRY: MARKETED UNAPPROVED DRUGS—COMPLIANCE POLICY GUIDE 12 (2011).

1. GRAS/GRAE STATUS

In 1973, the Supreme Court approved FDA's position that "general recognition" of safety and effectiveness must be based upon the same quantity and quality of scientific evidence that would be needed to obtain an NDA. This holding arose in the context of the complex process by which FDA imposed the 1962 effectiveness requirement to drugs already on the market—a process that will be discussed in more detail later in this chapter. *See infra* p. 775. Because of this decision, the GRAS/GRASE exception to the "new drug" definition can never be used as a shortcut to market.

Weinberger v. Hynson, Westcott & Dunning, Inc.

412 U.S. 609 (1973).

■ MR. JUSTICE DOUGLAS delivered the opinion of the Court.

. . . The 1938 Act, which established a system of premarketing clearance for drugs, prohibited the introduction into commerce of any "new drug" unless a new drug application (NDA) filed with the Food and Drug Administration (FDA) was effective with respect to that drug. § 505(a). Under the 1938 Act a "new drug" was one not generally recognized by qualified experts as safe for its intended use. § 201(p)(1). . . .

The 1962 Act amended § 201(p)(1) of the 1938 Act to define a "new drug" as a drug not generally recognized among experts as *effective* as well as safe for its intended use. A new drug, as now defined, still may not be marketed unless an NDA is in effect. FDA is now directed to refuse approval of an NDA and to withdraw any prior approval if "substantial evidence" that the drug is effective for its intended use is lacking. 21 U. S. C. §§ 355(d) and (e). Thus, the basic clearance system, requiring FDA approval of an NDA before a "new drug" may be lawfully marketed, was continued, except that FDA now either must approve or disapprove an application within 180 days. 21 U. S. C. § 355(c). (Under the 1938 Act an application automatically became effective if it was not disapproved.) . . .

Since the Act as amended requires affirmative agency approval, all NDA's "effective" prior to 1962 were deemed "approved" under the new definition, and manufacturers were given two years to develop substantial evidence of effectiveness, during which previously approved NDA's could not be withdrawn by FDA for a drug's lack of effectiveness. The 1962 amendments also contain a "grandfather" clause. . . .

Between 1938 and 1962 FDA had permitted 9,457 NDA's to become effective. Of these, some 4,000 were still on the market. . . .

To aid in its task of fulfilling the statutory mandate to review all marketed drugs for their therapeutic efficacy . . . FDA retained the National Academy of Sciences–National Research Council (NAS–NRC) to create expert panels to review by class the efficacy of each approved drug. Holders of NDA's were invited to furnish the panels with the best available data to establish the effectiveness of their drugs. The panels reported to FDA; and on January 23, 1968, FDA announced its policy of applying the NAS–NRC efficacy findings to all drugs. . . .

. . . [Before 1962, Hynson, Westcott & Dunning, Inc.,] had filed an application under the 1938 Act for a drug called Lutrexin, recommended by Hynson for use in the treatment of premature labor, threatened and habitual abortion, and dysmenorrhea. [Also before 1962,] FDA informed Hynson that Hynson's studies submitted with the application were not sufficiently well controlled to justify the claims of effectiveness and urged Hynson not to represent the drug as useful for threatened and habitual abortion. But FDA allowed the application to become effective, since the 1938 Act permitted evaluation of a new drug solely on the grounds of its *safety*.... When the 1962 amendments became effective and NAS–NRC undertook to appraise the efficacy of drugs theretofore approved as safe, Hynson submitted a list of literature references, a copy of an unpublished study, and a representative sample testimonial letter on behalf of Lutrexin. The panel of NAS–NRC working in the relevant field reported to FDA that Hynson's claims for effectiveness of the drug were either inappropriate or unwarranted in the absence of submission of further appropriate documentation. At the invitation of the Commissioner of Food and Drugs, Hynson submitted additional data. But the Commissioner concluded that this additional information was inadequate and published notice of his intention to withdraw approval of the NDA's covering the drug, offering Hynson the opportunity for a prewithdrawal hearing [in accordance with section 505(e) of the Act].

    ... The Commissioner denied the request for a hearing and withdrew the NDA for Lutrexin. He ruled that Lutrexin is not exempt from the 1962 amendments and that Hynson had not submitted adequate evidence that Lutrexin is not a new drug or is effective....

    The general contours of "substantial evidence" are defined by § 505(d) of the Act to include "evidence consisting of adequate and well-controlled investigations, including clinical investigations, by experts qualified by scientific training and experience to evaluate the effectiveness of the drug involved, on the basis of which it could fairly and responsibly be concluded by such experts that the drug will have the effect it purports or is represented to have under the conditions of use prescribed, recommended, or suggested in the labeling or proposed labeling thereof." Acting pursuant to his "authority to promulgate regulations for the efficient enforcement" of the Act, § 701(a), the Commissioner has detailed the "principles ... recognized by the scientific community as the essentials of adequate and well-controlled clinical investigations. They provide the basis for the determination whether there is 'substantial evidence' to support the claims of effectiveness for 'new drugs'...." 21 CFR § 130.12(a)(5)(ii) [similar language now at § 314.126(a)].... [T]he regulation provides that "[u]ncontrolled studies or partially controlled studies are not acceptable as the sole basis for the approval of claims of effectiveness. Such studies, carefully conducted and documented, may provide corroborative support.... Isolated case reports, random experience, and reports lacking the details which permit scientific evaluation will not be considered." 21 C.F.R. § 130.12(a)(5)(ii)(c) [now § 314.126(e)].

    ... [I]t is not disputed here that [these regulations] express well-established principles of scientific investigation. Moreover, their strict and demanding standards, barring anecdotal evidence indicating that doctors "believe" in the efficacy of a drug, are amply justified by the legislative history....

    ... As indicated above, Hynson in requesting an administrative hearing also asked FDA to decide that Lutrexin is not a "new drug" within the meaning of § 201(p) as amended, 21 U. S. C. § 321(p).... Finding that Hynson had failed to present any evidence of adequate and well-controlled investigations in support of Lutrexin's effectiveness, [the

Commissioner] concluded that "there is no data base upon which experts can fairly and responsibly conclude that the safety and effectiveness of the drugs has been proven and is so well established that the drugs can be generally recognized among such experts as safe and effective for their intended uses." . . .

The thrust of § 201(p) is both qualitative and quantitative. The Act, however, nowhere defines what constitutes "general recognition" among experts. Hynson contends that the "lack of substantial evidence" is applicable only to proof of the *actual* effectiveness of drugs that fall within the definition of a new drug and not to the initial determination under § 201(p) whether a drug is "generally recognized" as effective. It would rely solely on the testimony of physicians and the extant literature, evidence that has been characterized as "anecdotal." We agree with FDA, however, that the statutory scheme and overriding purpose of the 1962 amendments compel the conclusion that the hurdle of "general recognition" of effectiveness requires at least "substantial evidence" of effectiveness for approval of an NDA. In the absence of any evidence of adequate and well-controlled investigation supporting the efficacy of Lutrexin, *a fortiori* Lutrexin would be a "new drug" subject to the provisions of the Act.

. . . [T]he 1962 amendments for the first time gave FDA power to scrutinize and evaluate drugs for effectiveness as well as safety. The Act requires the Commissioner to disapprove any application when there is a lack of "substantial evidence" that the applicant's drug is effective. § 505(d). Similarly, he may withdraw approval for any drug if he subsequently determines that there is a lack of such evidence. § 505(e). Evidence may be accepted only if it consists of "adequate and well-controlled investigations, including clinical investigations, by experts qualified by scientific training and experience to evaluate the effectiveness of the drug involved. . . ." § 505(d). The legislative history of the Act indicates that the test was to be a rigorous one. The "substantial evidence" requirement reflects the conclusion of Congress, based upon hearings, that clinical impressions of practicing physicians and poorly controlled experiments do not constitute an adequate basis for establishing efficacy. This policy underlies the regulations defining the contours of "substantial evidence": "Uncontrolled studies or partially controlled studies are not acceptable as the sole basis for the approval of claims of effectiveness. Such studies, carefully conducted and documented, may provide corroborative support of well-controlled studies. . . . Isolated case reports, random experience, and reports lacking the details which permit scientific evaluation will not be considered." 21 CFR § 130.12 (a)(5)(ii)(c) [now 314.126(e)].

These efficacy requirements were not designed to be prospective only. Clearly, after the initial two-year moratorium on existing drugs, FDA has the power to withdraw an application which became effective prior to the adoption of the 1962 amendments, if the applicant has not provided "substantial evidence" of the drug's efficacy. The Act plainly contemplates that such drugs will be evaluated on the basis of adequate and well-controlled investigations. Hynson would have us hold that withdrawal proceedings can be thwarted by a showing of general recognition of effectiveness based merely on expert testimony and reports with respect to investigations and clinical observation regardless of the controls used. But, we cannot construe § 201(p) to deprive FDA of jurisdiction over a drug which, if subject to FDA regulation, could not be marketed because it had not passed the "substantial evidence" test. To do so "would be to impute to Congress a purpose to paralyze with one hand what it sought to promote with the other."

. . . . We have held [elsewhere in this opinion], however, that the Commissioner was not justified in withdrawing Hynson's NDA without a prior hearing on whether Hynson had submitted "substantial evidence" of Lutrexin's effectiveness. Consequently, any ruling as to Lutrexin's "new drug" status is premature and must await the outcome of this hearing.

It is well established that our task in interpreting separate provisions of a single Act is to give the Act "the most harmonious, comprehensive meaning possible" in light of the legislative policy and purpose. We accordingly have concluded that a drug can be "generally recognized" by experts as effective for intended use within the meaning of the Act only when that expert consensus is founded upon "substantial evidence" as defined in § 505(d). We have held . . . however, that the Commissioner was not justified in withdrawing Hynson's NDA without a prior hearing on whether Hynson had submitted "substantial evidence" of Lutrexin's effectiveness. Consequently, any ruling as to Lutrexin's "new drug" status is premature and must await the outcome of this hearing. . . .

NOTE

1. *Other Holdings of Hynson.* Another portion of this opinion, in which the Court upheld, in general, the agency's use of a summary judgment procedure to deny drug withdrawal hearings but reversed the use of summary judgment against Hynson in particular, is reproduced *infra* at p. 848.

2. *Implications.* The *Hynson* decision effectively renders every new chemical entity drug introduced since 1962 a "new drug," for it holds that no drug can be generally recognized as effective in the absence of the "adequate and well controlled" clinical studies that are required for approval of an NDA.

3. *The Supreme Court's 1973 Quartet. Hynson* was one of four major opinions the Supreme Court issued in June 1973 upholding FDA's approach to implementing the 1962 effectiveness requirement with respect to drugs already on the market. The others were *Ciba Corp. v. Weinberger,* 412 U.S. 640 (1973), *Weinberger v. Bentex Pharmaceuticals,* 412 U.S. 645 (1973), and *USV Pharmaceutical Corp. v. Weinberger,* 412 U.S. 655 (1973). *Hynson* itself addressed multiple issues in addition to the meaning of the GRAS/GRASE exception. A portion of *Bentex* is reproduced later in this section. *Infra* p. 667. The quartet will be discussed further *infra* at p. 779.

4. *The "Bentex Exception."* In *Bentex,* 412 U.S. at 652–653, *infra* p. 667, the Supreme Court stated that, in some cases, general recognition that a drug is effective might be made without the kind of scientific support necessary to obtain approval of an NDA. No court has ever applied this

"*Bentex* exception," however. *See United States v. 50 Boxes More or Less*, 909 F.2d 24, 27–28 (1st Cir. 1990) (remarking on non-use of the exception); *see also United States v. 225 Cartons . . . Fiorinal*, 871 F.2d 409, 418–419 (3d Cir. 1989). Despite the courts' consistent rejection of claims that drugs subject to enforcement actions are GRAE, drug manufacturers continue to advance this defense. *See, e.g., United States v. 675 Cases . . . "Damason-P,"* Food Drug Cosm. L. Rep. (CCH) ¶ 38,156 (C.D. Calif. 1989); *United States v. Vital Health Products, Ltd.*, 786 F. Supp. 761 (E.D. Wisc. 1992); *United States v. Nine Cases . . . Endodontic Formula*, Food Drug Cosm. L. Rep. (CCH) ¶ 38,460 (D. Conn. 1996).

2.   THE "GRANDFATHER" CLAUSES

When Congress, in 1938, first required that new drugs be proved safe for the conditions of their intended use, it specified in section 201(p)(1) that this requirement would not apply to any drug marketed under the 1906 Pure Food and Drugs Act (i.e., prior to 1938) so long as its labeling continued to contain "the same representations concerning the conditions of its use." This "grandfather" clause for pre-1938 drugs in section 201(p)(1) was not changed in 1962.

The 1962 Amendments contained their own so-called transitional provisions designed to provide either permanent or temporary exemption from the new effectiveness requirement for certain classes of drugs first marketed after 1938. These transitional provisions appeared in section 107(c) of the Drug Amendments of 1962, 76 Stat. 780, 788–789, but are not codified in the FD&C Act.

> In the case of any drug which, on the day immediately preceding the enactment date, (A) was commercially used or sold in the United States, (B) was not a new drug as defined by section 201(p) of the basic Act as then in force, and (C) was not covered by an effective application under section 505 of that Act, the amendments to section 201(p) made by this Act shall not apply to such drug when intended solely for use under conditions prescribed, recommended, or suggested in labeling with respect to such drug on that day.

As is the case with the GRAS/GRASE exception, FDA and the courts have whittled down the grandfather clauses into insignificance. According to FDA:

> The two grandfather clauses in the FD&C Act have been construed very narrowly by the courts. FDA believes that there are very few drugs on the market that are actually entitled to grandfather status because the drugs currently on the market likely differ from the previous versions in some respect, such as formulation, dosage or strength, dosage form, route of administration, indications, or intended patient population. If a firm claims that its product is grandfathered, it is that firm's burden to prove that assertion. See 21 CFR 314.200(e)(5); *see also United States v. An Article of Drug (Bentex Ulcerine)*, 469 F.2d 875, 878 (5th Cir. 1972); *United States v. Articles of Drug Consisting of the Following: 5,906 Boxes*, 745 F.2d 105, 113 (1st Cir 1984).

GUIDANCE FOR FDA STAFF AND INDUSTRY: MARKETED UNAPPROVED DRUGS—COMPLIANCE POLICY GUIDE 12 (2011).

As suggested in this Compliance Policy Guide (CPG), courts have strongly supported the agency's stringent application of the grandfather clauses. In addition to the cases cited by FDA, consider also the court's statement in *United States v. Allan Drug Corp.*, 357 F.2d 713, 718–19 (10th Cir. 1966):

> Since we are dealing with a Grandfather Clause exception, we must construe it strictly against one who invokes it. . . .

> Judged in this context, we construe the critical language of the Grandfather Clauses to exempt drugs . . . if on the effective date of the Act the labeling contained the same representations concerning its use, and thus confine the exemption to drugs intended solely for use under conditions prescribed on the effective date of the Act. . . .

No drug has ever been judicially determined to fall within the 1938 or 1962 grandfather clause.

3. JURISDICTION TO DETERMINE NEW DRUG STATUS

The following case is another of the quartet of June 1973 Supreme Court decisions upholding FDA's approach to applying the 1962 effectiveness requirement to pre-1962 products. The decision ensures that a drug manufacturer cannot attempt to circumvent FDA's new drug approval process by trying to persuade a court, in the first instance, that a product is not a "new drug" under FD&C Act 201(p) and thus not required to have an approved NDA. More broadly, the decision has been of crucial importance in establishing FDA as a strong and authoritative administrative agency.

Weinberger v. Bentex Pharmaceuticals, Inc.
412 U.S. 645 (1973).

■ MR. JUSTICE DOUGLAS delivered the opinion of the Court.

In this case Bentex and some 20 other firms . . . filed this suit for a declaratory judgment that their [pre-1962] drugs containing pentylenetetrazol are generally recognized as safe and effective, and thus not "new drugs" within the meaning of § 201(p)(1). . . . They also sought exemption from the new effectiveness requirements by reason of § 107(c)(4) [the "Grandfather clause"] of the 1962 amendments. . . .

. . . [T]hree separate National Academy of Sciences–National Research Council (NAS–NRC) panels reviewed the evidence concerning these drugs, and each concluded that the drug was "ineffective" for the indicated use. The Commissioner concluded there was a lack of substantial evidence that these drugs were effective for their intended uses and gave notice of his intention to initiate proceedings to withdraw approval of the new drug applications (NDA's). . . .

The Court of Appeals . . . held that FDA has no jurisdiction, either primary or concurrent, to decide in an administrative proceeding what is a "new drug" for which an NDA is required. In its view the 1962 Act established two forums for the regulation of drugs: an administrative one for premarketing clearances for "new drugs" or withdrawal of previously approved NDA's, with the right of appeal; and, second, a judicial one for enforcement of the requirement that "new drugs" be cleared as safe and effective before marketing by providing the Government with judicial remedies of seizure, injunction, and criminal prosecution available solely in the District Court.

We reverse the Court of Appeals. . . .

. . . The line sought to be drawn by the Court of Appeals is FDA action on NDA's pursuant to § 505(d) and § 505(e), on the one hand, and the question of "new drug" determination on the other. We can discern no such jurisdictional line under the Act. The FDA . . . may deny an NDA where there is a lack of "substantial evidence" of the drug's effectiveness, based . . . on clinical investigation by experts. But the "new drug" definition under § 201(p) encompasses a drug "not generally recognized, among experts qualified by scientific training and experience to evaluate the safety and effectiveness of drugs, as safe and effective for use." Whether a particular drug is a "new drug," depends in part on the expert knowledge and experience of scientists based on controlled clinical experimentation and backed by substantial support in scientific literature. One function is not peculiar to judicial expertise, the other to administrative expertise. The two types of cases overlap and strongly suggest that Congress desired that the administrative agency make both kinds of determination. Even where no such administrative determination has been made and the issue arises in a district court in enforcement proceedings, it would be commonplace for the court to await an appropriate administrative declaration before it acted. It may, of course, be true that in some cases general recognition that a drug is efficacious might be made without the kind of scientific support necessary to obtain approval of an NDA. But . . . the reach of scientific inquiry under both § 505(d) and § 201(p) is precisely the same.

. . . We are told that FDA is incapable of handling a caseload of more than perhaps 10 or 15 *de novo* judicial proceedings a year. Clearly, if FDA were required to litigate, on a case-by-case basis, the "new drug" status of each drug now marketed, the regulatory scheme of the Act would be severely undermined, if not totally destroyed. Moreover, a case-by-case approach is inherently unfair because it requires compliance by one manufacturer while his competitors marketing similar drugs remain free to violate the Act. . . .

. . . The determination whether a drug is generally recognized as safe and effective within the meaning of § 201(p)(1) necessarily implicates complex chemical and pharmacological consideration. Threshold questions within the peculiar expertise of an administrative agency are appropriately routed to the agency, while the court stays its hand. . . .

NOTES

1. *Concurrent Decisions.* In *Ciba Corp. v. Weinberger*, 412 U.S. 640, 644 (1973), the Supreme Court reiterated its position on this issue:

> . . . [T]he Act does not create a dual system of control—one administrative, and the other judicial. Cases may arise where there

has been no formal administrative determination of the "new drug" issue, it being first tendered to a district court. Even then, however, the district court might well stay its hand, awaiting an appropriate administrative determination of the threshold question. Where there is, however, an administrative determination, whether it be explicit or implicit[,] in the withdrawal of an NDA, the tactic of "reserving" the threshold question (the jurisdictional issue) for later judicial determination is not tolerable. . . . [P]etitioner, having an opportunity to litigate the "new drug" issue before FDA and to raise the issue on appeal to a court of appeals, may not relitigate the issue in another proceeding.

The decision in another case in the quartet added: "The heart of the new procedures designed by Congress is the grant of primary jurisdiction to FDA, the expert agency it created. . . ." *Weinberger v. Hynson, Westcott & Dunning, Inc.*, 412 U.S. at 627.

2. *Primary Jurisdiction.* The Supreme Court's holding in *Bentex* and *CIBA* that FDA has "primary jurisdiction" to determine new drug status was a major victory for the agency. For additional discussion of the doctrine of primary jurisdiction, see *supra* p. 66.

C. DRUG DEVELOPMENT AND FDA LICENSURE OF NEW DRUGS

1. NONCLINICAL FORMULATION AND TESTING

Before clinical (human) testing may begin on an investigational new drug, substantial nonclinical testing must be completed. FDA does not directly regulate nonclinical testing, but it indirectly shapes all preclinical work because drug sponsors must ultimately conduct whatever nonclinical testing FDA determines to be necessary to justify allowing the drug to proceed to human testing. This initial phase of testing requires at least two years and can last much longer.

a. SYNTHESIS AND PURIFICATION

The first step in the lengthy and costly process of the development of a new drug is the synthesis and purification of an active pharmaceutical ingredient (API).

Preclinical Research: Synthesis and Purification
in THE CDER HANDBOOK, *The New Drug Development and Review Process*
FDA Website.

The research process is complicated, time-consuming, and costly and the end result is never guaranteed. Literally hundreds and sometimes thousands of chemical compounds must be made and tested in an effort to find one that can achieve a desirable result. . . .

There is no standard route through which drugs are developed. A pharmaceutical company may decide to develop a new drug aimed at a specific disease or medical condition. Sometimes, scientists choose to pursue an interesting or promising line of research. In other cases, new findings from university, government, or other laboratories may point the way for drug companies to follow with their own research.

New drug research starts with an understanding of how the body functions, both normally and abnormally, at its most basic levels. The questions raised by this research help determine a concept of how a drug might be used to prevent, cure, or treat a disease or medical condition. This provides the researcher with a target. Sometimes, scientists find the right compound quickly, but usually hundreds or thousands must be screened. In a series of test tube experiments called assays, compounds are added one at a time to enzymes, cell cultures, or cellular substances grown in a laboratory. The goal is to find which additions show some effect. This process may require testing hundreds of compounds since some may not work, but will indicate ways of changing the compound's chemical structure to improve its performance.

Computers can be used to simulate a chemical compound and design chemical structures that might work against it. Enzymes attach to the correct site on a cell's membrane, which causes the disease. A computer can show scientists what the receptor site looks like and how one might tailor a compound to block an enzyme from attaching there. But even though computers give chemists clues as to which compounds to make, a substance must still be tested within a living being.

Another approach involves testing compounds made naturally by microscopic organisms. Candidates include fungi, viruses and molds, such as those that led to penicillin and other antibiotics. Scientists grow the microorganisms in what is known as a "fermentation broth," with one type of organism per broth. Sometimes, 100,000 or more broths are tested to see whether any compound made by a microorganism has a desirable effect.

It is important to purify and characterize the API even at this early stage, in order to make certain that nonclinical and clinical studies on the compound are conducted using the same active moiety.

b.   NONCLINICAL TESTING

Nonclinical testing is conducted prior to human trials for three reasons. First, computer and animal modeling are pursued to obtain preliminary confirmation that the API has the potential for effectiveness. Second, chemical analysis and manufacturing controls are further refined to assure that the drug can be reliably reproduced. Third, toxicity testing in laboratory systems and in animals is essential to obtain sufficient safety data to justify human testing.

Preclinical Research

in THE CDER HANDBOOK, The New Drug Development and Review Process
FDA Website.

Under FDA requirements, a sponsor must first submit data showing that the drug is reasonably safe for use in initial, small-scale clinical studies. Depending on whether the compound has been studied or marketed previously, the sponsor may have several options for fulfilling this requirement: (1) compiling existing nonclinical data from past *in vitro* laboratory or animal studies on the compound; (2) compiling data from previous clinical testing or marketing of the drug in the United States or another country whose population is relevant to the U.S. population; or (3) undertaking new preclinical studies designed to provide the evidence necessary to support the safety of administering the compound to humans.

During preclinical drug development, a sponsor evaluates the drug's toxic and pharmacologic effects through *in vitro* and *in vivo* laboratory animal testing. Genotoxicity screening is performed, as well as investigations on drug absorption and metabolism, the toxicity of the drug's metabolites, and the speed with which the drug and its metabolites are excreted from the body. At the preclinical stage, the FDA will generally ask, at a minimum, that sponsors: (1) develop a pharmacological profile of the drug; (2) determine the acute toxicity of the drug in at least two species of animals, and (3) conduct short-term toxicity studies ranging from 2 weeks to 3 months, depending on the proposed duration of use of the substance in the proposed clinical studies.

NOTES

1. *FDA Guidance.* FDA has issued a GUIDANCE FOR INDUSTRY: NONCLINICAL SAFETY STUDIES FOR THE CONDUCT OF HUMAN CLINICAL TRIALS AND MARKETING AUTHORIZATION FOR PHARMACEUTICALS (January 2010). *See also* Geoff Goodfellow, *Nonclinical Safety Assessment of New Drugs and Therapeutic Proteins*, 10 Reg. Affairs Focus, No. 12, at 7 (Dec. 8, 2005).

2. *Animal Welfare.* All animal testing must be conducted in accordance with the requirements established in the Animal Welfare Act, 80 Stat 350 (1966), 84 Stat. 1560 (1970), 7 U.S.C. Chapter 54, as implemented by USDA regulations in 9 C.F.R. Subchapter A. *See* Adam I. Mandelbaum, *The Origin and Development of the Animal Welfare Act* (1999), in Chapter I(J) of the Electronic Book.

3. *Animal Rights Activists.* Activists for animal rights, such as the People for the Ethical Treatment of Animals (PETA) and the Animal Liberation Front, believe that animals have the same rights as humans and should not be the subject of experimentation. *See, e.g.*, PETA website. Some more extreme activists have threatened scientists and their families, raided laboratories to free test animals, and engaged in other illegal activities in order to dramatize their position. To protect companies and individuals against terrorism by animal rights activists, Congress enacted the Animal Enterprise Protection Act of 1992, 106 Stat. 928, and the Animal Enterprise Terrorism Act, 120 Stat. 2652 (2006).

4. *Federal Efforts to Establish Alternatives to Animal Testing.* In 2000, Congress enacted the ICCVAM Authorization Act, 114 Stat 2721, formally recognizing the previously-established Interagency Coordinating Committee on the Validation of Alternative Methods. The purpose of the ICCVAM is to identify and validate alternative testing methods. In spite of substantial international effort to develop validated alternatives to animal toxicity testing, progress over the past two decades has been modest.

c.   GOOD LABORATORY PRACTICES

In 1976, FDA discovered substantial fraud in a prominent animal testing laboratory. *See United States v. Keplinger*, 775 F.2d 678 (7th Cir. 1985). The agency subsequently established comprehensive good laboratory practice (GLP) regulations governing all forms of preclinical testing, codified at 21 C.F.R. Part 85. Any report of preclinical testing submitted with an Investigational New Drug (IND) Application or NDA must either comply with GLP or explain why compliance could not be achieved. The failure to comply may result in the report being rejected by FDA.

d.   REQUEST FOR DESIGNATION

In many instances, the classification of a product as a "drug" under the FD&C Act and its regulation by the Center for Drug Evaluation and Research (CDER) are clear. However, because of the often uncertain jurisdictional lines that divide drugs, biological products, and medical devices—particularly when two of these categories are combined into a single product—FDA has sought to clarify in what agency center particular types of products are regulated and to establish a mechanism for determining the proper locus of regulation when it is unclear or is disputed.

Beginning in the 1980s, the centers responsible for drugs, biological products, and medical devices entered into Intercenter Agreements with respect to their individual jurisdiction. These agreements, which have been revised over the years, are available on the FDA website.

As combination products became more numerous, however, Congress determined that the matter should be handled on a more comprehensive basis. The Safe Medical Devices Act of 1990 therefore added section 503(g) to the FD&C Act to require that FDA establish a mechanism for assigning primary jurisdiction for a combination product to a particular FDA center according to the product's "primary mode of action." In 1991, FDA issued regulations implementing this new statutory mandate. 21 C.F.R. Part 3. Under these regulations, the sponsor of any combination product may submit a request for designation (RFD) to the Office of Combination Products to clarify where the product is to be regulated within FDA. That office will issue a "letter of designation" within 60 days after the request is filed.

In many instances, companies find that it is more efficient to work informally with a particular center to determine where a product should be regulated rather than to submit a formal request for designation. An RFD does not always provide a satisfactory result, and FDA's determination is sometimes challenged. *See, e.g., Prevor v. Food and Drug Administration*, 895 F. Supp. 2d 90 (D.D.C. 2012) (excerpted *infra* p. 1207. Nonetheless, the existence of 21 C.F.R. Part 3 has helped greatly in clarifying the jurisdiction of the individual centers in situations in which disputes have slowed product development in the past. For a comprehensive review of the history and current status of this subject, see Danielle C. Schillinger, *The Office of Combination Products: Its Roots, Its Creation, and Its Role* (2005), in Chapter IX(A)(7) of the Electronic Book.

NOTE

Disparate Treatment. FDA strives to ensure that similar products are treated in the same way so as to avoid competitive inequity, but it is not always successful. This problem is illustrated by *Bracco Diagnostics, Inc. v. Shalala*, 963 F. Supp. 20 (D.D.C. 1997), where three manufacturers of injectable contrast imaging agents for use with diagnostic ultrasound equipment in the diagnosis of cardiac dysfunction brought suit against FDA on the ground that they were required to obtain NDAs while a competitor with virtually identical technology was regulated as a medical device. The District Court found that CDER and CDRH (the device center) were applying very different standards to assess safety and effectiveness of essentially identical products. It granted the plaintiffs' motion for injunctive relief, concluding that FDA has discretion under section 503(g) of the FD&C Act to determine whether to regulate these products as drugs or devices, but that "what the FDA is not free to do . . . is to treat them dissimilarly and to permit two sets of similar products to run down two separate tracks, one more treacherous than the other, for no apparent reason." *Id.* at 28. Because the "disparate treatment of functionally indistinguishable products is the essence of the meaning of arbitrary and capricious," *id.*, the District Court enjoined FDA from continuing any approval or review procedure with respect to the medical device product until the agency determined how all of the products should be regulated. The court also enjoined the agency from taking any further review action with respect to the three drug products until the jurisdictional issue was resolved. FDA subsequently declared that it would regulate all ultrasound contrast agents as drugs, after which the District Court determined that all of the pending lawsuits were moot and should be dismissed. Food Drug Cosm. L. Rep. (CCH) ¶ 38,537 (D.D.C. 1997).

2. CLINICAL TESTING: INVESTIGATIONAL NEW DRUG APPLICATION (IND)

All of the clinical testing requirements discussed in this subsection apply to biological products subject to the biologics license (BLA) procedure established by section 351 of the Public Health Service Act, as well as to drugs subject to the NDA requirement of FD&C Act 505. Biologics manufacturers use the very same IND procedure as the small molecule drugs considered in this chapter. Much of the discussion below also applies to clinical investigations of medical devices in connection with section 510(k) "substantial equivalence" filings and section 515 premarket approval applications (PMAs). Medical device investigations, however, are subject to a separate FDA oversight process called the Investigational Device Exemption (IDE). FD&C Act 520(g); *see infra* p. 1230. Biologics and medical devices will be covered in Chapters 9 and 10, respectively. The following detailed discussion of FDA clinical trials regulation will not be repeated in those chapters, although the medical devices chapter will describe the basics of the IDE process.

a. PURPOSE AND FORM OF THE IND

In order to market a new drug, a manufacturer must first obtain FDA approval of a new drug application (NDA). Before submitting an application, the manufacturer must conduct, or arrange to be conducted, clinical studies designed to demonstrate that the drug is safe and effective under the criteria established in section 505(d) of the FD&C Act. Usually this will require shipment of the drug in interstate commerce, e.g., to researchers at medical schools across the country. But section 505(a) prohibits the shipment of any new drug for which FDA has not approved an NDA. To enable sponsors of new drugs to carry out the clinical testing necessary to support FDA approval of an NDA, Congress in section 505(i) permitted FDA to exempt a drug from this prohibition for the limited purpose of conducting clinical investigations.

The procedure FDA has created to implement this exemption is the investigational new drug application (IND), governed by 21 C.F.R. Part 312. The IND content and format is set forth in 21 C.F.R. 312.23. Under 21 C.F.R. 312.40(b)(1), an IND goes into effect 30 days after FDA receives it, unless FDA notifies the sponsor that the IND is subject to a "clinical hold." The agency will issue such a hold, among other reasons, if the "[h]uman subjects . . . would be exposed to an unreasonable and significant risk of illness or injury," if the named investigators "are not qualified by reason of their scientific training and experience to conduct the investigation," or if the protocol for a Phase II or Phase III study "is clearly deficient in design to meet its stated objectives." 21 C.F.R. 312.42(b)(1)(i), (ii); (b)(2)(ii). In many instances, FDA officials will raise informal questions about an IND within the 30-day post-submission period but will not institute a formal clinical hold. Companies often delay starting a clinical trial until these informal discussions are completed.

The clinical investigation of a new chemical entity (NCE) new drug requires five to ten years. It is often estimated that, for every 5,000 chemicals screened, five will proceed to clinical testing and one will survive to approval of an NDA. And for every 100 drugs for which an IND is submitted to FDA, 70 will successfully complete Phase I clinical testing and proceed to Phase II, 33 will proceed Phase III, and 20 will be approved for marketing.

NOTES

1. *Consent of Test Subjects.* Section 505(i) requires that FDA's regulations condition the IND exemption upon assurance by the sponsor of an investigation that all investigators:

> will inform any human beings to whom such drugs, or any controls used in connection therewith, are being administered, or their representatives, that such drugs are being used for investigational purposes and will obtain the consent of such human beings or their representatives, except where they deem it not feasible or, in their professional judgment, contrary to the best interests of such human beings.

Based upon this language, and the remainder of section 505(i), FDA has established an elaborate system of controls over the conduct of clinical drug investigations. The present regulations, which require written consent of test subjects in virtually all cases and the approval of a local institutional review board (IRB) for any study conducted in an institutional setting, appear at 21 C.F.R. Part 312. In 1987, after a decade of consideration, FDA promulgated a comprehensive revision of these regulations. In general, the new IND regulations codified existing practice and reorganized the old regulations to make them more easily understandable, but did little to reduce regulatory requirements or to speed up the investigation and approval of new drugs.

2. *Development of IND Regulations.* Prior to 1962, the IND regulations were brief and basic. No IND application was required to be submitted to FDA. Following enactment of the Drug Amendments of 1962, FDA promulgated extensive regulations governing the submission and review of an IND and the obligations of sponsors and investigators. Twenty years later, as part of the IND–NDA review undertaken when the attempt to revise all of section 505 under the Drug Regulation Reform legislation of 1977–1980 failed, FDA promulgated the current IND regulations, codified at 21 C.F.R. Part 312.

3. *Responsibility to Test.* The FD&C Act places responsibility for testing new drugs on the manufacturer who desires FDA approval for marketing. Manufacturers in turn fund independent medical experts, most of whom are affiliated with teaching hospitals, to conduct these tests. Suspicion of manufacturer bias has prompted some critics of FDA and of the industry to advocate that responsibility for testing be removed from private hands and taken over by the government or some other independent testing institution.

4. *Exemptions.* Under 21 C.F.R. 312.2(b), FDA exempts from the requirement of an IND a clinical investigation of a drug product that is already lawfully marketed in the U.S. if it meets five conditions. In 21 C.F.R. 312.2(d), FDA exempts from the requirements of an IND the use of an approved new drug for an unlabeled indication in the practice of medicine. FDA has adopted a guidance for industry on IND EXEMPTIONS FOR STUDIES OF LAWFULLY MARKETED CANCER DRUG OR BIOLOGICAL PRODUCTS. 68 Fed. Reg. 53984 (Sept. 15, 2003) (availability of guidance).

5. *Financial Disclosure.* To minimize bias in clinical studies, FDA regulations require the disclosure of the financial arrangements between sponsors and clinical investigators and of any financial interests the clinical investigators have in the product under study or in the sponsor of the study. 21 C.F.R. Part 54. *See* Kevin W. Williams, *Managing Physician Financial Conflicts of Interest in Clinical Trials Conducted in the Private Practice Setting*, 59 FOOD & DRUG L.J. 45 (2004).

6. *FDA Power to Mandate Testing.* FDA has no authority to require any person to investigate a new drug, however promising the drug may be, nor can any citizen compel FDA or the federal government to undertake studies of a drug. For an understanding of the frustration felt by physicians and patients when a manufacturer declines to develop what they believe is

a promising drug, see Amy Dockser Marcus, *Different Rx: A Doctor's Push for Drug Pits Him Against Its Maker*, WALL ST. J., Nov. 13, 2006, at. A1.

7. *CDER Guidance.* CDER continually issues a very large number of guidances about specific and general subjects involving the investigation and development of new drugs. In addition to following the FDA Good Guidance Practice (GGP) Policy, 21 C.F.R. 10.115, CDER has its own process for developing guidance. CDER Manual of Policies and Procedures (MAPP) No. 4000.2. CDER MAPP No. 6030.1 (May 1, 1998) governs *IND Process and Review Procedures.*

8. *IND Safety Reporting.* FDA regulations require an investigator to "immediately report to the sponsor any serious adverse event, whether or not considered drug related . . . and must include an assessment of whether there is a reasonable possibility that the drug caused the event." 21 C.F.R. 312.64(b). The sponsor, in turn, must report any "serious and unexpected adverse reaction" within 15 days of determining it is reportable, but only if there is evidence to suggest a causal relationship between the drug and the event. *Id.* 312.32(c)(1). The sponsor must report "unexpected fatal or life-threatening suspected adverse reactions within seven days of receiving the information." *Id.* 312.32(c)(2).

b. MEETINGS WITH FDA

Perhaps the most important determinant of the success of the IND/NDA development process is the frequency and candor of meetings with FDA. Both experience and actual studies have determined that open communication with the agency is essential for an efficient and effective IND/NDA process.

Since enactment of the Drug Amendments of 1962, FDA policy regarding meetings with the pharmaceutical industry has varied from commissioner to commissioner. At some times, FDA has sought to distance itself from the regulated industry and thus has kept meetings both infrequent and formal. At other times, FDA has understood that meetings are essential to the regulatory process and has been more open and forthcoming in granting meetings.

In March 1996, CDER adopted MAPP No. 4512.4, governing formal meetings between CDER and the regulated industry. As part of the FDA Modernization Act of 1997, section 505(b)(4)(B) was added to the FD&C Act, directing FDA to meet with the pharmaceutical industry for the purpose or reaching agreement on the design and size of clinical trials intended to form the primary basis for NDA approval. This provision, which resulted in the FDA Special Protocol Assessment (SPA) program, is discussed further *infra* at page 691. The pharmaceutical industry also reached agreement with FDA in conjunction with the 1997 reauthorization of the Prescription Drug User Fee Act (PDUFA) on specific performance goals for the management of meetings. As a result, in February 2000, FDA issued the following guidance.

Guidance for Industry: Formal Meetings
With Sponsors and Applicants for PDUFA Products

February 2000.

. . . .

There are three categories of meetings between sponsors or applicants for PDUFA products and CDER or CBER staff: Type A; Type B; and Type C. Each type of meeting will be subject to different procedures, as described below.

A. Type A Meeting

A Type A meeting is one that is immediately necessary for an otherwise stalled drug development program to proceed (i.e., a critical path meeting).

Type A meetings generally will be reserved for dispute resolution meetings, meetings to discuss clinical holds, and special protocol assessment meetings that are requested by sponsors after FDA's evaluation of protocols in assessment letters. . . .

B. Type B Meeting

Type B meetings are (1) pre-IND meetings (21 CFR 312.82), (2) certain end of Phase I meetings (21 CFR 312.82), (3) end of Phase 2/pre-Phase III meetings (21 CFR 312.47), and (4) pre-NDA/BLA meetings (21 CFR 312.47). . . .

C. Type C Meeting

A Type C meeting is any meeting other than a Type A or Type B meeting between FDA and a sponsor or applicant regarding the development and review of a product in a human drug application. . . . Meetings that do not pertain to the review of human drug applications for PDUFA products (e.g., most meetings about advertising and promotional labeling for approved drug products except meetings about launch activities and materials, postmarketing safety evaluation meetings) are not Type C meetings and are not addressed in this guidance document. . . .

NOTES

1.   *Schedule for Meetings.* Under the guidance, a Type A meeting will occur within 30 calendar days, Type B within 60 calendar days, and Type C within 75 calendar days.

2.   *Additional Guidance.* The guidance, in addition to establishing the three types of meetings, gives detailed advice regarding procedures for requesting meetings, the information to be included in a request, the timing of the submission of information for the meeting, procedures for the conduct of meetings, documentation by minutes, and dispute resolution.

3.   *Criticism of the FDA Meeting Policy.* Critics have argued that the 30, 60, and 75-day waiting times for a meeting with FDA are unconscionably long. No private business would ever conduct discussions on that type of lengthy schedule. The impact on the cost of new drugs is substantial. If one of the roughly 5000 small biotechnology companies in the United States must wait two months to discuss a protocol with FDA,

and the company's burn rate (i.e., the amount of money needed simply to keep the doors open) is $1 million per month, the cost of just a simple meeting with FDA is $2 million. And if, as often happens, a second meeting is needed, the total cost becomes extremely high. Indeed, the cost of meetings with FDA to discuss a protocol for a clinical trial can exceed the cost of the clinical trial itself. Because it is essential to meet with FDA to discuss clinical protocols, however, pharmaceutical companies have no option other than to follow the February 2000 guidance.

c.   PHASES OF CLINICAL TESTING

At one time, clinical testing proceeded through three very distinct and separate phases: Phases I, II, and III. In recent years, however, the distinctions between these phases have broken down. Some trials have characteristics of two phases at the same time. Nonetheless, it is useful to describe the basic concepts of these three phases—as well as the new Phase Zero—to understand the types of clinical trials that must be undertaken in order to obtain sufficient safety and effectiveness information for NDA approval.

i.   *Phase Zero*

FDA created a new category of clinical trial, termed "exploratory IND studies," in a draft guidance announced in 70 Fed. Reg. 19764 (Apr. 14, 2005). The final guidance, excerpted below, was released the following year.

Guidance for Industry, Investigators, and Reviewers: Exploratory IND Studies
January 2006.

. . . .

For the purposes of this guidance the phrase exploratory IND study is intended to describe a clinical trial that

— is conducted early in phase 1,

— involves very limited human exposure, and

— has no therapeutic or diagnostic intent (e.g., screening studies, microdose studies).

Such exploratory IND studies are conducted prior to the traditional dose escalation, safety, and tolerance studies that ordinarily initiate a clinical drug development program. The duration of dosing in an exploratory IND study is expected to be limited (e.g., 7 days). This guidance applies to early phase 1 clinical studies of investigational new drug and biological products that assess feasibility for further development of the drug or biological product.

. . . .

Typically, during pharmaceutical development, large numbers of molecules are generated with the goal of identifying the most promising candidates for further development. These molecules are generally structurally related, but can differ in important ways. Promising candidates are often selected using in vitro testing models that examine binding to receptors, effects on enzyme activities, toxic effects, or other in vitro pharmacologic parameters; these tests usually require only small amounts of the drug. Candidates that are not rejected during these early tests are prepared in greater quantities for in vivo animal testing for efficacy and safety. Commonly, a single candidate is selected for an IND application and introduction into human subjects, initially healthy volunteers in most cases.

Before the human studies can begin, an IND must be submitted to the Agency containing, among other things, information on any risks anticipated based on the results of pharmacological and toxicological data collected during studies of the drug in animals (21 CFR 312.23(a)(8)). These basic safety tests are most often performed in rats and dogs. The studies are designed to permit the selection of a safe starting dose for humans, to gain an understanding of which organs may be the targets of toxicity, to estimate the margin of safety between a clinical and a toxic dose, and to predict pharmacokinetic and pharmacodynamic parameters. These early tests are usually resource intensive, requiring significant investment in product synthesis, animal use, laboratory analyses, and time. Many resources are invested in, and thus wasted on, candidate products that subsequently are found to have unacceptable profiles when evaluated in humans—less than 10 percent of INDs for new molecular entities (NME) progress beyond the investigational stage to submission of a marketing application (NDA). In addition, animal testing does not always predict performance in humans, and potentially effective candidates may not be developed because of resource constraints.

Existing regulations allow a great deal of flexibility in terms of the amount of data that need to be submitted with any IND application, depending on the goals of the proposed investigation, the specific human testing proposed, and the expected risks. The Agency believes that sponsors have not taken full advantage of that flexibility. As a result, limited, early phase 1 studies, such as those described in this guidance, are often supported by a more extensive preclinical database than is required by the regulations.

This guidance describes preclinical and clinical approaches, and the chemistry, manufacturing, and controls information that should be considered when planning exploratory IND studies in humans, including studies of closely related drugs or therapeutic biological products, under a single IND application (21 CFR 312).

Exploratory IND studies . . . can help sponsors

- Determine whether a mechanism of action defined in experimental systems can also be observed in humans (e.g., a binding property or inhibition of an enzyme)
- Provide important information on pharmacokinetics (PK)
- Select the most promising lead product from a group of candidates designed to interact with a particular therapeutic target in humans, based on PK or pharmacodynamic (PD) properties

- Explore a product's biodistribution characteristics using various imaging technologies

Whatever the goal of the study, exploratory IND studies can help identify, early in the process, promising candidates for continued development and eliminate those lacking promise. As a result, exploratory IND studies may help reduce the number of human subjects and resources, including the amount of candidate product, needed to identify promising drugs. The studies discussed in this guidance involve dosing a limited number of subjects with a limited range of doses for a limited period of time.

. . . .

ii.   Phase I

Phase I Clinical Studies

in THE CDER HANDBOOK, *The New Drug Development and Review Process*
FDA Website.

Phase 1 includes the initial* introduction of an investigational new drug into humans. These studies are closely monitored and may be conducted in patients, but are usually conducted in healthy volunteer subjects. These studies are designed to determine the metabolic and pharmacologic actions of the drug in humans, the side effects associated with increasing doses, and, if possible, to gain early evidence on effectiveness. During Phase 1, sufficient information about the drug's pharmacokinetics and pharmacological effects should be obtained to permit the design of well-controlled, scientifically valid, Phase 2 studies.

Phase 1 studies also evaluate drug metabolism, structure-activity relationships, and the mechanism of action in humans. These studies also determine which investigational drugs are used as research tools to explore biological phenomena or disease processes. The total number of subjects included in Phase 1 studies varies with the drug, but is generally in the range of twenty to eighty.

NOTES

1.   *Phase I Safety.* Phase I is regarded as the safest phase of human testing, because it customarily begins with low doses and is conducted under close medical supervision. However, two recent Phase I incidents, involving one death and six very serious adverse events, have served to remind clinical pharmacologists that human experimentation with highly active modern drugs can produce unexpected toxic reactions. S. E. Raper et al., *Fatal Systemic Inflammatory Response Syndrome in an Ornithine Transcarbanylase Deficient Patient Following Adenoviral Gene Transfer*, 80 MOLECULAR GENETICS METABOLISM 148 (2003) (the death of Jesse Gelsinger at the University of Pennsylvania); Ganesh Suntharalingam et al., *Cytokine Storm in a Phase I Trial of the Anti–CD28 Monoclonal*

---

*   [This description was prepared before the development by FDA of Phase Zero.]

Antibody TGN1412, 355 NEW ENG. J. MED. 1018 (Sept. 7, 2006) (serious adverse reactions in six healthy volunteers in England).

2. *Reasons for Clinical Hold*. In Phase I studies, CDER can impose a clinical hold (i.e., prohibit the study from proceeding or stop a trial that has started) for reasons of safety, or because of a sponsor's failure accurately to disclose the risk of the study to investigators. Although CDER often provides advice on nonsafety aspects of protocols, investigators may choose to ignore any advice regarding the design of Phase 1 studies in areas other than patient safety.

3. *Deregulation of Phase I*. It has been proposed that regulation of Phase I clinical testing be subject only to IRB supervision, and that an IND be required only for Phases II and III. *See* Kingsley L. Taft, *Deregulation of Investigational New Drug Applications* (1996), in Chapter VI(C)(1) of the Electronic Book.

iii. Phase II

Phase II Clinical Studies
in THE CDER HANDBOOK, *The New Drug Development and Review Process*
FDA Website.

Phase 2 includes the early controlled clinical studies conducted to obtain some preliminary data on the effectiveness of the drug for a particular indication or indications in patients with the disease or condition. This phase of testing also helps determine the common short-term side effects and risks associated with the drug. Phase 2 studies are typically well-controlled, closely monitored, and conducted in a relatively small number of patients, usually involving several hundred people.

iv. Phase III

Phase III Clinical Studies
in THE CDER HANDBOOK, *The New Drug Development and Review Process*
FDA Website.

Phase 3 studies are expanded controlled and uncontrolled trials. They are performed after preliminary evidence suggesting effectiveness of the drug has been obtained in Phase 2, and are intended to gather the additional information about effectiveness and safety that is needed to evaluate the overall benefit-risk relationship of the drug. Phase 3 studies also provide an adequate basis for extrapolating the results to the general population and transmitting that information in the physician labeling. Phase 3 studies usually include several hundred to several thousand people.

In both Phase 2 and 3, CDER can impose a clinical hold if a study is unsafe (as in Phase 1), or if the protocol is clearly deficient in design in meeting its stated objectives. Great care is taken to ensure that this determination is not made in isolation, but reflects current scientific knowledge, agency experience with the design of clinical trials, and experience with the class of drugs under investigation.

———

FD&C Act section 505(d) states that FDA must deny an NDA unless it contains "substantial evidence" of effectiveness, and the provision defines "substantial evidence" as "adequate and well-controlled investigations, including clinical investigations, by experts qualified by scientific training and experience to evaluate the effectiveness of the drug involved." As discussed below, *infra* p. 725, note 2, approval of an NDA ordinarily requires at least two "adequate and well-controlled studies" demonstrating effectiveness. These pivotal trials on which approval is based are usually Phase III studies. Consequently, in designing their Phase III studies, sponsors must pay close attention to FDA's regulatory definition of "Adequate and Well-Controlled Studies," which is excerpted below.

21 C.F.R. § 314.126 Adequate and Well-Controlled Studies

(a) The purpose of conducting clinical investigations of a drug is to distinguish the effect of a drug from other influences, such as spontaneous change in the course of the disease, placebo effect, or biased observation. . . . Reports of adequate and well-controlled investigations provide the primary basis for determining whether there is "substantial evidence" to support the claims of effectiveness for new drugs and antibiotics. Therefore, the study report should provide sufficient details of study design, conduct, and analysis to allow critical evaluation and a determination of whether the characteristics of an adequate and well-controlled study are present.

(b) An adequate and well-controlled study has the following characteristics:

(1) There is a clear statement of the objectives of the investigation and a summary of the proposed or actual methods of analysis in the protocol for the study and in the report of its results. . . .

(2) The study uses a design that permits a valid comparison with a control to provide a quantitative assessment of drug effect. The protocol for the study and report of results should describe the study design precisely; for example, duration of treatment periods, whether treatments are parallel, sequential, or crossover, and whether the sample size is predetermined or based upon some interim analysis. Generally, the following types of control are recognized:

(i) *Placebo concurrent control.* The test drug is compared with an inactive preparation designed to resemble the test drug as far as possible. A placebo-controlled study . . . usually includes randomization and blinding of patients or investigators, or both.

(ii) *Dose-comparison concurrent control.* At least two doses of the drug are compared. . . . Dose-comparison trials usually include randomization and blinding of patients or investigators, or both.

(iii) *No treatment concurrent control.* Where objective measurements of effectiveness are available and placebo effect is negligible, the test drug is compared with no treatment. No treatment concurrent control trials usually include randomization.

(iv) *Active treatment concurrent control.* The test drug is compared with known effective therapy; for example, where the condition treated is such that administration of placebo or no treatment would be contrary to the interest of the patient.... Active treatment trials usually include randomization and blinding of patients or investigators, or both.

(v) *Historical control.* The results of treatment with the test drug are compared with experience historically derived from the adequately documented natural history of the disease or condition, or from the results of active treatment, in comparable patients or populations. Because historical control populations usually cannot be as well assessed with respect to pertinent variables as can concurrent control populations, historical control designs are usually reserved for special circumstances. Examples include studies of diseases with high and predictable mortality (for example, certain malignancies) and studies in which the effect of the drug is self-evident (general anesthetics, drug metabolism).

(3) The method of selection of subjects provides adequate assurance that they have the disease or condition being studied, or evidence of susceptibility and exposure to the condition against which prophylaxis is directed.

(4) The method of assigning patients to treatment and control groups minimizes bias and is intended to assure comparability of the groups with respect to pertinent variables such as age, sex, severity of disease, duration of disease, and use of drugs or therapy other than the test drug.... Ordinarily, in a concurrently controlled study, assignment is by randomization....

(5) Adequate measures are taken to minimize bias on the part of the subjects, observers, and analysts of the data....

(6) The methods of assessment of subjects' response are well-defined and reliable....

(7) There is an analysis of the results of the study adequate to assess the effects of the drug....

NOTES

1.   *Government–Sponsored INDs.* The federal government has a long history of supporting academic and industry scientists in the development of new drugs and of licensing new drugs to industry for commercialization. *See, e.g.,* John P. Swann, *Biomedical Research and Government Support: The Case of Drug Development,* 31 PHARMACY IN HISTORY, No. 3, at 103 (1989). The National Cancer Institute (NCI) has participated in the development of a number of important anticancer drugs. The Department of Commerce's National Technical Information Service (NTIS) and the National Institutes of Health (NIH) regularly publish notices in the Federal Register of the availability of federal government patents on pharmaceutical products available for licensing and of exclusive licenses subsequently granted to pharmaceutical companies to develop the drugs

involved. The exclusive license for a particularly important anticancer drug was renewed over the objections of competitors who argued that any license should be nonexclusive. 48 Fed. Reg. 5313 (Feb. 4, 1983), 48 Fed. Reg. 53177 (Nov. 25, 1983). NIH has made a number of potential AIDS drugs available for licensing. *E.g.,* 53 Fed. Reg. 40134 (Oct. 13, 1988), 54 Fed. Reg. 39815 (Sept. 28, 1989).

2. *Regulations Governing Drug Tests.* FDA proposed new regulations governing the responsibilities of sponsors and monitors of clinical investigations in 42 Fed. Reg. 49612 (Sept. 17, 1977) and new regulations governing the obligations of clinical investigators in 43 Fed. Reg. 35210 (Aug. 8, 1978), but they have never been promulgated in final form. A guideline for monitoring clinical investigators was made available in 53 Fed. Reg. 4723 (Feb. 17, 1988). Regulations governing institutional review boards were promulgated in 21 C.F.R. Part 56. FDA has also published good laboratory practice (GLP) regulations governing preclinical testing of food additives, human drugs, and animal drugs in 21 C.F.R. Part 58. *See generally* Richard F. Kingham, *History of FDA Regulation of Clinical Research,* 22 DRUG INFO. J. 151 (1988).

3. *Contractual Right to Investigational Drug.* In *Dahl v. HEM Pharmaceuticals Corp.,* 7 F.3d 1399 (9th Cir. 1993), the plaintiffs contracted to enroll in a double-blind study of an investigational drug in return for a promise that, if the study found the drug to be effective, those on the drug would receive a free supply of the drug for a year after the test ended and those on placebo would be switched to the drug. At the conclusion of the study, FDA denied a treatment IND but allowed an open label study. The District Court ordered the defendant to honor the contract, and the Court of Appeals affirmed the decision. Absent an explicit contractual provision stating that the trial will be continued or that the investigational drug will continue to be provided to the test subjects, however, no such obligation exists. *See, e.g., Abney v. Amgen, Inc.,* 443 F.3d 540 (6th Cir. 2006).

4. *Suits against the Government.* An individual who was terminated from a federally funded clinical trial has no cause of action against the government or government employees. *Kraemer–Katz v. Public Health Service,* 872 F. Supp. 1235 (S.D.N.Y. 1994). The District Court went on to discuss the existence of compassionate use of investigational drugs for treatment purposes, however, and stated that a "federal agency's denial of permission to obtain such [investigational] medications would support standing to seek review of the decision." *Id.* at 1240–41.

5. *No "Practice of Medicine" Exemption.* In *Cowan v. United States,* 5 F. Supp. 2d 1235 (N.D. Okla. 1999), the District Court held that the "practice of medicine exception" from the IND/NDA requirements of the FD&C Act only applies to a drug substance that is subject to an approved NDA for a different use and that "[n]othing in the FDCA or the case law suggests that the exception was intended to be expanded to permit doctors to test unapproved drugs," citing *United States v. Algon Chemical, Inc.,* 879 F.2d 1154 (3d Cir. 1989).

6. *Ambiguity of FDA's Role.* There has long been controversy over whether the FDA's responsibility is solely to protect the safety of human subjects, or also to assure that the clinical protocol is adequately designed

to yield data that can support ultimate approval of an NDA. The revised IND regulations, 21 C.F.R. 312.22(a), state:

> FDA's primary objectives in reviewing an IND are, in all phases of the investigation, to assure the safety and rights of subjects, and in Phase 2 and 3, to help assure that the quality of the scientific evaluation of drugs is adequate to permit an evaluation of the drug's effectiveness and safety.

This declaration notwithstanding, FDA reviewers often comment on the scientific adequacy of protocols for Phase I studies, as well.

7. *Protocol Guidelines and Guidance.* Since enactment of the 1962 Drug Amendments, FDA has repeatedly stated that one of the major reasons for the length of time required for development and approval of new drugs has been the failure of sponsors and clinical investigators to utilize adequate protocols for clinical trials. The agency in the early 1970s began to develop model protocols for clinical trials for different therapeutic classes of drugs. To forestall concern that these model protocols would stifle innovation in clinical investigation, FDA initially issued the protocols as "guidelines." They are now issued as "guidance."

8. *Enriched Trials.* An "all-comers" clinical trial enrolls anyone in the trial who meets relatively general inclusion criteria, without regard to whether they are more or less likely to benefit from the investigational drug. In an enriched trial, however, the inclusion criteria are narrowed in an attempt to enroll only those patients who are most likely to benefit from the drug, with the intent of demonstrating a stronger proof of effectiveness with fewer people in the trial. Some enriched trials have an initial run-in period after which only the responders are randomized into the trial. *See* FDA, DRAFT GUIDANCE FOR INDUSTRY ON ENRICHMENT STRATEGIES FOR CLINICAL TRIALS TO SUPPORT APPROVAL OF HUMAN DRUGS AND BIOLOGICAL PRODUCTS (December 2012).

9. *Adaptive Trials.* In a traditional clinical trial, patients are randomized to one or more dose levels of the investigational drug or to a placebo (the "arms" of the trial), and no one knows which patients are on which regimen. In an adaptive trial, an independent Data Monitoring Committee (DMC) reviews the patient responses to their regimens and can alter the number of patients in each arm to reflect the interim results. If one arm shows poor results and another shows excellent results, patients in the former arm can be added to the latter to obtain a faster and more reliable determination of effectiveness. There is controversy about how strongly FDA can rely on this trial design. *See* Bridget M. Kuehn, *Industry, FDA Warm to "Adaptive" Trials,* 296 J.A.M.A. 1955 (Oct. 25, 2006); PhRMA Working Group on Adaptive Designs, *White Paper* and related articles, 40 DRUG INFO. J. 421–484 (2006). *See* FDA, DRAFT GUIDANCE FOR INDUSTRY ON ADOPTIVE DESIGN CLINICAL TRIALS FOR DRUGS AND BIOLOGICS (Feb. 2012).

10. *Noninferiority Trials.* Rather than testing an investigational drug against a placebo, a noninferiority trial tests it against an approved effective agent. This is often required where use of a placebo would be unethical. If the investigational drug is shown to be superior, there is no issue. If it is only shown not to be inferior, however, there is scientific

debate whether this is adequate for approval, because the investigational drug might be slightly less effective but still within the statistical definition of equivalence. *See* FDA, DRAFT GUIDANCE FOR INDUSTRY ON NON–INFERIORITY FOR CLINICAL TRIALS (Mar. 2012).

11. *Patient Reported Outcomes.* FDA issued GUIDANCE FOR INDUSTRY ON PATIENT–REPORTED OUTCOME MEASURES: USE IN MEDICAL PRODUCT DEVELOPMENT TO SUPPORT LABELING CLAIMS (Dec. 2009) for studies intended to support the clinical effectiveness of a drug.

d. INSTITUTIONAL REVIEW BOARD APPROVAL AND HUMAN SUBJECT PROTECTION

An Institutional Review Board (IRB) is an independent committee tasked with protecting the welfare of human research subjects. An IRB reviews a clinical protocol before it is initiated and exercises general supervision over the trial as it is conducted. The primary function of an IRB, which is comprised of lay people as well as scientists, is to assure compliance with local community ethical standards. FDA regulations provide that, with rare exceptions, a study subject to the IND requirement may not be initiated "unless that investigation has been reviewed and approved by, and remains subject to continuing review by, an IRB meeting the requirements of this part." 21 C.F.R. 56.103(a).

Part 56 of the regulations establishes the functions and operations of an IRB, required records and reports, and FDA administrative action for noncompliance with the regulations. Over the three decades since these regulations were promulgated, the duties and responsibilities of IRBs have substantially increased. Whereas once an IRB simply reviewed a protocol to assure that the clinical testing met ethical standards, today an IRB is expected to give a much harder look at protocols, assure that the written informed consent form is sufficiently simple and clear to be understood by the test subjects, monitor the progress of the testing, and maintain substantial records of these activities. An IRB must meet in person, not by telephone, and must devote substantial time to its responsibilities.

Ensuring informed consent is perhaps the most important function of an IRB. Indeed, the FD&C Act itself requires that FDA's IND regulations provide that a sponsor must "inform any human beings to whom such drugs, or any controls used in connection therewith, are being administered, or their representatives, that such drugs are being used for investigational purposes and will obtain the consent of such human beings or their representatives, except where it is not feasible or it is contrary to the best interests of such human beings." FD&C Act 505(i)(4). Accordingly, an IRB may not approve an FDA-regulated study unless informed consent is sought and documented in accordance with agency regulations. 21 C.F.R. 56.111(a)(4)–(5). In turn, FDA's rules governing the protection of human subjects set out the mandatory elements of informed consent.

21 C.F.R. § 50.25 Elements of Informed Consent

(a) *Basic elements of informed consent*. In seeking informed consent, the following information shall be provided to each subject:

(1) A statement that the study involves research, an explanation of the purposes of the research and the expected duration of the subject's participation, a description of the procedures to be followed, and identification of any procedures which are experimental.

(2) A description of any reasonably foreseeable risks or discomforts to the subject.

(3) A description of any benefits to the subject or to others which may reasonably be expected from the research.

(4) A disclosure of appropriate alternative procedures or courses of treatment, if any, that might be advantageous to the subject.

(5) A statement describing the extent, if any, to which confidentiality of records identifying the subject will be maintained and that notes the possibility that the Food and Drug Administration may inspect the records.

(6) For research involving more than minimal risk, an explanation as to whether any compensation and an explanation as to whether any medical treatments are available if injury occurs and, if so, what they consist of, or where further information may be obtained.

(7) An explanation of whom to contact for answers to pertinent questions about the research and research subjects' rights, and whom to contact in the event of a research-related injury to the subject.

(8) A statement that participation is voluntary, that refusal to participate will involve no penalty or loss of benefits to which the subject is otherwise entitled, and that the subject may discontinue participation at any time without penalty or loss of benefits to which the subject is otherwise entitled.

. . . .

NOTES

1. *History*. There is a lengthy history of the development of protection of human subjects by FDA. When Congress enacted the Drug Amendments of 1962, it required in section 505(i)(4) that any IND be conditioned upon informed consent by human subjects. FDA initially implemented this obligation by publishing a statement of policy concerning consent for use of investigational new drugs on humans. FDA promulgated more comprehensive Institutional Review Board (IRB) requirements by amending the IND regulations, and later promulgated a separate set of institutional review regulations to cover all clinical investigations subject to FDA jurisdiction, 21 C.F.R. Parts 50, 56. *See* Christi J. Williams, *A History of Institutional Review at the U.S. Food and Drug Administration: 1960–2001* (2001), in Chapter VI(C)(1) of the Electronic Book.

2. *IND Deregulation*. Some have argued that Phase I studies should only require approval by a local IRB. This is the approach used for

investigational studies of non-significant risk medical devices. *See infra* p. 1231; 21 C.F.R. 812.2. Although it entertained this possibility in its preamble to a proposed revision of the IND regulations, 48 Fed. Reg. 26720, 26722 (June 9, 1983), FDA expressed the preliminary view that the other changes might make it unnecessary. In the preamble to the final regulations, 52 Fed. Reg. 8798, 8805–8806 (Mar. 19, 1987), the agency concluded that the issue required additional study. *See* Kingsley L. Taft, *Deregulation of Investigational New Drug Applications* (1996) in Chapter VI(C)(1) of the Electronic Book.

3.   *Investigational Research on Prisoners.* In 45 Fed. Reg. 36386 (May 30, 1980) FDA promulgated regulations severely limiting the use of prisoners in drug clinical trials. FDA stayed the effective date of these regulations in 46 Fed. Reg. 35085 (July 7, 1981) and later reproposed them with fewer restrictions in 46 Fed. Reg. 61666 (Dec. 18, 1981), but then revoked the regulations completely in 62 Fed. Reg. 39439, 39440 (July 23, 1997). The Department of HHS has promulgated regulations governing the use of prisoners as research subjects where the research is conducted or supported by the Department. 45 C.F.R. Part 46, Subpart C. *See* Caitlin N. Fitzpatrick, *The Prisoner's Dilemma: The History, Ethical Dimensions, and Evolving Regulatory Landscape of Clinical Trials on Inmates* (2012), in the Electronic Book.

4.   *Recruiting Clinical Trial Subjects.* FDA has no regulations or guidance regarding the recruitment of individuals to participate in a clinical trial. Accordingly, the methods used to recruit trial subjects, the compensation to be paid them, and related matters are within the discretion of the IRB.

5.   *IRB Ethical Standards.* Each IRB may impose its own ethical standards. It is not unusual for one IRB to approve a clinical trial that another IRB has disapproved. This is consistent with the concept that IRBs reflect local community ethical standards. FDA proposed in 67 Fed. Reg. 10115 (Mar. 6, 2002) to require that an IRB be informed of any prior IRB reviews, but then withdrew the proposal in 71 Fed. Reg. 2493 (Jan. 17, 2006).

6.   *False Claims Act.* In *United States ex rel. Gross v. AIDS Research Alliance–Chicago*, 415 F.3d 601 (7th Cir. 2005), a clinical trial subject alleged fraudulent negligence by the IRB supervising the study. The Court of Appeals affirmed the District Court in dismissing the complaint for failure to plead negligence with specificity. *See Primum Non Nocere: The Continuing Evolution of Safety Monitoring in Human Subjects Research* (2006), in Chapter VI(C)(1) of the Electronic Book.

7.   *Inadequate Informed Consent.* In *Iron Cloud v. Sullivan*, Food Drug Cosm. L. Rep. (CCH) ¶ 38,287 (D.S.D. 1993), the District Court held that a person alleging that inadequate information was provided to participants in a clinical trial of a hepatitis A vaccine on Native American children had to request FDA action through a citizen petition before resorting to the courts. The Court of Appeals declared the matter moot because the clinical trial was terminated before it heard the case. 984 F.2d 241 (8th Cir. 1993).

8.   *Placebo-Controlled Trials.* There is a long-running debate about the ethics of using a placebo rather than an active drug as the control in a

clinical trial. FDA adheres to the position that placebo-controlled trials are the gold standard. When the Declaration of Helsinki was amended in October 2000 to require the use of an active control unless none exists, FDA revised its regulations in 73 Fed. Reg. 22800 (April 28, 2008) to delete the requirement that foreign clinical studies be conducted in accordance with the Declaration of Helsinki and to substitute a requirement that foreign studies must comply with good clinical practice. 21 C.F.R. 312.120. *See* GUIDANCE FOR INDUSTRY AND FDA STAFF ON FDA ACCEPTANCE OF FOREIGN CLINICAL STUDIES NOT CONDUCTED UNDER AN IND: FREQUENTLY ASKED QUESTIONS (March 2012).

9. *Investigational Drugs in the Military.* In 1997, Congress provided that the President may, in connection with a particular military operation, waive the informed consent requirement with respect to members of the armed forces. 111 Stat. 1629, codified at 10 U.S.C. 1107(f). Originally, this statute mandated that waivers be granted solely according to standards and criteria established by FDA regulation. Thus, in 1990, in advance of the 1991 Operation Desert Shield/Desert Storm military operations in Kuwait, FDA published, in response to a request from the Department of Defense, an interim final regulation authorizing the FDA Commissioner to determine that obtaining informed consent from individual military personnel is not feasible in specific situations involving combat or the immediate threat of combat. 21 C.F.R. 50.23(d). The regulation was upheld in *Doe v. Sullivan*, 756 F. Supp. 12 (D.D.C. 1991), *aff'd*, 938 F.2d 1370 (D.C. Cir. 1991). FDA revised this regulation by interim rule in 1999. 64 Fed. Reg. 54180 (Oct. 5, 1999). *See also* Brenda Jarrell, *FDA Regulation and the Military: Is There a Compromise in the Battle Over Investigational Drugs* (1997), and Christopher J. Lovrien, *Investigational Drug Use Among the Troops: The Waiver of Informed Consent in Cases of Military Combat Exigencies* (1997), in Chapter VI(C)(1) of the Electronic Book.

10. *Emergency Research.* In 1996, FDA established regulations governing the narrow circumstances under which emergency clinical research may be conducted without informed consent, e.g., because of a life-threatening condition for which there is no available alternative and the person is unconscious. 21 C.F.R. 50.24. A decade later, on the basis of approximately 60 INDs for emergency research, FDA issued a DRAFT GUIDANCE and then a FINAL GUIDANCE FOR INSTITUTIONAL REVIEW BOARDS, CLINICAL INVESTIGATORS, AND SPONSORS ON EXCEPTION FROM INFORMED CONSENT REQUIREMENTS FOR EMERGENCY RESEARCH (April 2013). *See* Robert V. Ciccone, *Medical Research and the Protection of Individuals Incapable of Providing Consent* (1999), in Chapter XI(C)(1) of the Electronic Book.

11. *FDA Clinical Research.* In 2006, the Inspector General of HHS subjected the clinical research conducted by FDA itself to a critical review. OFFICE OF INSPECTOR GENERAL, REVIEW OF CORRECTIVE ACTIONS CONCERNING THE HUMAN SUBJECT RESEARCH PROGRAM, No. A–06–06–00042 (2006).

e.   PROTOCOL AMENDMENTS

In practice, a sponsor ordinarily submits only one IND for each new drug. A distinct process called "protocol amendment" is used for significant changes in an investigation subsequent to the start of human trials—including the commencement of Phase II and Phase III studies, if they are not included in the initial protocol. According to 21 C.F.R. 312.30:

> (a) *New protocol.* Whenever a sponsor intends to conduct a study that is not covered by a protocol already contained in the IND, the sponsor shall submit to FDA a protocol amendment containing the protocol for the study. Such study may begin provided two conditions are met: (1) The sponsor has submitted the protocol to FDA for its review; and (2) the protocol has been approved by the Institutional Review Board (IRB) with responsibility for review and approval of the study in accordance with the requirements of part 56. The sponsor may comply with these two conditions in either order.

The rule also provides that a protocol amendment must be submitted when significant changes are made to an existing protocol or a new investigator is added to a protocol. 21 C.F.R. 312.30(b), (c).

Whereas an IND goes into effect only after 30 days have elapsed, an investigator using the protocol amendment procedure can commence the new protocol immediately upon receiving IRB approval.

f.   THE CLINICAL HOLD

Although FDA has used clinical holds since 1962 to prevent trials from beginning or to stop trials that are already underway, the statutory authority for a clinical hold in section 505(i)(3) was not added to the FD&C Act until the FDA Modernization Act did so in 1997.

Clinical Hold Decision

in THE CDER HANDBOOK, *The New Drug Development and Review Process*
FDA Website.

A clinical hold is the mechanism that CDER uses when it does not believe, or cannot confirm, that the study can be conducted without unreasonable risk to the subjects/patients. If this occurs, the Center will contact the sponsor within the 30-day initial review period to stop the clinical trial. CDER may either delay the start of an early-phase trial on the basis of information submitted in the IND, or stop an ongoing study based on a review of newly submitted clinical protocols, safety reports, protocol amendments, or other information. When a clinical hold is issued, a sponsor must address the issue that is the basis of the hold before the order is removed.

CDER's authority concerning clinical holds is outlined in Federal regulations. The regulations specify the clinical hold criteria that CDER applies to various phases of clinical testing. In addition, all clinical holds are reviewed by upper management of CDER to assure consistency and scientific quality in the Center's clinical hold decisions.

NOTES

1. *FDA Regulations.* The FDA regulations governing clinical holds and requests for modification are codified at 21 C.F.R. 312.42. CDER MAPP Nos. 6030.1 & 6031.1 govern FDA policy relating to the issuance, monitoring and resolution of clinical holds. Following enactment of section 505(i)(3) in 1997, FDA promulgated a direct final regulation amending 21 C.F.R. 312.42 to require that the agency respond to a request to lift a clinical hold within 30 days of receiving a complete response to the FDA clinical hold letter.

2. *FDA Guidance.* In 63 Fed. Reg. 26809 (May 14, 1998), FDA announced the availability of GUIDANCE FOR INDUSTRY: SUBMITTING AND REVIEWING COMPLETE RESPONSES TO CLINICAL HOLDS, which was updated in October 2000. *See also FDA Guidance for Industry and Investigators on the Use of Clinical Holds Following Clinical Investigator Misconduct* (September 2004).

3. *Frequency of Clinical Holds.* Between 1980 and 1988, FDA placed between 5 and 15 percent of new commercial INDs on clinical hold. Letter from Robert Temple, Director, FDA CDER Office of Drug Evaluation, to Dr. E. Stonehill, National Cancer Institute (Sept. 28, 1989). In 1992, FDA promulgated regulations that expanded its authority to impose clinical holds and to terminate an IND, for the stated purpose of exerting control over protocols for expanded use of investigational drugs in general and AIDS drugs in particular. 21 C.F.R. 312.42. *See infra* p. 674.

g.   SPECIAL PROTOCOL ASSESSMENT

For the first 35 years of operating under the Drug Amendments of 1962, the pharmaceutical industry was constantly frustrated by what came to be known as the "moving target syndrome," i.e., repeated changes in agency advice about the studies needed to obtain FDA approval of an NDA. A number of factors contributed to this problem, including (1) recurring changes in personnel, (2) poor records of prior FDA advice, (3) the lack of significant written FDA guidance, (4) the lack of consistent supervision by higher FDA officials over the decisions of lower officials, (5) the ability of lower-level FDA personnel to take any position on a matter without supervisory control, (6) the pharmaceutical industry's fear of retaliation if a lower decision was appealed to a higher level, and (7) the lack of any realistic deadlines for FDA decisions on INDs and NDAs.

This situation changed partly with enactment of the Prescription Drug User Fee Act of 1992, which brought significant deadlines to the process, and partly with the enactment of the FDA Modernization Act of 1997, which added section 505(b)(5)(B) and (C) to the FD&C Act, establishing what is now referred to as the "Special Protocol Assessment" (SPA) program. Section 505(b)(5)(B) states that FDA "shall" meet with a sponsor or applicant "if the sponsor or applicant makes a reasonable written request for the purpose of reaching agreement on the design and size of clinical trials intended to form the primary basis of an effectiveness claim." Section 505(b)(5)(C) states: "Any agreement regarding the parameters of the design and size of clinical trials a new drug under this paragraph that is reached between

[FDA] and a sponsor or applicant shall be reduced to writing and . . . shall not be changed after the testing begins" except in specified limited circumstances. FDA implemented these statutory provisions through the following guidance, issued in 67 Fed. Reg. 35122 (May 17, 2002).

Guidance for Industry: Special Protocol Assessment
May 2002.

. . . .

The PDUFA goals for special protocol assessment and agreement [performance goals agreed to by FDA in conjunction with PDUFA reauthorization in 1997] provide that, upon request, FDA will evaluate within 45 days certain protocols and issues relating to the protocols to assess whether they are adequate to meet scientific and regulatory requirements identified by the sponsor. Three types of protocols related to PDUFA products are eligible for this special protocol assessment under the PDUFA goals: (1) animal carcinogenicity protocols, (2) final product stability protocols, and (3) clinical protocols for phase 3 trials whose data will form the primary basis for an efficacy claim if the trials had been the subject of discussion at an end-of-phase 2/pre-phase 3 meeting with the review division, or in some cases, if the division agrees to such a review because the division is aware of the developmental context in which the protocol is being reviewed and the questions are being answered. The clinical protocols for phase 3 trials can relate to efficacy claims that will be part of an original new drug application (NDA) or biologics license application (BLA) or that will be part of an efficacy supplement to an approved NDA or BLA. . . .

Section 119(a) of the Modernization Act amends section 505(b) of the Act (21 U.S.C. 355(b)). New section [505(b)(5)(B)] of the Act directs FDA to meet with sponsors, provided certain conditions are met, for the purpose of reaching agreement on the design and size of clinical trials intended to form the primary basis of an efficacy claim in a marketing application submitted under section 505(b) of the Act or section 351 of the Public Health Service Act (42 U.S.C. 262). Such marketing applications include NDAs, BLAs, and efficacy supplements to approved NDAs and BLAs.

Under new sections [505(b)(5)(B) and (C)] of the Act, if a sponsor makes a reasonable written request to meet with the Agency for the purpose of reaching agreement on the design and size of a clinical trial, the Agency will meet with the sponsor. If an agreement is reached, the Agency will reduce the agreement to writing and make it part of the administrative record. An agreement may not be changed by the sponsor or FDA after the trial begins, except (1) with the written agreement of the sponsor and FDA, or (2) if the director of the FDA reviewing division determines that "a substantial scientific issue essential to determining the safety or effectiveness of the drug" was identified after the testing began (section [505(b)(5)(C)] of the Act). If a sponsor and the Agency meet regarding the design and size of a clinical trial under section [505(b)(5)(B)] of the Act and the parties cannot agree that the trial design is adequate to meet the goals of the sponsor, the

Agency will clearly state the reasons for the disagreement in a letter to the sponsor. However, the absence of an articulated disagreement on a particular issue should not be assumed to represent an agreement reached on that issue. . . .

CDER and CBER generally recommend that a sponsor submit a protocol intended for special protocol assessment to the Agency at least 90 days prior to the anticipated start of the study. The protocol should be complete, and enough time should be allowed to discuss and resolve any issues before the study begins. *SPECIAL PROTOCOL ASSESSMENT WILL NOT BE PROVIDED AFTER A STUDY HAS BEGUN.* Protocols for studies that have already begun can be evaluated by CDER and CBER, but they do not qualify for the 45-day time frame described in the PDUFA goals. . . .

As stated in the PDUFA goals for special protocol assessment and agreement,

having agreed to the design, execution, and analyses proposed in protocols reviewed under this process [i.e., carcinogenicity protocols, stability protocols, and phase 3 protocols for clinical trials that will form the primary basis of an efficacy claim], the Agency will not later alter its perspective on the issues of design, execution, or analyses unless public health concerns unrecognized at the time of protocol assessment under this process are evident.

Thus, documented special protocol assessments should be considered binding on the review division and should not be changed at any time, except as follows:

- Failure of a sponsor to follow a protocol that was agreed upon with the Agency will be interpreted as the sponsor's understanding that the protocol assessment is no longer binding on the review division.

- If the relevant data, assumptions, or information provided by the sponsor in a request for special protocol assessment change are found to be false statements or misstatements or are found to omit relevant facts, the review division will not be bound by any assessment that relied on such data, assumptions, or information.

- A documented special protocol assessment can be modified if (1) FDA and the sponsor agree in writing to modify the protocol (section [505(b)(5)(C) of the Act) and (2) such modification is intended to improve the study. A special protocol assessment modified in this manner will be considered binding on the review division, except under the circumstances described below.

- A clinical protocol assessment will no longer be considered binding if the director of the review division determines that a substantial scientific issue essential to determining the safety or efficacy of the drug has been identified after the testing has begun (section 505(b)(5)(C) of the Act). If the director of the review division makes such a determination, (1) the determination should be documented in writing for the administrative record and should be provided to the sponsor, and (2) the sponsor should be given an opportunity for a meeting at which the review division director will discuss the scientific issue involved (section 505(b)(5)(D) of the Act).

NOTES

1. *Impact on the IND/NDA Process*. The SPA is the most important reform of the IND/NDA process since 1962. By providing certainty about the regulatory requirements for drug development, it gives assurance to sponsors and investors that FDA-approved protocols will in fact be accepted as pivotal studies. There has been no documented instance where FDA has rejected an SPA-approved protocol after the trial met its endpoints when analyzed in accordance with the SPA-approved statistical analysis plan.

2. *SPA Deadline*. In the early years of the SPA process, the statutory 45-day deadline for FDA review of the SPA frequently was not met. Under Section VII of the PDUFA Reauthorization Performance Goals and procedures implementing user fee provisions of the FDA Safety and Innovation Act of 2012, FDA commits to responding in writing to 90 percent of SPA submissions within 45 days.

h.   CLINICAL ENDPOINTS, SURROGATE ENDPOINTS, AND BIOMARKERS

In designing a clinical trial, it is important to determine the endpoints that will be evaluated in the course of the study. There are two types of endpoints relevant to determining the effectiveness of a new drug: (1) clinical endpoints, such as mortality and serious morbidity, and (2) surrogate endpoints, which are physiological assessments that are recognized as validated indicators of clinical benefit. Clinical endpoints are the gold standard for demonstrating the effectiveness of a drug, but for many diseases it is not feasible to test for changes in clinical endpoints, and surrogate endpoints must therefore suffice. In both situations, biomarkers—objectively measured indicators of normal biological or pathogenic processes or pharmacologic responses to a therapeutic intervention—are used in studies to evaluate activity and develop dose-response relationships. Thus, a surrogate endpoint is a biomarker that has been sufficiently validated to substitute for a clinical endpoint.

James Bilstad, M.D.,* Surrogate Endpoints

Talk at the Institute of Medicine AIDS Roundtable (March 12, 1990).

Faced with the tragic consequences of HIV infection and AIDS, we all want to determine as efficiently as possible which investigational agents effectively treat the disease and which do not. A discussion of the role of surrogate endpoints is a very important step in examining the drug evaluation process for potential therapeutic agents for HIV infection. . . .

To be considered for a surrogate endpoint, the parameter being measured or evaluated must be therapeutically rational and biologically

---

*   [Dr. Bilstead was Director of the FDA CDER Office of Drug Evaluation when he gave this talk.]

plausible. It must be consistent with what is known about the pathophysiology and pathogenesis of the disease. . . .

Although the vast majority of drugs that are approved by the FDA for marketing are approved on the basis of efficacy demonstrated by significant clinical benefits, there are a number of drug classes in which we have accepted surrogate markers as a basis for approval. Anti-hypertensive drugs have long been approved on the basis of demonstrated effect in lowering blood pressure. It had been known for decades that untreated hypertension was associated with increased cardiovascular mortality and morbidity, primarily from accelerated atherosclerosis but also from end organ damage related to the hypertension itself. Although demonstrating a decrease in cardiovascular mortality and morbidity were the obvious endpoints of interest in evaluating the effects of anti-hypertensive therapy, these studies were very difficult to carry out. They required large numbers of patients to be followed over prolonged periods. . . .

Another area in which we have accepted endpoints other than the clinical endpoint of most interest is for drugs to treat osteoporosis. The clinical endpoint of primary interest is the reduction of the incidence of fractures. . . .

Again, we have the problem that the event rate is relatively low, and a large number of patients need to be followed over a prolonged period. . . .

Based on a number of studies evaluating the techniques for assessing bone structure, we did accept measurements of bone density using photon absorption in the case of estrogens and total body calcium by neutron activation analysis in the case of calcitonin. These studies involved multiple measurements over relatively long periods, at least two years. In these cases, we considered the data convincing that the drugs were having an effect directly on maintaining the bone structure.

A third area in which we have used surrogate endpoints, the vaccines. I will use influenza vaccine as an example. The initial clinical trials with the crude vaccine were started in the 1940's. A number of antibodies to the virus were evaluated for correlation with disease prevention. After considerable testing, the one that seemed to correlate the best with prevention was the antibody to the hemagglutinin glycoprotein on the viral envelope which is responsible for the attachment of the virus to receptor cells. . . .

A fourth drug class in which we have accepted surrogate endpoints, the lipid altering drugs. The FDA has long approved drugs that lower serum cholesterol based only on demonstrated efficacy at lowering cholesterol levels. Epidemiologic studies have established the association between elevated cholesterol level and increased cardiovascular mortality and morbidity. Obviously, the endpoints of interest in evaluating the effects of lowering serum cholesterol by drug therapy relate to demonstrating a decrease in cardiovascular mortality and morbidity. However, these studies are very difficult to do because of the relatively low number of events in the study population and therefore the large number of patients that must be followed for prolonged periods. . . .

A fifth class in which the agency has accepted surrogate markers of effectiveness is for the anti-arrhythmic drugs. The most important clinical benefit expected from these drugs is again to decrease the frequency of sudden death. Approval for anti-arrhythmics has not been based on demonstration of decreased cardiac mortality but rather approval has relied heavily on 24-hour holter monitoring for the frequency and duration of arrhythmias. These studies may involve either symptomatic or asymptomatic individuals but at least some information has also been required for recent approvals on symptom reduction. For example, decreased frequency of palpitations or syncopal episodes. . . .

A sixth area in which we have accepted a surrogate endpoint is with the alpha one proteinase inhibitor. Alpha one antitrypsin deficiency is a hereditary disease that in the more serious aphenotryptic variants can lead to severe emphysema starting in the third and fourth decades of life. There are only about 400 patients affected with the severe variant in the United States. The alpha one antitrypsin, the proteinase inhibitor blocks the action of an elastase released by nutraphils in the lower respiratory track. In absence of the inhibitor, elastase leads to breakdown of the structural integrity of the alveolae.

The FDA recently approved an alpha one proteinase inhibitor derived from pooled plasma to be given intravenously weekly to patients with the deficiency and early evidence of emphysema. The approval was based not on a demonstration of maintenance of pulmonary function and prevention of emphysema but on demonstrated levels of the proteinase inhibitor in blood and on evaluation of bronchial alveolar washings for proteinase inhibitor activity as reflected by elastase activity. Secondly, on decrease nutraphil counts and thirdly a decrease in other inflammatory mediators. . . .

Tissue plasminogen activator or TPA is an example of a therapeutic agent in which we did not accept a surrogate endpoint as a basis for approval. The initial application included only data demonstrating an effect on thrombolysis by coronary arteriography. In the agency's judgment, there was insufficient evidence to correlate these findings with clinical benefit. The product license application was later approved on the basis of a decreased incidence of overt congestive heart failure and an increase in the ventricular ejection fraction.

In addition to establishing that there is a correlation between a surrogate endpoint and a significant clinical endpoint, the surrogate endpoint must be carefully validated. This usually means that the drug must be studied for its effect on the clinical endpoint and on the surrogate market in well-designed prospective studies. This process is helped if other drugs in the same class demonstrate similar effects.

NOTES

1. *Cancer Drug Endpoints* For discussion of FDA's views on appropriate endpoints for approval of new cancer drug NDAs over the last thirteen years, see John R. Johnson et al., *Endpoints and United States Food and Drug Administration Approval of Oncology Drugs*, 21 J. Clinical Oncology 1404 (2003).

2. *FDA Commentary. See also* Robert J. Temple, *A Regulatory Authority's Opinion about Surrogate Endpoints, in* CLINICAL MEASUREMENT IN DRUG EVALUATION (Walter S. Nimmo & Geoffrey Tucker eds., 1995); Robert J. Temple, *Are Surrogate Markers Adequate to Assess Cardiovascular Disease Drugs?*, 282 J.A.M.A. 790 (1999).

i. CLINICAL TESTING ON SUBPOPULATIONS

Clinical testing of new drugs has traditionally been conducted on white, middle-aged males on the premise that they are less vulnerable to potential harm, are relatively reliable test subjects, and are more likely to be available for follow up. Consequently, few drugs have been tested in children, women, the elderly, and racial subgroups. Both FDA and Congress have taken steps to change this paradigm.

i. *Children*

By not testing on children, the pharmaceutical industry made them therapeutic orphans. Any use of a drug in children was inherently experimental. The pharmaceutical industry, however, was reluctant to test investigational drugs in children before it had full safety information in adults, because of fear that it could seriously harm this vulnerable population. Sponsors therefore chose simply to label their products with statements that the safety and effectiveness of the drug in children had not yet been established.

FDA's first step in addressing this problem was to promulgate a regulation in 1994 clarifying that to qualify for a pediatric label, a manufacturer did not necessarily have to complete pediatric clinical tests. 59 Fed. Reg. 64240 (Dec. 13, 1994), codified at 21 C.F.R. 201.57. FDA stated that adult studies in combination with pharmacokinetics, safety, and pharmacodynamics data could satisfy pediatric labeling requirements. This regulation was unsuccessful, however, for two reasons. First, it did not resolve the ethical concerns about testing in children. Second, it did not address the fact that the patents for many drugs were near or beyond expiration and thus sponsors had no economic incentive to undertake even limited efforts to qualify for pediatric labeling.

In 1998, FDA promulgated a new regulation requiring pediatric testing of new and marketed drugs. 63 Fed. Reg. 66632 (Dec. 2, 1998). At the same time that FDA was pursuing an administrative approach to the matter, Congress created in the FDA Modernization Act of 1997 a new section 505A of the FD&C Act to provide six months of market exclusivity, beginning at the end of the patent term, for any drug for which pediatric testing was conducted at the request of FDA. This was a substantial incentive for many drugs, and it resulted in a major increase in pediatric studies. *See* FDA GUIDANCE FOR INDUSTRY ON QUALIFYING FOR PEDIATRIC EXCLUSIVITY UNDER SECTION 505A OF THE FEDERAL FOOD, DRUG, AND COSMETIC ACT (Sept. 1999). In its January 2000 report to Congress on pediatric exclusivity, FDA stated, "The pediatric exclusivity provision has done more to generate clinical studies and useful prescribing information for the pediatric population than any other regulatory or legislative process to date." *See* FDA DRAFT GUIDANCE FOR INDUSTRY AND REVIEW STAFF ON PEDIATRIC

INFORMATION INCORPORATED INTO HUMAN PRESCRIPTION DRUG AND BIOLOGICAL PRODUCTS LABELING (Feb. 2013). Because section 505A was subject to a five-year sunset provision, Congress extended it for another five years under the Best Pharmaceuticals for Children Act, 115 Stat. 1408, and the FDA Amendments Act of 2007, 121 Stat. 876, before making it permanent in the FDA Safety and Innovation Act of 2012, 126 Stat. 1039. As of April 2006, FDA had received 467 proposed pediatric study requests from manufacturers, issued 320 written requests, granted six-month exclusivity to 118 drugs, and added new pediatric information to 109 labels. CDER, REPORT TO THE NATION 2005, 23 (2006).

In its December 1998 regulations, FDA had broadly asserted the legal authority to require pharmaceutical manufacturers to conduct any form of testing that the agency concluded to be justified. This conflicted with prior FDA statements, including a speech by Commissioner David Kessler. A physicians group dedicated to deregulating medicine filed suit challenging the FDA regulations. In *Association of American Physician & Surgeons, Inc. v. FDA*, 226 F. Supp. 2d 204 (D.D.C. 2002), the District Court declared the December 1998 pediatric regulations unlawful and enjoined enforcement. FDA decided not to appeal the matter and instead to seek a legislative solution. Congress responded by enacting the Pediatric Research Equity Act of 2003, 117 Stat. 1936, which added section 505B to the FD&C Act. This section requires all new NDAs to contain a pediatric assessment unless FDA grants a waiver or deferral, and it also authorizes FDA to require holders of already-approved NDAs to conduct pediatric studies for marketed drugs. FDA issued draft guidance on these provisions in 2005. 70 Fed. Reg. 53233 (Sept. 7, 2005),

As part of the 2002 Best Pharmaceuticals for Children Act, Congress also included a mechanism for pediatric testing of drugs whose patents have expired. NIH is required to publish an annual list of these drugs, and FDA then issues requests for testing proposals to be supported by government funds.

NOTES

1. *FDA Regulations.* In 2001, FDA published regulations to provide additional safeguards for children in clinical investigations. 21 C.F.R. Part 50, Subpart D. FDA issued draft guidance for implementation of this process in May 2006.

2. *Scope of Market Exclusivity.* FDA interpreted the market exclusivity provisions for pediatric testing in section 503B of the FD&C Act to extend to a manufacturer's entire line of drug products having the same active moiety. This interpretation was upheld in *National Pharmaceutical Alliance v. Henney*, 47 F. Supp. 2d 37 (D.D.C. 1999).

3. *Availability of Information.* All of the information regarding requests for pediatric testing under the Best Pharmaceuticals for Children Act and the Pediatric Research Equity Act is readily available on the FDA website. As required by the Best Pharmaceuticals for Children Act, FDA periodically publishes notices announcing the availability of summaries of medical and clinical pharmacology reviews of pediatric studies conducted

pursuant to that statute. *E.g.,* 71 Fed. Reg. 61484 (Oct. 18, 2006). But publication of pediatric studies in the medical literature remains limited. Daniel K. Benjamin et al., *Peer–Reviewed Publication of Clinical Trials Completed for Pediatric Exclusivity,* 296 J.A.M.A. 1266 (2006).

ii. The Elderly

FDA has also recognized that separate information on geriatric use of a new drug may be important to the elderly. In 1997, FDA established a "geriatric use" subsection in the physician labeling. 21 C.F.R. 201.57(c)(9)(v). Although specific testing on the elderly is not required, age is one of the categories that must be broken out separately in all clinical trial reports submitted to FDA under the agency's February 1998 revision of the IND and NDA regulations. As FDA stated in 58 Fed. Reg. at 39410, "Patients in clinical trials should, in general, reflect the population that will receive the drug when it is marketed."

iii. Women

During the past decade, FDA has made progress on the inclusion of women in clinical trials. In 1977, FDA adopted a policy restricting the participation of women with childbearing potential in early clinical trials. In 1993, FDA withdrew the 1977 policy and published a GUIDELINE FOR THE STUDY AND EVALUATION OF GENDER DIFFERENCES IN THE CLINICAL EVALUATION OF DRUGS. 58 Fed. Reg. 39406 (July 22, 1993). The 1993 FDA policy affirmatively encouraged inclusion of women in clinical trials and stated that researchers were expected to analyze potential gender-related differences in the patients included in clinical studies.

Four years later, FDA published a proposal that would have authorized the agency to place a clinical hold on any clinical trial relating to a life-threatening illness if men or women with reproductive potential who have the disease are excluded from any phase of the trial because of a risk of reproductive toxicity. 62 Fed. Reg. 49946 (Sept. 24, 1997). While this proposal was pending, Congress added section 505(b)(1) to the FD&C Act as part of the FDA Modernization Act of 1997. This provision directed FDA, in consultation with NIH and the pharmaceutical industry, to "review and develop guidance, as appropriate, on the inclusion of women and minorities in clinical trials." In 1998, FDA amended its IND and NDA regulations to require that reports of studies for both safety and effectiveness present data by gender, age, and racial subgroups. 63 Fed. Reg. 6854 (Feb. 11, 1998). This is required even if the study is not sufficiently powered to permit statistical analysis. See Patricia F. Kaufman, A Critique of the Food and Drug Administration's 1993 Guideline Concerning the Inclusion of Fertile Women in Early Clinical Testing of New Drug Therapies (1994), Jonathan A. Roskes, The Inclusion of Women in Clinical Studies: Yesterday and Today (1994), and Stacey E. Parker, From Protectionism to Access: Women's Participation in Clinical Trials—Conflict, Controversy and Change (2002), in Chapter VI (C)(1) of the Electronic Book.

iv. Ethnic and Racial Groups

Although there is no statutory or regulatory requirement that special testing be conducted in ethnic or racial subpopulations, FDA expects that members of these groups will be included in clinical trials and requires, as noted above, that they be separated out for purposes of analysis in study reports submitted to the agency.

In June 2005, FDA approved a new drug, BiDil, for severe heart failure. The FDA-approved labeling provides that the drug is intended "for the treatment of heart failure as an adjunct to standard therapy in self-identified black patients." This is the only drug approved by FDA for a discrete racial group. For thoughtful analyses of the issues raised by this approval, see Alpana Gupta, *The Emerging Field of Race–Based Genetic Research: Can We Trust It?* (2006), and Stephanie A. Yonker, *FDA Drug Approval: A Black and White Issue?* (2006), in Chapter VI(C)(3) of the Electronic Book. In 68 Fed. Reg. 4788 (Jan. 30, 2003), FDA announced a Draft Guidance on COLLECTION OF RACE AND ETHNICITY DATA IN CLINICAL TRIALS. For scientific criticism of FDA's suggestion that ethnicity and race data will "enhance the early identification of differences in physiological response among racial and ethnic subgroups," see Susanne B. Haga & J. Craig Venter, *FDA Races in Wrong Direction*, 301 SCIENCE 466 (July 25, 2003).

NOTE

FDA Study. Section 907 of the Food and Drug Administration Safety and Innovation Act (FDASIA) of 2012 directed FDA to study issues surrounding demographic subgroups (sex, age, race, and ethnicity) in clinical trials, specifically the level of their participation in clinical trials, the reporting of subgroup data, and the dissemination of such data to the public. The resulting study, published in August 2013, generally reported positively on the collection and reporting of demographic subgroup information but concluded that nonwhite racial subgroups were underrepresented in many studies. FDA REPORT, COLLECTION, ANALYSIS, AND AVAILABILITY OF DEMOGRAPHIC SUBGROUP DATA FOR FDA-APPROVED MEDICAL PRODUCTS (Aug. 2013).

j.   GMP FOR INVESTIGATIONAL DRUGS

Collection of the chemical, manufacturing, and controls (CMC) information ultimately needed to assure compliance with good manufacturing practice (GMP) of the finished pharmaceutical product begins even before an IND is submitted. This process continues during the investigational studies. In effect, GMP is on a continuum of improved compliance, beginning with preclinical work and extending through to final validation studies during NDA review or even after NDA approval.

FDA issued a GUIDELINE ON PREPARATION OF INVESTIGATIONAL NEW DRUG PRODUCTS in 1991, which required drugs under an IND to meet the commercial GMP standards established in 21 C.F.R. Part 211. This guideline made no distinction in the GMP requirements for the three different phases of clinical investigation. As a practical matter, however, FDA never enforced full Part 211 GMP compliance on Phase I clinical trials, nor would such compliance have been achievable.

In 71 Fed. Reg. 2458 (Jan. 17, 2006), FDA issued a direct final regulation to exempt investigational drugs for Phase I clinical trials from the commercial GMP requirements. At the same time, the agency announced the availability of a Draft Guidance on INDs: APPROACHES TO COMPLYING WITH CGMP DURING PHASE I. According to this draft guidance, the pharmaceutical industry should implement:

> . . . manufacturing controls that are appropriate for the stage of development. The use of this approach recognizes that some controls and the extent of controls needed to achieve appropriate product quality differ not only between investigational and commercial manufacture, but also among the various phases of clinical studies.

Because FDA received significant adverse comments to the January 2006 direct final rule, the agency withdrew it and reissued it as a final rule using APA procedures. 73 Fed. Reg.40453 (July 15, 2008). It concurrently finalized the guidance. GUIDANCE FOR INDUSTRY: CGMP FOR PHASE I INVESTIGATIONAL DRUGS (July 2008).

NOTE

In the FDA Modernization Act of 1997, Congress added section 505(c)(4) to the FD&C Act to provide that a drug manufactured in a pilot or other small facility may be used for clinical investigation to demonstrate safety and effectiveness and to obtain NDA approval prior to manufacture of the drug in a larger facility. This reflected the concern of Congress that small companies cannot afford to build large manufacturing facilities in full compliance with drug GMP requirements prior to NDA approval.

k. DATA MONITORING COMMITTEE

Beginning in the 1960s, consideration was also given to the need for independent review of the data emerging from large clinical studies to determine whether the study should be stopped, either because of safety problems or because the drug was so effective that it would be unethical not to give it to the control group as well. The sponsors themselves could not perform this role, because it would unblind their trials. IRBs did not have the pharmacological and statistical competence to conduct adequate safety reviews. Thus, drug sponsors began to use what came to be called Data and Safety Monitoring Boards (DSMBs) to perform this function. FDA now calls this type of group a Data Monitoring Committee (DMC).

Guidance for Clinical Trial Sponsors:
Establishment and Operation of Clinical Trial Data Monitoring Committees

March 2006.

. . . .

A clinical trial DMC is a group of individuals with pertinent expertise that reviews on a regular basis accumulating data from one or more ongoing clinical trials. The DMC advises the sponsor regarding the continuing safety of trial subjects and those yet to be recruited to the trial, as well as the continuing validity and scientific merit of the trial. When a single DMC is responsible for monitoring multiple trials, the considerations for establishment and operation of the DMC are generally similar to those for a DMC monitoring a single trial, but the logistics may be more complex. For example, multiple conflict of interest determinations may be needed for each DMC member.

Many different models have been proposed and used for the operation of DMCs. Although different models may be appropriate and acceptable in different situations, experience has shown that some approaches have particular advantages or disadvantages. In this document, we highlight these advantages and disadvantages, with particular attention to the setting in which investigational products are being evaluated for possible marketing approval in well-controlled clinical trials. The intent of this guidance document is to ensure wide awareness of acceptable practices and of potential concerns regarding operation of DMCs that may arise in specific situations. . . .

Few trials sponsored by the pharmaceutical/medical device industry incorporated DMC oversight until relatively recently. The increasing use of DMCs in industry-sponsored trials is the result of several factors, including:

- The growing number of industry-sponsored trials with mortality or major morbidity endpoints;
- The increasing collaboration between industry and government in sponsoring major clinical trials, resulting in industry trials performed under the policies of government funding agencies, which often require DMCs;
- Heightened awareness within the scientific community of problems in clinical trial conduct and analysis that might lead to inaccurate and/or biased results, especially when early termination for efficacy is a possibility, and need for approaches to protect against such problems;
- Concerns of IRBs regarding ongoing trial monitoring and patient safety in multicenter trials. . . .

NOTES

1. *Mandatory DMC.* Although some clinical trials sponsored by NIH are required to incorporate a DMC, FDA has no requirement for the use of a DMC other than under 21 C.F.R. 50.24(a)(7)(iv), for research studies in an emergency setting in which informed consent is not required.

2. *Commentary. See* Susan S. Ellenberg et al., DATA MONITORING COMMITTEES IN CLINICAL TRIALS: A PRACTICAL PERSPECTIVE (2002), Joseph Corkery, *Primum Non Nocere: The Continuing Evolution of Safety Monitoring in Human Subjects Research* (2005), in Chapter VI(C)(1) of the Electronic Book.

3. *Patient Advocates.* Because of the increasing focus on protection of human subjects in clinical trials, some sponsors have also begun to use an ombudsperson or patient advocate whose duty it is to ensure the well-being of the research subjects, from the time that the protocol is first reviewed by the IRB, through the actual conduct of the study, and including the post-trial period as well.

l. CLINICAL TESTING CONDUCTED OVERSEAS

An investigational new drug may be used in clinical trials abroad under either of the following two circumstances. First, if the drug is manufactured abroad by or for a United States company, it is not subject to the FD&C Act and must meet only the requirements of the foreign country. Second, if the drug is manufactured in the United States, it may be exported under section 802(c) of the FD&C Act, as added by the FDA Drug Export Reform and Enhancement Act of 1996, to any of the countries listed in section 802(b)(1)(A) without the need to comply with any of the United States investigational drug provisions.

When the Drug Amendments of 1962 were first implemented, it was unusual for a sponsor to conduct clinical studies abroad. FDA officials were at first reluctant to accept the results of foreign clinical trials, but they gradually came to consider them similar to United States trials. In 1975, FDA made it clear that there would be no discrimination against foreign clinical trials submitted to support NDAs as long as the trials were conducted under the ethical standards of the Declaration of Helsinki. 40 Fed. Reg. 16053 (Apr. 9, 1975), codified at 21 C.F.R. 312.120.

In the 1980s, the pharmaceutical industry began to move many of its early stage clinical trials abroad because the regulatory requirements were substantially less onerous than those in the United States. FDA responded by attempting to streamline the information required for a United States IND. In the past decade, however, an increasing number of clinical trials have been conducted abroad for both regulatory and cost reasons. Not only are the regulatory requirements less burdensome in some foreign countries, but the cost is only a fraction of what a clinical trial costs in the United States. Clinical testing abroad has therefore spread from Western Europe to Eastern Europe and now to India and China. Fewer trials are conducted in the United States. Recognizing this trend, many have raised concerns about the protection of human subjects overseas and the quality of the trials themselves. *E.g.,* OFFICE OF DHHS INSPECTOR GENERAL, THE GLOBALIZATION OF CLINICAL TRIALS: A GROWING CHALLENGE IN PROTECTING HUMAN SUBJECTS, No. OEI–01–00–00190 (2001).

As part of the FDA Safety and Innovation Act of 2012, Congress enacted two new sections of the FD&C Act to address the increased use of foreign drug trials by United States companies. Section 569A requires FDA to work with foreign entities to foster and encourage "scientifically driven clinical trial standards" around the world. Section 569B provides that data from foreign clinical trials shall be accepted by FDA if the data are adequate to meet FDA standards. Neither of these provisions changes what FDA is already doing.

m.   INVESTIGATOR FRAUD

Ever since Congress enacted the Drug Amendments of 1962, requiring proof of the effectiveness of a drug before FDA will approve an NDA, the pharmaceutical industry has been plagued by sporadic instances of investigator fraud during clinical trials, especially Phase III trials. On occasion, the sponsoring company has uncovered this fraud. FDA investigators have also occasionally been the first to find such problems. Regardless of how the fraud is discovered, it can have a devastating effect on drug development and thus on the economic viability of both the drug and the company involved. FDA has issued GUIDANCE FOR INDUSTRY AND CLINICAL INVESTIGATORS: THE USE OF CLINICAL HOLDS FOLLOWING CLINICAL INVESTIGATOR MISCONDUCT (2004).

Virtually every type of fraud imaginable has been uncovered by companies and the FDA. Some investigators have fabricated the names and data for some or all of the trial subjects. Others have used the names of deceased patients. Still others have used the names of actual patients but have "penciled" (i.e., made up) the data, either without administering the test drug at all or by substituting fraudulent data for the actual data.

On occasion, it has been difficult to determine whether questionable data are in fact valid or fraudulent. Attempts to validate data after the trial is complete can be extremely time-consuming and costly, and thus can have a major impact on a trial even if the data are in fact validated. Whenever data are found by FDA to be suspect, it is unlikely that the agency will rely upon those data as pivotal evidence for an NDA in the absence of unequivocal validation.

The clinical monitoring that has commonly been used for the past 40 years to assure the integrity of clinical trials offers only modest safeguards against fraudulent investigator activity. For the most part, sponsoring companies rely upon clinical research associates (CRAs) to talk to investigators periodically and to review the clinical report forms (CRFs) for individual patients. A clever and determined investigator, however, can easily hide fraudulent material from random and relatively superficial oversight of this type. Indeed, even a relatively rigorous inquiry by a CRA can easily miss systematic and continuing fraud in clinical research.

Because FDA has encountered fraudulent reporting of clinical studies of investigational new drugs, the IND regulations provide for disqualification of clinical investigators who have submitted false information to FDA or to the sponsor. 21 C.F.R. 312.70. This rule also provides for disqualification of investigators who violate the regulations regarding protection of human subjects and the use of IRBs. FDA has recommended criminal prosecution of several clinical investigators for violation of the False Reports to the Government Act, 18 U.S.C. 1001, and the mail fraud statute, 18 U.S.C. 1341 & 1346. The agency has also initiated prosecutions for fraudulent animal testing of new drugs. In 47 Fed. Reg. 52228 (Nov. 19, 1982), FDA published guidelines for reinstating previously disqualified clinical investigators.

n. CLINICAL TRIALS DATABANK (CLINCIALTRIALS.GOV)

During the 1980s, FDA began publishing a list of all AIDS drugs in clinical trial under an IND. In the AIDS Amendments of 1988, enacted as part of the Health Omnibus Programs Extension of 1988, 102 Stat. 3048, 3062, 3072, 42 U.S.C. 300cc–17(d) & (e), Congress directed FDA to establish, as part of a databank on AIDS drugs, a registry of clinical trials of AIDS drugs conducted under an IND.

The FDA Modernization Act (FDAMA) of 1997 added section 402(j) to the Public Health Service Act, 42 U.S.C. 282(j), to require the Director of NIH to establish a databank of information on clinical trials for drugs for serious or life-threatening diseases and conditions. In March 2002, FDA issued a GUIDANCE FOR INDUSTRY: INFORMATION PROGRAM ON CLINICAL TRIALS FOR SERIOUS OR LIFE–THREATENING DISEASES AND CONDITIONS to address statutory and procedural issues relating to the databank, called ClinicalTrials.gov, but pharmaceutical industry participation in the databank was been hindered by the absence of enforcement remedies for noncompliance. *See* FDAMA SECTION 113: STATUS REPORT ON IMPLEMENTATION (2005) (available on FDA website) (reporting that only 35 percent of the trials that should have been listed in the database had been).

Almost immediately after the enactment of FDAMA, patients and physicians began to call for a more expanded clinical trials databank, to cover all diseases and to provide more information on the clinical trial protocols involved, as well as to cover the results of trials as soon as they became available. A consortium of respected medical journals announced that they would not publish the results of clinical trials that were not fully registered in the databank. Catherine D. DeAngelis et al., *Clinical Trial Registration: A Statement from the International Committee of Medical Journal Editors*, 292 J.A.M.A. 1363 (Sept. 15, 2004). The Pharmaceutical Research and Manufacturers of America published *Principles for the Conduct of Clinical Trials and the Communication of Clinical Trial Results* in 2002, launched a *Clinical Study Results Database* in 2004, and adopted a Policy Paper on *Principles Regarding the Disclosure of Clinical Trial Information* in 2005. Individual companies have also established their own databanks. Nonetheless, submission to all of these other clinical trial databanks remains voluntary, and they vary widely in the type and detail of the information they contain.

The FDA Amendments Act of 2007 (FDAAA) mandated expansion of the ClinicalTrials.gov databank and added enforcement provisions to help ensure compliance. Under the revised section 402(j)(2) of the PHSA, the registry data bank must include all "applicable" drug (and device) clinical trials. "Applicable" drug clinical trials include all controlled clinical investigations of a product subject to section 505 of the FDCA or section 351 of the PSHA, other than phase I clinical investigations. The sponsor of the investigation must submit the required information within 21 days after the first patient is enrolled in a clinical trial. FDAAA also expands the information about the trial required to be posted at this stage.

FDAAA also added new PHSA section 402(j)(3), which requires ClinicalTrials.gov to include information regarding the results of completed trials, but only for approved products. (NIH is permitted, in its implementing regulations, to require that such data be posted for unapproved products as well). Results data must be posted "for those clinical trials that form the primary basis of an efficacy claim or are conducted after the drug involved is approved." The required data, which must be posted within twelve months of completion of the trial or within 30 days after approval of the application, include both a technical and nontechnical summary of the trial and its results, information on the protocol, and "[s]uch other categories as the Secretary determines appropriate." PHSA 402(j)(3)(D)(iii).

FDAAA also added measures to ensure compliance. Applicants must certify compliance with 402(j) when they submit their applications, and failure to submit the required information and submission of false or misleading information is a prohibited act subject to civil monetary penalties.

As of July 2013, NIH had not yet developed a proposed rule implementing the FDAAA requirements for ClinicalTrials.gov, despite FDAAA's mandate to do so by 2010. A 2012 study estimated that approximately 40% of industry-sponsored trials likely to be subject to the FDAAA requirements had results posted on ClinicalTrials.gov. AP Prayle et al., *Compliance with Mandatory Reporting of Clinical Trial Results on ClinicalTrials.gov: Cross Sectional Study*, 344 BRIT. MED. J. d7373 (2012). In 2012, the Secretary of HHS delegated to FDA the authority to implement section 402(j)(5)(C)(ii) of the Public Health Service Act, concerning the submission of false or misleading information to ClinicalTrials.gov. 77 Fed. Reg. 59196 (Sept. 26, 2012).

o.   FDA/SEC COOPERATION

The rise of venture capital-financed biotechnology companies resulted in a substantial increase in initial public offerings (IPOs) to gain sufficient funding to support the heavy research and development costs leading to submission and approval of an NDA. The documents submitted to the Securities and Exchange Commission (SEC) supporting these IPOs and subsequent financings typically made representations about the status of INDs and NDAs pending at FDA and about discussions with agency officials. While prior to 2004, FDA and the SEC cooperated informally in reviewing these documents, during that year the two agencies announced a more formal collaborative program.

FDA and SEC Work to Enhance Public's Protection From False and Misleading Statements
FDA NEWS No. P04–15 (February 5, 2004).

The Food and Drug Administration (FDA) is announcing new measures designed to improve the manner by which FDA assists the Securities and Exchange Commission (SEC), whose primary mission is to protect the investing public and maintain the integrity of the securities market. In addition to implementing administrative improvements to make FDA technical and scientific support of the SEC and its staff more efficient, FDA is for the first time establishing a centralized procedure for FDA personnel to use in referring to the SEC statements by FDA-regulated firms that may be false or misleading.

"The SEC and its staff have primary responsibility for enforcing the rules requiring truth in the securities market, which is essential for its proper functioning," said Commissioner of Food and Drugs Mark B. McClellan, M.D., Ph.D. "Unfortunately, companies sometimes violate the public trust by issuing false or misleading statements about FDA-related issues, such as the progress of FDA's premarket review. When we identify suspected misstatements, we have a new process to bring them to the attention of the SEC staff as quickly and efficiently as possible."

Under the new referral procedure, any FDA employee who believes a publicly held, FDA-regulated firm has made a false or misleading statement to the investment public concerning a matter within FDA's authority can initiate a process for referring the matter to the SEC Division of Enforcement. FDA's mission is to promote and protect the public health, and FDA employees will not be expected routinely to police statements by publicly held, FDA-regulated companies. However, FDA can be in a position to identify statements that may be of interest to the SEC and its staff, and FDA employees will now have a centralized procedure to make SEC referrals if, in the normal course of their activities, they come to believe that a company may have made a false or misleading statement to the investing public.

NOTES

1. *FDA Referrals.* Since the establishment of the new cooperative procedure, FDA has in fact referred matters to the SEC for investigation and the SEC has requested FDA to review company securities documents for accuracy.

2. *Commentary.* For a review of SEC disclosure requirements, see Mikko Heinonen, *Disclosure of the Dealings between Drug Developing Companies and the FDA Under the Federal Securities Laws* (2002), in Chapter I(G)(9) of the Electronic Book.

3. THE NEW DRUG APPLICATION

Richard A. Merrill, *The Architecture of Government Regulation of Medical Products*
82 VIRGINIA LAW REVIEW 1753 (1996).

. . . .

3 key changes

The 1962 Amendments transformed the new drug review process that Congress had first authorized in 1938. Three changes were critically important. First, the 1962 Amendments converted what had been a premarket *notification* system, under which the maker of a new

① Must be approved

drug could commence marketing after the statutorily prescribed 180 days unless FDA challenged its safety, into a premarket *approval* system, in which the maker was obliged to wait for agency officials to affirm the drug's safety *and* effectiveness. The law thus gave FDA an effective veto over the marketing of any drug about which it had reservations. Not only was it harder for a manufacturer to satisfy FDA because effectiveness as well as safety had to be shown, the agency now had to be *convinced* before a drug could be marketed. Drug makers thus were held hostage to reviewers' indecision, to their preoccupation with other work, or to Congress's failure to provide FDA the resources necessary to handle its workload.

② Raised standards

Second, the Amendments obviously raised the standard that a new drug had to satisfy by explicitly directing FDA to confirm its effectiveness as well as its safety. FDA now had express authority to examine the evidence supporting all therapeutic claims made for a drug. Congress accordingly broadened the statutory definition of "new drug" to include any drug that was not generally recognized by experts as safe *and* effective.

The effectiveness requirement dramatically expanded the scope of the new drug approval process. Once FDA was convinced that a new therapeutic agent was safe for a particular indication, the manufacturer could reasonably conclude—and FDA might even agree—that it was "generally recognized as safe" for other uses. But for any active ingredient, novel or familiar, many therapeutic uses are possible, each of which, under the law's broadened definition of a "new drug," potentially required FDA review.

The 1962 Amendments enlarged the fixed time limit for FDA to rule on an application to 180 days, after which the applicant could, in theory, demand a final decision. And, if that decision was adverse, the applicant could take the matter to court. These procedural safeguards proved to be empty promises; FDA made it a practice to restart the clock each time an applicant submitted new information, even if the agency had requested the information. Reviewers resisted any pressure to rush to rule on completed applications. Almost without exception, applicants for approval have been unwilling to press for a timely decision when the answer might be "no," and they have displayed no inclination whatever to challenge in court an agency refusal to approve drugs.

③ Enlarge authority over clinical trials

The third important change made by the 1962 Amendments was to enlarge FDA's authority over the design and conduct of clinical trials of new drugs, the experiments undertaken to generate the data that the agency requires to decide whether a drug is safe and, centrally, effective. Section 505(d) of the Act specifies that the effectiveness of a drug must be shown by "substantial evidence," which the statute defines as "evidence consisting of adequate and well-controlled investigations, including clinical investigations, by experts qualified . . . to evaluate the effectiveness of the drug involved. . . ." The 1962 Amendments also gave FDA explicit authority to establish standards under which experimental drugs may be shipped to investigators who agree to conduct clinical trials.

These two grants of authority have made FDA the ultimate arbiter of how clinical trials should be designed. In interpreting the "substantial evidence" requirement and in reviewing applications for "investigational exemptions" from the premarket approval requirement, the agency has inevitably played a dominant role in deciding how to determine whether new drugs work as claimed. At the end of the day, drug makers must persuade FDA reviewers that they have submitted sufficient evidence to prove that a drug works. As a result, the agency has become the most influential source of guidance on the design of clinical drug studies in the country, and perhaps in the world.

Under the 1906 law, FDA had relatively little influence over the therapeutic claims made for drugs. Its authority was exerted, if at all, after a drug was on the market and evidence had accumulated that it might not work. The 1938 Act gave the agency a gatekeeper role, which permitted officials to examine and sometimes question a drug's clinical utility. The 1962 Amendments completed the law's reversal of the burden of proof. Since the passage of the Amendments, FDA has been responsible for judging, on the basis of evidence that it prescribed and makers supplied, whether new drugs worked. This shift in responsibility transformed the way in which drugs are developed, tested and marketed.

With the shift came a more subtle change in FDA's own view of its consumer protection role. Citizens may complain when local police fail to curtail unlawful or violent activity, but few believe that even the best-functioning police force can solve, much less prevent, all crimes. FDA is believed to have a different role, a responsibility to prevent harm before it occurs. The law makes it unlawful, without proof of intent or demonstration of actual injury or deception, to market drugs that the agency has not approved. In some sense, the agency becomes a warrantor of manufacturer compliance with the rules that govern drug development and marketing. This responsibility is implicitly acknowledged in the agency's own publications, is frequently referred to in press accounts of its performance, and historically has permeated the dialogue between the agency and congressional oversight committees. FDA is repeatedly reminded, and often reminds us, that it shares responsibility for any drug that causes harm. Many observers claim that this perception of FDA's role has made agency officials responsible for allowing drugs to reach the market exceptionally, and inappropriately, cautious. . . .

a.   PURPOSE AND FORM OF THE NDA

Peter Barton Hutt, *The Regulation of Drug Products by the United States Food and Drug Administration*

in THE TEXTBOOK OF PHARMACEUTICAL MEDICINE (John P. Griffin & John O'Grady, eds., 5th ed. 2006).

After the sponsor has completed all non-clinical and clinical testing necessary to demonstrate the safety and effectiveness of the drug, the test results must be compiled in an NDA for submission to FDA. As with the IND, the content and format of the NDA are set forth in the FDA regulations and must be followed in detail. The NDA must begin with a summary, to be followed by technical sections relating to (1) chemistry, manufacturing and controls, (2) non-clinical pharmacology and toxicology, (3) human pharmacokinetics and bioavailability, (4) microbiology, (5) clinical data and (6) statistics. Proposed labeling must also be included. The typical NDA comprises tens of thousands or even hundreds of thousands of pages.

The statute requires that a new drug should be shown to be both safe and effective. Because no drug has ever been shown to be completely safe or effective, in all cases this has been interpreted to mean that the benefits of the drug outweigh its risks under the labeled conditions of use for a significant identified patient population. The statute is very broadly worded with respect to the required proof for safety and effectiveness, and FDA has exercised substantial discretion in applying these requirements. New drugs have been approved on the basis of only one study, on the basis of Phase II studies that have never progressed to Phase III, on the basis of foreign studies alone and with results that could not be regarded as definitive from a scientific standpoint.

In most instances, FDA requires more than one adequate and well-controlled clinical trial. In the FDA Modernization Act of 1997 however, Congress clarified the law by providing that FDA may base the approval of an NDA on data from one adequate and well-controlled clinical investigation and confirmatory evidence.

The FDA has in practice implemented this provision only when the single adequate and well-controlled clinical investigation has statistical significance that is an order of magnitude greater than is normally required, that is, 0.005 or greater than 0.05.

Under the FD&C Act, FDA has always been required to evaluate the NDA and approve or disapprove it within 180 days. Until 1992, this almost never occurred. The average time for approval of an NDA was between 2 and 3 years. This time remained largely unchanged for the years between 1962 and 1994, in spite of repeated promises and attempts by FDA to speed up the process. FDA was able to avoid the 180-day statutory time deadline in several ways. First, the agency started the clock when it accepted the NDA for filing, not when it was submitted. Second, FDA stopped the clock, and restarted it, whenever new submissions were made. Third, FDA requested an extension of time from the applicant, who had no choice but to agree. Fourth, FDA simply ignored the 180-day deadline, and there was nothing that the applicant could do about it anyway.

NOTES

1. *NDA Regulations.* Following its success in the four Supreme Court cases in 1973, FDA planned to undertake a total revision of its IND and NDA regulations. This work was interrupted, first by investigations growing out of allegations of improper FDA handling of new drug decisions during the fall of 1974, "Examination of the Pharmaceutical Industry, 1973–74," Joint Hearings before the Subcommittee on Health of the Senate Committee on Labor and Public Welfare and the Subcommittee on

Administrative Practice and Procedure of the Senate Committee on the Judiciary, 93rd Cong., 2nd Sess., Part 7 (1974), and later by Congressional consideration of the Drug Regulation Reform legislation in 1977–1980. FDA promulgated new NDA regulations in 50 Fed. Reg. 7452 (Feb. 22, 1985), completely revising 21 C.F.R. Part 314. Thereafter, FDA made available several guidelines on compliance with the new provisions.

2. *NDA Filing.* An NDA is not "filed" when it is submitted to FDA. It becomes "filed" only after it has been reviewed and the agency concludes that it is complete enough to be acted on. This procedure, which dates back to 1938, was upheld in *Newport Pharmaceuticals International, Inc. v. Schweiker,* Food Drug. Cosm. L. Rep. (CCH) ¶ 38,148 (D.D.C. 1981).

3. *Data Supporting Approval.* In an unusual situation, one party to a joint venture to develop recombinant erythropoietin (EPO) for two separate indications sued the other to require that the data supporting both indications be submitted to FDA. *Ortho Pharmaceutical Corp. v. Amgen, Inc.,* 709 F. Supp. 504 (D. Del. 1989). The court granted the requested injunction, which was honored by the defendant, but the agency approved the drug for only one of the two requested indications.

4. *Electronic Format Submissions.* Almost all NDAs are now submitted in electronic format. The format recommended by the agency is the International Conference of Harmonisation of Technical Requirements for Registration of Pharmaceuticals for Human Use (ICH) electronic common technical document (eCTD). *See* GUIDANCE FOR INDUSTRY: PROVIDING REGULATORY SUBMISSIONS IN ELECTRONIC FORMAT—HUMAN PHARMACEUTICAL PRODUCT APPLICATIONS AND RELATED SUBMISSIONS USING THE ECTD SPECIFICATIONS (June 2008). The ICH is a cooperative joint effort by the United States, Europe, and Japan, and an eCTD can be submitted to regulatory agencies throughout the world.

5. *International Harmonization of Drug Approval Process.* International cooperation in drug development extends beyond the development of the eCTD. As part of the integration of countries into the European Union (EU), the EU established in January 1995 the European Medicines Evaluation Agency (EMEA), located in London, to centralize European evaluation of novel drugs. In September 2003, FDA and the EMEA issued a public statement relating to confidentiality arrangements to allow closer collaborative discussion. In 70 Fed. Reg. 69977 (Nov. 18, 2004) this was extended to the European Commission as well. Beginning in January 2005, FDA and the EMEA established a parallel scientific advice program under which a drug sponsor seeking marketing approval from both agencies can obtain a telephone conference with both to discuss a harmonized approach. At the same time, ICH has been working on detailed guidance on all aspects of the drug development process. For the past 25 years, these remarkably successful cooperative efforts have proceeded both on a formal level and through informal communications among medical review officials in countries everywhere.

These efforts are consistent with section 803(c) of the FD&C Act, added by the FDA Modernization Act of 1997, which encourages international harmonization efforts in general and mutual recognition agreements in particular. Harmonization is a realistic goal at this time, although mutual recognition by one country of another country's regulatory determination on a new drug is unlikely to be realized in the near future, if ever.

6.   *The Applications Integrity (Fraud) Policy.* In the generic drug scandal of the late 1980s, generic drug manufacturers submitted fraudulent data and bribed FDA officials in connection with abbreviated new drug applications (ANDAs). *See infra* p. 1011, note 10. As a result of this scandal, FDA adopted a "fraud policy" in September 1991. *See* 56 Fed. Reg. 46191 (Sept. 10, 1991), Compliance Policy Guide No. 120.100. This policy, later called the Applications Integrity Policy, covers situations in which FDA concludes that an applicant has engaged in a wrongful act and needs to take corrective action to establish the reliability of data submitted to FDA in support of a pending application and/or to support the integrity of a product already on the market. Under this policy, FDA issues a formal letter invoking the policy and requiring the applicant to cooperate fully with the FDA investigation. The applicant is required to identify all individuals associated with the wrongful act and to ensure that they are removed from any substantive authority on matters under FDA jurisdiction. A credible internal review must be conducted to identify all instances of wrongful acts, to supplement FDA's own investigation. Finally, the applicant must commit in writing to developing and implementing a correction action operating plan. Although this fraud policy was developed in response to the generic drug scandal, it also applies to pioneer drug companies and to data in full NDAs.

Although companies are given the opportunity to meet with FDA and make submissions demonstrating that they should not be placed under the fraud policy, FDA has not provided any specific administrative or judicial remedy to contest a fraud policy determination. Presumably such a determination could be contested in a District Court under the Administrative Procedure Act, but no company has chosen to pursue that remedy.

7.   *Studies of NDA Process.* The new drug approval process has been the subject of dozens of studies and reports. *See* Peter Barton Hutt, *Investigations and Reports Respecting FDA Regulation of New Drugs,* 33 CLINICAL PHARMACOLOGY AND THERAPEUTICS 537 (Part I), 674 (Part II) (1983). The early implementation of section 505 is discussed in numerous books, articles, congressional hearings, and GAO reports. Since the investigations and reports described in Hutt, there have been an equally large number of studies and reports on reforming the NDA approval system.

b.   USER FEES

The General Accounting Office had long favored the imposition of user fees to finance the increasingly expensive IND/NDA process outside the annual FDA appropriations. The Office of Management and Budget raised the question in the early 1970s and in 1982, the President's Private Sector Survey on Cost Control issued a task force report recommending FDA user fees in 1983, and the Reagan administration proposed FDA user fees as part of the fiscal year budgets of both 1985 and 1986. In 1985, pursuant to administration policy to raise additional funds without new taxes, FDA—in a reversal of its longstanding opposition to user fees—proposed to establish user fees in the amount of $126,200 for a full NDA, $16,400 for a supplemental NDA, and $9900 for an abbreviated NDA. 50 Fed. Reg. 31726 (Aug. 6, 1985). From the mid-1980s to 1992, the administration routinely requested user fees as part of the FDA appropriations process, but the pharmaceutical industry opposed them and Congress consistently rejected them. The industry's resistance to these early user fee proposals was based largely on the fact that revenue from the fees would have substituted for, rather than supplemented, revenues appropriated from general funds.

By 1992, it was apparent that Congress would not provide sufficient funding to allow timely review of INDs and NDAs and adequate opportunity for industry-FDA interaction on these applications. Average NDA review and approval times reached a high of three years. Thus, industry put aside its antipathy toward user fees and agreed to cooperate on a workable legislative approach.

There was agreement between FDA and industry that the fees must supplement, rather than replace, existing FDA baseline appropriations. There was also agreement that, in return for industry paying user fees to support the IND/NDA process, FDA would commit to improved performance goals in the operation of this process. Industry wanted those goals to be included in the legislation, but FDA insisted that they be set forth in a separate letter from the Commissioner or the HHS Secretary to the appropriate House and Senate Committees. The first Prescription Drug User Fee Act (PDUFA) was passed in 1992, 106 Stat. 4491. *See* Bruce N. Kuhlik, *Industry Funding of Improvements in the FDA's New Drug Approval Process: The Prescription Drug User Fee Act of 1992*, 47 FOOD & DRUG L.J. 483 (1992). PDUFA was initially authorized for five years, and it was reauthorized for another five years under the Food and Drug Administration Modernization Act of 1997, 111 Stat. 2296, the Prescription Drug User Fee Amendments of 2002, 116 Stat. 594, the FDA Amendments Act of 2007, 121 Stat. 823, and the FDA Safety and Innovation Act of 2012, 126 Stat. 993. *See* James L. Zelenay, Jr., *The Prescription Drug User Fee Act: Is a Faster Food and Drug Administration Always a Better Food and Drug Administration?*, 60 FOOD & DRUG L.J. 261 (2005); Alusheyi J. Wheeler, *The Prescription Drug User Fee Act: A Solution to the Drug Lag?* (2003), in Chapter III(G) of the Electronic Book.

The legislation provides for three types of user fees: (1) drug applications, (2) drug products, and (3) drug establishments. These fees have allowed FDA to more than double the number of personnel reviewing NDAs. The average time for NDA approval under user fees was initially halved. In 1999 and 2000, however, this trend was reversed and the time for approval began to increase. As a response to this increase in approval time, FDA began its current practice of issuing "approvable" letters within the user-fee time guidelines and then taking substantial additional time to negotiate remaining issues, often including labeling, before a final approval letter is sent.

The initial performance goals focused on the time required for FDA review of an NDA. Industry realized, however, that the amount of time required for nonclinical and clinical testing was increasing at a greater rate than the NDA review time was being reduced. Consequently, subsequent performance goals have focused on pre-NDA requirements as well. FDA issued the following White Paper in November 2005, summarizing the agency performance goals under the first three successive PDUFA statutes.

FDA White Paper, Prescription Drug User Fee Act (PDUFA): Adding Resources and Improving Performance in FDA Review of New Drug Applications

November 11, 2005.

The Prescription Drug User Fee Act (PDUFA) program is the cornerstone of modern FDA drug review. User fees currently fund about half of new drug review costs. By providing needed funds, PDUFA ended slow and unpredictable review and approval of new drug applications, while keeping FDA's high standards.

PDUFA funds allowed FDA to accomplish a number of important goals. FDA hired more review and support staff to speed review. The number of full-time equivalent (FTE) staff devoted to the new drug review process has nearly doubled, growing from 1,277 FTE in 1992 to 2,503 FTE in 2004. FDA upgraded its data systems and gave industry guidance to help minimize unnecessary trials and generally improve drug development. FDA gave industry guidance on how to improve the quality of applications, with the goal to reduce misunderstandings and the need for sponsors to rework and resubmit applications. Finally, FDA improved procedures and standards to make review more rigorous, consistent, and predictable.

Taken together, all of these steps ensure that the time and effort patients put in to clinical trials provide useful data. They also lowered drug development costs and shortened review times. For example, the median approval time for priority new drug applications and biologics license applications decreased from 13.2 months on 1993 to 6.4 months in 2003. Ultimately these developments enabled FDA to ensure that needy American patients get fast access to novel drugs—faster, in fact, than citizens of other countries. Since the start of PDUFA, FDA has approved over 1,000 new drugs and about 100 new biologics. Under the currently authorized program (PDUFA 3) 50 percent of new drugs are launched first in the United States, compared to only 8 percent in the years pre-PDUFA. . . .

FDA funding and staffing levels for drug review activities have significantly increased under PDUFA. At the same time, the performance focus of the program has continued to expand, as summarized in the Table 4.1 below. The user fees performance goals for the 2007 and 2012 programs are too numerous and complex to capture in tabular form, and are discussed in the following sections.

Table 4.1 Expansion of FDA Performance Commitments Since Enactment of PDUFA

PDUFA 1 Goals by FY97	PDUFA 2 Goals by FY02	PDUFA 3 Goals by FY07
Backlog: Eliminate **Priority Reviews**: 90% in 6 months **Standard Reviews**: 90% in 12 months	**Priority Reviews**: 90% in 6 months **Standard Reviews**: 90% in 10 months **Formal Meetings**: schedule 90% within 14 days, convene 90% within 30/60/75 days **Clinical hold response**: 90% in 30 days **Special protocol evaluation**: 90% in 45 days **Electronic submissions**: Able to receive by end of FY02	**Priority Reviews**: 90% in 6 months **Standard Reviews**: 90% in 10 months **Formal Meetings**: schedule 90% within 14 days, convene 90% within 30/60/75 days **Clinical hold response**: 90% in 30 days **Special protocol evaluation**: 90% in 45 days **Electronic submissions**: Able to receive by end of FY02 **Continuous Marketing Application** **Pre- and Peri-NDA/BLA Risk Management** Plan Activities **Independent Consultants for Clinical Trials** **Good Review Management Principles (GRMPs)** for First Cycle Review Performance **Improved Performance Management** **Electronic Applications & Submissions**

The user fees established under the PDUFA program have increased substantially.

	1993	1997	2002	2007	2012
Product	$12,000	$13,200	$21,630	$49,750	$98,380
Establishment	$60,000	$115,700	$140,109	$313,100	$526,000
NDA	$100,000	$205,000	$313,320	$896,200	$1,958,000

Under all PDUFA statutes, congressional appropriations have been required to be maintained at the 1992 level, indexed for inflation. In reality, however, PDUFA fees have gradually become the predominant source of the FDA budget for the review of human new drugs.

	User Fees %	Appropriations %
1992	0	100
1993	7	93
1994	23	77
1995	35	65
1996	36	64
1997	36	64
1998	40	60
1999	43	57
2000	47	53
2001	50	50
2002	47	53
2003	49	51
2004	53	47
2005	56	44
2006	58	42
2007	56	44
2008	63	37
2009	60	40
2010	62	38
2011	61	39
2012	62	38

Steve Usdin, *Cinderella's Glass Slipper*, BIOCENTURY, Sept. 18, 2006, at A1, A2 (updated by Eds.). The IOM Report, A DRUG SAFETY SYSTEM PROMOTING AND PROTECTING THE HEALTH OF THE PUBLIC (2006), recommended that the IND/NDA regulatory system be funded by congressional appropriations rather than by user fees.

Steve Usdin, *Diminishing Returns*

BIOCENTURY, Feb. 13, 2006, at A1.

PDUFA must again be reauthorized in 2007, which will require the development of new performance goals. It will also provide the opportunity for other statutory reforms of the IND/NDA process to be added to the legislation.

Data from the Prescription Drug User Fee Act are clear in one respect: most of the progress in reducing review and approval times was made in the first two years—between 1993 and 1995. Since then, despite ever-larger infusions of cash and increasing requirements that are intended to make FDA more responsive and collaborative, the agency and industry have been treading water.

Drugs aren't getting developed or approved any faster than when user fees were much lower and FDA's workload, as measured by new drug and biologics applications, was larger. In part, this is because user fees have replaced taxpayer funding, even though PDUFA income was designed to supplement government investments in the agency.

During the first five-year PDUFA round, the $292.3 million paid by drug sponsors covered about 30% of the costs for reviewing human drug applications. For the first two years of PDUFA III, user fees covered 49% and 53% of the costs in fiscal years 2003 and 2004, respectively.

Thus, all signs lead to the conclusion that the easy gains have been made.

As industry and FDA now prepare for PDUFA IV, some efficiency still could be squeezed out of the system. There is scope for cutting approval times for standard applications, particularly by reducing the number of review cycles. Review practices could be made more consistent across divisions. And it is important to remain vigilant to detect backsliding.

But to get more drugs approved faster, the focus of regulatory innovation must widen to include the entire time from preclinical to marketing. A sea change, something on the order of the 60% reduction accomplished through PDUFA in review and approval times for priority new molecular entities, can come only by attenuating the period from preparing an IND to submitting an NDA or BLA.

Although proposals to add user fees to improve sponsor-agency dialog during the development process will be discussed as part of PDUFA IV, most of the big ideas for cutting drug development times require forging consensus among FDA, industry and academic researchers, rather than the enactment of legislation.

c.   MEETINGS WITH FDA

Just as it is important to have substantive meetings between sponsors and FDA throughout the IND process, *supra* p. 676, it is equally important to continue having these meetings while the NDA is in preparation and under review. These meetings are used to help prepare an NDA that will meet the expectations of the agency, to respond to questions that arise during FDA's review of the NDA, and to maintain continuing dialogue about all aspects of the review process.

See Joseph A. DiMasi & Michael Manocchia, *Initiatives to Speed New Drug Development and Regulatory Review: The Impact of FDA–Sponsor Conferences*, 31 DRUG INFO. J. 771 (1997).

One indicator of a successful NDA review process is whether the NDA review is completed, and final action by FDA is taken, within the performance goal established by PDUFA, e.g., within 10 months for a standard NDA. At the end of the time established by PDUFA for review of the NDA, the agency is obligated to send the applicant a letter either approving the NDA or stating what needs to be done in order to obtain approval. The first ten-month period is called the first cycle. Subsequent review periods are called the second cycle, the third cycle, and so on.

As one of the performance goals under PDUFA III, FDA agreed to retain an independent expert consultant to evaluate the factors that contribute to first cycle approval. In 71 Fed. Reg. 6284 (Feb. 7, 2006), FDA announced the availability of the resulting final report, excerpted below:

Booz Allen Hamilton, Inc., *Independent Evaluation of FDA's First Cycle Review Performance— Retrospective Analysis*
January 2006.

. . . .

FDA reviewer team members agree that early on-going dialog with sponsors is the most important factor in identifying issues and potentially providing an opportunity for timely resolution, ideally before first action is taken. All divisions interviewed routinely strive to start discussions with sponsors before the submission. These efforts meet with mixed success: End-of-Phase 2 meetings appear to significantly contribute to first-cycle approval while Pre-NDA/BLA meetings had a lesser impact. In some instances, substantial deficiencies were not documented/identified until the review phase, potentially preventing first-cycle approval despite the possible availability of pertinent information at the time of Pre-BLA/NDA meetings. This finding may be attributed to the general focus of these meetings on application formatting rather than review of development results. When issues are identified, there is often insufficient time to adequately address these as submission timelines are generally not delayed. This may be due to sponsors' unwillingness to adopt FDA suggestions or lack of clarity in FDA communications on the severity of the issues raised. There are also examples where sponsors are able to resolve issues via a different path than originally recommended by the FDA. These findings point to broad issues around coverage of problem areas prior to submission, ineffective communication between the FDA and sponsors, and unclear prioritization of issues and/or problem resolution requirements.

An approach to address this challenge is the development of an open and accountable communication system centered around issue resolution. This system may include a pre-submission check-list and follow-up responsibilities that will guide FDA–Sponsor discussions and ensure that these communications are better leveraged to achieve agreement on issue resolution. This system—termed in this report as check-and-follow up communication—will increase consistency and reduce the risk of overlooking key issues at pre-submission stages. . . .

———

FDA has stated that meetings require FDA personnel to spend extensive time in preparation and attendance—time that is not adequately reflected in PDUFA funding. It is the uniform experience of the pharmaceutical industry, however, that between ten and twenty FDA personnel typically attend these meetings, but only two or three people actually participate in the discussion. If FDA were to limit meetings to the agency employees who will actually participate, and were to communicate the results through accurate and detailed minutes, the agency could hold far more meetings with the same amount of resources.

In the past quarter century, the pharmaceutical industry has been successful in two important areas relating to meetings. First, the number of meetings between FDA and drug sponsors has increased. Second, the ability of a drug sponsor to obtain detailed information relating to the FDA positions on critical regulatory aspects of the development of a drug have greatly increased.

The following types of meetings between FDA and the sponsor are routinely available prior to submission of an NDA.

- Pre-nonclinical
- Post-nonclinical
- Pre-IND
- End of Phase II
- Pre-SPA
- SPA
- Pre-Phase III
- End of Phase III
- Pre-NDA

Where unanticipated events occur, moreover, FDA is often accommodating in scheduling additional meetings, often by telephone.

Once the NDA is filed, there is now routine interaction between FDA and the sponsor, in writing, by telephone, or in person.

- The Day 74 Letter (74 calendar days from receipt of the NDA), identifying any review issues.
- The Mid-Cycle Telephone Call, to provide an update on the status of the review.
- Information Letters from FDA requesting any additional information not in the NDA.
- Discipline Review Letters, identifying any issues.
- FDA GCP, GLP, and GMP inspections.
- Late-Cycle Meeting with the FDA signatory authority for the NDA, to discuss any substantive issues that have been identified

and the FDA review package for any advisory committee meeting.

Depending on the NDA and the FDA reviewers, there may also be additional emails and telephone calls.

For all formal meetings, the sponsor's briefing package must be received by FDA at least 30 days before the scheduled meeting date and may include an unlimited number of specific questions to which the sponsor is seeking answers. About two days before the meeting, FDA will provide to the sponsor written answers to all of these questions. These answers are usually written in very clear and direct terms that often begin with a blunt "yes" or "no." It is these answers that are invaluable to the sponsor in understanding the status and future requirements for the drug. The sponsor may then keep the meeting or cancel it.

This process does not always work perfectly. But it is far more interactive and informative than at any time in the past.

d.   REFUSAL TO FILE

From the inception of the NDA review process under the 1938 Act, it was FDA practice to declare as "incomplete" any application it regarded as inadequate and not to take any form of action on it until the applicant submitted a new application that the agency deemed to be complete. When FDA promulgated the current NDA regulations as part of the IND/NDA rewrite in 1985, it included, at 21 C.F.R. 314.101, a detailed regulation governing its refusal to file an application because it is not "sufficiently complete to permit a substantive review." 50 Fed. Reg. 7452 (Feb. 22, 1985). FDA issued a guidance on its refuse-to-file policy in July 1993. Around the same time, the agency established a Refuse-to-File (RTF) Review Committee. The Review Committee held two pilot meetings and then two regular meetings, 58 Fed. Reg. 28983 (May 18, 1993), 58 Fed. Reg. 52497 (Oct. 8, 1993), but there have been no further announced meetings. In general, if a sponsor has held adequate pre-NDA meetings with FDA, it should have little concern the agency will refuse to file the NDA.

e.   THE SAFETY STANDARD

Section 505(d) of the FD&C Act directs FDA to withhold approval of an NDA unless the sponsor's evidence shows the drug to be safe "by all methods reasonably applicable to show whether or not such drug is safe for use under the conditions of use prescribed, recommended, or suggested" in the proposed labeling. The Act does not say how safety is to be determined, and FDA has never attempted to spell out in regulations the criteria that it employs.

The term "safety" appears in many provisions of the FD&C Act. With respect to food, for example, FDA has always applied it as an absolute standard, ignoring any potential benefit that the food may have. *See supra* p. 580. With respect to drugs, on the other hand, FDA has relatively consistently taken into account a product's potential benefit. As the following testimony by former FDA Commissioner George Larrick illustrates, even before enactment of the Drug Amendments of 1962 (when FDA could disapprove an NDA on safety grounds alone), the agency implicitly considered the effectiveness of the product in making its safety decisions.

Testimony of FDA Commissioner George Larrick

"Drug Safety," Hearings Before a Subcommittee of the House Committee on
Government Operations, 88th Congress 2d Session (1964).

The 1938 new drug section of the law did not require a manufacturer to prove that his new drug would yield the benefits claimed on its label. It spoke only of safety. Thus, many of the Government's decisions allowing drugs to be marketed had to be made without access to the full facts a physician would want in deciding whether to use the product. . . .

Of course the question of benefit was an integral part of the safety question in dealing with a product to be used in a life-threatening disease such as pneumonia or in dealing with a drug presenting grave risks. We required information about effectiveness for such drugs in order to reach a decision about safety. But many fairly innocuous new drugs offered for ailments that were not life-threatening were presented to us for evaluation without evidence that they would do what the label claimed. We had no power in such case to require submission of efficacy data. . . .

In evaluating risk we need, to the extent it is available, and in many of these areas the extent of the available science is quite deficient, information on such things as:

    1.   The interaction of the drug with body processes, including: hormonal, enzymic, metabolic, and reproductive processes.

    2.   The manner in which the drug is absorbed, distributed in body tissues, and inactivated or excreted. . . .

    3.   Whether active compounds arise from the metabolism of the drug by the body.

    4.   The influence of other chemicals, such as other drugs or even articles of food or drink upon the activity of the drug in question.

    5.   How the activity of the drug in animals compares with its activity in man. . . .

No plan of clinical investigation, even the most expensive, can be expected to give all of the information that will be revealed by general marketing and use of a new drug. . . . General use involves more patients than can possibly be employed in clinical trial. Whereas the clinical trial may expose hundreds or at most thousands of people to a new product, general use may involve several million. Physicians who investigate a drug before it is marketed, even in the widespread tests just before marketing, are generally selected because of their specialized superior training and skill and because of their interest in clinical testing. After release the drug will be used by some physicians with less training, less skill, and less opportunity to make sure they are adhering to all of the suggestions in the labeling of the drug.

In fact, the early period following general marketing of a new drug must be regarded as a final step in the testing of the product. There is no way to duplicate fully in clinical trials the great variety of use conditions under which a new drug will be employed when it is finally approved. . . .

NOTE

Pre-1962 Effectiveness Review. In his monumental history of FDA drug regulation, Daniel Carpenter shows how even before 1962, the agency systematically took effectiveness into account, as well as safety, when reviewing NDAs.

> As the pharmacological regime began to populate and govern FDA drug regulation, its officers transformed the standards by which new drugs were reviewed. The most visible and durable of these shifts was the stable emergence of an efficacy standard in new drug review years before Congress explicitly authorized FDA rulings on pharmaceutical "effectiveness" in the Kefauver-Harris Amendments of 1962. Considerations of efficacy and therapeutic value had been in play since the first drug reviews following the 1938 Act. What changed was the emergence of protocol—a systematic, planned, and sequentially ordered assay of efficacy issues in drug development and new drug review.

DANIEL CARPENTER, REPUTATION AND POWER 149–50 (2010). Carpenter remarks that FDA officials were generally reluctant to acknowledge a formal efficacy calculus in drug review even as the agency applied it in practice. *Id.* 152.

———

Four decades after Commissioner Larrick's testimony, the safety decision had not fundamentally changed.

Bernadine Healy, M.D., *What Is a 'Safe' Drug?*
U.S. NEWS & WORLD REPORT, Dec. 13, 2004, at 37.

One of the most vivid lessons I learned in medical school came from an otherwise dry course in pharmacology. Our professor sobered a class of eager 20–somethings just aching to have prescription pads in their hands with his opening pronouncement: "Drugs are dangerous." If there's any lesson for the public in the current firestorm surrounding the recalled anti-inflammatory drug Vioxx, it should be that. Whether it's the century-old aspirin or the recently disgraced Vioxx—designed as a safer form of aspirin—all drugs come with unwanted and often unexpected side effects.

Unfortunately, the public theater of Vioxx's demise omits such messy details. Within moments of the recall, media stories rushed to sing good riddance to a "bad drug," tort lawyers set out in hot pursuit of the injured "class," and critics assailed the drug maker for greed and deception and the FDA for lack of vigilance. Wall Street analysts wrapped the entire COX-2 drug class in black crepe. Would that it were this simple.

I predict that the COX-2 inhibitors will survive. They are too important a tool to be dumped from the medicine chest. In addition to their pain-relieving capabilities, they show great promise in preventing and treating a wide array of deadly tumors, including those of the colon, lung, pancreas, stomach, brain, and breast. There's reason for this: To take hold and spread, some cancer cells have learned how to hijack the body's inflammatory pathways by producing overactive COX-2 genes. The COX-2 inhibitors offer a unique and targeted weapon against this banditry. Celebrex has already been approved for the prevention of colon cancer. Remember thalidomide? Once a notorious drug because it caused birth defects, it is now a lifesaver for those with certain cancers, like multiple myeloma.

Vioxx is no demon drug. And the FDA does not turn a blind eye to danger. Were safety the only measure, the agency's job would be easy— and our medicine chests would be empty. As we watch the Vioxx fallout, we should be wary of a scalping party that could leave us so safe we are not safe at all.

NOTES

1. *Procedures for Disapproval.* A notable example of FDA disapproval of an NDA for a prescription drug on the ground of lack of safety is medroxyprogesterone acetate (Depo–Provera). In 1974, in anticipation of approval of the NDA for Depo–Provera for use as an injectable contraceptive, FDA established patient package inserts for the drug. 39 Fed. Reg. 32907 (Sept. 12, 1974), codified as 21 C.F.R. 310.501a. Soon thereafter, however, the FDA commissioner delayed approval of the drug based on concerns it presented a risk of cancer. 39 Fed. Reg. 38226 (Oct. 30, 1974) (delaying approval), 40 Fed. Reg. 12830 (Mar. 21, 1975) (announcing open meeting). In 43 Fed. Reg. 28555 (June 30, 1978), FDA published a notice of opportunity for hearing on its intent to disapprove the NDA, based on its carcinogenicity. The applicant elected a hearing before a public board of inquiry, 44 Fed. Reg. 44274 (July 27, 1979), which recommended against approval of the NDA. Food Drug Cosm. L. Rep. (CCH) ¶ 39,291 (Oct. 17, 1984); 49 Fed. Reg. 43507 (Oct. 29, 1984) (announcement of availability of decision). The company then withdrew its NDA. 51 Fed. Reg. 37651 (Oct. 23, 1986). FDA revoked the PPI for Depo–Provera in 54 Fed. Reg. 22585 (May 25, 1989). In 1992, however, the carcinogenicity issue was resolved and FDA approved the NDA.

2. *Withdrawal of NDA Approval for Safety Reasons.* The separate issue of FDA withdrawal of an NDA approval for safety reasons after the drug has been marketed is discussed *infra* at p. 848.

3. *Competitive Safety Studies.* On occasion, companies will conduct safety studies on each other's drugs and submit the results to FDA, in an attempt to slow down the NDA approval for competitive products. Companies have made presentations to advisory committees arguing that a competitor's drug was unsafe and should be disapproved or at least bear a strong warning label, perhaps with a black box. Some of these efforts have been successful. Others have been viewed as competitive tactics that should be given little or no weight.

4. *Private Right of Action With Regard to Safety*. In *Hawkins v. Upjohn Company*, 890 F. Supp. 609 (E.D. Tex. 1994), plaintiffs alleged a fraudulent conspiracy by the defendants to withhold safety information from FDA for the purpose of inducing the agency to approve the marketing of two drugs. The District Court held that, although plaintiffs could not assert a private right of action for enforcement of the FD&C Act, they could properly allege a conspiracy both to commit fraud and to market a known unreasonably dangerous product.

5. *FDA's Risk Management System*. In 1999, Public Citizen Health Research Group charged that time pressures caused by the PDUFA performance goals and the FDA initiatives to speed up the review and approval of new drugs was resulting in an increased number of unsafe drugs being introduced onto the market, and thus an increased number of unsafe drugs required to be taken off the market. In response, FDA Commissioner Jane Henney established a Task Force on Risk Management to evaluate this allegation. The resulting report, MANAGING THE RISKS FROM MEDICAL PRODUCT USE: CREATING A RISK MANAGEMENT FRAMEWORK (1999), rejected the allegations. But the Task Force report went on to review the FDA mechanisms for risk management in the approval of NDAs and concluded that the agency could do a more effective job of risk management. The report identified numerous ways that FDA could improve these programs.

The Task Force report had an immediate impact on FDA requirements for clinical trials. The pharmaceutical industry soon found that FDA was requesting more nonclinical studies and more clinical trials, of longer duration, with more subjects, containing more arms for additional dosage levels, with more diverse subjects, and longer follow up. The result was a significant reduction in NDAs submitted to the agency and an approximate doubling of the average cost of an NDA. In June 2001, stock analysts at SalomonSmithBarney, citing ten negative developments at FDA, headed its analysis: "FDA Goes Hostile."

In 2005, FDA issued three final guidances as part of its risk management program, 70 Fed. Reg. 15866 (Mar. 29, 2005) and CDER made available MAPP No. 6700.1 on RISK MANAGEMENT PLAN ACTIVITIES IN OND AND ODS (Sept. 8, 2005). Because this array of risk management policies is still relatively recent, it is unclear how much of an impact they will have on drug development in the United States.

f.   THE EFFECTIVENESS STANDARD

Section 505(d) also specifies that the FDA shall withhold approval of a new drug unless the sponsor provides "substantial evidence that the drug will have the effect it purports or is represented to have under the conditions of use prescribed, recommended, or suggested in the proposed labeling." The section defines "substantial evidence" of effectiveness as

> evidence consisting of adequate and well-controlled investigations, including clinical investigations, by experts qualified by scientific training and experience to evaluate the effectiveness of the drug involved, on the basis of which it could fairly and responsibly be

concluded by such experts that the drug will have the effect it purports or is represented to have under the conditions of use prescribed, recommended, or suggested in the labeling or proposed labeling thereof.

In 1970, FDA promulgated a regulation defining adequate and well-controlled clinical studies. 21 C.F.R. 314.126. This regulation is excerpted above, *supra* p. 682, in the discussion of clinical testing. The agency issued this rule not to provide guidance to the pharmaceutical industry in designing protocols for future NDAs, but rather to enable the agency to withdraw pre-1962 new drugs from the market as ineffective under the DESI Review without the need for an administrative hearing. *See infra* pp. 776–779. Nonetheless, these regulations have remained unchanged for more than 35 years and continue to guide both FDA and the pharmaceutical industry in their daily decisions.

NOTES

1. *Meaning of Substantial Evidence.* The Senate Report on the 1962 Drug Amendments provides this description of the proof of effectiveness requirement:

> When a drug has been adequately tested by qualified experts and has been found to have the effect claimed for it, this claim should be permitted even though there may be preponderant evidence to the contrary based upon equally reliable studies. There may also be a situation in which a new drug has been studied in a limited number of hospitals and clinics and its effectiveness established only to the satisfaction of a few investigators qualified to use it. There may be many physicians who deny the effectiveness simply on the basis of a disbelief growing out of their past experience with other drugs or with the diseases involved. Again the studies may show that the drug will help a substantial percentage of the patients in a given disease condition but will not be effective in other cases. What the committee intends is to permit the claim for this new drug to be made to the medical profession with a proper explanation of the basis on which it rests.
>
> In such a delicate area of medicine, the committee wants to make sure that safe new drugs become available for use by the medical profession so long as they are supported as to effectiveness by a responsible body of opinion.

S. Rep. No. 1744, 87th Cong., 2nd Sess., Part. 1 at 16 (1962).

2. *One or More Studies.* Prior to 1997, section 505(d) referred only to "investigations," including clinical "investigations." This wording raised the question whether there must be at least two clinical investigations to support approval of an NDA. The regulations FDA promulgated immediately following the 1962 Drug Amendments stated, that "ordinarily" more than one clinical study would be required. 28 Fed. Reg. 1449 (Feb. 14, 1963), 28 Fed. Reg. 6377 (June 20, 1963). In implementing the DESI program, however, FDA summarily withdrew approval of an NDA only where there was *no* adequate and well-controlled clinical study. In 39 Fed.

Reg. 9750, 9755 (Mar. 13, 1974), FDA declined to adopt a requirement that two, rather than just one, adequate and well-controlled clinical studies be identified in order to demonstrate a drug's effectiveness. When it revised the NDA regulations in 1985, FDA retained the provision that summary revocation of an NDA will not occur where at least one adequate and well-controlled clinical investigation has been identified. 21 C.F.R. 314.200(g)(1). In the years prior to 1997, FDA officials testified more than once that the agency has authority to approve an NDA on the basis of a single adequate and well-controlled clinical study. "Use of Advisory Committees by the Food and Drug Administration," Hearings before a Subcommittee of the House Committee on Government Operations, 93rd Cong., 2nd Sess. 122 (1974); "The Regulation of New Drugs by the Food and Drug Administration: The New Drug Review Process," Hearings before a Subcommittee of the House Committee on Government Operations, 97th Cong., 2nd Sess. 37 (1982). Nonetheless, for most NDAs, FDA required at least two adequate and well-controlled clinical studies.

In the FDA Modernization Act of 1997, Congress added to section 505(d) a new sentence stating that:

> If the Secretary determines, based on relevant science that data from one adequate and well-controlled clinical investigation and confirmatory evidence (obtained prior to or after such investigation) are sufficient to establish effectiveness, the Secretary may consider such data and evidence to constitute substantial evidence for purposes of the preceding sentence.

This provision has been applied by FDA only in situations where a single study demonstrates statistical significance at the .005–.001 level. FDA has issued no guidance on this matter. A significant number of NDA and supplemental NDA submissions have been based on a single controlled trial since 1997. *See, e.g.,* TUFTS CENTER FOR THE STUDY OF DRUG DEVELOPMENT, 3 IMPACT REPORT, No. 5 (Sept./Oct. 2001).

3. *Clinical Testing Guidelines.* To advise manufacturers and investigators on testing protocols that will satisfy the agency's requirements for adequate and well-controlled clinical studies, FDA began issuing clinical testing guidelines for several types of drugs in the 1970s. *E.g.,* 44 Fed. Reg. 20796 (Apr. 6, 1979). All of these have now been converted to guidance, and numerous other guidances have been issued by FDA on appropriate clinical testing.

4. *Relative Efficacy.* The history of the 1962 Amendments reveals a Congressional decision that FDA not refuse to approve a drug on the ground of "relative efficacy," i.e., that a more effective drug is available. While FDA has formally observed this mandate, it has taken other actions that have a similar impact. First, it has disapproved drugs on the ground of relative safety. Second, it has stated that the labeling of a less effective drug may be required to specify the drug of choice. Third, it has taken the position that, to be found "effective," a drug must be shown to have a clinically significant effect.

5. *Combination Drugs.* In 1971, FDA promulgated a policy for evaluating the effectiveness of combination prescription drugs. 36 Fed. Reg. 20037 (Oct. 15, 1971), codified at 21 C.F.R. 300.50.

6. *Statistical Analysis.* To minimize bias and maximize statistical power, FDA relies on the so-called "intent-to-treat" analysis of large clinical trials. Under this approach, all patients who are included in the control or treatment group, without exception, must be included in the ultimate analysis of the results, regardless of whether additional information reveals that they failed to follow the protocol instructions or otherwise do not represent appropriate subjects. For example, patients who are instructed to take the drug according to a specified regimen, but who fail to take it, are included in the analysis even though they obviously could not have exhibited any benefits from the drug. Accordingly, the results of an "intent-to-treat" analysis provide an average of those subjects who comply with the protocol and those who do not. Depending upon the extent of noncompliance with the protocol, the results may accurately reflect the effectiveness of the drug or may be seriously misleading. More accurate analysis can be obtained by stratifying the clinical data according to the level of patient compliance with the prescribed drug regimen. The physician package insert for Questran (cholestyramine), for example, provides information on the reduction in cholesterol in relation to the amount of the drug taken in a clinical trial, i.e., the patient compliance with the drug regimen established in the protocol:

Packet Count	Total Cholesterol Lowering	Reduction in Coronary Heart Disease Risk
0–2	4.4%	10.9%
2–5	11.5%	26.1%
5–6	19.0%	39.3%

7. *Clinical and Surrogate Endpoints.* In determining effectiveness, the ultimate endpoint of interest is the survival of the patient. Clinical trials studying only patient survival may, however, require large numbers of subjects and take many years to complete. For that reason, researchers seek "surrogate" endpoints that will demonstrate, at a much earlier stage, whether the drug is effective. These surrogate endpoints are typically physiological parameters that correlate with the progress of the disease. For some diseases, the correlation between particular physiological parameters and the disease is sufficiently well-established that the parameters are accepted as surrogate endpoints. For example, reduction in serum cholesterol is now accepted as a surrogate endpoint to demonstrate the effectiveness of a drug in reducing the risk of coronary heart disease. For cancer and AIDS, however, there is substantial debate whether any surrogate endpoints have been sufficiently validated to permit approval of drugs for these indications without more direct evidence of their effect on morbidity and mortality. For a more detailed discussion of this topic, see *supra* p. 694.

8. *The "Animal Rule".* FDA has always recognized that there are some drugs for which human clinical trials, and particularly controlled clinical trials, cannot be conducted ethically. The paradigm example is a

snake bite remedy. Such drugs have been approved by FDA on the basis of animal studies. In 1999, FDA proposed what has come to be known as the "animal rule," under which the effectiveness of a new drug to reduce or negate the toxicity of chemical, biological, radiological, or nuclear substances is permitted to be tested only in animals because it would be unethical to expose individuals to these lethal or permanently disabling toxic substances in clinical trials. Following the September 11, 2001 attacks, FDA promulgated a final regulation, codified at 21 C.F.R. Part 314, Subpart I. The animal rule removes a major obstacle to the development of new drugs to counter bioterrorism. *See* Carrie Campbell, *No Humans Have Been Injured in the Testing of this Drug: The New Animal Efficacy Rule* (2004), in Chapter VI(C)(2) of the Electronic Book. Nonetheless, the pharmaceutical industry has expressed concern about its potential liability arising from the development or use of drugs for which only animal models are available to support effectiveness. In the Public Readiness and Emergency Preparedness Act, 119 Stat. 2680, 2818 (2005), Congress conferred immunity from tort liability for the clinical investigation or marketing of any antiterrorism drug used under a declaration of emergency by the Secretary of HHS pursuant to section 564 of the FD&C Act. This immunity is lost only if the company has engaged in willful misconduct and enforcement action has been brought by FDA and resolved in favor of the agency.

9.   *Exemptions.* The FDA regulations permit the agency to exempt a drug, in writing, from the requirement for controlled studies. FDA granted one of these rare exemptions for the approval of AZT for use in children with AIDS.

10.   *Effectiveness of Oncology Drugs.* There is no more controversial field in the FDA review of NDAs than oncology. Many believe that the agency has been too strict and that promising drugs have inappropriately been held back from approval, thus denying potential relief to thousands of cancer victims every year. Yet there has been a significant decline in cancer in the United States, undoubtedly in part due to improved cancer detection and treatment. FDA has repeatedly defended its record of cancer drug approvals. For a different view of FDA policy on cancer drugs, see a remarkable series of editorials by Antonio J. Grillo–Lopez, published under the title *The ODAC Chronicles*, beginning in 4 EXPERT REV. OF ANTICANCER THERAPEUTICS (2004), which provide rare insight into the work of the FDA Oncology Drugs Advisory Committee. *See also* Benjamin M. Hron, *Placebo or Panacea: The FDA's Rejection of ImClone's Erbitux Licensing Application* (2003), and Andrew J. Sung, *Expediting Oncology Drug Approvals: The Public Backlash Against the FDA and Opportunities to Reform* (2005), in Chapter VI(C)(3) of the Electronic Book.

11.   *Longer Term Studies.* The length of a clinical trial to study the effectiveness of a new drug is almost always determined by FDA. There is no objective way to set the required length of a trial. It is a matter of subjective judgment. For example, drugs to treat major depressive disorder are typically studied in a placebo-controlled trial for six to twelve weeks. Longer-term effectiveness studies are then routinely conducted following NDA approval to confirm safety but not to study effectiveness. When FDA proposed to require longer-term effectiveness trials prior to NDA approval,

the pharmaceutical industry strongly objected, and an advisory committee of experts voted 12–0 against the proposal because it would result in patients being denied important new medication.

g.   BALANCING BENEFIT AND RISK

Under the 1938 Act, an applicant had to submit sufficient data to demonstrate the safety of the new drug. That requirement was not amended when Congress enacted the Drug Amendments of 1962. Under the 1962 Amendments, a separate and independent provision was added to require the applicant also to submit substantial evidence of effectiveness. The new provision made no reference to the preexisting safety requirement.

Confronted with these two independent and separate requirements in 1962, FDA could have interpreted section 505 in two different ways. First, the agency could have interpreted the statute the way it was written. That is, the agency could have concluded that Congress intended FDA separately to evaluate the safety information and the evidence of potential benefit presented in the NDA, to require that information regarding both be set forth in the physician labeling in a truthful and non-misleading way, and then to allow the physician and the patient jointly to make a benefit-risk judgment whether the doctor should prescribe the drug for the patient, in light of the individualized disease situation confronting the patient. In other words, the physician and patient would make the benefit-risk determination, not FDA. Second, FDA could have decided to take the benefit-risk determination away from the physician and patient, and to make that decision itself. Under this approach, the agency would deny patients access to drugs that they might rationally want to use for their own individualized disease situations, even if the drug might be regarded as unsafe or ineffective for other patient populations or for the country as a whole.

Without public participation of any type, FDA Commissioner George Larrick announced how the agency would implement its new authority under the Drug Amendments of 1962 at a Congressional hearing held in March 1964.

Testimony of FDA Commissioner George Larrick

"Drug Safety," Hearings before a Subcommittee of the House Committee on
Government Operations, 88th Congress 2d Session 150, 153, 154 (1964).

The decisionmaking process can conveniently be regarded as a three-step operation. . . .

Step 1. Determine the benefit to be derived from the drug;

Step 2. Determine the risk; and

Step 3. Weigh the benefit against the risk and decide whether it is in the public interest to approve the drug for marketing or to withdraw approval if the product is already on the market. . . .

The decision to approve a drug for marketing, or to withdraw an earlier approval requires a weighing of the benefit to be expected from use of the product against the risk inherent in its use. . . . The Government must make a judgment as to the hazards likely to be encountered when the drug is employed: by physicians of varying skills and abilities, in patients with a multitude of disease processes, many occurring concurrently, and in patients incorrectly diagnosed or inadequately tested with accepted laboratory procedures. . . .

We seek to make decisions about drugs solely on the basis of scientific consideration. But over a period of time, the direction of Government's decisions will inevitably be influenced by public reaction. . . . The judgments of society are not necessarily consistent with scientific facts. Neither are they always logical. They can be and sometimes are arbitrary. Even so, neither the executive nor the legislative branches of government can long ignore them. If it should become the overwhelming public view that society should drastically limit the risk no matter how much good a drug can do, then we would be forced to remove from the market many drugs whose good far outweighs their harm. Carried too far, such developments would seriously impede the progress of medicine. . . .

NOTES

1. *Risk v. Benefit.* David L. Cavers, *The Legal Control of Clinical Investigation of Drugs: Some Political, Economic, and Social Questions,* 98 DAEDALUS 427 (1969), characterized the agency's analytical process as follows:

> . . . [T]his evaluation does not call for a simple "yes" or "no" judgment. One dosage level may be safe, another questionable, but the safer dosage level may be of doubtful efficacy. A satisfactory answer may lie in between. Negotiation follows. The reports of clinical trials may include some evidence of hazard, but was the reported condition the consequence of the drug's administration or of other factors? There may have been side effects disclosed in the trials, but ought these merely to be listed as such or was their association with a given condition such as to require its listing in the labeling as a contraindication? The FDA must evaluate the sponsor's statistical work; it may have to decide whether a sponsor was justified in downgrading a side effect as "rare" or "infrequent."

2. *The FDA Judgment Factor.* The benefit-risk decision embodied in the choice whether to approve an NDA is purely impressionistic and judgmental. It cannot be justified by modeling or other objective criteria. It is, pure and simple, an "I know it when I see it" type of decision. For that reason alone, patient advocacy groups and individual patients often question the authority of FDA to make a decision that may determine whether they will live or die.

———

Regulation of antidepressant drugs presents a particularly useful illustration of the difficulty in making benefit-risk judgments for drugs used in serious diseases. FDA must balance the risk that an antidepressant drug may increase suicide against the risk that the failure to use the drug may also increase the risk of suicide. There are no hard data documenting the degree of either of these risks, but the latter appears to be larger than the former. *See, e.g.,* "FDA's Role in

Protecting the Public Health: Examining FDA's Review of Safety and Efficacy Concerns in Anti–Depressant Use by Children." Hearing before the Committee on Oversight and Investigations of the House Committee on Energy and Commerce, 108th Cong. 2d Sess. (2004).

Thomas M. Burton, *Risk vs. Benefit: FDA Weighs Antipsychotic*

WALL STREET JOURNAL, Oct. 14, 1996, at B1.

"I think that this is a dangerous drug," declared senior Food and Drug Administration official Raymond Lipicky at an FDA advisory committee hearing in July.

As head of the FDA's division of cardio-renal drug products, Dr. Lipicky used this unusually harsh language to describe sertindole, a new antipsychotic drug from Abbott Laboratories. The drug, trade-named Serlect, may cause sudden cardiac death, he contended. Yet earlier this month, North Chicago, Ill.-based Abbott received an FDA letter suggesting that the agency will soon approve marketing of the drug.

This case illustrates the FDA's dilemma in balancing potentially lethal side effects against possibly powerful therapeutic benefits— particularly when no existing drug cures an illness. The FDA evaluates "safety and efficacy" in a delicate risk-benefit analysis and sometimes makes decisions before the full scope of potential risk can be known. "Safety in our terms," says Robert Temple, an FDA director of drug evaluation, means that a drug's "benefits outweigh its risks when used as labeled."

Sertindole is among the first of a new class of antipsychotic medications that offer hope for millions of people. About 1% of the world's population, including some 2.5 million adult Americans, suffer from schizophrenia. They are tormented by hallucinations, such as voices torturing them or visions of dead relatives. They're plagued by delusions of persecution and of being followed by strangers. Such terrors are alleviated to varying degrees by older generic medications like haloperidol, and by newer drugs like Sandoz AG's Clozaril and Johnson & Johnson's Risperdal.

But an estimated 40% to 60% of patients develop drug-induced side effects such as debilitating tremors or muscle rigidity. Perhaps half of those with side effects drop off medication as a result, psychiatrists estimate. Clozaril, generically called dozapine, tends to be effective in patients who aren't helped by other drugs, but it can lead to a sometimes-fatal condition called agranulocytosis, a blood disorder characterized by fever and weakness.

As a result, psychiatrists and pharmaceutical companies are searching for new therapies. "We need all the help we can get," says Harvard University psychiatry professor William M. Glazer. And University of Maryland psychiatry professor Carol A. Tamminga says sertindole holds promise because of its "potent antipsychotic effects."

But during Abbott's clinical trials on 2,194 patients using sertindole for an average of about six months, 27 patients died. Of these, Dr. Lipicky identified at least six as possible sudden cardiac deaths . . .

Ultimately, the FDA's advisory committee voted, 4 to 2, that sertindole was safe enough to allow it on the U.S. market; the FDA usually follows the directives of its advisory committees. . . .

Among the options now available for the FDA regarding sertindole is to put restrictions in the labeling of the drug, warning of a possibly fatal side effect—though researchers don't yet know whether they pose more risks for some types of patients than others. . . .

NOTES

1. *Recent Statutory Developments.* In section 904 of the FDA Amendments Act of 2007, Congress required Congress to submit a report of Congress within one year on how best to communicate to the public the risks and benefits of new drugs. As part of the FDA Safety and Innovation Act of 2012, Congress amended section 505(d) of the FD&C Act to require FDA to implement a "structured risk-benefit assessment framework" in the NDA approval process.

2. *Environmental Considerations.* Under the National Environmental Policy Act of 1969, all federal agencies must consider the environmental impact of any major action that may significantly affect the quality of the environment. *See infra* p. 1526. FDA has promulgated regulations in 21 C.F.R. Part 25 to implement this statutory requirement. 21 C.F.R. 25.20(1) requires the preparation of an environmental assessment for every NDA unless it is subject to a categorical exclusion under 21 C.F.R. 25.31. Section 411 of the FDA Modernization Act of 1997 added section 746 to the FD&C Act to confirm that an environmental impact statement prepared in accordance with 21 C.F.R. Part 25 meets the requirements for a detailed environmental statement under section 102(2)(C) of the National Environmental Policy Act. FDA formerly periodically published notices of the availability of these environmental assessments in the Federal Register, but in 1999, FDA announced that it would no longer publish these notices because all environmental assessments are now available through the CDER Electronic Reading Room. 64 Fed. Reg. 25046 (May 10, 1999).

3. *Ozone.* In accordance with the Montreal Protocol on Substances that Deplete the Ozone Layer of September 16, 1987, FDA has promulgated regulations for an orderly phaseout of the use of chlorofluorocarbons in inhaled drugs administered by metered dose inhalers. 21 C.F.R. 2.125.

4. *Request for Designation.* In most instances, the proper FDA center for regulating a product is determined at the investigational stage, as described *supra* at p. 672, because one center asserts jurisdiction or the sponsor files a request for designation pursuant to 21 C.F.R. Part 3. It is entirely possible, however, that this intercenter jurisdictional issue will only arise when a product application is submitted. In that event, the matter can still be resolved either by informal agreement or through a request for designation.

h.   INTERNAL AGENCY REVIEW PROCESS

No two NDAs are alike, and thus no two review processes are similar. Each is an ad hoc negotiation which varies widely among different FDA review divisions, within a single review division, and among individual reviewers. Each is fact dependent, i.e., it depends on the specific data and information contained in the particular NDA for the product. All clinical trials are different, all manufacturing information is highly specific to the individual company and the specific drug, and the labeling claims sought in the NDA are unique because they depend solely on the data in the application. It is therefore treacherous to generalize from one NDA to the other. The most that can be done is to describe, in broad terms, the overall process.

Before and after the NDA is submitted, there should have been a series of meetings of the type described earlier. *Supra* pp. 676 & 717. When the NDA is submitted, the first issue is whether it will survive a refuse-to-file screening by the agency. Assuming the drug is subject to a standard review rather than a priority review, there is almost always a period of complete silence from the agency. At some point, the agency will communicate with the sponsor to ask various questions, relying on every known form of communication—letter, telephone, e-mail, and fax. These inquiries will intensify as the PDUFA date approaches. There may also be personal meetings between the applicant and FDA. The hope is that, when the first cycle is complete, the drug will be approved. If it is not, FDA will send the applicant a "complete response letter" to indicate that the review cycle is complete and that the application is not ready for approval. Before the agency adopted the use of the "complete response letter" at 73 Fed. Reg. 39588 (July 10, 2008), it would send letters under a variety of titles (e.g., "approvable" and "not approvable") to applicants whose NDAs it did not approve in the first cycle.

Whatever title the letter bears, two points are clear. First, the letter is no more than a tentative position of the agency and an invitation to begin a serious negotiation. Second, the burden is on the company to respond to all issues raised in the letter if it hopes to persuade FDA that the NDA should be approved.

The most difficult letter the applicant may receive is one stating that one or more additional lengthy and expensive clinical trials must be conducted in order to demonstrate effectiveness. Particularly for a small biotechnology company, this can be devastating news, requiring substantial additional financing in the face of a falling stock price caused by the SEC-required disclosure of the FDA request. Even if there is no request for an additional trial, this does not mean that the remaining issues are easily resolved. It may still take months to gather all of the information requested by FDA. Fortunately, the FDA letters are detailed and candid, spelling out every issue needed to resolve FDA's remaining questions and thus obtain NDA approval. But from beginning to end, this dialogue is a riveting, exhausting, and all-consuming process that is frightening even for those who have gone through it on more than one occasion because ultimately it determines the success or failure of the entire enterprise.

NOTES

1. *Good Review Management Principles and Practices.* The FDA Modernization Act of 1997 added section 505(d)(4)(A) to the FD&C Act. This provision requires FDA to issue guidance for the individuals who review NDAs, which shall relate to promptness in conducting the review, technical excellence, lack of bias and conflict of interest, and knowledge of regulatory and scientific standards. In response to this statutory requirement, FDA issued GUIDANCE FOR REVIEW STAFF AND INDUSTRY: GOOD REVIEW MANAGEMENT PRINCIPLES AND PRACTICES FOR PDUFA PRODUCTS (2005). The Guidance breaks down the typical NDA first cycle review to five phases: (1) filing determination and review planning, (2) review, (3) advisory committee meeting, (4) action, and (5) post-action. The Guidance offers an excellent list of references to the FDA regulations, guidance, and other policies that apply throughout the NDA review process.

2. *Preapproval Inspection.* Beginning in 1980, FDA conducted a preapproval inspection (PAI) of the drug manufacturer before approving any NDA, to assure compliance with GMP and with the CMC (chemistry, manufacturing, and controls) sections of the NDA, under Compliance Program Guidance Manual No. 7346.832 (Oct. 1, 1980). This new policy of mandatory preapproval inspection (PAI) was not codified in the FD&C Act or FDA regulations at that time or subsequently. It was first formally announced in preambles to regulations requiring every NDA applicant to submit a review copy of the CMC section of the NDA for use by FDA field investigators during the PAI to audit application commitments and statements against actual manufacturing practices used by the applicant. 56 Fed. Reg. 3180 (Jan. 28, 1991), 58 Fed. Reg. 47340 (Sept. 8, 1993). The PAI program inevitably led to delays in approval of NDAs. Congress directly addressed this issue in the FDA Modernization Act of 1997, adding a provision, now FD&C Act 505(b)(5)(F), stating: "No action by the reviewing division may be delayed because of the unavailability of information from or action by field personnel unless the reviewing division determines that a delay is necessary to assure the marketing of a safe and effective drug." As a result of improved electronic communications within FDA, up to 90 percent of NDA approvals no longer require a PAI because the agency can determine from the GMP compliance history that an inspection is not warranted.

3. *Antagonistic Medical Review Officer.* As occasionally occurs in all organizations, an FDA medical review officer can be biased and antagonistic. Higher FDA officials have gone so far as to remove an abusive member of a medical review team.

4. *FDA Regulatory Briefing.* When an NDA raises an issue that CDER regards as novel, important, or particularly difficult, or simply the subject of substantial public controversy, top CDER officials will participate in a "regulatory briefing" to analyze the matter and reach a conclusion. Regulatory briefings are relatively uncommon but can be an important mechanism for resolving difficult matters.

5. *Company Resubmissions.* FDA has issued GUIDANCE FOR INDUSTRY: CLASSIFYING RESUBMISSIONS IN RESPONSE TO ACTION LETTERS (1998) that sets forth the PDUFA performance goals regarding FDA review of these second cycle and subsequent submissions relating to an NDA.

i.   ADVISORY COMMITTEE REVIEW

FDA has several permanent prescription drug advisory committees. The agency has discretion whether to require advisory committee review of any NDA.

Peter Barton Hutt, *The Regulation of Drug Products by the United States Food and Drug Administration*

in THE TEXTBOOK OF PHARMACEUTICAL MEDICINE (John P. Griffin & John O'Grady, eds., 5th ed. 2006).

There is no statutory requirement that FDA review the approval of an NDA with an advisory committee before final action is taken. Since the 1970s, however, this has been the customary practice, particularly with important new drugs. This prompted Congress to enact a specific provision dealing with the establishment of drug advisory committees under the FDA Modernization Act of 1997.

The review of an NDA by an advisory committee is an extremely important step in the approval process. It represents the best opportunity that the applicant has to address the agency and the public about the evidence of safety and effectiveness and the importance of the drug to public health. In the vast majority of cases, FDA accepts the recommendation of the advisory committee for approval, further testing or outright disapproval. Where the advisory committee recommends approval and FDA disagrees, however, the agency will almost always take a long time to implement the advisory committee recommendations, or may even add additional testing requirements before approval is eventually obtained. The importance of advisory committee review is widely recognized in the pharmaceutical industry, and it is common for a company to engage in extensive preparation for the company presentation and to seek supportive statements from independent outside experts and patients as well.

NOTES

1.   *FDA Statutory Authority and Guidance.* The FDA Modernization Act of 1997 added section 505(n) to the FD&C Act explicitly to authorize scientific advisory committees to provide expert advice on IND and NDA issues. FDA has issued a Guidance for Industry on ADVISORY COMMITTEES: IMPLEMENTING SECTION 120 OF THE FOOD AND DRUG ADMINISTRATION MODERNIZATION ACT OF 1997 (Oct. 1998). The general FDA advisory committee regulations are codified in 21 C.F.R. Part 14. *See infra* p. 1488.

2.   *Disclosure of Materials Sent to Advisory Committee.* In *Public Citizen Health Research Group. v. FDA*, Food Drug Cosm L. Rep. (CCH) ¶ 15,427 & ¶ 38,614 (D.D.C. 1999), FDA entered into a stipulation that it

would make publicly available all the materials provided to advisory committee members prior to or at the committee meetings, subject to applicable exemptions under the Freedom of Information Act (FOIA). In accordance with these stipulations, FDA issued a GUIDANCE FOR INDUSTRY ON DISCLOSING INFORMATION PROVIDED TO ADVISORY COMMITTEES IN CONNECTION WITH OPEN ADVISORY COMMITTEE MEETINGS CONVENED BY THE CENTER FOR DRUG EVALUATION AND RESEARCH, BEGINNING ON JANUARY 1, 2000 (Nov. 1999).

3. *Financial Conflict of Interest.* There has been substantial controversy about possible conflicts of interest among advisory committee members. Experts in a particular medical discipline are often consultants to, or investigators for, the pharmaceutical industry. As a consequence, they would be precluded from serving on advisory committees if FDA did not grant a waiver that allowed them to participate. The appropriations legislation for fiscal years 2006 and 2007 contained provisions requiring all FDA waivers of conflict of interest to be made public. Public Citizen Health Research Group published an article analyzing the voting patterns of drug advisory committee members and concluded that a "weak relationship between certain types of conflict and voting behaviors was detected, but excluding advisory committee members and voting consultants with conflicts would not have altered the overall vote outcome at any meeting study." Peter Lurie et al., *Financial Conflict of Interest Disclosure and Voting Patterns at Food and Drug Administration Drug Advisory Committee Meetings*, 295 J.A.M.A. 1921 (2006). Analyzing the data in that report, FDA released a "comment" concluding that "Advisory committee members and voting consultants with financial ties to pharmaceutical companies tend to vote against the financial interest of those companies. This result suggests that fears that disclosed conflicts of interest are leading to tainted, unreliable recommendations are unfounded."

4. *Strengthening the Advisory Committee Process.* In July 2006, FDA announced several steps to help make its advisory committee processes more effective: (1) the issuance of a guidance identifying more clearly the conditions under which conflict of interest waivers are granted, (2) the issuance of a guidance specifying when waivers of conflict of interest will be disclosed to the public and what information will be made available, (3) the issuance of a guidance specifying when briefing materials used at advisory committees will be made publicly available, (4) greater public dissemination of advisory committee schedules through increased mailing to public groups and electronic notifications, and (5) implementation of a more streamlined approach to the appointment of members of the advisory committees. FDA's use of advisory committees is examined in detail in Chapter 15, *infra* p. 1488.

j.   LABELING REVIEW

Every NDA must include proposed labeling for physicians. FDA invariably leaves negotiation about the exact wording of this labeling until the last few days before NDA approval. As added by the Drug Amendments of 1962, section 505(d)(7) of the FD&C Act provides that FDA shall disapprove an NDA if "based on a fair evaluation of all material facts, such labeling is false or misleading in any particular period." Prescription drug labeling will be examined in greater detail later in this chapter. *See infra* p. 860.

House of Representatives

107 CONGRESSIONAL RECORD 21065 (Sept. 27, 1962).
87th Congress, 1st Session.

Mr. JARMAN. Mr. Chairman, I rise to propound an inquiry in respect to one provision of section 102 which will sharply modify long-established relationships between industry and the Food and Drug Administration. . . .

The distinguished chairman of our committee will recall that, when we substituted the Senate-approved language for the original provisions of section 102, included in that language was an entirely new provision which gives the Secretary of Health, Education, and Welfare a new basis for disapproving a new-drug application, even when the drug is unquestionably safe and unquestionably effective. Under section 102, the Secretary may now disapprove a new-drug application on the ground that a proposed labeling is "false or misleading." A parallel provision, authorizes the Secretary to withdraw already-approved applications on the same ground.

Today, where the safety of a drug is clearly established, compliance with the broadly phrased statutory rules on labeling remains the manufacture's responsibility. A charge that any label wording is "false or misleading" must be judicially determined on objective facts produced in open court. Under this bill, however, a manufacturer can be stopped from marketing a new drug, not because the drug is unsafe or ineffective, but because the proposed label of an acknowledgedly safe and effective drug is considered "false or misleading."

Now, in committee we recognized that the granting to FDA of a new authority of this kind could open the door to possible administrative abuse. To meet this contingency, we adopted an amendment requiring that a finding that a proposed label is "false or misleading" have an objective base—that is, the finding by the Secretary must be based on a fair evaluation of all material facts.

The question I now raise with the distinguished chairman of our committee is our intent in adopting this amendment. I construe it to mean this—that we have precluded a refusal of a new drug application or a revocation of an effective application on false or misleading grounds if the departmental objection is merely a subjective interpretation of a proposed label or any particular word appearing therein. We have required that there must be, to warrant a disapproval or a revocation, objective facts of record which make the proposed labeling demonstrably false or demonstrably misleading.

May I inquire of the distinguished chairman of our committee if this construction of this particular amendment fairly and accurately explains what our committee has sought to do? . . .

Mr. HARRIS. Mr. Chairman, if I understand correctly the question of the gentleman I would answer in the affirmative. However, I think if you read the language it is self-explanatory. The language provides a new basis for refusing to approve a new drug application. The gentleman quoted the language correctly "based on a fair evaluation of all material facts." I think that would be the prevailing language in the interpretation. It is true that to warrant a disapproval or a revocation of the application objective facts of record which makes the proposed labeling is false or misleading would be necessary—demonstrably false or misleading. That is true. That must be a part of the consideration which would be given to this particular problem.

Mr. JARMAN. The concern that I have had, Mr. Chairman, is the danger that the departmental objection might be merely a subjective interpretation. My own understanding of the words that we put into the bill with this amendment is that we intended that it be based on objective facts of record that are clear and more definite than simply a matter of individual interpretation.

Mr. HARRIS. We must presume and certainly the Congress expects any Secretary of Health, Education and Welfare Administering this program to be fair in his decision and the administration of the law. The gentleman raises the question of subjective decisions and objective decisions. We expect the Secretary to have wide latitude in his decisions. Certainly we do not expect by this language for any Secretary in the administration of the law to be arbitrary in his decisions but to be objective, after consideration of all the material facts then to make the best decision objectively that he can make on it. . . .

NOTE

First Amendment. Although Representative Jarman did not justify his position in First Amendment terms, his emphasis on "objective facts" as opposed to a "subjective interpretation" foretells current First Amendment jurisprudence. *See infra* p. 951.

k. FINAL APPROVAL OR DENIAL

Section 505 does not require FDA to explain its approval of an NDA. In its public information regulations, however, FDA announced that, beginning in July 1975, it would release a summary of the basis of approval (SBA) for every NDA, instead of disclosing internal agency memoranda prepared in the course of reaching its decision. 39 Fed. Reg. 44602, 44635–44636 (Dec. 24, 1974). Under FOIA, FDA is also required to release non-confidential records reflecting the administrative review of the NDA. Since 1996, FDA has posted the SBA and supporting materials on its website. Under section 505(l)(2) of the FD&C Act, as added by the FDA Amendments Act of 2007, FDA is now required to make the "action package for approval" of an NDA immediately available on the FDA website following NDA approval. This provision also applies retroactively for any drug for which the action package is requested three times under FOIA.

An FDA decision to *approve* a drug has seldom been contested in court. When FDA approved an NDA for an OTC version of ibuprofen, two competitors of the applicant challenged this action. *See supra* p. 964, note 2. Neither was successful. Patients injured by an approved drug have similarly failed in attempts to obtain damages from FDA for wrongfully approving the drug. *See infra* p. 742, note 9.

Perhaps surprisingly, court challenges to decisions refusing approval have been equally rare. No sponsor has successfully sought reversal of an FDA refusal to approve its drug. The lesson has not been lost on applicants, who understand that the only way to secure approval of an NDA is to satisfy the agency. Manufacturers who anticipate denial focus all their efforts on attempting to persuade the agency to change its mind, realizing that recourse to judicial review of an adverse determination is almost certain to be futile.

Ubiotica Corp. v. FDA
427 F.2d 376 (6th Cir. 1970).

■ COMBS, CIRCUIT JUDGE. . . .

Petitioner originally filed its new drug application and claim for investigational exemption in June, 1963. The new drug is proposed for treatment of mongolism. . . .

In November, 1963, the Commissioner notified petitioner that, since certain conditions had not been met, the investigational exemption allowing clinical testing of the drug was terminated. Petitioner unsuccessfully sought to enjoin and vacate this order in *Turkel v. Food and Drug Administration,* 334 F.2d 844 (6th Cir. 1964). We held there that 21 U.S.C. § 355(h) does not permit review of the withdrawal of an investigational exemption except on appeal from a subsequent order of the Secretary refusing to approve a new drug application. However, prior to our decision in *Turkel,* petitioner withdrew the new drug application which it had submitted in June, 1963.

Then, in June, 1966, petitioner submitted a second new drug application which was designated as supplemental to the previously withdrawn new drug application. After extended correspondence, petitioner was notified that the Commissioner proposed to issue an order refusing approval of the new drug application. A hearing was held, and subsequently the order was issued which is the subject of this appeal. The record before us consists of numerous exhibits and in excess of 6,000 pages of transcript. On this appeal we are asked to review the Commissioner's action in refusing to approve the new drug application and also in terminating petitioner's investigational exemption. . . .

In enacting section 355, Congress clearly placed on the applicant the burden of establishing that the drug proposed to be distributed in interstate commerce is both safe and effective for the intended use. Here, the hearing examiner properly phrased the issues in terms of the statutory grounds for rejection set forth in section 355(d), and the Government came forward with proof as to why petitioner had not satisfied the burden of proof required of a new drug applicant under section 355. The Commissioner adopted the findings of the hearing examiner and concluded that the new drug application should not be approved in that it was deficient in each of the five respects enumerated above under section 355(d). The question here is whether those findings are supported by substantial evidence. We conclude that they are and that the Commissioner properly refused to approve the new drug application. . . .

NOTES

1.   *Exhaustion of FDA Procedures.* The ruling earlier in the same case, *sub. nom. Turkel v. FDA,* that the sponsor of a clinical investigation whose IND is terminated may only obtain judicial review of that action by filing an NDA and then seeking review of FDA's subsequent denial of approval, seems questionable. Other "exhaustion" cases suggest that it would not be followed today. *E.g., Rosado v. Wyman,* 397 U.S. 397 (1970); *Leedom v. Kyne,* 358 U.S. 184 (1958). *See also AMP, Inc. v. Gardner,* 275 F. Supp. 410 (S.D.N.Y. 1967), *aff'd,* 389 F.2d 825 (2d Cir. 1968).

2.   *Judicial Review of FDA Denial of NDA.* The Court of Appeals' perfunctory scrutiny of FDA's denial of Ubiotica's NDA is paralleled in one of the two other court challenges to FDA's refusal to approve a drug. In *Unimed, Inc. v. Richardson,* 458 F.2d 787 (D.C. Cir. 1972), the Court of Appeals' full opinion, after describing the applicant's argument, consisted of the following paragraph:

> We have examined the record of the administrative hearing on this point with care, particularly with a view to grasping as best we can the nature of the divergences between the differing expert witnesses. Although the matter seems to us one not entirely free from doubt, we remind ourselves that our role in the Congressional scheme is not to give an independent judgment of our own, but rather to determine whether the expert agency entrusted with regulatory responsibility has taken an irrational or arbitrary view of the evidence assembled before it. We are unable to say that it has; and, accordingly, the petition for review is denied.

3.   *The Cothyrobal Litigation.* The third court challenge to FDA's refusal to approve a drug has a unique history. A physician, Dr. Murray Israel, developed an injectable drug, Cothyrobal, for hypercholesterolemia and hypothyroidism. Frustrated by the agency's skeptical and desultory handing of his NDA, he unsuccessfully sued the agency and a competitor, alleging a conspiracy to keep the drug off the market. *Israel v. Baxter Laboratories, Inc.,* 466 F.2d 272 (D.C. Cir. 1972). Following FDA's eventual denial of approval and its refusal to grant an administrative hearing, the court set aside the agency's decision and ordered it to hold an evidentiary hearing on the issue. *Edison Pharmaceutical Co., Inc. v. FDA,* 513 F.2d 1063 (D.C. Cir. 1975). The agency's ultimate denial of the NDA, following the hearing, was upheld. *Edison Pharmaceutical Co., Inc. v. FDA,* 600 F.2d 831 (D.C. Cir. 1979).

4.   *Proper Court for Judicial Review.* Challenges to FDA's final decisions under sections 505(d) and (e) must be filed in the United States Court of Appeals for the appropriate circuit. A District Court thus lacks jurisdiction to order FDA to approve an NDA, but it may entertain a case seeking to force FDA to rule on an NDA within a specified period of time. *IMS Limited v. Schweiker,* Food Drug Cosm. L. Rep. (CCH) ¶ 38, 104 (C.D. Cal. 1981).

5.   *Grounds for Disapproval.* A 1980 FDA analysis of NDA rulings during the 1970s produced the surprising findings that 61 percent of the deficiencies cited in nonapproval letters during 1977 and 1978 related to

the chemistry, manufacturing, and controls (CMC) portions of the NDA, and that nearly 90 percent of such letters identified such deficiencies. Only 22 percent of the deficiencies related to the applicant's evidence of safety and effectiveness. Jonathan D. Cook et al., *Approvals and Non–Approvals of New Drug Applications During the 1970s*, FDA OPE STUDY No. 57 (Dec. 1980). A 1988 FDA report examined the fate of 174 new chemical entity (NCE) drugs for which INDs were filed during 1976–1978. Nine percent had been discontinued before the commencement of Phase I studies, 20 percent had been discontinued during Phase I studies, 39 percent during Phase II studies, and 5 percent during Phase III studies. Twenty-seven percent had become the subject of a submitted NDA, and nearly all of these—85 percent—ultimately gained approval. Steven A. Tucker et al., *The Outcome of Research on New Molecular Entities Commencing Clinical Research in the Years 1976–1978*, FDA OPE STUDY No. 77 (May 1988).

6. *NDAs Invited by FDA.* On rare occasions, FDA has formally announced that it would approve NDAs for particular drugs if and when they were submitted. In 40 Fed. Reg. 5351 (Feb. 5, 1975), FDA stated that NDAs would be approved for diethylstilbestrol (DES) as a postcoital contraceptive. FDA had hoped that this announcement would induce DES manufacturers to submit abbreviated NDAs to add postcoital contraception as an approved indication, but the plausible fear of liability deterred all potential applicants. In 1989, FDA deleted this provision because there were still no marketed drugs approved for this use. 54 Fed. Reg. 2285 (May 25, 1989). DES products approved for other uses thus continue to be prescribed for this still unapproved use as well. In 1997, FDA announced that combined oral contraceptives containing ethinyl estradiol and norgestrel or levonorgestrel are safe and effective for use as post-coital emergency contraceptives and requested submission of NDAs for this use. 62 Fed. Reg. 8610 (Feb. 25, 1997).

In 1980, FDA announced that it had approved two NDAs for potassium iodide as a thyroid-blocking agent for use in radiation emergencies. 45 Fed. Reg. 11912 (Feb. 22, 1980). These NDAs were received after the agency had invited manufacturers to seek approval as part of an emergency preparedness program for possible accidents at nuclear facilities. 43 Fed. Reg. 58798 (Dec. 15, 1978). The agency later announced the availability of draft recommendations for administering potassium iodide to the general public in a radiation emergency. 46 Fed. Reg. 30199 (June 5, 1981), 47 Fed. Reg. 28158 (June 29, 1982).

7. *FDA Control Over Packaging.* FDA control over the safety and effectiveness of a new drug extends to the packaging as well. See FDA GUIDANCE FOR INDUSTRY ON CONTAINER CLOSURE SYSTEMS FOR PACKAGING HUMAN DRUGS AND BIOLOGICS (May 1999).

8. *Publicity about NDA Approvals.* Section 301(l) of the 1938 Act prohibited any representation that FDA has approved an NDA for a drug. Despite repeated arguments that this provision was an anachronism, attempts to repeal it prior to 1997 failed. *E.g.,* H.R. Rep. No. 98–431, 98th Cong., 1st Sess. (1983), H.R. Rep. No. 99–143, 99th Cong, 1st Sess. (1985). Section 421 of the FDA Modernization Act of 1997 finally repealed this provision. 111 Stat. 2296, 2380.

9.	*Federal Tort Claims Act.* In *Forsyth v. Eli Lilly & Co.*, 904 Fed. Supp. 1153 (D. Haw. 1995), the District Court dismissed an action for damages against FDA for negligently approving the NDA for a new antidepressant drug that allegedly caused a man to kill his wife and then commit suicide, on the ground that the approval of an NDA falls within the discretionary function exception to the Federal Tort Claims Act. The District Court in *Nichols v. FDA*, Food Drug Cosm. L. Rep. (CCH) ¶ 38,325 (S.D. Ohio 1993), held that, before suing FDA for damages because his health deteriorated after taking an FDA-approved drug, the plaintiff must first file a claim with FDA and receive a denial. Plaintiff's request for an injunction to remove the drug and related drugs from the market was dismissed for failure to exhaust administrative remedies.

10.	*Suits to Force FDA Approval.* FDA cannot be sued by a private party to force the agency to approve an NDA. *Garlic v. FDA*, 783 F. Supp. 4 (D.D.C. 1992), *appeal dismissed* 986 F.2d 546 (D.C. Cir. 1993).

11.	*FDA Alert List.* Any drug establishment found by FDA inspection not to be in compliance with GMP regulations is placed by the agency on an "alert list." It is standard FDA procedure not to approve any NDA or abbreviated NDA of any firm which is on the alert list. FDA's immediate withdrawal of approval of an abbreviated NDA on the same day an inspection resulted in placing the company on the alert list was upheld in *American Therapeutics, Inc. v. Sullivan,* Food Drug Cosm. L. Rep. (CCH) ¶ 38,159 (D.D.C. 1990).

12.	*Judicial Enforcement of 180-Day Deadline.* Section 505(c)(1) of the FD&C Act unequivocally states that FDA shall, within 180 days after the filing of an NDA, either approve the application or give notice of opportunity for an administrative hearing on the question of whether the application is approvable. This provision is mandatory, not discretionary. Its enforceability has been considered in two cases. In *In re Barr Laboratories, Inc.,* 930 F.2d 72 (D.C. Cir. 1991), the Court of Appeals concluded that, although section 505(c)(1) is mandatory, the Court would not issue an injunction against FDA where the delay was roughly 489 days and FDA demonstrated that it did not have sufficient resources to act faster. In *Sandoz, Inc. v. Leavitt,* 427 F. Supp. 2d 29 (D.D.C. 2006), the District Court concluded that a delay of roughly 1000 days justified a court order requiring FDA to take action on the pending NDA in light of the fact that FDA now has sufficient funds under PDUFA. FDA promptly approved the NDA and did not appeal the District Court's ruling.

13.	*Rationing a Newly Approved Drug.* On occasion, the demand for an important new drug outpaces the manufacturing capacity. In these situations, it is common to conduct a lottery to determine which patients will receive the drug. *E.g.*, Michael Manocchi & Louis Lasagna, *Issues in Pharmaceutical Lotteries: The Case of Interferon Beta–1b,* 62 CLINICAL PHARMACOLOGY & THERAPEUTICS 241 (Sept. 1997).

Richard J. Crout,* *The Nature of Regulatory Choices*

33 FOOD DRUG COSMETIC LAW JOURNAL 413 (1978).

. . . .

There was a time, not very long ago, when I thought the quality of public discussion on our drug regulatory system in the United States was extraordinarily low. In those days it was typical for most critics of the FDA to cast all criticism into one of two models, depending upon their point of view. The first of these might be called the "political" model and is highly popular among physicians, clinical investigators, and the drug industry. According to this construct, the regulation of drugs is conducted by slow, unimaginative bureaucrats who are intent on disapproving drugs so as to avoid criticism by Congressional committees for approving anything with risks. By combining such qualities as lack of perspective, overconcern with safety, and inefficiency, they manage to bog down all of drug regulation into a mire of technicalities. Admirers of this model tend to see regulatory decisions as contests between science and politics, and they plead for an FDA which is "more scientific" and "more reasonable."

The other model might be called the "sellout" model and is particularly popular among consumer activists, certain congressional committees, and the press. According to this formulation, the Agency is also slow and bureaucratic—a point on which all critics seem to agree— but largely because it lacks commitment in enforcing the law. Because of personal allegiance to the medical profession and the drug industry, the regulator is seen as quick to approve new drugs without adequate evidence for safety or effectiveness but as slow and inept in withdrawing drugs from the market. The new effect is an industry-dominated Agency which fails to enforce the law. . . .

Each of these models has the virtue of being readily understandable and is inherently plausible. It appeals to the biases of nearly everyone to view regulatory controversies as basically one-on-one contests between the virtuous and the untrustworthy. . . .

If drug development is to move faster in this country, the public must come to accept the idea that less control over research is, in the long run, safer than the alternative, because freedom is essential to discovery and insight. This is a sophisticated concept, not easily explained to the public, and certainly not about to be readily accepted by those already suspicious of science and technology, and of physicians. The challenge to those concerned about the innovative process is to defend that point of view in public on its merits, not to promote some simplistic, extraneous "solution" such as repeal of the effectiveness requirement. . . .

---

*   [Dr. Crout was Director of the FDA Bureau of Drugs, now CDER.]

Scott Gottlieb, M.D., *The Price of Too Much Caution*

NEW YORK SUN, Dec. 22, 2004, at 8.

... Over the last 50 years, we have added successive layers of testing and monitoring before new drugs are approved for sale to patients, to the point where the average development time for a new drug can span 10 years and cost almost $1 billion.

The result is that today we have the safest system in the world, but few glaring gaps to easily improve on. When it comes to making new drugs safer, most of the obvious solutions are already accounted for and we have reached the flat part of a curve that measures incremental safety against the additional cost. We can make our drug development system a little safer, but only at a very big cost.

This trade-off is at issue, after the pain medications Vioxx and Celebrex, known as Cox–2 inhibitors, were traced to small but higher risks of heart attacks among patients who use them. ...

Consumers are angry that these problems were not unearthed earlier. But the higher risk of heart attacks caused by Vioxx, for example, was on the order of about six or seven heart attacks for every 1,000 patients who took the drug. In an older-patient population that already suffered more heart attacks, such a risk could have been easily missed, even with a clinical trial that included 10,000 patients or more. With this additional testing, the benefits of an off chance of discovering a rare side effect before a new drug is approved is eventually outweighed by the cost of keeping promising drugs from patients.

Even delaying seemingly ordinary drugs can have dramatic consequence on the public health. The first non-sedating anti-allergy medicine, Claritin, took almost seven years to get approved, while sleepy drivers with sniffles continued to cause car accidents. Each of the popular anti-cholesterol drugs known as statins that today prevent 15% to 30% of heart attacks took several years to get approved. How many people died waiting? The math is straightforward.

Or consider this math: It's estimated more than 20,000 people died between 1985 and 1987 waiting for streptokinase, the first drug that could be intravenously administered to reopen the blocked coronary arteries of heart attack victims. Between 1988 and 1992, about 3,500 kidney cancer patients died waiting for Interleukin–2, which was available in several European countries. In 1988 alone, it is estimated between 7,500 and 15,000 people died from gastric ulcers caused by aspirin and other non-steroidal anti-inflammatory drugs, waiting for the FDA to approve misoprostol, which was already available in 43 countries. ...

4. THE EFFECTS OF THE NDA REQUIREMENT

a. THE "DRUG LAG"

Within a few years after enactment of the Drug Amendments of 1962, physicians began to complain that, because of the new drug approval process, drugs were being introduced into foreign markets substantially earlier than into the United States. This phenomenon became known as the "drug lag."

Statement of Sam Peltzman*

"Competitive Problems in the Drug Industry," Hearings before the Subcommittee on
Monopoly of the Senate Small Business Committee, 93d Cong., 1st Sess. (1973).

[T]he benefits provided by the [1962] amendments seem clearly outweighed by the costs they have engendered. . . . As I hope to make clear, consumers could not have avoided losses under the most efficient and well-intentioned administration of the law. . . .

It is beyond dispute that new drug innovation in the United States has declined since 1962. The 15 years prior to 1962 saw an average of 42 new chemical entities marketed per year compared to 16 in the subsequent decade. What is in dispute is the connection of this decline to the 1962 amendments. Innovation was declining from 1959 to 1962, and it is sometimes thought that the post-1962 experience might simply be a continuation of a previous trend. However, my research has led me to reject this explanation. I found that prior to 1962 there was a regular, highly predictable relationship between the rate of drug innovation in any year and previous growth in the market for drugs. . . . Subnormal growth in prescription sales led—with a lag of about two years, that being the average development time for new drugs—to subnormal innovation. That relationship held closely in the 1959–62 period and accounts fully for the decline in innovation: growth of the drug market peaked in the mid 1950's and declined to about 1960. However, unlike the pre-1962 period, the resumption of drug market growth in the early 1960s did not subsequently lead to increased innovation. . . .

. . . [I]t appears that the Amendments are preventing development of something like 25 new chemical entities for the U.S. drug market annually. I will argue subsequently that only a small fraction of the sales of those drugs would likely prove ineffective. . . . [This] means that the amendments' proof of efficiency and clinical testing requirements impose costs on the drug development process which discourage new drug development. I have estimated that the R.&D. costs for developing a new chemical entity have been about doubled by the added testing and information requirements of the Amendments. . . . It is simply unreasonable to expect a cost increase of this magnitude not to discourage development of new drugs, effective as well as ineffective. . . . Even if an effective new drug could be developed, neither the FDA nor the consumer will hear of it if its prospective returns cannot defray added development costs. . . .

. . . If the pre-1962 rate of innovation had been maintained, annual sales of new drugs in their initial full year of marketing would, given the larger size of today's drug market, approximate $125 million. . . . The comparable post-1962 figure is about $50 million. . . . [I]f one assumes that about 10 percent of the pre-1962 drug sales were for ineffective drugs . . . and that none of the post-1962 drugs are

---

*   [Sam Peltzman is a Professor of Economics at the University of Chicago Graduate School of Business.]

ineffective . . . then the decline in sales of effective new drugs due to the Amendments is over $60 million per year. My net benefit estimate of 50 percent of sales then applies a benefit loss exceeding $30 million on new drugs in their initial year of marketing. This loss will recur each year that new drugs remain on the market and sales remain $60 million lower. . . . [A]ssuming that these new drugs have level sales and a market life of 15 years . . . , the total benefits sacrificed due to reduced innovation in a single year would exceed $450 million into a present value of about $250 million. . . . In addition . . . because the amendments have been such an effective barrier to new competition for existing drugs, price rivalry in the drug market has been weakened. My estimate of the consumer cost of the resulting high prices for old and new drugs is about $50 million per year.

The benefits attributable to the Amendments must, of course, be set against this . . . cost. I used two approaches to estimate the waste on ineffective new drugs prior to 1962. One was the test of the marketplace. . . . If a new drug is ineffective, one would expect some reduction in prescribing for it as physicians accumulate evidence . . . of its ineffectiveness. . . . If the Amendments screened ineffective drugs out, one would then find sales of pre-1962 new drugs taken together growing more slowly over time than their post-1962 counterparts. . . . I will not burden the committee with this calculation, because the plain fact is that the difference in market acceptance between pre- and post-1962 drugs is trivial. . . .

. . . I turned to drug evaluations by experts—specifically the AMA Council on Drugs. A highly skeptical layman's reading of their *Drug Evaluations* turned up 16 of 80 new chemical entities introduced 1960–62 which could be labeled either ineffective, or no more effective than a cheaper alternative. The total consumer waste on these drugs—expenditures on the eight ineffective drugs, and the price premium for the eight equally effective but more expensive drugs—scaled to the 1970 drug market was under $20 million annually. . . . [U]nlike most new drugs, sales of the ineffective drugs decline markedly over time. . . . Taking both this decline and the difference between present and future losses into account, I arrive at a present value of well under $100 million for the total waste imposed on consumers. . . .

The extravagant potential costs of the risk-tradeoff in the Amendments can be illustrated by first examining its potential benefits in forestalling something like the thalidomide tragedy. . . . [T]he thalidomide tragedy was, in fact, forestalled in the United States without the Amendments. But if we . . . consider what might have been, and . . . assume that the thalidomide tragedy here might have been as widespread as it was in West Germany . . . we could have expected the birth of about 20,000 phocomelic infants on a 1970 population base. . . . If we further make the extreme assumption that none of these infants would be at all productive in adulthood, I estimate the present value of the economic cost of this hypothetical event at between $150 and $500 million. . . . Now, if we are going to assume that the Amendments completely eliminate the potential for such tragedies, we must gauge the frequency with which such a tragedy could otherwise be expected to occur in order to evaluate the prospective benefits. . . . Since a tragedy as profound as thalidomide has in fact never occurred in the United

States, this must be largely conjectural. . . . [W]e could attribute to the Amendments a potential for preventing something like 10,000 deaths or serious disabilities and an economic loss of something like $300 million perhaps once per decade. . . .

NOTES

1. *FDA Risk Aversion.* Peltzman's study prompted Professor Milton Friedman to write in the January 8, 1973 issue of *Newsweek:*

> Put yourself in the position of an FDA official charged with approving or disapproving a new drug. You can make two very different kinds of serious mistakes:
>
> > 1. Approve a drug that turns out to have unanticipated side effects resulting in death or serious impairment of a sizable number of persons.
> >
> > 2. Refuse approval of a drug that is capable of saving many lives or relieving great distress and has no untoward side effects. . . .
>
> With visions of the thalidomide episode dancing in your head and the knowledge of the fame and acclaim that came to the woman who held up approval of thalidomide in the U.S., is there any doubt which mistake you will be more anxious to avoid? With the best will in the world, you will be led to reject or postpone approval of many a good drug in order to avoid even a remote possibility of approving a drug that will have newsworthy side effects. . . .

2. *Drug Lag Literature.* The literature dealing with the "drug lag" is extensive, and the conclusions reached about the impact of FDA's implementation of the 1962 Amendments conflicting. For statements of both sides of the issue, compare Donald Kennedy, *A Calm Look at "Drug Lag,"* 239 J.A.M.A. 423 (1978), with William M. Wardell, *A Close Inspection of the "Calm Look,"* 239 J.A.M.A. 2004 (1978). In addition to Peltzman's work, see William M. Wardell and Louis C. Lasagna, REGULATION AND DRUG DEVELOPMENT (AEI, 1975).

3. *Congressional Budget Office.* For a thorough study of all aspects of the economics of drug development, see CBO, RESEARCH AND DEVELOPMENT IN THE PHARMACEUTICAL INDUSTRY (2006).

4. *Impediments to Contraceptive Research.* For a discussion of the political, social and regulatory (including liability) climate that inhibits contraceptive research in the United States, see Carl Djerassi, *The Bitter Pill,* 245 SCIENCE 356 (July 28, 1989).

b. IND/NDA STATISTICS

To understand the impact of the Drug Amendments of 1962 and the regulatory requirements that law has spawned, it is necessary briefly to review the statistics relating to the average cost of an approved NDA, the annual number of approved NDAs, and the time devoted to IND testing and NDA review. Together, these statistics illustrate the enormous investment in time and money that is required to obtain FDA approval of an NDA for a new molecular entity (NME) new drug.

i.   Cost of an Approved NME Drug

There is as much debate about the cost of an approved NDA as there is about other aspects of the impact of the Drug Amendments of 1962. The most rigorous studies conducted on this issue make two key assumptions. First, they include all the research and development costs from failed or abandoned research along with the costs of successful research. Second, they include the opportunity costs, i.e., the interest expense of the money invested in this research that could have been deployed elsewhere. Under these assumptions, researchers have arrived at the following figures:

Year of Survey	Author	Average Cost of NME NDA
1976	Hansen	$137 million
1987	DiMasi	$319 million
1990	U.S. OTA	$445 million
1996	Lehman Brothers	$608 million
2000	DiMasi	$802 million
2000–2002	Bain & Co.	$1.7 billion

DiMasi also conducted a study, based on a 2005 survey, which determined that the average cost to develop a new biotechnology drug is $1.2 billion. Joseph A. DiMasi & Henry G. Grabowski, *The Cost of Biopharmaceutial R&D: Is Biotech Different?* 28 MANAGERIAL & DECISION ECON. 469 (2007). Regardless of how each of these was calculated, it is apparent that the cost of an approved NME NDA has risen far faster than inflation in the past three decades.

ii.   Number of Approved NME NDAs

The number of approved NME NDAs from 1990 to 2012, according to the published FDA statistics, is disappointing when viewed in the light of the amount invested in research and development by the pharmaceutical industry and NIH, as shown on their respective websites.

Year	Approved NME NDAs	Total PhRMA Members R&D Foreign & Domestic ($Millions)	Total NIH Budget ($Millions)
1990	23	8.4	7.6
1991	30	9.7	8.3
1992	26	11.5	8.9
1993	25	12.7	10.3
1994	21	13.4	11.0
1995	29	15.2	11.3
1996	53	17.0	12.0

Year	Approved NME NDAs	Total PhRMA Members R&D Foreign & Domestic ($Millions)	Total NIH Budget ($Millions)
1997	39	19.0	12.7
1998	30	21.0	13.6
1999	35	22.7	15.6
2000	27	26.0	17.8
2001	24	29.8	20.4
2002	17	31.0	23.3
2003	21	34.4	27.0
2004	36	37.0	27.9
2005	20	39.4	28.5
2006	18	43.0	–
2007	16	47.9	–
2008	21	47.4	–
2009	17	46.4	–
2010	15	50.7	–
2011	24	48.6	–
2012	33	48.5	–

These statistics confirm that the productivity of pharmaceutical research has declined substantially, although there appears to be a trend toward improvement in the last two years.

iii. Time Devoted to IND Testing and NDA Review

The median number of months taken by FDA to review and approve an NME NDA over the past quarter of a century shows that user fees—first imposed in 1993—have had a substantial impact.

Year	Months
1986	32.9
1987	29.8
1988	34.1
1989	29.8
1990	27.9
1991	22.9
1992	22.4
1993	23.0
1994	17.4
1995	17.1
1996	15.4
1997	14.4
1998	12.0

Year	Months
1999	12.0
2000	15.6
2001	14.3
2002	16.3
2003	9.9
2004	13.7
2005	8.5
2006	10.0
2007	9.7
2008	12.4
2009	12.9
2010	10.0
2011	10.0
2012	9.8

Thus, under PDUFA, FDA has cut the NME NDA review time by more than 50 percent. The NME NDA review time is, however, the smaller portion of the entire development time for a drug. Total development time must also take into consideration the time for nonclinical and clinical testing. The following table, provided to the authors by Joseph A. DiMasi, Ph.D., the Director of Economic Analysis the Tufts Center for the Study of Drug Development, shows the average clinical time alone—without considering the time for nonclinical testing required by FDA before an IND can be submitted.

Period	Months of IND Time
1971–1973	34.9
1974–1976	53.5
1977–1979	48.4
1980–1982	57.0
1983–1985	58.0
1986–1988	56.9
1989–1991	58.0
1992–1994	60.4
1995–1997	64.7
1998–2000	60.3
2001–2003	56.6
2004–2006	73.6
2007–2009	69.8
2010–2012	73.4

One study shows that the total drug development time—including nonclinical research and development as well as the IND/NDA time—was 8.1 years in 1960, 11.6 years in the 1970s, and 14.2 years in the 1980s and 1990s. Joseph A. DiMasi, *New Drug Development in the*

United States 1963 to 1999, 69 CLINICAL PHARMACOLOGY & THERAPEUTICS 286 (2001).

D. VARIATIONS AND EXCEPTIONS TO THE STANDARD DRUG DEVELOPMENT, INVESTIGATION, AND APPROVAL PROCESS

1. EXPEDITED DEVELOPMENT OF LIFESAVING DRUGS AND DRUGS FOR SERIOUS CONDITIONS

FDA currently administers a confusing bundle of four programs designed to speed the development and approval of drugs addressing serious unmet medical needs. A useful source is DRAFT GUIDANCE FOR INDUSTRY ON EXPEDITED PROGRAMS FOR SERIOUS CONDITIONS—DRUGS AND BIOLOGICS (June 2013), in which the agency helpfully summarizes these programs.

a. FAST TRACK

i. *The FDA Regulations*

Faced with the AIDS epidemic in the mid-1980s, FDA promulgated an interim regulation to establish an official policy on expedited development of new drugs for life-threatening and severely debilitating diseases. 53 Fed. Reg. 41516 (Oct. 21, 1988), codified at 21 C.F.R. Part 312, Subpart E.

Investigational New Drug, Antibiotic, and Biological Drug Product Regulations: Procedures for Drugs Intended to Treat Life–Threatening and Severely Debilitating Illnesses

53 Fed. Reg. 41516 (October 21, 1988).

. . . The purpose of these new procedures (§ 312.80) is to expedite the development, evaluation, and marketing of new therapies intended to treat persons with life-threatening or severely-debilitating illnesses, especially where no satisfactory alternative therapies exist. . . .

The scope of the new procedures (§ 312.81) will apply to new drugs, antibiotics, and biological products that are being studied for their safety and effectiveness in treating life-threatening or severely-debilitating illnesses. Within the context of these procedures, the term "life-threatening" is defined to include diseases where the likelihood of death is high unless the course of the disease is interrupted (e.g., AIDS and cancer), as well as diseases or conditions with potentially fatal outcomes where the end point of clinical trial analysis is survival (e.g., increased survival in persons who have had a stroke or heart attack). The term "severely-debilitating" refers to diseases or conditions that cause major irreversible morbidity (e.g., blindness or neurological degeneration).

A key component of the procedures is early consultation between FDA and drug sponsors (§ 312.82) to seek agreement on the design of necessary preclinical and clinical studies needed to gain marketing approval. Such consultation is intended to improve the efficiency of the process by preventing false starts and wasted effort that could otherwise result from studies that are flawed in design. Most important, at the end of early (phase 1) clinical testing, FDA and the sponsor will seek to reach agreement on the proper design of phase 2 controlled clinical trials, with the goal that such research will be adequate to provide sufficient data on the product's safety and effectiveness to support a decision on its approvability for marketing. . . .

If the preliminary analysis of test results appears promising, FDA may ask the sponsor (§ 312.83) to submit a treatment protocol to be reviewed under the treatment IND regulations. Such a treatment protocol, if submitted and granted, would serve as a bridge between the completion of early stages of clinical trials and final marketing approval.

Once phase 2 testing and analysis is completed by the sponsor and a marketing application is submitted, FDA will evaluate the data utilizing a medical risk-benefit analysis (§ 312.84). As part of this evaluation, FDA will consider whether the benefits of the drug outweigh the known and potential risks of the drug and the need to answer remaining questions about risks and benefits of the drug, taking into consideration the severity of the disease and the absence of satisfactory alternative therapy. In making decisions on whether to grant marketing approval for products that have been the subject of an end-of-phase 1 meeting under this rule, FDA will usually seek the advice of outside expert scientific consultants or advisory committees. . . .

Finally, when approval or licensing of a product is being granted, FDA may seek agreement from the sponsor (§ 312.85) to conduct certain postmarketing (phase 4) studies to delineate additional information about the drug's risks, benefits, and optimal use. These studies could include, but would not be limited to, studying different doses or schedules of administration than were used in phase 2 studies, use of the drugs in other patient populations or other stages of the disease, and use of the drug over a longer period of time. . . .

ii. The Congressional Statute

As part of the FDA Modernization Act of 1997, Congress added section 506 to the FD&C Act to codify the FDA's 1988 regulations establishing an expedited development initiative. Congress gave the term "Fast Track" to this program, although the program remained unchanged from the original October 1988 FDA Subpart E regulations. Under the FDA Safety and Innovation Act of 2012, Congress clarified and expanded the designation and advantages of Fast Track drugs.

Section 506(b) of the FD&C Act governs Fast Track drugs. A Fast Track designation request may be submitted to FDA with an IND or at any time thereafter. Unlike FDA 1988 regulations, which have not been amended, it includes any drug intended to treat a serious unmet medical need that has supporting nonclinical or clinical data, whether or not it relies on a surrogate endpoint. The Fast Track program has two dimensions. The first is frequent scientific feedback from and interaction with FDA, which facilitates expedited development during the IND phase of a new drug, as discussed *supra* at p. 676. The second provides the opportunity to submit what is called a "rolling NDA," which allows FDA to receive and review parts of the NDA as they become available.

A Fast Track designation applies only to a specific drug for a specific indication. The indication must be for a serious or life-threatening condition and must be intended to meet an unmet medical need not adequately addressed by existing therapy. Although a Fast Track designation is independent from priority review, *infra* p. 756, the definitions are sufficiently similar that a Fast Track NDA will almost always be able to obtain priority review. Separate requests must be submitted for each of these programs.

NOTE

Drugs to Combat Terrorism. Following the events of September 11, 2001, Congress enacted the Public Health Security and Bioterrorism Preparedness and Response Act of 2002, 116 Stat. 594. Section 122 authorizes the Secretary of HHS to designate an antiterrorism drug, including one whose approval may be sought solely on the basis of animal studies, as a Fast Track product under section 506 that will be given priority review. Section 123 ordered FDA to complete its rulemaking regarding drugs approved solely on the basis of animal trials. *See supra* p. 727, note 8. Both the Bioterrorism Act of 2002 and the Project BioShield Act of 2004, 118 Stat. 835, were intended to stimulate research and development of drugs to combat terrorism. For critiques of these statutes, see Sara Kasper, *The National Strategic Stockpile: Will it Really Protect the Nation Against Bioterrorism?* (2006), and Janet Temko, *The Project Bioshield Act of 2004: An Innovative Failure* (2006), in Chapter II(Y) of the Electronic Book.

b. BREAKTHROUGH THERAPY

Section 506(a) of the FD&C Act, which was added by the FDA Safety and Innovation Act of 2012, governs Breakthrough Therapy. A drug is eligible for the breakthrough therapy designation if it is intended to treat a serious or life-threatening disease or condition and preliminary clinical evidence indicates that the drug may demonstrate substantial improvement on a clinically significant endpoint over available therapies. A request for designation is submitted to FDA, which has 60 calendar days to respond. FD&C Act 506(a)(1). Section 506(a)(3)(B) describes five types of actions that FDA may take to expedite the development and review of a breakthrough therapy. These possible measures include increased meetings and communications with the sponsor, efficiency-enhancing changes to the agency review process, and the provision of assistance in designing efficient clinical trials. As of August 23, 2013, 25 breakthrough therapy designations had been granted by FDA and 32 had been denied. The details and benefits of this new program remain to be seen.

c.   ACCELERATED APPROVAL

i.   *The FDA Regulations*

In 1992, FDA promulgated regulations establishing two forms of accelerated approval of an NDA: (1) approval based on evidence of the drug's effect on a surrogate endpoint that reasonably suggests clinical benefit or on evidence of the drug's effect on a clinical endpoint other than survival or irreversible morbidity, and (2) approval of an effective drug that can be used safely only if distribution or use is modified or restricted. 57 Fed. Reg. 58942 (Dec. 11, 1992), codified at 21 C.F.R. Part 314, Subpart H. In both situations, the approval is determined by FDA to meet the requirements for safety and effectiveness and thus is a full NDA approval under section 505 of the FD&C Act.

(a) Approval Based on a Surrogate Endpoint

As the discussion *supra* at p. 694 showed, FDA has for many years approved NDAs on the basis of *validated* surrogate endpoints. Accelerated approval, however, is based on an *unvalidated* surrogate endpoint that nonetheless is reasonable likely, in light of epidemiologic, therapeutic, pathophysiologic, or other evidence, to predict clinical benefit or on an effect on a clinical endpoint other than survival or irreversible morbidity. 21 C.F.R. 314.510. NDA approval will therefore be subject to the requirement of a further clinical trial to verify clinical benefit when there is uncertainty as to the relation of the surrogate endpoint to clinical benefit or of the observed clinical benefit to ultimate outcome. As the following article authored by five FDA officials with responsibility for the regulation of oncology drug products reflects, this accelerated approval mechanism has been very successful. If there is any criticism, it is that it has not been used as often as it could be. *E.g., FDA's Handling of UFT Raises Questions about Agency's Isolation, Grasp of Science,* 26 THE CANCER LETTER, No. 29 (July 21, 2000); Jacob W. Stahl, *A History of Accelerated Approval: Overcoming the FDA's Bureaucratic Barriers in Order to Expedite Desperately Needed Drugs to Critically Ill Patients,* in Chapter IX(C)(2) of the Electronic Book.

Ramzi Dagher et al., *Accelerated Approval of Oncology Products: A Decade of Experience*

96 JOURNAL OF THE NATIONAL CANCER INSTITUTE 1500 (2004).

In 1992, Accelerated Approval Subpart H was added to the new drug application regulations. This addition allows accelerated approval of drugs for serious or life-threatening diseases if the drug appears to provide a benefit over available therapy [and] the benefit is determined by the drug's effect on a surrogate endpoint that is reasonably likely to predict clinical benefit or on evidence of an effect on a clinical benefit other than survival. . . .

In general, the FDA has considered an effect on survival or relief of patient symptoms as evidence of clinical benefit in oncology. Objective tumor response rates and time-to-progression have often been viewed as surrogate endpoints that are reasonably likely to predict clinical benefit. Objective response rates and/or time-to-progression have been accepted as evidence of clinical benefit in some circumstances—for example, when relatively nontoxic products are evaluated, such as hormonal therapies for breast cancer and some biologic products. Durable complete responses have been accepted as evidence of clinical benefit in hematologic malignancies when response has been associated with an established clinical benefit parameter, such as improved survival, reduced rate of infection, or reduced need for transfusion (3–5). These endpoints have also been accepted for other malignancies, such as testicular cancer, because the response was of sufficient magnitude and duration that it appeared to be associated with improved survival. . . .

From January 1992 through January 2004, 18 different anticancer drugs or biologic products for 22 indications were approved under Subpart H regulations. Since the first accelerated approval for an oncology drug was granted in 1995, six accelerated approval oncology drugs have subsequently been converted to regular approval. Of the remaining 16 applications, 11 accelerated approvals were granted on the basis of studies without an active comparator group (i.e., single-arm studies or studies comparing two dose levels) and five accelerated approvals were granted on the basis of randomized studies with an active or placebo control group. . . .

In conclusion, the accelerated approval program in oncology has been successful in making 18 different products available to patients for 22 different cancer treatment indications. The use of single-arm studies for accelerated approval allows for the rapid evaluation of novel agents, usually in patients with refractory disease. Randomized studies allow for the evaluation of populations with less refractory disease, add-on designs, confirmation of clinical benefit in the same population as that used for accelerated approval, a larger and more precise safety database, and the examination of time-to-event endpoints.

Both single-arm studies and randomized studies may provide evidence to support accelerated approval. It is useful to discuss development plans including the design, conduct, and analysis of confirmatory studies with the FDA early in the development process. These studies are viewed as part of a comprehensive drug development plan that includes studies that might lead to accelerated approval and the confirmatory studies.

(b) Approval Conditioned on Restricted Distribution

The second provision in Subpart H authorizes FDA to approve an effective drug that can be used safely only if distribution or use is modified or restricted. As discussed below, *infra* p. 829, FDA gained formal authority in 2007 to restrict the distribution of a drug using a process called Risk Evaluation and Mitigation Strategies (REMS). When the agency promulgated Subpart H in 1992, however, courts had interpreted the FD&C Act as then written to provide FDA with no authority to restrict distribution as a condition of NDA approval. *American Pharmaceutical Association v. Weinberger*, 377 F. Supp. 824 (D.D.C. 1974), *aff'd per curiam*, 530 F.2d 1054 (D.C. Cir. 1976).

Consequently, this provision of Subpart H can be applied by FDA only at the request or with the agreement of the NDA applicant. FDA has approved fewer than ten drugs with restricted distribution programs under subpart H. Examples include thalidomide, RU–486, GHB (the "date rape" drug), and a highly addictive pain medication. Each of the restricted distribution programs is uniquely tailored to the specific drug, and is described in detail on the FDA website. It is unlikely that this provision will be invoked in the future because of the now predominant use of REMS.

NOTES

1.   *Listing of Approvals.* The FDA website lists all Subpart H NDA accelerated approvals based on a surrogate endpoint.

2.   *FDA Approval of Promotional Materials.* 21 C.F.R. 314.550 requires that all promotional materials intended to be used within 120 days after approval of an NDA under Subpart H be approved by FDA prior to NDA approval, and that all subsequent promotional materials be submitted to FDA at least 30 days prior to use. *See* GUIDANCE FOR INDUSTRY: ACCELERATED APPROVAL PRODUCTS—SUBMISSION OF PROMOTIONAL MATERIALS (1999).

ii.   The Congressional Statute

Five years after FDA promulgated its accelerated approval regulations, Congress enacted its own version of accelerated approval in Section 506 of the FD&C Act as part of the FDA Modernization Act of 1997. The statutory provisions were different from the FDA regulations in two important respects. First, although the regulations limited accelerated approval to drugs whose evidence of benefit was based on a surrogate endpoint, section 506 explicitly allowed both a clinical and a surrogate endpoint. Second, section 506 did not authorize restricted distribution. Nonetheless, FDA did not amend its regulations and continued to implement accelerated approval solely under the terms of the regulations, not section 506. This approach has contributed to criticism that FDA has not used accelerated approval as widely as Congress directed.

As part of the FDA Safety and Innovation Act of 2012 (FDASIA), Congress expanded accelerated approval further. First, section 901(a) of FDASIA, 126 Stat. 1082–1083, which is not codified in the FD&C Act, includes both Findings and a Sense of Congress encouraging FDA to make greater use of accelerated approval. Second, Section 506(c) of the FD&C Act, which now governs accelerated approval, was amended to provide even greater flexibility and discretion to grant accelerated approval for drugs intended to treat a serious condition.

d.   PRIORITY REVIEW

FDA has always regularly accorded expedited consideration to applications for important new medicines. In 1974, FDA formalized this sensible, if not expressly authorized, practice by establishing a complex matrix to classify NDAs according to chemical type and therapeutic potential to determine their priority for review. In 1996, FDA replaced the 1974 priority system with the following, much simpler approach.

CDER Manual of Policies and Procedures 6020.3, Priority Review Policy
April 22, 1996.

BACKGROUND

The NDA classification system provides a way of describing drug applications upon initial receipt and throughout the review process and prioritizing their review.

DEFINITIONS

Review Priority Classification. A determination that is made based on an estimate of its therapeutic preventive or diagnostic value. The designations "Priority" (P) and "Standard" (S) are mutually exclusive. Both original NDAs and effectiveness supplements receive a review priority classification but manufacturing supplements do not.

- *P—Priority review*

The drug product, if approved, would be a significant improvement compared to marketed products [approved (if such is required), including non-"drug" products/therapies] in the treatment, diagnosis, or prevention of a disease. Improvement can be demonstrated by, for example: (1) evidence of increased effectiveness in treatment, prevention, or diagnosis of disease; (2) elimination or substantial reduction of a treatment-limiting drug reaction; (3) documented enhancement of patient compliance; or (4) evidence of safety and effectiveness of a new subpopulation.

- *S—Standard review*

All non-priority applications will be considered standard applications.

POLICY . . .

- Because the review priority classification determines the review time frame the application receives, the review priority classification should be determined and assigned at the 45-day meeting if the application is to be filed.

- The final review classification of a new drug may change from "P" to "S" during the course of the review of a marketing application (NDA), either because of the approval of other agents or because of availability of new data; however, the review priority classification assigned at the time of filing will not change during the first review cycle and the user fee time frame of the original review cycle will be that based on the original priority.

- The review priority classification determines the overall approach to setting review priorities and user fee review time frames but is not intended to preclude work on other projects. It does not imply that staff working on a priority application cannot work on other projects, such as 30-day safety reviews of a newly submitted investigational new drug application (IND), preparation for end-of-phase 2 conferences, etc. . . .

NOTES

1. *Authority to Prioritize.* A priority review policy necessarily means that NDAs for drugs assigned a low classification will be reviewed more slowly than those with a higher classification, even though they may be economically important to the applicant. Section 505 makes no reference to prioritizing NDAs for review. It does specify that FDA is to reach a final decision on any NDA within 180 days, a schedule the agency rarely meets even for drugs of great therapeutic promise.

2. *Challenge to FDA Priorities.* FDA did not establish this priority classification system by public rulemaking, and the agency has not provided a procedure by which an applicant may dispute its initial classification of a drug. Nor has any applicant formally contested FDA's classification of its NDA or the agency's review in accordance with its priority classification.

2. ORPHAN DRUGS

The requirements for approval of a new drug present special obstacles for the development of drugs intended to treat rare diseases whose potential sales are not large enough to justify funding the necessary nonclinical and clinical tests. For several years, FDA kept many such drugs indefinitely in "orphan IND" status, contrary to the intent of section 505(i), while allowing them to be used for patient treatment. One goal of FDA's revision of the IND regulations in the late 1970s was to establish a formal regulatory status for these orphan INDs.

A 1979 report of an HHS interagency task force, SIGNIFICANT DRUGS OF LIMITED COMMERCIAL VALUE, outlined new mechanisms for spurring the development of orphan drugs. Soon after, Congress enacted the Orphan Drug Act, 96 Stat. 2049 (1983), to provide two types of incentives for the development of orphan drugs. First, the Act amended the Internal Revenue Code to provide tax credits for expenditures for clinical testing. 26 U.S.C. 44H. Second, it added four new sections, 525–528, to the FD&C Act. These provisions require FDA to provide orphan drug sponsors written recommendations for the animal and clinical investigations needed for approval of an NDA, authorize FDA to designate those drugs that qualify as orphan drugs, provide seven years of postapproval market exclusivity for any unpatentable orphan drug (during which even a full NDA for an identical drug cannot be approved by FDA), and direct the agency to encourage open label INDs for orphan drugs under which patients suffering from the disease can obtain the drug for treatment. The pharmaceutical industry's response to the 1983 Act surpassed expectations, in part because several orphan drugs had already been identified and were thus available for immediate development.

To provide additional incentives for manufacturers to expand research into new clinical areas, Congress made two other important changes to the FD&C Act in the mid-1980s. In the Health Promotion and Disease Prevention Amendments of 1984, 98 Stat. 2815, 2817, section 526(a)(2) was revised to define a "rare disease or condition" as one that affects fewer than 200,000 persons in the United States. This change greatly expanded the number of diseases that could be regarded as "rare" and thus the number of drugs that could qualify as orphan drugs. The Orphan Drug Amendments of 1985, 99 Stat. 387, expanded the provision for market exclusivity to include patented as well as unpatentable drugs. As a result, pharmaceutical companies began to compete to become the first to obtain FDA approval of NDAs for lucrative orphan drugs.

Genentech, Inc. v. Bowen

676 F. Supp. 301 (D.D.C. 1987).

■ STANLEY S. HARRIS, DISTRICT JUDGE.

This matter is before the Court on the separate, but similar, motions of plaintiff Genentech, Inc. (Genentech) [and] intervenor-defendant Ares–Serono, Inc. (Serono) . . . for partial summary judgment. In its complaint, Genentech, the manufacturer and marketer of a synthetic human growth hormone produced through recombinant DNA technology, alleges that the recent decision of the Food and Drug Administration (FDA) . . . to approve a recombinant DNA human growth hormone product manufactured by intervenor-defendant Eli Lilly and Company (Lilly) violated the Administrative Procedure Act, the Orphan Drug Act, and the Fifth Amendment to the United States Constitution. The pending motions challenge the validity of the FDA's designation, prior to marketing approval, of Lilly's drug as an orphan drug. . . . [T]he motions for partial summary judgment are denied. . . .

Human growth hormone (hGH) is a protein naturally produced and secreted by the human pituitary gland. In some children, between 6,000 and 15,000 in the United States, the pituitary gland does not produce enough hGH, resulting in stunted growth. Since 1958, the condition had been treated by supplementing a patient's natural hGH with hGH derived from the pituitary glands of human cadavers. However, in 1985, use of pituitary-derived hGH was effectively eliminated by the discovery that three hGH patients who had been treated with hGH provided by NHPP had developed Creutzfeldt–Jakob Disease, an extremely rare but fatal condition, apparently due to exposure to a pathogen transmitted by the pituitary-derived hGH. Although no cases of Creutzfeldt–Jakob Disease have ever been linked to hGH distributed by Serono or KabiVitrum, neither has distributed pituitary-derived hGH in the United States since 1985.

On October 17, 1985, the FDA granted Genentech, a pharmaceutical developer that specializes in the use of biotechnology (popularly known as "gene splicing"), marketing approval for a human growth product known commercially as Protropin. Genentech's product differs from pituitary-derived hGH in two important respects. First, it is synthesized through a recombinant DNA process utilizing *E. coli* bacteria, rather than produced in a human gland. Second, Genentech's "r-hGH" product includes an amino acid group not commonly found in pituitary-derived hGH. In terms of chemical structure, Genentech's r-hGH has the same sequence of 191 amino acids found in hGH, with an additional methionine amino acid group attached to one end of the molecule. Because Genentech's drug apparently does not present the risk of Creutzfeldt–Jakob Disease associated with pituitary-derived hGH, its approval in 1985 filled an important health need. On December 12, 1985, the FDA designated Protropin as an orphan drug, thus granting Genentech marketing exclusivity, pursuant to 21 U.S.C. § 360cc, until December 12, 1992. . . .

On June 12, 1986, the FDA designated an r-hGH drug developed by intervenor-defendant Lilly as an orphan drug for the treatment of human growth hormone deficiency. Unlike Genentech's r-hGH product, the chemical structure of Lilly's product is identical to that of natural, pituitary-derived hGH; that is, Lilly's drug does not contain the additional methionyl group found in Protropin. On October 15, 1986, Lilly submitted to the FDA a New Drug Application (NDA) for its r-hGH product, seeking permission to market the drug commercially.

On November 3, 1986, Genentech submitted a "citizen petition" to the FDA. In it, Genentech took the position that Lilly's drug was, for the purposes of the Orphan Drug Act, the same as Protropin and therefore ineligible for marketing approval until 1992. . . . Genentech . . . requested an administrative stay of approval of any new r-hGH products. . . .

When Genentech learned that the FDA was preparing to approve the NDA for Lilly's methionyl-free r-hGH product, known commercially as Humatrope, Genentech sought an emergency stay from the FDA. When that request was denied, Genentech filed suit in this Court on March 6, 1987, seeking temporary, preliminary, and permanent injunctive relief, in addition to a declaratory judgment that the FDA's application of the Orphan Drug Act violated Genentech's statutory and constitutional rights.

. . . On March 8, the FDA approved Lilly's NDA for Humatrope, thereby authorizing Lilly to market the drug commercially and triggering the orphan drug exclusivity provision of 21 U.S.C. § 360cc. . . .

Movants contend that Humatrope's orphan drug designation violated both the Orphan Drug Act and the FDA's binding regulations implementing the Act. Their argument is based on the contention that Humatrope and pituitary-derived hGH are the same drug. In light of the peculiar facts of this case, the Court cannot accept movants' contention, and therefore must uphold the Humatrope designation. . . .

Two related aspects of this particular case convince the Court that if Congress had been presented with the facts of this case, it would have considered Humatrope and pituitary-derived hGH different drugs for the purposes of § 360bb(a). First, Humatrope, by virtue of its synthetic origin, does not present the danger of contamination with the Creutzfeldt–Jakob prion that is associated with hGH obtained from human cadavers. . . . [A]ny pituitary-derived hGH product presents a risk (albeit unquantifiable) of lethal side effects not associated with r-hGH products such as Protropin and Humatrope.

Second, the industry's response to the linking of Creutzfeldt–Jakob Disease to pituitary-derived hGH—withdrawal from the United States market—meant that regardless of the status of the Serono and Kabi

NDAs, methionyl-free hGH would not be available to hGH-deficient children in this country. The legislative history is replete with references to the fundamental need to provide treatment for presently untreated patients; the fact that NDAs for pituitary-derived hGh were technically still valid would not have convinced Congress that growth hormone deficiency was not a condition in need of new treatments. One need only imagine a world without methionyl r-hGH (plaintiff's Protropin) to appreciate the unacceptable ramifications of movants' argument when applied to this case. Without Protropin, children in need of supplemental hGH would go without treatment, while movants offered assurances that no additional orphan drug designations were necessary because valid, but unused, NDAs remained in effect. In enacting the Orphan Drug Act, Congress clearly focused on the availability of treatments, not the existence of prior NDAs. . . .

In finding that Humatrope and pituitary-derived hGH are different drugs for the purposes of orphan drug designation under 21 U.S.C. § 360bb, and that therefore the Humatrope designation is valid, the Court's holding is narrow and confined to the particular facts of this case. The Court expresses no opinion on the still-pending issue of whether Protropin's orphan drug exclusivity barred approval of Humatrope, and, in particular, sets down no universal rule for determining whether two drugs are "different: for the purposes of the Orphan Drug Act. . . .

NOTES

1. *Consistent Decisions.* In two other cases, the courts reached the same conclusion as the District Court in *Genentech.* In *Berlex Laboratories, Inc. v. Food and Drug Administration,* 942 F. Supp. 19 (D.D.C. 1996), Berlex was given market exclusivity for its drug under the Orphan Drug Act, but FDA approved an NDA for a competitor's product on the ground that it was "clinically superior" because the pioneer drug had a higher rate of injection site necrosis. The court upheld the FDA's decision. In *Sigma–Tau Pharmaceuticals, Inc. v. Schwetz,* 288 F.3d 141 (4th Cir. 2002), FDA approved a generic version of the pioneer drug in spite of the seven-year period of orphan exclusivity for the pioneer because the FDA approval was only for an indication that was no longer protected by market exclusivity. The Court of Appeals held that the seven-year period of orphan drug exclusivity applies on an indication basis, not for the entire drug and all of its uses. As the Court of Appeals stated, the market exclusivity granted under the orphan drug is "disease-specific, not drug-specific."

2. *Implementing Regulations.* FDA published regulations to implement the Orphan Drug Act in 57 Fed. Reg. 62076 (Dec. 29, 1992), codified at 21 C.F.R. Part 316.

3. *Timing of Claim of Orphan Status.* FDA initially concluded that a drug was eligible for orphan drug designation if a petition was received before the agency *approved* an NDA for use of the drug to treat the rare disease. The Orphan Drug Amendments of 1988, 102 Stat. 90, amended section 526 to require that a petition for orphan drug designation be made before the *submission* of an NDA for the orphan drug use.

4. *List of Orphan Drugs.* FDA formerly periodically published a cumulative list of orphan drug designations. That list is now available only on the FDA website.

5. *Orphan Products Board.* As originally enacted, the Orphan Drug Act created an Orphan Products Board, composed entirely of officials of the Department of HHS, to promote the development of drugs and devices for rare diseases and conditions. 96 Stat. 2049, 2052 (1983). The Orphan Drug Amendments of 1985 substituted a new National Commission on Orphan Diseases, with nongovernmental membership, to assess governmental and nongovernmental activities with respect to rare diseases. 99 Stat. 387, 388. FDA has generally heeded the recommendations of the National Commission.

6. *Seven-Year Exclusivity.* As illustrated in the *Genentech* case, the assurance of seven years of market exclusivity is of major commercial importance. An amendment to allow exceptions to this provision passed by Congress was vetoed by President George H. W. Bush on the ground that it would undermine the commercial incentive to develop orphan drugs. 26 WEEKLY COMP. OF PRES. DOC. 1796 (Nov. 8, 1990).

7. *Proposed Legislation.* Because some orphan drugs have been very profitable, legislation has been proposed to revise various provisions of the law. *See, e.g.*, "Anticompetitive Abuse of the Orphan Drug Act: Invitation to High Prices," Hearing before the Subcommittee on Antitrust, Monopolies and Business Rights of the Senate Committee on the Judiciary, 102d Cong., 2d Sess. (1992).

Marlene E. Haffner, *Adopting Orphan Drugs—Two Dozen Years of Treating Rare Diseases*
354 NEW ENGLAND JOURNAL OF MEDICINE 445 (2006).

In the 24 years since this law was passed, 282 [orphan] drugs and biologic products, providing treatment for more than 14 million patients in the United States, have come to market under its aegis. In the 8 to 10 years before 1982, by contrast, only 10 treatments for rare diseases had been approved by the FDA and brought to market. . . .

Orphan drugs must go through the same development process as any other drug and must be shown to meet the same standards for effectiveness and safety as a drug for a common condition. Indeed, because of the small number of patients available to be enrolled in clinical trials of orphan drugs, these products must be even more effective than the average drug if a statistically significant benefit is to be established. . . .

The research and development encouraged by the Orphan Drug Act have brought needed therapies to millions of patients in the United States, but these products are not free from controversy. One criticism concerns the high cost of some orphan drugs—although other drugs developed by means of biotechnology are equally expensive. . . .

NOTE

A study conducted by the National Organization for Rare Disease evaluating all 135 non-cancer new chemical entity orphan drugs approved by FDA from 1983 (when the Orphan Drug Act was enacted) to June 30, 2010, showed that 90 (67 percent) were approved on the basis of some exercise of regulatory flexibility by FDA—i.e. the evidence of effectiveness did not meet the conventional FDA standard. F. Sasinowski, QUANTUM OF EFFECTIVENESS EVIDENCE IN FDA'S APPROVAL OF ORPHAN DRUGS: CATALOGUING FEA'S FLEXIBILITY IN REGULATING THERAPIES FOR PERSONS WITH RARE DISORDERS, 46 Drug Information J. 238 (2012).

3. USE OF INVESTIGATIONAL DRUGS FOR THERAPY

a. INTRODUCTION

Section 505(i) of the FD&C Act was included in the statute in 1938, and expanded in 1962, solely to authorize clinical trials designed to obtain data relating to safety and effectiveness sufficient to justify FDA approval of an NDA. It was never intended to authorize the use of investigational drugs for the treatment of ill patients outside a clinical trial. From the very beginning, however, it has been widely used to provide therapy for sick patients in situations in which there is little or no pretense of gathering data for an NDA.

Since 1938, FDA has consistently taken the position that an unapproved new drug may not lawfully be "commercialized" prior to approval. Before the Drug Amendments of 1962, the agency's regulations specified that investigational drugs were to be made available "solely for investigational use by or under the direction of, an expert qualified by scientific training and experience to investigate the safety of such drug." 21 C.F.R. 130.2(a)(2) (1962). The use of investigational drugs for therapy, rather than for investigational purposes, was not specifically addressed in FDA publications or contemporary articles describing the new drug process. The original IND regulations provided that the sponsor must not "commercially distribute nor test-market" the drug prior to approval and that an IND could be terminated if FDA found that the drug "is being or is to be sold or otherwise distributed for commercial purposes not justified by the requirements of the investigation." 28 Fed. Reg. 179 (Jan. 8, 1963), codified at 21 C.F.R. 130.3(a)(11), 130.3(d)(8). The IND form itself, beginning in 1963, required that the sponsor provide

> [i]f the drug is to be sold, a full explanation why sale is required and should not be regarded as the commercialization of a new drug for which an application is not approved.

FDA thus embraced two related enforcement principles. First, investigational drugs were to be used solely for investigational purposes and not for treatment. Second, investigational drugs were to be made available without charge, except under unusual circumstances that were fully justified in the IND.

As new drugs began to be developed to treat serious diseases for which no alternative therapy was available, FDA discarded the rule that an investigational drug could not be used for treatment purposes.

Although the agency did not amend the IND regulations to reflect this change in policy, it allowed the use of investigational drugs in patient treatment while clinical trials were ongoing, on various terms.

One goal of FDA's revision of the IND regulations in the 1980s was to rationalize these exceptions to the general ban on commercialization of an investigational drug. The agency's 1983 proposal, 48 Fed. Reg. 26720 (June 9, 1983), contained new sections on "treatment use" and "emergency use" that did no more than codify existing agency practice. By the time the final regulation was promulgated in March 1987, however, the AIDS epidemic had forced FDA to reevaluate these provisions. 52 Fed. Reg. 8798 (Mar. 19, 1987). The emergency use provision was retained as it appeared in the March final rule, 21 C.F.R. 312.310, but the treatment use provision was reproposed in more detailed form and promulgated just two months later as a final regulation. 52 Fed. Reg. 19466 (May 22, 1987), codified as 21 C.F.R. 312.320.

As part of the FDA Modernization Act of 1997, Congress added section 561 to the FD&C Act to permit expanded access to unapproved new drugs. This provision authorizes three types of expanded access programs: emergency access, individual patient access, and treatment INDs.

In August 2009, FDA published a final rule creating a new 21 C.F.R. Part 312, Subpart I to clarify the existing regulations and create additional types of expanded access for treatment use. 74 Fed. Reg. 40900 (Aug. 13, 2009). Under Subpart I, expanded access to investigational drugs for treatment use is available to (i) individual patients, (ii) individual patients in emergency situations; (iii) intermediate-size patient populations; and (iv) larger populations under a treatment protocol or treatment investigational new drug application (IND). FDA subsequently issued a guidance reflecting the structure of Subpart I. DRAFT GUIDANCE FOR INDUSTRY ON EXPANDED ACCESS TO INVESTIGATIONAL DRUGS FOR TREATMENT USE—QS & AS (May 2013). Each category of expanded access can be pursued through either an "access IND" or an "access protocol," depending on the situation. A protocol, rather than an IND, should be used when an IND for the drug is already in effect.

At 21 C.F.R. 312.305, FDA sets out requirements applicable to all expanded access uses:

(a) *Criteria.* FDA must determine that:

(1) The patient or patients to be treated have a serious or immediately life-threatening disease or condition, and there is no comparable or satisfactory alternative therapy to diagnose, monitor, or treat the disease or condition;

(2) The potential patient benefit justifies the potential risks of the treatment use and those potential risks are not unreasonable in the context of the disease or condition to be treated; and

(3) Providing the investigational drug for the requested use will not interfere with the initiation, conduct, or completion of clinical investigations that could support marketing approval of the

expanded access use or otherwise compromise the potential development of the expanded access use.

The use of investigational drugs for active therapy, rather than for clinical trials, is common. There is no single term used to designate this phenomenon, but "expanded access" is a fair description. The only thing that can be said with certainty is that the purpose of each of the programs described below is to provide active therapy to sick patients, not to obtain data to justify approval of an NDA.

b. THE VARIETY OF EXPANDED ACCESS PROGRAMS

i. Individual Patient IND or Protocol

FDA has long granted "single patient exceptions" to allow the use of investigational drugs outside the protocols of the approved IND. In 1978, a program for compassionate use of marijuana was established as a single patient IND to settle a civil lawsuit against the government. The program grew to 13 participants in 1992, when HHS decided to add no new participants and to phase out the program as people died or voluntarily left. In *Kuromiya v. United States*, 37 F. Supp. 2d 717, 78 F. Supp. 2d 367 (E.D. Pa. 1999), the HHS action was upheld. In *Smith v. Shalala*, 954 F. Supp. 1 (D.D.C. 1996), the court held that where a terminally ill cancer patient had failed to try available FDA-approved drugs for his condition, the agency could, under 21 C.F.R. 312.42(b)(1)(i), properly disallow a single patient exception for an investigational drug.

Under section 561(b) of the FD&C Act, added in 1997 by the FDA Modernization Act, any person may ask a sponsor for access to an investigational drug for the treatment of a serious disease or condition if there is no satisfactory alternative therapy available, there is sufficient evidence of safety and effectiveness to support the use of the investigational drug, FDA determines that provision of the investigational drug will not interfere with clinical investigations to support NDA approval, and the sponsor or clinical investigator submits to FDA a clinical protocol consistent with the IND regulations. This provision of the statute is consistent with FDA practice since 1962, and it thus did not expand access to investigational drugs beyond what already existed.

The 2009 rule adding Subpart I of Part 312 expressly allows physicians to request the use of an investigational drug for the treatment of an individual patient. 21 C.F.R. 312.310. This procedure ordinarily requires a written submission by the physician.

ii. Emergency Use IND or Protocol

Under section 561(a) of the FD&C Act, also added by the FDA Modernization Act, FDA may authorize the shipment of investigational drugs (or devices) for the treatment of a serious disease or condition in emergency situations. Like section 561(b), this provision codifies prior FDA practice extending back to 1962. FDA first promulgated regulations formally establishing the emergency use IND in 1987. 52 Fed. Reg. 8798, 8820–8821 (Mar. 19, 1987), codified at 21 C.F.R. 312.36. The 2009 Subpart I regulations replaced this provision with one that treats the emergency IND as a particular version of the individual patient IND. 21 C.F.R. 312.310(d). The rule provides that in an emergency situation, FDA may grant a physician's telephone request to immediately begin expanded access for an individual patient.

An emergency use IND is exempt from prior IRB approval and, in some instances, from informed consent. 21 C.F.R. 56.104(c), 50.23(a). The physician must, however, submit a report of the emergency use to the IRB within five days after the use of the unapproved article. *Id.* 50.23(c).

NOTES

1. *Planned Emergency Research.* In another regulation, FDA creates an exemption from informed consent for emergency research. 21 C.F.R. 50.24. This rule addresses situations in which an investigator of an unapproved drug or device knows in advance that trial subjects in a life-threatening situation will be unable to give informed consent. Use of this provision requires both prior IRB approval and the submission of a separate IND.

2. *National Security Emergency.* Following the terrorist attacks of September 11, 2001, Congress enacted the Project BioShield Act of 2004, 108 Stat. 276, which added section 564 to the FD&C Act to allow FDA to authorize the use of an unapproved new drug during a declared domestic, military, or national security emergency. FDA has twice issued an authorization of emergency use of anthrax vaccine by military personnel at the request of the Department of Defense. *See* 70 Fed. Reg. 5450 (Feb. 2, 2005), 70 Fed. Reg. 44657 (Aug. 3, 2005).

iii. Treatment IND or Protocol

The agency first promulgated a final treatment use regulation in 52 Fed. Reg. 19466 (May 22, 1987), just as the AIDS crisis reached a peak in the United States. This regulation (21 C.F.R. 312.34) authorized access to investigational drugs for a broad population under a treatment protocol or treatment IND when certain criteria were met. In the FDA Modernization Act of 1997, Congress added section FD&C Act 561(c), which expressly authorizes FDA to permit the use of an investigational drug under a treatment protocol (referred to in the provision as an "expanded access protocol") for the treatment of a serious or immediately life-threatening disease or condition. This provision simply codified the prior FDA regulation.

In the 2009 Subpart I regulation, section 312.34 was replaced by 312.320, which continues prior practice. The rule specifies that FDA will approve a treatment IND or protocol only if the drug is being investigated in a controlled clinical trial under an IND designed to support a marketing application for the same use, or if such trials are already complete. 21 C.F.R. 312.320(a)(1). Moreover, the sponsor must be "actively pursuing marketing approval" with "due diligence." *Id.* 312.320(a)(2).

NOTES

1. *Publication of Treatment INDs.* FDA used to periodically publish a list of all drugs subject to treatment INDs. *E.g.*, "Treatment Investigational New Drugs (INDs) Allowed to Proceed, June 22, 1987—February 19, 2002," available on FDA website. The agency has abandoned this practice, however.

2. *The AIDS Amendments.* The AIDS Amendments of 1988 essentially ratified the treatment IND policy previously adopted by FDA. The Amendments, 102 Stat. 3048, 3066–3067, codified at 42 U.S.C. 300cc–12, require FDA to encourage submission of an IND for clinical trials, and submission of a treatment IND for individuals not in clinical trials, for any investigational drug when there is "preliminary evidence that the drug has effectiveness in humans" in the prevention or treatment of AIDS. FDA is specifically authorized to provide technical assistance, directly or through grants or contracts, to facilitate submission of INDs for these purposes.

3. *Continuing Demands.* FDA's official recognition of Treatment INDs by rule in 1987 did not satisfy all the agency's critics. *See* "FDA Responds to Act Up Demands," FDA Talk Paper No. T88–74 (Oct. 5, 1988). Some contended that the agency applied the treatment IND regulations more restrictively than their wording promised. These critics claimed that rather than allowing a treatment IND for any drug that "may" be effective for some AIDS victims, FDA approved a treatment IND for a drug only after the sponsor had already submitted substantial evidence of safety and effectiveness, as a "bridge" to NDA approval. Many argued that treatment INDs should be granted much earlier, even if this allowed the use of some drugs that were later found to be unsafe or ineffective. At the same time, others contended the widespread use of unapproved drugs threatened the development of legitimate, effective AIDS treatments. According to a news article:

> Although FDA officials dispute the notion, some experts are concerned that the use of unproven medications may be getting out of control. So many AIDS patients are taking a pharmacological stew of approved and experimental drugs and potions that it is difficult to gauge the effectiveness of any single drug. Underground studies of experimental drugs ... confuse an already complex situation and frustrate scientists. "They're violating all the standards of safe testing of new compounds," says Dr. Paul Volberding, an AIDS specialist at the University of California at San Francisco. The haphazard use of experimental drugs may help some AIDS patients in the short run, but it will slow down the quest to discover the best ways to treat the many people who will contract the disease in the future.

Drugs from the Underground, TIME MAG., July 10, 1989, at 49.

iv. *Intermediate-Size Patient Population IND or Protocol*

The most significant innovation of the 2009 regulations is the creation, in 21 C.F.R. 312.315, of an "intermediate-size patient population IND" to "formally bridge the gap between individual patient access, on the one hand, and large population access under treatment

INDs, on the other." 74 Fed. Reg. 40900, 40926 (Aug. 13, 2009). In promulgating the rule, FDA explained: "The primary purpose of the intermediate-size patient population IND or protocol is to consolidate expanded access under a single IND to promote better monitoring, oversight, and ease of administration for an expanded access use compared to multiple individual patient INDs." 74 Fed. Reg. at. 40926. The agency envisions this procedure being used not only for drugs currently under development, but also drugs not being developed "for example, because the disease or condition is so rare that the sponsor is unable to recruit patients for a clinical trial." 21 C.F.R. 312.315(a)(1).

NOTES: OTHER EARLY ACCESS PROGRAMS

1.   *Parallel Track IND.* In 1990, as a result of continuing pressure from the AIDS community, and at the personal recommendation of NIH–NIAID Director Anthony Fauci, the Public Health Service and FDA announced a "parallel track mechanism" permitting the use of investigational drugs by people with AIDS and HIV-related diseases who are both unable to benefit from existing standard therapies and unable to participate in ongoing clinical trials. 57 Fed. Reg. 13250 (Apr. 15, 1992). This policy can be found only in the Federal Register; it is not codified in the C.F.R. An investigational new drug may not be released under a parallel track protocol before patient enrollment in an FDA-approved Phase II clinical trial for that drug is initiated. A parallel track protocol must comply with the requirements generally applicable to other protocols for investigational new drugs.

2.   *Group C Cancer Treatment IND.* The National Cancer Institute (NCI) plays a major role in the discovery and development of anticancer drugs. Since 1976, NCI has furnished qualified physicians the most promising investigational drugs, called "Group C" drugs, to treat their patients outside any clinical trial. These drugs appear in a Master File submitted to FDA. NCI includes on this list only those drugs that it concludes are likely to obtain NDA approval. This is an informal program, not codified in regulations. The program was incorporated into a Memorandum of Understanding between the two agencies published in 44 Fed. Reg. 25510 (May 1, 1979). Beginning in October 1980, Group C drugs were made eligible for Medicare reimbursement, despite their investigational status.

In 1988, FDA determined that NCI would continue to use the designation "Group C" for these drugs, that FDA would use the designation "treatment IND/Group C," and that FDA "will treat NCI applications for Group C status as treatment IND requests, no matter what name they come under, and utilize the standards that we would ordinarily use for such a request." Under the program, NCI may submit an application to FDA for authorization to distribute the investigational new drug for a specific indication. If approved, NCI ships the drug to appropriately trained physicians who have provided adequate assurance that their patients qualify under the protocol. Patients are not charged for the investigational new drugs they receive pursuant to a Group C IND. To facilitate the exchange of clinical research information between NCI and FDA, the two agencies entered into a Memorandum of Understanding establishing a secure electronic database for clinical investigator information. 71 Fed. Reg. 54286 (Sept. 14, 2006).

3. *Open Label IND.* Open label INDs trace their origin back to 1962, but they have never been codified in FDA regulations. There are two types of open label INDs. First, when a placebo-controlled clinical trial is completed and there is no formal follow-up as part of the protocol, it is common to continue the treatment arm, and switch the placebo arm to treatment, under an open label protocol. Second, an open label protocol is used under a wide variety of other circumstances for the treatment of ill patients. In both instances, safety data are collected and reported to FDA under the IND and as part of the NDA.

4. *Compassionate Use IND.* Like the term "expanded access," "compassionate use" is a broad and undefined term. It applies to situations in which the use of an investigational new drug for patient therapy does not fall within any other specific expanded access IND program. Since 1962, FDA has taken a very liberal and flexible approach to compassionate use INDs where there is a clear medical need. The term "compassionate IND" is regarded by some as synonymous with an "open protocol." Section 2312 of the Public Health Service Act, 42 U.S.C. § 300cc–12, provides that FDA shall encourage "an application to use the drug in the treatment of individuals" as part of the IND where "there is preliminary evidence that a new drug has effectiveness in humans with respect to the prevention or treatment of acquired immune deficiency syndrome."

5. *Orphan Drug IND.* Prior to the enactment of the Orphan Drug Act of 1983, orphan drugs (i.e., drugs for rare diseases or conditions) seldom proceeded from an IND to an approved NDA. In some instances, there were too few patients to satisfy FDA testing requirements for an NDA, and in other instances, the market for the drug was too small to justify the investment needed to obtain an approved NDA. As a result, orphan drugs were relegated to a continuing IND status that FDA and the sponsor tacitly agreed would probably be permanent. Section 528 of the FD&C Act requires FDA to encourage the sponsor of an orphan drug to design "open protocols" for "persons with the disease or condition who need the drug to treat the disease or condition and who cannot be satisfactorily treated by available alternative drugs." Although the Orphan Drug Act has reduced the number of permanent orphan drug INDs, they have not been eliminated completely. In the future, they may all be categorized as intermediate-size population INDs, the new category created by regulation in 2009, which explicitly applies to such rare disease situations. 21 C.F.R. 312.315(a)(1).

6. *Tropical Drug IND.* Although FDA has long permitted drugs for tropical diseases to be the subject of clinical trials in the United States, the agency, until fairly recently, rarely approved NDAs for exclusively tropical new drugs, on the ground that there was no need for such drugs in this country. Thus, like the orphan drug INDs, a tropical drug IND was tacitly assumed to be permanent. With increased international travel and immigration, the rationale for not approving NDAs for tropical drugs has now largely disappeared.

7. *Special Exception IND.* When an individual is ineligible to enroll in a clinical trial of an investigational drug, the sponsor may request that FDA permit a special exception from the IND protocol to permit the excluded individual to receive treatment. Although this special exception IND is not reflected in any FDA regulation or guidance, the agency does permit such exceptions. Because the patient falls outside the inclusion criteria for the study, the data regarding the patient are excluded from the reported study results.

8. *Non-Programmatic Enforcement Discretion.* In the 1980s, FDA declined to initiate regulatory action against various activities by organized nonprofit AIDS groups that would almost surely have triggered enforcement immediately if engaged in by commercial enterprises. For example, on July 23, 1988, in a speech to the Second International Lesbian and Gay Health Conference & Aids Forum in Boston, FDA Commissioner Frank Young declared:

> Traditionally, FDA has not interfered with individuals that use unproven substances in self-treatment. Nor have we interfered, when doctors prescribed drugs for other than their approved use. On the other hand, we have acted against promoters or seized products when there was a fraudulent promotion, or when the product represented an unreasonable risk. FDA's new policy regarding self-help, nonprofit clinics is similar to our policy regarding the use of unproven substances in self-treatment—that is, not to interfere as long as patients are not being harmed, clinics do not promote unproven products outside the clinic, and the clinic does not serve as a subterfuge for a commercial enterprise.

The previous month, the agency had acted to stop two companies from selling AL–721, a substance made from eggs and soybeans that, although marketed as a food, was widely used as a possible treatment against the AIDS virus. The use of the substance was promoted and organized by an impressive network of activists, many of whom formed buyers clubs. FDA's enforcement actions against AL–721 triggered a firestorm.

> As word of the action spread through the AIDS community, people felt panicked and outraged. Almost immediately, lawyers for gay support groups called the agency, and some AIDS patients began stockpiling AL–721. By Thursday, the agency called off the embargo and informed Nutricology that if it would comply with agency regulations and stop implying that the substance is useful against AIDS, it could resume selling the product.

Gina Kolata, *An Angry Response to Actions on AIDS Spurs F.D.A. Shift,* N.Y. TIMES, June 26, 1988, at 1. Compare FDA's actions with respect to AIDS treatments to its efforts to shut down for-profit cancer clinics using unproven cancer drugs. *United States v. Hoxsey Cancer Clinic,* 198 F.2d 273 (5th Cir. 1952); *United States v. Burzynski Cancer Research Institute,* 819 F.2d 1301 (5th Cir. 1987).

c.   CHARGING FOR EXPANDED ACCESS

A prominent feature of FDA's initial expanded access regulation, 52 Fed. Reg. 19466 (May 22, 1987), was the authority for sponsors to charge for investigational drugs under a treatment IND if they requested and received written authorization from the agency. This opportunity was available only if the drug was not being commercially promoted or advertised and the sponsor of the drug was pursuing marketing approval with due diligence. The rule made clear that the sponsor could not commercialize an investigational drug by charging a price larger than necessary to recover the costs of manufacture, research, development, and handling of the drug. Although several drug sponsors successfully filed and implemented treatment INDs early in the program's history, when CMS and third party payors refused to reimburse for any drugs administered under a treatment IND on the ground that it represented experimental use, this approach fell into disuse. The regulatory provision prohibiting drug manufacturers from profiting on the sale of experimental drugs, even in under a treatment protocol, was a focus of the constitutional attack rejected in *Abigail Alliance v. Von Eschenbach*, 495 F.3d 695 (D.C. Cir. 2007), *supra* p. 654.

In August 2009, on the same day it issued its new expanded access rule, FDA also promulgated a revised regulation on charging for investigational drugs under an IND. 74 Fed. Reg. 40872 (Aug. 13, 2009), codified at 21 C.F.R. 312.8. In one respect, this rule slightly expands the opportunities for companies to charge for treatment access; it extends the relevant provisions to the new category of intermediate-size patient population INDs and protocols as well to treatment INDs and protocols. *Id.* 312.8(d)(2). But the overall effect is to reduce the possible cost recovery available to such sponsors. The old regulation was sometimes interpreted as permitting sponsors to charge for the costs of research and development of investigational drugs. *See* 71 Fed. Reg. 75168, 75170 (Dec. 14, 2006). The new regulation was written to clarify that such costs are *not* recoverable; it permits charging only for "direct costs" (e.g., the cost per unit to manufacture the drug and to ship and handle it) and excludes all indirect costs (e.g., research, development, facilities, and equipment). 21 C.F.R. 312.8(d). The rule does permit a sponsor to recover the costs of monitoring the expanded access use, complying with IND reporting requirements, and other administrative costs directly associated with making a drug available for treatment use. *Id.* 312.8(d)(2).

In short, it remains infeasible for a small company to engage in expanded access without losing money. Instead of encouraging expanded access, FDA has made it prohibitively expensive. *See* Benjamin R. Rossen, *FDA's Proposed Regulations to Expand Access to Investigational Drugs for Treatment Use: The Status Quo in the Guise of Reform*, 64 FOOD AND DRUG L.J. 183 (2009).

d.   IMPORTATION OF INVESTIGATIONAL DRUGS FOR PERSONAL USE

FDA first adopted a personal import policy for drugs in 1954. Faced with a large number of unapproved AIDS drugs being imported for personal use, the agency, in July 1988, issued a guidance stating that it would exercise enforcement discretion with respect to unapproved products imported by mail for personal use in limited quantities. FDA Office of Regional Operations, PILOT GUIDANCE FOR RELEASE OF MAIL IMPORTATIONS (1988). Meanwhile, ever since 1977, the FDA Regulatory Procedures Manual has stated that the agency will not detain unapproved new drugs imported for personal use by mail or personal baggage. The current statement of this policy, which remains essentially unchanged since 1989, follows.

Coverage of Personal Importations

Regulatory Procedures Manual Ch. 9–2 (updated Apr. 2013).

. . . [I]ndividuals seek medical treatments that are not available in this country. Drugs are sometimes mailed to this country in response to a prescription-like order to allow continuation of a therapy initiated abroad. With increasing international travel and world trade, we can anticipate that more people will purchase products abroad that may not be approved, may be health frauds or may be otherwise not legal for sale in the United States.

In addition, FDA must be alert to foreign and domestic businesses that promote or ship unapproved, fraudulent or otherwise illegal medical treatments into the United States or who encourage persons to order these products. Such treatments may be promoted to individuals who believe that treatments available abroad will be effective in the treatment of serious conditions such as AIDS or cancer. Because some countries do not regulate or restrict the exportation of products, people who mail order from these businesses may not be afforded the protection of either foreign or U.S. laws. . . .

FDA personnel may use their discretion to allow entry of shipments of violative FDA regulated products when the quantity and purpose are clearly for personal use, and the product does not present an unreasonable risk to the user. Even though all products that appear to be in violation of statutes administered by FDA are subject to refusal, FDA personnel may use their discretion to examine the background, risk, and purpose of the product before making a final decision. Although FDA may use discretion to allow admission of certain violative items, this should *not* be interpreted as a license to individuals to bring in such shipments.

Commercial and promotional shipments are not subject to this guidance. Whether or not a shipment is commercial or promotional may be determined by a number of factors including, for example, the type of product, accompanying literature, size, value, and/or destination of the shipment. FDA personnel may also consider whether an importation of drugs or medical devices is a commercial shipment by evaluating whether the article appears to have been purchased for personal use or whether the quantity suggests commercial distribution (i.e., the supply exceeds what one person might take in approximately three months).

. . . .

In deciding whether to exercise discretion to allow personal shipments of drugs or devices, FDA personnel may consider a more permissive policy in the following situations:

1. when the intended use is appropriately identified, such use is not for treatment of a serious condition, and the product is not known to represent a significant health risk; and

2. when a) the intended use is unapproved and for a serious condition for which effective treatment may not be available domestically either through commercial or clinical means; b) there is no known commercialization or promotion to persons residing in the U.S. by those involved in the distribution of the product at issue; c) the product is considered not to represent an unreasonable risk; and d) the individual seeking to import the product affirms in writing that it is for the patient's own use (generally not more than 3 month supply) and provides the name and address of the doctor licensed in the U.S. responsible for his or her treatment with the product, or provides evidence that the product is for the continuation of a treatment begun in a foreign country.

. . . .

NOTES

1. *Recent Change in Attitude, but not Policy.* With the increased availability of FDA-approved cancer and AIDS drugs in the United States and the substantial problem of foreign counterfeit drugs, FDA has, since the turn of the new century, contemplated either drastically reducing or eliminating the personal import policy. Although the agency discussed this possibility with the Secretary of HHS, for obvious political reasons it has taken no action.

2. *Congressional Steps.* In the 2000s, Congress, in light of the price differential between domestic and foreign drugs, enacted two statutes designed to increase imports of less expensive drugs from abroad. *See infra* p. 1026. Those two statutes failed because the Secretaries of HHS in three administrations refused to certify that importation of drugs not approved by FDA would pose no additional risk to public health and would result in a significant reduction in cost to consumers. As political pressure increased prior to the November 2006 elections, it became clear that a compromise was essential in order to forestall more sweeping legislation. Congress therefore enacted section 535 of the FY 2007 appropriations statute for the Department of Homeland Security, 120 Stat. 1355 (2006), to provide, for one year, that an individual entering the country from Canada could bring up to a 90-day supply of any drug except a controlled substance or a biological product.

3. *Drugs on Import Alert.* The FDA importation policy does not apply to drugs that have been made the subject of an Import Alert, which FDA sometimes issues for medical products that are unsafe or clearly fraudulent. *See* "Policy on Importing Unapproved AIDS Drugs for Personal Use," FDA Talk Paper No. T88–51 (July 27, 1988).

4. *Importation of Unapproved RU–486.* In June 1989, under pressure from antiabortion members of Congress, the agency issued an import alert stating that the French abortifacient pill RU–486 (mifepristone) was subject to automatic detention. Three years later, a

pregnant woman who sought to import a single dose of RU–486 from Great Britain for personal use had her supply seized at airport customs in accordance with the import alert. The woman obtained a preliminary injunction in U.S. District Court requiring the government to return the drug to her. The District Court accepted her argument that she was entitled to the return of her RU–486 because FDA issued the import alert without notice-and-comment procedures. *Benten v. Kessler*, 799 F. Supp. 281, 288–90 (E.D.N.Y. 1992). The Second Circuit stayed the injunction, and the United States Supreme Court, *per curiam*, refused to vacate the stay. *Benten v. Kessler*, 505 U.S. 1084 (1992). Justice Stevens, dissenting, contended that the government's seizure of Benten's RU–486 constituted an undue burden on the woman's constitutional due process right to liberty. *Id.* at 1085–86. The majority declined to express any view on the merits of Steven's assertion. In 2000, FDA approved mifepristone for termination of early pregnancy.

5. *FDA Denial of Personal Use Import.* The district court in *Garlic v. FDA*, 783 F. Supp. 4 (D.D.C. 1992), held that a person denied permission to import an investigational drug for personal use must first exhaust administrative remedies by submitting a citizen petition to FDA requesting the agency to reverse its refusal to permit importation before bringing an injunction and declaratory judgment action in court. The district court also held that a person with Alzheimer's disease has no constitutional right to obtain unapproved medications. *See also Sifre v. Robles*, 917 F. Supp. 133 (D.P.R. 1996).

6. *Illegal Commercial Importation.* In *United States v. Haas*, 171 F.3d 259 (5th Cir. 1999), the court of appeals affirmed the conviction of a defendant for illegally importing unapproved versions of approved prescription drugs. The court held that the importation was for commercial purposes that did not fall within the FDA personal use exception. In *In re: Canadian Import Antitrust Litigation*, Civil No. 05–3873 (8th Cir. 2006), the court of appeals affirmed the district court's dismissal of an antitrust case brought against nine large pharmaceutical companies alleging a conspiracy to suppress the importation of Canadian prescription drugs for personal use.

7. *Compound Q.* In the midst of the AIDS crisis in the late 1980s, buyers clubs and other nonprofit organizations not only purchased unapproved products domestically, *see supra* p. 770, note 8, but also imported them from abroad. In June 1989, FDA announced it was investigating the distribution of GLQ–223, or "Compound Q," a putative treatment for AIDS:

> Trichosanthin is a plant protein, which researchers think may be an effective agent against the AIDS virus. An FDA-sanctioned clinical study of GLQ–223, a refined form of trichosanthin, was started at San Francisco General Hospital in May 1989. This initial human study is designed to test the safety of this drug's use in treating AIDS patients. . . .

> According to media reports, Project Inform, a San Francisco-based AIDS activist group initiated distribution of a trichosanthin-based preparation imported from China, supposedly to test its efficacy in

AIDS patients. . . . There have been several media reports that the death of one patient and the serious adverse reactions of other patients participating in this informal study have been either directly or indirectly linked to this trichosanthin-based product. . . .

The agency feels that the concerns raised by this operation point out the need to conduct clinical studies in a scientific manner, that includes careful study design, institutional monitoring mechanisms and consistent reporting channels. Such studies assure the acquisition of good clinical data in the shortest possible time, and ensure the safety of patients.

"FDA Statement on Unauthorized AIDS Drug Study," FDA Talk Paper No. T89–40 (June 28, 1987).

4. PRE-1962 DESI DRUGS

In this subsection, we summarize the history of FDA's efforts to apply the 1962 Drug Amendments, with their requirement of a showing of efficacy, to the large universe of products that were already on the market at the time the Amendments were enacted. Obviously, the agency could not practically subject each of these thousands of drugs to the full investigation and approval process examined earlier in this Chapter. The alternative process established by FDA to accomplish this massive task is known as the Drug Efficacy Study Implementation (DESI). Remarkably, the DESI process is not yet complete, and food and drug lawyers therefore still occasionally confront the legal issues surrounding a "DESI Drug."

Marketing of Drugs Under the 1938 FD&C Act

Although section 505 of the 1938 Act did not mandate affirmative FDA approval prior to marketing, it gave the agency the authority to refuse to let a new drug application (NDA) become effective if there was an insufficient demonstration of safety. By 1941, 4128 NDAs had been submitted to FDA. Because it was unable to cope with this volume, the agency began in 1942 to examine each application to determine whether the product covered was indeed a "new drug," i.e., whether it was generally recognized as safe (GRAS) and thus excluded from the section 201(p) definition of new drug as then written. FDA did not require (and, indeed, refused to accept for filing) NDAs for drugs that the agency concluded were generally recognized as safe (GRAS) and thus not new drugs. Manufacturers responded by seeking FDA's opinion as to their products' GRAS status prior to submitting an NDA, or by making their own GRAS determinations. These practices ultimately led to a reduction in the number of full NDAs submitted, though the agency's workload still remained substantial. By June 30, 1962, NDAs for 9457 individual products had become effective for nonprescription and prescription human and animal drugs.

In addition to the new drug products with effective NDAs that entered the market between 1938 and 1962, many thousands of similar formulations entered the market without NDAs during this period because they were deemed to be "old drugs" (i.e., not "new drugs"). Manufacturers of these products either concluded independently that they were GRAS because an NDA was in effect for a version manufactured by another company or obtained an opinion from FDA that their drugs were GRAS and thus not "new." Though the agency kept no record of these "old drug" opinions, it issued several thousand between 1942 and 1962. An original NDA'd drug product came to be referred to as the "pioneer," and all subsequent versions were described as generic or "me-too" drugs. By 1962, for every pioneer drug with an effective NDA, many additional me-too copies were on the market without an effective NDA.

The Drug Amendments of 1962 and the NAS Review

The 1962 Amendments required FDA, going forward, to allow post-amendment new drugs to enter the market only after the agency affirmatively determined that the NDA for the product demonstrated not only that the drug was safe, but also (by "substantial evidence") that it was effective. Furthermore, the Amendments required FDA to review all NDAs that had become effective during the previous 24 years to determine whether the products met the new effectiveness standard.[†] No one inside or outside the agency fully appreciated the consequences of this requirement when President Kennedy signed the Amendments into law on October 10, 1962.

Because the 1962 Amendments expanded the coverage of section 505, FDA immediately began to receive an increased volume of NDAs and investigational new drug (IND) submissions, which soon overwhelmed its review capacity. The agency at first did nothing to implement Congress's mandate to review NDAs that had previously become effective. In 1964, however, FDA issued regulations requiring the submission of reports on those pre-1962 drugs. 29 Fed. Reg. 7019 (May 28, 1964). The major pharmaceutical manufacturers promptly contested the regulations insofar as they might apply to drugs that the firms regarded as grandfathered or GRAS (and thus not "new drugs") under the 1962 Amendments. FDA stayed the reporting requirements pending the outcome of the manufacturers' court challenge. 29 Fed. Reg. 12872 (Sept. 12, 1964).

Although the companies provided some of the requested information in 1965, they argued that any review of pre-1962 NDAs should be performed by an independent scientific authority, not by FDA. In June 1966, FDA contracted with the National Academy of Sciences/National Research Council (NAS/NRC) to conduct such a review. Holders of NDAs were requested to submit information supporting the claims for their products. 31 Fed. Reg. 13014 (Oct. 6, 1966). The manufacturers thereafter withdrew their lawsuit.

Of the 9457 pre-1962 effective NDAs, about 400 were for human nonprescription drugs and the rest were evenly divided between human prescription drugs and animal drugs. Although the DESI program

---

[†] There actually was no direct requirement that FDA review all pre-1962 NDAs for effectiveness. Section 107(c)(2) of the statute provided that a pre-amendments drug for which an NDA was effective on the day prior to enactment of the new law was deemed to be "approved" by FDA under the revised law. Under Section 107(c)(3)(A) of the statute, the "deemed approved" status of a pre-1962 effective NDA remained in effect until FDA withdrew approval of the NDA. Thus, unless and until FDA reviewed a pre-amendments NDA and determined whether the drug was effective, the NDA was deemed approved in perpetuity. Accordingly, FDA had no choice but to begin a process of reviewing each pre-1962 NDA to determine whether it was shown to be an effective as well as a safe drug.

reviewed animal drugs too, this discussion will focus exclusively on its treatment of human drugs. FDA would ultimately deal with the application of the 1962 requirements to pre-1962 over-the-counter drugs (most of which were not "covered" by an effective NDA) primarily through a separate procedure, discussed later in this chapter, called the OTC Drug Review. *See infra* p. 973.

The NAS DESI review was performed by thirty panels of experts in specific drug categories. The NAS established guidelines delineating the functions of the panels and identifying the following sources of evidence for evaluation of effectiveness: (1) information available in the scientific literature; (2) information available from FDA, from the manufacturer, or other sources; and (3) the experience and informed judgment of the members of the panels. The NAS also established six ratings to serve as the basis for evaluating each claim made for a drug:

(1) *Effective.*

(2) *Probably effective.* Additional evidence required to be determined. Remedy could be additional research or modification of claims or both.

(3) *Possibly effective.* Little evidence of effectiveness, but possibility of additional evidence should not be ruled out.

(4) *Ineffective.* No acceptable evidence to support claim of effectiveness.

(5) *Effective, but* . . . Effective for claimed indication but not approved form of treatment because better, safer or more conveniently administered drugs available.

(6) *Ineffective as a fixed combination.* Combination drugs for which there is no substantial reason to believe that each ingredient adds to the effectiveness of the combination.

The NAS transmitted its first evaluation to FDA in October 1967, and continued to submit monthly reports until midsummer 1968. *See* NAS, DRUG EFFICACY STUDY: FINAL REPORT TO THE COMMISSIONER OF FOOD AND DRUGS (1969). The panels reviewed approximately 4000 different human drug formulations. The panels found roughly seven percent of the drugs ineffective for all claims, many effective for all claims, and the majority somewhere in between. The breakdown of ratings was as follows:

Rating	No. of Claims	% of Claims
Ineffective	2,442	14.7
Possibly effective	5,778	34.9
Probably effective	1,204	7.3
Effective	3,159	19.1
Effective, but	3,990	24.0
Total	16,573	100%

As the body with ultimate responsibility for determining drug effectiveness, FDA undertook to review the NAS findings. It refused, however, to release the panel reports before completing its own evaluations.

The Commencement of NDA–Withdrawal Proceedings

The agency's first implementation notice, covering all bioflavonoid drugs, was published in 1968. FDA announced that, based on NAS's finding that these drugs were ineffective, the agency intended—in conformance with the procedures of FD&C Act 502(e)—to publish a notice of opportunity for a hearing on a proposal to withdraw approval of all bioflavonoid NDAs. 33 Fed. Reg. 818 (Jan. 23, 1968). (FDA's subsequent withdrawal of approval for these drugs without a hearing was later overturned in *USV Pharmaceutical Corp. v. Secretary of HEW*, 466 F.2d 455 (D.C. Cir. 1972).) FDA next turned its attention to fixed dosage combination antibiotic products. In 33 Fed. Reg. 12904 (Dec. 24, 1968), the agency proposed to initiate proceedings to withdraw approval of Panalba, the first of many of these drugs that NAS had rated "ineffective as a fixed combination." In 34 Fed. Reg. 7687 (May 15, 1969), FDA withdrew approval of the drug and offered an opportunity for an administrative hearing, as required by FD&C Act 505(e). The manufacturer promptly obtained a judicial order enjoining FDA from withdrawing approval of the drug until after it had ruled on the firm's request for a formal evidentiary hearing. *Upjohn Co. v. Finch,* 303 F. Supp. 241 (W.D. Mich. 1969). One month later, another manufacturer obtained a similar injunction. *American Home Products Corp. v. Finch,* 303 F. Supp. 448 (D. Del. 1969).

Thus, by mid-1969, FDA confronted the prospect of having to conduct a long series of formal administrative hearings before it could implement the 1962 effectiveness standard. The agency therefore decided to adopt a new policy. In 34 Fed. Reg. 14598 (Sept. 19, 1969), FDA concluded that Upjohn had failed to show reasonable grounds for an evidentiary hearing and immediately withdrew approval of Panalba. Simultaneously, the agency published regulations embodying two features that became central in its subsequent efforts to implement the 1962 Amendments. First, the regulations defined the essential elements of an "adequate and well-controlled clinical investigation" necessary to constitute substantial evidence of effectiveness under sections 505(d) and (e). Second, they required the submission of at least two such studies to avoid summary judgment, *i.e.,* withdrawal of approval without a hearing. 34 Fed. Reg. 14596 (Sept. 19, 1969). In the initial court test of its new approach, FDA's order withdrawing approval of Panalba was sustained. *Upjohn Co. v. Finch,* 422 F.2d 944 (6th Cir. 1970).

Meanwhile, the major pharmaceutical manufacturers challenged FDA's regulations defining adequate and well-controlled clinical studies. In *Pharmaceutical Manufacturers Association v. Finch,* 307 F. Supp. 858 (D. Del. 1970), the District Court held that FDA had violated section 553 of the Administrative Procedure Act by failing to provide an opportunity to comment on the regulations. The agency thereupon reproposed the regulations and after receiving comments, promulgated them in final form, 35 Fed. Reg. 7250 (May 8, 1970), 21 C.F.R. 314.126 (excerpted *supra* p. 682). In *Pharmaceutical Manufacturers Association v. Richardson,* 318 F. Supp. 301 (D. Del. 1970), the regulations were upheld on their merits.

Armed with this decision, FDA began publishing hundreds of so-called DESI (Drug Effectiveness Study Implementation) notices. Orders withdrawing approval of combination antibiotic drugs were upheld in *Pfizer, Inc. v. Richardson,* 434 F.2d 536 (2d Cir. 1970) and *Ciba–Geigy Corp. v. Richardson,* 446 F.2d 466 (2d Cir. 1971). In two other cases, *American Cyanamid Co. v. Richardson,* 456 F.2d 509 (1st Cir. 1971), and *Bristol Laboratories v. Richardson,* 456 F.2d 563 (1st Cir. 1971), the companies withdrew their appeals after failing to obtain a judicial stay of the agency's withdrawal order.

Manufacturers Challenge DESI in Court

By the end of 1971, FDA had disposed of dozens of requests for hearings on the revocation of NDAs. In no instance had it found a manufacturer's supporting data sufficient to justify a hearing. One explanation for this striking consistency is that the agency's substantial evidence regulations embodied requirements for clinical investigations that few pre-1962 studies could meet. The drugs it initially selected for withdrawal—those evaluated by the NAS as "ineffective" (rather than "possibly effective")—also presented the easiest targets. But it was becoming obvious that the manufacturer of any drug would have to make an overwhelming showing to persuade FDA to expend the resources even one hearing would demand.

In 1972, three rulings by the U.S. Court of Appeals for the Fourth Circuit threatened to undermine FDA's basic approach. The agency sought and obtained certiorari in all three of these cases, and it also supported the successful petition for certiorari in a Second Circuit case in which the agency had prevailed. In June 1973, the Supreme Court issued a group of cases in which it sustained FDA on all of the legal issues involved. (These cases are known alternatively as the *"Hynson* quartet" or the *"Weinberger* trilogy," depending on how many are included.) In *Weinberger v. Hynson, Westcott & Dunning, Inc.,* 412 U.S. 609 (excerpted *infra* p. 848), the Court upheld FDA's "summary judgment" procedure, under which it denied hearings to companies that failed to proffer at least some evidence meeting the standard of "adequate and well-controlled investigations." In *Weinberger v. Bentex Pharmaceuticals, Inc.,* 412 U.S. 645 (1973) (excerpted *supra* p. 667), the Court held that FDA had primary jurisdiction to determine, with administrative finality, the "new drug" status of a product and thus that manufacturers could not raise the issue *de novo* in declaratory judgment suits in District Court and thus involve the agency in a deluge of litigation. In *U.S.V. Pharmaceutical Corp. v. Weinberger,* 412 U.S. 655, the Supreme Court decided that the NDAs of pre-1962 pioneer drugs also "covered" these products' pre-1962 "me-too" counterparts, thus excluding the me-too drugs from the grandfather clause in the 1962 Drug Amendments and subjecting them to the same requirement of proof of effectiveness as the pioneers. Finally, in *CIBA Corp. v. Weinberger,* 412 U.S. 640 (1973), the Court, in affirming the Second Circuit, echoed its holding on primary jurisdiction in *Weinberger.*

The Supreme Court decisions did not end litigation or resolve all of FDA's problems in implementing the 1962 Amendments. For example, the Supreme Court concluded, in *Weinberger v. Hynson,* that Hynson itself had presented sufficient evidence to justify a hearing. Several subsequent agency denials of hearings were upheld, but others were reversed with instructions to hold a hearing. *Cf., e.g., Agri-Tech, Inc. v. Richardson,* 482 F.2d 1148 (8th Cir. 1973); *with E.R. Squibb & Sons, Inc. v. Weinberger,* 483 F.2d 1382 (3d Cir. 1973).

Attempts to Speed Implementation

Even before the Supreme Court vindicated FDA's basic approach, some consumer groups had become impatient with FDA's slow progress in implementing the 1962 Amendments and sued to force prompter action. In *American Public Health Association v. Veneman,* 349 F. Supp. 1311 (D.D.C. 1972), the district court held FDA's performance unlawful in several respects and issued a detailed order requiring it to complete the DESI process within four years. This ruling imposed a new and, as it developed, unachievable demand on the agency, a demand ironically inflated by FDA's own decision to extend the NAS findings to all pre-1962 me-too drugs.

The Problem of "Me-Too" Drugs

FDA addressed the issue of pre-1962 "me-too" drugs for the first time in 1968. At a government-industry conference, the agency announced that it would apply NAS findings not only to the pioneer NDA drug, but also to all subsequently marketed me-too products. FDA realized, however, that the "old drug" opinions it had issued for me-too versions of NDA drugs before 1962 presented a major obstacle to its efforts to exert control over these copies. The agency therefore issued a statement of policy withdrawing all those opinions. 33 Fed. Reg. 7758 (May 28, 1968), codified at 21 C.F.R. 310.100. At the same time, it proposed to establish a new procedure for determining old drug status, under which many me-too products would presumably be held not to require NDAs. 33 Fed. Reg. 7762 (May 28, 1968).

FDA had difficulty developing a consistent approach to the "me-too" facet of the problem. The agency ruled in 1970 that me-too drugs that had been found to be effective under the DESI program could be the subject of an "abbreviated" NDA, which was required to contain bioavailability, labeling, and manufacturing information, but not data relating to safety and effectiveness. 35 Fed. Reg. 6574 (Apr. 24, 1970). This approach rested on the theory that the active ingredients in such products had become generally recognized as safe and effective and thus that FDA only had to require assurance that individual versions were properly labeled and manufactured.

The agency then issued a general notice establishing uniform conditions for the marketing of all drugs covered by a DESI determination that a drug was effective for one or more indications. 35 Fed. Reg. 11273 (July 14, 1970). According to these procedures, pre-1962 NDA holders covered by the DESI notice would be required, promptly after issuance of the notice, to submit supplemental NDAs containing only basic information and revised labeling. These supplemental applications would be automatically approved assuming they met the minimal requirements. *Id.* Meanwhile, "me-too" drugs covered by the notice would have to provide similar basic information, and generally also bioavailability data, in abbreviated NDAs. Although FDA did not explicitly state so, it informally embraced a policy of requiring only a submission—not an approval—of an abbreviated NDA for the marketing of a me-too product. *See* 40 Fed. Reg. 26142, 26145

(June 20, 1975) (retrospectively describing this policy). This approach applied regardless of whether the abbreviated NDA was for a me-too product introduced prior to the issuance of the relevant DESI notice or one marketed by a new manufacturer subsequent to the notice.

In 1972, the agency adopted a regulation explicitly stating that every DESI notice and notice of opportunity for hearing applied both to the pioneer drug and to all identical, related, and similar "me-too" drug products. 37 Fed. Reg. 23185 (Oct. 31, 1972), codified at 21 C.F.R. 310.6. Because it was having difficulty learning what me-too drugs were marketed, FDA persuaded Congress to enact the Drug Listing Act of 1972, 86 Stat. 559. This legislation, which amended section 510 of the FD&C Act, requires all manufacturers to submit lists of their drugs and thus provides the agency a complete inventory of all marketed products. *See infra* p. 834.

As the DESI program progressed, and more and more DESI notices were issued finding pre-1962 drugs to be effective, abbreviated NDAs began to swamp the agency. By June 1975, it had received over 6000 abbreviated NDAs, of which roughly 1100 had been acted on. Therefore, in 40 Fed. Reg. 26142 (June 20, 1975), FDA proposed comprehensive regulations governing the status of me-too drugs. In the June 1975 proposal, the agency stated that it would soon propose a new procedure for establishing "old drug monographs" for drugs that had been found safe and effective through the DESI program. More important, FDA announced that it would immediately embrace an "interim enforcement policy" under which any me-too version of a drug covered by a DESI notice could be lawfully marketed without even *submitting* an abbreviated NDA unless evidence existed to suggest it presented a bioavailability, bioequivalence, or special manufacturing problem. *See* Robert L. Spencer, *New Concepts in Abbreviated NDAs,* 30 FOOD DRUG COSM. L.J. 426 (1975).

FDA's 1970 policy of allowing the marketing of me-too drugs covered by a DESI "effective" determination even prior to approval of an abbreviated NDA—and, implicitly, also the agency's still more permissive 1975 policy—was challenged in *Hoffmann–LaRoche, Inc. v. Weinberger,* 425 F. Supp. 890 (D.D.C. 1975). The court ruled that FDA could not sanction the marketing of me-too drugs without an individualized determination of old drug status. The agency therefore withdrew its 1975 interim enforcement policy and also abandoned its 1970 approach of permitting the marketing of abbreviated NDA drugs prior to approval. 41 Fed. Reg. 9001 (Mar. 2, 1976).

In 1976, FDA announced the availability of a guideline explaining the agency's policy for implementing the *Hoffman–LaRoche* decision. This document, codified as Compliance Policy Guide 7132c.02, set forth the agency's process for bringing regulatory action against me-too drugs being marketed without an approved NDA or abbreviated NDA. 41 Fed. Reg. 41770 (Sept. 23, 1976). This enforcement policy was in turn challenged by the manufacturers of generic me-too drugs. Two courts of appeals split on the question whether a generic version of an approved pioneer drug was a "new drug" in the first place, and thus whether it required either an approved NDA or abbreviated NDA to be marketed. In *United States v. Generix Drug Corp.,* 460 U.S. 453 (1983) (excerpted *infra* p. 999), the Supreme Court resolved this conflict, holding that the

Act's definition of "drug" includes inactive as well as active ingredients and therefore that a generic version of a pioneer drug requires its own NDA or abbreviated NDA if it differs in any significant respect from the pioneer. The Supreme Court did not, however, reach the issue of what sorts of differences would be significant.

As the end of the 1970s approached, therefore, FDA had adopted the following enforcement policy with respect to generic drugs. First, the agency was prepared to approve an abbreviated NDA for any generic version of a pre-1962 pioneer drug that had been found effective under the DESI program. Second, it would initiate regulatory action against any generic drug on the market without an approved NDA or abbreviated NDA.

Paper NDAs and Abbreviated NDAs for Post-1962 Generics

A final facet of the agency's enforcement policy at the time was its decision to insist on a full NDA, rather than an abbreviated NDA, for a generic version of any post-1962 new drug. This reflected the requirements of data confidentiality. From 1938, FDA had consistently taken the position that each NDA was an individual license, and that the accompanying safety and effectiveness information constituted confidential commercial information that was not disclosable to the public or available for use by another applicant under section 301(j) of the FD&C Act, the Freedom of Information Act, or the Federal Trade Secrets Act, 18 U.S.C. 1905. The proposed Drug Regulation Reform Act, considered by Congress during 1977–1980, would have authorized abbreviated NDAs for post-1962 new drugs, but this measure was not enacted. The agency thus found itself caught between two important and longstanding policies. It required an NDA or abbreviated NDA for every prescription drug on the market. But it could not approve abbreviated NDAs for post-1962 new drugs without violating the confidentiality provisions of the law.

In an attempt to break the impasse, the agency announced in July 1978 that it would approve "paper" NDAs for generic copies of pioneer new drugs, whether pre-1962 or post-1962, based upon *published* scientific data concerning the pioneer products' safety and effectiveness. This new policy was upheld in the face of claims that it had not been adopted through APA informal rulemaking. *Burroughs Wellcome Co. v. Schweiker,* 649 F.2d 221 (4th Cir. 1981). In *Upjohn Manufacturing Co. v. Schweiker,* 681 F.2d 480 (6th Cir. 1982), the Court of Appeals sustained the policy's application to a specific drug product. Despite these victories, FDA recognized that its paper NDA policy could not apply to more than a small fraction of the ever-increasing number of post-1962 new drugs. For most post-1962 new drugs, the published literature contained inadequate data on animal toxicity and human clinical trials to justify approval of a paper NDA.

After the collapse of efforts in Congress to amend the new drug provisions of the FD&C Act in the late 1970s, FDA, in 1983, began to work on a proposed regulation to establish the basis for some form of abbreviated NDA procedure for post-1962 new drugs. When this proposal did not surface quickly, the National Association of Pharmaceutical Manufacturers, an association of generic drug manufacturers, brought suit seeking a declaratory judgment that the agency could lawfully approve abbreviated NDAs for post-1962 new drugs without any change to the FD&C Act.

Meanwhile, makers of innovative new drugs had become increasingly concerned about the gradual shrinkage of the effective patent life for pioneer products after they completed the rigorous development and testing program and emerged from the NDA approval process. In 1984, Representative Henry Waxman introduced a proposal that combined patent term restoration, favored by pioneer manufacturers, with authority for FDA to approve abbreviated NDAs (ANDAs) for post-1962 new drugs, favored by the generic industry. This legislation was ultimately enacted as the Drug Price Competition and Patent Term Restoration Act of 1984, 98 Stat. 1585. This statute, commonly referred to as "Hatch–Waxman," finally broke the two-decade-old impasse over the marketing of generic versions of post-1962 drugs. It will be examined in detail later in this chapter. *Infra* p. 1000.

The Elusive Goal of DESI Completion

Throughout these events, FDA continued, albeit in desultory fashion, to press ahead with implementation of the DESI Review. Having missed the original four-year deadline imposed by the court in *American Public Health Association v. Veneman,* 349 F. Supp. 1311 (D.D.C. 1972), *infra* p. 780, the agency entered into an agreement with the plaintiffs establishing a new timetable. *American Public Health Association v. Harris,* Food Drug Cosm. L. Rep. (CCH) ¶ 38,068 (D.D.C. 1980). The semiannual reports that FDA submitted to the district court through 1989, when the case was formally closed, confirmed that the agency continued to be in violation of the new agreement, as well as the court's 1972 order. Today, 50 years after the DESI process began, it still has not yet been fully implemented. About 20 DESI matters remain unfinished.

In response to court orders in specific cases, and on its own initiative in others, FDA has held a number of hearings on the withdrawal of approval of pre-1962 NDAs. *See, e.g.,* 49 Fed. Reg. 50788 (Dec. 31, 1984) (Mepergan Fortis); 51 Fed. Reg. 20551 (June 5, 1986) (Deprol). The process of withdrawing approval of a pre-1962 NDA can be protracted, to put it mildly. For example, in 1989, an Administrative Law Judge (ALJ) upheld the FDA's withdrawal of approvals of NDAs and abbreviated NDAs for pentaerythritol tetranitrate, a process commenced in 1972. FDC L. Rep. ¶ 38,120 (May 10, 1989). The appeal to the Commissioner has not yet been acted upon, however, and the drug thus remains on the market. In no instance has a manufacturer challenging the withdrawal of an NDA prevailed before an ALJ or the Commissioner. In the few cases appealed to the courts, the Commissioner's rulings have been sustained. *Warner–Lambert Co. v. Heckler,* 787 F.2d 147 (3d Cir. 1986) (oral proteolytic enzymes); *E.R. Squibb and Sons, Inc. v. Bowen,* 870 F.2d 678 (D.C. Cir. 1989) (mysteclin).

Of course, the new drug requirements enacted in the Drug Amendments of 1962 also apply to post-1962 drugs. Indeed, all new prescription entities introduced since 1962 have been required to go through the new drug approval process. In this respect, the coverage of the law has ceased to be an important issue. Nor, typically, has FDA, with respect to post-1962 drugs, confronted claims to procedural rights—such as demands for hearings—like those advanced against its implementation of the effectiveness standard with respect to pre-1962 drugs. The controversial issues have involved the agency's internal processes for evaluating and acting on NDAs and the impact of those requirements on the availability of drugs and the health of patients.

NOTE

Federal Reimbursement for Less-Than-Effective Drugs. Congress included in the Omnibus Budget Reconciliation Act of 1981, 95 Stat. 357, 787, an amendment to the Social Security Act prohibiting the expenditure of federal funds under Medicare and Medicaid for Pre-1962 drugs for which FDA has published a notice of opportunity for hearing to withdraw approval of the NDA. That provision, codified at 42 U.S.C. 1395y(c), was implemented by HCFA in 46 Fed. Reg. 48550 (Oct. 1, 1981), 46 Fed. Reg. 51646 (Oct. 21, 1981), 46 Fed. Reg. 53664, 54304 (Oct. 30, 1981), codified at 42 C.F.R. 410.29.

5. NON-DESI UNAPPROVED NEW DRUGS

Even though FDA successfully took the position that all related, similar, and identical me-too drugs were also automatically covered by the DESI Review of a pre-1962 pioneer NDA, there were six categories of drug products remaining on the market without an NDA that never went through the DESI Review: (1) drugs grandfathered under the 1938 grandfather clause, (2) drugs grandfathered under the 1962 grandfather clause, (3) drugs marketed prior to 1962 on the basis of an FDA determination that they were "old drugs," (4) drugs marketed prior to 1962 on the manufacturer's determination that they were "old drugs," (5) drugs marketed subsequent to 1962 on the manufacturer's determination that they were "old drugs," and (6) drugs marketed subsequent to 1962 on the manufacturer's determination that they were the same or closely related to drugs in any of the prior categories. All of these drugs, collectively, are known as non-DESI unapproved new drugs. FDA has always known of their existence, but the agency was so overwhelmed by the DESI Review and other priorities that it had never had an opportunity or the resources necessary to address them on a systematic basis. A niche drug industry thus continued (and still continues) to manufacture these products.

In CPG 7132c.02 (1976), FDA stated that it would systematically handle each one of these non-DESI, unapproved new drugs on a priority basis. The CPG was expanded and reissued in 1981, revised several additional times, and codified as section 440.100 of the FDA Compliance Policy Guides.

Ever since the publication of the April 1981 version of CPG 7132c.02, FDA has clearly stated an enforcement position that (1) all of these non-DESI unapproved new drugs are in fact new drugs for which FDA can require an NDA or force the products off the market at any time, (2) an unapproved non-DESI drug product first marketed prior to the Drug Amendments of 1962 and still on the market may be copied by any competitor, and will be subject to the same requirements imposed on the original drug product, (3) each of these products may remain on the market until FDA makes a final determination relating to the class of drugs under which the product falls, and (4) if any manufacturer obtains some form of an NDA for one of these products, FDA will promptly remove all other products in that category from the market. Although the agency hoped that the fourth aspect of this approach would provide an incentive for the manufacturers of these products to submit NDAs, no such application was submitted until the early 2000s.

In early 1984, prescription drugs that were on the market despite never having been the subject of any form of NDA became a high priority for FDA. E–Ferol, an intravenous vitamin E product marketed without an NDA produced serious adverse reactions that required a nationwide recall. In response to this incident, and the subsequent congressional investigation, the agency gathered information about marketed unapproved drugs. Using information obtained under the Drug Listing Act, FDA estimated that there were approximately 5000 prescription drugs marketed without an approved NDA of any kind. Some 1800 of these products were identical or similar to drugs reviewed by NAS under the DESI program, but 2400 had avoided DESI review altogether. The remainder fell into a variety of additional categories. Lacking the resources to require an NDA for all of these drugs, FDA promulgated a regulation requiring the maintenance of records and submission of reports of adverse drug reactions for all prescription drugs marketed without approved NDAs. 51 Fed. Reg. 24476 (July 3, 1986), codified at 21 C.F.R. 310.305.

A few non-DESI unapproved new drugs were sufficiently important to prompt FDA to institute regulatory action to require NDAs. Three prominent examples are Digoxin, 39 Fed. Reg. 2491 (Jan. 22, 1974), 62 Fed. Reg. 43535 (Aug. 14, 1997); levothyroxine, 62 Fed. Reg. 43535 (Aug. 14, 1997); and exocrine pancreatic insufficiency products, 69 Fed. Reg. 23410 (Apr. 28, 2004). When FDA determined in its final OTC monograph for nonprescription wart remover drug products that no existing products were effective, the agency pulled all the prescription non-DESI unapproved new drugs from the market as well. 55 Fed. Reg. 33246 (Aug. 14, 1990). FDA has proposed to take the same regulatory action for all nonprescription and prescription skin bleaching drug products. 71 Fed. Reg. 51146 (Aug. 29, 2006). And the agency has opportunistically removed individual non-DESI unapproved new drugs from the market when taking enforcement action against them for other reasons, even while leaving equally illegal competitive products alone. *United States v. Sage Pharmaceuticals, Inc.*, 210 F.3d 475 (5th Cir. 2000). But no program has been established by FDA to review all of the non-DESI unapproved new drugs on a comprehensive or systematic basis.

In 2002, FDA finally received an NDA for a non-DESI unapproved new drug—specifically, a section 505(b)(2) NDA for an extended release guaifenesin product. The company promptly requested FDA to take all of the other unapproved competitive products off the market, in accordance with the agency policy established in CPG 7132c.08. In October 2002, FDA issued approximately 66 warning letters to implement this policy, prompting a citizen petition requesting that the agency reopen the DESI program to review all non-DESI unapproved new drugs on a systematic basis. FDA Docket No. 02P–0483 (Nov. 12, 2002). In February 2003, FDA issued a second letter to the 66 recipients of the warning letters, providing a final date of November 30, 2003, by which all of the products had to be completely removed from the market.

The companies who received these 66 warning letters lobbied Congress to pass legislation barring FDA from taking enforcement action against them. They were not successful in this effort, but they did succeed in having a paragraph inserted in the House and Senate Reports accompanying the FDA appropriations legislation for fiscal year 2004. That paragraph requested a report from FDA regarding the feasibility and cost of the type of systematic review of non-DESI unapproved drugs that the citizen petition requested. H.R. Rep. 108–193, 108th Cong., 1st Sess. 86 (2003); S. Rep. No. 108–107, 108th Cong., 1st Sess. 157 (2003). FDA responded with a report dated July 2004 concluding that the approach advocated by the citizen petition would be "scientifically infeasible . . . and the costs would be prohibitive." The Senate Appropriations Committee Reports for 2005 and 2006 therefore simply directed FDA to devise an alternative approach. S. Rep. No. 109–92, 109th Cong., 1st Sess. 155 (2005); S. Rep. No. 109–266, 109th Cong., 2d Sess. 146 (2006).

In June 2006, FDA designated this mandated effort as the Unapproved Drugs Initiative. After an article stated that almost two percent of prescriptions, or as many as 73 million, were for non-DESI unapproved new drugs, and two members of Congress sent letters to FDA demanding detailed information on this category of products, FDA announced a public workshop on the matter. *See* Justin Blum, *Drugs Slip Through FDA Cracks, Sell Unapproved by the Millions*, BLOOMBERG NEWS (Oct. 11, 2006); letters from Senator Charles E. Grassley & Representative Edward J. Markey to Andrew C. von Eschenbach, FDA Acting Commissioner (Oct. 11, 2006); 71 Fed. Reg. 64284 (Nov. 1, 2006) (announcing Jan. 2007 workshop).

Following the FDA workshop, FDA reissued Compliance Policy Guide Section 440.100 in June 2006 and resumed its enforcement work. The agency released this document as part of a new initiative against the "several thousand drug products," both prescription and OTC, that are "marketed illegally without required FDA approval." 71 Fed. Reg. 33466, 33467 (June 9, 2006) (announcing availability of the guidance). Some of the drugs it has targeted in this initiative are carbinoxamine, quinine, ergotamine, trimethobenzamide, hydrocodone, colchicine, pilocarpine, codeine, and morphine. When FDA realized that its Compliance Policy Guide was still advising companies that they could legally market new copies of existing non-DESI unapproved drugs, it revised the CPG and reissued it on September 19, 2011. The revised GPG states that no new versions of existing non-DESI unapproved new drugs may be marketed after that date. *See* GUIDANCE FOR FDA STAFF AND INDUSTRY: MARKETED UNAPPROVED DRUGS—COMPLIANCE POLICY GUIDE (SEPT. 2011).

NOTES

1. *Increase in Non-DESI Unapproved New Drugs.* Because FDA has not systematically enforced the FD&C Act with respect to non-DESI unapproved new drugs, the number of these products has grown from an estimated 2400 in 1984 to about 12,000–16,000 at the present. These drugs have fueled the growth of the niche drug industry in the United States.

2. *Exocrine Pancreatic Insufficiency Drugs.* In 1995, when FDA issued its final determination that all nonprescription exocrine pancreatic insufficiency drugs have not been determined to be safe and effective, it stated that similar non-DESI unapproved new drug products marketed by prescription should also have an approved NDA and promised to address the subject further in a future Federal Register notice. It was ten years before FDA returned to this matter and required NDAs for the prescription products. 69 Fed. Reg. 23410 (Apr. 28, 2004). Manufacturers were given four years to obtain an approved NDA.

3. *Hormone Drugs.* In 68 Fed. Reg. 17953 (Apr. 14, 2003), FDA published a notice of opportunity for hearing on the removal of estrogen-androgen combination drugs and other non-DESI unapproved hormone drugs remaining on the market without an NDA. No further action has been taken on this matter.

4. *Lanham Act Cases.* It has become common for generic drug companies to market "generic" versions of "branded" non-DESI unapproved new drugs, because at least until FDA revised the CPG in 2011, there was no need to obtain FDA approval of an abbreviated NDA, and the cost of knocking off the "branded" non-DESI unapproved new drug was thus trivial. Not surprisingly, the "generic" version is promoted as equivalent to the "branded" drug and soon cannibalizes its market. In order to preserve its market, the "branded" version of the drug is forced to initiate protracted litigation under the Lanham Act, with highly unpredictable results. *See, e.g., Florida Breckenridge, Inc. v. Solvay Pharmaceuticals,* 174 F.3d 1227 (11th Cir. 1999). In *Florida Breckenridge,* a case involving two non-DESI unapproved new drugs, the court of appeals criticized both parties for failing to inform the district court that neither drug was the subject of an approved NDA. *Id.*

5. *FD&C Act Preemption.* In *Autin v. Solvay Pharmaceuticals, Inc.,* 2006 WL 889423 (W.D. Tenn. 2006), the District Court dismissed a consumer suit alleging that the company's non-DESI unapproved new drug, Estratest, was being illegally marketed, on the ground that the FD&C Act preempted the suit.

6. *Levothyroxine.* In 62 Fed. Reg. 43535 (Aug. 14, 1997), FDA announced that NDAs would be required for all currently marketed orally administered levothyroxine sodium drug products. The original deadline of August 14, 2000 was extended by a year in 65 Fed. Reg. 24488 (Apr. 26, 2000). Knoll, the original manufacturer of the leading levothyroxine drug, Synthroid, and Abbott Laboratories, the company that purchased Knoll, missed the original 2000 deadline for submitting an NDA. On July 12, 2001 FDA ordered Abbott to cut its distribution of Synthroid pills to wholesalers as a novel penalty for missing the deadline.

Following approval of an NDA for one levothyroxine product, Unithroid, FDA posted on its website information from the NDA that constituted trade secrets. Thereafter, FDA again postponed the NDA deadline for an additional two years. 66 Fed. Reg. 36794 (July 13, 2001). The manufacturer of Unithroid, Jerome Stevens Pharmaceuticals, brought suit against FDA challenging the further delay and seeking damages for disclosure of trade secrets. In *Jerome Stevens Pharmaceuticals, Inc. v. FDA*, 402 F.3d 1249 (D.C. Cir. 2005), the Court of Appeals affirmed the District Court's dismissal of the count relating to FDA's continuing extension of time for competitors to submit NDAs, but it reversed the dismissal of the counts relating to unlawful disclosure of the company's trade secrets. The case was settled in 2008. Stipulation for Compromise Settlement and Release of FTCA Claims Pursuant to 28 U.S.C. 2677 and APA Claims, Jerome Stevens Pharmaceuticals, Inc. v. FDA, No. 102–CV–01939 (D.D.C. Sept. 12, 2008), 2008 WL 6982535.

7. *Digoxin.* When Bertek Pharmaceutical obtained an approved NDA for digoxin and FDA failed to remove competitive unapproved digoxin products from the market, the company sued the agency, requesting a declaratory judgment and injunctive relief. The parties agreed to a consent decree in the form of a declaratory judgment that FDA would take action against the unapproved products "within a reasonable time." *Bertek Pharmaceuticals Inc. v. Henney*, Civ. No. 1:00CV02393 (D.D.C. Oct. 4, 2000).

8. *Criteria for NDAs.* In letters from CDER Director Steven Galson to Peter Barton Hutt dated May 25, 2005 and December 23, 2005, FDA promised not to target a firm or a marketed non-DESI unapproved drug for enforcement action simply because the firm meets with FDA to discuss an NDA for the product. The agency expressed a flexible procedure to discuss NDAs for these products.

6. SPECIAL CATEGORIES OF DRUGS

a. RADIOPHARMACEUTICAL DRUGS

Radiopharmaceutical drugs receive distinctive regulatory treatment. Few of these drugs have been the subject of NDAs, and it is not feasible to regulate all radioactive-tagged drugs through the new drug process. FDA has established an old drug monograph approach, 21 C.F.R. 310.503 & Part 361, in cooperation with the Nuclear Regulatory Commission (NRC). The NRC regulations governing licensing of individuals and institutions for medical use of radioactive material are codified in 10 C.F.R. Part 35. The NRC has established training and experience criteria for physicians who request authorization to engage in nuclear medicine.

When FDA sought to increase its regulation of one form of radiopharmaceutical product, positron emission tomography (PET), in response to the forthcoming INSTITUTE OF MEDICINE, RADIATION IN MEDICINE: A NEED FOR REGULATORY REFORM (1996), it met with strong opposition from the nuclear medicine industry.

Syncor International Corporation v. Shalala

127 F.3d 90 (D.C. Cir. 1997).

■ SILBERMAN, CIRCUIT JUDGE: . . .

Positron emission tomography (PET) is a diagnostic imaging method that uses a subset of radioactive pharmaceuticals, called PET drugs, to determine biochemistry, physiology, anatomy, and pathology within various body organs and tissues by measuring the concentration of radioactivity in a targeted area of the body. The active component of PET drugs is a positron-emitting isotope. This component has a short half-life, so the drug remains effective for only brief periods of time. As a consequence, PET drugs are not manufactured by pharmaceutical companies; instead, they are prepared by physicians and pharmacists operating accelerators in facilities known as nuclear pharmacies, which most often are part of major teaching hospitals or their adjacent universities, and always are located very near to the place where the PET drug will be administered to patients. These nuclear pharmacists compound the isotope with a chemical solution called a substrate. The substrate is used to carry the isotope to the targeted organ or tissue, and the precise solution used depends on the targeted area. For example, a nuclear pharmacist might combine an isotope with a glucose substrate if the brain was being targeted, since the brain is an area of high glucose uptake. In part for this reason, PET drugs are compounded pursuant to a prescription.

On February 25, 1995, FDA announced that PET radiopharmaceuticals "should be regulated" under the drug provisions of the Federal Food, Drug, and Cosmetic Act. In this publication, labeled a "Notice," and referred to alternatively in its text as "guidance" and a "policy statement," FDA indicated that it would require PET "radiopharmaceutical manufacturers" to comply with the adulteration provision of § 501(a)(2)(B) of the Act (drugs are considered adulterated unless manufactured in conformance with current good manufacturing practices); the misbranding provision of § 502 of the Act (drugs are considered misbranded if the product labeling is false or misleading, if the drug is dangerous to health when used as suggested in the labeling, or if the labeling fails to include certain required information); the new drug provision of § 505 of the Act (new drugs must be the subject of approved new drug applications or abbreviated new drug applications before marketing); and the registration and listing provisions of § 510 of the Act (drug establishment must register with FDA, and file a list of all drugs that it makes or processes). *See* Regulation of Positron Emission Tomography Radiopharmaceutical Drug Products; Guidance; Public Workshop, 60 Fed. Reg. 10594, 10595 (1995).

FDA indicated that its 1995 publication was to supersede its prior 1984 publication—which had been directed at all nuclear pharmacies, not just those compounding PET radiopharmaceuticals—entitled "Nuclear Pharmacy Guideline; Criteria for Determining When to Register as a Drug Establishment." The 1984 Guideline had unequivocally stated that nuclear pharmacists who operated an accelerator to produce radioactive drugs to be dispensed under a prescription—which precisely describes the process by which nuclear pharmacies compound PET radiopharmaceuticals—were not required to register under § 510 of the Act. The Guideline also indicated that if a nuclear pharmacist was not required to register, that other of the Act's requirements, including the new drug provision and compliance with current good manufacturing practices, would not apply.

Syncor filed suit in the district court challenging FDA's 1995 publication. Syncor brought three claims, alleging that: (1) FDA lacked jurisdiction over PET drugs under the new drug provision of § 505 of the Act, which requires premarket approval for drugs introduced or delivered for introduction into interstate commerce, because PET drugs do not move in interstate commerce; (2) FDA violated the Tenth Amendment to the United States Constitution by regulating pharmacies in the absence of clear congressional authorization to do so, since pharmacy is an area traditionally reserved for state regulation; and (3) FDA violated the Administrative Procedure Act's requirement that an agency engaged in rulemaking give notice of its proposed rulemaking to the public and "give interested persons an opportunity to participate in the rule making through submission of written data, views, or arguments." The district judge granted summary judgment in FDA's favor on all three claims. We consider the APA claim first since if notice and comment are required we think it prudent to defer deciding the other two issues which presumably would be explored in a future rulemaking. . . .

The APA exempts from notice and comment interpretative rules or general statements of policy. 5 U.S.C. § 553(b)(3)(A). . . .

We have long recognized that it is quite difficult to distinguish between substantive and interpretative rules. . . . An agency policy statement does not seek to impose or elaborate or interpret a legal norm. It merely represents an agency position with respect to how it will treat—typically enforce—the governing legal norm. By issuing a policy statement, an agency simply lets the public know its current enforcement or adjudicatory approach. The agency retains the discretion and the authority to change its position—even abruptly—in any specific case because a change in its policy does not affect the legal norm. We thus have said that policy statements are binding on neither the public nor the agency. The primary distinction between a substantive rule—really any rule—and a general statement of policy, then, turns on whether an agency intends to bind itself to a particular legal position.

An interpretative rule, on the other hand, typically reflects an agency's construction of a statute that has been entrusted to the agency to administer. The legal norm is one that Congress has devised; the agency does not purport to modify that norm, in other words, to engage in lawmaking. . . .

A substantive rule has characteristics of both the policy statement and the interpretative rule; it is certainly in part an exercise of policy, and it is a rule. But the crucial distinction between it and the other two techniques is that a substantive rule modifies or adds to a legal norm based on the agency's own authority. That authority flows from a congressional delegation to promulgate substantive rules, to engage in supplementary lawmaking. And, it is because the agency is engaged in lawmaking that the APA requires it to comply with notice and comment.

It is apparent to us, in light of the foregoing discussion, that FDA's 1995 publication is not an interpretative rule. It does not purport to construe any language in a relevant statute or regulation; it does not interpret anything. Instead, FDA's rule uses wording consistent only with the invocation of its general rulemaking authority to extend its regulatory reach. . . .

The reasons FDA has advanced for its rule—advancement in PET technology, the expansion of procedures in which PET is used, and the unique nature of PET radiopharmaceuticals—are exactly the sorts of changes in fact and circumstance which notice and comment rulemaking is meant to inform. . . .

Accordingly, we reverse and remand to the district court with instructions to enter summary judgment in Syncor's favor, and to vacate FDA's rule as not in accordance with law. The district court should also dismiss Syncor's substantive claims without prejudice.

NOTES

1. *Congressional Direction.* Section 121 of the FDA Modernization Act of 1997, 111 Stat. 2296, 2320, added section 201(ii) to the FD&C Act to define the term "compounded positron emission tomography drug" and added section 501(a)(1)(C) to authorize FDA to promulgate GMP requirements for these drugs. Congress explicitly revoked the notices and regulations that were the subject of the litigation. Congress also directed the agency to adopt appropriate procedures for the approval of PET drugs under section 505 of the FD&C Act, taking into account the "special characteristics of positron emission tomography drugs and the special techniques and processes required to produce these drugs."

2. *Implementation.* FDA promulgated final GMP regulations for PET drug products in December 2009, 21 C.F.R. Part 212. Under section 121 of the FDA Modernization Act of 1997, an NDA or abbreviated NDA must be submitted to FDA by December 2011 for any PET drug marketed for clinical use in the United States, and must be approved by December 2015. *See* FDA GUIDANCE ON FDA OVERSIGHT OF PET DRUG PRODUCTS: QUESTIONS AND ANSWERS (Dec. 2012).

b. INSULIN AND ANTIBIOTIC DRUGS

The 1938 Act contained no provisions relating specifically to insulin or antibiotic drugs. Congress added section 506 to provide for the individual batch certification of insulin, 55 Stat. 851 (1941), and section 507 to provide for certification of the first antibiotic drug, penicillin, 59 Stat. 463 (1945). Section 507 was later amended to include streptomycin in 61 Stat. 11 (1947), aureomycin, chloramphenicol, and bacitracin in 63 Stat. 409 (1949), and to substitute chlortetracycline for aureomycin in 67 Stat. 389 (1953). The Drug Amendments of 1962, 76 Stat. 780, 785 amended section 507 to include all antibiotic drugs.

Because antibiotics are produced from microorganisms, individual batch certification was thought necessary to assure the identity, and thus the safety and effectiveness, of these drugs. Antibiotic drugs were also subject to the same IND and NDA requirements as other new drugs under 21 C.F.R. Parts 312 and 314. Because of the high level of manufacturer compliance with antibiotic standards, in 1982 FDA exempted all classes of antibiotic drugs from batch certification. Ever since, antibiotic new drugs have been regulated on the same terms as non-antibiotic new drugs.

Recognizing that there was no longer a reason to distinguish insulin or antibiotics from other new drugs, Congress repealed sections 506 and 507 in the FDA Modernization Act of 1997, 111 Stat 2296, 2325. As a result, these drugs are now regulated as new drugs, except that Congress specifically provided that they could continue to be exported solely under the requirements of Section 801(e)(1). FDA is presently determining what standards should be applied for abbreviated NDAs for insulin, a naturally derived protein.

NOTES

1. *Regional Compounding.* In *United States v. Baxter Healthcare Corp.*, 901 F.2d 1401 (7th Cir. 1990), the courts reviewed antibiotic manufacturers' practice of obtaining an approved NDA for antibiotics in powder and liquid form and then reconstituting, repackaging, and freezing those drugs in final dosage form at regional compounding facilities for distribution to hospitals. Both courts upheld the FDA position that an NDA was needed for the final products produced at the regional compounding facilities. Under these decisions, all preparation of final dosage form antibiotics must be undertaken by the hospitals.

2. *Antibiotic Resistance.* As a result of antibiotic overuse and improper use, bacteria can develop resistance to existing antibiotic drugs, making infections difficult if not impossible to treat. As addressed in Chapter 8, the primary focus of regulation to limit antibiotic use has been the veterinary arena. Some contend that the use of antibiotics in livestock is the primary promoter of antibiotic resistance. Furthermore, FDA has more authority to limit off-label uses of animal drugs than of human drugs. *See infra* p. 1071.

3. *Promoting Antibiotic Development.* Legislative and other solutions have been proposed to stimulate research and development on new antibiotic drugs that would help address the antibiotic resistance problem. In 2012, Congress responded to the need for developing new antibiotics by enacting the Generating Antibiotic Incentives Now (GAIN) Act as part of the FDA Safety and Innovation Act, 126 Stat. 1077. Under the GAIN Act, FDA is required to create a list of "qualifying pathogens." Any antibacterial or antifungal drug approved by FDA that the agency designates as a "qualified infectious disease product" because it treats serious infections caused by a qualifying pathogen or drug resistant pathogen receives another five years of market exclusivity added on to the end of the current five years, for a total of ten years of market exclusivity.

c. MEDICAL GAS

Until Congress enacted a Medical Gas Product Regulation section as part of the FDA Safety and Innovation Act of 2012, 126 Stat. 1108, FDA took the position that all medical gases were unapproved new drugs that must be handled under the Unapproved Drugs Initiative announced by FDA in June 2006. The industry, conversely, took the position that medical gases are grandfathered or are GRAS and GRAE and thus are not new drugs. The new provisions, enacted as sections 575–577 of the FD&C Act, resolve the matter without invoking the new drug authorities of the Act.

The new provisions list "designated medical gases" and "approved uses" for each listed medical gas. FDA may expand each list. A manufacturer must file with FDA a simple Request for Certification to produce a designated gas that meets the standards of an official compendium for an approved use. The certification is deemed to be granted unless FDA, within 60 days, determines that the gas is not a designated gas, or the request is inadequate, or denial is necessary to protect the public health. No user fees are imposed. A certification covers the manufacturer of the gas and all people who subsequently distribute and use it for one of the listed approved uses. In effect, a certification substitutes for an approved NDA. *See* FDA, GUIDANCE FOR INDUSTRY ON CERTIFICATION PROCESS FOR DESIGNATED MEDICAL GASES (Dec. 2012).

7. THE PRACTICE OF PHARMACY

Long before there were independent drug manufacturers, apothecaries, now known as pharmacists, compounded drugs both for their own patients and in response to prescriptions of physicians. Companies engaged in the manufacture and distribution of drugs did not emerge in the United States until the latter half of the 19th century. Today, the vast majority of prescription drugs are produced in finished form by drug manufacturers and only dispensed by pharmacists, but the compounding of prescription drugs still occupies a distinctive place under the FD&C Act.

Nothing in the FD&C Act of 1938 excluded pharmacy compounding from the requirements of the statute. In the Act as amended, the only pertinent provisions from which some pharmacies are expressly exempted are the establishment registration section and one sentence of the establishment inspection provisions. FD&C Act 510(g)(1), 704(a)(2)(A). Nonetheless, the regulation of traditional pharmacy compounding—that is, compounding performed to fill a prescription for a specific patient—has always been almost exclusively the domain of the states. When FDA has exercised authority over compounding, it has almost always been in larger operations that function more like drug manufacturers. Indeed, the line between traditional compounders, on the one hand, and commercial scale compounders that operate more like manufacturers, on the other, is built into the two exceptions mentioned above. They each apply only to

> pharmacies which maintain establishments in conformance with any applicable laws regulating the practice of pharmacy and which are regularly engaged in dispensing prescription drugs . . . upon

prescriptions of practitioners licensed to administer such drugs . . . to patients under the care of such practitioners in the course of their professional practice, and which do not manufacture, prepare, propagate, compound, or process drugs . . . for sale other than in the regular course of their business of dispensing or selling drugs . . . at retail.

FD&C Act 501(g)(1), 704(a)(2)(A).

In 1992, concerned that some rogue pharmacies were undertaking commercial-scale compounding, FDA issued Compliance Policy Guide No. 7132.16 (Mar. 16, 1992), which stated that the agency would exercise its enforcement discretion only with regard to traditional compounders. Nevertheless, even since then, the agency has asserted its authority over large-scale compounders only sporadically. One action it did take was a 2002 inspection of the New England Compounding Center (NECC) in Framingham, Massachusetts, following adverse events reports of patients experiencing meningitis-like symptoms after receiving injections of a drug produced by the facility. Further complaints about the company's products and practices followed, as did additional inspections, in 2002 and 2004. Pursuant to the 2004 inspection, FDA issued a warning letter to NECC in 2006. The letter stated, among other things, that the company was engaging in activities outside the scope of traditional pharmacy compounding by (among other actions) compounding copies of commercially available drugs and distributing drugs without patient-specific prescriptions. Finally, in 2012, NECC caused a full-scale public health disaster, which compelled FDA publicly to address the scope of its power over compounding.

FDA's Oversight of NECC and Ameridose: A History of Missed Opportunities

Preliminary Majority Staff Report, Comm. on Energy & Commerce, U.S. House of Rep.
113th Cong., Apr. 16, 2013.

In the summer and fall of 2012, a Massachusetts company, the New England Compounding Center (NECC), shipped over 17,000 vials of an injectable steroid solution from three contaminated lots to healthcare facilities in 23 states. The sterility of this drug product is critical. To relieve chronic pain, it is often injected into patients' spinal columns. After receiving injections of NECC's contaminated steroid, over 50 people have died from complications associated with fungal meningitis and almost 700 others have been stricken with meningitis or other persistent fungal infections. This outbreak ranks as one of the worst public health crises associated with contaminated drugs in the history of the United States, and exposed a fundamental failure in drug safety oversight.

. . . . On November 14, 2012, the Subcommittee on Oversight and Investigations held a hearing to examine the meningitis outbreak and determine whether it could have been prevented. The Subcommittee . . . invited FDA Commissioner Margaret Hamburg, M.D. . . . to testify about [her agency's] oversight of NECC. . . .

During the Commissioner's testimony . . . and in numerous statements made by her and other FDA officials since, FDA has maintained that uncertainty over its authority prevented the agency from pursuing enforcement actions against companies involved in compounding. For example, in her written statement for the Subcommittee's hearing on November 14, the Commissioner asserted that "FDA's ability to take action against compounding that exceeds the bounds of traditional pharmacy compounding and poses risks to patients has been hampered by gaps and ambiguities in the law." She repeatedly mentioned that FDA's authority over compounding pharmacies—even when such entities were engaged in activities that closely resembled those of a drug manufacturer—was questionable. The Commissioner stated . . . that FDA has "ambiguous, fragmented, unclear, and contested authorities in this particular realm of pharmacy and drug manufacturing practice. . . ." Citing these issues as impediments to FDA's ability to act in the face of mounting patient safety and public health concerns associated with NECC and Ameridose, the Commissioner proposed a new framework for regulating drug compounding operations and asked Congress for additional "authorities to support this new regulatory paradigm."

FDA has long been steadfast in its assertions of authority over drug manufacturing being conducted under the guise of pharmacy compounding. . . . That being said, internal FDA documents do show that the agency has been grappling with its authority over compounding for decades and that this debate came to a head in early 2009, after two different Circuit Courts of Appeals had issued conflicting opinions on the matter. What is troubling, though, is that FDA allowed this uncertainty to essentially paralyze the agency's oversight efforts from 2009 through 2012, even with respect to companies operating well outside the bounds of traditional pharmacy compounding, including NECC and Ameridose.

. . . .

FDA has long defined traditional pharmacy compounding as the combining, mixing, or altering of ingredients by a pharmacist in response to a physician's prescription to create a medication for an individual patient. In 1992, due to FDA's concerns that certain compounding pharmacies were producing and distributing unapproved new drugs in a manner that was clearly outside the bounds of traditional pharmacy compounding, the agency issued Compliance Policy Guide 7132.16 (1992 CPG). FDA asserted that compounded drugs were not exempt from the requirements of the Food, Drug, and Cosmetic Act, and while the agency did not intend to initiate enforcement actions against entities involved in traditional pharmacy compounding, it did plan to do so in situations where a company's activities resembled those of a drug manufacturer. A list of non-exhaustive factors the agency would consider in making these determinations was included.

In 1997, based on concerns from compounding pharmacists that, according to the 1992 CPG, they were operating in per se violation of the FDCA, Congress added section 503A to the Act as part of the Food and Drug Administration Modernization Act of 1997 (FDAMA). Congress's intent in doing so was to "bring the legal status of compounding in line with FDA's longstanding enforcement policy of regulating only drug manufacturing, not ordinary pharmacy compounding." Section 503A exempts compounded drugs from the new drug requirements and certain adulteration and misbranding provisions of the FDCA so long as certain conditions are met. The conditions listed in the statute parallel the factors included in the 1992 CPG and are intended to limit the exemptions from the FDCA's requirements to traditional pharmacy compounding. These conditions include that the compounding be performed by a licensed pharmacist or physician, that it is done in response to a patient-specific prescription, and that the compounded product is necessary for an identified patient. Section 503A also required that the physician's prescription must be unsolicited and the pharmacy must not advertise or promote the compounding of any particular drug.

The provisions related to solicitation and advertising were challenged in court by a group of pharmacists as impermissible regulation of commercial speech. In February 2001, the U.S. Court of Appeals for the Ninth Circuit agreed and declared that the speech-related provisions were non-severable from the remainder of section 503A and, therefore, the entire section was invalid. In *Thompson v. Western States Medical Center*, 535 U.S. 357 (2002), the U.S. Supreme Court affirmed the Ninth Circuit's decision with respect to the First Amendment restrictions, but did not rule on the issue of severability.

Because of the uncertainty caused by the Supreme Court's decision in *Western States*, FDA re-issued an updated version of its 1992 CPG in May 2002. Compliance Policy Guide Section 460.200 (2002 CPG) was very similar to the 1992 CPG; it reaffirmed FDA's authority over compounding under the FDCA and listed nine non-exhaustive "factors the Agency will consider in exercising its enforcement discretion regarding pharmacy compounding," including compounding copies of drugs that are commercially available and compounding drugs for third parties who resell to individual patients. According to the document: "FDA believes that an increasing number of establishments with retail pharmacy licenses are engaged in manufacturing and distributing unapproved new drugs in a manner that is clearly outside the bounds of traditional pharmacy practice and that violates the Act. Such establishments and their activities are the focus of this guidance. . . . Pharmacies engaged in activities analogous to manufacturing and distributing drugs for human use may be held to the same provisions of the Act as manufacturers."

In early 2005, another group of pharmacies brought suit—this time in Texas—contesting FDA's authority to regulate compounded drugs under the FDCA. On appeal, the case reached the Fifth Circuit. In *Medical Center Pharmacy v. Mukasey*, 536 F. 3d 383 (5th Cir. 2008), the U.S. Court of Appeals for the Fifth Circuit refused to be bound by the Ninth Circuit's decision in *Western States*, and held in July 2008 that the unconstitutional restrictions on commercial speech were in fact severable from the rest of section 503A, which should remain in effect. Therefore, in the Fifth Circuit, compounded drugs are exempt from the new drug, manufacturing, labeling, and other requirements of the FDCA, but only to the extent that the pharmacy complies with the restrictions set out in section 503A. Until the *Medical Center Pharmacy* decision, FDA had been operating under the assumption that section 503A was invalid in its entirety; therefore, as the agency stated in litigation and various correspondence over the previous six years, compounded drugs were subject to the FDCA requirements but FDA would continue to exercise enforcement discretion nationwide, as articulated in the 2002 CPG. After the decision, FDA publicly took the position that it would apply the non-commercial speech related provisions of section 503A in the Fifth Circuit and continue to exercise enforcement discretion with respect to entities located outside the Fifth Circuit. Within FDA, however, debate about the soundness of this approach would continue. . . .

Publicly, FDA has consistently asserted authority over compounding pharmacies engaged in activities more analogous to those of a drug manufacturer. In fact, . . . in a . . . letter sent to one large-scale compounding pharmacy [on June 29, 2012], FDA stated that the agency is "applying its normal enforcement policies for compounded drugs" and that the compounding of large volumes of drugs that are essentially copies of FDA-approved products is one factor "the Agency considers in deciding whether to initiate enforcement action with respect to compounding." The letter highlighted that these factors are addressed "in both section 503A of the . . . FDCA and the Agency's compliance policy guide on pharmacy compounding (CPG Sec. 460.200)." The letter then included a footnote discussing the fact that "the Fifth and Ninth Circuit Courts of Appeals have reached different conclusions regarding whether section 503A is invalid or remains in effect."

In her written statement for the November 14, 2012, Oversight Subcommittee hearing, Commissioner Hamburg cited this Circuit Court split as having "amplified the perceived gaps and ambiguity associated with FDA's authority over compounding pharmacies." While there were challenges to FDA's authority, at no point in time did the agency lack sufficient authority under the FDCA to take enforcement action against companies that were clearly manufacturing under the guise of compounding and jeopardizing patient safety in the process. Regardless of whether FDA applied and cited to the factors listed in section 503A or the CPG, NECC and Ameridose were operating well outside the scope of traditional compounding pharmacies and squarely within FDA's authority to take action in response to violations of the FDCA. . . .

Compliance Policy Guides Section 460.200: Pharmacy Compounding

May 2002.

. . . [W]hen the scope and nature of a pharmacy's activities raise the kinds of concerns normally associated with a drug manufacturer and result in significant violations of the new drug, adulteration, or misbranding provisions of the Act, FDA has determined that it should seriously consider enforcement action. In determining whether to initiate such an action, the Agency will consider whether the pharmacy engages in any of the following acts:

1. Compounding of drugs in anticipation of receiving prescriptions, except in very limited quantities in relation to the amounts of drugs compounded after receiving valid prescriptions.

2.   Compounding drugs that were withdrawn or removed from the market for safety reasons. . . .

3.   Compounding finished drugs from bulk active ingredients that are not components of FDA approved drugs without an FDA sanctioned investigational new drug application (IND). . . .

4.   Receiving, storing, or using drug substances without first obtaining written assurance from the supplier that each lot of the drug substance has been made in an FDA-registered facility.

5.   Receiving, storing, or using drug components not guaranteed or otherwise determined to meet official compendia requirements.

6.   Using commercial scale manufacturing or testing equipment for compounding drug products.

7.   Compounding drugs for third parties who resell to individual patients or offering compounded drug products at wholesale to other state licensed persons or commercial entities for resale.

8.   Compounding drug products that are commercially available in the marketplace or that are essentially copies of commercially available FDA-approved drug products.

9.   Failing to operate in conformance with applicable state law regulating the practice of pharmacy. . . .

NOTES

1.   *Legislation under Consideration.* As this book goes to press, Congress is deliberating on whether to address FDA authority over pharmacy compounding by new legislation. Bills explicitly granting the agency power to regulate large-scale compounders have been introduced in both houses of Congress. In the meanwhile, FDA has belatedly launched a major investigation of large scale pharmacies and has bought numerous enforcement actions based on serious GMP violations.

2.   *Judicial Support for FDA Authority over Compounding.* In *Cedars North Towers Pharmacy, Inc. v. United States,* 1978–1980 FDLI Jud. Rec. 668 (S.D. Fla. 1978), a pharmacy which prepared, packaged, and shipped to physicians throughout the country various drugs formulated by a physician sought a declaratory judgment that these activities fell within the practice of pharmacy. The court held that the pharmacy was a drug manufacturer and that the drugs were new drugs under the FD&C Act. *See also United States v. Sene X Eleemosynary Corp., Inc.,* 479 F. Supp. 970 (S.D. Fla. 1979), *aff'd per curiam,* 1983–1984 FDLI Jud. Rec. 123 (11th Cir. 1983) (rejecting a defense to an injunction action based upon the practice of pharmacy); *In the Matter of Establishment Inspection of: Wedgewood Village Pharmacy, Inc.,* 270 F. Supp. 2d 525 (D.N.J. 2003), *aff'd sub nom. Wedgewood Village Pharmacy, Inc. v. United States,* 421 F.3d 263(3d Cir. 2005) (holding that FDA has a statutory right to inspect a pharmacy where there is probable cause to conclude that the pharmacy's compounding constitutes commercial manufacturing). *Cf. United States v. Herold,* 136 F. Supp. 15 (E.D.N.Y. 1955) (upholding FDA's authority to inspect a drug store under the FD&C Act).

3.   *U.S. v. Franck's Lab.* Although *United States v. Franck's Lab, Inc.,* 816 F. Supp. 2d 1209 (M.D. Fla. 2011), concerns the compounding of

animal drugs, not human drugs, the case also has much to say about the latter. Most important, the court suggests the FD&C Act does *not* give FDA the authority to regulate traditional compounding (as opposed to large-scale quasi-manufacturing). *Franck's Lab* is excerpted extensively in Chapter 8, *infra* p. 1112.

4. *Parenteral Nutrition.* As part of the practice of pharmacy, a parenteral nutrition solution may be modified by adding one or more prescription drugs pursuant to the order of a physician for a particular patient. Beginning in the mid-1980s, one company undertook to perform this function in regional compounding centers rather than at local pharmacies, reasoning that this would reduce the possibility of compounding error and product contamination. However, in an enforcement action by the United States, the court held that this was outside the practice of pharmacy and that, because the new drugs being added to the parenteral nutrition solutions were being used outside the approved NDAs, the practice violated the FD&C Act. *United States v. Baxter Healthcare Corp.*, 712 F. Supp. 1352 (N.D. Ill. 1989), *aff'd*, 901 F.2d 1401 (7th Cir. 1990). In mid-1986, FDA commenced a nationwide inspection of pharmacies manufacturing large volume parenteral solutions to determine if they were exceeding the practice of pharmacy.

5. *Mail Order Pharmacy.* The FD&C Act does not distinguish among the various types of pharmacy practice, and it thus acknowledges mail order pharmacy, an activity that community and hospital pharmacy organizations have gone to great efforts to discourage.

6. *Compounding for Other Pharmacists.* In Regulatory Letter No. CHI–379–85 (June 27, 1985), FDA took the position that "compounding and dispensing prescription drug products specifically compounded on the basis of a valid prescription issued by a duly licensed practitioner for a specific patient" was within the practice of pharmacy, but that performing this function for other pharmacies falls outside the practice of pharmacy.

8. NDA-EXEMPT PRODUCTS

a. HOMEOPATHIC DRUGS

The concept of homeopathy was invented in Germany by Samuel Hahnemann in the late 1700s. Homeopathy is based on the principle that "like cures like" and thus a drug that produces symptoms in a healthy subject is capable of curing the illness underlying the same symptoms in a sick patient. This concept came to be known as the "law of similars." Homeopathic drugs are subject to "provings," in which healthy volunteers take doses of the agent and record their symptoms to help establish the drug's full remedy picture.

Homeopathic drugs were not mentioned in the 1906 Pure Food and Drugs Act. Because Senator Royal S. Copeland, M.D., the Senate sponsor of the legislation that ultimately became the 1938 FD&C Act, was a homeopathic physician, the Homeopathic Pharmacopeia was included in section 501(b) of the Act as one of the three official drug compendia recognized by statute. Although this single reference to the Homeopathic Pharmacopeia does not technically require FDA to exempt homeopathic drugs from any of the drug provisions of the FD&C Act, FDA has as a practical matter always interpreted it that way.

By 1972, when FDA initiated its OTC Drug Review, *infra* p. 973, homeopathic drugs had almost disappeared from the United States market. FDA could locate only five homeopathic pharmacies in the entire country, and no other drug stores sold homeopathic drugs. FDA therefore exempted homeopathic drugs from the Review. Three factors have contributed to the remarkable growth in homeopathic drugs since that decision was made. First, all forms of complementary and alternative medicine have had a resurgence in public interest, as individuals seek more natural and holistic approaches to personal health. For example, the March 2002 publication of a final report by the White House Commission on Complementary and Alternative Medicine Policy led to the establishment of an Office of Complementary and Alternative Medicine in the National Institutes of Health. Second, FDA has, as a matter of policy, not required NDAs for homeopathic drugs and has declined to take action against homeopathic drugs directly competing with drug products that are subject to an approved NDA. *See, e.g.*, Citizen Petition, FDA Docket No. 98P–0084/CP1 (Feb. 10, 1998) (complaining to FDA about a homeopathic drug for smoking cessation, marketed in competition with drugs for that indication approved through the NDA process). Third, because homeopathic drugs were also exempted from the FDA OTC Drug Review, their manufacturers need not be concerned about compliance with an OTC drug monograph.

In 1988, as commercial and public interest in homeopathic drugs rose, FDA published Compliance Policy Guide No. 7132.15, stating its regulatory position on these products. The CPG imposed the same labeling and manufacturing requirements on OTC and prescription homeopathic drugs as those that apply to allopathic drugs, but it did not mention compliance with OTC drug monographs or with the IND/NDA approval system. The FDA policy has not changed since this CPG was issued.

NOTE

FDA's authority to regulate homeopathic drugs was confirmed in *United States v. Writers & Research, Inc.*, 113 F.3d 8 (2d Cir. 1997).

b. TRADITIONAL CHINESE MEDICINE

Like homeopathy, traditional Chinese medicine (TCM) is a form of complementary and alternative medicine. TCM drugs have long been sold in the United States, almost exclusively in Chinese pharmacies. They are labeled in Chinese and bear little or none of the labeling information the FD&C Act requires for drugs. No TCM drug has ever been approved by FDA through an NDA, and none has been considered under the OTC Drug Review. FDA has traditionally ignored TCM products except when some type of safety problem has emerged. Because virtually all of these products come from China, the agency has simply informed the Chinese government whenever there has been a problem, and the shipment of the products has immediately stopped. Because there has been no interest in expanding TCM products beyond the traditional Chinese market, FDA has not found it necessary to issue a compliance policy guide or any other form of policy statement about these products.

NOTES

1. *FDA Guidance for Botanical NDAs.* For several years, FDA promised to provide guidance on a flexible approach toward NDAs for botanical drug products. When GUIDANCE FOR INDUSTRY: BOTANICAL DRUG PRODUCTS was issued in 65 Fed. Reg. 49247 (Aug. 11, 2000), 69 Fed. Reg. 32359 (June 9, 2004), it was widely regarded as providing only slight relief from the normal NDA requirements. Between 1982 and 2006, FDA received almost 300 INDs for botanical drugs. After at least three companies tried and failed to develop botanical drugs through the IND/NDA process, the first botanical drug NDA—for Polyphenon E, an extract of green tea leaves for topical use to treat external and perianal genital warts—was approved on October 31, 2006. *See FDA Botanical Review Team Clears Green Tea–Based Drug As First Approval,* 14 TAN SHEET, No. 45, at 10 (Nov. 6, 2006).

2. *Dietary Supplements.* Some botanical ingredients used in TCM products have been marketed to the general public as dietary supplement products and are thus regulated as food.

c. SPECIFICALLY EXCLUDED PRODUCTS

As originally enacted, the FD&C Act contemplated substantial overlap among the various categories of products defined in the Act. In the intervening years, however, Congress has amended the Act to reduce this overlap.

Food: Under the Nutrition Labeling and Education Act of 1990, Congress added section 403(r)(i)(B) to the FD&C Act to authorize FDA to promulgate regulations permitting the use of disease claims in food labeling. *See supra* p. 409. In order to prevent these disease claims from converting the food into a drug, Congress also amended the drug definition in section 201(g)(i) to exclude these claims.

Dietary Supplements: In order to emphasize that dietary supplements are to be regulated as food and not as drugs, the Dietary Supplement Health and Education Act of 1994 included in the definition of a dietary supplement under section 201(ff) of the FD&C Act that these products are to be regulated as food unless they meet the definition of a drug, i.e., unless they bear claims to prevent or treat disease. *See supra* p. 443.

Cosmetics: When the Drug Amendments of 1962 were enacted, Congress added section 509 to the FD&C Act to confirm that cosmetics are not drugs unless they meet the definition of a drug, i.e., unless they bear claims to prevent or treat disease or to affect the structure or function of the human body.

Medical Devices: As part of the Medical Device Amendments of 1976, Congress revised the definition of a "device" in section 201(h) of the FD&C Act in order to differentiate between a drug and a device. *See infra* p. 1205.

E. RESTRICTIONS ON DISTRIBUTION AND PRESCRIBING

1. LIMITATION TO PRESCRIPTION SALE

a. LEGAL BASIS

Until the end of the 19th century, professional pharmacists dominated the compounding of drugs and had equal status with physicians in prescribing their use. In the late 1800s, however, two groups arose to challenge this authority. Commercial firms were organized to manufacture and sell drug products, usually without prescription. Organized medicine also began to assert itself, contending that only licensed physicians were qualified to prescribe drugs, as part of the practice of medicine.

Federal laws enacted by Congress to regulate drugs during the 19th century and the first half of the 20th century were designed to assure the integrity of drug products and did not address the prescription/nonprescription issue. The legislative histories of the Vaccine Act of 1813 and the Import Drugs Act of 1848 reveal a congressional concern only with the quality of the drugs made available to the Americans public. Under the Biologics Act of 1902 and the 1906 Pure Food and Drugs Act, the status of a drug as prescription or nonprescription was left entirely to the manufacturer. Even in the FD&C Act of 1938, Congress made no attempt to resolve this matter. Only in the Harrison Narcotic Act of 1914 and subsequent statutes controlling narcotics did Congress specifically designate drugs as available only on the prescription of a licensed physician.

FDA invented the concept of mandatory prescription status in regulations promulgated in 1938. The key provision was FD&C Act 502(f) which states that a drug is misbranded

> Unless its labeling bears (1) adequate directions for use . . . except that where any requirement of clause (1) . . . is not necessary for the protection of the public health, the Secretary shall promulgate regulations exempting such drug . . . from such requirement.

"Adequate directions for use" was always assumed to be directions for the *layperson*, although FDA did not explicitly state this by regulation until 1952. 17 Fed. Reg. 1130 (Feb. 5, 1952). *See* 21 C.F.R. 201.5 (current definition of "adequate directions for use"). In its 1938 regulations, as described in the excerpt below, the agency declared that drugs sold by prescription were exempt from this requirement. Congress subsequently confirmed FDA's policy in the Durham–Humphrey Amendments of 1951.

Peter Temin, *The Origin of Compulsory Drug Prescriptions*
22 JOURNAL OF LAW & ECONOMICS 91 (1979).

. . . The FDA promulgated regulations to enforce the [FD&C Act] before the end of 1938. And among these regulations were those making clear the scope of the exemption from labeling requirements set forth in section 502(f) of the act. . . . The FDA said a shipment or delivery of a drug or device was exempt from these requirements:

> If the label of such drug or device bears the statement *"Caution: To be used only by or on the prescription of a* _____ (the blank to be filled in by the word *"Physician," "Dentist,"* or *"Veterinarian,"* or any combination of such words), and all representations or suggestions contained in the labeling thereof with respect to the conditions for which such drug or device is to be used appear only in such medical terms as are not likely to be understood by the ordinary individual, and if such shipment or delivery is made for use exclusively by, or on the prescription of, physicians, dentists, or veterinarians licensed by law to administer or apply such drug or device; but such exemption shall expire when such shipment or delivery, or any part thereof, is offered or sold or otherwise disposed of for any use other than by or on the prescription of such a physician, dentist, or veterinarian. [3 Fed. Reg. 3168 (Dec. 28, 1938)]. . . .

It seems simple enough. The law said that the FDA could exempt drugs or devices from the requirement to include recommended usages and the dangers of misuses when these regulations were "not necessary for the public health." The FDA interpreted this to mean that—among other conditions—the usage and danger labels were not needed for drugs sold by prescription. . . .

The act said elsewhere (section 503) that drugs sold by prescription were exempt from the labeling requirements, but it did not say which drugs were to be sold by prescription or that there were any drugs that could not be sold without a prescription. This regulation is different. It says that drugs with certain kinds of labels—"*Warning* . . ."—can only be sold by prescription. It allows the drug companies to create a class of drugs that cannot legally be sold without a prescription by putting the appropriate label on them.

This is a stunning change in the ways drugs were to be sold. Before this regulation took effect, consumers could get any nonnarcotic drug they desired without going to see a doctor. . . . After this regulation became effective, the consumer could no longer buy some drugs without seeing a doctor first and getting his approval. Which drugs were now beyond the consumer's reach? The drug companies would decide, although the FDA could sue them for mislabeling if it disagreed with their choices. The consumers became passive recipients of this decision. . . .

The FDA's assumptions were new to the drug market. Had they arisen from a change in the technology of producing drugs, from the availability of many new and complex drugs? The answer is no. The drug revolution came after 1938. . . . The FDA's *Annual Report* for 1939 identifies the regulation as the result of "an administrative conclusion of some moment." The conclusion resulted from a conflict the FDA saw within the new law. On the one hand, the law said that all drugs must be labeled adequately, adding that any drug that was dangerous to health when used as the label suggested was automatically misbranded. On the other hand, the report asserted, "Many drugs of great value to the physician are dangerous in the hands of those unskilled in the uses of drugs. The statute obviously was not intended to deprive the medical profession of potent but valuable medicaments."

The conflict was created by the assumption underlying the first of the two sentences quoted. The FDA assumed that adequate directions for self-medication could not be written for some drugs. . . .

The 1938 regulation does not seem to have aroused much discussion at the time, and its effect on the function of prescriptions was never tested in the courts. . . . [T]he distinction between prescription and "over-the-counter" drugs was simply accepted. . . .

———

The courts upheld FDA's approach of creating mandatory prescription status by regulation even before the agency received express authority to do so in the Humphrey—Durham Amendments of 1951.

United States v. El–O–Pathic Pharmacy

192 F.2d 62 (9th Cir. 1951).

■ McALLISTER, CIRCUIT JUDGE.

This is an appeal from an order of the district court denying permanent injunctions in consolidated cases in which the government sought to restrain appellees from introducing certain allegedly misbranded drugs, known as hormones, into interstate commerce. . . .

. . . It appears that the hormones in question are manufactured by pharmaceutical corporations in the eastern part of the United States and shipped to appellees in California with labeling that states, in part, "Caution: To be dispensed only by or on the prescription of a physician." Thereafter, the appellees relabel the drugs to eliminate this prescription statement; and the new labeling, it was claimed, caused the drugs to become misbranded within the meaning of the statute. . . .

The district court held that the warnings on the cartons containing the drugs were sufficient in that they stated that . . . before taking, [sic] the hormone, a physician should be consulted, since the hormone would not aid or relieve symptoms not associated with male hormone deficiency; and that children and young adults must not use the hormone except under constant, direct supervision of a physician. . . .

It is the claim of the government that it has sustained the burden of proving that the hormones in this case are inherently dangerous; that they are not safe and efficacious for use except under the supervision of a physician; that they are not suitable for self-medication, since a layman could not know when they should be used and when they should not be used; that adequate directions for unsupervised lay use cannot be written; and that such drugs, if sold legally in interstate commerce, must be dispensed only upon prescription of a physician, in accordance with the regulations of the Federal Security Administrator. . . .

. . . [I]t is to be remarked that appellees' labels themselves . . . clearly demonstrate that adequate directions for unsupervised use can not be written; and the testimony of the government's medical witnesses, which we accept, only strikingly emphasizes this important and crucial fact. Obviously, in such cases, the direction on the label that "a physician should be consulted" . . . [is] not enough to constitute "adequate directions for use" within the meaning of the statute. . . .

NOTE

"Consult a Physician." In this case, the court of appeals held that the label direction that "a physician should be consulted" did not constitute adequate directions for use. By contrast, a requirement for physician diagnosis of disease prior to use of an OTC drug has been included in the labeling for cholecystokinetic OTC drugs, 48 Fed. Reg. 27004 (June 10, 1983), codified at 21 C.F.R. 357.250(d)(1); anti-asthmatic bronchodilator OTC drugs, 47 Fed. Reg. 47520 (Oct. 26, 1982), codified at 21 C.F.R. 341.76(c)(1); and other OTC drugs pursuant to the OTC Drug Review.

————

In 1951 Congress enacted the Durham–Humphrey Amendments, 65 Stat. 648, revising section 503(b) of the FD&C Act to codify the FDA regulations distinguishing between prescription and nonprescription drugs. The primary purpose of the 1951 Amendments was to prevent the same drug from being marketed simultaneously as a prescription drug and as a nonprescription drug. The amended section 503(b) provided:

(1) A drug intended for use by man which—

(A) is a habit-forming drug to which section 502(d) applies; or

(B) because of its toxicity or other potentiality for harmful effect, or the method of its use, or the collateral measures necessary to its use, is not safe for use except under the supervision of a practitioner licensed by law to administer such drug; or

(C) is limited by an approved application under section 505 to use under the professional supervision of a practitioner licensed by law to administer such drug;

shall be dispensed only [upon prescription] . . . The act of dispensing a drug contrary to the provisions of this paragraph shall be deemed to be an act which results in the drug being misbranded while held for sale.

The subparagraph concerning habit-forming drugs was deleted in 1997, but section 503(b)(1) otherwise remains unchanged since 1951.

NOTES

1.   *Misbranding Violation.* Under section 503(b)(1)(B) of the FD&C Act, dispensing a drug in contravention of section 503(b) "shall be deemed to be an act which results in the drug being misbranded while held for sale." This provision reaches a pharmacist who dispenses a drug without the required labeling long after it has moved in interstate commerce. *See United States v. Sullivan,* 332 U.S. 689 (1948).

2.   *The Rx/OTC Line.* The actual application of these criteria for determining when a drug should be limited to prescription sale will be

explored in detail in the section on OTC drugs later in this chapter. *Infra* p. 957.

3.   *NDA Approvals and Rx Status.* Section 503(b)(1)(C) provides that FDA may require a new drug to be sold only on prescription as part of its decision to approve a new drug application. Virtually all new chemical entity new drugs are approved initially as prescription drugs, in case safety issues not discovered in the clinical trials emerge once the drug is on the market.

4.   *Senate Report.* The Senate Report on the Durham–Humphrey Amendments, S. Rep. No. 946, 82d Cong., 1st Sess. 4 (1951), provides this explanation:

> The word "safe," as used in the definition, is intended to have its ordinary meaning. For example, nontoxic drugs like quinidine sulfate, intended for heart disease, or penicillin, for infections, are not safe for self-medication because their unsupervised use may indirectly cause injury or death. The language of the definition clearly shows that toxicity is only one factor to be considered by the courts in determining whether a particular drug is safe for use without medical supervision. The definition requires the court to consider also other potentialities for harmful effect, the method by which the drug is used, and the collateral measures that may be necessary in order to use the drug safely. . . .

> . . . S. 1186 would have authorized the Federal Security Administrator to list by name or class the drugs which he considered within the statutory definition. The grant of such administrative authority was objected to as an unnecessary regulation of the drug industry, and the committee concluded that administrative listing is not necessary at this time. It was felt that the statutory definition, together with the authority to make interpretative regulations, could bring an end to the existing confusion in drug labeling and that uniformity can be achieved through cooperative efforts of the drug industry and the Food and Drug Administration working under the statutory plan.

5.   *Different Dosages.* FDA's initial administrative exception to Durham–Humphrey was to acknowledge that the same drug could be sold as both a prescription and nonprescription product at different dosages. E.g., under the OTC Drug Review a panel recommended that the antihistamine doxylamine—formerly limited to prescription status—be switched to nonprescription use at a dosage level of 7.5 to 12.5 mg, but retained as a prescription drug at higher levels. 41 Fed. Reg. 38312, 38385 (Sept. 9, 1996). FDA ultimately embraced this recommendation. 59 Fed. Reg. 4216 (Jan. 28, 1994), 21 C.F.R. 341.72(d)(8).

6.   *Different Indications.* In 1989, FDA for the first time agreed that it could approve, at the same dosage level, one indication of a drug as prescription only and another indication as nonprescription, when it initially approved the switch of some—but not all—indications of clotrimazole from prescription to nonprescription status in 1989. A year later, all of the remaining indications were switched.

7. *Different Ages.* In considering the switch of the emergency contraceptive Plan B from prescription to nonprescription status, FDA held a public meeting in 2005 to consider whether the agency could designate the drug, at the same dosage level and for the same indication, as prescription for women under 17 years of age and nonprescription for 17 years and older. 70 Fed. Reg. 52050 (Sept. 1, 2005). The agency subsequently approved the NDA with an age restriction of 18 rather than 17, but required that for adults, the drug be made available "behind-the-counter" rather than "over-the-counter." As discussed in detail below, *infra* p. 972, a court ordered FDA to lower the age cutoff to age 17 and later forced it to make Plan B available to women of all ages over-the-counter.

8. *Different Genders.* In 2013, FDA made Oxytrol, a treatment for overactive bladder, OTC for women while maintaining the prescription requirement for men.

9. *Simultaneous Rx and OTC Status.* FDA has consistently taken the position that a drug cannot be marketed both Rx and OTC in the same dosage form and strength for the same indication, population, and conditions of use. Consequently, after it switched MiraLAX®, the brand name version of PEG 3350, to OTC status in 2006 pursuant to a supplemental NDA submitted by the manufacturer, the agency sent letters to generic manufacturers of the prescription version of drug informing them that their prescription PEG 3350 products were now misbranded, despite their approved ANDAs. When the agency issued a Notice of Opportunity for Hearing on its proposal to withdraw the PEG 3350 ANDAs, 73 Fed. Reg. 63491 (Oct. 24, 2008), several ANDA sponsors requested a hearing. The hearing has not yet been scheduled, and the prescription generic version of PEG 3350 remains on the market.

10. *The Prescription Legend.* As enacted in 1951, section 503(b)(4) required a prescription drug to bear the legend "Caution: Federal law prohibits dispensing without prescription." 65 Stat. 648, 649. The legend was changed in 1997 to "Rx only." 111 Stat. 2296, 2327.

11. *Establishing Rx Status for Drug Class by Regulation.* In *National Nutritional Foods Association v. Weinberger,* 512 F.2d 688 (2d Cir. 1975), *supra* p. 31, FDA's authority to issue substantive regulations restricting an entire class of drugs to prescription sale was in principle upheld.

b. AUTHORITY TO PRESCRIBE AND THE REQUIREMENT OF A VALID PRESCRIPTION

Section 503(b) relies upon state law to determine what professional training is required for licensure to administer prescription drugs. *See United States v. Shock,* 379 F.2d 29 (8th Cir. 1967) (holding that a district court should look to state law to determine whether a chiropractor is an authorized practitioner). Physicians and dentists have prescription authority in every state. Advanced practice registered nurses do, also, although states vary in their requirements for physician involvement. States also vary in the prescribing authority, if any, that they extend to various other categories of professionals, such as physician assistants and psychologists. Some types of practitioners, such as podiatrists and optometrists, have prescription authority in every state, but their scope of practice is delimited by state law. Practitioners of naturopathy have been unsuccessful in their attempts to force FDA and state agencies to recognize their discipline as a healing art separate from but of equal standing with orthodox medicine. *See Idaho Association of Naturopathic Physicians, Inc. v. FDA,* 582 F.2d 849 (4th Cir. 1978), and cases cited therein.

Although federal law is silent as to the types of practitioners that can prescribe drugs, it does touch on the relationship that must exist between a practitioner and a patient for a prescription to be valid. There is substantial judicial precedent interpreting this aspect of the prescription requirements in federal drug abuse statutes, as well in the FD&C Act itself.

The first statute specially to regulate narcotic drugs was the Harrison Narcotic Act of 1914. The 1914 Act required that the doctor issue a prescription "in the course of his professional practice only." After upholding the validity of the Act in *United States v. Deremus,* 249 U.S. 86 (1918), the Supreme Court decided two cases which interpreted and defined the prescription requirement. According to these two decisions, narcotic drugs regulated by the Act could be dispensed only under a valid doctor/patient relationship and in the course of legitimate medical treatment. *Webb v. United States,* 249 U.S. 96 (1919); *Jin Fuey Moy* v. *United States,* 254 U.S. 189 (1920). In *Webb,* the Court opined, with respect to a doctor who prescribed morphine to habitual users merely to satisfy their addictions: " '[T]o call such an order . . . a physician's prescription would be so plain a perversion of meaning that no discussion of the subject is required." 249 U.S. at 100.

The Fifth Circuit later relied on *Webb* in deciding a case under the prescription drug provisions of the FD&C Act. In *Brown* v. *United States,* 250 F.2d 745 (5th Cir. 1958), the court of appeals relied on the professional practice standard to uphold the conviction of a doctor who issued amphetamines to truck drivers. The court highlighted several key facts, including that the doctor did not inquire into the physical health of the driver, that he issued the drugs without a physical examination, and that he issued drugs without a dosage restriction. The court emphasized that the absence of a professional relationship "bears on the question whether there had been a 'prescription.' " *See also DeFreese* v. *United States,* 270 F.2d 730 (5th Cir. 1959).

In 1965, Congress enacted the Drug Abuse Control Amendments of 1965, 79 Stat. 226, which amended the FD&C to forbid any person acting outside "the ordinary and authorized course of his business, profession, occupation, or employment" to "sell, deliver, or otherwise dispose of any depressant or stimulant drug." In *White v. United States,* 399 F.2d 813 (8th Cir. 1968), the Eighth Circuit continued to rely on the prescription requirements articulated under the case law interpreting earlier statutes. In *White,* a doctor issued amphetamines to federal agents without a prescription and without any inquiry into their medical condition. The doctor also issued a prescription for one individual whom he had never met and who was not present at the time of the prescription. The court of appeals upheld the doctor's conviction, accepting the precedent that subjected doctors to punishment when they act outside of a bona fide doctor/patient relationship.

In 1970, Congress enacted the Comprehensive Drug Abuse Prevention and Control Act of 1970, 84 Stat. 1236. Included in the 1970 Act was the Controlled Substances Act (CSA), which established requirements relating to the manufacture, prescription, and distribution of any controlled substance. Under section 829 of the CSA, 21 U.S.C. 829, "except when dispensed directly by a practitioner, other than a pharmacist, to an ultimate user, no controlled substance in schedule II [or III or IV] which is a prescription drug as determined under the Federal Food, Drug, and Cosmetic Act, may be dispensed without the written prescription of a practitioner." In regulations implementing the statute, the Department of Justice stated: "A prescription for a controlled substance . . . must be issued for a legitimate medical purpose by an individual practitioner acting in the usual course of his professional practice." 21 C.F.R. 1306.04.

In *United States v. Rosen*, 582 F.2d 1032 (5th Cir. 1978), the Fifth Circuit relied on prior case law to determine the liability under the CSA of a doctor who prescribed amphetamine diet pills to individuals without an examination or a legitimate doctor/patient relationship. The court of appeals noted that the doctor conducted only a cursory examination of the individual, prescribed large quantities of the controlled substances, and often used street slang in describing the substances. Relying on these factors, the Fifth Circuit upheld the finding that the doctor acted without a legitimate medical purpose in violation of the CSA. In *United States v. Kaplan*, 895 F.2d 619 (9th Cir. 1990), the Ninth Circuit upheld the conviction of a physician under the CSA, holding that a doctor may be liable for prescribing controlled substances outside the usual bounds of professional practice. The evidence showed that the doctor issued numerous prescriptions for controlled substances without conducting a physical examination. The defendant in *United States v. Nelson*, 383 F.3d 1227 (10th Cir. 2004) was convicted under the CSA for selling controlled substances over the internet.

FDA relied on the "legitimate medical purpose" theory to prosecute physicians who distributed anabolic steroids and androgenic hormones to athletes outside a genuine doctor-patient relationship. *See, e.g., Doe v. United States,* 801 F.2d 1164 (9th Cir. 1986). The Anti–Drug Abuse Act of 1988, 102 Stat. 4181, 4230, added section 303(e) to the FD&C Act to prohibit distribution of any anabolic steroid for use in humans other than by prescription for the treatment of disease and provided for imprisonment of up to three years (up to six years for distribution to a minor). In 104 Stat. 4789, 4853 (1990), Congress reclassified anabolic steroids as Schedule III controlled substances while enacting a new, similarly worded FD&C Act 303(e) to regulate the distribution of human growth hormone.

Thus, according to the relevant case law, a valid prescription is one granted after a sufficient medical examination and consideration of the patient's individual needs. There must be a valid doctor/patient relationship as well as a good faith determination that the prescribed medication is medically necessary.

A pharmacist also bears a burden for not dispensing a drug where the pharmacist knows that there is no valid prescription. In *Webb*, the Supreme Court upheld the indictment under the Harrison Narcotic Act of the pharmacist as well as the doctor in a scheme to provide morphine to habitual users. Similarly, in *United States* v. *Guerrero,* 650 F.2d 728 (5th Cir. 1981), the Fifth Circuit found under the Controlled Substances Act that, although "the responsibility for the proper prescribing and dispensing of controlled substances is upon the prescribing practitioner, . . . a corresponding responsibility rests with the pharmacist who fills the prescription." The court of appeals found that such responsibility arose only in the case where a pharmacist knew that the prescription was invalid. *See also United States* v. *Green,* 511 F.2d 1062 (7th Cir. 1975); *United States v. Leal,* 75 F.3d 219 (6th Cir. 1996); *United States v. Munoz,* 430 F.3d 1357 (11th Cir. 2005); *United States v. Kim,* 298 F.3d 746 (9th Cir. 2002), 2006 WL 903214, 1421115 (9th Cir. 2006).

NOTES

1. *Dependent Pharmacist Prescribers.* To allow immediate access to emergency contraception or other prescription medication, some states have enacted laws authorizing a pharmacist to dispense drugs pursuant to a protocol established in advance with a collaborating physician. *See* Heather M. Field, *Increasing Access to Emergency Contraceptive Pills Through State Law Enabled Dependent Pharmacist Prescribers*, 11 U.C.L.A. WOMEN'S L.J. 141 (2000).

2. *Refills for Schedule II Prescription Drugs.* The Controlled Substances Act prohibits a prescription for more than a 30 day supply, and the refilling of a prescription, for a Schedule II drug. In 2007, the Drug Enforcement Administration (DEA) promulgated a final rule established a policy of allowing a physician to provide a patient with three 30-day prescriptions at one office visit. 72 Fed. Reg. 64921 (Nov. 19, 2007).

2. PRESCRIPTION DRUG CONTROLLED SUBSTANCES

Before 1970, federal control of narcotic drugs, marijuana, and other drugs used for recreational and nonmedical purposes was shared among several agencies and rested on a haphazard cluster of laws enacted since the Harrison Narcotic Act of 1914, 38 Stat. 785. FDA was responsible for enforcement of the Drug Abuse Control Amendments of 1965, 79 Stat. 226, to prevent abuse of depressant and stimulant drugs, such as the amphetamines and barbiturates, which also have legitimate medical use. In 1970, Congress repealed the earlier statutes and enacted a new comprehensive law, the Controlled Substances Act (CSA), 84 Stat. 1236, 1242, 21 U.S.C. 801 *et seq.* Responsibility for enforcement of the Controlled Substances Act rests with the Drug Enforcement Administration (DEA) of the Department of Justice, which has the statutory obligation to consult with FDA on the scheduling of controlled substances. FDA's recommendations are binding on scientific and medical matters, and DEA may not schedule a drug if FDA recommends against it. 21 U.S.C. 201(b). FDA is required to request public comment on drug scheduling. *E.g.,* 70 Fed. Reg. 73775 (Dec. 13, 2005).

The CSA establishes five schedules of controlled substances, which can be summarized as follows: Schedule I includes drugs with a high potential for abuse that have no currently accepted medical use (e.g., heroin). Schedule II includes drugs with a high potential for abuse with a currently accepted medical use. Schedule III includes drugs with a moderate potential for abuse and a currently accepted medical use. Schedule IV includes substances with a low potential for abuse and a currently accepted medical use. Schedule V includes substances with the lowest potential for abuse and a currently accepted medical use.

The CSA prohibits domestic distribution of all Schedule I drugs. The controls used to regulate distribution of drugs on Schedules II–V are calibrated to the degree of risk of abuse. Because the controls over scheduled drugs increase with the schedule to which they are assigned, scheduling decisions are of major importance to the pharmaceutical industry. DEA may also establish production quotas for Schedule I and Schedule II drugs. Although the requirements established under the CSA may impose extra burdens upon manufacturers, physicians, and pharmacists, they do not prevent FDA from approving an NDA for any controlled substance that has a legitimate medical use. *See generally* Anthony Vieux, *Regulatory Requirements under the Controlled Substances Act*, CRS REP. No. RX22487 (Aug. 2, 2006).

NOTES

1. *Medical Marijuana.* Marijuana has been a Schedule I controlled substance since 1970. The efforts of the National Organization for the Reform of Marijuana Laws (NORML) are reflected in more than four decades of administrative and judicial procedures concerning the appropriate scheduling of the drug. In 1972, DEA denied a NORML petition to remove marijuana and its components from Schedule I, but the D.C. Circuit ordered the DEA to hold hearings and reconsider the petition. *NORML v. Ingersoll*, 497 F.2d 654 (D.C. Cir. 1974). After DEA again denied the petition following a hearing, the D.C. Circuit remanded the matter with instructions to refer the petition to the Secretary of HHS for medical and scientific evaluation. *NORML v. DEA*, 559 F.2d 735 (D.C. Cir. 1977).

After receiving FDA's recommendation that marijuana remain in Schedule I, DEA again denied the NORML petition in 44 Fed. Reg. 36123 (June 20, 1979). The Court of Appeals again disagreed, remanding with directions that FDA take into account new evidence concerning medical use of THC. *NORML v. DEA*, No. 79–1660 (D.C. Cir., October 16, 1980). In 1988, a DEA administrative law judge recommended that marijuana be rescheduled from Schedule I to Schedule II, but the DEA Administrator rejected this recommendation and denied the NORML petition in 54 Fed. Reg. 53767 (Dec. 29, 1989). Still NORML did not surrender; it and the Alliance for Cannabis Therapeutics challenged the DEA's final order again, and the D.C. Circuit ordered a remand for further explanation. *Alliance for Cannabis Therapeutics v. DEA*, 930 F.2d 936 (D.C. Cir. 1991). After the DEA once again denied the petition, the D.C. Circuit finally put an end to the matter. 15 F.3d 1131 (D.C. Cir. 1994).

Various constitutional challenges to the classification of marijuana in Schedule I have also failed. *NORML v. Bell*, 488 F. Supp. 123 (D.D.C. 1980); *Hartz v. Bensinger*, 461 F. Supp. 431 (E.D. Pa. 1978).

State attempts to legalize medical marijuana were thwarted by the decision in *Gonzales v. Raich,* 545 U.S. 1 (2005), which upheld Congress's power, through the Controlled Substances Act, to prohibit intrastate, noncommercial cultivation and possession of cannabis for personal medical purposes as recommended by a patient's physician pursuant to California law. So although sixteen states now have laws legalizing marijuana for medical purposes, and two have also legalized it for recreational use, it remains an illegal Schedule I controlled substance under federal law.

2.   *THC.* Tetrahydrocannabinol (THC), the principal active ingredient in marijuana, has its own regulatory history. In 47 Fed. Reg. 10080 (Mar. 9, 1982), FDA recommended to the Department of HHS that THC remain in Schedule I until an NDA was approved for medical purposes. In 1985, FDA approved an NDA for a drug, Marinol®, containing synthetic THC. DEA reclassified this formulation into Schedule II in 1986 and into Schedule III in 1999. 51 Fed. Reg. 17476 (May 13, 1986); 64 Fed. Reg. 35928 (July 2, 1999).

3.   *Peyote for Religious Use.* The use of an otherwise banned Schedule I controlled substance as part of a religious ceremony has also provoked litigation. The plaintiff in *Peyote Way Church of God, Inc. v. Smith,* 922 F.2d 1210 (5th Cir. 1991), was unsuccessful in gaining permission to use peyote in its ceremonies despite its claims of discrimination because members of the Native American Church could use the drug pursuant to federal and state statutory exceptions intended to protect Native American culture. *See also Employment Div. v. Smith,* 494 U.S. 872 (1990) (state is not barred by the First Amendment from prohibiting sacramental use of peyote); *Olsen v. DEA,* 878 F.2d 1458 (D.C. Cir. 1989) (rejecting a religious use exemption for marijuana). In *Gonzales v. O Centro Esprita Beneficente Uniao Do Vegetal,* 544 U.S. 973 (2005), however, the Supreme Court interpreted the Religious Freedom Restoration Act of 1993, 107 Stat. 1488, which prohibits the federal government from substantially burdening a person's exercise of religion unless it represents the least restrictive means of advancing a compelling interest, to require DEA to allow a bona fide religious sect to receive communion by drinking a sacramental tea, hoasca, brewed from plants that naturally contain DMT, a Schedule I hallucinogen under the Controlled Substances Act.

4.   *Hemp.* In *Hemp Industries Association v. DEA,* 333 F.3d 1082 (9th Cir. 2003) & 357 F.3d 1012 (9th Cir. 2004), the Court of Appeals held that DEA may not regulate naturally-occurring THC not contained within or derived from marijuana, i.e., nonpsychoactive hemp products.

5.   *Control of Methamphetamine.* In recent decades, the United States has been subject to an epidemic of illegal methamphetamine use. Because methamphetamine can be derived from common over-the-counter cold remedies containing pseudoephedrine, Congress enacted various measures to fight diversion of such medicines to illicit methamphetamine production. The Domestic Chemical Diversion Control Act of 1993, 107 Stat. 2333, 2333–34, required companies to report all transactions in FDA-approved drug products containing various listed chemicals, including ephedrine and norpseudoephedrine. The Methamphetamine Anti-Proliferation Act of 2000, 114 Stat. 1227, allocated funding to combating

methamphetamine production, imposed stiffer penalties on the operators of methamphetamine laboratories, and limited the amount of pseudoephedrine that could lawfully be purchased at retail. When those restrictions proved inadequate and the epidemic continued to grow, Congress enacted the Combat Methamphetamine Epidemic Act of 2005, 120 Stat. 192, 256, imposing still tighter restrictions on the retail sale of lawful nonprescription drugs containing ephedrine, pseudoephedrine, or phenylpropanolamine. *See United States v. Kim*, 298 F.3d 746 (9th Cir. 2002) & 449 F.3d 933 (9th Cir. 2006); *PDK Laboratories, Inc. v. DEA*, 438 F.3d 1184 (D.C. Cir. 2006); *United States v. Youngblood*, 949 F.2d 1065 (10th Cir. 1991).

6. *Pain Medication*. Many important prescription drugs for serious pain are scheduled under the Controlled Substances Act. This has provoked repeated confrontations between DEA, which wants to reduce the use of these drugs, and the medical profession, which wants to assure that patients receive adequate medication for chronic pain. *See* Lars Noah, *Challenges in the Federal Regulation of Pain Management Technologies*, 31 J. LAW, MED. & ETHICS 55 (2003); Ronald T. Libby, *Treating Doctors as Drug Dealers: The DEA's War on Prescription Pain Killers*, CATO Institute Policy Analysis No. 545 (June 16, 2005); "OxyContin and Beyond: Examining the Role of FDA and DEA in Regulating Prescription Pain Killers," Hearing before the House Subcommittee on Regulatory Affairs of the Government Reform Committee, 109th Cong., 1st Sess. (2005). In 2012, FDA established a Risk Evaluation and Mitigation Strategy (REMS) for opioid analgesics that requires professional education and patient labeling on the safe use of these products. In September 2013, FDA announced the imposition of physician labeling changes (to combat addiction and abuse) and mandatory postmarket study requirements on all extended-release and long-acting opioid analgesics intended to treat pain.

In 2010, after the approval of a supplemental NDA for a new version of OxyContin, reformulated to be abuse-resistant, the manufacturer, Purdue, informed FDA that it had ceased shipment of the original version. In 2013, the agency announced that it would not accept or approve any ANDAs for products referencing the original NDA because the product was voluntarily withdrawn from the market "for reasons of safety or effectiveness." 21 C.F.R. 314.62; 78 Fed. Reg. 23273 (Apr. 18, 2013).

As this book went to press, FDA announced its intention, by December 2013, to formally recommend the reclassification of hydrocodone combination products (e.g., Vicodin, which combines hydrocodone with acetaminophen) from Schedule III into Schedule II. *See* Statement on Proposed Hydrocodone Reclassification from Janet Woodcock, M.D., Director, CDER (Oct. 24, 2013).

7. *GHB*. While GHB was being developed as a treatment for narcolepsy under an IND, Congress scheduled it as a controlled substance in Schedule I because of its notoriety as a "date rape" drug but determined that it would be rescheduled to Schedule III upon approval of an NDA. 114 Stat 7 (2000). GHB was subsequently approved by FDA and rescheduled. The sponsor agreed to a risk management plan to prevent diversion of the drug. *See* Ariel Neuman, *GHB's Path to Legitimacy: An Administrative and*

Legislative History of Xyrem (2004), in Chapter VI(C)(3) of the Electronic Book.

8.   *Direct To Consumer (DTC) Advertising.* DEA has objected to several DTC advertisements for products scheduled under the Controlled Substances Act, but it has taken no formal legal action. FDA had previously cleared each of the advertisements in question, and it has not supported the DEA position.

3.   THE (NON–)REGULATION OF THE PRACTICE OF MEDICINE

a.   OFF-LABEL PRESCRIBING PRACTICES

As defined by the FD&C Act, a prescription drug is a drug for which adequate directions for use cannot be written, because laypersons lack the scientific understanding needed to diagnose their disease or to use the drug in treating it. This rationale for restricting drugs to sale only by prescription is beginning to erode. With the spread of patient labeling and other educational materials, combined with direct-to-consumer advertising and the internet, patients have become more knowledgeable about prescription drugs and often participate with their physicians in treatment decisions. *See infra* p. 876.

Since 1939, when FDA created a mandatory category of prescription drugs, the agency has sought to protect consumers of these products in two distinct ways. First, it has attempted to assure through the new drug approval process and other regulatory controls that prescription drugs are safe and effective. Second, the agency has sought to provide physicians, through labeling addressed specifically to them, increasingly detailed information about the use of drugs in patients. The FDA-approved physician labeling has now become a summary of all that is known about the safety and effectiveness of a drug. It represents a distillation of the results of testing arrived at through negotiations between agency officials and the drug's sponsor. Both FDA and pharmaceutical manufacturers assume that this labeling will influence the physician's decisions about use of the drug. The wisdom of FDA's reliance upon the physician labeling thus depends on the validity of that assumption.

There seems little doubt that the FDA-approved physician labeling significantly influences how prescription drugs are used. But it is also clear that every prescription drug is sometimes administered for conditions that fall outside the FDA-approved labeling, and that many are frequently used this way. There are several reasons for this. The physician labeling describes only those conditions that have been systematically studied, not all possible conditions of use. Physicians who routinely confront the duty to care for seriously ill patients are impelled to try new methods of treatment. Medical need invariably outpaces controlled clinical evaluation. New uses of established drugs often gain acceptance before controlled studies are launched, supplemental NDAs submitted, and FDA approval obtained. Once a drug goes off patent, there is no economic incentive for either the pioneer or a generic company to invest in clinical trials for off-label uses.

But use of a drug for an unapproved indication can also represent poor judgment, inattention to warnings, or inadequate medical training. Thus, FDA is often faced with the following dilemma. Some unapproved uses represent sound medical care, sometimes even the only promising treatment. Other unapproved uses are ill-advised or even reckless. Initially, the agency took the position that only the information contained in the FDA-approved physician labeling represented reliable information about a new drug and cautioned physicians not to stray beyond it. When pressed, however, FDA backed away from the proposition that prescribing a new drug for an indication not approved in the FDA-approved physician labeling constitutes a violation of the FD&C Act. Instead, the agency took the more limited position that the manufacturer may not promote an approved drug for unapproved uses.

NOTES

1. *Extent of Unapproved Use.* In its report on OFF–LABEL DRUGS: REIMBURSEMENT POLICIES CONSTRAIN PHYSICIANS IN THEIR CHOICE OF CANCER THERAPIES (1991), the GAO found that 44 of the 46 FDA-approved cancer drugs were sometimes prescribed for off-label uses, that almost all types of cancer were treated by unapproved uses of approved drugs, and that 56 percent of cancer patients were given at least one drug off-label. A 2003 study found that among 160 common drugs, off-label use accounted for approximately 21 percent of prescriptions. *See* Randall S. Stafford, *Regulating Off–Label Drug Use: Rethinking the Role of the FDA*, 358 N. ENGL. J. MED. 1427, 1427 (2008). Off-label prescription is also particularly common in pediatrics.

2. *Use of Anticancer Drugs in Combination.* Few cancer drugs have been approved by FDA with labeling that explicitly recommends use in combination with any other cancer drug. The National Cancer Institute (NCI) not only recommends and makes available a number of Group C investigational cancer drugs for routine cancer therapy, *see supra* p. 768, note 2, but also recommends that virtually all cancer drugs be used in various combination in order to achieve the most effective therapy. In distributing or referring to standard NCI materials, pharmaceutical manufacturers are thus clearly recommending their drugs for unapproved uses. For years FDA has taken no action to prevent this activity, but in early 1991 the agency issued a letter objecting to the practice. Letter from K. R. Feather, Acting Director, FDA CDER Division of Drug Advertising and Labeling, to R. L. Gelb (Jan. 25, 1991). In light of current First Amendment jurisprudence, it is unlikely that FDA would take the same position today.

b. FDA AUTHORITY OVER OFF-LABEL PRESCRIBING

FDA initially sought to prevent any unapproved use of an approved new drug.

New Drugs Used for Nonapproved Purposes
(Methotrexate for Psoriasis)

Hearings Before a Subcomm. of the House Comm. on Government Operations, 92d
Congress, 1st Sess. (1971).

Mr. [Benjamin] Rosenthal [Congressman from N.Y.]. . . . If you find . . . that physicians who are not part of the IND studies are dispensing a drug improperly, is it also your attitude that nothing can be done?

Mr. [William] Goodrich [FDA Chief Counsel]. We could have done more than we did. The problem here was the physicians were using the drug on the basis of literature reports. The company was saying that it was not promoting the drug. We examined the evidence; we thought they did.

. . . We found out that when a physician out in the prescribing territory asked the detail man about Methotrexate for psoriasis then that would be reported back to Lederle and Lederle would send the physician a letter and reprints. They would send a disclaimer that they were not promoting the drug for that purpose, but that they would supply the information that it had been used; it had been used successfully by simply reporting out of the literature, and they would give him some information about the dose.

Mr. Rosenthal. That was not legal, what they were doing?

Mr. Goodrich. No, it was not. . . .

And Dr. Ley's approach, Mr. Rosenthal, was that it should be dealt with as an educational program with the profession. He encouraged the American Medical Association Journal to run an editorial on this. . . .

Mr. Grant [FDA Deputy Commissioner]. . . . Methotrexate is not the only drug that is being used for conditions for which it is not approved or labeled. Drugs approved for marketing for one purpose sometimes are found in ingenuity or by accident or have other uses. . . .

Our problem in dealing with the use of drugs for conditions in which they are not approved involves both the manufacturer and the prescribing physician. We have direct control over the manufacturer. We can take legal and administrative actions to assure that any drug is labeled for all of the conditions for which it is intended to be used, whether that intent is openly expressed in the promotional literature and promotional practices, or whether it is demonstrated by the manufacturer supplying a drug for purposes not covered in the approved labeling.

As to the physician, no less a group than the Council on Drugs of the American Medical Association has taken the position that it is within the physician's sole discretion to choose and to prescribe a drug for his own patient. . . .

What physicians need to know is that when they prescribe outside the limits of safety and effectiveness that have been established through the adequate and well-controlled clinical investigations required by the new drug procedures, they are using the drug investigationally on their patients. If any untoward reaction or adverse effect occurs, the physician may well be called upon to defend the reasonableness of his therapy. . . .

Following this hearing, FDA's position changed in two respects. First, FDA agreed that a company could properly respond with information about an off-label use of a drug to an unsolicited question by a physician. *See infra* p. 939. Second, the agency published the following proposed regulation to state its policy on physician prescribing for off-label uses.

Legal Status of Approved Labeling for Prescription Drugs; Prescribing for Uses Unapproved by the Food and Drug Administration: Notice of Proposed Rule Making

37 Fed. Reg. 16503 (August 15, 1972).

The widespread use of certain prescription drugs for conditions not named in the official labeling has led to questions concerning the legal responsibilities of the prescribing physicians and the position of the Food and Drug Administration with respect to such use. . . .

Section 505 of the Federal Food, Drug, and Cosmetic Act prohibits the introduction or delivery for introduction into interstate commerce of any new drug without the filing of an investigational new drug plan or approval of a new drug application. Unlike the adulteration and misbranding provisions of the Act, the new drug provisions apply only at the moment of shipment in interstate commerce and not to action taken subsequent to shipment in interstate commerce. In *United States v. Phelps Dodge Mercantile Co.,* 157 F.2d 453 (9th Cir. 1946) [*supra* p. 277], the court held that violations while products are held for sale after interstate shipment did not come within the jurisdiction of the Act. As a result of that decision, Congress enacted the Miller amendment of 1948, amending section 301(k) of the Act to extend the reach of the adulteration and misbranding provisions of the Act to violations after interstate shipment. The 1948 amendment did not, however, also extend the reach of the new drug provisions of the Act, which are separate from the adulteration and misbranding provisions, to action taken after interstate shipment.

The major objective of the drug provisions of the Federal Food, Drug, and Cosmetic Act is to assure that drugs will be safe and effective for use under the conditions of use prescribed, recommended, or suggested in the labeling thereof. . . . When a new drug is approved for marketing, the conditions of use that have been approved are required to be set forth in detail in the official labeling. This labeling must accompany the drug in interstate shipment and must contain adequate information for safe and effective use of the drug. . . . It presents a full disclosure summarization of drug use information, which the supplier of the drug is required to develop from accumulated clinical experience, and systematic drug trials consisting of preclinical investigations and adequate well-controlled clinical investigations that demonstrate the drug's safety and the effectiveness it purports or is represented to possess.

If an approved new drug is shipped in interstate commerce with the approved package insert, and neither the shipper nor the recipient intends that it be used for an unapproved purpose, the requirements of section 505 of the Act are satisfied. Once the new drug is in a local pharmacy after interstate shipment, the physician may, as part of the practice of medicine, lawfully prescribe a different dosage for his patient, or may otherwise vary the conditions of use from those approved in the package insert, without informing or obtaining the approval of the Food and Drug Administration.

This interpretation of the Act is consistent with congressional intent as indicated in the legislative history of the 1938 Act and the drug amendments of 1962. Throughout the debate leading to enactment, there were repeated statements that Congress did not intend the Food and Drug Administration to interfere with medical practice and references to the understanding that the bill did not purport to regulate the practice of medicine as between the physician and the patient. . . .

[A]lthough it is clear that Congress did not intend the Food and Drug Administration to regulate or interfere with the practice of medicine, it is equally clear that it did intend that the Food and Drug Administration determine those drugs for which there exists substantial evidence of safety and effectiveness and thus will be available for prescribing by the medical profession, and additionally, what information about the drugs constitutes truthful, accurate, and full disclosure to permit safe and effective prescription by the physician. As the law now stands, therefore, the Food and Drug Administration is charged with the responsibility of judging the safety and effectiveness of drugs and the truthfulness of their labeling. The physician is then responsible for making the final judgment as to which, if any, of the available drugs his patient will receive in the light of the information contained in their labeling and other adequate scientific data available to him.

Although the Act does not require a physician to file an investigational new drug plan before prescribing an approved drug for unapproved uses, or to submit to the Food and Drug Administration data concerning the therapeutic results and the adverse reactions obtained, it is sometimes in the best interests of the physician and the public that this be done. The physician should recognize that such use is investigational, and he should take account of the scientific principles, including the moral and ethical considerations, applicable to the safe use of investigational drugs in human patients. . . .

Where the unapproved use of an approved new drug becomes widespread or endangers the public health, the Food and Drug Administration is obligated to investigate it thoroughly and to take whatever action is warranted to protect the public. Several alternative courses of action are available to the Food and Drug Administration under these circumstances, depending upon the specific facts of each case. These actions include: Requiring a change in the labeling to warn against or to approve the unapproved use, seeking substantial evidence to substantiate the use, restricting the channel of distribution, and even withdrawing approval of the drug and removing it from the market in extreme cases. When necessary, the Food and Drug Administration will not hesitate to take whatever action of this nature may be required to bring possible harmful use of an approved drug under control.

Section 1.106 of the regulations [now 21 C.F.R. § 201.5] requires the labeling to contain appropriate information with respect to all intended uses of the drugs. Thus, where a manufacturer or his representative, or any person in the chain of distribution, does anything that directly or indirectly suggests to the physician or to the patient that an approved drug may properly be used for unapproved uses for which it is neither labeled nor advertised, that action constitutes a direct violation of the Act and is punishable accordingly. . . .

NOTES

1. *Subsequent Proceedings.* FDA first announced this policy in response to a question posed during a congressional hearing. "Regulation of Diethylstibestrol (DES)," Hearings before a Subcommittee of the House Committee on Government Operations, 92d Cong., 1st Sess., Part 1, at 102–103 (1971). The agency has taken no further action on the proposed regulation, but it has not been revoked and the agency has occasionally referred to this proposal as expressing its established policy. *See, e.g.,* "Use of Approved Drugs for Unlabeled Indications," 12 FDA DRUG BULL. 4 (Apr. 1982); 40 Fed. Reg. 15392, 15393–15394 (Apr. 7, 1975). When FDA undertook its comprehensive revision of the IND regulations in the 1980s, it incorporated this policy. 52 Fed. Reg. 8798 (Mar. 19, 1987), codified at 21 C.F.R. 312.2(d) ("This part does not apply to the use in the practice of medicine for an unlabeled indication of a new drug. . . ."). The Supreme Court recognized the legitimacy and medical importance of off-label uses in *Buckman Co. v. Plaintiffs' Legal Comm.*, 531 U.S. 341, 350 (2001). Various other courts have also done so, for example in the cases concerning First Amendment protections for speech about off-label uses. *See infra* pp. 942–956.

2. *Prohibition of Unapproved Use.* The only drug for which Congress has expressly prohibited all off-label use is human growth hormone (HGH). Section 303(e)(1) of the FD&C Act makes it a criminal offense for a physician to distribute HGH for any use other than the FDA-approved labeled use.

3. *Unapproved New Drugs.* Although unapproved uses of an FDA-approved new drug are lawful, any sale, distribution, or dispensing of an unapproved new drug is unlawful. *See, e.g., United States v. Hiland*, 909 F.2d 1114 (8th Cir. 1990).

4. *State Law.* A related issue is whether the unapproved use of an approved new drug complies with state law. Relying upon FDA's position, states that have considered the matter have determined that the physician is not bound by the approved physician package insert. *E.g.,* Opinion of California Attorney General E. J. Younger, CV 76/212 and 77/236 (May 2, 1978); Opinion of California Legislative Counsel B. M. Gregory No. 8182 (May 26, 1981). But in 2011, the Oklahoma legislature passed a law requiring mifepristone, the "abortion pill," be administered strictly in accordance with the protocol established by FDA in the drug's labeling and in a risk evaluation and mitigation strategy (REMS). In 2012, the

Oklahoma Supreme Court struck down this law on substantive due process grounds, applying the abortion rights decision *Planned Parenthood of SE Pa. v. Casey*, 505 U.S. 833 (1992). *Oklahoma Coalition for Reproductive Justice v. Cline*, 292 P.3d 27 (Okla. 2012). As this book went to press, the U.S. Supreme Court had certified two statutory interpretation questions to the Oklahoma to assist its decision as to whether to grant certiorari.

5.   *Depo-Provera.* The Department of HHS has itself officially used approved drugs for unapproved purposes. The Indian Health Service prescribed Depo-Provera for contraceptive use even after FDA specifically disapproved this indication. *See* "Use of the Drug, Depo Provera, by the Indian Health Service," Oversight Hearing before the Subcommittee on General Oversight and Investigations of the House Committee on Interior and Insular Affairs, 100th Cong., 1st Sess. (1987). The military also uses approved drugs for unapproved purposes. *See, e.g.*, Matthew A. Hoffman, *The Military's Need for "Speed:" A Case Study on the FDA's Regulation of Off–Label Prescriptions* (2003), in Chapter VI(B)(5) of the Electronic Book.

6.   *Generic Drugs.* Relying upon the FDA policy, the Chairman of the Subcommittee on Health and the Environment of the House Committee on Energy and Commerce took the position that a generic drug may lawfully be prescribed for a use for which only the pioneer drug has been approved, without added risk of liability on the part of the pharmacist or the physician. *See* letter from Representative Henry A. Waxman to F. S. Mayer (Nov. 25, 1985).

7.   *Reimbursement for Unapproved Uses.* Even though FDA has stated that a physician may lawfully prescribe a new drug for an unapproved use, reimbursement for such uses under Medicare, Medicaid, and private insurance programs is not available unless a special rule states otherwise. *See* 42 U.S.C. § 1396r–8(k)(6) (providing Medicare and Medicaid coverage for drug uses included in one or more specified compendia); GAO, OFF-LABEL DRUGS: REIMBURSEMENT POLICIES CONSTRAIN PHYSICIANS IN THEIR CHOICE OF CANCER THERAPIES, Rep. No. PEMD–91–14 (1991). These coverage limitations have caused the federal government to bring cases under the False Claims Act against drug manufacturers who promote unapproved uses. *See infra* p. 934.

8.   *Physician Distribution.* Although a physician does not violate section 505 of the FD&C Act by *prescribing* an approved new drug for an unapproved use, a physician who distributes either unapproved drugs or approved drugs for unapproved uses is fully subject to the requirements of section 505. *See, e.g., United States v. Sartori*, Food Drug Cosm. L. Rep. (CCH) ¶ 38,196 (D. Md. 1982). Where the requisite interstate commerce is lacking, misbranding or adulteration charges may properly be brought.

9.   *Diversion of Drugs Exempted for Studies in Animals.* FDA's August 1972 policy apparently does not provide a basis for the diversion of experimental drugs from animal testing to human use. In 1983, FDA discovered that interferon, a biological drug which was being shipped for investigational use only in laboratory animals or in vitro studies, was being diverted to human use. The agency published a notice warning that such diversion constituted a violation of section 351 of the Public Health Service Act. 48 Fed. Reg. 52644 (Nov. 21, 1983).

10. *FTC Enforcement.* When physicians began to advertise unapproved uses of approved new drugs, the FTC sought to prevent it. In 1975, the FTC sought to enjoin a weight reduction clinic from advertising human chorionic gonadotropin or any other unapproved drug for use in its treatment program. Citing FDA's August 1972 policy, however, the District Court ruled that advertising a treatment program that utilizes an unapproved new drug does not violate the FD&C Act. *F.T.C. v. Simeon Management Corp.,* 391 F. Supp. 697 (N.D. Cal. 1975), *aff'd,* 532 F.2d 708 (9th Cir. 1976).

11. *DEA Concern.* Just as DEA has attempted to discourage DTC advertising of scheduled prescription drugs, *infra* p. 924, note 6, it has also threatened to penalize physicians who prescribe these drugs off-label. 51 Fed. Reg. 17476 (May 13, 1986).

———

On occasion, FDA has—even after its 1972 policy statement— sought to prevent physicians from systematic off-label prescribing.

In the late 1960s and early 1970s, Ray Evers was one of the nation's most prominent practitioners of "chelation therapy." This therapy, roundly rejected by orthodox medicine, involved the intravenous injection of ethylenediaminetetraacetic acid (EDTA). Although FDA had approved EDTA only for treatment of heavy metal poisoning, practitioners promoted it as a cure for a range of ailments, including arteriosclerosis. Dr. Evers ran Meadowbrook Hospital in Belle Chasse, Louisiana, where he performed chelation therapy. In 1976, the United States government brought a successful action in U.S. district court in Louisiana. The court condemned the EDTA seized at the hospital and also enjoined Evers and the hospital from administering the substance. *United States v. An Article of Drug . . . Diso–Tate,* 1975– 1977 FDLI Judicial Record 239 (E.D. La. 1976). Evers then moved his operation to Alabama, where he opened the Ra–Mar Clinic in Montgomery. The federal government sought an injunction preventing Evers and the clinic from receiving EDTA or any other chelating drug or administering chelation therapy. This time, a U.S. district court in Alabama rejected the request, citing the FDA's 1972 policy statement, *supra* p. 817, disclaiming any authority to prohibit off-label prescription. The court stated: "Congress did not intend the [FDA] to interfere with medical practice as between the physician and the patients." *United States v. Evers,* 453 F. Supp. 1141, 1149 (M.D. Ala. 1978). Indeed the court suggested that a prohibition of off-label prescribing might exceed the federal government Commerce Clause power. *Id.* 1144.

In the following decision, the Fifth Circuit (which at the time included both Louisiana and Alabama) confirmed the holding of the U.S. district court in Alabama, but on different grounds.

United States v. Evers

643 F.2d 1043 (5th Cir. 1981).

■ RANDALL, CIRCUIT JUDGE:

In this action the government charges a licensed Alabama physician with a violation of section 301(k) of the Federal Food, Drug, and Cosmetic Act. That section prohibits, *inter alia,* the misbranding of a drug which is held for sale after shipment in interstate commerce. The government charges that the drug at issue, which is a prescription drug, was misbranded under section 502(f)(1) of the Act, which deems a drug to be misbranded unless its labeling contains "adequate directions for use." In particular, the government alleges that the physician promoted and administered a drug for a use that is not approved by the Food and Drug Administration (the FDA), without providing adequate directions for such use to his patients. The district court found that the physician had indeed failed to provide adequate directions for the intended use of the drug, but held that the physician's actions were within "the practice of medicine" and therefore beyond the constitutional reach of federal power and beyond the intended reach of the Act. . . .

We do not reach the issue on which the district court's opinion rests, for we find that the government has not established a violation of section 301(k) of the Act. Since prescription drugs are required by regulations promulgated pursuant to section 502(f)(1) of the Act to bear adequate information for use by physicians but not for use by patients, and since the physician charged in this case was administering the drug to his own patients but not distributing it to other physicians, we hold that Dr. Evers has not violated section 301(k) of the Act by his failure to provide such "adequate directions for use" as are required by section 502(f)(1) of the Act. . . .

The government contends that Dr. Evers violated section 301(k) of the Act, which prohibits any act with respect to a drug which "is done while such [drug] is held for sale (whether or not the first sale) after shipment in interstate commerce and [which] results in such article being . . . misbranded." The government must therefore establish two separate elements: (1) that the act in question occurred while the drug was held for sale after shipment in interstate commerce; and (2) that the act resulted in the article being misbranded. The focus of the government's case, as well as of Dr. Evers' defense and of the district court's opinion, is the second of these elements. In order to establish this element, that is, to demonstrate that Dr. Evers has "misbranded" Calcium EDTA, the government relies solely on section 502(f)(1) of the Act. That section deems a drug to be misbranded "unless its labeling bears . . . adequate directions for use." In brief, the government contends that Dr. Evers failed to provide "adequate directions for use" when he promoted and prescribed Calcium EDTA for the treatment of circulatory disorders, a use for which the drug has not been approved by the FDA.

In response to this charge, Dr. Evers (as well as certain of his patients, as intervenors) argues that as a licensed physician he has a right to prescribe any lawful drug for any purpose, whether or not that purpose has been approved by the FDA. The district court agreed with Dr. Evers and held that no misbranding could result from a doctor's prescription of a lawful drug to his own patients. . . .

However, the analysis urged by Dr. Evers and adopted by the district court misapprehends the thrust of the government's case against Dr. Evers, for the FDA has at no point contended, and the government does not argue on appeal, that the misbranding provisions of the Act prohibit a doctor from prescribing a lawful drug for a purpose for which the drug has not been approved by the FDA. To the contrary, the FDA has explicitly informed Dr. Evers that he could legally prescribe chelating drugs for the treatment of circulatory disorders. . . .

The object of the government's case against Dr. Evers is not, therefore, his *prescription* of Calcium EDTA for use in the treatment of circulatory disorders. Instead, the government seeks to challenge Dr. Evers' *promotion* and *advertising* of chelating drugs for that use. According to the government, Dr. Evers "misbranded" Calcium EDTA when he publicly advocated his use of chelating drugs for an unapproved purpose without providing "adequate directions" for such a use. . . .

The government argues that Dr. Evers' prescription and promotion of Calcium EDTA for the treatment of circulatory disorders meets both of the above requirements of section 301(k) of the Act. In the first place, the government contends that Dr. Evers "held (Calcium EDTA) for sale" when he maintained a supply of the drug for use on his own patients at the Ra–Mar Clinic. To support this position, the government relies on cases . . . which did indeed hold that a doctor who had held drugs for use in his practice had held those drugs for sale within the meaning of the Act. In the second place, the government contends that Dr. Evers misbranded Calcium EDTA within the meaning of section 502(f)(1) of the Act by failing to provide "adequate directions for use". . . . It is undisputed that Dr. Evers did in fact fail to provide adequate directions for either lay or professional use; Dr. Evers does not contend that his booklets contained "adequate directions for lay use" within the meaning of the regulations, and he does not appear to have made any attempt to meet the terms of either the regulatory or the statutory exception for prescription drugs.

When each of the two elements of the offense with which Dr. Evers is charged is examined individually, Dr. Evers does indeed seem to have violated the statute. A different picture emerges, however, when the two elements are considered together. Since Calcium EDTA is a prescription drug, the FDA can establish an act of misbranding under section 502(f)(1) of the Act only by proving that Dr. Evers did not provide adequate information *for use by physicians,* as is required by the exceptions to that section. The information provided by Dr. Evers to his patients is irrelevant to the question at hand, for according to FDA regulations there is *no* information which could have been provided about this prescription drug which would have constituted "adequate directions for [lay] use." However, the government argues that Dr. Evers "held [Calcium EDTA] for sale" within the meaning of section 301(k) because he maintained a supply of the drug for use *on his own patients;* the government does not contend that Dr. Evers was distributing Calcium EDTA to other licensed physicians. The government therefore must find itself in an awkward position: while the misbranding violation it urges is based on Dr. Evers' failure to provide adequate information to licensed physicians, it seeks to include his actions within the reach of section 301(k) of the Act by virtue of his distribution to patients.

The requirement which the FDA seeks to impose is nonsensical. Since Calcium EDTA is a prescription drug, the misbranding provision under which Dr. Evers was charged requires him to provide adequate information for use by prescribing physicians. However, Dr. Evers was the only physician who used the Calcium EDTA in question. The government's application of the statute may therefore be reduced to the following proposition: Dr. Evers did not provide adequate information to himself. It is doubtful at best that this interpretation was intended by the drafters of the statute.

In more specific terms, the government's interpretation of the Act breaks down over its use of the phrase "held for sale after shipment in interstate commerce." Although Dr. Evers was holding Calcium EDTA for sale in the sense that he was distributing it *to his own patients,* he was not holding it for sale *to physicians.* Section 301(k) of the Act cannot reasonably be read to require a physician who is holding a drug for sale only to patients to provide adequate information to physicians to whom he is not distributing the drug. We think it clear that a single doctor may be holding drugs for sale to one group of purchasers but not to another. If the doctor is not holding the drug for sale to the party to whom he owes a statutory obligation of full disclosure (in this case other prescribing physicians), then it makes no sense to impose the requirements of the statute. No legitimate purpose is served when a statutory provision requiring disclosure to one particular group of purchasers is invoked on the basis of sales made to a different group. Since Dr. Evers was holding Calcium EDTA, a prescription drug, for sale only to his patients, and since section 502(f)(1) of the Act does not require any disclosure to patients regarding prescription drugs, we conclude that Dr. Evers did not violate section 301(k) of the Act.[16]

---

[16] One might argue that although Dr. Evers did not distribute Calcium EDTA to other physicians, he nevertheless "labeled" the drug to the medical community at large through his public promotional and advertising efforts, and that he therefore caused the drug to be "misbranded" because the drug's label did not meet the full disclosure requirements of the regulatory exception to section 502(f)(1) with respect to the new use advocated for the drug by Dr. Evers. This seems to be the theory on which the District Court for the Eastern District of Louisiana found a misbranding violation in the government's earlier suit against Dr. Evers. *See United States v. An Article of Drug . . . Diso-tate.* This approach relies on the promotion *per se* of the drug, and seems to ignore altogether the fact that misbranding under section 301(k) of the Act can occur only with respect to particular drugs "held for sale after shipment in interstate commerce." At base, this theory equates *promotion* with sale, and therefore brings into question the legality of a physician's advocacy of any medical program involving drugs not approved for the advocated use by the FDA, even when the physician does not himself sell or even dispense the drug. But the Act was intended to regulate the distribution of drugs in interstate commerce, not to restrain physicians from public advocacy of medical opinions not shared by the FDA. We believe, therefore, that a doctor who merely advocates to other doctors a lawful prescription drug for a use not approved by the FDA, and does not distribute that drug to other doctors, is not holding that drug for sale within the meaning of the statute and therefore is not in violation of section 301(k) of the Act.

4. CONTROLS OVER PRESCRIPTION DRUG DISTRIBUTION

a. PRE-2007

As discussed in the next subsection, the Food and Drug Administration Amendments Act of 2007 (FDAAA) gave the agency important new authority to restrict the distribution of approved drugs pursuant to a mechanism known as the Risk Evaluation and Mitigation Strategy (REMS). The notion of imposing a limited distribution scheme was not a new one, however.

The addictive drug methadone was originally approved by FDA as an analgesic. When it was discovered that methadone was effective in blocking the euphoria caused by heroin and therefore could be used in the treatment of heroin addiction, physicians throughout the country began to prescribe it for this off-label use without adequate consideration of the drug's own addictive properties. To bring the drug's use back under control, FDA promulgated regulations restricting distribution to hospital pharmacies. 37 Fed. Reg. 26790 (Dec. 15, 1972).

American Pharmaceutical Association
v. Weinberger

377 F. Supp. 824 (D.D.C. 1974).

■ PRATT, DISTRICT JUDGE. . . .

. . . Plaintiffs challenge the validity of certain provisions of the Food and Drug Administration's methadone regulations. . . . Specifically, plaintiffs object to those parts of the regulations which purport to restrict the distribution of methadone to direct shipments from the manufacturer to (a) approved maintenance treatment programs, (b) approved hospital pharmacies, and (c) in cases where hospital pharmacies are unavailable in a particular area, to selected community pharmacies. Plaintiffs include the American Pharmaceutical Association (APhA), a professional association of pharmacists with a membership in excess of 50,000, three individual professional pharmacists and an individual physician. . . .

The drug methadone, a synthetic substitute for morphine, is a "new" drug within the meaning of section 201(p) of the Federal Food, Drug and Cosmetic Act and, as a new drug, requires FDA's approval of a NDA, filed with the Commissioner of Food and Drugs pursuant to section 505(b) of the Act. The drug was first approved by FDA in the 1950's as safe for use as an analgesic and antitussive agent as well as for short-term detoxification of persons addicted to heroin. Subsequently, investigation of methadone for use in long-term maintenance of narcotic addicts (methadone maintenance) was approved by FDA pursuant to its authority under 21 U.S.C. § 355(i), the investigational new-drug (IND) exemption. . . . [In 1972] FDA determined that "retention of the drug [methadone] solely on an investigational status appears to be no longer warranted" and published a notice of proposed rulemaking which resulted, with certain modifications, in the regulations now in question.

The final regulation gave notice that pursuant to FDA's authority under 21 U.S.C. § 355(c), the Commissioner was withdrawing approval of all outstanding NDA's because of "a lack of substantial evidence that methadone is safe and effective for detoxification, and analgesia, or antitussive use *under the conditions of use that presently exist.*" Having withdrawn all approved NDA's, the Commission's new regulatory scheme is presently the exclusive means of distribution for the drug methadone. The Commissioner has thereby created an admittedly unique classification for methadone since on the one hand he has determined that methadone should not be limited solely to investigational status while at the same time concluding that the drug is inappropriate for regular NDA approval. As statutory support for this novel solution to the methadone dilemma, defendants rely on an expansive interpretation of the Commissioner's NDA authority under § 355 of the Act. . . .

The defendants point . . . out that § 355(d) gives the Secretary the authority to refuse to approve an NDA where the reports of the investigations submitted do not include adequate tests showing whether the new drug is "safe for use under the conditions prescribed, recommended, or suggested in the proposed labeling thereof." Defendants argue that the term "safe" should be interpreted with reference not only to the inherent qualities of the drug under consideration but also in the sense of the drug's being secure from possible misuse. Such a broad interpretation would, according to defendants' theory, serve as the statutory foundation for FDA's exercise of authority in restricting methadone's channels of distribution because FDA's principal rationale for restricting distribution was "to help reduce the likelihood of diversion."

. . . As noted above, the term "safe" is used in conjunction with the phrase "for use under the conditions prescribed, recommended, or suggested in the proposed labeling thereof. When taken in this context, a determination of whether a drug is "safe" is premised on the drug's use in the "prescribed, recommended, or suggested" manner. Thus the context of the statute indicates that the term "safe" was intended to include only the inherent safety of the drug when used in the manner intended. Moreover, . . . [§ 355(d)(3)] extends the Secretary's authority to pass on the adequacy of methods, facilities and *controls* only with respect to *manufacturing, processing* and *packaging.* Under the doctrine of "expressio unius est exclusio alterius" any stage of the drug's genesis not specifically mentioned in provision (3) was presumably intended to be excluded from the Secretary's authority. Thus . . . the Court concludes that the term "safe" was intended to refer to a determination of the inherent safety or lack thereof of the drug under consideration when used for its intended purpose.[9] . . .

---

[9]   Even if the Court were to agree with defendant's interpretation of the term "safe," this alone would not provide a statutory basis for the regulations challenged herein. At most such an interpretation would authorize FDA to deny or withdraw any methadone NDA based on a finding that the drug could not be "safely" distributed. As outlined in the Court's opinion, FDA's discretion under the Act's NDA provisions is limited to either approving or denying NDA's and nowhere is FDA empowered to approve an NDA upon the condition that the drug be distributed only through specified channels.

In addition to being a "new" drug and thus within the jurisdiction of the FDA, methadone is a controlled substance within Schedule II of the Controlled Substances Act, 21 U.S.C. § 812. Under this Act the Attorney General is made responsible for the registration of any person who manufactures, distributes or dispenses any controlled substance. . . .

The Court concludes that Congress intended to create two complementary institutional checks on the production and marketing of new drugs. At the production or pre-marketing stage, the FDA is given the primary responsibility in determining which new drugs should be permitted to enter the flow of commerce. . . . When an IND exemption is approved, the Commissioner may, of course, severely restrict the distribution of the exempted drug to bona fide researchers and clinicians. But once a drug is cleared for marketing by way of an NDA-approval, for whatever uses the Commissioner deems appropriate, the question of permissible distribution of the drug, when that drug is a controlled substance, is one clearly within the jurisdiction of the Justice Department. . . . To allow the challenged portions of the methadone regulations to stand, therefore, would be to abrogate the collective judgment of Congress with regard to the appropriate means of controlling unlawful drug diversion. . . .

NOTES

1. *Subsequent Proceedings.* On appeal, the District Court decision was affirmed *per curiam,* 530 F.2d 1054 (D.C. Cir. 1976). Although he concurred in the judgment, Judge McGowan was not content simply to affirm the lower court's opinion:

> . . . The FDA contends that where there exists a documented pattern of drug misuse contrary to the intended uses specified in the labelling, the drug is unsafe for approval unless controls over distribution are imposed. As a corollary, it asserts that for a drug such as methadone, for which there is substantial evidence of misuse, the FDA must have the power to restrict distribution to avoid the dilemma of either disapproving a drug with important therapeutic benefits or of placing on the market a drug likely to be misused. The FDA claims that . . . the regulations at issue differ only in degree from a prescription-only restriction. . . .

> Although these arguments have some weight, I do not find them ultimately convincing. The word "safe" in section 355(d) is, to my mind, best interpreted as requiring the labelling to include the evidence from drug testing, and the inferences therefrom, indicating the therapeutic benefits, possible dangers, and uncertainties involved in use of a drug, as an aid to a conscientious physician in determining appropriate medical treatment. That view seems to me to accord with both the most reasonable interpretation of the statutory language and the common understanding of the FDA's mission. Thus, methadone is safe for its intended use notwithstanding the possibility that it will be employed in unintended fashions. . . .

There would be almost no limit to the FDA's authority were its view adopted. If, for example, it had concluded before 1970 that without restrictions on methadone of the sort now contained in the Controlled Substances Act the possibility of drug misuse remained high, there would be no barrier under its argument to its having established a regulatory scheme of the complexity of that ultimately adopted in that Act. . . .

2.   *Methadone Regulations.* FDA subsequently revised its methadone regulations by deleting the restrictions on distribution. 41 Fed. Reg. 28261 (July 9, 1976). In 2001, HHS repealed the narcotic treatment regulations enforced by FDA and created a new regulatory system based on an accreditation model, under the oversight of the Substance Abuse and Mental Health Services Administration (SAMHSA). 66 Fed. Reg. 4076 (Jan. 17, 2001).

3.   *Distribution Restrictions.* The Drug Regulation Reform Act of 1979, which passed the Senate but was never adopted by the House, would have explicitly authorized FDA to restrict distribution of drugs. S. Rep. No. 96–321, 96th Cong., 1st Sess. (1979).

————

Although *American Pharmaceutical Association v. Weinberger* held that FDA could not restrict distribution as a condition of approving an NDA, it did not state that a pharmaceutical manufacturer could not *voluntarily* limit distribution or that FDA could not approve labeling that incorporated such voluntary controls. Facing the alternative of the agency rejecting its NDA, a manufacturer would, even after *American Pharmaceutical Association*, sometimes "voluntarily" accept such conditions. Therefore, even before 2007, FDA approved physician labeling for some drugs containing various limitations on the type of pharmacy at which the drug is available, the conditions under which pharmacies are permitted to stock the drug, or the qualifications of the physicians who are permitted to prescribe the drug. For example, in addition to providing stringent warnings for the acne drug Accutane® (isotretinoin) to reduce teratogenic side effects (birth defects), *see infra* p. 872, note 5, the manufacturer implemented a restricted distribution program called iPLEDGE,. This program involves education and registration of physicians and pharmacists and also requires female patients to sign a patient information/informed consent form in which they agree to use two forms of birth control one month before, during, and one month after the administration of the drug. Before 2007, FDA sometimes called such strategic safety programs risk minimization action plans (RiskMAPs).

Prior to 2007, FDA also imposed restricted distribution regimes on drugs approved pursuant to Subpart H accelerated approval. *See supra* p. 754. In 2006, FDA granted accelerated approved to thalidomide (the drug whose side effects launched the 1962 Drug Amendments) for treatment of multiple myeloma while subjecting it to a restricted distribution program. Other pre-2007 examples include RU–486 ("the abortion pill") and GHB (the "date rape" drug, approved for narcolepsy). Because the request for accelerated approval is voluntary on the part of the manufacturer, these programs are not inconsistent with *American*

Pharmaceutical Association v. Weinberger. If the applicant were to refuse to agree on the conditions, FDA would likely refuse to approve the NDA on an accelerated basis.

b. RISK EVALUATION AND MITIGATION STRATEGIES (REMS)

The Food and Drug Administration Amendments Act of 2007 (FDAAA) added a new section to the FD&C Act, section 505–1, authorizing the imposition of risk evaluation and mitigation strategies (REMS). Under 505–1(a)(1), a new drug applicant must submit, as part of its application, a proposed risk evaluation and mitigation strategy if FDA determines that a REMS is necessary to ensure that the benefits of the drug outweigh its risks. Moreover, even after the approval of an NDA, the agency may demand such a submission if it makes the same determination on the basis of new safety information. *Id.* 505–1(a)(2).

Less burdensome REMS may include a Medication Guide, patient package insert, or a plan for communication to healthcare providers. *Id.* 505–1(e). (For more discussion on Medication Guides and patient package inserts, see *infra* p. 886.) But FDA may also require "elements to assure safe use" of a drug (i.e., use and distribution restrictions) upon a determination that: (1) the drug, which is associated with a serious adverse drug experience, "can be approved only if, or would be withdrawn unless, such elements are required as part of a strategy to mitigate a specific serious risk listed in the labeling of the drug," and (2) if the drug was initially approved without such restrictions in place, other potential REMS elements are not sufficient to mitigate this risk. *Id.* 505–1(f)(1).

The Act lists a number of possible elements of a REMS, including requirements that: (1) healthcare providers who prescribe the drug have particular training, experience, or certification; (2) patients be monitored; (3) patients be enrolled in registries; (4) pharmacies and others dispensing the drug be specially certified; (5) the drug be dispensed to patients only in certain settings, such as hospitals; and (6) patients have evidence of "safe-use conditions" (e.g., laboratory test results).

The Act requires the agency to engage in "discussions" with the manufacturer about the proposed REMS. *Id.* 505–1(h)(2). If a proposed REMS is submitted as part of an initial NDA (or BLA), and the manufacturer and FDA cannot agree on the strategy, the applicant must use the major dispute resolution procedures set forth in FDA's user fee reauthorization goals letter. *Id.* 505–1(h)(4). In all other cases, if the discussions do not resolve disagreements regarding the particular elements of the REMS, the applicant may request another form of dispute resolution, namely, review of the strategy in a meeting of the Drug Safety Oversight Board. (The agency's decision to require a REMS is not itself reviewable in this proceeding.) *Id.* 505–1(h)(5). The Board's final recommendation is published but is not binding on FDA. *Id.* 505–1(h)(5)(F)–(G). REMS may be established for classes of drugs as well as for individual products. *Id.* 505–1(h)(7).

FD&C Act 505(p) states that a person may not introduce a drug with a required REMS into interstate commerce unless the person complies with the REMS. Failure to comply with a REMS is a misbranding violation. *Id.* 502(y). Moreover, a violator is subject to civil money penalties. *Id.* 303(f)(4).

In theory, the use of REMS should increase the number of drug approvals, because the management of risks through a REMS alters the calculus of the risk-benefit balance. It is not at all obvious that the advent of REMS has had this effect, however—perhaps because FDA was already mitigating risks through the use of RiskMAPs prior to 2007.

As of July 2013, approximately 70 approved REMS are in effect, some of which are converted pre-2007 RiskMAPs. (FDA has imposed and later lifted about 140 additional REMS.) About half of the REMS in effect consist only of communication plans or medication guides, but the other half also include elements to assure safe use. Some of these more restrictive REMS directly regulate the practice of medicine. Consider, for example, the following REMS for Entereg®, a drug indicated to accelerate the time of recovery following partial large or small bowel resection surgery.

Risk Evaluation and Mitigation Strategy (REM) for NDA 21–775 Entereg (alvimopan)

I.   GOAL

To reduce the risk of myocardial infarction observed with longer use, Entereg (alvimopan) will be used only for short-term use (not to exceed 15 doses) in inpatient settings.

II.   REMS ELEMENTS

A.   Communication Plan

Cubist Pharmaceuticals, Inc. will implement a communication plan to healthcare providers to support implementation of this REMS.

Cubist will provide educational materials for distribution to healthcare professionals involved in the prescribing, dispensing, or administration of Entereg. This includes surgeons who perform bowel resection surgery, hospitalists, anesthesiologists, nurse anesthetists, pharmacists, nurses, and physicians assistants. . . .

• Dear Hospital Pharmacist Letter

The Dear Hospital Pharmacist Letter, to be distributed on product launch, will state that Entereg can be used for no more than 15 doses in inpatients, and that Entereg is not available for outpatient use. Additionally, the letter will provide a description of and directions on how to enroll in the E.A.S.E. program, the program that incorporates elements for safe use as shown in the appended Dear Hospital Pharmacist Letter.

• Entereg Access Support and Education (E.A.S.E.) educational materials

Cubist will use the E.A.S.E. educational materials (available in printed form . . . and on-line as part of the . . . registration system), to educate all hospital-based healthcare professionals that are involved in the prescribing, dispensing, or administration of Entereg.

The E.A.S.E. printed materials include:

- E.A.S.E. Program Overview
- E.A.S.E. Hospital Brochure
- E.A.S.E. Kit Folder
- Registration Form
- Prescribing Information Brochure

Additional educational materials include:

- Dear Hospital Pharmacist Letter(at product launch)
- Professional Labeling

The educational materials will prominently feature the safety-related message that because of the risk of myocardial infarction observed with longer use, Entereg can be used for no more than 15 doses in inpatients, and Entereg cannot be prescribed for outpatients as shown in the appended printed material and web shots.

B.   Elements to Assure Safe Use

1.   Drug Dispensed Only in Hospitals

Entereg will be dispensed to patients only in hospitals. The hospital will not dispense Entereg for outpatient use.

2.   Drug Dispensed in Specially Certified Hospitals

Entereg will be dispensed only in hospitals that perform bowel resection surgery and that are specially certified by enrollment in the E.A.S.E. program. The specially certified hospital will not transfer Entereg to any hospital not registered with the E.A.S.E. Program. To register in the E.A.S.E. program, responsible hospital personnel must attest that:

- E.A.S.E. educational materials have been received by the hospital and distributed to healthcare professionals who are responsible for the ordering, prescribing, dispensing, or administering of Entereg;

- The hospital has systems, order sets, protocols, or other measures in place to ensure that Entereg is dispensed only to patients with evidence of safe use conditions. . . .

Entereg will be distributed to registered hospitals via a drop-ship program through which Cubist retains direct control over who purchases Entereg. . . .

3.   Drug Dispensed Only to Patients with Evidence of Safe–Use Conditions

Entereg will be dispensed only to patients in hospitals performing bowel resections; each patient will receive no more than 15 doses of the drug.

C.   Implementation System

The Implementation System includes the following:

- Cubist will maintain a database of all specially certified hospitals;

- Cubist will monitor distribution to determine whether the drug is only dropshipped to certified hospitals and will conduct audits to verify;

- Cubist will monitor dispensing of Entereg to ensure that it is dispensed only for inpatient use;

- Cubist will monitor the duration of therapy to determine whether Entereg is being dispensed to patients with evidence that the patient is hospitalized for bowel resection surgery and has received no more than 15 doses;

. . . .

NOTE

Drug Safety Oversight Board. As noted above, disputes over REMS are considered by a body called the Drug Safety Oversight Board (DSOB). Following the controversy about the Cox–2 inhibitor drugs, FDA announced on February 15, 2005 that the agency it was creating this independent entity to oversee the management of important drug safety issues within CDER. "FDA Improvements in Drug Safety Monitoring," FDA Fact Sheet (Feb. 15, 2005). CDER issued MAPP No. 4151–3 (May 4, 2005) to describe the organizational structure, roles, and responsibility of the DSOB. The DSOB is comprised only of government employees and thus is not subject to the Federal Advisory Committee Act requirements for open public meetings. Its meetings are closed except when it invites representatives of a pharmaceutical company to discuss a specific safety issue relating to one of its products. A public summary of each meeting is available on the FDA website.

———

Even before 2007, some commentators expressed concern about the implications of risk mitigation programs for the practice of medicine.

Speech by Scott Gottlieb, M.D.,* Before the American Medical Association
June 12, 2006.

. . . One of the questions that the public has is whether or not the FDA is doing enough to find out about new safety issues that marketed drugs might have, and whether we are communicating these things quickly enough. Those are fair concerns, and we have been doing a lot at FDA to address them. . . .

But there is a second question that I am equally concerned with, and it has to do with how we confront situations where we already know that a drug has a certain side effect at the time of approval, or shortly after. Especially in cases where we know there are some common sense precautions physicians and patients can take to mitigate, or even nearly eliminate the chances of someone suffering these side effects. . . .

———

* Dr. Gottlieb was the FDA Deputy Commissioner for Medical and Scientific Affairs.

This challenge cuts directly to issues related to the practice of medicine, and sometimes tugs at where the boundary is between our role at FDA and the role of practicing doctors. I am worried that this boundary has become increasingly blurry to an outside view, and we at FDA are being increasingly asked by some groups and by political bodies to occasionally step across it, when drug safety issues arise and where our role in influencing how a drug is prescribed can be reasonably assumed to cut down on that risk. I am talking in particular about the increasing number of risk management plans that are becoming part of new drug approvals. These plans attempt to mitigate a certain risk by directly influencing or controlling how a drug is used. Now I think if you look at the places where we have implemented these plans, I think you would agree we have been balanced and careful to respect practice issues. These plans also allow us to often put drugs on the market or keep drugs on the market that otherwise we would not feel comfortable with. But I worry about the future.

My concern is that ... these plans ... are ... becoming an increasingly prominent condition of certain approvals as we negotiate final labeling over newly approved drugs. It is fair to say, I believe, that these plans are sometimes a less-than-optimal response to more systemic systems problems in the delivery of medical care. . . . [T]here are ... some real challenges we face if these plans continue to become a common feature of drug approvals. In particular, there is a cumulative burden they impose that could encroach on medical practice decisions that doctors make and on patient discretion. This could be especially true when it comes to patients who already have a hard time getting access to specialty care or to the most innovative safe and effective medicines. Patients for example who may receive care in urban settings where busy clinics may not have the time and resources to comply with these plans, or patients who do not have access to specialists who are favored prescribers under some of these plans, or access to pharmacies able to subsidize all of the requirements. We are especially sensitive to these kinds of concerns when working on the design of these plans.

The good news is I think there are some steps we can take working together to make sure that the laudable medical safety goals that these risk management plans aim to achieve can be accomplished without FDA being directly involved every time. But addressing these healthcare systems problems is going to require a lot more involvement and collaboration of organized medical bodies as well as individual physicians in our work than we have enjoyed in the past. . . .

. . . A lot of these drug safety questions are difficult for us to address directly at FDA, because they deal with personal prescribing decisions. The more we promulgate plans that attempt to guide or even control these decisions, the more we encroach on professional autonomy, and the responsibilities doctors have as a profession to address these kinds of practice issues through their own vehicles so that they can continue to personalize care to their patients' individual preferences.

NOTE

Minimizing REMS' Negative Effects. The FD&C Act, as amended by the FDAAA, requires FDA to seek input from patients, physicians, pharmacists, and other healthcare providers regarding how REMS can be standardized so that they are not unduly burdensome on patient access and minimize (to the extent practicable) the burden on the healthcare delivery system. FD&C Act 505–1(f)(5). It also requires the agency annually to evaluate at least one REMS to assure that these prerogatives are being met. *Id.*

F. POSTAPPROVAL ISSUES

Following NDA approval, the manufacturer of a new drug becomes subject to a new set of regulatory requirements and prohibitions.

1. POSTAPPROVAL SUBMISSIONS TO FDA

a. DRUG ESTABLISHMENT REGISTRATION AND DRUG PRODUCT LISTING

The Drug Amendments of 1962 added section 510 to the FD&C Act, which requires the annual registration of all establishments engaged in the "manufacture, preparation, propagation, compounding, or processing of" drugs or devices. 76 Stat. 780, 793; FD&C Act 510(b)(1). The Drug Listing Act of 1972, 86 Stat. 559, added section 510(j) to require the submission to FDA of lists of the drug products made in those establishments. It took almost a decade before the information submitted under the Drug Listing Act became computer-accessible.

The drug establishment registration and drug product listing regulations are codified in 21 C.F.R. Part 207. A report by the HHS Office of Inspector General, *The Food and Drug Administration's National Drug Code Directory*, No. OEI–06–05–00060 (Aug. 2006), found that FDA's list of marketed drug products is seriously deficient. In response, FDA published a proposed complete revision of its regulations, under which drug establishment registration and drug product listing would be required to be done electronically through the internet. 71 Fed. Reg. 51276 (Aug. 29, 2006). In 2007, FDAAA required that drug establishment and listing information be submitted electronically unless a waiver is granted. FD&C Act 510(p). *See* GUIDANCE FOR INDUSTRY: PROVIDING REGULATORY SUBMISSIONS IN ELECTRONIC FORMAT—DRUG ESTABLISHMENT REGISTRATION AND LISTING (May 2009).

The registration and listing requirements apply equally to foreign establishments manufacturing drugs or devices for import into the United States. FD&C Act 510(i)(1)–(2).

For an unusual case sustaining a criminal conviction for failure to register a drug establishment, see *United States v. Antosh*, 1999 WL 132252 (9th Cir. 1999).

b. SUPPLEMENTAL NDAS (SNDAS)

Under 21 C.F.R. 314.70, any significant variance from the detailed terms and conditions specified in the approved NDA must be the subject of a supplemental NDA (SNDA) and may not be put into effect until approved by FDA. The only changes that an NDA holder may make without such prior approval are set forth in the FDA regulations, and those exceptions must be reflected in the annual report for the NDA submitted to agency, discussed below. If FDA finds that significant changes have been made to a drug without approval of an SNDA, it may take very stringent regulatory action, including recall of the product and the suspension of manufacture until the unapproved changes are eliminated or approved.

FDA rigorously enforces the requirement for a supplemental NDA. *See, e.g., United States v. Sardesai*, Food Drug Cosm. L. Rep. (CCH) ¶ 38,536 (4th Cir. 1997) (criminal prosecution for failure to submit and obtain approval of a supplemental NDA prior to making manufacturing changes); *United States v. Marcus*, 82 F.3d 606 (4th Cir. 1996) (criminal prosecution for failure to submit and obtain approval of a supplemental NDA prior to making a change in the inactive ingredients of the drug); *United States v. 1500 90–Table Bottles . . . Genendo Pharmaceutical N.V.*, 384 F. Supp. 2d 1205 (N.D. Ill. 2005) (seizure for repackaging without an approved supplemental NDA).

Two types of supplemental NDAs are particularly important: (1) labeling changes and (2) manufacturing changes.

i. *Labeling Changes*

FDA maintains control and surveillance over product labeling and advertising in three ways. First, any change in the actual labeling of the product—e.g., a new indication for the drug, a change in the dosing schedule, or any other significant change in the physician labeling—must be the subject of a supplemental NDA. Second, under 21 C.F.R. 314.81(b)(3)(i), the NDA holder is required to submit specimens of all promotional labeling and advertising at the time of initial dissemination, accompanied by form FDA 2253. Third, under 21 C.F.R. 314.81(b)(2), the NDA holder must submit each year an annual report containing currently used professional labeling, patient brochures, package inserts, and package labels. Thus, FDA maintains a file of the complete history and current status of all prescription drug labeling used under the NDA. For more discussion of labeling changes, see *infra* p. 874.

ii. *Manufacturing Changes*

The pharmaceutical industry has long felt that FDA has been too stringent in requiring supplemental NDAs for manufacturing changes. Prior to 1997, the industry found it easier to continue obsolete manufacturing methods in establishments producing drugs for the U.S. market rather than seek FDA approval of an SNDA. In contrast, manufacturers were free to make substantial manufacturing changes, reflecting the latest technology, in establishments producing the same drugs for foreign markets. In the FDA Modernization Act of 1997, Congress added section 506A to the FD&C Act to make changes in manufacturing more flexible. Under section 506A, a major manufacturing change may be made only pursuant to a supplemental NDA, but all other manufacturing changes may be made based on the manufacturer's validation, so long as the change is reported to FDA either at the time it is made or as part of the NDA annual report. The implementation of this new provision, as reflected in 21 C.F.R. 314.70 and FDA guidance, has substantially streamlined the regulatory process for manufacturing changes.

c.　Adverse Event Reporting

Under 21 C.F.R. 314.80, an NDA holder must report to FDA any adverse event "associated with the use of a drug in humans, whether or not considered drug related," in one of the following ways. First, an adverse event that is both serious and unexpected, whether foreign or domestic, must be reported as soon as possible but in no event later than 15 calendar days after initial receipt of the information. The company is required to promptly investigate all 15-day alert reports and submit additional new information to FDA. Second, all other adverse drug experiences must be reported to FDA at quarterly intervals for the first three years under the NDA and at annual intervals thereafter. These reports should not include information that would identify individual patients.

NOTES

1.　*Economic Impact.* In compliance with the requirements for OMB review and clearance under the Paperwork Reduction Act of 1995, 44 U.S.C. 3507, FDA must prepare a yearly analysis of the economic burden of its recordkeeping and reporting requirements. For an analysis of the adverse drug experience reporting requirements, see 71 Fed. Reg. 6281 (Feb. 7, 2006).

2.　*The MedWatch Program.* The FD&C Act requires drug manufacturers to submit adverse reports to FDA, but FDA has no authority to require physicians or medical institutions to submit such reports. Nevertheless, for many years FDA has maintained and widely publicized a MedWatch program for voluntary reporting of adverse drug events by health care professionals and institutions.

3.　*Preemption of Confidentiality.* In a product liability case, a Texas trial judge ordered Eli Lilly to disclose the names and addresses of all persons who submitted adverse reaction reports relating to the drug. In *Eli Lilly and Co. v. Marshall*, Food Drug Cosm. L. Rep. ¶ 38,304 (Sup. Ct. Tex. 1993), the Texas Supreme Court, taking into account an FDA statement of interest supporting the Eli Lilly position, reversed the trial court. Because this issue arose repeatedly in product liability litigation throughout the country, FDA determined in 60 Fed. Reg. 16962 (Apr. 3, 1995), 21 C.F.R. 20.63(f)(2), to preempt all state and local requirements that permit or require disclosure of the identities of a voluntary reporter or any other person named in an adverse event report.

4.　*Different Types of Adverse Reactions.* In *Post Marketing Surveillance and Adverse Drug Reactions: Current Perspectives and Future*

Needs, 281 J.A.M.A. 824 (Mar. 3, 1999), Timothy Brewer and Graham A. Colditz argue that adverse drug reactions should be divided into two categories: (1) events that otherwise occur rarely in the population and (2) events that represent an increased frequency over a relatively common rate in the general population. Adverse event reports are extremely helpful in revealing the former, but controlled studies are needed to find the latter type of adverse events. The increased risk of heart disease attributed to some Cox–2 inhibitors could not be found with the former type of reporting but came to light in the 2000s when controlled studies were conducted.

5. *Field Alert Reports and Annual Reports.* FDA regulations require two types of postmarket reports in addition to adverse event reports. Under 21 C.F.R. 314.81, the NDA holder must submit to FDA a "field alert report" within three working days of receipt of information concerning (1) the drug being mistaken for another article or (2) bacteriological or other change or deterioration in a distributed drug product or any failure to meet specifications. 21 C.F.R. 314.81(b)(1). In addition, the NDA holder must submit each year an "annual report" that summarizes all significant new information from the previous year that might affect the safety, effectiveness, or labeling of the drug, as well as the distribution data; labeling and advertising; changes in chemistry, manufacturing, and controls (CMC); nonclinical studies; clinical data; and the status of any postmarketing study commitments. 21 C.F.R. 314.81(b)(2).

2. POSTAPPROVAL TESTING COMMITMENTS

In 2007, FDAAA gave FDA explicit power, for the first time, to require a drug manufacturer to conduct postapproval (Phase IV) trials. Even before then, however, the agency frequently made the performance of additional nonclinical or clinical studies a condition for NDA approval, starting in the late 1960s. On the rare occasions when the agency specified the statutory basis for these actions, it cited section 505(e) (the provision for withdrawal of approval of an NDA) and 505(k) (the provision authorizing FDA to require NDA applicants to establish and maintain records). Although in 1972 FDA published a still-extant regulation allowing the establishment of postapproval testing obligations by rule, 37 Fed. Reg. 201 (Jan. 7, 1972), codified at 21 C.F.R. 310.303, the agency has done so on only two occasions (for levodopa and methadone) and never since 1976. In all other instances, postapproval testing commitments prior to 2007 were a matter of informal negotiation between the applicant and the agency.

Pre-FDAAA Phase IV testing commitments were generally established in the following way. At the very end of the NDA review process, one or more of the FDA review team would inform the applicant that the application was ready for approval, but that FDA would like assurance that additional specified Phase IV testing would be undertaken. The unmistakable implication was that the NDA would be approved immediately if the commitments were made, but that otherwise, the NDA review would continue and there would be no certainty when or whether the NDA would be approved. Under these circumstances, applicants understandably committed to any postapproval testing suggested by FDA personnel. There was little consistency in or managerial oversight over this practice of strong-arming Phase IV commitments from companies.

Not surprisingly, the result of this approach was chaotic. Applicants frequently agreed to undertake tests for which there was no reasonable possibility of patient accrual once the drug was marketed. Many of the Phase IV tests had little or no scientific rationale or became moot once the drug was marketed without significant adverse events. There was no mechanism for systematic review of these commitments either before or after the NDA was approved, no appeal procedure that would not hold up NDA approval, and no mechanism for reconsideration of these commitments after the drug was marketed.

In Office of Inspector General, *FDA's Monitoring of Postmarketing Study Commitments*, OIG REP. No. OEI–01–04–00390 (June 2006), the OIG reported that 48 percent of NDAs approved during 1990–2004 involved at least one Phase IV commitment and 74 percent of these commitments were for clinical studies. The OIG concluded that the FDA tracking of these commitments was lax and not a high priority. In 71 Fed. Reg. 10978 (Mar. 3, 2006), FDA reported that, as of September 2005, there were 154 NDAs with 1231 open Phase IV commitments. Less than a month later, FDA announced a study of the entire Phase IV program. *See* "FDA Awards Contract to Assess Postmarketing Study Commitment Decision-making Process: Analysis Will Lead to More Standardized Approach," FDA News No. PO6–52 (Apr. 5, 2006). Then Congress stepped in.

Under FD&C Act 505(*o*)(3), added by FDAAA, the agency is explicitly authorized to require postapproval clinical trials or other studies to evaluate the risks of a drug as a condition of NDA approval. If a sponsor fails to comply with its postapproval testing obligations under this section, it commits a misbranding violation. *Id.* 502(z). Furthermore, FDA may, after notice and an opportunity for a hearing, impose civil money penalties on the sponsor for shirking its commitments. *Id.* 303(f)(4).

Under FD&C Act 505(*o*)(3)(C), FDA may establish mandatory postapproval studies for a drug after approval if it "becomes aware of new safety information." Regardless of whether FDA acts to impose the obligation on the company prior to or after approval of the NDA, the only recourse for a disgruntled sponsor is to engage in dispute resolution procedures established by the agency. *Id.* 505(*o*)(3)(F).

In accordance with section 506B of the FD&C Act, the annual report for an NDA drug must identify each Phase IV commitment and describe the progress being made until the commitment is completed or terminated. The reasons for any delay in fulfilling a study commitment must be specified. 21 C.F.R. 314.81(b)(2)(vii).

3.   CURRENT GOOD MANUFACTURING PRACTICE (CGMP)

In contrast to the food sanitation provisions of the FD&C Act, which do not expressly mandate good manufacturing practice, section 501(a)(2)(B) of the Act, added by the Drug Amendments of 1962, explicitly declares a drug to be adulterated if it is not manufactured "in conformity with current good manufacturing practice." FDA initially implemented this authority in 1963. 28 Fed. Reg. 6385 (June 20, 1963). The rules are codified at 21 C.F.R. Parts 210 & 211.

a. BACKGROUND

United States v. An Article of Drug . . . White Quadrisect

484 F.2d 748 (7th Cir. 1973).

■ PER CURIAM.

. . . The lower court condemned the shipment because the defendant's production procedure violated the "current good manufacturing practice" (GMP) provision of the Act, 21 U.S.C. § 351(a)(2)(B). Appellant contends that that provision is unconstitutional under the Due Process Clause of the Fifth Amendment because of its alleged vagueness.

The GMP provision stems from congressional concern over the danger that dangerously impure drugs might escape detection under a system predicated only on seizure of drugs shown to be in fact adulterated. In order to insure public safety, Congress determined in 1962 that it was necessary to regulate the means of production themselves. . . . By way of implementation, the FDA has promulgated detailed regulations to spell out the precise requirements of the section.

The district court found violations of GMP standards by defendant which include the failure to keep basic production records, inadequate testing of active ingredients before use, and insufficient tests of the finished product prior to shipment. These findings are not contested on appeal and we therefore consider them established. . . .

. . . We conclude that the term "current good manufacturing practice" adequately defines a standard which the Administrator was authorized to particularize in interpretative regulations. Defendant does not deny that the regulations, which he has plainly violated, were adequate to notify him that his conduct was prohibited.

Defendant's argument is based on attacks on the statutory terms "current" and "good." . . . We have no trouble with the use of the words in § 351(a)(2)(B). The term "current" fixes the point in time when the acceptability of the relevant production practices must be determined. Thus, the statute does not permit prosecution for failure to follow safety practices which were not recognized prior to the production of the subject drugs.[4] The term "good" likewise acquires adequate meaning when read in context even though, as defendant observes, a good dictionary lists a good many definitions of the word. Alternative definitions do not create impermissible ambiguity if the relevant definition is capable of interpretation by reference to objective

---

[4] Appellant also argues that even if the section has a definite meaning, it creates a standard subject to such rapid change that a drug manufacturer is unable to ascertain at any point in time what is expected of him. This argument overlooks the interpretative regulations. In our opinion it is appropriate for the statute to authorize changes in regulations to reflect the Administrator's evaluation of "current" practice. We think the GMP standard is sufficiently fixed.

criteria. . . . The word "good," as used in the GMP provision, is not unduly subjective.

The Constitution requires only a reasonable degree of certainty in statutory language. . . . Appellant also ignores the detailed regulations promulgated by the FDA which considerably illuminate the statutory language.[5]

In view of the customary presumption of constitutionality and the established high regard for the purposes of the Act, we readily sustain the GMP provision. The language utilized by Congress in this statute is neither less certain nor more difficult to interpret than language elsewhere in the same Act which has been upheld. . . .

Moreover, an argument identical to defendant's was made and rejected in *United States v. Bel–Mar Laboratories, Inc.,* 284 F. Supp. 875 (E.D.N.Y. 1968). Judge Mishler's treatment of the constitutional question in that case is thorough and persuasive; we adopt his views. . . . We hold that defendant violated reasonably stable, definite, and ascertainable standards of current good manufacturing practice designed to insure the production of unadulterated drugs. . . .

Once the constitutionality of the original GMP regulations was upheld, FDA moved to expand them.

Human and Veterinary Drugs: Current Good Manufacturing Practice in Manufacture, Processing, Packing, or Holding

43 Fed. Reg. 45014 (September 29, 1978).

In the FEDERAL REGISTER of February 13, 1976 (41 FR 6878), the Commissioner of Food and Drugs proposed to revise the CGMP regulations, Parts 210 and 211, issued under section 501(a)(2)(B) of the Federal Food, Drug, and Cosmetic Act, to update them in light of current technology and to adopt more specific requirements to assure the quality of finished drug products. . . .

A number of comments addressed the so-called "how to" versus the "what" argument; that is, the proposed CGMP regulations describe "how" a particular requirement should be achieved rather than specifying "what" it is that is to be achieved. Many comments recommended that the regulations establish only objectives or specifications and allow each manufacturer to determine the best method of attaining the objective or meeting the specification. . . .

The Commissioner believes that, with relatively few exceptions, the CGMP regulations do describe "what" is to be accomplished and provide great latitude in "how" the requirement is achieved. For example, written records and procedures are required, but FDA will recognize as

---

[5] "[T]he Secretary's interpretative regulations as to good manufacturing practice for purposes of judging the adequacy of the methods, facilities, and controls would be prima facie evidence of what constitutes current good manufacturing practice in any proceeding involving [§ 351(a)(2)] of the Food, Drug, and Cosmetic Act as amended by the bill." 1962 U.S. Cong. & Admin. News, p. 2890.

satisfactory any reasonable format that achieves the desired results. Because of the need for uniformity in certain areas of the CGMP regulations that have presented problems in the past, however, there are some instances where it is desirable to specify the manner in which requirements are to be accomplished. . . .

The requirement for written procedures is intended to provide additional assurance of effective communication of appropriate information from firm management to line personnel and of regular performance of a firm's established programs and procedures. It is not enough that employees "know their jobs." Key personnel may be absent without warning; personnel substitutions involving less experienced employees may be necessary; and new or revised instructions to employees must be adequately conveyed to those who need to know. These situations are not usual, but may occur frequently. The most appropriate method for reliably relating policies and procedures to those who must know them is to have them set down in writing, readily available, and presented in a manner easily understood. The Commissioner does not believe this is a burdensome requirement. . . .

Several comments argued that § 210.1 [stating that failure to comply with any of the CGMP requirements shall render a drug adulterated under FD&C Act 501(a)(2)(B)] should be deleted because it is based on the erroneous proposition that CGMP regulations can be substantive. The comments urged that regulations issued under section 501(a)(2)(B) of the act are only interpretive.

Because of the fervor reflected by these objections and because the Commissioner foresees identical objections being made to proposals to issue binding CGMP regulations for specific classes of drug products in the future, the Commissioner has decided that a lengthy exposition of the basis for his concluding that FDA has legal authority to promulgate such regulations is warranted. . . .

Based on . . . complete review of the legislative history of section 501(a)(2)(B) of the act, the Commissioner concludes that there is no support for the proposition that Congress intended that CGMP regulations should be merely interpretive. At the least, Congress wanted CGMP regulations to have the same force and effect as other regulations issued under section 701(a) of the act. To the extent that a stronger Congressional mandate can be gleaned from the various reports, amendments, and debates, it appears that binding standards were to be issued by FDA and issued through the less cumbersome-notice-and-comment rulemaking procedures of section 701(a) of the act rather than the more complex section 701(e) mechanism. Therefore, the Commissioner rejects the argument that § 210.1 exceeds the authority conferred by Congress under sections 501(a)(2)(B) and 701(a) of the act. . . .

. . . [I]f each CGMP requirement has to receive a de novo hearing in each and every enforcement proceeding, the burden of litigation that would result would not be in the public interest, nor would it be equitable to competing manufacturers who were not involved in such litigation. . . .

. . . The Commissioner notes that [*National Confectioners' Association*, 569 F.2d 690, and *Nova Scotia, supra* p. 529] dealt specifically with the validity of CGMP regulations issued under the statutory standards relating to adulterated foods, which do not explicitly refer to "current good manufacturing practice." It would indeed be anomalous that those regulations could be issued as legally binding if regulations amplifying section 501(a)(2)(B) could not be. . . .

With regard to the alleged lack of flexibility in the enforcement of "binding" CGMP regulations, the Commissioner believes that the comments have confused the question of whether a violation exists with the question of whether FDA will take action upon the violation. . . . It should be noted, however, that even in the absence of any CGMP regulations, whether binding or not, the doing of or failure to do any particular act which is inconsistent with current good manufacturing practice results in the product being legally adulterated, even if no legal action is brought. . . .

NOTES

1.   *Drug GMP Cases.* FDA has in most instances found the courts to be receptive to its GMP cases, even when criminal charges are included. *See, e.g., United States v. Dianovin Pharmaceuticals, Inc.,* 342 F. Supp. 724 (D.P.R. 1972), *aff'd,* 475 F.2d 100 (1st Cir. 1973); *United States v. Jamieson–McKames Pharmaceuticals, Inc.,* 651 F.2d 532 (8th Cir. 1981); *United States v. Bhutani,* 175 F.3d 572 (9th Cir. 1999).

2.   *History of Drug GMP Regulations.* FDA first published final current good manufacturing practice (CGMP) regulations for drugs in 1963. 28 Fed. Reg. 6385 (June 20, 1963). They were revised in 36 Fed. Reg. 601 (Jan. 15, 1971), 43 Fed. Reg. 45014 (Sept. 29, 1978), 58 Fed. Reg. 41348 (Aug. 3, 1993), and 77 Fed. Reg. 16158 (Mar. 20, 2012). The GMP regulations were held to have the force of law in *National Association of Pharmaceutical Manufacturers v. FDA,* 637 F.2d 877 (2d Cir. 1981). For the origin of the concept of drug GMP, see John P. Swann, *The 1941 Sulfathiazole Disaster and the Birth of Good Manufacturing Practices,* 40 PHARMACY IN HIST., No. 1, at 17 (1999).

3.   *Denial of NDA Approval.* In a relatively unusual action, FDA refused to approve three NDAs for failure to comply with GMP in 53 Fed. Reg. 18905 (May 25, 1988). The agency has also successfully withdrawn approval of NDAs for failure to comply with GMP. *See* 52 Fed. Reg. 29274 (Aug. 6, 1987), *aff'd, Copanos and Sons, Inc. v. Food and Drug Administration,* 854 F.2d 510 (D.C. Cir. 1988).

4.   *Other Drug Adulteration.* Section 501 also lists other ways in which a drug may be adulterated, including, for example, "[i]f it consists in whole or in part of any filthy, putrid, or decomposed substance," "if it has been prepared, packed, or held under insanitary conditions whereby it may have been contaminated with filth," if it contains an unlisted color additive, and if any substance has been mixed with the drug "so as to reduce its quality or strength." FD&C Act 501(a)(1), (a)(2)(A), (a)(4), (d).

5.   *Compendial Standards.* The FD&C Act establishes a special, but very limited, status for three official compendia: the United States Pharmacopeia (which incorporates the National Formulary) and the Homeopathic Pharmacopeia. Section 501(b) provides that a drug that

purports to be or is represented as a drug the name of which is recognized in one of the official compendia is adulterated if its strength differs from, or its quality or its purity falls below, the standards set in the compendium. The provision specifically authorizes USP or HP to establish tests or methods of assays to determine the strength, quality, or purity of a drug. The compendia have no authority, however, to issue regulations or any other form of binding guidance regarding the labeling, methods of manufacture, or other aspects of a drug. Any compendial requirements must be in a drug standard and must be limited to determinations of strength, quality, or purity.

Under sections 501(b) and 502(e)(3)(B), a drug that does not meet a compendial standard with respect to strength, quality, or purity has two options. First, if it chooses to use the official compendial name, the label must state that the drug differs from the standard of strength, quality, or purity set forth in the compendium. Second, it may choose to use a different established name, in which case the label need not state that the drug differs from the compendial standard.

At one time, section 501(b) was an important regulatory tool. Although the constitutionality of the provision was questioned, *see* Thomas W. Christopher, *Validity of Delegation of Power to a Private Agency—The Pharmacopoeia Provisions,* 6 FOOD DRUG COSM. L.J. 641 (1951), the compendial standards were the basis for hundreds of FDA regulatory actions under both the 1906 Act and the 1938 Act. *See, e.g., United States v. King & Howe, Inc.,* 78 F.2d 693 (2d Cir. 1935); *Woodard Laboratories, Inc. v. United States,* 198 F.2d 995 (9th Cir. 1952). As FDA has relied increasingly upon specifications established through the new drug approval process, compendial standards have declined in regulatory importance.

b. CGMP ENFORCEMENT

In spite of the substantial success of FDA GMP enforcement, courts remain reluctant to cripple a drug manufacturer by completely closing down its manufacturing establishment, as the following strongly contested case illustrates.

United States v. Barr Laboratories, Inc.
812 F. Supp. 458 (D.N.J. 1993).

■ WOLIN, DISTRICT JUDGE

Currently before the Court is plaintiff's application for a preliminary injunction directing defendants to suspend, recall or revamp numerous products in their current product line. . . .

The current conflict . . . is best characterized as a confrontation between a humorless warden and his uncooperative prisoner. Exchanging heavy blows, the parties generated a record of more than twenty-three hundred pages of testimony, almost four hundred exhibits and numerous lengthy declarations. . . .

The divergent views presented to the Court reflect not only a difference of perspective, but also the changes made at Barr Laboratories since the first threat of this litigation. As a result, the record is a composite of two trials: the case that was and the case that is. As such, the bases upon which some of the government's criticisms rest have disappeared during the course of this litigation. Wary of this timing element, the Court has reviewed the lengthy record and the parties' proposed findings with the dual desire to protect an unsuspecting public and to avoid unnecessarily burdensome rules and now makes the following findings of fact and conclusions of law. . . .

Courts entering injunctions under the Act have required the government to show: (1) violations of the Act on the part of the defendant; and (2) a cognizable danger of recurrent violations. . . .

. . . With regard to past violations, there can be no dispute that Barr has violated the Act by failing to follow manufacturing practices that comply with CGMP as required under section 351(a)(2)(B) and, therefore, has introduced adulterated drugs into commerce in violation of section 331(a). Until recently, for example, Barr did not conduct failure investigations, released batches on the basis of selective data, and refused to validate its cleaning processes, thereby ignoring specific provisions of the CFR. Barr's own attempts to remake itself through a vigorous overhaul prevents any other conclusion.

Turning to future violations, the government has demonstrated that a threat of recurrence exists, as a consideration of the appropriate factors illustrates. First, defendants' violations properly are characterized as "recurrent" and not "isolated." Problems at Barr persisted despite repeated criticism from the FDA over at least a four-year period.

Barr's reluctance to ameliorate its methods in the face of these warnings is troublesome. This behavior requires the Court to attach a greater degree of scienter to Barr's actions. Further, Barr's refusal to comply with the recommendations of the government casts doubt on Barr's recognition of the wrongful nature of its conduct as well as the genuineness of its efforts to conform to the law.

While defendant has made many improvements, these efforts are long overdue. Because the threat of this litigation served as the catalyst for Barr's renovation, the Court cannot with confidence conclude that Barr's current efforts are the product of a new philosophy rather than a reflection of a desire to deflect this suit.

Due to established past violations and the risk of future violations, the Court now must consider whether an injunction is required under the particular facts of this case.

The Court concludes that injunctive relief is necessary to safeguard the public interest. Many of the practices the Court condemns today are used in the day-to-day operations of Barr and memorialized in standard operating procedures. Examples include Barr's blend sampling strategy, retesting procedure, outlier technique and reliance on averaging. Only through an injunction can the Court be confident that these forbidden methods, defended with vigor by Barr's employees, will be abandoned and the products made under their auspices shielded from the public. . . .

The government cites Barr for general CGMP-compliance problems. Although the Court recognizes that Barr has had much difficulty satisfying the often reasonable demands of the FDA, injunctive relief must be used sparingly, to prevent future harm, and not to punish past violations.

In light of Barr's recent makeover, both personal and physical, the Court is unwilling to order a temporary shut-down. While Barr's transformation from an ugly duckling to a swan is neither natural nor complete, the Court cannot ignore Barr's remedial efforts, as reflected in the satisfaction of many of the concerns of its experts.

Of more concern, however, are the specific products. To the extent that Barr relied upon investigations which do not satisfy section 211.192, as construed by the Court, to release batches or to complete retrospective and prospective validation studies, these actions and studies are invalid. Reliance on faulty methods cannot be cured by subsequent compliance. . . .

Based on these findings, the Court will order Barr to validate its products. This order will reach only those products of particular concern to the government. . . .

The Court may recall any drug product found to be manufactured in violation of the Act that has been released to the public for distribution. Although not authorized expressly in the Act, this remedy is consistent with the broad equitable relief powers district courts enjoy.

Citing a variety of failures, the government asks the Court to recall fifteen batches of ten different drug products. In a batch-by-batch defense, Barr attempts to refute these charges. [The District Court then determined which batches must and need not be recalled.]

NOTES

1. *Neither Party Satisfied.* Both FDA and Barr—as well as most of the pharmaceutical industry—regarded this decision as a setback. FDA failed to get the type of injunction it sought, and Barr did not prevail on a number of the detailed GMP issues. The District Court set a standard of judicial inquiry that made both parties uncomfortable.

2. *Consent Decrees.* After *Barr*, FDA began its current practice of striving to avoid protracted and expensive GMP litigation by negotiating consent decrees of injunction for GMP violations. They negotiated such agreements with Warner–Lambert (1993), Eli Lilly (1995), Abbott Laboratories (1999), Wyeth–Ayerst (2000), Schering–Plough (2002), and GlaxoSmithKline (2005). Most recently, the agency has entered into consent decrees of permanent injunction for GMP violations with, for example, McNeil Consumer Healthcare, a subsidiary of Johnson & Johnson (2011) (OTC), Ranbaxy Laboratories, an overseas generic drug manufacturer (2012), and Ben Venue Laboratories, a unit of Boehringer Ingelheim (2013). Both the McNeil and Ben Venue consent decrees required the shutdown of manufacturing of facilities pending compliance.

3. *International Cooperation.* In June 1997, the United States and the European Community entered into an Agreement on Mutual Recognition. Under that agreement, FDA promulgated regulations to govern mutual recognition of GMP inspections where FDA determines that the specific EU country involved has an inspection system equivalent to the

FDA inspection system. 63 Fed. Reg. 60122 (Nov. 6, 1998), codified at 21 C.F.R. Part 26.

c.   CGMP MODERNIZATION

After *Barr*, FDA had the opportunity to revise its GMP regulations to incorporate both the guidance documents that it had periodically issued (in particular, the guidance on process validation) and the lessons learned from *Barr* itself. It chose not to do so. Nonetheless, both FDA and the pharmaceutical industry realized that, because the GMP regulations had not significantly been altered since 1979, it was time for a thorough review to determine policy for the future. In August 2002, FDA released the following concept paper covering a new agency initiative to enhance pharmaceutical GMP.

Pharmaceutical CGMPs for the 21st Century: A Risk–Based Approach
August 21, 2002.

FDA oversees the quality of drug products using a two-pronged approach involving review of information submitted in applications as well as inspection of manufacturing facilities for conformance to requirements for current Good Manufacturing Practice (cGMP). These two programs have served the country well by helping to ensure the quality of drug products available in the US. Now, as we approach the 25th anniversary of the last major revision to the drug cGMP regulations, it is time to step back and evaluate the currency of these programs so that:

- the most up-to-date concept of risk management and quality systems approaches are incorporated while continuing to ensure product quality;
- the latest scientific advances in pharmaceutical manufacturing and technology are encouraged;
- the submission review program and the inspection program operate in a coordinated and synergistic manner;
- regulation and manufacturing standards are applied consistently;
- management of the program encourages innovation in the pharmaceutical manufacturing sector; and
- FDA resources are used most effectively and efficiently to address the most significant health risks.

To these ends, FDA is undertaking an initiative, "Pharmaceutical cGMPs for the 21st Century: A Risk–Based Approach."

. . . The following principles will guide implementation of the reappraisal:

Risk-based orientation In order to provide the most effective public health protection, FDA must match its level of effort against the magnitude of risk. Resource limitations prevent uniformly intensive coverage of all pharmaceutical products and production. Although the agency has been implementing risk-based programs, a more systematic and rigorous risk-based approach will be developed.

Science-based policies and standards Significant advances in the pharmaceutical sciences and in manufacturing technologies have occurred over the last two decades. While this knowledge has been incorporated in an ongoing manner into FDA's approach to product quality regulation, the fundamental nature of the changes dictates a thorough evaluation of the science base to ensure that product quality regulation not only incorporates up-to-date science, but also encourages further advances in technology. Recent science can also contribute significantly to assessment of risk.

Integrated quality systems orientation Principles from various innovative approaches to manufacturing quality that have been developed in the past decade will be evaluated for applicability, and cGMP requirements and related pre-approval requirements will be evaluated according to applicable principles. In addition, interaction of the pre-market CMC [chemistry, manufacturing, and controls] review process and the application of cGMP requirements will be evaluated as an integrated system.

International cooperation The globalization of pharmaceutical manufacturing requires a global approach to regulation. FDA will collaborate with other regulatory authorities, via ICH and other venues.

Strong Public Health Protection The initiative will strengthen the public health protection achieved by FDA's regulation of drug product manufacturing and will not interfere with strong enforcement of the existing regulatory requirements, even as we are examining and revising our approach to these programs. . . .

NOTE

Implementation. FDA decided to implement its "Pharmaceutical CGMPs for the 21st Century" initiative through guidance and related documents rather than through amendment of the GMP regulations themselves. FDA's progress reports continued to emphasize a "risk-based" and "science-based" approach to GMP, but none articulated what those phrases mean in practice. The final report on the initiative was issued in September 2004. In 71 Fed. Reg. 31194 (June 1, 2006), FDA withdrew five GMP guidances and revised two others to make them consistent with the GMP initiative. The agency issued its final GMP Guidance, QUALITY SYSTEMS APPROACH TO PHARMACEUTICAL CURRENT GOOD MANUFACTURING PRACTICE (CGMP) REGULATIONS, in September 2006. *See also* GUIDANCE FOR INDUSTRY: Q10 PHARMACEUTICAL QUALITY SYSTEM (April 2009). The now–25-year-old GMP regulations remain largely unchanged. The pharmaceutical industry has seen no difference in the way that FDA inspects pharmaceutical manufacturing facilities or enforces GMP requirements. And the agency has continued to negotiate consent decrees in the same way that it did before the initiative was announced.

4. WITHDRAWAL OF NDA APPROVAL AND VOLUNTARY WITHDRAWAL FROM THE MARKET

Companies quite frequently voluntarily withdraw their drugs from sale, based either on efficacy/safety concerns or business considerations. Involuntary withdrawals of approval of NDA's by FDA, by contrast, are a rare event. Almost all such withdrawals have occurred under the DESI program.

a. INVOLUNTARY WITHDRAWAL OF NDA

The following opinion, from the Supreme Court's 1973 *"Weinberger* Trilogy" (or *"Hynson* Quartet") of cases, *supra* p. 779, considers the procedures for NDA withdrawal, and in particular the FDA's "summary judgment" practice of denying hearings to NDA holders who do not present sufficient evidence of effectiveness. Other portions of this opinion were excerpted earlier in this chapter, *supra* p. 662.

Weinberger v. Hynson, Westcott & Dunning, Inc.

412 U.S. 609 (1973).

■ MR. JUSTICE DOUGLAS delivered the opinion of the Court.

. . . Hynson, Westcott & Dunning, Inc., had filed an application under the 1938 Act for a drug called Lutrexin, recommended by Hynson for use in the treatment of premature labor, threatened and habitual abortion, and dysmenorrhea. FDA informed Hynson that Hynson's studies submitted with the application were not sufficiently well controlled to justify the claims of effectiveness and urged Hynson not to represent the drug as useful for threatened and habitual abortion. But FDA allowed the application to become effective, since the 1938 Act permitted evaluation of a new drug solely on the grounds of its *safety.* . . . When the 1962 amendments became effective and NAS–NRC undertook to appraise the efficacy of drugs theretofore approved as safe, Hynson submitted a list of literature references, a copy of an unpublished study, and a representative sample testimonial letter on behalf of Lutrexin. The panel of NAS–NRC working in the relevant field reported to FDA that Hynson's claims for effectiveness of the drug were either inappropriate or unwarranted in the absence of submission of further appropriate documentation. At the invitation of the Commissioner of Food and Drugs, Hynson submitted additional data. But the Commissioner concluded that this additional information was inadequate and published notice of his intention to withdraw approval of the NDA's covering the drug, offering Hynson the opportunity for a prewithdrawal hearing [in accordance with section 505(e) of the Act]. Before the hearing could take place, Hynson brought suit in the District Court for a declaratory judgment that the drugs in question were exempt from the *efficacy* review provisions of the 1962 amendments or, alternatively, that there was no lack of substantial evidence of the drug's *efficacy*. The Government's motion to dismiss was granted, the District Court ruling that FDA had primary jurisdiction and that Hynson had failed to exhaust its administrative remedies.

While the District Court litigation was pending, FDA promulgated new regulations establishing minimal standards for "adequate and well-controlled investigations" and limiting the right to a hearing to those applicants who could proffer at least some evidence meeting those standards. Although Hynson maintained that it was not subject to the new regulations because its initial request for a hearing predated their issuance, it renewed its request and submitted the material which it claimed constituted "substantial evidence" of Lutrexin's effectiveness. The Commissioner denied the request for a hearing and withdrew the NDA for Lutrexin. He ruled that Lutrexin is not exempt from the 1962 amendments and that Hynson had not submitted adequate evidence that Lutrexin is not a new drug or is effective. The Court of Appeals reversed, holding that while the drug in question was not exempt, Hynson was entitled to a hearing on the substantial-evidence question.

Section 505(e) directs FDA to withdraw approval of an NDA if the manufacturer fails to carry the burden of showing there is "substantial evidence" respecting the *efficacy* of the drug. . . . The Act and the Regulations, in their reduction of that standard to detailed guidelines, make FDA's so-called administrative summary judgment procedure appropriate.

The general contours of "substantial evidence" are defined by § 505(d) of the Act to include "evidence consisting of adequate and well-controlled investigations, including clinical investigations, by experts qualified by scientific training and experience to evaluate the effectiveness of the drug involved, on the basis of which it could fairly and responsibly be concluded by such experts that the drug will have the effect it purports or is represented to have under the conditions of use prescribed, recommended, or suggested in the labeling or proposed labeling thereof." Acting pursuant to his "authority to promulgate regulations for the efficient enforcement" of the Act, § 701(a), the Commissioner has detailed the "principles . . . recognized by the scientific community as the essentials of adequate and well-controlled clinical investigations. They provide the basis for the determination whether there is 'substantial evidence' to support the claims of effectiveness for 'new drugs'. . . ." 21 CFR § 130.12(a)(5)(ii) [now § 314.126(a)]. . . . [T]he regulation provides that "[u]ncontrolled studies or partially controlled studies are not acceptable as the sole basis for the approval of claims of effectiveness. Such studies, carefully conducted and documented, may provide corroborative support. . . . Isolated case reports, random experience, and reports lacking the details which permit scientific evaluation will not be considered."

. . . [I]t is not disputed here that [these regulations] express well-established principles of scientific investigation. Moreover, their strict and demanding standards, barring anecdotal evidence indicating that doctors "believe" in the efficacy of a drug, are amply justified by the legislative history. . . .

To be sure, the Act requires FDA to give "due notice and opportunity for hearing to the applicant" before it can withdraw its approval of an NDA. FDA, however, by regulation, requires any applicant who desires a hearing to submit reasons "why the application . . . should not be withdrawn, together with a well-organized and full-factual analysis of the clinical and other investigational data he is prepared to prove in support of his opposition to the notice of opportunity for a hearing. . . . When it clearly appears . . . from the reasons and factual analysis in the request for the hearing that there is no genuine and substantial issue of fact . . ., *e.g.*, no adequate and well-controlled clinical investigations to support the claims of effectiveness," the Commissioner may deny a hearing and enter an order withdrawing the application based solely on these data. 21 C.F.R. 130.14(b) [now worded slightly differently, at 21 C.F.R. 314.200(g)(1).] What the agency has said, then, is that it will not provide a formal hearing where it is apparent at the threshold that the applicant has not tendered *any* evidence which *on its face* meets the statutory standards as particularized by the regulations. The propriety of such a procedure was decided in *United States v. Storer Broadcasting Co.,* 351 U.S. 192, and *FPC v. Texaco, Inc.,* 377 U.S. 33. We said in *Texaco:*

> "[T]he statutory requirement for a hearing under § 7 [of the Natural Gas Act] does not preclude the Commission from particularizing statutory standards through the rulemaking process and barring at the threshold those who neither measure up to them nor show reasons why in the public interest the rule should be waived."

There can be no question that to prevail at a hearing an applicant must furnish evidence stemming from "adequate and well-controlled investigations." We cannot impute to Congress the design of requiring, nor does due process demand, a hearing when it appears conclusively from the applicant's "pleadings" that the application cannot succeed[17] . . .

Our conclusion that the summary judgment procedure of FDA is valid does not end the matter, for Hynson argues that its submission to FDA satisfied its threshold burden. In reviewing an order of the Commissioner denying a hearing, a court of appeals must determine whether the Commissioner's findings accurately reflect the study in question and if they do, whether the deficiencies he finds conclusively render the study inadequate or uncontrolled in light of the pertinent regulations. There is a contrariety of opinion within the Court concerning the adequacy of Hynson's submission. Since a majority are of the view that the submission was sufficient to warrant a hearing, we affirm the Court of Appeals on that phase of the case. . . .

---

[17] This applies, of course, only to those regulations that are precise. For example, the plan or protocol for a study must include "[a] summary of the methods of analysis and an evaluation of data derived from the study, including any appropriate statistical methods." 21 CFR § 130.12(a) [314.111(a)(5)(ii)(a)(5)]. A mere reading of the study submitted will indicate whether the study is totally deficient in this regard. Some of the regulations, however, are not precise, as they call for the exercise of discretion or subjective judgment in determining whether a study is adequate and well-controlled. For example, § 130.12(a) [314.111(a)(5)(ii)(a)(2)(i)] requires that the plan or protocol for the study include a method of selection of the subjects that provide [sic] "*adequate* assurance that they are suitable for the purposes of the study." (Emphasis added.) The qualitative standards "adequate" and "suitable" do not lend themselves to clear-cut definition, and it may not be possible to tell from the face of a study whether the standards have been met. Thus, it might not be proper to deny a hearing on the ground that the study did not comply with this regulation.

NOTES

1. *Subsequent Proceedings.* Following this decision, FDA published a notice of hearing in 39 Fed. Reg. 15341 (May 2, 1974) and subsequently held a formal evidentiary hearing. The Commissioner's ultimate decision withdrawing approval of the NDAs for Lutrexin, 41 Fed. Reg. 14406 (Apr. 5, 1976), was not challenged.

2. *Withdrawal by Statute.* Congress has only once ordered FDA to withdraw approval of an NDA. The agency took this action to ban methaqualone (Quaalude) after the sponsor had already discontinued marketing. 98 Stat. 280 (1984); 49 Fed. Reg. 36441 (Sept. 17, 1984).

3. *NDA Withdrawal for Untrue Statements of Material Fact.* In 60 Fed. Reg. 32982 (June 26, 1995), FDA proposed to withdraw approval of three abbreviated NDAs because the applicants had submitted false and misleading information in the applications. The agency withdrew approval in 1998, after KV Pharmaceutical, the holder of the applications, requested a hearing and then withdrew the request when it stopped marketing the products. 63 Fed. Reg. 30765 (June 5, 1998).

4. *Withdrawal of Obsolete NDAs.* In 1998, FDA withdrew approval of Seldane® on the ground that it was no longer shown to be safe because a safer version, Allegra®, containing the primary active derivative of Seldane produced in the body when Seldane is taken, was shown to be a safer drug. 63 Fed. Reg. 53444 (Oct. 5, 1998). In 2000, at FDA's request, the manufacturer of the diabetes drug Rezulin® agreed to withdraw it from the market voluntarily because newer drugs had a better safety profile. *See* "Rezulin is Outmoded Drug, Not an Example of System Failure—FDA's Lumpkin," 12 HEALTH NEWS DAILY, No. 96, at 1 (May 19, 2000).

5. *Rescission of NDA Approval Because of a Mistake.* In a very unusual case, *American Therapeutics, Inc. v. Sullivan*, Food Drug Cosm. L. Rep. (CCH) ¶ 38,159 (D.D.C. 1990), FDA approved an NDA on June 23 and then rescinded the approval on August 3 on the ground that approval had issued through "an inadvertent mistake." The District Court held that even though FDA lacked statutory authority to correct a mistake of this kind, it would defer to the agency and thus dismiss the complaint.

b. VOLUNTARY WITHDRAWAL FROM MARKET

As the *Hynson* case illustrates, lack of substantial evidence of effectiveness was the chief reason for withdrawal of FDA approval of many pre-1962 new drugs pursuant to the DESI program. By contrast, a number of effective drugs approved since 1962 have been voluntarily withdrawn from the market by their manufacturers because of infrequent but serious adverse reactions that occurred following approval. In 1964, Parnate®, an antidepressant, was the first drug to be withdrawn from the market because of a safety issue following enactment of the Drug Amendments of 1962. *See* Statement of Joseph F. Sadusk, Jr., FDA Med. Dir., "Drug Safety," Hearings before the Intergovernmental Relations Subcommittee of the House Committee on Government Operations, 89th Congress, 1st Session (1965).

The Parnate scenario has been reoccurred numerous times since 1964, most prominently with regard to the Cox-2 inhibitor drugs.

Statement of Sandra L. Kweder, Deputy Director, CDER Office of New Drugs

"FDA, Merck, and Vioxx: Putting Patient Safety First?" Hearing before the Senate Committee on Finance, 108th Cong., 2d Sess. (2004).

FDA approved Vioxx in May, 1999 for the reduction of signs and symptoms of osteoarthritis, as well as for acute pain in adults for the treatment of primary dysmenorrhea. Vioxx received a 6-month priority review because the drug potentially provided a significant therapeutic advantage over existing approved drugs due to fewer gastrointestinal side effects, including bleeding. A product undergoing a priority review is held to the same rigorous standards for safety, efficacy, and quality that FDA expects from all drugs submitted for approval.

As with many other new molecular entities, this product was taken before the Arthritis Advisory Committee, April 20, 1999, prior to its approval. It was the second of a new class (Cox-2 selective) of non-steroidal anti-inflammatory drugs (NSAIDs) approved by FDA. The original safety database for this product included approximately 5,000 patients on Vioxx and did not show an increased risk of heart attack or stroke.

In the clinical trials conducted before approval, the risk of gastrointestinal (GI) side effects was determined through the use of endoscopy. At the time that FDA approved Vioxx, the available evidence from these endoscopy studies showed a significantly lower risk of gastrointestinal ulcers, a significant source of serious side effects such as bleeding and death, in comparison to ibuprofen.

After Vioxx was approved in 1999, Merck continued studies of Vioxx designed to look at clinically meaningful GI effects, such as stomach ulcers and bleeding (Vioxx Gastrointestinal Outcomes Research, or VIGOR study). . . .

VIGOR did not have a placebo group because to do so would have meant patients with rheumatoid arthritis would have been randomized to receive no pain relief. Use of a placebo would have been intolerable, because untreated patients would have suffered and left the study. The study also excluded subjects taking low dose aspirin for cardiovascular (CV) prevention because use of aspirin might have contributed to increased rates of GI bleeding in the study and confound the results. However, the exclusion of patients on low dose aspirin may have influenced CV events in the study, since low dose aspirin has been shown to reduce CV risk

In April, 2002, FDA approved extensive labeling changes to reflect the findings from the VIGOR study. These labeling changes included detailed information about the increase in risk of cardiovascular events relative to naproxen, including heart attack. . . .

In the years following the 1999 FDA approval of Vioxx, Merck began conducting a serious of clinical trials exploring other potential indications of this product. All trials for chronic use were designed to monitor carefully for CV safety, and included data safety monitoring committees as well as blinded experts to assess all CV events in the trials. . . .

Merck contacted FDA on September 27, 2004, to request a meeting to discuss with the Agency the Data Safety Monitoring Board's decision to halt Merck's long-term study of Vioxx in patients at increased risk of colon polyps. Merck and FDA officials met the next day, September 28, and during that meeting the company informed FDA of its decision to remove Vioxx from the market voluntarily. The data presented demonstrated an increase in cardiovascular risk and stroke starting at the 18-month time-point compared to placebo. This was the first demonstration of a difference in comparison to a placebo group, and supported the previous signal seen in the VIGOR trial and some of the epidemiologic studies. . . .

NOTES

1. *Cox–2 Inhibitor Actions.* At a subsequent FDA Advisory Committee hearing, the committee voted 17 to 15 to bring Vioxx® back to the market. The same advisory committee voted 31 to 1 to retain a second Cox–2 inhibitor, Celebrex® on the market, and 17 to 13 to retain a third, Bextra® on the market. Because of the widespread publicity surrounding the withdrawal of Vioxx and the results of this Advisory Committee meeting, FDA took the unprecedented step of releasing a memorandum prepared jointly by FDA CDER Office of New Drugs Director John K. Jenkins and FDA CDER Office of Pharmacoepidemiology and Statistical Science Director Paul J. Seligman (Apr. 6, 2005) recommending that FDA: (1) allow Celebrex to remain on the market, (2) request Pfizer voluntarily to withdraw Bextra from the market or face a formal withdrawal procedure, and (3) carefully review any proposal from Merck for resumption of the marketing of Vioxx. Pfizer immediately agreed to voluntarily withdraw Bextra from the market, and Merck has made no attempt to return Vioxx to the market. Pfizer's Celebrex remains available for sale. *See generally* Lan Tran, *Untangling the Vioxx–Celebrex Controversy: A Story About Responsibility* (2005), Daniel Zahler, *Preventing the Next Public Health Crisis: New Drug Approval After Vioxx* (2005), and McCauley Mancinelli, *Placing Blame for the Vioxx Debacle* (2006), in Chapter VI(C)(3) of the Electronic Book.

2. *Return to the Market.* Parnate was returned to the market with revised labeling less than a year after its withdrawal. It was the first drug to be taken off the market and later returned. In the 2000s, Lotronex and Tysabri similarly were withdrawn from marketing and then returned; both of these drugs were returned to market under pre-REMS risk mitigation programs.

3. *Congressional Reactions.* The discovery of serious adverse reactions after a drug is marketed, and thus in wide use, is not an uncommon event, and its occurrence almost invariably prompts outraged reactions from members of Congress, who view FDA as responsible.

4. *Postmarketing Adverse Reactions.* Because an investigational new drug is tested in only a relatively few patients before an NDA is approved,

low frequency adverse reactions will almost certainly be discovered when use becomes widespread. In FDA DRUG REVIEW: POSTAPPROVAL RISKS 1976–85, PEMD–90–15 (1990), the General Accounting Office found that of 198 drugs approved by FDA during this period, about half had serious postapproval risks as evidenced by labeling changes or market withdrawal. All but six of the drugs studied were still being marketed in 1989, based upon the agency's determination that the benefits continued to outweigh the risks.

5.   *Approval Speed v. Safety Withdrawal.* A study has shown no link between NDA approval speed and subsequent withdrawal for safety reasons. Tufts Center for Study of Drug Development, *Drug Safety Withdrawals in the U.S. Not Linked to Speed of FDA Approval*, 7 IMPACT, No. 5 (Sept./Oct. 2005). The study found that the rate of drug safety withdrawals has not increased since the user fee era began in 1993 and that faster approval times do not correlate with increased drug safety withdrawals.

6.   *Impact of Tort Liability.* In recent years, it has no longer been necessary for FDA to take legal action to remove an unsafe drug from the market. As soon as serious toxicity is encountered—often discovered by the company rather than by FDA—the manufacturer will voluntarily remove the product from the market as quickly as possible to avoid, or at least reduce, product liability exposure.

7.   *Patients' Need for Unsafe Drugs.* Drugs removed from the market for safety reasons frequently have an extremely low rate of serious adverse events. Moreover, these drugs are often very effective, and in some people they are uniquely effective. FDA has frequently requested that companies continue to serve unmet medical needs with these drugs on a compassionate IND basis, but companies are reluctant to do so. Patients do everything they can to keep obtaining some drugs that have been removed from the market, often turning to rogue internet sources. *See, e.g., Ill Patients Fight to Keep Receiving Banned Drug*, N.Y. TIMES, December 12, 2000, at F9 (Propulsid); Denise Grady, *F.D.A. Pulls a Drug, and Patients Despair*, N.Y. TIMES, January 30, 2001, at F1 (Lotronex); Bill Saporito, *My Most Difficult Choice*, TIME, May 23, 2005, at 64 (Vioxx).

8.   *Voluntary Withdrawal of Life–Supporting Drug.* Because of concern about sudden interruptions in the availability of important drugs, the FDA Modernization Act of 1997 added section 506C to the FD&C Act to require that a sole manufacturer of a drug that is life-supporting, live-sustaining, or used in the prevention of a debilitating disease or condition must notify FDA at least six months prior to the date of discontinuance unless there are good reasons for a shorter notification.

9.   *Sales Abroad.* Voluntary removal of a drug from the United States market does not necessarily result in removal from markets in other countries. Different countries can make different benefit-risk judgments. *See, e.g.,* Joanne McManus & Trish Saywell, *Not in Our Backyard: Medicines Deemed Unsafe for Americans by Federal Regulators are Still Being Sold and Prescribed Throughout Asia*, FAR EASTERN ECON. REV. (Aug. 3, 2000).

10. *FDA Determination of Basis for Withdrawal.* When a brand-name drug is voluntarily withdrawn from the market, and FDA has approved ANDAs for one or more generic products that reference the drug's listing in the Orange Book, *see infra* p. 1006, the agency must make a determination of whether the brand-name manufacturer withdrew the drug from sale for "safety or effectiveness reasons." 21 C.F.R. 314.161(a)(2). The agency must also make such a determination if it receives the first ANDA referencing a drug's Orange Book listing after the drug's voluntary removal from sale. If FDA determines that the pioneer drug was withdrawn for safety or effectiveness reasons, it will, pursuant to 314.162(d), suspend any previously approved ANDAs under procedures set forth in 21 C.F.R. 314.153(b). Moreover, it will remove the withdrawn drug from the Orange Book, making approval of additional ANDAs impossible.

c.   SUMMARY BAN OF AN "IMMINENT HAZARD" DRUG

As part of the Drug Amendments of 1962, Congress provided to the Secretary of HEW (now HHS) nondelegable authority to suspend the NDA approval for any drug determined to be an "imminent hazard" to health. The following is the only occasion in which a human drug has been banned under this provision.

Forsham v. Califano

442 F. Supp. 203 (D.D.C. 1977).

■ CORCORAN, DISTRICT JUDGE.

Plaintiffs are seven physicians who specialize in the treatment of diabetes and six diabetic patients taking phenformin hydrochloride (phenformin) prescribed by their physicians as part of their diabetic therapy. Phenformin is an orally administered drug designed to control blood sugar levels in patients with adult-onset diabetes who are not dependent on insulin and who cannot or will not reduce their daily caloric intake. . . .

The defendant is the Secretary of Health, Education and Welfare (the Secretary) who, pursuant to section 505(e) of the Federal Food, Drug and Cosmetic Act, has suspended new drug applications for phenformin on grounds that the drug poses an "imminent hazard." . . .

Plaintiffs seek to enjoin the Secretary from implementing his suspension order. They also seek a declaratory judgment that the suspension order is outside the scope of the Secretary's authority, is arbitrary and capricious, and violates their Fifth Amendment due process rights, the Administrative Procedure Act and the Food and Drug Administration's regulations. . . .

In considering the likelihood of success on the merits, it should be noted at the outset that the review by this Court of the Secretary's decision to suspend phenformin pursuant to his authority under 21 U.S.C. § 355(e) is limited to a determination of whether that decision was arbitrary and capricious, an abuse of discretion, or otherwise not in accordance with the law. . . . In other words, [the plaintiffs] must demonstrate the substantial likelihood that the decision was "a clear error of judgment" by the Secretary and that he failed to articulate any rational connection between the facts submitted to him and the choice he made. . . .

While acknowledging the existence of "conflicting testimony" on the incidence of lactic acidosis among phenformin patients and the view expressed by the manufacturers that labeling changes made in January, 1977 would reduce the incidence of phenformin-related lactic acidosis, the Secretary nonetheless deemed that the following factors necessitated his decision to suspend:

1.   The discontinued marketing of phenformin in Norway and Canada based on the experience in those countries with phenformin related lactic acidosis cases.

2.   Adverse reports of phenformin-related lactic acidosis in Finland, Sweden, New Zealand, and Australia.

3.   The discontinued use of phenformin by several diabetes clinics in major U.S. hospitals.

4.   The unanimous October, 1976 recommendation by the FDA Endocrinology and Metabolism Advisory Committee that phenformin be removed from the market.

5.   The May 6, 1977 decision by the FDA's Bureau of Drugs to seek withdrawal of approval of NDA's for phenformin.

6.   Calculations submitted by the FDA's Bureau of Drugs based on information it had received from phenformin manufacturers, research conducted in other countries, studies conducted in a group of university based medical centers and reports from individual hospitals. Those calculations indicated that:

   a.   Between 0.25 and four cases of lactic acidosis arose per 1,000 phenformin users per year with an approximate mortality rate of fifty per cent.

   b.   That the estimated incidence of death due to lactic acidosis in phenformin users is between 0.125 and 2 deaths annually per 1,000 patients—a rate 5 to 80 times higher than that of other widely used drugs known to cause fatalities even when properly used.

   c.   That between four and 60 patients would die each month from phenformin-induced lactic acidosis.

   d.   That final administrative action on withdrawal of the NDA's for phenformin could take from six to twelve months during which time anywhere from 10 to 700 people could die from phenformin associated lactic acidosis.

   . . . . [P]laintiffs allege that the standards used by the Secretary in determining that phenformin posed an imminent hazard under the statute do not comport either with the standards dictated by Congress[4] or with those set forth in the FDA's own regulation.[5]

---

[4]   Plaintiffs cite the Senate Judiciary Report accompanying the 1962 Amendments . . . which added the imminent hazard provision to the effect that the Secretary's power should be exercised "only in the exceptional case of an emergency which does not permit the Secretary to correct it by other means." S. Rep. No. 1744, Pt. 2, 87th Cong., 2d Sess. p. 7 (1962).

As recited in the Order, the criteria used by the Secretary to determine the imminence of the hazard included:

1.   The severity of the harm that could be caused by the drug during the completion of customary administrative proceedings to withdraw the drug from the general market.

2.   The likelihood that the drug will cause such harm to users while the administrative process is being completed.

3.   The risk to patients currently taking the drug that might be occasioned by the immediate removal of the drug from the market taking into account the availability of other therapies and the steps necessary for patients to adjust to these other therapies.

4.   The likelihood that after the customary administrative process is completed, the drug will be withdrawn from the general marketing.

5.   The availability of other approaches to protect the public health.

Upon reviewing these criteria, the Court is not persuaded either that they improperly reflect the intent of Congress or are at substantial variance with the FDA regulation. And, even if there may exist some discrepancy between the Secretary's criteria and those set forth in 21 CFR § 2.5, we would note that the regulation was designed to guide the FDA Commissioner in making his *recommendations* to the Secretary with respect to the existence of an imminent hazard, and would not necessarily bind the Secretary in making his nondelegable decision to suspend. Further we are not inclined to adopt plaintiff's "crisis" interpretation of imminent hazard. Rather we are more persuaded by defendant's suggested analogy to cases interpreting the imminent hazard provisions of the Federal Insecticide, Fungicide and Rodenticide Act which caution "against any approach to the term imminent hazard . . . that restricts it to a concept of crisis" and adopt the view that "It is enough that there is substantial likelihood that serious harm will be experienced during . . . any realistic projection of the administrative process." *See Environmental Defense Fund v. Environmental Protection Agency,* 510 F.2d 1291 (1975) (E.D.F. II); *Environmental Defense Fund v. Environmental Protection Agency,* 465 F.2d 528 (1972) (E.D.F. I).

We decide accordingly that the Secretary's criteria for evaluating the existence of an imminent hazard were not improper. There remains to be determined whether a rational connection exists between the facts on which he relied and his decision to suspend. Keeping in mind that "invocation of this emergency power is a matter which is peculiarly one

---

Reference is also made to the consideration of the amendments by the Senate where it was noted that the imminent hazard authority "should only be exercised under the most extreme conditions and with the utmost care." 108 Cong. Rec. 16304 (Aug. 23, 1962).

⁵   The FDA regulation defines imminent hazard as one, "(1) that should be corrected immediately to prevent injury and (2) that should not be permitted to continue while a hearing or other formal proceeding is being held. The 'imminent hazard' may be declared at any point in the chain of events which may ultimately result in harm to the public health. The occurrence of the final anticipated injury is not essential to establish that an 'imminent hazard' of such occurrence exists." 21 C.F.R. § 2.5(a).

The regulation also noted [sic] that in determining the existence of an imminent hazard, the number, nature, severity and duration of the injury will be considered. 21 C.F.R. § 2.5(b).

of judgment," this Court cannot say that the facts on which the Secretary relied, particularly the calculations provided by the Bureau of Drugs, do not adequately support his decision to suspend. . . .

Assuming, as we must at this juncture, the validity of the Bureau of Drug's projection of between four and 60 phenformin related deaths each month, we cannot find that the Secretary's conclusion that labeling changes "cannot be expected to achieve a needed reduction in the usage of phenformin within any reasonable time frame . . . with so many lives at stake," was either arbitrary or unreasonable. Nor was it made so by his decision to act first on phenformin rather than some other drug which may pose a hazard of similar magnitude. . . .

. . . [P]laintiffs also object to what it [sic] alleges is the unprecedented and unlawful attempt by the Secretary to create within the suspension order a voluntary system of limited distribution to those small number of patients for whom it may be determined that phenformin's benefits outweigh its risks. Plaintiffs voice similar objections to the Secretary's 90 day delay in implementing his order. In view of the fact that the Secretary's power to suspend under section 355(e) has never been exercised, it is obvious that any method of implementation used would be unprecedented. . . . It appears to us that the Secretary's dual concerns of an orderly withdrawal of the use of the drug from the majority of patients now using it, and of accommodating the small number of patients for whom the benefits outweighed the risks were eminently reasonable and that the power to deal with them in the manner in which he did could fairly be implied from his power to suspend.

. . . [T]he Court concludes that it must deny plaintiffs' Motion for a Preliminary Injunction. . . .

NOTES

1. *Background.* As the District Court noted, Secretary Califano's suspension of the NDAs for phenformin was the first time this nondelegable suspension authority had ever been exercised. The action came in response to a petition and threatened lawsuit by the Public Citizen Health Research Group, and it followed FDA's publication of a notice proposing to withdraw approval of the NDAs. 42 Fed. Reg. 23170 (May 6, 1977).

2. *Standing to Challenge NDA Withdrawal.* After the District Court declined to overturn Secretary Califano's suspension order, a full evidentiary hearing was held on the proposed withdrawal of the NDAs, following which the Commissioner ordered the NDAs withdrawn. 43 Fed. Reg. 54995 (Nov. 24, 1978). Forsham subsequently sought review of this order as well as review of the District Court's original ruling. The Court of Appeals dismissed the appeal regarding the suspension order as moot and ruled that Forsham and his co-plaintiffs (prescribing physicians and patients) lacked standing to seek review of the Commissioner's withdrawal order under section 505(h) of the FD&C Act because "only an 'applicant' may petition a Court of Appeals to review the . . . withdrawal of his approval of a new drug application." *Forsham v. Califano,* Food Drug Cosm. L. Rep. (CCH) ¶ 38,241 (D.C. Cir. 1979).

3. *Petition to Suspend Propoxyphene.* Secretary Califano's willingness to exercise the previously dormant "imminent hazard" authority prompted a similar petition in 1978 from the Public Citizen Health Research Group, which this time sought suspension of the drug propoxyphene because of fatalities attributed to overdose. The Secretary denied the petition pending consideration of rescheduling of the drug under the Controlled Substances Act and strengthened label warnings, including patient labeling, against the risks of misuse. *In re Petition to Suspend New Drug Applications for Propoxyphene: Order of the Secretary Denying Petition* (Feb. 15, 1979). After a public hearing on the safety and effectiveness of the drug, 44 Fed. Reg. 11837 (Mar. 2, 1979), the company voluntarily agreed to revise the drug's labeling and distribute a patient package insert (PPI).

To show its persistence, more than 25 years later, on February 28, 2006, the Public Citizen Health Research Group submitted a citizen petition to FDA again requesting that the agency immediately begin the phased removal from the market of propoxyphene. FDA Docket No. 2006P–0090/CP1. This time, however, Public Citizen did not invoke the "imminent hazard" provision but simply called for a standard NDA withdrawal. In 2010, Xanodyne Pharmaceuticals, the manufacturer of brand-name propoxyphene, agreed to withdraw it from the market voluntarily, and FDA asked generic manufacturers to do the same.

4. *Butazolidin, Tandearil, and Feldene.* In response to a petition to ban the nonsteroidal anti-inflammatory drugs Butazolidin® (phenyllbutazone) and Tandearil® (oxyphenbutazone), FDA conducted a hearing to develop recommendations for the HHS Secretary. 49 Fed. Reg. 1939 (Jan. 16, 1984). On FDA's recommendation, the Secretary denied the petition. FDA Docket No. 84N–0014 (Aug. 7, 1984). In response to a petition to ban Feldene® (prioxicam), FDA again conducted a public hearing to develop recommendations for the Secretary. 51 Fed. Reg. 3658 (Jan. 29, 1986). In this case, too, the Secretary adopted FDA's recommendation and denied the petition. FDA Dkt No. 86P–0023 (July 7, 1986). Since 1986, there have been no other petitions to the Secretary that have invoked the imminent hazard provision.

5. *Imminent Hazard Criteria.* FDA's definition of "imminent hazard" is codified at 21 C.F.R. 2.5. 36 Fed. Reg. 12516 (July 1, 1971). In 44 Fed. Reg. 48979 (Aug. 12, 1979) the Secretary of HHS proposed new criteria and procedures for implementing the imminent hazard provisions of the Act, but no further action was taken on this proposal, and it was withdrawn at 59 Fed. Reg. 3042, 3043 (Jan. 20, 1994).

G. PHYSICIAN LABELING AND PATIENT LABELING OF PRESCRIPTION DRUGS

1. PHYSICIAN LABELING (PRESCRIBING INFORMATION)

a. CONTENT

FDA requires a prescription drug manufacturer to prepare an information sheet for physicians and provide this labeling "on or within the package from which the drug is to be dispensed." 21 C.F.R. 201.100(c)(1). This sheet, known alternatively as "physician labeling," "prescribing information," and the "package insert," must present "adequate information for [the drug's] use, including indications, effects, dosages, routes, methods, and frequency and duration of administration, and any relevant hazards, contraindications, side effects, and precautions under which practitioners . . . can use the drug safely and for the purposes for which it is intended. . . ." *Id.*

FD&C Act 505(b)(1)(F) requires every NDA to contain the proposed labeling for the new drug, and section 505(d)(7) authorizes FDA to disapprove an NDA if the labeling is false or misleading in any particular. For any prescription drug on the market pursuant to an approved NDA, FDA regulations state that the physician labeling "on or within the package" must be "the labeling authorized by the approved new drug application." 21 C.F.R. 201.100(c)(2). Moreover, the regulations state that any additional labeling furnishing information regarding the use of a drug (whether or not it is on or within the package) must present this information with the same language and emphasis as the approved labeling, must be otherwise "consistent with and not contrary to" the approved labeling, and must be accompanied by the full approved labeling. 21 C.F.R. 201.100(d). Because virtually all marketed prescription drugs require some form of NDA, FDA thus has almost complete control over the content of the labeling of these products. The FDA-approved physician labeling also constitutes the bounds of permissible advertising for the drug.

Before the rise of the internet, the primary place in which doctors could find the approved physician labeling for drugs was a compilation of this information titled *The Physicians' Desk Reference (PDR)*. Today, physicians (and patients) can easily obtain the approved prescribing information for drugs online, at manufacturers' web sites.

Because of the central importance of the physician labeling, FDA, the medical profession, and the pharmaceutical industry have focused substantial attention on the appropriate form and content of this information. The agency conducted a major revision of its physician labeling requirements in 1979. 44 Fed. Reg. 37434 (June 26, 1979). Another major revision, resulting in the current requirements, occurred in 2006. 71 Fed. Reg. 3922 (Jan. 24, 2006), codified at 21 C.F.R. 201.56–7.

FDA-mandated physician labeling has become increasingly extensive and complex over time. The following mandatory headings and subheadings required for the labeling of all new and recently

approved prescription drug products provide some sense of the length
and detail of today's physician package inserts:

Highlights of Prescribing Information

Product Names, Other Required Information

Boxed Warning

Recent Major Changes

Indications and Usage

Dosage and Administration

Dosage Forms and Strengths

Contraindications

Warnings and Precautions

Adverse Reactions

Drug Interactions

Use in Specific Populations

Full Prescribing Information: Contents

Full Prescribing Information

Boxed Warning

1   Indications and Usage

2   Dosage and Administration

3   Dosage Forms and Strengths

4   Contraindications

5   Warnings and Precautions

6   Adverse Reactions

7   Drug Interactions

8   Use in Specific Populations

8.1 Pregnancy

8.2 Labor and delivery

8.3 Nursing mothers

8.4 Pediatric use

8.5 Geriatric use

9   Drug Abuse and Dependence

9.1 Controlled substance

9.2 Abuse

9.3 Dependence

10   Overdosage

11   Description

12   Clinical Pharmacology

12.1 Mechanism of action

12.2 Pharmacodynamics

12.3 Pharmacokinetics

13   Nonclinical Toxicology

13.1 Carcinogenesis, mutagenesis, impairment of fertility

13.2 Animal toxicology and/or pharmacology

14   Clinical Studies

15   References

16   How Supplied/Storage and Handling

17   Patient Counseling Information

21 C.F.R. 201.56(d)(1).

The more notable features of the January 2006 revisions include: the requirement of a "highlights" section at the beginning of the insert, which is limited to one-half of a page; a requirement of a table of contents that must list all of the headings and subheadings mandated by the regulation; a requirement that any FDA-approved patient labeling must either be reprinted at the end of the insert or accompany the insert; and detailed requirements for format and font size. In addition, in the preamble to the final rule, FDA stated that the labeling requirements were intended to preempt all conflicting state law requirements. As discussed below, however, the Supreme Court ultimately rejected this assertion with respect to product liability actions in *Wyeth v. Levine*, 555 U.S. 555 (2009). *Infra* p. 894.

NOTES

1.   *FDA Approval of Drug Labeling.* See Richard A. Merrill, *Compensation for Prescription Drug Injuries*, 59 VA. L. REV. 1 (1973):

> The FDA not only decides whether a drug may be marketed, it also determines how it may be promoted and sold. The agency approves, and for practical purposes prescribes, the labeling that the drug must bear. The label typically includes information concerning dosages, directions for administration, conditions for which the drug is effective, contraindications (disease conditions in which the drug may be harmful), and warnings about known or suspected side effects and adverse reactions. In this critical part of the approval process the FDA attempts to refine and articulate its initial weighing of hazards and benefits. It believes . . . that the information conveyed by the labeling will effectively control the use of a drug and thereby limit risks and enhance benefits. . . .

2.   *Physician's Desk Reference.* In *United States v. Abbott Laboratories,* 1965–1968 FDLI Jud. Rec. 315 (N.D. Ill. 1968), a prosecution for misbranding, FDA charged that the information about a drug that the defendants supplied to the *Physician's Desk Reference* was not "substantially the same" as the FDA-approved package insert, as required by agency regulations. The District Court held that the *PDR* is labeling, but it concluded that FDA had failed to prove beyond a reasonable doubt that the *PDR* monograph differed significantly from the approved labeling in this case. The regulations were subsequently changed to require, as mentioned above, that all labeling containing such information be presented "in the same language and emphasis" and in the same format, as

the approved physician labeling. 33 Fed. Reg. 15023 (Oct. 8, 1968), codified as amended at 21 C.F.R. 201.100(d).

3. *The Drug Label.* The FD&C Act defines "label," as opposed to "labeling," to be "upon the immediate container of [the] article." FD&C Act 201(m). Section 502(b) of the Act requires that every drug in package form—that is, in the commercial stream from the manufacturer to the pharmacy—bear a label "containing (1) the name and place of business of the manufacturer, packer, or distributor and (2) an accurate statement of the quantity of the contents in terms of weight, measure or numerical count." Section 502(e) mandates that every drug's label bear the established (nonproprietary) name of the drug, the established name and quantity of each active ingredient, and the established name of each inactive ingredient. FDA has elaborated on these requirements at 21 C.F.R. Part 201. The agency requires the labels of drugs used in hospitals to bear a scannable bar code that contains at least the product's National Drug Code (NDC) number in order to reduce medication errors. 69 Fed. Reg. 9120 (Feb. 26, 2004), codified at 21 C.F.R. 201.25.

The above requirements apply to both prescription and OTC drugs. Rx and OTC drugs are subject to distinct label requirements, as well. OTC requirements will be addressed later in this chapter. *Infra* p. 985. The most notable label requirements particular to prescription drugs are listed at 21 C.F.R. 201.100(b). This regulation requires each prescription drug label to include, among other things, the statement "Rx only," the recommended or usual dosage, the route of administration (if not oral), an identifying lot or control number, and a statement directed to the pharmacist specifying the type of container to be used in dispensing the product. 21 C.F.R. 201.100(b)(1), (2), (3), (6), (7).

4. *Name of Manufacturer.* As noted above, section 502(b) of the FD&C Act requires that the label of a drug bear the name and place of business of the manufacturer, packer, or distributor. With the advent of specialized manufacturing techniques in the pharmaceutical industry, this seemingly simple requirement became a matter of some complexity. FDA adopted an informal policy that any of the firms which perform an important manufacturing operation could be identified as *the* manufacturer. In addition, the agency established a "man-in-the-plant" policy, under which a drug company could lease the facilities of, or contract with, another firm to manufacture a drug and still identify itself as the manufacturer if it placed its own employees in the manufacturing facility to supervise production. Both policies came in for criticism, and they provoked multiple congressional hearings. Faced with this chorus of dissent, FDA in 1978 proposed a new regulation to clarify who may be considered the "manufacturer" of a drug. 43 Fed. Reg. 45614 (Oct. 3, 1978). After some administrative twists and turn, FDA promulgated a final regulation in 1983, which is still in effect. 48 Fed. Reg. 37620 (Aug. 19, 1983), codified at 21 C.F.R. 201.1. This complex rule abolishes the "man-in-the-plant" policy and allows a firm to be designated as the manufacturer of a drug only if it performs *all* manufacturing operations (with certain limited exceptions). A firm that performs more than half of the important manufacturing operations may be designated as the manufacturer if the label also states that "certain manufacturing operations have been performed by other

firms." Alternatively, all firms that contribute to production may be listed as "joint manufacturers," or a single firm may simply be listed as the distributor.

b.   DRUG NAMES

From December 1959 until his death in August 1963, Senator Estes Kefauver presided over extensive hearings investigating pricing, promotion, and patent practices of the pharmaceutical industry. One of the few of Kefauver's original proposals that survived the legislative process culminating in the 1962 Drug Amendments was the requirement in section 502(e) of the FD&C Act that manufacturers disclose the generic name of the active ingredient in their products in labeling and in advertising. Kefauver explained the reason for this provision as follows:

Administered Prices—Drugs

Senate Report No. 448, 87th Congress, 1st Session (1961).

In addition to patent controls and the vast amounts spent on advertising and promotion, the control of the market by the large drug companies stems from a third source of power; this is their remarkable success in persuading physicians to prescribe by trade names rather than generic names. Where this is done the small manufacturer is automatically excluded from the market, regardless of whether the drugs are patented or nonpatented, and the opportunity for price competition disappears. This state of affairs is furthered by anything which causes the physician to be apprehensive of, or have difficulty in, prescribing by generic names. . . .

The new so-called synthetic penicillin illustrates the problem. The chemical name for this product is alpha-phenoxyethyl penicillin potassium. This set of syllables is also used as a generic name. In addition, there are two other generic names—potassium penicillin 152 and phenethicillin potassium. Since the product is protected by patent, there are only six sellers, each of whom markets under his own trade name. Thus the prescribing physician is bombarded with promotional material for Syncillin, Darcil, Alpen, Chemipen, Dramcillin–S, and Maxipen. All of these are, of course, the same chemical compound. . . .

In this example the busy practitioner is confronted with three generic names, six brand names used as the name of the drug itself, and at least five different colors. Thus, there are 14 different identification symbols for the identical drug. In terms of nomenclature, each product stands isolated: indeed, there is an attempt to conceal the identical nature of the drug. . . .

———

Pharmaceutical manufacturers opposed adoption of section 502(e). When FDA adopted regulations to implement the provision in 1963, the major drug companies promptly took the agency to court. *See* Harry A. Sweeney, Jr., *The "Generic Every Time" Case: Prescription Drug Industry In Extremis,* 21 FOOD DRUG COSM. L.J. 226 (1966). The regulations would have required manufacturer labeling and advertising to disclose the generic name of the drug—termed the "established name" in section 502(e)—every time the trade name was used. The manufacturers sought a declaratory judgment that the regulations were invalid and an injunction against their enforcement in advance of any attempt by FDA to initiate compliance proceedings against any firm or drug. The District Court held the regulations invalid. *Abbott Laboratories v. Celebrezze,* 228 F. Supp. 855 (D. Del. 1964). Neither the Court of Appeals for the Third Circuit, which reversed the District Court, 352 F.2d 286 (1965), nor the U.S. Supreme Court reached the merits of the case. The Supreme Court's decision in the matter, *Abbott Laboratories v. Gardner,* 387 U.S. 136 (1967) (excerpted *supra* p. 34) remains the seminal judicial discussion of "ripeness" of agency action for judicial review. The Court held that the regulations were reviewable in a pre-enforcement suit and remanded the case for consideration of the legality of FDA's "every time" requirement.

Following the Supreme Court's remand, the parties reached a settlement a few days before the case was scheduled for reargument before the Third Circuit. The resulting regulation, 21 C.F.R. 201.10(g), requires that the generic name appear, in type at least half the size as the brand name, whenever the brand name is "featured," and at least once when the brand name is used "in the running text."

NOTES

1. *Official Names.* The Drug Amendments of 1962 also added section 508 to the FD&C Act, which authorizes FDA, when necessary, to designate a drug's official name. FDA established a procedure for designating official names in 21 C.F.R. Part 299 and initially promulgated a number of official names. The agency later revoked these names, however, and adopted the policy of relying upon the drug names established by United States Adopted Names (USAN). 49 Fed. Reg. 37574 (Sept. 25, 1984), 53 Fed. Reg. 5368 (Feb. 24, 1988). USAN is published by a consortium of private organizations, in consultation with FDA and international organizations.

2. *FDA Change in Official Name.* In *Novartis v. Leavitt,* 435 F.3d 344 (D.C. Cir. 2006), the Court of Appeals held that FDA may lawfully change an official name without notice-and-comment rulemaking.

3. *Brand Name.* The manufacturer of a drug may choose any brand name that is not false or misleading. FDA has successfully challenged brand names as misleading. *E.g., United States v. 70 1/2 Dozen Bottles . . . "666",* 1938–1964 FDLI Jud. Rec. 89 (M.D. Ga. 1944). If disclaimers are adequate to prevent a brand name from being misleading, however, the manufacturer has the right to use the disclaimer. *E.g.,* 39 Fed. Reg. 11298 (Mar. 27, 1974). For many years, FDA officials quite commonly objected to trademarks that they believed could be misleading. Reacting in part to recent First Amendment decisions, however, FDA has substantially reduced this practice. Nonetheless, based on a full factual record, the Court of Appeals in *Kos Pharmaceuticals, Inc. v. Andrx Corp.,* 369 F.3d 700 (3rd Cir. 2004) determined that the Andrx trademark Altocor® was confusingly similar to the Kos trademark Advicor and thus should be enjoined. *See* Angela A. Sun, *A Drug by Any Other Name: The Power of Naming and the*

Medical and Regulatory Impact of Misnaming Prescription Drugs (2001), in Chapter (VI)(B)(1) of the Electronic Book.

c.   WARNINGS

Section 502(f)(2) of the Act requires, in addition to adequate directions for use, "such adequate warnings against use in those pathological conditions or by children where its use may be dangerous to health, or against unsafe dosage or methods or duration of administration or application, . . . as are necessary for the protection of users. . . ." This logical requirement presents difficult problems of implementation.

Section 201.57(c)(6) of the FDA regulations establishes the requirements for the warnings that must be contained in the physician package insert for a prescription drug.

> (6) *Warnings and precautions.* (i) *General.* This section must describe clinically significant adverse reactions (including any that are potentially fatal, are serious even if infrequent, or can be prevented or mitigated through appropriate use of the drug), other potential safety hazards (including those that are expected for the pharmacological class or those resulting from drug/drug interactions), limitations in use imposed by them (*e.g.,* avoiding certain concomitant therapy), and steps that should be taken if they occur (*e.g.,* dosage modification). The frequency of all clinically significant adverse reactions and the approximate mortality and morbidity rates for patients experiencing the reaction, if known and necessary for the safe and effective use of the drug, must be expressed. . . . A specific warning relating to a use not provided for under the "Indications and Usage" section may be required by FDA in accordance with sections 201(n) and 502(a) of the act if the drug is commonly prescribed for a disease or condition and such usage is associated with a clinically significant risk or hazard.

FDA regulations further provide that "[c]ertain contraindications or serious warnings, particularly those that may lead to death or serious injury, may be required by the FDA to be presented in a box. . . . The box must contain, in uppercase letters, a heading inside the box that includes the word 'WARNING' and conveys the general focus of the information in the box." 21 C.F.R. 201.57(c)(1). Such warnings, known as "black box warnings," appear in the "Warnings and Precautions" or "Contraindications" section of the physician package insert, as appropriate. *Id.* Moreover, a concise summary of the black box warning must appear (also in a box) in the highlights section of the insert. 21 C.F.R. 201.57(a)(4).

Ordinarily such a warning must be based on clinical data, but serious animal toxicity may also suffice. Other than the general statements in 201.57(c)(6), FDA has issued no guidance on the criteria applied by FDA in imposing a black box warning. In Judith E. Beach et al., *Black Box Warnings in Prescription Drug Labeling: Results of a Survey of 206 Drugs*, 53 FOOD & DRUG L.J. 403 (1998), the authors reviewed all 206 black box warnings for drugs that were listed in the 1995 Physician's Desk Reference. As a result of FDA's heightened interest in risk management, there has been a substantial increase in black box warnings.

In addition to information specifically designated as "warnings and precautions" or "contraindications," the physician package insert is also required to contain warning-related sections devoted to adverse reactions; drug interactions; effect on pregnancy, labor, delivery, and lactation; pediatric and geriatric use; and nonclinical toxicology including carcinogenesis, mutagenesis, and impairment of fertility. These requirements result in a lengthy, complex, and highly conservative summary of the drug's safety. The prescribing brochure has been described as a "conservative consensus" between two parties with an interest in not omitting any possible hazards: the manufacturer (worried about tort liability) and FDA (worried about Congressional and public criticism). *See* Peter Barton Hutt, *Regulation of the Practice of Medicine under the Pure Food and Drug Laws*, 33 J. OF THE ASS'N OF FOOD AND DRUG OFFICIALS OF THE U.S. 3 (1969).

Organized medicine and individual practitioners have no role in determining the content of the warnings in the package insert. It is therefore not surprising that the leading court challenge to an FDA-required warning was brought by a group of physicians, not by the affected drug manufacturers. The following opinion describes the inception of one of the most contentious episodes in FDA's administration of federal drug law.

Bradley v. Weinberger

483 F.2d 410 (1st Cir. 1973).

■ COFFIN, CHIEF JUDGE.

Plaintiffs, 178 physicians who treat diabetes and one diabetes patient who use oral hypoglycemic agents to control the disease by lowering the blood sugar level, brought suit to enjoin the defendants Secretary of Health, Education and Welfare and the Commissioner of the Food and Drug Administration (FDA) from enforcing and the defendant drug companies from complying with the FDA's proposal for altering the labeling of those drugs. . . .

This controversy revolves around a long-term, federally funded study undertaken by the University Group Diabetes Program (hereafter the UGDP study) to determine the effects of oral hypoglycemic agents on vascular complications in patients with adult-onset diabetes. . . . [T]he study concluded that the combination of diet and either tolbutamide or phenformin [two oral hypoglycemic agents] was no more effective than diet alone in prolonging life but that those oral agents might be more hazardous than diet or diet plus insulin insofar as cardiovascular mortality was concerned. . . .

After the study received much publicity and criticism . . . the FDA concluded that protection of the public required a strong warning to physicians recommending use of an oral agent only if other treatments were inadvisable and noting the UGDP's findings regarding the apparently increased danger of cardiovascular mortality. This evaluation and proposed labeling change was first formally published in the FDA *Drug Bulletin* of June, 1971.

On October 7, 1971, the Committee on the Care of the Diabetic, consisting of eminent doctors and experts in the field including some of the plaintiff doctors, submitted through its counsel a petition to the FDA. It asked the FDA to rescind its labeling recommendation, insure that all future FDA comments on the UGDP study include references to its alleged deficiencies and controversial nature, provide petitioners with the complete raw data of the study, and, "in accord with its policy of fair balance," disseminate with equal emphasis and frequency studies and individual expert opinions differing with the study. . . .

In the May, 1972, *Drug Bulletin,* the FDA published the "Final Labeling Approved for Oral Hypoglycemic Drugs," which proposed changes in the "indications" section of the label and the addition of a "special warning" section. . . .

This suit was filed [by the Committee] on August 11, 1972 and a temporary restraining order issued that day. After a hearing and submission of affidavits of experts by both sides, the emergency district judge denied the preliminary injunction. . . .

On October 17, 1972, the litigation entered an entirely new phase. On that date, plaintiffs filed a motion for leave to amend their complaint, supported by 13 affidavits by diabetes experts attesting to the controversy over the UGDP study, and new motions for a temporary restraining order and a preliminary injunction. The motions presented for the first time the argument that the FDA's proposed label was itself misleading and thus rendered the drug misbranded in violation of the statute, because it failed to reveal the existence of a "material weight of contrary opinion" among "experts qualified by scientific training and experience" as allegedly required by the agency's own regulation, 21 C.F.R. § 1.3. After oral argument . . . the district court in a Memorandum and Order granted on November 3, 1972, the motions to amend the complaint and for a preliminary injunction. It . . . stated that "the court is satisfied plaintiffs have made a showing that there is reasonable likelihood upon a full hearing on the merits they would be successful in establishing the defendants . . . have not in the order described in the May 1972 Bulletin complied with 21 C.F.R. § 1.3.; 21 U.S.C. § 321(n) and 21 U.S.C. § 352(a). . . ."

. . . Courts are not best equipped, as both sides here readily agree, to judge the merits of the scientific studies and the objections to them. Specialized agencies like the FDA are created to serve that function . . .

. . . [S]everal factors in this case lead us to insist that the specific argument now pressed be first thrashed out in the administrative arena.

Most significantly, this is an unprecedented argument. As plaintiffs' counsel readily admitted in oral argument before the district court, there appears to be no prior case in which an FDA drug labeling decision was challenged not by the producer but by concerned medical practitioners, and no case in which the misbranding statutes and regulations were sought to be applied not to the manufacturer's label but to the FDA's proposal for alteration of the label in light of new information. . . .

. . . The . . . statute (21 U.S.C. § 321(n)) provides: "If an article is alleged to be misbranded because the labeling is misleading, then in determining whether the labeling is misleading there shall be taken into account (among other things) not only representations made or suggested . . . but also the extent to which the labeling fails to reveal facts material in light of such representations or material with respect to consequences which may result from the use of the article to which the labeling relates." Implementing [this] definition is regulation 1.3:

> "The existence of a difference of opinion, among experts qualified by scientific training and experience, as to the truth of a representation made or suggested in the labeling is a fact (among other facts) the failure to reveal which may render the labeling misleading, if there is a material weight of opinion contrary to such representation."

. . . .

The Commissioner never considered the meaning of this regulation, . . . the intersection of the safety, effectiveness, and misbranding requirements, or the applicability of the misbranding requirements, both statutory and regulatory, to an FDA proposal for re-labeling, for the simple reason that the issue was not presented to him. . . .

Because the plaintiffs failed to exhaust their administrative remedies regarding the issues they now present and, consequently, the district court reviewed the agency decision on something other than the administrative record, we must vacate the injunction. . . .

NOTES

1. *Physician Opposition.* It is notable that it was a group of physicians, rather than the manufacturers of tolbutamide and phenformin, who initially resisted FDA's efforts to require label warnings about the increased risk of cardiovascular mortality ostensibly revealed by the UGDP study. The opposition of the Committee for the Care of the Diabetic reflected profound disagreement with the findings of the study and suspicion about the way in which it had been conducted. Clinicians specializing in the treatment of diabetes, and known for their espousal of the oral hypoglycemic drugs, believed that the UGDP findings were unreliable. Committed as they were to continued use of the drugs, the *Bradley* plaintiffs were obviously also concerned about the liability implications of an FDA-prescribed warning cautioning against their routine use and alluding to a heightened risk of cardiovascular disease—a condition that besets many diabetics anyway.

2. *UGDP Study Records.* From the time of the earliest reports of the UGDP study, the Committee on the Care of the Diabetic had . . . sought access to all of the study records. Ultimately this demand was submitted to NIH and FDA in the form of a Freedom of Information Act request, which the agencies denied on the ground that they did not have custody of the records—which were kept by the study coordinator, a biostatistician at the University of Maryland Medical School. This denial was upheld in *Forsham v. Califano,* 587 F.2d 1128 (D.C. Cir. 1978), *aff'd Forsham v. Harris,* 445 U.S. 169 (1980). The Court of Appeals expressly left open the question whether FDA could validly mandate final labeling for the oral

hypoglycemic drugs based upon the UGDP findings without affording critics access to the study records.

———

The *Bradley* ruling, and the subsequent failure to reach agreement with the plaintiffs on labeling for the drugs, caused FDA to alter its legal approach. As a first step, the agency proposed to revise 21 C.F.R. 1.3 (now 21 C.F.R. 1.21), its regulation interpreting section 201(n) of the Act.

Labeling: Failure to Reveal Material Facts
39 Fed. Reg. 33229 (September 16, 1974).

. . . Drug warnings, by their very nature, warn only about possible danger. Although they are often the subject of intense debate, the Food and Drug Administration has never permitted drug labeling to reflect such debate. That debate and disagreement is properly the subject of scientific discussion in professional journals and symposia, but not in drug labeling. . . .

. . . 21 CFR 1.3 is inconsistent with relevant statutory requirements and contemporary medical and scientific principles. The Commissioner has concluded that the use of medical opinion in product labeling must be limited and particularized accordingly.

. . . § 1.3 is inconsistent with the statutory standard established in section 502(f) of the act. An adequate warning of possible danger must appear in all such labeling. Without such a warning, a product is misbranded. The statute presupposes a difference of medical opinion since the danger need not be established and absolute, but rather merely potential. Thus, there is no basis to permit warnings to be discounted by an opinion that the warning is really not necessary at all. Providing for medical controversy with respect to a warning undermines the public health impetus of section 502(f) of the act. Where potential danger is the statutory standard, a warning must be unencumbered and unambiguous.

The degree of scientific uncertainty about a possible hazard, or its frequency of occurrence, or other similar related information may, of course, accompany or be part of a warning. It is common for a warning to state the product "may" cause a hazard, where the relationship is not yet conclusively proven, or to point out that the relationship between adverse animal findings and human consequences has not yet been determined. However, presentation of such factual information, which is helpful to the physician in evaluating the significance of a warning, does not permit additional statements of conflicting medical opinion relating to the warning.

. . . The Commissioner concludes that, where warnings are required, disclamatory opinions necessarily detract from the warning in such a manner as to be confusing and misleading. In this way, differences of medical opinions regarding warnings for foods and cosmetics would render the products to be misbranded within the meaning of section 402(a) and 602(a) of the act. . . .

Therefore ... the Commissioner proposes that [the C.F.R.] be amended by revising § 1.3 to read as follows: ...

(c) Paragraph (a) of this section does not:

(1) Permit or require a statement of differences of opinion with respect to warnings (including contraindications, precautions, adverse reactions, and other information relating to possible product hazards) required in labeling for food, drugs, devices, or cosmetics under the act.

. . . .

NOTES

1. *Final Regulation on "Failure to Reveal Material Facts".* The final version of this regulation—identical to the proposed version except for the deletion of the superfluous phrase "or require"—was promulgated in 40 Fed. Reg. 28582 (July 7, 1975). The regulation remains in force today, now numbered 21 C.F.R. 1.21.

2. *Differences of Opinion Regarding Effectiveness.* The preamble excerpted above also asserted:

> Congress has determined that the effectiveness of new drugs and new animal drugs must be established by substantial evidence. Thus, a difference of medical opinion with respect to a labeling claim of effectiveness for these products is legally insufficient and is not a material fact, within the meaning of section 201(n) of the act, unless such opinion is itself supported by evidence which meets the statutory standard. . . .

39 Fed. Reg. at 33232. In the same document, FDA thus also proposed to revise 21 C.F.R. 1.3 to also prohibit "a statement of differences of opinion with respect to the effectiveness of a drug unless each of the opinions expressed is supported by substantial evidence of effectiveness as defined in sections 505(d) and 512(d) of the act." *Id.* at 33233. This provision, too, was finalized at 40 Fed. Reg. 28582 (July 7, 1975). It is now at 21 C.F.R. 1.21(c)(2).

3. *Relabeling of Oral Hypoglycemic Drugs.* At the same time that FDA published its final regulation interpreting section 201(n), it published comprehensive proposed labeling requirements for oral hypoglycemic drugs, 40 Fed. Reg. 28587 (July 7, 1975). The comments to this proposal, as well as presentations made in an August 1975 legislative-style hearing, continued to advance accusations of poor design and recording errors in the UGDP study. Finally, FDA and the sponsor of the study, NIH, undertook an audit of the accuracy of the transcription of the study's "raw data"—the actual patient records—into the published reports. The agencies completed this audit in 1978, concluding:

> ... [W]hile there are certain errors and discrepancies between the data file of the UGDP study and the published reports, none of these appears of sufficient frequency or magnitude to invalidate the finding that cardiovascular mortality was higher in the groups of patients

treated with tolbutamide plus diet and phenformin plus diet compared to the groups treated with placebo or insulin.

43 Fed. Reg. 52732, 52733 (Nov. 14, 1978). FDA reopened the comment period on the proposed labeling. *Id.* at 52734.

More than five years later, FDA published its final regulation—still in effect—establishing a warning for this class of drugs. *See* 49 Fed. Reg. 14303, 14441 (Apr. 11, 1984), codified at 21 C.F.R. 310.517. The prescribed warning, citing the UGDP study, states that oral hypoglycemic drugs have been "reported to be associated with increased cardiovascular mortality as compared to treatment with diet alone or diet plus insulin," and that:

> [d]espite controversy regarding the interpretation of these results, the findings of the UGDP study provide an adequate basis for this warning. The patient should be informed of the potential risks and advantages of (name of drug) and of alternative modes of therapy.

Finally, the regulation states that the warning is applicable to all marketed oral hypoglycemic drugs even though only one, tolbutamide, was included in the UGDP study. (Phenformin, the other drug involved in the UDGDP study, was banned by the Secretary of HEW as an "imminent hazard" on other grounds in 1977. *See supra* p. 855.) The adverse results found in the UGDP trial have not been confirmed in subsequent studies. *See, e.g.*, Francis M. Collins, *Current Treatment Approaches to Type 2 Diabetes Mellitus: Successes and Shortcomings*, 8 AM. J. OF MANAGED CARE S460 (Oct. 2002).

4.   *Other Drug Warnings by Regulation.* Other examples of warnings for prescription drugs imposed by FDA regulations appear in 21 C.F.R. Part 201, Subpart G. This method for mandating warnings is largely a remnant of the complex DESI process by which FDA imposed the 1962 effectiveness requirements on extant drug products. *See infra* p. 776. Today, the agency prescribes warnings for prescription drugs almost exclusively through the NDA process. Although one goal of the DESI approach was achieving uniform, indeed near-identical, labeling ("class labeling") for all identical, similar, or related drugs, the agency currently pursues the goal of labeling uniformity almost exclusively through the NDA and abbreviated NDA process.

5.   *Accutane Labeling.* Because of the substantial toxicity, and consequent narrow benefit/risk ratio, of many modern prescription drugs, their labeled contraindications and warnings can be quite frightening. Accutane (isotretinoin) is uniquely effective in treating severe cystic acne, but is teratogenic (causes birth defects). As part of a comprehensive program (originally a RiskMAP, now a REMS) to assure its safe use, the physician labeling bears the following information:

**CAUSES BIRTH
DEFECTS**

**DO NOT GET
PREGNANT**

> **CONTRAINDICATIONS AND WARNINGS**
> Accutane must not be used by female patients who are or may become pregnant. There is an extremely high risk that severe birth defects will result if pregnancy occurs while taking Accutane in any amount, even for short periods of time. Potentially any fetus exposed during pregnancy can be affected. There are no accurate means of determining whether an exposed fetus has been affected.
> Birth defects which have been documented following Accutane exposure include abnormalities of the face, eyes, ears, skull, central nervous system, cardiovascular system, and thymus and parathyroid glands. Cases of IQ scores less than 85 with or without other abnormalities have been reported. There is an increased risk of spontaneous abortion, and premature births have been reported.
> Documented external abnormalities include: skull abnormality; ear abnormalities (including anotia, micropinna, small or absent external auditory canals); eye abnormalities (including microphthalmia); facial dysmorphia; cleft palate. Documented internal abnormalities include: CNS abnormalities (including cerebral abnormalities, cerebellar malformation, hydrocephalus, microcephaly, cranial nerve deficit); cardiovascular abnormalities; thymus gland abnormality; parathyroid hormone deficiency. In some cases death has occurred with certain of the abnormalities previously noted.
> If pregnancy does occur during treatment of a female patient who is taking Accutane, Accutane must be discontinued immediately and she should be referred to an Obstetrician-Gynecologist experienced in reproductive toxicity for further evaluation and counseling.
>
> **Special Prescribing Requirements**
> Because of Accutane's teratogenicity and to minimize fetal exposure, Accutane is approved for marketing only under a special restricted distribution program approved by the Food and Drug Administration. This program is called iPLEDGE™. Accutane must only be prescribed by prescribers who are registered and activated with the iPLEDGE program. Accutane must only be dispensed by a pharmacy registered and activated with iPLEDGE, and must only be dispensed to patients who are registered and meet all the requirements of iPLEDGE (see **PRECAUTIONS**).

6. *Antibiotic Resistance Warning*. In 2003, FDA promulgated a regulation requiring new warning information in the labeling of all systemic antibacterial drug products. 68 Fed. Reg. 6062 (Feb. 6, 2003), codified at 21 C.F.R. 201.24. Directly under the product name, the labeling must state:

"To reduce the development of drug-resistant bacteria and maintain the effectiveness of [insert name of antibacterial drug product] and other antibacterial drugs, [insert name of antibacterial drug product] should be used only to treat or prevent infections that are proven or strongly suspected to be caused by bacteria."

In the "precautions" section of the physician labeling, under "information for patients," the labeling is required to state that patients should be counseled that antibacterial drugs should only be used to treat bacterial infections, not viral infections such as the common cold, and that the drug should be taken exactly as directed because skipping doses decreases the effectiveness of the immediate treatment and increases the likelihood that bacteria will develop resistance.

7. *"Dear Doctor" Letters.* Sometimes, emergency notices regarding a drug's safety problems are disseminated in the form of "Dear Doctor" letters sent directly to physicians. In *Bernhardt v. Pfizer, Inc.*, Food Drug Cosm. L. Rep. (CCH ¶ 38,639 (S.D.N.Y. 2000)), the District Court denied tort plaintiffs' motion to require such a letter on the ground that the matter was within the primary jurisdiction of FDA, and it referred the matter to the agency.

8. *Effectiveness of Warnings.* There is substantial controversy about the effectiveness of the warnings required by FDA to be included in drug product labeling. Studies have shown that changing the labeling on a drug does not necessarily change prescribing practices. For example, Walter Smalley et al., *Contraindicated Use of Cisapride: Impact of Food and Drug Administration Regulatory Action*, 284 J.A.M.A. 3036 (2000), concluded that a warning about life-threatening cardiac arrhythmias caused by cisapride through a boxed warning and a "Dear Healthcare Professional" letter from the drug manufacturer "had no material effect on contraindicated cisapride use." Others argue that the lack of an impact of a drug warning on prescribing practices may indicate that the use of the particular drug remains important to doctors and patients in spite of the potential adverse events. Although FDA continues to recognize the importance of labeling changes and other communications with the medical profession about new safety information, the agency recognizes that physicians often base their decisions on their own experience and therefore discount agency warnings. Accordingly, FDA has sought alternative means of risk management for drug safety problems, most notably REMS.

d.   REVISIONS TO WARNINGS BASED ON POSTMARKET SAFETY INFORMATION

FDA's prescription drug labeling regulations require the agency to respond to risks that emerge after the drug is already on the market. The provision on "warnings and precautions" states: "[T]he labeling must be revised to include a warning about a clinically significant hazard as soon as there is reasonable evidence of a causal association with a drug; a causal relationship need not have been definitely established." 21 C.F.R. 201.57(c)(6). Pursuant to this provision, FDA often requires warnings in prescription drug labeling where there is in fact no evidence of a causal relationship; sometimes a single known case of an adverse event prompts agency action.

Until 2007, the only formal power FDA possessed to force a labeling change for an approved new drug was the threat of withdrawal of the

NDA approval. Nonetheless, the agency frequently persuaded manufacturers to submit supplemental NDAs adding or enhancing warnings. With the passage of FDAAA in 2007, in the wake of the crisis surrounding the safety of COX–2 inhibitors, the agency gained the authority to mandate labeling changes reflecting new safety information. FD&C Act 505(o)(4). Under this provision, FDA must first request a voluntary change. The agency may require a labeling revision only after conducting dispute resolution procedures, if the manufacturer requests them. *Id. See* GUIDANCE FOR INDUSTRY: SAFETY LABELING CHANGES—IMPLEMENTATION OF SECTION 505(O)(4) OF THE FEDERAL FOOD, DRUG, AND COSMETIC ACT (JULY 2013). FDA posts its "Safety Labeling Change Order Letters" on its website.

Sometimes a manufacturer need not wait for FDA approval of an SNDA before voluntarily adding a warning to a prescription drug label. The "changes being effected" (CBE) regulation permits a manufacturer, in specified circumstances, to revise the labeling immediately upon submitting an SNDA to the agency. According to 21 C.F.R. 314.70(c):

> (6) The agency may designate a category of changes for the purpose of providing that, in the case of a change in such category, the holder of an approved application may commence distribution of the drug product involved upon receipt by the agency of a supplement for the change. These changes include, but are not limited to:
>
> . . . .
>
> (iii) Changes in the labeling to reflect newly acquired information. . . . to accomplish any of the following:
>
> (A) To add or strengthen a contraindication, warning, precaution, or adverse reaction for which the evidence of a causal association satisfies the standard for inclusion in the labeling of under § 201.57(c) of this chapter;
>
> (B) To add or strengthen a statement about drug abuse, dependence, psychological effect, or overdosage;
>
> (C) To add or strengthen an instruction about dosage and administration that is intended to increase the safe use of the drug product. . . .

21 C.F.R. 314.70(c)(6)(iii)(A).

The requirement in 314.70(c)(6)(iii) that the labeling change "reflect newly acquired information" was added to the CBE regulation in 2008, and at first glance, this amendment may appear to limit the application of the rule to situations in which totally new safety data emerges. 73 Fed. Reg. 49603 (Aug. 22, 2008). In the preamble to the final rule amending the regulation, however, FDA made clear that "newly acquired information" includes "new clinical studies, reports of adverse events, and *new analyses of previously submitted data.*" *Id.* at 49604.

As you will see below, the CBE regulation was an important factor in the Supreme Court's rejection of federal preemption of state failure-to-warn tort suits against brand-name drug manufacturers in *Wyeth v. Levine*, 555 U.S. 555 (2009) (excerpted *infra* p. 894).

2.   PATIENT LABELING FOR PRESCRIPTION DRUGS

a.   INTRODUCTION

The last half century has witnessed a general shift in society's view of the patient, from a passive subject of the physician's beneficent ministrations to an informed and empowered participant in one's own treatment. This development is reflected in the evolution of FDA's regulation of the information provided to patients about prescription drugs. A patient cannot have significant agency in the decision to use a prescription drug unless she has access to detailed facts about the drug itself. Since 1970, FDA has become dramatically more willing than it once was to permit, and sometimes require, drug manufacturers to provide prescription drug labeling to patients. A parallel change has occurred in the agency's approach to direct-to-consumer advertising of these products. *See infra* p. 915.

The older, submissive understanding of the patient's role is well illustrated by an FDA rule issued shortly after the passage of the FD&C Act in 1938. As discussed previously, *supra* p. 802, although the Act did not originally establish compulsory prescription status, the agency effectively did so through regulation. These regulations contained a provision stating, in effect, that a prescription drug was misbranded unless "all representations or suggestions contained in the labeling thereof with respect to the conditions for which such drug . . . is to be used appear only in such medical terms as are *not* likely to be understood by the ordinary individual." 21 C.F.R. 2.106(b)(2) (1938) (emphasis added). In other words, after 1938, it was illegal to sell a prescription drug with labeling that a layperson could easily comprehend!

Neither the Durham–Humphrey Amendments of 1951, in which Congress codified compulsory prescription status, nor the regulations FDA issued pursuant to these Amendments contained such a provision. Nevertheless, the agency continued to maintain its position that prescription drug information should be directed only to physicians and other medical professionals. Indeed, many inside and outside the agency considered the act of giving a layperson the approved labeling of a prescription drug to be a violation of federal law.

For the first three decades following the passage of the FD&C Act, consumers were thus largely ignorant about the prescription drugs they took. Notably, the Act does not require the dispensing label attached to the container in which a prescription drug is delivered to the patient to include the name of the drug. *See* FD&C Act 503(b)(2). Through the late 1960s, many state pharmacy laws not only did not compel this information to appear on the prescription bottle, but actually forbade it. *See* JEREMY A. GREENE THE SAME BUT NOT THE SAME: A HISTORY OF GENERIC DRUGS (forthcoming 2014). Even as states embraced the now universal requirement that the dispensing label identify the drug, the minimal additional data on the bottle was not particularly enlightening. Section 503(b)(2) requires only the following information to appear on the dispensing label: the name and address of the dispenser, the serial number and date of the prescription, the name of the prescriber, the name of the patient, and the directions for use and any cautionary statements contained in the doctor's scrip. Until the 1970s, patients' knowledge about the prescription drugs they took was usually limited to this information and whatever else their physicians chose to tell them. There was no additional labeling directed to patients and no easy way for patients to acquire the physician labeling. Moreover, there were no mass market guides to prescription drugs and, of course, no internet.

b.   THE INTRODUCTION OF MANDATORY PATIENT LABELING:
     PATIENT PACKAGE INSERTS (PPIS)

The FDA did not mandate any patient-directed labeling for prescription drugs until 1968, when it required a two sentence warning statement to appear on the container of a self-administered inhalation drug product. Two years later, FDA began to embrace direct-to-patient labeling in earnest when it proposed to require a "patient package insert" (PPI) for oral contraceptives. This insert would set out, "in lay language," the risks and possible side effects associated with the use of the pill, primarily the risk of abnormal blood clotting. As indicated in the preamble to the final rule excerpted below, the agency's proposal faced significant opposition.

Statement of Policy Concerning Oral Contraceptive Labeling Directed to Users

35 Fed. Reg. 9001 (June 11, 1970).

On April 10, 1970, there was published in the FEDERAL REGISTER, 35 F.R. 5962, a notice of proposed rule-making to establish new labeling requirements for oral contraceptives which would assure that the user is provided information necessary for her safe use of these drugs. . . .

Organized medicine . . . generally opposed the statement of policy, on the grounds that (1) it would interfere with the physician-patient relationship by introducing a barrier, and by exerting an undue influence on the physician's prescribing decision and the patient's acceptance of the drugs; (2) that it would confuse and alarm the patient to the extent that persons who should take the drugs for health reasons would not do so; (3) that the package insert cannot provide all of the needed information and is not an appropriate means of informing patients; (4) that the physician is the proper person to provide the kind of information to his own patient on an individualized, need-to-know, basis; and (5) that the regulations should not control what information the prescriber gives to the patient by a labeling statement that certain points had been discussed with the patient when the drug was prescribed. . . .

A number of individual physicians also commented that providing information of this type was an unnecessary government intrusion into medical practice. . . . It was contended that the doctor's judgment as to what the patient should be told should prevail.

A number of physicians took the opposite view, that information about the hazards of the use of oral contraceptive drugs would serve the cause of patient protection, would enable the patient to make a conscientious choice of this method of contraception, and would not be unduly alarming. . . .

Consumer spokesmen also were divided. Most supported much more extensive patient information to assure informed consent to the use of the drugs, but a few spoke of the need to encourage the use of oral contraceptives in family planning among persons for whom unwanted pregnancy would pose a special hazard. . . .

The Pharmaceutical Manufacturers Association . . . opposed the concept of requiring patient information in the labeling of prescription drugs on the ground that this is the responsibility of the physician who must deal with it on an individualized basis. . . .

The Commissioner . . . conclu[des] . . . [i]t will be no undue intrusion into the physician-patient relationship to require a brief warning notice in the dispensing package. . . .

Therefore . . . the following new section is added. . .

§ 130.45 Oral contraceptive preparations; labeling directed to the patient.

(a) The Food and Drug Administration is charged with assuring both physicians and patients that drugs are safe and effective for their intended uses. . . . [T]he Administration has reviewed the oral contraceptive products, taking into account the following factors: The products contain potent steroid hormones which affect many organ systems; they are used for long periods of time by large numbers of women who, for the most part, are healthy and take them as a matter of choice for prophylaxis against pregnancy, in full knowledge of other means of contraception; and there is no present assurance that persons for whom the drugs are prescribed or dispensed are uniformly being provided the necessary information for safe and effective use of the drugs.

(b) In view of the foregoing, it is deemed in the public interest to present to users of the oral contraceptives a brief notice of the nature of the drugs, the fact that continued medical supervision is needed for safe and effective use, that the drugs may cause side effects and are contraindicated in some cases, that the most important complication is abnormal blood clotting which can have a fatal outcome, that the physician recognizes an obligation to discuss the potential hazards of using the drugs with the patient, that he has available for the patient written material discussing the effectiveness and the hazards of the drugs, and that users of the oral contraceptives should notify their physicians if they notice any unusual physical disturbance or discomfort.

(c) The Commissioner agrees that the physician is the proper person for providing use information to his patients, and these regulations will provide him a balanced discussion of the effectiveness and the risks attendant upon the use of oral contraceptives for his use in discussing the drugs with his patients.

(d)(1) . . . [T]he Commissioner conclude[s] that it is necessary in the best interests of users that the following printed information for patients be included in or with the package dispensed to the patient: . . .

Do Not Take This Drug Without Your Doctor's Continued Supervision

The oral contraceptives are powerful and effective drugs which can cause side effects in some users and should not be used at all by some women. The most serious known side effect is abnormal blood clotting which can be fatal.

Safe use of this drug requires a careful discussion with your doctor. To assist him in providing you with the necessary information, (firm name) has prepared a booklet (or other form) written in a style understandable to you as the drug user. This provides information on the effectiveness and known hazards of the drug including warnings, side effects and who should not use it. Your doctor will give you this booklet (or other form) if you ask for it and he can answer any questions you may have about the use of this drug.

Notify your doctor if you notice any unusual disturbance or discomfort.

. . . .

NOTES

1.   *Content of Patient Labeling.* This patient package insert (PPI) for oral contraceptives represented a dramatic contraction of the agency's proposed 600-word version, which itself fell far short of the scope and detail of the labeling then directed at physicians. The current, more comprehensive requirements for patient labeling of oral contraceptives are codified at 21 C.F.R. 310.501.

2.   *Oral Contraceptive Labeling.* In *Turner v. Edwards,* 1969–1974 FDLI Jud. Rec. 471, 493 (D.D.C. 1970 & 1971), the plaintiffs sought an injunction against FDA's original oral contraceptive PPI regulation on the ground that the short warning was inadequate. The plaintiffs asked the court to require that a longer pamphlet be placed in all oral contraceptive packages. The court granted FDA's motion for summary judgment. In *Kushner v. Mathews,* 1975–1977 FDLI Jud. Rec. 537 (S.D.N.Y. 1977), the court declined to order the agency to complete a pending rulemaking to revise the patient labeling for oral contraceptives, despite a claim that the agency had failed to meet commitments for prompter action made before Congress.

———————

Neither the Pharmaceutical Manufacturers Association (PMA) nor any individual company challenged mandatory patient labeling for oral contraceptives in court. However, PMA and various other trade and professional associations filed suit when FDA, later in the decade, promulgated a regulation requiring patient labeling for prescription drug products containing estrogens. 42 Fed. Reg. 37636 (July 22, 1977), codified at 21 C.F.R. 310.515. The agency took this action on the basis of reports of an increased risk of endometrial cancer associated with the long-term use of estrogens in postmenopausal women. *See* 41 Fed. Reg. 43108 (Sept. 29, 1976).

Pharmaceutical Manufacturers Association v. FDA

484 F. Supp. 1179 (D. Del. 1980), *aff'd per curiam* 634 F.2d 106 (3d Cir. 1980).

■ STAPLETON, DISTRICT JUDGE:. . . .

The regulation . . . outlined several categories of information which must be included in a patient package insert, and required that such an insert be provided to a patient every time the drug was dispensed or administered (i.e. injected). . . . The agency's action came as a result of several studies published in 1975 which indicated an association between the use of conjugated estrogens and an increased risk of endometrial cancer in women. . . .

Plaintiffs and plaintiff-intervenors raise a number of challenges to the regulation. First, they contend that the FDA lacks statutory authority to require patient packaging inserts for prescription drugs. They next assert that such a requirement is an unconstitutional interference with the practice of medicine. Finally, they challenge the adequacy of the FDA's findings and conclusions embodied in the preamble to the regulation and argue that, based on the administrative record, the regulation is "arbitrary, capricious, an abuse of discretion, or otherwise not in accordance with law." Because I find that the FDA does have statutory authority to require patient labeling, that such a requirement does not interfere with any constitutionally protected rights of physicians, that the agency's reasoning is sufficiently articulated and that the record adequately supports its judgment, I will grant the defendants' motion for summary judgment and deny that of the plaintiffs. . . .

. . . [Sections 502(a), 502(f), and 201(n) of the FD&C Act], combined with section 701(a), provide direct support for the challenged regulation. Among other things, they reflect a clear Congressional objective that the users of drugs, whether prescription or non-prescription, shall receive facts "material . . . with respect to consequences which may result from the use of the . . . [drug] under the conditions of use prescribed in the labeling thereof or under such conditions of use as are customary or usual." [FD&C Act 201(n).] The Commissioner, in furtherance of this objective, has seen fit in the challenged regulation to require that information concerning consequences which may result from the use of estrogen drugs be provided to the users thereof on their labeling. I think it clear that section 701(a) authorizes him to do so. . . .

. . . [T]he plaintiffs argue that . . . Section 502(a) . . . and Section 201(n) require affirmative disclosures in the form of warnings or qualifying information only when affirmative claims of curative effect are made on the labeling which, in the absence of additional information, would be misleading. . . .

While it is true that one of the important applications of section 201(n) relates to the problem of misleading affirmative claims, nothing in the [1938 House] Report suggests that the section is limited in its application to such claims. Indeed, the text of section 201(n) itself demonstrates that its scope is not so limited. Plaintiffs focus on that portion of the section which defines as misleading any failure to "reveal facts material in light of . . . [the] representations" made on the labeling. But section 201(n) goes on to require the disclosure of "facts . . . material with respect to consequences which may result from the use" of the drug. This language would be rendered meaningless if this Court were to adopt the construction favored by the plaintiffs.

Finally, plaintiffs argue that any authority which the FDA may have had under the 1938 Act with respect to patient labeling of prescription drugs was withdrawn by Congress in 1951. One of the amendments adopted in that year exempted prescription drugs from the "warnings against misuse" requirement and the "adequate directions for use" requirement of Section 502(f) in those situations where the label contains certain specified information. . . . According to plaintiffs, the adoption of this exemption as Section 503(b)(2) of the Act was intended by Congress to deprive the Secretary of authority to require that patient labeling for prescription drugs contain information regarding possible undesirable effects of the prescribed use. I do not agree. . . .

It is . . . true that the 1951 exemption of prescription drugs from the requirements of section 502(f) was enacted with the idea that prescribing physicians would be the primary source of adequate directions for use and adequate warning against misuse or overuse. It does not necessarily follow, however, that Congress meant to strip the Commissioner of the regulatory authority he had possessed for thirteen years over prescription drug labeling. Plaintiffs' argument glosses over the fact that while prescription drugs were exempted from the requirements of section 502(f) in 1951, they were not exempted from the requirement of section 502(a) that their labels not be misleading. . . .

. . . Plaintiffs argue that the mandatory nature of the regulation interferes with the doctor-patient relationship, and thus with the practice of medicine, by requiring the physician to communicate information emanating from Washington without regard to his or her professional judgment concerning the accuracy of the advice or the desirability of the patient being exposed to it.

To the extent that the plaintiffs' claim of unconstitutional interference with the right to practice medicine is founded on a notion of federalism which reserves all rights over such regulation to the states, it is without merit. . . .

. . . The fact that the practice of medicine is an area traditionally regulated by the states does not invalidate those provisions of the [FD&C Act] which may at times impinge on some aspect of a doctor's practice.

Turning to plaintiff's view of a physician's right to exercise professional judgment, it is important to focus on what the challenged regulation does not do. The regulation at issue here does not forbid a physician from prescribing conjugated estrogen drugs, or limit the physician's exercise of professional judgment in that regard. Nor does it limit the information the physician may impart to his or her patients concerning estrogens. If the physician disagrees with a perceived "slant" of the labeling provided by the manufacturer, or with the facts stated therein, he or she is free to discuss the matter fully with the patient, noting his own disagreement and views. The sample labeling encourages the patient to have this kind of open discussion with her doctor.

When these limitations on the effect of the challenged regulation are considered, it becomes apparent that the plaintiffs urge recognition not of a right to exercise judgment in prescribing treatment, but rather of a right to control patient access to information. . . . There simply is no constitutional basis for recognition of a right on the part of physicians to control patient access to information concerning the possible side effects of prescription drugs. The cases cited by plaintiffs do contain language referring to a doctor's right to practice medicine, but the rights there recognized were only those necessary to facilitate the exercise of a right which patients were found to possess. The physician rights discussed are thus derivative of patient rights and do not exist independent of those rights. . . .

The patient rights recognized in the line of cases relied upon by plaintiffs flow from a constitutionally protected right of privacy. As the Supreme Court noted in *Whalen v. Roe* [429 U.S. 589 (1977)], this right encompasses the individual's "interest in independence in making certain kinds of important decisions". . . . To the extent these cases have any bearing on the present issue, then, their rationale would appear to support the challenged regulation. . . . The asserted right to limit patient access to such information can hardly be said to facilitate the patient's "interest in independence" in decision making.[15] . . .

. . . I do not overlook the affidavits of numerous experienced physicians who foresee patient anxiety and ruptured physician-patient relationships as a result of the implementation of the regulation. These matters are clearly relevant to an evaluation of the wisdom of the regulation. They do not, however, render it constitutionally infirm. . . .

NOTE

1. *Estrogen PPI.* The rule requiring a PPI for estrogens, 21 C.F.R. 310.515, has since been revised. 55 Fed. Reg. 18722, 18761 (May 4, 1990). Oral contraceptives and estrogens are the only drugs for which Part 310 regulations currently require PPIs. As described below, FDA has in recent years generally mandated patient labeling (now known as "medication guides") through product-by-product orders in connection with NDA approvals and/or as part of REMS, rather than through notice-and-comment rulemaking.

2. *Women's Rights and Patient Labeling.* It is no coincidence that the first two mandatory PPIs were for women's drugs; the women's rights and patients' rights movements of the 1970s overlapped significantly. Feminists expressed general dissatisfaction with the treatment of women by a paternalistic, male-dominated, technocratic medical system, and they sought greater agency for women patients in all health decisions. Indeed, even before FDA proposed to require patient labeling for estrogenic drug products, three major women's organizations joined consumer groups in petitioning the agency to mandate patient labeling for several broad classes

---

[15] The "important decisions" referred to in *Whalen* were decisions involving marriage, procreation, contraception, family relationships, and child rearing and education. . . .

of drugs, including drugs that posed a danger to pregnant or lactating women, widely used hazardous drugs such as hypnotics and tranquilizers, and drugs such as amphetamines that were overprescribed and had serious side effects. 40 Fed. Reg. 52075 (Nov. 7, 1975).

c.   THE RISE OF VOLUNTARY PATIENT LABELING

In the 1979 notice excerpted below, FDA proposed to require PPIs for all prescription drugs except in a few specified situations. As the subsequent materials illustrate, however, FDA soon thereafter abandoned this approach in favor of encouraging private labeling efforts.

Prescription Drug Products: Patient Labeling Requirements

44 Fed. Reg. 40016 (July 6, 1979).

The Food and Drug Administration (FDA) is proposing regulations that would require manufacturers to distribute labeling to patients for most prescription drug products for human use, including biological products licensed under the Public Health Service Act of 1944 [42 U.S.C. 262]. The regulations would require dispensers of prescription drug products to provide the labeling to patients when the products are dispensed. This action is being taken because FDA believes that prescription drug labeling that is directed to patients will promote the safe and effective use of prescription drug products and that patients have a right to know about the benefits, risks, and directions for use of the products. . . .

The proposed regulations set forth general patient labeling requirements that would apply to most prescription drug products. The regulations would require the manufacturer of the product to prepare and distribute patient labeling that physically accompanies the product. The labeling would be written in nontechnical language, would not be promotional in tone or content, and would be based primarily on the physician labeling for the drug product. The patient labeling would contain both a summary of information about the product and more detailed information that identifies the product and the person responsible for the labeling, the proper uses of the product, circumstances under which it should not be used, serious adverse reactions, precautions the patient should take when using the product, information about side effects, and other general information about the proper uses of prescription drug products. The agency would be permitted to exempt the labeling for a particular drug product from any of the specific requirements. The regulations would also establish minimum printing specifications for patient labeling.

Patient labeling for a prescription drug product would be required to be based primarily on the physician labeling required for the product under § 201.100(d). . . . As a legal matter, statements in patient labeling cannot conflict with statements in physician labeling without misbranding the drug product. At the same time, the proposed requirements recognize that there may be substantial differences between the physician and patient labeling for a particular product. For example, the patient labeling may not discuss each of the subjects discussed in the product's physician labeling; and may not contain as thorough a discussion of a subject as the physician labeling. On the other hand, some information that does not appear in physician labeling may be required to appear in patient labeling, such as the consequences of the patient's failure to follow the prescribed regimen. . . .

The patient labeling would also be required to contain a statement that the physician labeling for the drug product (. . . that is, the drug product's "package insert") is available from the patient's pharmacist or physician. Many persons, including some pharmacists and physicians, erroneously believe that State or Federal law prohibits providing a drug product's official package insert to patients. No such prohibition exists. . . . Although the package insert for a drug product may be too technical for most patients to easily understand, patients should not be denied access to this information. . . .

———

The next year, FDA published final regulations establishing requirements for the preparation and distribution of patient package inserts (PPIs) for 10 high priority classes of human prescription drugs as a three-year pilot program. 45 Fed. Reg. 60754 (Sept. 12, 1980), and it also asked for comments on 10 draft guideline PPIs, *id.* at 60785. In late 1980 and early 1981, FDA issued a series of final rules mandating PPIs for specified drugs and drug classes and announced the availability of final guideline PPIs for these products. *See, e.g.,* 46 Fed. Reg. 28, 160 (Jan. 2, 1981).

About that time, however, a RAND Corporation study sponsored by the agency concluded that patients could be provided with information about prescription drugs more effectively and efficiently by the private sector than by a mandatory PPI program. Shortly after President Reagan took office in January 1981, FDA temporarily stayed the effective dates of the PPI requirements for the drugs for which final guidelines had been published, pending "additional review of these requirements" under President Reagan's Executive Order No. 12291. 46 Fed. Reg. 23739, 23815 (Apr. 28, 1981). In early 1982, FDA proposed to revoke the PPI regulation, 47 Fed. Reg. 7200 (Feb. 17, 1982), and following an opportunity for public comment, it issued the following final decision.

Prescription Drug Products: Revocation of Patient Package Insert Requirements

47 Fed. Reg. 39147 (September 7, 1982).

. . . .

In the proposal to revoke the final rule, the agency explained that the Commissioner of Food and Drugs had carefully reviewed the entire administrative record of the patient package insert program, the results of a 3-year study conducted under contract for the agency by the RAND Corp. on the effects of prototype PPI's, and information presented at public meetings FDA held . . . to solicit views on PPI's.

Based on this review, the proposal noted, the agency believed it could no longer justify the PPI pilot program. First, the agency had been persuaded that the program would not likely have achieved a principal objective, that of enabling FDA to determine whether a mandatory, pharmacy-oriented, drug leaflet program was the most practical way of increasing patient knowledge about prescription drugs. Secondly, the agency pointed out that, since the promulgation of the pilot program, the private sector had provided new initiatives in patient information and was currently developing others. The various private sector initiatives, if effectively implemented, were considered likely to provide consumers with the same type of information about prescription drugs as would have been provided by the agency's pilot program. Moreover, as these initiatives would not be limited to 10 drugs or drug classes, or to pharmacy-distributed leaflets, it was believed possible that they would be capable of providing more information than the agency's pilot program. Also, the agency stressed that cooperation with the private sector would encourage experimentation with diverse systems for delivering patient information, thereby promoting innovation in delivery systems. . . .

The agency received 602 comments on the proposal. . . . On the basis of the information in the proposal, a review of the comments, and other information received by the agency through its Committee on Patient Education (COPE), the agency believes that encouraging diverse private sector efforts for providing consumers with adequate prescription drug information is now preferable to implementing a single, mandated Federal program. . . .

The agency has repeatedly affirmed that patients have both a right and a need to know about the drugs they use. Further, the agency acknowledges that consumers have not traditionally had available to them adequate information about prescription drug use. The agency believes, however, that private sector efforts to provide consumers with drug educational materials have increased and, therefore, that the mandatory Federal program is not now needed and may have a restrictive effect on private sector efforts. . . .

The agency agrees with the comments that written information, which the patient can retain and refer to later, is very useful to most patients. It stresses, however, that most current and planned private sector programs will provide this type of written information, to be available either at the pharmacy in the form of pamphlets, tear-off sheets, etc., or directly from the prescribing physician. . . .

Revocation of the program will have a reasonable effect. Patients will have access to a variety of programs of drug education and information. Pharmacists will not bear an undue share of the managerial and cost burdens associated with patient information services. At least one alternative program under development—the AMA's—will provide patient information at the time a drug is prescribed. This means of patient education, which is recognized as superior to providing patient labeling at the time of dispensing, would likely not be used if PPI's were Federally mandated.

Revocation of the PPI program is consistent with the law. The argument that absence of PPI's misbrands prescription drugs is based on a misunderstanding of the manner in which FDA utilizes its broad statutory authority in support of specific regulations. A regulation, such as the PPI program, is issued under FDA's authority to promulgate regulations for the efficient enforcement of the Federal Food, Drug, and Cosmetic Act. Such a regulation must also be justified by other, more specific, authority in the act, in this case the prohibition against misbranding. After a regulation is promulgated, failure to adhere to the regulation causes a violation of the specific statutory authority on which the regulation is based. In the absence of the regulation, however, violation of that specific authority does not necessarily occur by conduct that the regulation would have covered. To suggest that it does is tantamount to saying that all regulations issued under section 701(a) of the act are merely interpretive, for substantive regulations would be redundant of the legal requirements inherent in other provisions of the act. This view is plainly wrong. FDA has issued numerous substantive regulations under section 701(a) of the act. Most of these regulations created new legal requirements of general applicability and did not simply explain existing requirements. . . .

NOTES

1.   *Revocation of Guidelines.* At the same time, FDA revoked the five final guideline PPIs and withdrew the five draft guideline PPIs that it had previously published. 47 Fed. Reg. 39249 (Sept. 7, 1982).

2.   *Voluntary PPIs.* Since 1982, pharmaceutical manufacturers have voluntarily distributed PPIs for a number of drugs that present unique safety questions. Patient labeling is now commonly provided by entities other than the manufacturers of the drugs, such as pharmacies, private vendors, and healthcare associations. In 71 Fed. Reg. 40724 (July 18, 2006), FDA announced the availability of a guidance titled USEFUL WRITTEN CONSUMER MEDICATION INFORMATION, which is intended to assist these entities in developing third-party patient labeling, which neither FDA nor the drug manufacturer approves or reviews.

3.   *Success of Voluntary Patient Labeling Programs.* In 1995, FDA embraced, as a measure of the success of voluntary labeling efforts, the following goals: by the year 2000, 75 percent of consumers should be receiving "useful written patient information" about their medication when they first pick up their new prescriptions, and by 2006, this number should increase to 95 percent. 60 Fed. Reg. 44182, 44199 (Aug. 24, 1995). According to FDA surveys, the percentage of consumers actually receiving written information about their prescriptions at the pharmacy reached 74 percent in 2000 and 77 percent in 2004. A smaller percentage (21 percent in 2004) received written information at the physician's office. *See* National Surveys of Prescription Medicine, Information Received by Consumers (available on FDA website).

d.   MANDATORY PATIENT MEDICATION GUIDES

In 1995, FDA, expressing concern that "[i]nadequate access to appropriate patient information is a major cause of inappropriate use of prescription medications, resulting in serious personal injury," proposed to establish a new, limited program for mandatory patient package inserts, renamed "medication guides," or "MedGuides" for short. 60 Fed. Reg. 44182, 44199 (Aug. 24, 1995). The agency finalized this rule in 1998. 63 Fed. Reg. 66378 (Dec. 1, 1998), codified at 21 C.F.R. Part 208. The regulation, at 21 C.F.R. 208.3(h), defines a medication guide as "FDA-approved patient labeling"; in effect, it is a patient package insert by a different name. At 21 C.F.R. 208.20, the rule establishes general requirements for the content and format of a medication guide.

The MedGuide requirement in Part 208 is far from universal; it is intended to apply only to "certain products that pose a serious and significant public health concern requiring immediate distribution of FDA-approved patient information." 60 Fed. Reg. at 44184. Under the rule, the agency will mandate a MedGuide only in the following circumstances:

(1) The drug product is one for which patient labeling could help prevent serious adverse effects.

(2) The drug product is one that has serious risk(s) (relative to benefits) of which patients should be made aware because information concerning the risk(s) could affect patients' decision to use, or to continue to use the product.

(3) The drug product is important to health and patient adherence to directions for use is crucial to the drug's effectiveness.

21 C.F.R. 208.1(c). In the preamble to its final regulations, FDA estimated that it would mandate a medication guide for only five to ten drugs per year. For the next decade, the agency stayed at the lower end of this estimate.

The passage of the Food and Drug Administration Amendments Act of 2007 triggered a new wave of MedGuides. The FDAAA REMS provisions state that the risk evaluation and mitigation strategy for a drug may require the dissemination of either "a Medication Guide, as provided for under part 208" or "a patient package insert." FD&C Act 505–1(e)(2). In practice, MedGuides have become by far the most common element—and frequently the only element—of REMS. FDA observed in 2011: "Between March 25, 2008, when the REMS provisions of FDAAA took effect and January 1, 2011, FDA has approved over 150 Medication Guides for products approved under new drug applications (NDAs) and biologic license applications (BLAs) as part of a REMS. One hundred and eight of these REMS included only a Medication Guide. . . ." *See* GUIDANCE: MEDICATION GUIDES—DISTRIBUTION REQUIREMENTS AND INCLUSION IN RISK EVALUATION AND MITIGATION STRATEGIES (REMS) 4 (Nov. 2011).

FDA may still compel the use of a MedGuide under part 208 separately from the imposition of a REMS. *Id.* at 4. In fact, however, REMS have become the new standard vehicle for mandating patient labeling of a prescription drug.

NOTES

1.   *Other Sources of Drug Information for Patients.* In 1979, Bantam released the first edition of *The Pill Book*, subtitled *The Illustrated Guide to the Most Prescribed Drugs in the United States.* Ever since the introduction of this publication, which is still regularly updated, bookstore shelves (and

now Amazon search results) have been replete with various publications that provide information about prescription drugs to laypersons. The PHYSICIAN'S DESK REFERENCE, which contains the full physician's package insert and is republished yearly, is also sold in substantial numbers in bookstores throughout the country.

Today, of course, the significance of these books about prescription drugs pales in comparison to that of the internet. The internet revolution has made it easy for anyone to find detailed medical information, including information about prescription drugs. As early as 1998, there were more than 14,000 health-related websites. WebMD, an internet portal consolidating health information for consumers as well as physicians, launched in 1998, followed by major competitor sites such as Yahoo Health, Mayoclinic.com, and About.com Health. Advanced search engine technology has reduced the importance of websites such as WebMD, however. In a 2012 survey, 59 percent of American adults reported looking for health information on the internet in the previous year, and 35 percent said they had used the internet to diagnose a medical condition for themselves or someone else, but many more of these "online health seekers" started their research on internet search engines (77%) than on a site that specializes in health information (13%).

Another important modern source for consumer information about prescription drug products is the "brief summary" of the physician labeling that must accompany all direct-to-consumer print advertising of these products. *See infra* p. 916, note 2.

2.   *Child Resistant Packaging.* The Poison Prevention Packaging Act of 1970, 84 Stat. 1670, 15 U.S.C. 1471, was enacted to prevent poisoning of children through accidental ingestion of toxic household substances, including drugs. Experience, particularly with aspirin, had demonstrated that label warnings were inadequate to prevent such poisonings. Congress therefore authorized the requirement of special "child-restraint" packaging designed to prevent young children from inadvertently obtaining access to dangerous household substances. The Consumer Product Safety Commission (CPSC), which administers the Poison Prevention Packaging Act, has promulgated regulations requiring essentially all prescription drugs, as well as aspirin and a relatively small number of other nonprescription drugs, to comply with the Act. 21 C.F.R. 1700.14(a)(10), 1700.15. The CPSC interprets this provision to apply to all investigational drugs whose clinical trials involve household use. *See* letter from Geri Niebauer, CPSC Compliance Officer, to Daphne Allen (June 22, 2000).

3.   FDA REGULATION OF PRESCRIPTION DRUG LABELING AND "FAILURE TO WARN" TORT SUITS

a.   THE LEARNED INTERMEDIARY DOCTRINE AND EXCEPTIONS

The duty of a manufacturer of prescription drugs to warn about its risks is a duty owed the patient, the ultimate consumer, but fulfilled by communication with the prescribing physician, the so-called "learned intermediary." Nearly every state has embraced this doctrine as a governing principle. *See Larkin v. Pfizer, Inc.*, 153 S.W. 3d 758 (Ky.

2004). A drug manufacturer thus usually fulfills its legal obligation to warn by providing adequate warnings to the health-care provider. At the same time there has been a growing willingness to recognize exceptions—and hold that the consumer is entitled to be warned directly—in at least two, and perhaps three, circumstances.

First, where a drug is administered in a setting where individual physician diagnosis and attention to individual patients cannot be expected, the manufacturer has a duty to ensure that patients get warned directly. The leading case is *Reyes v. Wyeth Laboratories*, 498 F.2d 1264 (5th Cir. 1974), which imposed liability on Wyeth for failing to take steps to ensure that parents of youngsters who were vaccinated at a public health clinic were alerted to the slim but real possibility that the polio vaccine could actually cause the disease.

Second, the courts, as well as the American Law Institute, have also endorsed the proposition that users of birth control pills (and no doubt other drugs that serve health needs or personal goals, but do not treat or prevent disease) are entitled to be warned about their risks. Restatement (Third) of Torts § 6 Comment; *Odgers v. Ortho Pharm. Corp.*, 609 F. Supp. 867 (E.D. Mich. 1985). It is not entirely clear whether this "exception" to the learned intermediary doctrine rests on the distinctive characteristics of these products or on the fact that FDA for 30 years has required oral contraceptives to be accompanied by a detailed "patient insert." The leading case establishing this exception, *MacDonald v. Ortho*, 475 N.E.2d 65 (Mass. 1985), is reproduced below.

Finally, there is some support for the proposition that when a manufacturer of a prescription drug chooses to promote the product in advertisements directed at consumers, it should be obligated to provide adequate warnings to them in labeling. *See Perez v. Wyeth Laboratories, Inc.*, 734 A.2d 1245 (N.J. 1999).

Those who assert the need for adequate warnings directly to consumers contend that manufacturers that communicate directly with consumers should not escape liability simply because the decision to prescribe the drug was made by the health-care provider. Proponents of the learned intermediary rule argue that, notwithstanding direct communications to the consumer, drugs cannot be dispensed unless a health-care provider makes an individualized decision that a drug is appropriate for a particular patient, and that it is for the health-care provider to decide which risks are relevant to the particular patient. The Restatement leaves to developing case law whether exceptions to the learned intermediary rule in these or other situations should be recognized.

MacDonald v. Ortho Pharmaceutical Corporation

475 N.E.2d 65 (Mass. 1985).

■ ABRAMS, JUSTICE

This products liability action raises the question of the extent of a drug manufacturer's duty to warn consumers of dangers inherent in the use of oral contraceptives. The plaintiffs brought suit against the defendant, Ortho Pharmaceutical Corporation (Ortho), for injuries allegedly caused by Ortho's birth control pills, and obtained a jury verdict in their favor. The defendant moved for a judgment notwithstanding the verdict. The judge concluded that the defendant did not owe a duty to warn the plaintiffs, and entered judgment for Ortho. The plaintiffs appealed. We transferred the case to this court on our own motion and reinstate the jury verdict.

We summarize the facts. In September, 1973, the plaintiff Carole D. MacDonald (MacDonald), who was twenty-six years old at the time, obtained from her gynecologist a prescription for Ortho–Novum contraceptive pills, manufactured by Ortho. As required by the then effective regulations promulgated by the United States Food and Drug Administration (FDA), the pill dispenser she received was labeled with a warning that "oral contraceptives are powerful and effective drugs which can cause side effects in some users and should not be used at all by some women," and that "[t]he most serious known side effect is abnormal blood clotting which can be fatal."[3] The warning also referred MacDonald to a booklet which she obtained from her gynecologist, and which was distributed by Ortho pursuant to FDA requirements. The booklet contained detailed information about the contraceptive pill, including the increased risk to pill users that vital organs such as the brain may be damaged by abnormal blood clotting.[4] The word "stroke" did not appear on the dispenser warning or in the booklet.

MacDonald's prescription for Ortho–Novum pills was renewed at subsequent annual visits to her gynecologist. The prescription was filled annually. On July 24, 1976, after approximately three years of using the pills, MacDonald suffered an occlusion of a cerebral artery by a blood clot, an injury commonly referred to as a stroke. The injury caused the death of approximately twenty per cent of MacDonald's brain tissue, and left her permanently disabled. . . .

---

[3] FDA regulations in effect during the time period relevant to this litigation required that the following warning be included in or with the pill dispenser:

"Do Not Take This Drug Without Your Doctor's Continued Supervision.

   The oral contraceptives are powerful and effective drugs which can cause side effects in some users and should not be used at all by some women. The most serious known side effect is abnormal blood clotting which can be fatal. . . . "

[4] Applicable FDA regulations required that the booklet contain "information in lay language, concerning effectiveness, contraindications, warnings, precautions, and adverse reactions," including a warning "regarding the serious side effects with special attention to thromboembolic disorders and stating the estimated morbidity and mortality in users vs. nonusers." Ortho's booklet contained the following information:

"About blood clots

   Blood clots occasionally form in the blood vessels of the legs and the pelvis of apparently healthy people and may threaten life if the clots break loose and then lodge in the lung or if they form in other vital organs, such as the brain. It has been estimated that about one woman in 2,000 on the pill each year suffers a blood clotting disorder severe enough to require hospitalization. The estimated death rate from abnormal blood clotting in healthy women under 35 not taking the pill is 1 in 500,000; whereas for the same group taking the pill it is 1 in 66,000. For healthy women over 35 not taking the pill, the rate is 1 in 200,000 compared to 1 in 25,000 for pill users. Blood clots are about three times more likely to develop in women over the age of 34. For these reasons it is important that women who have had blood clots in the legs, lungs or brain not use oral contraceptives. Anyone using the pill who has severe leg or chest pains, coughs up blood, has difficulty breathing, sudden severe headache or vomiting, dizziness or fainting, disturbances of vision or speech, weakness or numbness of an arm or leg, should call her doctor immediately and stop taking the pill."

MacDonald testified that, during the time she used the pills, she was unaware that the risk of abnormal blood clotting encompassed the risk of stroke, and that she would not have used the pills had she been warned that stroke is an associated risk.[6] The case was submitted to a jury on the plaintiffs' theories that Ortho was negligent in failing to warn adequately of the dangers associated with the pills and that Ortho breached its warranty of merchantability. These two theories were treated, in effect, as a single claim of failure to warn. [T]he jury found . . . that Ortho was negligent and in breach of warranty because it failed to give MacDonald sufficient warning of such dangers.

After the jury verdict, the judge granted Ortho's motion for judgment notwithstanding the verdict, concluding that, because oral contraceptives are prescription drugs, a manufacturer's duty to warn the consumer is satisfied if the manufacturer gives adequate warnings to the prescribing physician, and that the manufacturer has no duty to warn the consumer directly.

The rule in jurisdictions that have addressed the question of the extent of a manufacturer's duty to warn in cases involving prescription drugs is that the prescribing physician acts as a "learned intermediary" between the manufacturer and the patient, and "the duty of the ethical drug manufacturer is to warn the doctor, rather than the patient, [although] the manufacturer is directly liable to the patient for a breach of such duty." Oral contraceptives, however, bear peculiar characteristics which warrant the imposition of a common law duty on the manufacturer to warn users directly of associated risks. Whereas a patient's involvement in decision making concerning use of a prescription drug necessary to treat a malady is typically minimal or nonexistent, the healthy, young consumer of oral contraceptives is usually actively involved in the decision to use "the pill," as opposed to other available birth control products, and the prescribing physician is relegated to a relatively passive role.

Furthermore, the physician prescribing "the pill," as a matter of course, examines the patient once before prescribing an oral contraceptive and only annually thereafter. Thus, the patient may only seldom have the opportunity to explore her questions and concerns about the medication with the prescribing physician. Even if the physician, on those occasions, were scrupulously to remind the patient of the risks attendant on continuation of the oral contraceptive, "the patient cannot be expected to remember all of the details for a protracted period of time."

Last, the birth control pill is specifically subject to extensive Federal regulation. The FDA has promulgated regulations designed to ensure that the choice of "the pill" as a contraceptive method is informed by comprehensible warnings of potential side effects. These regulations, and subsequent amendments, have their basis in the FDA commissioner's finding, after hearings, that "[b]ecause oral

---

[6] Subsequent to the events in this case, the FDA regulation was amended by 43 Fed. Reg. 4221 (1978), which replaced the regulation requirement of a specified warning on the pill dispenser, see note 3, *supra*, with a requirement that the dispenser contain a warning "of the serious side effects of oral contraceptives, such as thrombophlebitis, pulmonary embolism, myocardial infarction, retinal artery thrombosis, *stroke*, benign hepatic adenomas, induction of fetal abnormalities, and gallbladder disease" (emphasis added).

contraceptives are ordinarily taken electively by healthy women who have available to them alternative methods of treatment, and because of the relatively high incidence of serious illnesses associated with their use . . . users of these drugs should, without exception, be furnished with written information telling them of the drug's benefits and risks." The FDA also found that the facts necessary to informed decisions by women as to use of oral contraceptives are "too complex to expect the patient to remember everything told her by the physician," and that, in the absence of direct written warnings, many potential users of "the pill" do not receive the needed information "in an organized, comprehensive, understandable, and handy-for-future-reference form."

The oral contraceptive thus stands apart from other prescription drugs in light of the heightened participation of patients in decisions relating to use of "the pill"; the substantial risks affiliated with the product's use; the feasibility of direct warnings by the manufacturer to the user; the limited participation of the physician (annual prescriptions); and the possibility that oral communications between physicians and consumers may be insufficient or too scanty standing alone fully to apprise consumers of the product's dangers at the time the initial selection of a contraceptive method is made as well as at subsequent points when alternative methods may be considered. We conclude that the manufacturer of oral contraceptives is not justified in relying on warnings to the medical profession to satisfy its common law duty to warn, and that the manufacturer's obligation encompasses a duty to warn the ultimate user.

. . . Ortho contends initially that its warnings complied with FDA labeling requirements, and that those requirements preempt or define the bounds of the common law duty to warn. We disagree. The regulatory history of the FDA requirements belies any objective to cloak them with preemptive effect. In response to concerns raised by drug manufacturers that warnings required and drafted by the FDA might be deemed inadequate by juries, the FDA commissioner specifically noted that the boundaries of civil tort liability for failure to warn are controlled by applicable State law. Although the common law duty we today recognize is to a large degree coextensive with the regulatory duties imposed by the FDA, we are persuaded that, in instances where a trier of fact could reasonably conclude that a manufacturer's compliance with FDA labeling requirements or guidelines did not adequately apprise oral contraceptive users of inherent risks, the manufacturer should not be shielded from liability by such compliance. Thus, compliance with FDA requirements, though admissible to demonstrate lack of negligence, is not conclusive on this issue, just as violation of FDA requirements is evidence, but not conclusive evidence, of negligence. We therefore concur with the plaintiffs' argument that even if the conclusion that Ortho complied with FDA requirements were inescapable, an issue we need not decide, the jury nonetheless could have found that the lack of a reference to "stroke" breached Ortho's common law duty to warn.

The common law duty to warn, like the analogous FDA "lay language" requirement, necessitates a warning "comprehensible to the average user and . . . convey[ing] a fair indication of the nature and extent of the danger to the mind of a reasonably prudent person."

Whether a particular warning measures up to this standard is almost always an issue to be resolved by a jury; few questions are "more appropriately left to a common sense lay judgment than that of whether a written warning gets its message across to an average person." . . .

Ortho argues that reasonable minds could not differ as to whether MacDonald was adequately informed of the risk of the injury she sustained by Ortho's warning that the oral contraceptives could cause "abnormal blood clotting which can be fatal" and further warning of the incremental likelihood of hospitalization or death due to blood clotting in "vital organs, such as the brain." We disagree. . . . We cannot say that this jury's decision that the warning was inadequate is so unreasonable as to require the opposite conclusion as a matter of law. The jury may well have concluded, in light of their common experience and MacDonald's testimony, that the absence of a reference to "stroke" in the warning unduly minimized the warning's impact or failed to make the nature of the risk reasonably comprehensible to the average consumer. Similarly, the jury may have concluded that there are fates worse than death, such as the permanent disablement suffered by MacDonald, and that the mention of the risk of death did not, therefore, suffice to apprise an average consumer of the material risks of oral contraceptive use.

Ortho's argument that, as a matter of law, there was insufficient evidence that MacDonald's injury was proximately caused by a deficiency in the warnings is substantially similar to its argument on the issue of the adequacy of the warnings, and is likewise unavailing. . . .

NOTES

1. *Rejection of Learned Intermediary Defense.* The *MacDonald* court's rejection of Ortho's claim that it had no duty to warn consumers directly about the risk of stroke is consistent with the Restatement and with other judicial authority. The reasons the court offers for holding that Ortho had a duty to warn patients as well as physicians are similar to those on which FDA relied when it decided to require makers of oral contraceptives to provide "patient package inserts." Of course, as a result of FDA's decision, Ortho had no choice in the matter. Federal law required the very communication Mrs. MacDonald claimed that Massachusetts common law mandated. It is therefore not clear whether this obligation arises from federal or state law.

2. *Rejection of FDA's Mandated Labeling.* More problematic, perhaps, is the court's holding that the jury was entitled to conclude that Ortho's unquestioned compliance with FDA's mandatory form and wording was not sufficient to satisfy its common law duty to warn. The court's reasoning does not quite do justice to the company's defense. FDA had considered the very risk that Mrs. MacDonald experienced. The risk of stroke had long been apparent. Furthermore, the agency wrestled with the question of how best to warn patients about this risk. It prescribed the words Ortho used after considering other possibilities. Consumers may have understood other words, including the word "stroke," more readily,

but the court offers no reason to believe that a jury would be better equipped than FDA to select the best verbal formula.

b.   FEDERAL PREEMPTION OF PRIVATE TORT SUITS

Wyeth v. Levine
555 U.S. 555 (2008).

■ JUSTICE STEVENS delivered the opinion of the Court.

Directly injecting the drug Phenergan into a patient's vein creates a significant risk of catastrophic consequences. A Vermont jury found that petitioner Wyeth, the manufacturer of the drug, had failed to provide an adequate warning of that risk and awarded damages to respondent Diana Levine to compensate her for the amputation of her arm. The warnings on Phenergan's label had been deemed sufficient by the federal Food and Drug Administration (FDA) when it approved Wyeth's new drug application in 1955 and when it later approved changes in the drug's labeling. The question we must decide is whether the FDA's approvals provide Wyeth with a complete defense to Levine's tort claims. We conclude that they do not.

I

Phenergan is Wyeth's brand name for promethazine hydrochloride, an antihistamine used to treat nausea. The injectable form of Phenergan can be administered intramuscularly or intravenously, and it can be administered intravenously through either the "IV-push" method, whereby the drug is injected directly into a patient's vein, or the "IV-drip" method, whereby the drug is introduced into a saline solution in a hanging intravenous bag and slowly descends through a catheter inserted in a patient's vein. The drug is corrosive and causes irreversible gangrene if it enters a patient's artery.

Levine's injury resulted from an IV-push injection of Phenergan. On April 7, 2000, as on previous visits to her local clinic for treatment of a migraine headache, she received an intramuscular injection of Demerol for her headache and Phenergan for her nausea. Because the combination did not provide relief, she returned later that day and received a second injection of both drugs. This time, the physician assistant administered the drugs by the IV-push method, and Phenergan entered Levine's artery, either because the needle penetrated an artery directly or because the drug escaped from the vein into surrounding tissue (a phenomenon called "perivascular extravasation") where it came in contact with arterial blood. As a result, Levine developed gangrene, and doctors amputated first her right hand and then her entire forearm. In addition to her pain and suffering, Levine incurred substantial medical expenses and the loss of her livelihood as a professional musician.

After settling claims against the health center and clinician, Levine brought an action for damages against Wyeth, relying on common-law negligence and strict-liability theories. Although Phenergan's labeling warned of the danger of gangrene and amputation following inadvertent intra-arterial injection,[3] Levine alleged that the labeling was defective because it failed to instruct clinicians to use the IV-drip method of intravenous administration instead of the higher risk IV-push method. More broadly, she alleged that Phenergan is not reasonably safe for intravenous administration because the foreseeable risks of gangrene and loss of limb are great in relation to the drug's therapeutic benefits.

Wyeth filed a motion for summary judgment, arguing that Levine's failure-to-warn claims were pre-empted by federal law. The court found no merit in either Wyeth's field pre-emption argument, which it has since abandoned, or its conflict pre-emption argument. . . .

[T]he jury found that Wyeth was negligent, that Phenergan was a defective product as a result of inadequate warnings and instructions, and that no intervening cause had broken the causal connection between the product defects and the plaintiff's injury. It awarded total damages of $7,400,000, which the court reduced to account for Levine's earlier settlement with the health center and clinician. . . .

II

Wyeth makes two separate pre-emption arguments: first, that it would have been impossible for it to comply with the state-law duty to modify Phenergan's labeling without violating federal law, and second, that recognition of Levine's state tort action creates an unacceptable "obstacle to the accomplishment and execution of the full purposes and objectives of Congress," because it substitutes a lay jury's decision about drug labeling for the expert judgment of the FDA. As a preface to our evaluation of these arguments, we identify two factual propositions decided during the trial court proceedings, emphasize two legal principles that guide our analysis, and review the history of the controlling federal statute.

The trial court proceedings established that Levine's injury would not have occurred if Phenergan's label had included an adequate warning about the risks of the IV-push method of administering the drug. . . . That the inadequate label was both a but-for and proximate cause of Levine's injury is supported by the record and no longer challenged by Wyeth.

---

[3] The warning for "Inadvertent Intra-arterial Injection" stated: "Due to the close proximity of arteries and veins in the areas most commonly used for intravenous injection, extreme care should be exercised to avoid perivascular extravasation or inadvertent intra-arterial injection. Reports compatible with inadvertent intra-arterial injection of Phenergan Injection, usually in conjunction with other drugs intended for intravenous use, suggest that pain, severe chemical irritation, severe spasm of distal vessels, and resultant gangrene requiring amputation are likely under such circumstances. Intravenous injection was intended in all the cases reported but perivascular extravasation or arterial placement of the needle is now suspect. There is no proven successful management of this condition after it occurs. . . . Aspiration of dark blood does not preclude intra-arterial needle placement, because blood is discolored upon contact with Phenergan Injection. Use of syringes with rigid plungers or of small bore needles might obscure typical arterial backflow if this is relied upon alone. When used intravenously, Phenergan Injection should be given in a concentration no greater than 25 mg per mL and at a rate not to exceed 25 mg per minute. When administering any irritant drug intravenously, it is usually preferable to inject it through the tubing of an intravenous infusion set that is known to be functioning satisfactorily. In the event that a patient complains of pain during intended intravenous injection of Phenergan Injection, the injection should be stopped immediately to provide for evaluation of possible arterial placement or perivascular extravasation."

.... [T]he dissent incorrectly assumes that the state-law duty at issue is the duty to contraindicate the IV-push method. But, as the Vermont Supreme Court explained, the jury verdict established only that Phenergan's warning was insufficient. It did not mandate a particular replacement warning, nor did it require contraindicating IV-push administration. . . . We therefore need not decide whether a state rule proscribing intravenous administration would be pre-empted. The narrower question presented is whether federal law pre-empts Levine's claim that Phenergan's label did not contain an adequate warning about using the IV-push method of administration.

Our answer to that question must be guided by two cornerstones of our pre-emption jurisprudence. First, "the purpose of Congress is the ultimate touchstone in every pre-emption case." *Medtronic, Inc. v. Lohr,* 518 U.S. 470 (1996). Second, "[i]n all pre-emption cases, and particularly in those in which Congress has 'legislated . . . in a field which the States have traditionally occupied,' . . . we 'start with the assumption that the historic police powers of the States were not to be superseded by the Federal Act unless that was the clear and manifest purpose of Congress.' " *Lohr,* 518 U.S., at 485.

In order to identify the "purpose of Congress," it is appropriate to briefly review the history of federal regulation of drugs and drug labeling. . . .

As it enlarged the FDA's powers to "protect the public health" and "assure the safety, effectiveness, and reliability of drugs," Congress took care to preserve state law. The 1962 amendments added a saving clause, indicating that a provision of state law would only be invalidated upon a "direct and positive conflict" with the FDCA. § 202, 76 Stat. 781, 793.* Consistent with that provision, state common-law suits "continued unabated despite . . . FDA regulation." And when Congress enacted an express pre-emption provision for medical devices in 1976, it declined to enact such a provision for prescription drugs.

In 2007, after Levine's injury and lawsuit, Congress again amended the FDCA. For the first time, it granted the FDA statutory authority to require a manufacturer to change its drug label based on safety information that becomes available after a drug's initial approval. In doing so, however, Congress did not enact a provision in the Senate bill that would have required the FDA to preapprove all changes to drug labels. Instead, it adopted a rule of construction to make it clear that manufacturers remain responsible for updating their labels.

III

Wyeth first argues that Levine's state-law claims are pre-empted because it is impossible for it to comply with both the state-law duties underlying those claims and its federal labeling duties. The FDA's premarket approval of a new drug application includes the approval of the exact text in the proposed label. Generally speaking, a manufacturer may only change a drug label after the FDA approves a supplemental application. There is, however, an FDA regulation that permits a manufacturer to make certain changes to its label before

---

* [Although the saving clause appeared in the 1962 statute, that law did not add the clause to the FD&C Act itself. EDS.]

receiving the agency's approval. Among other things, this "changes being effected" (CBE) regulation provides that if a manufacturer is changing a label to "add or strengthen a contraindication, warning, precaution, or adverse reaction" or to "add or strengthen an instruction about dosage and administration that is intended to increase the safe use of the drug product," it may make the labeling change upon filing its supplemental application with the FDA; it need not wait for FDA approval. 21 C.F.R. §§ 314.70(c)(6)(iii)(A), (C).

Wyeth argues that the CBE regulation is not implicated in this case because a 2008 amendment provides that a manufacturer may only change its label "to reflect newly acquired information." Resting on this language (which Wyeth argues simply reaffirmed the interpretation of the regulation in effect when this case was tried), Wyeth contends that it could have changed Phenergan's label only in response to new information that the FDA had not considered. And it maintains that Levine has not pointed to any such information concerning the risks of IV-push administration. Thus, Wyeth insists, it was impossible for it to discharge its state-law obligation to provide a stronger warning about IV-push administration without violating federal law. Wyeth's argument misapprehends both the federal drug regulatory scheme and its burden in establishing a pre-emption defense.

We need not decide whether the 2008 CBE regulation is consistent with the FDCA and the previous version of the regulation, as Wyeth and the United States urge, because Wyeth could have revised Phenergan's label even in accordance with the amended regulation. As the FDA explained in its notice of the final rule, "'newly acquired information'" is not limited to new data, but also encompasses "new analyses of previously submitted data." 73 Fed. Reg. 49603, 49604 (Aug. 22, 2008). The rule accounts for the fact that risk information accumulates over time and that the same data may take on a different meaning in light of subsequent developments: "[I]f the sponsor submits adverse event information to FDA, and then later conducts a new analysis of data showing risks of a different type or of greater severity or frequency than did reports previously submitted to FDA, the sponsor meets the requirement for 'newly acquired information.'" *Id.* at 49607.

. . . Levine . . . present[ed] evidence of at least 20 incidents prior to her injury in which a Phenergan injection resulted in gangrene and an amputation. After the first such incident came to Wyeth's attention in 1967, it notified the FDA and worked with the agency to change Phenergan's label. In later years, as amputations continued to occur, Wyeth could have analyzed the accumulating data and added a stronger warning about IV-push administration of the drug.

Wyeth argues that if it had unilaterally added such a warning, it would have violated federal law governing unauthorized distribution and misbranding. Its argument that a change in Phenergan's labeling would have subjected it to liability for unauthorized distribution rests on the assumption that this labeling change would have rendered Phenergan a new drug lacking an effective application. But strengthening the warning about IV-push administration would not have made Phenergan a new drug. *See* 21 U.S.C. § 321(p)(1) (defining "new drug"). Nor would this warning have rendered Phenergan misbranded. The FDCA does not provide that a drug is misbranded simply because the manufacturer has altered an FDA-approved label; instead, the misbranding provision focuses on the substance of the label and, among other things, proscribes labels that fail to include "adequate warnings." 21 U.S.C. § 352(f). . . . And the very idea that the FDA would bring an enforcement action against a manufacturer for strengthening a warning pursuant to the CBE regulation is difficult to accept—neither Wyeth nor the United States has identified a case in which the FDA has done so.

Wyeth's cramped reading of the CBE regulation and its broad reading of the FDCA's misbranding and unauthorized distribution provisions are premised on a more fundamental misunderstanding. Wyeth suggests that the FDA, rather than the manufacturer, bears primary responsibility for drug labeling. Yet through many amendments to the FDCA and to FDA regulations, it has remained a central premise of federal drug regulation that the manufacturer bears responsibility for the content of its label at all times. It is charged both with crafting an adequate label and with ensuring that its warnings remain adequate as long as the drug is on the market. *See, e.g.*, 21 CFR § 201.80(e) (requiring a manufacturer to revise its label "to include a warning as soon as there is reasonable evidence of an association of a serious hazard with a drug").

. . . Thus, when the risk of gangrene from IV-push injection of Phenergan became apparent, Wyeth had a duty to provide a warning that adequately described that risk, and the CBE regulation permitted it to provide such a warning before receiving the FDA's approval.

Of course, the FDA retains authority to reject labeling changes made pursuant to the CBE regulation in its review of the manufacturer's supplemental application, just as it retains such authority in reviewing all supplemental applications. But absent clear evidence that the FDA would not have approved a change to Phenergan's label, we will not conclude that it was impossible for Wyeth to comply with both federal and state requirements.

Wyeth has offered no such evidence. It does not argue that it attempted to give the kind of warning required by the Vermont jury but was prohibited from doing so by the FDA. And while it does suggest that the FDA intended to prohibit it from strengthening the warning about IV-push administration because the agency deemed such a warning inappropriate in reviewing Phenergan's drug applications . . . the trial court found "no evidence in this record that either the FDA or the manufacturer gave more than passing attention to the issue of" IV-push versus IV-drip administration. The Vermont Supreme Court likewise concluded that the FDA had not made an affirmative decision to preserve the IV-push method or intended to prohibit Wyeth from strengthening its warning about IV-push administration. . . . We accordingly cannot credit Wyeth's contention that the FDA would have prevented it from adding a stronger warning about the IV-push method of intravenous administration.

Impossibility pre-emption is a demanding defense. On the record before us, Wyeth has failed to demonstrate that it was impossible for it to comply with both federal and state requirements. The CBE regulation permitted Wyeth to unilaterally strengthen its warning, and the mere fact that the FDA approved Phenergan's label does not establish that it would have prohibited such a change.

IV

Wyeth also argues that requiring it to comply with a state-law duty to provide a stronger warning about IV-push administration would obstruct the purposes and objectives of federal drug labeling regulation. Levine's tort claims, it maintains, are pre-empted because they interfere with "Congress's purpose to entrust an expert agency to make drug labeling decisions that strike a balance between competing objectives." We find no merit in this argument, which relies on an untenable interpretation of congressional intent and an overbroad view of an agency's power to pre-empt state law.

Wyeth contends that the FDCA establishes both a floor and a ceiling for drug regulation: Once the FDA has approved a drug's label, a state-law verdict may not deem the label inadequate, regardless of whether there is any evidence that the FDA has considered the stronger warning at issue. The most glaring problem with this argument is that all evidence of Congress' purposes is to the contrary. Building on its 1906 Act, Congress enacted the FDCA to bolster consumer protection against harmful products. Congress did not provide a federal remedy for consumers harmed by unsafe or ineffective drugs in the 1938 statute or in any subsequent amendment. Evidently, it determined that widely available state rights of action provided appropriate relief for injured consumers.[7] It may also have recognized that state-law remedies further consumer protection by motivating manufacturers to produce safe and effective drugs and to give adequate warnings.

If Congress thought state-law suits posed an obstacle to its objectives, it surely would have enacted an express pre-emption provision at some point during the FDCA's 70-year history. But despite its 1976 enactment of an express pre-emption provision for medical devices, see § 521, 90 Stat. 574 (codified at 21 U.S.C. § 360k(a)), Congress has not enacted such a provision for prescription drugs. Its silence on the issue, coupled with its certain awareness of the prevalence of state tort litigation, is powerful evidence that Congress did not intend FDA oversight to be the exclusive means of ensuring drug safety and effectiveness. . . .

Despite this evidence that Congress did not regard state tort litigation as an obstacle to achieving its purposes, Wyeth nonetheless maintains that, because the FDCA requires the FDA to determine that a drug is safe and effective under the conditions set forth in its labeling, the agency must be presumed to have performed a precise balancing of risks and benefits and to have established a specific labeling standard that leaves no room for different state-law judgments. In advancing this argument, Wyeth relies not on any statement by Congress, but instead on the preamble to a 2006 FDA regulation governing the content and format of prescription drug labels. In that preamble, the FDA declared that the FDCA establishes "both a 'floor' and a 'ceiling,' " so that "FDA

---

[7]   Although the first version of the bill that became the FDCA would have provided a federal cause of action for damages for injured consumers, witnesses testified that such a right of action was unnecessary because common-law claims were already available under state law.

approval of labeling . . . preempts conflicting or contrary State law." It further stated that certain state-law actions, such as those involving failure-to-warn claims, "threaten FDA's statutorily prescribed role as the expert Federal agency responsible for evaluating and regulating drugs." 71 Fed. Reg. 3922, 3935 (Jan. 24, 2006). . . .

In prior cases, we have given "some weight" to an agency's views about the impact of tort law on federal objectives when "the subject matter is technica[l] and the relevant history and background are complex and extensive." *Geier v. American Honda Motor Co.,* 529 U.S., 861 (2000). Even in such cases, however, we have not deferred to an agency's *conclusion* that state law is pre-empted. Rather, we have attended to an agency's explanation of how state law affects the regulatory scheme. While agencies have no special authority to pronounce on pre-emption absent delegation by Congress, they do have a unique understanding of the statutes they administer and an attendant ability to make informed determinations about how state requirements may pose an "obstacle to the accomplishment and execution of the full purposes and objectives of Congress."

Under this standard, the FDA's 2006 preamble does not merit deference. When the FDA issued its notice of proposed rulemaking in December 2000, it explained that the rule would "not contain policies that have federalism implications or that preempt State law." In 2006, the agency finalized the rule and, without offering States or other interested parties notice or opportunity for comment, articulated a sweeping position on the FDCA's pre-emptive effect in the regulatory preamble. The agency's views on state law are inherently suspect in light of this procedural failure.

Further, the preamble is at odds with what evidence we have of Congress' purposes, and it reverses the FDA's own longstanding position without providing a reasoned explanation, including any discussion of how state law has interfered with the FDA's regulation of drug labeling during decades of coexistence. . . . Not once prior to Levine's injury did the FDA suggest that state tort law stood as an obstacle to its statutory mission. To the contrary, it cast federal labeling standards as a floor upon which States could build and repeatedly disclaimed any attempt to pre-empt failure-to-warn claims. . . .

In keeping with Congress' decision not to pre-empt common-law tort suits, it appears that the FDA traditionally regarded state law as a complementary form of drug regulation. The FDA has limited resources to monitor the 11,000 drugs on the market, and manufacturers have superior access to information about their drugs, especially in the postmarketing phase as new risks emerge. State tort suits uncover unknown drug hazards and provide incentives for drug manufacturers to disclose safety risks promptly. They also serve a distinct compensatory function that may motivate injured persons to come forward with information. Failure-to-warn actions, in particular, lend force to the FDCA's premise that manufacturers, not the FDA, bear primary responsibility for their drug labeling at all times. Thus, the FDA long maintained that state law offers an additional, and important, layer of consumer protection that complements FDA regulation. The agency's 2006 preamble represents a dramatic change in position. . . .

... [T]he FDA's newfound opinion, expressed in its 2006 preamble, that state law "frustrate[s] the agency's implementation of its statutory mandate," does not merit deference for the reasons we have explained. . . .

In short, Wyeth has not persuaded us that failure-to-warn claims like Levine's obstruct the federal regulation of drug labeling. Congress has repeatedly declined to pre-empt state law, and the FDA's recently adopted position that state tort suits interfere with its statutory mandate is entitled to no weight. . . .

V

We conclude that it is not impossible for Wyeth to comply with its state and federal law obligations and that Levine's common-law claims do not stand as an obstacle to the accomplishment of Congress' purposes in the FDCA. Accordingly, the judgment of the Vermont Supreme Court is affirmed.

It is so ordered.

■ JUSTICE ALITO, With whom THE CHIEF JUSTICE and JUSTICE SCALIA join, dissenting.

PLIVA, Inc. v. Mensing
131 S. Ct. 2567 (2011).

■ JUSTICE THOMAS delivered the opinion of the Court . . .

These consolidated lawsuits involve state tort-law claims based on certain drug manufacturers' alleged failure to provide adequate warning labels for generic metoclopramide. The question presented is whether federal drug regulations applicable to generic drug manufacturers directly conflict with, and thus pre-empt, these state-law claims. We hold that they do.

I

Metoclopramide is a drug designed to speed the movement of food through the digestive system. . . . The drug is commonly used to treat digestive tract problems such as diabetic gastroparesis and gastroesophageal reflux disorder.

Evidence has accumulated that long-term metoclopramide use can cause tardive dyskinesia, a severe neurological disorder. . . .

Accordingly, warning labels for the drug have been strengthened and clarified several times. . . . [I]n 2009, the FDA ordered a black box warning—its strongest—which states: "Treatment with metoclopramide can cause tardive dyskinesia, a serious movement disorder that is often irreversible. . . . Treatment with metoclopramide for longer than 12 weeks should be avoided in all but rare cases."

Gladys Mensing and Julie Demahy, the plaintiffs in these consolidated cases, were prescribed Reglan [brand name metoclopramide] in 2001 and 2002, respectively. Both received generic metoclopramide from their pharmacists. After taking the drug as prescribed for several years, both women developed tardive dyskinesia.

In separate suits, Mensing and Demahy sued the generic drug manufacturers that produced the metoclopramide they took. Each alleged . . . that long-term metoclopramide use caused her tardive dyskinesia and that the Manufacturers were liable under state tort law (specifically, that of Minnesota and Louisiana) for failing to provide adequate warning labels. . . .

In both suits, the Manufacturers urged that federal law pre-empted the state tort claims. . . .

The Courts of Appeals for the Fifth and Eighth Circuits rejected the Manufacturers' arguments and held that Mensing and Demahy's claims were not pre-empted. We . . . now reverse each.

II

. . . The parties do not dispute that, if [the plaintiffs' factual] allegations are true, state law required the Manufacturers to use a different, safer label.

. . . Under the 1962 Drug Amendments to the Federal Food, Drug, and Cosmetic Act, a manufacturer seeking federal approval to market a new drug must prove that it is safe and effective and that the proposed label is accurate and adequate.[4] *See, e.g.*, 21 U.S.C. §§ 355(b)(1), (d). . . .

Originally, the same rules applied to all drugs. In 1984, however, Congress passed the Drug Price Competition and Patent Term Restoration Act, 98 Stat. 1585, commonly called the Hatch–Waxman Amendments. Under this law, "generic drugs" can gain FDA approval simply by showing equivalence to a reference listed drug that has already been approved by the FDA. 21 U.S.C. § 355(j)(2)(A). This allows manufacturers to develop generic drugs inexpensively, without duplicating the clinical trials already performed on the equivalent brand-name drug. A generic drug application must also "show that the [safety and efficacy] labeling proposed . . . is the same as the labeling approved for the [brand-name] drug." § 355(j)(2)(A)(v); *see also* § 355(j)(4)(G).

As a result, brand-name and generic drug manufacturers have different federal drug labeling duties. A brand-name manufacturer seeking new drug approval is responsible for the accuracy and adequacy of its label. *See, e.g.,* 21 U.S.C. §§ 355(b)(1), (d). A manufacturer seeking generic drug approval, on the other hand, is responsible for ensuring that its warning label is the same as the brand name's. *See* 21 CFR §§ 314.94(a)(8), 314.127(a)(7).

. . . What is in dispute is whether, and to what extent, generic manufacturers may change their labels *after* initial FDA approval. Mensing and Demahy contend that federal law provided several avenues through which the Manufacturers could have altered their metoclopramide labels in time to prevent the injuries here. The FDA, however, tells us that it interprets its regulations to require that the warning labels of a brand-name drug and its generic copy must always be the same—thus, generic drug manufacturers have an ongoing federal duty of "sameness." . . . The FDA's views are "controlling unless plainly

---

[4] All relevant events in these cases predate the Food and Drug Administration Amendments Act of 2007, 121 Stat. 823. We therefore refer exclusively to the pre-2007 statutes and regulations and express no view on the impact of the 2007 Act.

erroneous or inconsistent with the regulation[s]" or there is any other reason to doubt that they reflect the FDA's fair and considered judgment. *Auer* v. *Robbins*, 519 U.S. 452, 461, 462.

First, Mensing and Demahy urge that the FDA's "changes-being-effected" (CBE) process [21 CFR § 314.70(c)(6)(iii)(A)] allowed the Manufacturers to change their labels when necessary. . . . When making labeling changes using the CBE process, drug manufacturers need not wait for preapproval by the FDA, which ordinarily is necessary to change a label. *Wyeth v. Levine*, 555 U.S. at 568. . . .

The FDA denies that the Manufacturers could have used the CBE process to unilaterally strengthen their warning labels. The agency interprets the CBE regulation to allow changes to generic drug labels only when a generic drug manufacturer changes its label to match an updated brand-name label or to follow the FDA's instructions. The FDA argues that CBE changes unilaterally made to strengthen a generic drug's warning label would violate the statutes and regulations requiring a generic drug's label to match its brand-name counterpart's. *See* 21 U.S.C. § 355(j)(4)(G); 21 CFR §§ 314.94(a)(8)(iii), 314.150(b)(10) (approval may be withdrawn if the generic drug's label "is no longer consistent with that for [the brand-name]").

We defer to the FDA's interpretation of its CBE and generic labeling regulations. . . . [W]e do not find the agency's interpretation "plainly erroneous or inconsistent with the regulation." *Auer, supra*, at 461. . . .

Next, Mensing and Demahy contend that the Manufacturers could have used "Dear Doctor" letters to send additional warnings to prescribing physicians and other healthcare professionals. Again, the FDA disagrees, and we defer to the agency's views.

The FDA argues that Dear Doctor letters qualify as "labeling." *See* 21 U.S.C. § 321(m); 21 CFR § 202.1(*l*)(2). Thus, any such letters must be "consistent with and not contrary to [the drug's] approved . . . labeling." 21 CFR § 201.100(d)(1). . . . Moreover, if generic drug manufacturers, but not the brand-name manufacturer, sent such letters, that would inaccurately imply a therapeutic difference between the brand and generic drugs and thus could be impermissibly "misleading."

As with the CBE regulation, we defer to the FDA. . . .

Though the FDA denies that the Manufacturers could have used the CBE process or Dear Doctor letters to strengthen their warning labels, the agency asserts that a different avenue existed for changing generic drug labels. According to the FDA, the Manufacturers could have proposed—indeed, were required to propose—stronger warning labels to the agency if they believed such warnings were needed. If the FDA had agreed that a label change was necessary, it would have worked with the brand-name manufacturer to create a new label for both the brand-name and generic drug.

The agency traces this duty to 21 U.S.C. § 352(f)(2), which provides that a drug is "misbranded . . . [u]nless its labeling bears . . . adequate warnings against . . . unsafe dosage or methods or duration of administration or application, in such manner and form, as are necessary for the protection of users." By regulation, the FDA has interpreted that statute to require that "labeling shall be revised to include a warning as soon as there is reasonable evidence of an association of a serious hazard with a drug." 21 CFR § 201.57(e).

According to the FDA, these requirements apply to generic drugs. As it explains, a " 'central premise of federal drug regulation is that the manufacturer bears responsibility for the content of its label at all times.' " U.S. Brief 12–13 (quoting *Wyeth* 555 U.S., at 570–571). The FDA reconciles this duty to have adequate and accurate labeling with the duty of sameness in the following way: Generic drug manufacturers that become aware of safety problems must ask the agency to work toward strengthening the label that applies to both the generic and brand-name equivalent drug.

The Manufacturers and the FDA disagree over whether this alleged duty to request a strengthened label actually existed. . . . Because we ultimately find pre-emption even assuming such a duty existed, we do not resolve the matter.

. . . .

III

. . . We have held that state and federal law conflict where it is "impossible for a private party to comply with both state and federal requirements."[5]

We find impossibility here. It was not lawful under federal law for the Manufacturers to do what state law required of them. And even if they had fulfilled their federal duty to ask for FDA assistance, they would not have satisfied the requirements of state law.

If the Manufacturers had independently changed their labels to satisfy their state-law duty, they would have violated federal law. . . . [I]t was impossible for the Manufacturers to comply with both their state-law duty to change the label and their federal law duty to keep the label the same.

The federal duty to ask the FDA for help in strengthening the corresponding brand-name label, assuming such a duty exists, does not change this analysis. Although requesting FDA assistance would have satisfied the Manufacturers' federal duty, it would not have satisfied their state tort-law duty to provide adequate labeling. State law demanded a safer label; it did not instruct the Manufacturers to communicate with the FDA about the possibility of a safer label. Indeed, Mensing and Demahy deny that their state tort claims are based on the Manufacturers' alleged failure to ask the FDA for assistance in changing the labels.

Mensing and Demahy contend that, while their state-law claims do not turn on whether the Manufacturers asked the FDA for assistance in changing their labels, the Manufacturers' federal affirmative defense of pre-emption does. Mensing and Demahy argue that if the Manufacturers had asked the FDA for help in changing the

---

[5] The Hatch–Waxman Amendments contain no provision expressly pre-empting state tort claims. Nor do they contain any saving clause to expressly preserve state tort claims. Although an express statement on pre-emption is always preferable, the lack of such a statement does not end our inquiry. Contrary to the dissent's suggestion, the absence of express pre-emption is not a reason to find no conflict pre-emption.

corresponding brand-name label, they might eventually have been able to accomplish under federal law what state law requires. That is true enough. The Manufacturers "freely concede" that they could have asked the FDA for help. If they had done so, and if the FDA decided there was sufficient supporting information, and if the FDA undertook negotiations with the brand-name manufacturer, and if adequate label changes were decided on and implemented, then the Manufacturers would have started a Mouse Trap game that eventually led to a better label on generic metoclopramide.

This raises the novel question whether conflict pre-emption should take into account these possible actions by the FDA and the brand-name manufacturer. . . .

Mensing and Demahy assert that . . . the Manufacturers cannot bear their burden of proving impossibility because they did not even *try* to start the process that might ultimately have allowed them to use a safer label. This is a fair argument, but we reject it.

The question for "impossibility" is whether the private party could independently do under federal law what state law requires of it. *See Wyeth*, 555 U.S., at 573 (finding no pre-emption where the defendant could "unilaterally" do what state law required). Accepting Mensing and Demahy's argument would render conflict pre-emption largely meaningless because it would make most conflicts between state and federal law illusory. We can often imagine that a third party or the Federal Government *might* do something that makes it lawful for a private party to accomplish under federal law what state law requires of it. In these cases, it is certainly possible that, had the Manufacturers asked the FDA for help, they might have eventually been able to strengthen their warning label. Of course, it is also *possible* that the Manufacturers could have convinced the FDA to reinterpret its regulations in a manner that would have opened the CBE process to them. Following Mensing and Demahy's argument to its logical conclusion, it is also *possible* that, by asking, the Manufacturers could have persuaded the FDA to rewrite its generic drug regulations entirely or talked Congress into amending the Hatch–Waxman Amendments.

If these conjectures suffice to prevent federal and state law from conflicting for Supremacy Clause purposes, it is unclear when, outside of express pre-emption, the Supremacy Clause would have any force. We do not read the Supremacy Clause to permit an approach to pre-emption that renders conflict pre-emption all but meaningless. . . .

. . . To decide these cases, it is enough to hold that when a party cannot satisfy its state duties without the Federal Government's special permission and assistance, which is dependent on the exercise of judgment by a federal agency, that party cannot independently satisfy those state duties for pre-emption purposes. . . .

. . . Mensing and Demahy's tort claims are pre-empted.

Wyeth is not to the contrary. . . . The Court held that the lawsuit was not pre-empted because . . . the CBE regulation, 21 CFR § 314.70(c)(6)(iii), permitted a brand-name drug manufacturer like Wyeth "to unilaterally strengthen its warning" without prior FDA approval. . . .

We recognize that from the perspective of Mensing and Demahy, finding pre-emption here but not in *Wyeth* makes little sense. Had Mensing and Demahy taken Reglan, the brand-name drug prescribed by their doctors, *Wyeth* would control and their lawsuits would not be pre-empted. But because pharmacists, acting in full accord with state law, substituted generic metoclopramide instead, federal law pre-empts these lawsuits. We acknowledge the unfortunate hand that federal drug regulation has dealt Mensing, Demahy, and others similarly situated.

But . . . [i]t is beyond dispute that the federal statutes and regulations that apply to brand-name drug manufacturers are meaningfully different than those that apply to generic drug manufacturers. . . . [D]ifferent federal statutes and regulations may, as here, lead to different pre-emption results. We will not distort the Supremacy Clause in order to create similar pre-emption across a dissimilar statutory scheme. As always, Congress and the FDA retain the authority to change the law and regulations if they so desire.

The judgments of the Fifth and Eighth Circuits are reversed, and the cases are remanded for further proceedings consistent with this opinion.

■ JUSTICE SOTOMAYOR, with whom JUSTICE GINSBURG, JUSTICE BREYER, and JUSTICE KAGAN join, dissenting.

NOTES

1. *Preemption of Design Defect Claims.* In *Mutual Pharmaceutical Co., Inc. v. Bartlett*, 133 S. Ct. 2466 (2013), the Supreme Court held that many, if not all, design-defect claims against generic drug manufacturers are also preempted by the FD&C Act under the theory of impossibility preemption. It reasoned:

> New Hampshire requires manufacturers to ensure that the products they design, manufacture, and sell are not "unreasonably dangerous." The New Hampshire Supreme Court has recognized that this duty can be satisfied either by changing a drug's design or by changing its labeling. . . .

> In the present case . . . redesign was not possible for two reasons. First, the FDCA requires a generic drug to have the same active ingredients, route of administration, dosage form, strength, and labeling as the brand-name drug on which it is based. 21 U. S. C. §§ 355(j)(2)(A)(ii)–(v) and (8)(B); 21 CFR § 320.1(c). . . . Indeed, were Mutual to change the composition of its sulindac, the altered chemical would be a new drug that would require its own NDA to be marketed in interstate commerce. . . . Second, because of sulindac's simple composition, the drug is chemically incapable of being redesigned.

> Given the impossibility of redesigning sulindac, the only way for Mutual to ameliorate the drug's "risk-utility" profile—and thus to escape liability—was to strengthen "the presence and efficacy of [sulindac's] warning" in such a way that the warning "avoid[ed] an unreasonable risk of harm from hidden dangers or from foreseeable uses." . . .

As PLIVA made clear, federal law prevents generic drug manufacturers from changing their labels. . . . Thus, federal law prohibited Mutual from taking the remedial action required to avoid liability under New Hampshire law. . . .

2. *Regulatory Fix?* In July 2013, immediately on the heels of *Bartlett*, a rulemaking agenda on the website of the Office of Management and Budget showed that FDA planned, by September 2013, to propose a rule that would allow generic manufacturers, like pioneer manufacturers, to add or strengthen a warning or contraindication to reflect new safety information. Presumably, this change would subject generic drugs to the reasoning of *Wyeth v. Levine* and end the federal preemption of product liability suits against them.

H. ADVERTISING AND PROMOTION OF PRESCRIPTION DRUGS

1. INTRODUCTION

FDA, rather than FTC, has primary authority over the advertising of prescription drugs. It exercises this power through the Division of Drug Marketing, Advertising, and Communications (DDMAC).

FDA acquired jurisdiction over prescription drug advertising when the Drug Amendments of 1962 added 502(n) to the FD&C Act. Until recently, however, the Act required that regulations to implement this grant of authority be promulgated in accordance with the formal rulemaking procedures of section 701(e). Consequently, FDA has issued general regulations for prescription drug advertising on only two occasions, and then only after it agreed to revisions that persuaded the Pharmaceutical Manufacturers Association (now the Pharmaceutical Research and Manufacturers of America) to withdraw its demand for a formal hearing. The 2007 Amendments (FDAAA) removed the formal hearing requirement, but FDA has not yet issued any significant additional advertising regulations.

As discussed below, the rules that FDA has promulgated generally require that drug advertisements be accurate, fair, and balanced and contain sufficient warnings regarding side effects and contraindications. In addition, the regulations forbid advertisers from implicitly or explicitly expanding the uses of the drug beyond the approved indications in the labeling. The question of off-label promotion in advertising, labeling, and other modes of communication will be explored in more detail in the following section of this chapter. *Infra* p. 925.

FDA has a regulatory mechanism for monitoring a company's use of promotional labeling and advertising for a new drug. Under 21 C.F.R. 314.81(b)(3)(i), at the time of initial dissemination of promotional labeling or initial publication of an advertisement, manufacturers must submit a specimen of the material to FDA with a transmittal form, Form FDA 2253. As discussed further below, *infra* p. 919, note 1, FDA can also now require particular drugs to submit any television advertisements to the agency for review prior to airing them.

2. PRINT ADVERTISING TO PROFESSIONALS

Until the mid-1980s, with very few exceptions, advertising of prescription drugs was directed exclusively to medical professionals and appeared primarily in professional journals. This mode of advertising remains very important to drug companies today, although, as discussed later in this chapter, it is now supplemented by substantial direct-to-consumer (DTC) advertising.

FDA's original prescription drug advertising regulations, promulgated in 1964, were thus drafted with professional advertising in mind. 28 Fed. Reg. 10993 (Oct. 15, 1963), 29 Fed. Reg. 257 (Jan. 10, 1964). Later in the decade, as a result of FDA Commissioner James L. Goddard's strong personal concerns about pharmaceutical advertising, FDA revised those regulations to prohibit specific practices to which the agency had strong objections. 34 Fed. Reg. 7802 (May 16, 1969). *See* James L. Goddard, *The Administrator's View,* 22 FOOD DRUG COSM. L.J. 449, 452 (1967). The revised regulations are excerpted below; the unabridged version of this rule contains no less than 33 specific features that always or sometimes render an advertisement "false, lacking in fair balance, or otherwise misleading."

21 C.F.R. § 202.1 Prescription-Drug Advertisements

. . . .

(e) True statement of information in brief summary relating to side effects, contraindications, and effectiveness:

(1) *When required.* All advertisements for any prescription drug . . . except advertisements described in paragraph (e)(2) of this section, shall present a true statement of information in brief summary relating to side effects, contraindications (when used in this section "side effects, contraindications" include side effects, warnings, precautions, and contraindications and include any such information under such headings as cautions, special considerations, important notes, etc.) and effectiveness.

(2) *Exempt advertisements.* The following advertisements are exempt from the requirements of paragraph (e)(1) of this section under the conditions specified:

(i) *Reminder advertisements.* Reminder advertisements are those which call attention to the name of the drug product but do not include indications or dosage recommendations for use of the drug product. . . .

(3) *Scope of information to be included; applicability to the entire advertisement.*

(i) The requirement of a true statement of information relating to side effects, contraindications, and effectiveness applies to the entire advertisement. Untrue or misleading information in any part of the advertisement will not be corrected by the inclusion in another distinct part of the advertisement of a brief statement containing true information relating to side effects, contraindications, and effectiveness of the drug. . . .

(iii) The information relating to side effects and contraindications shall disclose each specific side effect and contraindication . . . contained in required, approved, or permitted labeling for the advertised drug dosage form(s). . . .

(4) *Substance of information to be included in brief summary.* (i)(a) An advertisement for a prescription drug covered by a new-drug application approved pursuant to section 505 of the act after October 10, 1962 . . . shall not recommend or suggest any use that is not in the labeling accepted in such approved new-drug application or supplement. . . .

(5) *"True statement" of information.* An advertisement does not satisfy the requirement that it present a "true statement" of information in brief summary relating to side effects, contraindications, and effectiveness if:

(i) It is false or misleading with respect to side effects, contraindications, or effectiveness; or

(ii) It fails to present a fair balance between information relating to side effects and contraindications and information relating to effectiveness of the drug in that the information relating to effectiveness is presented in greater scope, depth, or detail than is required by section 502(n) of the act and this information is not fairly balanced by a presentation of a summary of true information relating to side effects and contraindications of the drug. . . .

(6) *Advertisements that are false, lacking in fair balance, or otherwise misleading.* An advertisement for a prescription drug is false, lacking in fair balance, or otherwise misleading, or otherwise violative of section 502(n) of the act if it:

(i) Contains a representation or suggestion, not approved or permitted for use in the labeling, that a drug is better, more effective, useful in a broader range of conditions or patients . . ., safer, has fewer, or less incidence of, or less serious side effects or contraindications than has been demonstrated by substantial evidence or substantial clinical experience . . . whether or not such representations are made by comparison with other drugs or treatments, and whether or not such a representation or suggestion is made directly or through use of published or unpublished literature, quotations, or other references.

(ii) Contains a drug comparison that represents or suggests that a drug is safer or more effective than another drug in some particular when it has not been demonstrated to be safer or more effective in such particular by substantial evidence or substantial clinical experience.

(iii) Contains favorable information or opinions about a drug previously regarded as valid but which have been rendered invalid by contrary and more credible recent information, or contains literature references or quotations that are significantly more favorable to the drug than has been demonstrated by substantial evidence or substantial clinical experience.

. . . .

(xviii) Uses headline, subheadline, or pictorial or other graphic matter in a way that is misleading.

. . . .

(7) *Advertisements that may be false, lacking in fair balance, or otherwise misleading.* An advertisement may be false, lacking in fair balance, or otherwise misleading or otherwise violative of section 502(n) of the act if it:

(i) Contains favorable information or conclusions from a study that is inadequate in design, scope, or conduct to furnish significant support for such information or conclusions.

. . . .

(vii) Fails to provide sufficient emphasis for the information relating to side effects and contraindications, when such information is contained in a distinct part of an advertisement, because of repetition or other emphasis in that part of the advertisement of claims for effectiveness or safety of the drug.

(viii) Fails to present information relating to side effects and contraindications with a prominence and readability reasonable comparable with the presentation of information relating to effectiveness of the drug, taking into account all implementing factors such as typography, layout, contrast, headlines, paragraphing, white space, and any other techniques apt to achieve emphasis.

. . . .

NOTES

1. *Brief Summary.* The requirement in 21 C.F.R. 202.1(e)(1) that each prescription drug advertisement contain a brief summary relating to side effects, contraindications, and effectiveness in effect mandates the familiar second page of every print advertisement for a prescription drug, summarizing the physician labeling information.

2. *Fair Balance.* The requirement in 21 C.F.R. 202.1(e)(5)(ii) that the text of the advertisement present a "fair balance" between information relating to side effects and contraindications and information relating to effectiveness is the one that is probably cited most often in warning letters sent by FDA to prescription drug advertisers.

3. *Comparative Claims.* Pharmaceutical companies seldom test their own drugs against competitive products in direct head-to-head comparative clinical trials, as would generally be required to make a comparative claim consistent with 21 C.F.R. 202.1(e)(6)(ii). To obtain this type of information, Congress included section 1013 in the Medicare Prescription Drug, Improvement, and Modernization Act of 2003, 117 Stat. 2066, 2438, 42 U.S.C. 2996–7, to require the HHS Agency for Healthcare Research and Quality (AHRQ) to conduct and support research on the comparative clinical effectiveness of prescription drugs.

4. *Reminder Advertisements.* Section 202.1(e)(2)(i) of the regulations recognizes a category of "reminder advertisements," which "call attention to the name of the drug product but do not include indications or dosage recommendations. . . ." Such advertisements need not include a summary of information about side effects and contraindications unless the agency has specifically required that a drug's labeling and promotional literature

contain a boxed warning relating to a serious hazard associated with its use.

5. *Corrective Advertisements.* On occasion, FDA has effectively compelled drug manufacturers to run corrective advertisements in medical journals. For example, in January 2003, FDA issued a warning letter to Purdue Pharma regarding two professional medical journal advertisements for OxyContin® that minimized its risks, overstated its efficacy, and omitted important information about the limitations on the drug's indicated use. In response to FDA's request that it provide a plan of corrective action, Purdue issued a corrective advertisement. This remedial advertisement, which ran for 3 months and appeared in approximately 30 journals, called attention to the warning letter and the cited violations and directed the reader to the prominently featured boxed warning and indication information for OxyContin. *See* GAO, OXYCONTIN ABUSE AND DIVERSION AND EFFORTS TO ADDRESS THE PROBLEM 26 (2003).

6. *Tort Liability Based on Overpromotion.* In *Love v. Wolf,* 38 Cal. Rptr. 183 (Cal. Ct. App. 1964), the court held that the manufacturer of Chloromycetin®, then the only marketed version of the potent antibiotic chloramphenicol, could be held liable for the plaintiff's bone marrow depression if the jury were persuaded that the company's heavy promotion of the drug effectively submerged its own warnings about the hazard. Following a retrial, Parke Davis was found liable for Mrs. Love's injuries and appealed without success.

7. *Constitutionality of Prescription Drug Advertising Regulations.* Section 505(d) of the FD&C Act provides that FDA must withhold approval of an NDA unless the sponsor provides "substantial evidence that the drug will have the effect it purports or is represented to have under the conditions of use, prescribed, or recommended or suggested in the proposed labeling." Section 505(d)(5) defines "substantial evidence" to mean "evidence consisting of adequate and well-controlled investigations." Under the FDA regulations set forth above, drug product claims supported by some lesser quantum of evidence categorically violate the law, whether or not they are in fact misleading, whether or not the statements are qualified with appropriate disclaimers, and whether or not the nature of the supporting evidence and the existence of countervailing evidence are made clear. Under the landmark decision in *Pearson v. Shalala,* 164 F.3d 650 (D.C. Cir. 1999) (excerpted *supra* p. 430), there is a reasonable argument that qualified prescription drug claims should be permitted on the same basis that qualified food disease claims are permitted.

3.   OTHER FORMS OF PROMOTION TO PROFESSIONALS

The pharmaceutical industry is highly competitive. It is a unique market, which relies on a limited group of "learned intermediaries"— healthcare professionals who are authorized under state law to prescribe prescription drugs. Pharmaceutical companies thus employ diverse tactics, in addition to print advertising in medical journals, to convince physicians to prescribe their products.

a. FDA'S LEGAL AUTHORITY

To the extent that promotional practices involve the distribution of materials that can be characterized as "labeling," FDA has direct power over their content. FDA defines drug labeling extremely broadly.

> Brochures, booklets, mailing pieces, detailing pieces, file cards, bulletins, calendars, price lists, catalogs, house organs, letters, motion picture films, film strips, lantern slides, sound recordings, exhibits, literature, and reprints and similar pieces of printed, audio, or visual matter descriptive of a drug and references published (for example, the "Physicians Desk Reference") for use by medical practitioners, pharmacists, or nurses, containing drug information supplied by the manufacturer, packer, or distributor of the drug and which are disseminated by or on behalf of its manufacturer . . . are hereby determined to be labeling as defined in section 201(m) of the act.

21 C.F.R. 202.1(*l*)(2).

Under 21 C.F.R. 201.100(d), a prescription drug will be deemed misbranded under FD&C Act 502(f)(1) unless:

> Any labeling . . . that furnishes or purports to furnish information for use or which prescribes, recommends, or suggests a dosage for the use of the drug . . . contains:

> (1) Adequate information for such use, including indications, effects, dosages, routes, methods, and frequency and duration of administration and any relevant warnings, hazards, contraindications, side effects, and precautions, under which practitioners licensed by law to administer the drug can use the drug safely and for the purposes for which it is intended, including all conditions for which it is advertised or represented; and if the article is subject to section 505 of the act, the parts of the labeling providing such information are the same in language and emphasis as labeling approved or permitted, under the provisions of section 505, and any other parts of the labeling are consistent with and not contrary to such approved or permitted labeling; and

> . . . .

> (3) The information required, and in the format specified, by §§ 201.56 [i.e., the full approved package insert].

By contrast, FDA does not have direct legal authority over the oral statements made by the pharmaceutical company sales representatives who call on physicians millions of times each year. Such oral statements are neither "labeling" nor "advertising." As discussed in detail below, the only way FDA can reach these and other oral statements is indirectly, through a tactic known as the "squeeze play." *See infra* p. 927.

b. CONTROVERSIES REGARDING THE CONTENT OF DRUG PROMOTION

The most prominent disputes regarding the substantive content of prescription drug promotion involve off-label promotion, a topic that will be considered separately below. *See infra* p. 925. But commentators have criticized other aspects of drug promotion, as well, even when the information transmitted is technically accurate and concerns approved uses. For example:

Incomplete Information. There is a perception that drug companies provide physicians with incomplete information, or manipulate that information, in order to influence physician prescribing choices. It is thus argued that greater restrictions should be placed on these interactions.

Designer Diseases. Some critics suggest that drug companies manipulate or invent disease states in order to increase prescribing. It is contended that the medical profession should maintain a tighter control over the designation of new diseases. *See* JEREMY GREENE, PRESCRIBING BY NUMBERS: DRUGS AND THE DEFINITION OF DISEASE (2007).

Newly Marketed Drugs. It is argued that drug companies focus marketing efforts on newer and more expensive drugs, causing doctors to abandon older and less expensive generic drugs even where there is little evidence that the new drug provides a meaningful advantage.

Continuing Medical Education (CME). There is controversy about whether any pharmaceutical industry grant to even an independent CME organization can be regarded as anything other than product promotion, even when it is not off-label promotion. It has been pointed out that drug companies would not support CME if they were not expecting an increase in their sales.

NOTE

Cost Effectiveness Claims. Although economic considerations do not play an explicit role in FDA drug approvals, pharmaceutical companies attempting to persuade health insurers to cover their products sometimes gather data to demonstrate the overall cost-saving potential of these drugs. In 2007, Congress amended section 502(a) of the FD&C Act to state:

> Health care economic information provided to a formulary committee, or other similar entity, in the course of the committee or the entity carrying out its responsibilities for the selection of drugs for managed care or other similar organizations, shall not be considered to be false or misleading under this paragraph if the health care economic information directly relates to an [approved] indication . . . and is based on competent and reliable scientific evidence.

This provision has had only a modest impact on the number of pharmacoeconomic studies undertaken by the pharmaceutical industry.

c.   MATERIAL INDUCEMENTS TO PHYSICIANS

Critics of prescription drug marketing efforts also focus much attention on material benefits that drug companies provide to physicians, allegedly to encourage doctors to prescribe their products. These inducements—some of which are also directed to medical students and residents—include the provision of meals by sales representatives, the conferral of small to modest gifts, support for travel to conferences, and consultant arrangements. FDA has also alleged in warning letters that companies contract with physicians to conduct uncontrolled studies as a form of inducement to increase their prescribing of the products involved. Critics contend that these practices lead to prescribing decisions based at least in part on financial considerations rather than strictly on scientific evidence. *See, e.g.,* MARCIA ANGELL, THE TRUTH ABOUT DRUG COMPANIES: HOW THEY DECEIVE US AND WHAT TO DO ABOUT IT (2005).

1. Statutory Responses

The provision of gifts to physicians to induce them to prescribe particular therapies is severely restricted by the federal Anti–Kickback Statute, 42 U.S.C. 1320a–7b(b). This law makes it a felony either to pay or to receive any remuneration of any kind to induce the order or purchase of a drug for which reimbursement is made under Medicare or Medicaid. Because it is not feasible to determine in advance whether a particular drug will be subject to Medicare or Medicaid reimbursement, all current pharmaceutical industry promotional practices are potentially subject to these provisions. The statute is administered by the HHS Office of Inspector General (OIG).

Section 1320(a)–7b(b), which replaced a comparable prohibition enacted in 1977, derives from the Medicare and Medicaid Patient Protection Act of 1987, 101 Stat. 680. The 1987 law also added a civil sanction and ordered OIG to establish safe harbors for practices determined not to constitute illegal kickbacks. The OIG Regulations to implement the statute are at 42 C.F.R. Part 1001.

A more recent Congressional response to the issue of physician inducements is the Physician Payment Sunshine Act, section 6002 of the 2010 Affordable Care Act. 124 Stat. 119. This section of the ACA added section 1128G to the Social Security Act. Section 1128G requires manufacturers of drugs and other medical products covered under Medicare, Medicaid, or the Children's Health Insurance Program to report annually to HHS certain payments or other transfers of value to physicians and teaching hospitals. HHS is required to publish the reported data—which is physician-specific—on a public web site. In February 2013, HHS issued complex final rules implementing these requirements. 78 Fed. Reg. 9458 (Feb. 8, 2013), codified at 42 C.F.R. Part 403.

2. Organizational Responses

Three organizations have prepared guidance to address such issues. In May 2003, the HHS Office of Inspector General issued a *Compliance Program Guidance for Pharmaceutical Manufacturers,* 68 Fed. Reg. 23731 (May 5, 2003). This Guidance advises companies on establishing compliance programs with respect to all federal health care program requirements, but it focuses especially on avoiding kickbacks and other illegal remuneration to induce or reward the referral or generation of federal health care business.

In 2002, the Pharmaceutical Research and Manufacturers of America (PhRMA) adopted a voluntary *Code on Interactions with Healthcare Professionals.* The most recently revised version of this document went into effect in January 2009. The document addresses fourteen basic aspects of the relationship between the pharmaceutical

of text, an affordable option only in commercials run during television programs after midnight.

In 1995, FDA, faced with threats of legal challenge to its policy regarding DTC advertising, published a background document and asked for comments. 60 Fed. Reg. 42581 (Aug. 16, 1995). Two years later, following a public hearing, the agency announced the availability of a draft guidance that effectively permitted broadcast advertising of prescription drugs for the first time.

Draft Guidance for Industry: Consumer-Directed Broadcast Advertisements

62 Fed. Reg. 43171 (August 12, 1997).

Section 502(n) of the Federal Food, Drug, and Cosmetic Act requires that advertisements for prescription drugs for humans and animals and human biological products include information in brief summary relating to side effects, contraindications, and effectiveness. This is known as the "brief summary" requirement. The prescription drug advertising regulations in § 202.1(e)(1) and (e)(3)(iii) further require that the brief summary disclose all the risk-related information in a product's approved package labeling (package insert or product package insert).

The regulations for advertising prescription drugs through broadcast media, such as radio, television, or telephone communications systems, however, modify the disclosure requirements somewhat. All prescription drug broadcast advertisements must include information about the major risks of the advertised drug (the "major statement") in either the audio or audio and visual parts of the presentation. Instead of presenting a "brief summary" in connection with the broadcast advertisement, a sponsor may make adequate provision for the dissemination of the approved package labeling in connection with the broadcast presentation (§ 202.1(e)(1)). This alternative requirement is referred to as the "adequate provision" requirement.

The "adequate provision" requirement recognizes the inability of broadcast advertisements of reasonable length to present and communicate effectively the extensive information that would be included in a brief summary; it instead specifies that presentation of the advertised product's most important risk information as part of the "major statement," together with "adequate provision" for the dissemination of the approved labeling, can fulfill the risk information disclosure mandated by the act. . . .

Previously, FDA had not described how prescription drug and biological product sponsors could fulfill the "adequate provision" requirement for consumer-directed broadcast advertising. . . .

. . . In light of the agency's increased experience and recent public input, FDA has reconsidered the issue of adequate provision as it relates to consumer-directed broadcast advertising. Therefore, FDA is publishing a draft guidance entitled, "Consumer–Directed Broadcast Advertisements." . . . This draft guidance is intended to provide consumers with adequate communication of required risk information, while facilitating the process used by sponsors to advertise their products to consumers.

———

Two years later, FDA issued the following final guidance, which contains effectively the same provisions for satisfying the "adequate provision" requirement as the 1997 draft guidance:

Guidance for Industry: Consumer–Directed Broadcast Advertisements
August 1999.

. . . .

III. FULFILLING THE ADEQUATE PROVISION REQUIREMENT

A sponsor wishing to use consumer-directed broadcast advertisements may meet the adequate provision requirement through an approach that will allow most of a potentially diverse audience to have reasonably convenient access to the advertised product's approved labeling. This audience will include many persons with limited access to technologically sophisticated outlets (e.g., the Internet) and persons who are uncomfortable actively requesting additional product information or are concerned about being personally identified in their search for product information. One acceptable approach to disseminating the product's approved labeling is described below. This approach includes the following components.

A. Disclosure in the advertisement of an operating toll-free telephone number for consumers to call for the approved package labeling. Upon calling, consumers should be given the choice of:

• Having the labeling mailed to them in a timely manner (e.g., within 2 business days for receipt generally within 4–6 days); or

• Having the labeling read to them over the phone (e.g., by offering consumers a selection of prerecorded labeling topics).

B. Reference in the advertisement to a mechanism to provide package labeling to consumers with restricted access to sophisticated technology, such as the Internet, and those who are uncomfortable actively requesting additional product information or are concerned about being personally identified in their search for product information. One acceptable mechanism would be to provide the additional product information in the form of print advertisements appearing concurrently in publications that reach the exposed audience. The location of at least one of these advertisements would be referenced in the broadcast advertisement. If a print advertisement is part of an adequate provision procedure, it should supply a toll-free telephone number and an address for further consumer access to full package labeling. This mechanism of providing access to product labeling has the advantage of also providing considerable information in the form of the required brief summary and in the advertising text itself.

. . . [P]rint advertisements associated with broadly disseminated broadcast advertisements should be comparably broadly disseminated in terms of the targeted audiences.

C. Disclosure in the advertisement of an Internet web page (URL) address that provides access to the package labeling.

D. Disclosure in the advertisement that pharmacists, physicians (or other healthcare providers), or veterinarians (in the case of animal drugs) may provide additional product information to consumers. This statement should communicate clearly that the referenced professional is a source of additional product information.

. . . .

NOTES

1. *FDA Pre-Broadcast Review of TV Advertisements.* Under 21 C.F.R. 314.81(b)(3)(i), manufacturers must submit broadcast advertisements (along with all other Rx drug advertisements) to FDA at the time of initial dissemination, using Form FDA 2253. In only certain instances, however, is a sponsor required to submit a TV ad to FDA *before* it airs.

The 2007 Amendments (FDAAA) added FD&C Act 503B, which provides that FDA may require submission for review of any television advertisement for a particular drug (or group of drugs) at least 45 days prior to broadcast. After reviewing the advertisement, the agency can mandate the inclusion of (1) specific disclosures of serious risks listed in the labeling and (2) the date of approval of the drug (for up to two years after the date of approval). Otherwise, in this review, FDA is limited to making recommendations. Although the agency has no authority to require additional types of changes to the television advertisements it reviews, the Act elsewhere states that in assessing the amount of a civil penalty for a false or misleading DTC advertisement, FDA shall take into account "whether the person incorporated any comments made by the Secretary [after section 503B review] with regard to the advertisement." FD&C Act 303(g)(3)(D).

In a 2012 Draft Guidance, FDA announced that it intends to require six categories of television advertisements to undergo pre-dissemination review under section 503B: (1) the initial TV ad for a new drug or an expanded indication; (2) ads for drugs subject to REMS; (3) ads for Schedule II controlled substances; (4) the first TV ad for a drug following a safety labeling update; (5) the first TV ad for a drug following receipt by the sponsor of an enforcement letter citing another TV ad for the same product; and (6) "[a]ny TV ad that is otherwise identified by FDA as subject to the pre-dissemination review provision." DRAFT GUIDANCE FOR INDUSTRY: DIRECT-TO-CONSUMER TELEVISION ADVERTISEMENTS—FDAAA DTC TELEVISION AD PRE-DISSEMINATION REVIEW PROGRAM (2012).

2. *Aborted User Fee Program.* FDAAA also added FD&C Act 736A, which established a user-fee based voluntary program to review DTC television advertising prior to broadcast. However, 736A(f) required FDA to collect a specified amount in fees before the program could commence, and

because the agency failed to meet this amount, the program was cancelled before it ever started. Section 736A sunset on October 1, 2012.

————

In 2008, FDA sent Bayer HealthCare the following warning letter regarding two television commercials for YAZ, a birth-control pill. (The excerpt is edited to focus on one of the two advertisements.) After receiving this letter, Bayer agreed not only to pull the commercials, but also to run a corrective TV advertisement. While the violative ads are not available online, the corrective ad can be found at http://www.you tube.com/watch?v=EO–G8O0lHq0.

Warning Letter From Thomas Abrams, Dir., DDMAC to Reinhard Franzen, Pres. & CEO, Bayer HealthCare Pharmaceuticals, Inc.

October 3, 2008.

Dear Mr. Franzen

The Division of Drug Marketing, Advertising, and Communications (DDMAC) has reviewed two 60–second direct-to-consumer (DTC) broadcast television advertisements entitled "Not Gonna Take it" and "Balloons" for YAZ® (drospirenone and ethinyl estradiol) Tablets submitted by Bayer . . . under cover of separate Forms FDA–2253. The TV Ads are misleading because they broaden the drug's indication, overstate the efficacy of YAZ, and minimize serious risks associated with the use of the drug. Thus, the TV Ads misbrand the drug in violation of the Federal Food, Drug, and Cosmetic Act (the Act), 21 U.S.C. 352(n), 352(f)(1) & 321 (n), and FDA's implementing regulations. 21 CFR 201.100(c)(1); 201.128; 202.1(e)(5)(iii) & (e)(6)(i). . . .

BACKGROUND

According to the INDICATIONS AND USAGE section from the FDA-approved product labeling (PI), YAZ is approved for the following indications . . . :

> [F]or the prevention of pregnancy in women who elect to use an oral contraceptive. . . .

> [F]or the treatment of symptoms of premenstrual dysphoric disorder (PMDD) in women who choose to use an oral contraceptive as their method of contraception. . . .

> [F]or the treatment of moderate acne vulgaris in women at least 14 years of age, who have no known contraindications to oral contraceptive therapy and have achieved menarche. YAZ should be used for the treatment of acne only if the patient desires an oral contraceptive for birth control.

. . . .

The PI for YAZ includes a BOXED WARNING that [cigarette smoking increases the risk of serious cardiovascular side effects from oral contraceptive use, particularly among heavy smokers and women over 35 years of age.]

Additionally, there are numerous warnings associated with the use of YAZ including, but not limited to, venous and arterial thrombotic and thromboembolic events (such as myocardial infarction, thromboembolism, stroke), hepatic neoplasia, gallbladder disease, and hypertension. . . .

BROADENING OF INDICATION

Premenstrual Dysphoric Disorder (PMDD)

The TV Ads misleadingly suggest that YAZ is effective in a broader range of patients and conditions than has been demonstrated by substantial evidence or substantial clinical experience. Specifically, given the overlap in certain symptoms between premenstrual syndrome (PMS) and PMDD . . . the TV Ads misleadingly suggest that YAZ is appropriate for treating women with PMS, who may not be appropriate candidates for this drug. . . .

. . . [T]he TV Ad "Balloons" starts by stating:

- "All birth control pills are 99% effective and can give you shorter, lighter periods. But there's one Pill that goes beyond the rest. It's YAZ."

It then displays numerous balloons throughout the ad with symptoms, such as, "IRRITABILITY," "MOODINESS," "FEELING ANXIOUS," "BLOATING," "FATIGUE," "MUSCLE ACHES," "HEADACHES," "INCREASED APPETITE," and "ACNE."

The symptoms displayed . . . are commonly seen in women with PMS, which is a less serious and more common condition than PMDD. . . .

The TV Ads entirely omit the material limitation from the PI of the drug's PMDD indication—i.e., that "YAZ has not been evaluated for the treatment of premenstrual syndrome (PMS)"—and fail to convey that the drug is only indicated for women who experience the symptoms presented to such a degree that they have PMDD, rather than PMS. . . .

We note that the list of symptoms displayed in the TV Ads are accompanied by the text "YAZ treats PMDD" along with a SUPER reading "PMDD is a mood disorder related to the menstrual cycle." However, these disclosures do not suffice to communicate the material fact that YAZ is not approved for treatment of PMS or to overcome the implication created by the totality of the visuals and images in the ads that YAZ is appropriate for any woman who experiences the symptoms presented. . . .

Acne

In addition, the TV Ads suggest that YAZ is approved for acne of all severities when this is not the case. Specifically, in . . . "Balloons," the "ACNE" balloon is prominently displayed on the screen, as it floats by a smiling woman with obviously clear skin, along with the audio claim that YAZ ". . . also helps keep skin clear." These presentations fail to adequately convey that, as noted in the PI, "YAZ is indicated for the treatment of <u>moderate</u> acne vulgaris . . ." (emphasis added). While the TV Ads do include a SUPER which refers to "improvement in . . . moderate acne" in small, unbolded print, this does not mitigate the misleading impression created by the prominent audio and visual claims in the TV Ads that YAZ is indicated for acne of all severities.

OVERSTATEMENT OF EFFICACY

PMDD

The ["Balloons"] TV Ad is misleading because it suggests that YAZ is more effective than has been demonstrated by substantial evidence or substantial clinical experience. The totality of the audio and visual claims and presentations misleadingly suggests that treatment with YAZ will allow women to say "good-bye" to their symptoms completely. For example, the TV Ad's theme song "Good–Bye to you" [sic] plays in the background as energetic, euphoric, playful women release balloons into the air displaying certain symptoms. . . . The balloons then float up and away from the women misleadingly suggesting that these women are saying, [sic] "goodbye" to their symptoms and are now symptom-free, when such an elimination of symptoms has not been demonstrated by substantial evidence or substantial clinical experience. . . .

Acne

The TV Ads include close-up images of women with completely clear, acne-free skin. . . . In "Balloons," a woman with obviously clear skin smiles and acknowledges the "ACNE" balloon as it floats away from the center of the screen and disappears into the sky, in conjunction with, the background song "Good-bye to you" and the audio claim that YAZ ". . . also helps keep skin clear." The overwhelming impression conveyed by the TV Ads is that treatment with YAZ results in clear, acne-free skin for those women suffering from acne when this has not been demonstrated by substantial evidence or substantial clinical experience. . . .

MINIMIZATION OF RISK

The audio communication of serious risk disclosures during the "major statement" is minimized by distracting visuals, numerous scene changes, and other competing modalities such as the background music which combine to interfere with the presentation of the risk information. . . . [I]n "Balloons," the background music plays as fast-paced visuals depict various women running in a park, sitting on a scenic waterfront, smiling, walking out of a coffee shop, driving and singing, walking out on a balcony, using an elevator, walking through the street to join friends, in addition, to a pigeon on a building ledge and balloons being released and floating away. These complex presentations distract from and make it difficult for viewers to process and comprehend the important risks being conveyed. This is particularly troubling as some of the risks being conveyed are serious, even life-threatening. The overall effect . . . is to undermine the communication of important risk information, minimizing these risks and misleadingly suggesting that YAZ is safer than has been demonstrated by substantial evidence or substantial clinical experience.

CONCLUSION AND REQUESTED ACTION

For the reasons discussed above, the promotional piece misbrands YAZ in violation of the Act . . . and FDA implementing regulations. . . .

DDMAC asks Bayer to immediately cease dissemination of violative promotional materials for YAZ that are the same as or similar to those described above. Please submit a written response to this letter on or before October 20, 2008, describing your intent to comply with this request. . . . Because the violations described above are serious, we request, further, that your submission include a comprehensive plan of action to disseminate truthful, non-misleading, and complete corrective messages about the issues discussed in this letter to the audience(s) that received the violative promotional materials. . . .

c.   GENERAL ISSUES SURROUNDING DTC ADVERTISING

The United States is extremely unusual in permitting full-scale DTC advertising of prescription drugs; New Zealand is the only other developed nation that does so. Not surprisingly, DTC advertising— especially television advertising—has been a matter of controversy. The pros and cons of the practice are summarized in the following FDA web publication:

Keeping Watch Over Direct-to-Consumer Ads
FDA CONSUMER HEALTH INFORMATION (May 2010).

. . . .

A Topic of Debate

While DTC advertising has many supporters, it raises concerns for many people.

Proponents say that the ads

- provide useful information to consumers that may result in better health
- can advance public health by encouraging more people to talk with health care professionals about problems, particularly undertreated conditions such as high blood pressure and high cholesterol
- can help remove the stigma associated with diseases that in the past were rarely openly discussed (including erectile dysfunction and depression)
- can remind patients to get their prescriptions refilled and help them adhere to their medication regimens

However, many people are concerned that such promotion

- may contain false or misleading information
- does not provide enough information about the risks and negative effects of the advertised drugs
- may not advance—and may even threaten—the public health
- encourages overuse of prescription drugs
- encourages use of the most costly treatments, instead of less expensive treatments that would be just as satisfactory

NOTES

1. *Relationship to Drug Prices.* The relationship of DTC advertising to the increased price of prescription drugs has provoked heated debate. Some argue that drug prices have been substantially increased because of this advertising. Others argue that prices either have not been affected or have been kept down as a result the increase in sales attributed to DTC advertising.

2. *The Doctor-Patient Relationship.* There is an equally heated debate about the impact of DTC advertising on the doctor-patient relationship. Some argue that patients pressure their doctors into prescribing drugs that the patients have heard about on TV, even if they do not need these drugs. Others argue that advertising informs patients about new drugs that may help them and drives them into the doctor's office to have useful and meaningful discussions about the utility of additional medication.

3. *Lack of Fair Balance.* One of the strongest attacks on DTC advertising, both by FDA and by critics, has been its emphasis on effectiveness and its inadequate mention of risk information. As a result, the industry trade association, PhRMA, has issued voluntary *Principles on Direct-to-Consumer Advertising,* and the pharmaceutical industry has improved its balance in DTC advertising between risk information and effectiveness claims.

4. *Legal Challenge by Third-Party Payer.* Third-party payers are understandably concerned that DTC advertising informs patients about the availability of potentially helpful prescription drugs and thus increases reimbursement payments. In *Pennsylvania Employee Benefit Trust Fund v. Zeneca, Inc.,* 2005 WL 2993937 (D. Del. 2005), the plaintiffs brought suit against the manufacturer of Prilosec® and Nexium® on the ground that, after the Prilosec patent had expired and was subject to generic competition which substantially reduced the price, the company used misleading DTC advertising to persuade consumers that the more expensive new Nexium was an improved drug. The District Court determined that the Nexium DTC advertising was consistent with its FDA-approved labeling and that the action was preempted by the FDA jurisdiction over the labeling of Nexium.

5. *Moratorium on DTC Advertising for Selected Drugs?* Critics have argued that all DTC advertising is inappropriate for some categories of drugs. Examples include: (1) newly-marketed drugs for the first year after launch, (2) drugs with black box warnings, (3) narrow therapeutic index drugs, (4) drugs subject to risk management programs, and (5) other drugs with significant toxicity. Some pharmaceutical companies have decided not to advertise such products on a voluntary basis. There is a serious question, however, whether such restrictions would survive First Amendment scrutiny if the government made them mandatory.

6. *DTC Advertising for Controlled Substances.* FDA regulations and guidance regarding DTC advertising do not distinguish between prescription drugs that are scheduled under the Controlled Substances Act and prescription drugs that are not so scheduled. The Drug Enforcement

Administration (DEA) has sent letters objecting to DTC advertising for various controlled substances. Some companies have agreed to discontinue their DTC advertising for controlled substances, but others have continued to advertise. The DEA relies on the Convention on Psychotropic Substances of 1971, which states in article 10 that "[e]ach Party shall, with due regard to its constitutional provisions, prohibit the advertisement of such substances to the general public." A government ban on DTC advertising for all prescription drug controlled substances would be unlikely to withstand judicial scrutiny under the First Amendment, however.

7. *Growth of DTC Advertising.* DTC prescription drug advertising has undergone phenomenal growth. From a base of about $12 million in 1997, it grew to approximately $4.1 billion in 2005. Rich Thomaselli, *Ten Years Later: Direct to Consumer Drug Advertising*, 77 ADVERTISING AGE 51 (Oct. 1, 2006).

I. REGULATING OFF-LABEL PROMOTION

1. INTRODUCTION

The dissemination by manufacturers of information about unapproved uses of approved drugs has long presented vexing problems for FDA. The dilemmas derive from the fact that once the agency approves a drug for one use, physicians may prescribe it for any other use they deem appropriate. *See supra* p. 817.

If off-label promotion (also known as extralabel promotion) were legal, the manufacturer of an approved drug would have little incentive ever to invest the substantial resources necessary to seek FDA approval of an additional indication not contained in the initial NDA. Instead, it would simply attempt to persuade physicians to prescribe the drug for this unapproved use, often with less supportive evidence in hand than would be required to support a supplemental NDA. The drug industry would fund fewer well-controlled clinical studies, and the system as a whole would be denied the benefit of this research.

Conversely, a total prohibition against manufacturers discussing off-label uses would raise its own problems. Doctors prescribing drugs off-label sometimes need information from the manufacturer—the entity that knows the drug best—about how to do so safety and effectively. Moreover, FDA does not want to stifle legitimate scientific and educational discussion about off-label uses. After all, extralabel uses of drugs occur frequently in all fields of medicine and characterize the majority of prescriptions in some, such as oncology.

Over the years, FDA has struggled to fashion a delicate compromise that permits drug manufacturers to engage in scientific and educational communication about unapproved indications while simultaneously banning companies from conducting off-label promotional activities that, even if technically accurate, would threaten the integrity of the NDA process and, in FDA's view, potentially mislead physicians and patients.

This precarious balance is illustrated, for example, by section 312.7(a) of the Investigational New Drug Application (IND) regulations.

This rule applies both to investigations of new molecular entities and to studies of new uses for already-approved drugs. On the one hand, the rule prohibits any sponsor or investigator from "represent[ing] in a promotional context that an investigational new drug is safe or effective for the purposes for which it is under investigation." On the other hand, the rule then goes on to state:

> This provision is not intended to restrict the full exchange of scientific information concerning the drug, including dissemination of scientific findings and scientific or lay media. Rather, its intent is to restrict promotional claims of safety or effectiveness of the drug for a use for which it is under investigation. . . .

Over the years, FDA has established a compromise approach to the off-label communication conundrum through regulations, guidances, policy statements, and enforcement patterns. The agency's policies in this area have often been blurry and sometimes controversial. Recently, as examined below, the agency's regulation of off-label promotion has faced a new attack, from opponents of such restrictions wielding the commercial speech doctrine of the First Amendment. The courts have accepted these free speech arguments in a manner that has expanded the scope of protected off-label communications and may, ultimately, eviscerate FDA's power in this area.

2. THE LEGAL BASES FOR PROHIBITING OFF-LABEL PROMOTION UNDER THE FD&C ACT

The FD&C Act provisions governing labeling and advertising do not explicitly and directly prohibit off-label promotion. The ban on such activity is thus based largely on agency regulations interpreting the Act. The government invokes different statutory and regulatory provisions, depending on whether the off-label promotion occurs in the context of labeling, advertising, or oral statements.

At the outset of this discussion, it is important to recognize that the FD&C Act does not prohibit any person other than the person(s) marketing a drug from promoting an unapproved use. Indeed, even federal agencies—in particular, the National Institutes of Health— routinely recommend off-label uses of new drugs.

a.   OFF-LABEL PROMOTION IN LABELING

When off-label promotion occurs in "labeling," the relevant FD&C Act provisions include: (1) 505(a), which prohibits the introduction or delivery for introduction into interstate commerce of a "new drug" that has not been approved by FDA; (2) 201(p), which, as interpreted, defines "new drug" to include any drug that FDA has not approved for "use under the conditions prescribed, recommended, or suggested in the labeling;" and (3) 201(m), which defines "labeling" broadly to include "all labels and other written, printed, or graphic matter" upon the drug or "accompanying such article." The government cites these provisions to undergird an accusation that the off-label promoter has violated FD&C Act 301(d), which prohibits interstate commerce in unapproved new drugs. Moreover, the government may allege a misbranding violation under section 301(a) or 301(k) because the labeling is "false or misleading in any particular" (502(a)), or fails to include "adequate directions for use" (502(f)(1)), or both.

FDA regulations interpret these provisions so as to make a large universe of off-label communications illegal. Most important, the agency has interpreted the definition of "labeling" in FD&C Act 201(m) extremely broadly with respect to drugs, to embrace everything from brochures to films to sound recordings. 21 C.F.R. 202.1(*l*)(2) (quoted *supra* p. 912).

Another regulation that enhances FDA's reach in the off-label promotion area is 201.100(d)(1), which states that a drug is eligible for the prescription drug exemption from FD&C Act 502(f)(1) (and thus avoid a misbranding violation under that provision) only if the labeling information presenting "adequate information" for use by practitioners, including information about "indications, effects, dosages, routes, methods, and frequency and duration of administration," uses the "same language and emphasis" as the approved labeling. 21 C.F.R. 201.100(d)(1). Moreover, any other parts of the labeling must be "consistent with and not contrary to" the approved labeling. *Id.* For a discussion of the prescription drug exemption from the 502(f)(1) requirement of adequate directions for use by a layman, see *supra* p. 802.

b.   OFF-LABEL PROMOTION IN ADVERTISING

As discussed previously, *supra* p. 907, FDA has used its section 502(n) power over prescription drug advertising to promulgate thoroughgoing regulations concerning the required and permissible content of advertisements. 21 C.F.R. Part 202. One provision of these regulations unambiguously declares:

> An advertisement for a prescription drug is false, lacking in fair balance, or otherwise misleading, or otherwise violative of section 502(n) . . . if it [c]ontains a representation or suggestion, not approved or permitted for use in the labeling, that a drug is better, more effective, [or] useful in a broader range of conditions or patients . . . than has been demonstrated by substantial evidence or substantial clinical experience. . . .

21 C.F.R. 202.1(e)(6)(i). Furthermore, another section of the advertising regulations states that an advertisement for a prescription drug "shall not recommend or suggest any use that is not in the labeling accepted in [the] new-drug application or supplement." 21 C.F.R. 202.1(e)(4)(i)(a).

c.   OFF-LABEL PROMOTION THROUGH ORAL STATEMENTS AND FDA'S "SQUEEZE PLAY"

The most complex scenario occurs when the alleged off-label promotion occurs in oral statements that qualify as neither "labeling" nor "advertising"—such as assertions made by sales representatives during visits to doctors. This situation does not support a charge of selling an unapproved new drug, because the statutory definition of "new drug" refers only to "conditions prescribed, recommended, or suggested *in the labeling*." FD&C Act 201(p)(emphasis added). Because they are not labeling, the oral statements similarly cannot be deemed to violate section 502(a)'s prohibition against "false or misleading" labeling. And assuming they cannot be characterized as "advertising," such statements also cannot be deemed to violate section 502(n). How, then, does FDA find illegality in this situation? The answer lies in an indirect use of section 502(f)(1)'s requirement that the labeling itself include "adequate directions for use." This tactic is commonly known as the "squeeze play."

As discussed above, prescription drugs are exempt from section 502(f)(1) if they satisfy certain other labeling requirements. The legal basis for the "squeeze play" in the context of prescription drugs is thus rather complex. It is helpful first to grasp the concept as applied to a nonprescription product.

i.   The "Squeeze Play" in the OTC Context

United States v. Articles of Drug . . . Foods Plus, Inc.

239 F. Supp. 465 (D.N.J. 1965).

■ WORTENDYKE, DISTRICT JUDGE

In its libel of information praying seizure and condemnation of certain articles of drug therein particularized, in the possession of Foods Plus, Inc., (hereinafter Foods Plus or claimant) in this District, the United States of America charges that the articles described were misbranded when introduced into, while in, and while held for sale after such shipment in interstate commerce, within the meaning of 21 U.S.C. § 352(a) and § 352(f)(1). . . . Claimant denies the misbranding charged. . . .

Libelant charges that the articles seized were misbranded under § 352(a) in that their labeling, i.e., the labels upon their containers and the booklet entitled 'Foods Plus 1962 Vitamin Catalog' (hereinafter catalog) which accompanied the articles, contain statements which represent and suggest that the articles are superior to similar products available on the market because they were formulated by one Carlton Fredericks, Ph.D., who is alleged in the catalog to be an internationally prominent nutritionist; that vitamins are more effective in combination with each other and with minerals; and that the nutritional requirements of old people differ from those of adults generally.

. . . .

Finally, the libel alleges that all of the seized articles were misbranded under § 352(f)(1) because Foods Plus, through its intimate relationship with Carlton Fredericks, a radio commentator in the field of nutrition, represented the various articles to be effective in the prevention and mitigation of disease conditions, but that neither he nor any labeling (the catalog included) prescribed 'adequate directions for use' of the articles as required by § 352(f)(1).

. . . . [S]ince the articles in question are clearly misbranded under § 352(f)(1), the question as to their misbranding under § 352(a) has not been further considered.

. . . .

The Government's charge of misbranding under § 352(f)(1) of the Act is predicated upon its assertion that the seized vitamins, minerals and dietary supplements are drugs and that their 'labeling' failed to disclose adequate directions for their use 'for the many disease conditions for which Carlton Fredericks represented them as being effective in his radio broadcasts, which were merely disguised advertisements for the Foods Plus products.' The Government does not claim that Fredericks' broadcasts should be treated as incorporated by reference in or forming a part of the 'labeling' of the drug. Nevertheless, oral representations, such as these broadcasts, may be considered in determining the intended use of the vitamins. The reasoning upon which this claim of misbranding rests may be outlined as follows:

(1) the Food and Drug Act (specifically 21 U.S.C. § 352(f)(1)) requires that 'adequate directions for use' of a drug be borne by its 'labeling';

(2) the articles seized, which comprise various quantities of some 43 different formulas of vitamin, mineral and other dietary preparations, are drugs; and

(3) the labeling associated with the formulations does not contain adequate directions for the use of the articles seized. . . .

The initial question here presented is whether the seized articles are drugs under the Act and so within the proscription of § 352(f)(1). In § 321(g)(2) the term drug is defined as 'articles intended for use in the diagnosis, cure, mitigation, treatment, or prevention of disease in man or other animals.' . . .

Concededly accurate transcripts of radio broadcasts by Carlton Fredericks . . . clearly disclose that . . . Fredericks extolled the value of vitamin and mineral supplementation for use by the layman in the prevention, treatment and cure of disease.

 . . . .

This Court is impelled to the conclusion that these radio broadcasts of Carlton Fredericks, in which he presented abstracts of articles on nutrition together with his own comments thereon, were intended to urge or encourage the regular ingestion of vitamins as medicaments for the prevention, mitigation or cure of diseases in man. The question remains whether Foods Plus was a party to such intention. . . . Whenever a listener responded to one of his offers to send the listener nutritional literature on . . . any of a host of . . . subjects alluded to in the course of Fredericks' radio broadcasts, the listener received a catalog from Foods Plus. . . . This catalog left no doubt that Foods Plus and Carlton Fredericks were very closely related. . . . His picture, name and title appeared in the upper right hand corner of the first page of the catalog, which expressly and emphatically exhorted the inquiring radio listener in the following vein:

 . . . .

'Carlton Fredericks, Ph.D., internationally prominent nutritionist, is FOODS PLUS' Chief Consultant. He has scientifically formulated the exclusive formulas in this catalog. . . .

'FOODS PLUS is the only vitamin company privileged to carry Carlton Fredericks' name and receive his endorsement.'

Once this catalog was read . . . a close relationship between Fredericks and Foods Plus became a natural inference in the listener's mind.

Such a relationship was more than purely inferential; it was actually contractual, as appears from . . . [a] written agreement, dated August 1, 1960, between Foods Plus, Inc. and Carlton Fredericks. . . .

The remaining issue is whether the labeling of the seized articles satisfied the required 'adequate directions for use.' This phrase has been considered by the courts before and an excellent explanation of its meaning is included in *United States v. Various Quantities of Articles of Drug, etc.*, D.C.D.C.1949, 83 F. Supp. 882, at page 885, as follows:

> The words, 'adequate directions for use,' necessarily relate to some purpose which is to be served by the use. . . . It seems . . . obvious that no drug can be said to contain in its labeling adequate directions for its use, unless every ailment of the body for which it is, through any means, held out to the public as an efficacious remedy be listed in the labeling, together with instructions to the user concerning the quantity and frequency of dosage recommended for each particular ailment. * * *

Another construction of the meaning of this statute is given in *Alberty Foods Products v. United States*, 9 Cir. 1952, 194 F.2d 463, 464:

> In order for the labeling of a drug to bear 'adequate directions for use' within the meaning of 21 U.S.C.A. § 352(f)(1) it must, among other things, state the purposes and conditions for which the drug was intended and sufficient information to enable a layman to intelligently and safely attempt self medication. * * *

The relevant regulations under § 352(f)(1) which were in effect at the time this seizure was made . . . are found at 21 C.F.R. 1.106(a)(1) and read:

> . . . (a) Directions for use may be inadequate by reason (among other reasons) of omission, in whole or in part, or incorrect specification of:
>
> (1) Directions for use in all conditions for which such drug or device is prescribed, recommended, or suggested in its labeling, or in its advertising disseminated or sponsored by or on behalf of its manufacturer, packer, or distributor, or in such other conditions, if any there be for which such drug or device is commonly and effectively used.

All of these interpretations indicate that adequate directions within the meaning of the statute require at the very least a recitation of the diseases or conditions for which the drug is prescribed. Since the labeling of the seized articles did not contain this information the Government's case is complete.

The articles seized . . . are condemned for misbranding. . . .

NOTES

1. *The "Squeeze Play."* If Foods Plus had sought to comply with section 502(f)(1) by including the disease indications in the labeling of its products, FDA would then have claimed that the products were misbranded

under section 502(a) because the claims were "false or misleading." For activity that occurred after the effective date of the 1962 Drug Amendments, FDA would also have charged Foods Plus under section 505(a) for introducing an unapproved new drug into interstate commerce. Thus, FDA was leveraging its authority over the labeling to indirectly sanction the company for Fredericks' radio broadcasts even though the agency did not have direct jurisdiction over these broadcasts. (Even if these broadcasts were aggressively classified as "advertisements," they would have been outside the agency's bailiwick in this case because the products were OTC drugs.) The FDA approach reflected in this case has come to be referred to as the "squeeze play."

2.   *Appellate History.* The District Court's opinion was upheld by the Third Circuit. *United States v. Article of Drug . . . Designated B–Complex Cholinos Capsules*, 362 F.2d 923 (3d Cir. 1966).

3.   *Current Regulations.* Oral statements that cannot be categorized as "labeling" or "advertising" are nonetheless relevant evidence for determining a drug's "intended uses" for which "adequate directions" must be provided. The current regulations interpreting FD&C Act 502(f)(1) state this more clearly than did the earlier rule quoted in *Foods Plus.*

> *Adequate directions for use* means directions under which the layman can use a drug safely and for the purposes for which it is intended . . . Directions for use may be inadequate because, among other reasons, of omission, in whole or in part, or incorrect specification of:
>
> (a) Statements of all conditions, purposes, or uses for which such drug is intended, including conditions, purposes, or uses for which it is prescribed, recommended, or suggested in its oral, written, printed, or graphic advertising, and conditions, purposes, or uses for which the drug is commonly used; except that such statements shall not refer to conditions, uses, or purposes for which the drug can be safely used only under the supervision of a practitioner licensed by law and for which it is advertised solely to such practitioner. . . .

21 C.F.R. 201.5. Meanwhile, 21 C.F.R. 201.128 illuminates the meaning of 201.5, in part by stating:

> The words *intended uses* or words of similar import in [§ 201.5] . . . refer to the objective intent of the persons legally responsible for the labeling of drugs. The intent is determined by such persons' expressions or may be shown by the circumstances surrounding the distribution of the article. This objective intent may, for example, be shown by labeling claims, advertising matter, or oral or written statements by such persons or their representatives.

4.   *The "Squeeze Play" and OTC Drug Advertising.* As a formal matter, FDA has jurisdiction over the advertising of prescription drugs only; the FTC has authority over OTC drug advertising. However, FDA can exert indirect power over OTC drug advertising through its use of the "squeeze play," because advertising is one of the types of evidence that the agency can use to determine the "intended uses" for which "adequate directions" are required in the labeling by FD&C Act 502(f)(1).

ii. The "Squeeze Play" in the Prescription Context

The government's use of the "squeeze play" to prevent off-label promotion of prescription drugs is even less straightforward. The complication arises from the fact that the term "adequate directions for use" in FD&C Act 502(f)(1) is interpreted to mean "directions under which the *layman* can use a drug safely and for the purposes for which it is intended." 21 C.F.R. 201.5 (emphasis added). A prescription drug can *never* bear such adequate directions; after all, the very reason for imposing prescription status on a drug is that a layman cannot use it safely and effectively without a physician's supervision. This fact explains why FDA found it necessary to promulgate 21 C.F.R. 201.100, which, if followed, explicitly *exempts* a prescription drug from the 502(f)(1) "adequate directions for use" requirement.

But the fact that a layman is incapable of sufficiently comprehending any directions for use of a drug does not excuse the manufacturer from providing any instructions at all; after all, the prescribing physician must understand how to use the drug. Therefore, to qualify for such a 502(f)(1) an exemption under 21 C.F.R. 201.100, a prescription drug must satisfy (among other conditions) the following requirement:

> (1) Labeling on or within the package from which the drug is to be dispensed bears adequate *information* for its use, including indications, effects, dosages, routes, methods, and frequency and duration of administration, and any relevant hazards, contraindications, side effects, and precautions under which practitioners licensed by law to administer the drug can use the drug safely and for the purposes for which it is intended, including all purposes for which it is advertised or represented; and
>
> (2) If the article is subject to section 505 of the act, the labeling bearing such information is the labeling authorized by the approved new drug application. . . .

21 C.F.R. 201.100(c) (emphasis added).

This "adequate information for use" requirement creates its own "squeeze play" opportunity. The legal theory behind the government's employment of this tactic is outlined well in the following excerpt from a memorandum of law by the drug manufacturer Allergan. The company filed this memorandum in a suit it brought seeking an injunction, on both statutory and constitutional grounds, that would permit it to communicate certain off-label information about the prescription drug Botox® to physicians. Allergan later voluntarily dismissed the suit as part of a broad settlement.

Memorandum of Law in Support of Motion for Preliminary Injunction

Allergan, Inc. v. United States, No. 1:09–cv–01879 (D.D.C. filed Oct. 1, 2009).

. . . .

FDA Regulations Prohibit a Manufacturer from Communicating About or Having Constructive Knowledge of the Off-Label Use of a Prescription Drug

Under the Act, a drug generally is "misbranded" unless its labeling contains "adequate directions for use." 21 U.S.C. § 352(f)(1). However, the Act exempts drugs dispensed by prescription from the "adequate directions" requirement of § 352(f)(1). 21 U.S.C. § 353(b)(2). The FDA has nullified this broad statutory exemption by a regulation that limits the exemption from the "adequate directions" requirement to prescription drugs with labeling that contains "adequate *information*" for use. 21 C.F.R. § 201.100(c)(1) (emphasis added). "Adequate information" for use, in turn, means adequate directions *"for the purposes for which [the drug] is intended, including all purposes for which it is advertised or represented." Id.* (emphasis added). FDA regulations thus require a prescription drug's "labeling" to contain directions for all "intended uses."

If the "intended uses" for which § 352(f)(1) required manufacturers to provide adequate directions in labeling were defined to match up with the uses for which § 355(a) permitted the manufacturer to provide adequate directions in labeling—namely, the FDA-approved on-label uses—those provisions would operate harmoniously. But the FDA has set §§ 352(f)(1) and 355(a) on a collision course by adopting the broadest possible conception of "intent." The FDA broadly defines a drug's "intended uses" to include not only FDA-approved on-label uses, but also any use "objective[ly] inten[ded]" by the manufacturer. 21 C.F.R. § 201.128. And a manufacturer's "objective intent" may be shown via its expression in labeling, advertisement, or other "oral or written statements." *Id.* An "objective intent" is also shown if, with the knowledge of the manufacturer, the drug is "offered and used for a purpose for which it is neither labeled nor advertised." *Id.* Most broadly, if a manufacturer merely "knows, or has knowledge of facts that would give notice" that its drug "is to be used" off-label, it "is required to provide adequate labeling for such a drug which accords with [those] uses." *Id.* (emphasis added).

21 C.F.R. §§ 201.100 and 201.128, along with the misbranding statute to which they are linked, prohibit virtually all manufacturer expression and knowledge about the off-label use of a prescription drug. The manufacturer commits a "springing" misbranding violation whenever its speech reflects its "objective intent" that a drug be used off-label, because the drug's labeling by definition does not contain "adequate directions" for that off-label use. *See* 21 C.F.R. §§ 201.100, 201.128; 21 U.S.C. § 352(f)(1). Although the drug was properly labeled when introduced into commerce, the violation springs into being if the manufacturer speaks about the off-label use in any forum, to any audience, even if the speech is neither "labeling" nor an "advertisement." And the manufacturer cannot avoid this misbranding violation, because changing the "labeling" to add directions for an off-label use is itself unlawful: "suggest[ing]" an off-label use on a drug's "labeling" transforms that drug into a "new drug" that cannot be sold. 21 U.S.C. §§ 321(p), 355(a). Any speech by a manufacturer about an off-label use thus places the manufacturer in a Catch–22: It violates § 355(a) to change the labeling to add adequate directions for that off-label use, but it violates the "intended use" regulations and § 352(f)(1) not to change the labeling to add adequate directions for that use.

. . . .

———

d.   THE GOVERNMENT'S USE OF OTHER STATUTES TO ENFORCE THE PROHIBITION AGAINST OFF-LABEL PROMOTION

Various statutes in addition to the FD&C Act can be used against a drug manufacturer engaged in off-label promotion. The most important of these is the False Claims Act (FCA). Claims can be brought pursuant to this statute by either the government or by private individuals as *qui tam* relators. "Qui tam" (standing for "qui tam pro domino rege quam pro se ipso"—"he who as much on behalf of the king as on behalf of himself") is a common-law action in which a private individual, the "relator," sues on behalf of himself and the government, and the two share the proceeds. The following case was a seminal one in this area.

United States ex. rel. Franklin v. Parke–Davis

147 F. Supp. 2d 39 (D. Mass. 2001).

■ SARIS, J.

In this *qui tam* action under the False Claims Act ("FCA"), 31 U.S.C. § 3729–33, Relator Dr. David Franklin alleges, among other things, that his former employer engaged in a fraudulent scheme to promote the sale of the drug Neurontin for "off-label" uses (i.e., uses other than those approved by the Food and Drug Administration) and that this illegal marketing campaign caused the submission of false claims to the Veterans Administration and to the federal government for Medicaid reimbursement. The Defendant has moved for dismissal. . . .

Whether a drug is FDA-approved for a particular use will largely determine whether a prescription for that use of the drug will be reimbursed under the federal Medicaid program. Reimbursement under Medicaid is, in most circumstances, available only for "covered outpatient drugs." 42 U.S.C. § 1396b(i)(10). Covered outpatient drugs do not include drugs that are "used for a medical indication which is not a medically accepted indication." *Id.* § 1396r–8(k)(3). A medically accepted indication, in turn, includes a use "which is approved under the Federal Food Drug and Cosmetic Act" or which is included in specified drug compendia. *Id.* § 1396r–8(k)(6). Thus, unless a particular off-label use for a drug is included in one of the identified drug compendia, a prescription for the off-label use of that drug is not eligible for reimbursement under Medicaid.

Neurontin, which is the brand name for the drug gabapentin, was approved by the FDA in 1994 for use as an adjunctive treatment for epilepsy in doses from 900 to 1800 mg per day. Neurontin is also used for a number of off-label purposes. For example, Neurontin is prescribed for pain control, as mono-therapy for epilepsy, for control of bipolar disease, and as treatment for attention deficit disorder. According to Relator, 50% of Neurontin's sales in 1996 are attributable to off-label uses. Of those sales, Relator estimates that 50% (or 25% of Neurontin's total sales) were reimbursed by the government either indirectly through Medicaid or directly through purchases by the Veterans Administration.

. . . .

The crux of Relator's allegations is that the Defendant engaged in an extensive and far-reaching campaign to use false statements to promote increased prescriptions of Neurontin and Accupril for off-label uses which caused the filing of false claims for reimbursement by the federal government.

Relator alleges that he was hired by Parke–Davis onto a team of "medical liaisons." While medical liaisons are ordinarily connected to the research divisions of the manufacturer, Parke–Davis's medical liaisons were exclusively employed as sales and promotion personnel.

Parke–Davis's medical liaisons, including Relator, were instructed to make exaggerated or false claims concerning the safety and efficacy of Parke–Davis drugs for off-label uses. . . . To bolster their representations to physicians, medical liaisons were encouraged to misrepresent their scientific credentials and to pose as research personnel, rather than as sales representatives.

. . . .

Relator filed this nine-count *qui tam* action under seal on August 13, 1996. The case remained in limbo and under seal for several years while the United States mulled over its option to intervene. The seal on the complaint was finally lifted on December 21, 1999, and the litigation began in earnest. To date, the government has elected to participate only in the capacity of *amicus curiae* while reserving its right to intervene as a plaintiff at a later point.

. . . .

The FCA provides:

Any person who—

(1) knowingly presents, or causes to be presented, to an officer of employee of the United States Government a false or fraudulent claim for payment or approval;

(2) knowingly makes, uses, or causes to be made or used, a false record or statement to get a false or fraudulent claim paid or approved by the Government; is liable to the United States Government for a civil penalty . . ., plus 3 times the amount of damages which the Government sustains because of the act of that person. . . .

31 U.S.C. § 3729(a) (emphasis added). An action may be brought under the False Claims Act only if there is "(1) . . . a false statement or fraudulent course of conduct; (2) made or carried out with the requisite scienter; (3) that was material; and (4) that caused the government to pay out money or to forfeit moneys due (i.e., that involved a 'claim')." . . .

Here, the Relator has alleged . . . that Parke–Davis has caused the submission of numerous off-label prescription [sic] for Neurontin to the Medicaid program through . . . its fraudulent statements about the safety and efficacy of Neurontin. . . .

Defendant does not dispute that an off-label prescription submitted for reimbursement by Medicaid is a false claim within the meaning of the FCA. Instead, Defendant's response is a four-fold attack on the viability of a claim under the FCA against a pharmaceutical manufacturer that did not itself submit false claims in the form of off-label prescriptions directly to the government.

First, Defendant argues that Relator cannot use the FCA as an end-run around the enforcement provisions of the FDCA by creating a cause of action for money damages. Although the FDCA forbids the marketing of drugs for off-label uses, it does not provide the government with a civil damage remedy to enforce the ban on off-label marketing.[6] The FDCA provides for enforcement of the off-label marketing prohibition only by the FDA and only through certain channels. The FDA may take administrative actions against a manufacturer such as seizing the violative drugs or seeking a court order enjoining the unlawful promotional activities. The FDA may also institute criminal proceedings for off-label marketing violations.

It is true that the FCA cannot be used to enforce compliance with every federal law or regulation.

Nonetheless, the FCA *can* be used to create liability where failure to abide by a rule or regulation amounts to a material misrepresentations [sic] made to obtain a government benefit. Thus, the failure of Congress to provide a cause action for money damages against a pharmaceutical manufacturer for marketing off-label drugs does not preclude an FCA claim where the manufacturer has knowingly caused a false statement to be made to get a false claim paid or approved by the government in violation of 31 U.S.C. § 3729(a).

Second, Defendant argues that an impermissible off-label promotion does not necessarily include a false statement or fraudulent conduct. For example, it points out, off-label promotion of a drug might simply consist of a representative of a pharmaceutical company distributing the finding of one doctor's experience with an off-label use of a particular drug to other physicians. However, Relator alleges more than a mere technical violation of the FDA's prohibition on off-label marketing. The gravamen of Relator's claim is that Parke–Davis engaged in an unlawful course of fraudulent conduct including knowingly making false statements to doctors that caused them to submit claims that were not eligible for payment by the government under Medicaid. Thus, the alleged FCA violation arises—not from unlawful off-label marketing activity itself—but from the submission of Medicaid claims for uncovered off-label uses induced by Defendant's fraudulent conduct. . . . A much closer question would be presented if the allegations involved only the unlawful—yet truthful—promotion of off-label uses to physicians who provide services to patients who are covered by Medicaid, as well as patients who are not, without any fraudulent representations by the manufacturer.

Third, Defendant argues that Relator has not stated a claim because he has not accounted for the independent actions of the physicians who wrote the off-label prescriptions and the pharmacists

---

[6]   Likewise, the FDCA does not contain a provision creating private enforcement of the off-label marketing ban by way of a civil damages action.

who accepted and filled the off-label prescriptions. In other words, Defendant argues that—as a matter of law—Relator's allegations cannot establish the causation requirement of the FCA because the actions of these professionals were an intervening force that breaks the chain of legal causation. . . . Under black letter law, however, such an intervening force only breaks the causal connection when it is unforeseeable. In this case . . . the participation of doctors and pharmacists in the submission of false Medicaid claims was not only foreseeable, it was an intended consequence of the alleged scheme of fraud.

Finally, Defendant argues that Relator's claim fails because he does not allege that false statements made by Parke–Davis to doctors were material to the government's decision to pay the claim for off-label prescriptions of Neurontin. Liability under the FCA, however, is not limited only to false statements or claims made directly by the Defendant to the government. The Act "reaches beyond claims which might be legally enforced, to all fraudulent attempts to cause the Government to pay out sums of money." Relator has adequately alleged that Parke–Davis knowingly caused the submission of these false claims through a fraudulent course of conduct in violation of 31 U.S.C. § 3729(a). The fact that such prescriptions are for an off-label use is material because, as the Defendant does not dispute, the government would not have paid the claims if it had known of the use for which they were being submitted. . . .

NOTES

1. *No Double-Falsehood Requirement.* Later in the litigation, when denying the defendant's motion for summary judgment, the court revisited the "much closer question" of whether Parke–Davis could be liable under the FCA even if the off-label statements were entirely true.

> . . . Under Parke–Davis's interpretation, the FCA contains a double falsehood requirement: An FCA plaintiff must prove a false statement that led to a false claim. Parke–Davis contends that Relator has failed to show that Parke–Davis made any material false statements.
>
> Parke–Davis's legal argument is inconsistent with the text of the FCA. While § 3729(a)(2) contains a double-falsehood requirement ("knowingly makes, uses, or causes to be made or used, *a false record or statement* to get a *false or fraudulent claim* paid or approved by the Government") (emphasis added), FCA liability under § 3729(a)(1) arises when a defendant "knowingly presents, or causes to be presented . . . *a false or fraudulent claim*" (emphasis added). Thus, there is no double falsehood requirement under § 3729(a)(1): One will suffice.
>
> . . . Under § 3729(a)(1), Relator is not required to present evidence that Parke–Davis lied to physicians about Neurontin's off-label efficacy or safety to induce them to prescribe Neurontin for uses ineligible under Medicaid. . . .

United States ex rel. Franklin v. Parke–Davis, 2003 U.S. Dist. LEXIS 15754 (D. Mass. 2003).

2.   *The Plaintiff's Burden of Proof.* Franklin faced another hurdle in establishing the dollar value of the claims he alleged were false. He had to identify which prescriptions and related claims for reimbursement were for off-label, non-compendium use. That information does not appear on the prescription form itself. Physicians presumably know why they want a patient to use a drug and may record this information in the patient's record, but the form they sign for delivery to the pharmacist does not call for any description of the purpose for which the drug is prescribed. Moreover, Medicaid reimbursement claim forms for prescription drugs do not require the claimant to list the indication for which the drug is being prescribed. Franklin claimed to have solved this problem by developing an instrument or algorithm that permitted estimates of the share of any drug's use that is off-label. Yet another challenge Franklin faced was finding a way to estimate the share of the off-label use that was attributable to Parke–Davis's unlawful promotion rather than to physicians' self-informed decisions.

3.   *Settlement.* Franklin and Parke–Davis (a division of Warner–Lambert) ultimately settled the dispute. A Stipulation of Dismissal stated that the United States would pay Relator Franklin $24,640,000 (in accordance with the Relator Share Agreement between the U.S. and Franklin) after defendant Parke–Davis paid the agreed upon settlement amount. In 2004, after Pfizer acquired Warner–Lambert, Pfizer announced that it was taking a charge of $427 million dollars in connection with investigations into Warner–Lambert's promotion of Neurontin to "resolve all outstanding federal and state governmental investigations related to Neurontin as well as the pending civil qui tam suit concerning this matter." In April 2013, the U.S. Court of Appeals for the First Circuit upheld a $142 million jury verdict in a RICO suit by HMO operator Kaiser against Pfizer based on allegations of off-label marketing of Neurontin. *Kaiser Found. Health Plan, Inc. v. Pfizer, Inc.*, 712 F.3d 21 (1st Cir. 2013).

4.   *Other Notable Settlements.* Although the Parke–Davis settlement was the first under the False Claims Act for off-label promotion, there have since been numerous additional settlements under the same theory, some with payouts surpassing the billion dollar mark. In July 2012, GlaxoSmithKline paid over $3 billion in criminal and civil penalties, in part to resolve off-label promotion allegations under the False Claims Act for Paxil, Wellbutrin, and other products. Abbott Labs paid more than $1.5 billion in May 2012 to settle claims about the off-label promotion of Depakote. In September 2009, Pfizer paid a combined $2.3 billion in criminal and civil penalties to settle claims regarding off-label promotion of Bextra and other drugs. Eli Lilly and Company settled for $1.4 billion for off-label marketing of Zyprexa in January 2009.

5.   *State Unfair Competition and Consumer Deception Laws.* State Attorneys General can bring cases on the ground that dissemination of off-label information represents an unfair business practice under state laws.

6.   *Lanham Act.* Competitors can bring lawsuits charging that a company engaged in off-label marketing is making unwarranted claims that result in competitive harm under 15 U.S.C. 1125(a).

3. PERMISSIBLE OFF-LABEL COMMUNICATIONS BY DRUG MANUFACTURERS

Despite FDA's firm stance against off-label promotion of drugs, it has long allowed manufacturers to communicate with physicians about off-label uses in certain limited circumstances. The two main categories of permissible off-label communication, both discussed below, are (1) responses to unsolicited requests for information and (2) scientific exchange. As this section will also explore, however, litigants wielding the First Amendment have forced the agency to expand the zone of permissible manufacturer statements concerning off-label indications. It is unclear just how far this expansion will go.

a. RESPONSES TO UNSOLICITED REQUESTS FOR INFORMATION

Since the early 1980s, FDA has taken the position that the agency does not forbid a pharmaceutical company to provide scientific information about extralabel uses to a physician in response to an unsolicited request. *E.g.*, 59 Fed. Reg. 59820, 59823 (Nov. 18, 1994). As part of the FDA Modernization Act of 1997, Congress added section 557(a) to the FD&C Act to affirm this policy. Although this section sunsetted in 2006, FDA has not abandoned its longstanding policy on this issue. In fact, the following 2011 guidance seems to liberalize the policy by allowing responses to unsolicited requests by patients as well as physicians.

Draft Guidance for Industry: Responding to Unsolicited Requests for Off-Label Information About Prescription Drugs and Medical Devices (2011)

. . . .

Scientific or medical departments within drug or medical device firms often maintain a large body of information about their products. This information ... may ... include off-label information for their products. . . . [A]lthough dissemination of off-label information can be used as evidence of new intended uses for products in distribution, such information may also be of use to individuals seeking information about a medical product for themselves, patients, family members, or friends. . . .

This draft guidance provides FDA's recommendations to firms wishing to respond to unsolicited requests for off-label information, including both requests made directly and privately to firms and requests made in public forums, including through emerging electronic media. FDA recognizes that firms are capable of responding to requests about their own named products in a truthful, non-misleading, and accurate manner. Furthermore, as these firms are regulated by FDA and have robust and current information about their products, FDA recognizes that it can be in the best interest of public health for a firm to respond to unsolicited requests for information about off-label uses of the firm's products that are addressed to a public forum, as other participants in the forum who offer responses may not provide or have access to the most accurate and up-to-date information about the firm's products.

If a firm responds to unsolicited requests for off-label information in the manner described in this draft guidance, FDA does not intend to use such responses as evidence of the firm's intent that the product be used for an unapproved or uncleared use. Such responses would also not be expected to comply with the disclosure requirements related to promotional labeling and advertising. . . .

Unsolicited requests are those initiated by persons or entities that are completely independent of the relevant firm. (This may include many health care professionals, health care organizations, members of the academic community, and formulary committees, as well as consumers such as patients and caregivers). Requests that are prompted in any way by a manufacturer or its representatives are not unsolicited requests. . . .

Example . . . If a firm's sales representative mentions a use of a product that is not reflected in the product's approved labeling and invites a health care professional to request more information, resulting requests would be considered solicited requests.

Example . . . If a firm issues to health care professionals business reply cards that are intended for use in requesting off-label information, presents statements or contact information in promotional pieces in a manner that solicits requests for off-label medical or scientific information . . . or displays a commercial exhibit panel suggesting a new indication . . . requests made in response to these types of prompts would be considered solicited requests.

Example . . . A firm asks or otherwise encourages users to post videos about their own uses of its product on third-party video-sharing sites (e.g., YouTube), which may result in video postings about an off-label use of its product. If . . . any off-label video posting made in response to the firm's encouragement of video postings results in questions about the product's off-label use, these questions would be considered solicited requests.

Example . . . If a firm sends out packets of information to known bloggers or online consumer reviewers and encourages them to write about an off-label use of its product on third-party sites and this then provokes a discussion about that off-label use, any requests inquiring about the product's off-label use as a result of these blogs, whether posted as comments to the third-party site or directed to the firm, would be considered solicited requests.

Example . . . If a firm announces results of a study via a microblogging service (e.g., Twitter) and suggests that an off-label use of its product is safe and effective, any comments and requests received as a result of the original message about the off-label use would be considered solicited requests. . . .

RESPONDING TO NON-PUBLIC UNSOLICITED REQUESTS FOR OFF-LABEL INFORMATION DIRECTED TO DRUG OR MEDICAL DEVICE FIRMS

. . . .

FDA makes the following recommendations to a firm that is responding to a non-public unsolicited request for off-label information about its product that was specifically directed to the firm privately through a one-on-one communication.

1.   Information distributed in response to an unsolicited request should be provided only to the individual making the request directly to the firm as a private, one-on-one communication.

2.   Information distributed in response to an unsolicited request should be tailored to answer only the specific question(s) asked.

. . . If an unsolicited question is broad in nature, the firm should appropriately narrow the question. . . .

3.   Information distributed in response to an unsolicited request should be truthful, non-misleading, accurate, and balanced.

. . . A response should provide non-biased information or data relating to the particular off-label use that is the subject of the request, including applicable data that are not supportive or that cast doubt on the safety or efficacy of that use. For example, when conclusions of articles or texts that are disseminated have been specifically called into question by other articles or texts, a firm should disseminate representative publications that reach contrary or different conclusions regarding the use at issue. . . . The response can include unpublished data on file if they are responsive to the specific request. . . . However, to the greatest extent possible, a firm should rely on published peer-reviewed journal articles, medical texts, or data derived from independent sources. . . .

4.   Information distributed in response to an unsolicited request should be scientific in nature.

When responding to an unsolicited request for information, a firm should respond with material that is scientific in tone and presentation. The material should not be promotional in tone or presentation. Furthermore, the responsive material should not be distributed along with other material or information that is promotional in nature or tone.

5.   Responses to unsolicited requests for information should be generated by medical or scientific personnel independent from sales or marketing departments.

. . . .

RESPONDING TO PUBLIC UNSOLICITED REQUESTS FOR OFF-LABEL INFORMATION, INCLUDING THOSE ENCOUNTERED THROUGH EMERGING ELECTRONIC MEDIA BY DRUG OR MEDICAL DEVICE FIRMS

. . . [B]ecause product information posted on websites and other public electronic forums is likely to be available to a broad audience and for an indefinite period of time, FDA is concerned that firms may post detailed public online responses to questions about off-label uses of their products in such a way that they are communicating unapproved or uncleared use information about FDA-regulated medical products to individuals who have not requested such information. . . .

1.   If a firm chooses to respond to public unsolicited requests for off-label information, the firm should respond only when the request pertains specifically to its own named product (and is not solely about a competitor's product).

. . . .

2.   A firm's *public* response to public unsolicited requests for off-label information about its named product should be limited to providing the firm's contact information and should *not* include any off-label information.

- The firm's public response should convey that the question pertains to an unapproved or uncleared use of the product and state that individuals can contact the medical/scientific representative or medical affairs department with the specific unsolicited request to obtain more information.

- The firm's public response should provide specific contact information for the medical or scientific personnel or department . . . so that individuals can follow up independently with the firm to obtain specific information about the off-label use of the product through a non-public, one-on-one communication.

. . . .

3.   Representatives who provide public responses to unsolicited requests for off-label information should clearly disclose their involvement with a particular firm.

4.   Public responses to public unsolicited requests for off-label information . . . should not be promotional in nature or tone.

In addition to a firm's contact and disclosure information, a public response should include a mechanism for providing readily accessible current FDA-required labeling, if any, for the product (e.g., FDA-approved package insert and, if the response is for a consumer, FDA-approved patient labeling . . .). The public response should not provide any promotional information. . . .

NOTE

This draft guidance also includes additional detailed instructions regarding what must accompany enduring materials distributed in response to unsolicited requests. These requirements closely echo those in the 2009 *Good Reprint Practices Guidance* excerpted *infra* at p. 948.

b.   MANUFACTURER-INITIATED DISTRIBUTION OF SCIENTIFIC INFORMATION

FDA has long been ambivalent about curbing the promotional dissemination of scientific information about off-label uses because of its awareness of the First Amendment issues that would arise from a complete ban on such communications. When FDA issued guidance documents to restrict industry-supported continuing medical education (CME) programs, 62 Fed. Reg. 64074 (Dec. 3, 1997) and industry distribution of textbooks and medical journal articles, 61 Fed. Reg. 52800 (Oct. 8, 1996), its actions indeed provoked a First Amendment challenge. The Washington Legal Foundation (WLF), a conservative nonprofit legal organization, successfully argued in the U.S. District Court for the District of Columbia that these guidances violated the First Amendment rights of its physician members by unduly limiting drug manufacturers' ability to disseminate information regarding unapproved uses to them. *Washington Legal Foundation v. Friedman*, 13 F. Supp. 2d 51 (D.D.C. 1998). The court enjoined FDA from enforcing the guidances except to the extent permitted by the injunction.

By the time the court issued this decision in July 1998, section 401 of the Food and Drug Administration Modernization Act of 1997 (FDAMA) had already added FD&C Act 551, governing off-label communications. This section went into effect later in 1998, along with FDA's implementing regulations. 63 Fed. Reg. 64556 (Nov. 20, 1998), codified at 21 C.F.R. Part 99. The WLF then filed a constitutional challenge to FDAMA and these regulations as well.

Washington Legal Foundation v. Henney

56 F. Supp. 2d 81 (D.D.C. 1999).

■ LAMBERTH, DISTRICT JUDGE . . .

The provisions of the FDAMA perpetuate in part and modify in part the policies contained in the Guidance Documents. In particular, the FDAMA permits a drug manufacturer to disseminate journal articles and reference texts only under certain conditions, including the following:

1.   The drug must be the subject of an approved application or otherwise lawfully marketed.

2.   The disseminated information must be unabridged, not false or misleading, and not pose a significant risk to the public health.

3.   The information must not be derived from clinical research by another manufacturer without that manufacturer's permission.

4.   The manufacturer must submit an advance copy of the information to be disseminated to FDA along with any clinical trial information and reports of clinical experience.

5.   The manufacturer must submit a supplemental new drug application for the off-label use or have certified that such an application will be submitted within the applicable statutory deadline, unless the Secretary determines that the manufacturer is exempt from this requirement because a) such supplemental application would be prohibitively expensive or b) it would be unethical to conduct the necessary studies.

6.   The disseminated information must include a prominent disclosure that a) the material concerns an off-label use not approved by the FDA; b) the material is disseminated at the manufacturer's expense; c) identifies the authors of the information that have received compensation from or have financial interests in the manufacturer; d) includes the product's current approved labeling; e) includes a statement that there exist products approved for the particular intended use (if applicable); f) identifies the person providing funding for a study of the off-label use; and g)

gives a bibliography of other scientific articles concerning the off-label use.

7. The manufacturer must prepare and submit semi-annually to the FDA lists of the articles and reference publications disseminated and the categories of recipients.

21 U.S.C. § 360aaa [FD&C Act 551]. The plaintiff objects to most of these requirements (most forcefully to the last four) as unconstitutional and inconsistent with this Court's . . . 1998 order and injunction. . . .

As in its previous decision of July, 30, 1998 [*WLF v. Friedman*, 13 F. Supp. 2d 51 (D.D.C. 1998], the Court will analyze the constitutionality of the FDA's policies (as now contained in the FDAMA) under the four-prong inquiry articulated by the Supreme Court in *Central Hudson Gas & Electric Corp. v. Public Service Commission of New York*, 447 U.S. 557 (1980). Under *Central Hudson*, the court looks first to determine whether the speech at issue is false or inherently misleading. If the speech is truthful and nonmisleading, the government must demonstrate a substantial interest that is directly advanced by the regulation without burdening substantially more speech than necessary. . . .

The Speech is Neither Unlawful Nor Inherently Misleading

First, the Court reiterates its prior holding that the speech at issue here is neither false nor inherently misleading. It is a difficult contention indeed that the medical and scientific articles and reference texts at issue in this case are "inherently misleading." To the contrary, the defendants themselves admit to the importance of ensuring the availability of such information to physicians and health care providers making prescription and treatment decisions. Rather, the defendants argue that the manufacturers' dissemination of such information is likely to be misleading because manufacturers have an incentive to disseminate information that presents their drugs only in a positive light, omitting negative information and failing to provide the "balance" that the FDA would prefer.

This argument must fail, for at least two reasons. . . . First, "potentially misleading" speech is not proscribable under the First Amendment. The FDA may not restrict speech based on its perception that the speech could, may, or might mislead. Rather, for the protections of the First Amendment to fall away, the government must demonstrate that the restricted speech, by nature, is more likely to mislead than to inform, a demonstration which the defendants have not made here. Second, defendants' true perception of the speech at issue here is revealed by their attitude toward the same speech disseminated under other circumstances. For example, defendants have no concern over the exchange of article reprints and reference texts among physicians; more telling, defendants do not even object to a manufacturer providing such information to a health care provider upon such person's request. Only when the manufacturer initiates the exchange does the FDA choose to label the speech false or inherently misleading. . . .

The Government Has A Substantial Interest

In its July 30, 1998 decision, this Court identified two governmental interests at issue in this case: 1) ensuring that physicians receive accurate and unbiased information upon which to make prescription decisions, and 2) encouraging drug manufacturers to seek FDA-approval of off-label uses. The Court found the first of these interests unavailing and the second substantial, a determination that the Court reaffirms today. . . .

However forcefully the FDA argues the need to ensure a "balanced" flow of information to health care providers, . . . [t]he government . . . simply cannot justify a restriction of truthful nonmisleading speech on the paternalistic assumption that such restriction is necessary to protect the listener from ignorantly or inadvertently misusing the information. . . . [T]his axiom is particularly powerful where the recipient of information is a sophisticated listener trained extensively in the use of such information—as are the doctors and other health care providers in this case. . . .

The second interest advanced by defendants, and accepted by the Court in its previous ruling, is that of encouraging manufacturers to seek FDA approval of uses not yet on the labels of their products. Congress has determined that mandatory FDA approval of all drug uses benefits the public health, and . . . the Court accepts Congress's judgment on this matter. . . .

Only One of the Policies Contained in the FDAMA Directly Advances the Substantial Government Interest in Encouraging Manufacturers to Seek FDA Approval of Off-label Uses

The majority of [the FDAMA] provisions . . . directly advance the FDA's stated goal of ensuring that physicians receive accurate and balanced information. As explained above, however, that is not a substantial interest that might justify the FDA's restrictions on speech.

In contrast, only one requirement of the FDAMA can be said to directly advance the substantial governmental interest in encouraging supplemental drug applications. The FDAMA states that a manufacturer may disseminate information on off-label uses only if it has met one of the following three requirements: 1) it has submitted a supplemental application for approval of the off-label use, 2) it has certified to the FDA that such supplemental application will be forthcoming as provided in the statute, or 3) the Secretary has determined that the manufacturer is exempt from this requirement because the supplemental application would be economically prohibitive or would require unethical studies. It is abundantly clear that this requirement directly advances the interest in encouraging supplemental applications. Indeed, any manufacturer that wishes to disseminate article reprints or reference texts (on its own initiative) has no choice but to submit a supplemental application.

The Supplemental Application Requirement Is Unconstitutional Because It Burdens Substantially More Speech Than Necessary

The problem with FDAMA is not its effectiveness in encouraging supplemental drug applications, but rather the means by which it encourages such applications. The supplemental application requirement of the act amounts to a kind of constitutional blackmail—comply with the statute or sacrifice your First Amendment rights. It should go without saying that the tactic cannot survive judicial scrutiny.

. . . [I]t is worth noting here a few of the means that Congress and the FDA have *not* chosen to effectuate the substantial interest in encouraging manufacturers to seek FDA approval of off-label uses. The government has not chosen to ban the prescription of drugs for off-label uses. It has not chosen to prohibit manufacturers from profiting from off-label prescriptions. It has not chosen to impose a fine or other pecuniary penalty on manufacturers for failure to seek supplemental applications, nor has it chosen to more stringently enforce its statutory authority to prosecute misbranding. Instead, Congress and the defendants have chosen to condition the exercise of rights guaranteed by the United States Constitution upon the submission of a supplemental drug application. Such a gross imposition upon free speech is in clear violation of the First Amendment, and it cannot stand.

It also bears repeating that there currently do exist numerous incentives for manufacturers to seek approval of off-label uses. Under the Court's narrowly applicable injunction, manufacturers are still much more limited in their promotion of off-label uses than in the promotion of approved uses. The manufacturers are also undoubtedly aware of the value of FDA approval as an indication of safety and reliability, certainly important factors for health care providers choosing between competing products as they make prescription decisions.

The existing factors encouraging supplemental applications, along with the many non-speech-restrictive alternatives available to the government, highlight the degree to which the FDAMA unduly burdens commercial speech. The supplemental application requirement burdens substantially more speech than necessary to advance the government's legitimate interest, and it therefore violates the First Amendment. . . .

Having found the Food and Drug Administration Modernization Act and its implementing regulations unconstitutional, the Court hereby AMENDS, sua sponte, its Order Granting Summary Judgment and Permanent Injunction, issued July 30, 1998, to explicitly declare the FDAMA and its implementing regulations unenforceable. . . .

FINAL AMENDED ORDER GRANTING SUMMARY JUDGMENT AND PERMANENT INJUNCTION

. . . .

THE COURT HEREBY ENJOINS Defendants . . . and all persons . . . purporting to act on behalf of the United States (collectively "Defendants") from application or enforcement of any regulation, guidance, policy, order or other official action, as follows:

1.   Defendant SHALL NOT in any way prohibit, restrict, sanction or otherwise seek to limit any pharmaceutical or medical device manufacturer or any other person:

a) from disseminating or redistributing to physicians, or other medical professionals any article concerning prescription drugs or medical devices precious published in a bona fide "peer-reviewed professional journal, regardless of whether such article includes a significant or exclusive focus on unapproved uses for drugs or medical devices that are approved by FDA for other uses and regardless of whether such article reports, the original study on which FDA approval of the drug or device in question was based;

b) from disseminating or redistributing to physicians or other medical professionals any reference textbook (including any medical textbook or compendium) or any portion thereof published by a bona fide independent publisher and otherwise generally available for sale in bookstores or other distribution channels where similar books are normally available, regardless of whether such reference textbook or portion thereof includes a significant or exclusive focus on unapproved uses for drugs or medical devices that are approved by FDA for other uses.

. . . .

5. Nothing herein shall be construed to limit Defendants' application or enforcement of any rules, regulations, guidances, statutes or other provisions of law that sanction the dissemination of redistribution of any material that is false or misleading. In addition, Defendants may require any pharmaceutical or medical device manufacturer that sponsors or provides financial support for the dissemination or redistribution of articles or reference textbooks or for seminars that include references to unapproved uses for drugs or medical devices that are approved by FDA for other uses to disclose (i) its interest in such drugs or devices, and (ii) the fact that the use discussed has not been approved by FDA.

. . . .

NOTES

1. *Continuing Medical Education.* The injunction excerpted above also included provisions limiting the extent to which FDA could prohibit drug manufacturers from involvement in Continuing Medical Education (CME) Programs concerning off-label uses. (The injunction addressed this issue because one of the three FDA guidance documents challenged in 1998 concerned industry support of educational activities.) The injunction forbade any restrictions on drug and device manufacturers "suggesting content or speakers to an independent program provider in connection with a continuing medical education seminar program or other symposium regardless of whether unapproved uses for drugs or medical devices that are approved by FDA for other uses are to be discussed."

2. *Decisions and Injunction Vacated.* During oral argument before the court of appeals, FDA—reversing its former position—contended that both FD&C Act 551 and the FDA CME guidance were only "safe harbors" and did not independently authorize FDA to prohibit or to sanction speech. Accordingly, the court dismissed FDA's appeal and vacated the district court decisions and injunction, explaining, "[W]e do not think it at all appropriate to rule on the constitutionality of a hypothetical interpretation

of a statute." *Washington Legal Foundation v. Henney*, 202 F.3d 331, 336 (D.C. Cir. 2000). Nonetheless, the court remarked, "In disposing of the case in this manner, we certainly do not criticize the reasoning or conclusions of the district court." *Id.* at 337 n. 7.

3. *FDA Embrace of Injunction.* After some initial hedging, criticized in *Washington Legal Foundation v. Henney*, 128 F. Supp. 2d 11 (D.D.C. 2000), FDA in 2002 determined as a matter of policy that it would not bring legal action against any off-label promotion that complied with the now-dissolved injunction of the District Court. "Because FDA must choose carefully where to deploy its limited resources, FDA is unlikely to initiate an enforcement action where the only evidence of an unapproved intended use is the distribution of enduring materials or sponsorship of CME." Letter from Margaret M. Dotzel, FDA Associate Commissioner for Policy, to Daniel J. Popeo & Richard A. Samp (Jan. 28, 2002).

4. *Independently Published and Distributed Journal Articles.* In Compliance Policy Guide Sec. 400.700 (1989), FDA determined that an article about a prescription drug in an independent publication is generally not to be regarded as advertising (or labeling) for the drug—whether or not the drug is also separately advertised in the same publication—if the manufacturer makes no contribution to the article and does not use the article for promotional purposes.

———

FD&C Act 551, recognized by both FDA and industry after the *WLF* litigation as merely a "safe harbor" provision, *see supra* note 2, sunsetted in 2006. FDA then issued the following guidance document.

Guidance for Industry: Good Reprint Practices for the Distribution of Medical Journal Articles and Medical or Scientific Reference Publications on Unapproved New Uses of Approved Drugs and Approved or Cleared Medical Devices

January 2009.

... In light of [FD&C Act 401's] sunset, FDA is providing its current views on the dissemination of medical journal articles and medical or scientific reference publications on unapproved uses of approved drugs and approved or cleared medical devices to healthcare professionals and healthcare entities.

. . . .

... When a manufacturer disseminates such medical and scientific information, FDA recommends that the following principles of "Good Reprint Practices" be followed.

A. *Types of Reprints/Articles/Reference Publications*

A scientific or medical journal article that is distributed should:

• be published by an organization that has an editorial board that uses experts who have demonstrated expertise in the subject of the article under review by the organization and who are independent of the organization to review and objectively select, reject, or provide comments about proposed articles; and that has a publicly stated policy, to which the organization adheres, of full disclosure of any conflict of interest or biases for all authors, contributors, or editors associated with the journal or organization;

- be peer-reviewed and published in accordance with the peer-review procedures of the organization; and

- not be in the form of a special supplement or publication that has been funded in whole or in part by one or more of the manufacturers of the product that is the subject of the article.

A scientific or medical reference publication that is distributed should not be:

- primarily distributed by a drug or device manufacturer but should be generally available in . . . independent distribution channels. . . .

- written, edited, excerpted, or published specifically for, or at the request of, a drug or device manufacturer; or

- edited or significantly influenced by a drug or device manufacturer or any individuals having a financial relationship with the manufacturer.

The information contained in the scientific or medical journal article or reference publication should address adequate and well-controlled clinical investigations that are considered scientifically sound by experts with scientific training and experience to evaluate the safety or effectiveness of the drug or device. . . .

The information must not:

- be false or misleading. For example, a distributed journal article or reference text should not be characterized as definitive or representative of the weight of credible evidence derived from adequate and well-controlled clinical investigations if it is inconsistent with that weight of credible evidence or a significant number of other studies contradict the article or reference text's conclusions; . . .

- pose a significant risk to the public health, if relied upon.

The following publications are examples of publications that would not be considered consistent with the "Good Reprint Practices" outlined in this guidance:

- letters to the editor;

- abstracts of a publication;

- reports of Phase 1 trials in healthy subjects; or

- reference publications that contain little or no substantive discussion of the relevant investigation or data.

B.   *Manner in which to Disseminate Scientific and Medical Information*

Scientific or medical information that is distributed should:

- be in the form of an unabridged reprint, copy of an article, or reference publication;
- not be marked, highlighted, summarized, or characterized by the manufacturer in any way (except to provide the accompanying disclosures discussed in this section);
- be accompanied by the approved labeling for the drug or medical device;
- be accompanied, when such information exists, by a comprehensive bibliography of publications discussing adequate and well-controlled clinical studies published in medical journals or medical or scientific texts about the use of the drug or medical device covered by the information disseminated. . . . ;
- be disseminated with a representative publication, when such information exists, that reaches contrary or different conclusions regarding the unapproved use . . . ; and
- be distributed separately from information that is promotional in nature. For example, if a sales representative delivers a reprint to a physician in his office, the reprint . . . should not be the subject of discussion between the sales representative and the physician during the sales visit. Similarly, while reprints may be distributed at medical or scientific conferences in settings appropriate for scientific exchange, reprints should not be distributed in promotional exhibit halls or during promotional speakers' programs.

The journal reprint or reference publication should be accompanied by a prominently displayed and permanently affixed statement disclosing:

- that the uses described in the information have not been approved or cleared by FDA, as applicable to the described drug or medical device;
- the manufacturer's interest in the drug or medical device that is the subject of the journal reprint or reference text;
- any author known to the manufacturer as having a financial interest in the product or manufacturer or who is receiving compensation from the manufacturer . . . and the nature and amount of any such financial interest . . . or compensation. . . .
- any person known to the manufacturer who has provided funding for the study; and
- all significant risks or safety concerns known to the manufacturer concerning the unapproved use that are not discussed in the journal article or reference text.

. . . . FDA does not intend to consider the distribution of such medical and scientific information in accordance with the recommendations in this guidance as establishing intent that the product be used for an unapproved new use. . . .

c. OTHER SPEECH ABOUT UNAPPROVED USES PROTECTED BY THE
FIRST AMENDMENT

With the following 2012 opinion, the U.S. Court of Appeals for the
Second Circuit cast uncertainty over the question of what other types of
communication from manufacturers about off-label uses might be
protected by the First Amendment.

United States v. Caronia

703 F.3d 149 (2nd Cir. 2012).

■ CHIN, CIRCUIT JUDGE

Defendant-appellant Alfred Caronia appeals from a judgment of
conviction entered in the United States District Court for the Eastern
District of New York ... following a jury trial at which Caronia was
found guilty of conspiracy to introduce a misbranded drug into
interstate commerce, a misdemeanor violation of 21 U.S.C. §§ 331(a)
and 333(a)(1). Specifically, Caronia, a pharmaceutical sales
representative, promoted the drug Xyrem for "off-label use," that is, for
a purpose not approved by the U.S. Food and Drug Administration.
Caronia argues that he was convicted for his speech—for promoting an
FDA-approved drug for off-label use—in violation of his right of free
speech under the First Amendment. We agree. . . .

STATEMENT OF THE CASE . . .

Orphan Medical, Inc., ... manufactured the drug Xyrem, a
powerful central nervous system depressant. In 2005, after Jazz
Pharmaceuticals acquired Orphan, Jazz continued to manufacture and
sell Xyrem. . . .

Xyrem can cause serious side effects, including difficulty breathing
while asleep, confusion, abnormal thinking, depression, nausea,
vomiting, dizziness, headache, bedwetting, and sleepwalking. If abused,
Xyrem can cause additional medical problems, including seizures,
dependence, severe withdrawal, coma, and death.

Xyrem's active ingredient is gamma-hydroxybutryate ("GHB").
GHB has been federally classified as the "date rape drug" for its use in
the commission of sexual assaults.

. . . In July 2002, the FDA approved Xyrem to treat narcolepsy
patients who experience cataplexy, a condition associated with weak or
paralyzed muscles. In November 2005, the FDA approved Xyrem to
treat narcolepsy patients with excessive daytime sleepiness
("EDS"). . . .

To protect against its serious safety concerns, in 2002, the FDA
required a "black box" warning to accompany Xyrem ... stat[ing],
among other things, that the drug's safety and efficacy were not
established in patients under 16 years of age, and the drug had "very
limited" experience among elderly patients.

To identify patients suffering side effects from the drug, the FDA
also regulated Xyrem distribution, allowing only one centralized
Missouri pharmacy to distribute Xyrem nationally.

In March 2005, Orphan hired Caronia as a Specialty Sales Consultant to promote Xyrem. . . .

In July 2005, Caronia started Orphan's "speaker programs" for Xyrem. Speaker programs enlist physicians, for pay, to speak to other physicians about FDA-approved drug use. Orphan's speaker programs for Xyrem presented the benefits of the drug among patients with cataplexy and narcolepsy. Orphan hired Dr. Peter Gleason to promote Xyrem through its speaker programs.

. . . .

In the spring of 2005, the federal government launched an investigation of Orphan and Gleason. . . . Caronia and Gleason were audio-recorded on two occasions as they promoted Xyrem for unapproved uses, including unapproved indications and unapproved subpopulations. . . . [to] Dr. Stephen Charno, a physician who, as a government cooperator, posed as a prospective Xyrem customer.

On October 26, 2005, Caronia plainly promoted the use of Xyrem in unapproved indications with Charno:

[Caronia]: And right now the indication is for narcolepsy with cataplexy . . . excessive daytime . . . and fragmented sleep, but because of the properties that . . . it has it's going to insomnia, Fibromyalgia[,] periodic leg movement, restless leg, ahh also looking at ahh Parkinson's and . . . other sleep disorders are underway such as MS.

[Charno]: Okay, so then so then it could be used for muscle disorders and chronic pain and . . .

[Caronia]: Right.

[Charno]: . . . and daytime fatigue and excessive sleepiness and stuff like that?

[Caronia]: Absolutely. Absolutely. Ahh with the Fibromyalgia.

Caronia further directed Charno to list different "diagnosis codes" when prescribing Xyrem, for insurance purposes, including Fibromyalgia, chronic fatigue, or chronic pain.

On separate occasions, Caronia and Gleason each explained to prospective physician-customers that Xyrem could be used with patients under age sixteen, an unapproved Xyrem subpopulation. . . .

On October 23, 2008, the jury found Caronia guilty as to . . . conspiracy to introduce a misbranded drug into interstate commerce under 18 U.S.C. § 371(a) and 21 U.S.C. § 331(a). . . .

. . . [T]he district court sentenced Caronia to one year of probation, 100 hours of community service, and a $25 special assessment.

. . . .

DISCUSSION

On appeal, Caronia principally argues that the misbranding provisions of the FDCA prohibit off-label promotion, and therefore, unconstitutionally restrict speech. Caronia argues that the First Amendment does not permit the government to prohibit and criminalize a pharmaceutical manufacturer's truthful and non-misleading promotion of an FDA-approved drug to physicians for off-label use where such use is not itself illegal and others are permitted to engage in such speech.

. . . We agree that Caronia's conviction must be vacated, but for narrower reasons than he urges.

. . . [U]nder the principle of constitutional avoidance, explained *infra*, we construe the FDCA as not criminalizing the simple promotion of a drug's off-label use because such a construction would raise First Amendment concerns. Because we conclude from the record in this case that the government prosecuted Caronia for mere off-label promotion and the district court instructed the jury that it could convict on that theory, we vacate the judgment of conviction.

. . . .

I.   *Speech versus Evidence of Intent*

The government contends—and the dissent agrees—that the First Amendment is not implicated in this case. Specifically, the government argues that . . . "the promotion of off-label uses plays an *evidentiary* role in determining whether a drug is misbranded under 21 U.S.C. § 352(f)(1)." The government contends that Caronia was not prosecuted for his speech, but that Caronia's promotion of Xyrem for off-label use served merely as "evidence of intent," or evidence that the "off-label uses were intended ones[ ] for which Xyrem's labeling failed to provide any directions."

Even assuming the government can offer evidence of a defendant's off-label promotion to prove a drug's intended use and, thus, mislabeling for that intended use,[9] that is not what happened in this case.

. . . [T]he government's assertion . . . that it used Caronia's efforts to promote Xyrem for off-label use only as evidence of intent is simply not true. Even if the government could have used Caronia's speech as evidence of intent, the district court record clearly shows that the government did not so limit its use of that evidence. . . . The government never suggested that Caronia engaged in any form of misbranding other than the promotion of the off-label use of an FDA-approved drug.

. . . [T]he government clearly prosecuted Caronia for his words—for his speech. . . .

II.   *The Prosecution of Caronia's Speech*

To the extent there is any ambiguity as to whether off-label promotion is tantamount to illegal misbranding, we construe the FDCA narrowly to avoid a serious constitutional question. . . .

As we now explain, we decline . . . to construe the FDCA's misbranding provisions to criminalize the simple promotion of a drug's off-label use by pharmaceutical manufacturers and their representatives because such a construction . . . would run afoul of the First Amendment.

---

[9] *See Wisconsin v. Mitchell*, 508 U.S. 476, 489 (1993) (concluding First Amendment "does not prohibit the use of speech to establish . . . intent"); *Whitaker v. Thompson*, 353 F.3d 947 (D.C. Cir. 2004) (holding product's labeling may be used to infer its intended use and, thus, whether it is an unapproved drug under FDCA).

A. *Applicable First Amendment Doctrine . . .*

In applying [First Amendment] principles, we have a benefit not available to the district court: the Supreme Court's decision in *Sorrell v. IMS Health, Inc.,* 131 S. Ct. 2653 (2011), a case involving speech restrictions on pharmaceutical marketing. In *Sorrell,* the Vermont Prescription Confidentiality Law (the "VPCL") prohibited pharmaceutical companies and similar entities from using prescriber-identifying information for marketing purposes; it was challenged on First Amendment grounds.

The *Sorrell* Court held that "[s]peech in aid of pharmaceutical marketing . . . is a form of expression protected by the . . . First Amendment. . . ." The Court held that the Vermont statute set forth content- and speaker-based restrictions, and that the statute was therefore subject to heightened scrutiny. Because the VPCL disfavored speech with a particular content (marketing) when expressed by certain disfavored speakers (pharmaceutical manufacturers), the Court held that it unconstitutionally restricted speech.

. . . The Court did not decide the level of heightened scrutiny to be applied, that is, strict, intermediate, or some other form of heightened scrutiny. *Id.* Rather, after observing that "[i]n the ordinary case, it is all but dispositive to conclude that a law is content-based," the Court concluded that the Vermont statute was unconstitutional even under the lesser intermediate standard set forth in *Central Hudson. . . .*

B. *Application*

First, we conclude that the government's construction of the FDCA's misbranding provisions imposes content- and speaker-based restrictions on speech subject to heightened scrutiny. Second, we conclude the government cannot justify a criminal prohibition of off-label promotion even under Central Hudson's less rigorous intermediate test.

1. *Heightened Scrutiny*

. . . [T]he government's interpretation of the FDCA's misbranding provisions to prohibit off-label promotion is content-based because it distinguishes between "favored speech" and "disfavored speech on the basis of the ideas or views expressed." Under this construction, speech about the government-approved use of drugs is permitted, while certain speech about the off-label use of drugs—that is, uses not approved by the government—is prohibited, even though the off-label use itself is not. . . .

. . . [T]his construction is speaker-based because it targets one kind of speaker—pharmaceutical manufacturers—while allowing others to speak without restriction. . . .

Accordingly, the government's construction of the FDCA's misbranding provisions to prohibit and criminalize off-label promotion is content- and speaker-based, and subject to heightened scrutiny under *Sorrell.*

2. *Central Hudson*

The first two prongs of *Central Hudson* are easily satisfied here. First, promoting off-label drug use concerns lawful activity (off-label drug use), and the promotion of off-label drug use is not in and of itself false or misleading.[11] Second, the government's asserted interests in drug safety and public health are substantial. Specifically, the government asserts an interest in preserving the effectiveness and integrity of the FDCA's drug approval process, and an interest in reducing patient exposure to unsafe and ineffective drugs.

. . . We turn to the third and fourth prongs. . . .

a. *Direct Advancement*

The government's construction of the FDCA as prohibiting off-label promotion does not . . . withstand scrutiny under *Central Hudson's* third prong. First . . . [a]s off-label drug use itself is not prohibited, it does not follow that prohibiting the truthful promotion of off-label drug usage by a particular class of speakers would directly further the government's goals of preserving the efficacy and integrity of the FDA's drug approval process and reducing patient exposure to unsafe and ineffective drugs.

Second, prohibiting off-label promotion by a pharmaceutical manufacturer while simultaneously allowing off-label use "paternalistically" interferes with the ability of physicians and patients to receive potentially relevant treatment information; such barriers to information about off-label use could inhibit, to the public's detriment, informed and intelligent treatment decisions. . . . In fact, in granting safe harbor to manufacturers by permitting the dissemination of off-label information through scientific journals, the FDA itself "recognizes that public health can be served when health care professionals receive truthful and non-misleading scientific and medical information on unapproved uses" of approved drugs. [Citing Guidance on Good Reprint Practices (2009), excerpted *supra* p. 948].

Here, as the FDA recognizes, it is the physician's role to consider multiple factors, including a drug's FDA-approval status, to determine the best course of action for her patient. . . . [I]n the fields of medicine and public health, "where information can save lives," it only furthers the public interest to ensure that decisions about the use of prescription drugs, including off-label usage, are intelligent and well-informed.

The government's construction of the FDCA essentially legalizes the outcome—off-label use—but prohibits the free flow of information that would inform that outcome. If the government's objective is to shepherd physicians to prescribe drugs only on-label, criminalizing manufacturer promotion of off-label use while permitting others to promote such use to physicians is an indirect and questionably effective means to achieve that goal. Thus, the government's construction of the FDCA's misbranding provisions does not directly advance its interest in reducing patient exposure to off-label drugs or in preserving the efficacy of the FDA drug approval process because the off-label use of such drugs continues to be generally lawful. . . .

---

[11] The government does not contend that off-label promotion is in and of itself false or misleading. Of course, off-label promotion that is false or misleading is not entitled to First Amendment protection. . . .

The government did not argue at trial, nor does it argue on appeal, that the promotion in question was false or misleading.

b.   *Narrowly Drawn*

The last prong of *Central Hudson* requires the government's regulation to be narrowly drawn to further the interests served. Here, the government's construction of the FDCA to impose a complete and criminal ban on off-label promotion by pharmaceutical manufacturers is more extensive than necessary to achieve the government's substantial interests. Numerous, less speech-restrictive alternatives are available, as are non-criminal penalties.

To advance the integrity of the FDA's drug approval process and increase the safety of off-label drug use, the government could pursue several alternatives without excessive First Amendment restrictions. For example, if the government is concerned about the use of drugs off-label, it could more directly address the issue. If the government is concerned that off-label promotion may mislead physicians, it could guide physicians and patients in differentiating between misleading and false promotion, exaggerations and embellishments, and truthful or non-misleading information. The government could develop its warning or disclaimer systems, or develop safety tiers within the off-label market, to distinguish between drugs. The government could require pharmaceutical manufacturers to list all applicable or intended indications when they first apply for FDA approval, enabling physicians, the government, and patients to track a drug's development. To minimize off-label use, or manufacturer evasion of the approval process for such use, the government could create other limits, including ceilings or caps on off-label prescriptions. The FDA could further remind physicians and manufacturers of, and even perhaps further regulate, the legal liability surrounding off-label promotion and treatment decisions. Finally, where off-label drug use is exceptionally concerning, the government could prohibit the off-label use altogether. . . . The possibilities are numerous indeed.

. . . The government contends that these alternative means of reducing patient exposure to unsafe, untested drugs and maintaining the integrity of the FDA-approval process are "indefensible," because they are not administrable, feasible, or otherwise effective. In the absence of any support, such conclusory assertions are insufficient to sustain the government's burden of demonstrating that the proposed alternatives are less effective than its proposed construction of the FDCA in furthering the government interests identified.

Accordingly, even if speech can be used as evidence of a drug's intended use, we decline to adopt the government's construction of the FDCA's misbranding provisions to prohibit manufacturer promotion alone as it would unconstitutionally restrict free speech. We construe the misbranding provisions of the FDCA as not prohibiting and criminalizing the truthful off-label promotion of FDA-approved prescription drugs. . . .

CONCLUSION

For the reasons set forth above, we VACATE the judgment of conviction and REMAND the case to the district court.

4. PREAPPROVAL PROMOTION

As NDA approval approaches, a company may wish to begin advising the medical profession that the drug may soon be available. However, 21 C.F.R. 312.7(a) prohibits a sponsor from representing "in a promotional context" that an investigational new drug is safe or effective and from otherwise promoting the drug. FDA takes the position that there may be a "full exchange of scientific information" relating to an investigational drug prior to NDA approval, but that promotion of the drug constitutes illegal commercialization. *Id.* Nonetheless, press releases that simply announce events in the regulatory approval process are unlikely to raise FDA concern. Similarly, press releases that merely report factual data relating to scientific studies, and that avoid any statement that the drug is safe or effective, have raised no FDA objections.

In a 1989 speech, an FDA representative voiced what appears to be the agency's main concern with preapproval promotion: "Many times it appears these activities are designed, not for scientific dialogue, but to try to get a drug used for a wide variety of uses which the company knows they will not get approval for." Speech by Kenneth R. Feather, Acting Dir. FDA Div. of Drug Advert. & Labeling (Mar. 14, 1989). Such communications may also lack warnings and contraindications that FDA will require in the labeling when it approves the drug.

In PRE-APPROVAL PROMOTION, a guidance originally issued in 1982 and revised and reissued in April 1986, FDA stated that preapproval promotion is not allowed except in one of the following two ways: (1) institutional promotions stating that a specifically named drug company is conducting research in a therapeutic area to develop new and important drugs without mentioning any drug name, and (2) "coming soon" promotions announcing the name of a new product that will be available soon, but without any direct or implied representations concerning the safety, effectiveness, or intended use of the product. FDA stated that a sponsor could not use both types of advertisements simultaneously or switch types during the promotional campaign prior to product approval. This guidance was issued before recent judicial decisions applying the First Amendment to FDA advertising policy, however, and it is uncertain that it would withstand constitutional scrutiny.

J. OVER-THE-COUNTER DRUGS

1. DISTINGUISHING BETWEEN PRESCRIPTION AND NONPRESCRIPTION DRUGS

Section 503(b)(1) of the FD&C Act, added by the Durham–Humphrey Amendments of 1951, makes the act of dispensing a prescription drug without a valid prescription a statutory violation. *See supra* p. 805. Furthermore, section 503(b)(1)(A) sets forth the factors FDA must consider in determining whether a drug should be limited to prescription sale in the first place. Applying the criteria in section 503(b)(1) to a particular drug is not always a simple matter, however, as demonstrated by the following case.

United States v. Article of Drug . . . "Decholin"

264 F. Supp. 473 (E.D. Mich. 1967).

■ FREEMAN, DISTRICT JUDGE. . . .

The Government commenced the case by filing a libel of information for condemnation of seventy-three packages bearing approximately ten thousand tablets, each of which contained 250 milligrams (3 3/4 grains) of dehydrocholic acid and was marketed under the trade name "Decholin." Ames Company, Inc., the manufacturer of Decholin, intervened in this in rem proceeding as claimant of the seized articles. . . .

The only substantive provision of concern is Federal Food, Drug and Cosmetic Act, § 503 . . . reading in pertinent part:

(b)(1) A drug intended for use by man which—

. . . .

(B) because of its toxicity or other potentiality for harmful effect, or the method of its use, or the collateral measures necessary to its use, is not safe for use except under the supervision of a practitioner licensed by law to administer such drug . . .*

(C) . . . . shall be dispensed only [upon prescription]. . . .

The reverse side of the containers gives this . . . information: "INDICATIONS: Indigestion . . . after-meal discomfort and fullness (particularly after fatty meals) . . . excessive belching . . . constipation. . . . CAUTION: Consult your physician should symptoms persist or severe abdominal pain, nausea and vomiting appear." . . .

There is only one fundamental issue presented by these [cross] motions [for summary judgment]: is Decholin unsafe as a drug intended for human use without a prescription? Nevertheless, recognizing that in section 503(b)(1)(B) Congress listed a number of ostensibly different reasons why a drug may be unsafe for self-medication and attempting to deal with the parties' arguments in an organized fashion, the motions will be viewed as raising two issues. First, is the pharmacological effect of Decholin such that, unless it is taken pursuant to and in accordance with a physician's directions, reactions sufficient to cause the product to be unsafe may result from its ingestion? This will be called the "toxicity question." Second, does the fact that Decholin may be taken by a person who, although experiencing the indications set out on the label, has an ailment which Decholin cannot cure, coupled with the fact such an individual may postpone a visit to his physician in reliance upon the over-the-counter availability of Decholin, cause the drug to be unsafe? Because the gist of the Government's argument on this issue is that an immediate professional diagnosis to detect the underlying cause of the symptoms in a particular case is a step which must precede or accompany use in order for the drug to be considered safe, this point will be called the collateral measures question. . . .

At the basis of both questions lies the fact that the indications mentioned on the Decholin container can stem from any one of what, for present purposes, will be considered as three types of causes: biliary

---

*   [This language now appears at FD&C Act 503(b)(1)(A). EDS.]

tract obstruction, organic disease and various minor factors. These last include a host of elements ranging from pregnancy through dietary indiscretions, such as skipping meals, and on to old age. Claimant willingly agrees with the Government that Decholin would not be prescribed by a physician to cure either a tract obstruction or an organic disease.

Toxicity Question

If the record showed clearly why a practitioner would not order Decholin for a person suffering from an obstruction or an organic disease, the toxicity question could be in better posture for summary disposition. However, the affidavits of the experts suggest different reasons which may be grounded upon conflicting views on a factual issue, the pharmacological effect of the drug. The statements of claimant's authorities suggest that they would not prescribe Decholin in the presence of one of these major ailments primarily, if not exclusively, just because the drug would do no good for the patient. However, these experts are quick to point out that they have never heard of an instance in which a person with either an obstruction or an organic disease sustained any ill effect from self-medication with Decholin; and at least several of them doubt that harm would ever come to an individual who takes the drug under these circumstances. . . .

. . . [T]he affidavit of Dr. Manuel Sklar . . . is most helpful in showing why the Government considers the drug properly dispensed only on prescription. . . . [I]n his opinion, the product solely by virtue of its composition can be injurious to an individual with an ailment giving rise to Decholin's indications but beyond Decholin's power to cure. . . .

Even the Government's most helpful spokesman, Dr. Sklar, did not mention that he knew or had heard of a case in which Decholin or any article of similar composition had done harm in any perceptible degree to a layman who had taken the preparation, without consulting a physician upon experiencing the indications listed on the Decholin label. This is not surprising since the Government admitted in answer to interrogatories that it knew of no actual cases of harm attributable to the product.[5] On the other hand, statements made by three of the claimant's experts leave the strong impression that the principal reason why they would consider Decholin safe for self-medication is the fact that their experiences have taught them that a person suffering from an organic disease or a biliary tract obstruction will feel so ill that, as a matter of course, he will seek professional help. Therefore, claimant's experts do not seem to be so much of the opinion that home treatment with Decholin *cannot* cause harm as they do of the view that it *will not*; whereas the Government's affiants stress that Decholin could cause harm to the uninformed lay user, while the Government itself all but concedes that if future unadvised laymen act as their predecessors have, the drug will not be responsible for any serious consequences. . . .

Even if it were apparent from the record that both sides conceded the theoretical possibility of harm from self-medication with Decholin but admitted that, as a practical matter, the likelihood of ill effects is

---

[5]   The record shows that the use of Decholin type medicines has been extensive. Since 1926, claimant and its predecessor corporations alone have sold over six tenths of a billion dehydrocholic acid tables under one or another tradename.

virtually nonexistent, the Court would not feel confident in granting either motion until it has been made aware of the nature of the factors which claimant would say separate the practical order from the theoretical. . . .

The legislative history of the 1951 amendment, which gave birth to section 503(b)(1)(B), shows that Congress did not desire to proscribe self-medication with a product just because under some set of circumstances—and especially hypothetical conditions—the drug may be harmful if taken without professional supervision. . . .

Collateral Measures Question. . . .

The Government in this case has raised the point that a layman cannot determine whether he is suffering from a disorder such as a tract obstruction or a disease like jaundice, although he can compare his symptoms with the indications mentioned on the Decholin label. However, . . . the pertinent question is not whether an individual is able to detect the cause of his ailment, but rather whether the symptoms described on the package as reasons for him to visit a physician are sufficient to alert him to the possibility that his illness may require professional attention. . . .

As the foregoing discussion indicates, there are not only differences of opinion in the record concerning pertinent factual issues, but also an absence from the record at this time of evidence relating to many of the factors which must be considered before the outcome of this case can be decided. For these reasons, both motions for summary judgment are denied.

NOTE

Following the denial of the cross-motions for summary judgment, the case was dismissed with prejudice to FDA and the seized drug was ordered released to Ames. 2 FDA Papers, No. 9, at 34 (Nov. 1968). *See also United States v. General Nutrition, Inc.,* 638 F. Supp. 556 (W.D.N.Y. 1986).

2.   SWITCH FROM PRESCRIPTION TO NONPRESCRIPTION STATUS

Section 503(b)(1)(B) provides that FDA may require a new drug to be sold only on prescription as part of its decision to approve a new drug application. Virtually all new chemical entity drugs enter the market initially as prescription drugs and become eligible for consideration for a switch to OTC status only after at least five years of marketing. This waiting period assures FDA that there are unlikely to be major undiscovered adverse events. Switches of Rx drugs to OTC status will provide virtually all new nonprescription drugs in the future.

A drug may be switched from Rx to OTC status in four ways. First, FDA can implement a switch through notice-and-comment rulemaking, either on its own initiative or in response to a petition. This mechanism, set forth at 21 C.F.R. 310.200, implements FD&C Act 503(b)(3), which provides that the agency may, by regulation, change a drug to over-the-counter status when the prescription status mandated by its NDA approval is no longer "necessary for the protection of the public health."

A first wave of OTC switches occurred pursuant to this method between 1955 and 1971. Most or all of the resulting "switch regulations"—which are listed in 21 C.F.R. 310.201—were initiated by the agency. Probably the most prominent of the medications switched in this manner was acetaminophen (Tylenol®). 20 Fed. Reg. 3499 (May 19, 1955), now codified at 21 C.F.R. 310.201(a)(1).

Second, a switch in status may occur through the mechanisms of the OTC Drug Review, examined in detail below. *Infra* p. 973. Although the Review was established in the early 1970s primarily to determine the effectiveness of drug ingredients that were already sold over-the-counter prior to passage of the 1962 Drug Amendments, the resulting "monographs" listing legal OTC ingredients also embraced some previously Rx-only products. The OTC Drug Review was responsible for a second surge of switches, which commenced in the early 1970s. Between the 1970s and the early 1990s, FDA switched approximately 32 active drug ingredients through this mechanism, including, for example, hydrocortisone and various cough and cold products. With the near-completion of the OTC Drug Review, this mode of switching has become largely irrelevant today.

Third, the holder of an NDA (including a section 505(b)(2) NDA or an abbreviated NDA for a generic drug) may submit a supplemental NDA requesting FDA to approve a switch to OTC status. Most of the switches that have occurred since the late 1980s have been implemented in this way, almost always through approval of SNDAs filed by name-brand manufacturers. The many important drugs switched from prescription to OTC status by this method include, for example, ibuprofen (Advil®), loperamide (Imodium®), clotrimazole (Gyne-Lotrimin®), famotidine (Pepcid AC®), nicotine polacrilex (Nicorette®), and loratadine (Claritin®).

Fourth, after a prescription drug goes off patent, any person may submit a section 505(b)(2) NDA to switch the drug from Rx to OTC. This is the method by which generic versions of OTC Claritin reached the market. *See infra* p. 972, note 2. Section 505(b)(2) NDAs are discussed *infra* at p. 1012.

Peter Barton Hutt, *A Legal Framework for Future Decisions on Transferring Drugs From Prescription to Nonprescription Status*

37 FOOD DRUG COSMETIC LAW JOURNAL 427 (1982).

. . . FDA has never enunciated either in published regulations or in other written documents the kind of operational rules that would provide clear policy and result in consistent decisions on the prescription/nonprescription status of drugs in this country. . . .

[Section 503(b)(1)(A)] contains three factors to be considered in determining the prescription/nonprescription status of a drug: (1) toxicity, (2) potentiality for harmful effect, and (3) the method of use or collateral measures necessary to use . . .

1. Toxicity. The first factor, toxicity, is perhaps the most easily understood and applied. Drugs that have a low margin of safety, and which must therefore be titrated carefully to achieve an adequate level of effectiveness without endangering patient safety, are appropriately placed in prescription status. With increasing scientific sophistication in the field of pharmacology, and the recognition that life-threatening drugs may be needed to treat life-threatening disease, there will undoubtedly always be at least some drugs too toxic for OTC marketing.

At the same time, it must be recognized that the mere possibility that a drug could be misused, with toxic results, is not sufficient by itself to retain that drug in prescription status. As the court recognized in the *Decholin* case, virtually any drug can be misused with some toxic results. . . .

As with all of the factors described in this paper, it is not feasible now, and undoubtedly will not be feasible in the future, to derive operational definitions or empirical formulas for determining appropriate margins of safety. Toxicity, like each of the other factors described below, is simply one factor to be considered as part of an integrated decision. . . .

2.   Other potentiality for harmful effect. The statute does not limit FDA to questions simply relating to toxicity. . . . Rather, FDA is permitted a broad inquiry into other potentiality for harmful effects as well. . . .

It is undoubtedly not feasible to anticipate all of the various possible considerations that fall within this factor of potential for other harmful effects. It is important, however, to note that some considerations that represent valid public health concerns do not properly fall within this factor. Two that immediately come to mind are the potential for tampering with OTC drug products and the possibility that some OTC drug ingredients might be substituted for serious drugs of abuse in counterfeit drug sales on the street. . . .

3.   Method of use and collateral measures necessary to use. Congress intended this factor to have the broadest possible scope. It encompasses all aspects of the circumstances under which a drug is used, including broad questions of social policy. There is perhaps no issue involving drug use that cannot properly be brought into consideration under this factor.

a.   Self-diagnosis. Many people erroneously believe that a drug must be placed on prescription status for any condition for which self-diagnosis is not feasible. In fact, self-diagnosis is not a statutory prerequisite for OTC status and the law has not been applied by FDA in that way. . . .

Numerous OTC drugs are presently available for conditions that are not susceptible to self-diagnosis to lay people. The classic example is insulin. No lay person would be trusted to diagnose diabetes. Nor is that an isolated example. Many minor conditions for which OTC drugs are available could be the result of a wide variety of diseases. . . . Upset stomach . . . could be caused by food poisoning, gastric cancer, too much alcoholic beverage or rich food, excess stomach acid, or an ulcer. Yet no one questions the OTC status of appropriate home remedies for this condition. And analgesics are available for headaches even though no lay person is capable of diagnosing the difference between a headache caused by simple stress and a headache caused by a concussion or a brain tumor. . . .

    b.   Self-treatment and self-care. Another consideration frequently mentioned as a major element in any prescription/nonprescription determination is the need for a doctor to supervise the administration of the drug and to monitor the patient's progress. . . . Today, it remains one consideration, but not nearly as important as it once was. . . .

    With rare exception, self-administration of any drug by a lay person is entirely feasible. It is useful to remember that a major OTC drug, insulin, is administered by injection. . . .

    The vast majority of our population is now fully capable of listening to, understanding, and complying with instructions for self-treatment and self-care. Most people—and particularly those suffering from chronic illness, who must take drugs for long periods of time and perhaps the rest of their lives—are quite capable of appreciating the interaction of daily self-treatment and periodic visits to a physician who can then monitor overall progress. . . .

    c.   Adequate labeling. This consideration is receiving more attention than ever before, and undoubtedly will become, with toxicity and abuse potential, the most important consideration in determining prescription/nonprescription status in the future. The quintessential requirement for any OTC drug must be adequate directions for use. . . .

    d.   Social policy. Neither the FD&C Act nor its legislative history includes, in specific terms, any reference to broad social policy. It is readily apparent, however, that many determinations of prescription/nonprescription status depend in large measure upon unarticulated principles of social policy.

    Societal concerns must always be considered in any decision on prescription/nonprescription status. The panel that considered the prescription/nonprescription status of oral contraceptives, as part of the OTC Drug Review, undoubtedly spent more time discussing broad questions of social policy than narrow questions of toxicity. The status of drugs used to treat venereal disease would undoubtedly raise similar considerations.

    The importance of having particular drugs available readily and cheaply for public use is also a major consideration. . . . The cost of adequate professional care for the poor and the elderly will undoubtedly be a major factor in future decisions about the possibility of transferring drugs used in chronic disease from prescription to OTC status. These are valid considerations, to be encouraged rather than discouraged, as society attempts to come to grips with the need to provide the best possible medical care for its divergent population at the least possible cost.

    The concerns of the medical and pharmacy professions must also be considered. Physicians are torn between their concern about permitting important prescription drugs to leave their control, and their realization that many unproductive and unrewarding routine office visits could be avoided if, after a disease was once diagnosed, appropriate medication were readily available on an OTC basis. . . .

Pharmacists, like physicians, are concerned about their eroding position as recognized experts in drug therapy. Ultimately, however, that position must be stabilized and rebuilt not on the basis of a legalized monopoly, but on the basis of demonstrated ability and hard-won public confidence. . . .

Finally, industry concerns must also be appreciated. The relative profitability of a drug when sold on prescription and nonprescription status will have a significant impact on the approach of the drug industry to any particular decision in this area. The relationship of the drug industry to physicians and pharmacists, and their concern about the potential impact of any prescription/nonprescription decision upon that relationship, is too important to be ignored. Nor is the potential change in product liability when a drug is transferred from prescription to prescription status a matter of insignificance. . . .

NOTES

1. *Benylin.* The process of switching an Rx drug to OTC status can be treacherous, contentious, and prolonged. For example, the switch of the expectorant drug Benylin®, through approval of an SNDA in 1981, took more than a decade. The story is detailed in 44 Fed. 51512 (Aug. 31, 1979) and 47 Fed. Reg. 18669 (Apr. 30, 1982).

2. *Ibuprofen.* FDA's much-publicized decision in May 1984 to switch ibuprofen from Rx to OTC status by approving SNDAs for Nuprin® and Advil®, was immediately subjected to two different types of legal challenge. A competitor unsuccessfully challenged FDA's decision to effect this switch by approval of NDAs rather by amendment of the OTC drug monograph. *Chattem, Inc. v. Heckler,* Food Drug Cosm. L. Rep. (CCH) ¶¶ 38,293, 38,294, 38,339 (D.D.C. 1984, 1985), *aff'd per curiam* 1985–1986 FDLI Jud. Rec. 326 (D.C. Cir. 1986). Consequently, ibuprofen can now be marketed only under FDA approval of an abbreviated NDA. In *McNeilab, Inc. v. Heckler,* Food Drug Cosm. L. Rep. ¶¶ 38,290 & 38,317 (D.D.C. 1984, 1985), the District Court held that another competitor could challenge the legal basis of FDA's switch of ibuprofen from Rx to OTC but upheld the agency on the merits.

3. *Metaproterenol.* FDA has had to be sensitive to the views of physicians and pharmacists when it considers an Rx to OTC switch. Without consulting either the medical profession or the manufacturer, in the tentative final monograph for OTC bronchodilator drugs, the agency announced that metaproterenol sulfate in a metered-dose inhaler for use as a bronchodilator could immediately be switched from Rx to OTC status. 47 Fed. Reg. 47520 (Oct. 26, 1982). Following objections from the medical community and an adverse vote by an advisory committee, the agency rescinded the switch. 48 Fed. Reg. 24925 (June 3, 1983).

4. *Considerations for Switch.* FDA CDER Office of Drug Evaluation Director Robert DeLap offered the following 12 considerations for a switch:

"Fundamentals"

• Can the condition be adequately self-diagnosed?

• Can the condition be successfully self-treated?

• Is the self-treatment product safe and effective for consumer use, under conditions of actual use?

"Points to Consider"

• Is there a need for physician evaluation of the condition?

• What is the nature and severity of adverse effects of consumer misdiagnosis, and delay in correct diagnosis?

• Regarding effective product use, what is the nature of consumer understanding of product use?

• What is the consumer understanding of the expected benefit?

• Does the consumer have the ability to assess treatment effect?

"Safe Product Use"

• What is the consumer understanding of product directions for safe use?

• What is the consumer understanding of what to do if the product isn't working?

• What is the consumer ability to identify adverse effects, and the consumer ability to determine when adverse events may require professional care?

• What is the consumer expectation of safety?

DeLap's "12 Principles of OTCness," NDMA EXECUTIVE NEWSLETTER 3 (Nov. 20, 1998). *See also* Mark B. Gelbert, *Making the Rx-to-OTC Switch: What You Need to Know,* 1 REG. AFFAIRS FOCUS, No. 10, at 18 (October 1996); Eric P. Brass, *Changing the Status of Drugs from Prescription to Over-the-Counter Availability,* 345 NEW ENG. J. MED 810 (Sept. 13, 2001).

5. *Reimbursement.* Prescription drugs are reimbursed by government and private medical insurance, but OTC drugs generally are not. Section 503(b) does not include reimbursement or any other economic factor as a criterion for consideration of a potential switch. Yet reimbursement is often raised by interested parties. FDA and its advisory committees, although not addressing this issue directly, could easily be influenced by it in evaluating a potential switch.

6. *Unsuccessful Attempts to Switch.* FDA and its advisory committees have thus far declined to approve switch petitions filed by the pioneer manufacturers of two types of very successful Rx drugs. Burroughs Wellcome (now part of GlaxoSmithKline) proposed to switch its very successful drug, Zovirex®, for herpes, but was turned down after two advisory committees failed to support the switch. Merck proposed to switch its anticholesterol statin drug, Mevacor®, and Bristol Myers proposed to switch its statin, Pravachol®, but both were unsuccessful after two

advisory committee meetings. *See* Brian L. Strom, *Statins and Over-the-Counter Availability*, 352 NEW ENG. J. MED. 1403 (Apr. 7, 2005); Niteesh K. Choudry & Jerry Avorn, *Over-the-Counter Statins*, 142 ANNALS OF INTERNAL MED. 910 (June 7, 2005).

7. *Required Testing for Switch.* Before it will consider switching a prescription drug to OTC status, FDA almost always requires (1) a label comprehension study to demonstrate that consumers can understand the indications, warnings, and directions for use and (2) a home use study to demonstrate that consumers will follow the label information. A home use study has been determined by FDA to qualify the applicant for 3 years of market exclusivity. *See* Letter from Janet Woodcock, Director, FDA CDER, to Gary L. Yingling (Oct. 31, 1996). Exclusivity periods are discussed *infra* at p. 1003.

8. *State Reverse Switch.* A state cannot on its own switch a drug from Rx to OTC status, but it can do the reverse. In *Northwest Connection, Inc. v. Board of Pharmacy*, 814 P.2d 191 (Or. Ct. App. 1991), the court upheld a decision of the Oregon State Board of Pharmacy to switch ephedrine from nonprescription to prescription status. Section 751(c)(1)(B) of the FD&C Act, added in 1997, implicitly acknowledges the legality of such state-law reverse switches by explicitly excluding them from the requirement of national uniformity for nonprescription drugs. *But see Carey v. Population Services International*, 431 U.S. 678 (1977) (invalidating, on substantive due process grounds, a New York statute making it a crime for anyone other than a pharmacist to distribute contraceptives).

———

No Rx/OTC switch in history has attracted more attention than the switch of the emergency contraceptive, Plan B, from prescription to nonprescription status.

Tummino v. Hamburg

2013 WL 1348656 (E.D.N.Y Apr. 5, 2013).

■ KORMAN, U.S. DISTRICT COURT JUDGE

I. Overview

Plan B and Plan B One–Step are emergency contraceptives that can be taken to reduce the risk of pregnancy after unprotected intercourse. In 1999, Plan B became the first emergency contraceptive drug approved for prescription-only use in the United States. In 2006, the Food and Drug Administration approved non-prescription access to Plan B for women 18 and older, and with a prescription to adolescents under the age of 18. Subsequently, the FDA was ordered to make it available without a prescription to adolescents aged 17. *Tummino v. Torti,* 603 F. Supp.2d 519 (E.D.N.Y.2009). Even for women 17 and older, Plan B can only be purchased at a pharmacy and requires government-issued proof of age. Plan B One–Step was approved by the FDA in 2009 and is available without a prescription subject to the same restrictions. . . .

Both contraceptives contain the same total dose of levonorgestrel, a synthetic hormone similar to the naturally occurring hormone progesterone; Plan B consists of two pills . . . while Plan B One–Step consists of one pill. . . . Both Plan B and Plan B One–Step are most effective when taken immediately after intercourse and preferably no later than 24 hours later, though they may retain some effectiveness if taken within 72 hours. Neither drug has any known serious or long-term side effects, though they may have some mild short-term side effects. . . .

Levonorgestrel-based emergency contraception "interferes with prefertilization events. . . ." These contraceptives "have not been shown to cause a postfertilization event—a change in the uterus that could interfere with implantation of a fertilized egg." . . . Nevertheless, because it would be "unethical and logistically difficult to conduct the necessary research" . . . "the possibility of a postfertilization event cannot be ruled out."

Plaintiffs in this case—organizations and individuals concerned with women's health, as well as minors and their parents—seek to expand the availability of Plan B and all emergency contraceptives. This action was originally brought in January 2005 to challenge the FDA's denial of a Citizen Petition seeking over-the-counter ("OTC") access to Plan B for women of all ages. . . .

In light of the overwhelming evidence of political pressure underlying the agency's actions, I vacated the FDA's denial of the Citizen Petition and remanded for the agency to exercise its discretion without impermissible political intrusion. I also directed the FDA to make Plan B available to 17-year-old women without a prescription. . . .

The FDA did not rule on the remanded Citizen Petition for almost three years. During this time, the agency again considered a proposal—referred to as a supplemental new drug application ("SNDA")—from Plan B's manufacturer; this proposal would have allowed over-the-counter access to Plan B One–Step . . . for all ages. The FDA agreed to approve this SNDA. FDA Commissioner Margaret Hamburg explained . . .

> . . . Based on the information submitted to the agency, CDER determined that the product was safe and effective in adolescent females, that adolescent females understood the product was not for routine use, and that the product would not protect them against sexually transmitted diseases. Additionally, the data supported a finding that adolescent females could use Plan B One–Step properly without the intervention of a healthcare provider.

> . . . Our decision-making reflects a body of scientific findings, input from external scientific advisory committees, and data contained in the application that included studies designed specifically to address the regulatory standards for nonprescription drugs. CDER experts . . . reviewed the totality of the data and agreed that it met the regulatory standard for a nonprescription drug and that Plan B One–Step should be approved for all females of child-bearing potential.

Statement from FDA Commissioner Margaret Hamburg, M.D., on Plan B One–Step (Dec. 7, 2011). Commissioner Hamburg . . . expressly agreed that . . . [the SNDA] should be approved. . . .

Nevertheless, she explained that Kathleen Sebelius, the Secretary of Health and Human Services . . . disagreed with the agency's decision . . . and ordered Commissioner Hamburg to deny the Plan B One–Step SNDA. Secretary Sebelius . . . observed:

> The label comprehension and actual use studies submitted to FDA do not include data on all ages for which the drug would be approved and available over-the-counter. Yet, it is commonly understood that there are significant cognitive and behavioral differences between older adolescent girls and the youngest girls of reproductive age, which I believe are relevant to making this determination as to non-prescription availability of this product for all ages. Although the average age of the onset of menses for girls in the United States is 12.4 years of age, about ten percent of girls reach menarche by 11.1 years of age. . . .

Memorandum from Kathleen Sebelius, Sec'y Health and Human Servs., to Margaret Hamburg, Comm'r of Food and Drugs (Dec. 7, 2011). The President endorsed this decision, explaining that "the reason [Secretary Sebelius] made this decision was she could not be confident that a 10-year-old or an 11-year-old go into a drugstore, should be able—alongside bubble gum or batteries—be able to buy a medication that potentially, if not used properly, could end up having an adverse effect."
. . .

This case is not about the potential misuse of Plan B by 11-year-olds. These emergency contraceptives would be among the safest drugs sold over-the-counter, the number of 11-year-olds using these drugs is likely to be miniscule, [and] the FDA permits drugs that it has found to be unsafe for the pediatric population to be sold over-the-counter subject only to labeling restrictions. . . . Instead, the invocation of the adverse effect of Plan B on 11-year-olds is an excuse to deprive the overwhelming majority of women of their right to obtain contraceptives without unjustified and burdensome restrictions.

. . . This case has proven to be particularly controversial because it involves access to emergency contraception for adolescents who should not be engaging in conduct that necessitates the use of such drugs and because of the scientifically unsupported speculation that the drug could interfere with implantation of fertilized eggs. Nevertheless, the issue in this case involves the interpretation of a general statutory and regulatory scheme relating to the approval of drugs for over-the-counter sale. The standards are the same for aspirin and for contraceptives. While the FDA properly recognizes that cognitive and behavioral differences undermine "the ability of adolescents to make reasoned decisions about engaging in sexual intercourse," the standard for determining whether contraceptives or any other drug should be available over-the-counter turns solely on the ability of the consumer to understand how to use the particular drug "safely and effectively."

II. Discussion

. . . .

In *INS v. Yang*, 519 U.S. 26 (1996), the Supreme Court held: "Though the agency's decision is unfettered at the outset, if it announces and follows—by rule or by settled course of adjudication—a general policy by which its exercise of discretion will be governed, an irrational departure from that policy (as opposed to an avowed alteration of it) could constitute action that must be overturned as 'arbitrary, capricious, [or] an abuse of discretion' within the meaning of the Administrative Procedure Act." The denial of the SNDA and the Citizen Petition was accomplished by unexplained departures from a number of established policies and practices followed by the FDA.

The Unprecedented Intervention of the Secretary

Perhaps the most significant departure from agency practice was the intervention of the Secretary of Health and Human Services. . . .

. . . The motivation for the Secretary's action was obviously political. "It was the first time a cabinet member had ever publicly countermanded a determination by the F.D.A. . . ." Gardiner Harris, *White House and the FDA Often at Odds*, N.Y. TIMES, Apr. 3, 2012 at A1. And it was an election-year decision that "many public health experts saw as a politically motivated effort to avoid riling religious groups and others opposed to making birth control available to girls."
. . .

. . . [E]ven with eyes shut to the motivation for the Secretary's decision, the reasons she provided are so unpersuasive as to call into question her good faith. . . .

The Secretary . . . observed that there are "significant cognitive and behavioral differences between older adolescent girls and the youngest girls of reproductive age," which she believes "are relevant to making this determination as to non-prescription availability of this product for all ages." She fails to explain why. . . . [T]he Director of the Office of New Drugs at the FDA . . . explained that such concerns are beyond the scope of the FDA's review because they are "more applicable to the ability of adolescents to make reasoned decisions about engaging in sexual intercourse, not their ability to understand how to use Plan B safely and effectively as an emergency contraceptive should they engage in unprotected sexual intercourse." . . .

On the other hand . . . if the "cognitive differences" to which she referred affected the ability of the youngest adolescents to understand the label and use the drug appropriately, then it would be impossible for any drug to be approved for over-the-counter sales without a prescription. . . .

. . . [T]he Secretary has never demanded "data . . . [that] conclusively establish" that 100% of the potential users of a drug can understand the label. Nor has she or the FDA precluded the over-the-counter sale of drugs for that reason.

The Secretary finally observed that, if the SNDA were granted, Plan B One–Step would be available "without a prescription or other point-of-sale restrictions, even to the youngest girls of reproductive age," including the ten percent of girls who "reach menarche by 11.1

years of age." Nevertheless, the Secretary does not define any harm that could result from the use of levonorgestrel-based emergency contraceptives by this population. . . . [T]he FDA approves drugs for over-the-counter sale which have either not been shown to be safe for use by the pediatric population or have been shown to be unsafe for such use. The policy of the FDA is to rely on . . . age-based labeling restrictions. . . .

Moreover, the likelihood of unsafe use or misuse with respect to levonorgestrel-based emergency contraceptives is extremely low, and much lower than the dangers of misuse of common over-the-counter medications that are known to be abused by minors and adults, even though these drugs cause hundreds of deaths every year in the United States. . . .

Extrapolation

Extrapolation is the use of studies in one age group to support approval of a drug in another age group. The FDA's failure to extrapolate involves the next and perhaps the most significant unexplained deviation from FDA practice ordered by the Secretary. . . .

. . . As early as April 2002, the FDA informed the Plan B sponsor that results from trials in the adult population could be extrapolated to the postmenarcheal pediatric population. . . .

. . . Moreover, responding directly to concerns that the label comprehension and actual use studies enrolled too few young adolescents, the Director of the Office of New Drugs . . . wrote, "the Agency has a long history of extrapolating findings from clinical trials in older patients to adolescents in both prescription and nonprescription approvals. . . ."

There was . . . evidence in the record that the FDA routinely extrapolated such data when considering new drug applications or switch applications seeking over-the-counter status for contraceptives. . . .

. . . [W]hen the FDA has declined to extrapolate because of safety concerns, it used [sic] labeling to indicate that the drug was not to be made available to children. . . . [A]s [the Director] testified, age-based labeling restrictions have "been [the FDA's] long-standing way of handling instructing consumers whether they should or should not use a product in a young age group, and [the Plan B marketing regime is] a substantial deviation from that practice." . . .

Point-of-Sale Departure from Policy

. . . [T]he current regime . . . which the Secretary forced the FDA to retain . . . requires that the product be sold only at pharmacies and health clinics and that it be kept behind the counter at pharmacies. This point-of-sale restriction not only limits young adolescents' access to Plan B, it limits the access of individuals 17 and older to the product.

. . . In 1984, more than 20 years before the Plan B sponsor submitted the initial SNDA, the FDA denied a citizen petition urging it to establish a class of non-prescription drugs products to be sold only by a pharmacist. . . . [T]he FDA Commissioner at the time wrote:

. . . Under the [FDCA] there is no provision for an intermediate class of drugs between OTC and prescription products. The statutory requirement that a drug either be limited to prescription dispensing or available OTC with adequate directions for use seems to preclude the agency from establishing a class of drugs whose labeling would need to be supplemented by a pharmacist's instructions.

Consistent with this policy, the FDA has voiced concerns in this proceeding about its authority to impose an age-restricted marketing regime on an approved drug. . . .

I agree that the FDA did not have the authority to mandate point-of-sale restrictions on drugs approved for nonprescription sale that it found to be safe and effective for all women of childbearing age. Nevertheless, even if it had such authority, it clearly deviated from the policy here. This is demonstrated . . . by the drugs that were either not shown to be safe or were unsafe for the pediatric population . . . which were dealt with through labeling, not point-of-sale restrictions. . . .

Standard of Review

. . . The only decision subject to review here is the denial of the Citizen Petition; I do not have any authority to review the denial of the Plan B One–Step SNDA for the purpose of granting relief. Nevertheless . . . the two were clearly linked together. . . . [O]nce the Secretary directed the FDA to deny the Plan B One–Step SNDA, the FDA had no possible basis on which to approve the Citizen Petition. . . .

. . . The decision that the agency was forced to make, contrary to its own policies and judgment, is not entitled to any deference. Indeed, it is hardly clear that the Secretary had the power to issue the order, and if she did have that authority, her decision was arbitrary, capricious, and unreasonable.

. . . Because the Secretary's action was politically motivated, scientifically unjustified, and contrary to agency precedent, it cannot provide a basis to sustain the denial of the Citizen Petition. The Citizen Petition Denial Letter, which came five days after the denial of the Plan B One–Step SNDA, was clearly prompted by the Secretary's action, despite the FDA's fanciful effort to make it appear that it undertook an independent review of the Citizen Petition.

. . . .

III. Conclusion

The decisions of the Secretary with respect to Plan B One–Step and that of the FDA with respect to the Citizen Petition, which it had no choice but to deny, were arbitrary, capricious, and unreasonable. . . . Consequently, the decision of the FDA denying the Citizen Petition is reversed, and the case is remanded to the FDA with the instruction to grant the Citizen Petition and make levonorgestrel-based emergency contraceptives available without a prescription and without point-of-sale or age restrictions within thirty days. . . . [I]f the FDA actually believes there is any significant difference between the one- and two-pill products, it may limit its over-the-counter approval to the one-pill product.

I do not grant the application of the FDA to remand for the commencement of administrative rulemaking proceedings. In my previous opinion . . . I described two methods by which the FDA could change a drug's status: first, by promulgating a regulation through rulemaking initiated by either the Commissioner herself or a citizen petition, or by approving a drug sponsor's request for an over-the-counter switch. I observed, "[u]nlike the first mechanism, this process does not require rulemaking." On further review, I believe that no statute or regulation requires the FDA to engage in administrative rulemaking upon approval of a citizen petition or *sua sponte* reconsideration of a drug's prescription-only status. . . .

Finally, even if the defendants' arguments would be sufficient to carry the day in the run-of-the-mill case, the bad faith that has permeated consideration of the Citizen Petition, not to speak of the Plan B sponsor's applications, should rule out such relief here. . . .

REVERSED and REMANDED

NOTES

1. *Resolution.* On June 10, 2013, the U.S. Attorney sent Judge Korman a letter proposing to comply with his order by inviting the NDA holder for Plan B One-Step, Teva, to submit an SNDA for a complete, unfettered OTC switch that FDA would "approve without delay." Although this plan of action did not conform exactly to Korman's order—which mandated approval of the citizen petition—the judge deemed it sufficient. *Tummino v. Hamburg*, 2013 WL 2631163 (E.D.N.Y June 12, 2013). However, he urged FDA to not grant three-year market exclusivity for Teva—and thus to promptly approve any SNDAs submitted by generic manufacturers—unless the FDA determined that the study submitted by Teva in support of its SNDA was truly essential to FDA approval of the application. *Id.* Later in June, FDA approved Teva's Plan B One-Step as an OTC product for all ages, and in July granted Teva a three-year exclusivity period. Consequently, no generic versions of OTC Plan B One-Step will appear on the market until at least 2016.

2. *Switch in Response to Third Party Petition.* Apparently, FDA has never issued a switch regulation in response to a petition by an interested third party. The Plan B controversy illuminates FDA's apparent reluctance to do so. Instead of approving the citizen petition, FDA requested that Teva file a new SNDA requesting OTC status for Plan B One-Step and then approved this application.

A prior effort by an interested third party to initiate a switch concluded similarly. In June 1998, Wellpoint Health Networks, a medical insurance company, filed a citizen petition with FDA (Docket No. 1998P–0610/CPI) requesting that the agency switch the three largest selling allergy drugs (Claritin, Allegra, and Zyrtec) from Rx to OTC. Wellpoint had a major economic interest in obtaining a switch because, if the three drugs were switched, they would no longer be reimbursable. All three drugs still enjoyed patent protection, and the manufacturers opposed the petition. When the companies rebuffed the agency's pressure to cooperate with a switch, FDA threatened to grant the Wellpoint petition and do a "forced switch" by rulemaking under 21 C.F.R. 310.200. The three companies responded that any action to force a switch would require a notice of opportunity for a formal evidentiary hearing under section 505(e). To add to the pressure, other companies submitted section 505(b)(2) NDAs to switch Claritin to OTC status upon expiration of the patent.

The matter was resolved in 2002, when, just prior to the expiration of the patent for Claritin, its manufacturer (Schering–Plough) filed an SNDA requesting a switch and FDA approved the application. The pending section 505(b)(2) NDAs were promptly approved when the patent expired. It appears that the FDA threat of a forced switch was only the agency's way of increasing the pressure for a voluntary switch, and that the agency had no intention of actually devoting the resources necessary to implement such a contentious approach. FDA's authority to force a switch through rulemaking therefore remains unresolved. *See* Holly M. Spencer, Comment: *The RX-to-OTC Switch of Claritin, Allegra, and Zyrtec: An Unprecedented FDA Response to Petitioners and the Protection of the Public Health*, 51 AM. U. L. REV. 999 (2002)

3. *Switch Regulations without Rulemaking.* Judge Korman ordered FDA to issue a switch regulation without notice-and-comment rulemaking. The judge's interpretation of the FD&C Act and FDA regulations to permit the issuance of such a regulation without rulemaking was a novel one, representing a change in Judge Korman's own prior understanding of the switch procedure. The agency would almost certainly have challenged the judge's interpretation on appeal, but the agency abandoned its appeal upon resolution of the controversy.

3. THE OTC DRUG REVIEW

a. RATIONALE AND PROCEDURES OF THE REVIEW

Congress's mandate in the Drug Amendments of 1962 to review all previous effective NDAs extended to OTC as well as prescription drugs. Most OTC drugs could not be considered to be "covered" by effective NDAs, however, and FDA concluded that case-by-case challenges to individual OTC products on the ground that they were not generally recognized as safe and effective (and thus were unapproved "new drugs") would exhaust its resources. In 1972, FDA proposed a new approach that featured expert advisory committees and relied on the agency's claim to primary jurisdiction to determine new drug status.

Over-the-Counter Drugs: Proposal Establishing Rule Making Procedures for Classification
37 Fed. Reg. 85 (January 5, 1972).

. . . .

Estimates of the number of OTC drug products on the market vary from 100,000 to one-half million. Extremely few of these drugs have been approved through the new-drug procedures set forth in section 505 of the act. Some OTC drugs may be excluded from the definition of a new drug by reasons of the so-called 1938 grandfather clause in section

201(p)(1) of the act, and others may be excluded from application of the Drug Amendments of 1962 by reason of the so-called 1962 grandfather clause in section 107(c) of those amendments. Any OTC drug excluded from new-drug status by reason of the 1938 or 1962 grandfather clause is, however, subject to other requirements for drugs in Chapter V of the act, and in particular may not be misbranded under section 502.

The Food and Drug Administration intends to require that all unapproved new drugs and misbranded drugs either be reformulated and/or relabeled to meet all requirements of the act or be removed from the market. In carrying out its responsibilities in this area, the Food and Drug Administration may either initiate a separate court action with respect to each violative OTC drug or deal with all OTC drugs through rulemaking by therapeutic classes on an industry wide basis. It has been determined that the latter approach should be pursued. In making this decision, the following factors were considered:

1.   The limited resources of the Food and Drug Administration would be overwhelmed by attempting to review separately the labeling and the data on the safety and effectiveness for each OTC drug now on the market. . . .

2.   Litigation to remove violative OTC preparations from the market would necessarily be on a drug-by-drug basis. . . . Such litigation is time-consuming and expensive and is sometimes ineffective because manufacturers may change the formulation of the drug in question and/or its labeling claims and reintroduce the product into the market, thus requiring still further litigation.

3.   Litigation to delineate the precise scope of the 1938 and 1962 grandfather clauses in order to determine exactly which of the thousands of OTC drugs on the market may validly claim exemption from new-drug status under those clauses and then to determine on a drug-by-drug basis which of those grandfathered claims and formulations are safe and effective under the prescribed, recommended, or suggested conditions of use, and thus not misbranded, would more than exhaust all present resources of the agency. . . .

4.   Of paramount concern is the inadequate consumer protection produced by a product-by-product review and case-by-case litigation against each drug. . . .

5.   It is impossible to proceed simultaneously by litigation against all manufacturers of similar preparations or their drugs. . . .

6.   Practically all of the thousands of OTC drugs now marketed are compounded from only an estimated 200 active ingredients which are used either alone or in varying combinations. Many thousands of these drugs are readily comparable in that the labeling is similar and the active ingredients are the same, or are essentially the same, but are present in slightly different dosages. Although each is a separate product, the same scientific and medical evidence is relevant in reviewing all OTC drugs within a given therapeutic class. . . .

Accordingly, the Commissioner proposes to establish procedures for rule making which will result in classifying some OTC drugs as generally recognized among qualified experts as safe and effective and not misbranded under prescribed, recommended, or suggested conditions of use. Any OTC drug not meeting the requirements established for such drugs pursuant to this procedure will have to be the subject of an approved new-drug application prior to marketing. (Since a grandfathered drug that is found to be misbranded would be required to change its formulation and/or labeling and thus lose its grandfathered status, any such product must either meet the applicable monograph or be the subject of an approved new-drug application in order to be legally marketed.) . . . Shipment of a non-conforming OTC drug (one neither classified as generally recognized as safe and effective and not misbranded, nor subject to an approved NDA) in interstate commerce will be prohibited. . . .

————

The agency made modifications in only a few provisions in the proposed regulations and quickly promulgated the final regulations at 37 Fed. Reg. 9464 (May 11, 1972), currently codified at 21 C.F.R. Part 330. Section 330.10, excerpted below, lays out the procedures for classification of OTC drugs. Today, more than forty years later, the process described below is still not entirely completed. *See infra* p. 979. An example of an "OTC monograph," the term used for the final rules produced by the OTC Drug Review, is included below. *Infra* p. 980.

Over-the-Counter Human Drugs Which Are Generally Recognized as Safe and Effective and Not Misbranded

21 C.F.R. Part 330.

§ 330.10 Procedures for classifying OTC drugs as generally recognized as safe and effective and not misbranded, and for establishing monographs

. . . .

(a) *Procedure for establishing OTC drug monographs.* (1) *Advisory review panels.* The Commissioner shall appoint advisory review panels of qualified experts to evaluate the safety and effectiveness of OTC drugs, to review OTC drug labeling, and to advise him on the promulgation of monographs establishing conditions under which OTC drugs are generally recognized as safe and effective and not misbranded. A single advisory review panel shall be established for each designated category of OTC drugs. . . . The members of a panel . . . may include persons from lists submitted by organizations representing professional, consumer, and industry interests. . . .

(3) *Deliberations of an advisory review panel.* An advisory review panel will . . . review the data submitted to it and . . . prepare a report containing its conclusions and recommendations to the Commissioner with respect to the safety and effectiveness of the drugs in a designated category of the OTC drugs. A panel may consult any individual or group. Any interested person may request an opportunity to present oral views to the panel; such request may be granted or denied by the panel. . . . Any interested person may present written data and views which shall be considered by the panel. . . .

(4) *Standards for safety, effectiveness, and labeling.* The advisory review panel . . . shall apply the following standards . . .:

(i) Safety means a low incidence of adverse reactions or significant side effects under adequate directions for use and warnings against unsafe use as well as low potential for harm which may result from abuse under conditions of widespread availability. Proof of safety shall consist of adequate tests by methods reasonably applicable to show the drug is safe under the prescribed, recommended, or suggested conditions of use. This proof shall include results of significant human experience during marketing. General recognition of safety shall ordinarily be based upon published studies which may be corroborated by unpublished studies and other data.

(ii) Effectiveness means a reasonable expectation that, in a significant proportion of the target population, the pharmacological effect of the drug, when used under adequate directions for use and warnings against unsafe use, will provide clinically significant relief of the type claimed. Proof of effectiveness shall consist of controlled clinical investigations as defined in § 314.111(a)(5)(ii) of this chapter, unless this requirement is waived on the basis of a showing that it is not reasonably applicable to the drug or essential to the validity of the investigation and that an alternative method of investigation is adequate to substantiate effectiveness. Investigations may be corroborated by partially controlled or uncontrolled studies, documented clinical studies by qualified experts, and reports of significant human experience marketing. . . . General recognition of effectiveness shall ordinarily be based upon published studies which may be corroborated by unpublished studies and other data.

(iii) The benefit-to-risk ratio of a drug shall be considered in determining safety and effectiveness.

. . . .

(5) *Advisory review panel report to the Commissioner.* . . . Included within this report shall be:

(i) A recommended monograph or monographs covering the category of OTC drugs and establishing conditions under which the drugs involved are generally recognized as safe and effective and not misbranded (Category I). . . .

(ii) A statement of active ingredients, labeling claims or other statements, or other conditions reviewed and excluded from the monograph on the basis of the panel's determination that they would result in the drug's not being generally recognized as safe and effective or would result in misbranding (Category II).

(iii) A statement of active ingredients, labeling claims or other statements, or other conditions reviewed and excluded from the monograph on the basis of the panel's determination that the available data are insufficient to classify such condition under either paragraph (a)(5)(i) or (ii) of this section and for which further testing is therefore required (Category III). . . . .

(6) *Proposed monograph.* After reviewing the conclusions and recommendations of the advisory review panel, the Commissioner shall publish in the FEDERAL REGISTER a proposed order containing:

(i) A monograph or monographs establishing conditions under which a category of OTC drugs or a specific or specific OTC drugs are generally recognized as safe and effective and not misbranded (Category I).

(ii) A statement of the conditions excluded from the monograph on the basis of the Commissioner's determination that they would result in the drug's not being generally recognized as safe and effective or would result in misbranding (Category II).

(iii) A statement of the conditions excluded from the monograph on the basis of the Commissioner's determination that the available data are insufficient . . . (Category III).

(iv) The full report(s) of the panel to the Commissioner. . . . Any interested person may, within 90 days after publication of the proposed order . . . file . . . written comments. . . .

(7) *Tentative final monograph.* (i) After reviewing all comments, reply comments, and any new data and information or, alternatively, after reviewing a panel's recommendations, the Commissioner shall publish in the FEDERAL REGISTER a tentative order containing a monograph establishing conditions under which a category of OTC drugs or specific OTC drugs are generally recognized as safe and effective and not misbranded. Within 30 days, any interested party may file . . . written objections specifying with particularity the omissions or additions requested. . . . A request for an oral hearing may accompany such objections. . . .

(8) *Oral hearing before the Commissioner.* After reviewing objections filed in response to the tentative final monograph, the Commissioner, if he finds reasonable grounds in support thereof, shall . . . schedule an oral hearing. . . .

(9) *Final monograph.* After reviewing the objections . . . and considering the arguments made at any oral hearing, the Commissioner shall publish in the FEDERAL REGISTER a final order containing a monograph establishing conditions under which a category of OTC drugs or a specific or specific OTC drugs are generally recognized as safe and effective and not misbranded. . . .

NOTES

1. *Legality of OTC Drug Review.* Surprisingly, the legality of the OTC Drug Review, while questioned, has never been squarely challenged in the courts. Several court opinions have referred approvingly to the Review. *E.g. Weinberger v. Bentex Pharmaceuticals, Inc.,* 412 U.S. 645 (1973). FDA's initial use of closed panel meetings, with confidential transcripts, was upheld by one court and declared unlawful by another before the issue was mooted by the enactment of the Federal Advisory Committee Act. *See infra* p. 1488. The agency's approval for continued marketing of Category III drugs was enjoined in *Cutler v. Kennedy. See infra* p. 979, note 8.

2. *FDA Request for Data.* Because FDA has no statutory power to require a manufacturer to submit any information to, or otherwise participate in, the OTC Drug Review, the agency feared that companies might submit only favorable information. FDA's initial requests for data on

specific drug categories therefore stated that if the data submission was by a manufacturer, it must include:

> . . . a statement signed by the person responsible for such submission, that to the best of his knowledge it includes unfavorable information, as well as any favorable information, known to him pertinent to an evaluation of the safety, effectiveness, and labeling of such a product. Thus, if any type of scientific data is submitted, a balanced submission of favorable and unfavorable data must be submitted. . . .

E.g., 37 Fed. Reg. 26842 (Dec. 16, 1972) (antimicrobial drugs).

3.   *The Work of the Panels.* The OTC Drug Review panels reviewed some 722 active ingredients for approximately 1,454 specific uses. They rated roughly 30 percent as Category I for the intended use, 34 percent as Category II, and 36 percent as Category III. The agency later upgraded many Category III active ingredients to Category I based upon new information. William Gilbertson, THE PRESCRIPTION TO OTC SWITCH: FDA VIEW 5 (Apr. 1986).

4.   *FDA Enforcement Policy.* A well-understood premise of the OTC Drug Review was that FDA would tolerate continued marketing of most OTC drug products pending completion of the Review. But FDA added two caveats. It would take action against an individual OTC product if it believed the product posed a significant health hazard or was likely to defraud consumers. *See* Compliance Policy Guide No. 7132b.15 (Oct. 1, 1980). In addition, the agency made clear that it would not hesitate to act outside the scope and schedule of the review to deal with ingredients that were found by the panels, or otherwise demonstrated, to be health hazards. FDA has done so on various occasions, and the drugs so deemed by separate rulemaking to be new drugs are listed at 21 C.F.R. 310.502. The agency has also transferred to category II, and thus banned, a number of active ingredients for which the OTC drug industry expressed no further interest. These ingredients are listed at 21 C.F.R. 310.545.

5.   *Encouraged Reformulation.* FDA encouraged manufacturers to reformulate and re-label their products to conform to proposed monographs even before the monographs were promulgated in final form. The agency adopted a regulation, 21 C.F.R. 330.12(d), stating that it would not take action against such products, pending promulgation of a final monograph, if such changes resulted in loss of grandfather protection.

6.   *Premature Marketing.* Once the nonprescription drug industry began to appreciate the commercial opportunities created by the OTC Drug Review, companies closely followed each panel and anticipated the results of the Review by marketing new products that previously were not permitted (e.g., drugs previously limited to prescription status or marketed for a different indication or containing less of the active ingredient) even before the panel submitted its report. After FDA forced the nationwide recall of Benylin, a prescription product marketed OTC in anticipation of a panel conclusion with which the agency disagreed, it promulgated a rule governing the conditions under which manufacturers may safely follow the recommendations of an OTC drug panel before a final monograph has been promulgated. 41 Fed. Reg. 32580 (Aug. 4, 1976), codified at 21 C.F.R.

330.13. The FDA policy was amended in 47 Fed. Reg. 17738 (Apr. 23, 1982) to provide that when the Commissioner agrees that a new product meets all the requirements for Category I and provides notice of that determination in the Federal Register, marketing may begin before promulgation of a final monograph.

7. *The Flexibility of the OTC Drug Review.* Although criticized as rigid, in truth the OTC Drug Review exhibited notable flexibility. For example, 21 C.F.R. 330.10(a)(5) authorized a panel to recommend in a monograph any conditions of any kind relating to an OTC drug. Panels routinely considered and recommended approval of conditions for which the drugs under review were not marketed prior to May 1972.

8. *Legality of Category III.* A controversial feature of the OTC Drug Review was the provision allowing continued marketing of products containing ingredients classified by final FDA monographs in Category III (insufficient data) while additional testing was being conducted. Category III was designed as a bridge between the status quo and GRAS/GRAE status for ingredients for which the requisite evidence could eventually be obtained. However, in *Cutler v. Kennedy*, 475 F. Supp. 838, 854 (D.D.C. 1979), the court held that the agency's allowance of continued marketing of such drugs "is nothing less than a frontal assault on the premarket licensing scheme of the [FD&C Act]." FDA revised its regulations to comply with the decision. 46 Fed. Reg. 47730 (Sept. 29, 1981). The revised regulations deleted the authorization to market Category III ingredients after publication of a final monograph. At the same time, however, FDA published a policy statement announcing that it would meet with industry representatives and comment on the adequacy of studies of Category III ingredients prior to the completion of the monograph process. 46 Fed. Reg. 47740 (Sept. 29, 1981). In substance, therefore, the *Cutler* decision resulted in Category III ingredients being tested and FDA decisions on those ingredients reached before, rather than after, the publication of the final monograph.

b.　COMPLETION OF THE OTC DRUG REVIEW

The OTC Drug Review has been one of the most challenging rulemaking efforts undertaken by any government agency. FDA passed one landmark in the OTC Drug Review on October 7, 1983, when it published the last of the 58 reports prepared by the 17 advisory panels. The 17 panels held 508 meetings over 1047 days and reviewed some 20,000 volumes of data on more than 700 active ingredients used in over 300,000 nonprescription drug products. HHS News No. P83–22 (Oct. 7, 1983). Because most OTC drugs were reformulated and relabeled to comply with the panel reports soon after, and sometimes even before, their publication, the major impact of the OTC Drug Review was already reflected in the marketplace by the mid-1980s.

In 1982, consumers of OTC drugs asserted in U.S. District Court that FDA's lack of progress in completing the OTC Drug Review infringed the provisions of the Administrative Procedure Act prohibiting unreasonable agency delay. The court granted FDA's motion for summary judgment, 549 F. Supp. 1341 (D.D.C. 1982), but the D.C. Circuit remanded the case, ordering the agency to justify the delay. *Cutler v. Hayes*, 818 F.2d 879 (D.C. Cir. 1987). On remand, at the request of the District Court, FDA submitted document titled *A Historical Examination of FDA's Review of the Safety and Effectiveness of Over-the-Counter Drugs* (Sept. 22, 1987).

The agency passed a second landmark when it published the last of the tentative final monographs in the early 1990s. Nonetheless, even today, about a dozen final monographs remain to be published.

NOTE

Reopening the OTC Drug Review. In 68 Fed. Reg. 75585 (Dec. 31, 2003), FDA published a request for data and information on categories of products it characterized as OTC drugs eligible for the original OTC Drug Review but that had not been reviewed by FDA to date. Many companies did not respond to the notice, and others who did respond objected to the list. In 2008, FDA proposed to expand 21 C.F.R. 310.545, a list of non-GRASE OTC drug ingredients requiring NDAs, by adding those categories and ingredients for which it did not receive any data in response to its 2003 request. 73 Fed. Reg. 34895 (June 19, 2008).

c.   FINAL MONOGRAPHS

A final monograph is published as a rule in the Code of Federal Regulations. In addition to complying with the relevant specific monograph, products must also conform to general requirements for monograph drugs at 21 C.F.R. 330.1. The following monograph is included as an example.

Topical Acne Drug Products

21 C.F.R. Part 333 ("Topical Antimicrobial Drug Products for OTC Human Use"),
Subpart D.

§ 333.301   Scope.

(a) An over-the-counter acne drug product in a form suitable for topical application is generally recognized as safe and effective and is not misbranded if it meets each of the conditions in this subpart and each general condition established in § 330.1 of this chapter. . . .

§ 333.303   Definitions

As used in this subpart:

(a) *Acne.* A disease involving the oil glands and hair follicles of the skin which is manifested by blackheads, whiteheads, acne pimples, and acne blemishes.

(b) *Acne blemish.* A flaw in the skin resulting from acne.

. . . .

(d) *Acne pimple.* A small, prominent, inflamed elevation of the skin resulting from acne.

(e) *Blackhead.* A condition of the skin that occurs in acne and is characterized by a black tip.

(f) *Whitehead.* A condition of the skin that occurs in acne and is characterized by a small, firm, whitish elevation of the skin.

§ 333.310   Acne active ingredients

The active ingredient of the product consists of any of the following:

(a) Benzoyl peroxide, 2.5 to 10 percent.

(b) Resorcinol, 2 percent, when combined with sulfur in accordance with § 333.320(a).

(c) Resorcinol monoacetate, 3 percent, when combined with sulfur in accordance with § 333.320(b).

(d) Salicylic acid, 0.5 to 2 percent.

(e) Sulfur, 3 to 10 percent.

(f) Sulfur, 3 to 8 percent, when combined with resorcinol or resorcinol monoacetate in accordance with § 333.320.

§ 333.320   Permitted combinations of active ingredients

(a) Resorcinol identified in § 333.310(b) may be combined with sulfur identified in § 333.310(f).

(b) Resorcinol monoacetate identified in § 333.310(c) may be combined with sulfur identified in § 333.310(f).

§ 333.350   Labeling of acne drug products

(a) *Statement of identity.* The labeling of the product contains the established name of the drug, if any, and identifies the product as an "acne medication," "acne treatment," "acne medication" (insert dosage form, e.g., "cream," "gel," "lotion," or "ointment"), or "acne treatment" (insert dosage form, e.g., "cream," "gel," "lotion," or "ointment").

(b) *Indications.* The labeling of the product states, under the heading "Indications," the phrase listed in paragraph (b)(1) of this section and may contain any of the additional phrases listed in paragraph (b)(2) of this section. Other truthful and nonmisleading statements, describing only the indications for use that have been established and listed in paragraph (b) of this section, may also be used, as provided in § 330.1(c)(2) of this chapter. . . .

(1) "For the" (select one of the following: "management" or "treatment") "of acne."

(2) In addition to the information identified in paragraph (b)(1) of this section, the labeling of the product may contain any one or more of the following statements:

(i) (Select one of the following: "Clears," "Clears up," "Clears up most," "Dries," "Dries up," "Dries and clears," "Helps clear," "Helps clear up," "Reduces the number of," or "Reduces the severity of") (select one or more of the following: "acne blemishes," "acne pimples," "blackheads," or "whiteheads") which may be followed by "and allows skin to heal."

(ii) "Penetrates pores to" (select one of the following: "eliminate most," "control," "clear most," or "reduce the number of") (select one or more of the following: "acne blemishes," "acne pimples," "blackheads," or "whiteheads").

. . . .

(v) "Helps prevent the development of new" (select one or more of the following: "acne blemishes," "acne pimples," "blackheads," or "whiteheads").

(c) *Warnings.* The labeling of the product contains the following warnings under the heading "Warnings":

(1) *For products containing any ingredients identified in § 330.310.*

(i) The labeling states "For external use only."

(ii) The labeling states "When using this product [bullet] skin irritation and dryness is more likely to occur if you use another topical acne medication at the same time. If irritation occurs, only use one topical acne medication at a time."

. . . .

(d) *Directions.* The labeling of the product contains the following information under the heading "Directions":

(1) *For products applied containing any ingredient identified in § 333.310.* The labeling states "[bullet] clean the skin thoroughly before applying this product [bullet] cover the entire affected area with a thin layer one to three times daily [bullet] because excessive drying of the skin may occur, start with one application daily, then gradually increase to two or three times daily if needed or as directed by a doctor [bullet] if bothersome dryness or peeling occurs, reduce application to once a day or every other day."

. . . .

NOTES

1.   *The NDA Deviation.* A final OTC drug monograph represents only the state of the evidence provided to FDA at the time the monograph is promulgated. FDA recognized that improvements in OTC drugs would occur continuously. The agency therefore included in 21 C.F.R. 330.11 a procedure for an "NDA deviation" from an applicable monograph. This provision specifically authorizes the use of an NDA to request approval of an OTC drug deviating in any respect from a final monograph. The NDA need address only the requirement of the monograph for which the deviation is requested, and it may omit all information except that pertinent to the deviation. The concept is analogous to a section 505(b)(2) NDA for a prescription drug. *See infra* p. 1012. FDA granted one NDA deviation to permit an aerosol pediculicide, where the final monograph permitted only a non-aerosol dosage formulation. In response to a citizen petition requesting that the cough and cold monograph be amended to include a chewing gum dosage form for a topical antitussive drug, FDA responded that the appropriate mechanism would be to submit an NDA deviation under 21 C.F.R. 330.11. Letter from FDA Associate Commissioner for Regulatory Affairs Dennis E. Baker to David L. Rosen (Nov. 9, 2001), FDA Docket No. OIP–0253/CPI.

2.   *Combination OTC Drugs.* The conditions under which combination OTC drugs are permitted have long been in dispute. 21 C.F.R. 330.10(a)(4)(iv), stating the prerequisites for a permissible OTC combination, paraphrases the prescription combination drug regulation (21

C.F.R. 300.50). Many more combinations have been permitted for OTC drugs than for Rx drugs, however.

Because most new OTC drug products utilize combinations of active ingredients, FDA has paid particular attention to the marketing of new combinations not explicitly recognized in an OTC drug monograph. For example, when a company attempted to market a toothpaste containing both an anticaries active ingredient and a tooth desensitizer, a combination not sanctioned by the report of the OTC Dental Drug Panel, the Seventh Circuit upheld FDA's seizure of the product as an unapproved new drug. *United States v. Articles of Drug . . . Promise Toothpaste for Sensitive Teeth,* 826 F.2d 564 (7th Cir. 1987).

3. *OTC Drug "Time and Extent" Applications.* In 2002, FDA promulgated regulations establishing a new mechanism for adding foreign ingredients to OTC drug monographs. 67 Fed. Reg. 3060 (Jan. 23, 2002), codified at 21 C.F.R. 330.14. The agency did so in response to the 1983 *Fmali Herb* decision, *supra* p. 581, which held that marketing experience abroad must be considered in determining whether a food ingredient fits the "generally recognized as safe" exception to "food additive," and in recognition of the fact that there are safe and effective OTC drug ingredients that have been marketed abroad for decades. Under in section 201(p)(2) of the FD&C Act, a drug is a "new drug" even if it is generally recognized as safe and effective based on scientific investigations if it has not been used "to a material extent or for a material time." Thus, the application under the new procedure is called a "time and extent application" (TEA). The information that must be included with a TEA is voluminous, and the procedure established by FDA for consideration of a TEA is complex. Nonetheless, at least ten companies have submitted these applications and some have met with success. *E.g.,* 70 Fed. Reg. 72447 (Dec. 5, 2005); 70 Fed. Reg. 72449 (Dec. 5, 2005)

4. *Daytime Sedatives.* In 44 Fed. Reg. 36378 (June 22, 1979), FDA issued a final order dealing with OTC daytime sedative products. The document set forth FDA's conclusion that "any ingredient when labeled for use as an over-the-counter daytime sedative is not generally recognized as safe and effective for this intended use." The agency's conclusion, which precludes the marketing of any OTC product for use as a daytime sedative, was based on findings that the ingredients used in such products were either ineffective at the dosages used (and potentially toxic at higher dosages) or only capable of rendering the user sleepy. The agency's ruling relied on concerns about potential societal abuse as a basis for its conclusion that no daytime OTC sedative can be generally recognized as safe and effective.

5. *Professional Labeling.* Some OTC drugs have prescription as well as nonprescription indications. In such instances, the applicable monographs specifically provide for "professional labeling" containing these prescription indications. *See, e.g.,* 21 C.F.R. 331.80 (relating to peptic ulcer claims for antacid products); 21 C.F.R. 332.31 (permitting postoperative gas pain claims for antiflatulent products).

6. *First Amendment Considerations.* In two final monographs, serious First Amendment issues were raised. When the final monograph for

OTC sunscreen drug products was promulgated in 64 Fed. Reg. 27666 (May 21, 1999), the affected companies threatened to bring a lawsuit to contest the constitutionality of restrictions on truthful and nonmisleading labeling claims. The monograph was stayed for other reasons, and the agency rejected the First Amendment arguments when it published proposed amendments to the final monograph. 72 Fed. Reg. 49070, 49077–80 (Aug. 27, 2007). Similarly, when the OTC antiperspirant drug product final monograph was promulgated in 68 Fed. Reg. 34273 (June 9, 2003) an affected manufacturer objected on the ground that it permitted only 48-hour duration claims even if longer durations were fully supported by scientific data. In the face of a constitutional objection, FDA stayed the effectiveness of that portion of the final monograph. No further action has been taken on the matter.

7. *Nanotechnology.* A citizen petition filed by environmental organizations requested FDA to determine that nanomaterial versions of traditional OTC sunscreen drug active ingredients manufactured with the use of nanotechnology constitute new drugs requiring a separate NDA. FDA Docket No. 2006P0210 (May 17, 2006). Other interested persons have submitted substantial responses disputing this petition. FDA held a public meeting announced in 71 Fed. Reg. 19523 (Apr. 14, 2006) on the impact of nanotechnology on the agency's regulatory programs. *See also* NATIONAL ACADEMY OF SCIENCES, A MATTER OF SIZE: TRIENNIAL REVIEW OF THE NATIONAL NANOTECHNOLOGY INITIATIVE (2006).

8. *Homeopathic Drugs.* FDA decided to defer consideration of homeopathic drugs, for which there is scant evidence of effectiveness, because they represented such a small volume. *See* 37 Fed. Reg. 9464, 9466 (May 11, 1972). In the interim, *Meserey v. United States,* 447 F. Supp. 548 (D. Nev. 1977), confirmed that homeopathic drugs are subject to all the drug provisions of the FD&C Act. Compliance Policy Guide 7132.15 (May 31, 1988) sets forth FDA's policy on the conditions under which homeopathic drugs may be marketed. *See supra* p. 800.

d.   INACTIVE INGREDIENTS

FDA deferred review of inactive ingredients used in OTC drug products until evaluation of all active ingredients was completed. As one of the general conditions for recognition of an OTC drug as safe, effective, and not misbranded under 21 C.F.R. 330.1(e), all inactive ingredients must be suitable, safe in the amounts administered, and not interfere with the effectiveness or with suitable tests or assays to determine if the product meets its professed standards. In 42 Fed. Reg. 19156 (Apr. 12, 1977), the agency proposed general conditions for use and labeling of inactive ingredients. No further action was taken on this proposal. In 1984, the nonprescription drug industry established its own voluntary program for the labeling of inactive ingredients on OTC drug labels. *See* PROPRIETARY ASSOCIATION, GUIDELINES FOR DISCLOSURE OF INACTIVE INGREDIENTS IN OTC MEDICINES (1984). As part of the FDA Modernization Act of 1997, Congress amended section 502(e)(1)(A)(iii) of the FD&C Act to require all inactive ingredients to be listed on an OTC drug label in alphabetical order. *See* 21 C.F.R. 201.66(c)(8).

There are three types of inactive ingredients: (1) those that are inert and serve no functional purpose in the product, (2) those that facilitate the activity of the active ingredients but that exert no activity of their own, and (3) those that serve as a pharmacological adjuvant and therefore are regulated as an active ingredient. Although the line between each of these categories is not always clear, the preambles to several proposed, tentative final, and final monographs discuss these three categories and draw distinctions among them.

4. OTC DRUG LABELING

Two aspects of OTC drug labeling must be considered: (1) the restrictions established under the OTC Drug Review and (2) the "Drug Facts" format established in 1999.

a. OTC DRUG REVIEW RESTRICTIONS

At the outset of the OTC Drug Review, FDA intended that the only label claims that could lawfully be made for an OTC drug were those specified in a final monograph for the class of drugs or approved by the agency in a new drug application. The agency took the position on several occasions that a manufacturer must use the precise terminology set forth in the monograph in describing the indications for use of a product or in providing warnings about misuse. *E.g.*, 38 Fed. Reg. 31260, 31261, 31264 (Nov. 12, 1973); 39 Fed. Reg. 19862, 19868 (June 4, 1974). This so-called "exclusivity" policy did not prevent the use of accurate and non-misleading descriptive phrases or adjectives, e.g., "sparkling" antacid. 40 Fed. Reg. 11718 (Mar. 13, 1975).

Manufacturers of OTC drugs opposed FDA's exclusivity policy for a decade, arguing that greater flexibility should be permitted for both legal and policy reasons. After a public hearing announced in 47 Fed. Reg. 29002 (July 2, 1982), the FDA published the following proposal.

Labeling of Drug Products for Over-the-Counter Human Use

50 Fed. Reg. 15810 (April 22, 1985).

. . . .

The policy of limiting monograph labeling terminology to specific words and phrases considered and approved by FDA has been the subject of comment throughout the OTC drug review process. With the publication of the tentative final monograph for OTC antacid drug products in the Federal Register of November 12, 1973 (38 FR 31280), FDA responded to comments proposing that terms other than those specified in the monograph should be allowed in the product labeling. The agency concluded that the terms recommended by the panel fully met the intent of the regulation. The agency also stated that allowing each manufacturer to select words other than those set forth in the monograph would result in continued consumer confusion and deception (38 FR 31264). . . .

The objections to the exclusivity policy were resubmitted with respect to nighttime sleep-aid and stimulant drug products after publication of the tentative final monographs for these products, and an oral hearing was requested. . . .

The notice of hearing defined the scope of the hearing broadly as encompassing all aspects, both practical and legal, of the exclusivity policy and its possible alternatives. . . .

The agency has decided . . . that the present exclusivity policy, while legally supportable, should not be continued for policy reasons. FDA specifically rejects the assertions in the submitted comments that the present policy is legally deficient on constitutional grounds, is in violation of the Administrative Procedure Act (APA), or contrary to the Federal Food, Drug, and Cosmetic Act. . . .

The agency believes that labeling established in an OTC drug monograph would continue to serve a vital purpose. It would represent the agency's determination, following extensive notice and comment rulemaking, of the specific indications for which an OTC drug product would be generally recognized as safe and effective, and not misbranded. Because the monographs would provide a definitive explanation of those uses a particular drug is good for, FDA would be able to determine whether nonmonograph language is an accurate description of a drug's properties. . . .

The agency emphasizes, as described below in the discussion of the proposed regulation, that it will use the monograph language as a regulatory benchmark. FDA will carefully examine any alternative language to ensure that it does not go beyond the approved indications, thereby causing the drug to become a "new drug" or misbranded, or both, under the act. Language that is so nondescriptive as to be meaningless, or that indicates uses for a new indication, would cause the product to be misbranded, a new drug, or both. . . .

NOTE

Although the proposed rule would have allowed the use of alternative wording throughout the label, the final regulation, promulgated in 51 Fed. Reg. 16258 (May 1, 1986), specified that flexibility was allowed only for labeled "indications" and not for any other required features of OTC drug labeling. That provision, which has since been simplified, 64 Fed. Reg. 13254 (Mar. 17, 1999), currently reads:

> The "Uses" section of the label and labeling of the product shall contain the labeling describing the "Indications" that have been established in an applicable OTC drug monograph or alternative truthful and nonmisleading statements describing only those indications for use that have been established in an applicable monograph, subject to the provisions of section 502 of the act relating to misbranding and the prohibition in section 301(d) of the act against the introduction or delivery for introduction into interstate commerce of unapproved new drugs in violation of section 505(a) of the act. Any other labeling . . . shall be stated in the exact language where exact language has been established and identified by quotation marks in an applicable OTC drug monograph or by regulation (e.g., § 201.63 of this chapter), except as provided in paragraphs (i) and (j) of this section

[listing interchangeable terms that may be used and connecting terms that may be deleted].

21 C.F.R. 330.1(c)(2).

b.   OTC "DRUG FACTS" FORMAT

Drawing on its "nutrition facts" food labeling initiative, in February 1997 FDA proposed to standardize OTC drug labeling. The rule, proposed in the excerpt below, was finalized at 64 Fed. Reg. 13254 (Mar. 17, 1999) and codified at 21 C.F.R. 201.66.

Over-the-Counter Human Drugs; Proposed Labeling Requirements

62 Fed. Reg. 9024 (February 27, 1997).

Under the Federal Food, Drug, and Cosmetic Act, OTC Drug products must be safe and effective in order to be marketed. The agency is conducting a comprehensive review of these drug products, which are available to consumers without a prescription. As a result of this review, the agency has required specific language to be included in the labeling of many OTC drug products, describing the uses, directions, warnings, drug interaction precautions, active ingredients, and other information, so that consumers can use these products safely and effectively.

As a result of escalating health care costs and the increasing availability of OTC drug products, some of which were once available only by prescription, more consumers are engaging in self-medication. Thus, it is increasingly important that consumers read and understand the information on drug product labeling.

On January 6, 1993, the agency issued final regulations to help consumers read and understand the information on food product labeling. . . .

FDA believes it is equally important for consumers to be able to make reasoned decisions about the drugs they take. On August 24, 1995 (60 FR 44182), FDA proposed a comprehensive program to increase the distribution and quality of easy to read and easy to understand written information about prescription drugs to patients. Recently enacted legislation provides that various private entities will work to transform these goals into a satisfactory program. FDA is now proposing to improve the way that information on the labeling of OTC drug products is communicated.

The design, format, and placement of required labeling information varies considerably among OTC drug products. As a result, consumers often have difficulty finding, reading, and understanding this labeling information. Modifying and simplifying the manner in which the information is presented can improve the legibility and understandability of OTC drug product labeling. FDA is, therefore, proposing to establish a standardized format for the labeling of all marketed OTC drug products. This action is intended to enable consumers to better read and understand OTC drug product labeling and to apply this information to the safe and effective use of OTC drug products.

The agency is proposing five types of labeling changes for OTC drug products. First, the proposal would require that OTC drug product labeling include standardized headings and subheadings presented in a standardized order, as well as standardized graphical features such as the Helvetica type style, minimum standards for type size, leading (i.e., space between two lines of text), kerning (spacing between letters), upper and lower case letters, and graphical highlights.

Second, the proposal would permit manufacturers, packers, or distributors to delete specific terms, referred to for purposes of this rulemaking as "connecting terms," that are currently required in OTC drug product labeling. . . . Typically, such terms are found within quotation marks in OTC drug monographs and in specific regulations. Deletion of these terms would only be permitted where deletion would not change the meaning of the information. . . .

Third, the proposal would expand the list of "interchangeable terms" found in the current regulations, to facilitate the use of more concise, easier to understand statements on the labeling of OTC drug products. . . .

Fourth, the proposal would amend specific warning language required under current monographs and regulations (the pregnancy-nursing warning, the "keep out of reach of children" warning, and the overdose/accidental ingestion warning) make the warnings easier to understand and more concise.

Finally, in order to ensure OTC drug product labeling is easier to read and understand, and to ensure the safe and effective use of OTC drug products, FDA is proposing to preempt State and local rules that establish different or additional format or content requirements than those in this proposed rule. . . .

————

The final regulations, promulgated in 65 Fed. Reg. 13254 (Mar. 17, 1999), closely followed the proposal, except that FDA deleted the preemption provision. It did so because in 1997, FDAMA added FD&C Act 751 ("National Uniformity for Nonprescription Drugs"), which accomplishes the same objective. One of the sample OTC drug labels used by FDA to illustrate the new format follows.

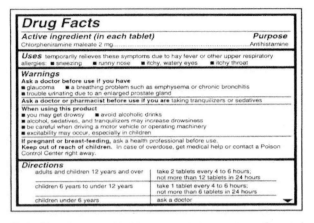

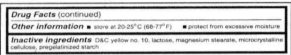

c. OTC DRUG LABEL WARNINGS

There is a substantial difference between the standards for a labeling warning for a prescription and a nonprescription drug. The standard for a prescription drug warning in 21 C.F.R. 201.57(c)(6) states that:

> . . . The labeling must be revised to include a warning about a clinically significant hazard as soon as there is reasonable evidence of a causal association with a drug; a causal relationship need not have been definitely established.

FDA thus often requires warnings of potential adverse events in prescription drug labeling where causality has not been established. In contrast, label warnings for nonprescription drugs—which are directed at consumers, not physicians—are required to address only proven risks. FDA has stated that nonprescription label warnings must be "scientifically documented, clinically significant, and important for the safe and effective use of the products by the average consumer." 47 Fed. Reg. 54750, 54754 (Dec. 3, 1982); 53 Fed. Reg. 46204, 46213 (Nov. 16, 1988). Accordingly, when a drug is switched from prescription to nonprescription status it is entirely possible that the labeled warnings will change. *See* R. William Soller, *When To Warn*, 2 REG. AFFAIRS FOCUS, No. 10 at 18 (Oct. 1997).

NOTES

1. *Extra-Monograph Warnings.* In 21 C.F.R. Part 201, Subparts C & G, FDA has, outside the monograph process, mandated various OTC drug warnings. *See, e.g.,* 21 C.F.R. 201.63 (pregnancy/breast-feeding warning), 201.70(c), 71(c) & 72(c) (calcium, magnesium, and potassium warnings), 201.308 (ipecac syrup warning), 201.325 (nonoxynol 9 vaginal contraceptive products warnings).

2. *Aspirin Warnings.* In *Public Citizen Health Research Group v. Commissioner,* 740 F.2d 21 (D.C. Cir. 1984), the Court of Appeals declined to order FDA to require a warning on aspirin-containing products about the risk of Reye's Syndrome. FDA ultimately did prescribe such a warning. 51 Fed. Reg. 8180 (Mar. 7, 1986), 53 Fed. Reg. 21633 (June 9, 1988), codified at 21 C.F.R. 201.314(h). A warning against the use of aspirin in the last 3 months of pregnancy was mandated in 55 Fed. Reg. 27776 (July 5, 1990), codified at 21 C.F.R. 201.63.

3. *Proposition 65 Warnings.* Under California Proposition 65, nicotine products are required to bear a warning about reproductive toxicity. Under the NDA for nicotine smoking cessation products, however, FDA concluded that such a warning was inappropriate and could not be used. In *Dowhal v. Smithkline Beecham Consumer Healthcare,* 88 P.3d 1 (Cal. 2004), the California Supreme Court held that, under these circumstances, the FDA determination preempted the California law.

4. *Adverse Event Reporting.* In late 2006, Congress enacted the Dietary Supplement and Nonprescription Drug Consumer Protection Act, 120 Stat. 3469, which added sections 760 and 761 to the FD&C Act to require the reporting to FDA of serious adverse events for both dietary supplements and nonprescription drugs. The law provides that such a report does not constitute an admission that the product caused the adverse event, and it preempts any non-identical state law.

5. FTC REGULATION OF OTC DRUG ADVERTISING

Congress declined in 1938 to give FDA jurisdiction to regulate drug advertising and instead confirmed the advertising authority of the Federal Trade Commission. *See* David Cavers, *The Food, Drug, and Cosmetic Act of 1938: Its Legislative History and Its Substantive Provisions,* 6 LAW & CONTEMP. PROBS. 2 (1939). Congress granted FDA authority to regulate advertising for prescription drugs in the Drug Amendments of 1962. FD&C Act 502(n); *see supra* p. 907. With respect to OTC drugs, however, FTC retains the jurisdiction that Congress conferred in 1938.

The two agencies are supposed to cooperate in exercising their abutting responsibilities. *See* FDA–FTC Memorandum of Understanding, 36 Fed. Reg. 18539 (Sept. 16, 1971). FDA's commencement of the OTC Drug Review promised new opportunities for collaboration. In determining what label claims for OTC drugs were supported by legally adequate evidence of effectiveness and would not render drugs misbranded, FDA would inevitably examine evidence that might be pertinent to a determination of whether advertising claims for a drug were deceptive. Both agencies hoped that the FTC would be able to make use of FDA's monographs in a fashion that would limit claims in advertising to those approved for labeling.

Based on FDA's adoption of the "exclusivity" policy in the 1970s, *see supra* p. 985, the FTC proposed a trade regulation rule (TRR) under sections 5 and 12 of the Federal Trade Commission Act, 15 U.S.C. 45, 52, that would have translated FDA's OTC drug monographs into commensurate restrictions on advertising. 40 Fed. Reg. 52631 (Nov. 11, 1975). Under the terms of the rule as proposed, it would have been a violation of the FTC Act to disseminate an advertisement for an OTC drug in any drug category

> for which an applicable final monograph has been established by the Food and Drug Administration . . . which advertisement makes any claim, directly or by implication, which the Commissioner of Food and Drugs has determined, in a final order accompanying such monograph, may not appear in the labeling of such drug.

FTC staff supporting the proposed rule argued that in the course of approving label claims in a final monograph, FDA necessarily concluded that other terminology would not convey the same message to consumers, and accordingly that drugs bearing other terminology would not be generally recognized as safe and effective and not misbranded. From this premise, it was a small step to the conclusion that advertising using nonconforming terminology to describe a drug's performance would be deceptive.

The presiding officer's report largely rejected the staff position. 44 Fed. Reg. 1123 (Jan. 4, 1979). Although the staff persevered, 44 Fed. Reg. 31241 (May 31, 1979), the full Commission terminated the proceeding in 46 Fed. Reg. 24584 (May 1, 1981) with the following explanation:

> The Commission has concluded that in advertising a drug for a permissible (i.e., FDA-approved) purpose, advertisers should not always be limited (as they would have been under the original proposed rule) to the labeling language approved by FDA.

The Commission declared that it would continue to review advertising for OTC drugs, in the light of FDA monographs, to determine whether further action was necessary. As discussed above, FDA itself abandoned the exclusivity policy with respect to the statement of indications in 1986. *Supra* p. 985.

NOTES

1. *Indirect FDA Authority.* Although FTC has primary jurisdiction over OTC drug advertising, FDA regulations state that monograph drugs are generally recognized as safe and effective and not misbranded only if "[t]he advertising for the product prescribes, recommends, or suggests its use only under the conditions stated in the labeling." 21 C.F.R. 330.1(d).

2. *FDA Label Warnings in Advertising.* The FTC proposed a second TRR to require that some of the label warnings required by the final FDA monograph for antacid drugs also appear in advertising. 41 Fed. Reg. 14534 (Apr. 6, 1976), 43 Fed. Reg. 38851 (Aug. 31, 1978). Following a public hearing, publication of the staff report, and an oral hearing before the Commissioners, the FTC terminated this proceeding. 49 Fed. Reg. 46156 (Nov. 23, 1984). The Commission concluded that the record did not support the staff's contention that antacid advertisements would be deceptive or unfair if they failed to contain warnings similar to those required by FDA in labeling.

3. *Defensive Use of OTC Panel Report.* For an unsuccessful attempt by a respondent before the FTC to use the tentative conclusions of an OTC

Drug Review panel defensively, see *Warner–Lambert Co. v. FTC*, 562 F.2d 749 (D.C. Cir. 1977).

4. *Claim Substantiation.* In *Pfizer, Inc.*, 81 F.T.C. 23 (1972), the FTC enunciated the policy that it is unfair and deceptive for a manufacturer to make any affirmative drug product claim without having a "reasonable basis" for it. Relying on the prevailing view of experts in the field, the Commission has required at least two clinical studies to substantiate OTC drug advertising claims. *See Thompson Medical Co., Inc.*, 104 F.T.C. 648 (1984), *aff'd*, 791 F.2d 189 (D.C. Cir. 1986); *Bristol-Myers Co.*, 102 F.T.C. 21 (1983), *aff'd*, 738 F.2d 554 (2d Cir. 1984); *American Home Products Corp.*, 98 F.T.C. 136 (1981), *aff'd*, 695 F.2d 681 (3d Cir. 1982).

5. *Corrective Advertising.* In *Warner–Lambert Co. v. FTC*, 562 F.2d 749 (D.C. Cir. 1977), the FTC for the first time required corrective advertising for an OTC drug. It was not until *Novartis Corp. v. FTC*, 223 F.3d 783 (D.C. Cir. 2000), that the FTC used this remedy a second time.

6. *Options for Competitors.* Not infrequently a company finds that competitors' advertisements are making unjustified comparison against the company's own product. There are a limited number of actions that the company can take to contest such claims.

• *Complain to FDA.* One option is to bring the matter to the attention of FDA and request that the agency take appropriate regulatory action. Unfortunately, even in egregious cases, FDA often replies that it has very few resources and that this type of competitive problem is a low priority for the agency. If FDA does take action, it is almost always limited to a warning letter, and the competitive claim usually remains in place for a lengthy period of time.

• *Complain to the FTC.* As with the FDA, it is not easy to persuade the FTC to challenge a competitive claim. Even if the FTC ultimately decides to act, it may take months to persuade the agency and much longer before final agency action occurs.

• *Complain to the NAD.* The National Advertising Division of the Better Business Bureau conducts a program under which a company may initiate a proceeding in which the NAD reviews a competitive claim and offers an opinion on it. In most instances, the party making the competitive claim will comply with the NAD opinion. If it does not, the NAD will then refer the matter to the FTC or the FDA, where it receives a much higher priority than if the complaining company went to these agencies in the first place. An NDA proceeding can, however, take several months, during which the claim may continue to be made. *See generally* Jeffrey S. Edelstein, *Self–Regulation of Advertising: An Alternative to Litigation and Government Action*, 43 IDEA: THE J. OF LAW AND TECH. 509 (2003).

• *Complain to the Broadcast Media.* A complaint to the broadcast media can produce faster action if the matter is clear-cut. The FTC has been known to include advertising agencies and broadcast companies in false advertising proceedings. The media must therefore take seriously complaints about clearly misleading advertising.

• *A Lanham Act Lawsuit.* Finally, the company may have a cause of action against a competitor under section 43(a) of the Lanham Act. This statute provides a private right of action for unfair competition based on false or misleading claims in labeling or advertising. It does not provide a remedy for failure to adhere to the FD&C Act or FDA regulations per se, but it does offer a strong remedy against false or misleading competitive claims. *E.g., Zeneca Inc. v. Eli Lilly and Co.,* 1999 WL 509471 (S.D.N.Y. 1999).

6. OTC DRUG PRODUCT PACKAGING

In 1982, in response to purposeful cyanide contamination of Tylenol resulting in the death of several persons in Chicago, FDA promptly promulgated final regulations to require tamper-resistant packaging for non-prescription drugs and cosmetics. 21 C.F.R. 211.132 (OTC drugs), 700.25 (cosmetics).

Tamper-Resistant Packaging Requirements for Certain Over-the-Counter Human Drug and Cosmetic Products

47 Fed. Reg. 50442 (November 5, 1982).

FDA is issuing final regulations to require tamper-resistant packaging for certain over-the-counter (OTC) drug and cosmetic products. OTC drug products subject to these regulations include all OTC drug products except dermatologics (i.e., products applied to the skin), dentifrices, and insulin. The OTC drug products that are covered by these regulations include oral (except dentifrices), nasal, otic, ophthalmic, rectal, and vaginal drug products. Cosmetic products covered by these regulations are liquids that are used orally, such as mouthwashes, gargles, breath fresheners, etc., and vaginal cosmetic products. The agency is requiring that the packaging of these products be capable of providing consumers with visible evidence of package tampering. . . .

On September 30, 1982, FDA was advised that several persons living in the Chicago metropolitan area had died from cyanide poisoning after taking Extra–Strength Tylenol capsules. Capsules taken from bottles of Extra–Strength Tylenol in the possession of the victims were chemically analyzed by local authorities, and some of the capsules in these bottles were found to contain lethal amounts of potassium cyanide. By October 1, several more Chicago area residents had died from cyanide poisoning after ingesting Tylenol Extra–Strength capsules, bringing the total of deaths to seven.

On September 30, government authorities and the manufacturer of Tylenol, McNeil Consumer Products, Fort Washington, PA, began an investigation to determine the manner in which the capsules had become contaminated with cyanide. The capsules involved in the seven deaths were manufactured in two plants, one in Pennsylvania and one in Texas. FDA investigators immediately inspected both plants. Based on the plant inspections, FDA concluded that the contamination had not occurred at either plant, but rather was the result of tampering after the capsules had been shipped to distribution points and, most likely, after they had reached the retail shelves. . . .

The poisoning fatalities make plain the gravity of the risk to which the nation's population is exposed from malicious tampering with drug products sold over-the-counter to the consumer. . . . [T]he need for adequate product security is national in scope and requires an industrywide response. . . .

The agency defines a tamper-resistant package as one having an indicator or barrier to entry which, if breached or missing, can reasonably be expected to provide visible evidence to consumers that tampering has occurred. Tamper-resistant packaging may involve immediate-container/closure systems or secondary-container/carton systems or any combination thereof intended to provide a visual indication of package integrity when handled in a reasonable manner during manufacture, distribution, and retail display. The visual indication is required to be accompanied by appropriate illustrations or precautionary statements to describe the safeguarding mechanism to the consumer. To reduce the possibility that the security mechanism can be restored after tampering, the agency is also requiring that either the tamper-resistant feature be designed from materials that are generally not readily available (*e.g.*, an aerosol system) or that barriers made from readily obtainable material (*e.g.*, plain tape, paper seals, clear plastic) carry a distinctive design or logo.

The agency stresses that tamper-*proof* packaging is not possible. Although the requirements in this final rule will reduce the potential for tampering, they cannot eliminate it. Neither the agency nor manufacturers can guarantee protection against malicious tampering but can only make tampering more difficult by making product packaging more *resistant* to tampering. For this reason, the agency will consider any labeling statement suggesting that the package is tamper-proof, as contrasted with tamper-resistant, to be false and misleading. . . .

Under the Federal Food, Drug, and Cosmetic Act, FDA is authorized to impose requirements necessary to assure that drugs meet the requirements of the act for identity, strength, quality, and purity. Such requirements may be imposed as current good manufacturing practice (CGMP) (21 U.S.C. 351(a)(2)(B)). . . .

. . . The requirements set forth in FDA's CGMP regulations for pharmaceutical products represent those measures needed to ensure that drugs purchased by the people of this country meet all statutory requirements at the time of purchase. Such measures must now include provision for container and package design that provides protection against intentional product adulteration by means of tampering.

FDA's authority to issue Federal standards for tamper-resistant drug packaging is also derived from other provisions of the act relating to drug adulteration. Under section 501(b) of the act, drugs are required to meet applicable compendial standards for strength, quality, and purity. Under section 501(c) of the act, drugs not subject to compendial standards are required to possess the strength, quality, and purity they are represented to have. Because contamination of drugs by tampering causes these requirements to be violated, FDA is authorized to impose packaging requirements reasonably designed to prevent such contamination. . . .

NOTES

1. *Preemption.* In order to make certain that state and local governments would not enact different or additional anti-tampering requirements, FDA included a specific administrative determination of federal preemption. 47 Fed. Reg. at 50447–50448.

2. *Anti-Tampering Act.* In response to the Chicago Tylenol poisonings, Congress enacted the Federal Anti–Tampering Act, 97 Stat. 831 (1983), codified at 18 U.S.C. § 1365, which makes it a crime to tamper with a consumer product with reckless disregard for the risk of persons or with intent to cause injury to a business. The statute also prohibits the communication of false information that a consumer product has been tainted and threats to tamper with a consumer product. For examples of prosecution under this statute, see *United States v. Garnett*, 122 F.3d 1016 (11th Cir. 1997); *United States v. Moyer*, 985 F. Supp. 924 (D. Minn. 1997); *United States v. Acosta*, Food Drug Cosm. L. Rep. (CCH) ¶ 38,294 (S.D.N.Y. 1992).

3. *The PPPA and Child-Resistant Packaging.* The Consumer Product Safety Commission (CPSC) administers the Poison Prevention Packaging Act of 1970 (PPPA), 84 Stat. 1670. In addition to requiring poison prevention packaging for almost all oral prescription drugs, *see supra* p. 888, note 2, the PPPA regulations also requires poison prevention packaging for some OTC drugs. FDA was responsible for implementing the PPPA before the Consumer Product Safety Commission was established, and in 1972 it issued a regulation requiring that aspirin products be marketed in child-resistant packaging. 37 Fed. Reg. 3127 (Feb. 6, 1972). In *Nutritional Health Alliance v. FDA*, 318 F.3d 92 (2d Cir. 2003), the Court of Appeals held that CPSC has exclusive jurisdiction over poison prevention packaging and therefore that FDA has no jurisdiction to require unit dose packaging for drugs and dietary supplements.

Under section 4(a) of the PPPA, 15 U.S.C. 1473(a), manufacturers have the right to package a nonprescription drug in one size of non-child-resistant packaging if the company also supplies the drug in child-resistant packaging of a popular size and the noncomplying package bears a conspicuous statement that "this package for households without young children." This exception does not apply to prescription drugs, but samples distributed to physicians are not required to be in child-resistant packaging. 49 Fed. Reg. 8008 (Mar. 5, 1984). The Drug and Household Substance Mailing Act of 1990, 104 Stat. 1184, prohibits the mailing of a "household substance" (which includes OTC drugs) that does not comply with any special child-resistant packaging requirements established for the product under the Poison Prevention Packaging Act of 1970. In 2001, the CPSC promulgated a requirement of child resistant packaging for all drugs approved by FDA for OTC sale that contain active ingredients formerly available only by prescription. 66 Fed. Reg. 40111 (Aug. 2, 2001), codified at 16 C.F.R. 1700.14(a)(30).

K. GENERIC DRUGS

1. FDA AND GENERIC DRUGS BEFORE HATCH-WAXMAN (1984)

FDA has been required to confront the issue of generic, or "me-too," drugs ever since the advent of the NDA in 1938. As discussed previously, *supra* p. 780, in addition to the new drug products that entered the market between 1938 and 1962 with effective NDAs, many thousands of similar formulations entered the market without NDAs during this period. Manufacturers of these products either concluded independently that they were GRAS (and thus not "new drugs") because an NDA was in effect for another version, or they obtained an opinion from FDA that their drugs were GRAS. Though the agency kept no record of these "old drug" opinions, it issued several thousand between 1942 and 1962. By 1962, for every pioneer drug with an effective NDA, many additional me-too copies were on the market without an effective NDA.

The enactment of the 1962 Drug Amendments, adding the requirement that drug demonstrate substantial evidence of effectiveness, forced the agency to grapple with these numerous me-too products in a daunting new context. (You might find it useful to review the earlier discussion of the DESI Review's treatment of me-too drugs before proceeding with this subsection. *Supra* p. 780.)

Soon after the NAS began to deliver its DESI reports to FDA in 1967, FDA devised the "abbreviated NDA" to secure control over, and at the same time allow marketing of, generic copies of pre-1962 prescription drugs that had been deemed by the DESI review to be effective for one or more indications. 34 Fed. Reg. 2673 (Feb. 27, 1969), 35 Fed. Reg. 6574 (Apr. 24, 1970). An abbreviated NDA was required to contain information only on biological availability (to demonstrate bioequivalence) and manufacturing controls. No court ever ruled on the legality of the core of the abbreviated NDA policy—namely, the fact that under this approach, the agency approved the marketing of me-too versions of pre-1962 NDA'd drugs without the submission of full reports of safety and effectiveness and without formal release of the safety and effectiveness data supporting the pioneer product. The Drug Price Competition and Patent Term Restoration Act of 1984 (Hatch–Waxman) ultimately codified this policy.

Nonetheless, both pioneer and generic manufacturers challenged certain aspects of FDA's use of the abbreviated NDA in court. The pioneer industry struck first. As discussed *supra* at p. 780, in 1970 FDA, foreseeing an ever-growing mountain of abbreviated NDAs for drugs deemed to be effective in final DESI notices, informally embraced the practice of permitting me-too drugs to be marketed upon *submission* of an abbreviated NDA, even before the application was approved. This approach applied regardless of whether the abbreviated NDA was for a me-too product introduced prior to the issuance of the relevant DESI notice or one marketed by a new manufacturer subsequent to the notice. A pioneer manufacturer successfully challenged FDA's interim policy in the case below.

Hoffman–LaRoche, Inc. v. Weinberger

425 F. Supp. 890 (D.D.C. 1975).

■ June L. Green, District Judge. . . .

Plaintiff, Hoffmann–LaRoche, Inc., has brought suit for declaratory and injunctive relief. . . . Specifically, Hoffmann–LaRoche challenges the FDA's policy of permitting the introduction of a new drug in interstate commerce without first approving a new drug application for such drug as required by 21 U.S.C. §§ 331, 355 (1970). . . .

. . . Hoffmann–LaRoche is the holder of three approved new drug applications for compounds which contain chlordiazepoxide or chlordiazepoxide hydrochloride (both hereafter referred to as "chlordiazepoxide"). Plaintiff markets these drugs under the trademark "Librium." Since 1959, when Hoffmann–LaRoche first filed a new drug application for chlordiazepoxide, Hoffmann–LaRoche has marketed the drug only after it has obtained approval by the FDA of its new drug applications.

. . . In March 1973, Zenith filed an abbreviated new drug application with the FDA on chlordiazepoxide. On February 27, 1975, plaintiff filed this action in district court. . . .

The crux of this controversy is the use by the FDA of the new drug application procedure as a sort of administrative holding action to regulate the sale and manufacture of "me-too" drugs. Me-too drugs are drugs which are chemically equivalent to a pioneer drug for which a full new drug application is in effect. It is estimated that five to thirteen me-too drugs exist for every new drug that has a FDA approved new drug application. It is the present policy of the FDA, termed an interim policy, to require the filing of an abbreviated new drug application by the manufacturers of each me-too drug where the pioneer drug has a full new drug application approved pursuant to 21 U.S.C. § 355 (1970). The FDA's position is that marketing of these drugs may be permitted without the approval of each individual [abbreviated] new drug application.

The FDA advances two principal arguments to justify its policy. First, it claims that its compliance resources are limited and must be concentrated primarily in those areas where a potential health problem exists. Thus, the FDA has directed its compliance activities toward those drug products which have been found ineffective rather than toward those which have been found effective. Second, for those drugs that the NAS/NRC have found effective and are widely recognized as safe and effective and no bioavailability or special manufacturing problem is known or suspected, the need to police their distribution is minimal. Additionally, the FDA claims that it would have a difficult time in court contending that a specific version is a new drug within the meaning of 21 U.S.C. § 321(p) (1970).

On the contrary, Hoffmann–LaRoche argues that the FDA's action is another example of its failure to follow the 1962 New Drug Amendment. . . . Plaintiff contends that the plain meaning of section 355 dictates that once the FDA requires a new drug application to be filed, then the approval process must be completed before such drug can be marketed. . . .

Reaching the merits of plaintiff's statutory argument, the Court holds that the FDA's policy of permitting new drugs to be marketed without an approved new drug application contravenes the clear statutory requirement of preclearance mandated by 21 U.S.C. § 355 (1970). The FDA's choice of policy is not within the intendment of the 1962 New Drug Amendments and the legislative scheme they embody.

. . . The Court recognizes that the FDA is to be given the administrative flexibility to make regulations and to determine the new drug status of individual drugs or classes of drugs. Certainly it has the power to promulgate regulations that adopt a monograph procedure for human prescription drugs similar to that adopted for over-the-counter drugs whereby a drug or drugs may be declared to be no longer new drugs. *See* 21 C.F.R. § 330.10 (1974). The FDA can regulate the bioequivalence and special manufacturing problems through its general rule-making power. However, the argument that the FDA lacks the administrative resources to insure compliance with section 355 cannot be permitted to postpone to some indefinite future date the implementation of the required preclearance approval of new drug applications. . . .

Summary judgment will therefore be entered for the plaintiff. Defendants will be permanently enjoined from implementing its policy which permits the introduction into interstate commerce without an approved new drug application of prescription drugs which the FDA has previously declared to be new drugs within the meaning of 21 U.S.C. § 321(p).

––––––

FDA did not appeal Judge Green's ruling that FDA could not sanction the marketing of me-too drugs without an individualized determination of old drug status. In 1976, FDA announced the availability of a new guideline explaining the agency's policy for implementing the *Hoffman–LaRoche* decision. This document, codified as Compliance Policy Guide 7132c.02, set forth the agency's process for bringing regulatory action against me-too drugs being marketed without an approved NDA or abbreviated NDA. 41 Fed. Reg. 41770 (Sept. 23, 1976). This enforcement policy was in turn challenged by generic manufacturers, who contended that generic drugs were not "new drugs" and thus not required to have abbreviated NDAs—let alone full NDAs—approved prior to marketing.

Two courts of appeals split on the question whether a generic version of an approved pioneer drug was a "new drug" in the first place. In the case excerpted below, the Supreme Court resolved this conflict, holding that the Act's definition of "drug" includes inactive as well as active ingredients and therefore that a generic version of a pioneer drug requires its own NDA or abbreviated NDA if it differs in any significant respect from the pioneer—a principle that still holds true today.

United States v. Generix Drug Corp.

460 U.S. 453 (1983).

■ JUSTICE STEVENS delivered the opinion of the Court.

The question presented is whether the statutory prohibition against the marketing of a "new drug" without the prior approval of the Food and Drug Administration (FDA) requires respondent Generix Drug Corp. to have approved new drug applications (NDA's) before it may market its generic drug products. In statutory terms, we are required to determine whether the term "drug" as used in the relevant sections of the Federal Food, Drug, and Cosmetic Act (Act), as amended, 21 U.S.C. § 301 *et seq.* (1976 ed. and Supp. V), refers only to the active ingredient in a drug product or to the entire product. We hold that Congress intended the word to have the broader meaning. . . .

In examining [FD&C Act 201(g)(1), the statutory definition of the term "drug"], the Court of Appeals was persuaded that only active ingredients come within the terms of subsection (A). Unfortunately, the [Court of Appeals] did not analyze the entire definition. If it had done so, it would have noted both that the terms of subsections (A), (B), and (C) are plainly broad enough to include more than just active ingredients, and that they *must* do so unless subsection (D) is to be superfluous. Because the definition is disjunctive, generic drug products are quite plainly drugs within the meaning of the Act.

In this case we are not required to determine what types of differences between drugs would be significant or insignificant under the statute. Respondent Generix argued only that its products are not new drugs under the theory that "drug" means "active ingredient"; it does not argue that its complete products—active ingredients and excipients together—are the same as previously approved products. The latter argument would, of course, have been unavailing on the facts before us; for the respondent has not questioned the District Court's finding of a reasonable possibility that its products are not bioequivalent to any previously approved products. We thus do not reach the issue of whether two demonstrably bioequivalent products, containing the same active ingredients but different excipients, might under some circumstances be the same "drug."

In summary, a generic drug product is a "drug" within the meaning of § 201(g)(1) of the Act. Such a product is therefore a "new drug," subject to the requirements of § 505, until the product (and not merely its active ingredient) no longer falls within the terms of § 201(p). . . .

NOTES

1. *Post-1962 Drugs.* This decision prompted FDA officials to begin development of a policy for approval of abbreviated NDAs for post-1962 generic drugs and eventually provoked a suit by generic drug manufacturers to force the agency to issue such a policy. One year after *Generix*, the legislation ultimately enacted as the Drug Price Competition and Patent Term Act of 1984 was introduced.

2. *Exceptions to Generix?* In *United States v. Atropine Sulfate 1.0 Mg. (Article of Drug),* 843 F.2d 860 (5th Cir. 1988), the Court of Appeals

rejected the claimant's argument that its generic product was "uniquely equivalent" to the pioneer new drug and thus fell within the exception left open by the Supreme Court in the *Generix* decision.

3.   *"Paper NDAs" for Post-1962 Drugs.* Prior to the enactment of the Drug Price Competition and Patent Term Restoration Act of 1984, FDA refused to accept abbreviated NDAs for generic copies of post-1962 new drugs. The agency was, however, concerned that an approach that required redundant preclinical and clinical testing of generic equivalent products would not increase protection of consumers and would burden scarce testing facilities. In 1978, it announced the following "paper NDA" policy for approval of duplicates of post-1962 new drugs:

> A drug marketed for the first time after 1962 under an approved New Drug Application may be marketed by a second firm only after the second firm has received the approval of a full New Drug Application for that purpose. Current Agency policy does not permit ANDAs for this purpose. Present interpretation of the law is that no data in the NDA can be utilized to support another NDA without express permission of the original NDA holder. Thus, in the case of duplicate NDAs for already approved post-62 drugs, the Agency will accept published reports as the main supporting documentation for safety and effectiveness. The Agency will not interpret the "full reports of investigations" phrase in the law as requiring either case reports or an exhaustive review of all published reports on the drug. Depending upon the quality of the published data, selected preclinical and perhaps additional clinical studies may be required of the new sponsor prior to NDA approval.

Memorandum from FDA Bureau of Drugs Associate Director of New Drug Evaluation (July 31, 1978). This policy was upheld in *Burroughs Wellcome Co. v. Schweiker,* 649 F.2d 221 (4th Cir. 1981), and *Upjohn Manufacturing Co. v. Schweiker,* 681 F.2d 480 (6th Cir. 1982), and later revoked (as superseded) by the preamble to FDA's proposed regulations to implement the 1984 Act. 54 Fed. Reg. 28872, 28890 (July 10, 1989).

2.   THE DRUG PRICE COMPETITION AND PATENT TERM RESTORATION ACT OF 1984 (HATCH–WAXMAN)

All of the requirements for an abbreviated NDA that FDA had developed as part of the implementation of the Drug Amendments of 1962, and all of the proposed changes that FDA considered to adapt those requirements to post-1962 new drugs, were eliminated when Congress enacted the Drug Price Competition and Patent Term Restoration Act of 1984. The 1984 Act established detailed requirements that supersede everything that went before.

a.   THE HATCH–WAXMAN SCHEME

Hatch–Waxman represents a grand bargain between the generic and pioneer drug industries. Before 1984, generic companies were dissatisfied with their inability to take advantage of the safety and effectiveness data contained in the NDAs of approved post-1962 new drugs. As a result of this limitation, manufacturers of generic versions of such drugs could not reach the market using abbreviated NDAs; the best they could hope for, short of having to submit a full NDA with original data, was successfully to take advantage of FDA's "paper NDA" policy. *See supra* p. 1000, note 3. Meanwhile, pioneer manufacturers were frustrated about the fact that much of their products' patent life was consumed before they could even legally market the drugs, because of the prolonged nature of the NDA approval process. Hatch–Waxman, the brainchild of a conservative Utah Senator and a liberal California Representative, attempted to address both sides' concerns.

Under the 1984 Act, FDA may approve an abbreviated NDA (now commonly called an ANDA) for a generic version of a pioneer new drug after (1) all relevant product and use patents have expired for the pioneer drug and (2) all relevant periods of market exclusivity for the pioneer drug have also expired. The statute contains detailed and complex rules for determining precisely how this system works. No attempt will be made here to discuss all the specific provisions, but they are extremely important in determining the commercial value of a pioneer new drug, because they govern when the drug will become subject to generic competition.

There are basically two types of situations in which an abbreviated NDA may be submitted. The first situation is where the generic version is the same as the pioneer version in all material respects. In these instances, the sponsor of the generic product simply submits the ANDA, and FDA may approve it without further consideration about the basic safety and effectiveness of the drug. The second situation is where the generic version is different from the pioneer drug in any significant respect (e.g., a different active ingredient, route of administration, dosage form, or strength). In these circumstances, the generic applicant must first submit to FDA a "suitability petition" demonstrating that the difference between the drugs is not sufficient to preclude an ANDA and that additional studies to show safety and effectiveness are not needed. If FDA grants the suitability petition, an ANDA may be submitted. If the agency denies the suitability petition, the applicant must submit either (1) a "section 505(b)(2) NDA," the 1984 version of a paper NDA or (2) a full NDA. In all other respects, the regulations and requirements for an abbreviated NDA are the same as those for a full NDA.

In exchange for allowing the use of pioneer data to support ANDAs, the innovator industry received various forms of patent term extension and non-patent market exclusivity, as described in the excerpt below.

Peter Barton Hutt, *Landmark Pharmaceutical Law Enacted*

1 HEALTH SCAN, No. 3, p. 11 (1984).

. . . [T]he Drug Price Competition and Patent Term Restoration Act of 1984 . . . caps fifteen years of controversy about the procedures to be used by the Food and Drug Administration (FDA) in approving the marketing of *generic* drugs, and about the incentives for developing important new pioneer drugs, given the erosion of patent protection resulting from lengthy regulatory processes. . . . The legislation applies to all drugs marketed in the United States and to all patents granted in the United States, regardless of whether the drug is imported, or the new drug application (NDA) or patent is owned abroad. . . .

The new statute keeps abbreviated NDAs and paper NDAs [i.e., section 505(b)(2) NDAs] separate, but applies the . . . same rules to both. . . . Accordingly, the rest of this article refers only to abbreviated NDAs, but must be understood to encompass paper NDAs as well.

The statute amends the FD&C Act to establish a new procedure for abbreviated NDAs. Unlike a pioneer NDA, which must contain full animal and human data to establish the safety and effectiveness of the drug, an abbreviated NDA need only contain sufficient information to demonstrate that the generic version of the drug is bioavailable and is bioequivalent to the pioneer drug. In return, however, the statute provides three new statutory protections for manufacturers of pioneer new drugs; protection against release of safety and effectiveness information, protection against an abbreviated NDA becoming effective before all relevant product and use patents for the pioneer drug have expired, and protection against an abbreviated NDA becoming effective during specified periods of market exclusivity that are independent of the patent status of the pioneer drug.

Part of the disagreement about abbreviated NDAs for post-1962 drugs during the past several years has been a dispute about the status of the safety and effectiveness information submitted in the pioneer NDA. The FDA has consistently stated . . . that this information constitutes trade secrets which cannot be released to the public or used to approve a generic drug. The new statute provides that such information will retain its trade secret status and cannot be released to the public at least up to the point where an abbreviated NDA for a generic version could be made effective by FDA. Thereafter, the status of such information continues to enjoy protection against disclosure as trade secrets or other confidential commercial information. Under all circumstances, however, such information—even if not disclosable to the public—can be used by FDA to approve an abbreviated NDA for a generic drug.

Although FDA can approve an abbreviated NDA for a patented pioneer drug, that approval cannot be made effective (and thus the generic version cannot be marketed) until all relevant product and use patents have expired. Thus, a patented product or use (but not a patented process) will be protected by FDA until the relevant patents expire, because FDA is precluded from making an abbreviated NDA for a generic drug effective during the life of those patents. This is an entirely new concept under the FD&C Act. Previously, FDA approved all forms of NDAs without any consideration of patent status.

The new statute does permit a generic company to challenge a product or use patent which the pioneer NDA holder identifies as precluding the marketing of generic versions. The generic company which wishes to initiate such a challenge must submit an abbreviated NDA to FDA certifying that any relevant patent is invalid or will not be infringed, must notify the patent owner of that certification, and must specify the legal and factual basis for it. If the patent owner takes no action within 45 days, FDA may proceed to handle the abbreviated NDA like any other abbreviated NDA and the patent owner remains free to initiate or not initiate any form of patent litigation once the drug is approved by FDA and marketed. If the patent owner chooses to challenge the certification of patent invalidity or noninfringement and keep the generic version off the market, however, it must bring suit within 45 days of receiving the generic company's notification. If that is done, FDA is precluded from making the abbreviated NDA effective for a period of 30 months while the matter is being litigated or until the trial court decides the matter. If at the end of that 30 months the litigation is not concluded, an approved abbreviated NDA will become effective, and the generic drug can be marketed subject to the outcome of the pending litigation, unless the court itself enjoins marketing.

In addition to protection of trade secret data and product and use patents, the statute sets specified time periods during which abbreviated NDAs for generic drugs cannot become effective and thus generic versions cannot be marketed. . . .

- All pioneer drugs approved by FDA during 1962–1981 are subject to abbreviated NDAs immediately. . . .
- Abbreviated NDAs for post-enactment NCE drugs cannot be submitted to (or accepted by) FDA for five years following the date of approval of the pioneer NDA, except that an abbreviated NDA challenging a patent for a pioneer drug can be submitted after four years.
- Abbreviated NDAs for post-enactment, non-NCE drugs cannot become effective for three years following the date of approval of the pioneer NDA if the FDA approval of the pioneer NDA is based upon new clinical investigations.
- Abbreviated NDAs covering changes in pioneer NDAs (*e.g.*, new uses, new dosages, or new processes) approved by FDA after the date of enactment cannot become effective for three years after such FDA approval if the supplemental NDA submitted by the pioneer NDA holder to obtain approval of those changes is based upon reports of new clinical investigations.

All of these provisions also apply, as already noted, to paper NDAs. These time periods apply regardless of the status of any patents for the pioneer drug. If, at the end of the applicable period of market exclusivity, any product or use patent for the pioneer drug remains unexpired, however, no approval of an abbreviated NDA could be made effective by the FDA for that drug until the last such patent expires.

. . . .

Under the new statute (which amends the patent law) the patent for any drug approved by FDA after the date of enactment is potentially eligible for patent term extension. . . .

Any product, use, or process patent is potentially subject to extension. The patent may be a broad genus patent, or a narrow species patent. The decision as to which patent to extend is up to the patent owner. No patent may be extended more than once, and only one patent may be extended for any regulatory review. Moreover, the marketing or use of the product permitted by the regulatory review must represent the first permission for that marketing or use, and cannot previously have been permitted by an earlier regulatory review. The only exception to this rule is for a new process using recombinant DNA technology, where the production of the product permitted by an earlier regulatory review does not preclude the extension of a process patent for making the product through recombinant DNA technology as a result of a second regulatory review.

Patent term extension may be obtained for the length of the regulatory review period as defined in the statute, subject to three important limitations. The regulatory review period for a drug is defined as half the IND (human clinical study) time, plus the whole time during which FDA is reviewing the NDA. Thus, if the IND time is eight years and the NDA time is two years, the regulatory review period would be 6 years (half the 8-year IND time *plus* the full two-year NDA time).

The three important limitations to the length of patent term extension are as follows. First, under no circumstances may it exceed five years. . . . Second, the total effective patent life (defined as the time from the date of the pioneer NDA approval to the conclusion of patent protection, including the extended patent term) may not exceed a total of fourteen years. Third, the regulatory review period is to be reduced by any amount of time during which the NDA applicant has not exerted "due diligence" in attempting to obtain FDA approval of the NDA. The statute defines "due diligence" in terms of usual industry practice and requires FDA to initiate a due diligence investigation only upon petition of an interested person showing good cause.

In order to obtain patent term restoration, the patent holder must submit an application to the Patent Office within sixty days of approval of the NDA. The Patent Office is directed to take action upon the application solely on the basis of information contained in the application, in order to reduce the burden placed on it by the legislation.

NOTES

1. *Implementing Regulations.* For a more detailed discussion of the 1984 statute, see Ellen J. Flannery & Peter Barton Hutt, *Balancing Competition and Patent Protection in the Drug Industry: The Drug Price Competition and Patent Term Restoration Act of 1984*, 40 FOOD DRUG COSM. L.J. 269 (1985); Elizabeth Stotland Weiswasser & Scott D. Danzis, *The Hatch–Waxman Act: History, Structure, and Legacy*, 71 ANTITRUST L.J. 585 (2003). FDA promulgated detailed regulations to implement the generic drug provisions of the statute in 57 Fed. Reg. 17950 (Apr. 28, 1992), codified at 21 C.F.R. Part 314, Subpart C.

2. *Length of Patent Term.* At the time that the Drug Price Competition and Patent Term Restoration Act was enacted, the statutory patent term was 17 years from the date of issue. In 1994, to comply with an international treaty, Congress enacted the Uruguay Round Agreements Act, 108 Stat. 4809 (1994), 35 U.S.C. 156, to extend the patent term in the United States to 20 years from the filing of the patent.

3. *Administration of Patent Provisions.* The Patent and Trademark Office (PTO) has promulgated regulations implementing the patent provisions of the 1984 statute. 37 C.F.R. 1.710 et seq. FDA promulgated regulations implementing the patent provisions of the 1984 statute for

which it is responsible in 53 Fed. Reg. 7298 (Mar. 7, 1988), codified at 21 C.F.R. Part 60. FDA and the PTO entered into a Memorandum of Understanding to coordinate implementation of these regulations. 52 Fed. Reg. 17830 (May 12, 1987). FDA regularly publishes in the Federal Register notices of the determinations of regulatory review periods for purposes of patent term extension.

4. *Due Diligence.* Under 35 U.S.C. 156(d)(2)(B), any interested person may request a hearing to determine whether an NDA applicant seeking patent term extension has failed to act with "due diligence" in pursuing FDA approval. It appears that this provision has never formally been invoked.

5. *Eligibility for Patent Extension.* In the first cases it decided under the 1984 Act, the United States Court of Appeals for the Federal Circuit held that 35 U.S.C. 156(a)(5)(A) precludes patent term restoration for a second approved use after the new drug was initially approved for another use, and that the provisions in 35 U.S.C. 271(e)(1) allow a manufacturer to test a patent holder's device (or drug) to obtain information to support FDA approval of a substitute product prior to expiration of the patent. *Fisons plc v. Quigg*, 876 F.2d 99 (Fed. Cir. 1989); *Eli Lilly and Co. v. Medtronic, Inc.*, 872 F.2d 402 (Fed. Cir. 1989), *aff'd* 496 U.S. 661 (1990).

6. *Statutory Extensions for Particular Products.* In addition to the general statutory patent term restoration provided by the 1984 statute, specific patent term extensions have been granted by congressional enactment for Forane in 97 Stat. 831, 832–833 (1983), Impro in 98 Stat. 3430 (1984), glyburide in 98 Stat. 3434 (1984), and Lopid in 102 Stat. 1107, 1569–1570 (1988).

7. *Bases for Additional Market Exclusivity.* Several provisions other than those in Hatch–Waxman entitle NDA holders to an additional period of statutory market exclusivity period independent of patent law—that is, a period in which FDA cannot approve an ANDA regardless of the patent status of the pioneer. In the FDA Modernization Act of 1997, as extended by the Best Pharmaceutical for Children Act of 2002, Congress provided an extra six months of market exclusivity at the end of the extended patent term (or market exclusivity term, if the patent has already expired) when the sponsor conducts pediatric testing requested and approved by FDA. Under the Orphan Drug Act, if a product designated by FDA as an orphan drug receives the first FDA approval for the disease for which it was designed, it is entitled to seven years of additional market exclusivity. Most recently, the Generating Antibiotic Incentives Now (GAIN) Act of 2012 gives companies manufacturing a "qualified infection disease product" seven years of additional marketing exclusivity.

8. *Market Exclusivity for a New Indication.* Section 505(j)(5)(F)(iv) provides that a supplemental NDA containing reports of new clinical investigations (other than bioavailability studies) "essential" to the approval of the supplement and conducted by the sponsor is entitled to three years of market exclusivity from the date of approval of the supplemental NDA. In *Upjohn Co. v. Kessler*, 938 F. Supp. 439 (W.D. Mich. 1996), the District Court held that the administrative record supported the

conclusion that the study conducted by the company was not "essential" to approval.

9. *Copyright.* In *SmithKline Beecham Consumer Healthcare v. Watson Pharmaceuticals, Inc.*, 211 F.3d 21 (2d Cir. 2000), the pioneer drug company sought to prevent a generic competitor from using copyrighted materials developed for its nonprescription drug product that was subject to an NDA. The Court of Appeals held that the Drug Price Competition and Patent Term Restoration Act of 1984 requires generic drug manufacturers to use the same labeling as the pioneer drug even if that use may infringe a copyright held by the pioneer drug company. The Court of Appeals further held that the pioneer company may not obtain damages. *But see* John C. O'Quinn, *Protecting Private Intellectual Property from Government Intrusion: Revisiting SmithKline and the Case for Just Compensation*, 29 PEPP. L. REV. 435 (2002).

10. *The Research Use Exemption.* The Supreme Court has broadly interpreted the research use exemption from the patent law in 35 U.S.C. 271(e)(1), which allows a manufacturer to test a competitor's patented drug prior to expiration of the patent to obtain information to support FDA approval of a generic product. In *Eli Lilly and Co. v. Medtronic, Inc.*, 496 U.S. 661 (1990), the Supreme Court held that this exemption applies to medical devices as well as to drugs. In *Merck KGaA v. Integra Lifesciences I, Ltd.*, 545 U.S. 193 (2005), the Supreme Court held that drug discovery using a patented research tool is similarly eligible for this exemption. The lower courts have also provided broad interpretations of this exemption.

11. *Patent Notice in Labeling.* In order to prevent innocent infringement of patents, Congress enacted 35 U.S.C. 287 to provide for notice that an article is patented by placing on the article the word "patent" or the abbreviation "pat." together with the number of the patent. Absent such notice, no damages may be recovered by the patentee in any action for infringement unless the infringer was notified of the infringement.

b.   THE ORANGE BOOK

The "Orange Book," formally known as *Approved Drug Products with Therapeutic Equivalence Evaluations*, is a central tool in the administration of Hatch–Waxman. The Drug Price Competition and Patent Term Restoration Act of 1984 added section 505(j)(6) to the FD&C Act to require FDA to publish a list of all drugs approved on the basis of safety and effectiveness as a way of identifying drugs eligible for ANDAs. In accordance with that provision, the agency published a yearly list of approved drugs, with monthly revisions, commonly referred to as the "Orange Book," which has now been replaced with an electronic version on the FDA website.

In addition to identifying all NDA'd drugs, the Orange Book also lists every patent purported by the brand-name manufacturer to protect each drug. As described below, every ANDA must make an assertion regarding the applicability of each listed patent to the generic aspirant. With judicial approval, FDA has taken the position that its task of listing submitted patents in the Orange Book is ministerial and that it is not obligated to determine the relevance or accuracy of the patent information submitted to it.

Finally, the Orange Book, through a coding system, indicates the "therapeutic equivalents"—that is, generic copies—for each drug. This information is intended to help state health agencies, physicians, and pharmacists to control costs through generic substitution; this function of the Orange Book explains why its first edition (1979) actually predated Hatch–Waxman. The Orange Book contains two types of therapeutic equivalence evaluations. A drug given an "A" rating is considered by FDA to be "therapeutically equivalent to other pharmaceutically equivalent products." Drugs that "FDA at this time considers NOT to be therapeutically equivalent to other pharmaceutically equivalent products, i.e., drug products for which actual or potential bioequivalence problems have not been resolved by adequate evidence of bioequivalence," are rated "B." FDA arrives at these ratings without consultation with manufacturers and without notice-and-comment rulemaking.

NOTE

Removal from Orange Book. When a pioneer drug is voluntarily withdrawn from marketing by its manufacturer for reasons of safety or effectiveness, it is automatically withdrawn from the FDA-approved drug list and can no longer be the subject of an abbreviated NDA. 21 C.F.R. 314.161. *See supra* p. 855, note 10.

c.   THE ANDA AND "BIOEQUIVALENCE"

FD&C Act 505(j)(2) sets forth the required content of an ANDA. Normally, the abbreviated application includes information to show that the proposed labeling, the active ingredient, the route of administration, and the strength of the new drug are all identical to those of an already-approved drug listed in the Orange Book. FD&C Act 505(j)(2)(A)(i)–(iii), (v). In addition, the ANDA must include "information to show that the new drug is bioequivalent to the listed drug." *Id.* 505(j)(2)(A)(iv). Finally, the ANDA must include:

> a certification, in the opinion of the applicant and to the best of his knowledge, with respect to each patent which claims the listed drug . . . or which claims a use for such listed drug for which the applicant is seeking approval
>
> (I) that such patent information has not been filed,
>
> (II) that such patent has expired,
>
> (III) of the date on which such patent will expire, or
>
> (IV) that such patent is invalid or will not be infringed by the manufacture, use, or sale of the new drug for which the application is submitted.

Id. 505(j)(2)(A)(vii). As discussed below, a "Paragraph IV" certification triggers the special patent litigation procedure established by Hatch Waxman.

The bulk of an ANDA comprises the bioequivalence data. The task of demonstrating bioequivalence was not invented by Hatch–Waxman.

"Biological availability" was a requirement for approval of the earlier version of the abbreviated NDA, invented by FDA as part of its DESI implementation. In the 1970s and early 1980s, manufacturers of pioneer drugs questioned the quality, and thus the clinical effectiveness, of generic products. In Drug Bioequivalence (1974), the Office of Technology Assessment concluded that "current standards and regulatory practices do not insure bioequivalence for drug products" and that "present compendial standards and guidelines for Current Good Manufacturing Practice do not insure quality in uniform bioavailability for drug products." In 1977, FDA promulgated general regulations defining important terms and setting forth procedures and methods for establishing drug bioequivalence. 42 Fed. Reg. 1624 (Jan. 7, 1977), 42 Fed. Reg. 42311 (Aug. 23, 1977), codified at 21 C.F.R. Part 320. As amended, the current version of 21 C.F.R. 320.1 defines the critical terms as follows:

(a) "Bioavailability" means the rate and extent to which the active drug ingredient or therapeutic moiety is absorbed from a drug product and becomes available at the site of drug action.

(b) "Drug product" means a finished dosage form, *e.g.*, tablet, capsule, or solution, that contains the active drug ingredient, generally, but not necessarily, in association with inactive ingredients.

(c) "Pharmaceutical equivalents" means drug products that contain identical amounts of the identical active drug ingredient, i.e., the same salt or ester of the same therapeutic moiety, in identical dosage forms, but not necessarily containing the same inactive ingredients, and that meet the identical compendial or other applicable standard of identity, strength, quality, and purity, including potency and, where applicable, content uniformity, disintegration times and/or dissolution rates.

(d) "Pharmaceutical alternatives" means drug products that contain the identical therapeutic moiety, or its precursor, but not necessarily in the same amount or dosage form or as the same salt or ester. . . .

(e) "Bioequivalent drug products" means pharmaceutical equivalents or pharmaceutical alternatives whose rate and extent of absorption do not show a significant difference when administered at the same molar dose of the therapeutic moiety under similar experimental conditions, either single dose or multiple dose. Some pharmaceutical equivalents or pharmaceutical alternatives may be equivalent in the extent of their absorption but not in their rate of absorption and yet may be considered bioequivalent because such differences in the rate of absorption are intentional and are reflected in the labeling, are not essential to the attainment of effective body drug concentrations on chronic use, or are considered medically insignificant for the particular drug product studied.

In 1977, FDA also began to propose regulations establishing bioequivalence requirements for eleven drug clusters, the first for anticonvulsants, 42 Fed. Reg. 39675 (Aug. 5, 1977), and the last for quinidine, 45 Fed. Reg. 72200 (Oct. 31, 1980). The agency later determined simply to set bioequivalence requirements through the abbreviated NDA process rather than by regulations. 54 Fed. Reg. 28823, 28872, 28911 (July 10, 1989).

NOTES

1. *Complex Mixtures.* For generic versions of several complex mixtures, FDA has required the submission of a section 505(b)(2) NDA or a full NDA rather than an abbreviated NDA, because the generic version could not be shown to be the same as the pioneer drug. Examples include digoxin, Premarin, and levothryoxine. In *Serono Laboratories, Inc. v. Shalala*, 158 F.3d 1313 (D.C. Cir. 1998), however, the Court of Appeals upheld the legality of an abbreviated NDA for a complex mixture extracted from the urine of post-menopausal women where the generic version had demonstrable differences from the pioneer drug.

2. *The Active Ingredient.* In *Glaxo Operations UK Limited v. Quigg*, 894 F.2d 392 (Fed. Cir. 1990), the Court of Appeals concluded that, in determining whether an active ingredient is the same as a previously-approved active ingredient or is a new active ingredient, the statute refers to the substance as it is formulated in the drug product and not as it is subsequently metabolized in the gut.

3. *New Indications for Use.* It is common for a pioneer drug manufacturer to seek FDA approval of new indications through submission of supplemental NDAs following FDA approval of the original NDA. In *Bristol–Myers Squibb Co. v. Shalala*, 91 F.3d 1493 (D.C. Cir. 1996), the Court of Appeals held that FDA may approve an abbreviated NDA for the original indication, for which the patent and market exclusivity have expired, even if later indications retain patent protection or market exclusivity. The approved abbreviated NDA must be limited to indications for which there is no patent or market exclusivity protection. As a practical matter, however, this means that a physician may prescribe the generic drug for all of the indications, including those protected by a patent or market exclusivity, and thus the additional indications obtained by the pioneer company's supplemental NDAs are of little value. It is for this reason that pioneer manufacturers do not submit supplemental NDAs for new indications unless there is a substantial amount of patent protection time remaining on the original NDA.

4. *In Vivo Bioequivalence Test.* The conventional test to determine the bioequivalence of a generic drug involves giving a single oral dose to 24–36 healthy human volunteers. The 90 percent confidence intervals for the peak serum concentration (Cmax) and area under the plasma concentration-time curve (AUC) of a generic formulation must fall within 80 percent to 125 percent of those of the reference listed drug (RLD) specified in the Orange Book. In a letter from FDA Associate Commissioner for Regulatory Affairs Dennis Baker to Sharon W. Brown & Mary Mathisen, FDA Docket No. 98P–0434/CPI & PSAI (Mar. 17, 2000), the agency defended the use of these criteria to determine bioequivalence.

5. *Change in Bioavailability Standards.* FDA has on occasion sought to relax the bioequivalence requirements for generic drugs. For example, FDA previously required in vivo testing to demonstrate the bioequivalence

of antibiotic drugs that treat serious life-threatening infections. In a letter from CDER Office of Generic Drugs Director Gary J. Buehler to Timothy J. Smith (Mar. 7, 2006), FDA announced that it would waive in vivo bioequivalence testing if the generic drug is rapidly dissolving under the conditions specified in an FDA guidance. The manufacturer of the pioneer reference listed drug (RLD) contested this decision by submitting a citizen petition. FDA Docket No. 2006P–0124 (May 31, 2006).

6. *Citizen Petitions.* It is common for the manufacturer of a pioneer drug to submit a citizen petition asking FDA to adopt rigorous testing requirements for a generic applicant to demonstrate bioequivalence to the pioneer drug. In 64 Fed. Reg. 66822 (Nov. 30, 1999), FDA proposed significantly to restrict the use of citizen petitions. Because citizen petitions are the very heart of the FDA administrative procedure regulations, however, the agency took no further action on this proposal. Nonetheless, the agency continued to consider ways in which citizen petitions for bioequivalence requirements could be limited. Primarily to address this issue, FDAAA (2007) added new section 505(q), which provides that FDA "shall not delay approval of a pending [ANDA or 505(b)(2)] application" because of a request in a citizen petition to "take any form of action relating to the application" unless the agency "determines . . . that a delay is necessary to protect the public health." FD&C Act 505(q)(1)(A). *See* GUIDANCE FOR INDUSTRY: CITIZEN PETITIONS AND PETITIONS FOR STAY OF ACTION SUBJECT TO SECTION 505(q) OF THE FEDERAL FOOD, DRUG, AND COSMETIC ACT (June 2011).

7. *Alternative Methods of Demonstrating Bioequivalence.* Section 505(j)(8)(A)(ii) provides: "For a drug that is not intended to be absorbed into the bloodstream, the Secretary may assess bioavailability by scientifically valid measurements intended to reflect the rate and extent to which the active ingredient . . . becomes available at the site of drug action." *See Schering Corp. v. FDA*, 782 F. Supp. 645 (D.D.C. 1992), 994 F.2d 1103 (D.C. Dir. 1993), 51 F.3d 390 (3rd Cir. 1995).

For an absorbed drug, section 505(j)(8)(B) provides it shall be considered to be bioequivalent to a listed drug either if the rate *and* extent of absorption of the drug do not show a significant difference from the listed drug or if the extent of absorption does not show a significant difference and the difference in the rate of absorption is intentional, reflected in the proposed labeling, and medically insignificant. In *Pfizer, Inc. v. Shalala*, 1 F. Supp. 2d 38 (D.D.C. 1998), the District Court held that FDA was justified in finding that a generic version of a sustained-release drug provided the "same" dosage as the listed drug despite a different release mechanism.

8. *FDA Waiver.* Under 21 C.F.R. 320.22(b), FDA may waive the submission of evidence demonstrating in vivo bioequivalence. The courts have upheld the authority of FDA to grant such a waiver. *E.g., Fisons Corp. v. Shalala*, 860 F. Supp. 859 (D.D.C. 1994). *See also Somerset Pharmaceuticals, Inc. v. Shalala*, 973 F. Supp. 443 (D. Del. 1997).

9. *History of Bioequivalence.* For a fascinating history, see Daniel Carpenter, *Bioequivalence: The Regulatory Career of a Pharmaceutical Concept*, 85 BULL. HIST. MED. 93 (2011).

10. *The Generic Drug Scandal.* In 1988, the House Subcommittee on Oversight and investigations launched an investigation into allegations by some manufacturers of generic drugs that their applications were not being processed fairly or expeditiously by FDA. "FDA's Generic Drug Approval Process (Parts 1–3)," Hearings before the Subcommittee on Oversight and Investigations of the House Committee on Energy and Commerce, 101st Cong., 1st Sess. (1989). The Subcommittee found that some employees of the FDA Division of Generic Drugs of the Office of Drug Standards had accepted illegal gratuities from manufacturers, that some manufacturers conducted (and submitted) bioavailability and bioequivalence studies using the pioneer drug rather than their own generic products, and that significant discrepancies occurred in the testing and manufacture of some generic drugs. The agency employees and responsible officials of the implicated manufacturers were prosecuted and the suspect products were recalled. FDA withdrew, or proposed to withdraw, the approval of the abbreviated NDAs for the suspect products, and it undertook investigations of manufacturing facilities and testing of products to verify the quality and clinical effectiveness of the generic drug supply. FDA also made management changes and upgraded the Division of Generic Drugs.

On August 18, 1989, the Secretary of HHS and the FDA Commissioner issued statements announcing intensified analyses of generic drugs and their manufacturers, strengthened generic drug review procedures, and the creation of an independent ombudsman to assure fairness in decisionmaking on product approval. As part of its program to reassure the public about the safety and effectiveness of generic drugs, FDA, among other actions, issued AN INTERIM REPORT ON GENERIC DRUGS (Nov. 17, 1989), established an advisory committee on generic drugs, 55 Fed. Reg. 5838 (Feb. 20, 1990), and held a public meeting on new policies and procedures for generic drugs, 55 Fed. Reg. 38583 (Sept. 19, 1990). The agency published an interim regulation on retention of bioavailability and bioequivalence testing samples in 55 Fed. Reg. 47034 (Nov. 8, 1990). By early 1991, five FDA employees had been convicted of bribery or perjury and eight generic drug companies had been found to have submitted applications to FDA containing fraudulent data. Companies that did not engage in the fraudulent activities sued for damages for the harm done by their competitors in submitting fraudulent applications and bribing FDA officials to approve them. *E.g., Mylan Laboratories, Inc. v. Azko*, 770 F. Supp. 1053 (D. Md. 1991), *aff'd* 2 F.3d 56 (4th Cir. 1993); *Mylan Laboratories, Inc. v. Matkari*, 7 F.3d 1130 (4th Cir. 1993).

For a personal recollection of the generic drug scandal by an FDA employee reassigned as temporary Director of the Generics Review Division to solve the problems created by the episode, see Richard A. Terselic, *The Generic Drugs Scandal Revisited*, 11 DICKINSON'S FDA REVIEW, No. 7, at 2 (July 2004).

11. *Legislative Response to the Generic Drug Scandal.* In 1992, Congress passed legislation, the Generic Drug Enforcement Act, 106 Stat. 149, to provide increased penalties, including debarment, against individuals and corporations who defrauded FDA in generic drug applications. *See supra* p. 252.

d. SECTION 505(b)(2) NDAs

When Congress enacted the Drug Price Competition and Patent Term Restoration Act of 1984, it added FD&C Act 505(b)(2), a provision modeled after, and arguably meant to codify, the concept of a paper NDA. *See supra* p. 1000, note 3. The former paper NDA is therefore now called a section 505(b)(2) NDA. Section 505(b)(2) expressly permits the agency to rely, for approval of an NDA, on data not developed by the applicant.

FDA has interpreted this provision expansively. As did the paper NDA, section 505(b)(2) covers situations in which the applicant relies to any extent on published literature. But it also provides for applications that rely on FDA's own previous finding of safety or effectiveness for a previously approved drug. This type of 505(b)(2) application may be used when changes (anything from dosage form to strength to Rx/OTC status to indications) are made to an existing drug which has lost patent protection and market exclusivity. A section 505(b)(2) NDA relies on the pioneer NDA for all required information except the data needed to support the difference. Thus, a section 505(b)(2) NDA need not include any data supporting the basic safety and effectiveness of the drug, except insofar as the difference between the pioneer drug product and the applicant's modification of that drug product bears upon safety or effectiveness.

As discussed *supra* at p. 1001, FDA may approve an abbreviated NDA for a generic drug that differs in minor ways from the listed pioneer drug in response to the filing of a "suitability petition". If the differences are substantial, however, FDA will deny the suitability petition and require a more complete application. In these circumstances, the section 505(b)(2) application will suffice, and a full NDA will not be required. Thus, the section 505(b)(2) NDA is mid-way between a full NDA and an abbreviated NDA.

FDA interprets section 505(b)(2) to authorize the agency to rely on confidential commercial information in a pioneer NDA in order to approve a generic competitor's new version of the drug. The pioneer pharmaceutical industry takes the position that this would be unlawful under the FD&C Act. This disagreement must ultimately be resolved in the courts.

NOTES

1.   *Frequency of Use.* For the decade following its enactment, section 505(b)(2) was rarely used. Since the 1990s, however, generic drug companies have sought to use it in innovative ways. Competitors to a pioneer prescription drug have sought to switch the drug to OTC status using the section 505(b)(2) NDA. They have also sought to use 505(b)(2) to add a new indication, change the dosage or delivery form, or make other changes to a pioneer drug.

2.   *Substitution.* As noted *supra* at p. 1007, a generic drug that is the "same" as and "bioequivalent" to a pioneer drug is rated "A" and thus can be substituted by doctors and pharmacists for the pioneer drug. In contrast, a drug approved under section 505(b)(2) cannot be rated "A" because it is

not therapeutically equivalent to the pioneer drug and thus cannot be substituted in the same way as an abbreviated NDA drug.

3. *Non-Application of Hatch–Waxman to Biological Products.* Congress explicitly determined to exclude biological products from sections 505(b)(2) and (j) when it enacted the Drug Price Competition and Patent Term Restoration Act of 1984. This was confirmed with the passage of the FDA Modernization Act of 1997, in which Congress added section 351(j) to the Public Health Service Act stating that a biological product is not subject to the NDA provisions of FD&C Act 505 and, in an uncodified provision, mandated that FDA minimize differences in the review and approval of products required to have an approved biologics license under section 351 of the Public Health Service Act and products required to have an approved NDA under section 505(b)(1) of the FD&C Act, but not sections 505(b)(2) or (j). FDA Modernization Act 123(f), 111 Stat. 2296, 2324. In 2009, Congress established a separate abbreviated pathway for biosimilars, which will be examined below in the chapter on Biologics. *See infra* p. 1135.

4. *Biological Products Subject to an NDA.* A small number of biological products are marketed pursuant to an NDA rather than a biological products license (BLA). These include human growth hormone (HGH), for which an NDA was obtained as one of the earliest approvals for a drug made through recombinant DNA technology, and insulin, which became subject to an NDA when Congress repealed former section 506 of the FD&C Act as part of the FDA Modernization Act of 1997. Because these products are subject to NDAs, FDA must handle applications for generic versions of them and a few others. On May 30, 2006, FDA approved a section 505(b)(2) NDA for a generic version of recombinant HGH.

e.   HATCH-WAXMAN, DRUG PRICES, AND INDUSTRY PROFITS

Development of the average new chemical entity (NCE) NDA drug takes some 15 years from preclinical research through NDA approval and costs in excess of $1.5 billion. The average generic drug takes only 3 to 5 years from formulation through FDA approval of an abbreviated NDA and costs up to $500,000. Thus, a generic drug can be sold at a fraction of the cost of the pioneer drug. This difference in application burden and cost is due to the fact that all of the research and development must be undertaken by the pioneer company. The generic company relies on that information and need only prove that its version of the drug is bioequivalent.

In 2006, FDA conducted a study, *Generic Competition and Drug Prices,* in which the agency determined that the first generic competitor results in only about a 5 percent reduction in price, whereas the second brings the price down to about 50 percent of the pioneer drug price. By the sixth competitor, the price is only about 25 percent of the pioneer price. With a large number of competitors it can reach 10 percent or lower.

In the first twenty years after enactment of the 1984 statute, FDA approved over 8000 abbreviated NDAs. As more major pioneer drugs lose patent protection and are displaced by generic versions, and fewer pioneer drugs are being approved by FDA to take their place, some commentators have questioned whether the pioneer drug industry can sustain its current level of research and development. Even after patent term restoration under the 1984 Act, the current average effective patent life of an NCE NDA drug is only 11–12 years. This relatively brief period of market protection may not be long enough for a drug's sponsor to recoup the full research and development investment made in the drug other than by charging extremely high prices. At some point, Congress may reconsider the compromise made in the 1984 Act. *See* "Improving Access to Generic Drugs," Hearing before the Senate Special Committee on Aging, 109th Cong. 2d Sess. (2006).

f.   PATENT INFRINGEMENT LITIGATION UNDER HATCH WAXMAN

i.   *The Commencement of Litigation and the 30-Month Stay*

Under Hatch–Waxman, the filing of an ANDA with a Paragraph IV certification (alleging that a patent listed in the Orange Book is "invalid or will not be infringed," FD&C Act 505(j)(2)(A)(vii)), is itself made a technical act of patent infringement. 35 U.S.C. 271(e)(2)(A). The pioneer manufacturer is notified of the Paragraph IV certification, and it has 45 days to file a patent infringement suit; otherwise, the ANDA approval is made effective immediately. FD&C Act 505(j)(5)(B)(iii). If the pioneer manufacturer brings such a suit, FDA may not make approval of the ANDA effective for a 30-month period, unless a court decides before that time that the patent is invalid or not infringed. *Id.*

This 30-month stay has been the subject of a fair amount of controversy and, some would claim, abuse. Pioneer companies would obtain multiple patents covering different features or variants of the same drug, list them in the Orange Book at different (tactically calculated) times, and thus enjoy numerous sequential 30-month stays. Faced with criticism from the FTC and the generic drug industry, FDA amended its regulations on Orange Book listings and 30-month stays in 2003. 68 Fed. Reg. 36676 (June 18, 2003). The amended regulations accomplished the following objectives. First, they permitted only one 30-month stay per NDA or section 505(b)(2) NDA. Second, they prevented the submission of information on patents claiming packaging, intermediates, or metabolites. Third, they permitted the submission of patents claiming alternate polymorphic forms of the active ingredient found in the NDA and required information demonstrating that a drug product containing the polymorph will perform the same as the drug product described in the NDA. Fourth, they amended the patent information required to be submitted to FDA and provided declaration forms for submitting that information to ensure that only those patents claiming the approved drug product and its approved uses are listed in the Orange Book. Fifth, except in the case of method-of-use-patents, the regulations did not require a claim-by-claim declaration. All of these changes were designed to reduce what FDA regarded as abuse of the 1984 Act by the pioneer pharmaceutical industry.

Congress then amended the Drug Price Competition and Patent Term Restoration Act of 1984 as part of the Medicare Prescription Drug, Improvement, and Modernization Act of 2003, 117 Stat. 2066, 2448. First, Congress codified the FDA regulation providing that only one 30-month stay is permitted for each abbreviated NDA. Second, an abbreviated NDA applicant who makes a Paragraph IV certification must give notice to the pioneer manufacturer and the patent owner within 20 days after FDA files the abbreviated NDA. (It is this notice that starts the 45-day period during which the pioneer manufacturer must bring suit in order to obtain a 30-month stay.) Third, if the pioneer manufacturer does not exercise its right to bring a patent infringement suit within the 45-day period, the statute permits an abbreviated NDA applicant to bring a declaratory judgment action to determine the validity of the patent. Fourth, if the pioneer manufacturer sues the generic drug manufacturer, the latter may bring a counterclaim seeking an order requiring the pioneer manufacturer to delete from the Orange Book any patent that does not claim the approved drug or method of using the drug.

NOTES

1. *Guidance.* FDA published a draft guidance to implement the 2003 regulations and statutory amendments. DRAFT GUIDANCE FOR INDUSTRY: LISTED DRUGS, 30-MONTH STAYS, AND APPROVAL OF ANDAS AND 505(b)(2) APPLICATIONS UNDER HATCH–WAXMAN, AS AMENDED BY THE MEDICARE PRESCRIPTION DRUG, IMPROVEMENT, AND MODERNIZATION ACT OF 2003— QUESTIONS AND ANSWERS (October 2004).

2. *Case or Controversy.* In *Teva Pharmaceuticals USA, Inc. v. Pfizer, Inc.*, 395 F.3d 1324 (Fed. Cir. 2005), the Court of Appeals held that there was no constitutionally-required case or controversy where the pioneer manufacturer did not sue the generic applicant within the 45-day period.

3. *"Use Codes" and the* Caraco *Decision.* FDA regulations authorize the pioneer manufacturer to submit to the agency, for inclusion in the Orange Book, not only any substance or product patents it claims for the NDA'd drug, but also any "method-of-use" patents or particular indications. The NDA holder's submission must, for any claimed method-of-use patent, contain a "description" of the patent, along with "identification of the specific section of the . . . labeling for the drug product that corresponds to the method of use claimed by the patent submitted." 21 C.F.R. 314.53(c)(2)(i)(O), 314.53(c)(2)(ii)(P). Based on this description, FDA assigns the method of use patent a use code number that it lists in the Orange Book.

To avoid infringing a pioneer's method of use patent, a generic applicant may seek marketing approval of fewer than all of the pioneer drug's labeled uses. To do so, it files as part of its ANDA a "section viii" statement, according to which it seeks approval only for those methods of use not protected by the listed patent, while "carving out" from the approved labeling those portions covered by the listed use code. FDA will not approve such an ANDA if the generic's proposed carve-out label overlaps at all with the brand's use code, and the agency will not independently assess the accuracy of the pioneer manufacturer's description of the scope of the patent.

But what recourse does the ANDA filer have if the NDA holder overstates the scope of the methods of use covered by the patent in question? In *Caraco Pharmaceutical Laboratories v. Novo Nordisk*, 132 S. Ct. 1670 (2012), the Supreme Court held that ANDA applicants could use the counterclaim provision of FD&C Act 505(j)(5)(C)(ii)(I) to force correction in the Orange Book of a pioneer's use code that wrongly describes the brand-name drug's method of use patent. This is the same counterclaim provision that an ANDA filer can use to try to force deletion from the Orange Book of any patents that do not actually claim the approved drug.

ii.   180-Day First-Filer Generic Exclusivity and "Pay-to-Delay"

To encourage generic companies to challenge invalid and weak patents, Hatch Waxman provides the following incentive: the first generic applicant to file a successful ANDA with a "Paragraph IV certification"—a certification in the ANDA that the pioneer's listed patent is invalid or will not be infringed—receives 180 days of generic market exclusivity for its generic drug, during which no other abbreviated NDA for the same generic drug product may be approved. FD&C Act 505(j)(5)(B)(iv). This period of market exclusivity is extremely valuable. As noted above, generic manufacturers typically undercut the price of the pioneer drug by only about 5 percent during their exclusive marketing period, but then are forced to reduce the price by 50 percent or more as other generic manufacturers receive approvals of their abbreviated NDAs.

The dramatic loss of market share and profits experienced by pioneer drugs upon the entry of generic competitors has driven innovator manufacturers to enter financial arrangements with generic companies designed to induce the latter to stay out of the market. In these "reverse payment" or "pay-to-delay" agreements, a pioneer drug manufacturer typically pays a first-filing paragraph IV generic challenger not to market a generic version of the drug in question for a specified period of time. Reforms to Hatch–Waxman enacted in 2003 were designed in part to limit the effectiveness of this tactic, but the approach persists.

Reverse payment deals have long been controversial. The Federal Trade Commission (FTC), which enforces the antitrust laws in the pharmaceutical industry, has been leery of them for years. In the following recent Supreme Court case, the FTC successfully repelled industry's contention that these agreements are immune from antitrust attack. This casebook obviously cannot begin to familiarize students with the complexities of antitrust law. The case is edited so as to highlight the dynamics of generic drug competition and the system of incentives established by Hatch–Waxman. The opinion also provides a useful overview of the scheme for pharmaceutical patent litigation established by the 1984 statute.

FTC v. Actavis, Inc.

2013 U.S. LEXIS 4545; 2013 WL 2922122 (2013).

■ JUSTICE BREYER delivered the opinion of the Court.

Company A sues Company B for patent infringement. The two companies settle under terms that require (1) Company B, the claimed infringer, not to produce the patented product until the patent's term expires, and (2) Company A, the patentee, to pay B many millions of dollars. Because the settlement requires the patentee to pay the alleged infringer, rather than the other way around, this kind of settlement agreement is often called a "reverse payment" settlement agreement. And the basic question here is whether such an agreement can sometimes unreasonably diminish competition in violation of the antitrust laws.

In this case, the Eleventh Circuit dismissed a Federal Trade Commission (FTC) complaint claiming that a particular reverse payment settlement agreement violated the antitrust laws. . . . We . . . hold that the Eleventh Circuit should have allowed the FTC's lawsuit to proceed.

I

A

Apparently most if not all reverse payment settlement agreements arise in the context of pharmaceutical drug regulation. . . . We consequently describe four key features of the relevant drug-regulatory framework established by the Drug Price Competition and Patent Term Restoration Act of 1984, 98 Stat. 1585, as amended. That Act is commonly known as the Hatch–Waxman Act.

First, a drug manufacturer, wishing to market a new prescription drug, must submit a New Drug Application to the federal Food and Drug Administration (FDA) and undergo a long, comprehensive, and costly testing process, after which, if successful, the manufacturer will receive marketing approval from the FDA.

Second, once the FDA has approved a brand-name drug for marketing, a manufacturer of a generic drug can obtain similar marketing approval through use of abbreviated procedures. The Hatch–Waxman Act permits a generic manufacturer to file an Abbreviated New Drug Application specifying that the generic has the "same active ingredients as," and is "biologically equivalent" to, the already-approved brand-name drug. 21 U.S.C. § 355(j)(2)(A)(ii), (iv). In this way the generic manufacturer can obtain approval while avoiding the "costly and time-consuming studies" needed to obtain approval "for a pioneer drug." The Hatch–Waxman process, by allowing the generic to piggyback on the pioneer's approval efforts, "speed[s] the introduction of low-cost generic drugs to market," thereby furthering drug competition.

Third, the Hatch–Waxman Act sets forth special procedures for identifying, and resolving, related patent disputes. It requires the pioneer brand-name manufacturer to list in its New Drug Application the "number and the expiration date" of any relevant patent. *See* 21 U.S.C. § 355(b)(1). And it requires the generic manufacturer in its Abbreviated New Drug Application to "assure the FDA" that the generic "will not infringe" the brand-name's patents.

The generic can provide this assurance in one of several ways. *See* 21 U.S.C. § 355(j)(2)(A)(vii). It can certify that the brand-name manufacturer has not listed any relevant patents. It can certify that any relevant patents have expired. It can request approval to market beginning when any still-in-force patents expire. Or, it can certify that any listed, relevant patent "is invalid or will not be infringed by the manufacture, use, or sale" of the drug described in the Abbreviated New Drug Application. *See* § 355(j)(2)(A)(vii)(IV). Taking this last-mentioned route (called the "paragraph IV" route), automatically counts as patent infringement, *see* 35 U.S.C. § 271(e)(2)(A), and often "means provoking litigation." If the brand-name patentee brings an infringement suit within 45 days, the FDA then must withhold approving the generic, usually for a 30-month period, while the parties litigate patent validity (or infringement) in court. If the courts decide the matter within that period, the FDA follows that determination; if they do not, the FDA may go forward and give approval to market the generic product. *See* 21 U.S.C. § 355(j)(5)(B)(iii).

Fourth, Hatch–Waxman provides a special incentive for a generic to be the first to file an Abbreviated New Drug Application taking the paragraph IV route. That applicant will enjoy a period of 180 days of exclusivity (from the first commercial marketing of its drug). *See* § 355(j)(5)(B)(iv). During that period of exclusivity no other generic can compete with the brand-name drug. If the first-to-file generic manufacturer can overcome any patent obstacle and bring the generic to market, this 180-day period of exclusivity can prove valuable, possibly "worth several hundred million dollars." Indeed, the Generic Pharmaceutical Association said in 2006 that the " 'vast majority of potential profits for a generic drug manufacturer materialize during the 180-day exclusivity period.' " The 180-day exclusivity period, however, can belong only to the first generic to file. Should that first-to-file generic forfeit the exclusivity right in one of the ways specified by statute, no other generic can obtain it. *See* § 355(j)(5)(D).

B

In 1999, Solvay Pharmaceuticals, a respondent here, filed a New Drug Application for a brand-name drug called AndroGel. The FDA approved the application in 2000. In 2003, Solvay obtained a relevant patent and disclosed that fact to the FDA, as Hatch–Waxman requires. *See* § 355(c)(2) (requiring, in addition, that FDA must publish new patent information upon submission).

Later the same year another respondent, Actavis, Inc. (then known as Watson Pharmaceuticals), filed an Abbreviated New Drug Application for a generic drug modeled after AndroGel. Subsequently, Paddock Laboratories, also a respondent, separately filed an Abbreviated New Drug Application for its own generic product. Both Actavis and Paddock certified under paragraph IV that Solvay's listed patent was invalid and their drugs did not infringe it. . . .

Solvay initiated paragraph IV patent litigation against Actavis and Paddock. Thirty months later the FDA approved Actavis' first-to-file generic product, but, in 2006, the patent-litigation parties all settled. Under the terms of the settlement Actavis agreed that it would not bring its generic to market until August 31, 2015, 65 months before Solvay's patent expired (unless someone else marketed a generic sooner). Actavis also agreed to promote AndroGel to urologists. The other generic manufacturer[ ] made roughly similar promises. And Solvay agreed to pay millions of dollars to each generic—$12 million in total to Paddock; . . . and an estimated $19–$30 million annually, for nine years, to Actavis. The companies described these payments as compensation for other services the generics promised to perform, but the FTC contends the other services had little value. According to the

FTC the true point of the payments was to compensate the generics for agreeing not to compete against AndroGel until 2015.

. . . [T]he FTC filed this lawsuit against all the settling parties. . . . The FTC's complaint . . . alleged that respondents violated § 5 of the Federal Trade Commission Act, 15 U.S.C. § 45, by unlawfully agreeing "to share in Solvay's monopoly profits, abandon their patent challenges, and refrain from launching their low-cost generic products to compete with AndroGel for nine years." The District Court held that these allegations did not set forth an antitrust law violation. . . .

The Court of Appeals for the Eleventh Circuit affirmed the District Court. It wrote that "absent sham litigation or fraud in obtaining the patent, a reverse payment settlement is immune from antitrust attack so long as its anticompetitive effects fall within the scope of the exclusionary potential of the patent." 677 F.3d, at 1312. . . .

II

Solvay's patent, if valid and infringed, might have permitted it to charge drug prices sufficient to recoup the reverse settlement payments it agreed to make to its potential generic competitors. And we are willing to take this fact as evidence that the agreement's "anticompetitive effects fall within the scope of the exclusionary potential of the patent." But we do not agree that that fact, or characterization, can immunize the agreement from antitrust attack.

. . . The patent here may or may not be valid, and may or may not be infringed. A *valid* patent . . . may permit the patent owner to charge a higher-than-competitive price for the patented product. But an invalidated patent carries with it no such right. And even a valid patent confers no right to exclude products or processes that do not actually infringe. The paragraph IV litigation in this case put the patent's validity at issue, as well as its actual preclusive scope. The parties' settlement ended that litigation. . . . [T]he plaintiff agreed to pay the defendants many millions of dollars to stay out of its market, even though the defendants did not have any claim that the plaintiff was liable to them for damages. That form of settlement is unusual. And . . . there is reason for concern that settlements taking this form tend to have significant adverse effects on competition.

. . . [I]n *United States v. Line Material* . . . rather than measure the length or amount of a restriction solely against the length of the patent's term or its earning potential, as the Court of Appeals apparently did here, this Court answered the antitrust question by considering traditional antitrust factors such as likely anticompetitive effects, redeeming virtues, market power, and potentially offsetting legal considerations present in the circumstances, such as here those related to patents. *United States v. Line Material Co.*, 333 U. S. 287, 310 (1948).

. . . [T]his Court's precedents make clear that patent-related settlement agreements can sometimes violate the antitrust laws. . . .

. . . These cases . . . seek to accommodate patent and antitrust policies, finding challenged terms and conditions unlawful unless patent law policy offsets the antitrust law policy strongly favoring competition.

. . . Finally, the Hatch–Waxman Act itself does not embody a statutory policy that supports the Eleventh Circuit's view. Rather, the general procompetitive thrust of the statute, its specific provisions facilitating challenges to a patent's validity, and its later-added provisions requiring parties to a patent dispute triggered by a paragraph IV filing to report settlement terms to the FTC and the Antitrust Division of the Department of Justice, all suggest the contrary. Those interested in legislative history may also wish to examine the statements of individual Members of Congress condemning reverse payment settlements in advance of the 2003 amendments.

The Eleventh Circuit's conclusion finds some degree of support in a general legal policy favoring the settlement of disputes. The Circuit's related underlying practical concern consists of its fear that antitrust scrutiny of a reverse payment agreement would require the parties to litigate the validity of the patent in order to demonstrate what would have happened to competition in the absence of the settlement. Any such litigation will prove time consuming, complex, and expensive. The antitrust game, the Circuit may believe, would not be worth that litigation candle.

. . . [W]e nonetheless conclude that this . . . factor should not determine the result here. Rather, five sets of considerations lead us to conclude that the FTC should have been given the opportunity to prove its antitrust claim.

First, the specific restraint at issue has the "potential for genuine adverse effects on competition." . . . Suppose, for example, that the exclusive right to sell produces $50 million in supracompetitive profits per year for the patentee. And suppose further that the patent has 10 more years to run. Continued litigation, if it results in patent invalidation or a finding of noninfringement, could cost the patentee $500 million in lost revenues, a sum that then would flow in large part to consumers in the form of lower prices.

. . . [S]ettlement on the terms . . . at issue here—payment in return for staying out of the market—simply keeps prices at patentee-set levels, potentially producing the full patent-related $500 million monopoly return while dividing that return between the challenged patentee and the patent challenger. The patentee and the challenger gain; the consumer loses. . . .

But, one might ask, as a practical matter would the parties be able to enter into such an anticompetitive agreement? Would not a high reverse payment signal to other potential challengers that the patentee lacks confidence in its patent, thereby provoking additional challenges, perhaps too many for the patentee to "buy off?" Two special features of Hatch–Waxman mean that the answer to this question is "not necessarily so." First, under Hatch–Waxman only the first challenger gains the special advantage of 180 days of an exclusive right to sell a generic version of the brand-name product. . . . Subsequent challengers cannot secure that exclusivity period, and thus stand to win significantly less than the first if they bring a successful paragraph IV challenge. . . . [T]hat litigation victory will free not just the challenger to compete, but all other potential competitors too (once they obtain FDA approval). . . . Second, a generic that files a paragraph IV after learning that the first filer has settled will (if sued by the brand-name) have to wait out a stay period of (roughly) 30 months before the FDA may approve its application, just as the first filer did. *See* 21 U.S.C. § 355(j)(5)(B)(iii). These features together mean that a reverse payment settlement with the first filer . . . "removes from consideration the most motivated challenger, and the one closest to introducing competition." . . . It may well be that Hatch–Waxman's unique regulatory framework . . . does much to explain why in this context, but not others, the patentee's ordinary incentives to resist paying off challengers (i.e., the fear of provoking myriad other challengers) appear to be more frequently overcome.

Second, these anticompetitive consequences will at least sometimes prove unjustified. As the FTC admits, offsetting or redeeming virtues are sometimes present. . . . But that possibility does not justify dismissing the FTC's complaint. An antitrust defendant may show in the antitrust proceeding that legitimate justifications are present, thereby . . showing . . . lawfulness . . . under the rule of reason.

Third, where a reverse payment threatens to work unjustified anticompetitive harm, the patentee likely possesses the power to bring that harm about in practice. . . . [T]he Commission has referred to studies showing that reverse payment agreements are associated with the presence of higher-than-competitive profits—a strong indication of market power.

Fourth, an antitrust action is likely to prove more feasible administratively than the Eleventh Circuit believed. . . . That is because it is normally not necessary to litigate patent validity to answer the antitrust question. . . . An unexplained large reverse payment itself would normally suggest that the patentee has serious doubts about the patent's survival. . . . In a word, the size of the unexplained reverse payment can provide a workable surrogate for a patent's weakness, all without forcing a court to conduct a detailed exploration of the validity of the patent itself.

Fifth, the fact that a large, unjustified reverse payment risks antitrust liability does not prevent litigating parties from settling their lawsuit. They may, as in other industries, settle in other ways, for example, by allowing the generic manufacturer to enter the patentee's market prior to the patent's expiration, without the patentee paying the challenger to stay out prior to that point. Although the parties may have reasons to prefer settlements that include reverse payments, the relevant antitrust question is: What are those reasons? If the basic reason is a desire to maintain and to share patent-generated monopoly profits, then, in the absence of some other justification, the antitrust laws are likely to forbid the arrangement.

. . . In our view, these considerations, taken together, outweigh the single strong consideration—the desirability of settlements—that led the Eleventh Circuit to provide near-automatic antitrust immunity to reverse payment settlements.

III

The FTC urges us to hold that reverse payment settlement agreements are presumptively unlawful and that courts reviewing such agreements should proceed via a "quick look" approach, rather than applying a "rule of reason." We decline to do so. . . . [T]he likelihood of a reverse payment bringing about anticompetitive effects depends upon its size, its scale in relation to the payor's anticipated future litigation costs, its independence from other services for which it might represent payment, and the lack of any other convincing justification. . . . These complexities lead us to conclude that the FTC must prove its case as in other rule-of-reason cases.

. . . We reverse the judgment of the Eleventh Circuit. And we remand the case for further proceedings consistent with this opinion.

It is so ordered.

■ CHIEF JUSTICE ROBERTS, with whom JUSTICE SCALIA and JUSTICE THOMAS join, dissenting.

. . . It is especially disturbing here, where the Court discerns from specific provisions [of Hatch–Waxman] a very broad policy—a "general procompetitive thrust," in its words—and uses that policy to unsettle the established relationship between patent and antitrust law. . . .

The majority . . . points out that the first challenger gets a 180-day exclusive period to market a generic version of the brand name drug, and that subsequent challengers cannot secure that exclusivity period— meaning when the patent holder buys off the first challenger, it has bought off its most motivated competitor. There are two problems with this argument. First, according to the Food and Drug Administration, all manufacturers who file on the first day are considered "first applicants" who share the exclusivity period. Thus, if ten generics file an application to market a generic drug on the first day, all will be considered "first applicants." *See* 21 U. S. C. § 355(j)(5)(B)(iv)(II)(bb); *see also* FDA, Guidance for Industry: 180-Day Exclusivity When Multiple ANDAs Are Submitted on the Same Day 4 (July 2003). This is not an unusual occurrence. *See* Brief for Generic Pharmaceutical Association as Amicus Curiae 23–24 (citing FTC data indicating that some drugs "have been subject to as many as sixteen first-day" generic applications [and] that in 2005, the average number of first-day applications per drug was 11. . . .).

Second . . . [e]ven if a subsequent generic would not be entitled to this additional incentive, it will have as much or nearly as much incentive to challenge the patent as a potential challenger would in any other context outside of Hatch–Waxman. . . . And a patent holder who gives away notably large sums of money because it is . . . concerned about the strength of its patent, would be putting blood in water where sharks are always near.

The majority also points to the fact that, under Hatch–Waxman, the FDA is enjoined from approving a generic's application to market a drug for 30 months if the brand name sues the generic for patent infringement within 45 days of that application being filed. According to the majority, this provision will chill subsequent generics from challenging the patent . . . But this overlooks an important feature of the law: the FDA may approve the application before the 30 months are up "if before the expiration of [the 30 months,] the district court decides that the patent is invalid or not infringed." § 355(j)(5)(B)(iii)(I). . . .

The irony of all this is that the majority's decision may very well discourage generics from challenging pharmaceutical patents in the first place. . . . Taking the prospect of settlements off the table—or limiting settlements to an earlier entry date for the generic, which may still be many years in the future—puts a damper on the generic's expected value going into litigation, and decreases its incentive to sue in the first place. . . .

NOTES

1. *Authorized Generic Drugs.* When a pioneer NDA drug approaches the end of its patent coverage, another common response by the pioneer manufacturer is to license a generic drug company immediately to begin marketing a generic version in order to preserve as much of the market as possible. If another generic company has challenged the pioneer company's patent for the drug and as a result obtained the statutory right to a 180-day period of market exclusivity before any other generic product may be approved by FDA, the licensing of the authorized generic drug substantially reduces the value of this period of market exclusivity. Nonetheless, the courts have upheld the legality of immediate marketing of an authorized generic. *E.g., Teva Pharmaceuticals, Inc. v. Crawford*, 410 F.3d 51 (D.C. Cir. 2005).

2. *180-Day Exclusivity Reform.* The impact of a reverse payment deal with the first filer used to be more dramatic than it is now, because the first-filer could, by not commercializing its generic product, prevent the 180-day period from ever commencing and thus preclude the entry of all other generics. Congress's 2003 amendments, 117 Stat. 2066, 2448, addressed this issue, as well. Now, if the generic manufacturer fails to market its drug in a timely manner, the 180-day market exclusivity period is subject to forfeiture, as it is under other specified conditions. FD&C Act 505(j)(5)(D).

The 2003 amendments also reformed other aspects of first-filer exclusivity. It provided that when two abbreviated NDAs are submitted on the same day, each will share the 180-day market exclusivity, which will begin whenever either first begins marketing. It stated that the 180-day market exclusivity begins on the date of first commercial marketing of either the abbreviated NDA product or the NDA product (in the event that the generic manufacturer enters into an agreement with the pioneer manufacturer to market the NDA product instead of the generic version). Finally, to permit monitoring under the antitrust laws, agreements between pioneer and generic manufacturers that could violate the antitrust laws are required to be filed with the FTC and the Department of Justice within ten days of their execution.

L. THE COST OF DRUGS

1. INTRODUCTION

Patients living in the United States pay a higher price for new prescription drugs than patients living anywhere else in the world. This is because the United States is the only country where the market, rather than the government, sets drug prices. Consequently, the cost of the research and development for a new drug is borne by United States citizens. We subsidize, through the higher prices we pay, the research and development for products used throughout the world.

With an annual budget of more than $30 billion, the National Institutes of Health (NIH) provides funds, often supplemented by university funds, for substantial university research that results in exclusive licenses to private companies who turn that research into profitable drugs. Some view this as an appropriate use of public tax dollars and academic funds, but others complain that the government and universities should control the price of the drugs resulting from their funding and should receive a larger royalty. To assure that government-sponsored research is translated into useful products for the country, Congress has passed a number of statutes, including the Stevenson–Wydler Technology Innovation Act of 1980, 94 Stat 2311, the Bayh–Dole Act, 94 Stat 3015 (1980), the Federal Technology Transfer Act of 1986, 100 Stat 1785, and the National Technology Transfer Competitiveness Act of 1989, 103 Stat 1352, 1674.

Surprisingly, once a drug loses its patent protection and market exclusivity in the United States, generic competition drives the price down to a point below the generic drug prices in virtually all other countries. Thus, we have a system that features very high prices for patented new drugs and very low prices for generic old drugs.

Malcolm Gladwell, *High Prices*

THE NEW YORKER, October 25, 2004, at 86.

. . . .

The problem with the way we think about prescription drugs begins with a basic misunderstanding about drug prices. The editorial board of the *Times* has pronounced them much too high; Marcia Angell calls them "intolerable." The perception that the drug industry is profiteering at the expense of the American consumer has given pharmaceutical firms a reputation on a par with that of cigarette manufacturers.

In fact, the complaint is only half true. The "intolerable" prices that Angel writes about are confined to the brand-name sector of the American drug marketplace. As the economists Patricia Danzon and Michael Furukawa recently pointed out in the journal *Health Affairs,* drugs still under patent protection are anywhere from twenty-five to forty per cent more expensive in the United States than in places like England, France, and Canada. Generic drugs are another story. Because there are so many companies in the United States that step in to make drugs once their patents expire, and because the price competition among those firms is so fierce, generic drugs here are among the cheapest in the world. And, according to Danzon and Furukawa's analysis, when prescription drugs are converted to over-the-counter status no other country even comes close to having prices as low as the United States.

It is not accurate to say, then, that the United States has higher prescription-drug prices than other counties. It is accurate to say only that the United States has a different pricing system from that of other countries. Americans pay more for drugs when they first come out and less as the drugs get older, while the rest of the world pays less in the beginning and more later. Whose pricing system is cheaper? It depends. If you are taking Mevacor for your cholesterol, the 20–mg. pill is two-twenty-five in America and less than two dollars if you buy it in Canada. But generic Mevacor (lovastatin) is about a dollar a pill in Canada and as low as sixty-five cents a pill in the United States. Of course, not every drug comes in a generic version. But so many important drugs have gone off-patent recently that the rate of increase in drug spending in the United States has fallen sharply for the past four years. And so many other drugs are going to go off-patent in the next few years—including the top-selling drug in this country, the anti-cholesterol medication Lipitor—that many Americans who now pay more for their drugs than their counterparts in other Western countries could soon be paying less.

The second misconception about prices has to do with their importance in driving up over-all drug costs. In one three-year period in the mid-nineteen-nineties, for example, the amount of money spent in the United States on asthma medication increased by almost a hundred per cent. But none of that was due to an increase in the price of asthma drugs. It was largely the result of an increase in the *prevalence* of usage—that is, in the number of people who were given a diagnosis of the disease and who then bought drugs to treat it. Part of that hundred-per-cent increase was also the result of a change in what's known as the *intensity* of drug use: in the mid-nineties, doctors were becoming far more aggressive in their attempts to prevent asthma attacks, and in those three years people with asthma went from filling about nine prescriptions a year to filling fourteen prescriptions a year. Last year, asthma costs jumped again, by twenty-six per cent, and price inflation played a role. But, once again, the big factor was prevalence. And this time around there was also a change in what's called the therapeutic mix; in an attempt to fight the disease more effectively, physicians are switching many of their patients to newer, better, and more expensive drugs, like Merck's Singulair.

Asthma is not an isolated case. In 2003, the amount that Americans spent on cholesterol-lowering drugs rose 23.8 per cent, and similar increases are forecast for the next few years. Why the increase? Well, the baby boomers are aging, and so are at greater risk for heart attacks. The incidence of obesity is increasing. In 2002, the National Institutes of Health lowered the thresholds for when people with high cholesterol ought to start taking drugs like Lipitor and Mevacor. In combination, those factors are having an enormous impact on both the prevalence and the intensity of cholesterol treatment. All told, prescription-drug spending in the United States rose 9.1 per cent last year. Only three of those percentage points were due to price increases, however, which means that inflation was about the same in the drug sector as it was in the over-all economy. Angell's book and almost every other account of the prescription-drug crisis take it for granted that cost increases are evidence of how we've been cheated by the industry. In fact, drug expenditures are rising rapidly in the United States not so much because we're being charged more for prescription drugs but because more people are taking more medications in more expensive combinations. It's not price that matters; it's volume.

This is a critical fact, and it ought to fundamentally change the way we think about the problem of drug costs. Last year, hospital expenditures rose by the same amount as drug expenditures—nine percent. Yet almost all of that (eight percentage points) was due to inflation. That's something to be upset about: when it comes to hospital services, we're spending more and getting less. When it comes to drugs, though, we're spending more and we're getting more, and that makes the question of how we ought to respond to rising drug costs a little more ambiguous. . . .

The fact that volume matters more than price also means that the emphasis of the prescription-drug debate is all wrong. We've been focussed on the drug manufacturers. But decisions about prevalence, therapeutic mix, and intensity aren't made by the producers of drugs. They're made by the consumers of drugs. . . .

NOTES

1. *Antitrust Issues.* For an unsuccessful attempt to attack under the antitrust laws the legality of a 478 percent increase in the price of an AIDS drug, see *Schor v. Abbott Laboratories Inc.*, 457 F.3d 608 (7th Cir. 2006).

2. *The Medicare Prescription Drug Benefit.* Under the Medicare Prescription Drug, Improvement, and Modernization Act of 2003, 117 Stat. 2066, 2071, Congress created an outpatient prescription drug benefit under Part D of the Social Security Act. Previously, only an inpatient prescription drug benefit was available under Part B. Private plans may negotiate prices with pharmaceutical manufacturers for drugs listed on their formularies, but the federal government (with some exceptions, including the Department of Veterans Affairs) may not do so.

3. *Makena.* One of the most prominent of recent controversies regarding drug pricing concerned Makena®, a drug for the prevention of premature birth. In 2011, FDA approved KV Pharmaceutical's NDA for Makena as an orphan drug, with seven years of marketing exclusivity. KV charged $1,500 per injection, which amounted to approximately $25,000 per treatment. But for many years, the same active ingredient, compounded by pharmacists, had been available for only about $15 per injection. In response the outcry over the stunning increase in the price of the drug, FDA announced that it did not intend to take enforcement action against pharmacies compounding it based on a valid prescription for an individually identified patient. *See FDA Statement on Makena* (Mar. 30, 2011) (available on FDA website).

2. IMPORTATION OF CHEAPER DRUGS

The high price of drugs in the United States has frustrated and angered citizens. Because of the large differential between the price of new drugs in the United States and in all other countries, many consumers have sought to find sources of cheaper drugs from abroad. Americans' desire for more affordable foreign drugs has led to legislation permitting the lawful import of unapproved versions of

NDA'd drugs, the creation of organized programs to obtain these drugs, and an increased use of internet pharmacies.

Congress has on three occasions enacted legislation to address this matter: (1) the Medicine Equity and Drug Safety Act of 2000, 114 Stat. 1549A–35, adding section 804 to the FD&C Act, (2) the Medicare Prescription Drug, Improvement and Modernization Act of 2003, 117 Stat. 2066, 2464, which replaced section 804 with a virtually identical substitute provision, and (3) section 535 of the FY 2007 appropriations statute for the Department of Homeland Security, 120 Stat. 1355 (2006), which for one year permitted individuals personally to bring up to a 90-day supply of any drug from Canada, except for a biological product or a controlled substance. In both of the first two statutes, Congress required that, before the provision could take effect, the Secretary of HHS had to certify to Congress that its implementation would impose no risk to the public health and safety and that it would result in a significant reduction of the cost of prescription drugs to the American consumer. The Secretaries of HHS in the Clinton, Bush, and Obama Administrations have determined that these certifications could not be made, and thus these laws have never been implemented. Nonetheless, Congress has continued to consider legislation of this type, particularly in election years. Interest has been particularly high among members of Congress from border states, whose constituents can see lower drug prices just a few miles away. The third provision simply codified the FDA personal import policy first adopted by the agency in 1954. For a more detailed discussion of these legislative measures, see the chapter on the Regulation of Foreign Commerce, *infra* p. 1458.

A wide variety of illegal programs have been established to import cheaper drugs into the United States. Some have been set up by counties and states, and others have relied on internet pharmacies in Canada and elsewhere. FDA considers all of these programs illegal. In the cases brought by state and local governments to obtain declaratory judgments, and in the cases brought by FDA to shut down rogue pharmacies, the agency has been uniformly successful. *See, e.g., In Re: Canadian Import Antitrust Litigation*, 385 F. Supp. 2d 930 (D. Minn. 2005), *aff'd* 2006 WL 3436309 (8th Cir. 2006); *United States v. Rx Depot, Inc.*, 290 F. Supp. 2d 1238, 297 F. Supp. 2d 1306 (D. Okla. 2003) (excerpted *infra* p. 1464).

3. Promotion of the Use of Generics

The primary goal of the investigations begun by Senator Estes Kefauver in 1959 was to reduce drug prices by increasing competition in the pharmaceutical industry. Although the only element of Kefauver's proposed legislation that became part of the Drug Amendments of 1962 was the requirement that drug labeling and advertising disclose the generic name, the federal government's growing financial responsibility for drug purchases has led FDA to assume a role in promoting the use of generic drugs that extends beyond its narrow statutory mandate. The costs to both federal and state governments for reimbursing prescription drug purchases have continued to increase, and accordingly the incentive to encourage price competition and contain costs has been substantial.

In the 1970s, the Department of HEW (the predecessor to HHS) established procedures for fixing the maximum allowable cost (MAC) that the federal government would reimburse for any multi-source drug dispensed to patients under Medicare and other programs. 40 Fed. Reg. 32284 (July 31, 1975). Under these procedures, a new body, the Pharmaceutical Reimbursement Board, would establish a "MAC" for a drug based on the "lowest unit price at which the drug is widely and consistently available from any formulator or labeler." The MAC did not apply where "the prescriber has certified in his own handwriting [that a particular brand] is medically necessary for that patient." For a single-source drug, reimbursement was based on the actual cost of the product. The MAC regulations withstood legal challenge. *American Medical Association v. Mathews,* 429 F. Supp. 1179 (N.D. Ill. 1977); *Hoffmann–LaRoche, Inc. v. Califano,* 453 F. Supp. 900 (D.D.C. 1978). Nonetheless, following a public meeting on the MAC regulations, 48 Fed. Reg. 35506 (Aug. 4, 1983), HHS later revoked them, on the grounds that they had had little impact on drug costs and that alternative approaches to encouraging generic prescribing under Medicaid would be more cost-effective. 52 Fed. Reg. 28648 (July 31, 1987)

During the 1970s, many states also sought to promote the use of generic drugs under Medicaid. To assist the states in developing formularies listing drugs appropriate for reimbursement, FDA initially disseminated lists of all drugs it had approved for marketing. 41 Fed. Reg. 5539 (Feb. 5, 1976), 43 Fed. Reg. 28557 (June 30, 1978). Soon afterwards, it prepared a list of "therapeutically equivalent drugs," including prices, and proposed that it be distributed to all physicians and pharmacists to aid them in making comparisons among products containing the same generic active ingredients. 44 Fed. Reg. 2932 (Jan. 12, 1979). Following an unsuccessful attempt to halt the rulemaking, *Pharmaceutical Manufacturers Association v. Kennedy,* 471 F. Supp. 1224 (D. Md. 1979), FDA issued a final regulation in 45 Fed. Reg. 72582 (Oct. 31, 1980), codified at 21 C.F.R. 20.117(a)(3), making available a list of all approved drugs together with "an evaluation of the therapeutic equivalence of the drug products covered by such applications." This list, known as the Orange Book also plays a central role in the administration of Hatch–Waxman. *See supra* p. 1006.

M. COUNTERFEIT, IMITATION, STREET ALTERNATIVE, AND DIVERTED PRESCRIPTION DRUGS

As drug prices have increased, the problems of counterfeit drugs, diverted drugs, and imitation drugs have grown exponentially.

1. COUNTERFEIT DRUGS

FDA has been concerned about the illicit distribution of legitimate drugs and the distribution of counterfeit drugs ever since the mid-1960s, when it was responsible for enforcement of the Drug Abuse Control Amendments of 1965, 79 Stat. 226 (superseded by the Controlled Substances Act, 84 Stat. 1236, 1242, 1281–1282 (1970), enforced by DEA). The 1965 Amendments added to the FD&C Act section 201(g)(2), defining the term "counterfeit drug," and section

301(i)(2), prohibiting counterfeiting and the distribution of counterfeit drugs. FDA vigorously enforced these provisions. *See, e.g., United States v. Jamieson–McKames Pharmaceuticals, Inc.,* 651 F.2d 532 (8th Cir. 1981); Counterfeit Drug Cases, FDA Talk Paper, T87–42 (Sept. 30, 1987) (describing cases involving counterfeit contraceptives, analgesic, and antibiotic drug products).

Congress addressed the growing issue of counterfeit drugs by enactment of the Prescription Drug Marketing Act (PDMA) of 1987, 102 Stat. 95, as modified by the Prescription Drug Amendments of 1992, 106 Stat. 941.

Prescription Drug Marketing Act Pedigree Requirements; Effective Date and Compliance Policy Guide; Request for Comment

71 Fed. Reg. 34249 (June 14, 2006).

The Prescription Drug Marketing Act of 1987 (the PDMA), as modified by the Prescription Drug Amendments of 1992, establish, among other things, requirements related to the wholesale distribution of prescription drugs. A primary purpose of the PDMA was to increase safeguards to prevent the introduction and retail sale of substandard, ineffective, and counterfeit drugs in the U.S. drug supply chain.

Section 503(e)(1)(A) of the act establishes the so-called "pedigree" requirement for prescription drugs. A drug pedigree is a statement of origin that identifies each prior sale, purchase, or trade of a drug, including the dates of those transactions and the names and addresses of all parties to them. Under the pedigree requirement, each person who is engaged in the wholesale distribution of a prescription drug in interstate commerce, who is not the manufacturer or an authorized distributor of record for that drug, must provide to the person who receives the drug a pedigree for that drug. The PDMA states that an authorized distributor of record is a wholesaler that has an "ongoing relationship" with a manufacturer to distribute that manufacturer's drug. However, the PDMA does not define "ongoing relationship."

In 1999, FDA published final regulations implementing the PDMA. The regulations were to take effect in December 2000. . . . Based on concerns raised by various stakeholders, the agency delayed the effective date . . . several times.

Most recently, in February 2004, FDA delayed the effective date . . . until December 1, 2006, in part because we were informed by stakeholders in the U.S. drug supply chain that the industry would voluntarily implement electronic track and trace technology by 2007. If widely adopted, this technology could create a de facto electronic pedigree documenting the sale of a drug product from its place of manufacture through the U.S. drug supply chain to the final dispenser. If properly implemented, an electronic record could thus meet the pedigree requirements in section 503(e)(1)(A) of the act. Based on a recent fact-finding effort by FDA to assess the use of e-pedigree across the supply chain, however, it appears that industry will not fully implement track and trace technology by 2007.

Today, the agency is announcing that it does not intend to delay the effective date . . . beyond December 1, 2006. . . .

We are issuing a draft CPG [Compliance Policy Guide] that describes how we plan to prioritize our enforcement actions during the next year with respect to these new requirements. To this end, FDA is announcing the availability of a new CPG section 160.900, entitled "Prescription Drug Marketing Act Pedigree Requirements Under 21 CFR Part 203." This CPG, which the agency is publishing in draft for comment, lists factors that FDA field personnel are expected to consider in prioritizing FDA's pedigree-related enforcement efforts during the next year. Consistent with our risk-based approach to the regulation of pharmaceuticals, these factors focus our resources on drug products that are most vulnerable to counterfeiting and diversion or that are otherwise involved in illegal activity.

FDA has not provided in the CPG a list of drug products that have been counterfeited in the past. We solicit comment on the merit of providing such a list. . . .

NOTES

1. *Proposed Amendment to Regulations.* In 2011, FDA proposed to remove a section of the PDMA regulations requiring unauthorized distributors to provide full pedigree information to wholesale purchasers. 76 Fed. Reg. 41434 (July 14, 2011).

2. *FD&C Act 505D.* The 2007 amendments to the FD&C Act (FDAAA) created new section 505D, which requires FDA to develop standards and identify and validate technologies that can be used to secure the drug supply chain against counterfeited, diverted, subpotent, substandard, adulterated, misbranded, and expired prescription drugs. These technologies may include radio frequency identification technology (RFID), nanotechnology, and encryption technology, among others. FD&C Act 505D(b)(3). The agency is required to work with the Department of Justice, the Department of Homeland Security, the Department of Commerce, other appropriate federal and state agencies, manufacturers, distributors, pharmacies, and other supply chain stakeholders to prioritize and develop standards for identification, validation, authentication, and tracking and tracing of prescription drugs. The Secretary is also required to expand and enhance the resources and facilities of FDA components involved with regulatory and criminal enforcement of the FD&C Act to secure the drug supply chain and must undertake related enhanced and joint enforcement activities with other federal and state agencies.

3. *Standardized Numeral Identifier.* Section 505D(b)(2) obligates FDA, no later than 30 months after enactment of the FDAAA, to develop a standardized numerical identifier to be applied to every prescription drug at the package or pallet level. In 2010, following the 2009 promulgation of a draft guidance, the agency published a final guidance regarding the development of such a system for prescription drug packages. GUIDANCE FOR INDUSTRY: STANDARDS FOR SECURING THE DRUG SUPPLY CHAIN— STANDARDIZED NUMERICAL IDENTIFICATION FOR PRESCRIPTION DRUG PACKAGES (March 2010).

4. *The FDA Counterfeit Drug Task Force.* FDA established a Counterfeit Drug Task Force in 2003. The Task Force issued its first report in February 2004 and its second report in May 2005. Following a public meeting in February 2006 to gather additional information, the Task Force issued its most recent report in June 2006. All of these documents are available on the FDA website.

5. *The Federal Criminal Code.* A statutory provision outside the FD&C Act, 18 U.S.C. 2320, broadly prohibits any traffic in counterfeit goods. This provision has been applied to counterfeit prescription drugs. *See, e.g., United States v. Milstein*, 401 F.3d 53, 59 (2d Cir. 2005). In *United States v. Cambra, Jr.*, 933 F.2d 752 (9th Cir. 1991), the Court of Appeals upheld a sentence based on the crime of fraud and deceit, a more serious offense than the violation of the counterfeit drug provisions of the FD&C Act.

6. *Liability for Counterfeit Drugs.* As the problem of counterfeit drugs has escalated, patients harmed by these drugs have sought remedies in the courts. In *Fagan v. Amerisourcebergen Corp.*, 356 F. Supp. 2d 198 (E.D.N.Y. 2004), a patient who was prescribed Epogen following a liver transplant, and who received a counterfeit drug, brought suit against the manufacturer of Epogen, the wholesale drug distributor, and the pharmacy, to recover damages for personal injuries under common law theories of tort and contracts.

7. *State Law.* In *Ferndale Laboratories, Inc. v. Cavendish*, 79 F.3d 488 (6th Cir. 1996), the Court of Appeals upheld an Ohio registration requirement imposed on out-of-state drug wholesalers on the ground that it was not an impermissible burden on interstate commerce.

2. DIVERTED DRUG SAMPLES

In two early cases, courts held that diverted prescription drugs labeled as "physician's sample—not to be sold" did not become misbranded in the possession of wholesalers who obtained them with the intention of selling them to retail druggists to fill prescriptions. *United States v. Various Articles of Drugs Consisting of Unknown Quantities of Prescription Drugs,* 332 F.2d 286 (3d Cir. 1964); *United States v. Various Articles of Drugs Consisting of Unknown Quantities of Prescription Drugs,* 207 F. Supp. 480 (S.D.N.Y. 1962). Similarly, a company that repackaged tablets from the manufacturer's original package and resold them was not required to obtain separate FDA approval when the manufacturer already had an approved NDA. *United States v. Kaybel, Inc.* 430 F.2d 1346 (3d Cir. 1970). These decisions made it very difficult for FDA to prevent the adulteration and misbranding of diverted samples.

Congressional investigations brought to light a related problem involving pharmaceutical products exported from the United States and later reimported. *See* "Dangerous Medicine: The Risk to American Consumers from Prescription Drug Diversion and Counterfeiting," Report by the Subcommittee on Oversight and Investigations of the House Committee on Energy and Commerce, 99th Cong., 2nd Sess., Comm. Print 99–Z (1966). In September 1985, FDA adopted a policy of automatic detention of imports of U.S.-produced drugs in order to confirm that they had not become adulterated or misbranded while abroad. 52 Fed. Reg. 706 (Jan. 8, 1987). Because this policy was adopted without the opportunity for public comment, it was declared invalid in *Bellarno International Ltd. v. FDA,* 678 F. Supp. 410 (E.D.N.Y. 1988).

The Prescription Drug Marketing Act of 1987, 102 Stat. 95, added section 801(d)(1) to the FD&C Act, making the importation of American drugs by anyone other than the manufacturer illegal. The PDMA also added section 503(c), prohibiting the sale of drug samples and the resale of drug products initially sold to health care institutions; 503(d), allowing the distribution of drug samples by pharmaceutical manufacturers, but only in response to a written request and if a receipt is obtained; and 503(e), requiring state licensure of wholesale distributors of prescription drugs. FDA's steps to implement these provisions can be traced in 53 Fed. Reg. 29776 (Aug. 8, 1988), 53 Fed. Reg. 35325 (Sept. 13, 1988), 53 Fed. Reg. 44954 (Nov. 7, 1988), 55 Fed. Reg. 7778 (Mar. 5, 1990).

NOTES

1. *Drug Samples.* For post-1987 cases involving illegal distribution of drug samples, *see United Sates v. Dino,* 919 F.2d 72 (8th Cir. 1990); *Parke–Davis & Co. v. Ricci,* 587 So.2d 589 (Fla. Dist. Ct. App. 1991).

2. *Kaybel.* The *Kaybel* decision applies only to solid oral dosage forms of a drug, and does not apply when a liquid drug is diluted or pooled. *United States v. Baxter Healthcare Corp.,* 712 F. Supp. 1352 (N.D. Ill. 1989), *aff'd* 901 F.2d 1401 (7th Cir. 1990); FDA Compliance Policy Guide No. 7132c.06 (January 18, 1991).

3. *State Registration.* Ohio's law requiring registration of all prescription drug wholesalers was upheld against the charge that it represented an unconstitutional burden on out-of-state distributors. *Ferndale Laboratories, Inc. v. Cavendish,* 79 F.3d 488 (6th Cir. 1996).

3. INTERNET PHARMACY

The extraordinary growth of the internet in the past 15 years has produced a nightmare for the regulation of drug products and an enormous growth in the distribution of counterfeit and imitation drugs. So-called "rogue" internet sites bombard the country with advertising for inexpensive versions of costly new drugs. Most of the drugs are counterfeit drugs that are made abroad and have no approved NDA. Many have no active ingredient. For most, there is no pretense of a doctor's prescription. When a prescription is written, it is done over the telephone without a valid doctor-patient relationship.

In 2011, Pfizer determined that about 80 percent of pills sold online as Viagra®, its erectile dysfunction treatment, were counterfeit and often contained much less active ingredient than the actual product. *See* Katie Thomas, *Turning to the Internet to Sell Viagra,* N.Y. TIMES, May 7, 2013, at 1. Recently, Pfizer, in an attempt to stanch the loss of sales to this black market, announced that it would begin selling Viagra to consumers on its website.

Because rogue internet sites are difficult to trace and can easily move their location, enforcement is a complex matter.

Jody Feder, *Legal Issues Related to Prescription Drug Sales on the Internet*

Congressional Research Service (CRS) Report No. RS–21711 (June 7, 2006).

With the advent of the Internet, many individuals have turned to online pharmacies to purchase prescription drugs, and an increasing number of physicians have incorporated the Internet and email into their medical practice. Use of this technology has many advantages for both the doctor and the patient, including cost savings, convenience, accessibility, and improved privacy and communication. Although many online pharmacies are legitimate businesses that offer safe and convenient services similar to those provided by traditional neighborhood pharmacies and large chain drugstores, other online pharmacies—often referred to as "rogue sites"—engage in practices that are illegal, such as selling unapproved or counterfeit drugs or dispensing drugs without a prescription. Some rogue sites operate in a legal gray area in which the online pharmacy, as mandated by federal law, requires a prescription before dispensing prescription drugs, but allows patients to secure a prescription by completing an online questionnaire that is reviewed by a doctor who never examines or speaks to the patient. . . .

Current regulation of online pharmacies and doctors consists of a patchwork of federal and state laws in an array of areas. At the federal level, the Food and Drug Administration regulates prescription drugs under the Federal Food, Drug, and Cosmetic Act (FFDCA), which governs, among other things, the safety and efficacy of prescription medications, including the approval, manufacturing, and distribution of such drugs. It is the FFDCA that requires that prescription drugs may be dispensed only with a valid prescription. The Drug Enforcement Agency enforces the Controlled Substances Act, which is a federal statute that establishes criminal and civil sanctions for the unlawful possession, manufacturing, distribution, or importation of controlled substances. At the state level, state boards of pharmacy regulate pharmacy practice, and state medical boards oversee the practice of medicine. Thus, some of the laws that govern online pharmacies and doctors vary from state to state. . . .

The current legal framework for regulating online pharmacies and doctors is a patchwork of federal and state laws regarding controlled substances, prescription drugs, pharmacies, and the practice of medicine. Although many doctors and pharmacies who use the Internet prescribe and dispense drugs in a safe and legal fashion, others have exploited gaps in the current system to prescribe and dispense potentially dangerous quantities of highly addictive prescription drugs. To combat such abuses, legislators and interest groups have proposed an array of solutions, including establishing a federal definition of what constitutes a valid prescription, requiring doctors to conduct in-person examinations, mandating that online pharmacies disclose identifying information about themselves and their employees, establishing state prescription drug monitoring programs to track data regarding the prescription and use of controlled substances, giving state prosecutors the authority to seek nationwide injunctions against rogue sites, educating consumers about the potential dangers of buying drugs online, establishing certification programs to identify legitimate online pharmacies, and regulating search engines and shipping companies that enable rogue sites to do business.

NOTES

1.   *Conviction of Physician.* In *United States v. Nelson*, 383 F.3d 1227 (10th Cir. 2004), a physician who operated an internet pharmacy was convicted for a conspiracy to distribute controlled prescription drugs outside the usual course of professional practice. Although all patients requesting prescription drugs were required to fill out a medical history questionnaire, the defendant signed thousands of prescriptions without ever examining a patient.

2.   *Congressional Hearings.* Congress has examined the problem of internet sales of prescription drugs on several occasions, but thus far has enacted no substantive legislation to address the matter. The FDA Safety and Innovation Act (2012) required the U.S. Comptroller General, within one year, to submit to Congress a report on the issues raised by internet pharmacy websites.

4.   IMITATION DRUGS AND STREET DRUG ALTERNATIVES

Section 502(i)(2), as enacted in 1938, prohibits the sale of any imitation drug. FDA has enforced this provision against a variety of drugs made in imitation of, and sold on the street in substitution for, illegal controlled substances. In April 1984, for example, the government seized from Midwest Pharmaceuticals, Inc. fifteen tons of imitation amphetamines which contained primarily caffeine and ephedrine. *See United States v. Articles of Drug*, 633 F. Supp. 316 (D. Neb. 1986). In addition to condemning the mountain of tablets and capsules, the district court imposed an injunction prohibiting the defendant from marketing imitation drugs. The court of appeals rejected the defendant's claim that the statute was void for vagueness because it did not define the term "imitation." *United States v. Articles of Drug*, 825 F.2d 1238 (8th Cir. 1987). It held that a product is an imitation if it is identical in shape, size and color, or similar or virtually identical in gross appearance, or similar in effect to a controlled substance, but not if it is only "similar in concept." The court of appeals remanded the case, however, instructing the district court to more clearly define the prohibited acts. For the decision on remand, see *United States v. Articles of Drug*, Food Drug Cosm. L. Rep. (CCH) ¶ 38,089 (D. Neb. 1988). On a second appeal, *United States v. Midwest Pharmaceuticals, Inc.*, 890 F.2d 1004 (8th Cir. 1989), the court of appeals upheld the scope of the revised injunction. In *New Mexico v. Castleman*, 863 P.2d 1088 (Ct. App. N. Mex. 1993), the New Mexico Court of Appeals upheld the state imitation drug statute against a charge that it was unconstitutionally vague.

FDA has also been confronted with the problem of street drug alternatives that do not fit the narrow definition of an imitation drug.

In 65 Fed. Reg. 17512 (Apr. 3, 2000), the agency announced the availability of a guidance stating its position on these products. FDA explained that street drug alternatives are herbal products that claim to mimic the euphoric effects of illegal street drugs. The agency took the stance that these products constitute unapproved new drugs and misbranded drugs and that they do not fall within the definition of a dietary supplement because they are intended to modify the psychological states of the user rather than to supplement the diet. The FDA's position was upheld in *United States v. Undetermined Quantities of Articles of Drug, Street Drug Alternatives*, 45 F. Supp. 2d 692 (D. Md. 2001).

N. PRESENT AND FUTURE CHALLENGES

1. RESTORING INNOVATION

Concerned by the slowdown in the industry's submission of INDs and NDAs, in March 2004, FDA issued a report titled CHALLENGE AND OPPORTUNITY ON THE CRITICAL PATH TO NEW MEDICAL PRODUCTS "to address the growing crisis in moving basic discoveries to the market where they can be made available to patients." The report "highlights examples of Agency efforts that have improved the critical path and discusses opportunities for future efforts." *See also* 29 Fed. Reg. 21839 (Apr. 22, 2004); Janet Woodcock, *FDA's Approach to the Pipeline Problem*, 9 REG. AFFAIRS FOCUS, No. 9, at 6 (Sept. 2004). When, as part of its critical path initiative, FDA announced a public workshop "to explore approaches and potential obstacles to developing drugs," 70 Fed. Reg. 44660 (Aug. 3, 2005), it stated that the 2004 Critical Path report was "aimed at identifying potential problems and solutions to ensure that breakthroughs in medical science can be efficiently translated to safe, effective, and available medical products." After the workshop, FDA published a CRITICAL PATH OPPORTUNITIES REPORT AND LIST (Mar. 2006), identifying "targeted research that we believe, if pursued, will increase efficiency, predictability, and productivity in the development of new medical products." As one example of such a research project, FDA has established with Duke University the Cardiac Safety Research Consortium, to identify indicators of cardiac risk, predict adverse cardiovascular events, and improve biomarkers as diagnostic and assessment tools that will facilitate the development of safer and more effective cardiovascular drugs and diagnostic products. 71 Fed. Reg. 60732 (Oct. 16, 2006).

Despite these efforts, the perception remains that the development of important new drugs remains sluggish. And many have asked both whether FDA is part of the problem and whether it can be part of the solution.

"The FDA and the Next Generation of Drug Development"

Remarks by FDA Commissioner Margaret Hamburg at the Consensus Science Conference (Nov. 30, 2011).

Thank you all—from industry, academia, and government—for joining us for this important discussion on *"Consensus Science: New Tools and Tactics for Next–Gen Drug Development."* Ultimately, this is a discussion aimed at helping translate new drugs from discovery to delivery . . . and into the hands of those who need them.

. . . Today I'd like to speak to you about two areas of concern for the FDA that are also essential for the creation of new tools and tactics for next-generation drug development. They are strengthening regulatory science . . . and supporting innovation. . . .

All of us here understand the extraordinary importance of regulatory science. A bench scientist may develop a new approach to a disease. A clinician may be able to show that it works. But regulatory scientists develop the knowledge and tools to translate discovery and innovation into hope—into those products that hold so much promise.

We are at an incredible moment for discovery—and as we look ahead at the scientific landscape, there are so many areas that hold tremendous promise for progress, including genomics, synthetic biology, systems biology, advanced therapies like stem cells, and emerging technologies, like nanotechnology. But we all recognize that—as a scientific community—we are not effectively translating these scientific discoveries into therapies, prevention, or cures. Despite unprecedented spending on basic research and development by government as well as the biotechnology and pharmaceutical industries—to the tune of more than $80 billion this past year—the pipeline of new drugs is disturbingly dry.

There are numerous reasons for this—scientific, economic, and regulatory—but among other factors, there must be a shift in how we think about drug candidates and discover new ones . . . and how we evaluate emerging therapies when it comes to their benefit/risk profile. A big part of the solution is having the right regulatory and product development tools—which is why regulatory science is such an essential component of the scientific enterprise. A robust field of regulatory science would enable us to use our knowledge of biological pathways and gene variants to help identify promising new drug candidates and new potential targets for treatment. A robust field of regulatory science would help prevent promising therapies from being discarded during development because we lack the tools to recognize their potential or because outdated review methods delay their access. And a robust field of regulatory science would save significant dollars and many years by ensuring that we have the tools to detect unsafe or ineffective therapies at an early stage.

Additionally . . . [t]he knowledge generated from such studies informs a whole body of innovation—and entire classes of drugs—rather than single products. With more advanced regulatory science, we could usher in an era of personalized medicine, by linking advanced genetic data and biomarkers with targeted therapies. We could make significant strides in the science of safety, including predictive toxicology. We could develop and optimize innovative clinical trial designs and analytics that facilitate the possibilities of targeted therapy and that require smaller patient populations, shorter timeframes, and lower costs. And we could find better ways of mining and applying the information and knowledge that resides in the vast quantities of data housed at the FDA and other agencies around the world.

. . . .

Through our strategic plan, *Advancing Regulatory Science at the FDA*, we're devoting time and resources to help lead the effort to ensure that the necessary investments are made. The plan's core strategies are strengthening the science base at the FDA . . . and—perhaps most important for our discussions today—scientific collaboration. We're building partnerships—across government and with academia, industry, and the non-profit community—to help fill the critical gap between promising discoveries and approved products, while accelerating the development and reducing the costs of innovative products.

For example . . . last month, we announced two new regional Centers for regulatory science and innovation, one at Georgetown University, and the other at the University of Maryland. The two pilot programs will support targeted research in FDA's strategic priority areas and strengthen cutting edge training in areas important to drug, biologic, and medical device review—as well as scientific collaboration. . . .

The Centers for Scientific Excellence approach builds on and supports FDA's regulatory science strategic plan—as well as our Critical Path Initiative. . . . [T]he Critical Path Initiative . . . [has] created a nationwide network of scientists who search for ways to accelerate drug development, testing, and review. And it's helping the FDA to drive innovation in scientific processes through which medical products are developed, evaluated, and manufactured. The Initiative was launched in March 2004, with the release of FDA's landmark report *"Innovation/Stagnation: Challenge and Opportunity on the Critical Path to New Medical Products."* The publication diagnosed the reasons for the widening gap between scientific discoveries that have unlocked the potential to prevent and cure some of today's biggest killers, such as diabetes, cancer, and Alzheimer's, and their translation into innovative medical treatments. The report concluded that collective action was needed to modernize scientific and technical tools as well as to harness information technology to evaluate and predict the safety, effectiveness, and manufacturability of medical products.

. . . .

Ultimately, though, harnessing science on behalf of the public health is about more than adequate tools. It's about applying a new way of thinking about how we do research and development from the get-go. . . . That brings me to my second area for discussion: the FDA as catalyst for innovation.

. . . .

We know that if we want to continue to help foster the kind of innovation that we saw with the AIDS epidemic, we must continue to find new and better ways of doing things—while always maintaining a gold standard of safety and effectiveness. Just last month FDA outlined some of our plans and progress in a new report: *"Driving Biomedical Innovation: Initiatives for improving Products for Patients."* . . . [T]he report outlines how FDA is focused on implementing major reforms in a number of areas.

Among our initiatives, we're working to build the infrastructure to support personalized medicine . . . to create a rapid drug development pathway for targeted therapies . . . to harness the potential of data mining and information gathering . . . and to streamline FDA regulations.

I'd like to take a closer look at what we're doing in just one of these areas. . . : Developing tools and strategies to accelerate drug review and approval, while consistently ensuring drug safety and effectiveness.

Our expedited drug approval pathways now include Fast Track . . . Accelerated Approval . . . Priority Review . . . and Expanded Access programs. All are designed to speed the testing, availability, and approval of drugs in different ways—while never neglecting safety—and they've made a real difference. For example, as outlined in our *"Innovative Drug Report"* which we released last month, in Fiscal Year 2011 we approved 35 novel medicines. These new drugs are targeting diseases such as late-stage lung cancer, metastatic breast cancer, and hepatitis C. They also include the first new drug to treat lupus in 50 years . . . the first to treat Hodgkin's lymphoma in 30 years . . . and the very first drug ever shown to be effective in extending the lives of patients with metastatic melanoma. All are compounds that have never been marketed before in the United States.

Sixteen of these new drugs were reviewed within six months. And we also evaluated nearly 70% of these 35 drugs for quality, safety and effectiveness—and approved their use for patients—before they were available in any other nation in the world. . . .

We've also demonstrated considerable regulatory flexibility. In reviewing and approving the 35 new drugs . . . we streamlined clinical requirements to permit smaller, shorter or fewer studies wherever possible. . . .

Of course, as we continually strive to accelerate innovation and speed up development, we must also continually work to strengthen our ability to identify and resolve drug safety issues. Innovation for innovation sake is not in anyone's interest. For patients and consumers, newer does not necessarily mean better—if drugs are not safe and effective.

. . . .

Meeting these challenges will not be easy. But they are necessary if we want to further our common cause: Generating innovative tools to develop efficacious medicines with optimal risk profiles. . . .

2. GENETICS, GENOMICS, AND PERSONALIZED MEDICINE

Drugs behave differently in different people. A drug may be effective in some and ineffective in others. It may be safe in some but toxic in others. These variations among individuals are potentially explainable by the genetic differences among individuals in a large population. The emergence of the science of genetics and genomics therefore has important implications for clinical trials for drugs, as the following article by two respected FDA drug officials relates.

Larry J. Lesko & Janet Woodcock,
Pharmacogenomic–Guided Drug Development:
Regulatory Perspective
2 PHARMACOGENOMICS JOURNAL 20 (2002).

Pharmacogenetics (PGt) and now the more global term, pharmacogenomics (PGx), have come to the forefront after an evolutionary period of more than 30 years. Several transforming events in the past 5 years, not the least of which was the completion of the human genome sequence in 2001, have created an expectation that genetic and genomic information will produce sweeping changes in the practice of medicine and the prescribing of drugs. The almost daily press reports of new gene discoveries lend credence to the argument that personal genetic/genomic profiles will have a tremendous impact on health by the year 2010.

Genomic information has the potential to revolutionize pharmacologic therapies at many levels. The process of drug discovery may be transformed by this knowledge. Extensive genetic data will promote understanding of the molecular genetic contribution to many diseases. Genes and gene products suspected of being involved in disease pathogenesis will become new targets for intervention, and will stimulate new drug discovery programs. Conversely, gene expression profiling is being used currently to gain new insights into the molecular mechanism of drug actions, and the drug-disease interaction. Taken together, these techniques are expected to yield major advances in identifying drug candidates.

Genomic information will be increasingly used in the preclinical phases of drug development. There is great interest in using gene expression profiling to develop markers for both desired pharmacologic actions and toxic effects. Batteries of markers will then be used to characterize drug candidates and to aid in selection of those with optimal properties for further development, thus improving the effectiveness of drug development.

At the clinical level, the hope is for true individualization of therapy, which would maximize benefit and minimize toxicity. Currently, clinicians have few tools for predicting who will respond to a drug, or who will suffer ill effects. Although such differential responses have long been characterized as 'idiosyncratic', clearly there are underlying reasons for them, and many have a genetic component. It is believed then most chronic diseases represent a heterogeneous group of disorders at the molecular level. This heterogeneity is one of the reasons that not all people with a disease respond to a given drug. One contribution of genomic science could be to provide a much more precise diagnosis, based either on underlying genotype, or on gene expression profiles. Similarly, some differences in drug efficacy response, and some toxicities, are based on variability in exposure or in pharmacodynamic response, caused by genetic differences. The ability to predict and account for such differences could markedly improve the therapeutic index of many drug interventions. Finally, it is hoped that genetically-based mechanisms of toxicity can be elucidated, and adverse effects avoided, by application of pharmacogenomic information.

We are not aware of any consensus on the definition of PGt and PGx, and in fact there are many different definitions in the scientific literature. Occasionally, these terms are used interchangeably. For the purposes of this article, we will consider PGx to be the global science of using genetic information from an individual or population for the purpose of: (1) explaining interindividual differences in pharmacokinetics (PK) and pharmacodynamics (PD); (2) identifying responders and non-responders to a drug; and (3) predicting the efficacy and/or toxicity of a drug. Also, we will consider PGt to be a scientific subset of PGx in which there are genetic variations (e.g., polymorphism in cytochrome P–450 metabolizing enzymes) to drug doses and dosing regimens that result in different systemic drug exposure patterns (PK) in individuals or populations.

Over the past 5 years, many have expressed the concern that human clinical efficacy and safety trials in a traditional drug development program are challenging, time-consuming and increasingly more expensive to conduct. The relatively high rate of failure of drug candidates entering the clinical phases of drug development add significantly to these estimated costs. More recently, new drug candidates have been filtered from the discovery and development pipeline because their hepatic metabolism requires CYP–450 enzymes subject to genetic polymorphism. Several experts in the science of drug development perceive the increasing costs, and recent decreasing return on investment, as a significant threat to the viability of the pharmaceutical industry in the next 10 years.

Conventional wisdom suggests that PGx-guided clinical trials would shift the drug development paradigm toward a more efficient and informative process, resulting in a lower attrition rate of new drug candidates, and an overall lower development cost to the sponsor, albeit in the long-run. Furthermore, many believe that drug therapy based on the genetic profile of individuals could provide public health benefits such as better management of post-approval risks, and a decreased incidence of drug-induced morbidity and mortality. PGx could also reduce the incidence of drug product market withdrawals due to serious or fatal adverse events by allowing pre-selection, in advance of prescribing the drug, those patients who will be predisposed to toxicity.

It is hoped that more extensive use of PGx/PGt information will be utilized in future clinical trials. However, there are many unanswered questions about the FDA's regulation of clinical development programs using various elements of PGx/PGt. The following issues and questions, which need further discussion, are among the major concerns of the industry with regard to drug development:

- What are the regulatory implications of genetic profile screening of patients during investigational drug therapy?

- Is it acceptable to the FDA to stratify patients entering into a clinical trial *a priori* based on a PGx/PGt test?

- What are the statistical ramifications when using PGx/PGt to define patient subsets?

- If a PGx/PGt test is used to enrich a patient cohort receiving a certain dose and dosing interval during a clinical trial, will the label for that drug require a PGx/PGt diagnostic test?

- Would the Agency require the drug sponsor to submit an application for approval for the PGx/PGt diagnostic test at the time of approving the drug?

- What are the performance and statistical requirements for the PGx/PGt diagnostic that would be used for this purpose?

- What use would the Agency allow for a *post hoc* subset analysis based on a PGx/PGt diagnostic test in a clinical trial that failed to demonstrate efficacy or had an unacceptably high rate of adverse events?

- What information would be expected in those patient subgroups excluded from the pivotal clinical trials based on a PGx/PGt test?

- What PGx/PGt testing might be required for drugs currently approved and in the marketplace as new "genetic/genomic information is discovered?

- When is it appropriate to prescreen in, or out, subjects for bioavailability, bioequivalence, drug interaction and other clinical pharmacology studies?

Ideally, a regulatory agency should be able to meet its public health mandate without stifling new technology that might lead to better drugs including the "customized medicines" of the PGx/PGt era. It should be noted that the FDA went on record of supporting the basic idea of "customized medicines" for a patient subset, back in 1998, as evidenced by its approval of trastuzumab (Hercept). The approved indication of trastuzumab, a recombinant DNA-derived humanized monoclonal antibody, was for the treatment of only those patients with metastatic breast cancer whose tumors overexpress the protein, HER2, in large amounts. This patient subset represents up to 30% of all women with breast cancer. The FDA has also approved one prognostic PGt assay and two PGx immunohistochemical assays to measure HER2/neu protein overexpression to be used in patient selection before prescribing trastuzumab treatment. It is likely that FDA would not have approved Hercept without the accompanying diagnostic test. Also, the recent approval of Gleevec (imatinib mesylate) in May 2001 for late phase chronic myelogenous leukemia (CML) is another example that the CDER is well aware of, and open to, individualization of drug therapy using PGx or other research strategies. The discovery and development of imatinib, while not strictly PGx-driven, is a good example of the type of molecular targeting to abnormal proteins, in this case in CML cells, that is possible with the help of PGx information. In addition, the Center for Biological Evaluation and Research (CBER) has extensive experience with gene therapy development for over 10 years and has reviewed applications for genetically engineered protein drugs for such indications as sepsis and hemophilia.

At present, patient genomic/genetic data from prospective clinical and clinical pharmacology studies are necessary to: (1) evaluate the role that PGx can play in drug development; (2) identify issues that will trigger more urgent and extensive discussion between the Agency and industry; (3) focus the regulatory review on the important science/clinical questions and determine what evidence is necessary to support label claims. We continue to be concerned that despite the widespread availability of simple PGx/PGt tests to determine a patient's phenotype and/or genotype with regard to polymorphism in drug metabolizing enzymes, there has been little use of this information to tailor drug doses and dosing regimens to individual patient subgroups in clinical practice before using the drug. Together, all of the stakeholders in PGx/PGt need to work on ways to assure that this does not happen with the second and third generation of PGx/PGt diagnostic tests. We conclude that the bridge between the current and emerging PGx/PGt research in drug development and regulatory review practices, and related policy, needs to be built systematically and on a sound scientific foundation. The gap between research and the use of PGx/PGt in clinical practice remains very wide, but we are encouraged with the progress that is being made to close this gap.

NOTES

1. *FDA Guidance.* FDA announced its GUIDANCE FOR INDUSTRY: PHARMACOGENOMIC DATA SUBMISSIONS in 70 Fed. Reg. 14698 (Mar. 23, 2005) and issued a Draft Concept Paper, *Recommendations for the Generation and Submission of Genomic Data*, in November 2006. Other FDA documents relevant to the developing field of personalized medicine include GUIDANCE FOR INDUSTRY: E16 BIOMARKERS RELATED TO DRUG OR BIOTECHNOLOGY PRODUCT DEVELOPMENT: CONTEXT, STRUCTURE, AND FORMAT OF QUALIFICATION SUBMISSIONS (August 2011) and GUIDANCE FOR INDUSTRY: E15 DEFINITIONS FOR GENOMIC BIOMARKERS, PHARMACOGENOMICS, PHARMACOGENETICS, GENOMIC DATA AND SAMPLE CODING CATEGORIES (Apr. 2008). As this casebook was going to press, FDA issued a major report titled PAVING THE WAY FOR PERSONALIZED MEDICINE: FDA'S ROLE IN A NEW ERA OF MEDICAL PRODUCT DEVELOPMENT (Oct. 2013).

2. *Biomarkers in Drug Labels.* On its website, FDA has posted a table of more than 120 drugs whose labels currently contain information on particular genomic biomarkers. This pharmacogenomics information relates, depending on the drug, to drug exposure and clinical response variability; risk for adverse events; genotype-specific dosing; mechanisms of drug action; and polymorphic drug target and disposition genes. *See Table of Pharmacogenomic Biomarkers in Drug Labels* (available on FDA website).

3. *CDER–CDRH Cooperation.* In vitro diagnostic devices that can identify biomarkers are necessary adjuncts to personalized drug therapy. FDA is working to optimize the development and review of such co-developed devices and drugs. *See* DRAFT GUIDANCE FOR INDUSTRY AND FDA

Staff: In Vitro Companion Diagnostic Devices (July 14, 2011); *Drug–Diagnostic Co–Development* (Draft Concept Paper, Apr. 2005) (available on FDA website).

3. Drug Shortages

Executive Order 13588—Reducing Prescription Drug Shortages
October 31, 2011

By the authority vested in me as President by the Constitution and the laws of the United States of America, it is hereby ordered as follows:

Section 1. Policy. Shortages of pharmaceutical drugs pose a serious and growing threat to public health. While a very small number of drugs in the United States experience a shortage in any given year, the number of prescription drug shortages in the United States nearly tripled between 2005 and 2010, and shortages are becoming more severe as well as more frequent. The affected medicines include cancer treatments, anesthesia drugs, and other drugs that are critical to the treatment and prevention of serious diseases and life threatening conditions.

For example, over approximately the last 5 years, data indicates that the use of sterile injectable cancer treatments has increased by about 20 percent, without a corresponding increase in production capacity. While manufacturers are currently in the process of expanding capacity, it may be several years before production capacity has been significantly increased. Interruptions in the supplies of these drugs endanger patient safety and burden doctors, hospitals, pharmacists, and patients. They also increase health care costs, particularly because some participants in the market may use shortages as opportunities to hoard scarce drugs or charge exorbitant prices.

[The FDA] . . . has been working diligently to address this problem through its existing regulatory framework. While the root problems and many of their solutions are outside of the FDA's control, the agency has worked cooperatively with manufacturers to prevent or mitigate shortages by expediting review of certain regulatory submissions and adopting a flexible approach to drug manufacturing and importation regulations where appropriate. As a result, the FDA prevented 137 drug shortages in 2010 and 2011. Despite these successes, however, the problem of drug shortages has continued to grow.

Many different factors contribute to drug shortages, and solving this critical public health problem will require a multifaceted approach. An important factor in many of the recent shortages appears to be an increase in demand that exceeds current manufacturing capacity. While manufacturers are in the process of expanding capacity, one important step is ensuring that the FDA and the public receive adequate advance notice of shortages whenever possible. The FDA cannot begin to work with manufacturers or use the other tools at its disposal until it knows there is a potential problem. Similarly, early disclosure of a shortage can help hospitals, doctors, and patients make alternative arrangements before a shortage becomes a crisis. However, drug manufacturers have not consistently provided the FDA with adequate notice of potential shortages.

As part of my Administration's broader effort to work with manufacturers, health care providers, and other stakeholders to prevent drug shortages, this order directs the FDA to take steps that will help to prevent and reduce current and future disruptions in the supply of lifesaving medicines.

Sec. 2. Broader Reporting of Manufacturing Discontinuances. To the extent permitted by law, the FDA shall use all appropriate administrative tools, including its authority to interpret and administer the reporting requirements in 21 U.S.C. 356c, to require drug manufacturers to provide adequate advance notice of manufacturing discontinuances that could lead to shortages of drugs that are life supporting or life sustaining, or that prevent debilitating disease.

Sec. 3. Expedited Regulatory Review. To the extent practicable, and consistent with its statutory responsibility to ensure the safety and effectiveness of the drug supply, the FDA shall take steps to expand its current efforts to expedite its regulatory reviews, including reviews of new drug suppliers, manufacturing sites, and manufacturing changes, whenever it determines that expedited review would help to avoid or mitigate existing or potential drug shortages. In prioritizing and allocating its limited resources, the FDA should consider both the severity of the shortage and the importance of the affected drug to public health.

Review of Certain Behaviors by Market Participants. The FDA shall communicate to the Department of Justice (DOJ) any findings that shortages have led market participants to stockpile the affected drugs or sell them at exorbitant prices. The DOJ shall then determine whether these activities are consistent with applicable law. Based on its determination, DOJ, in coordination with other State and Federal regulatory agencies as appropriate, should undertake whatever enforcement actions, if any, it deems appropriate.

. . . .

BARACK OBAMA

THE WHITE HOUSE

NOTE

Recent Developments. As this casebook went to press, FDA announced that it was taking two further actions with respect to drug shortages. First, it released a strategic plan called for in the Food and Drug Administration Safety and Innovation Act (FDASIA) of 2012 to improve the agency's response to imminent or existing shortages, and for longer term approaches for addressing the underlying causes of drug shortages. Second, the agency issued a proposed rule requiring all manufacturers of certain medically important prescription drugs to notify the FDA of a permanent discontinuance or a temporary interruption of manufacturing likely to disrupt their supply. 78 Fed. Reg. 65904 (Nov. 4, 2013). This proposed rule implements the expanded early notification requirements included in FDASIA.

CHAPTER 8

FOOD AND DRUGS FOR ANIMALS

A. INTRODUCTION

As originally drafted, the 1938 FD&C Act, like the 1906 statute, drew no distinction between food and drugs for human beings and food and drugs for animals. Indeed, to the present day, the FD&C Act's definitions of both "food" and "drug" explicitly embrace articles for use by "man or other animals." FD&C Act 201(f) & (g). For the first thirty years of the statute's existence, food and drugs for animals were subject not only to the same definitions as food and drugs for people, but also to the same statutory regimes. This continues to be the case, for the most part, with respect to animal food. Since the passage of the Animal Drug Amendments of 1968, however, animal drugs have, in certain critical respects, been governed by animal-drug-specific statutory provisions. *See, e.g.,* FD&C Act 201(v), 503(f), 504, 512. Nonetheless, many of the general drug adulteration and misbranding provisions continue to apply to animal drugs.

NOTES

1. *Animal Food Versus Animal Drugs.* The elusive statutory boundary between human food and drugs also separates animal food from animal drugs. For example, in *United States v. Articles of Drug for Veterinary Use*, 50 F.3d 497 (8th Cir. 1995), the court held that whether certain promotional literature converted six cattle-feed products made from dried cow colostrum into new animal drugs was a question of fact properly submitted to the jury. And *United States v. Pro–Ag, Inc.*, 968 F.2d 681 (8th Cir. 1992), held that the defendants' promotional literature demonstrated that its whey-based products were intended to improve feed efficiency and increase milk production, thus making them drugs.

2. *Medicated Feed.* Many animal drugs are intended for use in animal feed. The statutory definition of "new animal drug" makes clear that animal drugs intended for use in animal feed are encompassed by the definition, but that the feed itself is not. *See* FD&C Act 201(v).

B. ANIMAL FOOD AND FEED

In the world of animal products, the terms "food" and "feed" are somewhat imprecise. As a practical matter, FDA and other regulators use the word "food" mainly in connection with pet food for dogs, cats, and other household creatures, from fish to ferrets. They use the term "feed" to embrace the articles fed to all other types of animals—most importantly livestock and poultry, but also, for example, research animals and circus animals. It is important to be aware, however, that as a formal matter, the statutory term "food" embraces all of these products, and, conversely, that FDA sometimes uses the word "feed" broadly to include pet food.

As mentioned above, animal food and feed are, for the most part, regulated pursuant to the same provisions of the FD&C Act as human food, including the provisions concerning food additives. Nevertheless, FDA has promulgated various labeling and safety regulations specific to animal food and feed. *See* 21 C.F.R. Parts 501–09, 570–89. Many of these provisions precisely echo corresponding provisions in the human food regulations, because FDA simply created duplicate sets of many requirements when it first split human and animal food regulations in 1976. *See* 41 Fed. Reg. 38618 (Sept. 10, 1976).

States have primary responsibility for regulating animal food and feed. An influential institution in this sphere is the Association of Animal Feed Control Officials (AAFCO), a voluntary membership organization comprising local, state, and federal regulators. Among other activities, AAFCO establishes model laws and regulations for animal food and feed that most states have adopted. Because animal food and feed labels must generally comply with the same labeling requirements under the FD&C Act as human food, FDA must establish regulatory exemptions from these requirements when they are inconsistent with the uniform AAFCO standards. *See, e.g.,* 36 Fed. Reg. 6891 (Apr. 10, 1971) (now codified at 21 C.F.R. 501.110) (allowing the use of AAFCO-defined collective names in ingredient listing for livestock and poultry feed). *Cf.* 51 Fed. Reg. 11456 (Apr. 3, 1986) (denying an industry request for the use of collective names for pet food ingredients).

NOTES

1. *Safety Review of Ingredients.* AAFCO administers a process called the "New and Modified Feed Ingredient Definitions Process" to identify the suitability of ingredients used in animal feed (including pet food) as well as to establish a common or usual name for the ingredients. FDA provides AAFCO with scientific and technical assistance in the operation of this process in accordance with a Memorandum of Understanding between the two organizations. *See* MOU Between FDA and AAFCO (April 2012). FDA has long recognized AAFCO definitions and given great deference to AAFCO determinations of safety, customarily stating "no objection" to such determinations.

In 2010, FDA, at 75 Fed. Reg. 31800 (June 4, 2010), established a voluntary pilot GRAS notice system for animal food ingredients parallel to the GRAS notification procedure for human foods described in Chapter 6. *Supra* p. 575 The agency's introduction of this procedure was likely a reaction to the 2007 melamine pet food crisis and Congress's response to it, discussed *infra* p. 1047. This pilot program is available for substances used in any animal feed, including pet food. Through September 25, 2013, FDA's Center for Veterinary Medicine (CVM) had received fifteen such notices, only four of which received "FDA has no questions at this time" responses. According to recent rumors, CVM is planning to abandon its recognition of

AAFCO reviews within the next few years and instead rely exclusively on the new GRAS notice procedure.

1. PET FOOD

Until very recently, the federal government had a relatively minimal role in the regulation of pet food. State regulators and, especially, AAFCO were the dominant actors in this field. In the late 2000s, however, this longstanding allocation of responsibility was called into question in response to a tragic adulteration episode. In 2007, many—perhaps thousands—of dogs and cats around the nation were killed by pet food tainted with melamine, a toxic industrial chemical intentionally added to an ingredient imported from China. This crisis led to a massive FDA-monitored recall of pet food, widespread public outrage, a Senate hearing, and ultimately an amendment to the FD&C Act (described below) that compels FDA to assume a more prominent role in ensuring pet food safety.

The excerpt that follows is the indictment of the officials of the American company that imported the tainted pet food ingredients and of the corporation itself. Observe how the legal theories underlying the indictment are identical to those that the agency likely would have invoked had the adulterated articles been human food rather than pet food. The company and its owners ultimately pled guilty to one misdemeanor count of selling adulterated food and one misdemeanor count of selling misbranded food. *Guilty in Pet-Food Tainting*, CHI. TRIB., June 17, 2009, at C19. The indictment also included a federal wire fraud charge, which is redacted from the excerpt.

Indictment in United States v. Sally Miller, Stephen S. Miller, and ChemNutra, Inc.

W.D. Mo. 2007 (Feb. 6, 2008).

Indictment

THE GRAND JURY CHARGES THAT:

At times material and relevant to this Indictment:

INTRODUCTION AND BACKGROUND
The Defendants

1.   Defendant ChemNutra, Inc. (ChemNutra), was located in Las Vegas, Nevada. ChemNutra was engaged in the business of buying food and food components in China, importing those Chinese items into the United States, and then selling those items to companies in the United States. ChemNutra represented itself as "the China source experts" with respect to importing Chinese products into the United States. Defendant Sally Miller, a/k/a Sally Q. Miller, a/k/a Sally Qing Miller was the corporate President of ChemNutra and owned 51% of its stock. Defendant Stephen S. Miller was the Chief Executive Officer of ChemNutra and owned 49% of its stock. Sally Qing Miller and Stephen S. Miller were married to each other and were the sole owners of ChemNutra.

. . . .

<u>The Chinese Business Entities . . .</u>

3. Xuzhou Anying Biologic Technology Development Co., Ltd (XAC), was located in Pei County, Xuzhou City, Jiangsu Province, China. Selling products to companies in the United States was XAC's business. . . .

4. Suzhou Textiles, Silk, Light Industrial Products, Arts and Crafts I/E Co., Ltd. (SSC), was located in Suzhou, China. SSC was registered as an export broker by the Chinese Ministry of Foreign Trade Bureau and the Chinese Department of Commerce and Industry. . . . XAC used SSC to export products to the United States. . . .

<u>Chinese Government Agency Responsible for Safety of
Exported Food</u>

5. The General Administration of Quality Supervision, Inspection and Quarantine of the People's Republic of China (AQSIQ) was a government agency under the State Council of the People's Republic of China. . . . According to the Food Hygiene Law of the People's Republic of China and the law of the People's Republic of China on Import and Export Commodity Inspection, AQSIQ was responsible for inspecting, supervising and administering the safety, hygiene and quality of imported and exported foods. . . .

<u>The Scheme to Introduce, Deliver, and Sell
Adulterated/Misbranded Food</u>

11. Defendants Sally Qing Miller and Stephen S. Miller caused ChemNutra to enter into contracts and agreements with various pet food manufacturers in the United States for the purpose of supplying wheat gluten to the pet food manufacturers. Wheat gluten is the natural protein derived from wheat or wheat flour. . . . So unique is the functionality of wheat gluten and so persistent is the structural integrity after cooking, that wheat gluten appears to have no functional competitor. Pet food manufacturers used wheat gluten as a binding agent in the manufacture of certain types of pet food. ChemNutra was required to supply the pet food manufacturers with food grade wheat gluten that contained a minimum protein content of 75%.

12. Defendants Sally Qing Miller and Stephen S. Miller caused ChemNutra to enter into an agreement with SSC to purchase the wheat gluten that ChemNutra intended to supply to pet food manufacturers in the United States. The agreement required SSC to supply food grade wheat gluten with a minimum protein content of 75%.

13. SSC contracted with XAC to manufacture and supply the wheat gluten SSC needed to fulfill its contract with ChemNutra.

. . . .

16. Between November 6, 2006, and February 21, 2007, XAC used SSC to export at least 13 shipments of XAC-manufactured wheat gluten to defendant ChemNutra in the United States, totaling more than 800 metric tons.

17. Wheat gluten was on the AQSIQ list of food products that were subject to mandatory inspection prior to being exported from China.

. . . .

25. By using [the wrong product nomenclature code] for the XAC-manufactured wheat gluten, SSC falsely declared to the Chinese government that the product being exported was not subject to mandatory inspection by AQSIQ prior to leaving China. By using [this wrong code] for the XAC-manufactured wheat gluten, SSC, among other things, avoided triggering an AQSIQ inspection of the facilities XAC used for manufacturing wheat gluten.

26. ... Based on Sally Qing Miller's training and experience, she knew that products exported from China and imported into the United States with [this wrong code] would not be subjected to mandatory inspection by AQSIQ prior to leaving China. . . .

27. Defendants . . . sold the XAC wheat gluten to customers in the United States. Defendants . . . knew that their customers would use the XAC wheat gluten to manufacture pet food.

28. Defendants . . . did not disclose to said customers the material fact that the XAC wheat gluten had been exported out of China and imported into the United States with the use of a code that avoided subjecting the product to mandatory inspection by AQSIQ prior to leaving China.

29. Throughout the United States, countless pets suffered serious illness and death after eating pet food manufactured with the above-described wheat gluten that XAC [and] SSC, . . . aided and abetted by defendants . . ., introduced and delivered, and caused to be introduced and delivered, into interstate commerce.

30. By March 29, 2007, the FDA's Forensic Chemistry Center had determined that melamine was present in the above-described wheat gluten. . . .

31. Melamine had and has a number of commercial and industrial uses, and can be used, for example, to create products such as plastics, cleaning products, counter tops, glues, inks, and fertilizers. Melamine had and has no approved use as a food additive in the United States. . . . Adding melamine to wheat gluten was a way to fraudulently create the appearance that the wheat gluten had a higher protein level than was actually present. Adding melamine to wheat gluten in this fashion was cheaper for the manufacturer than increasing the actual protein content. The presence of melamine in the XAC-manufactured wheat gluten contributed to serious illness in, and the deaths of, countless pets after they ate pet food manufactured with the above-described wheat gluten. . . .

32. XAC added melamine to the wheat gluten production process in order to make it appear to meet the minimum 75% protein content requirement specified in the contract with ChemNutra. . . .

COUNTS ONE thru THIRTEEN

(Introduction of Adulterated Food Into Interstate Commerce)

. . . .

The Charge

On or about the dates set forth below, in Kansas City, Jackson County, within the Western District of Missouri and elsewhere, the defendants . . . introduced, delivered for introduction, and caused the introduction and delivery for introduction, into interstate commerce from China to Kansas City, Missouri, of a quantity of adulterated food, as the term food is defined in 21 U.S.C. § 321(f): specifically, said defendants caused wheat gluten to be adulterated pursuant to 21 U.S.C. § 342(a)(1), in that the wheat gluten contained melamine, a deleterious substance that rendered the wheat gluten injurious to health; pursuant to 21 U.S.C. § 342(a)(2)(C)(i), in that the wheat gluten contained melamine, an unsafe food additive; pursuant to 21 U.S.C. § 342(b)(2) in that melamine was substituted wholly or in part for the protein requirement of the wheat gluten; and pursuant to 21 U.S.C. § 342(b)(4) in that melamine had been added to the wheat gluten and mixed therewith so as to make it appear the wheat gluten was better or of greater value than it was.

. . . .

All in violation of 21 U.S.C. §§ 331(a) and 333(a)(1) and 18 U.S.C. § 2.

COUNTS FOURTEEN thru TWENTY-SIX
(Introduction of Misbranded Food Into Interstate Commerce)

. . . .

On or about the dates set forth below, in Kansas City, Jackson County, within the Western District of Missouri and elsewhere, the defendants . . . introduced, delivered for introduction, and caused the introduction and delivery for introduction, into interstate commerce from China to Kansas City, Missouri, of a quantity of misbranded food, as the term food is defined in 21 U.S.C. § 321(f): specifically, said defendants caused wheat gluten to be misbranded pursuant to 21 U.S.C. § 343(a)(1), in that the labeling of the wheat gluten was false and misleading because the wheat gluten was represented to have a minimum protein level of 75% when in fact it did not; and pursuant to 21 U.S.C. § 343(i)(2), in that the food labeled as wheat gluten contained two or more ingredients, including melamine, but melamine was not listed on the label.

. . . .

All in violation of 21 U.S.C. §§ 331(a) and 333(a)(1) and 18 U.S.C. § 2.

. . . .

Dated this day of February 6, 2008.

A TRUE BILL:

_____

FOREPERSON OF THE GRAND JURY

_____

Joseph Marquez
Assistant United States Attorney

NOTE

Congressional Response in the FDAAA. Title X of the sprawling Food and Drug Administration Amendments Act, 121 Stat. 823, signed on September 27, 2007, includes section 1002, titled "Ensuring the Safety of Pet Food." Section 1002(a) states:

> (a) Processing and Ingredient Standards.—Not later than 2 years after the date of the enactment of this Act, the Secretary of Health and Human Services . . . in consultation with the Association of American Feed Control Officials and other relevant stakeholder groups, including veterinary medical associations, animal health organizations, and pet food manufacturers, shall by regulation establish—

> (1) ingredient standards and definitions with respect to pet food;

> (2) processing standards for pet food; and

> (3) updated standards for the labeling of pet food that include nutritional and ingredient information.

Despite the mandated completion date, FDA had not even issued proposed rules at the time of publication of this casebook.

Section 1002(b) instructed FDA to establish an "early warning and surveillance system to identify adulteration of the pet food supply and outbreaks of illness associated with pet food." In response, the agency has implemented a "Pet Event Tracking Network" (PETNet) that allows FDA, other federal agencies, and the states to share information about outbreaks of illness in companion animals associated with pet food. *See* 75 Fed. Reg. 43990 (July 27, 2010).

2. LIVESTOCK FEED AND THE MAD COW DISEASE CRISIS

The regulation of feed for human-food-producing animals must address an important issue irrelevant to the regulation of pet food— namely, the safety of the animal feed to the ultimate human consumer of the meat, milk, or eggs. Notably, none of the food provisions in the FD&C Act limit safety considerations to the immediate consumer of the food, and FDA therefore must assess the safety of animal feed to the ultimate human consumers as well as to the target animals themselves. Furthermore, section 409(c)(5)(A) instructs the agency, when considering a food additive petition, to consider "the probable consumption of the additive and of any substance formed in or on food because of the use of the additive." Even though this provision, from the Food Additive Amendments of 1958, probably was not drafted specifically to address the problem of "pass-through" additives in feed for food-producing animals, it clearly applies to that situation.

The most dramatic recent example of FDA's approach to regulating animal feeds' risk to human health was its response to "mad cow disease." In the late 1980s, Great Britain was swept by fear that a newly-identified disease in cattle, bovine spongiform encephalopathy (BSE), which erodes an animal's nervous system, could be transmitted to humans who drank milk or ate meat from afflicted cows. It was soon learned that cattle could contract BSE from feed that included bone meal from diseased ruminants, usually sheep. In 1989, a working party established by Britain's Ministries of Health and Agriculture concluded that "the risk of transmission of BSE to humans appears remote," but it acknowledged that the possibility "cannot be ruled out." Report of the Working Party on Bovine Spongiform Encephalopathy 14 (Feb. 1989).

Events soon shattered this sanguine assessment. By the mid-1990s, the British government had ordered (and paid for) the destruction of more than 100,000 head of potentially diseased cattle and stringently limited the permissible source of feed for livestock. By the end of the decade, BSE had been reported among cattle in most European countries as well as Japan and Canada. Japan, a major customer for imported beef, announced that it would not accept imports from any country that had not established a fail-safe system for preventing the disease—including the United States.

It was not the risk to livestock that prompted government action; it was the fear, and soon the realization, that consumption of meat from BSE-infected animals could produce an analogous form of the disease—dubbed "mad cow disease" and officially labeled variant Creutzfeld–Jacob Disease (vCJD)—in humans. By the end of the decade, British health authorities had identified more than 100 cases of vCJD, most of them attributed to consumption of meat from diseased cattle. Isolated cases had also been discovered in other countries. In the United States, FDA and USDA adopted a series of measures—summarized in the following Federal Register excerpt—designed to prevent the occurrence of BSE in domestic cattle and sheep. In addition, FDA imposed restrictions on blood donations by persons who had resided in Britain for six months or more since 1989, during which time they might have consumed meat from diseased animals.

As of September 2013, there have been no reports of cases of vCJD linked to consumption of meat from BSE-infected cows in the United States. Three cases of vCJD have been reported in this country, but the Centers for Disease Control concluded that the victims were most likely exposed to the BSE agent while living overseas. Four cases of BSE in cows have been confirmed in the United States, most recently in April 2012.

To safeguard the country against BSE, FDA finalized new ruminant feed requirements in 1997. 62 Fed. Reg. 30936, codified at 21 C.F.R. 589 (1997). The press coverage accorded the discovery of the first two cases of BSE in American cows in 2003 and 2005 contributed to the following additional measures that FDA and USDA announced in 2005.

Substances Prohibited From Use in Animal Food or Feed
70 Fed. Reg. 58570 (October 6, 2005).

SUMMARY: The Food and Drug Administration (FDA) is proposing to amend the agency's regulations to prohibit the use of certain cattle origin materials in the food or feed of all animals. . . . These measures will further strengthen existing safeguards designed to help prevent the spread of bovine spongiform encephalopathy (BSE) in U.S. cattle. . . .

I.   Background

   A.   *Bovine Spongiform Encephalopathy*

BSE belongs to the family of diseases known as transmissible spongiform encephalopathies (TSEs). In addition to BSE, TSEs also include scrapie in sheep and goats, chronic wasting disease (CWD) in deer and elk, and Creutzfeldt–Jakob disease (CJD) in humans. The agent that causes BSE and other TSEs has yet to be fully characterized. The most widely accepted theory in the scientific community is that the agent is an abnormal form of a normal cellular prion protein. . . . There is currently no available test to detect the disease in a live animal.

Since November 1986, there have been more than 180,000 confirmed cases of BSE in cattle worldwide. Over 95 percent of all BSE cases have occurred in the United Kingdom, where the epidemic peaked in 1992/1993, with approximately 1,000 new cases reported per week. In addition to the United Kingdom, the disease has been confirmed in native-born cattle in 22 European countries and in some non-European countries, including Japan, Israel, Canada, and the United States.

   . . . .

In 1996, a newly recognized form of the human disease CJD, referred to as variant CJD (vCJD), was reported in the United Kingdom. Scientific and epidemiological studies have linked vCJD to exposure to the BSE agent, most likely through human consumption of beef products contaminated with the agent. To date, approximately 150 probable and confirmed cases of vCJD have been reported in the United Kingdom, where there had likely been a high level of contamination of beef products. It is believed that in the United States, where measures to prevent the introduction and spread of BSE have been in place for some time, there is far less potential for human exposure to the BSE agent. The Centers for Disease Control and Prevention (CDC) . . . has [sic] not detected vCJD in any resident of the United States that had not lived in or traveled to the United Kingdom for extended periods of time. . . .

   B.   *Current Animal Feed Safeguards in the United States*

In the Federal Register of June 5, 1997 (62 FR 30936), FDA published a final rule to provide that animal protein derived from mammalian tissues is prohibited for use in ruminant feed. . . .

The 1997 ruminant feed final rule (§ 589.2000) prohibits the use of mammalian-derived proteins in ruminant feed, with the exception of certain proteins believed at that time not to pose a risk of BSE transmission. These exceptions to the definition of "protein derived from mammalian tissues" included: Blood and blood products; gelatin; inspected meat products which have been cooked and offered for human food and further heat processed for feed (such as plate waste and used cellulosic food casings); . . . milk products (milk and milk protein); and any product whose only mammalian protein consists entirely of porcine or equine protein. . . .

C.   Risk of BSE in North America

. . .

[A 2001] Harvard–Tuskegee Study [commissioned by USDA] concluded that the most effective measures for reducing potential introduction and spread of BSE are as follows: (1) The ban placed by USDA's Animal and Plant Health Inspection Service on the importation of live ruminants and ruminant meat-and-bone meal from the United Kingdom since 1989 and all of Europe since 1997 and (2) the feed ban instituted in 1997 by FDA to prevent recycling of potentially infectious cattle tissue. . . .

The Harvard–Tuskegee Study also . . . evaluated the impact of a specified risk materials (SRMs) ban that would prohibit high risk materials such as the brain, spinal cord, vertebral column and animals that die on the farm, from inclusion in human and animal food. The analysis predicts that this measure would reduce potential new BSE cases in cattle following a hypothetical introduction of ten infected animals by 90 percent (from 4.3 to 0.53 cases).

. . . .

On December 23, 2003, [following the detection of BSE in a native-born cow in Canada,] USDA announced that a dairy cow in Washington State had tested positive for BSE. . . . Immediately after the diagnosis was confirmed, USDA, FDA, and other Federal and State agencies initiated an epidemiological investigation, and began working together to trace any potentially infected cattle, trace potentially contaminated rendered product, increase BSE surveillance, and take additional measures to address risks to human and animal health. The epidemiological investigation and DNA test results confirmed that the infected cow was born and most likely became infected in Alberta, Canada, before Canada's 1997 implementation of a ban on feeding mammalian protein to ruminants. . . .

In December 2004, Canada announced that a third North American cow tested positive for BSE. . . .

In June 2005, USDA announced that a 12-year-old beef cow, born and raised in Texas, was confirmed BSE positive. The BSE-positive cow most likely became infected before FDA's implementation of the 1997 ruminant feed final rule. . . .

D.   Additional Measures Considered to Strengthen Animal Feed Safeguards

. . . .

In response to the BSE case identified in Washington State, USDA published an interim final rule in the Federal Register of January 12, 2004 (69 FR 1861), excluding high-risk tissues from human food. The interim final rule prohibited the use of SRMs and certain other cattle material in USDA-regulated human food. USDA defined SRMs as brain, skull, eyes, trigeminal ganglia, spinal cord, vertebral column (excluding [certain sections]), and dorsal root ganglia (DRG) of cattle 30 months of age and older, and the tonsils and distal ileum of the small intestine of cattle of all ages. . . .

On January 26, 2004, FDA announced its intention to implement additional measures to strengthen existing BSE safeguards for FDA-regulated products. . . . The interim final rule would have implemented four specific measures related to animal feeds. These measures included the elimination of the exemptions for blood and blood products and "plate waste" from the 1997 ruminant feed rule, a prohibition on the use of poultry litter in ruminant feed, and a requirement for dedicated equipment and facilities to prevent cross-contamination.

. . . .

Consistent with measures implemented by USDA to exclude high-risk cattle tissues from human food (69 FR 1861), FDA published an interim final rule on July 14, 2004 (69 FR 42255), prohibiting a similar list of risk materials from FDA-regulated human food, including dietary supplements, and cosmetics.

. . . .

In the Federal Register of July 14, 2004 (69 FR 42287), FDA published an ANPRM (2004 ANPRM) jointly with USDA in which FDA announced its tentative conclusion that it should propose banning SRMs in all animal feed. . . .

II.   Proposed Measures to Strengthen Animal Feed Safeguards

   A.   FDA Response to Comments to the 2004 ANPRM

FDA agrees with the numerous comments saying that it is important to keep the BSE risk in the United States in proper perspective. FDA acknowledges that the risk is likely low, and acknowledges that it is inappropriate to compare the BSE situation in the United States to the situation in Europe. However, FDA disagrees with comments concluding that for these reasons no additional measures are needed. Even though strong control measures have been put in place and compliance with the current BSE feed regulation is high by renderers, protein blenders and feed mills, the Agency is concerned, as discussed further below, about such issues as the presence of high risk material in the non-ruminant feed supply and cross-contamination of ruminant feed during the rendering or feed manufacturing process. . . . In addition, resource constraints limit FDA's ability to assure full compliance by all segments of the industry that are subject to the current BSE feed regulation. For example, resources are not available to the FDA and its state counterparts to fully verify compliance on over 1 million farms where cattle are being fed.

. . . .

   B.   Additional Measures to Further Strengthen Feed Protection

   . . . While FDA continues to believe that compliance with the [1997] feed regulation has provided strong protection against the spread of BSE, the agency believes that the recent cases are an indication that additional animal feed protections are needed to remove residual infectivity that may be present in the animal feed supply. FDA also believes that . . . excluding the highest risk tissues from all animal feed is the best approach to address the risks of BSE in the United States. In the 2004 ANPRM, FDA announced its tentative conclusion that it should propose a prohibition on the use of SRMs in all animal feed.

. . . The agency proposes to prohibit from use in all animal feed the brains and spinal cords from cattle 30 months of age and older, the brains and spinal cords from all cattle not inspected and passed for human consumption, and the entire carcass of cattle not inspected and passed for human consumption from which brains and spinal cords were not removed. The agency also proposes to prohibit from use in all animal feed mechanically separated beef and tallow that are derived from materials prohibited by the rule. However, the rule proposes to exempt tallow from this requirement if it contains no more than 0.15 percent insoluble impurities. . . .

C.   Basis for Proposing to Apply Additional Measures to All Animal Food and Feed

The current U.S. ruminant feed regulation prohibits the use of certain mammalian-origin proteins in ruminant feed, but allows the use of these materials in feed for non-ruminant species. FDA believes that the presence of high-risk materials in the non-ruminant feed supply presents a potential risk of BSE to cattle in the United States.

. . . [R]emoval of the highest risk tissues from animal feed channels should serve to address noncompliance with the [2007] rule that could result in cattle exposure to prohibited material through cross-contamination, mislabeling, or intentional or unintentional misfeeding.

D.   Cattle Materials Proposed to be Prohibited From Use in All Animal Food and Feed

. . . [I]nfectivity is not present in most tissues that harbor BSE infectivity until more than 30 months after the animal was exposed to the agent. . . . The agency continues to believe that the rationale for the 30-month age criterion described previously for human food and cosmetics is appropriate and proposes that it be applied to animal feed as well.

. . . FDA considered prohibiting from animal feed the same materials defined as SRMs that are currently prohibited from use in food for humans, but decided that proposing to require the removal of brain and spinal cord is the most appropriate approach at this time.

In reaching the decision to propose to exclude only the brain and spinal cord from animal feed, FDA considered information regarding the tissue distribution of BSE infectivity. . . . Although available data are limited on the distribution of tissue infectivity, data from both naturally infected and experimentally infected cattle support the finding that the brain and spinal cord are the tissues with the highest level of infectivity.

Because available data indicate that the brain and spinal cord contain about 90 percent of BSE infectivity, FDA believes that the most appropriate course of action is to concentrate efforts on excluding these highest risk tissues from animal feed. . . . The measures proposed by this rule will effectively reinforce existing ruminant feed protection measures by removing the tissues with the highest infectivity from all animal feed. As a result, these measures greatly minimize BSE risks if cross-contamination of ruminant feed with non-ruminant feed, or diversion of non-ruminant feeds to ruminants, were to occur.

. . . [T]he term "cattle not inspected and passed for human consumption" includes cattle not inspected and passed for human consumption by the appropriate regulatory authority as well as nonambulatory disabled cattle.

European surveillance data indicate that cattle found dead or culled onsite, where the carcass was submitted to rendering (fallen stock), and cattle with health-related problems unfit for routine slaughter (emergency slaughter) have a greater incidence of BSE than healthy slaughter cattle. These findings suggest that cattle not inspected and passed for human consumption are more likely to test positive for BSE than healthy cattle that have been inspected and passed for human consumption.

Because cattle not inspected and passed for human consumption are included in the population of cattle at highest risk for BSE, and processes are currently not established in the rendering industry for verifying the age of such cattle through inspection, the agency is proposing to define brains and spinal cords from all cattle not inspected and passed for human consumption, regardless of age, to be cattle materials prohibited in animal feed. . . .

III. . . .

E.   Legal Authority

FDA is issuing this proposed regulation on animal feed under the food adulteration provisions in sections 402(a)(2)(C), (a)(3), (a)(4), (a)(5), 409, and 701(a) of the Federal Food, Drug, and Cosmetic Act. The term "food" is defined to include articles used for food "for man or other animals." See section 201 of the act. We note that the material that would be prohibited under this proposed rule from use in animal feed continues to meet the definition of food. Therefore, this material would be adulterated or misbranded under the act based on violations of the proposed rule, as well as any animal feed or feed ingredients that were manufactured from, processed with, or otherwise contained, the prohibited material.

. . . "Otherwise unfit for food" is an independent clause in section 402(a)(3). The statute does not require that a food be filthy, putrid, or decomposed for it to be "otherwise unfit for food." . . . Because of the possibility of intentional or unintentional use of the materials that would [be] prohibited under this proposed rule in ruminant feed and the risk of BSE to ruminants and humans from these materials, we have tentatively concluded that these materials would be "otherwise unfit for food" under section 402(a)(3) of the act.

Under section 402(a)(5) of the act, food is deemed adulterated "if it is, in whole or in part, the product . . . of an animal which has died otherwise than by slaughter." Some cattle are not inspected and passed because they are diseased or have died before slaughter. Material from these cattle that are diseased or that die otherwise than by slaughter that is used as animal feed would render that feed adulterated under section 402(a)(5) of the Act. FDA has traditionally exercised enforcement discretion with regard to the use of such animals in animal feed. FDA intends to continue exercising such discretion for the use in animal feed of the remaining material from cattle that are diseased or that die other than by slaughter when the brain and spinal cord are removed.

We are also relying on the adulteration provision in section 402(a)(2)(C)(i) of the act. Section 402(a)(2)(C)(i) deems a food adulterated if it is or bears or contains a food additive that is unsafe under section 409 of the act. . . .

For the reasons discussed in other sections of this document, the agency is tentatively concluding that cattle materials prohibited in animal feed under this proposed rule are not GRAS by qualified experts for use in animal food and, therefore, would be food additives. . . . Under section 409(a), a food additive is unsafe unless a food additive regulation or an exemption is in effect with respect to its use or its intended use. . . .

NOTES

1.   *Final Regulations.* FDA issued final regulations in 2008. 73 Fed. Reg. 22719 (Apr. 25, 2008), codified at 21 C.F.R. 589.2001. Based on comments, the agency made a few minor changes from the proposed rule. Most notably, the final rule prohibits the use in animal feed of the entire carcass of BSE-free cattle not inspected and passed for human consumption from which the brain and spinal cord have not been removed, but *only* if the cattle are 30 months of age or older. *See* 21 C.F.R. 589.2001(b)(iii). It remains the case, of course, that the entire carcass of any BSE-positive cattle, regardless of age, is prohibited for use in feed. *Id.* 589.2001(b)(i).

2.   *Other Prohibited Ingredients.* As of September 2013, 21 C.F.R. Part 589, Subpart B prohibits the use of four substances in animal food and feed: animal proteins in ruminant feed, 589.2000 (discussed above), cattle materials in all animal feed, 589.2001 (discussed above), gentian violet in all animal feed (589.1000), and propylene glycol in cat food, 589.1001. FDA once proposed to prohibit the use of trichloroethylene, a carcinogen in test animals, but it ultimately withdrew this proposal. 42 Fed. Reg. 49468 (Sept. 27, 1977).

3.   *Salmonella.* In July 2013, FDA released a Compliance Policy Guide that explains the conditions under which FDA will consider taking regulatory action concerning *Salmonella* in animal feed. GUIDANCE FOR FDA STAFF: COMPLIANCE POLICY GUIDE SEC. 690.800, *SALMONELLA* IN ANIMAL FEED (July 2013). This guidance document states that FDA deems any strain of *Salmonella* to render non-heat-treated pet food and pet treats to adulterated. *Id.* at 5. The agency justifies this strict policy as necessary because these products come into direct contact with human beings, including vulnerable populations. *Id.* at 4. With respect to other types of animal feed, however, the guidance document notably lists only eight serotypes of *Salmonella* that render poultry or livestock feed adulterated because of pathogenicity in the animals intended to consume the feed. Moreover, each of these eight serotypes is identified as adulterating feed for only one type of animal. *Id.* at 6. The document indicates, however, that *Salmonella* adulteration is not limited to the listed serotype-feed combinations; it declares that cases of contamination involving other serotypes will be considered on a case-by-case basis. *Id.* at 5.

4. *Animal Feed Safety System.* The 2011 Food Safety Modernization Act, discussed in Chapter 6, applies to animal food as well as human food. In response to the law's passage, FDA, in 2011, published a revised Framework Document describing all the elements of the agency's safety program for animal feed. OVERVIEW OF FDA ANIMAL FEED SAFETY SYSTEM (2011) (available on FDA website). Whereas FDA's feed program historically focused on specific safety issues, such as BSE and *Salmonella*, the AFSS is intended to address feed safety in a comprehensive, risk-based manner. In October 2013, shortly before this casebook went to press, FDA issued its proposed FSMA rule for animal food and feed. Current Good Manufacturing Practice and Hazard Analysis and Risk-Based Preventive Controls for Food for Animals, 78 Fed. Reg. 64736 (Oct. 29, 2013).

5. *Misbranding.* For examples of FDA's successful enforcement of the Act's misbranding provisions against animal feed, see, e.g., United States v. Dr. David Roberts Veterinary Co., 104 F.2d 785 (7th Cir. 1939); United States v. 14 105 Pound Bags . . . Mineral Compound, 118 F. Supp. 837 (D. Idaho 1953); United States v. 18 Cases . . . "Barton's Cannibalism Remedy," 1938–1964 FDLI Jud. Rec. 1335 (D. Neb. 1956). As in other areas, FDA relies on rulemaking to correct label deceptions. FDA's requirements for animal food labeling are at 21 C.F.R. Part 501. In addition, the agency regulates the use of terms such as "tonic," "toner," or "conditioner" in the labeling of preparations intended for use in or on animals. 21 C.F.R. 500.52.

C. ANIMAL DRUGS

Prior to the enactment of the 1968 Animal Drug Amendments, new drugs for animal use were subject to the same premarket approval requirements as new drugs for human use. Similarly, before 1968, new animal drugs used in food-producing animals that left residues in meat, milk, or eggs were subject to the requirements applicable to food additives for human food use. Thus, unless GRAS or prior sanctioned, a drug added to feed of animals raised for human food required an approved food additive regulation under section 409 of the Act.

1. NEW ANIMAL DRUG APPROVAL

To eliminate the overlapping regulatory requirements imposed by section 409, section 505, and the antibiotic drug provisions of section 507, Congress, in 1968, enacted the Animal Drug Amendments, 82 Stat. 342 (1968), which added section 512 to the Act. These Amendments led to the use of a unitary application known as a New Animal Drug Application (NADA). In broad terms, the criteria and procedures for approval of new animal drugs remained similar to those for new human drugs, but the 1968 Amendments introduced some important formal distinctions reflecting differences in the way animal drugs are manufactured, distributed, and administered. The following excerpt from the legislative history describes Congress' basic objectives.

Animal Drug Amendments

H.R. Rep. No. 875, 90th Cong., 1st Sess. (1967).

The bill would consolidate into one place in the law all of the principal provisions of the Federal Food, Drug, and Cosmetic Act which relate to premarketing clearance of new drugs for administration to animals, either directly or in their feed and water. . . .

In many cases, the requirements for clearance of new drugs for administration to animals are more complicated than the clearance procedures for new human drugs. These complexities have in some instances led to long delays in the clearance of new animal drugs, and the purpose of the bill is to provide a single procedure for clearance of these drugs. . . .

In the past 15 years the animal feed industry in the United States has been virtually revolutionized through the use of drugs and other additives in the feed of animals. Drugs are used to promote growth and combat disease, and as a result of the increasing use, animals today add more meat per pound to feed in a much shorter time than has ever been true in the past. This means that the price of meat and poultry is much less than it otherwise would be. For example, in 1950 broiler production was about 630 million birds whereas in 1965 it was well over 2 billion. The average retail price of broilers has dropped from 57 cents a pound in 1950 to approximately 39 cents today. This results from two factors. First, a few years ago, broiler producers had 15 to 20 percent of their chicks die before they reached maturity whereas today it is not unusual for broiler producers to raise 99 to 100 percent of the chicks started.

In addition, broilers are ready for market weeks earlier today than a few years ago, and they consume less feed per pound of added body weight than was true a few years ago. Similar developments have taken place in the beef producing industry and in the production of swine, lambs, and other animals.

. . . Yet the farmer even today suffers enormous losses in disease, parasites, and insects, losses estimated by the Department of Agriculture at $2.8 billion per year. These losses not only reduce farm income, but, by reducing the supply of food, affect the availability of meat, poultry, eggs, and milk and increase the cost of the basic foods to the consumer. Each delay in the clearance of safe and effective products for animal health perpetuates these losses. Every duplication of unnecessary controls adds to the ultimate cost of providing food for the consumer. Every lack of administrative coordination adds needlessly to the time required to provide the farmer with the resources he needs to feed an ever-growing population. . . .

Subsection (a) of the proposed new section 512 provides in general that a new animal drug shall be considered as adulterated unless there is in effect an approval of an application with respect to the drug. In general, this subsection follows corresponding provisions in sections 409(a), 505, and 507 of the act.

Subsection (b) corresponds to section 505(b) of the act, and details the requirements for an application with respect to a new animal drug. . . .

Subsection (i) requires publication of a notice in the Federal Register of information with respect to approved applications for use of new animal drugs in manufacture of animal feed. The application must refer to the regulation published pursuant to subsection (i) on which the application relies, together with other information. . . .

In general, the procedure prescribed in this subsection for approval of an application is similar to that set out for approval of the basic application, and the same is true with respect to withdrawal of approval, except that an order granting approval for use of an animal drug in feed manufacture shall be disapproved automatically when the basic animal drug application is disapproved. Since disapproval of the basic application may occur only after notice and opportunity for a hearing, the feed manufacturer may intervene in that proceeding. . . .

Eugene I. Lambert, *The Reformation of Animal Drug Law: The Impact of 1996*

52 FOOD & DRUG LAW JOURNAL 277 (1997).

Before 1968, there was no separate "animal drug" law. There was only "new drug" law, "antibiotic" law, and "food additive" law, because drugs used in animals were subject to one or more of these regulatory provisions. . . . This system involved three separate statutory provisions; three separate administrative procedures; three separate parts of the agency. Especially for drugs intended to be used in food-producing animals, it was an administrative maelstrom.

As a result of efforts that began in 1962, the Animal Drug Amendments were passed in 1968, coalescing the three regulatory systems into a single provision governing approvals for drugs used in animals.

The basic licensing system came from the new drug provisions, with an overlay of antibiotic batch certification for certain antibiotics, and an interweaving of food additive concepts, including the Delaney anticancer clause and its diethylstilbestrol (DES) proviso. In addition to the Delaney Clause, food additive concepts included the requirements that animal drugs be used only in accordance with their approval, that optimal doses be determined, and that approvals be published as regulations. . . .

Enactments in 1988 and 1994 started the process of looking at animal drug law as separate from other drug regulation. These initial steps recognized some unique aspects of animal drug regulation that were distinct from human drug regulation.

[The Generic Animal Drug and Patent Term Restoration Act of 1988, 102 Stat. 3971] recognized the distinction between drugs used in food producing animals and other animal drugs, by providing, both in the drug approval process and in the patent extension process, that an applicant first obtaining an approval for nonfood-animal use, could waive the "new chemical entity" period of exclusivity and the right to obtain an extended patent, and exercise those rights upon the later approval of the same drug in food-producing animals. Second, it repealed the then-obsolete antibiotic certification provisions; all animal drugs that are or contain antibiotics are controlled simply as new animal drugs. Third, it granted the Food and Drug Administration (FDA) additional authority to require human safety information concerning the inactive ingredient composition of generic animal drugs. Fourth, it created new safeguards against the use of data submitted in support of new animal drug approvals being used by a competitor to obtain foreign approval for the use of the drug. . . . Finally, it created a separate provision defining veterinary drugs limited to use by or on the order of a licensed veterinarian. . . .

Another major step forward was the 1996 passage of the [Animal Drug Availability Act, 110 Stat. 3151]. . . . [T]he ADAA altered the efficacy criteria, including the definition of "substantial evidence" of effectiveness, altered the approval criteria for combination drugs, created a process for achieving greater certainty in drug research and development, created a new class of feed drugs limited to use under the "directive" of a veterinarian, permitted the establishment of residue tolerances for animal drugs not approved in the United States, and changed the regulation of medicated feed from product licenses to establishment licenses. . . .

In borrowing the definition of "substantial evidence" from the new drug provision of the Act, and the "optimal dose" provision from the food additive provision of the Act, animal drug producers were faced (as was FDA) with restrictions and requirements that went beyond what was necessary, especially in the case of food producing animals, to establish that the drug worked. The substantial evidence definition always required a minimum of two studies, one of which had to be a field trial; for some kinds of drugs, a single well-designed study in the target species, but not under field conditions, could establish efficacy. The optimal dose provision—that no approval could exceed what was reasonably necessary to achieve the drug's intended effect—led to laborious dose titrations that were as exact as they were misleading. . . .

What both industry and the agency sought was more flexibility in designing the right studies to evaluate efficacy, without a "punchlist" that had to be completed. This was achieved in the amendments made by the ADAA. First, the definition of "substantial evidence" was rewritten to reflect the range of studies, from *in vitro* laboratory studies through laboratory animal studies (including in the target species), to other target species studies, including a field trial when needed. Second, the optimal dose provision was rewritten to focus on a safety cap, *i.e.*, the effective dose must not leave a residue in excess of the established tolerance. . . .

While "fixed combination drugs" are well recognized in both human and animal medicine, animal drugs also are combined in feed, and so fed in combination, even if the drugs have different sponsors and uses. Chickens may receive an anticoccidial drug together with a growth promotant; swine may be treated for scours while fed for efficiency and growth promotion. In most cases, the individual drugs had been approved previously, and users—that is, animal producers—wanted to be able to use various combinations, often for disparate purposes. The FDA approval process provided no flexibility or alternative; producers were faced with redoing both safety and efficacy studies.

The ADAA created an entirely new approach to combination drug approvals, whether in dosage form or as feed-use recommendations. By starting with the requirement that each component will previously have been approved, the new provision of the Act specifies just what new or additional data are needed to ensure safety and effectiveness. Thus, on the safety side, the ADAA focuses on interference with methods of analysis, or altering residue patterns, or any safety issue raised by submitted studies or newly-identified in the scientific literature. On the efficacy side, the new provision distinguishes between dosage form products and drugs intended to be used in animal feed or drinking water.

There is one major difference between dosage form and feed drugs: the new rules do not apply when a systemic combination dosage form— e.g., injectable, implant, or bolus—contains an "antibacterial" drug. If that limitation does not apply, and each of the drugs has at least one use different than the other drugs in the combination, the issue is solely whether the [dosage form] combination "provides appropriate concurrent use for the intended target population." If all of the uses are the same, the issue is whether there is "substantial evidence," as newly defined, that each drug "makes a contribution to the labeled effectiveness." If, based on "scientific information," FDA determines that the drugs are physically incompatible in the combination, or if their dosing schedules are "disparate," e.g., one of the drugs is to be administered before feeding and the other after, the combination can be disapproved.

The two basic criteria are the same in the case of combinations of drugs to be used in feed: if the uses are different, the issue is "appropriate concurrent use," and where the uses are the same, the issue is "substantial evidence" of "contribution to effectiveness." Similarly, if "scientific information" shows a combination in drinking water to be "physically incompatible," the combination may be disapproved. . . .

Over the years, drug sponsors have been concerned by the concept of a "moving target" for approval. Studies would be planned and executed. Then, between the time of planning and results, new FDA reviewers would make "suggestions" for additional data. Sometimes testing concepts would change, with questions raised concerning the adequacy of the design. One of the provisions of the ADAA was intended to provide greater certainty to the research process; a new provision was added to the Act to provide for *binding* presubmission conferences.

The language of the new provision makes clear, as does the congressional report, that what is provided is a *process* for reaching agreement, rather than an *event* called a "presubmission conference." The new provision grants an applicant "one or more conferences . . . to reach an agreement acceptable to [CVM] establishing a submission or an investigational requirement. . . ." This is "a forum for the applicant and FDA to discuss what studies the applicant needs to conduct to support FDA's finding that the new animal drug is safe and effective. . . . The binding nature of the . . . agreement gives the sponsor assurance that development time and resources will be used efficiently and predictably." . . .

Before there was an animal drug law, FDA took the position that mixing an active ingredient into feed form was manufacturing a final dosage form drug, requiring a new drug approval if the active ingredient was a new drug. Although the Animal Drug Amendments of 1968 changed that system, it left feed mills with the requirement for medicated feed applications for each new animal drug mixed into feed. Both FDA and industry chafed under the administrative burden of those applications, and FDA by successive administrative actions reduced the number of drugs and persons subject to the application requirement. The ADAA further reduces both the industry and FDA burden by eliminating individual drug applications for feed mills.

In its place, the ADAA calls for the licensing of feed mills based on their compliance with current good manufacturing practices. In addition, the FDCA now specifically authorizes FDA to exempt mills from licensing. Each licensed mill will be able to mix any drug, limited by its approval to mixing in a licensed facility, *i.e.*, the "Category II" drugs under the Second Generation of Medicated Feed Controls. Every current holder of any approved medicated feed application is deemed to have a license for the manufacturing site of the feed, and is required in the eighteen months after enactment to submit a feed mill license application that "shall be deemed to be approved upon receipt by" FDA.

NOTES

1.   *New Drug Status Pre-1968*. As with human drugs, FDA often found itself, prior to the enactment of the 1968 Animal Drug Amendments, enmeshed in protracted litigation over the "new" status of veterinary drugs. *See, e. g., United States v. 7 Cartons . . . "Ferro–Lac Swine Formula Concentrate (Medicated),"* 293 F. Supp. 660 (S.D. Ill. 1968), *aff'd on other grounds*, 424 F.2d 1364 (7th Cir. 1970). Animal drugs that FDA had approved between 1938 and 1962 were subject to the National Academy of Sciences review and the FDA drug efficacy study implementation (DESI) program.

2.   *New Drug Status Post-1968*. The 1968 Amendments did not end litigation over the new drug status of particular products. *E.g., United States v. An Article of Drug Consisting of 4,680 Pails*, 725 F.2d 976 (5th Cir. 1984); *United States v. Undetermined Quantities of Various Articles of Drug . . . Equidantin Nitrofurantoin Suspension*, 675 F.2d 994 (8th Cir. 1982); *United States v. Western Serum Co.*, 666 F.2d 335 (9th Cir. 1982); *United States v. An Article of Drug . . . "Cap–Chur–Sol,"* 661 F.2d 742 (9th Cir. 1981).

3.   *Publication of Approval*. Section 512 requires approvals of new animal drugs, unlike approvals of new human drugs, to be published in the Federal Register. Such notices appear regularly and are codified in 21 C.F.R. Subchapter E.

4.   *Investigational Animal Drugs*. Under 21 C.F.R. 511.1, an investigational new animal drug application (INAD) is required only for field trials and not for laboratory animal research, which can include research on the target species.

5. *Animal Feed Additives.* The 1968 Amendments did not eliminate the need for petitions requesting approval, under section 409, of non-drug additives to animal feed.

6. *Antibiotic Certification.* Section 507 of the FD&C Act, which was added to the statute in 1945 to require FDA to certify individual batches of penicillin and later other antibiotics, did not distinguish between human and animal drugs. The 1968 Amendments incorporated the provisions of section 507 into new section 512. FDA later determined that batch-by-batch certification was no longer required to assure the safety of animal antibiotics, and it revoked the requirement for certification. 47 Fed. Reg. 39155 (Sept. 7, 1982). In the Generic Animal Drug and Patent Term Restoration Act of 1988, 102 Stat. 3971, Congress repealed all antibiotic certification requirements for animal drugs.

7. *Good Manufacturing Practice.* Animal feed and drugs are also subject to FDA's general GMP regulations for food and for drugs. The agency has brought court enforcement action against animal products that violated these requirements and has withdrawn approval of NADAs for non-compliance. *See United States v. Articles of Drug . . . Manufactured or Labeled by Goshen Laboratories, Inc.,* Food Drug Cosm. L. Rep. (CCH) ¶ 38,174 (S.D.N.Y. 1982); *United States v. Bronson Farms, Inc.,* Food Drug Cosm. L. Rep. (CCH) ¶ 38,354 (M.D. Fla. 1986). *See also* 52 Fed. Reg. 29274 (Aug. 6, 1987).

8. *Drugs for Minor Uses and Minor Species.* Many animal drugs have "minor uses" or are for "minor species" for which development of full-blown NADAs cannot be justified economically. The Minor Use and Minor Species Animal Health Act of 2004, 117 Stat. 1006, added a new subchapter to the FD&C Act titled "New Animal Drugs for Minor Use and Minor Species." FD&C Act 571–73. This statute provides FDA with flexibility in approving such drugs, including the possibility of granting them "conditional approval" prior to a final showing of effectiveness. FD&C Act 571. The statute also provides limited funding and exclusive marketing rights to specially "designated" new animal drugs to help support their development. FD&C Act 573; *see* GUIDANCE FOR INDUSTRY: FDA APPROVAL OF NEW ANIMAL DRUGS FOR MINOR USES AND MINOR SPECIES (May 29, 2008). The Minor Use and Minor Species Animal Health Act defined "minor species" to include animals other than cattle, horses, swine, chickens, turkeys, dogs, and cats. FD&C Act 201(nn), (oo).

9. *Animal Drugs and FIFRA.* There is substantial overlap between the new animal drug provisions of the FD&C Act and the pesticide registration provisions of the Federal Insecticide, Fungicide, and Rodenticide Act (FIFRA) administered by EPA. *See United States v. Articles of Drug in Possession of Nip-Co Mfg., Inc.,* Food Drug Cosm. L. Rep. (CCH) ¶ 38,233 (S.D.N.Y. 1979). The two agencies have entered into a Memorandum of Understanding to reduce duplication. 36 Fed. Reg. 24234 (Dec. 22, 1971); 38 Fed. Reg. 24233 (Sept. 6, 1973). In 41 Fed. Reg. 26734 (June 29, 1976), FDA assumed exclusive jurisdiction of new animal drugs that are also pesticides. Nonetheless, EPA adopted a statement of policy, 44 Fed. Reg. 62940 (Nov. 1, 1979), respecting the application of FIFRA to veterinarians who use or dispense pesticides in the course of their practice.

A new MOU published in 48 Fed. Reg. 22799 (May 20, 1983) gave FDA exclusive jurisdiction over new animal drugs that are also pesticides, but it was stayed in 48 Fed. Reg. 37077 (Aug. 16, 1983) and remains unexecuted.

10. *Animal Biologic Drugs.* In 1913 Congress enacted a separate animal Virus-Serum-Toxin Act to regulate animal biological drugs, 37 Stat. 832, 21 U.S.C. 151–58. This statute is administered by USDA, not FDA. To avoid regulatory duplication, 21 C.F.R. 511.1(b)(5) and 510.4 exempt animal biologics from section 512 of the FD&C Act if they comply with the provisions of the 1913 statute. Because the 1913 statute applied only to the interstate shipment of finished products, FDA asserted jurisdiction over animal biological drugs that were not shipped in interstate commerce but contained components that were so shipped. *Animal Health Institute v. USDA,* 487 F. Supp. 376 (D. Colo. 1980); *Grand Laboratories, Inc. v. Harris,* 660 F.2d 1288 (8th Cir. 1981) (en banc), *aff'g* 644 F.2d 729 (8th Cir. 1981). FDA and USDA subsequently entered into a Memorandum of Understanding defining their respective jurisdictions. 47 Fed. Reg. 26458 (June 18, 1982). The Food Security Act of 1985, 99 Stat. 1354, 1654, made all animal biologics, whether sold intrastate or interstate, subject to the 1913 statute and strengthened USDA's enforcement authority. This statute thus ousted FDA from jurisdiction over animal biological products, which are now USDA's exclusive responsibility.

2. THE EFFECTIVENESS STANDARD

Until 1996, the statutory definition of "substantial evidence" for animal drugs, FD&C Act 512(d)(3), almost exactly paralleled its definition for human drugs, except that the animal drug provision required at least one "field investigation" for approval (as opposed to the "clinical investigations" required for human drug approval). Both the animal drug and human drug definitions of "substantial evidence" generally required at least two "adequate and well-controlled investigations." FDA's implementation of this pre-1996 effectiveness requirement closely paralleled its implementation of section 505's effectiveness standard for new human drugs. *See, e.g., Masti–Kure Products Co. v. Califano,* 587 F.2d 1099 (D.C. Cir. 1978); *Agri-Tech, Inc. v. Richardson,* 482 F.2d 1148 (8th Cir. 1973); *Diamond Laboratories, Inc. v. Richardson,* 452 F.2d 803 (8th Cir. 1972).

The Animal Drug Availability Act of 1996 (ADAA), 110 Stat. 3151, revised the definition of "substantial evidence" for animal drugs at FD&C Act 512(d)(3) to explicitly provide that only one adequate and well-controlled study may provide substantial evidence of effectiveness. (The following year, section 505(d) was similarly amended to state that for human drugs, "substantial evidence" may be satisfied by "one adequate and well-controlled clinical investigation and confirmatory evidence.") The ADAA also removed the requirement that at least one field study be performed, although FDA may still mandate such studies when necessary. *Id.*

The ADAA directed FDA to issue final regulations to further define the term "substantial evidence" and also to define the term "adequate and well controlled studies." The agency issued a regulation defining the latter term in 1998. 63 Fed. Reg. 10765 (Mar. 5, 1998), codified at

21 C.F.R. 514.117. Among other things, this rule addresses the difference between studies conducted in the laboratory and those conducted under field conditions, particularly with regard to the level of control to be used. 21 C.F.R. 514.117(c). FDA's final regulatory definition of "substantial evidence" gives the agency further flexibility to make case-specific scientific determinations regarding the number and types of studies required. 64 Fed. Reg. 40746 (July 27, 1999), codified at 21 C.F.R. 514.4.

3. THE SAFETY STANDARD

Whereas the effectiveness standard for animal drugs is similar to that for human drugs, the safety standard differs substantially, because the law requires the agency to take into account not only safety for the target animal but also, in the case of food-producing animals, safety for human consumers.

The safety standard for animal drugs is initially stated in terms identical to that for human drugs. FD&C Act 512(d)(1)(A), like 505(d)(1), requires FDA to deny a NADA if "the investigations, reports of which are required to be submitted to the Secretary pursuant to subsection (b) of this section, do not include adequate tests by all methods reasonably applicable to show whether or not such drug is safe for use under the conditions prescribed, recommended, or suggested in the proposed labeling thereof." But section 512 goes on to elaborate:

> In determining whether such drug is safe for use under the conditions prescribed, recommended, or suggested in the proposed labeling thereof, the Secretary shall consider, among other relevant factors, (A) the probable consumption of such drug and of any substance formed in or on food because of the use of such drug, (B) the cumulative effect on man or animal of such drug, taking into account any chemically or pharmacologically related substance, (C) safety factors which in the opinion of experts, qualified by scientific training and experience to evaluate the safety of such drugs, are appropriate for the use of animal experimentation data, and (D) whether the conditions of use prescribed, recommended, or suggested in the proposed labeling are reasonably certain to be followed in practice.

FD&C Act 512(d)(2).

Because the human food safety standard of section 512 originated from the food additives provisions in section 409, FDA uses the same "reasonable certainty of no harm" standard when reviewing whether food from an animal treated with a new animal drug is safe for human consumption. Moreover, the animal drug section of the Act, like the food additive and color additive sections, has its own anticancer "Delaney Clause," requiring denial of a NADA if the drug "induces cancer when ingested by man or animal or, after tests which are appropriate for the evaluation of the safety of such drug, induces cancer in man or animal." FD&C Act 512(d)(1)(I). As discussed later in the book, the Delaney Clause in section 512 contains a provision, known as the "DES proviso," regarding how much residue of an animal drug must be found in food to trigger application of the clause. *See infra* p. 1388.

For more than 40 years, FDA has devoted substantial attention to regulating carcinogenic animal drugs that are used in food-producing animals and thus may leave carcinogenic residues in human food derived from the animals. This effort has been an important component in the evolution of FDA's comprehensive approach to regulating carcinogens, which is the subject of Chapter 13.

The special case of the application of the NADA safety standard to antibiotics used in livestock production will be examined in detail later in this chapter. *Infra* p. 1081.

NOTES

1. *Residue Monitoring.* USDA shares responsibility with FDA for monitoring the residues of animal drugs in livestock. *See, e.g.*, 53 Fed. Reg. 52177 (Dec. 27, 1988) (recording FDA's and USDA's concern about the continuing occurrence of above-tolerance sulfamethazine residues in swine); 55 Fed. Reg. 7472 (Mar. 2, 1990) (adding 9 C.F.R. 310.21, relating to USDA post-mortem inspection of carcasses suspected of containing sulfamethazine and antibiotic residues). *See also United States v. Nelson Farms, Inc.*, Food Drug Cosm. L. Rep. (CCH) ¶ 38,019 (D. Vt. 1987). Animal drug residues are a subject of constant FDA interest. In 52 Fed. Reg. 165 (Jan. 2, 1987), FDA announced the availability of funds to support studies on the development and improvement of analytical methodologies for residues of high priority animal drugs in tissues. *See* Gary E. Stefan, *FDA's Role in Combatting Animal Drug Residues*, 52 J. AFDO, No. 3, at 45 (July 1988). FDA, USDA, and EPA have a Memorandum of Understanding covering monitoring for, and control of, drug and pesticide residues in food. 50 Fed. Reg. 2304 (Jan. 16, 1985).

2. *Sulfonamide Drugs.* Sulfonamide drugs are a class of synthetic antibacterials. Thirty-five years ago, FDA required residue depletion data to permit the establishment of an adequate withdrawal period to assure that edible products from animals treated with sulfonamide-containing drugs were safe for consumption. 35 Fed. Reg. 16538 (Oct. 23, 1970). Interim marketing was permitted while approved NADAs were being obtained for all sulfonamide drugs. FDA ended interim marketing and announced the requirement of an approved NADA for these drugs in 49 Fed. Reg. 27543 (July 5, 1984). After sulfamethazine was found to be carcinogenic in both mice, 53 Fed. Reg. 9492 (Mar. 23, 1988), and rats, 53 Fed. Reg. 17850 (May 18, 1988), FDA announced a public hearing in 53 Fed. Reg. 17852 (May 18, 1988) to determine a proper course of action on that drug. Following the hearing, FDA acted to prevent further use of any sulfonamide-containing drugs in food-producing animals. It refused to approve all the pending NADAs for sulfonamide drugs, not on the specific ground of carcinogenicity, but on the more general ground that the data were inadequate to support the safety of the drug either in animals or in people who consumed edible products from treated animals. 53 Fed. Reg. 46050 (Nov. 15, 1988) (NOOH); 54 Fed. Reg. 10725 (Mar. 15, 1989) (example of denial order).

3 *Abbreviated NADAs for Generics.* During the 1980s, FDA approved abbreviated NADAs for generic versions of pre-1962 animal drugs

that had been rated effective in the DESI review, *e.g.*, 46 Fed. Reg. 36254 (July 14, 1981), but it did not adopt a formal policy allowing abbreviated or paper NADAs for copies of post-1962 animal drugs. Congress, however, was eventually persuaded to fill this gap, as explained in the following excerpt by the leading expert on animal drug regulation:

> The Generic Animal Drug and Patent Term Restoration (GADPTR) Act [of 1988] differs in a number of respects from the 1984 human drug legislation [i.e., Hatch-Waxman]. The principal differences recognized the human food safety concerns inherent in using drugs in food producing animals, as well as the greater expenditure of time normally required to obtain the initial approval of such drugs. This led to changes in both the FDA approval process for abbreviated applications as well as the availability of additional options for patent term restoration. In the case of the approval process, for example, the FDA was authorized to go beyond requiring bioavailability and bioequivalence data to demonstrate that a generic applicant's product was equivalent to the pioneer drug it was emulating. FDCA section 512(c)(2)(H) authorizes the FDA to require (as scientific principles dictate) bioequivalence studies in each species for which the drug is approved, tissue residue studies in each such species, "or such other data or studies as [the FDA] considers appropriate based on scientific principles." Under the patent term restoration provisions, a company could choose between an initial companion animal approval and a subsequent food animal approval in seeking a patent term extension.

> There also was a total exclusion from both the generic approval process and the patent extension process of animal drugs produced by biotechnology. This exclusion was to permit the biotechnology industry to demonstrate that patents in their area did not provide the same protection, and thus different incentives, as patents on chemically defined drugs. . . .

> The GADPTR Act also contained a special provision dealing with the release of data on the safety and efficacy of drugs that are eligible for abbreviated applications; both the initial requester and any person to whom the data are transferred must submit verified statements to the FDA that the data will not be used to market the drug outside the United States. . . .

Eugene I. Lambert, *Food and Drugs for Animals Other than Man*, *in* 1 Fundamentals of Law and Regulation: An In–Depth Look at Foods, Veterinary Medicines, and Cosmetics 295–96 (1997).

4. PRESCRIPTION STATUS AND VETERINARY FEED DIRECTIVES

Prior to 1988, the animal drug provisions of the FD&C Act did not contain a counterpart to section 503(b), which specifies that some human drugs are available only with a doctor's prescription. Nonetheless, FDA created a class of prescription animal drugs by regulation. After an initial setback, the agency's regulation was upheld as a valid interpretation of section 502(f)(1)'s requirement for "adequate directions for use." *United States v. Colahan*, 635 F.2d 564 (6th Cir. 1980), *rev'g* Food Drug Cosm. L. Rep. (CCH) ¶ 38,004 (N.D. Ohio 1979).

In the Generic Animal Drug and Patent Term Restoration Act of 1988, 102 Stat. 3971, Congress for the first time formally recognized prescription status for animal drugs. The prescription provisions for animal drugs, now codified at FD&C Act 503(f), closely mirror the parallel provisions for human drugs in section 503(b) in both language and organization. The very same factors for determining prescription status apply to an animal drug as to a human drug, namely, "toxicity or other potentiality for harmful effect, or the method of its use, or the collateral measures necessary for its use." *Id.* 503(f)(1)(A)(i). Moreover, as with human drugs, animal drugs must be limited to prescription use if FDA so orders when approving the drug's application. *Id.* 503(f)(1)(A)(ii).

A prescription animal drug may be dispensed only "by or upon the lawful written or oral order of a licensed veterinarian in the course of the veterinarian's professional practice." FD&C Act 503(f)(1)(B). The Act provides that an order is "lawful" if it:

> (i) is a prescription or other order authorized by law,

> (ii) is, if an oral order, promptly reduced to writing by the person lawfully filling the order, and filed by that person, and

> (iii) is refilled only if authorized in the original order or in a subsequent oral order promptly reduced to writing by the person lawfully filling the order, and filed by that person.

Id.

Even after 1988, however, all animal drugs mixed in feed remained available without veterinarian control. FDA simply could not come up with a practical method for requiring that mixed feeds be dispensed by pharmacies. Finally, facing growing FDA pressure for veterinarian control over the use of some new antibiotics, industry groups proposed the administrative, and then the legislative, creation of a new set of controls for feed-administered drugs. Congress established these new controls under the name "veterinary feed directives" (VFDs) in the Animal Drug Availability Act of 1996, 110 Stat. 3151.

According to FD&C Act 504, "veterinary feed directive drugs" are animal drugs "intended for use in or on animal feed" that are limited by their terms of approval to "use under the professional supervision of a licensed veterinarian." FD&C Act 504(a). The statute states, "[A]ny animal feed bearing or containing a [VFD drug] shall be fed to animals only by or upon the lawful [VFD] issued by a licensed veterinarian in the course of the veterinarian's professional practice." *Id.* Although VFD drugs thus require the intervention of a veterinarian before they can be fed to an animal, they are not limited to special channels of distribution, as are section 503(f) veterinarian-order (i.e., prescription) drugs. The veterinarian issuing the VFD, the seller of the feed, and the purchaser-user of the feed all must retain a copy of the VFD, and these records are subject to FDA inspection. *Id.* 504(a)(3)(A)–(B). Furthermore, the label, labeling, and advertising for a VFD drug must contain a uniform notification that the drug is limited to use pursuant to a VFD. *Id.* 504(b). Although VFD drugs seem very much like "prescription" drugs, the Act specifies that neither these drugs nor feeds containing them "shall be deemed to be a prescription article under any Federal or State law." *Id.* 504(c).

NOTE

Rx to OTC Switch. In 41 Fed. Reg. 51078 (Nov. 19, 1976), FDA issued a notice of opportunity for hearing on its proposal to reject a supplemental NADA seeking to switch a new animal drug from Rx to OTC status. Although the agency concluded that a hearing was not warranted and rejected the NADA , 42 Fed. Reg. 46595 (Sept. 16, 1977), this decision was overturned. *American Cyanamid Co. v. FDA*, 606 F.2d 1307 (D.C. Cir. 1979). Following the court-ordered hearing, the Administrative Law Judge and subsequently the Commissioner upheld the agency's initial decision. 49 Fed. Reg. 26311 (June 27, 1984), *aff'd, American Cyanamid Co. v. Young*, 770 F.2d 1213 (D.C. Cir. 1985). *See also* 46 Fed. Reg. 46396 (Sept. 18, 1981) (FDA denial of another petition to switch an animal drug from Rx to OTC status). In October 1988, the agency's Veterinary Medicine Advisory Committee recommended to FDA criteria for determining Rx and OTC status.

5. EXTRALABEL USE OF ANIMAL DRUGS AND USE OF HUMAN DRUGS IN ANIMALS

The FD&C Act's regulation of the off-label use of animal drugs contrasts strikingly with the Act's non-regulation of the off-label prescription of human drugs. *See supra* p. 814. In 1994, the FD&C Act was amended to reduce FDA's authority over the off-label prescribing of animal drugs, but the agency still exercises more authority over such practices in the animal drug arena than in the human drug arena.

A new animal drug is "unsafe" under section 512(a)(1) "with respect to any particular use or intended use of the drug" unless FDA has approved an application for the drug with respect to such use or intended use, and "such drug, its labeling, and such use conform to such approved application." An animal drug that is "unsafe" under section 512(a)(1) is deemed to be an "adulterated" drug under section 501(a)(5), and any food containing such an unapproved animal drug or its residues is "adulterated food" under section 402(a)(2)(C)(ii). A veterinarian who prescribes or administers an animal drug for an unapproved use can be viewed as violating the FD&C Act by causing the drug to be adulterated while it is "held for sale . . . after shipment in interstate commerce" under section 301(k). Moreover, if the target animal is a food-producing animal, the veterinarian can also be charged with adulterating the food. FDA has interpreted the Act to give it similar power to ban the off-label use of approved *human* drugs in animals—a common practice.

Nevertheless, even before the 1994 amendments, FDA never wielded its theoretical authority to prohibit all off-label use of animal drugs and all unapproved use of human drugs in animals. In 1996, in *Takhar v. Kessler*, the U.S. Court of Appeals for the Ninth Circuit described the history of the agency's approach to this issue:

By . . . 1977, the FDA took the position that while extra-label drug use by veterinarians was technically illegal under the FDCA, its Bureau of Veterinary Medicine did not object to such use in non-food-producing animals as long as the veterinarian legally obtained the drug and had no approved alternative drug available, and as long as the use posed no obvious hazard to the animal's health. The FDA stated that extra-label drug use by veterinarians in food-producing animals was not sanctioned and was the responsibility of the veterinarian, and advised that it would take regulatory action where such use resulted in illegal drug residues in edible animal tissue.

In 1984, the FDA revised its compliance policy and issued CPG 7125.06 regarding extra-label use of animal drugs in food-producing animals. CPG 7125.06 announced that a finding of illegal drug residues in food would no longer be a prerequisite to regulatory action against extra-label drug use by veterinarians. "Nevertheless," the agency stated, "extra-label drug use in treating food-producing animals may be considered by a veterinarian when the health of animals is immediately threatened and suffering or death would result from failure to treat the affected animals." The agency then provided criteria and precautions for such extra-label drug use and announced that as long as those criteria were met and those precautions followed, the FDA "would not ordinarily" consider regulatory action against veterinarians' extra-label drug use. The current version of those criteria and precautions provides that regulatory action will not ordinarily be considered where:

1) a medical diagnosis is made by an attending veterinarian within a valid veterinarian-client-patient relationship;

2) no approved drug or dosage is available to treat the condition effectively in the animals affected;

3) the animals treated are carefully identified;

4) an extended withdrawal period is assigned and observed before the marketing of food produced by the animal and no illegal residues occur in the food; and

5) the extra-label drug is adequately labeled by the prescribing veterinarian.

In addition, the FDA indicated that certain drugs could not be used in food-producing animals even when the outlined criteria and precautions were met and followed. . . .

In 1991, the FDA issued CPG 7125.35 regarding the use of human drugs in animal medicine. The agency noted that most such use occurs in non-food pets and that "many of the maladies of pets cannot be treated in accordance with current standards of veterinary practice without the use of human drugs since veterinary versions of many human drugs do not exist." Concern was expressed about increasing promotion and distribution of human drugs for use in, and actual use of such drugs in, food-producing animals. The criteria and precautions in CPG 7125.06 for extra-label animal-drug use in food-producing animals were incorporated by reference to guide enforcement of extra-label human-drug use in such animals, and the FDA announced its intent to take aggressive regulatory action to discourage such use, while stating that extra-label human-drug use in non-food-producing animals would not ordinarily prompt regulatory action. . . .

Takhar v. Kessler, 76 F.3d 995, 997–98 (9th Cir. 1996).

Despite FDA's promulgation of these Compliance Policy Guides, the ostensible illegality of extra-label drug use, even in companion and exotic animals—and the consequent risk of *per se* malpractice exposure—sparked concern among veterinarians. This led to the passage of the Animal Medicinal Use Clarification Act of 1994 (AMDUCA); 108 Stat. 4153, which largely established the lawfulness of the practices the FDA was already permitting under its CPGs.

New section 512(a)(4) of the FD&C Act, added by AMDUCA, provides that a drug with an approved NADA is not rendered "unsafe" (and thus adulterated) with respect to an unapproved use if such use is by prescription "within the context of a veterinarian-client-patient relationship" and the use complies with FDA's implementing regulations. New section 512(a)(5) contains similar language with regard to the use in animals of human drugs with approved NDAs. According to FDA's implementing regulations, the following extralabel uses of animal drugs (or human drugs in animals) remain illegal: extralabel use by a lay person, extralabel use in animal feed, and extralabel use resulting in any residue that "may present a risk to the public health" or that is "above an established safe concentration or tolerance." 21 C.F.R. 530.11.

The new AMDUCA regime is applied in the following recent case.

———

United States v. Scenic View Dairy, L.L.C.

2011 WL 3879490 (W.D. Mich. 2011).

■ QUIST, DISTRICT JUDGE:

In this case, the United States of America seeks to enjoin Scenic View Dairy, L.L.C. [and named individual defendants] . . . from violating the Federal Food, Drug, and Cosmetic Act. . . . For the reasons set forth below, the Court concludes that the United States' . . . motion for summary judgment should be granted. . . .

FACTS

. . . Scenic View owns and operates three separate dairy farms in West Michigan: the "Fennville Farm," the "Freeport Farm," and the "Gowen Farm." . . . The individual Defendants are Michael D. Geerlings, who is president and majority owner of Scenic View, and Mark A. Lucas and Michael J. Van Dam, who manage the Fennville Farm and Freeport Farm, respectively, and are responsible for the daily operations at those farms, including the diagnosis and treatment of animals. . . .

Although Scenic View's primary business is the sale of Grade A milk, it also sells cull cows for beef, shipping approximately 70 cows to slaughter for human consumption per week. The cows are sold, either directly or by auction, to slaughterhouses both in Michigan and in other states. . . . Since 2002, the United States Department of Agriculture Food Safety and Inspection Service has detected above-tolerance levels of new animal drug residues in the edible tissues of slaughtered animals alleged to have originated from Scenic View on eleven occasions. . . .

DISCUSSION

The United States alleges that Defendants have violated three separate provisions of the FDCA—§ 331(a), (k), and (u). . . .

A.   Whether Defendants Have Violated 21 U.S.C. § 331(a) by Delivering Adulterated Food for Introduction into Interstate Commerce

Section 331(a) prohibits "[t]he introduction or delivery for introduction into interstate commerce of any food . . . that is adulterated." 21 U.S.C. § 331(a). . . . Defendants do not contest that their cattle qualify as "food" within the meaning of the Act nor that they deliver their cattle for introduction into interstate commerce.[2] Instead, the dispute here lies in whether the food is "adulterated" under the Act. . . .

Under 21 U.S.C. § 342(a)(2)(C)(ii) [FD&C Act 402(a)(2)(C)(ii)], food is adulterated "if it is or if it bears or contains . . . a new animal drug (or conversion product thereof) that is unsafe within the meaning of section 360b of this title." As a threshold matter, § 360b [FD&C Act 512] provides that a new animal drug is automatically considered unsafe prior to receiving FDA approval for its intended use. *See* 21 U.S.C. § 360b(a)(1)(A). . . . To obtain FDA approval, a new animal drug must undergo an extensive application and approval process that requires the applicant to demonstrate that the drug is safe and effective when used in accordance with the proposed labeling. *See id.* § 360b(b) and (d); *see also* FDA, Proper Drug Use and Residue Avoidance by Non–Veterinarians, Compliance Policy Guide ("CPG") § 615.200 ("The pre-market approval process ensures that when animal drugs are used in accordance with the labeled directions . . . milk, eggs, and the edible tissues of slaughtered animals treated with a drug will not contain potentially harmful or violative drug residues."). When an approved new animal drug is not used in accordance with its labeling, the use is referred to as being "extralabel." *See* 21 C.F.R. § 530.3(a). . . . Extralabel use "includes, but is not limited to, use in species not listed in the labeling, use for indications (disease or other conditions) not listed in the labeling, use at dosage levels, frequencies, or routes of administration other than those stated in the labeling, and deviation from the labeled withdrawal time based on these different uses." *Id.*

In its motion for summary judgment, the United States initially took the position that a drug is unsafe under § 360b if the actual use varies from the FDA-approved use (i.e., an extralabel use) *and* such different use "(1) is not by or under the lawful order from a licensed veterinarian; or (2) results in any drug residue above an established safe level, safe concentration, or safe tolerance." Thus, the opening brief

---

[2]   Animals intended for slaughter have been held to constitute food within the meaning of the Act. *See United States v. Tuente Livestock*, 888 F. Supp. 1416, 1424 (S.D. Ohio 1995) (holding that live hogs raised for food and intended to be offered for slaughter are "food" as used in § 331(a)) . . . .

focused solely on extralabel uses. In their response, Defendants asserted that a drug that is used in accordance with the label, but nonetheless results in an above-tolerance residue level, is not "unsafe" under § 360b. In its reply, the United States expanded its position somewhat by arguing that "whether Defendants' use of new animal drugs is on-label or extra-label, those drugs are unsafe under § 360b, and Defendant's food is adulterated under § 342(a)(2)(C)(ii), if such use results in an illegal drug residue." The parties cite no case law, and chambers research reveals none, interpreting the Act with respect to either position.

In paragraph (1), § 360b begins with the following position:

> A new animal drug shall, with respect to any particular use or intended use of such drug, be deemed unsafe for purpose of . . . section 342(a)(2)(C)(ii) of this title unless . . . there is in effect an approval of an application filed [with the FDA] with respect to such use or intended use of such drug, and such drug, its labeling, and such use conform to such approved application.

§ 360b(a)(1)(A). Paragraph (4) addresses the safety of a drug when used in an extralabel manner:

> (A) Except as provided in subparagraph (B), if an approval of an application filed [with the FDA] is in effect with respect to a particular use or intended use of a new animal drug, the drug shall not be deemed unsafe for purposes of paragraph (1) . . . with respect to a different use or intended use of the drug . . . if such use or intended use—
>
> (i) is by or on the lawful written or oral order of a licensed veterinarian within the context of a veterinarian-client-patient relationship, as defined by the Secretary; and
>
> (ii) is in compliance with the regulations promulgated by secretary that establish the conditions for such different use or intended use.
>
> * * *
>
> (B) If the Secretary finds that there is a reasonable probability that a use of an animal drug authorized under subparagraph (A) may present a risk to the public health, the Secretary may—
>
> (i) establish a safe level for a residue of an animal drug when it is used for such different use authorized by subparagraph (A); and
>
> (ii) require the development of a practical, analytical method for the detection of residues of such drug above the safe level established under clause (i).
>
> The use of an animal drug that results in residues exceeding a safe level established under clause (i) shall be considered an unsafe use of such drug under paragraph (1).

21 U.S.C. §§ 360b(a)(4)(A)–(B) [FD&C Act 512(a)(4)(A)–(B)].

Turning to the regulations, 21 CFR Part 530 deals with extralabel uses of new animal drugs. Section 530.10, entitled "Provision permitting extralabel use of animal drugs," explains that a drug is not unsafe with respect to an extralabel use so long as such use is "[b]y or on the lawful written or oral order of a licensed veterinarian within the context of a valid veterinarian-client-patient relationship [which the regulations also define] . . . *and* in compliance with this part." The very next section, entitled "Limitations," explains that "*[i]n addition* to uses that do not comply with the provisions set forth in § 530.10, the following specific extralabel uses are not permitted and result in a drug being deemed unsafe . . . (d) Extralabel use resulting in any residue above an established safe level, safe concentration or tolerance." 21 C.F.R. § 530.11 (emphasis added).

As to extralabel uses, therefore, the Act and its regulations are clear. Any extralabel use results in the drug being deemed unsafe under § 360b unless it is by order of a licensed veterinarian in the context of a valid veterinarian-client-patient relationship ("VCPR"), as it is defined in the Act; and even if it is by order of a veterinarian in the context of a VCPR, it is still unsafe under§ 360b if it results in an illegal tissue residue. . . .

As to uses that accord with the drug's approved labeling, the only references to tolerance levels in § 360b and the related regulations are found in the provisions dealing with extralabel uses. Also, the pre-approval process itself is designed to ensure that the drug is safe when used in accordance with its approved label. Thus, a new animal drug is not legally deemed to be unsafe with respect to uses that accord with the drugs approved labeling simply because there was a violative tissue residue.

Given this legal framework, what follows is a discussion of the evidence presented as to each alleged residue violations on a farm-by-farm basis. . . .

(i) The Freeport Farm

On November 26, 2008, the USDA–FSIS collected a tissue sample from a cow . . . in which laboratory tests identified a Penicillin residue of 0.10 ppm in the animal's kidney, which exceeds the 0.05 ppm tolerance level codified at 21 § C.F.R. § 556.510(a). The FDA identified the cow as having been delivered from Defendants' Freeport Farm on November 25, 2008, to a livestock auction in Michigan for sale for use in human food, where it was purchased by a Pennsylvania slaughterhouse.

. . . Defendant Van Dam admitted in a sworn affidavit that the identified cow had originated from Scenic View and had been treated with 40 cc of Penicillin on November 10, 2008, and 20 cc each of the following three days, even though, given the cow's weight, it should not have received more than 14 cc according to the labeled dosage. . . .

Defendants do not contest having administered extralabel dosages of Penicillin, but assert that they did so based upon protocols in place at the time, which were established in conjunction with veterinarians. . . . The Court need not determine whether Defendants' have presented sufficient evidence to meet their burden of establishing the existence of a valid VCPR, however. As set forth above, even where an extralabel use is by order of a veterinarian in the context of a VCPR, the drug is still deemed unsafe under § 360b if the extralabel use results in an illegal tissue residue. 21 U.S.C. § 360b(a)(4)(A)–(B); 21 C.F.R. §§ 530.10 and 530.11(d). Because Defendants' extralabel use of Penicillin resulted in an above-tolerance residue, the drug is deemed "unsafe" under

§ 360b, and the food containing that drug "adulterated" under 21 U.S.C. § 342(a)(2)(C)(ii), regardless of whether a VCPR relationship existed.

. . . .

(ii) Gowen Farm

. . . .

Defendants . . . argue that even if the three cows did originate from Scenic view, the cows were treated under the verbal orders of the Gowen Farm's veterinarian. Again, the Court assumes that Defendants are attempting to assert that their extralabel use falls within the VCPR exception. The Court need not determine whether Defendants' have presented sufficient evidence to meet their burden in this regard, however, because even where an extralabel use is under order of a veterinarian in the context of a VCPR, the drug is still deemed unsafe under § 360b if it results in an illegal tissue residue. 21 U.S.C. § 360b(a)(4)(A)–(B); 21 C.F.R. §§ 530.10 and 530.11(d).

. . . .

(iii) Fennville Farm

On August 12, 2009, the USDA–FSIS identified an above-tolerance Sulfadimethoxine residue in a tissue sample collected from a cow that had been delivered from the Fennville Farm to a livestock auction in Michigan where it was purchased by a Pennsylvania slaughterhouse for use in human food. . . .

Defendants assert that the label-required dosage and withdrawal times were followed. . . .

The Court finds that, as to the August 12, 2009 sample, a genuine issue material fact exists about whether Defendants' use of Sulfadimethoxine was, in fact, extralabel. Given the Court's conclusion that a drug is not "unsafe" under § 360b with respect to uses that accord with the drug's label, but nonetheless results in a violative tissue level, the Court will ignore the August 12, 2009 sample for purposes of determining whether Defendants' food is adulterated under § 342(a)(2)(C)(ii). . . .

. . . .

Accordingly, the Court finds that Defendants have delivered for introduction into interstate commerce food that is adulterated in violation of 21 U.S.C. § 331(a).

B. Whether Defendants have violated 21 U.S.C. § 331(k)

The United States next asserts that Defendants have violated § 331(k) by adulterating drugs while held for sale and after shipment in interstate commerce. . . .

. . . Under 21 U.S.C. § 351(a)(5), a drug is deemed adulterated if "it is a new animal drug which is unsafe within the meaning of section 360b." Because, as discussed above, the Court finds that Defendants' extralabel use of new animal drugs results in the drugs being deemed unsafe under § 360b, those acts also result in the drugs being adulterated for purposes of § 331(k).

. . . Defendants argue that the "held for sale" element is not satisfied because (1) the first time their cows can be considered "held for sale" is after they have been shipped to auction, which is *after* Defendants have administered drugs, and (2) they do not "sell" drugs to their cows.

To begin, the question is not whether the offending conduct took place while Defendants' *cows* were held for sale, but while Defendants held the *drugs* for sale. The United States' claim here is that Defendants adulterated *drugs* while held for sale and after shipment in interstate commerce. In addition, "[i]t is well established that the terms 'while held for sale' as they appear in the Federal Food, Drug, and Cosmetic Act have been given by courts an expansive rather than technical construction." . . . Indeed, several Courts have agreed with the United States' interpretation that the "held for sale" language is satisfied if the item is used for any purpose other than personal consumption.

Given these broad interpretations of § 331(k), as well as the FDCA in general, the Court finds that the drugs Defendants administer to their cattle are "held for sale" within the meaning of § 331(k). . . .

C. Whether Defendants have Violated § 331(u)

Section 331(u) prohibits "[t]he failure to comply with any requirements of the provisions of, or any regulations or orders of the Secretary, under section 360b(a)(4)(A)." As discussed above, § 360b(a)(4)(A) authorizes the extralabel use of new animal drugs only where such use is (1) by written or oral order of a veterinarian in the context of a valid VCPR *and* (2) such use complies with the regulations establishing conditions for extralabel use, including 21 C.F.R. § 530.11(d)'s prohibition of any extralabel use that results in violative tissue residues. Regardless of whether Defendants have met their burden with regard to the former, because their extralabel use results in violative tissue residues they have failed to comply with the latter. Accordingly, the Court finds that Defendants have failed to comply with 21 U.S.C. § 331(u).

In addition, the Court finds Defendants have not established that their extralabel use of new animal drugs is by order of a licensed veterinarian within the context of a valid VCPR. The regulations define a valid VCPR as one in which:

> (1) a veterinarian has assumed the responsibility for making medical judgments regarding the health of (an) animal(s) and the need for medical treatment, and the client (the owner of the animal or other caretaker) has agreed to follow the instructions of the veterinarian;

> (2) There is sufficient knowledge of the animal(s) by the veterinarian to initiate at least a general or preliminary diagnosis of the medical condition of the animal(s); and

> (3) The practicing veterinarian is readily available for followup in case of adverse reactions or failure of the regimen of therapy. Such a relationship can exist only when the veterinarian has recently seen and is personally acquainted with the keeping and care of the animal(s) by virtue of examination of the animal(s), and/or by medically appropriate and timely visits to the premises where the animal(s) are kept.

21 C.F.R. 530.3(i).

Defendants assert that, in consultation with veterinarians, they have established protocols for treating certain ailments, which the farm managers and herdsmen use to diagnosis the animal, elect treatment options, and provide drug-specific information such as route of administration, dosage, and withdrawal times. In addition, veterinarians visit the farms approximately once every two weeks and as necessary to address specific health issues. . . .

. . . The United States alleges that the protocols are inadequate to support Defendants' extralabel use. Specifically, the United States points to 21 C.F.R. § 530.20(a)(2)(i), entitled "Conditions for permitted extralabel animal and human drug use in food-producing animals." That regulation provides that, before any extralabel use may be permitted, the veterinarian must "[m]ake a careful diagnosis and evaluation of the conditions for which the drug is to be used." By virtue of this regulation, the United States alleges, veterinarians must be substantially involved in the diagnosis of the animals before extralabel use may permitted. The United States concedes this may be done through implementation of both diagnostic and treatment protocols along with regular follow-up to ensure that the protocols are being properly applied. Yet, Defendants' protocols contain no diagnostic criteria whatsoever. . . .

The Court finds that the United States has the better side of the argument based upon the language of the regulations requiring the veterinarian's "careful diagnosis," 21 C.F.R. § 530.20(a)(2)(i), as well as other regulations such as 21 C.F.R. § 530.5(a)(6), which requires the veterinarian to keep records of the number of animals treated in an extralabel manner, which could not be done if the diagnosis are made by laypersons without sufficient involvement of the veterinarian.

D. *Injunctive Relief*

. . . .

The Court finds that injunctive relief is warranted in this case. . . .

NOTES

1. *Veterinarians Compared to Physicians.* AMDUCA and its implementing regulations maintain the effective distinction between the prescribing authority of veterinarians and physicians by recognizing the public health significance of off-label use of drugs in food-producing animals, and thus the limitations on the discretion of veterinarians in those circumstances. While extralabel use of approved animal and human drugs in nonfood-animals is permitted with minimal restrictions, extralabel use in food-producing animals is subject both to current limitations and prospective ones.

2. *Recordkeeping.* FDA has conditioned extralabel use on the maintenance of fairly detailed records of these uses by veterinarians and the availability of those records to FDA. 21 C.F.R. 530.5.

3. *Extralabel Uses of Animal Drugs in Food-Producing Animals.* Current limitations include, among others, the requirements (1) that where data do not exist to provide for an extended safe withdrawal time, the

animal be withheld from the food supply and (2) that there be "an appropriate medical rationale" for the extralabel use. 21 C.F.R. 530.20. FDA may adopt residue requirements based on existing or required new analytical methods (or prohibit extralabel use if such methods are not developed). 21 C.F.R. 530.21–24. The list of such residue tolerances is at 21 C.F.R. Part 556. In addition, the agency may issue orders that certain drugs not be used at all in an extralabel fashion in food-producing animals. 21 C.F.R. 530.25. This list appears at 21 C.F.R. 530.41.

4. *Use of Human Drugs in Animals.* Prior to the Animal Drug Amendments of 1968, veterinarians routinely used drugs that had been developed and approved for human use. After 1968, FDA continued to condone the use of human drugs in veterinary medicine as long as veterinarians took responsibility for the decisions to use these agents. *See* FDA, Compliance Policy Guide Sec. 608.100, "Human–Labeled Drugs Distributed and Used in Animal Medicine" (Mar. 19, 1991) (withdrawn July 7, 2006). But the agency also took the position that the use of human drugs in food-producing animals was improper unless the veterinarian met a series of tests designed to give an assurance that an "extra-label use" will not result in unsafe residues in meat, milk, or eggs. Compliance Policy Guide Sec. 615.100, "Extra Label Use of New Animal Drugs in Food Producing Animals." No. 7125.06 (Mar. 9, 1984). The FDA's position became increasingly strict in part due to congressional criticism. *E.g., "Regulation of Animal Drugs by the Food and Drug Administration," Hearings Before a Subcomm. of the House Comm. on Government Operations,* 99th Cong., 1st Sess. 221–75 (1985). The requirements set forth in the Compliance Policy Guide included establishing what the American Veterinary Medical Association refers to as a valid veterinarian-client-patient relationship (requiring actual and continued oversight of the animal), determining that the unapproved usage is medically necessary, and ensuring that a prolonged withdrawal time is observed to protect against residues. Today, AMDUCA and its regulations apply equally to human drugs used in animals and extralabel use of animal drugs. *See* FD&C Act 512(a)(5); 21 C.F.R. 530.1.

5. *FDA Enforcement.* In *Cowdin v. Young,* 681 F. Supp. 366 (W.D. La. 1987), the court granted FDA's motion to dismiss a court action challenging the 1984 compliance policy guide on the grounds that the issues were not ripe and that veterinarians did not have standing to challenge the guide. In *United States v. Blease,* Food Drug Cosm. L. Rep. (CCH) ¶ 38,095 (D.N.J. 1988), FDA obtained an injunction in a case involving the extra-label use of a new animal drug. In *United States v. Jacobs,* Food Drug Cosm. L. Rep. CCH ¶ 38,113 (E.D. Cal. 1989), the agency successfully opposed a motion to dismiss a criminal indictment in another such case.

6. *Withdrawal of Chloramphenicol.* Because of evidence of widespread extra-label use in food-producing animals, FDA withdrew approval of the NADAs for chloramphenicol oral solution. The drug had been approved only for use in dogs because of its known human toxicity. 51 Fed. Reg. 1367, 1441 (Jan. 13, 1986).

6. THE SAFETY OF ANTIBIOTICS USED IN LIVESTOCK PRODUCTION

The subtherapeutic use of antibiotics in livestock feed for growth promotion is widespread in the United States and several other countries. For more than three decades, FDA officials have wrestled with assertions that this practice poses a risk to human health by inducing resistance to disease-producing organisms the drugs might otherwise combat. The attempt to assess the risk posed by this practice has taken the agency to the frontiers of science, while action to restrict the use of these drugs probes the limits of the concept of "safety" in section 512 of the FD&C Act.

Harold C. Hopkins, *Keeping the Kick in Antibiotics*
FDA Papers (June 1972).

The dual use of antibiotics—at concentrated or therapeutic dosages in humans and animals to treat diseases, and at low levels in feeds to promote faster growth in food-producing animals—has been widely discussed in recent years. The problem is that some bacteria exposed to low levels of antibiotics for prolonged periods in animals develop a resistance to some of these drugs. . . . If the resistant bacteria find their way into the human system, they may successfully fight off antibiotic treatment, making it less effective for treatment of humans. . . . Humans may become exposed to these large numbers of antibiotic-resistant bacteria from animals which are a major source of our food. After this resistance develops, antibiotic treatment may be less effective in humans. . . .

———

The concern described by Mr. Hopkins was first identified by public health authorities in the United Kingdom in the late 1960s and elaborated in a famous document titled the Swann Report. In 1972, FDA took what turned out to be the first of several halting steps to characterize and manage the risk. *See* Antibiotic and Sulfonamide Drugs in Animal Feed: Proposed Statement of Policy, 37 Fed. Reg. 2444 (Feb. 1, 1972) (declaring that the agency would revoke "currently permitted uses of subtherapeutic and/or growth promotant uses of antibacterial agents in feeds . . . when such drugs are also used in human clinical medicine unless data are submitted which establish their safety and effectiveness").

The following year the agency sounded a more cautious note, acknowledging that the withdrawal of all antibacterial approvals for subtherapeutic uses could have significant economic impact, but at the same time directing sponsors of such drugs to undertake field studies to determine the reality and magnitude of the risk. Continued attention to the issue, coupled with accumulation of research findings, seemed to enlarge rather than narrow the uncertainty. Years passed without any decisive regulatory action.

Antibiotic and Sulfonamide Drugs in the Feed of Animals

38 Fed. Reg. 9811 (April 20, 1973).

The commercial animal and poultry production practices used in this country today, including the use of medication in feed administered to the entire herd or flock, have made it possible to effectively concentrate large numbers of animals into small areas without serious losses in production efficiency. From such concentration and intensified production, benefits accrue in terms of efficient land usage, labor savings, and more efficient conversion of animal feed to animal protein, thereby making a major contribution to the abundance of food from animals. . . . Immediate and total withdrawal of these drugs from animal feeds could seriously disrupt the quality and quantity of an important portion of our total human diet. . . .

It would be chaotic, and is clearly not feasible, to withdraw approval of all food or drug substances merely because new questions have arisen, new testing is considered scientifically appropriate, or new studies raise issues that require further exploration. That is the situation involved here. . . .

1. The antibacterial drugs commonly used in animal feed and which are recognized to cause transferable drug resistance and are commonly used to treat human and animal diseases include the tetracyclines, streptomycin, dihydrostreptomycin, the sulfonamides, and penicillin. The use of these drugs in feeds may also affect the reservoir of salmonella organisms in food animals. An assessment of the effect of subtherapeutic levels of these drugs in feed on the salmonella reservoir can be completed in a relatively short time. Therefore, continued marketing of products containing any of these named drugs will be dependent on completion of salmonella reservoir studies by no later than 1 year following the effective date of this order. A determination that the drug promotes a significant increase in the salmonella reservoir will be considered sufficient grounds for proceeding to withdrawal [sic] approval of that drug.

2. The approval for the use of antibiotic and sulfonamide drugs in animal feeds at subtherapeutic levels will be withdrawn, unless by no later than 2 years following the date of this order there has been submitted conclusive evidence demonstrating that no human or animal health hazard exists which can be attributed to such use. . . .

———

Three years later, FDA withdrew product approvals held by firms that had not complied with the information requirements of this regulation. 41 Fed. Reg. 8282 (Feb. 25, 1976). The next year, Donald Kennedy, Stanford Professor of Human Biology, became FDA Commissioner. Within a month, FDA announced that the Bureau of Veterinary Medicine would soon propose:

1. To terminate all subtherapeutic use of penicillin in all feed;

2. To restrict the use of the tetracyclines to situations where there are no viable alternatives;

3. To impose restrictions on the distribution and use of the remaining uses of penicillin and tetracycline; and

4. To expedite implementation of the drug efficacy study implementation (DESI) notices proposing to withdraw approval of all penicillin and tetracycline combination products that lack evidence of effectiveness. . . .

42 Fed. Reg. 27264 (May 27, 1977).

FDA published detailed notices of opportunity for hearing (NOOHs) on its intent to withdraw approval for subtherapeutic uses of penicillin and tetracycline in animal feed in 42 Fed. Reg. 29999 (June 10, 1977), 42 Fed. Reg. 43772 (Aug. 30, 1977), and 42 Fed. Reg. 56264 (Oct. 21, 1977), and the agency announced its intention to conduct hearings in 43 Fed. Reg. 53827 (Nov. 17, 1978). The agency never held these hearings, however. Remarkably, FDA's failure to complete these withdrawal proceedings would become the topic of litigation in 2012. The history of this controversy is set forth in *Natural Resources Defense Council, Inc. v. FDA*, 884 F. Supp. 2d 127 (S.D.N.Y. 2012) (excerpted immediately following this discussion).

In the meantime the General Accounting Office issued a report criticizing FDA's failure to disapprove the subtherapeutic use of several antibiotics. NEED TO ESTABLISH SAFETY AND EFFECTIVENESS OF ANTIBIOTICS USED IN ANIMAL FEEDS, HRD–77–81 (1977). However, the House Appropriations Committee, sensitive to the needs of agriculture, instructed the agency to delay any regulatory action pending a study by the National Academy of Sciences. The NAS concluded that it was not possible to conduct a single comprehensive epidemiological study to resolve the issues, but it suggested studies that could advance understanding of the potential risk. NAS, THE EFFECTS ON HUMAN HEALTH OF SUBTHERAPEUTIC USE OF ANTIMICROBIALS IN ANIMAL FEED (1980).

Opening another legal front, the Animal Legal Defense Fund of Boston sued a Wisconsin veal producer, alleging that the defendant raised calves in confined pens, fed them iron-deprived diets, and gave them subtherapeutic doses of drugs that might promote antibiotic resistance in human beings. The Fund asserted that the veal producer's failure to tell consumers about these practices was unfair and deceptive under Massachusetts law. The court entered summary judgment for the defendant, finding that there is no private right of action under the Massachusetts animal cruelty statutes and that FDA regulation of animal drugs preempted Massachusetts law on this subject. *Animal Legal Defense Fund Boston, Inc. v. Provimi Veal Corp.*, 626 F. Supp. 278 (D. Mass. 1986), *aff'd without opinion* 802 F.2d 440 (1st Cir. 1986).

In February 1989, the Institute of Medicine, a unit of the NAS, issued yet another report, HUMAN HEALTH RISKS WITH THE SUBTHERAPEUTIC USE OF PENICILLIN OR TETRACYCLINES IN ANIMAL FEED. The IOM committee concluded that it was "unable to find data directly implicating the subtherapeutic use of feed antimicrobials in human illness and that much of the available evidence was primarily circumstantial, often ambiguous, and sometimes conflicting," but it put forward a novel risk assessment model that estimated the possible number of excess deaths per year under a variety of assumptions.

As detailed below, *infra* p. 1098, in 2005, FDA withdrew approval of the NADA for enroflaxacin in poultry on the basis of the promotion of antibiotic resistance. It is the only NADA the agency has ever withdrawn for this reason. The rest of the history of FDA's approach to subtherapeutic uses of antibiotics in food-producing animals is reviewed by the court below in an action brought against the FDA by the Natural Resources Defense Council (NRDC). The NRDC sought to compel the FDA to begin to withdraw antibiotics for subtherapeutic uses in accordance with the regulations and the NOOHs promulgated in the 1970s.

Natural Resources Defense Council, Inc. v. Food and Drug Administration

884 F. Supp. 2d 127 (S.D.N.Y. 2012).

■ KATZ, UNITED STATES MAGISTRATE JUDGE.

Plaintiffs . . . bring this action . . . alleging that the FDA withheld agency action in violation of the Food, Drug, and Cosmetic Act and the Administrative Procedure Act ("APA"). . . . Presently before the Court are the parties' cross-motions for summary judgment. For the reasons that follow, Plaintiffs' motion is granted and Defendants' motion is denied.

BACKGROUND

For over thirty years, the FDA has taken the position that the widespread use of certain antibiotics in livestock for purposes other than disease treatment poses a threat to human health. In 1977, the FDA issued notices announcing its intent to withdraw approval of the use of certain antibiotics in livestock for the purposes of growth promotion and feed efficiency, which the agency had found had not been proven to be safe. The FDA issued the notices pursuant to 21 U.S.C. § 360b(e)(1), which states that

> [t]he Secretary shall, after due notice and opportunity for hearing to the applicant, issue an order withdrawing approval of an application . . . with respect to any new animal drug if the Secretary finds . . . (B) that new evidence not contained in such application or not available to the Secretary until after such application was approved, or tests by new methods, or tests by methods not deemed reasonably applicable when such application was approved, evaluated together with the evidence available to the Secretary when the application was approved, shows that such drug is not shown to be safe for use under the conditions of use upon the basis of which the application was approved. . . .

21 U.S.C. § 360b(e)(1)(B). Although the notices were properly promulgated and over twenty drug sponsors requested hearings on the matter, the FDA never held hearings or took any further action on the proposed withdrawals.

In the intervening years, the scientific evidence of the risks to human health from the widespread use of antibiotics in livestock has grown, and there is no evidence that the FDA has changed its position that such uses are not shown to be safe. In May 2011, after the FDA failed to respond to two Citizen Petitions urging the agency to follow through with the 1977 notices, Plaintiffs filed this action seeking a court order compelling the FDA to complete the withdrawal proceedings for antibiotics included in the 1977 notices. In December 2011, the FDA withdrew the original notices on the grounds that they were outdated, and it now argues that Plaintiffs' claim is moot.

Antibiotics, also known as antimicrobials, are drugs used to treat infections caused by bacteria. Although antibiotics have saved countless lives, the improper use and overuse of antibiotics has led to a phenomenon known as antibiotic resistance. Specifically, the misuse of antibiotics creates selective evolutionary pressure that enables antibiotic resistant bacteria to increase in numbers more rapidly than antibiotic susceptible bacteria, increasing the opportunity for individuals to become infected by resistant bacteria. People who contract antibiotic-resistant bacterial infections are more likely to have longer hospital stays, may be treated with less effective and more toxic drugs, and may be more likely to die as a result of the infection. The FDA considers antibiotic resistance "a mounting public health problem of global significance."

In the 1950s, the FDA approved the use of antibiotics to stimulate growth and improve feed efficiency in food-producing animals, such as cattle, swine, and chickens. Antibiotics used for growth promotion are typically administered through animal feed or water on a herd- or flock-wide basis. The approved doses of antibiotics for growth promotion are typically lower than the approved doses for disease treatment. The administration of "medically important"[2] antibiotics to entire herds or flocks of food-producing animals, at "subtherapeutic"[3] levels, poses a qualitatively higher risk to public health than the administration of such drugs to individual animals or targeted groups of animals to prevent or treat specific diseases. Research has shown that the use of antibiotics in livestock leads to the development of antibiotic-resistant bacteria that can be—and has been—transferred from animals to humans through direct contact, environmental exposure, and the consumption and handling of contaminated meat and poultry products. Consequently, the FDA has concluded that "the overall weight of evidence available to date supports the conclusion that using medically important antimicrobial drugs for production purposes [in livestock] is not in the interest of protecting and promoting the public health."

The present action pertains to the use of three different antibiotics in animal feed: penicillin and two forms of tetracycline—chlortetracycline and oxytetracycline ("tetracyclines"). Pursuant to the FDCA, any "new animal drug" that is introduced into interstate commerce must be the subject of an FDA approved new animal drug application ("NADA") or, with respect to generic drugs, an abbreviated NADA ("ANADA"). See 21 U.S.C. § 360b(b)–(c). . . . The FDA lawfully issued NADAs and ANADAs for penicillin and tetracyclines in the mid-

---

[2] The term "medically important antibiotics" refers to antibiotic drugs that are important for therapeutic use in humans.

[3] The term "subtherapeutic" was commonly used in the 1960s and 1970s to refer to any use of antibiotics for purposes other than disease treatment and prevention, including growth promotion and feed efficiency in animals. Although FDA no longer uses the term, in this Opinion the Court uses the term "subtherapeutic" to refer to the use of antibiotics in food-producing animals for growth promotion and feed efficiency.

1950s. Since that time, penicillin has been used to promote growth in chickens, turkeys, and swine, and tetracyclines have been used to promote growth in chickens, turkey, swine, cattle, and sheep.

In the mid-1960s, the FDA became concerned that the long-term use of antibiotics, including penicillin and tetracyclines, in food-producing animals might pose threats to human and animal health. As a result, in 1970, the agency convened a task force to study the risks associated with the use of antibiotics in animal feed. . . .

In response to the findings of the task force, the FDA, in 1973, issued a regulation providing that the agency would propose to withdraw approval of all subtherapeutic uses of antibiotics in animal feed unless drug sponsors and other interested parties submitted data within the next two years "which resolve[d] conclusively the issues concerning [the drugs'] safety to man and animals . . . under specific criteria" established by the FDA. . . . The FDA regulation required that "[a]n antibacterial drug fed at subtherapeutic levels to animals must be shown not to promote increased resistance to antibacterials used in human medicine." . . .

Over the next two years, the Bureau of Veterinary Medicine ("BVM"), a subdivision of the FDA, reviewed the data submitted by drug sponsors to support the subtherapeutic use of antibiotics. By April 20, 1975, all data concerning the safety and efficacy criteria for antibiotic drugs had been received. The BVM was assisted by a sub-committee of the FDA's National Advisory Food and Drug Committee ("NAFDC") in its review of the data. . . .

After carefully considering the recommendations of the NAFDC and the NAFDC sub-committee, the Director of the BVM issued notices of an opportunity for hearing ("NOOHs") on proposals to withdraw approval of all subtherapeutic uses of penicillin in animal feed and, with limited exceptions, all subtherapeutic uses of oxytetracycline and chlortetracycline in animal feed. In the Penicillin Notice, the Director reported that "[n]one of the specified human and animal health safety criteria [for the subtherapeutic use of antibiotics in animal feed] have been satisfied. . . ." With respect to the transfer of antibiotic-resistant bacteria, the Director surveyed the available data and found that (1) the pool of bacteria carrying transferrable resistance genes was increasing; (2) the increase was due in part to the subtherapeutic use of penicillin in animal feed; and (3) antibiotic-resistant bacteria were transferred from animals to humans as a result of direct human-animal contact, the consumption of contaminated food, and the widespread presence of resistant bacteria in the environment. . . .

Similarly, the Director of the BVM . . . concluded that he "is unaware of evidence that satisfies the requirements for demonstrating the safety of extensive use of subtherapeutic tetracycline-containing premixes. . . ." . . .

In response to the 1977 NOOHs, approximately twenty drug firms, agricultural organizations, and individuals requested hearings. On November 9, 1978, the Commissioner of the FDA granted the requests for hearings. . . . The Commissioner stated that a date for the hearing would be set "as soon as practicable." According to the statutory and regulatory scheme, at the hearing, the drug sponsors would have the burden of proving that the drugs were in fact safe.

The Commissioner never set a date for the hearings on the BVM's proposal to withdraw approval of the use of penicillin and tetracyclines in animal feed. In the late 1970s and early 1980s, Congressional committees issued three reports that contained statements that the FDA interpreted as requests to postpone the withdrawal hearings pending further research. . . . Importantly, none of these recommendations was adopted by the full House or Senate, and none was passed as law.

Regardless of the legal effect of these Congressional statements, the FDA never held hearings on the proposed withdrawals, and instead engaged in further research on the risks associated with the subtherapeutic use of antibiotics in food-producing animals. . . .

. . . In 1983, the Commissioner denied requests from several drug sponsors to rescind the 1977 NOOHs. The Commissioner explained that the 1977 NOOHs "represent[ed] the Director's formal position that use of the drugs is not shown to be safe" and that the Commissioner "concur [red]" with the decision of the Director. . . . In 2004, the BVM, now known as the Center of Veterinary Medicine ("CVM"), sent letters to several manufacturers of approved animal feed products containing penicillin and tetracyclines, explaining that "[t]he administrative record does not contain sufficient information to alleviate the CVM's concerns about the use of [these] product[s] and [their] possible role in the emergence and dissemination of antimicrobial resistance." . . .

On June 28, 2010, the FDA released a non-binding Draft Guidance entitled The Judicious Use of Medically Important Antimicrobial Drugs in Food–Producing Animals ("2010 Draft Guidance") (Guidance No. 209). In the Draft Guidance . . . [a]fter reviewing the scientific evidence, the FDA concluded that "the overall weight of evidence available to date supports the conclusion that using medically important antimicrobial drugs for production purposes is not in the interest of protecting and promoting the public health." The FDA announced two non-mandatory principles to guide the use of antibiotics in animal feed: (1) "[t]he use of medically important antimicrobial drugs in food-producing animals should be limited to those uses that are considered necessary for assuring animal health[;]" and (2) "[t]he use of medically important antimicrobial drugs in food-producing animals should be limited to those uses that include veterinary oversight or consultation."

On December 16, 2011, nearly twenty-five years after their initial publication and during the pendency of this action, the FDA rescinded the 1977 NOOHs. The FDA explained that it was rescinding the NOOHs because the "FDA is engaging in other ongoing regulatory strategies developed since the publication of the 1977 NOOHs" and that if the FDA were to move forward with the NOOHs it would need to "update the NOOHs to reflect current data, information, and policies" and "prioritize any withdrawal proceedings." The FDA noted that "although [it] is withdrawing the 1977 NOOHs, FDA remains concerned about the issue of antimicrobial resistance." . . .

Plaintiffs filed the present action on May 25, 2011, alleging that the FDA's failure to withdraw approval of the subtherapeutic use of penicillin and tetracyclines pursuant to the 1977 NOOHs constituted an agency action unlawfully withheld or unreasonably delayed in violation of the APA, 5 U.S.C. § 706(1), and the FDCA, 21 U.S.C. § 360b(e)(1). Plaintiffs seek a Court order compelling the FDA to withdraw approval for the subtherapeutic use of penicillin and tetracyclines in animal feed, unless, after a hearing, the drug uses at issue are determined to be safe. Plaintiffs further request that the Court set a deadline by which the FDA must hold hearings and issue a final decision on the withdrawals. Plaintiffs maintain that under the FDCA, 21 U.S.C. § 360b(e)(1), once the FDA found that the subtherapeutic use of penicillin and tetracyclines in animal feed was not shown to be safe to humans, the agency was statutorily obligated to withdraw approval of those uses, unless the drug sponsors demonstrated the safety of the drugs. Defendants contend that withdrawal was not legally required, and, in any event, the issue is now moot because the 1977 NOOHs have been withdrawn. . . .

DISCUSSION

. . . Section 706(1) [of the APA] provides relief for an agency's failure to act by empowering reviewing courts to "compel agency action unlawfully withheld or unreasonably delayed[.]" The Supreme Court has made clear that § 706(1) applies only when an "an agency failed to take a discrete agency action that it is required to take." *Norton v. S. Utah Wilderness Alliance*, 542 U.S. 55, 64 (2004). The limit to discrete actions precludes a court from authorizing "broad programmatic attack[s]" on agency policy, and the limit to legally required actions ensures that a court will not interfere with an agency's discretionary functions. *See id*. at 64–65. . . .

Here, the Director of the BVM issued the penicillin and tetracyclines NOOHs pursuant to 21 U.S.C. § 360b(e)(1), which governs the withdrawal of [sic] approval of NADAs/ANADAs. . . . In order to obtain the relief they seek, Plaintiffs must establish that § 360b(e)(1) legally requires the FDA to take a discrete action. . . .

Defendants argue that given the procedural complexity of issuing a notice and holding a hearing, which may take months or years to complete, the relief sought by Plaintiffs is not discrete. The Court disagrees. Upon a finding that a new animal drug has not been shown to be safe, § 360b(e)(1) and the accompanying regulations require the FDA to implement several related discrete actions: (1) provide notice of the FDA's finding and intent to withdraw approval; (2) provide an opportunity for a hearing to the relevant animal drug sponsors; (3) if an applicant timely requests a hearing and raises a genuine issue of fact, hold a hearing; and (4) if the applicant fails to show that the drug is safe, the Commissioner must issue an order withdrawing approval of the drug. The first three steps are statutory precursors to issuing the final withdrawal order. . . . The fact that § 360b(e)(1) requires notice and an opportunity for a hearing prior to the issuance of a withdrawal order does not undermine the fact that the requested relief is a discrete agency action. Plaintiffs are not launching a "broad programmatic attack" on the FDA's animal drug policies; rather, Plaintiffs have identified certain new animal drugs that the agency has publicly concluded are "not shown to be safe" and is requesting that the agency move forward with its statutory duty to hold the requested hearings and withdraw approval if the drug sponsors fail to show that the drugs are safe.

The parties dispute whether, given the facts of this case, § 360b(e)(1) legally requires the Commissioner of the FDA to hold withdrawal proceedings for the relevant penicillin and tetracyclines NADAs/ANADAs. . . . Defendants contend that the statute only requires the Secretary to withdraw approval of a NADA/ANADA if the Secretary makes a finding after a formal hearing. Since the FDA never held hearings and has now withdrawn the 1977 NOOHs, Defendants argue that no findings have been made and no further action is required. Plaintiffs contend that under § 360b(e)(1) the Secretary makes a finding prior to a hearing, and that upon making such a finding, the Secretary is legally required to withdraw approval of a drug, unless the drug sponsor requests a hearing and shows that the drug is safe. They further argue that the FDA's recent withdrawal of the 1977 NOOHs does not disturb the agency's original findings and that the FDA is legally required to hold withdrawal proceedings for the relevant penicillin and tetracyclines NOOHs.

. . . .

The Court finds that Plaintiff's interpretation provides a common sense reading of the statute based on its text and grammatical structure. The statute states that "[t]he Secretary shall, after due notice and opportunity for hearing to the applicant, issue an order withdrawing approval of a[ ] [NADA/ANADA] . . . if the Secretary finds . . . [that a drug is not shown to be safe]. . . ." The "after due notice and opportunity for hearing" clause is setoff [sic] by commas and immediately precedes the words "issue an order withdrawing approval," indicating that the "notice" clause modifies the "issue an order" clause and not the findings clause. Accordingly, the statute only requires the Secretary to give notice and provide an opportunity for a hearing before issuing an order of withdrawal and not before making findings. Under this reading, if the Secretary finds that an animal drug has not been shown to be safe, he is statutorily required to withdraw approval of that drug, provided that the drug sponsor has notice and an opportunity for a hearing. If, after a hearing, the drug sponsor has not met his burden of proving the drug to be safe, the Secretary must issue a withdrawal order.[11]

. . . .

[B]ased on the text and grammar of § 360b(e)(1), as well as the structure of § 360b as a whole and the overriding purpose of the FDA, the Court finds that the plain meaning of § 360b(e)(1) requires the Secretary to issue notice and an opportunity for a hearing whenever he finds that a new animal drug is not shown to be safe. If the drug sponsor does not meet his burden of demonstrating that the drug is safe at the hearing, the Secretary must issue an order withdrawing approval of the drug.

This interpretation is consistent with how courts have interpreted 21 U.S.C. § 355(e), the human drug parallel to § 360b(e). . . .

---

[11] Admittedly, the Secretary will make a second set of findings after a hearing, but the initial findings trigger the mandatory withdrawal process and, if not rebutted, provide a basis for mandatory withdrawal.

Were the Court to conclude that § 360b(e)(1) is ambiguous as to when the Secretary makes findings, the Court would defer to the agency's reasonable interpretation of the statute. See *Chevron*, 467 U.S. at 842–43. Although in this litigation the FDA has maintained that findings pursuant to § 360b(e)(1) can only be made after a hearing, the agency's implementing regulation, 21 C.F.R. § 514.115, interprets § 360b(e)(1) to require the agency to make findings prior to a hearing. The regulation reads: "The Commissioner shall notify in writing the person holding [a NADA/ANADA] and afford an opportunity for a hearing on a proposal to withdraw approval of such [NADA/ANADA] if he finds ... that such drug is not shown to be safe...." 21 C.F.R. § 514.115(b)(3)(ii). ... Accordingly, if the Court were to defer to the agency's interpretation of the statute it would reach the same conclusion: findings pursuant to § 360b(e)(1) are made before a hearing and trigger the withdrawal process.

. . . .

Having found that the Director of the BVM is authorized to make findings under § 360b(e)(1), the question becomes whether the Director made such findings for the subtherapeutic use of penicillin and tetracycline. ... [I]n both the Penicillin and the Tetracycline Notices, the Director explicitly concluded that the drugs had not been shown to be safe and cited § 360b. Such a conclusion is the statutory trigger for the FDA to institute withdrawal proceedings, which it in fact did. Based on the language of the 1977 Notices, the Director made the findings necessary to trigger mandatory withdrawal proceedings for the subtherapeutic uses of penicillin and tetracyclines in animal feed.

... Defendants maintain that Plaintiffs' claim is now moot because, during the pendency of this case, the FDA rescinded the 1977 NOOHs for the subtherapeutic use of penicillin and tetracyclines in animal feed.

... Plaintiffs contend, and the Court agrees, that upon a finding by the FDA that a new animal drug has not been shown to be safe, the FDA is required to withdraw approval of that drug after providing notice and an opportunity for a hearing. Therefore, the trigger for FDA to initiate mandatory withdrawal proceedings is not the issuance of a NOOH but a finding that a drug has not been shown to be safe.... Accordingly, Plaintiffs are still entitled to relief and their claim is not moot if they can establish that the rescission of the NOOHs did not rescind the FDA's findings that the subtherapeutic use of penicillin and tetracyclines in animal feed has not been shown to be safe.

The record makes clear that the FDA did not rescind its findings when it rescinded the 1977 NOOHs. In the official notice rescinding the 1977 NOOHs, the FDA provided three justifications for the rescission:

(1) FDA is engaging in other ongoing regulatory strategies developed since the publication of the 1977 NOOHs with respect to addressing microbial food safety issues; (2) FDA would update the NOOHs to reflect current data, information, and policies if, in the future, it decides to move forward with withdrawal of the approved uses of the new animal drugs described in the NOOHs; and (3) FDA would need to prioritize any withdrawal proceedings....

None of these reasons addresses the initial findings that prompted the NOOHs or suggests that the FDA is rescinding those findings.

Rather, in the notice rescinding the 1977 NOOHs, the FDA emphasized ... "... FDA remains concerned about the issue of antimicrobial resistance. Today's action should not be interpreted as a sign that FDA no longer has safety concerns or that FDA will not consider re-proposing withdrawal proceedings in the future, if necessary." This public announcement of the FDA's continuing safety concerns and its attempts at other strategies support the view that the FDA has not rescinded its original findings that use of the drugs has not been shown to be safe.[16]

In addition, the 2010 Draft Guidance, which represents the FDA's current strategy to address microbial food safety issues, emphasizes the FDA's continuing concerns about the safety of the subtherapeutic use of penicillin and tetracyclines in animal feed. . . . The FDA has not issued a single statement since the issuance of the 1977 NOOHs that undermines the original findings that the drugs have not been shown to be safe. . . .

Lastly, the fact that the FDA "is engaging in other ongoing regulatory strategies," does not relieve it of its statutory obligation to complete withdrawal proceedings. Upon a finding that the use of a drug under certain conditions has not been shown to be safe, § 360b(e)(1) prescribes a clear course of conduct: issue notice and an opportunity for a hearing, and, if the drug sponsor does not demonstrate that the drug use is safe at the hearing, withdraw approval of such use. The statute does not empower the agency to choose a different course of action in lieu of withdrawal proceedings, such as that embodied in the 2010 Draft Guidance. . . .

Accordingly, because the rescission of the 1977 NOOHs did not rescind the original findings that the subtherapeutic use of penicillin and tetracyclines in food-producing animals has not been shown to be safe, Plaintiffs' claim is not moot.

CONCLUSION

For the foregoing reasons, Plaintiffs' Motion for Summary Judgment on their first claim for relief is granted and Defendants' Motion for Summary Judgment is denied. Defendants are hereby ordered to initiate withdrawal proceedings for the relevant NADAs/ANADAs. Specifically, the Commissioner of the FDA or the Director of the CVM must re-issue a notice of the proposed withdrawals (which may be updated) and provide an opportunity for a hearing to the relevant drug sponsors; if drug sponsors timely request hearings and raise a genuine and substantial issue of fact, the FDA must hold a public evidentiary hearing. If, at the hearing, the drug sponsors fail to show that the use of the drugs is safe, the Commissioner must issue a withdrawal order.

---

[16] Any claim that the 1977 NOOHs are out-of-date does not relieve the FDA of its obligation to proceed with the withdrawal process. First, the agency cannot, through its own prolonged inaction, create obstacles to its statutorily mandated obligation. Second, while there have been additional scientific studies since the 1977 NOOHs were issued, they all appear to support the FDA's original finding that the use of these drugs has not been shown to be safe. Finally, nothing precludes the FDA from updating the NOOHs, so long as it does so in a reasonably prompt manner.

The following month, April 2013, FDA tried to avert further court action by finalizing the following guidance (originally disseminated as a draft guidance in 2010), setting out voluntary compliance measures as an alternative to instituting formal withdrawal proceedings.

Guidance for Industry: The Judicious Use of Medically Important Antimicrobial Drugs in Food–Producing Animals

April 13, 2012.

. . . .

RECOMMENDED PRINCIPLES REGARDING JUDICIOUS USE IN ANIMALS

The continued availability of effective antimicrobial drugs is critically important for combating infectious disease in both humans and animals. This includes the continued availability of feed and water uses of such drugs for managing disease in animal agriculture. Therefore, it is in the interest of both human and animal health that we take a more proactive approach to considering how antimicrobial drugs are being used, and take steps to assure that such uses are appropriate and necessary for maintaining the health of humans and animals. Using medically important antimicrobial drugs as judiciously as possible is key to minimizing resistance development and preserving the effectiveness of these drugs as therapies for humans and animals. Although FDA applauds the efforts to date by various veterinary and animal producer organizations to institute guidelines for the judicious use of antimicrobial drugs, the agency believes additional, voluntary steps are needed.

To further address this public and animal health concern, FDA is recommending two additional principles about the appropriate or judicious use of medically important antimicrobial drugs in food-producing animals. . . .

PRINCIPLE 1: *The use of medically important antimicrobial drugs in food-producing animals should be limited to those uses that are considered necessary for assuring animal health.*

In light of the risk that antimicrobial resistance poses to public health, FDA believes the use of medically important antimicrobial drugs in food-producing animals for production purposes (e.g., to promote growth or improve feed efficiency) represents an injudicious use of these important drugs. Production uses are not directed at any specifically identified disease, but rather are expressly indicated and used for the purpose of enhancing the production of animal-derived products. In contrast, FDA considers uses that are associated with the treatment, control, or prevention[6] of specific diseases, including administration through feed or water, to be uses that are necessary for assuring the health of food-producing animals.

---

[6] Disease prevention involves the administration of an antimicrobial drug to animals, none of which are exhibiting clinical signs of disease, in a situation where disease is likely to occur if the drug is not administered.

Some may have concerns that the use of medically important antimicrobial drugs in food-producing animals for disease prevention purposes is not an appropriate or judicious use. However, FDA believes that some indications for prevention use are necessary and judicious as long as such use includes professional veterinary involvement. . . . For example, if a veterinarian determines, based on the client's production practices and herd health history, that cattle being transported or otherwise stressed are more likely to develop a certain bacterial infection, preventively treating these cattle with an antimicrobial approved for prevention of that bacterial infection would be considered a judicious use. Another example would be the prevention of necrotic enteritis in broiler chickens. In this case, the prevention use of an antimicrobial is important to manage this disease in certain flocks in the face of concurrent coccidiosis, a significant parasitic disease in chickens. On the other hand, FDA would not consider the administration of a drug to apparently healthy animals in the absence of any information that such animals were at risk of a specific disease to be a judicious use. The decision to use a specific drug or combination drug is generally based on factors that veterinarians are uniquely qualified to consider. . . .

PRINCIPLE 2: *The use of medically important antimicrobial drugs in food-producing animals should be limited to those uses that include veterinary oversight or consultation.*

Most of the feed-use antimicrobial drugs are currently approved for over-the-counter use in food-producing animals for purposes that include the treatment, control, and prevention of disease as well as for production purposes (i.e., for growth promotion uses such as increased rate of weight gain). In addition to instituting voluntary measures that would limit use of medically important antimicrobial drugs in food-producing animals to uses that are considered necessary to assure the animals' health, FDA also believes it is important to phase-in the voluntary practice of including veterinary oversight or consultation in the use of these drugs. . . . FDA recognizes that the nature of veterinary involvement can vary due to numerous factors such as geographic location and animal production setting. In fact, there are limited numbers of large animal veterinarians, which can make consultation or oversight challenging in certain situations. For example, some animal disease events require immediate attention. In some cases, veterinarians may be directly diagnosing and administering therapies, while in other cases they are visiting and consulting with producers periodically to establish customized disease management protocols for that producer's herd or flock. Of key importance to FDA is the fact that, in both of these cases, the veterinarian is involved in the decision-making process regarding antimicrobial drug use. FDA recognizes that increasing veterinary involvement in the use of antimicrobial drugs has significant practical implications for animal producers, veterinary practitioners, and the veterinary profession as whole. Therefore, FDA is particularly interested in receiving comments on strategies for effectively promoting the voluntary adoption of such a change.

. . . .

NOTES

1. *"Judicious Use."* The FDA's focus on attaining voluntary compliance with "judicious use" of antibiotics for subtherapeutic uses seems to be a compromise between agency inaction and the proposed hearings and complete withdrawals of the drugs for those uses. It is important to observe, however, that the "judicious use" principle, if followed, constitutes a hard-line ban on subtherapeutic uses.

> "Judicious use" is using an antimicrobial drug appropriately and only when necessary. Based on a thorough review of the available scientific information, FDA recommends that use of medically important antimicrobial drugs in food-producing animals be limited to situations where the use of these drugs is necessary for ensuring animal health, and their use includes veterinary oversight or consultation. FDA believes that using medically important antimicrobial drugs to increase production in food-producing animals is not a judicious use.

FDA's STRATEGY ON ANTIMICROBIAL RESISTANCE—QUESTIONS AND ANSWERS (April 11, 2012) (available on FDA website).

2. *Second Ruling in NRDC Case.* In June 2012, three months after the first ruling, and two months after FDA issued the above "judicial use" guidance, Judge Katz ruled on a claim by other plaintiffs in the suit who had filed citizen petitions in 1999 and 2005 requesting that FDA withdraw approval for subtherapeutic uses of antibiotics in livestock. The judge held that the agency's 2011 denial of these petitions was arbitrary and capricious. *Natural Resources Defense Council, Inc. v. FDA*, 872 F.Supp.2d 318, 338–42 (S.D.N.Y. 2012). The opinion remarked:

> ... In an eleventh hour response, the Agency pointed to a guidance program that encourages industry to use these drugs "judiciously," with no hard evidence that the drug sponsors have agreed or will agreed [sic] to the proposed measures. . . .

> Although the Agency argues that the Court should defer to its decision to implement a voluntary program in lieu of evaluating the safety of the drugs and initiating withdrawal proceedings if necessary, the Court cannot defer because the statute clearly commands a different course of action. Moreover, the Agency has failed to explain the basis for its claim that the voluntary program will more effectively achieve the same results as formal withdrawal proceedings. The Agency points to the time and resources involved in holding public hearings. However, if any credence is to be given to the Agency's position that the drug industry intends to comply with the voluntary program, then it is unclear why the industry would contest formal withdrawal notices or require time consuming hearings. Here, the statutory scheme requires the Agency to ensure the safety and effectiveness of all drugs sold in interstate commerce, and, if an approved drug is not shown to be safe or effective, the Agency must begin withdrawal proceedings. The Agency has forsaken these obligations in the name of a proposed voluntary program and acted contrary to the statutory language.

Id. at 340–41.

———

In August 2012, following Judge Katz's retirement, the NRDC and FDA were back in court quarreling over the timeframe within which the agency was required to take action. Despite FDA's 30-year delay in scheduling the NADA withdrawal proceedings, the court approved the agency's proposed timeline over a quicker schedule requested by NRDC.

Natural Resources Defense Council v. Food and Drug Administration

884 F.Supp.2d 108 (S.D.N.Y. 2012).

■ JAMES C. FRANCIS IV, UNITED STATES MAGISTRATE JUDGE.

. . . .

In compliance with the March 22 Order, the parties have submitted briefs on the issue of a schedule for the FDA's withdrawal proceedings. The Government asks that I refrain from imposing any deadlines, stating that "subject to any future direction by the appellate courts, it intends to abide by the orders of the Court." In the alternative, the Government proposes a timeline—derived from an "analysis to estimate the time and resources that would be required"—that requires reissuance of the NOOHs within 11 to 17 months, with an additional period of years to complete the withdrawal process, including administrative appeals. NRDC, in contrast, asserts that a schedule is essential, and that the Government's "protracted" timing estimate should be slashed so that the NOOHs are required to be issued within 125 days of commencement of the process and withdrawal proceedings are complete in an additional two years.

1. Authority to Impose a Schedule

Even in the area of administrative law, district courts have "broad equitable powers" to order "any appropriate relief" that is not prohibited by Congress. However, a court must be careful not to intrude "into the domain which Congress has set aside exclusively for the administrative agency." . . . However, it is clear that if an agency has unreasonably delayed dispatching its duty, it is permissible for a court to impose a timetable for compliance.

. . . In granting NRDC's motion for summary judgment, Judge Katz did not make an explicit finding that the FDA unreasonably delayed action. However, he did mark the agency's "prolonged inaction" and repeatedly referred to its decades-long failure to commence withdrawal proceedings. . . . The fact that the March 22 Order lacks a discussion of unreasonable delay does not indicate, as the Government would have it, that it is "[not] present here" as a factual matter. Nor does it mean that I cannot consider whether the agency has in fact unreasonably delayed institution of withdrawal proceedings in deciding how to exercise the court's "broad equitable powers" to order relief.

To decide whether there has been unreasonable delay meriting the imposition of a schedule or deadline, I am guided by "six principles that have helped courts determine when mandamus is an appropriate remedy for agency delay":

(1) the time agencies take to make decisions must be governed by a "rule of reason"; (2) where Congress has provided a timetable or other indication of the speed with which it expects the agency to proceed in the enabling statute, that statutory scheme may supply content for this rule of reason; (3) delays that might be reasonable in the sphere of economic regulation are less tolerable when human health and welfare are at stake; (4) the court should consider the effect of expediting delayed action on agency activities of a higher or competing priority; (5) the court should also take into account the nature and extent of the interests prejudiced by the delay; and (6) the court need not find any impropriety lurking behind agency lassitude in order to hold that agency action is unreasonably delayed.

In re Barr Laboratories, Inc., 930 F.2d 272 (D.C. Cir. 1991) (citing *Telecommunications Research & Action Center v. FCC*, 750 F.2d 70 (D.C. Cir. 1984).

As the March 22 Order makes clear, the finding that triggered the FDA's duty to commence withdrawal proceedings was memorialized in the 1977 NOOHs. This lawsuit was filed over thirty years later, in 2011. During the intervening decades, the FDA did not perform its statutorily-prescribed duty to initiate, let alone complete, withdrawal proceedings. Although Congress has not provided guidance on the issue, I have no difficulty concluding that thirty-plus years is an unreasonable delay.

The Government complains that imposing a timetable will impermissibly re-order its priorities, citing *Barr Laboratories*. In that case, a drug manufacturer sought a writ of mandamus compelling the FDA to act on its generic drug applications. Although the law required action within 180 days of receipt of the applications, the FDA admitted that action on such applications took significantly longer and estimated that in the future, it could take almost two years. Nonetheless, the court refused to issue the writ, explaining that "a judicial order putting Barr at the head of the queue simply moves all others back one space and produces no net gain."

This case is easily distinguishable. In *Barr Laboratories,* the writ of mandamus would have effectively controlled the agency's generic drug approval process, benefitting one enterprise at the expense of others, failing to improve the efficiency of the process of approving (or disapproving) generic drugs, and having no effect on human health and welfare. Here, the FDA has utterly failed in its duty to initiate congressionally-mandated withdrawal proceedings. Requiring it to do so promptly is not reordering the FDA's priorities; it is correcting the agency's misprision of its duty. In *Barr Laboratories,* the court found that the contemplated order would have no effect on human health and welfare. Here, in contrast, compelling the FDA to timely fulfill its obligations will speed adjudication on the issue of whether the non-therapeutic use of certain antibiotics in animal feed threatens human health and, if the sponsors or other interested parties cannot demonstrate the drugs' safety, accelerate their compulsory withdrawal.

The Government repeatedly asserts that a schedule should not be imposed because the FDA did not believe it had "a legal duty to proceed with hearings." However, as the District of Columbia Circuit makes clear, "the court need not find any impropriety lurking behind agency lassitude in order to hold that agency action is unreasonably delayed." . . . Moreover, the FDA seems to have a pattern of attempting to avoid instituting proceedings to withdraw approval of the non-therapeutic use of antibiotics in animal feed. As detailed in the June 1 Order, in 1999 and 2005 certain plaintiffs (as well as other entities) filed citizen petitions with the FDA seeking such proceedings. The FDA delayed final action on the petitions for "thirteen and seven years, respectively." It was not until November 7, 2011, during the pendency of this litigation, that the agency issued final responses denying the petitions, citing the time and expense of holding withdrawal proceedings. . . .

2. Schedule for Compliance

The Government has conducted an analysis to determine the likely amount of time it will take to perform each of the tasks required to comply with the March 22 Order and supports the schedule with a declaration from Dr. William T. Flynn, the CVM's Deputy Director for Science Policy. NRDC objects to the proposed time estimates as "protracted", "leisurely", "vague", "excessive", and "generous", and suggests a significantly abbreviated schedule. While the government's position draws on its expertise, including experience with prior withdrawal proceedings, plaintiffs' arguments are largely speculative.

. . . .

The agency is in the best position to analyze the issue and propose a realistic schedule that is not based on unsupported assumptions, but rather on its expertise, and it has done so. Therefore, I adopt the Government's proposed schedule, which requires issuance of revised NOOHs for penicillin and tetracyclines in 17 months, and provides an additional 41 months for the hearing process.

. . . .

NOTE

Proposed Legislation. Legislation has been introduced in both houses of Congress aimed at preserving the efficiency of antibiotics by eliminating the subtherapeutic uses in food-producing animals. The Preservation of Antibiotics for Medical Treatment Act of 2013 (PAMTA) was introduced in the House of Representatives in March 2013, and the Preventing Antibiotic Resistance Act of 2013 was introduced in the Senate in June 2013. Both bills would allow the use of antibiotics in food-producing animals only to treat disease, thereby eliminating subtherapeutic uses.

Despite the narrative of agency neglect contained in the opinions above, in one instance, FDA has taken a concrete regulatory step to address the problem of antibiotic resistance. In 1996, FDA approved a NADA submitted by Bayer for enrofloxacin to reduce *Campylobacter* infections in chickens and turkey. Almost immediately, the agency became concerned about the development of *Campylobacter* resistance in humans, and four years later it proposed to withdraw approval. Bayer demanded the evidentiary hearing to which the Act entitled it.

This hearing concluded with the ruling of an Administrative Law Judge upholding the withdrawal. In the following decision, the Acting FDA Commissioner, Dr. Lester Crawford, affirmed the ALJ.

Withdrawal of Approval of the New Animal Drug Application for Enrofloxacin in Poultry: Final Decision of the Commissioner

FDA Docket No. 2000N–1571 (July 27, 2005).

Enrofloxacin is an antimicrobial drug belonging to a class of drugs known as fluoroquinolones. On October 31, 2000, the Center for Veterinary Medicine (CVM) of the U.S. Food and Drug Administration (FDA) published a Notice of Opportunity for Hearing (NOOH) proposing to withdraw the approval of the new animal drug application (NADA) 140.828 for the use of enrofloxacin in chickens and turkeys. 65 Fed. Reg. 64,954 (2000). On November 29, 2000, Bayer Corporation (Bayer), the sponsor of enrofloxacin (sold under the trade name Baytril® 3.23% Concentrate Antimicrobial Solution), requested a hearing on the proposed withdrawal. . . . On March 21, 2002, the Animal Health Institute (AHI) submitted a Notice of Participation pursuant to 21 CFR § 12.45, identifying itself in part as "the national trade association representing research based manufacturers of animal health products."

. . . .

On March 16, 2004, the ALJ [Administrative Law Judge] issued an Initial Decision pursuant to 21 CFR § 12.120. The ALJ found, among other things, that more than a million people annually suffer from infections caused by Campylobacter, a genus of bacteria; that poultry is a source of *Campylobacter* infections; that the use of enrofloxacin in poultry results in the emergence and dissemination of fluoroquinolone-resistant *Campylobacter*; that fluoroquinolone-resistant *Campylobacter* in poultry can be transferred to humans and "can contribute to" fluoroquinolone-resistant *Campylobacter* infections in humans; and that fluoroquinolone-resistant *Campylobacter* infections in humans "have the potential to adversely affect human health." . . . Based on these and other findings, the ALJ determined that "Bayer has not shown Baytril use in poultry to be safe" as set out in § 512(e)(1)(B) of the Federal Food, Drug, and Cosmetic Act (FDCA), 21 U.S.C. § 360b(e)(1)(B).

. . . .

After reviewing the evidentiary record of the hearing, I find that the record supports the ALJ's determination. . . . However, my reasoning varies in several regards from that of the ALJ. I therefore am withdrawing the approval of the NADA for use of enrofloxacin in poultry for the reasons set forth more fully in this Final Decision. . . .

CVM proposed to withdraw approval of enrofloxacin pursuant to § 512(e)(1)(B) of the FDCA, which provides:

> The Secretary shall, after due notice and opportunity for hearing to the applicant, issue an order withdrawing approval of an application filed pursuant to subsection (b) with respect to any new animal drug if the Secretary finds . . .

(B) that new evidence not contained in such application or not available to the Secretary until after such application was approved, or tests by new methods, or tests by methods not deemed reasonably applicable when such application was approved, evaluated together with the evidence available to the Secretary when the application was approved, shows that such drug is not shown to be safe for use under the conditions of use upon the basis of which the application was approved. . . .

I agree with the Initial Decision's general description of the allocation of the burdens between CVM and Bayer. CVM, as the proponent of withdrawal of approval of the use of enrofloxacin in poultry, has the burden of making the first showing; in other words, CVM has the initial burden of production. Once this threshold burden has been satisfied, the burden passes to Bayer, as the sponsor of enrofloxacin, to demonstrate its safety. *Rhone–Poulenc, Inc. v. FDA*, 636 F.2d 750, 752 (D.C. Cir. 1980) (*per curiam*); *Hess & Clark*, 495 F.2d at 992; 21 CFR § 12.87(d).

. . . Bayer, as the sponsor of enrofloxacin, has the ultimate burden of persuasion regarding the safety of the drug. . . .

DISCUSSION

. . . .

A. *Human Campylobacter Infections in the United States*

. . . *Campylobacter* is a genus of bacteria with many different species, a number of which are known to cause illness in humans, although two, *Campylobacter jejuni* (abbreviated as *C. jejuni*) and *Campylobacter coli* (*C. coli*), are identified as the cause of almost all cultured human infections. *Campylobacter* is recognized as a leading cause of gastroenteritis in many developed and developing countries. In the United States, the most important, in terms of human infection, is *C. jejuni*. . . .

Based on data from 1996–1997 (adjusted for underreporting), in 1999 CDC [U.S. Centers for Disease Control and Prevention] estimated that 2.4 million illnesses in the United States each year are caused by *Campylobacter*, of which approximately 80% were food borne infections. In that analysis, CDC estimated that about 14.2% of food borne illness in the United States annually is caused by *Campylobacter* infection, making it the leading bacterial source of food borne illness in this country.

. . . [A]lthough the incidence of these infections has declined in recent years, I find that the record demonstrates that *Campylobacter* infections remain a major cause of food borne illness in the United States.

Campylobacter infections in humans are characterized by fever, headache, abdominal pain, and diarrhea (bloody or watery), usually 24–72 hours after ingestion of the contaminated food. Less frequently, patients may suffer from muscle aches and vomiting.

Campylobacter infection in humans ... may resolve without antibiotics or other pharmaceutical treatment. However, in some patients the illness may be prolonged or more severe. In addition, *Campylobacter* infections can occasionally result in significant and sometimes long term adverse health outcomes. . . .

Finally, there is a very low possibility of death associated with *Campylobacter* infections. Mortality in the United States associated with *Campylobacter* is low, with estimates ranging from 8 per 10,000 to 24 per 10,000. . . .

I find that the record demonstrates that fluoroquinolones, such as ciprofloxacin, are widely used to treat gastroenteritis, because they are generally well-tolerated, can be prescribed on an outpatient basis, and are effective against a broad range of bacteria. . . .

B.   *Enrofloxacin Use and Campylobacter in Poultry*

On October 4, 1996, FDA approved NADA 140–828 under § 512 of the FDCA, authorizing the use of enrofloxacin (Baytril® 3.23% Concentrate Antimicrobial Solution) to control mortality in chickens associated with *Escherichia coli* (*E. coli*) and mortality in turkeys associated with *E. coli* and *Pasteurella multocida* (fowl cholera). FDA approved the use of enrofloxacin only by prescription and under veterinary supervision, and only for therapeutic treatment (*i.e.*, not for growth promotion). FDA prohibited the extra-label use of enrofloxacin for all food-producing animals, including poultry. . . .

. . . I find that commercially produced chickens and turkeys in the United States are frequently colonized with *Campylobacter*, and that the colonization of *Campylobacter* persists until slaughter. I further find that the selection for fluoroquinolone-resistant *Campylobacter* occurs rapidly in poultry following initiation of fluoroquinolone treatment, and that fluoroquinolone-resistant *Campylobacter* persist until slaughter.

In contrast, I find the absence of fluoroquinolone treatment of poultry to be associated with a very low level of fluoroquinolone resistance in such untreated poultry, despite the fact that the actual mutation occurs spontaneously. This is important evidence linking the use of enrofloxacin in poultry to the emergence of resistant *Campylobacter* infections in poultry and exposure of humans to resistant *Campylobacter*.

C.   *Poultry Consumption as a Risk Factor for Human Campylobacter Infection*

In addition to the data on persistent colonization of live poultry with susceptible *Campylobacter* and resistant *Campylobacter*, the presence of susceptible and resistant *Campylobacter* in and on broilers and turkeys presented for slaughter, and the frequency of contamination of poultry carcasses with susceptible and resistant *Campylobacter*, there is substantial other evidence supporting my determination that, in the United States, poultry consumption is a primary risk factor for human infections with *Campylobacter*, including fluoroquinolone-resistant *Campylobacter*. . . .

      . . . .

In sum, the record shows that illness can occur at very low levels of exposure to *Campylobacter*. I find that there is no scientific justification for disregarding the retail meat studies because they do not provide a measure of bacterial load. The retail meat studies show that the contamination of poultry meat persists to and after the point of purchase, providing further evidence in the link between fluoroquinolone use in poultry and fluoroquinolone-resistant *Campylobacter* infections in humans. We know from these studies that, in different areas of the country and over a range of recent years, all researchers investigating retail meat contamination have found that a large proportion of retail poultry products is contaminated with *Campylobacter*. Moreover, recent studies consistently have shown that a large proportion of the products is contaminated with *Campylobacter* that are resistant to fluoroquinolones. This is important evidence linking human infections to poultry consumption. . . .

Several case-control studies from the United States and elsewhere have shown that the risk of *Campylobacter* infection is significantly elevated with respect to: consumption of poultry generally; poultry consumption in restaurants; consumption of undercooked or raw poultry; handling of raw chicken; and failure to clean food preparation or cutting board surfaces. The association between poultry and *Campylobacter* infections in humans is generally consistent across studies, despite broad differences in size, methodology, and sample population. . . .

The epidemiologic studies I have described thus far identified risk factors for acquiring *Campylobacter* infections, without consideration of the susceptibility or resistance of the bacteria to fluoroquinolones. However, the record demonstrates, and I find, that there are no significant biologic reasons that transmission of fluoroquinolone-resistant *Campylobacter* infections from animals to humans is different from transmission of fluoroquinolone-susceptible infections. As a result, it can be expected that when resistance to fluoroquinolones emerges in *Campylobacter* in animals, resistant *Campylobacter* will be transmitted to humans, and investigations have shown temporally that this in fact occurs.

. . . .

I also find that data from several countries, including the United States, indicate that a rise in human *Campylobacter* infections that are resistant to fluoroquinolones has consistently followed the introduction of enrofloxacin in poultry production in that country. . . . [A]n indication that an exposure precedes the outcome of interest is consistent with a causal association. . . .

CVM introduced into evidence a quantitative assessment of the human health impact of fluoroquinolone-resistant *Campylobacter* infections attributed to the consumption of contaminated chicken. The question the risk assessment addresses was whether the use of fluoroquinolones in poultry introduced a significant human health burden associated with a specific prevalence of fluoroquinolone resistance in poultry carcasses, and, if so, whether any action by CVM would significantly reduce that burden. Using the risk assessment model, CVM estimated that in 1998 about 8,678 people and in 1999 about 9,261 people were expected to be infected with fluoroquinolone-resistant *Campylobacter* from consuming chicken, receive fluoroquinolone treatment, and experience a longer duration of illness because of the decreased effectiveness of the antibiotic.

. . . .

The risk assessment was not published in a peer reviewed journal. It was, however, subject to extensive public review and layers of expert review within and outside of FDA. . . .

Although I have found that the [Information Quality Act] does not afford Bayer any legal basis to challenge the reliability of any of CVM's evidence in the context of this administrative proceeding, under the unique circumstances of this proceeding, I now have pending before me [the Animal Health Institute's] IQA request for correction and request for reconsideration . . . I am therefore taking the unusual step of also resolving, in this Final Decision, AHI's request for correction of the CVM risk assessment. . . .

Based on several factual findings set forth in this Final Decision, I find that, even assuming that the risk assessment is properly considered "influential" under FDA's Guidelines, and is otherwise subject to the IQA, the process by which the risk assessment was produced (which predated the enactment of the IQA and the issuance of OMB, HHS, and FDA guidelines), was nonetheless consistent with the FDA Guidelines, even those for influential information, and that no correction of the risk assessment is warranted.

. . . .

DISCUSSION OF LEGAL ISSUES

A.   *New evidence*

. . . § 512(e)(1)(B) of the FDCA requires withdrawal of a new animal drug application if the Commissioner finds that "new evidence not contained in [a new animal drug] application or not available to the [Commissioner] until after such application was approved, or tests by new methods, or tests by methods not deemed reasonably applicable when such application was approved, evaluated together with the evidence available to the [Commissioner] when the application was approved" shows that the new animal drug is no longer shown to be safe. . . .

In its exceptions, Bayer contests whether there is "new evidence" on enrofloxacin use in poultry. Bayer argues that evidence about a drug that is generated after approval of the drug cannot be "new evidence" under § 512(e)(1)(B) of the FDCA unless it "points to a different conclusion that was not contained in the original application. . . ." In effect, Bayer argues that if FDA is aware that a human health risk could occur or exists when it approves a new animal drug, then post-approval evidence relating to that risk cannot be "new evidence."

. . . While it is clear that the content of the evidence is critical to my determination of whether CVM has met its burden to produce evidence raising serious questions about enrofloxacin's safety, I do not find support for such a content-driven definition of "new" in the statute or its legislative history. To the contrary, § 512(e)(1)(B) requires that I must make my determination about whether an animal drug "is not shown to be safe" based on "new evidence . . . evaluated together with the evidence available to [me] when the application was approved." 21 U.S.C. § 360b(e)(1)(B). In other words, I must find both that there is "new" evidence, and that the collective weight of the evidence in front of me, old and new, shows that the drug in question is no longer shown to be safe.

. . . .

B. *The meaning of "safe"*

. . . I agree with the ALJ that when assessing whether food from animals treated with a new animal drug is safe for human consumption, it is correct to frame the meaning of "safe" as presenting a "reasonable certainty of no harm." I conclude, as FDA has before, that an assessment of the human health impacts of the use of a particular drug in food-producing animals under the "reasonable certainty of no harm" standard involves a straightforward evaluation of the human safety of the animal drug; it does not encompass any weighing of costs and benefits, including any weighing of human safety concerns (in other words, health risks) against human health benefits. I find that the FDCA as a whole, as well as its legislative history, makes clear that Congress did not intend to allow FDA to weigh costs or benefits associated with the use of a new animal drug in deciding whether its use has been shown to be safe for humans when used in food-producing animals.

When FDA reviews an application for approval of a use of a new animal drug in a food-producing animal, the agency must find: 1) that the drug is safe and effective in the target animal, and 2) that food from the animal is safe for human consumption. . . .

The target animal safety standard of § 512 originated from the new drug safety standard used in § 505 which, until 1968, applied to both human and animal drugs. Thus, FDA, when implementing the 1968 Animal Drug Amendments, continued to use, and still uses, this same standard when it is reviewing whether a new animal drug is safe for use in or on the target animal. Thus, FDA may, in evaluating a NADA, look at both the risks and benefits a new animal drug will have with respect to the target animal. Section 505 however, provides no direct insight into the process by which FDA evaluates the human food safety of animal drugs. . . .

. . . Section 409(a), 21 U.S.C. 348(a), requires that uses of "food additives" be approved by FDA as safe prior to their use in food. . . . This broad definition of food additive included drugs used in animal feed and food-producing animals. Therefore, these animal drugs were subject to § 409's safety standard.

Congress defined "safe" for purposes of § 409. Section 201(t) (now § 201(u)) provided: "The term 'safe' as used in paragraph(s) of this section [the definition of food additive] and in section 409, has reference to the health of man or animal." . . .

By framing the safety standard as "reasonable certainty of no harm," [the] legislative history [of § 409] makes it clear that weighing costs and benefits, including any weighing of health risks and benefits, was not envisioned by Congress as part of the assessment of the safety of food additives.

Furthermore, Congress explicitly rejected consideration of benefits as part of the food additive approval process.

. . . .

Because the human food safety standard of § 512 originated from the "reasonable certainty of no harm" standard used in § 409, FDA, when implementing the 1968 Animal Drug Amendments, continued to use, and still uses, this same standard when it is reviewing whether food from an animal treated with a new animal drug is safe for human consumption. Thus, in making a determination . . . whether food from animals treated with a new animal drug is safe for human consumption, FDA looks only at whether there are human health risks from the use of the drug and does not consider whether there are any benefits to humans from the use of the drug.

. . . .

Bayer relies on two D.C. Circuit cases, *Hess & Clark, Inc. v. FDA*, 495 F.2d 975 (D.C. Cir. 1974), and *Rhone–Poulenc, Inc. v. FDA*, 636 F.2d 750 (D.C. Cir. 1980), in support of its argument that, in assessing human food safety, I must weigh all of these alleged benefits of enrofloxacin's use in poultry against the human health risks such use poses. The ALJ found that these D.C. Circuit cases implicitly have been overruled by two Supreme Court rulings, *Donovan*, 452 U.S. 490 (1981), and *American Trucking*, 531 U.S. 457 (2001). . . .

. . . Based on my review, I conclude that the Supreme Court has effectively overruled those parts of *Hess & Clark* and *Rhone–Poulenc* that address consideration of costs and benefits as part of a withdrawal of approval of a new animal drug based on human food safety risks.

Hess & Clark involved a challenge to FDA's decision to withdraw, without a hearing, the approval of the new animal drug diethylstilbestrol (DES) for use in cattle and sheep. After ruling that FDA had not given the sponsors adequate notice of the grounds for withdrawal, the D.C. Circuit stated:

> Outside of the *per se* rule of the Delaney Clause, the typical issue for the FDA is not the absolute safety of a drug. Most drugs are unsafe in some degree. Rather, the issue for the FDA is whether to allow sale of the drug, usually under specific restrictions. Resolution of this issue inevitably means calculating whether the benefits which the drug produces outweigh the costs of its restricted use. In the present case, DES is asserted to be of substantial benefit in enhancing meat production. . . .

In *Rhone–Poulenc*, the D.C. Circuit . . . the court noted that it was "bound by the holding of the *Hess & Clark* court until we are instructed otherwise by the Supreme Court or an *en banc* decision of this court."

A year after *Rhone–Poulenc* was decided, the Supreme Court decided *Donovan*. At issue was whether the Occupational Safety and Health Administration (OSHA) was required to compare costs and benefits when setting a standard for harmful agents under § 6(b)(5) of the Occupational Safety and Health Act (OSH Act), 29 U.S.C. § 655(b)(5). This provision states that OSHA is to set a standard "which most adequately assures that, to the extent feasible . . . no employee will suffer material impairment of health or functional capacity even if such employee has regular exposure to the hazard dealt with by the standard for the period of his working life." The Supreme Court concluded that this provision did not permit comparison of costs and benefits. . . . [T]he Court said, "[w]hen Congress has intended that an agency engage in cost-benefit analysis, it has clearly indicated such intent on the face of the statute." . . . In the *Nitrofurans* Final Decision, FDA Commissioner David Kessler concluded that *Donovan* is "ample authority for the proposition that clauses like the [FDCA's] general safety clause do not permit, much less invite, cost/benefit analysis." I agree.

. . . .

C.   Bayer's Evidence on Costs and Benefits

Because I conclude that CVM has met its initial burden of coming forward with evidence to show that there are serious questions about enrofloxacin's safety, the burden then shifts to Bayer to show that the use of enrofloxacin in chickens and turkeys is safe and that FDA should continue to approve such use. I conclude . . . that Bayer has not met its burden.

7.   BIOENGINEERED ANIMALS

Whereas FDA regulates genetically modified food plant organisms pursuant to its food authorities, *see supra* p. 458, it regulates genetically modified animals—whether or not they are used for food—under its animal drug authorities.

The press has devoted much attention in recent years to the NADA filed by AquaBounty for the AquaAdvantage® Salmon. This is an Atlantic salmon that includes a gene from the Pacific Chinook salmon and a gene from an eel-like fish called the ocean pout, which together allow the bioengineered fish to grow to market size in half the time of conventional salmon. AquaBounty submitted this application in 1995, and it remains unapproved today. As discussed in Chapter 15, *infra* p. 1529, much of the hesitation about allowing the marketing of the AquaAdvantage Salmon concerns the environmental impact it might have if it were to escape and breed with wild salmon. If FDA ultimately approves the NADA, the AquaAdvantage Salmon will be the first bioengineered animal approved by FDA pursuant to the scheme described in the following guidance.

Guidance for Industry: Regulation of Genetically Engineered Animals Containing Heritable Recombinant DNA Constructs
January 15, 2009.

I.   Introduction and Background

. . . GE [genetically engineered] animals have been produced since the early 1980s when Brinster et al. (1982) and Palmiter et al. (1982) reported on the development of GE mice. . . . Now, more than two decades later, many different species, including those traditionally consumed as food, have been genetically engineered with various rDNA constructs.

For the purpose of this guidance, FDA defines "genetically engineered (GE) animals" as those animals modified by rDNA techniques, including the entire lineage of animals that contain the modification. The term GE animal can refer to both animals with heritable rDNA constructs and animals with non-heritable rDNA constructs (e.g., those modifications intended to be used as gene therapy). Although much of this guidance will be relevant to non-heritable rDNA constructs . . . this guidance only pertains to GE animals containing heritable rDNA constructs. . . .

GE animals currently being developed can be divided into six broad classes based on the intended purpose of the genetic modification: (1) to enhance production or food quality traits (e.g., pigs with less environmentally deleterious wastes, faster growing fish); (2) to improve animal health (e.g., disease resistance); (3) to produce products intended for human therapeutic use (e.g., pharmaceutical products or tissues for transplantation; these GE animals are sometimes referred to as "biopharm" animals); (4) to enrich or enhance the animals' interactions with humans (e.g., hypo-allergenic pets); (5) to develop animal models for human diseases (e.g., pigs as models for cardiovascular diseases); and (6) to produce industrial or consumer products (e.g., fibers for multiple uses).

The Center for Veterinary Medicine ("CVM") of the United States Food and Drug Administration has been working on applications submitted by developers of GE animals under the New Animal Drug provisions of the Federal Food Drug and Cosmetic Act. This guidance is intended to clarify our requirements and recommendations for producers and developers ("sponsors," "you") of GE animals and their products. . . .

II. Statutory and Regulatory Authority

. . . The definition of a drug, in section 201(g) of the [FD&C Act], includes "articles intended for use in the diagnosis, cure, mitigation, treatment, or prevention of disease in man or other animals;" and "articles (other than food) intended to affect the structure or any function of the body of man or other animals." The definition of "new animal drug" in section 201(v) of the Act includes that it is a drug intended for use in animals that is not generally recognized as safe and effective for use under the conditions prescribed, recommended, or suggested in the drug's labeling, and that has not been used to a material extent or for a material time.

Generally under the Act, a new animal drug is "deemed unsafe" unless FDA has approved a new animal drug application (NADA) for that particular use, unless the drug is only for investigational use and conforms to specified exemptions for such use under an Investigational New Animal Drug (INAD) exemption, or unless the drug is used in conformance with regulations promulgated under sections 512(a)(4) or (5) of the Act [concerning off-label uses on the order of a veterinarian].

The rDNA construct in a GE animal that is intended to affect the structure or function of the body of the GE animal, regardless of the intended use of products that may be produced by the GE animal, meets the FFDCA drug definition. . . .

In most cases, the methods used to introduce a new rDNA construct into the germline of an animal do not control the site in the genome where the construct will end up. Therefore, animals derived from different introductions of rDNA constructs (referred to as "transformation events") will likely have their rDNA constructs at different sites in the genome. The rDNA construct at a specific site in the genome is the subject of the NADA.

Because the site at which an rDNA construct is located can affect both the health of the animal and the level and control of expression of the construct (i.e., its effectiveness), in general, each animal lineage derived from a separate transformation event (or series of transformation events) is considered to contain a separate new animal drug subject to a separate new animal drug approval. However, during the investigational phase, a single INAD file may be established containing information on investigational GE animals that contain different numbers or types of rDNA constructs, or rDNA constructs at different integrations sites, prior to selecting the GE animal intended for commercialization.

Each new animal drug approval covers all animals containing the same rDNA construct (the regulated article or new animal drug) derived from the same transformation event, including, for example, animals containing that rDNA construct as a result of breeding between a non-GE animal and a GE animal. We consider all GE animals derived from the same transformation event to contain the same article and to be subject to evaluation under a single NADA. . . .

Because GE animals that are being used for commercial purposes are likely to be descendents [sic] of the initial GE animal, rather than the initial GE animal itself, the NADA safety and effectiveness evaluations should be focused on a generation as close to those animals to be used for commercial purposes as possible. . . .

Although all GE animals are subject to premarket approval requirements, in certain circumstances, based on the risk(s) they pose, we intend to exercise enforcement discretion with regard to INAD and NADA requirements for certain GE animals. . . . For example, FDA has not and does not intend to take enforcement action with respect to INAD and NADA requirements for: (1) GE animals of non-food-species that are regulated by other government agencies or entities, such as GE insects being developed for plant pest control or animal health protection, and that are under APHIS oversight; and (2) GE animals of non-food-species that are raised and used in contained and controlled conditions such as GE laboratory animals used in research institutions. . . .

Based on evaluation of risk factors, we may exercise enforcement discretion over INAD and NADA requirements for additional kinds or uses of non-food-species GE animals, as we did after reviewing information about *Zebra danio* aquarium fish genetically engineered to fluoresce in the dark (GloFish) (*Int'l Ctr. for Tech. Assessment v. Thompson*, 421 F. Supp. 2d 1 (D.D.C. 2006)). . . .

When FDA reviews and approves an INAD or NADA, it complies with the requirements of the National Environmental Policy Act (NEPA), including a review of environmental risks where required. When FDA exercises its enforcement discretion over the INAD or NADA requirements, no NEPA review would take place. As a result, environmental risks are among the factors we intend to consider in determining whether to exercise enforcement discretion. . . .

III. Investigational Use of GE Animals

. . . The INAD requirements in 21 CFR 511.1(b) apply to investigational GE animals. Further, the development of GE animals constitutes clinical investigation because it involves studying the effectiveness of the drug in the target species and the effects of the rDNA construct, including those of its expression product(s), on the animal containing it.

. . . Section 511.1(b) . . . requires that prior to shipping a new animal drug for clinical tests, a sponsor must submit a Notice of Claimed Investigational Exemption for a New Animal Drug (INAD Notice) containing specified information.

. . . [W]e strongly recommend that you submit an INAD Notice early in your development of GE animals. We will then establish an INAD file that will enable you to begin discussions with us on how best to develop the data and information that will be needed for an NADA, and to provide such data and information to us for evaluation and comment. . . .

A primary goal during the investigational phase of development of the GE animal is to ensure that edible products from the GE animals do not enter the food or feed supply without prior FDA authorization. . . . We recommend that all surplus investigational animals and their biological products be disposed of by incineration, burial, or composting, and that appropriate records be kept of animal identification and disposition. . . .

Actions on INADs are considered federal actions under the National Environmental Policy Act (NEPA), and as such may require preparation of an environmental assessment (EA) (21 CFR 511.1(b)(10), 21 CFR 25.15) or environmental impact statement (EIS) (21 CFR 25.22).

Through the preparation of an EA or EIS, FDA will examine the potential for environmental impacts, including the potential for inadvertent release or escape of the GE animal and/or its products into the environment, and whether certain measures may mitigate any potential significant impacts that would adversely affect the human environment. . . .

IV. FDA Approval of GE Animals

Other than for investigational uses, section 512(a)(1) of the Act requires that a new animal drug be the subject of an approved new animal drug application (NADA) based on a demonstration that it is safe and effective for its intended use.

When submitting an NADA, you should include the results of any investigations you conducted under an INAD. We will evaluate the

NADA to determine whether you have demonstrated that the new animal drug is safe and effective for its intended use. To demonstrate effectiveness of an article intended to express an extractable protein (e.g., for use as a human biologic), generally you would simply have to show that the expression product is in fact expressed in the animal. To demonstrate effectiveness of an article intended to alter a characteristic of the resulting GE animal, in general you would have to show that the GE animal had the claimed altered characteristic (e.g., that its rate of growth was as claimed or that it was indeed resistant to a disease).

. . . [W]e intend to hold public advisory committee meetings prior to approving any GE animal. We may revisit that policy in the future as we gain more experience with reviews of GE animals.

. . . .

Section 514.1(b)(3) requires that an NADA include three copies of each piece of labeling to be used for the new animal drug.

. . . Labeling should include a summary description of the article, the animal into which the article is introduced (e.g., common name/breed/line; genus and species), the name of the resulting GE animal line, and the intended use of the GE animal containing the article. Where the labeling for a GE animal contains animal care or safety information (e.g., husbandry or containment), we recommend that the labeling accompany the animal throughout all stages of its lifecycle. . . .

We note that labeling of food from GE animals would be subject to the same requirements as food from non-GE animals, and that as with food from GE plants, the fact that the animal from which food was obtained was genetically engineered would not be material information with respect to labeling. However, if food from a GE animal is different from that of its non-engineered counterpart, for example if it has a different nutritional profile, in general that difference would be material information that would have to be revealed in labeling.

. . . .

To facilitate the evaluation of GE animals under the existing regulatory framework for new animal drugs, we have developed the following approach for submitting data for an NADA for GE animals. . . .

Step 1: Product Identification

Product identification (21 CFR 514.1(b)(1)), which many molecular biologists would refer to as product definition, forms the foundation for the evaluation process and drives subsequent data generation and review. It encompasses the specific GE animal (that is, the article as well as the GE animal containing it) and the purpose (i.e., intended use) of the article that is the subject of the NADA. . . .

Step 2: Molecular Characterization of the Construct

This step of the process serves to describe the components and composition of the article. (21 CFR 514.1(b)(4).) For this step, we recommend that you provide information for identifying and characterizing the rDNA construct that will be introduced into the progenitor of the GE animal that will be marketed. . . .

In order to determine whether any risks exist that would make the product unsafe, we expect to evaluate whether the rDNA construct contains any potentially mobilizeable DNA sequences, or whether sequences are present that encode pathogens, toxins (including allergens), or substances likely to dysregulate the growth control of cells, tissues, or organs, except by explicit design.

Step 3: Molecular Characterization of the GE Animal Lineage

This step continues the analysis of the rDNA construct in the resulting GE animal, as well as the production of the GE animal(s) intended to be used in commerce and any potential hazards that may be introduced into those animals as part of their production. As such, this step addresses the identity and some manufacturing requirements of your NADA. 21 CFR 514.1(b)(1) and (b)(5). We recommend that you provide data and information describing the method by which you introduced the rDNA construct into the initial GE animal. . . . In addition, we recommend that you describe the breeding strategy you used to produce the lineage progenitor (the GE animal that contains the final stabilized version of the initial event and from which the GE animals to be used for commercial purposes are derived). You should fully characterize the final stabilized rDNA construct in the GE animal.

Step 4: Phenotypic Characterization of GE Animal

The previous steps of the review process have concentrated on establishing and characterizing the rDNA construct and its integration into the resulting GE animals. Information in this and the following steps helps establish whether the GE animal poses any risks to humans, risks to health of the GE animal, or risks to the environment.

With regard to health of the GE animal, including the target animal safety requirements of 21 CFR 514.1(b)(8), we recommend that you submit data regarding whether the rDNA construct or its expression product(s) cause any direct or indirect toxicity. In general, we recommend that you compile and submit data and information addressing the health of the GE animals, including veterinary and treatment records, growth rates, reproductive function, and behavior. In addition, we recommend that you submit data on the physiological status of the GE animals. . . .

Step 5: Genotypic and Phenotypic Durability Assessment

As in Step 3, this step also addresses some additional components of the manufacturing requirements codified in 21 CFR 514.1(b)(5). It is intended to provide information to ensure that the rDNA construct in the GE animal resulting from the specific transformation event and defining (identifying) the GE animal being evaluated is durable—that there is a reasonable expectation that the rDNA construct is stably inherited, and the phenotype is consistent and predictable. . . .

For genotypic durability, we recommend that you use the results of studies demonstrating that the rDNA construct is stably inherited. For the phenotypic durability portion of the plan, we recommend that you submit data on the consistency of the expressed trait (based on the intended use) over multiple generations. . . .

Step 6: The Food/Feed Safety and Environmental Safety Assessments

Food/Feed Safety

This part of Step 6 addresses the food and feed safety requirements in 21 CFR 514.1(b)(8). It focuses on the issue of whether food or feed derived from a GE animal is safe for humans or animals consuming edible products from the animals.

The risk issues involved in determining food and feed safety can be divided into two overall categories. The first addresses whether there is any direct toxicity, including allergenicity, via food or feed consumption of the expression product of the article. The second category addresses potential indirect toxicity associated with both the article and its expressed product (e.g., whether location or expression of the article affects physiological processes in the resulting animal such that unintended food/feed consumption hazards are created, or whether existing food/feed consumption risks are increased). . . .

In the end, if the expression product(s) is shown to be safe, and the composition of edible tissues from the GE animal is shown to be as safe as those from animals of the same or comparable type that are commonly and safely consumed, then we expect to view this as evidence that food and feed derived from the GE animal is safe (i.e., there is a reasonable certainty of no harm from consumption of the food or feed).

. . . .

Environmental Safety

This portion of Step 6 addresses the environmental component of your NADA. 21 CFR 514.1(b)(14). We expect that, at least until we have more experience, most GE animal applications would have to be evaluated to determine whether such an application individually or cumulatively affects the environment. . . . 21 CFR 25.21. An EA that demonstrates the GE animal will not significantly affect the quality of the human environment leads to a finding of no significant impact (FONSI).

. . . The appropriate scope and content of the EA may vary widely depending on the GE animal product, claim, and conditions of use (e.g., aquatic vs. terrestrial animal species). . . .

Step 7: Effectiveness/Claim Validation

The previous steps of the review process primarily address identity and safety issues. This last step of pre-market review addresses effectiveness, i.e., whether you have validated your claims for the characteristics that the GE animal is intended to exhibit. 21 CFR 514.1(b)(8). For example, in the case of a GE animal that is intended to resist disease, you should demonstrate that the GE animals were indeed resistant to that disease. In the case of GE animals that are intended to produce a non-food product, you should demonstrate that the animal indeed produces the claimed product. If that product is . . . a drug or component of a drug intended for use in humans, the safety and effectiveness of that drug would be evaluated separately by Center for Drug Evaluation and Research. . . .

V. Post-Approval Responsibilities

Once a GE animal is approved, sponsors have on-going responsibilities including registration and drug listing, recordkeeping, filing supplements, and periodic reporting. (21 USC 360, 21 USC 356a, 21 CFR 514.80, 21 CFR 514.8). . . .

NOTES

1. *Cloned Animals.* In January of 2008, FDA's CVM issued a risk assessment on animal cloning, concluding that meat and milk from clones of cattle, swine, and goats, and the offspring of clones from any species traditionally consumed as food, are as safe to eat as food from conventionally bred animals. However, FDA recommended that edible products from clones of animals other than cattle, swine, sheep, or goats not be introduced into the human food supply due to insufficient data to support a safety conclusion. FDA and the Department of Agriculture requested that the animal cloning industry continue for another year a voluntary moratorium on the sale of food from cloned animals, reflecting an undetermined transition period needed to fully address marketing concerns regarding labeling and other issues. 73 Fed. Reg. 2923–2924 (Jan. 16, 2008).

2. *Use of GMO Crops in Animal Feed.* In 2006, at least 70 percent of the corn and soybean crops fed to farm animals were obtained from genetically modified crops. The Council for Agricultural Science and Technology concluded that this does not present a human or animal safety concern. CAST, *Safety of Meat, Milk, and Eggs from Animal Fed Crops Derived from Modern Biotechnology*, Issue Paper No. 34 (July 2006).

3. *Animal Biologics.* USDA's licensure under the Virus–Serum–Toxin Act of an animal vaccine produced through recombinant DNA technology was the subject of a congressional hearing into whether the department and the company had acted properly. "USDA Licensing of a Genetically Altered Veterinary Vaccine," Joint Hearing Before the Subcommittee on Investigations and Oversight of the House Committee on Science and Technology and the Subcommittee on Department Operations, Research, and Foreign Agriculture of the House Committee on Agriculture, 99th Cong. 2nd Sess. (1986). USDA has undertaken public reviews of genetically engineered animal vaccines. 54 Fed. Reg. 161 (Jan. 4, 1989); 54 Fed. Reg. 9241 (Mar. 6, 1989).

8. ANIMAL DRUG COMPOUNDING

United States v. Franck's Lab, Inc.

816 F. Supp.2d 1209 (M.D. Fla. 2011).

■ TIMOTHY J. CORRIGAN, DISTRICT JUDGE.

In the seventy-plus years since Congress created the Food and Drug Administration, the FDA has never before sought to enjoin a state-licensed pharmacist from engaging in the traditional practice of bulk compounding of animal drugs. Here, the FDA seeks just such an injunction. This case of first impression implicates matters of statutory construction, federalism, and the proper deference to be afforded to the FDA in interpreting its enabling statute.

... Mr. Franck, a Florida-licensed pharmacist in good standing since 1981, ... open[ed a] ... retail pharmac[y] ... in Ocala in 1985. That same year, Franck began to compound medications at the Ocala location for humans and "non food-producing animals" (such as horses). The Ocala pharmacy was later expanded into two practices which now comprise Franck's: Franck's Lab, which operates as a compounding pharmacy, and Franck's Pharmacy, which is a traditional retail pharmacy. . . .

... Franck's compounds the majority of its animal medications from "bulk" active ingredients, which it receives from suppliers outside the state of Florida. The company also receives prescription orders from customers outside Florida and ships its compounded products to those out-of-state customers. Franck's holds a valid pharmacy license in each of the 47 states in which it is required to do so, and, nationwide, fills approximately 37,000 animal drug prescriptions per year.

The FDA first inspected Franck's compounding facilities between September 29 and October 4, 2004 and, in January 2005, issued a warning letter expressing concern that Franck's was impermissibly manufacturing drugs. . . .

In April 2009, a veterinarian commissioned Franck's to compound an injectable solution of the prescription drug Biodyl for the Venezuelan national polo team. Due to a mathematical error in the conversion of an ingredient (which went unnoticed by the prescribing veterinarian), the compounded medication was too potent and 21 polo horses died. The incident was thoroughly investigated by the Florida Board of Pharmacy, which imposed fines and reprimanded Franck's for the misfilled prescription. Despite the reprimand, the Board voted to allow Franck's to continue its pharmacy compounding practice without restriction, and Franck's remains in good standing in Florida. . . .

... [T]he Venezuelan polo pony incident prompted the FDA to reinspect Franck's facilities three times [in 2009]. . . .

... FDA initiated this action in April of 2010, seeking to enjoin Franck's practice of distributing animal drugs compounded from bulk substances. . . .

... [T]he FDA has taken the bright-line position that *any* compounding of animal medications from bulk substances violates ... the Federal Food, Drug, and Cosmetic Act, even when conducted by a state-licensed pharmacist for an individual animal patient pursuant to a valid veterinary prescription. Franck's admits that it routinely engages in this practice, but contends that it does not violate the FDCA. . . .

Because no material facts are in dispute, the parties' cross-motions present this Court with a pure question of law. . . .

Background

... Because the practice of pharmacy is state-governed, the States, including Florida, regulate compounding as part of their regulation of pharmacists.

. . . When a drug is not commercially available, or the commercially available drug is unsuitable for a particular patient, compounding is often the only way for a human or animal patient to obtain necessary medication for the safe and effective treatment of their condition. This is especially so for non food-producing animals because limited commercially available products exist and the available products are often inadequate due to the animal patient's size, species, and/or intolerance to active ingredients.

A pharmacist can compound a medication requested by the prescribing veterinarian from either a finished drug product or from bulk drug substances. Between the two, compounding from bulk substances has become the "widely preferred" method among veterinarians due to "concerns about the quality, safety, and efficacy of animal medications compounded from finished products." Pharmacists also favor compounding from bulk because use of bulk ingredients ensures that the compounded medicine is of the expected purity, potency, and quality; further, it is often not practical or possible to compound a medically necessary animal drug from an FDA-approved finished drug product. . . .

Under Florida law, traditional compounding from bulk substances is an approved part of the practice of pharmacy. As a result, many, if not all, compounding pharmacies in Florida compound drug products from bulk ingredients. Florida is not an outlier in this regard; the practice of compounding from bulk ingredients is expressly recognized by many states and is a "widespread practice performed by the majority of licensed compounding pharmacy professionals throughout the country, and has been for decades."

. . . .

In the wake of *Western States,* 535 U.S. 357 (2002), the FDA issued revised Compliance Policy Guides addressing compounding of human and animal drugs. Like the 1992 and 1996 Guides before them, the 2002 and 2003 Guides assert that compounded human and animal drugs are not exempt from the FDCA's new drug approval, adulteration, or misbranding provisions. And the updated Guides continue to assure pharmacists that the FDA will use its enforcement [powers] against a compounding pharmacy only where the pharmacy's activities raise the kinds of concerns normally associated with manufacturing. Despite these overarching parallels, however, the new Guides make a number of policy departures from their predecessors.

. . . .

The 2003 Guide, which addresses animal drug compounding, was, according to the FDA, issued "to ensure the consistency of its policies with regard to compounding of drugs intended for use in humans and in animals." From the outset, however, the 2003 Guide strikes a decidedly more hostile tone toward compounding than its human drug counterpart (as well as its 1996 predecessor). . . . Unlike the 1996 Guide . . . the 2003 Guide makes no distinction between food and non food-producing animals. . . .

. . . [T]he most noticeable departure in the 2003 Guide is the FDA's policy regarding the use of bulk drug substances in compounded animal medications. While the 1996 Guide acknowledged the occasional utility of compounding from bulk, the circumstances under which doing so would not subject a pharmacist to potential regulatory action, and the permissibility of the practice for non food-producing animals, such statements are absent—without explanation—from the 2003 Guide. And despite the 2002 Guide's allowance of compounding from bulk for human drugs so long as the bulk ingredients are FDA-approved, the 2003 Guide lists "[c]ompounding finished drugs [for animals] . . . from bulk substances" among the factors which "raise[ ] the kind[ ] of concern normally associated with a manufacturer."

. . . [T[he 2003 Guide [does not] draw any distinctions based upon the scale of bulk compounding activity, implying that a pharmacist who compounds one animal medication from bulk for a non food-producing animal has committed a *per se* violation of the FDCA. Thus, under the 2002 and 2003 Guides, *a pharmacist who compounds medication from bulk for ingestion by a horse is akin to a manufacturer and subject to an FDA enforcement action, while the same pharmacist compounding medication from bulk for ingestion by the human rider of that horse is not.* . . .

Now, for the first time, the FDA has brought an enforcement action under the FDCA seeking to enjoin a pharmacist from compounding veterinarian-prescribed medications from bulk.

The Court's Decision

The FDA says this is a simple case: the literal, plain language of the original FDCA, enacted in 1938, gives it the enforcement authority to prevent pharmacists from bulk compounding medications for non food-producing animals. . . .

Although the FDA's complaint and declarations contain allegations that Franck's has engaged in conduct indicative of a "manufacturer" of drugs, such as compounding commercially available drugs or compounding drugs in advance of a valid prescription, it has provided no factual support for such claims and ultimately does not rely on them to maintain this action. Further, despite the FDA's allusions to Franck's "large" and "interstate" operation, it has not sought to prove a statutory violation based on the size or breadth of Franck's operation. Nor does the FDA contend that Franck's has compounded from bulk substances so as to produce animal drugs which are actually unsafe for animal consumption or are not efficacious. Finally, though the FDA references the deaths of the Venezuelan polo horses, that tragic event was unrelated to the bulk compounding that the FDA targets in this suit. Thus, each of these matters proved to be irrelevant. Given the undisputed record in this case and the FDA's broad view of its authority under the FDCA, this enforcement action could just as easily have been brought against a state-licensed "Mom–and–Pop" pharmacy for filling, through bulk compounding, one veterinary prescription for one horse.

. . . .

Franck's says that Congress, in passing the FDCA, never intended to allow the FDA to prohibit the long-standing and widespread practice of bulk compounding when done by a state-licensed, state-regulated pharmacist, acting on an individual prescription written by a veterinarian for a non food-producing animal. . . .

The FDA acknowledges that, for over a half-century after enactment of the FDCA, it did not assert authority to regulate traditional pharmacy compounding. Despite this, the agency's position is that the FDCA has always provided the FDA with authority to bring enforcement actions against pharmacists who compound animal drugs, and that its failure to do so in the past was merely the exercise of prosecutorial discretion. . . .

1. The FDCA's Language and the New Animal Drug Approval Process

The FDCA broadly defines "drug" to include "articles intended for use in the diagnosis, cure, mitigation, treatment, or prevention of disease in man or other animals." The term "new animal drug" is also broadly defined as

> *any* drug intended for use for animals other than man . . . the composition of which is such that such drug is not generally recognized, among experts qualified by scientific training and experience to evaluate the safety and effectiveness of animal drugs, as safe and effective for use under the conditions prescribed, recommended, or suggested in the labeling thereof.

This definition provides no general exception for drugs created by compounding, nor a specific exemption for compounding by pharmacists. . . .

Before introducing or distributing a "new animal drug," a person must file an application. . . .

Thus, read literally, the type of bulk compounding performed by Franck's (and hundreds of other pharmacists across the country on a daily basis) creates "new animal drugs" within the FDCA's broad definition of that term. According to the FDA, the Court's inquiry ends here. Franck's compounds animal medications from bulk substances (and in so doing implicates the interstate nexus); those medications are "new animal drugs" within the plain language of the FDCA; no statutory exceptions apply which would exempt compounded animal drugs from the FDCA's misbranding or adulteration provisions; the FDA has authority to enforce the new drug approval scheme; and it has chosen to do so here. Thus, FDA urges this Court to "follow the holdings of the Third, Fifth, and Seventh Circuits that compounded animal drugs are 'new animal drugs' within the meaning of the FDCA. . . ."

2. Algon, 9/1 Kg. Containers, and Medical Center

United States v. Algon, 879 F.3d 1154 (3rd Cir.1989) and *United States v. 9/1 Kg. Containers*, 854 F.2d 173 (7th 1988), each addressed the enforceability of an FDA regulation that exempted bulk drug sales from the FDCA's labeling requirements but limited the exemption to holders of new drug approval applications, thereby excluding veterinarians from the exemption. In so doing, the Third and Seventh Circuits analyzed the FDCA and noted that "[t]he statutory definition of a 'new drug' . . . does not exempt drugs that are compounded by veterinarians." As a result, the courts concluded that "[t]he effect of § 352(f) [the FDCA's misbranding provision] and § 201.122 [the bulk drug exemption] is that ingredients that can be used to produce 'new' drugs may be sold only to firms that hold approved (or have filed) new animal drug applications."

There is no doubt that *Algon* and *9/1 Kg. Containers* favor a broad reading of the FDA's authority under the FDCA. However, though *Algon* and *9/1 Kg. Containers* certainly have implications for this case, they are not on all fours either factually or procedurally. Both cases were enforcement actions against *suppliers* to prohibit them from supplying unapproved bulk ingredients to *veterinarians* for use in compounding. Neither case mentioned pharmacists or the practice of pharmacy. Thus, neither court had occasion to consider the FDA's asserted authority to enjoin the practice of traditional pharmacy compounding.

. . . .

Medical Center v. Mukasey, 536 F.3d 383 (5th Cir. 2008) . . . though more similar to this case, is also different in important ways. First, *Medical Center* was not an FDA enforcement proceeding aimed at a specific target. Rather, the plaintiff pharmacies in that case sought broad-based prospective declaratory relief, i.e., to be excluded *entirely* from the FDCA's new drug approval regime . . .

The pharmacies' position [in *Medical Center*] . . . was simply untenable because, as Franck's concedes, the FDA *does* have the authority to prohibit pharmacists from manufacturing under the guise of compounding. Thus, the Fifth Circuit was understandably reluctant to issue a blanket declaration that the FDA could not regulate pharmacists who compromised the FDCA's new drug approval scheme, especially in light of the agency's "promised self-restraint" in bringing enforcement proceedings and its "demonstrated willingness to accommodate traditional compounding's continued existence."

. . . Here, however, the FDA is taking the "maximalist" position that any pharmacy compounding of animal drugs from bulk substances pursuant to a valid veterinary prescription—which, according to the undisputed record evidence, would qualify as "traditional compounding"—is *per se* unlawful under the FDCA. Thus, the Fifth Circuit's faith that the FDA would not seek to enforce a "maximalist" interpretation of its authority turned out to be misplaced.

There is an additional problem with the Fifth Circuit's disposition when overlaid upon this case. Not only did the Court in *Medical Center* presume that the FDA would continue to demonstrate its historical willingness to accommodate traditional compounding, but it also presumed that the FDA drew no distinction between human and animal compounding, even though the manifest differences in the 2002 and 2003 Guides belie such a presumption. Here, the FDA is not only asserting its authority to regulate traditional compounding, but is drawing an enforcement line between human and animal drugs. Although Franck's compounds medications for both humans and animals, the FDA is not seeking to enjoin Franck's' human compounding business. . . .

3.   *Chevron Step One: Whether Congress Intended to Grant the FDA Authority to Regulate Traditional Compounding*

The FDA argues that, even if *Algon, 9/1 Kg. Containers,* and *Medical Center* are distinguishable, this Court must find that the plain terms of the FDCA encompass compounded drugs because the FDCA grants the FDA "broad authority" to regulate drugs "to ensure public health and safety." . . .

Franck's concedes that the literal language of the "new animal drug" provision read without any other context is sufficiently capacious to encompass pharmacists and compounding, but argues that . . . Congress never meant the FDCA to reach so broadly as to allow the FDA to enjoin the long-standing practice of a state-licensed pharmacist using traditional bulk compounding to fill a veterinarian's prescription for a non food-producing animal. Stated differently, Franck's position is not that Congress left open an implied exception for traditional pharmacy compounding; rather, Franck's argues that Congress never intended to regulate the practice in the first place. . . .

Franck's finds support in *FDA v. Brown & Williamson Tobacco Corp.*, 529 U.S. 120 (2000). . . . In *Brown & Williamson,* the FDA asserted jurisdiction to regulate tobacco products based on its conclusions that nicotine was a "drug" and that cigarettes and smokeless tobacco were "drug delivery devices" under the FDCA. While tobacco products appeared at first blush to be encompassed by the FDCA's literal definitions, which might have rendered the statute unambiguous on the question, the Court cautioned that " '[a]mbiguity is a creature not of definitional possibilities but of statutory context.' " As such, the Court stated that "[i]n determining whether Congress has specifically addressed the question at issue, a reviewing court should not confine itself to examining a particular statutory provision in isolation." . . . After interpreting the FDCA "as a symmetrical and coherent regulatory regime," the Court declared that "Congress could not have intended to delegate a decision of such economic and political significance to an agency in so cryptic a fashion." *Id.* at 133 (citation omitted), 160. . . .

Th[is] . . . doctrine is equally applicable here: it is not at all clear that Congress meant to hide the elephant of the FDA's regulation of traditional pharmacy compounding in the mousehole of the FDCA's new drug approval process. Every court that has addressed the issue—no matter the context—has recognized that the FDA new drug approval process is an "especially poor fit" for regulating traditional pharmacy compounding, one that would potentially eradicate traditional compounding despite the recognized importance, historical acceptance, and decades-long state regulation of the practice. Likewise, despite the literal language of the statute, this Court cannot find that Congress has "directly and plainly" said that traditional pharmacy compounding of animal drugs must meet the requirements of the FDCA's new drug approval provisions.

. . . [F]urther review is warranted to determine whether the statute is "ambiguous in such a way as to make the [agency's] decision worthy of deference under the second step of *Chevron.* . . . The Court must therefore proceed with a review of the structure and legislative history of the FDCA, using recognized canons of statutory construction, to determine whether deference to the FDA's statutory construction is appropriate here.

Though nothing in the FDCA or its amendments actually *prohibits* compounding by a state-licensed pharmacist. . . . FDA argues that because the statute includes no *exemption* for state-licensed pharmacists or for compounded medications, traditional pharmacy compounding practices are subject to the same regulatory requirements as new drugs that are manufactured, marketed, and distributed in interstate commerce. . . .

However, "if we were to *presume* a delegation of power from the absence of 'an express *withholding* of such power, agencies would enjoy virtually limitless hegemony." And while pharmacists do not enjoy a uniform exemption from the FDCA's new drug approval scheme, the 1962 amendments to the FDCA do exempt from certain FDA registration and inspection requirements "pharmacies which maintain establishments in conformance with any applicable local laws regulating the practice of pharmacy" and dispense drugs "upon prescriptions of practitioners" for their patients, "and which do not manufacture . . . [or] compound . . . drugs . . . for sale *other than in the regular course of their business of dispensing or selling drugs.*" Interestingly, these provisions contain the FDCA's only mention of compounding, and arise in a context which expressly distinguishes drug manufacturers from pharmacists engaged in the practice of traditional compounding. The presence of these exemptions could be interpreted as a congressional policy decision to distinguish compounding from manufacturing. . . .

The legislative history of the FDCA also supports the view that manufacturers, not compounding pharmacists, were the intended target of the FDCA's new drug approval scheme. Because Congress appeared to be focused on the fact that manufacturing—unlike the practice of pharmacy—was conducted by unlicensed, unregulated nonprofessionals, it seems unlikely that it would have intended to subject professionally dispensed drugs to the same regulatory scheme. This distinction is even more compelling when one considers the FDCA scheme's poor fit with a traditionally compounded animal medication. . . . Given that traditionally compounded medications are prepared for individual animal patients in response to a valid veterinary prescription, meaning each compounded medication has unique components and is ill-suited for "adequate and well-controlled studies," it just does not seem plausible that Congress would have intended to subject pharmacy compounded drugs to the lengthy and expensive new animal drug approval process. The statutory "fit" is especially poor when compounded medications are the best—and sometimes only—way to treat an animal.

However, . . . [w]hile the FDCA might not have been focused on pharmacists behaving badly, it was without question enacted to protect the public from the distribution of unapproved drugs which have been mass-produced without any assurances of safety or quality control. To the extent that a pharmacist's bulk compounding activity moves beyond the bounds of traditional compounding and begins to approximate the "manufacturing" of unapproved drugs, there seems little question that this activity is squarely within the crosshairs of the FDCA.

. . . .

What the Supreme Court recognized [in *Western States*] is that Congress delegated to the FDA the authority to *draw a line* distinguishing between compounded drugs that *must* undergo the new drug approval process because they bear the attributes of having been "manufactured" and "compounded drugs *created to meet the unique needs of individual patients,*" because it "would not make sense" for the latter "to undergo the testing required for the new drug approval process."

. . . .

Though it certainly has the statutory authority to do so, the FDA has chosen not to draw the line between manufacturing and traditional compounding with formal regulations. . . . Rather, beginning with the 1992 Guide, it has utilized Compliance Policy Guides to disseminate its policy determinations vis-a-vis the acceptability of compounding animal and human drugs. Along the way those non-binding guidance documents have made clear that "traditional pharmacy compounding" was not the subject of the FDA's guidance. In addition, the agency has continued to recognize that because of an "insufficient variety of approved medications," certain compounded medications are medically necessary for the treatment of animals. . . . But although the FDA generally deferred to the states with regard to "traditional compounding," and brought no enforcement actions against the numerous pharmacies nationwide engaged in bulk compounding for non food-producing animals, the agency has, since *9/1 Kg. Containers,* asserted that it possessed the statutory authority to regulate the practice. As a result, state-licensed veterinarians and pharmacists have, with the FDA's blessing, been "living in sin" (according to the FDA) for over twenty years.

The FDA says that it does adequately account for the continued practice of traditional pharmacy compounding through the judicious exercise of its enforcement discretion. . . . [T]he FDA says, "the specter that [D]efendants present of the whole [pharmacy] industry behind bars is farfetched hyperbole. FDA has consistently exercised its enforcement discretion against compounding pharmacies in a manner that clearly demonstrates that it has no intention of shuttering the entire industry."

Although that argument was appropriately accepted by the Fifth Circuit under the procedural posture of that case, it cannot prevail here. . . .

Here, the FDA's authority to regulate pharmacy compounding as a disguise for manufacturing is not at issue. Rather,. . . [U]tilizing this first-of-its-kind enforcement action, the FDA seeks to expand its statutory authority by enjoining an individual pharmacy which is engaged in traditional pharmacy compounding of animal drugs in compliance with state law. In so doing, the FDA overreaches.

Another potential anomaly (not presented to the Fifth Circuit) is in sharp relief here. . . . If the FDA's position is correct, Congress intended to give the agency the authority to require traditionally compounded medications for non food-producing animals to go through the FDA's lengthy and involved new drug approval process but declined to require it for compounded medications prescribed for human beings. This is simply too much for a public health statute like the FDCA to bear.

As a result, though § 321(v)'s "new animal drug" definition affords the FDA license to enforce against pharmacists who manufacture in the guise of compounding, Congress did not, by any remaining contextual ambiguity, give the FDA the authority to enjoin traditional pharmacy compounding of animal drugs, a practice never before regulated by a federal agency and never mentioned in the FDCA. The FDA is certainly statutorily authorized to draw clear distinctions between manufacturing and compounding generally. However, what the FDA seeks to do here is reinterpret the FDCA to allow it to *eradicate* the line between manufacturing and traditional compounding of animal medications. Its wholesale assertion of authority over traditional pharmacy compounding in the context of a pharmacist-veterinarian-patient relationship is contrary to congressional intent. Thus, the Court concludes that the FDA lacks the statutory authority it seeks to exercise here.

4.   *Chevron Step Two*

. . . [T]o the extent that the FDCA could be interpreted as being ambiguous in such a way as to allow deference to the FDA's statutory construction, the agency's interpretation would fail, for many of the same reasons, at *Chevron* Step Two. . . .

. . . Because the FDA seeks to enforce a prohibition that it has not delineated through notice-and-comment rule-making, *Skidmore* deference is appropriate here. . . . FDA's statutory interpretation lacks the "power to persuade."

. . . .

CONCLUSION

. . . The Court holds that, in enacting the FDCA in 1938, Congress did not intend to give the FDA *per se* authority to enjoin the long-standing, widespread, state-regulated practice of pharmacists filling a veterinarian's prescription for a non food-producing animal by compounding from bulk substances.

Accordingly, it is hereby ORDERED:

1.   The United States' Motion for Summary Judgment is DENIED.

2.   Defendants' Motion for Summary Judgment is GRANTED to extent described in this Order.

3.   The United States is not entitled to the injunction it seeks.

CHAPTER 9

BIOLOGICAL PRODUCTS: VACCINES, BLOOD, TISSUE TRANSPLANTS, AND CELLULAR THERAPIES

A. HISTORICAL BACKGROUND

Smallpox was once the most feared disease, with the highest mortality rate in human history. Its devastating effects are widely chronicled. Near the end of the Middle Ages halting efforts began to prevent the disease. Based on the observation that victims who survived never got smallpox again, the practice known as "variolation"—inoculation with smallpox puss or scabs—arose in the Far East. By the 16th century the practice had spread to Europe. During a severe smallpox epidemic in Boston in 1721, Cotton Mather persuaded Dr. Zabdiel Boylston to use variolation for the first time in North America. Though initially resisted by the medical profession, variolation eventually became common practice in this country too.

In the late eighteenth century, English physician Edward Jenner, observing that milkmaids rarely got smallpox, vaccinated several Gloucestershire children with cowpox taken from an infected milkmaid and then inoculated them with live smallpox. All displayed resistance to smallpox. Following publication of Jenner's results in 1798, Dr. Benjamin Waterhouse conducted confirmatory tests in Boston by inoculation with the cowpox vaccine and subsequent challenge with injection of live smallpox. Thereafter, the use of Jenner's vaccine spread rapidly. *See* FRANK FENNER ET AL., SMALLPOX AND ITS ERADICATION (1988).

Inevitably, spurious smallpox vaccine appeared in the market. Frequently, neither physicians nor the general public could distinguish the genuine product. A crusading Baltimore physician, James Smith, persuaded the Maryland legislature to establish a public lottery to raise funds so that he could distribute "genuine vaccine matter" free to everyone. L. Md., Ch. 123 (1809). Dr. Smith later persuaded Congress to enact similar legislation. 2 Stat. 806 (1813). The federal law gave the President authority to appoint a Vaccine Agent "to preserve the genuine vaccine matter, and to furnish the same to any citizen of the United States, whenever it may be applied for, through the medium of the post office." Smith was appointed the first (and only) Vaccine Agent of the United States. Following an outbreak of smallpox in North Carolina that was attributed to a vaccine Smith had furnished, H.R. Rep. Nos. 48 & 93, 17th Cong., 1st Sess. (1822), Congress repealed the 1813 Act on the premise that it was "better to commit the subject altogether to the local authorities." 3 Stat. 677 (1822).

By the late 19th century diphtheria had become the third most common cause of death in the United States. The causative agent was identified and, through injection into animals who built up an immunity, an "antitoxin" was produced. In 1902, an outbreak of tetanus in St. Louis was traced to contaminated diphtheria antitoxin. This followed an outbreak of tetanus in Camden, New Jersey, the previous year that was traced to contaminated smallpox vaccine. *See* JONATHAN LIEBENAU, MEDICAL SCIENCE AND MEDICAL INDUSTRY: THE FORMATION OF THE AMERICAN PHARMACEUTICAL INDUSTRY (1987). Spurred by these episodes, Congress enacted the law that today still underpins federal regulation of biological products for human use, commonly called the Biologics Act. 32 Stat. 728 (1902). The Biologics Act was reenacted in 1944 as part of the recodification of the Public Health Service Act, 58 Stat. 682, 702 (1944) and further revised by the FDA Modernization Act of 1997, 111 Stat. 2296. It is now codified at 42 U.S.C. 262.

The past 25 years have been a period of dramatic advances in understanding of human biology, which have in turn made possible major improvements in human health and welfare. A cursory listing provides a glimpse of the technological advances that FDA has confronted: human cloning, prenatal genetic diagnosis, germ line engineering, embryonic stem cell research, xenotransplantation, and various aids to human reproduction. FDA has not attempted to regulate all of these technologies. Some have not reached the stage at which the agency could plausibly assert jurisdiction. Others have reached the clinical trial stage but not yielded commercial products whose safety and effectiveness the agency might assess. But many of these new technologies are recognized subjects of governmental regulation.

B. FDA ACQUIRES RESPONSIBILITY FOR BIOLOGICS

When the omnibus Public Health Service Act was recodified in 1944, a major issue was the status of biological products under the FD&C Act. During hearings on the recodification bill, Alanson W. Willcox, Acting General Counsel of the Federal Security Agency, predecessor of the Department of Health, Education, and Welfare (HEW), initially recommended the addition of the following language:

The persons and the products to which this section is applicable shall be subject also to the provisions of the Federal Food, Drug, and Cosmetic Act.

Later, Willcox went on to explain:

That, I am convinced, is the present law, though there has been some difference of opinion on the subject. The wording has caused some alarm in the industry for fear it would mean duplication of administrative control, which is the last thing we want or anybody else wants. I am going to suggest that subsection be revised to read this way:

Nothing contained in this Act shall be construed as in any way affecting, modifying, repealing, or superseding the provisions of the Federal Food, Drug, and Cosmetic Act.

We are making that suggestion only because we are confident that it does now apply. The controls which the Public Health

Service exercises are, I think, very effective but there is also a possibility in anything of that sort that some product which is dangerous to life may inadvertently get out into the market. The Federal Food and Drug [Act], unlike this act, contains seizure of power [sic]. We are very firmly of the opinion that the authority in law to pick up off the market any dangerous product that might have gotten out despite the most rigid controls should be continued and, as I say, it is only because of our confidence that this revised wording would continue that, that we are willing to suggest the revised wording. . . .

Hearings Before a Subcomm. of the S. Comm. on Educ. & Labor, 78th Cong., 2d Sess. 48 (1944).

The language added by Willcox survives today as section 351(g) of the Public Health Service Act (PHSA). It thus continues to be the case that the regulation of biologics under the PHSA is supplemented by regulation of them as "biological drugs" pursuant to the relevant provisions of the FD&C Act.

The biological products licensing section of the PHSA has been amended several times since 1944, most significantly in 1997. The relevant provisions are found in section 351 of the PHSA and codified at 42 U.S.C. 262. Another section of the PHSA pertinent to FDA's mission is section 361, which empowers the agency to promulgate regulations to prevent the spread of communicable diseases and is codified in 42 U.S.C. 264.

During its first half century, the biologics control program was the responsibility of the director of the Hygienic Laboratory, the predecessor of the National Institutes of Health (NIH). In 1948 the program was made a part of the National Microbiological Institute, a unit of NIH. In 1955, after several cases of polio resulted from vaccine containing undetected live virus, the need for closer oversight became clear and a new organization, the Division of Biologics Standards (DBS), was established within NIH.

In early 1972, Dr. Anthony Morris, a DBS scientist, charged publicly that the DBS's combination of research and regulatory functions created an inherent conflict of interest. According to Nicholas Wade, *Division of Biologics Standards: Scientific Management Questioned*, 175 SCIENCE 966 (1972):

The common theme of the . . . charges is that in numerous instances, amounting to a "pattern of administrative insensitivity," the DBS management has suppressed or ignored scientific findings that would adversely affect the vaccine market. The motive for this alleged behavior is ascribed . . . to a "passionate commitment to vaccine therapy" on the part of the DBS leadership. . . .

In a later article, *Division of Biologics Standards: The Boat That Never Rocked*, 175 SCIENCE 1225 (1972), Wade described the DBS decision-making environment:

. . . Federal responsibility for vaccines does not rest solely on the DBS, but is diffused over a handful of committees with interlocking memberships. Thus, if the mass annual inoculations against influenza were indeed the "forcing on the public [of] a bogus situation . . . ," it is not too clear whether responsibility would lie with the DBS for certifying an inefficacious vaccine or with a second body, the Center for Disease Control's Advisory Committee on Immunization Practices (ACIP), whose function is to decide who should be vaccinated against what. . . .

. . . [F]ederal responsibility for vaccine development should be clarified, in a way that ensures the DBS does not develop vaccines in-house. There should be some court of appeal against the director's decisions. Since the DBS acts, in effect, for the academic community on behalf of the public, there should be a stronger connection with the academic world than occasional ad hoc conferences and a rubber-stamp board of scientific counselors. . . .

A contemporaneous General Accounting Office investigation resulted in charges of improper certification of influenza vaccine:

. . . The GAO investigators discovered that on the evidence of the DBS's own records, 130 of the 221 lots of influenza vaccine released by the DBS in 1966 failed to meet the standards of potency required by the agency's own regulations. One hundred and fifteen of these lots were subpotent according to the test results submitted to the DBS by the manufacturers themselves. Another 15 lots were potent according to the manufacturers' tests and failed the tests conducted by DBS scientists, yet were released for public use by the DBS management. . . .

The precise effect of the DBS policy of releasing subpotent vaccines is hard to estimate but probably some 67 million doses of influenza vaccine were used in the United States during the 3 years covered by the GAO report. If half of these vaccines failed the DBS's own standards, and the cost to each recipient was $1 a head (a conservative estimate), then the DBS has allowed citizens to spend more than $30 million on subpotent vaccines. . . .

Nicholas Wade, *DBS: Agency Contravenes Its Own Regulations*, 176 SCIENCE 34 (1972).

As a result of these criticisms, the Secretary of HEW transferred DBS from NIH to FDA in 1972 and renamed it the Bureau of Biologics. 37 Fed. Reg. 12865 (June 23, 1972). *See Consumer Safety Act of 1972: Hearings Before the Subcomm. on Exec. Reorganization of the S. Comm. on Gov't Affairs*, 92d Cong., 2d Sess. (1972); *Hearings Before the Subcomm. on Health of the S. Comm. on Labor & Human Res.*, 92d Cong., 2d Sess. (1972); *see also* Margaret Pittman, *The Regulation of Biologic Products, 1902–1972*, NAT'L INST. OF ALLERGY & INFECTIOUS DISEASE, INTRAMURAL CONTRIBUTIONS, 1887–1987 (1987).

The Bureau of Biologics remained a separate administrative unit within FDA from the time of its transfer from NIH in 1972 until it was merged with the Bureau of Drugs in 1982. 47 Fed. Reg. 26913 (June 22, 1982). The combined unit was named the National Center for Drugs and Biologics, later shortened to the Center for Drugs and Biologics. In 1988, the two parts were again separated and the biologics unit given its present title, the Center for Biologics Evaluation and Research (CBER). 52 Fed. Reg. 38275 (Oct. 15, 1987); 53 Fed. Reg. 8978 (Mar. 18, 1988).

NOTES

1.   *Commercial Sale.* Unlike the FD&C Act, the Biologics Act applies only to commercial production or sale of biologics. For that reason, investigational biologics are subject to the IND requirements of section 505(i) of the FD&C Act prior to their licensure for marketing. 21 C.F.R. 312.2(a).

2.   *Veterinary Biologics.* Congress enacted a separate Animal Virus, Serum, and Toxin Act to regulate veterinary biological products in 1914, 37 Stat. 828, 832, codified at 21 U.S.C. 151, *et seq.* The law is administered by the U.S. Department of Agriculture.

C. FDA REGULATION OF THERAPEUTIC BIOLOGICS

The 1972 GAO report cited above concluded that DBS had failed to apply the FD&C Act's requirements for proof of effectiveness. According to Nicholas Wade:

> The GAO report states that . . . 75 of the 263 products licensed by the DBS are generally not recognized as effective by most of the medical profession. The GAO report reveals that [DBS] . . . was advised by HEW counsel in February 1969 that the DBS possessed authority under . . . [the Drug Amendments of 1962] to enforce vaccine efficacy. Murray [Director of DBS] refused to use the [FD&C] act . . . on the grounds that to do so would strengthen the argument of those who wished to merge the DBS with the FDA into a single control agency. . . .

Wade, *DBS: Agency Contravenes Its Own Regulations*, 176 SCIENCE at 34.

1.   THE BIOLOGICS REVIEW

In anticipation of the GAO findings, HEW Secretary Richard Schweiker redelegated authority to apply the drug provisions of the FD&C Act with respect to all biological drugs concurrently to FDA and DBS. 37 Fed. Reg. 4004 (Feb. 25, 1972). NIH then announced its intention to have DBS review the effectiveness of all licensed biological products, and it called for manufacturers to submit "substantial evidence of effectiveness" meeting the requirements of FDA's Bureau of Drugs. 37 Fed. Reg. 5404 (Mar. 15, 1972). When, later that year, DBS was transferred to FDA and the responsibility for administering the Biologics Act was thus delegated to FDA alone, FDA revoked NIH's notice and proposed new procedures for the review of the safety, effectiveness, and labeling of all licensed biological products, modeled on the OTC Drug Review.

Biological Products: Procedures for Review of Safety, Effectiveness, and Labeling
37 Fed. Reg. 16679 (August 18, 1972).

This proposal will establish a procedure under which the safety, effectiveness, and labeling of all biological products presently licensed under section 351 of the Public Health Service Act will be reviewed. Advisory review panels comprised of independent experts will provide their conclusions and recommendations to the Commissioner of Food and Drugs, who then will review and implement them. . . .

The review procedure proposed in this notice relies for legal authority on both the Federal Food, Drug, and Cosmetic Act and section 351 of the Public Health Service Act. . . .

The Commissioner of Food and Drugs is aware of the unique problems involved in applying the requirement of "substantial evidence of effectiveness" to biological products, under the Federal Food, Drug, and Cosmetic Act. Where adequate and well-controlled studies are not feasible, and acceptable alternative scientific methods of demonstrating effectiveness are available, the latter will be sufficient. The advisory review panels convened under the procedure proposed in this notice will initially develop the standard and methodology for effectiveness for a particular class of biological products, . . . subject to review by the Commissioner of Food and Drugs. . . . Each review panel will determine those biological products that are and are not safe, effective, and not misbranded, as well as those for which further study is required. The applicable product licenses will then be confirmed, revoked, or permitted to remain in effect on an interim basis pending further study. . . .

———

The process that FDA set in motion took much longer than the agency originally forecast.

Biological Products: Bacterial Vaccines and Toxoids; Implementation of Efficacy Review

70 Fed. Reg. 75018 (December 19, 2005).

I.　Introduction. . . .

The purpose of this document is to: (1) categorize those bacterial vaccines and toxoids licensed before July 1972 according to the evidence of their safety and effectiveness, thereby determining whether they may remain licensed and on the market; (2) issue a final response to recommendations made in the Panel's report.[7] These recommendations concern conditions relating to active components, labeling, tests required before release of product lots, product standards, or other conditions considered by the Panel to be necessary or appropriate for assuring the safety and effectiveness of the reviewed products; and (3) revise the standard for potency of Tetanus Immune Globulin in § 610.21.

II.　Background

In the Federal Register of February 13, 1973 (38 FR 4319), FDA issued procedures for the review by independent advisory review panels of the safety, effectiveness, and labeling of biological products licensed

---

[7]　The Panel was convened on July 12, 1973, in an organizational meeting, followed by multiple working meetings until February 2, 1979. The Final Report of the Panel was completed in August 1979.

before July 1, 1972. This process was eventually codified in § 601.25 (21 CFR 601.25) (38 FR 32048 at 32052, November 20, 1973). Under the panel assignments published in the Federal Register of June 19, 1974 (39 FR 21176), FDA assigned the biological product review to one of the following groups: (1) bacterial vaccines and bacterial antigens with "no U.S. standard of potency," (2) bacterial vaccines and toxoids with standards of potency, (3) viral vaccines and rickettsial vaccines, (4) allergenic extracts, (5) skin test antigens, and (6) blood and blood derivatives.

Under § 601.25, FDA assigned responsibility for the initial review of each of the biological product categories to a separate independent advisory panel consisting of qualified experts to ensure objectivity of the review and public confidence in the use of these products. Each panel was charged with preparing an advisory report to the Commissioner of Food and Drugs which was to: (1) Evaluate the safety and effectiveness of the biological products for which a license had been issued, (2) review their labeling, and (3) identify the biological products that are safe, effective, and not misbranded. Each advisory panel report was also to include recommendations classifying the products reviewed into one of three categories.

• Category I, designating those biological products determined by the panel to be safe, effective, and not misbranded.

• Category II, designating those biological products determined by the panel to be unsafe, ineffective, or misbranded.

• Category III, designating those biological products determined by the panel not to fall within either Category I or Category II on the basis of the panel's conclusion that the available data were insufficient to classify such biological products, and for which further testing was therefore required. Category III products were assigned to one of two subcategories. Category IIIA products were those that would be permitted to remain on the market pending the completion of further studies. Category IIIB products were those for which the panel recommended license revocation on the basis of the panel's assessment of potential risks and benefits.

. . . .

III. Categorization of Products—Final Order

Category I. Licensed biological products determined to be safe and effective and not misbranded. Table 1 of this document is a list of those products proposed in December 2004 by FDA for Category I.

. . . .

Category II. Licensed biological products determined to be unsafe or ineffective or to be misbranded and which should not continue in interstate commerce. FDA did not propose that any products be placed in Category II and in this final rule and final order does not categorize any products in Category II.

Category IIIB. Biological products for which available data are insufficient to classify their safety and effectiveness and should not continue in interstate commerce. Table 2 of this document is a list of those products proposed by FDA for Category IIIB. . . .

IV. FDA's Responses to Additional Panel Recommendations

. . . .

The Panel recommended that actions be taken to improve the reporting and documentation of adverse reactions to biological products. The Panel particularly noted the need to improve the surveillance systems to identify adverse reactions to pertussis vaccine.

Since publications of the Panel's report, the Vaccine Adverse Event Reporting System (VAERS) was created ... and is administered by FDA and the Centers for Disease Control and Prevention (CDC). VAERS accepts from health care providers, manufacturers, and the public, reports of adverse events that may be associated with the U.S.-licensed vaccines. Health care providers must report certain adverse events included in a Reportable Events Table and any event listed in the vaccine's package insert as a contraindication to subsequent doses of the vaccine. Health care providers also may report other clinically significant adverse events. FDA and CDC receive about 1,000 reports each month under the VAERS program. . . .

NOTE

Anthrax Vaccine. One of the products reviewed by the Panel on Review of Bacterial Vaccines and Toxoids was Anthrax Vaccine Adsorbed (AVA), which had been produced by the Michigan Department of Public Health and distributed pursuant to a license issued by the Division of Biologics Standards in 1970. 50 Fed. Reg. 51002, 51059 (Dec. 13, 1985). After lengthy evaluation, the panel recommended and FDA proposed in 1985 to assign AVA to Category I (safe and effective). Some nineteen years would pass before the agency acted on this proposal and confirmed that the vaccine was effective as well as safe. Various circumstances slowed and complicated FDA's decision making. First, in the late 1990s the product's sponsor, the Michigan Department of Public Health, sold its facility and business to a private firm, BioPort, which took over all dealings with FDA. Then, those dealings became contentious when FDA inspectors reported that BioPort's facilities and operation failed to satisfy the agency's good manufacturing practice requirements. Finally, while FDA and BioPort were in discussions over GMP requirements, the company, and indirectly FDA, came under pressure to confirm AVA's safety and effectiveness so that it could lawfully be administered to U.S. military personnel who faced deployment in the first Gulf War. INSTITUTE OF MEDICINE, THE ANTHRAX VACCINE: IS IT SAFE? DOES IT WORK? (2004). The controversy surrounding the Defense Department's determination to administer the vaccine—despite FDA's reluctance to confirm its safety and effectiveness until relevant studies were concluded and GMP requirements were met—is chronicled in *Doe v. Rumsfeld*, 297 F. Supp. 2d 119 (D.D.C. 2003), 341 F. Supp. 2d 1 (D.D.C. 2004).

2. FDA APPROVAL OF NEW BIOLOGICS

Section 123(f) of the FDA Modernization Act of 1997, 111 Stat. 2296, 2324, which is not codified, requires FDA's processes for reviewing BLAs and NDAs to be parallel. This provision culminated 25 years of biologics law assimilation into FDA. The section reads:

> The Secretary of Health and Human Services shall take measures to minimize differences in the review and approval of products required to have approved biologics license applications under section 351 of the Public Health Service Act (42 U.S.C. 262) and products required to have approved new drug applications under section 505(b)(1) of the Federal Food, Drug, and Cosmetic Act (21 U.S.C. 355(b)(1)).

111 Stat. at 2324.

An application for approval of a biologics license (BLA) resembles a new drug application described in detail in Chapter 7, and the agency's criteria are similar even if couched in the language—"safe, pure, and potent"—of the Biologics Act. The user fee legislation that has fueled FDA's approval process for drugs applies to biologics as well. Clinical trials of investigational biologics must satisfy the agency's IND standards. And biologics are eligible for orphan drug status if they satisfy that law's requirements.

For many years, FDA's requirements for obtaining marketing approval of a biologic differed from the requirements for drugs in one important respect: the agency required approval of both a biologics product license application (PLA) and an establishment license application (ELA). This approach reflected the agency's long-standing concern about whether a biologic applicant's production processes would assure identity and consistency from batch to batch. In the 1990s this dual requirement came to be regarded as unnecessarily burdensome. The Clinton administration, as part of its "Reinventing Government" initiative to simplify government operations, chaired by Vice President Gore, proposed to conflate the two licenses into one.

Reinventing Regulation of Drugs Made From Biotechnology

FDA Press Release, November 9, 1995.

The Food and Drug Administration today is proposing several measures that will reduce costs for manufacturers of biotechnology derived pharmaceuticals, increase the agency's efficiency and continue to protect the public health. The six proposals—which constitute FDA's most significant overhaul of biotech regulations to date—complement and build on the drug and medical device reforms announced last spring as part of the Clinton Administration's National Performance Review.

. . . .

The proposals include the following changes:

• Elimination of establishment license application (ELA) for well-characterized therapeutic biotech drugs. . . .

• Elimination of FDA's lot-by-lot release for well-characterized therapeutic biologic drugs that are licensed for marketing. . . .

• Consolidation of 21 different approval application forms into a single, user-friendly format. . . .

• Elimination of the need for approval of promotional labeling before launching a new product. . . .

• FDA commitment to review and respond within 30 days to information submitted in response to a clinical hold on a study of an investigational drug or biologic. . . .

Elimination of Establishment License Application for Specified Biotechnology and Specified Synthetic Biological Products

61 Fed. Reg. 24227 (May 14, 1996).

In the Federal Register of January 29, 1996, FDA proposed to amend the biologics regulations to eliminate the ELA requirement for well-characterized biotechnology products licensed under the PHS Act. In that document, FDA proposed to use the general phrase "well-characterized biotechnology product," to describe products that would be eligible for a single license application so that the regulatory language would accommodate categories of products that might later be considered to be well-characterized as scientific knowledge progresses. . . .

The agency noted that technical advances over the last 15 years have greatly increased the ability of manufacturers to control and analyze the manufacture of many biotechnology-derived biological products. After over a decade of experience with these products, the agency has found that it can review the safety, purity, potency, and effectiveness of most well-characterized biotechnology products without requiring submission of a separate ELA. Accordingly, FDA proposed procedures under which CBER would approve most well-characterized biotechnology products by requiring a single biologics license application. FDA noted that the proposed procedures would significantly reduce burdens without reducing the safety or effectiveness of these products. . . .

After considering the public comments received on the interim definition, the discussion at the workshop, and the many requests the agency has received for further clarification of the term "well-characterized," FDA has determined that it may not be possible to achieve a sufficiently clear and specific understanding of this term to adequately apprise potential applicants of the applicability of the new procedures. Accordingly, in this final rule, FDA is specifying, in lieu of the term "well characterized biotechnology product," the categories of products to which this final rule will be applicable. . . .

FDA agrees that blood and blood components, including plasma, plasma derivatives, and stem cells, are products which should not fall within the scope of this rule. FDA believes that license applications for these and other naturally derived products should continue to include establishment information at this time. FDA believes that a license application that includes detailed information on the facilities and controls may be necessary to assess the continued safety, purity, and potency of these products. Because these products involve complex issues, such as a risk of contamination with infectious agents, their review requires special expertise and adequate time in order to assess the adequacy of controls in place at the facility. In addition, end product testing of naturally derived products may not be sufficient to detect contamination with infectious agents. . . .

————

This reform was endorsed and expanded by Congress in the FDA Modernization Act of 1997 and soon thereafter implemented by the agency.

Biological Products Regulated Under Section 351 of the Public Health Service Act; Implementation of Biologics License; Elimination of Establishment License and Product License

64 Fed. Reg. 56441 (October 20, 1999).

. . .

On November 21, 1997, the President signed into law FDAMA (Pub. L. 105–115). Section 123 of FDAMA, in pertinent part, amended section 351 of the PHS Act to specify that a biologics license shall be in effect for a biological product prior to such product's introduction into interstate commerce. FDAMA thereby statutorily codified FDA's administrative BLA/biologics license "Reinventing Government" initiative. Section 123(a)(1) of FDAMA further states that the Secretary of Health and Human Services (the Secretary) (delegated to the Commissioner of Food and Drugs at 21 CFR 5.10(a)(5)) shall approve a "biologics license application" on the basis of a demonstration that the biological product that is the subject of the application is safe, pure, and potent; and the facility in which the biological product is manufactured, processed, packed, or held meets standards designed to ensure that the biological product continues to be safe, pure, and potent.

With the consolidation of the ELA's and PLA's into a single BLA, the amount of information formerly included in the ELA will be reduced, but not eliminated. Much of the information previously reviewed in an ELA at FDA will be reviewed by FDA investigators at the manufacturing site during a preapproval inspection. Some information formerly included in the ELA will now be submitted as "chemistry, manufacturing, and controls" (CMC) information or under the "establishment description" . . . .

————

After President George W. Bush took office, his appointees to HHS and FDA implemented another reform designed to exploit what they saw as CDER's superior performance in meeting the product approval targets adopted pursuant to the Prescription Drug User Fee Act. On June 30, 2003, FDA transferred some of the therapeutic biological products that had been reviewed and regulated by CBER to the Center for Drug Evaluation and Research (CDER).

Categories of Therapeutic Biological Products Transferred to CDER

   • Monoclonal antibodies for in vivo use.

• Proteins intended for therapeutic use, including cytokines (*e.g.* interferons), enzymes (*e.g.* thrombolytics), and other novel proteins, except for those that are specifically assigned to CBER (*e.g.*, vaccines and blood products). This category includes therapeutic proteins derived from plants, animals, or microorganisms, and recombinant versions of these products.

• Immunomodulators (non-vaccine and non-allergenic products intended to treat disease by inhibiting or modifying a pre-existing immune response).

• Growth factors, cytokines, and monoclonal antibodies intended to mobilize, stimulate, decrease or otherwise alter the production of hematopoietic cells in vivo.

Categories of Therapeutic Biological Products Remaining in CBER

• Cellular products, including products composed of human, bacterial or animal cells (such as pancreatic islet cells for transplantation), or from physical parts of those cells (such as whole cells, cell fragments, or other components intended for use as preventative or therapeutic vaccines).

• Gene therapy products. Human gene therapy/gene transfer is the administration of nucleic acids, viruses, or genetically engineered microorganisms that mediate their effect by transcription and/or translation of the transferred genetic material, and/or by integrating into the host genome. Cells may be modified in these ways ex vivo for subsequent administration to the recipient, or altered in vivo by gene therapy products administered directly to the recipient.

• Vaccines (products intended to induce or increase an antigen specific immune response for prophylactic or therapeutic immunization, regardless of the composition or method of manufacture).

• Allergenic extracts used for the diagnosis and treatment of allergic diseases and allergen patch tests.

• Antitoxins, antivenins, and venoms.

• Blood, blood components, plasma derived products (for example, albumin, immunoglobulins, clotting factors, fibrin sealants, proteinase inhibitors), including recombinant and transgenic versions of plasma derivatives, (for example clotting factors), blood substitutes, plasma volume expanders, human or animal polyclonal antibody preparations including radiolabeled or conjugated forms, and certain fibrinolytics such as plasma-derived plasmin, and red cell reagents.

Transfer of Therapeutic Products to the Center for Drug Evaluation and Research, FDA–CBER Website (updated Feb. 22, 2010).

NOTE

Investigational Products. FDA clarified the relationship between the Biologics Act and section 505(i) of the FD&C Act insofar as they relate to investigational products in 45 Fed. Reg. 73922 (Nov. 7, 1980).

3. FDA REVIEW OF BLAS

The process followed by CBER in reviewing BLAs for compliance with the requirements of 21 U.S.C. 262 does not differ in any fundamental way from that followed by CDER in evaluating NDAs. CDER's process is reviewed in detail in Chapter 7.

4. BIOSIMILAR BIOLOGICAL PRODUCTS

As many therapies produced through genetic engineering approached the end of their patent protection, interest focused on the question whether Hatch–Waxman applied to biologics, i.e., whether ANDAs could be approved for copies of biologic drugs. Some FDA officials had signaled their hope for an affirmative response, but Acting Commissioner Lester Crawford stated the following in testimony before Congress, providing this summary of the law:

> The FD&C Act provides the ANDA and 503(b)(2) abbreviated approval pathways for drugs approved under section 505 of the Act. However, the PHS Act has no similar provision. That is, unlike section 505 of the FD&C Act, there is no provision under the PHS Act for an abbreviated application that would permit approval of a "generic" or "follow-on" biologic based on the Agency's earlier approval of another manufacturer's application.

The Law of Biologic Medicine: Hearing Before the S. Comm. on the Judiciary, 108th Cong., 2d Sess. 11 (2004). Crawford went on to suggest that for a few biological products for which FDA had approved marketing under section 505, such as "simple peptide or protein products," the agency might have the authority to accept abbreviated applications for generic versions. But some thought FDA could go further. *E.g.*, David Dudzinski, *Reflections on Historical, Scientific, and Legal Issues Relevant to Designing Approval Pathways for Generic Versions of Recombinant Protein-Based Therapeutics and Monoclonal Antibodies*, 60 FOOD & DRUG L.J. 143 (2005).

After years of debate about the matter, Congress settled the issue by enacting the Biologics Price Competition and Innovation Act of 2009 under Title VII, Subtitle A, sections 7001–7003 of the Patient Protection and Affordable Care Act, 124 Stat. 119, 804–821 (2010), codified at section 351(k) of the Public Health Services Act, 42 U.S.C. 262(k). This statute, commonly referred to as the Biosimilars Act, establishes a new regulatory pathway for FDA to approve biological products that are intended to be highly similar to biological products that have previously been approved by FDA under a full BLA. Because biological products are made from complex natural materials that, unlike synthesized drugs, cannot be made to be identical to the pioneer product, these "follow-on" biological products are called "biosimilar" products, not "generic" products. The Biosimilars Act is very different from the Hatch–Waxman Act under which FDA approves abbreviated NDAs for generic new drugs. The legislative history is analyzed in detail in Krista Hessler Carver et al., *An Unofficial Legislative History of the Biologics Price Competition and Innovation Act of 2009*, 65 FOOD & DRUG L.J. 671 (2010).

A biosimilar is defined as a biological product that is "highly similar" to a pioneer biological product approved by FDA "notwithstanding minor differences in clinically inactive compounds" where there are no "clinically meaningful differences" in safety, purity, and potency. There are two types of biosimilars. A standard biosimilar is not substitutable for the pioneer product by a pharmacist. An interchangeable biosimilar is substitutable.

For all biosimilars, the BLA must prove that the biosimilar (1) has the same mechanism of action as the pioneer, (2) is intended for the same conditions of use, (3) has the same route of administration, dosage form, and strength, and (4) complies with FDA GMP requirements. Any change from the pioneer with respect to any of these features requires a full BLA. In other words, there is no regulatory approval mechanism comparable to section 505(b)(2) for generic new drugs. A biosimilar application must contain analytical studies to show similarity, toxicity studies to show safety, and clinical studies for safety and effectiveness, unless FDA waives them as unnecessary. In contrast, generic new drugs are required only to show bioequivalence to the pioneer.

For an interchangeable biosimilar, there are two additional requirements. First, the application must show that the biosimilar can be expected to provide the same clinical result as the pioneer "in any given patient." Second, for a biological product given more than once to a patient, the application must show that the risk of switching between the biosimilar and the pioneer is no greater than the risk of the pioneer alone.

The FDA review process for both types of biosimilar applications is essentially the same as for a full BLA or NDA. A biosimilar application must be reviewed by the same FDA regulatory division that reviewed the pioneer BLA, and all the other procedures (e.g., Special Protocol Assessments, accelerated approval, REMS, Phase IV requirements and mandatory labeling change) and user fees apply.

A biosimilar application cannot be submitted to FDA earlier than four years after FDA approval of the pioneer BLA. Approval of a biosimilar application cannot be made effective earlier than 12 years after approval of the pioneer BLA. A new indication for a pioneer BLA receives no additional protection unless there is a structural change in the pioneer product.

The 12 years of market protection for a pioneer biological product cannot be challenged in the courts. It is similar to the five years of market protection for a pioneer new drug or the seven years for a pioneer orphan drug. It is much stronger than the patent term restoration available under the Hatch–Waxman Act for pioneer new drugs, which is very frequently challenged in the courts, often successfully.

FDA has long disliked its role in enforcing patents under the Hatch–Waxman Act and was relieved that it did incur this responsibility under the Biosimilars Act. Instead, the Biosimilars Act establishes an entirely new four-step process for resolving biosimilar patent issues. First, the biosimilar applicant must disclose to the pioneer BLA holder detailed information about its application. Second, the two parties must identify and evaluate all relevant patents. Third, if they cannot agree on the scope and validity of the patents, they must agree on a subset of patents for expedited litigation. Fourth, the biosimilar applicant must inform the pioneer BLA holder 180 days before marketing begins, and the pioneer can then sue the biosimilar on the remaining patents. Meanwhile, FDA can approve the biosimilar application when the 12-year statutory market protection expires, regardless of any patent issues or litigation. Because no biosimilar application has yet been submitted to FDA, and there is no precedent for this novel procedure, it is unclear how it will work in practice.

5. USER FEES

When user fees were first imposed on prescription drugs under the Prescription Drug User Fees Act of 1992, both new drugs and biological products were included. Following enactment of the Biosimilars Act of 2009, separate user fees were also enacted for biosimilar biological products in Title IV of the Food and Drug Administration Safety and Innovation Act, 126 Stat. 993, 1026 (2012), codified at 21 U.S.C. 379j–51.

D. REGULATING AND PROMOTING VACCINES

The most prominent activity of the Division of Biologics Standards, which became FDA's Bureau of Biologics in 1972, dealt with vaccines. The DBS's responsibility for vaccine safety was just one element of a larger public health effort to promote the development and use of agents to prevent infectious disease. This has been a goal of the federal public health apparatus for more than a century and, as later excerpts illustrate, it has achieved some dramatic successes. Consider, for example, FDA's approval of a new vaccine to prevent cervical cancer. *FDA Licenses New Vaccine for Prevention of Cervical Cancer and Other Diseases in Females Caused by Human Papillovirus*, FDA News, No. P06–77 (June 8, 2006).

Edward Mortimer, *Immunization Against Infectious Disease*

200 SCIENCE 902 (1978).

. . . In the United States since the turn of the century life expectancy has increased remarkably. Expected duration of life for individuals born in 1900 was 47.3 years; in 1970 it was 70.9 years. The age-adjusted death rate in 1900 was 17.2 deaths per thousand population, whereas in 1970 it was 9.5 per thousand, a reduction in mortality of 45 percent. . . .

. . . [T]he decrease in mortality has been most pronounced in younger age groups. . . . The mortality rate in children 1 to 4 years of age declined 96 percent between 1900 and 1970, whereas that in the population aged between 65 and 74 years declined by only a little more than a third. . . . [M]uch of this change in mortality in younger age groups is due to a decrease in deaths from certain infectious diseases, including the common contagious diseases of childhood, tuberculosis, meningitis, pneumonia, and epidemic diseases such as typhoid fever, plague, and smallpox. . . . [I]n children older than 1 year of age, approximately two-thirds of the decreased mortality can be attributed to a decline in deaths from the above-specified infectious diseases.

. . . .

In view of the above, what has been the contribution of immunization to the decreased mortality from infectious disease in the United States? In the case of a number of diseases, immunization—though available and of some effect—has been of negligible importance. These diseases include typhoid fever, cholera, epidemic typhus fever, and plague. Far more important than immunization has been control of transmission of the infecting organism. Thus, immunization against these diseases is reserved for those who, because of occupation or travel, cannot avoid exposure.

The disappearance of mortality from one disease (smallpox) and the rarity of deaths from two others (tetanus and poliomyelitis) can be attributed almost entirely to active immunization. . . .

1. GOVERNMENT SUPPORT FOR IMMUNIZATION

The federal vaccine program involves more than FDA review and approval of the agents used in immunization programs. Through many organizations, the federal and state governments help develop vaccines; encourage and in some cases require their use (*see Jacobson v. Commonwealth of Massachusetts*, 197 U.S. 11 (1905)); subsidize their distribution; and assume responsibility for anticipating disease threats for which prophylactic agents should be used or, if need be, devised. Currently, officials confront two major challenges. Scientists at the Centers for Disease Control and Prevention anticipate the possibility of a major flu pandemic in the near future, possibly the result of the spread of an avian flu virus, first to humans in Asia and then, inexorably, around the world. The last major flu pandemic, at the end of World War I, claimed more than 10 million lives in the U.S. alone. The other threat is a possible sequel to 9/11, the purposeful exposure of the U.S. population to an infectious agent for which no reliable prevention is now available. Anthrax and smallpox are two of several agents that lawmakers have directed public health authorities to address.

In short, vaccines represent a technology that government not only regulates but promotes. The responsible agencies often face conflicts in the performance of their regulatory functions because some of the most effective vaccines are capable, in rare cases, of causing the very disease they are supposed to prevent. One result has been legal claims brought by individuals who suffered adverse reactions from vaccines. These claims in turn have generated programs designed to compensate the "victims" of government-sponsored or encouraged immunization programs and, in various ways, to cushion the impact of potential liability on the dwindling number of private firms still engaged in manufacturing vaccines.

Frank A. Sloan, et al., *The Fragility of the U.S. Vaccine Supply*

351 NEW ENGLAND JOURNAL OF MEDICINE 23 (2004).

The number of companies that produce vaccines for the United States has declined markedly since the 1960s. Today only five companies produce all routine vaccines for this market, and for each of eight of these vaccines—including the measles, mumps, and rubella (MMR); diphtheria, pertussis, and tetanus (DPT); and polio vaccines—there is only one supplier. Should one of these suppliers cease production, it could take years to have a replacement vaccine licensed and publicly available.

The dearth of suppliers has decreased the availability of vaccines. In 2001–2002, the United States had shortages of 8 of the 11 recommended childhood vaccines: DPT, MMR, varicella, and pneumococcal conjugate vaccines. In 2004, the country again had a shortage of pneumococcal conjugate vaccine, prompting the Centers for Disease Control and Prevention (CDC) to recommend suspension of the third and fourth doses.

Several explanations for the small number of vaccine suppliers seem plausible. Developing a new vaccine is costly and risky. It can cost $700 million to bring a new vaccine from concept to market. Phase 3 trials for pneumococcal vaccines and *Haemophilus influenzae* type b vaccine required tens of thousands of subjects. Some observers have suggested that the licensure requirements of the Food and Drug Administration (FDA) are excessively stringent and unnecessarily limit the entry of new suppliers into the market. Unlike pharmaceutical manufacturers, vaccine producers must obtain a license in advance to produce a vaccine at a particular site, and the FDA encourages creation of commercial production capacity before the license is granted, a stipulation that puts the company at substantial financial risk.

Vaccine suppliers also face increasingly stringent regulation of production. Suppliers undergo frequent FDA inspections of their production facilities, individual product batches require separate approval for release, and slight modifications to production processes or even the packaging of products may trigger expensive product reviews. The FDA requires frequent upgrades of vaccine production to reflect state-of-the-art manufacturing processes. In the mid-1990s, the FDA implemented Team Biologics, a new inspection process that imposed new record-keeping and administrative requirements. This regulatory approach is likely to increase the costs of producing vaccines, add to the uncertainty of rewards for investment in research and development and in production capacity, and discourage the entry of new suppliers.

. . .

Despite intensive regulation of quality, vaccine companies are vulnerable to product-liability lawsuits. A surge of lawsuits in the 1980s resulted in a serious concern about the supply of DPT and other vaccines. . . .

Pharmaceutical companies cannot justify investment in vaccines if their risk-adjusted returns on investment are low, and vaccine profitability appears to be relatively low. . . .

Institute of Medicine, Financing Vaccines in the 21st Century: Assuring Access and Availability

National Academies Press, 2003

. . . .

The federal government currently purchases between 52 and 55 percent of the childhood vaccines distributed in the United States, primarily for children who are uninsured or Medicaid-eligible. Nearly 20 doses of vaccines against 11 diseases are required for childhood immunization, at a cost of about $400 at the discounted prices available to the public sector (up to $600 at private-sector prices). This investment strains the ability of both the public and private sectors to immunize a daily birth cohort of more than 11,000 babies. Additional funds are required for the administration of the vaccines, as well as the vaccine shipping and storage costs.

. . . .

Recent vaccine shortages that were unprecedented in their scope and severity, as well as diminishing numbers of vaccine suppliers for the U.S. market, are early warning signs of other problems that require systemic remedies to assure a healthy and reliable vaccine supply system. While temporary production problems appear to have eased, the potential for disruption remains. The problem of vaccine shortages has raised concerns about the relationships among the size of the government vaccine market, low vaccine prices, and the scale of investment in the production of current vaccines and the development of new vaccine products. The ability of the government to negotiate low prices for recommended vaccines is important to public health agencies and others that are trying to stretch tight budgets to cover both traditional vaccines and a growing array of new and higher-priced vaccine products. On the other hand, adequate financial incentives are necessary to sustain private investment in the vaccine production and licensing processes if the vaccine industry is to remain competitive and have the capacity to innovate within a global vaccine market.

. . . .

Ultimately, the [Institute of Medicine] committee determined that the best strategy would be to formulate a comprehensive plan that can address multiple goals. This plan would encompass a mandated insurance benefit strategy that includes a subsidy for insurers; a decentralized, private market for vaccines; and a voucher program for the uninsured. . . .

The prospect of a guaranteed public subsidy for selected vaccines would provide economic incentives that would encourage manufacturers to invest in the clinical trial, licensing, and production processes necessary to move a vaccine product from the early stage of discovery to its use in routine medical care. Reducing the financial uncertainties associated with these processes would stimulate the market and encourage the development of new and effective vaccine products. . . .

2. MANUFACTURER LIABILITY FOR VACCINE INJURIES

Reyes v. Wyeth Laboratories

498 F.2d 1264 (5th Cir. 1974).

■ WISDOM, CIRCUIT JUDGE:

. . . .

I.

Twenty or thirty years ago poliomyelitis was a dread disease that especially attacked the very young. In 1952 alone, there were 57,879 reported cases of polio in the United States; 21,269 of these resulted in crippling paralysis to the victims. By 1970, when Anita Reyes contracted polio, the number of those stricken by polio had diminished dramatically; she was one of just 33 individuals to be afflicted during that year. Credit for this precipitous decline must go primarily to the medical researchers who discovered the viral nature of the disease, and were able to isolate and reproduce the virus in an inactivated or an attenuated form. But credit for this remarkable achievement must also be given to such laboratories as Wyeth, which processed the polio vaccine, and to massive federal-state public health programs for the administration of the vaccine.

On May 8, 1970, Anita Reyes was fed two drops of Sabin oral polio vaccine by eye-dropper at the Hidalgo County Department of Health clinic in Mission, Texas. The vaccine was administered to Anita by a registered nurse; there were no doctors present. Mrs. Reyes testified that she was not warned of any possible danger involved in Anita's taking the vaccine. Mrs. Reyes has a seventh grade education, but her primary language is Spanish. She signed a form releasing the State of Texas from "all liability in connection with immunization". The form contained no warning of any sort, and it is apparent from her testimony that she either did not read the form or lacked the linguistic ability to understand its significance. About fourteen days after the vaccine was administered, Anita Reyes became ill. On May 23, 1970, she was admitted to the McAllen (Texas) General Hospital, where her disease was diagnosed as Type I paralytic poliomyelitis. As a result of the polio, at the time of trial Anita was completely paralyzed from the waist down, her left arm had become atrophied, and she was unable to control her bladder or bowel movements.

. . . Included with every vial, each of which contained ten doses of vaccine, was a "package circular" provided by Wyeth which was intended to warn doctors, hospitals, or other purchasers of potential dangers in ingesting the vaccine. Mrs. Lenore Wiley, the public health nurse who administered the vaccine to Anita Reyes, testified that she had read the directions on this package insert, but that it was not the practice of the nurses at the Mission Health Clinic to pass on the warnings to the vaccinees or to their guardians. She testified that she gave Mrs. Reyes no warning before she administered the vaccine to Anita.

On October 7, 1970, Epifanio Reyes, individually and as next friend of his minor daughter, brought this action on theories of strict products

liability, breach of warranty, and negligence. In his complaint he
alleged that his daughter had contracted polio from the live virus in
Wyeth's vaccine, and that Wyeth's failure to warn him or his wife that
this might occur rendered it liable for Anita's injuries. . . .

II.

. . . Texas courts recognize both tort and warranty theories of
products liability. This case was tried, briefed, and argued on appeal
entirely on the tort theory of strict liability. . . .

We begin the inquiry by asking whether the vaccine was
unreasonably dangerous, that is, in a defective condition when Anita
Reyes received it. It is clear, of course that the vaccine was not itself
defective. Wyeth Vaccine Lot No. 15509 was exactly what its makers
and the Texas public health authorities intended it to be: trivalent live-
virus Sabin oral polio vaccine. The live virus which the jury concluded
caused Anita's poliomyelitis was not inadvertently included in the
mixture. Indeed, it is the presence of the living but attenuated Type I,
II, and III viruses which makes the Sabin vaccine so effective.

Although the living virus in the vaccine does not make the vaccine
defective, it does make it what the Restatement calls an "unavoidably
unsafe product", one which cannot be made "safe" no matter how
carefully it is manufactured. Such products are not necessarily
"*unreasonably* dangerous", for as this Court has long recognized in
wrestling with product liability questions, many goods possess both
utility and danger. Rather, in evaluating the possible liability of a
manufacturer for injuries caused by his inevitably hazardous products,
a two-step analysis is required to determine first, whether the product
is so unsafe that marketing it at all is "unreasonably dangerous per se",
and, if not, whether the product has been introduced into the stream of
commerce without sufficient safeguards and is thereby "unreasonably
dangerous as marketed". . . .

Since Sabin oral polio vaccine is not "unreasonably dangerous per
se", we move to the second step of our analysis to determine whether it
is "unreasonably dangerous as marketed", for to conclude that the
maker of an unavoidably unsafe product did not act unreasonably in
placing it on the market is not to relieve him of the responsibility to
market it in such a way as to prevent unreasonable danger. In the case
of a product such as Sabin oral polio vaccine, this translates into a duty
to provide proper warnings in selling the product. . . . Consequently, the
Restatement requires a seller who has reason to believe that danger
may result from a particular use of his product to provide adequate
warning of the danger in order that the product's potential for harm
may be reduced. Failure to give such a warning when it is required will
itself present a "defect" in the product and will, without more, cause the
product to be "unreasonably dangerous as marketed".

. . . .

Wyeth does not deny that its vaccine is "unavoidably unsafe", or
contend that it was unaware of the danger. Rather, the appellant
contends that if it had a duty to warn at all, that duty was discharged
by the warning contained on the package insert which accompanied the
vials of vaccine sold to the Texas State Department of Health. This is
so, Wyeth asserts, because the Sabin trivalent oral polio vaccine in

issue here is a "prescription drug", and those who prepare such drugs are not required to warn the ultimate consumer. If the warning to the dispensing physician or authorities (here the Texas and Hidalgo County Public Health Departments) was adequate, Wyeth is not liable for any harm caused by the vaccine. Resolution of these contentions is crucial; Wyeth concedes in its brief that "since it is undisputed that Wyeth did not warn Reyes, but only the Texas State Department of Health, a finding that the vaccine was not a prescription drug establishes as a matter of law the defectiveness of the vaccine for purposes of a prima facie case in strict products liability."

We cannot quarrel with the general proposition that where *prescription* drugs are concerned, the manufacturer's duty to warn is limited to an obligation to advise the prescribing physician of any potential dangers that may result from the drug's use. . . .

Although there is no question that Sabin oral vaccine is licensed for sale only as a prescription drug, the district court, in its charge to the jury, noted that the vaccine was not administered as a prescription drug at the Mission Clinic. The court charged: "if you [the jury] find that a warning should have been given, the warning had to be given to Anita and her parents, not to Mrs. Wiley, that Public Health nurse, somebody else[.] . . . The ultimate consumer is the one that had to be warned." The district court apparently based this instruction on the leading federal case in the area, *Davis v. Wyeth Laboratories,* 399 F.2d 121 (9th Cir. 1968). In *Davis,* the plaintiff had allegedly contracted polio from Wyeth oral vaccine distributed at a public clinic. The Ninth Circuit held that where no individualized medical judgment intervenes between the manufacturer of a prescription drug and the ultimate consumer, "it is the responsibility of the manufacturer to see that warnings reach the consumer, either by giving warning itself or by obligating the purchaser to give warning. Where there is no physician to make an "individualized balancing . . . of the risks", the Court reasoned, the very justification for the prescription drug exception evaporates. Thus, as in the case of patent drugs sold over the counter without prescription, the manufacturer of a prescription drug who knows or has reason to know that it will not be dispensed as such a drug must provide the consumer with adequate information so that he can balance the risks and benefits of a given medication himself. . . .

Wyeth does not resist the Ninth Circuit's holding in *Davis,* but asserts that the instant case can be distinguished on four grounds. First, the appellant argues, Davis received his vaccine during a mass immunization program, whereas Anita Reyes ingested her vaccine at her parents' request. Second, Wyeth stresses the fact that Davis received his vaccine from a pharmacist, but Reyes's was administered by a public health nurse. Third, Wyeth's active participation in the mass immunization program involved in the *Davis* case is contrasted to its relatively passive role here. Finally, Wyeth urges that unlike the situation in *Davis,* here it had no knowledge that the vaccine would not be administered as a prescription drug.

None of these asserted grounds for distinguishing *Davis* justifies a different result here. The first two arguments are admittedly distinctions between *Davis* and the instant controversy, but they have no bearing on the *rationale* of the *Davis* opinion. Whether vaccine was received during a mass immunization or an on-going program, whether it was administered by nurse or pharmacist, it was, in both these cases, dispensed without the sort of individualized medical balancing of the risks to the vaccinee that is contemplated by the prescription drug exception. The third and fourth asserted bases for distinguishing *Davis* from this case are essentially the same: Wyeth took no active part in the vaccination process here, and did not know that its vaccine would be dispensed without procedures appropriate for distribution of prescription drugs.

Were we to conclude that Wyeth neither knew nor had reason to know that its vaccine would be dispensed without prescription drug safeguards, we might be required to hold that the *rationale* in *Davis* is inapplicable here. But Wyeth had ample reason to foresee the way in which its vaccine would be distributed. . . .

Viewed in this light, the present controversy, however it differs from *Davis* factually, invites application of the *Davis* principles, and the conclusion that Wyeth was under a duty to warn Anita Reyes's parents of the danger inherent in its vaccine. . . .

. . . Aware of its unavoidable dangers and cognizant that it foreseeably would not be dispensed as a prescription drug, Wyeth nonetheless failed to warn Mrs. Reyes that its vaccine could cause polio in some few of the millions receiving the medication. Administered without a warning, the vaccine was "defective", hence unreasonably dangerous. . . . [W]e must assume in the absence of evidence to the contrary that Anita's parents would have acted on the warning, had it been given. Perhaps this would have prevented her polio. It unquestionably would have avoided Wyeth's liability.

V.

In closing, we feel that we should comment on the important policy considerations raised in the briefs of the amici curiae, the American Academy of Pediatrics [AAP] and the Conference of State and Territorial Epidemiologists [CSTE]. Both insist that the holding we reached is "dangerous" to the nation's preventive medicine programs and contravenes a strong public policy favoring large-scale participation in immunization efforts to combat infectious disease. . . .

Citing a recent Texas statute which requires that all Texas schoolchildren receive polio vaccine, the AAP insists that this renders any warnings futile. This argument assumes, of course, that the only options available are to ingest the oral vaccine at the clinic or to eschew immunity. Obviously, however, one can choose to be inoculated with killed-virus Salk vaccine, either to provide complete immunity or as a precautionary prelude to ingesting oral vaccine. The AAP also insists that the warnings would be so complex or misleading as to confuse and frighten potential vaccinees. This is possible. Yet we believe that a warning advising a patron of a public health clinic of the relative risk of contracting polio from a "wild" source against the slight chance of contracting it from the vaccine would not be terrifying or confusing. . . .

[AAP's] position raises a policy consideration scarcely less urgent than the need for mass immunization from disease; the right of the individual to choose and control what risk he will take, in the absence of an individualized medical judgment by a physician familiar with his needs and susceptibilities. Recognition of this right counters the argument advanced in the CSTE's brief that once an epidemiological balancing of the risks of immunization has been made, no warning is required. Clearly, the rationale excusing warnings to ultimate consumers of prescription drugs whose physicians have balanced the risk for them, cannot be extended to a medical determination that statistical probabilities justify universal immunization. . . .

Here, the qualitative risk was great, the quantitative risk minute. The end sought to be achieved—immunization—is important both to the individual and society. Striking the balance in this case is difficult, but . . . two elements . . . lend strong policy support to our holding. First, the risk here was foreseeable statistically, although unknowable individually. Thus, unlike the abreaction cases, here there was a basis for rational choice. Second, a choice here, if given, had an opportunity to be efficacious, since reasonable alternatives to taking the oral vaccine were available. . . .

. . . Statistically predictable as are these rare cases of vaccine-induced polio, a strong argument can be advanced that the loss ought not lie where it falls (on the victim), but should be borne by the manufacturer as a foreseeable cost of doing business, and passed on to the public in the form of price increases to his customers.

. . . [W]e hold that in the case of a prescription drug which is unavoidably unsafe, and as to which there is a certain, though small, risk throughout the population, there must be *either* a warning—meaningful and complete so as to be understood by the recipient—*or* an individualized medical judgment that this treatment or medication is necessary and desirable for this patient. Anita's parents received neither. Wyeth is therefore liable for the consequence of its failure to market its unavoidably unsafe product in such a way as to warn Anita's parents of its unreasonably dangerous condition.

NOTE

Congressional Response to the Reyes *Decision.* In the National Childhood Vaccine Injury Compensation Act of 1986, discussed *infra* p. 1150, Congress overrode *Reyes* by declaring that childhood vaccine manufacturers need provide warnings of unavoidable side effects only to the administering physician or nurse.

3. GOVERNMENT LIABILITY FOR VACCINE INJURIES

As the *Reyes* case illustrates, public campaigns to achieve wide immunization can produce cases of diseases that are attributable to the vaccine itself. In addition to seeking recovery from vaccine manufacturers, victims of these "accidents" have occasionally sought recovery from the government agencies responsible for a vaccine's release and use. In the following opinion, the Supreme Court addresses this issue and at the same time provides a close look at the workings of FDA's vaccine approval process.

The case provides a window on a distinctive facet of the regulatory process for vaccines. Because most vaccines are the byproduct of natural biological processes, successive batches may differ in their composition and thus in their effects. This means that a batch produced today by the same process used to produce the doses used in clinical trials may diverge, slightly or even significantly, from the tested formula. To deal with this problem, DBS (and later FDA) called for individual testing of each successive batch—both by the manufacturer and then by the agency itself. In short, FDA often plays two roles to assure the safety of vaccines: it evaluates and approves the results of tests on the "model" of the product, and then, repeatedly over time, it examines successive reproductions to assure that—as closely as can be—they mimic the "model."

Berkovitz v. United States

486 U.S. 531 (1988).

■ MARSHALL, J., delivered the opinion for a unanimous Court.

The question in this case is whether the discretionary function exception of the Federal Tort Claims Act (FTCA or Act), 28 U.S.C. § 2680(a), bars a suit based on the Government's licensing of an oral polio vaccine and on its subsequent approval of the release of a specific lot of that vaccine to the public.

On May 10, 1979, Kevan Berkovitz, then a 2-month-old infant, ingested a dose of Orimune, an oral polio vaccine manufactured by Lederle Laboratories. Within one month, he contracted a severe case of polio. The disease left Berkovitz almost completely paralyzed and unable to breathe without the assistance of a respirator. . . .

Berkovitz, joined by his parents as guardians, subsequently filed suit against the United States in Federal District Court. The complaint alleged that the United States was liable for his injuries under the FTCA, because the Division of Biologic Standards (DBS), then a part of the National Institutes of Health, had acted wrongfully in licensing Lederle Laboratories to produce Orimune and because the Bureau of Biologics of the Food and Drug Administration (FDA) had acted wrongfully in approving release to the public of the particular lot of vaccine containing Berkovitz's dose. According to petitioners, these actions violated federal law and policy regarding the inspection and approval of polio vaccines.

The Government moved to dismiss the suit for lack of subject-matter jurisdiction on the ground that the agency actions fell within the discretionary function exception of the FTCA. . . .

FTCA, 28 U.S.C. § 1346(b), generally authorizes suits against the United States for damages

> "for injury or loss of property, or personal injury or death caused by the negligent or wrongful act or omission of any employee of the Government while acting within the scope of his office or employment, under circumstances where the United States, if a private person, would be liable to the claimant in accordance with the law of the place where the act or omission occurred."

The Act includes a number of exceptions to this broad waiver of sovereign immunity. The exception relevant to this case provides that no liability shall lie for "[a]ny claim . . . based upon the exercise or performance or the failure to exercise or perform a discretionary function or duty on the part of a federal agency or an employee of the Government, whether or not the discretion involved be abused." 28 U.S.C. § 2680(a).

. . . [T]he discretionary function exception will not apply when a federal statute, regulation, or policy specifically prescribes a course of action for an employee to follow. In this event, the employee has no rightful option but to adhere to the directive. And if the employee's conduct cannot appropriately be the product of judgment or choice, then there is no discretion in the conduct for the discretionary function exception to protect.

Moreover, assuming the challenged conduct involves an element of judgment, a court must determine whether that judgment is of the kind that the discretionary function exception was designed to shield. . . . The exception, properly construed, . . . protects only governmental actions and decisions based on considerations of public policy. . . .

Petitioners' suit raises two broad claims. First, petitioners assert that the DBS violated a federal statute and accompanying regulations in issuing a license to Lederle Laboratories to produce Orimune. Second, petitioners argue that the Bureau of Biologics of the FDA violated federal regulations and policy in approving the release of the particular lot of Orimune that contained Kevan Berkovitz's dose. . . .

Under federal law, a manufacturer must receive a product license prior to marketing a brand of live oral polio vaccine. . . .

In deciding whether to issue a license, the DBS is required to comply with certain statutory and regulatory provisions. . . .

Petitioners' first allegation with regard to the licensing of Orimune is that the DBS issued a product license without first receiving data that the manufacturer must submit showing how the product, at the various stages of the manufacturing process, matched up against regulatory safety standards. The discretionary function exception does not bar a cause of action based on this allegation. The statute and regulations described above require, as a precondition to licensing, that the DBS receive certain test data from the manufacturer relating to the product's compliance with regulatory standards. The DBS has no discretion to issue a license without first receiving the required test data; to do so would violate a specific statutory and regulatory directive. . . .

Petitioners' other allegation regarding the licensing of Orimune is difficult to describe with precision. Petitioners contend that the DBS licensed Orimune even though the vaccine did not comply with certain regulatory safety standards. This charge may be understood in any of three ways. . . .

If petitioners aver that the DBS licensed Orimune either without determining whether the vaccine complied with regulatory standards or after determining that the vaccine failed to comply, the discretionary function exception does not bar the claim. Under the scheme governing the DBS's regulation of polio vaccines, the DBS may not issue a license except upon an examination of the product and a determination that the product complies with all regulatory standards. The agency has no discretion to deviate from this mandated procedure. . . .

If petitioners' claim is that the DBS made a determination that Orimune complied with regulatory standards, but that the determination was incorrect, the question of the applicability of the discretionary function exception requires a somewhat different analysis. In that event, the question turns on whether the manner and method of determining compliance with the safety standards at issue involve agency judgment of the kind protected by the discretionary function exception. . . . We . . . leave it to the District Court to decide, if petitioners choose to press this claim, whether agency officials appropriately exercise policy judgment in determining that a vaccine product complies with the relevant safety standards.

The regulatory scheme governing release of vaccine lots is distinct from that governing the issuance of licenses. The former set of regulations places an obligation on manufacturers to examine all vaccine lots prior to distribution to ensure that they comply with regulatory standards. These regulations, however, do not impose a corresponding duty on the Bureau of Biologics. Although the regulations empower the Bureau to examine any vaccine lot and prevent the distribution of a noncomplying lot, they do not require the Bureau to take such action in all cases. The regulations generally allow the Bureau to determine the appropriate manner in which to regulate the release of vaccine lots, rather than mandating certain kinds of agency action. . . .

Given this regulatory context, the discretionary function exception bars any claims that challenge the Bureau's formulation of policy as to the appropriate way in which to regulate the release of vaccine lots. . . . The discretionary function exception, however, does not apply if the acts complained of do not involve the permissible exercise of policy discretion. . . .

Viewed in light of these principles, petitioners' claim regarding the release of the vaccine lot from which Kevan Berkovitz received his dose survives the Government's motion to dismiss. Petitioners allege that, under the authority granted by the regulations, the Bureau of Biologics has adopted a policy of testing all vaccine lots for compliance with safety standards and preventing the distribution to the public of any lots that fail to comply. Petitioners further allege that notwithstanding this policy . . . employees of the Bureau knowingly approved the release of a lot that did not comply with safety standards. . . . If those allegations are correct—that is, if the Bureau's policy did not allow the official who took the challenged action to release a noncomplying lot on the basis of policy considerations—the discretionary function exception does not bar the claim. . . .

NOTES

1. *Proceedings on Remand.* The court of appeals denied the government's motion to dismiss and remanded the case for a trial on the merits. 858 F.2d 122 (3d Cir. 1988). The case was then consolidated with several other suits seeking damages for injuries resulting from the

administration of Orimune. *In re Sabin Polio Vaccine Products Liability Litigation*, 743 F. Supp. 410 (D. Md. 1990).

2. *Related Theory of Government Liability.* In *Griffin v. United States*, 500 F.2d 1059 (3d Cir. 1974), the court sustained recovery against the government for the severe injuries suffered following administration of a dose of Sabin polio vaccine that the Division of Biological Standards had licensed. The DBS had promulgated a regulation establishing specifications that its employees were to apply in determining nonvirulence of batches of the vaccine—specifications that many outside experts had criticized as unnecessarily stringent. The DBS had released the batch of vaccine administered to Mrs. Griffin even though it did not meet these specifications. The court disagreed with the government's contention that the decision whether to release the vaccine was discretionary and that the DBS regulation required a judgmental determination.

4. COMPENSATING VACCINE INJURIES

Michael Greenberger, *The 800 Pound Gorilla Sleeps: The Federal Government's Lackadaisical Liability and Compensation Policies in the Context of Pre-Event Vaccine Immunization Programs*

8 JOURNAL OF HEALTH CARE LAW & POLICY 7 (2005).

. . . .

The United States government has implemented three primary vaccine liability and compensation schemes over recent years. . . .

A. The National Swine Flu Immunization Program of 1976

The National Swine Flu Immunization Program of 1976 [hereinafter the Swine Flu Act] was the federal government's first foray into a vaccine liability and compensation program. Fear of a flu pandemic began in January of 1976 when four cases of swine flu were discovered at Fort Dix, New Jersey. This raised grave concerns in the public health community because the community feared a repeat of the swine flu pandemic that had killed millions in 1918–1919. While neither a swine flu epidemic nor a pandemic materialized in the early months of 1976 (the flu season generally runs from September through March), Congress quickly authorized the procurement of nearly 200 million doses of the swine flu vaccine in April of 1976.

Concerns over vaccine manufacturer liability did not arise until insurers declared that they would end coverage for vaccine manufacturers as of June 30, 1976. This refusal stemmed in large part from the case of *Reyes v. Wyeth Laboratories*, 498 F.2d 1264 (5th Cir. 1974), which held polio vaccine manufacturers strictly liable for failing to provide product warnings directly to vaccinees which would have allowed vaccinees to assess the risks of the vaccine. . . .

. . . As a result, swine flu manufacturers stopped producing the vaccine that would potentially save the lives of thousands, if not millions, of Americans if the swine flu returned for the fall flu season.

However, Congress eventually passed the Swine Flu Act on August 12, 1976 . . . .

. . . .

The Swine Flu Act protected manufacturers and distributors of the swine flu vaccine, as well as those who administered the vaccine. Plaintiffs asserted claims directly against the United States through the Federal Tort Claims Act rather than against the alleged "wrongdoer," and the United States assumed the liability of manufacturers, distributors, and vaccinators, "based on any theory of liability . . . including negligence, strict liability in tort, and breach of warranty." In addition, the courts consistently interpreted the "any theory of liability" language as establishing a no-fault compensation system that made the government liable to all plaintiffs who could demonstrate that their injuries were caused by the swine flu vaccine. However, the United States would seek indemnification from negligent organizations or individuals covered by the Swine Flu Act's liability protections.

. . . .

The swine flu vaccination program was successful in terms of getting a large number of people vaccinated in a short period. During the two-month run of the program, over 40 million Americans—nearly a third of the adult population of the United States—received the swine flu vaccination. However, a vast field of vaccine injury litigation subsequently began in which attorneys and medical experts readily attributed injuries to the vaccine. By 1985, the government had paid out $90 million to those that developed Guillain–Barre syndrome, an often reversible, but sometimes fatal, form of paralysis, which had been attributed to the swine flu vaccine. . . .

B.   National Childhood Vaccine Injury Act of 1986

Prior to 1986, the number of manufacturers making childhood vaccines had "declined significantly." In addition, the early 1980s exhibited an increase in vaccine tort litigation, which in part grew out of the fact that injuries previously unrecognized as arising from childhood vaccines were starting to be connected to those vaccines. . . . At the time, vaccine manufacturers faced grave difficulty in obtaining liability insurance, which caused one vaccine manufacturer to stop producing vaccines temporarily in 1984. Others were threatening to follow suit. . . . Congress once again involved the federal government in vaccine liability and compensation through the National Childhood Vaccine Injury Act of 1986 (NCVIA). However, NCVIA's liability and compensation provisions were crafted differently from the Swine Flu Act, largely due to the government's increasing reluctance to accept financial responsibility.

Specifically, NCVIA established a two-staged, no fault compensation system for specific childhood vaccines (exclusive of the smallpox vaccine). The first stage was a mandatory "no-fault" system, administered by a special master of the federal district court, which compensated specific injuries resulting from childhood vaccination. This administrative hearing provided compensation regardless of the party alleged to have caused the injury, and the respondent was always the United States.

However, unlike the Swine Flu Act of 1976, which did not limit awards, NCVIA capped certain types of awards. . . .

If unsatisfied with an administrative award, the plaintiff could enter NCVIA's second stage and commence traditional tort litigation against the vaccine manufacturer. . . . If a plaintiff chose litigation, Congress made certain alterations to traditional tort law to protect vaccine manufacturers, as the government would not pay awards that arose from litigation. First, the manufacturer was not liable for injuries or death that resulted from "unavoidable" side effects that were inherent in properly prepared, labeled, and administered vaccines. Next, Congress legislatively altered the rule established in *Reyes* by declaring that childhood vaccine manufacturers were not liable for failing to provide such warnings. Rather, simply providing those warnings to the administering physician or nurse was adequate. . . . Finally, a manufacturer was immune from punitive damages in a civil trial if it complied with the Federal Food, Drug, and Cosmetic Act and the Public Health Service Act when manufacturing the vaccine, unless the manufacturer engaged in fraudulent, wrongful, or criminal action when submitting information for the vaccine's approval. . . .

A final retreat from the generosity of the Swine Flu Act was that NCVIA made its compensation secondary to state and private sources of compensation as well as federal sources. NCVIA clearly stated that the federal government had liability in this area secondary to state compensation programs; private or public health benefits; private insurance; state "health benefits programs." . . .

C. Phase I Smallpox Vaccination Program

Believing that regimes and persons hostile to the United States may possess *Variola major*, the etiological agent of smallpox, President Bush announced the Phase I smallpox vaccination program in December of 2002—a program which aspired to vaccinate 500,000 first responders against smallpox. While the smallpox vaccine had been used routinely in America until 1972, few in today's medical field have any experience administering the smallpox vaccine. In addition, the smallpox vaccine . . . has been referred to as the "least safe human vaccine" available today.

. . . Congress and the President knew they had to protect a variety of entities and persons from liability and compensate those injured or killed by the vaccine. Otherwise, the Phase I smallpox vaccination program would likely fail. . . .

Initially, the Phase I smallpox vaccination program relied upon Section 304 of the Homeland Security Act of 2002 (passed in November 2002) as its vehicle for providing liability protection and compensation to injured vaccinees. However, the liability protection afforded was ambiguous and the compensation available to those injured was inadequate.

. . .

It was not until April 2003—three months after Phase I began—that Congress passed a law, the Smallpox Emergency Personnel Protection Act of 2003 (SEPPA), to improve upon the compensation provisions of Section 304. Specifically, SEPPA aimed to "provide benefits and other compensation for certain individuals with injuries resulting from administration of smallpox countermeasures." Like the Swine Flu Act and NCVIA, SEPPA created a no-fault compensation program for vaccinees injured or killed by the smallpox vaccine. SEPPA supplied medical benefits, death benefits, and lost income benefits for covered injuries, resulting from countermeasures administered to those volunteering before a confirmed active case of smallpox is discovered anywhere in the world.

However, there are limits to SEPPA's compensation. For example, like NCVIA, SEPPA's benefits are also secondary to all other sources of compensation . . . . In addition, SEPPA imposed caps on any award, which are more stringent than previous federal vaccine compensation and liability laws. . . .

Ultimately . . . [e]ven SEPPA's no-fault compensation package and added liability protections were not enough to invigorate the [federal Phase I vaccination] program. As of January 31, 2005 (the most recent data available online as of this writing), only 39,608 first responders have been vaccinated—far short of the government's goal of 500,000. . . .

D. The Support Anti-Terrorism by Fostering Effective Technologies Act

Cognizant of SEPPA's shortcomings, some experts are belatedly suggesting that the solution to the dilemma of vaccine liability protection and compensation lies in the Support Anti-Terrorism by Fostering Effective Technologies Act (SAFETY Act]. Congress passed the SAFETY Act in November of 2002 (as part of the Homeland Security Act of 2002) as a response to the growing concern of liability protection for technologies developed to combat terrorism. Through passage of the Act, Congress aimed to ensure that the threat of liability would not discourage potential development of technologies that could significantly reduce the risks or mitigate the effects of large-scale acts of terrorism.

However, the SAFETY Act is not an attractive option for a viable biodefense vaccine liability and compensation scheme for the following three reasons. First, as its legislative history illustrates, the Act was not drafted with biodefense vaccines in mind. Rather, the purpose of the Act was to encourage the development of anti-terrorism hardware such as computer systems, explosion detection services, and audio/video identifiers. Accordingly, the drafters gave little—if any—thought to the issue of injury compensation because, unlike biodefense vaccines, SAFETY Act technologies do not involve intimate contact with people. Second, even if the SAFETY Act were applicable to biodefense vaccines, the Act's procedural and insurance requirements are overly burdensome. In fact, the entire basis of liability protection in the SAFETY Act context hinges upon the ability to obtain insurance, which is virtually impossible in the vaccine context. Thus, it would be extremely difficult to obtain protection for pre-event biodefense vaccination programs under the Act. Third, even if the procedural and insurance requirements are satisfied, the level of liability protection available under the Act is far too broad and would be provided at the expense of those injured by the vaccine. . . .

... The Phase I smallpox vaccination program taught us an important lesson: that without adequate compensation, it will be difficult to attract volunteer vaccinees. Indeed, days before President Bush formally announced the Phase I vaccination program, Service Employees International Union (SEIU), America's largest health care worker union, demanded that a "simple and fair compensation system—like [NCVIA]—should be made available to assist anyone who is injured from receiving the vaccine or coming into contact with someone who received it." The limited compensation package offered by Section 304 failed to encourage first responders to volunteer for vaccination. Furthermore, even SEPPA's improved compensation scheme did little to increase participation in the program. In particular, the limits and caps SEPPA placed on awards were more stringent than the previous federal vaccination programs, and thus less attractive to first responders.

Compensation should also restore an injured vaccinee to their pre-injury positions. As mentioned above, SEPPA generally offered benefits that were less generous than either NCVIA or the Swine Flu Immunization Program. . . .

NOTE

In *Bruesewitz v. Wyeth LLC*, 131 S. Ct. 1068 (2011), the Supreme Court held that the NCVIA preempts all design defect claims against manufacturers brought by plaintiffs who seek compensation in court for injury caused by vaccine side effects, and thus that the NCVIA is their only source of compensation.

E. BLOOD AND BLOOD PRODUCTS

1. REGULATORY JURISDICTION

Prior to 1970, the Biologics Act did not expressly cover blood or blood products. Two earlier cases had produced conflicting answers to the question of whether blood products are "biological products." In *United States v. Steinschreiber*, 219 F. Supp. 373 (S.D.N.Y. 1963), *aff'd per curiam*, 326 F.2d 759 (2d Cir. 1964), the court held that human blood plasma is analogous to a therapeutic serum and is thus properly regulated under the Biologics Act. The court also concluded that processing and drying liquid blood constituted sufficient steps in the "manufacture" or "preparation" of the final product to subject those activities to the Act. But *Blank v. United States*, 400 F.2d 302 (5th Cir. 1968), held that citrated whole human blood and packed human red blood cells were not analogous to a therapeutic serum. The court concluded that only immunological agents were covered by the Biologics Act. However, it sustained the defendant's conviction under the FD&C Act for interstate shipment of a misbranded drug. Following the Fifth Circuit's ruling, Congress amended the Biologics Act specifically to include blood and blood components or derivatives in the definition of "biological product." 84 Stat. 1297, 1308 (1970), codified at 42 U.S.C. 262(i)(1) (section 351(i)(1) of the PHS Act).

Although BLA requirements of section 351(a) apply only to products introduced or delivered for introduction into interstate commerce, the provision of the Biologics Act prohibiting false labeling, section 351(b), contains no interstate commerce requirement. Moreover, the power FDA has under section 361 Public Health Service Act to promulgate regulations to prevent the spread of communicable diseases has no interstate commerce limitations, either. Consequently, the agency's authority over the blood supply extends even to the most local blood banks.

2. THE REGULATORY MECHANISM

Blood and processed blood derivatives, such as plasma and clotting factors, are licensed biological products under the PHS Act. Prior to 1997 the statute prescribed two types of licensure for blood products, as for other biologics. A processor—such as a blood bank—required an establishment license from FDA confirming that its facilities and procedures could produce products that, in the statute's words, were "safe, pure, and potent." However, it also needed a license for each product that it manufactured or distributed, specifying requirements designed to assure satisfaction of that statutory standard. Now, pursuant to the FDA Modernization Act's directive to combine establishment and product licenses, a distributor of a blood product needs only a single biologics license, but approval of a BLA requires proof that its facilities are equipped to produce a compliant product. While many BLAs are proprietary, like an NDA, those for blood products typically are generic. Thus, numerous establishments can hold essentially identical licenses for the same generic product, such as "source plasma, human."

The reason why licenses for similar blood products are essentially identical should be obvious. Distributors all draw upon the same source of supply—donated or in some circumstances purchased whole human blood or blood fractions. In this respect blood is more like a commodity than a proprietary product. To be sure, units of whole blood are not all identical, as is demonstrated by the division of blood into different types—A, AB, B, and O, each in two forms, – and +. But within these categories, units of whole blood are essentially interchangeable.

The primary goals of blood regulation are easy to state but hard to achieve. For most blood products, clinical utility is established by long clinical experience. Safety is the central concern. And the task for regulators is to assure that the source material does not transmit disease infecting the donor and to enforce measures that prevent blood and blood products from being contaminated in the distribution process. Thus, much of the regulatory effort is focused on the screening and testing of donors and tracking the distribution of individual units.

A relatively small share of blood is used in the form in which it was collected, i.e., as single units transfused into individual patients. Here the risk of disease transmission is confined; only the recipient of a contaminated unit of blood is potentially vulnerable. But most blood is fractionated, pooled, and processed to yield a variety of useful products. For example, factor H, a product used to stimulate clotting in hemophiliacs, is produced in batches that combine several thousand individual donations. If only one donor to the pool has a transmissible disease, the entire population receiving the contaminated product is at risk.

A unique concern for blood regulators is potential scarcity of source material. The United States is nearly self-sufficient when it comes to blood. Less than three percent of total annual usage comes from foreign sources. This margin between need and supply, however, is not evenly spread across the country or during the calendar year. During bad weather, for example, donations typically decline while demand for blood rises. Thus, regulators are sometimes faced with circumstances in which measures to prevent the transmission of life-threatening disease may lead to an inadequate supply of life-sustaining material.

United States General Accounting Office, Blood Supply: FDA Oversight and Remaining Issues of Safety

February 1997.

. . . The Commissioner of the Food and Drug Administration . . . described "five layers of safety" that were present throughout the blood industry to help ensure safe blood:

1.   screening donors,

2.   maintaining donor deferral registries to eliminate unsuitable donors from the rolls,

3.   testing blood,

4.   quarantining blood until tests and control procedures establish its safety, and

5.   monitoring and investigating adverse incidents to ensure that deficiencies are corrected.

. . . .

About 8 million volunteers donate approximately 14 million units of whole blood each year. This whole blood is rarely transfused into patients. Instead, blood services in the blood industry separate each unit of whole blood into an average of 1.8 specialized components that, in blood-banking terminology, are "products" consisting of various types of blood cells, plasma, and special preparations of plasma. Health care facilities transfuse the resulting 23 million components—4 to 5 units at a time, on average—into as many as 4 million patients to treat specific conditions such as anemia and hemophilia. Donors give an additional 12 million units of plasma each year, for a total of approximately 26 million annual blood donations.

. . . .

In addition to separating blood into component products, plasma facilities manufacture "derivative products" by fractioning plasma chemically into concentrated proteins. These include albumin, used to treat shock; immune globulin, used to prevent certain infectious diseases and to treat deficiencies of protein; clotting factor concentrates, used to control bleeding in patients with clotting factor deficiencies; and specific immune globulins, prepared from plasmas collected from donors with antibodies to specific diseases and then used to prevent those diseases in others. Derivatives are commonly made by commercial manufacturers. Depending on the product, they may pool plasma from as many as 60,000 donors for fractionation in order to produce sufficient amounts of the final concentrated material cost-effectively. These therapies processed from plasma also undergo viral and bacterial removal and inactivation procedures that are effective in destroying most of these agents.

The blood services industry has both volunteer and commercial sectors. Voluntary donors are unpaid and usually donate whole blood. Commercial facilities collect plasma from paid donors for manufacturing various derivatives. . . .

The three types of facilities in the volunteer section are (1) regional and community blood centers, which usually collect and distribute blood and blood components to hospitals within circumscribed geographical areas; (2) hospital blood facilities, which collect and transfuse whole blood and blood components; and (3) hospitals, which primarily store and transfuse blood but do not collect it.

. . . .

The volunteer sector is represented by three organizations: the American Association of Blood Banks (AABB), the American Red Cross (ARC), and America's Blood Centers (ABC), formerly known as the Council of Community Blood Centers (CCBC). ABC member centers collect approximately 45 percent of all blood, ARC collects another 45 percent, and independent facilities collect the remaining 10 percent. The members of the AABB include both ARC and the majority of ABC member centers.

AABB is the professional society of blood facilities and transfusion services and it also includes individual members such as physicians, scientists, nurses, and administrators, among others. ABC is a council of community based blood-collection facilities. ARC is a single corporation consisting of all ARC blood centers. Until 1994, ARC served as an organizational framework for its centers, each operating somewhat independently and self-sufficiently. In an organizational change that began in 1994 and was completed in 1995, ARC centralized and standardized its operations, reducing the number of regions and limiting testing to a few centralized laboratories.

The commercial sector, which is generally called the "source plasma sector" and receives plasma from paid donors, has three main components: (1) collectors, or plasmapheresis centers; (2) fractionators; and (3) brokers. (Brokers do not collect source plasma.) The plasmapheresis centers collect plasma that they either sell to U.S. fractionators (who manufacture derivatives such as albumin from it) or export to fractionators in Europe, Japan, and South America. . . .

Plasma brokers purchase and market recovered plasma from whole-blood facilities (that is, the volunteer section) and sell this directly to fractionators. Plasma is "recovered" after components have been removed from whole blood or after whole blood has become outdated.

. . . .

The five layers of safety are designed to overlap so that they will prevent the distribution of contaminated blood and blood products. . . .

Following its assumption of responsibility for the Biologics Act in 1972, FDA took steps to apply several provisions of the FD&C Act to blood products:

1. *Establishment Registration and Inspection.* FDA required registration of blood establishments. The frequency of the inspection of blood establishments was changed from at least once every year to at least once every two years.

2. *Good Manufacturing Practice.* FDA promulgated regulations governing current good manufacturing practices (GMP) in the collection, processing, and storage of human blood and blood components. 40 Fed. Reg. 53532 (Nov. 18, 1975). By combining the jurisdictional and regulatory provisions of the Biologics Act and the FD&C Act, FDA brought all blood and blood products produced and used in the United States under uniform federal requirements.

3. *Container Regulation.* Responsibility for regulation of containers for collection or processing of blood and blood components, with or without ingredients such as anticoagulant solutions, was established in 40 Fed. Reg. 33971 (Aug. 13, 1975). FDA's current regulations governing the composition and configuration of containers for blood appear at 21 C.F.R. Part 606.

4. *Adverse Reaction Reports.* Regulations requiring the submission of error and accident reports by licensed and unlicensed blood establishments appear at 21 C.F.R. 606.171.

5. *FDA/HCFA Collaboration.* FDA and the Health Care Financing Administration (the predecessor to CMS) executed a Memorandum of Understanding, published at 45 Fed. Reg. 19316 (Mar. 25, 1980), to coordinate their inspection of blood banks and transfusion services. FDA exempted from its establishment registration requirements all transfusion services and clinical laboratories that are regulated by HCFA (now CMS) under Medicare. 45 Fed. Reg. 85727 (Dec. 30, 1980). HCFA in turn adopted FDA's blood regulations, 46 Fed. Reg. 41059 (Aug. 14, 1981), to assure uniform regulation of these facilities.

3. PROTECTING THE SAFETY OF THE BLOOD SUPPLY

The biggest public health risk presented by blood and blood products is the spread of communicable diseases, such as hepatitis and AIDS. Because communicable diseases know no borders, FDA must regulate local as well as interstate transactions in blood and blood products. Fortunately, neither section 351(b) of the PHS Act (prohibiting "false labeling" of biological products) nor section 361 of the PHS Act (authorizing FDA to issue regulations necessary to prevent the spread of communicable diseases) has an interstate commerce requirement.

In 1975, FDA relied on both of these provisions, as well as various provisions of the FD&C Act, to propose mandatory label statements (1) distinguishing blood from volunteer donors and blood from paid donors and (2) warning that blood collected from paid donors is associated with a higher risk of transmitting hepatitis. 40 Fed. Reg. 53040 (Nov. 14, 1975). The agency re-proposed the rule two years later, omitting the warning statement concerning hepatitis, 42 Fed. Reg. 11018 (Feb. 25, 1977), and it finalized that version the following year, 43 Fed. Reg. 2142 (Jan. 13, 1978), now codified at 21 C.F.R. 606.121.

Blood Donor Classification Statement, Paid or Volunteer Donor

Food and Drug Administration Compliance Policy Guide Sec. 230.150
(updated Nov. 1, 2011).

. . . .

In a Federal Register notice dated January 13, 1978 (43 FR 2142), the Agency issued a final rule which required that blood and blood components intended for transfusion include a donor classification statement on the labels to indicate whether the products were collected from paid or volunteer donors. This labeling requirement appears at 21 CFR 606.121(c)(5). The regulation defines a "paid donor" as a person who receives monetary payment for a blood donation [21 CFR 606.121(c)(5)(i)]. A volunteer donor is a person who does not receive monetary payment for a blood donation.

. . . As used in this document, the term incentive means anything a donor receives for donating blood other than those items a donor would ordinarily receive during the blood donation process. For example, refreshments provided by the blood collection facility would not be considered to be a donor incentive.

. . . .

All monetary payments to the donor would require the blood and blood components to be labeled with a "paid donor" classification statement, regardless of the dollar value of the incentive. The nature of the population (the type of people) attracted by the incentive should not be considered in determining whether an incentive is a monetary payment. . . .

––––––––

FDA's blood product regulations address every step in collection, delivery, and use, including: donor recruitment and screening; the procedures collecting entities must use in handling whole blood and other source material; the maintenance of records and reporting of "errors and accidents;" the obligation to comply with good manufacturing practice; and the reporting of adverse events.

The agency's expectations for blood collecting, processing, and distribution facilities are set forth in detailed regulations, 21 CFR Part 600 *et seq.* While it would be wrong to say that violations of FDA's elaborate requirements are common, the reality is that most of the major organizations involved in collecting, processing and distributing blood have from time to time had conflicts with FDA. In 1997, for example, organizations responsible for fully 70 percent of the nation's blood supply were operating under judicially monitored consent decrees. Lawrence K. Altman, *Blood Center to Shut Down Screening Lab*, N.Y. TIMES, May 15, 1997, at B3. The organization responsible for nearly half of all blood collected and used in the United States, the American Red Cross, has been a particular target of FDA scrutiny and enforcement.

As the following case illustrates, FDA has two different broad responsibilities in the efforts to assure the safety of blood and blood products. First, as discussed above, it regulates the entities that collect, process, and distribute blood, and in that capacity ultimately determines—under the Biologics Act—what screening and testing procedures must be followed. Second, because most test methods are themselves diagnostic products subject to regulation under the Medical Device Amendments of 1976, FDA is responsible for confirming their reliability and sensitivity.

R.F. and R.F. v. Abbott Laboratories
745 A.2d 1174 (N.J. 2000).

■ GARIBALDI, J.

In September 1986, plaintiff, R.F., received a transfusion of blood incident to surgery, that was infected with the human immunodeficiency virus ("HIV"), causing her to subsequently test positive for the presence of that virus. The blood which was transfused into R.F. had been previously screened for HIV infection at the Bergen Community Blood Center ("BCBC") with the first commercially-available HIV blood screening test, manufactured by defendant, Abbott Laboratories ("Abbott"). . . .

R.F. and her husband (collectively, "plaintiffs"), claim that the HIV blood test used by the BCBC was defective under [New Jersey law] because its package insert failed to provide adequate instructions or warnings regarding the sensitivity limitations allegedly inherent in Abbott's test. Specifically, plaintiffs contend that in light of its knowledge that the test was not 100% sensitive, Abbott should have instructed blood banks to retest samples that were negative yet "borderline," meaning samples that had yielded results close to the test's "cutoff value." The cutoff value was a value defined by the federal Food and Drug Administration ("FDA") in the test's instructional pamphlet, to be used by blood bank technicians to measure whether the HIV antibody was present in a donated blood sample.

. . . The primary issue presented in this appeal is whether federal regulation of Abbott's HIV blood screening test preempts plaintiffs' cause of action for defective design and failure to warn. . . .

Although the FDA considered the blood screening test as a "device" under the Medical Device Amendments of 1976, the development, manufacturing, and field performance of the HIV test, was overseen by the FDA's Office of Biologics Research and Review ("OBRR"). That is consistent with the FDA's 1982 designation of the Bureau of Biologics as "the lead Bureau for regulating certain medical devices used in the processing or administration of biological products," such as the test kit. Therefore, although the test kit was largely regulated by the OBRR as a biologic (because the virus was the main component of the test) the OBRR required that the test be listed as a medical device, and its package insert drafted pursuant to Labeling for In Vitro Diagnostic Products, 21 C.F.R. § 809.10(b) (1985), a medical device regulation.

. . . .

As part of the product license application, Abbott submitted a draft of the test's package insert. In the December 19, 1984 draft, Abbott suggested that the package insert state: "*Specimens with absorbance values within a ± 10% range of the Cutoff Value should be retested to confirm the initial results.*" (emphasis added). However, in their January 29, 1985 response, . . . the FDA "mandated that [this provision] be deleted." Dr. Heller [Abbott's lead scientist in the development of the HIV assay] testified that the FDA decided not to instruct blood banks to retest "borderline" negative samples because: (1) there was no scientific basis for the belief that samples close to the borderline were more likely to be *false*-negative than negative samples with results well-below the cutoff; and (2) such a provision would effectively redefine the cutoff to the lower value for which there would be associated a new set of "borderline samples."

. . . .

On March 1, 1985, after the package insert was completed, the OBRR issued a license that "authorized Abbott to manufacture and sell in interstate and foreign commerce HTLV III in an *in vitro* ELISA test," hereinafter referred to as the "Test" or the "First Generation Test." . . .

. . . [T]he FDA's letter accompanying the license specifically indicated that if Abbott sought to amend the labeling or package insert of the Test, "it would be necessary . . . to submit an amendment to either [the] product or establishment license application for review and approval prior to implementation." Moreover, the Test's labeling was subject to a similar, promulgated FDA regulation for biologics [concerning changes to labeling]. . . .

. . . [P]rior to the introduction of the Test onto the market, the FDA conducted a mass-mailing campaign to blood banks and physicians regarding the use and limitations of the first HIV blood screening tests. . . . The FDA's memorandum, summarizing an attached copy of the CDC's January 11, 1985 newsletter, explicitly described the limitations of the tests as follows:

> . . . [A] negative antibody test result does not necessarily mean that one is free from virus. Antibody may not have developed, or be undetectable, if infection was recent. There is at least one report that 4 of 96 individuals carried the virus for 6 months without developing detectable antibodies.

Soon thereafter, the FDA sent out a similar "Dear Doctor" letter to *all* licensed physicians in the United States, including R.F.'s physician, expressly warning of the above limitations.

. . . .

In this case, both (1) the FDA's exercise of control and initiative over the Test's development, packaging, and field performance monitoring, and (2) the unique circumstances under which the Test arose (a national health crisis surrounding the emergence of the AIDS epidemic and the loss of a safe national blood supply), give rise to implied preemption of the plaintiffs' state law claims under each of the three categories of implied preemption.

. . . .

First, the extensive control and continuous scrutiny of the Test by the FDA was so pervasive as to make reasonable the inference "that [the FDA] left no room for the states to supplement it." Secondly, requiring blood banks to retest the "borderline" samples, and to warn that borderline results were inherently dangerous, would have been in direct conflict with the specific mandates of the FDA. The FDA dealt directly with the issue of how to define the cutoff, and concluded that false-negative results were not clustered around the cutoff, but were randomly spread over the entire scale of negative results. Additionally, the FDA did not only scrutinize the language required in the package insert warning, but also in large part, dictated the wording of the insert. Moreover, the FDA's regulations and its specific mandates restricted Abbott's ability to amend the package insert.

The plaintiffs' state law cause of action based on a claim of inadequate warnings, where those warnings are dictated by the FDA, is "inconsistent" with federal regulation, and is therefore preempted. . . .

■ STEIN, J., dissenting.

. . . .

This Court's willingness to rest its "field" preemption analysis solely on the basis of the comprehensiveness of the FDA's regulation of Abbott's test prior to licensure is suspect on two grounds. First, it disregards the Supreme Court's admonition in *Hillsborough County v. Automatic Med. Labs.*, 471 U.S. 707 (1985) that "we will seldom infer, solely from the comprehensiveness of federal regulations, an intent to pre-empt in its entirety a field related to health and safety." . . . Although the Court's opinion attempts to justify federal preemption not on the basis of Congressional action but rather on the basis of a national health emergency concerning a safe blood supply, experience informs us that Congress knows how to mandate federal preemption in the context of a national health emergency. . . . *See National Swine Flu Immunization Program of 1976*, Pub. L. No. 94–380, 90 Stat. 1113 (1976). . . .

Second, the Court either overlooks or disregards that the plaintiffs' focus is *not* on the FDA's regulation *prior* to licensure, but on Abbott's after-acquired knowledge in the summer of 1986 that its test's tendency to record false negatives around the cutoff required prompt remediation. The record demonstrates that during this post-licensure period Abbott was concerned about its test . . . because the blood tests of competitors appeared, according to some research reports, to be more sensitive in detecting HIV contaminated blood. Abbott knew enough about its test's deficiencies to propose to the FDA in July 1986 a modified test that "would be better able to detect positive samples that were 'borderline or negative' by the First Generation Test." . . .

———

The New Jersey Supreme Court's opinion reveals the technical complexity of testing for the presence of pathogens in blood (and indirectly for the presence of disease in donors). It took several years and much effort for testing to move beyond the search for antibodies to the detection of the HIV virus itself. And complicating this essentially scientific inquiry is the realization that improvement in the test methodology may shrink the available supply of blood. This gloomy possibility is at the heart of Justice Stewart Pollock's opinion in the next case.

Snyder v. American Association of Blood Banks

676 A.2d 1036 (N.J. 1996).

■ The opinion of the Court was delivered by POLLOCK, J.

Plaintiff William Snyder contracted Acquired Immune Deficiency Syndrome (AIDS) from a transfusion of blood that the Bergen Community Blood Center (BCBC), a non-profit blood bank, had provided to St. Joseph's Hospital. The BCBC is a member of defendant, the American Association of Blood Banks (AABB), an association of blood banks and blood-banking professionals. . . .

I

. . . .

At the time, no direct test existed to determine whether blood was infected with Human Immunodeficiency Virus (HIV), the cause of AIDS. Other means of making that determination, however, were available. Starting in 1985, the enzyme-linked immunoabsorbent-assay-screening test (the ELISA test) enabled blood banks to screen for HIV.

Under a nation-wide "look-back" program instituted that year, blood banks could determine whether a prospective donor who tested positive for HIV had donated blood before the development of the ELISA test. As part of the "look-back" program sponsored by the AABB, BCBC ascertained in 1986 that the donor of unit 29F0784 was HIV positive. That same year BCBC so informed St. Joseph's Hospital. St. Joseph's, in turn, informed Snyder's doctor, who notified him in 1987. . . .

Ultimately, all defendants other than the AABB either settled or obtained dismissals. At the trial, the critical issue was whether the AABB had breached a duty of care to Snyder. Hence, the trial focused on the AABB's role in the blood-banking industry and the reasonableness of its response to increasing evidence that blood or blood products could transmit AIDS.

. . . .

II

Crucial to the assessment of the AABB's alleged duty of care is its role in the blood-banking industry in 1983–84. . . .

The AABB describes itself as a "professional, non-profit, scientific and administrative association for individuals and institutions engaged in the many facets of blood and tissue banking, and transfusion and transplantation medicine." . . . In the early 1980s, the AABB centers collected about half of the nation's blood supply and transfused eighty percent of the blood to patients. Its institutional members were mainly hospitals and non-profit blood centers.

According to the AABB's executive director . . . the general purpose of the AABB is "to develop and recommend standards on the practice of blood banking, to help promote the public health, . . . and to conduct numerous programs for communication and education among organization members and the public at-large." The AABB discharges its educational mission by conducting workshops and seminars, and by publishing books, newsletters, pamphlets, and a peer-review journal, *Transfusion.* . . .

Significantly, the AABB annually inspects and accredits member institutions. It conditions accreditation on compliance with standards published in its *Standards for Blood Banks and Transfusion Services* and procedures outlined in its *Technical Manual.* According to the annual report, AABB standards often become FDA standards. . . .

Both the state and federal government, as well as the blood-banking industry, generally accept AABB standards as authoritative. Consequently, blood banks throughout the nation rely on those standards. . . .

III

. . . .

By words and conduct, the AABB invited blood banks, hospitals, and patients to rely on the AABB's recommended procedures. The AABB set the standards for voluntary blood banks. At all relevant times, it exerted considerable influence over the practices and procedures over its member banks, including BCBC. On behalf of itself and its member banks, the AABB lobbies legislatures, participates in administrative proceedings, and works with governmental health agencies in setting blood-banking policy. In many respects, the AABB wrote the rules and set the standards for voluntary blood banks.

. . . The severity of the risk of transfusion-related AIDS is a function of the mortality rate and the infection rate. In 1984, the overall mortality rate of AIDS was forty percent, but for those who had AIDS for more than three years, the rate approached nearly 100%. The infection rate was increasing exponentially. . . . Thus, the risk that blood transfusions could transmit AIDS was severe.

The risk also was foreseeable. Epidemiologists at the CDC believed as early as 1982 that the AIDS virus could be transmitted by blood and blood products. In January 1984, Dr. Curran's article in the *New England Journal of Medicine* confirmed that belief. Thus, before Snyder received his transfusion, the AABB should have foreseen that a blood transfusion could transmit AIDS.

We are unpersuaded by the AABB's argument that because the evidence was inconclusive, it owed no duty to Snyder. The foreseeability, not the conclusiveness, of harm suffices to give rise to a duty of care. By 1983, ample evidence supported the conclusion that blood transmitted the AIDS virus. In early 1984, the AABB knew that AIDS was a rapidly spreading, fatal disease and that apparently healthy donors could infect others. The AABB also knew that blood and blood products probably could transmit AIDS and that each infected blood donor could infect many donees. Thus, the AABB knew, or should have known, in 1984 that the risk of AIDS infection from blood transfusions was devastating. We agree with the lower courts that the record establishes that the AABB owed Snyder a duty of care.

. . . .

Relevant also to the determination of the AABB's duty of care is its role in the governmental regulation of the blood-banking industry. In 1984, the AABB was more than a trade association. It was the governing body of a significantly self-regulated industry. . . .

V

. . . .

The record reveals that the AABB led the charge against direct questioning of donors and surrogate testing. Viewed most favorably to the AABB, the evidence suggests that it was concerned that such questioning and testing would be of limited effectiveness and could diminish the supply of blood and blood products. A less favorable view suggests that the AABB resisted surrogate testing because it did not want to suffer the added inconvenience and costs of such testing. . . .

On the record, the jury could have concluded that the AABB in 1984 unreasonably resisted recognizing that blood transmits HIV. That resistance led the AABB to sacrifice an uncontaminated supply of blood for one that was contaminated, but more readily available. The jury could have found that if the AABB had not been so intransigent, its members, particularly the BCBC, would have instituted surrogate testing. Further, the jury could have found that if the BCBC had instituted surrogate testing, it would have rejected Unit 29F0784. Rejecting that unit could have prevented the transfusion of contaminated blood to William Snyder. It could have saved his health and his life. Against this background, we believe that the imposition of liability on the AABB is both fair and reasonable. . . .

[The dissenting opinion of Justice Garibaldi is omitted.]

NOTES

1. *Deciding Whether to Screen for AIDS.* The AABB's decision-making process was the focus of a critical report by the Institute of Medicine, which recommended major reforms. INSTITUTE OF MEDICINE, HIV AND THE BLOOD SUPPLY: AN ANALYSIS OF CRISIS DECISION MAKING (1995).

2. *Umbilical Cord Blood.* Blood circulating in the placenta prior to birth and thus present in—and recoverable from—the umbilical cord following birth is a rich source of stem cells, which might later be used in the treatment of diseases displayed by the newborn or discovered as late as adulthood. In the early 1990s, entrepreneurs offered recovery and long-term storage services to expectant parents as a form of insurance. Calls for regulation of this activity led FDA to assert jurisdiction, but instead of simply applying the requirements of the Biologics Act, the agency declared cord blood a type of human tissue transplant subject to its general plan for tissue and cellular therapies, described *infra* at p. 1172.

F. HUMAN TISSUES AND CELLS

1. WHOLE ORGANS

Since the 1960s, transplantation of organs (e.g., heart, liver, and kidneys) has become common. However, government oversight of organs has lagged behind their medical use. FDA has played essentially no role in their regulation.

In 1983, Congress asked FDA to address its authority under existing law to oversee whole organ transplantation. In the following statement, unnamed FDA officials tried to explain why the agency had not asserted jurisdiction over these products.

Statement by the Food and Drug Administration Concerning Its Legal Authority to Regulate Human Organ Transplants and to Prohibit Their Sale

Submitted to the Subcommittee on Investigations and Oversight, House Committee on Science and Technology, 98th Congress,1st Session (1983).

... The Food and Drug Administration has never had occasion formally to address the issue of its authority to regulate the sale of human organs. This statement constitutes the FDA's first examination of that issue.

The Federal Food, Drug, and Cosmetic Act defines the term "drug" in part as "articles intended for use in the diagnosis, cure mitigation, treatment, or prevention of disease in man ...", and "articles (other than food) intended to affect the structure or any function of the body of man...."

A human organ intended for use in transplantation arguably could be regulated as a drug because it falls within the literal language of these provisions. Although Congress could not have had human organ transplants in mind when it defined the term "drug" in 1938, the case law suggests that the definition is not limited to the types of substances used as drugs prior to 1938....

Although the case law has interpreted the term "drug" very broadly, no court has held that a human organ intended for use in transplantation is a drug. Such an interpretation, while arguably supportable, would extend the legal definition well beyond the traditional medical concept of the term "drug." The unprecedented nature of this interpretation necessarily means that considerable uncertainty would be associated with a conclusion by FDA that the definition of the term "drug" includes human organ transplants. Adding to this uncertainty is FDA's current administrative interpretation of the term "drug," which cannot be read to include human organs. That interpretation states: "[a] drug ... is a chemical or a combination of chemicals in liquid, paste, powder, or other drug dosage form that is ingested, or instilled into body orifices, or rubbed or poured onto the body in order to achieve its intended medical purpose." 47 FR 46139. Although this administrative interpretation would not be conclusive, it would be given deference by a reviewing court.

Section 201(h) of the FDC Act, as amended by the Medical Device Amendments of 1976, defines the term "device" as "an instrument, apparatus, implement, machine, contrivance, implant, in vitro reagent, or other similar or related article . . . which is . . . intended for use in the diagnosis of disease or other conditions, or in the cure, mitigation, treatment, or prevention of disease" or which is "intended to affect the structure or any function of the body," *and* "which does not achieve any of its principal intended purposes through chemical action within or on the body" or by "being metabolized." 21 U.S.C. 321(h). A human organ transplant could be regarded as within the literal language of the statute, for a transplanted organ is a type of "implant."

On the other hand, the definition's list of things that are "devices"—"instrument, apparatus, implement, machine, contrivance, implant, in vitro reagent"—implies that Congress understood the term "device" to refer to the product of human artifice. Except for implants and in vitro reagents, the items in the list are man-made products that generally are constructed of materials such as metal or plastic. Although some devices regulated by FDA consist in part of organic material, the material is usually either a part of a man-made device, or it is treated to make it useful for its intended purpose rather than simply being substituted for its equivalent material in the human body. In vitro reagents often use organic material, but as part of a system designed to diagnose diseases or conditions. There are many man-made devices that are "implants." Cardiac pacemakers, artificial joints, and intraocular plastic lenses fall into this category. The legislative intent underlying the definition of "device" is, therefore, probably limited to artificial implants. This view is consistent with the principle of statutory construction that a word is known by the company it keeps (*noscitur a sociis*).

     . . . .

The Public Health Service Act, 42 U.S.C. 262, *et seq.*, authorizes the licensure of a class of products that has come to be known as "biological products." Although the term is undefined, the Act includes the following as subject to licensure: ". . . any virus, therapeutic serum, toxin, antitoxin, vaccine, blood, blood component or derivative, allergenic product, or analogous product . . . applicable to the prevention, treatment, or cure of diseases or injuries of man. . . ."

Whether a human organ transplant is a biological product depends on whether solid organs, such as the heart, liver, or kidneys, are "analogous" to blood or blood derivatives. If the term "analogous" is interpreted in its broadest sense, FDA arguably could regulate human organ transplants as biological products. Blood is essentially a liquid organ. Blood performs vital functions comparable to the functions performed by solid organs. Blood is composed of tissue cells, which are similar but not identical to the tissue cells of solid organs.

The legislative history of the PHS Act suggests, however, that a narrower interpretation of the term "analogous" would be more in keeping with the legislative design for the regulation of "biological products." The predecessor of the PHS Act, the Viruses, Serums, and Toxins Act of 1902 ("VSTA"), defined a biological product as "any virus, therapeutic serum, toxin, antitoxin, or analogous product." In 1970,

Congress amended the VSTA by adding to the definition the terms "blood" and "blood component or derivative." The legislative history of the 1970 amendment states that Congress added these terms because ". . . the products and processes involved in blood transfusions were not known in 1902 when the "Virus–Toxin law," which preceded section 351 [42 U.S.C. § 262], was enacted . . . [and] Congress [therefore] could not have intended that they be included." 116 Cong. Rec. 31017 (1970) (remarks of Sen. Dominick). Under this rationale, the definition of "analogous products" would be limited to those human organs for which transplantation had become known at the time of the enactment of the 1970 amendments to the VSTA. By 1970, kidney and bone marrow transplants had become fairly common and liver and heart transplants had been performed, but were still in the experimental stages.

. . . .

NOTES

1. *Analogous to Blood?* It is by no means clear that, by adding the words "blood, blood component or derivative" to the definition of "biological product" in 1970, Congress intended to include as "analogous" products the entire range of human organs then known to be capable of transplantation. Kidney and bone marrow transplants were known to be part of the developing field of organ transplants, yet those organs were not mentioned by name in the 1970 amendment. Although as a matter of human physiology blood is correctly regarded as a "liquid organ," it seems improbable that those who drafted the amendment viewed blood as simply one of the several organs or organ systems that make up the human body. The more plausible assumption is that Congress believed that blood in particular should be subject to regulation and thus included it in the list of biological substances for which a license was required as a means of authorizing necessary governmental controls. Under this view, the term "analogous product" would include analogous blood products, not solid organs that are "analogous" only because blood is also, in a broad sense, a human "organ."

2. *National Organ Transplant Act.* The year after FDA submitted this statement, Congress enacted the National Organ Transplant Act, 98 Stat. 2339 (1984), which established the framework for whole organ recovery and allocation that operates today. The system, described in IOM, ORGAN DONATION: OPPORTUNITIES FOR ACTION (2006), does not deal with tissue recovery, processing, or use, and it accords no role to FDA. The statute is administered by the Health Resources and Services Administration (HRSA), another division of HHS.

2. FDA'S REGULATION OF TISSUES AND CELLS

a. INTRODUCTION

In addition to the few thousand recipients of organ transplants each year, more than one million Americans receive allogeneic (from another) tissue transplants. Bone is the most common transplanted tissue. Thoroughly cleansed, demineralized, and then pulverized, cadaver bone is widely used in reconstructive dental surgery. Intact bone segments are used by orthopedic surgeons in spinal restoration and joint repair. Soft tissues—such as tendons—are the material of choice in some procedures to repair joint damage. Consider, for example, the widely reported surgical repair of the knee of Cincinnati Bengals' quarterback Carson Palmer with the Achilles tendon of a deceased victim of an automobile accident. N.Y. TIMES, Aug. 9, 2006, at D2.

Like organs, almost all of the tissues in question come from deceased donors. Some donors may have willed their bodies to medical research or for use in treatment. More commonly, it is the families of persons who die abruptly from traumatic injury who consent to recovery of usable body parts. To be transplantable, organs must be recovered within a few hours of death. Other tissues do not deteriorate as quickly, but most must be recovered within 24 hours. Most tissue banks are affiliated with organ procurement organizations (OPOs), and it is routine for teams representing both to collaborate in the recovery operation.

Until the 1980s, the surgical use of cadaver tissue was regarded as a facet of the "practice of medicine" that FDA did not regulate. Many of the earliest tissue "banks" were established by surgical teams and maintained as part of hospital operations. In time, however, these surgeon-managed operations took on independent status. Supplying tissues for surgery was out-sourced. Contemporaneously, innovations in tissue preservation and manipulation expanded the procedures in which human-source materials could be used. Demand expanded and tissue banks responded. What had been an in-hospital service for surgeons became an independent industry—a source of materials that offered unique functionality or served as alternatives to man-made replacement parts.

In some respects the regulatory regime that FDA has constructed for tissue resembles the agency's program for blood. Prevention of disease transmission has been a primary goal of the agency's requirements. But blood is collected from living donors who can be tested again after donation. Testing of cadaveric donors of tissue is more complicated, and investigation of their experience and habits prior to death must generally rely on surrogates—the same next of kin whose consent must be obtained. More similar to blood regulation is the regulation of reproductive tissues (such as semen)—the most important type of tissue ordinarily provided by living donors.

The following excerpt relates the history leading up to FDA's creation, in the 1990s, of a special regulatory scheme for regulating human cellular and tissue-based products. The scheme itself will be examined in more detail in the subsequent subsections.

Richard A. Merrill, *Human Tissues and Reproductive Cloning: New Technologies Challenge FDA*

3 HOUSTON JOURNAL OF HEALTH LAW & POLICY 1 (2002).

. . . .

The question whether FDA could regulate human tissue apparently first arose in 1973. . . . This was an era when FDA rarely shrank from new challenges, and the response of the Chief Counsel to whom the question was first put, Peter Barton Hutt, was predictable: Human tissues as well as whole organs, could be considered "analogous" to materials such as blood, over which FDA had authority under section 351 of the Public Health Service Act. Hutt went further:

> In any event, whether human semen, human tissues and organs are or are not biological products, they clearly are drugs when used for therapeutic purposes or to affect any bodily function and accordingly are subject to the requirements of the FD&C Act. The decision as to which Bureau within FDA handles these products is entirely an administrative matter that raises no legal issue.

Several years were to pass before FDA took any formal position regarding its authority to regulate tissue. . . . According to FDA's one-time Associate Commissioner for Health Affairs, Stuart Nightingale, representatives of the three bureaus (now "Centers") responsible for regulating medical products in 1976 "met to discuss possible regulation of tissue banks." They apparently were not able to identify clear criteria that could justify and at the same time limit FDA's assertion of jurisdiction: "[N]o one system seemed applicable to all of the potential products that fall under the rubric of transplantable tissues. It was [therefore] decided that FDA jurisdiction over tissues would be asserted only in response to an immediate need."

. . . .

In 1979, two incidents occurred which led the agency to again review the possible need to regulate the banking of allogeneic materials. In one incident, gonorrhea had been transmitted by contaminated fresh semen used in artificial insemination, and in the other incident a thirty-seven year old woman contracted rabies and died a month after she had received a corneal transplant.

Once again the question of legal authority was referred to FDA's Chief Counsel, then Richard Cooper, who declared that "any residual doubt about (FDA's) authority can be put aside," implying that whether and how to regulate were questions of science and policy. Once more, the decision was made not to assert jurisdiction. . . .

. . . Nightingale records that during the 1980s some officials were of the view that the Agency was obliged to regulate tissue. They may have recognized that tissue transplants were being used for purposes identical to those for which man-made—and comprehensively regulated—product were being used. . . .

Others recognized, however, that regulating by analogy would have far-reaching implications. The statutory definition of "device" is very broad. It would not be easy to confine regulation to tissue implants that resembled artificial products designed for similar use. . . .

Furthermore, the requirements FDA would be obliged to impose if tissues were drugs or medical devices did not seem well-matched for the operations of tissue recovery and processing or well-suited to address the concerns that might justify regulation in the first place. If human tissues were "drugs," virtually every one would be a "new drug" for which FDA approval was required. Few tissue banks had the resources to fund the sort of clinical studies that FDA would require. . . .

Classifying tissues as "devices" would also present problems for FDA. Not all medical devices require premarket approval by FDA; only those classified in Class III, and then only after the Agency calls for applications. The device law would thus appear to afford a "window" during which suppliers could conduct the studies needed to gain Agency approval. But this avenue was available only for devices that were in commercial distribution prior to 1976 or were "substantially equivalent" to a device then in distribution. For any tissue first provided to surgeons after 1976, it would have been difficult for FDA to fashion even a temporary exemption from the Act's premarket approval requirement.

. . . .

In 1985 the family of a 22-year old Virginia man, who had died from gunshot wounds, agreed to donate his organs and tissues for transplantation. Tests of the donor for HIV were negative. His tissues were processed and distributed by LifeNet Transplant Services of Virginia Beach. Over the next few years several dozen individuals received grafts from the Virginia donor. Some time thereafter seven of them tested positive for the HIV antibody. Their infections were attributed to the common donor, who at the time he died had been infected but apparently fell within the "window" between exposure to the AIDS virus and the development of detectable antibodies.

. . . [I]n December 1993, FDA published general regulations governing human tissue intended for transplantation. "To help prevent the transmission of AIDS and hepatitis through human tissue used in transplantation," the Agency mandated screening of tissue donors, testing of individual tissues for infectious disease, and maintenance of records to enable FDA inspectors to confirm compliance with the requirements for screening and testing. Thus, in a single stroke, FDA asserted control over as many as 200 institutions whose activities had previously largely escaped federal regulation. . . .

. . . FDA defined the category [of "human tissue"] as including "musculoskeletal and integumentary materials that may be recovered from living or cadaveric donors," which "largely consist of bone, ligaments, tendons, fascia, cartilage, corneas, and skin" used in disease treatment or reconstructive surgery. The new regulations did not apply to "tissues already regulated . . . as drugs, biological products, or medical devices," or to vascularized organs and bone marrow (overseen by other parts of the Public Health Service) and human milk. Significantly, FDA also specifically excluded "semen [and] other reproductive tissue," without identifying any other federal agency with oversight authority.

From the outset a critical issue for tissue banks was whether processing that altered the appearance or form, or facilitated the use, of a tissue would cause it to fall outside the coverage of the new regulations—and under the more stringent requirements for drugs or medical devices. FDA's treatment of this issue was not altogether reassuring. The Agency stated that its regulations applied to tissue processed or stored "by methods not intended to change tissue structure or functional characteristics." . . .

Perhaps the most significant feature of FDA's "interim" regulations was its decision not to rely on the FDCA for legal authority. Instead, the Agency invoked Section 361 of the Public Health Service Act, an old provision of awesome breadth. In its current form, Section 361 reads:

> The Surgeon General [i.e., FDA] . . . is authorized to make and enforce such regulations as in his judgment are necessary to prevent the introduction, transmission, or spread of communicable diseases from foreign countries into the States or possessions, or from one State or possession into any other State or possession. For purposes of carrying out and enforcing such regulations, the Surgeon General may provide for such inspection fumigation, disinfection, sanitation, pest extermination, destruction of animals or articles found to be so infected or contaminated as to be sources of dangerous infection to human beings, and other measures, as in his judgment may be necessary.
>
> . . . .

The interim regulations that FDA promulgated in December 1993 proved to be just the first installment in the Agency's development of an elaborate program for regulating human tissue and "tissue-based products." . . .

. . . [In February 1997, FDA] released for discussion an unusual document, titled "A Proposed Approach to the Regulation of Cellular and Tissue-Based Products." . . .

FDA's plan set forth the Agency's thinking about a critical issue: When should a tissue-based product require premarketing proof of safety and effectiveness? In other words, when should a product be regulated as a new drug or Class III medical device? . . .

. . . Essentially, FDA embraced the principle of familiarity. If a donated tissue was expected to perform in the recipient the same function it performed in the donor, its effectiveness could be assumed and its safety could be assured if appropriate screening and testing were conducted. In an effort to capture this concept, the Agency said it would ask whether a tissue had been more than "minimally manipulated" and whether it was intended for other than a "homologous use." Significant changes in the form of a tissue or implantation in a different part of the body to perform a novel function would, the Agency suggested, undermine the presumption of clinical utility and safety. . . .

b.   DISTINGUISHING BETWEEN "SECTION 361 HCT/PS" AND HCT/PS
REGULATED AS BIOLOGICAL DRUGS OR DEVICES

FDA released its "Proposed Approach to the Regulation of Cellular
and Tissue-Based Products" for comment in February 1997 and held a
public meeting on the proposed approach in March 1997. The following
year, the agency described this risk-based approach when proposing
new establishment registration and listing rules premised on the
approach. 63 Fed. Reg. 26744 (May 14, 1998). A final rule on "Human
Cells, Tissues, and Cellular and Tissue-Based Products" (HCT/Ps) was
published in 2001. 66 Fed. Reg. 5447 (Jan. 19, 2001), codified at 21
C.F.R. Part 1271. As subsequently amended, it comprises not only the
registration and listing requirements, but also separately proposed
donor eligibility requirements and current good tissue practice (CGTP)
requirements.

The HCT/P rule embraces FDA's proposed approach by formally
distinguishing between HCT/Ps regulated solely under section 361 of
the Public Health Service Act, on the one hand, and those regulated
more intensively as "drugs, devices, and/or biological products under
section 351 of the PHS Act and/or the Federal Food, Drug, and Cosmetic
Act," on the other hand. *Id.* at 1271(b). Products in the former category
are subject only to Part 1271. HCT/Ps in the latter category, by
contrast, must follow not only the Part 1271 rules, but also all the
obligations applicable to drugs, devices, or licensed biologics—including
the requirement to demonstrate safety and clinical effectiveness prior to
marketing.

FDA uses two criteria—so called "kick-up factors"—to distinguish
between "section 361 HCT/Ps" and HCT/Ps regulated as drugs, devices,
and/or biological products: (1) "homologous use" versus "nonhomologous
use" and (2) "minimal manipulation" versus "more than minimal
manipulation." The agency defines "homologous use" as "the
replacement or supplementation of a recipient's cells or tissues with a
HCT/P that performs the same basic function or functions in the
recipient as in the donor." 21 C.F.R. 1271.3(c). The agency defines
"minimal manipulation" of structural tissue as "processing that does not
alter the original relevant characteristics of the tissue relating to the
tissue's utility for reconstruction, repair, or replacement." 21 C.F.R.
1271.3(f)(1). It defines "minimal manipulation" with respect to cells and
nonstructural tissues as "processing that does not alter the relevant
biological characteristics of cells or tissues." 21 C.F.R. 1271.3(f)(2).

In September 2006, FDA issued guidance describing its approach to
the question of "minimal manipulation." Its brief discussion includes
the following paragraph:

> Accordingly, FDA's determination of whether structural tissue is
> eligible for regulation solely under section 361 of the PHS Act has
> encompassed a consideration of all the potential effects, both
> positive and negative, of the alteration of a particular characteristic
> on the utility of the tissue for reconstruction, repair or replacement,
> *i.e.*, changing the characteristic could improve or diminish the
> tissue's utility. Once FDA has determined, based on the data and
> information before it, that processing has altered an original
> characteristic of a structural tissue, and that the characteristic is

relevant in that it has a potential effect on the utility of the tissue for reconstruction, repair, or replacement, the agency has considered the tissue to be more than minimally manipulated and not eligible for regulation solely under section 361 of the PHS Act. In such a case the structural tissue will be regulated as a drug, device and/or biological product under the Federal Food, Drug and Cosmetic Act and/or section 351 of the PHS Act.

GUIDANCE FOR INDUSTRY AND FDA STAFF: MINIMAL MANIPULATION OF STRUCTURAL TISSUE (JURISDICTIONAL UPDATE) (Sept. 2006).

FDA has established an institutional mechanism for determining whether a tissue product implicates either of the "kick-up factors." In guidance, the agency describes the composition and processes of this mechanism, known as the Tissue Reference Group (TRG). This working group responds to inquiries regarding whether a HCT/P meets the criteria for regulation solely under section 361, whether it is a device or a biologic, and what the primary mode of action of a combination product including an HCT/P is.

> The TRG is composed of three members from CBER and three members from CDRH, including the respective product jurisdiction officers. Liaisons from CBER's Office of Compliance and Biologics Quality (OCBQ), CDRH's Office of Compliance (OC), and Office of the Chief Counsel (OCC) assist with evaluation of the inquiries and drafting responses as needed. A liaison from the Office of Combination Products (OCP) may participate to provide information about previous Requests for Designation (RFDs) when pertinent. An executive secretary provides administrative support. Additional FDA staff provide consultative reviews and attend meetings on an as-needed basis.

Biologics Procedures, SOPP 8044: Tissue Reference Group (May 3, 2013) (available on FDA website).

NOTES

1. *Exempt Products and Procedures.* Some analogous products are explicitly excluded from FDA's definition of HCT/Ps and are thus not required to comply with the Part 1271 regulations. These articles include, among others, vascularized human organs for transplantation; blood and blood products; human milk; minimally manipulated bone marrow for homologous use; and cells, tissues and organs derived from non-human animals. 21 C.F.R. 1271.3(d). Moreover, the regulations provide: "You are not required to comply with the requirements of this part if you are an establishment that removes HCT/P's from an individual and implants such HCT/P's into the same individual during the same surgical procedure" or if "you are an establishment that only recovers reproductive cells or tissue and immediately transfers them into a sexually intimate partner of the cell or tissue donor." *Id.* 1271.15(b), (e).

2. *Cord Blood.* FDA has chosen to treat umbilical cord blood as transplantable human tissue subject to its general requirements for tissue, rather than as donated whole blood subject to the Biologics Act. David A. Suski, *Frozen Blood, Neonates, and FDA: The Regulation of Placental Umbilical Cord Blood*, 84 VA. L. REV. 715 (1998). FDA's implicit reliance on

section 361—the legal predicate for its tissue regulations—suggests that it is chiefly concerned about disease transmission rather than clinical performance. When the agency made this decision, most uses of cord blood were thought to contemplate autologous administration, i.e., return of blood to its original donor. *See* Eligibility Determination for Donors of Human Cells, Tissues, and Cellular and Tissue–Based Products, 69 Fed. Reg. 29786 (May 25, 2004). However, FDA held out the possibility of more rigorous regulation if recovered blood underwent significant manipulation to enhance its therapeutic properties.

c.   SECTION 361 REGULATION OF HCT/Ps

Current Good Tissue Practice for Human Cell, Tissue, and Cellular and Tissue–Based Product Establishments; Inspection and Enforcement

69 Fed. Reg. 68612 (November 24, 2004).

In February 1997, FDA proposed a new, comprehensive approach to the regulation of human cellular and tissue-based products (now called human cells, tissues, and cellular and tissue-based products or HCT/Ps). . . .

Since that time, the agency has published two final rules and one interim final rule to implement aspects of the proposed approach. On January 19, 2001, we issued regulations to create a new, unified system for registering HCT/P establishments and for listing their HCT/Ps (registration final rule, 66 FR 5447). . . . On January 27, 2004 (69 FR 3823), we issued an interim final rule to except human dura mater and human heart valve allografts from the scope of that definition until all of the tissue rules became final. On May 25, 2004, we issued regulations requiring most cell and tissue donors to be tested and screened for relevant communicable diseases (donor-eligibility final rule, 69 FR 29786). . . .

FDA is issuing these new regulations under the authority of section 361 of the PHS Act. . . .

Section 361 of the PHS Act authorizes FDA to issue regulations necessary to prevent the introduction, transmission, or spread of communicable diseases. Certain diseases, such as those caused by the human immunodeficiency virus (HIV) and the hepatitis B and C viruses (HBV and HCV respectively), may be transmitted through the implantation, transplantation, infusion, or transfer of HCT/Ps derived from infected donors. . . . However, donor screening and testing, although crucial, are not sufficient to prevent the transmission of disease by HCT/Ps. Rather, each step in the manufacturing process needs to be appropriately controlled. Errors in labeling, mix-ups of testing records, failure to adequately clean work areas, and faulty packaging are examples of improper practices that could produce a product capable of transmitting disease to its recipient. Similarly, . . . improper handling of an HCT/P can lead to bacterial or other pathogenic contamination of the HCT/P, or to cross-contamination between HCT/Ps, which in turn can endanger recipients. The agency has determined that the procedural provisions of this rule are necessary to ensure that the important protections created by these regulations are actually effected and are not simply empty promises. Only manufacturing conducted in accordance with established procedures can assure that HCT/Ps meet the standards in these rules. . . .

The record requirements of this rule are similarly necessary. A single donor may be the source of a large number of HCT/Ps. . . . Unless adequate records were maintained, and maintained for the period of time throughout which infections may be identified, it would be impossible to identify the recipients potentially infected by the donor's HCT/Ps. . . .

The CGTP [Current Good Tissue Practices] regulations govern the methods used in, and the facilities and controls used for, the manufacture of HCT/Ps. CGTP requirements are a fundamental component of FDA's risk-based approach to regulating HCT/Ps. HCT/Ps regulated solely under section 361 of the PHS Act and the regulations in part 1271 are not regulated under the [FD&C] act or section 351 of the PHS Act (42 U.S.C. 262). By requiring that HCT/Ps meeting the criteria listed in Sec. 1271.10 (361 HCT/Ps) be manufactured in compliance with CGTP, in combination with the other requirements in part 1271, the agency can ensure that 361 HCT/Ps are subject to sufficient regulatory controls to protect the public health.

HCT/Ps regulated as drugs, devices, and/or biological products, and not as 361 HCT/Ps, must be manufactured in accordance with CGTP, in addition to existing requirements. The CGTP regulations supplement the current good manufacturing practice (CGMP) and quality system (QS) regulations applicable to drugs, devices, and biological products in parts 210, 211, and 820 (21 CFR parts 210, 211, and 820). . . . Thus, . . . those HCT/Ps regulated as drugs, devices, and/or biological products are subject to CGMP regulations as well as to CGTP regulations. . . .

NOTE

FDA's tissue regulations rely on section 361 of the PHS Act for legal authority. That provision allows FDA to use virtually any means to accomplish the congressional objective—prevention of disease transmission. But that goal arguably limits the measures that FDA might adopt. Unless a requirement can be justified as contributing to the prevention of communicable disease, section 361 presumably does not provide the necessary legal support.

G. OTHER CELLULAR TECHNOLOGIES

This concluding section of the chapter surveys a series of emerging medical technologies over which FDA exercises some level of regulatory authority. The technologies have two things in common. Each of them utilizes materials recovered from living organisms, human or animal. And though the case for FDA jurisdiction in each instance seems plausible, the agency was at first slow to respond to claims that it could or should exert control.

1. GENE THERAPY

The remarkable advances in mapping the human genome and understanding the role of specific genes in the genesis of disease have spurred development of therapeutic applications of genetic material. These efforts have raised questions on several fronts. What agency or agencies should be responsible for overseeing attempts at gene therapy? What controls should public entities impose to protect patients and at the same time facilitate promising research? And, more recently, are the early applications of gene therapy yielding evidence to support the optimistic predictions of the technology's pioneers?

Joseph M. Rainsbury, *Biotechnology on the RAC: FDA/NIH Regulation of Human Gene Therapy*

55 FOOD & DRUG LAW JOURNAL 575 (2000).

Gene therapy, a procedure in which healthy genes are spliced into the cells of sick patients, represents the cutting edge of medical research. If successful, it will constitute a revolution in medicine. It already has pushed the limits of regulatory science. . . .

On April 11, 1983, the RAC [Recombinant DNA Advisory Committee at NIH] established a Working Group on a Response to the Splicing Life Report. . . .

. . . FDA began to take notice of the emerging technology of gene therapy. In 1984, the agency announced that it intended to regulate rDNA-derived products. In 1986, it specifically asserted jurisdiction over human gene therapy products, while acknowledging that it might share regulatory duties with NIH. . . .

The opening salvo in the regulatory battles to get particular gene therapy treatments approved occurred on April 24, 1987, when Dr. W. French Anderson submitted what he styled a Preclinical Data Document to the RAC that detailed his proposal to treat Severe Combined Immunodeficiency (SCID) with ex vivo modification of extracted blood cells. Anderson sought to use a retroviral vector to splice a functioning copy of the defective gene into the blood cells of a SCID victim, thus enabling the patient herself to manufacture the protein. In this initial quasi-protocol, Anderson targeted blood cells in the bone marrow, hoping to transduce blood stem cells with copies of the healthy gene. Unfortunately, the results from Anderson's animal studies were less than promising. Among other things, half of the (otherwise healthy) monkeys subjected to the treatment died. Professional reaction to the Phonebook (the name given to Anderson's 500-page document) was withering, and at its December 7, 1988 meeting the RAC made it clear that it was nowhere near approving Anderson's protocol. . . .

Not long after gene therapy trials began, it became clear that the technique could be employed to fight diseases other than rare, single-gene, hereditary defects like SCID. In particular, cancer and AIDS began to emerge as potential targets. Consequently, the number of gene therapy protocols approved by the RAC rose exponentially. With these diseases came large and, particularly with AIDS, well-organized, vocal, and powerful activist groups. Because the RAC and its Human Gene Therapy Subcommittee met only three or four times a year, the work soon began to exceed their processing capacity. More importantly, many of the new protocols raised no new ethical or safety issues. The work was becoming mundane, stuff for full-time regulators at FDA, not for the all-star staff assembled at the RAC.

. . .

As the RAC's role in overseeing human gene therapy clinical trials gradually waned, FDA's responsibility correspondingly waxed. . . . FDA had asserted jurisdiction over human gene therapy products as early as 1986. The agency, however, was vague about both the legal authority underlying this jurisdiction and the content of the technical standards the ʼagency intended to deploy. As human gene therapy trials commenced, FDA began to clarify both.

Unlike NIH, FDA was not a source of funding for human gene therapy clinical trials. Thus, it could not ensure compliance with its gene therapy policies simply by withholding funding from violator researchers/institutions. Instead, it had to rely on its statutory authority to prevent the shipment of misbranded drugs, devices, or biologics. Human gene therapy products defy easy classification under the existing regulatory schemata of drugs, devices, or biologics. Nevertheless, FDA determined early that it would regulate this class of therapeutic agents as biologics. By doing so, FDA maximized its control over such products. . . . Moreover, under the Public Health Service Act (PHS Act), FDA did not need to demonstrate an interstate nexus to exert its regulatory power.

. . .

The gene therapy field lost its innocence on September 17, 1999. On that date, eighteen year-old Jesse Gelsinger died from complications arising out of a Phase I safety trial of a gene therapy treatment for ornithine transcarbamylase (OTC) deficiency. Unlike previous gene therapy fatalities, researchers ascribed Gelsinger's death to his treatment, not to the underlying disease being treated. Worse, Gelsinger was a (reasonably) healthy volunteer. The incident therefore cast a harsh spotlight on the legal safeguards in place to protect patients at the frontier of medicine.

. . . The actual cause of [Gelsinger's] death was acute respiratory distress syndrome brought on by a severe immunological response to the adenovirus vector. . . . Although there is little evidence that [the investigators'] deviations [from the approved protocol] contributed to Gelsinger's death, their revelation in the wake of the disaster provided a lightning rod for those critical of . . . the conduct of gene therapy researchers. . . .

Public attention also focused on the institutions responsible for regulating gene therapy. An issue that dominated headlines was widespread industry non-compliance with NIH disclosure requirements. . . . This is not to say the researchers were keeping adverse events hidden from regulators. FDA has nearly identical requirements for adverse-event reporting, and had reported no serious compliance problems among gene therapy researchers. A major explanation for this difference appears to have been industry concerns about proprietary information. Unlike the RAC, FDA treats sponsor-provided clinical data as confidential information that cannot be disclosed publicly without prior sponsor approval. . . . Whatever the motives, the failure of so many researchers to comply with NIH requirements gave the appearance of a major regulatory breakdown. . . .

———

In addition to causing regulators to reassess their requirements, the death of Jesse Gelsinger and the manifestation of cancer among gene therapy patients in France prompted some critics to question the early predictions of the promise of gene therapy.

This doubt was well-founded: as of June 2013, not a single gene therapy had won approval from the FDA. A promising development occurred in November 2012, however, when a Dutch company received regulatory approval in Europe for a gene therapy called Glybera, used to treat patients with a rare metabolic disorder. *See Gene Therapy Shows New Signs of Promise*, BOSTON GLOBE, June 2, 2013, at G3.

2. STEM CELLS

Stem Cells and the Future of Regenerative Medicine

Institute of Medicine and National Research Council (2001).

. . . .

The conditions listed below occur in many forms and thus not every person with these diseases could potentially benefit from cell-based therapies. Nonetheless, the widespread incidence of these conditions suggests that stem cell research could help millions of Americans.

Condition	Number of patients
Cardiovascular disease	58 million
Autoimmune diseases	30 million
Diabetes	16 million
Osteoporosis	10 million
Cancers	8.2 million
Alzheimer's disease	5.5 million
Parkinson's disease	5.5 million
Burns (severe)	0.3 million
Spinal-cord injuries	0.25 million
Birth defects	0.15 million/year

. . . .

The Committee placed off limits the issue of reproductive cloning, which is sometimes linked to stem cell research because in both cases, the somatic cell nuclear transfer (SCNT) technique can be used to create embryos. The interest in this technique for stem cell research is related to the possibility of producing stem cells for regenerative therapy that are genetically matched to the person needing a tissue transplant. The immune system is poised to reject tissue transplants from genetically non-identical people, and immunological rejection poses serious clinical risks that can be life-threatening. Overcoming the threat of immunological rejection is thus one of the major scientific challenges to stem cell transplantation—and, indeed, for transplantations of any sort. The SCNT technique offers the possibility of deriving stem cells for transplantation from the recipient's own cells. Such cells would produce only the patient's own proteins and would not cause an immunological reaction when transplanted into their patient.

. . . .

Embryonic stem cells (ESCs) are derived from an early-stage embryo. Fertilization of an ovum by a sperm results in a zygote, the earliest embryonic stage. . . . To be useful for producing medical therapies, cultured ESCs will need to be differentiated into appropriate tissues for transplantation into patients. Researchers are just beginning to learn how to achieve this differentiation.

Fetal stem cells are primitive cell types in the fetus that eventually develop into the various organs of the body, but research with fetal tissue so far has been limited to only a few cell types: neural stem cells, including neural crest cells; hematopoietic stem cells, and pancreatic islet progenitors. . . .

. . . Finally, multipotent cells called primordial germ cells have been isolated from the gonadal ridge, a structure that arises at an early stage of the fetus that will eventually develop into eggs or sperm in the adult. Germ cells can be cultured in vivo and have been shown to give rise to multiple cell types of the three embryonic tissue layers.

Adult stem cells are undifferentiated cells that occur in a differentiated tissue, such as bone marrow or the brain, in the adult body. They can renew themselves in the body, making identical copies of themselves for the lifetime of the organism, or become specialized to yield the cell types of the tissue of origin. Sources of adult stem cells include bone marrow, blood, the eye, brain, skeletal muscle, dental pulp, liver, skin, the lining of the gastrointestinal tract, and pancreas. Studies suggest that at least some adult stem cells are multipotent. . . . Finding ways to culture adult stems cells outside the body is a high priority of stem cell research. . . .

United States v. Regenerative Sciences, LLC

878 F. Supp. 2d 248 (D.D.C. 2012).

■ COLLYER, DISTRICT JUDGE.

MEMORANDUM OPINION

Drs. Christopher J. Centeno and John R. Schultz developed the Regenexx™ Procedure, by which they use stem cell therapies to aid healing for their orthopedic patients. They formed Regenerative Sciences LLC for this endeavor. . . . They are . . . now facing an enforcement action by the Food and Drug Administration, which charges them with "causing articles of drug to become adulterated" and "misbranded" within the meaning of the Federal Food, Drug, and

Cosmetic Act ("FFDCA"), 21 U.S.C. § 301 *et seq.* Defendants respond that they practice medicine wholly within the State of Colorado and under its oversight and that the Regenexx™ Procedure is not a "drug" subject to regulation by the federal government.

It is a close question but ultimately the Court concludes that the Regenexx™ Procedure is subject to FDA enforcement because it constitutes a "drug" and because a drug that has been shipped in interstate commerce is used in the solution through which the cultured stem cells are administered to patients. This acknowledged connection to interstate commerce renders the Regenexx™ Procedure subject to the FFDCA even though the doctors themselves are practicing medicine under Colorado law. Summary judgment will be granted to the United States and an injunction will be issued precluding the continued use of the Regenexx™ Procedure without compliance with the FFDCA.

I.   FACTS

... The Regenexx™ Procedure is a non-surgical procedure for patients suffering from moderate to severe joint, muscle, tendon or bone pain due to injury or other conditions.

The Regenexx™ Procedure begins with a licensed physician taking a small bone marrow sample from the back of a patient's hip through a needle. Blood samples are also taken from a vein in the patient's arm. These samples are then sent to the Regenerative laboratory which is also in Broomfield, Colorado, just a few miles from the Clinic where the mesenchymal stem cells (MSCs) are isolated from the bone marrow and then grown to greater numbers. This process uses the natural growth factors found in the patient's blood to grow the MSCs.

After approximately 2 weeks, the expanded stem cells are sent to the University of Colorado affiliated Colorado Genetics Laboratory for testing. . . .

Once the cells pass quality assurance testing, they are placed back into the patient's injured area (i.e. knee, hip, rotator cuff), typically 4–6 weeks after they were removed. The stem cells then begin to repair the patient's degenerated or injured area. . . .

Of critical importance here is the process by which Regenerative expands the mesenchymal cells taken from a patient's bone marrow and delivers a syringe with the cells in solution to the Clinic.

1.   A doctor at the Clinic obtains a tissue sample from the patient's bone marrow by inserting a needle into the hip bone and drawing a thick blood like liquid into a syringe; the sample is then sent to the laboratory.

2.   The marrow sample is centrifuged to separate out fractions of the bone marrow and the middle layer ("buffy coat") is taken off with a pipette.

3.   The cells from the buffy coat are placed in a plastic flask and kept in a warm environment to incubate with the patient's own blood platelets that contain growth factors, as well as a nutrient solution. Over a few days, the mesenchymal stem cells adhere to the plastic flask while the rest of the cells do not adhere.

4.   The non-adherent cells are discarded and the mesenchymal stem cells are collected using Trypsin, an enzyme, to detach the cells from the plastic flask.

5.   The process is repeated to grow the cells.

6.   The cells undergo a visual inspection by the Colorado Genetics Laboratory to make sure that there are no genetic mutations or other genetic problems. The treating doctor then approves the cells.

"[T]he expanded cells, along with a drug product that has been shipped in interstate commerce and other additives, are placed into syringes. Regenerative Sciences [sends] the filled syringes in sterile bags to the Clinic, where they are injected into patients."

. . . .

III. ANALYSIS

. . . .

A. *Federalism and the Commerce Clause*

. . . By long tradition, the health and safety of the people is left to the States as matters of local concern. Accordingly, Defendants state that Congress has left the practice of medicine to the States to regulate. FDA does not disagree with these principles but asserts that their exercise of jurisdiction over Defendants' Regenexx™ Procedure is a permissible exercise of federal power under the Commerce Clause.

Congress may regulate the practice of medicine or rather, certain aspects of it, when it does so pursuant to its Commerce Clause powers. . . . The FFDCA provisions at issue in this case require an interstate commerce nexus, ensuring that regulation under the FFDCA is consistent with the Commerce Clause. 21 U.S.C. § 331(k) (applying only if the drug is held for sale "after shipment in interstate commerce"). Thus, the question here is one of statutory interpretation— whether Defendants' cell product is subject to the terms of the FFDCA.

B. *The Regenexx™ Procedure is a "Drug" Under the FFDCA*

1.   Definition of a "Drug"

. . . .

Defendants' pleadings confirm their intentions to use the Regenexx™ Procedure for "mitigation" and "treatment," among others, of disease and injury. . . . These statements of "intended use" fully satisfy the statutory definition for a "drug." [21 U.S.C. § 321(g).] Similarly, Defendants' admissions that the Regenexx™ Procedure is based on mesenchymal stem cells derived from the patient's bone marrow and that it is intended to treat orthopedic conditions fully satisfy the definition of "biological product" under the PHSA because it is a "blood, blood component or derivative, . . . or analogous product . . . applicable to the prevention, treatment, or cure of a disease or condition of human beings." 42 U.S.C. § 262(i). In sum, the cell product used in the Regenexx™ Procedure meets the statutory definition for both a "drug" under the FFDCA and a "biological product" under the PHSA.

2.   The Regulations at 21 C.F.R. Part 1271 Do Not Exempt the Regenexx[™] Procedure

. . . .

The development of research and medical treatments using human cells, tissues, and cellular or tissue-based products (human cell or tissue products or "HCT/Ps") caused the FDA to announce in 1997 a tiered, risk-based approach for their regulation. . . . Part 1271.3 defines HCT/Ps as "articles containing or consisting of human cells or tissues that are intended for implantation, transplantation, infusion, or transfer into a human recipient." 21 C.F.R. § 1271.3(d). Those HCT/Ps that meet the set of criteria listed in 21 C.F.R. § 1271.10 are only regulated under section 361 of the PHSA and Part 1271 of the C.F.R. In contrast, those HCT/Ps that do not meet these criteria are regulated as "a drug, device, and/or biological product." 21 C.F.R. § 1271.20.

One of these criteria is that the HCT/Ps be "minimally manipulated." 21 C.F.R. § 1271.10(a)(1). Minimal manipulation is defined as "processing that does not alter the relevant biological characteristics of cells or tissues." 21 C.F.R. § 1271.3(f)(2). Defendants admit that "[t]he processing of the cultured cell product involves many steps, including selective culture and expansion of a multitude of different types of blood-forming and rare bone marrow stromal cells using plastic flasks, additives and nutrients, and environmental conditions such as temperature and humidity, to determine the growth and biological characteristics of the resulting cell population." This admission supports the conclusion that the biological characteristics of the cells change during the process employed by Defendants, resulting in more than minimal manipulation of the HCT/Ps originally extracted from the patient. Moreover, the FDA's conclusion that the Regenexx™ Procedure does not meet the regulatory definition of "minimal manipulation" is entitled to "substantial deference." . . . As a result, Defendants fail to meet at least one of the criteria listed in 21 C.F.R. § 1271.10, and the HCT/Ps in the Regenexx™ Procedure must be regulated as a "drug" under the FFDCA.

C. *Defendants Violated 21 U.S.C. § 331(k)*

1. The Regenexx™ Procedure Is Subject to the Commerce Clause

. . . Defendants do not contest the "held for sale" requirement [of FD&C Act 301(k)] but instead argue that the Regenexx™ Procedure does not meet the "interstate commerce" requirement because the entire process takes place intrastate at Defendants' medical facilities in Colorado. The FFDCA defines "drug" to include "articles intended for use as a *component* of any article. . . ." 21 U.S.C. § 321(g)(1)(D) (emphasis added). Courts have held that the "interstate commerce" element is met if any component of that drug moved in interstate commerce. *See Baker v. United States*, 932 F.2d 813, 816 (9th Cir. 1991). Defendants combine an antibiotic, doxycycline, with the cell product before the drug is administered to the patients through a syringe. Defendants do not dispute that the doxycycline is shipped from out of state to their facilities in Colorado. Therefore, because a component of the drug in this case is shipped through interstate commerce prior to its administration to the patient, the "interstate commerce" requirement is also met.

2. Adulteration

. . . The FDA performed two separate inspections, one in 2009 and the other in 2010, which revealed a number of CGMP violations. Having concluded that the cell product used in the Regenexx™ Procedure is a "drug" that is subject to regulation by the FFDCA and that the drug has been "held for sale after shipment in interstate commerce," the fact that the Regenexx™ Procedure does not comply with CGMP renders the drug adulterated in violation of the FFDCA.

3. Misbranding

. . . The FDA asserts that the cultured cell product is misbranded because it is a prescription drug that does not bear the "Rx only" symbol or carry "adequate directions for use." . . .

A prescription drug is misbranded "if at any time prior to dispensing the label of the drug fails to bear, at a minimum, the symbol "Rx only." 21 U.S.C. § 353(b)(4)(A). It is undisputed that the label of the cultured cell product does not bear this symbol. On this basis, Defendants misbrand the cultured cell product in violation of the FFDCA.

The FDA further alleges that Defendants have misbranded the cultured cell product because its label does not bear "adequate directions for use," which the FFDCA requires. 21 U.S.C. § 352(f)(1). The FDA defines "adequate directions for use" as "directions under which the layman can use a drug safely and for the purposes for which it is intended." 21 C.F.R. § 201.5. However, a prescription drug by its very definition cannot bear "adequate directions for use" by a layman. As a result, a prescription drug must qualify for an exemption to avoid violating the FFDCA's misbranding provision.

. . . The FDA has . . . created a regulatory exemption to the misbranding provision, which exempts prescription drugs with a label bearing, *inter alia*, information regarding dosage, administration, and ingredients. 21 C.F.R. § 201.100. . . .

The label for the cultured cell product contains only the [sic] "the patient's name, date of birth, laboratory notebook number, cell passage number, day in culture, cell number, number of cells cryo-preserved, and condition of cell suspension." The information on this label does not satisfy the disclosure requirements under either the statutory or the regulatory exemptions. For this reason also, Defendants have violated the misbranding provision of the FFDCA.

D. The Regenexx™ Procedure Does Not Avoid FDA Regulation Because Defendants Are Engaged in the Practice of Medicine

Defendants rely heavily on their argument that the FDA cannot regulate the Regenexx™ Procedure because it constitutes the practice of medicine. However, "[w]hile the [FFDCA] was not intended to regulate the practice of medicine, it was obviously intended to control the availability of drugs for prescribing by physicians." *United States v. Evers*, 643 F.2d 1043, 1048 (5th Cir. 1981). There is a difference between a licensed physician's use of an FDA-approved drug such as doxycycline in an off-label way, which is permissible within the "practice of medicine," and adding doxycycline to a cell product to be administered to patients, which renders the latter a "drug" that has connections to interstate commerce. The question of interstate commerce is not relevant to the first issue but controls the second. Likewise, the fact that off-label use of an FDA-approved drug is permissible within the practice of medicine does not speak to whether the drug traveled in interstate commerce, which provides the nexus for regulation under the provision of the FFDCA relevant here.

Where, as here, a product meets the definition of "drug" under the [F]FDCA, it comes under the ambit of this law and is thus subject to its provisions. This is true even if its regulation will affect the practice of medicine. Consequently, Defendants' argument that the cell product cannot be regulated by the FDA because the Regenexx™ Procedure constitutes the "practice of medicine" is unavailing.

E.   Defendants' Counterclaims Will Be Dismissed

. . . Defendants allege in Counterclaim VIII that the FDA lacks the authority to enact the "entire regulatory scheme governing stem cells" because the autologous use of stem cells carries no risk of spreading communicable diseases. . . . FDA may enact regulations to prevent the spread of communicable diseases pursuant to section 361 of the PHSA, 42 U.S.C. § 264(a). When issuing these regulations, FDA carefully explained its determination that the manufacturing of HCT/Ps, including autologous stem cells, presents a risk of spreading communicable disease:

> . . . Errors in labeling, mixups of testing records, failure to adequately clean work areas, and faulty packaging are examples of improper practices that could produce a product capable of transmitting disease to its recipient . . . [and] improper handling of an HCT/P can lead to bacterial or other pathogenic contamination of the HCT/P, or to cross-contamination between HCT/Ps, which in turn can endanger recipients.

69 Fed. Reg. 68612, 68613 (Nov. 24, 2004). . . . Counterclaim VIII will be dismissed.

. . . .

NOTES

1.   *"Autologous" Procedures.* Procedures in which the cell or tissue product is put back into the donor are known as "autologous" use of HCT/Ps. 21 C.F.R. 1271.3(a).

2.   *Critical Analysis.* For a critical analysis of FDA enforcement policy under the tissue regulations regarding autologous use by physicians of adult stem cells, see Andrew S. Ittleman, *Enforcement Discretion: How Can FDA More Reasonably Regulate Autologous Stem Cell Procedures*, 2 FDLI FOOD AND DRUG POLICY FORUM, No. 24 (Dec. 26, 2012).

3. ASSISTED REPRODUCTION

Lars Noah, *Assisted Reproductive Technologies and the Pitfalls of Unregulated Biomedical Innovation*
55 FLORIDA LAW REVIEW 603 (2003).

. . . .

ART [Assisted Reproductive Technology] now encompasses several distinct methods, though they often are used in combination. Artificial insemination (AI), also referred to as intrauterine insemination (IUI), has the longest history and requires the least technological sophistication: the procedure introduces sperm (spermatozoa)—from either the husband or a donor—into the woman's uterus. Gamete intrafallopian transfer (GIFT), which delivers the sperm and harvested eggs (ova or oocytes) directly into the woman's fallopian tube, represents a more complicated method of insemination requiring the use of a laparoscope through an abdominal incision. . . .

In vitro fertilization (IVF), first accomplished a quarter of a century ago, represents the paradigmatic form of ART. Basically, the procedure involves harvesting oocytes from the patient, mixing them with sperm in a petri dish containing a culture medium in order to achieve extracorporeal fertilization, and then transferring one or more embryos back into the patient. Several permutations are, however, possible: the sperm and/or eggs may come from donors, the embryos may be transferred into a woman shortly after fertilization or cryopreserved (frozen) for possible future use, they may be transferred back into the woman who supplied the eggs or into an unrelated surrogate, and they may be transferred into the woman's uterus or, typically at an earlier stage of embryonic development, into her fallopian tubes.

. . . .

In recent years, ARTs have become an increasingly popular medical intervention. . . . Almost 400 fertility clinics currently operate in the United States. Some of these are free-standing entrepreneurial facilities, while other clinics are housed within larger health care institutions. Much like other fee-for-service operations such as elective cosmetic surgery, hospitals may establish fertility clinics as lucrative profit centers. . . .

Unlike other medical technologies, ARTs arrive[d] on the scene with little or no rigorous testing of their safety and effectiveness. . . .

As a number of researchers have documented, fertility drugs and IVF increase the incidence of multiple births. Such pregnancies pose a variety of significant health risks to both mothers and children. . . .

. . . In addition, ART procedures raise a variety of other safety concerns for the mother, ranging from acute and chronic side effects associated with the use of fertility drugs, including a suspected increased risk of ovarian cancer, to complications involved in the harvesting procedure, and higher rates of ectopic pregnancies. . . .

Until recently, the FDA had not asserted regulatory jurisdiction over IVF or other fertility procedures. Indeed, scholars who wrote about the regulation of ARTs had paid no attention to the agency, and, when Congress passed the Fertility Clinic Success Rate and Certification Act of 1992, it suggested no role for the FDA. . . .

Nonetheless, in 1998, the FDA announced, and subsequently reiterated, that its proposed rule governing cellular and tissue-based products would apply to ARTs as well:

> Most aspects of cellular and tissue product manufacturing in the reproductive tissue industry would become newly regulated under the proposed CGTP [current good tissue practices] rule. The affected establishments within this industry include sperm banks and ART facilities. Reports of the sensitivity of product quality to variations in tissue collection, technician skill, processing methods, environmental conditions, and other factors, indicate that the risk of communicable disease transmission would be reduced by improving the proposed overall product quality, and economic benefits would be seen through improved patient outcomes from facility compliance with the proposed CGTP requirements. . . . Despite the increasing effectiveness of infertility treatment through ART, problems can occur in tissue processing. Adverse outcomes owing to problems with product quality can result from contamination that produces infection (*e.g.*, HIV transmission) in the infertility patient. Problems with ART facility processing of sperm or oocytes can also lead to reduced rates of fertilization. . . . [66 Fed. Reg. 1508, 1542–43 (Jan. 8, 2001).]

> . . . .

More controversially . . . the FDA also asserted jurisdiction over other aspects of ARTs, claiming that it had the authority to subject human reproductive tissues to premarket review—and to demand proof of their safety and effectiveness—in the event that they had undergone more than minimal manipulation. After the publication of its proposed CGTP rule, the agency sent warning letters to several fertility clinics ordering them to cease using techniques that entail any kind of alteration of human genetic material, including cloning, genetic engineering, and ooplasmic transfer (a.k.a. IVONT). . . .

4. REPRODUCTIVE CLONING

Richard A. Merrill, *Human Tissues and Reproductive Cloning: New Technologies Challenge FDA*

3 HOUSTON JOURNAL OF HEALTH & POLICY 1 (2003).

. . . The first signal that FDA would seek to regulate cloning was sent during a radio interview of Acting FDA Commissioner Dr. Michael Friedman. . . . He went on to say that FDA viewed human cloning as analogous to gene therapy, over which the Agency had years before asserted regulatory control.

     . . . .

[Later, in congressional testimony, the head of CBER] described the Agency's concerns and outlined the regulatory requirements that, she asserted, existing law imposed. . . .

FDA has the authority to regulate medical products, including biological products, drugs, and devices. The use of cloning technology to clone a human being would be subject to both the biologics provisions of the Public Health Service (PHS) Act and the drug and device provisions of the Federal Food, Drug, and Cosmetic (FD&C) Act. . . . Before such research could begin, the researcher must submit an IND request to FDA, which FDA would review to determine if such research could proceed. FDA believes that there are major unresolved safety questions on the use of cloning technology to clone a human being and therefore would not permit any such investigation to proceed at this time.

Advocates for FDA regulation [had earlier] suggested that the Agency could rely on [section 361 of the PHSA] to regulate human cloning because of the risk of transmission of HIV and other infectious diseases from the donor(s) of cellular material to a clone or its "mother." While not facially implausible, this theory would have confronted two difficulties that may explain FDA's failure to adopt it. First, while the measures authorized by Section 361 are broadly described, the end at which such measures must be aimed is not; the only goal that Congress has authorized the Agency to pursue is the prevention of communicable disease—a narrower target than the manifold concerns about cloning. Moreover, and more importantly, FDA could have invoked Section 361 only if it had been prepared to initiate rulemaking in accordance with the APA. . . .

A second option pressed on FDA . . . was to rely on the "FDA plan for cellular and tissue-based products." . . .

FDA's "plan for cellular and tissue-based products" does contemplate that some tissues will require clinical studies to demonstrate safety and effectiveness—a requirement that would be triggered by a determination that a tissue is a biological drug or Class III device. FDA's plan can therefore be read as predicting how the Agency might view human cloning but, standing alone, it cannot provide authority for the restrictions the Agency later sought to impose.

In 1998, an unidentified FDA employee prepared the following analysis of the agency's legal authority to regulate—and prohibit—human cloning.

FDA's Jurisdiction Over Human Cloning Activities

April 16, 1998.

. . . The conclusion that FDA has jurisdiction over somatic cell clones under the PHS Act and the FD&C Act is consistent with the statutory purpose of public health protection. Courts have recognized that remedial statutes, such as the FD&C Act and the PHS Act, are to be liberally construed consistent with their public health purpose. See

United States v. An Article of Drug . . . Bacto–Unidisk, 394 U.S. 784 (1968).

FDA regulates biological products under section 351 of the PHS Act. 42 U.S.C. § 262. That section applies to "any virus, therapeutic serum, toxin, antitoxin, vaccine, blood, blood component or derivative, allergenic product, or analogous product, or arsphenamine or its derivatives (or any other trivalent organic arsenic compound), applicable to the prevention, treatment or cure of diseases or injuries of man . . ." Section 123(d) of the Food and Drug Administration Modernization Act of 1997 (FDA Modernization Act) amends the PHS Act by including within the definition of biological products "conditions" as well as diseases. 42 U.S.C. § 262(I) (effective February 19, 1998).

. . . A somatic cell clone used to create a cloned human being for an infertile individual is a product applicable to the treatment of infertility. Likewise, a somatic cell clone used to create a cloned human being to avoid transmission of a genetic disease from a prospective parent is a product applicable to the prevention of that genetic disease in the cloned human being. In addition, significant safety questions have been raised regarding whether the cloning process will produce a healthy human being who will develop normally. For example, the cloned human being might have defects from the donor or during development, such as genetic, biochemical, or cellular defects.

A somatic cell clone is not one of the specifically listed products in section 351 of the PHS Act. It is, however, an "analogous product" under the PHS Act and thus falls within the scope of this section.

. . . A somatic cell clone has similarities in composition and function with blood and blood components. A somatic cell clone is analogous to white blood cells, a component of blood, in that both cells are similarly composed because they are somatic cells that contain a nucleus. A somatic cell clone is also like blood and blood components in that they contain cellular elements derived from a living human being and are applicable to diseases or conditions of human beings.

. . . .

Under the FD&C Act, the term "drug" is defined as "articles (other than food) intended to affect the structure or any function of the body." . . . As described above, a somatic cell clone is a product intended to affect the structure or function (including the diseases or conditions) of the cloned human being. The continued growth and development of the cloned human being are the result of the maturation of the somatic cell clone. In addition, a somatic cell clone could be viewed as a product intended to affect the structure or function of the woman into whose uterus the somatic cell is to be implanted.

A product also is a "drug" if it is "intended for use in the diagnosis, cure, mitigation, treatment, or prevention of disease in man or other animals." A somatic cell clone used to create a cloned human being in order to avoid transmission of a genetic disease from a prospective parent with the disease would be an article intended to prevent the transmission of disease to the cloned human being and thus would fall within this definition. A somatic cell clone used with the intent to create a cloned human being for an infertile couple also could fall within this drug definition in that the product would be used to treat infertility.

. . . .

In the regulatory approach [the agency had proposed for tissue in 1997], FDA addressed reproductive tissues and noted that such tissues have a long history of use in the medical community. FDA also recognized that such tissues raised a number of less substantial issues than those raised by other tissues that have a systemic effect on the body. As a result, FDA stated that such tissues would be subject to less regulation than other tissues that have a systematic effect on the body. Unlike the reproductive tissues discussed in the regulatory approach, tissues and cells for cloning of human beings raise additional significant health concerns not raised by processes in place for the reproductive tissues used in the past. Consistent with the tiered approach for cellular and tissue-based products, a somatic cell clone would be subject to FDA premarket review and approval because it is more than minimally manipulated.

Under the authorities of both Acts, FDA promulgated regulations to allow clinical research on investigational drugs and biological products. Clinical research on these products can proceed only when an investigational new drug application (IND) is in effect. Before such research may begin, the sponsor of the research is required to submit to FDA an IND describing the proposed research plan. The sponsor also is required to obtain authorization to proceed from an institutional review board (an independent group of experts and consumers which reviews the proposed study from a scientific and ethical perspective). Thus, before an egg is removed from a woman or the cell containing the nucleus to be inserted into the egg is removed from the prospective genetic parent for the purpose of creating a cloned human being, an IND should be in place and informed consent obtained.

5. XENOTRANSPLANTATION

When FDA asserted jurisdiction over human heart valves as medical devices in 1990, it had already ordered the manufacturers of artificial heart valves and providers of porcine (pig) valves to submit premarket approval applications for these "devices." 52 Fed. Reg. 18162 (May 13, 1987). FDA's later approval of PMAs for porcine valves is clear evidence that the agency has jurisdiction over at least some implants derived from animals—known as xenotransplants. Although the technology is still in the investigational stage, there continues to be interest in the possibility that animals may be, or may be made to become, sources of tissues or possibly even organs for humans. The scarcity of cadaver organs for transplantation helps fuel this interest. The development of drugs to suppress the body's rejection of foreign materials, which has been key to the success of human organ transplants, has also stimulated xenotransplantation research. More than two dozen clinical trials using animal source materials have been undertaken in the United States, pursuant to INDs approved by FDA. None has yet led to an application for marketing approval.

Because this research involves human subjects, there has been little question that it is subject to FDA oversight. Whether categorized as drugs, biologics, or medical devices, materials derived from animals implanted in human subjects fall under FDA's authority to regulate the clinical investigation of medical products.

Jodi K. Frederickson, *He's All Heart . . . and a Little Pig Too: A Look at the FDA Draft Xenotransplant Guideline*
52 FOOD AND DRUG LAW JOURNAL 429 (1997).

The recent transplant of baboon bone marrow into an AIDS patient . . . has . . . thrust the potential of xenotransplantation into the realm of medical possibility. In the wake of the . . . transplant, the Food and Drug Administration (FDA) collaborated with the Centers for Disease Control and Prevention (CDC), the National Institutes of Health (NIH), and the Health Resources and Services Administration (HRSA) in the development and publication for comment of its Draft Guideline on Infectious Disease Issues in Xenotransplantation [(1996)]. This draft guideline would require an investigational new drug (IND) application prior to proceeding with a xenotransplant, set forth parameters for a xenotransplantation protocol, define animal sources, and address clinical issues, as well as other public health considerations.

. . . .

Xenotransplantation is the transplanting of organs or tissues across species, and is by no means a new concept. Xenotransplantation was first attempted in 1905. Advances in scientific technology and increasing efficacy of antirejection therapy in allogeneic transplants allowed xenotransplants to come closer to being a reality in the 1960s. Early efforts involved attempts to transplant baboon organs into human recipients. The baboons were chosen because the similarity between human and baboon physiology gave rise to the hope that the two species could accept one another's organs with minimal rejection. These early attempts were largely unsuccessful, but laid the groundwork and identified the issues researchers needed to confront in future attempts.

. . . .

In 1995, the University of Pittsburgh Medical Center performed the first baboon-to-human liver transplants on two patients dying of Hepatitis B. The first recipient lived for seventy-one days before dying of a brain hemorrhage stemming from a fungal infection, and the second recipient died of sepsis, a common cause of death in transplant patients, twenty-six days after the transplant. According to surgeons, neither death was attributable to the source of the livers, but rather was due to complications associated with transplants in general. The surgeons used a combination of four drugs intended to prevent hyper-acute rejection, at levels that may have contributed to the patients' deaths. In 1984, Baby Fae received a baboon heart to replace her congenitally defective heart, in hopes that her immune system would be too immature to mount an immune response. She died a mere twenty days later of graft rejection and infection.

Human organ transplants have become almost commonplace due to the arsenal of drugs designed to combat rejection of transplanted tissues. The increasing efficacy of these agents has made the transplantation of organs that are not closely matched a realistic option, and it permits science to move one step closer to utilizing organs that are not only non-HLA [human leukocyte antigen] matched, but also are harvested from entirely different species.

. . . .

The potential of xenotransplants is phenomenal, but does not come without associated, and potentially catastrophic, risks. The issue of paramount concern is the potential for viruses to use transplanted organs as vehicles into the human body, where they may develop into new diseases with epidemic potential. The gravity of these concerns escalates when viewed in light of the recent outbreaks of HIV, Ebola virus, and hantavirus that have killed thousands, and the looming possibility of unknown viruses waiting for an opportunity to strike. . . .

The development of a draft guideline was deemed an acceptable compromise between competing interests—those representing the risks and the promise of xenotransplantation. . . . The decision to use a guideline rather than a regulation is indicative of FDA's policy to allow for greater flexibility as the industry develops, while providing insight into FDA views. . . . Although draft guidelines do not carry the force and effect of law, they provide strong evidence of the standard FDA will apply in compliance considerations. . . .

The draft guideline suggests that patients be informed of specific risks associated with xenotransplants. The recipient should be informed that there is the potential for infection from zoonotic agents, including those infections known to be associated with the donor species and those yet to be identified. Furthermore, the patient must be made aware of the uncertainty as to the risks, including the likelihood of a latency period with any infectious agents, and that any resulting clinical diseases may be unknown. The draft guideline also suggests that the recipient should be adequately informed that there exists a risk of transmission of xenogeneic infectious agents to his or her close contacts, including family members and particularly sexual contacts. Recipients must be informed and understand that they may be isolated while hospitalized and that there are special precautions to be adhered to after discharge from the hospital.

The patient will be required to consent to life-long surveillance, including physical examinations and tissue sampling, and the recipient and his/her close contacts will be required to report to a physician immediately the event of any unexplained physical illnesses. The recipient must keep the transplant investigator abreast of address and telephone number changes to facilitate life-long surveillance. The team also should discuss the eventual need to perform a complete autopsy on the recipient; this discussion should include family members so as to ensure that the recipient's wishes ultimately are carried out. The recipient must understand that his or her medical records will be accessible by public health authorities, but that confidentiality of those records will be maintained. Finally, the recipient should never donate blood, tissues, or fluids. . . .

NOTES

1. *FDA Guidance for Xenotransplantation.* In 2001, the FDA and its sister agencies issued a final version of the guideline discussed in the article excerpt above. PHS GUIDELINE ON INFECTIOUS DISEASE ISSUES IN XENOTRANSPLANTATION (2001). In addition, FDA has published its advice on the design and conduct of clinical studies employing animal tissues in a series of guidances. *E.g.*, GUIDANCE FOR INDUSTRY: SOURCE ANIMAL, PRODUCT, PRECLINICAL AND CLINICAL ISSUES CONCERNING THE USE OF XENOTRANSPLANTATION PRODUCTS IN HUMANS (Apr. 2003); GUIDANCE FOR INDUSTRY: PUBLIC HEALTH ISSUES POSED BY THE USE OF NONHUMAN PRIMATE XENOGRAFTS IN HUMANS (Apr. 1999).

2. *Clinical Studies.* As of October 1, 2006, FDA acknowledged having received approximately two dozen INDs for clinical applications of xenotransplantation, of which perhaps fifteen were still active. *Cf. Campaign for Responsible Transplantation v. U.S. Food and Drug Administration*, 219 F. Supp. 2d 106 (D.D.C. 2002).

CHAPTER 10

MEDICAL DEVICES

FDA regulation of medical devices has gone through two distinct phases. The first phase began with enactment of the FD&C Act in 1938 and extended to the mid-1970s. The second, and still evolving phase, opened with enactment of the Medical Device Amendments of 1976. This chapter reviews FDA enforcement of the medical device provisions of the 1938 Act; explores the reasons why the 1976 Amendments were enacted; and examines the first three and a half decades of FDA's implementation of the new regulatory regime.

A. HISTORICAL BACKGROUND

Congress made medical devices subject to the 1938 Act largely because of its concern about the growing number of fraudulent—and in many instances implausible—instruments being marketed during the 1930s. This problem was not new.

Wallace F. Janssen, *The Gadgeteers*
Chapter 16 of Barrett & Knight, THE HEALTH ROBBERS (1980).

When Benjamin Franklin published his discoveries on electricity he also helped open the door for two of the most famous frauds in medical history. . . . In 1784, while representing the United States in France, Franklin was appointed to a royal commission to investigate the hypnotist Antoine Mesmer, whose treatments had become the rage of Paris. Mesmer, clad in a lilac suit, carrying a metal wand and playing a harmonica, healed by what he called "animal magnetism." Patients sat around a huge vat or "battery," holding iron rods which were immersed in a solution. The treatments went on for hours, accompanied by shouts, hysterical laughter and convulsions. The Franklin commission, after conducting some experiments, reported no electricity in Mesmer's tub. Nor could they detect the current known as "animal magnetism." A royal decree banned further treatments, but Mesmer was allowed to take his winnings to England. . . .

Ten years later, Elisha Perkins, a mule trader turned physician, secured a patent for "Perkins Tractors." . . . The tractors, two pointed rods about three inches long, one gold-colored, the other silver, were simply drawn downward across the afflicted part of the anatomy, in a sort of scratching motion. This, it was theorized, would draw off the "noxious fluid" (electricity) which was alleged to cause disease. "Tractoration," of course, was universal therapy—good for everything. For a time, the Perkins treatment enjoyed amazing popularity. Ministers, college professors and Congressmen gave enthusiastic endorsement. The Chief Justice of the Supreme Court bought a pair and President Washington himself is supposed to have been a customer. The medical profession was initially impressed; but in 1796 the Connecticut Medical Society condemned the treatment as "gleaned from the miserable remains of animal magnetism." In the following year the

Society expelled Dr. Perkins from membership. In 1799, Dr. Perkins voluntarily served in a yellow fever epidemic in New York, caught the disease, and died. Tractoration withered away.

But electrical health gadgetry marched on—through the 19th century and into the 20th. . . . In the 1920's, Albert Abrams, M.D., invented the system of diagnosis and healing he called "Radionics." Soon more than 3,000 local practitioners, mainly chiropractors, were sending dried blood specimens from patients to be inserted in Abrams' "Radioscope." The diagnosis would come back on a postcard, with recommended dial settings for treatment with other Abrams machines. . . .

Albert Abrams had many imitators, among them Ruth Drown, a Los Angeles chiropractor. One of her many nonsensical inventions was the Drown Radio-therapeutic Instrument. With this little black box and *two* blood spots, Mrs. Drown claimed to be able to "tune in" specific organs of the body and treat a patient by remote control anywhere in the world! . . .

Wilhelm Reich, M.D., one-time pupil of psychiatrist Sigmund Freud, claimed to have discovered "orgone energy," the most powerful force in the universe, and wrote extensively of its manifestations. . . . Soon after coming to the United States in 1934, Reich designed and built "orgone accumulators." Most of them were boxes of wood, metal and insulation board about the size of a telephone booth. Disease, he claimed, could be cured simply by sitting inside the box and absorbing the orgone. Hundreds of the boxes were sold or leased to practitioners and laymen for treatment of all kinds of diseases including cancer. Rentals were around $250 per month. . . .

NOTE

For a history of device regulation, see Peter Barton Hutt, *A History of Government Regulation of Adulteration and Misbranding of Medical Devices*, 44 FOOD DRUG COSM. L.J. 99 (1989). The key legislative history of the device provisions of the 1938 Act is summarized in *United States v. An Article of Drug . . . Bacto–Unidisk*, 394 U.S. 784 (1969).

B. REGULATION OF DEVICES UNDER THE FD&C ACT BEFORE 1976

The 1938 Act gave FDA jurisdiction over medical devices, but did not give the agency authority to review them for safety or effectiveness prior to marketing, to require premarket testing, or to establish and enforce performance standards. FDA power over devices prior to 1976 was thus limited primarily to pursuit of postmarket judicial remedies by actions brought in federal district court charging violations of the 1938 Act's basic misbranding and adulteration provisions. Probably the most important provision was section 502, which declares a drug or device to be misbranded "if its labeling is false or misleading in any particular." The Medical Device Amendments of 1976 gave FDA important new authorities, including premarket review, but the 1938 Act's basic adulteration and misbranding provisions remain important regulatory tools.

1. BACKGROUND

Medical Device Legislation—1975

House Committee on Interstate and Foreign Commerce. 94th Congress,
1st Session (1975).

The medical devices in use during the 1930's and through the late 1940's were of relatively simple and basic design. Seizure and injunction actions by FDA were generally limited to actions against a persistent series of "quack" devices. Legitimate devices were generally only reviewed for the accuracy of labeling. Between 1939 and 1941, the FDA initiated roughly 100 seizure actions against devices. At that time, several dangerous devices, such as lead nipple shields which caused nursing infants to incur lead poisoning, contraceptives which often caused genital infection and injury, and vaporizers which caused sinus and eustachian tube infections were removed from the market. . . .

The post-[World War II] years brought forth a wide variety of "quack" devices utilizing colored lights, dangerous gases such as ozone and chlorine, radio waves, heat, and vibration with claims of treatment and cure for virtually every disease known to man. One such device was a simple galvanometer which was encased in an impressive box and purportedly could diagnose any illness known to man. But when tested by the FDA on a corpse, the device registered a reading. It cost only a few dollars to produce, yet sold for hundreds of dollars.

The post-war revolution in biomedical technology also resulted in the introduction of a wide variety of sophisticated but legitimate devices. New developments in the electronic, plastics, metallurgy, and ceramics industries, coupled with progress in design engineering, led to invention of the heart pacemaker, the kidney dialysis machine, defibrillators, cardiac and renal catheters, surgical implants, artificial vessels and heart valves, intensive care monitoring units, and a wide spectrum of diagnostic and therapeutic devices. The increased sophistication of medical products, coupled with a stronger authority to regulate drugs, caused FDA to classify some of the new products as drugs. During the 1950s and 1960s, FDA encountered increasing difficulty in proving why certain dangerous or ineffective medical devices should be removed from the market. Device manufacturers were increasingly inclined to challenge FDA actions in the courts as the Diapulse Litigation illustrates.

2. DIAPULSE LITIGATION

In November 1965, FDA instituted its first seizure of a Diapulse, beginning litigation that lasted more than 20 years and exposed central deficiencies of the 1938 Act. The Diapulse was designed to produce a high frequency electrical pulse, similar to a conventional diathermy unit, but with lower output. FDA took the position that it was a misbranded device because it did not produce sufficient heat to provide the claimed therapeutic benefit. Although the government prevailed at trial, *United States v. An Article of Device . . . Diapulse Manufacturing Corp. of America*, 269 F. Supp. 162 (D. Conn. 1967), and on appeal, 389 F.2d 612 (2d Cir. 1968), the violations continued. FDA, therefore, secured a permanent injunction against further sales. *United States v. Diapulse Corp. of America*, 457 F.2d 25 (2d Cir. 1972). *See* Comment, *United States. v. The Diapulse Corp. of America*, 8 New Eng. L. Rev. 111 (1972).

In October 1973, FDA advised Congress: "The *Diapulse* cases require us to expend an inordinate amount of the resources allocated to device regulation, and thereby restrict investigative effort with respect to other dangerous or useless devices." "Medical Devices," Hearings before the Subcomm. on Public Health and Environment of the House Comm. on Interstate and Foreign Commerce, 93d Cong., 1st Sess. 155 (1973). Indeed, the litigation did not end with the Second Circuit's 1972 decision. FDA enforcement activities continued into 1976. A criminal contempt action failed, but the court strengthened the injunction. *United States v. Diapulse Corp. of America*, 365 F. Supp. 935 (E.D.N.Y. 1973), 514 F.2d 1097 (2d Cir. 1975). FDA then lost a seizure action in a District Court, but won on appeal. *United States v. Articles of Device . . . "Diapulse,"* 527 F.2d 1008 (6th Cir. 1976), *reh'g denied*, 532 F.2d 1056 (6th Cir. 1976). When FDA again initiated seizures, the claimant, a physician, acknowledged misbranding violations, but the District Court declined to condemn the devices and instead allowed them to be relabeled over the agency's objections. The Court of Appeals ruled that the trial court had incorrectly conducted a de novo trial on the validity of the relabeling rather than first requiring the claimant to submit a compliance proposal to FDA. *United States v. An Article of Device . . . Diapulse*, 650 F.2d 908 (7th Cir. 1981). On remand, the District Court affirmed FDA's refusal to accept the relabeling. *See United States v. An Article of Device . . . Diapulse*, 768 F.2d 826 (7th Cir. 1985).

In the interim, based on FDA's approval (pursuant to the Medical Device Amendments of 1976) of a higher-powered diathermy device marketed by a competing company, the Diapulse Corporation persuaded the District Court to permit it to market a modified Diapulse device similar to the newly approved device. That ruling against FDA was upheld on appeal. *United States v. Diapulse Corp. of America*, 748 F.2d 56 (2d Cir. 1984). Rather than market a Diapulse identical to the approved competitor device, however, the Diapulse Corporation continued research on its own lower-powered version. It ultimately obtained FDA's agreement to a narrower claim, "for adjunctive use in the palliative treatment of post-operative edema and pain in superficial tissues." 13 Medical Devices, Diagnostics & Instrumentation Rep. (the "Gray Sheet"), No. 16, at I & W–12 (Apr. 20, 1987).

3. SCIENTOLOGY'S E-METER

In 1950, L. Ron Hubbard, a science-fiction writer, published a bestselling book titled *Dianetics: The Modern Science of Mental Health*. Dianetics was a secular approach to self-improvement. Hubbard soon added religious elements to his theory, however, and in 1953, he founded the Church of Scientology. Over ensuing decades, the Church of Scientology grew into a global organization.

The Hubbard Electrometer, or E-meter, is used in the Church of Scientology's "auditing" process, by which adherents strive to purge from their minds negative memories known as "engrams." The Church of Scientology's assertion that the E-meter plays an essential part in the practice of religion complicated FDA's attempts to enforce the FD&C Act against what the agency saw as a worthless device.

Founding Church of Scientology v. United States

409 F.2d 1146 (D.C. Cir.), *cert. denied*, 396 U.S. 963 (1969).

■ J. SKELLY WRIGHT, CIRCUIT JUDGE.

This is an appeal from a judgment and decree of condemnation and destruction against several electrical instruments and a large quantity of literature owned by claimants-appellants, The Founding Church of Scientology of Washington, D.C. and various individual adherents of that organization. The instruments and literature were seized by the Food and Drug Administration as "devices" with accompanying "false and misleading labeling" subject to condemnation under the Food, Drug and Cosmetic Act. The Government further charged that the instruments were "devices" lacking "adequate directions for use," in further violation of the Act. After a jury trial, a general verdict "for the Government" was returned, and a judgment and decree of condemnation was entered.

Appellants contend that ... the proceedings interfered with the free exercise of their religion, and that the evidence was insufficient to sustain the verdict. Because we find that much of the literature relied on by the Government to establish misbranding was not "labeling" within the meaning of the statute as interpreted in the light of the First Amendment, we reverse. . . .

. . . The Government has charged that the instruments seized, Hubbard Electrometers or "E-meters," are "devices" as defined in the Act, that the literature seized constitutes "labeling" of the device, in that it is "written, printed, or graphic matter . . . accompanying" the device; and that this "labeling" is false or misleading. . . .

In its legal arguments the Government has contended from the outset that whether or not Scientology is a religion, and whether or not auditing or processing is a practice of that religion, are entirely irrelevant to the case. Religious beliefs, it is argued, are entirely protected by the First Amendment, but action in the name of religion is susceptible to legal regulation under the same standards and to the same degree as it would be if entirely secular in purpose.

Appellants have argued from the first that the entire case must fall as an unconstitutional religious persecution. In their view, auditing or processing is a central practice of their religion, akin to confession in the Catholic Church, and hence entirely exempt from regulation or prohibition. They have made no attempt to contradict the expert testimony introduced by the Government. They have conceded that the E-meter is of no use in the diagnosis or treatment of disease as such, and have argued that it was never put forward as having such use. Auditing or processing, in their view, treats the spirit of man, not his body, though through the healing of the spirit the body can be affected. . . .

The principles enunciated in [prior decisions of the Supreme Court] . . . at least raise a constitutional doubt concerning the condemnation of instruments and literature apparently central to the practice of religion. That doubt becomes more serious when we turn to the decision of the Supreme Court in *United States v. Ballard*, 322 U.S. 78 (1944). . . .

. . . Here the E-meter has been condemned, not because it is itself harmful, but because the representations made concerning it are "false or misleading." And the largest part of those representations is contained in the literature of Scientology describing the process of auditing which appellants have claimed, without contest from the Government, is part of the doctrine of their religion and central to its exercise. Thus if their claims to religious status are accepted, a finding that the seized literature misrepresents the benefits from auditing is a finding that their religious doctrines are false. To construe the Food, Drug and Cosmetic Act to permit such a finding would . . . present the gravest constitutional difficulties. . . .

Finally, we come to the vexing question: is Scientology a religion? On the record as a whole, we find that appellants have made out a *prima facie* case that the Founding Church of Scientology is a religion. . . .

(1) We do not hold that the Founding Church is for all legal purposes a religion. Any *prima facie* case made out for religious status is subject to contradiction by a showing that the beliefs asserted to be religious are not held in good faith by those asserting them, and that forms of religious organization were erected for the sole purpose of cloaking a secular enterprise with the legal protections of religion.

(2) We do not hold that, even if Scientology is a religion, all literature published by it is religious doctrine immune from the Act.

(3) We do not hold that public health laws in general, or the Food, Drug and Cosmetic Act in particular, have no application to the activities of religion. For instance, it may well be that adulterated foods, drugs or devices used in religious practices can be condemned under the Act. It may be that a drug or device used in religion is subject to condemnation as "misbranded" if its labeling is found to lack, for instance, adequate directions for use, as was charged in this case. Our holding prevents only a finding of false labeling on the basis of doctrinal religious literature.

(4) Finally, we made no holding concerning the power of Congress to deal generally with the making of false claims by religions deemed injurious to the public health or welfare. . . .

■ McGOWAN, CIRCUIT JUDGE (DISSENTING):

. . . .

This proceeding did not involve an inquisition into the validity of any personal religious beliefs, or the infliction of a punishment upon any person for holding or disseminating such beliefs. It was a proceeding against property under a Congressional statute aimed at protecting the unsophisticated against not only wasting their money but, more importantly, endangering their lives by relying upon misbranded machines. There is, as the majority points out, a well-recognized distinction between the good faith holding of a religious belief, however bizarre, and unlimited freedom to implement that belief by conduct. I do not believe that the Government was required, at least in a statutory *in rem* proceeding of the kind here involved, to show that, over and above the misbranding of the device, the religious pretensions of its sponsors were fraudulent.

NOTES

1. *Subsequent Proceedings.* Upon retrial following remand, the District Court held that the Founding Church of Scientology had met its burden of establishing its status as a genuine religion. It also found the E-meter to be misbranded. The court's decree returned the devices and literature to the church for use only in bona fide religious counseling. *United States v. An Article of Device . . . "Hubbard Electrometer,"* 333 F. Supp. 357 (D.D.C. 1971). Its order, designed to assure observance of this limitation, would have required the following statement to be affixed to every E-meter:

> The E-meter is a device which has been condemned by Order of a Federal Court for misrepresentation and misbranding, in violation of the Federal Food, Drug, and Cosmetic Act. Use of the E-meter is permitted only as part of bona-fide religious activity. The E-meter is not medically or scientifically useful for the diagnosis, treatment, or prevention of any disease. It is not medically or scientifically capable of improving the health or bodily functions of anyone. Any person using, selling or distributing the E-meter is forbidden by law to represent, state or imply that the E-meter is useful in the diagnosis, treatment, or prevention of any disease.

The court order would also have required a similar version of the statement to be signed by every recipient of auditing services and to appear in the Church's E-meter literature. 1969–1974 FDLI Jud. Rec. 90 (D.D.C. 1971).

Upon appeal once more, the Court of Appeals, per curiam, concluded that the lower court's order "would involve the Government and the courts in an excessive entanglement with religion . . . in circumstances in which the legitimate governmental interest in law enforcement can be protected by a narrower remedy." It therefore modified the order to read as follows:

1. E-meters shall be used or sold or distributed only for use in bona fide religious counseling.

2. Each E-meter shall bear the following warning, printed in 11-point leaded type, permanently affixed to the front of the E-meter so that it is clearly visible when the E-meter is used, sold, or distributed:

> The E-meter is not medically or scientifically useful for the diagnosis, treatment, or prevention of any disease. It is not medically or scientifically capable of improving the health or bodily functions of anyone.

3. Any and all items of written, printed, or graphic matter which directly or indirectly refers [sic] to the E-meter or to Dianetics and/or Scientology and/or auditing or processing shall . . . bear the following prominent printed warning . . . :

WARNING

The device known as a Hubbard Electrometer, or E-meter, used in auditing, a process of Scientology and Dianetics, is not medically or scientifically useful for the diagnosis, treatment, or prevention of any disease. It is not medically or scientifically capable of improving the health or bodily functions of anyone.

1969–1974 FDLI Jud. Rec. 131 (D.C. Cir. 1973).

2. *Enforcement Against Quack Devices.* FDA actions against so-called "quack" devices under the 1938 Act often precipitated protracted litigation. *See, e.g., United States v. Urbuteit,* 335 U.S. 355 (1948).

3. *Organizational Responsibility.* The same FDA unit was responsible for regulating drugs and medical devices until the device program was transferred from the Bureau of Drugs to the Office of the Associate Commissioner for Medical Affairs in 1971. David M. Link & Larry R. Pilot, *FDA's Medical Device Program,* FDA Papers, May 1972, at 24 (1972). In 1974, in anticipation of the enactment of the Medical Device Amendments, the device program was transferred to a new Bureau of Medical Devices and Diagnostic Products. 39 Fed. Reg. 5812 (Feb. 15, 1974). In 1982, this Bureau was combined with the Bureau of Radiological Health to form the National Center for Devices and Radiological Health (CDRH), 47 Fed. Reg. 44614 (October 8, 1982).

4. THE DRUG–DEVICE DISTINCTION BEFORE 1976

According to Professor David F. Cavers, *The Food, Drug, and Cosmetic Act of 1938: Its Legislative History and Its Substantive Provisions,* 6 LAW & CONTEMP. PROBS. 2 (1939):

The definition of "drug" in the old [1906] Act was defective in two respects. It did not cover (1) products designed to affect the structure or functioning of the body where disease was not involved or (2) mechanical devices used either for such purposes or in the diagnosis or treatment of disease. Consequently the [FDA] was powerless to combat a host of both types of products which appeared on the market under misleading claims and which in some instances were positively dangerous to the user. Accordingly the term "drug" was redefined in S.1944 so as to include these products. The simple tactic, far from uncommon in statutory definition, of giving a special meaning to an ordinary term, evoked unexpected opposition, and ultimately separate definitions were provided for "drug" and "device" [in the 1938 Act]. . . .

Under the 1938 Act, the definition of "device" in section 201(h) was: "instruments, apparatus [sic], and contrivances, including their components, parts, and accessories, intended (1) for use in the diagnosis, cure, mitigation, treatment, or prevention of disease in man or other animals; or (2) to affect the structure or function of the body of man or other animals." The distinction between a drug and a device was unclear, because the definition of "device" did not yet include the proviso, added by the Medical Device Amendments of 1976, that a device "does not achieve any of its principal intended purposes through chemical action within or on the body of man or other animals and which is not dependent upon being metabolized for the achievement of any of its principal intended purposes."

Before the enactment of the 1976 Amendments, devices, unlike new drugs, were never required to obtain premarket approval from FDA. The agency thus classified a handful of device-like products as drugs rather than devices in order to exercise this higher level of regulatory control over them. In *AMP, Inc. v. Gardner*, 389 F.2d 825 (2d Cir. 1968), *cert. denied*, 393 U.S. 825 (1968), the Second Circuit upheld FDA's contention that the two products described below were drugs:

> Both of the products are intended to be used in a new method of tying off, or ligating, severed blood vessels during surgery. The conventional ligating method is to hand-tie ligatures around severed vessels by means of a surgeon's knot (which is a reef knot). AMP's products both consist of a disposable applicator, a nylon ligature loop, and a nylon locking disk. . . . The ligature is applied by inserting the hemostat or tube into the body and placing the loop around the severed vessel, then tightening the loop and locking it in place with the disk. The excess nylon thread is cut off, and the disk and the rest of the thread remain in the patient's body.

In *United States v. An Article of Drug . . . Bacto–Unidisk*, 394 U.S. 784 (1969), *supra* p. 78, the Supreme Court upheld FDA's categorization of an antibiotic sensitivity disc as a drug rather than as a device. With the Court's endorsement of the agency's authority to categorize products so as to protect the public health, FDA's chief counsel announced that with regard to medical products falling "in the middle ground or the grey area, where they are not clearly one or the other, [the agency has] complete discretion at this time to decide whether it will handle those products as drugs or devices. . . ." Remarks by Peter Barton Hutt at the FDA Medical Device Conference of April 11, 1972, 34 FDC Reports (the "Pink Sheet"), No. 16, at 18–20 (April 17, 1972).

The following are examples of device-like products that FDA classified as drugs before 1976: surgical sutures, contact lenses, injectable silicone, pregnancy test kits, and bone cement. The 1976 Amendments labeled these products as "transitional devices." For a complete list, see 56 Fed. Reg. 57960, 57961–62 (Nov. 14, 1991). Because the 1976 Amendments permit FDA to require premarket approval for many devices, the decision of whether to classify a product as a drug or device, while still significant, is less critical than it used to be.

Following its victory in the *Bacto–Unidisk* decision, FDA considered the possibility of demanding the submission of NDAs for all in vitro diagnostic products. Instead, mindful of both the resources it would need and the impact on the industry and the public health, FDA explicitly declined to determine whether these products would be regulated as drugs or devices. Rather, the agency prescribed detailed labeling requirements to assure that users would have accurate and reliable information. 38 Fed. Reg. 7096 (Mar. 15, 1973). Because of the importance of reliable diagnoses of gonorrhea and cancer, however, FDA announced that any diagnostic test for these diseases would require an approved NDA. 38 Fed. Reg. 10488 (Apr. 27, 1973), 39 Fed.

Reg. 3705 (Jan. 29, 1974). All of these diagnostic products were subsequently included within the new definition of a device under the 1976 Amendments.

C. INTRODUCTION TO THE MODERN DEVICE REGULATORY REGIME

1. BACKGROUND TO THE 1976 MEDICAL DEVICE AMENDMENTS

Medical Device Amendments of 1976
House Report No. 853, 94th Congress, 2d Session (1976).

FDA began focusing more attention on hazards from legitimate medical devices around 1960. . . . New developments in the electronic, plastic, metallurgy, and ceramics industries, coupled with progress in design engineering, led to invention of the heart pacemaker, the kidney dialysis machine, defibrillators, cardiac and renal catheters, surgical implants, artificial vessels and heart valves, intensive care monitoring units, and a wide spectrum of other diagnostic and therapeutic devices. Although many lives have been saved or improved by the new discoveries, the potential for harm to consumers has been heightened by the critical medical conditions in which sophisticated modern devices are used and by the complicated technology involved in their manufacture and use. In the search to expand medical knowledge, new experimental approaches have sometimes been tried without adequate premarket clinical testing, quality control in materials selected, or patient consent.

An example . . . is the Dalkon Shield. In November 1970, the Dalkon Shield was introduced to the medical profession as a safe effective contraceptive device. . . . In less than two years the Shield had been adopted by 1,497 family planning clinics in the United States and was also being used in world population control programs. The manufacturer reported that more than one million Shields had been sold. In May of 1972, the Family Planning Digest, an official HEW publication, reported that, based on an eighteen month study of 937 patients in family planning programs in California, the pregnancy rate with the Shield was 5.1%, the removal rate for medical reasons was 26.4%, the infection rate was 5%, and the continuation rate after eighteen months was under 60%. By mid-1975 the Shield had been linked to sixteen deaths and twenty-five miscarriages. Presently, more than 500 lawsuits seeking compensatory and punitive damages totalling more than $400 million are pending against the manufacturer of the Shield, which is no longer being marketed. . . .

Experience with two other types of devices further demonstrates the need for increased statutory authority. Significant defects in cardiac pacemakers have necessitated 34 voluntary recalls of pacemakers, involving 23,000 units, since 1972. A recent investigation in four states of eleven patients who experienced unusual eye infections following implantation of intraocular lenses revealed serious impairment of vision in all patients and the necessity to remove the eyes of five patients. . . .

———

Congress first seriously considered device legislation in 1962. Following the thalidomide tragedy, Congress focused on enacting the Drug Amendments of 1962 and deferred device legislation. After years of congressional consideration and FDA discussion, the Department of HEW established a Study Group on Medical Devices to consider what form such legislation should take. The Study Group (the "Cooper Committee") issued its report in September 1970.

Study Group on Medical Devices, Medical Devices: A Legislative Plan

Department of Health, Education and Welfare (1970).

The variety of medical devices already in use are produced from an equally wide variety of materials. Moreover, the bases of scientific data range from almost pure empiricism to reasonably well systematized information. As a result, there are many scientific and technical issues involved in the evaluation of medical devices that require judgment by expert professionals all along the developmental continuum from research through development to testing, evaluation, and preparation for sale. Accordingly, unilateral decisions by government agencies without expert advice would be as unwise as unilateral decisions by developers or producers. . . .

The study group agrees that definition and classification are important, and that there are inherent differences between drugs and devices—differences in the state of the art, and the size and scope of manufacture. Therefore, the study group believes that a new regulatory plan is needed, one which is specifically adapted to the needs of devices. . . . By drawing upon the advice of appropriate scientific organizations, the Department can determine an appropriate basis for decisions about which devices are so well recognized as safe and effective as to require neither standards nor pre-clearance. It can also identify devices or characteristics of devices for which *standards* should and can be developed and applied. With continuing assistance of the scientific and medical community, a system for *review of objective data prior to clinical application* can be devised for new and unproven critical devices that are at the leading edge of technological innovation and biomedical explorations to assure the safety and reliability of devices offered to the profession.

NOTES

1. *Anticipatory Implementation.* FDA began to implement the recommendations of the Cooper Committee even before enactment of the 1976 Amendments.

2. *Legislative History.* The House Report's explanation of the 1976 Amendments consumes 87 pages, H.R. Rep. No. 853, 94th Cong., 2d Sess.

(1976). The legislation itself runs 45 pages, 90 Stat. 539 (1976), more than doubling the length of the original FD&C Act.

3. *Additional Sources.* For more on the history leading up to the passage of the 1976 Amendments, see Theodore H. Cooper, *Device Legislation*, 26 FOOD DRUG COSM. L.J. 165 (1971); Peter Barton Hutt, *A History of Government Regulation of Adulteration and Misbranding of Medical Devices*, 44 FOOD DRUG COSM. L.J. 99 (1989).

2. OVERVIEW OF THE MODERN REGIME

The 1976 Amendments created a complex and novel system for regulating the development, introduction, and marketing of medical devices. Later statutes have made numerous adjustments to the 1976 structure without modifying the basic framework that it established. *See* Safe Medical Devices Act of 1990, 104 Stat. 4511; Medical Device Amendments of 1992, 106 Stat. 238; Food and Drug Administration Modernization Act of 1997, 111 Stat. 2296; Medical Device User Fee and Modernization Act of 2002, 116 Stat. 1588; Medical Device Technical Corrections Act, 118 Stat. 572 (2004); Medical Device User Fee Stabilization Act of 2005, 119 Stat. 439; Food and Drug Administration Amendments Act of 2007, 121 Stat. 823; Food and Drug Administration Safety and Innovation Act of 2012, 126 Stat. 993. These statutes are generally referred to in this chapter simply by their year of enactment (e.g., the 2007 Act) rather than by their name or acronym.

The new regime established by the 1976 Amendments can best be understood by focusing on six key features.

First, the 1976 Amendments revised the definition of a "device." The new definition was intended to convert some medical products then being regulated as drugs into devices. The definition was also broadened to include products intended to diagnose physiological conditions that are not ordinarily regarded as diseases, such as pregnancy.

Second, FDA was required to classify all medical devices in accordance with the relative degree of assurance of their safety and effectiveness. Class I includes those devices for which neither special controls nor premarket approval is warranted because the general regulatory controls available under the FD&C Act are sufficient to assure safety and effectiveness. Class II includes those devices for which general controls are not sufficient but for which enough information exists to develop special controls. Class III includes those devices for which general controls are not sufficient to assure safety and effectiveness and for which there is not sufficient information to establish special controls. Class III also includes all devices introduced after the enactment of the 1976 Amendments (postamendments devices) that are not substantially equivalent to a device marketed prior to enactment (preamendments devices), unless they are down-classified under a "de novo" procedure.

Third, the 1976 Amendments, as amended, provide for comprehensive control over the market introduction of all medical devices. After 1976, a new device may lawfully be marketed in one of four ways: (1) all Class III devices must be the subject of an approved premarket approval (PMA) application under Section 515; (2) most Class II and some Class I devices must be the subject of a cleared premarket notification (PMN) to FDA under section 510(k) demonstrating that they are "substantially equivalent" to a preamendments device (or to a postamendments device that is itself substantially equivalent to a preamendments device); (3) most Class I and some Class II devices are exempt from the 510(k) requirement and thus do not have to make any submission at all prior to market introduction; and (4) upon petition to FDA under section 513(f)(2)(A), a Class III device may be reclassified to Class II or I and subjected to the requirements applicable to a device in its new classification.

Fourth, two classes of preamendments medical devices are subject to special requirements. A Class II medical device must comply with any special controls established by FDA for that device under section 514. A Class III device must be the subject of an approved PMA demonstrating its safety and effectiveness and submitted once the agency promulgates a regulation requiring the submission of applications for that type of device.

Fifth, all medical devices, regardless of class and regardless of the manner of market introduction, are subject to the general regulatory controls established under the 1938 Act and amplified by the 1976 and subsequent amendments. These "general controls" include the basic adulteration and misbranding provisions as well as applicable good manufacturing practice (GMP) regulations, banned device regulations, and notification and repair, replacement, or refund requirements.

Sixth, Congress has enacted special rules for specific types of devices. Examples include requirements for custom devices and provisions for extending the patent term for certain Class III devices.

D. THE DEFINITION OF "DEVICE" SINCE 1976

1. THE LINE BETWEEN A "DRUG" AND A "DEVICE"

As discussed in the chapter on product definitions, *supra* p. 89, the definition of a "device" at FD&C Act section 201(h) closely mirrors the definition of "drug" at section 201(g)(1). This has been the case ever since the device definition was added to the Act in 1938. Indeed, subsequent amendments to the definition have been designed largely to address the distinction between these two categories of products.

The definition of "device" at section 201(h) of the 1938 FD&C Act embraced "instruments, apparatus, and contrivances . . . intended (1) for use in the diagnosis, cure, mitigation, treatment, or prevention of disease in man or other animals; or (2) to affect the structure or any function of the body of man or other animals." In 1976, Congress amended the device definition to provide that a device could not achieve "any of its principal purposes" through chemical action or metabolization. It also expanded the list of device types to any "instrument, apparatus, implement, machine, contrivance, implant, in vitro reagent, or similar or related article." The 1990 Act further amended the definition to state that an article is a device only if it does not achieve "its primary intended purposes" (rather than "any of its principal purposes") through chemical action within or on the body or by being metabolized. Moreover, the 1990 Act removed an explicit exclusion of devices from the definition of "drug."

The current definition of "device" does not always make clear whether an article will be regulated as a drug or as a device. However, FDA must regulate similar products consistently. *Bracco Diagnostics, Inc. v. Shalala*, 963 F. Supp. 20(D.D.C. 1997). In *Bracco*, FDA had treated some injectable contrast imaging agents as drugs and others as devices. Manufacturers challenged the agency's actions, complaining that it was applying different standards to assess the safety and effectiveness of these similar products. The District Court agreed, stating:

> The MBI products and plaintiffs' products all likely meet both the definition of a drug and the definition of a device under the Federal Food, Drug and Cosmetic Act, and the FDA therefore has discretion in determining how to treat them. . . . What the FDA is not free to do, however, is to treat them dissimilarly and to permit two sets of similar products to run down two separate tracks, one more treacherous than the other, for no apparent reason. Plaintiffs merely maintain that the same tests and studies should be required of each product before it is approved and that the result is impossible so long as the FDA treats one as a device subject to the regimen established by the CDRH and the other three as drugs subject to the more rigorous regimen established by the CDER. The Court agrees.

Id. at 28.

In June 2011, FDA issued two draft guidances on the distinction between a device and a drug. DRAFT GUIDANCE FOR INDUSTRY AND FDA STAFF: INTERPRETATION OF THE TERM "CHEMICAL ACTION" IN THE DEFINITION OF DEVICE UNDER SECTION 201(h) OF THE FEDERAL FOOD, DRUG, AND COSMETIC ACT (June 2011); DRAFT GUIDANCE FOR INDUSTRY AND FDA STAFF: CLASSIFICATION OF PRODUCTS AS DRUGS AND DEVICES AND ADDITIONAL PRODUCT CLASSIFICATION ISSUES (June 2011).

2. DRUG–DEVICE COMBINATIONS

Medical products that combine a device with a drug (or combine a device with a biologic) present special challenges. One important type of combination product is a device (such as a stent or catheter) coated with a drug (such as an antibiotic). Another prominent type is a prefilled drug delivery device, such as a syringe, metered dose inhaler, transdermal patch, or implanted pump.

Section 503(g), added by the 1990 Act, directs FDA to assign "primary jurisdiction" to regulate combination products to the agency's drug, device, or biologics center based on the product's "primary mode of action." The 2002 Act modified section 503(g) to require the establishment of an Office of Combination Products within the Office of the Commissioner. FDA created the office that year. The purpose of the Office of Combination Products is to ensure the prompt assignment of combination products to agency components, the timely and effective premarket review of such products, and consistent and appropriate postmarket regulation of combination products. The center to which a specific combination product is assigned (CDER, CBER, or CDRH) retains primary regulatory responsibility for the product.

In 2005, FDA amended its combination product regulations to define "mode of action" and "primary mode of action." 21 C.F.R. 3.2(k), (m). The regulation also sets forth the principles the agency will use to assign combination products to a center when the agency cannot determine with reasonable certainty which mode of action provides the most important therapeutic effect. 70 Fed. Reg. 49848 (August 25, 2005).

As the following case shows, questions concerning the appropriate classification and assignment of possible drug-device (or biologic-device) combinations may require FDA and the courts to wrestle simultaneously with both section 503(g) and the section 201 product definitions.

Prevor v. Food and Drug Administration

895 F. Supp. 2d 90 (D.D.C. 2012).

■ COLLYER, DISTRICT JUDGE.

PREVOR . . . developed a product called Diphoterine™ Skin Wash ("DSW") to mitigate chemical burn injuries in the industrial workplace. PREVOR sues the Food and Drug Administration for declaratory and injunctive relief to change FDA's designation of DSW as a drug-device combination product with a "drug" primary mode of action. . . .

The Court concludes that FDA acted arbitrarily and capriciously in designating DSW as a drug-device combination product with a drug primary mode of action. Accordingly, the Court will grant PREVOR's motion for summary judgment and deny the cross-motion of the FDA.

PREVOR developed DSW to prevent and minimize chemical burn injuries that occur in the industrial workplace due to accidental exposure to chemicals. . . . When a water shower is not available, DSW provides an alternative "first-response" to chemical exposure. "DSW consists of a liquid substance contained in a canister propelled by pressurized gas." The liquid substance is colorless and odorless and is comprised of roughly 96% water and 4% diphoterine. . . . "DSW is intended to: (1) remove splashes of acidic or basic substances off the skin by physically and mechanically washing the chemicals away from the skin, and (2) neutralize and dilute acids and bases." PREVOR states that "[t]he first use is a physical/mechanical mode of action (comprises approximately 90% of DSW's overall effect), while the second one is a chemical mode of action (comprises approximately 10% of DSW's overall effect)." "Dissolution of the acids and bases has a minor, incidental effect, comprising less than 1/2% of DSW's overall effect."

. . . The critical distinguishing element [between the definitions of "drug" and "device" at FD&C Act 201(g) and 201(h)] applicable in this case is that a product that "achieve[s] its primary intended purposes through chemical action within or on the body" is excluded from the definition of a device.

The FFDCA recognizes that a product may be both a drug and a device, which the law labels a "combination product." 21 U.S.C.

§ 353(g). A combination product is defined by regulation as: "A product comprised of two or more regulated components, i.e., drug/device, biologic/device, drug/biologic, or drug/device/biologic, that are physically, chemically, or otherwise combined or mixed and produced as a single entity." 21 C.F.R. § 3.2(e)(1). FDA considers the DSW canister/liquid solution, as a whole, to be a combination product. . . .

. . . To determine which agency component will regulate a given combination product, FDA assesses a product's primary mode of action ("PMOA"). See 21 U.S.C. § 353(g)(1). Each constituent part of a combination product contributes a "mode of action"—"the means by which a product achieves an intended therapeutic effect or action." 21 C.F.R. § 3.2(k). "A constituent part has a device mode of action if it meets the [FFDCA] definition of device . . . and it does not achieve its primary intended purposes through chemical action within or on the body of man or other animals. . . ." 21 C.F.R. § 3.2(k)(2). "A constituent part has a drug mode of action if it meets the [FFDCA] definition of drug . . . and it does not have a . . . device mode of action." 21 C.F.R. § 3.2(k)(3). A primary mode of action is defined as:

> [T]he single mode of action of a combination product that provides the most important therapeutic action of the combination product. The most important therapeutic action is the mode of action expected to make the greatest contribution to the overall intended therapeutic effects of the combination product.

21 C.F.R. § 3.2(m).

For those combination products whose primary mode of action is that of a drug, the Center for Drug Evaluation and Research ("CDER") has jurisdiction. See 21 C.F.R. § 3.4(a)(1). For those combination products whose primary mode of action is that of a device, the Center for Devices and Radiological Health ("CDRH") has jurisdiction. See 21 C.F.R. § 3.4(a)(2). Assignment to a specific agency component will determine the regulatory requirements for that product and the cost of approval. . . .

On August 13, 2009, PREVOR submitted a Request for Designation ("RFD") to the Office of Combination Products ("OCP") at FDA, requesting that it "confirm that DSW is a device to be regulated by the Center for Devices and Radiological Health." Alternatively, PREVOR asked that if the Office of Combination Products determined DSW to be a combination product, "OCP confirm that DSW should be regulated as a device by CDRH.". . . .

On October 16, 2009, the Office of Combination Products sent a letter to PREVOR designating DSW as a combination product assigned to the Center for Drug Evaluation and Research for regulation. The Office of Combination Products concluded:

> The liquid appears to have two primary intended purposes: to wash the chemical off the skin and neutralize the chemical that is on the skin. Since this liquid achieves its primary intended purposes, at least in part, through chemical action, it does not meet the definition of device. The liquid does, however, meet the definition of drug at section 201(g) of the Act (21 U.S.C. 321(g)). Accordingly, we have concluded that the liquid is a drug.

The Office of Combination Products also concluded that the pressurized canister that delivers the DSW solution constitutes a device. Thus, "because the product is comprised of both drug and device constituent parts," the Office of Combination Products determined that DSW is a combination product. The Office of Combination Products also determined that the drug constituent part of DSW "provides the greater contribution to the overall therapeutic effect of the combination product and, thereby, the product's PMOA," so it assigned DSW to the Center for Drug Evaluation and Re-search. . . .

PREVOR timely sought review of this determination from FDA's Office of Special Medical Programs ("OSMP"). . . .

On April 25, 2011, the Office of Special Medical Programs "affirm[ed] OCP's designation of DSW as a combination product to be assigned to CDER" for regulation. . . .

FDA did not address the necessary action of the compressed gas in the canister to expelling the solution under pressure.

. . . .

PREVOR first claims that FDA misapplied the statutory definition of device. Under the statute, a product is not a device if it "achieve[s] its primary intended purposes through chemical action within or on the body of man." 21 U.S.C. § 321(h). . . . PREVOR disagrees with FDA's conclusion that the neutralization of chemicals is one of the DSW solution's primary intended purposes.

. . . FDA states that it determines whether an intended purpose for a product is primary . . . "based on scientific information . . . on a case-by-case basis, as it is dependent on the specific characteristics of the article being examined." Here, however, FDA failed to provide any details regarding its "qualitative evaluation" or the "scientific information" on which it based the particular decision that one of the primary purposes of the DSW solution is achieved through chemical action.

. . . While FDA rejected the studies that supported PREVOR's position that neutralization of chemicals is not a primary intended purpose of the DSW solution, FDA did not rely on any studies or other scientific analysis in its classification letters to support its contrary conclusion.

This lack of scientific analysis may be explained by FDA's substitution of a new expansive interpretation of an exclusion from the statutory term "device." The Office of Combination Products decided, "Since this liquid achieves its primary intended purposes, at least in part, through chemical action, it does not meet the definition of device" (emphasis added). The Office of Special Medical Programs agreed that "if an article depends, even in part, on chemical action . . . to achieve any of its primary intended purposes, it does not meet the definition of a device" (emphasis added). . . .

. . . Inasmuch as the statute seeks to identify primary intended purposes that are achieved through chemical action, it would be magnificently expanded if a primary purpose could automatically be achieved "at least in part" or "even in part" by chemical action. Primary means principal, first among others, foundational. . . . The addition of such language when applying the statute substantively modifies the standard to be applied by expanding the reach of the exclusionary language. The Court agrees with PREVOR's argument that "FDA now prevents a device from having even a *de minimus* chemical effect because the 'at least in part' or 'even in part' language is so encompassing." . . .

While FDA asserts that its interpretation of "primary intended purposes" is "not new," the case it cites in support states only that a product can have more than one primary intended purpose, which is not in dispute, not that the standard includes the language "even in part" or "at least in part." Indeed, FDA fails to cite a single prior instance in which it has applied an "even in part" standard.

The fact that FDA has changed its interpretation becomes most apparent when examining products that are analogous to DSW but regulated as devices by FDA. "An agency must treat similar cases in a similar manner unless it can provide a legitimate reason for failing to do so." . . . "The disparate treatment of functionally indistinguishable products is the essence of the meaning of arbitrary and capricious." *Bracco Diagnostics, Inc. v. Shalala*, 963 F. Supp. 20, 28 (D.D.C. 1997).

. . . PREVOR highlighted Reactive Skin Decontamination Lotion ("RSDL") as the product most like DSW that FDA regulates as a device. "RSDL consists of a drug constituent (lotion) and a device constituent (sponge applicator) and is intended to remove and/or neutralize chemicals . . . from the skin." FDA concluded that the sponge (device) provides the primary mode of action, not the lotion, so it regulates RSDL as a combination product with a device primary mode of action. To distinguish RSDL from DSW [in this matter], the Office of Special Medical Programs stated:

> The sponge applicator is not only used to apply the drug (lotion) but it is also physically scrubbed over the contaminated skin and through this action, loosens and removes toxic chemicals from the skin. . . . [W]hile the sponge applicator in RSDL directly re-moves chemicals from the body, with DSW, it is not the canister that directly removes chemicals from the body but the solution. It is the solution in DSW that washes off the chemicals from the body as well as neutralizes and dilutes the chemicals.

The Court does not question FDA's expertise, but this explanation makes a most ephemeral distinction. Both the sponge applicator in RSDL and the canister in DSW are used to apply the relevant material and to remove chemicals from the skin. FDA recognizes that "the canister sprays the solution onto the body," but then ignores the necessary force of propulsion in washing off harmful chemicals. Given the almost identical roles played by the device (sponge) in RSDL and the device (canister) in DSW, FDA's attempt at distinguishing them appears to treat similar products differently without a reasoned explanation. . . .

FDA's designation decision here relied on a doubly grandiose interpretation of the phrase "primary intended purposes" from 21 U.S.C. § 321(h). First, FDA treated any purpose of DSW as a primary intended purpose, contrary to the more limited language of the statute and the agency's distinction between primary and secondary in prior precedent. Second, FDA treated achievement even in part of any purpose through chemical action as achievement of a primary intended purpose through chemical action. There may be solid scientific reasons for FDA's new approach but these remain unexplained, at least without defining "primary" in a manner consistent with the law. . . .

Whether FDA would come to the same conclusions without resort to its extra-statutory interpretations remains to be seen. The case will be remanded for the agency to make that determination in compliance with this Opinion.

3. DIAGNOSTIC DEVICES

Prior to 1976, FDA had declared some diagnostic products to be drugs, as in *Bacto–Unidisk*, *supra* p. 78. *See* 38 Fed. Reg. 10488 (Apr. 27, 1973) (test for cancer regulated as drug); 39 Fed. Reg. 3705 (Jan. 29, 1974) (test for gonorrhea regulated as drug). In 1975, however, the agency confronted the limits of this approach when a federal district court ruled that a pregnancy test was not a drug. *U.S. v. An Article of Drug . . . Ova II*, 414 F. Supp. 660 (D.N.J. 1975), *aff'd* 535 F.2d 1248 (3d Cir. 1976). The case was a seizure action against a pregnancy test kit sold for home use. The government claimed that this *in vitro* diagnostic product, consisting of vials of sodium hydroxide and hydrochloric acid, was a new drug under the Act. The trial court disagreed, concluding that it fell outside all three dimensions of the Act's definition of "drug," even though both its ingredients appear in the U.S. Pharmacopeia and the National Formulary. The Court stated that, "The OVA II kit is not . . . related to the diagnosis of disease," since "the existence or non-existence of pregnancy . . . is not of itself a disease." The Court also held that, because the product was to be used *in vitro*, it was not intended "to affect the structure or any function of the body."

The *OVA II* decision threatened to undermine FDA's efforts to assert control over the reliability, and thus the safety, of a host of *in vitro* diagnostics. Accordingly, the 1976 Amendments broadened the definition of "device" in section 201(h)(2) to include articles "intended for use in the diagnosis of disease *or other conditions*." In addition, the Amendments added "in vitro reagent" to the list of articles categorized as devices. Finally, the Amendments imposed a premarket approval regime on many types of medical devices.

Today FDA regulates most diagnostic products (and all articles that diagnose "conditions" rather than "diseases") as medical devices. *E.g.*, 44 Fed. Reg. 10133 (Feb. 16, 1979) (pregnancy test kits). But in 55 Fed. Reg. 5892 (Feb. 20, 1990), FDA announced that *in vitro* diagnostic test kits that are used to detect total antibody to hepatitis B core antigen in blood would be regulated as biologics rather than as medical devices, because the major use had changed from clinical diagnostic use to screening blood intended for transfusion.

E. CLASSIFICATION OF DEVICES INTO CLASS I, CLASS II, AND CLASS III

1. PROCEDURE

Following enactment of the 1976 Amendments, FDA promulgated new classification procedures to meet the requirements of new section 513 of the FD&C Act. 43 Fed. Reg. 32988 (July 28, 1978), codified at 21 C.F.R. Part 860.

Medical Devices: Classification Procedures

42 Fed. Reg. 46028 (September 13, 1977).

Anticipating eventual enactment of medical device legislation, FDA initiated in 1973 a preliminary classification of medical devices. A list of approximately 8,000 devices had been compiled in 1971, and 13 classification panels, plus a Diagnostic Products Advisory Committee, had been established by 1975. The panels made recommendations for classifying medical devices into different classes of regulatory control using criteria contained in legislative proposals before Congress during this period. . . .

Under section 513(b) of the act, the Commissioner may either establish classification panels or use panels established before the date of enactment of the amendments. The Commissioner finds that the objectives of the 13 classification panels established before enactment satisfy the requirements of the amendments. He has, however, rechartered each panel and directed it to reconsider its previous recommendations in light of the statutory classification criteria and other requirements of the legislation. . . .

Section 513 of the act establishes three classes of regulatory control for medical devices and requires FDA to classify all devices intended for human use into one of those classes. They are: Class I, General Controls; Class II, Performance Standards; and Class III, Premarket Approval.

Section 513(a)(1)(A) of the act defines Class I devices as those devices (1) for which there is sufficient information to determine that the provisions of the act with respect to adulteration; misbranding; registration; banning; defect notification; repair, replacement, or refund; records and reports; and good manufacturing practices (referred to as "general controls" hereafter) will provide reasonable assurance of the safety and effectiveness of the device or (2) for which there is insufficient information to determine that general controls are sufficient to provide reasonable assurance of the safety and effectiveness of the device or to establish a performance standard to provide such assurance but which are not purported or represented to be for a use in supporting or sustaining human life or for a use which is of substantial importance in preventing impairment of human health and do not present a potential unreasonable risk of illness or injury. Class I devices are to be regulated under the general controls provisions of the act.

Section 513(a)(1)(B) of the act defines Class II devices as those devices for which general controls alone are insufficient to provide reasonable assurance of safety and effectiveness and for which there is sufficient information to establish a performance standard to provide such assurance. Class II devices will be subject to performance standards to be established under section 514 of the act. . . .

Section 513(a)(1)(C) of the act defines Class III devices as those devices for which there is insufficient information to determine that general controls will assure their safety and effectiveness and for which there is insufficient information to establish a performance standard to provide such assurance, and which are purported or represented to be for a use in supporting or sustaining human life or for a use which is of substantial importance in preventing impairment of human health, or which present a potential unreasonable risk of illness or injury. Class III devices are subject, under section 515 of the act, to premarket approval. . . .

The classification procedures contained in section 513(b)–(d) of the act . . . apply to the initial classification of "old" devices, *i.e.*, those which either were in commercial distribution before the date of enactment of the amendments or are substantially equivalent to devices in commercial distribution before that date. Section 513(f) of the act contains special provisions for the classification of "new" devices, *i.e.*, those which were not in commercial distribution before the date of enactment and are not substantially equivalent to any which were in distribution. Such a device is automatically classified in Class III unless it is substantially equivalent to another new device that has been reclassified to Class I or II. . . .

Section 513(d) of the act requires the Commissioner to publish in the Federal Register panel recommendations and proposed classification regulations. After providing an opportunity for comment, the Commissioner must by final regulation classify the device. . . .

2. THE CLASSIFICATION REGULATIONS

FDA began the process of classifying devices even before enactment of the 1976 Amendments, but it then had to start over again, following the procedures prescribed by the new statute. Classification of the diverse universe of devices took longer than either FDA or Congress had anticipated. By 1984, FDA had completed classification of products in 11 out of 19 categories (comprising about 1,700 types) of devices and had issued proposed classifications for the other eight. Of these 1,700 types, roughly 30 percent were placed in Class I, 60 percent in Class II, and 10 percent in Class III. Office of Technology Assessment, Federal Policies and the Medical Devices Industry, OTA–H–230, at 105–106 (Oct. 1984) (hereinafter OTA Devices Report). FDA completed the classification process with a final rule classifying general and plastic surgery devices. 53 Fed. Reg. 23856 (June 24, 1988). There have been no formal legal challenges to the results of this classification process, perhaps because in the vast majority of cases, a device's classification does not control when and on what terms it can be marketed.

FDA has issued rules identifying and classifying almost 1,800 types of medical devices. Excerpted below are just three of these classification regulations, all from the category of dental devices. They offer examples of a Class I, Class II, and Class III device and hint at the range of technological sophistication illustrated by the universe of devices regulated by FDA.

21 C.F.R. Part 872—Dental Devices

. . . .

Sec. 872.3570 OTC denture repair kit.

(a) Identification. An OTC denture repair kit is a device consisting of a material, such as a resin monomer system of powder and liquid glues, that is intended to be applied permanently to a denture to mend cracks or breaks. The device may be available for purchase over-the counter.

(b) Classification. Class II. The special controls for this device are FDA's:

(1) "Use of International Standard ISO 10993 'Biological Evaluation of Medical Devices—Part I: Evaluation and Testing," and

(2) "OTC Denture Reliners, Repair Kits, and Partially Fabricated Denture Kits."

. . . .

Sec. 872.3940 Total temporomandibular joint prosthesis.

(a) Identification. A total temporomandibular joint prosthesis is a device that is intended to be implanted in the human jaw to replace the mandibular condyle and augment the glenoid fossa to functionally reconstruct the temporomandibular joint.

(b) Classification. Class III.

(c) Date PMA or notice of completion of a PDP is required. A PMA or a notice of completion of a PDP is required to be filed with the Food and Drug Administration on or before March 30, 1999, for any total temporomandibular joint prosthesis that was in commercial distribution before May 28, 1976, or that has, on or before March 30, 1999, been found to be substantially equivalent to a total temporomandibular joint prosthesis that was in commercial distribution before May 28, 1976. Any other total temporomandibular joint prosthesis shall have an approved PMA or a declared completed PDP in effect before being placed in commercial distribution.

. . .

Sec. 872.6390 Dental floss.

(a) Identification. Dental floss is a string-like device made of cotton or other fibers intended to remove plaque and food particles from between the teeth to reduce tooth decay. The fibers of the device may be coated with wax for easier use.

(b) Classification. Class I (general controls). The device is exempt from the premarket notification procedures in subpart E of part 807 of this chapter subject to Sec. 872.9.

NOTE

PDPs. The "total temporomandibular joint prosthesis" rule refers to "notice of completion of a PDP" as a path to market entry. PDP stands for "Product Development Protocol," a rarely-used form of PMA approval mentioned in every Class III device regulation. The concept will be discussed below, *infra* p. 1242.

F. CHANGEOVER ISSUES: THE 1976 MEDICAL DEVICE AMENDMENTS AND THE REGULATION OF PREAMENDMENTS DEVICES

1. EQUITABLE TREATMENT OF OLD AND NEW DEVICES

When FDA officials were engaged in drafting the legislation that became the 1976 Amendments, they faced an issue that is common in the design of new health and safety legislation—whether to discriminate between old and new products. (For a discussion of the law's propensity to apply more stringent standards to new technologies, see Peter Huber, *The Old–New Division in Risk Regulation*, 69 VA. L. REV. 1025 (1983)). Congress was not prepared to require that every preamendments Class III device be pulled from the market immediately upon classification, to be reintroduced only when the manufacturer established safety and effectiveness through a PMA. Such an approach would keep many well-established and important devices off the market for years while creating an enormous backlog of unapproved PMAs.

But if Congress postponed the imposition of the new PMA requirement for preamendments Class III devices only, and not for similar products introduced after 1976, the result would be an untenable discrimination between old and new devices. A preamendments Class III device would remain *on* the market while the manufacturer gathered and FDA evaluated evidence of safety and effectiveness. But a counterpart postamendments device would remain *off* the market while the same evidence was being obtained and evaluated. Furthermore, once the postamendments device was approved by FDA, it might enter the market to compete with preamendments counterparts whose safety and effectiveness FDA had not yet approved.

To avoid this result, FDA advocated, and Congress endorsed, the following policy. Sections 513(f)(1)(A) and 515(b)(1) and (2) provide that a preamendments Class III device, and any postamendments Class III device that is substantially equivalent to a preamendments Class III device, need not secure FDA approval of safety and effectiveness through a PMA until FDA promulgates a regulation triggering the approval requirement for that type of device. Thus, a postamendments Class III device that is substantially equivalent to a preamendments Class III device of a type not yet subject to a "PMA call" can go on the market immediately, with only the submission of a section 510(k) notification. Once on the market, the post-1976 device will be subject only to the same general controls as its preamendments counterpart (and other medical devices). When FDA orders the submission of PMA applications for devices of that type, the requirement applies equally to both preamendments and postamendments products. An understanding of this process clarifies subsection (c) of the "total temporomandibular joint prosthesis" rule reprinted above. 21 C.F.R. 872.3940(c), *supra* p. 1214.

2. THE STILL-UNFINISHED IMPLEMENTATION OF THE 1976 AMENDMENTS WITH RESPECT TO PREAMENDMENTS CLASS III DEVICES

Congress did not anticipate the relatively large number of preamendments device types that FDA would place in Class III, nor the wave of postamendments Class III devices of these types that would successfully take advantage of the section 510(k) substantial equivalence route to market entry. Moreover, Congress certainly did not expect FDA to take as long as it did to commence, let alone complete, PMA proceedings for preamendments Class III devices and their postamendment equivalents. FDA did not even issue a final regulation setting forth PMA procedures until 1986. 45 Fed. Reg. 81769 (July 22, 1986). Many Class III devices, both old and new, thus remained on the market for years without establishing safety and effectiveness through a PMA.

As an alternative to issuing PMA calls, FDA could have completed the transition process for some preamendments class III device types by reclassifying them to Class I or II, and thus releasing them from the PMA requirement altogether. Section 513(e) authorizes FDA, upon the petition of any interested person or upon its own initiative, to change the classification of a preamendments device. The agency rarely took advantage of this option, however; it has only reclassified about ten types of preamendments devices under this provision.

In 1990, Congress, unhappy with FDA's progress in implementing the 1976 Amendments, required the agency to act with respect to the preamendments class III device types. More specifically, new section 515(i) required FDA to order the submission of safety and effectiveness data for every one of these device types not yet subject to a PMA call and, by December 1995, either to downclassify it to Class I or Class II or to retain it in Class III and schedule it for imposition of the PMA requirement.

The agency completely failed to meet these deadlines. In 1994, it calculated there were about 149 Class III device types not yet subject to the PMA requirement. 59 Fed. Reg. 23731 (May 6, 1994). It dealt fairly promptly with the 43 of these products that were no longer used or were in very limited use, publishing a final rule requiring the filing of a PMA for most of them in 1996. 61 Fed. Reg. 50704 (Sept. 27, 1996). FDA was not nearly as efficient with respect to the 73 remaining class III device types, however. The agency did not start publishing significant numbers of final rules downclassifying them into Class I or II or retaining them in Class III and imposing the PMA requirement until 1999.

A decade later, the process was still not finished. In April 2009, FDA stated that there remained 27 types of preamendments class III devices that the agency had neither required the submission of PMAs for nor reclassified into class I or II. 74 Fed. Reg. 16214, 16215 (Apr. 9, 2009). These products—new versions of which continued to be introduced onto the market through the use of the 510(k) process—included widely used devices such as pacemakers and hip replacements. The agency required the manufacturers of 25 of these 27 devices to submit safety and effectiveness information to FDA by August 2009. *Id.* In the 2012 Act, Congress facilitated the completion of the process by amending section 515 to authorize FDA to require a PMA for a preamendments device by a simple "order" rather than by notice-and-comment rulemaking. As of the summer of 2013, the agency has completed the changeover process with respect to seven of these 25 preamendments class III devices; it has issued PMA calls for six of them and reclassified one. Moreover, the agency has proposed either PMA calls or reclassification for approximately ten others. As for the two (of 27) devices that FDA decided to treat separately, both have been reclassified into class II. 75 FR 59670 (Sept. 28, 2010); 76 Fed. Reg. 22805 (Apr. 25, 2011). The end of the changeover process finally seems to be in sight.

3. "TRANSITIONAL" DEVICES PREVIOUSLY REGULATED AS DRUGS

As discussed above, *supra* p. 1201, FDA had regulated approximately twenty types of devices as new drugs prior to enactment of the 1976 Amendments. In the legislation, Congress, at the agency's urging, automatically assigned these devices, generally referred to as "transitional" devices, to Class III under section 520(l)(1). The agency, which identified the transitional devices in 42 Fed. Reg. 63472 (Dec. 16, 1977), took the position that these products and their postamendments counterparts would remain in Class III unless and until reclassified. Moreover, in a major exception to the nondiscrimination policy between old and new Class III devices discussed above, FDA determined that no postamendments version of any Class III transitional device could come on the market without FDA approval of a PMA application, even if it were substantially equivalent to a preamendments product not yet required to submit a PMA.

The resulting treatment of transitional devices was unsatisfactory in several respects. First, many of these types products did not seem to raise safety and effectiveness concerns sufficient to warrant their placement into Class III. Second, the discriminatory treatment of postamendments transitional devices created a disincentive for new manufacturers and technological improvements. Finally, the requirement that manufacturers of new transitional devices gain PMA approval before entering the market overburdened FDA. Some 60 percent of PMAs filed with the agency were for transitional devices, and about 50 percent of these were for contact lens products. These proportions were strikingly high, not only because transitional devices represented only a small portion of the total device market (and transitional contact lens products an even smaller portion), but also because many transitional devices presented fewer risks than most of preamendments nontransitional Class III products for which FDA had not yet demanded PMAs.

Section 520(l)(2) offered a potential escape from this quandary, namely the reclassification of low-risk transitional devices from Class III to Class II or Class I. But by 1991, FDA had downclassified only seven types of transitional devices, and it had considered and explicitly declined to downclassify about eight others. In the 1990 Act, Congress attempted to resolve the transitional device problem by requiring FDA to reconsider the classification of each Class III transitional device and, by December 1, 1993, to issue a regulation either downclassifying it or keeping it in Class III. FD&C Act 520(l)(5). Moreover, section 4(b)(3) of the 1990 Act specified that two types of transitional device—soft and rigid daily wear contact lenses—had to be downclassified to Class II unless FDA affirmatively ruled otherwise by November 28, 1993.

Although FDA nearly satisfied the deadline for contact lenses, it did not come close to meeting the deadline for the other transitional devices. As of June 2013, the agency had issued post-1990 rules classifying or reclassifying only about ten types of transitional devices. In each instance, FDA either placed a transitional device it had never considered into Class II or downclassified a transitional device it had earlier placed into Class III. However, there remain numerous transitional devices that FDA expressly classified into Class III prior to 1990 that the agency has not reconsidered, and even some transitional devices that remain automatically in Class III because FDA has never classified them at all.

G. REGULATION OF MARKET ENTRY

1. INTRODUCTION

Under the regulatory structure established by the 1976 Amendments, there were only four ways a new medical device could lawfully be introduced: (1) as a Class III device for which FDA had approved a premarket approval (PMA) application under section 515; (2) as a device for which FDA had cleared a section 510(k) premarket notification (PMN) demonstrating, under section 513(f)(1), that the device was substantially equivalent to a preamendments Class I or Class II device; (3) as a device for which FDA had, pursuant to section 515(b)(1), cleared a section 510(k) notification demonstrating that the device was substantially equivalent to a preamendments Class III device on which the agency had not yet imposed the PMA requirement; or (4) as a device that FDA had reclassified from Class III (the class by default of all new devices without a substantially equivalent predicate) into Class I or Class II pursuant to a section 513(f) reclassification petition.

After the implementation of the new regime, the section 510(k) notification demonstrating substantial equivalence became the dominant route of market entry. Between 1976 and 2012, more than 98 percent of new medical devices entered the market by demonstrating substantial equivalence to a preamendments device.

In the 1997 Act, Congress established two additional paths for introducing a device onto the market. First, new section 513(f)(2) established, as a supplement to the reclassification petition process, a procedure for requesting that FDA *initially* (de novo) classify a device with no substantially equivalent predicate into Class I or Class II instead of Class III (the default classification in this situation). Congress eased this path in the 2012 Act by authorizing FDA to reclassify devices by a simple "order" rather than by notice-and-comment rulemaking, and by allowing sponsors to submit a reclassification petition before filing a section 510(k) notification. Second, and more important, Congress in 1997 automatically exempted most Class I devices from the section 510(k) premarket notification requirement and authorized FDA also to exempt Class II devices where appropriate. Consequently, today FDA does not oversee the market entry of most low-risk devices at all.

For those devices for which premarket filings are still required, section 510(k) remains the dominant mode of market entry. In 2011, FDA cleared 3,072 premarket notifications while approving only 37 PMAs. In other words, approximately 98.8 percent of new devices cleared for marketing by FDA that year were cleared under section 510(k) rather than by a PMA. The number of devices initially marketed pursuant to reclassification petitions or initial classification requests is negligible. In 2005, for example, FDA granted only eight section 513(f)(2) de novo requests, and it granted no section 513(f)(3) reclassification petitions. In 2009, only three de novo petitions were approved. This may change, however, under the new provisions in the 2012 Act.

Each of these premarket pathways is examined below. For now, it is important to grasp the basic features of the different pathways and to recognize that section 510(k) offers a route to market that is usually faster and smoother than any other.

Jonathan S. Kahan, *Premarket Approval Versus Premarket Notification: Different Routes to the Same Market*

39 FOOD DRUG COSMETIC LAW JOURNAL 510 (1984).

. . . .

. . . Unless the device is a nonsignificant risk device, a company must first obtain FDA approval to conduct a clinical investigation of the device. . . .

Once the investigational data are gathered, they must be analyzed by the sponsor, and then reported to FDA in some statistically meaningful way. . . .

Once FDA decides that the PMA is complete, the agency will refer the approval question to one of several expert outside panels. . . .

After the panel issues its report on the device, FDA also conducts its own in-depth review. In addition to a careful examination of the safety and effectiveness data, this review will include close scrutiny of the labeling claims. . . . If FDA ultimately decides to grant the application, that decision is published in the *Federal Register*, and a summary of the evidence must be prepared.

. . . Some companies have elected to seek reclassification of a device. Essentially, this mechanism allows a device that would otherwise be placed into Class III to be regulated as a Class II or Class I device. This obviates the need for a PMA. . . . However, the common perception is that the data required by FDA for approval of a petition to reclassify may in many cases be tantamount to the data required for a PMA. This may be one reason that this procedure has been invoked infrequently. . . .

The simplest, least costly, and fastest way to place a new device into commercial distribution is to file a "510(k) notification." For these reasons, the 510(k) submission has become the option of choice for bringing a new device to market. . . .

A.   Less Information is Required in a 510(k) Submission

In implementing the Medical Device Amendments, FDA has adopted regulations that delineate, to some extent, the data requirements for a 510(k) notification. Compared to the PMA, comparatively little is directly required by FDA regulation.

One of the few substantive requirements in the regulation is that the applicant provide information supporting the claim of substantial equivalence to a pre-amendment device. . . .

B.   510(k)s Have a Better Chance of Gaining FDA Acceptance

. . . Over the years, FDA has consistently had a very high rate of finding post-amendment devices to be substantially equivalent to pre-amendment devices. Of the approximately 20,650 510(k)s FDA had reviewed by the end of 1983, only 2 percent were found not to be substantially equivalent.

Comparable statistics for PMA approval rates are not readily available. However, PMAs plainly fare less well. . . .

NOTES

1.   *Recent Data.* In the five years from 2000 to 2004, FDA received 20,652 premarket notifications claiming substantial equivalence and rejected only 369 of these (approximately 1.8 percent). In the same period, FDA made 338 approval decisions on original PMAs, of which 41 (approximately 12.1 percent) were "not approvable." (Some sponsors receiving "not approvable" letters may have corrected the identified deficiencies and ultimately received PMA approval.) In the years between 2000 and 2004, the average amount of time that elapsed between submission of a section 510(k) premarket notification and a substantial equivalence decision by FDA ranged from 96 days (2001 and 2003) to 102 days (2000). By contrast, the average total time from submission to decision for PMAs ranged from 359 days (2003) to 436 days (2004).

In 2007 and 2008, approximately 3 percent of section 510(k) notifications were rejected and 30 percent of PMAs were deemed not approvable. In 2012, after reviewing the section 510(k) process and implementing a Plan of Action for improvement, FDA announced in a report that the time for 510(k) clearance, the backlog, and the percent rejected were all declining. FDA, *Improvements in Device Review* (Nov. 2012).

2.   *Least Burdensome.* The 1997 Act added section 513(a)(3)(D)(ii) to provide that FDA must consider the "least burdensome" means of establishing the effectiveness of a device. This provision had no discernible impact. Congress therefore clarified in the 2012 Act that this phrase means the minimum information necessary for clearance or approval. It is doubtful that this clarification will result in any change in CDRH policy.

3.   *Required FDA Explanation of Action.* Under new section 517A, added by the 2012 Act, upon request FDA is required to provide a "substantive summary of the scientific and regulatory rationale for any significant division" regarding an investigational device exemption (IDE), PMN, or PMA.

4.   *Patent Term Restoration.* The Drug Price Competition and Patent Term Restoration Act of 1984 (Hatch-Waxman), *supra* p. 1000, provides patent term restoration of up to five years for medical devices that have been subject to a regulatory review period that has reduced their effective patent life. Some PMA devices have, in fact, been awarded extensions of their patent term under this statute. *E.g.*, 63 Fed. Reg. 24557 (May 4, 1998); 58 Fed. Reg. 42560 (Aug. 10, 1993).

5.   *Use of Patented Device in Preparation of Premarket Application.* 35 U.S.C. 271(e)(1) states that research conducted with a patented drug to develop information for a submission to FDA does not constitute infringement. *Eli Lilly & Co. v. Medtronic, Inc.*, 496 U.S. 661 (1990), held that this provision also applies to the use of a patented medical device to develop information in connection with an application for marketing approval.

2.   THE 510(k) REVIEW PROCESS AND "SUBSTANTIAL EQUIVALENCE"

a.   BACKGROUND

The regulatory structure created by the 1976 Amendments was organized around three principles. First, a postamendments device that is substantially equivalent to a preamendments device (a predicate device) should meet the same standards of safety and effectiveness as the predicate device, on the same schedule. Second, a postamendments device that has no preamendments counterpart, and thus cannot establish substantial equivalence to a predicate device, should presumptively be class III and required to obtain approval of a PMA before it is allowed on the market. Third, a mechanism should be established to allow FDA to review the basis for a manufacturer's decision to introduce a device and thereby prevent the introduction of novel devices that have not undergone an official assessment. This third principle is embodied in the section 510(k) premarket notification (PMN) process.

FD&C Act 510(k) requires the seller of a new device, at least 90 days prior to marketing, to notify FDA of the proper classification of the device and the manufacturer's "basis for [this] determination." (As discussed below, the manufacturers of many low-risk devices are now exempt from this obligation.) Meanwhile, section 513(f)(1) states that the seller can avoid classification into Class III—and the attendant PMA approval requirement—if its device is "substantially equivalent" to an already-marketed Class I or Class II device. The section 510(k) PMN is the vehicle by which device manufacturers try to demonstrate "substantial equivalence." Consequently, this path to market has come to be known as the "510(k) process," although it might be less confusing to call it the "513(f)(1) process."

Most recently, FDA issued a draft guidance in December 2011 summarizing the history and current status of the agency's implementation of the 510(k) program.

b.   MEANING OF "SUBSTANTIAL EQUIVALENCE"

The 1976 Amendments did not include a definition of "substantially equivalent." The legislative history, however, indicates that substantial equivalence was meant to be assessed not merely in terms of physical characteristics and intended use, but also in terms of safety and effectiveness:

> The term "substantially equivalent" is not intended to be so narrow as to refer only to devices that are identical to marketed devices nor so broad as to refer to devices which are intended to be used for the same purposes as marketed products. The Committee believes that the term should be construed narrowly where necessary to assure the safety and effectiveness of a device but not so narrowly where differences between a new device and a marketed device do not relate to safety and effectiveness.

H.R. Rep. No. 853, 94th Cong., 2d Sess. 36–37 (1976). Thus, the concept of substantial equivalence was left for FDA to interpret, but it was clearly intended to embrace some inquiry into the safety and effectiveness of a new device.

When FDA issued regulations governing the PMN process soon after enactment of the 1976 Amendments. 42 Fed. Reg. 42520 (Aug. 23, 1977), these regulations did not include any definition of "substantial equivalence." In 1986, FDA issued a guidance that, for the first time, spelled out in detail the agency's approach to assessing substantial equivalence. GUIDANCE ON THE CENTER OF DEVICES AND RADIOLOGICAL HEALTH'S PREMARKET NOTIFICATION REVIEW PROGRAM (1986). According to this document, one device could be substantially equivalent to another only if it had the same intended use. If a new device had the same intended use as a predicate device, and also the same technological characteristics, it was substantially equivalent. Moreover, a new device could be substantially equivalent to a predicate device even if it had different technological characteristics—but only if the section 510(k) notification demonstrated that these new technological characteristics did not diminish safety or effectiveness.

In the 1990 Amendments, Congress defined "substantial equivalence" in section 513(i) of the FD&C Act in a manner that essentially codifies the substantial equivalence policy stated in FDA's 1986 document. Soon thereafter, FDA issued a rule incorporating these requirements into the existing medical device regulations. 57 Fed. Reg. 58400 (Dec. 10, 1992), codified at 21 C.F.R. 807.100. *See generally* Benjamin A. Goldberger, *The Evolution of Substantial Equivalence in*

FDA's Premarket Review of Medical Devices, 56 FOOD & DRUG L. J. 317 (2001).

c.   "PIGGYBACKING"

To enter the market without a PMA, must a postamendments device be substantially equivalent to a preamendments device, or is it sufficient to be substantially equivalent to an earlier postamendments device that itself was found to be equivalent to a device on the market prior to 1976? The latter approach, especially if carried through several generations, may lead to the marketing of new devices that bear little resemblance to any preamendment products. Nevertheless, FDA permitted PMNs to take this approach prior to 1990 even though the agency did not have explicit statutory authorization to do so. This interpretation led to a phenomenon known colloquially as "piggybacking" or "equivalence creep."

The 1990 Act specifically authorized piggybacking. The current statutory definition of "substantial equivalence," added in 1990, states that a device with technological characteristics different from a predicate device is nonetheless substantially equivalent if the PMN "contains information . . . that demonstrates that the device is as safe and effective as a *legally marketed device* and does not raise different questions of safety and effectiveness than the predicate device" (emphasis added). FD&C Act 513(i)(1)(A)(ii).

d.   EXEMPTIONS FROM THE PMN REQUIREMENT

In 1976, Congress concluded that the manufacturer of a new device should not have the authority to resolve the issue of substantial equivalence unilaterally, without FDA oversight, and it thus imposed the 510(k) PMN requirement on manufacturers of all devices without PMAs. In the 1997 Amendments, however, Congress revolutionized the section 510(k) process by automatically exempting many devices from the PMN requirement. According to new section 510(l): "A report under subsection (k) is not required for a device that . . . is within a type that has been classified into Class I," unless the device "is intended for a use which is of substantial importance in preventing impairment of human health, or . . . presents a potential unreasonable risk of illness or injury." The 1997 Act also authorized FDA to identify types of Class II devices for which a PMN is not necessary. FD&C Act 510(m).

Today, under this regime, most Class I devices and some Class II devices are exempt from the premarket notification requirement. Under the current system, manufacturers of less risky devices routinely determine substantial equivalence for themselves.

e.   REVOKING A 510(k) CLEARANCE

The FD&C Act does not authorize FDA to revoke a prior clearance of a PMN. FDA has nonetheless asserted that this power is inherent in the statutory scheme. The following case upholds the agency's view, at least in the circumstances at issue.

Ivy Sports Medicine, LLC v. Sebelius

2013 WL 1455271 (D.D.C 2013).

■ ROBERT L. WILKINS, CIRCUIT JUDGE.

. . . .

The meniscus is made of tissue and is found between the knee bones. . . . Unfortunately, meniscus injuries are quite common, and often result in a surgical procedure known as a partial meniscectomy. That procedure removes torn meniscus cartilage interfering with knee joint function. The product at issue in this litigation is a Collagen Scaffold ("CS") manufactured by Ivy that was marketed in the United States as Menaflex. According to Ivy, the CS is intended "to reinforce damaged or weakened meniscal soft tissue in the knee and to provide a resorbable scaffold for replacement by a patient's own soft tissue." . . . According to Ivy, although debated by the FDA as explained below, use of the CS is limited to repairing and reinforcing tissue, and the CS is not intended to replace tissue.

ReGen began clinical research on the safety of the CS around 1997, and sought premarket approval in 2004. Later, instead of pursuing premarket approval, ReGen submitted its first 510(k) application in 2005, describing the CS as "a resorbable collagen-based surgical mesh" that "serves to reinforce and repair soft tissue." The FDA rejected the 510(k) application in February 2006 as not substantially equivalent to a predicate surgical mesh, stating its "decision is based on the fact that the performance data you have provided did not demonstrate your device to be as safe and effective as legally marketed devices." The agency reconsidered its rejection . . . but in July 2006 . . . again rejected the 510(k) application, "based on the fact that your device has a new indication (i.e., the reinforcement and repair of soft tissue where weakness exists, including, but not limited to . . . meniscus defects) that alters the therapeutic effect, impacting safety and effectiveness, and is therefore a new intended use." . . .

ReGen submitted a second 510(k) application in December 2006, describing the device's use as "repairing and reinforcing meniscal defects." The FDA's lead reviewer found the device not substantially equivalent to a predicate device, and wrote that the CS "was not used to repair and reinforce a repair but to replace tissue that has been removed after partial meniscectomy." . . . [I]n August 2007 the FDA ultimately again rejected ReGen's application. . . .

In December 2007, both of New Jersey's United States Senators, and two members of its United States House of Representatives delegation, wrote to the FDA on behalf of ReGen, asking for the FDA's review of the current submission and requesting a meeting to "discuss this situation." ReGen's principal place of business is in New Jersey.

Following the suggestion of Dr. Daniel G. Schultz, the then Director of the FDA's Center for Devices and Radiological Health ("CDRH"), ReGen later submitted a third 510(k) premarket notification to the FDA on July 22, 2008 for its CS, noting an indication that the device "is intended for use in surgical procedures for the reinforcement and repair of soft tissue injuries of the meniscus." . . .

By letter dated December 18, 2008, Dr. Schultz informed ReGen of the agency's decision to classify the CS as a Class II device under the FDCA, because the agency had "determined the device is substantially equivalent (for the indications for use stated in the enclosure) to legally marketed predicate devices . . . or to devices that have been reclassified in accordance with the provisions of the Federal Food, Drug, and Cosmetic Act (Act) that do not require approval of a premarket approval application (PMA)." The agency at that time determined the CS to be substantially equivalent to an approved surgical mesh. Surgical meshes are regulated as Class II devices. *See* 21 C.F.R. § 878.3300 (a mesh is "intended to be implanted to reinforce soft tissue or bone where weakness exists"). As a result, ReGen began commercial distribution of the CS in the United States, and first distributed the device in April 2009. . . .

Shortly before they began distribution, however, an article about the approval of ReGen's CS appeared on the front page of the *Wall Street Journal*. Alicia Mundy, *Political Lobbying Drove FDA Process*, WALL ST. J., Mar. 6, 2009, at A1. . . . That day Senator Charles Grassley contacted the FDA about the substantial equivalence determination for the CS device. . . . The agency began an internal review at the end of April 2009.

        . . . .

On October 14, 2010, the FDA (via [new CDRH Director]Dr. Jeffrey Shuren) informed ReGen of its intention to rescind the CS's Class II designation, noting "[t]he review team concluded that the CS device is intended to replace meniscal tissue that has been surgically excised rather than to repair and reinforce soft tissue or bone." Dr. Shuren also wrote that, "even if the CS device had the same intended use as any of the identified predicate devices, the differences between the technological characteristics of the CS device and each of the predicate devices raise different questions of safety and effectiveness." On March 30, 2011 . . . the FDA wrote to ReGen that . . . it was "rescinding our determination of substantial equivalence." This caused reclassification of the CS to Class III, meaning the device could not be marketed in the United States without approval of the FDA. . . .

As a threshold matter, this Court must decide whether the FDA acted properly in how it reclassified the CS device. Ivy argues that the FDA had only one option: to use the statutory procedure for reclassification found at 21 U.S.C. § 360c(e). Because it did not do so, Ivy argues, the agency acted in violation of the law, and this ends the litigation in their favor. The FDA disagrees that § 360c(e) was its only option, and instead argues that it properly used its inherent authority to reclassify the CS. The agency argues that because of serious procedural irregularities in the approval process, and because there is no statutory limitation on their power to reconsider, the agency acted properly. . . .

One of the key cases on the issue of inherent authority, if not the key case, is *American Methyl Corp. v. EPA*, 749 F.2d 826 (D.C. Cir. 1984). . . . The court stated that because "Congress has provided a mechanism capable of rectifying mistaken actions . . . it is not reasonable to infer authority to reconsider agency action." . . .

But *American Methyl* is distinguishable in several critical ways. . . .

. . . [I]n a situation in which the integrity of an approval process can reasonably be challenged, *American Methyl* does not necessarily apply to an agency exercising its inherent authority. . . . The key point is whether some form of misconduct "taint[ed] the original record" and "affect[ed] the integrity" of the FDA proceedings.

In this case, the FDA internal review concluded that there were multiple "procedural irregularities" that called into question the basis of the agency's decision and Dr. Shuren said "the integrity of our process for reaching a decision was compromised in this case. . . ."

One of the reasons for an agency to invoke inherent authority . . . is ex parte contacts, and the Administrative Record in this case includes several communications that fit into this category. For example, the FDA found that the agency violated its "usual practice" when it met with Ivy "without members of the review team present." The FDA allowed Ivy to have "unusual access to the Commissioner and his Principal Deputy." The FDA violated their "[t]ypical[ ]" procedures and allowed members of Congress to speak "directly to both the FDA Commissioner and the Principal Deputy Commissioner."

. . . .

Because of the numerous departures from normal agency practice, the circumstances of this case present the rare situation where the FDA was justified in exercising its inherent authority to reevaluate the approval of the CS device. . . .

. . . .

The agency's substantial equivalence determination of a 510(k) submission is limited to the "intended use" of a device set forth in "the proposed labeling submitted in a report for the device under section 510(k)." 21 U.S.C. § 360c(i)(1)(E)(1). Ivy argues that the FDA acted arbitrarily and capriciously because it failed properly to limit its review of the CS device to the description provided in the device's Indications for Use statement, which states its use "is intended for use in surgical procedures for the reinforcement and repair of soft tissue injuries of the medial meniscus . . . and is not intended to replace normal body structure." The agency counters that Dr. Shuren properly based his decision on "the labeled description of the device," including material outside the Indications for Use statement.

. . . Dr. Shuren found that "the Instructions for Use make clear that upon implantation the CS device is intended to replace damaged meniscal tissue that has been removed." . . . Simply because Ivy stated [in the "Indications for Use"] that the CS device is "not intended to replace normal body structure" does not mean it is not intended to replace anything. As Dr. Shuren noted, "this disclaimer does not counter plain statements in both the Indications for Use statement and in the instructions for use that the device is intended to replace something, namely, damaged meniscal tissue that has been surgically removed." He later added: "The indications for use statement purporting to indicate the device for use in repair and reinforcement seems to be an attempt to manipulate language to conform the indications for the CS device to those of predicate meshes." Whether Ivy is correct that looking beyond the Indications for Use Statement is not "[t]ypically" what is done is irrelevant: there is nothing improper about doing so, *see* 21 U.S.C. § 321(m).

Others at the FDA besides Dr. Shuren shared the view that the CS device was intended to replace tissue rather than simply reinforce and repair damaged tissue. . . .

Dr. Shuren's examination of predicate devices adequately explains why their differences from the CS device indicate the agency did not treat the CS device unfairly. . . . Dr. Shuren . . . concluded that

> [n]one of these devices in any of their iterations have an intended use of replacing tissue in the knee that has been surgically excised. The review team considered all predicates indicated by ReGen in its 510(k) submission and concluded that none were suitable predicates for the CS device. I agree with that conclusion.

. . . Dr. Shuren's . . . argument . . . cannot reasonably be called arbitrary or capricious, which is the standard at issue here. . . .

The FDCA also states that whether a new device is substantially equivalent to a predicate depends on the device's "technological characteristics"—they need to either be the same or, if different, the manufacturer must demonstrate that the device is as safe and effective as a predicate. 21 U.S.C. § 360c(i)(1)(A). The agency argues, independently from its argument about intended use, that it found the device not substantially equivalent to a predicate because "differences between the technological characteristics of the CS device and each of the predicate devices raise different questions of safety and effectiveness." . . .

Dr. Shuren found that the "CS device has different technological characteristics from other [predicate devices] because of differences in shape," and that these different characteristics "raise new types of safety and effectiveness questions." Ivy states that Dr. Shuren offered "no reason" for his concerns about the shape of the CS device. But Dr. Shuren stated that "new types of safety and effectiveness questions are raised based on the shape of the CS device in terms of biomechanical properties, composition, and possible chondral changes in the knee joint from the presence of the device." Again, Dr. Shuren is not alone: the review team also found "different technological characteristics from other meshes because of differences in shape."

Because of the technological differences, Ivy needed to submit data demonstrating the CS device was as safe and effective as the proposed predicates. A number of people, including Dr. Shuren, found the company failed to do so. . . .

For the foregoing reasons, Defendants' Motion for Summary Judgment is granted.

NOTES

1. *Distinct Analyses.* The question of whether a new device is "substantially equivalent" to a particular predicate device is distinct from the question of whether it falls within a generic type of device as defined by

FDA in a classification regulation. Sometimes both questions arise with respect to a single product. For example, in this case, FDA had to separately determine (1) whether the CS device could properly be categorized as "surgical mesh," a type of device identified (and placed in Class II) by 21 C.F.R. 878.3300, a classification regulation within the CFR Part on "General and Plastic Surgery Devices," and (2) whether the CS device was "substantially equivalent" to another device of that type already on the market.

2. *Safety and Effectiveness Data.* The 1990 Act specifically authorized FDA to require clinical data in a section 510(k) notification. Many PMN's include such data. Indeed, FDA would be unlikely to clear a PMN for a product incorporating new technologies that could affect safety or effectiveness if the notification did not contain clinical investigation data. Nevertheless, FDA assiduously avoids mentioning safety or effectiveness in letters clearing PMNs, and the agency clings to its position that a 510(k) clearance reflects a determination of equivalence, not safety and effectiveness. This distinction was critical in the Supreme Court's conclusion that a PMN clearance does not preempt a state tort action based on a device's allegedly defective design. *Medtronic v. Lohr*, 518 U.S. 470, 492–94 (1996) (excerpted *infra* at 1283).

3. *PMN Summary Versus PMN Statement.* A section 510(k) notification must include either a "510(k) Summary" or a "510(k) Statement." The former is a summary of the information upon which the person filing the notification bases a claim of substantial equivalence. A 510(k) statement is a certification that the 510(k) owner will provide safety and effectiveness information supporting the FDA finding of substantial equivalence to any person within 30 days of a written request. 21 C.F.R. 807.92 & 807.93.

4. *User Fees.* Under the authority granted to it by the Medical Device User Fee and Modernization Act of 2002 (MDUFMA) and the statutes enacted in 2007 and 2012 to reauthorize the program, FDA assesses fees for the review of 510(k)s and PMAs.

5. *Abbreviated PMN.* In FDA's "New 510(k) Paradigm: Alternate Approaches to Demonstrating Substantial Equivalence in Premarket Notifications (1998)," the agency invites any device manufacturer submitting a PMN to include a "summary report" outlining its product's compliance with an FDA guidance document or special control, or a declaration of conformity to a national or international standard that FDA has recognized pursuant to section 514(c). Such a notification is known as an "Abbreviated 510(k)." While FDA does not put Abbreviated 510(k)s on a special processing track, it states that their review will generally be more efficient than the review of traditional section 510(k) submissions.

6. *Special 510(k)s.* FDA regulations have long required the submission of a PMN for devices that are already in commercial distribution but are about to be "significantly changed or modified in design, components, method of manufacture, or intended use." 21 C.F.R. 807.81(a)(3). FDA's 1998 "New 510(k) Paradigm" established the use of "Special 510(k)s" for some device modifications. The previous year, FDA had begun to require manufacturers of Class I, Class II, and some Class III

devices to follow design control procedures when introducing devices or when modifying them. 21 C.F.R. 820.30. In establishing the "Special 510(k)" process, FDA recognized that many of the questions traditionally addressed in a section 510(k) notification for a device modification could now be addressed in the verification and validation studies performed by the manufacturer pursuant to these new design control procedure requirements. A Special 510(k) contains a declaration of conformity with design control requirements. FDA promises to process Special 510(k)s within 30 days of receipt. The agency will not, however, accept Special 510(k)s for modifications that affect the intended use of the device or alter its fundamental scientific technology.

7. *Third Party Review.* The 1997 Act added section 523 to establish a five year program under which FDA would accredit external organizations to review section 510(k) notifications and make recommendations to FDA regarding the agency's response to these submissions. (FDA began experimenting with this approach prior to 1997 under a pilot program.) This third party review authority was extended in section 221 of the 2007 Act and section 611 of the 2012 Act despite tepid use of the program by device sponsors. The accredited third parties, which may be used only at the request of the person submitting the PMN, are not authorized to review Class III devices or specified types of Class II devices. According to FDA, in 2002, PMNs reviewed by Accredited Persons received FDA marketing clearance, on average, 29 percent faster than comparable PMNs reviewed entirely by FDA. Another advantage to using third-party review is that submissions reviewed by Accredited Persons are not subject to a FDA user fee for PMNs, which increased from $3502 in 2005 to $4960 in 2013.

8. *Continuing 510(k) Controversy.* From its inception the section 510(k) process was controversial. In 2009, CDRH established internal committees to review possible changes to improve the PMN process, and in 2010, FDA asked the Institute of Medicine to undertake a parallel review. The CDRH internal committees made 55 recommendations, the most significant of which were strongly criticized by the regulated industry. FDA immediately dismissed the IOM Report, set aside the internal proposals that had been strongly opposed by the industry, and focused on a Plan of Action with 36 specific actions designed to improve the device premarket review system. In *Improvements in Device Review: Results of CDRH's Plan of Action for Premarket Review of Devices* (Nov. 2012), the agency reported that major improvements had been achieved. Throughout this entire time, no one has put forth a viable alternative to the PMN process as originally established in the 1976 Amendments. It is therefore likely that this process will remain in place for the foreseeable future, with occasional small modifications of the type that have occurred periodically since 1976.

f.   510(k) AND REPROCESSED SINGLE-USE DEVICES

Traditionally, most medical devices used in hospital settings were considered to be reusable. Users would routinely clean, disinfect, and sterilize glass, rubber, and metal devices and use them again and again. In the 1970s, however, manufacturers increasingly began to sell devices labeled as "single-use devices" (SUDs). The market for these products developed in response to the emergence of new plastics and a demand for disposable equipment. Hospitals and health care facilities, to save costs and prevent the accumulation of medical waste, often chose to reprocess SUDs and reuse them. Hospitals reprocessed many SUDs themselves, but by the late 1970s, a new industry of third-party reprocessors developed.

Through the 1990s, FDA left hospital reprocessing operations virtually unregulated, despite declaring in a Compliance Policy Guide that "there is a lack of data to support the general reuse of disposable medical devices," and that "any [health care] institution or practitioner who resterilizes and/or reuses a disposable medical device must bear full responsibility for its safety and effectiveness." REUSE OF MEDICAL DISPOSABLE DEVICES, Compliance Policy Guide 300.500 (1977). As for third-party reprocessors, the agency considered them to be subject to the full panoply of requirements applicable to original device manufacturers, including premarket notification. Nevertheless, although FDA issued warning letters to third-party reprocessors for some types of violations, it exercised its enforcement discretion with regard to section 510(k) notification and never took action against a third-party reprocessor for failing to comply with this requirement. FDA PROPOSED STRATEGY ON REUSE OF SINGLE–USE DEVICES 2–5 (1999).

The age of unregulated device reprocessing ended at the turn of the millennium. In 2000, FDA announced its intention to phase in enforcement of the premarket submission requirements on third-party and hospital reprocessors. 65 Fed. Reg. 49583 (Aug. 14, 2000). Reprocessors of Class III devices would have to file premarket applications, and reprocessors of nonexempt Class II and Class I devices would have to file PMNs. Then, the 2002 Act added section 510(o) to the FD&C Act. This provision, which assumes that reprocessed single use devices are fully subject to the premarket submission requirements, instructs FDA to identify SUDs for which PMNs must include validation data concerning cleaning, sterilization, and functional performance. The validation data are intended to ensure that the reprocessed devices are substantially equivalent to their predicate devices. The provision further provides that the PMN requirement, including validation data, will apply to formerly exempt critical and semi-critical devices identified by the agency. FDA has since promulgated a list of SUD types requiring validation data and a list of critical and semicritical SUDs whose PMN exemption has been terminated.

3. INVESTIGATIONAL DEVICES

a. GENERAL REQUIREMENTS

All PMAs for Class III devices require clinical data demonstrating safety and effectiveness. Section 515(c)(1)(A). Moreover, as noted above, some PMNs require such data. In most instances, a manufacturer seeking to introduce a device to the market by either route must itself generate the necessary clinical data.

Like new drugs, the FD&C Act and FDA regulations allow the investigational use of a new device in order to obtain the safety and effectiveness data required to support a PMA application or section 510(k) notification. A sponsor seeking to perform clinical studies on an uncleared/unapproved device must qualify for an investigational device exemption (IDE). The IDE system resembles the IND system for clinical testing of new drugs (discussed *supra* p. 673), with one major difference: the manufacturers of some lower risk investigational devices are not required to submit IDE applications to the agency.

The FD&C Act states that FDA may require agency approval of an IDE application, in addition to approval by a local institutional review board (IRB), if the agency "finds that the process of review by such committee is inadequate." Section 520(g)(3)(A). FDA has implemented this provision by dividing investigational devices into two categories: those that represent a "significant risk" and those that do not. The IDE application requirements for a device in the "significant risk" category are similar to the IND process for new drugs, except that FDA must explicitly approve the IDE application before testing may begin. For a device in the second category, however, an investigation will be "considered to have" an approved IDE based solely on IRB approval and the satisfaction of several other requirements, and the sponsor need not submit an application to FDA. 21 C.F.R. 812.2(b). A sponsor has the authority initially to determine whether its device is a "significant risk" device, but either the IRB or FDA may disagree and redesignate it. 21 C.F.R. 812.2(b)(1), 812.20(a), 812.66. FDA Information Sheet Guidance, SIGNIFICANT RISK AND NONSIGNIFICANT RISK MEDICAL DEVICE STUDIES (1995).

b.   FEASIBILITY STUDIES

Often only a limited "feasibility" study is conducted on a significant risk investigational device, to determine whether a full investigation is warranted. As FDA has explained:

> In a developmental process, a device is designed to meet a clinical need and testing begins in the laboratory using animal and/or bench methodology. Once the design and operating parameters have been subject to adequate preclinical tests, the developer may wish to conduct an initial limited study in humans to confirm the design and operating specifications before beginning an extensive clinical trial. The initial study may indicate that minor or major changes in the device or its manufacture are necessary before proceeding. It may also indicate that the device does not meet expectations and it will be terminated. The performance of the device in the limited study serves to establish the parameters for the larger clinical study, such as sample size and indices of measurement.

> Inherent in the utility of the limited study is the importance of maintaining sufficient flexibility for the researcher to make adjustments in the device, its manufacture or the investigational plan in the early stages of clinical testing without the need for repeated prior FDA approval.

GUIDANCE MEMORANDUM: REVIEW OF IDES FOR FEASIBILITY STUDIES (1989).

c.   "RESEARCH USE ONLY" EXEMPTION FOR DIAGNOSTIC DEVICES

An exemption from the IDE requirements in 21 C.F.R. 812.2(c)(2) allows the sale of a diagnostic device labeled "For Research Use Only" or "For Investigational Use Only" if the testing is noninvasive, does not require an invasive sampling procedure that presents a significant risk, does not introduce energy into a subject, and is not used without confirmation by another established diagnostic product or procedure. In a consent decree entered in *United States v. Centocor, Inc.*, Civ. No. 85–5613 (E.D. Pa. 1986), 22 FDA Consumer, No. 7, at 44 (Sept. 1989), the defendant agreed not only to label a diagnostic device "For Research Use Only," but also to obtain from each researcher a written agreement that the device would not be used for investigation involving clinical use, including diagnosis or monitoring, and that results of tests would not be used in conjunction with any patient records or treatment. The consent decree prohibited shipment to any researcher before this agreement was executed. FDA has since used this consent decree as a model for regulating diagnostic products sold for research use only. *See* DRAFT COMPLIANCE POLICY GUIDE, COMMERCIALIZATION OF IN VITRO DIAGNOSTIC DEVICES LABELED FOR RESEARCH USE ONLY OR INVESTIGATIONAL USE ONLY 14 (Jan. 1998).

NOTES

1.   *Other IDE Exemptions*. In addition to exempting some diagnostic devices from the IDE requirement, 21 C.F.R. 812(c) also exempts, with some qualifications: preamendments nontransitional devices being investigated in accordance with their 1976 labeling; devices determined to be substantially equivalent to such preamendments devices; devices undergoing nonrisky consumer preference testing; veterinary devices; devices shipped solely for research on laboratory animals; and custom devices. In accordance with section 520(g)(6) (added by the 1997 Act), the regulations do not require FDA approval of "developmental changes" in a device subject to an IDE if these changes "do not constitute a significant change in design or in basic principles of operation" and are "made in response to information gathered during the course of an investigation." 21 C.F.R. 812.35(a)(3)(i).

2.   *Early Collaboration on IDEs*. In 1995, FDA established a "Pre-IDE" program to increase the approval rate and reduce the time to approval. This informal program encourages IDE sponsors to meet with agency staff before submitting IDE applications for review, to submit portions of the IDE to FDA preliminarily for guidance before making the formal submission, and to communicate frequently with the agency during the review process. *See Goals and Initiatives for the IDE Program* (1995) (IDE Memorandum D95–1). The informal Pre-IDE program is still in effect, but it now coexists with a formal system of "early collaboration meetings" established by the 1997 Act. These meetings are also intended to take place prior to submission of the IDE. FDA must grant requests for formal early collaboration meetings, reduce the resulting determinations or agreements to writing, and generally treat these written conclusions as binding. Meetings under FD&C Act section 513(a)(3)(D) (termed "Determination Meetings" by FDA), between the agency and individuals intending to

submit PMAs, address what type of scientific evidence will be necessary to establish the effectiveness of the device in question. Meetings under FD&C Act 520(g)(7) ("Agreement Meetings") are between FDA and individuals intending to file PMAs or PMNs for Class III or implantable devices. Agreement Meetings are meant to reach agreement regarding the key parameters of the investigational plan. *See* FINAL GUIDANCE: EARLY COLLABORATION MEETINGS UNDER FDAMA (Feb. 2001).

3. *Clinical Holds.* The 2012 Act amends section 520(g) to authorize FDA to issue a clinical hold if an IDE presents an "unreasonable risk" to the trial subjects.

4. *Criteria for IDE Disapproval.* Section 520(g)(4)(C), added by the 2012 Act, states that FDA shall not disapprove an IDE because the agency believes that the trial will not support clearance or approval.

d. EMERGENCY INVESTIGATIONAL USE

The IDE system appears to work satisfactorily for routine long term investigations of new devices, but it seems less well-suited to studies of devices that are deployed infrequently and usually in an emergency. For example, FDA had approved an IDE for the Jarvik–7 artificial heart, setting stringent protocol conditions, months before Dr. William DeVries implanted it in Barney Clark on December 1–2, 1982. After four permanent implants of the Jarvik–7 heart, however, an FDA advisory committee reviewed the program and recommended that "FDA should assume a more direct oversight role as the clinical trial proceeds, and should approve subsequent implants on a case-by-case basis." "FDA Sets New Requirements For Permanent Artificial Heart Program," FDA Talk Paper No. T86–3 (Jan. 7, 1986).

In the interim, however, the exigencies of patient care overcame FDA's IDE requirements for another type of artificial heart.

Cristine Russell, *Temporary Heart Implanted: Tucson Operation Lacked FDA Approval*

WASHINGTON POST, March 7, 1985, at A1.

Doctors at a University of Arizona teaching hospital yesterday implanted a new type of temporary artificial heart in a dying 32-year-old man while they tried to locate a human heart for transplant. . . . Dr. Allan Beigel, a university vice president and spokesman for the University Medical Center hospital, said last night that the mechanical device, designed by a Chinese dentist, "had not been tested in humans" and does not have government approval, but was implanted anyway because "the alternative was that the patient would die." The recipient . . . had rejected a human heart transplant earlier in the day and had been placed on a heart-lung machine. Beigel said time was of the utmost concern because the patient was reaching the point where continued use of the machine risked causing irreparable damage.

The patient was reported in critical but stable condition after the three-hour implant procedure, which has not been approved by the federal Food and Drug Administration. Asked at a news briefing last night whether FDA approval was needed for the operation, Dr. Jack Copeland, head of the hospital's heart-transplant team, said: "Ideally, they should have, but you can't think of everything." Later, he added, "We did not set out to do a human experiment. We set out to do a heart transplant. We were faced with a patient who had no alternative except death."

The mechanical heart used, called the Phoenix heart, was developed at St. Luke's Hospital in Phoenix, where it has been under study for about two years, Beigel said. It was one of three devices—including the Jarvik–7 artificial heart, which has been implanted into three permanent artificial-heart recipients—rushed to Tucson when the patient's condition began deteriorating.

An FDA spokesman said last night that the agency had informed the university yesterday that federal permission was needed for human experimentation with unproven medical devices, but that the university failed to obtain the approval. . . .

FDA spokesman David Duarte said the agency "is waiting to hear the facts from the university." He said the FDA response could range from a reprimand to taking the matter to court.

———

On May 10, 1985, after FDA completed an investigation of the Phoenix heart episode, John Villforth, Director of CDRH, wrote to the administrator of the University of Arizona's hospital:

Although the Medical Device Amendments to the Food, Drug, and Cosmetic Act do not provide for the emergency use of unapproved devices, FDA has discretion to withhold consideration of regulatory action in appropriate circumstances. Because we believe that the situation at the University of Arizona Hospital constitutes such a circumstance, no further action by FDA is indicated and we consider the matter closed.

To govern future emergencies of this sort, FDA then published a guidance permitting emergency use of unapproved devices without an IDE when the patient is in a life-threatening condition and no alternative treatment is available. GUIDANCE FOR THE EMERGENCY USE OF UNAPPROVED MEDICAL DEVICES (1985).

In 1996 FDA finalized a rule, discussed *supra* p. 689, note 10, permitting IRBs to approve emergency protocols for investigational drugs or devices with an exception to the informed consent requirement when obtaining such consent is not feasible. 21 C.F.R. 50.24. A manufacturer may thus prospectively obtain an IDE for emergency use of an unapproved device. Nevertheless, situations may still arise in which a device with no approved IDE represents a patient's final chance. A revised version of FDA's Guidance for Emergency Use of Unapproved Devices thus remains in effect:

Information Sheet Guidance For IRBs, Clinical Investigators, and Sponsors, Frequently Asked Questions About Medical Devices (2006)

. . . .

Can a physician use an unapproved device in an emergency?

In general, an unapproved medical device may be used only on human subjects when the device is under clinical investigation and when used by investigators participating in a clinical trial. Section 561 of the Act, however, recognizes that there may be circumstances under which a health care provider may wish to use an unapproved device to save the life of a patient or to prevent irreversible morbidity when there exists no other alternative therapy. For investigational devices under an IDE, the IDE regulation permits deviations from the investigational plan without prior approval when necessary to protect the life or physical well-being of a subject in an emergency. (See 21 CFR 812.35(a)). A physician may treat a patient with an unapproved medical device in an emergency situation if he/she concludes that:

- The patient has a life-threatening condition that needs immediate treatment;
- No generally acceptable alternative treatment for the condition exists; and
- Because of the immediate need to use the device, there is no time to use existing procedures to get FDA approval for the use.

FDA expects the physician to make the determination that the patient's circumstances meet the above criteria, to assess the potential for benefit from the use of the unapproved device, and to have substantial reason to believe that benefits will exist. In the event that a device is used in circumstances meeting the criteria listed above, the physician should follow as many of the patient protection procedures listed below as possible:

- Informed consent from the patient or a legal representative;
- Clearance from the institution as specified by their policies;
- Concurrence of the IRB chairperson;
- An assessment from a physician who is not participating in the study; and
- Authorization from the IDE sponsor, if an IDE exists for the device.

While prior approval for shipment or emergency use of the investigational device is not required, the use must be reported to FDA by the IDE sponsor within 5 working days from the time the sponsor learns of the use. 21 CFR 812.35(a)(2) and 812.150(a)(4). The report should contain a summary of the conditions constituting the emergency, patient outcome information, and the patient protection measures that were followed. If no IDE exists, the physician should follow the above procedures and report the emergency use to CDRH or CBER.

4. PREMARKET APPROVAL APPLICATIONS

After the sponsor of a novel Class III device has obtained the requisite safety and effectiveness data, it must submit a PMA application to FDA for review and approval. FDA promulgated regulations governing the PMA process in 51 Fed. Reg. 26342 (July 22, 1986), codified at 21 C.F.R. Part 814.

a. COMPARISON OF PMAS AND NDAS

The PMA process is similar to the new drug application (NDA) process discussed in Chapter 7. After FDA determines that the PMA is complete and accepts it for filing, the agency performs a comprehensive review of the information contained within. As discussed below, FDA must refer the PMA to an advisory committee if the applicant requests, and it may do so on its own initiative. As is the case with new drugs, the primary questions for the advisory committee, and ultimately for FDA itself, are safety and effectiveness under the conditions of use in the proposed labeling.

Despite these similarities, the statutory standards for determining the safety and effectiveness of devices differ from the comparable standards for drugs in several respects. First, section 513(a)(1)(C) of the FD&C Act provides that premarket approval of devices is intended to provide "reasonable assurance" of safety and effectiveness. The drug provisions do not contain similar qualifying language.

Second, section 513(a)(2) explicitly mandates that when assessing the safety and effectiveness of a device, FDA consider: (1) the persons for whose use the device is intended, (2) the "conditions of use" prescribed in the labeling, and (3) the "probable benefit to health from the use of the device [weighed] against any probable risk of injury or illness." Such enumerated factors do not appear in the new drug provisions of the Act, although FDA routinely takes them into account when reviewing NDAs.

Third, the Act sets a standard for establishing the effectiveness of devices that seems more flexible than the "substantial evidence" standard applicable to drugs. Section 513(a)(1)(C) states that effectiveness may be established "on the basis of well-controlled investigations, including clinical investigations *where appropriate. . . .*" Section 513(a)(3)(A) (emphasis added). Paragraph (B) then provides an alternative method for proving a device's effectiveness.

If the Secretary determines that there exists valid scientific evidence (other than evidence derived from [well-controlled investigations])—

(i) which is sufficient to determine the effectiveness of a device, and

(ii) from which it can fairly and responsibly be concluded by qualified experts that the device will have the effect it purports or is represented to have under the conditions of use prescribed, recommended, or suggested in the labeling of the device,

then . . . the Secretary may authorize the effectiveness of the device to be determined on the basis of such evidence.

There are a number of reasons why Congress, when drafting the 1976 Amendments, may have been inclined to subject medical device manufacturers seeking premarket approval to a more flexible standard of proof of safety and effectiveness than new drug sponsors. Because devices are not metabolized, their interaction with the body tends to be less complex than is the case with drugs. Moreover, as noted by one witness at hearings preceding the enactment of the 1976 Amendments: "In the determination of efficacy, drug studies permit measurements of dosages, biological levels, and responses in relation to these, whereas in devices these relationships are not present and effectiveness must often be evaluated by professional judgment rather than measurable responses." "Medical Device Amendments of 1975," Hearings before the Subcomm. on Health and the Environment of the House Comm. on Interstate and Foreign Commerce, 94th Cong., 1st Sess. 298–99 (1975) (statement by Vallee I. Willman, M.D). Finally, double-blind, placebo-controlled clinical investigations are sometimes simply not feasible or appropriate for medical devices. Surgically implanting a nonfunctioning dummy device in a patient obviously raises different issues than does administering a sugar pill.

The House Report accompanying the bill that was eventually enacted in 1976 stated the following when discussing the section 513(a)(3)(B) alternative to well-controlled investigations:

> Devices vary widely in type and in mode of operation, as well as in the scope of testing and experience they have received. Thus, the Committee has authorized the Secretary to accept meaningful data developed under procedures less rigorous than well-controlled investigations in instances in which well-documented case histories assure protection of the public health or in instances in which well-controlled investigations would present undue risks to subjects or patients.

H.R. Rep. No. 853, 94th Cong., 2d Sess. 17 (1976).

During the first 15 years of the new device regime, FDA frequently approved devices based on evidence that would have been deemed insufficient for approval of a new drug. Richard A. Merrill, *The Architecture of Government Regulation of Medical Products*, 82 VA. L. REV. 1753, 1823 (1996). In the mid-1990s, however, the agency began to assert that it expected studies for Class III devices to be as rigorous, and often as elaborate, as those required for new drugs. This apparent shift in policy followed the 1993 publication of an FDA internal committee report critical of the device review process. Final Report of the FDA Committee for Clinical Review (1993), *reprinted in* "Less Than the Sum of Its Parts: Reforms Needed in the Organization, Management, and Resources of the Food and Drug Administration's Center for Devices and Radiological Health," Subcomm. on Oversight and Investigations, House Comm. on Energy and Commerce, 103d Cong., 1st Sess., 98–163 (Comm. Print 1993). The committee was chaired by Dr. Robert Temple, the Director of CDER's Office of Drug Evaluation, and was composed almost entirely of CDER scientists. FDA Commissioner David Kessler established the Temple Committee in the midst of widespread criticism of the agency's regulation of silicone breast implants and commentary alleging a lack of rigor in CDRH's assessment of devices.

Based on its examination of a small sample of pending and approved applications for medical devices, the Temple Committee identified "certain patterns of deficiencies in the design, conduct, and analysis of clinical studies . . . in enough of the applications to suggest that these deficiencies represent a common problem." Although the committee did not directly criticize CDRH's performance, the very fact that the center had approved such flawed applications raised questions about the center's thoroughness and competence. The committee's formal recommendations included more systematic integration of biostatisticians into the review process, development of "guidance" on clinical study design for manufacturers and agency reviewers, and "adherence to the principles of sound study design throughout the review of device applications and in final decisionmaking." Importantly, the committee stated: "The fundamental principles underlying evaluation of any therapeutic intervention, whether it is a drug [or a] device . . . are the same." Commissioner Kessler endorsed the report and promised that its recommendations would be implemented.

Although the conclusion is difficult to document, it seems fair to say that FDA sets the bar higher for PMA sponsors today than it did in the years following the enactment of the Medical Device Amendments. Nevertheless, the device approval process remains less rigorous than the drug approval process. After all, the differences in the statutory standards remain. *See* Peter Barton Hutt, Richard A. Merrill & Alan M. Kirschenbaum, *The Standard of Evidence Required for Premarket Approval Under the Medical Device Amendments of 1976*, 77 FOOD & DRUG L.J. 605 (1992).

NOTE

Patient Preference Initiative. On September 18–19, 2013, FDA hosted a public workshop entitled "The Patient Preference Initiative: Incorporating Patient Preference Information into the Medical Device Regulatory Processes." According to the Federal Register notice announcing the meeting: "The purpose of the workshop is to discuss ways to incorporate patient preferences on the benefit-risk tradeoffs of medical devices into the full spectrum of the Center for Devices and Radiological Health (CDRH) regulatory decision making. It also aims to advance the science of measuring treatment preferences of patients, caregivers, and health care providers." 78 Fed. Reg. 45538 (July 29, 2013).

b.   ADVISORY COMMITTEE REVIEW

Whereas FDA's use of advisory committees in the review of NDAs, BLAs, and food additive petitions is discretionary, the agency ordinarily must refer a PMA to an advisory committee if the applicant asks that it do so. Under section 515(c)(3), added by the 1990 Act, FDA may refer a PMA application to an expert panel on its own initiative, and it must do so on the request of the applicant unless the agency finds that the information in the application substantially duplicates information which has previously been reviewed by a panel. FDA describes its implementation of this provision of the Act as follows:

In general, all PMAs for the first-of-a-kind device are taken before the appropriate advisory panel for review and recommendation. However, as soon as FDA believes that (1) the pertinent issues in determining the safety and effectiveness for the type of medical device are understood and (2) FDA has developed the ability to address those issues, future PMAs for devices of that type are not [to] be taken before an advisory panel unless a particular application presents an issue that can best be addressed through panel review.

FDA Website, Device Advice: Review Process (Sept. 3, 2013).

The panel to which FDA must refer a PMA is the appropriate classification panel organized by clinical category pursuant to section 513(b). The workload of these panels originally was dominated by the task of classifying the universe of preamendments devices into Class I, Class II, or Class III, but they now dedicate much of their time to making reports and recommendations respecting approval of PMAs.

c.   FDA ACTION ON PMAS

By statute, FDA has only 180 days after receipt of a PMA to issue an order approving or denying approval. In fact, the time from initial submission of a PMA to ultimate approval or denial can be much longer. First, FDA measures the 180-day period from the date it files the PMA, having made a threshold determination that the application is sufficiently complete to permit a substantive review. 21 C.F.R. 814.40–42. Second, the submission of any "major" PMA amendment restarts the 180-day clock, and FDA may request such an amendment. 21 C.F.R. 814.37(a)–(c). Finally, FDA does not commit itself to issuing an actual approval or denial order within the mandatory period. It deems itself compliant with the 180-day requirement if it issues an "approvable letter" or a "not approvable letter" within that time. 21 C.F.R. 814.40. An approvable letter is sent if the PMA "substantially meets the requirements [of the PMA regulations] and the agency believes it can approve the application if specific additional information is submitted or specific conditions are agreed to by the applicant." 21 C.F.R. 814.44(e). A not approvable letter, which is sent if "the agency believes that the application may not be approved," "describes the deficiencies" and, "where practical . . . identif[ies] measures required to place the PMA in approvable form." 21 C.F.R. 814.45(f). An applicant may respond to either type of letter by amending its PMA, withdrawing its PMA, or considering the letter to be a denial of approval and requesting administrative review of that denial. 21 C.F.R. 814.44(e)(2) & (f).

NOTES

1.   *Use of Data from a Prior PMA Application.* Under the 1976 Amendments, the data contained in a PMA application were considered confidential and thus could not be used by FDA or relied on by another applicant to support approval of a different PMA application for an identical or similar device. The 1990 Act added new section 520(h)(4), which, as amended by the 1997 Act, authorizes FDA, six years or more after a PMA approval, to refer to clinical and preclinical data in the

application, but not to descriptions of methods of manufacture or product composition, in approving a subsequent PMA application.

2. *Administrative Review of a PMA Decision.* If FDA denies or withdraws approval of a PMA, the applicant may petition for review of the decision. Section 515(d)(4), (e)(2). Moreover, any interested person, including any member of the public, may petition the agency for reconsideration of a PMA approval. A petitioner may seek one of two types of administrative review. First, under section 515(g)(1) the petitioner may request a formal evidentiary public hearing. *E.g.*, 47 Fed. Reg. 7877 (Feb. 23, 1982) (announcing a public hearing on a petition to withdraw premarket approval of three gonorrhea antibody test kits). Alternatively, under section 515(g)(2), the petitioner may request review by an independent advisory committee of experts. *E.g.*, 51 Fed. Reg. 19610 (May 30, 1986) (granting advisory committee review of FDA denial of a PMA for antibiotic bone cement). The reviewing committee provided in the second option must be distinct from the section 513(b) panels that advise FDA on classification and initial PMA decisions. Section 515(g)(2)(B). *See* 52 Fed. Reg. 3865 (Feb. 6, 1987) (establishing special committee for reconsideration of antibiotic bone cement PMA). FDA may deny a request for either type of review if it concludes that a hearing is not warranted.

3. *Temporary Suspension of Approval.* The 1990 Act added new section 515(e)(3), which authorizes FDA to suspend approval of a PMA application if, after providing an opportunity for an informal hearing, it determines there is a reasonable probability that use of the device would cause serious adverse health consequences or death. The agency must then proceed "expeditiously" to provide an opportunity for a hearing on whether to withdraw approval of the PMA permanently. 21 C.F.R. 814.47.

4. *Breast Implants.* Silicone gel-filled breast implants are preamendments devices. In 1988, the agency classified them into Class III, and in 1991, it required their manufacturers to file PMAs. Four manufacturers submitted applications. In October 1992, concerned about reports of a possible association between the implants and autoimmune disorders, FDA denied the PMAs for cosmetic augmentation of healthy breasts. With respect to the use of silicone gel-filled breast implants for reconstructive purposes, however, FDA invoked section 515(d)(1)(B)(i), which permits the agency to delay action on a PMA if "he finds that the continued availability of the device is necessary for the public health." The commissioner extended the review period indefinitely.

During the extended review period, FDA permitted the use of silicone gel-filled implants in any woman seeking breast reconstruction, so long as she enrolled in an open scientific protocol. Manufacturers distributed the devices for purely cosmetic purposes only under an approved IDE. 57 Fed. Reg. 45812 (Oct. 5, 1992); FDA Commissioner David A. Kessler, Statement Regarding FDA's Decision on the Distribution and Use of Silicone Gel–Filled Implants (Apr. 16, 1992). In 2002–03, FDA received two new PMAs for silicone gel-filled implants. FDA sent both manufacturers "approvable" letters in 2005 and approved both on November 17, 2006. In 2011, the agency, based on a review of data from mandatory post-approval studies, decided that silicone-gel filled breast implants should remain on the market for both breast reconstruction and enhancement. In 2013, FDA approved the PMA for a new version of the device.

d. EFFORTS TO QUICKEN THE PMA REVIEW PROCESS

FDA's implementation of the premarket approval provisions of the 1976 Amendments proved largely uncontroversial for the first decade of the new device regime. The time required for FDA review of a PMA application was approximately half that for review of an NDA. No doubt the agency's prompt processing of PMAs was in part attributable to the relatively small number of Class III postamendments devices required to go through the premarket approval process. By the late 1980s, however, these time frames had begun to lengthen significantly. The device industry and its supporters in Congress began to call for measures to quicken the PMA review process. An obvious model for achieving this goal appeared with the enactment of the Prescription Drug User Fee Act (PDUFA) of 1992, in which Congress authorized user fees to fund the drug review process and tied these fees to the achievement of performance goals. It took almost a decade, however, for Congress to institute a parallel system for devices.

The Medical Device User Fee and Modernization Act (MDUFMA) of 2002, 116 Stat. 1588, amended the FD&C Act to provide FDA with the authority to assess fees for the premarket review of PMAs and PMNs, as well as various other types of premarket submissions, for the five year period between 2002 and 2007. According to section 101(3) of the 2002 Act, "the fees authorized by this title will be dedicated to meeting the goals identified in the letters from the Secretary of Health and Human Services to the [appropriate House and Senate Committees], as set forth in the Congressional Record." This same procedure can be found in the 2007 and 2012 acts reauthorizing the fees. The FDA 20-page performance goals under the 2012 Medical Device User Fee Amendments (MDUFA III) are available on the agency's website. In addition to containing specific time goals for decisions on each type of submission and application, this document establishes procedures for presubmission meetings and telephone conferences, in an attempt to have a more interactive and timely process.

Another innovation used to speed the PMA review process is the use of "Modular" PMAs. In 1998, FDA began to allow applicants to submit discrete completed sections, or "modules," of a PMA before completing the entire PMA. This approach permitted applicants to submit, and the agency to review, preclinical data and manufacturing information while clinical data were still being collected and analyzed. The 2002 Act sanctioned this policy by adding section 515(c)(4), which provides: "Prior to submission of [a PMA], the Secretary shall accept and review any portion of the application that the applicant and the Secretary agree is complete, ready, and appropriate for review."

In spite of attempts to reform the PMA process and provide greater resources through user fees, the time required for PMA review has steadily increased. A study conducted in 2012 found that median approval times for PMAs initially declined from 610 days in 1996 to 305 days in 1997, but then increased to 400 days in 2005 and 540 days in

2008. However, a subsequent analysis suggested that the PMA review time was improving.

NOTES

1. *Expedited Review.* FDA has had some form of expedited review for medical devices used for serious conditions since 1994. The practice was mandated by Congress in the 1997 Act:

> In order to provide for more effective treatment or diagnosis of life-threatening or irreversibly debilitating human diseases or conditions, the Secretary shall provide review priority for devices—
>
> (A) representing breakthrough technologies,
>
> (B) for which no approved alternatives exist,
>
> (C) which offer significant advantages over existing approved alternatives, or
>
> (D) the availability of which is in the best interest of the patients.

Section 515(d)(5). Although this provision applies only to PMAs, the agency performs expedited review of all types of premarket submissions for devices that satisfy the statutory criteria. In 2013, FDA replaced the term "expedited review" with "priority review" to echo the statutory language. GUIDANCE FOR INDUSTRY AND FDA STAFF: PRIORITY REVIEW OF PREMARKET SUBMISSIONS FOR DEVICES (May 2013). The submitter may request priority review, but it is FDA that determines whether the device qualifies for such treatment. A PMA, PMN, or other submission granted priority review status is moved to the front of the review queue and may receive additional review resources.

2. *Product Development Protocols.* At the urging of manufacturers of cardiac pacemakers, FDA acquiesced in 1976 to the inclusion of section 515(f), which provides an alternative track for the consideration of a Class III device, termed a "product development protocol" (PDP). Under this rarely-used approach, one regulatory mechanism embraces both the investigation of the device and its marketing approval. FDA and the applicant agree in advance upon a testing program which, if completed with successful results, will result in approval. FDA may not declare a protocol complete (the equivalent of PMA approval) if it finds that "there is a lack of a showing of reasonable assurance of the safety and effectiveness of the device under the conditions of use prescribed, recommended, or suggested in the proposed labeling." Section 515(f)(6)(B)(iii). Section 513(C)(2), elaborating on the calculation of safety and effectiveness under section 515, applies equally to PDPs and PMAs. The PDP is in many respects the model for the SPA used for new drugs, *supra* p. 691, but it is used far less frequently.

Despite early expectations, only a few Class III devices have completed—or even started down—the PDP path to market. In 1991, the author of an article on the PDP process reported that, since 1976, FDA had declared only two devices appropriate for PDP treatment, and neither manufacturer had completed the PDP procedure. From 1995 to 2005, 13

PDPs were received and approved by FDA, but only two were ultimately declared completed. From 2007 to 2008, no PDPs were declared completed.

e. POSTAPPROVAL REQUIREMENTS

Section 515(d)(1)(B)(ii) of the Act explicitly provides that an order approving a PMA "may require as a condition to such approval that the sale and distribution of the device be restricted . . . to the extent [they] may be restricted under a regulation under section 520(e)." Section 520(e), examined *infra* at p. 1264, empowers FDA to issue regulations that restrict a device to sale, distribution, or use only upon prescription or "upon such other conditions as the Secretary may prescribe in such regulation."

FDA believes that its authority to impose postapproval requirements under the 1976 Amendments is not limited to restrictions on the sale, distribution, or use of a device. In its PMA regulations, the agency asserts the power to impose a wide variety of postapproval requirements, either in the PMA order itself or by regulation. 21 C.F.R. 814.82. The most common type of postapproval requirement imposed by FDA is mandatory postmarketing evaluation, reporting, or both regarding the safety and effectiveness of a device. According to its regulations, FDA may also require the prominent display of warnings or other information in the labeling of any device and in the advertising of a restricted device; the use of identification codes; the maintenance of records, including patient records; batch testing; and "[s]uch other requirements as FDA determines are necessary to provide reasonable assurance, or continued reasonable assurance, of the safety and effectiveness of the device."

When FDA proposed its initial PMA regulations, some comments challenged the agency's right to impose postapproval requirements other than restrictions on sale or distribution. FDA dismissed these arguments. 51 Fed. Reg. 26342, 26359 (July 22, 1986). Subsequent amendments to the FD&C Act have provided FDA with explicit authority to impose various types of postapproval requirements. For example, the 1997 Act amended section 522 to authorize FDA to order a manufacturer to conduct postmarketing surveillance of a Class III or Class II device if the device's failure is "reasonably likely to have serious adverse health consequences," and the device is either (1) intended to be implanted for more than one year or (2) is a life sustaining or life supporting device used outside a device user facility. 21 C.F.R. 822; GUIDANCE FOR INDUSTRY AND FDA STAFF: POSTMARKET SURVEILLANCE UNDER SECTION 522 (Apr. 2006).

5. REGULATION OF IN VITRO DIAGNOSTIC DEVICES

FDA defines "in vitro diagnostic products" (IVDs) as "those reagents, instruments, and systems intended for use in the diagnosis of disease or other conditions, including a determination of the state of health, in order to cure, mitigate, treat, or prevent disease or its sequelae. Such products are intended for use in the collection, preparation, and examination of specimens taken from the human body." 21 C.F.R. 809.3(a). The regulation of IVDs presents distinctive issues, and a separate office within CDRH, the Office of In Vitro

Diagnostic Device Evaluation and Safety (OIVD), is dedicated to these products. The Center for Biologics Evaluation and Research (CBER), rather than CDRH, regulates IVD devices involved in the collection, processing, testing, manufacture, and administration of blood, blood components, and cellular products. CBER also regulates all HIV test kits used either to screen blood and cellular products or to diagnose and treat people with HIV and AIDS.

FDA has issued regulations focused solely on IVD devices. For example, as noted previously, FDA rules establish an exemption from the IDE requirements for diagnostic devices labeled "For Research Use Only" or "For Investigational Use Only." *Supra* p. 1232. FDA has also, by regulation, created a special labeling regime for IVD products. 21 C.F.R. 809.10. Moreover, the agency has issued two restricted device regulations regulating the sale, distribution, and use of particular types of IVD devices. 21 C.F.R. 809.30 & .40.

On its website, FDA recognizes that a PMA for an IVD presents unique issues:

> PMA approval is based on scientific evidence providing a reasonable assurance that the device is safe and effective for its intended use or uses. For IVDs, there is a unique link between safety and effectiveness since the safety of the device is not generally related to contact between the device and patient. For IVD products, the safety of the device relates to the impact of the device's performance, and in particular on the impact of false negative and false positive results, on patient health.

"Overview of IVD Regulation," FDA Website (Sept. 3, 2010). Although the agency has not formally established any special PMA, BLA, or PMN requirements for IVDs, it has published numerous guidance and draft guidance documents advising manufacturers on the investigation of IVD products and the preparation of successful premarket submissions for them.

In 1988, Congress enacted the Clinical Laboratory Improvement Amendments (CLIA), 102 Stat. 2903, which established quality standards for laboratory testing and an accreditation program for clinical laboratories. Although the Centers for Medicare & Medicaid Services (CMS) (formerly the Health Care Financing Administration (HCFA)) has primary responsibility for overseeing the CLIA program, OIVD also has an important role in implementing the law.

Under CLIA, it is illegal for a laboratory that has not been federally certified to "solicit or accept materials derived from the human body for . . . examination." Laboratories are subject to different levels of regulation depending on the nature of the tests they perform. CLIA and its implementing regulations, 43 C.F.R. Part 493, establish three categories of testing based on the complexity of the testing methodology: (1) waived tests, (2) tests of moderate complexity, and (3) tests of high complexity. Laboratories performing only waived tests are subject to minimal regulation, whereas laboratories performing moderate or high complexity tests are subject to specific laboratory standards governing personnel, proficiency testing, patient test management, quality assurance, quality control, and inspections. Although FDA was initially given the task of categorizing commercially marketed IVD products for

CLIA purposes, it delegated it to the Centers for Disease Control and Prevention (CDC) in 1994. In 2000, FDA reassumed this responsibility. 64 Fed. Reg. 73561 (Dec. 30, 1999). OIVD determines the appropriate complexity categories for clinical laboratory devices as it evaluates premarket submissions.

One area of recent controversy has been FDA's authority over "laboratory developed tests" (LDTs), a class of in vitro diagnostics that are developed, manufactured, validated, and offered within a single laboratory. The laboratories performing such tests are subject to CLIA. Although FDA has long maintained that LDTs are medical devices subject to the agency's authority, until recently it usually stated that it would exercise its "enforcement discretion" over LDTs and not regulate them pursuant to the FD&C Act. However, various FDA communications in June 2010, including untitled letters sent to genetic testing companies and an opinion piece in the *New England Journal of Medicine* coauthored by Commissioner Margaret Hamburg, suggested a change in this position. On June 17, FDA published a notice of a July public meeting on "Oversight of Laboratory Developed Tests." 75 Fed. Reg. 34463 (June 17, 2010). In this notice, FDA explained that "[i]n response to . . . public health concerns, the agency believes it is time to reconsider its policy of enforcement discretion over LDTs." *Id.* at 34464. At the July 19–20 workshop itself, FDA officials indicated that they planned to regulate at least some LDTs as medical devices, although they had not yet determined the details of the regulatory scheme. FDA's next step remains unclear.

6. HUMANITARIAN DEVICE EXEMPTIONS

In the 1990 Act, Congress added section 520(m), to encourage the development of devices intended to benefit patients in the diagnosis and treatment of diseases that affect fewer than 4,000 individuals in the United States. FDA regulations implementing this section call these Class III products "humanitarian use devices" (HUDs). 21 C.F.R. Part 814, Subpart H. Under these regulations, a device manufacturer may apply for a "humanitarian device exemption" (HDE) that allows a HUD to be marketed "notwithstanding the absence of reasonable assurance of effectiveness that would otherwise be required under sections 514 and 515 of the act." 21 C.F.R. 814.100(a)(2).

To acquire an HDE, a sponsor must first request a formal designation of HUD status from FDA's Office of Orphan Products Development. To receive such designation, the sponsor must provide sufficient evidence to establish that the disease or condition intended to be treated or diagnosed by the device affects fewer than 4,000 people in the United States per year. If the agency designates the product as a HUD, the sponsor then files an HDE application with CDRH. The application generally must contain all the information required to be in a PMA, except that it need only include "reasonably obtainable" clinical data. 21 C.F.R. 814.104(b)(4). The HDE applicant must aver that no "comparable" device is available to treat or diagnose the condition. Like a PMA applicant, a person submitting an HDE application must provide "reasonable assurance that the device is safe under the conditions of use prescribed, recommended, or suggested in the labeling." But instead of also providing reasonable assurance of effectiveness, a HDE application need only satisfy FDA that "the probable benefit to health from the use of the device outweighs the risk of injury or illness from its use, taking into account the probable risks and benefits of currently available devices or alternative forms of treatment." *Id.* 814.104(b)(3).

Section 520(m)(3) limits the price of an HUD to "the costs of research and development, fabrication, and distribution of the device." Under the 2007 Act, however, this limitation does not apply to pediatric HUDs. The 2012 Act extends this exemption to any HUD device where development of the device would otherwise be "impossible, highly impracticable, or unsafe."

An HDE constitutes full marketing approval. Unlike a device with an approved IDE, an approved HUD is not an investigational device and does not require informed consent. Section 520(m)(4) requires, however, that except in emergency situations, a device granted an HDE may be used only in facilities in which an IRB has approved its use.

NOTE

Orphan Devices. As discussed previously, *supra* p. 758, the Orphan Drug Act of 1983 provided for financial assistance, in the form of grants and contracts, to defray the cost of developing "orphan drugs" for rare diseases (diseases suffered by fewer than 200,000 Americans). The Orphan Drug Amendments of 1988, 102 Stat. 90, extended this provision to medical devices. Consequently, under 21 U.S.C. 360ee, FDA "may make grants to and enter into contracts with public and private entities and individuals to assist in . . . (2) defraying the costs of developing medical devices for rare diseases or conditions. . . ."

7.   CUSTOM DEVICES

As amended in 2012, Section 520(b) of the FD&C Act provides that the requirements of sections 514 (performance standards) and 515 (premarket approval) do not apply to any device which, to comply with the order of an individual physician or dentist, necessarily deviates from an otherwise applicable performance standard or approved PMA application. This "custom device" exemption applies only if the device is not generally available for commercial distribution in finished form and is made pursuant to a physician's or dentist's order "on a case-by-case basis to accommodate the unique needs" of either the physician or dentist or an individual patient. FDA regulations exempt custom devices from the IDE requirement "unless the device is being used to determine safety or effectiveness for commercial distribution." 21 C.F.R. 812.2(c)(7).

In *Contact Lens Manufacturers Ass'n v. FDA*, 766 F.2d 592 (D.C. Cir. 1985), the manufacturers contended that soft lenses were custom devices and thus exempt from the classification scheme. The court, interpreting the pre-2012 version of 520(b), upheld FDA's rejection of this claim. It noted that soft lenses, as a class, are generally available "within an approved range of powers ... and contours," and that most prescriptions are likely to be replicated. *Id.* at 599. *Cf. Sharp v. Artifex*, 110 F. Supp. 2d 388, 395 (W.D. Pa. 1999) ("We hold that given the narrow reading of the statute in *Contact Lens Manufacturers Association*, there is a material issue of fact as to whether the Defendant's [pedical screw fixation] device falls within the custom device exemption."). In a 1983 advisory opinion, FDA took the position that a custom device may not be a "standardized modification" of a marketed device, may not be "commercially distributed," and must be "made in a specific form for a patient named in the order of a physician or intended to meet the special needs of such physician in the course of his or her professional practice." FDA Associate Commissioner for Regulatory Affairs J.P. Hile to B. Gersh, FDA Docket No. 82A–0264 (March 7, 1983).

Congress rewrote section 520(b) in 2012 because of continuing controversy about the scope of the custom device exception. In the amended version, some of the requirements appear to be loosened and others to be tightened. Many ambiguities remain. Under the revised provision, production of a custom device is limited to five per year "of a particular device type." FD&C Act 520(b)(2)(B).

8. RECLASSIFICATION AND *DE NOVO* CLASSIFICATION OF NOVEL DEVICES

Under section 513(f)(3)(A), the manufacturer of a postamendments device that is not substantially equivalent to a preamendments device, and thus is presumptively a Class III product required to obtain premarket approval under 513(f)(1), may instead petition FDA to reclassify the device into Class II or I. If reclassified, the device may be marketed immediately. A successful reclassification petition results in a new classification regulation for that device, published in the Federal Register and later inserted into the Code of Federal Regulations.

The 1997 Act created another procedural option for the manufacturer of a postamendments device with no substantially equivalent predicate. Under section 513(f)(2), if FDA responds to a PMN for a new device with a "not substantially equivalent" (NSE) determination, presumptively classifying it into Class III, the manufacturer may, within 30 days, request FDA instead to classify the device into Class I or Class II. This is called the "*de novo* process." Within 60 days of receiving such a request, the agency must classify the device by rulemaking. If the agency classifies the device into Class I, the manufacturer is free to start marketing the device immediately. If it is classified into Class II, marketing cannot begin until the PMN is cleared by FDA. Moreover, the device becomes a predicate for other PMN submissions. Like a successful section 513(f)(3) reclassification petition, this procedure results in the addition of a new classification regulation for the device in the CFR. However, the section 513(f)(2) process, as a formal matter, is not one of "reclassification," because the Act states that a classification under this provision "shall be the initial classification of the device." GUIDANCE FOR INDUSTRY AND CDRH STAFF: NEW SECTION 513(F)(2): EVALUATION OF AUTOMATIC CLASS III DESIGNATION (Feb. 1998).

The 2012 Act further streamlined the *de novo* process, in two respects. If the sponsor knows that there is no predicate, the sponsor can proceed directly to request reclassification without having first to submit a pointless PMN. Moreover, initial classification into Class I or Class II can now be accomplished by FDA through a simple "order" without the need for formal notice-and-comment rulemaking. FD&C Act 513(f)(2)(A)(ii), (B)(i).

Even with the advent of the section 513(f)(2) procedure, a manufacturer may still choose instead to file a reclassification petition under section 513(f)(3). The reclassification petition process does not require prior submission of a PMN, nor is it limited to requests submitted within 30 days following receipt of an NSE determination.

For the manufacturer of a new device with no substantially equivalent predicate, the key question, of course, is whether section 513(f)(3) reclassification or section 513(f)(2) *de novo* classification can be accomplished more speedily or with less safety and effectiveness data than approval of a PMA application. The section 513(f)(2) process, with its 60-day time limit, may lead to quicker classifications into Class I or Class II than the older reclassification petition procedure, which presumes that FDA will routinely refer petitions to an expert panel and gives FDA up to 210 days to reach a final decision. Section 513(f)(3)(B)(i), (C)(i). In its guidance document on section 513(f)(2), FDA retains the option of requesting input from an advisory panel but recognizes that the agency must nonetheless complete its review within 60 days. Despite its time advantages, however, the new section 513(f)(2) process does not reduce the manufacturer's burden of providing data. A manufacturer making a section 513(f)(2) request must present FDA with the same types of information submitted in a traditional reclassification petition.

Reclassification of a new postamendments device by petition has rarely provided a shortcut to the market. FDA granted three such petitions in 2003, but that was the only year in the past 20 in which the agency granted more than one. Many years, FDA has granted no section 513(f)(3) reclassification petitions. For a time, the section 513(f)(2) *de novo* approach appeared to be a somewhat more successful strategy, but FDA grants of such classification requests have slowed to a trickle. In short, entry into the market through either initial classification into Class I or Class II or reclassification into one of these classes remains a minor feature in the overall scheme of device regulation. This may change, however, with enactment of the 2012 Act.

If the statutory definition of Class I had been read literally, sections 513(f)(2) and 513(f)(3) might have become popular methods for bringing harmless but unproven postamendments devices onto the market. That definition embraces low-risk devices for nonserious conditions, regardless of the amount of safety and effectiveness data available. FD&C Act 513(a)(1)(A)(ii). One clever manufacturer believed that the reclassification petition offered a potential loophole by which he could introduce a new device onto the market as a Class I product.

Lake v. FDA

Med. Devices Rep. (CCH) ¶ 15,117, 1989 WL 71554 (E.D. Pa. 1989).

■ AHN, DISTRICT JUDGE.

Mr. Lake was the inventor of the Inductive Nasal Device ("IND"), which he maintained could cure the common cold and allergies. Despite these extraordinary claims and the appropriately august name attached to the invention, the IND is, essentially, a nose clip. Mr. Lake repeatedly attempted to obtain Food and Drug Administration approval to market the IND. The FDA, however, was unconvinced of the efficacy of the invention and refused to approve its sale as a cure for colds and allergies. Plaintiff now challenges the FDA decision. . . . [F]or the reasons that follow, defendants' motion for summary judgment will be granted.

The FDA was first called on to review the IND in 1979. The invention was automatically considered a Class III device pursuant to 21 U.S.C. § 360c(f)(1). . . . In order to sell the IND, Mr. Lake either had to procure approval of the PMA or get the IND reclassified out of Class III.

In 1983, Mr. Lake filed a PMA, but the FDA denied his application. The FDA cited numerous deficiencies, including a lack of scientific evidence demonstrating the safety and effectiveness of the device. Mr. Lake amended the PMA, but the FDA still found the petition lacking because no clinical trials had been held.

Realizing that the first route to market, the PMA process, had been foreclosed, Mr. Lake tried the second route; he filed a reclassification petition. He asserted the IND was properly a Class I device. Under 21 U.S.C. § 360c(f)(2) [now 360c(f)(3)], the Secretary is empowered to review reclassification petitions for "deficiencies," and if none are found, then the Secretary must refer the petition to a panel of experts for consideration. The FDA rejected Mr. Lake's original petition because it failed . . . to provide valid scientific evidence of the safety and effectiveness of the device. . . . Mr. Lake's attorney then wrote to the FDA, which responded:

> Not only is the petition devoid of "valid scientific evidence", but even if a reclassification was possible, the agency would regulate the device as misbranded. The agency's view is that no device will prevent or cure the common cold and that such a claim would be false or misleading.

> . . . .

[The plaintiff argues] that the FDA violated the Medical Device Amendments of 1976, 21 U.S.C. §§ 360c–360k, by making it too difficult to procure reclassification into Class I.

[The FD&C Act defines "Class I" to include not only a device for which general controls are sufficient to provide reasonable assurance of safety and effectiveness, but also a device for which insufficient information exists to provide this assurance if the device:]

> (I) is not purported or represented to be for use in supporting or sustaining human life or for a use which is of substantial importance in preventing impairment of human health, and

(II) does not present a potential unreasonable risk of illness or injury. . . .

21 U.S.C. § 360c(a)(1)(A). . . .

Plaintiff raises an interesting question of statutory interpretation. § 360c(a)(1)(A)(ii) provides for the marketing of devices which are unproven to be "safe and effective" and which do not provide an "unreasonable risk of illness or injury." Thus, it is possible that a small Class of devices unproven as safe, but without demonstrable risks could be reclassified into Class I. As one court has recognized: "Congress contemplated that a device not both safe and effective might be able to enter the stream of commerce, although such a device has to meet conditions so narrow that no actual device may fall into the category." *General Medical Co. v. United States Food and Drug Admin.*, 770 F.2d 214, 222 (1985). . . . In applying [360c(a)(1)(A)(ii)] to the facts of the case, the *General Medical* court held that because there was some minimal evidence of minor harm and no benefits, the harm outweighed the benefits, and the risk of injury was therefore unreasonable.

The case at bar, however, goes one step beyond *General Medical*. There is nothing in the record demonstrating even minor harm from the IND. The FDA stands solely only on its interpretation of the statute that a lack of evidence presents an unreasonable risk.

The FDA's interpretation is valid. It could not have been the intent of Congress to allow the marketing of unproven medical devices about which no scientific evidence is available. To hold otherwise would allow people to market all manner of fraudulent devices. We are long past the day when snake oil can be sold with impunity. Plaintiff's reading of the statute would shift the burden of proof to the FDA and that is not how our public health laws are designed to work. When there is no valid scientific evidence of efficacy, and the risks are unknown, the risk is unreasonable.

. . . [T]he legislative history defined "potential unreasonable risk of illness or injury" [in FD&C Act 513(a)(1)(A)(ii)] as a risk which is "simply foreseeable" and "[t]he fact that a device is being marketed without sufficient testing is an adequate basis for the Secretary's conclusion that the device presents a potential unreasonable risk to health." H.R. Rep. 853, at 36. . . .

In this case it is not hard to see why additional proof of safety is required. The closing of an infected or irritated nose may well have negative, not positive effects on the course of illness. In addition, anyone who fails to see an allergist because he believes the IND will help, may harm himself. Anyone who avoids bed rest believing the IND will cure him, may suffer all manner of subsequent illnesses caused by inattention to a cold. Attorneys are trained to pose hypotheticals like these, but only medical experts can answer them. I am a jurist, not a physician. It is uniquely within the ken of the FDA to make determinations of the safety and effectiveness of medical devices. For this reason, I will defer to the FDA's decision on the IND. Defendants' motion for summary judgment will be granted. . . .

NOTES

1. *Effect of Change in Law?* The court in *Lake* remarks on the absurdity of referring a petition containing no evidence to an expert panel. At the time of the decision, the FD&C Act required FDA to refer all nondeficient reclassification petitions to an advisory committee. The 1990 Act, however, made referral to a panel discretionary rather than mandatory. Section 513(f)(3)(B)(i).

2. *Distinction from Reclassification of Preamendments Devices.* The section 513(f) procedures discussed in this subsection concern the *de novo* classification and reclassification of postenactment devices with no substantially equivalent preamendments predicate. They are alternative methods for a manufacturer to get a completely new postenactment device onto the market. Section 513(f) reclassification should not be confused with section 513(e) and 515(i) reclassification of already-classified preamendments devices, discussed *supra* at p. 1216.

H. SPECIAL CONTROLS FOR CLASS II DEVICES

Class II devices are those "which cannot be classified as a Class I device because . . . general controls by themselves are insufficient to provide reasonable assurance of [safety and effectiveness], and for which there is sufficient information to establish special controls to provide such assurance." FD&C Act 513(a)(1)(B). As originally enacted in 1976, this provision referred not to "special controls" in general but only to "performance standards." In the 1990 Act, Congress revised section 513(a)(1)(B) to authorize a broad array of "special controls," of which performance standards are only one listed example. Today, as discussed below, other kinds of special controls, particularly guidance documents, are far more important than performance standards in the regulation of Class II devices.

1. PERFORMANCE STANDARDS

a. INTRODUCTION

FDA's reliance on performance standards predates the enactment of the 1976 Amendments. Prior to 1976, FDA promulgated a standard for impact-resistant lenses in eyeglasses and sunglasses. 37 Fed. Reg. 2503 (Feb. 2, 1972), presently codified at 21 C.F.R. 801.410. In 1972, as part of its decision to regulate *in vitro* diagnostic products without ruling whether they were drugs or devices, *supra* p. 1200, FDA established a procedure for establishing "product Class standards," as well as detailed labeling requirements, for IVD products. 33 Fed. Reg. 7096 (Mar. 15, 1973). In 1976, the agency made available a draft standard for IVD products intended for the detection or measurement of glucose or total sugars. 41 Fed. Reg. 22394 (June 3, 1976). FDA also published notices requesting information to establish standards for other in vitro diagnostic products.

The 1976 Amendments established a procedure for the formal promulgation of performance standards under new section 514, modeled on the provisions governing standards under the Consumer Product

Safety Act, 15 U.S.C. 2056 & 2058. As enacted in 1976, section 514 provided that FDA "may" establish performance standards. FDA officials involved in drafting the original legislation carefully chose this language to negate any implication that the agency was obligated to establish a performance standard for every Class II device or to adopt standards in accordance with any fixed schedule. It was their expectation that the provision for performance standards, like the requirement for approval of preamendments Class III devices, would be implemented in accordance with priorities to be determined in the future and in light of the resources then available to the agency. Even if FDA had been inclined to quickly issue a large number of performance standards, it could not practically have done so. The procedure originally established by section 514 for the promulgation of performance standards was extraordinarily complex and drawn-out.

Indeed, by the time Congress enacted the 1990 Act, FDA had not finalized a single performance standard. The 1990 Act amended section 514 to permit the agency to promulgate performance standards through ordinary notice-and-comment rulemaking, with a few special requirements. *See* FD&C Act 514(b)(1)(B) (mandating specific content in a notice of proposed rulemaking for the establishment of a performance standard); 514(b)(5)(A)(ii) (FDA must, upon request of interested person demonstrating "good cause," refer proposed performance standard to advisory committee). To date, however, FDA has published only one final performance standard. This standard, published in 1997, applies to electrode lead wires and patient cables, which are components of devices such as breathing frequency monitors and electrocardiographs. 21 C.F.R. Part 898. The regulation, intended to prevent patient contact with power sources, states: "Any connector in a cable or electrode lead wire having a conductive connection to a patient shall be constructed in such a manner as to comply with subclause 56.3(c) of [International Electrotechnical Commission (IEC) standard 601–1, Medical Electrical Equipment, general requirements for safety]." 21 C.F.R. 898.12.

FDA has proposed, but then withdrawn, performance standards for a few additional devices, including vascular graft prostheses and continuous ventilators, 59 Fed. Reg. 3042 (Jan. 20, 1994) (withdrawal of proposed rule), and infant apnea monitors, 65 Fed. Reg. 57303 (Sept. 22, 2000) (withdrawal of proposed rule).

b.   VOLUNTARY MEDICAL DEVICE STANDARDS

Shortly after enactment of the 1976 Amendments, FDA described its activities to encourage and support the development of performance standards for devices by private organizations and associations:

> The Food and Drug Administration intends to continue to promote such voluntary efforts because they contribute to assuring the safety and effectiveness of marketed devices. Voluntary or privately recognized performance standards will not be a substitute for the formal promulgation of standards under section 514 of the act for any device that is classified in the performance standard category. However, voluntary or privately recognized standards can serve as informal standards prior to classification as well as during the development of formal standards for devices that are not

candidates for immediate attention, and they may be the basis for subsequent formal FDA standards.

41 Fed. Reg. 34099, 34100 (Aug. 12, 1976).

Four years later, when FDA issued final regulations establishing its procedures for developing performance standards, it simultaneously acknowledged that it lacked the resources to establish performance standards for all Class II devices. 45 Fed. Reg. 7474 & 7490 (Feb. 1, 1980). The agency proposed a policy of endorsing particular voluntary standards, encouraging manufacturers of devices conforming to these standards to label them as such, and deferring development of mandatory standards if there were adequate voluntary compliance. Subsequently, however, FDA abandoned its proposal to endorse voluntary standards, because manufacturers might mistake such standards as mandatory. The agency also discarded its suggestion that it might defer the establishment of a formal performance standard for a Class II device based solely on adequate compliance with an agency-endorsed voluntary standard. 50 Fed. Reg. 43060 (Oct. 23, 1985). "FDA now believes that it should focus its limited resources on setting priorities for, and initiating proceedings to establish, performance standards, rather than on endorsement and promotion of voluntary standards."

In the 1997 Act, Congress, for the first time, required FDA to recognize voluntary device standards, but as an aid to premarket submissions, not as a substitute for mandatory performance standards. Under new section 514(c), FDA "shall, by publication in the Federal Register, recognize all or part of an appropriate standard established by a nationally or internationally recognized standard development organization for which a person may submit a declaration of conformity in order to meet a premarket submission requirement or other requirement under this Act to which such standard is applicable." FDA refers to section 514(c) standards as "consensus standards" and maintains a list of those it has recognized on the CDRH website. Under section 514(c), a manufacturer filing a PMN, PMA, or other premarket submission may include a "declaration of conformity" to a recognized standard. Conformity to a recognized standard usually conclusively establishes substantial equivalence of safety and effectiveness for those aspects of a device addressed by the standard. *See* GUIDANCE FOR INDUSTRY AND FDA: RECOGNITION AND USE OF CONSENSUS STANDARDS (Sept. 2007); GUIDANCE FOR INDUSTRY AND FDA STAFF: FREQUENTLY ASKED QUESTIONS ON THE RECOGNITION OF CONSENSUS STANDARDS (Sept. 2007).

In the past 15 years, FDA has increasingly designated voluntary standards as special controls for Class II devices. At first blush, this approach seems effectively identical to the incorporation of a voluntary standard into a mandatory performance standard. There is an important difference, however. Whereas failure to comply with a formal performance standard automatically adulterates a device under section 501(e)(1), the same is not true for violations of other types of special controls, which are discussed in more detail below.

2. OTHER SPECIAL CONTROLS

While FDA has largely abandoned formal performance standards, it has liberally embraced other types of special controls for Class II devices. Although the agency acquired the statutory authority to impose special controls other than performance standards in 1990, as late as 1997 it had implemented such special controls only sparingly. Today, by contrast, approximately three-fourths of the classification regulations for Class II devices incorporate one or more special controls.

Special controls other than performance standards include: "postmarket surveillance, patient registries, development and dissemination of guidelines (including guidelines for the submission of clinical data in premarket notification submissions in accordance with section 510(k)), recommendations, and other appropriate actions." Section 513(a)(1)(B). FDA uses guidance documents far more than any other type of special control. It has issued guidances as special controls for the majority of Class II devices. The second most common type of special control is a voluntary standard set by a private standard-setting organization. FDA has also, more rarely, used other types of special controls, either alone or in combination with guidance, standards, or both. *See, e.g.* 21 C.F.R. 864.9245(b) (annual report requirement for "automated blood cell separator"); 21 C.F.R. 866.3332(b)(2) (limitation of distribution of "reagents for detection of specific novel influenza A viruses" to laboratories with specified training, expertise and procedures); 21 C.F.R. 870.5550(b)(2) (limitations on the maximum pulse amplitude and duration for "external transcutaneous cardiac pacemaker"); 21 C.F.R. 872.1745(b) (restriction to prescription sale and special PMN content and labeling requirements for "laser fluorescence caries detection device").

I. GENERAL CONTROLS APPLICABLE TO ALL DEVICES

All marketed devices, regardless of their date of introduction or classification, are subject to the following general regulatory controls, unless specifically exempted from them.

1. TRADITIONAL ADULTERATION AND MISBRANDING

The device regime established in 1976 is enforced through sections 501 and 502, the FD&C Act's adulteration and misbranding provisions for drugs and devices. For example, a device is adulterated if it is a Class II device that fails to comply with a performance standard or a Class III device that fails to conform to the premarket approval requirement. FD&C Act 501(e) & (f). Similarly, a device is misbranded if its manufacturer fails to comply with the section 510(k) premarket notification requirement. *Id.* 502(o). Failure to comply with other statutory requirements, to be discussed below, also constitutes adulteration or misbranding.

Misbranding and adulteration also retain the meanings they had under the 1938 Act. For instance, section 501(a) declares that a device is adulterated "[i]f it consists in whole or in part of any filthy, putrid, or decomposed substance; or if it has been prepared, packed, or held under insanitary conditions whereby it may have been contaminated with filth, or whereby it may have been rendered injurious to health." Section 502(a) provides that a device is misbranded "[i]f its labeling is false or misleading in any particular," and section 502(f) states that it is misbranded "[u]nless its labeling bears adequate directions for use." These provisions apply to all medical devices, but they can be difficult to enforce. It is much easier for FDA to establish a violation of the PMA requirement, for example, than a violation of one of the broadly-phrased adulteration and misbranding prohibitions. The traditional adulteration and misbranding provisions are thus relatively unimportant regulatory tools for Class III devices, which are subject to the PMA mandate. By contrast, for preamendments Class I and Class II devices (and their postamendments substantial equivalents), the agency sometimes has no choice but to rely on traditional, and often difficult to prove, charges of adulteration or misbranding.

United States v. An Article . . . Acu–Dot

483 F. Supp. 1311 (N. D. Ohio 1980).

■ LAMBROS, DISTRICT JUDGE.

This action is the result of a libel of information brought by the United States of America for the condemnation of numerous cases of an over-the-counter medical device called an Acu-dot . . .

. . . [T]he sole issue presented to this Court at trial was this: are the Acu-dot devices "misbranded" within the meaning of 21 U.S.C. § 352?

In simple terms, the Acu-dot is a small, pin-head sized magnet attached to the underside of a circular, adhesive patch. It is sold to the public in sheets of ten, packaged in a flat, cardboard box. Inside the box, in addition to the sheet of ten Acu-dots, can be found a four-page pamphlet, purporting to be instructions for the use of the device. The . . . cardboard box reads in this way:

ACU–DOT Magnetic Analgesic Patch

For temporary relief of occasional minor aches and pains of
muscles and joints.

Contains 10 Patches

. . . .

Directions for use:

Apply fingertip pressure to sensitive area to determine point or points of sharpest pain or discomfort. Thoroughly clean and dry area and apply an adhesive-backed ACU–DOT to each such point.

. . . .

I.

The majority of the evidence presented both by the government and by claimant-intervenor went to the first of the two "misbranding" issues—is the labeling "false or misleading in any particular"? 21 U.S.C. § 352(a). Libellant, in presenting its case, specifically attacked the descriptions of the devices as "magnetic analgesic patch(es)" and "for temporary relief of occasional minor aches and pains of muscles and joints".

Libellant offered the testimony of three experts—one biophysicist and two medical doctors. These experts were adduced to show that none of the theories offered by claimant-intervenor were valid explanations for the mechanism by which the devices were to achieve their results. Further, each expert testified to his belief that the devices could not achieve the effect alleged by the labeling, other than through a placebo effect.

On behalf of the effectiveness of the res, claimant-intervenor presented several theories for the mechanism of the device. At various times, it was suggested that the magnetic action of the device "drew" blood to the affected area, which action had the therapeutic effect; that the blood, being composed in part of iron-based chemicals, produced an electromotive force within the body when passing through the field of the magnet, much in the way electric generators produce electricity by moving an electric wire through a magnetic field; that the pressure of the device against the skin creates therapeutic effects in a way analogous to acupuncture techniques; that the ionization of molecules in the skin area under the magnet caused the therapeutic effect claimed; and, finally, that the claimed beneficial effect of the device was achieved largely as a result of the psychosomatic placebo response.[3] These various theories were suggested by the teachings of the patent said to include the res, by the theories presented in an article written by Kyoichi Nakagawa, M.D., one of a number of Japanese researchers attempting to analyze the mechanism of an identical device now in wide currency in Japan, and, most importantly, by the empirical results of an experiment conducted by Rocco Antenucci, M.D., an Akron area family physician who testified at the hearing.

The most impressive evidence on behalf of the res was the result of the Antenucci study. That study purported to be a double-blind comparison of the Acu-dots with non-magnetized facsimiles. Of the 70 patients receiving the facsimiles, 10 indicated some degree of pain relief. Of the 152 patients receiving the Acu-dots, 138 reported some degree of pain relief. These figures are impressive and argue strongly for the therapeutic claims.

However, each of the government witnesses was able to suggest major flaws in the conception and execution of the test protocol. Considerable doubt was also cast on the Nakagawa study and the Court was finally left with this problem: libellant could demonstrate that the therapeutic claims of the device could not be explained by any reasonable theory that did not rely on a "placebo" explanation, but had no empirical evidence of the lack of efficacy; claimant-intervenor had very weak theoretical support for the mechanism of the device, and vested its claims in unexplained empirical evidence. . . .

After careful consideration of all of the evidence, this Court finds that any therapeutic value of the res is the result of its placebo effect,

---

[3] This last theory—the "placebo effect"—cannot be dismissed lightly. Expert witnesses testified that current medical theory explains the placebo relief of pain as being mediated by the release of "endorphins" within the body. . . . This explanation suggests to the Court that a placebo cannot be dismissed as "ineffective" simply because it works its effect in a way more oblique than standard therapeutic treatments. As is seen *infra* in this opinion, the real difficulty of this case is that a "placebo" can work only by means of the artifice of its presentation to the patient—the patient must be misled as to its inherent effectiveness. . . .

and that this placebo effect is very strong in the case of ailments for which the device is claimed effective. Thus, the device often can achieve its claims of providing "temporary relief of occasional minor aches and pains of muscles and joints"; but this effect is the result of nothing more than sophisticated marketing chicanery.

This Court hastens to affirm here its belief in the right of the American public to seek any treatment it wishes, especially when that treatment is a harmless, if ineffective, drug or device. The Court further wishes to make plain that it in no way desires to allow a governmental agency to emasculate the constitutional right to seek desired medical treatment enunciated in *Roe v. Wade*, 410 U.S. 113 (1973). There is a difference, however, between the right to use a harmless, ineffective drug or device and a claimed right to promote and profit from the drug or device. . . . Judge Bohanon, speaking for the district court for the Western District of Oklahoma, explained this distinction in *Rutherford v. United States*, 438 F. Supp. 1287 (1977), at 1300–1301:

> . . . By denying the right to use a nontoxic substance in connection with one's own personal health-care, FDA has offended the constitutional right of privacy.

> This court's decision in this case in no way portends the return of the traveling snake oil salesman. . . . [T]he right to use a harmless, unproven remedy is quite distinct from any alleged right to promote such. FDA is fully empowered under other statutory provisions to combat false or fraudulent advertising of ineffectual or unproven drugs.

This Court resists the impulse to allow claimant to market a product that works only by means of a placebo effect on the basis that it nevertheless often achieves a relief of pain as claimed. The strong placebo effect may save the res from claims of "false labeling" under 21 U.S.C. § 352(a), but it does not protect the device from the charge that the labeling is "misleading" under 21 U.S.C. § 352(a), and that is all that is required to warrant condemnation of the res. The device's label is "misleading" because the device is not inherently effective, its results being attributable to the psychosomatic effect produced by the advertising and marketing of the device. A kiss from mother on the affected area would serve just as well to relieve pain, if mother's kisses were marketed as effectively as the Acu-dot device.

This Court finds that the device is "misbranded" under 21 U.S.C. § 352, and properly subject to seizure and condemnation under 21 U.S.C. § 334, even though the claims are not technically false, because the claims are inherently misleading. . . .

———

Under its section 701(a) authority "to promulgate regulations for the efficient enforcement of this Act," FDA has issued rules setting forth specific labeling that must be used to avoid misbranding of particular types of devices. *E.g.*, 21 C.F.R. 801.405 (labeling for denture repair and refitting products); 801.420 (hearing aid labeling); 801.435 (latex condoms). FDA used this approach in prescribing labeling for menstrual tampons. Following discovery of the association between tampons, which are Class II devices, and toxic shock syndrome (TSS), FDA mandated a strong warning statement on the package label and the provision of detailed consumer information in a package insert. 47 Fed. Reg. 26982 (June 22, 1982), codified at 21 C.F.R. 801.430(a)–(d). The following year, FDA asked the American Society for Testing and Materials (ASTM) to devise a performance standard for tampons regarding absorbency testing and labeling, but the ASTM task force was unable to reach agreement. The principal tampon manufacturers then each consented to take voluntary action, but while they agreed on an absorbency testing method, they adopted different approaches to providing label information about absorbency. FDA thus proposed to establish a uniform test for absorbency and a uniform letter designation, from A (the lowest degree of absorbency) to F (the highest degree of absorbency), for purposes of product labeling. 53 Fed. Reg. 37250 (Sept. 23, 1988). Comments from the public, however, caused the agency to revise this approach.

Medical Devices; Labeling for Menstrual Tampons; Ranges of Absorbency; Reproposed Rule
54 Fed. Reg. 25076 (June 12, 1989).

... The Food and Drug Administration (FDA) is reproposing amendments to its tampon labeling regulation. The reproposed rule would require that manufacturers of menstrual tampons determine tampon absorbency using a test method specified in the reproposal, and, based on the results of that testing, express absorbency on tampon labeling by using one of six specified absorbency terms, each of which corresponds to a range of absorbency set forth in the reproposal. The reproposed rule would enable consumers to compare the absorbency of one brand and style of tampons with the absorbency of other brands and styles before purchasing them. . . .

... [O]mission of uniform absorbency information does render tampons misbranded within the meaning of sections 201(n) and 502(a) and (f)(1) of the act. But, rather than act against individual tampons to remedy the deficiency, FDA has proposed, consistent with its authority, to address the misbranding by requiring a uniform labeling system through rulemaking. . . . [A]ny tampon that is not labeled as required by any final rule and that is initially introduced or initially delivered for introduction into commerce after the effective date of the final rule would be misbranded under sections 201(n) and 502(a) and (f)(1) of the act. . . .

FDA received many comments on the use of letters to designate ranges of absorbency. One manufacturer, one consumer group, and several individual consumers, opposing the use of letters, contended that their use would create confusion because consumers are accustomed to numbers, not letters, representing quantity or size, because the use of letters would require that consumers learn two systems (the letters and the numerical ranges to which they refer), and because consumers would not know whether "A" were high or low. A comment from an individual consumer argued that "A" commonly indicates "most desirable" and, thus, would be misinterpreted by consumers. By contrast, comments from two manufacturers, two consumer groups, and most individual consumers supported the use of letter designations. . . .

. . . [T]he use of [numerical] sun protection factors on labeling for sunscreens is effective and appropriate . . . because the public understands that the higher the number, the greater the blockage of ultraviolet radiation and the greater the health benefit. In the case of tampons and TSS, the reverse would be true: the higher the number the higher the risk of TSS and the lower the public health benefit. FDA, therefore, believes that the analogy to sunscreen labeling is unpersuasive. Also, the agency continues to believe that the use of single numbers to represent grams of fluid absorbed by tampons is not feasible at this time.

FDA agrees, however, with the comments that the use of letters representing numerical ranges might be confusing and that consumers might not be able to readily ascertain which letters represented high or low absorbency. . . . The agency has tentatively concluded, therefore, that letter designations would not provide to consumers the clear, nonmisleading absorbency information that was intended in the proposed rule, and, accordingly, has removed letter designations from the reproposal.

. . . The agency has tentatively concluded that a system in which a new set of standardized, clear, nonmisleading terms of absorbency, corresponding to standardized nonoverlapping ranges of absorbency, would best facilitate interbrand comparison of tampon absorbencies and selection of the least absorbent tampon needed. Accordingly, FDA now proposes to further revise § 801.430(e)(1) to require the use of the following absorbency terms in lieu of letters: low absorbency, medium absorbency, medium-high absorbency, high absorbency, very high absorbency, and highest absorbency, each corresponding to one of the six nonoverlapping ranges provided for in the initial proposal. . . . In addition, reproposed § 801.430(e)(2) would permit a manufacturer to include on tampon labeling the numerical range of absorbency corresponding to the applicable term of absorbency. . . .

NOTE

The final regulations, 54 Fed. Reg. 43766 (Oct. 26, 1989), codified at 21 C.F.R. 801.430, once again changed the required absorbency terms, settling upon junior absorbency, regular absorbency, super absorbency, and super plus absorbency. In 2000, FDA required the term "ultra absorbency" for a new category of more absorbent tampons introduced to the market in 1989. 65 Fed. Reg. 62282 (Oct. 18, 2000). Finally, in 2004, the agency amended the rule to change the "junior" designation to "light," to combat perceptions that the previous term meant "the tampon is only for younger or teenage women when, in fact, it may be appropriate for women of any age with light menstrual flow." 69 Fed. Reg. 52170, 52171 (Aug. 25, 2004).

2.   ESTABLISHMENT REGISTRATION AND PRODUCT LISTING

Section 510 of the Act requires that "every person who owns or operates any establishment in any State engaged in the manufacture, preparation, propagation, compounding, or processing of . . . a device or devices" must register the establishment with FDA at the commencement of device production and on December 31 of each year. Sections 510(b) & (c). Registration of foreign establishments, which was originally voluntary, has been mandatory since 1997 under section 510(i). Every person who registers one or more device establishments must also, at the time of registration and semiannually thereafter, file with the agency a list of devices produced in these establishments. Section 510(j); 21 C.F.R. 807.20–.65.

3. ADVERSE EVENT REPORTING

Section 519 authorizes FDA to promulgate regulations requiring device manufacturers, importers, and user facilities to maintain records and submit reports necessary to assure the safety and effectiveness of devices. Under section 502(t)(2), failing to furnish information required by section 519 automatically makes a device misbranded.

FDA's regulations, borrowing language directly from the Act, require manufacturers and importers to make a medical device report (MDR) whenever they receive information from any source that "reasonably suggests" that one of their devices "[m]ay have caused or contributed to a death or serious injury" or "has malfunctioned and such device or similar device marketed by the manufacturer would be likely to cause or contribute to a death or serious injury, if the malfunction were to recur." 21 C.F.R. 803.40(a) & (b) (importers) & 803.50(a) (manufacturers). Manufacturers and importers must submit an MDR within 30 days of acquiring such information, except that manufacturers must do so within five days if the reportable event "necessitates remedial action to prevent an unreasonable risk of substantial harm to the public health." 21 C.F.R. 803.40, 50, & 53.

The 1976 Amendments authorized FDA to require medical device distributors also to file adverse event reports. For many years, the agency chose not to impose such a requirement on distributors, but the 1990 Act added a new provision to section 519 mandating that distributors report adverse events to FDA and submit copies of these reports to manufacturers. The agency never issued a final rule regarding distributor reporting, but its tentative final rule became final by operation of law in 1993. 56 Fed. Reg. 60024 (Nov. 26, 1991), 58 Fed. Reg. 46514 (Sept. 1, 1993). Distributors thus bore this obligation from 1993 until 1997, when the 1997 Act eliminated distributors from the list of entities required to report adverse device events.

The 1990 Act also mandated for the first time that device user facilities make adverse event reports. This requirement survives today. By regulation, user facilities include hospitals, ambulatory surgical facilities, nursing homes, outpatient diagnostic facilities, and outpatient treatment facilities, but not physicians' offices. 21 C.F.R. 803.3(f). User facilities must make a report to both FDA and the device manufacturer within ten days of receiving information that "reasonably suggests" that a device "has or may have caused or contributed to the death of a patient of the facility." Section 519(b)(1)(A); 21 C.F.R. 803.30(a)(1). Within the same time frame, user facilities must make reports of serious injury, rather than death, to the manufacturer of the device, if known, and otherwise to FDA. FD&C Act 519(b)(1)(B); 21 C.F.R.

803.30(a)(2). Moreover, user facilities must make annual reports to the agency summarizing all the reportable events that occurred in the facility during the year. *Id.* 519(b)(1)(C); 21 C.F.R. 803.33.

The 1997 Act directed FDA, at some indefinite time in the future, to convert the current user facility MDR system from a universal one to one involving only a subset of user facilities. Section 519(b)(5). In response to this requirement, since February 2002 CDRH has been collecting data about medical device problems from a sample of cooperating facilities. The goal of this initiative, called the Medical Product Surveillance Network (MedSun), is to determine the impact of various incentives and types of feedback on the quantity and quality of reports. The agency has not yet implemented a nonuniversal MDR system, however, and for the time being all user facilities not specifically exempted from the MDR requirements must continue to comply with them.

Commentators have noted: "In 2004 alone, nearly 152,000 MDR submissions were posted. While this number may seem high, underreporting of adverse events concerns FDA. The agency estimates that as few as one in every 100 medical device adverse events actually is reported to FDA, although there is no hard data to support this estimate." Edward M. Basile & Beverly H. Lorell, *The Food and Drug Administration's Regulation of Risk Disclosure for Implantable Cardioverter Defibrillators: Has Technology Outpaced the Agency's Regulatory Framework?*, 61 FOOD & DRUG L.J. 251, 257–58 (2006). The General Accounting Office has criticized FDA's device reporting regulations and its implementation of them on multiple occasions.

4. GOOD MANUFACTURING PRACTICE/QUALITY SYSTEM

Section 520(f) of the Act authorizes FDA to "prescribe regulations requiring that the methods used in, and the facilities and controls used for, the manufacture, pre-production design validation . . ., packing, storage, and installation of a device conform to current good manufacturing practice, as prescribed in such regulations, to assure that the device will be safe and effective and otherwise in compliance with this Act." FDA first established regulations governing current good manufacturing practices (GMPs) for devices in 1978. 43 Fed. Reg. 31508 (July 21, 1978), codified at 21 C.F.R. Part 820. These regulations governed, among other things, production and process controls; packaging and labeling controls; distribution; and recordkeeping. Notably lacking, however, were any preproduction design controls. The original GMP regulations distinguished between "critical" and "noncritical" devices, and the most rigorous requirements applied only to the former.

In the 1990s, FDA substantially revised 21 C.F.R. Part 820 and renamed it the "Quality System" regulation. The excerpt below, from the proposed rule, highlights the most important changes.

Medical Devices; Current Good Manufacturing Practice (CGMP) Regulations; Proposed Revisions; Request for Comments

58 Fed. Reg. 61952 (November 23, 1993).

. . . Except for editorial changes to update organizational references in the regulations and revisions to the list of critical devices that was included in the preamble to the final regulations, the device CGMP requirements have not been revised since 1978. This proposed rule is the result of an effort begun in 1990 to revise these regulations.

On November 28, 1990, the Safe Medical Devices Act of 1990 became law. The SMDA amended section 520(f)(1)(A) of the act to provide clear authority to add preproduction design validation controls to the device CGMP regulations and also added a new section 803 to the act which encourages FDA to work with foreign countries toward mutual recognition of CGMP requirements. . . .

Thus, FDA's decision to revise the CGMP regulations is based on changes in the law by the SMDA, the agency's discussions with others including its Device Good Manufacturing Practice Advisory Committee, responses to . . . Federal Register notices on this matter, FDA's analysis of recall data, its experience with the regulatory application of the current device CGMP regulations, and its assessment of international quality standards. . . .

Design Controls

Over the last 9 years, FDA has identified lack of design controls as one of the major causes of device recalls. The intrinsic quality of devices, including their safety and effectiveness, is established during the design phase. Thus, FDA believes that unless appropriate design controls are observed during preproduction stages of development, a finished device may be neither safe nor effective for its intended use. . . . Based on its experience with administering the CGMP regulations, which currently do not include preproduction design validation controls, the agency is concerned that the current regulations provide less than an appropriate level of assurance that devices will be safe and effective. . . .

. . . Therefore, FDA has concluded that it is essential that those firms and individuals who design Class II, Class III, and certain Class I medical devices . . . do so under formal controls that will ensure that, for each intended use of a device, specifications are established and validated to be adequate and that the final design actually meets these validated specifications.

Purchasing Controls

. . . Many device failures due to problems with components that result in recall are due to unacceptable components provided by suppliers. Therefore, FDA believes that the purchasing of components, finished devices, packaging, labeling, and manufacturing materials must be conducted with the same level of planning, control, and verification as internal activities.

The appropriate level of control should be achieved, FDA believes, through a proper mix of supplier and in-house controls. Purchasing contracts, orders, or other purchasing documents must clearly and unambiguously specify the necessary requirements for the product or service ordered. This means, of course, that a manufacturer must establish and validate component requirements prior to purchasing the component. . . .

Harmonization

FDA is proposing to reorganize the structure of the device CGMP regulations and modify some of their language in order to harmonize them with international quality standards. Thus, FDA is proposing to relocate and combine certain requirements to better harmonize the requirements with specifications for quality systems in the ISO [International Standards Organization] 9001 quality standard and to use as much common language as possible to enhance conformance with ISO 9001 terminology.

. . . .

FDA believes that revising the device CGMP regulations so they are comparable to the ISO 9001 specifications for quality systems will, once harmonization is achieved, reduce a source of competitive disadvantage to U.S. manufacturers attempting to market devices in the EC. Harmonization of FDA's device CGMP regulations with the medical device good manufacturing practice rules of the EC, and with comparable device good manufacturing practice rules being developed by Canada and Japan, will minimize the number of quality systems with which the U.S. industry must comply to compete in the international market. . . .

NOTES

1. *Final Rule.* In the final rule, FDA changed the title of the regulations from "Current Good Manufacturing Processes" to "Quality System" regulations. The agency embraced this terminology because it is used by international standard setting organizations and reflects the expansion of the GMP regulations to cover a comprehensive quality system, including preproduction design and purchasing and postproduction servicing. 61 Fed. Reg. 52602, 52605 (Oct. 7, 1996).

In the final rule, FDA also eliminated the term "critical device" from the rule, noting that this deletion would bring the regulation in closer harmony with ISO 9001 (an International Organization for Standardization standard) and the quality system standards of other countries. Despite the abandonment of the "critical device" terminology, however, FDA clung to the critical/noncritical distinction in one respect:

> . . . FDA has retained the concept of distinguishing between devices for the traceability requirements in § 820.65. As addressed in the discussion under that section, FDA believes that it is imperative that manufacturers be able to trace, by control number, any device, or where appropriate component of a device, that is intended for surgical implant into the body or to support or sustain life whose failure to perform when properly used in accordance with instructions for use

provided in the labeling can be reasonably expected to result in a significant injury to the user.

Id.

2. *Exemptions from Quality System Requirements.* FDA's final Quality System regulation exempts all Class I devices from the design control requirements, except for those "automated with computer software" and a few others specifically listed in the rule. 21 C.F.R. 820.30(a). The classification regulations for many types of Class I devices exempt them from all the other Quality System requirements, too, besides the general recordkeeping requirements and those concerning complaint files. *E.g.*, 21 C.F.R. 880.6085 (hot/cold water bottle).

5. RESTRICTED DEVICES

a. INTRODUCTION

Section 520(e) of the Act provides that FDA may:

By regulation require that a device be restricted to sale, distribution, or use—

(A) only upon the written or oral authorization of a practitioner licensed by law to administer or use such device, or

(B) upon such other conditions as the Secretary may prescribe in such regulation, if, because of its potentiality for harmful effect or the collateral measures necessary to its use, the Secretary determines that there cannot otherwise be reasonable assurance of its safety and effectiveness. . . .

A restricted device is thus analogous to a prescription drug, but the statutory language was crafted to allow FDA to control distribution of a device in ways that at that time it could not control distribution of a drug. *See supra* p. 825. Only in 2007, with the establishment of REMS by FDAAA, did the agency obtain the same formal power to restrict the distribution of drugs that it has had over devices ever since 1976.

FDA has issued restricted device rules pursuant to this provision in only a few instances. For example, hearing aids are "restricted devices" whose sale, distribution, and use are subject to FDA requirements governing the clinical context in which they are used and the professional and patient labeling that must be provided with them. 21 C.F.R. 801.420–21. *See also* 21 C.F.R. 809.30 (restrictions on the sale, distribution, and use of analyte specific reagents). The fact that a "restricted device" is not necessarily synonymous with a "prescription device" is illustrated by FDA's restricted device rule for over-the-counter test sample collection systems for drugs of abuse testing. 21 C.F.R. 809.40. The restrictions imposed by this rule include a requirement that sample testing be performed by a laboratory that satisfies several conditions, that the collection system bear certain specified labeling, and that there be "an adequate system to communicate the proper interpretation of test results from the laboratory to the purchaser."

The paucity of restricted device rules issued pursuant to section 520(e) does not reflect the frequency with which FDA actually restricts the sale, distribution, and use of devices. Although a section 520(e) rule is the only way FDA can impose such restrictions on a Class I device, the agency has other options in regulating Class II and Class III products. The Act provides that a performance standard for a Class II device may include "a provision requiring that the sale and distribution of the device be restricted but only to the extent [they] may be restricted under a regulation under section 520(e)." FD&C Act 514(a)(2)(B)(v). Moreover, permissible special controls for Class II devices include "other appropriate actions as the Secretary deems necessary to provide" reasonable assurance of safety and effectiveness. *Id.* 513(a)(1)(B). Finally, and most importantly, the Act states that an order approving a PMA for a Class III device may "require as a condition to such approval that the sale and distribution of the device be restricted" to the extent they may be restricted under a section 520(e) regulation. Thus, many Class III devices are prescription devices, or their distribution is otherwise restricted, as a condition of their PMA approval.

———

b.   HEARING AIDS

In the early 1970s, FDA became concerned about widespread abuses in the marketing of hearing aids. Hearing aid sales were regulated only by the states, and the state regulatory schemes were inconsistent. Some states required that a customer, before purchasing a hearing aid, receive an examination by a physician specializing in hearing disorders or by an audiologist. Other states applied such requirements only to certain age segments of the population. Still other states required no examination at all.

In 1974, the Department of HEW established a Task Force to study problems relating to the marketing of hearing aids throughout the United States. As a result of the Task Force findings, FDA undertook to develop national rules. In April 1976, just prior to the enactment of the Medical Device Amendments, the agency published proposed rules requiring an examination by a licensed physician prior to the issuance of a hearing aid. This requirement was subject to waiver in certain instances. 41 Fed. Reg. 16756 (Apr. 21, 1976). The agency maintained that it had the legal authority to impose such a requirement under the misbranding provisions of the Act combined with its section 701(a) power to promulgate regulations for the "efficient enforcement" of the Act. FDA also noted, however, that after the forthcoming enactment of the 1976 Amendments, it would consider hearing aids to be restricted devices and base its power to place conditions on their sale and distribution on the restricted device provision.

In 1977, FDA published the final hearing aid rules. 42 Fed. Reg. 9286 (Feb. 15, 1977), codified 21 C.F.R. 801.420–.421. The final regulations retained the proposed rule's requirement, subject to waiver, concerning an examination by a physician. The American Speech and Hearing Association (ASHA), a national association of audiologists and speech pathologists, challenged the final rules. ASHA contended that the requirement that the presale evaluations be conducted by physicians, rather than by any practitioners licensed to administer hearing aid devices, including audiologists, violated the 1976 Amendments and was arbitrary and capricious.

American Speech and Hearing Ass'n v. Califano
Civ. No. 77–1327 (D.D.C. 1977).

■ GESELL, DISTRICT JUDGE.

. . . .

At the very heart of the substantive dispute is the fact that FDA's requirement of examination by a physician as opposed to an audiologist has threatened an important facet of the audiologist's role in the hearing aid delivery system. . . . A clinical audiologist is a graduate-school-trained "individual qualified to provide professional assistance concerning communication problems associated with hearing impairment." . . .

. . . Plaintiffs argue that the regulation in question is invalid under subsection (A) [of section 520(e)(1)] which, in plaintiffs' opinion, requires any regulation mandating pre-sale authorization by a licensed practitioner to apply equally to all licensed practitioners. In most states audiologists, physicians, and hearing aid dealers are all licensed practitioners within the meaning of the statute. . . .

Plaintiffs' argument has several flaws. First, it is incorrect to characterize it as one of exclusion: neither audiologists nor dealers are barred from doing anything, nor are they deprived of their status as practitioners. Second, at least in the context of hearing aid sales, plaintiffs' construction of the term "practitioner" leaves subsection (A) devoid of meaning. Hearing aids are always sold by "licensed practitioners" who, by the very act of selling have "authorized" the sale. The type of restriction comprehended by plaintiffs' interpretation of subsection (A) imposes no restriction at all. . . . [T]he Court . . . find[s] that subsection (A) permits the FDA to distinguish among different types of practitioners and thus to authorize the type of regulation at issue.

This result accords with plain sense. The purpose of the Amendments was to empower the Secretary or his designate to root out the abuses extant under state regulation of medical devices. The regulation at issue is so obviously directed toward that goal that the Court would have to ignore the most fundamental tenets of statutory interpretation to void it. . . .

Plaintiffs argue that . . . the regulation . . . is nonetheless arbitrary and capricious and thus voidable under section 10 of the APA, 5 U.S.C. § 706(2)(A). Under the Amendments the regulation is valid only if "there cannot otherwise be reasonable assurance of [the] safety and effectiveness" of hearing aid devices. Yet if this is so is it not irrational to make the examination requirement waivable in a large number of cases? And is it not irrational to allow the required examination to be performed by any physician, a Class that include podiatrists, gynecologists, and others with little familiarity with hearing disorders, yet at the same time exclude audiologists, whose expertise is in this area?

These are thoughtful questions. The record shows, however, that they were carefully considered by the FDA prior to enactment. The regulation is accompanied by detailed and conscientious findings of fact that justify the rule adopted. The seeming contradictions are actually the result of compromises between the competing demands of economy and safety. . . . The Court is far from convinced of the wisdom of the compromise adopted, but is mindful of the limited scope of its review and the deference due to the "informed experience and judgment of the agency to whom Congress delegated appropriate authority." Because the regulatory choice made in this case cannot be termed unconsidered, it is upheld. . . .

———

c.   In Vitro Diagnostic Devices

Today, dozens of tests are available over-the-counter for use in the diagnosis and screening of a growing number of conditions and symptoms, including, for example, cholesterol, the presence of drugs of abuse, glucose levels in diabetics, and HIV. Most of these tests provide results for the consumer at home, but a few require the consumer to deposit a specimen in a collection device and send it to a laboratory, which then contacts the consumer with the results. On its website, FDA's Office of In Vitro Diagnostic Device Evaluation and Safety (OIVD) lists no fewer than 70 types of tests it has approved or cleared for over-the-counter sale.

When to permit the sale of in vitro diagnostic devices for home use has long been a difficult issue for FDA. In 1985, in recognition of "the growing interest in home-use in vitro devices," FDA held a public meeting of the chairpersons and the consumer and industry representatives of four of its advisory committees to help develop "uniform evaluation criteria for home-use in vitro devices to help insure that these devices are regulated in a consistent fashion and that consumers are provided with reliable, adequately labeled products." 50 Fed. Reg. 32641 (Aug. 13, 1985). In 1988, the agency released a draft "points to consider" in formulating labeling and premarket submissions for home use in vitro diagnostic devices.

Since that time, FDA has issued restricted device regulations with regard to two types of in vitro diagnostic products. The first covers analyte specific reagents (ASRs). As described by FDA, ASRs are:

> reagents composed of chemicals or antibodies that may be thought of as the "active ingredients" of tests that are used to identify one specific disease or condition. ASR's are purchased by manufacturers who use them as components of tests that have been cleared or approved by FDA and also by clinical laboratories that use the ASR's to develop in-house tests used exclusively by that laboratory.

62 Fed. Reg. 62243 (Nov. 21, 1997). In 1997, FDA published a final rule classifying ASRs as Class I, II, or III, depending on their intended use. 21 C.F.R. 864.4020. At the same time, the agency designated all ASRs as restricted devices under section 520(e) and promulgated a restricted device rule for them. Under this rule, ASRs intended for clinical use can

be sold only to in vitro diagnostic manufacturers and to certain categories of laboratories qualified to perform high-complexity testing. 21 C.F.R. 809.30. Moreover, the regulation restricts ordering the use of in-house developed tests using ASRs to physicians or other health care practitioners authorized by applicable state law to access such tests. FDA explained this latter requirement as follows:

> FDA disagrees with comments that have suggested that results from in-house assays developed using ASR's are no different from other IVD test results and that OTC access to the use of ASR's in these settings does not raise issues of their safety and effectiveness. Traditionally, IVD test results are evaluated in the context of a patient's history, physical examination and other sources of diagnostic information. In many cases, those tests are approved or cleared by FDA and their performance criteria have been established. . . . By contrast, results of IVD tests using ASR's may be particularly difficult for lay persons to interpret correctly without the guidance of a physician because the performance characteristics of the individual tests often have not been cleared or approved by FDA.

62 Fed. Reg. at 62255.

The other category of IVD products subject to a restricted device rule is "OTC test sample collection systems for drugs of abuse testing." 21 C.F.R. 864.3260 (device classification regulation); 21 C.F.R. 809.40 (restrictions). As revealed by the name of the device, however, FDA has not made these prescription products. Rather, the restricted device regulation requires that sample testing be performed only in qualified laboratories using FDA-approved or FDA-cleared screening tests and that the systems "provide an adequate system to communicate the proper interpretation of test results from the laboratory to the lay purchaser." 21 C.F.R. 809.40. This rule applies only to sample collection devices; FDA allows complete drug of abuse test systems to be sold to consumers over-the-counter without any restrictions on sale, distribution, or use.

For several years, perhaps the most contentious question in this area was whether test kits for HIV (the virus that causes AIDS) should be approved for home use. Although regulated as medical devices, HIV tests are under the authority of FDA's biologics center (CBER). In 1996, FDA approved a PMA for the first home collection HIV testing system. The approved device consists of materials for specimen collection, instructions, an educational booklet, and a mailing envelope to send the specimen to a laboratory for analysis. The distributor of the kit, which anonymizes the results and provides them over the telephone, also provides counseling and referral services. As a condition of PMA approval, the company agreed to conduct postmarketing surveillance studies and lot acceptance testing.

d.   CIGARETTES

As discussed in Chapter 12, in 1996 FDA published "Regulations Restricting the Sale and Distribution of Cigarettes and Smokeless Tobacco to Protect Children and Adolescents." 61 Fed. Reg. 44396 (Aug. 28, 1996). In this rule, the agency categorized cigarettes as combination drug-devices and determined to regulate them pursuant to its device authorities. Because the agency did not immediately classify these products under section 513, however, the only controls it could apply to them initially were the general controls applicable to all devices. FDA purported to apply the Act's full panoply of general controls, although, in the rule, it exempted cigarettes from the adequate directions for use requirement of section 502(f)(1); required adverse event reports from manufacturers "only for serious adverse events that are not well-known or well-documented by the scientific community;" and wholly exempted distributors from the registration and listing, GMP, and adverse event reporting requirements. Most of the rule consisted of restrictions on sale designed to prevent youth from gaining access to tobacco products, and restrictions on advertising and promotion designed to limit the targeting of children and adolescents. To support these controls, FDA relied on section 520(e).

The tobacco industry challenged the legality of FDA's rule in federal district court. What follows is an excerpt from the district court ruling on the industry's summary judgment motion. Earlier in this opinion, Judge Osteen held that the agency could exercise jurisdiction over tobacco products and could regulate them as medical devices rather than as drugs. In the excerpt below, he assesses whether section 520(e) permits the particular restrictions imposed by FDA. On appeal, majorities on both the Fourth Circuit and the Supreme Court held that FDA lacked jurisdiction over tobacco products, and consequently neither addressed the legality of the agency's specific restrictions under 520(e).

Coyne Beahm, Inc. v. United States Food & Drug Administration

966 F. Supp. 1374 (M.D.N.C. 1997).

■ OSTEEN, DISTRICT JUDGE.

. . . .

The court has found that FDA properly regulated tobacco products pursuant to its device authorities. The question remains whether FDA has properly applied its device authorities to tobacco products. The Regulations' requirements fall into essentially three categories: restrictions on advertising and promotion, restrictions on access, and labeling requirements. FDA promulgated the first two categories of restrictions pursuant to 21 U.S.C. § 360j(e), and the last pursuant to 21 U.S.C. § 352.

a. Section 360j(e) Does Not Authorize Restrictions on the Promotion and Advertisement of Tobacco Products.

. . . FDA determined that tobacco products are restricted devices within the meaning of § 360j(e) because, due to the "unique circumstances surrounding the use of tobacco products, the only way to provide a reasonable assurance of the safety of these products is to prevent children and adolescents from using and becoming addicted to them" and that, "without the restrictions contained in the Regulations, there cannot be a reasonable assurance of the safety and effectiveness of these products." FDA asserts that since tobacco products are restricted devices, it may restrict their "sale, distribution, or use," pursuant to § 360j(e). FDA further asserts that it may restrict the advertising and promotion of tobacco products, explaining that advertising and promotion constitutes an "offer of sale" and, moreover, that an "offer of sale" is part of the "sale" of a product.

Plaintiffs contend, and the court agrees, that FDA may not restrict advertising and promotion pursuant to § 360j(e). First, both as ordinarily defined and as used in the phrase "may ... be restricted to sale, distribution, or use," the word "sale" does not encompass the advertising or promotion of a product. Second, as Plaintiffs note, although Congress expressly used the words "offer for sale" and "advertising" or "advertisements" elsewhere in the FDCA, it chose not to use such language in § 360j(e).

. . . .

In addition ... Congress ... gave FDA authority to regulate the advertising of [restricted] devices in §§ 352(q) and 352(r). . . . [T]he fact that Congress has specifically granted to FDA the authority to regulate advertising of restricted devices in a separate section supports the court's finding that Congress did not intend to grant FDA such authority under § 360j(e). . . .

b.   Section 360j(e) Authorizes the Food and Drug Administration to Impose Restrictions on Access to Tobacco Products.

The court finds that § 360j(e) can be construed to authorize the access restrictions imposed by FDA. First, the access restrictions imposed by FDA, unlike its advertising and promotion restrictions, directly restrict the sale or distribution of tobacco products within the meaning of § 360j(e). Second, the court finds that such conditions on the sale or distribution of tobacco products fit within what Congress intended for FDA to impose pursuant to its authority to impose "other conditions." Thus, FDA's access restrictions will stand.

c.   Section 352 Authorizes the Food and Drug Administration to Impose Labeling Restrictions on Tobacco Products.

FDA, pursuant to § 352(r), requires tobacco products to have a statement of intended use and the established name printed on the packages. The court finds that § 352(r) clearly authorizes FDA to require restricted devices to bear the product's established name and a statement of intended use.

. . . .

NOTES

1.   *Explicit Authority Over Restricted Device Advertising.* Even if Judge Osteen was correct in holding that section 520(e) does not authorize advertising limitations of the type FDA attempted to impose on cigarettes, the agency indisputably has some power over advertising for restricted devices. Section 502(r) requires that advertisements for restricted devices contain "a true statement of the device's established name" and "a brief statement of the intended uses of the device and relevant warnings, precautions, side effects, and contraindications." Moreover, section 502(q)

provides that a restricted device is misbranded if "its advertising is false or misleading in any particular."

2. *Explicit Authority Over Tobacco Product Advertising.* The Family Smoking Prevention and Tobacco Control Act of 2009 unambiguously gives the agency authority to regulate the advertising and promotion of "tobacco products." *See* FD&C Act 903(a)(7), 906(d). To avoid the interpretive problem identified by Judge Osteen, the parallel to the restricted device provision for tobacco products states that FDA may "require restrictions on the sale and distribution of a tobacco product, including restrictions on the access to, *and the advertising and promotion of,* the tobacco product. . . ." *Id.* 906(d) (emphasis added).

6. BANNED DEVICES

Section 516 authorizes FDA, by regulation, to ban a device that "presents substantial deception or an unreasonable and substantial risk of illness or injury." It was included in the 1976 Amendments primarily to enable FDA to deal with the "quack" devices that occupied so much of the agency's attention in the past. The agency has adopted procedural regulations to implement this provision. 44 Fed. Reg. 29214 (May 18, 1979), codified at 21 C.F.R. Part 895. In 1984, FDA promulgated its first, and thus far only, regulation under this provision, banning prosthetic hair fibers intended for implantation into the human scalp to simulate natural hair or conceal baldness. 49 Fed. Reg. 1177 (Jan. 10, 1984), codified at 21 C.F.R. 895.101.

7. ADMINISTRATIVE DETENTION

Section 304(g), governing seizures, gives FDA authority to detain by administrative order potentially adulterated and misbranded devices discovered during a section 704 inspection for up to 30 days. FDA has established procedural regulations for such detentions. 44 Fed. Reg. 13234 (Mar. 9, 1979), codified at 21 C.F.R. 800.55. Administrative detentions are intended to prevent the distribution of devices that an inspector has reason to believe are adulterated or misbranded until the agency has had the opportunity to consider whether to institute a seizure action. This provision, too, has rarely been used.

8. NOTIFICATION AND REPAIR, REPLACEMENT, OR REFUND

Sections 518(a)–(d) authorize FDA to order a manufacturer, importer, or distributor to notify the public of an unreasonable risk of substantial harm from a marketed device. After offering the opportunity for an informal hearing, the agency may order a manufacturer, importer, or distributor of a device presenting an unreasonable risk to repair or replace the device or refund the purchase price. Under section 502(t)(1), a device is misbranded in the event of a failure or refusal to comply with any requirement in a section 518 order.

Section 518 was patterned on similar grants of authority to the National Highway and Traffic Safety Administration, to the Consumer Product Safety Commission, and to FDA itself under the Radiation Control for Health and Safety Act. FDA considers the section self-executing and therefore has not promulgated implementing regulations. In 49 Fed. Reg. 11716 (Mar. 27, 1984), however, FDA did make available for public comment a draft guideline on Medical Device Notification and Voluntary Safety Alert, which sets forth the procedure that it follows in implementing section 518.

FDA has invoked its authority under these provisions on several occasions. For example, in 1980, a Minnesota public health study and a CDC study both found that users of Rely® tampons, manufactured by Procter & Gamble, were at a higher risk for toxic shock syndrome than users of other tampons. After FDA threatened to issue a section 518 notification and refund order against the company, the agency and Procter & Gamble entered the following consent agreement:

In re Procter & Gamble Co.: Consent Agreement

U.S. Food and Drug Administration, September 26, 1980.

. . . .

2.   Rely brand tampon ("Rely") is a device. . . .

3.   Toxic Shock Syndrome ("TSS") is a recently recognized disease. The exact cause of and cure for TSS are not known, although *Staphylococcus aureus* may play an important role in the etiology of the disease. TSS is a rare disease which progresses rapidly and, in some instances, has resulted in death. The Food and Drug Administration ("FDA") believes that TSS is a significant public health problem. The Center for Disease Control ("CDC") and FDA believe there is an association between use of Rely and occurrence of TSS, a proposition which P&G vigorously disputes.

4.   On September 23, 1980, FDA advised P&G that FDA was contemplating the possibility of invoking the provisions of 21 U.S.C. § 360h [FD&C Act 518] to compel the firm to engage in a notification and retrieval/refund program.

5.   In settlement of actions contemplated by FDA under 21 U.S.C. § 360h, P&G and FDA enter into this Agreement. . . .

Therefore, IT IS AGREED that P&G shall:

8.   Discontinue all sale and commercial distribution of Rely.

9.   Make every reasonable effort to withdraw from all media any advertisement for Rely placed prior to September 22, 1980.

10. Conduct the consumer notification program set forth and explained as follows. . . .

11. Conduct a retrieval/refund program as follows. . . .

IT IS FURTHER AGREED that P&G shall not reintroduce for commercial distribution nor export nor offer for export the products covered by this Agreement or identical products under any name without the prior written permission of the Director of FDA's Bureau of Medical Devices.

NOTES

1. *Private Lawsuits.* After 1980, more than 1000 injury and death claims were brought against P&G by users of Rely tampons and their relatives. The leading reported case is *Kehm v. Procter & Gamble*, 724 F.2d 613 (8th Cir. 1983) (affirming judgment awarding compensatory damages to husband and children of Rely user who died of TSS).

2. *Medtronic Pacemakers.* On February 19, 1979, Medtronic submitted a section 510(k) notification to FDA for the Model 6972 bipolar pacemaker lead. On April 19, 1979, FDA concurred that the device was substantially equivalent to a preamendments device. Experience with the device, however, disclosed a high failure rate, which led to a full FDA investigation and a congressional hearing. After extensive deliberation, FDA decided not to pursue possible action under section 518(b) for repair, replacement, or refund.

> This decision is based on the absence here of any ongoing public health problem or concern which could be addressed by such an action. The pacemaker leads of concern are no longer being manufactured or sold, unimplanted leads have been recalled, and the firm has a program for reimbursement or elimination of out-of-pocket costs to patients who require surgery or increased monitoring because they rely on Model 6972 leads.

Memorandum from FDA Commissioner Frank E. Young to CDRH Director John C. Villforth (Aug. 19, 1985).

3. *Dalkon Shield.* In *National Women's Health Network, Inc. v. A.H. Robins Co., Inc.*, 545 F. Supp. 1177 (D. Mass. 1982), the District Court dismissed a class action for injunctive relief to require the manufacturer of the Dalkon Shield intrauterine contraceptive device (IUD) to conduct a nationwide notification and refund program. The Court held that the FD&C Act creates no private right of action and that any state cause of action would be preempted by the 1976 Amendments.

4. *Alternative Approaches.* On its website, FDA explains its approach to section 518:

> The procedures for repair, replacement, or refund are complex and could result in multiple orders, regulatory hearings, and much delay if FDA and the manufacturer, or other responsible person, are unable to agree on a plan for addressing a risk. The Agency must consider available alternatives. . . . Before ordering notification, FDA must determine that no more practical means are available under the FD&C Act to eliminate the risk. . . . FDA must determine that notification alone is insufficient before ordering repair, replacement or refund.

The agency then identifies civil and criminal enforcement actions, the promulgation of regulations, and recalls as potential alternatives to section 518.

5. *1990 Act Response to Under-Use of Section 518.* In 1990, concerned about FDA's reluctance to use its authority under section 518, Congress added a number of additional postmarket powers for FDA, including postmarket surveillance, mandatory recall, device tracking, and

the requirement that manufacturers notify FDA of corrective actions. These new postmarket authorities are discussed below.

9. POSTMARKET SURVEILLANCE

Under section 522, FDA may order the manufacturer of any Class II or Class III device to conduct postmarket surveillance if the failure of the device would be "reasonably likely to have serious adverse health consequences," if it is intended to be implanted in the body for more than one year, or if is intended to be used outside a user facility to support or sustain life. 21 C.F.R. 822.1. As defined by FDA regulations, "postmarket surveillance" is "the active, systematic, scientifically valid collection, analysis, and interpretation of data or other information about a marketed device." 21 C.F.R. 822.3(h).

Congress first gave FDA the authority to order postmarket surveillance in the 1990 Act. Section 522 was meant to compensate for underreporting of adverse events under the MDR system and for the agency's reluctance to use its postmarket authorities under section 518. 65 Fed. Reg. 52376, 52377–78 (Aug. 29, 2000). Before FDA issued a final rule implementing section 522, Congress, in the 1997 Act, revised the section, giving the agency more discretion in imposing postmarket surveillance and setting a presumptive limit of three years on studies.

FDA has issued rules implementing section 522 as amended by the 1997 Act. 67 Fed. Reg. 38878 (June 6, 2002), codified at 21 C.F.R. Part 822. After receiving a postmarket surveillance order, a manufacturer must submit a surveillance plan for FDA approval within 30 days. Failure to submit such a plan, to resubmit if FDA rejects the plan, or to conduct surveillance in accordance with the plan constitutes a misbranding violation and is prohibited under sections 301(q)(1)(C) and 502(t)(3). *See* GUIDANCE FOR INDUSTRY AND FDA STAFF: POSTMARKET SURVEILLANCE UNDER SECTION 522 (Apr. 2006).

10. DEVICE TRACKING

Section 519(e) authorizes FDA to issue an order requiring the manufacturer of a Class II or Class III device to adopt a method of tracking it from manufacturer to patient if the failure of the device would be "reasonably likely to have serious adverse health consequences," if it is intended to be implanted in the body for more than one year, or if it is intended to be used outside a user facility to support or sustain life. The subset of devices potentially subject to device tracking is precisely the same as that for which FDA may order postmarket surveillance under section 522. Failure to comply with a tracking requirement constitutes a misbranding violation and is prohibited under sections 301(e), 301(q)(1)(C), and 502(t)(2).

FDA has issued device tracking regulations implementing section 519(e). 67 Fed. Reg. 5943 (Feb. 8, 2002), codified at 21 C.F.R. Part 821. As stated by the agency in these regulations: "Effective tracking of devices from the manufacturing facility, through the distributor network (including distributors, retailers, rental firms and other commercial enterprises, device user facilities, and licensed practitioners) and, ultimately, to the patient is necessary for the effectiveness of remedies prescribed by the act, such as patient notification (section 518(a) of the act) or device recall (section 518(e) of the act)." 21 C.F.R. 821.1(b). The list of device types that the agency has ordered to be tracked is published in GUIDANCE FOR INDUSTRY AND FDA STAFF: MEDICAL DEVICE TRACKING 8–9 (Jan. 2010).

The device tracking provision was first added to the FD&C Act by the 1990 Act. Originally, section 519(e) tracking was mandatory for the manufacturers of all devices fitting the statutory criteria. The 1997 Act amended section 519(e) to give FDA discretion as to whether or not to require tracking for such devices. Accordingly, starting in 1998, the agency rescinded the tracking orders for fourteen types of devices. 67 Fed. Reg. 5943, 5944 (Feb. 8, 2002). According to the 2010 guidance, the additional criteria FDA uses to determine whether to compel tracking for a device meeting the statutory criteria are "likelihood of sudden, catastrophic failure," "likelihood of significant adverse clinical outcome," and "the need for prompt professional intervention."

The 2007 Amendments to the FD&C Act added section 519(f), which requires the agency to issue regulations establishing a Unique Device Identification (UDI) system for medical devices to facilitate tracking. In 2012, FDA issued a proposed rule implementing this provision, just as Congress passed a law requiring it to do so by the end of the year. 77 Fed. Reg. 40736 (July 10, 2012). The agency issued the final rule at 78 Fed. Reg. 58786 (Sept. 24, 2013). The introduction to the preamble summarized the rule as follows:

> This rule requires the label of medical devices to include a unique device identifier (UDI), except where the rule provides for an exception or alternative placement. The labeler must submit product information concerning devices to FDA's Global Unique Device Identification Database (GUDID), unless subject to an exception or alternative. The system established by this rule requires the label and device package of each medical device to include a UDI and requires that each UDI be provided in a plain-text version and in a form that uses automatic identification and data capture (AIDC) technology.

Id.

11. MANDATORY RECALLS

Another aspect of Congress's effort to bolster FDA's postmarketing authority was the 1990 Act's addition of new subsection 518(e), giving the agency power to order device recalls. Under this provision, if FDA finds there is "a reasonable probability that [a device] would cause serious adverse health consequences or death," it must order the manufacturer, importer, distributor, or retailers to cease distribution of the device and to notify health professionals and device user facilities that they should stop using it. After providing the person subject to such an order an opportunity for an informal hearing, FDA may amend the order to require a recall. The agency may not order the recall of a device from individuals, but it must provide that notice be given to those subject to the risks associated with the device. FDA has published regulations governing the mandatory recall process. 61 Fed. Reg. 59004 (Nov. 20, 1996), 21 C.F.R. Part 810.

When one of its devices presents a serious risk, a manufacturer will usually agree to conduct a voluntary recall, thus obviating FDA to issue a section 518(e) order. Nonetheless, FDA has found it necessary to order device recalls about ten times, though never since 1994. Section 518A, added by the 2012 Act, requires FDA to analyze device recalls in order to improve the recall process.

12. REPORTS OF REMOVALS AND CORRECTIONS

Under section 519(f), added by the 1990 Act, FDA must promulgate regulations requiring the manufacturer, importer, or distributor of a device to report to the agency any correction or removal of a device undertaken to reduce a risk to health or to remedy a violation of the FD&C Act which may present a risk to health. FDA has published a regulation implementing this subsection. 62 Fed. Reg. 27183 (May 19, 1997), 21 C.F.R. Part 806. As the agency explained in the preamble to this rule:

> Section 519(f) of the act was enacted because Congress was concerned that device manufacturers, distributors, and importers were carrying out product corrections or removals without notifying FDA, or not notifying the agency in a timely fashion Congress explained that industry's failure to report corrections and removals, particularly those undertaken to reduce risks associated with the use of a device, "denies the agency the opportunity to fulfill its public health responsibilities by evaluating device-related problems and the adequacy of corrective actions." . . .

Section 519(f) supplements rather than duplicates the previously-discussed MDR system implemented pursuant to section 519(a). According to FDA:

> Generally, there is expected to be little overlap between these reporting requirements. This is because MDR's are based on adverse events that have occurred (*i.e.*, deaths, serious injuries, and malfunctions) regardless of whether a remedial action (*i.e.*, correction or removal) has been undertaken by the manufacturer or distributor. Moreover, the MDR report, which is tied to the adverse event itself and its possible association with the device, will only rarely address any remedial action taken by the manufacturer because, in most cases, no such remedial action has yet occurred.

62 Fed. Reg. at 27183. The one area of potential overlap between sections 519(a) and 519(f) concerns the former's requirement that a manufacturer file an MDR within five days of becoming aware that a reportable event "necessitates remedial action to prevent an unreasonable risk of substantial harm to the public health." 21 C.F.R. 803.53. To avoid duplication, FDA has provided that a section 519(f) report is not required for an event that has already been reported under section 519(a). 21 C.F.R. 806.10(f).

13. CIVIL PENALTIES

Finally, the 1990 Act added a new provision to the FD&C Act's section on penalties, stating that any person who violates the device provisions of the FD&C Act may be liable for a civil penalty in an amount not to exceed $15,000 for each violation and $1 million for all such violations adjudicated in a single proceeding. Section 303(f). FDA may assess civil penalties only after affording the person to be assessed an opportunity for a formal adjudicatory hearing. For more on civil penalties as an enforcement tool, see *supra* p. 262.

J. MOBILE MEDICAL DEVICES

In 2011, FDA published a DRAFT GUIDANCE FOR INDUSTRY AND FOOD AND DRUG ADMINISTRATION STAFF: MOBILE MEDICAL APPLICATIONS (July 11, 2011). This document provoked a flurry of protest questioning the appropriateness of FDA regulation of software used to support patient and physician health care decisions, as well as congressional efforts to mandate further consideration of the policy and collaborative approaches between FDA, stakeholders, and other agencies. *See* Scott Gottlieb & J. D. Kleinke, *There's a Medical App for That—Or Not*, WALL ST. J., May 30, 2012, at A11. The Food and Drug Administration Safety and Innovation Act ("FDASIA"), enacted in July 2012, requires FDA, in consultation with other relevant agencies, to issue a report by January 9, 2014, that contains a "proposed strategy and recommendations on an appropriate, risk-based regulatory framework pertaining to health information technology, including mobile medical applications, that promotes innovation, protects patient safety, and avoids regulatory duplication." Pub. L. No. 112–144, § 618(a). In September 2013, FDA issued the following final guidance, although it had not yet published the FDASIA-mandated report.

Guidance for Industry and FDA Staff: Mobile Medical Applications

September 25, 2013

I. Introduction

The Food and Drug Administration (FDA) recognizes the extensive variety of actual and potential functions of mobile apps, the rapid pace of innovation in mobile apps, and the potential benefits and risks to public health represented by these apps. The FDA is issuing this guidance document to inform manufacturers, distributors, and other entities about how the FDA intends to apply its regulatory authorities to select software applications intended for use on mobile platforms (mobile applications or "mobile apps"). Given the rapid expansion and broad applicability of mobile apps, the FDA is issuing this guidance document to clarify the subset of mobile apps to which the FDA intends to apply its authority.

Many mobile apps are not medical devices (meaning such mobile apps do not meet the definition of a device under section 201(h) of the Federal Food, Drug, and Cosmetic Act (FD&C Act)), and FDA does not regulate them. Some mobile apps may meet the definition of a medical device but because they pose a lower risk to the public, FDA intends to exercise enforcement discretion over these devices (meaning it will not enforce requirements under the FD&C Act). The majority of mobile apps on the market at this time fit into these two categories.

Consistent with the FDA's existing oversight approach that considers functionality rather than platform, the FDA intends to apply its regulatory oversight to only those mobile apps that are medical devices and whose functionality could pose a risk to a patient's safety if the mobile app were to not function as intended. This subset of mobile apps the FDA refers to as mobile medical apps.

. . . .

II. Background

As mobile platforms become more user friendly, computationally powerful, and readily available, innovators have begun to develop mobile apps of increasing complexity to leverage the portability mobile platforms can offer. Some of these new mobile apps are specifically targeted to assisting individuals in their own health and wellness management. Other mobile apps are targeted to healthcare providers as tools to improve and facilitate the delivery of patient care.

. . . .

IV. Scope

This guidance explains the FDA's intentions to focus its oversight on a subset of mobile apps. Mobile medical apps as defined in section III include only those mobile apps that meet the statutory definition of a device and either are intended:

•   to be used as an accessory to a regulated medical device; or

•   to transform a mobile platform into a regulated medical device.

. . . .

This guidance does not address the approach for software that performs patient-specific analysis to aid or support clinical decision-making.

. . . .

V. Regulatory approach for mobile medical apps

As described in this guidance, FDA intends to apply its regulatory oversight to only those mobile apps that are medical devices and whose functionality could pose a risk to a patient's safety if the mobile app were to not function as intended. This approach to overseeing mobile medical apps is consistent with our existing approach to overseeing medical device functionality of a product and the risks it poses to patients regardless of the shape, size or the platform. The FDA believes that this subset of mobile medical apps poses the same or similar potential risks to the public health as currently regulated devices if they fail to function as intended.

. . . .

For mobile medical apps, manufacturers must meet the requirements associated with the applicable device classification. If the mobile medical app, on its own, falls within a medical device classification, its manufacturer is subject to the requirements associated with that classification. A mobile medical app, like other devices, may be classified as class I (general controls), class II (special controls in addition to general controls), or class III (premarket approval).

A. Mobile medical apps: Subset of mobile apps that are the focus of FDA's regulatory oversight

Mobile apps may take a number of forms, but it is important to note that the FDA intends to apply its regulatory oversight to only the subset of mobile apps identified below . . . .

1. Mobile apps that are an extension of one or more medical devices by connecting to such device(s) for purposes of controlling the device(s) or displaying, storing, analyzing, or transmitting patient-specific medical device data. . . .

2. Mobile apps that transform the mobile platform into a regulated medical device by using attachments, display screens, or sensors or by including functionalities similar to those of currently regulated medical devices. Mobile apps that use attachments, display screens, sensors or other such similar components to transform a mobile platform into a regulated medical device are required to comply with the device classification associated with the transformed platform. . . .

3. Mobile apps that become a regulated medical device (software) by performing patient-specific analysis and providing patient-specific diagnosis, or treatment recommendations. These types of mobile medical apps are similar to or perform the same function as those types of software devices that have been previously cleared or approved. . . .

B. Mobile Apps for which FDA intends to exercise enforcement discretion (meaning that FDA does not intend to enforce requirements under the FD&C Act)

FDA intends to exercise enforcement discretion for mobile apps that:

-   Help patients (i.e., users) self-manage their disease or conditions without providing specific treatment or treatment suggestions;

-   Provide patients with simple tools to organize and track their health information;

-   Provide easy access to information related to patients' health conditions or treatments;

-   Help patients document, show, or communicate potential medical conditions to health care providers;

-   Automate simple tasks for health care providers; or

-   Enable patients or providers to interact with Personal Health Record (PHR) or Electronic Health Record (EHR) systems.

Some mobile apps in the above categories and listed below may be considered mobile medical apps, and others might not. For those mobile apps listed below that are devices, FDA intends to exercise enforcement discretion because they pose a low risk to patients. . . .

1. Mobile apps that provide or facilitate supplemental clinical care, by coaching or prompting, to help patients manage their health in their daily environment.—These are apps that supplement professional clinical care by facilitating behavioral change or

coaching patients with specific diseases or identifiable health conditions in their daily environment. . . .

2. Mobile apps that provide patients with simple tools to organize and track their health information.—These are apps that provide patients with tools to organize and track health information without providing recommendations to alter or change a previously prescribed treatment or therapy. . . .

3. Mobile apps that provide easy access to information related to patients' health conditions or treatments (beyond providing an electronic "copy" of a medical reference).—These are apps that provide contextually-relevant information to users by matching patient-specific information (e.g., diagnosis, treatments, allergies, signs or symptoms) to reference information routinely used in clinical practice (e.g., practice guidelines) to facilitate a user's assessment of a specific patient. . . .

4. Mobile apps that are specifically marketed to help patients document, show, or communicate to providers potential medical conditions.—These are apps that in their labeling or promotional materials are not promoted for medical uses but which, by virtue of other circumstances surrounding their distribution, may meet the definition of a medical device. These products either pose little or no risk, or are the sole responsibility of the health care providers who have used them in medical applications. . . .

5. Mobile apps that perform simple calculations routinely used in clinical practice.—These are apps that are intended to provide a convenient way for clinicians to perform various simple medical calculations taught in medical schools and are routinely used in clinical practice. These apps are generally tailored for clinical use, but retain functionality that is similar to simple general purpose tools such as paper charts, spread sheets, timers or generic mathematical calculators. . . .

6. Mobile apps that enable individuals to interact with PHR [Personal Health Record] systems or EHR [Electronic Health Record] systems.—These are apps that provide patients and providers with mobile access to health record systems or enables them to gain electronic access to health information stored within a PHR system or EHR system. Applications that only allow individuals to view or download EHR data are also included in this category. These mobile apps are generally meant to facilitate general patient health information management and health record-keeping activities.

K. PREEMPTION OF STATE LAW BY THE MEDICAL DEVICE AMENDMENTS OF 1976

In the 1976 Medical Device Amendments, Congress attempted to define the federal and state roles in the regulation of medical instrumentation. The result is section 521 of the FD&C Act, which reads:

> Sec. 521(a) Except as provided in subsection (b), no State or political subdivision of a State may establish or continue in effect with respect to a device intended for human use any requirement

(1) which is different from, or in addition to, any requirement applicable under this Act to the device, and

(2) which relates to the safety or effectiveness of the device or to any other matter included in a requirement applicable to the device under this Act.

(b) Upon application of a State or a political subdivision thereof, the Secretary may, by regulation promulgated after notice and opportunity for an oral hearing, exempt from subsection (a), under such conditions as may be prescribed in such regulation, a requirement of such State or political subdivision applicable to a device intended for human use if

(1) the requirement is more stringent than a requirement under this Act which would be applicable to the device if an exemption were not in effect under this subsection; or

(2) the requirement

(A) is required by compelling local conditions, and

(B) compliance with the requirement would not cause the device to be in violation of any applicable requirement under this Act.

Soon after passage of the Amendments, FDA promulgated regulations describing its understanding of section 521(b), governing exemptions. The following are excerpts from the preamble to the final rule.

Exemptions From Federal Preemption of State and Local Device Requirements

43 Fed. Reg. 18661 (May 2, 1978).

. . . [F]rom a plain reading of section 521 of the act it is clear that the scope of preemption is limited to instances where there are specific FDA requirements applicable to a particular device or class of devices. . . . [A] prime example is the preemption of divergent State or local requirements relating to hearing aid labeling and conditions for sale, which occurred when the new FDA hearing aid regulations took effect on August 25, 1977. Here, only requirements relating to labeling and conditions for sale were preempted, not all State or local requirements regulating other facets of hearing aid distribution. . . .

. . . [T]he [agency's] interpretation . . . allows State and local requirements to continue in effect until FDA establishes a national policy on the regulation of specific devices. Thus, since there is no duplication between FDA and State programs, there is no greater burden on interstate commerce than if the Amendments had not been enacted.

Several comments stated that there is no basis in the act or in the legislative history for the statement in proposed § 808.1(d)(2) that section 521(a) does not preempt State or local requirements that are equal to, or substantially identical to, requirements imposed by or under the Act. . . . The Commissioner believes that a common sense reading of section 521 of the act supports the "substantially identical" concept in § 808.1(d)(2). Thus, while a State or local requirement may differ in some nonessential manner from an FDA requirement, if it is substantially identical to an FDA requirement it is not "different from" the FDA requirement within the meaning of section 521, and therefore not preempted. . . .

The Commissioner also cannot accept the argument that an identical State or local requirement is preempted because it is "in addition to" the FDA requirement. Such an interpretation of section 521 renders meaningless the "different from" language of section 521 because under this theory any State and local requirement would be preempted whether or not it was actually "different from" an FDA requirement. . . .

The Commissioner believes that State laws relating to inspection, registration, and licensing usually are not requirements "with respect to a device" within the meaning of section 521 of the act because they generally pertain either to persons who manufacture or distribute devices or to places where devices are manufactured, and not directly to devices. In order for a State provision to be a requirement with respect to a device within the meaning of section 521 of the act—and thereby a candidate for preemption—it must relate to the device itself. . . .

NOTES

1. *FDA Exemption Regulations.* FDA's regulations governing exemptions from preemption of state medical device laws, and the specific exemptions that have been granted, are codified in 21 C.F.R. Part 808.

2. *Hearing Aid Controls.* Massachusetts challenged FDA's denial of its application for an exemption for two provisions of its statute governing the sale of hearing aids, contending that the agency's published criteria for exemptions were invalid because they permit broad consideration of "the best interest of public health, taking into account the potential burden on interstate commerce." 21 C.F.R. 808.25(g)(3). The First Circuit approved both FDA's criteria for exemptions from preemption and its action on the Massachusetts application. *Commonwealth of Massachusetts v. Hayes,* 691 F.2d 57 (1st Cir. 1982). For a discussion of the circumstances under which state hearing aid requirements are not preempted, see 55 Fed. Reg. 23984 (June 13, 1990). State hearing aid requirements were upheld in *Smith v. Pingree,* 651 F.2d 1021 (5th Cir. 1981); *New Jersey Guild of Hearing Aid Dispensers v. Long,* 75 N.J. 544, 384 A.2d 795 (1978).

———

The most controversial question concerning section 521 was whether it was intended to preempt state tort actions. The United States Supreme Court visited this problem twice, first in connection with devices holding cleared 510(k)'s and then in connection with devices holding approved PMAs. Excerpts from both decisions follow.

Medtronic, Inc. v. Lohr

518 U.S. 470 (1996).

■ JUSTICE STEVENS announced the judgment of the Court and delivered the opinion of the Court with respect to Parts I, II, III, V, and VII, and an opinion with respect to Parts IV and VI, in which JUSTICE KENNEDY, JUSTICE SOUTER, and JUSTICE GINSBURG join.

Congress enacted the Medical Device Amendments of 1976, in the words of the statute's preamble, "to provide for the safety and effectiveness of medical devices intended for human use." 90 Stat. 539. The question presented is whether that statute pre-empts a state common-law negligence action against the manufacturer of an allegedly defective medical device. . . .

I.

Throughout our history the several States have exercised their police powers to protect the health and safety of their citizens. . . .

Despite the prominence of the States in matters of public health and safety, in recent decades the Federal Government has played an increasingly significant role in the protection of the health of our people. . .

In response to the mounting consumer and regulatory concern, Congress enacted the statute at issue here: the Medical Device Amendments of 1976 (MDA or Act). The Act classifies medical devices in three categories based on the risk that they pose to the public. . . . Pacemakers are Class III devices.

Before a new Class III device may be introduced to the market, the manufacturer must provide the FDA with a "reasonable assurance" that the device is both safe and effective. Despite its relatively innocuous phrasing, the process of establishing this "reasonable assurance," which is known as the "premarket approval," or "PMA" process, is a rigorous one.

Not all, nor even most, Class III devices on the market today have received premarket approval because of two important exceptions to the PMA requirement. First, Congress realized that existing medical devices could not be withdrawn from the market while the FDA completed its PMA analysis for those devices. The statute therefore includes a "grandfathering" provision which allows pre-1976 devices to remain on the market without FDA approval until such time as the FDA initiates and completes the requisite PMA. Second, to prevent manufacturers of grandfathered devices from monopolizing the market while new devices clear the PMA hurdle, and to ensure that improvements to existing devices can be rapidly introduced into the market, the Act also permits devices that are "substantially equivalent" to pre-existing devices to avoid the PMA process.

II.

As have so many other medical device manufacturers, petitioner Medtronic took advantage of § 510(k)'s expedited process in October 1982, when it notified the FDA that it intended to market its Model 4011 pacemaker lead as a device that was "substantially equivalent" to devices already on the market. (The lead is the portion of a pacemaker that transmits the heartbeat-steadying electrical signal from the "pulse generator" to the heart itself.) On November 30, 1982, the FDA found that the model was "substantially equivalent to devices introduced into interstate commerce" prior to the effective date of the Act, and advised Medtronic that it could therefore market its device subject only to the general control provisions of the Act, which could be found in the Code of Federal Regulations. . . .

Cross-petitioner Lora Lohr is dependent on pacemaker technology for the proper functioning of her heart. In 1987 she was implanted with a Medtronic pacemaker equipped with one of the company's Model 4011 pacemaker leads. On December 30, 1990, the pacemaker failed, allegedly resulting in a "complete heart block" that required emergency surgery. . . .

In 1993 Lohr and her husband filed this action in a Florida state court. Their complaint contained both a negligence count and a strict liability count. The negligence count alleged a breach of Medtronic's "duty to use reasonable care in the design, manufacture, assembly, and sale of the subject pacemaker" in several respects, including the use of defective materials in the lead and a failure to warn or properly instruct the plaintiff or her physicians of the tendency of the pacemaker to fail, despite knowledge of other earlier failures. The strict-liability count alleged that the device was in a defective condition and unreasonably dangerous to foreseeable users at the time of its sale. . . .

Medtronic removed the case to Federal District Court, where it filed a motion for summary judgment arguing that both the negligence and strict-liability claims were pre-empted by 21 U.S.C. § 360k(a). . . .

III.

. . . While the pre-emptive language of § 360k(a) [FD&C Act section 521] means that we need not go beyond that language to determine whether Congress intended the MDA to pre-empt at least some state law, we must nonetheless "identify the domain expressly pre-empted" by that language. Although our analysis of the scope of the pre-emption statute must begin with its text, our interpretation of that language does not occur in a contextual vacuum. Rather, that interpretation is informed by two presumptions about the nature of pre-emption.

First, because the States are independent sovereigns in our federal system, we have long presumed that Congress does not cavalierly pre-empt state-law causes of action. . . .

Second, our analysis of the scope of the statute's pre-emption is guided by our oft-repeated comment that the purpose of Congress is the ultimate touch-stone" in every pre-emption case. . . .

IV.

In its petition, Medtronic argues that the Court of Appeals erred by concluding that the Lohrs' claims alleging negligent design were not pre-empted by 21 U.S.C. § 360k(a). That section provides that "no State or political subdivision of a State may establish or continue in effect with respect to a device intended for human use any requirement (1) which is different from, or in addition to, any requirement applicable under this chapter to the device, and (2) which relates to the safety or effectiveness of the device or to any other matter included in a requirement applicable to the device under this chapter." Medtronic suggests that any common-law cause of action is a "requirement" which alters incentives and imposes duties "different from, or in addition to," the generic federal standards that the FDA has promulgated in response to mandates under the MDA. In essence, the company argues that the plain language of the statute pre-empts any and all common-law claims brought by an injured plaintiff against a manufacturer of medical devices.

Medtronic's argument is not only unpersuasive, it is implausible. Under Medtronic's view of the statute, Congress effectively precluded state courts from affording state consumers any protection from injuries resulting from a defective medical device. Moreover, because there is no explicit private cause of action against manufacturers contained in the MDA, and no suggestion that the Act created an implied private right of action, Congress would have barred most, if not all, relief for persons injured by defective medical devices. Medtronic's construction of § 360k would therefore have the perverse effect of granting complete immunity from design defect liability to an entire industry that, in the judgment of Congress, needed more stringent regulation in order "to provide for the safety and effectiveness of medical devices intended for human use," 90 Stat. 539 (preamble to Act). It is, to say the least, "difficult to believe that Congress would, without comment, remove all means of judicial recourse for those injured by illegal conduct," and it would take language much plainer than the text of § 360k to convince us that Congress intended that result.

. . . .

An examination of the basic purpose of the legislation as well as its history entirely supports our rejection of Medtronic's extreme position. The MDA was enacted "to provide for the safety and effectiveness of medical devices intended for human use." Medtronic asserts that the Act was also intended, however, to "protect innovations in device technology from being 'stifled by unnecessary restrictions,'" and that this interest extended to the pre-emption of common-law claims. While the Act certainly reflects some of these concerns, the legislative history indicates that any fears regarding regulatory burdens were related more to the risk of *additional* federal and state regulation rather than the danger of pre-existing duties under common law. Indeed, nowhere in the materials relating to the Act's history have we discovered a reference to a fear that product liability actions would hamper the development of medical devices. . . .

V.

Medtronic asserts several specific reasons why, even if § 360k does not pre-empt all common-law claims, it at least pre-empts the Lohrs' claims in this suit. In contrast, the Lohrs argue that their entire complaint should survive a reasonable evaluation of the pre-emptive scope of § 360k(a). . . .

Design Claim

The Court of Appeals concluded that the Lohrs' defective design claims were not pre-empted because the requirements with which the company had to comply were not sufficiently concrete to constitute a pre-empting federal requirement. Medtronic counters by pointing to the

FDA's determination that Model 4011 is "substantially equivalent" to an earlier device as well as the agency's continuing authority to exclude the device from the market if its design is changed. These factors, Medtronic argues, amount to a specific, federally enforceable design requirement that cannot be affected by state-law pressures such as those imposed on manufacturers subject to product liability suits.

The company's defense exaggerates the importance of the § 510(k) process and the FDA letter to the company regarding the pacemaker's substantial equivalence to a grandfathered device. . . . "[S]ubstantial equivalence determinations provide little protection to the public. These determinations simply compare a post-1976 device to a pre-1976 device to ascertain whether the later device is no more dangerous and no less effective than the earlier device. If the earlier device poses a severe risk or is ineffective, then the later device may also be risky or ineffective." The design of the Model 4011, as with the design of pre-1976 and other "substantially equivalent" devices, has never been formally reviewed under the MDA for safety or efficacy.

The FDA stressed this basic conclusion in its letter to Medtronic finding the 4011 lead "substantially equivalent" to devices already on the market. That letter only required Medtronic to comply with "general standards"—the lowest level of protection "applicable to all medical devices," and including "listing of devices, good manufacturing practices, labeling, and the misbranding and adulteration provisions of the Act." It explicitly warned Medtronic that the letter did "not in any way denote official FDA approval of your device," and that "any representation that creates an impression of official approval of this device because of compliance with the premarket notification regulations is misleading and constitutes misbranding."

Thus, even though the FDA may well examine § 510(k) applications for Class III devices (as it examines the entire medical device industry) with a concern for the safety and effectiveness of the device, it did not "require" Medtronic's pacemaker to take any particular form for any particular reason; the agency simply allowed the pacemaker, as a device substantially equivalent to one that existed before 1976, to be marketed without running the gauntlet of the PMA process. In providing for this exemption to PMA review, Congress intended merely to give manufacturers the freedom to compete, to a limited degree, with and on the same terms as manufacturers of medical devices that existed prior to 1976.

Identity of Requirements Claims

. . . Although the precise contours of [the Lohrs'] theory of recovery have not yet been defined (the pre-emption issue was decided on the basis of the pleadings), it is clear that the Lohrs' allegations may include claims that Medtronic has, to the extent that they exist, violated FDA regulations. At least these claims, they suggest, can be maintained without being pre-empted by § 360k, and we agree.

Nothing in § 360k denies Florida the right to provide a traditional damages remedy for violations of common-law duties when those duties parallel federal requirements. Even if it may be necessary as a matter of Florida law to prove that those violations were the result of negligent conduct, or that they created an unreasonable hazard for users of the product, such additional elements of the state-law cause of action would make the state requirements narrower, not broader, than the federal requirement. While such a narrower requirement might be "different from" the federal rules in a literal sense, such a difference would surely provide a strange reason for finding pre-emption of a state rule insofar as it duplicates the federal rule. The presence of a damages remedy does not amount to the additional or different "requirement" that is necessary under the statute; rather, it merely provides another reason for manufacturers to comply with identical existing "requirements" under federal law.

The FDA regulations interpreting the scope of § 360k's pre-emptive effect [21 CFR 808.1] support the Lohrs' view, and our interpretation of the pre-emption statute is substantially informed by those regulations.... Congress has given the FDA a unique role in determining the scope of § 360k's pre-emptive effect.... [P]re-emption under the MDA does not arise directly as a result of the enactment of the statute; rather, in most cases a state law will be pre-empted only to the extent that the FDA has promulgated a relevant federal "requirement." Because the FDA is the federal agency to which Congress has delegated its authority to implement the provisions of the Act, the agency is uniquely qualified to determine whether a particular form of state law "stands as an obstacle to the accomplishment and execution of the full purposes and objectives of Congress," and, therefore, whether it should be pre-empted.... The ambiguity in the statute—and the congressional grant of authority to the agency on the matter contained within it—provide a "sound basis" for giving substantial weight to the agency's view of the statute. *See Chevron U.S.A. Inc. v. Natural Resources Defense Council, Inc.,* 467 U.S. 837 (1984).

The regulations promulgated by the FDA expressly support the conclusion that § 360k "does not preempt State or local requirements that are equal to, or substantially identical to, requirements imposed by or under the act."...

Manufacturing and Labeling Claims

... The Court of Appeals believed that these claims would interfere with the consistent application of general federal regulations governing the labeling and manufacture of all medical devices, and therefore concluded that the claims were pre-empted altogether.

The requirements identified by the Court of Appeals include labeling regulations that require manufacturers of every medical device, with a few limited exceptions, to include with the device a label containing "information for use, ... and any relevant hazards, contraindications, side effects, and precautions." Similarly, manufacturers are required to comply with "Good Manufacturing Practices," or "GMP's," which are set forth in 32 sections and less than 10 pages in the Code of Federal Regulations....

While admitting that these requirements exist, the Lohrs suggest that their general nature simply does not pre-empt claims alleging that the manufacturer failed to comply with other duties under state common law. In support of their claim, they note that § 360k(a)(1) expressly states that a federal requirement must be "applicable to the device" in question before it has any pre-emptive effect. Because the labeling and manufacturing requirements are applicable to a host of different devices, they argue that they do not satisfy this condition. They further argue that because only state requirements "with respect to a device" may be pre-empted, and then only if the requirement "relates to the safety or effectiveness of the device or to any other matter included in a requirement applicable to the device," § 360k(a) mandates pre-emption only where there is a conflict between a specific state requirement and a federal requirement "applicable to" the same device.

The Lohrs' theory is supported by the FDA regulations, which provide that state requirements are pre-empted "only" when the FDA has established "specific counterpart regulations or . . . other specific requirements applicable to a particular device." 21 C.F.R. 808.1(d). They further note that the statute is not intended to pre-empt "State or local requirements of general applicability where the purpose of the requirement relates either to other products in addition to devices . . . or to unfair trade practices in which the requirements are not limited to devices." . . .

Although we do not believe that this statutory and regulatory language necessarily precludes "general" federal requirements from ever pre-empting state requirements, or "general" state requirements from ever being pre-empted, it is impossible to ignore its overarching concern that pre-emption occur only where a particular state requirement threatens to interfere with a specific federal interest. . . . The statute and regulations, therefore, require a careful comparison between the allegedly pre-empting federal requirement and the allegedly pre-empted state requirement to determine whether they fall within the intended pre-emptive scope of the statute and regulations.

Such a comparison mandates a conclusion that the Lohrs' common-law claims are not pre-empted by the federal labeling and manufacturing requirements. The generality of those requirements make this quite unlike a case in which the Federal Government has weighed the competing interests relevant to the particular requirement in question, reached an unambiguous conclusion about how those competing considerations should be resolved in a particular case or set of cases, and implemented that conclusion via a specific mandate on manufacturers or producers. Rather, the federal requirements reflect important but entirely generic concerns about device regulation generally, not the sort of concerns regarding a specific device or field of device regulation that the statute or regulations were designed to protect from potentially contradictory state requirements.

Similarly, the general state common-law requirements in this suit were not specifically developed "with respect to" medical devices. Accordingly, they are not the kinds of requirements that Congress and the FDA feared would impede the ability of federal regulators to implement and enforce specific federal requirements. The legal duty that is the predicate for the Lohrs' negligent manufacturing claim is the general duty of every manufacturer to use due care to avoid foreseeable dangers in its products. Similarly, the predicate for the failure to warn claim is the general duty to inform users and purchasers of potentially dangerous items of the risks involved in their use. These general obligations are no more a threat to federal requirements than would be a state-law duty to comply with local fire prevention regulations and zoning codes, or to use due care in the training and supervision of a work force. These state requirements therefore escape pre-emption, not because the source of the duty is a judge-made common-law rule, but rather because their generality leaves them outside the category of requirements that § 360k envisioned to be "with respect to" specific devices such as pacemakers. As a result, none of the Lohrs' claims based on allegedly defective manufacturing or labeling are pre-empted by the MDA.

VI.

In their cross-petition, the Lohrs present a final argument, suggesting that common-law duties are never "requirements" within the meaning of § 360k and that the statute therefore never pre-empts common-law actions. . . .

. . . [W]e do not respond directly to this argument for two reasons. First, since none of the Lohrs' claims is pre-empted in this suit, we need not resolve hypothetical cases that may arise in the future. Second, given the critical importance of device specificity in our (and the FDA's) construction of § 360k, it is apparent that few, if any, common-law duties have been pre-empted by this statute. It will be rare indeed for a court hearing a common-law cause of action to issue a decree that has "the effect of establishing a substantive requirement for a specific device." Until such a case arises, we see no need to determine whether the statute explicitly pre-empts such a claim. Even then, the issue may not need to be resolved if the claim would also be pre-empted under conflict pre-emption analysis, see *Freightliner Corp. v. Myrick*, 514 U.S. 280 (1995).

NOTES

1. *Deference to FDA's Interpretation of Section 521.* At the time that FDA issued its regulations interpreting section 521, 43 Fed. Reg. 18861 (May 2, 1978), it was already aware that years, even decades, would pass before the agency could fully deploy and enforce all of the authorities the Medical Device Amendments provided. The agency thus knew that an expansive interpretation of section 521—one that displaced numerous state regulations—would leave consumers less well-protected than if the Device Amendments had never been passed.

2. *Did Congress Intend to Preempt State Civil Causes of Actions?* In *Medtronic v. Lohr*, the Supreme Court was faced with a claim that the Device Amendments preempted a major slice of the states' common law of torts, a body of judge-made law whose fate had never been mentioned in the legislative history and that could be said to embody the states' front line of protection of consumers of medical products. Justice Stevens makes no secret of his unwillingness, absent a very clear directive from Congress, to recognize such a claim. And there is little doubt that the draftsmen of section 521 had only statutory and administrative "requirements" in mind. Nevertheless, Justice Stevens, in the final section of the opinion, declines to resolve this issue. However, five justices in *Lohr* supported the idea that common-law causes of action impose "requirements" that might be

preempted, and in the following case, *Riegel v. Medtronic*, the Court identified a situation in which such preemption in fact occurs.

Riegel v. Medtronic, Inc.

552 U.S. 312 (2008).

■ JUSTICE SCALIA delivered the opinion of the Court, in which JUSTICE ROBERTS, JUSTICE KENNEDY, JUSTICE SOUTER, JUSTICE THOMAS, JUSTICE BREYER, and JUSTICE ALITO join.

We consider whether the pre-emption clause enacted in the Medical Device Amendments of 1976, 21 U.S.C. § 360k, bars common-law claims challenging the safety and effectiveness of a medical device given premarket approval by the Food and Drug Administration (FDA). . . .

I.

The device at issue is an Evergreen Balloon Catheter marketed by defendant-respondent Medtronic, Inc. It is a Class III device that received premarket approval from the FDA in 1994; changes to its label received supplemental approvals in 1995 and 1996.

Charles Riegel underwent coronary angioplasty in 1996, shortly after suffering a myocardial infarction. His right coronary artery was diffusely diseased and heavily calcified. Riegel's doctor inserted the Evergreen Balloon Catheter into his patient's coronary artery in an attempt to dilate the artery, although the device's labeling stated that use was contraindicated for patients with diffuse or calcified stenoses. The label also warned that the catheter should not be inflated beyond its rated burst pressure of eight atmospheres. Riegel's doctor inflated the catheter five times, to a pressure of 10 atmospheres; on its fifth inflation, the catheter ruptured. Riegel developed a heart block, was placed on life support, and underwent emergency coronary bypass surgery.

Riegel and his wife Donna brought this lawsuit in April 1999, in the United States District Court for the Northern District of New York. Their complaint alleged that Medtronic's catheter was designed, labeled, and manufactured in a manner that violated New York common law, and that these defects caused Riegel to suffer severe and permanent injuries. . . . The District Court held that the MDA pre-empted Riegel's claims of strict liability; breach of implied warranty; and negligence in the design, testing, inspection, distribution, labeling, marketing, and sale of the catheter. It also held that the MDA pre-empted a negligent manufacturing claim insofar as it was not premised on the theory that Medtronic violated federal law. . . .

The United States Court of Appeals for the Second Circuit affirmed these dismissals. . . .

II.

Since the MDA expressly pre-empts only state requirements "different from, or in addition to, any requirement applicable . . . to the device" under federal law, § 360k(a)(1), we must determine whether the Federal Government has established requirements applicable to

Medtronic's catheter. If so, we must then determine whether the Riegels' common-law claims are based upon New York requirements with respect to the device that are "different from, or in addition to," the federal ones, and that relate to safety and effectiveness. § 360k(a). . . .

. . . While § 510(k) is "'focused on *equivalence*, not safety,'", *Lohr v. Medtronic, Inc.*, 518 U.S., at 493, premarket approval is focused on safety, not equivalence. While devices that enter the market through § 510(k) have "never been formally reviewed under the MDA for safety or efficacy," the FDA may grant premarket approval only after it determines that a device offers a reasonable assurance of safety and effectiveness, § 360e(d). And while the FDA does not " 'require' " that a device allowed to enter the market as a substantial equivalent "take any particular form for any particular reason," *Lohr v. Medtronic, Inc.*, 518 U.S., at 493, the FDA requires a device that has received premarket approval to be made with almost no deviations from the specifications in its approval application, for the reason that the FDA has determined that the approved form provides a reasonable assurance of safety and effectiveness.

III.

We turn, then, to . . . whether the Riegels' common-law claims rely upon "any requirement" of New York law applicable to the catheter that is "different from, or in addition to," federal requirements and that "relates to the safety or effectiveness of the device or to any other matter included in a requirement applicable to the device." § 360k(a). Safety and effectiveness are the very subjects of the Riegels' common-law claims, so the critical issue is whether New York's tort duties constitute "requirements" under the MDA.

A.

In *Lohr,* five Justices concluded that common-law causes of action for negligence and strict liability do impose "requirement[s]" and would be pre-empted by federal requirements specific to a medical device. *See Lohr*, 518 *U.S., at 512*. We adhere to that view. . . .

. . . In the context of this legislation excluding common-law duties from the scope of pre-emption would make little sense. State tort law that requires a manufacturer's catheters to be safer, but hence less effective, than the model the FDA has approved disrupts the federal scheme no less than state regulatory law to the same effect. Indeed, one would think that tort law, applied by juries under a negligence or strict-liability standard, is less deserving of preservation. A state statute, or a regulation adopted by a state agency, could at least be expected to apply cost-benefit analysis similar to that applied by the experts at the FDA: How many more lives will be saved by a device which, along with its greater effectiveness, brings a greater risk of harm? A jury, on the other hand, sees only the cost of a more dangerous design, and is not concerned with its benefits; the patients who reaped those benefits are not represented in court. . . .

B.

The dissent would narrow the pre-emptive scope of the term "requirement" on the grounds that it is "difficult to believe that Congress would, without comment, remove all means of judicial recourse" for consumers injured by FDA-approved devices. But, as we have explained, this is exactly what a pre-emption clause for medical devices does by its terms. . . . It is not our job to speculate upon congressional motives. If we were to do so, however, the only indication available—the text of the statute—suggests that the solicitude for those injured by FDA-approved devices, which the dissent finds controlling, was overcome in Congress's estimation by solicitude for those who would suffer without new medical devices if juries were allowed to apply the tort law of 50 States to all innovations.

. . . .

C.

The Riegels contend that the duties underlying negligence, strict-liability, and implied-warranty claims are not pre-empted even if they impose " 'requirements,' " because general common-law duties are not requirements maintained " 'with respect to devices.' " . . . Nothing in the statutory text suggests that the pre-empted state requirement must apply *only* to the relevant device, or only to medical devices and not to all products and all actions in general.

The Riegels' argument to the contrary rests on the text of an FDA regulation which states that the MDA's pre-emption clause does not extend to certain duties, including "[s]tate or local requirements of general applicability where the purpose of the requirement relates either to other products in addition to devices (e.g., requirements such as general electrical codes, and the Uniform Commercial Code (warranty of fitness)), or to unfair trade practices in which the requirements are not limited to devices." 21 CFR § 808.1(d)(1). . . .

All in all, we think that § 808.1(d)(1) can add nothing to our analysis but confusion. . . .

IV.

State requirements are pre-empted under the MDA only to the extent that they are "different from, or in addition to" the requirements imposed by federal law. § 360k(a)(1). Thus, § 360k does not prevent a State from providing a damages remedy for claims premised on a violation of FDA regulations; the state duties in such a case "parallel," rather than add to, federal requirements. . . .

For the foregoing reasons, the judgment of the Court of Appeals is affirmed.

L. RADIATION CONTROL

FDA's responsibility for assuring the safety and effectiveness of medical equipment is not confined to the device provisions of the FD&C Act. Under the Radiation Control for Health and Safety Act of 1968, 82 Stat. 1173, originally codified as 42 U.S.C. 263b *et seq.*, recodified and integrated into the FD&C Act by the 1990 Act as FD&C Act sections 531 *et seq.*, the agency is also responsible for regulating products that emit radiation, many of which fit the definition of a medical device. This responsibility was transferred to FDA in 1971, 36 Fed. Reg. 12803 (July 7, 1971), and combined with the medical devices program in 1982, 47 Fed. Reg. 44614 (Oct. 8, 1992).

The radiological health provisions of the FD&C Act give FDA primary authority for protecting the public from "electronic product radiation." The Act defines this term as "(A) any ionizing or non-ionizing electromagnetic or particulate radiation, or (B) any sonic, infrasonic, or ultrasonic wave, which is emitted from an electronic product as the result of the operation of an electronic circuit in such product." Section 531(1). In its regulations, FDA provides a lengthy list of examples of electronic products subject to the Radiation Control for Health and Safety Act. 21 C.F.R. 1000.15. Many of the listed products are medical devices, but the majority are not. Medical products subject to the provisions include, among others, x-ray machines, tanning and therapeutic lamps, diathermy units, cauterizers, electromedical equipment, and medical lasers. Some of the nonmedical products on FDA's list are television receivers, accelerators, black light sources, welding equipment, infrared alarm systems, microwave ovens, radar devices, remote control devices, vibrators, sound amplification equipment, and "art-form" lasers. This list, published in 1973, does not include important new categories of radiation-emitting electronic products over which FDA has authority, such as cell phones, for example.

FDA's ability to minimize the risks of medical devices without nullifying their benefits depends in many instances on its power to control the ways in which they are put to use by medical professionals. This theme of utilization review and control pervades the field of medical radiation.

1. PERFORMANCE STANDARDS

FDA's most important power under the radiation provisions of the FD&C Act is the authority to issue performance standards, by regulation, "to control the emission of electronic product radiation . . . if [it] determines that such standards are necessary for the public health and safety." Section 534(a)(1). The statute provides that radiation safety standards "may include provisions for the testing of such products and the measurement of their electronic product radiation emissions, may require the attachment of warning signs and labels, and may require the provision of instructions for the installation, operation, and use of such products." Unstated, but assumed, is FDA's power through such standards to control the physical characteristics of electronic products. The Act requires FDA, before issuing a radiation safety standard, to consult with an advisory committee known as the "Technical Electronic Product Radiation Safety Standards Subcommittee." Every manufacturer of an electronic product subject to a standard must, upon delivery to the dealer or distributor, certify that the product conforms to the applicable standard. 21 C.F.R. 1010.2.

Although FDA has published only one medical device performance standard under Section 514, it has finalized 13 radiation safety standards under section 534. *See* 21 C.F.R. Parts 1020–50.

Electronic Products; Performance Standard for Diagnostic X–Ray Systems and Their Major Components; Final Rule

70 Fed. Reg. 33998 (June 10, 2005).

The Food and Drug Administration is issuing a final rule to amend the Federal performance standard for diagnostic x-ray systems and their major components (the performance standard). The agency is taking this action to update the performance standard to account for changes in technology and use of radiographic and fluoroscopic x-ray systems. . . .

The purpose of the performance standard for diagnostic x-ray systems is to improve the public health by reducing exposure to and the detriment associated with unnecessary ionizing radiation while assuring the clinical utility of the images produced.

In order for mandatory performance standards to continue to provide the intended public health protection, the standards must be modified when appropriate to reflect the changes in technology and product usage. When the performance standard was originally developed, the only means of producing a fluoroscopic image was either a screen of fluorescent material or an x-ray image intensifier tube. Therefore, the standard was written with these two types of image receptors in mind. A number of technological developments have been implemented for radiographic and fluoroscopic x-ray systems, such as solid-state x-ray imaging (SSXI) and new modes of image recording (*e.g.*, digital recording to computer memory or other media). These developments have made the application of the current standard to systems incorporating these new technologies cumbersome and awkward. FDA is therefore amending the performance standard for diagnostic x-ray systems and their major components in 21 CFR 1020.30, 1020.31, and 1020.32 to address the recent changes in technology. . . .

These amendments will require that newly-manufactured x-ray systems include additional features that physicians may use to minimize x-ray exposures to patients. Advances in technology have made several of these new features feasible at minimal additional cost.

. . . .

The benefits that are expected to result from these amendments are reductions in acute skin injuries and radiation-induced cancers. These benefits will result from two types of changes to the performance standard that should reduce patient dose and associated radiation detriment without compromising image quality.

The first type of change involves several new equipment features that will directly affect the intensity or size of the x-ray field. . . .

The second type of change . . . involves the information to be provided by the manufacturer or directly by the system itself that may be utilized by the operator to more efficiently use the x-ray system and thereby reduce patient dose. . . .

Projected benefits are quantified in table 3 of this document in terms of: (1) Collective dose savings, (2) numbers of lives spared premature death associated with radiation-induced cancer, (3) collective years of life spared premature death, (4) numbers of reports of fluoroscopic skin burns precluded, and (5) pecuniary estimates associated with the preceding four items. . . .

Costs to manufacturers of fluoroscopic and radiographic systems will increase due to these proposals. FDA will also experience costs for increased compliance activities. Some costs represent one-time expenditures to develop new designs or manufacturing processes to incorporate the regulatory changes. Other costs are the ongoing costs of providing improved equipment performance and features with each installed unit. . . .

The cost-effectiveness of the final regulation using a 7-percent discount rate has a modal value of $184,400 within an estimated range of between $50,900 and $667,600 per cancer avoided. . . .

NOTES

1.   *CT Scanners.* As a result of the development and widespread use of computed tomography (CT) diagnostic x-ray systems, FDA revised the x-ray standard to include a section on this equipment. 49 Fed. Reg. 34698 (Aug. 31, 1984), codified at 21 C.F.R. 1020.33.

2.   *Mammography.* In the Mammography Quality Standards Act of 1992 (MQSA), 106 Stat. 3547, section 263b of the Public Health Service Act, 42 U.S.C. 2636, Congress gave FDA responsibility for certifying mammography (radiology of the breast) facilities. Under the statute, it is unlawful to operate any mammography facility in the United States, with the exception of a Department of Veterans Affairs facility, without FDA certification. To obtain FDA certification, a mammography facility must meet quality standards set forth in agency regulations and be accredited by an approved accreditation body. 21 C.F.R. Part 900.

3.   *Baggage Screening Machines.* FDA regulations contain a separate performance standard for "cabinet x-ray systems," which include systems "designed primarily for the inspection of carry-on baggage at airline, railroad, and bus terminals, and in similar facilities." 21 C.F.R. 1020.40(a)(3).

———

FDA has established a radiation safety standard for sunlamps and ultraviolet lamps intended for use in sunlamps. 44 Fed. Reg. 65352 (Nov. 9, 1979), codified at 21 C.F.R. 1040.20. The standard regulates "irradiation ratio limits," timer systems, shut-off switches, protective eyewear, lamp compatibility, and labeling. Ultraviolet lamps for tanning are also regulated as Class I medical devices. 21 C.F.R. 878.4635. This classification reflects the fact that FDA relies more on its radiation safety authorities than on its device authorities to regulate these products. Nonetheless, in 2013, the agency proposed to reclassify sunlamp products into Class II. 78 Fed. Reg. 27117 (May 9, 2013).

In the 1980s, the rapid growth of commercial suntanning facilities led the agency to revise the radiation safety standard, to reflect the changes in product technology and design. The following excerpts from the preamble to the final rule focus on the labeling aspects of the revised standard.

Sunlamp Products; Performance Standard

50 Fed. Reg. 36548 (September 6, 1985).

. . . .

FDA believes that irradiation of the skin with ultraviolet radiation to induce skin tanning is hazardous. The performance standard for sunlamp products was established to protect the consumer from acute burns (as evidenced by erythema) and from exposure to hazardous radiation that is unnecessary for skin tanning (in this case, UV radiation of wavelengths in air of less than 260 nanometers (nm)) and to warn the consumer of the known adverse effects to the body after exposure to ultraviolet radiation. FDA believes that the user of a sunlamp product can take appropriate action when informed of the possible adverse effects to the body from exposure to ultraviolet radiation, if the product is equipped with necessary safety performance features. . . .

A comment suggested that the warning statement required by § 1040.20(d)(1)(i) should utilize the signal word "CAUTION" rather than "DANGER." The comment contended that the word "DANGER" implies an immediate and serious threat to life, a hazard not associated with UVA sunlamp products, *i.e.*, sunlamp products that operate in the wavelength region of 320 to 400 nm. The comment stated that there is a need for an appropriate warning label cautioning the user that certain safeguards need to be observed to avoid injury and that prolonged use has long-term risk.

The agency believes that the word "DANGER" as used on the warning statement is appropriate. Exposure to ultraviolet radiation can be an immediate threat to life for people using photosensitizing medications or cosmetics and for people with a medical condition that causes them to be sensitive to ultraviolet radiation, for example, photoallergies.

One comment urged that UVA lamps should be exempt from the provisions of § 1040.20(d) that require the warning: "As with natural sunlight, overexposure can cause eye and skin injury and allergic reactions. Repeated exposure may cause premature aging of the skin and skin cancer." The comment argued that radiation at wavelengths in air longer than 320 nm cannot induce skin cancer and that only radiation at wavelengths in air shorter than 320 nm is responsible for premature skin aging. The comment argued further that UVA radiation that does not contain measurable UVB radiation (280 to 320 nm) has positive effects, for example, a UVA tan can protect a person against the harmful UVB radiation of the sun. . . .

FDA disagrees that it has been proven that UVA does not cause skin cancer or premature skin aging, or that UVA radiation can protect humans against UVB radiation. Relatively few studies have been carried out on the long-term biological effects of UVA radiation in humans or in animals. Further studies are needed to establish clearly the long-term biological effects of UVA radiation. There are, however, reports that, under long-term continuous exposure, UVA radiation can induce skin cancer in test animals. Also, there is evidence that the incidence of skin tumors induced in animals by irradiation with a combination of UVB and UVA radiation can be increased by subsequent irradiation with UVA alone. . . .

Based on available evidence, FDA concludes that to exempt UVA lamps from the warning statement required by the standard would not promote the public health and safety.

Therefore, . . . Part 1040 is amended . . . [b]y revising § 1040.20, to read as follows:

§ 1040.20 Sunlamp products and ultraviolet lamps intended for use in sunlamp products.

(d) *Label requirements*. . . .

(1) *Labels for sunlamp products.* Each sunlamp product shall have a label(s) which contains:

(i) A warning statement with the words "DANGER—Ultraviolet radiation. Follow instructions. Avoid overexposure. As with natural sunlight, overexposure can cause eye and skin injury and allergic reactions. Repeated exposure may cause premature aging of the skin and skin cancer. WEAR PROTECTIVE EYEWEAR; FAILURE TO MAY RESULT IN SEVERE BURNS OR LONG–TERM INJURY TO THE EYES. Medications or cosmetics may increase your sensitivity to the ultraviolet radiation. Consult physician before using sunlamp if you are using medications or have a history of skin problems or believe yourself especially sensitive to sunlight. If you do not tan in the sun, you are unlikely to tan from the use of this product."

NOTES

1. *Further Revisions?* In 1999, FDA published an advance notice of proposed rulemaking in which it stated its intent to propose amendments to the performance standard for sunlamp products. 64 Fed. Reg. 6288 (Feb. 9, 1999). The notice explained:

> The agency is taking this action to address concerns about the adequacy of the warnings on sunlamp products, current recommended exposure schedule to minimize risk to customers who choose to produce and maintain a tan, current labeling for replacement lamps, and current health warnings which do not reflect recent advances in photobiological research.

FDA has not issued a proposed regulation amending the standard.

Pursuant to a requirement in section 230 of the 2007 Act, FDA submitted a report to Congress on labeling information regarding the relationship of indoor tanning devices to skin cancer and other skin damage. When it proposed to reclassify sunlamp products from Class I to Class II devices in 2013, FDA also proposed a variety of special controls (under its device authorities), including a mandatory warning against use on persons under the age of 18. 78 Fed. Reg. 27117 (May 9, 2013).

2. *Violations of Sunlamp Standards.* In lengthy litigation, FDA successfully obtained an injunction and civil penalties for violations of the

sunlamp standard in 47 separate suntanning booths. *Throneberry v. FDA*, 1983–1984 FDLI Jud. Rec. 242 (E.D. Tenn. 1983), 1983–1984 FDLI Jud. Rec. 382 (E.D. Tenn. 1984).

3. *Relationship to Device Statute.* The precise relationship between the standard-setting and premarket approval authority of the Medical Device Amendments and the Radiation Act's standard-setting authority is uncertain. It does seem clear that FDA is obligated to regulate radiation-emitting medical devices under the 1976 Amendments and has discretion to regulate them under the Radiation Act as well. Because all new radiation-emitting medical devices are subject to the premarket approval requirement of section 515, the agency may have few if any occasions to establish additional radiation safety standards for medical devices under the Radiation Act.

4. *Variances.* Under 21 C.F.R. 1010.4, FDA may, upon application of a manufacturer, grant a variance from all or part of any electronic product performance standard. After 20 years of publishing these variances in the Federal Register, many of them for laser light shows, FDA observed that it had never received comment on any of them and announced it was discontinuing publication. 53 Fed. Reg. 52683 (Dec. 29, 1988).

2. ENFORCEMENT OF RADIATION STANDARDS

The Radiation Act, now incorporated into the FD&C Act, provides FDA with various tools in addition to performance standards to ensure the radiation safety of electronic products. For example, section 537 states that FDA may inspect any "factory, warehouse, or establishment in which electronic products are manufactured or held" if the agency "finds for good cause that the methods, tests, or programs related to electronic product radiation safety in [the facility] may not be adequate or reliable." Section 537(a). The broad sweep of this provision is epitomized by FDA's declaration, on its website, that it may "inspect displays of laser light shows to ensure the public is protected. Producers of laser light shows are required to tell the FDA where they are planning a show so that the agency can inspect it if possible and take action if required."

Section 535(f) requires manufacturers of electronic products to notify purchasers when they discover safety defects related to the emission of radiation and to repair the defect, replace the product, or refund the cost. Sections 535(a) & (f). When Congress gave these same additional authorities to FDA with respect to medical devices in the 1990 Act, the Radiation Act served as a model. *See supra* p. 1271.

For many years, the Radiation Act was the only statute administered by FDA that authorized civil penalties. As discussed in the chapter on enforcement, *supra* p. 262, Congress has, since the 1980s, given FDA the power to impose civil penalties for an assortment of other types of violations, including, under the 1990 Act, violations of the FD&C Act's device requirements. There is an important distinction, however, between the civil penalties authorized by the Radiation Act and those authorized elsewhere. Under the Radiation Act, the United States must file an action in federal district court to obtain an order imposing civil money penalties. Under all the later civil penalty provisions, FDA can impose the monetary penalties itself, through administrative order, after notice and an administrative hearing.

FDA's civil penalties policy under the Radiation Act is set forth in Compliance Policy Guide No. 7133.23 (Mar. 1, 1983) (rev. Apr. 2005). Although the agency has not recently pursued civil penalties under the Radiation Act, it has sought and collected civil fines from mammography facilities under the Mammography Quality Standards Act.

3. COLLECTION AND DISSEMINATION OF INFORMATION

Section 532(a) requires FDA to establish and carry out an "electronic product radiation control program designed to protect the public health and safety from electronic product radiation." As part of this program, the agency must not only develop and administer performance standards for electronic products, but also, for example, conduct, coordinate, and support testing and research and collect information from other agencies, industry, and professional organizations.

One important authority FDA has in this area is to "(A) collect and make available, through publications and other appropriate means, the results of, and other information concerning, research and studies relating to the nature and extent of the hazards and control of electronic product radiation; and (B) make such recommendations relating to such hazards and control as [FDA] considers appropriate." FD&C Act 532(b)(1)(A). Pursuant to this provision, through the 1980s FDA issued numerous recommendations relating to safe exposure to radiation. These recommendations were initially codified in the Code of Federal Regulations. In 1983, however, the agency ceased publishing its radiation exposure recommendations in the C.F.R. and instead started merely to announce their availability.

CDRH apparently has not issued a radiation exposure recommendation or guidance document since 1992. Moreover, FDA has neither affirmed nor withdrawn two radiation exposure recommendations it announced, but did not publish, in the Federal Register in the mid-1980s. Today, most of the guidance documents issued by the agency in the radiological health area concern manufacturer reporting requirements or procedures for the FDA field force. Occasionally, CDRH provides radiation exposure risk information and prevention advice on the FDA website.

FDA's primary initiative in the collection of radiological health data is a 30-year old survey program called the Nationwide Evaluation of X-ray Trends (NEXT). Under this program, CDRH collaborates with the Conference of Radiation Control Program Directors, an organization made up primarily of radiation professionals in state and local government. Each year, the NEXT program selects a particular radiological examination for study. State radiation control personnel then collect radiation exposure data from a nationally representative sample of U.S. clinical facilities, and CDRH compiles, analyzes, and publishes the survey results.

Because FDA has never had significant amounts of money to fund radiological health research and only occasionally publishes radiation exposure recommendations, the NEXT program and the issuance and administration of performance standards are the most important components of the "electronic product radiation control program" mandated by section 532(a).

4. OTHER FEDERAL RADIATION CONTROL PROGRAMS

Several federal agencies in addition to FDA regulate exposure to radiation. While far from exhaustive, this comment describes some of these other authorities and their relationship to FDA's authority under the Radiation Act.

FCC. The Federal Communications Commission (FCC) authorizes and licenses products, transmitters, and facilities that generate radiofrequency (RF) and microwave radiation. The FCC does not itself develop radiation exposure guidelines, but instead adopts standards promulgated by other agencies and by private organizations. FCC and FDA both regulate wireless telephones. FCC ensures that all wireless phones sold in the United States follow safety guidelines that limit RF energy, while FDA monitors the health effects of wireless telephones. Each agency has the authority to take action if a wireless phone produces hazardous levels of RF energy.

NRC. The Nuclear Regulatory Commission (NRC), in addition to regulating the medical use of radioactive byproduct material, 10 C.F.R. Part 35, *see supra* p. 788, also regulates the manufacture and transfer of other types of products containing byproduct material. 10 C.F.R. Part 32.

FAA. Laser light radiation projected into navigable airspace, in connection with a laser light show or scientific operations, can damage the eyesight of aircraft pilots and passengers. The Federal Aviation Administration (FAA) and FDA have entered into a memorandum of understanding to coordinate their regulatory programs to prevent this danger. FAA–FDA Memorandum of Understanding (1998).

EPA. The Environmental Protection Agency (EPA), on its website, describes itself as "the primary federal agency for protecting people and the environment from harmful and avoidable exposure to radiation." EPA has authority to advise the president and other agencies on the health hazards of radiation under 42 U.S.C. 2021(h). It produces guidances and technical reports for use by both federal and state agencies responsible for radiation safety. EPA's radiation protection activities include, among others: running radioactive waste management programs; disseminating information and issuing regulations concerning naturally occurring radioactive sources in the ground, air, and water; overseeing the cleanup of radioactive sites; and participating in nuclear emergency response plans.

Interagency Working Groups. Over the years, various interagency working groups have been established to address issues of radiation safety in a coordinated manner.

CHAPTER 11

COSMETICS

A. HISTORICAL AND STATUTORY BACKGROUND

Peter Barton Hutt, *A History of Government Regulation of Adulteration and Misbranding of Cosmetics*

In COSMETIC REGULATION IN A COMPETITIVE ENVIRONMENT (Norman F. Estrin & James M. Akerson eds., 2000).

The use of cosmetics began long before recorded history. The earliest cosmetics found by archaeologists are dated from about 10,000 B.C. Aboriginal societies have painted their bodies for centuries for a variety of reasons—as camouflage, a mark of status or achievement, for sexual attraction, to obtain spiritual protection, for community celebrations, and other purposes.

Historical evidence demonstrates widespread use of virtually all of the types of cosmetic products available today beginning about 5,000 B.C. in Egypt and later in ancient Greece and Rome. The best documentation of this comes from Pliny the Elder (23–79 A.D.), who recorded the use in Roman society of every form of cosmetic known to us today: hair dye, eyelash dye, eyebrow dye, freckle removers, rouge, deodorants and antiperspirants, depilatories, wrinkle removers, hair preservatives and restorers, bust firmers, sunburn products, complexion aids, moisturizers, mouthwashes and breath fresheners, toothpaste, face powder, and of course, perfume, to name only some. Pliny also described their sources, which were primarily readily available plant and animal materials.

From these ancient times to the present, cosmetics have continued to be widely used. Following Guttenberg's invention of the printing press in the fifteenth century, books began to appear on how to make and use cosmetics. At the same time, however, a Puritan movement was developing whose philosophy opposed the use of cosmetics. Books were published beginning in the late 1500s strongly criticizing those who sought to enhance their natural beauty. As the Puritan movement waned a century later, however, beauty specialists advertised their products and skills and cosmetic products appeared as commercial products in retail stores. Widely read books were also published advising women how to make their own cosmetics.

From 1700 on, cosmetic products of all types have been marketed and used throughout the world. The specific types of cosmetic products in greatest use at any time are influenced by current beauty and fashion trends and popular philosophy as well as personal taste. Some books stress the importance of personal appearance and others criticize any societal emphasis on beauty. Critics have attacked the cosmetic industry generally or offer selective reviews of particular products. Yet over the past century, hundreds of beauty books have been best-sellers, beauty magazines have been widely read, the founders of cosmetic companies and the models who appear in their advertising have become well-recognized celebrities, and a number of the largest and most successful consumer marketing companies have helped increase the annual retail sales of cosmetics in the United States from about $350,000 in 1850 to $7 million in 1900, $150 million in 1940, $1 billion in 1960 and close to $35 billion today.

———

FDA first acquired authority to regulate cosmetics in the 1938 Act. The safety of cosmetics, however, had been a concern in Congress as early as 1881. *See* H.R. Rep. No. 199, 46th Cong., 3d Sess. 2 (1881). Following the example of a Massachusetts statute (L. Mass. 1886, c. 171), Congress in 1898 amended the District of Columbia food and drug law to define the term "drug" to include cosmetics. 30 Stat. 246. The original 1897 bill to create a federal law similarly "included cosmetics in the definition of drugs, but this portion was dropped in 1900 as partial payment for support from the National Pure Food and Drug Congress." Oscar E. Anderson, *Pioneer Statute: The Pure Food and Drugs Act of 1906*, 13 J. Pub. L. 189, 195 (1964).

Senate Report No. 361
74th Congress, 1st Session (1935).

While the definition of the term cosmetic does not include devices, it is drawn in broad terms to include all substances and preparations, other than ordinary toilet or household soap, intended for cleansing, or altering the appearance of, or promoting the attractiveness of the person. Cosmetics may be used externally, orifically, or even internally as in the case of arsenic for clearing the complexion. The definition therefore must be sufficiently broad to cover potential abuses no matter how the substance or preparation is used. While soaps sold only for ordinary toilet or household use are specifically exempted from the definition of cosmetic and will not be subject to the definition of drug, soaps for which claims concerning disease are made or which are sold as pharmacopoeial articles will come within the definition of drug and will thus be subject to regulation. Likewise soaps intended for other than ordinary toilet or household use and represented, for instance, as beautifying agents, will come within the definition of cosmetic. . . .

Section [601(a)] deals with adulterated cosmetics. . . . There are on the market a number of preparations, notably hair dyes, eyelash and eyebrow dyes, complexion bleaches and depilatories, which have caused serious impairment to the health of users and, in a number of instances, have resulted in such injuries as blindness and paralysis. These injuries have been caused by such toxic substances as certain coal-tar dyes and metals like lead, arsenic, mercury, and thallium, upon which the beautifying "action" of the preparations depends. Paragraph (a) is intended to protect the user against such hazards to health.

It will be noted that in drafting this paragraph the same general form has been used, to avoid complications arising from allergic reaction to wholesome products, as was employed in dealing with food under section [401](a)(2). . . . [O]nly those products are considered as adulterated which contain poisonous and deleterious substances, and then only when those substances are present in such quantity which may render the product injurious. This would not prevent the marketing of a face powder or cream or any other cosmetic which did not contain poisonous or deleterious ingredients, even though such cosmetics might contain ingredients to which a certain class of unfortunate people are allergic. . . .

Paragraph (a) of . . . section [602] is identical with the general misbranding provision on food. . . . Paragraphs (b) and (c) . . . are merely an extension to cosmetics of provisions in the food and drug chapters. . . .

NOTES

1.   *History.* For a broad history of cosmetic regulation, see Peter Barton Hutt *A History of Government Regulation of Adulteration and Misbranding of Cosmetics, in* Cosmetic Regulation in a Competitive Environment (Norman F. Estrin & James M. Akerson eds., 2000).

2.   *Commentary.* For a treatment of cosmetic regulation in historical context, see Hugo Mock, *Cosmetic Law: History and Observation,* 1 Food Drug Cosm. L.Q. 61 (1946). Accounts of the dangers of cosmetics, which led to their inclusion in the 1938 Act, may be found in Arthur Kallet & F. J. Schlink, 100,000,000 Guinea Pigs, Ch. V. (1933); Ruth deForest Lamb, American Chamber Of Horrors, Ch. 2 (1936). A defense of the industry was published by Everett G. McDonough, Truth About Cosmetics (1937).

3.   *State Regulation.* The constitutionality of an early state law requiring the registration of cosmetic preparations was upheld in *Bourjois, Inc. v. Chapman,* 301 U.S. 183 (1937).

George P. Larrick,* *Some Current Problems in the Regulation of Cosmetics Under the Federal Food, Drug, and Cosmetic Act*

3 FOOD DRUG COSMETIC LAW QUARTERLY 570 (1948).

We do recognize that a great deal of progress has been made, but the principal object of this short talk is to emphasize the need for universal acceptance in the industry of the fact that a real scientific appraisal of the safety and suitability of materials used should be made before an ingredient is included in the composition of products designed to enhance the attractiveness of users. The same scientific approach should, of course, be followed in deciding what claims can legitimately be made. . . .

There is still, in our opinion, too much secrecy concerning the precise composition of some ingredients of beautifying agents. We encounter instances wherein manufacturers or distributors of finished products do not know the composition of the preparations which they sell. . . .

---

*   [Mr. Larrick was an FDA Associate Commissioner in 1948 and served as Commissioner from 1954 to 1965.]

This situation encourages changes in composition of the basic ingredients without the knowledge of the cosmetic firm. Scarcities or price variations are sometimes an invitation to change these compositions without notice. Occasionally, these circumstances have led to the introduction of dangerous ingredients. . . .

———

The Select Committee to Investigate the Use of Chemicals in Food Products, chaired by Representative James Delaney of New York, was established on June 20, 1950, pursuant to House Resolution 323, 81st Cong., 1st Sess. *See supra* p. 552. On October 15, 1951, the House extended the scope of the Delaney Committee's authority to include "an investigation and study of the nature, extent, and effect of the use of chemicals, compounds, and synthetics in the production, processing, preparation, and packaging of cosmetics to determine the effect of the use of such chemicals, compounds, and synthetics upon the health and welfare of the Nation. . . ." A year later, the Committee issued its final report.

Investigation of the Use of Chemicals in Foods and Cosmetics

House Report No. 2182, 82d Congress, 2d Session (1952).

. . . The partial regulation of cosmetics . . . has appreciably decreased the incidence of serious harm, but insufficiently tested cosmetics still constitute a source of considerable annoyance, discomfort, and disability.

Under existing law, a dangerous cosmetic can be removed from the market by the institution of seizure proceedings. Unfortunately, the protection offered the public by this procedure is somewhat illusory. Before the government can avail itself of this remedy, data must first be assembled which will sustain the Government's burden of establishing to the satisfaction of a court and jury, by a preponderance of the evidence, that the cosmetic may cause injury to users. . . . It is clear that substances and combinations of substances have been used in cosmetics which, because of their injurious effects, would have been excluded if a law had existed requiring that adequate information concerning their safety be obtained before the cosmetics were sold to consumers. . . .

There is probably no cosmetic ingredient which can be used with impunity by every human being. In the case of virtually every cosmetic preparation, some particular person or limited number of persons may experience an unfavorable reaction, although all others may suffer no ill effects. Allowance must necessarily be made, therefore, for some incidence of untoward effects. . . .

1. Pretesting

Most of the representatives of the cosmetic industry took the position that existing legislation was adequate to protect the public fully. . . . The incongruity of the position of some industry representatives is exemplified by their testimony that the companies they represent conduct rigorous and exhaustive tests, and maintain strict controls over their products, as a necessary precaution to protect both themselves and the health of their customers. Nevertheless, they were opposed to a requirement that all cosmetic manufacturers observe essentially the same safety standards. . . .

. . . Your committee recommends . . . that the Federal Food, Drug, and Cosmetic Act be amended to require that cosmetics be subjected to essentially the same safety requirements as now apply to new drugs. Under such an amendment, data would not be required to be submitted to the Food and Drug Administration with respect to cosmetics which are generally recognized by qualified experts as safe under the conditions of use for which they are sold. . . .

2. Soaps

. . . Soaps which have been on the market for years, and are generally recognized by competent authorities as being safe, would be unaffected by pretesting legislation. As indicated, however, inadequately tested hair shampoos have caused injury to the eye. There is an even greater possibility of injury from soaps containing new ingredients, for soaps are used to wash the face and, therefore, more readily make contact with the eye than do shampoos. . . . Your committee is of the opinion that the Federal Food, Drug, and Cosmetic Act is in need of amendment to bring soaps within the definition of cosmetics.

3. Labeling of Ingredients

. . . Physicians who specialize in the fields of allergy and dermatology testified that the labeling of cosmetic ingredients would be most helpful in their diagnosis and treatment of patients who may be suffering from the effects of some cosmetic ingredient. . . . Industry representatives testified, generally, in opposition to the labeling of ingredients, on the ground that cosmetics are composed of a large number of ingredients and that a long list affixed to the product would destroy the attractiveness of the package. The committee recognizes the importance of packaging attractiveness in the sale of cosmetics, and that in some instances it would be most difficult to set forth on the label of a cosmetic preparation a list of its numerous ingredients. It is the committee's view, however, that a list of ingredients need not in all cases be physically affixed to the cosmetic. Where the number of ingredients is quite large, the list can be contained, in most instances, in the cosmetic package in the form of an accompanying circular. . . .

4. Coal–Tar Hair Dyes

Coal-tar hair dyes have long been a source of difficulty for cosmetic users. Paraphenylenediamine, a coal-tar color base for a large number of hair dyes, has a high sensitizing potential. There was considerable testimony that there have been reactions to this substance varying from slight dermatitis around the forehead, eyes, scalp, face, and neck, to generalized dermatitis requiring hospitalization. . . .

Coal-tar hair dyes are permitted special privileges under [section 601(a)]. . . . These provisions of the law have proven inadequate to provide the protection intended. . . .

The cosmetic industry made the following response.

S. L. Mayham,* *Chemicals in Cosmetics*
7 FOOD DRUG COSMETIC LAW JOURNAL 184 (1952).

. . . The provisions of the present law, as they affect cosmetics, are entirely adequate to control any situation which is controllable with any type of law whatever. . . .

. . . I have surveyed the 189 (and there are only 189) adjudicated cases on cosmetics since the enactment of the law in 1938. During those 13 years there have been 95 adjudicated cases brought under the adulteration provisions of the Act. One of these was won by the defendant, leaving 94 such cases. Of these 94 cases, only 59 were brought because of the presence of harmful or deleterious ingredients used in the manufacture of the cosmetics. The other 35 were because of the presence of filth, products being held under insanitary conditions, and for other reasons technically and legalistically classified as adulterations. Of these 59 which were brought because of the presence of a harmful ingredient, 22 came in the very early stages. . . . [L]et us be generous and say there were 34 cases where the presence of a chemical in a cosmetic was brought to court and proved to have done a harm.

This was over the period of 13 years since the law went into effect. During that time, the Toilet Goods Association has estimated that . . . 26,301,000,000 packages of cosmetics [have been] sold and consumed in the United States. I contend that to find only 34 cases where harm has arisen from the presence of a poisonous ingredient in over 26 billion packages of cosmetics sold is not only *de minimis* but is really "much ado about nothing." . . .

The first [proposal] is to write into the cosmetic section of the present law something akin to the new-drug application provision of the present law. . . . From my observation of the industry, I would say that more than two thirds of the present cosmetic manufacturers do not have sufficient resources to file one single new-cosmetic application should there be such a provision in the law. . . .

The second proposal . . . is to list all ingredients of every cosmetic on the label. . . . Let us look at this proposal for a moment and consider how it would work. First, I have examined a great many cosmetic formulas. Few of them contain less than 15 ingredients and many of them contain 50 or more. Just where on the label or in the labeling would this list appear in distinguishable form? If you consider the perfume ingredients used in some of these products, you might well have to list 150 items on the label. The names of most of these would be completely unfamiliar to anyone who might want to read them. . . .

. . . [L]et us go back now for a moment to the lady who is allergic. She goes to a dermatologist who discovers that she is allergic possibly to lanolin, so she wants to avoid lanolin in cosmetics. If her dermatologist

---

*   [Mr. Mayham was Executive Vice–President of The Toilet Goods Association, now renamed The Cosmetic, Toiletry, and Fragrance Association.]

really knows his business he is aware of the fact that there are already a number of cosmetic manufacturers making hypo-allergenic cosmetics which exclude every possible known allergen and that these companies are willing to make up on special order at very, very reasonable prices cosmetics excluding the ingredients to which the individual may be allergic. So, the industry itself has made provision [sic] to take care of these cases of allergy and it would seem folly to insist on listing all the ingredients of a cosmetic, when absolutely nothing in the way of public protection would be accomplished by doing it. . . .

. . . I would call attention to the record of the hearings of the Delaney Committee to date. Practically every industry witness who has appeared has shown how carefully he insists upon control of the product from the time of purchase of the raw material until the ultimate consumer actually uses it. He tests the raw materials, he tests the products in process, he tests the finished product and he does so without any great love for the public, but because he knows that if a manufacturer puts out something that is harmful and poisonous he will not stay in business. . . .

————

A quarter of a century later, the issues dividing proponents and opponents of new cosmetic legislation had not changed.

U.S. General Accounting Office, Lack of Authority Hampers Attempts to Increase Cosmetic Safety

GAO Report No. HRD–78–139 (August 8, 1978).

About 125 ingredients available for use in cosmetics are suspected of causing cancer, according to studies. In addition, about 25 are suspected of causing birth defects and 20 may cause adverse effects on the nervous system, including headaches, drowsiness, and convulsions. . . . Although many of the reported adverse effects have not been verified, 12 of the ingredients are known to cause cancer in humans or contain impurities known to cause cancer in humans. Another 18 ingredients have been found to cause cancer in animals. . . .

Although there is increasing evidence that some cosmetic products and ingredients may carry a significant risk of injury to consumers, the Food and Drug Administration does not have an effective program for regulating cosmetics. . . . The act . . . does NOT authorize the Food and Drug Administration to require manufacturers to

- register their plants or products,
- file data on the ingredients in their products,
- file reports of cosmetic-related injuries, or
- test their products for safety. . . .

. . . [I]n 1972 and 1973 the agency asked cosmetic manufacturers, packers, and distributors to register their plants and file information on the ingredients used in their products and the injuries reported from their use. As of December 1977, about 40 percent of the manufacturers and packers had registered their plants; less than 20 percent of the manufacturers, packers, and distributors had filed ingredient listings, and less than 4 percent had filed injury reports. A Food and Drug Administration regulation requires that labeling of cosmetics that have not been adequately tested for safety include a warning to that effect. This regulation cannot be effectively enforced because the agency is not authorized to require manufacturers to test their products for safety or to make their test available to the agency. In addition, many manufacturers have refused Food and Drug Administration inspectors access to manufacturing records, such as qualitative and quantitative formulas, sales or shipping records, and consumer complaint files. The agency lacks authority to require that such records be made available. . . .

The Food and Drug Administration has not inspected most manufacturers' plants or sampled most of their products for compliance with the Federal Food, Drug, and Cosmetic Act. Only about half the cosmetic establishments were inspected between fiscal years 1969 and 1975. Since 1975 the agency identified about 1,000 additional manufacturers, which it had never inspected because they had been unknown to the agency. The Food and Drug Administration also has not established criteria to determine whether adequate methods, facilities, and controls are used in all phases of manufacturing and distribution of cosmetics. According to an agency official, about 75 percent of a sample of over 300 firms inspected since 1976 had deficiencies in their manufacturing practices. Between 1974 and 1976 Food and Drug Administration inspectors and laboratories identified over 400 violations of the cosmetic provisions of the act which they believed warranted some form of regulatory action. Yet only 141 regulatory actions were taken; 54 involved 1 violative product. No prosecutions were started.

Establishing regulations to prohibit or limit the use of an individual ingredient or requiring the use of a specific warning on the label is an effective way to increase consumer safety with regard to a specific product or class of products. However, as of January 1, 1978, the Food and Drug Administration had established regulations governing the use of only 11 ingredients used in cosmetics and had required precautionary labeling only on feminine deodorant sprays, aerosols containing chlorofluorocarbon propellants, and aerosol cosmetics in self-pressurized containers. . . .

Although the Food and Drug Administration cannot require cosmetic manufacturers to test the safety of their products, it can establish regulations identifying appropriate tests which should be used by manufacturers in evaluating safety. The agency said that development of appropriate tests is both difficult and resource demanding.

Some coal tar hair dyes may pose a significant risk of cancer to consumers because they contain colors known to cause or suspected of causing cancer in humans or animals. However, exemptions granted to coal tar hair dyes under the Federal Food, Drug, and Cosmetic Act prevent the Food and Drug Administration from regulating hair dyes effectively. . . . The Congress should repeal these exemptions. . . .

———

The cosmetic industry again responded.

Statement of the Cosmetic, Toiletry and Fragrance Association, Inc.

"Cancer–Causing Chemicals—Part 1 (Safety of Cosmetics and Hair Dyes)," Hearings Before the Subcommittee on Oversight and Investigations of the House Committee on Interstate and Foreign Commerce, 95th Congress, 2d Session (January 26, 1978).

Cosmetic products have an enviable safety record. In September 1973, the panel on chemicals and health of the President's Science Advisory Committee issued a report published by the National Science Foundation which concluded with respect to cosmetics:

> From what may be judged from human experience, the incidence of injury is small.
>
> In the total pattern of environmental risks, those from cosmetics are both infrequent and slight.
>
> While there are no formal pretesting or preclearance requirements for cosmetics, the total effect of individual and informal review—usually private rather than governmental—together with the innocuousness of most materials used, has made the injury rate fairly low by comparison with other widely prevalent sources of hazard.
>
> It seems likely, though solid information is lacking, that the actual injury rate from cosmetics has declined, while the complaint rate has increased as a result of greater consumer awareness of the Food and Drug Administration as a regulatory agency, and of the existence of legal and insurance remedies.

Company records show that reactions to cosmetics are rarely serious and are almost invariably transient and reversible. We are unaware that any case of cancer has ever been shown to have been caused by any cosmetic. . . .

The FDA regulation requiring ingredient labeling for cosmetics is effective. The regulation requires that all retail cosmetic packaging list the ingredients in descending order of predominance with the exception of flavor and fragrance. It is more informative than food ingredient labeling because it requires specific designation of color ingredients, and is far more informative than drug ingredient labeling which requires declaration only of active ingredients.

Any cosmetic which has not been adequately substantiated for safety prior to marketing is required by an FDA regulation to bear the warning statement that "the safety of this product has not been determined." . . . CTFA strongly supports the concept of safety substantiation, firmly believing that it is the obligation of every manufacturer and distributor not to market any cosmetic which has not been substantiated for safety. CTFA has not challenged the legal authority of FDA to promulgate its regulation requiring safety substantiation, and has over the years established many programs designed to help industry meet its obligation to the public even before it became a legal requirement. . . .

CTFA inaugurated its scientific program 30 years ago with the establishment of analytical standards for ingredients commonly used in cosmetics. In the past 10 years it has formed scientific committees of qualified experts to analyze and resolve scientific questions dealing with microbiology, pharmacology, and toxicology, quality assurance, color safety, hair coloring, ingredient nomenclature, and a wide variety of other subjects. CTFA regularly develops and disseminates standards for raw material specifications, testing methods, and ingredient descriptions, as well as technical guidelines to help insure the quality and safety of finished products.

CTFA initiated and submitted three major petitions to FDA, on the basis of which FDA has promulgated regulations governing voluntary registration of cosmetic product manufacturing plants, filing of cosmetic product formulas, and filing of cosmetic product experience reports. The following statistics reflect voluntary industry participation in these three programs as of September 30, 1977. About 900 cosmetic plants have been registered with FDA, representing about 85 percent of the volume of cosmetics sold in the United States. Some 23,500 cosmetic formulas have been submitted to FDA, representing about 80 percent of the volume of cosmetics sold in the United States. About 125 companies were participating in the product experience reporting program, representing about 50 percent of the volume of cosmetics sold in the United States. . . .

CTFA has recently undertaken a major program to review the safety of cosmetic ingredients. All available published and unpublished data on individual ingredients will be compiled and submitted for review by an independent expert panel of eminent scientists. The expert panel members have been required to meet the same strict conflict-of-interest standards as are applied to members of Federal Government advisory committees. The review process is modeled directly after current FDA safety review programs, and includes a consumer liaison selected by consumer organizations, an industry liaison, and an FDA contact person. . . .

NOTES

1. *Reprise.* The same debate was replayed a decade later. *See* "Potential Health Hazards of Cosmetic Products," Hearings Before the Subcomm. on Regulation and Business Opportunities of the House Comm. on Small Business, 100th Cong., 2d Sess. (1988).

2. *Legislative Proposals.* Since 1938, many bills have been introduced in Congress to amend and strengthen the cosmetic provisions of the FD&C Act. *See, e.g.,* Vincent A. Kleinfeld, *What Kind of Cosmetic Legislation?*, 19 Food Drug Cosm. L.J. 87 (1964); Vincent A. Kleinfeld, *The Role of Government in the Field of Cosmetics*, 20 Food Drug Cosm. L.J. 480 (1965); Selma M. Levine, *Cosmetics: Is New Legislation Needed?*, 29 Food Drug Cosm. L.J. 564 (1974); Vincent A. Kleinfeld, *Cosmetic Legislation: Benefit–Risk*, 29 Food Drug Cosm. L.J. 308 (1974); Joseph A. Page & Kathleen A. Blackburn, *Behind the Looking Glass: Administrative, Legislative and Private Approaches to Cosmetic Safety Substantiation*, 24 UCLA L. Rev. 795 (1977). However, these proposals only received serious consideration in the Senate in 1974 and 1975. *See* "Cosmetic Safety Act of 1974," Hearings Before the Subcomm. on Health of the Senate Comm. on Labor and Public Welfare, 93d Cong., 2d Sess. (1974); "Cosmetic Safety

Amendments, 1975," Hearing Before the Subcomm. on Health of the Senate Comm. on Labor and Public Welfare, 94th Cong., 1st Sess. (1975). Cosmetic legislation was reported out of committee, S. Rep. No. 94–1047, 94th Cong., 2d Sess. (1976), and passed the Senate, 122 Cong. Rec. 24629 (July 30, 1976), but was never taken up by the House. *See also* "Cancer–Causing Chemicals—Part 1: Safety of Cosmetics and Hair Dyes," Hearings before the Subcomm. on Oversight and Investigations of the House Comm. on Interstate and Foreign Commerce, 95th Cong., 2d Sess. (1978).

3. *Enforcement History.* For a summary of the 205 notices of judgment in legal actions by FDA against cosmetics between 1938 and 1959, see James C. Munch & James C. Munch, Jr., *Notices of Judgment— Cosmetics*, 14 Food Drug Cosm. L.J. 399 (1959).

4. *Commentary.* For general discussion of the adequacy of FDA regulation of cosmetic safety, see Margaret Gilhooley, *Federal Regulation of Cosmetics: An Overview*, 33 Food Drug Cosm. L.J. 231 (1978); Thomas O. Henteleff, *A Cosmetic Legal Update*, 33 Food Drug Cosm. L.J. 252 (1978); Stephen H. McNamara, *FDA Regulation of Cosmetics in 1979: Industry Concerns*, 34 Food Drug Cosm. L.J. 236 (1979); Jacqueline A. Greff, *Regulation of Cosmetics That Are Also Drugs*, 51 Food & Drug L.J. 243 (1996); Laura A. Heymann, *The Cosmetic/Drug Dilemma: FDA Regulation of Alpha–Hydroxy Acids*, 52 Food & Drug L.J. 357 (1997); Bryan A. Liang & Kurt M. Hartman, *It's Only Skin Deep: FDA Regulation of Skin Care Cosmetics Claims*, 8 Cornell J.L. & Pub. Pol'y 249 (1999); Nakia Elliott, *Cosmetic Regulation: The Case for Reform* (2006) and Sarah Schaffer, *Reading Our Lips: The History of Lipstick Regulation in Western Seats of Power* (2006), in Chapter X of the Electronic Book.

B. DEFINITION OF "COSMETIC"

The definition of a "cosmetic," and its relation to the definition of a "drug," are discussed in Chapter 3, *supra*.

C. ADULTERATED COSMETICS

United States v. An Article of Cosmetic . . . "Beacon Castile Shampoo"

1969–1974 FDLI Jud. Rec. 160 (N.D. Ohio 1974).

As the case was finally submitted to me for determination, the claim of the Government narrowed to a contention that the article of commerce is adulterated in that it contains deleterious substances, namely, potassium oleate and Neutronyx 600, which may render it injurious to users under such conditions of use as are customary or usual. Thus the claim is based on the wording of Section 361(a), which declares that "a cosmetic shall be deemed to be adulterated (A) if it bears or contains . . . any deleterious substance which may render it injurious to users under the conditions of use prescribed in the labeling thereof, or under such conditions of use as are customary or usual."

Government's counsel has correctly noted that the meaning of the words "may render the deleterious substance injurious" actually bears the same meaning as given or interpreted by the United States Supreme Court in the case of *United States vs. Lexington Mill and Elevator Company* [*supra* p. 495]. . . . Further, I think it is correct and appropriate to observe and to determine here that the word "injurious" is understood to mean capable of causing physical harm when the cosmetic is rubbed or poured on or otherwise applied on the human body as intended. However, it is concluded that the physical harm which may result from the deleterious substance may be temporary as well as permanent.

However, if temporary, it should be objectively and medically demonstrable that it is damaging either externally or internally to a part of the body, including but not limited to the skin, tissues, or vessels of the body. It should be added that, as I construe the term, pain alone without objective injury would not be enough to establish the injurious character of the deleterious substance.

. . . Under the evidence in this case it develops that the potential harm of the subject Beacon Castile Shampoo relates to its full strength concentrate getting into the eyes of a human being. Hence it is essential to determine whether, within the second condition of 361(a), the Beacon Castile Shampoo is injurious to a user who is using the shampoo in a customary or usual manner. I, therefore, conclude that it is part of the government's burden of proof in this case to show that getting the full concentrate of shampoo into one's eyes would occur under a condition of use that is customary or usual.

There is no evidence in this record that shows exactly what condition of use is customary or usual in applying shampoo to the hair. But certainly the evidence in this record does not disclose any basis for inferring that one is likely to apply shampoo to the hair without water and, if so, that the full strength of the shampoo would trickle down undiluted into the eyes. . . . Similarly, I think there is no evidence here that it is a customary and usual use to apply the shampoo so closely to the eyes that it would enter the eye in a full concentrated condition.

But the Government's burden goes further. Assuming that full strength shampoo got into a user's eyes while washing his hair, it is my conclusion that it is the Government's further burden to show that the user would not then flush or wash out the eye in the customary and usual use of the shampoo.

The burden which I feel is imposed on the Government in this respect immediately takes us . . . to the results of the Harris study. . . . [T]he Harris report shows, with reference to each of the instillations, whether it be quarter strength, half strength, or full strength, that there was ocular burning and irritation. Surely, in the customary and usual use of shampoo, if by accident some shampoo got into one's eye and caused ocular burning and irritation, the autonomic response of a human being would be to wash out his eye. Hence the Harris report, the keystone of the Government's case, fails to show that it was conducted under circumstances that represented the customary and usual use of the Beacon Castile Shampoo.

The significance of the omission of washing as a step in the protocol of the Harris human studies becomes quite apparent when the Marzulli studies are considered together with Dr. Marzulli's oral testimony of last Saturday. Dr. Marzulli's tests of March 25th, 1970, showed corneal epithelial damage to the eye of one of two rabbits where eyes were washed 30 seconds after the instillation of full strength Beacon, and significant iritis of the eyes of two rabbits washed after 30 seconds. It was quite clear in Dr. Marzulli's testimony of last Saturday that these findings were regarded by him as essential to his conclusions, for he testified in substance as follows—and these are my notes, but in substance this is the way I took down his testimony:

> We were concerned that shampoo that causes damage despite washing should not be marketed. If an eye is unwashed and produces injury to the cornea, that shampoo should not be marketed. If, in addition, flushing the eye 30 seconds after does not prevent injury, that shampoo should not be marketed.

The absence of the washing step from the protocol of the Harris studies thus has this added result: It negatives the extrapolation of this key portion of the Marzulli rabbit studies, and thus the relevancy of the principal point in Dr. Marzulli's testimony is impaired. . . . Thus it is not the ocular burning that represents an injury.

There is also evidence in the human studies of mild-to-moderate injection of the conjunctiva; yet this is not deemed sufficient to constitute an injury within the contemplation of 361(a). Surely there are many soaps that might cause temporary redness to the conjunctiva, and yet I don't believe they would be subject to condemnation. Surely it is clear in the Harris studies that there is no injury to the iris of any of the 22 human subjects. And thus up to this point the human studies do not disclose any injury that I think would fall within the contemplation of 361(a).

There is, however, destruction of the corneal epithelium of Joan Hughes. This, it turned out, was a temporary destruction; and in accordance with the medical testimony that I received, the epithelium of Joan Hughes was reported by Dr. Harris as being restored in 72 hours. The evidence in the case seems to indicate that, when epithelium is destroyed, one third of it will be restored within the first 24 hours, the second third within the second 24 hours, and the third third within the third 24 hours.

This destruction of corneal epithelium is deemed to be and determined to be a sufficient injury to meet the meaning of the word "injurious" in 361(a), especially because there is certainly a basis for believing that there is a susceptibility to infection, though the evidence indicates that it is a very small possibility. And yet the possibility remains, and presumably within that very broad language of 361(a), the definition of "injurious," if there is a possibility of injury, this would constitute an injury within that term.

Then there were also two other persons of the 22 who had slight corneal staining, which is indicative of some slight corneal epithelial injury. But the significant point is that the injury of Joan Hughes occurred only when full strength shampoo was applied to her eye. And likewise, the slight corneal staining occurred only when the full strength Beacon shampoo was applied to the eyes of those two other subjects. . . . Thus the only evidence in this record that would sustain the Government's burden is the human studies as to the temporary injury that occurred to the cornea of Joan Hughes when full strength Beacon Castile Shampoo was applied to one of her eyes. Yet it is this full concentration that has previously not been proved by the Government, as I evaluate the evidence, as being shown to be a condition customary or usual in the use of a shampoo. . . .

On the entire record, as I previously have shown, the Government has not proved that the use of the full concentrate in a manner that would get into the human eye while shampooing the hair represents a customary and usual use of the shampoo. In fact, that in the usual and customary use of this shampoo the full shampoo has not gotten into the eyes of the user is certainly a fair inference to draw from the facts set forth in the stipulation.

Those facts show that the Claimant, Consolidated Royal Chemical Company, has manufactured and sold over two million gallons of shampoo of this formulation from August 11th, 1958, to the date of seizure in January, 1971. Approximately eight to ten million bottles of this product have been sold, usually in 16, 32 and 64 ounce containers. During this period neither Claimant nor its insurers received any claim of injury to the eyes of a user.

And, therefore, on the entire record, I conclude and determine that the Government has failed to establish its requisite burden of proof. . . .

NOTES

1. *Baby Shampoo.* On April 4, 1979, FDA's Associate Commissioner for Compliance sent the following letter to R. C. Stites, President, Johnson & Johnson Baby Product Company:

On June 17, 1978, you submitted a petition requesting that the Commissioner of Food and Drugs propose regulations . . . defining the term "baby shampoo" for the purpose of cosmetic labeling and requiring that shampoos so designated comply with prescribed animal testing requirements to demonstrate ocular safety. . . . For the reasons stated below, the agency is denying your petition. . . .

. . . Your petition contains no data to support the allegation that baby shampoos contain a deleterious substance that may render them injurious to babies' eyes under customary conditions of use. It simply notes society's emphasis upon the safety of products designed for use on babies and young children and asserts that baby shampoos should be subject to more stringent safety requirements. It is argued that baby shampoos may accidentally spill into babies' eyes. While this may be true, you have not submitted data to support your conclusion. . . .

. . . You presented a 1976 consumer perception survey to support the allegation that a "baby shampoo" that is a potential eye irritant is misbranded because, to consumers, a "baby shampoo" is expected to be "more gentle and mild and less irritating to eyes and scalp than a product labeled 'shampoo.'" This comparative definition of the term "baby shampoo" is not adequately supported by the results of the survey. Furthermore, in our view, the survey results are undermined by the possibility of bias because an inherently comparison-oriented situation was used in conducting the survey. . . .

Finally, we agree that a rabbit eye irritation test similar to the one you propose would be capable of distinguishing between moderately or strongly irritating shampoos and those which possess little or no potential for ocular irritancy. However, it is generally recognized that the rabbit eye irritation test is not capable of making fine distinctions between degrees of irritancy. Our understanding of the standard your petition sets forth includes the requirement that "baby shampoos" are, among other characteristics, free of stinging and burning qualities. . . . These characteristics cannot be measured by the rabbit eye irritation test. . . .

21 CFR 10.30(e)(1) provides that the Commissioner shall review and rule upon a petition, taking into consideration, inter alia, the agency resources available to handle the category of subject matter involved and the priority assigned to the petition in relation both to the category of subject matter involved and the overall work of the agency. . . . This means that a petition such as yours must establish, by adequate supporting documentation, that a health problem exists which, in comparison with health problems that are currently being addressed by the agency, warrants the reallocation of FDA resources. Your petition fails to do this. . . .

Johnson & Johnson submitted a new citizen petition (FDA Docket No. 80P–0139/CP) on April 8, 1980, with additional information supporting its request that all baby shampoos be required to pass a standard rabbit eye safety test, but FDA again denied the petition on October 5, 1981, concluding that there was no basis for requiring baby shampoos to be safer than other shampoos, that no evidence demonstrated that baby eyes are different from adult eyes, and that available data did not demonstrate a significant difference between babies and other age groups in injury frequency from shampoos.

2. *Cosmetics for Children.* The U.S. Public Interest Research Group submitted a citizen petition to FDA requesting a ban on the use of xylene, toluene, and dibutyl phthalate in nail polish marketed for children under the age of 14. FDA Docket No. 2005P–0487/CPI (Dec. 6, 2005). FDA has taken no action on this matter.

3. *GMPs for Cosmetics.* On the need for cosmetic GMP regulations, see Edward Milardo, *Quality Assurance Guidelines—The Industry's Viewpoint*, 31 Food Drug Cosm. L.J. 105 (1976); Michael A. Pietrangelo, *Cosmetic Quality Assurance—Alias Cosmetic Good Manufacturing Practices*, 31 Food Drug Cosm. L.J. 167 (1976); John A. Wenninger, *Quality Assurance Procedures for the Cosmetic Industry—The FDA's Viewpoint*, 31 Food Drug Cosm. L.J. 101 (1976). CTFA submitted a citizen petition (FDA Docket No. 77P–0315) on July 28, 1977, requesting the promulgation of cosmetic GMP regulations. No action has been taken by FDA on this petition. In October 1977, FDA stated that it intended to propose GMP regulations with respect to preservative systems in mascara and other eye area cosmetic products, 42 Fed. Reg. 54837 (Oct. 11, 1977), but no action

has been taken on this matter. Current FDA views with respect to cosmetic GMP are reflected in the yearly revisions to the cosmetic provisions of the FDA Inspection Operations Manual and Compliance Program Guidance Manual and in cosmetic GMP guidance on the agency's website.

4. *GMPs for Cosmetic–Drugs.* In response to a CTFA comment urging that products that fall within both the cosmetic and the drug provisions of the Act be subject to different GMP requirements than other drug products, FDA defended the need for uniform drug GMP requirements:

> . . . A number of comments, including a petition to the Commissioner, were received regarding the applicability of the proposed general CGMP regulations to a class of products identified as cosmetic-drug products and described as those which: (1) Meet the definitions of both "drug" and "cosmetic" under section 201 of the act; (2) represent a minimum health or safety risk; and (3) are marketed over-the-counter for regular and frequent consumer use without dosage limitations. Examples of these products are described as medicated skin creams, antibacterial soap, antiperspirants, and topical sunburn prevention products. Specifically, the comments requested separate CGMP regulations for this alleged class of drugs. . . .

> The Commissioner has concluded that these regulations . . . must apply to all products meeting the definition of drug products, whether the drug products are highly potent prescription drugs or are OTC drugs of the type described as "cosmetic-type." Past experience of the agency has demonstrated that the public has been put in a hazardous situation because of manufacturing errors in OTC products. . . . That many of the general CGMP regulations are applicable to and reasonable for the cosmetic-type drug products is evidenced by the fact that a majority of the specific suggestions submitted by the petitioner and others as applicable for cosmetic-type drug products duplicated in substance, a number of comments submitted by other OTC manufacturers and manufacturers of prescription drug products. . . .

43 Fed. Reg. 45014, 45027–28 (Sept. 29, 1978).

5. *Commentary.* For an early FDA review of potential toxicity problems raised by cosmetics, see Arnold J. Lehman, *Toxicological Aspects of Certain Types of Cosmetics*, 15 Food Drug Cosm. L.J. 399 (1960).

———

In the course of the OTC Drug Review, *supra* p. 973, FDA determined that some ingredients used in both cosmetic and OTC drug products were unsafe, and it took action to ban these ingredients in both types of products.

Aerosol Drug and Cosmetic Products Containing Zirconium

42 Fed. Reg. 41374 (August 16, 1977).

... In the Federal Register of June 5, 1975 (40 FR 24328), the Commissioner proposed that any aerosol drug or cosmetic product containing zirconium is a new drug or an adulterated cosmetic. ...

The June 5, 1975 proposal was in response to a report submitted to the Commissioner by the over-the-counter (OTC) Panel on Review of Antiperspirant Drug Products. This panel concluded in their report that zirconium compounds have caused skin granulomas and toxic effects in the lungs and other organs of experimental animals and expressed concern about the potential toxicity of such compounds when used in humans over an extended period of time. Although extensive animal toxicity data were received, these data failed to provide a basis for establishment of a safe level for long-term use. The panel also concluded that the benefit likely to be derived from the use of zirconium-containing aerosol antiperspirants is unsupportable in view of the risks involved. ...

Because it appears that conclusive testing to establish the safety of zirconium-containing aerosol antiperspirants would take years to accomplish, and because during that time millions of consumers would be unnecessarily subjected to risk, the Commissioner has decided to stop movement of these agents in interstate commerce until safety testing adequate for approval of a new drug application has been done, as recommended in the proposed rule making.

The available toxicological data indicate that zirconium compounds may be responsible for human skin granulomas as well as toxic effects in the lungs and other internal organs of test animals. Accordingly, these ingredients in aerosol formulations are not generally recognized as safe, and the Commissioner considers any drug product containing zirconium in aerosol form to be a new drug. Furthermore, the Commissioner believes that the available information is sufficient to show that aerosol cosmetic products containing zirconium may be injurious to users. The regulation as proposed stated that regulatory action was being taken with respect to cosmetic products "[b]ased upon the lack of toxicological data adequate to establish a safe level for use. ...." The final regulation relating to cosmetic products has been revised to delete this phrase, to identify the risks from zirconium use that are of concern, and to refer to the statutory test for determining when a product is adulterated. ...

§ 700.16 Use of aerosol cosmetic products containing zirconium

(a) Zirconium-containing complexes have been used as an ingredient in cosmetics and/or cosmetics that are also drugs, as, for example, aerosol antiperspirants. Evidence indicates that certain zirconium compounds have caused human skin granulomas and toxic effects in the lungs and other organs of experimental animals. When used in aerosol form, some zirconium will reach the deep portions of the lungs of users. The lung is an organ, like skin, subject to the development of granulomas. Unlike the skin, the lung will not reveal the presence of granulomatous changes until they have become advanced and, in some cases, permanent. It is the view of the Commissioner that zirconium is a deleterious substance that may render any cosmetic aerosol product that contains it injurious to users. . . .

NOTES

1.   *Other Ingredients Banned from Cosmetics.* Other substances banned by FDA under the cosmetic adulteration provisions of the FD&C Act are listed at 21 C.F.R. 700.11–23. Examples include: hexachlorophene, 37 Fed. Reg. 20160 (Sept. 27, 1972); vinyl chloride, 39 Fed. Reg. 30830 (Aug. 26, 1974); halogenated salicylanilides, 40 Fed. Reg. 50527 (Oct. 30, 1975); chloroform, 41 Fed. Reg. 26842 (June 29, 1976); chlorofluorocarbon propellants, 43 Fed. Reg. 11301 (Mar. 17, 1978); and methylene chloride, 54 Fed. Reg. 27328 (June 29, 1989). FDA also proposed to ban 2-mercaptoimidazoline, 39 Fed. Reg. 15306 (May 2, 1974), and trichloroethylene 42 Fed. Reg. 49467 (Sept. 27, 1977). Both of these proposed regulations were withdrawn by FDA in 56 Fed. Reg. 67440 (Dec. 30, 1991).

2.   *Cattle Materials.* Because of the concern about transmission of "mad cow disease" (bovine spongiform encephalopathy), FDA banned specified cattle materials from use in cosmetics and promulgated recordkeeping requirements to enforce the ban. 69 Fed. Reg. 42256 & 42275 (July 14, 2004), 70 Fed. Reg. 53063 (Sept. 7, 2005), 71 Fed. Reg. 59653 (Oct. 11, 2006), codified at 21 C.F.R. 700.27.

3.   *OTC Drug Review.* The impact of the OTC Drug Review on the status of substances also used in cosmetic products is discussed in Robert P. Giovacchini, *The Significance of the Over-the-Counter Drug Review with Respect to the Safety Considerations of Cosmetic Ingredients*, 30 Food Drug Cosm. L.J. 223 (1975); Gary L. Yingling, *The Effect of the FDA's OTC Drug Review Program on the Cosmetic Industry*, 33 Food Drug Cosm. L.J. 78 (1978).

4.   *Tattoos.* FDA has issued a formal advisory opinion stating that dyes and pigments for temporary or permanent tattooing are both color additives and cosmetics, and are not drugs. *See* letter from John Taylor, Associate Commissioner for Regulatory Affairs, FDA, to Robert E. Carpenter, Docket No. 81A–0315/AP (July 21, 1986). The agency has taken no action to enforce that position. *See* Carrie Griffin, *Henna Tattooing: Cultural Tradition Meets Regulation* (2002), in Chapter X of the Electronic Book. FDA has placed information on tattoos and permanent makeup on its website and has on occasion issued consumer alerts about these products. *E.g.,* "FDA Alerts Consumers About Adverse Events Associated With 'Permanent Makeup'," FDA Talk Paper No. T04–20 (July 2, 2004). Regulation of tattooing varies widely among the states. Robert Louis Stauter, *Tattooing: The Protection of the Public Health*, 6 Health Matrix, No. 2 (1988).

5.   *Cosmetics Sold at Flea Markets and Electronic Auctions.* In a letter from Linda M. Katz, Director, FDA CFSAN Office of Cosmetics and Colors, to Peter Barton Hutt (Nov. 25, 2003), the agency confirmed that cosmetic products resold at flea markets and electronic auctions are held to full compliance with all requirements under the FD&C Act.

6. *EC Regulation.* The European Community adopted Council Directive 76/768/EEC relating to cosmetic products, which requires that cosmetic products "must not be liable to cause damage to human health when they are applied under normal conditions of use." Official Journal of the European Communities No. L 262, at 169 (July 27, 1976). In contrast to the United States, where the only cosmetic ingredients requiring approval before they may be used are color additives, the EC directive adopts a listing approach for all cosmetic ingredients. Thus, the EC has issued several annexes listing provisional, permanent, and restricted (including banned) substances, and substances left to regulation by individual countries.

7. *Environmentally Protected Ingredients.* On occasion, ingredients are prohibited from cosmetics for reasons other than safety. The use of spermaceti (a substance taken from the oil in the head of a sperm whale or dolphin) is prohibited under the Mammal Protection Act of 1972 and the Endangered Species Act of 1973.

———

At the same time that FDA expressed concern about the safety of nitrosamines in the food supply, *supra* p. 601, the agency sought to control their occurrence in cosmetics.

Nitrosamine-Contaminated Cosmetics; Call for Industry Action; Request for Data
44 Fed. Reg. 21365 (April 10, 1979).

The agency is concerned about contamination of cosmetic products with nitrosamines, particularly N-nitrosodiethanolamine (NDELA). . . .

Some nitrosamines are potent animal carcinogens. The carcinogenicity of NDELA at high dose levels has been established in two animal species. . . .

A limited number of cosmetic products have been analyzed for NDELA in both private and FDA laboratories. A number of these products were found to be contaminated with NDELA. The contamination is believed to be caused by the chemical reaction between the amines used to formulate the products and a nitrosating agent. . . . Analytical methods for identifying nitrosamines such as NDELA at concentrations of parts per million (ppm) and parts per billion (ppb) are quite new. . . . Analyses were made of 29 cosmetics thought likely to contain such contamination. It was found that 27 of the 29 contained up to 48 ppm of NDELA. . . .

Recent studies have also been conducted in FDA laboratories to determine whether NDELA penetrates the skin. The agency now has evidence that NDELA penetrates excised human skin from an aqueous vehicle. One study that has been completed demonstrated that NDELA penetrates the skin of live monkeys. . . .

The Commissioner of Food and Drugs has therefore determined that cosmetics containing nitrosamines may be considered adulterated under section 601 of the Federal Food, Drug, and Cosmetic Act.

Cosmetic manufacturers are put on notice that cosmetic products may be analyzed by FDA for nitrosamine contamination and that individual products could be subject to enforcement action. However, the Commissioner is still considering whether a compliance program is needed to reduce or eliminate nitrosamine contamination in cosmetics, and, if so, what the nature of the program should be. Three factors will influence the Commissioner's decision on how to proceed in this matter:

1.   The results of FDA's continuing efforts to understand better the nature of the problem and the means of reducing or preventing it. . . .

2.   The extent to which the public health risk is alleviated by industry reformulation of products.

3.   The results of FDA's continuing efforts to determine the extent of the formation of, and human exposure to, nitrosamines in cosmetics. . . .

NOTES

1.   *Nitrosamines.* FDA has continued to express concern about nitrosamines in cosmetics (as well as in food and drugs), but it has not adopted a specific tolerance level or taken formal regulatory action against products containing nitrosamines. The Cancer Prevention Coalition petitioned FDA in 1996 to require a cancer warning on the label of any cosmetic containing diethanolamine (DEA), a commonly used ingredient, because it could react with nitrosating agents to form nitrosomines (FDA Docket No. 96P–0404). FDA has taken no action on this petition.

2.   *Alpha Hydroxy Acid Labeling.* Because of concern that cosmetic products containing alpha hydroxy acids may increase skin sensitivity to the sun, FDA issued a guidance on a labeling statement for these products alerting consumers to take appropriate action. 70 Fed. Reg. 1721 (Jan. 10, 2005).

3.   *Enforcement History.* The following summary illustrates the variety of circumstances in which FDA has brought court enforcement action or requested recalls to protect consumers against unsafe cosmetics:

> Early in 1978, FDA received about 50 complaints of hair breakage and scalp irritation associated with a hair straightener. An investigation disclosed that a compounding error had resulted in one batch of the product containing 60% more than the intended level of free caustic (sodium hydroxide). During the course of the FDA investigation the firm recalled the product.

> In 1974 consumer complaints of fingernail injuries associated with the use of certain nail extenders led FDA to investigate the problem. It was determined that the methyl methacrylate monomer used in these products was causing the injuries. The FDA obtained a court order to seize the offending product. Similar products were voluntarily recalled by the distributors and some have since been reformulated. . . .

During 1976 and 1977, a number of consumer complaints that a nail hardener had caused serious allergic and irritant effects were received. An investigation and subsequent laboratory analyses demonstrated that the product contained formaldehyde at a potentially harmful concentration. The product was seized in August 1977.

Fifteen consumer complaints of axillary irritation from a new deodorant were received during 1976. During the course of the investigation of the problem, FDA was notified by the firm that distribution of the product had been terminated. The adverse experiences reported to FDA were not serious enough to warrant regulatory action.

During 1976–1978 an unusually large number of consumer complaints concerning one brand of suntan product were received. The ensuing investigation disclosed that the firm also had received many complaints. Many of the adverse experiences appeared to be a form of photocontact dermatitis. Research sponsored by the firm and investigations by FDA identified 6–methylcoumarin (6–MC), a fragrance ingredient in the suntan products, as a potent photocontact allergen.

When FDA learned that 6–MC was commonly used in suntan or sunscreen products, telegrams were sent to all known domestic firms which either market suntan/sunscreen products or distribute fragrance compounds to the cosmetics industry, requesting that they immediately terminate the use of 6–MC in all topical products and recall existing stocks of suntans or sunscreen products containing 6–MC. . . .

Martin Greif et al., *Cosmetics Regulation*, 7 FDA By–Lines 331, 333–334 (Sept. 1979).

4. *Child Resistant Packaging.* Because of a report of accidental poisoning from ingestion of a solvent product intended for use in the removal of sculptured nails, E. Martin Caravati & Toby L. Litovitz, *Pediatric Cyanide Intoxication and Death from an Acetonitrile–Containing Cosmetic*, 260 J.A.M.A. 3470 (1988), CTFA submitted a petition and the Consumer Product Safety Commission promulgated a regulation requiring child-resistant packaging under the Poison Prevention Packaging Act to protect against accidental ingestion of acetonitrile contained in glue removers. 55 Fed. Reg. 1456 (Jan. 16, 1990), 55 Fed. Reg. 51897 (Dec. 18, 1990), codified at 16 C.F.R. 1700.14(a)(18). The Drug and Household Substance Mailing Act of 1990, 104 Stat. 1184, prohibits the mailing of any cosmetic that fails to comply with an applicable requirement for child-resistant packaging.

5. *Opposition to Animal Testing.* At the same time that the public and FDA are demanding greater assurance of safety of all FDA-regulated products, animal rights activists are demanding an end to the type of animal testing used to evaluate product toxicity. The cosmetic industry has been a principal target of animal rights proponents. For a discussion of the issues involved, see National Academy of Sciences, Use of Laboratory

Animals in Biomedical and Behavioral Research (1988); Office of Technology Assessment, Alternatives to Animal Use in Research, Testing, and Education, OTA–BA–273 (1986); and articles in Chapter I(J) of the Electronic Book. Faced with these attacks, some cosmetic industry officials have promised to end animal testing, and some firms have promoted their products as not tested on animals (e.g., "beauty without cruelty"). In a decision handed down in December 1988 by a Higher Regional Court in Frankfurt, Germany, however, the representation of "beauty without cruelty" was held to be misleading, and thus illegal, unless the manufacturer can demonstrate that neither the finished product nor any of the ingredients has *ever* been tested in animals by itself or by anyone else. Such a showing would be impossible for any ingredient in any consumer product.

6.   *Mailing Fragrances.* The Drug and Household Substance Mailing Act of 1990, 104 Stat. 1184, prohibits the mailing of any fragrance advertising sample unless it is sealed or otherwise prepared to prevent individuals from being unknowingly or involuntarily exposed to the sample.

7.   *California Statute.* The California Safe Cosmetics Act of 2005, California Health and Safety Code Division 104, Part 5, Chapter 7, Article 3.5, Section 111791, requires companies with aggregate worldwide cosmetic sales of more than $1 million to submit to the state a list of any cosmetics sold in California that contain an ingredient listed by the state as causing cancer or reproductive harm. The state is authorized to investigate the safety of any product containing a listed ingredient and to require manufacturers to submit pertinent requested information. The results of an investigation may be referred to the California Division of Occupational Safety and Health, which is required to establish occupational health standards if an ingredient poses an occupational safety hazard.

D. COAL-TAR HAIR DYES

Section 601(a) of the FD&C Act exempts from the prohibition against any poisonous or deleterious substance in cosmetics a coal-tar hair dye if it is labeled with a statutorily prescribed caution statement advising that the consumer should first conduct a test for skin irritation. The special treatment accorded coal-tar hair dyes by section 601(a) has been a continuing source of frustration for FDA, which periodically has sought to circumvent the provision.

Toilet Goods Association v. Finch
419 F.2d 21 (2d Cir. 1969).

Nine years ago Congress amended the Food, Drug, and Cosmetic Act by enacting the Color Additive Amendments of 1960. Nearly three years later, after appropriate rule-making proceedings, the Food and Drug Administration (FDA) published its Regulations thereunder, 28 F.R. 6439. This litigation about the validity of their provisions concerning diluents, finished cosmetics and hair-dyes has continued ever since. . . .

The two provisions of § 361 relevant to the FDA's hair-dye regulation are subdivisions (a) and (e). They say that a cosmetic shall be deemed adulterated

(a) If it bears or contains any poisonous or deleterious substance which may render it injurious to users under the conditions of use prescribed in the labeling thereof, or under such conditions of use as are customary or usual: *Provided*, That this provision shall not apply to coal-tar hair dye, the label of which bears the following legend conspicuously displayed thereon: "Caution—This product contains ingredients which may cause skin irritation on certain individuals and a preliminary test according to accompanying directions should first be made. This product must not be used for dyeing the eyelashes or eyebrows; to do so may cause blindness," and the labeling of which bears adequate directions for such preliminary testing. . . .

(e) If it is not a hair dye and it is, or it bears or contains, a color additive which is unsafe within the meaning of section 376(a) of this title.

. . . .

The Regulation held invalid by the district court, 21 C.F.R. § 8.1(u), provides:

(u) The "hair-dye" exemption in section 601(a) of the act applies to those articles intended for use in altering the color of the hair and which are, or which bear or contain, color additives with the sensitization potential of causing skin irritation in certain individuals and possible blindness when used for dyeing the eyelashes or eyebrows. The exemption is permitted with the condition that the label of any such article bear conspicuously the statutory caution and adequate directions for preliminary patch-testing. If the poisonous or deleterious substance in the "hair dye" is one to which the caution is inapplicable and for which patch-testing provides no safeguard, the exemption does not apply; nor does the exemption extend to poisonous or deleterious diluents that may be introduced as wetting agents, hair conditioners, emulsifiers, or other components in a color shampoo, rinse, tint, or similar dual-purpose cosmetics that alter the color of the hair. . . .

Taking first things first, we agree with the invalidation of so much of the Regulation as sought to deprive coal-tar hair dyes of the exemption conferred by § 361(a) in cases where, in the view of FDA, the coal-tar color ingredient carries a danger for which patch-testing provides no safeguard. The Government's argument should indeed be appealing to a legislator—what good is the warning to make a patch test if the test will not disclose the danger? But a court must take the statute as it is, and Congress wrote with great specificity. . . .

It is equally plain that the exemption of § 361(a) does not apply to coloring agents in hair dyes not derived from coal-tar. . . . We likewise see no basis for invalidating the portion of the Regulation which says that the exemption does not apply to poisonous or deleterious diluents. It is inconceivable that Congress meant to deprive the FDA of its ordinary powers with respect to other ingredients simply because they are combined with a coal-tar dye.

We think the court also erred in excluding from § 361(e) color additives in hair dyes other than those made from coal tar. The 1938 Act applied only to coal-tar colors, and the exemption of hair dyes in subdivision (e) was logical since coal-tar colors were dealt with by subdivision (a) in a supposedly adequate fashion. The modification of subdivision (e) in 1960 was part of a program to regulate all colors, and not merely coal-tar colors. But, if the statute be read with entire literalness, the unaltered introductory provision in subsection (e) now would have the effect of excluding any sanction for the use in a hair dye of an unlisted or uncertified coloring ingredient although not within the proviso to § 361(a). In the absence of any legislative history indicating an intention to broaden the exemption in § 361(e), the most sensible construction is that, despite the retention of the introductory words "if it is not a hair dye," Congress did not mean to exempt non-coal-tar color additives used in hair dyes from the requirement of listing and certification. . . .

NOTES

1.   *Origin of Exemption.* The coal-tar hair dye exemption in Section 601(a) was the product of intensive lobbying during consideration of the 1938 Act by thousands of beauty shop operators and employees who were concerned that the pending legislation would require FDA to ban coal-tar hair dye products and thus seriously injure their business. The allegation that some ingredients in coal-tar hair dyes are carcinogenic prompted Congressional hearings in 1978 and 1979. "Cancer-Causing Chemicals—Part 1 (Safety of Cosmetics and Hair Dyes)," Hearings Before the Subcommittee on Oversight and Investigations of the House Committee on Interstate and Foreign Commerce, 95th Cong., 2nd Sess. (1978); "Safety of Hair Dyes and Cosmetic Products," Hearing before the Subcommittee on Oversight and Investigations of the House Committee on Interstate and Foreign Commerce, 96th Cong., 1st Sess. (1979). *See also* Anatasia Menechios, *Sixty Years Later: The Survival of the 1938 Coal Tar Hair Dye Exemption* (2000), in Chapter X of the Electronic Book. FDA regulation of carcinogenic coal tar hair dye substances is treated in depth *infra* in Chapter 9.

2.   *Scope of Exemption.* The coal-tar hair dye exemption extends only to products intended to dye the hair and explicitly excludes products for dyeing eyebrows and eyelashes. FD&C Act 601(a). *See Byrd v. United States*, 154 F.2d 62 (5th Cir. 1946).

3.   *Deletion of Caution Statement.* FDA Trade Correspondence 103 (Feb. 29, 1940), 1938–49 FDLI Jud. Rec. at 610, states that hair dyes containing harmless coal tar colors need not bear the caution statements specified in Section 601(a) of the FD&C Act. Failure to use the statutory caution statement subjects a coal tar hair dye to Section 601(a), but as long as the product does not contain any poisonous or deleterious substance it is not unlawful. Under Section 601(e), a coal tar hair dye is exempt from the color additive requirements of Section 706 whether or not it bears the statutory caution statement.

4.   *Roux Litigation.* FDA has been continually frustrated in efforts to establish that ingredients used in Roux Lash & Brow Tint Kits are

hazardous color additives. Not long after enactment of the FD&C Act, FDA seized this product, contending that it contained three poisonous or deleterious substances. The first jury to hear the case was unable to agree on a verdict. A second jury returned a verdict for Roux. *See* James C. Munch & James C. Munch, Jr., *Notices of Judgment—Cosmetics*, 20 Food Drug Cosm. L.J. 399, 400–01 (1959). In 1968, FDA instituted another seizure of the product, charging that the three ingredients were unapproved color additives. The district court dismissed the case on the ground that it was controlled by the decision in *TGA v. Gardner*, 278 F. Supp. 786 (S.D.N.Y. 1968). This ruling was reversed on appeal and the case was remanded for trial. *United States v. Roux Labs., Inc.*, 437 F.2d 209 (9th Cir. 1971). The district court ultimately dismissed the action on the ground that a 1963 Federal Register notice exempted the substances from color additive requirements. *Roux Lash & Brow Tints*, FDA Consumer, Nov. 1974, at 42. In 1974, FDA brought yet another seizure, again alleging the use of unapproved color additives. The trial judge this time ruled that the 1963 Federal Register notice did not exempt the substances. Following trial on the factual question of whether the ingredients were color additives or diluents, the jury returned a verdict for the claimant. *Roux Lash & Brow Tint Kits*, FDA Consumer, Dec. 1977–Jan. 1978, at 37.

E. MISBRANDED COSMETICS

1. LABEL WARNINGS

FDA has no specific statutory authority to require label warnings for cosmetics. Under Sections 201(n) and 602(a) of the FD&C Act, however, the agency has determined that the failure of a label to bear an appropriate warning constitutes misbranding.

Preservation of Cosmetics Coming in Contact With the Eye: Intent to Propose Regulations and Request for Information

42 Fed. Reg. 54837 (October 11, 1977).

. . . FDA has received several reports of corneal ulceration associated with the use of cosmetic mascaras containing pathogenic microorganisms. . . . Mascaras can become contaminated with various microorganisms when the consumer uses the product and re-inserts the applicator wand into the container after application of the mascara to the eye lashes. The re-insertion of the applicator wand into the mascara is part of the intended or customary conditions of use of the products. Without an adequate preservative system, microorganisms introduced into the mascara with the applicator wand can survive and multiply inside the container. When the mascara is used again, if the microorganisms on the applicator wand come into contact with a scratched or damaged cornea, the eye may become infected. . . .

The reported incidents all involve mascaras in which the microorganism *Pseudomonas aeruginosa* has been found. *Pseudomonas aeruginosa* is an ubiquitous bacterium that may be present on the skin as a transient microorganism. It may readily grow in a cosmetic unless the cosmetic contains a preservative adequate to prevent contamination. *Pseudomonas aeruginosa* infections, if not recognized and treated immediately, can cause corneal ulceration that leads to partial or total blindness in the injured eye. . . .

The Commissioner believes that the preservative systems used in mascara and other eye-contact products should be adequate not only to prevent the further growth of microorganisms introduced during use but also to reduce significantly the number of microorganisms introduced during use. The Commissioner expects to promulgate all-inclusive regulations delineating good manufacturing practice for cosmetics at some point, and he intends to propose regulations regarding microbial preservation of cosmetics coming in contact with the eye as a first step. . . .

The Commissioner also advises that he considers inadequately preserved cosmetics to be in violation of the Act. Under section 601 of the act, a cosmetic is considered adulterated if it is prepared under conditions whereby it may have been rendered injurious to health, as well as if it bears any poisonous or deleterious substance that may render it injurious to users under the conditions of use. Furthermore, under sections 201(n), 601, and 602 of the act and 21 CFR 740.10, the label must bear any warning statements that are necessary or appropriate to prevent a health hazard that may be associated with the product. Manufacturers and distributors should be advised that FDA . . . does not intend to await the completion of the rule making proceeding announced in this notice of intent before taking needed regulatory action. . . .

NOTES

1. *Update.* FDA has taken no further action on this matter.

2. *Commentary. See* Anthony D. Hitchins, *Cosmetic Preservatives and Safety*, 57 J. Ass. of Food and Drug Officials, No. 3, at 42 (July 1993).

———

In addition to requiring specific cosmetic product warnings, FDA has promulgated 21 C.F.R. 740.10, a requirement that a warning appear on the label of all cosmetics whose safety has not been adequately substantiated.

Food, Drug, and Cosmetic Products: Warning Statements
40 Fed. Reg. 8912 (March 3, 1975).

The Commissioner of Food and Drugs is establishing required warnings for certain food, drug, and cosmetic products. Products packaged in self-pressurized containers are required to bear warnings to ensure their safe use and storage. Aerosol products containing halocarbon or hydrocarbon propellants are required to bear warnings against the dangers of deliberate concentration and inhalation.

Cosmetic products whose safety has not been adequately substantiated are required to warn of that fact on the label. . . .

The Commissioner concludes that section 201(n) of the act applies in those situations where abuse has become sufficiently frequent to constitute a hazard of widespread public concern. Section 201(n) of the act is applicable to require affirmative disclosures in the light of representations and also to reveal consequences of customary or usual conditions of use. The very act of representing a product for food, drug, or cosmetic use constitutes an inherent implied representation of its safety. Warnings to ensure safe use are therefore within the scope of section 201(n) of the act. Moreover, the customary or usual conditions of use of such products often involve little or no protection against their misuse, where no warning exists. Accordingly, section 201(n) of the act is applicable to assure that consumers will understand, and guard against, the potential consequences of inadvertent misuse under conditions of such customary or usual conditions of use. In addition, the Commissioner advises that "conditions of use" is not a narrow term limited to the active handling, operation, and application of a product, but rather includes the entire setting and circumstances in which a product is used. The usual conditions of use of aerosol products are, that once purchased, they are freely available to all members of a household. Thus, warnings against misuse of aerosol products may alert parents of adolescent children to take precautions to ensure that such products in the household are not misused. . . .

The availability of section 201(n) of the act to require an explicit warning against misuse was upheld in *United States v. 12 Bottles of Esterex* (E.D. Mo. 1946), reported in V. Kleinfeld & C. Dunn, Federal Food, Drug and Cosmetic Act 1938–1949 at 523, 525. . . .

Several comments request clarification of the term "adequately substantiated for safety" as used in § 740.10.

The Commissioner advises that the safety of a product can be adequately substantiated through (a) reliance on already available toxicological test data on individual ingredients and on product formulations that are similar in composition to the particular cosmetic, and (b) performance of any additional toxicological and other tests that are appropriate in the light of such existing data and information. Although satisfactory toxicological data may exist for each ingredient of a cosmetic, it will still be necessary to conduct some toxicological testing with the complete formulation to assure adequately the safety of the finished cosmetic. . . .

The Commissioner recognizes that a manufacturer of a cosmetic ingredient cannot always foresee, much less control, the uses of the ingredient in cosmetic products, and therefore cannot be held responsible for the safety of the ingredient under every possible condition of use. The manufacturer is responsible, however, for the safety of the ingredient under the conditions of use recommended in its labeling as well as reasonably expected related uses, and the safety of the ingredient must be adequately substantiated for use under these conditions if the label does not bear the warning statement required by § 740.1. . . .

One comment argued that substantiation of safety amounts to premarketing review of cosmetics since the manufacturer would have to meet the "vague" standard of adequate substantiation for safety before his cosmetics could be marketed, and would bear the burden of meeting this standard in a court review.

. . . It is the manufacturer, not the Food and Drug Administration, who is responsible for having his product in compliance with the act and regulations promulgated thereunder. The act necessarily contemplates that the manufacturer has assured itself of the safety of its product, but in no way does this imply Food and Drug Administration approval or review prior to marketing. . . .

Part 740—Cosmetic Product Warning Statements

§ 740.1   Establishment of warning statements

(a) The label of a cosmetic product shall bear a warning statement whenever necessary or appropriate to prevent a health hazard that may be associated with the product.

(b) The Commissioner of Food and Drugs, either on his own initiative or on behalf of any interested person who has submitted a petition, may publish a proposal to establish or amend, under Subpart B of this part, a regulation prescribing a warning for a cosmetic. . . .

§ 740.10 Labeling of cosmetic products for which adequate substantiation of safety has not been obtained

(a) Each ingredient used in a cosmetic product and each finished cosmetic product shall be adequately substantiated for safety prior to marketing. Any such ingredient or product whose safety is not adequately substantiated prior to marketing is misbranded unless it contains the following conspicuous statement on the principal display panel:

Warning—The safety of this product has not been determined.

(b) An ingredient or product having a history of use in or as a cosmetic may at any time have its safety brought into question by new information that in itself is not conclusive. The warning required by paragraph (a) of this section is not required for such an ingredient or product if:

(1) The safety of the ingredient or product had been adequately substantiated prior to development of the new information;

(2) The new information does not demonstrate a hazard to human health; and

(3) Adequate studies are being conducted to determine expeditiously the safety of the ingredient or product.

(c) Paragraph (b) of this section does not constitute an exemption to the adulteration provisions of the act or to any other requirement in the act or this chapter.

§ 740.11 Cosmetics in self-pressurized containers

(a)(1) The label of a cosmetic packaged in a self-pressurized container and intended to be expelled from the package under pressure shall bear the following warning:

Warning—Avoid spraying in eyes. Contents under pressure. Do not puncture or incinerate. Do not store in temperature above 120 deg. F. Keep out of reach of children.

. . . .

NOTES

1. *Judicial Affirmance.* FDA's aerosol warning was upheld in *Cosmetic, Toiletry and Fragrance Ass'n, Inc. v. Schmidt,* 409 F. Supp. 57 (D.D.C. 1976).

2. *Feminine Deodorant Sprays.* At the same time, FDA prescribed a warning statement for feminine deodorant sprays. 40 Fed. Reg. 8926 (Mar. 3, 1975), codified at 21 C.F.R. 740.12. FDA concluded that "the reported adverse reactions do not demonstrate a health hazard which is serious enough to justify removal of these products from the market" but agreed with comments that "these sprays offer no medical usefulness or hygienic benefits" and therefore stated that the use of the term "hygienic" would render the products misbranded under Section 602(a).

3. *Talcum Powders.* A citizen petition (No. 83P–0404) submitted on December 2, 1983, requesting that FDA require a label warning for cosmetic talcum powders because of their potential asbestos content, was denied by FDA on July 21, 1986.

4. *Bubble Bath.* The need for a label warning for bubble bath products provoked dispute between FDA and the cosmetic industry for a decade. FDA proposed a label warning about irritation of the skin and urinary tract from bubble bath products in 42 Fed. Reg. 5368 (Jan. 28, 1977). Manufacturers responded that the incidence of problems was trivial. Nonetheless, FDA promulgated a final regulation requiring a warning, stating that the number of reported reactions was "sufficiently large enough to indicate a public hazard." 45 Fed. Reg. 55172 (Aug. 19, 1980), codified at 21 C.F.R. 740.17. In response to an industry petition, FDA stayed the regulation and requested further comment in 48 Fed. Reg. 7169 and 7203 (Feb. 18, 1983). After further comment, FDA reinstated the warning but excluded products labeled exclusively for adults. 51 Fed. Reg. 20471 (June 5, 1986). Industry again petitioned FDA for reconsideration, but the petition was denied and the regulation became effective.

5. *Disclosure to Dermatologists.* It is common practice for cosmetic companies to provide the components of their products to dermatologists to use in skin patch tests on patients to determine sensitivity to particular substances. *See* Cyril H. March, *Editorial: Cosmetic Formula Information,* 216 J.A.M.A. 1337 (May 24, 1971); CTFA, Cosmetic Industry On Call (annual publication providing dermatologists with contact information for company personnel who can provide these components). FDA encourages this practice. 21 C.F.R. 720.4(b)(4). In 51 Fed. Reg. 33664 (Sept. 22, 1986), FDA took the position that all skin patch test kits "intended for commercial marketing" are drugs or biologics that require FDA approval. The "commercial marketing" proviso allows cosmetic companies to continue their present practice.

6. *Failure to Warn as Misbranding.* See 16 C.F.R. 1500.81(a), originally promulgated by FDA under the Federal Hazardous Substances Act before it was transferred to the Consumer Product Safety Commission, which provides that where a cosmetic "offers a substantial risk of injury or illness from any handling or use that is customary or usual it may be regarded as misbranded under the Federal Food, Drug, and Cosmetic Act because its label fails to reveal material facts with respect to consequences that may result from use of the article (21 U.S.C. 321(n)) when its label fails to bear information to alert the householder to this hazard."

2. MISLEADING LABELING

FDA failed in its attempt to establish by rule when use of the claim "hypoallergenic" in cosmetic labeling is misleading.

Almay, Inc. v. Califano

569 F.2d 674 (D.C. Cir. 1977).

■ MARKEY, CHIEF JUDGE, United States Court of Customs and Patent Appeals:. . . .

On February 25, 1974, appellee Food and Drug Administration (FDA) in accordance with 21 U.S.C. §§ 321(m), 362(a), and 371(a), initiated informal rulemaking proceedings by publishing a proposed regulation governing hypoallergenic cosmetics, under which:

> A cosmetic may be designated in its labeling by words that state or imply that the product of any ingredient thereof is "hypoallergenic" if it has been shown by scientific studies that the relative frequency of adverse reactions in human subjects from the test product is significantly less than the relative frequency of such reactions from each reference product(s). [39 F.R. 7291.]

The lynch-pin of the regulation was its requirement for employment of "comparison testing," *i.e.*, for testing the labeled product against "reference product(s)" defined in the regulation as "similar-use competitive products in the same cosmetic product category" and representing a market share of 10%. Adoption of the comparison testing method rested entirely on the Commissioner's adoption of a comparative definition: "the term 'hypoallergenic' means to the consumer that the product causes fewer adverse reactions than other, similar-type use products" and the feeling that, while use of "hypoallergenic" has expanded over the years, the difference between "hypoallergenic" cosmetics and those not so labeled has become less distinct.

Included in the preamble were comments of the Cosmetic, Toiletry and Fragrance Association (CFTA), the Bureau of Consumer Protection of the Federal Trade Commission (FTC), and appellant Almay Corporation (Almay). CFTA alleged that "there is no demonstrated need nor is it practicable for the minimizing of allergic reactions to be an overriding consideration in all aspects of production and marketing of every cosmetic product". . . . Almay objected to the comparison testing method because the composition of the selected reference products could not be predicted. . . . [T]he FTC filed the results of a consumer survey on hypoallergenic cosmetics, and . . . comments thereon by the Director of FTC's Bureau of Consumer Protection. . . .

Comments were also submitted by a number of dermatologists, consumer groups, and individual consumers. Eight dermatologists favored testing in which a product would have to demonstrate an extremely low potential for allergic reaction to qualify as hypoallergenic. Seven dermatologists opposed the comparison test method, and one was non-committal. Four consumer groups took issue with the comparative definition as likely to cause confusion among users of hypoallergenic cosmetics. One consumer group was in general agreement with the FDA proposal. . . .

FDA justified its decision to define "hypoallergenic" as meaning less allergenic than some competing products on what it considered confusion in the use of the term. . . . The district court found the Commissioner's definition supported by two factors in the administrative record: (1) a significantly greater number of consumers believed that "hypoallergenic" meant "safer than competitors" rather than "very safe," and (2) a comparative definition would be more helpful to consumers because adverse reactions to cosmetic products are relatively rare today overall. . . .

Involved here is an informal rulemaking proceeding, in which no hearing is required. The scope of review is therefore governed by the "arbitrary or capricious" standards set out in the Administrative Procedure Act, 5 U.S.C. § 706(2)(A). . . .

The fact that an "arbitrary and capricious" standard applies to informal rulemaking, rather than a "substantial evidence" requirement, cannot mean that *nothing* of an evidentiary nature is needed in the administrative record to support an agency decision. On the contrary, there being no evidentiary hearing, informal rulemaking proceedings are much more susceptible to abuse, and it becomes all the more important that a rational basis for the agency's decision be found in the facts of record. . . .

FDA relies first on the preamble to its own proposed regulation in support of the Commissioner's conclusion. Respecting the definition of "hypoallergenic," the preamble is conclusory. The only authorities cited are a dictionary which defines "hypo" to mean "under," "beneath," "down," "less than normal," of "the lowest position in a series of compounds;" and the statement of an AMA Committee on Cutaneous Health and Cosmetics that "the term 'hypoallergenic' as applied to cosmetics has outlived its usefulness, is misleading, and should be dropped from the labeling of cosmetic products."

. . . The dictionary definition clearly does not support the Commissioner's decision to define "hypoallergenic" as causing "fewer reactions than *some* [10% of the market] products."

. . . In light of the AMA report's conclusion that "hypoallergenic" should be dropped entirely, and of its further statement that "little distinction can be made between established cosmetic products as to their sensitization potential," it was inappropriate to cite the AMA report in support of any use whatever of "hypoallergenic," no matter how defined.

FDA relied also on [an FTC survey on hypoallergenic cosmetics]. . . . In drawing inference from the FTC survey, the Commissioner failed to consider a relevant factor—the comments of the FTC's Director of the Bureau of Consumer Protection. . . . The Director . . . stated on the record that the survey: (1) was limited in population, sample and number of questions; (2) was silent in important respects; (3) lacked a breakdown between users and non-users; (4) lacked a tabulation; (5) established that consumers lacked medical knowledge sufficient to distinguish skin reactions; (6) produced results which should be used with caution; and (7) probably produced fewer "correct" definitions because it was not limited to consumers interested in the subject, *i.e.*, hypoallergenic cosmetic users. Finally, the survey defined the "correct" definition as "less likely to cause irritation than regular cosmetics," yet the Commissioner chose a different definition: "less likely to cause adverse reactions than some [10% of market] similar-use competitive products in the same category."

We are fully aware of the caveat that we must not substitute our judgment for that of the regulator, nor shall we. We are equally aware, however, of the need for rationality, in the interest not only of justice, our major concern, but in the interest of the continued viability and public acceptance of the federal regulatory scheme itself. . . .

An aura of unreality surrounds the creation of a definition in the present case. In the apparent belief that most products are today non-allergenic, it may have been thought that producers could not find 10% of marketed products producing more reactions and that use of "hypoallergenic" would thereupon cease. If so, the cumbersome method here chosen to achieve that result is an irrational substitute for a direct prohibition of all use of "hypoallergenic." . . .

NOTE

FDA revoked this regulation in 43 Fed. Reg. 10559 (Mar. 14, 1978), and it has not since initiated regulatory action against cosmetic products labeled as hypoallergenic.

―――――――

The scope of legitimate cosmetic claims has been a source of controversy for the past forty years. The line between cosmetic claims and drug claims is examined in greater detail in Chapter 3. *Supra* p. 110.

Peter Barton Hutt, *The Legal Distinction in the United States Between a Cosmetic and a Drug*

In COSMECEUTICALS (Peter Elsner & Howard I. Maibach eds., 2000).

The Wrinkle Remover Cases of the 1960s

In the early 1960s, the cosmetic industry developed a line of products, broadly characterized as "wrinkle remover" products, containing ingredients intended to smooth, firm, and tighten the skin temporarily and thus to make wrinkles less obvious. In 1964, the FDA seized several of these products, alleging that they were drugs under the FD&C Act. The resulting litigation produced three decisions by U.S. District Courts and two decisions by U.S. Courts of Appeals involving three products: Line Away, Sudden Change, and Magic Secret. . . .

The OTC Drug Review

The OTC Drug Review inherently raised issues relating to the distinction between a cosmetic and a drug. All of the traditional cosmetic drug products—sunscreens, antiperspirants, antidandruff shampoos, anticaries toothpaste, skin protectants, hormone creams, acne products, and so forth—were reviewed under the OTC Drug Review. The FDA made clear that only the drug and not the cosmetic aspects of cosmetic drugs were subject to review and evaluation, and ultimately a final monograph, under this program. Thus, in many of the advisory committee meetings and subsequent reports, as well as in the preambles of the tentative final and final monographs, there has been substantial discussion about the dividing line between a drug claim and a cosmetic claim for a cosmetic drug. In several instances, the FDA has explicitly stated that a final monograph covered only products making drug claims and did not cover cosmetic claims for the product or products making only cosmetic claims. . . .

The Warning Letters of the Late 1980s

For a period of 15 years following the conclusion of the wrinkle remover cases, the FDA pursued cosmetic/drug issues largely through the OTC Drug Review and seldom, if ever, through Regulatory Letters or direct court action. Based upon new product technology and the conclusion that the consuming public was becoming increasingly sophisticated about skin-care products and their claims, the cosmetic industry gradually became more aggressive with cell rejuvenation and other antiaging promotional claims. As a result of research and development in the intervening years, new and more effective products were now on the market.

Two defining events served to initiate a new round of FDA enforcement activities against skin-care claims in the late 1980s. First, in 1986 the well-known South African heart surgeon, Christian Barnard, made a tour of the United States on behalf of a cosmetic company to promote its skin care product, Glycel. Barnard made extravagant claims for Glycel on the television program, Nightline, with FDA Commissioner Frank Young participating on the same program. Second, an attorney for a major cosmetic company wrote Dr. Young to protest the claims being made for Glycel. As a result, the FDA began to issue Regulatory Letters not only to manufacturer of Glycel but also to other leading members of the industry. More than 20 Regulatory Letters were sent in the first wave, and when the FDA concluded that the response was unsatisfactory the agency sent another 20. . . .

The Alpha–Hydroxy Acid (AHA) Products of the 1990s

In the early 1990s, the cosmetic industry developed and marketed a line of products containing alpha-hydroxy acids such as glycolic, lactic, and citric acid that occurred in natural food products, to cleanse dead cells from the surface of the skin and assist moisturization. The AHAs have been used in consumer products at relatively modest levels, usually at 10% or lower, in contrast with very high levels used in professional skin peeling products. It is universally accepted that the AHA products are the most effective skin-care beauty products that the industry has ever developed. As a result, they have become extremely popular with consumers and gained substantial media and regulatory attention.

The FDA has raised two questions about the AHA products. First, the agency has questioned the claims being made. The FDA has sought to adhere to the guidelines established in the November 1987 letter on the antiaging and cell rejuvenation products. Second, the FDA has also questioned the safety of these products, not on the ground that there are known toxicological concerns but rather on the ground that their safety is unproven. In contrast with the cell rejuvenation claims of the 1980s, however, the FDA has not launched another wave of Warning Letters. A company that had obtained FDA approval of NDAs for antiaging drugs, frustrated by this lack of FDA action, brought a private false advertising case under section 43(a) of the Lanham Act against a competitor making aggressive claims for a cosmetic product, but lost in both the District Court and the Court of Appeals. . . .

NOTES

1. *Regulation of Claims.* For discussion of FDA regulation of cosmetic claims, see Stephen H. McNamara, *Performance Claims for Skin Care Cosmetics or How Far May You Go in Claiming to Provide Youthfulness?*, 41 Food Drug Cosm. L.J. 151 (1986); Laura A. Heymann, *The Cosmetic/Drug Dilemma: FDA Regulation of Alpha–Hydroxy Acids*, 52 Food & Drug L.J. 357 (1997); Bryan A. Liang & Kurt M. Hartman, *It's Only Skin Deep: FDA Regulation of Skin Care Cosmetics Claims*, 8 Cornell J.L. & Pub. Pol'y 249 (1999). For a list of cosmetic claims that FDA regarded as false or misleading in 1939, see FDA Trade Correspondence 10 (Aug. 2, 1939), 1938–1949 FDLI Jud. Rec. at 566.

2. *"See Through" Labels.* FDA once proposed to ban, as misbranded, all "see-through" cosmetic labels (*i.e.*, labels that can be read only through the container and its contents), 39 Fed. Reg. 25328 (July 10, 1974), but later relented, 44 Fed. Reg. 47547 (Aug. 14, 1979).

3. *FDA Budget for Cosmetics.* The ability of the FDA to monitor and bring regulatory action with respect to claims for cosmetic products depends on the resources available to the agency for this purpose. Because of budgetary factors, FDA announced in 1998 that it was reducing the staff of the Office of Cosmetics and Colors by 50 percent and cutting back or eliminating many cosmetic regulatory programs. This reduction was so substantial that it propelled the cosmetic industry to request and obtain restoration by Congress of adequate funds to assure that the FDA has a credible cosmetic regulatory program.

4. *NAD Review of Cosmetic Claims.* The National Advertising Division (NAD) of the Better Business Bureau, *see supra* p. 992, note 6, frequently reviews the substantiation for cosmetic product claims. *See, e.g.*, *Coty, Inc.* 34 NAD/CARU Case Reports 368 (July 2004).

5. *Organic Cosmetics.* USDA has determined that cosmetic products that meet the requirements established under the Organic Foods

Production Act of 1990, *see supra* p. 453, are eligible for certification in accordance with that statute. *See* Memorandum on Certification of Agricultural Products that Meet NOP Standards from Barbara C. Robinson, Deputy Administrator, USDA Agricultural Marketing Service Transportation and Marketing Programs (Aug. 23, 2005).

F. COSMETIC INGREDIENT LABELING

The FD&C Act contains no provision authorizing FDA to require ingredient labeling on cosmetics. FDA initially established a recommended format for voluntary cosmetic ingredient labeling. 37 Fed. Reg. 16208 (Aug. 11, 1972). The next year, the agency promulgated the following regulation imposing mandatory cosmetic ingredient labeling under Section 5(c) of the Fair Packaging and Labeling Act (FPLA) of 1966, 15 U.S.C. 1451 *et seq.*

Cosmetic Ingredient Labeling
38 Fed. Reg. 28912 (October 17, 1973).

In the Federal Register of February 7, 1973 (38 FR 3523), the Commissioner of Food and Drugs published two proposals concerning the labeling of cosmetic ingredients. . . .

Several comments questioned the legal basis for the proposals, contending that [Section 5(c) of] the Fair Packaging and Labeling Act grants authority to establish ingredient labeling only on a commodity-by-commodity basis, and only as necessary to prevent consumer deception or to facilitate value comparisons.

. . . For the purposes of ingredient labeling, the Commissioner concludes that all cosmetics are appropriately considered a single "commodity." . . .

The Commissioner also concludes that cosmetic ingredient labeling is necessary to prevent the deception of consumers and to facilitate value comparisons. Ingredient labeling can be meaningful in preventing consumer deception by precluding product claims that are unreasonable in relation to the ingredients present and by providing consumers with additional information that can contribute to a knowledgeable judgment regarding the reasonableness of the price of the product. Furthermore, while ingredient identity may not be the sole determinant of a product's value to a consumer, it is one important criterion of a product's value in comparison with others. The presence of a substance to which a consumer is allergic or sensitive, for example, may render the product worthless to that consumer. . . .

The Commissioner recognizes that section 5(c)(3) of the act does not grant authority for promulgating ingredient labeling regulations that require the divulgence of trade secrets. However, because quantitative formulas are not revealed, he does not agree that the mere listing of ingredients in descending order of their predominance is tantamount to the divulgence of a trade secret. Furthermore, the final regulation does not require declaration by name of flavors or fragrances, the two types of cosmetic ingredients which would be the most likely of any to create trade secret issues. Nevertheless, in consideration of the possibility that there may be some legitimate trade secret issues regarding the mere identity of other ingredients, the final regulation provides for an administrative review of any such claims of trade secret status and for exemption from label declaration by name for any legitimate trade secret identity. . . .

The Commissioner recognizes that many consumers may initially be unfamiliar with certain cosmetic ingredients, but concludes that increasing familiarity will be acquired. Certain ingredients have become known to consumers who, for example, are aware of their sensitivity to specific substances and who will quickly learn to utilize the ingredient statement. Ingredient labeling will have to be accompanied by the acquisition of additional information by consumers if they are to be fully informed. Ingredient labeling will, however, directly provide some of the necessary information and should help to motivate consumers to acquire the necessary additional information. . . .

Therefore, pursuant to provisions of the Fair Packaging and Labeling Act and the Federal Food, Drug, and Cosmetic Act (sec. 701(e)), Part 1 is amended by adding the following new section: [The regulation that follows is the current, slightly revised version of the rule promulgated by FDA in the above Federal Register notice.]

21 C.F.R. § 701.3 Designation of Ingredients

(a) The label on each package of a cosmetic shall bear a declaration of the name of each ingredient in descending order of predominance, except that fragrance or flavor may be listed as fragrance or flavor. An ingredient which is both fragrance and flavor shall be designated by each of the functions it performs unless such ingredient is identified by name. . . . Where one or more ingredients is accepted by the Food and Drug Administration as exempt from public disclosure pursuant to the procedure established in § 720.8(a) of this chapter, in lieu of label declaration of identity the phrase "and other ingredients" may be used at the end of the ingredient declaration.

(b) The declaration of ingredients shall appear with such prominence and conspicuousness as to render it likely to be read and understood by ordinary individuals under normal conditions of purchase. The declaration shall appear on any appropriate information panel in letters not less than 1/16 of an inch in height and without obscuring design, vignettes, or crowding. In the absence of sufficient space for such declaration on the package, or where the manufacturer or distributor wishes to use a decorative container, the declaration may appear on a firmly affixed tag, tape, or card. In those cases where there is insufficient space for such declaration on the package, and it is not practical to firmly affix a tag, tape, or card, the Commissioner may establish by regulation an acceptable alternate, *e.g.*, a smaller type size. A petition requesting such a regulation as an amendment to this paragraph shall be submitted pursuant to part 10 of this chapter.

(c) A cosmetic ingredient shall be identified in the declaration of ingredients by:

(1) The name specified in § 701.30 as established by the Commissioner for that ingredient for the purpose of cosmetic ingredient labeling pursuant to paragraph (e) of this section;

(2) In the absence of the name specified in § 701.30, the name adopted for that ingredient in the following editions and supplements of the following compendia, listed in order as the source to be utilized:. . . .

(3) In the absence of such a listing, the name generally recognized by consumers.

(4) In the absence of any of the above, the chemical or other technical name or description.

(d) Where a cosmetic product is also an over-the-counter drug product, the declaration shall declare the active drug ingredients as set forth in § 201.66(c)(2) and (d) of this chapter, and the declaration shall declare the cosmetic ingredients as set forth in § 201.66(c)(8) and (d) of this chapter.

. . . .

NOTES

1. *Final Regulations.* FDA received objections to the cosmetic ingredient labeling rule as originally promulgated. It accommodated these objections and issued a revised final order. 39 Fed. Reg. 27181 (July 25, 1974), 40 Fed. Reg. 8918, codified at 21 C.F.R. 701.3.40. The procedure followed by the agency in promulgating these regulations, without conducting an evidentiary hearing, *see* 40 Fed. Reg. 8924 (Mar. 3, 1975), 40 Fed. Reg. 23458 (May 30, 1975), was upheld by a divided court. *Independent Cosmetic Mfrs. & Distribs., Inc. v. Califano,* 574 F.2d 553 (D.C. Cir. 1978).

2. *Determination of Trade Secret Status.* The process used by FDA to determine whether a cosmetic ingredient represents a trade secret and is therefore exempt from required label declaration was challenged in *Zotos Int'l, Inc. v. Kennedy,* 460 F. Supp. 268 (D.D.C. 1978). The district court ruled that the procedure, which did not afford an opportunity for a hearing or other form of "focused dialogue" with the agency, violated the due process clause of the Constitution. In *Carson Prods. Co. v. Califano,* 594 F.2d 453 (5th Cir. 1979), the court agreed with the *Zotos* decision but held that the revised procedures afforded Carson satisfied due process, and that the facts justified FDA's conclusion that the ingredient involved was not a trade secret. The court in *Del Labs., Inc. v. United States,* 86 F.R.D. 676 (D.D.C. 1980), overturned, on procedural grounds, FDA's preliminary refusal to recognize the trade secret status of an ingredient of the plaintiff's products. To remedy the deficiencies discovered by the courts, FDA established a new procedure for considering requests for confidentiality of cosmetic ingredient identity. 47 Fed. Reg. 38353 (Aug. 31, 1982), 51 Fed. Reg. 11441 (Apr. 3, 1986). Even following these new regulations, FDA had difficulty justifying its decisions. In the continuing *Zotos* litigation, FDA again rejected trade secret status after reconsideration under the new regulations, and the District Court affirmed the FDA decision. However, the Court of Appeals reversed and remanded the matter for yet additional proceedings because the agency had given inconsistent reasons for its decision. *Zotos Int'l, Inc. v. Young,* 830 F.2d 350 (D.C. Cir. 1987).

3. *Ingredient Names.* In 45 Fed. Reg. 3574 (Jan. 18, 1980), FDA recognized the second edition of the CTFA Cosmetic Ingredient Dictionary as the primary source for cosmetic ingredient terminology, but refused to adopt the CTFA names for 34 listed substances and required the description of the chemical composition of 16 listed substances. Because of the Office of the Federal Register rule that federal regulations may not incorporate documents by prospective reference, the cosmetic ingredient labeling regulations must be revised whenever a new edition of or supplement to the CTFA Cosmetic Ingredient Dictionary is published. Since 1980, FDA has failed to respond to CTFA petitions recognizing these new editions and supplements but has not taken regulatory action against use of the terminology contained in the most current edition.

4. *Color Additive Names.* In 50 Fed. Reg. 23815 (June 6, 1985), FDA permitted color additives to be designated in product labeling without their prefix, *i.e.*, "Yellow 5" rather than "FD&C Yellow No. 5," and proposed to change its regulations to reflect this policy.

5. *Commentary.* For differing views about the cosmetic ingredient labeling regulations, see Eugene I. Lambert, *Working Out Cosmetic Ingredient Labeling*, 30 Food Drug Cosm. L.J. 228 (1975); Murray Berdick, *Cosmetic Ingredient Labeling—The Nomenclature Problem*, 31 Food Drug Cosm. L.J. 125 (1976); Walter E. Byerley, *Cosmetic Ingredient Labeling— An FDA Chimera*, 31 Food Drug Cosm. L.J. 109 (1976); Heinz J. Eiermann, *Cosmetic Ingredient Labeling Requirements*, 31 Food Drug Cosm. L.J. 115 (1976); Margaret Gilhooley, *Status Report on Cosmetic Ingredient Labeling*, 31 Food Drug Cosm. L.J. 121 (1976).

6. *Scope of Ingredient Labeling.* The FPLA applies only to retail packaging and contains no criminal enforcement sanctions. Ingredient labeling for cosmetics is thus required to appear only on the outside labeling and only on retail packages (not on packages sold to beauty salons or institutions for use on the premises), and the requirement is enforceable only by civil action. On December 16, 1988, following congressional hearings that criticized the lack of ingredient labeling for professional cosmetic products, *see supra* p. 1310, note 1, five cosmetic industry trade associations announced a voluntary program to provide ingredient information for all professional products manufactured on or after December 31, 1989. Under this voluntary program, the ingredient information for professional cosmetic products may be provided on the product label or in accompanying labeling, and may be provided in descending order of predominance or in alphabetical order.

G. VOLUNTARY "REGULATION" OF COSMETICS

The FD&C Act does not authorize FDA to require registration of cosmetic manufacturing establishments, submission of lists of cosmetic products and their ingredients, or filing of adverse event reports. In the early 1970s, in response to petitions from the cosmetic industry, FDA promulgated regulations governing the voluntary registration of cosmetic establishments (21 C.F.R. Part 710), voluntary filing of cosmetic product ingredient statements (21 C.F.R. Part 720), and voluntary filing of product experience reports (21 C.F.R. Part 730). The product experience report regulations were revoked in 1997.

Voluntary Registration of Cosmetic Product Establishments; Voluntary Filing of Cosmetic Product Ingredient and Cosmetic Raw Material Composition Statements
37 Fed. Reg. 7151 (April 11, 1972).

. . . [A] member of Congress urged that the registration and filing of ingredient statements by producers of cosmetics be mandatory [and] that foreign producers of cosmetics be subjected to the regulations. . . . Two other comments challenged the legality of establishing voluntary regulations under section 701(a) of the Federal Food, Drug, and Cosmetic Act and urged that the regulations issued be mandatory. . . .

The Commissioner has considered these comments and concludes that under section 701(a) of the act he is authorized to accept the voluntary registration of cosmetic product establishments and the voluntary filing of cosmetic product ingredient statements and cosmetic raw material composition statements as set forth in the regulations established below. He also agrees that foreign producers should be included in this voluntary registration. He concludes however that promulgation of a mandatory regulation could result in lengthy litigation that would seriously delay FDA from obtaining the type of information expected as a result of this promulgation. . . .

A dermatologist commented that the proposed regulations . . . did not go far enough, particularly in the provision for providing coded samples to physicians treating persons suffering from allergic reaction. He urged establishment of a "Register" that would list all ingredients of all cosmetic products used in the United States and would be made available to every practicing dermatologist. The Commissioner concludes that a "Register" of cosmetic ingredients goes beyond the scope of the proposal and cannot be implemented by these regulations. The Commissioner considers that promulgation of labeling requirements for cosmetic ingredients will substantially satisfy the need of dermatologists for this type of data. . . .

Voluntary Filing of Cosmetic Product Experiences
38 Fed. Reg. 28914 (October 17, 1973).

In the Federal Register of November 1, 1972 (37 FR 23344) a notice of proposed rulemaking to establish a procedure for the voluntary filing of cosmetic product experience was published by the Commissioner of Food and Drugs. The notice included the text of regulations suggested in a petition filed by the Cosmetic, Toiletry, and Fragrance Association, Inc. (CTFA) . . . as well as regulations proposed by the Commissioner. . . .

A number of comments agreed with the FDA proposal that all complaints alleging bodily injury received by a manufacturer, packer, or distributor should be submitted to the Food and Drug Administration.

The petitioner opposed the request for the submission of all complaints and suggested that provision be made for a manufacturer, packer, or distributor to use a screening procedure for determining reportable experiences and in the absence of such a procedure to submit all alleged injury complaints received.

The Commissioner of Food and Drugs concludes that the submission of complaints that have been screened by a procedure appropriately designed to eliminate any unfounded or spurious complaints would be more meaningful and, therefore, adopts the suggestion of the petitioner. However, in order to protect against the use of screening procedures which might eliminate valid experience reports, the regulation provides that any procedure used to screen such reports should be filed with the agency and that it will be subject to public inspection. . . .

Several comments argued for a broad definition of "reportable experience." It was asserted that any bodily injury resulting from the accidental or deliberate misuse of a cosmetic product is a valid reportable experience. The petitioner, on the other hand, opposed the inclusion of any experience not in association with the intended use of a cosmetic product.

The Commissioner is of the opinion that any information he can obtain in regard to injuries involving cosmetic products, including adverse reactions resulting from the accidental or deliberate misuse of cosmetic products, may be of use in protecting the public health, and therefore he has concluded that all such experiences should be considered reportable.

. . . [T]he rules governing confidentiality granted to voluntarily submitted data on cosmetic product experiences should be the same as the rules governing confidentiality for other data submitted to the agency on a voluntary basis [set forth in 21 C.F.R. 20.111]. . . .

A public interest group requested that FDA obtain testing data on products for which complaints have been received. The regulation provides that the Commissioner may request additional information in response to reports received. . . .

Both the Industry member and the petitioner opposed the provision in the FDA proposal for submitting a negative report for each cosmetic product by brand name for which no reportable experience had been received during a reporting period.

The Commissioner is of the opinion that statistical data obtained from the submission of reportable experiences will be meaningful only if the agency obtains sufficient information to relate the number of the reportable experiences in a product category to the total number of cosmetic product units sold in that particular product category. Such information by product categories can be obtained, however, without the need for filing a separate negative report for each product by brand name. The regulation now provides for the submission of a "Summary Report of Cosmetic Product Experience by Product Categories." The person submitting this report need not list products by brand name, but only the total number of product units in each product category estimated to have been distributed to consumers during the reporting period, together with the number and rate of reportable experiences in each category. . . .

NOTES

1. *Confidentiality of Reports.* FDA subsequently issued final regulations under the Freedom of Information Act, granting confidentiality to product experience reports. 39 Fed. Reg. 44602 (Dec. 24, 1974).

2. *Simplification of Reporting Requirements.* In an effort to improve compliance with the voluntary reporting regulations, FDA reduced the reporting burdens. 50 Fed. Reg. 47760 (Nov. 20, 1985), 51 Fed. Reg. 25687 (July 16, 1986). On May 15, 1989, CTFA submitted a citizen petition to FDA (No. 89P–0180) requesting that the voluntary filing of cosmetic formulas be simplified by eliminating the requirement for semi-quantitative information, thus permitting manufacturers to submit a simple list of ingredients. FDA proposed amendments to the regulations in accordance with this petition and stated that they could be implemented immediately. 55 Fed. Reg. 42993 (Oct. 29, 1990). FDA has announced that establishment registration, and product and ingredient listing may be accomplished electronically.

3. *Industry Compliance.* The industry record of compliance with the voluntary reporting regulations was a subject of debate during the 1988 House hearings on cosmetic product safety. *See supra* p. 1310, note 1. *See also* GAO, Cosmetics Regulation Information on Voluntary Actions Agreed to by FDA and the Industry, HRD–90–58 (1990).

4. *Revocation of Adverse Experience Reporting.* As part of President Clinton's "Reinventing Government" initiative, FDA revoked the voluntary adverse experience reporting regulation in 1997. 62 Fed. Reg. 43071 (Aug. 12, 1997). FDA stated that, after 23 years of adverse event reporting, even with limited industry participation, the agency now had sufficient data to calculate the baseline adverse reactions that occur for each cosmetic category and thus that the program no longer provided useful new information. FDA promised to provide "an in depth report that will be useful to both the cosmetic industry and the public in understanding adverse reaction trends for different product categories and the baseline rates for adverse reactions," but no such report has been published.

5. *Commentary.* For a description of cosmetic experience reporting from FDA's perspective, see John A. Wenninger, *Voluntary Cosmetic Product Experience Reporting—The FDA Viewpoint*, 30 Food Drug Cosm. L.J. 204 (1975). For discussion of cosmetic industry concerns about product experience reporting, see Eugene I. Lambert, *Carrot and Stick: Product Experience Reporting and Cosmetic Ingredient Labeling*, 29 Food Drug Cosm. L.J. 78 (1974); George L. Wolcott, *Cosmetics Workshop—Product Experience Reporting*, 29 Food Drug Cosm. L.J. 284 (1974); Michael Pietrangelo, *Product Experience Reporting—An Industry View*, 30 Food Drug Cosm. L.J. 219 (1975).

In 1975, after FDA promulgated section 740.10 of its regulations, requiring safety substantiation (or a warning statement) for cosmetic ingredients, *see supra* p. 1326, CTFA initiated meetings to request FDA to undertake a review of the safety of cosmetic ingredients similar to the agency's reviews of GRAS food ingredients and OTC drugs. When FDA declined to do this, CTFA, in 1976, undertook its own comprehensive review of the safety of ingredients used in cosmetic products.

Robert L. Elder, *The Cosmetic Ingredient Review—A Safety Evaluation Program*
11 JOURNAL OF THE AMERICAN ACADEMY OF DERMATOLOGY 1168 (1984).

The Cosmetic Ingredient Review (CIR) was established in 1976 by the Cosmetic, Toiletry and Fragrance Association to review and document information on the safety of ingredients as used in cosmetic products. . . .

CTFA recognized that acceptance of the program and its results would depend on three major factors: (1) the safety review process had to be conducted with no cosmetic industry bias; (2) the Panel of Experts who would review the safety test data on each ingredient had to be given complete independence; and (3) the review process, the reports, and all of the data used in the safety evaluation had to be available for public and scientific scrutiny.

These three major requirements were codified into formal, written procedures that established CIR as an independent, nonprofit organization. CIR staff and all consultants were to be separate from CTFA and the cosmetic industry and must pass the same conflict of interest requirements stipulated for special federal government employees. All reports were to be discussed and voted on in a public meeting before being released for a 90-day public comment period without prior industry review. And finally, all data, published or unpublished, used by the CIR Expert Panel would be available for public review.

Policy guidance for the CIR program is provided by a five-person Steering Committee chaired by the president of CTFA [and including two scientists] . . . appointed by the American Academy of Dermatology . . . [and] the Society of Toxicology. Two scientists from industry—the current chairman of CTFA's Scientific Advisory Committee and CTFA's senior vice-president for Science—also serve on the Committee. The Steering Committee has no input into the scientific evaluations of the CIR Expert Panel. One of the Steering Committee's major responsibilities is the selection of the seven-member CIR Expert Panel. This is done following a public announcement requesting nominees. . . .

Three nonvoting members assist the Expert Panel and attend the public meetings. These include a consumer representative (appointed by the Consumer Federation of America), an industry liaison, and a Food and Drug Administration (FDA) "contact person." . . .

The priority order of ingredient review is established by using a weighted formula that includes factors for: ingredient concentration in cosmetic products, number of products containing the ingredient, frequency of consumer use, area of use, use by sensitive population subgroups, biologic activity, estimate of penetration, and frequency of consumer complaints about products containing the ingredient. . . . Ingredients specifically regulated by the FDA, such as color additives, are exempt from CIR review. Any ingredient that is being evaluated by the FDA under the Over-The-Counter Drug Review (OTC) or for use as a Direct Food Additive is deferred until that review is completed. Fragrance materials are being evaluated separately in a program sponsored by the Research Institute for Fragrance Materials (RIFM) and are not included in the CIR review program. The CIR ingredient review list is developed as described and then issued for public comment before it is forwarded with all the comments to the Expert Panel for their review and approval. The Expert Panel may at any time add, delete, or change the order of ingredient review without requesting concurrence by the Steering Committee. . . .

. . . [T]he review of each ingredient goes through several stages. The staff of CIR prepares a Scientific Literature Review summarizing the published information and publicly requests any relevant published or unpublished data that the review does not already include.

Individually, ingredient suppliers and cosmetic manufacturers have tested ingredients, as well as formulations, for many years. Although much of these data have been published, a significant portion are in industry files and not available for public or scientific review. The collection of these data and the test protocols used to produce the data are critical to the success of the program. At the end of a 90-day public comment period, all submitted data are incorporated into a document for consideration by a subgroup (Team) of the Expert Panel. From 25% to 75% of the data included in the CIR reports has not been published previously. Teams meet in a series of closed working sessions to evaluate the report and determine whether there are sufficient data upon which to base a conclusion. A document reflecting those considerations is then prepared for review by the full Expert Panel. After discussion of this document in public meetings of the full Panel, a Tentative Report is issued with one of three conclusions: (1) that the ingredient is safe as currently used, (2) that the ingredient is unsafe, or (3) that there is insufficient information for the Panel to make a determination of safety. It is significant that CIR procedures require documented evidence giving reasonable assurance of safety before reaching the final determination. Lack of adverse information about an ingredient is not sufficient to justify a determination of safety.

The Tentative Report is then made available for a 90-day public comment period. . . . A Final Report, incorporating any substantive changes resulting from public comment, is then released by the Expert Panel. . . .

Statement of Robert L. Elder, SC.D.*

"Potential Hazards of Cosmetic Products," Hearing before the Subcommittee on
Regulation and Business Opportunities House Committee on Small Business
(September 15, 1988).

The CTFA Ingredient Dictionary currently lists 5000 nonfragrance ingredients. These are ingredients that are offered for use by the

---

*   [Dr. Elder was the Director of CIR.]

cosmetic industry. Many are not used in a cosmetic at any given time. It is estimated that about 2300 of these nonfragrance ingredients are in actual use at any one time. Data from the FDA cosmetic voluntary reporting program indicate that approximately 700 of these 2300 ingredients have been reported to be used in 20 or more cosmetic formulations. The 700 ingredients whose reported frequency of use is greater than 20 are the ingredients that have thus far been prioritized for CIR review. Although we have prioritized only those cosmetic ingredients used in 20 or more formulations, in going through this process we have actually considered a much larger number of ingredients. We considered all ingredients in 10 or more formulations when we established the 1984 priority list, to make sure that important chemicals were not missed. And in 1987 FDA provided to the Expert Panel a list of all chemicals used in *any* cosmetic formulation, again to be sure that any important chemical was included. Thus, we have cast a wide net. One-third of these 700 ingredients are already regulated by FDA for use in food or drug products or as color additives. . . .

Wilma F. Bergfeld* et al., *Safety of Ingredients Used in Cosmetics*

52 Journal of the American Academy of Dermatology 125 (2005).

. . . From 1976 to September 2004, the CIR Expert Panel completed safety assessments of 1194 ingredients. These ingredients are estimated to be used in more than 100,000 cosmetic products. . . .

For 683 ingredients (approximately 58%), the conclusion was safe as used. In this context, "as used" refers to the practices of use and concentrations described in each safety assessment . . .

For 114 ingredients (approximately 33%) the conclusion was that they could be used safely in cosmetic products with qualifications. Ingredients found safe with qualifications fall into one or more of the following groups: concentration limits, inhalation or other product-use restrictions, and nitrosamine formation. Ingredients may be listed more than once if there are multiple qualifications on their safe use. . . .

For 114 ingredients (approximately 9%), the available data were insufficient to support safety. If the panel reaches an insufficient data conclusion, it does not state whether the ingredient is safe or unsafe. The panel is, however, describing a situation in which the available data do not support safety. . . .

Only 9 ingredients were found to be unsafe for use in cosmetic products (<1%). These are ingredients with specific adverse effects that make them unsuitable for use in cosmetics, in the view of the panel.

———

As of December 31, 2005, the CIR has reviewed 1,284 cosmetic ingredients and has made the following determinations.

———

*   [Dr. Bergfeld is the Chair of the CIR Expert Panel.]

Safe	766
Safe with qualifications	408
Insufficient data for a safety determination	120
Unsafe	9

Cosmetic Ingredient Review, 2005 Annual Report 10 (2006).

———

In 1991, the Consumer Federation of America petitioned FDA to ban urocanic acid, one of the ingredients found by CIR to lack sufficient data for a safety determination.

Letter From Ronald G. Chesemore, Associate Commissioner for Regulatory Affairs, FDA, to Consumer Federation of America

FDA Docket No. 91P–0114/CP (October 25, 1996).

This replies to your citizen petition (91P–0114CP), of March 20, 1991, and filed March 21, 1991, requesting that the Food and Drug Administration (FDA) find that the cosmetic ingredient urocanic acid is a deleterious substance which may render any cosmetic product containing it injurious to users and that FDA declare any cosmetic products containing urocanic acid to be adulterated under the Federal Food, Drug and Cosmetic Act (FD&C Act). . . .

We conclude that the scientific evidence does not establish that the low level of immunosuppression by urocanic acid in humans presents a safety concern to humans. Thus, we cannot conclude that urocanic acid is a deleterious substance which, when used as a component of a cosmetic product, may render the product injurious to the user under the conditions of use prescribed in the labeling or under such conditions of use as are customary or usual. As a result, we are not prepared to say that cosmetic products containing urocanic acid are adulterated under the FD&C Act. Therefore, FDA is denying your petition.

We also conclude, however, that, while the scientific evidence reviewed for your petition does not demonstrate that use of urocanic acid is unsafe, it does raise questions whether the evidence exists to conclude that the use of this ingredient in cosmetic products is safe. These questions are significant under 21 CFR 740.10—a regulation that FDA adopted under the misbranding provisions of the FD&C Act. . . .

The safety of urocanic acid as a cosmetic ingredient has been previously reviewed by the Cosmetic Ingredient Review (CIR) Expert Panel. The CIR Expert Panel is a group of scientists that reviews the safety of cosmetic ingredients under the aegis of the Cosmetic, Toiletries and Fragrance Association (CTFA), a trade association of the cosmetics industry. As such, the CIR Expert Panel is the focus for the evaluation of the safety of ingredients by the cosmetic industry. In 1995, the CIR Expert Panel published a report of its review of the safety of urocanic acid (J. Am. Coll. Toxicol., 14 386–423 (1995).) In its report, the CIR Expert Panel concluded that the safety of urocanic acid as a cosmetic ingredient has not been documented and substantiated. . . .

Based on the Expert Panel's report, it would seem that manufacturers that use urocanic acid would have to provide notice on the labels of those products that contain this ingredient that its safety has not been established. We recognize that additional, unpublished, studies to substantiate the safety of urocanic acid may have been performed by individual companies. If cosmetic manufacturers have not done so, then the safety of urocanic acid in cosmetic products has not been substantiated, and there may be questions about the labeling of products that contain this ingredient. . . .

NOTE

FDA subsequently sent letters to manufacturers of cosmetic products containing urocanic acid, informing them of their obligation to include the warning statement under Section 740.10, and the industry discontinued use of the ingredient.

———

In 2004, the Environmental Working Group (EWG) surveyed the labeling for cosmetic products. EWG concluded that many products contain ingredients determined by CIR to be unsafe, to have insufficient data to determine safety, or to have qualifications not followed by the manufacturer. EWG issued a report, available on its website, and, on June 14, 2004, petitioned FDA to take appropriate regulatory action (Docket No. 2004P–0266/CP).

Letter From Robert E. Brackett, Director, FDA Center for Food Safety and Applied Nutrition, to CTFA
February 3, 2005.

. . . In December 2004, the Center for Food Safety and Applied Nutrition released its 2005 Program Priorities. These priorities include two items specifically aimed at ensuring that cosmetic products being marketed in the United States remain safe.

The first of these priorities addresses a citizen petition received from the Environmental Working Group (EWG) alleging that cosmetic products are currently being marketed in the United States with ingredients that have been determined by the Cosmetic Ingredient Review Expert Panel (CIR) to be unsafe, or to have insufficient data for a determination of safety, or to fall outside the qualifications for safe use. . . . We are preparing a response to the EWG citizen petition. Additionally, you should know that FDA intends to consider taking compliance action, where appropriate, regarding cosmetic products that contain ingredients that we determine have not been shown to be safe, based on findings of the CIR Expert Panel and other sources of information available to the Agency, but that are not currently labeled with the warning statement ("Warning—The safety of this product has not been determined.") required under 21 CFR 740.10. In the past we have taken appropriate action based in part on the CIR Expert Panel determination for safety.

FDA regards the CIR Expert Panel determination an important element in ensuring the safety of the cosmetic supply in the United States. Indeed, we have provided a Liaison Representative to the Expert Panel since approximately 1980 and plan to continue to provide a representative.

The second 2005 Program Priority related specifically to cosmetics is the development of draft guidance to implement 21 CFR 740.10. The guidance is intended to provide information to manufacturers on determining the adequacy of safety substantiation of ingredients in cosmetic products and on determining when the 21 CFR 740.10 warning statement would be necessary. . . .

NOTES

1. *Update.* FDA denied the EWG petition, stating that requests for enforcement action are not appropriate for a citizen petition, that EWG did not provide sufficient information for FDA to evaluate the safety of the ingredients which EWG identified, and that FDA takes enforcement action based on "the agency's priorities and available resources." Letter from Margaret O'K. Glavin, Associate Commissioner for Regulatory Affairs, FDA, to Jane Houlihan & Arianne Callender (Sept. 29, 2005).

2. *Section 740.10 Guidance.* The guidance to implement Section 740.10, promised in Dr. Brackett's letter to CTFA, never appeared and has been removed from the CFSAN annual priority list.

3. *Challenge to FDA's Role.* Before the CIR commenced, Consumers Union brought suit against FDA, contending that discussions between CTFA and FDA about plans for the program were advisory committee meetings that must comply with all of the requirements of the Federal Advisory Committee Act. *See infra* p. 1491. In *Consumers Union of United States, Inc. v. Department of HEW*, 409 F. Supp. 473 (D.D.C. 1976), *aff'd without opinion*, 551 F.2d 466 (D.C. Cir. 1977), the court concluded that CTFA was not "advising" FDA but that "CTFA in its own discretion was ultimately to decide whether or not to initiate a testing program." The District Court observed that FDA "appears to lack statutory authority to require initiation of an ingredient testing program."

4. *Fragrance Ingredients.* Fragrance ingredients used in cosmetics are exempt from the CIR program because they are subject to a separate safety review conducted by the Research Institute for Fragrance Materials. *See* Richard A. Ford, *Criteria for Development of a Database for Safety Evaluation of Fragrance Ingredients*, 31 Reg. Toxicology & Pharmacology 166 (2000).

5. *Commentary.* The objectives of the cosmetic industry's self-regulation program are discussed in Murray Berdick, *The Cosmetic Industry's Approach to Voluntary Regulation—Scientific Aspects*, 27 Food Drug Cosm. L.J. 208 (1972); J. Richard Edmondson, *Cosmetic Industry Self–Regulation*, 27 Food Drug Cosm. L.J. 45 (1972). For contrasting assessments of the effectiveness of the cosmetic industry self-regulation program, compare Murray Berdick, *Cosmetic Industry Initiatives*, 33 Food Drug Cosm. L.J. 239 (1978), with Joseph A. Page & Kathleen A. Blackburn, *Behind the Looking Glass: Administrative, Legislative and Private*

Approaches to Cosmetic Safety Substantiation, 24 UCLA L. Rev. 795 (1977). *See also* Casey Daum, *Self–Regulation in the Cosmetic Industry: A Necessary Reality or a Cosmetic Illusion?* (2006), in Chapter X of the Electronic Book.

H. THE PRESENT AND FUTURE OF COSMETICS REGULATION

Peter Barton Hutt, *"Examining the Current State of Cosmetics"*

Testimony before the Health Subcomm. of the Comm. on Energy & Commerce, U.S. House of Representatives, 112th Cong., 2nd Sess. (March 27, 2012).

Thank you for the opportunity to appear before you today on behalf of the Personal Care Products Council, the trade association representing the cosmetic industry in the United States and globally. . . .

The American cosmetic industry has an estimated $60 billion in annual retail sales, and employs 8.5 million people, directly and indirectly, in the United States. This industry is a net product exporter. It is innovative and entrepreneurial. The industry launches over 2,000 new products every year. Over 90 percent of cosmetic companies are small businesses that have 50 or fewer employees.

I will make three points . . . .

First, the Federal Food, Drug, and Cosmetic Act of 1938 creates a strong framework for FDA regulation of cosmetics. Under this law, it is a crime to market an unsafe or mislabeled cosmetic. Under FDA regulations, cosmetic companies are responsible for substantiating the safety of their products, and each of the individual ingredients, before marketing to the public. FDA has the responsibility to provide regulatory oversight through the creation and enforcement of safety and labeling requirements that hold industry accountable and to conduct postmarket surveillance to determine whether a cosmetic is in violation of these requirements. FDA collects samples for examination and analysis as part of its plant inspections and conducts follow-up inspections to investigate complaints of adverse reactions.

Cosmetic products imported into the United States are subject to the same substantive standards as those produced here. They face an even higher regulatory threshold upon entry into the country, because even the "appearance" of adulteration or misbranding subjects them to detention at the border. All labeling and packaging must be in compliance with United States regulations.

. . . .

Second, like many industries, the cosmetic industry continues to be affected by rapid globalization of supply chains, expansion in foreign markets, new technology, and increased consumer interest in product information. In much the same way that market changes require companies to adjust business plans, these global challenges justify the modernization of regulatory structures.

The basic statutory provisions that govern FDA regulatory authority over cosmetics today were put in place in 1938. Since 1938, FDA and the cosmetic industry have worked together to keep pace with changing technology by promulgation of creative regulations and the establishment of new regulatory programs. FDA issued regulations requiring safety substantiation of all cosmetic products and ingredients prior to marketing. Based on industry petitions, FDA established programs for the registration of cosmetic manufacturing establishments, the listing of cosmetic products and ingredients, and the submission of adverse reaction reports. At the request of FDA, industry established the Cosmetic Ingredient Review under which the safety of cosmetic ingredients is reviewed by independent expert academic scientists. These are only a few examples of the many FDA and cosmetic industry collaborations to assure product safety. But even though FDA has repeatedly stated that cosmetics are the safest products they regulate, it is time to bring FDA's statutory authority up to date.

Third, we believe that Congress can address these developments by making simple but important changes in the statutory authority over cosmetics. We offer the following 7 principles to guide this effort. We support enactment of legislation that includes all of them.

1. Enacting into law the existing FDA programs for registration of manufacturing establishments and listing of cosmetic products.

2. Requiring submission of reports on adverse reactions that are serious and unexpected.

3. Mandating FDA regulations establishing good manufacturing practices for cosmetics.

4. Establishing programs to require FDA to review and determine whether controversial cosmetic ingredients and constituents are or are not safe, followed by strong FDA enforcement.

5. Requiring FDA review of all Cosmetic Ingredient Review determinations on cosmetic ingredient safety and either acceptance or rejection of those determinations, followed by strong FDA enforcement.

6. FDA establishment of a national cosmetic regulatory databank for use by everyone.

7. An unambiguous Congressional determination that, as modernized, the revised statute will apply uniformly through the country.

Concerns about cosmetic ingredient safety must be addressed as rapidly as possible by FDA scientists, who can then advise consumers about the safety of products they use every day. We believe Congress should enact a statute that defines a clear path for any person, organization, state or local official, or company, to request that FDA review the safety of a cosmetic ingredient or constituent and make their findings public in an enforceable specified time period. We believe this will allow concerns about cosmetic ingredients and constituents to be resolved expeditiously by the appropriate expert federal agency—FDA.

It is essential in this legislation that FDA's regulatory authority over cosmetics is firmly established as comprehensive and paramount. It is extremely important for the vitality of the industry that FDA establish national standards on safety that apply in every state. It is impossible to formulate innovative products if different safety standards apply in different states. And FDA's authority is undermined if states create regulatory régimes for cosmetics that are different from FDA regulation of cosmetics. That is why national uniformity of these regulatory changes is critical to our support of this legislation.

. . . .

CHAPTER 12

TOBACCO PRODUCTS

A. INTRODUCTION

Almost a decade after the Supreme Court struck down FDA's attempt to regulate cigarettes and smokeless tobacco as combination drugs/medical devices in *FDA v. Brown & Williamson Tobacco Corp.*, 529 U.S. 120 (2000) (excerpted *supra* p. 141), Congress gave the agency explicit authority to regulate tobacco products. In June 2009, President Obama signed the Family Smoking Prevention and Tobacco Control Act (FSPTCA), 123 Stat. 1776 (2009) with the stated goal of reducing the number of children and adolescents using tobacco products and preventing tobacco-related disease. The new act establishes FDA's authority to regulate tobacco products as a category separate from the traditional spheres of FDA regulatory power—food, drugs, devices, and cosmetics. It also explicitly designates the FDA as the "primary Federal regulatory authority with respect to the manufacture, marketing, and distribution of tobacco products."

The Family Smoking Prevention and Tobacco Control Act reinstates FDA's 1996 regulations on the distribution, promotion, and advertising of cigarettes and smokeless tobacco products. The statute goes much further than the 1996 regulations, however, by also establishing a comprehensive regulatory regime for tobacco products.

The new law defines tobacco products as "any product made or derived from tobacco that is intended for human consumption, including any component, part, or accessory of a tobacco product (except for raw materials other than tobacco used in manufacturing a component, part, or accessory of a tobacco product)." FD&C Act 201(rr)(1). The statute goes on to specify that "the term 'tobacco product' does not mean an article that is a drug under subsection (g)(1), a device under subsection (h), or a combination product described in section 503(g)." *Id.* 201(rr)(2). The new tobacco sections of the FD&C Act apply automatically to cigarettes, cigarette tobacco, roll-your-own tobacco products, and smokeless tobacco. FD&C Act 901(b). They will also apply to any other type of tobacco product (e.g., cigars, pipe tobacco, or e-cigarettes) that FDA "by regulation deems to be subject to" the new law. *Id.*

The Family Smoking Prevention and Tobacco Control Act directs FDA to establish a new Center for Tobacco Products (CTP), which is responsible for implementing FSPTCA and reporting to the Commissioner of Food and Drugs in the same manner as other agency centers. FSPTCA also amends the FD&C Act to, among other things:

- define misbranding and adulteration of tobacco products (FD&C Act 901 & 902);

- require annual establishment registration and product listing (FD&C Act 905);

- permit FDA to establish "tobacco product standards" that may include provisions regarding nicotine yields, reduction or elimination of other harmful constituents, product construction, and product testing, but may not require the reduction of nicotine yields to zero or completely ban cigarettes, smokeless tobacco products, cigars, little cigars, pipe tobacco, or roll-your-own tobacco (FD&C Act 907);

• prohibit the use of all added characterizing flavors (other than tobacco or menthol) in cigarettes (FD&C Act 907(a)(1)(A));

• allow new tobacco products that are "substantially equivalent" to products that were commercially marketed in the United States as of February 15, 2007 to enter or remain on the market on a showing of substantial equivalence to these older products (FD&C Act 905(j), 910(a));

• allow new tobacco products that are not "substantially equivalent" to enter the market only with FDA approval of a detailed new tobacco product application showing that "permitting such tobacco product to be marketed would be appropriate for the protection of the public health" (FD&C Act 910);

• allow "modified risk tobacco products" to enter the market only with FDA approval of a distinct type of application for modified risk tobacco products (FD&C Act 911);

• forbid the use of the terms "light," "mild," or "low" after June 22, 2010;

• reinstate FDA's 1996 final regulation establishing restrictions on the distribution, promotion, and advertising of cigarettes and smokeless tobacco.

Through the FSPTCA, FDA is given "primary regulatory authority with respect to the manufacture, marketing, and distribution of tobacco products" as "appropriate for the protection of the public health."

The regulatory scheme established by the FSPTCA is, in some ways, modeled on the FD&C Act's provisions for medical device regulation. Just as market entry for a medical device can be through a PMA application or by a less rigorous 510(k) application demonstrating substantial equivalence, new tobacco products can enter the market either through a premarket tobacco product application (PMTPA) or by demonstrating substantial equivalence to a tobacco product already on the market. Furthermore, "tobacco product standards" are parallel to performance standards for Class II devices. Many of the FSPTCA's prohibitions against misbranding and adulteration are, on their face, not so different from corresponding provisions in the FD&C Act regarding not only medical devices, but also food, drugs, and cosmetics.

Nonetheless, tobacco products pose dramatically different regulatory issues than do the other products under FDA's authority. Unlike these other articles, tobacco products unequivocally and inevitably harm the health of both users and non-users. To address the special problems raised by tobacco products, the FSPTCA subjects them to a new "public health" standard that does not apply to any other FDA-regulated products. The agency recognizes the distinctiveness of tobacco product regulation on its website:

Tobacco products are a unique addition to the FDA's regulatory authorities because they are harmful yet widely used consumer products, responsible for severe health problems in both users and non-users, including cancer, lung disease, and heart disease, which often lead to death. FDA's traditional "safe and effective" standard for evaluating medical products does not apply to tobacco. FDA evaluates new tobacco products based on a public health standard that considers the risks and benefits of the tobacco product on the population as a whole, including users and non-users.

Tobacco Products, *Tobacco Product Review & Evaluation*, http://www. fda.gov/TobaccoProducts/Labeling/TobaccoProductReviewEvaluation/ default.htm (last visited June 4, 2013).

B. TOBACCO PRODUCT REVIEW

Section 910 of the FD&C Act establishes a review process for tobacco products. New tobacco products and tobacco products that make claims about modified risks are subject to FDA review and clearance or approval prior to marketing. Products that were already on the market prior to February 15, 2007 are not subject to any review measures, although if such a product makes claims using the words "light", "mild", "low" or similar descriptors, the manufacturer is required to submit a Modified Risk Tobacco Product Application (MRTA) or discontinue the use of those words in labeling.

The FSPTCA establishes three methods by which a company can get permission from the FDA to market a new tobacco product: a demonstration of substantial equivalence, an exemption from a demonstration of substantial equivalence, or a premarket tobacco application. FD&C Act 905(j), 910. It also establishes a distinct review process for modified risk tobacco products. *Id.* at 911.

1. SUBSTANTIAL EQUIVALENCE REPORTS

One regulatory path for introducing a new tobacco product to market is parallel to the 510(k) process for medical devices. FD&C Act 905(j) provides that a manufacturer may show that its new tobacco product is substantially equivalent to a tobacco product that was on the market prior to February 15, 2007 or to a product that has been found to be substantially similar itself to a product on the market before February 15, 2007. Section 910(a)(3) states that a tobacco product is "substantially equivalent" to a predicate tobacco product if it has the same characteristics as the predicate, or if it has different characteristics but the new product "does not raise different questions of public health."

In January 2011, the FDA released a draft guidance for industry discussing how to demonstrate substantial equivalence for tobacco products.

Guidance for Industry and FDA Staff; Section 905(j) Reports: Demonstrating Substantial Equivalence for Tobacco Products

Jan. 5, 2011.

... This guidance provides recommendations and information related to the submission and review of reports under section 905(j) of the Federal Food, Drug, and Cosmetic Act. ... In the future, FDA intends to initiate a rulemaking that would establish requirements and standards for substantial equivalence under sections 905(j) and 910 of the Act. ... This guidance ... explains, among other things, FDA's interpretation of the statutory sections related to substantial equivalence, and provides recommendations on the form and content of section 905(j) reports. ...

In general, a tobacco product manufacturer must obtain an order under section 910(c)(1)(A)(i) (order after review of a premarket application) before the manufacturer may introduce a new tobacco product into interstate commerce. An order under section 910(c)(1)(A)(i) is not required, however, if a manufacturer submits a report under section 905(j) for the new tobacco product and FDA issues an order finding that the tobacco product is (1) substantially equivalent to a tobacco product commercially marketed in the United States as of February 15, 2007, and (2) in compliance with the requirements of the Act.

... A tobacco product may not be found to be substantially equivalent to a predicate tobacco product that has been removed from the market at the initiative of the FDA or that has been determined by a judicial order to be misbranded or adulterated (section 910(a)(3)(C) of the Act). ...

At this time, FDA does not intend to enforce the requirements of sections 910 and 905(j) for tobacco blending changes required to address the natural variation of tobacco (e.g., blending changes due to variation in growing conditions) in order to maintain a consistent product. Blending changes that are intended to alter the chemical or perception properties of the new product (e.g., nicotine level, pH, smoothness, harshness, etc.) compared to the predicate should be reported under 910 or 905(j). ...

For the purposes of this guidance document, FDA refers to predicate tobacco products that were commercially marketed ... in the United States as of February 15, 2007 as "grandfathered tobacco products."

. . . .

The 905(j) report should provide side-by-side quantitative and qualitative comparisons of the new tobacco product with the predicate tobacco product with respect to all product characteristics. In addition, if the predicate to which the new tobacco product is being compared is a product for which FDA has issued an order of substantial equivalence, FDA recommends that the 905(j) report also include a side-by-side comparison to the grandfathered tobacco product (the tobacco product to which the predicate was compared). ...

. . . It is important . . . that you submit sufficient information to enable FDA to determine whether the new tobacco product has the same characteristics (defined [in 910(a)(3)(B)] as the materials, ingredients, design, composition, heating source, or other features of a tobacco product) as the predicate tobacco product, in accordance with 910(a)(3)(A)(i), or has different characteristics but it is not necessary to regulate the product under section 910(c)(1)(A)(i) because it does not raise different questions of public health, as required by 910(a)(3)(A)(ii). . . .

. . . [F]or 905(j) reports for products with different characteristics, but which you do not believe raise different questions of public health under 910(a)(3)(A)(ii), FDA may request additional data needed to make a substantial equivalence determination.

Examples of additional data that may be requested include:

Consumer Perception Studies—data comparing consumer perceptions with respect to the new tobacco product and the predicate that could affect initiation, cessation, frequency of use, patterns of use, smoking behavior, and perceptions of harm or addictiveness.

Clinical data—data comparing the biomarkers of exposure and biomarkers of potential harm and human toxicity. . . .

Abuse liability data—data comparing the abuse liability. . . .

Toxicology data—data comparing the toxicity. . . .

———

NOTES

1. *Changes in Labeling.* In a subsequent draft guidance, FDA stated: "The label and packaging of a tobacco product is considered a 'part' of that product. A change to any part of a tobacco product after February 15, 2007 makes that product a 'new tobacco product.' " The agency then explained that it does not intend to enforce the section 905(j) and section 910 premarket requirements with respect to products for which the only change from the predicate product is the elimination of descriptors such as "light," "mild," or "low"; the addition of FDA-mandated graphic warnings; a switch from a soft pack to a hard pack (or vice-versa); or a change in the font size, ink color, or background color of the packaging or label that does not raise different questions of public health. The agency further explained that a change in the name of a cigarette brand renders the cigarette a new product subject to the premarket requirements. DRAFT GUIDANCE FOR INDUSTRY AND FDA STAFF DEMONSTRATING THE SUBSTANTIAL EQUIVALENCE OF A NEW TOBACCO PRODUCT: RESPONSES TO FREQUENTLY ASKED QUESTIONS 3–6 (Sept. 2011).

2. *First Marketing Order Decisions Based on Substantial Equivalence (SE).* On June 25, 2013, the FDA released its first set of decisions on substantial equivalence claims for new tobacco products. FDA authorized the marketing of two new tobacco products as substantially equivalent, while denying four others. FDA also noted that 136 905(j) SE reports had been voluntarily withdrawn by manufacturers at some point in the review process. FDA News Release, *FDA Announces First Decisions on*

New Tobacco Products Through the Substantial Equivalence Pathway (June 25, 2013). By its actions, FDA demonstrated that while it is not impossible to demonstrate substantial equivalence, the burden on the manufacturer to demonstrate there are no new questions of public health is significant. In the order letters to Lorillard Tobacco, the company that had two new Newport Gold Box® products cleared for market entry, FDA emphasized that the company may not in any way represent these products as being "FDA-approved."

2.   EXEMPTION FROM DEMONSTRATION OF SUBSTANTIAL EQUIVALENCE

Under Section 905(j)(3) of the FD&C Act, as implemented by 21 C.F.R. 1107.1, the agency can exempt a new tobacco product from the requirement that its manufacturer demonstrate substantial equivalence. To be granted such an exemption, a manufacturer must submit an "exemption request" demonstrating that its new tobacco product features only a minor modification from a predicate tobacco product; that a 905(j)(1) SE report is unnecessary for the protection of public health; or that an exemption is otherwise appropriate. According to section 905(j)(3)(A), the only types of new products that may qualify for an exemption are "tobacco products that are modified by adding or deleting a tobacco additive, or increasing or decreasing the quantity of an existing tobacco additive." When it announced its first two SE clearances in June 2013, FDA also mentioned that it had refused to accept 20 SE Exemption Requests, in some cases because the requests "were not limited to changes in additives." *FDA Announces First Decisions on New Tobacco Products Through the Substantial Equivalence Pathway* (June 25, 2013).

3.   PREMARKET TOBACCO PRODUCT APPLICATION (PMTA)

If a new tobacco product is not substantially equivalent to a predicate tobacco product and does not qualify for an exemption, the manufacturer must file a Premarket Tobacco Product Application (PMTA). In September 2011, the FDA released a draft guidance regarding such applications.

Draft Guidance for Industry Applications for Premarket Review of New Tobacco Products
September 2011.

... Section 910(c)(1)(A)(ii) of the FD&C Act requires that FDA deny a PMTA and issue an order that the product may not be introduced or delivered for introduction into interstate commerce where FDA finds that:

- You have not shown that the product is appropriate for the protection of the public health;

- The manufacturing methods, facilities, or controls do not conform to manufacturing regulations issued under section 906(e);

- The proposed labeling is false or misleading; or
- You have not shown that the product complies with any tobacco product standard in effect under section 907.

. . . As defined in section 910(a)(1) of the FD&C Act, a new tobacco product is any tobacco product that was not commercially marketed in the United States as of February 15, 2007 or any product that was commercially marketed as of February 15, 2007 but which was subsequently modified.

Section 910 of the FD&C Act provides that manufacturers of new tobacco products may submit a substantial equivalence report under section 905(j) and obtain a substantial equivalence order under section 910(a)(2)(A)(i) as an alternative to submitting a PMTA and obtaining a marketing authorization order under section 910(c)(1)(A)(i). Furthermore, a new tobacco product may be exempted from the requirement to obtain a substantial equivalence order or a marketing authorization order if the product is exempt from the requirements of section 905(j) pursuant to a regulation issued under section 905(j)(3).

. . . Section 910(b)(1)(A) of the FD&C Act requires that a PMTA contain "full reports of all information, published or known to, or which should reasonably be known to, the applicant, concerning investigations which have been made to show the health risks of such tobacco product and whether such tobacco product presents less risk than other tobacco products." FDA interprets the information required under this provision to include, not only investigations that support the application, but also any investigations that do not support, or are adverse to, the application. Information on both nonclinical and clinical investigations should be provided. . . .

The information provided in the application described in . . . this guidance should present data and information sufficient to enable FDA to make a finding that the marketing of a new tobacco product is "appropriate for the protection of the public health" (section 910(c)(4) of the FD&C Act). The statute provides that the basis for this finding shall be determined:

with respect to the risks and benefits to the population as a whole, including users and nonusers of the tobacco product, and taking into account—

(A) the increased or decreased likelihood that existing users of tobacco products will stop using such products; and

(B) the increased or decreased likelihood that those who do not use tobacco products will start using such products.

Section 910(c)(2)(A) of the FD&C Act requires that FDA deny applications where "there is a lack of a showing that permitting such tobacco product to be marketed would be appropriate for the protection of the public health."

Under section 910(c)(5)(A) of the FD&C Act, whether a new tobacco product is appropriate for the protection of public health shall be determined "when appropriate . . . on the basis of well-controlled investigations." . . .

FDA . . . recommends you provide a detailed explanation of how the data and information provided in the application support a finding that introducing your new tobacco product to the market is appropriate for the protection of the public health. FDA recommends that your explanation include a comparison of the new tobacco product to tobacco products currently on the market.

. . . We request comment on what product chemistry, nonclinical, and adult human subject studies could be used to demonstrate that the marketing of the product is appropriate for the protection of the public health. We also request comment on establishing a baseline for determining whether a new product affects the likelihood that tobacco users will quit or the likelihood that non-users will start using such products.

. . . .

FDA plans to issue regulations pursuant to section 910(g) providing conditions under which tobacco products may be exempted from the requirements of section 910 when used for investigational purposes. Until these regulations are issued, FDA will consider exercising discretion in enforcing the premarket review requirements . . ., in some circumstances, for the purposes of investigational use of new tobacco products. Applicants who would like to study their new tobacco products should contact the Office of Science at the Center for Tobacco Products to discuss submission of a study protocol and/or study endpoints for investigations intended to support a PMTA.

———

NOTE

It is not yet clear how or whether a novel form of tobacco product could be considered "appropriate for the protection of the public health" if it is not also a "modified risk tobacco product," as described immediately below.

4. MODIFIED RISK TOBACCO PRODUCT APPLICATION (MRTPA)

a. DEFINITION OF MODIFIED RISK TOBACCO PRODUCT

A modified risk tobacco product is "any tobacco product that is sold or distributed for use to reduce harm or the risk of tobacco-related disease associated with commercially marketed tobacco products." FD&C Act 911(b)(1). If a manufacturer wants to claim that its tobacco product is safer, healthier, or a lower risk than conventional tobacco products, the product must have a modified risk tobacco product application (MRTPA) approved by the FDA.

Section 911(b)(1) elaborates on the definition of an MRTP by specifically providing that the term includes any tobacco product (1) whose label, labeling, or advertising represents, explicitly or implicitly, that it presents a lower risk than or is less harmful than other products, or that the product is free of, contains less of, or presents reduced exposure to a substance, (2) whose label, labeling, or advertising contains the descriptors "light," "mild," "low," or similar words, or (3) whose manufacturer suggests reduced risk or reduced exposure to a substance outside of the label, labeling, or advertising.

For a tobacco product that is already on the market, the manufacturer must have an approved MRTPA before using language indicating a reduced risk associated with the use of its product. For a new tobacco product, a manufacturer would today have to submit an MRTPA in addition to either a substantial equivalence report, request for exemption, or premarket tobacco product application. However, FD&C Act 911(*l*)(4) requires FDA to issue a regulation or guidance that will permit the filing of a single application in such instances.

Letter From Lawrence R. Deyton, Dir., Center for Tobacco Products, to Tobacco Manufacturers on Tobacco Products Labeled or Advertised With the Descriptors "Light," "Low," "Mild," or Similar Descriptors

June 17, 2010.

Dear Tobacco Manufacturer:

The Food and Drug Administration is providing this notice to remind manufacturers, including importers of finished tobacco products, that . . . on or after July 22, 2010, manufacturers, including importers of finished tobacco products, may not introduce into the domestic commerce of the United States any tobacco product for which the label, labeling, or advertising contains the descriptors "light," "low," or "mild," or any similar descriptor, irrespective of the date of manufacture, without an FDA order in effect [approving a MRTPA under FD&C Act 911(g).]

Tobacco use is the leading preventable cause of death in the United States. In prohibiting the use of "light," "mild," and "low," Congress found that many smokers mistakenly believe that cigarettes marketed with those descriptors cause fewer health problems than other cigarettes, and that those mistaken beliefs can reduce the motivation to quit smoking. Studies have demonstrated that there has been no reduction in health risk from such products, and such products may actually increase the risk of tobacco use. Congress has determined that prohibiting the use of "light," "mild," and "low" and similar descriptors is necessary to protect the public health and important to ensure that tobacco product label, labeling, and advertising are truthful and not misleading.

. . . Under section 301(pp) of the Act, the introduction or delivery for introduction into interstate commerce of a tobacco product in violation of section 911 is a prohibited act. Under section 902(8) of the Act, a tobacco product shall be deemed to be adulterated if it is in violation of section 911 of the Act. Under the Act, adulterated products sold or held for sale in the United States may be subject to seizure under section 304 of the Act. In addition, manufacturers, including importers of finished tobacco products, may be subject to injunction actions, civil money penalty proceedings, and/or criminal prosecution for violating the requirements of the Act. . . . FDA intends to use the full range of enforcement tools within the Agency's authority to ensure compliance with the new requirement. . . .

NOTE

Since July 2010, manufacturers have sought clever ways to retain the differentiation between products within their brands without using terms like "light," "mild," and "low." Marlboro, for example, utilizes a color system that it had already incorporated into its branding. Marlboro Lights (sold with gold accents on the packaging) became Marlboro Gold and Marlboro Ultralights (sold with silver accents on the packaging) became Marlboro Silver.

b.   STANDARDS FOR APPROVAL OF AN MRTPA

Scientific Standards for Studies on Modified Risk Tobacco Products

Institute of Medicine of the National Academies, Board on Population Health and Public Health Practice Committee on Scientific Standards for Studies on Modified Risk Tobacco Products (2011).

Preface

. . . The prospect of a less hazardous tobacco product is not in and of itself problematic. The fundamental issue is that if a product is going to be marketed as being "safer," then the claim must be true.

Section 911 of the Family Smoking Prevention and Tobacco Control Act of 2009 directly addresses the problem of false and unfounded claims for modified risk tobacco products (MRTPs). The law remains open to the possibility that less hazardous products that reduce harm to public health may enter the market, but it gives the government the authority and the power to assure that they are actually reducing risk and harm. The law also directed [FDA] to develop, in consultation with the Institute of Medicine (IOM), regulations and guidance on the design and conduct of scientific studies of MRTPs, which was the task of the committee.

Regulating tobacco products creates unique challenges. Unlike most products regulated by the FDA, tobacco is inherently hazardous and offers primarily risks rather than any significant physiological benefit to the user's health. Recognizing this . . ., [f]irst, the law creates a public health standard that requires the FDA to evaluate the effect of the MRTP on not only users of the product, but also nonusers and the entire population as a whole. Second, the law requires postmarket observational studies of the MRTPs as a condition of approval, and also requires the annual submission of data about the MRTPs to the FDA. Finally, the law sets expiration dates on the orders to market the MRTPs. In addition, the FDA can revoke an order for any failure to comply with regulatory requirements or if there is evidence that the product is in fact harmful to public health.

The evaluation of the effect of MRTPs on public health will require a wide range of evidence and therefore will require many different types of study designs, including studies of the composition of MRTPs and studies of human exposure, human health effects, the likelihood of addiction and abuse, and the perception and understanding of the product by the public. Furthermore, the evidence must be able to reliably support predictions about the effect of marketing the product on public health, and therefore these studies must be properly designed and rigorously conducted. Study designs will need to include all relevant populations including populations at a high risk for tobacco use. Study designs must be able to support not only inferences about the mechanisms of the products [sic] effects, but also predictions about the products' effects in the real world.

Also, relevant to the committee's deliberations as it considered the conduct of studies is the history of the tobacco industry's past behavior. The tobacco industry has a long and well-documented history of illegal and improper conduct, and its practices have only recently been regulated. Because of the health impact of its products and the opaque practices that have been engaged by the tobacco industry, many academic institutions and their faculty that would normally be involved in a product's evaluation have been separated from conducting research related to tobacco products for many years. Thus, the committee concluded that the tobacco industry currently lacks not only the trustworthiness, but also the expertise, infrastructure, and other resources needed to independently produce the scientific evidence necessary to meet the public health standards set by the law. In the report, the committee explores the possibility of new governance mechanisms to address this problem, including the potential creation of a third-party governance entity. . . .

———

There are two bases on which FDA may approve an MRTPA. First, if the product as actually used by consumers will (A) significantly reduce the harm and risk of tobacco-related disease, and (B) benefit the health of the population as a whole, including non-users of the product, then the agency is required to issue a marketing order for the product. FD&C Act 911(g)(1). Such an order is known as a "risk modification order."

Second, when a product cannot demonstrate the above without conducting long-term epidemiological studies, and the reduced risk claims are limited to a representation that the product or its smoke contains a reduced level of or is free of a particular substance, then a "special rule" applies. FD&C Act 911(g)(2). The manufacturer must demonstrate that the overall reduction in exposure to the harmful substance is substantial and that the available scientific evidence demonstrates that it is reasonably likely that subsequent studies will demonstrate reduced morbidity or mortality from use of the product. In addition, the applicant must show that the product will benefit the health of the population as a whole, including both users and non-users. FD&C Act 911(g)(2). When the FDA grants a MRTPA on this basis, it is known as an "exposure modification order."

In March 2012, the FDA issued a draft guidance for industry about submitting MRTPAs. As part of an MRTPA, a manufacturer must submit a description of the proposed tobacco product and any proposed advertising and labeling, the conditions for using the tobacco product, the formulation of the tobacco product, sample product labels and labeling, all documents relating to research findings and data, and information on how consumers actually use the product. Manufacturers must also conduct postmarket surveillance and studies and submit the results to the FDA so it may assess the impact of the product on consumer behavior and health. *See* DRAFT GUIDANCE FOR INDUSTRY: MODIFIED RISK TOBACCO PRODUCT APPLICATIONS (Mar. 2012).

C. TOBACCO PRODUCT STANDARDS

FSPTCA added FD&C Act 907, which gives FDA the authority to adopt tobacco product standards appropriate for the protection of public health. Tobacco product standards are modeled on section 514 performance standards, a form of special control for Class II medical devices. However, whereas a device performance standard includes provisions "necessary to provide reasonable assurance of safety and effectiveness," a tobacco product standard contains provisions "appropriate for the protection of the public health." FD&C Act 514(a)(2)(A); 907(a)(3). Again, this public health standard takes into consideration the effect of tobacco products on both users and non-users of tobacco products.

Tobacco product standards may be used to regulate a broad range of product characteristics. Perhaps most important, section 907(a)(4) allows FDA to regulate nicotine yields—although, according to 907(d)(3)(B), the agency cannot reduce nicotine yields to zero. Under section 907(a)(4), tobacco product standards may also address the levels of other constituents and ingredients, product construction, and labeling. They may also mandate product testing and impose restrictions on sale and distribution. *Id.* However, FDA may not ban an entire class of tobacco products under this authority—for example, all cigarettes or all pipe tobacco. FD&C Act 907(d)(3)(A).

Two self-executing standards ("special rules") were included directly in section 907. These product standards went into effect without FDA rulemaking. First, manufacturers cannot use tobacco that contains a level of pesticide chemical residue greater than permitted by any federal tolerance. FD&C Act 907(a)(1)(B). In addition, a special rule bans all characterizing flavors from cigarettes, with the exception of menthol. *Id.* 907(a)(1)(A).

FDA may eventually ban menthol, as well. Section 907(a)(1)(A) preserves the agency's power to do so. In compliance with section 907(e), the FDA Tobacco Products Scientific Advisory Committee submitted a report and recommendation to the agency in 2011 on the impact of the use of menthol in cigarettes, particularly among children, African Americans, Hispanics, and other racial/ethnic minorities. FDA also prepared an independent review of the public health effects of menthol and submitted this report to peer review. FDA is still considering what action is appropriate. In May 2013, the African American Tobacco Control Leadership Council encouraged the FDA to take steps to ban menthol. In July 2013, FDA announced the availability of its preliminary scientific evaluation indicating that there is a "likely public health impact" of menthol in cigarettes, and it issued an ANPR to obtain comments regarding "regulatory actions FDA might take with respect to" the issue. 78 Fed. Reg. 44484 (July 24, 2013).

NOTES

1.   *Good Manufacturing Practices.* Tobacco product manufacturers are subject to good manufacturing practices. FD&C Act 906(e). In 2012, thirteen tobacco companies submitted joint recommendations for cGMP regulations to FDA, and the agency has opened a docket to receive input on these recommendations. 78 Fed. Reg. 16824 (Mar. 19, 2013).

2.   *Reporting of HPHCs.* FD&C Act 904(a)(3) requires tobacco product manufacturers to report the quantities of harmful and potentially harmful constituents (HPHCs) in each of their products. Although there are more than 7,000 chemicals in tobacco products and tobacco smoke, this reporting requirement applies only to HPHCs that FDA has listed. In 2012, the agency promulgated a list of 96 HPHCs, but rather than simultaneously requiring the testing and reporting of all of them, the agency also released a draft guidance containing an abbreviated list of approximately 20 HPHCs with respect to which FDA would enforce 904(a)(3) initially. 77 Fed. Reg. 20034 (April 3, 2012); DRAFT GUIDANCE FOR INDUSTRY: REPORTING HARMFUL AND POTENTIALLY HARMFUL CONSTITUENTS IN TOBACCO PRODUCTS AND TOBACCO SMOKE UNDER SECTION 904(a)(3) OF THE FD&C ACT (Mar. 2012).

D. TOBACCO PRODUCT LABELING AND ADVERTISING

The FSPTCA gives authority to FDA to regulate the labeling, advertising, and marketing of tobacco products in various ways. In the case below, a group of tobacco companies challenged, on First Amendment grounds, the Act's: (1) requirement that tobacco manufacturers reserve a significant portion of tobacco packaging for the display of health warnings, including graphic images intended to illustrate the hazards of smoking; (2) restrictions (discussed *supra* p. 1358) on the commercial marketing of "modified risk tobacco products;" (3) ban of statements that implicitly or explicitly convey the impression that tobacco products are approved by, or safer by virtue of being regulated by, the FDA; (4) restriction on the advertising of tobacco products to black text on a white background in most media; and (5) bar on the distribution of free samples of tobacco products in most locations, brand-name tobacco sponsorship of any athletic or social event, branded merchandising of any non-tobacco product, and distribution of free items in consideration of a tobacco purchase (i.e., "continuity programs"). The excerpt only includes the court's discussion of the first and fourth of these restrictions.

Discount Tobacco City & Lottery, Inc. v.
United States

674 F. 3d 509 (6th Cir. 2012).

■ CLAY, CIRCUIT JUDGE. . . .

Plaintiffs Discount Tobacco City & Lottery, Inc., *et al.,* comprised of manufacturers and sellers of tobacco products . . . claim that certain provisions of the Family Smoking Prevention and Tobacco Control Act violate their rights to free speech under the First Amendment.

. . . .

Now challenged are the Act's requirements (1) that tobacco manufacturers reserve a significant portion of tobacco packaging for the display of health warnings, including graphic images intended to illustrate the hazards of smoking; (2) restrictions on the commercial marketing of so-called "modified risk tobacco products;" (3) ban of statements that implicitly or explicitly convey the impression that tobacco products are approved by, or safer by virtue of being regulated by, the FDA; (4) restriction on the advertising of tobacco products to black text on a white background in most media; and (5) bar on the distribution of free samples of tobacco products in most locations, brand-name tobacco sponsorship of any athletic or social event, branded merchandising of any non-tobacco product, and distribution of free items in consideration of a tobacco purchase (i.e., "continuity programs").

. . . We review the Act's restrictions on commercial speech, subject to the framework initially set forth in *Central Hudson Gas & Elec. Corp. v. Public Serv. Comm'n of N.Y.,* 447 U.S. 557 (1980), and *Zauderer v. Office of Disciplinary Counsel of the Sup. Ct. of Ohio,* 471 U.S. 626 (1985). . . .

Because the *Central Hudson* test does not govern commercial speech that is false, deceptive or misleading, if commercial speech is so categorized, we apply a different test to determine whether a restriction, or disclosure requirement, is unconstitutional. . . . We have recently clarified . . . [that] *Zauderer* applies where a disclosure requirement targets speech that is inherently misleading . . . [it also] also controls our analysis where . . . the speech at issue is potentially misleading."

. . . As set forth in *Zauderer*, in the case of misleading or potentially misleading commercial speech, "an advertiser's rights are adequately protected as long as disclosure requirements are reasonably related to the State's interest in preventing deception of consumers," and not "unjustified or unduly burdensome." *Zauderer*, 471 U.S. at 651. . . .

Restriction on the Use of Color and Imagery in Tobacco Product Advertising

. . . .

The FSPTCA adopts the language of the 1996 FDA regulation, and provides that:

[E]ach manufacturer, distributor, and retailer advertising or causing to be advertised, disseminating or causing to be disseminated, any labeling or advertising for cigarettes or smokeless tobacco shall use only black text on a white background. This section does not apply to [certain subsequently described facilities and publications]. . . .

21 C.F.R. § 1140.32(a) (adopting 21 C.F.R. § 897.32(a), as amended).

. . . .

In this case, the government contends that the tobacco industry's graphic color advertisements are deceptive because "[t]obacco imagery . . . seeks to distract potential users from the fact that tobacco products are lethal and addictive." Consequently, the government's claim is not that tobacco advertisements make deceptive or misleading claims, but that they create positive associations in the minds of consumers, such as linking the use of tobacco products to "part of a desirable lifestyle that includes activities such as mountain biking, tug-of-war, and sex," along with concepts such as "fun" and "relaxation."

. . . .

It is worth quoting the Supreme Court, at some length, on this issue of the constitutionality of blanket bans of color and imagery in advertising:

> . . . We are not persuaded that identifying deceptive or manipulative uses of visual media in advertising is so intrinsically burdensome that the State is entitled to forgo that task in favor of the more convenient but far more restrictive alternative of a blanket ban on the use of illustrations. . . . Given the possibility of policing the use of illustrations in advertisements on a case-by-case basis, the prophylactic approach taken by [the State] cannot stand.

Zauderer, 471 U.S. at 649.

All use of color and imagery in tobacco advertising, of course, is not deceptive or manipulative. As Plaintiffs underscore, some advertising, like that for the "Camel Crush" product, is largely informational. Other tobacco advertising is used to reinforce consumer preference "by simply showing the package" of the customer's preferred brand. Finally, some uses of color imagery are simply attention grabbing in a crowded marketplace, letting consumers know that their preferred brand or product is available at a particular retailer. Furthermore, there are surely certain color graphic tobacco ads that have nominal to zero appeal to the youth market. Each of these forms of advertising has great expressive value for the tobacco industry, and its suppression would be an undue burden on Plaintiffs' free speech.

. . . .

Instead of instituting a blanket restriction on color and graphics in tobacco advertising, the government may instead restrict only the speech necessary to effect its purposes. . . . As the district court correctly stated, instead of instituting such a sweeping and complete ban, "Congress could have exempted large categories of innocuous images and colors—e.g., images that teach adult consumers how to use novel tobacco products, images that merely identify products and producers, and colors that communicate information about the nature of a product, at least where such colors and images have no special appeal to youth."

There is no doubt that identifying and targeting certain advertising practices will be more arduous than banning all color and graphics in tobacco advertising. . . . But this is the exact work required by the First Amendment. . . .

■ JANE B. STRANCH, CIRCUIT JUDGE.

I write for the majority in concluding that the warnings mandated by the Family Smoking Prevention and Tobacco Control Act . . . are constitutional under the First Amendment. . . .

Laws that restrict speech are fundamentally different than laws that require disclosures, and so are the legal standards governing each type of law. *Compare Central Hudson Gas & Elec. Corp. v. Public Serv. Comm'n of N.Y.,* 447 U.S. 557, 563–66 (1980) (setting forth the standard for restricting commercial speech), *with Zauderer v. Office of Disciplinary Counsel,* 471 U.S. 626, 650–53 (setting forth the standard for requiring commercial-speech disclosures). Since the Act's warnings require the disclosure of factual information, *Zauderer* governs the warnings. . . .

If a commercial-speech disclosure requirement fits within the framework of *Zauderer* and its progeny, then we apply a rational-basis standard. *Zauderer,* 471 U.S. at 651. If it does not, then we treat the disclosure as compelled speech under *Wooley v. Maynard,* 430 U.S. 705 (1977) and its ilk and apply strict scrutiny. . . .

Zauderer relied on the distinction between a fact and a personal or political opinion to distinguish factual, commercial-speech disclosure requirements, to which courts apply a rational-basis rule, from the type of compelled speech on matters of opinion that is "as violative of the First Amendment as prohibitions on speech."

With these principles in mind, we now turn to whether the *Zauderer* framework governs the constitutionality of disclosure requirements in this case. The Act mandates nine new textual and graphic warnings for packaging and advertising of cigarettes and four new textual warnings for packaging and advertising of smokeless-tobacco products. Act §§ 201(a), 204(a). The Act requires that the warnings comprise the top 50% of the front and back of cigarette packaging, 30% of the front and back of smokeless-tobacco-products packaging, and 20% of the advertising for cigarettes and smokeless-tobacco products. *Id.* §§ 201(a), 203(a). All of the warnings address the negative health consequences of using tobacco. *See id.* The factual content of the textual warnings is undisputed. It is beyond cavil that smoking presents the serious health risks described in the warnings, and Plaintiffs do not contend otherwise. . . . Because the textual warnings require disclosing factual information rather than opinions, *Zauderer*'s rational-basis rule applies.

The Act's graphic-warnings provision mandates that the FDA "require color graphics depicting the negative health consequences of smoking" to accompany the textual warnings on cigarette packaging and advertising. Act § 201(a). Because Plaintiffs bring a facial challenge to the warning requirements, our concern is not the specific images the FDA chose—those are under review elsewhere—but rather whether Plaintiffs can show that "no set of circumstances exists under which [the statute] would be valid, or that the statute lacks any plainly legitimate sweep." To satisfy this burden, Plaintiffs would have to establish that a graphic warning cannot convey the negative health consequences of smoking accurately, a position tantamount to concluding that pictures can never be factually accurate, only written statements can be. . . .

. . . We can envision many graphic warnings that would constitute factual disclosures under *Zauderer*. A nonexhaustive list of some that would include a picture or drawing of a nonsmoker's and smoker's lungs displayed side by side; a picture of a doctor looking at an x-ray of either a smoker's cancerous lungs or some other part of the body presenting a smoking-related condition; a picture or drawing of the internal anatomy of a person suffering from a smoking-related medical condition; a picture or drawing of a person suffering from a smoking-related medical condition; and any number of pictures consisting of text and simple graphic images.

. . . The next step in the analysis is to determine whether the Act's required warnings survive *Zauderer's* rational-basis rule.

The Act's required textual and graphic warnings are constitutional if there is a rational connection between the warnings' purpose and the means used to achieve that purpose. The warnings' purpose is to prevent consumers from being misled about the health risks of using tobacco. . . .

The question we are thus faced with is whether graphic and textual warnings that convey factual information about the health risks of tobacco use are reasonably related to the purpose of preventing consumer deception. We find they are. . . .

Faced with evidence that the current warnings ineffectively convey the risks of tobacco use and that most people do not understand the full risks, the Act's new warnings are reasonably related to promoting greater public understanding of the risks. A warning that is not noticed, read, or understood by consumers does not serve its function. The new warnings rationally address these problems by being larger and including graphics.

. . . [A]bundant evidence establishes that larger warnings incorporating graphics promote a greater understanding of tobacco-related health risks and materially affect consumers' decisions regarding tobacco use. Drawing on the available scientific evidence, the IOM concluded in its 2007 Report that "graphic warnings of the kind required in Canada, Brazil, and Thailand would promote greater public understanding of the risks of using tobacco and would help reduce consumption" in the United States. . . .

NOTES

1. *Divided Opinion.* The complicated structure of this decision is due to the fact that Judges Stranch and Barrett agreed with much of Judge Clay's opinion, but disagreed with his reasoning with respect to the Act's mandatory warnings and rejected both his reasoning and result with respect to graphic warnings in particular. (Judge Clay would have held the graphic warning requirement to be unconstitutional.)

2. *Decision with Respect to Other FSPTCA Provisions.* The court in *Discount Tobacco City* also upheld the other challenged labeling, advertising, and marketing provisions, with one exception: it struck down the ban on continuity or loyalty programs, reasoning that the government did not meet its burden of showing that the prohibition of such programs advances the interest of preventing youth from smoking or has a material effect on youth tobacco use.

———

Although the graphic warnings requirement withstood a facial challenge in *Discount Tobacco City*, the specific graphic warnings selected by the FDA to fulfill this FSPTCA provision were successfully challenged in the case below.

R.J. Reynolds Tobacco Co. v. Food & Drug Administration

696 F.3d 1205 (D.C. Cir. 2012).

■ BROWN, CIRCUIT JUDGE

The Family Smoking Prevention and Tobacco Control Act . . . directed the Secretary of the U.S. Department of Health and Human Services to issue regulations requiring all cigarette packages manufactured or sold in the United States to bear one of nine new textual warnings, as well as "color graphics depicting the negative health consequences of smoking." Pursuant to this authority, the Food and Drug Administration initiated a rulemaking proceeding through which it selected the nine images that would accompany the statutorily-prescribed warnings. Five tobacco companies challenged the rule, alleging that FDA's proposed graphic warnings violated the First Amendment. The district court granted the Companies' motion for summary judgment . . . and we affirm.

I. Background

. . . FDA promulgated the final set of nine images—one for each warning statement—by regulations issued on June 22, 2011. . . . *See* Required Warnings for Cigarette Packages and Advertisements, 76 Fed. Reg. 36,628 (June 22, 2011) (hereinafter Final Rule). FDA also required each graphic image to bear the phone number of the National Cancer Institute's "Network of Tobacco Cessation Quitlines," which uses the telephone portal "1–800–QUIT–NOW."

. . . .

II. Level of Scrutiny

The Companies do not dispute Congress's authority to require health warnings on cigarette packages, nor do they challenge the substance of any of the nine textual statements mandated by the Act. The only question before us is whether FDA's promulgation of the graphic warning labels . . . violates the First Amendment. We begin our analysis by determining the applicable level of scrutiny.

Both the right to speak and the right to refrain from speaking are "complementary components of the broader concept of individual freedom of mind" protected by the First Amendment. *Wooley v. Maynard,* 430 U.S. 705, 714 (1977). Any attempt by the government either to compel individuals to express certain views, or to subsidize speech to which they object, is subject to strict scrutiny. The general rule "that the speaker has the right to tailor the speech[ ] applies not only to expressions of value, opinion, or endorsement, but equally to statements of fact the speaker would rather avoid." . . .

This case contains elements of compulsion and forced subsidization. The Companies contend that, to the extent the graphic warnings go beyond the textual warnings to shame and repulse smokers and denigrate smoking as an antisocial act, the message is ideological and not informational. "[B]y effectively shouting well-understood information to consumers," they explain, "FDA is communicating an ideological message, a point of view on how people should live their lives: that the risks from smoking outweigh the pleasure that smokers derive from it, and that smokers make bad personal decisions, and should stop smoking." In effect, the graphic images are not warnings, but admonitions: "[D]on't buy or use this product." No one doubts the government can promote smoking cessation programs; can use shock, shame, and moral opprobrium to discourage people from becoming smokers; and can use its taxing and regulatory authority to make smoking economically prohibitive and socially onerous. And the government can certainly require that consumers be fully informed about the dangers of hazardous products. But this case raises novel questions about the scope of the government's authority to force the manufacturer of a product to go beyond making purely factual and accurate commercial disclosures and undermine its own economic interest—in this case, by making "every single pack of cigarettes in the country [a] mini billboard" for the government's anti-smoking message.

Even assuming the Companies' marketing efforts (packaging, branding, and other advertisements) can be properly classified as commercial speech, and thus subject to less robust First Amendment protections, a thorny question remains: how much leeway should this Court grant the government when it seeks to compel a product's manufacturer to convey the state's subjective—and perhaps even ideological—view that consumers should reject this otherwise legal, but disfavored, product? . . .

Courts have recognized a handful of "narrow and well-understood exceptions" to the general rule that content-based speech regulations—including compelled speech—are subject to strict scrutiny. There are two primary exceptions in the commercial speech context. First, "purely factual and uncontroversial" disclosures are permissible if they are "reasonably related to the State's interest in preventing deception of consumers," provided the requirements are not "unjustified or unduly burdensome." *Zauderer,* 471 U.S. at 651. Second, restrictions on commercial speech are subject to less stringent review than restrictions on other types of speech. . . . *See Cent. Hudson Gas & Elec. Corp. v. Pub. Serv. Comm'n,* 447 U.S. 557, 566 (1980). While this test is not quite as demanding as strict scrutiny, it is significantly more stringent than *Zauderer's* standard, which is akin to rational-basis review.

    . . . .

The Supreme Court has never applied *Zauderer* to disclosure requirements not designed to correct misleading commercial speech. FDA argues that *Zauderer's* lenient standard of scrutiny applies to regulations that serve a different governmental interest: disclosure of the health and safety risks associated with commercial products.

But by its own terms, *Zauderer's* holding is limited to cases in which disclosure requirements are "reasonably related to the State's interest in preventing deception of consumers." . . .

Zauderer [and other cases] . . . establish that a disclosure requirement is only appropriate if the government shows that, absent a warning, there is a self-evident—or at least "potentially real"—danger that an advertisement will mislead consumers. In this case, the proposed disclosure requirements would apply to both cigarette advertisements and cigarette packages. The Act bans any labeling or advertising representing that any tobacco product "presents a lower risk of tobacco-related disease or is less harmful than one or more other commercially marketed tobacco products," "contains a reduced level of a substance or presents a reduced exposure to a substance," or "does not contain or is free of a substance." The Act also bans advertising or labeling using the descriptors "light," "mild," "low," or similar descriptors. In light of these restrictions, and in the absence of any congressional findings on the misleading nature of cigarette packaging itself, there is no justification under *Zauderer* for the graphic warnings.

The dissent's argument that cigarette packages and other advertisements that fail to prominently display the negative health consequences of smoking are misleading, seems to blame the industry for playing by the government's rules. The Companies have never argued that *no* disclosure requirements are warranted; they merely object to the form and content of the specific requirements proposed by the FDA. . . .

Moreover, the graphic warnings do not constitute the type of "purely factual and uncontroversial" information or "accurate statement[s]" to which the *Zauderer* standard may be applied. . . .

The FDA's images are a much different animal. FDA concedes that the images are not meant to be interpreted literally, but rather to symbolize the textual warning statements, which provide "additional context for what is shown." But many of the images chosen by FDA could be misinterpreted by consumers. For example, the image of a man smoking through a tracheotomy hole might be misinterpreted as suggesting that such a procedure is a common consequence of smoking—a more logical interpretation than FDA's contention that it symbolizes "the addictive nature of cigarettes," which requires significant extrapolation on the part of the consumers. Moreover, the graphic warnings are not "purely" factual because—as FDA tacitly admits—they are primarily intended to evoke an emotional response, or, at most, shock the viewer into retaining the information in the text warning.

In fact, many of the images do not convey *any* warning information at all, much less make an "accurate statement" about cigarettes. For example, the images of a woman crying, a small child, and the man wearing a T-shirt emblazoned with the words "I QUIT" do not offer any information about the health effects of smoking. And the "1–800–QUIT–NOW" number, when presented without any explanation about the services provided on the hotline, hardly sounds like an unbiased source of information. These inflammatory images and the provocatively-named hotline cannot rationally be viewed as pure attempts to convey information to consumers. They are unabashed attempts to evoke emotion (and perhaps embarrassment) and browbeat consumers into quitting. Consequently, the images fall outside the ambit of *Zauderer*.

Because this case does not fall within the narrow enclave carved out by *Zauderer*, we must next determine which level of scrutiny—strict or intermediate—is appropriate. The district court held that compelled speech that falls outside the *Zauderer* framework is subject to strict scrutiny. Despite the contrary views of other circuits, our governing precedent makes clear that *Central Hudson* is the appropriate standard.

III. Evaluating the Graphic Warnings Under Intermediate Scrutiny

Under *Central Hudson,* the government must first show that its asserted interest is "substantial." If so, the Court must determine "whether the regulation directly advances the governmental interest asserted, and whether it is not more extensive than is necessary to serve that interest. . . .

FDA has not provided a shred of evidence—much less the "substantial evidence" required by the APA—showing that the graphic warnings will "directly advance" its interest in reducing the number of Americans who smoke. FDA makes much of the "international consensus" surrounding the effectiveness of large graphic warnings, but offers no evidence showing that such warnings have *directly caused* a material decrease in smoking rates in any of the countries that now require them. While studies of Canadian and Australian youth smokers showed that the warnings on cigarette packs caused a substantial number of survey participants to think—or think more—about quitting smoking, and FDA might be correct that intentions are a "necessary precursor" to behavior change, it is mere speculation to suggest that respondents who report increased *thoughts* about quitting smoking will actually follow through on their intentions. And at no point did these studies attempt to evaluate whether the increased thoughts about smoking cessation led participants to actually quit. . . .

. . . FDA claims that Canadian national survey data suggest that graphic warnings may reduce smoking rates. . . . But . . . FDA concedes it cannot directly attribute *any* decrease in the Canadian smoking rate to the graphic warnings because the Canadian government implemented other smoking control initiatives, including an increase in the cigarette tax and new restrictions on public smoking, during the same period. . . .

FDA has . . . presented us with only two studies that directly evaluate the impact of graphic warnings on actual smoking rates, and neither set of data shows that the graphic warnings will "directly" advance its interest in reducing smoking rates "to a material degree." And one of the principal researchers on whom FDA relies recently surveyed the relevant literature and conceded that "[t]here is no way to attribute . . . declines [in smoking] to the new health warnings." . . .

Alternatively, FDA asserts an interest in "effectively communicating health information" regarding the negative effects of cigarettes. But . . . FDA's interest in "effectively communicating" the health risks of smoking is merely a description of the means by which it plans to accomplish its goal of reducing smoking rates, and not an independent interest capable of sustaining the Rule.

. . . The First Amendment requires the government not only to state a substantial interest justifying a regulation on commercial speech, but also to show that its regulation directly advances that goal. FDA failed to present any data—much less the substantial evidence required under the APA—showing that enacting their proposed graphic warnings will accomplish the agency's stated objective of reducing smoking rates. The Rule thus cannot pass muster under Central Hudson. . . . We therefore vacate the graphic warning requirements and remand to the agency. . . .

CHAPTER 13

REGULATION OF CARCINOGENS

Perhaps the most famous provision of the FD&C Act is the Delaney Clause, a provision of the 1958 Food Additives Amendment that prohibits FDA approval of any food additive that has been shown to "induce cancer in man or other animal. . . ." Its presence in the law is largely attributable to the persistence of New York Representative James Delaney, who from 1950 to 1953 presided over a House select committee established to investigate the use of man-made chemicals in producing and marketing food. *See supra* p. 552. Representative Delaney became convinced that chemical additives—or some of them—posed serious risks to humans. And he was particularly concerned that chemicals shown to cause cancer in experimental animals could be responsible for the reported increase in U.S. cancer incidence.

When Delaney's committee concluded its work, only a small number of chemicals were believed to be carcinogenic, and few of these could be found in food. Hence, Delaney's endorsement of a clause that flatly prohibited the approval of any "food additive" that induces cancer in animals was seen as noncontroversial. A generation later, however, a different picture emerged. As the result of more comprehensive and thorough testing, increasing numbers of chemicals used or found in food exhibited carcinogenic potential. Moreover, dramatic advances in the sensitivity of chemical analysis were revealing the presence in food of small, often very small, quantities of hitherto unsuspected residues of chemicals used in its production, processing, and packaging. In this more complex world, the Delaney Clause presented a mounting regulatory challenge.

A. HISTORICAL BACKGROUND

Although more is discovered each year about the causes of cancer in humans, complete understanding of the disease remains elusive. Percivall Pott, an English physician, published the first epidemiological report identifying one cause of cancer in 1775. Pott described what he termed "chimney-sweepers' cancer," a disease "which always makes its first attack on, and its first appearance in the inferior part of the scrotum. . . ." He advocated immediate surgery upon discovery of the lesion "for when the disease has got head, it is rapid in its progress, painful in all its attacks, and most certainly destructive in its event." PERCIVALL POTT, CHIRURIGICAL OBSERVATIONS 64–68 (1775). Notwithstanding Pott's prescient finding, knowledge about the causes and mechanisms of cancer remained primitive throughout the 19th century. Only after researchers began using large colonies of inbred strains of rodents in toxicity studies in the early 20th century did scientific investigation of the processes of carcinogenesis itself begin in earnest.

Many ancient Greek and Roman writers recognized that consumption of different amounts of the same substance had quite different effects. But it was Paracelsus, an enigmatic alchemist writing in the first half of the 16th century, who documented the relationship between dose and response: "Poison is in everything, and nothing is without poison. The dosage makes it either a poison or a remedy." H. M. PACHTER, MAGIC INTO SCIENCE: THE STORY OF PARACELSUS 86 (1951). Paracelsus' insight did not immediately advance societal decision making. He correctly pointed out that there is a line dividing safe from unsafe doses, but he offered no criteria for determining how to draw that line. It took several centuries before dose-response relationships assumed their present importance in regulatory risk assessment.

B. EARLY FDA POLICY

The advent of systematic toxicity testing in laboratory animals made possible, for the first time, the formulation of an *operational* definition of safety. During the 1940s, FDA scientists adopted the rough rule of thumb that a safe human dose of a substance was 1/100th of the highest dose that produced no toxic effects in test animals (the "no effect level," now known as the "no observed adverse effect level" (NOAEL)).

Arnold Lehman et al., *Procedures for the Appraisal of the Toxicity of Chemicals in Foods*
4 FOOD DRUG COSMETIC LAW JOURNAL 412 (1949).

While it is not especially difficult to evaluate a set of pharmacological data which lead to the conclusion that the substance being investigated is a poison, it is extremely difficult to conclude that any chemical is safe for human consumption.

It is possible to compare the effects of the chemical with a drug or compound which has a known history on both man and animals. In other cases, the comparative biochemistry of man and the various species of animals used will serve as a guide for evaluating the data obtained. Finally, there are compounds which produce effects in animals that are so alarming that one has no hesitation in excluding such compounds from further consideration. For example, if a chemical has been shown to possess carcinogenic properties, there would be no question in applying animal data to man. . . .

The second factor that must be kept in mind is the apparent heterogeneity of man as compared with the relative homogeneity of experimental animals. Normally, laboratory animals exist under controlled conditions, are fed adequate diets, and are in good health. If a chemical is added to human food, however, it is eaten by all people, the young and old, those suffering from various pathological conditions, and those existing in borderline states of nutrition.

The third consideration which is all too often overlooked is the other sources of exposure to a given chemical.

––––––––

As Dr. Lehman relates, a finding that a substance caused cancer in experimental animals was regarded as so "alarming" as to exclude it from consideration for human exposure. Accordingly, FDA used (and continues to use) the 100:1 safety factor to set permissible exposure levels only for substances that cause adverse effects other than cancer. For chemicals that caused cancer, no safety factor was ever used. The agency's goal was to prevent any use of carcinogens in human food or drugs.

C. Evolution of Legislative Policy

1. The Incidence and Causes of Cancer

Based upon evidence of variations in cancer frequency among different populations, epidemiologists have contended that up to 90 percent of all cancers are "environmental" in origin. But this label can be misleading; "environmental causes" of cancer include not only air and water pollutants, but also lifestyle factors such as smoking, dietary patterns, consumption of alcoholic beverages, and sexual habits.

Factors in Cancer, as Summarized by the Conference on the Primary Promotion of Cancer, New York, 1979

	Men	Women
	Percent of Cancers Involving the Listed Factors	
Smoking	25–35	5–10
Alcohol	7	2
Occupation	6	2
Nutrition	30	30–50
Food contaminants	0	0
Drugs	1	1
Air pollution	0	0
Ionizing radiation	3	3
Ultraviolet radiation	(skin 50)[1]	(skin 50)[1]
Heredity	10–25	10–25
Viruses	1	1
Immunodeficiency	1	1

[1] Excluded from total cancers.

M. Shimkin, Industrial and Life–Style Carcinogens 10 (1980).

In a comprehensive study commissioned by the Office of Technology Assessment, two prominent British epidemiologists reached similar conclusions:

Proportions of Cancer Deaths Attributed to Various Different Factors

	Percent of all Cancer deaths	
Factor or class of factors	Best estimate	Range of acceptable estimates
Tobacco	30	25–40
Alcohol	3	2–4
Diet	35	10–70
Food additives	1	–5[1]–2
Reproductive and sexual behavior	7	1–13

Occupation	4	2–8
Pollution	2	1–5
Industrial products	1	1–2
Medicines and medical	1	0.5–3
Geophysical factors[2]	3	2–4
Infection	10?	1–?
Unknown	?	?

[1] Allowing for a possibly protective effect of antioxidants and other preservatives.

[2] Only about 1%, not 3%, could reasonably be described as "avoidable".

Sir Richard Doll & Richard Peto, *The Causes of Cancer: Quantitative Estimates of Avoidable Risks of Cancer in The United States Today*, 66 J. NAT'L CANCER INST. 1191, 1256 (1981).

While these tables represent estimates rather than measured frequencies, they have elicited agreement from other experts, and thus provide a consensus picture of the major causes of cancer among Americans.

2. THE ORIGINAL DELANEY CLAUSE

As the number of Americans dying from cancer rose in the 1930s and 1940s, reflecting the increased longevity of the population, public anxiety about the disease grew. Inevitably, this concern stimulated congressional consideration of measures to reduce potential cancer risks. One expression of this effort was the enactment of the Delaney Clause in 1958.

A version of the Clause appears in three places in the Act: the Food Additives Amendment of 1958 (section 409(c)(3)(A)), the Color Additive Amendments of 1960 (section 721(b)(5)(B)), and the Animal Drug Amendments of 1968 (section 512(d)(1)(I)). While the three versions differ slightly in their language, their basic thrust is similar—to prohibit the addition to human food of any defined substance that has been found to induce cancer in man or laboratory animals. The language of section 409(c)(3)(A) is exemplary:

> [N]o such regulation [authorizing use of a food additive] shall issue if a fair evaluation of the data before the Secretary—
>
> (A) fails to establish that the proposed use of the food additive, under the conditions of use to be specified in the regulation, will be safe: *Provided*, That no additive shall be deemed to be safe if it is found to induce cancer when ingested by man or animal, or if it is found, after tests which are appropriate for the evaluation of the safety of food additives, to induce cancer in man or animal. . . .

While the Delaney Clause attracted attention during congressional deliberations on the Food Additives Amendment and Color Additive Amendments, it was not the central focus of debate either time. The accompanying legislative history, therefore, can be frustrating for one who wishes to divine Congress' contemporaneous understanding of the provisions that have excited so much interest since. Even now there is no agreement on how the key passages should be interpreted.

In 1950, the House of Representatives established a Select Committee to Investigate the Use of Chemicals in Food Products, chaired by Representative James Delaney. The reports of that committee did not make specific recommendations about carcinogens. No special consideration was given to carcinogens during the enactment of the Miller Pesticide Amendments of 1954, which added section 408 to the FD&C Act. Nor did the initial versions of the legislation that ultimately became the Food Additives Amendment of 1958 contain anticancer language. In 1957, however, as Congress began to focus on requirements for food additives, Delaney introduced a revised bill (H.R. 7798, 85th Cong., 1st Sess.), which contained the following clause: "The Secretary shall not approve for use in food any chemical additive found to induce cancer in man, or, after tests, found to induce cancer in animals."

FDA's parent, the Department of Health, Education, and Welfare (HEW), initially objected to this provision on the following grounds:

> We, of course, agree that no chemical should be permitted to be used in food if, as so used, it may cause cancer. We assume that this, and no more, is the aim of the sponsor. No specific reference to carcinogens is necessary for that purpose, however, since the general requirements of this bill give assurance that no chemical additive can be cleared if there is reasonable doubt about its safety in that respect.

> On the other hand, the above-quoted provisions are so broadly phrased that they could be read to bar an additive from the food supply even if it can induce cancer only when used on test animals in a way having no bearing on the question of carcinogenicity for its intended use. This, we think, would not be in the public interest.

"Food Additives," Hearings before a Subcomm. of the House Comm. on Interstate and Foreign Commerce, 85th Cong. 38–39 (1958).

In July 1958, the House Commerce Committee reported out a bill requiring premarketing clearance of food additives but containing no anticancer clause. Accordingly, Representative Delaney urged the addition of the following anticancer proviso:

> *Provided*, That no additive shall be deemed to be safe if it is found to induce cancer when ingested by man or animal, or if it is found, after tests which are appropriate for the evaluation of the safety of food additives, to induce cancer in man or animal.

Thus, on its face the Clause Delaney championed applies only to "food additives" and does not apply to food itself or to food substances excluded from the statutory definition of a "food additive" because they are generally recognized as safe (GRAS) or were sanctioned by FDA or USDA between 1938 and 1959.

Rather than risk possible defeat of the legislation, HEW agreed to this amendment, which became part of the statute. Assistant HEW Secretary Elliot Richardson, in a letter to the committee chairman, at once embraced Delaney's goal and stated that the anticancer language would not change the bill's meaning:

> . . . This Department is in complete accord with the intent of these suggestions—that no substance should be sanctioned for uses in food that might produce cancer in man. H.R. 13254, as approved by your committee, will accomplish this intent, since it specifically

instructs the Secretary not to issue a regulation permitting use of an additive in food if a fair evaluation of the data before the Secretary fails to establish that the proposed use of the additive will be safe. The scientific tests that are adequate to establish the safety of an additive will give information about the tendency of an additive to produce cancer when it is present in food. Any indication that the additive may thus be carcinogenic would, under the terms of the bill, restrain the Secretary from approving the proposed use of the additive unless and until further testing shows to the point of reasonable certainty that the additive would not produce cancer and thus would be safe under the proposed conditions of use. This would afford good, strong public health protection.

. . . .

At the same time, if it would serve to allay any lingering apprehension on the part of those who desire an explicit statutory mandate on this point, the Department would interpose no objection to appropriate mention of cancer in food additives legislation. If the specific disease were referred to in the law, it would however, be important for everyone to have a clear understanding that this would in no way restrict the Department's freedom in guarding against other harmful effects from food additives.

Richardson welcomed the amendment's reference to "appropriate tests."

[T]he language suggested by some to bar carcinogenic additives would, if read literally, forbid the approval for use in food of any substance that causes any type of cancer in any test animal by any route of administration. This could lead to undesirable results which obviously were not intended by those who suggested the language. Concentrated sugar solution, lard, certain edible vegetable oils, and even cold water have been reported to cause a type of cancer at the site of injection when injected repeatedly by hypodermic needle into the same spot in a test animal. But scientists have not suggested that these same substances cause cancer when swallowed by mouth.

The enactment of a law which would seem to bar such common materials from the diet on the basis of the evidence described above, would place the agency that administered it in an untenable position. The agency would either have to try to enforce the law literally so as to keep these items out of the diet—evidently an impossible task—*or it would have to read between the lines of the law an intent which would make the law workable*, without a clear guide from Congress as to what was meant.

104 Cong. Rec. 17415 (Aug. 13, 1958) (emphasis supplied). The bill was passed by the House with the revised amendment.

In the Senate, the House-passed bill was favorably reported without hearings. Commenting on the anticancer clause, the Senate Report declared:

We applaud Congressman Delaney for having taken this, as he has every other opportunity, to focus our attention on the cancer-producing potentialities of various substances, but we want the record to show that in our opinion the bill is aimed at preventing the addition to the food our people eat of any substances the ingestion of which reasonable people would expect to produce not just cancer but any disease or disability. In short, we believe the bill reads and means the same with or without the inclusion of the clause referred to. This is also the view of the Food and Drug Administration.

S. Rep. No. 2422, 85th Cong., 2d Sess. 10–11 (1958). The bill passed the Senate and, after minor amendments were agreed to by the House, was signed into law as the Food Additives Amendment of 1958.

3.   THE COLOR ADDITIVES DELANEY CLAUSE

The 1960 Color Additive Amendments, at FD&C Act 721(b)(5)(B)), contain a Delaney Clause similar in language to the clause that appears in section 409. This clause precludes approval for food use (or any other use that may result in ingestion) of any color additive shown to induce cancer when ingested by animals or people. (The clause also prohibits the listing of color additives for external uses when "appropriate" tests demonstrate carcinogenicity in animals or people.) Because the Amendments do not recognize a category of "generally recognized as safe" colors or exclude substances that were sanctioned or used prior to 1960, the Delaney Clause in section 721 applies to all food coloring agents except those that are only provisionally listed while further safety testing is being conducted.

The original House bill contained an anticancer clause, while the bill initially introduced in the Senate was silent on the point. Both bills contained language comparable to the food additive law, requiring proof of the safety of a color before FDA could list it. Then, just before Thanksgiving in 1959, HEW Secretary Arthur Flemming issued a statement advising the public about the possible contamination of substantial quantities of cranberries with a pesticide, aminotriazol, which FDA had recently determined was a carcinogen. Although the Act's pesticide residue provisions contain no anticancer clause, the agency determined that use of this pesticide could not be approved as safe, and that the public should be warned of the potential hazard. During the same period, FDA determined that the previously-approved use of the drug diethylstilbestrol (DES) in poultry resulted in detectable residues in liver and skin fat. *See infra* p. 1382. Although the 1958 Delaney Clause did not apply, because DES for poultry was subject to a prior sanction and therefore not a "food additive," FDA proposed to withdraw the new drug application for this use on the ground that the finding of residues confirmed that it was unsafe.

On the heels of these two events, Secretary Flemming appeared before the House Commerce Committee in January 1960 to testify in support of the proposed color additive legislation. Anticipating that a major issue would be the desirability of including an anticancer clause, he had requested the National Cancer Institute to summarize the prevailing scientific knowledge about the etiology of cancer. The NCI report concluded:

No one at this time can tell how much or how little of a carcinogen would be required to produce cancer in any human being, or how long it would take the cancer to develop.

"Color Additives," Hearings Before the House Comm. on Interstate and Foreign Commerce, 86th Cong., 2d Sess. 45, 52 (1960). After offering the NCI report for the record, Secretary Flemming testified:

Unless and until there is a sound scientific basis for the establishment of tolerances for carcinogens, I believe the Government has a duty to make clear—in law as well as in administrative policy—that it will do everything possible to put persons in a position where they will not unnecessarily be adding residues of carcinogens to their diet.

Flemming contended that the anticancer clause allowed greater room for scientific judgment than its critics claimed:

It has been suggested that once a chemical is shown to induce a tumor in a single rat, this forecloses further research and forever forbids the use of the chemical in food. This is not true. The conclusion that an additive "is found to induce cancer when ingested by man or animal" is a scientific one. The conclusion is reached by competent scientists using widely accepted scientific testing methods and critical judgment. An isolated and inexplicable tumor would not be a basis for concluding that the test substance produces cancer. . . .

This, I believe, is as far as our discretion should go in the light of present scientific knowledge. We have no basis for asking Congress to give us discretion to establish a safe tolerance for a substance which definitely has been shown to produce cancer when added to the diet of test animals. We simply have no basis on which such discretion could be exercised because no one can tell us with any assurance at all how to establish a safe dose of any cancer-producing substance.

In a subsequent colloquy with Committee Chairman Oren Harris, Flemming returned to the distinction between the exercise of scientific judgment in identifying carcinogenic activity and the discretion to set tolerance levels for carcinogens:

When the time comes that our research reaches the place where that threshold can be identified, where a tolerance can be established that we know will not induce cancer in man, then we will come back and ask the Congress to give us authority to identify the threshold or to establish the tolerance.

Even with Flemming's assurances, however, some feared that the Delaney Clause was too rigid. In early 1960, the President's Special Assistant for Science and Technology convened a panel of prominent scientists to consider the regulation of carcinogens in food. The panel's report was released by the White House on May 14, 1960, just before the 1960 Amendments were to be voted on by the House and Senate. *See* President's Scientific Advisory Committee, Report of the Panel on Food Additives (May 1960), *reprinted in* 106 CONG. REC. 15380 (July 1, 1960).

It is to be emphasized that the present difficulty in establishing whether there are permissible levels for certain possibly carcinogenic food additives is accentuated by the limited relevant scientific information available. From the experience obtained in animal experiments and study of humans who have been exposed to carcinogens in the course of their work such as cited above, the panel believes that the probability of cancer induction from a particular carcinogen in minute doses may be eventually assessed by weighing scientific evidence as it becomes available.

The special emphasis placed by the Congress on the protection of the public from the dangers resulting from the addition of possible carcinogens to food calls for prudent administration of section 409(c). . . . Since an area of administrative discretion based on the rule of reason is unavoidable if the clause is to be workable, it is essential that this discretion be based on the most informed and expert scientific advice available. Until the causes of carcinogenesis are better understood, each situation must be judged in the light of all applicable evidence. In this way the protection of public health can best be assured.

. . . If existing legislation does not permit the Secretary of Health, Education, and Welfare to exercise discretion consistent with the recommendations of this report, it is recommended that appropriate modifications in the law be sought.

Id. at 8–9. This report was widely disseminated during the congressional debate on the 1960 Delaney Clause.

The House Commerce Committee, reporting the bill ultimately enacted, H. R. Rep. No. 1761, 86th Cong., 2d Sess. 13–14 (1960), discussed several proposed amendments to the Color Additives anticancer clause and explained why no changes were made:

One industry witness objected to any anticancer clause. Another witness argued that it is possible to establish safe tolerance levels for substances that produce cancer when fed to test animals. Some would have the ban on cancer producers apply only to colors that induce cancer when ingested in an amount and under conditions reasonably related to their intended use. And another witness proposed that the cancer clause be taken out of its present position in the bill and added with material language changes to section 706(b)(5)(A) so that it would become simply one of the factors for the Secretary to consider in evaluating the safety of a color additive.

It is evident that such proposed changes are intended to give the Secretary the right to establish tolerances for presumed safe levels of colors that produce cancer when tested under appropriate laboratory conditions. Thus, any of the proposals, if adopted, would weaken the present anticancer clause in the reported bill. For this reason all of the proposed changes were rejected by the committee. . . .

Some of the panel members have suggested that despite these difficulties, in extraordinary cases, the Secretary of Health, Education, and Welfare should have the authority to decide that a minute amount of a cancer-producing chemical may be added to man's food after a group of scientists consider all the facts and conclude that the quantity to be tolerated is probably without hazard. . . .

In view of the uncertainty surrounding the determination of safe tolerances for carcinogens, the committee decided that the Delaney anticancer provision in the reported bill should be retained without change.

A qualification that any test demonstrating carcinogenicity be appropriate was incorporated in the enacted version of the anticancer clause. The clause contains two parts: A color additive that will or may result in ingestion is deemed unsafe if it is found to cause cancer when ingested or if it is found to cause cancer after tests "which are appropriate for the evaluation of the safety of additives for use in food." A color additive that will not be ingested, on the other hand, falls within the proscription of the anticancer clause only if it is found to cause cancer "after tests which are appropriate for the evaluation of the safety of additives for such [non-ingestion] use, or after other relevant exposure of man or animal to such additive."

Prior to the 1970s FDA invoked either Delaney Clause only twice, both times to ban insignificant indirect food additives. *See* 32 Fed. Reg. 5675 (Apr. 7, 1967) (1,2-dihydro-2, 2, 4-trimethylquinoline, polymerized), and 34 Fed. Reg. 19073 (Dec. 2, 1968) (4,4-methylenebis(2-choroanaline)). In that era, few substances were systematically tested for carcinogenicity, the customary test protocols were less rigorous than those now in use, and available analytical methods were not sufficiently sensitive to detect trace amounts of known or suspected carcinogens in consumer products. The 1970s, however, brought changes on several fronts: more chemicals were subjected to toxicological evaluation in accordance with better designed and more carefully executed study protocols; a significant percentage of these exhibited the capacity to produce tumors in one or more test species; and analytical chemists improved by several orders of magnitude their methods for detecting and measuring trace chemicals in environmental media—including food. The collective result of these developments was to expand the universe of chemicals to which one of the versions of the Delaney Clause might apply.

D. REGULATION OF DIETHYLSTILBESTROL

In the 1940s and 1950s, FDA approved a number of new drug applications for the use of diethylstilbestrol (DES) as a growth promotant in poultry, cattle, and sheep. As discussed in Chapter 8, new drugs for animal use were, prior to the passage of the Animal Drug Amendments of 1968, subject to the same section 505 licensure requirements as new drugs for human use. After the enactment of the Food Additive Amendments of 1958, animal drugs intended for food-producing animals were also subject to the food additive regime of section 409. Therefore, when FDA became highly concerned about the carcinogenicity of DES residues in meat in the late 1950s, section 409's Delaney Clause was an obvious tool to address the problem.

After 1958, FDA took the position that the Delaney Clause precluded it from approving any new DES uses or products. This tool was unavailable with respect to the NDAs for DES that had been approved before section 409 went into effect, however, because FDA concluded that these uses of DES were "prior sanctioned" uses exempt from the food additive definition and thus from the Delaney Clause as well. In withdrawing approval of a pre-1958 NDA for DES pellets for use in poultry, FDA thus had to rely on the general drug safety standard of section 505, a tactic upheld against a challenge by the NDA holder in *Bell v. Goddard*, 366 F.2d 177 (7th Cir. 1966).

But even after *Bell v. Goddard* upheld the withdrawal of approval of DES pellets for poultry, various pre-1958 NDAs covering DES implants and feed premixes for cattle and sheep remained in effect as "prior sanctioned" uses. Faced with the discrepancy in treatment between pre-1958 and post-1958 NDAs for DES, Congress in 1962 enacted the so-called "DES proviso" to allow FDA to resume approving DES for use in livestock as long as no residue could be found in human food produced from the animals. *See* 108 Cong. Rec. 21077–81 (Sept. 27, 1962). The proviso appears in section 409(c)(3)(A) of the Act and reads as follows:

> [E]xcept that [the Delaney] proviso shall not apply with respect to the use of a substance as an ingredient of feed for animals which are raised for food production, if the Secretary finds (i) that, under the conditions of use and feeding specified in proposed labeling and reasonably certain to be followed in practice, such additive will not adversely affect the animals for which such feed is intended, and (ii) that no residue of the additive will be found (by methods of examination prescribed or approved by the Secretary by regulations, which regulations shall not be subject to subsections (f) and (g)) in any edible portion of such animal after slaughter or in any food yielded by or derived from the living animal.

Congress, in 1962, also added essentially identical language to the color additive Delaney Clause. *See* FD&C Act 721(b)(5)(B).

The Animal Drug Amendments of 1968 contain their own Delaney Clause, with the same DES proviso. FD&C Act 512(d)(1)(I). In the early 1970s, after the enactment of these Amendments, USDA monitoring of livers of slaughtered steers detected small residues of DES deriving from their feed. FDA therefore ordered that the withdrawal period for DES (i.e., the time between the last use of DES in the feed of an animal and the date of slaughter) be extended from 48 hours to seven days. 36 Fed. Reg. 23292 (Dec. 8, 1971). USDA simultaneously required written certification that this new withdrawal period was in fact followed. On March 11, 1972, FDA announced the opportunity for a hearing on a proposal to withdraw approval for use of DES in liquid animal feed premixes, 37 Fed. Reg. 526 (Jan. 13, 1972). Because of continuing reports of residues, the agency announced the opportunity for a hearing to determine whether *any* approvals for DES uses in animal feed or as implants could be continued, 37 Fed. Reg. 12251 (June 21, 1972).

Meanwhile, USDA undertook new analytic studies using a more sensitive radioactive tracer method to determine whether DES residues occurred only when the prescribed withdrawal period was not adhered to. When the new studies revealed residues even under the approved conditions of use, FDA withdrew all approvals of DES for use in animal feed while denying requests for a hearing. 37 Fed. Reg. 15747 (Aug. 4, 1972). Formal revocation of the applicable regulations was accomplished in 37 Fed. Reg. 26307 (Dec. 9, 1972). The agency later obtained similar results from a study using radioactive tagged DES implants and therefore summarily withdrew approval of all NADAs for this use as well. 38 Fed. Reg. 10485 (Apr. 27, 1973). A week later it also revoked the regulation prescribing the official method for detection of DES residues. 38 Fed. Reg. 10926 (May 3, 1973).

Various manufacturers of DES sought direct review of the agency's orders in the District of Columbia Circuit. In *Hess & Clark, Division of Rhodia, Inc. v. FDA*, 495 F.2d 975 (D.C. Cir. 1974), the court overturned FDA's withdrawal of approval of DES implants on the ground that the agency had not afforded the petitioners the evidentiary hearing that the Act guaranteed if material factual issues were in dispute.

> . . . If the FDA, using an approved test method, detected residues of DES in edible portions of slaughtered animals, then it could show a violation of the Delaney Clause.

> . . . [T]he USDA did not detect the residues while using an "approved" test method as required by the Delaney Clause. In its regulations, the FDA has approved only the "mouse-uterine" test. Using this test, no residues have been found in the tissues of slaughtered animals. Rather, the only method by which residues have been detected is the radioisotope tracer test, but that method has not been approved. For that reason, the Delaney Clause is plainly inapplicable . . . .

> Because he is not using the Delaney Clause, it is not enough for the Commissioner merely to show that animal carcasses contain residues and that DES is a carcinogen. Instead, the FDA must show that two different issues are resolved in its favor before it can shift to petitioners the burden of showing safety: (1) whether the detected residues are related to the use of DES implants; (2) if so, whether the residues, because of their composition, and in the amounts present in the tissue, present some potential hazard to the public health.

>   . . . .

In 39 Fed. Reg. 11323 (Mar. 27, 1974), FDA reinstated the NADAs for DES and encouraged further precautions to reduce the possibility of residues. Simultaneously, the agency took the first step toward final revocation of the NADAs by proposing to revoke the currently approved mouse uterine test method of detecting DES residues. 39 Fed. Reg. 11299 (Mar. 27, 1974). In 1976, FDA published a notice of opportunity for a hearing on a proposal to withdraw approval of all NADAs for DES. 41 Fed. Reg. 1804 (Jan. 12, 1976). Later that year, it ordered a hearing with respect to those NADAs for which a hearing was requested. 41 Fed. Reg. 52105 (Nov. 26, 1976). After a lengthy hearing, FDA's lone Administrative Law Judge issued an Initial Decision concluding that the Delaney Clause did not require withdrawal of the NADAs but that DES had not been shown to be safe. Food Drug Cosm. L. Rep. (CCH)

¶ 38,198 (Sept. 21, 1978). This ruling was appealed to Commissioner Donald Kennedy who rendered the following decision.

Diethylstilbestrol: Withdrawal of Approval of New Animal Drug Application

44 Fed. Reg. 54852 (September 21, 1979).

. . . [This] Decision discusses what might at first appear to be very small amounts of DES in edible tissues of meat from treated animals. Yet, as a respected cancer expert has testified, we have no data upon which to base the conclusion that any amount of a carcinogen above the single-molecule level would not produce a response. The risk of cancer would, of course, be expected to be lower the smaller the number of molecules of a carcinogen that are ingested. . . .

. . . I may not approve (and must withdraw approval of) the NADA for any animal drug that induces cancer when ingested by animals unless the drug comes within the DES exception to the Delaney clause, 21 U.S.C. 360b(e)(1)(B); (d)(1)(H) [now (d)(1)(I)]. A drug comes within the DES exception only if it is found that (1) the animals treated with the drug will not be adversely affected by it and (2) no residue of the drug will be found, by methods prescribed or approved by the Commissioner by regulation, in the edible products of the treated animals.

. . . I am now revoking the [mouse uterine] analytical method for DES. My decision to do so is supported by the evidence in the record that no analytical method is acceptable for DES. Because there is now no approved method of analysis for DES, I conclude that the Delaney Clause applies to the drug. I therefore withdraw approval of the DES NADA's on that ground. . . .

The manufacturing parties argue that the DES exception remains in effect unless and until the FDA finds illegal residues, using an approved analytical method, in the edible tissues of animals. They content that if there is no approved analytical method to measure residues, the Delaney Clause does not authorize withdrawal of NADA approvals, no matter how high the residue levels may be. . . .

The legislative history of the DES exception does not support the manufacturing parties' argument. . . .

. . . [T]he operation of the DES exception depends on the Commissioner making a finding of no residue (by use of a method approved by regulation). The DES exception does not begin to operate without that prerequisite finding. . . .

. . . I find that evidence in the record concerning the incidence of clear cell adenocarcinoma in daughters of mothers treated with DES (the Herbst data) supports the conclusion (which may also be drawn from animal carcinogenicity data) that DES presents a human cancer risk. The evidence from the treatment of women with DES provides no basis for concluding that there is a no-effect level for DES with respect to cancer. These findings warrant the conclusions that DES has not been shown to be safe and that it is unsafe. . . .

The Administrative Law Judge held that . . . consideration of the alleged social benefits of the use of DES is not an appropriate part of the decision whether approval of the new animal drug application should be withdrawn. This interpretation of the statute is supported by the legislative history of the statute, is consistent with positions the agency has taken previously on this issue, and reflects sound public policy.

. . . There are persuasive policy arguments against having an administrative agency such as the FDA make the kind of risk-benefit analysis sought by the manufacturing parties here. It may be that preliminary issues in this analysis are of the type that the FDA is qualified by experience and expertise to resolve. The agency is equipped, for instance, to evaluate calculations of the risk from a drug such as DES if the necessary data are available (they are not here). Once the risk and the benefits of an animal drug are determined, however, the ultimate issues require pure value judgments. . . .

Perhaps society is willing to expose all of its meat-consuming members to a relatively small risk of cancer and other adverse effects in order to provide a small economic benefit to those consumers and a larger economic benefit to DES producers and, potentially, users. The FDA is not, however, qualified in any particular way to make that value judgment for society. The value judgment could not be supported by a record; a record could support only factual findings not value judgments. Nor could the value judgment be effectively reviewed by a court, which in general is limited to consideration of facts, law, and procedures. In a democratic system, the appropriate place for value judgments to be made is the legislature.

    . . . .

NOTES

1. *Judicial Affirmation.* In *Rhone–Poulenc, Inc. v. Food and Drug Administration*, 636 F.2d 750 (D.C. Cir. 1980), the Commissioner's withdrawal of the NADAs for DES was upheld.

2. *Subsequent Proceedings.* While the *Rhone–Poulenc* case was pending, FDA formally withdrew approval of the NADAs for DES in 44 Fed. Reg. 39387, 39388 & 39618 (July 6, 1979). While partial stays of the effective date of these regulations were granted, 44 Fed. Reg. 42679, 42781 (July 20, 1979), 44 Fed. Reg. 45618, 45764 (Aug. 3, 1979), the ban of DES became effective on November 1, 1979, and USDA therefore also revoked its DES certification requirements, 44 Fed. Reg. 59498 (Oct. 16, 1979).

3. *Nitrofurans.* FDA has also taken action to revoke the NADAs for animal drugs containing nitrofurans on the ground that they are carcinogenic. The Administrative Law Judge handed down his Initial Decision in favor of the agency on November 12, 1986 and the manufacturer appealed to the Commissioner. The ALJ's decision was affirmed with modifications and two NADs ordered withdrawn. 56 Fed. Reg. 41902 (Aug. 23, 1991).

E. FDA EMBRACES QUANTITATIVE RISK ASSESSMENT

Prior to 1972, the possibility that the magnitude of the risk presented by a carcinogen could be reliably estimated had been discussed in the scientific literature but had not received serious attention from regulators. In response to the challenge posed by DES, however, FDA adopted quantitative risk assessment as a tool for regulating carcinogenic animal drugs. By 1980, the agency was also relying on quantitative risk estimation in evaluating carcinogenic constituents in food, drugs, medical devices, and cosmetics.

Simply summarized, quantitative risk assessment is the mathematical extrapolation from high-dose laboratory animal data to estimate the cancer risk associated with much lower human exposures from the consumer products. It is the key step in a four-step process: identifying a hazard, generally on the basis of animal studies; extrapolating from the high animal doses to estimate human response at lower doses; measuring or estimating human exposure to the substance; and characterizing the risk faced by exposed humans. This process is explained in a seminal report by the NAS. RISK ASSESSMENT IN THE FEDERAL GOVERNMENT: MANAGING THE PROCESS (1983).

Because of uncertainties in this process, assumptions must be made to fill gaps in the data or in the underlying scientific knowledge. Regulators generally rely on conservative assumptions at each stage of the process. For example, they assume that laboratory animals are appropriate models for human risk; choose data from the most sensitive sex of the most sensitive animal species; count benign tumors as malignant tumors; assume the relationship between dose and response to be linear; select upper bound estimates of human exposure and absorption; and assume away the uncertainties at each stage of the process at the next stage. Thus, risk assessment typically produces "worst-case" estimates that may be orders of magnitude higher than the actual risk.

As the following examples illustrate, FDA found in quantitative risk assessment an intellectual framework for estimating the magnitude of the cancer risk associated with human exposures to chemicals believed capable of causing cancer in humans. But as several of the examples show, FDA has repeatedly been forced to wrestle with the question of whether the applicable statutory language permits the agency to apply the framework at all. After all, the unqualified wording of the Delaney Clause does not, on its face, permit FDA to tolerate the presence of carcinogens simply because the agency has determined, using quantitative risk analysis, that the amount of the carcinogen does not pose a significant risk of actually causing cancer. Therefore, the agency can employ quantitative risk analysis with respect to carcinogens only in situations in which it finds that no Delaney Clause applies or—as with the animal drug Delaney Clause discussed immediately below—it finds some flexibility in the applicable clause itself.

1. APPLIED TO ANIMAL DRUGS (THE "DES PROVISO")

In the 1970s, FDA discovered in the "DES proviso" of section 512(d)(1)(I) the flexibility it needed to apply quantitative risk analysis to carcinogenic animal drug residues. The common name of this provision may generate unfortunate confusion, because—as explained by Commissioner Kennedy when he withdrew approval of the DES New Animal Drug Applications—the agency ultimately concluded that the "DES proviso" did not apply to DES itself. *See supra* p. 1385.

Section 512(d)(1)(I) of the FD&C Act allows FDA to approve a carcinogenic animal drug for use in food-producing animals if it concludes that, when the drug is used in accordance with its label directions, "no residue" will be found in human food derived from the animals using the detection method prescribed by the agency. Obviously, the sensitivity of the detection method that FDA prescribes will influence the likelihood of finding residues.

Until the 1970s, FDA had no uniform criteria for determining the level of sensitivity it should require for methods to monitor drug residues. Sometimes it simply approved the best method available for the drug in question. More often it insisted that a drug's sponsor submit a method capable of detecting a specified level of residues, typically 2 ppb. In 1973 FDA decided to rely on quantitative risk assessment to determine the sensitivity of the detection method required to allow approval of any carcinogenic animal drug. In short, the agency decided to correlate the required level of sensitivity to the risk posed by the residues of a drug that might escape detection.

The key to FDA's "sensitivity of method" (SOM) approach is the conduct of a quantitative risk assessment for the specific drug under review. In proposed regulations, 38 Fed. Reg. 19226 (July 19, 1973), the agency prescribed a modified version of the Mantel–Bryan method as the appropriate mathematical extrapolation model. It specified that residues presenting no more than one in 100 million lifetime individual risk of cancer could be considered "acceptable." Using the agency's proposed formula, one could calculate the residue level that, were it to occur undetected in the food derived from the animal, could be regarded as essentially "safe." The drug's sponsor would then be required to submit a detection method capable of measuring any residues that exceeded this level.

Chemical Compounds in Food-Producing Animals: Criteria and Procedures for Evaluating Assays for Carcinogenic Residues

44 Fed. Reg. 17070 (March 20, 1979).

. . . .

Two interpretations of the [DES] proviso are, in theory, possible. The first interpretation, which in the Commissioner's judgment is the less probable, is that Congress intended to allow FDA to approve the use of a carcinogenic compound in food-producing animals only if the agency could be absolutely positive that no traces whatever—no matter how small—would remain in edible tissues.

This interpretation presents several difficulties, all stemming from the fact that any introduction of a compound, whether or not carcinogenic, is likely to leave in edible tissues minute residues, which are below the level of detection of any known or likely to be developed method of analysis, *i.e.*, assay. . . . Although different assays may have different lowest limits of measurement, all assays are subject to the same type of limitation. Thus, when a tissue is examined with an assay having a lowest limit of measurement of 1 ppb and no interpretable response is observed, the analyst can conclude only that the compound under analysis is not present at a level of 1 ppb or above. It can never be concluded that the compound is "not present" in the absolute sense. It is thus impossible to determine the conditions under which edible tissues derived from food-producing animals that have received a carcinogen will contain no residue if the phrase "no residue" is to be interpreted literally. . . .

. . . [T]he "absolutely no molecules" interpretation seems, at the very least, an improbable interpretation of an amendment enacted by Congress precisely because it wanted to relieve animal drugs from the rigid strictures of the anticancer clauses. Moreover, any interpretation of a statutory provision that would render it totally inoperative should be rejected unless considerations of overwhelming persuasiveness require that interpretation. . . .

A second, and in the Commissioner's view more plausible, interpretation of the DES proviso accepts the words of the amendment and focuses on the . . . language, "no residue of such drug will be found . . . by methods of examination prescribed or approved by the Secretary by regulations. . . ." Under this interpretation, a sponsored compound that is carcinogenic may be approved for use in animals if examination of edible tissues by an assay approved by FDA reveals no residues. . . .

The Commissioner believes that the criteria to be applied in evaluating assays for carcinogenic residues in the edible tissue of food-producing animals must further the congressional intent to minimize public exposure to carcinogens, without nullifying the decision reflected in the DES proviso, as the first interpretation of the proviso would do. As explained more fully below, the criteria set forth in these regulations for evaluating assays for carcinogenic residues are minimum requirements. They are designed to identify assays that are (1) reliable and practical for use by a regulatory agency and (2) capable of measuring residues at levels that have been determined, on the basis of animal toxicity tests, to present no significant increase in human risk of cancer. An assay that does not meet both criteria cannot be approved. . . .

. . . By enacting and twice re-enacting the Delaney clause, Congress made clear its willingness to ban entirely from the human food supply food additives, color additives, and animal drugs that present a carcinogenic risk to man. It enacted the DES proviso with the intent and expectation that the provision that "no residue . . . will be found" would sufficiently protect the human food supply from any significant cancer risk from food additives, color additives, and animal drugs. Thus, in enacting the DES proviso, Congress did not change in any way the policy of the Delaney clause to protect the human food supply from carcinogenic additives and animal drugs; it merely eliminated an application of the clause that it considered unnecessary to the complete achievement of that policy.

The Commissioner has considered three basic alternative approaches to an operational definition of the phrase ["no residue"]. Under one approach, the term "no residue" might be operationally defined as satisfied when the levels of residues fall below those that can be measured by available analytical methodology. A second approach would be to establish some low finite level (*e.g.*, 1 part per billion) as a "practical zero" and to require assays that can reliably measure this zero, and to insist on the development of new assays if available assays are not adequate. Finally, "no residue" might be operationally defined on the basis of quantitative carcinogenicity testing of residues and the extrapolation of test data using one of a number of available procedures to arrive at levels that are safe in the total diet of test animals and that would, if they occurred, be considered safe in the total diet of man. Under this approach, the Commissioner would require assays that can reliably measure that safe level in edible tissues. For the reasons discussed below in this preamble, the Commissioner has concluded that alternative 3 should be adopted. . . .

By adopting this approach to implementing the no-residue standard, the Commissioner has assumed that: (i) The dose-response relationship between chemical compounds and carcinogenesis can be quantified, and (ii) a dietary level of a carcinogen can be identified at which no significant human risk of carcinogenesis would derive from consuming food containing residues below this level.

. . . Of the three general procedures recommended by the comments or available in the literature (the curvilinear models, linear extrapolation and the Mantel and Bryan procedure), the Commissioner has now decided that for purposes of this regulation, linear extrapolation best meets the above criteria:

(1) Of the available procedures, the linear procedure is least likely to underestimate risk. That is, at the level of acceptable risk (1 in 1 million over a lifetime), the maximum permissible dose of residues calculated by use of the linear extrapolation is usually lower than that obtained by the use of the other procedures.

(2) Linear extrapolation does not require the use of complicated mathematical procedures and can be carried out without the aid of complex computer programs. . . .

(3) No arbitrary selection of slope is required to carry out linear extrapolation. . . .

The 1973 proposal suggested that an acceptable level of risk for test animals, and thus for man, could be 1 in 100 million over a lifetime. In the February notice the Commissioner concluded that the 1 in 100 million level of risk was unduly limiting without substantial compensation in terms of public health. Consequently, the notice established the maximum risk to be used in the Mantel–Bryan calculation as 1 in 1 million. . . .

In the Commissioner's opinion, the acceptable risk level should (1) not significantly increase the human cancer risk and (2) subject to that constraint, be as high as possible in order to permit the use of carcinogenic animal drugs and food additives as decreed by Congress. . . . In addition to protecting the public health and satisfying the congressional directive, the Commissioner believes the selected level of risk should be consistent with acceptable levels of risk for other materials that are considered safe, and should prevent any false sense of security in the calculations. After reviewing data on acceptable levels of risk and knowing the limitations on the procedures, the Commissioner has concluded that a level of risk of 1 in 1 million over a lifetime satisfies all of these criteria. . . .

NOTES

1. *Translating Risk Estimates.* The product of any quantitative risk assessment for a carcinogen is the correlation of a level of risk with a given dose. This risk level is usually stated in terms of the lifetime risk of cancer faced by an exposed individual and in terms of the increased number of cancers that would occur annually in the exposed population. An individual risk of one in 100,000 means that an exposed individual faces that additional risk of developing cancer from this exposure alone during his lifetime. Roughly 4,000,000 persons are born each year in the United States. An individual lifetime risk of one in 100,000 associated with exposure to a substance would mean that 40 of these might develop cancer at some point in their lifetimes if they do not die of other causes—including cancers with other causes—first. Assuming an average lifetime of 70 years, this cohort would experience an average maximum risk of 4/7 of one cancer case each year.

2. *"Acceptable" Risk.* The level of risk that a regulatory agency ought to consider "acceptable" or "insignificant" is, as could be expected, controversial. The level of risk considered "acceptable," moreover, must be keyed to a specified mathematical extrapolation model. The more conservative the model, the higher the risk it will project for a given level of exposure. For example, it has been estimated that the risk projected by the Mantel–Bryan procedure may differ from the risk estimated by the linear model by an order of magnitude (*i.e.*, a factor of 10). It should be noted, however, that any of the mathematical extrapolation models provides the so-called "upper bound" risk, and does not purport to predict the number of cancers that will occur. Each of these mathematical models incorporates so many conservative assumptions that it is unlikely that the actual number of cancers would approach the upper-bound "worst case." For that reason, the result of a risk assessment is often depicted as a range of potential risk from zero to the number given by the quantitative risk assessment.

3. *Commentary.* For a scientific discussion of the SOM approach, see M.K. Perez, *Human Safety Data Collection and Evaluation for the Approval of New Animal Drugs*, 3 J. Toxicol. & Envt'l Health 837 (1977). *See also* George Gass, *A Discussion of Assay Sensitivity Methodology and Carcinogenic Potential*, 30 Food Drug Cosm. L.J. 111 (1975); David S. Salsburg, *Mantel–Bryan—Its Faults and Alternatives Available After Thirteen More Years of Experimentation*, 30 Food Drug Cosm. L.J. 116 (1975); Robert G. Zimbelman, *Biological Perspectives on Approaches to Sensitivity of Analytical Methods for Tissue Residues*, 30 Food Drug Cosm. L.J. 124 (1975). For illustrations of the application of the SOM approach to individual animal drugs, see the notices of opportunity for hearing on

proposals to withdraw approval of various NADAs in 41 Fed. Reg. 19907 (May 13, 1976), 41 Fed. Reg. 34891, 34899, 34908 (Aug. 17, 1976), and 44 Fed. Reg. 1463 (Jan. 5, 1979).

————

Several years later, FDA published the following revised proposal.

Sponsored Compounds in Food–Producing Animals; Criteria and Procedures for Evaluating the Safety of Carcinogenic Residues

50 Fed. Reg. 45530 (October 31, 1985).

The comments, however, as discussed below, failed to demonstrate that any higher level satisfied FDA's responsibility under the statute to protect the public health. FDA has . . . concluded that the 1 in 1 million level represents an insignificant level of risk.

FDA emphasizes that the 1 in 1 million level of risk . . . does not mean that 1 in every 1 million people will contract cancer as a result of this regulation. Rather, as far as can be determined, in all probability no one will contact [sic] cancer as a result of this regulation. The 1 in 1 million level represents a (1) 1 in 1 million increase in risk over the normal risk of cancer and (2) a lifetime—not annual—risk. Furthermore, because of a number of assumptions used in the risk assessment procedure and the extrapolation model used, FDA expects that the actual risk to an individual will be between 1 in 1 million and some much lower, but indeterminable, level.

Some comments on the 1979 proposal suggested . . . that a level of risk should be chosen for each compound on an individual basis. FDA disagrees. Under the suggested procedure sponsors would receive no guidance about the likelihood of approval of a compound during the expensive stage of drug development or about the factors consider[ed] in determining whether the compound should be approved. This unstructured ad hoc approach would be contrary to the interests of the public health and would result in inequitable treatment of sponsors.

. . . Although FDA has considered the comments and information provided, FDA concludes that the sole use of social preferences and the magnitude of involuntary risks to select an insignificant level of risk provides an incomplete basis for determining the level of risk to which the public should be exposed by substances permitted in the food supply. FDA also concludes that an increase in the level of risk to 1 in 15,000 might significantly increase the risk of cancer to people, and, until better information is provided, such a level must be viewed as unacceptable in light of current knowledge and legal standards.

. . . The question that logically follows is whether a level of 1 in 100,000 presents a significant risk to people. If FDA were to propose 1 in 100,000 as the insignificant level of risk, the permitted concentration of residue would increase by a factor of 10. . . .

The 1 in 100,000 level does not carry with it the degree of concern presented by the 1 in 15,000 level. Similarly, it is not as insignificant as the 1 in 1 million level. The approval of a carcinogenic sponsored compound, at any level of risk, does not include consideration of the potential interaction or synergy between an approved compound and any other substance or substances to which people are exposed. Certainly, the more approved carcinogenic compounds that are marketed the greater is the likelihood of cancer induction in people.

In the presence of these uncertainties, FDA cannot, with assurance, state that the 1 in 100,000 level would pose an insignificant level of risk of cancer to people. FDA can state, and comments agree, that the 1 in 1 million level presents an insignificant level of risk of cancer to people. Furthermore, FDA has developed confidence in the merit of the 1 in 1 million level because in recent years the agency has considered that level as its benchmark in evaluating the safety of carcinogenic compounds administered to food-producing animals. . . .

. . . Pervasive uncertainty is the primary analytical difficulty in making a risk assessment that involves trying to define the human health effects of exposure to harmful residues. There is uncertainty in types, probability, and magnitude of the health effects that will be associated with a given compound and its residues. These problems have no immediate solutions because of the many gaps in FDA's ability to ascertain the nature or extent of the effects associated with specific exposures.

   . . . .

The risk assessment procedure used by FDA requires that the upper 95 percent confidence limit on the tumor incidence data be used to estimate the carcinogenic potency of a substance. Assuming a typical bioassay conducted on a sponsored compound (*e.g.*, 50 animals per sex per dose) and a 20 percent incidence of tumors, this requirement causes an overestimate of the most probable potency by a factor of two. In addition, data from the most sensitive species and the most sensitive sex are used, resulting in an overestimate of the most probable potency by a factor of one to four.

The risk assessment procedure used by FDA assumes that each residue is as potent as the most potent compound detected in the bioassay. This is unlikely to be true, but in the absence of a bioassay on each residue and of knowledge of the quantity of each residue in the tissue, the effect on risk to the consuming public cannot be quantified. . . .

The risk assessment procedure used by FDA assumes that a lower frequency of dosing has no effect on carcinogenic potency. This is unlikely to be true. Because the animals used in the bioassay receive a constant and daily dose, but people will most likely be exposed to sporadic doses, the carcinogenic potency to people is most likely overestimated. However, FDA has no data that will allow a reliable prediction of the magnitude of this overestimate. . . .

NOTES

1. *A Risk of One in One Million.* FDA adopted the one in one million level of risk without guidance from Congress or any clear empirical justification. It emphasized that a one in one million level of risk is an "extremely small, perhaps non-existent, theoretical risk" that "represents a

calculated statistical upper bound estimate of a conservative model" and "does not represent a documented experience or a real expectation." Letter from FDA Acting Commissioner Mark Novitch to Representative Theodore Weiss (Dec. 28, 1983) at 9, 10. According to the agency, a one in one million level of risk over a lifetime "imposes no additional risk of cancer to the public," 44 Fed. Reg. 17070, 17093 (Mar. 20, 1979), and "is consistent with the likelihood that no cancers will result," 46 Fed. Reg. 15500, 15501 (Mar. 6, 1981), 47 Fed. Reg. 49628, 49631 (Nov. 2, 1982).

> This computed level of risk is ... not an actuarial risk. An actuarial risk is the risk determined by the actual incidence of an event. In contrast, the computed risk is a projection based on certain assumptions that enable the agency to estimate a risk that is too small to actually be measured. The agency uses conservative assumptions to ensure that the computation does not understate the risk.

50 Fed. Reg. 51551, 51557 (Dec. 18, 1985).

FDA has variously characterized a one in one million risk as "represent[ing] no significant carcinogenic burden in the total diet of man," 42 Fed. Reg. 10412, 10422 (Feb. 22, 1977); "for all practical purposes, zero," 50 Fed. Reg. 51551, 51557 (Dec. 18, 1985); "the functional equivalent of no risk at all," 51 Fed. Reg. 28331, 28344 (Aug. 7, 1986); "so low as to be effectively no risk," *id.;* assuring that "in all probability no one will contract cancer," 50 Fed. Reg. 45530, 45541 (Oct. 31, 1985); and "so low that there is a reasonable certainty of no harm." 51 Fed. Reg. 4173, 4174 (Feb. 3, 1986).

2. *Department of Justice Views.* In 1995, the views of the Department of Justice Office of Legal Counsel regarding FDA's and EPA's interpretation of the DES proviso were sought. In responding, Deputy Assistant Attorney General Christopher Schroeder addressed three questions:

• Could the agencies demand, as a condition of approval of a carcinogenic animal drug, that there be an analytical method capable of detecting any residues that could present a significant human cancer risk? In providing an affirmative answer, Schroeder made clear that the agencies need not require a method capable of detecting any residues at all. In this respect, he concluded, the DES proviso for animal drugs implicitly qualified the mandate of the Delaney Clause itself, as interpreted in *Public Citizen v. Young, infra* p. 1410.

• Having once approved an analytical method as adequate to detect (and thus prevent human consumption of) any residue that could present a significant risk, could the agencies decline to mandate the adoption of a more sensitive method if one were developed? Schroeder advised that the law did not require the agencies to continue to press for the adoption of the most sensitive method of detection.

2. APPLIED TO CONTAMINANTS OF FOOD

Aflatoxins in Shelled Peanuts and Peanut Products Used as Human Foods: Proposed Tolerance

39 Fed. Reg. 42748 (December 6, 1974).

. . . .

Aflatoxins may contaminate foods whenever the producing molds grow on foods under favorable conditions of temperature and humidity. . . .

Aflatoxins are present in peanuts and peanut products because of these contaminating molds. They are, therefore, added substances within the meaning of [section 402(a)(1) of the] Act. . . .

Of primary concern, data . . . indicate that these substances, particularly aflatoxin B_1, in some species of test animals are among the most potent liver carcinogens known. . . .

Epidemiological studies bearing on the possible effects of aflatoxin in man have been performed on specific population groups in Southeast Asia and Africa, where there is a known high incidence of primary liver cancer. . . .

. . . [W]hile it is not certain that aflatoxins are a cause of primary liver cancer in the United States, the Commissioner concludes that the observations of severe carcinogenic effects in experimental animals and positive correlations between dietary aflatoxins and primary human liver cancer seen in other parts of the world are sufficient justification to regard aflatoxins as poisonous or deleterious substances and to take actions to hold the human exposure to aflatoxins in the United States to the lowest level possible. . . . In 1965, the FDA established an informal action level of 30 ppb total aflatoxins. In 1969, it was reduced to the current level of 20 ppb total aflatoxins. . . .

It is impossible at this time totally to eliminate all of the breakdowns that can occur in the total process of growing, harvesting, and storing peanuts. . . .

Survey data . . . indicate that since 1971 an average of 93 percent of sampled peanut products contained aflatoxins below the 20 ppb level. The Commissioner concludes that current agricultural and manufacturing technology is capable of meeting a level below that which it is now being asked to meet.

Setting a level at 5 or 10 ppb was considered by the Commissioner. Eleven of the 12 major U.S. manufacturers of peanut butter could meet a 10 ppb level in 90 percent of their products. The Canadian government survey of 1972 indicated that 95 percent of the samples of peanut butter could meet this standard. However, there is year-to-year variability in aflatoxin contamination of the peanut crop. The FDA survey of 1973 evidenced the fact that only 89 percent of the peanut butter samples and 82 percent of the establishments surveyed met a 10 ppb level. Of the 12 largest establishments surveyed, only seven met a 5 ppb limit in 90 percent of their samples. There are also data showing that in some years only about 60 percent of the peanut butter produced met a 5 ppb level. One bad crop year could effectively eliminate a large percentage of peanut products from the market. Thus, a move to 5 or 10 ppb could result in significant losses to producers, manufacturers, and consumers alike.

Setting a tolerance level of 5 or 10 ppb for aflatoxins in peanut products would have the effect of requiring manufacturers to employ an analytical limit of less than 1 to 5 ppb for quality control purposes. Because present sampling and analytical methodologies have considerable error at the 1–5 ppb range, analytical results obtained for such quality control samples would not accurately represent the production lot from which the sample was drawn. Therefore, the capability of manufacturers to control their production at these levels is extremely questionable, and to guard against the release of products containing levels of aflatoxins in excess of 5 or 10 ppb is not possible. . . .

The Commissioner concludes that existing agricultural and industrial technology can combine to yield finished peanut products at or below a 15 ppb level without causing significantly increased losses of food. This level will also allow manufacturers to maintain capability for monitoring their products during processing with nearly as much reliability as could be attained with a 20 ppb level . . .

There are no new procedures pending, either agronomic or technical, that will alter the present unavoidability of aflatoxins. Furthermore, it is unlikely that any new pertinent information will become available in the near future. Therefore, it is the Commissioner's preliminary conclusion that the most reasonable approach to regulating aflatoxin, in shelled peanuts and peanut products, would be a formal tolerance established under section 406.

NOTES

1. *Withdrawal of Proposed Tolerance.* FDA has never finalized the proposed tolerance for aflatoxins in peanuts and peanut products, and it formally withdrew the proposal in 1991. 56 Fed. Reg. 67440 (Dec. 30, 1991). The 20 ppb informal action level, first instituted in 1969, remains in effect. *See* CPG 570.375.

2. *Risk Assessment for Aflatoxins.* FDA later released its formal assessment of the cancer risk posed by aflatoxin in peanuts. 43 Fed. Reg. 8808 (Mar. 3, 1978). The agency's estimate of the human risk of liver cancer based on animal test data using the Mantel-Bryan mathematical model (rather than the linear model) substantially exceeded the reported incidence of liver cancer in the United States from all causes. FDA speculated that "possible explanations for these differences are: (1) the level of human exposure to aflatoxin has been overestimated; (2) the Mantel-Bryan extrapolation procedure is overly conservative in this case; and/or (3) rats may not be an appropriate model for predicting aflatoxin-induced primary liver cancer in humans." FDA, Assessment of Estimated Risk Resulting From Aflatoxins in Consumer Peanut Products and Other Food Commodities (1978).

3. *Contamination Variability.* FDA's concern about the variability of aflatoxin contamination proved correct. In 1980, the corn crop in

southeastern United States contained a higher than usual level of aflatoxin due to an unusual combination of early drought and late rains. At the request of the States of South Carolina, North Carolina, and Virginia, FDA agreed to an exemption raising the action level for aflatoxin in corn for use solely as feed for mature nonlactating livestock and poultry from 20 ppb to 100 ppb, 46 Fed. Reg. 7447 (Jan. 23, 1981). The Community Nutrition Institute challenged this decision, both on procedural grounds and on the substantive grounds that the higher level of aflatoxin was unsafe and that the FDA policy of permitting farmers to blend corn containing high levels of aflatoxin with corn containing lower levels was illegal. In *Community Nutrition Institute v. Novitch*, 583 F. Supp. 294 (D.D.C. 1984), the 100 ppb level was upheld as "safe for consumption" and the FDA authorization for blending was held to be lawful. Following the Supreme Court's decision upholding FDA's reliance on action levels rather than tolerances, *Young v. Community Nutrition Institute*, 476 U.S. 974 (1986) (excerpted *supra* p. 512), the Court of Appeals held that the intentional blending of contaminated corn constitutes adulteration but, citing *Heckler v. Chaney, supra* p. 171, upheld FDA's discretion not to initiate enforcement proceedings. *Community Nutrition Institute v. Young*, 818 F.2d 943 (D.C. Cir. 1987). In 54 Fed. Reg. 22622 (May 25, 1989), FDA issued revised action levels for aflatoxin and its enforcement policy with respect to the blending of contaminated and noncontaminated corn from the 1988 harvest.

4. *Acrylonitrile.* In 1977, FDA banned acrylonitrile for use in formulating plastic beverage containers because of the possibility that some small amount could migrate from the container wall to the food it contained. In *Monsanto Co. v. Kennedy*, 613 F.2d 947 (D.C. Cir. 1979) (excerpted *supra* p. 610), the court overturned this ban because FDA had not considered the possibility that the risk faced by beverage consumers might be *de minimis*.

Upon reconsideration, FDA estimated that the human cancer risk was 1 in 3 million and therefore approved the use of acrylonitrile in plastic bottles for food use, 49 Fed. Reg. 36635 (Sept. 19, 1984), and for alcoholic beverage use, 52 Fed. Reg. 33802 (Sept. 8, 1987).

5. *Polyvinyl Chloride.* After concluding that vinyl chloride monomer (VCM) was carcinogenic, FDA banned the use of vinyl chloride in aerosol cosmetic products starting in 1975, 39 Fed. Reg. 30830 (Aug. 26, 1974), and proposed to ban or severely restrict the use of polyvinyl chloride (PVC) in food packaging, 40 Fed. Reg. 40529 (Sept. 3, 1975). Following the decision in *Monsanto*, however, the agency reassessed its position, withdrew the 1975 proposal, 51 Fed. Reg. 4173 (Feb. 3, 1986), and published a new proposal to set limits on the use of PVC in food packaging that would assure a cancer risk from VCM of less than 1 in 10 million, 51 Fed. Reg. 4177 (Feb. 3, 1986).

3. APPLIED TO "CONSTITUENTS" OF ADDITIVES

Questions about the Delaney Clause's coverage lurk around many corners. For example, how (if at all) does it apply to a naturally-occurring carcinogenic constituent of a raw agricultural commodity? FDA offered the following analysis:

> . . . [T]he detection of a trace amount of a known carcinogenic substance naturally present in a food, or unavoidably added to a food in the course of its manufacture or processing, does not invoke the anticancer clauses. It has been pointed out, for example, that there are small amounts of estrogenic substances, which are regarded as carcinogenic, naturally present in many foods. The anticancer clauses would be applicable, however, only if the food itself (containing the naturally-occurring substance) were, upon feeding to test animals or some other appropriate test, found to induce cancer. If this were to happen, the food itself would then be prohibited for use as a "food additive"—*i.e.*, for any use other than as an unprocessed raw agricultural commodity. . . .

"Agriculture–Environmental and Consumer Protection Appropriations for 1975," Hearings before a Subcomm. of the House Comm. on Appropriations, 93d Cong., 2d Sess. (1974).

Policy for Regulating Carcinogenic Chemicals in Food and Color Additives: Advance Notice of Proposed Rulemaking

47 Fed. Reg. 14464 (April 2, 1982).

During the two decades that FDA has administered the food and color additive provisions, the agency has, with a few exceptions, interpreted the Food and Color Additive Amendments to ban the use of any additive that was found to contain or was suspected of containing minor amounts of carcinogenic chemicals, even if the additive as a whole had not been found to cause cancer.

Over the past 20 years, there have been rapid developments in analytical capabilities that make it possible to decrease by orders of magnitude the levels at which the components of a substance such as a food additive or color additive are detectable and identifiable. . . . Coupled with this development has been a large increase in the number of substances that have been studied for carcinogenicity in animal bioassays. For example, Tomatis has reported that 828 chemical substances were under test for cancer throughout the world in 1975. Many of these bioassays have resulted in positive findings for carcinogenesis. . . .

. . . It is the agency's frank expectation that a growing number of additives will be found to contain a carcinogenic chemical in future years. If FDA continues to implement the regulatory approach that it has followed in recent years, it will be forced to refuse to approve or to terminate the approval of the use of each of these additives, even though they themselves may be safe.

However, the agency believes that there are alternatives to its current policy that will adequately protect the public health. Not all of the additives that have been or will be found to contain carcinogenic chemicals will themselves be shown to induce cancer in appropriate tests (*e.g.* D&C Green No. 6). The agency believes that a distinction can be drawn between additives that contain a carcinogenic chemical but that have not themselves been shown to be carcinogenic. Two recent developments support the agency's belief that such a distinction is appropriate.

One development was the 1979 decision by the United States Court of Appeals for the District of Columbia in *Monsanto Co. v. Kennedy*, 613 F.2d 947 (D.C. Cir. 1979). In discussing whether a substance that migrates into food is a food additive, that court expressed the view that there is "administrative discretion, inherent in the statutory scheme, to deal appropriately with *de minimis* situations." If FDA has discretion to disregard low-level migration into food of substances in indirect additives because the migration of the particular additive presents no public health concern, then the agency may also disregard, after appropriate tests, a carcinogenic chemical in a noncarcinogenic food additive or color additive, if FDA determines that there is a reasonable certainty of no harm from the chemical.

Second, the agency is now confident that it possesses the capacity, through the use of extrapolation procedures, to assess adequately the upper level of risk presented by the use of a non-carcinogenic additive that contains a carcinogenic chemical.... Many theoretical models have been developed to extrapolate from animal experimental data to the relatively low levels of possible human exposure, but they can vary widely in the risk values that they predict. Thus, knowledge of the true risk at relatively low exposures is elusive.

In the decision on D&C Green No. 6, FDA is approving a color additive that has not been shown to be a carcinogen in appropriate tests, even though it contains a carcinogenic impurity. In this advance notice of proposed rulemaking, FDA is announcing its intent to formally adopt the principles on which that decision is based as the general policy of the agency....

The policy consist of three elements:

1.   Clarifying exactly what an "additive" is;

2.   Interpreting the Delaney Clause to apply only when the additive itself has been shown to cause cancer; and

3.   Using risk assessment as one of the tools for determining whether the additive is safe under the general safety clause....

Conceivably, each chemical in the complex mixture that constitutes a food additive could itself be considered to be a food additive. Each of these chemicals in some sense becomes a component of the food of which the additive is a part. For example, in the case of an indirect food additive used in food packaging or the like, any chemical impurity that migrates from the indirect additive into food could be considered to be an additive. In the *Monsanto* case, the agency argued that the food additive definition applied to the residual acrylonitrile monomer used to fabricate the final bottle, as well as to the bottle itself, because the monomer was intended for use and was used to manufacture the copolymer bottle. However, the *Monsanto* court held that the statute does not compel the Commissioner of Food and Drugs to declare that each chemical in an additive is itself an additive....

The constituents approach ... distinguishes between the additive as a whole and its constituents for the purpose of determining when the Delaney Clause is triggered. Using this approach, the food additive would be the substance that is actually intended for use in food or for food contact. All nonfunctional chemicals present in that substance would be called the "constituents" of the additive. Similarly, the term "color additive" would mean only those substances intended for use as a dye, pigment, or other substance that is capable of imparting color. . . . The constituents would include residual reactants, intermediates, and manufacturing aids, as well as products of side reactions and chemical degradation. A constituent, although part of the additive as a whole, would not itself be considered to be an additive for regulatory purposes. . . .

The Delaney Clause requires the disapproval of any food additive that has been shown to be a carcinogen in appropriate testing. . . . However, it does not state that an additive shall not be deemed safe if the additive "or any of the chemicals present in the additive" is found to induce cancer. . . . A natural reading of the language that does appear in the statute establishes that the Delaney Clause does not apply to a carcinogenic chemical in a food additive absent a finding, after appropriate tests, that the additive as a whole induces cancer. Similar reasoning would apply to the Delaney Clause in the color additive provisions of the act.

. . . The risk assessment procedure discussed in this advance notice would not modify currently applied requirements under the general safety clause other than to provide a procedure for determining whether a noncarcinogenic additive that contains minor amounts of a proven carcinogenic chemical is safe. The risk assessment procedure would provide a method for estimating the levels of such chemicals that meet the general safety clause standard of safety. The upper limit of acceptable exposure would be determined by carcinogenic potency and risk extrapolation by the best current scientific methods available. FDA believes that any risk assessment procedure should yield such low acceptable levels that nothing but minor levels of carcinogenic chemicals would be able to pass the screen. . . .

FDA believes that this general policy is a sensible, scientific means of limiting the circumstances in which it will be necessary for the government to act to ban the use of a food additive or color additive, without compromising the public health protection afforded by the act. This policy, if finally adopted, is intended to be implemented solely in those instances (e.g., in the case of D&C Green No. 6) where data demonstrate that there is a reasonable certainty that no harm will result from the use of an additive that contains a carcinogenic chemical. . . .

————

The Natural Resources Defense Council objected to FDA's approval of D&C Red No. 6, but, when the agency denied a hearing, 48 Fed. Reg. 34463 (July 29, 1983), did not seek court review. However, FDA's reliance on the "constituents policy" to approve a second color additive, D&C Green No. 5, 47 Fed. Reg. 14138 (Apr. 2, 1982), 47 Fed. Reg. 24278 (June 4, 1982), triggered a court challenge.

Scott v. Food and Drug Administration

728 F.2d 322 (6th Cir. 1984).

■ Per Curiam . . .

D&C Green No. 5 contains another color additive, D&C Green No. 6, manufactured through the use of p-toluidine, which has been proven to be a carcinogenic when tested separately, and which is present in minute quantities as a chemical impurity in D&C Green No. 5. After extensive tests, the FDA determined that D&C Green No. 5, as a whole, did not cause cancer in test animals. It also determined that p-toluidine was not itself a color additive. It concluded, therefore, that the Delaney Clause . . . did not bar the permanent listing of D&C Green No. 5. . . .

The FDA first . . . determined that the maximum life-time average individual exposure to p-toluidine from use of D&C Green No. 5 would be 50 nanograms per day. The FDA then extrapolated from the level of risk found in animal bioassays to the conditions of probable exposure for humans using two different risk assessment procedures. Under the first procedure, the upper limit individual's life time risk of contracting cancer from exposure to 50 nanograms per day of p-toluidine through the use of D&C Green No. 5 was 1 in 30 million; the second procedure resulted in a calculation of a 1 in 300 million risk. The agency concluded "that there is a reasonable certainty of no harm from the exposure of p-toluidine that results from the use of D&C Green No. 5."

. . . Petitioner does not contest the validity of the tests employed by the FDA in determining that D&C Green No. 5 was safe for its intended uses but rather asserts that the Delaney Clause, as a matter of law, prohibits approval of a color additive when it contains a carcinogenic impurity in any amount and that the FDA has no discretion to find D&C Green No. 5 "safe" under the General Safety Clause because "[it is not] possible to establish a safe level of exposure to a carcinogen." . . .

We affirm the judgment of the Food and Drug Administration. . . . The FDA's finding that the Delaney Clause is inapplicable to the instant case because D&C Green No. 5 does not cause cancer in humans is in accordance with the law. In its final order, the FDA stated its rationale for its conclusion, and it was fully mindful of the Delaney Clause in making its decision:

> [T]he Agency does not believe that it is disregarding the Delaney Clause. In drafting the Delaney Clause, Congress implicitly recognized that known carcinogens might be present in color additives as intermediaries or impurities but at levels too low to trigger a response in conventional test systems. Congress apparently concluded that the presence of these intermediaries or impurities at these low levels was acceptable. This legislative judgment accounts for the absence of any requirement in the Delaney Clause that the impurities and intermediaries in a color additive, rather than the additive as a whole, be tested or otherwise evaluated for safety. Thus, Congress drew a rough, quantitative distinction between a color additive that is deemed unsafe under the Delaney Clause because it causes cancer, and an additive that is not subject to the Delaney Clause because it does not cause

cancer even though one of its constituents does. FDA's decision on D&C Green No. 5 is consistent with this distinction.

This interpretation of the Delaney Clause case is a reasonable one, and it is consistent with its legislative history. Congress distinguished between "pure dye" and its "impurities" in its list of factors for the FDA to consider under the General Safety Clause, but omitted "impurities" as a factor under the Delaney Clause. Although the Agency's regulatory interpretation of the Delaney Clause contains the words, "color additive *including its components*," it is clear that this regulation was aimed only at those additives containing impurities that produced cancer when tested together. . . .

Since in the instant case it was determined by the FDA that D&C Green No. 5, after testing as a whole, did not cause cancer in test animals, under the plain language of the Delaney Clause and the FDA's interpretation of that Clause, the FDA was not prohibited from permanently listing D&C Green No. 5.

. . . We agree with the FDA's conclusion that since it "has discretion to find that low-level migration into food of substances in indirect additives is so insignificant as to present no public health or safety concern . . . it can make a similar finding about a carcinogenic constituent or impurity that is present in a color additive." Accordingly, we hold that the FDA did not abuse its discretion under the General Safety Clause in determining that the presence of p-toluidine in D&C Green No. 5 created no unreasonable risk of harm to individuals exposed to the color additive.

NOTES

1. *Characterization of Other Carcinogenic "Constituents."* Although FDA said that it intended to publish the constituents policy as a final regulation, it has not done so. Since the decision in *Scott* the agency has approved more than 30 color additives and indirect food additives containing trace amounts of carcinogenic constituents.

2. *Indirect Additives.* FDA in 43 Fed. Reg. 56247 (Dec. 1, 1978) proposed to ban the use of 2-nitropropane as an indirect additive for use in food packaging because of its carcinogenicity. No further action has been taken on that proposal, but the agency has approved another indirect food additive, 2-amino-2-methyl-1-proponol which contains 2-nitropropane as a constituent, 52 Fed. Reg. 29665 (Aug. 11, 1987).

4. APPLIED TO ADDITIVES "STRAIGHT UP"

a. ARTIFICIAL SWEETENERS

FDA's 1969 ban of the nonnutritive sweetener, cyclamate, on the ground that it had been shown in animal tests to be carcinogenic, 34 Fed. Reg. 17063 (Oct. 21, 1969), disrupted the diet food industry. The agency's effort to soften the blow by reclassifying cyclamate-containing dietary foods as drugs, and therefore not subject to the Delaney Clause, provoked ridicule and was soon abandoned. In 1985, FDA's Cancer Assessment Committee concluded that cyclamate is not a carcinogen, but a report by the National Academy of Sciences stating that cyclamate may be a tumor promoter or co-carcinogen led to yet another reassessment. *See* "Cyclamate Update," FDA Talk Paper T89–35 (May 16, 1989).

Following cyclamate's removal from the market, saccharin remained the only nonnutritive sweetener approved in the U.S. Two years later FDA had before it the results of two animal studies which suggested that saccharin was a carcinogen. With candor that could not be expected of any regulator while still in office, Dr. Charles Edwards, the FDA Commissioner who declined to ban saccharin, later explained his decision:

> Technically, I could have banned saccharin immediately under the Delaney Clause, in early 1972, on the basis of those animal studies. I did not take that step because, once again, it was clear to me that the law should not be interpreted to yield absurd results. Saccharin was, at that time, the only remaining nonnutritive sweetener on the market. American consumers demand the availability of diet food products. It is irrelevant whether these diet products produce quantifiable health benefits or whether consumers simply like them. The point is that saccharin, like nitrite and many other important food substances, has come to be accepted and expected by the American public, and any law which does not recognize this simply will not work.

"Oversight of Food Safety, 1983," Hearings Before the Senate Comm. on Labor and Human Resources, 98th Cong., 1st Sess. 20–21 (1983).

By 1977, after Dr. Edwards had retired, FDA once again faced a threat to saccharin's continued approval in the form of a third study, sponsored by the Canadian government, which appeared to confirm the earlier findings that saccharin induced cancer in experimental animals. This time FDA officials concluded that they had no choice but to ban the sweetener. The agency defended its action in the following terms:

> . . . Public reaction to recent publicity about the Canadian study suggests considerable misunderstanding about the nature of toxicity testing in animals and the interpretation of results. For example, it has been widely publicized that the dose of saccharin found to be carcinogenic in rats is about 1,000 times that ingested by a human in a single diet beverage (when both doses are adjusted for the difference in body weight between rats and humans). Since this amount of saccharin would clearly never be ingested chronically by any person, some have suggested that these results have no pertinence whatsoever to human risk. In the judgment of FDA, this conclusion is not valid. . . .

> Current scientific methods are not capable of determining the exact risk to humans of a chemical found to be carcinogenic in animals. However, techniques are available for estimating the upper limits of the risk. The Food and Drug Administration estimates that the lifetime ingestion of the amount of saccharin in one diet beverage per day results in a risk to the individual of somewhere between zero and 4 in 10,000 of developing a cancer of the bladder. If this risk is transposed to the population at large and if everyone in the United States drank one such beverage a day,

this would result in somewhere between zero and 1,200 additional cases of bladder cancer each year. . . .

The estimated increase in risk from this moderate use of saccharin cannot be detected in human epidemiological studies. Such studies usually can only detect increased risks of 200 to 300 percent (*i.e.*, 2 to 3 times the baseline rate) or greater. Even the best feasible epidemiologic study is not likely to detect an increased risk of only 2 to 4 percent over background incidence. . . . The Food and Drug Administration thus considers the animal data and the human epidemiological data on saccharin to be compatible. . . .

. . . [T]he human risk of cancer indicated by these findings is significant and cannot be ignored. The Commissioner believes that conscientious protection of the public health is not consistent with continued general use in foods of a compound shown to present the kind of risk of cancer that has been demonstrated for saccharin— regardless of the asserted benefits of its use for some individuals in the population.

Section 409(c) of the act requires that any food additive must be found to be safe for human consumption before it can be approved or, in case of an additive already approved, continue to be used in foods. Based on the accumulated evidence of hazard associated with ingestion of saccharin, culminated by the Canadian study, the Commissioner concludes that the finding required by the statute can no longer be made. . . .

Therefore, under both the general safety requirement of the Food Additives Amendment of 1958 and the Delaney anticancer clause, the Commissioner concludes that saccharin may no longer be approved as a food additive. . . .

Saccharin and Its Salts: Proposed Rule Making, 42 Fed. Reg. 19996 (Apr. 15, 1977).

Within days of FDA's proposal, it became apparent that Congress would not permit a ban to become effective. Congress soon passed, and the President signed, the Saccharin Study and Labeling Act, 91 Stat. 1451, which forbade FDA, for a period of eighteen months, to take any action to prohibit or restrict the sale of saccharin sweetened foods. The Act also instructed the Department of HEW to conduct or arrange for studies of the health benefits and risks of saccharin and of the current national food safety policy. The legislation added to the FD&C Act sections 403(o) and (p), which required that warnings about the risk of cancer be placed on all food containing saccharin and in all retail stores selling food containing saccharin. 42 Fed. Reg. 59119 (Nov. 15, 1977), 42 Fed. Reg. 62209 (Dec. 9, 1977) (guidelines for labeling warning); 42 Fed. Reg. 62160 (Dec. 9, 1977), 43 Fed. Reg. 8793 (Mar. 3, 1978) (retail store warning).

NOTES

1.   *Other Studies of Saccharin.* An epidemiologic study of 9000 people sponsored by the National Cancer Institute found no overall added risk from the use of nonnutritive sweeteners, but did reveal the possibility of a slightly increased risk to some subgroups. FDA took the position that this

study and two others were consistent with its 1977 judgment. A congressional report observed that most epidemiological studies are only capable of detecting increased risks on the order of 200 percent and concluded that the available studies of the effects of saccharin would probably fail to detect as many as 20,000 additional cases of cancer per year. H.R. Rep. No. 348, 96th Cong., 1st Sess. 27–28 (1979).

2. *Rescission of the Saccharin Ban.* The statutory moratorium on any ban of saccharin was reenacted seven times, six times for two years each, and a seventh (in 1996) for five years. During this period, concern that saccharin might cause cancer in humans declined as questions about the relevance of the original animals studies were raised and research into the experience of long-time saccharin users failed to uncover a heightened cancer risk. In supporting the 1996 extension of the moratorium, Senator Orrin Hatch declared . . .

> Frankly, Congress long ago recognized, based on the established science on the issue, that the benefits of saccharin exceed the risk. . . . Because . . . no evidence has come to light that the risk of saccharin is greater than previously thought, I see no more reason to ban this product today than existed in 1977. In fact, I understand that more recent studies indicate saccharin does not pose the cancer risk in animals that it was thought to pose 20 years ago.

142 Cong. Rec. S8608 (July 24, 1996).

b.   COLOR ADDITIVE (LEAD ACETATE) IN HAIR DYE

Lead Acetate; Listing as a Color Additive in Cosmetics That Color the Hair on the Scalp

45 Fed. Reg. 72112 (October 31, 1980).

. . . .

Lead acetate is a metallic salt color additive which had been used in cosmetic hair dyes before the enactment of the [Color Additive] Amendments. . . .

By 1978 . . . it had been established conclusively through animal feeding testing in the 1950's and 1960's that lead acetate was an animal carcinogen in two species, the mouse and the rat. Yet, because the limited human epidemiological data were considered equivocal, a definitive conclusion whether lead was a human carcinogen could not be reached.

. . . In addition to passing muster under the general safety clause, a color additive must also pass the test laid down by the color additive anticancer (Delaney) clause in section 706(b)(5)(B) [now 721(b)(5)(B)] of the Amendments. . . . The applicable provision is the second section of the color additive Delaney Clause (section 706(b)(5)(B)(ii) of the Amendments), which states that a color additive:

> . . . shall be deemed unsafe, and shall not be listed, for any use which will not result in ingestion of any part of such additive, if, after tests which are appropriate for the evaluation of the safety of

additives for such use or after other relevant exposure of man or animal to such additive, it is found by the Secretary to induce cancer in man or animal.

. . . [T]he "non-ingestion clause," does not make an animal ingestion study demonstrating carcinogenicity an absolute bar to the approval of a petition for a non-ingested color additive. Instead, it requires the agency to make one of two additional findings:

1. That the tests relied upon to conclude that the substance is an animal or human carcinogen are "appropriate for the evaluation of the safety of additives" for the particular use under review; or,

2. That other exposure of man or animal "relevant" to the substance shows it to be a carcinogen.

. . . As discussed below, after a thorough evaluation of all available scientific evidence relevant to the issue, the agency cannot find that the animal feeding studies are either "appropriate" or "relevant" for making the safety determination for lead acetate hair dyes under section 706(b)(5)(B)(ii) of the Amendments. This conclusion is based upon the unusual combination of scientific facts peculiar to lead acetate in hair dyes, a combination which will rarely, if ever, be presented again in this context. . . .

1. The Combe, Inc. radioactive tracer skin absorption study, in attempting to identify whether systemic absorption of lead occurred following the application of the hair dye, demonstrated that on an average only 0.5 ug of lead per application penetrates the skin. Conventional analytical methods could not detect so small an amount of lead. Indeed, the agency believed prior to the performance of the study that absorption would not be considered significant, in an analytical sense, unless found to be greater than 1 ug. On the basis of that study, it is estimated that frequent users of lead acetate hair dyes who might apply the hair dye as often as twice per week, could have an average daily absorption of lead from that source of 0.3 ug (3/10 of one millionth of a gram). . . . [T]his compares to an average human absorption of lead from air, food, and water of approximately 35 ug/per day. Thus, the average user of lead acetate hair dye might increase his or her body lead burden by less than 1 percent. Such an increase of absorbed lead from hair dyes over the normal human "background" levels of lead does not augment the existing risk of acute or chronic lead toxicity, including cancer, in any clearly discernible, much less significant, manner.

2. The scientific data submitted to FDA concerning the issue of whether lead is a human carcinogen are not sufficient for substantiating a direct correlation between lead exposure and human carcinogenicity. Using "worst case" risk estimates (i.e., assuming carcinogenicity), the agency calculated that the upper limit of lifetime cancer risk from the use of lead acetate in hair dyes was approximately two in ten million lifetimes. Dr. Wilson's risk assessment calculated that the upper limit lifetime cancer risk from lead acetate in hair dyes was about one in eighteen and one half million lifetimes.

. . . .

The reasoning that leads FDA to conclude that lead acetate is safe and that the Delaney Clause cannot be invoked also justifies the conclusion that lead acetate hair dyes satisfy the general safety provisions under section 706(b)(5)(A)(i) through (iv) of the Amendments.

NOTE

Aftermath of Lead Acetate Decision. Six months later, FDA rejected, as inadequate to require an evidentiary hearing, the objections filed by several consumer groups, 46 Fed. Reg. 15500 (Mar. 6, 1981).

> The objection stated "if the risk is 1 in a million and if more than 1 million persons use hair dyes with lead acetate, then at least 1 person will die as a direct consequence of the FDA's decision." . . .

> Upper limit estimates of risk using "worst case" assumptions cannot be used to predict with mathematical precision what will actually occur. . . . The agency's conclusion that less than 1 out of 5 million persons would be at risk from the use of this color additive in hair dyes based upon the "worst case estimates" is consistent with the likelihood that no cancers will result from the topical use of this color additive. . . .

FDA's decision was not challenged in court. Noting that "there is a healthy new skepticism about how far regulators should go without first proving the extent of risk or the value of a ban," the *New York Times* editorialized that "The F.D.A.'s restraint in this case is welcome." *A Carcinogen Passes*, N.Y. Times, Nov. 9, 1980, at 18E.

C. COLOR ADDITIVE (ORANGE NO. 17) IN EXTERNALLY APPLIED DRUGS AND COSMETICS

Listing of D&C Orange No. 17 for Use in Externally Applied Drugs and Cosmetics
51 Fed. Reg. 28331 (August 7, 1986).

. . . .

Because FDA considers D&C Orange No. 17 to be a carcinogen when ingested by laboratory animals, . . . the Delaney Clause (section 706(b)(5)(B)(i) of the act [now 721(b)(5)(B)(i)]) is applicable. A strictly literal application of the Delaney Clause would prohibit FDA from finding that D&C Orange No. 17 is safe and, therefore, prohibit FDA from permanently listing the color for externally applied uses in drugs and cosmetics. However . . . the calculated risk for these uses of D&C Orange No. 17 is extremely low. In fact, the level is three to four orders of magnitude lower than that level of risk which the agency accepts in other areas concerning carcinogens. . . . With such a negligible risk, there is no gain to the public and the statutory purpose is not implemented or served by an agency action delisting the substance.

. . . Therefore, FDA has decided to exercise its inherent authority under the *de minimis* doctrine and concludes that the Delaney Clause does not require a ban in the case of the externally applied uses of D&C Orange No. 17. Because there are no other safety problems with this use of D&C Orange No. 17, FDA finds that the externally applied uses are safe.

. . . .

Two conditions must apply to justify an agency's exercise of its authority to interpret a legal requirement as not requiring action in *de minimis* situations. First, it must be consistent with the legislative design for the agency to find that a situation is trivial and, therefore, one that need not be regulated. *Alabama Power Co. v. Costle*, 636 F.2d 323, 360 (D.C. Cir. 1979). Second, it must be clear that the situation is in fact trivial, and that no real benefit will flow from regulating the particular situation. Both conditions apply here.

1.   The establishment of a *de minimis* exception to the Delaney Clause is consistent with the legislative design.

In *Alabama Power Co. v. Costle*, the court stated that the implication of *de minimis* authority is consistent with most statutes. The court stated that unless Congress has been extraordinarily rigid, there is likely a basis for an implication of such authority. . . .

. . . [T]he Senate agreed to adopt the color additive Delaney Clause only with the understanding that the clause would be administered with "a rule of reason," premised on the expectation that scientists would be able to determine the "probability of cancer induction." Thus, far from having been "extraordinarily rigid," Congress clearly contemplated that those administering the Delaney Clause would have discretion to implement that provision in a reasonable way.

This interpretation of the Delaney Clause finds support in recent case law. In *Monsanto v. Kennedy*, the [D.C. Circuit] held that not all chemicals that become components of food need be considered food additives. . . .

The court also held in *Monsanto* that the "*de minimis*" concept, applied to the threshold "food additive" definition, could be utilized to allow the marketing of a substance that presents no real public health risk. Thus, the court's decision in *Monsanto* has the practical effect of shielding substances that present effectively no carcinogenic risk from the Delaney Clause. Although the court did not explicitly interpret the Delaney Clause as inapplicable to such substances, the court presumably knew that if a carcinogenic chemical was disregarded as *de minimis* in relation to the food additive definition, the chemical would not be subject to the Delaney Clause, which applies only when that definition is met. Necessarily, therefore, the court regarded this consequence as legally warranted.

Moreover, in *Scott v. FDA*, the Sixth Circuit upheld the so-called constituents policy. . . .

In addition to the foregoing precedents, the state of scientific knowledge about cancer when the Delaney Clause was passed also supports the implication of *de minimis* authority under the Delaney Clause and the fact that the provision could not possibly have been meant to be "extraordinarily rigid." In 1958, there were only four substances that were known to induce cancer in humans: soot, radiation, tobacco smoke, and *beta*-naphthylamine. Only 20 years later, scientists had identified 37 human carcinogens and over 500 animal carcinogens.

. . . .

Under these circumstances, it would not be consistent with the legislative design for FDA, today, to attempt to prohibit all added carcinogens from the food supply provided the risks presented by permitted levels are trivial. . . .

2.   The risk from the use of D&C Orange No. 17 in externally applied drugs and cosmetics is, in fact, so trivial as to be effectively no risk.

According to the [agency] panel's revised risk estimates, the highest lifetime level of risk presented by the external uses of D&C Orange No. 17 is 1 in 19 billion, *i.e.*, 5.1×10^{-11}. . . . The risk from the use of D&C Orange No. 17 in externally applied drugs and cosmetics will not exceed 1 in 19 billion and is likely to be somewhere between that level and zero. The 1 in 19 billion level represents a 1 in 19 billion increase in risk over the normal risk of cancer in a lifetime—not annual—risk. FDA emphasizes that the 1 in 19 billion level of risk does not mean that 1 in every 19 billion people will contract cancer as a result. Rather, in all likelihood, no one will contract cancer as a result of this exposure. In light of the level of risk presented by the external uses of D&C Orange No. 17, FDA finds that the uses are safe, that they impose no additional risk of cancer to the public, and that any risk they may present is of no public health consequence.

The Environmental Protection Agency (EPA) in recent years has . . . relied upon the 1 in 1 million lifetime level as a reasonable criterion for separating high risk problems from low risk problems presented by the wide ranging environmental contaminants EPA must regulate. . . . For example, under the Safe Drinking Water Act (42 U.S.C. 300f et seq.), EPA sets drinking water standards that contain maximum contaminant levels for toxicants, including carcinogens. Maximum contaminant levels for carcinogens that have been promulgated or proposed to date by EPA generally fall into lifetime risk ranges of 1 in 10,000 to 1 in 1 million. Similarly, EPA recently proposed to establish the 1 in 1 million level as the "point of departure" in determining the level of control for all known and possible carcinogenic constituents compounds resulting from hazardous waste contamination (51 FR 1602, 1635; January 14, 1986). . . .

Although comparisons between the safety decisions made by OSHA and EPA with those made by FDA must be tempered by the fact that the decisions are made under different statutory frameworks, the decisions support the consensus proposition that a lifetime level of 1 in 1 million presents an extremely small risk.

———

When the listing of Orange No. 17 was challenged in court, the Department of Justice expressed reluctance to defend FDA's decision on the grounds the agency had originally advanced. FDA was instructed to issue the following clarification.

Correction of Listing of D&C Orange No. 17 for Use in Externally Applied Drugs and Cosmetics
52 Fed. Reg. 5081 (February 19, 1987).

. . . .

[In the preamble to the permanent listing of D&C Orange No. 17, a]fter summarizing the animal toxicity studies for this color additive as part of its explanation of this conclusion, FDA observed that the "data and information regarding the safety of D&C Orange No. 17 support FDA's conclusion that the substance induces cancer when tested in laboratory animals." This clarification of the Final Rule is being published to make clear that FDA was not, by this observation, concluding that this additive induces cancer in animals within the meaning of the Delaney Clause. As explained in the permanent listing document, in calculating the risk to man presented by the expected use of D&C Orange No. 17, FDA concluded that absorption of the color additive through the human skin was essentially the same as oral exposure in the rat. By virtue of this essentially one-to-one correspondence in absorption between rodent and man, a conclusion for purposes of the Delaney Clause that a substance at a given level poses a *de minimis* risk to humans implicitly includes the conclusion that a *de minimis* level of risk at a comparable level of exposure is presented to animals. Accordingly, D&C Orange No. 17 cannot be said to induce cancer in animals, as well as in man, within the meaning of the Delaney Clause. When a substance causes only a *de minimis* level of risk in animals, it cannot be said to induce cancer in animals within the meaning of the Delaney Clause. . . .

. . . The words "induce cancer in man or animal" as used in the Delaney Clause are terms of art intended to convey a regulatory judgment that is something more than a scientific observation that an additive is carcinogenic in laboratory animals. To limit this judgment to such a simple observation would be to arbitrarily exclude from FDA's consideration developing sophisticated testing and analytical methodologies, leaving FDA with only the most primitive techniques for its use in this important endeavor to protect public health. Certainly the language of the Delaney Clause itself cannot be read to mandate such a counterproductive limit on FDA's discharge of its responsibilities. Moreover, nothing in the legislative history indicates that Congress intended to impose such a scientifically anachronistic meaning on the words of the statute, stopping the technological clock and relegating FDA's expert regulatory judgment to outdated analytical tools. . . .

Public Citizen v. Young
831 F.2d 1108 (D.C. Cir. 1987).

■ WILLIAMS, CIRCUIT JUDGE:

. . . Assuming that the quantitative risk assessments are accurate, as we do for these purposes, it seems altogether correct to characterize these risks as trivial. For example, CTFA notes that a consumer would run a one-in-a-million lifetime risk of cancer if he or she ate *one* peanut with the FDA-permitted level of aflatoxins once every *250* days (liver cancer). Another activity posing a one-in-a-million lifetime risk is spending 1,000 minutes (less than 17 hours) every year in the city of Denver—with its high elevation and cosmic radiation levels—rather than in the District of Columbia. Most of us would not regard these as high-risk activities. Those who indulge in them can hardly be thought of as living dangerously. Indeed, they are risks taken without a second thought by persons whose economic position allows them a broad range of choice.

According to the risk assessments here, the riskier dye [D&C Orange No. 19] poses one ninth as much risk as the peanut or Colorado hypothetical; the less risky one [D&C Orange No. 17] poses only one 19,000th as much.

. . . .

The Delaney Clause of the Color Additive Amendments provides as follows:

> a color additive . . . (ii) shall be deemed unsafe, and shall not be listed, for any use which will not result in ingestion of any part of such additive, if, after tests which are appropriate for the evaluation of the safety of additives for such use, or after other relevant exposure of man or animal to such additive, it is found by the Secretary to induce cancer in man or animal. . . . 21 U.S.C. § 376(b)(5)(B) [now 21 U.S.C. § 379e(b)(5)(B)].

The natural—almost inescapable—reading of this language is that if the Secretary finds the additive to "induce" cancer in animals, he must deny listing. Here, of course, the agency made precisely the finding that Orange No. 17 and Red. No. 19 [another color additive approved by FDA on a similar rationale] "induce[ ] cancer when tested in laboratory animals." . . .

Courts (and agencies) are not, of course, helpless slaves to literalism. One escape hatch, invoked by the government and CTFA here, is the *de minimis* doctrine, shorthand for *de minimis non curat lex* ("the law does not concern itself with trifles"). The doctrine—articulated in recent times in a series of decisions by Judge Leventhal—serves a number of purposes. One is to spare agency resources for more important matters. But that is a goal of dubious relevance here. The finding of trivial risk necessarily followed not only the elaborate animal testing, but also the quantitative risk assessment process itself; indeed, application of the doctrine required additional expenditure of agency resources.

More relevant is the concept that "notwithstanding the 'plain meaning' of a statute, a court must look beyond the words to the purpose of the act where its literal terms lead to 'absurd or futile results.'" Imposition of pointless burdens on regulated entities is obviously to be avoided if possible, especially as burdens on them almost invariably entail losses for their customers: here, obviously, loss of access to the colors made possible by a broad range of dyes.

. . . Assuming as always the validity of the risk assessments, we believe that the risks posed by the two dyes would have to be characterized as "acceptable." Accordingly, if the statute were to permit a *de minimis* exception, this would appear to be a case for its application.

    . . . .

    Judge Leventhal articulated the standard for application of *de minimis* as virtually a presumption in its favor: "Unless Congress has been extraordinarily rigid, there is likely a basis for an implication of *de minimis* authority to provide [an] exemption when the burdens of regulation yield a gain of trivial or no value." But the doctrine obviously is not available to thwart a statutory command; it must be interpreted with a view to "implementing the legislative design." Nor is an agency to apply it on a finding merely that regulatory costs exceed regulatory benefits.

    Here, we cannot find that exemption of exceedingly small (but measurable) risks tends to implement the legislative design of the color additive Delaney Clause. The language itself is rigid; the context—an alternative design admitting administrative discretion for all risks other than carcinogens—tends to confirm that rigidity. . . .

    [Judge Williams then examined the legislative history of the 1960 Color Additive Amendments, searching for indications that Congress might not have intended the Delaney Clause to be applied literally in all cases.]

    Like all legislative history, this is hardly conclusive. But short of an explicit declaration in the statute barring use of *de minimis* exception, this is perhaps as strong as it is likely to get. Facing the explicit claim that the Clause was "extraordinarily rigid," a claim well supported by the Clause's language in contrast with the bill's grant of discretion elsewhere, Congress persevered.

    Moreover, our reading of the legislative history suggests some possible explanations for Congress's apparent rigidity. One is that Congress, and the nation in general (at least as perceived by Congress), appear to have been truly alarmed about the risks of cancer. . . .

    A second possible explanation for Congress's failure to authorize greater administrative discretion is that it perceived color additives as lacking any great value. . . . [T]here is evidence that Congress thought the public could get along without carcinogenic colors, especially in view of the existence of safer substitutes. Thus the legislators may have estimated the costs of an overly protective rule as trivial.

    So far as we can determine, no one drew the legislators' attention to the way in which the Delaney Clause, interacting with the flexible standard for determining safety of non-carcinogens, might cause manufacturers to substitute more dangerous toxic chemicals for less dangerous carcinogens. But the obviously more stringent standard for carcinogens may rest on a view that cancer deaths are in some way more to be feared than others.

    Finally, . . . the House committee (or its amanuenses) considered the possibility that its no-threshold assumption might prove false and contemplated a solution: renewed consideration by Congress. . . .

    Apart from their contentions on legislative history, the FDA and CTFA assert two grounds for a *de minimis* exception: an analysis of two cases applying *de minimis* concepts in the food and drug regulation context, and contentions that, because of scientific advances since enactment, the disallowance of *de minimis* authority would have preposterous results in related areas of food and drug law. . . .

. . . The opinion [in *Monsanto v. Kennedy*] makes no suggestion that anyone supposed acrylonitrile to be carcinogenic, or that the Delaney Clause governing food additives was in any way implicated. Thus the case cannot support a view that the food additive Delaney Clause (or, obviously, the color additive one) admits of a *de minimis* exception.

Scott v. Food and Drug Administration involved the color additive Delaney Clause, but is nonetheless distinguishable. . . . Application of a *de minimis* exception for *constituents* of a color additive . . . seems to us materially different from use of such a doctrine for the color additive itself. As the *Scott* court noted, the FDA's action was completely consistent with the plain language of the statute, as there was no finding that the *dye* caused cancer in animals. Here, as we have observed, application of a *de minimis* exception requires putting a gloss on the statute qualifying its literal terms. . . .

The CTFA also argues that in a number of respects scientific advance has rendered obsolete any inference of congressional insistence on rigidity. . . . If the color additive Delaney Clause has no *de minimis* exception, it follows (they suggest) that the food additive one must be equally rigid. The upshot would be to deny the American people access to a healthy food supply.

As a historical matter, the argument is overdrawn: the House committee was clearly on notice that certain common foods and nutrients were suspected carcinogens. Beyond that, it is not clear that an interpretation of the food additive Delaney Clause identical with our interpretation of the color additive clause would entail the feared consequences. The food additive *definition* contains an exception for substances "generally recognized" as safe (known as the "GRAS" exception), an exception that has no parallel in the color additive definition. That definition may permit a *de minimis* exception at a stage that logically precedes the FDA's ever reaching the food additive Delaney Clause. Indeed, *Monsanto* so holds—though, as we have noted, in a case not trenching upon the food additive Delaney Clause. . . .

The relationship of the GRAS exception and the food additive Delaney Clause clearly poses a problem: if the food additive definition allows the FDA to classify as GRAS substances carrying trivial risks . . . but the food additive Delaney Clause is absolute, then Congress has adopted inconsistent provisions. . . . On the other hand, if (1) the GRAS exception does not encompass substances with trivial carcinogenic effect (especially if its special provision for substances used before 1958 does not do so for long-established substances), and (2) the food additive Delaney Clause is as rigid as we find the color additive clause to be, conceivably the consequences identified by the CTFA, or some of them, may follow. All these are difficult questions, but they are neither before us nor is their answer foreordained by our decision here.

Moreover, we deal here only with the color additive Delaney Clause, not the one for food additives. Although the clauses have almost identical wording, the context is clearly different. Without having canvassed the legislative history of the food additive Delaney Clause, we may safely say that its proponents could not have regarded as trivial the social cost of banning those parts of the American diet that CTFA argues are at risk. . . .

[The FDA clarification notices on the listing of Orange No. 17, *supra* p. 1407, and Red No. 19] effectively apply quantitative risk assessment at the stage of determining whether a substance "induce[s] cancer in man or animal." They assert that even where a substance does cause cancer in animals in the conventional sense of the term, the FDA may find that it does not "induce cancer in man or animal" within the meaning of 21 U.S.C. § 376(b)(5)(B).

The notices acknowledged that the words "to induce cancer" had not been "rigorously and unambiguously" so limited in the previous notices. This is a considerable understatement. The original determinations were quite unambiguous in concluding that the colors induced cancer in animals in valid tests. . . .

The plain language of the Delaney Clause covers all animals exposed to color additives, including laboratory animals exposed to high doses. It would be surprising if it did not. High-dose exposures are standard testing procedure, today just as in 1960; such high doses are justified to offset practical limitations on such tests: compared to expected exposure of millions of humans over long periods, the time periods are short and the animals few. Many references in the legislative history reflect awareness of reliance on animal testing, and at least the more sophisticated participants must have been aware that this meant high-dose testing. A few so specified.

All this indicates to us that Congress did not intend the FDA to be able to take a finding that a substance causes only trivial risk in humans and work back from that to a finding that the substance does not "induce cancer in . . . animals." This is simply the basic question—is the operation of the clause automatic once the FDA makes a finding of carcinogenicity in animals?—in a new guise. The only new argument offered in the notices is that, without the new interpretation, only "primitive techniques" could be used. In fact, of course, the agency is clearly free to incorporate the latest breakthroughs in animal testing; indeed, here it touted the most recent animal tests as "state of the art." The limitation on techniques is only that the agency may not, once a color additive is found to induce cancer in test animals in the conventional sense of the term, undercut the statutory consequence. As we find the FDA's construction "contrary to clear congressional intent," *Chevron USA v. NRDC*, 467 U.S. 837, 843 n. 9 (1984), we need not defer to it.

NOTES

1. *Subsequent Proceedings.* Following the Supreme Court's denial of certiorari, FDA delisted the color additives involved in the litigation and two other color additives that had been approved on the same basis in the interim, 53 Fed. Reg. 26766, 26768, 26881, 26884, 26885 (July 15, 1988).

2. *FDA Discretion.* A former FDA Chief Counsel later suggested that the agency erred when it attempted to reinterpret the legal meaning of the

Delaney Clause rather than taking its language at face value and reaching the same result by exercising the scientific judgment inherent in "induces cancer" to treat

> tumor development in experimental animals dosed at the level of maximum tolerated dose as insufficient to prove that the additive induces cancer when ingested. The observation of tumors, even malignant ones, at this extreme boundary of the experiment should have been regarded only as part of the total scientific evidence about carcinogenicity of the color additive, and a rule of reason judgment should have been reached that the colors do not fall within the ban of the Delaney Clause. I do not believe that FDA has ever had a policy of basing a judgment on the issue of cancer causation upon the results of a study in only one strain, gender, and species, at one dose in one experiment. Indeed, that is what Secretary Flemming warned against.

Letter from W. W. Goodrich to D. W. Sigelman, Counsel to the Human Resources and Intergovernmental Relations Subcomm., House Comm. on Government Operations (Sept. 11, 1987).

3. *Dimethyl Dicarbonate.* In 53 Fed. Reg. 41325 (Oct. 21, 1988), FDA approved the use of dimethyl dicarbonate for direct use as a yeast inhibitor in wines. FDA noted that the additive could react with naturally occurring ammonia in wine to form trace amounts of methyl carbamate, a carcinogen in rats, but concluded that the risk was less than one in 42 million and thus that the additive was safe. The agency declined to apply the Delaney Clause, commenting, "An additive that has not been shown to cause cancer but that contains a carcinogenic constituent, or whose use will lead to the formation of trace amounts of a carcinogenic substance in or on food, may be properly evaluated under the general safety clause of the statute." *Id.* at 41325.

4. *Methylene Chloride.* At the same time that FDA proposed to ban the use of methylene chloride in cosmetics, it announced that it was not proposing to revoke the existing food additive regulation, 21 C.F.R. 173.255, authorizing the use of methylene chloride for decaffeination of coffee because the residue of the additive in coffee represents less than a one in one million risk, 50 Fed. Reg. 51551 (Dec. 18, 1985). In *Public Citizen v. Bowen*, 833 F.2d 364 (D.C. Cir. 1987), the court determined that this decision was not ripe for judicial review.

5. *Coverage of the Delaney Clause.* Section 409 empowers FDA to promulgate a food additive regulation under two circumstances. First, the agency is required by section 409(c) to act on any petition submitted by an interested person under section 409(b). Second, under section 409(d) FDA may promulgate a food additive regulation on its own initiative. The Delaney Clause appears in section 409(c) and not in section 409(d). Does this mean that FDA is not bound by the Delaney Clause when it acts on its own initiative?

6. *Color Additive Advisory Committee.* Section 721(b)(5)(C) provides a unique opportunity for the petitioner or any person adversely affected to trigger advisory committee review of any question involving application of the Delaney Clause to a color additive. FDA has issued regulations

governing this procedure, 21 C.F.R. 14.140 *et seq.*, but it has not been used in more than 45 years. *See* Robert Becker, *The Scientific Advisory Committee and the Administration of Color Additives*, 15 Food Drug Cosm. L.J. 801 (1960).

5. APPLIED TO NATURAL FOODS

Many natural foods have been found to be carcinogenic in laboratory animals. *See, e.g.*, B. Toth & J. Erickson, *Cancer Induction in Mice by Feeding of the Uncooked Cultivated Mushroom of Commerce, Agaricus bisporue*, 46 Cancer Res. 4007 (Aug. 1986). In addition, many chemicals found to be carcinogenic in laboratory animals are constituents in important foods. For example, the NTP announced in 48 Fed. Reg. 4557 (Feb. 1, 1983) that allyl isothiocyanate, which was shown to be carcinogenic, is:

> the major component in volatile oil of mustard, a flavoring agent prepared from seed of black mustard. Allyl isothiocyanate may be present in syrups, meats, condiments, baked goods, candy, ice cream and ices, and nonalcoholic beverages. Allyl isothiocyanate is found in cabbage, broccoli, kale, cauliflower and horseradish.

In 55 Fed. Reg. 26016 (June 26, 1990), NTP announced clear evidence of the carcinogenicity of d-Limonene, "a naturally occurring monoterpene found in many volatile oils, especially citrus oils which are used as a flavor and fragrance additive for food. . . ." *See also* Bruce Ames et al., *Ranking Possible Carcinogenic Hazards*, 236 Science 271 (Apr. 17, 1987); Bruce Ames, *Dietary Carcinogens and Anticarcinogens*, 221 Science 256 (Sept. 23, 1983).

FDA scientists have pointed out that traditional methods of cooking and preserving food often contaminate food with carcinogens. For example, charbroiling and smoking contaminate food with polynuclear aromatic hydrocarbons, and pickling produces nitrosamines.

> This is just the tip of the iceberg. The spectrum of natural carcinogenic contaminants at low levels in food is far larger than these two examples can suggest. These "added" carcinogens are officially ignored because the exposures are ubiquitous and they would be extraordinarily difficult if not impossible to control and regulate.

Robert Scheuplein et al., *New Approaches to the Regulation of Carcinogens in Foods: The Food and Drug Administration*, in HANDBOOK OF CARCINOGEN TESTING 556, 563 (Harry A. & Elizabeth Weisburger, eds., 1985). *See also* M. J. Prival, *Carcinogens and Mutagens Present as Natural Components of Food or Induced by Cooking*, 6 NUTR. CANCER 236 (1985). Dr. Scheuplein, at one time Director of the Office of Toxicological Sciences in CFSAN, has concluded that, although "we should continue to minimize exposure to carcinogens from any major source," the data suggest that almost 98% of the cancer risk from food is natural in origin.

> [E]ven a modestly effective attempt to lessen the dietary risk of natural carcinogens would probably be enormously more useful to human health than regulatory efforts devoted to eliminating traces

of pesticide residues or contaminants. The risk from natural carcinogens appears to be so much greater that just reducing it a few percent . . . promises a greater decrease in absolute cancer risk than the total elimination of the lesser risks.

Perspectives on Toxicological Risk: An Example: Food-Borne Carcinogenic Risk 25 (1989) (unpublished manuscript).

As early as 1954, FDA banned the use of natural tonka beans as food because of the carcinogenicity of a constituent, coumarin, 19 Fed. Reg. 1239 (Mar. 5, 1954). FDA published an order banning the use of safrole and oil of sassafras in 25 Fed. Reg. 12412 (Dec. 2, 1960) based on animal studies demonstrating carcinogenicity. This ban was extended to include natural sassafras bark marketed for use in making sassafras tea in the home in 38 Fed. Reg. 20040 (July 26, 1973), 39 Fed. Reg. 26748 (July 23, 1974), 39 Fed. Reg. 34172 (Sept. 23, 1974), 41 Fed. Reg. 19207 (May 11, 1976), 21 C.F.R. 189.180. Although a 1973 seizure of sassafras bark was initially contested, the claimant subsequently withdrew the claim and thus the validity of FDA's position was not litigated. *United States v. Articles of Food . . . Select Natural Herb Tea, Sassafras, etc.*, Civ. No. 73–1370–RF (C.D. Cal., June 15, 1973). Since then, the agency has not sought to ban natural food products containing carcinogenic constituents. Although FDA has quietly ignored carcinogenicity studies of long-established food products, it has consistently taken the position that a substance found to be carcinogenic in animals *cannot* be regarded as GRAS, although a substance containing a carcinogenic constituent *can* be regarded as GRAS. *See, e.g.,* "Agriculture, Rural Development and Related Agencies Appropriations for 1984," Hearings Before a Subcomm. of the House Comm. on Appropriations, 98th Cong., 1st Sess., Part 4, at 475 (1983).

F. DECIDING WHETHER AN ADDITIVE "INDUCES CANCER"

1. CARCINOGENICITY THRESHOLDS

The supporters of the Delaney Clause assumed that any chemical capable of causing cancer at high doses could cause cancer at low doses, albeit less frequently. In other words, carcinogens exhibited no threshold; any exposure carried some risk of cancer. As knowledge of cancer induction progressed, the scientific community came to believe that this generalization did not fit all carcinogens. Some were probably threshold-limited, though it was far from certain whether these could be reliably identified.

Selenium in Animal Feed; Proposed Food Additive Regulation
38 Fed. Reg. 10458 (April 27, 1973).

The Commissioner of Food and Drugs . . . proposes that the food additive regulations should be amended as set forth below to provide for the safe use of selenium as a nutrient in the feed of chickens, turkeys, and swine. . . .

Selenium is an element essential for normal growth and metabolism in animals. The minimum dietary requirements for selenium in poultry and swine range from 0.1 to 0.2 p/m of available selenium in the form of sodium selenite or sodium selenate. A dietary intake of less than these quantities of available selenium may result in a variety of debilitating conditions. . . .

It has been estimated that 70 percent of domestic basic feedstuffs (corn and soybeans) contain less selenium than that required to meet the animals' nutritional needs. . . .

The applicability of the anticancer clause (sec. 409(c)(3)(A)) of the act to the addition of selenium to animal feed has been thoroughly considered. . . . Available data have been evaluated by the Food and Drug Administration and the National Cancer Institute. Based on these evaluations, it has been concluded that the judicious administration of selenium derivatives to domestic animals would not constitute a carcinogenic risk. In three of the six studies available on the subject, test animals were found to have developed neoplastic lesions. These lesions were concluded to be a consequence of the liver cirrhosis produced by frank selenium toxicity. Further evaluation of the results of these three studies was complicated by the unusually high levels of selenium that had been administered, faulty experimental design, and, or infectious conditions present in the animal colonies used. Results of the remaining three studies, all of which were well controlled investigations, were negative for carcinogenic activity.

Selenium at high dietary levels (above 2 p/m for experimental animals) is a proven hepatotoxic agent. Early studies at dietary levels of 5, 7, and 10 p/m showed liver damage and regeneration in rats and an increased incidence of hepatoma in treated animals as compared with controls. Hepatoma did not occur in the absence of severe hepatotoxic phenomena. In more recent studies, hepatotoxicity was observed in rats fed selenium at 2 p/m. At 16 p/m, more severe liver damage was observed but was not associated with hepatoma. No hepatotoxic effects were noted at 0.5 p/m or below.

In this respect, selenium is no different from a number of foods and drugs available in the marketplace today. Beverage alcohol, for example, is associated with a higher incidence of liver cirrhosis, which, in turn, is associated with a higher incidence of liver cancer.

The Commissioner is of the opinion that these foods and drugs are not, by reason of their capacity to induce liver damage when abused by being consumed at high levels, properly classified as carcinogenic because of their potential association with a higher rate of liver cancer. The various anticancer clauses contained in the act were predicated on the theory that, since we do not know the mechanisms of carcinogenesis, even one molecule of a carcinogen should not be allowed into the food supply. The anticancer clauses do not apply in the case of an agent that (1) occurs naturally in practically all foods, (2) is used in a manner such that the natural level in food is not increased, (3) has a definite hepatotoxic effect/no-effect level, and (4) has a possible carcinogenic effect which is associated only with the hepatotoxic effect.

Accordingly, the Commissioner has concluded that: (1) The available information does not support classification of selenium or its compounds as having carcinogenic activity, (2) the use of selenium as set forth below constitutes no carcinogenic risk, and (3) the limitations set forth below, while satisfying the animals' dietary need for selenium, will assure safety to animals treated with sodium selenite or sodium selenate and to consumers of edible products of such treated animals.

NOTES

1. *No Court Challenge.* FDA's selenium ruling was never challenged in court.

2. *Agency Discretion to Reject Linearity.* EPA is responsible for administering the Safe Drinking Water Act. The Act requires the agency to establish two sets of limitations on concentrations of toxic materials in public drinking water systems—one pair for each contaminant. First, the agency is to establish a "maximum contaminant level goal" (or MCLG) at a level sufficient to protect consumers from any adverse health effect. Then, because achievement of that goal might not be practical, EPA is to prescribe an enforceable "maximum contaminant level" (MCL). For contaminants the agency considered carcinogenic, it had routinely set MCLGs at zero.

In the late 1990s EPA undertook to reassess several contaminants of drinking water, including chloroform, a byproduct of chlorination, for which it had established an MCLG of zero based on the premise that any level of exposure posed a finite risk of cancer. In the meantime, however, further toxicological studies had suggested that chloroform's mode of action might not be linear. A group of independent experts surveyed the data and came to the conclusion that, while carcinogenic at higher concentrations, chloroform exhibited a threshold below which it presented no risk of cancer. EPA said it agreed with this assessment. "Employing the threshold approach that it found was entailed by chloroform's mode of action, EPA then calculated an MCLG of 600 parts per billion based solely on carcinogenicity." 206 F.3d at *1288*. However, when it resumed rulemaking in 1998, the agency retained its old MCLG of zero. The Chlorine Chemistry Council promptly challenged EPA's rule in court.

The D.C. Circuit upheld the challenge. *Chlorine Chemistry Council v. Environmental Protection Agency*, 206 F.3d 1286 (D.C. Cir. 2000). It held that EPA's adherence to the no-threshold premise for carcinogenicity, in the face of its own agreement with the expert panel's assessment, violated the Drinking Water Act's directive to set MCLs and MCLGs at levels supported by "the best available evidence." By the agency's own admission, the "best available evidence" showed that chloroform's cancer-producing effects were threshold-limited. Its reluctance to take the precedent-setting step of recognizing that one carcinogen did not fit the linear model provided no justification for EPA's failure to adhere to the conclusion dictated by the science.

In 2006, the Office of Management and Budget announced that it expected all agencies responsible for regulating chronic health hazards to use quantitative risk assessment in analyzing the potential adverse health effects of products and processes. OMB made clear that it expected agencies to adhere to the "best available evidence" standard in characterizing putative health hazards, thus making the distinctive language of the Safe Drinking Water Act a universal standard for regulatory decision making. *See* Office of Management and Budget, Office of Information and Regulatory Affairs, Proposed Risk Assessment Bulletin, Jan. 9, 2006. *See also* Occupational Safety and Health Act § 6(b)(5), 29 U.S.C. 655 (b)(5).

2. FDA SCIENTIFIC ASSESSMENT

FDA has never embraced the proposition that a mere temporal association between administration of a chemical to test animals and an elevation in tumor incidence inexorably requires a finding that the chemical "induces cancer." The agency has generally subjected study results to critical scientific assessment. It considers information on other biological parameters, such as dose response, tumor progression, and tumor latency, as well as the results of other bioassays. *See, e.g.*, 51 Fed. Reg. 41765 (Nov. 19, 1986) (Yellow No. 6); 48 Fed. Reg. 5252 (Feb. 4, 1983) (Blue No. 2); 47 Fed. Reg. 24278, 24281–82 (June 4, 1982) (Green No. 5).

The agency considers whether the effects observed in an animal study are biologically significant:

> Determining that the incidence of neoplasms increases as a result of exposure to the test compound requires a full biological, pathological, and statistical evaluation. Statistics assist in evaluating the biological conclusion, but a biological conclusion is not determined by the statistical result.

52 Fed. Reg. at 49577 (quoting with approval from a report of the Interdisciplinary Panel on Carcinogenicity entitled Criteria for Evidence of Chemical Carcinogenicity, 225 SCIENCE 682, 683 (1984)). *See also* 50 Fed. Reg. at 10415 (STP guidelines emphasizing the need for biological as well as statistical significance); 45 Fed. Reg. 61474, 61478 (Sept. 16, 1980).

In approving the color additive FD&C Blue No. 2, FDA declared that it had "consistently asserted that statistical factors must be analyzed in conjunction with biological factors" in determining what conclusions can be drawn from a study. 48 Fed. Reg. at 5257. FDA based its decision that the food additive acesulfame potassium is not a carcinogen on "the weight of all of the evidence; no single point provided complete proof in determining the question of carcinogenicity." 57 Fed. Reg. 6667, 6675 (Feb. 27, 1992). In denying a subsequent petition for a hearing, FDA defended, *inter alia*, its conclusion that the incidence of mammary gland tumors in female rats was not treatment-related by pointing out that these tumors are common in old age rats of the strain used in the bioassays, that the incidence of these tumors was in the range for historical controls, and that there was no evidence of progressive tumor stages. 57 Fed. Reg. at 6674–75.

In the 2000 edition of CFSAN's RED BOOK, FDA emphasizes the importance of scientific judgment in weighing all the evidence when deciding whether a chemical is carcinogenic.

> FDA's guidance for toxicity studies for food ingredients continue [sic] to emphasize that there is no substitute for sound scientific judgement [sic]. This guidance presents recommendations—not

hard and fast rules. If an investigator believes that he/she can provide the Agency with useful toxicological information by modifying a recommended study protocol, and is able to support the modification with sound scientific arguments, then the investigator should propose the modified protocol to the appropriate program division within OFAS [the Office of Food Additive Safety].

CFSAN, RED BOOK 2000: TOXICOLOGICAL PRINCIPLES FOR THE SAFETY ASSESSMENT OF FOOD INGREDIENTS, Ch. I, Introduction (rev. July 2007).

In describing FDA's approach to evaluating toxicological evidence, the *Red Book* implies that a statistically significant increase in tumors by itself without the support of corroborative evidence, would not support a finding of carcinogenicity.

There are no universally agreed upon ways of evaluating carcinogenicity data. It is necessary that there be interaction between pathologist, toxicologist and statistician. The role of pathologist is to decide whether an observed lesion is . . . cancerous or noncancerous. The role of the toxicologist is to determine whether the lesion is related to the treatment. The statistician's role is to analyze the mathematical probability of occurrence of the tumors by chance or as a result of treatment. . . .

Because the power of carcinogenesis bioassays that use groups of a few dozen animals is relatively weak for determining carcinogenic activity, it is not surprising that evidence of carcinogenicity is something difficult to establish [from] a single bioassay. This is so for several reasons, including problems of historical diagnosis, sensitivity of the bioassay, and variability of the background tumor incidence. For these reasons, other correlative information may be necessary to add to the weight of evidence of carcinogenicity of a chemical. In general, the extent of the evidence for carcinogenicity can be determined by considering the following evidence: the number of species or strains with an increased tumor incidence; the number of positive studies (with different routes of administration and/or doses), if tested in more than one bioassay; the degrees of tumor response (incidence, site, type, multiplicity, etc.); evidence of structure-activity relationship; prevalence of dose-response relationship; the results of short-term tests for genetic toxicity; the presence of preneoplastic lesions; and a reduced latency for tumor development or increase in the severity (malignancy) of the neoplasia.

Id. Ch. II.

FDA has frequently noted the difficulties involved in determining whether the tumors have been caused by exposure to the test chemical or by some other factor. In its evaluation of acesulfame potassium, FDA explained that "the presence of extensive, severe chronic respiratory disease in the lungs of rats of all groups confounded diagnosis and interpretation of lung lesions in these animals." 53 Fed. Reg. 28379, 28380 (July 28, 1988) (adding that there were "inconsistencies in the diagnostic criteria applied to the observation reported in the study"). The agency continued, "Although the data appeared to show treatment-related differences in a few of the observations, these were subsequently found to be due to the different way categories of lesions were summarized."

FDA has declined to classify a chemical as a carcinogen if its observed effects in treated animals fall within the expected range from historical controls. The preamble to the agency's listing of the color additive D&C Green No. 5 explains its reasons for ignoring statistically significant findings:

> [T]he tumor incidence in the D&C Green No. 5 high-dose group is within the expected range for controls. On the basis of this analysis, FDA has concluded that the tumor incidence found in the high-dose group is attributable to random variation. . . . FDA believes that, in this instance, the p-value calculated using the concurrent controls for the trend in the incidence of hepatocellular tumors in the mouse bioassay of D&G Green No. 5 is not a crucial factor in determining whether this bioassay has shown the color additive to be a carcinogen.

47 Fed. Reg. 49628, 49630 (Nov. 2, 1982).

FDA routinely takes into account whether a compound is genotoxic or exhibits structural alerts. The majority of chemicals that are recognized carcinogens are capable of directly altering the DNA, and FDA has held that negative findings in genotoxicity tests are relevant when determining whether a chemical "induces cancer" in animals. *See, e.g.*, 51 Fed. Reg. 41765, 41773 (Nov. 19, 1986) ("the predominantly negative results [in short-term tests] with FD&C Yellow No. 6 support the conclusion that the color additive is not a carcinogen."); 48 Fed. Reg. 5252, 5258 (Blue No. 2) (Feb. 4, 1983); 47 Fed. Reg. 24278, 24282 (June 4, 1982) (Green No. 5).

FDA accords evidence of decreased lifespan substantial weight, as illustrated by its decision on Green No. 5:

> A shortening of this period is considered to be one of the primary indicators of an induced carcinogenic event, and studies with many bona fide carcinogens have indicated a more dramatic relationship between latency period and treatment than between tumor incidence and treatment.

47 Fed. Reg. 24278, 24283 (because the size and type of liver neoplasms was similar in the treatment and control groups, FDA concluded that "the small increased incidence of liver tumors in the high dose group was a spurious and nonreproducible occurrence"); *see also* 50 Fed. Reg. at 10416 (STP guidelines); 43 Fed. Reg. 18258 (April 28, 1978) (rejecting statistically significant reduced time-to-tumor findings for lymphomas in mice tested with Red. No 40).

As a general rule, FDA demands corroborative evidence before it finds that a chemical "induces cancer." *See, e.g.*, 51 Fed. Reg. 41765, 41773 (Nov. 19, 1986) ("None of the other chronic studies in rats, mice, and dogs displayed a suggestion of treatment-related carcinogenic effects of FD&C Yellow No. 6 of the kidney."). As a former FDA Chief Counsel later explained, the agency has never had a policy of basing a judgment on the issue of cancer causation upon the results of a study in only one strain, gender, and species, at one dose in one experiment. Letter from William B. Goodrich, former FDA Chief Counsel, to D.W.

Sigelman, Counsel to the Human Resource & Intergovernmental Relations Subcomm., House Comm. On Government Operations (Sept. 11, 1987).

FDA's willingness to consider evidence relating to mechanism extends beyond selenium. In a report to Congress, the agency wrote:

> The issue has arisen whether the substance tested, or some other intervening factor, has caused the cancer. If a food additive causes a pathologic change at a particular level (*e.g.*, liver damage), and it is that pathologic change (rather than the additive directly) which in turn leads to cancer, the anti-cancer clause does not preclude approval of that additive for use at levels which provide an adequate margin of safety below the point at which it causes the pathologic change involved.

FDA Study of the Delaney Clause and Other Anti–Cancer Clauses in "Agriculture—Environmental and Consumer Protection Appropriations for 1975," Hearings Before a Subcomm. of the Comm. On Appropriations, House of Representatives, 93rd Cong., 2nd Sess. Part 8 at 219 (1974).

FDA has relied on mechanistic evidence in assessing the carcinogenicity of other chemicals. A notable example is the antioxidant BHA, which in 1982 was found to be associated with a statistically-significant increase in tumors in the forestomach of the rat. To evaluate this finding, FDA convened a working group of international scientists to evaluate the test results. The scientists commented on the evidence illuminating BHA's mechanism of action.

> The available evidence indicates that BHA is not a carcinogen in the classical sense, *i.e.*, it is not a primary or direct-acting carcinogen, but instead exerts and expresses its activity through some as yet unknown mechanism.

Report of the Participants of the Four Nations (Canada, Japan, United Kingdom and United States) on the Evaluation of the Safety of BHA 2 (1982). The group's report noted the steep dose-response curve in the BHA study, BHA's lack of genotoxicity, and the evidence suggesting a possible link between a marked increase in cell proliferation at high doses of BHA and consequent hyperplasia. Based on this analysis, FDA took no action to restrict the use of BHA.

FDA also considers the "appropriateness" or "relevance" of particular test species both in recommending test protocols and in assessing whether elevated tumor occurrence warrants a finding that an additive "induces cancer." For example, it is established agency policy that positive results for certain synthetic steroids do not trigger the Delaney Clause if "tumors are observed only in endocrine-sensitive tissue and no adverse data are obtained from . . . genetic toxicity tests." *See* 52 Fed. Reg. 49572, 49578 (Dec. 31, 1987). Similarly, FDA has questioned the relevance of tumors observed in the forestomach of the male rat because humans do not have a corresponding organ. Based partly on this distinction, FDA in 1982 declined to find that BHA "induces cancer" in the face of a statistically significant increase in this tumor type in the rat.

In 1981, FDA received evidence that D&C Green No. 5 caused a statistically significant increase in the incidence of liver carcinomas in male mice. However, the agency concluded that, notwithstanding the statistical significance of the increase in tumor incidence, other factors led to the conclusion that Green No. 5 did not induce cancer.

> [C]ollectively there exists a significant body of "biological" evidence that strongly supports the conclusion that D&C Green No. 5 is not a carcinogen. FDA finds that this evidence, when considered in conjunction with the results of the analysis of variance conducted by the agency, refutes any inference from the low p-values found in the statistical analysis of the data on D&C Green No. 5 that this color additive is a carcinogen.

47 Fed. Reg. 24278 (June 4, 1982).

FD&C Yellow No. 6 provides another illustration of FDA's reliance upon biological factors in evaluating what otherwise would appear to be statistically significant bioassay findings. Female rats fed doses of Yellow No. 6 exhibited a statistically significant increase in renal tubular adenomas. FDA concluded, however, that the effect could not be directly attributed to Yellow No. 6 for three reasons: (1) the animals exhibited an underlying kidney disease that could have been exacerbated by consumption of large doses of the color additive; (2) male rats, though known to be more susceptible than females to the effect of renal carcinogens, did not exhibit any form of treatment-related changes in their kidneys; and (3) the test animals may have suffered from chronic progressive nephrosis, a disease which is generally associated with the presence of tubular cell proliferative lesions. 51 Fed. Reg. 41765 (Nov. 19, 1986).

NOTES

1. *FD&C Red No. 3.* In 52 Fed. Reg. 29728 (Aug. 11, 1987), FDA released a report by a panel of government scientists the agency had convened to evaluate FD&C Red No. 3. This color has been shown to cause cancer in experimental animals, but the proponents of listing sought to persuade FDA that its mechanism of carcinogenic action posed no cancer risk for humans who might ingest it. Three years earlier the Director of CFSAN summarized the questions the agency would have to resolve before it could approve Red No. 3:

> Even if sufficient evidence of a secondary mechanism is developed, the agency would still need to consider other scientific questions in deciding on the safety of this color additive. Among the relevant questions are: (a) whether valid scientific data demonstrate that the cancer caused by the color additive has a clearly established threshold below which cancer will not be induced; (b) whether there is an adequate margin of safety between that threshold and expected consumption levels; and (c) whether FD&C Red No. 3 has otherwise been shown to be safe for its uses.

"The Regulation by the Department of Health and Human Services of Carcinogenic Color Additives," Hearing Before a Subcomm. Of the House Comm. On Government Operations, 98th Cong.; 2d Sess. 84–85 (1984)

(Letter from Sanford A. Miller, Ph.D., to National Food Processors Association) (Apr. 16, 1984). In 55 Fed. Reg. 3516 (Feb. 1, 1990), FDA terminated the provisional listing of FD&C Red No. 3 for cosmetics and external drugs, and of Red No. 3 lakes (insoluble variants) for all purposes, stating that industry had failed to prove the hypothesis that the color is a secondary carcinogen.

2. *Dioxin.* There has been continuing controversy about whether 2,3,7,8–TCDD (dioxin) is a secondary, rather than primary, carcinogen. FDA and EPA have determined that it has not yet been satisfactorily shown to be a secondary carcinogen and have continued to regulate it as a no-threshold carcinogen, relying on quantitative risk assessment. Members of the EU have accepted the evidence of a secondary mechanism and thus have set dioxin exposure limits based on safety factors. In consequence, there is a 1000-fold difference between U.S. limits on exposure to dioxin and those observed in Europe. *See* Michael Gough, *Science Policy Choices and the Estimation of Cancer Risk Associated with Exposure to TCDD,* 8 Risk Analysis 337 (1988). In the interim, the paper industry reduced dioxin contamination to an insignificant level. "Progress in Eliminating Dioxin from Packaging," FDA Talk Paper T90–21 (Apr. 30, 1990).

3. *Other Putative Secondary Carcinogens.* FDA found that the scientific evidence is insufficient to characterize either chloroform or methylene chloride as a secondary, rather than primary, carcinogen. 41 Fed. Reg. 26842, 26843 (June 29, 1976), 54 Fed. Reg. 27328, 27333 (June 29, 1989). But the agency has agreed with EPA that melamine is a secondary carcinogen. 49 Fed. Reg. 18120 (Apr. 27, 1984), 53 Fed. Reg. 23128 (June 20, 1988), 54 Fed. Reg. 12912 (Mar. 29, 1989).

G. RESOLVING THE "DELANEY PARADOX"

As part of the Food Additives Amendment, Congress added to the Act language codifying FDA's practice in regulating pesticides on processed foods. Section 402(a)(2)(C) said that a residue on processed food would not render the food adulterated if the level did not exceed the tolerance that had been established under section 408 for the raw form. The statute did not say specifically what was to happen if, in processing, the concentration of pesticide did exceed the level allowed on the raw food, but there is little doubt that Congress expected the agency to regulate this elevated residue under section 409. However, section 409 contains the Delaney Clause. This meant that if the pesticide, whose level was elevated by processing, was shown to induce cancer in animals, EPA could not approve its presence—and thus any food in which residues concentrated would be adulterated.

The next case, *Les v. Reilly,* exposes the implications of this statutory arrangement. The practical consequences were amplified because EPA took the position that, if a food additive tolerance could not—because of Delaney—be approved for any processed form of a food, it would be obliged to revoke its 408 tolerance for the raw commodity. The agency reasoned that it could not permit marketing of a raw commodity some of which could be converted into unlawful processed food.

Les v. Reilly

968 F.2d 985 (9th Cir. 1992).

■ SCHROEDER, CIRCUIT JUDGE.

Petitioners seek review of a final order of the Environmental Protection Agency permitting the use of four pesticides as food additives although they have been found to induce cancer. Petitioners challenge the final order on the ground that it violates the provisions of the Delaney clause, 21 U.S.C. § 348(c)(3), which prohibits the use of any food additive that is found to induce cancer.

. . . A food "additive" is defined broadly as "any substance the intended use of which results or may reasonably be expected to result . . . in its becoming a component . . . of any food." A food additive is considered unsafe unless there is a specific exemption for the substance or a regulation prescribing the conditions under which it may be used safely.

Before 1988, the four pesticide chemicals with which we are here concerned—benomyl, mancozeb, phosmet and trifluralin—were all the subject of regulations issued by the EPA permitting their use. In October 1988, however, the EPA published a list of substances, including the pesticides at issue here, that had been found to induce cancer.

The FFDCA . . . contains special provisions which regulate the occurrence of pesticide residues on raw agricultural commodities. Section 402 of the FFDCA provides that a raw food containing a pesticide residue is deemed adulterated unless the residue is authorized under section 408 of the FFDCA, which allows tolerance regulations setting maximum permissible levels and also provides for exemption from tolerances under certain circumstances. When a tolerance or an exemption has been established for use of a pesticide on a raw agricultural commodity, then the FFDCA allows for the "flow-through" of such pesticide residue to processed foods, even when the pesticide may be a carcinogen. This flow-through is allowed, however, only to the extent that the concentration of the pesticide in the processed food does not exceed the concentration allowed in the raw food. The flow-through provisions are contained in section 402 which provides:

> That where a pesticide chemical has been used in or on a raw agricultural commodity in conformity with an exemption granted or a tolerance prescribed under section 346a of this title [section 408] and such raw agricultural commodity has been subjected to processing such as canning, cooking, freezing, dehydrating, or milling, the residue of such pesticide chemical remaining in or on such processed food shall, notwithstanding the provisions of sections 346 and 348 of this title [sections 406 and 409], not be deemed unsafe if such residue in or on the raw agricultural commodity has been removed to the extent possible in good manufacturing practice and the concentration of such residue in the processed food when ready to eat is not greater than the tolerance prescribed for the raw agricultural commodity.

It is undisputed that the EPA regulations at issue in this case allow for the concentration of cancer-causing pesticides during processing to levels in excess of those permitted in the raw foods.

The proceedings in this case had their genesis in October 1988 when the EPA published a list of substances, including these pesticides, that were found to induce cancer. Simultaneously, the EPA announced a new interpretation of the Delaney clause: the EPA proposed to permit concentrations of cancer-causing pesticide residues greater than that tolerated for raw foods so long as the particular substances posed only a "de minimis" risk of actually causing cancer. Finding that benomyl, mancozeb, phosmet and trifluralin (among others) posed only such a de minimis risk, the Agency announced that it would not immediately revoke its previous regulations authorizing use of these substances as food additives.

. . . The Agency acknowledges that its interpretation of the law is a new and changed one. From the initial enactment of the Delaney clause in 1958 to the time of the rulings here in issue, the statute had been strictly and literally enforced. The EPA also acknowledges that the language of the statute itself appears, at first glance, to be clear on its face.

The language is clear and mandatory. The Delaney clause provides that no additive shall be deemed safe if it induces cancer. The EPA states in its final order that appropriate tests have established that the pesticides at issue here induce cancer in humans or animals. The statute provides that once the finding of carcinogenicity is made, the EPA has no discretion. . . .

This issue was litigated before the D.C. Circuit in connection with the virtually identical "color additive" prohibition of 21 U.S.C. § 376(b)(5)(B). . . . *Public Citizen v. Young*, 831 F.2d 1108. The court concluded that the EPA's de minimis interpretation of the Delaney clause in 21 U.S.C. § 376 was "contrary to law." The *Public Citizen* decision reserved comment on whether the result would be the same under the food additive provisions as it was under the food color provisions, but its reasoning with respect to the language of the statute is equally applicable to both.

The Agency asks us to look behind the language of the Delaney clause to the overall statutory scheme governing pesticides, which permits the use of carcinogenic pesticides on raw food without regard to the Delaney clause. Yet section 402 of the FFDCA, 21 U.S.C. § 342(a)(2)(C), expressly harmonizes that scheme with the Delaney clause by providing that residues on processed foods may not exceed the tolerance level established for the raw food. The statute unambiguously provides that pesticides which concentrate in processed food are to be treated as food additives, and these are governed by the Delaney food additive provision contained in section 409. If pesticides which concentrate in processed foods induce cancer in humans or animals, they render the food adulterated and must be prohibited.

. . . .

The EPA contends that the legislative history shows that Congress never intended to regulate pesticides, as opposed to other additives, with extraordinary rigidity under the food additives provision. The

Agency is indeed correct that the legislative history of the food additive provision does not focus on pesticides, and that pesticides are regulated more comprehensively under the Federal Insecticide, Fungicide, and Rodenticide Act (FIFRA), 7 U.S.C. §§ 136–136y. . . . Congress intended to regulate pesticides as food additives under section 409 of the FFDCA, at least to the extent that pesticide residues concentrate in processed foods and exceed the tolerances for raw foods.

Finally, the EPA argues that a de minimis exception to the Delaney clause is necessary in order to bring about a more sensible application of the regulatory scheme. It relies particularly on a recent study suggesting that the criterion of concentration level in processed foods may bear little or no relation to actual risk of cancer, and that some pesticides might be barred by rigid enforcement of the Delaney clause while others, with greater cancer-causing risk, may be permitted through the flow-through provisions because they do not concentrate in processed foods. *See* National Academy of Sciences, REGULATING PESTICIDES IN FOOD: THE DELANEY PARADOX (1987). The EPA in effect asks us to approve what it deems to be a more enlightened system than that which Congress established.

The EPA is not alone in criticizing the scheme established by the Delaney clause. *See, e.g.,* Richard A. Merrill, *FDA's Implementation of the Delaney Clause: Repudiation of Congressional Choice or Reasoned Adaptation to Scientific Progress*, 5 YALE J. ON REG. 1, 87 (1988) (concluding that the Delaney clause is both unambiguous and unwise: "at once an explicit and imprudent expression of legislative will"). Revising the existing statutory scheme, however, is neither our function nor the function of the EPA. . . . If there is to be a change, it is for Congress to direct.

. . . .

———

The Ninth Circuit's rejection of EPA's effort to resolve this paradox prompted Congress to amend both the FD&C Act and the Federal Insecticide, Fungicide, and Rodenticide Act (FIFRA). The following excerpts explain the source of EPA's dilemma and the compromise that Congress adopted.

James Smart, *All the Stars in the Heavens Were in the Right Places: The Passage of the Food Quality Protection Act of 1996*

17 STANFORD ENVIRONMENTAL LAW JOURNAL 273 (1998).

. . . .

Section 408 required EPA to reduce pesticide tolerances for raw agricultural commodities "to the extent necessary to protect the public health," but the provision also instructed the Administrator to "give appropriate consideration . . . to the necessity for the production of an adequate, wholesome and economical food supply." In implementing this standard, EPA first calculated the theoretical maximum residue contribution (TMRC) for use of a pesticide on a given commodity. . . . If the pesticide was one for which a threshold or "no observable effect level" (NOEL) could be identified for any ill effect, EPA considered the dietary residue contribution of the pesticide on the crop for which a new tolerance was sought in conjunction with all other dietary residue contributions for the pesticide on other crops. Regulators then compared this aggregate total maximum residue contribution to EPA's reference dose—the acceptable exposure level.

EPA arrived at the reference dose by applying an uncertainty factor to the level at which no observable effect could be found, the NOEL. The uncertainty factor consisted of one factor of ten to account for the uncertainty in "extrapolating data from animals to humans." Another factor of ten was meant to cover "variation within the human population." A third factor of ten applied whenever testing revealed fetal developmental effects.

If the reference dose was greater than the aggregate TMRC, the pesticide use would be approved. If the commodity-specific TMRC pushed the aggregate TMRC above the reference dose, EPA usually denied a new tolerance. Nevertheless, in some instances, EPA would allow consideration of the benefits of a pesticide to tip the scales the other way.

If the pesticide were only oncogenic, EPA simply considered the magnitude of the risk posed by the use's TMRC. If the risk were below a lifetime mortality risk of one in a million, and the crop had no processed form that concentrated the pesticide to trigger the Delaney Clause, the agency would approve the use. If the risk were greater than one in ten thousand, the agency typically disallowed the use. When the risk fell between these two numbers, consideration of the benefits of the pesticide was crucial to the outcome.

Thus, the FDCA created a discrepancy between the absolute prohibition on Delaney pesticides and the risk-benefit regime for pesticide residues that do not fall under Delaney. Delaney pesticides were those cancer-inducing pesticides that concentrated during food processing. Pesticides that either did not induce cancer or did not concentrate avoided Delaney. . . .

Allison D. Carpenter, *Impact of the Food Quality Protection Act of 1996*

3 ENVIRONMENTAL LAWYER 479 (1997).

. . . .

The Act resolves the Delaney Paradox by establishing a single standard for pesticide residues in all types of food. The Act does not repeal or amend the Delaney Clause, but redefines "food additive" and "pesticide chemical residue" to ensure that pesticide residue in all foods, including processed foods, are covered by . . . section 408 of the FFDCA. The Act then amends section 408 to provide a general safety standard to govern pesticide tolerances, defined as "reasonable certainty that no harm will result from aggregate exposure to the pesticide chemical residue."

When a pesticide residue does not meet the general safety standard, EPA still may establish a tolerance for it if it qualifies as an "eligible pesticide chemical residue." To determine that a residue qualifies as an "eligible pesticide chemical residue," EPA must (1) appropriately assess the "non-threshold" health risks associated with the pesticide through a quantitative risk assessment, and (2) determine that the "threshold" health risks for the expected level of exposure are safe.

Once a pesticide residue qualifies as an "eligible pesticide chemical residue," EPA then may establish a tolerance for it if the Agency determines that use of the pesticide is necessary to avoid a significant disruption in production of an adequate, safe and wholesome food supply, or that the health benefits from using the pesticide outweigh the risks involved.

The Act, however, establishes three limitations on EPA's authority to issue tolerances in such circumstances. First, the yearly non-threshold risk may not exceed ten times the general safety standard, and the lifetime non-threshold risk may not be greater than twice the general safety standard. Second, EPA must review tolerances established under a risk-benefit analysis after five years and, if necessary, revoke or modify the tolerances if the foregoing requirements have not been met. Third, tolerances established under the risk-benefit analysis must be consistent with the special provisions for infants and children set out in the Act.

The Act responds to the findings of a study performed by the National Academy of Sciences Board on Agriculture, *Pesticides in the Diets of Infants and Children* ("the NAS Report"). The Act requires EPA to assess risk based on children's dietary patterns, including their higher consumption of fruits and vegetables, when setting a pesticide tolerance. In addition, the Act requires EPA to consider the special susceptibility of infants and children to pesticides, and to publish a special determination regarding the safety of each pesticide for infants and children. The Act also requires EPA to use an additional tenfold margin of safety when assessing threshold risks for infants and children. . . .

NOTE

Mandate to Protect Children. As the previous excerpts reveal, the Food Quality Protection Act was a classic legislative compromise. A coalition of chemical companies and agricultural interests sought, above all, to escape the "Delaney paradox" and were rewarded by amendments to Sections 402 and 408 of the Act that excluded pesticide residues from the category of food additives to which Delaney might apply. The several groups that sought stricter limits on pesticide residues in food wished to curtail if not eliminate EPA's authority to take account of the benefits of pesticide use in setting tolerances, a victory more symbolic than substantive. But they were even more eager to have the law ensure that tolerances would be low enough to protect infants and children. The amended statute accomplished this in two steps. First, it required EPA to find that any tolerance would reflect analysis of the size, maturity, and dietary exposure of these populations. And then, by way of emphasis, it instructed the agency, in setting a tolerance, to apply an additional "safety" or "uncertainty" factor of 10 unless available data supported a different safety factor.

The latter provision was soon recognized as a potential threat to pesticide use (and thus sale) and, indirectly, to agricultural practice. Rigorous application of an "extra" 10 in computing an "acceptable daily intake" (ADI, or reference dose) for a pesticide could require that allowable residues be reduced by an order of magnitude, *i.e.*, a factor of 10. This would not only cut into chemical sales to farmers but could render pesticide use futile to cope with the pest. Environmental groups grasped the practical implications of this analysis and began to lobby EPA vigorously to accept and follow a protective—and arguably literal—interpretation of the crucial statutory language.

No definitive interpretation of the "10-X" provision has thus far been endorsed by any court. *See New York v. U.S. E.P.A.*, 350 F. Supp. 2d 429 (S.D.N.Y. 2004) (challenge to EPA position for lack of subject matter jurisdiction), *aff'd NRDC v. Johnson*, 461 F.3d 164 (2d Cir. 2006) (challenge may be brought in Court of Appeals, but only after exhaustion of administrative review). *See also* Alexandra Klass, *Pesticides, Children's Health Policy, and Common Law Tort Claims*, 7 Minn. J.L. Sci. & Tech. 89 (2005). EPA has approved tolerances for several crop-pesticide combinations based on analyses that reflect special attention to infants and children, and none has so far been overturned. It is too early to venture any definitive assessment of the impact of Congress' preoccupation with the risks faced by the youngest consumers of pesticide-treated food.

H. OTHER EFFORTS TO IDENTIFY OR REGULATE CARCINOGENS

1. IARC AND NTP

The International Agency for Research on Cancer (IARC), a component of the World Health Organization, helps coordinate research into the causes of cancer and monitors trends in cancer incidence worldwide. IARC has produced a series of "monographs" describing the evidence for the carcinogenicity of individual chemicals. It recognizes four categories or tiers of animal evidence of carcinogenicity: (1) sufficient evidence, (2) limited evidence, (3) inadequate evidence, and (4) evidence suggesting lack of carcinogenicity. IARC Monographs on the Evaluation of Carcinogenic Risks to Humans, IARC Int'l Tech. Rep. No. 87/001, at 30–31 (1987).

IARC classifies substances according to carcinogenic potential under four headings: Group 1 (substances carcinogenic to humans), Group 2A (substances probably carcinogenic to humans), Group 2B (substances possibly carcinogenic to humans), and Group 3 (substances not classifiable). Like the National Toxicology Program, discussed below, IARC draws no distinctions based on mechanism of action. In 1986, EPA adopted a similar classification system, which includes an additional category: Group A (human carcinogens), Group B (probable human carcinogens), Group C (possible human carcinogens), Group D (not classifiable as to human carcinogenicity), and Group E (evidence of noncarcinogenicity for humans). 51 Fed. Reg. 33992 (Sept. 24, 1986). Only for substances in Group A and Group B will EPA prepare a quantitative risk assessment.

In the United States, the National Toxicology Program (NTP), part of the National Institute of Environmental Health Sciences, has adopted a five-tier system for describing the "strength of evidence" of the experimental findings from its animal carcinogenicity studies. 51 Fed. Reg. 2579 (Jan. 17, 1986), 51 Fed. Reg. 11843 (Apr. 7, 1986). The five categories are: (1) clear evidence, (2) some evidence, (3) no evidence, (4) equivocal evidence, and (5) inadequate study. The first two categories (clear evidence and some evidence) represent positive results. Based upon the "weight" of the animal evidence, as well as any relevant human or in vitro data, NTP then classifies the substances as "known" or as "reasonably anticipated" to be human carcinogens. NTP's refusal to consider a chemical's mechanism of action in compiling the required annual report under 42 U.S.C. 241(b)(4) was upheld in *Synthetic Organic Chemical Mfrs. Ass'n v. Secretary, Dept. of HHS*, 720 F. Supp. 1244 (W.D. La. 1989).

In 1978 Congress enacted legislation that requires the Secretary of Health and Human Services to compile and annually, later biannually, publish a list of known and suspected carcinogens. Pub. L. 95–622, 92 Stat. 3412. The responsibility to discharge this duty had been assigned to NTP, now a function of the National Institute of Environmental Health Sciences. NTP's decisions whether to list a chemical and what to say about the evidence relating to chemicals that are listed are often a matter of intense interest to firms that make, sell, or use a chemical. Some NTP choices have provoked legal challenges by affected industry groups. Government claims that such decisions are not actions subject to judicial review under the Administrative Procedure Act have not been successful, but the two courts that have entertained challenges have upheld NTP's procedures and its findings on the merits. *The Fertilizer Institute v. U.S. Department of Health and Human Services*, 355 F. Supp. 2d 123 (D.D.C. 2004) (challenging listing of sulfuric acid mist); *Tozzi v. U.S. Department of Health and Human Services*, 271 F.3d 301 (D.C. Cir. 2001) (challenging NTP's listing of dioxin as a "known human carcinogen").

2. AGENCY CANCER GUIDELINES

FDA is not the only federal agency with responsibility to protect consumers and others from chemicals that may cause cancer. As the previous section illustrates, EPA has been active in this field—and probably more active than even FDA—since its creation in 1970. Over time EPA has been given authority to discover and control toxic chemicals in a wide range of exposure settings, under a long list of health-protective statutes: the Clean Air Act; the Federal Water Pollution Control Act; the Safe Drinking Water Act; the Toxic Substances Control Act; the Hazardous Waste Act (part of the Resource Conversation and Recovery Act); and, most prominently, the Federal Insecticide, Fungicide, and Rodenticide Act (along with the companion provisions of the FD&C Act that apply to pesticides on food).

With so vast a range of authorities, EPA almost from its beginning found it useful to formulate and adhere to an agency-wide set of criteria for identifying substances that might cause cancer and a set of standards for assessing the risks posed by those that displayed this potential. In 1974, the agency announced its first "interim guidance and procedures" governing its assessment of the health risks of carcinogens and the economic impact of possible regulatory responses. 41 Fed. Reg. 21402 (May 25, 1974). This comparatively brief document provided the intellectual framework within which EPA formulated risk assessments for the next decade. By the late 1980s, however, experience had added so many refinements and qualifications that the agency was impelled to develop an updated and far more sophisticated set of "cancer guidelines." This project has undergone several iterations, resulting in the release of successive drafts coupled with invitations for public comment. The most recent, and possibly "final" (for the moment) version was released—again for comment—in 70 Fed. Reg. 10616 (Mar. 4, 2005). *See also* Questions and Answers: EPA's Guidelines for Carcinogen Risk Assessment and Supplemental Guidance from Assessing Susceptibility from Early-Life Exposure to Carcinogens, March 29, 2005.

The Occupational Safety and Health Administration (OSHA) has likewise been active in assessing and regulating carcinogenic chemicals to which workers are exposed on the job. The agency is empowered to establish and enforce workplace exposure limits for chemicals that threaten worker health under statutory language that directs it to assure, "to the extent feasible," that workers exposed to toxic chemicals experience no adverse effects on health.

Like EPA, OSHA's appreciation of its potential caseload led it to attempt to formulate criteria for carcinogen risk assessment that it could apply in case after case. In 1978, the agency launched the most ambitious effort to codify these criteria—and the remedial response that should automatically follow—through rulemaking. OSHA's criteria were to be binding rules, not simply hortatory guidelines. 45 Fed. Reg. 5002 (Jan. 22, 1980), 29 C.F.R. Part 1990. In essence, the agency accepted the no-threshold premise for all cancer-causing chemicals and said it would require that workplace exposure to any chemical found to be carcinogenic be reduced to as near zero as the affected industry could achieve by engineering methods and afford, short of bankruptcy, to pay for. In the most famous case in this field, *Industrial Union Department, AFL–CIO v. American Petroleum Institute*, 448 U.S. 607 (1980), the Supreme Court essentially rejected OSHA's decision to dispense with any attempt to quantify the risk of a carcinogen. The agency did not abandon its effort to codify its cancer criteria, but instead amended its published generic cancer policy to require risk assessment. 46 Fed. Reg. 5878 (Jan. 21, 1981) (amending 29 C.F.R. 1990 to require OSHA to demonstrate that existing levels of worker exposure to a chemical pose a significant risk before it can regulate). Although OSHA later announced that it was reconsidering further changes, 47 Fed. Reg. 187 (Jan. 5, 1982), 48 Fed. Reg. 241 (Jan. 4, 1983), the agency has taken no further steps to revise its 1980 regulation. OSHA's workplace standards for particular carcinogens reflect explicit reliance on quantitative risk assessment. *E.g., International Union, United Automobile, Aerospace and Agricultural Implement Workers of America v. Pendergrass*, 878

F.2d 389 (D.C. Cir. 1989) (formaldehyde); *Building and Construction Trades Department, AFL–CIO v. Brock*, 838 F.2d 1258 (D.C. Cir. 1988) (asbestos); *Public Citizen Health Research Group v. Tyson*, 796 F.2d 1479 (D.C. Cir.1986) (ethylene oxide); *ASARCO, Inc. v. Occupational Safety and Health Administration*, 746 F.2d 483 (9th Cir. 1984) (airborne arsenic); *Asbestos Information Association / North America v. Occupational Safety and Health Administration*, 727 F.2d 415 (5th Cir. 1984) (ambient asbestos fibers). For a thoughtful discussion of regulatory risk assessment by EPA and OSHA, see Matthew D. Adler, *Against "Individual Risk": A Sympathetic Critique of Risk Assessment*, 153 U. Pa. L. Rev. 1121 (2005).

Of the principal federal safety agencies, the Consumer Product Safety Commission (CPSC) has had the least experience identifying or regulating carcinogens. On the one occasion it explicitly relied on quantitative risk assessment to justify action, a ban of urea-formaldehyde foam insulation, a court set aside the Commission's action. *Gulf South Insulation v. U.S. Consumer Product Safety Commission*, 701 F.2d 1137 (5th Cir. 1983). *See generally* Richard A. Merrill, *CPSC Regulation of Cancer Risks in Consumer Products*: 1972–1981, 67 Va. L. Rev. 1261 (1981). *See* 57 Fed. Reg. 46626 (1992) (the Commission's art materials rule).

3. GOVERNMENT-WIDE POLICIES

In 1977, FDA, EPA, CPSC, and OSHA established the Interagency Regulatory Liaison Group (IRLG) whose goal was to develop common approaches to the regulation of toxic chemicals. One of the IRLG's first projects was the establishment of a Work Group on Risk Assessment. The efforts of the Work Group were complicated by interagency policy differences. Although FDA and EPA strongly supported quantitative risk assessment for carcinogens and had been using this technique for some years, OSHA had recently proposed an approach to classifying carcinogens that explicitly refrained from giving weight to carcinogenic potency or risk assessment, 42 Fed. Reg. 54148 (Oct. 4, 1977). The final IRLG report, 44 Fed. Reg. 39858 (July 6, 1979), was therefore muted. While acknowledging its limitations, the report nevertheless endorsed the use of quantitative risk assessment.

On February 1, 1979, the Office of Science and Technology Policy (OSTP) of the Executive Office of the President issued a staff paper, Identification, Characterization, and Control of Potential Human Carcinogens: A Framework for Federal Decision–Making, which explicitly endorsed use of quantitative risk assessment. The since-defunct Regulatory Council, representing the four IRLB agencies and others, likewise issued a statement on regulation of chemical carcinogens in 44 Fed. Reg. 60038 (Oct. 17, 1979). It declared that, except where a statute "explicitly indicates which substances are to be controlled and how, every regulatory proposal will be accompanied by some form of risk assessment." The statement went on to say, however, that all carcinogens "will be considered capable of causing or contributing to the development of cancer even at the lowest doses of exposure."

Several years later, OSTP convened an Interagency Staff Group on Chemical Carcinogenesis, and prepared a comprehensive review of a science and associated principles governing the assessment of chemical carcinogens, 49 Fed. Reg. 21594 (May 22, 1984), 50 Fed. Reg. 10372 (Mar. 14, 1985). Most recently OMB, in consultation with OSTP, released a risk assessment bulletin to guide rulemaking agencies, 71 Fed. Reg. 2600 (Jan. 17, 2006). OMB said it relied specifically on OSTP's 1985 report. Office of Management and Budget, Proposed Risk Assessment Bulletin, Jan. 9, 2006.

I. ISSUES

Peter Barton Hutt, *Food and Drug Law: A Strong and Continuing Tradition*

37 FOOD DRUG COSMETIC LAW JOURNAL 123 (1982).

. . . In 1960, at the time Congress enacted the Food Additives Amendment, the Color Additive Amendments, and the Drug Amendments, [U.S. life expectancy] stood at 69.7 years. In 1978 . . . it reached 73.3 years. . . .

Food and drug regulation was designed, from its inception, to deal with the acute causes of death. . . . The 1906 Act was directed against poisons in food and food-borne disease. Regulatory strategy dictated elimination of dangerous ingredients and contaminating microorganisms. It was a sound strategy then, it remained a sound strategy when the law was modernized in 1938, and it continues to be a sound strategy today.

. . . [T]raditional regulatory strategy involves elimination of dangerous substances from the food and drug supply. This clearly works for such substances as salmonella, botulism, and other pathogenic microorganisms. It works equally well for frank poisons that can produce demonstrable injury, such as diethylene glycol and thalidomide. The question being raised today, however, is whether that regulatory strategy applies equally well to protect the public health against the causes of chronic disease. . . .

The burden of demonstrating safety has changed for some categories of substances but not for others. For food and color additives, and new human and animal drugs, the burden of demonstrating safety has been shifted to the regulated industry. For many other ingredients used in food and drugs, however, the burden of demonstrating a lack of safety remains on the government, where it has been for centuries. This change in strategy, however, does not seem at all related to any attempt to prevent chronic disease. There is no evidence whatever that the principal causes of heart disease and cancer fall into those categories that now require premarket approval rather than into those categories that are exempt from premarket approval. One can persuasively argue, indeed, that the reverse is likely to be true. Heart disease and cancer have existed for centuries. To the extent that these diseases are attributable to any particular substances, therefore, those substances are more likely to be in the categories of old substances that are exempt from premarket approval than in the categories of new substances that now require premarket approval. . . .

The credibility of regulatory agencies has been severely damaged by the mounting evidence that some of the most popular items in our food supply are carcinogenic by some form of scientific test. The public is not prepared to give up charcoal-broiled steak and hamburgers, pepper, nutmeg, mustard, and coffee, much less the essential nutrients that have been implicated by this scientific evidence. The failure of traditional regulatory techniques to deal with these problems was definitely demonstrated when regulatory action was threatened against artificially sweetened food containing saccharin and cured meat containing nitrites. The government quickly learned that the public simply did not intend the food and drug laws to be applied literally when it meant the elimination of important items from the food supply.

Evidence mounts that to reduce either heart disease or cancer there must be major lifestyle changes. Where this is true, it radically alters the prospects for regulatory intervention. Regulation can require some modifications in individual items in the food supply, but it cannot reform the entire American diet. If it is the way we eat and live that is associated with cancer, rather than specific substances in our environment, the traditional approaches of a regulatory agency are obviously inappropriate. . . .

Perhaps most devastating, the eradication of cancer and heart disease would have a much smaller impact on longevity than is commonly assumed. If all cancer, from all sources, were eliminated from the United States, average life expectancy at birth would still be increased by only 2.5 years. If a 30% reduction in cancer were achieved—an obviously more realistic but still extremely difficult goal— average life expectancy at birth would be increased by 0.71 year. A 30% reduction in major cardiovascular disease would produce an increase in average life expectancy at birth of 1.98 years. Application of the same 30% reduction to the working ages, 15 to 70 years, would result in a gain for them of 0.43 year from major cardiovascular disease and 0.26 year from cancer. . . .

The question, then, is whether the heroic personal, societal, and regulatory measures that would be required to make a substantial reduction in cancer—assuming that they would be effective, an assumption that is entirely conjectural—would be worth an additional 0.26 to 0.71 year added to the end of our lives. The smallest part of the sacrifice necessary to make that effort would entail the economic cost of regulation. Much more important would be the foregone pleasures of life-style, dietary habits, and individual food items that we have all learned to enjoy.

NOTES

1. *Life Style Changes.* J.F. Fries et al., *Health Promotion and the Compression of Morbidity*, 1 LANCET 481 (1989), point out that the substantial increase in life expectancy, and our lack of ability to achieve overall life extension, require "a change of focus from quantity to quality of life—'Add Life to Your Years, Not Years to Your Life.'"

As life-style practices continue to improve and as mortality rates at advanced years decline more slowly, there may be disillusionment about the link between risk factors and health. It is critically important to recognize that the dividends of prevention are mainly in reduction of the population illness burden and enhancement of the quality of life, and that these are very large dividends indeed. . . . The primary purpose of population interventions, risk assessment, and risk reduction in developed societies is to compress morbidity and to improve the quality and vigor of life.

2.   *More and More Carcinogens.* Of 86 chronic bioassays conducted by NTP and reported between July 1981 and July 1984, half showed the chemical was carcinogenic. J.K. Haseman et al., *Results From 86 Two–Year Carcinogenicity Studies Conducted By the National Toxicology Program*, 14 J. TOX. & ENVIRON. HEALTH 621, 634 (1984). FDA has stated that the sensitivity of analytical detection methodology increased in the period from 1958 to 1979 "between two and five orders of magnitude," *i.e.*, between 100 and 100,000 times. 44 Fed. Reg. 17070, 17075 (Mar. 20, 1979). The increase in the number of chemicals found to be carcinogenic, their easy detection, and the expenditures required to control human exposure have led some cancer experts to suggest that the strategy of regulatory control has been overemphasized. *See, e.g.*, John Higginson, *Changing Concepts in Cancer Prevention: Limitations and Implications for Future Research in Environmental Carcinogenesis*, 48 CANCER RES. 1381 (Mar. 15, 1988).

3.   *Costs of Regulation.* In 1987 the Office of Management and Budget (OMB) questioned the cumulative impact of conservative assumptions used in quantitative risk assessment.

Often each conservative assumption is made by a different scientist or analyst responsible for a portion of the risk assessment. Each may think that erring on the side of caution or conservatism is reasonable. However, the effect of these individual conservative assumptions is compounded in the final estimate of risk presented to the decisionmaker. For example, if at each of two different steps in an analysis, estimates are chosen that have a 5 percent chance of being less than the true risk, then the final risk estimate will have only a 0.25 percent chance of being less than the true risk (0.05 + 0.05 = 0.0025). That is, the risk estimate will have a 99.75 percent chance of being greater than the true risk. If there were 5 steps in the analysis instead of 2 and a conservative estimate at the 5 percent level were chosen for each step then the final risk estimate would have a 0.00003 percent (0.05^5) chance of being less than the true risk, or 3 chances in 10 million. In other words, the estimate has a 99.99997 percent chance of overstating the true risk.

In practice, there may be as many as 20 distinct stages in a risk assessment where conservative assumptions are made. A typical risk assessment would probably contain about 10. The final risk estimate derived from these compounded conservative assumptions may be more than a million times greater than the best estimate and may, thus, have a probability of being accurate that is virtually zero. . . .

OMB, Regulatory Program of the United States government, Apr. 1, 1986–Mar. 31, 1987, xx & xxv (1987).

   4.   *Proposition 65.* On November 4, 1986, the voters of California by a large majority enacted Proposition 65 as an initiative measure under Article II, Section 8 of the California Constitution. Codified in the California Health and Safety Code 25249.5–25249.13, Proposition 65 requires the governor to publish, and periodically revise, a list of chemicals "known to the state to cause cancer. . . ." Any listed chemical is presumed to be a health hazard, and any individual exposed to a listed chemical must be given a "clear and reasonable warning" about the exposure by the person responsible for the exposure unless that person can prove that the exposure represents "no significant risk," assuming lifetime exposure at the level in question. Within three years, more than 370 natural and synthetic chemicals had been listed as carcinogens, including some essential nutrients and many natural constituents of food. The impact of this experiment in risk communication is discussed in Peter Barton Hutt, *Application of Proposition 65 to Food, Drugs, Medical Devices, and Cosmetics, in* CLEAN WATER AND TOXIC WASTE: AT WHAT COST FOR WHAT GAIN? 23 (National Legal Center for the Public Interest, 1989); Matt Kuryla, *California Proposition 65 and the Chemical Hazard Warning: Risk Management Under the New Code of Popular Outrage,* 8 VA. J. NAT. RES. L. 103 (1988).

CHAPTER 14

REGULATION OF FOREIGN COMMERCE

A. IMPORTATION INTO THE UNITED STATES

1. FDA'S GENERAL AUTHORITY OVER IMPORTATION

FDA works closely with Customs and Border Protection of the Department of Homeland Security (formerly the Customs Service of the Department of Transportation) to prevent the importation of adulterated or misbranded products, and unapproved drugs, into the United States. FDA's primary source of authority to keep such products out of the country is section 801(a) of the FD&C Act:

> The [Secretary of Homeland Security] shall deliver to the Secretary of Health and Human Services, upon his request, samples of food, drugs, devices, tobacco products, and cosmetics which are being imported or offered for import into the United States, giving notice thereof to the owner or consignee, who may appear before the Secretary of Health and Human Services and have the right to introduce testimony. . . . If it appears from the examination of such samples or otherwise that (1) such article has been manufactured, processed, or packed under insanitary conditions or, in the case of a device, [in violation of the cGMP requirements for devices], or (2) such article is forbidden or restricted in sale in the country in which it was produced or from which it was exported, or (3) such article is adulterated, misbranded, or in violation of section 505 [the new drug approval requirement] or the importer . . . is in violation of [the foreign supplier verification program for foods in] section 805 . . . or (4) the recordkeeping requirements under section 204 of the FDA Food Safety Modernization Act (other than the requirements [for farms] under subsection (f) of such section) have not been complied with regarding such article, then such article shall be refused admission, except as provided in subsection (b) of this section [providing for reconditioning]. . . .

As the case immediately following illustrates, the FDA enjoys wide discretion in determining whether to grant or refuse admission of imported products pursuant to section 801(a).

Sugarman v. Forbragd
405 F.2d 1189 (9th Cir. 1968).

■ MERRILL, CIRCUIT JUDGE:

Appellant seeks by suit for injunction to review an order of the Food and Drug Administration excluding from import as adulterated certain damaged coffee beans. In entering its order the Food and Drug Administration was acting . . . pursuant to the terms of the Food, Drug and Cosmetic Act, 21 U.S.C. § 381(a) [FDCA § 801(a)]. The question presented is whether (absent arbitrary or capricious action which clearly is lacking here) such an order excluding material from import under § 381(a) is subject to judicial review. The District Court held that it was not. We agree.

Appellant contends that the Administrative Procedure Act applies to require agency notice and hearing and provide judicial review. By the terms of that Act, § 701(a)(2), it is not to apply where "agency action is committed to agency discretion by law." In our judgment that is the situation here; by 21 U.S.C. § 381(a) exclusion from import as there provided is committed to the discretion of the Secretary of Health, Education and Welfare.

We note that the prescribed procedure suggests final discretionary authority in the Secretary. His judgment must be accepted and acted upon by the Secretary of the Treasury. Further, the language of the section "if it appears" suggests discretion to be tested by a standard of arbitrariness rather than error. These suggestions in our view are compellingly borne out by the fact that the Secretary's judgment may be founded solely upon his examination of the material in question.[3] While the superficiality of tests and inspections or an arbitrary refusal to accept their results may be appropriate subjects for judicial review, a dispute as to what an examination has established or disclosed is more appropriately left to agency expertise.

The material in question was determined to be adulterated under the statutory definition for the reason that it was found to be "unfit for food." Appellant contends that to preclude arbitrary action the Secretary should promulgate regulations spelling out fitness for food. The [FDA] here determined from its examination that due to its damage the material in question was wholly lacking in recognized food values. A determination of unfitness under these facts cannot, in our judgment, be regarded as arbitrary even in absence of more explicit definition by regulation.

Judgment affirmed.

NOTES

1. *Similar Holdings.* See also *K&K Merchandise Group, Inc. v. Shalala,* 1996 U.S. Dist. LEXIS 4880 (S.D.N.Y. 1996) (citing *Sugarman* and noting "the wide discretionary power FDA enjoys to determine the factors regarding its decision to grant or refuse admission of imported goods"); *Goodwin v. United States,* 371 F. Supp. 433 (S.D. Cal. 1972) (FDA may bar the importation of all shellfish from the waters of a particular nation without determining that each shellfish is actually contaminated, because it is sufficient that the shellfish "appear" to have been grown under insanitary conditions).

---

[3]   While provision is made to supplement the Secretary's examination with a hearing, his decision need not be determined exclusively on the record of a formal hearing. The District Court held, and we agree, that to exclude imports, no formal hearing is required either by the Food, Drug and Cosmetic Act, 21 U.S.C. § 381(a), by the Administrative Procedure Act, 5 U.S.C. §§ 551–558, or by the Constitution, congressional power over foreign commerce being absolute.

2. *Nature of Hearing.* Although FDA is not required to give an importer a formal evidentiary hearing on the record before refusing admission to the owner's product, the agency is, in accordance with section 801(a), obligated to provide the owner notice and an opportunity to "introduce testimony." This procedure is set forth at 21 C.F.R. § 1.94(a), which states: "If it appears that the article may be subject to refusal of admission, the district director [having jurisdiction over the port of entry] shall give the owner or consignee a written notice to that effect, stating the reasons therefor. The notice shall specify a place and a period of time during which the owner or consignee shall have an opportunity to introduce testimony."

3. *Requirement of Adequate Notice.* In *L&M Industries, Inc. v. Kenter*, 458 F.2d 968 (2d Cir. 1972), FDA issued a Notice of Detention and Hearing informing an importer that its detained shipment of food was misbranded. After the hearing, FDA issued a Notice of Refusal, based on its conclusion that the shipment was adulterated (rather than misbranded). The Second Circuit held: "L&M was effectively denied the opportunity to be heard or to introduce testimony as to this central issue for it never received a Section 381 notice that adulteration was in question. Therefore, we find that the F.D.A. exceeded its statutory authority when it determined [the shipment] to be adulterated without first providing the appellant with the opportunity to be heard on that issue."

4. *A Double Standard?* FDA's ability to interdict imports of products into the United States—in effect to prevent commercial distribution before any charge of misbranding or adulteration is adjudicated—arguably permits discrimination against foreign products.

———

Despite the broad discretion that courts have generally granted FDA in implementing section 801(a), the U.S. District Court for the District of Columbia recently limited the agency's discretion to allow the importation of a violative product in a striking context—the importation of a drug used for lethal injections. The holding was particularly notable because the leading case establishing the principle of administrative enforcement discretion, *Heckler v. Chaney*, 470 U.S. 821 (1985) (excerpted *supra* p. 171) itself concerned a demand that the agency enforce the FD&C Act against a drug used in executions.

Cook v. FDA

2013 WL 3799987 (D.C. Cir. 2013)

■ GINSBURG, SENIOR CIRCUIT JUDGE:

A group of prisoners on death row ... sued the Food and Drug Administration ... for allowing state correctional departments to import sodium thiopental (thiopental), a misbranded and unapproved new drug used in lethal injection protocols, in violation of the Food, Drug, and Cosmetic Act, 21 U.S.C. § 381(a), and the Administrative Procedure Act, 5 U.S.C. § 706(2)(A). The district court entered summary judgment for the plaintiffs .... For the reasons that follow, we affirm the judgment of the district court ....

The FDCA ... regulates the importation of drugs. 21 U.S.C. § 381(a) provides:

> The Secretary of the Treasury shall deliver to the Secretary of [HHS], upon his request, samples of ... drugs ... being imported or offered for import into the United States. ... The Secretary of [HHS] shall furnish to the Secretary of the Treasury a list of establishments registered [with the FDA] ... and shall request that if any drugs ... manufactured, prepared, propagated, compounded, or processed in an establishment not so registered are imported or offered for import into the United States, samples of such drugs ... be delivered to the Secretary of [HHS]. ... If it appears from the examination of such samples or otherwise that ... such article is adulterated, misbranded, or [an unapproved new drug] ..., then such article shall be refused admission.

The duties of the Secretary of the Treasury under § 381(a) are administered by Customs and Border Protection, a unit of the Department of Homeland Security ....

Each of the plaintiffs in this action has been sentenced to death under the laws of Arizona, California, or Tennessee. At the time of the complaint those states and many others executed prisoners by injecting them with a sequence of three drugs: (1) sodium thiopental, which induces anesthesia; (2) pancuronium bromide, which causes paralysis; and (3) potassium chloride, which stops the heart. The administration of thiopental is critical because absent "a proper dose ... render[ing] the prisoner unconscious, there is a substantial, constitutionally unacceptable risk of suffocation from the administration of pancuronium bromide and pain from the injection of potassium chloride." Although thiopental has been used as an anesthetic since the 1930s, it is presently an unapproved new drug.

In 2009 the last domestic manufacturer of thiopental stopped making it. Several state departments of correction then began ordering thiopental from Dream Pharma Ltd., a wholesaler located in the United Kingdom. The thiopental sold by Dream was prepared and marketed by Archimedes Pharma UK, Ltd., which obtained unfinished thiopental from a facility in Austria; neither Dream nor Archimedes was registered with the FDA. The FDA therefore detained the first two shipments from Dream because, per § 381(a), the thiopental appeared to be a misbranded and unapproved new drug. After state officials explained the purpose of the imported thiopental, however, the FDA released the shipments. Several states, including Arizona, California, and Tennessee, thereafter imported thiopental from Dream without interference from the FDA.

In 2011 the FDA issued a policy statement concerning the importation of thiopental for the execution of state prisoners. The FDA stated that ... in "defer[ence] to law enforcement" agencies, henceforth it would exercise its "enforcement discretion not to review these shipments and allow processing through [Customs'] automated system for importation."

. . . .

The FDA's principal contention on appeal is that its "determination whether to invoke [§ 381(a)] and refuse admission to any particular drug offered for import is . . . not subject to judicial review.". . .

A. *Justiciability*

Judicial review under the APA is unavailable insofar as "agency action is committed to agency discretion by law." 5 U.S.C. § 701(a)(2). This "very narrow exception" to the general rule applies only "in those rare instances where 'statutes are drawn in such broad terms that in a given case there is no law to apply.' " *Citizens to Preserve Overton Park, Inc. v. Volpe*, 401 U.S. 402, 410 (1971). . . .

1. The relevance of *Heckler v. Chaney*

The leading Supreme Court case applying § 701(a)(2), *Heckler v. Chaney*, is factually quite similar to the present case. 470 U.S. 821 (1985). There, too, a group of death row inmates claimed the drugs used for lethal injection were misbranded and unapproved new drugs. . . . The Supreme Court held "an agency's decision not to take enforcement action should be presumed immune from judicial review under § 701(a)(2)." *Id.* at 832. Although "the presumption may be rebutted where the substantive statute has provided guidelines for the agency to follow in exercising its enforcement powers," *id.* at 832–33, the Court found no such guidance in the relevant provisions of the FDCA; for example, "the Act's general provision for enforcement, [21 U.S.C.] § 372, provides only that '[t]he Secretary is *authorized* to conduct examinations and investigations,' " *id.* at 835.** Similarly, the Court refused to read the section "stat[ing] baldly that any person who violates the Act's substantive prohibitions 'shall be imprisoned . . . or fined,' " as requiring "criminal prosecution of every violator of the Act." *Id.* (quoting 21 U.S.C. § 333).

Here the FDA argues *Chaney* applies straightforwardly to § 381(a), which provides that "[i]f it appears" an article offered for import violates a substantive prohibition of the FDCA, then "such article shall be refused admission." According to the agency, it has unreviewable discretion under both the antecedent and the consequent phrases: The antecedent "if it appears" implies the FDA may choose whether to "make a formal determination that a statutory obligation has been violated," and the consequent "shall be refused admission" provides a permissive sanction, as did the criminal provision in Chaney itself.

. . . [E]ven assuming the presumption against judicial review announced in *Chaney* does apply to the FDA's refusal to enforce § 381(a), that presumption is rebutted by the specific "legislative direction in the statutory scheme." *Chaney*, 470 U.S. at 833. Contrary to the FDA's interpretation, § 381(a) sets forth precisely when the agency must determine whether a drug offered for import appears to violate the FDCA, and what the agency must do with such a drug.

2. Textual analysis

Section 381(a) provides the FDA "shall furnish" to Customs a list of registered establishments and "shall request" from Customs samples of

---

** Chaney concerned the FDCA's enforcement provisions governing "the use of drugs in interstate commerce," 470 U.S. at 828, not the provision governing importation, § 381(a), at issue here.

drugs offered for import that are "manufactured, [etc.,] in an establishment not so registered." Customs, in turn, "shall deliver" to the FDA the requested samples. *Id.* "If it appears from the examination of such samples or otherwise" that a drug violates a substantive prohibition of the FDCA, then the drug "shall be refused admission." *Id.* The plaintiffs argue each of these directives is unambiguously binding . . . . We agree.

The plaintiffs begin by arguing simply that "the ordinary meaning of 'shall' is 'must.'" The case law provides ample support. Citing *Chaney*, the FDA objects that "in the enforcement context . . . [the word 'shall'] may not be properly read to curtail the agency's discretion." In *Chaney*, however, the word "shall" appeared in the consequent of a section providing for criminal sanctions: A violator "shall be imprisoned . . . or fined." 470 U.S. at 835 (quoting 21 U.S.C. § 333). The criminal statute in Chaney did not use "shall" in connection with the antecedent condition of prosecution; in fact, the Court emphasized that "[t]he Act's general provision for enforcement, [21 U.S.C.] § 372, provides only that '[t]he Secretary is *authorized* to conduct examinations and investigations;'" thus, "the Act charges the Secretary only with recommending prosecution; any criminal prosecutions must be instituted by the Attorney General." *Id.* The "enforcement" discretion held unreviewable in *Chaney*, therefore, was whether to recommend prosecution.... Here, by contrast, the word "shall" appears in both an antecedent ("shall request . . . samples") and the consequent ("shall be refused admission").

The plaintiffs further argue, and again we agree, that reading "shall be refused admission" as mandatory gives meaning to the exception to that command, "except as provided in subsection (b)." That subsection provides "[i]f it appears to the [FDA] that . . . an article . . . can, by relabeling or other action, be brought into compliance," then "final determination as to admission of such article may be deferred" while the owner posts a bond and takes remedial action. A permissive construction of "shall be refused admission" would render "the express exception . . . insignificant, if not wholly superfluous.". . .

The FDA next objects that even if the agency lacks discretion under the consequent "shall be refused admission," it at least has discretion under the antecedent condition "if it appears." . . . The FDA, however, omits the second half of the relevant clause: "If it appears from the examination of such samples or otherwise." § 381(a). The clear implication is the FDA must examine the samples that it must request and determine whether they appear to violate the FDCA. Indeed, it would make no sense for the Congress to mandate the collection, but not the examination, of samples of drugs made in an unregistered facility.

Of course, the clause "[i]f it appears from the examination of such samples or otherwise" may leave the FDA enforcement discretion in other respects. For example, the open-ended phrase "or otherwise" implies the FDA may examine drugs it is not obligated to sample, such as those made in a registered establishment. Indeed, the FDA interprets § 381(a) as giving it general authority to examine "drugs . . . offered for entry into the United States." The same phrase also implies the FDA may detect a violation through a method other than "examination," such as electronic screening of entry data that importers submit to Customs. Moreover, the phrase "if it appears" implies discretion in making the substantive determination whether a drug appears to violate the FDCA; a drug may appear to violate the FDCA to one examining officer but not to another.

We identify these oases of possible agency discretion not to suggest they are beyond judicial review, a question not before us, but rather to delineate the bounds of our interpretation. We do not say the FDA must sample and examine every article under its jurisdiction that is offered for import but only that it must sample and examine drugs "manufactured, [etc.,]" in an unregistered establishment. Nor do we say the FDA must find any type of drug "appears" to violate a substantive prohibition of the FDCA but only that, having found a drug apparently violates the Act, the FDA must "refuse[ ] [it] admission."

3. Policy considerations

Ordinarily, if a statute is "plain and unambiguous," as is the FDCA in relevant respects here, "our analysis ends with the text." We may, however, in rare instances depart from the plain text when "adherence to the plain text leads to an 'absurd' result." Although the FDA does not use the word "absurd," perhaps because the doctrine of avoiding absurd results is so rarely applied, the FDA does argue the practical consequences of reading § 381(a) as we do should give us pause.

The FDA argues the court should not read § 381(a) to require enforcement because the agency is better able to determine "how to most effectively allocate scarce resources."... Our reading of § 381(a), however, does not require the FDA to inspect 21 million articles offered for import; rather, it requires only the FDA examine the samples of articles that it is obligated to collect because they were "manufactured, [etc.,]" in an unregistered facility....

The FDA next argues it must have discretion not to enforce § 381(a) in order to combat domestic shortages of medically necessary drugs. According to a report cited by both parties, the FDA has allowed "controlled importation of similar products approved abroad but not approved in the United States in 5% of" the drug shortages it studied. FDA, A REVIEW OF FDA'S APPROACH TO MEDICAL PRODUCT SHORTAGES 4 (2011). By its own account, however, the FDA has ways short of allowing importation of inadmissible drugs to counteract a drug shortage, including: "Asking other firms to increase production (31%)," "Working with manufacturers" to mitigate quality problems (28%), and "Expediting review of regulatory submissions (26%)." *Id.* The FDA may exercise enforcement discretion to allow the domestic distribution of a misbranded or unapproved new drug, as the Supreme Court recognized in *Chaney*, 470 U.S. at 837, and in some cases may invoke its express statutory authority to permit the importation of an unapproved new drug. For example, the FDA may designate an unapproved foreign manufactured drug as an investigational new drug (IND), thereby allowing its lawful importation. 21 C.F.R. § 314.410(a)(1)(ii). In any event, even if reading § 381(a) by its terms, as we do, deprives the FDA of one possible response to five percent of all drug shortages, that is hardly an absurd result.

In an effort to bolster its drug shortage argument, the FDA points to two provisions in a 2012 statute that it says reveal the Congress's "understanding that FDA already has authority to exercise enforcement discretion." 21 U.S.C. § 356d(c) instructs the Secretary of HHS to "evaluate the risks associated with the impact" of a drug shortage before taking an enforcement action that "could reasonably cause or exacerbate a shortage," and § 356c–1(a)(5) directs the Secretary to issue an annual report listing, among other things, "instances in which the [FDA] exercised regulatory flexibility and discretion to prevent or alleviate a drug shortage." The Congress enacting these directives may have implicitly—and correctly—assumed the FDA already had some discretion in combating a drug shortage, but the agency gives us no reason to think the Congress was referring to the discretion to ignore § 381(a) and not to the discretion to allow the domestic distribution of a violative drug or to admit an unapproved foreign manufactured drug as an IND.

Finally, the FDA argues it must have discretion to ignore § 381(a) in order to allow the "importation of drugs that are clearly for personal use." As evidence that the Congress is aware of and agrees with this view, the FDA points to a 2003 statute, not yet in effect, directing the Secretary of HHS to "exercise discretion to permit individuals to make . . . importations" of prescription drugs for personal use. 21 U.S.C. § 384(j)(1)(B). The FDA, however, conveniently overlooks the very next subsection, which effectuates the statute by authorizing the Secretary to grant individual waivers to import prescription drugs. § 384(j)(2). The Congress would have had no reason to grant the FDA explicit waiver authority if, as the FDA argues, the agency was already authorized not to enforce § 381(a).

* * *

In sum . . . [b]ecause [the requirements of 21 U.S.C. § 381(a)] are clear statutory "guidelines for the agency to follow in exercising its enforcement powers," *Chaney*, 470 U.S. at 833, the FDA's compliance with § 381(a) is subject to judicial review under the standards of the APA.

B. The APA on the Merits

From the foregoing analysis it follows apodictically that the FDA's policy of admitting foreign manufactured thiopental destined for state correctional facilities, as well as the several individual admissions of such shipments challenged by the plaintiffs, were "not in accordance with law." 5 U.S.C. § 706(2)(A). The FDA's policy was not in accordance with law because § 381(a) requires the agency to sample and examine for violations any drug offered for import that has been prepared in an unregistered facility; as the FDA acknowledges, the preparer of the finished thiopental identified in this case, Archimedes Pharma UK, Ltd., is not registered with the FDA. The FDA's individual admissions of thiopental shipments were not in accordance with law because § 381(a) requires the FDA to refuse admission to any drug that appears to violate the substantive prohibitions of the FDCA, and the FDA conceded before the district court that the thiopental in these shipments "clearly 'appears' to be an unapproved new drug."

. . . [W]e affirm the judgment of the district court. . . .

NOTES

1. *Legal Challenges to FDA Importation Procedures.* Particular procedures under which FDA has regulated importation have been sharply questioned in several cases. In *Caribbean Produce Exchange, Inc. v. Secretary of HHS*, Food Drug Cosm. L. Rep. (CCH) ¶ 38,100 & ¶ 38,110 (D.P.R. 1988), *rev'd*, 893 F.2d 3 (1st Cir. 1989), the District Court enjoined the FDA detention procedure for imported garlic because its requirements had not been established through rulemaking. The Court of Appeals, however, remanded the case for an evidentiary hearing. In *Bellarno International Ltd. v. FDA*, 678 F. Supp. 410 (E.D.N.Y. 1988), the court invalidated an FDA "import alert" that provided for automatic detention of drugs that had been exported and then reimported, because of the agency's failure to engage in notice-and-comment rulemaking. In *United States v. Articles of Drugs Consisting of 203 Paper Bags*, 634 F. Supp. 435 (N.D. Ill. 1985), *vacated*, 818 F.2d 569 (7th Cir. 1987), the District Court allowed reexportation of illegal animal drugs, over FDA's protest, because the agency had failed to establish its requirements for imported drugs through rulemaking. The Court of Appeals vacated this decision as moot after the drugs had been reexported.

2. *Coordination with Customs Service.* In a Memorandum of Understanding (MOU) between the Customs Service and FDA, published in 44 Fed. Reg. 53577 (Sept. 14, 1979), FDA was given the authority under section 801 of the FD&C Act to collect samples at ports, issue notices of sampling, and issue notices of refusal of admission. The MOU stated that the FDA Commissioner would designate certain FDA officers as Customs Officers with the responsibility for performing these functions.

The Bioterrorism Act of 2002 added section 801(m) to the FD&C Act, requiring food importers to give FDA prior notice of each article of imported food. FDA's implementing regulations, which went into effect in 2003, require this notice to be submitted electronically and to identify, among other things, the article, the manufacturer or grower of the article, and the country of origin. 21 C.F.R. 1.281 (implementing section 801(m)). Even before 2003, importers and brokers provided much of this information to the Customs Service, but the Bioterrorism Act mandates notice directly to FDA so it can determine whether to inspect the imported food. The introduction of this requirement impelled FDA and Customs and Border Protection to increase their level of cooperation even further. The two agencies entered an MOU allowing FDA to commission all CBP officers it deems necessary to enforce section 801(m) and the implementing regulations. Memorandum of Understanding Between CBP and FDA (Dec. 3, 2003).

2. RECONDITIONING, DESTROYING, OR REEXPORTING GOODS REFUSED ADMISSION

Section 801(a) of the FD&C Act provides:

The Secretary of [Homeland Security] shall cause the destruction of any . . . article refused admission unless such article is exported, under regulations prescribed by the Secretary of [Homeland

Security], within ninety days of the date of notice of such refusal or within such additional time as may be permitted pursuant to such regulations, except that the Secretary of Health and Human Services may destroy, without the opportunity for export, any drug refused admission under this section, if such drug is valued at an amount that is $2,500 or less (or such higher amount as the Secretary of [Homeland Security] may set by regulation . . .) and was not brought into compliance as described under subsection (b) [providing for reconditioning]."

Section 801(b) creates an alternative mechanism by which FDA may defer its final determination as to the admission of a violative article and allow the importer to attempt to correct the problem ("reconditioning"):

If it appears to the Secretary of Health and Human Services that (1) [an article that appears to be adulterated, misbranded, or in violation of the Act's new drug approval requirements or in violation of the foreign supplier verification program for foods] can, by relabeling or other action, be brought into compliance with the Act or rendered other than a food, drug, device, or cosmetic, or (2) with respect to [a nonprescription drug or a dietary supplement, the manufacturer, packer, or distributor] can take action that would assure . . . compliance with [serious adverse event reporting requirements], final determination as to admission of such article may be deferred and, upon filing of timely written application by the owner or consignee and the execution by him of a bond . . ., the Secretary may, in accordance with regulations, authorize the applicant . . . to perform such relabeling or other action specified in such authorization (including destruction or export of rejected articles or portions thereof, as may be specified in the Secretary's authorization).

As the following case shows, FDA's discretion under section 801(a) and (b) is not unlimited.

Carl Borchsenius Co. v. Gardner

282 F. Supp. 396 (E.D. La. 1968).

■ CASSIBRY, DISTRICT JUDGE:

The shipment of 5,000 bags of coffee, weighing 665,000 pounds with an estimated invoice value of $227,000, arrived at the Port of New Orleans from Paranagua, Brazil aboard the Mario D'Almeida on November 21, 1967. . . .

A wharf examination of the shipment by a United States Food and Drug Inspector on December 1 disclosed damp, moldy coffee in four of the six samples taken in the inspection. Approximately 1,500 bags were wet and some contained moldy coffee. The entire shipment of 5,000 bags was detained by the Food and Drug Administration. . . .

On December 1, plaintiff filed an application for authorization pursuant to 21 U.S.C. § 381(b) to attempt to bring the 5,000 bags of coffee into compliance with the Act by the procedure of "skimming the coffee to remove molded beans" and "drying the coffee out to remove wet beans." This authorization was given on December 4. . . .

Of the 5,000 bags, examination showed 2,325 to be sound, and upon request of plaintiff's representatives these bags were released under a partial release of the shipment on December 8. . . . [T]he Import Inspector's examination showed on December 21 that, of the 2,789 bags received for reconditioning, 1,730 bags were made sound and thus brought into compliance with the law, 270 bags were poor skims, 231 bags were sweepings, and 1,053 bags were too poor to skim due to mold.

On December 26, the defendant C. C. Freeman, Acting Director of the Food and Drug Administration for this District, advised the plaintiff's representative by letter that a "Release Notice" on the 1,730 bags made sound would be issued upon receipt of proof of destruction of the remaining 270 bags of poor skims, 231 bags of sweepings and 1,053 bags of moldy coffee in original bags. The plaintiff had no objection to destruction of the 270 bags of poor skims and the 231 bags of sweepings, but its representative requested on January 2, 1968 that the 1,730 bags of "made sound" coffee be released for import and that it be allowed to burnish, rebag and export the 1,053 bags which had not been reconditioned. The request to burnish, rebag and export was denied by Acting Director Freeman by letter of January 3. . . .

The only issue before the Court is whether the defendants acted within the limits of their statutory authority in this case, and to resolve that issue the Court must determine whether the defendants have the discretion under 21 U.S.C. § 381(b) to require destruction of articles offered for import, which are rejected because they cannot be brought into compliance with the Act, without giving the applicant an opportunity to export the rejected articles. . . .

The defendants agree that the owner or consignee could choose to export articles refused admission under the language in subsection (a) that "The Secretary of the Treasury shall *cause the destruction of any such article refused admission unless such article is exported*, . . .," and they agree that had the plaintiff in this case not chosen to attempt to bring the coffee into compliance under subsection (b), it would have had the choice of exporting the entire shipment of 5,000 bags. (Italics here and elsewhere mine). They argue that such a choice is not available to an owner or consignee as to rejected articles from the attempt at compliance under the language of subsection (b) that "the Secretary of Health, Education and Welfare may, in accordance with regulations authorize the applicant to perform such relabeling or other action specified in such authorization (*including destruction or export of rejected articles or portions thereof*, as may be specified in the Secretary's authorization)," and that the rejected articles may be ordered destroyed at their discretion.

This contention of defendants as to their discretion under 381(b) is not only at variance with the policy set by Congress as to the disposition of articles rejected for admission set out in 381(a), but is at variance with a continuing policy of Congress as to the disposition of articles refused admission for import. . . .

There is nothing in 381(b) to indicate that the taking advantage of the opportunity to bring articles into compliance with standards for import makes those rejected from the compliance operation products involved in illegal import activity. Interpreting that statute as giving administrative discretion to destroy rejected articles would be a radical departure from the policy of Congress on this matter, and such a major change in policy could hardly be expected to appear as a parenthetical insertion in a statute. I find nothing from policy considerations to support the argument of defendants that Congress intended when a consignee elects to avail himself of the compliance provisions of 381(b) to deprive him of the choice under 381(a) to export rejected articles. From this viewpoint the contention of plaintiff that 381(a) and (b) should be read together, and that the parenthetical phrase regarding disposition of rejecting articles in (b) was not intended to depart from the disposition provision of (a) and deprive the consignee of the choice of export is logical and persuasive. . . .

The Court concludes that the defendants do not have the discretion under 381(b) to require the destruction of articles offered for import, which are rejected because they cannot be brought into compliance with the Act, without giving the applicant an opportunity to export the rejected articles upon compliance with the applicable statutes; therefore, the action in this case in refusing to grant the request for permission to export the rejected coffee, and in requiring its destruction as a condition of release of the sound coffee, was beyond their statutory authority. Judgment is rendered in accordance with these views granting to plaintiff the relief prayed for.

3.   REFUSAL OF ADMISSION COMPARED TO SEIZURE

An imported article that is adulterated, misbranded, or unapproved might be detained by the government under section 801 or seized by the government under section 304. Which remedy the government pursues has important practical implications for the importer or consignee. First of all, section 801 creates a purely administrative procedure, whereas section 304 requires the United States to seek a condemnation order from a federal district court. Second, the two procedures can potentially lead to different ultimate dispositions of the goods in question. Under either section, an importer may be given an opportunity to bring the goods into compliance with the FD&C Act. FD&C Act 304(d)(1), 801(b). Suppose, however, that the importer is not provided such an opportunity to cure, or is unable to do so. As discussed above, section 801 requires U.S. Customs and Border Protection to permit the reexportation of the goods, as an alternative to their destruction. By contrast, under section 304(d)(1), as revised in 1997, a court may permit exportation of a seized and condemned imported good only if the person seeking to export it can "establish that the article was intended for export at the time the article entered commerce." The regulation of "import for export" will be explored in more detail *infra* at p. 1483. For purposes of the current discussion, the important thing to recognize is that, for goods imported for sale in the United States, reexportation is often an option under section 801 but never an option under section 304.

United States v. Food, 2,998 Cases

64 F.3d 984 (5th Cir. 1995).

■ E. GRADY JOLLY, CIRCUIT JUDGE:

This appeal presents complex, difficult, and close questions. It is, however, a case that is unlikely to arouse widespread passion. . . .

In October 1989, the Food and Drug Administration issued an "import alert"[2] for all canned mushrooms processed in China in response to a food-borne illness caused by staphylococcal enterotoxin found in canned mushrooms produced in nine China factories. Appellee First Phoenix Group Limited, Inc., an importer of food products, purchased several orders of canned mushrooms supposedly packaged at Hwa Chen Industrial Corporation in Taiwan. In late spring 1992, First Phoenix attempted to enter two shipments of mushrooms—3,000 cases and 6,000 cases—into the United States. . . . The United States Customs Service conditionally released these mushrooms under bond pending review by the FDA. . . .

On July 10, 1992, the FDA issued a second import alert advising its field offices to detain shipments of canned mushrooms from specified Taiwanese manufactures, including Hwa Chen. The FDA issued this import alert because mushrooms labelled [sic] as packaged and produced from these specified manufacturers actually were processed and packaged in an unknown factory in China. Because of this import alert, the FDA issued Notices of Detention and Hearing for the 3,000–case shipment on July 29, and for the 6,000–case shipment on December 14. In these notices, the FDA indicated that it was acting under its power in § 381(a) of the Federal Food, Drug, and Cosmetic Act. . . . FDA . . . concluded that an unknown factory in China used Hwa Chen's can codes in a deliberate attempt to circumvent the broad import alert on canned mushrooms originating in China. The FDA then advised First Phoenix that it would likely refuse admission of the mushrooms and allow reexport only under very strict conditions. The FDA, however, issued no formal notice of refusal of admission. The FDA then conducted additional testing of a separate lot of mushrooms ostensibly packaged at Hwa Chen and shipped into the United States by First Phoenix, but not at issue in this appeal. Based on staphyloccal enterotoxin found in these mushrooms, the FDA informed First Phoenix of its decision to destroy the mushrooms, rather than allow reexport. Thus, the FDA decided to proceed under the authority provided in 21 U.S.C. § 334, instead of proceeding under 21 U.S.C. § 381.

Accordingly, on November 3, 1993, the government filed a complaint in the United States District Court for the Eastern District of Louisiana seeking seizure and condemnation of both [the 3,000–case and 6,000–case] shipments of mushrooms as adulterated and misbranded goods in interstate commerce under its authority in 21 U.S.C. § 334(a) of the FDCA. Under the district court's warrant for the arrest of both shipments, the United States Marshals Service seized and attached the shipments at the New Orleans warehouse where they

---

[2] An import alert advises FDA field offices of ongoing problems with a specific product offered for import and suggests appropriate action, such as detention for inspection and sampling.

were stored upon entry into New Orleans and continue to be held at the present time. On April 19, 1994, the district court granted summary judgment in favor of First Phoenix and dismissed the government's case. The district court held that the mushrooms had never entered interstate commerce as required for an action under § 334(a) because they had continually remained under Customs Service transit bonds. The district court thus determined that the Customs Service remained in control of the mushrooms since their import into the United States. Finally, the court concluded that § 381(a) was the government's exclusive authority with respect to the mushrooms and gave First Phoenix the opportunity to reexport the two shipments before being destroyed by the FDA. . . .

On appeal, the government argues that because the mushroom shipments fall within the statutory definition of "interstate commerce," it had the authority to bring a § 334 seizure and condemnation action in the district court. The government further contends that its authority to act under this statute is unaffected by the fact that the administrative remedy in § 381 is also available to it in this case. . . .

. . . We hold that the interstate commerce requirement has been satisfied in this case and that goods seized at the port of entry may be the proper subject of an action under § 334. We therefore reverse the judgment of the district court and remand for further proceedings not inconsistent with this opinion.

We first examine whether the mushrooms in this case were introduced into "interstate commerce," as required to initiate a seizure and condemnation action under § 334. . . . [T]o initiate an action for seizure and condemnation, the FDA must prove only that the goods have been introduced into interstate commerce, notwithstanding the fact that the goods may be removed at some later time from interstate commerce. The FDCA expansively defines interstate commerce as "commerce between any State or Territory and any place outside thereof." 21 U.S.C. § 321(b). Here, each shipment was shipped from a place outside the United States—Taiwan—and entered the United States at Savannah, Georgia, and Long Beach, California, respectively, where they arrived and were unloaded. There is some suggestion, however, that these mushrooms may have been effectively detained at sea by the import alert and thus were removed from the stream of commerce before they actually entered the United States. If, however, goods are destined for sale in a state other than the place from which they are shipped, then goods are in "interstate commerce" without the necessity of physically crossing a state boundary. Thus, we conclude that the mushrooms in this case undoubtedly constituted an interstate shipment from the moment they left Taiwan.

The question remaining is whether these goods, which were never released for sale in the United States from the Customs Service, were also in "commerce," as required by § 321(b). First Phoenix argues that these mushrooms could not possibly be in commerce because from the moment the goods were placed on alert, even before they arrived in the United States, and at all times thereafter, sale of these goods in the United States was prohibited by the FDA. First Phoenix additionally argues that because the mushrooms were held under Customs Service bonds[8] since arriving in the United States, they were never introduced into interstate commerce as required in § 334 for a condemnation action. First Phoenix attempts to place an impossibly narrow construction on a very broad statute. Regardless of the government's impediments to the sale of these goods once they reached the United States, these goods nevertheless had been shipped to the United States for the express purpose of sale when they left Taiwan. . . . In sum, we hold that these mushrooms had been introduced into interstate commerce at the time they were detained by the Customs Service, given the expansive and unrestricted definition of § 321(b).

Having determined that the mushrooms had been introduced into interstate commerce, it is plain on the face of the statute that § 334 is a judicial remedy available to the FDA in this case. We now must address, however, First Phoenix's argument that Congress intended § 334 to apply only to seizures of goods that have been released from the Customs Service. In short, First Phoenix argues that only the administrative procedures under § 381 may be invoked by the FDA when the goods are seized at the port of entry and not yet admitted into the United States. We now turn to consider this question of whether § 334 and § 381 create two mutually exclusive statutory remedies for goods under the FDCA.

As earlier discussed, § 334(a) is a judicial remedy available to the FDA allowing it to seize and condemn any goods that have been introduced into or are already in interstate commerce or after shipment is in interstate commerce, but if the FDA chooses to proceed under this statute it must prove in a court of law by a preponderance of the evidence that the goods are indeed adulterated or misbranded. Section 381, on the other hand, is purely an administrative procedure, which allows a quick and efficient means of protecting the American public from unhealthy or mislabeled imported goods. . . .

Clearly no provision of § 381 expressly restricts the authority of the FDA from proceeding judicially under § 334 when it seizes and holds goods at the port of entry in the United States.[10] If goods are, in point of time, both "in interstate commerce" [§ 334] and "being imported or offered for import into the United States," [§ 381] as the mushrooms here, the plain words of the statutes permit the government the option of proceeding under either § 334 or § 381.[11] . . .

---

[8] A Customs Service bond includes any bond required under Customs laws or regulations in order to perform a particular Customs activity. 19 C.F.R. § 113.61 (1994). Under 19 U.S.C. § 1553, "any merchandise, other than . . . merchandise the importation of which is prohibited, . . . may be entered for transportation in bond through the United States by a bonded carrier without appraisement or the payment of duties." Here, both shipments were transported under bond and to New Orleans based on § 1553. These bonds were obtained to secure duties, taxes, and other charges due on the shipments of the imported mushrooms. *See* 19 C.F.R. § 113.62 illust. a (requiring bond securing duties, taxes, and charges imposed or estimated to be due if merchandise is released from Customs custody).

[10] We point out that § 381 undoubtedly only applies to goods detained at the port of entry and any seizure of imported goods after release by the Customs Service must submit to judicial proceedings under § 334. The question here is whether these statutes provide overlapping remedies for goods seized at the port of entry so that the government, at that point, may choose to proceed under either § 334 or § 381.

[11] First Phoenix argues that the express language of § 381 mandates that adulterated goods being imported or offered for import, as here, shall be refused admission. Once admission is refused, First Phoenix argues, § 381 grants the importer an unqualified right to

We therefore hold that the plain language of § 334 permits the FDA to initiate a seizure and condemnation action, such as the one before us, when goods are seized at the port of entry. The district court is REVERSED and the case REMANDED for further proceedings not inconsistent with this opinion.

NOTES

1. *Reexportation of Imported Goods Seized Under Section 304.* FD&C Act 304(d)(1) authorizes courts, at their discretion, to permit reexportation of seized and condemned imported articles under certain conditions, as an alternative to their destruction or reconditioning. A claimant seeking to reexport condemned imported goods must show that the adulteration, misbranding, or violation did not occur after importation; that it had no reason to believe that the articles were adulterated, misbranded, or in violation before they were released from customs custody; and that it can and will satisfy the requirements in section 801(e), applicable to exported goods generally. Section 304(d)(1) explicitly forbids reexportation with regard to certain types of adulteration and misbranding that render an article dangerous to health. *See, e.g., United States v. 76,552 Pounds of Frog Legs*, 423 F. Supp. 329 (S.D. Tex. 1976) (reexportation not allowed because claimant offered part of shipment for sale in domestic commerce in violation of section 801(e)(1)(D) and because the food was injurious to health).

Despite these conditions, courts could, prior to 1997, permit reexportation of a wide variety of seized imported goods that could not legally have been sold in the United States. *E.g., United States v. Articles of Drug . . . 203 Paper Bags*, 634 F. Supp. 435 (N.D. Ill. 1985) (permitting reexportation of adulterated and misbranded animal drugs). However, in the FDA Modernization Act of 1997 Congress added a further requirement that severely reduced the availability of section 304(d)(1) reexportation, namely, that the person seeking to reexport must "establish that the article was intended for export at the time the article entered commerce." Section 304 reexportation is now thus restricted to goods "imported for export." Perhaps the last ever application of the earlier, broader version of the reexportation provision was a 1998 district court order permitting the claimant to reexport three lots of adulterated frozen shrimp that were originally imported in 1997, before the new version of 304(d)(1) went into effect. The court refused to apply the amendment retroactively. *United States v. 302 Cases . . . Frozen Shrimp*, 25 F. Supp. 2d 1358 (M.D. Fla. 1998).

---

reexport the goods within ninety days of this refusal. First Phoenix contends, and the district court agreed, that allowing the FDA the option of proceeding under § 334 or § 381 when the imported goods meet the prerequisites of both would emasculate its unqualified right granted by § 381 to reexport goods within ninety days of refusal of admission.

We acknowledge that this plain language projects a forceful argument that importers have an unequivocal right to a notice of refusal of admission. And it is true that if the FDA proceeds under § 334, as they have in this case, the importer does not receive a notice of refusal of admission and the concomitant right to reexport. Nevertheless, we are convinced that the more compelling view of the statutory scheme, for reasons we express in this opinion, is that the FDA has an option to proceed under either statute with respect to goods detained at the port of entry, and if the government chooses to proceed under § 334, the right to a notice of refusal and opportunity to reexport provided in § 381 simply is inoperative.

2. *FDA Guidance.* FDA has published a draft guidance to help importers establish practices and procedures to ensure that the products they import comply with U.S. safety and security requirements. DRAFT GUIDANCE FOR INDUSTRY: GOOD IMPORTER PRACTICES (Jan. 2009).

3. *GAO Oversight.* The Government Accountability Office has been a frequent critic of FDA's enforcement against imported products. *See, e.g.,* FOOD SAFETY: FEDERAL EFFORTS TO ENSURE THE SAFETY OF IMPORTED FOODS ARE INCONSISTENT AND UNRELIABLE, No. RCED–98–103 (Apr. 30, 1998); PRESCRIPTION DRUGS: ENHANCED EFFORTS AND BETTER AGENCY COORDINATION NEEDED TO ADDRESS ILLEGAL IMPORTATION, No. GAO–06–175T (Dec. 13, 2005); FOOD AND DRUG ADMINISTRATION: OVERSEAS OFFICES HAVE TAKEN STEPS TO HELP ENSURE IMPORT SAFETY, BUT MORE LONG–TERM PLANNING IS NEEDED, No. GAO–10–960 (Sept. 30, 2010).

4. *Commentary. See generally* F. K. Killingsworth, *Import Control Under Federal Laws,* 2 FOOD DRUG COSM. L.Q. 498 (1947), 5 FOOD DRUG COSM. L.J. 205 (1950), and 8 FOOD DRUG COSM. L.J. 117 (1953); D. Joe Smith Jr., *Detention and Seizure of Imports by the Food and Drug Administration,* 33 FOOD DRUG COSM. L.J. 726 (1978); Paul M. Hyman, *Legal Overview of FDA Authority over Imports,* 49 FOOD & DRUG L.J. 525 (1994); Christine M. Humphrey, *The Food and Drug Administration's Import Alerts Appear to Be "Misbranded",* 58 FOOD & DRUG L.J. 595 (2003).

4.   IMPORTATION OF FOOD

An estimated fifteen percent of the U.S. food supply is imported, including fifty percent of fresh fruits, twenty percent of fresh vegetables, and eighty percent of seafood. According to the U.S. Government Accountability Office (GAO), imported food as a percentage of all food consumed in the United States rose from about nine percent to over sixteen percent between 2000 and 2011. Recognizing this increasing globalization of our food supply and the insufficiency of relying on inspections at ports of entry to assure the safety of imported food, Congress enacted Title III of the FDA Food Safety Modernization Act (FSMA), Pub. L. No. 111–353 (2011). FSMA is a sweeping reform of U.S. food safety laws, representing a shift from a reaction-based food safety system to a prevention-based food regulatory regime. The food import provisions contained in Title III of the FSMA provide FDA with new tools to ensure that imported food meets the same standards as domestic food. They aim to assure food import safety by moving controls upstream in the supply chain, closer to the source of the food.

FSMA grants five major new import authorities to the FDA. First, under a new section 805 of the FD&C Act, food importers are required to verify that their foreign suppliers have sufficient risk-based preventive controls in place to assure the safety of their food. FD&C Act 805. This verification activity of an importer is called a foreign supplier verification program (FSVP). Specifically, the importer must verify that the food it imports has been produced in compliance with section 418 HACCP requirements and section 419 standards for produce safety. *Id.* 805(a)(1)(A). It must also verify that the food is not adulterated and is labeled for the presence of major food allergens in accordance with section 403(w). *Id.* 805(a)(1)(A). An importer must keep records related to a FSVP for two years and be made available promptly to the FDA on request. *Id.* 805(d). Section 805(g) requires the FDA to maintain a current list of participating importers on its website.

Second, new section 806 sets up a "voluntary qualified importer program" (VQIP). This program offers expedited review and importation of food by the participating importer from a foreign facility with a "facility certification." FD&C Act 806(a)(1). To participate in the program, an importer must submit a notice and application to FDA. *Id.* 806(c). In reviewing the application, the agency must consider the risk of the food to be imported. *Id.* 806(d). Section 806(d) lists several risk factors that must be considered, including (1) the known safety risks of the food to be imported; (2) the compliance history of the foreign supplier used by the importer; (3) the capability of the regulatory system of the country of export to ensure compliance with U.S. food safety standards; (4) compliance of the importer with section 805 foreign supplier verification program; (5) the importer's recordkeeping, testing, inspection, auditing and other practices; (6) potential risk for intentional adulteration of the food; and (7) any other factor that the Secretary determines appropriate. If a qualified importer is later found not to be in compliance with the eligibility criteria, the qualified importer status will be revoked. § 806(e). Section 806(e) also requires the Secretary to reevaluate the qualified status of any importer at least every three years.

Third, the FSMA authorizes the FDA to require certification for the import of particular high-risk food under a new subsection 801(q). This certification may be shipment-specific, facility-specific, or in some other form. 801(q)(1). It may be provided by an agency of the country of origin designated by FDA or by a third-party auditor accredited pursuant to section 808 (discussed in the next paragraph). A determination by FDA that an article of food is required to have such certification must be based on the risk of the imported food. *Id.* 801(q)(2). Factors to be considered are (1) the known safety risks associated with the food; (2) the known food safety risks associated with the country, territory, or region of origin of the food; (3) a finding by the agency, supported by scientific risk-based evidence, that the food safety system of the food's country of origin is inadequate to ensure that the food is as safe as a similar article of food manufactured, processed, packed, or held in the United States; and (4) information submitted to FDA by a nation previously determined to have an inadequate food safety system about improvements in the system. *Id.*

Fourth, a new section 808 of the FD&C Act establishes a system for accrediting third-party auditors of foreign food facilities. Section 808(b) requires FDA to implement a system for the recognition of accreditation bodies that accredit third-party auditors. The statute, however, authorizes the agency to directly accredit third-party auditors if no accreditation body has been recognized by January 4, 2013. *Id.* 808(b)(1)(A)(ii). Third-party auditors may be a foreign government, an agency of a foreign government, a foreign cooperative, or any other third party. *Id.* 808(a)(3). To be accredited, a third-party auditor must meet model accreditation standards as developed by the agency. *Id.* 808(b)(2). Foreign governments and foreign cooperatives seeking accreditation must also satisfy additional requirements. *Id.* 808(c)(1).

Accredited third-party auditors may conduct consultative and regulatory audits on behalf of the FDA. FD&C Act 808(c)(4)(B). A "consultative audit" is a compliance investigation of a foreign facility for internal purposes only. *Id.* 808(a)(5). A regulatory audit, by contrast, is a compliance investigation for purposes of issuing a "facility certification" under section 806(a) or a "food certification" pursuant to section 801(q). *Id.* 808(a)(7), (c)(2). If, at any time during an audit, an accredited third-party auditor discovers a condition that could cause or contribute to a serious risk to public health, the auditor must immediately notify the Secretary. *Id.* 808(c)(4)(A).

Fifth, under a new section 807, the FDA has the authority to refuse admission of a food from a foreign facility if a U.S. or other designated inspector has been denied entry into the foreign facility. FD&C Act 807(b).

In addition to these five key new import authorities, FSMA contains other significant requirements and mandates regarding FDA's regulation of imported food. Section 308 of FSMA requires the Secretary to establish FDA offices in foreign countries. Pub. L. No. 111–353, § 308. The purpose of these offices is "to provide assistance to appropriate governmental entities of such countries with respect to measures to provide for the safety of articles of food and other products regulated by the [FDA] . . ., including by directly conducting risk-based inspections of such articles and supporting such inspections by such governmental entity." *Id.* FSMA further directs the FDA to help build the capacity of foreign governments with respect to food safety. Pub. L. No. 111–353, § 305.

FSMA also updates a requirement to provide prior notice of imported food pursuant to section 801(m), which was added by the Bioterrorism Act of 2002. Pub. L. No. 111–353, § 304(a). Section 801(m)(1) requires food importers to give FDA prior notice of each article of food imported or offered for import into the United States. In addition to the previously required information, FSMA adds that the notice must identify "any country to which the article has been refused entry." Pub. L. No. 111–353, § 304(a). *See* GUIDANCE FOR INDUSTRY: ENFORCEMENT POLICY CONCERNING CERTAIN PRIOR NOTICE REQUIREMENTS (June 2011); COMPLIANCE POLICY GUIDE: SEC. 110.310 PRIOR NOTICE OF IMPORTED FOOD UNDER THE PUBLIC HEALTH SECURITY AND BIOTERRORISM PREPAREDNESS AND RESPONSE ACT OF 2002 (May 2009).

Lastly, the FSMA requires the Secretary to develop and implement a strategy to better identify smuggled food and to prevent entry of such food into the United States, in coordination with the Secretary of Homeland Security. Pub. L. No. 111–353, § 309(a).

NOTES

1. *International Food Safety Capacity–Building Plan.* Under section 305 of FSMA, FDA must "develop a comprehensive plan to expand the technical, scientific, and regulatory food safety capacity of foreign governments [that export to the United States], and their respective food industries." Pub. L. No. 111–353, § 305. In February 2013, the FDA issued its International Food Safety Capacity–Building Plan. The plan sets forth

the agency's strategic framework for enhancing the food safety capacities of foreign governments and manufacturers. *See* FDA, FDA's INTERNATIONAL FOOD SAFETY CAPACITY–BUILDING PLAN: FOOD SAFETY MODERNIZATION ACT SECTION 305 (Feb. 2013).

2. *FDA's Foreign Offices and Posts.* The FDA began establishing foreign posts and offices in late 2008. It installed its first foreign post in Beijing, China. As of March 2013, the FDA has foreign offices in China, India, Costa Rica, Jordan, South Africa, Belgium, England, and Italy. Their primary purpose is to engage foreign counterpart regulatory authorities and industries to help prevent unsafe products from reaching the United States and to gather information for better decision making at ports of entry. Specifically, FDA staff overseas aims to build stronger relationships with foreign counterpart regulatory authorities by holding regular meetings, improving information exchanges, and engaging in technical cooperation and capacity building. Foreign FDA staff also conducts training workshops on FDA's regulatory policies and scans the environment for any adverse conditions and events in a country that might affect the safety and quality of FDA-regulated products designated for the United States. FDA investigators abroad conduct inspections and investigations of high-risk facilities and high-risk products. *See* FDA, REPORT TO CONGRESS ON THE FDA FOREIGN OFFICES (Feb. 2012).

5. IMPORTATION OF PRESCRIPTION DRUGS AND DEVICES

a. COMMERCIAL IMPORTATION

Because of the significant price differential, it became common in the early 2000s to import from Canada, for sale in the United States, cheaper unapproved versions of FDA-approved drugs.

Warning Letter From David J. Horowitz, Dir., CDER Office of Compliance, to Harry Lee Jones, Store Manager, Rx Depot, Inc.

March 21, 2003.

Dear Mr. Jones:

The Food and Drug Administration (FDA) has learned that you are assisting United States consumers in obtaining prescription drugs from Canada. Specifically, you are running a storefront operation that sends U.S. prescriptions, credit card information, and paperwork (including a "Patient Profile" and "Release & Limited Power of Attorney") to a Canadian pharmacy. According to information provided by you and your store, a prescription is then obtained from a medical doctor in Canada, and Canadian drugs are shipped by a pharmacy in the Canadian province of Manitoba directly to the U.S. consumer. As discussed in greater detail below, your actions violate the Federal Food, Drug and Cosmetic Act. Your actions also present a significant risk to public health, and you mislead the public about the safety of the drugs obtained through Rx Depot.

Legal Violations

Your actions violate the FD&C Act because virtually every shipment of prescription drugs from Canadian pharmacies to consumers in the U.S. violates the Act. Even if a prescription drug is approved in the U.S., if the drug is also originally manufactured in the U.S., it is a violation of the Act for anyone other than the U.S. manufacturer to import the drug into the United States (21 U.S.C. 381(d)(1)). We believe that virtually all drugs imported into the U.S. from Canada by or for individual U.S. consumers also violate U.S. law for other reasons. Generally, such drugs are unapproved (21 U.S.C. 355), labeled incorrectly (21 U.S.C. 353(b)(2)), and/or dispensed without a valid prescription (21 U.S.C. 353(b)(1)). Thus, their shipment into the U.S. from Canada violates the Act. *See, e.g.,* 21 U.S.C. 331(a), (d), (t).

The reason that Canadian or other foreign versions of U.S.-approved drugs are generally considered unapproved in the U.S. is that FDA approvals are manufacturer-specific, product-specific, and include many requirements relating to the product, such as manufacturing location, formulation, source and specifications of active ingredients, processing methods, manufacturing controls, container/closure system, and appearance. 21 C.F.R. 314.50. Frequently, drugs sold outside of the U.S. are not manufactured by a firm that has FDA approval for that drug. Moreover, even if the manufacturer has FDA approval for a drug, the version produced for foreign markets usually does not meet all of the requirements of the U.S. approval, and thus it is considered to be unapproved. 21 U.S.C. 355.

In order to ensure compliance with the Act when they are involved in shipping prescription drugs to consumers in the U.S., businesses and individuals must ensure, among other things, that they only sell FDA-approved drugs that are made outside of the U.S. and that comply with the FDA approval in all respects, including manufacturing location, formulation, source and specifications of active ingredients, processing methods, manufacturing controls, container/closure system, and appearance. 21 C.F.R. 314.50. They must also ensure that each drug meets all US. labeling requirements, including that it bears the FDA-approved labeling. 21 C.F.R. 201.100(c)(2). The drug must also be dispensed by a pharmacist pursuant to a valid prescription. 21 U.S.C. 353(b)(1).

Practically speaking, it is extremely unlikely that a pharmacy could ensure that all of the applicable legal requirements are met. Consequently, almost every time an individual or business ships a prescription drug from Canada to a U.S. consumer, the individual or business shipping the drug violates the FD&C Act. Moreover, individuals and businesses, such as Rx Depot, Inc. and its responsible personnel, that cause those shipments also violate the Act. 21 U.S.C. 331 ("The following acts and the causing thereof are hereby prohibited . . .").

Rx Depot's web site . . . misleadingly claims that, "United States FDA policy allows importation of approved products for personal use in quantities not to exceed three months." This is not correct. Under FDA's Personal Importation policy, as a matter of enforcement discretion in certain defined circumstances, FDA allows consumers to import otherwise illegal drugs. However, contrary to your statement, this policy is not intended to allow importation of foreign versions of drugs of which there is an FDA-approved version. This is especially true when the foreign versions of such drugs are being "commercialized" to U.S. citizens through operations such as yours.

Moreover, the policy simply describes the agency's enforcement priorities. It does not change the law, and it does not give a license to persons to import or export illegal drugs into the United States. See FDA Regulatory Procedures Manual, Chapter 9, Subchapter: Coverage of Personal Importations.

FDA's Public Health Concerns and Your Misleading Statements about Drug Safety

. . . Prescription drugs purchased from foreign countries generally are not FDA-approved, do not meet FDA standards, and are not the same as the drugs purchased in the United States. Drugs from foreign countries do not have the same assurance of safety as drugs actually regulated by the FDA. Because the medications are not subject to FDA's safety oversight, they could be outdated, contaminated, counterfeit or contain too much or too little of the active ingredient. In addition, foreign dispensers of drugs to American citizens may provide patients with incorrect medications, incorrect strengths, medicines that should not be used in people with certain conditions or with other medications, or medications without proper directions for use. These risks are exacerbated by the fact that many of the products you are soliciting United States consumers to buy are indicated for serious medical conditions. . . .

FDA is also very concerned about the importation of prescription drugs from Canada and other foreign counties because, in our experience, many drugs obtained from foreign sources that purport or appear to be the same as U.S.-approved prescription drugs are, in fact, of unknown quality. Recent examples of counterfeit products entering the U.S. marketplace also raise substantial safety questions about drugs from foreign countries. Moreover, there is a possibility that drugs which come to U.S. consumers through Canada or purport to be from Canada may not actually be Canadian drugs. In short, drugs delivered to the American public from foreign countries may be very different from products approved by FDA and may not be safe and effective. For all of these reasons, FDA believes that operations such as yours expose the public to significant potential health risks.

. . . .

Sincerely,

David J. Horowitz, Esq.

United States of America v. Rx Depot, Inc.

290 F. Supp. 2d 1238 (N.D. Okla. 2003).

■ EAGAN, DISTRICT JUDGE.

. . . .

I. *FINDINGS OF FACT*

A. *Procedural History*

1. The plaintiff [United States] instituted this suit on September 11, 2003, by filing a complaint for injunction and a motion for a preliminary injunction. Plaintiff's complaint alleged violations by defendants of the Federal Food, Drug, and Cosmetic Act.

2. Defendants . . . moved for their own preliminary injunction against the plaintiff's attempt to enforce the FDCA. . . .

. . . .

D. *Operation of Rx Depot/Rx Canada*

11. Rx Depot assists individuals in procuring prescription medications from pharmacies in Canada. Each Rx Depot/Rx Canada location has one or two employees who accept prescriptions from U.S. customers. Customers also are asked to fill out a medical history form and other forms provided by Rx Depot. Customers can deliver these documents to defendants' stores in person, or can mail or fax to the nearest Rx Depot/Rx Canada store.

12. Once an Rx Depot/Rx Canada customer has submitted the required forms and prescription to defendants, the papers and the customer's credit card information or a certified check are transmitted to a cooperating pharmacy in Canada. A Canadian doctor rewrites the prescription, and the Canadian pharmacy fills the prescription, ships the prescription drugs directly to the U.S. customer, and bills the U.S. customer's credit card.

13. Defendants receive a 10 to 12 percent commission for each sale they facilitate for the Canadian pharmacies. The defendants also receive commissions for refill orders, which generally are arranged directly between customers and the Canadian pharmacies.

14. Defendants are essentially commissioned sales agents for Canadian pharmacies.

. . . .

E. *Prescription Drugs from Foreign Countries*

18. Although defendants presented evidence that the amount of prescription drugs shipped from Canadian pharmacies never exceeds a ninety-day supply, that defendants do not allow Canadian pharmacies to ship temperature-sensitive drugs, and that defendants do not deal with any third parties, unapproved prescription drugs and drugs imported from foreign countries by someone other than the U.S. manufacturer do not have the same assurance of safety and efficacy as drugs regulated by the Food and Drug Administration ("FDA"). Because the drugs are not subject to FDA oversight and are not continuously under the custody of a U.S. manufacturer or authorized distributor, their quality is less predictable than drugs obtained in the United States. For instance, the drugs may be contaminated, counterfeit, or contain erratic amounts of the active ingredient or different excipients. Also, the drugs may have been held under uncertain storage conditions, and therefore be outdated or subpotent.

19. Prescription drugs obtained through Rx Depot frequently are dispensed in greater quantities than are requested by the prescribing physician. Although defendants presented evidence that the amount of prescription drugs shipped from Canadian pharmacies never exceeds a ninety-day supply, Rx Depot advertises the availability of, and causes the importation of, preset quantities of drugs and dispenses these preset quantities regardless of the quantity of the drug the patient's U.S. physician prescribed and without directions to take the drug for only the number of days prescribed by the U.S. physician. American patients could, therefore, take a drug for many days more than their physicians intend without supervision. This practice can be dangerous in instances where drugs have potentially life-threatening side effects with continued use.

20. Prescription drugs obtained through Rx Depot also do not contain the FDA-approved patient package inserts included with certain prescription drugs in the United States. Nor are prescription drugs obtained through Rx Depot shipped in FDA-approved unit-of-use packaging. This type of packaging is used in the United States to help ensure that certain drugs received by customers arrive in designated dosages with the approved patient package insert.

21. The fact that there are currently no known cases of someone being harmed by a drug received as a result of using Rx Depot, or that plaintiff is currently unaware of anyone being harmed by prescription medications ordered through Rx Depot and imported from Canada, does not diminish the legitimate safety concerns of the FDA with unregulated commercial reimportation of U.S.-manufactured drugs by someone other than the manufacturer and importation of foreign-manufactured drugs not approved by the FDA.

. . . .

H.   *Cost of Prescription Drugs . . .*

43. Because of the high cost of prescription drugs in the United States, some citizens cannot afford their medications at U.S. prices. Defendants presented three highly credible witnesses to testify to this effect at the preliminary injunction hearing. These witnesses use or used Rx Depot to purchase their medications at a significantly lower price. The high cost of prescription drugs in the United States especially impacts those on fixed incomes, such as senior citizens and the disabled. . . .

46. Not only is Congress the best forum to address the high cost of prescription drugs for U.S. citizens, but also Congress is currently considering legislation which could allow prescription drug importation from Canada.

I.   *FDA Personal Use and Enforcement Discretion Policies*

47. The FDA has a personal importation policy which allows entry of foreign drugs by U.S. citizens who bring prescription drugs from foreign countries for personal use.

48. The FDA also has an "enforcement discretion policy" whereby the FDA allows small quantities of prescription drugs to be brought into the U.S. by individuals for personal use without recourse. In this regard, the FDA does not enforce the FDCA against individuals who travel to

Canada or use the Internet to purchase prescription drugs from Canada for personal use. . . .

II. CONCLUSIONS OF LAW

. . . .

3. The defendants violate 21 U.S.C. § 331 by causing the importation of prescription drugs from Canadian pharmacies. . . .

7. Defendants violate 21 U.S.C. § 331(t) each time they cause the importation of prescription drugs in violation of 21 U.S.C. § 381(d)(1). Specifically, the defendants cause the reimportation of the U.S.-manufactured drugs, such as Sporanox, listed on their website. Reimportation of U.S.-manufactured drugs, even those approved for use in the United States, violates the FDCA, because only the manufacturer of a drug can reimport that drug into the United States. 21 U.S.C. § 381(d)(1). . . .

18. The Court recognizes that individual customers of the defendants believe that they benefit from the low prescription drug prices offered by Rx Depot/Rx Canada. This Court is not unsympathetic to the predicament faced by individuals who cannot afford their prescription drugs at U.S. prices. However, the defendants are able to offer lower prices only because they facilitate illegal activity determined by Congress to harm the public interest. Congress, not this Court, is the best forum for weighing all of the costs and benefits of the national statutory scheme regulating prescription drug importation. . . .

28. Plaintiff's motion for a preliminary injunction is granted.

29. For the same reasons described herein, defendants' motion for a preliminary injunction is denied.

NOTES

1. *Subsequent History.* The following week, the court denied Rx Depot's emergency motion to stay the order of preliminary injunction pending appeal. *United States v. Rx Depot*, 297 F. Supp. 2d 1306 (N.D. Okla. 2003). The parties then agreed to, and the district court approved, a consent decree of permanent injunction. In the consent decree, Rx Depot admitted to violating the FDCA and agreed not to resume its business operations. The consent decree left "to the discretion of [the district court] the issue of what, if any, equitable relief, including restitution and/or disgorgement, should be awarded to [the United States]." As explained at *supra* p. 230, note 1, in *United States v. Rx Depot, Inc.*, 438 F.3d 1052 (10th Cir. 2006), the Tenth Circuit held that a court may, pursuant to its equity power under the FDCA, impose the remedy of disgorgement.

2. *Other Plans to Import Drugs from Canada.* The defendant in *Rx Depot* was not alone in trying to import prescription drugs from Canada at the time the case was decided. In 2003 and 2004, FDA exchanged a significant amount of correspondence with various types of public and private entities interested in taking advantage of lower prices for prescription drugs in our neighbor to the north. *See, e.g.*, Letter from William K. Hubbard, FDA Associate Commissioner for Policy and Planning, to Robert P. Lombardi (Feb. 12, 2003) (responding to letter of

inquiry from Lombardi, an attorney representing sponsor and administrators of employer-sponsored health plans, considering including coverage for prescription drugs purchased outside the U.S.); Letter from Hubbard to Gregory Gonot, Deputy Attorney General, California (Aug. 25, 2003) (responding to letter of inquiry asking whether California citizens can purchase drugs from Canada and whether California public pension funds can negotiate Canadian prescription drug prices for their members); Letter from Hubbard to Ram Kamath & Scott McKibbon, Illinois Special Advocates for Prescription Drugs (Nov. 6, 2003) (unsolicited letter regarding report presented to Illinois governor regarding feasibility of Illinois employees and retirees purchasing prescription drugs from Canada); Letter from Hubbard to Charlie Ryan, Mayor, Springfield, Massachusetts (Aug. 4, 2004) (denying citizen petition in which Springfield asked FDA to exercise its enforcement discretion to allow importation of Canadian drugs). In all of this correspondence, FDA, in language similar to that used in the Rx Depot warning letter, observed (1) that 21 U.S.C. § 381(d) forbids anyone other than the manufacturer to reimport drugs originally manufactured in the U.S. and (2) that virtually all foreign versions of U.S.-approved drugs are illegal under the FD&C Act because they are unapproved variants, incorrectly labeled, or dispensed without a valid prescription.

b.   IMPORTATION FOR PERSONAL USE

As noted in the *Rx Depot* decision, FDA exercises its enforcement discretion with regard to personal-use quantities of imported drugs, devices, and biologics in baggage and mail. The agency instituted this policy in 1954 and updated it in 1988 with respect to mailed imports of AIDS and cancer treatments. In February 1989, FDA set forth the broader, current version of the personal importation policy in a revision to its Regulatory Procedures Manual. The current version of this policy is excerpted in Chapter 7, on Human Drugs, *supra* p. 772.

In the early 2000s, some of the entities seeking to participate in systematic schemes for importing drugs from Canada invoked the personal importation policy in communications with FDA. In its correspondence with these and other entities, discussed above, FDA consistently emphasized that the policy does not change the law, but only reflects the agency's enforcement priorities. Moreover, the agency emphasized that the personal importation policy does not apply to situations in which foreign drugs are commercialized and promoted to U.S. consumers, or generally to foreign versions of U.S.-approved drugs.

c.   IMPORTATION PURSUANT TO WAIVER

At the end of 2003, a new potential avenue for legal importation of unapproved foreign versions of prescription drugs appeared. On December 8, President Bush signed into law the Medicare Prescription Drug Improvement and Modernization Act of 2003 ("MMA"), 117 Stat. 2066 (2003). This complex legislation created Medicare Part D, providing voluntary access to prescription drug coverage for senior citizens and individuals with disabilities. MMA also included various provisions addressing the cost of drugs. Section 1121 of the legislation amended section 804 of the FD&C Act to permit individuals to import prescription drugs and devices from Canada pursuant to waivers granted by FDA by regulation or on a case-by-case basis. FD&C Act 804(j). Congress also provided, however, that section 804 will become effective only if and when the Secretary of Health and Human Services certifies to Congress that the implementation of the section will "pose no additional risk to the public's health and safety" and will "result in a significant reduction in the cost of covered products to the American consumer." FD&C Act 804(l)(1). This certification requirement was carried over from the Medicine Equity and Drug Safety Act of 2000 (MEDS Act), which first added section 804 to the FD&C Act, but limited importation to pharmacists and wholesalers. 114 Stat. 1549, 1549A–36 (codified as amended in section 21 U.S.C. § 384). Under both the 2000 and 2003 statutes, successive HHS Secretaries in the Clinton, Bush, and Obama administrations have said they were unable to make this certification.

On December 12, 2003, just days after President Bush signed MMA, FDA received a citizen petition from the state of Vermont, asking the agency to permit the state's employee medical benefit plan to establish a program for the orderly importation, by its members, of prescription drugs from Canada. In addition to arguing that FDA should exercise its enforcement discretion, consistent with its Personal Importation Policy, Vermont urged the agency to establish regulations permitting importation from Canada under section 1121 of MMA. When FDA denied this citizen petition, Vermont challenged the denial in federal district court:

State of Vermont v. Leavitt

405 F. Supp. 2d 466 (D. Vt. 2005).

■ SESSIONS, CHIEF JUDGE.

In Beebe Plains, Vermont, there is a street, appropriately named Canusa Avenue, that runs right along the United States–Canada border. Houses on the northern side of the street are in Canada while houses on the southern side are in Vermont. If a resident of the northern side of Canusa Avenue needs medication to control high cholesterol, he or she can purchase a 90-day supply of 20 milligram Lipitor for $170. On the southern side of the street, Vermont residents will have to dig much deeper if they need to purchase the same drug. The same 90-day supply of Lipitor costs about $330 in the United States.

This price differential is far from unique. On average, brand-name drug prices are approximately 70% higher in the United States. It has been estimated that United States consumers would have saved $59.7 billion if, during 2004, they had purchased all brand-name drugs at Canadian prices. To put that figure in context, it is more than the gross national products of Kuwait, Iceland and Jamaica *combined*.

Given the dramatic difference between United States and Canadian drug prices, it is unsurprising that many Americans are interested in buying prescription drugs in Canada. . . .

Vermont regulators have been concerned about high domestic drug prices and the increase in ad-hoc, personal importation of Canadian drugs by Vermont residents. In response to these concerns, plaintiff Vermont Agency of Administration submitted a citizen petition to the Food and Drug Administration requesting that the FDA allow the Vermont State Employee Medical Benefit Plan ("VTSEMBP") to "establish a program for the orderly individual importation of prescription medications." The FDA denied this petition.

Plaintiffs . . . filed this lawsuit on August 19, 2004, challenging the FDA's denial of the citizen petition. Vermont claims that the denial was arbitrary and capricious in violation of the Administrative Procedure Act. Vermont also seeks a declaratory judgment that 21 U.S.C. § 384(*l*)(1) violates Article I, § 1 of the United States Constitution by improperly delegating legislative power to the Executive Branch.

. . . For the reasons set forth below, the Court grants the Defendants' Motion to Dismiss. . . .

A.   Importation Under the FDCA and the MMA

The MMA contains a provision that authorizes the Secretary of HHS to "promulgate regulations permitting pharmacists and wholesalers to import prescription drugs from Canada into the United States." 21 U.S.C. § 384(b). The MMA also provides that the Secretary "may grant to individuals, by regulation or on a case-by-case basis, a waiver of the prohibition of importation of a prescription drug or device or class of prescription drugs or devices, under such conditions as the Secretary determines to be appropriate." 21 U.S.C. § 384(j)(2)(A). Thus, the MMA contemplates both commercial and individual importation. These provisions of the MMA appear to become effective only if the Secretary certifies to Congress that importation will be safe and cost-effective. . . . 21 U.S.C. § 384(l). Secretary Leavitt and his predecessor, former Secretary Thompson, have declined to issue a certification under this subsection.

The MMA superseded the Medicine Equity and Drug Safety Act of 2000 ("MEDS Act"). Like the MMA, the MEDS Act authorized the Secretary of HHS to pass regulations allowing commercial importation of prescription drugs. The MEDS Act also contained a certification provision conditioning importation on a certification to Congress. Former Secretaries Thompson and Shalala declined to issue a certification to Congress under the MEDS Act. Thus, when Congress enacted the MMA's certification provision, it was aware that, during the previous three years, the Secretary of HHS had declined to issue a certification under a very similar provision.

B.   Vermont's Proposed Plan Violates the FDCA

There is no question that Vermont's proposed program would violate the FDCA. For example, whenever Vermont assisted in the re-importation of a drug manufactured in the United States, it would violate 21 U.S.C. § 331(t) [prohibiting the importation of a drug in violation of FD&C Act 801(d)(1) (21 U.S.C. § 381(d)(1)), which generally bans reimportation of finished prescription drugs by parties other than the manufacturer]. This will be true regardless of whether VTSEMBP or the members themselves import the drugs. VTSEMBP will violate section 331(t) if it "causes" its members to import drugs in violation of 21 U.S.C. § 381(d)(1). Thus, as Vermont's proposed plan would be highly likely to include drugs manufactured in the United States, it would lead to violations of section 331(t).

Similarly, Vermont's plan is likely to violate 21 U.S.C. § 331(a) [prohibiting interstate commerce in adulterated and misbranded products]. Many Canadian drugs will have packaging and labeling that is not approved by the FDA. Also, many Canadian drugs may not have been manufactured according to GMP (even if these drugs are pharmacologically identical to drugs approved by the FDA). Thus, VTSEMBP would violate 21 U.S.C. § 331(a) by causing these drugs to be introduced into interstate commerce.

C. The MMA Does Not Authorize Vermont's Plan

As Vermont's proposed plan violates the FDCA, the crucial issue is whether the MMA provides authorization for the plan. Vermont argues that its proposed program is permitted under the MMA. Vermont is incorrect. Under section 384(l), the relevant provisions of the MMA only become effective if the Secretary certifies to Congress that importation is safe and cost-effective. As the Secretary has not made this certification, the MMA offers no support for Vermont's program. . . .

NOTES

1. *HHS Report.* In December 2004, as mandated by MMA, the Department of Health and Human Services issued a report on its study of drug importation. HHS Task Force on Drug Importation, Report on Prescription Drug Importation (2004). The task force's findings included, among others: (1) "It would be extraordinarily difficult and costly for 'personal' importation to be implemented in a way that ensures the safety and effectiveness of the imported drugs," (2) "Overall national savings from legalized commercial importation will likely be a small percentage of total drug spending," and (3) "Legalized importation will likely adversely affect the future development of new drugs for American consumers." *Id.* at XII–XIII (Executive Summary: "Key Findings"). In light of these conclusions, it is hardly surprising that the Secretary of HHS has not certified to Congress that the implementation of section 804 importation would "pose no additional risk to the public's health and safety" and would "result in a significant reduction in the cost of covered products to the American consumer." FD&C Act 804(*l*)(1). Consequently, section 804, while still part of the FD&C Act, has never gone into effect.

2. *Partial Certification.* In *Vermont v. Leavitt, supra,* the district court explicitly declined to consider whether MMA allows a certification specific to a particular state or program. 405 F. Supp. 2d at 479. Apparently trying to exploit this potential loophole, in 2004, the governor of Oregon requested certification of the Oregon Pioneer Prescription Drug program, which would have allowed the state board of pharmacy to license and inspect Canadian pharmaceutical wholesalers, who would then have sold a limited formulary of prescription drugs to Oregon pharmacies. FDA declined to permit the program, observing, "The certification requirement in the MMA does not authorize a partial certification or a specific waiver for a discrete state pilot program." Letter from Randall W. Lutter, FDA Acting Association Commissioner for Policy and Planning, to Theodore R. Kulongoski, Governor of Oregon (Oct. 14, 2005). Using identical language,

FDA subsequently rejected similar requests from the County Executive of Montgomery County, Maryland, and the Washington State Board of Pharmacy. Letter from Lutter to Douglas M. Duncan, County Executive, Montgomery County (Nov. 8, 2005); Letter to Steven M. Saxe, Director, Washington State Board of Pharmacy (Mar. 17, 2006); *see also Montgomery County v. Leavitt*, 445 F. Supp. 2d 505 (D. Md. 2006) (dismissing Montgomery County's mandamus action against FDA regarding its denied request for waiver under the MMA to allow its residents and the county government to import prescription medications from Canada).

B. EXPORTATION FROM THE UNITED STATES

1. EXPORTATION PURSUANT TO FD&C ACT § 801(e)(1)

a. GENERAL

Section 801(e)(1) of the FD&C Act establishes an "intended for export" exception to the Act's adulteration and misbranding provisions. Under section 801(e)(1):

> A food, drug, device, tobacco product or cosmetic intended for export shall not be deemed to be adulterated or misbranded under this Act, and a tobacco product intended for export shall not be deemed to be in violation of section 906(e) [good manufacturing practice requirements], 907 [tobacco product standards], 911 [modified risk tobacco products], or 920(a) [origin labeling requirement], if it—
>
> (A) accords to the specifications of the foreign purchaser,
>
> (B) is not in conflict with the laws of the country to which it is intended for export,
>
> (C) is labeled on the outside of the shipping package that it is intended for export, and
>
> (D) is not sold or offered for sale in domestic commerce.

This section applies to all misbranding of every FDA-regulated product, to all adulteration of food, human drugs, and cosmetics, and to most adulteration of devices, animal drugs, and tobacco products. However, as discussed *infra* at p. 1472, section 801(e)(1) does not, by itself, legalize exportation of unapproved new drugs, unlicensed biologics, unapproved class III devices, or "banned" new animal drugs.

For a detailed account of the legislative history of Section 801(e)(1), see PETER BARTON HUTT & BRUCE N. KUHLIK, EXPORT EXPERTISE: UNDERSTANDING EXPORT LAW FOR DRUGS, DEVICES, AND BIOLOGICS, Chapter 1 (Washington Business Information, Inc. 1998).

United States v. An Article . . . Enriched Rice
FDA CONSUMER, October 1976, at 36 (S.D. Tex. 1975).

. . . [C]laimant argues that it has met its burden of proving the applicability of the exemption provided by § 381(d) [now 381(e)] because the evidence it has submitted in support of the motion demonstrates that the export of the seized product would not be in violation of the laws of Chile. In view of the fact that disposition of this argument will require a consideration of facts outside of the pleadings, the Court will consider the motion to dismiss as a motion for summary judgment pursuant to Rule 56, Fed. R. Civ. P.

There appears to be little dissention between both parties that the applicable provisions of the law of Chile may be summarized as follows: (1) the importation of foodstuffs requires notification of the proper governmental authorities who may then inspect the product upon its arrival and thereafter take appropriate action in accepting, rejecting or altering the condition of the imported goods; (2) all imported foodstuffs must be accompanied by a sanitation certificate issued by a competent authority of the exporting country; (3) the manufacture, sale, [or] storage for sale of altered, contaminated, adulterated or falsified foods with risk to the health of men or animals is prohibited.

Insofar as items (1) and (2) are concerned, the Court does not find that these would prohibit the application of the export exemption to the seized goods in question here. Claimant had secured the necessary sanitation certificate prior to the seizure of the article of food in question here. Furthermore, it must be presumed that claimant will comply with the provisions requiring notice to be given to appropriate Chilean authorities in the absence of any evidence to the contrary. However, item (3) does prohibit the sale or storage for sale of altered food products. It is clearly the intention of claimant to export the seized goods for sale. . . . [T]he sale and shipment of the goods seized in this action, if altered within the meaning of Chilean law, will conflict with the laws of the receiving country.

Thus, it will be necessary for the Court to hear further evidence with respect to the Government's contention that the seized goods are in fact adulterated under the laws of the United States. It will be necessary thereafter for the claimant to demonstrate that, even if the goods are adulterated under our laws, they are not altered or adulterated within the meaning of these provisions of the Chilean law. Because the above questions present issues of fact that cannot be determined on the basis of the record now before the Court, claimant's motion for summary judgment will be denied and this matter set for hearing at a later date.

United States v. Kanasco, Ltd.

123 F.3d 209 (4th Cir. 1997).

■ Motz, Circuit Judge:

The United States filed a complaint for forfeiture requesting the seizure and condemnation of approximately 104 drums of adulterated bulk antibiotics manufactured by Kanasco, Limited. . . . Following discovery, the Government moved for summary judgment maintaining that the drugs were adulterated because they were not manufactured according to "current good manufacturing practice," as defined in 21 U.S.C.A. § 351(a)(2)(B). Kanasco filed a cross-motion for summary judgment. The company did not dispute that the drugs were not manufactured according to "current good manufacturing practice;"

instead, it argued that the drugs were exempt from the manufacturing requirements of § 351 because they were intended for export, and thus fell within the export exemption to the Food, Drug, and Cosmetic Act. *See* 21 U.S.C.A. § 381(e)(1).

. . . [T]he district court rejected Kanasco's argument and granted summary judgment to the Government. . . . We affirm. . . .

. . . [A] drug is not "adulterated" (and thus not subject to forfeiture) if the drug is "intended for export" and meets a four factor test. *See* 21 U.S.C.A. § 381(e)(1). A drug "intended for export shall not be deemed to be adulterated" if it:

(A) accords to the specifications of the foreign purchaser,

(B) is not in conflict with the laws of the country to which it is intended for export,

(C) is labeled on the outside of the shipping package that it is intended for export, and

(D) is not sold or offered for sale in domestic commerce.

21 U.S.C.A. § 381(e)(1).

Kanasco claims that the drugs were "intended for export" and that they satisfy the four factor test. The burden of pleading and proving the applicability of § 381(e)(1) is on Kanasco—the party that seeks the benefit of the exemption.

John Capanos, president of Kanasco, filed an affidavit stating that the seized drugs were "intended for export." Based on this affidavit, the district court held that Kanasco raised a dispute of fact as to the "threshold requirement" of § 381(e)(1) that the drugs be "intended for export." The Government does not dispute this point, and we agree that there is a factual dispute as to Kanasco's intent.

We also concur with the district court, however, that this factual dispute is not "material" because Kanasco clearly cannot satisfy the requirements of § 381(e)(1)(A) or (B). Kanasco has come forward with no evidence that the drugs seized "accord[ ] to the specifications of the foreign purchaser" or are "not in conflict with the laws of the country to which [they are] intended for export." 21 U.S.C.A. § 381(e)(1)(A)–(B).

Kanasco contends that § 381(e)(1) does not require that the drugs be manufactured for a specific foreign purchaser, or that the drugs comply with "the laws of" a particular country. The company asserts that Capanos' affidavit, which stated that he could find a foreign purchaser, and that the drugs met the requirements of unnamed and unspecified "foreign countries," satisfies the first two prongs of § 381(e)(1).

. . . Sections 381(e)(1)(A) and (B) require that in order to be deemed not adultered [sic], drugs meet "the specifications of *the* foreign purchaser," and that drugs not be "in conflict with the laws of *the* country to which" they are "intended for export." 21 U.S.C.A. § 381(e)(1)(A)–(B) (emphasis added). By using the definite article "the," Congress signaled that § 381(e)(1) requires proof that a drug accords with both the specifications of a specific foreign purchaser and the laws of a specific foreign country.

The plain language of § 381(e)(1) thus requires a particular foreign buyer and country; not a generalized assertion that the drugs can be sold to some buyer and that sale is consistent with the laws of some foreign country. Kanasco maintains that this interpretation of § 381(e)(1) subverts the objective of the export exemption because drugs that could be sold in foreign markets will instead be destroyed. This argument, however, examines the export exemption in a vacuum, ignoring the fact that it is an exception to the Food, Drug, and Cosmetic Act. "Exceptions from a general policy which a law embodies should be strictly construed."

Moreover, it is particularly appropriate to construe the export exemption narrowly, because a broad interpretation could seriously damage the "overriding purpose" of the Food, Drug, and Cosmetic Act, "to protect the public health." *United States v. Bacto–Unidisk*, 394 U.S. 784 (1969). Kanasco's expansive interpretation would undermine this purpose by crippling the effectiveness of enforcement actions against violators. Drug manufacturers could ignore the statutory quality requirements and produce adulterated drugs for sale in the United States, secure in the knowledge that if caught they could claim the export exemption and subsequently find a foreign buyer for the drugs. Manufacturers could thus produce adulterated drugs with little fear of any effective sanction.

Facing a similar argument in a case involving adulterated food, the Second Circuit reached an interpretation of the export exemption identical to ours:

> The practical aspects of the situation would seem to support this construction, for there is nowhere disclosed an intention that a violator of the Act may avoid the consequences of his wrong by then exporting the outlawed goods to some foreign country which will receive them. However laudatory may be the purpose to conserve the food supply (perhaps even of a condiment or relish such as catsup), an attempt to rewrite the Act along these lines seems likely to have the effect of nullifying its chief purposes.

United States v. Kent Food Corp., 168 F.2d 632, 634 (2d Cir. 1948).

In sum, Kanasco's interpretation of the export exemption is contrary to the plain language of § 381(e)(1), and would create an unwarranted escape hatch for violators of the Act. The district court properly rejected that interpretation.

Compliance Policy Guide Sec. 587.200: Uncertified or Delisted Colors in Food for Export— (e.g., FD&C Red #2)

March 1995.

. . . .

Policy: Colors such as FD&C Red No. 2, which have been delisted, can be used in lots of food specifically manufactured for export to a country in which its use is legal, provided all the requirements of section 801(e) of the Act are followed and provided further, that a control system is followed which insures that there is no possibility of diversion by mistake or otherwise to domestic channels, of the food containing the color. Proper control can be achieved by following the procedure set forth below:

1.   Prior to start of production and for each lot produced a separate order, letter from the purchaser, and letter from an official of the country must be obtained.

The order from the purchaser must state the exact amount desired by the foreign purchaser and must state on the order or be accompanied by a letter from the purchaser stating that he desires that FD&C Red No. 2 or other specific color be used in the lot and that he is aware of its illegality in the United States. The letter from a responsible official of the country to which the lot is to be shipped shall state that the use of the color is legal in his country. Since the laws and regulations of countries are subject to change, a continuing order or letter will not be satisfactory.

2.   The stock of the color to be used for export production must be kept locked up at all times, except when actually being used. Complete records must be kept accounting for all use.

3.   During all stages of production, manufacture, processing and packing the lot must be kept segregated from all other production and must be clearly marked that it is "for export only."

The outside of each shipping package of the lot must be labeled [to] show it is for export.

4.   All records, pertaining to such lots, including orders and letters, must be kept for at least three years and made available to any Food and Drug Administration inspector upon oral or written request.

NOTE: This policy only applies to uncertified or delisted colors that have been manufactured in this country, or entered legally into this country prior to being uncertified or delisted, and are intended to be used in foods solely for export.

NOTES

1.   *Lacking Legal Authority?* FDA could point to no legal authority for the position asserted in this guide.

2.   *Commentary. See generally* Edward Brown Williams, *Regulation of Exports Under the Federal Food, Drug, and Cosmetic Act*, 3 FOOD DRUG COSM. L.Q. 382 (1948); Paul M. Hyman, *Legal Overview of FDA Authority over Imports and Exports*, 42 FOOD DRUG COSM. L.J. 203 (1987).

b.   EXPORTATION OF UNAPPROVED NEW DRUGS AND UNLICENSED BIOLOGICS

As discussed above, section 801(e)(1) can prevent a product intended for export from being deemed adulterated or misbranded. However, the act of introducing an unapproved new human drug into interstate commerce, though prohibited by the statute, is not an adulteration or misbranding violation. *See* FD&C Act 301(d), 505(a). The same is true for unlicensed biological products. *See* 42 U.S.C.

262(a)(1). Accordingly, FDA has always taken the position that section 801(e) does not legalize unapproved new drugs or unlicensed biological products intended for export, and the courts have upheld this interpretation. In 1986, as discussed *infra* at p. 1476, Congress amended the Act to allow some exportation of unapproved products under new section 802. To this day, however, section 801(e)(1) is not a vehicle for exportation of medical products requiring approval.

United States v. An Article of Drug . . . Ethionamide–INH

1965–1968 FDLI Jud. and Ad. Rec. 16 (E.D.N.Y. 1967).

■ DOOLING, DISTRICT JUDGE.

The government seized a large quantity of tablets of Ethionamide–INH in the possession of Amfre–Grant, Inc. on the ground that it was a "new drug" . . . and that no approval of an application . . . was effective for the drug. . . .

. . . The drug in question is a combination of equal quantities (125 mg.) of ethionamide and isoniazid or isononicotinic acid hydrazide (INH). . . . While use of ethionamide in conjunction with INH is known in the literature, it is not contended that the particular Amfre–Grant combination has been approved for use in the manner recommended in the insert included in the completed packages, or that it could qualify as not a "new drug" because it was generally recognized by qualified persons to be safe and effective for use as recommended.

Amfre–Grant has supplied the drug to Vietnam, where it has been approved for sale, in 1966 and early 1967, and the Agency for International Development has approved the drug for Vietnamese sale, and authorized the use of AID funds to pay for it. The packaging for the drug is entirely in French, and the package displays the Vietnamese registration number; the insertion sheet is in French and Vietnamese. The package indicates that the drug is to be sold on prescription only. . . .

. . . Section 381(d) [now section 381(e)] took its present form in the 1938 Act, and the legislative history is invoked to show that the primary concern of the Congress was to safeguard residents of the United States, and that the narrow focus of that concern resulted in the rejection of amendments to section 381(d) that would have required exports to be in compliance with some but not all of the standards of the Act. It is argued that the "new drug" provisions of 21 U.S.C. Sec. 355 were introduced late in the transit of the bill through the Congress, that no hearings and little debate accompanied the addition of section 355 to the Senate Bill in the House, and that the section was added under the goad of concern over deaths caused in 1937 by using "antifreeze," diethylene glycol, as the carrier in "Elixir Sulfanilamide." . . .

The argument must yield to the language of the statute. The exemption of section 381(d) [381(e)] applies to what would otherwise be "adulterated or misbranded" within the other sections of the Act. On those words hinge the operation of the Act as it applies to foods and drugs that are not "new drugs." The "new drug" provisions, although solidly embedded in the Act, operate separately, and it is not a necessary, nor even a probable, inference that the policy considerations that led to the enactment of section 381(d) would extend to the new drug provisions. . . .

NOTES

1.   *Supporting Authority.* See *United States v. Yaron Laboratories, Inc.*, 365 F. Supp. 917 (N.D. Cal. 1972) (granting preliminary injunction to enjoin defendant from exporting an unapproved new drug to Vietnam because the section 801 export exemption did not apply).

2.   *Partially Processed Biologics.* In 1996, Congress amended the Public Health Service Act to allow exportation of a limited category of unapproved biologic products, namely, "partially processed biologics." According to this amendment:

> A partially processed biological product which—
>
> (1) is not in a form applicable to the prevention, treatment, or cure of diseases or injuries of man;
>
> (2) is not intended for sale in the United States; and
>
> (3) is intended for further manufacture into final dosage form outside the United States,
>
> shall be subject to no restriction on the export of the product under this chapter or the Federal Food, Drug, and Cosmetic Act if the product is manufactured, processed, packaged, and held in conformity with current good manufacturing practice requirements or meets international manufacturing standards as certified by an international standards organization recognized by the Secretary and meets the requirements of section 801(e)(1) of the Federal Food, Drug, and Cosmetic Act.

42 U.S.C. 262(h).

3.   *Drug Intermediates.* 21 C.F.R. § 310.3(g) defines "new drug substance" to exclude "intermediates used in the synthesis of such substance." Such intermediates may therefore be exported without an IND or NDA.

c.   EXPORTATION OF UNAPPROVED NEW ANIMAL DRUGS

Prior to the passage of the 1968 Animal Drug Amendments (ADA), unapproved animal drugs fell outside the scope of FD&C Act 801(d) (now 801(e)) for the same reason that human drugs did, and thus could not be legally exported. The ADA potentially changed the equation, however. Under the regulatory scheme established by the ADA, an unapproved animal drug, unlike an unapproved human drug, is adulterated by virtue of being unapproved. *See* FD&C Act 501(a)(5), 512(a)(1). Consequently, section 801(e), if not amended, would have allowed the exportation of unapproved new animal drugs that met the provision's four requirements. Indeed, the initial version of the ADA would have permitted such exportation. In the final version, however, Congress maintained the status quo regarding the illegality of the exportation of unapproved new animal drugs by amending 801(e) to exclude them explicitly.

As discussed below, the Drug Export Amendments Act of 1986 added FD&C Act 802, which created a scheme for exporting unapproved animal drugs and other types of unapproved products. In 1996, when Congress loosened export requirements for unapproved products under section 802, it also broadened the opportunity to export unapproved new animal drugs under section 801(e). Now, instead of excluding all unapproved new animal drugs from the scope of section 801(e), the Act excludes only new animal drugs that have been "banned" in the United States. FD&C Act 801(e)(3). Because there is no "banned animal drugs" section of the Act parallel to the "banned devices" provision in section 516, it is unclear precisely what the exclusion of "banned" new animal drugs means. Indisputably, however, section 801(e) now permits exportation of unapproved animal drugs for which FDA has neither rejected an NADA nor withdrawn approval of an NADA.

d. EXPORTATION OF UNAPPROVED MEDICAL DEVICES

Like unapproved new animal drugs, unapproved class III devices subject to premarket approval under section 515 are "adulterated." FD&C Act 501(f)(1). When Congress enacted the Medical Device Amendments of 1976 (MDA), however, it determined that exportation of such unapproved devices should not be permitted under section 801(e). The MDA thus amended section 801(e) to state that the provision does not generally apply to devices that violate the section 515 PMA requirement. FD&C Act 801(e)(2). This revision to 801(e) also excludes devices that fail to comply with an applicable performance standard under section 514, investigational devices subject to an IDE under section 520(g), and devices that are banned under section 516. Under section 801(e)(2), an unapproved device for which a PMA is required will be deemed adulterated, even if intended for export and in compliance with section 801(e)(1), unless "either (i) [FDA] has determined that the exportation of the device is not contrary to public health and safety and has the approval of the country to which it is intended for export or (ii) the device is eligible for export under section 802."

Despite these limitations, section 801(e) remains a viable path for exportation of many unapproved devices, even when FDA has not made a "health and safety"/foreign approval determination under section 801(e)(2). The reason why section 801(e) exportation remains an option for many manufacturers of unapproved devices is that section 801(e)(2) does not exclude devices based on their failure to comply with 510(k) marketing clearance requirements. A new device does not have to get PMA approval prior to marketing if it is "substantially equivalent" to a class I or class II device already on the market. And for class II devices (and class I devices not exempt from 510(k)), FDA makes this substantial equivalence determination based on a manufacturer's 510(k) submission. How, then, should the agency treat a class II device intended for export for which neither a PMA nor a 510(k) has been filed? FDA has declared:

> The Act prohibits exportation of class III devices requiring premarket approval unless the criteria under section 801(e)(2) of

the Act are met (or the device qualifies for export under section 802 of the Act). FDA has exercised its enforcement discretion and, to date, has not taken enforcement action against a firm who has not complied with the export criteria in section 801(e)(2) of the Act, provided that the firm has reasonably concluded that FDA would have granted 510(k) marketing clearance if a report under section 510(k) of the Act had been submitted. FDA intends, on a case by case basis, to continue to consider the exercise of its enforcement discretion in this manner with respect to the requirements in section 801(e)(2) of the Act. FDA emphasizes, however, even if a firm reasonably believes that its device would receive a 510(k) marketing clearance, FDA does not intend to consider the exercise of its enforcement discretion in this manner with respect to the requirements in section 801(e)(1) of the Act.

GUIDANCE FOR INDUSTRY: EXPORTS UNDER THE FDA EXPORT REFORM AND ENHANCEMENT ACT OF 1996 (2007).

2. EXPORTATION OF UNAPPROVED MEDICAL PRODUCTS PURSUANT TO FD&C ACT § 802

Guidance for Industry: Exports Under the FDA Export Reform and Enhancement Act of 1996

July 23, 2007.

. . . .

IV. Statutory Background

. . . .

The 1938 act . . . defined the terms, "drug" and "new drug," and these definitions led to the conclusion that section 801(d) of the 1938 Act did not apply to new drugs that did not comply with section 505 of the Act. (See, e.g., *United States v. An Article of Drug, etc. . . . Ethionamide–INH*, No. 67 C 288 (E.D.N.Y. Aug. 19, 1967); *United States v. Yaron Laboratories, Inc.*, 365 F. Supp. 917, 919 (N.D. Cal. 1972); Compliance Policy Guide 7132c.01 (Oct. 1, 1980).) As a result, the Act was interpreted as permitting the export of approved drugs, but not permitting the export of unapproved new drugs. This interpretation was viewed as imposing hardships on the pharmaceutical industry (by impairing its ability to compete in international markets) without any accompanying public health benefits.

To remedy the situation, Congress enacted the Drug Export Amendments Act of 1986 (Pub. L. 99–660). For human drug products and biological products, the 1986 Amendments created section 802 of the Act. . . . Under [section 802], FDA was authorized to approve an application for the export of new human and animal drugs and biological products that were not approved in the United States, so long as the drug contained the same active ingredient(s) as a product for which marketing approval in the United States was being sought or the biological product was one for which licensing was actively being pursued. Exports . . . were confined to 21 specific countries listed in section 802 of the Act. . . .

The 1986 Amendments, however, presented several problems and concerns. One significant problem was that the 1986 Amendments limited exports of most unapproved drugs and biological products to 21 countries. Although the 1986 Amendments provided criteria for adding more countries to the list, it omitted any administrative mechanism for doing so. . . .

The requirement that the drug contain the same active ingredient as a drug for which marketing approval in the United States was being "actively pursued" also caused some concern in the industry. Questions arose concerning the degree to which the active ingredient had to be the "same" or how "actively" the manufacturer had to be seeking approval.

The requirements in the 1986 Amendments for FDA approval before a product could be exported generated criticism and debate as well. . . . Some firms charged that this approval process took too long; others questioned why the United States should have to approve the export of a product to a foreign country, particularly when the foreign country had its own public health authorities or had approved the product for marketing.

. . .

The FDA Export Reform and Enhancement Act of 1996 (Public Law 104–134, and amended by Public Law 104–180) addressed the industries' chief problems and concerns. . . . [T]he 1996 Amendments . . . [r]eplaced section 802 of the Act in its entirety with a new section 802. . . .

. . .

VII. Exports of Unapproved Drugs, Biological Products, and Devices Under Section 802(b) of the Act

. . . .

Section 802(f) of the Act imposes certain basic requirements for all drugs, biological products, and devices exported under section 802 of the Act. In brief, these requirements [include, among others, the following]:

• The product must be manufactured, processed, packaged, and held in "substantial conformity" with cGMP's or meet international standards as certified by an international standards organization recognized by FDA. . . .

• The product must have the strength, purity, and quality that it purports or is represented to possess. . . .

• The product must comply with the requirements in section 801(e)(1) of the Act. . . .

• The product cannot present an imminent hazard to the public health of the country to which it would be exported; and

• The product must be labeled in accordance with the requirements and conditions of use in the listed country (see part VII.D., below) in which it received valid marketing authorization, if applicable, and the country to which it would be exported, and must be labeled in the language and units of measurement used in or designated by the country to which the drug or device would be exported. Additionally, a product may not be exported if it is not promoted in accordance with these labeling requirements.

If the above requirements are not met, section 802(f) of the Act states that the drug or device may not be exported under section 802 of the Act. Furthermore, in determining whether a drug or device may present an imminent hazard to the public health of the foreign country or is improperly labeled or promoted, section 802(f) of the Act requires FDA to consult with the "appropriate public health official in the affected country."

. . .

The principal provision authorizing the exportation of unapproved new drugs, biological products, and devices is section 802(b)(1)(A) of the Act. Section 802(b)(1)(A) of the Act states that a drug or device "may be exported to any country, if the drug or device complies with the laws of that country and has valid marketing authorization by the appropriate authority" in Australia, Canada, Israel, Japan, New Zealand, Switzerland, South Africa, or any member nation in the European Union or the European Economic Area. As of July, 2007, the EU countries are: Austria, Belgium, Bulgaria, Cyprus, the Czech Republic, Denmark, Estonia, Finland, France, Germany, Greece, Hungary, Ireland, Italy, Latvia, Lithuania, Luxembourg, Malta, the Netherlands, Poland, Portugal, Romania, Slovakia, Slovenia, Spain, Sweden, and the United Kingdom. The EEA countries are the EU countries, Iceland, Liechtenstein, and Norway. The number of "listed countries" expands automatically as countries become members of the EU or the EEA.

This means that a firm whose drug or device has received marketing authorization in any of the countries listed above can export that drug or device to any country in the world, without submitting an export request to FDA or receiving FDA approval to export the drug or device, as long as the drug or device meets applicable requirements of the Act, including the laws of the country to which the product is being exported. . . .

FDA interprets the term "valid marketing authorization" as meaning an affirmative decision by the appropriate public health authority in a foreign country to permit the drug, biological product, or device to be sold in that country. For example, under this interpretation, if country D approves a drug for investigational use, the approval would not constitute "valid marketing authorization" because country D's decision did not extend to commercial marketing. . . . Some countries, however, have regulatory systems that permit marketing without an affirmative act or decision by the government. In such cases, FDA may consider a drug, biological product, or device to have "valid marketing authorization" if the listed country does not object to the product's marketing in that country. In these cases, FDA recommends that the firm obtain a document from the relevant authority in the listed country indicating that it does not object to the product's marketing.

As for the word "drug," the drug to be exported under section 802(b)(1)(A) of the Act should be the same product as the drug that received marketing authorization in the listed foreign country. Thus, the issue of whether the drug to be exported must be exactly identical to the drug authorized in the listed country may depend on the conditions surrounding market authorization in the foreign country. . . .

The list of countries in section 802(b)(1)(A) of the Act can expand. The 1996 Amendments contained a mechanism whereby the Secretary may add other countries to the list, provided that the country meets certain criteria. . . .

Under section 802(b)(1)(B) of the Act, the authority to add countries to the list rests solely in the Secretary of Health and Human Services. Thus, FDA has no authority to add countries to the list.

. . .

If a firm intends to export an unapproved new drug (including a biological product) to a foreign country not included in section 802(b)(1)(A) of the Act and the drug does not have valid marketing authorization in a listed country, the firm has two other options for exporting the product.

One option is in section 802(b)(2) of the Act. This section permits a firm to export an unapproved drug directly to an unlisted country if:

  • The drug complies with the laws of the foreign country and has valid marketing authorization by the "responsible authority" in that country, and

  • FDA determines that the foreign country has statutory or regulatory requirements:

    ○ Which require the review of drugs for safety and effectiveness by a government entity in that country and which authorize marketing approval of drugs which trained and experienced experts have determined to be safe and effective. . . .;

    ○ pertaining to cGMP's;

    ○ for reporting adverse events and for removing unsafe or ineffective drugs from the market; and

    ○ which require that the labeling and promotion be in accordance with the product's approval.

. . .

The second option is in section 802(b)(3) of the Act. This section permits a firm to petition the agency to authorize exportation to an unlisted country if the conditions for export under section 802(b)(1) and 802(b)(2) of the Act cannot be met. Under section 802(b)(3) of the Act, FDA shall allow exportation of the drug if:

  • The person exporting the drug: (1) Certifies that the drug would not meet the conditions for approval under the Act or the conditions for approval in a listed country; and (2) provides "credible scientific evidence" for the product to be exported that is acceptable to FDA to show that the drug would be safe and effective under the conditions of use in the country to which it is being exported . . .; and

  • the appropriate health authority in the foreign country that is to receive the drug: (1) Requests approval of the drug's exportation; (2) certifies that the health authority understands that the drug is not approved under the Act or by any listed country; and (3) concurs that the scientific evidence provided to FDA is credible scientific evidence that the drug would be reasonably safe and effective in the foreign country. . . .

VIII. Exports of Unapproved Drugs and Devices for Investigational Use to Listed Countries Under Section 802(c) of the Act

. . . .

The 1996 Amendments . . . creat[ed] a new section 802(c) of the Act. In brief, section 802(c) of the Act permits a firm to export an unapproved drug for investigational use in any of the listed countries without prior FDA approval or even an IND. The only requirements are that the drug be exported in accordance with the laws of the foreign country and comply with the basic export requirements in section 802(f) of the Act. . . .

It is important to note that section 802(c) of the Act allows exports of drugs and devices "intended for investigational use *in* any [listed] country . . . in accordance with the laws of that country" (emphasis added). The key statutory phrase is that the drug or device must be intended for investigational use *in* a *listed* country. FDA is aware that some firms have interpreted section 802(c) of the Act as allowing shipments of investigational drugs or devices to an *unlisted* country (a practice known as "transshipment") as long as the shipment passes through a listed country. FDA disagrees with such an interpretation because the unrestricted transshipment of investigational drugs and devices from listed to unlisted countries would undermine the express limitation in section 802(c) of the Act. There is no indication that Congress intended to make listed countries act as mere transfer points for investigational drugs or devices that are destined for unlisted countries.

. . . .

Additionally, as an alternative to section 802(c) of the Act in some circumstances, section 802(b)(1) of the Act authorizes exportation of an unapproved product, including an investigational new drug, to unlisted countries if the drug complies with the foreign country's laws and has valid marketing authorization in a listed country. Thus, exports under section 802(b)(1) of the Act may be made for investigational uses as well as for marketing purposes.

. . . .

The 1996 Amendments also significantly affected investigational device exports. Section 802(c) of the Act permits a firm to export an unapproved device for investigational use in any of the listed countries, without prior FDA approval or an IDE. As in the case for drugs, the device must be exported in accordance with the laws of the foreign country, and the exports are subject to the recordkeeping requirement in section 802(g) of the Act as implemented by 21 CFR 1.101(e).

Yet, unlike the situation for drug exports, the 1996 Amendments permit device firms to export a device either under section 801(e)(2) of the Act or under section 802 of the Act. The authority selected is important because each section of the Act carries its own statutory requirements.

XI. Export Notification and Recordkeeping Under Section 802(g) of the Act

Section 802(g) of the Act requires persons exporting a drug or device under section 802(b)(1) of the Act to provide a "simple notification . . . identifying the drug or device when the exporter first begins to export such drug or device" to any country listed in section 802(b)(1) of the Act. If the product is to be exported to an unlisted country, section 802(g) of the Act requires the exporter to provide a simple notification "identifying the drug or device and the country to which such drug or device is being exported."

With respect to all exports pursuant to section 802 of the Act, section 802(g) of the Act requires the exporter to maintain records of all drugs or devices exported and the countries to which they were exported.

. . .

NOTES

1. *Listed Countries.* The Secretary of Health and Human Services has not yet used his nondelegable authority to expand the list of countries in section 802(b)(1)(A).

2. *Tropical Diseases.* Section 802(e) permits the exportation, with FDA approval of an export application, of "a drug or device which is used in the diagnosis, prevention, or treatment of a tropical disease or another disease not of significant prevalence in the United States and which does not otherwise qualify for export under this section."

3. *Partially Processed Biological Products.* Section 802(h)(2), by reference to section 351 of the Public Health Service Act, permits the exportation of "partially processed biological product" as defined under 42 U.S.C. § 262(h) upon FDA approval of an export application.

4. *Export Certificates.* Firms exporting a product from the United States are often requested by foreign customers or foreign governments to supply a "certificate" containing information about the product's regulatory or marketing status. For exported human drugs, biologics, animal drugs, and devices, FDA is statutorily required, if requested, to issue a certification either that the product is exportable under the requirements of FD&C Act 801(e)(1) or 802 or that it satisfies the Act's requirements for marketing in the United States. FD&C Act 801(e)(4)(A). The Act permits FDA to charge a fee for this service. *Id.* 801(e)(4)(B). A certificate that a product meets domestic requirements for marketing is called a "Certificate to Foreign Government" with respect to biologics, animal drugs, and devices. A "Certificate of a Pharmaceutical Product" is for human drugs and conforms to a World Health Organization (WHO) format. A certificate for an unapproved product that may be legally exported under 801(e) or 802 is called a "Certificate of Exportability," except with respect to human drugs, for which FDA instead issues a "Certificate of a Pharmaceutical Product" with a special notation that the product is unapproved. For all these sorts of certification, FDA relies on the manufacturer's self-certification that it meets the applicable legal requirements.

FDA is not obligated to issue export certificates for foods, cosmetics, or dietary supplements, and is not empowered to charge a fee for such certificates. Nonetheless, so far as resources permit, the agency issues export certificates for these products, attesting that they are produced and marketed in the United States in general conformity with U.S. requirements. Interestingly, other agencies with jurisdiction over food, including the Department of Agriculture, have statutory authority to collect fees associated with the issuance of export certificates. FDA, with responsibility for the majority of the food supply, does not. The burden on FDA is particularly high with regard to seafood and dairy products, for which many foreign nations require export certificates. *See generally* 71 Fed. Reg. 4147 (Jan. 25, 2006); GUIDANCE FOR INDUSTRY: FDA EXPORT CERTIFICATES (July 2004).

3. INTERNATIONAL TRADE AGREEMENTS

The General Agreement on Tariffs and Trade (GATT) governed international trade in agricultural, consumer, and industrial products for more than 40 years, from 1947 until 1995. The agreement successfully reduced tariff barriers to trade, but because GATT permitted each country to enact its own health and safety laws, food and drug regulatory requirements remained non-tariff barriers to trade throughout the world. Although GATT prohibited members from using health and safety measures as disguised trade barriers, the agreement offered little guidance on applying this prohibition, and there were few GATT rulings holding that particular domestic health and safety measures violated the treaty.

In 1995, GATT was succeeded by the World Trade Organization (WTO). WTO member states establish global trade rules by entering into multilateral agreements. Contrary to GATT, the WTO has a formalized dispute settlement mechanism that requires its members to resolve trade disputes arising from the WTO agreements through its dispute settlement body. Perhaps the most important WTO agreement with respect to products regulated by FDA is the Agreement on the Application of Sanitary and Phytosanitary Measures (SPS Agreement), which addresses regulations regarding food safety and diseases carried by animals and plants. Agreement on the Application of Sanitary and Phytosanitary Measures, Apr. 15, 1994, Annex 1A to Agreement Establishing the World Trade Organization. The SPS Agreement encourages member states to adopt international standards, such as the food safety standards promulgated by the Codex Alimentarius Commission, a subsidiary of the United Nations' World Health Organization and Food and Agriculture Organization. The SPS Agreement permits individual members to set more rigorous standards, but only if there is a scientific justification for doing so, as established by approved risk assessment techniques. SPS Agreement, arts. 3.3, 5.1. In the absence of adequate scientific evidence, nations may provisionally impose precautionary measures pending the acquisition of additional information, but they must obtain this further evidence within a reasonable time. *Id.* art. 5.7. The North American Free Trade Agreement (NAFTA) contains similar, though not identical, provisions regarding SPS measures. Can.–Mex.–U.S.: North American Free Trade

Agreement, Chapter 7(B) ("Sanitary and Phytosanitary Measures"), Dec. 17, 1992.

In the late 1990s, the United States brought a successful complaint in the WTO against the European Community's ban on meat and meat products derived from hormone-treated animals. The WTO ruled that the EC ban violated the SPS agreement. *See* Panel Report, *EC Measures Concerning Meat and Meat Products (Hormones), Complaint by the United States*, WT/DS26/R/USA (18 Aug. 1997); Appellate Body Report, *EC—Measures Concerning Meat and Meat Products (Hormones)*, WT/DS26/AB/R, ST/DS48/AB/R (Jan. 16, 1998) (adopted Feb. 13, 1998). When the European Union failed to act on this adverse ruling by ending the ban on hormone-treated beef, the United States retaliated by imposing tariffs against several specific European food products, such as foie gras, Roquefort cheese, and Dijon mustard. *See* James F. Smith, *From Frankenfood to Fruit Flies: Navigating the WTO/SPS*, 6 U.C. DAVIS J. INT'L L. & POL'Y 1 (2000).

In the late 1990s, the European Union instituted a moratorium on the approval of agricultural biotechnology products. In August 2003, the United States, Argentina, and Canada challenged this moratorium in the WTO, contending that the policy impermissibly blocks imports without a valid scientific basis, in violation of the SPS and other agreements. In February 2006, the WTO preliminarily concluded in favor of the United States and the other complainants. *See* Rob Portman, U.S. Trade Rep., & Mike Johanns, U.S. Agric. Sec., Joint Statement on Agricultural Biotechnology and the WTO (Feb. 7, 2006). The final WTO panel reports, confirming the preliminary verdict, were released on September 29, 2006 and are available on the organization's website. Although the EU has approved some biotechnology applications since the institution of the case in 2003, the United States maintains that a partial moratorium remains in effect.

While the WTO SPS Agreement can be an effective tool for the United States to use on behalf of American exporters, other countries could potentially use it to challenge the United States' own food safety measures, including, for example, some of the new requirements contained in the 2002 Bioterrorism Act. *See* Richard T. Ting, *Food and Drug Administration Regulation of Imported Foods and Compliance with International Trade Obligations* (2005), in Chapter II(C)(2) of the Electronic Book; Robyn E. Ridler, *Cattle, Dolphins, and the WTO: The Potential Impact of the World Trade Organization Agreements on United States Food Regulation* (1998), in Chapter II(C)(4) of the Electronic Book.

C. IMPORT FOR EXPORT

FDA Regulatory Procedures Manual, Chapter 9–15: Import for Export

April 2013.

. . . The FDA Export Reform and Enhancement Act of 1996 (Export Reform Act), Public Law 104–134[,] amended section 801(d)(3) of the Act to allow the importation of certain articles that are unapproved or otherwise do not comply with the Act, provided that those imported articles are further processed or incorporated into products that will be exported from the United States, by their initial owner or consignee in accordance with section 801(e) or section 802 of the Act or section 351(h) of the Public Health Service Act (PHSA). . . . [T]he Public Health Security and Bioterrorism Preparedness and Response Act of 2002 (Bioterrorism Act), Public Law 107–188 . . . [further] amended section 801(d)(3) of the Act. . . .

When a drug or device component, food additive, color additive, or dietary supplement is imported under section 801(d)(3), the importer is required to submit a statement to FDA at the time of each importation with the following information:

1.   that such article (the components, parts, accessories, or articles) is intended to be further processed by the initial owner or consignee or incorporated by the initial owner or consignee into a drug, biological product, device, food, food additive, color additive, or dietary supplement that will be exported from the United States by the initial owner or consignee in accordance with section 801(e) or section 802 of the Act or section 351(h) of the PHSA; and

2.   identification of the manufacturer of such article and each processor, packer, distributor or other entity that had possession of the article in the chain of possession from the manufacturer to such importer of the article.

. . . .

The terms "further processed" and "incorporated" can cover a wide range of activities. These can include packaging or labeling of finished products and specialized processing (such as sterilization) of a product. FDA recognizes that in some instances, it may be advantageous to manufacture a product in a foreign country and then ship it to the United States for specialized packaging or labeling. Merely storing an article or product in the United States before export is not considered "further processing." . . .

Many manufacturers assemble their products in various stages. These manufacturing steps may include sending partially completed products to firms in the United States for further manufacturing or processing, but not into a finished product. Neither the statutory language of the amended section 801(d)(3) nor the legislative history of the Export Reform Act or the Bioterrorism Act require that violative components allowed to be imported must be incorporated into "finished products." Because components, or "subassemblies," are the finished product of the U.S. manufacturer (although not necessarily a consumer ready product) and would constitute a drug, biological product, device, food additive, color additive, or dietary supplement within the Act's meaning, the agency has concluded that articles imported for use in the manufacture of such products fall within the scope of the import for export provision. . . .

The new section 801(d)(3)(A)(iv) requires that the initial owner or consignee maintain records on the use or destruction of the imported articles or portions and to provide records when requested. The initial owner or consignee is also required to submit a report to FDA, upon request, that provides an accounting of the export or destruction of such imported article or portions and the manner in which such owner or consignee complied with the requirements of section 801(d)(3). . . .

CHAPTER 15

OTHER AGENCY PROCEDURES

A. REGULARIZING AGENCY PROCEDURES

In 40 Fed. Reg. 22950 (May 27, 1975), FDA published comprehensive regulations governing a wide range of administrative procedures. Consisting of 34 pages of preamble and 62 pages of codified rules, the regulations were made effective 60 days later, without time for comment, on the premise that, as procedural regulations, they were exempt from the APA's rulemaking requirements. Suit was promptly brought seeking a declaration that the regulations were unlawful because of the agency's failure to provide an opportunity for public comment. *American College of Neuropsychopharmacology v. Weinberger*, Food Drug Cosm. L. Rep. (CCH) ¶ 38,025 (D.D.C. 1975), held that even though exclusively concerned with agency procedures, the regulations were so substantial that they could not lawfully be issued without complying with 5 U.S.C. 553, the APA section governing rulemaking. 40 Fed. Reg. 33063 (Aug. 6, 1975).

Following this ruling, FDA republished the entire document as a proposal, 40 Fed. Reg. 40682 (Sept. 3, 1975). After receiving comments, the agency proceeded to promulgate final regulations in stages: 41 Fed. Reg. 26636 (June 28, 1976), codified at 21 C.F.R. Part 13 (public hearing before public board of inquiry); 41 Fed. Reg. 48258 (Nov. 2, 1976), codified at 21 C.F.R. Part 15, 16, 19 (public hearing before the commissioner; informal regulatory hearings; standards of conduct and conflict of interest), 41 Fed. Reg. 51706 (Nov. 23, 1976), codified at 21 C.F.R. Part 12 (formal evidentiary hearing); 41 Fed. Reg. 52148 (Nov. 26, 1976), codified at 21 C.F.R. Part 14 (public hearing before advisory committees); 42 Fed. Reg. 4680 (Jan. 25, 1977), codified at 21 C.F.R. Part 10 (general administrative practices and procedures). FDA had earlier promulgated procedural regulations governing environmental impact considerations and public information. 38 Fed. Reg. 7001 (Mar. 15, 1973), codified at 21 C.F.R. Part 25; 39 Fed. Reg. 44602 (Dec. 24, 1974), codified at 21 C.F.R. Part 20.

Because of their length and detail, it is not feasible to summarize even the important issues addressed by FDA's procedural regulations. We have discussed some of them earlier in this book, especially in Chapter 2. In this chapter, we will address three particularly important parts of the procedural regulations, namely, those concerning advisory committees, public information, and environmental assessment.

B. ADVISORY COMMITTEES

1.   FDA'S RELIANCE ON ADVISORY COMMITTEES

Food and Drug Administration
Advisory Committees

National Research Council and Institute of Medicine of the
National Academies (1992).

The FDA uses technical advisory committees of outside scientific experts to advise it on the approvability of specific products and on the scientific and clinical policy issues it confronts regarding product development and evaluation. The agency also uses these committees to legitimate the soundness of its analysis of a given product, as a public forum for discussion of controversial issues, and, on occasion, as an "appeals court" for disputed agency decisions.

. . . .

The FDA's use of agency-chartered advisory committees for drug evaluation has evolved over the three decades since the 1962 drug amendments to the Food, Drug, and Cosmetic Act. Those amendments required FDA to assess all new drugs for effectiveness, in addition to safety (as required by the 1938 amendments), and to reassess for effectiveness nearly 4,000 prescription drugs that had been introduced to the market between 1938 and 1962—before proof of effectiveness was required.

The FDA responded by seeking external advice from the National Academy of Sciences–National Research Council (NAS–NRC) on previously marketed prescription drugs, establishing its own review committees for over-the-counter drugs, and extending such committees to new prescription drugs. . . .

Over-the-Counter Drugs

. . . In 1972, the FDA faced the mammoth problem of reviewing all of the OTC drugs that had been marketed between 1938 and the enactment of the 1962 Drug Amendments. Its solution was to establish an OTC review system. . . . The regulatory product of this process was a series of monographs consisting of approved active ingredients, labeling, and other general requirements.

. . . .

This system . . . articulated some general principles of FDA advisory committees. Such committees should include nonvoting industry and consumer representatives, for example, to increase the likelihood that the results of the review would be accepted in both quarters. The participation of the former helped to avoid surprising the industry, to maintain contact with it, to detect problems early, and to minimize opposition.

Prescription Drug Review

In the early 1970s . . . an advisory committee system evolved for prescription drugs. Its purpose was to secure expert advice on the evaluation and approval of new therapeutic products. . . .

The FDA used internal memoranda to create these prescription drug advisory committees administratively. Subsequently, the agency promulgated general regulations governing the formation and operation of advisory committees, which are now codified in (21 CFR 14). . . .

The FDA created a system of standing, rather than ad hoc, committees so that committee members would see the fruits of their labor. Terms for advisory committee members were four years but were often shortened by such factors as slow appointments and early departures. Committee members were primarily academic physicians, although it soon became clear that other expertise was also needed.

Biologics

. . . .

During the years in which the biologics regulatory program was a component of the NIH, ad hoc advisory committees were sometimes formed to deal with matters of high public visibility, such as a major new product that was being considered for approval or an important problem that occurred with an existing marketed product. The membership of these committees generally include experts from government as well as the academic community. . . .

The transfer [to FDA in 1972] was followed by a number of management changes in the biologics organization and a decision to reexamine the efficacy of all existing licensed biological products. At that time, there were no standing committees for biologics regulatory decisions, and the ad hoc committees that were involved had a narrow focus. To carry out its regulatory functions, the [Bureau of Biologics] created a process similar to the comprehensive OTC drug review and formed six standing committees to review the principal categories of biological products: major vaccines, bacterial vaccines, blood products, and products for which the science base was substantially less, such as allergenic extracts.

The scale and scope of the review were substantial in both administrative and logistical terms. As the committees began their work, it became apparent that these same experts could be helpful to the agency in other ways: giving ongoing advice about new products (assuming the role of earlier ad hoc committees in this regard); advising on general problems that occurred with both marketed and experimental products; and reviewing intramural research similarly to the function of the NIH DBS Board of Scientific Counselors. As the agency completed its one-time comprehensive reviews of existing products, it reduced the number of these original committees and rechartered them to provide continuing advice on all of the organization's regulatory and research programs.

. . . .

Medical Devices

The use of advisory committees by the Center for Devices and Radiological Health (CDRH) differs from that of the CDER and CBER in one critical aspect: it is required by statute. . . .

The Medical Device Amendments . . . required the creation of advisory panels or committees for two purposes. The first was the classification of medical devices. Following adoption of the amendments, the FDA revisited the classification process in accordance with the act. The new classification advisory panels had the benefit of prior efforts, which were a useful point of departure.

The second purpose was the evaluation of medical devices regulated by risk tier. . . .

For product evaluation, the amendments called for establishment of permanent advisory committees. To these advisory committees the FDA was to appoint "persons qualified in the subject matter to be referred to the committee and of appropriately diversified professional backgrounds"; the agency was also mandated to appoint a chairman and provide necessary clerical support. The performance standards section called for the appointment of nonvoting consumer and industry members; this provision was omitted from the premarketing approval section, but the practice was adopted for the product review committees nevertheless and is the basis for current policy.

Although the Safe Medical Devices Act of 1990 modified the original 1976 legislation in certain respects giving the agency greater discretion in the use of advisory committees—it did not change the basic mandate to use such committees. . . .

In 1990, the CDRH recharged its advisory committees into a single Medical Device Advisory Committee with a number of panels. Concurrently, the agency implemented the combination products requirements of the Safe Medical Devices Act by issuing regulations on product jurisdiction (which encompassed combination products) and negotiating three intercenter agreements on this subject. The CDRH rechartering of its device advisory committees converged with these product jurisdiction efforts and led to a rechartering of CDER and CBER advisory committees as well. . . .

NOTES

1. *Uses of Advisory Committees.* FDA relies heavily on technical advisory committees for advice on such issues as the approval of new drugs and the adequacy of clinical test designs. 21 C.F.R. 14.160 *et seq.* The agency has also used advisory committees to hold public hearings on a wide variety of issues, including proposed approvals, or denials of approval, of new products. Committees have also reviewed proposed approval or denial of new uses for existing products, or new warnings, or even revocation of prior approvals. *E.g.*, 46 Fed. Reg. 14355 (Feb. 27, 1981) (announcing an advisory committee hearing on the proposed revocation of erythromycin estolate, which FDA had approved more than 20 years earlier). *See* M.S. Brown & B.W. Richard, *Advisory Committees and the Drug Approval Process*, 2 J. Clin. Res. & Drug Dev. 15 (1988). *See also* Thomas Burack, *Of Reliable Science: Scientific Peer Review, Federal Regulatory Agencies and the Courts*, 7 VA. J. OF NAT. RES. LAW 27 (1987).

2. *Number of Committees.* On July 17, 2012, FDA reported that it had 51 advisory committee and panels, and that in the fiscal year to date, 1048 committee members had participated in 63 advisory committee meetings. *See* "July 17, 2012: FDA–TRACK Advisory Committees Quarterly Briefing Summary" (available on FDA website).

3. *Authority to Create Advisory Committees.* Most of FDA's advisory committees have been established by the Secretary of HHS. However, section 903(c) of the FD&C Act, as added by the Food and Drug Administration Act of 1988, 102 Stat. 3048, 3120, and amended by the Food and Drug Administration Revitalization Act, 104 Stat. 4583 (1990), explicitly empowers the FDA Commissioner to "establish such technical and scientific review groups as are needed to carry out the functions" of FDA. A minority of FDA advisory committees are statutorily mandated. These include the Technical Electronic Product Radiation Safety Standards Committee, 42 U.S.C. 263t(f)(1)(A); the color additive advisory committees, 21 U.S.C. 376(b)(5)(C)(D); the Device Good Manufacturing Practice Advisory Committee, 21 U.S.C. 360j(f)(3); and the advisory review panels for medical devices, 21 U.S.C. 360c(b).

2. STATUTORY REQUIREMENTS FOR ADVISORY COMMITTEES

In 1972, Congress passed the Federal Advisory Committee Act (FACA), which governs the composition and behavior of all federal advisory committees. Questions about FACA's applicability have generated as much controversy as its particular procedural requirements. *Food Chemical News, Inc. v. Davis*, 378 F. Supp. 1048 (D.D.C. 1974), held FACA applicable to a series of meetings that the Director of the Bureau of Alcohol, Tobacco and Firearms had scheduled separately with consumer and industry groups to discuss proposals for alcoholic beverage labeling. The aim of the plaintiff, a weekly trade journal, was to force BATF to open the meetings to the public. A similar objective inspired the plaintiff in the following case.

Consumers Union of United States, Inc. v. Department of HEW

409 F. Supp. 473 (D.D.C. 1976) *aff'd*, 551 F.2d 466 (D.C. Cir. 1977).

■ JOHN LEWIS SMITH, JR. DISTRICT JUDGE.

This case involves a relatively narrow legal question: Were the meetings held on April 9 and September 17, 1975 between Food and Drug Administration (FDA) officials and representatives of the Cosmetic, Toiletry and Fragrance Association, Inc. (CTFA, Intervenor) advisory committee meetings within the meaning of the Federal Advisory Committee Act? If so, they were invalidly held since under FACA the meetings should have been open to the public and the "advising" group authorized through administrative approval and chartering. . . .

The FDA has considered the desirability of labeling and of testing cosmetic ingredients since 1960. The initiative in these areas has moved back and forth from agency to industry, with industry representatives (acting at times to forestall pending legislation) proposing certain voluntary programs and FDA calling for refinements and clarifications in procedures. There now exist procedures for voluntary registration of cosmetic product establishments, for voluntary filing of cosmetic product ingredients, and for voluntary filing of cosmetic product experiences. . . .

In the area of testing cosmetic ingredients, FDA–CTFA efforts have increased in the past two years. Speaking at CTFA's annual meeting on February 27, 1974, FDA Commissioner Schmidt discussed the need for establishment of an ingredient review program. Another FDA official, Dr. Mark Novitch, stated: "Certainly, this kind of approach [*i.e.*, cosmetic ingredient safety substantiation paralleling the drug review process] is something you should consider and we *will* consider in our common effort to increase our mutual assurance and the public's confidence in the safety of our cosmetic products." (Emphasis in original.) CTFA had been developing a safety review program since 1972, and planning and consultation moved forward rapidly. After three exploratory meetings between FDA and CTFA representatives in 1974 and two briefing meetings in early 1975, CTFA requested a meeting with FDA to discuss CTFA's draft proposal. This meeting was held on April 9, 1975, and detailed minutes were kept for the session. Plaintiff's counsel subsequently requested permission to attend or participate in future FDA–CTFA meetings on the ingredient review proposal, invoking the Federal Advisory Committee Act. Commissioner Schmidt denied the request on grounds that these were private, CTFA-initiated meetings. Following the filing of this lawsuit, a second meeting was held on September 17, 1975 to discuss CTFA's revised proposal. Minutes were also kept for this meeting.

Resolution of the issues in this case requires a careful examination of FACA and its administrative and judicial construction. The Federal Advisory Committee Act was aimed at eliminating useless advisory committees, strengthening the independence of remaining advisory committees, and preventing advisory groups from becoming self-serving. The Act defines advisory committee in a general, open-ended fashion. For purposes of this action, the term includes "any committee, board, commission, council, conference, panel, task force, or other similar group . . . which is . . . established or utilized by one or more agencies, in the interest of obtaining advice or recommendations for . . . [such] agencies. . . ."

Several recent cases have interpreted FACA and afford some guidance to the Court in determining what constitutes an advisory committee under the Act. In *Nader v. Baroody*, 396 F. Supp. 1231 (D.D.C. 1975), the court held that certain bi-weekly meetings with various constituent and interest groups at the White House did not come within FACA's reach. The meetings were found to be of a random nature, without formally organized groups, without presidential request for policy recommendations, and without any continuity or follow-up. Further, to have applied the Act so as to impinge upon the effective discharge of the President's business might have raised serious constitutional questions.

In *Food Chemical News, Inc. v. Davis*, 378 F. Supp. 1048 (D.D.C. 1974), the court held as subject to FACA an agency's informal meetings with consumer and distilled spirits industry representatives relative to drafting proposed ingredient labeling regulations. . . .

The matter before the Court involves a factual situation different from the above-mentioned cases. The meetings complained of here were not ad hoc, amorphous or casual group meetings as in *Nader v. Baroody*. The FDA–CTFA conferences were the culmination of many months of planning, consulting, and revising. On the other hand—and unlike *Food Chemical News*—the two meetings were not called to consider proposals dealing with impending agency action. They were essentially consultations concerning the group's own proposal. This is a crucial factor for determining the group's status under the Act. . . .

Based on the record, the Court finds that CTFA was not advising the FDA about the cosmetic ingredient testing program. CTFA was presenting a voluntary, industry-sponsored proposal and seeking the FDA's comments and advice. . . . Granting that FDA had frequently expressed its concern for cosmetic ingredient testing, the Court finds that planning had evolved beyond agency control. CTFA in its own discretion was ultimately to decide whether or not to initiate a testing program. Such a relationship of agency and group does not rise to the level of a FACA "advisory" relationship. . . .

———

In its regulations, FDA summarizes its interpretation of FACA's coverage as follows:

(b) In determining whether a group is a *public advisory committee* and thus subject to this part and the Federal Advisory Committee Act, the following guidelines will be used:

(1) An advisory committee may be a standing advisory committee or an ad hoc advisory committee. . . .

. . . .

(3) An advisory committee includes any of its subgroups when the subgroup is working on behalf of the committee. . . .

(4) A committee composed entirely of full-time Federal Government employees is not an advisory committee.

(5) An advisory committee ordinarily has a fixed membership, a defined purpose of providing advice to the agency on a particular subject, regular or periodic meetings, and an organizational structure, for example, a chairman and staff, and serves as a source of independent expertise and advice rather than as a representative of or advocate for any particular interest. The following groups are not advisory committees:

(i) A group of persons convened on an ad hoc basis to discuss a matter of current interest to FDA, but which has no continuing function or organization and does not involve substantial special preparation.

(ii) A group of two or more FDA consultants meeting with the agency on an ad hoc basis.

(iii) A group of experts who are employed by a private company or a trade association which has been requested by FDA to provide its views on a regulatory matter pending before FDA.

(iv) A consulting firm hired by FDA to provide advice regarding a matter.

(6) An advisory committee that is utilized by FDA is subject to this subpart even though it was not established by FDA. In general, a committee is "utilized" when FDA requests advice or recommendations from the committee on a specific matter in order

to obtain an independent review and consideration of the matter, and not when FDA is merely seeking the comments of all interested persons or of persons who have a specific interest in the matter.

21 C.F.R. 14.1(b).

National Nutritional Foods Ass'n v. Califano

603 F.2d 327 (2d Cir. 1979).

■ FRIENDLY, CIRCUIT JUDGE.

This is an appeal from an order of the District Court for the Southern District of New York, 457 F. Supp. 275 (1978), in an action by two trade associations whose members manufacture and sell protein supplements. . . . The action concerns FDA rulemaking designed to require warnings for protein supplements and other preparations that may be used as the sole or primary source of calories in order to lose weight. . . .

Liquid protein products have been available for direct retail sale to the consuming public for at least 12 years. Within the last five years new medical research has suggested the usefulness of a modified fasting diet, supplemented by protein, vitamins and minerals, in alleviating obesity. Prominent in this "Protein Sparing Modified Fast" (PSMF) research was Dr. George L. Blackburn of the Harvard University Medical School, who is Director of the Center for Nutritional Research in Boston. . . .

The controversy was heated by the publication in late 1976 of "The Last Chance Diet" by Robert Linn, a doctor of osteopathy, which popularized the use of liquid protein products for diet control. The ASBP [American Society of Bariatric Physicians] attacked the new widespread and uncontrolled use of PSMF programs and urged its members to help with the problem, through such means as writing letters to newspapers. . . .

Primary responsibility in the FDA for products such as those manufactured and sold by plaintiffs lay in Dr. Allan Forbes, Acting Associate Director for Nutrition and Consumer Sciences in the Bureau of Foods. In the spring of 1977 he and Dr. Blackburn had various conversations about Dr. Linn's book and the consequent popularity of liquid food protein products, including Dr. Blackburn's attempts to dissuade Dr. Linn from publishing. In a letter to Dr. Forbes dated May 25, 1977, Dr. Blackburn suggested that the Bureau of Foods might become involved. During the summer of 1977, the FDA received a report of a death believed to be associated with the use of liquid protein products in dieting; a second death was reported in September. At a conference of FDA officials held on or before October 3, 1977, it was decided, among other things, "to obtain the advice of experts in the field of obesity research among whom are Dr. George L. Blackburn, Dr. Theodore B. Van Itallie, and Dr. Sanford A. Miller." . . .

Later in October, Dr. Forbes learned that a conference on obesity was scheduled to take place on October 20–22, 1977, at the National Institutes of Health in Bethesda, Md., near the FDA's headquarters. Between October 18 and 22 he communicated with five clinicians who were attending the conference and arranged for them to meet with him and six other FDA officials.... The memorandum recites that the "ultimate purpose for the meeting" was to assist the FDA in selecting the best course of action "for regulating the production and promotion of [protein products used for weight reduction] and/or informing the public of their hazard potential." It described the five physicians as an "ad hoc advisory group." . . . The memorandum concluded by saying:

> The members of the ad hoc advisory group have graciously agreed to provide further assistance to FDA as the need may arise.

On November 9, 1977 the Commissioner of Food and Drugs held a press conference and issued a press release on the subject of protein supplements used to fight obesity. He declared the FDA was aware of 16 reported deaths and a number of severe illnesses possibly associated with the use of such products and expressed special concern about the "liquid protein diets now so popular," which were being promoted in the new media and in books such as Dr. Linn's. He said that his statements reflected not only the views of the FDA but also "the information provided by the Center for Disease Control and advice given us by leading experts in obesity and obesity control," two of whom, Drs. Blackburn and Van Itallie, were present and could answer questions.

As should have been expected, this publicity resulted in a drastic decline in the sale of protein products for use in weight reduction. On December 2, 1977, the FDA gave notice of a proposed rule, 42 F.R. 61285, whereby protein supplements intended for use in weight reduction or maintenance programs would be required to bear the following warning:

> *Warning.* Very low calorie protein diets may cause serious illness or death. DO NOT USE FOR WEIGHT REDUCTION OR MAINTENANCE WITHOUT MEDICAL SUPERVISION. Do not use for any purpose without medical advice if you are taking medication. Not for use by infants, children, or pregnant or nursing women.

The notice relied heavily on the October 20 meeting with the ad hoc advisory group, which was described in detail, and the memorandum of the meeting was placed on file with the Hearing Clerk. . . .

Appellants contend that the meeting of October 20, 1977, was of an advisory committee as defined in FACA and did not comply with the Act and the FDA's regulations thereunder, 21 C.F.R. 14.1 *et seq.*, in several respects. The FDA gave no notice of the meeting as required by 21 C.F.R. 14.20 and § 10(a)(2) of the Act. No advisory committee charter was filed as required by § 9(c). The meeting was not open to the public, nor were interested persons given any opportunity to appear before the committee or file statements with it, as required by § 10(a)(1) and (3). Most important, appellants claim that appointment of a group composed solely of physicians, understandably leaning in favor of medical supervision of the use of protein supplements to conquer obesity, did not comply with § 5(b)(2) and (3), made applicable to agencies by § 5(c), which require that membership of an advisory committee "be fairly balanced in terms of the points of view represented and the functions to be performed" and that suitable provision be made to assure that advice and recommendations "will not be inappropriately influenced . . . by any special interest." The FDA's principal answer is that the group convened on October 20 was not an advisory committee within the meaning of FACA. . . .

In the long run the Government's argument that the October 20 meeting was not within FACA rests mainly on what it conceives to be common sense. An agency dealing with technical matters ought to be able to get the advice of highly qualified technicians in the private sector before it even initiates proceedings or takes other action, and to get this speedily and informally. Yet the OMB guidelines require that before creating a new advisory committee, an agency must first consult with the OMB secretariat and, if the OMB concurs, a process that may be time consuming, must publish in the Federal Register a certification of need and a description of the nature and purpose of the committee at least 15 days (unless that period is shortened by the OMB secretariat) before the filing of the committee's charter, which under § 9(c) of the Act, is a precondition to the committee's meeting. Congress, the Government argues, could not have intended to place such obstacles in the way of what proved to be a one-time meeting, even though there may have been an intention to hold more. . . .

The two most relevant reported decisions are *Food Chemical News, Inc. v. Davis* . . . and *Nader v. Baroody* . . . [W]e find *Food Chemical News* to be more nearly in point. One factor weighing heavily with us is that the Commissioner leaned so strongly on the advisory group in his press release and, even more so, in his proposed regulation. If an agency wishes to rely publicly on the backing of an advisory committee it must do what the statute commands. Such a situation directly implicates the concern Congress addressed in § 5(c)(2) and (3) of the Act, that agency action might be dominated by one particular viewpoint. Some two months elapsed between the initial plan for the meeting and the publication of the proposal, in which the advisory group was mentioned on four occasions. Even if the calling of the meeting without reference to FACA was a pardonable inadvertence, there was ample time for compliance before December 7. All things considered, we believe this to be a situation wherein Congress meant FACA to apply. If the straitjacket is too tight, Congress is free to loosen it.

The question of remedy remains. So far as we are aware, no court has held that a violation of FACA would invalidate a regulation adopted under otherwise appropriate procedures, simply because it stemmed from the advisory committee's recommendations, or even that pending rulemaking must be aborted and a fresh start made. We perceive no sound basis for doing so. Applicable rulemaking procedures afford ample opportunity to correct infirmities resulting from improper advisory committee action prior to the proposal. . . . We likewise cannot fault the district judge for concluding that, in light of the Government's agreement not to reconvene this particular group, there was no need for an injunction. Whether it was proper to deny declaratory relief is a closer question. . . . In any event this opinion gives appellants substantially the same relief as a declaratory order. . . .

NOTES

1. *Second Judicial Thoughts.* Reflecting on this ruling, Judge Friendly later wrote:

No one seems even to have considered that in seeking to cure one trouble by imposing procedural requirements, the statute would create others. Just what is an advisory committee? In a recent opinion, where the FDA had consulted with a number of physicians who were attending a meeting of the nearby National Institute of Health, I regretfully found it impossible to accept the Government's position that simply by keeping things informal an agency can escape from a statute whose very purpose is to require formality.

Against this a judge would scarcely wish to say that if on the night of Three Mile Island the NRC wanted to telephone a few eminent atomic scientists, it could not legally have done so. Assuming that a talk with one scientist would not have been subject to FACA, what about a conference call with five? What about a couple of meetings in Harrisburg during the next few days? Beyond this the statute necessitates additional staff in each agency and in the Office of Management and Budget. Would we not have been better off with a bit more trust and less law?

Should We Be Turning Back the Law Flood?, LEGAL TIMES OF WASHINGTON, Oct. 8, 1979, at 7.

2.   *Application to Nongovernmental Bodies.* FACA has been held not to apply to committees formed by independent scientific bodies on whose conclusions the government may later rely to formulate federal policy. *Food Chemical News v. Young*, 900 F.2d 328 (D.C. Cir. 1990) (decided on the authority of *Public Citizen v. United States Department of Justice*, 491 U.S. 440 (1989)); *Lombardo v. Handler*, 397 F. Supp. 792 (D.D.C. 1975), *aff'd without opinion* 546 F.2d 1043 (D.C. Cir. 1976).

3.   *Open Committee Meetings.* During their first three years of operation, the OTC Drug Review panels began each meeting with an open session but conducted deliberations in closed session. Transcripts of closed meetings were made but were not released to the public. *See* 40 Fed. Reg. 40682 (Sept. 3, 1975). FDA's policy of withholding meeting transcripts was initially upheld in *Smart v. FDA*, Civ. No. C–73–118–RHS (N.D. Cal. 1974), but it was later held to contravene the Freedom of Information Act in *Wolfe v. Weinberger*, 403 F. Supp. 238 (D.D.C. 1975). In 1976 FDA reversed its policy and opened the deliberative portions of all advisory committee meetings. On September 13, 1976, Congress enacted the Government in the Sunshine Act, 90 Stat. 1241, which amended FACA to narrow the circumstances under which an advisory committee may be closed. FDA's final advisory committee regulations, 41 Fed. Reg. 52148 (Nov. 26, 1976), 21 C.F.R. 14.25 & 14.27, provide that all advisory committee meetings are to be open to the public except during consideration of trade secrets, investigatory files, sensitive internal documents, or matters involving personal privacy.

4.   *Committee Drafts.* In *Bristol Meyers Co. v. Kennedy*, Food Drug Cosm. L. Rep. (CCH) ¶ 38,224 (D.D.C. 1979), plaintiff sought the transcripts of the 1972–1976 closed sessions of an OTC drug panel and all drafts of the proposed monograph, and argued that the closed sessions violated FACA and thus invalidated the panel's report. FDA provided the requested transcripts but not the panel drafts. The District Court held that

the drafts as a whole reflected the deliberative process of the panel and thus were exempt from public disclosure. The court also ruled that any FACA violation was mooted by the release of the transcripts of the closed sessions and would in any event not be ripe for judicial review until a final regulation was promulgated.

5. *GSA Guidelines.* The General Services Administration has promulgated guidelines for federal agencies to follow in order to comply with FACA in 41 C.F.R. Part 101–6.

6. *Application to the National Academy of Sciences.* Congress has relaxed the open meeting requirements of FACA for study committees established by the National Academy of Sciences. 5 U.S.C. App. 2 § 15.

———

On occasion an FDA advisory committee has been challenged on the ground that its membership is not, as FACA requires, "fairly balanced."

Public Citizen v. National Advisory Committee
886 F.2d 419 (D.C. Cir. 1989).

■ Opinion, concurring in the [per curiam] judgment [of affirmance], filed by CIRCUIT JUDGE FRIEDMAN.

In November 1987, the United States Department of Agriculture (Department) announced plans to establish a National Advisory Committee on Microbiological Criteria for Foods (Committee). The purpose of the Committee was to provide advice and recommendations to the Secretaries of Agriculture and Health and Human Services (HHS) on the development of microbiological criteria by which the safety and wholesomeness of food could be assessed.

The Committee's mandate was primarily technical and scientific. Developing microbiological criteria for foods requires an understanding of the complex science in the area and an appropriate background and training. . . .

The Committee membership . . . consisted of two university professors, one state agriculture department official, one state department of agriculture and consumer services official, two persons employed by food research firms, six persons employed by federal agencies, and six persons employed by private food companies. . . .

The Committee held its first meeting on April 5, 1988. By letter dated May 12, 1988, the appellants requested the Secretary of Agriculture to "take immediate action to appoint consumer representatives with public health expertise to membership" on the Committee, and, further, offered to "recommend . . . individuals with appropriate credentials in public health and consumer concerns." . . . The Assistant Secretary replied:

Although the Committee is composed of scientific experts, the consumer perspective is also brought to the Committee by its membership. In particular, Dr. Martha Rhodes, Assistant Commissioner of the Florida Department of Agriculture and Consumer Services, was selected for the Committee because of her expertise in microbiology, public health, and consumer affairs, as well as her involvement with State governmental matters. If you would like to recommend others for membership on the Committee, we will be happy to review their qualifications and consider them when there is a vacancy

. . . .

The appellants then filed the present action in the district court seeking declaratory and injunctive relief against the government's alleged violation of the Federal Advisory Committee Act. . . .

The appellants originally contended that because the Committee's recommendations will directly affect the interest of consumers, the Act requires that the Committee contain representatives of consumers, and that the Committee lacks such representation because "not a single member of the Committee works for, or is associated with, a consumer or public health organization, despite the fact that there are such individuals who have expertise and backgrounds in the very issues to be scrutinized by the Committee."

. . . .

The appropriate inquiry in determining whether the Committee's membership satisfies the "fairly balanced" standard in section 5(b)(2) is whether the Committee's members "represent a fair balance of viewpoints given the functions to be performed." Since the Committee's function in this case involves highly technical and scientific studies and recommendations, a "fair balance" of viewpoints can be achieved even though the Committee does not have any members who are consumer advocates or proponents of consumer interests.

The statutory directive that membership of the Committee be "fairly balanced" does not mean that such balance can be provided only by individuals who work for, or are associated with, a consumer or public health organization. . . .

The determination of how the "fairly balanced" membership of an advisory committee . . . is to be achieved, necessarily lies largely within the discretion of the official who appoints the committee. In my view, the membership of the Committee that the Secretary of Agriculture appointed did not violate the "fairly balanced" requirement of the Act, and the secretary did not abuse his discretion by failing to include on the Committee direct representatives of consumer organizations. . . .

The appellants have not shown that the original Committee was dominated or "inappropriately influenced" by food industry representatives. Only six of the 18 members were employed by the food industry. The appellants' contention that four other members of the Committee—the two employees of independent food research firms and the two university professors—represent food industry interests is unconvincing. The mere fact that the individuals employed by independent food research firms have food company clients or that the professors have performed some consulting work for food companies in the past, does not demonstrate that they are a part of "special interest groups [that] may use their membership on [advisory committees] to promote their private concerns,". . . .

■ Opinion, concurring in the judgment, filed by CIRCUIT JUDGE SILBERMAN.

... For any claim under section 5(b)(2) of the FACA to be justiciable under the APA, we must first conclude that Congress provided "a meaningful standard against which to judge the agency's exercise of discretion." Where no such meaningful standard exists, "the statute ('law') can be taken to have 'committed' the decision making to the agency's judgment absolutely," thereby precluding judicial review under 5 U.S.C. 701(a)(2). I cannot discern any meaningful standard that is susceptible of judicial application in the formulation "fairly balanced in terms of the points of view represented and the functions to be performed." Therefore, I believe that judicial review is unavailable. . . .

■ EDWARDS, CIRCUIT JUDGE, concurring in part and dissenting in part. . . .

The Committee at issue in this case is charged with recommending regulations for a broad range of food products. These decisions have health and safety implications that directly affect consumers. Recommendations regarding these regulations involve complex policy choices, not merely—or even primarily—technical determinations. For these reasons, especially in light of the legislative history of section 5, I disagree with Judge Friedman's opinion that the Committee's mandate in this instance was "primarily technical and scientific," and I conclude that a fair balance of viewpoints cannot be achieved without representation of consumer interests. . . .

The Government argues that consumers are represented by Dr. Martha Rhodes, the Assistant Commissioner of Agriculture for the Florida Department of Agriculture and Consumer Affairs, and by Dr. Mitchell Cohen of the Centers for Disease Control. Both of these persons, however, are government employees with a variety of regulatory responsibilities. One of the dangers that Congress specifically identified in adopting FACA was the risk that governmental officials would be unduly influenced by industry leaders. That is, it is precisely the lack of representatives of the public interest independent of *both* government *and* industry that prompted Congress to enact the "fairly balanced" provision. The fact that Dr. Rhodes and Dr. Cohen are state rather than federal government officials does not demonstrate that they will be less amenable to influence by industry representatives. This is not to impugn the integrity of either individual. Rather, it is to say that it is unnecessary for the court to assess the individual viewpoints of Dr. Rhodes and Dr. Cohen in order to find that their presence does not mitigate the lack of consumer representation. . . .

————

FDA often has difficulty recruiting members for its drug and device advisory committees because many of the best regarded experts have served as consultants to manufacturers of regulated products.

Robert Steinbrook, M.D., *Financial Conflicts of Interest and the Food and Drug Administration's Advisory Committees*

353 NEW ENGLAND JOURNAL OF MEDICINE 126 (2005).

The FDA's management of conflicts of interest for its advisory committees is based on the Ethics Reform Act of 1989 and implementing regulations that were issued in 1996 by the Office of Government Ethics. Voting members of FDA advisory committees are considered "Special government employees." Before each meeting in which they may participate, these experts complete a detailed confidential financial disclosure report. The agency determines whether any of the reported relationships pose a potential conflict of interest, and some people are disqualified on this basis.

The FDA, like other federal agencies, is permitted to balance its needs for scientific expertise against the potential for a conflict and to grant a waiver when "the need for the individual's services outweighs the potential for a conflict of interest." If the FDA determines that only general topics are being discussed . . . it takes a different approach from that used when it determines that approval of a specific product is being considered.

. . . .

After granting a waiver, the FDA balances the public's right to the information against the privacy of its advisory committee members. According to the agency, "information to be disclosed will adequately enable a reasonable person to understand the nature of the conflict and the degree to which it could be expected to influence the recommendations the [special government employee] will make."

The disclosure is read into the record at the beginning of the meeting. The FDA usually does not provide specifics when it grants a general waiver. When it grants a specific waiver, it usually discloses the type of interest (such as stock, consulting, or contracts and grants) as well as the magnitude, which is expressed in terms of dollar ranges rather than as a specific amount. The disclosure notes whether the financial interest is related to the product under discussion or a competing product (without naming the competitor). The actual waiver statements are not released; they can be obtained only through a written request under the Freedom of Information Act.

In February, the FDA convened a joint meeting of the Arthritis Advisory Committee and the Drug Safety and Risk Management Advisory Committee to discuss the safety of cyclooxygenase-2 (COX-2) inhibitors. At the beginning of the meeting, an agency official read a conflict-of-interest statement indicating that in the FDA's judgment the topics were "issues of broad applicability and there [were] no products being approved." Although the FDA acknowledged the possibility of conflicts of interests on the part of committee members, it declared that "because of the general nature of the discussions before the committee, these potential conflicts are mitigated." The agency issued general waivers to the members who required them in order to participate; no specific information was provided.

After the meeting, it was disclosed that 10 of the 32 voting panel members had financial associations with the manufacturers of COX–2 inhibitors, such as the receipt of speaking or consulting fees or research support. Of the 30 votes cast by these 10 members on whether rofecoxib, celecoxib, and valdecoxib should continue to be marketed, 28 favored marketing the drugs. Of the 66 votes of the other 22 members, only 37 favored marketing the drugs. If the 10 panel members with the financial associations had not participated, the committee would have voted 12 to 8 that valdecoxib should be withdrawn and 14 to 8 that rofecoxib should not return to the market. With their votes included, the tally was 17 to 13 for keeping valdecoxib on the market and 17 to 15 for the return of rofecoxib. . . .

According to Dr. Alastair J.J. Wood of Vanderbilt University Medical School, the chair of the joint meeting, the FDA made a "judgment error" when it decided to issue a general waiver and not to disclose specific information about the potential conflicts of members of the committees. In an interview, Wood said: "Of all the FDA advisory committee meetings I have attended, there has never been more money on the table. Some potential panel members had already been excluded because of conflicts. The people who were chosen had disclosed their financial interests to the FDA, although it played out as though they had something to hide."

Concern about potential conflicts of interest arose again in April, when the General and Plastic Surgery Devices Panel of the Medical Devices Advisory Committee met to consider the safety of silicone gel-filled breast implants made by Inamed and Mentor, both of Santa Barbara, California. Before the meeting, the FDA told a plastic surgeon from George Washington University School of Medicine and Health Sciences that the $50,000 to $100,000 in stock he owned in a company that is seeking to purchase Inamed did not disqualify him, and he was designated as one of 10 voting members of the panel. Days later, the agency said that he could participate but not vote; he declined a nonvoting seat. The remaining plastic surgeon on the panel had a major role in the development of an educational CD–ROM about breast-reconstruction surgery, a project that had received funding from Inamed. At the beginning of the meeting, an FDA official said that the surgeon "reported his institution's past and current involvement with firms at issue." In the absence of personal financial interests, the Agency has determined that he may participate fully in the Panel's deliberations. . . .

. . . [T]he cases raise the specific concern that the agency's disclosure statements are opaque and lack detail. They also raise the general concern that waivers for potential conflicts are common and that the agency has paid insufficient attention to its—and the public's—interest in selecting scientific advisers who are independent of industry.

    . . . .

Some changes to the FDA's approach to financial conflicts of interest could probably be implemented by the agency or the Department of Health and Human Services. One possible approach would be for the FDA to publish the names and background information of proposed committee members in the *Federal Register* and on its Web site and to give the public several weeks to comment. The agency could then consider these comments before the roster of participants in an advisory meeting was made final. Such procedures for public comment are used by the National Academies and the Environmental Protection Agency. The FDA could also make public more complete financial disclosures for its outside advisers. A possible criticism of such a move is that potential advisers would be less willing to serve under these conditions. However, in recent years, detailed public disclosures have become widely accepted—for example, in articles in medical journals and in materials associated with continuing medical education activities.

NOTES

1. *Waivers of Conflict of Interest.* FDA is authorized by statute to grant waivers to allow individuals with potentially conflicting financial interests to participate in meetings where it concludes, after close scrutiny, that certain criteria are met. *See* 18 U.S.C. 208(b)(1), (b)(3). The most common reason for a waiver is a determination that the member's expertise is essential to the committee's discussion and recommendations. Most recently, in 2007, Congress enacted section 701 of FDAAA (section 712 of the Act), which, in addition to establishing a new conflict of interest prohibition, capped the numbers of waivers that the agency could grant in a given year. Section 712(c)(2)(C) required that FDA reduce the rate of waivers the agency issued each year by 5 percent, beginning with fiscal year 2008. By 2012, the agency was permitted to issue waivers at a maximum rate of 75 percent of the rate issued in 2007. *See* GUIDANCE FOR THE PUBLIC, FDA ADVISORY COMMITTEE MEMBERS, AND FDA STAFF ON PROCEDURES FOR DETERMINING CONFLICT OF INTEREST AND ELIGIBILITY FOR PARTICIPATION IN FDA ADVISORY COMMITTEES (Aug. 2008). In 2012, FDASIA amended section 712 to repeal any caps on conflict of interest waivers.

2. *Disclosure of Waivers.* FD&C Act 701(c)(3) sets out requirements by which the agency must disclose on its website all waivers, the underlying conflict of interest, and the reason for the waiver. *See* GUIDANCE FOR THE PUBLIC, FDA ADVISORY COMMITTEE MEMBERS, AND FDA STAFF: PUBLIC AVAILABILITY OF ADVISORY COMMITTEE MEMBERS' FINANCIAL INTEREST INFORMATION AND WAIVERS (March 2012). On its website, FDA also reports the percent of advisory committee members granted waivers who participated in the meetings that took place each month. According to this data, in 2012, a year for which the target was less than 11.5%, in nine of the twelve months not a single advisory committee meeting occurred that included a member granted a conflict-of-interest waiver, and the percent never exceeded 7% for any single month.

C. PUBLIC INFORMATION

1. THE FREEDOM OF INFORMATION ACT (FOIA)

The Freedom of Information Act (FOIA) is codified in 5 U.S.C. 552 as part of the expanded statutory guarantees of access to records maintained or compiled by federal agencies. FOIA significantly influences FDA's relationships with outside organizations and individuals—makers of regulated products, public advocacy organizations, professional associations, and the private bar. FDA is the recipient, and thus the custodian, of vast amounts of information from industry. For this reason it is the target of more FOIA requests than any other agency except the FBI and the Department of Defense, and a non-trivial slice of its budget is dedicated to processing responses to these requests

Briefly summarized, FOIA requires an agency to disclose to any requester—who need not disclose or justify his interest—any responsive records that it possesses, subject to a series of ten exceptions. These exceptions permit records to be withheld, inter alia, if they are related to ongoing law enforcement, if they are officially classified as secret, if they would invade personal privacy, or if they consist of or contain confidential commercial or trade secret information. FOIA's broad mandate, coupled with its express exceptions, give rise to numerous disputes, many of which have required judicial resolution. Exemption 4—for confidential commercial information or trade secrets—has been the main battleground between those who seek FDA documents and the firms that provide most of the materials that are requested.

The following prescient excerpt, authored by the then-Chief Counsel of the agency, anticipates FOIA's impact on access to information in FDA files.

Peter Barton Hutt, *Public Information and Public Participation in the Food and Drug Administration*

36 QUARTERLY BULLETIN OF THE ASSOCIATION OF FOOD AND DRUG OFFICIALS 212
(1972).

. . . The Food and Drug Administration is the largest repository of private scientific research in the world. [It] receive[s] mountains of important data and information on the safety, effectiveness, and functionality of foods and drugs, and undoubtedly will soon be receiving the same type of information for devices and cosmetics, that is available nowhere else. Since 1938, virtually none of it has been divulged. It is now proposed [by FDA] . . . that most of it will become available for public disclosure upon request.

The proposal takes precautions to protect the confidentiality of information that genuinely can be regarded as a trade secret, in that its disclosure would destroy the competitive advantage of the person who has submitted it. The safety and effectiveness data for a new drug or a new animal drug would not be released, for example, because to do so would destroy the competitive advantage obtained from that data by the holders of the NDA or the NADA. Once those products become subject to abbreviated applications or become old drugs, however, that competitive advantage no longer exists, and it is therefore proposed that the data would promptly be released to the public upon request. Similarly, since food additives, color additives, and antibiotics are subject to public regulations rather than private licenses, and thus permit any person to engage in the their manufacture, it is proposed that the scientific data underlying those regulations would promptly be released to the public upon request the moment that the regulation is promulgated.

In an area . . . involving inspectional and other regulatory efforts, equally important changes in policy are proposed. . . . [A]n FDA inspector provides a Form 483 to an establishment upon completion of an inspection, to inform them of significant violations. The inspector then prepares an Establishment Inspection Report (EIR), which is retained for our own files, and in many instances writes a top official in the company to bring to his personal attention any violations of the law. Samples may be taken, and later analyzed, and other evidence may be accumulated. . . .

. . . [FDA] propose[s] to make available to the public, upon request, the Form 483 and any correspondence with the company or the individual involved. These documents are in the nature of an informal warning, rather than an investigatory file for law enforcement purposes, and thus would not be exempt from disclosure. The remaining information, such as the EIR, sample analyses, and so forth would be retained as confidential until the file is closed or a decision is made not to pursue legal action. . . .

A third area of interest is the Agency's general correspondence with the outside world. The [FDA] proposal adopts the position that all such documents would be released unless they fall within a specific exemption. Thus, correspondence with members of Congress, complaints from consumers, minutes of meetings with trade associations, summaries of scientific conferences, and similar documents would be available upon request. . . .

NOTES

1. *FDA's FOIA Regulations.* FDA's public information regulations were proposed in 37 Fed. Reg. 9128 (May 5, 1972) and made effective immediately. The final regulations, which also took account of the Freedom of Information Act Amendments of 1974, 88 Stat. 1561, were promulgated in 39 Fed. Reg. 44602 (Dec. 24, 1974). Further amendments were adopted in 41 Fed. Reg. 9317 (Mar. 4, 1976) and 42 Fed. Reg. 3094 (Jan. 14, 1977). FDA's current FOIA regulations are codified in 21 C.F.R. Part 20.

2. *Processing Fees.* Pursuant to the Freedom of Information Reform Act of 1986, 100 Stat. 3207, OMB has promulgated regulations in 5 C.F.R. Part 1303 setting a uniform schedule of fees applicable to all Federal agencies. Section 731 of the FD&C Act authorizes FDA to retain fees paid for searching and copying to help fund the agency's FOI activities.

3. *What Documents Are "Agency Records?"* FOIA applies only to documents actually in the possession of FDA, and does not include material to which the agency has the right of access but of which it does not have custody. This proposition was established in a case brought to challenge FDA's refusal to provide access to the raw data from a long-term multi-center clinical study of drugs approved for the treatment of diabetes. The study had been funded by NIH, which had a right to review or obtain custody of the data but had never done so. On the basis of the study findings that one of the drugs increased users' risk of heart attack, FDA proposed to require new label warnings. A group of physicians who

questioned the study findings demanded access to the underlying patient records, claiming that even though neither agency had possession, they were "agency records" under FOIA. The Supreme Court affirmed a D.C. Circuit decision rejecting their claim. *Forsham v. Harris*, 445 U.S. 169 (1980). The lower court observed in passing, however, that FDA might have to arrange for access if the physicians' opportunity to comment on its proposed relabeling would otherwise be undermined. *Forsham v. Califano*, 587 F.2d 1128 (D.C. Cir. 1978).

4.   *Cost of Implementing FOIA.* In a 2012 annual report posted on the FDA website, the agency reports that the cost of processing FOIA requests in FY 2012 was $34,617,484.54, including litigation-related costs. It collected $505,467.28 (1.51% of total costs) in FOIA fees. The agency fully granted 7,513 requests, partially denied 195 based on an exemption, and fully denied 159 based on an exemption. The report also lists how often each exemption was applied; the most common by far were Exemption 4 (trade secrets and other confidential business information) and Exemption 7(a) (could reasonably be expected to interfere with enforcement proceedings). Finally, FDA reported that it had a backlog of 2,575 requests.

Pharmaceutical Manufacturers Association
v. Weinberger

401 F. Supp. 444 (D.D.C. 1975).

■ SIRICA, DISTRICT JUDGE.

This action was instituted by the plaintiff, an association of drug companies, on May 7, 1975, when a complaint seeking declaratory and injunctive relief was filed. The motion for a preliminary injunction was filed the same day seeking to prohibit the defendants, the Secretary of the Department of H.E.W. and the Commissioner of Food and Drugs, from applying and enforcing certain regulations published by the Commissioner. . . . Specifically, plaintiff seeks to require the F.D.A. to provide notice to an affected drug company of any proposed release of information pursuant to Freedom of Information Act (hereinafter F.O.I.A.) requests, in order to provide an opportunity for the affected company to consult with the F.D.A. concerning the propriety of the release of said information, and to provide an opportunity for judicial review of the F.D.A.'s decision.

. . . .

The plaintiff argues that the notice provision of the new regulations does not satisfy due process or the confidentiality requirement of the nondisclosure statutes and exemption four. . . . [T]he principal thrust of the motion for a preliminary injunction is that the F.D.A. must provide for some notice to affected drug companies before it releases any material from its files. . . .

The Court first notes that the regulations here disputed do provide for prior notice of the possible release of exempt material and judicial review of the same:

§ 4.45 [now 21 C.F.R. 20.47]. In situations where the confidentiality of data or information is uncertain and there is a request for public disclosure, the Food and Drug Administration will consult with the person who has submitted or divulged the data or information or who would be affected by disclosure before determining whether or not such data or information is available for public disclosure.

§ 4.46 [now 21 C.F.R. 20.46]. Where the Food and Drug Administration consults with a person who will be affected by a proposed disclosure of data or information contained in Food and Drug Administration records pursuant to § 4.45 and rejects the person's request that part or all of the records not be made available for public disclosure, the decision constitutes final agency action that is subject to judicial review pursuant to 5 U.S.C. chapter 7. The person affected will be permitted 5 days after receipt of notification of such decision within which to institute suit in a United States District Court to enjoin release of the records involved. If suit is brought, the Food and Drug Administration will not disclose the records involved until the matter and all related appeals have been concluded.

However, what plaintiff claims is constitutionally and legally required is that the F.D.A. must notify the drug companies of the proposed release of any and all information which they submitted or which concerns them before it is actually released. Plaintiff argues that the F.D.A. will not always know when the confidentiality of information is uncertain. Two or three incidents are noted in which allegedly confidential, nondisclosable, F.O.I.A.-exempt information was inadvertently released by the F.D.A. pursuant to F.O.I.A. requests. In those cases the affected drug companies were not notified, consulted, or given the opportunity for judicial review before the information was disclosed. . . .

The existence of such statutes as the one involved in *American Sumatra* [*v. SEC*, 93 F.2d 236 (D.C. Cir. 1937)] implies that general constitutional principles do not provide for the relief that the plaintiff here seeks, and that legislative action is needed if such procedures are to be assured. When Congress is persuaded that such measures are necessary in light of the disclosure provisions of the F.O.I.A., it has specifically acted to insure that sensitive information is not disclosed under F.O.I.A. requests. Indeed, counsel for the defendants has notified the court that there is presently pending before Congress legislation that would, in certain cases involving the F.D.A., create a right to prior notice and judicial review comparable to that which the plaintiff seeks to obtain by injunction here.

Recent cases have implied that individuals do not have a right under the F.O.I.A. to block disclosure of information that falls within the exemptions to the F.O.I.A. because those exemptions permit, rather than require, nondisclosure. If there is no right to nondisclosure under the F.O.I.A., the Court does not perceive how there could be a right, under the F.O.I.A., to notice before a decision regarding nondisclosure is made. . . .

Furthermore, it appears that the regulations here disputed were properly promulgated, with public notice, opportunity for public comment, etc. Thus, to the extent that it could be said that the plaintiff is deprived of property rights by operation of the regulations, at least it has been afforded due process by the considered and proper manner in which the regulations have been promulgated.

Moreover, if the regulations do not provide for the absolute right to notice before the disclosure of F.D.A. information, they do provide for substantial notice and opportunity for judicial review. Indeed, those provisions can be interpreted as providing for notice and opportunity for judicial review any time the issue of confidentiality reasonably arises under a request for F.O.I.A. information. The regulation provides that the notice provisions will be applied whenever the confidentiality of information is "uncertain." The Commissioner implies that only when the material is "clearly disclosable under law" will notice not be given. The Court may assume, absent a contrary showing, that those regulations will be generously and liberally interpreted.

The plaintiff here is not seeking to prevent the disclosure of specific information which has been requested under F.O.I.A. provisions. Rather, what it seeks to prevent is some type of speculative future harm—the possibility of accidental disclosure in the future of unidentified confidential information. The threat of harm alleged, then, is not specific or certain, rather it is conjectural and speculative. Nor is it certain that the injury, if it did occur, would be irreparable injury. . . .

NOTES

1.   *Reverse FOIA Suits.* Organizations that provide information to the government frequently have a strong interest in having their confidentiality protected and may not be confident that the agency will perform this role vigorously—or at all. In *Chrysler Corp. v. Brown*, 441 U.S. 281 (1979), the Supreme Court ruled that an owner of information submitted to the government could bring suit to review the agency's decision to release records that the owner claimed were exempt from disclosure. The Court rejected Chrysler's claim that the FOIA itself implicitly recognized a right of action to enforce any of the Act's exemptions, and it likewise refused to recognize a private right to sue under the Trade Secrets Act. But it acknowledged that an agency's final decision to release information could be challenged under the Administrative Procedure Act. However, this could be an empty remedy if the owner of the information had no knowledge that the agency had received and was prepared to comply with a request for disclosure.

In 1987 President Reagan issued Executive Order No. 12,600, which required all agencies subject to FOIA "to the extent permitted by law" to "establish procedures to notify submitters of records containing [arguably] commercial information . . . when those records are requested" if the agency "determines that it may be required to disclose those records." *See generally* Note, *Protecting Confidential Business Information from Federal Agency Disclosure After* Chrysler v. Brown, 80 COLUM. L. REV. 109 (1980).

Judicial Watch, Inc. v. Food & Drug Administration
449 F.3d 141 (D.C. Cir. 2006).

■ SENTELLE, CIRCUIT JUDGE.

Judicial Watch filed an action in the District Court for the District of Columbia, seeking enforcement of its Freedom of Information Act ("FOIA") request for all documents related to the Food and Drug

Administration's approval of the drug mifepristone. It now appeals from the District Court's grant of summary judgment in favor of the FDA. Although we affirm the District Court's decision in a number of respects, because the FDA produced an inadequately detailed *Vaughn* index, we remand for further explanation of some of the index's entries.

1. Background

In September 2000, the FDA approved the drug mifepristone, better known as RU–486, for "medical abortion" during the first 49 days of pregnancy. Shortly thereafter, Judicial Watch submitted a FOIA request seeking all mifepristone-related documents in the FDA's possession. A few months later, having not received any documents, Judicial Watch sought to enforce its request in the District Court. The FDA requested a stay, which the District Court granted. The District Court ordered the FDA to produce all responsive documents by October 15, 2001.

After searching about 250,000 pages of information, the FDA disclosed over 9,000 relevant pages to Judicial Watch on a compact disc. It withheld over 4,000 other relevant documents in their entirety and parts of almost 2,000 more. The FDA compiled and produced a 1,500– page Vaughn index to summarize the withholdings. See *Vaughn v. Rosen,* 484 F.2d 820 (D.C. Cir. 1973). In addition to its Vaughn index, the FDA filed a supporting declaration by Andrea Masciale, who supervised the FDA's search and review of documents for Judicial Watch's FOIA request. The Masciale declaration described the types of withheld information and defended the application of FOIA Exemptions 3, 4, 5, and 6 to that information. Danco Laboratories and Population Council—mifepristone's creator and manufacturer, respectively— intervened in the suit and filed two additional affidavits. The intervenors' affidavits supported the FDA's reasons for using Exemptions 4 and 6 to withhold information submitted to it during mifepristone's approval.

. . . .

II. Adequacy of the *Vaughn* Index

Judicial Watch primarily argues that the FDA has produced an inadequately detailed *Vaughn* index. In this section, we consider—and reject—the challenge in its broadest sense, as a facial attack on the structure of the *Vaughn* index. Although we find nothing structurally wrong with the FDA's submission, we find merit in the narrower part of Judicial Watch's adequacy argument, specifically that the FDA has vaguely described some individual documents. We defer discussion of the vagueness inquiries until Section III and its subsections dealing with each individual FOIA exemption at issue.

. . . .

A. Functions of the *Vaughn* Index Requirement

Because of its unique evidentiary configuration, the typical FOIA case "distorts the traditional adversary nature of our legal system's form of dispute resolution." When a party submits a FOIA request, it faces an "asymmetrical distribution of knowledge" where the agency alone possesses, reviews, discloses, and withholds the subject matter of the request. The agency would therefore have a nearly impregnable defensive position save for the fact that the statute places the burden "on the agency to sustain its action."

Possessing both the burden of proof and all the evidence, the agency has the difficult obligation to justify its actions without compromising its original withholdings by disclosing too much information. The *Vaughn* index provides a way for the defending agency to do just that. By allowing the agency to provide descriptions of withheld documents, the index gives the court and the challenging party a measure of access without exposing the withheld information. The *Vaughn* index thereby also serves three important functions that help restore a healthy adversarial process:

> [I]t forces the government to analyze carefully any material withheld, it enables the trial court to fulfill its duty of ruling on the applicability of the exemption, and it enables the adversary system to operate by giving the requester as much information as possible, on the basis of which he can present his case to the trial court.

Keys v. U.S. Dep't of Justice, 830 F.2d 337, 349 (D.C. Cir. 1987) (internal quotation marks and citation omitted).

As past cases demonstrate, we focus on the functions of the *Vaughn* index, not the length of the document descriptions, as the touchstone of our analysis. Indeed, an agency may even submit other measures in combination with or in lieu of the index itself. Among other things, the agency may submit supporting affidavits or seek in camera review of some or all of the documents "so long as they give the reviewing court a reasonable basis to evaluate the claim of privilege." Any measure will adequately aid a court if it "provide[s] a relatively detailed justification, specifically identif[ies] the reasons why a particular exemption is relevant and correlat[es] those claims with the particular part of a withheld document to which they apply."

B.   The Structure of the FDA's Index

In this case, the FDA took a combined approach. In response to Judicial Watch's FOIA request, it produced a 1,500–page *Vaughn* index and supplemented the index with the supporting declaration of Andrea Masciale. The index itself includes eleven categories, consisting of the following: (1) an index identification number; (2) the document's subject; (3) its date; (4) the author; (5) the recipient; (6) the total number of pages; (7) a category entitled "Attach Page"; (8) the disposition (that is, whether entirely or partially withheld); (9) the reason for being withheld; (10) the statutory authority for the withholding; and (11) the number of pages containing withheld information. Whereas the index takes a document-specific approach, the Masciale declaration steps through the claimed exemptions. It avoids discussion of individual documents, instead describing the kinds of information withheld and how they relate to the exemptions. The intervenors filed two additional affidavits. Each covers issues specific to the documents submitted to the FDA during mifepristone's approval process, including matters ranging from competition in the abortion market to confidentiality issues.

Judicial Watch argues that the FDA's index/affidavit combination fails because it does not treat each document individually. Context dictates our approach to the particularity required of agencies. An agency may not claim exemptions too broadly, thereby sweeping unprotected information within the statute's reach. Broad, sweeping claims of privilege without reference to the withheld documents would impede judicial review and undermine the functions served by the *Vaughn* index requirement. The agency must therefore explain why the exemption applies to the document or type of document withheld and may not ignore the contents of the withheld documents.

On the other hand, abstraction can aid court review when drawing from specific examples. We have never required repetitive, detailed explanations for each piece of withheld information—that is, codes and categories may be sufficiently particularized to carry the agency's burden of proof. Especially where the agency has disclosed and withheld a large number of documents, categorization and repetition provide efficient vehicles by which a court can review withholdings that implicate the same exemption for similar reasons. In such cases, particularity may actually impede court review and undermine the functions served by a *Vaughn* index.

Seizing on the distinction between these two approaches, Judicial Watch asserts that the FDA claimed exemptions only in sweeping and conclusory generalities. We disagree. The FDA explained itself through commonalities, not generalities. Unsurprisingly, among thousands of withheld documents, certain topics and exemptions arose on multiple occasions. The index tied each individual document to one or more exemptions, and the Masciale declaration linked the substance of each exemption to the documents' common elements. No rule of law precludes the FDA from treating common documents commonly

And we do not fault the FDA for using the language of the statute as part of its explanation for withholding documents. As long as it links the statutory language to the withheld documents, the agency may even "parrot [ ]" the language of the statute. There are only so many ways the FDA could have claimed Exemptions 4, 5, and 6 for the thousands of documents generated during mifepristone's approval. . . . The FDA's decision to tie each document to one or more claimed exemptions in its index and then summarize the commonalities of the documents in a supporting affidavit is a legitimate way of serving those functions.

III. The Claimed Exemptions: Vagueness and Merits Challenges

Our holding that the FDA produced a structurally sound *Vaughn* index does not address the entirety of Judicial Watch's challenge to the adequacy of the index. . . .

A. Exemption 4

Exemption 4 allows agencies to withhold documents containing matters that are "trade secrets and commercial or financial information obtained from a person and privileged or confidential." Unlike many other types of information subject to an agency's control, materials implicating Exemption 4 are generally not developed within the agency. Instead, it must procure commercial information from third parties, either by requirement or by request. The agency thus has an incentive to be a good steward of that information: Disclosure could result in competitive disadvantages to the submitting entity, discouraging them from giving quality information in the future. The agency may therefore withhold involuntarily submitted information as confidential if disclosure would (1) impair the agency's ability to get information in the future or (2) cause substantial competitive harm to the entity that submitted the information.

The same incentive applies to the FDA approval process. The FDA requires applying companies to submit volumes of information related to a drug's development, composition, safety, and manufacture. A company must submit this information in an Investigational New Drug application ("IND") even prior to conducting clinical trials of a drug. All the information from the IND also goes into the company's New Drug Application ("NDA"), the formal application for sale and marketing approval from the FDA. Each stage of the FDA's administrative processes therefore depends directly on submissions from outside the agency.

The submission-dependent nature of the approval process means Exemption 4 extends to at least some information contained in INDs and NDAs. If it did not, other companies "could make use of the information in the INDs in order to eliminate much of the time and effort that would otherwise be required to bring to market a product competitive with the product for which" the submitting company filed the IND. . . .

Exemption 4 does not categorically exempt all information in INDs and NDAs, however, and the FOIA requester must have adequate descriptions in order to distinguish between protected and unprotected information. Judicial Watch argues that the index contains many entries . . . with descriptions too vague to allow it to mount a merits challenge to the FDA's Exemption 4 claims

The FDA argues that each index entry must be considered in relation to surrounding entries and to the additional information listed in the index. . . .

[Some] entries defy the FDA's claim of definition by association, though. . . .

The FDA asserts that its affidavit, along with those of the intervenors, makes up for any deficiency in its document descriptions. We agree that the three affidavits do a number of positive things. They show that the documents containing information from INDs or NDAs likely include either trade secrets or commercial information that would be valuable to competitors. They provide evidence, sufficient to satisfy the requirements of Exemption 4, of competitive harm in the medical abortion market that would result from the release of information in the IND. Finally, they also provide sufficient evidence to satisfy Exemption 4 of actual competition in markets for nonapproved uses of mifepristone, including cancer treatment. However persuasive, though, each of these points goes to the merits and does little to flesh out the vague document descriptions. . . .

It is no surprise that the FDA labeled many index entries with scientific codes, lab jargon, or other identifications specific to the agency. But the FDA may not create its own cryptolect, unknown to the challenger and the court. Without a glossary or technical dictionary, any lay person would be hard pressed to understand the series of numbers and letters given as descriptions in this index. . . .

By using this shorthand, the FDA missed sight of the *Vaughn* index's purpose—to enable the court and the opposing party to understand the withheld information in order to address the merits of the claimed exemptions. Scientific lingo and administrative slang, when unfamiliar, often baffle the brightest among us. To prevent confusion and aid resolution of this case, the FDA should have endeavored to make its technical world appear a little less foreign—and its shorthand a little less short—to Judicial Watch and the court. This is not to say that the FDA could not demonstrate that it properly claimed Exemption 4 as to these documents. Rather, the FDA "has failed to supply us with even the minimal information necessary to make a determination." We accordingly remand the case for further explanation of these technical descriptions.

. . . .

B.   Exemption 5

Exemption 5 permits agencies to withhold "inter-agency or intra-agency memorandums or letters which would not be available by law to a party other than an agency in litigation with the agency." Such "memorandums or letters" include those protected by the attorney-client privilege and the deliberative process privilege. The FDA relied on both privileges but has since released all documents initially withheld under the attorney-client privilege. Accordingly, we only address the question of deliberative process privilege, which Judicial Watch challenges on both adequacy grounds and the merits.

The deliberative process privilege protects agency documents that are both predecisional and deliberative. We deem a document predecisional if "it was generated before the adoption of an agency policy" and deliberative if "it reflects the give-and-take of the consultative process." Judicial Watch contends that the FDA has not demonstrated the predecisional nature of documents without dates or with dates coming after the agency approved mifepristone. The entries without dates, it argues, can never prove that a document came before the agency's decision at issue. The entries with later dates, it contends, are by definition postdecisional.

Because we have previously approved the application of the deliberative process privilege for an "undated note," we cannot adopt Judicial Watch's proposed categorical rule on undated entries. Dates are but one way to illustrate a chronology, and the FDA may have other ways to prove that the undated documents were indeed predecisional. As an example, the FDA asserts that Documents 1645 and 1646, though undated, are predecisional because they concern mifepristone's IND, filed far in advance of the NDA and the FDA's subsequent approval of the NDA. Other undated documents in the index do not have the benefit of the FDA's explanation, though. We therefore remand so that the FDA may provide more information, including dates for documents that lack them or explanations where dates cannot be found.

Likewise, documents dated after mifepristone's approval for abortion may still be predecisional and deliberative with respect to other, nonfinal agency policies, including uses of the drug that the agency has not approved. A contrary rule would undermine the privilege's purpose to encourage "honest and frank communication within the agency" without fear of public disclosure.... The intervenors' affidavits affirm that the companies continue to pursue other avenues of medical uses for the drug and may later seek FDA approval, which would require further final action by the agency.

The FDA admits, though, that some of the postdated documents have nothing to do with unapproved uses but instead relate to other administrative decisions, including replies to correspondence. The FDA's failure to provide an adequate explanation prevents us from determining whether every piece of correspondence after a policy is decided constitutes a new final agency action of its own. It may be that reflections on an already-decided policy are neither predecisional nor indicative of the deliberative process of the government. After all, "Exemption five is intended to protect the deliberative process of government and not just deliberative material." *Mead Data Cent.*, 566 F.2d at 256 (citation omitted). On remand, the FDA must provide additional information regarding these postdated documents and the agency policies they predate and deliberate over.

Judicial Watch also challenges many Exemption 5 entries as vague, including the FDA's use of otherwise commonly understood words and phrases that it claims shed no light on the documents....

... Terms like "fax" and "q & a" standing alone give the court no way to determine whether the withheld information is of a deliberative nature. Accordingly, on remand the FDA must provide more informative descriptions of these commonly understood documents ....

IV. Conclusion

... On remand ... we do not expect the FDA to engage in a full reappraisal of its index. As we held above, the defects in the index are specific to the descriptions and not structural. The FDA can clarify many vague document descriptions by producing a technical lexicon for the benefit of Judicial Watch and the District Court. As always, the goal should be to allow the court to understand the withheld information to the extent necessary to address the merits. With these considerations in mind, we remand for further explanation of the entries in the *Vaughn* index for documents withheld, in their entirety, under Exemptions 4 and 5....

2. THE CONFIDENTIALITY OF TRADE SECRETS AND CONFIDENTIAL COMMERCIAL INFORMATION

The most controversial issues raised by FDA's FOIA policy revolve around the definition of, and scope of protection accorded to, trade secrets and confidential commercial information. Particular attention has been focused on the status of safety and effectiveness data submitted to the agency in new drug applications and other requests for marketing approval.

a. GENERAL ISSUES

Several statutes applicable to FDA preserve the confidentiality of trade secrets. Exemption (b)(4) of FOIA permits agencies, as a matter of discretion, to withhold trade secrets and privileged or confidential financial commercial information. The so-called Trade Secrets Act, 18

U.S.C. 1905, makes it a criminal offense for any employee of the U.S. government to publish or divulge any information he learns or receives in the course of his employment that "concerns or relates to trade secrets, processes, operations, style of work, or apparatus, or to the identity, confidential statistical data, amount or source of any income, profits, losses, or expenditures of any person, firm, partnership, corporation, or association. . . ." Finally, FD&C Act 301(j) prohibits the revelation, except to other HHS employees, the courts, or Congress, of any information acquired under the authority of various provisions of the Act (including all the premarket approval provisions) "concerning any method or process which as a trade secret is entitled to protection."

Prior to 1972, FDA took the position that under both section 301(j) and the Trade Secrets Act, 18 U.S.C. 1905, all safety and effectiveness data submitted in marketing approval applications constituted trade secret information that could not be released to the public. In 37 Fed. Reg. 9128 (May 5, 1972), the agency refined its position to state that data needed to obtain a private license for a product (e.g., a new drug) would be kept confidential, but that data relating to a product which did not need a private license (e.g., an "old" drug) or relating to a public regulation under which any firm could market its own product (e.g., a food or color additive) provided no competitive advantage and thus could not be regarded as trade secret information. Relying on the Restatement of Torts (Second), FDA arrived at and still adheres to the following definitions, codified at 21 C.F.R. 20.61:

§ 20.61 Trade secrets and commercial or financial information which is privileged or confidential.

(a) A trade secret may consist of any formula, pattern, device, or compilation of information which is used in one's business and which gives him an opportunity to obtain an advantage over competitors who do not know or use it.

(b) Commercial or financial information that is privileged or confidential means valuable data or information which is used in one's business and is of a type customarily held in strict confidence or regarded as privileged and not disclosed to any member of the public by the person to whom it belongs.

(c) Data and information submitted or divulged to the Food and Drug Administration which fall within the definitions of a trade secret or confidential commercial or financial information are not available for public disclosure.

In *Public Citizen Health Research Group v. FDA*, 704 F.2d 1280 (D.C. Cir. 1983), the Court of Appeals offered its own definitions. It defined a trade secret as "a secret, commercially valuable plan, formula, process, or device that is used for the making, preparing, compounding, or processing of trade commodities and that can be said to be the end product of either innovation or substantial effort." It held that commercial information could be accorded confidentiality if its disclosure would either "(1) . . . impair the Government's ability to obtain necessary information in the future; or (2) . . . cause substantial harm to the competitive position of the person from whom the information was obtained." This formulation did not prompt FDA to amend its regulation.

NOTES

1. *No Disclosure of Application Submissions or Denials.* The submission of a marketing approval application is deemed to be a trade secret unless and until the application is approved. Moreover, FDA does not disclose the content of denied applications, or even their existence. *See, e.g.,* 21 C.F.R. 314.430(b) (NDAs and ANDAs).

2. *Confidentiality of NDA Data.* In *Tri–Bio Laboratories, Inc. v. United States,* 836 F.2d 135 (3d Cir. 1987), the Court of Appeals held that the manufacturer of a generic new animal drug could not rely upon the safety and effectiveness data submitted by the manufacturer of the pioneer drug, upholding FDA's position that unpublished safety and effectiveness data may not be disclosed until the agency determines that they are no longer needed to support FDA approval of the product. *See also Webb v. Department of HHS,* 696 F.2d 101 (D.C. Cir. 1982).

3. *Confidentiality of Device Data.* The same issue arose during Congress' consideration of the Medical Device Amendments of 1976. Section 520(c) prohibits FDA from disclosing trade secret information or using trade secret information to approve or reclassify a class III device. This provision was modified by the Safe Medical Devices Act of 1990, 104 Stat. 4511.

4. *Access by Makers of Generic Drugs.* During consideration of the Drug Price Competition and Patent Term Act of 1984, *see supra* p. 1000, debate focused on the continuing trade secret status of data submitted for a pioneer drug after ANDAs for generic versions could be submitted. FDA Commissioner Frank Young submitted a letter declaring that safety and effectiveness data would be made public following approval of generic versions of a pioneer drug unless "extraordinary circumstances" were shown. Young explained this standard would require a demonstration that the data continued to represent trade secret or confidential commercial or financial information. 130 Cong. Rec. 24977–78 (Sept. 12, 1984). This position is now reflected in 21 C.F.R. 314.430(f).

5. *Adverse Reaction Reports.* The issue in *Public Citizen Health Research Group v. FDA,* 704 F.2d 1280 (D.C. Cir. 1983), involved disclosure of reports of adverse reactions to intraocular lenses. On remand, the District Court ruled that company-specific adverse reaction rates could be withheld but averaged adverse reaction data had to be disclosed. *See also Kennedy v. FDA,* 1985–1986 FDLI Jud. Rec. 471 (N.D. Ohio 1986), upholding FDA's refusal to disclose company-specific adverse reaction reports on intraocular lenses to a plaintiff suing the company. In 2001 FDA suggested that it was prepared to relax its protection for reports of adverse reactions from clinical trials involving two promising but controversial technologies—gene therapy and xenotransplants. 66 Fed. Reg. 4688 (Jan. 18, 2001). The agency acknowledged that such a shift would represent a retreat from its long-standing policy but argued that public acceptance of these technologies would depend on assurance that all safety issues had been thoroughly explored. FDA has taken no further action on this proposal.

6. *Disclosure to Other Agencies.* Section 301(j) of the FD&C Act prohibits disclosure of trade secret information to any person outside the Department of HHS. Because this appeared to bar FDA from sharing such information with contractors engaged to assist FDA (*e.g.*, to review an NDA), the Medical Device Amendments of 1976 added section 708 to permit such disclosures, with respect to all categories of FDA-regulated products, under appropriate safeguards. In 1978, the Attorney General determined that section 301(j) prohibited FDA from disclosing trade secret information to committees of Congress. "Federal Food, Drug and Cosmetic Act—Prohibition on Disclosure of Trade Secret Information to a Congressional Committee," 43 Op. Atty. Gen., No. 21 (Sept. 8, 1978). Section 301(j) was ultimately amended in the Omnibus Budget Reconciliation Act of 1990, 104 Stat. 1388, 1388–210 to permit disclosure to Congress.

7. *Discovery of IND Information by Criminal Defendant.* In *United States v. Wood*, 57 F.3d 733 (9th Cir. 1995), the conviction of the defendants for a conspiracy to dispense an unapproved drug, GHB (the so-called "date rape drug"), was remanded because the government violated its duty under *Brady v. Maryland*, 373 U.S. 83 (1963), by failing to make the contents of INDs that might have exonerated the defendants available to them. (The government based its refusal to disclose on trade secret protection.) On remand, the District Court determined that the failure of the government to disclose the IND information was not prejudicial to Wood, a ruling summarily reversed by the Court of Appeals. 112 F.3d 518 (9th Cir. 1995).

8. *What Constitutes a "Trade Secret"?* For examples of the difficulties involved in determining whether information constitutes a "trade secret," see *Zotos International, Inc. v. Kennedy*, 460 F. Supp. 268 (D.D.C. 1978); *Zotos International, Inc. v. Young*, 830 F.2d 350 (D.C. Cir. 1987).

b.   THE SCOPE OF EXEMPTION 4 OF FOIA

When a request for commercial information is made to FDA, the company that submitted the information usually steps forward to defend its confidentiality. If FDA refuses disclosure and is sued, the submitting company typically intervenes, as in the following case. *See also*, *e.g.*, *Washington Post v. Department of Justice*, 863 F.2d 96 (D.C. Cir. 1988); *Greenberg v. FDA*, 803 F.2d 1213 (D.C. Cir. 1986); *Public Citizen Health Research Group v. FDA*, 704 F.2d 1280 (D.C. Cir. 1983); *Webb v. Department of HHS*, 696 F.2d 101 (D.C. Cir. 1982); *Campbell v. Department of HHS*, 682 F.2d 256 (D.C. Cir. 1982).

Public Citizen Health Research Group v. Food & Drug Administration

185 F.3d 898 (D.C. Cir. 1999).

■ GINSBURG, CIRCUIT JUDGE:

Pursuant to the Freedom of Information Act, the Public Citizen Health Research Group asked the Food and Drug Administration for documents relating to drug applications that had been abandoned for health or safety reasons. The FDA denied this request and Public

Citizen sued the agency in district court, where Schering Corporation, which had submitted five investigational new drug applications (INDs) of the sort requested by Public Citizen, intervened as a defendant. The FDA and Schering claimed that certain of the documents in those five INDs contained confidential commercial information and therefore could be withheld under Exemption 4 of the FOIA, 5 U.S.C. 552(b)(4). Public Citizen argued that the documents could not be withheld under that exemption and that in any event disclosure was required under 21 U.S.C. 355(l), which it asserted sets a standard for nondisclosure higher than that in Exemption 4 of the FOIA.

. . . .

The FDA and Schering argue that the agency may under § 355(l) withhold any data pertaining to the safety and effectiveness of an abandoned drug that it may withhold under Exemption 4 of the FOIA—in other words, that the standards in the two statutes are the same. Public Citizen contends that § 355(l) imposes a more stringent standard for nondisclosure than that in Exemption 4. We need not resolve this dispute over the relationship between the two statutes, however, because we hold that § 355(l) does not apply to INDs. Viewing the documents solely through the lens of Exemption 4, we conclude that the FDA has justified withholding at least some information in four of the five INDs.

A.   Section 355(l)

Section 355(l) requires the FDA, upon request, to disclose "safety and effectiveness data and information which has been submitted in an application under subsection (b) [of § 355] for a drug" that subsequently was abandoned by its sponsor, "unless extraordinary circumstances are shown." 21 U.S.C. 355 (l)(1). No one disputes that an "application under subsection (b)" is an NDA. Schering argues that § 355(l), therefore, simply does not apply to information in an IND, which is submitted under subsection (i), not subsection (b). That is indeed the plain meaning of the provision, and we cannot understand how "submitted in an application under subsection (b)" could include anything other than information submitted in an NDA. Public Citizen's arguments to the contrary are not convincing.

First, Public Citizen contends that the agency applies § 355(l) to the disclosure of material submitted in an IND and that we should accord "substantial weight" to the FDA's view of its regulatory structure. As Schering notes, however, the FDA has never promulgated a regulation—nor are we apprised of any FDA decision or other document—so interpreting § 355(l). More important, it is apparent that the Congress has spoken to "the precise question at issue" here, *Chevron U.S.A. Inc. v. NRDC, Inc.,* 467 U.S. 837 (1984): § 355(l) by its terms applies only to "safety and effectiveness data and information" submitted in an NDA. . . .

. . . Public Citizen contends that a plain meaning approach to § 355(l) leads to an illogical result: data and information submitted in an IND which later, rather than being resubmitted in an NDA, are incorporated by reference into the NDA would not be "submitted in an application under subsection (b)," that is, an NDA. The FDA and Schering offer a more sensible view, however: to incorporate IND materials by reference into an NDA is indeed to submit those materials as part of the NDA. By the same token, once those materials are incorporated by reference into an NDA, their disclosure is subject to the standard in § 355(l) even if the FDA keeps them in an IND file.

Finally, Public Citizen argues that "it makes no sense to assume Congress enacted a statute mandating disclosure of safety and effectiveness data only when the sponsor had filed an NDA . . . but not when the sponsor had abandoned the drug earlier in the process." In this regard Public Citizen points out that the FDA accords the same treatment to such data regardless whether they were submitted in an NDA or an IND. Specifically, the FDA by regulation (21 C.F.R. 312.130(b)) provides that disclosure of information in an IND "will be handled in accordance with" the regulation governing disclosure of information in an NDA (21 C.F.R. 314.430(f)).

Nonetheless, when the Congress enacted § 355(l) it did not mandate disclosure of information in an IND. Moreover, Schering offers a perfectly sensible explanation why the Congress did not do so. The Drug Price Competition and Patent Term Restoration Act of 1984, of which § 355(l) was a part, established an abbreviated process through which a company could obtain approval to market the generic equivalent of a drug that the FDA had previously approved on the basis of an NDA. The statute, Schering continues, does "not deal with INDs at all, and Congress had no reason in this legislative context to extend [§ 355(l)] to them." . . .

In view of the above analysis, we hold that § 355(l) does not apply to data and information submitted solely in an IND; such information may be withheld if the agency carries its burden under Exemption 4 of the FOIA. Schering did not file an NDA for four of the five INDs at issue in this case, but concedes that it filed two NDAs relating to the drug at issue in IND No. 18113. We need not determine the import of Schering's concession, however, for we conclude that documents in that IND cannot be withheld under the allegedly more lenient standard in Exemption 4.

B.   Exemption 4

Exemption 4 of the FOIA permits an agency to withhold "commercial or financial information [that was] obtained from a person [and is] privileged or confidential." 5 U.S.C. 552(b)(4). Information that a person is required to submit to the Government is considered confidential only if its disclosure is likely either "(1) to impair the Government's ability to obtain necessary information in the future; or (2) to cause substantial harm to the competitive position of the person from whom the information was obtained." *National Parks I*, 498 F.2d at 770. In the present case the FDA and Schering invoke only the latter standard. Meanwhile, Public Citizen claims disclosure would prevent other drug companies "from repeating Schering's mistakes, thereby avoiding risk to human health," and relies upon dicta in several district court opinions in arguing that under Exemption 4 the court should gauge whether the competitive harm done to the sponsor of an IND by the public disclosure of confidential information "is outweighed by the strong public interest in safeguarding the health of human trial participants."

We reject Public Citizen's proposal because a consequentialist approach to the public interest in disclosure is inconsistent with the "balance of private and public interests" the Congress struck in Exemption 4. . . . That balance is accurately reflected in the test of confidentiality set forth in *National Parks I*, which was "known to and acquiesced in by Congress" when it enacted 5 U.S.C. 552b(c)(4), an exemption to the Government in the Sunshine Act that is identical to Exemption 4 of the FOIA.

In other words, the Congress has already determined the relevant public interest: if through disclosure "the public would learn something directly about the workings of the *Government*," then the information should be disclosed unless it comes within a specific exemption. . . . It is not open to Public Citizen, however, to bolster the case for disclosure by claiming an additional public benefit in that, if the information is disclosed, then other drug companies will not conduct risky clinical trials of the drugs that Schering has abandoned. That is not related to "what the[ ] government is up to" and the Court has clearly stated that "whether disclosure of a . . . document . . . is warranted must turn on the nature of the requested document and its relationship to the basic purpose of the Freedom of Information Act to open agency action to the light of public scrutiny . . . rather than on the particular purpose for which the document is being requested." In other words, the public interest side of the balance is not a function of the identity of the requester, or of any potential negative consequences disclosure may have for the public, nor likewise of any collateral benefits of disclosure.

. . . .

With respect to the first three INDs, Public Citizen contends that releasing health and safety information would only "save Schering's competitors the time Schering spent developing and testing a dangerous drug, and thus save human trial participants from being exposed to a dangerous drug." . . .

. . . According to the affidavit of its Dr. George H. Miller, the Company "has just commenced clinical testing on a successor [drug] which was designed based on information learned during development of [the drugs described in those INDs]." Further, Dr. Miller states that "Schering's basic research revealed that the particular type of fungal infection for which this product was designed was not one that was relatively well-controlled by existing products." He also states that "the development and marketing of new antifungal products is . . . being actively engaged in by a number of other drug companies," which could make use of the information in the INDs in order to eliminate much of the time and effort that would otherwise be required to bring to market a product competitive with the product for which Schering filed its most recent IND. This is clearly the type of competitive harm envisioned in Exemption 4, as our case law makes clear.

The fourth IND listed above concerned a drug "designed to suppress allergic inflammations and subsequent symptoms of asthma." Public Citizen concedes that Schering is now testing compounds related to the abandoned drug. Nonetheless, Public Citizen complains that the Company does not "explain with any specificity how the pre-clinical and clinical studies on the old compound would lead its competitors to the new compounds that Schering has subsequently identified."

In the affidavit Schering filed to support withholding the documents in this IND, Dr. Francis Cuss recounts that the Company initially believed the drug was a "leukotrine inhibitor," but that its "scientists observed certain unanticipated effects during toxicity and clinical testing . . . suggesting that the drug may have achieved its anti-inflammatory effects through a [different] mechanism." Therefore, states the affiant, the "toxicity and clinical data together could direct a competitor of Schering . . . to pursue the same avenues of research and development" that Schering has pursued since abandoning this IND. We think this explanation sufficiently specific to support Schering's argument that disclosure of information in this IND would cause it substantial competitive harm.

> . . . .

■ Garland, Circuit Judge, concurring in the result:

My colleagues hold that in determining whether a document comes within Exemption 4, the court may not "gauge whether the competitive harm" disclosure would cause to the company that submitted the document "is outweighed by the public interest in safeguarding" human health. This means that even if disclosure were the only way to prevent the loss of human life, that would count for nothing as against a showing by the company that disclosure would cause substantial harm to its competitive position. This is an important issue, and the kind that should be decided only after full briefing and argument.

. . . [A]lthough no party cited the relevant precedent on this point, we have twice held that Exemption 4 requires a balancing of the interest in nondisclosure "against the public interest in disclosure." *See Washington Post Co. v. HHS*, 690 F.2d 252 (D.C. Cir. 1982) (*Washington Post I*); *Washington Post Co. v. HHS*, 865 F.2d 320, 326–27 (D.C. Cir. 1989) (*Washington Post II*).

NOTE

Narrow Interpretation of Competitive Harm Requirement. In *AIDS Healthcare Foundation v. FDA*, CV 11–07925 (C.D. Cal. 2013), the District Court, in denying the application of Exemption 4, narrowly interpreted the *National Parks* standard (cited in *Public Citizen*) that information is "confidential" if it is "likely . . . to cause substantial harm to the competitive position of the person from whom the information was obtained."

In 2012, FDA approved an SNDA submitted by Gilead Sciences with respect to its AIDS treatment Truvada®. Gilead sought, and obtained, approval of the drug for the additional use of pre-exposure prophylaxis (PrEP) to prevent the transmission of HIV. Citing Exemption 4, FDA refused to provide the plaintiff with certain information it requested concerning the SNDA pursuant to FOIA. The District Court agreed with the plaintiff that Exemption 4 did not properly apply. The court explained that to withhold information under Exemption 4, FDA must demonstrate both "(1) actual competition and (2) a likelihood of substantial competitive injury." The court held that FDA failed to adduce sufficient evidence of present or future "actual competition," in light of the fact that Truvada was the first and only drug approved for PrEP and that no other drugs were in "advanced clinical trials" for that indication. The court also found that although there was actual competition in the HIV treatment (as opposed to PrEP) market, FDA had failed to offer evidence that Gilead would suffer "substantial competitive injury" in that market from the disclosure of the requested information.

c. NON-FOIA DISCLOSURE OF CLINICAL INFORMATION

The fact that FDA is required to preserve the confidentiality of trade secrets and confidential commercial information does not mean that product approvals are shrouded in complete secrecy. Along the path to approval (and, sometimes, denial) the agency reveals a fair amount. For example, under a 2008 guidance document, FDA will release the briefing materials for an advisory committee meeting no later than two business days before the meeting, but only to the extent that the materials do not contain information covered by Exemption 4 or another FOIA exemption. Guidance for Industry: Advisory Committee Meetings—Preparation and Public Availability of Information Given to Advisory Committee Members (Aug. 2008). Moreover, after the agency sends an NDA approval letter to the applicant, various data and information "become immediately available for public disclosure, unless the applicant shows that extraordinary circumstances exists." 21 C.F.R. 314.430(e). This information includes a document known as the "Summary Basis of Approval."

(ii) For an application approved on or after July 1, 1975, a Summary Basis of Approval (SBA) document that contains a summary of the safety and effectiveness data and information evaluated by FDA during the drug approval process. The SBA is prepared in one of the following ways:

(a) Before approval of the application, the applicant may prepare a draft SBA which the Center for Drug Evaluation and Research will review and may revise. The draft may be submitted with the application or as an amendment.

(b) The Center for Drug Evaluation and Research may prepare the SBA.

21 C.F.R. 314.430(e)(2)(ii).

Finally, FD&C Act 505(l) was amended by FDAAA (2007) to requiring publication on the FDA website of an "action package for approval" of each NDA or BLA. Within 48 hours after approval of the application, FDA must publish a "summary review that documents conclusions about the drug from all reviewing disciplines, noting any critical issues and disagreements with the applicant and within the review team and how they were resolved, recommendations for action, and an explanation of any non-concurrence with review conclusions." FD&C Act 505(l)(2)(B), (C)(iv). (The action package also includes other pieces, which must be posted later.) The new paragraph makes clear, however, that it does not authorize the disclosure of any trade secret, confidential commercial or financial information, or other matter protected from disclosure under FOIA. *Id.* 505(l)(2)(E). None of this is to say that FDA, with its personnel and resource limitations, always complies with the SBA or "summary review" requirements. CBER seems to comply with the "action package" requirements more consistently than CDER.

In addition, as discussed in Chapter 7, *supra* p. 706, FDAAA also added new PHSA section 402(j)(3), which requires ClinicalTrials.gov to include information regarding the results of completed trials for approved products. Both a technical and nontechnical summary of the trial and its results must be posted "for those clinical trials that form the primary basis of an efficacy claim or are conducted after the drug involved is approved." PHSA 402(j)(3)(D)(iii).

CVM has established guidelines for the preparation of a "Freedom of Information summary" of safety and effectiveness data that is to be made publicly available after a NADA is approved. *See* CVM Policy and Procedures Manual 1243.5761 (Feb. 29, 2012). Though the relevant regulation says that FDA may require the applicant to draft this FOI summary, 21 C.F.R. 514.11(e)(ii), today the agency itself generally takes responsibility for preparing it. *See id.* at 2; 72 Fed. Reg. 70331, 70333 (Dec. 11, 2007).

The approved application disclosure protocols for medical devices are less regularized, and the information provided is sparser, than is the case for drugs and biologics. (Medical devices are, however, subject to the ClinicalTrial.gov requirements.) The food additive approval process, by contrast, is quite transparent, because approvals are implemented via notice-and-comment rulemaking.

NOTES

1. *Transparency Initiative.* In 2009, HHS Secretary Kathleen Sebelius and FDA Commissioner Margaret Hamburg announced the formation of the FDA Transparency Task Force to develop recommendations for enhancing the transparency of the agency's operations and decision-making process. Phase II of the initiative focused on disclosing certain information about FDA-regulated products and firms. In May 2010, the Task Force released the Phase II Transparency Report, which contained 21 draft proposals that would expand the disclosure of information by FDA. Section 11 of this report proposed for comment various possibilities for releasing more information about product applications. No further action has been taken on these proposals, many of which would face inevitable opposition by companies committed to maintaining confidentiality for trade secrets.

2. *Masked Data.* In 2013, FDA proposed to make "masked" data from medical product applications available to clinical researchers. 78 Fed. Reg. 33421 (June 4, 2013). It defined "masked data" as data from which any information that could link it to a specific product application removed. The agency suggested that such data could be helpful, for example, in identifying potentially valid endpoints for clinical trials, understanding the predictive value of preclinical models, clarifying how medical products work in different diseases, and informing development of novel clinical designs and endpoints. *Id.* at 33422.

3. *FDA Confidentiality Policy Criticized.* For a critical assessment of FDA's aggressive protection of drug sponsor clinical research data, see Mitchell Oates, *Facilitating Informed Medical Treatment Through*

Production and Disclosure of Research into Off–Label User of Pharmaceuticals, 80 N.Y.U. L. Rev. 272 (2005).

3. OTHER RELEVANT STATUTES

While FOIA provides the basic framework for resolving claims to access and assertions of an agency's right or duty to withhold information, it has recently been joined by two other laws that can affect how regulatory agencies, like FDA, handle information generated by private parties.

a. THE SHELBY AMENDMENT

In appropriations legislation for fiscal year 1999, Congress included the "Shelby Amendment" to address public access to data produced by federal grant recipients. 112 Stat. 2681 (1998). The two-sentence provision did not amend the FOIA. Instead, it directed the Office of Management and Budget to amend OMB Circular A–110 to require awarding agencies to ensure that data produced under a federal grant will be made available to the public through the procedures established under the FOIA.

OMB published a final revision to Circular A–110 in October of 1999, 64 Fed. Reg. 54926 (Oct. 8, 1999). In pertinent part, the revised Circular states:

> [I]n response to a Freedom of Information Act (FOIA) request for research data relating to published research findings produced under an award that were used by the Federal Government in developing an agency action that has the force and effect of law, the Federal awarding agency shall request, and the recipient shall provide, within a reasonable time, the research data so that they can be made available to the public through the procedures established under the FOIA.

By its terms, the revised Circular applies only to data relied on by a federal agency to support action that has the force and effect of law. In issuing the revised Circular, OMB explained that it took an approach that balanced the public interest in obtaining information needed to validate federally-funded research with the need to minimize interference with the traditional scientific process.

b. THE INFORMATION QUALITY ACT

The other recent legislation concerning the dissemination of government information is the Information Quality Act (also known as the Data Quality Act). Congress included this provision in appropriations legislation for fiscal year 2001. It directed OMB to issue "guidelines" that provide "policy and procedural guidance to Federal agencies for ensuring and maximizing the quality, objectivity, utility and integrity of information (including statistical information) disseminated by Federal agencies[.]" 114 Stat. 2763 (2000) (codified as a note following 44 U.S.C. 3516).

OMB published final guidelines in 67 Fed. Reg. 8452 (Feb. 22, 2002). The guidelines set out four general responsibilities for the covered agencies: (1) to "adopt specific standards of quality that are appropriate for the various categories of information they disseminate"; (2) to "develop a process for reviewing the quality (including the objectivity, utility, and integrity) of information before it is disseminated"; (3) to "establish administrative mechanisms allowing affected persons to seek and obtain, where appropriate, timely correction of information maintained and disseminated by the agency that does not comply with OMB or agency guidelines"; and (4) to report annually to OMB "on the number and nature of complaints received by the agency regarding agency compliance with these OMB guidelines and how such complaints were resolved." OMB Guidelines § III (1)–(4).

Proponents of the Information Quality Act hoped that the Act would be interpreted to create a new right, independent of any under the APA, to challenge the accuracy and balance of information disseminated by government agencies. Unfortunately for them, the leading case holds that the IQA creates no standing or legal rights for third parties, *Salt Institute v. Leavitt*, 440 F.3d 156 (4th Cir. 2006), and no court has disagreed.

NOTE

FDA Minimization of Significance of the IQA. In the FDA Commissioner's affirmation of the withdrawal of approval of the NADA for enrofloxacin in poultry, excerpted *supra* p. 1098, she rejected an argument based on the IQA advanced by Bayer, the NADA holder:

> Bayer . . . asserts that the FDA and Office of Management and Budget (OMB) guidelines issued pursuant to the Information Quality Act (IQA), Pub. L. No. 106–554, § 515 (2000), provide "useful guideposts" for evaluating the testimony and evidence relied on by CVM. Bayer further argues that a risk assessment relied on by CVM, described in more detail below, must satisfy FDA's guidelines to be considered reliable evidence in this proceeding.

> I disagree with both arguments. The stated intent of the IQA is to ensure and maximize the quality of data "disseminated" by Federal agencies and to allow "affected persons" to request correction of such information—not to impose new evidentiary standards in administrative proceedings. Indeed, OMB's guidelines specify that such requests for correction should serve to address the genuine and valid needs of outside parties without disrupting agency processes, and information used in and findings made in adjudications are expressly exempted by the FDA Guidelines. Furthermore, on its face, the FDA guidance makes clear that it, like all FDA guidance documents, does not "create or confer any rights for or on any person or bind FDA or the public." *See also* 21 C.F.R § 10.115(d).

> . . . If I were to agree with Bayer's interpretation of the role of the FDA's IQA guidelines in this proceeding, I would in effect be ruling that in any formal administrative proceeding the IQA guidelines should replace longstanding and well-established statutory provisions and judicial doctrine about the admissibility and reliability of expert testimony and scientific evidence. Bayer's IQA argument would also require me to evaluate the evidence on which CVM relies differently from that on which Bayer relies. . . . I do not believe that Congress

would have chosen such an indirect means of changing the formal adjudication provisions of the APA and drug approval and withdrawal provisions of the FDCA. The factors I look to in evaluating the reliability of the scientific evidence do not change depending on which participant is relying on it. . . .

Withdrawal of Approval of the NADA for Enrofloxacin in Poultry: Final Decision of the Commissioner (July 27, 2005). Although Commissioner Hamburg found that the IQA did not afford Bayer any legal basis to challenge the reliability of CVM's evidence, "under the unique circumstances of this proceeding," she decided also to address the Animal Health Institute's request for correction of the CVM risk assessment under the IQA. She concluded that even if the risk assessment were properly considered subject to the IQA, no correction of the risk assessment was warranted.

D. ENVIRONMENTAL ASSESSMENT

The National Environmental Policy Act (NEPA), 83 Stat. 852 (1969), requires all federal agencies to consider the environmental impact of any major action they initiate that may significantly affect the quality of the environment. FDA adopted regulations to implement this requirement. 38 Fed. Reg. 7001 (Mar. 15, 1973), 21 C.F.R. Part 25. Initially, the agency took the position that NEPA required it to consider the environmental impact of every important action including, for example, the approval of a new drug or a food additive. Later, impressed with the impracticality of this policy, FDA announced, 40 Fed. Reg. 16662 (Apr. 14, 1975), that it had no legal authority to approve or disapprove a new drug or food additive on any ground other than those specified in the FD&C Act itself. The agency hoped thereby to precipitate a judicial challenge that would clarify its obligations under NEPA.

Environmental Defense Fund, Inc. v. Mathews
410 F. Supp. 336 (D.D.C. 1976).

■ PRATT, DISTRICT JUDGE

. . . NEPA does not supersede other statutory duties, but, to the extent that it is reconcilable with those duties, it supplements them. Full compliance with its requirements cannot be avoided unless such compliance directly conflicts with other existing statutory duties.

. . . In April, 1975, FDA promulgated an amendment . . . which is the subject of this action. Said amendment reads:

A determination of adverse environmental impact has no legal or regulatory effect and does not authorize the Commissioner to take or refrain from taking any action under the laws he administers. The Commissioner may take or refrain from taking action on the basis of a determination of an adverse environmental impact only to the extent that such action is independently authorized by the laws he administers.

In effect, the amending regulation limits the grounds on which the Commissioner of FDA can base any action to those expressly provided for in the Food, Drug and Cosmetic Act or in other statutes which FDA administers. He is prohibited from acting solely on the basis of environmental considerations not identified in those statutes. This limitation of the agency's discretion to act in accordance with environmental considerations directly contravenes the mandate of NEPA to all Federal agencies to consider the environmental effects of their actions "to the fullest extent possible."

Defendants contend that FDA's statutes, particularly the FDCA, dictate that it act only in accordance with specifically expressed criteria, and that to the extent that NEPA demands consideration of additional criteria, it is in direct conflict with those statutes. Accordingly, they maintain that such a direct statutory conflict exempts FDA from full compliance with NEPA.

It appears clear to us that, contrary to defendants' contention, FDA's existing statutory duties under the FDCA and its other statutes are not in direct conflict with its duties under NEPA. The FDCA does not state that the listed considerations are the only ones which the Commissioner may take into account in reaching a decision. Nor does it explicitly require that product applications be granted if the specified grounds are met. It merely lists criteria which the Commissioner must consider in reaching his decision. In the absence of a clear statutory provision excluding consideration of environmental factors, and in light of NEPA's broad mandate that all environmental considerations be taken into account, we find that NEPA provides FDA with supplementary authority to base its substantive decisions on all environmental considerations including those not expressly identified in the FDCA and FDA's other statutes. This conclusion finds support in the legislative history, the precise statutory language, the holdings of the courts, and the construction adopted by other Federal agencies.

This is not to say that NEPA requires FDA's substantive decisions to favor environment protection over other relevant factors. Rather, it means that NEPA requires FDA to *consider* environmental factors in its decision-making process and supplements its existing authority to permit it to act on those considerations. It permits FDA to base a decision upon environmental factors, when balanced with other relevant considerations. Since the contested regulation prohibits FDA from acting on the basis of such environmental considerations, it is directly contrary to the letter and spirit of NEPA. . . .

NOTES

1.   *FDA Response.* Following this decision FDA revoked the contested regulation, 41 Fed. Reg. 21768 (May 28, 1976).

2.   *Environmental Impact beyond Human Safety Considerations?* The agency has rarely taken action in which it has identified environmental effects not involving risks to human health as an influential consideration. When FDA denied a food additive petition on the ground that the environmental impact analysis report was insufficient, the court in *Marshall Minerals, Inc. v. FDA*, 661 F.2d 409 (5th Cir. 1981), reversed, holding that this raised no issue beyond the human safety questions

previously considered, that Marshall Minerals had complied with all environmental analysis requirements, and that no separate environmental concerns prevented approval of the petition. But in 1993, FDA stayed 1987 amendments to a food additive regulation for selenium in animal feed, because it concluded that the information sufficient to permit an adequate environmental analysis was not available. 58 Fed. Reg. 47962 (Sept. 13, 1993). The main concern in this case was the threat to aquatic fish and wildlife. *Id.* at 47964. FDA was later forced to suspend this stay on directions from Congress. 60 Fed. Reg. 53702 (Oct. 17, 1995); 62 Fed. Reg. 44892 (Aug. 25, 1997).

3. *Challenges to FDA's Failure to Conduct an Environmental Assessment.* NEPA has occasionally been invoked by parties opposing FDA action. See, e.g., *Calorie Control Council, Inc. v. Department of HEW*, Food Drug Cosm. L. Rep. (CCH) ¶ 38,124 (D.D.C. 1977), in which the District Court refused to enjoin FDA's proposed ban of saccharin on the ground that the agency had failed to file an environmental impact statement. The Court ultimately dismissed the action in *Calorie Control Council, Inc. v. Department of HEW*, Food Drug Cosm. L. Rep. (CCH) ¶ 38,218 (D.D.C. 1978). Other cases rejecting NEPA-based objections to FDA action include *Rhone–Poulenc, Inc. v. FDA*, 636 F.2d 750 (D.C. Cir. 1980); *National Pork Producers Council v. Bergland*, 631 F.2d 1353 (8th Cir. 1980); *American Meat Institute v. Bergland*, 459 F. Supp. 1308 (D.D.C. 1978). FDA's approval of recombinant bovine growth hormone (rBST) was unsuccessfully challenged on several grounds, including the agency's failure to prepare an environmental impact statement and its reliance on the environmental assessment prepared by the drug's sponsor, Monsanto. *Stauber v. Shalala*, 895 F. Supp. 1178 (W.D. Wis. 1995). In *Stauber*, the court also rejected claims that the agency should have weighed, as environmental effects, the potential economic impact of rBST's use on dairy producers. When FDA announced that it would presume, subject to evidence to the contrary, that genetically altered foods were GRAS (*see* the discussion in Chapter III), its statement of policy was challenged on several grounds, including failure to provide notice and invite comment and failure to prepare an environmental impact statement. These and other challenges were rejected in *Alliance for Bio–Integrity v. Shalala*, 116 F. Supp. 2d 166 (D.D.C. 2000). The court interpreted FDA's pronouncement as essentially an affirmation of the status quo, not an action that might trigger an obligation to undertake an environmental assessment.

4. *Plastic Bottles.* FDA initiated an inquiry into the environmental impact of food additive regulations for plastic beverage containers in 38 Fed. Reg. 24391 (Sept. 7, 1973). A draft environmental impact statement (EIS) was later made available, 40 Fed. Reg. 16708 (Apr. 14, 1975), and a final EIS was issued, 41 Fed. Reg. 43944 (Oct. 5, 1976). In 42 Fed. Reg. 9227 (Feb. 15, 1977), the agency stated that, in acting on food additive petitions, environmental considerations "carry no greater weight than the factors required to be considered in section 409 of the act." It concluded that "the adverse environmental effects of the action, to some extent offset by the potential beneficial effects, are not of sufficient magnitude to justify limitation or revocation of food additive regulations permitting plastic bottles for carbonated beverages and beer."

5. *Transgenic Fish.* Recent advances in the area of genetic engineering are requiring FDA directly to confront environmental issues to an unprecedented degree. Consider, for example, the following excerpts from a 2003 speech delivered to the American Enterprise Institute by Lester Crawford, the Deputy Commissioner (later Acting Commissioner) of the FDA.

The FDA has . . . ample experience, as well as legislated authority and guidance, for ensuring the safety and effectiveness of drugs, biological medications, and medical devices, and it would use all of these resources in evaluating such products manufactured with the help of transgenic animals. But what about other concerns, including the critical question whether, and to what extent, the safety of the environment would be put at risk by genetically altered animals? And what about risks that may be posed to the genetic animals themselves?

The FDA is yet to answer these questions by approving or disapproving the application for marketing of any transgenic animal, and I am not in a position to discuss specific decisions and policies that may be currently under consideration. But I can address this issue in general terms on the basis of existing laws and practices. I can also examine the provisions that would protect the public health and environment from harm that could result from the commercialization of one transgenic product that has repeatedly prompted media comments, as well as concerns among environmental and consumer groups. That product is an Atlantic salmon genetically engineered to contain additional fish hormone gene to make it grow faster and use feed more efficiently.

One variety of this salmon has been reported to reach the market weight of 7–9 pounds in about 18 months, as against 24–30 months for non-transgenic salmon. As you will hear from Mr. McGonigle, the Vice President of Aqua Bounty Farms, his firm has been preparing for more than a decade to put a hybrid salmon on the market. To avoid environmental damage, Aqua Bounty plans to raise brood stocks of this transgenic fish in conventional inland hatcheries, and treat them to produce 100 percent genetically female eggs. The eggs in turn would be treated to cause reproductive sterility. The reproductively sterile, all-female offsprings would be grown initially in hatcheries, and then would be transferred to ocean net pens, to mature and be harvested for food.

What are the hazards associated with this sort of enterprise? Although current methods provide high ensurance [sic] of reproductive sterility, they are not 100 percent effective. This raises the possibility that fish that would almost inevitably escape from the net pens would include some females capable of reproduction. This in turn could lead to interbreeding with wild Atlantic salmon, hybridization with the closely related brown trout, and disturbance of habitat as a consequence of competition for resources, predation, or mis-mating.

There are several federal and state agencies that would take measures to minimize the involved environmental hazards. They include the National Marine Fisheries Service, Fish and Wildlife

Service, Army Corps of Engineers, and Environmental Protection Agency, all of which probably would be involved in regulating various aspects of this enterprise, such as the location and security of the ocean pens. In addition, the FDA is authorized to exercise oversight of transgenic animals under the Federal Food, Drug and Cosmetic Act, which makes our agency responsible for the safety of drugs, and defines drugs as "articles . . . intended to affect the structure or any function of the body of man or other animals."

Because the genetic modification affects the structure and function of the salmon, and because it may produce a protein that is not generally recognized as safe for human consumption, the biotech salmon is, in the eyes of the law, a "new animal drug," and as such is subject to the FDA's science-based review and approval before it can be marketed. As part of this review, the FDA routinely considers evidence of a new animal drug's effect on, among other factors, animal health; diseases susceptibility; zoonotic potential; animal welfare; impact on domestic and wildlife populations; and the environment.

I am skipping a lot detail, but I want to emphasize that the FDA takes environmental issues seriously, and takes action when appropriate.

Lester M. Crawford, Deputy FDA Commissioner, FDA, at the American Enterprise Institute (June 12, 2003).

The NADA to which Crawford was alluding was that for the AquAdvantage Salmon, an Atlantic salmon that has been genetically engineered to grow more rapidly than other farmed and wild Atlantic salmon. In 2012, FDA announced the availability for public comment of a Draft Environmental Assessment and Preliminary Finding of No Significant Impact (FONSI) regarding the proposed conditions of use specified in materials submitted by AquaBounty in support of its NADA. 77 Fed. Reg. 76050 (Dec. 26, 2012). It later extended the comment period. 78 Fed. Reg. 10620 (Feb. 14, 2013).

INDEX

References are to Pages

ACRYLONITRILE
Use in plastic beverage containers, 1397

ADDITIVES
Generally, 88, 552–607
Accidental additives, 614–615
Approval process, deterioration of,
603–607
Aspartame, 565
Carcinogens, this index
Change in status, 576, 577
Color additive regulation
1906 Act, 617
1938 Act, 617
1960 Amendments, 618–627
generally, 618–627,
1379–1382
approval by product category, 619
deceptive coloring of human food,
624
provisionally listed additives, 618,
619
Red No. 3, 619, 620, 1424, 1425
uses, power to allocate, 620
Yellow No. 5, 625–627
Contaminant or food additive, 511, 512
Cosmetics, color additive names, 1338
Cyclamate, 564, 565
Defined, 555
Fluoride, 566
Food Additives Amendment, 554, 555, 581
Generally recognized as safe (GRAS)
substances, 574–592
Heat susceptors, 615
Housewares exemption, 615, 616
Hyperactivity and food additives, 626, 627
Incidental additives, 393
Indirect additives, 614, 615, 1402
Interim additives, 563, 564
Nitrite and nitrate, 601, 602
Patent term extension, 563
Polyvinyl chloride, 1397
Procedural rights, 577
Radiation, 565, 566
Raw agricultural commodities, 567, 568
Saccharin, 565
Shopping bags, 615
Specifications for food additives, 563
Sucralose, 565
Sulfites, 591
Testing guidelines, 564
Utility, consideration of, 562, 563

**ADMINISTRATIVE PRACTICE AND
PROCEDURE**
Generally, 29–75, 1487–1530
Advisory committees
generally, 1488–1503
authority to create, 1491
drafts, 1497, 1498

FDA's reliance on, 1488–1491
Federal Advisory Committee Act
(FACA), 1491, 1497
GSA guidelines, 1498
open committee meetings, 1497
statutory requirements, 1491–1503
APA requirements, 43–47
Concurrent jurisdiction, FDA and other
agencies, 21
Denial of hearing, 51
Disclosure. Public information, below
Environmental assessment, 1526–1530
Ex parte communications, 24
Exhaustion of remedies, 68, 69
Expert advice. Advisory committees,
above
FOIA overview
generally, 1503–1514
Freedom of Information Act, this
index
Formal hearing procedures, 52, 53
Guidance procedures and OMB oversight,
55, 56, 59, 60
Hearings
alternatives to trial–type hearings,
53–55
evidentiary hearing, when required,
49–53
formal hearing procedures, 52, 53
Informal rulemaking procedures, 43–47
Information Quality Act, 1524–1526
Judicial acknowledgment of FDA's
rulemaking authority, 33–41
Judicial review of agency implementation,
62–75
Jurisdiction, primary
generally, 66–68
court-mandated, 67, 68
private litigation, 68
Makers of regulated products, dealing
with
generally, 21–24
ex parte communications, 24
Mutually exclusive jurisdiction, FDA and
other agencies, 20, 21
OMB oversight, 47–49, 59
Other agencies, FDA's relations with
generally, 20–21
concurrent jurisdiction, 21
mutually exclusive jurisdiction, 20,
21
overlapping jurisdiction, 21
services to other agencies, FDA
providing, 21
Overlapping jurisdiction, FDA and other
agencies, 21
Public information
adverse reaction reports, 1516
FOIA overview, 1503–1514

generic drug makers, access by, 1516
Information Quality Act, 1524–1526
nondisclosure of commercial information, defending, 1516
Shelby Amendment, public access to data produced by federal grant recipients, 1524
trade secret confidentiality, 1514–1524
Regularizing agency procedure, 1487
Regulations, FDA's reliance on
generally, 29–75
overview, 29, 55–60
regularizing agency procedure, 1487
Rulemaking, below
Rulemaking
adopting binding rules, FDA's authority, 32–43
APA requirements, 43–47
delay, 74
discretion whether to issue rules, 62
environmental assessment, 1526–1530
evidentiary hearing, when required, 49–53
formal rulemaking, 49–55
guidance, rulemaking vs., 59, 60
HHS oversight, 47
informal procedures, 43–47
interpretive vs. legislative, 36
judicial acknowledgment of FDA's rulemaking authority, 33–41
notice requirements, 46, 47
obstacles to rulemaking, 55, 56
OMB oversight, 47–49
procedures, 43–55
record for judicial review, 64, 65
statutory framework, 32, 33
what constitutes a "rule," 61, 62
Services to other agencies, FDA providing, 21
Shelby Amendment, public access to data produced by federal grant recipients, 1524
Standing to demand hearing or seek judicial review, 52
Trial-type hearings, alternatives to, 53–55

ADULTERATION
Aesthetic adulteration. Food, this index
Economic adulteration. Food, this index
Medical devices, 1254–1259

ADVERTISING
Food advertising, FTC jurisdiction, 151, 456–458
Natural food claims, 453
Over–the–counter drugs, FTC regulation, 990–993
Prescription drug labeling, relevance of advertising claims, 931
Prescription drug promotion
generally, 864–987
brand names, 865, 866
brief summary requirement, 910

comparative claims, 910
constitutionality, advertising regulations, 911
continuing controversies, 912–915
controlled substances, direct–to–consumer advertising, 924, 925
corrective advertisements, 911
direct-to-consumer (DTC) advertising, 915–925, 814
fair balance requirement, 910, 924
FDA legal authority, 912
generic name disclosure, 864–866
gifts and other promotional practices, 913, 914
healthcare economic information, 913
official names, 865
oral promotion, 912
overpromotion, 911
preapproval promotion, 957
professionals, advertising and promotion to, 908–915
remainder advertisements, 910, 911
unapproved uses, promotion of, 925–987

ADVISORY COMMITTEES
Administrative Practice and Procedure, this index

AGRICULTURAL MARKETING ACT
Food grading, inspection, and certification, 454, 455

AIDS
Blood and blood products, screening for AIDS, 1164
Food service workers, AIDS–infected, 532, 533
Home tests for HIV, 1268
Investigational drugs, use for therapy, 767

ALCOHOLIC BEVERAGES
Ingredient labeling, 393, 394
Regulatory jurisdiction, 318, 319
Warnings, 402

ALLERGIES
Food labeling, 397–399

ALPHA HYDROXY ACIDS
Regulation of, 119

ANIMAL FOOD AND DRUGS
Generally, 1045–1121
Animal Drug Amendments of 1968, 1059–1066
Antibiotic certification, 1065
Biologicals, veterinary, 1066, 1112, 1127
Carcinogenic drugs administered to animals raised for human food, regulation of, 1068
Cosmetics
animal cosmetics, 110
opposition to animal testing, 1321, 1322

Effectiveness, proving, 1066, 1067
Export of unapproved new drugs, 1474, 1475
Feed additives, 1065
FIFRA, animal drugs and, 1065, 1066
Generic new animal drugs, abbreviated NAD, 1068, 1069
Genetically modified crops, use in animal feed, 1112
Good manufacturing practice, 1065
Investigational animal drugs, 1064
Livestock, this index
Minor uses, drugs for, 1065
New drug status, 1064
New drug testing, animal rule, 727, 728
OTC status, switching drug to, 1071
Pet Food, this index
Prescription drugs, regulation of use, 1069–1080
Publication of approval, new drugs, 1064
Quantitative risk assessment applied to animal drugs, 1388–1394
Regulatory framework, completion of, 1061–1064
Statutory requirements, food and drugs, 1045–1059

ANTHRAX
Product review, 1130

ANTIWRINKLE CREAMS
Regulatory letters, 115, 116

ARTIFICIAL COLORING
Color additive regulation. Additives, this index
Dairy products, ingredient labeling, 392
Economic adulteration, 378

ASPARTAME
Food additives, 565

BAGGAGE SCREENING
Radiation control, 1295

BALDNESS PREVENTION PRODUCTS
Generally, 116

BENYLIN
Switch to OTC status, 964

BENZENE
Soft drinks, benzene in, 501, 502

BIOLOGICAL PRODUCTS
Generally, 1123–1192
Biologics Act, FDA enforcement, 14, 286–289
Biosimilar biologics, 1135–1137
Blood and Blood Products, this index
Definition, 135–139
Diagnostic biologics, 1211
Dual classification, 138, 139
Export of unlicensed products, 1475, 1476
FDA responsibility, 286–289, 1124–1127
Historical background, 1123, 1124
Human cell and tissue products, 1165–1174

Jurisdiction, FDA's, 135–139
NDA, products marketed pursuant to, 1013
New biologics, FDA approval, 1130–1134
Therapeutic biologics, FDA regulation generally, 1127–1137
    biologics review, 1127–1130
    biosimilar biologics, 1135–1137
    BLAs, FDA review, 1135
    new biologics, FDA approval, 1130–1134
Vaccines, this index
Veterinary biologicals, 1066, 1112, 1127

BIOTERRORISM
Threat of, 638–639

BIRTH CONTROL
Contraceptives, this index

BLOOD AND BLOOD PRODUCTS
Generally, 1153–1164
AIDS screening, 1164
Establishment registration and inspection, 1157
Good manufacturing practice, 1157
Protecting safety of blood supply, 1157–1164
Regulatory jurisdiction, 1153
Regulatory mechanism, 1153–1157
State regulation, 298
Umbilical cord blood, 1164, 1173, 1174

BONDS
Condemnation proceedings, forfeiture of bond, 209

BREAST IMPLANTS
Extended review period, 1240, 1241

BURDEN OF PROOF
Insanitary conditions, 485

CAFFEINE
Generally recognized as safe (GRAS) substances, 590, 591
Prior sanction for, 601
Regulation of, 89

CANADA
Prescription drug imports, 1458–1464

CANCER
Agency guidelines, 1432–1434
Anticancer drugs, use in combination, 815
Carcinogens, this index
Effectiveness of oncology drugs, 728
Group C cancer treatment IND, 768, 769
Incidence and causes, 1375, 1376
Laetrile, use of, 67, 68, 650–653

CANDY
Food, this index

CARCINOGENS
Generally, 1373–1438
Acceptable risk, 1391
Acrylonitrile, use in plastic beverage containers, 1397

Additives
  additives "straight up," quantitative
    risk assessment applied to,
    1402–1416
  constituents of additives,
    quantitative risk assessment
    applied to, 1397–1402
  deciding whether additive "induces
    cancer," 1417–1425
  indirect additives, 1402
Aflatoxins, 1395, 1396
Agency cancer guidelines, 1432–1434
Animal drugs, quantitative risk
    assessment applied to, 1387–1394
Children, mandate to protect, 1430, 1431
Color Additives Amendments, 1379–1382
Contamination variability, 1396, 1397
Costs of regulation, 1437, 1438
Delaney Clause
  Color Additives Amendments,
    1379–1382
  coverage, 1415
  generally recognized as safe (GRAS)
    substances, applicability to,
    581
  original enactment, 1376–1379
  resolving "Delaney paradox,"
    1425–1431
DES
          generally, 1382–1386
  human use, 741
residues in food, 488, 497
Dimethyl dicarbonate, use as yeast
    inhibitor in wines, 1415
Dioxin, 1425
DOJ views, 1394
Early FDA policy, 1374, 1375
Evolution of legislative policy
          generally, 1375–1382
  Delaney Clause, above
  incidence and causes of cancer,
    1375, 1376
Food contaminants, quantitative risk
    assessment applied to, 1395–1397
Government–wide policies, 1434, 1435
Historical background, 1373, 1374
IARC, coordination of research worldwide,
    1431, 1432
Incidence and causes of cancer, 1375,
    1376
Life style changes, 1436, 1437
Linearity, agency discretion to reject,
    1419, 1420
Methylene chloride, use for decaffination
    of coffee, 1415
National Toxicology Program (NTP), 1431,
    1432
Natural foods, quantitative risk
    assessment applied to, 1416, 1417
Polyvinyl chloride, 1397
Proposition 65 (California), 402, 1438
Quantitative risk assessment
          generally, 1387–1417
  acceptable risk, 1391
  additives "straight up," applied to,
    1402–1416

  aflatoxins, 1395–1397, 1395, 1396
  animal drugs, applied to, 1388–1394
  constituents of additives, applied to,
    1397–1402
  contamination variability, 1396,
    1397
  DOJ views, 1394
  food contaminants, applied to,
    1395–1397
  natural foods, applied to, 1416, 1417
  one in one million risk, 1393, 1394
  translating risk estimates, 1391
Red No. 3, 1424, 1425
Saccharin studies, 1404, 1405
Scientific assessment, 1420–1425
Secondary carcinogens, 1425
Translating risk estimates, 1391

CELLULITE
Warning letters, 116

CHEMICALS AND CHEMISTRY
Additives, this index
Development of chemistry, 2, 3
Use of chemicals in foods and cosmetics,
    553

CHEWING GUM
Food, classification as, 84

CHOLESTEROL
Food labeling, 413–415

CIGARETTES
Tobacco, this index

CIVIL PENALTIES
FDA enforcement, 262, 263, 916, 1298,
    1299
Medical devices, 1276, 1277

CLINICAL TESTING
Human Drugs, this index

CLONING
FDA jurisdiction over human cloning
    activities, 288, 289, 1186–1189

COLOR
Artificial Color, this index

COMPUTER PRODUCTS
FDA regulation of, 128, 129

CONDEMNATION
Food and Drug Administration, this index

CONFIDENTIALITY
Cosmetics, confidentiality of produce
    experience reports, 1341
Device data, 1516
NDA data, 1516
Persons reporting adverse drug reaction,
    preemption of confidentiality, 836
Trade Secrets, this index

CONFLICTS OF INTEREST
New drug approval, advisory committee
    members, 736

CONSENT
Clinical test subjects, 674, 675

CONSUMER PROTECTION AND EDUCATION
Food labeling, 386, 387

CONTAINERS
Food Labeling, this index
Slack fill
    container standards, 387, 388

CONTAMINANTS
Action levels, 61
Food, this index

CONTEMPT
Violation of injunction, 220, 221

CONTRACEPTIVES
Dalkon Shield, 1273
Emergency contraceptives, switch to OTC
    status, 807, 966–972
Oral contraceptives, patient labeling,
    877–879

CONTROLLED SUBSTANCES
Direct–to–consumer advertising, 924, 925
Prescription drug controlled substances,
    new drug applications (NDAs),
    810–814
Refills for Schedule II prescription drugs,
    810
Regulatory jurisdiction, 129, 130

COPYRIGHT
Generic drugs, use of copyrighted
    materials, 1006

COSMETICS
    Generally, 1301–1350
Adulterated cosmetics, 1311–1322
Adverse experience reporting, revocation
    of, 1341
Alpha hydroxy acid labeling, 1320
Animal cosmetics, 110
Animal testing, opposition to, 1321, 1322
Antiwrinkle creams, 115, 116
Baby shampoo, 1314, 1315
Banned ingredients, 1317–1319
Bubble bath, 1329
Budget for cosmetics, FDA's, 1334
California statute, 1322
Child resistant packaging, 1321
Children, cosmetics for, 1315
Coal tar hair dye exemption, 1322–1325
Color additive names, 1338
Cosmeceuticals, 118
Cosmetic devices
    generally, 121–124
    approved cosmetic devices, 117
    are cosmetic devices "cosmetics,"
    121–124
Cosmetic–drug spectrum, 110–117
Defined, 109, 110
Deodorants, 116, 117, 120
Dermatologists, disclosure to, 1329

Electronic auctions, cosmetics sold at,
    1318
Enforcement history, 1311
Environmentally protected ingredients,
    1319
European Community regulation, 1319
Feminine deodorant sprays, 1329
Flea markets, cosmetics sold at, 1318
Foods, cosmetic, 110
Fragrances
    ingredients, 1347
    mailing samples, 1322
GMPs for cosmetics and cosmetic–drugs,
    1316
Hair care products, 116
Historical background, 1301–1311
Ingredients
    fragrances, 1347
    labeling, 1335–1338
    names, 1338
Intended use and cosmetic–drug
    spectrum, 110–117
Labeling
    alpha hydroxy acid, 1320
    ingredient labeling, 1335–1338
    misleading labeling, 1330–1335
    see-through labels, 1334
    warnings, 1325–1330
Legislative proposals, 1310, 1311
Misbranded cosmetics
    generally, 1325–1335
    failure to warn as misbranding,
    1330
    label warnings, 1325–1330
    misleading labeling, 1330–1335
Odors, products intended to mask or
    prevent, 109, 110, 116, 117, 120
Organic cosmetics, 1334, 1335
OTC drug review, 120, 121, 1318
Product experience reports,
    confidentiality, 1341
Product claims, 1334
Reporting requirements, simplification,
    1341
Soap exemption, 109, 110
Statutory background, 1301–1311
Talcum powders, 1329
Tattoos, 110, 1318
Thigh creams, 116
Trade secret status, determination of,
    1337
Voluntary regulation, 1338–1348

CRIMINAL LIABILITY
    Generally, 237–252
Authorized criminal penalties, 238
Civil and criminal proceedings,
    interaction of, 239
Decision to prosecute, 237–239, 248–250
Guaranty clause, 251, 252
Impossibility defense, 250, 251
Investigations, 183, 184
Lack of knowledge, 249
Other statutes invoked in FDA
    proceedings, 239
Record of conviction, 250

Regulations governing Section 305 hearings, 239
Responsible officer, 249, 250
Section 305 hearings, 239
Standard of liability, 240–251

CT SCANNERS
Radiation control, 1295

CYCLAMATE
Food additives, 564, 565

DAIRY PRODUCTS
Filled milk, 338
Labeling
    artificial coloring, 392
    federal preemption, 310
Oleomargarine Act, 289, 338, 339
Reduced fat products, 375

DEBARMENT
FDA enforcement, 252–257

DEFAMATION
Privilege in defamation suits against FDA officials, 269

DEFINITIONS
Generally, 77–162
Cosmetics, 109, 110
Drugs and Devices, this index
Food, 79–89
Food additive, 555

DELANEY CLAUSE
Carcinogens, this index

DEODORANTS
Regulation of, 109, 110, 116, 120

DES
Carcinogens, this index

DEVICES
Drug and Device Definitions, this index
Medical Devices, this index

DIET PRODUCTS
Protein diet products, warning labels, 401

DIETARY SUPPLEMENTS
        Generally, 101–109, 319–323
Adverse event reporting, 633
Benecol, 323
Combination of drug and dietary supplement, 108, 109
Conventional food vs. dietary supplements, 321, 322, 449–451
Deceptive marketing practices, 328
Dietary ingredients in supplements, 627–629
Dietary Supplement Health and Education Act of 1994, 88, 89, 101–109
Ephedra, 629–633
Examples of FDA interpretations, 106, 107
Form of, 322, 323
Good manufacturing practices (GMP), 533

Hazardous nutrients, regulation of, 572–574
Herbs in food, 574
High–dose vitamin supplements, 92, 93
Intended to supplement the diet, 107, 108
Judicial review, de novo, 628
Labeling, exemption from, 156
Metabolites, 107
Method of administration, 108
New dietary ingredients, 628, 629
Previously designated drugs, use of, 108
Scope of definition, dietary ingredient, 105, 106
Structure/function and disease claims generally, 445–451
    Food, this index
Toxic nutrients, actions against, 573, 574
Vitamin-mineral products, 96, 151, 152, 323, 330, 331

DIMETHYL DICARBONATE
Use as yeast inhibitor in wines, 1415

DIOXIN
Detection of, 518
Secondary carcinogens, 1425

DISGORGEMENT
FDA enforcement, 221–230

DRINKING WATER
Bottled water, E. coli in, 476, 477
Fluoride, 566
Regulatory jurisdiction, 319

DRUGS
Animal drugs. Animal Food & Drugs, this index.
Human drugs, this index.

DRUG AND DEVICE DEFINITIONS
Generally, 89–135
Antiwrinkle creams, 115, 116
Approved cosmetic drugs and devices, 117
Baldness prevention, 116
Common sense limitations, 124–131
Compendia, official, 90–92, 842, 843
Cosmeceuticals, 118
Cosmetic devices. Cosmetics, this index
Cosmetic–drug line, products on, 117
Device, defined, 90
Diagnostic biologics, 1211
Diagnostic devices
        defined, 98–101
        drugs of abuse testing, 101
Diagnostic drugs, 100
Drug, defined, 90
Dual classifications, 89, 138, 139
Dual use products, 130
First Amendment limits, 131–135
Hair care products, 116
Human cellular and tissue–based products, 138
Intended use
        cosmetic-drug spectrum, intended use and, 110–121
        food-drug spectrum, intended use and, 101–109

in absence of claims, 96–98
Leeches and maggots, 129
Lethal products, 129
Medical and nonmedical uses, 130
Medical gas pipeline systems, 128
New drugs. Human Drugs, this index
Nontherapeutic uses, other types of drugs
    with, 129, 130, 1034, 1035
Sterilizers, 129
Street drugs, 1034, 1035
Testing for drugs of abuse, 101
Thigh creams, 116
Tobacco products, 139–151
Vitamin supplements, high–dose, 92, 93

DUE PROCESS
Substantive due process, 336

ECONOMIC ADULTERATION
Food, this index

EGGS
Label warnings, 532
USDA regulation, 318

EMERGENCY CONTRACEPTIVES
Switch to OTC status, 966–972

ENFORCEMENT
Food and Drug Administration, this index

ENVIRONMENTAL ASSESSMENT
Impact of major actions, 1526–1530

ENVIRONMENTAL CONTAMINANTS
Food, this index

EPHEDRA
Dietary supplements, 629–633

ESTROGEN
Patient labeling for prescription drugs,
    882

ETHICAL STANDARDS
Clinical testing, 688

EXPORTS
Foreign Commerce, this index

FACTORY INSPECTION
Food and Drug Administration, this index

FALSE CLAIMS
Food labeling, 328, 330

FALSE CLAIMS ACT
Qui tam enforcement, 934–938

FEDERAL TORT CLAIMS ACT
Negligent approval of NDA, 742

FEDERAL TRADE COMMISSION
Advertising unapproved drug uses, 821
Food advertising, FTC jurisdiction, 11,
    456–458

FIFRA
Animal drugs and FIFRA, 1065, 1066
Pesticide residues in food, 633–637

FIRST AMENDMENT
Device definition, First Amendment
    limits, 131–135
Health claims, 424, 425
OTC drugs, First Amendment
    considerations, 983, 984

FISH
Mercury levels, 515–518
Shellfish, this index
Transgenic fish, 1529, 1530

FLAVORINGS
Ingredient labeling, 392

FLUORIDE
Water additive, 566

FOLATE
Health claims, 423

FOOD
Generally, 317–639
Acrylamide in cooked food, 501, 502
Action levels
    contaminants, 61
    defects, 475, 476
    mercury, 517, 518
    pesticide residues, 637
Additives, this index
Advertising, 11, 456–458
Aesthetic adulteration
    generally, 469–488
    decomposition, 470–482
    filth, 470–485
    insanitary conditions, 482–485
    otherwise unfit for food, 486–488
Aflatoxin contamination, blending for,
    518–521
AIDS–infected personnel, 532, 533
Alar ban, 636
Benzene in soft drinks, 501, 502
Bioterrorism, threat of, 638–639
Brand name, nutrient descriptor in, 418
Caffeine, 89, 590, 591, 601
Candy
    choking hazard, 488
    mixtures of candy and trinkets, 507
Canned food contamination, 540
Carbohydrate descriptors, 416
CDC monitoring, foodborne illness, 527
Chewing gum, 87
Claims about food. Food Labeling, this
    index
Codex Alimentarius food standards,
    359–361
Coloring
    Additives, this index
    standardized foods, colors in, 624
Confectionery containing alcohol, 507
Constituents. Safety of food constituents,
    below
Contamination
    action levels for contaminants, 61
    canned food, 540

carcinogens, quantitative risk
assessment applied to food
contaminants, 1395–1397
Environmental contaminants, below
lead contamination, 518, 616
listeria contamination, 523
Sanitation, below
Cosmetic foods, 110
Filth, 470–474
Decomposition, 470–482
Defect action levels, 475, 476
Defined
generally, 79–89
other applications of definition, 88
DES residues, 488, 497
Dietary Supplements, this index
Dioxin, detection of, 518
Disease claims. Structure/function and
disease claims, below
Drinking water, regulatory jurisdiction,
319
Dual classification, 89
Economic adulteration, 375–379
Eggs, this index
Emergency permit control, 539–540
Enriched standardized foods, 352
Environmental contaminants
generally, 507–521
contaminant or food additive, 511,
512
dioxin, detection of, 518
lead contamination, 518, 616
mercury, 515–518
FDA terminology, relation of diet to
disease and health, 419
Filth, 470–485
Fish species, naming, 347
Foodborne illness
CDC monitoring, 527
Fortification, 353–354
Fruits and Vegetables, this index
Generally recognized as safe (GRAS)
substances
generally, 574–599
caffeine, 590, 591
change in status, 576, 577
Delaney Clause, applicability, 581
FDA options before and after 1997,
575
indirect uses, 577
lack of GRAS status, 579
prior sanction exceptions, GRAS
and, 602
prior sanction status, 602
Genetically modified ingredients
generally, 592–599
consultation process, 596
existing regulatory statutes, 598,
599
FDA safety regulation, 592–599
safety evaluation, 596
USDA safety regulations, 598, 599
Good manufacturing practice (GMP),
528–533
Grandfather clause, prior sanctioned
substances, 599–602

Hand sanitizers, use of, 130, 131
Hazard Analysis and Critical Control
Points (HACCP), 540–552
Ice, regulatory jurisdiction, 319
Imitation food
collateral challenges, 372
labeling, 351, 352
redefinition of imitation, 368–372
Industry use of regulation, 336
Infant food, 324
Infant formulas, 235, 236, 324, 533
Inferiority, concealment of, 378, 379
Ingredients, safe and suitable, 350, 351
Insanitary conditions, 482–485
Intentional functional ingredients.
Additives, this index
Labeling. Food Labeling, this index
Lead contamination, 518, 616
Listeria contamination, 523
Marketing permits, temporary, 347
Meat and Poultry, this index
Medical food, 324, 325
Mercury levels
generally, 515–518
action level, 517, 518
Migrating food–contact materials, 84
Names, common or usual
generally, 362–375
enriched standardized foods, 352
fish species, 347
infant food, 324
meat, 361, 262
modified standardized foods,
362–375
nonstandardized foods, 363–365
nutritional content, regulation of,
372–375
peanut butter vs. peanut butter
spread, 367, 368
White House Conference, 328, 329
Natural foods
carcinogens, quantitative risk
assessment applied to, 1416,
1417
claims. Food Labeling, this index
Nitrite and nitrate, 601, 602
No longer "fit" food, 84
Nonconforming products, challenges to,
346, 347
Nonenforcement of Section 402(b), 379
Nonnutritive, 507
Nutrient content, regulation of
common or usual names, 373–375
descriptor bans, 416
facts box, 404
FDA responsibility, 442
fortification, 353–354
fresh fruits and vegetables, 404, 405
imitation redefined, 386–372
infant formulas, 235, 236, 324, 533
labeling, 325–332
medical food, 324, 325
nutrient content claims, 413–418
nutrigenomics, 325
nutritional status of Americans,
442, 443

serving size, 405
terms, restriction on, 416
Nutrigenomics, 325
Nutritional support, statements of, 412
Nutritive value for health claims, 423
Omission of valuable constituent,
vagueness of standard, 378
Orphan medical food, 324
Other agencies' roles in regulating food,
84, 85
Otherwise unfit for food, 486–488
Packaging. Food Labeling, this index
Pathogenic microorganisms, 521–552
Peanut butter, 345
Pesticide residues
generally, 633–637
Alar ban, 636
EPA actions, 634–635
FDA action levels, 637
FIFRA, 383, 384, 636
human testing, 636
imported food, pesticides in, 636
monitoring and enforcement, 637
Poisonous or deleterious substances
generally, 488–521
acrylamide in cooked food, 501, 502
added substances, 492–507
benzene in soft drinks, 501, 502
Environmental contaminants, above
legislative history, 1938 Act, 494,
495
mercury action level, 517, 518
mixed, not added, 507
nonadded substances, 492–495
proof of hazard, 497
Premises of regulation, 333–339
Prior sanctioned substances, 599–602
Product-specific GMP regulations,
revocation of, 532
Reconditioning adulterated food, 485
Risk assessments for pathogens, 552
Safety of food constituents
generally, 488–492
dietary ingredients in dietary
supplements, 627–629
Environmental contaminants, above
food processing and packaging
substances, 607–617
genetically modified ingredients,
592–599
historical background, 488–492
Intentional functional ingredients.
Additives, this index
Pesticide residues, above
Poisonous or deleterious substances,
above
statutory background, 488–492
Salmonella contamination, 502–505, 532
Sanitation
generally, 469–488
Aesthetic adulteration, above
aflatoxin contamination, blending
for, 519–521
blending, issue of, 476–482
compliance policy, 485

constitutionality of statutory terms,
474
decomposition, 470–482
defect action levels, 475, 476
emergency permit control, 539, 540
FDA cooperative food sanitation
programs, 527, 528
food inspection, FDA oversight,
524–528
good manufacturing practice (GMP),
528–533
hand sanitizers, use of, 130, 131
Hazard Analysis and Critical
Control Points (HACCP),
540–552
impact of contamination, 545
insanitary conditions, 482–485
National Shellfish Sanitation
Program (NSSP), 527
otherwise unfit for food, 486–488
pathogenic microorganisms,
521–552
predaceous insects, 478
reconditioning, 485
Sanitation codes, 281, 282
transport sanitation, 485
worms, 487, 488
Seafood HACCP, enforcement of, 187
Serving size, 405
Soft drinks, benzene in, 501, 502
Special dietary foods, 325
Standards of identity
generally, 339–362
adversely affected by food standard,
who is, 52
amendment of standards, 329
Codex Alimentarius food standards,
359–361
colors in standardized foods, 624
court challenges, 52
decline of food standards, 352–355
formal procedures, impact of, 343,
344
historical background, 325–332
modernization, 350, 351
nonconforming products, challenges
to, 346, 347
operation of food standards,
340–347
rise of food standards (1938–1970),
339–350
statutory standards of identity, 347
Structure/function and disease claims
generally, 89, 443–451
advertising, FTC regulation,
456–458
background, 443–448
dietary supplements vs.
conventional foods, 449–451
disease prevention claims
generally, 418–441
abbreviated disease
prevention claims, 428
authoritative body provision,
424, 425

disqualifying macronutrient
levels, 424
FDA use of enforcement
discretion, 436, 437
First Amendment challenge,
424
folate, 423
general principles, 418–419
nutritive value for disease
prevention claims, 423
qualified disease claims, 436,
437
treatment claims, 423, 424
unqualified disease claims,
419–425
folate, 423
general health claims and dietary
guidance, 441–443
health claims. Disease prevention
claims, above
jelly bean rule, 417, 418
natural state exception, 449
nutritional support, statements of,
443, 444
nutritive value for disease claims,
423
relation of diet to disease and
health, FDA terminology, 419
statutory disclaimer and
notifications, 444
structure/function claims, 443–451
unqualified disease claims, 419–425
Sweeteners, this index
Tampering, 639
Temporary marketing permits, 347
Transport sanitation, 485
Unfitness, 486–488
USDA regulation of meat, poultry, and
eggs, 318
Vegetables. Fruits and Vegetables, this
index
Whole grains, 416
Worms, 487, 488

**FOOD AND DRUG
ADMINISTRATION**
Administrative consistency, 168–176
Administrative detention authority, 211
Administrative Practice and Procedure,
this index
Authorities delegated to FDA, 16
Chief counsel's office, 19
Citizen committees, 25
Civil penalties
generally, 262–263
inflation adjustment, 263
medical devices, 1276, 1277
radiation and mammography, 1299
Compliance correspondence, informal,
263–268
Compliance policy, 167, 168
Condemnation
bond, forfeiture of, 209
final condemnation decrees and
salvaging, 207–210
jurisdiction and venue, 206, 207

litigation costs, 209, 210
proof required, 204–207
re-export, 210
Seizure, below
Criminal Liability, this index
Definitions, this index
EMEA, cooperation with, 711, 712
Enforcement
generally, 163–270
administrative consistency, 168–176
bailee, goods in possession of, 280,
281
biologics, 286–289
Civil penalties, above
clinical investigators, 183
compliance policy, 167, 168
components shipped in interstate
commerce, 280, 282–285
Condemnation, above
constitutional limitations, 179–184
Criminal Liability, this index
debarment, 252–257
discretion, 171–176
disgorgement, 221–230
DOJ, role of, 164
Factory inspection, below
HHS Inspector General, role of, 261,
262
industry-wide enforcement, 167, 168
informal compliance
correspondence, 263–268
Injunctions, below
inspections
Factory inspection, below
Inspections, below
interstate commerce
bailee, goods in possession of,
280, 281
components shipped in
interstate commerce,
280, 282–285
dispensing prescription drugs,
276, 277
held for sale after shipment in
interstate commerce,
277–282
holding prior to shipping, 275
introduction into interstate
commerce, 273–277
new drugs, 280
proof of shipment, 277
ultimate consumer, goods in
possession of, 281
jurisdiction
generally, 271–289
biologics, 286–289
human cloning, 288, 289,
1186–1189
Interstate commerce, above
introduction, 271, 272
medical devices, 285–289
restaurants and food stores,
281, 282
medical devices, 285–289

OCC clearance of enforcement correspondence, mandatory, 266, 267
publicity, 268–270
Recalls, below
regulatory delay, 74
regulatory philosophy, 167, 168
repair, replacement, and refund, 230
restitution, 221–230
rulemaking. Administrative Practice and Procedure, this index
Section 309 and enforcement discretion, 175
Section 301 prohibited acts, 163
Seizure, below
selective enforcement, 168–171
statistics, 164–166
ultimate consumer, goods in possession of, 281
warning letters, 264–268
Factory inspection
    generally, 176–192
    costs, 179
    duration, 178
    introduction, 176–179
    third-party inspection, 179
    time of day, 178, 179
Food-drug spectrum, 101–109
Food inspection, FDA oversight, 524–528
Food Labeling, this index
Food sanitation programs, cooperative, 527, 528
Food stores, FDA jurisdiction, 281, 282
Foreign Commerce, this index
Historical background, 3–5
Human biological products, 135–139
Informal compliance correspondence, 263–268
Injunctions
    generally, 211–230
    contempt, violation of injunction, 220, 221
    disgorgement, 221–230
    introduction, 211–213
    jury trial, 213
    permanent injunctions, 215–221
    preliminary injunctions, 213–215
    restitution, 221–230
    seizures, multiple, 201–205
Inspections
    contract laboratories, records inspection, 186
    Factory inspections, above
    food inspection, FDA oversight, 524–528
    medical practitioners, records exception, 186
    pharmacies, records exception, 185, 186
    records, 184–187
    recording devices, use of, 192
    samples and photographs, 188–192
    scope, 184–192
Interstate commerce. Enforcement, above

Jurisdiction
    generally, 77–162
    Definitions, this index
    Drugs and Devices, this index
    enforcement jurisdiction. Enforcement, above
Mission, 14–16
Nutrition programs, 442
Obesity, 442
Office of the Commissioner, 19, 20
Other laws enforced by FDA, 14
Prescription drug labeling, FDA approval, 862
Proof required for condemnation, 204–207
Publicity, 268–270
Qualified disease claims, FDA use of enforcement discretion, 436, 437
Recalls
    generally, 230–237
    mandatory recalls, 235–237, 1275, 1276
    procedures, 232, 233
Records, FDA inspections, 184–187
Regulatory delay, 74
Regulatory environment, 25–27
Regulatory philosophy, 167, 168
Resources, 24, 25
Restaurants, FDA jurisdiction, 281, 282
Risk-benefit decisionmaking, 26
Rulemaking. Administrative Practice and Procedure, this index
SEC, cooperation with, 706, 707
Section 301 prohibited acts, 163
Seizure
    generally, 194–198
    administrative detention, 211
    Condemnation, above
    effectiveness, 210, 211
    labeling, 198
    multiple seizures, 201–204
    non-closely regulated industries, seizures from, 198
    seizure process, 194–198
Selective enforcement, 168–171
Smoking cessation products, 150, 151
Structure and organization, 16–20
Tobacco, implicit limits on FDA's jurisdiction, 139–151
Warning letters, 264–268

FOOD LABELING
Generally, 379–469
Additives
    hyperactivity, 626, 627
    incidental, 393
Affirmative disclosures, 388, 389
Alcoholic beverages ingredient labeling, 393, 394
Allergies, 397–399
Brand name, misleading, 383
Chemical preservatives, 391
Cholesterol and fat labeling, 413–415
Collective ingredient labeling, 392, 393
Colors, 392
Consumers to be protected, 386, 387

Country–of–origin labeling, mandatory, 408, 409
Dairy products, artificial coloring, 392
Dietary guidance, 441, 442
Dietary supplement labeling exemption, 156
Disclaimers ineffective, 383
Economic adulteration, 388
Enforcement, private right, 383
Exemptions, ingredient labeling, 393
Fair Packaging and Labeling Act, 388
False or misleading claims, prohibition, 328, 330
Flavorings, 392
Fresh food claims, 453
Fruits and vegetables, drained weight, 390, 391
Genetically modified foods, 458–469
Geographic designation labeling, 456
Health claims, 441, 442
Historical overview, 325–332
Imitation food, 309, 347–350
Inborn errors of metabolism, 401
Ineffectiveness of truthful labeling, 378, 379
Ingredient labeling, 391–397
Jurisdictional reach, 152–156
Kosher labeling, 455, 456
Mandatory labeling, 326
Metric labeling, 391
Misbranded food
    historical background, 325, 326
    Section 403 labeling requirements, below
Natural food claims
    generally, 451, 452
    FDA position, 451, 452
    USDA policy, 451, 452
Nomenclature, ingredients, 396
Nutrition labeling, 403–409, 313, 314
Oral representations, 352, 353
Organic food claims, 453, 454
Other nutrition labeling, 324, 235
Packaging
    deceptive packaging, 387, 388
    economic adulteration, 388
    enforcement of Section 403(d), 387, 388
    Fair Packaging and Labeling Act, 388
    FDA regulations, 388
    size of package, weight labeling, 388, 456
    slack fill, 387, 388
Percentage ingredient labeling, 329
Predominance, order of, 392, 393
Private enforcement, 383
Proposition 65 (California), 402, 1438
Protein diet products, 401
Public health messages, 418
Saccharin, 401, 402
Safe use warning, 399
Scope of labeling, 152–156
Section 403 labeling requirements
    generally, 379–391
    affirmative disclosures, 388, 389

brand name, misleading, 383
consumers to be protected, 386, 387
country–of–origin labeling, mandatory, 408, 409
disclaimers ineffective, 383
geographic designation labeling, 456
kosher labeling, 455, 456
Packaging, above
private enforcement, 383
prohibited representations, 379–388
Side effects, 401
Size of package, weight labeling, 388, 456
Sodium, 425, 426, 591
Solid content labeling, voluntary, 391
Standardized foods, ingredient labeling, 331
USDA food grade labeling, 454, 455
Warnings, 399–402
Weight labeling
    generally, 390, 391
    descriptive weight or size labeling, 456
    drained weight, 390, 391
    metric labeling, 391
    moisture, gain and loss, 390
    package size, 388, 456
    voluntary solid content labeling, 391

FOREIGN COMMERCE
    Generally, 1439–1485
Animal drugs, unapproved, export of, 1474, 1475
Biologics, unlicensed, export of, 1472–1474
Canada, drug imports from, 1458–1464
Customs Service, coordination with, 1447
Export from U.S.
    generally, 1468–1483
    drug intermediates, 1474
    export certificates, 1481, 1482
    international trade agreements, 1482, 1483
    medical devices, 1475, 1476
    Section 801(e)(1), export pursuant to, 1468–1472
    unapproved medical products pursuant to Section 802, 1476–1482
    unapproved new animal drugs, export of, 1474, 1475
    unapproved new drugs and unlicensed biologics, export of, 1472–1474
FDA's general authority over importation, 1439–1447
Import for export, 1483-1485
Importation into U.S.
    generally, 1439–1468
    Customs Service, coordination with, 1447
    FDA's general authority, 1439–1447
    GAO oversight, 1455
    hearing rights, 1441
    legal challenges to FDA procedures, 1447
    notice requirements, 1441

Prescription drugs and devices,
  below
reconditioning, destroying, or
  reexporting goods refused
  admission, 1447–1450
refusal of admission compared to
  seizure, 1450–1455
International trade agreements, 1482,
  1483
Legal challenges to FDA importation
  procedures, 1447
Medical devices, export of, 1475, 1476
New drugs, unapproved, export of,
  1472–1474
Personal use, importation for, 1464
Prescription drugs and devices,
  importation of
    generally, 1458–1468
  Canada, imports from, 1458–1464
  commercial importation, 1458–1464
  partial certification, 1467, 1468
  personal use, importation for, 1464
  waiver, importation pursuant to,
    1464–1468
Reconditioning, destroying, or reexporting
  goods refused admission, 1447–1450
Reexportation of goods, 1447–1450, 1454
Refusal of admission compared to seizure,
  1450–1455
Unapproved medical products, export
  pursuant to Section 802, 1476–1482
Unapproved new drugs and unlicensed
  biologics, export of, 1472–1474
Waiver, importation pursuant to,
  1464–1468

FRAGRANCES
Cosmetics, this index

FRAUD
New drug applications, fraud policy, 712

FREE RANGE
Use of term, 455

FREEDOM OF INFORMATION ACT
  Generally, 1503–1514
Costs of implementing FOIA, 1506
Documents constituting "agency records,"
  1505, 1506
Processing fees, 1505
Reverse FOIA suits, 1508

FRUITS AND VEGETABLES
Drained weight, 390, 391
HACCP-based voluntary program, 546,
  547
Nutrition labeling, 404, 405

GENERIC DRUGS
  Generally, 996–1023
Abbreviated NDAs, 1000–1011
Authorized generic drugs, 1023
Bioequivalence, 1009, 1010
Biological products, 1013
Citizen petitions, 1010
Confidential information, access to, 1516
Copyrighted materials, use of, 1006

Due diligence, 1005
Economic impact, 1013, 1014
Generic drugs before 1984, 996–1000
Generic name disclosure, 864–866
Implementing regulations, 1004
Market exclusivity, 1005, 1006, 1016
Marketing generic versions of branded
    Non–DESI unapproved new drugs,
    787
New indications for use, 1009
Orange Book listing, 1006, 1007
Patents
    recalculation of extension, 1005
    research use exemption, 1006
    statutory patent term, 1004, 1005
    term restoration, 1005
Post-1962 generics, paper NDAs and
    abbreviated NDAs, 782, 783
Price, effect of generic drugs, 1013
Section 505(b)(2) NDAs, 1012, 1013
30-month stay, 1014, 1015

GENETICALLY MODIFIED FOODS
Labeling, 458–469

**GENETICALLY MODIFIED
  INGREDIENTS**
Food, this index

GENETICS
Gene therapy, 1176–1178
Genetics, genomics and personalized
    medicine, 1039–1043

GIFTS
Prescription drug promotional practices,
  913, 914

**GOOD MANUFACTURING
  PRACTICE (GMP)**
Blood and blood components, 1157
Cosmetics and cosmetic–drugs, 1315,
  1316
Dietary supplements, 533
Food, 528–533
Human drugs, 838–847
Investigational drugs, 700, 701
Medical devices, 1261–1264

GRADE LABELING
USDA food grade labeling, 454, 455

HAIR CARE PRODUCTS
Generally, 116

HAZARDOUS NUTRIENTS
Regulation of, 572–574

HEARING AID CONTROLS
State regulatory authority, 312

HEARINGS
Administrative Practice and Procedure,
    this index

HEAT SUSCEPTORS
Food additives, 615

HEMP
Use of, 812

HISTORICAL BACKGROUND
Generally, 1–27
Accum Treatise, 2, 3
Ancient times, 1, 2
Biological products, 1123, 1124
Carcinogens, 1373, 1374
Chemistry, development of, 2, 3
Cosmetics, 1301–1311
Early regulation of food and drugs, 1–3
English experience, 2
Evolution of federal food and drug
    legislation, 5–13
FDA. Food and Drug Administration, this
    index
Federal Food, Drug, and Cosmetic Act of
    1938, 10, 11, 494, 495
Federal Food and Drugs Act of 1906, 8–10
Food labeling, 325–332
Food sanitation, 469, 470
Human drugs, 641–660
Medical devices, 1193, 1194
Other laws enforced by FDA, 14
Post-1938 amendments, 11–13
Regulatory environment, 25–27
Safety of food constituents, 488–492
State and local laws, 19th century, 5, 6
Statutory and institutional history
    generally, 3–14
    evolution of federal food and drug
        legislation, 5–13
    federal Food, Drug, and Cosmetic
        Act of 1938, 10, 11, 494, 495
    federal Food and Drugs Act of 1906,
        8–10
    Food and Drug Administration, 3–5
    other laws enforced by FDA, 14
    post-1938 amendments, 11–13
    state and local laws, 19th century,
        5, 6

HIV
Home tests, 1268

HOUSEWARES
Food additives, housewares exemption,
    615, 616

HUMAN BIOLOGICAL PRODUCTS
Biological Products, this index

HUMAN CLONING
FDA jurisdiction, 288, 289, 1187–1189

HUMAN DRUGS
Generally, 641–1044
Adverse event reporting, 836, 837, 990,
    1516
Ages, different, prescription vs.
    nonprescription sales, 807
Antibiotic drugs, 791, 792
Applications. New drug applications,
    below
Brand names, 865, 866
Children, clinical testing on, 697–699

Claims. Therapeutic claims, regulation of,
    below
Clinical holds, 681, 690, 691
Clinical testing
    generally, 673–707
    adaptive trials, 685
    all comers trials, 685
    children, testing on, 697–699
    clinical endpoints, surrogate
        endpoints, ad biomarkers,
        694–697
    clinical holds, 681, 690, 691
    consent of test subjects, 674, 675,
        688
    data monitoring committee,
        701–703
    databank, 705, 706
    elderly, testing on, 699
    enriched trials, 685
    ethical standards, 688
    ethnic and racial groups, 700
    financial disclosure, 675
    Investigational new drug (IND)
        process, below
    Lifesaving drugs, below
    mandating testing, FDA power, 675,
        676
    noninferiority trials, 685, 686
    overseas testing, 703, 704
    oversight of clinical investigators,
        704, 705
    patient advocates, 703
    patient reported outcomes, 686
    phases
        generally, 678–686
        phase I, 680, 681
        phase II, 681
        phase III, 681–683
        Phase IV testing
            commitments, 837, 838
        phase zero, 678–680
    placebo–controlled trials, 688, 689
    prisoners, 688
    recruiting trial subjects, 688
    regulations governing drug tests,
        684
    responsibility to test, 675
    subpopulations, testing on, 697–700
    women, testing on, 699
Compassionate use IND, 769
Competitor suits to contest product
    claims, 992, 993
Confidentiality of persons reporting
    adverse reaction, preemption, 836
Conflicts of interest, advisory committee
    members, 736
Controlled substances, this index
Cosmetic drugs, 110–117
Cost of approved NME drug, 748
Cost of drugs for patients
    generally, 1023–1028
    importation of cheaper drugs, 1026,
        1027
    internet pharmacy sales, 1032–1034
Counterfeit drugs, 1028–1031

Definitions. Drug and Device Definitions, this index
Disclaimers, 649
Diagnostic drugs, 100
Diverted drugs, 1031, 1032
Dosages, different, prescription vs. nonprescription sales, 807
Drug Amendments of 1962, impact of
 generally, 744–751
 Cost of drugs for patients, above
 drug lag, 744–747
 IND/NDA statistics, 747–751
Durham–Humphrey Amendments, prescription vs. nonprescription drugs, 805–807
Elderly, clinical testing on, 699
Emergency research, 689
Ethnic and racial groups, clinical testing on, 700
FDA enforcement strategy, therapeutic claims, 649
Field alert reports, 837
Formulation and testing
 Clinical testing, above
 Nonclinical formulation and testing, below
Freedom of choice, patients', 649–660, 743, 744
Generic Drugs, this index
Genetics, genomics and personalized medicine, 1039–1043
Good manufacturing practice (GMP), 838–847, 700, 701
Group C cancer treatment IND, 768, 769
Historical background, 641, 642
Illegal commercial importation, 774
Imitation drugs, 1034, 1035
Imminent hazard, summary ban, 855–859
Import alert, drugs on, 773
Importation
 investigational new drugs, importation for personal use, 771–775
 statutory legalization of unapproved drugs, 1026, 1027
Indications, different, prescription vs. nonprescription drugs, 806
Insulin, 791, 792
Internet sales, 1032–1034
Investigational drugs, use for therapy
 generally, 763–775
 AIDS amendments, 767
 compassionate use IND, 769
 constitutional right to expanded access, 653, 654
 continuing demands, 767
 emergency research, 689, 766
 emergency use IND, 765, 766
 group C cancer treatment IND, 768, 769
 individual patient IND, 765
 open label IND, 769
 orphan drug IND, 769
 parallel track IND, 768
 publication of treatment INDs, 767
 special exception IND, 770

 treatment IND, 765, 766
 tropical drug IND, 769
 unproven drugs for terminally ill, 653, 654
Investigational new drug (IND) process
 CDER guidance, 676
 Clinical testing, above
 contractual right to investigational drugs, 684
 date of effectiveness of IND, 674
 development of IND regulations, 675
 emergency research, 689
 exemptions, 675
 FDA critical path initiative, 1035
 generic new drug process. Generic Drugs, this index
 GMP for investigational drugs, 700, 701
 government–sponsored INDs, 683, 684
 importation of investigational new drugs for personal use, 771–775
 IND deregulation, 687, 688
 institutional review board (IRB) approval, 686–689
 Lifesaving drugs, below
 meetings with FDA, 717–720
 no practice of medicine exemption, 684
 protocol guidelines and guidance, 685
 purpose and form of IND, 709–712
 special protocol assessment, 691–694
 statistics, 747–749
 therapeutic use. Investigational drugs, use for therapy, above
 time devoted to IND testing, 749–751
Labeling. Prescription Drug Labeling, this index
Licensure of new drugs
 generally, 669–751
 abbreviated NDAs, 782, 783
 background, 642–644
 botanical NDAs, FDA guidance, 801
 commencement of NDA–withdrawal proceedings, 778, 779
 cosmetics as excluded product, 801
 coverage of new drug provisions
  generally, 667–751
  abbreviated NDAs, 996
  general recognition, evidence of, 996
  grandfather clauses, 666, 667
  homeopathic drugs, 799, 800
  hormone drugs, 787
  jurisdiction to determine new drug status, 667–669
  non–DESI unapproved new drugs, 784–788
  parenteral nutrition, 799
  pharmacy exemption, 793–799

traditional Chinese medicine, 800, 801
criteria for NDAs, 788
dietary supplements as excluded product, 801
digoxin, 788
drug Amendments of 1962 and NAS review, 776–778
food as excluded product, 801
general recognition, evidence of, 661, 662
grandfather clauses, 606, 607
homeopathic drugs, 799, 800
hormone drugs, 787
jurisdiction to determine new drug status, 667–669
less-than-effective drugs, federal reimbursement, 784
levothyroxine, 787, 788
marketing drugs under 1938 Act, 775, 776
me-too drugs, 780–782
non–DESI unapproved new drugs, 784–788
paper NDAs, 782, 783, 1000
parenteral nutrition, 799
post-1962 generics, paper NDAs and abbreviated NDAs, 782, 783
premarket approval requirement, FDA implementation, 775–788
specifically excluded products, 801
traditional Chinese medicine, 800, 801
Lifesaving drugs, expedited development generally, 751–758
fast track, 751–753
Subpart E, 751, 752
Life-supporting drug, voluntary withdrawal, 854
Limitation to prescription sale, 802–807
Listing of drugs, 834
Medical marijuana, 811, 812
Medication guides, 886–888
MedWatch program, 836
Military, use of investigational drugs, 689
Names
brand names, 865, 866
generic name disclosure, 864–866
official names, 865
New drug applications (NDAs), 759
generally, 709–712
accelerated approval (Subpart H)
promotional materials, FDA approval, 756
surrogate endpoint, approval based on, 754, 755
advisory committee review, 735, 736
alert list, 742
animal rule, 727, 728
antibiotic drugs, 791, 792
benefit and risk, balancing, 729–732
combination drugs, 727
company resubmissions, 735
confidentiality of NDA data, 1516
cost of approved NME drug, 748
data supporting approval, 711

designation, request for, 732
disapproval, procedures for, 723
disclosure of materials sent to advisory committee, 735, 736
effectiveness standard
generally, 724–729
clinical and surrogate endpoints, 727
clinical testing guidelines, 726
combination drugs, 727
exemptions, 728
longer term studies, 728, 729
oncology drugs, 728
relative efficacy, 726
statistical analysis, 727
substantial evidence, meaning of, 725
environmental considerations, 732
exhaustion of FDA procedures, 740
Fast Track, 751–753
FDA statutory authority and guidance, 735
FDA/EMEA cooperation, 711, 712
FDA/SEC cooperation, 706, 707
filing, 711
final approval or denial, 738–744
financial conflicts of interest, advisory committee members, 736
fraud policy, 712
Generic Drugs, this index
grounds for disapproval, 740, 741
insulin, 791, 792
internal agency review process, 733–735
judicial enforcement of 180–day deadline, 742
judicial review of denial, 740
labeling review, 737, 738
meetings with FDA, 676–678
NDAs invited by FDA, 741
negligent approval, 742
number of approved NME NDAs, 748, 749
obsolete NDAs, withdrawal, 851
Orphan drugs, below
packaging, FDA control over, 741
poison prevention packaging, 995
Postapproval obligations, below
postapproval testing commitments, 837, 838
preapproval inspection, 734
preapproval promotion, 957
prescription drug controlled substances, 810–814
priority review, 756–758
private right of action with regard to safety, 724
publicity about NDA approvals, 741
purpose and form of NDA, 709–712
radiopharmaceutical drugs, 788–791
rationing newly approved drug, 742
reform of approval system, 712
refusal to file, 720
regulations, 710, 711
relative efficacy, 726

rescission of NDA because of
mistake, 851
safety standard
generally, 720–724
competitive safety studies, 723
private right of action with
regard to safety, 724
withdrawal of NDA approval
for safety reasons, 723
studies of NDA process, 712
substantial evidence, meaning of,
725
suits to force approval, 742
supplemental NDAs, 835, 836
terrorism, drugs to combat, 753
time devoted to NDA review,
749–751
user fees, 712–717
withdrawal of NDA approval
generally, 848–859
obsolete NDAs, 851
rescission because of mistake,
851
standing to challenge, 858
statute, withdrawal by, 851
untrue statements of material
fact, 851
New drugs
Clinical testing, above
export of unapproved new drugs,
1472–1474
Investigational new drug (IND)
process, above
NDAs
New drug applications, above
Postapproval obligations,
below
Nonclinical formulation and testing
generally, 669–673
good laboratory practices, 672
nonclinical testing, 670, 671
request for designation, 672
synthesis and purification, 669, 670
Official names, 865
Open label IND, 769
Orphan drugs
generally, 758–763
implementing regulations, 761
IND, 769
list of, 762
Orphan Products Board, 762
proposed legislation, 762
seven year exclusivity, 762
timing of claim of orphan status,
761
Overseas testing, 703, 704
Oversight Board, Drug Safety (DSOB),
832
Over–the–Counter Drugs, this index
Pain medication, 813
Personal use, importation of
investigational new drugs, 771–775
Peyote, religious use, 812
Physician prescribing, regulating
generally, 814–834

anticancer drugs, use in
combination, 815
controls over prescription drug
distribution, 825–834
FDA influence, 814–825
FTC enforcement, 821
habits of physicians, 814, 815
state law, 819, 820
unapproved use, 819
Postapproval obligations
generally, 834–859
adverse event reporting, 836, 837,
990
annual report, 837
applications integrity (fraud) policy,
712
Drug Safety Oversight Board
(DSOB), 832
field alert reports, 837
imminent hazard, summary ban,
855–859
labeling changes, 835
life-supporting drug, voluntary
withdrawal, 854
manufacturing changes, 835, 836
MedWatch program, 836
Phase IV testing commitments,
837–838
recordkeeping and reporting
obligations, economic impact,
836
supplemental NDAs, 835, 836
withdrawal of NDA approval. New
drug applications, above
Prescription drugs
Advertising, this index
dependent pharmacist prescribers,
810
dispensing, interstate commerce,
276, 277
distinguishing between prescription
and nonprescription drugs,
957–960
diverted drugs, 1031, 1032
import–export. Foreign Commerce,
this index
internet sales, 1032–1034
labels. Prescription Drug Labeling,
this index
Physician prescribing, above
radio frequency identification
(RFID), establishing pedigree
for prescription drugs, 1029,
1030
refills for Schedule II prescription
drugs, 810
samples, illegal distribution, 1032
state authorization to prescribe
drugs, 807, 808
street drug alternatives, 1034, 1035
Street drugs, 107, 108
switch from prescription to
nonprescription status,
960–973
valid prescription, requirement of,
807–810

warnings. Prescription Drug
Labeling, this index
Prisoners, investigational research, 688
Product claims. Therapeutic claims,
regulation of, below
Promotion of prescription drugs.
Advertising, this index
Publicity about NDA approvals, 741
Radiopharmaceutical drugs, 788–791
Rationing newly approved drug, 742
Refills for Schedule II prescription drugs,
810
Registration of drug establishments, 834
Samples, illegal distribution, 1032
Special exception IND, 770
Special protocol assessment, 691–694
Street drug alternatives, 1034, 1035
Subpopulations, testing on, 697–700
Summary ban, imminent hazard, 855–859
Switch from prescription to
nonprescription status, 960–973
Terminally ill, unproven drugs, 653, 654
Testing
Clinical testing, above
Nonclinical formulation and testing,
above
Therapeutic claims, regulation of
generally, 664–660
competitor suits to contest product
claims, 992, 993
disclaimers, 647
FDA enforcement strategy, 649
Tropical drug IND, 769
Unproven drugs for terminally ill, 653,
654
Unsafe drugs, patients' need for, 854
User fees, new drug applications (NDAs),
712–717
Warnings. Prescription Drug Labeling,
this index
Withdrawal of NDA. New drug
applications, above
Women, clinical testing on, 699

HUMAN TISSUE TRANSPLANTS
Generally, 1165–1175
Cells and tissues, FDA regulation,
1167–1175
Regulatory authority, 1165–1167
Umbilical cord blood, 1164

HYPERACTIVITY
Food additives, 626, 627

IBUPROFEN
Switch to OTC status, 964

ICE
Regulatory jurisdiction, 319

IMITATION FOOD
Food, this index

IMPORTATION
Foreign Commerce, this index

IMPORTATION OF DRUGS
Human Drugs, this index

IMPOSSIBILITY
Criminal liability, defense of
impossibility, 250, 251

IN VITRO FERTILIZATION
Generally, 1185–1186
Diagnostics, in vitro
generally, 1201, 1202
OTC devices, 1267, 1268
regulation of, 1243–1245

INFANT FORMULAS
FDA regulation, 235, 236, 324
Good Manufacturing Practices, 533

INFORMATION QUALITY ACT
Generally, 1524–1526

INGREDIENTS
Cosmetics, this index
Genetically modified ingredients. Food,
this index
Labeling, 391–397

INJUNCTIONS
Food and Drug Administration, this index

INSECTS
Predaceous insects, 478

INSPECTIONS
Continuous factory inspection for meat
and poultry, 526
Food and Drug Administration, this index
Food inspection, FDA oversight, 524–528
USDA inspection regime, 192, 193

INTERNET
Prescription drug sales, 1032–1034, 1026,
1027

INTERSTATE COMMERCE
FDA enforcement jurisdiction. Food and
Drug Administration, this index

INVESTIGATIONAL DRUGS
Human Drugs, this index

JUDICIAL REVIEW
Agency implementation, 62–75
Dietary supplements, 628
Exhaustion of remedies, 69
New drug application, denial of, 740
Record for judicial review, FDA
rulemaking, 64, 65
Ripeness, 65–66
Standing to seek, 52

JURISDICTION
Condemnation proceedings, 206
Enforcement jurisdiction. Food and Drug
Administration, this index
Food advertising, FTC jurisdiction, 11
New drug status, jurisdiction to
determine, 667–669
Primary jurisdiction, 66–68
Regulatory jurisdiction
generally, 77–162
Drugs and Devices, this index

JURY TRIAL
Injunctive relief, 213

KOSHER FOODS
Labeling, 455, 456

LABELING
Cosmetics, this index
Food Labeling, this index
Over-the-Counter Drugs, this index
Prescription Drug Labeling, this index

LAETRILE
Use for cancer, 67, 68, 650–653

LANHAM ACT
Competitor suits to contest product
claims, 938, 992, 993
Marketing generic versions of branded
non–DESI unapproved new drugs,
787

LEAD CONTAMINATION
Generally, 518, 616
Tin cans, lead in, 616

LEECHES
Medical devices, 129

LETHAL PRODUCTS
Seizure of, 129

LICENSING NEW DRUGS
Human Drugs, this index

LISTERIA
Food contamination, 523

LITIGATION COSTS
Condemnation proceedings, 209, 210

LIVESTOCK
Antibiotics used in livestock production,
1081–1105
Mad cow disease, 1051–1059
Production practices, human health
hazards
antibiotics used in livestock
production, 1081–1105
mad cow disease, 1051–1059
Residues of animal drugs, monitoring,
1068
Sulfonamide drugs, 1068
USDA production/marketing claims, 454,
455

MAD COW DISEASE
Generally, 1051–1059
Specified cattle materials, unfitness, 1318

MAGGOTS
Medical devices, 129

MAMMOGRAPHY
Radiation control, 1295, 1299

MARGARINE
Imitation margarine, 350
Oleomargarine Act, 289, 338, 339

MEAT AND POULTRY
Canned foods, 540
Continuous factory inspection, 526
Drugs used to color poultry, 625
Food names, 361, 362
Irradiation, 565, 566
Nitrite and nitrate, 601, 602
USDA regulation, 318

MEDICAL DEVICES
Generally, 1193–1300
Abbreviated PMN, 1228
Administrative detention, 1271
Administrative review of PMA decision,
1240
Adulteration, 1254–1259
Adverse event reporting, 1260, 1261
Advisory committee review, 1238, 1239
Banned devices, 1271
Breast implants, 1240, 1241
Cigarettes as restricted devices, 1268,
1269
Civil penalties, 1276, 1277
Class II devices, special controls
generally, 1251–1254
other special controls, 1254
performance standards, 1251–1253
voluntary medical device standards,
1252, 1253
Classification
generally, 1212–1215
equitable treatment of old and new
devices, 1215, 1216
novel devices, de novo classification
and reclassification,
1247–1251
procedure, 1212–1215
reclassification of preamendment
devices, 1216, 1217, 1251
transitional devices, regulation of,
1217, 1218
Comparison of PMAs and NDAs,
1236–1238
Confidentiality of device data, 1516
Cosmetic devices, 121–124
Custom devices, 1246, 1247
Definition of "device", Drug and Device
Definitions, this index
Definition of "device" since 1976
generally, 1205–1211
diagnostic devices, 1211
drug–device combinations,
1206–1211
line between drug and device, 1205,
1206
Device tracking, 1274, 1275
Diagnostic devices
defined, 98–100, 1211
drugs of abuse testing, 100
Diapulse litigation, 1195, 1196
Drug-device combinations, 1206–1211
Drug-device distinction, 1200–1202, 1205,
1206
E–meters, 1199, 1200
Equitable treatment of old and new
devices, 1215, 1216

Establishment registration, 1259, 1260
Exportation, 1475, 1476
FDA action on PMAs, 1239–1241
FDA enforcement jurisdiction, 285, 286
Feasibility studies, 1231
General controls applicable to all devices
    generally, 1254–1277
    administrative detention, 1271
    adulteration and misbranding,
      1254–1259
    adverse event reporting, 1260, 1261
    banned devices, 1271
    civil penalties, 1276, 1277
    device tracking, 1274, 1275
    establishment registration, 1259,
      1260
    good manufacturing practice,
      1261–1264
    notification and repair,
      replacement, or refund,
      1271–1274
    postmarket surveillance, 1274
    product listing, 1259, 1260
    recalls, mandatory, 1275, 1276
    removals and corrections, reports of,
      1276
    restricted devices, 1264–1271
Good manufacturing practice, 1261–1264
Historical background, 1193, 1194
Humanitarian device exemptions, 1245,
    1246
In Vitro Fertilization, this index
Investigational devices, 1230–1235
Market entry, regulation of
    generally, 1218–1251
    abbreviated PMN, 1228
    classification and reclassification of
      novel devices, 1247–1251
    humanitarian device exemptions,
      1245, 1246
    introduction, 1218–1221
    investigational devices, 1230–1235
    piggybacking, 1223
    PMN summary vs. PMN statement,
      1228
    Premarket approval applications,
      below
    premarket notification and
      approval, 1218–1221
    product development protocols,
      1242, 1243
    research use only exemption, 1232,
      1233
        safety and effectiveness data,
          1228
        substantial equivalence,
          1221–1230
        third party review, 1229
    user fees, 1228
Medical Device Amendments of 1976
    generally, 1202–1218
    background, 1202–1204
    overview of 1976 and later
      amendments, 1204, 1205
    statutory preemption, 1280–1292
Medical gas pipeline systems, 128

Misbranding, 1254–1259
Notification and repair, replacement, or
    refund, 1271–1274
Organizational responsibility, 1200
Orphan devices, 1246
Pacemakers, 1273
Patent term restoration, 1218–1221
Performance goals, 1241
Performance standards, Class II devices,
    1251–1253
PMA review times, 1241
PMN summary vs. PMN statement, 1228
Postapproval requirements, 1243
Postmarket surveillance, 1274
Premarket approval applications
    generally, 1236–1243
    advisory committee review, 1238,
      1239
    comparison of PMAs and NDAs,
      1236–1238
    FDA action on PMAs, 1239–1241
    prior PMA application, use of data
      from, 1239, 1240
    temporary suspension of approval,
      1240
    user fees, performance goals, and
      PMA review times, 1241
Premarket notification and approval,
    1218–1221
Prior PMA application, use of data from,
    1239, 1240
Private lawsuits, 1273
Product development protocols, 1242,
    1243
Product listing, 1259, 1260
Quack devices, enforcement against, 1200
Radiation control
    generally, 1292–1300
    collection and dissemination of
      information, 1299, 1300
    enforcement of standards, 1292,
      1293
    other radiation control programs,
      1300
    performance standards, 1293–1300
Recalls, mandatory, 1275, 1276
Regulation under 1938 Act, 1194–1200
Removals and corrections, reports of, 1276
Reprocessed single–use devices, 1229,
    1230
Research use only exemption, 1232, 1233
Restricted devices, 1264–1271
Safety and effectiveness data, 1228
Special controls. Class II devices, special
    controls, above
Sterilizers, 129
Temporary suspension of approval, 1240
Third party review, 1229
Transitional devices, regulation of, 1217,
    1218
User fees, 1228, 1241
Voluntary medical device standards,
    Class II devices, 1252, 1253

MEDICAL FOOD
Generally, 324, 325

MEDICAL GAS PIPELINE SYSTEMS
Generally, 128

MEDICAL MARIJUANA
Generally, 811, 812

MEDICARE/MEDICAID
Prescription drug benefit, 1026

MERCURY
Action level, 517, 518
Food and drugs, mercury in, 515–518

METABOLITES
Generally, 107

METHADONE
Regulation of, 828

METHAMPHETAMINE
Control of, 812, 813

METHYLENE CHLORIDE
Use for decaffeination of coffee, 1415

MILITARY
Use of investigational drugs, 689

MISBRANDING
Cosmetics, 1325–1335
Food Labeling, this index
Medical devices, 1254–1259

MISLEADING CLAIMS
Food labeling, 328, 330

MISTAKE
NDA, rescission because of mistake, 851

NAMES
Food, this index
Human Drugs, this index

NATURAL FOODS
Food Labeling, this index

NUTRITION
Americans, nutritional status, 442, 443
Labeling, 313, 314, 403–408
Nutrient content of food. Food, this index
White House Conference on Food,
    Nutrition, and Health, 328, 329,
    353, 354, 362, 403

OBESITY
FDA response, 442
Food labeling, 442
HHS/FTC report, 443

ODORS
Products intended to mask or prevent,
    109, 110, 116, 117, 120

ORAL CONTRACEPTIVES
Patient labeling, 877–879

**ORGANIC FOODS PRODUCTION
    ACT OF 1990**
Generally, 453, 454

ORPHAN DRUGS
Human Drugs, this index

ORPHAN MEDICAL DEVICES
Generally, 1246

OVER–THE–COUNTER DRUGS
Generally, 957–995
Advertising, FTC regulation, 990–993
Category III legality, 979
Claim substantiation, 992
Daytime sedatives, 983
Defensive use of OTC panel report, 991,
    992
Encouraged reformulation, 978
FDA authority over OTC drug
    advertising, 990, 991
FDA request for data, 977, 978
First Amendment considerations, 983, 984
Homeopathic drugs, 984
Inactive ingredients, 984, 985
Labeling
        generally, 985–990
        drug facts format, 987–989
        drug review restrictions, 985–987
        professional labeling, 983
        warnings, 989, 990, 991
Mailing OTC drugs, 995
Nanotechnology, 984
NDA deviation, 982
OTC drug review
        generally, 120, 121, 973–985
        Category III legality, 979
        combination drugs, 982, 983
        completion of review, 979, 980
        daytime sedatives, 983
        encouraged reformulation, 978
        FDA enforcement policy, 978
        FDA request for data, 977, 978
        flexibility of review, 979
        homeopathic drugs, 984
        legality, 977
        panels, 978
        premature marketing, 978, 979
        rationale and procedures, 973–979
Premature marketing, 978, 979
Professional labeling, 983
Switch from prescription to
        nonprescription status, 960–973
Tampering–resistant packaging, 993–995
Time and extent applications, 983
Warnings, 989, 990, 991

PACEMAKERS
Repair, replacement, or refund, 1273

PACKAGING
Child–resistant packaging, 888, 1321
Food packaging
        colors used in packaging, 620
        labeling. Food Labeling, this index
        safety of food constituents, 614
Poison Prevention Packaging, this index
Tamper–resistant packaging, 639

PARENTERAL NUTRITION
Generally, 799

PATENTS
Food additives, patent term extension, 563
Generic Drugs, this index
Medical devices, patent term restoration, 1218–1221

PATHOGENS
Generally, 521–552

PEANUT BUTTER
Food standards, 345
Peanut butter spread, 367, 368

PERMITS
Temporary marketing permits, 347

PESTICIDE RESIDUES
Food, this index

PET FOOD
Colors used in, 625
FDA and state regulation, 1047
Low acid canned food, 540

PEYOTE
Religious use, 812

PHARMACIES AND PHARMACISTS
Compounding, 797–799
Dependent pharmacist prescribers, 810
Drug establishment registration, pharmacy exemption, 793–799
FDA inspections, pharmacy exception, 185, 186

PHYSICIANS
Regulating physician prescribing. Human Drugs, this index

PLASTIC BOTTLES
Environmental impact, 1528

POISON PREVENTION PACKAGING
Generally, 995
New drug applications, 995

POLYVINYL CHLORIDE
Food additives, 1397

POULTRY
Meat and Poultry, this index

PREEMPTION
Anti–tampering requirements, 995
Conflict preemption, 299–310
Persons reporting adverse drug reaction, preemption of confidentiality, 836
State Regulatory Authority, this index

PREGNANCY
Assisted reproduction, 1185, 1186
Natural state exception and, 449

PRESCRIPTION DRUG LABELING
Generally, 860–907
Accutane labeling, 872, 873
Adequate directions for use
advertising claims, relevance, 930
consult a physician, 805
interpretive regulations, 931
new drug provisions, relation to, 817
Advertising claims, relevance, 930
Antibiotic resistance warning, 873, 874
Bar code on drug labels, 863
Black box warning, 866, 867
Class labeling, 872
Consult a physician, label direction, 805
FDA approval of drug labeling, 862
Hypoglycemic drugs, oral, relabeling, 871, 872
Legend, mandatory, 807
Limitation to prescription sale, 802–807
Manufacturer's name, 863, 864
Material facts, failure to reveal, 870–871
New drug applications, labeling review, 736, 737
Oral contraceptive labeling, 877–879
Package inserts, 884–886
Patient labeling for prescription drugs
generally, 876–888
content, 879
estrogen, 882
medication guides, 886–888
oral contraceptives, 877–879
package inserts, 884–886
voluntary patient information efforts, FDA promotion, 886
Physician labeling, 860–864
Physician request, unsolicited, unapproved information provided in response, 939–942
Physician's Desk Reference, 862, 863
Prescription drugs, generally. Human Drugs, this index
Warnings
generally, 866–875
antibiotic resistance warning, 873, 874
black box warning, 866, 867
Dear Doctor letters, 874
effectiveness, 874
nonprescription vs. prescription warnings, 989

PRESERVATIVES
Chemical preservatives, ingredient labeling, 392

PRISONERS
Drug clinical trials, 688

PROPOSITION 65 (CALIFORNIA)
Required warnings, 402, 1438

PROTEIN DIET PRODUCTS
Warning labels, 401

PUBLIC HEALTH
Food labels, messages on, 418

PUBLICITY
FDA enforcement, 268–270

QUI TAM SUITS
False Claims Act, qui tam enforcement, 934–938

RADIATION
Food additives, 565, 566
Radiation control, 1292–1300
Radiopharmaceutical drugs, 788–791

**RADIO FREQUENCY
    IDENTIFICATION (RFID)**
Prescription drugs, establishing pedigree
    for, 1029, 1030

RECALLS
Food and Drug Administration, this index

RECORDS
FDA inspections, 184–187
FOIA, what documents are "agency
    records," 1505, 1506

REGULATIONS
Administrative Practice and Procedure,
    this index

REPRODUCTION
Assisted reproduction, 1185, 1186

RESCISSION
NDA, rescission because of mistake, 851

RESTAURANTS
FDA jurisdiction, 281, 282
Nutrition labeling, 314, 407

RESTITUTION
FDA enforcement, 221–230

RIPENESS
Judicial Review, this index

RULEMAKING
Administrative Practice and Procedure,
    this index

SACCHARIN
Cancer studies, 1404, 1405
Food additives, 565
Food labeling, 401, 402

SAFE DRINKING WATER ACT
Generally, 319, 1419, 1420

**SAFE MEDICAL DEVICES ACT OF
    1990**
FDA enforcement, 14

SALMONELLA
Animal food contamination, 1058
Human food contamination, 502–505, 532

SANITATION
Food sanitation. Food, this index

SEAFOOD
Enforcement of seafood HACCP, 187
National Shellfish Sanitation Program
    (NSSP), 527

**SECURITIES AND EXCHANGE
    COMMISSION**
FDA/SEC cooperation, 706, 707

SEIZURE
Food and Drug Administration, this index

SHELBY AMENDMENT
Public access to data produced by federal
    grant recipients, 1524

SHELLFISH
Mercury levels, 516–518
National Shellfish Sanitation Program
    (NSSP), 527

SIDE EFFECTS
Food labeling, 401

SKIN CREAMS
Regulatory letters, 115, 116

SLACK FILL
Containers, this index

SMOKING CESSATION PRODUCTS
FDA approval, 150, 151

SOAP
Exemption for, 109, 110

SODIUM
Food labeling, 425, 426, 591

SOFT DRINKS
Benzene in, 501, 502

STANDING
Hearing, standing to demand or to seek
    judicial review, 52
Withdrawal of NDA, standing to
    challenge, 855

STATE REGULATORY AUTHORITY
1938 Act and state authority, 292–308
    Generally, 289–316
Blood products, 298
Dairy product labeling, 310
FDA Modernization Act, preemption
    under, 314–315
Federal regulations, prospective adoption,
    290
Hearing aid controls, 312
Historical background, 5, 6, 292–294
Medical Device Amendments, statutory
    preemption, 1280–1282
National uniformity, elusive goal,
    314–315
Nutrition Labeling and Education Act,
    preemption under, 313, 314
Pet food, 1047
Physician prescribing, regulating, 820
Preemption
    agency purpose to preempt, 307, 308
    blood products, 298
    dairy product labeling, 310
    FDA Modernization Act, 314–315
    hearing aid controls, 312
    Medical Device Amendments,
        1202–1205
    Nutrition Labeling and Education
        Act, 313, 314
    statutory preemption, 310–316
    tamper-resistant packaging, 639,
        993–995

Tamper-resistant packaging, 639, 993–995

STEM CELLS
Searching for, 1178–1184

STERILIZERS
Medical devices, 129

SUCRALOSE
Food additives, 565

SULFITES
Generally, 591

SUN LAMPS
Radiation control, 1296–1298

SUPPLEMENTS
Dietary Supplements, this index

SWEETENERS
Aspartame, 565
Cyclamate, 564, 565
Saccharin, 565
Sucralose, 565

TAMPERING
Food tampering, 639
Tamper-resistant packaging, 639, 993–995

TATTOOS
FDA advisory opinion, 1318
Regulation of, 110

TEA
Quality standards, 339

TERRORISM
Drugs to combat, 753

THIGH CREAMS
Warning letters, 116

TISSUE TRANSPLANTS
Human Tissue Transplants, this index

TOBACCO PRODUCTS
Generally, 1351–1372
Cigarettes as restricted devices, 1268, 1269
Implicit limits on FDA's jurisdiction, 139–151
Lozenges, 151

TRADE SECRETS
Confidentiality, 1514–1524
Cosmetics, determination of trade secret status, 1337
Other agencies, disclosure to, 1517

TRADITIONAL CHINESE MEDICINE
Generally, 800, 801

TRANSPLANTS
Human Tissue Transplants, this index

USDA
Food grade labeling, 454, 455
Genetically modified ingredients, USDA safety regulations, 592, 598, 599

Inspection regime, 192, 193
Livestock, production/marketing claims, 455
Meat, poultry, and eggs, USDA regulation, 318
Recall policy, 234

VACCINES
Generally, 1137–1153
Compensating vaccine injuries, 1149–1153
Government liability, 1145–1149
Government support for immunization, 1138–1140
Injuries from vaccines
compensating vaccine injuries, 1149–1153
government liability, 1145–1149
manufacturing liability, 1141–1145
Manufacturing liability, 1141–1145

VEGETABLES
Fruit and Vegetables, this index

VENUE
Condemnation proceedings, 206, 207

VITAMINS
Dietary Supplements, this index

WARNINGS
Label warnings, 399–402

WARRANTS
Food and Drug Administration, this index

WATER
Drinking Water, this index

WEIGHT LABELING
Food Labeling, this index

WORMS
Unfit for food, 487, 488

XENOTRANSPLANTATION
Generally, 1189–1192
FDA guidance, 1192

X–RAYS
Radiation control, 1294–1296